De SMITH'S JUDICIAL REVIEW

De SMITH'S JUDICIAL REVIEW

EIGHTH EDITION

THE Rt HON LORD WOOLF CH, GBS (HK), FBA (HON)
Former Chief Justice of England and Wales
Chief Justice of the Astana Financial Centre Court
Blackstone Chambers

PROFESSOR SIR JEFFREY JOWELL KCMG QC
Barrister, Blackstone Chambers
Former Director of the Bingham Centre for the Rule of Law
Emeritus Professor of Public Law, University College London

CATHERINE DONNELLY
Barrister, Law Library, Dublin and Blackstone Chambers
Fellow and Associate Professor, Trinity College, Dublin

IVAN HARE QC
Former Fellow of Trinity College Cambridge
Barrister, Blackstone Chambers

SWEET & MAXWELL

THOMSON REUTERS

Published in 2018 by Thomson Reuters (Professional) UK Limited,
trading as Sweet & Maxwell.
Thomson Reuters is registered in England & Wales,
Company number 1679046.
Registered office and address for Service:
5 Canada Square, Canary Wharf, London, E14 5AQ.

For further information on our products and services, visit *http://
www.sweetandmaxwell.co.uk.*

Computerset by Sweet & Maxwell.
Printed and bound by CPI Group (UK) Ltd, Croydon, CR0 4YY.
No natural forests were destroyed to make this product: only farmed timber
was used and replanted.
A CIP catalogue record for this book is available from the British Library.

ISBN: 978-0-414-06404-1

Thomson Reuters and the Thomson Reuters logo are trademarks of
Thomson Reuters.
Sweet & Maxwell ® is a registered trademark of Thomson Reuters
(Professional) UK Limited.

Crown copyright material is reproduced with the permission of the
Controller of HMSO and the Queen's Printer for Scotland.

Previous Editions

First edition	1959
Second edition	1968
Third edition	1973
Fourth edition	1980
Fifth edition	1995
Sixth edition	2007
Seventh edition	2013
Eighth edition	2018

Preface

This book was begun by Stanley de Smith in the 1950s as a doctoral thesis and then published in 1959. De Smith set out its aims in his original Preface as follows:

> "It is to be hoped that [this book] will be helpful to practitioners, to public administrators and their legal advisers, and to students and their teachers in England and elsewhere. And those students of government who are not lawyers may also find in it material that has a bearing on the larger issues inherent in the relationship between the Administration and the individual."

De Smith's book was the first in the United Kingdom to describe and analyse this field of law with coherence. It quickly established a groundbreaking reputation here and in the Commonwealth. Professor de Smith produced two further editions in 1968 and 1973. After de Smith's untimely death, Professor John M. Evans (later Mr Justice Evans of the Federal Court of Canada) edited the 4th edition in 1980.

When two of the present authors (Woolf and Jowell) were asked to prepare a 5th edition of the work in the early 1990s, it soon became clear that the initial intention, which was merely to update the existing edition, was insufficient. Prompted by reforms to the procedures and remedies, and also by a changing intellectual climate, the 1980s and early 1990s saw dramatic changes in judicial review: the number of applications increased from a few hundred a year to several thousand; the judicial reasoning which creates the grounds for challenging the validity of governmental action grew in its sophistication; and there was by then a burgeoning academic literature about this area of law. The 5th edition of the work (ISBN 0420466207) was published in 1995 (with the assistance of Andrew Le Sueur) and consisted of a substantial restructuring and supplementation of the 1980 edition. A supplement, updating the 1995 text, was published in 1998 (ISBN 0421607904)). An abridged version of the work, intended more as a student text, was published in 1999 under the title *Principles of Judicial Review* (ISBN 042162020X).

When work began on the 6th edition (with Le Sueur now a joint author and assisted by Catherine Donnelly and Ivan Hare: ISBN 0421690305, 9780421690301), we recognised that new work on the impact upon judicial review of the Human Rights Act 1998 would be required. We also agreed that the separate short surveys of the operation of the judicial review in different contexts at the end of the 5th edition, excellent though they were, would be better integrated into the main body of the work. In other respects, however, we again initially assumed that a mere updating of the previous edition would suffice. It soon became clear, however, that judicial review had altered in the past 12 years to an extent even more significant than between the previous editions and that a substantial rearrangement and major additions were again required. These changes were driven, in particular, by the explicit recognition that individuals in a democracy possess rights against the state—as enunciated both by the common law as well as the Human Rights Act 1998 and in European Union law. In addition, the relationships between the courts and other branches of government had been clarified in important ways. The principle of the sovereignty of Parliament has been, if not been fatally undermined, at least substantially weakened as a shield against either unlawful administrative action or legislation which offends the rule of law. Constitutional principles such as the rule of law and separation of powers had been explicitly articulated as such, and their status enhanced. Above all, it had become clear that judicial review is not merely about the way decisions are reached but also about the substance of those decisions themselves. The fine line between appeal on the merits of a case and review still existed but we had moved, as we emphasised in various sections of that edition, towards a "culture of justification". *A First Supplement to the Sixth Edition* was published in 2009 (ISBN 9780421691001), edited by Le Sueur, Donnelly and Hare.

The 7th edition (with Woolf, Jowell, Le Sueur, Donnelly and Hare as joint authors), was published in 2013 (ISBN 9780414042155), with three Supplements, the first in 2014 (ISBN 9780414036673); the second in 2015 (ISBN 9780414054509), and the third in 2016 (ISBN 9780414060104). Previous editions of the work were entitled *Judicial Review of Administrative Action*. The sixth edition dropped the reference to 'administrative action' as some of judicial review (that under European Union law and in the interpretation of the rights under the European Convention on Human Rights as incorporated by the Human Rights Act 1998) involves review not only of administrative action (or the exercise of public functions, as we now prefer to say), but also of primary legislation.

This 8th edition, is authored by Woolf, Jowell, Donnelly and Hare. Regrettably, Le Sueur has had to relinquish his role, due to onerous administrative responsibilities at Essex University. His fellow authors want to thank him heartily for his key role as both author and de facto co-ordinator of the work since his very able assistant role for the 5th edition.

This edition has been prepared in the context of great uncertainty in respect of our public law, in consequence of the UK's decision to leave the European Union. There is also some uncertainty as to the future of our Human Rights Act insofar as it incorporates rights set out in the European Convention on Human Rights. Nevertheless, we thought it appropriate to incorporate the changes since 2013.

No doubt, over the years, we have deviated from some of de Smith's standpoints and approaches but not, we believe, in ways of which he would have disapproved, in the changed circumstances of the times. In three respects at least, we have attempted wherever possible to be faithful to de Smith's distinctive approach. First, by setting out the principles underlying each area of judicial review: de Smith's hallmark was, above all, the elucidation of principle. Never content merely to describe a line of cases, he would invariably sum up their underlying rationale through a series of "propositions". We have sought to do the same. Second, we have retained key parts of de Smith's unmatched historical researches (updating them were necessary), which are so important to a proper understanding of the context of judicial review today. As he wrote in his first Preface, "many of the peculiarities of judicial review in English administrative law are unintelligible unless viewed in the light of their historical origins". Third, we have attempted to refer to the experience of other jurisdictions, yet again as in the previous editions, without any pretence at creating a work of comparative law. We have been struck by the increased readiness of our courts to consider (if not slavishly to follow) the decisions of courts in other countries. The requirement in some of the provisions of the European Convention on Human Rights that our decision-makers adhere to the necessary qualities of a "democratic society" is just one of the factors that have encouraged reference to the experience of democra- cies elsewhere. We have summarised at the end of a number of chapters the corresponding law and practice in some relevant Commonwealth countries.

Another of de Smith's hallmarks was his meticulous coverage of the case law. He took pride in the fact that he had cited 1,800 cases in the first edition. In the age before electronic databases this was a considerable achievement. Professor

Evans was equally meticulous in his comprehensive coverage of developments in judicial review between 1973 and 1979. In those times it may have been possible to refer to virtually every case relevant to the subject (although some critics of the 4th edition queried the need for the routine citation of all relevant cases). To cite the mass of case law that exists today is, we believe, even if possible, unnecessary in a work of this nature. We hope not to have neglected the need to be comprehensive where desirable. We have, however, consciously been prepared to sacrifice coverage where it might impede de Smith's prime goal of clarity of exposition of principle.

Scheme of the Work

In Chapter 1 we set out the context of judicial review and its scope, considering at the outset a number of issues that guide our approach in so many of the later chapters. A raging debate on the constitutional foundations of judicial review erupted shortly after the 5th edition went to press. Our position remains that courts in judicial review enunciate not merely the will of the legislature but the fundamental principles of a democratic (albeit unwritten) constitution. We also sketch at the outset another fundamental issue, namely, the respective roles of courts and other branches of government—the question of whether there are some matters that are simply beyond judicial review because they are not "justiciable".

In addition, we consider the context in which judicial review is but one of a number of possible avenues of redress for aggrieved citizens, which include internal complaints procedures, mediation and other forms of ADR, ombudsmen and (reinvigorated by the Tribunals, Courts and Enforcement Act 2007) tribunals.

In an era of "proportionate dispute resolution" there is a renewed appreciation that administrative justice may be achieved beyond the Administrative Court. As we argue, however, while other redress mechanisms may often provide cheaper, speedier and more convenient remedies, judicial review is usually best placed to ensure the rule of law is respected. Chapter 1 also considers government reaction to judicial review and the sometimes intemperate ministerial or press attacks on the courts' function of supervising the legality of executive action, which is so essential to preserving the rule of law. Chapter 2 examines those who may initiate a claim for judicial review (claimants); who have a right to be a party (interested parties) and those, often pressure groups, who may seek permission from the court to make submissions as interveners.

Whatever may have been the case in the past, the operation of the standing rule—the need for "a sufficient interest in the matter" to which the claim relates—now excludes few people with well-presented grounds of challenge from commencing a review. Where a claimant seeks to rely on a Convention right as a ground of review, s.7 of the Human Rights Act 1998 modifies the standing test to include a requirement that the claimant be "a victim" (a development that has been subject to academic criticism and some judicial fog in its practical application). We conclude this chapter will a survey of the approaches to standing in other jurisdictions.

In Chapter 3, we consider the often complex and controversial questions of which defendants and decisions are subject to judicial review. The court's choice as to whether to embark on an adjudication of an alleged unlawful action or omission depends on its jurisdiction to do so (guided by s.29 of the Senior Courts Act 1981), whether the subject-matter of the public authority's impugned decision is justiciable (on which, see Chapter 1) and whether there are any factors that indicate that the court should exercise its discretion to decline to review the matter (for example, because the would-be claimant has failed to use an available alternative remedy). We see that the source of the public authorities' power in statute or a prerogative power continues to provide a clear basis for the court's jurisdiction in most cases; the complementary "public function" test coined in *Datafin* is a useful supplement but has not led to a widespread expansion of the ambit of judicial review. The court's approach to determining whether action taken by a public authority in relation to a contract—generally requiring there to be an "additional public element"—is less than satisfactory; we suggest that so long as the courts, in this context, approach the issue of amenability on this basis there is much to be said for adopting a pragmatic method and reasoning by analogy from previously decided cases. The Human Rights Act has brought with it a new range of amenability problems as the courts have struggled with the concept of "functions of a public nature" under s.6. In this part of Chapter 3 we have sought, as best we can, to present an even-handed account of this important and controversial point of law. Towards of end of Chapter 3, we note that a controversy of former years—whether a litigant has to use the judicial review procedure rather than some other form of legal proceedings to raise a public law issue—has now subsided in the wake of the flexibility introduced by the Civil Procedure Rules.

Chapter 4, which deals with concepts of jurisdiction and unlawful administration, is significantly affected by the Human Rights Act and the recently endorsed common law right of access to justice. As we say, the cases

"demonstrate how carefully the courts will scrutinise any attempt to oust their ability to protect the citizen against abuse of power by public bodies and at the same time how important it is to the rule of law that Parliament does not attempt to do so inappropriately. In this area in a jurisdiction where there is no entrenched constitution, there is a very heavy responsibility for restraint on all the arms of government."

Part II of the book (Chapters 5–14) deals with the grounds of review. As in the previous edition, we largely retain the categories that Lord Diplock set out, namely illegality (Chapter 5), lack of procedural fairness (Chapters 6–10) and irrationality or unreasonableness (Chapter 11—rephrased, as set out below, as "substantive review"). Again, we recognise that these grounds are by no means comprehensive nor self-contained (the failure to satisfy a "legitimate expectation", for example, can fall into different grounds) and that other grounds may well emerge in the future (the term "abuse of power" is sometimes employed, either as a distinct ground of review, or as a general term for unlawful action).

In the 5th edition the notion of "illegality" as a ground of review was regarded as relatively free of conceptual difficulties. From the 6th edition, we devoted more attention to the process of interpretation of statutory purpose, or relevancy, in respect of a number of issues, including problems raised in *Pepper v Hart* (in respect of the relevance of ministerial and other statements in parliament to a statute's intent), and the interaction between matters which engage Convention rights, European Union law and international law. New distinctions have been drawn recently between powers and duties (some of which are regarded as mere "target duties") and changing judicial approaches to what in the past may have been regarded as unenforceable "policies". Similarly, there have been significant developments in the notion of "relevancy", particularly the extent to which cost, or financial considerations may be lawfully relevant. The Localism Act 2011 Pt 1 creates a "general power of competence" for local authorities, requiring revaluation of some previous case law.

Chapters 6–10 deal with the ground of procedural fairness. We retain the basic format of the 5th edition, dealing first with the history of the requirement that both sides be heard (Chapter 6), then proceeding to the situations giving rise to the fair decision-making process and the content of that entitlement (Chapter 7), then exceptions (Chapter 8). Perhaps the most pressing challenge faced by the courts in this context in recent times has been the balancing of the requirements of procedural fairness with the interests of national security. In particular, the issue of the appropriate limits to usage of closed material procedures has been exercising both the courts and the legislature.

Although there have perhaps been relatively few conceptual developments in the notion of fettering of discretion (Chapter 9), we were surprised at the degree of intense judicial examination given to the notion of bias and conflict of interest (as we now entitle Chapter 10).

In the 5th edition, the chapter that contained for us the most surprises was the one we entitled "The Unreasonable Exercise of Power". De Smith had previously devoted little attention to the notion of "unreasonableness", but when we assembled the cases we discovered far more than we had expected in which decisions were held invalid on the ground of their substance, rather than procedure and we sought to make some sense of the categories in which such review took place. Substantive review is now fully recognised, prompted in particular by the more intense scrutiny that has been accorded to cases where human rights (or "constitutional rights" as they are now explicitly called) are engaged, and where the concept of proportionality is applied. As a result, we retitled Chapter 11 "Substantive Review and Justification", and seek to show the relationship between the irrational, unreasonable and disproportionate decisions, the different senses of each of those terms, and how the courts have, in different circumstances, adopted different degrees of intensity of review and imposed different standards of justification.

Chapter 12 considers the legitimate expectation in both its procedural and substantive contexts (considered in the previous edition in two parts of the book—in the section on procedural fairness and then in respect of the unreasonable decision). The chapter also considers the extent to which an unlawful representation may give rise to a legally enforceable expectation (as has sometimes been suggested).

This work cannot possibly cover the approach of the courts to each of the specific Convention rights, or the administrative law of the European Union. Other specialist texts admirably cover that extensive ground. However, we must at least outline the essence of those important areas of judicial review and this is done in Chapter 13, which sets out the salient features of judicial review as it applies to Convention Rights under the Human Rights Act 1998, and in Chapter 14, which has the same purpose in respect of the law of the European Union. Both of these areas continue to account for a substantial part of the judicial review caseload and to affect almost all areas of law, procedure and practice. While Chapter 14 has been drafted on the basis that European Union law continues fully in force for the present, the future of its application is obviously subject to significant uncertainty.

Part III of the book is concerned with procedures and remedies. Since the 5th edition, the Civil Procedure Rules have been extended to claims for judicial review—RSC Ord.53 has been replaced by CPR Pt 54. In judicial review, as in other types of litigation, regard must now be had to "the overriding objectives" of the CPR. There have also been several changes in terminology: claims (rather than applications) for judicial review; the Administrative Court superseded the Crown Office List; the ancient remedies of prohibition, mandamus and certiorari became prohibiting, mandatory and quashing orders. In Chapter 16, we have included some discussion of alternative dispute resolution, an outline of the Freedom of Information Act 2000 and the Data Protection Act 1998, funding and costs. There have been substantial changes in relation to costs in recent years and in this edition we cover the introduction of a fixed-costs regime for environmental judicial review claims and government initiatives to limit legal aid and the availability of costs protection, discourage without merit applications and those where the grounds of review would not have made a difference to the outcome. Chapter 19 turns to monetary remedies against the background of a failed Law Commission project on financial remedies against public authorities.

We have sought to state the law as it stood on 30 October 2017 (although some later developments have been incorporated at proof stage).

Acknowledgements

The comparative material we incorporate into this edition has been brought to our attention by our distinguished panel of "foreign correspondents", to whom we express our gratitude for their prompt, detailed and expert guidance.

- Australia: Professor Mark Aronson (University of New South Wales), Dr Matthew Groves (La Trobe University), and Greg Weeks (Australian National University).
- Canada: Professor David Mullan (Queen's University, Ontario).
- India: Harish Salve (formerly Solicitor General of India).
- New Zealand: Dr Caroline Morris (Queen Mary University of London).
- South Africa: Professor Cora Hoexter (University of the Witwatersrand, Johannesburg).

One of the authors, Catherine Donnelly, covers Irish law.

We are grateful to Anna Hardiman-McCartney, Clare Duffy, Stephen Brittain, Caroline Carney, Brady Gordon and Róisín Costello for their able assistance with research and proof-reading.

Our publishers at Sweet & Maxwell have again been very supportive. We are particularly grateful to Taryn Dullisear for her efficiency, encouragement, tolerance and innovative use of technology to enhance communication between the authors and between the authors and publishers. She was succeeded when she took maternity leave by Gregory Smith, who was equally helpful, as was Stephen Hepplestone with the editing of proofs.

The usual disclaimers apply: the undersigned alone are responsible for any errors or infelicities.

Harry Woolf

Jeffrey Jowell

Catherine Donnelly

Ivan Hare

February 2018

TABLE OF CONTENTS

Preface

PART I THE CONTEXT OF JUDICIAL REVIEW

1. THE NATURE OF JUDICIAL REVIEW

3.   DEFENDANTS AND DECISIONS SUBJECT TO JUDICIAL REVIEW

PART II GROUNDS OF JUDICIAL REVIEW

4. CONCEPTS OF JURISDICTION AND LAWFUL ADMINISTRATION

5. ILLEGALITY

6. Procedural Fairness: Introduction, History and Comparative
   Perspectives

11. SUBSTANTIVE REVIEW AND JUSTIFICATION

13.   CONVENTION RIGHTS AS GROUNDS FOR JUDICIAL REVIEW

PART III PROCEDURES AND REMEDIES

15. THE HISTORICAL DEVELOPMENT OF JUDICIAL REVIEW REMEDIES AND
    PROCEDURES

16. CPR Pt 54 Claims for Judicial Review

17. Other Judicial Review Proceedings

18. JUDICIAL REVIEW REMEDIES

APPENDICES

TABLE OF CASES

TABLE OF STATUTES

TABLE OF STATUTORY INSTRUMENTS

TABLE OF CIVIL PROCEDURE RULES

TABLE OF INTERNATIONAL LEGISLATION

REGULATIONS

PART I THE CONTEXT OF JUDICIAL REVIEW

CHAPTER 1

The Nature of Judicial Review

TABLE OF CONTENTS

INTRODUCTION

The value and significance of judicial review

    Judicial review provides a set of legal standards, enforced through a process of litigation, to enable people to challenge the lawfulness of decisions made by public bodies and others exercising public functions. The legal standards may be summarised as follows.

(1)   Public bodies must have legal authority for their actions. This may be derived from statute, the common law or (in the case of some central government functions) a prerogative power. Public bodies must act within the scope of that legal authority.[1]

(2)   Powers must be exercised within the objects and purpose of the statute.[2]

(3)   Where a statute gives a public body discretionary power, that power must be used to further the scope and object of the statute—not for an extraneous purpose.[3]

(4)   Public bodies must take into account all legally relevant considerations and avoid taking into account those that are irrelevant.[4]

(5)   Where a statute gives decision-making power to a public body, that body (not another one) must exercise its discretion: except in some recognised circumstances, it is unlawful to delegate the power.[5]

(6)   Fair procedures must be followed: these may be found in legislation, the common law, European Union law, and the Human Rights Act 1998. They may,

1-001

---

[1]   5-019.
[2]   5-090.
[3]   5-090.
[4]   5-130.
[5]   5-159.

according to the context, include requirements: to give notice of a proposed decision before making it; to consult and receive written representations; to disclose information before a final decision is reached; to provide oral hearings; and to give reasons for a decision.[6]

(7) Where a statute gives a public body discretionary power, the public body acts unlawfully if it adopts a rigid policy, with no exceptions, as to how the discretion will be exercised.[7]

(8) Public bodies act unlawfully if they are actually biased. They also act unlawfully if a fair-minded and informed observer, having considered the facts, would conclude that there was a real possibility of bias.[8]

(9) A public body's decision is unlawful if its substance is "unreasonable" or "irrational". This may involve: giving manifestly inappropriate weight to a factor; being illogical, arbitrary, inconsistent or uncertain: giving inadequate or incomprehensible reasons; or making a decision based on inadequate or mistaken facts.[9]

(10) A public body's decision is unlawful if it is disproportionate. One test of proportionality is to assess whether the action pursues a legitimate aim recognised by the law, whether the action is capable of achieving that aim, and whether a less restrictive alternative could have been employed. Generally, that kind of "structured proportionality" review is confined to the assessment of whether rights under European Union law and the European Convention on Human Rights (ECHR) may be limited.[10] However, proportionality can also engage when a decision-maker manifestly fails to attain a fair balance of (relevant) considerations, or where the impact of the decision is unduly oppressive.

(11) Unless Parliament speaks clearly to the contrary in a statute, a decision-maker should act in compliance with the rule of law, including access to justice and the principle of equality.

(12) A public body acts unlawfully if it creates a legitimate expectation (for example, by giving a clear and unambiguous assurance) that a particular procedure will be followed or a lawful benefit conferred from which it later seeks to resile without an adequate justification.[11]

(13) Under the Human Rights Act 1998 s.6 it is unlawful for a public body, or a person exercising functions of a public nature, to breach one of the rights of the ECHR (Convention rights) incorporated into national law.[12]

(14) Public bodies must comply with the requirements of European Union law, in accordance with the European Communities Act 1972 and the European Union Act 2011.[13]

1-002　　The court's role,[14] when a dispute arises, is to adjudicate on whether a legal standard has been breached. This often involves interpreting the Act of Parliament or other legislation that purportedly authorised the impugned decision. The court

---

[6] Chs 6-8.
[7] Ch.9.
[8] Ch.9.
[9] 11-043.
[10] 11-090.
[11] Ch.12.
[12] Ch.13.
[13] Ch.14.
[14] In England and Wales at first instance this is the Administrative Court (part of the Queen's Bench Division of the High Court): see 16-003.

assumes that an Act of Parliament does not authorise a public body to infringe basic rights recognised by the common law (unless the Act expressly and unambiguously permits this).[15] Until now, Parliament's ultimate power to make, repeal or amend laws has been supported by the constitutional principle of parliamentary sovereignty and has not therefore been successfully challenged outside the situation under European Union law, where sovereignty has been delegated to the relevant European Union law-making institutions. Questions as to the correct interpretation of legislation are, however, always ultimately for judges to adjudicate on—not politicians or officials. This reflects the constitutional principles of separation of powers and the rule of law. Under the Human Rights Act s.4, courts may issue a declaration that legislation is incompatible with Convention rights, but it is for Parliament to decide to rectify that incompatibility.

Some of the legal standards of public administration rest on principles and rules developed by the courts as part of the common law. This is especially so in relation to procedural propriety and rationality requirements. Here the court's role is both to develop and apply standards. Since the 19th century, the British constitution has recognised the need for "the justice of the common law" to "supply the omission of the legislature".[16] Against a general background of increasing expectations of fairness, rationality and justification in public affairs, the courts have developed more exacting legal standards (especially since the 1960s) and have applied these to a wider variety of decision-makers.[17]   **1-003**

In addition to standards, judicial review must provide procedures though which individuals, groups and business enterprises[18] may bring public law disputes to court. A special procedure in England and Wales (known as claim for judicial review under the Civil Procedure Rules Pt 54) exists for this purpose,[19] though a variety of other procedures may also be used.[20] The challenge in designing a judicial review system is to balance competing interests: the rule of law requires that the courts be accessible to people with grievances; there is a legitimate public interest in preventing or minimising disruption to public administration from misguided challenges; and the court itself has an interest in efficiency to prevent delays. Over many years there have been debates as to how to strike a satisfactory balance.[21] The current system includes: (i) limited access to public funds for claimants who otherwise could not afford to make a challenge[22]; (ii) a pre-action protocol designed to encourage resolution of disputes before resort to judicial review; (ii) relatively short time limits for starting claims[23]; (iii) a permission requirement through which the court, usually in a paper-based procedure, determines which cases should be allowed to proceed to a full hearing in open court[24]; (iv) remedies which are discretionary, meaning a court finding that a decision is unlawful may nonetheless withhold a remedial order if it is necessary to do so to protect competing private or public interests.[25]   **1-004**

Notwithstanding these restrictions on access, in December 2012 the Ministry of Justice published a Consultation Paper setting out further proposals for reform in   **1-005**

---

[15] On the principle of legality, see 5-045–5-049.
[16] 6-017.
[17] Ch.3.
[18] Ch.2.
[19] Ch.16.
[20] Ch.17.
[21] Ch.15.
[22] 16-086.
[23] 16-055.
[24] 16-048.
[25] 18-047.

three areas: (i) shortening the three-month time limit for bringing proceedings in certain procurement cases to 30 days and in certain categories of planning decisions to six weeks, bringing them into line with the statutory appeal timetable which applied to those cases; (ii) tightening the procedural rules for granting permission to bring judicial review proceedings by removing the right to an oral renewal where there had already been a prior judicial process involving a hearing on substantially the same issue or where the judge, on written submissions, had determined the case to be "totally without merit"; and (iii) increasing the court fee for an oral renewal hearing where permission had already been refused by a judge on the papers but the claimant asked for the decision to be reconsidered at a hearing.[26] The Government expressed concern that the judicial review process was subject to abuse and was used as a delaying tactic, added to the cost of public services, stifled innovation and frustrated much needed reforms aimed at stimulating growth and promoting economic recovery. It sought to justify its proposals by reference in particular to the significant growth in judicial review applications: 160 applications in 1974, increasing to nearly 4,250 by 2000 and over 11,000 by 2011 (largely attributable to challenges in immigration and asylum matters). The proposals were heavily criticised by academics and practitioners.[27]

1-006   The Ministry of Justice subsequently published consultation papers proposing a number of further reforms.[28] Many of these reforms were enacted in the Criminal Justice and Courts Act 2015 (which substantially amended the Senior Courts Act 1981). Some of the reforms relate only to specialist areas of practice. For example, there is now a specialist Planning Court as part of the Administrative Court which deals with most judicial reviews and statutory challenges in the field of planning

---

[26] Ministry of Justice, *Judicial Review: Proposals for Reform* (CP25/2012) published in December 2012; 'Judicial Review' (written ministerial statement) *Hansard*, HC Vol.561, col.50WS (23 April 2013) (C. Grayling).

[27] For a critique of the proposals, see Public Law Project, *Briefing on response to consultation Judicial Review: Proposals for Reform* (9 January 2013); V. Bondy and M. Sunkin, "*Judicial Review Reform: Who is Afraid of Judicial Review? Debunking the Myths of Growth and Abuse*", UK Const. L. Blog, 10 January 2013; R. Gordon, "Judicial Review – Storm Clouds Ahead?" [2013] J.R. 1. The new time limits for bringing procurement or planning challenges where the grounds for review arose on or after 1 July 2013 and removal of the right to seek an oral hearing where the case was assessed by a judge as being without merit on the papers were given effect on 1 July 2013 by an amendment to the Civil Procedure Rules. See Civil Procedure (Amendment No. 4) Rules 2013 (SI 2013/1412). A Planning Fast-Track was also put in place in the Administrative Court in July 2013. The court fee for seeking an oral renewal hearing after the initial judicial review application has been turned down was increased from £60 to £215. Certain proposals were not pursued: where there was a series of linked administrative acts, commencement of time limit for seeking judicial review to be when the first such act was committed; and removal of the right to an oral renewal where there had already been a prior judicial process involving a hearing on substantially the same matter.

[28] Ministry of Justice, *Transforming Legal Aid: Delivering a More Credible and Efficient System*, CP14/2013; Ministry of Justice, *Judicial Review: Proposals for Further Reform*, Cm 8703. For a critique of the proposals, see Public Law Project, *Judicial Review: Proposals for Further Reform* (October 2013); V. Bondy and M. Sunkin, "*How Many JRs are Too Many? An Evidence Based Response to Judicial Review: Proposals for Further Reform*", UK Const. L. Blog (26 October 2013); Joint Committee on Human Rights, *The Implications for Access to Justice of the Government's Proposals to Reform Judicial Review*, 13th Report of the 2013–2014 Session, HL 74/HC 868; M. Elliott, "*Judicial Review Reform – The Report of the Joint Committee on Human Rights*", UK Const. L. Blog (1 May 2014); J. McGarry, "The Importance of an Expansive Test of Standing" [2014] J.R. 60; Bingham Centre for the Rule of Law, *Response to Ministry of Justice Consultation Paper CM 8703: Judicial Review: Proposals for Further Reform* (available at *http://www.biicl.org/files/6618_bingham_centre_response_jr-pffr_cm_8703__2013-11-01.pdf*); M. Fordham, M. Chamberlain, I. Steele and Z. Al-Rikabi, *Streamlining Judicial Review in a Manner Consistent with the Rule of Law* (Bingham Centre Report 2014/01, Bingham Centre for the Rule of Law, BIICL, London, February 2014).

and which has shorter time limits (six weeks) and its own Practice Direction.[29] Shorter time limits for challenges also now apply to claims for judicial review of a decision to award a contract to which the Public Contracts Regulations 2015 (SI 2015/102) apply (30 days)[30] and of decisions of the Upper Tribunal (16 days from the date on which the decision was sent to the applicant).[31] Other reforms are welcome rationalisations of the judicial review procedure: for example, extending the availability of leap frog appeals to the Supreme Court.[32] Further changes require the court to refuse permission (or to grant relief) where it is likely that the outcome for the applicant would not have been substantially different if the conduct complained of had not occurred[33] and remove the right of an applicant to have the refusal of permission reconsidered at an oral hearing where the judge certifies the application to be totally without merit.[34] Recent reforms have also very substantially undermined the usefulness of Protective Costs Orders (now called Costs Capping Orders and only available after permission has been granted)[35] and tightened the rules on the recovery of costs by interveners.[36] Proposals on the disclosure of sources of funding have not yet been implemented[37] and some other reforms (such as narrowing the test of standing and limiting the powers of local authorities to challenge certain infrastructure projects) have been abandoned. These reforms are considered in greater detail in Chapter 16.

Our approach

Since the first edition of this book in 1959,[38] the circumstances in which the courts have been prepared to provide relief for unlawful administrative action have expanded in spectacular fashion. In the chapters that follow we shall see how, over a relatively short period, English courts reduced the zone of immunity from legal challenge formerly surrounding a great deal of action by public authorities. That task involved the jettisoning of many of the conceptual barriers and disfiguring

1-007

---

[29] CPR Pt 54.21 and Practice Direction 54E.
[30] CPR r.54.5 (as amended by Public Contracts Regulations 2015/102 Sch.6(2) para.11(3))).
[31] CPR r.54.7A(3).
[32] Criminal Justice and Courts Act 2015 ss.63–68.
[33] Senior Courts Act 1981 s.31(3C)–(3F).
[34] CPR Pt 54.12(7).
[35] Criminal Justice and Courts Act 2016 s.88.
[36] Criminal Justice and Courts Act 2015 s.87.
[37] In July 2015, the Ministry of Justice opened a consultation on provision of financial information to the court, on applications for judicial review or when applying for a costs capping order: see Ministry of Justice, *Judicial Review: Proposal for the provision and use of financial information* (Cm 9117). The Ministry of Justice published a response to the consultation submissions in July 2016, indicating that the government intended to retain the general approach upon which it consulted and inviting further views on the provision of financial information to other parties: see Ministry of Justice, *Reform of judicial review: Proposals for the provision and use of financial information* (Cm 9303). New rules on when legally aided claimant solicitors will be paid in judicial review claims were brought into force under the Civil Legal Aid (Remuneration) (Amendment) (No.3) Regulations 2014 (SI 2014/607), reg.5A, which prevent legal aid payments unless permission is granted by the Administrative Court or no order is made and the Lord Chancellor considers it reasonable to make a payment.
[38] The 1st to 5th editions of this work were entitled *Judicial Review of Administrative Action*. Stanley de Smith's own editions were published in 1959 (1st edn), 1968 (2nd edn) and 1973 (3rd edn). The 4th edition (by J.M. Evans) was published in 1980. The 5th edition (Lord Woolf and J. Jowell) was published in 1995; an abridged and updated paperback version of that edition appeared in 1999 under the title *Principles of Judicial Review*. For the 6th edition (2007) and a supplement to the 6th edition (2009) the work was renamed *De Smith's Judicial Review*, as it appeared in the 7th edition (2013) under the authorship of Lord Woolf, Sir Jeffrey Jowell QC, Prof. Andrew Le Sueur, Catherine Donnelly and Ivan Hare.

archaisms which had inhibited the development of effective judicial review. It also required the articulation of acceptable principles governing the exercise of public functions and the vindication of the rights of the individual against the state. These principles and rights are now seen as fundamental features of a constitutional democracy.

European influences

1-008   A number of factors have influenced the development of coherent common law principles of judicial review. The effects of European integration have had and continue to have a profound impact. Since the United Kingdom's accession to the European Communities (now the European Union) in 1973, principles of law developed by the European Court of Justice, and directly effective rights contained in EU legislation, have provided grounds for judicial review in the national courts.[39] More recently, the enactment of the Human Rights Act 1998 has required our domestic courts to protect rights set out in the European Convention of Human Rights (ECHR or Convention rights), taking into account the case law of the European Court of Human Rights.[40] Both European influences have helped develop new approaches to statutory interpretation and the standards of judicial review. Recent judgments of the UK Supreme Court have, however, emphasised the continuing vitality and importance of common law principles and approaches in contexts where European law also applies.[41]

1-009   At the time of writing this edition negotiations are in train for the withdrawal of

---

[39] See Ch.14.
[40] See Ch.13.
[41] See, e.g. *Osborn v Parole Board* [2013] UKSC 61; [2014] A.C. 1115, [57] (Lord Reed: "The importance of the [Human Rights] Act is unquestionable. It does not however supersede the protection of human rights under the common law or statute, or create a discrete body of law based upon the judgments of the European court. Human rights continue to be protected by our domestic law, interpreted and developed in accordance with the Act when appropriate); *R. (on the application of HS2 Action Alliance Ltd) v Secretary of State for Transport* [2014] UKSC 3; [2014] 1 W.L.R. 324, [207] (Lord Neuberger PSC and Lord Mance JSC, lamenting at [158] that "the issues that have had to be addressed only arise as a result of decisions of the European Court of Justice, which we have found problematic and which call for some further observations" went on to say "The common law itself also recognises certain principles as fundamental to the rule of law. It is, putting the point at its lowest, certainly arguable (and it is for United Kingdom law and courts to determine) that there may be fundamental principles, whether contained in other constitutional instruments or recognised at common law, of which Parliament when it enacted the European Communities Act 1972 did not either contemplate or authorise the abrogation".); *Kennedy v The Charity Commission* [2014] UKSC 20; [2015] A.C. 455 (Lord Mance JSC at [46] "Since the passing of the Human Rights Act 1998, there has too often been a tendency to see the law in areas touched on by the Convention solely in terms of the Convention rights. But the Convention rights represent a threshold protection; and, especially in view of the contribution which common lawyers made to the Convention's inception, they may be expected, at least generally even if not always, to reflect and to find their homologue in the common or domestic statute law" and Lord Toulson JSC at [133] "The growth of the state has presented the courts with new challenges to which they have responded by a process of gradual adaption and development of the common law to meet current needs. This has always been the way of the common law and it has not ceased on the enactment of the Human Rights Act 1998, although since then there has sometimes been a baleful and unnecessary tendency to overlook the common law. It needs to be emphasised that it was not the purpose of the Human Rights Act that the common law should become an ossuary"); *Pham v Secretary of State for the Home Department (Open Society Justice Initiative intervening)* [2015] UKSC 19; [2015] 1 W.L.R. 1591, [97]–[98] (Lord Mance JSC: "The present appeal concerns a status which is as fundamental at common law as it is in European and international law, that is that status of citizenship ... It is therefore improbably that the nature, strictness or outcome of such a review would differ according to whether it was conducted under domestic principles or whether it was also required to be conducted by reference to a principle of proportionality derived from [European] Union law") and [110] (Lord Sumption JSC: urging

the UK from the EU, following the triggering of art.50 of the Treaty of the European Union after the referendum on 23 June 2016 in favour of withdrawal. Assuming that the status of the judgments of the European Court of Justice prevail prior to the UK's exit from the EU (scheduled for 29 March 2019), questions remain as to its status after that time whether on a transitional or permanent basis.

Common law comparative perspectives

The development of judicial review in these new contexts requires the courts to define and enunciate the necessary requirements of a democratic society. In so doing it is right to look to other democratic jurisdictions as aids to the development of domestic standards, as judicial review in England and Wales continues to share many features with others in the common law family of legal systems. While this book is not a fully-fledged work of comparative law, approaches adopted in other jurisdictions can provide useful reference points as we plot the development of our own law and practice. We therefore draw on the experience of other common law jurisdictions, especially those of Australia, Canada, India, Ireland, New Zealand and South Africa, in our accounts of modern judicial review.[42] In relation to some aspects of judicial review, particularly those topics dealt with in Part III of the book, we have taken the view that comparisons are either of limited value or would require an expansive treatment that cannot be accommodated in a book with a primarily national focus. In relation to other aspects of judicial review, we present comparative material with two necessarily limited purposes in mind. First, there are situations where the law in another jurisdiction is so similar to that of England and Wales that a case could be of practical value as persuasive authority. Secondly and more broadly, an approach adopted in another jurisdiction may simply cast an interesting light on how the law in England and Wales operates or how it might develop in the future. **1-010**

We also make reference to judicial review to the United Kingdom's other two distinct jurisdictions—Scotland[43] and Northern Ireland.[44] The three jurisdictions share the UK Supreme Court as their final court of appeal for judicial review proceedings but under the Constitutional Reform Act 2005 s.41(2) binding precedent is not set by judgments in cases from outside the particular jurisdiction: "A decision of the Supreme Court on appeal from a court of any part of the United Kingdom, other than a decision on a devolution matter, is to be regarded as the deci- **1-011**

SIAC "to take the common law test as its starting point and then say in what respects (if any) its conclusions are different applying art.8 of the Human Rights Convention or EU law").

[42] Thanks to our "foreign correspondents" in those countries, details of whom are recorded in the Preface. For an explanation of the law reports from those jurisdictions and the rules governing the use of foreign material in the Courts of England and Wales, see Appendix A. See H. Corder, *Comparing Administratie Justice Across the Commonwealth* (2008).

[43] See generally Lord Clyde and D. Edwards, *Judicial Review* (2000) and A. McHarg and T. Mullen (eds), *Public Law in Scotland* (2006). The historical roots of the Court of Session's supervisory jurisdiction of judicial review a different from those of the High Court in England and Wales. The main grounds of judicial review are broadly similar in the two jurisdictions but it should not be assumed that they are identical (see, e.g. *L v Angus Council* [2011] CSOH 196; 2012 S.L.T. 204 holding that the "precedent fact" approach of the UK Supreme Court in *R. (on the application of A) v Croydon LBC* [2009] UKSC 8; [2009] 1 W.L.R. 2557 did not apply). In Scotland there is no permission stage in the judicial review procedure nor is there a specified time limit for seeking review (see Ch.16), though Lord Gill's *Report of the Scottish Civil Courts Review* (2010) recommended the introduction of both. Recently, the approach to standing in Scotland has come to be regarded as too restrictive (in the Gill report) and has been relaxed by the UK Supreme Court: see 2-072. The legal test for amenability to review is conceptually distinct from that in England and Wales: see 3-118.

[44] See generally G. Anthony, *Judicial Review in Northern Ireland* (2008). As with Scotland, the grounds of review in Northern Ireland and England and Wales are similar.

sion of a court of that part of the United Kingdom". Some courts and tribunals operate on a UK-wide basis, including the UK Supreme Court in relation to devolution
matters and the Upper Tribunal.

Judicial review in the context of the administrative justice system

1-012   This book is not a general treatise on the whole of administrative law in England
and Wales. Nor is it a book on human rights and civil liberties. Nor even does it
purport to give a complete account of that part of administrative law which is
concerned with redress of citizens' grievances—though later in this chapter we
outline the range of avenues of complaint and redress which now exist, including:
internal complaints procedures; mediation; recourse to ombudsmen; and appeals to
tribunals.[45] Judicial review provides just one way to control the abuse of public
power. In the 5th edition of this book we retained the reference to Professor de
Smith's celebrated phrase that judicial review is "sporadic and peripheral", for the
reason that the administrative process is not, and cannot be, a succession of
justiciable controversies. Public authorities are set up to govern and administer, and
if their every act or decision were to be reviewable by the courts, the business of
administration could be brought to a standstill. Today, however, the principles
developed through judicial review have become central to all of public administration insofar as those principles seek to enhance both the way decisions are reached
and the quality of the decisions made.[46] Regrettably, in recent times, the contribution of judicial review to ensuring maintenance of the rule of law, respect for
parliamentary intent and purpose, and enhancement of the principles of good
administration have not always been well understood by some politicians who claim
that judicial review obstructs the wheels of the state and may impede economic
progress.[47]

From "administrative action" to all public functions

1-013   Until the 6th edition in 2007, the title of previous editions of this book was
Judicial Review of Administrative Action. Although this book still concentrates
judicial review of what may broadly be described as "administrative action",[48] we
omitted from the title the words "of Administrative Action". This is because of the
importance of review of high-level policy decisions and of legislation.[49] Local
authority byelaws have for many years been amenable to judicial review, but in
more recent years the courts have with increasing vigour exercised jurisdiction over
the lawfulness of other kinds of delegated legislation—including statutory instruments passed by affirmative resolution of Parliament—to ensure that ministers keep
within the ambit of the rule-making powers conferred on them by Act of
Parliament.[50] Moreover, while the UK continues to be a member of the EU, it is a
concomitant of membership that national courts are required to disapply legislative provisions, including those in Acts of Parliament, where they are incompat-

---

[45] See 1-096.
[46] See Chapter 11.
[47] See 1-053.
[48] On the once important classifications of functions as "legislative", "administrative", "judicial", "quasi
judicial" and "ministerial" (now of mainly historical interest), see Appendix B, below.
[49] See 3-011.
[50] See 3-011.

ible with EU law.[51] The Human Rights Act 1998 s.4 also provides the courts with power to make declarations of incompatibility in relation to primary legislation, which has given the higher courts a role in evaluating whether Parliament's enactments are consistent with Convention rights.[52] The courts have also been called upon to adjudicate on the application of the Parliament Acts.[53]

THE CONSTITUTIONAL CONTEXT OF JUDICIAL REVIEW

The purpose of judicial review

In a mature democracy, the courts and Parliament have distinct and complementary constitutional roles in securing good government according to the constitution.[54] The courts will no longer avoid adjudicating on the legality of a decision merely because it has been debated and approved in Parliament[55] or relates to nationally important policy pursued by a Minister accountable to Parliament.[56] The distinctive roles of judicial review and parliamentary (and other) oversight of executive action create opportunities for synergy, with aspects of a particular decision being scrutinised in different ways by different bodies. Thus, a government decision may be examined in judicial review proceedings, in an ombudsman complaint and by a parliamentary committee.[57] Judicial review proceedings may prompt parliamentary action, and vice versa.[58] Judicial review also goes some way to answering the age old question of "who guards the guards?" by ensuring that public authorities responsible for ensuring accountability of government do so within the boundaries of their own lawful powers.[59]

1-014

A distinction which is now less clear than it was is between administrative law

1-015

---

51 See 14-012.

52 See 13-047.

53 *Jackson v Attorney General* [2005] UKHL 56; [2006] 1 A.C. 262.

54 Lord Steyn, "The Weakest and Least Dangerous Department of Government" [1997] P.L. 84 (constitutionalism "is neither a rule or a principle of law. It is a political theory as to the type of institutional arrangements that are necessary in order to support the democratic ideal. It holds that the exercise of government power must be controlled in order that it should not be destructive of the very values which it was intended to promote"). For an analysis of the various meanings attributed to the term constitutionalism, see J. Murkens, "The Quest for Constitutionalism in Public Law Discourse" (2009) 29 O.J.L.S. 1.

55 See, e.g. *R. (on the application of Javed) v Secretary of State for the Home Department* [2001] EWCA Civ 789; [2002] Q.B. 129 (delegated legislation approved by affirmative resolution of both Houses of Parliament could be subject to judicial review on the grounds of illegality, procedural impropriety or irrationality).

56 See, e.g. *R. (on the application of Medway Council) v Secretary of State for Transport, Local Government and the Regions* [2002] EWHC 2516; [2003] J.P.L. 583 (challenge to decision to exclude Gatwick from proposals to expand airport capacity in southern England).

57 See, e.g. the scheme for ex gratia payments to Second World War Far East internees was judicially reviewed (*R. (on the application of Association of British Civilian Internees (Far East Region)) v Secretary of State for Defence* [2003] EWCA Civ 473; [2003] Q.B. 1397), investigated by the Parliamentary Commissioner for Administration and was the subject of a special report by a select committee (House of Commons, Public Administration Committee, "A Debt of Honour": the ex gratia scheme for British Groups interned by the Japanese in the Second World War HC Paper No.735 (Session 2005/06)).

58 See, e.g. *R. v Secretary of State for Foreign and Commonwealth Affairs Ex p. World Development Movement Ltd* [1995] 1 W.L.R. 386 was followed by an inquiry of the Foreign Affairs Select Committee, *Pergau Dam* HC paper No.271 (Session 1993/94).

59 Thus the Local Government Ombudsman and the Independent Police Complaints Commission (to name but two) are amenable to judicial review. Decisions relating to public inquiries have also been subject to judicial review, as have regulators of the privatised industries (see Ch.3).

and constitutional law. We discuss below the constitutional foundations of judicial review and contend that both the exercise of judicial review and the principles enunciated through judicial review are constitutionally based. The constitution shapes administrative law and in turn is shaped by it. In earlier years, however, the purposes of constitutional and administrative law were considered distinct. Constitutional law was intended to define the powers of the State. Administrative law then had a subsidiary purpose, which was to regulate the exercise of those constitutionally established powers by ensuring that public officials acted within their scope. Most of the attention of administrative law was therefore absorbed in the interpretation of the power—express or implied—conferred upon administrators. Two questions predominated: should the grant of wide discretion be construed literally or purposively? And to what extent should a general duty of fairness or reasonableness be subsumed within the grant of official power?

1-016   Initially, these questions were resolved within the overriding aim of enabling administrators to further the public interest. Public power should, it was said, self-evidently be exercised in the interest of the public as a whole, and not in the interest of any individual or group of individuals alone. Private concerns were not to obstruct that overall mission. A former Lord Chief Justice considered judicial review to be founded on the principle that courts are the mere "handmaidens of public officials"[60]; there to facilitate the work of bodies charged with acting in the public interest.

1-017   As judicial review gained in confidence, another aim asserted itself, most often described as the promotion of "good public administration". This notion shifted the perspective of administrative law in the direction of the consumer—those persons affected by official decisions. However, the qualities of "the good" in public administration were not grounded in any clear theoretical or constitutional foundation. Later the courts articulated the "grounds" of administrative law as a failure to observe the principles of lawfulness, fairness and reasonableness. These more specific criteria were useful as guides to the content of the "good" in administrative action, but they were still considered duties of the administrator to provide, rather than rights of the individual to receive.

1-018   In recent years, it is increasingly being realised that in a constitutional democracy the role of judicial review is to guard the rights of the individual against the abuse of public power.[61] This does not mean that the courts should necessarily be impeded in their ability to determine the public interest, or to achieve efficiency. Whether or not these rights are as clearly articulated as in countries with written constitutions, we have arrived at a situation described in an address by Lord Diplock delivered at a meeting to pay tribute to the work of Professor de Smith. He said that our system of administrative law is "in substance nearly as comprehensive in its scope as *droit administratif* in France and gives effect to principles which, though not derived from Gallic concepts of *légalité* and *détournement de pouvoir*, are capable of achieving the same practical results".[62] Shortcomings and lacunae no

---

[60]   A phrase used in 1962 by Lord Parker CJ, quoted in G. Williams, "The Donoughmore Report in Retrospect" (1982) 60 Pub.Admin. 273, 291.

[61]   See, e.g. T. Allan, *Law, Liberty and Justice* (1993). For a further account of the history of administrative law in the 19th and 20th century see C. Harlow and R. Rawlings, *Law and Administration*, 3rd edn (2009), Chs 1-2. For a further history see J. Jowell, "Administrative Law" in V. Bognador (ed), *The British Constitution in the Twentieth Century* (2004). See also M. Bevir, "The Westminster Model, Governance and Judicial Reform" (2008) 61 Parl. Aff. 559; R. Masterman, "Juridification, Sovereignty and Separation of Powers" (2009) Parl. Aff. 499; M. Bevir, "Juridification and Democracy" (2009) Parl. Aff. 493.

[62]   Lord Diplock, "Administrative Law: Judicial Review Reviewed" [1974] C.L.J. 233, 244; and *R. v*

doubt remain, but English administrative law is now one of the most celebrated products of our common law, and doubtless the fastest developing over the past half-century.

Constitutional justifications of judicial review

Justification by the ultra vires principle

It is surprising that, during this period of development of judicial review, although its general purposes were articulated in the way we have seen, its constitutional justification was rarely articulated. It was perhaps generally assumed that judicial supervision over the exercise of official discretion was justified by the "central principle" of ultra vires.[63] Under this principle the role of the courts is to ensure that Parliament's will is enforced. Judicial review therefore simply involves the implementation of the express or implied intent of the legislature. It was only in 1987 that the ultra vires justification for judicial review was questioned in England and Wales,[64] initially mainly on the ground that judicial review supervises not only decision-making power conferred by statute, but also other regulatory bodies performing public functions and decisions taken under the authority of prerogative powers. These powers were not expressly created by the legislature, so it is not possible to discover the legislative intent behind their creation which might otherwise enable the vires of their actions to be determined.

1-019

It is only possible in this introduction briefly to sketch the heated debate that then ensued on this issue.[65] The principal attack on the ultra vires theory was that judges were not in practice merely interpreting the intent of a particular statute, but themselves fashioning independent principles of good administration under traditional methods of common law reasoning.[66] Adherents of this "common law" justification of judicial review argued that it should be openly acknowledged that principles such as "natural justice" or the requirement of a "fair hearing" were imposed by the courts in the face of legislative silence. It was artificial—a "fig leaf" or a "fairy tale"[67]—to suppose that the legislature had implicitly directed those procedures. The "common law" school concede the need to resolve many cases by reference to express or implied parliamentary intent. However, they pointed out that in some cases the courts would deliberately obstruct or evade legislative intent. For example, a clear legislative intention to exclude access to the courts had been subverted by employing the technical distinction between jurisdictional and non-

1-020

Inland Revenue Commissioners Ex p. National Federation of Self Employed [1982] A.C. 617 at 641 (Lord Diplock: "the progress towards a comprehensive system of administrative law… I regard as having been the greatest achievement of the English courts in my judicial lifetime"); *Breen v Amalgamated Engineering Union* [1971] 2 Q.B. 175 at 189 (Lord Denning, himself an imaginative architect, "It may truly now be said that we have a developed system of administrative law"); cf. *Ridge v Baldwin* [1964] A.C. 40 at 72 (Lord Reid: "We do not have a developed system of administrative law—perhaps because until fairly recently we did not need it"). For the first appearance in an English statute of the term "administrative law", see State Immunity Act 1978 s.3(2).

[63] The late Professor Sir William Wade considered that the ultra vires doctrine was "the central principle of administrative law": H.W.R. Wade and C. Forsyth, *Administrative Law*, 9th edn (2009), p.27.

[64] D. Oliver, "Is the Ultra Vires Rule the Basis of Judicial Review?" [1987] P.L. 543.

[65] A number of articles on this debate are collected together in C. Forsyth (ed.), *Judicial Review and the Constitution* (2000).

[66] P. Craig, "Competing Models of Judicial Review" [1999] P.L. 428; Sir John Laws, "Law and Democracy" [1995] P.L. 72.

[67] See the defence: C. Forsyth, "Of Fig Leaves and Fairy Tales: The Ultra Vires Doctrine, Sovereignty of Parliament and Judicial Review" [1987] P.L. 543; C. Forsyth and M. Elliott, "The Legitimacy of Judicial Review" [2003] P.L. 286.

jurisdictional errors. The common law school also accused the ultra vires school of lack of clarity: If the notion of legislative intent is so broad and indeterminate as to permit the implication of principles yet unarticulated (such as that legitimate expectations should not be disappointed), then it is of little use as a practical guide.

1-021   In response, the adherents of the ultra vires approach contended that the common law school wrongly justifies unconstrained judicial law-making, contrary to the principle of the separation of powers. Taken to its logical conclusion it was said that the common law approach could lead to judicial challenge to the supremacy of Parliament.

1-022   An attempt to reconcile the ultra vires and "common law" justifications of judicial review is provided by the "modified ultra vires" theory[68] (which just as easily could be called the "modified common law" theory). This justification accepts that part of the "common law" theory which acknowledges that judges create principles of good administration independent of specific parliamentary intent. However, it maintains that those principles should be applied consistently with a *general* intention attributed to Parliament that power which it confers should be exercised in accordance with the rule of law. In other words, legislative silence or ambiguity is read in the context of a continuing consent by Parliament to be bound by the rule of law as interpreted by the courts.

Justification by constitutional principles

1-023   To the extent that the modified ultra vires justification seeks to weave judicial law-making into a constitutional context (under the principle of the rule of law) it is surely right. However, to the extent that it seeks to assign a general intent to Parliament, it is scarcely less artificial than the pure ultra vires justification. We prefer to place the justification of judicial review on a normative and constitutional basis: [i]n our view Parliament *ought* to abide by the necessary requirements of a modern constitutional democracy (one of which is the rule of law). From that proposition follows a second: that courts *ought* to make the assumption that the rule of law (and other necessary requirements of constitutional democracy) are followed by the legislature. These two propositions are qualified only to the extent that the courts (in a constitution in which the principle of parliamentary supremacy is strong) submit to the authority of Parliament when it seeks clearly and unambiguously to exclude the rule of law or other constitutional fundamentals.[69] Under what circumstances the courts are required so to submit depends upon the continuing validity of the sovereignty of Parliament as our governing constitutional principle.

1-024   In the chapters that follow we shall maintain that the standards applied by the courts in judicial review must ultimately be justified by constitutional principle,

---

[68]   M. Elliott, "The Ultra Vires Doctrine in a Constitutional Setting: Still the Central Principle of Administrative Law" [1999] C.L.J. 129. See T. Adams, "Ultra Vires Revisted" [2018] P.L.31.

[69]   This approach is supported by D. Dyzenhaus, *The Constitution of Law* (2006); J. Jowell, "Of Vires and Vacuums: The Constitutional Context of Judicial Review" [1999] P.L. 448; and "Beyond the Rule of Law: Towards Constitutional Judicial Review" [2000] P.L. 119; P. Joseph, "The Demise of Ultra Vires: Judicial Review in the New Zealand Courts" [2001] P.L. 354, 359 (who says "the concept of the rule of law has replaced ultra vires as the organising principle of administrative law", and cites in support the New Zealand Court of Appeal case *Peters v Davison* [1999] 2 N.Z.L.R. 164 at 188 where it was said that the court's judicial review powers "are based on the central constitutional role of the Court to rule on questions of law, rather than the ultra vires doctrine". For a view that partially shares this approach see T. Allan, "Constitutional Dialogue and the Justification of Judicial Review" (2003) 23 O.J.L.S. 563. For a more recent contribution, see J. Leslie, "Vindicating Common Law Constitutionalism" (2010) 30 L.S. 301.

which governs the proper exercise of public power in any democracy.[70] This is so irrespective of whether the principles are set out in a formal, written document. The rule of law is one such principle of the greatest importance. It acts as a constraint upon the exercise of all power. The scope of the rule of law is broad and it incorporates different values. It has managed to justify—albeit not always explicitly—a great deal of the specific content of judicial review, such as the requirements that laws as enacted by Parliament be faithfully executed by officials; that orders of courts should be obeyed; that individuals wishing to enforce the law should have reasonable access to the courts; that no person should be condemned unheard; that decisions should be communicated before they are enforced, and that power should not be arbitrarily exercised. In addition, the rule of law embraces some internal qualities of all public law: that it should be certain, that is, ascertainable in advance so as to be predictable and not retrospective in its operation; and that it be applied equally, without unjustifiable differentiation.[71]

Other constitutional principles are perhaps less clearly identified but nevertheless involve features inherent in a democratic state. These include the requirements of political participation,[72] equality of treatment and freedom of expression.[73] A constitutional principle achieves practical effect as a constraint upon the exercise of all public power. Where the principle is violated it is enforced by the courts which define and articulate its precise content. As we shall see, English common law now recognises three main "grounds" of judicial review, known as "procedural propriety", "rationality" and "legality".[74] A further ground of "proportionality" is applied by the courts where rights under EU law and the ECHR are at stake. These grounds are not isolated requirements of a discrete area of law; they refer to and attempt to impose upon all decision-makers standards that are inherent in a democracy. Procedural propriety imposes fair decision-making procedures necessary to the degree of participation which democracy requires. Rationality seeks the accuracy of decisions and prohibits arbitrariness and excessive burdens being imposed on individuals. The ground of legality involves the application both of the

1-025

---

[70] The passages asserting this position in the 5th edition of this work were cited with approval by the South African Constitutional Court in *Pharmaceutical Manufacturer's Association of SA Ex p. President of the RSA* 2000 (3) B.C.L.R. 241 at 252, CC ("the finding that he [the decision-maker] acted ultra vires is a finding that he acted in a manner that was inconsistent with the Constitution").

[71] On the rule of law, see 5-040; 11-059; 14-068 (in the context of EU law); and J. Jowell, "The Rule of Law and its Underlying Values", Ch.1 in J. Jowell and D. Oliver (eds), *The Changing Constitution*, 8th edn (2013); P. Craig, "Formal and Substantive Conceptions of the Rule of Law: An Analytical Framework" [1997] P.L. 467; T. Allan *Constitutional Justice: A Liberal Theory of the Rule of Law* (2001); Lord Bingham, "The Rule of Law" [2007] C.L.J. 67 and *The Rule of Law* (2010); European Commission for Democracy through Law (Venice Commission), Report on the Rule of Law (Adopted by the Venice Commission at its 86th plenary session, Venice, 25-26 March 2011). The first statutory reference to the rule of law as a constitutional principle is in the Constitutional Reform Act 2005 s.1, on which see House of Lords Select Committee on the Constitution, *Relations between the Executive, the Judiciary and Parliament*. HL Paper No.151 (Session 2006/07), para.23.

[72] An important debate about the USA Constitution, but which has relevance in the UK, is the extent to which the constitution seeks to further "process values" (permitting effective participation in the democratic process) or also deals in substantive or moral rights against the state. The argument for the former is put by J. Ely, *Democracy and Distrust* (1980); for criticism see P. Brest, "The Substance of Protest" (1982) 42 Ohio S.L.J. 131; L. Tribe, "The Puzzling Persistence of Process-based Constitutional Theories" (1980) 89 Yale L.J. 1037; R. Dworkin, "The Forum of Principle" (1982) 56 N.Y.U.L.R. 469; M. Tushnet, "Darkness on the Edge of Town" (1980) 89 Yale L.J. 1037. See also G. Richardson, "The Legal Regulation of Process", in Richardson and Genn (eds), *Administrative Law and Government Action* (1994), p.105.

[73] See 11-052.

[74] Terms employed by Lord Diplock in *Council of Civil Service Union v Minister for the Civil Service* [1985] A.C. 374 and since employed widely by the courts.

sovereignty of Parliament and the rule of law, by requiring Parliament's will to be respected and official action to be congruent with legislative purpose. In applying the ground of legality the courts are effectively acting as guardians of Parliament's intent.[75] Parliamentary sovereignty and the rule of law are therefore not inevitably mutually opposed, since a great deal of judicial review (and indeed the rule of law) is concerned with implementing Parliament's will.[76] It is unfortunate that critics of judicial review sometimes fail to differentiate as clearly as they might the difference between Parliament's intent (as expressed in statutory words) and the policies of the government of the day.[77]

Reconciliation between parliamentary sovereignty and the rule of law

1-026   In some cases, however, courts have been faced with the challenge of having to adjudicate when the principle of the rule of law and the principle of the sovereignty of Parliament are in competition. This can occur when Parliament attempts to oust or limit the jurisdiction of the courts to determine the scope of a public authority's powers.[78]

1-027   From time to time it has also been suggested that the English courts ought to be prepared to modify the principle of parliamentary sovereignty by refusing to recognise as a valid law a statutory provision that violates a fundamental right recognised by the common law. Those who advocate this view stress that this judicial redefinition of the limits of parliamentary power would be justified only in an extreme case where the very foundations of democracy were at risk, or the rule of law was being undermined, by a legislative provision. Sir Robin Cooke, while President of the New Zealand Court of Appeal, expressed the view that some "common law rights presumably lie so deep that even Parliament could not override them".[79] Sir John Laws, writing extra-judicially, has alluded to "higher order" law, which "confers ... and must of necessity limit" parliamentary sovereignty.[80] Lord Woolf has also recognised that, in extremis, the judiciary would have a constitutional responsibility to uphold the rule of law, even in the face of plain statutory

---

[75]   See 5-090.

[76]   A. Le Sueur, "The Influence of the House of Lords on the Administrative Court (and Vice Versa)", Ch.4 in R. Gordon (ed.), *Judicial Review in the New Millennium* (2003).

[77]   See J. Sumption, "Judicial and Political Decision-making: the Uncertain Boundary" [2011] J.R. 301 and a riposte by S. Sedley, "Judicial Politics" (2012) 34 *London Review of Books* 15 ("executive government exercises public powers which are created or recognised by law and have legal limits that it is the courts' constitutional task to patrol"). See further, J. Sumption, *"The Limits of Law"*, 27th Sultan Azlan Shah Lecture, 20 November 2013 (available at *http://www.supremecourt.uk/docs/speech-131120.pdf*).

[78]   See 4-015.

[79]   *Taylor v New Zealand Poultry Board* [1984] 1 N.Z.L.R. 394, 398—an observation of the New Zealand Parliament but no doubt apt to apply also the UK Parliament. Robin Cooke, as Lord Cooke of Thorndon, sat occasionally as a Lord of Appeal in the HL and PC 1996-2001. See further: J. Goldsworth, *The Sovereignty of Parliament* (1999), Ch.1; R. Mullender, "Parliamentary Sovereignty, the Constitution, and the Judiciary" (1998) 49 N.I.L.Q. 138; M. Fordham, "Common Law Illegality of Ousting Judicial Review" [2004] J.R. 86; D. Jenkins, "Common law declarations of unconstitutionality" (2009) 7 Int. J. Constitutional Law 183 (arguing that British courts have an inherent power to issue non-binding, common law "declarations of unconstitutionality" when Parliament legislates against constitutional norms); S. Lakin, "Debunking the Idea of Parliamentary Sovereignty: The Controlling Factor of Legality in the British Constitution" (2008) 28 O.J.L.S. 709 (contending that the idea of Parliamentary sovereignty is misconceived and arguing that the British constitution instead rests on the ideal of government under law or the principle of legality); Sir John Laws, "Constitutional Guarantees" (2008) 29 Stat. L.R. 1; and M. Gordon, "The Conceptual Foundations of Parliamentary Sovereignty: Reconsidering Jennings and Wade" [2009] P.L. 519.

[80]   J. Laws, "Law and Democracy" [1995] P.L. 72, 87 (and see also 92).

words.[81] Lord Donaldson, a former Master of the Rolls, speaking in relation to an ouster clause proposed by the Government, speculated that had it been passed by Parliament "the judges would have said, 'We're not having this'".[82]

The matter was considered in a number of obiter dicta in *Jackson v Attorney General*, a case in which the House of Lords was called on to consider the validity of the Hunting Act 2004, which had received Royal Assent under the Parliament Acts.[83] While Lord Bingham felt that Parliamentary sovereignty was still "the bedrock of the British constitution",[84] Lord Steyn said that while parliamentary sovereignty is the *general* principle of our constitution:

1-028

> "It is a construct of the common law. The judges created this principle. If that is so, it is not unthinkable that circumstances could arise where the courts may have to qualify a principle established on a different hypothesis of constitutionalism. In exceptional circumstances involving an attempt to abolish judicial review or the ordinary role of the courts, the Appellate Committee of the House of Lords or a new Supreme Court may have to consider whether this is a constitutional fundamental which even a sovereign Parliament acting at the behest of a complaisant House of Commons cannot abolish."[85]

Lord Hope, was even more unequivocal. He said that "The rule of law enforced by the courts is the ultimate controlling factor on which our constitution is based".[86] In a later case, Lord Hope said "The question whether the principle of the sovereignty of the United Kingdom Parliament is absolute or may be subject to limitation in exceptional circumstances is still under discussion".[87]

Without, however, directly challenging the primacy of parliamentary sovereignty, the courts have, as we have discussed, finessed the apparent inconsistency between the rule of law and parliamentary supremacy by making the presumption that Parliament intended its legislation to conform to the rule of law as a constitutional principle. This presumption is powerful and is not easily rebutted; only express words or possibly necessary implication will suffice.[88] If officials refuse an individual reasonable access to the courts, or discriminate against a class of

1-029

---

[81] H. Woolf, "Droit Public - English Style" [1995] P.L. 57, 68-69 ("However, if Parliament did the unthinkable, then I would say that the courts would also be required to act in a manner which would be without precedent. Some judges might choose to do so by saying that it was an unrebuttable presumption that Parliament could never intend such a result. I myself would consider there were advantages in making it clear that ultimately there are even limits on the supremacy of Parliament which it is the courts' inalienable responsibility to identify and uphold. They are limits of the most modest dimensions which I believe any democrat would accept. They are no more than are necessary to enable the rule of law to be preserved").

[82] *Hansard*, HL Vol.667, col.746 (7 December 2004). He continued: "How the judges could have done that is a different matter. One possibility would be that they might have grounded their opposition, and based their insistence on taking jurisdiction, on the rule of law. We have a tripartite constitution, unwritten though it may be, under which it is not open to any two of the three components simply to close down the third. I make that point because I would not like the statement to go uncontradicted that in all circumstances Parliament is superior to the rule of law. It is in 99 out of 100 cases, yes, but not in all circumstances". The proposed ouster clause, which was not enacted, is set out at 1-055 below.

[83] *Jackson v Attorney General* [2005] UKHL 56; [2006] 1 A.C. 262 at [102]; also Lord Hope at [120] and Baroness Hale at [36]. For analysis of the constitutional significance of *Jackson*, see J. Jowell, "Parliamentary Sovereignty under the New Constitutional Hypothesis" [2006] P.L. 562; A.L. Young, "Hunting Sovereignty: Jackson v Her Majesty's Attorney-General" [2006] P.L. 187; A. McHarg, "What is Delegated Legislation" [2006] P.L. 539.

[84] *Jackson* [2005] UKHL 56; [2006] 1 A.C. 262 at [9].

[85] *Jackson* [2005] UKHL 56; [2006] 1 A.C. 262 at [102]; also Baroness Hale at [36].

[86] *Jackson* [2005] UKHL 56; [2006] 1 A.C. 262 at [107].

[87] *AXA General Insurance Ltd and others v HM Advocate and others* [2011] UKSC 46; [2012] 1 A.C. 868 at [50].

[88] See 11-057.

individuals, the courts will usually intervene to correct such breaches of the rule of law or other constitutional principle unless the language of the statute clearly and unambiguously prohibits this.[89]

Certainty and flexibility

1-030   The concrete application and elucidation of broad constitutional principles are not self-evident or static. It is for the courts to articulate them. The general principles are specifically implemented in the context of contemporary standards of fairness as well as other values.[90] For example, that aspect of the rule of law that requires legal certainty and predictability is practically applied through the emerging requirement that "legitimate expectations" should be fulfilled in appropriate circumstances.[91] Values such as these are part of our general legal system, developed in accordance with accepted norms as to the proper role of the democratic state and the rights of individuals within it.[92]

1-031   However, many of the standards applied through judicial review are necessarily open-textured. It has been claimed that some of them, such as natural justice, fairness, or reasonableness, are so vague as to be practically meaningless. Lord Reid rightly regarded these claims as "tainted by the perennial fallacy that because something cannot be cut and dried or nicely weighed or measured therefore it does not exist".[93] Judicial review will naturally search for precision, as an aid to the prediction and prescription of administratively fair and correct practices. Yet it cannot afford entirely to abandon flexibility (a principle by no means inferior to that of certainty, aimed at individuated justice).[94] The search for precise standards will always need to be accompanied by a recognition of the particular circumstances of a special case, depending upon the breadth of the power conferred upon the decision-maker; the conditions of its exercise; the availability of alternative procedural protections, and the fairness to the parties involved (and to others affected by the decision). It is for these reasons that the courts themselves retain discretion in the grant of remedies in judicial review.[95]

Rights to administrative justice

1-032   The constitutional foundations of "administrative justice" are underlined by the fact that a number of national constitutions have embodied a right to "just" or

---

[89]   See, e.g. *R. v Secretary of State for the Home Department Ex p. Leech (No.2)* [1994] Q.B. 198; 5-041, and recently *R. (on the application of Unison) v Lord Chancellor* [2017] UKSC 51; [2017] 3 W.L.R. 409 (holding that excessive court fees violated access to employment tribunals (such access being a key ingredient of the rule of law).

[90]   See, e.g. Lord Diplock's definition of the ground of review of irrationality as reflecting "accepted moral standards" in *Council of Civil Service Union v Minister for the Civil Service* [1985] A.C. 374.

[91]   See Ch.12.

[92]   During the 1990s a series of English judges, writing extra judicially, sought to place judicial review within the context of democratic rights: Lord Scarman, "The Development of Administrative Law: Obstacles and Opportunities" [1990] P.L. 490; Lord Browne-Wilkinson, "The Infiltration of a Bill of Rights" [1992] P.L. 397; Sir John Laws, "Judicial Remedies and the Constitution" (1994) 57 M.L.R. 213, and "Law and Democracy" [1995] P.L. 72; Lord Woolf, "Droit Public - English Style" [1995] P.L. 57; Sir Stephen Sedley, "The Sound of Silence: Constitutional Law Without a Constitution" (1994) 110 L.Q.R. 270.

[93]   *Ridge v Baldwin* [1964] A.C. 40 at 64-65.

[94]   D. Galligan, *Discretionary Powers* (1986). For further discussion on discretion, see 5-017; and for the tension between rules and discretion, see Chs 9 and 12.

[95]   See 18-047.

"good" administrative action—including Namibia,[96] South Africa[97] and the Cayman Islands.[98] The Charter of Fundamental Rights of the European Union now incorporates the right to "good administrative practice".[99] Within the United Kingdom, there have been proposals for a right to administrative justice but none have come to fruition. The Human Rights Commission for Northern Ireland recommended that a new Bill of Rights for Northern Ireland include a right to "civil and administrative justice", which encompasses the right to "administrative action that is lawful, procedurally fair, rational, proportionate and taken within a reasonable time". It also includes the right of access to public information and imposes a duty on public authorities to give reasons for their decisions and, where feasible, provide appropriate mechanisms for internal review or appeal of their decisions.[100] In 2012, a right to administrative justice was also considered for the United Kingdom by the Commission on a Bill of Rights.[101]

In some jurisdictions, the grounds of judicial review have come to be codified in statute,[102] but as yet that has not been considered necessary here as there is thus far no quarrel that the incremental development of the common law has satisfactorily fashioned a balance between the need for efficiency and the need to prevent abuses of power. **1-033**

---

[96] Constitution of the Republic of Namibia 1990 (as amended) art.18: "Administrative bodies and administrative officials shall act fairly and reasonably and comply with the requirements imposed upon such bodies and officials by common law and any relevant legislation, and persons aggrieved by the exercise of such acts and decisions shall have the right to seek redress before a competent Court or Tribunal".

[97] Constitution of the Republic of South Africa 1996 s.33: "(1) Everyone has the right to administrative action that is lawful, reasonable and procedurally fair. (2) Everyone whose rights have been adversely affected by administrative action has the right to be given written reasons. (3) National legislation must be enacted to give effect to these rights, and must— (a) provide for the review of administrative action by a court or, where appropriate, an independent and impartial tribunal; (b) impose a duty on the state to give effect to the rights in subsections (1) and (2); and (c) promote an efficient administration".

[98] Cayman Islands Constitution Order 2009 (SI 2009/1379), Sch.2 art.19: "(1) All decisions and acts of public officials must be lawful, rational, proportionate and procedurally fair. (2) Every person whose interests have been adversely affected by such a decision or act has the right to request and be given written reasons for that decision or act".

[99] Charter of Fundamental Rights of the European Union (see 14-030). The right here includes the right to have one's affairs handled impartially, fairly and within a reasonable time and the right to reasons and the right of access to your case file. There is no directly comparable right in ECHR, though arts 6 and 13 go some way to ensuring effective judicial remedies (see 6-048, 7-031, 13-010 and 13-033).

[100] See Northern Ireland Human Rights Commission, *A Bill of Rights for Northern Ireland* (December 2008), p.44.

[101] Commission on a Bill of Rights, *A UK Bill of Rights? The Choice Before Us* (2012), para.8.33.

[102] e.g. in Australia: Administrative Decisions (Judicial Review) Act 1977 ss.5-7; in South Africa: Promotion of Administrative Justice Act, 2000; in Trinidad and Tobago: Judicial Review Act No.60 of 2000 s.5(3); in Barbados: Administrative Justice Act 1980. See further R. Ramlogen, *Judicial Review in the Commonwealth Caribbean* (2007). The EU Parliament has recently proposed codifying principles of good administration within EU institutions: see Committee on Legal Affairs, *Procedure of the European Union with recommendations to the Commission on a Law of Administrative* (2012/2024(INI)).

JUSTICIABILITY: THE LIMITS OF JUDICIAL REVIEW

1-034   Judicial review has developed to the point where it is possible to say that no power—whether statutory, common law or under the prerogative[103]—is any longer inherently unreviewable. Courts are charged with the responsibility of adjudicating upon the manner of the exercise of a public power, its scope and its substance.[104] As we shall see, even when discretionary powers are engaged, they are not immune from judicial review. Discretion has been described as the "hole in the [legal] doughnut",[105] but that hole is not automatically a lawless void. Nevertheless, there are certain decisions which courts cannot or should not easily engage. Courts are limited (a) by their constitutional role[106] and (b) by their institutional capacity.[107]

Limitations inherent in the courts' constitutional role

1-035   The principle of the separation of powers confers matters of social and economic policy upon the legislature and the executive, rather than the judiciary. Courts should, therefore, avoid interfering with the exercise of discretion by the legislature

---

[103] On the sources of public power, see Ch.5.

[104] See Ch.11; J. Jowell, "What Decisions Should Judges Not Take?" in M. Andenas and D. Fairgrieve (eds), *Tom Bingham and the Transformation of the Law* (2009), Ch.9; A. Kavanagh, "Judging Judges under the Human Rights Act: Deference, Disillusionment and the 'War on Terror' [2009] P.L. 287.

[105] R. Dworkin, *Taking Rights Seriously* (1977), p.82.

[106] In *Khaira v Shergill* [2014] UKSC 33; [2015] A.C. 359, the Supreme Court reviewed the application of the principle of non-justiciability in the context of the interpretation and validity of the trust deeds of Sikh religious charities. Lord Neuberger PSC observed: "[41] .... the term non-justiciability refers ... to a case where an issue is said to be inherently unsuitable for judicial determination by reason only of its subject matter. Such cases generally fall into one of two categories. [42] The first category comprises cases where the issue in question is beyond the constitutional competence assigned to the courts under our conception of the separation of powers. Cases in this category are rare, and rightly so, for they may result in a denial of justice which could only exceptionally be justified either at common law or under ECHR art.6. The paradigm cases are the non-justiciability of certain transactions of foreign states and of proceedings in Parliament. The first is based in part on the constitutional limits of the court's competence as against that of the executive in matters directly affecting the United Kingdom's relations with foreign states ... The second is based on the constitutional limits of the court's competence as against that of Parliament ...".

[107] In *Khaira v Shargill* [2014] UKSC 33 at [43] Lord Neuberger said that a matter could also be non-justiciable if it "comprises claims or defences which are based neither on private legal rights or obligations, nor on reviewable matters of public law. Examples include domestic disputes; transactions not intended by the participants to affect their legal relations; and issues of international law which engage no private right of the claimant or reviewable question of public law. Some issues might well be non-justiciable in this sense if the court were asked to decide them in the abstract. But they must nevertheless be resolved if their resolution is necessary in order to decide some other issue which is in itself justiciable. The best-known examples are in the domain of public law. Thus, when the court declines to adjudicate on the international acts of foreign sovereign states or to review the exercise of the Crown's prerogative in the conduct of foreign affairs, it normally refuses on the ground that no legal right of the citizen is engaged whether in public or private law: *R. (Campaign for Nuclear Disarmament) v Prime Minister* [2002] EWHC 2777 (Admin); *R. (Al-Haq) v Secretary of State for Foreign and Commonwealth Affairs* [2009] EWHC 1910 (Admin). ... But the court does adjudicate on these matters if a justiciable legitimate expectation or a Convention right depends on it: *R. (Abbasi) v Secretary of State for Foreign and Commonwealth Affairs* [2003] UKHRR 76; *R. (Guernsey) v Secretary of State for Environment, Food and Rural Affairs* [2016] EWHC 1847 (Admin); [2016] 4 W.L.R. 145. The same would apply if a private law liability was asserted which depended on such a matter. As Lord Bingham of Cornhill observed in *R. (Gentle) v Prime Minister* [2008] A.C. 1356, para.8, there are 'issues which judicial tribunals have traditionally been very reluctant to entertain because they recognise their limitations as suitable bodies to resolve them. This is not to say that if the claimants have a legal right the courts cannot decide it'."

or executive when its aim is the pursuit of policy.[108] It is not for judges to weigh utilitarian calculations of social, economic or political preference.[109] Courts will not, therefore, make decisions on: whether site A or B is suitable for the location of a new airport[110]; whether the United Kingdom should engage in a programme of nuclear disarmament[111]; whether there should be investment in a significant nuclear power programme[112]; whether the programme to produce Trident nuclear warheads should be abandoned[113]; whether there should be further regulation on the

---

[108] See, e.g. *R. v Secretary of State for Trade and Industry Ex p. Lonrho Plc* [1989] 1 W.L.R. 525 at 536 (Lord Keith: "These provisions [that the Secretary of State may act against a proposed merger after a report by the Monopolies and Mergers Commission has so advised to Parliament and the Secretary of State acts by a draft order laid before Parliament] ensure that a decision which is essentially political in character will be brought to the attention of Parliament and subject to scrutiny and challenge therein, and the courts must be careful not to invade the political field and substitute their own judgment for that of the Minister. The courts judge the lawfulness not the wisdom of the decision"); *Wilson v First County Trust Ltd (No.2)* [2003] UKHL 40; [2004] 1 A.C. 816 at [70] (Lord Nicholls: "The more the legislation concerns matters of broad social policy the less ready will be a court to intervene"); *R. (on the application of Hooper) v Secretary of State for Work and Pensions* [2003] EWCA Civ 813; [2003] 1 W.L.R. 2623 at [63]-[64] (Laws LJ: "A very considerable margin of discretion must be accorded to the Secretary of State. Difficult questions of economic and social policy were involved, the resolution of which fell within the province of the executive and the legislature rather than the courts"), reversed on appeal: [2005] UKHL 29; [2005] 1 W.L.R. 1681; *R. v Secretary of State for Education and Employment Ex p. Begbie* [2000] 1 W.L.R. 1115 at 1131 (Laws LJ, stating that less intrusive judicial review should apply to decisions in the "macropolitical field"); see further 11-086. In *R. (on the application of Reilly and Wilson) v Secretary of State for Work and Pensions* [2013] UKSC 68; [2014] A.C. 453; [2013] EWCA Civ 66; [2013] 1 W.L.R. 2239, in a successful challenge to the legality of the Jobseeker's Allowance (Employment, Skills and Enterprise Scheme) Regulations 2011, Sir Stanley Burnton stated in the Court of Appeal: "I emphasise that this case is not about the social, economic or other merits of the Employment, Skills and Enterprise Scheme. Parliament is entitled to authorise the creation and administration of schemes that ... are designed to assist the unemployed to obtain employment ... Parliament is equally entitled to encourage participation ... by imposing sanctions ... on those who without good cause refuse to participate in a suitable scheme. The appeal is solely about the lawfulness of the Regulations?..." Both the Court of Appeal and the Supreme Court held the regulations to be ultra vires.

[109] Dworkin's definition of policy: R. Dworkin, "Political Judges and the Rule of Law" (1978) 64 *Proceedings of the British Academy* 259. On his distinction between "principle" and "policy", see *Taking Rights Seriously* (1977), pp.82-87. Sometimes the term used is "political question", especially in the USA.

[110] *Essex CC v Ministry of Housing and Local Government* (1967) 66 L.G.R. 23 (it would be quite futile to impugn the government's decision that Foulness should be developed as the third London airport, merely by contending that the decision was unreasonable or that Cublington was more suitable); cf. *R. (on the application of Medway Council) v Secretary of State for Transport, Local Government and the Regions* [2002] EWHC 2516; [2003] J.P.L. 583 (decision to exclude Gatwick airport from consultation about expansion of air transport capacity in SE England was unreasonable).

[111] *Chandler v DPP* [1964] A.C. 763 at 798 (Lord Radcliffe said, that this was an issue of "policy" and that "the more one looks at it, the plainer it becomes, I think, that the question whether it is in the true interests of the country to acquire, retain or house nuclear armaments depends upon an infinity of considerations, military and diplomatic, technical, psychological and moral, and of decisions, tentative or final, which are themselves part assessments of fact and part expectations and hopes. I do not think that there is anything amiss with a legal ruling that does not make this issue a matter for judge or jury").

[112] *R. (on the application of Greenpeace Ltd) v Secretary of State for Trade and Industry* [2007] EWHC 311 (Admin); [2007] Env. L.R. 29 (a government review which, on the basis of a short period of consultation, recommended reversing the government's policy against nuclear power, was flawed for illegality; the consultation was not sufficient by the standards of the Aarhus Convention art.7 (UNECE Convention on Access to Information, Public Participation in Decision-making and Access to Justice in Environmental Matters); despite being a matter of "high policy", the review was so deficient in content and form that its process was "manifestly unfair").

[113] *R. (on the application of Marchiori) v Environment Agency* [2002] EWCA Civ 3; [2002] Eu. L.R.

environmental effects of crop-spraying[114]; or whether the British invasion of Iraq in 2003 was justified in international law.[115]

1-036   Speaking extra-judicially shortly before becoming a member of the Supreme Court, Lord Sumption argued that the "tendency of the courts to intervene in the making of 'macro policy' has become more pronounced in recent years", with "the whole process ... unduly influenced by the degree of judicial aversion to the policy in question"[116]—an assessment rejected as conflating government and legislature "to suggest that both ought to be equally immunised by the democratic credentials from judicial oversight".[117]

1-037   The constitutional status of the judiciary should not, however, excuse the courts from any scrutiny of policy decisions. Courts are able, and indeed obliged, to require that decisions, even in the realm of "high policy"[118] are within the scope of the relevant legal power or duty,[119] and arrived at by the legal standards of procedural fairness.[120] The courts display reserve in impinging upon the substance of policy decisions, but even here they may legitimately intervene if the decision is devoid of reason and not properly justified.[121] Judges always possess the capacity to probe the evidence and assess whether the reasons and motives for decisions are rationally related to their aims. As will be shown in the chapters that follow,

---

225.

[114] *Secretary of State for Environment, Food and Rural Affairs v Downs* [2009] EWCA Civ 664; (2009) 153(27) S.J.L.B. 29: this fell within a "difficult social and technical sphere in which a balance must be struck between the competing interests of the individual and the community as a whole".

[115] *R. (on the application of Gentle) v Prime Minister* [2008] UKHL 20; [2008] 1 A.C. 1356. Lord Bingham noting at [8] the "restraint traditionally shown by the courts in ruling on what has been called high policy—peace and war, the making of treaties, the conduct of foreign relations".

[116] J. Sumption, "Judicial and Politicial Decision-making: the Uncertain Boundary" [2011] J.R. 301, para.12.

[117] S. Sedley, "Judicial Politics" (2012) 34 *London Review of Books* 15 ("executive government exercises public powers which are created or recognised by law and have legal limits that it is the courts' constitutional task to patrol").

[118] *R. v Secretary of State for the Home Department Ex p. Everett* [1989] Q.B. 811 (Taylor LJ), such as making treaties, dissolving Parliament, mobilising the armed forces. See 3-034.

[119] On notion of "target duties", see 5-064; *R. (on the application of Bancoult) v Secretary of State for Foreign and Commonwealth Affairs* [2007] EWCA Civ 498; (2007) 104 (23) L.S.G. 31 at [46] (Sedley LJ considered that very broad latitude is given to the executive in deciding what makes for the "peace, order and good government" of a colony but that the executive must be open to challenge on grounds of jurisdictional error or malpractice or if the subject matter "is manifestly not the peace, order or good government of the colony"). In *R. (on the application of Reilly and Wilson) v Secretary of State for Work and Pensions* [2013] UKSC 68; [2014] A.C. 453, the Supreme Court upheld the decision of the Court of Appeal that the Jobseeker's Allowance (Employment, Skills and Enterprise Scheme) Regulations 2011 were ultra vires because the Scheme did not have a "prescribed description" as required by s.17A(1) of the Jobseekers Act 1995. Retrospective legislation (the Jobseekers (Back to Work Schemes) Act 2013) to negate the financial effects of that decision was subsequently made the subject of a declaration of incompatibility in *R. (on the application of Reilly (No.2) and Hewstone) v Secretary of State for Work and Pensions* [2014] EWHC 2182 (Admin) (4 July 2014) as being incompatible with ECHR art.6.

[120] See, e.g. *R. (on the application of Medway Council) v Secretary of State for Transport, Local Government and the Regions* [2002] EWHC 2516; [2003] J.P.L. 583; *R. (on the application of Greenpeace Ltd) v Secretary of State for Trade and Industry* [2007] EWHC 311 Admin. In other jurisdictions, see: *Peters v Davidson* [1999] 2 N.Z.L.R. 164 (New Zealand) and *Operation Dismantle v The Queen* [1985] 1 S.C.R. 441 (Canada).

[121] A. Barak, "Foreword: A Judge on Judging: The Role of a Supreme Court in a Democracy" (2002) Harv L.R. 16, 97-106 (the former President of the Israeli Supreme Court does not admit that any decisions are inherently non-justiciable for this reason).

public law has rapidly advanced recently from a "culture of authority" to a "culture of justification".[122]

Thus even where the courts recognise their lack of relative constitutional capacity to make the primary decision of policy, they should nevertheless not easily relinquish their secondary function of probing the quality of the reasoning and ensuring that assertions are properly justified. As Lord Nicholls said in *Ghaidan v Godin-Mendoza*[123] in respect of national housing policy:

1-038

> "Parliament has to hold a fair balance between the competing interests of tenants and landlords, taking into account broad issues of social and economic policy. But, even in such a field, where the alleged violation comprises differential treatment based upon grounds such as race or sex or sexual orientation the court will scrutinise with intensity any reasons said to constitute justification".

In addition, it should be borne in mind that under the Human Rights Act 1998 no public authority may interfere with Convention rights and even Parliament is expected to abide by their terms.[124] When adjudicating on the scope of interference with Convention rights, therefore, the courts need not defer to the executive on the ground of their responsibility to Parliament. Nor need they defer to Parliament on the ground that it is elected[125]; though deference to elected members may be legitimate on the ground that they, rather than the court, are better equipped at deciding particular questions requiring an assessment of the public interest.[126] The

1-039

---

[122] The words of the late Professor Etienne Mureinik describing the transformation in post-apartheid public law in South Africa: "A Bridge Too Far: Introducing the Interim Bill of Rights" (1994) 10 S. African J. of Human Rights 31. See further 11-100.

[123] *Ghaidan v Godin-Mendoza* [2004] UKHL 30; [2004] 2 A.C. 557 at [19].

[124] See Ch.13; and A.L. Young, "Is Dialogue Working Under the Human Rights Act 1998?" [2011] P.L. 773. And see, e.g. *R. (on the application of Lord Carlile) v Secretary of State for the Home Department* [2014] UKSC 60; [2015] A.C. 945, [28]–[29] (Lord Sumption: "The Human Rights Act 1998 did not abrogate the constitutional distribution of powers between the organs of the state which the courts had recognised for many years before it was passed. ... However, traditional notions of the constitutional distribution of powers have unquestionably been modified by the Human Rights Act 1998. In the first place, any arguable allegation that a person's Convention rights have been infringed is necessarily justiciable").

[125] *R. v Inland Revenue Commissioners Ex p. National Federation of Self-Employed and Small Businesses Ltd* [1982] A.C. 617 at 644 (Lord Diplock: "It is not, in my view, a sufficient answer to say that judicial review of the actions of officers or departments of central governments is unnecessary because they are accountable to Parliament for the way in which they carry out their functions. They are accountable to Parliament for what they do so far as regards efficiency and policy, and of that Parliament is the only judge; they are responsible to a court of justice for the lawfulness of what they do, and of that the court is the only judge"). This view towards judicial deference on constitutional grounds is shared by Lord Steyn, "Deference: A Tangled Story" [2005] P.L. 346; J. Jowell, "Judicial Deference and Human Rights: A Question of Competence", in P. Craig and R. Rawlings (eds), *Law and Administration in Europe, Essays in Honour of Carol Harlow* (2005), p.67; Jowell, "Judicial Deference: Servility, Civility to Institutional Capacity" [2003] P.L. 592. In respect of "common law" rights the courts may presume that Parliament did not intend to abrogate the right unless clearly enunciated—"the principle of "legality" (on which see 5-036). cf. *Rehman v Secretary of State for the Home Department* [2001] UKHL 47; [2003] 1 A.C. 153 at [62] (Lord Hoffmann contended that matters of national security "must be made by persons whom the people have elected and whom they can remove"). For a rather different take on deference, approaching the question from the perspective of the administrative decision maker, see M. Lewans, *Administrative Law and Judicial Deference* (2016).

[126] See, e.g. in relation to local authorities: *R. v Brighton Corp Ex p. Tilling (Thomas) Ltd* (1916) 85 L.J.K.B. 1552 at 1555 (public transport licensing); *Sagnata Investments Ltd v Norwich Corp* [1971] 2 Q.B. 614 (amusement arcade permit); *Cumings v Birkenhead Corp* [1972] Ch. 12 (local educational policy); *Cannock Chase DC v Kelly* [1978] 1 W.L.R. 1 (allocation of tenancies of council houses); *Pickwell v Camden LBC* [1983] Q.B. 962 (allocation of salaries and wages even though

courts possess the legitimacy to guard the invasion of those rights that now form the basis of our constitutional democracy.[127]

Limitations inherent in the courts' institutional capacity

1-040   In respect of the institutional capacity of the courts, there are some decisions which they are ill-equipped to review—those which are not ideally justiciable or, in other words, "not amenable to the judicial process",[128] or indeed those which are better able to be determined by other bodies, including Parliament.

Matters which are in essence matters of preference

1-041   These include decisions which cannot be impugned on the basis of any objective standard because their resolution is essentially a matter of individual (including political) preference. Where the Secretary of State had the power to decide whether the expenditure of local authorities had been "excessive" and to penalise them if it had been, the House of Lords held that decision not suited to judicial determination because of the lack of "objective criteria" by which to determine the

---

strike still in progress). But note the caution expressed in *Huang v Secretary of State for the Home Department* [2007] UKHL 11; [2007] 2 A.C. 167 at [17] (HL found unpersuasive the submission of the Secretary of State that the decision-maker and the court should assume that the immigration rules adopted by the responsible minister and laid before Parliament "had the imprimatur of democratic approval and should be taken to strike the right balance between the interests of the individual and those of the community"). In *R. (on the application of Sinclair Collis Ltd) v Secretary of State for Health* [2011] EWCA Civ 437; [2012] Q.B. 394 (on the lawfulness under EU law and Convention rights of delegated legislation banning the sale of tobacco from automatic vending machines) the CA accepted, with different nuances, that "the involvement of the legislature is a factor favouring a broader margin of appreciation than would be appropriate to a purely executive decision" (Lord Neuberger of Abbotsbury MR at [211]-[214]), though this was not inevitably the case when all the relevant factors were taken into account (Arden LJ at [151]-[155]).

[127] In *R. (on the application of Nicklinson) v Ministry of Justice* [2014] UKSC 38; [2015] A.C. 657 a nine-member Supreme Court engaged in a discussion of these issues in the context of the imposition of criminal liability under s.2 of the Suicide Act 1961 on those who assisted suicide. Lord Neuberger stated: "[72] ... even under our constitutional settlement, which acknowledges parliamentary supremacy and has no written constitution, it is, in principle, open to a domestic court to consider whether s.2 infringes art.8. The more difficult question ... is whether we should do so. ... [76] ... while I respect and understand the contrary opinion, so well articulated by Lord Sumption and Lord Hughes, I am of the view that, provided that the evidence and the arguments justified such a conclusion, we could properly hold that section 2 infringed article 8. ... More specifically, where the court has jurisdiction on an issue falling within the margin of appreciation, I think it would be wrong in principle to rule out exercising that jurisdiction if Parliament addresses the issue ... such an approach would be an abdication of judicial responsibility ... given the potential for rapid changes in moral values and medicine, it seems to me that such an approach may well turn out to be inappropriate in relation to this particular issue." Having said that, Lord Neuberger concluded that it would not be appropriate to grant a declaration of incompatibility at this time. Lords Sumption, Clarke, Reed and Hughes considered that it would be institutionally inappropriate, or only institutionally appropriate if Parliament refused to address the issue, for a domestic court to consider whether s.2 infringed the ECHR. Lady Hale and Lord Kerr, however, did consider it to be institutionally appropriate at the current time and concluded that s.2 was not Convention compliant. On 11 September 2015, the House of Commons rejected a private member's bill on assisted dying by 330 to 180. On 18 July 2015 the House of Lords was split in a debate on Lord Falconer's private member's bill. In *R. (Conway) v Secretary of State for Justice* [2017] EWHC 640 (Admin); [2017] A.C.D. 62, the Queen's Bench Division rejecting an application for permission to apply for judicial review, held that, following the consideration given to the issue by both the House of Commons and House of Lords, it remained inappropriate to issue a declaration of incompatibility.

[128] *Council for the Civil Service Unions v Minister for the Civil Service* [1985] 1 A.C. 374 at 418 (Lord Roskill).

content of excessive expenditure.[129] Following the events of September 2001, the Government sought to derogate from ECHR art.5 on the ground specified in art.15 that there was a "public emergency threatening the life of the nation". The majority of the House of Lords held this to be a "pre-eminently political question", on the ground that it involved a prediction of what people around the world would do. The basis of this view was less that it was a question which lay, constitutionally, with the executive, than it required a judgment which admitted of no objective challenge.[130] In *R. (on the application of Wheeler) v Office of the Prime Minister* the claimant sought judicial review of the Government's decision not to hold a referendum on whether the United Kingdom should ratify the Treaty of Lisbon. Dismissing the claim, the Divisional Court doubted whether the correctness of the Government's assessment that the Lisbon Treaty was materially different from the Constitution Treaty (in respect of which a referendum had been promised) was justiciable as that "depends on political perspective and political judgment", adding: "At best, it is a matter to be approached on a *Wednesbury* basis; and on that basis we are far from persuaded that the assessment is an unreasonable on a *Wednesbury* basis".[131] In a case incolving the UK's powers over an Overseas Territory, Lord Rodger of Earlsferry took the view that it is not for the courts to substitute their view for that of the Foreign Secretary advising Her Majesty in Council that executive legislation was for the "peace, order and good government" of the British Indian Ocean Territories.[132]

Matters in relation to which the court lacks expertise

A second institutional limitation of the courts is lack of relative expertise.[133]   **1-042**
Particularly as the review of fact, or the merits of a decision, is not routinely permit-

---

[129] *R. v Secretary of State for the Environment Ex p. Hammersmith and Fulham LBC* [1991] 1 A.C. 521 at 593, 597 (Lord Bridge); *Buttes Gas v Hammer* [1982] A.C. 888 (Lord Diplock, in a case involving relations with a foreign state, said that the court has "no justiciable or manageable standards by which to judge" the issue. To attempt such review, he said, the court would be in a "judicial no-man's land"); *Gillick v West Norfolk & Wisbech Area Health Authority* [1986] 1 A.C. 112 at 193 (the court should exercise its jurisdiction with the "utmost restraint" in cases involving "questions of social and ethical controversy"); *Airedale NHS Trust v Bland* [1993] A.C. 789 at 891 (Lord Mustill); *Roberts v Hopwood* [1925] A.C. 578 at 606–607 (Sumner LJ); S. Sorabjee, "Decisions of the Supreme Court in S.R. Rommai v Union of India " (1994) 3 S.C.C. (Jour) 2.

[130] *X v Secretary of State for the Home Department* [2004] UKHL 56; [2005] 2 A.C. 68 (Belmarsh detainees case). Lord Hoffmann, dissenting, held firmly that the events did not amount to a threat to the nation's life (which he considered included not only in the physical sense but in the sense of its entire cultural fabric, including its attachment to values of civil liberty).

[131] *R. (on the application of Wheeler) v Office of the Prime Minister* 2008 EWHC 936 (Admin); [2008] 2 C.M.L.R. 57 at [37]. See also *Wheeler v Office of the Prime Minister* [2014] EWHC 3815 (Admin); [2015] 1 C.M.L.R 46 at [44]–[47] (enforcement of a legitimate expectation that a parliamentary vote would be held concerning European Arrest Warrants would involve a breach of art.9 of the Bill of Rights 1689, a breach of parliamentary privilege and breach the separation of powers).

[132] *R. (on the application of Bancoult) v Secretary of State for Foreign and Commonwealth Affairs (No.2)* [2008] UKHL 61; [2006] 1 A.C. 453 at [130] ("it is not for the courts to declare the law invalid on that ground. Once they enter upon such territory they could very easily get into the area of challenging what is essentially a political judgment, which is not for the courts of law"). And see further D. McGoldrick, "The Boundaries of Justiciability" (2010) 59 I.C.L.Q. 981 (considering recent decisions on justifiability in the sphere of foreign affairs, international relations, defence and national security).

[133] See, e.g. *R. v Secretary of State for the Home Department Ex p. Swati* [1986] 1 W.L.R. 477; *R. v Chief Constable of the Merseyside Police Ex p. Calveley* [1986] 1 Q.B. 424; *Pulhofer v Hillingdon LBC* [1986] A.C. 484; *R. v Secretary of State for Social Services Ex p. Stitt* [1990] C.O.D. 288; *R. (on the application of W) v Thetford Youth Justices* [2002] EWHC 1252; (2002) 166 J.P. 453 at [40] (Sedley LJ: "A youth court has expertise which a higher court lacks"); *R. (on the application of Legal*

ted in judicial review,[134] there are some matters which are best resolved by those with specialist knowledge.[135] Connected with the issue of expertise is that of risk-assessment.[136]

1-043 National security was often said to be an area in which the courts should not readily intervene, not merely because the executive possess prime constitutional responsibility in this area, but because they may be best placed to assess, through their network of informers, the risk of the dangers involved.[137] However, here too the court will no longer unquestioningly accept the say-so of the executive or other experts, and will properly intervene if the decision is based on a material mistake of fact,[138] is incompatible with Convention rights contrary to the Human Rights Act 1998,[139] or is otherwise illegal or irrational, or is affected by procedural

---

Remedy UK Ltd) v Secretary of State for Health [2007] EWHC 1252 (Admin) (court wary of "donning the garb of policy maker" in challenge to restructuring of postgraduate medical training); M. Hunt "Sovereignty's blight: why public law needs 'due deference'" in N. Bamforth and P. Leyland (eds) *Public Law in a Multi-layered Constitution* (2003); A. Young "In defence of due deference" (2009) 72 M.L.R. 554; A. Kavanagh "Defending deference in public law and constitutional theory" (2010) 126 L.Q.R. 236; for a more sceptical approach see T. Allan "Human rights and judicial review: a critique of 'due deference'" (2006) 65 C.L.J. 671; T. Allan "Judicial deference and judicial review: legal doctrine and legal theory" (2011) 127 L.Q.R. 96.

[134] On precedent fact, see 4-051; on mistake of fact, see 11-041.

[135] See, e.g. *R. v Higher Education Funding Council Ex p. Institute of Dental Surgery* [1994] 1 W.L.R. 242 (Sedley J considered the question of rating the research of a university department not amenable to review on the ground of lack of the court's expertise); cf. *R. (on the application of Wooder) v Feggetter* [2002] EWCA Civ 554; [2003] Q.B. 219 at [40] (Sedley LJ doubted whether he would necessarily reach that decision again). In *R. (on the application of Mott) v Environment Agency* [2016] EWCA Civ 564; [2016] 1 W.L.R. 4338 the Court of Appeal reversed a finding by the court below that a decision by the Environment Agency had been unsupported by scientific evidence (Beatson LJ: "A reviewing court should be very slow to conclude that the expert and experienced decision-maker assigned the task by statute has reached a perverse scientific conclusion.") Lack of expertise on the part of the Administrative Court is one reason for the insistence that claimants use alternative means of legal challenge where they exist: 16-016.

[136] See, e.g. *R. (on the application of Farrakhan) v Secretary of State for the Home Department* [2002] EWCA Civ 606; [2002] Q.B. 1391; *R. v Secretary of State for the Home Department Ex p. Turgut* [2001] 1 All E.R. 719 at 729 (Simon Brown LJ: "The court is hardly less well placed than the Secretary of State himself to evaluate the risk once the relevant material is placed before it"); *X v Secretary of State for the Home Department* [2004] UKHL 56; [2005] 2 A.C. 68 (assessment of whether there was a public emergency threatening the life of the nation was "pre-eminently political in character, to be made by the executive and Parliament"); *R. (on the application of Lord Carlile) v Secretary of State for the Home Department* [2014] UKSC 60; [2015] A.C. 945, [49], in a case concerning the exclusion from the UK of a dissident Iranian politician resident in France (Lord Sumption: "There is no challenge to the primary facts. We have absolutely no evidential basis and no expertise with which to substitute our assessment of the risks to national security, public safety and A the rights of others for that of the Foreign Office. We have only the material and the expertise to assess whether the Home Secretary has set about her task rationally, by reference to relevant matters and on the correct legal principle. Beyond that, in a case like this one, we would be substituting our own decision for that of the constitutional decision-maker without any proper ground for rejecting what she had done. All the recent jurisprudence of this court has rejected that as an inappropriate exercise for a Court of review, even where Convention rights are engaged").

[137] See further A. Tompkins, "National Security and the Role of the Court: a Changed Landscape?" (2010) 126 L.Q.R. 543.

[138] See 11-043. First instance judicial control over some decisions relating to national security— including decisions to deport or exclude a person from the United Kingdom or deprive a person of his or her British citizenship—are made by the Special Immigration Appeals Commission (SIAC), a superior court of record; appeals on points of law only lie to the Court of Appeal: Special Immigration Appeals Commission Act 1997. The Proscribed Organisations Appeal Commission (POAC), a superior court of record created by the Terrorism Act 2000 Sch.2, hears appeals against decisions of the Secretary of State not to de-proscribe organisations believed to be involved in terrorism.

[139] See, e.g. *X v Secretary of State for the Home Department* [2004] UKHL 56; [2005] 2 A.C. 68

impropriety.[140] In recent years the courts have frequently been called upon to adjudicate on the legality of legislation and executive decisions designed to protect national security through a variety of means, including: preventative detention without charge or trial of non-nationals (who could not be deported)[141] suspected of involvement in terrorism under the Anti-terrorism, Crime and Security Act 2001 s.23[142]; "control orders" made under the Prevention of Terrorism Act 2005 s.1[143]; "TPIM notices" under the Terrorism Prevention and Investigation Measures Act 2011 s.2 (the replacement for control orders)[144]; deportation orders on grounds of national security[145]; deprivation of citizenship under the British Nationality Act 1981 s.40 and exercise of prerogative power to exclude a person from the United Kingdom[146]; "secret" trials in the context of terrorist prosecutions[147]; exclusion of "the public" from an inquest on grounds of national security[148]; prohibitions on persons in the UK financial sector from entering commercial transactions or relationships[149]; and asset freezing orders.[150] The result has been described as "a

---

(preventive detention for non-nationals, designed for purposes of national security, was not sufficiently justified under the terms of ECHR art.15).

[140] In relation to procedural fairness, see 8-007.

[141] In light of European Court of Human Rights jurisprudence, the Secretary of State (and any court reviewing a proposed deportation) of a non-national must not deport if there is a real risk that the actions of overseas authorities would subject the person to torture, inhuman and degrading treatment or punishment (ECHR art.3) or deprive him of liberty contrary to art.5 (*Chahal v United Kingdom* (1997) 23 E.H.R.R. 413); or that there was a real risk that a person's trial overseas would use evidence obtained by torture contrary to art.6 (*Abu Qatada v United Kingdom, Othman v United Kingdom* (2012) 55 E.H.R.R. 1).

[142] *X v Secretary of State for the Home Department* [2004] UKHL 56; [2005] 2 A.C. 68; and in subsequent proceedings before the European Court of Human Rights, see *A v United Kingdom* (2009) 49 E.H.R.R. 29. Preventative detention was replaced with control orders.

[143] See, e.g. *Secretary of State for the Home Department v JJ and others* [2007] UKHL 45; [2008] 1 A.C. 385; *Secretary of State for the Home Department v MB and AF* [2007] UKHL 46; [2008] 1 A.C. 440; *Secretary of State for the Home Department v E and another* [2007] UKHL 47; [2008] 1 A.C. 499; *Secretary of State for the Home Department v AF (No.3)* [2009] UKHL 28; [2010] 2 A.C. 269; *BX v Secretary of State for the Home Department* [2010] EWCA Civ 481; [2010] 1 W.L.R. 2463; *BG v Secretary of State for the Home Department* [2011] EWHC 1478 (Admin); [2011] 1 W.L.R. 2917; *Secretary of State for the Home Department v CB and another* [2012] EWCA Civ 418; [2012] 1 W.L.R. 3259. Control orders were made against 52 individuals.

[144] *Secretary of State for the Home Department v BM* [2012] EWHC 714 (Admin); [2012] 1 W.L.R. 2734.

[145] *RB (Algeria) v Secretary of State for the Home Department* [2009] UKHL 10; [2010] 2 A.C. 110; *R. (on the application of BB (Algeria)) v Special Immigration Appeals Commission and another* [2011] EWHC 336 (Admin); [2012] Q.B. 146; *W (Algeria) and other v Secretary of State for the Home Department* [2012] UKSC 8; [2012] 2 A.C. 115; *R. (on the application of Naik) v Secretary of State for the Home Department* [2011] EWCA Civ 1546; [2012] Imm.A.R. 381, esp. [83]–[88] (setting out principles to be applied); *R. (on the application of Lord Carlile) v Secretary of State for the Home Department* [2014] UKSC 60; [2015] A.C. 945.

[146] *R. (on the application of GI) v Secretary of State for the Home Department* [2011] EWHC 1975 (Admin); [2012] 1 W.L.R. 2568; *IR (Sri Lanka) v Secretary of State for the Home Department* [2011] EWCA Civ 704; [2012] 1 W.L.R. 232.

[147] *Guardian News and Media Ltd v AB*, Court of Appeal (Criminal Division), 12 June 2014; *The Times*, 18 June 2014. On the use of closed material procedures in recent years, see paras 8-009 to 8-014.

[148] *R. (on the application of the Secretary of State for the Home Department) v Inner West London Assistant Deputy Coroner and others* [2010] EWHC 3098 (Admin); [2011] 1 W.L.R. 2564.

[149] *Bank Mellat v Her Majesty's Treasury (No.2)* [2011] EWCA Civ 1; [2012] Q.B. 101.

[150] *Ahmed and others v Her Majesty's Treasury (JUSTICE intervening)(Nos 1 and 2)* [2010] UKSC 2 and [2010] UKSC 5; [2010] 2 A.C. 534 (Terrorism (United Nations Measures) Order 2006 (SI 2006/2657) and the Al-Qaida and Taliban (United Nations Measures) Order 2006 (SI 2006/2952) were ultra vires the United Nations Act 1946: in the former, "reasonable suspicion" provision went further than was necessary to expient to comply with UN Security Council measures and in the latter there was a denial of fundamental rights of access to a judicial remedy. The Terrorist Asset-Freezing

complex case law that accommodates significantly more intensive scrutiny that [sic] is commonly found in practice in judicial review".[151] Questions of national security also arise in proceedings other than CPR Pt 54 claims for judicial review, including civil claims for damages[152] and applications for habeas corpus.[153]

Matters which are polycentric

1-044   A third limitation on the court's institutional capacity occurs when a legal challenge is made on substantive grounds to a matter which is "polycentric"—where the decision-taker has broad discretion involving policy and public interest considerations. The limitation does not apply where the alleged flaw is one of procedural impropriety[154] or a failure to discharge a general duty, such as the public sector equality duty.[155]

1-045   Most "allocative decisions"—decisions involving the distribution of limited resources—fall into the category of polycentric decisions. If the court alters such a decision, the judicial intervention will set up a chain reaction, requiring a rearrangement of other decisions with which the original has interacting points of influence.[156] Thus where it was alleged that the proposals of the Boundary Commission resulted in an "excessive disparity" between the number of electors in each

---

(Temporary Provisions) Act 2010 and subsequently the Terrorist Asset-Freezing etc Act 2010 were enacted to provide the necessary powers to implement the UN Security Council measures. For EU law iterations, see *Kadi v Council of the European Union* (Joined Cases C–402/05P and C–415/05P) [2009] 1 A.C. 1225; *Othman v Council of the European Union* (T 318/01) [2009] E.C.R. II–1627.

[151] House of Lords Constitution Committee, *Terrorism Prevention and Investigation Measures Bill*, 19th Report of 2010–12, HL Paper 198, para.15.

[152] See, e.g. *Al Rawi and others v Security Service and others (JUSTICE and others intervening)* [2011] UKSC 34; [2012] 1 A.C. 531 (in tort claims, "closed material procedure" held to be a departure from fundamental features of common law fair trials); *Tariq v Home Office* [2011] UKSC 35; [2012] 1 A.C. 452 (close material procedure could be used in the Employment Tribunal); the Justice and Security Act 2013 now permits use of this procedure in civil litigation generally.

[153] *Rahmatullah v Secretary of State for Defence and another (JUSTICE intervening)* [2012] UKSC 48; [2013] 1 A.C. 614.

[154] See, e.g. *R. (on the application of Luton BC) v Secretary of State for Education* [2011] EWHC 217 (Admin); [2011] Eq.L.R. 481, [96] ("however pressing the economic problems, there was no 'overriding public interest' which precluded consultation or justifies the lack of any consultation" in relation to government decision to shut down national programme for refurbishing schools); *R. (on the application of Rahman) v Birmingham City Council* [2011] EWHC 944 (Admin); [2011] Eq.L.R. 705 (decision to end funding to voluntary agencies providing legal advice to ethnic minorities and disabled people unlawful because they had been made without due regard to public sector equality duties).

[155] Equality Act 2010 s.149 and the Equality Act 2010 (Specific Duties) Regulations 2011 (SI 226/2011).

[156] *Council of Civil Service Unions v Minister for the Civil Service* [1985] A.C. 374 at 411 (Lord Diplock: decisions involving "competing policy considerations", involving "a balancing exercise which judges by their upbringing and their experience are ill-qualified to perform"). See L. Fuller, "The Forms and Limits of Adjudication" (1978–79) 92 Harv. L.R. 395, who likens a polycentric problem to that of a spider's web: "A pull on one strand will distribute tensions after a complicated pattern throughout the web as a whole. Doubling the original pull will, in all likelihood, not simply double each of the resulting tensions but rather create a different complicated pattern of tensions. This would certainly occur, for example, if the double pull caused one or more of the weaker strands to snap." These words were quoted in *R. v Secretary of State for the Home Department Ex p. P* [1995] 1 All E.R. 870 (Neill LJ: non-statutory power establishing a scheme to provide compensation for criminal injuries was held not justiciable because it involved "a balance of competing claims on the public purse and the allocation of economic resources which the court is ill equipped to deal with"); J. Allison "Fuller's Analysis of Polycentric Disputes and The Limits of Adjudication" (1994) C.L.J. 367; A. Le Sueur, "Justifying Judicial Caution: Jurisdiction, Justiciability and Policy", Ch.8 in B. Hadfield (ed.), *Judicial Review: A Thematic Approach* (1995); A. Chayes, "The Role of the

constituency and the "electoral quota" (as required by the Rules), it was held that this was a question on which the courts should be reluctant to decide, there being "more than one answer", particularly since any adjustment to the boundaries would necessitate other compensating adjustments to the proposals (a typical polycentric problem, although not directly referred to as such).[157]

Another typical polycentric decision is one involving the allocation of scarce resources among competing claims.[158] As will be discussed in Chapter 5, courts are asked to determine (a) whether the cost of a project is material to a decision; (b) whether the cost of a project is too high, or (c) too low.[159] The first issue to decide when these claims are made is whether the alleged duty is a mere "target duty" (such as to provide for the needs of children or the disabled in general) or an enforceable duty (to provide a particular service to the claimant). Once it has been decided that there is a duty to be engaged, or that a power is being neglected or ignored, should it then be for the courts to dictate how the resources ought to be allocated between the fulfilment of that duty and other competing responsibilities? In *R. v Cambridge DHA Ex p. B (No.1)*, the decision of a hospital not to provide expensive treatment to a child with cancer was upheld by the Court of Appeal.[160] Similarly: the House of Lords refused to interfere in a decision of a chief constable to deploy his resources in a manner that gave only partial and sporadic protection to exporters at risk of disruption of their trade from animal rights protesters[161]; a local authority system for allocating housing was held not to be inherently absurd or arbitrary.[162]

1-046

One of the reasons why a polycentric decision is not ideally amenable to judicial review is that the re-allocation of resources in consequence of the court's judgment will normally involve the interests of those who were not represented in the initial litigation. Yet it should not always be assumed that the legislature always possesses an institutional capacity superior to that of the courts to take into account a wide variety of interests. In *Huang*,[163] the House of Lords acknowledged that in some areas the determination of policy by the legislative or executive branch is institutionally no better than that of the courts. Their Lordships distinguished

1-047

Judge in Public Law Litigation" (1976) 89 Harv. L.R. 1281, 1288; J. King, "Institutional Approaches to Judicial Restraint" (2008) 28 O.J.L.S. 409; J. King, "The Pervasiveness of Polycentricity" [2008] P.L. 101.

[157] *R. v Boundary Commission for England Ex p. Foot* [1983] Q.B. 600.

[158] J. King, "The Justiciability of Resource Allocation" (2007) 70 M.L.R. 197; E. Palmer, "Resource Allocation, Welfare Rights—Mapping the Boundaries of Judicial Control in Public Administrative Law" (2000) 20 O.J.L.S. 63; S. Fredman, "Positive Rights Transformed: Positive Duties and Positive Rights" [2006] P.L. 498.

[159] See 5-134.

[160] *R. v Cambridge DHA Ex p. B (No.1)* [1995] 1 W.L.R. 898 at 906 (Sir Thomas Bingham MR: "Difficult and agonizing judgments have to be made as to how a limited budget is best allocated to the maximum advantage of the maximum number of patients. That is not a judgment which a court can make"); R. James and D. Longley, "Judicial Review and Tragic Choices: Ex p. B" [1995] P.L. 367.

[161] *R. v Chief Constable of Sussex Ex p. International Traders Ferry Ltd* [1999] 2 A.C. 418; also *R. (on the application of Pfizer Ltd) v Secretary of State for Health* [2002] EWCA Civ 1566; [2003] 1 C.M.L.R. 19 (CA upheld decision to provide the drug Viagra to a limited category of patients); K. Syrett, "Impotence or Importance? Judicial Review in an Era of Explicit NHS Rationing" (2004) 67 M.L.R. 289. cf. *R. (on the application of Rogers) v Swindon NHS Primary Care Trust* [2006] EWCA Civ 392; [2006] 1 W.L.R. 2649 (policy on funding breast cancer treatment with an unlicensed drug called Herceptin was irrational); K. Syrett, "Opening Eyes to the Reality of Scarce Health Care Resources? R (on the application of Rogers) v Swindon PCT and Secretary of State for Health" [2006] P.L. 664.

[162] *R. (on the application of Ahmad) v Newham LBC* [2009] UKHL 14; [2009] P.T.S.R. 632.

[163] *Huang v Secretary of State for the Home Department* [2007] UKHL 11; [2007] 2 A.C. 167.

between a case which concerns established housing policy[164]—where the result represented "a considered democratic compromise", and where all parties were represented in the debate and where the issue involved the allocation of finite resources—and the situation in immigration policy where those elements were not present. In the latter case, the courts have far less institutional reason to be diffident about intervening in order to protect the rights or interests of those who were not represented in the decision-making process.

1-048 Prosecution decisions have also been described as polycentric.[165] In *R. (on the application of Corner House Research) v Director of the Serious Fraud Office*, the House of Lords reiterated that the courts should be slow to interfere in prosecutorial decisions outside of exceptional cases.[166] One of the reasons given by Lord Bingham in support of that proposition was, quoting a judgment of the Supreme Court of Fiji "The polycentric character of official decision-making in such matters including policy and public interest considerations are not susceptible of judicial review because it is within neither the constitutional function nor the practical competence of the courts to assess their merits".[167] With respect, the concept of polycentricity does not justify judicial abstinence on the ground that the decision involves taking into account a number of different considerations. The essence of the polycentric problem is the fact that it has interacting points of influence described above, and is therefore not easily amenable to an either/or, or yes/no decision. Nevertheless, the deference to the Director's decision in *Corner House* was ultimately based less on polycentricity than the fact that it involved government policy in the area of national security (albeit ignoring the implications of such an approach for the rule of law).

1-049 Furthermore, budgetary decisions are not, invariably regarded by the courts as matters for the authority alone. The matter depends upon the relevant statute and context. While in *R. v Gloucestershire CC Ex p. Barry*,[168] the House of Lords held that the authority was entitled to take into account its limited resources when it considered whether it could fulfil "needs", in *R. v Sussex CC Ex p. Tandy*[169] the House of Lords took the opposite view in holding that the authority could not take its limited resources into account in considering whether it could provide "suitable education". As we shall see further when we consider these issues in greater detail in Chapters 5 and 11, so much in public law depends upon the context.[170]

---

[164] As in *Kay v Lambeth LBC* [2006] UKHL 10; [2006] 2 A.C. 465.

[165] *Sharma v Antoine and others* [2006] UKPC 57; [2007] 1 W.L.R. 780; *R. (on the application of Cityhook (Cornwall) Ltd v Office of Fair Trading* [2009] EWHC 57 (Admin); [2009] A.C.D. 41 (quoting passages from the 6th edn of this work with approval).

[166] [2008] UKHL 60; [2009] 1 A.C. 756; see further R. Hopkins and C. Yeginsu, "Storm in a Teacup: Domestic and International Conservatism from the Corner House Case" [2008] J.R. 267; J. Jowell, "Caving In: Threats and the Rule of Law" [2008] J.R. 273.

[167] [2008] UKHL 60; [2009] 1 A.C. 756, [31].

[168] [1997] A.C. 206.

[169] [1998] A.C. 714.

[170] See, e.g. *R. (on the application of A) v Croydon LBC* [2009] UKSC 8; [2009] 1 W.L.R. 2557, where the question of whether a child is "in need" was considered non-justiciable, and see *R. (on the application of McDonald) v Kensington and Chelsea RLBC* [2011] UKSC 33; [2011] P.T.S.R. 1266, where *Barry* was doubted in the context of a fiercely divided Supreme Court over the question of needs assessment in the context of community care). And see T. Dyke, "Judicial Review in an Age of Austerity" [2011] J.R. 202.

THE INCIDENCE AND IMPACT OF JUDICIAL REVIEW

However crude a measure, the quantity of judicial review to some degree **1-050** determines its potency as a constitutional constraint on the powers of public authorities and its practical utility as a means of dealing with individuals' grievances. Commentators and the government have often pointed to the growth of judicial review in England and Wales. In a consultation on proposed reforms to judicial review in 2012, the Ministry of Justice stated that "In 1974 there were 160 applications for judicial review, but by 2000 this had risen to nearly 4,250, and by 2011 had reached over 11,000".[171] This appears to be dramatic, but this stark statistic masks important features of the case load which mean that care is needed before ascribing too much weight to this trend. Judicial review is a two-stage procedure: claimants are required first to obtain the permission (formerly "leave") of the court: in 2015, about one in six of claims commenced received permission (760 out of a total number of applications that year of 4,680). Only cases granted permission may proceed to a full hearing in open court but many are withdrawn before or after permission as parties reach out of court settlements, often favourable to the claimant.[172] The result is that relatively few claims having a full hearing in open court (fewer than 300 in 2015).

The case load

The quantity of litigation needs to put in context. In relation to the number of **1-051** governmental decisions made each year, the overall number of review challenges commenced is infinitesimal (and the number receiving a fully reasoned judgment is even smaller). The scale of judicial review activity in redressing grievances is also modest compared to other avenues of complaint: in 2016–17, the Parliamentary and Health Service Ombudsman dealt with 120,000 enquiries of which almost 8,000 were referred for in-depth consideration[173]; the Local Government and Social Care Ombudsman registered 19,077 new complaints, of which 11,526 were allocated to

---

[171] Ministry of Justice, *Judicial Review: proposals for reform* (CP25/2012), para.29; see also National Audit Office, *Citizen Redress: What citizens can do if thing go wrong with public services* (Report by the Comptroller and Auditor General, HC Paper No.21, Session 2004/05); M. Sunkin, "What is Happening to Applications for Judicial Review?" (1987) 50 M.L.R. 432; Sunkin, "The Judicial Review Case-Load 1987–1989" [1991] P.L. 491; Sunkin, "Trends in Judicial Review" [1993] P.L. 443; L. Bridges, G. Meszaros and M. Sunkin, *Judicial Review in Perspective* (1996).; M. Sunkin and V. Bondy "The Use and Effects of Judicial Review: Assumptions and Empirical Evidence" in J. Bell, M. Elliott and J. Varuhas *Public Law Adjudication in Common Law Systems* (2016).

[172] See Ch.16. On settlement of threatened and actual claims for judicial review, see V. Bondy and M. Sunkin, *The Dynamics of Judicial Review Litigation: the resolution of public law challenges before final hearing* (London: Public Law Project, 2009); "Accessing Judicial Review" [2008] P.L. 647; and "Settlement in Judicial Review Proceedings" [2009] P.L. 237. The findings of these studies include that "increasing numbers of judicial review claims are now being resolved in favour of claimants by settlement without the need for trial in the Administrative Court"; and there is "widespread conscientious concern amongst both claimant and defendant solicitors to resolve disputes in a timely fashion". They conclude that the reforms to the judicial review claim procedure introduced following recommendations of the Bowman Committee (on which, see para.15-096)—including the pre-action protocol and "acknowledgment of service" procedures (whereby defendants must respond in summary form to a claim if they wish to be heard on the permission application)—may well have led to "a significant change in the dynamics of judicial review litigation".

[173] Parliamentary and Health Service Ombudsman, *The Ombudsman's Annual Report and Accounts 2016–17* (2017), Appendix.

investigators[174]; and hundreds of thousands of applications are received each year by the First-Tier Tribunal.[175] The judicial review data also reveal that there has been a significant decrease in the proportion of claims permitted to proceed to a full hearing (though success rates at the full hearing have remained fairly constant).[176] Moreover, a large proportion of the annual judicial review caseload used to arise from two particular areas—claims brought in relation to immigration and asylum decision-making (in 2011, over 75 per cent)[177] and local authority decisions relating to housing.[178] Both of these areas have now been transferred (to Tribunals and to the County Court respectively). Since then, the volume of judicial review applications has declined dramatically: to around 4,000 in 2016.

1-052   Many people expected the coming into force of the Human Rights Act 1998 in October 2000 to lead to a significant increase in the number of judicial review claims. Reforms to the claim procedure and operation of the Administrative Court were in large made in order to "clear the decks" before October 2000 and have efficient systems in place to cope with this.[179] In fact, the impact of the HRA on case load numbers has been at most marginal. Research based on a sample of cases suggested that the HRA was cited in about half of claims, usually to supplement ordinary domestic law grounds of review rather than as the main ground; and that, typically, the inclusion of human rights arguments does not add significantly to the case or to the claimant's prospects of success.[180]

1-053   Judicial review is not confined to claims at first instance in the Administrative Court. Claimants and defendants appeal to the Court of Appeal (Civil Division) and the Supreme Court.[181] A considerable proportion of the appeals heard each year by the UK Supreme Court and previously by the House of Lords are from judicial review claims.[182] Although the precise criteria on which leave to appeal to the House of Lords are granted and refused are far from clear, the relatively high incidence of judicial review cases shows that administrative law matters are often regarded as constituting points of law of general public importance.[183]

Central government responses to judicial review

1-054   The growth of judicial review since the 1960s—in terms of more rigorous legal standards, its theoretical base, the range of government functions amenable to

---

[174] Local Government and Social Care Ombudsman, *Annual Report and Accounts 2016–17: Making a Difference* (2017).

[175] Ministry of Justice, *Tribunals and Gender Recognition Statistics Quarterly-July to September 2017* (2017).

[176] See further V. Bondy and M. Sunkin, "Accessing Judicial Review" [2008] P.L. 647. The authors chart a long-term decline in the grant of permission, with a particularly steep decline since 2000. They suggest that "despite the diminishing grant rate, the overall picture may be one in which access to substantive justice in terms of satisfactory outcomes has improved" (p.666). This is because of the high incidence of settlements in favour of claimants that occur prior to permission being considered.

[177] See further R. Thomas, "Mapping Immigration Judicial Review Litigation: An Empirical Legal Analysis" [2015] P.L. 652.

[178] See 17-004.

[179] See 15-095.

[180] Public Law Project (V. Bondy), *The Impact of the Human Rights Act 1998 on Judicial Review* (2003) (also published in summary at [2003] J.R. 14). See further on the impact of the HRA, 13-102.

[181] See 16-080. Prior to October 2009, the final court of appeal for judicial review claims was the House of Lords.

[182] In 2011–12, 22 of the 58 judgments were public law cases; the comparable figure in 2010–11 was 22 of the 57 judgments: see C. Knight and T. Cross, "Public Law in the Supreme Court 2011–2012" [2012] J.R. 330.

[183] A. Le Sueur, "Panning for Gold: Choosing Cases for Top-level Courts", Ch.12 in Le Sueur (ed), *Building the UK's New Supreme Court: National and Comparative Perspectives* (2004); T. Poole and S. Shah, "The Impact of the Human Rights Act on the House of Lords" [2009] P.L. 347.

review and the practical impact on governmental decisions—has not been universally welcomed. Although an approach of "partnership" between the courts and government has been advocated by the courts[184] (and often achieved), the potency of judicial review to constrain government policy has led to a range of responses. Some can be welcomed as constructive engagements between the courts and the executive; others are regrettable and have at times risked undermining the important constitutional principles that ought to govern the relationship between the judges and ministers.[185]

During the 1980s, central government became increasingly concerned at the number of successful judicial review challenges and that departments seemed ill-equipped to respond effectively to actual or potential judicial reviews. Writing in 1983, the Treasury Solicitor drew attention to the fact that "senior administrators show a surprising ignorance of elementary legal principles" and "a lack of appreciation of the impact of legal considerations on administrative problems involving either considerable financial loss or embarrassment to Ministers".[186] A Cabinet committee endorsed this view and a strategy was formulated to deal with these problems. One aspect of the response was for the Treasury Solicitor's department and the Cabinet Office to distribute over 35,000 copies of a pamphlet called *The Judge Over Your Shoulder* to civil servants in 1987.[187] This set out some basic information about the judicial review process and some of the precautions which administrators could take to avoid the risk of challenge. A programme of legal awareness training was also organised for civil servants. Another aspect of the strategy was that departments and parliamentary counsel were urged to ensure that legislation was "expressed in the clearest possible language, even at the cost of drafting terms that are presentationally or politically unattractive".[188] In the years which followed, a marked change in the ethos of departments seemed to have occurred. Law and lawyers were no longer seen as peripheral to the process of administration. Administrators became more aware of the legal implications of their decisions and departmental lawyers tended to become involved at earlier stages of the policy-making process.[189] This does not, however, mean that government will always choose to avoid the risk of challenge: there is some evidence of public authorities pursuing policies despite receiving advice that there were good grounds

1-055

---

[184] *R. v Lancashire CC Ex p. Huddleston* [1986] 2 All E.R. 941 at 945; *R. v Monopolies and Mergers Commission Ex p. Argyll Group* [1986] 1 W.L.R. 763 at 774; H. Woolf, "Public Law-Private Law: Why the Divide?" [1986] P.L. 220, 30.

[185] House of Lords Select Committee on the Constitution, *Relations between the Executive, the Judiciary and Parliament*. HL Paper No.151 (Session 2006/07), para.37.

[186] Sir Michael Kerry, "Administrative Law and the Administrator" (1983) 3 *Management in Government* 168, pp.170–171.

[187] A. Bradley, "The Judge Over Your Shoulder" [1987] P.L. 485. A second edition of the pamphlet was prepared in 1994, on which see D. Oliver [1994] P.L. 514. The 4th edn (January 2006) reflects changes following the coming into force of the Human Rights Act. There appear to two different versions of "JOYS", one for administrators and one for lawyers (Solicitor General, *Hansard*, HC col.101WA (4 July 2000)). For the Government's account of the training related to the HRA, see Joint Committee on Human Rights, *Government Responses to Reports from the Committee in the last Parliament*. HL Paper No.104/HC Paper No.850 (Session 2005/06), Appendix 2.

[188] A. Bradley, "The Judge Over Your Shoulder" [1987] P.L. 485.

[189] M. Sunkin and A. Le Sueur, "Can Government Control Judicial Review?" (1991) 44 C.L.P. 161 at p.171; A. Hammond, "Judicial Review: Continuing Interplay Between Law and Policy" [1998] P.L. 34 (where the former Treasury Solicitor writes of correction by the courts as being accepted in a "constructive spirit"). For an account of the provision of legal advice to Government, see T. Daintith and A. Page, *The Executive in the Constitution: Structure, Autonomy and Internal Control* (1999), Chs 7 and 9.

for thinking that they are unlawful.[190] Nonetheless, in 2012 the Ministry of Justice expressed the belief that "the threat of judicial review has an unduly negative effective on decision makers", leading "public authorities to be overly cautious in the way they make decisions, making them too concerned about minimising, or eliminating, the risk of a legal challenge".[191]

1-056   Another approach to judicial review by government is that from time to time senior ministers have thought it fit to encourage and engage in hostile public comment about particular judges, judgments or the role of judicial review in general. Three particular episodes—all radiating from the Home Office—are of particular note. During the mid-1990s, the Conservative Home Secretary Mr Michael Howard MP did little to hide his displeasure at judicial review judgments overturning government decisions and the tabloid newspapers poured venom over several named judges, portraying them as anti-democratic and contemptuous of public and parliamentary opinion.[192] Similar "ill-tempered outbursts" emanated from Labour Home Secretary Mr David Blunkett during 2003,[193] and again the tabloid press dispensed scorn on to some named judges and deplored "unaccountable and unelected judges" who were "usurping the role of Parliament, setting the wishes of the people at nought and pursuing a liberal, politically correct agenda of their own, in the zeal to interpret European legislation".[194] During 2006, while Mr John Reid was Home Secretary, further outbursts occurred. Following a decision of Sullivan J that Afghan hijackers, released from prison on appeal, should not be deported to almost certain death in their home country,[195] the Prime Minister (Mr Tony Blair MP) told the news media "We can't have a situation in which people who hijack a plane, we're not able to deport back to their country. It's not an abuse of justice for us to order their deportation, it's an abuse of common sense, frankly, to be in a position where we can't do this".[196] Mr Reid added fuel to the fire: "When decisions are taken which appear inexplicable or bizarre to the general public, it only reinforces

---

[190] A. Le Sueur, "The Judicial Review Debate: From Partnership to Friction" (1996) 31 Govt & Opp. 8, 23–24; and more recently see, e.g. *R. (Lumba) v Secretary of State for the Home Department (JUSTICE and another intervening)* [2011] UKSC 12; [2012] 1 A.C. 245 (as the headnote records, "It subsequently emerged that, despite senior officials and lawyers within the Home Office having expressed concern that the unpublished policy [relating to deportation of foreign national prisoners] was vulnerable to legal challenge, a deliberate decision had been taken by Home Office officials to continue that policy and caseworkers had been directed to conceal the fact that the true reason for detention was the unpublished policy and to give other reasons which conformed to the published policy").

[191] Ministry of Justice, *Judicial Review: proposals for reform* (CP25/2012), para.35; and see C. Elphicke MP, "Make Ministers Accountable to Parliament, not Judges" in 2020 Group of Conservative MPs, *2012 Vision: an Agenda for Transformation* (2013), p.9 (asserting that the Home Office "is hobbled by persistent interference by the judiciary").

[192] Le Sueur (1996) 31 Govt & Opp., 24–26. *The Times* wrote that "it is tempting to observe a pattern emerging, a potentially alarming hostility between an overmighty executive and an ambitious judiciary" (November 3, 1995).

[193] A. Bradley, "Judicial Independence Under Attack" [2003] P.L. 397. During a radio interview, Mr Blunkett said "Frankly, I'm personally fed up with having to deal with a situation where Parliament debates issues and the judges then overturn them" (quoted in *The Independent*, February 20, 2003).

[194] *Daily Mail*, February 21, 2003.

[195] *R. (on the application of S) v Secretary of State for the Home Department* [2006] EWHC 1111; [2006] A.C.D. 96.

[196] Press Conference with the French Prime Minister, May 10, 2006 (quoted in Joint Committee on Human Rights, *The Human Rights Act: The DCA and Home Office Reviews*, 32nd Report (HL 278/HC 1716, 2005–06), para.11.

the perception that the system is not working to protect, or in favour of, the vast majority of ordinary, decent hard-working citizens in this country".[197]

In the Conservative/Liberal Democrat coalition government formed after the May 2010 general election, ministers did nothing to improve the quality of political debate about judicial review and the role of the judiciary more broadly. Home Secretary Theresa May MP set the tone in a speech to the Conservative Party conference in October 2011 when she claimed that a tribunal judge had ruled against the deportation a violent drug dealer "because—and I am not making this up—he had a pet cat"; the case did not turn on the fact of cat ownership.[198] In a speech to the Confederation of British Industry in November 2012, the Prime Minister pledged the government to "cutting back on judicial reviews", saying they were a "growth industry" and "so many are completely pointless".[199] The subsequent Ministry of Justice consultation paper was rather less full of hyperbole (even acknowledging that "Judicial review is a critical check on the power of the State, providing an effective mechanism for challenging the decisions of public bodies to ensure they are lawful"), though strong on "anecdotal evidence".[200] In another development, ministers, along with most MPs, continued to oppose the ruling of the European Court of Human Rights—binding in international law—holding that a blanket ban on all prisoners voting was a disproportionate interference with rights to free elections under ECHR Protocol 1, art.3, and the "serious concerns" expressed by the Council of Europe Council of Ministers at the United Kingdom's substantial delay in implementing the judgment.[201] In November 2012, the Voting Eligibility (Prisoners) Bill was drafted to give Members of Parliament three options on which to vote.[202] In a letter to the chairman of the Joint Committee on the Bill dated 25 February 2014, the Secretary of State for Justice, Chris Grayling MP, gave an assurance that "the matter is under active consideration within Government". The Committee of Ministers of the Council of Europe deferred any

1-057

---

[197] "Government appeal over hijackers" (BBC News on line, 11 May 2006)
http://news.bbc.co.uk/1/hi/uk_politics/4760873.stm [Accessed 2 February 2013].

[198] A. Wagner, "What the first #catgate appeal judgment actually says" (UK Human Rights Blog, October 6, 2011)
http://ukhumanrightsblog.com/2011/10/06/what-the-first-catgate-appeal-judgment-actually-says/ [Accessed 2 February 2013].

[199] Prime Minister's speech to CBI, 19 November 2012
http://www.number10.gov.uk/news/speech-to-cbi/ [Accessed 21 December 2012]. For an early response, see J. Jowell, "Diminishing judicial review will reverse 50 years of legal progress" (Guardian online, 19 November 2012)
http://www.guardian.co.uk/law/2012/nov/19/diminishing-judicial-review-reverse-legal-progress [Accessed 2 February 2013].

[200] Ministry of Justice, Judicial Review: proposals for reform (CP25/2012).

[201] The litigation started with an unsuccessful judicial review claim in 2001 before moving to Strasbourg: see Hirst v United Kingdom (No.2) (2004) 38 E.H.R.R. 40; Interim Resolution CM/ResDH(2009)160, [2009] ECHR 2260; Hansard, HC Vol.553, col.745 (22 November 2012) (Statement by the Lord Chancellor, Voting Eligibility (Prisoners)). See also R. (on the application of Chester) v Secretary of State for Justice [2013] UKSC 63; [2014] A.C. 271, where the Supreme Court agreed that the blanket ban on convicted prisoners' rights was ECHR incompatible but dismissed the appeals of the particular applicants that their rights had been infringed and declined to make a further declaration of incompatibility. On 12 August 2014, the European Court of Human Rights found the United Kingdom to be in violation of ECHR Protocol 1 art.3 in having primary legislation preventing all prisoners voting in the June 2009 European Parliament elections; the court held that the finding of a violation constituted sufficient just satisfaction for any non-pecuniary damage sustained by the applicants and therefore declined to award compensation and also rejected the applicants' claim for legal costs (Firth v United Kingdom, Application no. 47784/09).

[202] Option 1 would retain the ban for prisoners jailed for over four years; option 2 would retain the ban for prisoners jailed for over six months; option 3 would retain the current ban with minor amendments.

further discussion of the issue until after September 2015. Prisoners had no right to vote in the General Elections of May 2015 or June 2017.

1-058   Most recently, the Government was conspicuous by its silence following the decision of the Divisional Court in *Miller*.[203] The judgment provoked a barrage of stringent media attacks on the judiciary, to which the Government made no response.[204] The failure of the Lord Chancellor, Liz Truss, to condemn media attacks on the judges prompted criticism that she was failing to uphold her duty to defend the rule of law under s.1 of the Constitutional Reform Act.[205] The Lord Chancellor defended her silence in evidence given to the House of Lords Constitution Committee, arguing that it "is dangerous for a government Minister to say this is an acceptable headline and that is not."[206] Her stance was subject to robust criticisms from the Lord Chief Justice, Lord Thomas, who, in his own evidence to the Committee, suggested that the Lord Chancellor was "constitutionally absolutely wrong".[207]

1-059   While such tactics of confrontation and denunciation of judicial review may enable politicians to vent frustration and a handful of journalists to fill column inches, they cannot provide a stable basis for a relationship between executive and judiciary. Of course it is not for the executive to censor the press, but censuring the lack of mutual respect for the constitutional principles of the rule of law and separation of powers is a different matter.[208]

1-060   In a constitutional system based on parliamentary supremacy, the government may be tempted to seek to oust the jurisdiction of the courts over some areas of decision-making. There is nothing new in this and for several decades the courts have taken a robust approach to minimising the practical effect of preclusive clauses

---

[203] *R. (Miller) v Secretary of State for Exiting the European Union* [2016] EWHC 2768 (Admin); [2017] 1 All E.R. 158. See now [2017] UKSC 5; [2017] 2 W.L.R. 583.

[204] In particular, the *Daily Mail*'s account of the judgment ran under the headline 'Enemies of the People', accusing the High Court judges in question of attempting to frustrate the outcome of the referendum. In similar vein, *The Daily Telegraph* presented the story as 'The judges versus the people'.

[205] Section 1 of the Constitutional Reform Act 2005 places the Lord Chancellor under a statutory obligation to defend the rule of law. The Lord Chancellor's failure to condemn attacks on the judiciary was criticised by inter alia: the Bar Council D. Boffey 'Brexit: lawyers confront Truss over 'dangerous' abuse of judges' (*The Observer*, 6 November 2016) *https://www.theguardian.com/politics/2016/nov/05/lawyers-war-liz-truss-over-abuse-judges-brexit-barristers* [Accessed 26 October 2017]; the shadow Secretary of State for Justice, Richard Burgon MP R. Burgon 'Liz Truss swore to defend the judiciary. But she stood by as they got a roasting' (*Guardian Online*, 8 November 2016) *https://www.theguardian.com/commentisfree/2016/nov/08/liz-truss-defend-judges-article-50-stood-by* [Accessed 26 October 2017]; and Lord Falconer, the former Lord Chancellor C. Falconer 'The vicious assault on UK judges by the Brexit press is a threat to democracy' (*Guardian Online*, 4 November 2016) *https://www.theguardian.com/commentisfree/2016/nov/04/assault-uk-judges-brexit-press-judiciary-constitution* [Accessed 26 October 2017].

[206] House of Lords Select Committee on the Constitution *Corrected oral evidence: oral evidence session with the Lord Chancellor and Secretary of State for Justice*, 1 March 2017.

[207] House of Lords Select Committee on the Constitution *Corrected oral evidence: oral evidence session with the Lord Chancellor and Secretary of State for Justice*, 22 March 2017.

[208] House of Lords Select Committee on the Constitution, *Relations between the Executive, the Judiciary and Parliament*. HL Paper No.151 (Session 2006/07), para.51. Jack Straw MP said in one of his first speeches after his appointment as Lord Chancellor in 2007 that what ministers "must not do is gratuitously to criticise individual judgements, nor show a lack of respect for the institution of the judiciary or its members. After all, it is we in Parliament who ultimately make the law, and therefore have to accept its consequences" (Lord Mayor of London's annual judges dinner, 17 July 2007). See Jeffrey Jowell, "Brexit Judicialised: Crown v Parliament Again" [2018] *The UK Supreme Court Yearbook*, Vol.8, 1–21.

in legislation.[209] In recent years it is the field of immigration and asylum policy that has given government most incentive and opportunity to introduce legislation restricting the scope of judicial review.[210] The Government's case (contested by many) has been that failed asylum-seekers "play the system" by making claims for judicial review tactically to delay their deportation from the United Kingdom. The Nationality, Immigration and Asylum Act 2002 created a greatly modified version of the claim for judicial review procedure for legal challenges to refusals of permission to appeal from one tier of the immigration appellate system to another.[211] Although this procedure appeared to be working well, in early 2003 the Government's Asylum and Immigration (Treatment of Claimants etc) Bill contained an ouster clause the like of which had never been seen. Amidst a great deal of criticism,[212] that the clause would undermine the rule of law, the Government withdrew it. The clause read as follows:

"Exclusivity and finality of Tribunal's jurisdiction

(1)   No court shall have any supervisory or other jurisdiction (whether statutory or inherent) in relation to the Tribunal.
(2)   No court may entertain proceedings for questioning (whether by way of appeal or otherwise)—[here are listed decisions that may be made by the Tribunal].
(3)   Subsections (1) and (2)—
    (a)   prevent a court, in particular, from entertaining proceedings to determine whether a purported determination, decision, or action of the Tribunal was a nullity by reason of—
        (i)   lack of jurisdiction,
        (ii)   irregularity,
        (iii) error of law,
        (iv)   breach of natural justice, or
        (v)   any other matter, but
    (b)   do not prevent a court from—
        (i)   reviewing a decision to issue a certificate under s.94 or s.95 of this Act or under Sch.3 to the Asylum and Immigration (Treatment of Claimants, etc) Act 2004 (removal to safe country), or
        (ii)   considering whether a member of the Tribunal has acted in bad faith.
(4)   A court may consider whether a member of the Tribunal has acted in bad faith, in reliance on subsection (3)(b)(ii), only if satisfied that significant evidence has been adduced of—
    (a)   dishonesty,
    (b)   corruption, or
    (c)   bias.
(5)   Section 7(1) of the Human Rights Act 1998 (claim that public authority has infringed Convention right) is subject to subsections (1) to (3) above.

---

[209] See Ch.4.
[210] A. Le Sueur, "Three Strikes and it's Out? The UK Government's Strategy to Oust Judicial Review from Immigration and Asylum Decision-making" [2004] P.L. 225; R. Rawlings, "Review, Revenge and Retreat" (2005) 68 M.L.R. 378.
[211] Time limits were significantly shortened.
[212] Including that of the authors of this book: Lord Woolf, "The Rule of Law and a Change in the Constitution" (2004) 63 C.L.J. 317 (the clause "would be so inconsistent with the spirit of mutual respect between the different arms of government that it could be a catalyst for a campaign for a written constitution"); J. Jowell, "Immigration Wars", *The Guardian*, March 2, 2004 (it was "no longer self-evident ... that our courts would inevitably concede Parliament's right to ride roughshod over fundamental rights and newly discovered constitutional principles"); A. Le Sueur. "Three Strikes and it's Out? The UK Government's Strategy to Oust Judicial Review from Immigration and Asylum Decision-making" [2004] P.L. 225.

(6)   Nothing in this section shall prevent an appeal under section 2, 2B or 7 of the Special Immigration Appeals Commission Act 1997 (appeals to and from Commission).

(7)   In this section "action" includes failure to act."

Local government responses

1-061   In local government, the 1980s also marked a greatly increased awareness on the part of local authority officers and councillors of the potency of judicial review as both a challenge to their decisions and as a weapon to be employed by them against central government.[213] As a result, relationships between central and local government altered, with increased emphasis being given to the definition of legal powers and duties, and adjudication given greater prominence alongside administrative bargaining and negotiation as a method of dispute resolution.[214] In short, "the courts and the legal process have become, seemingly, a necessary part of the political debate and decision-making".[215] In some authorities, this involved a trend towards greater formality in decision-making, particularly in committees, where councillors and officers are anxious to be able to demonstrate, should a decision be challenged, that all and only relevant factors were considered.[216] The opinions of independent counsel were frequently sought and some concern was expressed that "these can supplant the decision-making powers of an elected body unless there are members with the confidence and political will to resist".[217]

1-062   Research into judicial review claims against local authorities in England and Wales has revealed some striking patterns.[218] The findings show that during 2000–05, 80 per cent of judicial review claims against local authorities were made against a group of councils that are less than 20 per cent of the total number. The top 20 authorities are all in London and the highest incidence of judicial review challenge is in areas of high multiple deprivations where there are relatively high numbers of solicitors with expertise in public law. The authors conclude that "For the inner city authority judicial review litigation typically involves a daily response to challenges by claimants seeking to protect their basic housing needs often in emergency situations. In this sense it is one part of the daily toil of resource management. This is a far cry from the more leisured engagement between citizen and authority in the High Court that is generally associated with the process". According to the study, quantitative analysis shows that "judicial review litigation may act as a driver to improvements in the quality of local government services, at least in so far as quality is defined by the government's performance indicators"; drawing also on interview data, the authors conclude that "The image of judicial review that is provided by our research is rather more positive than is commonly presented".[219]

---

[213] D. Cooper, "Institutional Illegality and Disobedience: Local Government Narratives" (1996) 16 O.J.L.S. 255.

[214] M. Loughlin, *Local Government in the Modern State* (1986), pp.193–201.

[215] L. Bridges, C. Game, O. Lomas, J. McBride, *Legality and Local Politics* (1987), p.3.

[216] Bridges et al. (1987), p.92. They comment that members are "deluged with paper on all aspects of the subject" under consideration and matters previously implicitly understood are now recorded.

[217] Bridges et al (1987), p.99.

[218] M. Sunkin, K. Calvo, L. Platt and T. Landman, "Mapping the Use of Judicial Review to Challenge Local Authorities in England and Wales" [2007] P.L. 545.

[219] L. Platt, M. Sunkin, and K. Calvo, *Judicial Review Litigation as an Incentive to Change in Local Authority Public Services in England and Wales* (ISER Working Paper Series No.2009–05, 2009), pp.22–24.

A different aspect of the dynamics between judicial review and local govern- **1-063**
ment has been concern by central and local government that the courts have been
too narrowly insistent on the ultra vires principle, hampering innovation by
councils.[220] The Localism Act 2011 Pt 1 seeks to provide a broader legal base for
local government decision-making through a "general power of competence",
which allows councils to do anything an individual can do unless specifically
prohibited by law.[221]

The impact of judicial review on the quality of decision-making

Judicial review has a constitutional importance.[222] It may also have an **1-064**
instrumental role in changing the behaviour of public authorities. The extent and
character of that change is open to debate but, as we have noted, there is evidence
supporting the view that judicial review improves the quality of decisions and
decision-making processes by promoting compliance with law. Law, in this context,
encompasses both adherence to criteria and procedures stipulated in legislation and
the broad principles that are articulated through the common law. Judges who carry
out the practical task of developing and refining the judicial review case law
certainly appear to work on the assumption that judicial review is capable of having a beneficial impact, both in relation to particular decisions and administrative
processes more broadly.[223] The past decade has seen a burgeoning of studies of the
relationships between judicial review and the political and administrative behaviour
of public authorities and officials.[224] The impact of review is now understood for
the complex phenomenon that it is; we appreciate that the size of the judicial review
caseload, or the frequency with which government bodies are challenged, are not
sure guides to assessing the various kinds of influence that may be exerted by
judicial review. Nevertheless, there can be little doubt that the principles of judicial
review, together with the requirements of Convention rights, have caused most bodies performing public functions to review their procedures and practices to comply

---

[220] See Ch.5.

[221] The Localism Act 2011 was brought into force earlier than originally planned by the Secretary of
State for Communities and Government Minister, Eric Pickles MP, following the decision of the High
Court in *R. (on the application of the National Secular Society) v Bideford Town Council* [2012]
EWHC 175 (Admin); [2012] 2 All E.R. 1175, where Ouseley J held that the saying of Christian
prayers as part of the formal business at the start of council meetings was ultra vires the Local
Government Act 1972 s.111.

[222] See 1-014.

[223] D. Feldman, "Judicial Review: A Way of Controlling Government?" (1988) 66 Pub. Admin. 21. cf.
Justice/All Souls, Review of *Administrative Law in the UK, Administrative Justice: Some Necessary Reforms* (1988), Ch.2 on the need for codes setting out in positive form principles of good
administration.

[224] See the valuable collection of essays in M. Hertogh and S. Halliday (eds), *Judicial Review and
Bureaucratic Impact: International and Interdisciplinary Perspectives* (2004); S. Halliday, *Judicial
Review and Compliance with Administrative Law* (2004); T. Daintith and A. Page, *The Executive
in the Constitution: Structure, Autonomy and Internal Control* (1999), pp.335–340; G. Richardson
and M. Sunkin, "Judicial Review: Questions of Impact" [1996] P.L. 79; M. Sunkin and K. Pick, "The
Changing Impact of Judicial Review: The Independent Review Service of the Social Fund" [2001]
P.L. 736; R. Thomas, "The Impact of Judicial Review on Asylum" [2003] P.L. 479. R. Thomas
"Administrative justice, better decisions, and organisational learning" [2015] P.L. 111; V. Bondy, L.
Platt and M. Sunkin *The Value and Effects of Judicial Review: The Nature of Claims, their Outcomes
and Consequences* (2015). In 2014, the Nuffield Foundation granted funding for three years to multi-
disciplinary team of academics working at the University of Essex and elsewhere to create the UK
Administrative Justice Institute (UKAJI), which has a remit to link the policy, practice and research
communities, develop a coordinated research agenda, and identify and tackle capacity constraints
on empirical research about law and administration.

with the principles of administrative justice, if for no other reason than to avoid the possibility of judicial review.

1-065   Drawing on a study of decision-making by local authorities about homeless people, Halliday has developed a useful model which seeks to identify the conditions which determine the degree to which public officials are likely to comply with administrative law norms.[225] He postulates three main variables. The first is the degree to which the decision-maker has knowledge about the law, cares about complying with the law and has competence in applying the law with appropriate sophistication. The second factor is the decision-making environment—which means the extent to which legal norms are in competition with other demands (such as requirements to reduce expenditure). The third element is the law itself, especially the extent to which it provides clear and consistent guidance. We draw from this the view that if judicial review is to achieve improvements in the quality of administrative decision-making, to give effect to the ideals of the rule of law as institutional morality, there does indeed need to be a partnership between public authorities and the courts. If the spirit of their judgments is to be embraced and translated into administrative practice, they need to show sensitivity to the tasks of officials in particular contexts.[226] It is also important for the courts to articulate principles in such a way as to provide meaningful guidance to public officials.

1-066   The empirical evidence gathered so far tends to suggest that prudence is needed before we can safely generalise that judicial review has a beneficial influence on administrative behaviour. In some organisations knowledge of the law, and empathy with values relating to the rule of law, appears to be thin on the ground.[227] Where judicial review has had some general influence, this seems more likely to be in relation to modifications of administrative procedure rather than changes to substantive entitlements.[228]

---

[225] S. Halliday, *Judicial Review and Compliance with Administrative Law* (2004), esp. Ch.9.

[226] Lord Donaldson MR spoke in several judgments of the need to establish a partnership between the courts and the administration "based on a common aim, namely the maintenance of the highest standards of public administration": see *R. v Lancashire CC Ex p. Huddleston* [1986] 2 All E.R. 941 at 945; *R. v Monopolies and Mergers Commission Ex p. Argyll Plc* [1986] 1 W.L.R. 763 at 774.

[227] I. Loveland, "Housing Benefit: Administrative Law and Administrative Practice" (1988) 66 Pub. Admin. 57 and "Administrative Law, Administrative Processes, and the Housing of Homeless Persons: A View from the Sharp End" (1991) 13 J.S.W.F.L. 4—he notes in the former that in one of the authorities studied "decision-making processes are entirely uninformed by explicit reference to administrative law as such. Mention of the *Wednesbury* principles draws a blank stare from most officers" (at p.73). A similar, rather dismal picture of officials' view of law and lawyers emerges from other empirical studies: see S. Halliday, "Internal Review and Administrative Justice: Some Evidence and Research Questions from Homelessness Decision-making" (2001) 23 J.S.W.F.L 473; D. Cowan and J. Fionda, "Homelessness Internal Appeals Mechanisms: Serving the Administrative Process" (1998) 27 Anglo-American L.R. 66 (Pt 1) and 169 (Pt 2). G. Richardson and D. Machin, "Judicial Review and Tribunal Decision-Making: a Study of the Mental Health Review Tribunal" [2000] P.L. 494 conclude that "that the influence of judicial review on the decision making of MHRTs is patchy at best, even with regard to procedural fairness".

[228] But for more positive conclusions, see L. Platt, M. Sunkin, and K. Calvo, *Judicial Review Litigation as an Incentive to Change in Local Authority Public Services in England and Wales* (ISER Working Paper Series No.2009–05, 2009), pp.22–24.

ADMINISTRATIVE JUSTICE AND PROPORTIONATE DISPUTE RESOLUTION

Under the Labour government, in its 2004 White Paper *Transforming Public Services: Complaints Redress and Tribunals*,[229] the Department for Constitutional Affairs (since May 2007 called the Ministry of Justice) coined the phrase "proportionate dispute resolution".[230] The strategy behind this slogan seeks "to transform civil and administrative justice and the way that people deal with legal problems and disputes".[231] The goal is to reduce the risk of administrative error in the first place by clarifying rights and responsibilities. Where disputes do arise, public authorities should offer internal methods to handle complaints. There should be a range of alternative dispute resolution services "so that different types of dispute can be resolved fairly, quickly, efficiently and effectively without recourse to the expense and formality of courts and tribunals where this is not necessary".[232] There is a growing realisation that "redress systems should be purposefully targeted to deliver valued benefits to citizens in a timely way, rather than just following through on established procedures whose added value for citizens remains unclear".[233] Since 2010, the notion of proportionate dispute resolution has continued to be a goal for the Conservative-Liberal Democrat coalition government, now embedded as an objective in the Ministry of Justice strategy for administrative justice.[234]

1-067

The general ideal of proportionate dispute resolution chimes well with the approach followed by the courts over many years. The Civil Procedure Rules (CPR), governing all civil litigation including judicial review, have at their heart as an overriding principle the idea that dealing justly with a dispute, when litigation does occur, requires the court to deal with the case in ways which are proportionate to the

1-068

---

[229] Cm. 6243; see also National Audit Office, *Citizen Redress: What citizens can do if things go wrong with public services* (Report by the Comptroller and Auditor General, HC Paper No.21, Session 2004/05).

[230] For commentary, see M. Alder, "Tribunal Reform: Proportionate Dispute Resolution and the Pursuit of Administrative Justice" (2006) 69 M.L.R. 958; and A. Le Sueur, "Courts, Tribunals, Ombudsmen, ADR: Administrative Justice, Constitutionalism and Informality", Ch.13 in J. Jowell and D. Oliver (eds), *The Changing Constitution* (2007).

[231] Para.2.1.

[232] Cm. 6243, para.2.3.

[233] National Audit Office, *Citizen Redress: What citizens can do if thing go wrong with public services* (Report by the Comptroller and Auditor General, HC Paper No.21, Session 2004/05), para.8. During 2007 it became plain that the Administrative Court was beset with such serious difficulties in listing cases that the principle of the rule of law was at risk. In *R. (on the application of Casey) v Restormel BC* [2007] EWHC 2554 Admin); [2008] A.C.D. 1, Munby J spoke of the indefensible delay that had occurred in that case as amounting to a denial of justice in the sense in which that phrase was used in Ch.40 of Magna Carta (which declares that "to no one will we sell, to no one we will deny or delay, right or justice"). In late 2007, the Public Law Project (a national legal charity which aims to improve access to public law remedies for those whose access is restricted by poverty, discrimination or other similar barriers) sent a letter before claim to the Ministry of Justice arguing that the unacceptable level of delays was unlawful. In April 2008, Collins J, the Lead Judge of the Administrative Court, issued a statement that the number of courts sitting from April to the end of the Trinity term would be substantially increased (see
http://www.hmcourts-service.gov.uk/cms/admin.htm; and further C. Haley, "Action on Administrative Court Delays" [2008] J.R. 69 and R. Clayton, "New Arrangements for the Administrative Court" [2008] J.R. 164).

[234] Ministry of Justice, *Administrative Justice and Tribunals: a Strategic Work Programme 2013–16* (2012), para.70 ("To promote early and proportionate dispute resolution across Government").

importance and complexity of the case and the financial position of the parties.[235]
In *R. (on the application of Anufrijeva) v Southwark LBC*,[236] the Court of Appeal
considered what procedures should be followed to ensure that the costs of obtaining relief are proportionate to that relief. Although that case concerned a claim for
damages under the Human Rights Act 1998, the approach advocated by the court
has a general relevance.[237] Without intending to be prescriptive, the court suggested that in appropriate cases a claimant should expect to have to explain to the
Administrative Court why (if this be the case) any internal complaints procedure
has not been pursued and why a complaint to the Ombudsman is not thought to be
appropriate.[238]

1-069   The rationale for directing complaints to appropriate agencies (which on occasion may entail turning an aggrieved citizen away from pursing a judicial review
claim) is two-fold. First, it enables a match to be made between, on the one hand,
the nature of the complaint and on the other the techniques and remedies needed
to resolve it. Secondly, there is a growing recognition of the public interest in using collective resources wisely in the context of administrative justice. Attempts at
quantifying the typical costs of the various redress mechanisms are inevitably rather
impressionistic, but it has been suggested that the cost of an internal review by a
public authority is £115; an appeal to a tribunal costs £455; and that ombudsman
interventions typically cost in the region of £1,200–£1,500.[239] These are all
relatively modest costs compared to that of a claim for judicial review (in which a
non-publicly funded claimant also bears the risk of being ordered to pay the defendant public authority's legal costs in the event of losing).[240]

1-070   The notion of proportionate dispute resolution is still in its relative infancy, but
we nonetheless identify three practical propositions to guide aggrieved citizens and
their advisers. First, complainants should always seek a local resolution of disputes.
Many public authorities have in place processes for internal reconsideration of
specific decisions or dealing with broader complaints about the conduct of public
officials.[241] Complainants who fail to use such mechanisms and instead take matters to an external agency without first giving the public authority an opportunity
to put things right are likely to be turned away. Secondly, where a local resolution
of a dispute cannot be attained, there is a strong presumption that the complainant
must use any statutory appeals procedure that exists.[242] Thirdly, investigation by the
ombudsmen and a claim for judicial review are avenues of last resort. There may
however be some difficult questions as to which—ombudsmen or judicial review—
are most suitable in a particular case, a point we consider below.[243]

---

[235] CPR r.1.1; see 16-011.
[236] *R. (on the application of Anufrijeva) v Southwark LBC* [2003] EWCA Civ 1406; [2004] Q.B. 1124.
[237] *R. (on the application of Scholarstica UMO) v Commissioner for Local Administration* [2003]
     EWHC 3202 (Admin); [2004] E.L.R. 265 at [17].
[238] See 16-014.
[239] National Audit Office. HC Paper No.21 (Session 2004/05), para.14.
[240] See 16-085.
[241] The Local Government Ombudsman publish a useful guide to good practice "Running a Complaints
     System", available on *http://www.lgo.org.uk*.
[242] See 16-018.
[243] See 1-096; and V. Bondy and A. Le Sueur, *Designing Redress: a Study About Grievances against
     Public Bodies* (PLP 2012).

Internal complaint systems

Most public authorities provide some form of internal complaints procedures for **1-071** people dissatisfied with the outcome of a decision or the way in which the decision was made.[244] Indeed, it is safe to assume that relatively few grievances proceed beyond this kind of procedure. In some contexts such complaint systems are relatively formalised and required by legislation. Thus, the Housing Act 1996 s.202 confers a right to request a review by an officer of decisions relating to homelessness and regulations set out the procedure to be followed, including the circumstances in which an oral hearing must be provided.[245] The Local Authority Social Services and National Health Service Complaints (England) Regulations 2009 provides a detailed framework which must be followed by NHS bodies for the handling complaints.[246] In other contexts public authorities choose to provide internal complaints systems of their own volition: these may be relatively informal (for example simply adopting a practice at looking again at decisions when requested to do so) or more systematised and elaborate.

In 2013, the Department of Work and Pensions introduced a policy of manda- **1-072** tory reconsideration, requiring all benefit decisions to be re-examined internally before a claimant may appeal to the First-tier Tribunal.[247] This reform aims, inter alia, to promote early resolution of disputes and reduce demand on HMCTS.[248] A recent consultation conducted by the Social Security Advisory Committee suggests that, while mandatory reconsideration has potential, the process does not work as well as it should; and makes a series of recommendations for improvement.[249]

There are some obvious benefits to encouraging internal resolution of griev- **1-073** ances within public authorities—including the relative speed and the modest costs incurred in looking again at a decision or investigating a complaint. Internal complaints are particularly well suited to cases where the aggrieved person is seeking an explanation for what has been decided or done, or an apology for poor service. Sometimes re-consideration of an application may result in a different outcome to the original determination. This said, in some contexts it may be open to doubt whether internal complaint systems are imbued with the values necessary to promote justice.[250] It has also been suggested that exposure to judicial review may

---

[244] See further D. Cowan and S. Halliday, *The Appeal of Internal Review* (2003); J. Gulland, "Independence in complaints procedures: lessons from community care" (2009) 31 J.S.W.F.L. 59 ("Most people do not make formal complaints at all and very few people seek an independent review of their complaint. When they do seek such a review, they expect it to be transparently independent of the body complained about. The article concludes that the current system of local authority complaints review panels or committees does not provide the independent element that complainants seek").

[245] Allocation of Housing and Homelessness (Review Procedures) Regulations 1999 (SI 1999/71); Department for Communities and Local Government, *Homelessness Code of Guidance for Local Authorities* (2006).

[246] SI 2009/309; and see also the Local Authority Social Services and National Health Service Complaints (England) (Amendment) Regulations 2009 (SI 2009/1768).

[247] Empowered by the Welfare Reform Act 2012 s.102.

[248] Department for Work and Pensions, *Appeals Reform: An Introduction* (August 2013).

[249] Social Security Advisory Committee, *Decision Making and Mandatory Reconsideration* (July 2016).

[250] D. Cowan and J. Fionda, "Homelessness Internal Appeals Mechanisms: Serving the Administrative Process" (1998) 27 Anglo-American L.R. 169, in their study of internal procedures relating to homelessness came to "the depressing conclusion that such systems have become cheap ways of denying justice. Nearly all the systems had design faults that make the walls of Jericho seem well constructed. Thus, the appeals processes become, in some instances, self-serving or an opportunity to adopt a view of the personal characteristics of the applicant" (pp.185–6).

have the effect of reducing willingness to carry out informal self-scrutiny of decisions.[251]

1-074 The Administrative Court looks favourably on the provision of internal complaint systems. A would-be judicial review claimant is likely to be refused permission to proceed with a claim for judicial review if he has failed to use a reasonably satisfactory internal complaints procedure.[252] The pre-action protocol for judicial review, published to accompany CPR Pt 54, requires that the claimant must in most situations write a letter before claim to the public authority "to identify the issues in dispute and establish whether litigation can be avoided".[253] Such a letter, in the absence of an established internal review system, ought normally to elicit a reconsideration of the initial decision. Would-be claimants need to bear in mind that claims for judicial review must be filed with the Administrative Court "promptly and in any event not later than 3 months after the grounds to make the claim first arose".[254] Arguably, grounds might "first arise" at the time of the initial decision by the public authority rather than at the conclusion of an internal review. It would however be antithetical to the idea of proportionate dispute resolution for a public authority which had failed to deal with an internal complaint promptly, or even within three months, to press the point that a subsequent claim for judicial review is out of time. What is more, the court has the power to extend time and is likely to do so if the complainant has acted reasonably.

1-075 On occasion, claimants have sought to challenge the lawfulness of an internal complaint or appeal system (rather than the initial decision by the public authority). In the homelessness context, it has been held that an internal review by a local authority officer of a homelessness application under the process required by the Housing Act 1996 s.202 is not flawed by apparent bias on the ground that that officer had been involved in a previous review of the claimant's case.[255] Nor is there apparent bias where an officer refuses an application and the goes on to determine an application under s.184 for temporary accommodation pending a review.[256] But an internal appeal procedure that "was clearly not impartial" led to the quashing of a local authority's decision to withdraw a licence for a person to work with vulnerable people.[257] In cases where "civil rights and obligations" within the meaning of ECHR art.6(1) are at stake,[258] an internal review or appeal process cannot amount to a decision by an independent and impartial tribunal (which is the protection afforded by art.6(1)). The English courts have, however, emphasised that what needs to be judged is not merely the initial decision and internal review, but also the pos-

---

[251] S. Halliday, "The Influence of Judicial Review on Bureaucratic Decision-Making" [2000] P.L. 110; D. Cowan and J. Fionda, "Homelessness Internal Appeals Mechanisms: Serving the Administrative Process" (1998) 27 Anglo-American L.R. 169.

[252] See 16-014. See, e.g. *R. (on the application of Bhatti) v Bury MBC* [2013] EWHC 3093 (Admin); (2014) 17 C.C.L. Rep. 64 (application to reinstate judicial review proceedings in community care proceedings dismissed. It would not be right to grant permission for the proceedings where there was an adequate alternative remedy and where the proceedings could be used as a mechanism for a challenge to new decisions).

[253] See Appendix I.

[254] CPR r.54.5, discussed at 16-055. This is a general requirement. In certain cases, stricter time limits apply.

[255] *Feld v Barnett* [2004] EWCA Civ 1307; [2005] H.L.R. 9.

[256] *R. (on the application of Abdi) v Lambeth LBC* [2007] EWHC 1565 (Admin); *The Times*, 11 July 2007.

[257] *R. (on the application of N) v A Local Authority* [2010] EWHC 3602 (Admin).

[258] See 7-119.

sibility of any subsequent appeal or review by a court—and such composite processes has been held in several different contexts to comply with art.6(1).[259]

Mediation

The courts have expressed a wish that before commencing a claim for judicial review the parties consider carefully whether mediation may resolve the dispute (and if so, to engage in mediation).[260] Despite judicial exhortation, the use of mediation in connection with judicial review claims is negligible. In 2007 the Public Law Project commenced a study of the value and limits of mediation in this context.[261] The possibilities for mediation exist beyond judicial review. The ombudsmen now have express powers to appoint and pay for mediators.[262] And it is envisaged that mediation will play a role in the new tribunal system created by the Tribunals, Courts and Enforcement Act 2007.[263]

1-076

Ombudsmen

Over recent decades there has been a burgeoning of grievance-handling schemes independent of the public authority (or private enterprise) against which a complaint

1-077

---

[259] See, e.g. *Tower Hamlets LBC v Begum (Runa)* [2003] UKHL 5; [2003] 2 A.C. 430 (review officer clearly not independent and impartial for purposes of ECHR art.6(1), but compliance was to be judged by looking at the composite process of internal review plus the possibility of appeal on point of law to the county court); *R. (on the application of Beeson) v Dorset CC* [2002] EWCA Civ 1812; [2003] H.R.L.R. 11 at [29] (emphasising that "even though the first decision-maker does not independently satisfy art.6 the quality of his decision is by no means therefore rendered nugatory or valueless"). But see now the ECtHR ruling in *Tsfayo v UK* (Application No.60860/00) (2009) 48 E.H.R.R. 18. On the meaning of "civil rights and obligations", see *Ali v Birmingham City Council* [2010] UKSC 8; [2010] 2 A.C. 39 where, unlike the entitlement to benefits in *Tsfayo*, the provision of housing to the homeless under the 1996 Housing Act did not engage a "civil right" within ECHR art.6. The award of services or benefits in kind which was dependent upon a series of evaluative judgments by the provider as to whether the statutory criteria had been satisfied and how the need for it ought to be met did not give rise to "civil rights".

[260] *Cowl v Plymouth City Council* [2001] EWCA Civ 1935; [2002] 1 W.L.R. 803, discussed at 16-022 (applied in *R. (on the application of C) v Nottingham City Council* [2010] EWCA Civ 790; [2011] 1 F.C.R. 127); see M. Supperstone, D. Stilitz and C. Sheldon, "ADR in Public Law" [2006] P.L. 299; S. Boyron, "The Rise of Mediation in Administrative Law Disputes: Experiences from England, France and Germany" [2006] P.L. 320.

[261] See V. Bondy and L. Mulcahy, *Mediation and Judicial Review: an empirical research study* (2009). The study concluded that "there is no single explanation for why there are so few mediations of public law disputes, nor it is possible to create a checklist of factors that would identify public law cases that are suitable for mediation" (p.89). An important context is that the vast majority of situations in which a claimant threatens judicial review, as well as of issued claims, are resolved before reaching the point of a full hearing in the Administrative Court: it is estimated that of 1,000 letters before claim written, only 46 cases will reach a full adjudication (p.19). The study found that there was no evidence to support the view that lawyers' lack of use of mediation in public law cases might be motivated by financial considerations. In cases where mediation was used or contemplated, lawyers took the view that they should be present and involved in the process to protect their clients' rights and interests especially where the clients were individuals challenging powerful public bodies. They also believe that mediators needed to understand the legal framework to the dispute in the context of public law challenges (p.59). There was a view that mediation "took too long to be of any help in urgent cases" (p.63). The study found no clear evidence to support a view that mediation is cheaper than judicial review litigation and urged caution in drawing comparisons in the costs of mediation in commercial disputes (p.69).

[262] See, e.g. in relation to the Parliamentary Ombudsmen, see Parliamentary Commissioner Act 1967 s.3(1A) (inserted by Regulatory Reform (Collaboration etc between Ombudsmen) Order 2007 (SI 2007/1889)).

[263] Tribunals, Courts and Enforcement Act 2007 s.24.

is made.[264] Some schemes are established by statute, others are non-statutory schemes set up by public authorities, and others are self-regulatory schemes run by particular private sector industries. The popular term "ombudsman" has been informally adopted by the three main public sector bodies—the Parliamentary Commissioner for Administration (PCA or Parliamentary Ombudsman),[265] the Health Service Commissioner for England (HSO or Health Service Ombudsman)[266]; and the Commission for Local Administration in England (CLA or Local Government Ombudsman (LGO)). All these ombudsmen have powers to provide mediation to complainants and may work jointly.[267]

1-078   In 2015 the Gordon Report recommended reform of the ombudsman sector and the creation of a new Public Service Ombudsman (PSO) uniting the existing jurisdictions of the Parliamentary and Health Service Ombudsman, Local Government Ombudsman and Housing Ombudsman.[268] The report makes a range of recommendations as to the role and powers of the proposed PSO, among them giving the PSO the task of promoting standards in public sector complaint-handling and improving access to the Ombudsman, including the suggestion that the PSO be furnished with "own initiative" powers to investigate complaints.[269] In December 2016, the Cabinet Office published the draft Public Sector Service Ombudsman Bill. The Bill incorporates a range of reform proposals, but differs from the Gordon Report in several respects, notably: it does not include the Housing Ombudsman; the proposed PSO will not have "own initiative" powers.[270]

1-079   As a consequence of devolution, Wales now has its own statutory ombudsman— the Public Services Ombudsman for Wales—dealing with complaints arising from matters relating the Assembly Government, health care in Wales, the work of local authorities and housing associations in Wales.[271] Similarly, an Act of the Scot-

---

[264] See further Law Commission, *Public Services Ombudsmen* (Law Com No.329, 2011), recommending among other things that the government establish a wide-ranging enquiry into ombudsmen; T. Buck, R. Kirkham and B. Thompson, *The Ombudsman Enterprise and Administrative Justice* (2011); J. Halford, "It's Public Law, But Not As We Know It: Understanding and Making Effective Use of Ombudsman Schemes" [2009] J.R. 81.

[265] Not to be confused with the Parliamentary Commissioner for Standards, the non-statutory office established by the House of Commons in 1995 to oversee the Register of Members' Interests and offer guidance and training for MPs on matters of conduct, propriety and ethics; the activities of the PCS are not subject to judicial review as he is concerned with activities within Parliament: *R. v Parliamentary Commissioner for Standards Ex p. Al-Fayed* [1998] 1 W.L.R. 669.

[266] The offices of PCA and HSC are held by the same person and there is considerable integration of the two legally separate bodies.

[267] Regulatory Reform (Collaboration etc between Ombudsmen) Order 2007 (SI 2007/1889).

[268] R. Gordon *Better to Serve the Public: Proposals to restructure, reform, renew and reinvigorate public services ombudsman* (2015), at para.57.

[269] R. Gordon *Better to Serve the Public: Proposals to restructure, reform, renew and reinvigorate public services ombudsman* (2015), at paras 137–138. The Cabinet Office's Consultation Paper on the creation of a Public Service Ombudsman, while accepting the need for enhanced access, did not seek views on "own initiative" powers: see Cabinet Office, *A Public Service Ombudsman- A Consultation* (March 2015).

[270] For commentary on the Draft Bill, see: R. Kirkham and B. Thompson, "*An initial commentary on the draft public services ombuds bill*", UK Administrative Justice Institute Blog, 20 December 2016; G. McBurnie, "*The draft Public Service Ombudsman Bill: What recommendations are being taken forward?*" UK Administrative Justice Institute Blog, 12 January 2017; D. Reynolds, "*A service user perspective of the draft legislation for the new Public Service Ombudsman*" 26 January 2017; N. O'Brien, "*No end of searching: A comment on the draft Public Service Ombudsman Bill 2016*" 2 February 2017.

[271] Public Services Ombudsman (Wales) Act 2005. M. Seneviratne, "A new ombudsman for Wales" [2006] P.L. 6. A draft Public Services Ombudsman (Wales) Bill, published in March 2016, makes a number of reform proposals to enhance the power of the ombudsman, including expanding its

tish Parliament has established the Scottish Public Services Ombudsman with jurisdiction over complaints relating to the Scottish Parliament and Executive, local government in Scotland, health care, housing, further and higher education institutions and a range of other public authorities.[272] The Northern Ireland Ombudsman (the working-title of the Assembly Ombudsman for Northern Ireland and the Northern Ireland Commissioner for Complaints) provides a service in that part of the United Kingdom.[273] The European Ombudsman investigates complaints about maladministration by the institutions and bodies of the European Union.[274] As well as seeking to resolve individual grievance, the ombudsmen have a role in improving the quality of decision-making in the public bodies within their jurisdictions.[275]

The Parliamentary Ombudsman

The PCA was established in 1967 following a campaign for a new means of investigating complaints against administrative decisions where there was no tribunal or other procedure for dealing with complaints. The PCA is led by the Commissioner (who also leads the Health Service Ombudsman), with 422 FTE staff working in London and Manchester. The PCA lays annual and special reports before Parliament and has a relationship with the House of Commons Public Administration Select Committee (PASC), before whom the Commissioner appears at least once a year. This link with Parliament serves a dual function: it provides scrutiny of the PCA's work and PASC may support the PCA in pressing for government action.[276] **1-080**

The function of the PCA is to investigate complaints from persons who claim to have "sustained injustice in consequence of maladministration" by specified central government bodies—including departments, executive agencies and non-departmental public bodies, or persons or bodies acting on their behalf, performing or failing to perform administrative (as distinct from judicial or legislative) functions.[277] Where authorities which are subject to the PCA's jurisdiction contract out services which are provided by other bodies, the ombudsman has the same power to investigate maladministration by the private contractor. This is important because of the widespread practice of "contracting out" public service provision to businesses and the voluntary sector. **1-081**

---

jurisdiction and conferring "own initiative" powers.

[272] Scottish Public Services Ombudsman Act 2002.

[273] Ombudsman (Northern Ireland) Order 1996 (SI 1006/1298); Commissioner for Complaints (Northern Ireland) Order 1996 (SI 1996/1297).

[274] Decision of the European Parliament on the regulations and general conditions governing the performance of the Ombudsman's duties, adopted by Parliament on March 9, 1994 ([1994] OJ L113/15) and amended by its decision of 14 March 2002 deleting arts 12 and 16 ([2002] OJ L92/13).

[275] See further C. Gill, "Right first time: the role of ombudsmen in influencing administrative decision-making" (2011) 33 J.S.W.F.L. 181; C. Gill, "The evolving role of the ombudsman: a conceptual and constitutional analysis of the 'Scottish Solution'" to administrative justice [2014] P.L. 662

[276] For reform proposals, see O. Gay and B. Winetrobe, *Officers of Parliament – transforming the role* (UCL Constitution Unit, 2003). For views of a former PCA, see: A. Abraham, "The Ombudsman as Part of the UK Constitution: A Contested Role?" (2008) 61 Parl. Aff. 206; "The Ombudsman and Individual Rights" (2008) 61 Parl. Aff. 370; "The Ombudsman and the Executive: The Road to Accountability" (2008) Parl. Aff. 535; "The Future in International Perspective: The Ombudsman as Agent of Rights, Justice and Democracy" (2008) 61 Parl. Aff. 681; "The ombudsman and 'paths to justice': a just alternative or just an alternative?" [2008] P.L. 1.

[277] Parliamentary Commissioner Act 1967 s.5. The list of public authorities subject to investigation by the PCA is found in Sch.2 to the Act, and currently range from the Administration of Radioactive Substances Advisory Board to the Zoos Forum.

1-082   "Injustice" has been widely interpreted to include "the sense of outrage aroused by unfair or incompetent administration", even where the complainant has suffered no actual loss.[278] "Maladministration" was deliberately left undefined in the Parliamentary Commissioner Act 1967; the PCA was to work out its meaning in developing a body of case law. The term includes: corruption; bias and unfair discrimination; misleading a member of the public; failure to notify him of his rights; losing or mislaying documents; sitting on a decision or an answer to a request for information for an inordinate length of time; failing to explain why a decision was made or why a situation had arisen when it was unreasonable to refuse; making a decision on the basis of faulty information which should have been properly ascertained and assembled; the dilatory and superficial handling of complaints by public authorities; refusal to answer reasonable questions; offering no redress or manifestly disproportionate redress; omitting to notify those who thereby lose rights of appeal and failing to advise on rights of appeal; failure by management to monitor compliance with adequate procedures; cavalier disregard of guidance which is intended to be followed in the interest of equitable treatment of those who use the service; failure to mitigate the rigid adherence to the letter of the law where that produces manifestly inequitable treatment.[279]

1-083   Complaints must be made within 12 months of the occurrence of the events complained about, although this period may be extended. The PCA cannot conduct an investigation of its own initiative. Although the "filter" has been much criticised, it remains the case that a complaint may only be accepted for formal investigation if it is referred to the PCA by a Member of Parliament. The Gordon Report recommended the removal of the MP filter, allowing the public to address the proposed PSO directly.[280]

1-084   In recent years the PCA, like the other ombudsmen, has adopted a range of informal methods of working which are not expressly referred to by the 1967 Act. Formal statutory investigations are therefore the exception rather than the rule. Investigations are conducted in private. No set procedure is prescribed, but the officials concerned must be given an opportunity to comment on the relevant allegations. The PCA has power to administer oaths and to compel the attendance of witnesses and the production of documents. Wilful obstruction of their investigations is punishable in the same way as a contempt of court. The PCA has access to all relevant documents except those relating to the Cabinet and its committees. Public interest can be asserted to prevent further dissemination of information by the PCA, but not to prevent him from acquiring it in the first place.[281]

1-085   Gaps still remain in the PCA's terms of reference. There can be no investigation of: personnel matters in the public service; commercial or contractual transactions (subject to some exceptions relating to the acquisition and disposal of land); action taken for the investigation and prevention of crime and the institution and conduct of civil and criminal proceedings; external relations, the rendition of fugitive offenders or action taken for the protection of State security (including the withholding of passports).

1-086   The PCA has no power to make mandatory orders, merely recommendations.[282] Central government bodies under the jurisdiction of the PCA in almost all cases ac-

---

[278] *Hansard*, HC Vol.734, col.51 (18 October 1966) (R. Crossman).
[279] Annual Report 1993 H.C. Paper No.290 (Session 1993/94), para.7.
[280] para.131.
[281] Parliamentary Commissioner Act 1967 ss.7–9, 11(3).
[282] *R. (on the application of Bradley) v Secretary of State for Work and Pensions* [2007] EWHC 242; [2007] Pens. L.R. 87 at [50]. And on appeal, see *R. (on the application of Bradley) v Secretary of*

cept the findings of investigations and provide the recommended redress. In the rare cases where this does not happen, the PCA may publish a special report and the matter will be raised in Parliament.[283] Since 2007, the PCA has formal powers to work collaboratively with the Health Service Ombudsman and the Local Government Ombudsman.[284]

Health Service Ombudsman for England

1-087 The PCA does not have jurisdiction to deal with complaints arising from the National Health Service. Instead, such complaints are dealt with by the Health Service Ombudsman (HSO)—a post that is in practice combined with that of the PCA.[285] In Wales, health service complaints are dealt with by the Public Services Ombudsman for Wales.[286] The HSO's jurisdiction has since 1996 extended to investigating action taken in exercise of clinical judgment.

1-088 A simpler two-stage complaints process was introduced by the Health and Social Care Act 2008, removing the requirement to complain to the Health Service Commission (now abolished) before approaching the HSO. Under the new scheme, complaints are made first to the local NHS body or practice; thereafter, if a person is dissatisfied with the way in which the local NHS body or practice has dealt with the complaint, a complaint may be made to the HSO. The reforms also introduced an integrated approach to both health and social care complaints. Complaints about social care (which is a local authority rather than NHS function) not resolved locally may be brought to the attention of the Local Government Ombudsman, which can work together on complaints that cross the boundaries of both systems.

Local Government Ombudsman

1-089 The LGO investigates complaints of injustice resulting from maladministration, a failure in a service that it is a function of an authority to provide, or a failure to provide such a service.[287] The LGO's jurisdiction is over local authorities in England[288]; additionally it has jurisdiction over registered social care providers[289];

State for Work and Pensions [2008] EWCA Civ 36; [2009] Q.B. 114 (considered below); and see further R. Kirkham, B. Thompson and T. Buck, "When Putting Things Right Goes Wrong: Enforcing the Recommendations of the Ombudsman" [2008] P.L. 510.

[283] For example, the Ministry of Defence did not accept all the findings, or agree to implement all the recommendations, of the PCA's investigation of failings in the ex gratia compensation scheme for British subjects interned by the Japanese during the Second World War. *"A Debt of Honour": the ex gratia scheme for British groups interned by the Japanese during the Second World War*, HC Paper No.324 (Session 2005). In 2006 the Department for Work and Pensions rejected all but one of the recommendations made by the PCA in relation to 75,000 people who lost all or part of their final salary occupational pensions on the winding up of their pension schemes (*Trusting in the Pensions Promise* (Cm. 6961) and for subsequent litigation see *Bradley* [2007] EWHC 242; [2007] Pens. L.R. 87.

[284] Primary legislation amended by Regulatory Reform (Collaboration etc between Ombudsmen) Order 2007 (SI 2007/1889).

[285] Health Service Commissioners Act 1993 (as amended).

[286] Public Services Ombudsman (Wales) Act 2005.

[287] Local Government Act 1974 ss.25–26.

[288] Local Government Act 1974 Pt 3. Local government complaints in Wales are dealt with the by Public Services Ombudsman for Wales. For a critical assessment of the LGO, see House of Commons Communities and Local Government Committee, *The Work of the Local Government Ombudsman*, HC 431 (Session 2012/13).

[289] Local Government Act 1974 Pt 3A ("Investigation of complaints about privately arranged or funded adult social care").

responsibility for local authority tenant complaints is moving to the Independent Housing Ombudsman; and a pilot project on internal school complaints led to responsibility being transferred back to the Secretary of State. Initial advice may be obtained by telephone.[290] The LGO is led by two Commissioners, with 215 staff working in offices in London, Coventry and York. Cases are allocated on the basis of geographical area. In addition to complaints by members of the public, the LGO may investigate where a compliant is referred by a member of an authority[291] and where an apparent case of maladministration comes to light even though they have received no complaint about the matter[292]; complaints about the procurement of goods and services are now within jurisdiction; the LGO may issue a "statement of reasons" instead of a report if they are satisfied with the council's proposals to remedy its failures; there are powers to publish LGO's decisions other than reports; and complaints no longer need to be in writing. As well as handing individual complaints, the LGO issues guidance on and seeks to promote good administrative practice.

1-090   The formal legal powers of the LGO are to conduct investigations and issue reports recommending redress, including financial reparation if appropriate; and to decide not to investigate a matter or to discontinue an investigation of a matter if satisfied with the action the authority has taken or is taking.[293] As with the other ombudsmen, a complainant must use the local authority's internal complaints processes before asking the LGO to investigate. Decisions of local authorities from which an appeal lies to a Minister may normally not be investigated by the LGO.[294]

1-091   A local authority in respect of which the LGO reports that there has been maladministration or service failure has a duty to consider the report within three months.[295] If a local authority refuses to accept the recommendation, the LGO has power to issue a further report. As well as publicising the report and allowing it to be publicly available, the report has to be laid before and considered by the authority, which must notify the LGO what it intends to do within specified time limits. If no notice is given or the LGO remains dissatisfied, it may issue a further report. Similar provisions apply to that further report and an unsatisfactory outcome may lead to the LGO requiring the authority to publish a statement in agreed form in the local press. Where this is refused, the LGO may publish such a statement at the authority's expense. Further reports must be considered by the local authority where the action recommended in the report is not taken.

Judicial review of ombudsmen

1-092   The PCA, HSC and LGO are public authorities carrying out a public function and thus in principle amenable to judicial review.[296] The absence of any statutory right of appeal against the findings of the ombudsmen makes judicial review the only

---

[290] *http://www.lgo.org.uk/making-a-complaint/* [Accessed 2 February 2013].

[291] Local Government Act 1974 s.26C.

[292] Local Government Act 1974 s.26D.

[293] Local Government Act 1974 s.24A; *R. (on the application of Adams) v Commission for Local Administration (Public Law Project intervening)* [2011] EWHC 2972 (Admin); [2012] P.T.S.R. 1172 (LGO acted unlawfully in failing to issue a statement of reasons for discontinuing).

[294] Local Government Act 1974 s.26(2)(b); however, it has been held that the Local Government Ombudsman was entitled to investigate the decisions of bodies hearing school admission appeals even though it was claimed the decision was made on the merits; he was investigating the process of decision: *R. v Commissioner for Local Administration Ex p. Croydon BC* [1989] 1 All E.R. 1033.

[295] Local Government Act 1974 s.31.

[296] See Ch.3.

process for questioning the lawfulness of their activity. This said, the court has indicated that it will not readily be persuaded to interfere with the broad discretionary powers of the ombudsmen, given their width and the high degree of subjective judgment involved.[297] Where an ombudsman report expresses an opinion that adversely affects a person's reputation, "a process which resulted in almost bare conclusions without significant reasoning would be unfair to those criticised".[298] Successful judicial review claims against the ombudsmen have involved: an investigation which failed to regard a public authority's refusal to exercise a power as maladministration[299]; the provision of inadequate reasons to explain a refusal to conduct and inquiry and refusal to disclose interview notes[300]; issuing a report that went beyond the formal powers of the ombudsman[301]; failing to issue a statement of reasons for discontinuing an investigation[302]; applying the wrong standard of proof to the question whether a consultant surgeon had acted unreasonably in the management of a patient after his discharge from hospital[303]; and then recommendation of financial compensation following the investigation of a complaint where the complainant had a remedy in damages in a court of law.[304]

Judicial review of failure to implement ombudsman findings and recommendations

Generally, there is a high level of compliance by public authorities with ombudsmen reports. Occasionally, however, a public authority subject to a formal investigation by an ombudsman may be inclined to disagree with findings contained in a report, may be disinclined to implement recommendations made, or both.[305] The extent to which a public authority may reject findings and recommendations of the ombudsmen is governed by the different statutory and constitutional frameworks in which these ombudsmen operate (the Parliamentary Commissioner for Administration Act 1967 in the case of the PCA and the Local Government Act 1974 in relation to the LGO). The PCA has express power to lay a report before Parliament where "it appears ... that the injustice" investigated "has not or will not be remedied"[306] but there are no legal powers of enforcement. Other than publicity, the LGO has no powers to compel action from a public authority following an adverse report: the only express sanction for a local authority's failure to follow LGO recommendations is local publicity, "leaving the electors to determine whether

1-093

---

[297] *R. v Parliamentary Commissioner for Administration Ex p. Dyer* [1994] 1 W.L.R. 621. *R. v Commissioner for Local Administration Ex p. Eastleigh BC* [1988] Q.B. 855; *R. v Commissioner for Local Administration Ex p. Croydon LBC* [1989] 1 All E.R. 1033.

[298] *R. (on the application of Attwood) v Health Service Commissioner* [2008] EWHC 2315 (Admin); [2009] P.T.S.R. 1330 at [47].

[299] *R. v Parliamentary Commissioner for Administration Ex p. Balchin (No.1)* [1998] 1 P.L.R. 1; *R. v Parliamentary Commissioner for Administration Ex p. Balchin (No.2)* (2000) 2 L.G.L.R. 87.

[300] *R. (on the application of Turpin) v Commissioner for Local Administration* [2001] EWHC Admin 503; [2003] B.L.G.R. 133,

[301] *R. (on the application of Cavanagh) v Health Services Commissioner* [2005] EWCA Civ 1578; [2006] 1 F.C.R. 7.

[302] *R. (on the application of Adams) v Commission for Local Administration (Public Law Project intervening)* [2011[EWHC 2972 (Admin); [2012] P.T.S.R. 1172.

[303] *R. (on the application of Attwood) v Health Service Commissioner* [2008] EWHC 2315 (Admin); [2009] P.T.S.R. 1330.

[304] *JR55 v Northern Ireland Commissioner for Complaints* [2016] UKSC 22; [2016] 4 All E. R. 779.

[305] R. Kirkham, B. Thompson and T. Buck, "When Putting Things Right Goes Wrong: Enforcing the Recommendations of the Ombudsman" [2008] P.L. 510.

[306] Parliamentary Commissioner Act 1967 s.10(3).

the local authority had behaved acceptably in rejecting any recommendation designed to remedy an injustice to a local citizen".[307]

1-094   In relation to the PCA, the Court of Appeal in *R. (on the application of Bradley) v Secretary of State for Work and Pensions*[308] accepted what was common ground between the parties: that the PCA's *recommendations*, as opposed to findings of "maladministration" and "injustice", were not binding on the Secretary of State. The issue in contention was that the Secretary of State disagreed with the PCA's factual findings and conclusions (in relation to guidance issued about occupational pensions). Sir John Chadwick drew a distinction between the PCA and the LGO: "there is no separation of powers in local government which corresponds to the separation, in national government, between the powers of the executive and the powers of parliament" and "a Minister who rejects the Ombudsman's findings of maladministration will have to defend him or herself in Parliament, and will be subject to Parliamentary control".[309] The constitutional question was whether this should lead to the conclusion that, when enacting the Parliamentary Commissioner for Administration 1967 Act, "Parliament intended to preclude a Minister who was called to account before either House from explaining, as part of his justification for the decision to provide no remedy in respect of the complaint which has been the subject of investigation, his reasons for rejecting the Parliamentary Commissioner's finding of maladministration". Sir John Chadwick set out the following principles.[310]

"(i)   the decision maker whose decision is under challenge … is entitled to exercise his own discretion as to whether he should regard himself as bound by a finding of fact made by an adjudicative tribunal … in a related context;

(ii)   a decision to reject a finding of fact made by an adjudicative tribunal in a related context can be challenged on *Wednesbury* grounds;

(iii)   in particular, the challenge can be advanced on the basis that the decision to reject the finding of fact was irrational;

(iv)   in determining whether the decision to reject the finding of fact was irrational the court will have regard to the circumstances in which, and the statutory scheme within which, the finding of fact was made by the adjudicative tribunal;

(v)   in particular, the court will have regard to the nature of the fact found (e.g. that the immigrant was an adulterer), the basis on which the finding was made (e.g. on oral testimony tested by cross-examination, or purely on the documents), the form of the proceedings before the tribunal (e.g. adversarial and in public, or investigative with no opportunity for cross-examination), and the role of the tribunal within the statutory scheme."

The "fundamental point" was to recognise that the Court of Appeal judgment in *R. v Local Commissioner for Administration Ex p. Eastleigh BC*[311] was not authority for the proposition that "the Secretary of State is bound by the Parliamentary Ombudsman's findings of maladministration and must treat them as correct unless

---

[307] *R. (on the application of Gallagher and another) v Basildon DC* [2010] EWHC 2824 (Admin); [2011] P.T.S.R. 731 at [26].

[308] *R. (on the application of Bradley) v Secretary of State for Work and Pensions* [2008] EWCA Civ 36; [2009] Q.B. 114; J. Varuhas, "Governmental Rejections of Ombudsman Findings: What Role for the Courts?" (2009) 72 M.L.R. 102.

[309] *R. (on the application of Bradley) v Secretary of State for Work and Pensions* [2008] EWCA Civ 36; [2009] Q.B. 114 at [58] (Sir John Chadwick) and [137] (Wall LJ).

[310] *R. (on the application of Bradley) v Secretary of State for Work and Pensions* [2008] EWCA Civ 36; [2009] Q.B. 114 at [70], derived from the judgments in *R. v Warwickshire CC Ex p. Powergen Plc* (1998) 75 P. & C.R. 89 and *R. v Secretary of State for the Home Department Ex p. Danaei* [1997] EWCA Civ 2704; [1998] Imm. A.R. 84.

[311] *R. v Local Commissioner for Administration Ex p. Eastleigh BC* [1988] 1 Q.B. 855.

and until they are quashed in judicial review proceedings".[312] The question is not whether the Secretary of State himself "considers that there was any maladministration, but whether in the circumstances his rejection of the Ombudsman's finding to this effect is based on a cogent reason".[313] The court concluded in relation to one finding that the minister had advanced sound arguments but no such reasons existed in relation to another finding; accordingly, the Secretary of State's department was required to reconsider its response. The "cogent reasons" requirement "is not a precise test" but requires "a careful examination of the facts of the individual case—with the focus resting upon the decision to reject the findings of the Ombudsman, rather than the Ombudsman's findings themselves".[314]

The legal and constitutional position of the LGO is different from that of the PCA, so the scope for a local authority wanting to disagree with the findings and recommendations of the LGO may be more limited. The LGO, unlike the PCA, has no power to pursue a failure to implement a recommendation in Parliament. In *Bradley*, it was suggested that "the system ... depends on the convention that local authorities will be bound by the findings of the LGO. It must follow inexorably that if a local authority wishes to avoid findings of maladministration made by a LGO, it must apply for judicial review to quash the decision".[315] The Administrative Court subsequently rejected the notion that a requirement of "cogent reasons" for refusing to follow recommendations was superimposed on the statutory framework, reiterating that the only grounds of challenge were irrationality or that the decision was "otherwise flawed on a recognised public law ground".[316]

1-095

Overlap of jurisdiction between judicial review and the ombudsmen

Maladministration (the province of the ombudsmen) and unlawfulness (the jurisdiction of the Administrative Court) are overlapping categories of complaint[317]: for example, bias, fettering a discretion, taking into account irrelevant considerations, disproportionate decision, and failure to follow a code of practice may well constitute both maladministration and provide a basis for judicial review. The main public sector ombudsmen have no jurisdiction to investigate a complaint if the complainant has or had a remedy by way of proceeding in any court of law unless the ombudsman is satisfied that, in the particular circumstances, it is not reasonable to expect the person aggrieved to have resorted or to resort to court proceedings.[318] In such cases, if a claim for judicial review is actually com-

1-096

---

[312] *R. (on the application of Bradley) v Secretary of State for Work and Pensions* [2008] EWCA Civ 36; [2009] Q.B. 114 at [135](Wall LJ).

[313] *R. (on the application of Bradley) v Secretary of State for Work and Pensions* [2008] EWCA Civ 36; [2009] Q.B. 114 at [72] (Sir John Chadwick).

[314] *R. (on the application of Equitable Members Action Group) v Her Majesty's Treasury* [2009] EWHC 2495 (Admin) at [66].

[315] *R. (on the application of Bradley) v Secretary of State for Work and Pensions* [2008] EWCA Civ 36; [2009] Q.B. 114 at [139](Wall LJ).

[316] *R. (on the application of Gallagher) v Basildon DC* [2010] EWHC 2824 (Admin); [2011] P.T.S.R. 731.

[317] *R. v Local Commissioner for Local Government for North and North East England Ex p. Liverpool City Council* [2001] 1 All E.R. 462 (Henry LJ: "What may not have been recognised back in 1974 was the emergence of judicial review to the point where most if not almost all matters which could form the basis for a complaint of maladministration are matters for which the elastic qualities of judicial review might provide a remedy").

[318] Parliamentary Commissioner Act 1967 s.5(2); Local Government Act 1974 s.26(6); Health Service Commissioners Act 1993 s.4(1); Public Services Ombudsman (Wales) Act 2005 s.9. The Law Commission has recommended that these statutory bars be repealed and replaced with the discretion for

menced, the ombudsman will be deprived of jurisdiction to investigate the matter.[319] In cases where legal proceedings have not yet started, both the ombudsmen and the Administrative Court have considerable latitude to form judgments as to which avenue the complainant should reasonably pursue. The ombudsmen have for their parts adopted a flexible approach.[320] A practical approach is required. In cases where extensive fact-finding is needed to deal with the complaint, an ombudsman will generally be a better route.[321] So too where the redress sought is relatively modest compensation.[322] The ombudsmen may also have regard to the emotional and financial cost of a claim for judicial review.[323] In contrast, judicial review is likely to be the more suitable avenue where a case turns on a dispute about the correct interpretation of statutory provisions or where an interim remedy is needed; but an ombudsman is not required to decline to investigate a complaint merely because a question of disability law arises.[324] On occasion, the court has refused permission to proceed with a claim for judicial review on the ground that a complaint to an ombudsman is a satisfactory alternative remedy,[325] and the development of proportionate dispute resolution principles may well result in this becoming more common.[326]

1-097   The Law Commission has recommended that the Administrative Court should have an express power to stay a claim for judicial review in order to allow an ombudsman to investigate the matter in dispute.[327] In turn, the ombudsmen "should be given a specific power to make a reference to the Administrative Court asking a question on a point of law".[328]

---

an ombudsman to open an investigation: Law Commission, *Public Services Ombudsmen* (Law Com No.329, 2011), Recommendation 3. See *R. (on the application of ER) v Commissioner for Local Administration in England (Local Government Ombudsman)* [2014] EWCA Civ 1407; [2015] E.L.R. 36 (LGO has no jurisdiction to investigate the *consequences* of a decision if investigation of the decision itself is excluded by s.26(6) because of right of appeal to Special Educational Needs and Disability Tribunal).

[319] *R. (on the application of Scholarstica UMO) v Commissioner for Local Administration* [2003] EWHC 3202 (Admin); [2004] E.L.R. 265 (Beatson J: "Accordingly, those advising individuals regarding matters potentially giving rise to both local commissioner investigations and to judicial review should first seek an investigation by the local commission"); this perhaps overlooks the practical difficulty that claims for judicial review must be made promptly and in any event within three months (see 16-050) while there is a 12 month time limit for complaints to the ombudsmen.

[320] E. Osmotherly, "*The Local Government Ombudsman as an alternative to judicial review*" (statement previously published on LGO website but no longer there).

[321] *R. v Local Commissioner for Local Government for North and North East England Ex p. Liverpool City Council* [2001] 1 All E.R. 462.

[322] *R. (on the application of Anufrijeva) v Southwark LBC* [2003] EWCA Civ 1406; [2004] Q.B. 1124; discussed at 19-085.

[323] Parliamentary Ombudsman, "*A Debt of Honour": the ex gratia scheme for British groups interned by the Japanese during the Second World War.* HC Paper No.324 (Session 2005/06), para.26. The Government in its response to the draft report took a different view, arguing that the complainant could reasonably have pursued judicial review proceedings (as others had done in *R. (on the application of Association of British Civilian Internees (Far East Region)) v Secretary of State for Defence* [2003] EWCA Civ 473; [2003] Q.B. 1397). The PASC supported the PCA's view: PASC, "A Debt of Honour", HC Paper No.735 (Session 2005/06), para.20.

[324] *R. (on the application of Mencap) v Parliamentary and Health Service Commissioners (Equality and Human Rights Commission intervening)* [2011] EWHC 3351 (Admin); [2012] P.T.S.R. Digest D17.

[325] See 16-021; *R. v Lambeth LBC Ex p. Crookes* (1997) 29 H.L.R. 28.

[326] *R. (on the application of Anufrijeva) v Southwark LBC* [2003] EWCA Civ 1406; [2004] Q.B. 1124.

[327] Law Commission, *Public Services Ombudsmen* (Law Com No.329, 2011), Recommendation 4.

[328] Law Commission, *Public Services Ombudsmen* (Law Com No.329, 2011), Recommendation 7.

Tribunals

The tribunal system (now rationalised into the First-Tier Tribunal and the Up- **1-098** per Tribunal) intersects with judicial review in two main ways. First, the tribunal system provides a more specialised method of supervising the legality (and in many cases the merits) of decision-making by public authorities. Where an aggrieved person has the possibility of an appeal to a tribunal, the Administrative Court will be reluctant to grant permission to proceed with a claim for judicial review.[329] Secondly, judicial review may in some situations be used to challenge the lawfulness of decisions taken by a tribunal.[330]

In the design of an administrative justice system, a tribunal may be preferred to **1-099** an ordinary court because its members have specialised knowledge of the subject-matter, because it will be more informal in its trappings and procedure, because it may be better at finding facts, applying flexible standards and exercising discretionary powers, and because it may be cheaper, more accessible and more expeditious than the High Court. Many of the decisions given to tribunals concern the merits of cases with relatively little legal content, and in such cases a tribunal, usually consisting of a legally qualified tribunal judge and two lay members, may be preferred to a court. Indeed dissatisfaction with the over-technical and allegedly unsympathetic approach of the courts towards social welfare legislation led to a transfer of functions to special tribunals; the Workmen's Compensation Acts were administered by the ordinary courts, but the National Insurance (Industrial Injuries) scheme was applied by tribunals. It is, however, unrealistic to imagine that technicalities and difficult legal issues can somehow be avoided by entrusting the administration of complex legislation to tribunals rather than the courts.[331] Until the coming into force of the Tribunals, Courts and Enforcement Act 2007, a wide range of grievances against public authorities were dealt with by a system of about 70 statutory tribunals, deciding over 1 million cases each year. The case load is dominated by adjudication on welfare benefits and immigration and asylum.

In 1957, the Franks Committee considered that "tribunals should properly be **1-100** regarded as machinery provided by Parliament for adjudication rather than as part of the machinery of administration",[332] and it made a number of detailed recommendations (most of which were implemented) to achieve that object and to improve the procedure at statutory inquiries that preceded a ministerial decision.[333] The Franks Committee sought the qualities of "openness, fairness and impartiality" in tribunals. Nonetheless, until the 2007 Act there remained a great deal of dissatisfaction with the design and operation of tribunals. The structure of the system was widely regarded as haphazard and unnecessarily complex.[334] Doubts were also been expressed as to the degree of independence and impartiality of some tribunals, especially those that were administered by the government department against whose decisions they heard appeals.

---

[329] See 16-018.

[330] See 17-004.

[331] Research published by the Council on Tribunals suggests that tribunal users were often confused about procedures: M. Adler and J. Gulland, *Tribunal Users' Experience: Perceptions and Expectations: A Literature Review* (2003).

[332] *Report of the Committee on Administrative Tribunals and Enquiries*, Cmnd. 218 (1957), p.9.

[333] For the implementation of the Committee's recommendations, see esp. Tribunals and Inquiries Act 1958 (now Tribunals and Inquiries Act 1992) and the statutory rules of procedure promulgated for planning, compulsory purchase and highways inquiries.

[334] H. Woolf, "A Hotchpotch of Appeals—The Need for a Blender" [1988] C.J.Q. 44.

Tribunals after the Tribunals, Courts and Enforcement Act 2007

1-101   The 2007 Act amalgamated almost all the previously separate tribunal jurisdictions into a new structure comprising the First-tier Tribunal and the Upper Tribunal.[335] The Upper Tribunal is a superior court of record,[336] on which High Court judges may sit, concerned mainly with appeals from the First-tier Tribunal.[337] Under secondary legislation, the First-tier Tribunal and Upper Tribunal are divided into chambers (each one headed by a judicial figure called the Chamber President), with jurisdiction over a specified subject or geographical area or a combination of the two. The independence of tribunal judges is protected by a statutory guarantee.[338] A judge is Senior President of Tribunals, with overarching responsibility for the system.[339]

1-102   The 2007 Act has its origins in a report of a major review chaired by Sir Andrew Leggatt in 2001. A series of far-reaching recommendations were made.[340] The review was established because of concern by the then Lord Chancellor, Lord Irvine, that tribunals should provide "fair, timely and proportionate and effective arrangements for handling disputes" and a "coherent structure" for the delivery of administrative justice. Lord Justice Leggatt saw need for radical change. He observed that the present tribunal system had grown up in a "haphazard" way, providing no coherence and was "developed more to meet the needs and convenience of the departments and other bodies which run tribunals, rather than the needs of the user". He recommended that the tribunals should be rationalised and, in order to ensure their independence from government departments, administered by a new executive agency, reporting to the Department of Constitutional Affairs, in parallel with the new Court Service which has been established to administer the courts. He made a number of detailed arrangements for improvements to such matters as procedures, administration and routes of appeal.

1-103   Those recommendations were broadly accepted by the Government which issued a White Paper in July 2004.[341] The White Paper was not, however, content with simply preserving the existing procedures and proposed an approach which would "re-engineer processes radically so that just solutions can be found without hearings at all" and be able not only to provide authoritative rulings where those were needed but also to "resolve disputes fairly and informally". The 2007 Act contains express provision for mediation, but subject to the safeguards that "(a) mediation of matters in dispute between parties to proceedings is to take place only by agreement between those parties; and (b) where parties to proceedings fail to mediate, or where mediation between parties to proceedings fails to resolve disputed matters, the failure is not to affect the outcome of the proceedings".[342]

---

[335] See generally, R. Carnwath, "Tribunal Justice—a New Start" [2009] P.L. 48; P. Cane, "Judicial Review in the Age of Tribunals" [2009] P.L. 479; E. Laurie, "Assessing the Upper Tribunal's potential to deliver administrative justice" [2012] P.L. 288. Immigration and asylum adjudication, previously kept separate, was transferred to the First-Tier Tribunal and Upper Tribunal in 2010.

[336] TCEA s.3(5).

[337] It also hears appeals from other adjudicatory bodies, including the Traffic Commissioners.

[338] TCEA s.1.

[339] TCEA s.2. It is proposed that this responsibility will be transferred to the Lord Chief Justice of England and Wales.

[340] Sir Andrew Leggatt, *Report of the Review of Tribunals: Tribunals for Users—One System, One Service* (2001) *http://www.tribunals-review.org.uk*.

[341] DCA, *Transforming Public Services: Complaints, Redress and Tribunals*, Cm. 6243 (2004).

[342] TCEA s.24.

Review and appeal in the new tribunal system

Like other courts, the First-tier Tribunal and the Upper Tribunal are public authorities operating under the rule of law and it is important that parties aggrieved by their determinations are able to challenge them. There are three main ways of challenging decisions. First, "reviews" may be carried out to identify and correct errors without the need for a full appeal. The First-tier Tribunal has discretion to carry out a review of its decisions, either of its own motion or at the request of a party[343]; if a decision is set-aside, the First-tier Tribunal may make the decision again or refer the matter to the Upper Tribunal. The Upper Tribunal also has powers to review its own decisions on a similar basis.[344]   **1-104**

Secondly, there are rights of appeal. In most cases, parties have a right of appeal on point of law, subject to permission, from the First-tier Tribunal to the Upper Tribunal.[345] If the Upper Tribunal holds that the decision was subject to an error of law, it may set aside the First-tier Tribunal decision and either take the decision itself or remit the case to the First-tier Tribunal for redetermination.[346] There is a further appeal on point of law, subject to permission, from the Upper Tribunal to the Court of Appeal, which may if it allows the appeal remit the matter back to the Upper Tribunal for re-decision or re-make a decision itself.[347] The Upper Tribunal has no jurisdiction to review its own refusal of permission to appeal.[348] The approach of the Court of Appeal and Supreme Court to considering appeals on points of law from the First-tier Tribunal is "that judicial restraint should be exercised when the reasons that a tribunal gives for its decision are being examined".[349]   **1-105**

Thirdly, a decision of the Upper Tribunal to refuse permission to appeal against the First-Tier Tribunal may be subject to challenge by way of a claim for judicial review in the Administrative Court where the claim "raises an important point of principle or practice" or "there is some other compelling reason to hear it".[350]   **1-106**

"Judicial Review" by the Upper Tribunal

The Upper Tribunal carries out "judicial review"[351] Under this arrangement, the Upper Tribunal has a supervisory jurisdiction similar to that of the Administrative   **1-107**

---

[343] TCEA s.9.

[344] TCEA s.10.

[345] TCEA s.11.

[346] TCEA s.12.

[347] TCEA s.13. The grounds of appeal are the same as those applying in the court system: (a) that the proposed appeal would raise some important point of principle or practice, or (b) that there is some other compelling reason to hear the appeal. On the approach to be adopted by appellate courts see, e.g. *Cooke v Secretary of State for Social Security* [2001] EWCA Civ 734; [2002] 3 All E.R. 279, [16] (CA should be cautious in the exercise of its discretion before interpolating its own view into that of the specialist tribunal); *Secretary of State for the Home Department v AH (Sudan)* [2007] UKHL 49; [2008] 1 A.C. 678; *RB (Algeria) v Secretary of State for the Home Department* [2009] UKHL 10; [2010] 2 A.C. 110 at [219]–[221]; *VH (Malawi) v Secretary of State for the Home Department* [2009] EWCA Civ 645 at [73]; *British Broadcasting Corporation and another v Sugar (No.2)* [2010] EWCA Civ 715; [2010] 1 W.L.R. 2278 at [23]. For analysis of the degree of deference appellate courts should accord to tribunals, see further E. Laurie, "Assessing the Upper Tribunal's potential to deliver administrative justice" [2012] P.L. 288.

[348] *Samuda v Secretary of State for Work and Pensions* [2014] EWCA Civ 1; [2014] 3 All E.R. 201.

[349] *Jones (by Caldwell) (Respondent) v First Tier Tribunal* [2013] UKSC 19; [2013] 2 A.C. 48 at [25] per Lord Hope.

[350] CPR 54.7A; following clarification by the Supreme Court in *R. (Cart) v Upper Tribunal (Public Law Project and another intervening)* [2011] UKSC 28; [2012] 1 A.C. 663. See 17-006.

[351] TCEA ss.15–18. The quotation marks are used in the Act.

Court in terms of the grounds of review, the remedial orders that it may make and subject to similar limits on its jurisdiction. Four conditions have to be met before a case falls within the Upper Tribunal's "judicial review" jurisdiction[352]: (a) the applicant seeks relief of the type normally available on judicial review claims under CPR Pt 54[353]—and nothing else; (b) the application does not call into question anything done in the Crown Court[354] (c) the application falls within a class of cases specified by a direction made by the Lord Chief Justice of England and Wales or his nominee and approved by the Lord Chancellor; and (d) the judge sitting in the Upper Tribunal is a High Court or Court of Appeal judge, or a judge agreed by the Lord Chief Justice of England and Wales and the Senior President of Tribunals. "Judicial review" claims come to the Upper Tribunal either because it is mandatory for them to do so (under the Lord Chief Justice's direction) or as discretionary transfers from the Administrative Court (usually where it is thought that the Upper Tribunal has expertise in the subject matter or will be able to deal with the matter more flexibly).[355]

PUBLIC INQUIRIES AND INQUESTS

Town and country planning

1-108   One type of public inquiry provides a means of appealing to the Secretary of State (in England) or National Assembly for Wales (in Wales) against decisions of local authorities in relation to planning and highways and transport proposals, rights of way and compulsory purchase.[356] Most appeals are in fact dealt with without a public inquiry—by exchange of written representations or a hearing; only some four per cent of appeals result in an inquiry. They are conducted by planning inspectors employed by the Planning Inspectorate, which is an executive agency under the auspices of the Department for Communities and Local Government in England (and the Welsh Assembly Government in Wales). At an inquiry, the developer and opposers are able to put their case by submitting written evidence and calling and cross-examining witnesses. The inspector's report makes findings of fact and recommendations to the relevant minister advising how statutory discretion should be exercised on the basis of law and government policy. In the vast majority of cases ministers accept the inspectors' recommendations. Neither inspectors nor ministers in the planning inquiry process constitute an "independent and impartial" tribunal for the purposes of determining civil rights and obligations under ECHR art.6(1).[357] There is, however, a right of appeal to the Administrative Court, on point of law, and this has been held to provide sufficient judicial oversight of the lawfulness of decision-making to comply with art.6(1).[358] In relation to aspects of the inquiry

---

[352] TCEA s.18.

[353] A mandatory, prohibiting, or quashing order, a declaration or injunction; permission to apply for "judicial review"; costs; interest; and monetary remedies.

[354] 3-009; Note that this is wider than the prohibition on the Administrative Court hearing judicial reviews on matters "relating to trials on indictment".

[355] See further 17-004.

[356] See, e.g. Town and Country Planning (Inquiries Procedure) Rules 1992 (SI 1992/2038). At the time of writing (February 2013), the Growth and Infrastructure Bill is before Parliament; it will introduce a range of changes to the planning system.

[357] See 10-083.

[358] *R. v Secretary of State for the Environment, Transport and the Regions Ex p. Holdings & Barnes Plc (the Alconbury case)* [2001] UKHL 23; [2003] 2 A.C. 295; see 10-083.

process from which there is no statutory appeal, a claim for judicial review under CPR Pt 54 may be made.

Other public inquiries

A different type of public inquiry is those established by ministers to investigate and make recommendations about events that have caused public concern.[359] The main legal basis for such inquiries is the Inquiries Act 2005, though ministers (and indeed other public authorities) may continue to establish ad hoc non-statutory investigative inquiries without formal legal powers. The 2005 Act provides ministers with a broad discretion to decide whether or not to call an inquiry, to determine terms of reference, appoint panel members[360] and restrict public access to information. Several bodies, including Amnesty International and the Law Society of England and Wales, have expressed disquiet about the degree of ministerial control over inquiries under the 2005 Act. Inquiries established under the 2005 Act must avoid ruling on any person's civil or criminal liability, though an inquiry panel is not to be "inhibited in the discharge of its functions by any likelihood of liability being inferred from facts that it determines or recommendations that it makes".[361] In March 2014, a House of Lords Select Committee reported on post-legislative scrutiny of the Inquiries Act 2005. Noting that no inquiry had been set up under the 2005 Act since 2011, but a number of non-statutory inquiries had been established, the committee recommended: "Ministers have at their disposal on the statute book an Act and Rules which, subject to the reservations we have set out, in our view constitute a good framework for such inquiries. Ministers should be ready to make better use of these powers, and should set up inquiries under the Inquiries Act unless there are overriding reasons of security or sensitivity for doing otherwise."[362] The Government rejected this recommendation (and several others), arguing that "Ministers should not feel constrained from considering other options which may be better suited to the circumstances".[363]

1-109

Given the controversial contexts in which public inquiries arise it is perhaps unsurprising that decisions relating to public inquiries have been subject to judicial review challenges. The 2005 Act expressly anticipates such challenges and requires claims for judicial review of decisions made by a minister in relation to an inquiry or a by a member of an inquiry panel, must be brought within 14 days after the day on which the claimant became aware of the decision, unless that time limit is extended by the court.[364] The normal time limit for claims for judicial review (promptly and in any event within three months) applies to challenges to the contents of reports and decisions of which the claimant could not have become aware until the publication of the report.[365]

1-110

Judicial review may be directed at three main types of decisions relating to public

1-111

---

[359] I. Steele, "Judging judicial inquiries" [2004] P.L. 738; Lord Thomas of Cwmgiedd "The future of public inquiries" [2015] P.L. 225.

[360] Ministers have often chosen judges to chair inquiries: J. Beatson, "Should Judges Conduct Public Inquiries?" (2005) 121 L.Q.R. 221; R. Masterman, "A Supreme Court for the United Kingdom: Two Steps Forward, But One Step Back on Judicial Independence" [2004] P.L. 48.

[361] Inquiries Act 2005 s.1.

[362] House of Lords Select Committee on the Inquiries Act 2005, *The Inquiries Act 2005: Post-legislative Scrutiny*, HL Paper 143, para.300.

[363] Ministry of Justice, *Government Response to the Report of the House of Lords Select Committee on the Inquiries Act 2005*, Cm 8903 (June 2014). For commentary on the Select Committee recommendations see Lord Thomas, "The Future of Public Inquiries" [2015] P.L. 225.

[364] Inquiries Act 2005 s.38(1).

[365] Inquiries Act 2005 s.38(2). On normal provisions for time limits, see 16-053.

inquiries. First, a claimant may seek to challenge a decision to hold or not hold an inquiry, or the basis on which the inquiry is to operate. Relatives of victims of Dr Harold Shipman successfully claimed that the Secretary of State for Health's decision to hold an internal departmental inquiry in the circumstances surrounding the multiple murders was irrational and a statutory public inquiry under the Tribunals of Inquiry (Evidence) Act 1921 (now repealed by the 2005 Act) was subsequently held.[366] This ruling has, however, been distinguished in later cases and it would seem doubtful whether there is any general proposition of law favouring public inquiries over internal government inquiries.[367] In R. (on the application of Litvinenko) v Secretary of State for the Home Department, the Secretary of State refused the coroner's request to replace an inquest with an inquiry under the Inquiries Act 2005, to permit account to be taken of closed material that the coroner was not permitted to consider. The Divisional Court held that the Secretary of State's refusal was irrational.[368]

1-112 Secondly, judicial review challenges may be brought to question decisions relating to the procedures adopted by an inquiry (and it is in relation to this category that most challenges have been made).[369]

1-113 Thirdly, it may be possible to challenge the findings of a report made by a public inquiry.[370] In *Mahon v Air New Zealand*, the Privy Council set aside a costs order of a Royal Commission (Justice Peter Mahon) into the crash of aircraft in the Antarctic in 1977 in which 257 people died. The report stated that there had been "an orchestrated litany of lies" by executives of Air New Zealand, and on that basis the costs order had been made. The Privy Council held that there was no probative evidence of such lies and no opportunity had been given to those implicated by the findings to make representations before the report was published. *Mahon*, arguably, does not provide clear authority for the amenability to judicial review of findings by a public authority.[371] Even if findings of fact are amenable, the court will

---

366 *R. (on the application of Wagstaff) v Secretary of State for Health* [2001] 1 W.L.R. 292. The internal inquiry under the chairmanship of Lord Laming of Tewin was stopped and a public inquiry under the terms of the 1921 Act was subsequently held under the chairmanship of Dame Janet Smith.

367 See, e.g. *R. (on the application of Howard) v Secretary of State for Health* [2002] EWHC 396 (Admin); [2003] Q.B. 830 (no presumption inquiries ordered under National Health Service Act 1977 s.84(1) would be public); *R. (on the application of Persey) v Secretary of State for the Environment, Food and Rural Affairs* [2002] EWHC 371; [2003] Q.B. 794 (Government to set up three separate independent inquiries, receiving evidence mainly in private, into a serious outbreak of foot and mouth disease in the UK).

368 [2014] EWHC 194 (Admin); [2014] H.R.L.R. 6 (for criticism of the court's approach, see Jason N.E. Varuhas, "Ministerial Refusals to Initiate Public Inquiries: Review or Appeal?" [2014] C.L.J. 238, arguing that the court had erroneously approached its task "as though it was hearing an appeal from the Minister's decision rather than exercising a supervisory jurisdiction").

369 See, e.g. in relation to Lord Saville's Bloody Sunday inquiry: *R. v Lord Saville of Newdigate Ex p. B (No.1)*, The Times, 15 April 1999, CA; *R. v Lord Saville of Newdigate Ex p. B (No.2)* [2000] 1 W.L.R. 1855; *R. (on the application of Widgery Soldiers) v Lord Saville of Newdigate* [2001] EWCA Civ 2048; [2002] 1 W.L.R. 1249; see further L. Blom-Cooper, "Procedures in Public Inquiries" [2002] P.L. 391 and "What went wrong on Bloody Sunday: a critique of the Saville inquiry" [2010] P.L. 61; in relation to Leveson inquiry on the role of the press and policy in the phone-hacking scandal, *R. (on the application of Associated Newspapers Ltd) v Leveson* [2012] EWHC 57 (Admin); [2012] A.C.D. 23 (not unlawful to allow admission of anonymous evidence).

370 H. Quane, "Challenging the Report of an Independent Inquiry under the Human Rights Act" [2007] P.L. 529.

371 Quane [2007] P.L. 529, argues that findings of a report may not be a "decision" amenable to judicial review). But the court's broad supervisory jurisdiction is broad and extends, e.g. to guidance and policy documents which do not directly affect any person's legal rights (see 3-025).

be reluctant to intervene for the same reasons—and subject to the same caveats—as it is cautious about quashing findings of fact made by tribunals and ombudsmen.[372]

Coroners

The regime for investigation of deaths and holding of inquests is set out in the Coroners and Justice Act 2009 Pt 1.[373] The Coroners Act 1988, which previously governed inquests, has now largely been repealed, though the provision in s.13 setting out a statutory application procedure to the High Court where a coroner refuses to hold an inquest, or where justice requires that a further inquest be held and the coroner refuses, remains in force.[374] A claim for judicial review under CPR Pt 54 may be made about other matters to do with investigations and inquests.

1-114

CATEGORIES OF JUDICIAL REVIEW

So far in this chapter we have referred to judicial review in England and Wales in general terms. It is, however, useful to differentiate five different categories of review reflecting the sources of the rights and powers in issue. These categories are:

1-115

- where a ground of review in domestic law is advanced (other than a fundamental right);
- a fundamental right recognised by the common law is in issue;
- Convention rights are advanced;
- a directly effective right protected by European Union law exists;
- there is a "devolution issue".

As we shall see in more detail in the chapters which follow, although there may be increasing convergence between the legal standards applied under these different sources of review, the courts may take different approaches to each of them. For example damages may be available for breach of a European Union law right or a Convention right but not in relation to unlawful administrative action that is taken under domestic law. Other stark contrasts may arise in relation to statutory interpretation: the different obligations placed upon the court according to the rights in issue may in some cases result in the same legislation being given different meanings according to whether the matter is entirely one of domestic law or involves Convention rights or European Union law.[375]

1-116

Domestic situations

The first category may be regarded as the default position. The rights and duties at stake stem from English law: either statute, prerogative powers or a common law power. No "constitutional rights" (as defined in the next section) are in issue and no questions of European Union law or ECHR law arise. The grounds of judicial

1-117

---

[372] See 1-087.
[373] Provision in the Coroners and Justice Act 2009 s.40 for a new system of appeals to the Chief Coroner were repealed by the Public Bodies Act 2011 s.33.
[374] The procedure is considered at 17-034.
[375] *R. (on the application of Hurst) v HM Coroner for Northern District London* [2007] UKHL 13; [2007] 2 A.C. 189 at [12] (Lord Rodger: "legislation is interpreted differently, depending on whether or not Community rights are involved" and the same applies in relation to Convention rights). For a fascinating alternative analysis, see R. Rawlings, "Modelling Judicial Review" (2008) 61 C.L.P. 95 (arguing that judicial review in England and Wales is a "multi-streamed" jurisdiction).

review here are the product of English common law. The court's general approach to statutory interpretation is to seek the intention of Parliament as expressed in words of enactment.[376] Substantive review has traditionally been carried out under the head of review called "irrationality", according to the classic *Wednesbury* formula and its modern-day variants, focusing on the "reasonableness" (or otherwise) of the decision, though the present work advocates recognising a broader and more varied scope for review of the substance of decision making.[377] Nevertheless, the court's role in fact-finding and correcting errors of law is limited.[378]

1-118   The scope of judicial review is governed by the Senior Courts Act 1981 ss.29 and 31. Standing to bring a claim for judicial review is expressed in terms of having a "sufficient interest in the matter to which the application relates" (SCA 1981 s.31), a provision that has been interpreted so liberally by the courts in recent years that it has ceased to be a bar except for busybodies.[379] Amenability to review is determined using a source of power test (is the power in question derived from statute or a prerogative power) supplemented by the *Datafin* approach of inquiring whether a "public function" is being carried out.[380] The remedial orders available are those specified in SCA 1981 s.29 (as amended): quashing orders; prohibiting orders; mandatory orders; declarations; and injunctions.[381] There is no right to damages for unlawful administrative action in and of itself; a claimant seeking financial recompense must establish that a tortious or other civil wrong has been committed.[382]

Constitutional rights under the common law

1-119   A second category of judicial review is where the claimant relies on a fundamental right recognised by the common law. Where in a claim for judicial review a common law fundamental right such as these is at stake, the court will adapt its approach to the task of statutory interpretation. Rights such as these, recognised by the common law, are fundamental in a more limited sense than comparable rights in many other constitutional systems. As we have discussed,[383] while "[t]here are not, under English domestic law, any fundamental constitutional rights that are immune from legislative change",[384] the court applies the "principle of legality", by which it is assumed that Parliament intended to legislate against a background of existing common law rights; only a specific provision in an Act of Parliament, or in regulations given specific power under an Act, can remove or limit a constitutional right.[385] This is an important safeguard for individual liberty so long as the principle of parliamentary sovereignty remains the basic rule of the British constitution.

1-120   Secondly, the recognition of a right as having a constitutional character calls for the court to modify its approach to substantive review. Where irrationality is used

---

[376] See 5-032.
[377] See Chapter 11.
[378] See 4-005 (precedent fact) and 11-043 (mistake of fact).
[379] See Ch.2.
[380] See Ch.3.
[381] See Ch.18.
[382] See Ch.19.
[383] See 1-019.
[384] *Hooper v Secretary of State for Work and Pensions* [2005] UKHL 29; [2005] 1 W.L.R. 1681 at [92] (Lord Scott).
[385] See 5-045.

as a ground of review, the court adopts a stance of "anxious scrutiny".[386] Whereas in an ordinary domestic case, the burden of argument lies upon the claimant to demonstrate unreasonableness, here the public authority is called upon to justify its action. We consider later whether the courts ought also to recognise that proportionality is an appropriate basis on which to judge official conduct.[387]

Thirdly, in a tort claim against a public authority, unconstitutional behaviour may permit the award of exemplary damages.[388]   **1-121**

Convention rights protected by the HRA

A third category of judicial review is where Convention rights are in issue. Since   **1-122** October 2000, when the Human Rights Act 1998 came into force, claimants have been able to use a breach of Convention rights as a ground of judicial review.[389] The ECHR does not itself expressly include the right to administrative justice but it has influenced administrative law in two important respects. First, it requires all public officials to respect Convention rights. Some of these rights are procedural (such as the right to a fair trial under ECHR art.6), yet others are substantive (such as the right to free expression under ECHR art.10, or equality under ECHR art.14). The principles by which public officials act have therefore been expanded and specified to the extent that the ECHR provides. Although the courts do not have the authority under the HRA to strike down Acts of Parliament which do not conform to Convention rights, they may review such legislation and issue a declaration of incompatibility with Convention rights. This effect of the HRA has been said to provide a "new legal order"[390] and this is to a large extent true. Since even Parliament is expected, by virtue of its own concessions, to respect Convention rights, the notion of democracy as synonymous with majority rule is greatly weakened. The new model of democracy requires in accord with the rule of law that certain fundamental rights are respected, even in the face of popular opinion to the contrary.

The HRA has brought about a range of important practical changes to the scope   **1-123** and operation of judicial review. The rules of standing (who can be a claimant) are modified by the requirement of s.7 that only claimants who are "victims" of a breach of a Convention right may rely upon them. The question of what decisions "of a public nature" are subject to Convention right review under s.6 have proved to be complex and controversial (and is distinct from the issue of whether an activity is a "public function" amenable to judicial review).[391] Of great importance is the approach to statutory interpretation demanded by s.3, that the courts "so far as pos-

---

[386] See Chapter 11.
[387] See Chapter 11; *Persimmon Homes (Thames Valley) Ltd v Taylor Woodrow Homes Ltd* [2005] EWCA Civ 1365; [2006] 1 W.L.R. 334 at [30] (Laws LJ: "There are, of course, now familiar areas of our law in which the court's role in judicial review cases is much more intrusive than would be contemplated by the *Wednesbury* doctrine. In particular, we are accustomed to consider whether an executive decision is proportionate to a legitimate public interest aim; and it is elementary that the test of proportionality is closer to an adjudication of merits than is *Wednesbury*. But cases of that kind engage the court's duty to see to the protection of the citizen's constitutional rights (whether or not arising through the medium of the Human Rights Act 1998), where such a right is threatened by government action").
[388] See 19-062.
[389] See Ch.13. More precisely, those Convention rights contained at the relevant time in Sch.1 to the HRA.
[390] *Jackson v Attorney General* [2005] UKHL 56; [2006] 1 A.C. 262 at [102] (Lord Steyn).
[391] See 3-072.

sible" interpret legislation so that it conforms with Convention rights.[392] Review of fact tends to be more intensive than in purely domestic law situations.[393]

1-124   A pervasive effect of the HRA has been to shift the focus of our courts away from purely domestic standards.[394] Where Convention rights are relied upon directly, the courts must "take into account" the case law of the European Court of Human Rights (HRA s.2).[395] There are also broader influences on domestic law. As we shall see in Chapter 11, what we call the "structured proportionality test" used in relation to qualified Convention rights may also be applicable to purely domestic contexts.[396] Convention rights have had an important role in creating a "culture of justification" in which the task of the courts is to ensure in an increasingly broad and deep way that there is a proper legal and factual basis for public authorities' actions.[397]

European Union law

1-125   A fourth category is where EU law rights and duties arise. Since the United Kingdom's accession to the European Communities in 1973, judicial review has been one of the ways in which the domestic courts have been called upon to uphold EU law rights that are "directly effective" in our national legal system.[398] In a small number of cases this has required English courts to "disapply" provisions in primary legislation that are incompatible with such rights—a major modification to the principle of parliamentary sovereignty and the normal rule that courts do not question the validity of statute law.[399] New remedies have also been fashioned to ensure full protection of EU law rights, including damages where there has been a seri-

---

[392] HRA 1998 s.3(1); See 13-041.

[393] For example, in relation to proportionality see 11-081.

[394] But the courts are increasingly asserting the power of common law human rights protection independently of the Human Rights Act 1998 and the ECHR. See *Osborn v Parole Board; Booth v Parole Board* [2013] UKSC 61; [2014] A.C. 1115 at [57] per Lord Reed: "The importance of the [Human Rights] Act is unquestionable. It does not however supersede the protection of human rights under the common law or statute, or create a discrete body of law based on the judgments of the European Court. Human rights continue to be protected by our domestic law, interpreted and developed in accordance with the Act when appropriate." The Convention was not to be treated "as if it were Moses and the prophets" (at [56]); and other cases discussed at para.1-007, above. See also: Lady Hale, "UK Constitutionalism on the March?" [2014] J.R. 201 ("... there is emerging a renewed emphasis on the common law and distinctively UK constitutional principles as a source of legal inspiration"); and Lord Neuberger PSC, "The Role of Judges in Human Rights Jurisprudence: A Comparison of the Australian and UK Experience", Conference speech given at the Supreme Court of Victoria, Melbourne, 8 August 2014, para.29 (available at *http://www.supremecourt.uk/docs/speech-140808.pdf*) ("... the Judges have tried to bring the common law back to centre stage. The most dramatic example of this is ... *Kennedy v Charity Commission* ([2014] UKSC 20; [2015] A.C. 455. A journalist wished to see the results of a Charity Commission inquiry into the affairs of a charity ... and based the claim on article 10 ... we sent the claim back to the trial judge on the basis that we thought that there was a stronger case based on common law ..."). Compare however the recent decision of *Moohan v Lord Advocate (Advocate General for Scotland intervening)* [2014] UKSC 67; [2015] A.C. 901 in which both Lord Hodge (at [34]) and Baroness Hale (at [56]) rejected the existence of a common law right to vote. *Moohan*, together with other recent jurisprudence on s, is considered in M. Elliott, "Beyond the European Convention: Human Rights and the Common Law" (2015) 68 C.L.P.

[395] See 13-035.

[396] See 11-080.

[397] See 11-098.

[398] See 14-013.

[399] See 3-012.

ous breach of EU law by a public authority[400]—this too is a significant innovation for a legal system that has generally set its face against compensation for public law wrongs.[401] Even where a claimant does not have a *directly* effective right under EU law, the domestic courts are obliged to adapt normal methods of statutory interpretation by ensuring that national legislation that deals with the same subject as EU law is construed in a manner that is consistent with it.[402] The UK's impending exit from the European Union will inevitably impact upon this, though the precise nature of the impact, particularly in any transitional period, is yet to be worked out.

Devolution issues and devolution-related questions

A final category of judicial review claim is those which raise a "devolution issue".[403] Such issues are defined with some precision and differently (reflecting the asymmetric devolution arrangements) in each of the devolution Acts.[404] Devolution issues may relate to legislation (including primary legislation) made by the Scottish Parliament, National Assembly for Wales and the Northern Ireland Assembly. Devolution issues may also relate to the exercise of functions by the Scottish Executive, the Welsh Assembly Government and the Northern Ireland Executive. There are three main ways in which a devolved institution may act outside its powers by legislating or exercising functions, namely (a) beyond the boundaries of the subject-matter competences conferred by the relevant devolution Act; (b) in way which is incompatible with Convention rights (which has the same meaning as under the Human Rights Act 1998); and (c) contrary to European Union law.[405] The definitions of "devolution issues" exclude some challenges to the lawfulness of decisions by or relating to the devolved institutions; these are dealt with as ordinary proceedings in the legal system in which they arise.[406]

1-126

To date, no "devolution issue" judicial review claims have arisen in the legal system of England and Wales; they have been confined to litigation in Scotland and in Northern Ireland. If and when a devolution issue arises in England and Wales, special procedures apply, including a requirement that a devolution issue notice be given to the Attorney General (the UK Government's Law Officer) and the relevant devolved institution, unless they are already a party to the proceedings. There is also provision for the court in which proceedings were initiated to make a reference of

1-127

---

[400] See 14-075.

[401] See Ch.19.

[402] See 14-047.

[403] G. Gee, "Devolution in the Courts", Ch.8 in R. Hazell and R. Rawlings (eds), *Devolution, Law Making and the Constitution* (2005).

[404] Scotland Act 1998 s.103(2) and Sch.6; Government of Wales Act 2006 s.149 and Sch.9; Northern Ireland Act 1998 ss.79–83 and Sch.10.

[405] "Community law" is defined in Northern Ireland Act 1998 s.98 as "(a) all rights, powers, liabilities, obligations and restrictions created or arising by or under the Community Treaties; and (b) all remedies and procedures provided for by or under those Treaties".

[406] See, e.g. *Re Robinson's Application for Judicial Review* [2002] UKHL 32; [2002] N.I. 390 (time limits for election of First Minister and Deputy First Minister by the Northern Ireland Assembly); *Whaley v Lord Watson of Invergowrie* 2000 S.C. 340 (challenge to lawfulness of a member of the Scottish Parliament promoting, and introducing a bill to outlaw fox hunting on the grounds that the MSP had received legal, administrative and other assistance from a pressure group contrary to the Scotland Act 1998 (Members' Interests) Order 1999); *In the Matter of an application by Bairbre de Brun and Martin McGuinness for Judicial Review High Court of Northern Ireland*, unreported 30 January 2001. (Two Sinn Fein Ministers of the Executive Committee of the Northern Ireland Assembly successfully challenged the legality of a decision by First Minister David Trimble not to nominate them for meetings of the North-South Ministerial Council; the case turned mainly on the proper interpretation of the Northern Ireland Act 1998 s.52(1)) under which the First Minister and Deputy First Minister are required to make nominations).

a devolution issue to the Supreme Court; and Law Officers may also directly refer to the Supreme Court questions relating to the legislative competence of a devolved legislature.[407]

1-128   In many legal systems, special techniques have been adopted in interpreting constitutional legislation that allocates powers to different levels of government. The devolution Acts provide that legislation made by a devolved legislature "is to be read as narrowly as is required for it to be within competence, if such a reading is possible, and is to have effect accordingly".[408] Generally, the courts will "favour constructions which render the constitutional settlement coherent, stable and workable".[409] Lord Bingham of Cornhill held that the Northern Ireland Act 1998:

> "does not set out all the constitutional provisions applicable to Northern Ireland, but it is in effect a constitution. So to categorise the Act is not to relieve the courts of their duty to interpret the constitutional provisions in issue. But the provisions should, consistently with the language used, be interpreted generously and purposively, bearing in mind the values which the constitutional provisions are intended to embody".[410]

He concluded that

> "Where constitutional arrangements retain scope for the exercise of political judgment they permit a flexible response to differing and unpredictable events in a way which the application of strict rules would preclude".[411]

1-129   In a later case, Lord Reed observed that the "Scotland Act is not a constitution but an Act of Parliament", noting that "its provisions are dense and detailed"; its aim was "to create a rational and coherent scheme" and "the interpretation of any specific provision will depend upon the language used, and the context which is relevant to understanding the meaning of that language".[412]

Overlapping categories

1-130   A claimant's challenge to the lawfulness of a public authority's decision may be based on more than one of the categories set out above: a Convention right, a European Union law right and a right under ordinary domestic law may all form grounds within a single claim for judicial review. A court may therefore have to

---

[407] See, e.g. *Attorney General v National Assembly for Wales Commission and others* [2012] UKSC 53; [2012] 3 W.L.R. 1294 (reference to UK Supreme Court by Attorney General to determine whether provisions of the Local Government Byelaws (Wales) Bill was within the legislative competence of the National Assembly; they were).

[408] Scotland Act 1998 s.101; and for similar provisions see Government of Wales Act 2006 s.154; Northern Ireland Act 1998 s.83.

[409] *Imperial Tobacco Ltd v Lord Advocate* [2012] CSIH 9; 2012 S.C. 297 at [14].

[410] *Re Robinson's Application for Judicial Review* [2002] UKHL 32; [2002] N.I. 390 at [11]. See also Lord Hoffmann at [25]: "In choosing between these two approaches to construction, it is necessary to have regard to the background to the 1998 Act. ... The 1998 Act is a constitution for Northern Ireland, framed to create a continuing form of government against the background of the history of the territory and the principles agreed in Belfast"; at [33]: "According to established principles of interpretation, the Act must be construed against the background of the political situation in Northern Ireland and the principles laid down by the Belfast Agreement for a new start. These facts and documents form part of the admissible background for the construction of the Act just as much as the Revolution, the Convention and the Federalist Papers are the background to construing the Constitution of the United States". Lord Hutton and Lord Hobhouse dissented, stressing the need for an "ordinary construction of such a statutory provision".

[411] *Re Robinson's Application for Judicial Review* [2002] UKHL 32; [2002] N.I. 390 at [12].

[412] *Imperial Tobacco Ltd v Lord Advocate* [2012] CSIH 9; 2012 S.C. 297 at [72]; and see also [181]–[182] (Lord Brodie).

adapt its approach during the course of its consideration of a claim. The courts of England and Wales have often emphasised that application of ordinary domestic law may produce the same result as the application of Convention rights. In most cases, the categorisation of a ground of challenge will be relatively straightforward. Difficulties, however, occasionally arise.[413]

---

[413] For example, it may not be clear whether a claimant is entitled to rely upon a EU law right if a measure is wholly internal to the United Kingdom (*R. v Secretary of State for the Home Department Ex p. Phull* [1996] Imm. A.R. 72); and Convention rights may overlap with fundamental rights recognised by English common law (*R. v Secretary of State for the Home Department Ex p. Daly* [2001] UKHL 26; [2001] 2 A.C. 532).

CHAPTER 2

Claimants, Interested Parties and Interveners

TABLE OF CONTENTS

SCOPE

This chapter deals with the following issues.   **2-001**

- The requirement for a claimant to have standing in order to bring a claim for judicial review. Under CPR Pt 54, this is expressed as the need for the claimant to have "sufficient interest".[1] In relation to the ground of review that there is a breach of a Convention right, a further requirement that the claimant be a "victim" is imposed.[2] In some other forms of public law proceedings, the term "person aggrieved" is used.[3]
- The extent to which others, in addition to the claimant and defendant, may be involved in a claim for judicial review. They include "interested parties" who are directly affected by the claim and must be served with the claim form and may, as of right, participate in the proceedings.[4] Others (typically pressure groups and public authorities) may apply to the court for permission to intervene in proceedings to make written or oral submissions.[5] As with the requirement of standing, the approach adopted towards these interventions has an important impact on the constitutional purpose served by judicial review.

---

[1] See 2-006.
[2] See 2-044; and Ch.13 on Convention rights generally.
[3] See 2-059.
[4] See 2-067.
[5] See 2-068.

- Questions relating to the legal capacity of some claimants (for example, unincorporated associations) to institute proceedings.[6]
- Techniques used in some other jurisdictions to define standing.[7]

CONSTITUTIONAL SIGNIFICANCE OF STANDING RULES

2-002   All developed legal systems have had to face the problem of resolving the conflict between two aspects of the public interest: the desirability of encouraging people to participate actively in the enforcement of the law, and the undesirability of encouraging meddlesome interlopers invoking the jurisdiction of the courts in matters in which they are not concerned.[8] The conflict may be resolved by developing principles which determine who is entitled to bring proceedings; that is who has locus standi or standing to make a claim. If those principles are satisfactory they should only prevent a would-be litigant who has no legitimate reason for bringing proceedings from doing so.

2-003   In 2013, the Ministry of Justice expressed concern[9] that judicial review is sometimes used as a delaying tactic in cases that have little prospect of success. The Ministry of Justice claimed that unmeritorious applications could delay government reforms and the progress of major infrastructure projects intended to stimulate growth and promote economic recovery. The courts' wide approach to standing, it said, "has tipped the balance too far, allowing judicial review to be used to seek publicity or otherwise to hinder the process of proper decision-making".[10] The Ministry of Justice considered that claimants for judicial review should have a more direct interest in the matter to which the application related, to exclude those who had only a political or theoretical interest, such as campaigning groups. Faced with opposition from many quarters, including the senior judiciary, proposals for a stricter test of standing were abandoned.

2-004   To deprive a person of access to the courts because of lack of standing can raise issues of constitutional significance. At its heart is the question whether it can ever be right, as a matter of principle, for a person with an otherwise meritorious challenge to the validity of a public authority's action to be turned away by the court on the ground that his rights or interests are not sufficiently affected by the impugned decision. To put this another way, if a decision which is otherwise justiciable is legally flawed, should the court prevent its jurisdiction being invoked because the litigant is not qualified to raise the issue? To answer "yes" to these questions presupposes that the primary function of the court's supervisory jurisdiction is to redress individual grievances, rather than that judicial review is concerned, more broadly, with the maintenance of the rule of law.[11] In recent years the courts

---

6   See 2-012.
7   See 2-071.
8   How serious this conflict actually is, is open to question. As K. Scott has written, "The idle and whimsical plaintiff, a litigant who litigates for a lark, is a spectre which haunts the legal literature, not the courtroom": "Standing in the Supreme Court: A Functional Analysis" (1973) 86 Harv.L.R. 645.
9   Ministry of Justice, *Judicial Review: Proposals for Further Reform*, Cm 8703 (September 2013), paras 67–90. See further para.1-005 above. For a critique of the proposals, see J. McGarry, "The Importance of an Expansive Test of Standing" [2014] J.R. 60.
10   Ministry of Justice, *Judicial Review: Proposals for Further Reform*, Cm 8703, para.79.
11   J. Miles, "Standing under the Human Rights Act 1998: Theories of Rights Enforcement and the Nature of Public Law Adjudication" (2000) 59 C.L.J. 133, 148–155 on underlying theoretical models; I. Hare, "The Law of Standing in Public Interest Adjudication", Ch.22 in M. Andenas (ed),

have approached standing issues in a more flexible and liberal way than once was the case.

In favour of restricted access

A number of arguments are traditionally advanced for restricting access to the court by any member of the public for the purpose of challenging executive action of which he does not approve. First, it would be unwise to assume that the other safeguards that exist, the effect of the doctrine of precedent, the limited availability of public funding to assist would-be litigants,[12] and the power of the courts to award costs,[13] are sufficient to deter unmeritorious challenges.[14] Secondly, the courts' resources should not be dissipated by the need to provide a forum for frivolous or academic proceedings. Thirdly, central and local government and other public authorities should not be disrupted unnecessarily, to the disadvantage of other members of the public, by having to contest unmeritorious proceedings. Fourthly, as a matter of prudence, the courts should reserve their power to interfere with the workings of public authorities to those occasions when there is a claim before them by someone who has been adversely affected by the unlawful conduct of which complaint is made. Fifthly, particularly in relation to administrative action which can affect sections of the public, it is important that the claim should be brought by a person who, because he is sufficiently interested in the outcome of the proceedings or otherwise, is in a position to ensure that full argument in favour of the remedy which is sought is deployed before the court. Sixthly, it is important that the courts confine themselves to their correct constitutional role, and do not become involved in determining issues which are not justiciable by giving unlimited access to the courts.[15] Campaign groups will not necessarily properly reflect the interests or wishes of their members, or those they purport to protect, by undertaking legal action.[16]

2-005

In favour of a more open approach

On the other side of the argument there are substantial reasons for adopting a generous approach to standing in judicial review proceedings, seeking to exclude only the "mere busybody".[17] It is usually important, in the interests of the public generally, that the law should be enforced. The policy should therefore be to encourage and not discourage public-spirited individuals and groups, even though they are not directly affected by the action which is being taken or who can demonstrate no greater impact upon himself than upon other members of the public, to challenge unlawful administrative action. Other safeguards, besides restrictive rules as to standing, exist to protect the courts and administrators from unmeritorious chal-

2-006

Liber Amicorum in Honour of Lord Slynn of Hadley: Vol.II Judicial Review in International Perspective (2000); Baroness Hale, "Who guards the guardians?" [2014] C.J.I.C.L. 100.

[12] On funding, see 16-086.

[13] On costs, see 16-091.

[14] On recent government proposals to restrict standing for claimants without a direct interest, in particular pressure groups, see para.2-002 above.

[15] See further K. Schiemann, "Locus Standi" [1990] P.L. 342 and his judgment in *R. v Secretary of State for the Environment Ex p. Rose Theatre Trust Ltd* [1990] 1 Q.B. 504.

[16] C. Harlow, "Public Law and Popular Justice" (2002) 65 M.L.R. 1; P. Cane, "Standing, Representation and the Environment" in I. Loveland (ed), *A Special Relationship? American Influences on Public Law in the UK* (1995); M. Kirby, "Deconstructing the law's hostility to public interest litigation" (2011) 127 L.Q.R. 537.

[17] That is, "someone who interferes in something with which he has no legitimate concern" (*Walton v Scottish Ministers* [2012] UKSC 44; 2012 S.L.T. 1211 at [92] (Lord Reed)).

lenges (including the requirement that claimants obtain permission from the court,[18] the relatively short time limits for commencing claims,[19] and in extreme circumstances provisions to bar vexatious litigants[20]). Where there are strict rules as to standing there is always the risk that no one will be in a position to bring proceedings to test the lawfulness of administrative action. It is hardly desirable that a situation should exist where because all members of the public are equally affected no one is in a position to bring proceedings: such a situation would impede the rule of law.[21] The fears that are sometimes voiced of the courts being overwhelmed by a flood of frivolous claims due to broad standing rules are unsupported by any evidence of this happening in practice. The costs of litigation are now so heavy that it is only the most determined litigant who will indulge in legal proceedings which are without merit. The arguments in favour of a restrictive approach to standing nearly always confuse the question of the merits of the litigation with the question of who should be entitled to bring the proceedings. If there is a satisfactory mechanism for dealing with unmeritorious or frivolous claims most of the arguments for a restrictive approach to standing fall away.

THE "SUFFICIENT INTEREST" REQUIREMENT

2-007   Prior to the judicial review reforms of 1978, the standing rules (along with other matters such as time limits and procedural requirements) varied according to the particular remedy sought.[22] One of the objects of the new test was to save the courts from having to try to reconcile the multiplicity of conflicting authorities which governed the principles of locus standi under the previous procedure for obtaining the prerogative orders. For example, the old authorities indicate that the test varied depending on which prerogative order or area of the law was involved (the standard appeared to be higher if the application for the prerogative order related to a criminal cause or matter than if the application related to a planning matter).[23] In contrast, other old cases are of interest insofar as they indicate that prior to 1978 a very generous approach to standing was already being adopted in some contexts. Thus proceedings could be brought even by "strangers" for an order of prohibition.[24] In general on a modern day claim for judicial review, the old authorities provide only limited assistance and can be misleading. This said, the pre-1978 authorities should not always be ignored as being merely of historic interest. It can be stated with confidence that as the reforms introduced in 1978 were intended to liberalise the procedure for obtaining the prerogative orders, the approach to standing on a claim for judicial review is now at least as generous to the claimant as that which previously existed. So, if the pre-1978 authorities indicate that a claimant would have standing, this is almost certainly still the position.

---

[18] See 16-044.
[19] See 16-055. Time limits in certain procurement and planning cases have been shortened to 30 days and six weeks respectively by an amendment to the Civil Procedure Rules: Civil Procedure (Amendment No.4) Rules 2013 (SI 2013/1412).
[20] Senior Court Act 1981 s.42.
[21] *Walton v Scottish Ministers* [2012] UKSC 44; 2012 S.L.T. 1211 at [93] (Lord Reed).
[22] See Ch.15.
[23] Such a distinction could be justified perfectly logically because in criminal proceedings there are normally only two parties, the prosecutor and the defendant, whereas planning procedures under the planning legislation allow for generous representation before the inquiry which the legislation normally contemplated would precede a decision on an appeal. For a modern application of a restricted approach to standing in criminal matters, see *R. (on the application of Bulger) v Lord Chief Justice* [2001] EWHC Admin 119; [2001] 3 All E.R. 449 at [18]–[24].
[24] See 15-029.

The standing requirement for claims for judicial review made under CPR Pt 54 **2-008** is now set out in the Senior Courts Act 1981 s.31, which with interpolations to modernise the terminology reads as follows[25]:

> "No application [claim] for judicial review shall be made unless the leave [permission] of the court has been obtained in accordance with the Rules of Court [Civil Procedure Rules Pt 54]; and the court shall not grant leave [permission] to make such an application [a claim] unless it considers that the applicant [claimant] has a sufficient interest in the matter to which the application [claim] relates."

The requirement is repeated by CPR r.54.4. The test is expressed in terms of **2-009** interests rather than rights because "What modern public law focuses upon are wrongs–that is to say, unlawful acts of public administration. These often, of course, infringe correlative rights, but they do not necessarily do so: hence the test of standing for public law claimants, which is interest-based rather than rights-based".[26] In Northern Ireland, a similar test based on sufficient interest applies under s.18(4) of the Judicature (Northern Ireland) Act 1978.[27]

The issue of whether a claimant has sufficient interest in the matter to which the **2-010** claim relates goes to the court's jurisdiction to entertain the claim for judicial review, and is not merely a matter of discretion.[28] It follows that the defendant may not merely agree to the claimant having standing, as the parties are not entitled to confer jurisdiction, which the court may not have, by consent.[29] The court may also take the standing point of its own motion, even if not raised by the parties.[30] The interest must be "in relation to the matter to which the application relates". Assessment of the claimant's standing must therefore relate to the circumstances as they exist at the time at which permission from the court is sought. A would-be claimant may have standing at an earlier point but have lost it by the time legal proceedings begin.[31] It has sometimes been suggested that a claimant may have standing to argue some grounds of review but be debarred by insufficient interest from

---

[25] See 16-002.
[26] *R. (on the application of Bancoult) v Secretary of State for Foreign and Commonwealth Affairs* [2007] EWCA Civ 498; [2008] Q.B. 365 at [61] (Sedley LJ).
[27] On the approach in Scotland, see 2-072.
[28] *R. v Secretary of State for Social Services Ex p. Child Poverty Action Group* [1990] 2 Q.B. 540 at 556; *R. v Secretary of State for Foreign and Commonwealth Affairs Ex p. World Development Movement Ltd* [1995] 1 W.L.R. 386 at 395; *R. v Secretary of State for the Environment Ex p. Rose Theatre Trust Co Ltd* [1990] 1 Q.B. 504 at 520.
[29] *R. v Secretary of State for Social Services Ex p. Child Poverty Action Group* [1990] 2 Q.B. 540 at 556E; cf. *R. (on the application of Evans) v Secretary of State for Defence* [2010] EWHC 1445 (Admin); [2011] A.C.D. 11, [2] (government did not pursue issue of claimant's standing).
[30] See, e.g. *R. (on the application of Bulger) v Lord Chief Justice* [2001] EWHC Admin 119; [2001] 3 All E.R. 449 at [18].
[31] See, e.g. *R. v North West Leicestershire DC Ex p. Moses (No.1)* [2000] J.P.L. 733 (claimant objecting to extension of airport runway had moved six miles away); on appeal, permission was refused on grounds of delay rather than standing: [2000] EWCA Civ 125. cf. *R. v Secretary of State for the Home Department Ex p. Salem* [1999] 1 A.C. 450, where the HL held that it had a discretion to hear an appeal which concerned an issue involving a public authority as to a question of public law, even where there was no longer any live issue which would affect the rights and duties of the parties as between themselves. In *Lamot v Secretary of State for Justice* [2016] EWHC 2564 (Admin); [2016] A.C.D. 123, an application by three prisoners to challenge the Secretary of State's refusal to accept the Parole Board's recommendation to transfer them to open conditions was refused on the ground that the decision was academic, all three having subsequently been released or transferred; where a matter between the parties was academic, it should not be heard unless there was a good reason in the public interest for doing so. Note also provisions in Pt 19 of the CPR on the addition and substitution of parties.

advancing other related grounds. The better view is that a claimant who has standing for some grounds has it for all.[32]

CHARITY PROCEEDINGS

2-011   Charities may perform public functions that are amenable to judicial review.[33]
Where the would-be defendant is a charity, claimants in this context face a double
hurdle. First, the claimant must obtain permission from the Charity Commission for
England and Wales or a judge of the Chancery Division of the High Court before
commencing legal action ("charity proceedings") against a charitable organisation.
The purpose of this "protective filter" is to prevent charitable organisations from
being "harassed and put to expense by a multiplicity of claims, which may or may
not be well-founded".[34] A claim for judicial review may constitute "charity
proceedings".[35] Rules on standing are imposed by the Charities Act 1993 s.33(1),
which regulates who may commence charity proceedings.[36] This general requirement has been interpreted more narrowly than the sufficient interest requirement of
s.31(3) of the Senior Courts Act 1981[37] though in the particular context of an
anticipated judicial review claim it is difficult to see why the test should be different from that applied in judicial review given that the overall purpose of the permission requirement is similar. Secondly, the claimant must obtain the permission of
the Administrative Court to commence a judicial review claim.[38]

2-012   Bearing in mind the overriding aim of the CPR,[39] there are clear advantages in
combining both requirements into a single application dealt by a judge of the
Chancery Division who is a nominated judge of the Administrative Court. If the
permissions to proceed are granted, that judge can then decide whether the claim
is most appropriately continued in the Chancery Division under CPR Pt 7 or Pt 8
or in the Administrative Court under CPR Pt 54.[40] Because of the availability of a
procedure in the Chancery Division, and the greater experience of charity law in
that part of the High Court, there is likely be a preference against proceeding by way

---

[32]   *R. (on the application of Kides) v South Cambridgeshire DC* [2002] EWCA Civ 1370, [2003] 1 P.
& C.R. 19 at [132]–[136]. The court may, however, grant permission on certain grounds only but
this is on the basis that the others lack merit: CPR r.54.12(1)(b)(ii).

[33]   See 3-038. Charities may also perform "functions of a public nature" under s.6(3)(b) HRA, on which
see, e.g. *R. (on the application of Heather) v Leonard Cheshire Foundation* [2001] EWHC Admin
429; (2001) 4 C.C.L. Rep. 211 (Stanley Burnton J); on appeal the CA heard no argument and
expressed no view on the charity proceedings point: [2002] EWCA Civ 366; [2002] 2 All E.R. 936
at [38].

[34]   *Scott v National Trust for Places of Historic Interest or Natural Beauty* [1998] 2 All E.R. 705, 714J
(Robert Walker J).

[35]   *R. (on the application of Heather) v Leonard Cheshire Foundation* [2001] EWHC Admin 429; (2001)
4 C.C.L. Rep. 211 at [100].

[36]   "Charity proceedings may be taken with reference to a charity either by the charity, or by any of the
charity trustees, or by any person interested in the charity, or by any two or more inhabitants of the
area if it is a local charity, but not by any other person".

[37]   *Scott v National Trust for Places of Historic Interest or Natural Beauty* [1998] 2 All E.R. 705 at 714
(a person was "interested" in a charity within the meaning of s.33(1) of the 1993 Act if he had a
materially greater interest in ensuring the due administration of the charity than that possessed by
ordinary members of the public).

[38]   *R. (on the application of Heather) v Leonard Cheshire Foundation* [2001] EWHC Admin 429; (2001)
4 C.C.L. Rep. 211 at [102]; Scott [1998] 1 W.L.R. 226 at 229. On the permission stage, see 16-044.

[39]   See 16-011.

[40]   *R. (on the application of Heather) v Leonard Cheshire Foundation* [2001] EWHC Admin 429; (2001)
4 C.C.L. Rep. 211 at [103].

of judicial review,[41] unless on the particular facts CPR Pt 54 provides a particularly suitable process for addressing the factual and legal issues in question.

The Charity Commission for England and Wales, a non-ministerial government department, is the public authority to register and regulate charities in England and Wales. Where decisions of the Charity Commission are to be challenged, judicial review proceedings under CPR Pt 54 will not normally be appropriate, as there is an alternative avenue of redress. The Charities Act 2006 created a tribunal, since 2009 the First-tier Tribunal (Charity), to which appeals against specified decisions of the Charity Commission may be made. The tribunal "shall apply the principles which would be applied by the High Court on an application for judicial review".[42]   **2-013**

CAPACITY AND STANDING

Unincorporated associations and companies

In English law, unincorporated associations generally lack legal capacity to sue   **2-014**
or be sued in their own name.[43] In some claims for judicial review brought by unincorporated associations it has been held that this is a bar to permission being granted.[44] A different approach has been adopted in other cases, where either no issue as to the legal capacity of the claimant has been being taken,[45] or the chairman, secretary or other member of the association was recognised as representing the association.[46] Indeed, it is possible formally to seek an order under CPR Pt 19.6 that a claim be begun or continued with one party representing the interests of others who have the same interest in the claim.[47] Given that the unincorporated status of a defendant has not been regarded as a bar to being subject to and defending judicial review proceedings,[48] a flexible approach is appropriate.[49]

Pitfalls may also lie ahead for an unincorporated association that rushes to form   **2-015**

---

[41]   *Royal Society for the Prevention of Cruelty to Animals v Attorney General* [2002] 1 W.L.R. 448 at [22].

[42]   Charities Act 1993 Sch.1C.

[43]   *Halsbury's Laws*, 4th edn, Vol.9(2), para.1001.

[44]   *R. v Darlington BC Ex p. Association of Darlington Taxi Owners* [1994] C.O.D. 424; *Alwoodly Golf Club v Leeds CC* [1995] N.P.C. 149.

[45]   See, e.g. *R. v Director of Rail Franchising Ex p. Save Our Railways* [1996] C.L.C. 589 (strictly speaking the unincorporated association lacked capacity to sue but "no time should be taken up in this case resolving this somewhat arid issue"); *R. (on the application of Association of British Civilian Internees (Far East Region)) v Secretary of State for Defence* [2003] EWCA Civ 473; [2003] Q.B. 1397.

[46]   See, e.g. *R. v Tower Hamlets LBC Ex p. Tower Hamlets Combined Traders Association* [1994] C.O.D. 325; *R. v Traffic Commissioner for the North Western Traffic Area Ex p. BRAKE* [1996] C.O.D. 248.

[47]   In its 1994 report, *Administrative Law: Judicial Review and Statutory Appeals*, the Law Commission described recommended that unincorporated associations should be permitted to make claims for judicial review in their own name through one or more of their members applying in a representative capacity where the court is satisfied that members of the claimant association have been, or would be, adversely affected or are raising an issue of public interest warranting judicial review, and that the members of the association are appropriate persons to bring that challenge: Law Com. No.226, para.5.41.

[48]   See, e.g. *R. v Panel on Takeovers and Mergers Ex p. Datafin Plc* [1987] Q.B. 815.

[49]   Unincorporated associations have been allowed to be claimants in many cases, see e.g. *R. v Ministry of Agriculture, Fisheries and Food Ex p. British Pig Industry Support Group* [2000] Eu. L.R. 724; *R. (on the application of West End Street Traders Association) v Westminster City Council* [2004] EWHC 1167 (Admin); [2005] B.L.G.R. 143; *R. (on the application of Western International Campaign Group) v Hounslow LBC* [2003] EWHC 3112; [2004] B.L.G.R. 536; *R. (on the applica-*

itself into a company for the purpose of commencing a claim for judicial review.[50] First, it needs to be understood that incorporation will not of itself create a sufficient interest. One of the reasons why the Rose Theatre Trust Company Ltd was held to lack sufficient interest, in a challenge to a minister's refusal to designate a site as a protected ancient monument, was that it "would be absurd if two people, neither of whom had standing could, by an appropriately worded memorandum, incorporate themselves into a company which thereby obtained standing".[51] The judgment in *Rose Theatre* has been doubted, distinguished and not followed,[52] but on this point the case affirms the approach adopted by the majority of the House of Lords in *National Federation*.[53] Secondly, the courts have in some cases been wary of unincorporated associations giving themselves limited liability specifically for the purpose of conducting litigation with the intention of avoiding the full force of any adverse costs order that might be made.[54]

Capacity and standing of public authorities

2-016   Many public authorities have capacity to institute legal proceedings. The Attorney General has an ancient power to make legal claims in the name of the Crown as an aspect of his role as guardian of the public interest. Proceedings may be commenced by the Attorney General in the name of the Attorney General; alternatively, the Attorney General may "consent to the use of his name, so as to enable proceedings to be brought by another party clothed with his authority in what are known as relator proceedings for the protection of the public interest in the civil courts".[55] A refusal by the Attorney General to "lend his *fiat*" to consent to a relator action has been thought to be not amenable to judicial review.[56] The liberalisation of the court's approach to the sufficient interest test has more or less brought an end to the use of relator actions in the public law context as there is now no impediment on a citizen commencing a claim in his own name to enforce a public duty. For local authorities, the statutory authorisation to institute legal proceedings rests on s.222 of the Local Government Act 1972 which authorises councils to initiate and defend

---

tion of Association of British Civilian Internees (Far East Region)) v Secretary of State for Defence [2003] EWCA Civ 473; [2003] Q.B. 1397; *R. (on the application of British Aggregates Associates) v Customs and Excise Commissioners* [2002] EWHC 926 (Admin); [2002] 2 C.M.L.R. 51; *R. v Coventry City Council Ex p. Coventry Heads of Independent Care Establishments (CHOICE)* (1997–98) 1 C.C.L. Rep. 379.

50   See also 2-037.

51   *R. v Secretary of State for the Environment Ex p. Rose Theatre Trust Co Ltd* [1990] 1 Q.B. 504 at 521D.

52   Rose Theatre has been "not followed" in *R. v HM Inspectorate of Pollution Ex p. Greenpeace (No.2)* [1994] 4 All E.R. 329 and "distinguished" in *R. v Poole BC Ex p. Beebee* [1991] J.P.L. 643 and *R. v Somerset CC Ex p. Dixon* [1998] Env.L.R. 111. Although not overruled by the CA, there can be little doubt that a court faced with similar facts today would adopt a different approach. There were individuals who were involved in the Rose Theatre Co Ltd of acknowledged distinction in the field of archaeology who should, because of the nature of the issue before the court, have been regarded as being a significant factor in favour of there being standing.

53   *Inland Revenue Commissioners v National Federation of Self-Employed and Small Businesses* [1982] A.C. 617 at 633D (Lord Wilberforce).

54   *R. v Leicestershire CC Ex p. Blackfordby and Boothorpe Action Group Ltd* [2001] Env.L.R. 2 at [34]–[38] ("The costs position can be dealt with adequately by requiring the provision of security for costs in a realistically large sum"). In *R. (on the application of Legal Remedy UK Ltd) v Secretary of State for Health* [2007] EWHC 1252 (Admin) a pressure group of junior doctors was incorporated as a company limited by guarantee for the specific purpose of making a claim for judicial review and no point was taken on this).

55   *Attorney General v Blake* [1998] Ch. 439 (Lord Woolf MR).

56   *Attorney General v Gouriet* [1978] A.C. 435; cf. B. Hough, "Judicial review where the Attorney General refuses to act: time for a change" (1988) 8 L.S. 190.

civil proceedings where it is "expedient for the promotion or protection of the interests of the inhabitants of their area". The Commission for Equality and Human Rights is expressly stated to have capacity to institute and intervene in legal proceedings, whether for judicial review or otherwise.[57] The fact that the decision in question is one which a public authority could itself have made does not preclude the authority from bringing judicial review. A recent decision of the Administrative Court upheld the possibility of a challenge by an NHS Trust to a decision which the Trust was empowered to take but had delegated to another body.[58]

Child claimants and abuse of process

Where a decision affects a child (for example, in relation to schooling arrangements) questions have arisen as to whether the child (acting through his "litigation friend")[59] should be the claimant, or the parents of the child. Where the child is the claimant, legal aid may be available in circumstances in which the parent would not be eligible for public funding and, if a claim is lost, an adverse costs order against a child claimant will have no practical effect. The Court of Appeal held, obiter, that in disputes about parental preference on school admissions the relevant claimant is the parent rather than the child; and any claims made in the name of the child in order to avoid potential adverse costs orders would be viewed as an abuse of process in the absence of special circumstances.[60] This approach has been doubted in subsequent cases in which the courts have taken the view that issues as to entitlement to legal aid are for the legal aid authorities, not the courts.[61] Even if it has some continuing relevance in the education field, a distinction ought to be drawn between situations where (a) rights of a parent are in issue (for example, the statutory right to express a preference about which school a child will attend) and (b) rights of a child.[62] Clear evidence would also be needed to demonstrate that a parent's claim is an abuse of process.[63] There may be circumstances in which a child should be made a party to judicial review proceedings and even separately represented.[64]

2-017

HOW AND WHEN IS STANDING RELEVANT?

Questions relating to standing may be relevant (a) at the permission stage of the claim for judicial review[65]; (b) at the full hearing of the claim; and (c) in relation

2-018

---

[57] Equality Act 2006 s.30(1). cf. *Re Northern Ireland Human Rights Commission's Application for Judicial Review* [2002] UKHL 25; [2002] N.I. 236 (the NIHRC had been granted general powers to promote an understanding of human rights law and practice and to review its adequacy and effectiveness together with an incidental power to make, but not insist on making, submissions to courts and tribunals).

[58] *South Staffordshire and Shropshire Healthcare NHS Foundations Trust v St George's Hospital Managers* [2016] EWHC 1196 (Admin); [2017] 1 W.L.R. 1528. The claim failed on the merits.

[59] CPR Pt 21.

[60] *R. v Richmond LBC Ex p. C (A Child)* [2001] B.L.G.R. 146.

[61] *R. (on the application of Edwards) v The Environment Agency* [2004] EWHC 736 (Admin); [2004] 3 All E.R. 21 at [17].

[62] *In the matter of an application by JS for judicial review* [2006] NIQB 40 at [14].

[63] *R. (on the application of WB) v Leeds School Organisation Committee* [2002] EWHC 1927 (Admin); [2003] E.L.R. 67 at [37].

[64] See e.g. *E (A Child) v Chief Constable of Ulster* [2008] UKHL 66; [2009] A.C. 536 at [6], [42] (judicial review challenge to police handling of sectarian demonstrations outside a school in which the mother but not her young daughter was a party to the application).

[65] See 16-048.

to the nature of the remedial orders that should be granted to the claimant.[66] A "rolled-up" hearing, combining all these stages, may be ordered where a judge considers that there is or may be an arguable claim but a defence, such as lack of standing or delay, "should be kept open or some additional evidence is needed to show that the claim is indeed an arguable one and it is desirable that it should be dealt with substantively rather than rejected as unarguable".[67]

Standing at the permission stage

2-019   The language of s.31(3) SCA 1981 makes it clear that the statutory requirement for a claimant to have a sufficient interest is a threshold test of standing which applies when the claimant is seeking permission to apply.[68] If the claimant has an insufficient interest at that stage, the court is prohibited from granting permission. In the *National Federation* case, however, the House of Lords held that except in an obvious case, questions as to sufficient interest ought not to be dealt with as a preliminary issue at the permission stage but should be postponed until the full hearing of the claim. This is because except in the "simple" case "the question of sufficient interest cannot ... be considered in the abstract, or as an isolated point: it must be taken together with legal and factual context".[69] The threshold for standing at the permission stage should be "set only at the height necessary to prevent abuse"—in other words, to exclude "cranks", "meddlesome busybodies" and "troublemakers".[70] Generally speaking, a person or body with a bona fide concern about the subject matter of the proceedings will not be regarded as a mere busybody.[71]

2-020   When assessing whether there is abuse, the claimant's motives for making the claim may be relevant.[72] Regard may also be had to obvious weaknesses in the grounds of challenge: if they are totally without foundation or unarguable, any standing that a claimant might hypothetically have disappears.[73] Where the grounds of challenge are hopeless it is preferable for the court to refuse permission on that

---

[66] See 18-054.

[67] *R. (on the application of Hasan) v Secretary of State for Trade and Industry (now Business, Enterprise and Regulatory Reform)* [2007] EWHC 2630 (Admin) at [7] (Collins J).

[68] An empirical study of the permission stage has shown that it is extremely rare for permission to be refused on the sole ground that a claimant lacks standing: see A. Le Sueur and M. Sunkin, "Applications for Judicial Review: The Requirement of Leave" [1992] P.L. 102; V. Bondy and M. Sunkin, "Accessing judicial review" [2008] P.L. 647.

[69] *Inland Revenue Commissioners v National Federation of Self-Employed and Small Businesses* [1982] A.C. 617 at 630 (Lord Wilberforce). The majority (Lord Diplock dissenting on this point) held that one taxpayer does not have standing to challenge the lawfulness of the Inland Revenue's treatment of another taxpayer. Exceptions to this proposition have been recognised in later cases: *R. v HM Treasury Ex p. Smedley* [1985] Q.B. 657 at 670, 667 and *R. v Attorney General Ex p. ICI Plc* [1985] 1 C.M.L.R. 588. More broadly, it may be said that Lord Diplock's general approach to standing now better represents the law and practice today.

[70] *R. v Monopolies and Mergers Commission Ex p. Argyll Group Plc* [1986] 1 W.L.R. 763 at 773; *R. (on the application of Dixon) v Somerset CC* [1997] EWHC Admin 393; [1998] Env. L.R. 111 at [12].

[71] *Ex p. Argyll Group Plc* [1986] 1 W.L.R. 763 at 773.

[72] *R. (on the application of Feakins) v Secretary of State for Environment, Food and Rural Affairs* [2003] EWCA Civ 1546 at [23]: "If the real reason why a claimant wishes to challenge a decision in which, objectively, there is a public interest is not that he has a genuine concern about the decision, but some other reason, then that is material to the question whether he should be accorded standing" (Dyson LJ).

[73] *R. v Secretary of State for the Home Department Ex p. Amnesty International (No.2)* 2000 W.L. 461 (challenge by human rights groups to gain access to Senator Pinochet's medical records was without foundation: "In legal, if somewhat peremptory terms, it is none of their business", Maurice Kay J).

basis alone without making any ruling on standing. In this context, it may be noted that the tort of abuse of process does not apply to judicial review claims.[74]

A state not recognised by the United Kingdom government has no standing in the English courts.[75]   **2-021**

Standing at the full hearing

If a claimant has been granted permission, of what relevance is standing at the   **2-022**
subsequent full hearing of the claim? One answer is that examination of the standing issue may be necessary to ensure that the Administrative Court has jurisdiction: as noted above, the Senior Courts Act 1981 s.31 is regarded as making the claimant's "sufficient interest" a condition precedent to court having jurisdiction.[76] In practice, however, the courts rarely deal with the question of standing as a preliminary issue at hearings and many of the leading cases deal with the grounds of review first and relegate discussion of standing to the end of the judgment. Moreover, there are few if any reported cases in which the court has found for the claimant on the grounds of review while also holding that the claimant lacks sufficient interest. It is therefore perhaps open to question whether any practical purpose is served by discussion of standing at a full hearing (unless it is relevant to remedies), other than to prolong submissions and extend judgments.

The task of the court in assessing whether a particular claimant has standing has   **2-023**
been described as "a balancing act between the various factors",[77] and these are discussed below.

Standing in relation to the grant of remedial orders

Suggestions have also been made in the past that the degree of interest required   **2-024**
by a claimant will depend on the remedy which is claimed, for example a greater degree of interest is needed for a mandatory order than for a declaration. It is contended that this approach is misconceived and the test of standing is the same irrespective of the remedy which is claimed. This is, however, contrary to the views expressed by Lord Wilberforce and possibly Lord Scarman in *National Federation*.[78] It would be difficult in practice to apply different principles of standing to different remedies at the permission stage. This is because claimants tend to include all relevant remedies in an application for permission and it is often only after the full hearing, often after judgment, that a claimant decides which remedial order to request. It would also be inconsistent with the intended comprehensive nature of the procedure of judicial review to have to apply different tests of standing for the different remedies. If Lords Wilberforce and Scarman were referring to the end of the hearing, then their views are perfectly acceptable since when it comes to deciding in its discretion whether to grant relief—a court is going to be more hesitant in some situations in granting, for example, a mandatory order or an injunc-

---

74 *Land Securities Plc v Fladgagte Fielder (a firm)* [2009] EWCA Civ 1402; [2010] 1 Ch 467.
75 *City of Berne v Bank of England* (1804) 9 Ves. 347; cf. *Gur Corporation v Trust Bank of Africa* [1987] 1 Q.B. 599 at 605; *R. (on the application of North Cyprus Tourism Centre Ltd) v Transport for London* [2005] EWHC 1698 (Admin); [2005] U.K.H.R.R. 1231.
76 See 3-014.
77 *R. v North Somerset DC Ex p. Garnett* [1998] Env. L.R. 91 (Popplewell J).
78 *Inland Revenue Commissioners v National Federation of Self-Employed and Small Businesses* [1982] A.C. 617 at 648E (Lord Scarman). It is not clear to what stage of the proceedings these statements referred.

tion (the disobedience of which can amount to contempt) than a declaration.[79] At this stage of the hearing the extent of the interest of the claimant is a factor to be considered when deciding what, if any, relief to grant.[80]

2-025   The court always has discretion to refuse a particular form of relief, or any relief, on a claim for judicial review even if the public authorities' actions have been held to be unlawful. In deciding whether or not to grant relief, the court is required to have regard to all the circumstances. It is therefore sensible for the court not to isolate the question of the claimant's interest for separate treatment, but to take it into account when it comes to decide what, if any, relief it should grant, as a matter of discretion.[81] The ability of the court to consider standing when deciding on a remedy has been described as "to some extent a necessary counter balance to the widening of the rules of standing" to ensure the overall balance of the public interest in some cases.[82] The weight or importance which will be attached to the claimant's interest will differ depending on the circumstances.

ASSESSING THE CLAIMANT'S INTEREST

2-026   As Lord Roskill pointed out in *National Federation*, the phrase "sufficient interest" was selected by the Rules Committee in 1977 "as one which could sufficiently embrace all classes of those who might apply and yet permit sufficient flexibility in any particular case to determine whether or not 'sufficient interest' was in fact shown".[83] This is precisely the approach which has been adopted in the vast majority of the cases which have come before the courts since that time, even if it creates considerable scope for differing judgments on the same facts as to whether a claimant has standing.[84]

2-027   Section 31(3) SCA 1981 does not contain any express guidance as to the factors to be taken into account in determining whether a claimant has sufficient interest. The court will assess the claimant's interest against all the factual and legal circumstances of the case. It is a "mixed question of fact and degree".[85]

The legislative framework

2-028   The starting point for analysis of whether a claimant has sufficient interest will normally be the legislative framework within which the public authority's decision was taken. This may expressly or impliedly indicate that the claimant has an interest in the subject matter of the claim. Thus, if the statute gives the claimant the

---

79   See Ch.18.
80   See, e.g. *R. v Felixstowe Justices Ex p. Leigh* [1987] Q.B. 582 (after the full hearing, a journalist, who had not been present at the hearing, had sufficient standing to claim a declaration that a policy of not disclosing names of justices who had heard certain types of case was contrary to public interest and unlawful. On the other hand he was refused a mandatory order, ordering the court to reveal the names of the justices who had heard a particular case: the claimant was sufficiently interested in the point of principle but not in what had happened in the particular case which had given rise to the application).
81   *Walton v Scottish Ministers* [2012] UKSC 44; 2012 S.L.T. 1211 at [95] (Lord Reed).
82   *Walton v Scottish Ministers* [2012] UKSC 44; 2012 S.L.T. 1211 at [103] (Lord Carnwath).
83   *Inland Revenue Commissioners v National Federation of Self-Employed and Small Businesses* [1982] A.C. 617 at 658.
84   For example in *Inland Revenue Commissioners v National Federation of Self-Employed and Small Businesses* [1982] A.C. 617 Lord Diplock dissented on the issue of standing and held that the pressure group had standing; and in *Equal Opportunities Commission v Secretary of State for Employment* [1995] 1 A.C. 1 Lord Jauncey dissented on the issue whether the EOC had standing.
85   *R. v Sheffield City Council Ex p. Power* [1994] E.G.C.S. 101 (Turner J).

right to make representations before the decision is reached this will be a strong indication that he has standing to challenge the decision when it is made.[86] In *National Federation*, Lord Frazer considered that one should look at the statute under which the duty arises and see whether it gives any express or implied right to persons in the position of the claimant to complain of the alleged unlawful act or omission.[87] It is suggested that this is an unhelpful approach except in a limited class of cases where the claimant's interest would in any event be obvious. An example of this class of case is where the statute gives the public authority seeking to make the claim special responsibility in the field of activity to which the claim relates. Thus in a claim involving alleged sex discrimination the Equal Opportunities Commission would have standing.[88] However, claims for judicial review are usually made in situations where the statute does not provide a remedy for the unlawful exercise of the statutory discretion or power which is being challenged. In those situations it is difficult, if not impossible, to apply satisfactorily the implied right to complain test which Lord Frazer suggested.

Legislation may make express provision in relation to the scope of "sufficient interest" in order to clarify, restrict or expand the category of those who have "sufficient interest". For example, the Local Government Act 1988 s.19(7) provides that "in proceedings for judicial review … the persons who have a sufficient interest in the matter shall include any potential contractor" (in relation to challenges to decisions about the contracting-out of local authority service provision).[89] In a different context, considered below, the Human Rights Act 1998 s.7 restricts the scope of "sufficient interest" by introducing a requirement that a person who seeks to rely on a breach of a Convention right has standing only if he or she is a "victim".[90]   **2-029**

The legislative framework may, however, be relevant in another sense. It will sometimes be the case that legislation is intended to protect the section of the public whose interests the claimant is seeking to defend.[91]   **2-030**

Strength and importance of the grounds of challenge

The strength of the grounds of review is likely to be considered by the court in assessing whether or not the claimant has sufficient interest,[92] though this is not the   **2-031**

---

[86] If the language of the statute is being considered in determining standing then again the approach should not be too restrictive. Thus under the Immigration Act 1971 the Home Secretary gives directions to the airline in respect of the removal of immigrants who are to be deported, but the deportee is entitled to challenge the directions since the directions were clearly of concern to the deportee.

[87] *Inland Revenue Commissioners v National Federation of Self-Employed and Small Businesses* [1982] A.C. 617 at 646B.

[88] In the CA in *R. v Secretary of State for Employment Ex p. Equal Opportunities Commission* [1993] 1 W.L.R. 872, the majority of the Court took a different view from that expressed in the text, but in the HL [1995] 1 A.C. 1 the judgment of Dillon LJ was preferred and it was decided that the EOC had standing in view of its statutory responsibilities.

[89] See *First Real Estates (UK) Ltd v Birmingham City Council* [2009] EWHC 817 (Admin); *R. v Enfield LBC Ex p. TF Unwin (Roydon)* 46 B.L.R. 1; *R. v Bristol City Council Ex p. D L Barrett & Sons*, CO/4181/1999.

[90] See 2-055 below.

[91] See e.g., *R. (Nationwide Association of Fostering Providers) v Bristol CC and others* [2015] EWHC 3615 (Admin); [2016] P.T.S.R. 932 (in a challenge to local authorities' approach to decision-making under the Children Act 1989, s.22C about the "most appropriate placement" for looked after children, William Davis J held that the claimant trade association "can legitimately be said to have more than purely commercial interests at heart" in relation to the s.22C administrative process, and declined to refuse judicial review on the basis that the claimant did not have sufficient interest.

[92] *R. v Secretary of State for Foreign and Commonwealth Affairs Ex p. World Development Movement Ltd* [1995] 1 W.L.R. 386 at 395G.

dominant factor.[93] Indeed it is difficult to find any case where a claimant has been refused permission to proceed with a claim solely on the basis that he lacks sufficient interest where strongly arguable grounds of review are advanced. It is similarly hard to find cases where the court has at the full hearing refused to hear the substantive claim, on the grounds that he has no standing where relief would have been granted but for his lack of standing. Weight may also be attached to the importance of the point of law at issue and the public interest in the case.[94]

Impact and proximity interests

2-032   If the decision which the claimant wishes to challenge interferes directly with the claimant's personal or public rights or has adverse financial consequences for him then this will be an obvious case in which he will have standing. But as the Court of Appeal has made plain, the relevance of a claimant's personal rights is not that without them there would be no claim for judicial review. Any person or body with a sufficient interest can seek judicial review. The claimants' interest is that they say they were among those who suffered violations of their right not to be inhumanly or degradingly treated; but there is no requirement of law that their claim for judicial review must be confined to their private law or personal interests.[95]

2-033   The Court of Appeal held, finding that the Home Secretary had acted unlawfully in failing to meet obligations to fully investigate events during a disturbance at an immigration removal centre, that "arguments about the degree of involvement or suffering of the particular claimants, unless these were to found a submission that they are mere meddlers who lack standing, are largely irrelevant. What matters is whether the entirety of what they have now brought to the court's attention requires, or at some point required, the Home Secretary to set up an inquiry".[96] A public authority's treatment of a claimant's competitors or business rivals may also provide a sufficient interest.[97] A non-pecuniary concern may provide a claimant with sufficient interest. Thus, a claimant who uses public land in respect of

---

[93]   *R. v North Somerset DC Ex p. Garnett* [1998] Env. L.R. 91 at [11].

[94]   *World Development Movement Ltd* [1995] 1 W.L.R. 386 at 395F; *R. (on the application of Bulger) v Lord Chief Justice* [2001] EWHC Admin 119; [2001] 3 All E.R. 449 at [24].

[95]   *R. (on the application of AM) v Secretary of State for the Home Department* [2009] EWCA Civ 219; [2009] A.C.D. 38 at [34].

[96]   *R. (on the application of AM) v Secretary of State for the Home Department* [2009] EWCA Civ 219; [2009] A.C.D. 38 at [35].

[97]   See, e.g. *R. v Canterbury City Council Ex p. Springimage Ltd* (1994) 68 P. & C.R. 171 (claimant, who intended to apply for permission to develop its own land, had standing to challenge legality of grant of planning permission to another person in respect of other land); *R. v Attorney General Ex p. ICI Plc* [1985] 1 C.M.L.R. 588 (ICI had standing to seek judicial review of the way the Inland Revenue proposed to value business goods used by Shell, Esso and BP which ICI alleged would have provided its competitors with an artificially favourable fiscal regime); *R. v Department of Transport Ex p. Presvac Engineering Ltd* (1992) 4 Admin. L.R. 121 (a trade competitor would normally have sufficient interest in the subject matter of an order which was intended to benefit a rival). cf. *R. v Hereford Corporation Ex p. Harrower* [1970] 1 W.L.R. 1424 (would-be contractors excluded from tendering process had standing if they were ratepayers, but not if they were mere contractors; this pre-1978 judgment needs to be treated with caution: see 2-006); *R. v Pembrokeshire CC Ex p. Coker* [1999] 4 All E.R. 1007 at [15] (potential purchasers of council land had no standing to challenge the council's decision to sell to another party); *R. (on the application of Rockware Glass Ltd) v Chester City Council* [2005] EWHC 2250 (Admin); [2006] Env. L.R. 30; *R. (Project Management Institute) v Minister for the Cabinet Office* [2016] EWCA Civ 21; [2016] 1 W.L.R. 1737 (claimant had sufficient interest because it would be adversely affected by the grant of a Royal Charter to a competitor).

which a challenge is made may have standing.[98] A parish council has standing to challenge planning permission for development three miles outside its area.[99] A claimant affected by the wrong-doing or negligence of a public official may have standing to challenge the conduct of subsequent disciplinary proceedings.[100] An architect with a rural practice has an interest in the proper administration of planning law which directly impacts on his clients and on his business.[101] "Not without hesitation", the Northern Ireland Court of Appeal held that the mother of a youth murdered by members of the British Army had sufficient interest to challenge a decision of the Army Board to retain them after their release from prison.[102]

The following have been held not to have a sufficient interest. An agent for six musicians (which sought to hire their services to perform at a concert) who had been refused work permits or entry clearance in circumstances where the musicians had a statutory right of appeal or could themselves make a claim for judicial review.[103] In a challenge to the grant of a licence, a person who was not a contender for the grant of the licence may lack standing.[104] A regular user of a bridle-way adjacent to a ruined cottage was held to have no standing to challenge a decision of a local authority to take enforcement action to require repair and restoration work to the cottage to be dismantled.[105] A former student of the University of Oxford, who alleged that another student had raped her, was held at the permission stage not to have standing to challenge the application of a new policy adopted by the university on investigation of such complaints.[106]

2-034

Public interest

It may not be necessary for the claimant to show any personal proximity to the decision or special impact or interest over and above that "shared with the generality of the public".[107] The claimant does not necessarily need to come from the sec-

2-035

---

[98] *R. v Dyfed CC Ex p. Manson* [1994] C.O.D. 366 (claimant lived in a house which directly adjoined a beach to which the impugned byelaws applied and he used the beach for a number of purposes, some of which he was concerned might be affected by the byelaws). cf. *R. v North Somerset DC Ex p. Garnett* [1998] Env. L.R. 91 (two local residents lacked standing to challenge grant of permission for quarrying in a large public park).

[99] *R. v Cotswold DC Ex p. Barrington Parish Council* (1998) 75 P. & C.R. 515.

[100] *R. v North Thames RHA Ex p. L (An Infant)* [1996] 7 Med. L.R. 385.

[101] *Re Ward, Application for Judicial Review* [2006] NIQB 67 (application for leave).

[102] *In the Matter of an Application for Judicial Review by Jean McBridge (No.2)* [2003] NICA 23 at [27].

[103] *R. (on the application of R70 World Ltd) v Visa Section* [2006] EWHC 330 (Admin).

[104] *R. (on the application of Wildman) v Office of Communications* [2005] EWHC 1573; *The Times,* 28 September 2005.

[105] *R. (on the application of Friend) v East Devon DC* [2009] EWHC 1013 (Admin) (HH Judge Kirham: "His interest is essentially that of a passer-by and a lover of the local landscape. He has no interest in the land itself. Mr Friend has not demonstrated a sufficient direct personal interest in the outcome. Further, I am not persuaded that there is a serious issue of general or public importance to be considered here").

[106] *R. (on the application of Ramey) v University of Oxford* [2014] EWHC 4847 (Admin), Edis J ("It appears to me that it is inappropriate for the claimant to be granted permission to bring judicial review to question not the terms of the policy itself but its application in circumstances where it has never actually been applied so far as the court knows. No doubt it has been applied but the court has no evidence about the way in which that has been done or the circumstances in which it is being done or whether indeed its application has caused anybody to suffer any sense of grievance. So the court is ill-equipped to take a decision on that question and that directly relates to the question of standing").

[107] *R. (on the application of Dixon) v Somerset CC* [1997] EWHC Admin 393; [1998] Env. L.R. 111 at [13] (Sedley J).

tion of the community on which the alleged breach of public law has impacted.[108] The Court of Appeal has drawn a distinction between "a person who brings proceedings having no real or genuine interest in obtaining the relief sought" (who accordingly will not have sufficient interest) and one "who, whilst legitimately and perhaps passionately interested in obtaining the relief sought, relies as grounds for seeking that relief on matters in which he has no personal interest".[109] Thus, for example, a former editor of *The Times* was held to have standing to challenge the Foreign Secretary's decision to ratify the Treaty on European Union "because of his sincere concern for constitutional issues".[110] The World Development Movement, none of whose supporters were directly affected by a particular grant of overseas aid to the government of Malaysia, was held to have standing.[111] The Howard League for Penal Reform had standing to challenge the Home Secretary's policy guidance on the treatment of children less than 18 years of age held in young offender institutions.[112] A Palestinian farmer who lived in a village near Bethlehem, whose land was appropriated to the Israeli Land Department, was held to have standing to challenge ministerial decisions to grant Standard Individual Export Licences (SIELs) for Military List items exported to Israel.[113]

2-036   Importance may be attached to a track record of concern and activity by the claimant in relation to the area of government decision-making under challenge.[114] But in assessing whether a claimant has sufficient interest, a failure to make representations before a decision was made, or be actively involved in a campaign, is unlikely to be fatal.[115] Equally, the fact that a claimant has made representations to the public authority and has received responses may not in and of itself signify that the claimant has standing subsequently to commence a claim for judicial review.[116] The fact that a claimant appears to have been "put up" by others to bring a claim in order to secure public funding from the Legal Services Commission, or to avoid exposure to an adverse order for costs, is not generally relevant to the question of standing.[117]

Presence or absence of other challengers

2-037   The courts have also regarded the presence or absence of challengers—apart from the claimant in question—as relevant. The existence of other potential claimants who have consciously or unwittingly decided not to bring proceedings need not

---

[108] *R. (on the application of Williams) v Surrey CC* [2012] EWHC 516 (Admin).

[109] *R. (on the application of Kides) v South Cambridgeshire DC* [2002] EWCA Civ 1370, [2003] 1 P. & C.R. 19 at [132].

[110] *R. v Secretary of State for Foreign and Commonwealth Affairs Ex p Rees-Mogg* [1994] Q.B. 552 at 562.

[111] *Ex p. World Development Movement Ltd* [1995] 1 W.L.R. 386. On campaign groups see 2-036.

[112] *R. (on the application of on the application of the Howard League for Penal Reform) v Secretary of State for the Home Department (No.2)* [2002] EWHC 2497; [2003] 1 F.L.R. 484.

[113] *R. (on the application of Hasan) v Secretary of State for Trade and Industry* [2007] EWHC 2630 (Admin) (Collins J at [8]); on appeal, where standing was not considered, see [2008] EWCA Civ 1311.

[114] *R. v Secretary of State for Social Services Ex p. Child Poverty Action Group* [1990] 2 Q.B. 540 at 546; *World Development Movement Ltd* [1995] 1 W.L.R. 386.

[115] *R. (on the application of Edwards) v The Environment Agency* [2004] EWHC Admin 736; [2004] 3 All E.R. 21 at [16].

[116] *R. v Secretary of State for the Environment Ex p. Rose Theatre Trust Co Ltd* [1990] 1 Q.B. 504 (Schiemann J: "The very fact that the Secretary of State has answered with care the representations made by those whose will the applicant embodies gives them a sufficient interest for the purpose of this application").

[117] *Edwards* [2004] EWHC 736 (Admin); [2004] 3 All E.R. 21.

however be a bar to another claimant being recognised as having sufficient interest.[118] The fact that nobody else apart from the claimant is likely to be sufficiently concerned by the impugned decision to bring legal proceedings may weigh in the claimant's favour, the rationale being that otherwise there would be a gap in the vindication of the law.[119]

Standing of local taxpayers

For many years, taxation levied by local authorities in England and Wales, based on a notional rental value of domestic and business premises, was known as rates. Business rates continue to be levied, but taxation of domestic dwellings is now called Council Tax. Naturally, ratepayers and Council Tax payers have standing to challenge decisions about rates and Council Tax.[120] A ratepayer in one London borough was held to be aggrieved by the rateable value ascribed to premises situated in a neighbouring borough on the ground that part of the rates collected from both boroughs was used to maintain services supplied by the Greater London Council.[121] Beyond this, the courts have generally adopted a generous approach to the standing of ratepayers to challenge the legality of local authority action in judicial review proceedings.[122] It is said that "Local authorities are not, of course, trustees for their ratepayers, but they do ... owe an analogous fiduciary duty to their ratepayers in relation to the application of funds contributed by the latter".[123] Thus, even before 1978, standing was accorded to local ratepayers seeking to challenge a breach of standing orders relating to the placing of contracts even though they had suffered no more detriment qua ratepayers than other members of their class.[124] Reliance on the claimant's status as a ratepayer to obtain standing appears to have fallen somewhat out of fashion, no doubt because of the general relaxation of the "sufficient interest" test.

2-038

---

[118] See, e.g. *R. v Lambeth LBC Ex p. Crookes* (1999) 31 H.L.R. 59 (landlord had standing to challenge failure to pay housing benefits to tenants, who would have paid the money over to him); *R. v HM Pollution Inspectorate Ex p. Greenpeace Ltd (No.2)* [1994] 4 All E.R. 329 at 350E (residents of Cumbria would also have had standing); cf. *R. (on the application of Grierson) v Office of Communications (OFCOM)* [2005] EWHC 1899 (Admin); [2005] E.M.L.R. 37 at [20]–[23] (where a company had decided not to make a judicial review claim in respect of a licensing decision, the managing director and a minority shareholder of that company lacked sufficient interest to bring a claim). But in *R. (on the application of Al-Haq) v Secretary of State for Foreign and Commonwealth Affairs* [2009] EWHC 1910 (Admin) at [62] Cranston J expressed doubt whether a non-governmental organisation based in the Occupied Palestinian Territory/the West Bank would have standing in a claim seeking a declaration that the UK Government was in breach of its obligations in international law in respect of the Israeli Government's actions in Gaza; the application for permission was refused on grounds of non-justiciability.

[119] *World Development Movement Ltd* [1995] 1 W.L.R. 386 at 395; cf. *Rose Theatre Trust Co Ltd* [1990] 1 Q.B. 504 at 522.

[120] See, e.g. *R. v Waltham Forest LBC Ex p. Baxter* [1988] Q.B. 419; Local Government Finance Act 1982 s.4.

[121] *Arsenal Football Club Ltd v Ende* [1979] A.C. 1. A ratepayer's standing was stated to depend as much upon his interest in the uniformity and fairness of rating assessments as upon any increased financial burden resulting from an under-assessment; thus, it was not necessary that the ratepayer establish any demonstrable material loss beyond that suffered by other ratepayers. A taxpayer, however, is not aggrieved by an erroneous valuation, even though he contributes through his taxation to the rate support grant administered by central government on the basis of total rateable value.

[122] The position is different in other types of legal proceedings: *Barrs v Bethell* [1982] Ch. 294.

[123] *Prescott v Birmingham Corp* [1955] Ch. 210 at 234–6 (unlawful for local authority to charge differential bus fares without specific statutory powers to do so).

[124] *R. v Hereford Corp Ex p. Harrower* [1970] 1 W.L.R. 1424 (contractors excluded from tendering process had standing as ratepayers, but not as competitors of the firm awarded the contract).

The role of campaign and interest groups as claimants

2-039   Campaign and interest groups are the claimants in only a relatively small proportion of judicial review claims each year.[125] The basis on which they are accorded standing varies:

(a)   in some claims, they may themselves have been directly affected, as an organisation, by the challenged decision and so be afforded standing on the basis of impact and proximity[126];

(b)   they may be bringing the claim in a representative capacity, where some or all of the organisation's members are personally affected by the decision being challenged[127]; and

(c)   in some other cases, the group brings a "pure" public interest challenge in circumstances where neither the organisation itself, nor any of its members, are personally or directly affected.[128] As we have noted, individuals may be afforded standing on the basis of public interest but public interest challenges by groups requires further comment.[129]

2-040   In *National Federation*, Lord Wilberforce considered that a body which represents a group of claimants who are seeking to establish standing are in no better position than an individual, "since an aggregate of individuals, each of whom has no interest, cannot of itself have an interest".[130] In *Ex p. Rose Theatre*,[131] Schiemann J applied the same principle to a body of individuals who, because they

---

[125]   Claims bought in the name of an individual may be brought behalf of a campaign group, see e.g. *R. (on the application of Smeaton) v Secretary of State for Health* [2002] EWHC 610 (Admin); [2002] 2 F.L.R. 146 (claim by the Society for the Protection of Unborn Children).

[126]   See, e.g. *R. v Radio Authority Ex p. Amnesty International* [1998] Q.B. 294 (Radio Authority refused AI permission to advertise on the radio about the distress of victims of human rights violations overseas, on the basis that the objects of the organisation were "mainly of a political nature" within the meaning of the Broadcasting Act 1990); *R. (on the application of National Union of Journalists) v Central Arbitration Committee* [2004] EWHC 2612 (Admin); [2005] I.C.R. 493; [2005] I.R.L.R. 28 (judicial review of a decision of the Central Arbitration Committee denying NUJ's recognition under the Trade Union and Labour Relations (Consolidation) Act 1992 by an employer).

[127]   See, e.g. *R. (on the application of West End Street Traders Association) v Westminster City Council* [2004] EWHC 1167; [2005] B.L.G.R. 143 (judicial review of a decision of local authority to implement changes in relation to charges for street trading); *R. (on the application of National Association of Colliery Overmen Deputies and Shotfirers) v Secretary of State for Work and Pensions* [2003] EWHC 607 (Admin); [2004] A.C.D. 14 (judicial review of the Secretary of State's decision not to immediately modify and revise the guidance given in the Notes on the Diagnosis of Prescribed Diseases on the use of the Cold Water Provocation Test as a diagnostic tool for vibration induced white finger in claims for industrial injuries benefits under the Social Security Contributions and Benefits Act 1992); *R. (on the application of United Kingdom Renderers Association Ltd) v Secretary of State for the Environment, Transport and the Regions* [2002] EWCA Civ 749; [2003] Env. L.R. 7 (judicial review of a Process Guidance Note issued by the Secretary of State which recommended, in the case of authorisations to carry out the rendering of animals, the imposition of an "odour boundary condition"); *R. (on the application of Association of British Civilian Internees (Far East Region)) v Secretary of State for Defence* [2003] EWCA Civ 473; [2003] Q.B. 1397 (judicial review of Secretary of State's refusal to make ex gratia compensation payment to individuals had been interned by foreign powers as British civilians during World War II); *Greenpeace Ltd (No.2)* [1994] 4 All E.R. 329 (in a challenge to the grant of a licence for a nuclear reprocessing plant at Sellafield, importance attached to the fact that 2,500 members of Greenpeace lived in Cumbria); *Gibraltar Betting and Gaming Association Ltd v Secretary of State for Culture, Media and Sport* [2014] EWHC 3236 (Admin); [2015] C.M.L.R. 28 (a trade association's challenge to the introduction of a new regulatory framework for gambling). On representation orders under CPR r.19.6, see 2-012.

[128]   See, e.g. *World Development Movement Ltd* [1995] 1 W.L.R. 386.

[129]   See 2-032.

[130]   *National Federation* [1982] A.C. 617 at 633.

were interested in preserving a site of historical theatrical remains from development, formed a company to challenge the failure of the minister to prevent the development. The company failed in its claim on the merits but the judge carefully considered the question of standing before coming to the conclusion the company did not have standing. In his judgment Schiemann J identified eight principles which were "not inconsistent" with the speeches in *National Federation*. Two of those principles were "The fact that some thousands of people join together and assert that they have an interest does not create an interest if the individuals did not have an interest" and "The fact that those without an interest incorporate themselves and give the company in its memorandum power to pursue a particular object does not give the company an interest".

No doubt there can be circumstances where both of these principles can be ap- **2-041** plied without producing undesirable results. However it would be wrong to regard them as being of general application. The simple act of incorporation may not improve the status of a claimant. There is no magic in the act of incorporation for public law purposes.[132] However the fact that a group of persons combine to make a claim may give them enhanced authority to speak on a subject on behalf of a section of the public. As a group or a company they may acquire a special status of acknowledged expertise.[133] It is possible for there to be situations where there are persons who are directly affected by administrative action who are for reasons of poverty, ignorance or lack of an incentive incapable of bringing proceedings. In such situations an appropriate body or, if necessary, an appropriate individual should be regarded by the court as having the necessary standing.

In *Rose Theatre*, counsel for the claimant did not submit that an "agglomeration **2-042** of individuals might have a standing which any one individual lacked".[134] It is suggested he was wrong not to do so. Indeed that there were individuals who were involved in the Rose Theatre company of acknowledged distinction in the field of archaeology who should, because of the nature of the issue before the court, have been regarded as being a significant factor in favour of there being standing. A specialist body which has the authority to speak collectively on behalf of its membership can carry greater weight than any one individual, no matter how distinguished. Similarly a trade union or a professional body is the obvious litigant to make a claim as to an administrative decision which affects its members generally.

The preferable approach was adopted by Otton J in *R. v HM Inspectorate of Pol-* **2-043** *lution Ex p. Greenpeace Ltd (No.2)*.[135] He decided that Greenpeace was entitled to challenge the Secretary of State's decision as to the discharge and disposal of radioactive waste at Sellafield. He pointed out if Greenpeace did not have standing an application would have to be made by an employee or neighbour of the establishment who would not be as well qualified as Greenpeace to make the application. The judge declined to follow the decision in *Rose Theatre*.

A subsequent case took the trend of liberalising the requirement of standing a step **2-044** further. In *R. v Secretary of State for Foreign Affairs Ex p. World Development*

---

[131] *Ex p. Rose Theatre* [1990] 1 Q.B. 504. cf. *R. v Stroud DC Ex p Goodenough* (1980) 43 P. & C.R. 59.

[132] See 2-013.

[133] *Greenpeace Ltd (No.2)* [1994] 4 All E.R. 329; *R. v Secretary of State for Social Security Ex p. Joint Council for the Welfare of Immigrants* [1997] 1 W.L.R. 275.

[134] *Rose Theatre Trust Co Ltd* [1990] 1 Q.B. 504 at 521.

[135] *Ex p. Greenpeace Ltd (No.2)* [1994] 4 All E.R. 329: Greenpeace's primary objectives include the protection of wildlife and the elimination of threats to the environment.

Movement Ltd[136] the Divisional Court held that the claimant had sufficient interest to apply for judicial review. The WDM was a non-partisan pressure group, founded in 1970, which campaigned to improve the quality and quantity of overseas aid given by the British government. In the past it had given evidence to parliamentary select committees, had regular contact with the Overseas Development Administration (the government department responsible for overseas aid) and internationally it had consultative status with United Nations organisations. In one respect, however, the WDM differed from Greenpeace; whereas in the *Greenpeace* application challenging the legality of testing THORP, individual members of Greenpeace who lived in Cumbria would have been directly affected by the testing, and so have sufficient interest to make an application themselves, no individual member of the WDM was any more or less affected by the grant to build a power station on the Pergau dam in Malaysia than other members of the public. Nevertheless, the court held that the WDM had sufficient interest, referring to a range of factors: the merits of the application (here the impugned decision was held to be unlawful); the importance of vindicating the rule of law; the importance of the issue raised; the likely absence of any other challenger; the nature of the breach of duty against which relief was sought; and the prominent role of these claimants in giving advice, guidance and assistance with regard to all.

2-045   The process of liberalising the standing requirements for pressure groups has reached the stage where in *R. v Secretary of State for Trade and Industry Ex p. Greenpeace*[137] Laws J commented that litigation of this kind was now an "accepted and greatly valued dimension of the judicial review jurisdiction". The corollary of this, however, is that a pressure group bringing a public interest challenge had to "act as a friend to the court," meaning that its conduct in making an application has to be controlled with particular strictness—especially as regards the requirement that applications for permission be made promptly and in any event within three months of the impugned decision.[138] In summary, it can be said that today the court ought not to decline jurisdiction to hear a claim for judicial review on the ground of lack of standing to any responsible person or group seeking, on reasonable grounds, to challenge the validity of governmental action. The good

---

[136] *R. v Secretary of State for Foreign Affairs Ex p. World Development Movement Ltd* [1995] 1 W.L.R. 386.

[137] *R. v Secretary of State for Trade and Industry Ex p. Greenpeace* [1998] Env L.R. 415.

[138] In *R. (on the application of Plantagenet Alliance Ltd) v Secretary of State for Justice* [2013] Inquest L.R. 204, the claimant was a not-for profit entity comprised of the collateral descendants Richard III (king of England 1483-1485), which was formed in response to the discovery of the king's remains during an archaeological excavation in a local authority carpark. The Alliance was granted permission to apply for judicial review of the Secretary of State's decision to grant an exhumation licence on the ground that he had failed to comply with a duty to consult relevant interests as to how and where the remains should be reburied, either prior to issuing the licence or subsequently. Although the application was made after the three-month time limit, additional time was granted. The Alliance was held to have standing and to have an arguable case. *R. v Secretary of State for the Environment, Ex p. Rose Theatre Ltd* [1990] 1 Q.B. 504 was not cited. In *R. (on the application of Plantagenet Alliance Ltd) v Secretary of State for Justice* [2013] EWHC 3164 (Admin); [2014] A.C.D. 26, the court upheld a protective costs order made in respect of the judicial review proceedings brought by the Alliance (which had no assets) on the basis that the proceedings raised matters of general public importance. At the full hearing of the claim for judicial review, it was held that there were no public law grounds to interfere with the Secretary of State's decision and the application was dismissed: *R. (on the application of the Plantagenet Alliance Ltd) v Secretary of State for Justice* [2014] EWHC 1662 (QB); [2015] 3 All E.R. 261. The Ministry of Justice estimated its unrecoverable costs at around £90,000. The University of Leicester and Leicester City Council (the second and third defendants) were also unable to recover their costs from the Alliance. This case was used by the government to justify its proposed reforms to protective costs orders contained in the Criminal Justice and Courts Act 2015 (see below at 16-XXX).

sense of this approach is emphasised by the ability of the courts to give permission to a third party to intervene in the proceedings to assist the court, which is happening with increasing frequency.[139]

Public Contracts Regulations

The Public Contracts Regulations 2015 (SI 201510) make provision in domestic law for European Union rules on public procurement; breach of rules by a "contracting authority" may be challenged by way of a judicial review claim. The courts have taken the approach that in order to have standing in this context, a claimant must be an "economic operator". Thus, the fact that a would-be claimant was a mother of school-age children living in the London Borough of Camden did not provide her with sufficient interest to make a judicial review claim on the ground that the public procurement rules had not been followed in a decision under s.482 of the Education Act 1996 relating to the establishment of an Academy sponsored by UCL: "The nature of the legal protections conferred by the procurement regime created by the 2006 Regulations [one of the predecessor provisions to the 2015 Regulations] is such that they can be invoked only in private law proceedings by affected economic operators and no such has come forward".[140]

2-046

HUMAN RIGHTS ACT 1998 AND THE VICTIM REQUIREMENT

Where a claim for judicial review seeks to rely on breach of a Convention right as a ground of review, in relation to that ground the meaning of "sufficient interest" is modified by s.7 of the HRA, which provides:

2-047

"(1)   A person who claims that a public authority has acted (or proposes to act) in a way which is made unlawful by section 6(1) may—
   (a)   bring proceedings against the authority under this Act in the appropriate court or tribunal, or
   (b)   rely on the Convention right or rights concerned in any legal proceedings, but only if he is (or would be) a victim of the unlawful act".

Subsection 7(3) states: "If the proceedings are brought on an application for judicial review, the applicant is to be taken to have a sufficient interest in relation to the unlawful act only if he is, or would be, a victim of that act".

2-048

The effect is to incorporate into English law the approach adopted by the European Court of Human Rights under ECHR art.34 (formerly art.25), which sets out the standing requirement for access that court in the following terms: "The Court may receive applications from any person, non-governmental organisation or group of individuals claiming to be a victim of a violation ...". The requirement to follow Strasbourg case law appears to be stronger here, by virtue of s.7, than the general obligation under HRA s.2 that courts "must take into account" this case law.

2-049

The rationale for including the victim requirement in the HRA appeared to be two-fold. In part, it reflected the government's general aim for the HRA that it

2-050

---

[139] See 2-068.
[140] *R. (on the application of Chandler) v Secretary of State for Children, Schools and Families* [2009] EWHC 219 (Admin); [2009] A.C.D. 50 at [140], Forbes J. See also *R. (on the application of UNISON) v NHS Wiltshire Primary Care Trust* [2012] EWHC 624 (Admin); [2012] A.C.D. 84; and *Wylde v Waverley BC* [2017] EWHC 466 (Admin); [2017] A.C.D. 57.

should "bring rights home" by closely mirroring the ECHR and not creating new kinds of rights. The victim requirement was also clearly intended to restrict the capacity of campaign groups to use Convention rights as a ground for judicial review.[141] Under the Equality Act 2006 s.30 the Equality and Human Rights Commission (a non-departmental public body) has capacity to institute or intervene in legal proceedings, including judicial review claims, "if it appears to the Commission that the proceedings are relevant to a matter in connection with which the Commission has a function".

When is the victim requirement relevant?

2-051   There continues to be uncertainty as to when the victim requirement is brought into play. On one analysis it is necessary, by reason of the words of the HRA, to differentiate between claims (a) in which the claimant argues that there has been a breach by a public authority under HRA s.6 (to which the victim requirement applies) and (b) where a claimant is seeking a declaration of incompatibility under HRA s.4 in respect of a legislation (in which the victim requirement does not apply and the ordinary judicial review approach to standing should be used).[142] In other cases, however, the courts have held or assumed that the victim requirement applies to claims for a declaration of incompatibility.[143] In our view the former approach is the better one.

Strasbourg case law on meaning of "victim"

2-052   In transplanting the case law of the European Court of Human Rights into the domestic setting, it needs to be borne in mind that the Strasbourg rule and its interpretation have been crafted for the purposes of controlling access to an international tribunal. That is a rather different purpose from the role of the "sufficient interest" test used in judicial review. When determining individual applications, the ECtHR is concerned with concrete review and eschews abstract review

---

[141] See, e.g. *Re Application by the Family Planning Association of Northern Ireland for Judicial Review* [2003] NIQB 48 at [58]-[67] (Kerr J held that FBANI was prevented from making submissions in relation to whether Minister had contravened Convention rights).

[142] *R. (on the application of Countryside Alliance) v Attorney General* [2006] EWCA Civ 817; [2007] Q.B. 305 at [64]-[66] (Lord Phillips CJ, claim for declaration of incompatibility of the Hunting Act 2004: the HRA "does not purport to prescribe rules for standing if a declaration like this is sought, in contrast to the rule in s.7(1)(a), which entitles a person who claims that a public authority has acted (or proposed to act) in a way which is made unlawful by s.6(1) to bring proceedings against that authority in the appropriate court, but only if he is (or would be) a victim of the unlawful act". The claimant in a claim for judicial review must still satisfy the requirement of having "sufficient interest" albeit not modified to include a victim test. The question was not pursued in a subsequent appeal [2007] UKHL 52; [2008] 1 A.C. 719); cf. *R. (on the application of Morris) v Westminster City Council (No.3)* [2005] EWCA Civ 1184; [2006] 1 W.L.R. 505 at [54] (Sedley LJ, "Although the claim for a declaration of incompatibility requires a sufficient interest on the part of the claimant, the decision to make a declaration if the conditions are met depends not on the claimant's interest alone but on the general compatibility of the measure with the Convention right in question"). The issue was discussed obiter in *An application for judicial review by the Northern Ireland Commissioner for Children and Young People* [2009] NICA 10; [2009] NI 235 at [11]-[18].

[143] *R. (on the application of Rusbridger) v Attorney General* [2003] UKHL 38; [2004] 1 A.C. 357, discussed below. See also *Taylor v Lancashire CC* [2005] EWCA Civ 284; [2005] 1 W.L.R. 2668 (appellant sought to raise as a defence to an order for possession of an agricultural holding that certain provisions of the Agricultural Holdings Act 1986, which did not apply to his case, were incompatible with Convention rights; held not to be a victim because he "has not been and could not be personally adversely affected by the repealed legislation on which he seeks to rely").

of legislation, policy or administrative action. Moreover, applications that amount to an *actio popularis* are excluded.[144]

Generally, the term "victim" in ECHR art.34 denotes a person directly affected by the specific act or omission in issue. It is not however necessary that the victim have suffered damage, which is an issue in relation to "just satisfaction" under art.41.[145] If a national authority makes a decision or measure favourable to the applicant, that is not sufficient to deprive him of his status as a victim unless (a) the national authorities acknowledges, either expressly or in substance, and then (b) affords redress for, the breach of the Convention.[146] It is no answer for a national authority to say that the person has, in the end, suffered no detriment under national law.[147] Where, however, an administrative order is retrospectively quashed by a national court a person can no longer claim to be a victim of interference.[148] The ECtHR has regarded a person falling within the ambit of legislation affecting a Convention right to be a victim, even in the absence of enforcement of that legislation against the person.[149] The repeal of national legislation violating a Convention right does not preclude a person being a victim in subsequent proceedings before the ECtHR if he suffered disadvantage during the time the legislation was in force.[150]

2-053

Close family relationships may form the basis of a claim to be a victim; this is not a general principle, rather all the circumstances of a case must be considered. Where a person has died and a breach of ECHR art.2 is alleged, the test of whom may be a victim involves consideration of whether the relationship between the claimant and the dead person is such that the claimant has "suffered gravely".[151] The father of a son who had disappeared may himself be the victim of inhuman and degrading treatment under ECHR art.3, having regard to the way in which national authorities responded when the disappearance was brought to their attention.[152]

2-054

---

[144] An *actio popularis* is an action "in which any member of the public may be entitled as such to vindicate certain forms of public right" (*MacCormick v Lord Advocate* 1953 S.C. 396 at 413, Lord Cooper LP).

[145] *Ilhan v Turkey* (2002) 34 E.H.R.R. 36 (brother of person injured by police could make application; but ECtHR noted that it would generally be appropriate for an application to name the injured person as the applicant and for a letter of authority to be provided allowing another member of the family to act on his or her behalf). On just satisfaction and damages, see 19-088.

[146] *Eckle v Germany* (1983) 5 E.H.R.R. 1.

[147] *Posokhov v Russia* (2004) 39 E.H.R.R. 21 (P complained about appointment of judge, his conviction was quashed on the basis of an unrelated procedural irregularity); *Ryabykh v Russia* (2005) 40 E.H.R.R. 25 (R successfully claimed that the State had failed to fulfil a legal requirement to revalue her savings to counter the effects of inflation; she suffered detriment because of a period of uncertainty during the litigation caused by a review of the case contrary to art.6(1)).

[148] *Akkoc v Turkey* (2002) 34 E.H.R.R. 51; *Amuur v France* (1996) 22 E.H.R.R. 533.

[149] See, e.g. *Klass v Federal Republic of Germany* (1978) 2 E.H.R.R. 214 at [33] (secret surveillance legislation), *Dudgeon v United Kingdom* (1982) 4 E.H.R.R. 149 (law prohibiting sex between men) *Burden v United Kingdom* (2007) 44 E.H.R.R. 51 at [25] (liability to pay inheritance tax had not yet accrued, but there was "every high probability" that applicants would become liable). cf. *Leigh v United Kingdom* (1982) 38 D.R. 74 (journalist claiming to be affected by "chilling effect" of House of Lords' judgment on contempt of court was not a victim). In relation to art.8 and secret surveillance, the ECtHR has accepted that an applicant does not need to contend that measures of surveillance were actually applied to him and that it is therefore inappropriate to apply a reasonable likelihood test to determine whether he may claim to be a victim: *Case of the Association for European Integration and Human Rights v Bulgaria* (62540/00), para.58.

[150] *SL v Austria* (2003) 37 E.H.R.R. 3 (S was a victim of legislation prohibiting sex between males, since repealed, as he had suffered disadvantage during the time it was in force).

[151] *R. (on the application of Morgan) v Ministry of Justice* [2010] EWHC 2248 (QB) at [70].

[152] *Timurtas v Turkey* (2001) 33 E.H.R.R. 6. See also *Kurt v Turkey* (1999) 27 E.H.R.R. 373. cf. *Akdeniz v Turkey* (23954/94).

2-055   The ECtHR has not been particularly generous in its interpretation of "victim" in relation to the deportation of foreign nationals. An applicant cannot claim to be the victim of a deportation measure if the measure is not enforceable.[153] Similarly, where execution of the deportation order has been stayed indefinitely or otherwise deprived of legal effect and where an appeal lies to a court, the person will not be regarded as a victim.[154] Removal from a register of residents did not make applicants victims when this did not result in the applicants facing any real and imminent risk of deportation.[155]

2-056   The ECtHR has attached considerable importance to the legal personality of applicants. Piercing of the corporate veil or disregarding the company's personality is justified only in exceptional circumstances: where it is the interests of a company that have been affected, and that company (or its liquidators) are able to bring proceedings, shareholders of the company are unlikely to be regarded as victims.[156] A distinction was made between a national political party (which had applied to the court) and a regional organisation of that party (which had not, yet had been the legal entity directly affected).[157]

2-057   In several respects, the standing rule in ECHR art.34 is more limited than the Administrative Court's approach to the test for sufficient interest. Government bodies fall outside the ambit of art.34, cannot be victims and therefore cannot use violation of Convention rights as a ground of review.[158] Moreover, the European Court

---

[153] *Vijayanathan v France* (1993) 15 E.H.R.R. 62 (applicants remained in France beyond the time set for their deportation order; if they had been arrested, the order would be subject to annulment for obvious error of assessment on appeal within 24 hours to the French courts. Lodging an appeal had a suspensive effect on deportation orders).

[154] See cases cited in *Sisojeva v Latvia* (60654/00) (2007) 45 E.H.R.R. 33, para.93.

[155] *Sisojeva* (60654/00) (2007) 45 E.H.R.R. 33, para.100.

[156] *Agrotexim v Greece* (1996) 21 E.H.R.R. 250.

[157] *Vatan v Russia* (2006) 42 E.H.R.R. 7.

[158] *Ayuntamiento de M v Spain* (1991) 68 D. & R. 209; para.3-071 below; and H. Davis, "Public authorities as 'victims' under the Human Rights Act" [2005] 64 C.L.J. 315. On determining the governmental status of a body, see *Transpetrol v Slovakia* Application 28502/08 [2011] E.C.H.R 2004. Transpetrol was a joint-stock company which specialised in transporting, storing, buying and selling oil. At the time of the contested judgment of the national Constitutional Court, which the applicant complained had breached its ECHR art.6 right to a fair hearing, the state owned 51 per cent of the shares in the company. The remainder were owned by private parties. The applicant had features of both a governmental and a non-governmental body. The court noted, at [65], that the applicant was a commercial joint-stock company operating exclusively under the private-law regime, governed by the Commercial Code, with no privileges or special rights or rules concerning enforcement of judgments against it; subject to the jurisdiction of the ordinary courts; not participating in the exercise of any government power and, in the past, partly owned by private entities (it had since become entirely state-owned). On the other hand (at [66]), the state had always been a major shareholder and at present was the sole shareholder in the company; on account of its national strategic economic importance it used to be excluded by law from privatisation; it had a "natural monopoly" and an unrivalled market position in the state. However, rather than weighing these elements against each other, the decisive considerations for the determination of the applicant's standing under ECHR art.34 lay in "the assessment of the overall procedural and substantive context of the application and of its underlying facts". The genuine issue behind the proceedings was the ownership of the shares in the applicant company, which primarily concerned the rights and interests of other shareholders rather than those of the company itself. In the circumstances, the interests of the applicant company and the government were the same and the application did not strive to further interests other than those that were concurrent interests of the state. The state had also joined the applicant as an intervener in separate proceedings involving essentially the same issues. The application was declared inadmissible for lack of standing under art.34. The court noted, however, that this was without prejudice to the applicant company's art.34 standing should the relevant circumstances be different. But see *Olympic Delivery Authority v Persons Unknown* [2012] EWHC 1012 (Ch), where, in a claim in private and public nuisance, the ODA sought injunctions to restrain

does not permit pure public interest claims: to bring proceedings a non-governmental organisation (NGO) must itself be directly affected by the alleged violation of a Convention right.[159]

Application of "victim" requirement in the HRA

The meaning of "victim" in HRA s.7 has been considered in several cases.   **2-058**

Victim status

The House of Lords held (obiter) that a person who, in proceedings before the   **2-059**
European Court of Human Rights, obtained the award of a payment by way of just satisfaction, remained a "victim" for the purposes of claim made under the HRA in respect of a continuing breach of a Convention right.[160] Parents did not lose their victim status for a claim relating to ECHR art.2 by accepting damages in a negligence claim after a hospital permitted their daughter, a psychiatric patient, to go on a home visit where she committed suicide.[161]

In another case, in which a newspaper editor sought declarations in respect of the   **2-060**
Treason Felony Act 1848 s.3, which appeared to criminalise advocacy of republicanism in Britain, the House of Lords was divided as to whether the editor should be held to be a victim (an issue that had, in fact, been conceded by the defendant).[162] In *Hooper v Secretary of State for Work and Pensions* the claimant widowers challenging the lawfulness of refusal to pay them social security and pension payments, to which they would have been entitled had they been widows, were held to be victims because each claimant had done something which identified him

---

protestors from entering or occupying land that was being developed as part of the Olympic site. The ODA was established by statute under the London Olympic Games and Paralympic Games Act 2006 s.3. In exercising its functions it must obey any directions given by the Secretary of State (Sch.1, para.18(1)(b)) who appointed its members and chairman (Sch.1, para.1(1)). It was undoubtedly a public authority (whether core or hybrid) within HRA s.6. Arnold J, however, considered himself bound to balance the rights of the protestors under ECHR arts 10 and 11 with the ODA's rights to peaceful enjoyment of property under art.1 of Protocol 1 (which he did in favour of the ODA). This aspect of the decision is open to criticism on the basis that the ODA, as a public authority, could not argue Convention rights.

[159] See, e.g. *Norris and National Gay Federation v Ireland* (1984) 44 D.R. 132 (NGF was not itself directly affected by legislation prohibiting sex between males); *Purcell v Ireland* (1991) 70 D.R. 262 (broadcasting unions could not bring proceedings to challenge probation on transmissions of interviews with paramilitary groups); cf. *Open Door Counselling Ltd and Dublin Well Woman Centre v Ireland* (1993) 15 E.H.R.R. 244 (two Irish counselling organisations assisting clients to have abortions in England were restrained by an injunction claimed by the Attorney General; as directly affected NGOs, there were recognised as victims). An NGO may, however, be permitted to make an application on behalf of a group of named individuals who are themselves victims if it is acting on specific instructions from those named individuals.

[160] *Re McKerr's Application for Judicial Review* [2004] UKHL 12; [2004] 1 W.L.R. 807 (obiter, because the HL held that the HRA did not operate retrospectively to create a continuing obligation under ECHR art.2 to investigate unlawful killings that occurred before the HRA came into force).

[161] *Rabone and another v Pennine Care NHS Trust (Inquest and others intervening)* [2012] UKSC 2; [2012] 2 A.C. 72.

[162] *Rusbridger* [2003] UKHL 38; [2004] 1 A.C. 357: Lord Steyn, at [21], emphasised this was a threshold question and applied *Norris v Ireland* (1989) 13 E.H.R.R. 186 in which a "homosexual man complained that the criminalisation of homosexual conduct in Ireland violated his art.8 right to respect for his private life, although he accepted that the risk of being prosecuted was remote"; Lord Rodger of Earlsferry, at [55], described the present proceedings as "in substance an actio popularis" and stressed that *Norris* required "that an individual applicant should be able to claim to be actually affected by the measure of which he complains" (which was not so in the case of the editor).

as having wished to make a claim.[163] In *Eastaway v Secretary of State for Trade and Industry* the Court of Appeal reiterated that "A person can be a victim under Strasbourg jurisprudence even though the violation has been brought to an end".[164] The appellant had given an undertaking to the Secretary of State in May 2001 not to act as a company director for four and a half years. In 2004, the European Court of Human Rights had held that ECHR art.6 rights of the appellant had been breached by the length of proceedings; he was awarded compensation for his legal costs and non-pecuniary damage. In the present case the appellant sought to have the undertaken given in 2001 set aside, even though it had expired. Arden LJ, for the court, held that[165]:

> "The definition of 'victim' in s.7(7) turns on whether proceedings could be brought in the Strasbourg court in respect of the act complained of. The act complained of would be the continuance of the disqualification proceedings when no fair trial was possible. Thus the statutory hypothesis in s.7(7) of the HRA must, in my judgment, be applied not to the proceedings which have already been brought in the Strasbourg court, but to some new proceedings brought on the same basis as his new complaint and at the same time."

The appellant did not, however, have an arguable case.

2-061   In a Northern Irish case, the applicant for judicial review (a detained patient) challenged the compatibility of arts 32 and 36 of the Mental Health (Northern Ireland) Order 1986 relating to the appointment of his "nearest relative" with Convention rights. The applicant wanted to change his nearest relative from his sister to his cousin (who lived in Northern Ireland and with whom he had more regular contact) but the legislation did not provide a procedure for achieving this. Identically, legislation in England and Wales had been acknowledged to be incompatible but the respondent was reluctant to bring forward amendments in Northern Ireland. Surprisingly, the respondent contended that the applicant did not have victim status, a submission rejected by the court.[166]

Not a victim

2-062   In *Re Northern Ireland Commissioner for Children and Young People's Application for Judicial Review*, the Court of Appeal of Northern Ireland held that the Commissioner (a statutory body) was not a victim for the purposes of challenging the compatibility with Convention rights of delegated legislation which provided for a defence of reasonable chastisement of a child to a criminal charge of assault.[167]

---

163 *Hooper v Secretary of State for Work and Pensions* [2005] UKHL 29; [2005] 1 W.L.R. 1681 at [53]-[59] (Lord Hoffmann, obiter, citing *Cornwell v United Kingdom* (1999) 27 E.H.R.R. CD 62 in which the court treated an inquiry about the availability of benefits as sufficient).

164 *Eastaway v Secretary of State for Trade and Industry* [2007] EWCA Civ 425; [2007] B.C.C. 550 at [51].

165 *Eastaway v Secretary of State for Trade and Industry* [2007] EWCA Civ 425; [2007] B.C.C. 550 at [54].

166 *An Application by HM for Judicial Review v In the Matter of Articles 32 and 36 of the Mental Health (Northern Ireland) Order 1986* [2014] NIQB 43, Treacy J ("The applicant submits that his article 8 rights are infringed by the lack of a mechanism allowing him to apply to change his nearest relative as evidenced at sections 32 and 36 of the 1986 order. It is common case that the 1986 order does not in fact contain any such mechanism. Therefore, if it is found that the relevant sections do infringe the applicant's rights then clearly he will fulfil the victim requirement as his rights will actually have been infringed by the impugned provisions").

167 *An application for judicial review by the Northern Ireland Commissioner for Children and Young People* [2009] NICA 10; [2009] N.I. 235. Cf. *Re Northern Ireland Human Rights Commission's Application for Judicial Review* [2012] NIQB 77; [2012] Eq. L.R. 1135, where the Commission brought

In *Austin Hall Building Ltd v Buckland Securities Ltd*,[168] the client of a building contractor was held not to be a victim in a challenge to a decision of an adjudicator appointed under the Housing Grants, Construction and Regeneration Act 1996 as it had not objected to the manner of the decision-making process at the time. In *R. (on the application of Broadway Care Centre Ltd) v Caerphilly CBC*,[169] where a local authority decided to terminate a care home's contract, the care home was not a victim in bringing a claim to protect its residents' ECHR art.8 rights. Nor did the responsibilities in respect of closure of care homes give rise to a responsibility of the local authority towards the care home such that the care home would itself be a victim of any breach. In *Somerville v Scottish Ministers*, the House of Lords considered the Scotland Act 1998 s.100(1), which in similar terms to HRA 1998 s.7 restricts reliance on Convention rights in legal proceedings to those who are "victims". Lord Scott of Foscote commented that[170]:

> "Bearing in mind that Convention incompatibility is a ground on which any enactment of the Scottish Parliament, any subordinate legislation made by the Scottish Ministers or the Scottish Executives or any act of any member of the Scottish Executive may be held to be outside devolved competence and therefore ultra vires, the need to place a strict limit on those entitled to raise such a point in litigation seems to me easy to understand."

Criticism of the victim requirement in the HRA

The policy of HRA s.7(3) was opposed during the passage of the Human Rights Bill and has been subject to academic criticism.[171] It may be thought undesirable to have different standing rules for purely domestic and Convention right grounds of review—particularly as these two categories of ground will often be combined in a single claim. An environmental pressure group may therefore have standing to advance (say) a claim of illegality but not to argue that ECHR art.8 has been violated by a development. Similarly a group campaigning for the rights of immigrants and asylum seeks may have standing in relation to a procedural impropriety point but not (say) an allegation that there has been a breach of ECHR art.6(1). A policy that permits only individuals to advance Convention right points in judicial review claims undermines the pragmatic good sense of Otton J's recognition in *Ex p. Greenpeace (No.2)* of the advantages to the court of having a well-qualified claimant, rather than "an employee or neighbour", or other individual, bring the challenge.[172] The Commission for Equality and Human Rights may rely on Convention rights in judicial review claims it makes or intervenes in without itself being a victim or potential victim of the unlawful act, provided that there are one or more other people who are victims.[173] Moreover, a campaign group that is

2-063

---

an application on behalf of unmarried couples in a challenge to the Adoption (Northern Ireland) Order 1987 arts 14–15, which provided that adoption orders could only be made on the application of married couples or individuals who were neither married nor in a civil partnership. The Commission had standing under the Northern Ireland Act 1998 s.71(2B)(c) provided there was or would be one or more victims of the unlawful act (which was established).

[168] *Austin Hall Building Ltd v Buckland Securities Ltd* [2001] B.L.R. 272, QBD.

[169] *R. (on the application of Broadway Care Centre Ltd) v Caerphilly CBC* [2012] EWHC 37 (Admin); (2012) 15 C.C.L. Rep. 82.

[170] *Somerville v Scottish Ministers* [2007] UKHL 44; [2007] 1 W.L.R. 2734 at [75].

[171] J. Marriott and D. Nicol, "The Human Rights Act, Representative Standing and the Victim Culture" (1998) 6 E.H.R.L.R. 730; J. Miles, "Standing under the Human Rights Act 1998: Theories of Rights Enforcement and the Nature of Public Law Adjudication" [2000] C.L.J. 133.

[172] See 2-040.

[173] Equality Act 2006 s.30(3).

not a victim may nevertheless be able to seek permission to intervene to raise Convention right points in a claim begun by someone else.[174]

STANDING OF "PERSONS AGGRIEVED"

2-064   In some contexts, legislation provides a procedure distinct from a claim for judicial review under CPR Pt 54, enabling those affected by the activities of public authorities to appeal or make an application to quash an order or other administrative decision.[175] The legislation may specify who is entitled to bring the proceedings, and when this happens as long as the legislation is not ambiguous and sufficiently specific there should be no difficulty in determining who has standing.[176] It frequently happens, however, that the legislation uses some general description to describe who may bring proceedings and in this situation the courts have to determine who falls within that description. A longstanding favourite description in legislation of those who are entitled to challenge the validity of or appeal against administrative acts is a "person aggrieved".[177] Judicial protests against the continued use of this vague expression have gone unheeded[178]; and in its 1994 report, the Law Commission concluded that "we do not wish to widen the test of standing under these statutes and, in the circumstances, make no recommendations for reform".[179] A "person aggrieved" may authorise an agent to commence and conduct proceedings on his behalf.[180]

2-065   The task of interpretation has been left to the judge.[181] The results in the past have

---

[174]   A possibility anticipated by the Government during the passage of the Human Rights Bill: *Hansard*, HC col.1058 (24 November 1997). On interventions, see 2-068.

[175]   See 17-025. The Competition Appeal Tribunal, in a review under Enterprise Act 2002 s.120 of a decision of the Secretary of State for Business, Enterprise and Regulatory Reform not to refer to the Competition Commission under the 2002 Act s.45 a proposed merger of banks, held that although "the relevant tests for standing in claims for judicial review in England and Wales and under s.120 of the Act are phrased differently, and thus the ease with which an applicant can establish standing may well differ, we see no reason why the factors that inform the question of standing should be wholly different" (*Merger Action Group v Secretary of State for Business, Enterprise and Regulatory Reform* [2008] CAT 36; 2009 S.L.T. 10 at [41]). Moreover, "it would be undesirable to interpret 'person aggrieved' in this context in such a way as to limit the possibility of challenge to a merger decision by shutting out those with a less immediate connection to the subject-matter of the dispute than, for example, competitors in the market place but who may well also be adversely affected, albeit in a different way" (at [47]).

[176]   See, e.g. Town and Country Planning Act 1990 s.289(1), which provides that in respect of a decision by the Secretary of State in respect of an enforcement notice, the person who appealed to the Secretary of State, the local authority or any other person having an interest in the land to which the notice relates may appeal to the High Court. Standing cannot be assigned: see *Eco-Energy (GB) Ltd v First Secretary of State* [2004] EWCA Civ 1566.

[177]   See, e.g. Town and Country Planning Act 1990 ss.287 and 288; Planning and Compulsory Purchase Act 2004 s.100; Human Tissue Act 2004 s.22; Petroleum Act 1998 s.42. No doubt the reason for this is that at common law, before the introduction of the universal test of "sufficient interest" in the 1978 procedural reforms, it was generally the test for determining whether a person had standing to apply for certiorari and prohibition to ask whether he was a person aggrieved. The use of the term "person aggrieved" in relation to appeals to tribunals or courts other than the Administrative Court falls outside the scope of this chapter.

[178]   *Ealing Corp v Jones* [1959] 1 Q.B. 384 at 390; *Buxton v Minister of Housing and Local Government* [1961] 1 Q.B. 278 at 282-3.

[179]   *Administrative Law: Judicial Review and Statutory Appeals* (Law Com. 226), para.12.18.

[180]   *General Legal Council (on the application of Whitter) v Frankson* [2006] UKPC 42; [2006] 1 W.L.R. 2803.

[181]   See, e.g. *Swansea City and County Council v Davies* (2001) 165 J.P. 156.

not been entirely coherent. It is, of course, to be expected that the meaning attributed to such an expression will vary according to the context in which it is found,[182] and this partly explains why in the past there was an undesirable lack of consistency in decisions as to the meaning of this term. The sheer number of different statutes which use the term is also a contributing factor.[183] The purpose for which a right of appeal or to make an application was conferred in a particular situation will often be a decisive factor in answering the question who is entitled to exercise the right.[184]

The courts did for a time give an unduly restrictive interpretation to the expression "person aggrieved". They took the view that to be legally aggrieved a person must not be merely dissatisfied with or even prejudiced by an act or decision, but must have been deprived of or refused something to which he was legally entitled[185] or subjected to a legal burden (for example, a duty to pay costs or execute works).[186] In accord with the developments which were taking place on applications for judicial review, there was a clearly discernible trend away from the restrictive and highly technical approach to who is a person aggrieved.   **2-066**

Normally, "a public authority which has an adverse decision made against it in an area where it is required to perform public duties, is entitled to be treated as a person aggrieved".[187] A local authority may be a "person aggrieved"[188]; so also may the Crown or the Attorney General acting on its behalf.[189] However, it may still be the case that if the decision is in favour of the local authority and that body only objects to the reasons given for the decision the local authority is not a "person aggrieved".[190] It is suggested that this view underestimates the importance which can attach to the reasons for a decision being given. The absence of reasons or the provision of unsatisfactory reasons can result in a local authority having to adopt in another case an approach of which it disapproves, for example to maintain consistency. At least in some cases a local authority should be able to challenge the   **2-067**

---

182 *Arsenal Football Club Ltd v Ende* [1979] A.C. 1 at 27 (Viscount Dilhorne).

183 Examples appear in Annex 2 to the Law Commission's Consultation Paper No.126 *Administrative Law: Judicial Review and Statutory Appeals* (1993).

184 cf. *R. v Ministry of Health Ex p. Ellis* [1968] 1 Q.B. 84; *R. v Dorset Quarter Sessions Appeals Committee Ex p. Weymouth Corp* [1960] 2 Q.B. 230. See also *R. v Ipswich Justices Ex p. Robson* [1971] 2 Q.B. 340 (driver refused licence could not be person who "feels aggrieved" by decision if licensing authority had no power to grant licence on particular facts); *General and Municipal Workers' Union v Certification Officer* [1977] I.C.R. 183 (right of appeal to Employment Appeal Tribunal against a decision of Certification Officer limited to a "trade union aggrieved" by the refusal of its application for or revocation of its certificate of independence).

185 *Ex p. Sidebotham* (1880) 14 Ch.D. 458 at 465 (James LJ), cf. at 466 (Bramwell LJ); *Ex p. Official Receiver; Re Reed, Bowen & Co* (1887) 19 Q.B.D. 174; *R. v London Quarter Sessions Ex p. Westminster Corp* [1951] 2 K.B. 508 (overruled in *Cook v Southend BC* [1990] 2 Q.B. 1); *Burke v Minister of Housing and Local Government* (1957) 8 P. & C.R. 25 at 27-28.

186 *R. v Nottingham Quarter Sessions Ex p. Harlow* [1952] 2 Q.B. 601; *R. v Lancaster Quarter Sessions Ex p. Huyton-with-Roby UDC* [1955] 1 Q.B. 52; *Re Hurle-Hobbs' Decision* [1944] 2 All E.R. 261; *Ealing Corp v Jones* [1959] 1 Q.B. 384; *R. v Dorset Quarter Sessions Appeals Committee Ex p. Weymouth Corp* [1960] 2 Q.B. 230; *R. v Boldero Ex p. Bognor Regis UDC* (1962) 60 L.G.R. 292; *Phillips v Berkshire CC* [1967] 2 Q.B. 991. However, this approach was rejected in *Cook v Southend BC* [1990] 2 Q.B. 1 in respect of appeals from magistrates' courts.

187 *Cook v Southend BC* [1990] 2 Q.B. 1.

188 *R. v Surrey Quarter Sessions Ex p. Lilley* [1951] 2 K.B. 749.

189 *Attorney General of the Gambia v N'Jie* [1961] A.C. 617; *Buxton v Minister of Housing and Local Government* [1961] 1 Q.B. 278.

190 *GLC v Secretary of State for the Environment* [1985] J.P.L. 868 (Woolf J); a claim for judicial review (rather than a statutory application to quash under the Town and Country Planning Acts) may be possible.

reasons given for a decision in its favour, if those reasons create an undesirable precedent.

2-068   In some contexts the term "person aggrieved" necessarily has a wider meaning. Thus, if a local authority refuses in its discretion to grant or to renew a licence, or revokes such a licence, the applicant or licensee is entitled to appeal as a "person aggrieved" to a magistrates' court[191]; though in some circumstances where there has not been an actual refusal of a licence or the actual grant of a licence subject to a condition, a person fearing an adverse decision may not be a person aggrieved.[192]

2-069   The narrow view previously adopted[193] as to who may be regarded as a "person aggrieved" by a decision on a planning appeal has been rejected. A person will now ordinarily be regarded as aggrieved if they made objections or representations as part of the procedure which preceded the decision challenged and their complaint is that the decision was not properly made.[194] Where a person has not stated his objection at the appropriate stage of the statutory procedure, he may not be a person aggrieved "since that procedure is designed to allow objections to be made and a decision then to be reached within a reasonable time, as intended by Parliament".[195] A statutory remedy is available not only to those with a statutory right to appear at the inquiry but also those who have, in the discretion of the inspector, been permitted to make representations.[196] Furthermore a successor in title of the person who was involved at the outset in a planning application can be entitled to appeal to the

---

[191]   *Ferrant v Stepney BC* (1964) 62 L.G.R. 182.
[192]   *Peddubriwny v Cambridge City Council* [2001] EWHC Admin 200; [2001] R.T.R. 31.
[193]   See, e.g. *Ealing Corp v Jones* [1959] 1 Q.B. 384 and *R. v Dorset Quarter Sessions Appeals Committee Ex p. Weymouth Corp* [1960] 2 Q.B. 230; *R. v London Sessions Appeal Committee Ex p. Westminster Corp* [1951] 2 K.B. 508; *Buxton v Minister of Housing and Local Government* [1961] 1 Q.B. 278 (neighbour who appeared at planning appeal denied standing); *Gregory v Camden LBC* [1966] 1 W.L.R. 899.
[194]   *Walton v Scottish Ministers* [2012] UKSC 44; 2012 S.L.T. 1211 at [86]. Some members of the Supreme Court expressed the caveat that there was, however, also a wide discretion to refuse a remedy even though the applicant had successfully established a breach of European Union law, see R. McCracken, "Standing and Discretion in Environmental Challenges: Walton, a Curate's Egg" [2014] J.P.L. 304; Baroness Hale of Richmond, "Who Guards the Guardians?" (2014) 3 C.J.I.C.L. 100 at 101–104.
[195]   *Walton v Scottish Ministers* [2012] UKSC 44; [2013] P.T.S.R. 51 at [87]; *Ashton v Secretary of State for Communities and Local Government* [2010] EWCA Civ 600; [2011] 1 P & C.R. 5 (claimant had no standing under Town and Country Planning Act 1990 s.288 as he had not objected to the proposal in any formal sense nor had he made representations to the public inquiry; mere attendance was insufficient). In *R. (on the application of Cherkley Campaign Ltd) v Mole Valley DC* [2013] EWHC 2582 (Admin); [2014] 1 P. & C.R. 12 in a challenge to the grant of planning permission for the development of a luxury golf course in the Cherkley estate, an area of great landscape value and part of which was also within an area of outstanding natural beauty, proof of participation in the process of objection was said (per Haddon-Cave J) not to be a sine qua non to standing, but merely strong evidence that such persons would ordinarily be regarded as aggrieved. Numerous of the directors of and individual subscribers to Cherkley Campaign Ltd not only lived in the area (and could be said thereby to be "aggrieved") but were also involved in the process of objecting to the proposal through bodies such as the Surrey Branch of the Campaign for the Protection for Rural England. Further, there was nothing unfair or improper about a group of aggrieved individuals forming a limited company to bring a claim. Haddon-Cave J quashed the decision (reversed on appeal [2014] EWCA Civ 567; [2014] P.T.S.R. D14).
[196]   *Turner v Secretary of State for the Environment* (1974) 28 P. & C.R. 123 (local amenity group); *Bison v Secretary of State for the Environment* (1976) 239 E.G. 281 (preliminary objection to locus standi of neighbour rejected; the court was prepared to assume without deciding that the applicant was a person aggrieved); *Jones v Secretary of State for Wales* (1974) 28 P. & C.R. 280 at 287. In *Murphy (J) & Sons Ltd v Secretary of State for the Environment* [1973] 1 W.L.R. 560, the locus standi of a neighbour to challenge planning appeal and confirmation of a compulsory purchase order was not raised. In *Times Investment Ltd v Secretary of State for the Environment and Tower Hamlets LBC* (1990) 3 P.L.R. 111, the phrase was applied to a successor in title of an appellant.

High Court even if he did not appear at the planning inquiry.[197] These developments are, no doubt, influenced by the opportunities available to objectors at local public inquiries.[198] When statutory recognition has been given to the desirability of public participation in the administrative process, it would seem appropriate that those qualified to question the validity of the decision or order should include those who participated in the inquiry which preceded the order.[199] The availability of judicial review to impugn planning decisions may have helped to widen the categories of persons with standing, since it would be a nonsense to prevent a person from exercising a statutory right of appeal in circumstances where the same remedy would be available on a claim for judicial review.[200] Hence a householder anticipating a serious loss of amenity as a result of an administrative decision to permit the building of a high block of flats nearby was entitled to appeal against the decision as "a person aggrieved".[201]

REFORM OF STANDING

In its 1994 report on remedies in administrative law, the Law Commission noted that "the fluid nature of the requirement of sufficiency means that it is uncertain what precisely is required".[202] It recommended that rules of court and Supreme Court Act 1981 s.31 (now Senior Courts Act 1981) be amended to make special provision for the standing requirements in cases where the claimant is a representative or pressure group or where there is a public interest in a matter being litigated but no individual has standing. It proposed that a "two track" system be established.[203] The first track would cover situations where a person has a direct interest in the impugned decision, in the sense that he has had his legal rights or legitimate expectations affected or there has been a refusal to confer some discretionary benefit. Here standing should be accorded as a matter of course. The second track would cover public interest challenges, i.e. applications in which no person is affected more than the public generally and also challenges by a group rather than an individual where the decision nevertheless affects an individual.[204]

2-070

---

[197] *Times Investment Ltd* (1990) 3 P.L.R. 111. cf. *Eco-Energy (GB) Ltd v First Secretary of State* [2004] EWCA Civ 1566; [2005] 2 P. & C.R. 5 (a person may be denied the status of a "person aggrieved" if he did not take a sufficiently active role in the planning process and did not hold an interest in the land at the relevant time).

[198] *Turner* [1974] 28 P. & C.R. 123 at 134–5 (*Buxton* is not followed for this reason). It may be noted that Major Buxton was permitted to appear at the inquiry and that the applicants in Turner only did so at the discretion of the inspector. But the statutory basis of modern inquiry procedure and the broad range of factors relevant to the exercise of planning powers can be seen as conferring legal recognition to interests other than those of the applicant and the planning authority. Whether a person has a legally protected "right" may involve a more sophisticated appreciation of the purposes underlying the legislative scheme than was assumed in the earlier decisions.

[199] *Wilson v Secretary of State for the Environment* [1973] 1 W.L.R. 1083, where an appropriation certificate was quashed for lack of proper public notice at the instance of members of the public who would have objected had the statutory requirements for notice been observed.

[200] *Cook v Southend BC* [1990] 2 Q.B. 1 at 18.

[201] *Maurice v London CC* [1964] 2 Q.B. 362; cf. *Buxton* [1961] 1 Q.B. 278. In *Maurice* there was no question of interference with an easement or any other proprietary interest; and *R. v Surrey (Mid-Eastern Area) Assessment Committee* [1948] 1 All E.R. 856.

[202] Law Com. 226, para.5.16 (see 15-092).

[203] Law Com. 226, para.5.20. A proposal supported by Lord Woolf in Access to Justice: final report (1995), p.255.

[204] The report gives as an illustration of this type of challenge *R. v Chief Adjudication Office Ex p. Bland*

In such cases, the court would have regard to a wider range of factors than under the first track in deciding whether there is standing, including: the importance of the legal point: the chances of the issue being raised in any other proceedings; the allocation of scarce judicial resources; and the concern that in the determination of issues the courts should have the benefit of the conflicting points of view of those most directly affected by them. Implementation of the Law Commission proposals now seems unnecessary in the light of developments in the *WDM* and other cases mentioned above,[205] which have moved the court's approach to a position which is not dissimilar.

2-071   Finally, we need to remember that issues as to standing are issues of procedure of the court. Issues of procedure have a primary purpose and that is to facilitate the achievement of justice. Because of this, the rules always have to be applied with the degree of flexibility necessary to assist the achievement of this purpose.

INTERESTED PARTIES AND INTERVENERS

Interested parties

2-072   Persons other than the claimant and defendant may participate in a claim for judicial review. One important category is "interested parties", upon whom the claimant is obliged to serve the claim form,[206] and who should receive a letter before the claim is started.[207] An interested party "means any person (other than the claimant and defendant) who is directly affected by the claim".[208] Being inevitably or necessarily affected by the outcome of the claim for judicial review is insufficient to make a person *directly* affected; he must (also) be "affected without the intervention of any intermediate agency".[209] Interested parties are parties to the claim and may therefore appeal against the judgment of the court. Doubt has been expressed as to whether an interested party is entitled to advance a particular argument without the grant of permission.[210] Moreover, the court held that "In order to succeed with a claim for judicial review the interested party has to show a sufficient interest in the matter in issue" and went on to find that the interested party in that case (a challenge to publication of a guideline by the National Institute for Health and Clinical Excellence on the treatment of Chronic Fatigue Syndrome/Myalgic Encephalomyelitis) "fails for insufficiency of interest" because the ground of challenge was without legal merit.[211]

---

and the TUC, The Times, 6 February 1985 where the Trades Union Congress was held not to have standing to challenge the legality of reductions of state welfare benefits to striking miners.

[205] See 2-040.

[206] CPR rr.54.6 and 54.7. PD 54 provides "Where the claim for judicial review relates to proceedings in a court or tribunal, any other parties to those proceedings must be named in the claim form as interested parties".

[207] CPR r.54 Pre-Action Protocol.

[208] CPR r.54.1(2)(f). The term "interested party" has different meanings in other contexts, e.g. Licensing Act 2003 s.13(3) and Gambling Act 2005 s.158.

[209] *R. v Rent Officer Service Ex p. Muldoon* [1996] 1 W.L.R. 1103, interpreting a similar provision (RSC, Ord.53 r.5(3)) in the precursor to the current rules; the Secretary of State for Social Security reimbursed local authorities for up to 95% of their expenditure on housing benefit but was not "directly affected" by a judicial review of the refusal or failure of a local authority to determine claims for benefits where rent officers had been denied entry to the dwelling in circumstances where there had been no deliberate denial of entry by the applicant.

[210] *R. (on the application of Fraser) v National Institute for Health* [2009] EWHC 452 (Admin) at [114].

[211] *R. (on the application of Fraser) v National Institute for Health* [2009] EWHC 452 (Admin) at [115].

Interveners

Secondly, a person may apply for permission to make written and/or oral submis- **2-073**
sions—"interventions"—at the hearing of the judicial review.[212] Prior to the adoption of the CPR, the rules relating to first instance claims for judicial review
provided only for intervention by persons seeking to oppose the application for
judicial review, not to support it. Since 2000 there has been a noticeable increase
in the number of interventions, in judicial review and other proceedings in the
Administrative Court, Court of Appeal and before the House of Lords.[213] Interveners may include campaign groups, government departments,[214] the Commission for
Equality and Human Rights,[215] and business enterprises indirectly affected by the
outcome of the claim. This trend, especially the role of campaign groups,[216] has attracted both supporters[217] and critics.[218] On the one hand, the court's decision-
making may benefit from the perspectives of interveners, who typically will make
different or broader legal points, or provide additional facts, from those raised by
the claimant and defendant. On the other hand, the courts have only begun to
articulate the principles that should govern when interventions should be permitted and when refused. The main criterion ought to be whether would-be interveners, though their expertise, are likely to be able to assist the court in understanding
either the legal issues in question or the factual basis of the claim and the
consequences that may flow from the court's judgment.[219]

An intervener used to be able to seek a protective costs order in its application **2-074**
for permission to be heard and/or file evidence, though costs remained within the
court's discretion. The Criminal Justice and Courts Act 2015 s.88 has replaced

---

[212] CPR r.54.17(1). Such applications must be made promptly. PD 54, para.13.3: "An application for
permission should be made by letter to the Administrative Court office, identifying the claim,
explaining who the applicant is and indicating why and in what form the applicant wants to
participate in the hearing". See S. Knights, "Interventions in Public Law Proceedings" [2013] J.R.
200.

[213] See Sir Henry Brooke, "Interventions in the Court of Appeal" [2007] P.L. 401. See also S. Shah, T.
Poole and M. Blackwell, "Rights, Interveners and the Law Lords" (2014) 34 O.J.L.S. 295 which,
inter alia, tests the hypothesis that the HRA led to an increase in third party interventions. For a
comparative analysis with the Supreme Court of the United States and the Supreme Court of Canada,
see L. Neudorf, "Intervention in the UK Supreme Court" (2013) 2 C.J.I.C.L. 16.

[214] See, e.g. the Secretary of State for Health in *R. v North and East Devon HA Ex p. Coughlan* [2001]
Q.B. 213; M. Havers and C. Mellor, "Third Party Interventions for Government" [2004] J.R. 130.

[215] Equality Act 2006 s.30(1).

[216] Among the organisations intervening in judicial review claims in recent years are: Liberty; Joint
Council for the Welfare of Immigrants; Stonewall; League Against Cruel Sports.

[217] M. Arshi and C. O'Cinneide, "Third Party Interventions: the Public Interest Reaffirmed" [2004] P.L.
69; Sir Konrad Schiemann, "Interventions in Public Interest Cases" [1996] PL. 240. See also Baroness Hale of Richmond, "Who Guards the Guardians?" (2014) 3 C.J.I.C.L. 100 at 104: "Once a matter is in court, the more important the subject, the more difficult the issues, the more help we need
to try and get the right answer."

[218] S. Hannett, "Third Party Intervention: in the Public Interest?" [2003] P.L. 128; C. Harlow, "Public
Law and Popular Justice" (2002) 65 M.L.R. 1.

[219] See *E (A Child) v Chief Constable of Ulster* [2008] UKHL 66; [2009] AC 536 at [3] (Lord Hoffmann:
"An intervention is however of no assistance if it merely repeats points which the appellant or
respondent has already made. An intervener will have had sight of their printed cases and, if it has
nothing to add, should not add anything. It is not the role of an intervener to be an additional counsel
for one of the parties. This is particularly important in the case of an oral intervention. ... In future,
I hope that interveners will avoid unnecessarily taking up the time of the House in this way"). In *R.
(on the application of British American Tobacco UK Ltd) v Secretary of State for Health* [2014]
EWHC 3515 (Admin); [2015] C.M.L.R. 35 an application to intervene was refused where it was
considered that the interests of the proposed interveners were not discernibly different from those
of the claimant: as such, their intervention would offer little assistance to the court.

protective costs orders with costs capping orders which are only available after the grant of permission and only to applicants for judicial review.[220] The Criminal Justice and Courts Act 2015 s.87 introduced a provision that the applicant and defendant (or any interested party) to judicial review proceedings shall not be required to pay the intervener's costs in connection with the proceedings, although the court may make such an order if it considers there are exceptional circumstances. Further, on an application to the High Court or Court of Appeal by the applicant, defendant or interested party, the court must order the intervener to pay any costs specified in the application which the court considers have been incurred as a result of the intervener's involvement in the proceedings. Again, the court has a discretion in exceptional circumstances. During the Bill's second reading in the House of Lords, Lord Carlile commented: "The inevitable consequence of this is that charitable and not-for-profit organisations will no longer be prepared to provide their expertise to assist the court in cases of wide public importance"[221]

2-075   Instead of merely intervening, in some circumstances a person may seek to be joined as a second claimant or defendant.[222] The same criteria should apply. The advantages of becoming a party are that you may obtain relief if you succeed or appeal if you do not. The principle disadvantage is your possible liability for costs.

Joining the Crown as a party to proceedings

2-076   Where the court is considering whether to make a declaration of incompatibility under s.4 of the Human Rights Act 1998, the Crown is entitled to be given notice and thereafter a minister of the Crown is entitled to be joined as a party to the proceedings.[223] No award of damages may be made against the Crown under s.9(3) HRA unless the appropriate person is joined in the proceedings.[224]

COMPARATIVE PERSPECTIVES

2-077   In this section, we bring together summaries of the approaches to standing adopted in several other jurisdictions—Scotland, Australia, Canada, India, Ireland, New Zealand and South Africa. The purpose of doing so is to illustrate the variety of legislative and judicial techniques that are employed in common law jurisdictions.[225] The fact that a person or organisation has been held to have standing in one jurisdiction does not, of course, necessarily imply that the same outcome ought to follow in other legal systems. A range of constitutional, political and procedural factors may justify different outcomes.

---

[220] See 16-094.
[221] HL Deb, 30 June 2014, col.1604.
[222] *R. v Secretary of State for the Home Department Ex p. O'Byrne* [2000] C.P. Rep. 9 (local authority joined as second respondent, but attaching a restriction as to costs).
[223] HRA s.5; CPR r.19. The notice given under r.19.4A must be served on the person named in the list published under s.17 of the Crown Proceedings Act 1947 (typically but not invariably the Treasury Solicitor).
[224] HRA s.9(4).
[225] See 1-008.

Scotland

The approach to standing in Scotland has changed significantly recently. There **2-078** are no distinct rules governing standing in relation to judicial review in Scotland. Ordinary principles apply; the respondent may enter pleas of "no title to sue" (the petitioner must be a party, in the widest sense, to some legal relation which has been infringed) and "no interest to sue" (there must be a real rather than merely an academic question of law), though in some cases it has been recognised that these elements "very much run into each other".[226] The Scots law approach, based on private law principles, has in the past led to the Court of Session refusing to hear petitions in situations where, on similar facts, the Administrative Court in England applying the broadly interpreted rules of "sufficient interest" would have accepted jurisdiction. In 2011, the UK Supreme Court held that "the time has come to recognise that the private law rule that title and interest has to be shown has no place in applications to the court's supervisory jurisdiction that lie in the field of public law"; rather, the words "directly affected" capture "the essence of what is to be looked for" but "a personal interest need not be shown if the individual is acting in the general public interest and can genuinely say that the issue directly affects the section of the public that he seeks to represent".[227]

Australia

In Australia, the standing tests for common law remedies and the formula adopted **2-079** in the Administrative Decisions (Judicial Review) Act 1977 (Cth) (ADJR) do not differ in any key respect. The common law test that requires an individual to demonstrate a "special interest in the subject matter of the action" now operates to require essentially the same interests as the ADJR test of a "person aggrieved".[228] Standing remains problematic for representative associations and community groups, most commonly in environmental cases. Such groups are increasingly accorded standing if they can satisfy the court that their activities involve the physical area or activities affected by the decision. Standing in such cases usually arises from the collective effect of the many activities of the group.[229] Kirby J suggested that the High Court ought to revisit standing in environmental cases, to fashion a more coherent approach for cases brought by groups whose members were based largely in the affected area.[230] The High Court has not explored that possibility, but the Administrative Review Council recommended that the simpler standing test applicable to representative groups in the Administrative Appeals Tribunal be adopted in the ADJR Act.[231] The Administrative Appeals Tribunal Act 1975 (Cth) extends standing to representative organisations if the decision relates to a matter included

---

[226] Lord Clyde and D. Edwards, *Judicial Review* (2000), Ch.10; Lord Hope of Craighead, "Mike Tyson comes to Glasgow:A Question of Standing" [2001] P.L. 294.

[227] *AXA General Insurance Ltd v HM Advocate* [2011] UKSC 46 [2012] 1 A.C. 868 at [62]—[63] (Lord Hope of Craighead) and [170] (Lord Reed); see also *Walton v Scottish Ministers* [2012] UKSC 44; 2012 S.L.T. 1211 at [89]-[96].

[228] The common law test was affirmed in *Australian Conservation Foundation v Commonwealth* (1980) 146 C.L.R. 493 and *Bateman's Bay Local Aboriginal Land Council v Aboriginal Community Benefit Fund Pty Ltd* (1998) 194 C.L.R. 247, 256. The requirement of a "person aggrieved" is contained in ADJR ss.3(1), 5(1), 6(1) and 7(1).

[229] The most influential such case was *North Coast Environmental Council Inc v Minister for Resources* (1994) 55 F.C.R. 492.

[230] *South-West Forest Defence Foundation Inc v Department of Conservation and Land Management* (1998) 72 A.L.J.R. 837, 839.

[231] Administrative Review Council, *Federal Judicial Review* (Report No.50, 2012) 146–151.

in the purposes or objects of the organisation.[232] The Council's recommendations were not adopted by the Commonwealth but clearly influenced reforms to standing in the ACT judicial review statute which replaced "person aggrieved" with "eligible person" and simplified the standing of corporations and associations. The notable change is to allow standing in statutory review to an eligible person in some cases where the person's own interests are not adversely affected but the case raises a "significant issue of public importance".[233]

2-080   The High Court recently considered the standing requirement of the ADJR Act and showed no appetite to settle or simplify the standing of environmental and like groups, though it made some notable findings in *Argos Pty Ltd v Corbell, Minister for the Environment and Sustainable Development*.[234] The case held that adverse effect or practical impact on a person's business interest could make them aggrieved for standing purposes. The High Court plainly rejected adoption of the "zone of interests" approach used in many American standing cases. Finally, the case accepted that claims of standing often raised questions of judgment and degree. This focus on context and questions of fact suggest standing claims may often require detailed evidence, at least in cases based on claims of economic impact.

2-081   The Australian requirements for standing in federal proceedings cannot be wholly divorced from constitutional requirements for the presence of a "matter", regarded as an essential precondition for the exercise of Commonwealth judicial power.[235] While the elements of standing and a "matter" may ultimately be distinct, a claimant who lacks standing is likely to raise a hypothetical case or one that lacks the features of a true legal controversy.

2-082   Political considerations also influence standing in Australia. The Attorney General has standing at common law to seek equitable remedies to enforce any public rights.[236] The Attorney can exercise that role personally, or by granting a fiat to a third party to do so. The courts have acknowledged but not yet resolved the obvious conflict faced by an Attorney General, who is always a member of cabinet in Australia, yet is also expected to discharge the role of first law officer with neutrality.[237] McHugh J took a different view in *Bateman's Bay Local Aboriginal Land Council v Aboriginal Community Benefit Fund Pty Ltd*,[238] suggesting that the political obligations of an Attorney introduced a desirable measure of political realism into decisions to commence public law cases. Gaudron, Gummow and Kirby

---

[232] Administrative Appeals Tribunal Act 1975 (Cth) s.27(2). This rule does not apply to an association that is established after the decision is made, or one that alters its purposes or objects to encompass a decision after it was made. The benevolent approach to the standing of associations in merits review proceedings has not been reproduced in legislation governing state and territory tribunals.

[233] Administrative Decisions (Judicial Review) Act 1989 (ACT) s.4A(3)(b). The definition of "eligible person" provides the body must have come into existence before the proposed decision was made, which is the case with AAT legislation.

[234] *Argos Pty Ltd v Corbell, Minister for the Environment and Sustainable Development* (2014) 242 C.L.R. 394.

[235] In *Pape v Commonwealth* (2009) 238 C.L.R. 1, 68, Gummow, Crennan and Bell JJ suggested that standing requirements for equitable remedies were subsumed by the constitutional requirement for the presence of a matter in order for judicial power to be exercisable. *Pape* was one of several recent cases where standing to challenge the constitutional validity of federal legislative or executive action was interpreted broadly.

[236] *Bateman's Bay Local Aboriginal Land Council v Aboriginal Community Benefit Fund Pty Ltd* (1998) 194 C.L.R. 247, 259.

[237] A former Chief Justice of Australia suggested that the Attorney simply cannot be expected to act impartially when deciding whether to commence public law proceedings against a government: A Mason, "Access to Constitutional Justice" (2010) 22 *Bond Law Review* 1, 2.

[238] *Bateman's Bay Local Aboriginal Land Council v Aboriginal Community Benefit Fund Pty Ltd* (1998) 194 C.L.R. 247, 277.

JJ doubted the value of such political considerations and seemed to place more faith in the judicial rather than political resolution of cases.[239] The privileged position of the Attorney General came into sharp focus in *Re McBain; Ex p. Australian Catholic Bishops Conference*.[240] In that case the Attorney granted a fiat to the Bishops so that they could challenge a discrimination case which had the effect of allowing single woman to access IVF services. The Attorney then intervened in the Bishops' proceeding to made submissions that were largely at odds with the Bishops to whom he had granted a fiat. The High Court dismissed the Bishops' case on technical grounds, but several judges either strongly doubted or completely rejected the inconsistent conduct of the Attorney.[241]

Later cases acknowledge that the effect of the political obligations of an Attorney General are not limited to judicial review. The Victorian Court of Appeal recently held that government ministers, including an Attorney General, had no general "right to intervene in proceedings where questions of public policy arise."[242] The court also rejected the Attorney's attempt to intervene as amicus curiae because "the mere fact that a Minister is responsible for the administration of a statutory scheme does not … endow him or her with any particular expertise in the interpretation of the legislative provisions."[243] Such sentiments make clear that Attorneys General will struggle to defend their existing common law privileges. Any extensions are a forlorn hope. The sole legislative reform was made in Queensland, in the form of parliamentary accountability. The Queensland Attorney General must respond to all requests for a fiat within 60 days, and must also table in parliament an explanation of every decision to grant or refuse a fiat.[244] The Attorney's discretion itself remains unfettered but is subject to a requirement of justification.

2-083

Canada

In Canada, standing as of right depends on the applicant for judicial review being "directly affected" or some variant of that term. It is not only the common law standard but also has been given statutory recognition in the Federal Courts Act.[245] In that context, "directly affected" has been interpreted as requiring that the applicant demonstrate that the decision affects its legal rights, imposes legal obligations upon it, or otherwise prejudicially affects it.[246]

2-084

While public interest standing depends on very different criteria which are generally applied liberally or expansively, nonetheless, there are limits on the willingness of the courts to grant applications for public interest standing. In particular, the courts are generally hostile to applications by persons or groups who have no real connection with the decision that is in issue. There is also a reluctance to accord public interest standing to those who are seeking to vindicate the rights of others

2-085

---

[239] *Bateman's Bay Local Aboriginal Land Council v Aboriginal Community Benefit Fund Pty Ltd* (1998) 194 C.L.R. 247, 261–264.

[240] *Re McBain; Ex p. Australian Catholic Bishops Conference* (2002) 209 C.L.R. 372.

[241] *Re McBain; Ex p. Australian Catholic Bishops Conference* (2002) 209 C.L.R. 372 at 402–403 (Gaudron and Gummow JJ), 473–475 (Hayne J). Kirby J was not troubled by those issues: 452. The Bishops' case was dismissed because the lower court decision they had sought to challenge had been finally settled and was not therefore a live "matter" as required for the valid exercise of judicial power.

[242] *Priest v West* [2011] VSCA 186, [26].

[243] *Priest v West* [2011] VSCA 186, [40].

[244] Attorney-General Act 1999 (Qld) s.10.

[245] RSC 1985 c. F-7, s.18.1(1).

[246] *Forest Ethics Association v Canada (National Energy Board)* 2014 FCA 245; [2015] 4 F.C.R. 75 at [30].

especially if those others are also before the court as applicants. Thus, in *Forest Ethics Advocacy Association v Canada (National Energy Board)*,[247] the Federal Court of Appeal denied public interest standing to a public interest group that was seeking to challenge various interlocutory rulings by the Board, including rulings that denied intervener status to a specific individual. In characterising the public interest group as a "classic busybody",[248] the court pointed to the group's lack of involvement in the proceedings and the issues that were at stake before the Board as well as the presence before the court as an applicant of the person who had been denied participatory rights as an intervener. Similarly, in *Cabana v Newfoundland and Labrador*,[249] the Newfoundland and Labrador Court of Appeal denied public interest standing to challenge a hydroelectric development. The applicant had shown no interest in the matter other than having been a long time vocal opponent with a desire to protect the interests of those who would be directly affected by the project. This was not enough to qualify as a "real stake or genuine interest".[250] The Nova Scotia Court of Appeal in *Miner v Kings (County)*[251] also classified as "mere busybodies",[252] two applicants for the quashing of a land development by-law who were not directly affected by the by-law and had not placed on the record anything explaining why they had an interest in the proceedings. Moreover, the principal basis on which they were attacking the by-law was a lack of procedural fairness to landowners who were directly affected. Basically, the court's position was that it was not for the applicants to act as surrogates for those who were directly affected.[253]

2-086   Especially prominent in the evolving Canadian case law on intervention in public law litigation are decisions giving content to r.109 of the Federal Courts Rules.[254] This requires applicants for intervener status to detail how they want to participate and how that participation "will assist the determination of a factual or legal issue related to that proceeding." In fleshing out these provisions, the Federal Court of Appeal has emphasised that the rule must be interpreted and applied in a manner that is mindful of r.3 and the mandate of the Federal Court and Federal Court of Appeal to secure "the just, most expeditious and least expensive determination of every proceeding on its merits." This has led to a more rigorous examination of applications for intervener status[255] and an emphasis on the overall interests of justice including the objectives of r.3.[256]

2-087   Many of these same considerations animate the application of tribunal rules respecting intervention in hearings either by way of specification in the rules themselves or through the developing jurisprudence of the tribunal. In this context,

---

[247] *Forest Ethics Association v Canada (National Energy Board)* 2014 FCA 245; [2015] 4 F.C.R. 75.
[248] *Forest Ethics Association v Canada (National Energy Board)* 2014 FCA 245; [2015] 4 F.C.R. 75 at [33].
[249] 2016 NLCA 39, 401 DLR (4th) 113.
[250] *Forest Ethics Association v Canada (National Energy Board)* 2014 FCA 245; [2015] 4 F.C.R. 75 at [29].
[251] 2017 NSCA 5; 60 MPLR (5th) 1.
[252] *Forest Ethics Association v Canada (National Energy Board)* 2014 FCA 245; [2015] 4 F.C.R. 75 at [46].
[253] See also *Close v Treasury Board (Department of Citizenship and Immigration)* 2017 FCA 52, where the court denied public interest standing to an applicant for judicial review who had no more than a jurisprudential interest in the validity of a particular decision and where those directly affected had not commenced an application for judicial review.
[254] SOR 98-106.
[255] *Sport Maska, Canada (Attorney General) v Pictou Landing First Nation* 2014 FCA 21; [2015] 2 F.C.R. 253.
[256] See e.g. *Prophet River First Nation v Canada (Attorney General)* 2016 FCA 120.

the approach of courts reviewing tribunal or agency decisions respecting intervention is to accord the tribunal's exercise of discretion on an application for intervention deference in the form of "a significant margin of appreciation".[257]

India

In India, standing does not constitute a significant impediment in applications for judicial review. The remedy of judicial review is available by way of proceedings in the Constitutional Courts being the High Courts, and the Supreme Court.[258] Civil suits[259] are governed by the Code of Civil Procedure 1908. Although the general principles of standing apply in such actions, Ord.1 r.8A, which provides that the court may, if satisfied that a person or body of persons is interested in any question of law which is directly and substantially in issue in the suit and that it is necessary in the public interest to allow the person or body of persons to present his or its opinion on that question of law, permit that person or body of persons to present such opinion and to take such part in the proceedings of the suit as the court may specify. Since, the provisions of the Code of Civil Procedure 1908 do not apply (although the court may follow an analogous procedure[260]) the principles fashioned to ascertain locus standi are far more liberal and amorphous. The concept of locus standi, in relation to violation of constitutional rights, has been substantially relaxed.[261] In such matters, it has effectively become a matter of discretion of the court and not so much a matter of locus of the petitioner. In a case where a petitioner in the court seeks relief for a personal injury (as against a general injury to the public) the normal principles of locus standi would apply.[262] The courts also entertain petitions raising issues of violation of constitutional rights where the petitioner is acting bona fide, and where the petition raises an issue of importance and is filed to vindicate a genuine cause. The exception is where an application, ostensibly filed in public interest, is really for some undisclosed personal gain or political motivation or other oblique considerations, in which event the court will not allow its process to be abused.[263] The writ jurisdiction cannot be turned into an instrument to serve partisan ends.[264]

2-088

Ireland

The test applied by the Rules of the Superior Courts Order 84 r.20(5) is that the applicant for judicial review must demonstrate "a sufficient interest in the matter to which the application relates". It has been observed that the standing rules are "in reality flexible rules of practice which are ultimately concerned with the

2-089

---

[257] *Forest Ethics Association v Canada (National Energy Board)* 2014 FCA 245; [2015] 4 F.C.R. 75 at [72].

[258] Where remedies are sought for violation of the Fundamental Rights enshrined in Part III of the Constitution. In practice the Supreme Court is selective in entertaining such applications.

[259] Proceedings in the Civil Courts established under statutes', including the five High Courts which have "Original Jurisdiction".

[260] *Public Service Commission, Uttaranchal v Mamta Bisht* (2010) 12 S.C.C. 204 at 207, 208.

[261] *Guruvayoor Dewaswom Managing Committee v CK Rajan* (2003) 7 S.C.C. 546, 569(iv).

[262] See *Suresh Narayan Kadam v Central Bank of India* (2016) 11 S.C.C. 306, 311, *Anand Sharadchandra Oka v University of Mumbai*, (2008) 5 S.C.C. 217, 220 and *B. Srinivasa Reddy v Karnataka Urban Water Supply and Drainage Board Employees Assn* (2006) 11 S.C.C. 731.

[263] *Kushum Lata v Union of India* (2006) 6 S.C.C. 180, 187.

[264] See *State of Uttaranchal v Balwant Singh Chaufal* (2010) 3 S.C.C. 402 for a full discussion on public interest litigation jurisdiction; *State of MP v Narmada Bachao Andolan* (2011) 7 S.C.C. 639.

conservation and propoer use of judicial power".[265] Irish courts regard the question of standing as a mixed question of law and fact[266] and generally treat the issue separately from that of the merits.[267] The test of standing applicable in judicial review proceedings is the same as that found in challenges to the constitutionality of legislation[268]; the leading case is that of *Cahill v Sutton*, in which, in the context of a challenge to the constitutionality of legislation, it was held that an applicant must "show that the impact of the impugned law on his personal situation discloses an injury or prejudice which he has either suffered or is in imminent danger of suffering."[269] The court also pointed out that the applicant must "stand in real or imminent danger of being adversely affected".[270]

2-090 Exceptions to the general rule requiring personal adverse effect in *Cahill* have been applied most notably in challenges raising constitutional issues, such as where those prejudicially affected by an impugned statute may not be in a position to assert adequately or in time their constitutional rights[271] or if it is difficult to separate those affected from those not affected by the challenged provision.[272] The Supreme Court has also observed that, although it is also important to ensure that unfounded and vexatious challenges are not entertained,

> "it is not in the public interest that decisions by statutory bodies which are of at least questionable validity should wholly escape scrutiny because the person who seeks to invoke the jurisdiction of the court by way of judicial review cannot show that he is personally affected, in some sense peculiar to him, by the decision".[273]

Representative actions are recognised in Irish law, dependent upon the particular circumstances.[274] It may also suffice to satisfy the requirement of "sufficient inter-

---

[265] *Waterville Fisheries Development Ltd v Aquaculture Licences Appeals Board* [2014] IEHC 248; [2014] 1 I.R. 684 at [13].

[266] *State (Lynch) v Cooney* [1982] I.R. 337 at 369. See generally, H. Biehler, *Judicial Review of Administrative Action*, 3rd edn (2013) at pp.407–412; M. de Blacam, *Judicial Review*, 3rd edn (2017), Ch.3; G. Hogan and D.G. Morgan, *Administrative Law in Ireland*, 4th edn (2010) at paras 16-195–16-238; D.G. Hogan, *Hogan and Morgan's Administrative Law*, 4th edn (2012) at paras 16-81–16-110.

[267] Hogan and Morgan (2010) at para.16-201; *Lancefort v An Bord Pleanála (No.2)* [1999] 2 I.R. 270 at 318. Contrast, however, the approach in *Lancefort Ltd v An Bord Pleanála* [1998] 2 I.L.R.M. 401 at 440–441.

[268] *Lancefort (No.2)* [1999] 2 I.R. 270 at 310–311; *State (Sheehan) v Government of Ireland* [1987] I.R. 550 at 557.

[269] *Cahill v Sutton* [1980] I.R. 269 at 284.

[270] *Cahill* [1980] I.R. 269 at 286. For a restrictive application of the standing test, see, e.g. *Shannon v McGuinness* [1999] 3 I.R. 274 at 280 (victims of an assault were not parties to the proceedings and did not have locus standi to impugn dismissal of criminal proceedings against the accused). For relatively generous applications of the test, see, e.g. *Chambers v An Bord Pleanála* [1992] 1 I.R. 134; *Lancefort Ltd v An Bord Pleanála (No.1)* [1997] 2 I.L.R.M. 508. For examples of the courts' reluctance to recognise standing where the Court would be involved in determining hypothetical matters, see: *Lennon v Limerick City Council* [2006] IEHC 112; *John Paul Construction Ltd v Minister for the Environment, Heritage and Local Government* [2006] IEHC 255.

[271] *Cahill* [1980] I.R. 269 at 285; see also *Society for the Protection of Unborn Children (Ireland) Ltd v Coogan* [1989] I.R. 734 at 742.

[272] *Cahill* [1980] I.R. 269 at 285; see also *Crotty v An Taoiseach* [1987] I.R. 713; *McKenna v An Taoiseach (No.2)* [1995] 2 I.R. 10; *Mulcreevy v Minister for Environment, Heritage and Local Government* [2004] IESC 5; [2004] 1 I.R. 72.

[273] *Mulcreevy* [2004] IESC 5; [2004] 1 I.R. 72 at 78.

[274] See, e.g. *Rafferty v Bus Éireann* [1997] 2 I.R. 424 at 441; *Construction Industry Federation v Dublin City Council* [2005] IESC 16; [2005] 2 I.R. 496; *Christian v Dublin City Council* [2012] IEHC 163; [2012] 2 I.R. 506 (member of a class had standing).

est" to demonstrate that the applicant is genuinely interested in the subject matter and there is no obviously more suitable applicant.[275]

New Zealand

In New Zealand, standing as a threshold issue is almost a dead letter. In a small country with a judicial review caseload of fewer than a hundred cases a year the floodgates have not opened without any noticeable standing requirement operating since the mid-1980s.[276] (Moreover, there are no time limits, as the Limitation Act 2010 does not apply to judicial review proceedings and no requirement to obtain leave to bring review proceedings). The liberalising trend, in line with the *National Federation* case in England,[277] has meant that questions of standing will normally require examination of the substantive issues and does not preclude ventilation of the merits of the challenge. Concerns about standing are rolled into the exercise of judicial discretion at the end of the proceedings as to what if any remedy to grant.[278] Standing as a preliminary requirement remains theoretically available as a filter at the outset for unmeritorious cases, but is very rarely invoked.[279]

2-091

Standing in New Zealand has never recovered from the ill-fated attempt in 1985 of the New Zealand Rugby Union to defeat a challenge to the constitutionality of the Union's decision to accept an invitation to tour the (then) apartheid South Africa. In a somewhat controversial decision the Court of Appeal held two rugby players to have standing to challenge the decision.[280] The upshot was delay and ultimately the substantive litigation was settled and the 1985 tour abandoned by the Rugby Union.[281] One of the last significant cases where the courts refused judicial review for lack of standing was *Wall v Livingston*,[282] where a third party (a paediatrician who had seen the expectant mother in hospital on an matter unrelated to her pregnancy) sought unsuccessfully to challenge on review the certification of two consultants that an abortion was necessary on health grounds. The judicial review proceeding foundered at first instance on the ground that the applicant had no standing, a view upheld by way of obiter in the Court of Appeal. It was said there that only those involved in the statutory decision-making could be regarded as having sufficient interest and therefore standing to challenge the certification. Nearly 25 years later, a High Court judge in *Right to Life New Zealand Inc v Rothwell*[283] refused to strike out a wide-ranging challenge to the discharge of the Abortion Supervisory Committee's statutory obligations. The earlier case of *Wall v Livingston* was distinguished as that was a challenge to a particular abortion decision by

2-092

---

[275] *Murphy v Wicklow County Council* [1999] IEHC 225 (Kearns J); *Riordan v An Tánaiste* [1995] 3 I.R. 62 at 71 (point not determined by the Supreme Court: [1997] 3 I.R. 502 at 506); *Digital Rights Ireland Ltd v Minister for Communications, Marine and Natural Resources* [2010] IEHC 221; [2010] 3 I.R. 251.

[276] See Sir Ivor Richardson, "Public Interest Litigation" (1995) 3 Waikato L. R. 1, 12.

[277] See 2-040. On this trend in New Zealand, see J. Caldwell, "Judicial Review: The Fading of Remedial Discretion" (2009) 23(4) N.Z.U.L.R. 489, 507–509.

[278] See, e.g. *Murray v Whakatane District Council* [1997] N.Z.R.M.A. 433, 465—6 HC, Elias J and *Society for the Protection of Auckland City and Waterfront Inc v Auckland City Council* [2001] N.Z.R.M.A. 209, HC, Morris J.

[279] cf. *Easton v Human Rights Commission* [2009] N.Z.A.R 575, HC.

[280] *Finnigan v New Zealand Rugby Football Union Inc* [1985] 2 N.Z.L.R. 159, CA.

[281] See generally M. Taggart, "Rugby, the Anti-Apartheid Movement and Administrative Law" in R. Bigwood (ed), *Law, Social Policy and the Role of the Courts* (2006), p.69.

[282] *Wall v Livingston* [1982] 1 N.Z.L.R. 734, CA.

[283] *Right to Life New Zealand Inc v Rothwell* [2006] 1 N.Z.L.R. 531.

consultants whereas the pro-life charitable society in *Rothwell* was seeking review of the performance of the Committee' statutory functions to oversee the process and indirectly protect the interests of the unborn child.[284]

2-093   At the High Court level in the case reported on appeal as *Curtis v Minister of Defence*,[285] the Crown challenged the standing of the applicant-organiser of a "Save our Squadrons" campaign created to persuade the government to change its decision to disband the air combat wing of the air force. The trial judge, Heron J, said there was "some force" in his counsel's submission that the applicant represented "a responsible public interest group and that unless people like him had standing "there may be no effective way of establishing whether or not the executive is acting within its lawful powers".[286] The trial judge preferred to deal with the substantive challenge, which he struck out as non-justiciable (a finding upheld on appeal). The Court of Appeal endorsed the justiciability finding, saying "It is a question which is not suitable of determination by any legal yardstick. Furthermore it is one of Government policy into which it is constitutionally improper for the Courts to go".[287]

South Africa

2-094   In the pre-democratic era (i.e. before the coming into force of the interim Constitution in 1994), the common-law rules of standing imposed a strict requirement of "sufficient interest", which was a very significant impediment in the area of public law. The interest held had to be personal and direct.[288] But after 1994, the South African courts recognised that the rules of standing operated differently in the private and public arenas. In *Ferreira v Levin NO*, O'Regan J acknowledged that while the interest parties have in private litigation is often direct and intimate, the harm alleged in litigation of a public nature "may often be quite diffuse or amorphous".[289]

2-095   The Constitution adopted in 1996 offers very liberal grounds on which to approach courts for relief. Section 38 of the Constitution lists five classes of persons who may approach a competent court alleging that a right in the Bill of Rights has been infringed or is threatened. These classes include classes familiar to the common law, such as anyone acting in his or her own interest (s.38(a)), anyone acting on behalf of another who cannot act in his or her own name (s.38(b)), and an association acting on behalf of its members (s.38(e)). But s.38 also goes well beyond the common law: s.38(c) and (d) respectively allow that "anyone acting as a member of, or in the interest of, a group or class of persons" and "anyone acting in the public interest" may approach a court alleging that a breach of rights in the Bill of Rights has occurred or is imminent.

2-096   Significant progress has been made in clarifying the scope and requirements of a class action, including the need for certification.[290] However, s.38(d) has become especially prominent over the last few years, as non-governmental organisations are

---

284 *Right to Life New Zealand Inc v Rothwell* [2006] 1 N.Z.L.R. 531 at [39].
285 *Curtis v Minister of Defence* [2002] 2 N.Z.L.R. 744, CA.
286 *Curtis v Minister of Defence* 20 November 2001 (High Court Wellington) at [16].
287 *Curtis* [2002] 2 N.Z.L.R 744, [28], Tipping J for the court. Further cases on justiciability include: *Prebble v TVNZ* [1995] 1 A.C. 321; *Boscawen v Attorney General* [2009] NZCA 12.
288 *Jacobs v Waks* 1992 (1) S.A. 521 at 534–536, *Independent Food Processors (Pty) Ltd v Minister of Agriculture* 1993 (4) S.A. 294, C, *Verstappen v Port Edward Town Board* 1994 (3) S.A. 569, D.
289 *Ferreira v Levin NO* 1996 (1) S.A. 984, CC at [229].
290 See especially *Children's Resource Centre Trust v Pioneer Food (Pty) Ltd* 2013 (2) S.A. 213, SCA; *Mukaddam v Pioneer Foods (Pty) Ltd* 2013 (5) S.A. 89, CC.

increasingly relying on public-interest standing to challenge governmental action. For example, a coalition of civic organisations was permitted to apply for an interdict in order to prevent the President from granting pardons under a certain pardoning dispensation.[291] In another case in which the Judicial Service Commission had dismissed a complaint of gross misconduct against a judge, an organisation that promotes democracy and the rule of law was granted standing to challenge this decision.[292] In relation to this type of standing, the essential question is whether the person or organisation is genuinely acting in the public interest in an objective sense.[293]

Until recently there was doubt about whether s.38 operates only where a right in the Bill of Rights is being applied directly or whether, as academic commentators had argued, it also governs indirect applications for judicial review under the Promotion of Administrative Justice Act 3 of 2000 (PAJA), the statute enacted to give effect to the administrative-justice rights contained in s.33 of the Constitution. In *Giant Concerts* the Constitutional Court confirmed that the provisions of s.38 must indeed be read into the PAJA.[294]   **2-097**

The judgment of Cameron J also clarified the scope and demands of s.38(a), which is no doubt the type of standing most frequently relied on in cases of judicial review on PAJA grounds. Constitutional own-interest standing, although broad, is "not limitless".[295] Importantly, too, it does not arise from the unlawfulness of the challenged decision or law. Accordingly, there is no "unqualified capacity to litigate against illegalities", although there may be exceptional cases where the public interest demands scrutiny of the merits in spite of questionable standing.[296] This case concerned the sale of land by a municipality to a third party. While the applicant alleged that it had a commercial interest in the site, it failed to demonstrate that it had interests capable of being directly affected by the decision.[297] More recently, the Constitutional Court held that a party lacked standing to challenge the award of a tender where it had not been a bidder for the tender in its own right.[298] For the majority, at least, this was not a case where the interests of justice demanded a more indulgent and less technical approach.[299]   **2-098**

---

[291] *Albutt v Centre for the Study of Violence and Reconciliation* 2010 (3) S.A. 293, CC.

[292] *Freedom Under Law v Acting Chairperson: Judicial Service Commission* 2011 (3) S.A. 549, SCA.

[293] *Lawyers for Human Rights v Minister of Home Affairs* 2004 (4) S.A. 125, CC at [18], with reference to *Ferreira v Levin NO* 1996 (1) S.A. 984, CC at [234].

[294] *Giant Concerts CC v Rinaldo Investments (Pty) Ltd* 2013 (3) B.C.L.R. 251, CC at [29].

[295] At [50].

[296] At [34]–[35].

[297] See also e.g. *Tulip Diamonds FZE v Minister for Justice and Constitutional Development* 2013 (10) B.C.L.R. 1180, CC.

[298] *Areva NP Incorporated in France v Eskom Holdings Soc Ltd* 2017 (6) B.C.L.R. 675, CC.

[299] at [41], but cf. the dissenting judgment of Moseneke DCJ, Bosielo AJ concurring.

CHAPTER 3

Defendants and Decisions Subject to Judicial Review

TABLE OF CONTENTS

SCOPE

This chapter examines the law, principles and policy relating to the following **3-001** questions.

- Which functions[1] of public authorities are amenable to judicial review? A wide range of governmental decision-making is potentially challengeable by judicial review claims. The Administrative Court may, however, decline to review the exercise of a function on the basis that it lacks jurisdiction; challenges to some functions of public authorities may be regarded as non-justiciable; and the court may refuse to hear a case in the exercise of its discretion having regard to a range of factors including the existence of alternative remedies.

- In what circumstances may public functions of office-holders and bodies which are not formal institutions of the State be subject to judicial review?[2] In recent years challenges have been brought against the exercise of functions of (for example) non-statutory self-regulatory bodies, members' clubs,

---

[1] We use "functions" as a collective term for the whole array of decisions, actions, omissions, legislation, etc. that may be the subject of challenge in judicial review proceedings. As has been noted, "The question in any particular case is not whether the decision-maker is, in general terms, amenable to judicial review, but whether a particular decision is": M. Supperstone and E. Laing, "The Ambit of *Judicial Review*", Ch.5 in M. Supperstone, J. Goudie and P. Walker (eds), *Judicial Review*, 4th edn (2010).

[2] See 3-038.

religious organisations, universities, and front-line service providers with which public authorities have contracted.

- Which public functions may be subject to judicial review claims on the ground that they unlawfully interfere with a Convention right, contrary to s.6 of the HRA?[3]
- What is the territorial reach of the Administrative Court's supervisory jurisdiction and the HRA?
- "Procedural exclusivity" and "collateral attack": where a matter falls within the Administrative Court's judicial review jurisdiction, is it mandatory for a claimant to use CPR Pt 54 (the claim for judicial review procedure) or is it permissible to use one of the other ways of commencing a civil claim, to raise issues before a tribunal, or as a defence in criminal proceedings?[4]
- How, in outline, do other jurisdictions deal with issues of amenability to review?[5]

In the past these questions have often been addressed in terms suggesting that there is a divide separating public law and private law. For several years this distinction caused more controversy between distinguished commentators than any other aspect of English administrative law. While most, if not all, developed legal systems recognise some degree of distinction between public and private law,[6] in England and Wales the law and procedural rules relating to judicial review have now developed in ways which make broad references to "public law" and "private law" less helpful than they may have been in the past because these terms beg important questions. In contrast, the terms "public authority", "public function" and "functions of a public nature" are terms now recognised in the common law developments and legislation.[7] In many contexts with which we are concerned, the term "public" is a synonym for "governmental" rather than referring to a decision affecting the general public, though in many situation these two senses coincide.[8]

RANGE OF PUBLIC AUTHORITIES SUBJECT TO JUDICIAL REVIEW

3-002　British constitutional law does not have any single "juristic conception of the State".[9] Nor is there any precise concept of "the executive" or "executive power";

3　See 3-066.

4　See 3-098.

5　See 3-117.

6　See C. Szladits, *International Encyclopaedia of Comparative Law*, Vol.2, paras 25, 31, 57. As was pointed out by Lord Goff in *Re Norway's Application*, "the identification of public law matters differs from country to country, sometimes in minor respects and sometimes in major respects" [1990] 1 A.C. 723 at 802–803.

7　CPR Pt 54.1 and HRA ss.6–7. For recent statutory use of the terminology "public authority", see e.g: Health and Social Care Act 2008 Sch.4 para.3 (similar definition to that used in the Human Rights Act 1998); Human Fertilisation and Embryology Act 2008 ss.8–9 (the Human Fertilisation and Embryology Authority may give assistance to "a government department, a public authority or the holder of a public office"—but are these not all "public authorities"?); Education and Skills Act 2008 s.128 ("the Secretary of State, or such other public authority as may be prescribed").

8　*Aston Cantlow and Wilmcote with Billesley Parochial Church Council v Wallbank* [2003] UKHL 37; [2004] 1 A.C. 546 at [6]–[7] (Lord Nicholls of Birkenhead, in the context of HRA s.6); *Mullins v The Board of Appeal of the Jockey Club* [2005] EWHC 2197 (Stanley Burnton J, in the context of amenability to judicial review generally).

9　J. McLean, "The Crown in Contract and Administrative Law" (2004) 24 O.J.L.S. 129, 131.

central government is "more plural than unitary".[10] In recent times, governance is said to be "multi-level" and "fragmented", with interventions from central and local government, actions by the voluntary sector (charities) and much practical delivery of public services contracted out to business enterprises. Across many fields, laws and decisions taken at European Union level—and sometimes also at international level—also have influence. It is therefore unsurprising that a wide range of public authorities and other organisations carrying out public functions find themselves subject to judicial review claims. Almost all judicial review claims are brought against functions exercised by office-holders and institutions that are clearly part of the formal machinery of government,[11] though as we examine below in a relatively small number of cases issues arise as to the amenability of non-State actors.

Central government

The Secretary of State is the most commonly challenged office-holder in central government.[12] There is in constitutional law a single office of Secretary of State; unless stated otherwise in an Act, any of the various Secretaries of State in existence at a given time (… for the Home Department … for Health) may lawfully exercise powers conferred on "the Secretary of State".[13] Convention and practice may dictate otherwise, however. The office of Lord High Chancellor of Great Britain is distinct from that of Secretary of State,[14] though since 2003 the minister holding the post of Lord Chancellor has held office as Secretary of State as well (first, as Secretary of State for Constitutional Affairs then, since May 2007, as Secretary of State for Justice). The naming of the relevant Secretary of State as the defendant is different from the practice in relation to "civil proceedings" (typically claims for damages) where the defendant is normally the Department.[15] Since the 1980s, there has been a split throughout central government between policy-formation (dealt with by Departments directly) and the delivery of services and practical administration dealt with by "executive agencies", staffed by civil servants but working under a chief executive at arm's length from the Department. In

3-003

---

[10] T. Daintith and A. Page, *The Executive in the Constitution: Structure, Autonomy and Internal Control* (1999).

[11] In accordance with Crown Proceedings Act 1947 s.17, the Cabinet Office from time to time prepares a list (published on the Treasury Solicitor's Department website) of authorised government departments for the purpose of identifying the department by and against which "civil proceedings" may be brought. Claims for judicial review are not "civil proceedings" (see 18-007); the defendants specified on that list are in the main *Departments* whereas in judicial review the *Secretary of State*, as the person empowered to carry out the impugned function, should be the defendant; but that list contains useful information about addresses for service.

[12] For an overview of central government, see A. Le Sueur, "The Nature, Powers and Accountability of Central Government", Ch.3 in D. Feldman (ed), *English Public Law*, 2nd edn (2009). Overall, challenges to decisions taken by central government departments amount on average to 20% of the total case load (leaving aside immigration and asylum applications): see M. Sunkin, K. Calvo, L. Platt and T. Landman, "Mapping the Use of Judicial Review to Challenge Local Authorities in England and Wales" [2007] P.L. 545.

[13] A. Simcock, "One and Many: the Office of Secretary of State" (1992) 70 Pub. Admin. 535.

[14] Constitutional Reform Act 2005 ss.2, 17. Certain functions of the Lord Chancellor are, by the 2005 Act, entrenched and cannot be transferred to other ministers by order under the Ministers of the Crown Act 1975. A claimant proposing to seek judicial review of a decision taken within the Ministry of Justice, or one of its executive agencies, will need to identify whether the function in question is one that is exercised by the Lord Chancellor or the Secretary of State for Justice; on this division of responsibilities, see House of Lords Select Committee on the Constitution, *Relations Between the Executive, Judiciary and Parliament*, HL Paper No.151 (Session 2006/07), Appendix 7.

[15] Crown Proceedings Act 1947 s.17. Judicial review claims are not "civil proceedings": see 18-007.

some situations it may be appropriate for an executive agency rather than a Secretary of State to be the defendant.[16] Many different non-departmental public bodies (NDPBs) also find the exercise of their functions challenged by judicial review.[17] In cases of doubt as to which public authority is the appropriate defendant, claims may be made against the Attorney General.[18] In British constitutional law, the civil service have no legal or constitutional personality separate from the Government or ministers.[19]

Local and devolved government

3-004   There are, at the time of writing, over 400 local authorities in England and Wales, with plans to encourage more parish councils as a tier of decision-making in each local authority area.[20] Challenges to decisions taken by local authorities typically constitute some 46 per cent of the annual judicial review case load (leaving aside immigration and asylum applications). Local authorities exercise statutory functions across a broad spectrum, the most challenged being: housing; homelessness[21]; community care; environmental planning; education; housing benefit; and family-related.[22]

The National Assembly for Wales and the Welsh Assembly Government are amenable to judicial review.[23]

---

[16] See, e.g. *R. (Ann Summers Ltd) v Jobcentre Plus* [2003] EWHC 1416 (Admin) (defendant being an executive agency of the Department for Work and Pensions) and *R. v Vehicle Inspectorate Ex p. Healy* [2001] R.T.R. 17. Practice seems to vary; in many other cases a Secretary of State under whose Department the executive agency operates is the defendant. Some executive agencies have legal personality (and in these cases may be made the defendant) whereas others lack a distinct legal personality (and here the relevant Secretary of State should be the defendant). See *R. (on the application of National Association of Health Stores) v Secretary of State for Health* [2005] EWCA Civ 154 at [40]–[41], where the potential difficulties are noted.

[17] The following have all been subject to judicial review challenge in recent years: Agriculture Wages Board of England and Wales; Audit Commission; British Broadcasting Corporation; Boundary Commission for England; Central Arbitration Committee (responsible for adjudicating on the recognition of trade unions); Commissioners of Customs and Excise, Special Commissioners of Income Tax and the Inland Revenue Commissioners; Civil Aviation Authority; Competition Commission; Construction Industry Training Board; Criminal Cases Review Commission; Criminal Injuries Compensation Appeals Board; Housing Corporation; English Nature; Environment Agency; Food Standards Agency; Forestry Commissioners; Gaming Board for Great Britain; Home Office Policy Advisory Board for Forensic Pathology; Horseracing Betting Levy Board; Human Fertilisation and Embryology Authority; Independent Police Complaints Authority; Legal Services Commission; Licensing Authority established under the Medicines Act 1968; Postal Services Commission; Rent Assessment Committees and panels; Medical Referees; National Asylum Support Service; National Care Standards Commission (superseded by two other inspectorates in 2004); several of the National Park Authorities; NHS Trusts and Primary Care Trusts; Office of the Schools Adjudicator; Rail Regulator; Standards Board for England (promoting ethical conduct in local government). A database of all NDPBs is published by the Cabinet Office. The Public Bodies Act 2011 makes provision for many public bodies to be merged, modified or abolished.

[18] See, e.g. *R. (on the application of Countryside Alliance) v Attorney General* [2005] EWHC 1677 (Admin); [2006] Eu. L.R. 178 (whether Hunting Act 2005 breached Convention rights). This follows the practice specified by Crown Proceedings Act 1947 s.17(3) (though claims for judicial review are not "civil proceedings").

[19] On the *Carltona* principle, see 5-172.

[20] For an overview of local government, S.H. Bailey, "The Structure, Powers and Accountability of Local Government", Ch.4 in D. Feldman (ed), *English Public Law*, 2nd edn (2009).

[21] Despite the existence of a remedy in the form of an appeal on point of law to the county courts: see 17-037.

[22] M. Sunkin et al, "Mapping the use of Judicial Review to Challenge Local Authorities in England and Wales" [2007] P.L. 545; there is a concentration of challenges in the London Boroughs.

[23] So far, the challenges to the National Assembly for Wales (established by the Government of Wales

Criminal justice system

Where the dispute as to the lawfulness of the exercise of a public function relates   **3-005**
to the criminal justice system, in addition to the Secretary of State for the Home
Department and the Secretary of State for Justice (the ministers with responsibili-
ties for this field), defendants may include: Chief Constables of Police[24]; the Crown
Prosecution Service; the Director of Public Prosecutions (DPP); the Director of the
Serious Fraud Office[25]; prison governors; the National Parole Service; the Parole
Board; the Criminal Cases Review Commission; and the Serious Organised Crime
Agency.

Some of decisions made by HM Attorney General in relation to instituting and   **3-006**
stopping prosecutions may fall outside the court's supervisory jurisdiction
altogether.[26] Even where matters are within the court's jurisdiction, there is a marked
reluctance exercise that supervisory jurisdiction over police decisions to investigate,[27] charge, and administer cautions[28]; and decisions of the DPP to prosecute,
continue or discontinue criminal prosecutions.[29] The court will generally do so only
if there is a grave abuse of power or a clear breach of the police or prosecuting

---

Act 1998; now the Government of Wales Act 2006) have mainly concerned environmental planning matters. On judicial review and devolution, see 1-119 and 3-091.

[24] See, e.g. *R. (on the application of R) v Durham Constabulary* [2005] UKHL 21; [2005] 1 W.L.R.
1184 (whether warning given to young offender compatible with ECHR art.6).

[25] See, e.g. *R. (on the application of Corner House Research) v Director of the Serious Fraud Office*
[2008] UKHL 60; [2009] 1 A.C. 756 (challenge to the legality of a decision of the DSF to halt a
criminal investigation into allegations of bribery against a defence contractor after a threat was made
by an official of Saudi Arabia that, if the investigation continued, Saudi Arabia would cease to co-
operate with the UK on counter-terrorism and would not enter into the contract. Lord Bingham of
Cornhill stated (at [30]–[31]) that it was "accepted that the decisions of the Director are not immune from review by the courts, but authority makes plain that only in highly exceptional cases will
the court disturb the decisions of an independent prosecutor and investigator"); see further J. Jowell,
"Caving In: Threats and the Rule of Law" [2008] J.R. 273 (arguing that it was "surprising that the
House of Lords in *Corner House* positively encourages the view that the rule of law is on a par with
any other 'relevant consideration' taken into account by the prosecutor" and expressing hope "that
this does not signal an abrupt lapse into the unnecessarily deferential administrative law of
yesteryear"); R. Hopkins and C. Yeginsu, "Storm in a Teacup: Domestic and International
Conservatism from the Corner House Case" [2008] J.R. 267.

[26] See, 3-017. Proposals for reform of the Attorney General's role in relation to prosecutions were
included in the draft Constitutional Renewal Bill in 2008 but were not enacted.

[27] cf. *R. v Commissioner of Police of the Metropolis Ex p. Blackburn* [1968] 2 Q.B. 118 (unlawful for
Commissioner to issue instructions to officers not to enforce provisions of the Betting, Gaming and
Lotteries Act 1963, except with his approval, because of manpower constraints and legal
complexities).

[28] See, e.g. *R. (on the application of Mondelly) v Commissioner of Police of the Metropolis* [2006]
EWHC 2370 (Admin); (2007) 171 J.P. 121; *R. v Chief Constable of Kent Ex p. L* [1993] 1 All E.R.
756; *R. v Commissioner of Police of the Metropolis Ex p. Thompson* [1997] 1 W.L.R. 1519.

[29] *R. v DPP Ex p. Kebilene* [2000] 2 A.C. 326 (absent "dishonesty or mala fide or an exceptional
circumstance" decisions by the DPP to consent to a prosecution are not amenable to judicial review);
cf. *R. v DPP Ex p. Manning* [2001] Q.B. 330 (challenge to decision not to bring prosecution); *R. v
DPP Ex p. Duckenfield* [2000] 1 W.L.R. 55; *R. (on the application of Gujra) v Crown Prosecution
Service* [2011] EWHC 472 (Admin); [2012] 1 W.L.R. 254 (court "strongly discourages" judicial
review challenges to CPS decisions to take over conduct of private prosecutions in order to
discontinue them on grounds of no reasonable prospect of conviction). For an example of a successful challenge to a decision to prosecute, see *R. (on the application of E, S and R) v DPP* [2011]
EWHC 1465 (Admin); [2012] 1 Cr. App. R 6 (prosecutor's decision letter simply did not engage
with multi-agency strategy group report on safeguarding the interests of the three children involved).
R. (S) v Crown Prosecution Service; R. (S) v Oxford Magistrates' Court [2015] EWHC 2868
(Admin); [2016] 1 W.L.R. 804 (refusing permission to proceed and holding that procedural propriety
did not require consultation with the suspect when the prosecution decided to prosecute following
a request for review by an alleged victim under the Victims' Right to Review scheme).

authority's settled policy. Claimants will also be expected to use other alternative remedies (such as an application to the relevant criminal court to dismiss or stay the criminal proceedings on the ground that they are an abuse of the process, or to utilise any route of appeal that may exist).[30]

Administrative justice system

3-007   Public authorities that handle peoples' grievances also fall within the supervisory jurisdiction of the Administrative Court. Thus, judicial review claims may be brought against tribunals,[31] ombudsmen[32] and public inquiries.[33]

Courts

3-008   The Administrative Court's jurisdiction over other courts has historically extended only to courts and tribunals of "inferior jurisdiction"; decisions of the "superior courts of record"—notably, the Supreme Court (formerly the House of Lords), Court of Appeal and the High Court—are outside the scope of judicial review (though judges of the higher courts may be subject to judicial review when exercising specific statutory power separate from the courts in which they sit).[34] Decisions of the Upper Tribunal, designated as a "superior court of record" by Tribunal, Courts and Enforcement Act 2007 s.3(5), are nonetheless subject to judicial review (where there is no appeal to the Court of Appeal), but a "restrained approach" to judicial review is adopted[35]: where the challenge is to a decision of the Upper Tribunal to refuse permission to appeal to itself, the Administrative Court, when considering whether to grant permission for judicial review, applies the same criteria as applies when there is a "second-tier" appeal to the Court of Appeal i.e. permission should not be granted unless "(a) the proposed appeal would raise some important point of principle or practice; or (b) there is some other compelling reason for the relevant appellate court to hear the appeal".[36]

Criminal cases

3-009   A significant proportion of the Administrative Court's load is judicial review claims and appeals "by way of case stated" against the decisions of the criminal courts.[37] The prosecution and defence may challenge magistrates' courts' decision, or decisions of the Crown Court on appeal from the magistrates, by judicial review. It has been held that where the "magistrate is acting not as an Examining

---

30   16-014.
31   1-091.
32   1-071.
33   1-101.
34   See, e.g. *R. v Master of the Rolls Ex P. McKinnell* [1993] 1 W.L.R. 88 (Master of the Rolls exercising his powers in relation to appeals under the Solicitors Act 1974); *R. (on the application of Woolas) v Parliamentary Election Court* [2010] EWHC 3169 (Admin); [2012] Q.B. 1 (Parliamentary Election Court consisting of High Court judges); cf. *R. (on the application of Bulger) v Secretary of State for the Home Department* [2001] EWHC Admin 119; [2001] 3 All E.R. 449, [13]–[17] (decision of Lord Chief Justice of England and Wales recommending minimum number of years to be served by murderer before eligible for consideration for parole—court left open question whether amenable to judicial review).
35   *R. (on the application of Cart) v Upper Tribunal (Public Law Project and another intervening)* [2011] UKSC 28; [2012] 1 A.C. 663 and *R. (on the application of Jones) v First-tier Tribunal* [2013] UKSC 19; [2013] 2 A.C. 48.
36   1-099 and 17-004.
37   17-036.

Magistrate, but deciding a preliminary issue as to jurisdiction, his ruling upon that is final and can properly be challenged by way of case stated or judicial review".[38] There are, however, several different existing appeal routes and judicial review will only be permitted in the absence of such an appropriate alternative remedy.[39]

The position of the Crown Court (the highest level criminal trial court in England and Wales) requires special analysis. Although it is a superior court of record, some of its decisions are amenable to judicial review.[40] The situation is governed by the Senior Courts Act 1981 s.29(3), derived from the Courts Act 1971 s.10: "In relation to the jurisdiction of the Crown Court, other than its jurisdiction in matters relating to trial on indictment, the High Court shall have all such jurisdiction to make mandatory, prohibiting or quashing orders as the High Court possesses in relation to the jurisdiction of an inferior court".[41] The phrase "matters relating to trials on indictment" has proved to be problematic.[42] The restriction applies even when a claimant seeks only a declaration.[43] In 2001, Sir Robin Auld's review of the criminal courts of England and Wales recommended that the Administrative Court's supervisory jurisdiction over criminal courts be replaced with new routes of appeal to the Court of Appeal (Criminal Appeal).[44] The Government accepted this and the Law Commission subsequently made recommendations to create new avenues of appeal and bar judicial review of Crown Court criminal proceedings on indictment from the time the case goes to the Crown Court for trial to the end of the trail (except for refusals of bail).[45]

3-010

Civil cases

The Administrative Court has jurisdiction to determine judicial review claims against decisions of the county courts; the Access to Justice Act 1999 s.54(4), which

3-011

---

[38]   R. (on the application of Donnachie) v Cardiff Magistrates' Court [2007] EWHC 1846 (Admin) at [6], citing R. v Clerkenwell Metropolitan Stipendiary Magistrate Ex p. DPP [1984] 2 All E.R. 193.

[39]   See 16-014, 17-033 and 17-036. cf. R. v Hereford Magistrates' Court Ex p. Rowlands [1998] Q.B. 110 in which the Divisional Court held that the existence of a right of appeal by way of retrial in the Crown Court did not preclude a person convicted in a magistrates' court from applying for judicial review on the grounds of procedural impropriety, unfairness or bias.

[40]   The historical explanation for this is that the Crown Court was created by the amalgamation of one court that was and another that was not subject to the High Court's supervisory jurisdiction: see In re Smalley [1985] A.C. 622 at 640 (Lord Bridge).

[41]   R. Ward, "Judicial Review and Trials on Indictment" [1990] P.L. 50; R. v Crown Court at Leeds Ex p. Hussain [1995] 1 W.L.R. 1329; R. v Crown Court at Manchester Ex p. H [2000] 1 W.L.R. 760; I. Steele, "Judicial Review of the Crown Court and Section 29(3) of the Supreme Court Act 1981" [2008] J.R. 180; J. Horder, "Rationalising Judicial Review in Criminal Proceedings" [2008] J.R. 207. So, e.g. a decision of the Crown Court to issue the warrants to enter and search properties under the Police and Criminal Evidence Act 1984 is amenable to judicial review: see R. (on the application of Faisaltex Ltd) v Crown Court Sitting at Preston [2008] EWHC 2832 (Admin); [2009] 1 Cr. App. R. 37.

[42]   It has been considered by the House of Lords five times over the past 20 years; for detailed analysis see Law Commission, Judicial Review of Decisions of the Crown Court (July 2005). For a survey see R. (on the application of H) v Wood Green Crown Court [2006] EWHC 2683 (Admin); [2007] 2 All E.R. 259.

[43]   R. v Chelmsford Crown Court Ex p. Chief Constable of Essex [1994] 1 W.L.R. 359. Though note that the High Court has considered the restriction ineffective where the trial judge has acted without jurisdiction: R. v Maidstone Crown Court Ex p. Harrow LBC [2000] Q.B. 719; R. (DPP) v Sheffield Crown Court) [2014] EWHC 2014 (Admin); [2014] 1 W.L.R. 4639; R. (M) v Crown Court at Kingston upon Thames [2014] EWHC 2702 (Admin); [2016] 1 W.L.R. 1685 ("an error so severe that it deprived the [Crown Court] of jurisdiction" to make the impugned order).

[44]   Review of the Criminal Courts of England and Wales, Ch.12.

[45]   Law Commission, The High Court's Jurisdiction in Relation to Criminal Proceedings (Law Com No.324, July 2010); the Government's response is awaited.

provides for appeals from county courts and restricts *appeals* against the refusal of permission to pursue such an appeal, does not oust that jurisdiction.[46] But the statutory appeal routes will in almost all cases be a more appropriate remedy than judicial review, and the Administrative Court will refuse permission for a judicial review claim save in the most exceptional circumstances.[47]

Legislation

3-012   As noted in Chapter 1, whereas in the past judicial review challenges focused on administrative action, the court's supervisory jurisdiction now extends to legislation.[48] Byelaws made by local authorities and other public authorities have for many years been amenable to judicial review.[49] So too is delegated legislation in the form of Statutory Instruments made by ministers,[50] including those passed

---

[46] *R. (on the application of Sivasubramaniam) v Wandsworth County Court* [2002] EWCA Civ 1738; [2003] 1 W.L.R. 475.

[47] *Sivasubramaniam* [2002] EWCA Civ 1738; [2003] 1 W.L.R. 475; the "possibility remains that there may be very rare cases where a litigant challenges the jurisdiction of a circuit judge giving or refusing permission to appeal on the ground of jurisdictional error in the narrow, pre-*Anisminic* sense, or procedural irregularity of such a kind as to constitute a denial of the applicant's right to a fair hearing. If such grounds are made out we consider that a proper case for judicial review will have been established" (Lord Phillips of Matravers MR at [54]); see also *Gregory v Turner* [2003] EWCA Civ 183; [2003] 1 W.L.R. 1149 at [29]–[31], [37]–[46], where even though the CA expressed "serious concern that something may have gone wrong in connection with the district judge's handling of the case", and acknowledged that the judge refusing permission to appeal had not had the "crucial errors" drawn to his attention, the case was not one in which judicial review was appropriate. For a rare example of a (partly) successful challenge, see *R. (on the application of Srinivasans Solicitors) v Croydon County Court* [2011] EWHC 3615 (Admin) (county court purporting to exercise jurisdiction that properly belonged to the High Court only).

[48] See 1-011.

[49] See e.g. *R. (on the application of Mott) v Ministry of Agriculture, Fisheries and Food* [2000] C.O.D. 183 (National Salmon Byelaws 1999 made by the Environment Agency); *Boddington v British Transport Police* [1999] 2 A.C. 143 (British Railways Board Byelaws 1965, on smoking); *R. v Ministry of Agriculture, Fisheries and Food Ex p. Bray* [1999] C.O.D. 187 (byelaw made by the Sussex Sea Fisheries Committee regulating fishing vessels); *Tabernacle v Secretary of State for Defence* [2009] EWCA Civ 23; (2009) 106(7) L.S.G. 18 (byelaws made by the Ministry of Defence, which sought to prevent a long-established peace camp near the Atomic Weapons Establishment at Aldermaston, violated arts 10 and 11 ECHR).

[50] See, e.g. *R. (Middlebrook Mushrooms Ltd) v Agricultural Wages Board of England and Wales* [2004] EWHC 1447 (Admin) (Agricultural Wages Order 2003 (No.1)); *R. v Secretary of State for Education and Employment Ex p. National Union of Teachers* [2000] Ed. C.R. 603; *R. v Secretary of State for Employment Ex p. Seymour-Smith* [1996] All E.R. (EC) 1; *Ahmed v HM Treasury (JUSTICE intervening) (Nos 1 and 2)*[2008] EWCA Civ 1187; [2010] UKSC 2; [2010] UKSC 5; [2010] 2 A.C. 534 (whether Terrorism (United Nations Measures) Order 2006 (SI 2006/2657) and the Al-Qaida and Taliban (United Nations Measures) Order 2006 (SI 2006/2952) were ultra vires the United Nations Act 1946); *R. (on the application of the Law Society) v Lord Chancellor* [2010] EWHC 1406 (Admin); [2011] 1 W.L.R. 234 (Costs in Criminal Cases (General) (Amendment) Regulations 2008 unlawful: applying *Padfield* [1968] A.C. 997 (see 5-008), Lord Chancellor's objective in making regulations held not to be a legitimate one). *R. (on the application of Reilly and Wilson) v Secretary of State for Work and Pensions* [2013] UKSC 68; [2014] A.C. 453 (Jobseeker's Allowance (Employment, Skills and Enterprise Scheme) Regulations (SI 2011/917) were ultra vires because the Scheme did not have a "prescribed description" as required by s.17A(1) of the Jobseekers Act 1995); *R. (on the application of SG) v Secretary of State for Work and Pensions (Child Poverty Action Group intervening)* [2015] UKSC 16; [2015] 1 W.L.R. 1449 (Benefit Cap (Housing Benefit) Regulations 2012 (SI 2012/2994) held not incompatible with Convention rights); *R. (on the application of Cushnie) v Secretary of State for Health* [2014] EWHC 3626 (Admin); [2015] P.T.S.R. 384 (National Health Service (Charges to Overseas Visitors) Regulations 2011 (SI 2011/1556) unlawful due to the Secretary of State's failure to comply with the public sector equality duty).

by affirmative resolution of Parliament.[51] Challenges may be made to draft orders not yet considered by Parliament.[52] All grounds of review, substantive as well as procedural, may be invoked against secondary legislation.[53] The court is not confined to giving declaratory relief; a quashing order may be made,[54] either of the whole instrument or, if an offending provision is severable, of that provision.[55] The Immigration Rules (formally, the Statement of Changes in Immigration Rules (1994), HC 395, as amended from time to time) made by the Home Secretary under s.1(4) of the Immigration Act 1971 "do not constitute 'rules' in the sense that a statute or a statutory instrument do" and are not subject to all the public law constraints on policies and discretionary powers, including the non-fettering principle.[56]

Although parliamentary supremacy remains a general principle of the British constitution, the court's supervisory jurisdiction now—in important albeit limited ways—extends to primary legislation. European Union law requires national courts to disapply legislative provisions, including those in Acts of Parliament, where they are incompatible with EU law norms.[57] Human Rights Act 1998 s.4 also provides the courts with power to make declarations of incompatibility in relation to primary legislation: though this stops well short of creating judicial review of Acts of Parliament, it nonetheless has given the higher courts a role in evaluating whether Parliament's enactments are consistent with Convention rights.[58] The principle of parliamentary sovereignty does not prevent the courts reviewing primary legislation made under prerogative powers.[59]

3-013

---

[51]   See, e.g. *R. (on the application of Javed) v Secretary of State for the Home Department* [2001] EWCA Civ 789; [2002] Q.B. 129 (Asylum (Designated Countries of Destination and Designated Safe Third Countries) Order 1996). *Javed* was approved by the Privy Council in *Toussaint v Attorney General of St Vincent and the Grenadines* [2007] UKPC 48; [2007] 1 W.L.R. 2825 at [18]: "both art.9 of the Bill of Rights and the wider common law principle accommodate the right and duty of the court to review the legality of subordinate legislation. The court can review the material facts and form its own judgment on the legality of subordinate legislation tabled in both Houses of Parliament and approved there, even though the result might be discordant with statements made in parliamentary debate".

[52]   See e.g., *R. (Public Law Project) v Lord Chancellor (Office of the Children's Commissioner intervening)* [2016] UKSC 39; [2016] 3 W.L.R. 387 (draft order laid before Parliament concerning restrictions on legal aid).

[53]   *R. (on the application of Javed) v Secretary of State for the Home Department* [2001] EWCH Civ 789; [2002] Q.B. 129. In relation to illegality as a ground of review, the UK Supreme Court has approved the proposition that "[a]lthough Henry VIII powers are often case in very wide terms, the more general the words used by Parliament to delegate a power, the more likely it is that an exercise within the literal meaning of the words will nevertheless be outside the legislature's contemplation" (*R. (Public Law Project) v Lord Chancellor (Office of the Children's Commissioner intervening)* [2016] UKSC 39; [2016] 3 W.L.R. 387 at [26], citing D. Greenberg (ed), *Craies on Legislation* 10th edn (2012), para.1.3.9).

[54]   *R. v Secretary of State for Social Services Ex p. Association of Metropolitan Authorities* [1986] 1 W.L.R. 1 (quashing order refused in court's discretion); *R. v Secretary of State for Health Ex p. US Tobacco International* [1992] 1 Q.B. 353 (quashing order made).

[55]   *R. (on the application of Middlebrook Mushrooms Ltd) v Agricultural Wages Board of England and Wales* [2004] EWHC 1447 (Admin) at [90]. On severability, see 5-145.

[56]   *R. (Sayaniya v Upper Tribunal)* [2016] EWCA Civ 85; [2016] 4 W.L.R. 58.

[57]   See 14-012.

[58]   See 13-047.

[59]   *R. (on the application of Bancoult) v Secretary of State for Foreign and Commonwealth Affairs (No.2)* [2008] UKHL 61; [2009] 1 A.C. 453.

JURISDICTION, JUSTICIABILITY AND DISCRETION

3-014   There is an obvious need to set a boundary—for practical and constitutional reasons—on the reach of the Administrative Court's role. In the past, the development of English administrative law was impeded by rigid distinctions made by the court between functions which were classified as "legislative", "administrative", "judicial", and "quasi-judicial".[60] These categories no longer determine whether a function is amenable to judicial review. The boundary is now set using three main techniques by: defining the jurisdiction of the court; holding some functions to be "non-justiciable" (even though not falling outside the court's jurisdiction); and exercising the court's discretion to refuse permission to proceed with a claim.[61] The courts have regrettably not always maintained a clear distinction between these techniques, for example describing a function as "non-justiciable" when it is more properly to be thought of as falling outside the courts' jurisdiction.

Jurisdiction of the Administrative Court

3-015   A starting point for analysing which functions are, and are not, amenable to judicial review is to ascertain the extent of the Administrative Court's supervisory jurisdiction.[62] In this context the term jurisdiction means the "courts have power to enquire into such a claim and consider whether any relief is called for".[63] The court's jurisdiction stems from the common law, is subject to precedent, and may be restricted by statute. This constitutional arrangement is reflected in the Senior Courts Act 1981 s.29, as amended, which provides: "(1A) The High Court shall have jurisdiction to make mandatory, prohibiting and quashing orders in those

---

[60] See Appendix B, below.
[61] On these terms, see A. Le Sueur, "Justifying Judicial Caution: Jurisdiction, Justiciability and Policy", Ch.8 in B. Hadfield (ed), Judicial Review: A Thematic Approach (1995), where it was argued that the justification for not intervening in cases has shifted from reliance on the concept of jurisdiction to discretionary factors and non-justiciability; M. Beloff, "Judicial Review—2001: A Prophetic Odyssey" (1995) 58 M.L.R. 143.
[62] For a historical account of the development of the supervisory jurisdiction see Ch.15.
[63] *Bahamas District of the Methodist Church in the Caribbean and the Americas v Symonette* [2000] UKPC 31; (2002–03) 5 I.T.E.L.R. 311 at [32]. The recognition of jurisdiction is distinct from the question whether a claimant has a cause of action or grounds of judicial review (see [36]). In *Fun World Co Ltd v Municipal Council of Quatre Bornes* [2009] UKPC 8, Lord Scott (dissenting as to the outcome of the appeal) noted at [55] the "distinction between jurisdiction in the strict sense and procedural propriety", citing *Guaranty Trust Company of New York v Hannay & Co* [1915] 2 K.B. 536, in which Pickford LJ commented at 563: "The word 'jurisdiction' and the expression 'the court has no jurisdiction' are used in two different senses which I think often leads to confusion. The first and, in my opinion, the only really correct sense of the expression that the court has no jurisdiction is that it has no power to deal with and decide the dispute as to the subject matter before it, no matter in what form and by whom it is raised. But there is another sense in which it is often used, i.e. that although the court has power to decide the question it will not according to its settled practice do so except in a certain way and under certain circumstances". See also *R. (on the application of St Helens BC) v Manchester Primary Care Trust* [2008] EWCA Civ 931; (2008) 11 C.C.L. Rep. 774: "Judicial review is a flexible, but not entirely unfenced jurisdiction. This stems from certain intrinsic features. The court's relevant function is to review decisions of statutory and other public authorities to see that they are lawful, rational and reached by a fair and due process" (May LJ at [13]). On questions relating to so-called jurisdictional and non-jurisdictional errors *by public authorities*—where the focus is on the powers (or jurisdiction) of the decision-maker rather than of the court—see 4-003.

classes of case in which, immediately before 1st May 2004, it had jurisdiction to make orders of mandamus, prohibition and certiorari respectively."[64]

The forerunners of this statutory provision provided that judicial review remedial orders could be granted by the High Court "in those classes of case which it had power to do so immediately before the commencement of this Act".[65] This statutory statement is declaratory of the existing jurisdiction and should not be regarded as exhaustive. It is capable of development by the courts in response to changing circumstances because ultimately its source lies in the prerogative or inherent power of the judiciary of the High Court, which has never been comprehensively defined. **3-016**

As we shall discuss below, the main touchstones for determining that a function falls within the court's supervisory jurisdiction are now (a) that the source of the decision-maker's authority is a statutory provision or prerogative power[66] and (b) that the function has a public character.[67] The question is not so much whether there is power to award one of the public law remedial orders, but whether in a more general sense the matter in dispute falls within the court's public law supervisory jurisdiction. **3-017**

Public functions outside the court's jurisdiction

Despite the expansion of judicial review,[68] there are situations in which the court has no jurisdiction. Matters falling into these "forbidden areas"[69] or "Alsatia",[70] include the following categories in which, as a matter of law, the court may not embark on an inquiry into a claim beyond satisfying itself that the case does truly fall within the relevant no-go area. **3-018**

(a) Challenges to decisions relating to the internal procedures of the United Kingdom Parliament, reflecting the constitutional principles of parliamentary privilege (derived from the Bill of Rights 1689 art.9)[71] and exclusive cognisance or jurisdiction (a broader and older concept enabling each House

---

[64] The significance of the date 1 May 2004 is that it was on this day that the Supreme Court Act (now called the Senior Courts Act) 1981 was amended to alter the names of some of the remedies available on claims for judicial review: orders of certiorari became quashing orders; prohibition, prohibiting orders; and mandamus, mandatory orders. See The Civil Procedure (Modification of Supreme Court Act 1981) Order 2004.

[65] Supreme Court Act 1981 s.29 (before amendment and change of its short title); Administration of Justice (Miscellaneous Provisions) Act 1938.

[66] See 3-037.

[67] See 3-038.

[68] See 1-011.

[69] A term used in *R. (on the application of Abassi) v Secretary of State for Foreign and Commonwealth Affairs* [2002] EWCA Civ 1598; [2003] U.K.H.R.R. 76 at [106] (Lord Phillips MR); discussed in *Rahmatullah v Secretary of State for Foreign and Commonwealth Affairs* [2011] EWCA Civ 1540; [2012] 1 W.L.R. 1462 at [47]–[55].

[70] A reference to an area adjacent to the Temple in London where during the 15th–17th centuries the courts' writs did not run and which accordingly provided sanctuary for criminals. See, e.g. *R. (on the application of UMBS Online Ltd v Serious Organised Crime Agency* [2007] EWCA Civ 406; at [58] (Sedley LJ: "In setting up the Serious Organised Crime Agency, the state has set out to create an Alsatia—a region of executive action free of judicial oversight. Although the statutory powers can intrude heavily, and sometimes ruinously, into civil rights and obligations, the supervisory role which the court would otherwise have is limited by its primary obligation to give effect to Parliament's clearly expressed intentions. But, except where the statute prevents it, the scheme must also accommodate what Byles J in *Cooper v Wandsworth Board of Works* (1863) 14 C.B.N.S. 180 called the justice of the common law. That is the duality we have sought to recognise in deciding this case").

[71] *Prebble v Television New Zealand Ltd* [1995] 1 A.C. 321 at 332, PC (Lord Browne-Wilkinson) (parliamentary privilege prevents the use of statements made in Parliament being used as evidence

to "manage its own affairs without interference from the other or from outside Parliament").[72] Questions as to the extent of parliamentary privilege are ultimately for the court to decide.[73] For the purposes of parliamentary privilege, a distinction is drawn between the "core or essential business" of Parliament that are part of its proceedings (and therefore immune from challenge) and "an activity which is an incident of the administration of Parliament", which is not.[74] Parliamentary privilege did not impede the UK Supreme Court from considering in detail the hybrid bill procedure and whether it was in accordance with an EU directive.[75]

(b) Challenges to the validity of provisions contained in Acts of Parliament,[76] reflecting the constitutional principle of the supremacy of Parliament, or seeking to require or prevent a bills to be laid before Parliament.[77] This is now subject to several exceptions: the court's duty to disapply statutory provisions that are not in compliance with European Union law[78] the court's discre-

---

of justification in libel proceedings); Bill of Rights 1689 art.9 provides: "That the freedom of speech and debates or proceedings in Parliament ought not to be impeached or questioned in any court or place out of Parliament"; *R. (on the application of Bradley) v Secretary of State for Work and Pensions* [2007] EWHC 242 (Admin); [2007] Pens. L.R. 87 at [26]–[35] (Parliamentary Commission for Administration); *R. (on the application of Bradley) v Secretary of State for Work and Pensions* [2007] EWHC 242 (Admin); [2007] Pens. L.R. 87 at [26]–[35] (obiter: to allow the evidence of a witness to a select committee to be relied on in court would inhibit the freedom of speech in Parliament and thus contravene art.9 of the Bill of Rights but reference to a select committee report would not infringe art.9; not commented upon in the subsequent CA judgment at [2008] EWCA Civ 36; [2009] Q.B. 114); in *R. (on the application of Equitable Members Action Group) v Her Majesty's Treasury* [2009] EWHC 2495 (Admin), [70], the Divisional Court recorded that the claimant had quoted and relied upon evidence given to the Public Administration Select Committee by the Economic Secretary to the Treasury—the court put it out of their minds and no further reference was made to it; *R. (on the application of Wheeler) v Office of the Prime Minister* [2008] EWHC 936 (Admin); [2008] 2 C.M.L.R. 57 at [45]–[54] (introduction of a bill into Parliament clearly forms part of the proceedings within Parliament; for a court to order a minister to introduce a bill, or an amendment to a bill, "would plainly be to trespass impermissibly on the province of Parliament"); *Corporate Officer of the House of Commons v Information Commissioner* [2008] EWHC 1084 (Admin); [2008] A.C.D. 71 at [2] (claim about right under Freedom of Information Act 2000 to access to information about MPs' allowances did not engage with "proceedings in Parliament" and therefore art.9 of the Bill of Rights was not engaged); *Wheeler v Office of the Prime Minister* [2014] EWHC 3815 (Admin); [2015] 1 C.M.L.R 46 at [44]–[47] (enforcement of a legitimate expectation that a parliamentary vote would be held concerning European Arrest Warrants would involve a breach of art.9 of the Bill of Rights 1689, a breach of parliamentary privilege and breach the separation of powers).

[72] *R. v Chaytor (David)* [2010] UKSC 52; [2011] 1 A.C. 684. [63] (Lord Phillips of Worth Matravers), [129] (Lord Clarke of Stone-Cum-Ebony); *R. v Parliamentary Commissioner for Standards Ex p. Fayed* [1998] 1 W.L.R. 669 (it fell to Parliament, not the courts, to supervise the work of the PCS); *Re McGuiness's Application* [1997] N.I. 359 (no judicial review of decision of Speaker that those who had not complied with the Parliamentary Oaths Act 1866 were denied use of various facilities).

[73] *R. v Chaytor (David)* [2010] UKSC 52; [2011] 1 A.C. 684 at [15]–[16].

[74] *R. v Chaytor (David)* [2010] UKSC 52; [2011] 1 A.C. 684 at [62].

[75] *R. (on the application of Buckingham County Council) v Secretary of State for Transport* [2014] UKSC 3; [2014] 1 W.L.R. 324, [95] (Lord Reed SCJ: "I am mindful of the importance of refraining from trespassing upon the province of Parliament or, so far as possible, even appearing to do so. The court can however consider the effect of the Directive under EU law without in my opinion affecting or encroaching upon any of the powers of Parliament. The parliamentary authorities have not thought it necessary to seek to intervene in these proceedings, although the court was told that they have been kept informed of the parties' cases").

[76] *British Railways Board v Pickin* [1974] A.C. 765.

[77] See, e.g. *R. (on the application of Wheeler) v Office of the Prime Minister* [2008] EWHC 1409 (Admin); [2008] A.C.D. 70; *R. (on the application of Unison) v Secretary of State for Health* [2010] EWHC 2655 (Admin); [2011] A.C.D. 10.

[78] See 14-012.

tion to make a declaration of incompatibility with Convention rights under ;s.4 of the Human Rights Act 1998[79]; questions of implied repeal of an earlier statutory provision by a later one[80]; and questions relating to the application of the Parliament Acts 1911 and 1949.[81]

(c)   Challenges to decisions made by the senior courts of England and Wales (the High Court, Court of Appeal and House of Lords). Historically, the prerogative writs[82] extended only to inferior courts (today, principally in the form of magistrates' courts and the county courts) and tribunals.[83] The Crown Court is a superior court of record but is made amenable to judicial review to some extent by s.29(3) of the Senior Courts Act 1981.[84] The Upper Tribunal[85] and the Parliamentary Election Court[86] are however amenable to judicial review.

(d)   Matters falling outside the territorial reach of the High Court of England and Wales (of which the Administrative Court is part) and the ambit of the HRA.[87]

(e)   Questions over which the court's jurisdiction has been expressly removed or limited by statute. Statutory restrictions on judicial review in "ouster" or "preclusive" clauses are construed narrowly.[88]

(f)   Challenges to certain decisions made by the HM Attorney General may also fall outside the court's supervisory jurisdiction. These are the functions, some derived from prerogative powers, others from statute, in respect of which the Attorney General makes decisions independently of ministerial colleagues and for which he is responsible to Parliament including: entering a *nolle prosequi* to stop a prosecution on indictment (very rarely exercised, usually on the ground of the defendant's ill health); he may institute a prosecution; direct the Director of Public Prosecutions to take over a prosecution; and give or withhold his consent ("fiat") to a relator action brought by a person to enforce the law. The House of Lords in *Gouriet* held that "in the exercise of these powers he is not subject to direction by his ministerial colleagues or to control and supervision by the courts",[89] though the Privy Council has subsequently

---

[79]   See 13-047 (a declaration under s.4 does not, in formal terms, affect the validity of the provision in question).

[80]   See *Thoburn v Sunderland City Council* [2002] EWHC 195 (Admin); [2003] Q.B. 151.

[81]   *Jackson v Attorney General* [2005] UKHL 56; [2006] 1 A.C. 262. The Parliament Acts set out legal requirements as to the manner and form of an Act passed under their provisions and only the courts—not Parliament—can resolve any dispute as the validity of such an Act. The court's jurisdiction is necessary to guarantee the rule of law and involves no breach of constitutional propriety (see Lord Bingham at [51]).

[82]   See 18-023.

[83]   *In re A Company* [1981] A.C. 374 at 392. The Privy Council considered the characteristics of a "superior court" in *Suratt v Attorney General of Trinidad and Tobago* [2007] UKPC 55; [2008] 1 A.C. 655, Baroness Hale of Richmond citing with approval at [49] John Burke (ed), *Jowitt's Dictionary of English Law*, 2nd edn, (1977), p.493: "Courts are of two principal classes – of record and not of record. A court of record is one whereof the acts and judicial proceedings are enrolled for a perpetual memory and testimony, and which has the power to fine and imprison for contempt of its authority ... Courts are also divided into superior and inferior, superior courts being those which are not subject to the control of any other courts, except by way of appeal".

[84]   See 3-009.

[85]   *R. (on the application of Cart) (Public Law Project and another intervening)* [2011] UKSC 28; [2012] 1 A.C. 663.

[86]   *R. (on the application of Woolas) v Parliamentary Election Court* [2010] EWHC 3169; [2012] Q.B. 1.

[87]   3-088 and 13-063.

[88]   4-015.

[89]   *Attorney General v Gouriet* [1978] A.C. 435 at 487 (Viscount Dilhorne); *Bahamas Hotel Maintenance & Allied Workers Union v Bahamas Hotel Catering & Allied Workers Union* [2011] UKPC 4 at [36].

highlighted that since the *GCHQ* case put the matter beyond doubt, prerogative powers do generally fall within the court's jurisdiction,[90] and there is no inherent objection to the court's jurisdiction being invoked where the Attorney General is exercising a statutory power.[91]

3-019 A claimant's lack of standing goes to the jurisdiction of the court, but the liberalisation of the "sufficient interest" test means that this will rarely now be a practical bar for a claimant who in other respects has a meritorious case.[92] Until comparatively recently, the courts worked upon the assumption that they had no jurisdiction to review decisions taken under prerogative powers, but it is now understood that this is not so[93]: whether a function under a prerogative power is or is not reviewable is determined by inquiring whether the issue at stake is justiciable or not. Some aspects of the Crown's power, when exercised directly by the Sovereign, remain outside the reach of the courts' jurisdiction but this is of little practical importance in the field of public law.[94]

3-020 The Administrative Court operates subject to the general limits governing the capacity of the courts of England and Wales to deal with matters of international law. Questions of interpretation of international legal instruments, unless they relate to the court's determination of some domestic law right or interest, are not matters of English law and fall outside the courts' jurisdiction. This reflects the dualist character of the United Kingdom's constitution in which international treaties are not a source of law recognised by domestic courts, until such time as a treaty provision is expressly incorporated into domestic law.[95] In the UK Supreme Court, Lord Kerr of Tonaghmore JSC has, however, called into question the rationale for this "dualist conception" of the restriction on the use of unincorporated treaty provisions in the human rights context, holding that art.3.1 of the United Nations Convention on the Rights of the Child should be directly enforceable in UK domestic law (a minority view with which the other Justices did concur).[96] The English courts also avoid determining questions relating to actions by a foreign sovereign state,[97] reflecting the international law principle of comity. However, the conduct of foreign states in gross violation of established principles of international

---

[90] 3-030. *R. v Criminal Injuries Compensation Board Ex p. Lain* [1967] 2 Q.B. 864, Div. Ct.; *Council of Civil Service Unions v Minister for the Civil Service* [1985] A.C. 374 HL.

[91] *Mohit v The Director of Public Prosecutions of Mauritius* [2006] UKPC 20; [2006] 1 W.L.R. 3343 at [14] (Lord Bingham). In July 2007, the Attorney General announced that she would no longer make key prosecution decisions in individual cases except where the law or national security requires it: *The Governance of Britain: a Consultation on the Role of Attorney General* (Cm 7192).

[92] 2-040.

[93] 3-030.

[94] 3-034.

[95] 5-046.

[96] *R. (on the application of SG) v Secretary of State for Work and Pensions (Child Poverty Action Group intervening)* [2015] UKSC 16; [2015] 1 W.L.R. 1449, [256] ("Standards expressed in international treaties or conventions dealing with human rights to which the United Kingdom has subscribed must be presumed to be the product of extensive and enlightened consideration. There is no logical reason to deny to United Kingdom citizens domestic law's vindication of the rights that those conventions proclaim. If the Government commits itself to a standard of human rights protection, it seems to me entirely logical that it should be held to account in the courts as to its actual compliance with that standard").

[97] *R. (on the application of Abassi) v Secretary of State for Foreign and Commonwealth Affairs* [2002] EWCA Civ 1598; [2003] U.K.H.R.R. 76 (no enforceable duty on minister to take diplomatic action to assist British citizen detained in Guantanamo Bay the by US government without access to any tribunal or lawyer; *R. (on the application of Al Rawi) v Secretary of State for Foreign and Commonwealth Affairs (United Nations High Commissioner for Refugees intervening)* [2006] EWCA Civ 1279; [2008] Q.B. 289 (minister's refusal to make formal representations to US government on behalf of British nationals detained in Guantanamo Bay was not direct discrimination on racial

law or fundamental human rights can impact upon the legality of actions by the UK government.[98]

Procedural point

Where a claim and a defendant's acknowledgement of service reveal a dispute about court's jurisdiction, it may be convenient for court to grant permission and order the case to proceed by way of the preliminary issue as to jurisdiction.   **3-021**

Non-justiciable decisions

It is a "wholesome development"[99] that the Administrative Court deals with many matters that even in the recent past would have been regarded as inappropriate for judicial determination. The fact remains, however, that there are some issues which are inherently unsuited to adjudication. In this category of case, the court acknowledges that the litigation process and the expertise of the court are unsuited to resolving the question in hand. This constraint is most evident where the court is called on to review the exercise of a function on grounds of rationality and proportionality. We discuss non-justiciability in Chapter 1.[100] However, even if a particular issue is not ideally suited to the judicial determination of its substance, it may be amenable to the court's jurisdiction on the ground that it was insufficiently justified or has been made procedurally improperly.   **3-022**

Judicial discretion

Even if a matter falls within the supervisory jurisdiction of the Administrative Court and is justiciable, there are a number of good reasons why the court may quite   **3-023**

---

grounds or a breach of ECHR); cf. application for habeas corpus in *Rahmatullah v Secretary of State for Defence* [2012] UKSC 48; [2012] 3 W.L.R. 1087 (issue of writ of habeas corpus in respect of Pakistani national captured by British armed forces in Afghanistan and handed over to US forces would not transgress or modify principle that the courts should not make decisions affecting foreign policy); *R. (on the application of Khan) v Secretary of State for Foreign and Commonwealth Affairs* [2014] EWCA Civ 24; [2014] 1 W.L.R. 872 (refusal of permission to seek judicial review of the alleged provision of intelligence by GCHQ officers to the United States for use in drone strikes in Pakistan. The claims involved serious criticism of the acts of a foreign state and there were no exceptional circumstances to justify the court sitting in judgment on those acts); *R. (on the application of Sandiford) v Secretary of State for Foreign and Commonwealth Affairs* [2014] UKSC 44; [2014] 1 W.L.R. 2697 (the government's blanket policy of refusing to provide funding for legal representation of British nationals facing criminal proceedings abroad was lawful. There was no necessary implication that a blanket policy was inappropriate, or that there must always be room for exceptions, when a policy was formulated for the exercise of a prerogative and not a statutory power. However, the Secretary of State should review the blanket policy in the light of information that the Indonesian proceedings appeared to raise the most serious issues as to the functioning of the local judicial system). In *Belhaj v Straw* [2013] EWHC 4111 (QB) the High Court struck out claims for damages and declarations of illegality relating to alleged unlawful rendition from Bangkok to Libya by agents of the US in which the defendants had allegedly participated by providing intelligence.

[98] *Othman v Secretary of State for the Home Department* [2013] EWCA Civ 277 (the defendant, also known as Abu Qatada—a Jordanian national resident in the United Kingdom—could not be deported to Jordan to stand trial on terrorism charges as there was a real risk that evidence previously obtained by torture would be admitted at his trial. He was eventually deported to Jordan on 7 July 2013, after the United Kingdom and Jordanian governments agreed and ratified a treaty satisfying the requirement that evidence obtained through torture would not be used against him).

[99] *R. (on the application of the Howard League for Penal Reform) v Secretary of State for the Home Department (No.2)* [2002] EWHC 2497 (Admin); [2003] 1 F.L.R. 484 at [140] (Munby J: challenge to the legality of the Secretary of State's policy guidance on the treatment of children under 18 years of age held in young offender institutions).

[100] 1-032.

properly exercise its discretion to refuse to consider a claim for judicial review.[101] Ideally this is a decision that ought to be made at the permission stage of the claim procedure.[102] Perhaps the most common reason for declining to hear a claim— usually at the point of the application for permission[103]—is that there is another more appropriate court procedure[104] or the claimant has a satisfactory alternative remedy outside the court system (for example an appeal to a tribunal[105] or a complaint to an ombudsman[106]). Discretion may also be exercised to refuse to determine a case whether the claim is filed outside the time requirement of "promptly and in any event within 3 months".[107] Discretion is also important at the point when the court considers what if any remedial order to make.[108]

NO DECISION OR DECISIONS WITHOUT LEGAL EFFECT

3-024   In some cases it has been suggested that the court should not consider a claim for judicial review because the public authority has not actually taken any decision amenable to review.[109]

Informal action

3-025   First, there are situations where a public authority seeks to deal with a problem by informal action outside the expected statutory procedures[110] or in the absence of any statutory regime.[111] It is submitted that where a public authority takes such action to further its public functions this should, in principle, be reviewable.[112] Moreover, since the HRA, it should be clear that where action interferes with a qualified Convention right (such as ECHR art.8 on respect for family life), such action needs to be taken "in accordance with law".[113]

Decisions without direct legal effect

3-026   Judicial review is generally "concerned with actions or other events which have, or will have, substantive legal consequences: for example, by conferring new legal

---

[101] On the difference between discretion *and judgment*, see F. Bennion, "Distinguishing judgment and discretion" [2000] P.L. 368 ("What then is the difference, in summary? With judgment the requirement is to assess and pronounce upon a factual or legal question; with discretion it is to determine how to exercise a power of choice. Broadly, discretion is subjective while judgment is objective. Discretion is free, except for limitations placed upon it by the defining formula. Judgment is necessarily restricted, because its purpose is to arrive at a conclusion which registers reality. Discretion necessarily offers choice; judgment registers the functionary's assessment of a situation offering no choice. Discretion analytically presents a variety of possibilities; judgment but one. Discretion offers looseness of outcome and scope for variation; judgment does not").

[102] See 16-044.

[103] See 16-044.

[104] See 16-018.

[105] See 1-091 and 17-004.

[106] See 1-071.

[107] See 16-053.

[108] See 18-048.

[109] On binding effects of policy, see Ch.12.

[110] See, e.g. *R. v Devon CC Ex p. L* [1991] 2 F.L.R. 541; *R v Harrow LBC Ex p. D* [1990] Fam. 133; *R. v Norfolk CC Ex p. M* [1989] Q.B. 619 (all dealing with child protection).

[111] Ch.5.

[112] See, e.g. *R. v Liverpool CC Ex p. Baby Products Association* (2000) 2 L.G.L.R. 689 (issue of press release following investigation into safety of a product held to be reviewable).

[113] See 13-023.

rights or powers, or by restricting existing legal rights or interests".[114] In some cases, the court has been invited to decline exercise its powers of review because the public authority's action is characterised as being without legal effect. The courts now take a broad view and it is no longer necessary for a claimant to demonstrate that a decision or action has direct legal consequences upon the claimant. Thus, the courts have reviewed: statements contained a press release[115]; policy guidance issued by public authorities[116]; and statements of national policy on airports by a minister to Parliament, though their "high-level" character and preliminary nature of the decision limited the scope of review.[117] However, when a favourable decision has not been communicated to the affected party it may (depending on the context or legislative scheme) be revocable.[118] Similarly, where an adverse decision has not been communicated to the affected party, constitutional principle may require that no action may be taken in reliance on that decision, for the reason that the claimant would not have had the opportunity to challenge the decision in the courts or elsewhere.[119]

Chains of decisions

A series of decisions may be made on the way to reaching a final substantive decision; the question may arise as to which of them is amenable to review.   **3-027**

Thus, a preparatory step on the way to making a formal, legally binding decision may not be reviewable.[120] Another situation is where there is a decision to make a particular decision—for example, a local authority may pass a resolution to grant planning permission subject to fulfilment of certain conditions (the formal grant taking place some time later) or the government may decide that it will introduce a bill to Parliament to give effect to a policy when there is an opportunity to do so in the legislative timetable. Here, "the immediate challenge may be directed at decisions   **3-028**

---

[114] *R. (on the application of Shrewsbury and Atcham BC) v Secretary of State for Communities and Local Government* [2008] EWCA Civ 148; [2008] 3 All E.R. 548, [32] (Carnwath LJ).

[115] *Baby Products* (2000) 2 L.G.L.R.; *R. v Secretary of State for Trade and Industry Ex p. Greenpeace Ltd (No.1)* [1998] Eu. L.R. 48.

[116] See, e.g. *R. (on the application of Burke) v General Medical Council* [2005] EWCA Civ 1003; [2006] Q.B. 273 (review of guidance on withdrawal of artificial feeding, though noting that the "court should not be used as a general advice centre" [21]); *R. (on the application of Axon) v Secretary of State for Health* [2006] EWHC 37 (Admin); [2006] Q.B. 539 (review of guidance entitled "Guidance for Doctors and other Health Professionals on the Provision of Advice and Treatment to Young People under 16 on Contraception, Sexual and Reproductive Health"); *R. (on the application of BAPIO Action Ltd) v Secretary of State for the Home Department* [2008] UKHL 27; [2008] 1 A.C. 1003 (ministerial guidance issued to employing bodies in the NHS on recruitment of international medical graduates was unlawful); *R. (on the application of A) v Secretary of State for Health* [2009] EWCA Civ 225; (2009) 12 C.C.L. Rep. 213 (NHS guidance on how NHS trusts should exercise discretion to grant or withhold treatment to failed asylum seekers was unlawful for lack of clarity); *R. (on the application of Equality and Human Rights Commission) v Prime Minister and others* [2011] EWHC 2401 (Admin); [2012] 1 W.L.R. 1389 (guidance for intelligence officers and service personnel on detention and interviewing of detainees overseas); cf. *R. (on the application of United Cooperatives Ltd) v Manchester City Council* [2005] EWHC 364 at [21] (Elias J noting that. "the courts are in principle reluctant to permit mere advice to be the subject of review").

[117] *R. (on the application of Hillingdon LBC) v Secretary of State for Transport* [2010] EWHC 626 (Admin); [2010] A.C.D. 64 at [65]–[69].

[118] *Re 56 Denton Road* [1953] Ch. 51; *Rootkin v Kent CC* [1981] 1 W.L.R. 1186. On the ground that the decision-maker is not functus officio.

[119] *R. (on the application of Anufrijeva) v Secretary of State for the Home Department* [2003] UKHL 36; [2004] 1 A.C. 604. See 11-061.

[120] cf. *R. (on the application of The Garden and Leisure Group Ltd) v North Somerset Council* [2003] EWHC 1605; [2004] 1 P. & C.R. 39 (review permitted of resolution by local authority committee that planning permission should in principle be formally granted if certain conditions were met).

or actions which are no more than steps on the way to the substantive event" but the court may take the view that decisions preparatory a substantive decision are overtaken by the final decision.[121]

3-029 A decision may be part of a two-tier process, so that an initial determination is superseded by a later one, with the effect that the first decision may no longer be challenged[122]; what purports to be a second decision may in reality be only a confirmation of an initial decision and so not itself reviewable[123]; or the legislative framework may make it unnecessary for a decision-maker to wait for an inspector's report before taking a decision.[124] There is also the question whether a decision not to alter an earlier administrative decision is itself a reviewable decision. There is "no formulaic or straightforward answer", and each case must to an extent turn on its own particular facts.[125] If there has been no significant change of circumstances since the original decision, especially if the court views the request to the public authority to reconsider its earlier decision as a ploy to circumvent the time limit for commencing a judicial review claim,[126] the court is likely to decline to hear the matter.

AMENABILITY TESTS BASED ON THE SOURCE OF POWER

3-030 The courts have adopted two complementary approaches to determining whether a function falls within the ambit of the supervisory jurisdiction. First, the court considers the legal source of power exercised by the impugned decision-maker. In identifying the "classes of case in which judicial review is available",[127] the courts place considerable importance on the source of legal authority exercised by the defendant public authority. Secondly and additionally, where the "source of power" approach does not yield a clear or satisfactory outcome, the court may consider the characteristics of the function being performed. This has enabled the courts to extend the reach of the supervisory jurisdiction to some activities of non-statutory bodies (such as self-regulatory organisations). We begin by looking at the first approach, based on the source of power.

Statutory powers

3-031 The court now operates on the assumption that "If the source of power is a statute, or subordinate legislation under a statute, then clearly the body in question

---

[121] *R. (on the application of Shrewsbury and Atcham BC) v Secretary of State for Communities and Local Government* [2008] EWCA Civ 148; [2008] 3 All E.R. 548 at [33] Carnwath LJ (alleged flaws in non-statutory consultation process overtaken by enactment of Local Government and Public Involvement in Health Act 2007, which put the minister's decision on a statutory footing).

[122] *R. v Secretary of State for Education Ex p. B (A Child)* [2001] E.L.R. 333.

[123] See, e.g. *R. v Secretary of State for the Home Department Ex p. Kaygusuz (Ibrahim)* [1991] Imm. A.R. 300.

[124] See *R. (Cruelty Free International) v Secretary of State for the Home Department* [2015] EWHC 3631 (Admin); [2016] P.T.S.R. 431 (claimant unsuccessfully argued that it was necessary under the Animals (Scientific Procedures) Act 1986 for the Minister to wait for final report from Home Office's Animals in Science Regulation Unit before imposing sanctions on license holder).

[125] *R. (on the application of Lambeth LBC) v Secretary of State for Work and Pensions* [2005] EWHC 637 (Admin); [2005] B.L.G.R. 764 at [38] (fresh facts may justify the court intervening; but "A subsequent change of English law or a change of the policy of our government that is not retrospective to the earlier decision will not, in general, justify treating a refusal to alter a previously undisputed decision as a new decision").

[126] See 16-053.

[127] See 3-016.

will be subject to judicial review".[128] There must be some "compelling reason to infer that such a presumption is excluded".[129] In the large proportion of claims commenced, there is no doubt that the decision in question is susceptible to review because the source of power exercised is statutory.

Decisions of bodies deriving their power from Private Acts of Parliament (that is, legislation promoted through special procedure by organisations to obtain powers in excess or in conflict with the general law) are not, however, for this reason alone, subject to judicial review. Thus, Lloyd's of London and Cambridge University, both institutions established by Private Act of Parliament, are not for that reason alone susceptible to judicial review[130]; a particular public function must also be identified. If, however, they perform public functions those functions will be reviewable. This approach accords with one of the roles of judicial review, which is to ensure decisions are taken lawfully. When applied here this means in accordance with the statutory power and purpose.   **3-032**

Prerogative powers

Nature of prerogative powers

The courts recognise that the Crown (a term we consider shortly) possesses common law powers and immunities. There is no consensus about the overarching definition of prerogative powers. Some commentators take the view that only those governmental powers which are unique to the Crown should be called prerogative,[131] whereas others adopt a more all-encompassing definition and include all the non-statutory powers of the Crown.[132] A practical example of the difference is that the action of making ex gratia payments falls within the latter but not the former definition of prerogative powers, because it is open to any citizen to make donations of money. Prerogative powers are residual powers; new ones cannot be created,[133] and they "remain in existence to the extent that Parliament has not expressly or by implication extinguished them".[134]   **3-033**

Despite uncertainty about the definition of prerogative powers, as a prelude to   **3-034**

---

[128] R. v Panel on Take-overs and Mergers Ex p. Datafin Plc [1987] Q.B. 815 at 847 (Lloyd LJ).

[129] Mohit v The Director of Public Prosecutions of Mauritius [2006] UKPC 20 at [20] (Lord Bingham).

[130] See, e.g. R. v University of Cambridge Ex p. Evans (No.2) [1999] Ed. C.R. 556; R. (on the application of West) v Lloyd's of London [2004] EWCA Civ 506; [2004] 3 All E.R. 251.

[131] See, e.g. H.W.R. Wade and C. Forsyth, Administrative Law, 9th edn (2004), p.216 ("'Prerogative' power is, properly speaking, legal power that appertains to the Crown but not to its subjects"), drawing on Blackstone (Bl.Comm. 1.239). Wade stressed the requirement for there to be legal power to alter people's rights, duties and status and, thus, he did not regard the issue of passports as based on prerogative power (Constitutional Fundamentals (1980), p.46). See R. (on the application of Heath) v Home Office Policy and Advisory Board for Forensic Pathology [2005] EWHC 1793 (Admin) at [25] (Newman J drawing a distinction between prerogative power and "executive power" as the basis for setting up the Board).

[132] A. Dicey, Introduction to the Study of the Law of the Constitution, 8th edn (1915), p.421 ("The prerogative is the name for the remaining portion of the Crown's original authority, and is therefore, as already pointed out, the name for the residue of discretionary power left at any moment in the hands of the Crown, whether such power be in fact exercised by the King himself or by his ministers.") This definition was quoted with approval in Attorney General v de Keyser's Royal Hotel Ltd [1920] A.C. 508 at 526, and by Lord Fraser in Council of Civil Service Unions v Minister for the Civil Service [1985] A.C. 374. On non-statutory powers and the Ram doctrine, see 5-022.

[133] British Broadcasting Corp v Johns [1965] Ch. 32 (Diplock LJ: it was "three hundred and fifty years and a civil war too late for the Queen's courts to broaden the prerogative" in respect of the Crown's right to a monopoly).

[134] R. v Secretary of State for the Home Department Ex p. Fire Brigades Union [1995] 2 A.C. 513 at 552 (Lord Browne-Wilkinson).

reforms, in 2009 the Government published the findings of a survey of departments' views as to the prerogative powers possessed by ministers.[135]

(i)   Under the heading 'Government and the Civil Service', prerogative powers included: powers concerning the machinery of government including the power to set up a department or a non-departmental public body;
and a range of powers concerning the civil service, including the power
to appoint and regulate most civil servants (subsequently placed on a
statutory footing by the Constitutional Reform and Governance Act 2010
Pt 1).

(ii)   In relation to the justice system and law and order, prerogative powers
include: appointment of Queen's Counsel; power to make provisional and
full order extradition requests to countries not covered by the Extradition Act 2003 Pt 1; the prerogative power mercy; and power to keep the
peace.

(iii)   In relation to foreign affairs, prerogative powers include: power to send
ambassadors abroad and receive and accredit ambassadors from foreign
states; recognition of states; governance of British Overseas Territories;
making and ratifying treaties; the conduct of diplomacy; acquisition and
cession of territory; the issue, refusal and withdrawal of passports;
responsibility for the Crown Dependencies of Jersey, Guernsey and the
Isle of Man; and the grant of diplomatic protection to British citizens
abroad.

(iv)   Powers relating to armed forces, war and times of emergency include: the
right to make war or peace or institute hostilities falling short of war; the
deployment and use of armed forces overseas; maintenance of the Royal
Navy; use of armed forces within the United Kingdom to maintain peace
in support of the policy or civilian authorities; government and command of armed forces is vested in Her Majesty; control, organisation and
disposition of armed forces; requisition of British ships in times of urgent
national necessity; commissioning of officers in all three armed forces;
armed forces pay; the Crown's right to claim Prize (enemy ships or goods
captured at sea); the Crown's right of angary, in times of war, to appropriate the property of a neutral which is within the realm; powers in the
event of grave national emergency, such as entering, taking and destroying private property.

(v)   Personal prerogatives exercised directly by the monarch include: appointment and removal of ministers; appointment of the prime minister;
dismissal of government; the power to summon, prorogue and dissolve
Parliament (subsequently regulated by the Fixed-term Parliament Acts
2011)[136]; royal assent to bills; appointment of privy counsellors; grant-

---

[135] Ministry of Justice, *The Governance of Britain: Review of the Executive Royal Prerogative Powers:
Final Report* (Ministry of Justice 2009), Annex.

[136] The future of the Fixed-term Parliaments Act 2011 is at present uncertain. In the General Election
which took place on 9 June 2017, the Conservative Party manifesto committed to repealing the Act.
The impact of repeal of the statute upon the prerogative power which it superseded is a matter of
some debate: see, for example R. Craig, *'Zombie Prerogatives Should Remain Decently Buried:
Replacing the Fixed-term Parliaments Act 2011 (Part 1)'*, U.K. Const. L. Blog (24 May 2017) (available at *https://www.ukconstitutionallaw.org* [Accessed 26 October 2017]); R. Craig, *'Zombie Prerogatives Should Remain Decently Buried: Replacing the Fixed-term Parliaments Act 2011 (Part 2)'*,
U.K. Const. L. Blog (25th May 2017) (available at *https://www.ukconstitutionallaw.org/* [Accessed
26 October 2017])).

ing of honours, decorations, arms and regulating matters of precedence; a residual power to appoint judges to non-statutory public offices; a power to legislate by Order in Council or letters patent for British Overseas Territories; the grant of leave of appeal from certain non-UK courts to the Judicial Committee of the Privy Council; requiring personal services of subjects in case of imminent danger; grant of civil honours and civil dignities; approval for certain uses of Royal names and titles.

(vi)   The Attorney General has functions under prerogative powers: relating to charities; relating to criminal proceedings, including the power to enter a *nolle presequi*; and in relation to civil proceedings to protect a public right where a person would otherwise lack standing (relator proceedings).[137]

(vii)   Various prerogative powers described as "archaic" and "unclear" were listed.

(viii)   A final category were "privileges and immunities" (rather than powers) possessed by the monarch "as an embodiment of the Crown", including: the Crown is not bound by statute save by express words or necessary implication; Crown immunities in litigation "including that the Crown is not directly subject to the contempt jurisdiction[138] and the Sovereign has personal immunity from prosecution or being sued for a wrongful act; tax is not payable on income received by the Sovereign; the Crown is a preferred creditor in a debtor's insolvency; time does not run against the Crown; and the Crown has priority of property rights in certain circumstances.

In recent years, several reforms to prerogative powers have been introduced.[139]   **3-035**
The management of the civil service is now on a statutory footing after the enactment of the Constitutional Reform and Governance Act 2010 Pt 1. While the ratification of treaties remains a prerogative power, Pt 2 of the 2010 Act creates a statutory framework for parliamentary scrutiny of treaties. The Crown is now prohibited from dissolving the UK Parliament except in accordance with the Fixed-term Parliaments Act 2011.

Many exercises of prerogative powers are also regulated by constitutional   **3-036**
conventions (rules of political behaviour which are regarded as binding by those to whom they apply) and new conventions continue to emerge to accommodate new or changing political times. Under the royal prerogative, the Prime Minister has power to order the deployment of the armed forces overseas. However, it became a political practice to open up such decisions to Parliamentary debate. In February 2006, Tony Blair sought the approval of the House of Commons before authorising military intervention in Iraq. In September 2013, David Cameron sought the approval of the House of Common before deciding on military intervention in Syria.

---

[137] On standing in judicial review and other public law proceedings, see Ch.2. The liberalisation of standing for judicial review has lessened the need for litigants to bring relator proceedings.

[138] Ministers, on the other hand, are subject to contempt proceedings: see *M v Home Office* [1994] 1 A.C. 377.

[139] See *The Governance of Britain* Green Paper (Cm 7170) and *The Governance of Britain—War Powers and Treaties: Limiting Executive Powers* (CP 26/07). The Government's reform initiatives followed several years of calls for reform, e.g. by the House of Commons Public Administration Committee, *Taming the Prerogative: Strengthening Ministerial Accountability to Parliament*. HC Paper No.422; (Session 2003/04) *A Matter of Honour: Reforming the Honours System*, HC Paper No.212-I (Session 2003/04); *A Draft Civil Service Bill: Completing the Reform*. HC Paper No.128-I (Session 2003/04); *Hansard*, HL (3 March 2006): 2nd reading debate of Lord Lester's Constitutional Reform (Prerogative Powers and Civil Service etc.) Bill.

When the Commons did not vote in favour, Cameron declined to intervene militarily. In 2008 Gordon Brown's government had suggested that Parliament's role should be formalised in a resolution to be passed by the House of Commons, but that proposal was not implemented. In July 2013, the House of Lords Constitution Committee stated that there was now an "existing convention – that, save in exceptional circumstances, the House of Commons is given the opportunity to debate and vote on the deployment of armed forces overseas".[140]

3-037
It has long been clear that "the King hath no prerogative, but that which the law of the land allows him"[141]; the existence of a prerogative power is ultimately a question for the determination of the courts, not mere assertion by government.[142] Prerogative and statutory powers may both govern a field,[143] though where there is conflict statute prevails. There have been suggestions that the scope of a prerogative power cannot be extended by the representations of a public authority in ways which might, in other contexts, have created a legitimate expectation.[144]

3-038
Until the mid-1970s, the courts took the view that the exercise of prerogative powers fell outside the court's supervisory jurisdiction, except in the narrowest senses of determining whether a prerogative power existed, and if so, its extent, whether it was being exercised in the appropriate form and as to how far it has been superseded by statute.[145] The courts were not normally prepared to examine the appropriateness or adequacy of the grounds for exercising the power,[146] or the fairness of the procedure followed before the power was exercised,[147] and they would not allow bad faith to be attributed to the Crown.[148] The unwillingness of the courts to review prerogative powers could be explained partly on the basis of the close

---

[140] House of Lords Constitution Committee, *Constitutional Arrangements for the Use of Armed Force*, Second Report of 2013–2014, HL Paper 46, para.64.

[141] *Case of Proclamations* (1611) 12 Co. Rep. 74 at 76 (Sir Edward Coke).

[142] For recent illustration see *R. (Miller) v Secretary of State for Exiting the European Union* [2017] UKSC 5; [2017] 2 W.L.R. 583, in which the Supreme Court held that the Secretary of State's prerogative power to withdraw from a treaty (namely the Treaty on European Union) had been precluded by the European Communities Act 1972.

[143] For example, the Immigration Act 1971 s.33(5) expressly preserves prerogative powers relating to immigration control of aliens.

[144] *R. v Criminal Injuries Compensation Board Ex p. M (A Minor)* [1998] P.I.Q.R. P107; [1998] C.O.D. 128.

[145] See, e.g. *Willion v Berkley* (1561) Plow. 223; *Case of Monopolies* (1602) 11 Co.Rep. 84b; *Prohibitions del Roy* (1607) 12 Co.Rep. 63; *Case of Proclamations* (1611) 12 Co.Rep. 74; *Burmah Oil Co v Lord Advocate* [1965] A.C. 75; *Attorney General v De Keyser's Royal Hotel Ltd* [1920] A.C. 508; *Walwin (LE) and Partners Ltd v West Sussex CC* [1975] 3 All E.R. 604; *Laker Airways Ltd v Department of Trade* [1977] Q.B. 643.

[146] See, e.g. *R. v Allen* (1862) 1 B. & S. 850 (*nolle prosequi*); *Musgrove v Chun Teeong Toy* [1918] A.C. 272 (exclusion of alien); *Bugsier Reederei-und-Bergungs A/G v SS Brighton* [1951] 2 T.L.R. 409 (licence granted to enemy company to sue in British court); *Chandler v DPP* [1964] A.C. 763 at 790–792, 796, 800–801, 814 (disposition of forces); *Hanratty v Lord Butler of Saffron Walden* (1971) 115 S.J. 386 and *de Freitas v Benn y* [1976] A.C. 239 (prerogative of mercy); *Jenkins v Attorney General* (1971) 115 S.J. 674 (dissemination of official information); *Blackburn v Attorney General* [1971] 1 W.L.R. 1037 (treaty-making power); *Secretary of State for the Home Department v Lakdawalla* [1972] Imm. A.R. 26 (issue of passport). Lord Denning MR in *Laker Airways* [1997] Q.B. 643 at 705–707 anticipated a change in the law by assimilating a review in which the review of the prerogative with that of statutory power, so that its exercise may be impugned for "misdirection in fact or in law". The majority, however, proceeded on a narrower basis, concluding that the Civil Aviation Act 1971 had impliedly superseded the Crown's prerogative in foreign affairs, and that the holder of a licence under the statute could not be deprived of its commercial value by a decision on the part of the Secretary of State to revoke the licensee's status as a designated carrier under the Bermuda Agreement. In other respects the majority accepted the orthodox position on the unreviewability of the exercise of the prerogative: at 718 (Roskill LJ) and, it appears, at 727–728 (Lawton LJ).

[147] *de Freitas v Benny* [1976] A.C. 239 at 247–248.

[148] *Duncan v Theodore* (1917) 23 C.L.R. 510 at 544; *Australian Communist Party v Commonwealth*

relationship those powers were regarded as having with the monarch personally, the Crown being the source of the powers, and partly because the courts regarded prerogative powers as being those common law powers of the Crown which had no statutory source. In addition, there are some prerogative powers which were considered within the appropriate constitutional realm of the executive, or which required unrestricted discretion for their effective exercise (such as the power to declare war).

Shift from jurisdiction to justiciability to set limits on court's powers to supervise legality of prerogative powers

In the *GCHQ* case,[149] a decision of great constitutional importance, the majority of the House of Lords were of the opinion that it was no longer constitutionally appropriate to deny the court supervisory jurisdiction over a governmental decision merely because the legal authority for that decision rested on prerogative rather than statutory powers.[150] The courts' intervention should be governed by whether or not, in the particular case, the subject-matter of the prerogative power was justiciable.[151] Lord Roskill tentatively listed examples of non-justiciable decisions those "such as those relating to the making of treaties, the defence of the realm, the prerogative of mercy, the grant of honours, the dissolution of Parliament and the appointment of Ministers".[152]

3-039

It has been suggested judicially that a number of Lord Roskill's examples "could today be regarded as questionable: the grant of honours for reward, the waging of a war of manifest aggression or a refusal to dissolve Parliament[153] at all might well call in question an immunity based purely on subject-matter".[154] In the ensuing years, some of the fields mentioned by Lord Roskill have upon further analysis come to be regarded as potentially justiciable. The question "is simply whether the nature and subject matter of the decision is amenable to the judicial process. Are the courts qualified to deal with the matter or does the decision involve such questions of policy that they should not intrude because they are ill-equipped to do so?"[155] The general concept of justiciability is examined elsewhere[156]; here we can simply set out those prerogative powers which have been regarded as susceptible

3-040

(1951) 83 C.L.R. 1 at 257–258.

[149] *Council of Civil Service Unions v Minister for the Civil Service* [1985] A.C. 374. The case concerned the decision of the Minister for the Civil Service (a post held by the Prime Minister, at the time Mrs Thatcher) to give instructions to affect the terms and conditions of Civil Servants at GCHQ, the government agency responsible for signals intelligence, so as to exclude them from membership of any trade union other than a department staff association approved by the Director of GCHQ; it was held that the unions had a legitimate expectation of being consulted but that whether national security considerations outweighed the need for fair procedures was a matter for the executive rather than the courts. See further L. Blom-Cooper and R. Drabble, "GCHQ Revisited" [2010] P.L. 18 and A. Le Sueur and M. Sunkin, *Public Law* (1997) Chs 17, 28.

[150] Lords Scarman, Diplock and Roskill. The minority (Lords Fraser and Brightman) preferred to leave open the question as to whether prerogative powers were reviewable until it had to be determined.

[151] Lord Scarman, at 407 ("The controlling factor in determining whether the exercise of prerogative power is subjected to judicial review is not its source but its subject matter.").

[152] At 418.

[153] The prerogative power of dissolution of Parliament prior to a general election has been overtaken by the Fixed Term Parliaments Act 2011, though the future of the Act is uncertain: see para.3-030

[154] *R. (on the application of Bancoult) v Secretary of State for Foreign and Commonwealth Affairs* [2007] EWCA Civ 498; [2008] Q.B. 365 at [46] (Sedley LJ).

[155] *R. v Secretary of State for the Home Department Ex p. Bentley* [1994] Q.B. 349 at 453 (Watkins LJ) An example was given: "If... it was clear that the Home Secretary had refused to pardon someone solely on the grounds of their sex, race or religion, the courts would be expected to interfere and, in our judgment, would be entitled to do so".

to judicial review: civil servants' conditions of service[157]; ex gratia payments to victims of crime[158]; ex gratia payments to a person convicted and imprisoned and then subsequently acquitted on appeal[159]; the power to issue and withdraw passports[160]; excluding a person from the United Kingdom[161]; inclusion of a person on the United Nations Security Council's list of persons associated with terrorist organisations and the European Union's sanctions list[162]; the issue of a warrant to intercept telephone communications signed by the Secretary of State for the Home Department[163]; the prerogative of mercy[164]; the duty of the Foreign and Commonwealth Office to render diplomatic assistance to a British citizen abroad in respect of miscarriage or denial of justice[165]; the form of declaration to be made

---

[156] See 1-032.

[157] *Council of Civil Service Unions v Minister for the Civil Service* [1985] A.C. 374; see 3-036 below for discussion of review relating to employment.

[158] *R. v Criminal Injuries Compensation Board Ex p. Lain* [1967] 2 Q.B. 864 (pre-dating the landmark ruling in the *CCSU* case); *R. v Secretary of State for the Home Department Ex p. Fire Brigades Union* [1995] 2 A.C. 513. In Great Britain the scheme now operates on a statutory basis under the Criminal Injuries Compensation Act 1995.

[159] See, e.g. *R. v Secretary of State for the Home Department Ex p. Harrison* [1988] 3 All E.R. 86; *Re McFarland* [2004] UKHL 17; [2004] 1 W.L.R. 1289.

[160] *R. v Secretary of State for Foreign and Commonwealth Affairs Ex p. Everett* [1989] Q.B. 811 (Taylor LJ distinguished those acts at "the top of the scale of executive functions under the prerogative" involving "high policy", which were not justiciable, from "administrative decisions, affecting the rights of individuals and their freedom of travel", which are justiciable); *R. (on the application of Rahman) v Secretary of State for the Home Department* [2015] EWHC 1146 (Admin) (refusal to renew the claimant's passport was quashed as irrational given the findings of an Immigration Appeal Tribunal that his late father had been a British citizen).

[161] *R. (on the application of GI) v Secretary of State for the Home Department* [2011] EWHC 1879 (Admin); [2012] 1 W.L.R. 2568.

[162] *R. (on the application of Youssef) v Secretary of State for Foreign and Commonwealth Affairs* [2013] EWCA Civ 1302; [2014] Q.B. 728.

[163] *R. v Secretary of State for the Home Department Ex p. Ruddock* [1987] 1 W.L.R. 1482. The power was subsequently governed by the Interception of Communications Act 1985 and now the Regulation of Investigatory Powers Act 2000.

[164] *R. v Secretary of State for the Home Department Ex p. Bentley* [1994] Q.B. 349 (Home Secretary's failure to consider the grant of a posthumous pardon when the previous Home Secretary's decision had been wrong was held to be a clear error of law). *R. (on the application of Shields) v Secretary of State for Justice* [2008] EWHC 3102 (Admin); [2010] Q.B. 150 (point of law was whether Convention on the Transfer of Sentenced Persons 1983, art.13 prevented minister granting a free pardon—it did not; Mr Shields, convicted of attempted murder in Bulgaria, was subsequently pardoned). In an answer to a Written Question, the Secretary of State for Northern Ireland revealed that the Royal Prerogative of Mercy had been used "in Northern Ireland 365 times between 1979 and 2002, but this total does not include the period between 1987 and 1997 for which records cannot currently be found" and "There are no cases where the RPM has been granted since the current Government came to office in May 2010, and the records indicate that there are no instances where the RPM was granted after 2002" (HC Deb, 1 May 2014, c762W). It was not clear how many of those pardoned were members of paramilitary groups or members of the security services, but the Northern Ireland Office said that the vast majority were not terrorism-related and examples of use "included driving offences, assault, burglary, theft and non-payment of national insurance contributions" (BBC News, "*Royal Prerogative of Mercy: Over 350 issued in Northern Ireland*", 2 May 2014 (available at *http://www.bbc.co.uk/news/uk-northern-ireland–27260596*)). The NIO also highlighted that the prerogative of mercy had been used much more frequently before the establishment of the Criminal Cases Review Commission in 1997. In December 2013 the wartime code breaker, Alan Turing, was granted a posthumous pardon by the Queen at the request of the Secretary of State for Justice (Chris Grayling MP). Turing had been convicted of an offence of gross indecency in 1952 for engaging in homosexual activity and had been chemically castrated (Ministry of Justice, "*Press Release: Royal Pardon for WW2 code-breaker Dr Alan Turing*", 24 December 2013 (available at *https://www.gov.uk/government/news/royal-pardon-for-ww2-code-breaker-dr-alan-turing*)).

[165] *R. (on the application of Abassi) v Secretary of State for Foreign and Commonwealth Affairs* [2002] EWCA Civ 1470; [2003] 1 W.L.R. 741 at [106]. This duty does not extend to the provision of fund-

upon appointment as Queen's Counsel[166]; and an Order of Council (primary legislation made under the prerogative) in relation to a British Overseas Territory.[167] In Scotland, it has doubted whether the "achievement" of arms on payment of a fee can truly be viewed as the conferment of any "honour" in the sense meant by Lord Roskill in *GCHQ*.[168]

Prerogative powers in respect of which the court may not have supervisory jurisdiction

Despite the general shift away from jurisdiction to justiciability marked by the **3-041** *GCHQ* case, there may still be some areas where the supervisory jurisdiction of the court will still not run.[169] First, some prerogative powers are exercised in the sphere of international relations and the courts of England and Wales do not consider questions of pure international law as these are not, for the purposes of the national legal system, "law" at all.[170] Secondly, the prerogative power of Royal Assent to legislation may fall outside the court's jurisdiction as being concerned with the processes of Parliament.[171]

Thirdly, in some circumstances the court may lack jurisdiction because the **3-042** prerogative power in question has been exercised directly by the Sovereign (rather than by ministers) and as a matter of general constitutional principle, the Sovereign cannot be subject to legal process.[172] These powers, called "personal" or "direct" prerogatives, "can be exercised legally by the person of the monarch him or

---

ing for legal representation of British nationals facing criminal proceedings abroad. *R. (on the application of Sandiford) v Secretary of State for Foreign and Commonwealth Affairs* [2014] UKSC 44; [2014] 1 W.L.R. 2697.

[166] *Re Treacy's Application for Judicial Review* [2000] N.I. 330.

[167] *R. (on the application of Bancoult) v Secretary of State for Foreign and Commonwealth Affairs (No.2)* [2008] UKHL 61; [2009] 1 A.C. 453 affirmed that prerogative legislation (even though classified as primary legislation) was subject to review on ordinary principles of legality, rationality and procedural impropriety in the same way as any other executive action. See further M. Richard, "Judicial Review of Prerogative Orders in Council" (2009) 68(1) C.L.J. 14; M. Cohn, "Judicial Review of Non-Statutory Executive Powers after Bancoult: a Unified Anxious Model" [2009] P.L.260; M. Elliott and A. Perreau-Saussine, "Pyrrhic public law: Bancoult and the sources, status and content of common law limitations on prerogative power" [2009] P.L. 697.

[168] *Kerr of Ardgowan v Lord Lyon King Of Arms* [2009] CSIH 61; 2010 S.C. 1.

[169] Or, if the courts do have jurisdiction, they defer to the authority of those exercising the powers of the Crown. If the exercise of a prerogative power were to offend human rights or was clearly irrational, the courts would find it difficult not to intervene.

[170] See, e.g. in relation to treaty-making *R. v Secretary of State for Foreign and Commonwealth Affairs Ex p. Rees-Mogg* [1994] Q.B. 552 (no jurisdiction to consider ratification of Title V of the Treaty on European Union which established a common foreign and security policy and involved no question of domestic law); *Ex p. Molyneaux* [1986] 1 W.L.R. 331 (Anglo-Irish Agreement was akin to a treaty); cf. *R. v HM Treasury Ex p. Smedley* [1985] Q.B. 657 (review of draft Order in Council, domestic delegated legislation, that sought to bring treaty provisions into national law). The conduct of foreign policy through the United Nations is not amenable to judicial review in the domestic courts—but logically prior decisions of a Minister about an individual living in the United Kingdom was assumed not to be immune from judicial review, though it would be an area in which the courts should proceed with caution: see *R. (Youssef) v Secretary of State for Foreign and Commonwealth Affairs* [2016] UKSC 3; [2016] 2 W.L.R. 509.

[171] See 3-017. See generally A. Twomey, "The Refusal or Deferral of Royal Assent" [2006] P.L. 580; R. Blackburn, "The Royal Assent to Legislation and a Monarch's Fundamental Human Rights" [2003] P.L. 205.

[172] On the changing nature of the legal status of the Crown, see J. Jacob, *The Republican Crown: Lawyers and the Making of the State in Twentieth Century Britain* (1996); M. Sunkin and S. Payne (eds), *The Nature of the Crown* (1999); also P. Sales, "Crown Proceedings", Ch.13 in M. Supperstone, J. Goudie and P. Walker (eds), *Judicial Review*, 4th edn (2010).

herself".[173] The main examples are the appointment of the Prime Minister, the dissolution of Parliament, and the Royal Assent to legislation. The traditional constitutional justification for immunity of the Crown (as Sovereign) from public law remedies was "both because there would be an incongruity in the Queen commanding herself to do an act, and also because the disobedience to a writ of mandamus is to be enforced by attachment".[174] The Crown is, however, only the nominal claimant in claims for judicial review.[175] The provisions of the Crown Proceedings Act 1947, which permitted claims to be brought against the Crown in the more general sense of the Crown as executive government, do not apply to the Monarch personally[176]; nor do they apply to claims for judicial review or other public law proceedings on the Crown side of the Queen's Bench Division of the High Court.[177] Moreover, the principal norms regulating the exercise of these "sovereign acts" (in distinction to merely executive acts) are also more in the nature of constitutional conventions than legal principles; and conventions are, broadly speaking, not enforceable by the courts.[178]

3-043   To the extent that an area of sovereign immunity continues to exist, it causes few practical problems.[179] Whereas until 1714 (when George I acceded to the throne) it could be thought that "the King or Queen governed through Ministers, now Ministers govern through the instrumentality of the Crown".[180] Most prerogative powers are now exercised by ministers of the Crown. Here, "any amenability to judicial review in relation to the use of the royal prerogative is that of ministers, not of the Monarch in whose name they govern" and the theoretical source of executive action in the Crown does not protect it from judicial review.[181] For this reason, it is of little practical importance that neither the prerogative remedies (quashing orders, prohibiting orders and mandatory orders) nor injunctions can be obtained against the Crown directly because they will clearly issue against Ministers of the Crown. Ministers of the Crown do not share the immunity of the Crown as Sovereign.[182]

3-044   The mere fact that an institution has been incorporated by Royal Charter does not

---

[173] R. Blackburn, "Monarchy and the Personal Prerogatives" [2004] P.L. 546 at 548; R. Brazier, "'Monarchy and the Personal Prerogatives': a personal response to Professor Blackburn" [2005] P.L. 45.

[174] *R. v Powell* (1841) 1 Q.B. 352 at 361 (Lord Denman CJ) quoted with approval by Lord Woolf in *M v Home Office* [1994] 1 A.C. 377 at 415.

[175] *R. (on the application of Ben-Abdelaziz) v Haringey LBC* [2001] EWCA Civ 803; [2001] 1 W.L.R. 1485.

[176] s.40, in relation to tort claims.

[177] s.38(2). The confusion which arose as to whether the court had jurisdiction to order an interim injunction against a Minister on an application for judicial review was rectified by the HL in *M v Home Office* [1994] 1 A.C. 377.

[178] K. Keith, "The Courts and the Conventions of the Constitution" (1967) 16 I.C.L.Q. 542; J. Jaconelli, "Do Constitutional Conventions Bind?" [2004] C.L.J. 149.

[179] Note also, in relation to that statutory power, that Acts of Parliament only rarely impose public law duties or confer functions on "the Crown" (and where they do, it will normally relate to an executive act); instead it is normal for "the Secretary of State" to be given such responsibilities: *M v Home Office* [1994] 1 A.C. 377 at 417.

[180] Anson, *Law and Custom of the Constitution*, 3rd edn (1907), II.i, p.41 (cited by Sedley J. in *R. (on the application of Bancoult) v Secretary of State for Foreign and Commonwealth Affairs* [2007] EWCA Civ 498; [2008] Q.B. 365 at [32]).

[181] *R. (on the application of Bancoult) v Secretary of State for Foreign and Commonwealth Affairs* [2007] EWCA Civ 498; [2008] Q.B. 365 at [31]–[36] (Sedley LJ) (in relation to an Order in Council made under prerogative powers, which was held to be an act of the executive and as such is amenable to any appropriate form of judicial review, whether anticipatory or retrospective).

[182] *M v Home Office* [1994] 1 A.C. 377.

necessarily make its decisions susceptible to judicial review[183]; it will be necessary to show that its decision engages with a public function.

Other sources of power

Statute and the prerogative do not exhaust the possible sources of power for some office-holders in the public sphere. Powers may also be exercised pursuant to contracts, a subject examined below.[184] Ministers also claim under the so-called "Ram doctrine" to have at their disposal all the common law powers enjoyed by a corporation sole.[185] Where, however, a body is a "creature of statute", as is the case with local authorities, all powers are ultimately derived from Acts of Parliament. The existence of a "general power of competence", conferred by the Localism Act 2011 Pt 1, does not alter this.[186]

3-045

JUDICIAL REVIEW OF PUBLIC FUNCTIONS

The previous section considered susceptibility to judicial review based on the *source of the power*: statute or prerogative. The courts came to recognise that an approach based solely on the source of the public authority's power was too restrictive. Since 1987 they have developed an additional approach to determining susceptibility based on by the type of *function performed* by the decision-maker.[187] The "public function" approach is, since 2000, reflected in the Civil Procedure Rules: CPR.54.1(2)(a)(ii), defines a claim for judicial review as a claim to the lawfulness of "a decision, action or failure to act in relation to the exercise of a public function". (Similar terminology is used in the Human Rights Act 1998 s.6(3)(b) to define a public authority as "any person certain of whose functions are functions of a public nature", but detailed consideration of that provision is postponed until later).[188] As we noted at the outset,[189] the term "public" is usually a synonym for "governmental".

3-046

Bodies held to be amenable to judicial review

The public functions approach brings within the court's judicial review supervisory jurisdiction some actions of some bodies—including self-regulatory organisations, charities and business enterprises—which would otherwise fall outside public law scrutiny if only the traditional "source of power" approach were deployed. Applying a public functions test in this context, the courts have held decisions taken by the following, among others, to be susceptible to review: the Panel

3-047

---

[183] *R. v Royal Life Saving Society Ex p. Howe* [1990] C.O.D. 440; cf. *R. v Royal Pharmaceutical Society of Great Britain Ex p. Mahmood* [2001] EWCA Civ 1245; [2002] 1 W.L.R. 879.

[184] See 3-054.

[185] See 5-022.

[186] 5-100.

[187] Notably in *R. v Panel on Takeovers and Mergers Ex p. Datafin Plc* [1987] 1 Q.B. 815, CA. See further: C. Forsyth, "The Scope of Judicial Review: 'public duty' not 'source of power'" [1987] PL. 356; D. Pannick, "Who is Subject to Judicial Review and in Respect of What?" [1992] P.L. 1; N. Bamforth, "The Scope of Judicial Review: Still Uncertain" [1993] P.L. 239; N. Duxbury, "The Outer Limits of Judicial Review" [2017] P.L. 235.

[188] See 3-072.

[189] See 3-001.

on Takeovers and Mergers[190]; Advertising Standards Authority[191]; Press Complaints Commission[192]; the Code of Practice Committee of the Association of the British Pharmaceutical Industry[193]; Life Assurance Unit Trust Regulatory Organisation[194]; London Metal Exchange Ltd[195] the Office of the Independent Adjudicator for Higher Education[196]; the managers of a privately-owned psychiatric hospital[197]; Hampshire Farmers Markets Ltd[198]; the Law Society of Northern Ireland[199]; and a community interest company funded by central government.[200]

3-048   Sir John Donaldson MR urged that it is important for the courts to "recognise the realities of executive power" and not allow "their vision to be clouded by the subtlety and sometimes complexity of the way in which it can be exerted".[201] Non-statutory bodies are as capable of abusing their powers as is government.[202]

Bodies held not to be amenable to judicial review

3-049   The adoption of the public functions approach has not led to a widespread expansion of the ambit of judicial review. More often than not, submissions that a body's

---

190 *Datafin* [1987] 1 Q.B.815. The Panel is a non-statutory body, set up in 1968, which administers the City Code on Takeovers and Mergers; its central objective is to ensure equality of treatment and opportunity for all shareholders in takeover bids. Since *Datafin*, the Panel has been designated as a supervisory authority under the EC Directive on Takeover Bids (2004/25/EC) and has Statutory functions under the Companies Act 2006 Pt 28.

191 *R. v Advertising Standards Authority Ltd Ex p. Insurance Services Plc* [1990] C.O.D. 42. The ASA is the self-regulatory body of the advertising industry, hearing complaints from members of the public about adverts in the print media. Since 2004 Ofcom, the statutory regulator for radio and television, has contracted out some of its regulatory functions to the ASA.

192 *R. v Press Complaints Commission Ex p. Stewart-Brady* (1997) 9 Admin. L.R. 247. The PCC is a self-regulatory body dealing with complaints from members of the public about the editorial content of newspapers and magazines.

193 *R. v Code of Practice Committee of the Association of the British Pharmaceutical Industry Ex p. Professional Counselling Aids* [1991] C.O.D. 228. The ABPI is the trade association for about a hundred companies in the UK producing prescription medicines.

194 *R. v Life Assurance Unit Trust Regulatory Organisation Ex p. Ross* [1993] Q.B. 17. LAUTRO was a recognised self-regulating organisation for the purposes of s.8 of the Financial Services Act 1986. It functions are now part of the Personal Investment Authority (PIA), a directorate of the Financial Services Authority (FSA) established by the Financial Services and Markets Act 2000.

195 *R. v London Metal Exchange Ltd Ex p. Albatros Warehousing Ltd*, unreported 30 March 2000 Richards J. The LME is now a "recognised investment exchange" (RIE); regulated by the FSA.

196 *R. (on the application of Siborurema) v Office of the Independent Adjudicator* [2007] EWCA Civ 1365; [2008] E.L.R. 209. The OIA was formed as a company limited by guarantee in 2003, to fulfil the function of providing a procedure by which students could make a complaint about decisions of Higher Education Institutions (HEIs) affecting them, other than matters of academic judgment. The scheme of handling complaints was set up by statute and the OIA had been designated as the operator. The aspiration of the OIA to be an informal substitute for court proceedings was not inconsistent with the presence of supervision by way of judicial review.

197 *R. (on the application of A) v Partnerships in Care Ltd* [2002] EWHC 529 (Admin); [2002] 1 W.L.R. 2610. The impugned decision was to change the focus of the ward on which the claimant was accommodated from treatment of patients with personality disorders to the treatment of mental illness.

198 *R. (on the application of Beer (t/a Hammer Trout Farm)) v Hampshire Farmers Markets Ltd* [2003] EWCA Civ 1056; [2004] 1 W.L.R. 233. The company was set up on the initiative of Hampshire County Council to help producers in its area run farmers markets.

199 *Brangam, Re Judicial Review* [2008] NIQB 11. In the exercise of its power of attorney over the property of a deceased solicitor, to create a mortgage of the interest of the deceased in the former matrimonial home to the Law Society of Northern Ireland as trustees of the solicitors' compensation fund.

200 *R. (on the application of Jenkins) v Marsh Farm Community Development Trust* [2011] EWHC 1097 (Admin).

201 *Datafin* [1987] 1 Q.B. 815 at 838–839.

202 See J. Black, "Constitutionalising Self Regulation" (1996) 59 M.L.R. 24; A. Ogus, "Rethinking Self-Regulation" (1995) 15 O.J.L.S. 95.

decision falls within the sphere of public functions have been unsuccessful, leading to dismissal of claims against (for example): organisations regulating sports[203]: decisions by religious bodies, including the Chief Rabbi, an imam, and chancellors and bishops of the Church of England[204]: in the commercial sphere, self-described ombudsman schemes, a trade association, the Association of British Travel Agents and Lloyd's of London[205]; the Medical Defence Union[206]; and "pub watch" schemes (in which publicans cooperate through an unincorporated association to bar customers banned from one licenced premises from all others in the scheme).[207] In some of these cases what was fatal to the claim was the presence of a contractual nexus between the claimant and the defendant.[208] In others, the activity in question was assessed not to have the characteristics of a public function. Even though a body may not be amenable to judicial review, the High Court nonetheless has a supervisory jurisdiction in private law proceedings under CPR Pt 8 "and the approach to be adopted is essentially that which the Administrative Court would adopt in public law cases".[209]

There is much to commend a function-based approach to determining the scope of judicial review. Not only does it enable the courts to articulate more explicitly the modern constitutional role of judicial review—the common law control of public functions[210]—but it may provide redress for grievance where no other remedy exists. As it is through the principles of judicial review that the rule of law

3-050

---

[203] In relation to horse racing: see *Mullins v The Board of Appeal of the Jockey Club* [2005] EWHC 2197 (Admin), Burnton J; *R. v Disciplinary Committee of the Jockey Club Ex p. Massingberd-Mundy* [1993] 2 All E.R. 207, DC; *R. v Jockey Club Ex p. RAM Racecourses Ltd* (1990) [1993] 2 All E.R. 225, DC; *R. v Disciplinary Committee of the Jockey Club Ex p. Aga Khan* [1993] 1 W.L.R. 909, CA. The Jockey Club no longer has regulatory functions: these were transferred to the Horse Racing Regulatory Authority and then to the British Horse Racing Authority (a company limited by guarantee). In relation to other sports, see: *R. v Football Association Ltd Ex p. Football League Ltd* [1993] 12 All E.R. 833 (Rose J); *Law v National Greyhound Racing Club* [1983] 1 W.L.R. 1302; and see J. Anderson, "An Accident of History: Why the Decisions of Sports Governing Bodies are not Amenable to Judicial Review" (2006) 35 *Common Law World Review* 173; the position is different in Scotland: C. Munro, "Sports in the Courts" [2005] P.L. 681 and 3–118 below.

[204] *R. v Chief Rabbi of the United Hebrew Congregations Ex p. Wachmann* [1992] 1 W.L.R. 1036; *R. v London Beth Din (Court of Chief Rabbi) Ex p. Bloom* [1998] C.O.D. 131; *R. v Imam of Bury Park Mosque, Luton Ex p. Ali (Sulaiman)* [1994] C.O.D. 142; *R. v St Edmundsbury and Ipswich Diocese (Chancellor) Ex p. White* [1948] 1 K.B. 195. cf. *R. v Bishop of Stafford Ex p. Owen* [2001] A.C.D. 14.

[205] *R. v Insurance Ombudsman Ex p. Aegon Life Assurance Ltd* [1994] C.O.D. 426; *R. v Panel of the Federation of Communication Services Ltd Ex p. Kubis* [1998] C.O.D. 56; *R. v Association of British Travel Agents Ex p. Sunspell Ltd (t/a Superlative Travel)* [2001] A.C.D. 16; *R. v Lloyd's of London Ex p. Briggs* [1993] 1 Lloyd's Rep. 176; *R. (on the application of West) v Lloyd's of London* [2004] EWCA Civ 506; [2004] 3 All E.R. 251; *R. (on the application of Mooyer) v Personal Investment Authority Ombudsman Bureau Ltd* [2001] EWHC Admin 247; [2002] Lloyd's Rep. I.R. 45. In *R. (Holmcroft Properties Ltd) v KPMG LLP* [2016] EWHC 323 (Admin); [2016] A.C.D. 67, it was held that a company appointed by the Financial Services Authority to provide redress to customers who had been mis-sold financial products was not amenable to review.

[206] *R. (on the application of Moreton) v Medical Defence Union Ltd* [2006] EWHC 1948 (Admin); [2007] LS Law Medical 180.

[207] *R. (on the application of Proud) v Buckingham Pubwatch Scheme* [2008] EWHC 2224 (Admin); *R (on the application of Boyle) v Haverhill Pub Watch* [2009] EWHC 2441 (Admin), [56]: the case "has no sufficient public element, flavour or character to bring it within the purview of public law". Neither case dealt with the law on "common callings" on which, see A. Reichman, *Human Rights in Private Law* (2001), p.248.

[208] See 3-053.

[209] *Fallon v Horseracing Regulatory Authority* [2006] EWHC 2030, [12] (Davis J); see also *Mckeown v British Horseracing Authority* [2010] EWHC 508 (QB); *Bradley v Jock Club* [2005] EWCA Civ 1056; and from an earlier period, *Nagle v Feilden* [1966] 2 Q.B. 633 (review of practice of Jockey Club to refuse trainer's licences to women).

[210] See 1-021.

and other constitutional principles are given practical effect, the supervisory jurisdiction of the Administrative Court should ensure that bodies, whether nominally public or private, when performing public functions comply with the law and achieve acceptable standards of administration. While some public functions fall outside the scope of judicial review,[211] nevertheless there exists a wide and growing—if sometimes uncertain—range of public functions which are potentially subject to the supervisory scrutiny of the courts.

Various characteristics of a public function

3-051   Where the courts do employ the broad test based on the existence of public functions, it is not always clear what criteria are relevant. Some judgments focus on the nature of the specific task carried out (which ought to be the dominant consideration) whereas others examine the general characteristics of the decision-making body. In *Ex p. Datafin Plc*, Sir John Donaldson MR suggested that possibly "the only essential elements are what can be described as a public element, which can take many different forms, and the exclusion from jurisdiction of bodies where the sole source of power is the consensual submission to its jurisdiction".[212] He warned that even as the law then stood, in the law reports it was possible to find enumerations of factors giving rise to the jurisdiction, but it was a fatal error to regard the presence of all those factors as essential or as being exclusive of other factors. In subsequent cases, the courts have gone on to elaborate a variety of overlapping criteria designed to particularise the broad-based functional approach of the Master of the Rolls in *Datafin*. The following points are relevant.

"But for"

3-052   The "but for" test—whether, but for the existence of a non-statutory body, the government would itself almost inevitably have intervened to do or regulate the activity in question. Here the court poses a hypothetical question.[213] Evidence as to the position of comparable bodies in other countries has sometimes been regarded as relevant, and sometimes not.[214] Given the huge changes in the scope of government activity, and disputes about its proper scope, it is open to doubt whether this criterion is a satisfactory one.

---

[211]   On non-justiciability, see 1-032.

[212]   *Ex p. Datafin Plc* [1987] 1 Q.B. 815 at 838.

[213]   A factor present in, e.g. *R. v Advertising Standards Authority Ex p. Insurance Services Plc* [1990] C.O.D. 42 where it was held that in the absence of a self-regulatory body such as the ASA, its functions "would no doubt be exercised by the Director General of Fair Trading" (Glidewell LJ at 86). cf., e.g. *R. v Football Association Ltd Ex p. Football League Ltd* [1993] 2 All E.R. 833 (television or other commercial company more likely than government to step in to regulate football if the FA did not exist). The but-for test is not conclusive. In *Ex p. Aga Khan* [1993] 1 W.L.R. 909, the Master of the Rolls was "willing to accept that if the Jockey Club did not regulate horse racing the government would probably be driven to create a public body to do so," but went on to hold that the Club "is not in its origin, its history, its constitution or (least of all) its membership a public body" (at 923); the other members of the CA differed, holding that the government would not have intervened. See further C. Campbell, "The Nature of Power as Public in English Judicial Review" (2009) 68 C.L.J. 90 at 92.

[214]   The fact that outside England some governments regulated the sport of horse racing was not regarded as significant in *Ex p. Aga Khan* [1993] 1 W.L.R. 909 at 932. cf. *Datafin* [1987] 1 Q.B. 815 where the Panel's lack of a direct statutory base was regarded as "a complete anomaly, judged by the experience of other comparable markets world-wide" (at 835).

Statutory underpinning

Where the government has acquiesced or encouraged the activities of the body **3-053** under challenge by providing "underpinning" for its work, has woven the body into the fabric of public regulation[215] or the body was established under the authority of government",[216] this can constitute statutory underpinning. Here the court is concerned not with what might happen, but with what has actually occurred.[217] The mere fact that existence of the body is explicitly or implicitly recognised in legislation is insufficient.[218]

Extensive or monopolistic powers

The fact that the body was exercising extensive or monopolistic powers, for **3-054** instance by effectively regulating entry to a trade or profession can be significant.[219] The Takeover Panel was said to have "a giant's strength".[220] Decisions of Lough Neagh Fishermen's Co-operative Society Ltd, a friendly society that by historical accident owns the rights to eel fishing on Lough Neagh and the River Bann, was carrying out a public function when it refused a boat-owners licence to someone who had fished there as a boat-helper for 47 years.[221]

Monopolistic power is not, however, necessarily to be equated with the **3-055** performance of public functions; nor will increases in scale lead to a change in the nature of the function in question. Extensive power over others is often exercised in the private sphere and here judicial review is not available.[222] The seriousness of

---

[215] An expression used by Sir Thomas Bingham MR in *Ex p. Aga Khan* [1993] 1 W.L.R. 909 at 921. See further C. Campbell, "The Nature of Power as Public in English Judicial Review" (2009) 68 C.L.J. 90 at 96.

[216] *Ex p. Lain* [1967] 2 Q.B. 864 at 884 (Diplock LJ), cited with approval in *Ex p. Datafin Plc* [1987] 1 Q.B. 815 at 849 (Lloyd LJ).

[217] See, e.g. *R. (on the application of A) v Partnerships in Care Ltd* [2002] EWCH 529 (Admin). The claimant was compulsorily detained under Mental Health Act 1983 s.3(1), the defendant private hospital was registered as a mental nursing home under Registered Homes Act 1984 Pt 2, and a statutory instrument imposed a duty directly on the hospital to provide adequate professional staff and treatment facilities.

[218] See, e.g. *R. v Chief Rabbi of the United Hebrew Congregations of Great Britain and the Commonwealth Ex p. Wachmann* [1992] 1 W.L.R. 1036 (existence and some functions of Chief Rabbi recognised by United Synagogues Act 1870 and Slaughter Houses Act 1974); *R. v Insurance Ombudsman Bureau Ex p. Aegon Life Insurance Ltd* [1995] L.R.L.R. 101 (under Financial Services Act 1986 LAUTRO recognised by Secretary of State as self-regulatory organisation; rather than itself carrying out a complaints investigation function, as required by the Act, LAUTRO recognised the Insurance Ombudsman as performing that task); *Ex p. Football Association Ltd* [1993] 2 All E.R. 833 where the EA had been recognised by Football Spectators Act 1989 s.4. In none of these cases was the presence of the legislation sufficient to make the body reviewable.

[219] As with the other criteria, the existence of monopolistic power is not in itself sufficient to make a decision-maker subject to judicial review. Rose J accepted that the FA had "virtually monopolistic powers" (see *Ex p. Football League Ltd* [1993] 2 All E.R. 833 at 848), and so did the Court of Appeal in *Ex p. Aga Khan* [1993] 1 W.L.R. 909. Sporting-relating businesses may be subject to oversight by the Office of Fair Trading, which enforces competition law.

[220] *Datafin* [1987] 1 Q.B. 815 at 845, Lloyd LJ.

[221] *Re Wylie's Application for Judicial Review* [2005] NIQB 2 at [19] (Weatherup J: "the regulation of the fishing involves an implied duty to act in the public interest; the issues that arise are matters of public concern and interest and the regulatory control arises in a public sphere where direct governmental regulatory control is absent and the regulatory activities are providing a public service").

[222] See, e.g. *Ex p. Aga Khan* [1993] 1 W.L.R. 909 at 932–3 where Hoffmann LJ stated: "the mere fact of power, even over a substantial area of economic activity, is not enough. In a mixed economy, power may be private as well as public. Private power may affect the public interest and liveli-

the impact of the decision on those affected,[223] or the number of people affected by the action,[224] have not been regarded as necessarily significant; nor is the importance of the body in national life.[225]

Absence of consensual submission

3-056   Whether the aggrieved person has consensually submitted to be bound by the decision-maker, this is closely linked to the previous criterion. In considering the position of the Panel on Takeovers and Mergers in *Datafin*, Lloyd LJ stated that "the City is not a club which one can join or not at will ... The panel regulates not only itself, but all others who have no alternative but to come to the market in a case to which the code applies".[226] The question of whether there has been consensual submission ought not to be merged with that of whether a contract *entirely* regulates the relationship between the parties. It has always been the case that private or domestic tribunals are performing no public function when their "authority is derived solely from contract, that is the agreement of the parties concerned".[227] Their functions are therefore outside the scope of judicial review. Whether or not a contract exists between the aggrieved person and the body, in some situations the body may be performing regulatory or other functions which create a situation where the person is left with the stark choice of either submitting himself to the control of the body or not participating in the activity concerned.[228] Here, it is submitted, judicial review ought in principle to be available to an aggrieved person,

---

hoods of many individuals. But that does not subject it to the rules of public law. If control is needed, it must be found in the law of contract, the doctrine of restraint of trade, the Restrictive Trade Practices Act 1976, arts 85 and 86 of the EEC treaty and all the other instruments available in law for curbing excesses of private power." See also *Mullins* [2005] EWHC 2197 (Admin) at [31].

[223] See, e.g. *Ex p. Wachmann* [1992] 1 W.L.R. 1036 (whether or not a decision had "public law consequences" must be determined otherwise than by reference to the seriousness of its impact upon those affected).

[224] For example, *Ex p. Football League Ltd* [1993] 2 All E.R. 833 Rose J noted at 841 that "FA's powers extend beyond contract to affect the lives of many hundreds of thousands who are not in any contractual relationship ... though the same could be said about large public companies".

[225] See *Ex p. Football League Ltd* [1993] 2 All E.R. 833 where Rose J. at 840 notes that the important role of the EA. had been recognised by official government reports. cf. *Ex p. Massingberd-Mundy* [1993] 2 All E.R. 207, DC where Neill LJ stated that, had the matter been free of authority, he would have held that the Jockey Club was judicially reviewable because it held a position of major public importance and "near monopolistic powers in an area in which the public generally have an interest and many persons earn their livelihoods".

[226] *Datafin* [1987] 1 Q.B. 815 at 846.

[227] See, e.g. *R. v Criminal Injuries Compensation Board Ex p. Lain* [1967] 2 Q.B. 864 at 882 (Lord Parker CJ) and 884–5 (Diplock LJ). Many self-regulatory organisations include arbitration provisions in their contracts with members, which may involve a waiver of any rights under ECHR art.6 to a determination by an independent and impartial tribunal established by law: see, e.g. *Stretford v Football Association Ltd* [2007] EWCA Civ 238; *The Times,* 13 April 2007. When dealing with claims for breach of contract of terms relating to discipline, it would be "surprising and unsatisfactory if a private law claim in relation to the decision of a domestic body required the court to adopt a materially different approach from a judicial review claim in relation to the decision of a public body. In each case the essential concern should be with the lawfulness of the decision taken: whether the procedure was fair, whether there was any error of law, whether any exercise of judgment or discretion fell within the limits open to the decision-maker, and so forth": *Bradley v Jockey Club* [2004] EWHC 2164 (QB) at [37] (Richards J), considered by the CA [2005] EWCA Civ 1056; *The Times,* 14 July 2005; *Flaherty v National Greyhound Racing Club Ltd* [2005] EWCA Civ 1117; (2005) 102(37) L.S.G. 31.

[228] See, e.g. *Ex p. Wachmann* [1992] 1 W.L.R. 1036 (judicial review not excluded because the applicant had consensually submitted to the Chief Rabbi's jurisdiction; the exclusion from judicial review of those who consensually submit to some subordinate jurisdiction properly applied only to arbitrators or private and domestic tribunals. Other reasons were, however, given for not subject-

though if a contract exists a contractual claim will normally be an appropriate alternative remedy which may bar judicial review.

Public funding

The fact that a body receives substantial funding from government to carry out its activities is of only marginal relevance in determining whether it is carrying out a public—that is, governmental—function. Many cultural organisations are heavily subsidised from taxation, but quite clearly that does not, in and of itself, make them susceptible to judicial review.[229]

3-057

Impact on the court's caseload

Suggestions have also been made from time to time that the court ought to have regard to the limited number of judges and the growing judicial review case load in deciding whether a class of body is susceptible to judicial review.[230] To take account of this factor appears to be wrong in principle and creates potential problems as to the independence of the judiciary. The number of the judiciary is of no relevance to the scope of judicial review. By failing to fill vacancies the executive could reduce the number of judges and thus, if the factor is relevant, theoretically reduce the scope of judicial review.

3-058

Broad and flexible approach

Undue reliance upon any one of the above criteria, while perhaps helpful in promoting certainty in this area of law, should be avoided. The test of public function should be overriding and the qualities enumerated in the criteria should be weighed and balanced in the context of each specific case. This will avoid the formalism that might otherwise develop and that has, in the past, inhibited the proper development of so much of administrative law.[231] It may, however, be going too far in the other direction to suggest that "The boundary between public law and private law is not capable of precise definition, and whether a decision has a sufficient public law element to justify the intervention of the Administrative Court by judicial review is often as much a matter of feel, as deciding whether any particular criteria are met".[232]

3-059

The application of the principles of judicial review can have the effect of extending the rights of the individual. For example, it can give an individual a right to be

3-060

---

ing the Chief Rabbi's decision to judicial review). There is much to be said for this view. cf. the statement of Farquharson LJ in *Ex p. Aga Khan* [1993] 1 W.L.R. 909 at 928: "The fact is that if the applicant wishes to race his horses in this country he had no choice but to submit to the Jockey Club's jurisdiction. This may be true but nobody is obliged to race his horses in this country and it does not destroy the element of consensuality". See also *Ex p. Professional Counselling Aids Ltd* [1991] C.O.D. 228.

229   *Mullins v The Board of Appeal of the Jockey Club* [2005] EWHC 2197 (Admin) at [35].

230   *Ex p. Football League Ltd* [1993] 2 All E.R. 833 at 849 (Rose J) it would be "a misapplication of scarce judicial resources" to hold the FA. amenable to the court's public law supervisory jurisdiction" and dicta in *R. v Panel on Take-overs and Mergers Ex p. Guinness Plc* [1990] 1 Q.B. 146 at 177–8 (Lord Donaldson MR). cf. D. Pannick, "Who is Subject to Judicial Review and in Respect of What?" [1992] P.L. 1 at pp.6–7.

231   Consider, e.g. the judicial/administrative/quasi-judicial categories (on which see Appendix B).

232   *R. (on the application of Tucker) v Director General of the National Crime Squad* [2003] EWCA Civ 2; [2003] I.C.R. 599 at [13] (Scott LJ).

consulted which he would not have in private law.[233] On the other hand, the extent of redress that is available in judicial review may be less extensive than that available in private law.

3-061   English law recognises that a public body can act in more than one capacity. This is unlike the situation in most civil legal systems, such as the French system, where all the activities of public bodies are governed by public law; or in relation to Convention rights, which apply to all functions of a "core" public authority.[234] Conversely, not all the activities of private bodies (such as business enterprises) are subject only to private law. For example, the activities of a private body such as a privatised former state-owned enterprise, may be governed by the standards of public law when its decisions are subject to duties conferred by statute[235] or when, by virtue of the function it is performing or possibly its dominant position in the market, it is under an implied duty to act in the public interest.[236]

AMENABILITY OF FUNCTIONS RELATING TO PRE-CONTRACTUAL AND CONTRACTUAL POWERS

Contractual capacity of public authorities

3-062   Most public authorities in England and Wales have powers to make contracts. For statutory bodies, including local authorities, the legal capacity to enter into contractual relations can only stem from express or implied powers in legislation.[237] The powers of central government to enter into contracts may in some instances derive from specific statutory powers but may alternatively arise from the Crown's inherent common law powers as a corporation sole.[238] Some bodies (such as self-regulatory organisations and members' clubs) carrying out public functions are limited liability companies, the contractual powers of which are governed by the articles and memoranda of association; others are unincorporated associations which have no separate legal personality from that of their individual members and so cannot enter into contracts in their own name. It is important to note that some of the judicial review challenges brought have related not directly to a contract but to pre-contractual matters (such as tender processes) in relation to which the claimant may not have any other private law redress. Where a public authority lacks

---

[233] *Council for Civil Service Unions v Minister for the Civil Service* [1985] A.C. 374.

[234] See 3-067.

[235] See, e.g. Gas Act 1986 s.9 (to supply gas).

[236] *Mercury Energy Ltd v Electricity Corp of NZ Ltd* [1994] 1 W.L.R. 521.

[237] See, for example, the Local Government (Contracts) Act 1997, which sought to put the contracting powers of local authorities on a firmer legal footing; the Local Authorities (Goods and Services) Act 1970 enables local authorities to supply goods and services, subject to certain restrictions, to other local authorities and to public bodies; and see now the "general power of competence" under the Localism Act 2011 s.1, which provides that "A local authority has power to do anything that individuals generally may do". Legislation may also make provision for imposing charges for the provision of services pursuant to statutory powers, though not duties (e.g. Local Government Act 2003 s.92; Localism Act 2011 s.3), though this will not always lead to the creation of a contractual relationship. A police force may charge for services and goods under Police Act 1996 ss.18, 25, 26 (e.g. where policing is provided for football and other sports events or to agencies such as Immigration Service).

[238] Under the so-called "Ram doctrine": see 5-022.

power to make a contract, the contract may as a matter of *private* law be unenforceable.[239]

Variety of contracts entered into by public authorities

Public authorities enter into a wide range of contracts to equip themselves to carry out their basic functions, including employment contracts and commercial contracts for the supply of goods and services to the authority. In more recent years, contracts have also assumed a more important general role in governance in many Western democracies, including the United Kingdom. Planning agreements have a role in relation to environment and planning development control.[240] Between 1980 and 1998 local authorities were required by legislation to put out a range of activities and services (including refuse collection, grounds maintenance, personnel management and legal services) to competitive tender. As a result of this "contracting out", the practical delivery of statutory duties came to be done by businesses and not-for-profit organisations.[241] The Local Government Act 1999 replaced compulsory competitive tendering with a duty of to secure "best value" on a wider range of public authorities. The aim was no longer to achieve simply the lowest cost but "to make arrangements to secure continuous improvement in the way in which its functions are exercised, having regard to a combination of economy, efficiency and effectiveness".[242] The outcome of these developments is that local authorities now fulfil many of their core public functions by entering into contracts for services with businesses and charities (for example, in respect of making arrangements for providing residential accommodation to persons who by reason of age, illness, disability or any other circumstances are in need of care and attention which is not otherwise available under s.21 of the National Assistance Act 1948).

3-063

At national level, a strategic policy of "Public Private Partnerships" (PPP) has been promoted as one means of providing capital investment for public services. This entails various kinds of private sector ownership of formerly wholly state-owned functions; the Private Finance Initiative (PFI) under which private sector businesses takes responsibility for providing public services, including providing and maintaining the necessary infrastructure; and the marketing of government services to the private sector.[243] European Union law imposes obligations and rights in relation to public procurement, but consideration of that regime falls outside the scope of this book.[244]

3-064

---

[239] See 19-077.

[240] See, e.g. "planning obligations" entered into under Town and Country Planning Act 1990 s.106. Such agreements must be made by deed and constitute a local land charge.

[241] This has resulted in judicial review claims in three main kinds of situation: first, in relation to complaints of unlawful tendering processes (See, e.g. *R. v Secretary of State for the Environment, Transport and the Regions Ex p. Bury MBC* [1998] 2 C.M.L.R. 787 and *R. v Avon CC Ex p. Terry Adams Ltd* [1994] Env. L.R. 442); secondly, by citizens who deal directly with the business or not-for-profit organisation delivering services which a local authority or other public body is under a statutory obligation to provide (e.g. *R. (on the application of Heather) v Leonard Cheshire Foundation* [2002] EWCA Civ 366; [2002] 2 All E.R. 936); and thirdly where a contractor is aggrieved by a public body's decision taken under the terms of a contract (e.g. *R. (on the application of Bevan & Clarke LLP) v Neath Port Talbot County BC* [2012] EWHC 236 (Admin) relating to the weekly rate paid by a local authority to providers of residential accommodation).

[242] s.3(1).

[243] See HM Treasury, *Public Private Partnerships—the Government's Approach* (2000); for a critical account of PFIs, see House of Commons Treasury Select Committee, *Private Finance Initiative*, 17th report of session 2010–12 (HC 1146).

[244] See S. Arrowsmith, *The Law of Public and Utilities Procurement* 3rd edn (2013); Public Contracts

Amenability tests for contractual situations

3-065   The range and growth of contractual relationships in the public sector has presented a challenge for judicial review law. The current position on amenability to judicial review of situations involving contracts is the product of two policies. One is that judicial review, as a remedy of last resort, is inappropriate where there is another field of law governing the situation. Thus, contract disputes are normally to be left to the general law of contract and CPR Pt 7 proceedings (or, in relation to employment contracts, recourse to an Employment Tribunal) rather than judicial review.[245] The Unfair Terms in Consumer Contracts Regulations 1999 may apply to the contracting activities of public authorities, including those relating to housing.[246] The existence of a possibility of a private law claim does not by itself, however, make judicial review inappropriate.[247] The other policy is to recognise that some public functions may be carried out through the medium of contractual relationships, which justifies the use of the Administrative Court's judicial review supervisory jurisdiction. It should be noted that the contracting process may give rise to tort claims, including for misfeasance in public office.[248]

3-066   The tests applied by the courts to determine whether a function involving a contract is susceptible to judicial review have been criticised as overly complex and liable to divert the attention of the court away from the substance of the complaint.[249] In the orthodox approach, the court assumes that the fact that the source of a public authority's power is statutory is in and of itself insufficient to make a dispute about a contract amenable to judicial review; the court therefore goes on to consider whether there is some additional "sufficient public element, flavour or character" to the situation.[250] A more straightforward approach (though not one widely applied by the courts) would be to say that if the contractual decision in issue involves that exercise of a statutory power, then in principle it should be subject to judicial review and the court should consider whether any of the grounds of review have been made out.[251]

3-067   As in other contexts, in working out whether a decision is susceptible to judicial review the court considers two main factors. It will have regard to the source of the

---

Regulations 2006 (SI 2006/5).

[245] It is inappropriate to start two sets of proceedings seeking the similar remedies on similar grounds: *Cookson & Clegg Ltd v Ministry of Defence* [2005] EWCA Civ 811; [2006] Eu. L.R. 1092 (claimant commenced Pt 7 and Pt 54 claims).

[246] *R. (on the application of Khatun) v Newham LBC* [2004] EWCA Civ 55; [2005] Q.B. 37.

[247] *R. (on the application of London Corp) v Secretary of State for the Environment, Food and Rural Affairs* [2004] EWCA Civ 1765; [2005] 1 W.L.R. 1286 (a decision of the minister to give consent to the to grant leases for the purpose of selling meat or fish at New Covent Garden Market in London, a market set up as a horticultural market, was a public law matter).

[248] See, e.g. *Harmon CFEM Facades (UK) Ltd v Corporate Officer of the House of Commons* [1999] EWHC Technology 199; (2000) 2 L.G.L.R. 372 (unlawful tender award).

[249] S. Bailey, "Judicial Review of Contracting Decisions" [2007] P.L. 444.

[250] *R. (on the application of Beer (t/a Hammer Trout Farm)) v Hampshire Farmers Markets Ltd* [2003] EWCA Civ 1056; [2004] 1 W.L.R. 233 at [16] (Dyson J); and see, e.g. *R. v Lord Chancellor Ex p. Hibbit & Saunders* [1993] C.O.D. 326; *R. v Camden LBC Ex p. Hughes* [1994] C.O.D. 253; *R. v Bolsover DC Ex p. Pepper* (2001) 3 L.G.L.R. 20; *R. (on the application of Trafford) v Blackpool BC* [2014] EWHC 85 (Admin); [2014] P.T.S.R. 989 (decision not to renew lease to firm of solicitors who had acted for claimants in personal injuries claims against the council held to be amenable to judicial review). Per HH Judge Stephen Davies: "At the very least there is a sufficient public element or connection to render the decision amenable to judicial review on the ground of abuse of power, whether categorised as improper or unauthorised power." See also para.11-072 fn.259.

[251] S. Bailey, "Judicial Review of Contracting Decisions" [2007] P.L. 444, 451.

power under which the impugned decision is made.[252] If this is "purely" contractual, judicial review is unlikely to be appropriate; some close statutory (or prerogative) underpinning of the contract will normally be needed. Alternatively, the court may consider whether the function being carried out by the defendant is a public function. Having decided that a decision is susceptible to judicial review, the court will go on to examine the grounds advanced by the claimant for the decision's unlawfulness.[253]

Identifying the "additional public element"

So long as the courts approach the issue of amenability by requiring a sufficient "public element" in the contractual dispute, there is much to be said for adopting a pragmatic method and reasoning by analogy from previously decided cases rather than attempting to identify broad overarching principles (an exercise that soon risks imploding in a sea of generalisations). The cases set out in the following paragraphs demonstrate that different *types* of consideration are capable of providing the necessary "public element"—in some it is the intrinsic public importance of the contract-related decision; in others it is the ground of review ("bad faith" scoring more highly than irrationality, for example).

3-068

Situations where there was an insufficient "additional public element"

The courts have held the following contractual situations *not* to be susceptible to judicial review: where a pupil at an independent, fee-paying school was excluded following an alleged theft[254]; where a sports regulatory body disciplined a member with whom it is in a contractual relationship[255]; where a disappointed tenderer for court reporting services alleged that they had a legitimate expectation that other tenderers would not be invited to submit lower bids[256]; alleged irrationalities in a marking scheme used to assess pre-qualification questionnaires from prospective tenderers for options to lease land for a wind farm[257]; decisions of the Business Conduct Committee of Lloyd's of London to approve four minority buyouts of his

3-069

---

[252] See, e.g. *R. v Pembrokeshire CC Ex p. Coker* [1999] 4 All E.R. 1007 (whether the council had contravened the Local Government Act 1972 s.123 in failing to obtain the best consideration reasonably obtainable for the letting of land).

[253] The PC in *Mercury Energy v Electricity Corp of New Zealand* [1994] 1 W.L.R. 521 held that decisions of a "state enterprise" (as defined by NZ legislation) were in principle susceptible to review, though the court would not interfere with a decision to enter into or determine a commercial contract to supply goods or services "in the absence of fraud, corruption or bad faith" (at 530).

[254] *R. v Incorporated Froebel Educational Institute Ex p. L* [1999] E.L.R. 488 (although the school operated within a statutory framework, the relationship between the school and its students was founded on the contract between the school and the parents).

[255] *Law v National Greyhound Racing Club* [1983] 1 W.L.R. 1302; *R. v Disciplinary Committee of the Jockey Club Ex p. Aga Khan* [1993] 1 W.L.R. 909.

[256] *R. v Lord Chancellor Ex p. Hibbit & Saunders* [1993] C.O.D. 326.

[257] *R. (on the application of Gamesa Energy UK Ltd) v National Assembly for Wales* [2006] EWHC 2167 (Admin); at [76] (Gibbs J): ("the stated aims of the pre-qualification procedure are not and could not be criticised. It follows that the complaints on the basis of irrationality and unfairness are confined to the nuts and bolts of parts of the exercise and their effect on the individual application of the claimant"). See also *Mass Energy Ltd v Birmingham CC* [1994] Env. L.R. 298, CA; *R. (on the application of Menai Collect Ltd) v Department for Constitutional Affairs* [2006] EWHC 724 at [47] (McCombe J: "It is not every wandering from the precise paths of best practice that lends fuel to a claim for judicial review. It is, I think, for this reason that the examples given of cases where commercial processes such as these are likely to be subject to review are such as they are in the reported cases, namely bribery, corruption, implementation of unlawful policy and the like. In such cases, there is a true public law element").

memberships in four syndicates at Lloyd's[258]; other decisions by Lloyd's of London to make cash calls on members of certain syndicates[259]; a decision of the British Standards Institution to circulate a letter to the chief fire officers' association stating that the claimant manufacturer had made false claims that its door release mechanisms met BSI standards[260]; a decision of the British Council to withdraw a language school's accreditation under a scheme designed to identify schools of good quality[261]; where a mobile phone dealer was contractually bound by terms of an anti-theft scheme, supported by the police and promoted by a trade association (of which the dealer was not a member)[262]; a refusal of the local authority to sell certain land to the claimant on the basis that he had a legitimate expectation, either to be sold the land or at least to be allowed to make representations before any decision not to sell it was taken.[263]

Situations where there was a sufficient "additional public element"

3-070   In contrast, the courts have held (or assumed) there to be a sufficient public law element: in a challenge by a disappointed tenderer to the Legal Aid Board's decision to award a contract to represent claimants seeking compensation for Gulf War Syndrome to two other firms[264]; where a building contractor was removed from a local authority's approved list of contractors following disputes about the quality of work[265]; where a local authority terminated an informal arrangement permitting a hot-food take-away caravan to be located at a market[266]; where a local authority refused to vary a lease to permit the use of premises as a café after the council had lost an appeal against the change of use under planning legislation[267]; where a group of former tenants of market units sought to challenge a council's decision not to select them as tenants for a new smaller market which was to replace the existing market[268]; the Northern Ireland Department for Social Development's decision to terminate the claimant's appointment as a preferred developer for the Queen's Quay project, which is a "key strategic site in a development in which the citizens of Belfast have a major interest given the huge investment of public money and

---

[258] *R. (on the application of West) v Lloyd's of London* [2004] EWCA Civ 506; [2004] 3 All E.R. 251.

[259] *R. v Lloyd's of London Ex p. Briggs* [1993] 1 Lloyd's Rep. 176; and see also *Doll-Steinberg v Society of Lloyd's* [2002] EWHC 419 (Admin) (renewed application for permission—determinations of its Settlement Panel not subject to judicial review).

[260] *R. v British Standards Institution Ex p. Dorgard Ltd* [2001] A.C.D. 15 (the dispute arose from a commercial contract under which the BSI had agreed to test the claimant's product).

[261] *R. (on the application of Oxford Study Centre Ltd) v British Council* [2001] EWHC Admin 207; [2001] E.L.R. 803 (the scheme was voluntary; the British Council had acted in breach of an implied term in its contract to act fairly).

[262] *R. v Panel of the Federation of Communication Services Ltd Ex p. Kubis* (1999) 11 Admin. L.R. 43.

[263] *R. v Bolsover DC Ex p. Pepper* (2001) 3 L.G.L.R. 20.

[264] *R. v Legal Aid Board Ex p. Donn & Co* [1996] 3 All E.R. 1 at 10–11 (the board were allocating a very large sum of public money; there was an obvious public important in making the right decision; and the board is the sole and final arbiter of selection).

[265] *R. v Bristol City Council Ex p. DL Barrett & Sons* (2001) 3 L.G.L.R. 11, following *R. v Enfield LBC Ex p. TF Unwin (Roydon) Ltd* [1989] C.O.D. 466.

[266] *R. v Wear Valley DC Ex p. Binks* [1985] 2 All E.R. 699.

[267] *R. (on the application of Molinaro) v Kensington and Chelsea RLBC* [2001] EWHC Admin 896; [2002] B.L.G.R. 336 at [63] (Elias J) ("Manifestly, the council was not simply acting as a private body when it sought to give effect to its planning policy through the contract. Again, the decision not to permit a change of use, albeit one involving the exercise of discretion under a contract, was taken for the purpose of giving effect to its planning objectives").

[268] *R. (on the application of Western International Campaign Group) v Hounslow LBC* [2003] EWHC 3112 (Admin); [2004] B.L.G.R. 536 (the council had specific statutory powers in relation to the market, the market was on publicly-owned land, and the council's powers emanated not solely from the lease but also its byelaws).

land"[269]; and the decision of a local authority to set a weekly fee under a contract for the provision of residential care.[270] Also, where a sub-contractor to run a breakdown recovery service for the police was refused a vetting clearance without reasons.[271]

Where the contract-related decision is the promulgation of a broad policy, taken under the exercise of statutory powers, the courts have often assumed without argument that the decision is susceptible to judicial review. For instance: where a local authority resolved not to contract in future with a company, on the ground of its links with South Africa during the apartheid era[272]; and where a local authority boycotted the publications of a particular newspaper company on the ground of the company's employment practices.[273]   **3-071**

Employment situations

Where a public authority takes action in relation to an employee, such as disciplinary action or termination of an employment relationship, this will normally be matter for contract or employment law rather than judicial review.[274] Complications have arisen in relation to civil servants who hold office under the Crown, terminable at will, as it has not been clear whether a contract of employment exists in this context, but that is a rather different question to the one in hand, namely whether the Administrative Court should intervene.[275] Police officers, similarly are office-holders rather than employees under contract. Following precedent, the court also probably has jurisdiction over claims made by Church of England clergymen complaining about lack of fairness in the procedures adopted by their superiors,[276] though not in respect of employment-type issues arising in other religious organisations.[277]   **3-072**

It will perhaps be easiest to establish that an employment decision amounts to a   **3-073**

---

[269] *Sheridan Millennium Ltd, Re Judicial Review* [2008] NIQB 8.

[270] *R. (on the application of Bevan & Clarke LLP) v Neath Port Talbot County BC* [2012] EWHC 236 (Admin); [2012] B.L.G.R. 728 at [48] (Beatson J): "The mere fact that the decision concerns the setting of a fee under a contract does not mean that it is to be characterised as a private act". In setting fees in this context, local authorities must have regard to "Commissioning Guidance" issued by ministers.

[271] *R. (on the application of A) v Chief Constable of B* [2012] EWHC 2141 (Admin); [2012] A.C.D. 125.

[272] *R. v Lewisham LBC Ex p. Shell UK* [1988] 1 All E.R. 938. See also *Bromley LBC v GLC* [1983] 1 A.C. 768 at 813 and *Wheeler v Leicester CC* [1985] A.C. 1054. See further 5-083.

[273] *R. v Ealing LBC Ex p. Times Newspapers Ltd* (1987) 85 L.G.R. 316.

[274] *R. v BBC Ex p. Lavelle* [1983] 1 W.L.R. 23 (claimant sought stay of BBC disciplinary proceedings pending conclusion of a criminal trial); *R. v East Berkshire HA Ex p. Walsh* [1985] Q.B. 152; *R. v Derbyshire CC Ex p. Noble* [1990] I.C.R. 808 (local authority terminated appointment of deputy police surgeon without given reasons or allowing representations); *McLaren v Secretary of State for the Home Department* [1990] I.C.R. 824; *R. v Lord Chancellor's Department Ex p. Nangle* [1991] I.R.L.R. 343; *R. (on the application of Arthurworry) v Haringey LBC* [2001] EWHC Admin 698; [2002] I.C.R. 279; *Evans v University of Cambridge* [2002] EWHC 1382 (Admin); [2003] E.L.R. 8; *R. (on the application of Tucker) v Director General of the National Crime Squad* [2003] EWCA Civ 57; [2003] I.C.R. 599 (termination of secondment of police office to the NCS). *Tucker* was distinguished in *R. (on the application of Woods) v Chief Constable of Merseyside Police* [2014] EWHC 2784 (Admin); [2015] 1 W.L.R. 539, where the decision to subject a police officer to a "service confidence procedure" was held to have a sufficient public law element to be amenable to judicial review and was not merely a deployment or operational decision.

[275] See S. Fredman and G. Morris, "Judicial Review and Civil Servants: Contracts of Employment Declared to Exist" [1991] P.L. 485.

[276] *R. v Bishop of Stafford Ex p. Owen* [2001] A.C.D. 14 (CA, Schiemann LJ stating that he so assumed "without finally ruling on the point").

[277] *R. v Chief Rabbi of the United Hebrew Congregations of Great Britain and the Commonwealth Ex p. Wachmann* [1992] 1 W.L.R. 1036.

public function where what is at stake is a general policy, taken under statutory or prerogative powers. The following situations have been held to be susceptible to judicial review: a local authority's decision restricting how educational psychologists could consult other professionals before producing their advisory reports[278]; delegated legislation by which a minister sought to change teachers' contracts of employment to implement a system of performance-related pay[279]; an exercise of prerogative powers to change terms of employment to ban trade union membership at CGHQ[280]; a redeployment and redundancy policy adopted by a local authority[281]; a ministerial decision to close collieries without following an agreed consultation procedure[282]; a wage settlement when it is claimed that the authority exceeded or abused its conferred powers[283]; and a decision of the Army Board, pursuant to Queen's Regulations, to retain two guardsmen in the Army after they had been released from prison after conviction for murdering a youth while on duty.[284]

3-074   Judicial review may also be possible in relation to disciplinary proceedings against office-holders that are specifically provided for in legislation, as opposed to being wholly informal or domestic matters.[285] The principles of procedural propriety apply, so "an officer cannot be lawfully dismissed without first telling him what is alleged against him and hearing the defence or explanation".[286] As in other contexts, the claimant may, however, be expected to have exhausted internal grievance procedures and other available remedies before resorting to judicial review.[287] In "the great majority cases", a person will be expected to seek remedies for breach of contract or the statutory remedy of unfair dismissal in the Employment Tribunal.[288] Exceptional circumstances justifying the Administrative Court exercising discretion to allow a judicial review rather than tribunal proceedings include that a judicial review is more effective and convenient because it may lead to higher compensation, vindicate the office-holder's reputation more emphatically than a tribunal, allow claims against several public authorities to be dealt with at the same time, and avoid unnecessary legal costs.[289]

3-075   Judicial review may also be used to challenge the compatibility of UK employment legislation with European Union law.[290]

---

278 *R. v Sunderland City Council Ex p. Baumber* [1996] C.O.D. 211.

279 *R. v Secretary of State for Education and Employment Ex p. National Union of Teachers* [2000] Ed. C.R. 603.

280 *Council of Civil Service Unions v Minister for the Civil Service* [1985] A.C. 374; *McLaren v Secretary of State for the Home Department* [1990] I.C.R. 824 (obiter).

281 *R. v Hammersmith and Fulham LBC Ex p. NALGO* [1991] I.R.L.R. 249.

282 *R. v Secretary of State for Trade and Industry Ex p. Vardy* [1993] I.C.R. 720.

283 *Pickwell v Camden LBC* [1983] Q.B. 962.

284 *In the Matter of an Application for Judicial Review by Jean McBride (No.2)* [2003] NICA 23 at [25].

285 *McClaren v Home Office* [1990] I.C.R. 824; and, e.g. *R. (on the application of Bennion) v Chief Constable of Merseyside* [2001] EWCA Civ 638; [2001] I.R.L.R. 442; *R. v Ministry of Defence Police Ex p. Byrne* [1994] C.O.D. 429; *R. v Deputy Chief Constable of North Wales Ex p. Hughes* [1991] 3 All E.R. 414; *R. v Chief Constable of Merseyside Ex p. Merrill* [1989] 1 W.L.R. 1077; *Re The Prison Officers Association's Application for Judicial Review* [2008] NIQB 35.

286 *Ridge v Baldwin* [1964] AC. 40, 66 (Lord Reid).

287 *R. v Chief Constable of the Merseyside Police Ex p. Calveley* [1986] Q.B. 424.

288 *R. (on the application of Shoesmith) v Ofsted* [2011] EWCA Civ 642; [2011] P.T.S.R. 1459, [87] (Maurice Kay LJ).

289 *R. (on the application of Shoesmith) v Ofsted* [2011] EWCA Civ 642; [2011] P.T.S.R. 1459, [92]-[99].

290 See, e.g. *R. v Secretary of State for Employment Ex p. Seymour-Smith (No.2)* [2000] 1 W.L.R. 435; *R. v Secretary of State for Employment Ex p. Seymour-Smith (No.1)* [1997] 1 W.L.R. 473; *R. v Secretary of State for Employment Ex p. Equal Opportunities Commission* [1995] 1 A.C. 1.

AMENABILITY AND THE HUMAN RIGHTS ACT

Having examined issues relating to amenability to judicial review generally, we now turn to consider which functions may be subject to judicial review claims on the specific ground that they unlawfully interfere with a Convention right, contrary to the Human Rights Act 1998 (HRA) s.6.[291] Three basic categories can be distinguished: (a) functions of "core public authorities"[292]; (b) "functions of a public nature" carried out by other organisations and persons[293]; and (c) decisions of courts and tribunals.[294] Section 6 of the HRA provides: **3-076**

"**6.**–(1)   It is unlawful for a public authority to act in a way which is incompatible with a Convention right.

(2)   Subsection (1) does not apply to an act if—

(a)   as the result of one or more provisions of primary legislation, the authority could not have acted differently; or

(b)   in the case of one or more provisions of, or made under, primary legislation which cannot be read or given effect in a way which is compatible with the Convention rights, the authority was acting so as to give effect to or enforce those provisions.

(3)   In this section 'public authority' includes—

(a)   a court or tribunal, and

(b)   any person certain of whose functions are functions of a public nature, but does not include either House of Parliament or a person exercising functions in connection with proceedings in Parliament.

(4)   In subsection (3) 'Parliament' does not include the House of Lords in its judicial capacity.

(5)   In relation to a particular act, a person is not a public authority by virtue only of subsection (3)(b) if the nature of the act is private.

(6)   'An act' includes a failure to act but does not include a failure to—

(a)   introduce in, or lay before, Parliament a proposal for legislation; or

(b)   make any primary legislation or remedial order."

Core public authorities

It has been said that the HRA fails to provide an exhaustive definition of what is meant by the term "public authority" because "there are certain bodies that so obviously have the character of a public authority that it is not necessary to mention them".[295] These bodies have come to be called "core", "true", "pure", "standard" or "through-and-through" public authorities. Put in terms of the structure of the HRA, we can say that core public authorities are those public authorities falling within s.6 without reference to s.6(3)(b).[296]   **3-077**

Categorising an organisation or person as a core public authority has several consequences. Under ECHR law, such institutions of the State are bound to respect Convention rights *in all aspects* of their activities. This being so, for the purposes of the HRA it is unnecessary to consider whether a particular act or function of a   **3-078**

---

[291] See Ch.13.

[292] See 3-067.

[293] See 3-072.

[294] HRA s.6(3)(a).

[295] *R. (on the application of Quark Fishing Ltd) v Secretary of State for Foreign and Commonwealth Affairs (No.2)* [2005] UKHL 57; [2006] 1 A.C. 529 at [85] (Lord Hope of Craighead).

[296] *Aston Cantlow and Wilmcote with Billesley Parochial Church Council v Wallbank* [2003] UKHL 37; [2004] 1 A.C. 546 at [8] (Lord Nicholls).

core public authority is or is not "of a public nature".[297] Thus, if a local authority provides accommodation and nursing care for elderly people in a council-run home, that function—and all acts connected with that function—fall within the scope of s.6 of the HRA simply because the local authority is a "core public authority" and regardless of whether the function is regarded as being public or private. Another consequence of classifying a body as a core public authority is that it will fall outside the protective scope of the ECHR as the State cannot benefit from or exert the protections offered by Convention rights.[298]

3-079   As in the interpretation of other aspects of the HRA, the courts must, in determining whether a body is a core public authority, take into account the text of the ECHR and the case law of the European Court of Human Rights (ECtHR).[299] The purpose of the HRA was to "bring rights home",[300] and the national courts will accordingly attempt to define a core public authority as one that "carries out a function of government that would engage the responsibility of the United Kingdom before the Strasbourg organs"[301]—subject to the important qualification that Parliament and a person exercising functions in connection with proceedings in Parliament, are expressly excluded from the definition of public authority in s.6(3) and 6(6), in order to preserve the constitutional principle of parliamentary supremacy. The limitation of this approach, however, is that the ECtHR takes little general interest in the internal governance arrangements within Member States: "It is only the responsibility of the [contracting] State itself—not that of a domestic authority or organ—that is in issue before the Court. It is not the Court's role to deal with a multiplicity of national authorities or courts or to examine disputes between institutions or over internal politics".[302] The ECtHR has held that Convention rights bind "governmental organisations established for public administration purposes".[303] Responsibility is not confined to central government but extends to lower tiers as well.[304] Of particular importance is whether the organisation in question might be a "non-governmental organisation" for the purposes of ECHR art.34.[305] Non-governmental organisations have the right to invoke Convention rights before the ECtHR and cannot therefore be part of the State (which cannot benefit from the

---

[297] *YL v Birmingham City Council* [2007] UKHL 27; [2008] 1 A.C. 95 at [110] (Lord Mance: "All such functions and activities are subject to the Convention, because the authority is a core public authority. It only becomes necessary to analyse their nature, if and when they are contracted out to a person who is not a core public authority"); [at 131] (Lord Neuberger of Abbotsbury: "… there is therefore no need to distinguish between private and public acts or functions of a core public authority"). See further J. Landau, "Functional public authorities after YL" [2007] P.L. 630.

[298] *Aston Cantlow and Wilmcote with Billesley Parochial Church Council v Wallbank* [2003] UKHL 37; [2004] 1 A.C. 546 at [8].

[299] HRA s.2; and see, e.g. *YL v Birmingham City Council* [2007] UKHL 27; [2008] 1 A.C. 95 at [119] (Lord Mance).

[300] See 13-031.

[301] *Aston Cantlow and Wilmcote with Billesley Parochial Church Council v Wallbank* [2003] UKHL 37; [2004] 1 A.C. 546 at [160] (Lord Rodger).

[302] *Assanide v Georgia* [2004] E.C.H.R. 140 at [149].

[303] *Holy Monasteries v Greece* (1995) 20 E.H.R.R. 1 at [49] (holding that monasteries of the Greek Orthodox Church did not exercise governmental power: "Their objectives—essentially ecclesiastical and spiritual ones, but also cultural and social ones in some cases—are not such as to enable them to be classed with governmental organisations established for public administration purposes").

[304] *Ayuntamiento de Mula v Spain*, Application No.55346/00, 1 February 2001 (ECtHR) ("the Court reiterates that in international law the expression 'governmental organisations' cannot be held to refer only to the Government or the central organs of the State. When powers are distributed along decentralised lines, it refers to any national authority which exercises public functions").

[305] Discussed at 2-054.

protection of Convention rights).[306] The concept of "emanation of the State" in European Union law,[307] is not relevant in this context.[308]

There is relatively little national case law on the ambit of the concept of core public authority for the simple reason that in most cases the answer is fairly clear. "The most obvious examples are government departments, local authorities, the police and the armed forces".[309] In addition: "Health authorities and NHS trusts and their staff"[310]; a local education authority, the governing body of a maintained school and a head teacher.[311] The following has been held *not* to be a core public authority: parochial church councils (PCCs) of the Church of England, responsible for the financial affairs of the Church and the care and maintenance of the church fabric.[312]

3-080

Although (as noted above) for the purposes of liability under the HRA it is unnecessary to consider whether a core public authority is carrying out a public function (because all its functions are subject to the HRA), it may, however, still be necessary to consider whether *for the purposes of making a claim for judicial review* the act or function in question is a public function.[313] So, for example, an employment dispute with a local authority which raises an issue of Convention rights may lack a sufficient public element to make it amenable to judicial review; and in any event proceedings before the Employment Tribunal may be a more appropriate alternative remedy.[314] In short, we can say that while all acts and functions of core public authorities fall within HRA s.6, some disputes about whether they are compatible with Convention rights may fall outside the scope of judicial review and should be pursued in other forms of legal claim.

3-081

---

[306] *Aston Cantlow and Wilmcote with Billesley Parochial Church Council v Wallbank* [2003] UKHL 37; [2004] 1 A.C. 546 in holding a parochial church council of the Church of England was not a core public authority, the HL attached significance to the fact that if were such a public authority, it would be incapable of seeking protection for Convention rights, notably freedom of religion (which by HRA s.12 is afforded especial recognition in domestic law).

[307] See 14-024.

[308] *Aston Cantlow and Wilmcote with Billesley Parochial Church Council v Wallbank* [2003] UKHL 37; [2004] 1 A.C. 546 at [55].

[309] *Aston Cantlow and Wilmcote with Billesley Parochial Church Council v Wallbank* [2003] UKHL 37; [2004] 1 A.C. 546 at [7].

[310] *R. (on the application of Wilkinson) v Broadmoor Special Hospital Authority* [2001] EWCA Civ 1545; [2002] 1 W.L.R. 419 at [61]; *Grampian University Hospitals NHS Trust v Her Majesty's Advocate* [2004] ScotHC 10.

[311] *A v Headteacher and Governors of Lord Grey School* [2004] EWCA Civ 382; [2004] Q.B. 1231 at [36]-[38] (but Sedley J expressing "a visceral unease at the conclusion that the headteacher of a maintained school is a public authority"); decision on Convention rights issues reversed by HL: [2006] UKHL 14; [2006] 2 A.C. 363. In relation to "trust schools" established under the Education and Inspections Act 2006, the Government takes the view that they are within the ambit of the HRA, though it is not entirely clear whether this is because they are "core" or "functional": see *Hansard*, HL col.WA46 (31 January 2006) "The governing bodies of all maintained schools are public authorities for the purposes of the Human Rights Act 1998, and the governing bodies of trust schools will be no different in this respect. Although the matter has not been judicially determined, in the department's view academies exercise functions of a public nature by providing education at public expense and are therefore public authorities for the purposes of the Human Rights Act 1998".

[312] *Aston Cantlow and Wilmcote with Billesley Parochial Church Council v Wallbank* [2003] UKHL 37; [2004] 1 A.C. 546: despite its close links to the State, "the Church of England remains essentially a religious organisation" (at [13]), and its concerns were for the "congregation of believers in the parish" rather than the general public, (at [86]).

[313] See 3-038.

[314] See 16-018.

"Functions of a public nature" under the HRA

3-082   The second type of act falling within the ambit of s.6 of the HRA is where a person or organisation that is not a core public authority carries out a "function of a public nature". This phrase is used in other legislation with increasing frequency.[315] Convention rights regulate only that public function, not all functions of the body in question; "if the nature of the act is private" (HRA s.6(5)), then it falls outside the scope of s.6. The HRA does not create a system of direct "horizontal effect" for Convention rights (*unmittlebare Drittwirkung*) in which they can be invoked in purely private relationships. In respect of its private functions and acts, such a body is capable of being a victim of breaches of Convention rights.[316] "Functions of a public nature" are defined by HRA s.6(3)(b) and 6(5), which requires "a two-fold assessment, first of the body's functions, and secondly of the particular act in question".[317]

The YL decision in the House of Lords

3-083   The leading decision on the meaning of "functions of a public nature" is *YL*,[318] a test case (though the outcome was subsequently reversed by legislation). The claimant was an elderly woman suffering from Alzheimer's disease living in a residential home operated by Southern Cross Healthcare Ltd (a business providing accommodation and nursing services, subject to regulation under the Care Standards Act 2000). The claimant lived at the home under the terms of a contract. There were three parties to this "placement agreement": the claimant (through her daughter); Southern Cross; and Birmingham City Council (the local authority with statutory responsibilities in relation to the claimant for care in the community). There was a further contract (a "third party funding agreement") between Southern Cross and the council, under which the council undertook to pay a certain sum towards the fee charged to the claimant by Southern Cross (478 a week), the balance (35 a week) being paid by the claimant's daughter. The local NHS Trust contributed a further sum towards the claimant's nursing care.

3-084   Following a dispute with the claimant's family, Southern Cross exercised its contractual right to terminate for "good reason" the placement agreement by giv-

---

[315] See, e.g. Equality Act 2010 s.150 (public sector equality duty extends to "a function of a public nature for the purposes of the Human Rights Act 1998"); London Olympic Games and Paralympic Games Act 2006 s.35; Government of Wales Act 2006 s.63 and Sch.7; Education and Inspections Act 2006 Sch.13; Companies Act 2006 s.54; and Police and Justice Act 2006 s.28. And see *YL* [2007] UKHL 27; [2007] 3 W.L.R. 112 [106]. In *R. (on the application of Weaver) v London & Quadrant Housing Trust* [2009] EWCA Civ 587; [2010] 1 W.L.R. 363, Elias LJ noted that "The concept of 'functions' is not altogether straightforward, nor is the distinction between functions and acts", continuing "In *Hazell v Hammersmith and Fulham London BC* [1992] 2 A.C. 1 29F Lord Templeman said that the word 'functions', at least as to be construed in s.111 of the Local Government Act 1972, embraced 'all the duties and powers of a local authority; the sum total of the activities Parliament has entrusted to it'. This would suggest that a function is a sub-species of those duties and powers; although whether and when a specific power or duty can be equated with a function is more problematic" (at [29]).

[316] *Aston Cantlow and Wilmcote with Billesley Parochial Church Council v Wallbank* [2003] UKHL 37; [2004] 1 A.C. 546 at [11]. On the victim requirement, see 2-044.

[317] *Aston Cantlow and Wilmcote with Billesley Parochial Church Council v Wallbank* [2003] UKHL 37; [2004] 1 A.C. 546 [85] (Lord Hobhouse). His Lordship added "The nature of the person's functions are not to be confused with the nature of the act complained of, as s.6 makes clear" at [88]. See also *YL v Birmingham City Council* [2007] UKHL 27; [2008] 1 A.C. 95 at [25], [34] (Lord Scott).

[318] *YL v Birmingham City Council* [2007] UKHL 27; [2008] 1 A.C. 95.

ing four weeks' notice. The claimant's lawyers argued that the termination notice violated her rights under art.8 (right to respect for home). Clearly, Southern Cross could not be a "core" public authority. The council was, but it was not the organisation which had served notice on the claimant and nor was it suggested that the council had failed to carry out any of its statutory duties. The claimant's only recourse under the HRA was therefore to demonstrate that Southern Cross were carrying out functions and acts of a public nature. The rival contentions took place against the contractual background, described above, and the statutory duties and powers that government the arrangements. The council was required to (and did) carry out an assessment of the claimant's needs under Pt 3 of the National Health Service and Community Care Act 1990 in relation to "community care". The local NHS Primary Care Trust was also required to assess the claimant's health care needs under the National Health Service Act 1977 (and did so). The National Assistance Act 1948 placed a duty on the council to "make arrangements for providing" residential accommodation and nursing care for people assessed to be in need, to be paid in whole or in part by the council and the NHS according to means testing—payments being made directly to the operator of the care home (which it had done). Under the Health and Social Care Act 2001, the council agreed to fund most of the claimant's costs.

For the reasons examined below, Lords Scott of Foscote, Mance and Neuberger of Abbotsbury held that Southern Cross were not performing a pubic function; Lord Bingham of Cornhill and Baroness Hale of Richmond dissented. The division within the Appellate Committee in YL provides amble evidence that "There is room for doubt and for argument"[319] about the meaning of the phrase "function of a public nature" and thus the ambit of the HRA. There have been sharp differences of opinion within the judiciary and between the courts and parliamentarians.[320]   **3-085**

These differences of view, which are unlikely to be settled by the House of Lords' ruling in YL, is a particular instance of a broader debate the overall aims of the HRA. The narrower view is that purpose of the HRA is limited to making available through the UK courts the rights and remedies that previously had to be obtained by individual petition to the ECtHR. There should therefore, on this view, be as great an equivalence as possible between what can and cannot be obtained in Strasbourg and in the national courts. The broader view sees the ECHR as providing simply a minimum starting point from which national courts, applying the HRA, may extend in order to achieve a higher degree of respect for Convention rights in a domestic setting—which necessarily entails outcomes where Convention rights in the United Kingdom are not completely aligned with how those rights are applied and defined in by the ECtHR.   **3-086**

In the particular context of interpreting "functions of a public nature", those supporting a narrower interpretation eschew reliance on what was said about the scope of s.6 in parliamentary debates reported in *Hansard*.[321] Another methodological   **3-087**

---

[319] *Aston Cantlow and Wilmcote with Billesley Parochial Church Council v Wallbank* [2003] UKHL 37; [2004] 1 A.C. 546 [36] (Lord Hope).

[320] Two reports of the Joint Committee on Human Rights have been critical of the courts' approach: *The Meaning of Public Authority under the Human Rights Act*, HL Paper No.39/HC Paper No.382; (Session 2003/04) and *The Meaning of Public Authority under the Human Rights Act*, HL Paper No.77/HC (Session 2006/07) 410; and a Private Members Bill has sought to address the perceived problem: see *Hansard*, HC col.1036 (15 June 2007).

[321] *Aston Cantlow and Wilmcote with Billesley Parochial Church Council v Wallbank* [2003] UKHL 37; [2004] 1 A.C. 547 at [37] (Lord Hope), [161]-[162] (Lord Rodger); *YL v Birmingham City Council* [2007] UKHL 27; [2008] 1 A.C. 95 at [89]-[90] (Lord Mance). The point is that there is no ambiguity in the expression "functions of a public nature" that brings into play the limited rule in

concern is to avoid making simplistic assumptions about what is the preferable policy to pursued: while there may be policy arguments in favour of extending the protection of Convention rights (for example, as in *YL*, to people being cared for by charitable organisations or in privately-owned care homes under arrangements made and funded by local government), there are also countervailing considerations (for example, that extension of liability under the HRA may risk driving voluntary sector organisations and businesses away from contracting with the state to carry out functions, or may inhibit effective deployment of resources within organisations).[322] Another consideration is that all residents of a home—whether their places are arranged by government and publicly funded or arranged by themselves or their families and privately funded (or, as is often the case, a mix of the two)—should have similar rights and protections. This would not be so if those residents (and only those residents) whose places are arranged and funded by government were to have Convention rights directly enforceable the care home provider.[323] An important article by Professor Dawn Oliver has influenced the courts, especially her argument that the characteristics which give some functions (of non-core authorities) a public nature should be confined to "specifically legally authorised coercion or authority over others which would normally be unlawful for a private body to exercise".[324] Furthermore, the structure of some of the Convention rights is ill-suited to deal with claims against non-State bodies: where a qualified right exists (as in ECHR arts 8-11), most of the limitations on that right can only be relied upon by high-level institutions of the State.[325]

3-088   Critics—including the Government[326]—said that the decisions of the House of Lords in the test case of *YL*[327] and the Court of Appeal in *Leonard Cheshire*[328] was based on too narrow a conception of function of a public nature.[329] The Joint Committee on Human Rights in reports made in 2003-04 and 2006-07 argued for a broad interpretation, to give better effect to what was intended by the provision, as evidenced by the parliamentary debates at the time.[330] A failure to adopt such an approach has, it is said, led to a gap in human rights protection, especially for people vulnerable to ill-treatment.[331] The Joint Committee's view in 2003-04 was that "a function is a public one when government has taken responsibility for it" in the

---

Pepper v Hart [1993] A.C. 593 allowing *reference* to ministerial statements.

[322] *YL v Birmingham City Council* [2007] UKHL 27; [2008] 1 A.C. 95 at [152] (Lord Neuberger).

[323] *YL v Birmingham City Council* [2007] UKHL 27; [2008] 1 A.C. 95 at [151] (Lord Neuberger).

[324] D. Oliver, "Functions of a Public Nature under the Human Rights Act" [2004] P.L. 328 at 330, and "Frontiers of the State: Public Authorities and Public Functions under the Human Rights Act" [2000] P.L. 476.

[325] See 13-081.

[326] The Secretary of State for Constitutional Affairs was an intervener in *YL*, supporting a broad interpretation.

[327] *YL v Birmingham City Council* [2007] UKHL 27; [2008] 1 A.C. 95. And see Lord Pannick, "Functions of a Public Nature" [2009] J.R. 109.

[328] *R. (on the application of Heather) v Leonard Cheshire Foundation* [2002] EWCA Civ 366; [2002] 2 All E.R. 936.

[329] See *Hansard*, HC Vol.439, col.1311 (21 November 2005) (Vera Baird); col.1302 (Mr Burstow); col.1266 (Sandra Gidley); *Hansard*, HL Vol.678, col.WA70 (2 February 2006).

[330] See, e.g. *Hansard*, HL col.1232 (3 November 1997): "We also decided that we should apply the Bill to a wide rather than a narrow range of public authorities, so as to provide as much protection as possible to those who claim that their rights have been infringed" (Lord Irvine LC).

[331] See M. Sunkin, "Pushing Forward the Frontiers of Human Rights Protection: The Meaning of Public Authority under the Human Rights Act" [2005] P.L. 643; A. Williams, "A Fresh Perspective on Hybrid Public Authorities under the Human Rights Act 1998: Private Contractors, Rights-stripping and 'Chameleonic' Horizontal Effect" [2011] P.L. 139.

public interest.[332] In this context, it was argued that "institutional links with a public body are not necessary to identifying a public function"[333]; the question ought instead to be whether the activity has "its origins in governmental responsibilities, in such a way as to compel individuals to rely on that body for realisation of their Convention human rights".[334]

The debate over the amenability of social care provision to the Human Rights Act 1998 moved forward with enactment of the Health and Social Care Act 2008 s.145. This seeks to ensure that people who are receiving publicly arranged care in a private sector care home fall within the ambit of the Human Rights Act in relation to that provision: **3-089**

"Human Rights Act 1998: provision of certain social care to be public function

(1) A person ('P') who provides accommodation, together with nursing or personal care, in a care home for an individual under arrangements made with P under the relevant statutory provisions is to be taken for the purposes of subsection (3)(b) of section 6 of the Human Rights Act 1998 (c. 42) (acts of public authorities) to be exercising a function of a public nature in doing so.

(2) The "relevant statutory provisions" are—
   (a) in relation to England and Wales, sections 21(1)(a) and 26 of the National Assistance Act 1948 (c. 29),
   (b) in relation to Scotland, section 12 or 13A of the Social Work (Scotland) Act 1968 (c. 49), and
   (c) in relation to Northern Ireland, articles 15 and 36 of the Health and Personal Social Services (Northern Ireland) Order 1972 (S.I. 1972/1265 (N.I. 14)).

(3) In subsection (1) "care home"—
   (a) in relation to England and Wales, has the same meaning as in the Care Standards Act 2000 (c. 14), and
   (b) in relation to Northern Ireland, means a residential care home as defined by article 10 of the Health and Personal Social Services (Quality, Improvement and Regulation) (Northern Ireland) Order 2003 (S.I. 2003/431 (N.I. 9)) or a nursing home as defined by article 11 of that Order.

(4) In relation to Scotland, the reference in subsection (1) to the provision of accommodation, together with nursing or personal care, in a care home is to be read as a reference to the provision of accommodation, together with nursing, personal care or personal support, as a care home service as defined paragraph 2 of schedule 12 to the Public Services Reform (Scotland) Act 2010 (asp 8).

(5) Subsection (1) does not apply to acts (within the meaning of section 6 of the Human Rights Act 1998 (c. 42)) taking place before the coming into force of this section."

Although s.145 on the face of it applies only to care homes, the fact of Parliament's evident disapproval of the majority approach in *YL* must leave open the question

---

[332] Joint Committee on Human Rights, *HL Paper No.39/HC Paper No.302* (Session 2003/04) Ch.8.
[333] Joint Committee on Human Rights *HL Paper No.39/HC Paper No.302* (Session 2003/04) para.143. By way of illustration: "Under s.6 … there should be no distinction between a body providing housing because it itself is required to do so by statute, and a body providing housing because it has contracted with a local authority which is under a duty to provide the service" (para.142).
[334] HL Paper No.39/HC Paper No.382 (Session 2003/04) para.157. In the 2006-07 report the Joint Committee on Human Rights suggested that an interpretive statute could provide "For the purposes of s.6(3)(b) of the Human Rights Act 1998, a function of a public nature includes a function performed pursuant to a contract or other arrangement with a public authority which is under a duty to perform the function" (para.150). Would this cover the situation in *YL*? The local authority's duty under the National Assistance Act 1949 s.21 is to make arrangements, not to provide directly, accommodation and care.

whether that approach should be re-examined.[335] Until that time, s.145 "plainly does not in any way affect the binding nature of the reasoning of the majority of their Lordships" in *YL*.[336]

3-090   Section 145 is expressly about the question whether a care home is exercising a public function for the purposes of the Human Rights Act 1998. It does not have the result that "all arrangements, contractual or otherwise, between a care home provider and the local authority are to be treated as arrangements of a public nature" and, accordingly, a local authority's decision to terminate a contract to provide care is not amenable to judicial review.[337]

3-091   Section 145 afforded protection to those whose care was arranged under the National Assistance Act 1948 but not those whose care was arranged outside the 1948 Act—for example, those who receive care in a home but pay for it themselves and those who receive care at home by an independent provider. This loophole was closed by s.73 of the Care Act 2014.[338]

---

[335] See Lord Pannick, "Functions of a Public Nature" [2009] J.R. 109 at [16].

[336] *R. (on the application of Weaver) v London and Quadrant Housing Trust (Equality and Human Rights Commission intervening)* [2009] EWCA Civ 587; [2010] 1 W.L.R. 363, [32] (Elias LJ).

[337] *R. (on the application of Broadway Care Centre Ltd) v Caerphilly CBC* [2012] EWHC 37 (Admin); (2012) 15 C.C.L. Rep. 82.

[338] Section 73 reads:

"Human Rights Act 1998: provision of regulated care or support etc a public function

   (1) This section applies where—

        (a)   in England, a registered care provider provides care and support to an adult or support to a carer, in the course of providing—

           (i)   personal care in a place where the adult receiving the personal care is living when the personal care is provided, or

           (ii)   residential accommodation together with nursing or personal care;

        (b)   in Wales, a person registered under Part 2 of the Care Standards Act 2000 provides care and support to an adult, or support to a carer, in the course of providing—

           (i)   personal care in a place where the adult receiving the personal care is living when the personal care is provided, or

           (ii)   residential accommodation together with nursing or personal care;

        (c)   in Scotland, a person provides advice, guidance or assistance to an adult or support to a carer, in the course of providing a care service which is registered under section 59 of the Public Services Reform (Scotland) Act 2010 and which consists of the provision of—

           (i)   personal care in a place where the adult receiving the personal care is living when the personal care is provided, or

           (ii)   residential accommodation together with nursing or personal care;

        (d)   in Northern Ireland, a person registered under Part 3 of the Health and Personal Social Services (Quality, Improvement and Regulation) (Northern Ireland) Order 2003 provides advice, guidance or assistance to an adult or services to a carer, in the course of providing—

           (i)   personal care in a place where the adult receiving the personal care is living when the personal care is provided, or

           (ii)   residential accommodation together with nursing or personal care.

              In this section "the care or support" means the care and support, support, advice, guidance, assistance or services provided as mentioned above, and "the provider" means the person who provides the care or support.

   (2) The provider is to be taken for the purposes of section 6(3)(b) of the Human Rights Act 1998 (acts of public authorities) to be exercising a function of a public nature in providing the care or support, if the requirements of subsection (3) are met.

   (3) The requirements are that—

        (a)   the care or support is arranged by an authority listed in column 1 of the Table below, or paid for (directly or indirectly, and in whole or in part) by such an authority, and

Overview of the case law

The following table summarises the principal decisions on "functions of a public   **3-092**
nature".

Case	Date	Court	"function"	"act"	Outcome
Poplar Housing (a housing association)[339]	2001	CA	Social Landlord to which the local authority had transferred all its housing stock	Decision to issue proceedings for possession	Was a public authority (but no breach of Convention rights)
Austin Hall Building Ltd (case concerned an adjudicator)[340]	2001	QBD	Adjudication about payment for building works under the Housing Grants, Construction and Regeneration Act 1996 s.108	Had been given insufficient opportunity to present case etc.	Not a public authority
Partnerships in Care (a private hospital provider)[341]	2002	Admin Court	Provision of treatment in private psychiatric hospital to person compulsorily detained under Mental Health Act 1983	Decision of managers to "change the focus of one of its wards"	Was an act of a public nature
Leonard Cheshire Foundation[342] (a charity providing accommodation and care to the elderly)	2002	CA	Provision of accommodation plus care to elderly under contract with local authority (which is fulfilling duties to make such arrangements under National Assistance Act 1948)	Decision to close home where claimants had lived for more than 17 years and move them to alternative accommodation	Not a function of a public nature

(b)   the authority arranges or pays for the care or support under a provision listed in the corresponding entry in column 2 of the Table."

[339] *Poplar Housing & Regeneration Community Association Ltd v Donoghue* [2001] EWCA Civ 595; [2002] Q.B. 48; cf. e.g. *Smart v Sheffield City Council* [2002] EWCA Civ 4; [2002] H.L.R. 34 (possession proceedings by a local authority subject to the HRA because it was a "core" public authority).

[340] *Austin Hall Building Ltd v Buckland Securities Ltd* [2001] B.L.R. 272.

[341] *R. (on the application of A) v Partnerships in Care Ltd* [2002] EWHC 529 (Admin); [2002] 1 W.L.R. 2610; see also *R. (on the application of Wilkinson) v Broadmoor Special Hospital Authority* [2001] EWCA Civ 1545; [2002] 1 W.L.R. 419 at [61] (HRA s.6(3) "is apt to cover the actions of private doctors and others carrying out statutory functions under the Mental Health Act").

[342] *R. (on the application of Heather) v Leonard Cheshire Foundation* [2002] EWCA Civ 366; [2002] 2 All E.R. 936.

Case	Date	Court	"function"	"act"	Outcome
Parochial Church Council of the Parish of Aston Cantlow etc.[343]	2003	HL	Ensuring the maintenance and repair of Church of England churches	Decision to enforce a lay rector's obligation to meet the cost of chancel repairs	Not a function of a public nature
Hampshire Farmers Markets Ltd[344] (private company limited by guarantee set up by local authority to regulate markets)	2003	CA	Controlling the right of access to a public market	Decision to reject application by claimant trout farmer to participate in programme of farmers markets	Was a public function
Malcolm[345] (trustee in bankruptcy)	2005	CA	Role of insolvency practitioner appointed trustee of bankrupt's estate under Insolvency Act 1986	Decision to obtain a lump sum benefit of a retirement annuity contract	Was a public function
Network Rail Infrastructure Ltd (formerly Railtrack Plc)[346]	2006	QBD	Role as an "infrastructure controller" under the Railways (Safety Case) Regulations 2000 and owner and controller of track, signalling and bridge works on the stretch of line on which Potters Bar accident occurred	A failure to maintain points on the track	Was not a public function

---

[343] *Aston Cantlow and Wilmcote with Billesley Parochial Church Council v Wallbank* [2003] UKHL 37; [2004] 1 A.C. 546 (4:1 decision on this point, Lord Scott of Foscote dissenting).

[344] *R. (on the application of Beer (t/a Hammer Trout Farm)) v Hampshire Farmers Markets Ltd* [2003] EWCA Civ 1056; [2004] 1 W.L.R. 233. The judgment does not identify which Convention right was at stake. See further B. Hough, "Public Law Regulation of Markets and Fairs" [2005] P.L. 586.

[345] *Malcolm, Re; Malcolm v Benedict Mackenzie (A Firm)* [2004] EWCA Civ 1748; [2005] 1 W.L.R. 1238 at [30].

[346] *Cameron v Network Rail Infrastructure Ltd (formerly Railtrack Plc)* [2006] EWHC 1133 (QB);

Case	Date	Court	"function"	"act"	Outcome
YL[347] (challenge to Southern Cross Healthcare, a business running care homes for the elderly)	2007	HL	Provision of accommodation plus care to elderly people (arranged by and subsidised by local authorities under duties imposed by National Assistance Act 1948)	Decision to terminate elderly resident's contractual right to remain in care home	Was not a public function
R. (on the application of Weaver) v London & Quadrant Housing Trust[348]	2009	CA (Elias LJ and Lord Collins of Mapresbury; Rix LJ dissenting)	management and allocation of housing stock by a registered social landlord	termination of a tenancy on grounds of rent arrears	act of terminating a tenancy in social housing did not constitute an act of a private nature, and was in principle subject to human rights considerations
In re All Saints', Sanderstead[349]	2011	Southwark Consistory Court	Celebration of Holy Communion by priest of the Church of England	Decision to remove communion rail	Not a function of a public nature (Equality Act 2010 s.31(4)).

[2007] 1 W.L.R. 163 at [29]: the company was set up in 1994, when the British Rail Board was privatised, and the railway infrastructure was vested in it by the Railway Act 1993. At first the company had statutory powers to regulate safety (and may during that time have been a public authority) but those were removed in December 2000 and transferred to the Health and Safety Executive and subsequently to the Office of Rail Regulation. cf. *In the Matter of an Application for Judicial Review by Ronald Wadsworth* [2004] NIQB 8 (a dispute about the exclusion of a licensed public hire taxi driver from a designated taxi rank) where Weatherup J held that the Northern Ireland Railways Company Ltd, a railway company authorised under the Transport Act (Northern Ireland) 1967, and the Northern Ireland Transport Holding Company (owner of the lands at Central Station Belfast), established under the 1967, were carrying out "functions of a public nature" for the purposes of the HRA.

[347] *YL v Birmingham City Council* [2007] UKHL 27; [2008] 1 A.C. 95.

[348] *R. (on the application of Weaver) v London & Quadrant Housing Trust* [2009] EWCA Civ 587; [2010] 1 W.L.R. 363. See also *R. (on the application of Bevan & Clarke LLP) v Neath Port Talbot CBC* [2012] EWHC 236 (Admin); [2012] B.L.G.R. 728 (private sector operators of care homes applied for judicial review of local authority's decision to award a 5.7 per cent increase in the rate to be paid to them. The decision was amenable to judicial review. The mere fact that it concerned the setting of a fee under a contract did not characterise it as a private act. The application failed on other grounds).

[349] *In re All Saints', Sanderstead* [2012] Fam 51.

Step 1—assessing the body's functions

3-093   As we have noted, assessment of the reach of the HRA is a two-step process: assessing the body's functions and then considering the nature of the "act". Here we consider the first step, which involves examination of the overall work of the body in question. "Function" has a more conceptual and less specific meaning than "act" (which falls for consideration at step 2).[350] Only if the body is carrying out a mix of public and private functions does it fall within the scope of s.6 of the HRA.[351] If *none* of its functions are of a public nature then it is incapable of perpetrating breaches of Convention rights. The use of the terms "hybrid public authority" and "functional public authority"[352] has been deprecated,[353] but in relation to this stage of the inquiry it is useful shorthand for the kind of body that falls within ambit of the HRA. Certainly, it would be wrong to focus only on what is "done" without considering the institutional and relational context in which it is done.[354] How then do and should the courts approach the task of identifying functions of a public nature? There are two possible sources of assistance.

Relevance of the judicial review case law on public functions

3-094   The first is the case law following from *Datafin* on "public functions" for the purposes of amenability to judicial review.[355] The language is similar, as are the broad purposes of the tests—respectively, to extend the ambit of the HRA beyond core public authorities[356] and to extend judicial review generally beyond those public authorities exercising statutory and prerogative powers. Some early judgments assumed that the tests were the same.[357] On more mature reflection it can, however, be seen that the tests are in fact distinct.[358] In many cases a decision will be susceptible to judicial review and the HRA. There are, however, situations in which a decision will be subject to the HRA but judicial review will not be an appropriate way of making a challenge (e.g. an issue to do with whether a decision in relation to an official's employment is compatible with Convention rights ought

---

[350] *YL v Birmingham City Council* [2007] UKHL 27; [2008] 1 A.C. 95 at [130] (Lord Neuberger).

[351] "The body must be one of which at least some, but not all, of its functions are of a public nature", *Aston Cantlow* [2003] UKHL 37; [2004] 1 A.C. 547 at [85].

[352] The terms "functional public authority" and "hybrid public authority" have been coined in the context of the institutional approach (see *Aston Cantlow* [2003] UKHL 37; [2004] 1 A.C. 547 at [34]), which has now been disapproved.

[353] The Joint Select Committee on Human Rights has pointed out use of such terms is unhelpful as they deflect attention away from the nature of the functions performed to the intrinsic character of the body (HL Paper No.39/HC Paper No.382 (Session 2003/04) para.7).

[354] *YL v Birmingham City Council* [2007] UKHL 27; [2008] 1 A.C. 95 at [102] (Lord Mance: "There is, for example, a clear conceptual difference between the functions of a private firm engaged by a local authority to enforce the Road Traffic Regulation Act 1984, as amended, on a public road and the activities of the same firm engaged by a private land-owner or a local authority to enforce a private scheme or parking restrictions of which notice have been given on a private property or estate"). cf. *Akumah v Hackney LBC* [2005] UKHL 17; [2005] 1 W.L.R. 985.

[355] See 3-038.

[356] Joint Committee on Human Rights HL Paper No.39/HC Paper No.382 (Session 2003/04) para.4 ("to apply human rights guarantees beyond the obvious government bodies").

[357] *Poplar Housing & Regeneration Community Association Ltd v Donaghue* [2001] EWCA Civ 595; [2002] Q.B. 48 at [65(i)]; *R. (on the application of Heather) v Leonard Cheshire Foundation* [2001] EWHC Admin 429 at [65] (Stanley Burnton J).

[358] *R. (on the application of Heather) v Leonard Cheshire Foundation* [2002] EWCA Civ 366; [2002] 2 All E.R. 936 at [36] (Lord Woolf CJ); *R. (on the application of A) v Partnerships in Care Ltd* [2002] EWHC 529 (Admin); [2002] 1 W.L.R. 2610 at [27]; *Aston Cantlow* [2007] UKHL 27; [2007] 3 W.L.R. 112 at [52] (Lord Hope of Craighead); *YL v Birmingham City Council* [2007] UKHL 27; [2008] 1 A.C. 95 at [87] (Lord Mance).

to be taken on appeal to the Employment Tribunal).[359] Nonetheless, provided a cautious approach is adopted, the case law relating to judicial review may be helpful in identifying, though not determinative of, the factors that need to be taken into account.[360] Too great an emphasis on the institutional and relational characteristics of the decision-maker must, however, be avoided. In some of the early cases courts fell into this trap[361] and as a result perhaps focused insufficiently on the inherent characteristics of the function, which ought to be the main object of the inquiry under the HRA.[362]

Relevance of the ECtHR case law

A second source of assistance is the case law of the European Court of Human Rights.[363] As with the identification of "core" public authorities,[364] so too with the ambit of "functions of a public nature": there is a link to the responsibility of Member States under the ECHR.[365] That said, the concept of "functions of a public nature" is one of national law that has no exact counterpart in ECHR case law. In YL, two "relevant principles" in the ECHR case law were identified, though it was conceded that the ECtHR has not always distinguished clearly between them.[366] First, there are circumstances in which Member States are responsible for a failure to take positive steps to prevent a person or non-state body from directly and immediately affecting a person's Convention rights. An example of this is a local authority's failure to protect children known to be being ill-treated by relatives (contrary to ECHR art.2).[367] Another illustration might be where the management of a commercially-owned shopping centre refuses to allow a campaign group

3-095

---

[359] See 16-017.
[360] In *YL v Birmingham City Council* [2003] UKHL 37; [2004] 1 A.C. 547 at [12] (Lord Bingham: "it will not ordinarily matter whether the body in question is amenable to judicial review"); *R. (on the application of Weaver) v London & Quadrant Housing Trust* [2009] EWCA Civ 587; [2010] 1 W.L.R. 363 at [37], [83] (Elias LJ).
[361] For example, in *Poplar Housing* [2001] EWCA Civ 595; [2002] Q.B. 48. In *YL*, the HL criticised *Poplar Housing*: [105] (Lord Mance: "The deployment in *Poplar Housing*, apparently as a decisive factor in favour of the application of s.6(3)(b), of the close historical and organisational assimilation of Poplar Housing with the local authority is in my view open to the objection that this did not bear on the function or role that Poplar Housing was performing"); at [61] (Baroness Hale: "It is common ground that it is the nature of the function being performed, rather than the nature of the body performing it, which matters under s.6(3)(b).The case of *Poplar Housing* relied too heavily upon the historical links between the local authority and the registered social landlord, rather than upon the nature of the function itself which was the provision of social housing").
[362] An approach adopted by Lord Hope in *Aston Cantlow* [2003] UKHL 37; [2004] 1 A.C. 547 at [34]-[64]. See also *YL v Birmingham City Council* [2007] UKHL 27; [2008] 1 A.C. 95 at [148] (Lord Neuberger of Abbotsbury: "s.6(3)(b) appears to me to be concerned primarily with 'functions', or services, as such, rather than with the identity of the person who is paying for the provision of the services, or the reason for payment (although such factors are not, in my view, irrelevant)").
[363] H. Quane, "The Strasbourg Jurisprudence and the Meaning of 'Public Authority' under the Human Rights Act" [2006] P.L. 106; *R. (on the application of Beer (t/a Hammer Trout Farm)) v Hampshire Farmers Markets Ltd* [2003] EWCA Civ 1056; [2004] 1 W.L.R. 233 at [28]. In *R. (on the application of Weaver) v London & Quadrant Housing Trust* [2009] EWCA Civ 587; [2009] 1 All E.R. 17 at [118], Rix LJ (dissenting) attached importance to the fact that "there is no case, at any rate none has been cited, in Strasbourg jurisprudence in which the non-governmental provider of social housing has been the cause or object of a complaint of victimhood within the meaning of the Convention".
[364] See 3-067.
[365] See, e.g. *YL v Birmingham City Council* [2007] UKHL 27; [2008] 1 A.C. 95 at [87] (Lord Mance).
[366] *YL v Birmingham City Council* [2007] UKHL 27; [2008] 1 A.C. 95 at [92] (Lord Mance).
[367] *Z v United Kingdom* (29392/95) [2001] 2 F.L.R. 612 (failure of State in its positive obligation to prevent breaches of art.3 (prohibition of cruel and degrading treatment) by private third party).

permission to distribute leaflets to shoppers.[368] Secondly, a Member State may remain responsible for the activities of non-State body to which it has delegated state powers. An example here would be a privately-managed "contracted out" prison or probation services (which may engage a number of Convention rights).[369]

Possible factors indicating a "function of a public nature"

3-096   The approach of the national courts has been to enumerate various factors, in the light of the ECtHR case law, and drawing lightly upon some of the factors relevant to determining amenability to judicial review,[370] which may indicate that a function is a "function of a public nature". In doing so, the courts have been careful to stress that "there is no single litmus test".[371] In the following table we set out some of the main factors that may need to be considered. No list can be comprehensive as each case necessarily turns on its own facts. In any case where there is disagreement over whether a function is or is not public in nature, it will be important to identify whether the source of that disagreement is about the relevance of a factor, the application of a factor to the facts in the case in hand, or the overall (and somewhat impressionistic) assessment as to the outcome that is suggested by the overall mix of factors. These factors are summarised in the following table.

Factor	Comment
Public funding—often necessary but never sufficient	"The extent to which in carrying out the relevant function the body is publicly funded" (*Aston Cantlow* at [12]).[372] "The greater the State's involvement in making payment for the function in question, the greater (other things being equal) is its assumption of responsibility" (*Aston Cantlow* at [10]).[373]

---

[368] *Appleby v United Kingdom* (44306/98) (2003) 37 E.H.R.R. 38. The applicants argued that there was a breach of art.10 (freedom of expression). The ECtHR held: "The Court does not find that the authorities bear any direct responsibility for this restriction on the applicants' freedom of expression. It is not persuaded that any element of State responsibility can be derived from the fact that a public development corporation transferred the property to Postel or that this was done with ministerial permission. The issue to be determined is whether the respondent State has failed in any positive obligation to protect the exercise of the applicants' art.10 rights from interference by others—in this case, the owner of the Galleries" (para.41). The State had not so failed.

[369] See, e.g. Offender Management Act 2007. Examples given in *YL* are *Wós v Poland* (2005) (Polish-German Reconciliation Foundation, a private body, had powers to provide compensation provided from Germany to compensate Nazi victims engaged the responsibility of the State); *Sychev v Ukraine* (2005) (powers to execute court judgments delegated to private law commission; held that it exercised State powers).

[370] See 3-042.

[371] *YL v Birmingham City Council* [2007] UKHL 27; [2008] 1 A.C. 95 at [66]; *Aston Cantlow* [2003] UKHL 37; [2004] 1 A.C. 547 at [11]. See further C. Campbell, "The Nature of Power as Public in English Judicial Review" [2009] C.L.J. 90 at 102, where it is suggested that the courts' approach of relying on indicia is problematic as it may have the effect of creating a presumption that a function is private unless it is shown to be public.

[372] *Aston Cantlow and Wilmcote with Billesley Parochial Church Council v Wallbank* [2003] UKHL 37; [2004] 1 A.C. 546.

[373] *Aston Cantlow and Wilmcote with Billesley Parochial Church Council v Wallbank* [2003] UKHL 37; [2004] 1 A.C. 546.

Factor	Comment
	"It may well be that an activity of an entity which is not a core public authority is often unlikely to be a 'function of a public nature' if it is not ultimately funded by a core public authority, but, again as a matter of logic and language, it cannot be a sufficient condition, in my view" (*YL*, [142]).[374]
	In *YL*, the majority drew a distinction between public subsidy (which may imply a public function) and payment by a core public authority for a service provided by a third party (at [27]); "The injection of capital or subsidy into an organisation in return for undertaking a non-commercial role or activity of general public interest may be one thing; payment for services under a contractual arrangement with a company aiming to profit commercially thereby is potentially quite another" (*YL*, [105]). cf. Baroness Hale in *YL* at [67]).[375]
	"[T]here is a substantial public subsidy which enables the [registered social landlord] to achieve its objectives. This does not involve, as in YL, the payment of money by reference to specific services provided but significant capital payments designed to enable the [RSL] to meet its publicly desirable objectives" (*Weaver* at [68])[376]

[374] *YL v Birmingham City Council* [2007] UKHL 27; [2008] 1 A.C. 95.
[375] *YL v Birmingham City Council* [2007] UKHL 27; [2008] 1 A.C. 95.
[376] *R. (on the application of Weaver) v London and Quadrant Housing Trust (Equality and Human Rights Commission intervening)* [2009] EWCA Civ 587; [2010] 1 W.L.R. 363.

Factor	Comment
Statutory powers	"Whether the body is "exercising statutory powers" (*Aston Cantlow* at [12])[377]; whether the body possesses "special powers and enjoys immunities which might have been indications of "publicness" (*Railtrack* at [29])[378]; "Conversely, the absence of any statutory intervention will tend to indicate parliamentary recognition that the function in question is private and so an inappropriate subject for public regulation" (*Aston Cantlow* at [8]).[379] "The existence and source of any special powers or duties must on any view be a very relevant factor when considering whether State responsibility is engaged in Strasbourg or whether s.6(3)(b) applies domestically" (*YL* at [102]).[380] But "the mere possession of special powers conferred by Parliament does not by itself mean that a person has functions of a public nature. Such powers may have been conferred for private, religious or purely commercial purposes" (*YL* at [101]).[381]
	Registered Social Landlords "have certain statutory powers, identical to those enjoyed by local authorities but not private landlords, empowering them to take action in respect of the conduct of their tenants. For example, they may apply for anti-social behaviour orders under Pt 1 of the Crime and Disorder Act 1998, or for a parenting order under the Anti-Social Behaviour Act 2003 in respect of the parents of children causing a nuisance" (*Weaver* at [16]).[382]

---

[377] *Aston Cantlow and Wilmcote with Billesley Parochial Church Council v Wallbank* [2003] UKHL 37; [2004] 1 A.C. 546.

[378] *Cameron v Network Rail Infrastructure Ltd (formerly Railtrack Plc)* [2006] EWHC 1133 (QB); [2007] 1 W.L.R. 163.

[379] *Aston Cantlow and Wilmcote with Billesley Parochial Church Council v Wallbank* [2003] UKHL 37; [2004] 1 A.C. 546.

[380] *YL v Birmingham City Council* [2007] UKHL 27; [2008] 1 A.C. 95.

[381] *YL v Birmingham City Council* [2007] UKHL 27; [2008] 1 A.C. 95.

[382] *R. (on the application of Weaver) v London and Quadrant Housing Trust (Equality and Human Rights Commission intervening)* [2009] EWCA Civ 587; [2010] 1 W.L.R. 363.

Factor	Comment
Coercive and regulatory powers	"The use or potential use of statutory coercive powers is a powerful consideration in favour of this being a public function" (*YL* at [70]).[383] "The regulatory or coercive powers of the state" (*YL* at [63]).[384] In *YL*, the majority distinguished this factor from situations in which a person may have powers under the common law doctrine of necessity and where statutory powers of coercion applied to people working in both the public and private sector (at [84]).[385]
Delegation—standing in the shoes of a core public authority	Whether the body is "taking the place of central government or local authorities" (*Aston Cantlow* at [12]).[386] In *YL*, the majority held that "no delegation of that sort exists in relation to the council's functions under s.21 of the 1948 Act" (at [104]).[387] "[A]lthough not directly taking the place of local government, the [registered social landlord] in its allocation of social housing operates in very close harmony with it, assisting it to achieve the authority's statutory duties and objectives" (*Weaver* at [69]).
Public service	Whether the body "is providing a public service" (*Aston Cantlow* at [12]).[388] The majority on *YL* held "It is necessary to look *also* at *the reason why* the person in question, whether an individual or corporate, is carrying out those activities. A local authority is doing so pursuant to public law obligations. A private person, including local authority employees, is doing so pursuant to private law contractual obligations" (at [31]).[389] Provision of subsidised housing was "a public service" (*Weaver* at [70]); it followed that not all tenants of a registered social landlord would fall within the ambit of s.6—those who were paying market.[390]

383 *YL v Birmingham City Council* [2007] UKHL 27; [2008] 1 A.C. 95.
384 *YL v Birmingham City Council* [2007] UKHL 27; [2008] 1 A.C. 95.
385 *YL v Birmingham City Council* [2007] UKHL 27; [2008] 1 A.C. 95.
386 *Aston Cantlow and Wilmcote with Billesley Parochial Church Council v Wallbank* [2003] UKHL 37; [2004] 1 A.C. 546.
387 *YL v Birmingham City Council* [2007] UKHL 27; [2008] 1 A.C. 95.
388 *Aston Cantlow and Wilmcote with Billesley Parochial Church Council v Wallbank* [2003] UKHL 37; [2004] 1 A.C. 546.
389 *YL v Birmingham City Council* [2007] UKHL 27; [2008] 1 A.C. 95.
390 *R. (on the application of Weaver) v London and Quadrant Housing Trust (Equality and Human Rights Commission intervening)* [2009] EWCA Civ 587; [2010] 1 W.L.R. 363.

Factor	Comment
Public rights of access	The function relates to a building or land over which the public have rights of access (*Aston Cantlow* at [130]).[391] Markets held on publicly owned land to which the public have access (*Hampshire Farmers Markets* at [33]).[392]
Core State responsibilities	Whether the function is "intrinsically an activity of government" (*Railtrack* at [29])[393]; "the role and responsibility of the state in relation to the subject matter in question" (*Aston Cantlow* at [7])[394]; "the fact that a function is or has been performed by a core public authority for the benefit of the public" (*YL* at [72]).[395] In *YL*, the majority held that it was wrong to regard "the actual provision, as opposed to the arrangement, of care and accommodation for those unable to arrange it themselves as an inherently governmental function" (at [115]).[396] "While it would be wrong to be didactic in this difficult area, I suspect that it would be a relatively rare case where a company could be performing a 'function of a public nature' if it was carrying on an activity which could not be carried out by any core public authority. On the other hand, I would not accept that the mere fact that a core public authority, even where it is the body funding the activity, could carry out the activity concerned must mean that the activity is such a function. Apart from anything else, there must scarcely be an activity which cannot be carried out by some core public authority" (*YL* at [144]).[397]

[391] *Aston Cantlow and Wilmcote with Billesley Parochial Church Council v Wallbank* [2003] UKHL 37; [2004] 1 A.C. 546; Lord Scott of Foscote, dissenting.

[392] *R. (on the application of Beer (t/a Hammer Trout Farm)) v Hampshire Farmers Markets Ltd* [2003] EWCA Civ 1056; [2004] 1 W.L.R. 233.

[393] *Cameron v Network Rail Infrastructure Ltd (formerly Railtrack Plc)* [2006] EWHC 1133 (QB); [2007] 1 W.L.R. 163.

[394] *Aston Cantlow and Wilmcote with Billesley Parochial Church Council v Wallbank* [2003] UKHL 37; [2004] 1 A.C. 546.

[395] *YL v Birmingham City Council* [2007] UKHL 27; [2008] 1 A.C. 95.

[396] *YL v Birmingham City Council* [2007] UKHL 27; [2008] 1 A.C. 95.

[397] *YL v Birmingham City Council* [2007] UKHL 27; [2008] 1 A.C. 95.

Factor	Comment
	"[T]he provision of subsidised housing, as opposed to the provision of housing itself, is, ... a function which can properly be described as governmental. Almost by definition it is the antithesis of a private commercial activity. The provision of subsidy to meet the needs of the poorer section of the community is typically, although not necessarily, a function which government provides" (*Weaver* at [70]).[398] But cf. *R. (on the application of Ahmad) v The Mayor and Burgesses of Newham LBC* at [12] where Baroness Hale of Richmond emphasises that the provision of housing (as opposed to its allocation) is not a government function.[399]
	Re All Saints', Sanderstead: the celebration of marriage in the Church of England, unlike purely "religious" services, involves a public function: [66]–[67].[400]
Beyond core State responsibilities: the assumption of responsibility by the State	"Whether the State has assumed responsibility for seeing that this task is performed" (*YL* at [66]).[401]

---

[398] *R. (on the application of Weaver) v London and Quadrant Housing Trust (Equality and Human Rights Commission intervening)* [2009] EWCA Civ 587; [2010] 1 W.L.R. 363.

[399] *R. (on the application of Ahmad) v The Mayor and Burgesses of Newham LBC* [2009] UKHL 14; [2009] P.T.S.R. 632.

[400] *Re All Saints', Sanderstead* [2012] Fam 51.

[401] *YL v Birmingham City Council* [2007] UKHL 27; [2008] 1 A.C. 95.

Factor	Comment
The public interest	Whether there is an obligation "to conduct its operations in a manner subservient to the public interest" (*Railtrack* at [29]),[402] "The contrast is between what is 'public' in the sense of being done for or by or on behalf of the people as a whole and what is 'private' in the sense of being done for one's own purposes" (*YL* at [62], and [67])[403]; "Democratic accountability, an obligation to act only in the public interest and (in most cases today) a statutory constitution exclude the sectional or personally motivated interests of privately owned, profit-earning enterprises" (*YL* at [105]). It goes against a function being public where there is a "a clear commercial objective" of making profits for shareholders (*Railtrack* at [29]).[404] "The fact that a service can fairly be said to be to the public benefit cannot mean, as a matter of language, that it follows that providing the service itself is a function of a public nature. Nor does it follow as a matter of logic or policy. Otherwise, the services of all charities, indeed, it seems to me, of all private organisations which provide services which could be offered by charities, would be caught by s.6(1)" (*YL* at [135]).[405]
	A registered social landlord was "acting in the public interest and has charitable objectives" (*Weaver* at [70]).[406]
Democratic accountability	Whether the body is "democratically accountable to central or local government" (*Railtrack* at [29])[407]; "democratic accountability" (*YL* at [103]).
Government control	Whether those appointed to run the body are subject to government influence or control (*Railtrack* at [29]).[408]

---

[402] *Cameron v Network Rail Infrastructure Ltd (formerly Railtrack Plc)* [2006] EWHC 1133 (QB); [2007] 1 W.L.R. 163.

[403] *YL v Birmingham City Council* [2007] UKHL 27; [2008] 1 A.C. 95.

[404] *Cameron v Network Rail Infrastructure Ltd (formerly Railtrack Plc)* [2006] EWHC 1133 (QB); [2007] 1 W.L.R. 163.

[405] *YL v Birmingham City Council* [2007] UKHL 27; [2008] 1 A.C. 95.

[406] *R. (on the application of Weaver) v London & Quadrant Housing Trust* [2009] EWCA Civ 587; [2010] 1 W.L.R. 363.

[407] *Cameron v Network Rail Infrastructure Ltd (formerly Railtrack Plc)* [2006] EWHC 1133 (QB); [2007] 1 W.L.R. 163.

[408] *Cameron v Network Rail Infrastructure Ltd (formerly Railtrack Plc)* [2006] EWHC 1133 (QB); [2007] 1 W.L.R. 163.

Factor	Comment
Regulation	The "extent to which the state, directly or indirectly, regulates, supervises and inspects the performance of the function in question, and imposes criminal penalties on those who fall below publicly promulgated standards in performing it" (*Aston Cantlow* at [9]).[409] In *YL*, the majority doubted this factor: "Regulation by the State is no real pointer towards the person regulated being a state or governmental body or a person with a function of a public nature, if anything perhaps even the contrary" (at [161]).[410] "There is no identity between the public interest in a particular service being provided properly and the service itself being a public service. As a matter of ordinary language and concepts, the mere fact that the public interest requires a service to be closely regulated and supervised pursuant to statutory rules cannot mean that the provision of the service, as opposed to its regulation and supervision, is a function of a public nature" (at [134]).[411]
	"[T]he regulation to which [a registered social landlord] is subjected is not designed simply to render its activities more transparent, or to ensure proper standards of performance in the public interest. Rather the regulations over such matters as rent and eviction are designed, at least in part, to ensure that the objectives of government policy with respect to this vulnerable group in society are achieved and that low cost housing is effectively provided to those in need of it. Moreover, it is intrusive regulation on various aspects of allocation and management, and even restricts the power to dispose of land and property" (*Weaver* at [71]).[412]

[409] *Aston Cantlow and Wilmcote with Billesley Parochial Church Council v Wallbank* [2003] UKHL 37; [2004] 1 A.C. 546.
[410] *YL v Birmingham City Council* [2007] UKHL 27; [2008] 1 A.C. 95.
[411] *YL v Birmingham City Council* [2007] UKHL 27; [2008] 1 A.C. 95.
[412] *R. (on the application of Weaver) v London & Quadrant Housing Trust* [2009] EWCA Civ 587; [2010] 1 W.L.R. 363.

Factor	Comment
Risk of breaching rights	"The extent of the risk, if any, that improper performance of the function might violate an individual's Convention right" (*YL* at [11]).[413] "The close connection between [the] service and the core values underlying the Convention rights and the ... risk that rights will be violated unless adequate steps are taken to protect them" (*YL* at [71]).[414]

Step 2—assessing the nature of the particular act complained of

3-097   If the court's analysis leads to the conclusion that there is a "function of a public nature", a second step is then to consider the precise act in question. If "the nature of the act is private" (s.6(5)), then it falls outside the protective scope of the HRA. The following have been held to be private acts: the enforcement of a civil debt[415]; and the exercise of a contractual notice to terminate a licence.[416]

3-098   The following has been held to be acts of a public nature: the termination of a tenancy by a registered social landlord.[417] The Court of Appeal in that case rightly stressed that in deciding whether a particular "act" is public or private, the court must look at the context in which the act occurs. Both the source and nature of the "act" must be considered, but it would be wrong to think that a private (e.g. contractual) source inevitably has the consequence of characterising the "act" as private. As Elias LJ stated:

> "if an act were necessarily a private act because it involved the exercise of rights conferred by private law, that would significantly undermine the protection which Parliament intended to afford to potential victims of hybrid authorities. Public bodies necessarily fulfil their functions by entering into contractual arrangements. It would severely limit the significance of identifying certain bodies as hybrid authorities if the fact that the act under consideration was a contractual act meant that it was a private act falling within s.6(5)."[418]

TERRITORIAL REACH OF JUDICIAL REVIEW AND THE HRA

3-099   Almost all functions challenged in judicial review claims in the Administrative Court are exercised in England and Wales in respect of claimants based in England and Wales. In a small number of cases, however, the court has had to consider whether decisions relating to other geographical areas are amenable to review.

---

[413] *YL v Birmingham City Council* [2007] UKHL 27; [2008] 1 A.C. 95.
[414] *YL v Birmingham City Council* [2007] UKHL 27; [2008] 1 A.C. 95.
[415] *Aston Cantlow* UKHL 37; [2004] 1 A.C. 547 at [64] (Lord Hope).
[416] *YL v Birmingham City Council* [2007] UKHL 27; [2008] 1 A.C. 95 at [34] (Lord Scott).
[417] *R. (on the application of Weaver) v London & Quadrant Housing Trust* [2009] EWCA Civ 587; [2010] 1 W.L.R. 363.
[418] *R. (on the application of Weaver) v London & Quadrant Housing Trust* [2009] EWCA Civ 587; [2010] 1 W.L.R. 363, [77]; and [102] (Lord Collins of Mapesbury).

Public functions exercised in Scotland or Northern Ireland

Within the United Kingdom there are three separate legal jurisdictions[419]: **3-100** England and Wales (with which this book is primarily concerned)[420]; Scotland; and Northern Ireland. As we note, judicial review law in Scotland has in the past differed in some significant respects, for example in relation to the time limit for commencing proceedings (no general limit is set by legislation), standing[421] and as to amenability.[422] Despite this, attempts at tactical "forum shopping" have been rare.[423]

The questions that arise are (a) whether the Administrative Court has jurisdic- **3-101** tion and (b) if so, whether discretion should be exercised to allow or require the claim to be dealt with in another legal system. Where a conflict of laws situation does arise, the Administrative Court will not necessarily adopt the same approach to determining the most convenient forum as English courts do in private law disputes as there are constitutional considerations at stake, not merely issues of private expediency.[424] One such constitutional factor is the Treaty and Act of Union with Scotland 1706 art.19, which should make the English and Scottish courts wary of exercising jurisdiction over cases which properly belong to the other legal system.

Where the impugned decision is taken by a public authority with decision- **3-102** making powers stretching across Great Britain[425] or the whole United Kingdom, the approach of the English courts faced, for example, with a claimant with strong links to Scotland has, however, varied. In some cases, the English courts have accepted jurisdiction. Thus the Court of Appeal heard, without detailed discussion of the jurisdictional issue, an appeal in a judicial review claim brought by Scottish Power Plc (an electricity power supply company operating exclusively in Scotland) against a decision of the Director General of Electricity Supply, a regulator with a remit covering Great Britain (whose head office was in Birmingham, England).[426] If jurisdiction does exist, discretion may be exercised to refuse or stay English proceedings brought by a person whose circumstances have an insufficiently strong connection to England.[427] There are, however, also cases in which jurisdiction has been declined by the English court.[428]

In immigration and asylum matters the substantive law is uniform throughout the **3-103** United Kingdom. In this context, where a judicial review challenge is made to a decision of a tribunal which has jurisdiction in all parts of the United Kingdom, the superior courts in each part of the United Kingdom should correspondingly have jurisdiction; generally, the court in the part of the United Kingdom where the

---

[419] And on devolution, see 1-119.
[420] On the emerging differentiation between England and Wales, see T. Jones and J. Williams, "Wales as a Jurisdiction" [2004] P.L. 78; Welsh Government, *Consultation Document: A Separate Legal Jurisdiction for Wales* (2012); D.C. Gardner, "Public Law Challenges in Wales: the past and the present" [2013] P.L. 1.
[421] See 2-072.
[422] See 3-118.
[423] cf. *Sokha v Secretary of State for the Home Office, The Times,* 15 August 1991 (Outer House).
[424] *R. (on the application of Majead) v Immigration Appeal Tribunal* [2003] EWCA Civ 615; [2003] A.C.D. 70 at [13].
[425] Great Britain consists of England and Wales and Scotland.
[426] *R. v Director General of Electricity Supply Ex p. Scottish Power Plc*, unreported, 3 February 1997. Neither party took a point on jurisdiction.
[427] *R. v Special Commissioners Ex p. RW Forsyth Ltd* [1987] 1 All E.R. 1035.
[428] *R. v Secretary of State for Scotland Ex p. Greenpeace* unreported 24 May 1995, in which, citing art.19, Popplewell J held that he had no jurisdiction to hear a challenge to a decision by the minister to grant a licence to Shell UK to dispose of the Brent Spa oil platform in deep water off Scotland.

tribunal made its decision should hear any challenge.[429] In relation to criminal justice, there are some significant differences between different parts of the United Kingdom and where the court's jurisdiction is called into question it will be necessary to consider the particular decision that raises the jurisdiction issue.[430]

Devolution issues

3-104   There has been remarkably little cross-border litigation over "devolution issues" since the coming into force of the Scotland Act 1998, the Northern Ireland Act 1998 and the Government of Wales Act 1998.

Judicial review of public functions exercised outside the United Kingdom

3-105   The Administrative Court's jurisdiction to issue judicial review remedial orders in respect of the exercise of functions in the name of the Crown extends beyond the United Kingdom "to overseas territories subject to the Queen's dominion", at least where in substance (if not in form) the decision is taken on the orders or direction of United Kingdom Ministers.[431] Thus, it may be possible to commence judicial review proceedings in respect of functions exercised by Ministers based in the United Kingdom in respect of the Isle of Man, the Bailiwick of Jersey, the Bailiwick of Guernsey (which includes Guernsey, Alderney and Sark), and British Overseas Territories. Thus, the House of Lords reviewed the legality of prerogative legislation made by the Privy Council in respect of the British Indian Ocean Territory[432]; and the Supreme Court has heard a judicial review challenge to the legality of the Reform (Sark) Law 2008, which sought to create a new constitution for that Channel Island.[433] The Administrative Court may, however, exercise its discretion to

---

[429] *Tehrani v Secretary of State for the Home Department* [2006] UKHL 47; [2007] 1 A.C. 521; C. Himsworth, "Inter-jurisdictional questions in judicial review" (2007) 11 Edin. L.R. 277 (who argues that "it may yet be found preferable to seek solutions not in terms of choice of jurisdiction, but by ensuring that, whichever jurisdiction is adopted, the result to be obtained from both the substance and procedural rules is the same").

[430] *Re Surgenor's Application for Judicial Review* [2003] NIQB 62.

[431] *R. (on the application of Bancoult) v Secretary of State for the Foreign and Commonwealth Office (No.1)* [2001] Q.B. 1067 at [21]–[29] (granting judicial review of a decision of the Commissioner for the British Indian Ocean Territory to banish inhabitants from the Chagos Islands; overruled in other respects in *R. (on the application of Bancoult) v Secretary of State for the Foreign and Commonwealth Office (No.2)* [2008] UKHL 61; [2009] 1 A.C. 453. cf. *R. (on the application of Quark Fishing Ltd) v Secretary of State for Foreign and Commonwealth Affairs (No.1)* [2002] EWCA Civ 1409 where no jurisdictional issue arose in relation to the refusal of a fishing licence in relation to the South Georgia and South Sandwich Islands and the Court of Appeal quashed a direction given by the Foreign Secretary. On the jurisdictional position in relation to the HRA, see 3-093.

[432] *R. (on the application of Bancoult) v Secretary of State for the Foreign and Commonwealth Office (No.2)* [2008] UKHL 61; [2009] 1 A.C. 453.

[433] *R. (on the application of Barclay) v Lord Chancellor and Secretary of State for Justice* [2008] EWHC 1354 (Admin); [2008] EWCA Civ 1319; [2009] UKSC 9; [2010] 1 A.C. 464. Though note *R. (on the application of Barclay) v Lord Chancellor and Secretary of State for Justice (No.2) (Attorney General and another intervening)* [2014] UKSC 54; [2015] A.C. 276 in which the Supreme Court, although confirming its earlier conclusion that the UK courts *could* review the making of an Order in Council giving assent to legislation made by the Bailiwick of Guernsey, nevertheless considered that they should decline to do so in the circumstances before it. Per Baroness Hale at [37]: "For the courts of England and Wales to entertain challenges to the compatibility of Island legislation with the Convention rights would clearly be to subvert the scheme of the Islands' own human rights legislation. It would also be to subvert the method by which the United Kingdom extended the European Convention to the Channel Islands. This was not by extending the 1998 Act to them: amendments to that effect were resisted in the United Kingdom Parliament. It was by extending the scope of the Convention in international law by a declaration under article 56, and leaving it to the

decline to hear the claim on the ground the local courts provide a more convenient forum.[434]

The Administrative Court will not, as a matter of international comity, hear a claim for judicial review which amounts to an unwarranted interference in the affairs of an independent member of the British Commonwealth.[435]   **3-106**

Territorial jurisdiction and the HRA

Where a judicial review claim includes the ground of breach of s.6 of the HRA, further considerations must be taken into account where the impugned decision or failure to act has taken place or had its impact outside the United Kingdom.   **3-107**

By ECHR art.1, Convention rights extend to everyone within the "jurisdiction" of the signatory State. The concept of jurisdiction is essentially territorial. For present purposes, the signatory State and territorial area is that of the United Kingdom of Great Britain and Northern Ireland. The United Kingdom has acted under ECHR art.56, or the various Protocols to the ECHR, to extend the application of the ECHR to many of the territories which are not part of the United Kingdom but for whose international relations the United Kingdom is responsible (essentially the British Overseas Territories[436] and the Crown dependencies of the Isle of Man and Bailiwicks of Jersey and Guernsey).[437] If the ECHR or a Protocol has not been formally extended to a British Overseas Territory (whether by oversight or deliberately), there is no possibility of a claim under HRA s.6 and consequently for damages under s.7.[438] The reach of the HRA is the same as the ECHR.   **3-108**

The ECtHR recognises two general exceptional extensions to the principle of   **3-109**

Islands to legislate to incorporate the rights contained in the Convention into Island law. They happened to adopt the same model as the 1998 Act but they did not have to do so. It would be inconsistent with that scheme for the definition of 'primary legislation' in the 1998 Act to cover any form of primary Island legislation as defined in the Human Rights (Bailiwick of Guernsey) Law 2000."

[434] *R. (on the application of Bancoult) v Secretary of State for the Foreign and Commonwealth Office (No.1)* [2001] Q.B. 1067 at [27].

[435] *Fitzgibbon v Attorney General* [2005] EWHC 114 (Ch); *The Times,* 15 March 2005 (the claimant sought declarations in relation to the power of the Queen to issue letters patent in respect of her functions under the Commonwealth of Australia Constitution Act 1900 (Australia)).

[436] British Overseas Territories Act 2002.

[437] Jersey, Guernsey and the Isle of Man have each adopted human rights laws broadly similar to the HRA.

[438] *R. (on the application of Quark Fishing Ltd) v Secretary of State for Foreign and Commonwealth Affairs (No.2)* [2005] UKHL 57; [2006] 1 A.C. 529 (UK had not extended the application of ECHR Protocol 1 art.1 (right to enjoyment of property) to the South Georgia and South Sandwich Islands; accordingly, the claimant had no basis for a claim for damages under HRA s.7). The House of Lords held that, in giving the instruction under the 1985 Order, the Secretary of State was acting on behalf of Her Majesty exercising Her powers as sovereign of SGSSI, not the United Kingdom. See further A. Twomey, "Responsible Government and the Divisibility of the Crown" [2008] P.L. 742, who argues that in *Quark Fishing* the House of Lords failed to recognise that "the criterion for recognising the divisibility of the Crown in this sense is not the existence of a separate government, but rather the source of responsibility for advice to the monarch with respect to matters concerning the relevant territory" (p.743). Twomey argues that the court neglected the crucial questions in the case—"On whose advice was the Queen acting giving these instructions? To whom was that person responsible for the advice?" (p.761). The better analysis, she contends, is that the Secretary of State was acting in relation to the United Kingdom rather than "as the mouthpiece of the Queen of South Georgia". The ECtHR dismissed a complaint as inadmissible: *Quark Fishing Ltd v United Kingdom (Admissibility)* (15305/06) 22 B.H.R.C. 568. See also J. Finnis, *"Law Constraints: Whose Common Good Counts?"* Oxford Legal Studies Research Paper No.10/2008 (available at SSRN: *http://ssrn.com/abstract$AD1100628* [Accessed 21 April 2013]).

territoriality.[439] First, where a State exercises control though its agents (for example its armed forces or consular and diplomatic officers abroad) over persons or property outside its national borders. Second, where a State has "effective control" of an area outside its territory which is part of the territory of another contracting state.[440]

PUBLIC LAW ARGUMENTS IN CIVIL CLAIMS, TRIBUNALS AND CRIMINAL PROCEEDINGS

3-110   The primary focus of this chapter is on amenability to claims for judicial review under CPR Pt 54,[441] but some public authorities are subject to judicial review independently of CPR Pt 54. Several Acts of Parliament provide that various tribunals and courts other than the Administrative Court have specific powers to adjudicate by "applying the principles applied by the court on an application for

---

[439] *Chagos Islanders v United Kingdom* (35622/04) para.70; *Al-Skeini v United Kingdom* (55721/07) (2011) 53 E.H.R.R. 18 (ECtHR Grand Chamber, during the relevant period in south-east Iraq the United Kingdom had, through its soldiers, exercised such authority and control over civilians killed by British soldiers operating outside their base as to bring those civilians within the United Kingdom's Convention jurisdiction) cf. earlier HL judgment *R. (on the application of Al-Skeini) v Secretary of State for Defence (The Redress Trust intervening)* [2007] UKHL 26; [2008] A.C. 153); *Al-Jedda v United Kingdom* (27021/08) (2011) 53 E.H.R.R. 23 (ECtHR Grand Chamber, person detained in custody by British forces in Iraq was within United Kingdom jurisdiction) cf. earlier HL judgment in *R. (on the application of Al-Jedda) v Secretary of State for Defence (JUSTICE and another intervening)* [2007] UKHL 58; [2008] 1 A.C. 332; *Bankovic v Belgium* (52207/99)(2007) 44 E.H.R.R. SE5; see further M. Milanovic, *Extraterritorial Application of Human Rights Treaties: Law, Principles and Policy* (2011).

[440] *Al-Skeini v United Kingdom* (2011) 53 E.H.R.R. 18 at [132]–[150] and *Al-Jedda v United Kingdom* (2011) 53 E.H.R.R 23 at [74]–[86]. On the territorial reach of the HRA Ch.3. The decision of the ECtHR in *Al-Skeini* was applied in the UK by the SC in *Smith v Ministry of Defence* [2013] UKSC 41; [2014] A.C. 52, in which it was held that the requirement of "exceptionality" does not set an especially high threshold [46] and that the jurisdiction of the United Kingdom extends to securing the protection of art.2 to members of the armed forces when they are serving outside its territory [55]. *Al-Skeini* was also applied in *R. (on the application of Sandiford) v Secretary of State for Foreign and Commonwealth Affairs* [2014] UKSC 44; [2014] 1 W.L.R. 2697, in which it was held that the applicant was not within the jurisdiction of the UK for the purposes of art.1 in relation to the policy of refusing to fund legal representation for those facing capital charges overseas. The decisions in *Al-Skeini* and *Smith* are heavily criticised in the context of military operations by the CA in *Mohammed v Secretary of State for Defence* [2015] EWCA Civ 843; [2016] 2 W.L.R. 247 at [93]–[97] on the basis that they involve a substantial extension of the scope of the ECHR to all cases where the state exercises control over an individual as opposed to a territorial area. In *Mohammed v Secretary of State for Defence (No.2)* [2017] UKSC 2; [2017] 2 W.L.R. 327 at [48], Lord Sumption referred to the "serious analytical and practical difficulties" to which *Al-Skeini* gave rise since it extended the essentially regional scope of the ECHR and potentially brought it into conflict with other sources of international law. See also *Jaloud v Netherlands* (2015) 60 E.H.R.R. 29 at [152], where jurisdiction was established in respect of the Netherlands in circumstances where Mr Jaloud died when a vehicle in which he was a passenger was fired upon while passing through a checkpoint manned by personnel under the command and direct supervision of a Netherlands Royal Army officer. The ECtHR has stated that the matter is heavily fact sensitive (*Chiragov v Armenia* (2016) 63 E.H.R.R. 9 at [168]). In *R. (Keyu) v Secretary of State for Foreign and Commonwealth Affairs & Secretary of State for Defence* [2015] UKSC 69; [2016] A.C. 1355 at [64]–[65], the SC (while rejecting the claim on time grounds) accepted that under the constitutional arrangements then in force, the United Kingdom was in complete control of the State of Malaya and hence the relatives of victims of the 1948 massacre of 24 civilians by members of the British Army in the State of Selangor could potentially rely on art.2.

[441] See Ch.16.

judicial review". These include: the Information Tribunal[442]; the High Court exercising supervisory jurisdiction over the making of non-derogating control orders[443]; the Competition Appeal Tribunal[444]; the tribunal established by the Regulation of Investigatory Powers Act 2000[445]; the Proscribed Organisations Appeal Commission[446]; and the Pathongens Access Appeal Commission.[447]

There are also appeals on a point of law to the county courts in homelessness cases.[448] In addition, various applications and appeals can be made to the High Court.[449] They can be brought on grounds of appeal that are basically the same as the grounds for judicial review. The Tribunals, Courts and Enforcement Act 2007 empowers the Upper Tribunal to carry out "judicial review" (quotation marks are used in the Act) in respect of decisions of the First-tier Tribunal if certain conditions are met; not only is adjudication on the basis of the substantive principles of judicial review, but the Upper Tribunal follows a procedure similar to that of the Administrative Court and may grant judicial review remedies.[450]   **3-111**

Beyond these, there are two main situations in which litigants may try to use grounds of judicial review arguments. The first is where a claimant uses the CPR Pt 7 or Pt 8 civil claim procedure rather than CPR Pt 54. The problems encountered here are referred to as "procedural exclusivity". A second situation is where a person seeks to use grounds for judicial review arguments by way of a defence, submitting that the public authority's decision, or delegated legislation, is unlawful. This is referred to as "collateral challenge". In both situations, the courts have moved away from strict attitudes based on often difficult conceptual distinctions in the direction of more flexible approaches.   **3-112**

Procedural exclusivity

Between 1983 and 2000 (when the CPR Pt 54 claim for judicial review procedure came into force), issues relating to "procedural exclusivity" often arose, and still do even though a new approach of flexibility is required in cases involving both public and private law questions. This term referred to the issue of whether a litigant wishing to challenge the legality of a decision made by an authority amenable to judicial review was *required* to use the RSC Ord.53 application for judicial review procedure to challenge the lawfulness of a public authority's action,[451] or whether it was permissible to commence litigation using some other procedure (a writ action or originating summons). The extent to which public law submissions may be advanced outside RSC Ord.53 proceedings was highly contentious.   **3-113**

Under CPR.54.2 there remains a requirement that "the judicial review procedure must be used" if the claimant is seeking one or more of the distinctly "public law" remedies of a mandatory, prohibiting or quashing order or an injunction restraining a person from acting in an office in which he is not entitled to act. Although the   **3-114**

---

[442] Adjudicating on rights under the Data Protection Act 1998 and the Freedom of Information Act 2000 (on which, see 16-028 and 16-032).

[443] Prevention of Terrorism Act 2005 s.3(11).

[444] Enterprise Act 2002 ss.120, 179.

[445] s.67.

[446] Terrorism Act 2000 ss.5(3), 9(3).

[447] Anti-Terrorism, Crime and Security Act 2001 s.70.

[448] See 17-037. But note that the Lord Chancellor is prohibited from making Orders allocating claims for judicial review to the county court: see Courts and Legal Services Act 1990 s.1(10).

[449] See Ch.17.

[450] ss.15–21.

[451] The main features of the RSC Ord.53 procedure are examined at 15-087; on the CPR Pt 54 procedure which superseded it, see Ch.16.

language of CPR.54.2 is similar to that used in the former RSC Ord.54, a rather different approach now needs to be taken in the light of the overarching changes brought about the CPR. The CPR seek to end the old wholly unproductive demarcation disputes.[452]

The justification for procedural exclusivity under RSC, Ord.53

3-115　　When recommending in 1976 the creation of a new procedure for judicial review, the Law Commission contemplated the co-existence of judicial review proceedings and actions brought by issuing a writ or originating summons for a declaration (private law proceedings) in relation to public law issues.[453] This was not, however, a realistic approach. The application for judicial review procedures had the safeguard of the requirement for leave (now called "permission") and a limited period in which to make applications, which would serve no purpose if they could be bypassed by issuing an ordinary civil proceedings for a declaration that was not subject to the same safeguards.

3-116　　The much-criticised decision in the House of Lords in *O'Reilly v Mackman*[454] was therefore the logical consequence[455] of the procedure included in RSC Ord.53. In that case Lord Diplock set out the general rule.

> "Now ... all remedies for infringement of rights protected by public law can be obtained upon an application for judicial review, as can also remedies for infringement of rights under private law if such infringement should also be involved, it would in my view as a general rule be contrary to public policy, and as such an abuse of the process of the court, to permit a person seeking to establish that a decision of a public authority infringed rights to which he was entitled to protection under public law to proceed by way of ordinary action and by this means to evade the provisions of Ord.53 for the protection of such authorities. ... I have described this as a general rule; for, though it may normally be appropriate to apply it by the summary process of striking out the action, there may be exceptions, particularly where the invalidity of the decision arises as a collateral issue in a claim for infringement of a right of the plaintiff arising under private law, or where none of the parties object to the adoption of the procedure by writ or originating summons. Whether there should be other exceptions should, in my view, at this stage in the development of procedural public law, be left to be decided on a case to case basis."

3-117　　It is important to note that in the passage of his speech just cited Lord Diplock was setting out a general rule and a rule which was to be the subject of exceptions which were to be worked out on a case-by-case basis.[456] In addition *O'Reilly v Mackman* typified the sort of case which it could be expected would result in the misgivings which had been expressed in earlier cases about the undesirability of bypassing the judicial review procedure being reiterated. It involved four prisoners who, after the Hull Prison Riots, brought an action claiming declarations that

---

[452] *R. (on the application of Heather) v Leonard Cheshire Foundation* [2002] EWCA Civ 366; [2002] 2 All E.R. 936 at [36]–[39] (Lord Woolf CJ).

[453] *Remedies in Administrative Law* (Law Commission No.73 (1976)), paras 34, 58(a). (The issue of "writs" and "summons" has been replaced by "claim forms" in the Civil Procedure Rules enacted in 1999).

[454] *O'Reilly v Mackman* [1983] 2 A.C. 237. See also the companion case *Cocks v Thanet District Council* [1983] 2 A.C. 287 (where private law rights depended on prior public law decisions they too must ordinarily be litigated by judicial review).

[455] cf. e.g. Justice/All Souls, *Administrative Justice-Some Necessary Reforms* (1988), para.6.18, which describes it as "an unfortunate decision". Wade and Forsyth say it "must be accounted a serious setback for administrative law ... a step back towards the time of the old forms of action which were so deservedly buried in 1852." (*Administrative Law* 10th edn (2009), p.567.).

[456] *O'Reilly v Mackman* [1983] 2 A.C. 237 at 284-285.

the disciplinary awards which had been made against them by the Prison Visitors were invalid as being in breach of the Prison Rules and as contravening the principles of natural justice. If the proceedings had been by way of judicial review, it is most unlikely that permission would have been granted for them to be commenced since the applicants were short on merits.

O'Reilly v Mackman represented something of a high-water mark in the courts'   **3-118** insistence on procedural exclusivity. In a series of subsequent cases, encouraged by Lord Scarman's dicta, the courts identified exceptions to the rule, allowing arguments based on grounds of judicial review to be advanced outside the RSC Ord.53 procedure. The exceptions included: where public and private law decisions were not separate and distinct[457]; where the public law aspect of the claim was collateral to an issue which was the proper subject matter of private law proceedings[458]; where private law aspects of the claim dominated the proceedings[459]; where a person sought to challenge the validity of a public authority's decision as a defence in a civil claim[460]; and where the parties did not contest the appropriateness of the chosen procedure.[461] The courts stressed the general need for flexibility[462] and pragmatism.[463] Nevertheless, parties frequently engaged in ferocious litigation as to whether the right procedure has been adopted purely for tactical purposes. Their indulging in this activity was made worthwhile by the fact that, depending on the nature of the issue involved, there could be substantial advantages in an applicant choosing one form of procedure rather than another. Unfortunately, although the House of Lords had a number of opportunities to improve the situation, a case by case approach prevented the development of a formula which might have injected some common sense into the position.

Procedural exclusivity in the era of the Civil Procedure Rules

The replacement of RSC Ord.53 by the new CPR 54 claim for judicial review   **3-119** procedure in October 2000 called for a fresh approach to procedural exclusivity. In all types of civil proceedings, the CPR gave judges new powers to manage litigation and in several respects the differences between judicial review (Pt 54) and the other ways of starting civil proceedings (Pt 7 and Pt 8) have been significantly reduced.[464] The main difference nowadays is in the time period within which a claim must be made. For judicial review the standard requirement is that claims be made

---

[457] *An Bord Bainne Co-op Ltd v Milk Marketing Board* [1984] 2 C.M.L.R. 584 at 587–8.

[458] In *Davy v Spelthorne BC* (1983) 81 L.G.R. 580 the CA did not permit the plaintiff to proceed with a claim for an injunction in ordinary civil proceedings to prevent the implementation of an enforcement notice and the setting aside of the notice, but did allow a claim for damages for negligent advice by the Council to proceed arising out of the same matter. The HL dismissed the authority's appeal in relation to the claim for damages since liability for damages did not directly raise any question of public law [1984] A.C. 262. See also *Steed v Home Office* [2000] 1 W.L.R. 1169.

[459] *Roy v Kensington and Chelsea and Westminster Family Practitioner Committee* [1992] 1 A.C. 624 (GP brought civil action against his family practitioner committee for withholding part of his practice allowance).

[460] *Wandsworth LBC v Winder* [1985] A.C. 461. This principle applies even where the litigation is between two private parties: *Dwr Cymru Cyfyngedig v Corus UK Ltd* [2006] EWHC 1183 (Ch)— this point was not challenged on a subsequent appeal ([2007] EWCA Civ 285).

[461] This could be considered as being the explanation for the ability of the plaintiffs in *Gillick v West Norfolk and Wisbech AHA* [1986] A.C. 112 and *Royal College of Nursing v Department of Health and Social Security* [1982] A.C. 800 to make claims and not apply for permission to seek judicial review when challenging ministerial guidance.

[462] *Mercury Communications Ltd v Director General of Telecommunications* [1996] 1 W.L.R. 48.

[463] *Trustees of the Dennis Rye Pension Fund v Sheffield City Council* [1998] 1 W.L.R. 840.

[464] CPR Pt 7 ("How to start proceedings") and Pt 8 ("Alternative procedure for claims", used primarily where a claimant seeks "the court's decision on a question which is unlikely to involve a

"promptly and in any event within three months", or "three months" where EU law rights are in question, whereas in relation to other types of civil claim the limitation period will typically be three, six or even 12 years.[465] What matters under the CPR regime is not the mode of commencement of proceedings but whether the choice of procedure may have a material effect on the outcome. To prove an abuse of process, it is now necessary to do more than merely show that a civil claim started under Pt 7 or Pt 8 could have been brought by way of judicial review.[466] The Court of Appeal, doubting the continuing relevance of *O'Reilly v Mackman*, held[467]:

> "The court's approach to what is an abuse of process has to be considered today in the light of the changes brought about by the CPR. Those changes include a requirement that a party to proceedings should behave reasonably both before and after they have commenced proceedings. Parties are now under an obligation to help the court further the overriding objectives which include ensuring that cases are dealt with expeditiously and fairly. (CPR 1.1(2)(d) and 1.3) They should not allow the choice of procedure to achieve procedural advantages".

Adopting this approach, sterile and expensive procedural disputes, which may be of no practical significance to the outcome of a case, may be avoided in situations where private and public law principles overlap. There are many illustrations of the new flexible approach.[468] Where, however, a case raises only public law issues, a claim for judicial review remains the preferable procedure as it is more likely to serve "the public interest that the legality of formal acts of a public authority should

---

substantial dispute of fact"). Pt 54 takes Part 8 as its starting point but greatly modifies it: see 16-008.

[465] See 16-053.

[466] *Clark v University of Lincolnshire and Humberside* [2000] 1 W.L.R. 1988 (not abuse of process to bring challenge to defendant's finding of plagiarism by civil claim for breach of contract in county court); and see also, e.g. *Phonographic Performance Ltd v Department of Trade and Industry* [2004] EWHC 1795 (Ch); [2004] 1 W.L.R. 2893 (civil claim not necessarily an abuse just because it involved consideration of duties of the Crown under EU law that might have been brought by judicial review proceedings); *Saha v Imperial College of Science, Technology and Medicine* [2011] EWHC 3286 (QB) (not abuse of process for former student to bring civil claim for harassment and breach of contract against university).

[467] *Clark v University of Lincolnshire and Humberside* [2000] 1 W.L.R. 1988 [34] (Lord Woolf MR).

[468] See, e.g. *R. (on the application of Wilkinson) v Broadmoor Special Hospital Authority* [2001] EWCA Civ 1545; [2002] 1 W.L.R. 419 at [62] ("it cannot and should not matter whether proceedings in respect of forcible treatment of detained patients are brought by way of an ordinary action in tort, an action under s.7(1) of the [HRA], or judicial review"); *R. (on the application of P) v Secretary of State for the Home Department* [2001] EWCA Civ 1151; [2001] 1 W.L.R. 2002 at [120] (challenge to lawfulness of Prison Service policy on mother and baby units should be made in the Family Division unless relief which only the Administrative Court may grant is sought); *D v Home Office* [2005] EWCA Civ 38; [2006] 1 W.L.R. 1003 at [104] (civil claim for damages for false imprisonment); *Rhondda Cynon Taff CBC v Watkins* [2003] EWCA Civ 129; [2003] 1 W.L.R. 1864 (possession action); *Bunney v Burns Anderson Plc* [2007] EWHC 1240 (Ch) at [25] (direction of Financial Services Ombudsman); *Ford-Camber Ltd v Deanminster Ltd* [2007] EWCA Civ 458; (2007) 151 S.J.L.B. 713 (CA dealt with public law questions in civil claim about stopping-up of a private access road); *BA v Secretary of State for the Home Department* [2012] EWCA Civ 944 (in unusual circumstances of the case, brought about by Legal Aid franchising arrangements, not abuse of process to bring claim for damages for unlawful detention in separate civil claim after judicial review); *R. (on the application of Shoesmith) v Ofsted* [2011] EWCA Civ 642; [2011] P.T.S.R. (discussion of choice between judicial review claim and proceedings in Employment Tribunal); *R. (on the application of NE) v Birmingham Magistrates' Court* [2015] EWHC 688 (Admin); [2015] 1 W.L.R. 4771 (court was disadvantaged on a judicial review application in comparison with an appeal by way of case stated as it did not have a complete note of the evidence before the magistrate; noting that the similar case of *R. (on the application of Hamill) v Chelmsford Magistrates' Court* [2014] EWHC 2799 (Admin); [2015] 1 W.L.R. 1798 had proceeded by way of judicial review without comment, it would not have been appropriate to deprive the claimants of a remedy).

be established without delay".[469] Where the only remedy sought is damages or restitution, a civil claim will rarely be an abuse of process even if public law questions are a dominant issue[470]; though it will be an abuse of process to use a damages claim merely to reopen public law questions.[471]

Practical considerations

A practical question may arise as to what a claimant ought to do in a case where he asserts that the defendant is carrying out a public function amenable to judicial review and the defendant does not accept that this is so.[472] One option is to commence claims both a claim for judicial review and an ordinary civil claim, which the court could order be consolidated and heard together; alternatively, a claimant may commence a judicial review claim and—if unsuccessful on the jurisdiction point—seek an order transferring the matter to continue as if it had not been commenced under CPR Pt 54.[473] Where delay is an issue, it may be addressed by the court either in ordinary civil proceedings,[474] or under CPR Pt 54.

3-120

Procedural exclusivity and tribunal proceedings

Does a tribunal hearing a statutory appeal, a ground of which may that an official decision is "not in accordance with the law", have jurisdiction to consider whether the "law" itself is unlawful, which "is a more deep-rooted and fundamental challenge going beyond the legality" of the official decision itself?[475] In *Chief*

3-121

---

[469] *Trim v North Dorset DC* [2010] EWCA Civ 1446; [2011] 1 W.L.R. 1901 at [23] (Carnwath LJ citing previous edition of this work; abuse of process to seek declaration in civil claim that a breach of a planning conditions notice had been served on the claimant by the defendant after the statutory time limit for taking enforcement action had expired); and see, e.g. *R. (on the application of Townsend) v Secretary of State for Works and Pensions* [2011] EWHC 3434 (Admin) (abuse of process for claimant to bring civil claim seeking declaration of incompatibility relating to Child Maintenance and Enforcement Commission).

[470] See, e.g. *Bloomsbury International Ltd v Sea Fish Industry Authority and DEFRA* [2009] EWHC 1721 (QB); [2010] 1 C.M.L.R. 344 (Hamben J refused to strike out a restitutionary claim brought by ordinary civil claim by importers of sea fish and sea fish products who had paid a levy to the SFIA, which they now said was demanded under delegated legislation that was contrary to European Union law. DEFRA contended that the examination of the public law issue of the vires of the regulations was the "primary focus" or "dominant issue". The court noted that the claim was brought in an ordinary action because the only claim being made was a private law claim for a monetary remedy and under CPR Pt 54.3(2) a claim for judicial review cannot be made where only a monetary remedy is being sought; the case went to the Supreme Court: *Bloomsbury International Ltd and others v Department for Environment, Food and Rural Affairs (Sea Fish Industry Authority intervening)* [2011] UKSC 25; [2011] 1 W.L.R. 1546).

[471] See, e.g. *Jones v Powys Local Health Board* [2008] EWHC 2562 (Admin); (2009) 12 C.C.L. Rep. 68 (civil claim in the High Court which sought reimbursement of fees paid for the care and accommodation of the claimant's deceased father at a nursing home struck out as abuse of process: the defendant had previously decided that the father did not meet the eligibility criteria for free accommodation and health care except for a two-month period immediately preceding his death).

[472] *Mullins* at [47]–[49] (noting that this was an issue that deserves the attention of the Rules Committee); and see also *Cookson & Clegg Ltd v Ministry of Defence* [2005] EWCA Civ 811; [2006] Eu. L.R. 1092.

[473] On transfers, see CPR.54.20.

[474] In civil proceedings the court of its own motion or on the application of a party may, under CPR Pt 24, give summary judgment in the claim or on an issue if it considers that it has no real prospect of succeeding. See, e.g. *Dwr Cymru Cyfyngedig (Welsh Water) v Corus UK Ltd* [2006] EWHC 1183 (Ch).

[475] *IH (Eritrea) v Secretary of State for the Home Department* [2009] UKAIT 00012 at [92].

Adjudication Officer v Foster,[476] the House of Lords considered whether social security commissioners (an appellate tribunal) hearing an appeal on "a point of law" had jurisdiction to determine any challenge to the validity of delegated legislation.[477] It was held that the commissioners did have such jurisdiction whenever it is necessary to do so in determining whether a decision under appeal was erroneous in point of law.[478] Lord Bridge, for a unanimous House, held that such a conclusion avoided "a cumbrous duplicity of proceedings" and welcomed the prior view of one of the commissioners "who have great expertise in this esoteric area of the law", which would benefit the superior court upon appeal or review. He also explained why the commissioners (and indeed the tribunal against whose decisions appeals were brought) were not inappropriate bodies to determine such an issue where the Secretary of State's views could be put before the tribunal by the adjudicating officer.

3-122   Under the provisions of the Tribunals, Courts and Enforcement Act 2007 it is now possible for cases to be transferred from the Upper Tribunal (to which the commissioners' jurisdiction was moved in 2008)[479] to the Administrative Court, and vice versa, which will ensure that important questions relating to the lawfulness of delegated legislation can be decided by a tribunal or court with the best relevant expertise for a particular. The Upper Tribunal, panels of which may include a High Court judge, has "judicial review" powers and so may quash delegated legislation.[480]

Collateral Challenges

3-123   In principle it would seem wrong for a person to be sued or prosecuted for non-compliance with an official decision or delegated legislation that is unlawful. Although over the years the courts have not been entirely consistent on the point, in general, collateral challenges have been allowed.[481] Even after *O'Reilly v Mackman*,[482] which held that challenges to the validity of action by public authorities must be brought by way of judicial review, and that it is an abuse of process not to do so, it was recognised both in *O'Reilly v Mackman* and in *Cocks v Thanet BC*[483] that a public law challenge could be permitted if it arose collaterally in the course of an ordinary civil action.

3-124   Two difficulties, however, arise: first, civil proceedings or criminal trial may be inappropriate to handle public law questions (for example, because they do not, as in judicial review, possess discretion to refuse relief; or have short time limits

---

[476] *Chief Adjudication Officer v Foster* [1993] A.C. 754.
[477] Social Security Act 1975 s.101.
[478] *Chief Adjudication Officer v Foster* [1993] A.C. 754, 767; Lord Bridge also referred to the distinction between substantive and procedural invalidity in *Bugg* (discussed at 3-111), but considered it unnecessary to decide that point since the issue in *Foster* was "one of pure statutory construction unaffected by evidence".
[479] To the Administrative Appeals Chamber of the Upper Tribunal.
[480] Tribunals, Courts and Enforcement Act 2007 ss.15–18.
[481] See, e.g. *DPP v Head* [1959] A.C. 83; *Customs and Excise Commissioners v Cure & Deeley Ltd* [1962] 1 Q.B. 340; *R. v Commissioners of Customs and Excise Ex p. Hedges and Butler Ltd* [1986] 2 All E.R. 164; *Musson v Emile* [1964] 1 W.L.R. 337; *Heptulla Bros Ltd v Thakore* [1956] 1 W.L.R. 289; *R. v Pugh (Judge) Ex p. Graham* [1951] 2 K.B. 623; *R. v Sheffield Area Rent Tribunal Ex p. Purshouse* (1957) 121 J.P. 553. *West Glamorgan CC v Rafferty* [1987] 1 W.L.R. 457.
[482] *O'Reilly v Mackman* [1983] 2 A.C. 237.
[483] *Cocks v Thanet BC* [1983] 2 A.C. 286.

designed to protect the public interest in effective public administration, or because of lack of expertise on the part of the judge called upon to determine the issue).[484]

Secondly (as discussed in Ch.4), in the past there was a distinction between void   **3-125** and voidable decisions; and the only decisions open to collateral attack were void decisions. Errors of law within a public authority's jurisdiction—even including those on the face of the record—were regarded as valid and effective for all purposes unless successfully challenged through direct attack. Whatever the limits today upon collateral challenge (and we shall see these shortly), the distinction between void and voidable decisions is no longer one of them. In *London & Clydeside Estates v Aberdeen DC*, Lord Hailsham, attacking that "misleading" language, made it clear that except in "flagrant" and "outrageous" cases, delegated legislation remains effective until it is quashed.[485] The question today therefore is whether the court or tribunal in question is competent to be seised of a collateral challenge to the validity of an official decision, rather than whether the decision challenged is or is not a "jurisdictional error".[486]

The matter received attention in the context of criminal enforcement of official   **3-126** decisions and delegated legislation. In *Quietlynn Ltd v Plymouth City Council*[487] it was held that a licence for a sex establishment, challenged collaterally in a magistrates' court for procedural irregularity, was presumed to be valid unless it was invalid on its face, and that in the case of such a challenge the correct proceedings was for the matter to be adjourned to enable an application for judicial review to be made and determined. However, in *R. v Reading Crown Court Ex p. Hutchinson*,[488] the Court of Appeal held that "justices have always had jurisdiction to inquire into the validity of a byelaw. They are not only entitled, but bound to do so when the defendant relies on the invalidity of the byelaw by way of defence".[489]

In *Bugg v DPP*[490] the defendants, charged with entering a military area contrary   **3-127** to byelaws,[491] pleaded not guilty on the ground, inter alia, that the byelaws were not valid because of non-compliance with certain procedural requirements. The Divisional Court held that all delegated legislation, whether "void" or "voidable", was in principle open to collateral challenge on the grounds of "substantive invalidity" (where the byelaws were on their face outside the scope of their powers or patently unreasonable). A challenge, however, on the ground of "procedural invalid-

---

[484] See H. Woolf, *Protection of the Public: a New Challenge* (1990), p.80.

[485] *London & Clydeside Estates v Aberdeen DC* [1980] 1 W.L.R. 182 at 189–90. See also Lord Radcliffe in *Smith v East Elloe RDC* [1956] A.C. 736 at 769–70 who said that "An order, even if not made in good faith, is still an act capable of legal consequences. It bears no brand of invalidity upon its forehead. Unless the necessary proceedings are taken at law to establish the cause of invalidity and to get it quashed or otherwise upset, it will remain as effective for its ostensible purpose as the most impeccable of orders". See also *Hoffmann-La Roche and Co AG v Secretary of State for Trade and Industry* [1975] A.C. 295 at 366 (Lord Diplock: "the presumption that subordinate legislation is intra vires prevails in the absence of rebuttal, and ... cannot be rebutted except by a party to legal proceedings in a court of competent jurisdiction who has locus standi to challenge [its] validity)".

[486] 4-003.

[487] *Quietlynn Ltd v Plymouth City Council* [1988] Q.B. 114.

[488] *R. v Reading Crown Court Ex p. Hutchinson* [1988] Q.B. 384.

[489] *R. v Reading Crown Court Ex p. Hutchinson* [1988] Q.B. 384 at 391 (Lloyd LJ). This case went to the HL ([1990] 2 A.C. 783), but the issue of invalidity was not there considered, but see Lord Bridge at 804. See also *R. v Oxford Crown Court Ex p. Smith* (1989) 154 J.P. 422 (following the approach of Lloyd LJ in *Ex p. Hutchinson*, [1988] Q.B. 384; *R. v Parking Adjudicator for London Ex p. Bexley LBC* [1998] C.O.D. 116 (parking adjudicator exercising appellate functions under Road Traffic Act 1984 s.32 was entitled and bound to consider validity of byelaw; he had correctly held that a provision was *Wednesbury* unreasonable).

[490] *Bugg v DPP* [1993] Q.B. 473.

[491] RAF Alconbury Byelaws 1985 byelaw 29(b), the "*Greenham Common byelaws*" made under the Military Lands Act 1892 s.17(2).

ity" was not normally an appropriate matter to be investigated in a magistrates' court since such an investigation required evidence in proceedings to which the byelaw-making authority was not to be a party. In such a case, the byelaws were, until set aside, to be treated as valid.[492] However, strong doubts were expressed about *Bugg* in *R. v Wicks*[493] and in *Boddington v British Transport Police*[494] the House of Lords held that a defendant in criminal proceedings was entitled to challenge the invalidity of a byelaw whether on procedural or substantive grounds. Lord Steyn found the consequences of *Bugg* "too austere and indeed too authoritarian to be compatible with the traditions of the common law".[495] He thought that a person had a right to defend himself against an unlawful provision. In *Boddington*,[496] Lord Irvine said that the rule of law raised a "strong presumption" that individuals should have a "fair opportunity" to vindicate their rights in court proceedings. However, in respect of collateral challenge both the rule of law (in respect of its value of certainty and stability of decisions which on their face seem valid and which may have been acted upon by others) as well as other values, such as that of public confidence, may invite principled exceptions to the possibility of collateral review.

Exceptions to the permissive approach to collateral review

3-128   The approach in *Boddington* has been held not to apply where the object to the challenge is an order of the court (rather than an official decision or delegated legislation) against which there is the possibility of an appeal. Thus, a district judge had no jurisdiction at a hearing for a breach of an anti-social behaviour order (ASBO) to consider whether the ASBO, which is an order of the court, was invalid on grounds that it lacked clarity and was too widely drawn.[497]

3-129   There will be some cases where the proceedings are simply inappropriate to decide the public law matter in question, for example: where evidence is needed to substantiate the claim[498]; where the decision-maker is not a party to the proceedings[499]; where the claimant has not suffered any direct prejudice as a result of the alleged invalidity; or where a statutory tribunal lacks jurisdiction because a collateral challenge falls out with the grounds of appeal it is able to consider.[500]

3-130   An Act of Parliament may have established a scheme which precludes col-

---

[492] This distinction was adopted by Lord Taylor CJ in respect of regulations in *R. v Blackledge* [1996] 1 Cr. App. R. 326.

[493] *R. v Wicks* [1998] A.C. 92 (Wicks sought to argue that local authority's service of planning enforcement notice was unlawful because it had failed to consider whether it was "expedient" to do so, contrary to the relevant planning Act); A.W. Bradley, "Collateral Challenge to Enforcement Decisions–a Duty to Apply for Judicial Review?" [1997] P.L. 365.

[494] *Boddington v British Transport Police* [1999] 2 A.C. 143 (Boddington was prosecuted for smoking in a train contrary to British Railways Board Byelaws 1965, which he sought to argue were ultra vires).

[495] *Boddington v British Transport Police* [1999] 2 A.C. 143 at 173.

[496] *Boddington v British Transport Police* [1999] 2 A.C. 143 at 161.

[497] *Director of Public Prosecutions v T* [2006] EWHC 728 (Admin); [2007] 1 W.L.R. 209, [27] ("The policy consideration that influenced the finding in *Boddington's* case that the magistrates' court had jurisdiction to determine issues of validity of a byelaw or administrative decision is wholly absent when the issue is the validity of an order of the court").

[498] *Hunter v Chief Constable of the West Midlands Police* [1982] A.C. 529 (abuse of process for one of the "Birmingham Six" to bring civil action for damages relating to alleged assault by police when a criminal court had decided the issue). Several years later, the convictions were recognised to be miscarriages of justice.

[499] Although in *Dwr Cymru Cyfyngedig (Welsh Water) v Corus UK Ltd* [2006] EWHC 1183 (Ch), Hart J seems to imply that collateral challenge of this type is permissible.

[500] See, e.g. *R. (Camden LBC) v Parking Adjudicator and others* [2011] EWHC 295 (Admin); [2011] P.T.S.R. 1391. See the suggestion of Keene LJ that a powerful factor influencing the court's deci-

lateral attack, explicitly or implicitly. The latter arose in *R. v Wicks*, where the House of Lords held that the defendant, who was prosecuted for breach of planning restrictions, could not challenge a planning enforcement notice as the statute provided an exclusive and comprehensive scheme of appeal.[501]

Another exception to the possibility of collateral challenge relates to judges and other official decision-makers acting under "colour of authority". Where there is a flaw in the appointment or authority of some officer or judge, such that he has no legal power at all, his acts may nevertheless be unchallengeable. The term employed to describe such a judge or officer is "judge de facto".[502] The de facto holder of the office must have some basis for the office (variously expressed as "colourable title" or "colourable authority"),[503] but must not be a "usurper".[504] The doctrine "protects the individual citizen, who had good reason to think that he was appearing before a properly constituted court, acted accordingly and should not without more be deprived of the rights he has established as a result".[505] Or as put by Laws LJ in *Baldock v Webster*[506]:

3-131

"... the general reputation of the law and the public's confidence in it must be protected as surely as the interests of individual parties who have proceeded on the assumption that a judgment in their case is perfectly valid, where that is exactly how it seems to all the world. Public confidence as well as individual parties are, in my judgment, protected by the requirement ...".

Summary

The position in relation to collateral attack is as follows.

3-132

- Except possibly for a decision that is clearly invalid on its face, all official decisions and delegated legislation are presumed to be valid until impugned by a court of competent jurisdiction.
- There is a strong presumption, based on the rule of law, that an individual should in principle generally be able to rely on any invalidity of an official decision or delegated legislation as a defence in collateral proceedings (unless "either the raising of the defence is an abuse of process or it has no

sion whether to permit a collateral attack will be whether the attack is aimed at an instrument directed specifically at him (such as an enforcement notice under planning legislation) or a generally applicable instrument (such as a byelaw or statutory instrument): "Collateral Challenge: Some Observations" [1999] J.R. 170. In the former case he will generally have had the opportunity to challenge the validity of the instrument at the time of its service (by way of appeal or judicial review—as in *Quietlynn v Plymouth City Council* [1988] Q.B. 114 and *R. v Wicks* [1988] A.C. 92. However, in a respect of an instrument of general application, he may have been unaware of its existence, and the time limit in which to challenge it under judicial review may well have passed.

[501] See, e.g. *R. v Wicks* [1988] A.C. 92; *R. v Davey* [1899] 2 Q.B. 301 (validity of an order for the removal to a hospital of a person suffering from scarlet fever could to be inquired into on summons for obstructing the execution of the order); cf. *Dilieto v Ealing LBC* [2000] Q.B. 381 (claim that a planning permission condition was so vague and imprecise as to be a nullity could be advanced by simply looking at the face of the planning permission and construing the condition).

[502] See, e.g. *Scadding v Lorant* (1851) 3 H.L.C. 418; cf. *R. v Bedford Level Corp* (1805) 6 East 356; *Adams v Adams* [1971] P 188; A. Rubinstein, *Jurisdiction and Illegality* (1963), pp.205–8; Sir Owen Dixon, *Jesting Pilate* (1965), p.229.

[503] *Fawdry and Co v Murfitt* [2002] EWCA Civ 643; [2003] Q.B. 104 at [21] (Hale LJ).

[504] Described in *Coppard v Customs and Excise Commissioners* [2003] EWCA Civ 511; [2003] Q.B. 1428 at [18] as a person who knew he had no title or legal authority.

[505] *Fawdry and Co v Murfitt* [2004] EWCA Civ 1869; [2006] Q.B. 315 at [15] (Hale LJ, with whom Arden and Kennedy LJJ agreed).

[506] *Baldock v Webster* [2004] EWCA Civ 1869; [2006] Q.B. 315 at [15].

reasonable prospect of success").[507] This is so whether or not the source of invalidity is alleged to arise out of a jurisdictional or non-jurisdictional error, whether the decision or instrument is "void" or "voidable", or whether the challenge is based on substantive or procedural grounds.

- To avoid "cumbrous duplicity of proceedings", that challenge should where possible take place in the forum in which it is made, without having to adjourn the proceedings in order to enable a claim to be made for judicial review.[508]
- There are, however, a number of exceptions to the generally permissive approach to allowing collateral challenges.

COMPARATIVE PERSPECTIVES

3-133   In this section, we bring together summaries of the approaches to amenability to review adopted in several other jurisdictions—Scotland, Australia, Canada, India, Ireland, New Zealand and South Africa. The purpose of doing so is to illustrate the variety of legislative and judicial techniques that are employed in common law jurisdictions to draw the dividing line between what falls within and outside the courts' supervisory jurisdiction. The fact that a particular function has been held to be within the scope of the court's jurisdiction in one jurisdiction does not, of course, imply that it ought to be within the jurisdiction of courts of other legal systems. A range of constitutional, political and procedural factors may justify difference.[509]

Scotland

3-134   In 1992, the Inner House restated the scope of judicial review in Scotland in *West v Secretary of State for Scotland*.[510] Lord President Hope (as he then was) made it clear that the scope of the judicial review in Scotland depended not on a "public" element that determines the reach of English judicial review, but rather on the presence of what became known as a "tripartite" or "triangular" relationship. The three elements are (i) a body that delegates or entrusts power, whether by statute, agreement or other instrument to (ii) a person who exercises that power (iii) in relation to a person or persons. The approach adopted in *West*—which eschews reference to the public/private divide—has allowed judicial review in some situations in Scotland that would not be amenable to judicial review in England and Wales under CPR Pt 54. Thus, decisions of sports clubs[511] and religious associations[512] have been held to be reviewable. Commentators now argue that the formula laid down in *West*

---

[507] *Bunney v Burns Anderson Plc* [2007] EWHC 1240 (Ch); [2008] Bus. L.R. 22 at [47].

[508] Facilitated now by the provisions for transfer between the Upper Tribunal and the Administrative Court contained in the Tribunal, Courts and Enforcement Act 2007.

[509] See, e.g. *Aga Khan* [1993] 1 W.L.R. 909 (Hoffmann LJ notes that "different countries draw the line between public and private regulation in different places. The fact that certain functions of the Jockey Club could be exercised by a statutory body and that they are so exercised in some other countries does not make them governmental functions in England").

[510] *West v Secretary of State for Scotland* 1992 S.C. 385. The case concerned a prison officer who was refused discretionary reimbursement of removal expenses following the transfer from one prison to another. West lost: there was no tripartite relationship. See further S. Thomson, "Golf clubbing judicial review to death" (2008) 33 S.L.T. 221 (in which it is argued that "a tripartite relationship analysis is a false analysis which serves no useful purpose other than to explain prior case law which has provided redress in contexts other than public law cases"; the author argues that an "honest return to a private/public law distinction is the sensible and sustainable option").

[511] See C. Munro, "Sports in the Courts" [2005] P.L. 681. See, e.g. *Irvine v Royal Burgess Golfing*

"should not be treated as definitive"[513] and "scope of review in Scotland is thus every bit as vague and contradictory as it is in England",[514] but it continues to be applied.[515] Review of decisions of the Scottish inferior criminal courts falls outside the jurisdiction of the Court of Session; there are dealt with instead by the High Court of Justiciary.[516]

Australia

In Australia, judicial review of most federal administrative action other than migration decisions lies under the Administrative Decisions (Judicial Review) Act 1977 (Cth) (ADJR), with judicial review governed by common law principles operating as the safety net in circumstances where ADJR does not apply. In the federal sphere, ADJR has procedural advantages over the common law alternative, but it applies to a narrower range of decisions; these must be decisions of an administrative character made under an enactment. Common law judicial review of federal administrative action has no such restriction, but its defendant must be an officer of the Commonwealth.

3-135

The defendant in *NEAT Domestic Trading Pty Ltd v AWB Ltd*[517] was a private sector company that had inherited most of the business of a formerly government-owned enterprise for the collective marketing of Australia's bulk export wheat crop. Those seeking to compete in that export market needed the government regulator's permission, which could not be granted unless and until the regulator had first sought and obtained the company's consent. In effect, a private sector company could choose to be a monopolist of the bulk export wheat market. The company needed no statutory authorisation to withhold its consent, because in common with most other private sector companies, its incorporation sufficed to give it all the relevant powers of a natural person. The High Court held that the defendant's withholding of consent was therefore not a decision made "under an enactment" for ADJR purposes. It also said that even though common law judicial review is not limited to decisions under statutory powers, the common law's judicial review

3-136

Society of Edinburgh 2004 S.C.L.R. 386 (no recognised principle that the courts should refrain from exercising judicial review with regard to a sporting body); *Wiles v Bothwell Castle Golf Club* 2005 S.L.T. 785; *Crocket v Tantallon Golf Club* 2005 S.L.T. 663.

[512] This does not extend to the Church of Scotland, which has its own system of courts. But other religious bodies may fall within the supervisory jurisdiction of the Court of Session: see, e.g. *M'Milan v The Free Church* (1859) 22D. 290; *M'Donald v Burns* 1940 S.C. 376.

[513] Lord Clyde and D. Edwards, *Judicial Review* (2000), para.8.33.

[514] A. McHarg, "Border Disputes: the Scope and Purposes of Judicial Review" Ch.11 in A. McHarg and T. Mullen (eds), *Public Law in Scotland* (2006), p.236. McHarg argues that "It is not that one jurisdiction rejects while the other accepts the relevance of the distinction; rather each emphasises different aspects of publicness and privateness. Thus, while *West* stressed the importance of non-consensual relationships and decision-making constraints, the English courts are interested primarily in identifying decisions made on behalf of the public collectively, and which affect the public interest" (p.238).

[515] See, e.g. *C v Advocate General for Scotland* [2011] CSOH 124; 2012 S.L.T. 103 (widow of deceased soldier challenged decision of Service Personnel and Veterans Agency of the Ministry of Defence to release his body to his mother (executrix of his will): a tripartite relationship was absent. Lord Brodie at [27]: "I recognise that in similar circumstances in England the courts may take an approach to applications for judicial review which is more pragmatic and closer to what parties would have wished me to do here: *Burrows v HM Coroner for Preston* [2008] EWHC 1387 (Admin); [2008] 2 F.L.R. 1225, but the nature of the equivalent English jurisdiction is different from that in Scotland").

[516] *Law Hospital NHS Trust v Lord Advocate* 1996 S.C. 301 at 311.

[517] *NEAT Domestic Trading Pty Ltd v AWB Ltd* (2003) 216 C.L.R. 277.

principles would not have applied to a company that was entitled to be entirely self-regarding in the way it exercised its "natural person" powers.

3-137   The defendant university in *Griffith University v Tang*[518] was a public sector statutory body, but its disciplinary action against a PhD candidate was held not to fall within ADJR's requirement of a decision made under an enactment, because its consequences could not be sourced to a statute. The university disciplinary code had no legislative force. There was no statutory relationship between the parties, and the student had not alleged a contractual relationship. In any event, the court also indicated that government's commercial and contractual decisions would largely fall beyond the reach of common law judicial review.

3-138   Common law judicial review of federal administrative action lies only against an "officer of the Commonwealth", a phrase that has received a generally expansive interpretation. It remains to be seen, however, how far (if at all) it extends to government contractors. The High Court in *Plaintiff M61/2010E v Commonwealth (Offshore Processing Case)*[519] ordered the Minister not to act on a private sector contractor's assessment of an asylum claim, because the contractor had misunderstood the law and had also failed to accord procedural fairness. Because review lay against the Minister, the court was able to avoid any decision as to whether the contractor might be called an officer of the Commonwealth.[520]

3-139   The Administrative Review Council rejected calls to recommend the extension of ADJR's reach to non-government parties exercising public but non-statutory power. It instead took a watching brief on that issue, arguing that the present system of ADJR, under-pinned by the safety net of the general law, operates reasonably well.[521] The High Court has not yet decided whether to adopt the *Datafin* principle for common law judicial review; nor has the issue been resolved by any of the State Courts of Appeal.[522]

3-140   The public/private divide appears in the context of human rights legislation in two jurisdictions. Those Acts apply to private sector bodies to the extent that they are exercising "functions of a public nature" for or on behalf of the government.[523] The Acts themselves provide some examples, and have left it to the courts to develop the general test for "functions of a public nature". Both Acts exclude the courts, except so far as they are acting in an administrative capacity, and the same exclusion applies in Victoria to its tribunals. Whether a court or tribunal acts in an administrative or judicial capacity is not to be complicated by the introduction of the label "quasi-judicial". Tribunal decisions about guardianship and mental health have been held to be administrative.[524] Key decisions about these human rights instruments suggest they may not make significant inroads into public sector decision making because they impose obligations of a largely procedural rather than

---

[518] *Griffith University v Tang* (2003) 216 C.L.R. 277.
[519] *Plaintiff M61/2010E v Commonwealth (Offshore Processing Case)* (2010) 243 C.L.R. 319.
[520] *Plaintiff M61/2010E v Commonwealth (Offshore Processing Case)* (2010) 243 C.L.R. 319 at 345, [51].
[521] Administrative Review Council, *Federal Judicial Review in Australia* (Report No 50) (Canberra, 2012) Ch.5.
[522] M. Aronson, M. Groves and G Weeks, *Judicial Review of Administrative Action and Government Liability*, 6th edn (2017) para.3.6. State courts of appeal see the standing of *Datafin* in Australia as "controversial": *Agricultural Societies Council of NSW v Christie* (2016) 340 A.L.R. 560 at [89]. Such remarks hint the issue can only be resolved by the High Court.
[523] Human Rights Act 2004 (ACT) ss.40 and 40A; and Charter of Human Rights and Responsibilities Act 2006 (Vic) s.4.
[524] The cases are collected in *PJB v Melbourne Health (Patrick's Case)* (2011) 39 V.R. 373.

substantive nature.[525] If those instruments are held to take only small steps within government, it seems unlikely the courts will take larger steps in their application outside government.

Judicial review's grounds and its principles have frequently applied in contexts **3-141** where its remedies are clearly unavailable.[526] Contracts, for example, might be taken to have incorporated public law principles, and it is a commonplace to see the rules of natural justice applied to the disciplinary functions of major sporting associations and other bodies operating in the public arena.[527] But this reach of review outside government remains narrow in scope and weak in content. It is narrow because courts have not moved beyond extending the rules of natural justice. The content is arguably weak because even the natural justice principles applied in sporting associations and like bodies are more muted when compared to the standards applied to public officials.

Canada

In Canada, public law judicial review is confined to bodies exercising powers **3-142** derived from statute or the prerogative. However, not all exercises of statutory or prerogative power are subject to judicial review. For the purposes of determining whether a particular statutorily-derived or prerogative power is amenable to judicial review, the Canadian courts have indicated[528] that they are primarily interested in the nature of the power rather than its specific source. One related context in which these threshold issues have arisen is that of the Canadian Charter of Rights and Freedoms 1982 and the question of what constitutes a governmental function for the purposes of triggering the application of the Charter. In *McKinney v University of Guelph*,[529] the Supreme Court held that "government" as used in the Charter was not co-extensive with the reach of judicial review in holding that the mandatory retirement rules of a public university were not subject to direct attack; they did not constitute government action even though universities were in general subject to the remedies of judicial review. Subsequently, however, in *Eldridge v British Columbia*[530] the Supreme Court accepted that the Charter could reach a non-governmental body performing a truly governmental function under a legislative delegation of power. In *Greater Vancouver Transportation Authority v Canadian Federation of Students British Columbia Component*, the Supreme Court summarised the impact of *McKinney*, *Eldridge*, and other earlier case law.[531] For the purposes of the Canadian Charter of Rights and Freedoms, an entity could be "government" because of its "very nature or because the government exercises substantial control over it". A non-governmental entity could also be subject to the Charter to the extent that it "performs governmental functions". In this instance, the court held that a transportation service that was controlled by a statutorily constituted regional municipal authority itself constituted a government entity.

Wall v Highwood Congregation of Jehovah's Witnesses (Judicial Commit- **3-143**

---

[525] *Bare v Independent Broad-Based Independent Anti-Corruption Commission* (2015) 48 V.R. 129.
[526] M. Aronson and M. Groves, *Judicial Review of Administrative Action* 5th edn (2013), 3.7.
[527] See, e.g. *Bird v Campbelltown Anglican Schools Council* [2007] NSWSC 1419; and *Sturt v Farran* [2012] NSWSC 400 at [89]–[146].
[528] *Black v Canada (Prime Minister)* (2001) 54 O.R. (3d) 215.
[529] *McKinney v University of Guelph* [1990] 3 S.C.R. 229.
[530] *Eldridge v British Columbia* [1997] 3 S.C.R. 624.
[531] *Greater Vancouver Transportation Authority v Canadian Federation of Students* [2009] 2 S.C.R. 295 at [16].

tee),[532] currently on appeal to the Supreme Court of Canada, provides a puzzling example of a court holding that a religious congregation's membership decision was subject to an application for judicial review. At stake was a decision of a committee of the non-statutory, unincorporated religious Congregation to "disfellowship" a member for disciplinary reasons.

3-144   Among the categories of decision that Canadian courts have held to be non-justiciable are decisions taken in the exercise of parliamentary privileges.[533] More generally, the courts will not interfere in Parliamentary processes. Thus, in a case now under appeal in the Supreme Court of Canada, the Federal Court of Appeal refused to impose a duty to consult indigenous peoples as part of the process of preparing, introducing and passing legislation affecting their rights, claims or interests.[534]

Amenability of functions relating to pre-contractual and contractual powers

3-145   In *Irving Shipbuilding Inc v Canada (Attorney General)*, the Federal Court of Appeal accepted that government procurement decisions made on the basis of statutory authority and having public interest dimensions were appropriate targets of applications for judicial review.[535] However, it went on to find that the sub-contractor of a disappointed bidder could not assert an entitlement to procedural fairness in the contract tendering process. The court also acknowledged that, to the extent that the government awarded contracts on the basis of residual executive power, the less likely it was that judicial review was available to challenge the process.

3-146   In *Air Canada v Toronto Port Authority*,[536] the Federal Court of Appeal held that the Authority established under an Act of Parliament was not acting in a public capacity and therefore not amenable to judicial review in issuing Bulletins respecting the criteria on which it would allocate landing rights at Toronto City Airport. In reaching that conclusion, Stratas JA for the court, evaluated whether the issuing of the Bulletins engaged public law principles by reference to eight criteria.[537] In contrast, the Federal Court of Appeal held that a Ministerial decision not to enter into another contribution agreement for the provision of English language instruction was amenable to an application for judicial review albeit that it had contractual elements.[538]

3-147   In *Dunsmuir v New Brunswick*, the Supreme Court of Canada rejected the application of the principles of procedural fairness to the dismissal of a Justice Department functionary who served at pleasure and whose relationship with the Crown was statutorily defined by reference to the normal rules of contract.[539] The court held that, in such cases, the law of contract, not public law principles applied. The court also took pains to emphasise that its holding reached beyond the particular arrangements under which Dunsmuir served. After referring to the difficulties of distinguishing between public office holders and those who have a contractual employment relationship with the Crown, the court went on to state that, where a

---

[532] *Wall v Highwood Congregation of Jehovah's Witnesses (Judicial Committee)* 2016 ABCA 255; 404 DLR (4th) 48.

[533] See e.g. *Canada (House of Commons) v Vaid* 2005 SCC 30; [2005] 1 S.C.R. 667.

[534] *Mikisew Cree First Nation v Canada (Minister of Aboriginal Affairs and Northern Development)* 2016 FCA 311.

[535] *Irving Shipbuilding Inc v Canada (Attorney General)* 2009 FCA 116; [2010] 2 F.C.R. 488.

[536] *Air Canada v Toronto Port Authority* 2011 FCA 347; [2013] 3 F.C.R. 605.

[537] *Air Canada v Toronto Port Authority* 2011 FCA 347; [2013] 3 F.C.R. 605 at [60].

[538] *Canadian Arab Federation v Canada (Citizenship and Immigration)* 2015 FCA 168.

[539] *Dunsmuir v New Brunswick* [2008] 1 S.C.R. 190.

contractual relationship existed between a public employee and the Crown, the law of contract governed irrespective of that person's status as a public office holder. To the extent that *Knight v Indian Head School Division No.19* held otherwise,[540] it was no longer the law. The only exceptions where a public servant could rely on the public law principles of procedural fairness were situations where a public employee had no contract of employment or where the terms of the relationship between the Crown and a public servant either permitted summary dismissal or was silent on the matter. Read in the light of the facts of *Dunsmuir*, this suggests that, so long as the relevant legislation includes some form of grievance procedure or provides the normal contractual protections of access to damages in the event of wrongful dismissal or without adequate notice, a public employee, even if clearly an office holder, will not have any entitlement to public law procedural fairness or the protection of public law remedies.

In stark contrast, the court held very shortly after *Dunsmuir*, in *Société de l'assurance automobile du Québec v Cyr*, that an employee of a company licensed by the province to carry out motor vehicle inspections was entitled to procedural fairness before the state removed his certification as an accredited mechanic for vehicle inspection purposes: as the consequence of the loss of accreditation, the employee was no longer able to carry out inspections on behalf of his employer.[541] This state action was sufficiently public in nature as to carry with it an entitlement to public law relief on the basis of procedural fairness. It did not matter that the relationship between the state and the company was a contractual one. The employee was not a party to that contract.

3-148

Even more recently, in *Canada (Attorney General) v Mavi*,[542] the court held that judicial review was available to challenge on limited procedural fairness grounds, the government's decision to enforce contractual guarantees provided by those sponsoring foreign relatives relocating to Canada.

3-149

India

The position in India has been explained in the following way: "Although, it is not easy to define what a public function or public duty is, it can reasonably be said that such functions are similar to or closely related to those performable by the State in its sovereign capacity".[543] A body is performing a "public function" when it seeks to achieve some collective benefit for the public or a section of the public and is accepted by the public or that section of the public as having authority to do so.[544] Article 13 of the Constitution makes the fundamental rights binding on the State, and art.12 defines the expression "State" expansively. The tests, distilled over two decades of judgments, not all consistent, was that to fall within the notion of a State (and thus be subject to the rigour of the fundamental rights including the right to equality, and thus its conduct being subject to the constitutional rigour of non-arbitrariness and fairness) the body should be "… financially, functionally or administratively dominated by or under the control of the Government …".[545] Hold-

3-150

---

[540] *Knight v Indian Head School Division No.19* [1990] 1 S.C.R. 653.
[541] *Société de l'assurance automobile du Québec v Cyr* [2008] 1 S.C.R. 338.
[542] *Canada (Attorney General) v Mavi* [2011] 2 S.C.R. 504.
[543] *G. Bassi Reddy v International Crops Research Institute* (2003) 4 S.C.C. 225 at 237, affirmed in *K.K. Saxena v International Commission on Irrigation and Drainage* (2015) 4 S.C.C. 670 at 691.
[544] *Jatya Pal Singh v Union of India* (2013) 6 S.C.C. 452 at 474.
[545] *Pradeep kumar Biswas v Indian Institute of Chemical Biology* (2002) 5 S.C.C. 111 at 134.

ing the tests earlier articulated as not being "… a rigid set of principles"[546] the Supreme Court held that the "… control must be particular to the body in question and must be pervasive … mere regulatory control whether under a statute or otherwise would not be sufficient".[547]

3-151 However, in the two cases relating to judicial review petitions filed against the Board of Cricket Control of India[548] the Supreme Court declined to characterise the BCCI as a "State"[549] but held its functions to be public functions. In the Zee Telefilms case, the Supreme Court found that "… the Board does discharge some duties like the selection of the cricket team, controlling the activities of the players and others involved in the game of cricket". The Supreme Court thus held the BCCI amenable to judicial review since "… these activities can be said to be akin to public duties or state functions".[550] In the next judgment[551] the Supreme Court held that "… the functions of the Board are clearly public functions, which, till such time the State intervenes to takeover the same, remain in the nature of public functions, no matter discharged by a society registered under the Registration of Societies Act".[552] The Supreme Court applied public law principles to the conduct of the BCCI, and declared as illegal, a change in the Regulations that allowed office bearers to own teams in the Indian Premier League (a professional cricket league comprised of teams owned by private persons and featuring cricketers from across the world), and went on to hold that "… BCCI is a very important institution that discharges important public functions. Demands of institutional integrity are, therefore heavy and need to be met suitably in larger public interest".[553] The Supreme Court held that the decisions of the Disciplinary Committee of the BCCI were amenable to judicial review, and in the course of this case, the court appointed a Probe Committee, whose findings of guilt were substituted for the exoneration by the Committee appointed by the BCCI, and directions of far reaching nature were issue by the court exercising the judicial power of judicial review.

3-152 The main respondents in an application for judicial review are ordinarily the government or governmental agencies or a State or instrumentalities of a State.[554] A writ will not however lie to enforce private law rights.[555] Further, the court may exercise its discretion to decline jurisdiction where other remedies are available.[556]

Ireland

3-153 Whether an entity will be amenable to judicial review will generally be dependent on a number of factors, including the source of the power or function exercised, the nature of the decision (whether it falls within the public domain), the relationship between the parties and the consequences of the decision.[557] Judicial review will usually not be available if it is concluded that the applicant has an alternative

---

[546] *Pradeep kumar Biswas v Indian Institute of Chemical Biology* (2002) 5 S.C.C. 111.
[547] *Pradeep kumar Biswas v Indian Institute of Chemical Biology* (2002) 5 S.C.C. 111.
[548] The powerful albeit private body that controls the game of cricket in India.
[549] *Zee Telefilms v Union of India* (2005) 4 S.C.C. 649.
[550] *Board of Control for Cricket in India v Cricket Association of Bihar* (2015) 3 S.C.C. 251.
[551] *Board of Control for Cricket in India v Cricket Association of Bihar* (2015) 3 S.C.C. 251.
[552] *Board of Control for Cricket in India v Cricket Association of Bihar* (2015) 3 S.C.C. 251 at 282.
[553] *Board of Control for Cricket in India v Cricket Association of Bihar* (2015) 3 S.C.C. 251 at 320.
[554] *Shalini Shyam Shetty v Rajendra Shankar Patil* (2010) 8 S.C.C. 329 at 349.
[555] *K.K. Saxena v International Commission on Irrigation and Drainage* (2015) 4 S.C.C. 670 at 692.
[556] *Commissioner of Income Tax v Chhabil Dass Agarwal* (2014) 1 S.C.C. 603 at 611, 612.
[557] *Geoghegan v Institute of Chartered Accountants in Ireland* [1995] 3 I.R. 86 at 130-131 (issue of availability of judicial review not decided by a divided court); *Bane v Garda Representative Association* [1997] 2 I.R. 449 at 467; *Rafferty v Bus Éireann* [1997] 2 I.R. 424 at 439; *O'Donnell v Tipperary (South Riding) County Council* [2005] IESC 18; [2005] 2 I.R. 483 at 487; *Walsh v Irish*

contractual remedy in private law.[558] However, it was held in the case of *Beirne v Commissioner of An Garda Síochána* that this principle is confined to those situations where the duty performed by the decision-maker is "manifestly a private duty and where his right to make it derives *solely* from contract or solely from consent or the agreement of the parties affected".[559] In *Beirne*, judicial review was available to challenge the decision of the Commissioner to terminate the assignment of the applicant as a trainee garda on the basis that the investigation leading to the termination had not been compliant with natural and constitutional justice. Finlay CJ concluded that the Commissioner's power to terminate the assignment "might ordinarily be seen as coming within the public domain"[560] and that it was not solely derived from contract but vested in the Commissioner by reason of his office and the statutory powers attached to his office.[561] Moreover, on occasion, even where the power exercised has been derived solely from contract, the power may be subject to judicial review if there is a public dimension[562] or if the contractual relationship arose from a standard form contract which had not been the subject of negotiation.[563]

New Zealand

The New Zealand cases have followed *Datafin*[564] and in determining whether a body or particular decision is susceptible to judicial review the courts can look not only at the source of the power but also at the "public" function exercised and its public consequences. In *Royal Australasian College of Surgeons v Phipps*, the Court of Appeal said that over recent decades

3-154

"courts have increasingly been willing to review exercises of power which in substance

---

Red Cross Society [1997] 2 I.R. 479 at 484 (membership of the Society was in the public domain); *Eogan v University College Dublin* [1996] 1 I.R. 390 at 398; *Zhang v Athlone Institute of Technology* [2013] IEHC 390 (power derived from statute); *O'Connell v Turf Club* [2015] IESC 57 (where significant power is being exercised with the approval of the legislature, whether express or tacit, judicial review may lie: [41]); *EG v Society of Actuaries in Ireland* [2017] IEHC 392 (no public law element). For discussion, see, G. Hogan and D.G. Morgan, *Administrative Law in Ireland*, 4th edn (2010) at Ch.17; H. Biehler, *Judicial Review of Administrative Action*, 3rd edn (2013) at pp.8-18; M. de Blacam, *Judicial Review*, 3rd edn (2017) at Chs 4–5; D.G. Hogan, *Hogan and Morgan's Administrative Law*, 4th edn (2012) at Ch.17.

[558] *Becker v Duggan* [2005] IEHC 376; [2009] 4 I.R. 1 at 15; *Murphy v The Turf Club* [1989] I.R. 171 at 173; *Rajah v Royal College of Surgeons in Ireland* [1994] 1 I.R. 384 at 393-394; *Quinn v Honourable Society of King's Inns* [2004] IEHC 220; [2004] 4 I.R. 344 at 364. See also *Murtagh v Board of Governors of St Emer's National School* [1991] 1 I.R. 482 at 485.

[559] [1993] I.L.R.M. 1 at 2 (emphasis added); see also *Kelly v Board of Management of St Joseph's National School* [2013] IEHC 392.

[560] *Beirne* [1993] I.L.R.M. 1 at 2.

[561] *Beirne* [1993] I.L.R.M. 1 at 4.

[562] *Browne v Dundalk UDC* [1993] 2 I.R. 512 at 522 (politically-motivated rescission of a contract amenable to judicial review) but contrast *Healy v Fingal County Council*, High Court, 17 January 1997.

[563] See *Geoghegan* [1995] 3 I.R. 86 at 130 (noting that the method by which the contractual relationship between the Institute of Chartered Accountants in Ireland and the applicant was created was "an important factor as it was necessary for the individual to agree in a 'form' contract to the disciplinary process to gain entrance to membership of the Institute"). Contrast *Murphy* [1989] I.R. 171 and *Quinn* [2004] IEHC 220; [2004] 4 I.R. 344 at 363. For imposition of fair procedure duties outside the judicial review context, see: *Glover v BLN Ltd* [1973] I.R. 388 at 425 (judicial review applied to the dismissal of a company director as constitutional justice required that "statutes, regulations or agreements setting up machinery for taking decisions which may affect rights or impose liabilities should be construed as providing for fair procedures"); *McCord v Electricity Supply Board* [1980] I.L.R.M. 153.

[564] See 3-038.

are public or have important public consequences, however their origins and the persons or bodies exercising them might be characterised ... The Courts have made it clear that in appropriate cases, even although there may be no statutory power of decision or the power may in significant measure be contractual, they are willing to review the exercise of the power".[565]

In *Electoral Commission v Cameron*, the Advertising Standards Complaints Board, an unincorporated body set up under the rules of a self-regulatory incorporated society representing the major advertising industry groups, was held to be carrying out public regulatory functions and was subjected to judicial review.[566] In *Lab Tests Auckland v Auckland District Health Board*, the Court of Appeal held that a District Health Board's decision to enter into a contract for provision of services was judicially reviewable and that the courts should "look at the nature of the public body, the particular function being performed, the context within which that function was performed, and what it was said had gone wrong."[567] In the case of a contracting decision by a public body in a commercial context, "judicial review would be available where there was fraud, corruption or bad faith and, as a matter of principle, it might be available in analogous situations such as where an insider with significant inside information and a conflict of interest had used that information to further its interests and to disadvantage rivals in a tender."[568]

3-155   As Cooke P said in *Finnigan v New Zealand Rugby Football Union Inc* "in the New Zealand context, a sharp boundary between public and private law cannot be realistically be drawn".[569]

3-156   Three examples illustrate this point. *Dunne v CanWest TVWorks Ltd* goes further than any case so far, subjecting a publicly-licensed but privately-owned free-to-air broadcaster to judicial review.[570] In *Sky City Auckland Ltd v Wu*, but for explicit statutory override, Blanchard and Anderson JJ (McGrath J to the contrary) were inclined to accept that a monopolistic, state-licensed casino was a "business affected with a public interest" and therefore could not exclude patrons arbitrarily and without good reason.[571] In *Velich v Body Corporate No.164980* the issue was whether the owner of a top-level apartment could complete a partially constructed deck that had not been completed by a previous owner within the time stipulated by the body corporate.[572] The body corporate asserted an unfettered discretion under the rules to refuse to allow the deck to be completed. After construing the rules of the body corporate so as to avoid that result, William Young P said for the court that "a public law dimension" to the case had been overlooked. A decision by a body corporate to withhold consent under either rule would involve the exercise of a statutory power of decision under s.3 of the Judicature Amendment Act 1972 (NZ). This would bring into play administrative law principles that would require the body corporate to give proper effect to the rules and the statutory scheme. It could not exercise its consent power essentially to prevent a unit owner from exercising his

---

565 *Royal Australasian College of Surgeons v Phipps* [1999] 3 N.Z.L.R. 1 at 11-12. This aspect of the case is untouched by the UKPC's overturning on another point: *Phipps v Royal Australasian College of Surgeons* [2000] 2 N.Z.L.R. 513.
566 *Electoral Commission v Cameron* [1997] 2 N.Z.L.R. 241, CA.
567 *Lab Tests Auckland v Auckland District Health Board* [2009] 1 N.Z.L.R 776 at [85].
568 *Lab Tests Auckland v Auckland District Health Board* [2009] 1 N.Z.L.R 776, [91]. See generally D Mullan, "The State of Judicial Scrutiny of Public Contracting in New Zealand and Canada" (2012) 43 V.U.W.L.R. 173.
569 *Finnigan v New Zealand Rugby Football Union Inc* [1985] 1 N.Z.L.R. 159, 179.
570 *Dunne v CanWest TVWorks Ltd* [2005] N.Z.A.R. 577, HC.
571 *Sky City Auckland Ltd v Wu* [2002] 3 N.Z.L.R. 621, [33] CA.
572 *Velich v Body Corporate No.164980* (2005) 5 N.Z.Conv.C. 194,138 CA.

property right. It might be that it would also satisfy the *Wednesbury* test that no reasonable body corporate could object to the minor works necessary to complete the deck. Although William Young P added the caveat that the application of the 1972 Act "does not mean that the body corporate must act as if the rules provided that consent not be declined unreasonably", that is the logic of the application of administrative law principles and there is excellent authority for the proposition.[573]

The New Zealand Bill of Rights Act 1990 s.3   **3-157**

"applies only to acts done ... (a)[b]y the legislative, executive, or judicial branches of the government of New Zealand; or (b) [b]y any person or body in the performance of any public function, power, or duty conferred or imposed on that person or body by or pursuant to law".

For example, in *Television New Zealand Ltd v Viewers For Television Excellence Inc* the Broadcasting Standards Authority was held to be within s.3(b) when determining complaints made under a statutorily recognised and industry-created Code of TV Programme Standards.[574] In *Air Nelson Ltd v Minister of Transport* the Court of Appeal rejected submissions on behalf of the Minister that decisions to increase landing charges at Hawke's Bay airport, which is part owned by the Crown, were of a purely commercial nature and thus not subject to review. It held that the Minister's price-setting power had a public law aspect, having a dual commercial and regulatory focus.[575] In *Cropp v Judicial Committee*, a challenge to drug test rules applying to jockeys, the Court held that New Zealand Thoroughbred Racing Inc was performing a public function for the purposes of the NZBORA when making its rules and therefore those rules should comply with the NZBORA.[576]

Three recent decisions discuss the availability of alternative relief to the court's   **3-158** decision whether to exercise its supervisory powers on review. In *Re Hutt Mana Energy Trust* Wild J held that customers of an energy trust could not review certain decisions made by the trustees pursuant to the trust deed.[577] Key to this decision was the existence of equitable obligations similar or identical to those that would be imposed by judicial review, which indicated that it was neither necessary nor appropriate for the court to extend its review power to cover the trustees' conduct. In *Stratford Racing Club Inc v Adlam*[578] the Court of Appeal said that part of the courts' traditional reluctance to intervene in the running of clubs by way of judicial review was that members had a contractual remedy against the club for rule breaches. However, those refused membership did not have a contractual remedy, meaning their only recourse was judicial review. Decisions refusing memberships were considered amenable to review. In *Tannadyce Investments Ltd v Commissioner of Inland Revenue*, the Supreme Court said that the approach of New Zealand courts "has been in general to recognise that the full right of appeal to a court or a Review Authority that is required to act judicially is able to provide superior remedies to judicial review while also recognising that there will be exceptional

---

[573] See, e.g. *Webster v Auckland Harbour Board* [1983] N.Z.L.R. 646, 650 (Cooke and Jeffries JJ), CA; *Webster v Auckland Harbour Board* [1987] 2 N.Z.L.R. 129, 131 (Cooke P), CA; *R. v Tower Hamlets LBC Ex p Chetnik Developments Ltd* [1988] 1 A.C. 858, 872 (Lord Bridge).

[574] *Television New Zealand Ltd v Viewers For Television Excellence Inc* [2005] N.Z.A.R. 1, HC.

[575] *Air Nelson Ltd v Minister of Transport* [2008] N.Z.A.R. 139, CA.

[576] *Cropp v Judicial Committee* [2008] N.Z.L.R. 774 [5]-[6], SC.

[577] *Re Hutt Mana Energy Trust* [2009] N.Z.A.R. 111, HC.

[578] *Stratford Racing Club Inc v Adlam* [2008] N.Z.A.R. 329, CA.

situations where judicial review should be permitted, without regarding the class of cases where that is so as closed".[579]

3-159   *Falun Dafa Association of New Zealand Inc v Auckland Children's Christmas Parade Trust Board* concerned an application for judicial review by the Falun Dafa Association of the trust board's decision to decline their application to participate in an annual Christmas parade run by the board.[580] The proceedings were interlocutory and the association sought interim relief. The board was incorporated under the Charitable Trusts Act 1957, and its relevant decision was considered an exercise of statutory power. Randerson J cited the 6th edition of *De Smith's Judicial Review* for the proposition that charities are not necessarily immune from judicial review. However, he said that judicial review would only be available where "it is clearly established that the body in question is exercising significant public functions or with substantial public effects which warrant intervention on public law grounds".[581] He was not persuaded that there was a seriously arguable case that the trust board had exercised public powers in rejecting the association's application. While the parade was staged for the benefit of the public and occurs in a public place (downtown Auckland) it did not follow that the powers being exercised were of a public nature.

South Africa

3-160   In South African law all exercises of public power and public functions are reviewable. Some of these are reviewable as "administrative action" under the administrative-justice rights, s.33 of the Constitution, and the Promotion of Administrative Justice Act 3 of 2000 (PAJA), which gives effect to those rights and defines the concept of administrative action in considerable detail. In this regard, the Constitutional Court has emphasised that the source of the power is not determinative and that "what matters is not so much the functionary as the function".[582] But even action that does not qualify as administrative action remains reviewable under the constitutional principle of legality, which is an aspect of the rule of law—a value on which the South African state is founded.[583] In all instances, the first and most essential question is whether the power or function in question is "public". In the jurisprudence this question has been explored mainly in two contexts. The first is where private bodies may be exercising public powers or functions; and the second concerns the contractual relationships of public bodies.

Private bodies

3-161   South African common law has always recognised that private bodies may exercise public powers and must comply with principles of administrative justice when they do so.[584] The most important case of the constitutional era is *AAA Invest-*

---

[579] *Tannadyce Investments Ltd v Commissioner of Inland Revenue* [2012] 2 N.Z.L.R 153, [36], SC.

[580] *Falun Dafa Association of New Zealand Inc v Auckland Children's Christmas Parade Trust Boa* [2009] N.Z.A.R. 122 HC.

[581] At [33].

[582] *President of the Republic of South Africa v South African Rugby Football Union* 2000 (1) S.A. 1, CC at [141].

[583] Constitution of 1996 s.1(c).

[584] *Johannesburg Stock Exchange v Witwatersrand Nigel Ltd* 1988 (3) S.A. 132, A, *Dawnlaan Beleggings (Edms) Bpk v Johannesburg Stock Exchange* 1983 (3) S.A. 344, W, *Theron v Ring van Wellington van die NG Sendingskerk in Suid-Afrika* 1976 (2) S.A. 1, A, and *Turner v Jockey Club of South Africa* 1974 (3) S.A. 633, A.

ments (Pty) Ltd v Micro Finance Regulatory Council,[585] which considered whether an apparently private and voluntary body exercised public power when making rules regulating the micro-loan industry. The applicant submitted that in making such rules the Council exercised public power and had to comply with the principles of the doctrine of legality when doing so. In the Supreme Court of Appeal, however, it was held that the Council was not a "public regulator" but a "private regulator" of moneylenders who consented to its authority.[586]

The Constitutional Court rejected this rather formalistic approach. Recognising that traditionally governmental functions are to an increasing degree being outsourced to private entities, Yacoob J concluded that the Council had been exercising a public function when it made the rules in question:

3-162

> "The fundamental difference between a private company registered in terms of the Companies Act and the Council is that the private company, while it has to comply with the law, is autonomous in the sense that the company itself decides what its objectives and functions are and how it fulfils them. The Council's composition and mandate show that although its legal form is that of a private company, its functions are essentially regulatory of an industry. ... I strain to find any characteristic of autonomy in the functions of the Council equivalent to that of an enterprise of a private nature. The Council regulates in the public interest and in the performance of a public duty. Its decisions and Rules are subject to constitutional control. The Council is subject to the principle of legality."[587]

The judgment put to rest any notion that the exercise of a power or function can escape constitutional scrutiny simply because a private body is involved. It also established that a power or function need not be "governmental" in order to have a public nature.[588] In spite of this, the Supreme Court of Appeal adopted a distinctly "governmental" approach in *Calibre Clinical Consultants (Pty) Ltd v National Bargaining Council for the Road Freight Industry*.[589] In this case the court concluded that when procuring services to manage its AIDS programme, the Bargaining Council had been performing a "quintessentially domestic function" and had not exercised public power.[590] It is arguable, however, that the matter could have been characterised differently on the principles established in *AAA Investments*.[591]

More recently, in *AMCU v Chamber of Mines*, the Constitutional Court confirmed that "public powers and public functions are wider than governmental powers and governmental functions"[592]—though without adverting to the contrary approach in *Calibre*. The *AMCU* case concerned a decision by private actors (employers and mining unions) to extend a collective agreement to non-parties. The extension of the agreement was found to be public in nature on account of its legislative context, its mandatory and coercive effects on non-parties and the

3-163

---

585 *AAA Investments (Pty) Ltd v Micro Finance Regulatory Council* 2006 (11) B.C.L.R. 1255, CC.
586 *Micro Finance Regulatory Council v AAA Investment (Pty) Ltd* 2006 (1) S.A. 27, SCA at [24].
587 *AAA Investments (Pty) Ltd v Micro Finance Regulatory Council* 2006 (11) B.C.L.R. 1255, CC at [45].
588 At [39]–[41] in the judgment of Yacoob J, distinguishing the approaches of the US and Canadian courts.
589 *Calibre Clinical Consultants (Pty) Ltd v National Bargaining Council for the Road Freight Industry* 2010 (5) S.A. 457, SCA at [33], [38], [39].
590 At [46] in the unanimous judgment of Nugent JA.
591 See further C. Hoexter, "A Matter of Feel? Public Powers and Functions in South Africa" in M. Elliott, J.N.E. Varuhas and S. Wilson Stark (eds), *The Unity of Public Law? Doctrinal, Theoretical and Comparative Perspectives* (forthcoming in 2018).
592 *AMCU v Chamber of Mines of South Africa* 2017 (3) S.A. 242, CC at [69].

rationale behind extension, which was the "plainly public goal" of improving work-ers' conditions by means of collectively agreed bargains.[593]

Private powers of public bodies

3-164   The second situation concerns the extent to which contractual relationships of public entities are subject to the constraints and controls of administrative law. Historically the approach to this question was dominated by reliance on the source of the power: if the exercise of the power was authorised in the terms of a contract, or the contract explicitly conferred the power concerned, then the exercise of the power was to be considered private—even where a statutory or public power authorised the conclusion of the contract in the first place.[594]

3-165   The dominance of this categorical approach has been eroded in the constitutional era. In *Cape Metropolitan Council v Metro Inspection Services (Western Cape) CC*[595] the Supreme Court of Appeal held, unconvincingly, that although the appel-lant Council's power to enter into a contract with the respondent came from statute, the power to terminate the contract arose only from the terms of the contract and common law. The cancellation of the contract was thus not a public duty or func-tion, did not amount to a public power, and was not subject to the controls on public power. The court did hold, however, that an important element of the reason for this conclusion was that the terms of the contract were not prescribed by statute and "could not be dictated by the [the Council] by virtue of its position as a public authority".[596] In *Logbro Properties CC v Bedderson NO*[597] Cameron JA emphasised this nuanced approach, relying on the nature of the relationship between the contracting parties over the formalism of a contract per se. He stated that the *Cape Metro* case established the principle that

> "a public authority's invocation of a power of cancellation in a contract concluded on equal terms with a major commercial undertaking, without any element of superiority or authority deriving from its public position, does not amount to an exercise of public power".[598]

In the case before him, however, things were different: the principles of administra-tive justice "framed the parties' contractual relationship" and continued to govern the administrator's exercise of its contractual rights.[599]

3-166   The point of *Logbro* is that a contractual context does not by itself answer the question whether and to what extent powers exercised by a public body will be subject to the controls of administrative law. That general proposition has found support in a number of subsequent cases.[600] However, the formalism Cameron JA sought to banish in *Logbro* evidently retains a hold over South African legal

---

[593]   At [81].
[594]   *Mustapha v Receiver of Revenue, Lichtenburg*, 1958 (3) S.A. 343, A. See also C. Hoexter, "Contracts in Administrative Law: Life after Formalism?" (2004) 121 *South African Law Journal* 595; D. Pretorius, "The Defence of the Realm: Contract and Natural Justice" (2002) 119 *South African Law Journal* 374.
[595]   *Cape Metropolitan Council v Metro Inspection Services (Western Cape) CC* 2001 (3) S.A. 1013, SCA.
[596]   At [18].
[597]   *Logbro Properties CC v Bedderson NO* 2003 (2) S.A. 460, SCA.
[598]   At [10].
[599]   At [8].
[600]   See e.g. *Commissioner, South African Revenue Service v Trend Finance (Pty) Ltd* 2007 (6) S.A. 117, SCA at [25]; *Transnet Ltd t/a National Ports Authority v Owner of MV Snow Crystal* 2008 (4) S.A. 111, SCA at [21]; *Masetlha v President of the Republic of South Africa* 2008 (1) S.A. 566, CC at

reasoning. For example, in *Government of the Republic of South Africa v Thabiso Chemicals (Pty) Ltd*[601] Brand JA stated that he did not believe that the principles of administrative law have any role to play in the cancellation of a tender award. After a tender has been awarded, he went on, the case is governed by the principles of contract law.

> "The fact that the tender board relied on authority derived from a statutory provision to cancel the contract on behalf of the government, does not detract from this principle. Nor does the fact that the grounds of cancellation on which the tender board relied were inter alia, reflected in the regulation".[602]

The Constitutional Court seemed to take a similar view in another procurement case, where it described the issue of contract price adjustment as one falling "squarely within the domain of private law".[603] The categorical approach thus continues to feature in the case law.[604]

---

[198] (in a dissenting judgment); *Joseph v City of Johannesburg* 2010 (4) S.A. 55, CC at [23]-[24] and *President of the Republic of South Africa v Reinecke* 2014 (3) S.A. 205, SCA at [16].

[601] *Government of the Republic of South Africa v Thabiso Chemicals (Pty) Ltd* 2009 (1) S.A. 163, SCA at [18].

[602] At [18].

[603] *Trencon Construction (Pty) Ltd v Industrial Development Corporation of South Africa Ltd* 2015 (5) S.A. 245, CC at [75].

[604] For criticism see R. Cachalia, "Government Contracts in South Africa: Constructing the Framework" (2016) 27 *Stellenbosch Law Review* 88. In essence, Cachalia argues that government contracts should always be treated differently in order to take proper account of the state's uniqueness as a contracting party.

PART II GROUNDS OF JUDICIAL REVIEW

CHAPTER 4

Concepts of Jurisdiction and Lawful Administration

TABLE OF CONTENTS

SCOPE

The following issues are discussed in this chapter, which concludes with some comparative perspectives.[1]   **4-001**

- The historical development of the concepts of jurisdiction and vires of public authorities[2];
- Ouster clauses and similar statutory provisions which seek to exclude or restrict the powers of the court to carry out judicial review of some decisions[3];
- The *Anisminic* case and its aftermath[4];
- The concepts of jurisdiction and vires today—we argue that the foundation of judicial review is no longer ultra vires but rather the principles of lawful or legitimate administration[5];
- The distinction between "void and voidable" decisions, which has now largely been superseded by a more straightforward distinction between "lawful and unlawful"[6];

---

[1]   The 5th edition of this work considered here the power of the courts to review findings of fact. This section, as amended, is now at Ch.11, except for brief discussion of "precedent fact" at 4-051.
[2]   See 4-009.
[3]   See 4-016.
[4]   See 4-032.
[5]   See 4-047.
[6]   See 4-058; and on the effect of void decision, see 4-067.

- The effect of a judgment that official action or delegated legislation is unlawful.

INTRODUCTION

4-002   Judicial review of administrative action was founded upon the premise that a public body is entitled to decide wrongly, but is not entitled to exceed the jurisdiction it was given by statute. The statutory jurisdiction (later referred to also as "vires") permitted the public authority to make errors of fact, or errors of law *within* its jurisdiction, provided that such an error of law was not manifest "on the face of the record". In this respect judicial review is to be distinguished from an appeal. It was largely restricted to review for *excess* of jurisdiction, while an appeal would usually enable errors either of fact or of law to be rectified. Ultra vires, or excess of jurisdiction, in the narrow or strict sense, was thus the organising principle which both justified judicial review (by declaring all power to be derived power) and constrained it (by permitting a degree of autonomy to the reviewed public body).

4-003   The concept of jurisdictional error has become one of the most elusive in administrative law, largely because it calls for analytical distinctions which have, as judicial review has developed, become impossible to sustain. There is the vexed distinction between jurisdictional error and error of law within jurisdiction; this is now largely of academic rather than practical interest as almost all errors of law are now regarded as jurisdictional. There is also a related distinction between "preliminary" or "precedent" requirements that have to be fulfilled before a public body's jurisdiction exists (which therefore go to a public body's jurisdiction, being preliminary to the "merits" of the decision), and requirements (of law or fact or merits) which do not. Finally, there is the equally contested distinction between a "void" and "voidable" decision: that is, a decision which is invalid or void in the sense that it is a nullity, or voidable in that it can be set aside but until it is set aside gives rise to legal consequences.

4-004   The terms "jurisdiction" and "vires" are both at times confused by the fact that they can refer to the power either of the public body reviewed or of the reviewing court. The assertion that the courts have no "jurisdiction" to review "non-jurisdictional" error committed by a public body raises questions both about the power to review of the court and the power to err of the public body. When an Act of Parliament seeks to oust the jurisdiction of the courts to review decisions of a public body, the question arises as to whether the intention was to preclude the court reviewing even for a jurisdictional error committed by the public body. Here again two questions are raised: (a) the power of the court to review,[7] and (b) the kind of determination (or non-determination) that the public body is entitled to make with impunity. These different senses of jurisdiction interlock and overlap. Although they may be kept conceptually distinct, we believe that they require common treatment and cannot be fully understood in isolation one from the other.

4-005   At the heart of these seemingly technical distinctions there lie fundamental constitutional issues concerning the rule of law (to what extent should public bodies be able to determine the scope of their own powers? To what extent may Acts of Parliament prevent access to justice? To what extent ought invalid decisions be able to survive once successfully challenged?); the relationship between the courts and the administration (to what extent should courts exercising powers of review

---

[7]   See Ch.3.

refrain from correcting the administration's factual or legal errors?), and the sovereignty of Parliament (to what extent do the courts possess an inherent power to review the legality of official action despite parliamentary legislation purporting to exclude or limit such review?).

To understand judicial review today, familiarity as to how it developed can be of considerable significance. Its history explains its unique qualities which today make it such an effective method of controlling abuse of power by public bodies. Over the last 40 years its scope has developed dramatically. It has grown from being little more than a method of correcting the errors of law of inferior courts to its present eminence as the remedy for protecting individuals against unlawful action by the Government and other public bodies. **4-006**

In the early 1970s this was the staple diet of the Divisional Court of the Queen's Bench Division of the High Court. This Court alone had the power to grant the prerogative remedies of certiorari, mandamus and prohibition. The importance attached to this power was demonstrated by the fact that the Divisional Court was usually presided over by the Lord Chief Justice of the day sitting with two other High Court Judges. The Court had direct historical links to the role of the High Court Judges of the Queen's Bench Division who, from the Middle Ages, exercised the authority of the monarch to keep the peace and uphold law and order. The prerogative writs together with inherent jurisdiction derived from their association with the monarch gave them wide discretionary powers. Those powers still play a role in claims for judicial review today. As a result of reforms in 1979, in addition to the prerogative orders being available to the judges of the new Court, the judges hearing cases on the "Crown Office List" (the progenitor of the Administrative Court created in 2000) were also able to grant the declarations and injunctions which were the tools used by the judges of the Chancery Division when supervising the activities of public bodies.[8] Declarations and injunctions, like the prerogative orders, were discretionary remedies. The powers to provide both sets of remedies meant that judicial review became a very effective method of upholding the rights of the individual against public bodies. This also meant that the technicalities relating to the grant of the prerogative remedies receded in importance. Thus, although some of the technical issues are no longer individually of important, they still have a collectively importance in establishing the parameters of judicial review as it is today, as a procedure of last resort by which citizens are able to exercise their right of access to the courts to protect themselves against unlawful acts or omissions by public bodies; a procedure that goes to the heart of the rule of law. **4-007**

Another area which has in the past, on a great many occasions, given rise to issues that could be described as technical, is the extent to which it is proper and possible for Parliament to exclude judicial review. Here the individual decisions of the court are still of the greatest importance. However, again it will be seen that the cases in addition to their individual significance have a collective importance. They demonstrate how carefully the courts will scrutinise any attempt to oust their ability to protect the citizen against abuse of power by public bodies and at the same time how important it is to the rule of law that Parliament does not attempt to do so inappropriately. In this area in a jurisdiction where there is no entrenched constitution there is a very heavy responsibility for restraint on all the arms of government. **4-008**

---

[8] See Ch.15.

HISTORICAL DEVELOPMENT OF THE CONCEPT OF JURISDICTION

4-009   From the earliest times the influence of the common law permeated the local courts and the local communities, and proceedings instituted before borough courts were removable into the King's courts at Westminster.[9] Usurpations of authority by municipal corporations gave rise to actions to impugn the validity of byelaws,[10] *quo warranto* proceedings,[11] and later, applications for writs of *scire facias* to repeal borough charters. When the justices of the peace emerged as the principal organ of local administration, the Court of King's Bench (which of all the common law courts was the one most closely associated with the business of government) assumed superintendence over their proceedings—a superintendence that was facilitated by the fact that the administrative functions of the justices were discharged in a judicial form. During the course of the 17th century a distinction gradually came to be drawn, as we shall see, between acts done without jurisdiction, which might be collaterally impeached in civil proceedings brought against the justices for trespass and which could be quashed by a writ of certiorari, and erroneous acts done within jurisdiction, which could not ordinarily be impugned in collateral proceedings and which were immune from the reach of certiorari unless an error was apparent on the face of the "record". The essential features of this distinction survived to condition the scope of judicial control over the successors of the justices of the peace in the work of public administration.[12]

4-010   The courts of common law had at the outset asserted a right to determine the proper jurisdiction of courts administering other systems of law and to contain them within that jurisdiction by writs of prohibition.[13] But it was not until the 17th century that what was to become the modern conception of judicial review took shape.[14] In actions for trespass and other civil wrongs against the Commissioners of Sewers and the judges and officers of other inferior courts, a distinction began to be drawn between a court which proceeded erroneously or *inverso ordine* within its jurisdiction, and a court which proceeded without jurisdiction of the cause. Only in the latter class of case could the order of the court be collaterally impeached and its judges or officers subjected to civil liability.[15] The jurisdiction of a court might be limited with respect to place, persons or subject-matter; and the conferment of a limited or stinted jurisdiction, so Hale held, implied a negative, namely, that the court should not proceed at all in other cases. "But if they should commit a mistake in a matter that were within their power, that would not be examinable here".[16]

4-011   After 1700, certiorari to quash became the regular mode of impugning the decisions of inferior courts. At first it was not easy to distinguish between certiorari to

---

[9]   W. Holdsworth, *History of English Law*, ii, pp.395–405; Ch.15 below.
[10]   W. Holdsworth, *History of English Law*, ii, pp.398, 400, giving illustrations from the 14th and 15th centuries.
[11]   See 15-057.
[12]   See 15-020.
[13]   See 15-017.
[14]   A. Rubinstein, *Jurisdiction and Illegality* (1965), Ch.4; E. Henderson, *Foundations of English Administrative Law* (1963); L. Jaffe, *Judicial Control of Administrative Action* (1933), pp.205–208, 329–334, 624–629; L. Jaffe and E. Henderson, "Judicial Review and the Rule of Law" (1956) 72 L.Q.R. 345; L. Jaffe, "Judicial Review: Constitutional and Jurisdictional Fact" (1957) 70 Harv. L.R. 953.
[15]   See esp. Coke's dicta in the case of the *Marshalsea* (1613) 10 Co.Rep. 68b, 76. But Coke himself did not always follow this distinction; see *Dr Bonham's case* (1610) 8 Co.Rep. 113b.
[16]   *Terry v Huntington* (1668) Hardres 480 at 483; see also *Commins v Massam* (1643) March 196 at 197–198 (Heath J); *Groenvelt v Burwell* (1700) 1 Ld.Raym. 454 at 467–468 (Holt CJ).

quash for want of jurisdiction and certiorari to quash for a defect on the face of the record.[17] The inferior court was required to incorporate in its record all the facts which invested it with jurisdiction, and often a wide range of other facts besides,[18] and if any material fact was omitted the record was bad on its face. In so far as the exercise of the power to quash was clearly referable to jurisdictional defects, errors committed by inferior courts were almost invariably assumed to go to jurisdiction.[19] That a distinction between errors within jurisdiction and errors going to jurisdiction was still recognised was demonstrated by the establishment in the latter part of the 18th century of the practice that findings on jurisdictional matters, though not on other matters, could be impugned by affidavit evidence.[20] But it was not until the first half of the 19th century that a reaction set in against the prevalent tendency to treat nearly all of an inferior court's findings as touching its jurisdiction.[21] This reaction made it possible to construct a coherent theory of the concept of jurisdiction which, had it but prevailed, would have seriously limited the scope of judicial review both in magisterial law and in administrative law.

The pure theory of jurisdiction

This "pure" theory of jurisdiction may be stated as follows.[22] Jurisdiction means authority to decide. Whenever a judicial tribunal is empowered or required to inquire into a question of law or fact for the purpose of giving a decision, its findings cannot be impeached collaterally or on an application for judicial review but are binding until reversed on appeal. Moreover, "Where a court has jurisdiction to entertain an application, it does not lose its jurisdiction by coming to a wrong conclusion, whether it was wrong in law or in fact".[23] It does not lose its jurisdiction even if its conclusion on any aspect of its proper field of inquiry is entirely

4-012

---

17 See 15-014.
18 Both in summary convictions and in orders the adjudication had to be stated, and in summary convictions the court was also required to set out the evidence and its conclusions drawn therefrom.
19 Not until about 1720 was it clearly settled that not every statutory requirement was to be treated as jurisdictional (Henderson, (1963) p.157). For the development of the distinction between jurisdictional and non-jurisdictional matters in prohibition and in mandamus cases, see Henderson (1963), Ch.4.
20 As late as 1735 extrinsic evidence to disprove the existence of jurisdictional facts was held inadmissible (*R. v Oulton Inhabitants* (1735) Cas.t.Hard.169). The distinction between the two classes of errors came to be drawn more sharply in the second-half of the 19th century, when the recital of evidential facts was omitted from the records of summary convictions.
21 *Brittain v Kinnaird* (1819) 1 B. & B. 432; *Cave v Mountain* (1840) 1 Mon. & G. 257; *R. v Bolton* (1841) 1 Q.B. 66; *R. v Rotherham (Inhabitants)* (1842) 3 Q.B. 776; *R. v Buckinghamshire Justices* (1843) 3 Q.B. 800. The relevant authorities are examined in *R. v Mahony* [1910] 2 I.R. 695 and *R. v Nat Bell Liquors Ltd* [1922] 2 A.C. 128; see L. Jaffe, *Judicial Control of Administrative Action* (1965), pp.624–30.
22 D. Gordon, "The Relation of Facts to Jurisdiction" (1929) 45 L.Q.R. 459; D. Gordon, "Tithe Redemption Commission v Gwynne" (1944) 60 L.Q.R. 250; D. Gordon, "Conditional or Contingent Jurisdiction of Tribunals" (1960) 1 U. of B.C.L. Rev. 185. For a reply to criticisms of his views see: H.W.R. Wade, "Anglo-American Administrative Law: More Reflections" (1966) 82 L.Q.R. 263 at 515.
23 *R. v Central Criminal Court Justices* (1886) 17 Q.B.D. 598 at 602; *R. v Grant* (1850) 19 L.J.M.C. 59; *Kemp v Neville* (1862) 10 C.B.(n.s.) 523 at 549–552; *R. v St Olave's Southwark, District Board of Works* (1857) 8 E. & B. 659; *R. v Bradley* (1894) 70 L.T. 349; *Shridramappa Pasare v Narhari Bin Shivappa* (1900) L.R. 27 I.A. 216 at 225; *R. v Cheshire Justices Ex p. Heaver* (1913) 108 L.T. 374; *R. (Limerick Corp) v LGB* [1922] 2 I.R. 76, 93; *R. v Weston-Super Mare Justices. Ex p. Barkers (Contractors) Ltd* [1944] 1 All E.R. 747; *R. v Minister of Health* [1939] 1 K.B. 232; *R. v Minister of Transport Ex p. Beech-Allen (WH) Ltd* (1964) 62 L.G.R. 76; *Punton v Ministry of Pensions and National Insurance (No.2)* [1964] 1 W.L.R. 226.

without evidential support.[24] The question whether a tribunal has jurisdiction depends not on the truth or falsehood of the facts into which it has to inquire, or upon the correctness of its findings on these facts, but upon their nature, and it is determinable "at the commencement, not at the conclusion, of the inquiry".[25] A preliminary or collateral question is said to be one that is collateral to "the merits"[26] or to "the very essence of the inquiry"[27]; it is "not the main question which the tribunal have to decide".[28] Thus, a tribunal empowered to determine claims for compensation for loss of office has jurisdiction to determine all questions of law and fact relating to the measure of compensation and the tenure of the office, and it does not exceed its jurisdiction by determining any of those questions incorrectly; but it has no implied jurisdiction to entertain a claim for reinstatement or damages for wrongful dismissal, and it will exceed its jurisdiction if it makes an order in such terms, for it has no legal power to give any decision whatsoever on those matters. A tribunal may also lack jurisdiction if it is improperly constituted, or (possibly) if it fails to observe certain essential preliminaries to the inquiry.[29] But it does not exceed its jurisdiction by basing its decision upon an incorrect determination of any question that it is empowered or required (i.e. has jurisdiction) to determine.

The ultra vires doctrine

4-013   In essence, the doctrine of ultra vires permits the courts to quash decisions made by bodies exercising public functions which they have no power to make. Acting ultra vires and acting without jurisdiction have essentially the same meaning, although in general the term "vires" has been employed when considering administrative decisions and delegated legislation, and "jurisdiction" when considering judicial decisions, or those having a judicial flavour.[30]

4-014   The evolution of a specific concept of ultra vires did not take place in the context of the power of public authorities. The term was first generally used to denote excess of legal authority by independent statutory bodies and railway companies in the middle years of the 19th century[31]; though the main features of the doctrine to which this name was given had already been taking shape over a long period in

---

24   *R. v Shropshire Justices Ex p. Blewitt* (1866) 14 L.T. 598; *Ex p. Hopwood* (1850) 15 Q.B. 121; *R. v Mahony* [1910] 2 I.R. 695; *R. v Nat Bell Liquors Ltd* [1922] 12 A.C. 128; *R. v Ludlow Ex p. Barnsley Corp* [1947] K.B. 634 at 639.

25   *R. v Bolton* (1841) 1 Q.B. 66 at 74.

26   *Bunbury v Fuller* (1853) 9 Ex. 111 at 140; *R. v Lincolnshire Justices Ex p. Brett* [1926] 2 K.B. 192 at 202; *R. (Limerick Corp) v LGB* [1922] 12 I.R. 76 at 93.

27   *Ex p. Vaughan* (1866) L.R. 2 Q.B. 114 at 116.

28   *R. v Fulham, etc. Rent Tribunal Ex p. Zerek* [1951] 2 K.B. 1 at 6. A tribunal that proceeds in a matter that is res judicata has also been said to exceed its jurisdiction: *Jowett v Bradford (Earl)* [1977] 2 All E.R. 33.

29   *Colonial Bank of Australasia Ltd v Willan* (1874) L.R. 5 at 417, 422, PC. D. Gordon has even challenged the validity of the last-mentioned proposition in "Observance of Law as a Condition of Jurisdiction" (1931) 47 L.Q.R. 386, 557.

30   cf. *R. v Secretary of State for the Environment Ex p. Ostler* [1977] Q.B. 122 at 135, 138 (distinction drawn between the effect of a breach of the rules of natural justice and fraud upon the jurisdiction of a judicial tribunal and upon the vires of an administrative decision, albeit one to which the rules of natural justice applied).

31   H. Street, *A Treatise on the Doctrine of Ultra Vires* (1930), pp.1–3. Ultra Vires has been largely eroded in modern company law. H. Rajak, "Judicial Control: Corporations and the decline of Ultra Vires" [1995] Cambrian L.R. 9; *Gibb v Maidstone & Tunbridge Wells NHS Trust* [2010] EWCA Civ 678; [2010] I.R.L.R. 786 at [50].

relation to the powers of common-law corporations.[32] The term came to be used in relation to municipal corporations, then to the other new types of local government authorities,[33] and finally to the Crown and its servants and even to inferior judicial bodies.

The ultra vires doctrine has had a restricted application to corporations created **4-015** otherwise than by or under statute. Although such corporations are subject to the doctrine in areas regulated by legislation, they seem to be as capable of performing other transactions (e.g. entering into contracts, acquiring land or providing new services) as any natural person.[34] But they may be restrained from committing acts infringing their charter of incorporation[35]; they cannot perpetrate any direct interference with the rights of individuals without specific legal authority; and in the case of such municipal corporations as owed their origin to the royal prerogative, it was doubtful whether they could expend money save in circumstances defined by statute.[36] Delegated legislation, as well as administrative acts and decisions, may be ultra vires on substantive as well as procedural grounds.[37]

STATUTORY RESTRICTION OF JUDICIAL REVIEW

People who dispute whether public functions have been exercised in accord-   **4-016** ance with the law are able to seek resolution on the question of legality by an independent and impartial court or tribunal. This elementary proposition is recognised by the common law, in Convention rights and under European Union law. In matters of public law, the role of the courts is therefore of high constitutional importance. It is a function of the judiciary to determine the lawfulness of the acts and decisions and orders of public bodies exercising public functions, and to afford protection to the rights of the citizen. Legislation that deprives them of these powers is inimical to the principle of the rule of law.[38] The courts have, accordingly, long been zealous to resist restrictions on their jurisdiction imposed by legislation. The issue at principle is whether (a) the right has been removed or (b) only restricted and if restricted, the right is still sufficient to give the citizen a reasonable opportunity to obtain relief.

The courts draw a distinction between legislative attempts to oust judicial control   **4-017** over the legality of decisions and legislation that has the function of allocating jurisdiction to determine the lawfulness of a decision to a particular judicial body (provided that there is effective judicial control). Thus, there was no objection to statutory provisions prohibiting the magistrates' court in which a liability order was sought from re-opening the question whether a prior assessment was valid where Parliament had provided for appeals against the assessment to a tribunal[39]; or to a provision that conferred exclusive jurisdiction on the Investigatory Powers

---

[32] Holdsworth viii, pp.59–61.

[33] I. Jennings in H. Laski, I. Jennings and W. Robson (eds), *A Century of Municipal Progress* (1935), p.418.

[34] *Sutton Hospital case* (1612) 10 Co.Rep. 23a at 30b; *Wenlock (Baroness) v River Dee Co* (1887) 36 Ch.D. 675 at 685; *Attorney General v Manchester Corp* [1906] 1 Ch. 643 at 651; *Attorney General v Leeds Corp* [1929] 2 Ch. 291 at 295; *Attorney General v Leicester Corp* [1943] 1 Ch. 86 at 93. The authority of the rule was strongly criticised by Street (1930), pp.18–22.

[35] A member of the incorporated body may sue: *Jenkin v Pharmaceutical Society of Great Britain* [1921] 1 Ch. 392; *Dickson v Pharmaceutical Society of Great Britain* [1970] A.C. 403.

[36] Subject to the "Ram doctrine" discussed at 5-022.

[37] See 3-011.

[38] See further on the rule of law in chapters 1, 5 and 11.

[39] *Farley v Secretary of State for Work and Pensions (No.2)* [2006] UKHL 31; [2006] 1 W.L.R. 1817;

Tribunal.[40] By comparison, a provision that, in given circumstances, conferred jurisdiction over exclusion and naturalisation decisions on the Special Immigration Appeals Commission rather than the High Court, did not enable the Secretary of State to stay existing judicial review proceedings challenging such decisions and transfer them to SIAC. The statutory provisions were too general to confer such a power on the Secretary of State. Specific and express language was expected.[41] Similarly, the courts have been tolerant of legislation which imposes an even shorter time limit than applies to CPR Pt 54 claims for judicial review (for example, six weeks rather than the standard "promptly and in any event within three months).[42] "Conclusive evidence" provisions have also been held to be effective in restricting the court's judicial review power.[43]

4-018 Various means have been devised by Parliament to seek to restrict the Administrative Court's jurisdiction to determine judicial review claims. Indirect means include: (a) the establishment of an appeals procedure to a tribunal or another court[44]; and (b) conferring wide "subjective" discretion upon the decision-maker.[45] It is now clear, however, that merely designating an appellate body as a "superior court of record" does not necessarily render it immune from judicial review claims.[46]

4-019 Direct means have included legislation employing a variety of formulae over many years: these include "finality clauses", "no certiorari" clauses, "conclusive

---

R. (on the application of Vtesse Networks Ltd) v North West Wiltshire Magistrates' Court [2009] EWHC 3283 (Admin); [2010] R.A. 1.

[40] *R. (on the application of A) v Director of Establishments of the Security Service* [2009] UKSC 12; [2010] 2 A.C. 1.

[41] See *R. (on the application of Ignaoua) v Secretary of State for the Home Department* [2013] EWCA Civ 1498; [2014] 1 W.L.R. 651, reversing [2013] EWHC 2512 (Admin); [2014] A.C.D. 37 on the interpretation of the Justice and Security Act 2013 s.15, which reads:

"(1) Subsection (2) applies in relation to any direction about the exclusion of a non-EEA national from the United Kingdom which—
(a) is made by the Secretary of State wholly or partly on the ground that the exclusion from the United Kingdom of the non-EEA national is conducive to the public good,
(b) is not subject to a right of appeal, and
(c) is certified by the Secretary of State as a direction that was made wholly or partly in reliance on information which, in the opinion of the Secretary of State, should not be made public—
(i) in the interests of national security,
(ii) in the interests of the relationship between the United Kingdom and another country, or
(iii) otherwise in the public interest.
(2) The non-EEA national to whom the direction relates may apply to the Special Immigration Appeals Commission to set aside the direction.
(3) In determining whether the direction should be set aside, the Commission must apply the principles which would be applied in judicial review proceedings."

The judicial review proceedings were, however, subsequently stayed by the Divisional Court itself and transferred to SIAC: R. (on the application of Ignaoua) v Secretary of State for the Home Department [2014] EWHC 1382 (Admin).

[42] See 4-025.

[43] See 4-024.

[44] See 16-018 and Ch.17.

[45] See further Chapter 5.

[46] *R. (on the application of Cart) v Upper Tribunal (Public Law Project and another intervening)* [2011] UKSC 28; [2012] 1 A.C. 663 (in relation to the Upper Tribunal); for discussion of the initial proposals, see A. Le Sueur, "Three strikes and it's out? The UK government's strategy to oust judicial review from immigration and asylum decision-making" [2004] P.L. 225. See further on the meaning of "court of record" *R. (on the application of Woolas) v Parliamentary Election Court* [2010] EWHC 3169 (Admin); [2012] Q.B. 1, [34].

evidence" clauses, time-limited clauses and general formulae purporting to exclude review. Each can constitute a threat to the rule of law. These will now be considered in turn.

Finality clauses

A finality clause is a legislative provision that states that a particular decision "shall be final", "shall not be questioned" or uses a similar formulation. The courts have held that such provisions merely confirm that there is no appeal from the decision in question and do not oust the jurisdiction of the Administrative Court to consider a judicial review claim.[47] **4-020**

By the end of the 17th century it had been settled that a conviction or order made by any inferior tribunal could be removed by certiorari into the Court of King's Bench to be quashed for excess or want of jurisdiction or error on the face of the record. The court, viewing with disfavour the process of conviction without indictment[48] and applying the principle that statutes creating new jurisdictions ought to be strictly construed[49] tended to combine lack of discrimination with excess of zeal and quashed convictions and orders for minor technical defects. Parliament therefore incorporated into a number of statutes conferring summary jurisdiction provisions that were designed to take away the right to apply for certiorari to quash decisions, either by using express words to that effect,[50] or by providing that the matter was to be finally determined by the justices. **4-021**

The King's Bench, however, held that a general finality clause was insufficient to deprive the courts of their power to award the beneficial remedy of certiorari for patent errors of law[51] or for jurisdictional defects,[52] unless the right to a certiorari had itself been conferred by statute.[53] These precedents were followed in later cases, and it became settled law that a finality clause did not restrict in any way whatsoever the power of the courts to issue certiorari to quash either for jurisdictional defects[54] or for error of law on the face of the record.[55] It was clear, furthermore, that a finality clause did not affect their power to award a declaration that a decision or order **4-022**

---

[47] See, e.g. *R. (on the application of Woolas) v Parliamentary Election Court* [2010] EWHC 3169 (Admin); [2012] Q.B. 1, [43]–[47] ("Although it is plain that Parliament intended that a lawful decision of the election court must be final in all respects, we do not consider that Parliament intended to provide that a decision that had been made on a wrong interpretation of the law could not be challenged. An express provision to that effect would have been required"); *R. (on the application of Revenue and Customs Commissioners) v Machell* [2005] EWHC 2593 (Admin); [2006] 1 W.L.R. 609, [24].

[48] *R. v Corden* (1769) 4 Burr. 2279.

[49] *Warwick v White* (1722) Bunb. 106.

[50] This practice began towards the end of the 17th century, shortly after it had become usual to give a right of appeal from justices sitting out of sessions to Quarter Sessions: *W. Paley on Summary Convictions*, 9th edn (1926), p.800. See generally *R. v Mahony* [1910] 2 I.R. 695 at 730 and following (Gibson J).

[51] As distinct from errors on questions of fact: *R. v Plowright* (1685) 3 Mod. 94.

[52] See, e.g. *R. v Plowright* (1685) 3 Mod. 94; *R. v Moreley* (1760) 2 Burr. 1040; *R. v Jukes* (1800) 8 T.R. 542.

[53] *R. v Hunt* (1856) 6 E. & B. 408; D. Yardley, "Statutory Limitations on the Power of Prerogative Orders in England" (1957) 3 U. of Queensld L.J. 103.

[54] *R. v Nat Bell Liquors Ltd* [1922] A.C. 128 at 159–160; *R. v Minister of Transport Ex p. HC Motor Works Ltd* [1927] 2 K.B. 401; *R. v Minister of Health* [1939] 1 K.B. 232 at 246, 249; *R. v Medical Appeal Tribunal Ex p. Gilmore* [1957] 1 Q.B. 574 at 583–585–588.

[55] *Gilmore* [1957] 1 Q.B. 574; Notes [1957] P.L. 89; S.A. de Smith, "Administrative Finality and Judicial Review" (1957) 20 M.L.R. 394. As a result of this decision a right of appeal on questions of law was statutorily provided to the Industrial Injuries Commissioner by the Family Allowance and National Insurance Act 1959 s.2.

made by a statutory body is invalid.[56] Even such words as "final and conclusive" were ineffective to abridge or attenuate judicial review.[57] The only practical effects of a finality clause were to take away a right of appeal where one already exists—e.g. rights of appeal to the High Court by way of case stated from inferior courts[58]—and to preclude a public authority from rescinding or rectifying one of its own valid decisions.[59]

4-023   The Tribunals and Inquiries Act 1958 s.11 reinforced judicial attitudes towards "finality clauses" by enacting that, subject to four exceptions,[60] any provision in an Act passed before August 1958, to the effect that an order or determination was not to be "called into question in any court" (and any such provision which "by similar words" excluded any of the powers of the High Court), was not to prevent the issue of certiorari or mandamus.[61] This section was re-enacted as the Tribunals and Inquiries Act 1971 s.14 and the Tribunals and Inquiries Act 1992 s.12(1). The section applies to all forms of finality clauses, howsoever worded (subject to the exceptions listed), and covers other remedies (such as the declaratory judgment[62]) as well as certiorari and mandamus (now known as declaratory order, quashing order and mandatory order). It does not extend to exclusionary clauses contained in statutes passed after July 1958.

"No certiorari" clauses

4-024   These clauses seek to restrict the Administrative Court's jurisdiction by reference to the remedial orders that the court has at its disposal, which now include quashing orders (previously 'certiorari), prohibiting orders (previously 'prohibition') and mandatory orders (previously 'mandamus').[63] Relatively few of these clauses remain on the statute book.[64]

4-025   Even where the right to certiorari had been expressly taken away by statute, the

---

[56] *Taylor v National Assistance Board* [1956] P 470; [1957] P 101 at 111 (dictum); *Pyx Granite Co v Ministry of Housing and Local Government* [1958] 1 Q.B. 554; [1960] A.C. 260; *Ridge v Baldwin* [1964] A.C. 40; *Watt v Lord Advocate* 1977 S.L.T. 130; *Smith v East Sussex CC* (1977) 76 L.G.R. 332.

[57] *Fenwick v Croydon Union Rural Sanitary Authority* [1891] 2 Q.B. 216; *Attorney General v Hanwell UDC* [1900] 1 Ch. 51; [1900] 2 Ch. 377 ("binding and conclusive"). In so far as any effect at all was attributable to a finality clause, it could often be circumvented by limiting its operation to matters other than those in issue before court: see *St Lucia Usines Co v Colonial Treasurer* [1924] A.C. 508 at 513; *Gateshead Union Guardians v Durham CC* [1918] 1 Ch. 146; *Seabrooke v Grays Thurrock Local Board* (1891) 8 T.L.R. 19; *Gillow v Durham CC* [1913] A.C. 54 at 57.

[58] *Westminster Corp v Gordon Hotels Ltd* [1907] 1 K.B. 910; [1908] A.C. 142; *Hall v Arnold* [1950] 2 K.B. 543; *Kydd v Liverpool Watch Committee* [1908] A.C. 327; *Piper v St Marylebone Licensing Justices* [1928] 2 K.B. 221. See also *Re McCosh's Application* [1958] N.Z.L.R. 731; *Dean v District Auditor for Ashton-in-Makerfield* [1960] 1 Q.B. 149; cf. *Tehrani v Rostron* [1972] 1 Q.B. 182.

[59] *R. v Agricultural Land Tribunal (South Eastern Area) Ex p. Hooker* [1952] 1 Q.B. 182.

[60] Now there are only two exceptions under Tribunals and Inquiries Act 1992 s.12(3): (a) an order or determination of a court of law, and (b) where an Act makes special provision for application to the High Court within a specified time.

[61] The Franks Committee on Administrative Tribunals and Enquiries had recommended in 1957 that no statute should contain words purporting to oust certiorari, prohibition or mandamus in respect of statutory tribunals (Cmnd. 218 (1957), pp.27, 93). The House of Commons Select Committee on Statutory Instruments was already required to consider whether to draw the attention of the House to instruments made under statutes purporting to exclude them from challenge in the courts.

[62] *Anisminic Ltd v Foreign Compensation Commission* [1969] 2 A.C. 147, where the plaintiffs successfully claimed a declaration.

[63] On the development of remedies, see Ch.15; on modern uses of remedial orders, see Ch.18.

[64] But see, e.g. Senior Courts Act 1981 s.29(3A) stating that the "High Court shall have no jurisdiction to make orders of mandamus, prohibition or certiorari in relation" in relation to specified decisions of a court-martial.

courts relying on one or other of the restrictive rules of interpretation already mentioned, or upon the proposition that Parliament could not have intended a tribunal of limited jurisdiction to be permitted to exceed its authority without the possibility of direct correction by a superior court, persistently declined to construe the words of the statute literally. It was held that certiorari would issue, notwithstanding the presence of words taking away the right to apply for it, if the inferior tribunal was improperly constituted (as where some of its members had a disqualifying interest),[65] or if it lacked or exceeded jurisdiction because of the nature of the subject-matter or failure to observe essential preliminaries,[66] or if a conviction or order had been procured by fraud or collusion.[67] Such language would also be ineffective to exclude certiorari or a declaration of invalidity for breach of either rule of natural justice.[68] Legislation purporting to exclude review by other named remedies (e.g. prohibition, injunction) was equally ineffective to prevent the courts from containing inferior tribunals within the limits of their jurisdiction.[69]

Conclusive evidence clauses

In the early 20th century, a clause making the confirmation of a compulsory **4-026** purchase order final and of effect as if enacted in the Act and "conclusive evidence that the requirements of this Act have been complied with, and that the order is duly made and is within the powers of this Act," has been held to exclude any inquiry into the vires of the order on an application for certiorari,[70] despite the absence of any words expressly taking away the right to a certiorari. The Committee on Ministers' Powers doubted whether even this type of clause (which appeared in a

---

[65] *R. v Cheltenham Commissioners* (1841) 1 Q.B. 467; *R. v L & NW Ry* (1863) 9 L.T. (N.S.) 423.

[66] *R. v Somersetshire Justices* (1826) 5 B. & C. 816; *R. v St Albans Justices* (1853) 22 L.J.M.C. 142; *R. v Wood* (1855) 3 E. & B. 49; *Ex p. Bradlaugh* (1878) 3 Q.B.D. 509 at 512; *R. v Hurst Ex p. Smith* [1960] 2 Q.B. 133; *R. v Worthington-Evans Ex p. Madan* [1959] 2 Q.B. 145 at 152; *R. v Bloomsbury and Marylebone County Court Ex p. Villerwest Ltd* [1975] 1 W.L.R. 1175.

[67] *R. v Gillyard* (1848) 12 Q.B. 527; *Colonial Bank of Australasia Ltd v Willan* (1874) L.R. 5 PC 417. Nor does an express privative clause affect the right of the Crown, or of a private prosecutor in criminal proceedings, to apply for the order.

[68] *Ridge v Baldwin* [1964] A.C. 40 at 120–121.

[69] On prohibition, see *Jacobs v Brett* (1875) L.R. 20 Eq. 1. On injunctions, see *Andrews v Mitchell* [1905] A.C. 78; cf. *Catt v Wood* [1910] A.C. 404 (where the error of law did not go to jurisdiction); see also *Wayman v Perseverance Lodge* [1917] 1 K.B. 677. There appears to be no statute expressly excluding review by an action for a declaration, but the same principles would surely have applied; see *Ridge v Baldwin* [1964] A.C. 40; *Anisminic Ltd v Foreign Compensation Commission* [1969] 2 A.C. 147, although it was assumed throughout *Anisminic* that a no certiorari clause would remove the power to quash for patent error of law not going to jurisdiction.

[70] *Ex p. Ringer* (1909) 73 J.P 436; and *Reddaway v Lancs CC* (1925) 41 T.L.R. 422; *Minister of Health v R. Ex p. Yaffe* [1931] A.C. 494 at 520 at 532–533 (dicta): *Merricks v Heathcoat-Amory* [1955] Ch. 567 (unnecessary to consider the legal effect of a similar formula); *London Parochial Charities Trustees v Attorney General* [1955] 1 W.L.R. 42 (formula providing that an Order in Council approving a statutory scheme "shall be conclusive evidence that such scheme was within the scope of and made in conformity with" the Act, and that "the validity of such scheme and order shall not be questioned in any legal proceedings whatsoever," precluded the courts from undertaking any inquiry into vires); *Graddage v Haringey LBC* [1975] 1 W.L.R. 241 (statutory provision that subject to a right of appeal, a notice "shall be final and conclusive as to any matters which could have been raised on such an appeal" precluded a declaration of invalidity for latent defects, but not if flawed ex facie); *Armstrong v Whitfield* [1974] Q.B. 16 (declaration by Quarter Sessions conclusive on existence of public rights of way); *County and Nimbus Estates Ltd v Ealing LBC* (1978) 76 L.G.R. 624 (magistrates barred by conclusive evidence clause from considering alleged invalidity of proposal to increase rateable value); *Suffolk CC v Mason* [1979] A.C. 705 (definitive map conclusive evidence of status of public right of way).

number of statutes passed before 1931)[71] would protect an order that was manifestly unrelated to the scheme of the Act.[72] However, conclusive evidence clauses in statutes have been successful to endow with finality: an executive pronouncement as to the existence of a state of affairs peculiarly within the knowledge of the executive branch of government[73]; or to cure a defect in the proceedings of a statutory body[74]; to preclude such a public body from revoking or varying its own decisions[75]; in relation to a certificate of the registration of a charge by the Registrar of Companies[76]; and to prevent review of a certificate made by the Secretary of State under the State Immunity Act 1978 s.21 that a person is not a head of government or state.[77]

Time-limited clauses

4-027   A number of statutes, particularly in the areas of housing, town and country planning and compulsory acquisition, preclude challenge to the validity of decisions made outside a limitation period within which statutory appeals or applications to quash are available.[78] The Town and Country Planning Acts, for example, have, since their inception in 1947, allowed applications to the High Court within six weeks only, on the ground that the relevant decision is "not within the power of this Act" or that any of the Act's "relevant requirements" have been breached. After the six week period the validity of the action "shall not be questioned in any legal proceedings whatsoever".[79]

4-028   Once the period in which a statutory remedy is available has expired, the

---

[71]   J. Willis, *The Parliamentary Powers of English Government Departments* (1933), pp.101–106; Housing Act 1930 Sch.3, para.2.

[72]   Cmd. 4060 (1932), 40. Conclusive evidence clauses containing an element of ambiguity could be circumvented. See *Waterford Corp v Murphy* [1920] 2 I.R. 165; *Damodhar Gordhan v Deoram Kanji* (1875) 1 App. Cas. 332.

[73]   Some statutory schemes have exempted acts certified by the Minister to be in the interests of national security; cf. Employment Rights Act 1996 s.202 (minister can prohibit the disclosure of information where disclosure would be contrary to national security).

[74]   *Woollett v Minister of Agriculture and Fisheries* [1955] 1 Q.B. 103.

[75]   *R. v Agricultural Land Tribunal (South Eastern Area) Ex p. Hooker* [1952] 1 K.B. 1; *Broxbourne BC v Secretary of State for the Environment* [1980] Q.B. 1 (established use certificate conclusive of matters contained in it so as to preclude on appeal against enforcement notice further inquiry about actual use of land).

[76]   *R. v Registrar of Companies Ex p. Central Bank of India* [1986] Q.B. 1114, CA (certificate of the registration of a charge provided by the Registrar of Companies was "conclusive evidence" under the Companies Act 1948 s.98(2) and was therefore not reviewable by the court even if the Registrar had made an error of fact or law or mixed fact and law in the course of determining the question. The words of the statute were held thus to override Tribunals and Inquiries Act 1971 s.14(1) which in effect itself overrides provisions in a pre-1958 statute seeking to oust the court's jurisdiction. The court was informed in that case that there were about 300 such clauses ("conclusive evidence" clauses) in existence; *R. v Secretary of State for Foreign and Commonwealth Affairs Ex p. Trawnik* (1985) 82 L.S.G. 2739; *Bahamas Hotel Maintenance & Allied Workers Union v Bahamas Hotel Catering & Allied Workers Union* [2011] UKPC 4.

[77]   *R. (on the application of HRH Sultan of Pahang) v Secretary of State for the Home Department* [2011] EWCA Civ 616, *The Times,* 13 June 2011.

[78]   On the history of such provisions, see 15-076; on the procedure for making statutory appeals (which differs from the general CPR Pt 54 claim for judicial review), see 17-022.

[79]   New time limits for bringing a judicial review in certain planning cases (six weeks) and in certain procurement cases (30 days) were given effect on 1 July 2013 by an amendment to the Civil Procedure Rules. Part 54 now includes in (A1)

         "'the planning acts' has the same meaning as in section 336 of the Town and Country Planning Act 1990; 'decision governed by the Public Contracts Regulations 2015' means any decision the legality of which is or may be affected by a duty owed to an economic operator by virtue of regulations 89 or 90 of those Regulations (and for this purpose it does not matter that the claim-

circumstances in which a decision or order protected by a preclusive clause has been successfully challenged in proceedings other than specific statutory one are extremely limited, if they exist at all. In *Smith v East Elloe RDC*,[80] the House of Lords held a compulsory purchase order immune from judicial review on the ground of alleged bad faith after a time limit had expired.

The principal justification for regarding a clause containing a time limit as an ef-   **4-029**
fective bar to review after the time limit has expired is that the legislator, having created a statutory remedy, is entitled to limit the availability of that remedy. This can be the case even where the time limit is too short to enable the order or decision to be challenged in some situations. The use of limitation periods to prevent the assertion of legal rights is, after all, a perfectly familiar feature of the legal system. Furthermore, there can be an obvious public interest in enabling public or private works to be commenced and resources to be committed in reliance upon the legal invulnerability of an apparently valid order. In *Smith v East Elloe* it was suggested that an order that is patently ultra vires may be impugned outside the six-week period.[81]

Formulae purporting to exclude judicial review by general but comprehensive language

Formulae of this character were the principal statutory device adopted for giv-   **4-030**
ing the impress of finality to administrative action by the direct prohibition of judicial review. The legal effects attributable to such formulae varied according to the contexts in which they appeared.

Where exclusionary formulae were contained in statutes dealing with foreign   **4-031**
relations or the working of the parliamentary system, there was a much stronger probability that the courts would give the prohibitive words a literal interpretation.[82] In other contexts, however, the courts have declined to give literal effect to generally worded clauses apparently intended totally to exclude from judicial review the determinations of administrative tribunals. This question was raised in the case of *Anisminic*,[83] which also dealt a blow to the distinction between jurisdictional and non-jurisdictional error from which it has scarcely recovered.

---

ant is not an economic operator); and 'economic operator' has the same meaning as in regulation 2(1) of the Public Contracts Regulations 2015.'

In planning and Public Contracts Regulations cases, the ordinary time limits are displaced by CPR 54.5(4) and replaced by 54.5(5)–(6):

(5) Where the application for judicial review relates to a decision made by the Secretary of State or local planning authority under the planning acts, the claim form must be filed not later than six weeks after the grounds to make the claim first arose.

(6) Where the application for judicial review relates to a decision governed by the Public Contracts Regulations 2015, the claim form must be filed within the time within which an economic operator would have been required by regulation 92(2) of those Regulations (and disregarding the rest of that regulation) to start any proceedings under those Regulations in respect of that decision."

[80]   *Smith v East Elloe RDC* [1956] A.C. 736.

[81]   *Smith v East Elloe RDC* [1956] A.C. 736 (Viscount Simonds), 769–770 (Lord Radcliffe); cf. *Graddage v Haringey LBC* [1975] 1 W.L.R. 241 at 250; *R. v Secretary of State for the Environment Ex p. Ostler* [1977] Q.B. 122.

[82]   See, e.g. Parliament Act 1911 s.3 (making a certificate given by the Speaker under the Act conclusive for all purposes and immune from challenge in any court of law); cf. *Harper v Home Secretary* [1955] Ch. 238.

[83]   *Anisminic v Foreign Compensation Commission* [1969] 2 A.C. 147.

THE ANISMINIC CASE

4-032   The *Anisminic* case concerned decisions of the Foreign Compensation Commission (which heard and determined claims for compensation out of payments received by the Crown from foreign governments for measures taken by them against the property of British subjects). The statute stated that the Commission's decisions were not to be "called in question in any court of law".[84] The reasons for excluding judicial review were that payments awarded to claimants were discretionary and that it would be undesirable for the calculations made by the Commission for distribution of the limited sums at its disposal to be upset by successful applications to the courts. More important, perhaps, instituting judicial proceedings might seriously retard distribution to successful claimants. Nevertheless, the House of Lords held that the exclusionary formula did not apply to a purported "determination" that was a nullity because it was not one that the Commission had jurisdiction to make. The effect of the clause was merely to protect valid decisions that might otherwise have been impugned for a non-jurisdictional error of law on the face of the record.[85]

4-033   The most important breakthrough in *Anisminic* was the emphatic rejection by the House of Lords[86] of the idea[87] that the jurisdiction of an inferior tribunal was determinable only at the outset of its inquiry. It was observed[88] that a tribunal having jurisdiction over a matter in the first instance might exceed its jurisdiction by breaking the rules of natural justice,[89] applying a wrong legal test and answering the wrong question,[90] failing to take relevant considerations into account or basing the decisions on legally irrelevant considerations.[91] Although they accepted the survival of the rule that a judicial tribunal has power to err within the limits of its

---

84   Foreign Compensation Act 1950 s.4(4). The Tribunals and Inquiries Act 1958 s.11(3) exempted the Commission from the scope of the section.

85   The 1950 Act was subsequently amended to provide a right of appeal from the Commission to the CA on jurisdictional and other questions of law. Foreign Compensation Act 1969; the former provision exempting decisions of the Commission from the scope of the 1958 Act was omitted from the Tribunals and Inquiries Act 1971 s.14(3); see now Tribunals, Courts and Enforcement Act 2007 Sch.23.

86   *Anisminic v Foreign Compensation Commission* [1969] 2 A.C. 147, Lords Reid, Pearce and Wilberforce; Lords Morris and Pearson dissenting); see H.W.R. Wade (1969) 85 L.Q.R. 198, Lord Diplock (1971) 24 C.L.P 1; D.M. Gordon (1971) 34 M.L.R. 1; B. Gould [1970] P.L. 358; de Smith [1969] C.L.J. 161. For a recent and comprehensive analysis of the context and significance of *Anisminic* see D. Feldman "Anisminic v Foreign Compensation Commission (1968): In Perspective" in S. Juss and M. Sunkin (eds) *Landmark Cases in Public Law* (2017).

87   Already rejected in a number of earlier cases, e.g. *R. v Nat Bell Liquors Ltd* [1922] 2 A.C. 128 at 156.

88   Most of the observations about to be noted were strictly obiter, since their Lordships held that the appellants, who had claimed to be entitled to a share in a compensation fund for British-owned property nationalised in Egypt had established their claim on the true construction of the relevant legislation, and that the Commission had erred in applying to the claimants a test of eligibility that they were not required to comply with and had dismissed the claim on this preliminary point. However, Lord Morris and all the members of the CA ([1968] 2 Q.B. 862) agreed that if the Commission had erred, its error went to the merits and not to jurisdiction. See also Gordon, (1971) 34 M.L.R. 1.

89   *Anisminic Ltd v Foreign Compensation Commission* [1969] 2 A.C. 147 at 171, 195, 207, 215.

90   *Anisminic Ltd v Foreign Compensation Commission* [1969] 2 A.C. 147 at 171, 195, 215; cf. the more guarded formulation by Lord Wilberforce at 210.

91   *Anisminic Ltd v Foreign Compensation Commission* [1969] 2 A.C. 147 at 171, 195, 198, 215. See also *R. v Southampton Justices. Ex p. Green* [1976] Q.B. 11 (decision that recognisance should be forfeit held to be in excess of jurisdiction because magistrates ignored a relevant factor and took into account an irrelevant consideration: but Browne LJ (at 22) doubted whether an exercise of discretion on wrong legal principles could be brought within *Anisminic*). cf. *R. v Secretary of State for the*

jurisdiction, it was not easy to identify errors of law which, in the light of their analyses, would not be held to go to jurisdiction. The importance of *Anisminic* is that "it established that there was a single category of errors of law, all of which rendered a decision ultra vires"[92] even if "its full implications are still open to debate".[93]

Subsequent cases

In *Pearlman v Keepers and Governors of Harrow School*[94] the relevant statute provided that the determination of a county court judge on the question of the rate-able value of a house was to be "final and conclusive". The Court of Appeal nevertheless, by a majority, overruled the county court's holding that a new central heating system was not a "structural alteration or addition to the house'. The county court judge's misconstruction of those words was held to be an error of law which went to his jurisdiction. Lord Denning, however, made it clear that the difference between jurisdictional and non-jurisdictional error could not be sustained logically, and considered that no inferior court or administrative tribunal has jurisdiction to make an error of law "on which the decision of the case depends".[95]

4-034

Pearlman was considered in two cases decided within a short time of each other the following year. In the first, the Privy Council held[96] that a clause that provided that an award of the Industrial Court in Malaysia shall be "final and conclusive"[97] was effective to preclude judicial review if the inferior tribunal "made an error of law which does not affect its jurisdiction". Lord Denning's view in *Pearlman* of the coincidence of error of law and error of jurisdiction was therefore not accepted and Lord Lane's dissent in that case preferred. In the second case, *In re Racal Communications Ltd*,[98] the House of Lords considered a challenge to an order of the High Court under the Companies Act 1948 to authorise the inspection of the company's books. The majority held that the ouster clause[99] was effective to exclude the power of the Court of Appeal to review the High Court judge's decision. Lord Diplock made a distinction, however, between cases where a legal error is made by

4-035

Environment Ex p. Ostler [1977] Q.B. 122, where a distinction appears to have been drawn between the jurisdictional control exercised over judicial tribunals and the application of the ultra vires doctrine to administrative decisions made in the exercise of a wide discretion, although Lord Denning has extra-judicially expressed regret at "some unguarded" statements made by him in this case: *The Discipline of Law* (1979), p.108.

[92] *R. (on the application of Lumba) v Secretary of State for the Home Department (JUSTICE and another intervening)* [2011] UKSC 12; [2012] 1 A.C. 245, [67] (Lord Dyson).

[93] *R. (on the application of Lumba) v Secretary of State for the Home Department (JUSTICE and another intervening)* [2011] UKSC 12; [2012] 1 A.C. 245, [193] (Lord Walker of Gestingthorpe), suggesting that it was a "big step" to extend the rationale of *Anisminic* to the context of a claim for unlawful imprisonment.

[94] *Pearlman v Keepers and Governors of Harrow School* [1979] Q.B. 56.

[95] *Pearlman v Keepers and Governors of Harrow School* [1979] Q.B. 56, 69–70 (Lord Denning), 77 (Eveleigh LJ, agreeing, that "before the tribunal could embark on its inquiry, it was necessary for it to decide the meaning of the question it was required to answer. This was a collateral matter. It had nothing to do with the merits of the case"); but see the dissent of Geoffrey Lane LJ who said, at 75–6: "The question is not whether he had made a wrong decision, but whether he inquired into and decided a matter which he had no right to consider".

[96] *South East Asia Fire Bricks Sdn Bhd v Non-Metallic Mineral Products Manufacturing Employees Union* [1981] A.C. 363.

[97] Malaysian Industrial Relations Act 1967 s.29(3)(a) continuing that "no award shall be challenged, appealed against, reviewed, quashed or called in question in any court of law".

[98] *In re Racal Communications Ltd* [1981] A.C. 374.

[99] Companies Act 1948 s.441(3): "The decision of a judge of the High Court ... on an application under this section shall not be appealable".

an administrative tribunal or authority and the case of an error made by a court of law. In the former case, there is a presumption that Parliament did not intend the administrative body to be the final arbiter of questions of law. There is, however, no such presumption in relation to courts of law. In respect of administrative bodies the distinction between errors of law that went to jurisdiction and errors of law that did not "was for practical purposes abolished". In respect of inferior courts, however, the "subtle distinctions ... that did so much to confuse English administrative law before *Anisminic*" might survive and the superior court conducting the review "should not be astute to hold that Parliament did not intend the inferior court to have jurisdiction to decide for itself the meaning of ordinary words used in the statute involving, as many do, inter-related questions of law, fact and degree".[100]

4-036   It should be noted that *In re Racal Communications Ltd* by no means exempted all courts or judicial decisions from review for non-jurisdictional error of law.[101] The case was limited to a consideration of the scope of a statutory provision attempting to oust the jurisdiction of the courts to review mistakes of law made by a judge of the High Court, which it was held could only be corrected by means of appeal to an appellate court.[102]

4-037   Two years later, Lord Diplock, in his celebrated obiter in *O'Reilly v Mackman*,[103] emphasised this point. He referred to *Anisminic* as:

> "A landmark decision ... which has liberated English public law from the fetters that the courts had therefore imposed on themselves so far as determinations of *inferior courts and statutory tribunals* were concerned, by drawing esoteric distinctions between errors of law committed by such tribunals that went to their jurisdiction, and errors of law committed by them within their jurisdiction. The breakthrough that *Anisminic* made was the recognition by the majority of this House that if a tribunal ... mistook the law applicable to the facts as it had found them, it must have asked itself the wrong question, i.e. one into which it was not empowered to inquire and so had no jurisdiction to determine. Its purported "determination", not being a 'determination' within the meaning of the empowering legislation, was accordingly a nullity."[104]

4-038   In *R. v Manchester Coroner Ex p. Tal* the question was raised as to whether a decision of a coroner's inquest was subject to judicial review for jurisdictional error alone. Despite the statement by Lord Diplock in *Re Racal Communications* to the effect that courts would be so treated, his clearer statement in *O'Reilly v Mackman* was preferred, Goff LJ stating that "Lord Diplock did not intend to say [in *Racal Communications*] that the *Anisminic* principle did not extend to inferior courts as well as tribunals".[105] It was therefore held that all errors of law committed during the course of the coroner's inquest were reviewable by the court,[106] and that "as a matter of principle, the *Anisminic* principle applies to inferior courts as well as

---

[100] *In re Racal Communications Ltd* [1981] A.C. 374 at 383. In evaluating what was said in *Re Racal*, it is important to remember that decisions of High Court judges are not subject to judicial review and the CA's jurisdiction is statutory and so can be limited by statute.

[101] For judicial review of decisions of courts and tribunals, see 3-008.

[102] *Re Racal Communications* [1981] A.C. 374 at 386: Lord Salmon said that the *Anisminic* principle was confined "to decisions made by commissioners, tribunals or inferior courts which can now be reviewed by the High Court of Justice, just as the decisions of inferior courts used to be reviewed by the old Court of King's Bench under the prerogative writs".

[103] *O'Reilly v Mackman* [1983] 2 A.C. 237 at 278, and agreed to by the remainder of their Lordships.

[104] *O'Reilly v Mackman* [1983] 2 A.C. 237 at 278 (emphasis added). In *Racal Communications* [1981] A.C. 374 at 386.

[105] *R. v Manchester Coroner Ex p. Tal* [1985] Q.B. 67 at 81.

[106] Contrary to an earlier decision of the Divisional Court, *R. v Surrey Coroner Ex p. Campbell* [1982] Q.B. 661. In *Renfrew DC v McGourlick* [1987] S.L.T. 538 a total ouster clause did not present challenge to a decision of the Sheriff.

inferior tribunals, nevertheless we do not wish to be understood as expressing any opinion that the principle will apply with full force in the case of every inferior court".[107] Applying Lord Diplock's distinction between decisions of judges of the High Court "acting in that capacity" and a court of limited jurisdiction, the Divisional Court has held that an election court comprised of two High Court judges constituted under Representation of the People Act 1983 s.123 was a tribunal of limited jurisdiction "and therefore the right of judicial review is not excluded".[108]

University visitors

In *R. v Hull University Visitor Ex p. Page*[109] the majority of the House of Lords   **4-039**
accepted "the general rule that any misdirection or error of law made by an administrative tribunal or inferior court in reaching its decision can be quashed for error of law.[110] In the case of an ouster clause, however, the majority in *Page* accepted the distinction made by Lord Diplock in *Re Racal Communications* that the presumption that a "final and conclusive" clause was not intended to oust the power to review the decision (including errors of law) applied to administrative bodies but not to courts. These comments were, however, strictly obiter, since the question to be decided in *Page* was not that of an ouster clause but whether a University Visitor had exclusive jurisdiction to determine disputes arising under the domestic law of the university. It was held that the visitor of an eleemosynary charity, applying the internal laws of the charity, and not applying the general law of the land" occupied an "exceptional" and "anomalous" position and was therefore not subject to the general rule that judicial review would lie to impeach decisions taken within a public authority's jurisdiction in the narrow sense.[111] Judicial review would only lie to the visitor "in cases where he has acted outside his jurisdiction (in the narrow sense) or abused his powers or acted in breach of the rules of natural justice".[112] This body of case law, at least in its application to universities, is now of little more

---

[107] *R. v Ipswich Justices Ex p. Edwards* (1979) 143 J.P. 699 was cited, where the principle was not applied in the case of committing justices.

[108] *R. (on the application of Woolas) v Parliamentary Election Court* [2010] EWHC 3169 (Admin); [2012] Q.B. 1, [55].

[109] *R. v Hull University Visitor Ex p. Page* [1993] A.C. 682.

[110] Lord Browne-Wilkinson at 702. See also *R. v Chancellor of Chichester Consistory Court Ex p. News Group Newspapers* [1992] C.O.D. 48.

[111] A similar view has been taken in respect of decisions of judges of the High Court acting as visitors to the Inns of Court: *R. v Visitors to the Inns of Court Ex p. Calder* [1994] Q.B. 1 and *R. v Honourable Society of the Middle Temple Ex p. Bullock* [1996] C.O.D. 376 (in an educational matter the judges qualified to sit as Visitors did not have an unfettered power to overrule decisions made by an expert review body under statutorily approved regulations and the Visitor was therefore right to conclude that he should only interfere if satisfied that the review board has acted irrationally or unlawfully). On the powers of Visitors, see *R. v Visitor of the University of London Ex p. Vijayatunga* [1990] 2 Q.B. 444; *R. v University of Nottingham Ex p. Ktorides* [1998] C.O.D. 26; *R. v University College London Ex p. Christofi*, 12 September 1997, CA unreported; *R. (on the application of Deman) v Lord Chancellor's Department* [2004] EWHC 930 (Admin); [2004] E.L.R. 484.

[112] *R. v Hull University Visitor Page* [1993] A.C. 682 at 704, Lord Griffiths (692–694), would permit judicial review of the visitor decision which amounted to an "abuse of his powers" (a term he had used in *Thomas v University of Bradford* [1987] A.C. 795 at 825.) Abuse of power was contrasted by Lord Griffiths with a "mistake of law", which, in the case of the university visitor, was not reviewable. "In such a case the judge is not abusing his powers: he is exercising them to the best of his ability albeit some other court thinks he was mistaken. I used the phrase "abuse of his powers" to connote some form of misbehaviour that was wholly incompatible with the judicial role that the judge was expected to perform. I did not intend it to include a mere error of law"(at 693). cf. the dissent of Lord Slynn, with whom Lord Mustill agreed, who could see no reason in principle for limiting the availability of certiorari to a patent excess of power and "excluding review on other grounds recognised by law", and no reason for excluding review on grounds generally available in

than historical interest. In almost all universities in the United Kingdom complaints that in the past would have fallen to be determined by a visitor are now handled by the Independent Adjudicator for Higher Education.[113]

Criminal proceedings

4-040   There are other situations where some important principle will permit review for jurisdictional error alone. One such principle is the avoidance of double jeopardy in relation to criminal proceedings. Normally—subject now to the Criminal Justice Act 2003 Pt 10[114]—when a person has been acquitted, the prosecution is not entitled to go behind that acquittal, and if they do the defendant will be entitled to rely on a plea of autrefois acquit. This does not, however, apply where the previous proceedings were a nullity. For the proceedings to be a nullity they will have to be shown to be "no trial at all".[115] For this to happen the decision has to be made without jurisdiction in the narrow sense. Thus in *R. v Hendon Justices. Ex p. DPP*[116] the decision of the magistrate was held to be a nullity when the defendant was quite irrationally acquitted because of the late arrival in the court of the prosecuting lawyer through no fault of his own.

Habeas corpus

4-041   During the 1990s, there were suggestions that the scope of review in an application for habeas corpus (which continues to be a separate remedy outside the normal CPR Pt 54 claim for judicial review procedure) is confined to want of jurisdiction in the narrow sense.[117] In *R. v Secretary of State for the Home Department Ex p. Cheblak* Lord Donaldson MR drew a distinction, obiter, between habeas corpus and judicial review, suggesting that the reach of the former was less broad than the latter. In his view "A writ of habeas corpus will issue where someone is detained without any authority or the purported authority is beyond the powers of the person authorising the detention and so is unlawful".[118] This was followed in *R. v Secretary of State for the Home Department Ex p. Muboyayi*, in which it was held[119] that, where the applicant for habeas corpus was not alleging the absence of precedent fact[120] but was challenging the reasons for the underlying decision, then habeas corpus could not lie. This view was, however, contradicted by the Law Commission[121] and other strong authority to the effect that both habeas corpus and judicial review are dealt

---

the case of the decision of a visitor (at 710). He also said that "If the individual's rights are affected he should be entitled to the same protection by the courts as he would be in respect of the decisions of a wide range of other tribunals and bodies to whom decisions involving questions of law are assigned" (at 710).

[113]   Higher Education Act 2004; *http://www.oiahe.org.uk/*.

[114]   For the position in Scotland, see the Double Jeopardy (Scotland) Act 2011.

[115]   *Harrington v Roots* [1984] A.C. 743 at 753 (Lord Roskill).

[116]   *R. v Hendon Justices. Ex p. DPP* [1994] Q.B. 167.

[117]   On habeas corpus, see 17-007.

[118]   *R. v Secretary of State for the Home Department Ex p. Cheblak* [1991] 1 W.L.R. 890, CA at 894. Judicial review on the other hand was available where the decision "is within the power of the person taking it but, due to procedural error, a misappreciation of the law, failure to take account of relevant matters, a taking account of irrelevant matters or the unreasonableness of the decision or action, it should never have been taken" (at 894).

[119]   *R. v Secretary of State for the Home Department Ex p. Muboyayi* [1992] 1 Q.B. 244, CA at 254–255 (Lord Donaldson MR, with whom Glidewell and Taylor LJJ agreed); and see *R. v Oldham Justices v Cawley* [1997] Q.B. 1, CA.

[120]   See 4-055.

[121]   Law Com. No.226 *Administrative Law: Judicial Review and Statutory Appeals* (1994) Part XI.

with "under a common principle".[122] Moreover, it is difficult to see how limiting the scope of review in habeas corpus applications is compatible with the requirements of ECHR art.5. Since the coming into force of the HRA, the Administrative Court is now itself (as a public authority) under a duty to ensure compliance with Convention rights and this is likely to entail review of both law and fact.[123]

Review of courts and tribunals

The Access to Justice Act 1999 s.54(4) provides that "No appeal may be made against a decision of a court under this section to give or refuse permission" for an appeal from a District Court to the County Court. Did this statutory bar oust the jurisdiction of the Administrative Court on a challenge in judicial review to a refusal of such permission? The Court of Appeal held that judicial review should not be taken away except by clear and explicit words, which s.54(4) did not provide, and therefore held that Administrative Court's jurisdiction should not be taken away in the circumstances of this case.[124] It was made clear, however, that a challenge by way of judicial review could not normally be made on the merits of a refusal of permission for an appeal to the county court. This was because the Act had established a system of fair and proportionate protection against the risk of error. However, there may be exceptional circumstances of "jurisdictional error" in the narrow, pre-*Anisminic* sense or procedural irregularity such as to constitute a denial of the applicant's right to a fair hearing".[125] The Court of Appeal revisited this question in *Gregory v Turner*,[126] where Brooke LJ said that judicial review would only be available where the judge below had acted in complete disregard of his duties or in fundamental departure from the rules of natural justice.[127]

4-042

In relation to tribunals, the *Sivasubramaniam* approach was applied in some cases[128] and distinguished in others.[129] In *Cart*, the Supreme Court considering the new institutional arrangements for the First-tier Tribunal and Upper Tribunal, created by the Tribunals, Courts and Enforcement Act 2007, held that *Sivasubramaniam* was not the most satisfactory approach and instead applied criteria ap-

4-043

---

[122] *R. v Secretary of State for the Home Department Ex p. Khawaja* [1984] A.C. 74 at 99 (Lord Scarman).

[123] *R. (on the application of MH) v Secretary of State for Health* [2005] UKHL 60; [2006] 1 A.C. 441 at [31] (Baroness Hale, reviewing the relevant case law). In *Guisto v Governor of Brixton Prison* [2003] UKHL 19; [2004] 1 A.C. 101 at [62] Lord Hutton referred to the distinction between habeas corpus on judicial review without expressing a view on its correctness (on the facts, there was a jurisdictional error by the district judge in an extradition case).

[124] *R. (on the application of Sivasubramaniam) v Wandsworth County Court* [2002] EWCA Civ 1738; [2003] 1 W.L.R. 475 (the claimant had bought "bizarre" claims before two district judges).

[125] *Sivasubramaniam* [2002] EWCA Civ 1738; [2003] 1 W.L.R. 475 at [54].

[126] *Gregory v Turner* [2003] EWCA Civ 183; [2003] 1 W.L.R. 1149 (circuit judges refusing to grant permission to appeal against district judge in small claims proceedings).

[127] Citing *Re McC* [1985] A.C. 528, where the HL held that an action for false imprisonment could only lie against justices if they acted without jurisdiction or in excess of jurisdiction, which Lord Bridge described as "some gross and obvious irregularity of procedure". See R. Kellar [2005] J.R. 244 and *R. (on the application of G) v Immigration Appeal Tribunal* [2004] EWCA Civ 1731; [2005] 1 W.L.R. 1445 where the refusal of the High Court to review a decision of the IAT to refuse permission to appeal was upheld by the CA. Again here, it was held that statutory review provided adequate and proportionate protection of asylum seekers' rights.

[128] *R. (on the application of Sinclair Gardens Investments (Kensington) Ltd v Lands Tribunal* [2005] EWCA Civ 1305; [2006] 3 All E.R. 650 (refusal of permission to appeal from the Leasehold Valuation Tribunal to the Lands Tribunal).

[129] *Wiles v Social Security Commissioner* [2010] EWCA Civ 258 at [43] (appeal against refusal by Social Security Commission of permission to appeal against Social Security Appeal Tribunal; Dyson LJ held that it was impossible to find in the relevant legislation any indication that Parliament intended to oust, or even to limit, the jurisdiction to grant judicial review.).

plicable to "second appeals" in the courts of England and Wales.[130] The second-tier appeals test places the emphasis on important points of law or principle or other compelling reasons.[131]

4-044
Highly unusually, in the recent case of *R. (Privacy International) v Investigatory Powers Tribunal*, the Divisional Court held that an ouster clause contained in se.67(8) of the Regulation of Investigatory Powers Act 2000 had been effective to prevent judicial review of the decisions of the Investigatory Powers Tribunal (IPT).[132] Sir Brian Leveson, PQBD argued that the ouster clause had to be considered in context and as the IPT was effectively performing a supervisory function itself, the argument for subjecting it to the supervisory jurisdiction of the High Court was not strong.[133] The decision has been subject to criticism, inter alia, on the grounds that not all decisions of the IPT may be classified as supervisory in character; and that the Divisional Court "does too little to insist upon the rule of law implications of the availability of judicial review."[134]

The Court of Appeal dismissed an appeal in *R. (Privacy International) v Investigatory Powers Tribunal* [2017] EWCA Civ 1868.

Time-limited ouster clauses

4-045
In respect of time-limited ouster clauses, although the logic of *Anisminic* cast doubt upon their efficacy to preclude review for excess of jurisdiction (as defined in that case) the courts have been inclined to prevent all challenges after the expiration of a reasonable limitation period,[135] even in cases where the claimant does not or is not able to discover the grounds for challenging the decision until after the

---

[130] *R. (on the application of Cart) v Upper Tribunal (Public Law Project and another intervening)* [2011] UKSC 28; [2012] 1 A.C. 663; and see further 1-019 and 17-004.

[131] On the application of the second-tier appeals test, see *PR (Sri Lanka) v Secretary of State for the Home Department* [2011] EWCA Civ 988; [2012] 1 W.L.R. 73 (the "other compelling reasons" test was to be an exceptional remedy; "compelling" meant legally compelling, rather than politically or emotionally though extreme consequences might exceptionally add weight to the legal arguments); *JD (Congo) v Secretary of State for the Home Department* [2012] EWCA Civ 327; [2012] 1 W.L.R. 3273 (the fact that an appellant had succeeded in the First-tier Tribunal (FTT) but failed in the Upper Tribunal (UT) or that the FTT's decision had been set aside and remade by the UT could be a relevant factor in applying the "other compelling reason" test; further, approving *PR*, in the absence of a strongly arguable error of law on the part of the UT, extreme consequences could not of themselves amount to a free-standing "compelling reason"); *R. (on the application of HS) v Upper Tribunal (Immigration and Asylum Chamber)* [2012] EWHC 3126 (Admin); [2013] Imm. A.R. 579 (the second-tier appeals criteria were to be satisfied at the permission stage; it was not sufficient to establish that they would be satisfied at the substantive hearing; if permission was granted on that basis, the test was spent and the Court of Appeal had to apply the established grounds for judicial review in determining whether the decision of the UT to refuse permission to appeal should be set aside); cf. *A v Secretary of State for the Home Department* [2013] EWHC 1272 (Admin) (applicants wrongly treated as non-EU nationals and made subject to deportation orders; multiple failures by the FTT and the UT amounted to a "compelling reason").

[132] *R. (Privacy International) v Investigatory Powers Tribunal* [2017] EWHC 114 (Admin).

[133] At [42].

[134] P. Scott "Ouster clauses and national security: judicial review of the investigatory powers tribunal" [2017] P.L. 335.

[135] See, e.g. *R. v Secretary of State for the Environment Ex p. Ostler* [1977] Q.B. 122; *R. v Secretary of State for the Environment Ex p. Kent* [1988] J.P.L. 706; *R. v Cornwall CC Ex p. Huntington* [1994] All E.R. 694; *Martin v Bearsden and Milngavie DC* 1987 S.L.T. 300. cf. *Greater London Council v Secretary of State for the Environment* [1985] J.P.L. 868 (reasoning underpinning the decision which was otherwise in the applicant's favour could be challenged when it damaged some further interest of the applicant); *Lenlyn Ltd v Secretary of State for the Environment* (1985) 50 P & C.R. 129 (failure of the decision-maker to exercise his discretion by refusing to make a decision); *R. v Carmarthen DC Ex p. Blewin Trust Ltd* [1990] C.O.D. 5; cf. *Pollway Nominees Ltd v Croydon LBC* [1987] A.C. 79 (21-day limitations clause ineffective). But see *Renfrew DC v McGourlick* [1987]

statutory period has elapsed,[136] or because he does not learn of the decision until it is too late to challenge it.[137] In *Enterprise Inns Plc v Secretary of State for the Environment, Transport and the Regions*[138] the court rejected a challenge to the six-week statutory period for challenges under the Acquisition of Land Act 1981. Kay J held that ECHR art.6(1) was not an absolute right and that the interests of certainty and good public administration justified the time limit for challenges.

When the opportunity for judicial challenge is closed off after a period of time,   **4-046** the requirement of the rule of law is met to the extent that an affected person has some reasonable time to challenge the decision.[139] The time limit is imposed in order to accommodate the needs of legal certainty.[140] Nevertheless, and despite authority to the contrary,[141] not all decisions of lower courts, nor all decisions taken by other bodies after the expiry of a time-limited ouster clause, should be exempt from judicial review. It would seem right in principle that decisions that lack jurisdiction in "the narrow and original sense of not being entitled to enter on the inquiry in question"[142] (for example, if a public body is wrongly constituted) should be amenable to judicial review. It is also suggested, despite the authorities to the contrary,[143] that if it is not possible for a claimant to ascertain the existence of a ground for challenging a decision during the period in which a challenge is permitted, the claimant should be permitted, at least for excess of jurisdiction, to make a claim for judicial review. The court could then decide whether, in all circumstances, permission should be granted.

JURISDICTION AND VIRES TODAY

It has been suggested that *Anisminic* freed the courts to adopt a "functional"[144]   **4-047** or "pragmatic"[145] approach to the question of jurisdiction.[146] This approach, it will be suggested below, may be helpful in those few instances where those "subtle distinctions"[147] between jurisdictional or non-jurisdictional error survive today.[148]

There is, however, a preliminary question that must be asked: namely, under what   **4-048**

S.L.T. 538. See *Century National Merchant Bank Ltd v Davies* [1998] A.C. 628 (10-day appeal from minister's action to CA held "a necessary implication" of finality; *Barraclough v Brown* [1897] A.C. 615 applied). Time limitation clauses have also been held to be effective in excluding review *before* the commencement of a statutorily mandated period: *R. (Hillingdon London Borough Council) v Secretary of State for Transport* [2010] EWHC 626 (Admin); [2010] J.P.L. 976.

[136] *Smith v East Elloe* [1986] A.C. 736 and *R. v Secretary of State for the Environment Ex p. Ostler* [1977] Q.B. 122.

[137] *R. v Secretary of State for the Environment Ex p. Kent* [1988] J.P.L. 706.

[138] *Enterprise Inns Plc v Secretary of State for the Environment, Transport and the Regions* (2001) 81 P. & C.R. 18.

[139] See 17-022 on procedures for statutory review under "six week clauses" and similar.

[140] As in *Enterprise Inns Plc v Secretary of State for the Environment, Transport and the Regions*: six week statutory period for challenge held by Kay J not to offend ECHR art.6(1) and in the interest of certainty and good public administration.

[141] See 4-025.

[142] Lord Reid in *Anisminic* [1969] 2 A.C. 147.

[143] See, e.g. *R. v Secretary of State for the Environment Ex p. Ostler* [1977] Q.B. 122.

[144] L. Jaffe, "Judicial Review : Constitutional and Jurisdictional Fact" (1957) 70 Harv. L. Rev 953; *Judicial Control of Administrative Action* (1965), pp.631-663; J. Beatson, "The scope of judicial review for error of law" (1984) 4 O.J.L.S. 22.

[145] G. Peiris, "Judicial review and judicial policy: the evolving mosaic" (1987) 103 L.Q.R. 66; C. Emery and B. Smythe, "Error of Law in Administrative Law" (1984) 100 L.Q.R. 612.

[146] See 1-012 on the purpose of judicial review.

[147] *In re Racal Communications* [1981] A.C. 374 at 390-391 (Lord Diplock).

[148] See 4-052.

circumstance does the distinction between jurisdictional and non-jurisdictional error survive? That preliminary question, it is submitted, should not be approached on the basis of pragmatism. It should rather be based upon principle.[149] The apposite principles are deeply embedded in our constitutional law, but have rarely been explicitly applied to administrative law. The principle of the rule of law is one such, which addresses two relevant issues.[150] The first of these is the legality of decisions of public authorities; the rule of law does not permit bodies performing public functions by determining their own powers to alter their scope. Any excess of their powers should be subject to restraint. The second issue addressed by the rule of law relates to legal certainty; where possible, individuals ought to be able to rely upon the validity of official decisions.[151] Another constitutional principle is the sovereignty of Parliament.[152] Under this principle Parliament may (in the interest perhaps of certainty and finality) permit a public authority to determine its own powers. The courts should attempt to reconcile these various principles when they appear superficially to compete. The courts thus presume, in the absence of clear words to the contrary, that Parliament does not intend to offend the rule of law.[153]

4-049   Identifying the relevant principles does not of course automatically solve the difficult problems in this area, particularly those relating to interpretation of parliamentary intent and to the scope and context of particular powers. Nevertheless, reference back to these principles will allow the issues to be resolved in a more coherent manner than can be achieved through a purely functional or pragmatic approach that leads to confusion and a wilderness of single instances.[154] Attempting to refer to and utilise these principles in the light of the recent developments, the following propositions can now be advanced.

Foundation of judicial review no longer ultra vires

4-050   The doctrine of ultra vires, to the extent that it implies that all administrative power is derived from a specific statutory source, can no longer be considered the sole justification for review of the powers of bodies exercising public functions. Certain of these functions are today carried out under prerogative and other common law powers[155] or under powers, like that of self-regulatory bodies, with "no visible means of legal support".[156] These days an increasing amount of regulatory activity and provision of public services is carried out by the use of powers created by contract, or by means of the manipulation of rights to property. These powers "do not lend themselves to the language of ultra vires".[157] Insistence upon ultra vires as the basis for judicial review inhibits review when the powers of the public authority are not derived from a defined statutory source. The review of such pow-

---

[149] *R. v Manchester Coroner Ex p. Tal* [1985] Q.B. 67 (Goff LJ considered that "as a matter of principle" the *Anisminic* principle applied to both inferior courts and tribunals); Sir John Laws, "Illegality: The Problem of Jurisdiction" in M. Supperstone and J. Goudie (eds), *Judicial Review*, 2nd edn (2005), p.51.

[150] On rule of law generally, see chapters 1, 5 and 11.

[151] See Ch.12 on legitimate expectations.

[152] See 1-024.

[153] See further chapters 1, 5 and 11.

[154] H.W.R. Wade, "Crossroads in Administrative Law" (1968) 21 C.L.P 75, 85; D. Galligan, "Judicial Review and the Textbook Writers" (1982) 2 O.J.L.S. 257; J. Beatson, "The Scope of Judicial Review for Error of Law" (1984) 4 O.J.L.S. 22; R. Williams, "When is an error not an error? Reform of jurisdictional review of error of law and fact" [2007] P.L. 793.

[155] See chapters 3 and 5.

[156] *R. v Panel on Takeovers and Mergers Ex p. Datafin* [1987] 1 Q.B. 815 at 824 (Sir John Donaldson MR).

[157] D. Oliver, "Is the ultra vires rule the basis of judicial review?" [1987] P.L. 543 at 545.

ers cannot easily be justified by the ultra vires principle. Yet, the courts recognise that it is important to the rule of law that the abuse of those powers be controlled irrespective of their source and that the nature of the control should be the same as the control of more conventional administrative powers conferred by statute.[158] Accordingly, the foundation for judicial review should no longer be regarded as ultra vires.[159] In general, therefore, in a claim for judicial review it is no longer of any significance whether the source of alleged invalidity of administrative action is based upon an excess of jurisdiction or error of law within jurisdiction. Nor does it matter whether the error is or is not an error disclosed on the face of the record.[160]

Review in accordance with principles of lawful administration

All power can be appropriately reviewed today under what might be described as the principles of lawful or legitimate administration. These principles were enunciated as "grounds" of judicial review, by Lord Diplock in the *GCHQ* case[161] (a case itself involving review of prerogative power). As we have seen, the grounds he conveniently set out—"legality", "procedural propriety" and "rationality"— may not be watertight categories, and may include others such as proportionality and abuse of power.[162] However, these requirements of lawful administration, together with the Convention rights and rights under European Union law, form a firm foundation upon which to review the public functions of modern administration and do not depend upon the limited notion of jurisdiction or vires in its narrow sense.[163]

4-051

---

[158] See 3-038.

[159] See 1-017 and following on the constitutional foundations of judicial review. It is noteworthy that Lord Steyn appeared to favour the ultra vires approach in *Boddington v British Transport Police* [1999] 2 A.C. 143 at 173. However, in his article "Democracy Through Law" (2002) 6 E.H.R.L.R. 723 at 725 he says that "By overwhelming weight of reasoned argument the ultra vires theory of judicial review has been shown to be a dispensable fiction" and "In a democracy, the rule of law itself legitimises judicial review". See also J. Jowell, "Beyond the Rule of Law: Towards Constitutional Review" [2000] P.L. 110; P. Joseph, "The Demise of Ultra Vires - Judicial Review in the New Zealand Courts" [2001] P.L. 354.

[160] *R. v Hull University Visitor Ex p. Page* [1993] A.C. 682 at 701 (Lord Browne-Wilkinson): "In my judgment the decision in *Anisminic Ltd v Foreign Compensation Commission* ... rendered obsolete the distinction between errors of law on the face of the record and other errors of law by extending the doctrine of ultra vires. Thenceforward it was to be taken that Parliament had only conferred the decision making power on the basis that it was to be exercised on the correct legal basis: a misdirection in law in making the decision rendered the decision ultra vires".

[161] *Council for Civil Service Unions v Minister for the Civil Service* [1985] A.C. 374.

[162] See 1-001.

[163] This view has much support, e.g. Lloyd LJ in *R. v Panel on Takeovers and Mergers Ex p. Datafin* [1987] 1 Q.B. 815 ("The express powers conferred on inferior tribunals were of critical importance in the early days when the sole or main ground for intervention by the courts was that the inferior tribunal had exceeded its powers. But those days are long since past"); see also D. Oliver, "Is the Ultra Vires Rule the Basis of Judicial Review?" [1987] P.L. 543; Sir John Laws and B. Hooper, "Illegality: The Problem of Jurisdiction", in M. Supperstone, J. Goudie and P.Walker (eds) *Judicial Review*, 2nd edn (2005), p.91; I. Hare, "The Separation of Powers and Judicial Review for Error of Law", in C. Forsyth and I. Hare (eds) *The Golden Metwand and the Crooked Cord: Essays in Honour of Sir William Wade* (1998), p.112; Sir William Wade, "Habeas Corpus and Judicial Review" (1997) 113 L.Q.R. 55. cf. P Craig, "Ultra Vires and the Foundations of Judicial Review" [1998] C.L.J. 63. And see the helpful discussion by Lord Cooke of the concept of jurisdiction in *R. v Bedwellty Justices Ex p. Williams* [1997] A.C. 225 (although remedy for error of law at court's discretion, where a committal procedure was so influenced by inadmissible evidence as to amount to an irregularity, a remedy would normally follow (although express use of "jurisdiction" was avoided); M. Taggart, "The Contribution of Lord Cooke to Scope of Review Doctrine in Administrative Law: A Comparative Common Law Perspective", in P. Rishworth (ed), *The Struggle for Simplicity in the Law: Essays for*

Residual categories of exceptional and anomalous situations

4-052   There are, however, very exceptional situations where the court's powers of review may be limited to jurisdictional errors in the narrow sense. These include decisions involving the acquittal of a criminal offence (where the principle of double jeopardy is in play)[164] and cases governed by a special historical tradition in relation to a particular institution (such as university visitors).[165] These are, however, strictly exceptional and anomalous situations. Habeas corpus is not one of them.[166] In general the rule of law requires that "there must be no Alsatia in England where the King's writ does not run".[167] In these few remaining situations where the distinction between jurisdictional and non-jurisdictional error survives, the question as to what is a non-jurisdictional error cannot be based upon any clear predetermined criteria that will serve as a test for all bodies. The test must depend upon the context of the particular power and the function being performed.

4-053   After *Anisminic* virtually every error of law is a jurisdictional error, and the only place left for non-jurisdictional error is where the components of the decision made by the public authority include matters of fact and policy as well as law, or where the error was evidential (concerning for example the burden of proof or admission of evidence).[168] Perhaps the most precise indication of jurisdictional error is that advanced by Lord Diplock in *Racal Communications*, when he suggested that a tribunal is entitled to make an error when the matter "involves, as many do, inter-related questions of law, fact and degree".[169] Thus it was for the county court judge in *Pearlman*[170] to decide whether the installation of central heating in a dwelling amounted to a "structural alteration extension or addition". This was a

> "typical question of mixed law, fact and degree which only a scholiast would think it appropriate to dissect into two separate questions, one for decision by the superior court, viz. the meaning of these words, a question which must entail considerations of degree, and the other for decision by a county court, viz. the application of words to the particular installation, a question which also entails considerations of degree."

4-054   It is, however, doubtful whether any test of jurisdictional error will prove satisfactory. The distinction between jurisdictional and non-jurisdictional error is ultimately based upon foundations of sand. Much of the superstructure has already crumbled. What remains is likely quickly to fall away as the courts rightly insist that all administrative action should be simply, lawful, whether or not jurisdictionally lawful.

Precedent fact

4-055   In Chapter 11 we consider what is a question of fact, as opposed to a question of law, a question of mixed law and fact, a question of judgment or a question of degree.[171] These all depend greatly upon the particular statutory scheme and its context. For example, whether a councillor was "disqualified" has been held to be

---

Lord Cooke of Thorndon (1997), p.189; D. Dyzenhaus, "The Politics of Deference: Judicial Review and Democracy" in M. Taggart (ed), *The Province of Administrative Law* (1997), p.279.
[164] See 4-061.
[165] See 4-037; *R. v Visitors to the Inns of Court Ex p. Calder* [1994] Q.B. 1.
[166] See 17-008.
[167] *Czarnikow v Roth Schmidt and Co* [1922] 2 K.B. 478 at 488 (Scrutton LJ); and see 3-017.
[168] See 4-024.
[169] *In re Racal Communications* [1981] A.C. 374 at 390-1.
[170] *Pearlman v Keepers and Governors of Harrow School* [1979] Q.B. 56.
[171] See 11-058.

a precedent fact (which, in case of a dispute, will ultimately be determined by the court).[172] However, whether a person is a "refugee" was considered to be just one of a number of facts which the decision-maker could take into account.[173] And whether a project had "likely significant effects on the environment", so as to necessitate an environmental impact assessment, was held to be a matter of "judgment" only.[174] In these cases, the primary judgement is made by the public body and the court's role is confined to applying *Wednesbury* principles.[175]

One of the exceptions to the general prohibition on courts reviewing the facts upon which decisions of public authorities are based is where it is alleged that there is an absence of required "jurisdictional fact" (sometimes called "precedent fact"). Where a set of facts must exist for the exercise of the jurisdiction of the decision-maker (in the strict sense of permitting the decision-maker to enter into its inquiry) the courts are entitled to inquire into the existence of those facts.[176] The language of jurisdiction is not necessary to justify such intervention.[177] The statute in such a case imposes a condition as precedent to the exercise of the public authority's power and it is the duty of the court to ensure that the condition has been met. The exercise of the decision-maker's power is dependent upon the existence of a fact or set of facts; the court is entitled to ensure that those facts exist. This point was not fully appreciated in *Zamir v Secretary of State for Home Department*,[178] where the question for the House of Lords was whether an appellant was an "illegal entrant".[179] It was held that the matter was one for the immigration officer although the court could "see whether there was evidence on which the immigration officer, acting reasonably, could decide as he did".[180] This approach was, however, overruled in *R. v Secretary of State for the Home Department Ex p. Khawaja*[181] where it was held that it was the court's duty to inquire whether the immigration officer's belief that the entry had been illegal was correct.[182] Similarly, where a local authority had a duty to provide accommodation for a "child", the determination of a person's age

4-056

---

[172] *Islington LBC v Camp* [2004] L.G.R. 58, 67; *R. (on the application of Brittannic Asset Management Ltd) v Pensions Ombudsman* [2002] EWCA Civ 1405; [2002] 4 All E.R. 860 ("administrators of the pension scheme").

[173] *R v. Secretary of State for the Home Department ex p. Bugdaycay* [1987] A.C. 514 at 522–3 (Lord Bridge). In *R. v Hillingdon BC Ex p. Pulhofer* [1986] A.C. 484 at 513 ("accommodation" was not considered a precedent fact).

[174] *R. (on the application of Jones) v Mansfield DC* [2003] EWCA Civ 1408; [2004] Env. L.R. 21.

[175] See Ch.11.

[176] See, e.g. cases such as *White and Collins v Minister of Health* [1939] 2 K.B. 838.

[177] For support of this view see Sir John Laws and B. Hooper, "Illegality: The Problem of Jurisdiction", in M. Supperstone, J. Goudie and P.Walker (eds) *Judicial Review*, 2nd edn (2005).

[178] *Zamir v Secretary of State for Home Department* [1980] A.C. 930.

[179] Immigration Act 1971 s.33(1).

[180] *Zamir v Secretary of State for Home Department* [1980] A.C. 930 at 949 (Lord Wilberforce).

[181] *R. v Secretary of State for the Home Department Ex p. Khawaja* [1984] A.C. 74. But see *Re S (Minors)* [1995] E.L.R. 98, where Butler-Sloss LJ said that the decision in *Khawaja* is only applicable to cases involving the liberty of the person.

[182] Where precedent fact is a condition to the exercise of power, the courts are not confined to intervening only when the fact-finding body has acted "unreasonably". They should themselves assess whether the decision was sufficiently justified. Where precedent fact was held not to be present see *R. v Secretary of State for the Home Department Ex p. Naheed Ejaz* [1994] Q.B. 496, CA; *Silver Mountain Investments Ltd v Attorney General of Hong Kong* [1994] 1 W.L.R. 925, PC; *R. v Secretary of State for the Home Department Ex p. Onibiyo* [1996] Q.B. 768 (*Bugdaycay* and *Khawaja* considered; court had no power to review as an objective precedent fact whether fresh "claim for asylum" had been made). But see *Tan Te Lam v Superintendent of Tai A Chau Detention Centre* [1997] A.C. 97, PC (question whether applicant could be repatriated to Vietnam from Hong Kong is a matter of jurisdiction for the court) and *Re Rahman (Saidur)* [1998] Q.B. 136.

was an objective fact which the court would decide in case of dispute.[183] However, a mistaken but reasonable belief that a person was over 18 did not render detention pending removal from the United Kingdom in breach of the Home Secretary's statutory duty regarding the welfare of children unlawful.[184]

Presumption that all errors of law are reviewable

4-057   Where a statute seeks to oust the jurisdiction of the courts to review the decisions of a public authority, there is a compelling inference that Parliament did not intend that public authority to be the final arbiter of its own powers. There is therefore a presumption that any error of law committed by that public authority is reviewable, whether or not the error is one of jurisdiction in the narrow sense.[185] As has been noted, the rule of law and parliamentary sovereignty are both engaged as principles in these situations. The courts are loath to relinquish their inherent power to review for jurisdictional error.

FROM "VOID AND VOIDABLE" TO "LAWFUL AND UNLAWFUL"

The position in the past

4-058   Behind the simple dichotomy of void acts (void ab initio, invalid, without legal effect) and voidable acts (valid until held by a court to be invalid) lurk terminological and conceptual problems of excruciating complexity.[186] The problems arose from the premise that if a decision is ultra vires in the sense of outside jurisdiction, it was said to be void. If it is intra vires it was, of course, valid. If it was flawed

---

[183]   *R. (on the application of A) v Croydon LBC (Secretary of State for the Home Department and another intervening)* [2009] UKSC 8; [2009] 1 W.L.R. 2557; *R (on the application of PM) v Hertfordshire County Council* [2010] EWHC 2056 (Admin); [2011] P.T.S.R. 269 (finding on the claimant's age by the First-tier Immigration Tribunal (Immigration and Asylum Chamber) was not a judgment in rem or otherwise binding in law against any person not privy to the appeal); *R. (on the application of CJ) v Cardiff City Council* [2011] EWCA Civ 1590; [2012] P.T.S.R. 1235 (burden of proof does not fall to be discharged by claimant or the local authority, rather the court must decide on the balance of probability whether a claimant was or was not at the relevant time a child).

[184]   *R. (AA (Afghanistan)) v Secretary of State for the Home Department* [2013] UKSC 49; [2013] 1 W.L.R. 2224 (Borders, Citizenship and Immigration Act 2009 s.55, required the Home Secretary to make arrangements for ensuring that her immigration functions were discharged having regard to the need to safeguard and promote the welfare of children; an initial local authority age assessment had concluded that the person was over 19 years of age on which basis the Home Secretary refused an asylum claim and made a detention order; a subsequent local authority age assessment concluded that the person was 17 and the Home Secretary conceded that, had she known this, she would not have made the order).

[185]   *Jacmain v Attorney General of Canada* [1978] 2 S.C.R. 15 at 29 (Can.), [1978 2 S.C.R. 15 at 29 (Dickson J, dissenting): "It is hard to conceive that a legislature would create a tribunal with a limited jurisdiction and yet bestow on such tribunal an unlimited power to determine the extent of its jurisdiction". See I. Hare fn.137 above, who raises the principle of separation of powers in this context.

[186]   A. Rubinstein, *Jurisdiction and Illegality* (1963); D. Gordon, "Observance of Law as a Condition of Jurisdiction" (1931) 47 L.Q.R. 386 and (1931) 47 L.Q.R 557; H.W.R. Wade, "Unlawful Administrative Action: Void or Voidable" (1967) 83 L.Q.R. 499; Wade, "Unlawful Administrative Action" (1968) 84 M.L.R. 95; M. Akehurst, "Void or Voidable? Natural Justice and Unnatural Meanings" (1968) 31 M.L.R. 2 and (1968) 31 M.L.R.138.

by an error perpetrated within the area of jurisdiction, it was usually said to be void-able[187]; that is, valid till set aside.[188]

Is it correct to say that "there are no degrees of nullity"?[189] If so, does it follow **4-059** that "out of nothing comes nothing"? The notion that void acts are destitute of legal effect is and always has been subject to major qualifications. Thus, although the courts refused to entertain appeals against void decisions because they were nuga-tory,[190] and have even refused to award certiorari to quash such acts and deci-sions,[191] it was inappropriate for a court to decline to hear an appeal or an applica-tion to set aside an ostensibly valid act which was in reality void.[192]

Again, although an ultra vires decision was ineffective against the party ag- **4-060** grieved, he might need, for his own protection, a formal pronouncement of a court setting the decision aside or declaring it to be void. Meanwhile, he could be enjoined from disregarding the decision until its validity had been finally determined.[193] If he took no judicial proceedings at all within a prescribed statu-tory time limit, the void decision could become as impregnable as if it had been valid in the first place.[194] And until he obtained such a judicial pronouncement in an appropriate form of proceedings, third parties (unable to impugn the invalid deci-sion) would be obliged to treat it as if it were valid.[195]

In addition, the courts have in practice had sufficient room for manoeuvre to be **4-061** able to avoid being driven to reach unsatisfactory conclusions by the pressure exerted by conceptual reasoning. They often employed the elasticity provided by the discretionary nature of most of the judicial remedies, particularly where the claimant had not been prejudiced.[196]

The situation today

The erosion of the distinction between jurisdictional errors and non-jurisdictional **4-062** errors has, as we have seen, correspondingly eroded the distinction between void

---

[187] See the discussion on ultra vires in Chapter 1 and the interpretation of purpose in Chapter 5.

[188] Unless an error on the face of the record goes to jurisdiction, the decision in question was undoubt-edly voidable, not void (e.g. *Punton v Ministry of Pensions and National Insurance (No.2)* [1964] 1 W.L.R. 226; *DPP v Head* [1959] A.C. 83 at 109, 112); but in *R. v Paddington Valuation Officer Ex p. Peachey Property Corp Ltd* [1966] 1 Q.B. 380 at 402, Lord Denning MR appeared to assume that patent error would have rendered the impugned decision void.

[189] *Anisminic Ltd v Foreign Compensation Commission* [1969] 2 A.C. 147 at 170 (Lord Reid).

[190] *R. v Jones (Gwyn)* [1969] 2 Q.B. 33; and *Chapman v Earl* [1968] 1 W.L.R. 1315; *Metropolitan Properties Co (FGC) Ltd v Lannon* [1969] 1 Q.B. 577 (application for certiorari regarded as the ap-propriate means of challenge rather than an appeal); *Campbell v Rochdale General Commissioners* [1975] 2 All E.R. 385 (breach of rules of natural justice: court could only affirm or reverse on ap-peal, thus rendering the matter res judicata on the merits: certiorari regarded as the appropriate remedy); cf. B. Schwartz and H.W.R. Wade, *Legal Control of Government* (1972), pp.159-60. See also *Hanson v Church Commissioners for England* [1978] Q.B. 823 (relief both by way of appeal and certiorari was sought for breach of the rules of natural justice. Certiorari was granted, and the matter remitted to a differently constituted tribunal: semble the appeal was dismissed. An appeal was allowed for breach of the rules of natural justice by an industrial tribunal in *Wilcox v HGS* [1976] I.C.R. 306).

[191] See, e.g. *R. v Barnstaple Justices. Ex p. Carder* [1938] 1 K.B. 385.

[192] For example, where X has been invalidly removed from an office and Y has been appointed in his place; or where P's licence has been invalidly revoked and allocated to Q, it may be futile for X and P to carry on as if nothing has happened.

[193] *Hoffmann-La Roche (F) & Co AG v Secretary of State for Trade and Industry* [1975] A.C. 295 (defendants failed to rebut presumption of validity of ministerial order).

[194] *Re Gale* [1966] Ch. 236 at 242, 247. See also *Ridge v Baldwin* [1964] A.C. 40 at 125 (Lord Morris).

[195] *Re F (Infants)* [1977] Fam. 165.

[196] See 18-047.

and voidable decisions. The courts have become increasingly impatient with the distinction,[197] to the extent that the situation today can be summarised as follows.

Presumption of validity

4-063   All official decisions are presumed to be valid until set aside or otherwise held to be invalid by a court of competent jurisdiction.[198] Under the terminology of void and voidable decisions, this proposition raises a paradox, namely, that a decision, although technically void, is in practice voidable. Such a paradox is, however, circumvented if we abandon those terms which "lead to confusion"[199] and instead use the terms lawful and unlawful decisions.[200] Decisions are thus presumed lawful unless and until a court of competent jurisdiction declares them unlawful. There is good reason for this: the public must be entitled to rely upon the validity of official decisions and individuals should not take the law into their own hands.[201] These reasons are built into the procedures of judicial review, which requires for

---

[197] See, e.g. *Hoffmann-La Roche* [1975] A.C. 295 at 366 (Lord Diplock considered the terms "concepts developed in the private law of contract which are ill adapted to the field of public law". In *London and Clydeside Estates Ltd v Aberdeen DC* [1980] 1 W.L.R. 182 at 189-90 (Lord Hailsham considered the existence of "stark categories such as 'mandatory' and 'directory', 'void' and 'voidable', a 'nullity' and 'purely regulatory' ... useful but ... misleading in so far as it may be supposed to present a court with the necessity of fitting a particular case into one or other of mutually exclusive and starkly contrasted compartments, ... which in some cases (e.g. 'void' and 'voidable') are borrowed from the language of contract or status and are not easily fitted to the requirements of administrative law"). Lord Denning, as we have seen, initially supported the void-voidable distinction and terminology but in *Lovelock v Minister of Transport* (1980) 40 P. & C.R. 336 at 345 said "I have got tired of all the discussion about 'void' and 'voidable'. It seems to be a matter of words-of semantics-and that is all." See also Lord Denning, *The Discipline of Law* (1979) p.77 where he said: "I confess that at one time I used to say that such a decision was not void but only voidable. But I have seen the error of my ways"; see also his retraction of remarks in *R. v Secretary of State for the Environment Ex p. Ostler* [1977] Q.B. 122 p.108.

[198] Lord Radcliffe in *Smith v East Elloe RDC* [1956] A.C. 736; Lord Denning in *Lovelock* (1980) 40 P. & C.R. 336 went on to say that "The plain fact is that, even if such a decision as this is 'void' or a 'nullity', it remains in being unless and until some steps are taken before the courts to have it declared void". Lord Diplock in *Hoffmann-La Roche* [1975] A.C. 295 said that "the presumption that subordinate legislation is intra vices prevails in the absence of rebuttal, and ... it cannot be rebutted except by a party to legal proceedings in a court of competent jurisdiction who has locus standi to challenge the validity of the subordinate legislation in question" (at 366). See also the decision of the PC in *Calvin v Carr* [1980] A.C. 574 where Lord Wilberforce stated (at 589-590) that a decision made contrary to natural justice is void, "but that, until it is so declared by a competent body or court, it may have some effect, or existence, in law" He preferred the term "invalid or vitiated" to void, and felt that it would be "wholly unreal" to hold that the decision made was totally void in the sense of being legally non-existent. The Master of the Rolls in *R. v Panel on Takeovers and Mergers Ex p. Datafin Plc* [1987] Q.B. 815 at 840 referred to "a very special feature of public law decisions" to be the fact that "however wrong they may be, however lacking in jurisdiction they may be, they subsist and remain fully effective unless and until they are set aside by a court of competent jurisdiction". *Mossell (Jamaica) Ltd v Office of Utilities Regulations* [2010] UKPC 1, [44] "Subordinate legislation, executive orders and the like are presumed to be lawful. If and when, however, they are successfully challenged and found ultra vires, generally speaking it is as if they had never had any legal effect at all: their nullification is ordinarily retrospective rather than merely prospective" (Lord Phillips of Worth Matravers PSC). See also D. Feldman, "Error of Law and Flawed Administrative Acts" [2014] C.L.J. 273, where it is argued that seven principles operate alongside the proposition that all legal flaws make a decision void as a matter of law and "can mitigate its potential to operate in anti-social ways in some circumstances".

[199] *Hoffmann-La Roche* [1975] A.C. 295 at 366 (Lord Diplock).

[200] *Palacegate Properties Ltd v Camden LBC* (2000) 4 P.L.R. 59 at 80 (Laws LJ).

[201] For a consideration of the presumption of regularity (*ommia praesumantur rite et solemniter esse acta donec probetur in contrarium*), see *R. v Inland Revenue Commissioners Ex p. TC Coombs & Co* [1991] 2 A.C. 283. Although an individual in the case in which "a fundamental obligation may have been so outrageously and flagrantly ignored or defied", may "safely ignore what has been done

example an application to quash a decision to be brought within a limited time.[202] A decision not challenged within that time, whether or not it would have been declared unlawful if challenged, and whether or not unlawful for jurisdictional error, retains legal effect.[203] So does a decision found to be unlawful but where a remedy is, in the court's discretion, withheld.[204] The language of void and voidable cannot, however, accommodate such an effect, as it would insist that a void decision, being void ab initio, is devoid of legal consequences and that a voidable decision is capable of being set aside.

Nature of unlawfulness irrelevant

Outside of the rare exceptions we have identified,[205] decisions may be unlawful whether or not they exceed a public authority's jurisdiction in the narrow sense, or are flawed by an error of law within the public authority's jurisdiction or an error of law on the face of the record.

4-064

Residual categories

There are a limited number of situations where the use of the word "nullity", coupled with the distinction between jurisdictional and non-jurisdictional error, survives. Here, some important principle justifies the retention of these concepts. We have seen that one such principle is the need to avoid double jeopardy in relation to criminal proceedings.[206] Thus a previous acquittal may only be challenged where it is a nullity in the sense of being made without jurisdiction in the narrow sense.[207]

4-065

The concept of "nullity" was also invoked by the majority in the House of Lords relation to the role of courts reviewing decisions of the Secretary of State to make "control orders" against individuals suspected of involvement in terrorism.[208] The

4-066

---

and treat it as having no legal consequences upon himself. In such a case it may be that the subject is entitled to use the defect in procedure simply as a shield or defence without having taken any positive action of his own": *London and Clydeside Estates Ltd v Aberdeen DC* [1980] 1 W.L.R. 182 at 190 (Lord Hailsham). Where a decision or delegated legislation has been held by a court to be ultra vires, it is without legal effect regardless of whether or not the court formally makes a declaration to that effect or a quashing order: *Ahmed and others v HM Treasury (JUSTICE intervening)(Nos 1 and 2)* [2010] UKSC 2, [2010] UKSC 5; [2010] 2 A.C. 534. For criticism of *Ahmed* see T. Adams, "The standard theory of administrative unlawfulness" [2017] C.L.J. 289.

[202] See 16-055.

[203] *McLaughlin v His Excellency the Governor of the Cayman Islands* [2007] UKPC 50; [2007] 1 W.L.R. 2839 at [14] (Lord Bingham: "it is a settled principle of law that if a public authority purports to dismiss the holder of a public office in excess of its powers ... the dismissal is ... null, void and without legal effect, at any rate once a court of competent jurisdiction so declares or orders").

[204] *McLaughlin* [2007] UKPC 50; [2007] 1 W.L.R. 2839 at [16] ("since public law remedies are, for the most part, discretionary, it necessarily follows that a claimant may be disabled from obtaining the full relief he seeks whether on grounds of lack of standing, delay or his own conduct, or grounds pertaining to the facts of a particular case"). For examples of two such cases: *Chief Constable of the North Wales Police v Evans* [1982] 1 W.L.R. 1155; *Jhagroo v Teaching Service Commission* (2002) 61 W.I.R. 510.

[205] See 4-038–4-039.

[206] See 4-040–4-041.

[207] *Harrington v Roots* [1984] A.C. 743 at 753; *R. v Hendon Justices. Ex p. DPP* [1994] Q.B. 167. In planning law the distinction between "invalidity" and "nullity" survives. See, e.g. *McKay v Secretary of State for the Environment* [1994] J.P.L. 806.

[208] *Re JJ* [2007] UKHL 45; [2008] 1 A.C. 385, [27] "An administrative order made without power to make it is, on well-known principles, a nullity: see the recent decision of the Privy Council in *Dr Astley McLaughlin v A-G of the Cayman Islands* [2007] UKPC 50" (Lord Bingham); cf. Lord

Prevention of Terrorism Act 2005[209] makes a distinction between "derogating control orders" (imposing obligations incompatible with the right to liberty under ECHR art.5) which may be made by a court and "non-derogating control orders" which may be made by the Home Secretary with the permission of a court. In respect of non-derogating orders, the function of a court is to decide, applying "the principles applicable on an application for judicial review", whether any relevant decision of the Secretary of State was "obviously flawed" (s.3). The court's powers are to quash the order, to quash one or more obligations imposed by the order, or to give directions to the Secretary of State for the revocation of the order or for the modification of the obligations it imposes. In a series of cases, courts held that obligations the Home Secretary sought to impose in non-derogating orders— including 18-hour curfews and restrictions on visitors—were contrary to ECHR art.5 and quashed each order in its entirety (rather than giving directions to the Secretary of State for the modification of the orders in question).

THE EFFECT OF A JUDGMENT THAT A DECISION IS UNLAWFUL

4-067   When official action or delegated legislation is held to be unlawful, and if the effect of that holding is that the matter is void ab initio then there may be what has been called a "domino effect" on a number of other decisions which were made on the assumption that the first act or decision was lawful. For example, where byelaws have been successfully challenged as unlawful, are all persons who were previously convicted on the basis of those byelaws entitled to damages against the police for false arrest?[210] In *Percy*, the answer to that question was held to be no, due to the fact, as we have discussed, that at the time of the arrest the presumption of validity applied. In similar situations, however, damages for false imprisonment have been awarded despite the fact that the prison had been following the law as it reasonably seemed at the time.[211] Retrospective application could lead to administrative chaos and also deprive individuals of their benefits (albeit that those benefits, obtained under the colour of a void act, may not strictly be regarded as rights). In practice this conundrum does not cause much problem, because the courts have discovered other principles to deal with this situation, but it has engaged intense debate, particularly in the light of the possibility, after *Boddington*[212] of collateral attack on a decision via a court not subject to the time limits and other constraints of a the procedures of judicial review.

4-068   The Court of Appeal was recently faced with a domino effect scenario in *R. (on the application of Shoesmith) v Ofsted*.[213] The Secretary of State directed the removal of the claimant as director of children's services in a local authority following a much publicised death of a child on a child protection register. The local

---

Hoffmann, dissenting, at [53]. On control orders, see 1-f041.

209 Repealed by the Terrorism Prevention and Investigation Measures Act 2011, which replaced "control orders" with "Terrorism Prevention and Investigation Measures" (TPIMs).

210 *Percy v Hall* [1997] Q.B. 924.

211 *R. v Governor of Brockhill Prison Ex p. Evans (No.2)* [2001] 2 A.C. 19; see 19-055. See also *R. (Mohammed (Shapoor)) v Secretary of State for the Home Department* [2014] EWHC 4317 (Admin); [2015] 1 W.L.R. 3349, in which it was held that the Home Secretary could not have "reasonable grounds for suspecting" that the claimant could be removed from the United Kingdom, where those grounds were based on a mistake of law.

212 *Boddington v British Transport Police* [1999] 2 A.C. 143.

213 *R. (on the application of Shoesmith) v Ofsted* [2011] EWCA Civ 642; [2011] P.T.S.R. 1459.

authority then summarily dismissed the claimant on the basis of the Secretary of State's direction. The Secretary of State's direction was subsequently held to be unlawful on grounds of procedural impropriety. In the Court of Appeal, Maurice Kay LJ (in the minority on this point) held that there was an area "admittedly ill-defined", in which "the act of a public authority which is done in good faith on the reasonably assumed legal validity of the act of another public authority, is not ipso facto vitiated by a later finding that the earlier act of the other public authority was unlawful"; the present case, involving the termination of an employment relationship, is within that ill-defined area (though the local authority's decision was unlawful on other grounds). A different view was expressed by the other members of the Court. Stanley Burton LJ held that there was no urgency for the local authority to dismiss the claimant and it "proceeded on the basis that the direction was lawful and took the risk of it subsequently being held to be void"; therefore its decision was itself unlawful and void.[214] Lord Neuberger of Abbotsbury MR was "prepared to accept, without deciding" that there might in principle exist circumstances in which the decision of public body acting in good faith in reliance on an earlier act of another public body will not have its decision vitiated as a result of a subsequent find that the earlier act was unlawful. On the facts of the case, however, he held that a combination of factors prevented the local authority from relying on that principle: (i) "it should be easier for the principle to be invoked against the public body by a third party who has done something in reliance on the validity of the act, than against a third party by the public body"; (ii) by the time she was dismissed, the claimant had put the local authority on notice of her contention that the Secretary of State's direction was unlawful; (iii) there was no requirement for particularly urgent action by the local authority; and (iv) the local authority could have suggested to the claimant that she choose between promptly starting a judicial review claim against the Secretary of State or letting the local authority's disciplinary hearing and any appeal hearing proceed on the basis that the Secretary of State's direction was valid. The local authority's decision to dismiss the claimant was therefore itself unlawful and void.[215]

Forsyth suggests that where an initial act (in the above example of *Percy*, the byelaw) appears to be valid and people have acted on that assumption, then the validity of the later act (the arrest) depends on the legal powers of the "second actor" (the police who made the arrest).[216] By looking at the relationship between the two acts the question of the validity of the second actor's legal powers will be determined. In some cases (as in *Percy*[217]) the second act will be valid because it had not been challenged before the first act was struck down as void. Thus is the theoretical integrity of the void-voidable distinction preserved, and the domino effect avoided.

4-069

Forsyth's approach has been called "a tissue of pseudo-conceptualism behind which lurks what is in reality a *pragmatic* conclusion".[218] In *Percy*, it was clear that considerations of what was called "policy" were invoked to preserve the arrests

4-070

---

[214] *R. (on the application of Shoesmith) v Ofsted* [2011] EWCA Civ 642; [2011] P.T.S.R. 1459 at [138]-[139].

[215] *R. (on the application of Shoesmith) v Ofsted* [2011] EWCA Civ 642; [2011] P.T.S.R. 1459 at [140].

[216] C. Forsyth, "The Metaphysics of Nullity: Invalidity, Conceptual Reasoning and the Rule of Law" in C. Forsyth and I. Hare (eds), *The Golden Metwand and the Crooked Cord* (1998), p.141.

[217] *Percy v Hall* [1997] Q.B. 924.

[218] M. Elliott, *Beatson, Matthew and Elliott's Administrative Law, Text and Materials* 4th edn (2011), p.100.

from nullity.[219] Yet in some cases Forsyth's analysis may be helpful provided that (and it is a major proviso) the interpretation of the second actor's power is capable of a clear solution. Craig, while believing that retrospective nullity should be the rule, disapproves of the "mask" of the void-voidable distinction in favour of a frank admission on the part of the courts that the decision is void, but would then employ discretion to refuse or limit a remedy to ensure that it only operates prospectively in an appropriate case.[220] As Lord Browne-Wilkinson said in *Boddington*, an ultra vires act may be capable of having some legal effect and the "subsequent recognition of its invalidity cannot rewrite history as to all other matters done in the meantime in reliance on its validity".[221] There are four ways in which the courts are able to prevent history being rewritten, all of them perfectly within the realm of public law principle.

4-071   First, there is clear authority for a recognition of the saving of de facto authority, as we have seen in respect of judges and officials acting under the colour of authority. Surely the same justification applies outside the area of official appointments (such as the arrest carried out in *Percy*)? To seek to avert the hardship that a rigorous imposition of the de jure situation would impose on countless people is not, as Lord Wilberforce said in *Buttes* a mere matter of discretion, but a matter of applying principles of public law that seek to avoid needless unfairness. He regarded the application of these principles as "inherent in the very nature of the judicial process".[222] Of course that does not mean that there will not be occasions where an individual or authority who had acted apparently lawfully will have to pay for the legal mistakes of others.[223]

4-072   Secondly, the courts should take into account the context of invalidity. This was done in a case where certain procedural requirements were not complied with to the letter in an immigration appeal (a declaration of truth was omitted). Lord Woolf MR considered whether there had been substantial compliance with the requirements, whether non-compliance was capable of being waived, and the practical consequences of non-compliance.[224] In another immigration case, the Queen's Bench Division held that appeal decisions taken by the First Tier Tribunal could subsist despite the invalidity of Asylum and Immigration Tribunal (Fast Track Procedure) Rules 2005, under which the appeal decisions were made: the 2005 rules had not created the Tribunal's jurisdiction and its decisions were not all inevitably unfair.[225]

4-073   Thirdly, where the court has discretion to refuse to provide a remedy, or to provide a remedy that is prospective in effect (in the form of a declaration), it may in appropriate situations refuse to quash an unlawful decision. This can happen where there is a lack of prejudice to the claimant, or where to quash the decision

---

[219] See e.g. *Percy v Hall* [1997] Q.B. 924, 951-952 (Simon Brown and Schiemann LJJ).

[220] P. Craig, *Administrative Law* (7th edn 2011), para.24-022; P. Craig, "Collateral Attack, Procedural Exclusivity and Judicial Review" (1998) 114 L.Q.R. 535.

[221] *Boddington v British Transport Police* [1999] 2 A.C. 143 at 164; Lord Slynn at 165; *Mossell (Jamaica) Ltd v Office of Utilites Regulations* [2010] UKPC 1, [44]; *R. (on the application of Shoesmith) v Ofsted* [2011] EWCA Civ 642; [2011] P.T.S.R. 1459.

[222] *Buttes Gas and Oil Co v Hammer* [1982] A.C. 888 at 932.

[223] See, e.g. *R. v Governor of Her Majesty's Prison Brockhill Ex p. Evans (No.2)* [2001] A.C. 19.

[224] *R. v Immigration Appeal Tribunal Ex p. Jeyeanthan* [2000] 1 W.L.R. 354, CA.

[225] *R. (TN (Vietnam)) v Secretary of State for the Home Department* [2017] EWHC 59 (Admin); [2017] 1 W.L.R. 2595, Ouseley J commenting, at [72] that: "the granting of the application [that the appeal decision was a nullity] has to depend on a judgment as to whether the appeal decision in fact was fair or unfair ... and not on the remorseless logic of some jurisprudential theory erasing all that was touched by the nullified Rules."

would prejudice third parties who have relied on the validity of the decision.[226] The maintenance of "public confidence"[227] is, as we shall see in different parts of this book, an important value of public law.

Finally, in some cases a person who has been adversely affected by an unlawful official decision may be entitled to restitution for consequential loss.[228] The House of Lords have held that money paid to the Revenue pursuant to a demand based upon an invalid regulation was prima facie recoverable.[229] The majority of the Lords held that the claimant was entitled in "common justice" to restitution and that the court should seek to "do justice between the parties".[230] Lord Goff's obiter in that case, to the effect that the principle of recovery may not apply in cases where the authority had "misconstrued a relevant statute or regulation" or had "simply … paid the money under a mistake of law"[231] fails to recognise the full effect of the collapse of the distinction between jurisdictional and non-jurisdictional error. As Lord Slynn said in that case, it is where the demand is based upon a mistake of law that the principle of recovery is "most likely to be needed".[232]

4-074

COMPARATIVE PERSPECTIVES

Australia

Judicial review of most federal administrative action other than migration decisions lies under the Administrative Decisions (Judicial Review) Act 1977 (Cth) (ADJR), with judicial review governed by common law principles operating as the safety net in circumstances where the ADJR does not apply.

4-075

ADJR partially codifies the common law's particularised grounds of review, such as breach of natural justice, improper purpose, and taking irrelevant considerations into account. ADJR also allows for the adoption of any new grounds that may have been developed at common law.[233] One of ADJR's grounds is "that the person who purported to make the decision did not have jurisdiction to make the decision", and another is "that the decision was not authorized by the enactment in pursuance of which it was purported to be made". These latter grounds are the closest that ADJR comes to the terminology of "jurisdictional error", and the High Court used them to outflank a legislative attempt to withdraw the *Wednesbury* unreasonableness ground from the Federal Court's migration jurisdiction.[234] ADJR's

4-076

---

[226] See 18-047.

[227] *Baldock v Webster* [2004] EWCA Civ 1869; [2006] Q.B. 315 (Laws LJ).

[228] See 19-077.

[229] *Woolwich Equitable Building Society v Inland Revenue Commission (No.2)* [1993] A.C. 70.

[230] *Woolwich Equitable Building Society v Inland Revenue Commission (No.2)* [1993] A.C. 70 at 174 (Lord Goff).

[231] *Woolwich Equitable Building Society v Inland Revenue Commission (No.2)* [1993] A.C. 70 at 177 (Lord Goff).

[232] *Woolwich Equitable Building Society v Inland Revenue Commission (No.2)* [1993] A.C. 70 at 205 (Lord Slynn of Hadley).

[233] These are the "catch-all" grounds "that the decision was otherwise contrary to law" and that a power was exercised "in a way that constitutes abuse of the power": ss.5(1)(j) and 5(2)(j) respectively. These clauses have had little effect and seem now unlikely to serve as vehicles for the development of significant new principles.

[234] *Minister for Immigration and Multicultural Affairs v Yusuf* (2001) 206 C.L.R. 323.

"error of law" ground draws no distinction between jurisdictional and non-jurisdictional errors.[235]

4-077   Common law principles apply to judicial review outside of statutory review schemes such as ADJR. With only three exceptions, all grounds of judicial review at common law are now treated as sub-sets of "jurisdictional error". The exceptions apply for non-jurisdictional errors of law, and operate only for the remedies of certiorari (where the error must appear on the face of the record),[236] the declaration, and the injunction.[237] Errors of law are less likely to be jurisdictional if committed by a court, but there is no strict presumption in that regard.[238] Because (with those three exceptions) "jurisdictional error" now accommodates all of the grounds of judicial review at common law, the term itself is nowadays no more than a conclusory label.[239] It applies to any error that could lead a court to treat as a nullity the resulting decision, conduct or omission.

4-078   Despite its long antecedents, jurisdictional error became a ubiquitous term in Australian law only relatively recently.[240] It has a constitutional significance, because no legislature can validly oust the judicial review jurisdictions of either the High Court[241] or the State Supreme Courts.[242] A Commonwealth provision that set a potentially arbitrary deadline for instituting a challenge to migration decisions or even "purported" migration decisions was therefore invalid,[243] as was a State provision protecting "purported" decisions from judicial review.[244] The High Court has referred to "an entrenched minimum provision of judicial review",[245] and if that were to lead to the entrenchment of substantive principles, these would probably include a constitutional prohibition upon the Parliament giving advance authority for government parties to act fraudulently, maliciously, dishonestly, in bad faith, in return for a bribe, or for any other highly improper purpose.[246] Parliament can validly stipulate that breach of some of an Act's requirements will not result in invalidity,[247] but there is some debate as to how far it can go in giving advance authority to breach all of an Act's requirements.[248]

4-079   The grounds for judicial review at common law in Australia resemble those in

---

[235] s.5(1)(f).

[236] *Craig v South Australia* (2000) 184 C.L.R. 163.

[237] *Project Blue Sky Inc v Australian Broadcasting Authority* (1998) 194 C.L.R. 355 at 393; *Muin v Refugee Review Tribunal* (2002) 190 A.L.R. 601 at [47] and [169]; *Re Minister for Immigration and Multicultural Affairs; Ex parte Lam* (2003) 214 C.L.R. 1 at 21; and *Plaintiff M61/2010E v Commonwealth [Offshore Processing Case]* (2010) 243 C.L.R. 319 at 358-360.

[238] *Kirk v Industrial Court (NSW)* (2010) 239 C.L.R. 531 at 572-573. The High Court's judicial review jurisdiction over superior courts of record is best explained on constitutional grounds, as opposed to review for jurisdictional error; see *New South Wales v Kable* (2013) 252 C.L.R. 118.

[239] A view adopted by the Full Court of the Federal Court in *SDAV v Minister for Immigration and Multicultural and Indigenous Affairs* (2003) 199 A.L.R. 43 at [27], and described as "painfully accurate" in S Gageler, "Impact of Migration Law on the Development of Australian Administrative Law" (2010) 17 AJ Admin L 92 at 104.

[240] A detailed account appears in S Gageler, "Impact of Migration Law on the Development of Australian Administrative Law" (2010) 17 AJ Admin. L 92.

[241] *Plaintiff S157/2002 v Commonwealth* (2003) 211 C.L.R. 476.

[242] *Kirk v Industrial Court (NSW)* (2010) 239 C.L.R. 531.

[243] *Bodrudazza v Minister for Immigration and Multicultural Affairs* (2007) 228 C.L.R. 651.

[244] *Kirk v Industrial Court (NSW)* (2010) 239 C.L.R. 531.

[245] *Plaintiff S157/2002 v Commonwealth* (2003) 211 C.L.R. 476 at 513.

[246] *Plaintiff S157/2002 v Commonwealth* (2003) 211 C.L.R. 476 at 508; and *Federal Commissioner of Taxation v Futuris Corp Ltd* (2008) 237 C.L.R. 146 at 164-165.

[247] *Project Blue Sky Inc v Australian Broadcasting Authority* (1998) 194 C.L.R. 355; and *Re Minister for Immigration and Multicultural and Indigenous Affairs; Ex p. Palme* (2003) 216 C.L.R. 212.

[248] M. Aronson, M. Groves and G Weeks, *Judicial Review of Administrative Action and Government Liability*, 6th edn, (2017) 18.9; and L. McDonald, "The Entrenched Minimum Provision of Judicial Review and the Rule of Law" (2010) 21 *Public Law Review* 14.

England and Wales,[249] and they are not confined to different manifestations of errors of law.[250] Review lies for want of a "jurisdictional fact" (the equivalent of England's "precedent fact"),[251] and for seriously irrational or illogical fact-finding.[252] Despite their similarities, however, the Australian cases tend to focus much more than their English analogues on the particularities of each established generic review ground, and much less on normative principles such as "abuse of power", "good administration", or "rule of law". Indeed, the High Court said that whilst those concepts inform judicial review principles, any resort to them as free-standing review grounds in their own right would violate the constitutionally entrenched separation of powers.[253]

The terminology of "ultra vires" also appears in Australian judicial review. It **4-080** tends to be used in the context of challenges to the validity of subordinate legislation, but it also appears occasionally in other contexts. Unlike the position in England and Wales, it has no linkage to any debate as to which of various review grounds are properly sourced to the common law or Parliament, a debate which in any event is regarded as largely "unproductive" in the Australian context.[254]

The establishment of a jurisdictional error usually results in the court declaring **4-081** or treating the flawed decision as a nullity.[255] There are occasions, however, when terms such as "nullity" and "invalid" are unhelpful.[256] Nullity is a bundle of possible legal consequences of a finding of jurisdictional error.[257] The courts will try to undo some or all of the relevantly adverse legal effects of a jurisdictionally flawed decision, at least so far as they affect the applicant. Retrospective nullification, however, is not always possible or desirable. If it is too late to sue, for example, it makes little sense to characterise an adverse administrative decision as a nullity, because in the last resort, it takes a court to achieve the result of retrospective nullification.[258]

Canada

The place of jurisdictional error in Canadian judicial review law is in a state of **4-082** considerable uncertainty. It does, however, still exist as a category. In *Pushpanathan v Canada (Minister of Citizenship and Immigration)*, Bastarache J stated: "'[J]urisdictional error' is simply an error on an issue with respect to which, according to the outcome of the pragmatic and functional analysis, the tribunal must

---

[249] A non-exhaustive and merely indicative catalogue of the generic grounds appears in *Commissioner of Taxation v Futuris Corp Ltd* (2008) 237 C.L.R. 146 at 186.

[250] *Re Minister for Immigration and Multicultural Affairs; Ex p. Applicant S20/2002* (2003) 198 A.L.R. 59 at [53]-[54].

[251] *Enfield City Corp v Development Assessment Commission* (2000) 199 C.L.R. 135.

[252] *Minister for Immigration and Citizenship v SZMDS* (2010) 240 C.L.R. 611. There remains a debate as to whether a court will excuse serious irrationality in a decision-maker's fact-finding if there was sufficient material for him or her to have reached the end result by flawless reasoning: M. Aronson, M. Groves and G Weeks, *Judicial Review of Administrative Action and Government Liability*, 6th edn, (2017) 4.730.

[253] *Re Minister for Immigration and Multicultural Affairs; Ex p. Lam* (2003) 214 C.L.R. 1 at 12 and 23.

[254] *Plaintiff S10/2011 v Minister for Immigration and Citizenship* (2012) 246 C.L.R. 636 at 666.

[255] *Minister for Immigration and Multicultural Affairs v Bhardwaj* (2002) 209 C.L.R. 597 at 614-615.

[256] *Berowra Holdings Pty Ltd v Gordon* (2006) 225 C.L.R. 364 at 369-370; and *Bounds v R* (2006) 228 A.L.R. 190 at [10].

[257] *Swansson v R* (2007) 69 N.S.W.L.R. 406 at 416.

[258] *Jadwan Pty Ltd v Secretary, Department of Health* (2003) 145 F.C.R. 1 at 16; and *SZKUO v Minister for Immigration and Citizenship* (2009) 180 F.C.R. 438.

make a correct interpretation to which no deference will be shown".[259] In other words, it seemed as though the Supreme Court was accepting that the term "jurisdiction" was simply an ex post facto way of describing an issue that a statutory authority had to get correct on pain of being set aside, that status being determined by the series of factors that the Court had identified as relevant in the reaching of that conclusion. However, in *Dunsmuir v New Brunswick*, the Supreme Court of Canada revisited its entire approach to judicial review of the substantive decisions of statutory and prerogative authorities.[260] In the course of doing so, the court emphasised that the concepts of jurisdiction and vires remained part of Canadian judicial review law. On such issues, the standard of review was that of correctness. However, the court cautioned that it was not signalling a return to the broad conceptions of jurisdiction and vires that had proved so problematic in earlier Canadian decisions. Jurisdiction was "intended in the narrow sense of whether or not the tribunal had the authority to make the inquiry".[261] What is clear, however, is that the court has implicitly abandoned its previous position that the term "jurisdiction" was nothing more than a description of any category of question on which, after a standard of review analysis, the statutory or prerogative authority had to be correct.[262] Indeed, the court identified three specific categories of question that were jurisdictional in character or raised issues of vires: constitutional issues, the jurisdictional lines between competing tribunals, and the limits of the authority of municipalities to enact byelaws. Nonetheless, the court has continued to emphasise the exceptional nature of true questions of jurisdiction and has adopted a strong presumption that that label does not attach to tribunals interpreting their home or constitutive, or other frequently encountered statute related to their mandate.[263]

4-083   Ouster clauses remain one factor that the Courts take into account in conducting the standard of review analysis. Since *Crevier v Quebec (Attorney General)*[264] and *MacMillan Bloedel Ltd v Simpson*,[265] accepting that judicial review of administrative action at least for jurisdictional error is a constitutionally guaranteed right (arising out of ss.96–101 of the Constitution Act 1981), a right that cannot removed by either the provincial legislature or Federal Parliament, there is no incentive to enact privative clauses that have as their objective the total removal of access to judicial review.[266] It should, however, be noted that this constitutional guarantee has not led to the striking down of "impediments" to judicial review such as limitation periods, leave requirements, or procedural and evidential restrictions favouring the "government" in judicial review and statutory appeals. In *Dunsmuir* (above), the Supreme Court has nonetheless reaffirmed that privative or preclusive ("ouster") clauses remain a significant element in the standard of review analysis. They provide "a strong indication" of what is now the only deferential standard under Canadian common law judicial review: unreasonableness.[267]

4-084   In *Alberta (Information and Privacy Commissioner) v Alberta Teachers' Federa-*

---

[259] *Pushpanathan v Canada (Minister of Citizenship and Immigration)* [1998] 1 S.C.R. 982.

[260] *Dunsmuir v New Brunswick* [2008] 1 S.C.R. 190.

[261] At [59].

[262] *Pushpanathan v Canada (Minister of Citizenship and Immigration)* [1998] 1 S.C.R. 982.

[263] *Alberta (Information and Privacy Commissioner) v Alberta Teachers' Federation* [2011] 3 S.C.R. 654.

[264] *Crevier v Quebec (Attorney General)* [1981] 2 S.C.R. 220.

[265] *MacMillan Bloedel Ltd v Simpson* [1995] 4 S.C.R. 725.

[266] Quaere whether *Crevier* guarantees in some form the perpetuation of "jurisdictional error" as a ground of review in Canadian law.

[267] At [52].

tion,[268] the majority of the Supreme Court questioned whether there was still any place for "true" questions of vires and jurisdiction as exceptional correctness review categories. Subsequently, the majority judgment in *McLean v British Columbia (Securities Commission)*[269] reiterated this scepticism. Indeed, it is difficult to identify any post-*Dunsmuir* judgment in which the Supreme Court has pinpointed for review purposes a "true" question of jurisdiction. On the other hand, there have been instances in which the court has deployed a non-deferential ultra vires standard in dealing with a challenge to the validity of subordinate legislation.[270]

India

Finality clauses ordinarily oust the power of the court to review decisions of authorities except on grounds of lack of jurisdiction or where such decision is a nullity for the reason of gross illegality, irrationality, violation of constitutional mandate, mala fides, non-compliance with rules of natural justice and perversity.[271] Judicial review is part of the basic structure of the Constitution and cannot be excluded[272] by statute or even by a Constitutional amendment. Judicial Review is essential for resolving disputes relating to transgressions of constitutional limitations.[273]   **4-085**

Ireland

The Irish system of judicial review continues to be based primarily on the principle of ultra vires, but is bolstered in many important respects by the requirements of the Constitution.[274] It appears that the distinction between jurisdictional and non-jurisdictional errors has been abandoned, however, the position is not clear. The leading Supreme Court judgment, *State (Holland) v Kennedy* endorsed the position in *Anisminic* and held as follows: **4-086**

> "It does not necessarily follow that a court or tribunal, vested with powers of a judicial nature, which commences a hearing within jurisdiction will be treated as continuing to act within jurisdiction. For any one of a number of reasons it may exceed jurisdiction and thereby make its decisions liable to be quashed on certiorari. For instance, it may fail into an unconstitutionality, or it may breach the requirements of natural justice, or it may fail to stay within the bounds of the jurisdiction conferred on it by statute".[275]

Nonetheless, subsequent decisions, including Supreme Court decisions, have envis-

---

[268] *Alberta (Information and Privacy Commissioner) v Alberta Teachers' Federation* 2011 SCC 61; [2011] 3 S.C.R. 654 at [34].
[269] *McLean v British Columbia (Securities Commission)* 2013 SCC 67; [2013] 3 S.C.R. 895 at [25].
[270] See e.g. *Katz Group Canada Inc. v. Ontario (Health and Long-Term Care)* 2013 SCC 64; [2013] 3 S.C.R. 810.
[271] *Raja Ram Pal v Honourable Speaker, Lok Sabha*, (2007) 3 S.C.C. 184 at 373.
[272] *Madras Bar Association v Union of India* (2014) 10 S.C.C. 1 at 181.
[273] *State of West Bengal v Committee for Protection of Democratic Rights* (2010) 3 SCC 571 at 39, 51, 67, 68; *Shalini Shyam Shetty v Rajendra Shankar Patil* (2010) 8 S.C.C. 329 at 349.
[274] See generally, G. Hogan and D.G. Morgan, *Administrative Law in Ireland*, 4th edn (2012) at paras 10-02–10-40 and 10-93–10-130; M. de Blacam, *Administrative Law*, 3rd edn (2017) at Chs. 9-10; H. Biehler, *Judicial Review of Administrative Action*, 3rd edn (2013) at pp.47-56; D.G. Morgan, *Hogan and Morgan's Administrative Law*, 4th edn (2012) at paras 10-02–10-28 and 10-53–10-92. The impact of the Constitution is particularly notable in the context of procedural fairness, see further 6-055.
[275] [1977] I.R. 193 at 201. It has been suggested, however, that the decision could be interpreted as applying the collateral fact approach to jurisdictional error: Hogan and Morgan (2010) at para.10-114. For further Supreme Court authority suggesting that the distinction between jurisdictional and non-jurisdictional errors of law has been abandoned, see *Killeen v Director of Public Prosecutions*

aged the possibility of errors being committed within jurisdiction.[276] There have also been indications that the courts will only intervene where the error committed is significant.[277] Overall, although the law far from settled, the trend is towards treating all errors of law reviewable.[278]

4-087   Irish courts have generally refused to enforce ouster clauses, even prior to the *Anisminic* case. For example, provisions providing that decisions are "final and conclusive" have not been interpreted to exclude judicial review.[279] Judicial reluctance to uphold ouster clauses is reinforced by the Constitution, and it has been held that "[s]ave to the extent required by the terms of the Constitution itself, no justiciable matter or question may be excluded from the range of the original jurisdiction of the High Court".[280] A more common contemporary problem relates to what have been described as partial ouster clauses,[281] namely clauses which impose extremely short time limits on the entitlement to seek judicial review; such clauses are generally upheld.

New Zealand

4-088   The categories of "jurisdictional" and "non-jurisdictional error" no longer apply in New Zealand.[282] The concept of jurisdiction was effectively jettisoned in favour of an error of law standard of review in *Bulk Gas Users Group v Attorney General*,[283] a direction confirmed by the Court of Appeal.[284] Following Lord Diplock's lead, there is a suggestion in *Bulk Gas* that the concept of jurisdiction might still have some operation in relation to inferior courts of law of general jurisdiction, primarily to prevent appeal rights from being circumvented by judicial review,[285] but this has had no significant impact in subsequent case law.

4-089   In relation to ouster clauses, the New Zealand courts have consistently followed *Anisminic* and not given effect to privative clauses that purport to exclude judicial review altogether unless there is a good policy reason for the exclusion.[286] But they have upheld privative clauses delaying judicial review until appeal rights

---

[1997] 3 I.R. 218 at 228-229. In the High Court, see, e.g. *State (Healy) v Donoghue* [1976] I.R. 325 at 333.

[276] In the Supreme Court, see *State (Abenglen Properties Ltd) v Dublin Corporation* [1984] I.R. 381 at 399-400. In the High Court, see *Memorex World Trade Corporation v EAT* [1990] 2 I.R. 184 at 186. There is also a lack of clarity in *Ryanair v Labour Court* [2007] IESC 6; [2007] 4 I.R. 199. In the High Court see *Nyhan v Riordan* [2016] IEHC 170; *Croake v Coughlan* [2015] IEHC 515; *PD v Minister for Justice and Law Reform* [2015] IEHC 111; *SFA (a minor) v Minister for Justice & Equality* [2015] IEHC 364; *GO v The Refugee Applications Commissioner* [2015] IEHC 645.

[277] *Sweeney v Judge Brophy* [1993] 2 I.R. 202 at 211; *Cork County Council v Shackleton* [2007] IEHC 241 at [9.7]; *McKernan v Employment Appeals Tribunal* [2008] IEHC 40 at [4.10]; *Ruttledge v Clyne* [2006] IEHC 146; *Donoghue v O'Donoghue* [2016] IEHC 7 at [23]–[25].

[278] See also *Royal Dublin Society v Revenue Commissioners* [1999] IESC 45; [2000] 1 I.R. 270 (decision quashed where based on erroneous view of the law); *Kivaway v Revenue Commissioners* [2005] IEHC 106.

[279] *State (McCarthy) v O'Donnell* [1945] I.R. 126.

[280] *Tormey v Attorney General* [1985] I.R. 289 at 297: see also *O'Doherty v Attorney General* [1941] I.R. 569 at 580.

[281] Hogan and Morgan (2010) at paras 11-70–11-76; de Blacam (2017) at paras 9.28–8.30.

[282] See generally M. Taggart, "The Contribution of Lord Cooke to Scope of Review Doctrine in Administrative Law: A Comparative Common Law Perspective" in P. Rishworth (ed), *The Struggle for Simplicity in the Law: essays for Lord Cooke of Thorndon* (1998), p.189.

[283] *Bulk Gas Users Group v Attorney General* [1982] N.Z.L.R. 129, CA.

[284] *Hawkins v Minister of Justice* [1991] 2 N.Z.L.R. 530, CA; *Peters v Davison* [1999] 2 N.Z.L.R. 164, CA.

[285] *Martin v Ryan* [1990] 2 N.Z.L.R. 209, 225, HC, Fisher J.

[286] *New Zealand Rail Ltd v Employment Court* [1995] 3 N.Z.L.R. 179, CA; *Ramsay v Wellington District Court* [2006] NZAR 136, CA.

and the like are exhausted where this is sensible policy[287] or the outcome of a particular statutory setting.[288] Partial ouster clauses which impose extremely short time limits are generally upheld.[289]

In contrast to the position in Canada, New Zealand courts have disregarded the presence of privative clauses in "determining, as a matter of statutory interpretation, what questions of law, if any, have been remitted to the conclusive decision of the tribunal".[290] Extra-judicially, Sir Robin Cooke frequently expressed the view that privative clauses are ineffectual, useless and best repealed.[291] Two recent cases from 2015 have discussed the impact of the New Zealand Bill of Rights Act 1990 on such clauses: in *Attorney General v Spencer*,[292] the NZBORA was deployed successfully to overcome an ouster clause; in *Mangawhai Ratepayers and Residents Association v Kaipara District Council*,[293] it failed.

4-090

South Africa

The South African courts have largely followed the English example in collapsing the distinction between jurisdictional and non-jurisdictional errors. The case taking the decisive step in this regard is *Hira v Booysen*,[294] decided towards the end of the pre-democratic era. The approach taken in *Hira* was essentially that courts of review need to pay attention to the intention of the legislature in determining whether the tribunal or administrator had exclusive authority to decide the question of law concerned. Today, however, the focus of the inquiry as described in *Hira* has largely been superseded by the provisions of the Promotion of Administrative Justice Act 3 of 2000 (PAJA). Section 6(2)(d) allows a court to review an administrative action if it is "materially influenced by an error of law". The focus of the inquiry is thus whether the error materially influenced the decision, rather than whether the administrator was "empowered" to err.

4-091

As the Constitutional Court has made clear, an error will not be regarded as material unless it affects the outcome of the decision.[295] *Tantoush v Refugee Appeal Board*[296] illustrates the distinction between an error that is material and one that is not: the Board had misconstrued its appellate functions and had gone on to insist on the presence of a "real risk" of persecution rather than a "reasonable possibility" of persecution. The first error was found not to be material as it had not affected the outcome while the second was held to be material.

4-092

---

[287] *Love v Porirua City Council* [1984] 2 N.Z.L.R. 308, CA; *McGuire v Hastings District Council* [2002] 2 N.Z.L.R. 577, 25 PC, Lord Cooke of Thorndon.

[288] *Tannadyce Investments Ltd v Commissioner of Inland Revenue* [2012] 2 N.Z.L.R. 153 at [60].

[289] *New Zealand Rail Ltd v Employment Court* [1995] 3 N.Z.L.R. 179; *Parker v Silver Fern Farms Ltd* [2012] 1 N.Z.L.R. 256; *Tannadyce Investments Ltd v Commissioner of Inland Revenue* [2012] 2 N.Z.L.R. 153.

[290] *Bulk Gas Users Group v Attorney General* [1982] N.Z.L.R. 129 at 134 CA; and *Mobil Oil New Zealand Ltd v Motor Spirits Licensing Appeal Authority* (1985) 5 N.Z.A.R. 412, CA.

[291] See e.g. R. Cooke, "Administrative Law: The Vanishing Sphinx" [1975] N.Z.L.J. 529, 530; R. Cooke, "The Struggle for Simplicity" in M. Taggart (ed), Judicial Review of Administrative Action: Problems and Prospects (1986) 1, p.8 ("[t]heir disuse by legislative draftsmen would be a further advance in the struggle for simplicity").

[292] *Attorney General v Spencer* [2015] NZCA 143.

[293] *Association v Kaipara District Council* [2015] NZCA 612.

[294] *Hira v Booysen* 1992 (4) S.A. 69, A. For an account of this judgment and the English decisions relied on in the reasoning of Corbett JA, see C. Hoexter, *Administrative Law in South Africa*, 2nd edn (2012), pp.286-8.

[295] *Johannesburg Metropolitan Municipality v Gauteng Development Tribunal* 2010 (6) S.A. 182, CC at [91].

[296] *Tantoush v Refugee Appeal Board* 2008 (1) S.A. 232, T.

4-093   Section 6(2)(d) is a ground often relied upon in practice, and its application is usually uncontroversial.[297] In the *Genesis* case,[298] however, there was disagreement about its application where the administrator had based his decision on a High Court judgment that was subsequently found to have been wrongly decided. The minority view, that administrator's error had to arise from the misinterpretation or misapplication of relevant legislative provisions themselves, was judged to be an "inappropriately rigid" characterisation of the ground by Cameron J for the majority of the Constitutional Court.[299] He held:

> "By explicitly affording the right to just administrative action, the Constitution bestows on the courts the power to review every error of law, provided of course that it is "material". PAJA embodies this right, in explicit terms. There is nothing in the statute that narrows or stifles it."

4-094   In relation to ouster clauses, the right of access to court in s.34 of the Constitution provides that "everyone has the right to have any dispute that can be resolved by the application of law decided in a fair public hearing before a court or ... another independent and impartial tribunal". This right probably makes direct and unambiguous ouster clauses unconstitutional. Similarly, the right to lawful administrative action in s.33(1) of the Constitution would appear to outlaw ouster clauses covering administrative action. As to limitation clauses, the Constitutional Court has struck down time-bar provisions for unreasonably narrowing the opportunity to seek judicial redress.[300]

---

[297] Prominent recent examples of the application of this ground include *Security Industry Alliance v Private Security Industry Regulatory Authority* 2015 (1) S.A. 169, SCA and *Business Zone 1010 CC t/a Emmarentia Convenience Centre v Engen Petroleum Ltd* 2017 (6) B.C.L.R. 773, CC.

[298] *Genesis Medical Scheme v Registrar of Medical Schemes* [2017] ZACC 16 (6 June 2017).

[299] At [21].

[300] See e.g. *Mohlomi v Minister of Defence* 1997 (1) S.A. 124, CC, *Engelbrecht v Road Accident Fund* 2007 (8) S.A. 96, CC and *Brümmer v Minister for Social Development* 2009 (6) S.A. 323, CC.

CHAPTER 5

Illegality

TABLE OF CONTENTS

INTRODUCTION

An administrative decision or other exercise of a public function is unlawful **5-001**
under the broad chapter head of "illegality" if the decision-maker:

  (a) misinterprets a legal instrument relevant to the function being performed
  (b) has no legal authority to make the decision
  (c) fails to fulfil a legal duty
  (d) exercises discretionary power for an extraneous purpose
  (e) takes into account irrelevant considerations or fails to take account of
      relevant considerations
  (f) improperly delegates decision-making power.[1]

The task for the courts in evaluating whether a decision is illegal is essentially **5-002**
one of construing the content and scope of the instrument conferring the duty or
power upon the decision-maker. The instrument will normally be a statute or

---

[1] Compare this definition with the variety of instances of illegality specified under the South African
Promotion of Administrative Justice Act 3 of 2000, s.6 of which permits judicial review of an
administrative action if the administrator who took it was "not authorised to so by the empowering
provision" (s.6(2)(a)(i)); or "acted under a delegation of power which was not authorised by the
empowering provision" (s.6(2)(a)(ii)); or if " a mandatory and material procedure or condition
prescribed by an empowering provision was not complied with" (s.6(2)(b)); or "the action was
materially influenced by an error of law" (s.6(2)(d)); or the action was taken: "for a reason not
authorised by the empowering provision; for an ulterior purpose or motive; because irrelevant
considerations were taken into account or relevant considerations were not considered; because of
the unauthorised or unwarranted dictates of another person or body; in bad faith; or arbitrary or
capriciously (s.6(2)(e)(i)–(vi)). In addition, review is available if the action itself "contravenes the
law or is not authorised by the empowering provision" (s.6(2)(f) i)), and finally "if the action
concerned consists of a failure to take a decision" (s.6(2)(g)). Other provisions deal with irrationality and procedural fairness.

delegated legislation, but it may also be an enunciated policy, and sometimes a prerogative or other common law power.[2] The courts when exercising this power of construction are enforcing the rule of law, by requiring administrative bodies to act within the "four corners" of their powers or duties. They are also acting as guardians of Parliament's will, seeking to ensure that the exercise of power is in accordance with the scope and purpose of Parliament's enactments.

5-003   At first sight this ground of review seems a fairly straightforward exercise of statutory interpretation, for which courts are well suited. It is for them to determine whether an authority has made an error of law. Yet there are a number of issues that arise in public law that make the courts' task more complex. First, is the fact that power is often conferred, and necessarily so in a complex modern society, in terms which grant the decision-maker a broad degree of discretion. Statutes abound with expressions such as: "the Secretary of State may" (do some act); conditions may be imposed as the authority "thinks fit"; action may be taken "if the Secretary of State believes" circumstances to exist or "considers it appropriate" to take action; the public body "must have due regard to" a desirable factor. These formulae, and others like them, appear on their face to grant the decision-maker infinite power, or at least the power to choose from a wide range of alternatives, free of judicial interference. The courts, however, insist that such seemingly unconstrained power is confined by the purpose for which the statute conferred the power. This task is made easier where the purpose is clearly defined, or where the considerations which the body must take into account in arriving at its decisions are clearly spelled out. In such cases the courts require the decision-maker to take into account the specified considerations and ignore the irrelevant. But many statutes provide only the framework for subsequent decisions, or delegate power to the executive further to specify those considerations. In any event the distinction between considerations which are "relevant" from those which are not is not always immediately obvious.

5-004   Secondly, legislation does not exist in a vacuum.[3] It is located in the context of our contemporary European democracy. As has been discussed above, the rule of law and other fundamental principles of democratic constitutionalism should be presumed to inform the exercise of all public functions unless Parliament expressly excludes them.[4] There may even be some aspects of the rule of law and other democratic fundamentals which Parliament has no power to exclude.[5] The courts should therefore strive to interpret powers in accordance with these principles. International law, both customary and treaty obligations are also part of the context which cannot be ignored. Until the UK leaves the European Union, European Union Law is part of our law (via the European Communities Act 1972 and European Union Act 2011), as now is the European Convention on Human Rights (via the Human Rights Act 1998). Breach of European Union law and Convention rights thus amounts to illegality—but are dealt with in Chs 13 and 14.

5-005   It is because of these considerations that for a substantial part of this chapter it is necessary to focus closely on issues as to the appropriate manner in which legisla-

---

2   See 3-030 (on prerogative powers) and 5-024 (on the "Ram doctrine").
3   *R. v Secretary of State for the Home Department Ex p. Pierson* [1998] A.C. 539 at 587 (Lord Steyn: "Parliament does not legislate in a vacuum. Parliament legislates for a European liberal democracy based upon the traditions of the common law ... and ... unless there is the clearest provision to the contrary, Parliament must be presumed not to legislate contrary to the rule of law").
4   See 1-021, 5-040 and 11-059.
5   *Jackson v Attorney General* [2005] UKHL 56; [2006] 1 A.C. 262 at [120] (Lord Hope), [102] (Lord Steyn), [159] (Baroness Hale suggest that the rule of law may have become "the ultimate controlling factor in our unwritten constitution"; J. Jowell, "Parliamentary Sovereignty under the New Constitutional Hypothesis" [2006] P.L. 262.

tion should be construed. This is necessary in order to identify the all-important dividing line between decisions that have been reached lawfully and those that have not. There are two questions: (i) was the decision taken within the powers granted? and (ii) if it was, was the manner in which it was reached lawful?

DISCRETIONARY POWER: A BRIEF HISTORY OF JUDICIAL ATTITUDES

The concept of discretion in its legal context implies power to make a choice between alternative courses of action or inaction.[6] If only one course can lawfully be adopted, the decision taken is not the exercise of a discretion. To say that somebody has a discretion presupposes that there is no unique legal answer to a problem. There may, however, be a number of answers that are wrong in law. And even in cases where the power is discretionary, circumstances can exist which mean the discretion can only be exercised in one way. There are degrees of discretion, varying the scope for manoeuvre afforded to the decision-maker.[7]

5-006

At the outset it should be emphasised that the scope of judicial review of the exercise of discretion will be determined mainly by the wording of the power and the context in which it is exercised.[8] Legislation employs a great variety of different formulae to confer discretion and to guide the exercise of that discretion. Sometimes, a statute exhaustively specifies the ways in which a discretion may be deployed, such as by enumerating the types of conditions which an authority may attach to the grant of a licence. In such cases, the attachment of any other type of condition may be illegal. Or it may lay down general standards to which the exercise of a power must conform.[9] Sometimes, however, the exercise of a statutory discretion is not limited by the express provisions of the Act and in those cases

5-007

---

[6]   See K.C. Davis, *Discretionary Justice* (1969), p.4: "A public officer has discretion whenever the effective limits of his power leave him free to make a choice among possible courses of action or inaction".

[7]   Ronald Dworkin makes the distinction between "strong discretion" (the sergeant's discretion to pick "any five men" for a patrol) and "weak discretion" (the sergeant's discretion to pick "the most five experienced men"): *Taking Rights Seriously* (1977), p.32. See also: D. Galligan, *Discretionary Powers* (1986); G. Richardson, A. Ogus and P. Burrows, *Policing Pollution: A Study of Regulation and Enforcement* (1982); K. Hawkins, *Environment and Enforcement: Regulation and the Social Definition of Pollution* (1984); B. Hutter, *The Reasonable Arm of the Law: The Law Enforcement Procedures of Environmental Health Officers* (1988); K. Hawkins (ed), *The Uses of Discretion* (1992) and its review by D. Feldman, "Discretion, Choices and Values" [1994] P.L. 279; T. Buck, D. Bonner and R. Sainsbury, *Making Social Security Law: The Role and Work of the Social Security and Child Support Commissioners* (2005); F. Bennion, "Judgment and Discretion Revisited: Pedantry or Substance?" [2005] P.L. 368; T. Endicott, *Vagueness in Law* (2000); J. King, "The Justiciability of Resource Allocation" (2007) 70 M.L.R. 197, 201–207.

[8]   *Secretary of State for Education and Science v Tameside MBC* [1977] A.C. 1014 at 1047 (Lord Wilberforce: "there is no universal rule as to the principles on which the exercise of a discretion may be reviewed: each statute or type of statute must be individually looked at").

[9]   The extent to which discretionary power should be confined by rule in any particular context will not be considered here. For concern with the "optimal precision" of rules, see R. Posner, *An Economic Analysis of Law*, 6th edn (2003); T. Endicott, *Vagueness in Law* (2000); J. King, "The Justiciability of Resource Allocation" (2007) 70 M.L.R. 197 For earlier accounts of the need to confine discretion see: D. Oliver, "Regulating Precision" in A. Hawkins and J. Thomas (eds), *Making Regulatory Policy* (1985); C. McRudden, "Codes in a Cold Climate: Administrative Rule-Making by the Commissions for Racial Equality" (1988) 51 M.L.R. 409; R. Baldwin "Why Rules Don't Work" (1990) 53 M.L.R. 321; D. McBarnet and C. Whelan, "The Elusive Spirit of the Law: Formalisation and the Struggle for Legal Control" (1991) 54 M.L.R. 848; C. Reich, "The New Property" (1964) 73 Yale L.J. 733; J. Jowell, *Law and Bureaucracy* (1975) and "The Legal Control

the courts embark upon an interpretation of the objects and purposes of the statute in order to identify the limitations to which the discretion is subject.

5-008   As was said by Lord Upjohn in *Padfield*, even if legislation were to confer upon a decision-maker an "unfettered discretion":

> "[T]he use of that adjective [unfettered], even in an Act of Parliament, can do nothing to unfetter the control which the judiciary have over the executive, namely, that in exercising their powers the latter must act lawfully and that is a matter to be determined by looking at the Act and its scope and object in conferring a discretion upon the minister rather than by the use of adjectives."[10]

5-009   Those words are true today and to some extent have always been true, subject to some notable decisions to the contrary in the past, particularly during times of war or public emergency. The criteria by which the exercise of a discretion could be judged were indicated early in the 17th century. Lambard's advice to justices— "no way better shall the Discretion of a Justice of the Peace appear than if he (remembering that he is *lex loquens*) do contain himself within the listes of the law, and (being soberly wise) do not use his own discretion, but only where both the law permitteth, and the present case requireth it"[11]—was fortified by dicta and decisions of the courts. Discretion, said Coke, was *scire per legem quod sit justum*[12]; it was "a science or understanding to discern between falsity and truth, between right and wrong, between shadows and substance, between equity and colourable glosses and pretences, and not to do according to their wills and private affections".[13] In 1647 it was laid down by the King's Bench that "wheresoever a commissioner or other person hath power given to do a thing at his discretion, it is to be understood of sound discretion, and according to law, and that this Court hath power to redress things otherwise done by them".[14] The concept of a judicial discretion, which was not confined to courts in the strict sense, was later stated by Lord Mansfield to import a duty to be "fair, candid, and unprejudiced; not arbitrary, capricious, or biased; much less, warped by resentment, or personal dislike".[15] In 1591 the discretion of licensing justices was expressed to mean that they were to act "according to the rules of reason and justice, not according to private opinion ... according to law, and not humour". Their discretion was to be "not arbitrary, vague, and fanciful, but legal and regular".[16]

5-010   It follows that a discretionary power which is prima facie unfettered has always

---

of Administrative Discretion" [1973] P.L. 178; R. Baldwin and K. Hawkins, "Discretionary Justice: Davis Reconsidered" [1984] P.L. 570. cf. G. Mashaw, *Bureaucratic Justice* (1983).

[10] *Padfield v Minister of Agriculture Fisheries and Food* [1968] A.C. 997 at 1060. For interpretation of a statute which came close to conferring unfettered discretion, but which nevertheless permitted judicial review, see *R. v Secretary of State for the Environment Ex p. Norwich CC* [1982] Q.B. 808 ("Where it appears to the Secretary of State that tenants ... have or may have difficulty in exercising the right to buy [council houses]"; held that evidence of such difficulty existed); *R. (on the application of Mehanne) v Westminster Housing Benefit Review Board* [2001] UKHL 11; [2001] 1 W.L.R. 539 at [13] (the power to decide as the Board "considers appropriate" is the "language of discretion"); *R. (on the application of G) v Barnet LBC* [2003] UKHL 57; [2004] 2 A.C. 208 (local authority's duties in relation to children under Children Act 1989).

[11] W. Lambard, *Eirenarcha or of the Office of the Justices of Peace* (1581), p.58.

[12] *Keighley's case* (1609) 10 Co.Rep. 139a at 140a.

[13] *Rooke's case* (1598) 5 Co.Rep. 99b at 100a (assessment by Commissioners of Sewers); and R. Callis, *Readings upon the Statute of Sewers*, 2nd edn, pp.112–113; *Hetley v Boyer* (1614) Cro. Jac. 336: *case of Commendams* (1617) Hob. 140 at 158–159.

[14] *Estwick v City of London* (1647) Style 42 at 43 (suspension of a councillor).

[15] *R. v Askew* (1768) 4 Burr. 2186 at 2189 (determination by College of Physicians as to competence to practise medicine).

[16] *Sharp v Wakefield* [1891] A.C. 173 at 179 (Lord Halsbury LC, substantially recapitulating a dictum

been held to be subject to implied limitations set by the common law.[17] Indeed, at an early date the courts drew a distinction between judicial discretions and executive discretions, recognising that it would be inappropriate to apply the same criteria to all classes of discretions[18]; and the courts would sometimes characterise a discretion as judicial when they wish to assert powers of review,[19] but as executive or administrative when they wished to explain their inability or unwillingness to measure it by reference to any objective standard.[20]

Various formulae have been drafted over the years to stretch administrative discretion to its outer limits, and even with the intention of making public officials "judge-proof". Some authorise a public body to take a prescribed course of action if *satisfied* that the action is "necessary" or "appropriate". Initially in this situation the courts held that they could not go behind a statement by the competent authority (in the absence of proof of bad faith) that it was satisfied that the statutory condition for the exercise of the power existed.[21] But it was later conceded that if prima facie grounds could be established for the proposition that the authority could not have been so satisfied, a court will be entitled to hold the act or decision to be invalid unless the authority itself persuades the court that it did in fact genuinely form the opinion which it claims to have held.[22] However, in any event, the burden cast upon a person seeking to impugn such an act or decision was likely to be a heavy one to discharge.[23]

5-011

In *Liversidge v Anderson*[24] the House of Lords held that the Secretary of State's power to order the detention of any person whom he had "reasonable cause to

5-012

---

of Lord Mansfield CJ, in *R. v Wilkes* (1770) 4 Burr. 2528 at 2539, concerning discretions exercised by courts of justice). *Roncarelli v Duplessis* [1959] S.C.R. 122 at 140; *Ward v James* [1966] 1 Q.B. 273 at 293–295; and *Birkett v James* [1978] A.C. 297, 317 (discretion on interlocutory order reviewable on appeal to promote consistency).

[17] A. Barak, *Judicial Discretion* (1989); and *The Judge in a Democracy* (2006).

[18] D. Gordon, "Administrative Tribunals and the Courts" (1933) 49 L.Q.R. 419 (where, however, the degree of immunity of discretionary powers from judicial review is overstated).

[19] *R. v Manchester Legal Aid Committee Ex p. Brand (RA) & Co* [1952] 2 Q.B. 413.

[20] *Johnson (B) & Co (Builders) Ltd v Minister of Health* [1947] 2 All E.R. 395 at 399–400 (Minister's decision whether or not to confirm a compulsory purchase order); *Attorney General v Bastow* [1957] 1 Q.B. 514 (Attorney General's decision to sue for injunction to restrain continuance of criminal offence); *Robinson v Minister of Town and Country Planning* [1947] K.B. 702; *Holmes (Peter) & Son v Secretary of State for Scotland* 1965 S.C. 1 (designation of large areas as subject to comprehensive redevelopment and compulsory purchase); *Webb v Minister of Housing and Local Government* [1964] 1 W.L.R. 1295 at 1301. Cf. *R. v Secretary of State for the Environment Ex p. Ostler* [1977] Q.B. 122 (administrative nature of minister's discretion to confirm a compulsory purchase order offered as one reason for the court's inability to review its legality outside the statutory time limitation for impugning it).

[21] *Re Beck & Pollitzer's Application* [1948] 2 K.B. 339 (order stopping up a highway); *Land Realisation Co v Postmaster-General* [1950] Ch. 435 (compulsory purchase order); *Shand v Minister of Railways* [1970] N.Z.L.R. 615 (closure of railway line); *Secretary of State for Education and Science v Tameside MBC* [1977] A.C. 1014, 1025 (Lord Denning MR commenting to the effect that the statements in the wartime and post-war cases "do not apply to-day").

[22] cf. *R. v Brixton Prison Governor Ex p. Soblen* [1963] 2 Q.B. 243 at 302, 307–308 (Home Secretary alleged to have used his power to order the deportation of an alien, a power exercisable whenever he deemed it to be "conductive to the public good", for the ulterior purpose of effecting an unlawful extradition).

[23] In *R. v Brixton Prison Governor Ex p. Soblen* [1963] 2 Q.B. 243, evidence relating to intergovernmental communications was withheld from production when the Secretary of State certified that its production would be injurious to good diplomatic relations.

[24] *Liversidge v Anderson* [1942] A.C. 206; see Lord Atkin (at 225–247) who delivered a powerful dissenting judgment. The nature of the "objective" test that Lord Atkin thought appropriate has sometimes been misrepresented; see 246–247 of his judgment, in which he gave his reasons for agreeing with the other members of the HL in the analogous case of *Green v Home Secretary* [1942] A.C. 284.

believe" to be of hostile origins or associations, and over whom it was therefore necessary to exercise control, was validly exercised unless it was shown that he had not honestly considered that he had had reasonable cause for his belief.[25]

5-013   In 1970 powers were given to the tax authorities to issue a warrant to enter premises where they have "reasonable ground" for suspecting an offence. Having entered the premises they had the power to seize and remove items found there which they had "reasonable cause to believe" may be required as evidence of the offence.[26] Suspecting tax fraud, the Inland Revenue officials obtained search warrants, entered premises and seized documents without informing the applicants of the offences suspected or the persons suspected of having committed them. The House of Lords upheld the Inland Revenue's actions and held that the applicants had no right to be informed of the alleged offences, or of the "reasonable ground" for suspecting an offence.[27] Nevertheless, it was held that the existence of "reasonable cause to believe" was a question of objective fact, to be tried on evidence, and Lord Diplock said that "the time has come to acknowledge openly that the majority of this House in *Liversidge v Anderson* were expediently and, at that time perhaps, excusably wrong and the dissenting speech of Lord Atkin was right.[28]

5-014   In the immediate aftermath of the Second World War judicial deference to the executive and other public authorities was still the norm, even where the statutory purposes were defined with close precision. In cases involving public control over land use and housing accommodation, one could point to dicta to the effect that an order shown to be perverse or otherwise lacking in any evidentiary support might be held ultra vires because the competent authority could not be deemed to have been genuinely satisfied that it was appropriate for a purpose sanctioned by legislation.[29] Yet if persons claimed to be aggrieved they invariably failed in the courts; and the judgments persistently laid a heavier emphasis on the amplitude of the discretionary power than on the need to relate it to the purposes of the Act.[30] The incantation of statements denying the absoluteness of administrative discretion in such cases was little more than a perfunctory ritual to satisfy the consciences of the judges.

5-015   Sometimes the question before a court is whether words which apparently confer a discretion (words such as "may", or "it shall be lawful if") are instead to be interpreted as imposing a duty. The word "may" has, over the years, primarily been construed as permissive, not imperative.[31] However, exceptionally, it is construed as imposing a duty to act, and even a duty to act in one particular manner.[32]

---

25 The only other admissible ground for challenge was that the detention order was improperly made out; see *R. v Home Secretary Ex p. Budd* [1942] 2 K.B. 1 at 22.

26 Taxes Management Act 1970 s.20C (now Finance Act 2008).

27 *Inland Revenue Commissioners v Rossminster Ltd* [1980] A.C. 952.

28 *Inland Revenue Commissioners v Rossminster Ltd* [1980] A.C. 952, 1011.

29 *Robinson v Minister of Town and Country Planning* [1947] K.B. 702 at 724; *Demetriades v Glasgow Corp* [1951] 1 All E.R. 457 at 463.

30 *Minister of Agriculture and Fisheries v Price* [1941] 2 K.B. 116; *Robinson* [1947] K.B. 702; *Taylor v Brighton Corp* [1947] K.B. 736; *Swindon Corp v Pearce* [1948] 2 All E.R. 119; *Holmes (Peter) & Son v Secretary of State for Scotland* 1965 S.C. 1.

31 *Julius v Bishop of Oxford* (1880) 5 App.Cas. 214. Students may wish to consider the following problem: "I learned afterwards that in the scholarship examination another man had obtained more marks than I had, but Whitehead had the impression that I was the abler of the two. He therefore burned the marks before the examiners' meeting, and recommended me in preference to the other man" (*The Autobiography of Bertrand Russell, 1872–1914* (1967), p.57). Discuss. (Notes for Guidance: (1) Assuming that there were no formal rules prescribing criteria for the award of scholarships, do you think the examiners had an implied duty to award them to the highest placed candidates, or did they have a discretion? (2) If the former, what legal remedy, if any, would the

Conversely, an apparently absolute duty cast by legislation upon a public body **5-016** may be interpreted as granting a discretion as to the manner and extent of its performance. Thus, a local authority required by statute to provide suitable alternative accommodation for those displaced by a closing order was held not to be obliged to place them at the top of its housing waiting list.[33] The local authority was in effect given discretion in relation to which it had to use its best endeavours to deal with the result of a housing shortage in the most satisfactory way. Similarly, the manner and timing of the performance by a highway authority of its statutory duty to remove obstructions from the highway are to a large extent within the discretion of the authority.[34] Discretion, in other words, may be conferred implicitly as well as expressly.

Change of approach

More than a decade was to elapse after the Second World War before the **5-017** pendulum swung and the emphasis shifted. In New Zealand in 1959 a power vested in the Governor-General to make such regulations as he "thinks necessary in order to secure the due administration" of an Education Act was held to be invalidly exercised in so far as his opinion as to the necessity for such a regulation was not reasonably tenable.[35] More recently, in 2005, the New Zealand Supreme Court held that the New Zealand Bill of Rights Act was a substantive factor restraining the exercise of administrative discretion as opposed to a mandatory consideration.[36] In England in 1962 the power of the Commissioners of Customs and Excise to make regulations for "any matter for which provision appears to them necessary for the purpose of giving effect" to the Act was not construed as constituting them as the sole judges of what was in fact necessary for the purposes of the Act; and a regula-

---

candidate with higher marks have had, and against whom? (3) If the latter, did the exercise of Whitehead's discretion taint the subsequent proceedings with invalidity? (4) If not, why not? (5) If yes, what legal remedies would the other candidate have had, and against whom? (The answers to these questions are not provided in this book.)

[32] See, e.g. *R. (OneSearch Direct Holdings Ltd (trading as OneSearch Direct) v York City Council* [2010] EWHC 590 (Admin); [2010] P.T.S.R. 1481 at [22]–[24] ("It is a perfectly sensible and proper tenet of statutory construction that Parliament is unlikely to have intended that a power granted in a statute should be exercised in such a way as utterly to defeat the obvious wider purpose of that statute")—moreover, as a matter of principle, a court might "conclude that Parliament could not have intended that a power in one statute be exercised in a way that would utterly defeat the purpose of another statute", thought much would depend on the wording and even possibly the timing of the specific statutory provisions; *Alderman Blackwell's case* (1683) 1 Vent. 152; *Julius v Bishop of Oxford* (1880) 5 App. Cas. 214; *Shelley v LCC* [1949] A.C. 56; *Peterborough Corp v Holdich* [1956] 1 Q.B. 124; *Re Shuter* [1960] 1 Q.B. 142; *Annison v District Auditor for St Pancras BC* [1962] 1 Q.B. 489; *R. v Derby Justices Ex p. Kooner* [1971] 1 Q.B. 147; *Lord Advocate v Glasgow Corp* 1973 S.L.T. 33, HL; *Re Pentonville Prison Governor Ex p. Narang* [1978] A.C. 247; *R. v Secretary of State for the Home Department Ex p. Phansopkar* [1976] Q.B. 606. For an analysis of the uses of "may" and "shall", "duty" and "power" see *R. v Berkshire CC Ex p. Parker* [1997] C.O.D. 64; and authorities cited in *Stroud's Judicial Dictionary of Words and Phrases*, 8th edn (2012), under "May".

[33] *R. v Bristol Corp Ex p. Hendy* [1974] 1 W.L.R. 498; *Thornton v Kirklees MBC* [1979] Q.B. 626; cf. *Salford CC v McNally* [1976] A.C. 379; *R. v Kerrier DC Ex p. Guppys (Bridport) Ltd* (1976) 32 P. & C.R. 411, where it was held that local authorities have no discretion to serve abatement notices under the Public Health Act 1936 or to discharge their obligations under the Housing Act 1957 in respect of houses unfit for human habitation: the duties imposed by both statutes are cumulative. See also *R. v Hillingdon AHA Ex p. Wyatt* (1978) 76 L.G.R. 727 (duty to provide home nurses).

[34] *Haydon v Kent CC* [1978] 1 Q.B. 343.

[35] *Reade v Smith* [1959] N.Z.L.R. 996; *Low v Earthquake and War Damages Commission* [1959] N.Z.L.R. 1198 at 1207 (dicta).

[36] *Zaoui v Attorney General (No.2)* [2005] NZSC 38. See also H Wilberg "The Bill of Rights in Administrative Law Cases:Taking Stock and Suggesting Some Reassessment" (2013) N.Z.U.L.R. 866.

tion in which they gave themselves power to determine conclusively the amounts of tax payable was held to be ultra vires.[37] Again, in 1964, the courts were not deterred by a subjectively worded formula from holding that a compulsory purchase order made ostensibly for the purpose of coast protection work was invalid because the land in question was not in fact required for such a purpose.[38] As was observed in a leading Canadian case, "there is always a perspective within which a statute is intended to operate".[39]

5-018
The decision in 1968 of the House of Lords in *Padfield*[40] was an important landmark.[41] The minister had refused to appoint a committee, as he was statutorily empowered to do at his discretion, to investigate complaints made by members of the Milk Marketing Board that the majority of the Board had fixed milk prices in a way that was unduly unfavourable to the complainants. The House of Lords held that the minister's discretion was not unfettered and that the reasons that he had given for his refusal showed that he had acted ultra vires by taking into account factors that were legally irrelevant and by using his power in a way calculated to frustrate the policy of the Act.[42] The view was also expressed by four of their Lordships that even had the minister given no reasons for his decision, the court would not have been powerless to intervene: for once a prima facie case of misuse of power had been established, it would have been open to the court to infer that the minister had acted unlawfully if he had declined to supply any justification at all for his decision.[43] In the years that followed the Court of Appeal[44] and the House of Lords[45] set aside as ultra vires the exercise of discretion that included a substantial subjective element. The *Padfield* principle also applies to a failure to

---

[37] *Customs and Excise Commissioners v Cure and Deeley Ltd* [1962] 1 Q.B. 340. A number of the authorities referred to in the preceding pages were considered in the judgment at 366–368. But on different facts, a similarly worded provision of a subsequent Act was interpreted literally in *Marsh (B) (Wholesale) Ltd v Customs and Excise Commissioners* [1970] 2 Q.B. 206.

[38] *Webb v Minister of Housing and Local Government* [1964] 1 W.L.R. 1295; [1965] 1 W.L.R. 755 (a complicated case, in which the enabling legislation was couched partly in subjective and partly in objective terms); J. Bennett Miller, "Administrative Necessity and the Abuse of Power" [1966] P.L. 330; A.W. Bradley, "Judicial Review and Compulsory Purchase" [1965] C.L.J. 161.

[39] *Roncarelli v Duplessis* [1959] S.C.R. 122 at 140 (Rand J); *Rogers v Jordan* (1965) 112 C.L.R. 580 (dicta).

[40] *Padfield v Minister of Agriculture, Fisheries and Food* [1968] A.C. 997.

[41] For some critical comments upon this decision and, more generally, upon judicial willingness to imply limitations upon the scope of subjectively worded discretion, see R. Austin, "Judicial Review of Subjective Discretion" (1975) 28 C.L.P 150, 167–173. For a recent analysis of *Padfield* and its impact, see: M. Sunkin, "Padfield v Ministry of Agriculture, Fisheries and Food [1968]: Judges and Parliamentary Democracy" in S. Juss and M. Sunkin (eds) *Landmark Cases in Public Law* (2017).

[42] The minister's reasons for refusing to accede to the complainants' request had been that it was the purpose of the statutory scheme that issues of the kind raised by the complainants should be settled by the representatives of the producers from the different regions who sat on the Board, and that were the committee to uphold the complainants, it would be politically embarrassing for him if he decided not to implement the committee's recommendations. After the decision of the HL the minister complied with the order by referring the complaint to a committee of investigation. The committee reported in favour of the complainants; the minister declined to follow the recommendation.

[43] *Padfield v Minister of Agriculture, Fisheries and Food* 1968 A.C. 997 at 1032–1933 (Lord Reid), 1049 (Lord Hodson), 1053-1054 (Lord Pearce), 1061–1062 (Lord Upjohn).

[44] See, e.g. *Congreve v Home Office* [1976] Q.B. 629 (subjective power to revoke television licences not validly exercisable to prevent avoidance of prospectively announced fee increase); *Laker Airways Ltd v Department of Trade* [1977] Q.B. 643 (neither statutory power to give directions to Civil Aviation Authority nor non-statutory power conferred by treaty validly exercisable to defeat legislative scheme); *R. (on the application of Quark Fishing Ltd) v Secretary of State for Foreign and Commonwealth Affairs (No.1)* [2002] EWCA Civ 1409.

[45] See, e.g. *Daymond v Plymouth CC* [1976] A.C. 609 (statutory power to make charges for sewerage services as the authority thought fit did not authorise charging those not in receipt of the services): *Secretary of State for Education and Science v Tameside MBC* [1977] A.C. 1014 (minister

exercise a power.[46] It is interesting to note that important as the decision in *Padfield* has been in the evolution of judicial attitudes, the minister was ultimately able to uphold the Board's decision without resorting to legislation. Another feature of those decisions was the willingness of the courts to assert their power to scrutinise the factual basis upon which discretionary powers have been exercised.[47] Nonetheless, at least in the absence of special circumstances and subject to the general point in *Padfield*, it is "inappropriate for the court to treat a statutorily conferred discretion with no express limitations or fetters, as being somehow implicitly limited or fettered".[48]

---

improperly exercised power to give directions to a local education authority when satisfied that the authority was proposing to act unreasonably).

[46] In *M v Scottish Ministers* [2012] UKSC 58; [2012] 1 W.L.R. 3386 the Mental Health (Care and Treatment) (Scotland) Act 2003 enabled patients compulsorily detained in hospital to apply to a mental health tribunal for a declaration that they were being held in conditions of excessive security. The provisions applied, inter alia, to "qualifying patients" in "qualifying hospitals", to be defined in ministerial regulations. The Act provided that the provisions were to come into force no later than 1 May 2006 but no regulations were ever made. In an application for judicial review, the Scottish Ministers argued a distinction between a statute coming into force and a statute coming into operation and that the failure to make regulations had not defeated the intention of the Scottish Parliament in defining the date when the statute should come into force. The Lord Ordinary refused the petition and the Inner House of the Court of Session refused the petitioner's reclaiming motion. But the Supreme Court allowed the petitioner's appeal—in the judgment of the court, Lord Reed held at [42]–[43], [47]: "It has long been a basic principle of administrative law that a discretionary power must not be used to frustrate the object of the Act which conferred it ... it follows that, although the Ministers had a discretion as to the manner in which they exercised their power to make the necessary regulations, they were under a duty to exercise that power no later than 1 May 2006 ... although (the relevant sections) are technically in force, they have no more practical effect today than they had ... when the 2003 Act received the Royal Assent. The Ministers' failure to make the necessary regulations has thus thwarted the intention of the Scottish Parliament ... The importance of *Padfield's case* [1968] AC 997 was its reassertion that, even where a statute confers a discretionary power, a failure to exercise the power will be unlawful if it is contrary to Parliament's intention. That intention may be to create legal rights which can only be made effective if the power is exercised ... It may however be to bring about some other result which is similarly dependent upon the exercise of the power ... In the present case, the exercise of the power to make regulations by 1 May 2006 was necessary in order to bring (the relevant part) of the 2003 Act into effective operation by that date, as the Scottish Parliament intended. The Ministers were therefore under an obligation to exercise the power by that date." Cf. *R. (on the application of Great Yarmouth Port Co Ltd) v Marine Management Organisation* [2014] EWHC 833 (Admin) (a discretionary power to make a harbour revision order if certain preconditions were met did not compel the making of such an order once the preconditions were met. There remained a residual discretion to refuse to make an order).

[47] For review of "precedent fact" see 4-055 and following and for substantive review of mistake of fact, see 11-043. See *Secretary of State for Education and Science v Tameside MBC* [1977] A.C. 1014, especially at 1047 at 1065–1066, 1072; but the statutory standard on which the minister had to be satisfied was by no means wholly subjective. Their Lordships did not indorse the wider scope of inquiry into the underlying facts advanced in the CA by Scarman LJ at 1030–1031. cf. Sir Leslie Scarman, *English Law—The New Dimension* (1974), pp.48–50. See also *Laker Airways Ltd v Department of Trade* [1977] Q.B. 643 at 706. But see the "Draconian" powers given to the Secretary of State by the Housing Act 1980 s.23 to intervene to exercise the powers of a local housing authority to do "all such things as appear to him necessary or expedient" to enable tenants to exercise the right to buy. Under that statute he could exercise those powers "Where it appears [to him] that [the tenants] have or may have difficulty in exercising their right to buy effectively or expeditiously" (see now Housing Act 1985 Pt 5). In *R. v Secretary of State for the Environment Ex p. Norwich CC* [1982] Q.B. 808 (Kerr LJ, it was held that this formula did not require the Secretary of State to intervene only when the authority had acted "unreasonably" but, it seems, there had to be some objective evidence that the tenants were experiencing "difficulty").

[48] *R. (on the application of Rudewicz) v Secretary of State for Justice* [2012] EWCA Civ 499; [2012] 3 W.L.R. 901 (Secretary of State's discretion under Burial Act 1857 s.25 to grant licence for exhumation and re-interment).

STATUTORY INTERPRETATION

5-019   In *GCHQ*, Lord Diplock defined the chapter head of review known as "illegality" as ensuring that "the decision-maker must understand correctly the law that regulates his decision-making power and must give effect to it".[49] The initial and everyday interpretation of legislation is by public bodies rather than the courts. This gives rise to the question: to what extent does a public body have discretion to interpret the legislation enabling and controlling its functions? Where the concept referred to in legislation is broad (such as "substantial", "cooking a main meal" or "such telecommunication services as satisfy all reasonable demands for them"),[50] the courts have accorded public bodies leeway in applying these concepts to particular instances and will not routinely substitute judicial judgement for that of the public body. But "while respect must be accorded to agencies entrusted by Parliament with the task of administering legislation, it would not be conformable with the rule of law for them to be given free rein, subject only to an irrationality challenge, to interpret the legislation in whatever manner they wished".[51] Where there is a dispute, it is always ultimately for the court to determine the correct legal meaning of legislation.

5-020   The law reports abound with cases involving challenges to the interpretation by public officials of statutory power. Sometimes the exercise of interpretation by the courts of the statutory provision in question involves no more than a search for the "natural and ordinary meaning" of a word or term. For example, a number of cases under various statutes requiring local authorities to house the homeless have considered the meaning of terms such as "homelessness",[52] or "intentionally homeless".[53] Others have considered the duty to provide "adequate accommodation" to gypsies "residing in or resorting to the area"[54] and "ordinary residence".[55] The term "ordinarily resident in the United Kingdom" has also been construed in

---

[49]   *Council of Civil Service Unions v Minister for the Civil Service* [1985] A.C. 374, 410.

[50]   *R. v Monopolies and Mergers Commission Ex p. South Yorkshire Transport Ltd* [1993] 1 W.R.R. 23, *Moyna v Secretary of State for Work and Pensions* [2003] UKHL 44; [2003] 1 W.L.R. 1929 and *R. (on the application of T-Mobile (UK) Ltd) v Competition Commission* [2003] EWHC 1555 (Admin); [2003] Eu.L.R. 769.

[51]   *R. (on the application of Unison) v Monitor* [2009] EWHC 3221 (Admin); [2010] P.T.S.R. 1827 at [60] (Cranston J, considering the meaning of "income derived from private charges" in National Health Act 2006 s.44(2)).

[52]   See, e.g. *R. v Hillingdon LBC Ex p. Islam* [1983] 1 A.C. 688; *Waltham Forest LBC v Maloba* [2007] EWCA Civ 1281; [2008] 1 W.L.R. 2079 (interpretation of "A person shall not be treated as having accommodation unless it is accommodation which it would be reasonable for him to continue to occupy"; CA held that good sense could be made of Housing Act 1996 s.175(3) by construing the words "reasonable for him to continue to occupy" as synonymous with "reasonable for him to occupy for a continuing period", meaning for the future, whether or not he was in occupation at the moment of the application or the decision. *Begum (Nipa) v Tower Hamlets LBC* [2000] 1 W.L.R. 306 CA, not followed).

[53]   See, e.g. *R. v Secretary of State for the Environment Ex p. Tower Hamlets LBC* [1993] Q.B. 632.

[54]   Caravan Sites Act 1968 s.6 (repealed by the Criminal Justice and Public Order Act 1994 s.80); *W Glamorgan v Rafferty* [1987] 1 W.L.R. 457; *R. v Gloucester CC Ex p. Dutton* [1992] C.O.D. 1.

[55]   In *R. (on the application of Cornwall Council) v Secretary of State for Health* [2015] UKSC 46; [2015] 3 W.L.R. 213, the Supreme Court was required to determine the meaning of "ordinary residence" in s.24 of the National Assistance Act 1948, for the purpose of ascertaining which local authority had responsibility for a severely incapacitated adult, the majority coming to a conclusion that no party had contended for at any stage of the proceedings. Lord Carnwath held that in construing the relevant words, "context is critical" and drew a distinction between a provision the purpose of which is purely "administrative and fiscal" (allocating responsibility between local authorities) and a context where the provision was directed to a person's entitlement to a benefit (at [57]). Dissenting, Lord Wilson emphasised that "in deploying a phrase, Parliament understands the meaning

various contexts.[56] The Supreme Court was called upon to determine the meaning of "stateless" in the British Nationality Act 1981.[57] Planning authorities, when deciding whether to grant permission in conservation areas, are required to pay special attention to the desirability of "preserving or enhancing the character or appearance" of the designated conservation area.[58] Do those words require that permission be granted only for development which positively improves the area, or do they merely require that the standards of amenity in the area are maintained at their existing level and not harmed? The House of Lords, after various interpretations in the courts below,[59] held the latter interpretation to be correct.[60] Where wording of a statute is equivocal, the phrase is to be given a purposive construction.[61]

Where the Secretary of State appointed a trust special administrator to a failing NHS trust pursuant to the statutory regime contained in Ch.5A of the National Health Service Act 2006, the words "action ... in relation to the trust" meant the trust special administrator could make recommendations only in relation to that specific NHS trust and the Secretary of State accordingly acted unlawfully in accepting recommendations relating to a neighbouring NHS trust.[62] The Supreme Court has held (by a majority) that the phrase "a map drawn to the prescribed scale" in relation to an application for modification orders in respect of a local authority's definitive map and statement of vehicular rights of way under the Wildlife and Countryside Act 1981 s.53(5) was not confined to the restrictive meaning of "originally drawn" but should be given a meaning that embraced later map production techniques synonymous with "produced" or "reproduced".[63]   **5-021**

Where discretion is conferred on the decision-maker the courts, in addition to resolving disputes about the meaning of particular words and phrases, also have to determine the scope of that discretion and the purpose for which it has been conferred and therefore need to construe the legislation purposefully.[64] We have seen that the expression "may" can mean "must" in the context of the purpose of the   **5-022**

---

which the courts have ascribed to it ... No doubt Parliament understands that in the future the courts may refine and develop their interpretation of a phrase. Subject to that however, Parliament in 1948 intended that the courts should construe the phrase in s.24(1) by reference to its established meaning" (at [67]).

[56] See, e.g. *Shah v Barnet LBC* [1983] 2 A.C. 309 (in the context of a student seeking non-overseas status).

[57] *Al-Jedda v Secretary of State for the Home Department* [2013] UKSC 62; [2014] A.C. 253 (under s.40(2) of the British Nationality Act 1981, the Secretary of State may not make an order depriving a person of citizenship if "satisfied that the order would make a person stateless". It was not open to the Secretary of State to argue that the cause of statelessness was a failure on the part of the applicant to apply for restoration of Iraqi nationality rather than the making of the order).

[58] Planning (Listed Buildings and Conservation Areas) Act 1990 s.72.

[59] See, e.g. *Steinberg v Secretary of State for the Environment* (1988) 58 P. & C.R. 453.

[60] *South Lakeland DC v Secretary of State for the Environment* [1992] A.C. 141.

[61] See e.g., *R. (on the application of J) v Worcestershire County Council (Equality and Human Rights Commission intervening)* [2014] EWCA Civ 1518; [2015] 1 W.L.R. 2825 (Children Act 1989 s.17(1) was to promote the welfare and best interests of children in need; since it was not expressly limited as to where the services could be provided, a local authority had the power (but no duty) to provide services to a child who had been in its area at the time of assessment but who had subsequently moved).

[62] *R. (on the application of Lewisham LBC) v Secretary of State for Health; R. (on the application of Save Lewisham Hospital Campaign Ltd) v Secretary of State for Health* [2013] EWCA Civ 1409; [2014] 1 W.L.R. 514.

[63] *R. (on the application of Trail Riders Fellowship) v Dorset County Council (Plumbe intervening)* [2015] UKSC 18; [2015] 1 W.L.R. 1406.

[64] Sir Rupert Cross, *Statutory Interpretation*, 13th edn (1995), pp.172–75; J. Burrows, *Statute Law in New Zealand*, 3rd edn (2003), pp.177–99. For a recent example in Canada see *ATCO Gas and Pipelines Ltd v Alberta (Energy and Utilities Board)* [2006] S.C.R. 140. In New Zealand, see *Dotcom v Attorney General* [2014] NZSC 199; *Taylor v Chief Executive of Department of Corrections* [2015]

legislation as a whole, and we shall see below that the opposite may also apply.[65] Where the legislation gives power to the decision-maker to act as he "thinks appropriate", or as he "believes", or "thinks fit", the courts nowadays tend to require those thoughts or beliefs to be "reasonably and objectively justified by relevant facts".[66] Assessing the purpose for which legislation was enacted may require the court to consider the "premise of the legislation".[67] Where a Henry VIII clause seeks to empower a Minister to amend primary legislation by use of delegated legislation, a purported exercise of that power that is within the literal meaning of the general words may nevertheless be outside Parliament's contemplation and the court will resolve any doubt about its scope by a restrictive reading of the clause.[68]

5-023   Although in judicial review the courts should not put themselves into the position of the primary decision-maker and reassess the facts or decide the merits of the original decision, we shall see in Chapter 11 that there is growing "culture of justification",[69] where even the broadest discretionary formula will not justify an arbitrary decision, or one that is not demonstrably justified (or at least demonstrably unjustified).[70]

Non-statutory sources of power and the Ram Doctrine

5-024   Virtually all of interpretation of legality engages statutory sources, but to what extent is government permitted to achieve its aims by "extra-statutory" means? The power of the Executive is derived from statute, but also, as we have seen, in a limited range of situations from the royal prerogative.[71] However, there is another source of power, known variously as a "de facto",[72] or "common law discretionary"[73] power, which is employed for the kind of "incidental" activities which are required at the level of central government. This authority is derived from what is known as the "Ram doctrine",[74] which states that a minister of the Crown may exercise any powers that the Crown may exercise, except in so far as the minister is precluded from doing so, either expressly or by necessary implication.

NZCA 477.

[65] See 5-049-072.

[66] *Office of Fair Trading v IBA Health Ltd* [2004] EWCA Civ 142; [2004] 4 All E.R. 1103 at [45].

[67] See, e.g. *Wells v Parole Board* [2008] EWCA Civ 30; [2008] 3 All E.R. 104 at [72] (legislative framework governing indeterminate sentences for public protection (ISPPs) in the Criminal Justice Act 2003 was enacted on the assumption that prisoners serving ISPPs would be able to take part in the courses necessary for them to demonstrate to the Parole Board that they were no longer a risk to public safety. Instead, there had been "a systemic failure on the part of the Secretary of State to put in place the resources necessary to implement the scheme of rehabilitation necessary to enable the relevant provisions of the 2003 Act to function as intended").

[68] *R. (Public Law Project) v Lord Chancellor (Office of the Children's Commissioner intervening)* [2016] UKSC 39; [2016] A.C. 1531.

[69] See 11-003.

[70] Although sometimes the court will not consider decisions (e.g. of elected local authorities in respect of the issuance of taxi licenses) "with over-refinement": *R. v Great Yarmouth BC Ex p. Sawyer* [1989] R.T.R. 297 at [55]; *R. (on the application of Johnson) v Reading BC* [2004] EWHC 765 (Admin); [2004] A.C.D. 72.

[71] See Ch.3.

[72] M. Elliott, *The Constitutional Foundations of Judicial Review* (2001), p.166; P. Cane, *Administrative Law*, 4th edn (2004), p.50.

[73] P. Craig, *Administrative Law*, 8th edn (2016), p.559.

[74] After Sir Granville Ram, First Parliamentary Counsel 1937–47, who set out the doctrine in a memorandum of November 2, 1945; it was first made public in a written parliamentary answer on January 22, 2003, *Hansard*, HL Vol.643, col.WA98. See further: B. Harris, "The 'Third Source' of Authority for Government Action Revisited" (2007) 123 L.Q.R. 225; M. Cohn, "Medieval Chains, Invisible Inks: On Non-Statutory Powers of the Executive" (2005) 25 O.J.L.S.97; J. Howell, "What the Crown May Do" [2010] J.R. 36; R. McManus, "The Crown's Common Law Powers" [2010] J.R. 27.

In a written reply to Lord Lester's question in the House of Lords about the scope of the doctrine, Baroness Scotland of Asthal explained that under the Ram doctrine ministers and their departments, "like many other persons" have common law powers which derive from the Crown's status as a corporation sole. She said that to require parliamentary authority for every exercise of the common law powers exercisable by the Crown "either would impose upon Parliament an impossible burden or produce legislation in terms that simply reproduced the common law".[75] The Ram doctrine has also been commented on by the Cabinet Office's Performance and Innovation Unit which claimed that the doctrine permitted "a department [to] do anything a natural person can, provided it is not forbidden from doing so".[76]

5-025

As Lester and Weait point out,[77] these interpretations of the Ram doctrine appear to be based upon the approach taken in *Malone v Metropolitan Police Commissioner*, where Sir Robert Megarry VC permitted telephone tapping by the police on the ground that England "is not a country where everything is expressly permitted; it is a country where everything is permitted except what is expressly forbidden".[78] The European Court of Human Rights subsequently held that the actions of the police violated ECHR art.8.[79]

5-026

While central government must be able to carry out incidental functions that are not in conflict with its statutory powers, it is wrong to equate the principle pertaining to private individuals—that they may do everything which is not specifically forbidden—with the powers of ministers, where the opposite is true. Any action they take must be justified by a law which "defines its purpose and justifies its existence".[80] The extension of the Ram doctrine beyond its modest initial purpose of achieving incidental powers[81] should be resisted in the interest of the rule of law.[82] However, in any event it seems that the courts are, also in accordance with the rule

5-027

---

[75] *Hansard*, HL Vol.645, col.WA12 (25 February 2003).

[76] Cabinet Office, *Report on Privacy and Data Sharing* (2002).

[77] Lord Lester and M. Weait, "The Use of Ministerial Powers Without Parliamentary Authority: The Ram Doctrine" [2003] P.L. 415, 421.

[78] *Malone v Metropolitan Police Commissioner (No.2)* [1979] Ch. 344 at 357.

[79] *Malone v UK* (1984) 7 E.H.R.R. 14 at [67]–[68] (action was not "in accordance with law" for the purposes of ECHR art.8). The Interception of Communications Act 1985 was enacted to provide a statutory framework for telephone tapping.

[80] *R. v Somerset CC Ex p. Fewings* [1995] 1 All E.R. 513 at 524 (Laws LJ), where, in a case about local authority powers, he made the distinction between the powers of the private citizen "which are not conditional upon some affirmative justification for which he must burrow in the law books" and the powers of a public body, which has no rights of its own ... beyond its public responsibility which defines its purpose and justifies its existence"; also Sir Thomas Bingham MR in the CA [1995] 1 W.L.R. 1037 at 1042. *Fewings* must now be read in the light of the Localism Act 2011, Pt 1, which confers a "general power of competence" on local authorities (but which does not affect central government): see 5-100. The Australian High Court held in *Williams v Commonwealth* (2012) 248 C.L.R. 156 that much government spending was illegal for want of any authorisation beyond an Appropriation Act. The decision obliged the government to transpose many Executive spending schemes to the statute book. The government's remedial legislation was not entirely successful: *Williams v Commonwealth (No.2)* (2014) 252 C.L.R. 416. On Ram or "third source" powers in New Zealand, see *Quake Outcasts v Minister for Canterbury Earthquake Recovery* [2015] NZSC 27 and generally: B.V. Harris "The 'Third Source' of Authority for Government Action" (1992) L.Q.R. 626; B.V. Harris "Recent Judicial Recognition of the Third Source of Authority for Government Action" (2014) 26 N.Z.U.L.R. 60.

[81] Lester and Weait, "The Use of Ministerial Powers Without Parliamentary Authority: The Ram Doctrine" [2003] P.L. 415, 417, 421.

[82] Cases where the doctrine has been liberally construed are *R. v Secretary of State for Health Ex p. C* [2000] 1 F.L.R. 627 and *R. v Worcester CC Ex p. SW* [2000] 3 F.C.R. 174, both cases which considered the legality of the Consultancy Services Index (CSI), a database maintained by the Secretary of State for Health without statutory authority. In both cases the CA and High Court

of law, increasingly insisting that all powers, whatever their source, are reviewable.[83]

5-028   The Court of Appeal considered the extent of the Crown's common law powers and their relationship with statutory powers in *R. (on the application of Shrewsbury and Atcham BC) v Secretary of State for Communities and Local Government*, where local authorities challenged actions of the Secretary of State in developing and implementing a policy of local government reorganisation.[84] A statutory framework, in the form of the Local Government Act 1992, existed for carrying out local government reorganisation but the Secretary of State decided not to use this. Instead, her department published a White Paper and consulted with a view to introducing a bill to give effect to what was finally decided (which eventually happened in the form of Pt 1 of the Local Government and Public Involvement in Health Act 2007). The claimants argued that the Secretary of State had no power to consult without statutory authority and the 1992 Act regime covered the same field. All three Lords Justice agreed that the claimants' appeal should be dismissed but they expressed differing views on the scope and significance of the concept of a "third source" of power (beyond statutory and prerogative powers). Carnwath LJ held[85]:

> "Unlike a local authority, the Crown is not a creature of statute. As a matter of capacity, no doubt, it has power to do whatever a private person can do. But as an organ of government, it can only exercise those powers for the public benefit, and for identifiably 'governmental' purposes within limits set by the law. Apart from authority, I would be inclined respectfully to share the view of the editors of De Smith that 'The extension of the Ram doctrine beyond its modest initial purpose of achieving incidental powers should be resisted in the interest of the rule of law' (*De Smith's Judicial Review* (6th edn) para.5-025)".

5-029   It was, however, unnecessary to invoke the concept of a "third source" of power to explain the Secretary of State's powers to prepare and publish a White Paper; that was "simply a necessary and incidental part of the ordinary business of central government".[86] Dismissing the appeal, Carnwath LJ held that it was "a constitutional principle of some importance that local authorities should be able to rely on the safeguards of a statutory framework for the processes leading to decisions of this importance", however it was "impossible to avoid the conclusion that Parliament has (if only retrospectively) given its stamp of approval to the procedure in this case, and there is no evidence that the authorities have been prejudiced in presenting their opposition".[87] Richards LJ did not share Carnwath LJ's "reservations about the extent of the common law powers of the Crown":

> "it is still necessary to explain the basis on which that ordinary business of government is conducted, and the simple and satisfactory explanation is that it depends heavily on the 'third source' of powers, i.e. powers that have not been conferred by statute and are not

---

respectively held that the Secretary of State could maintain the database just as a natural person could (see 3-026). The database now operates on a statutory basis. See also *R. v Secretary of State, Ex p. Keen* (1990) 3 Admin. L.R. 180 and *R. (on the application of Cala Homes) v Secretary of State for Communities and Local Government* [2011] EWCA Civ 639 (the anticipated abolition of regional strategies—prior to Royal Assent—capable of being a "material" planning consideration).

[83] See Ch.3.

[84] *R. (on the application of Shrewsbury and Atcham BC) v Secretary of State for Communities and Local Government* [2008] EWCA Civ 148; [2008] 3 All E.R. 548.

[85] *R. (on the application of Shrewsbury and Atcham BC)* at [48].

[86] *R. (on the application of Shrewsbury and Atcham BC)* at [49].

[87] *R. (on the application of Shrewsbury and Atcham BC)* at [70].

prerogative powers in the narrow sense but are the normal powers (or capacities and freedoms) of a corporation with legal personality".[88]

It would be wrong to introduce qualifications to their exercise such as that they are only "for the public benefit" or for "identifiably 'governmental' purposes"; "any limiting principle would have to be so wide as to be of no practical utility or would risk imposing an artificial and inappropriate restriction upon the work of government".[89] Waller LJ said that he instinctively favoured "some constraint on the powers by reference to the duty to act only for the public benefit".[90]

Where legislation provides a comprehensive code for regulating a public func-   **5-030**
tion that "occupies the entire field", there can be no room for common law powers.[91] However, the issue arises in respect of the pre-emption of Parliament when, in advance of the Royal assent to a new Bill, measures are taken to implement the new legislation or to start dismantling the old under the assertion that the Treasury is the guardian of Parliament's interests in Whitehall.[92] Sometimes the spending of money in advance of a bill becoming an Act of Parliament is achieved by means of a "paving act",[93] but on other occasions this is not considered necessary and preparatory acts are undertaken after a bill's second reading. Practically, the executive should have the power to prepare for the implementation of new legislation, for example, by beginning a process of recruitment or seeking potential tenderers for contracts. However, the executive does not possess the power, under the principles of the rule of law and the separation of powers, to alter rights or significant interests established under a law that is still in existence or in anticipation of a law that is not yet passed.

The House of Lords Constitution Committee addressed this question[94] and found   **5-031**
no widespread or egregious use of pre-emption but made the following recommendations, which accord with the view put above:

(i)   All instances of pre-emption must be governed by certain fundamental constitutional principles, including the rule of law and effective parliamentary scrutiny.

(ii)   The Treasury plays an important role in policing this area within Government. However, the Treasury's practices carry no constitutional force, and should not be described so as to suggest otherwise. In particular, its practice of authorising certain expenditure once a bill has been given a second reading in the House of Commons is not a constitutional convention and has not been endorsed by Parliament.

(iii)   As there is no standard procedure at present, the Government must do

---

88 *R. (on the application of Shrewsbury and Atcham BC)* at [73].
89 *R. (on the application of Shrewsbury and Atcham BC)* at [74].
90 *R. (on the application of Shrewsbury and Atcham BC)* at [81].
91 See, e.g. *R. (on the application of Sessay) v South London and Maudsley NHS Foundation Trust and another* [2011] EWHC 2617 (QB); [2012] Q.B. 760 (Mental Health Act 1983 was a complete statutory code for detention of non-compliant mentally incapacitated patient for treatment in hospital; the common law doctrine of necessity did not apply); *R. (on the application of the Child Poverty Action Group) v Secretary of State for Work and Pensions* [2010] UKSC 54; [2011] 2 A.C. 15 (Secretary of State had no power to reclaim overpaid benefits except under Social Security Act 1992 s.71); *R. v Secretary of State for Work and Pensions Ex p. Hooper* [2003] 1 W.L.R. 2623 at [135] ("plainly implicit that Parliament intended the express statutory provisions for payment of benefits to widows to occupy the entire field of entitlement to payment of benefits as a result of the death of a spouse"; on appeal [2005] UKHL 29; [2005] 1 W.L.R. 1681 at [46]–[47] Lord Hoffmann, without deciding, saw the force in the argument that common law powers could not be exercised).
92 Based upon a concordat agreed between Her Majesty's Treasury and the Public Accounts Committee in 1932, reflected in HM Treasury, *Managing Public Money* (2012), Ch.2.
93 e.g. the Planning-gain Supplement (Preparations) Act 2007.
94 *The pre-emption of Parliament*, 13th Report of 2012–2013, HL Paper 165.

more to inform Parliament of their pre-emptive activities. Written statements should be made to Parliament in a timely manner, setting out
details of each instance of pre-emption and justifying it; and a statement
should be made at the end of each session giving an annual summary of
pre-emptive activities.

(iv)   Similarly, a written ministerial statement should be made at the end of
        each session on the number of ministerial directions issued in the session.

(v)   Where pre-emption occurs, the Government must always state clearly the
        power under which they consider themselves authorised to act.

(vi)   The principles and practices governing pre-emption should be consoli-
        dated into a single, authoritative restatement for inclusion in the Cabinet
        Manual.

(vii)   The common law powers of the Crown are restrained by public law and
        constitutional principle. This should be made clear in all Government
        publications mentioning these powers.

(viii) The so-called "Ram doctrine", which has been invoked to support pre-
        emption, is misleading and inaccurate, and should no longer be used.

(ix)   Pre-emption of Parliament should not be undertaken when it would
        threaten the principle of effective parliamentary scrutiny.[95]

The discovery of Parliament's intent and use of Hansard

5-032   Because a body like Parliament can have no mind, it is not possible to
"consolidate individual intentions into a collective, fictitious group intention".[96]
Therefore the provisions of a statute need to be understood in the context of the
purpose of the statute as a whole. This first requires an understanding of the context
in which it was enacted and the "mischief" at which it was aimed. In *Pepper v
Hart*,[97] the term in dispute was that of "cost" in s.63 of the Finance Act 1976. The
question was whether teachers at independent schools whose children were
educated at the school at much reduced fees should be taxed on the "marginal cost"
to the school of educating those children (which would be a small sum), or on the
"average cost" (which would be significantly higher). The issue had implications
for the in-house benefits of many other employees as well. It was decided that the
statutory purpose favoured the interpretation most favourable to the teachers.
Departing from previous authority,[98] the House of Lords referred to parliamentary
material to assist the construction of the ambiguous provision. Reference may now
therefore be made to the parliamentary record to aid the construction of legislation.[99]
However, as Lord Browne Wilkinson made plain the exclusionary rule should be

---

[95] The government's response was that the advice in the Ram opinion was "necessarily incomplete
      because it predates important developments in public law, as well as the Human Rights Act. Nor can
      it have the force of law", although "the opinion does remain valid. That is, the Crown does have com-
      mon law powers which may be exercised subject to overarching legal constraints". *http://
      www.parliament.uk/documents/lords-committees/constitution/GovernmentResponse/Government
      %20response%20-%20report%20on%20pre-emption%20of%20parliament.pdf* [XXX Link not valid].

[96] R. Dworkin, *Law's Empire* (1986), pp.335–336.

[97] *Pepper v Hart* [1993] A.C. 593.

[98] *Practice Statement (Judicial Precedent)* [1966] 1 W.L.R. 1234; *Davis v Johnson* [1979] A.C. 264;
      Hadmor Productions Ltd v Hamilton [1983] A.C. 191. *Hansard* reports have been directly referred
      to in some cases, e.g. *Pickstone v Freemans Plc* [1989] A.C. 66, and *Owens Bank v Bracco* [1992]
      A.C. 443 and in others (mainly involving national security issues) the Crown has referred to *Hansard*
      see, e.g. *R. v Secretary of State for the Home Department Ex p. Brind* [1991] 1 A.C. 696.

[99] Online versions of *Hansard* are available at
      http://www.parliament.uk/business/publications/hansard/ (for the Commons back to November 1988
      and for the Lords back to 1995–96); earlier reports are at *http://hansard.millbanksystems.com*. In

relaxed to permit reference to parliamentary materials only where: "(a) legislation is ambiguous or obscure, or leads to an absurdity; (b) the material relied on consists of one or more statements by a minister or other promoter of the Bill together if necessary with such other parliamentary material as is necessary to understand such statements and their effect; (c) the statements relied on are clear".[100]

Contrasting illustrations of the court's willingness (or otherwise) to have regard to *Hansard* can been seen in two recent cases. In *A v HM Treasury*, the Supreme Court closely examined the parliamentary record relating to the United Nations Bill in 1946 in a challenge to the lawfulness of delegated legislation seeking to give effect to United Nations Security Council measures on asset freezing of terrorist suspects on grounds that they impinged on common law rights.[101] But in *R. v Forsyth and Mabey*, the Supreme Court held that there was no reason to refer to *Hansard* in a challenge to a prosecution for making funds available to Iraq, contrary to delegated legislation also made under the United Nations Act 1946; the appellants sought to rely on passages in *Hansard* to show that the power to make the delegated legislation had expired by the effluxion of time. *A v HM Treasury* was distinguished: in *A*, the challenge was based on fundamental rights going to the content of the legislation whereas in *Forsyth* the issue related to the time within which the power was properly exercisable.[102] Where *Hansard* is examined, it is a common experience that the court derives little or no assistance from it.[103]   **5-033**

Reference to *Hansard* may aid the "purposive" or "teleological" approach to statutory interpretation. There are, however, dangers: it encourages the artificial manufacture of parliamentary intent. Lobby groups seeking a particular interpretation of a statutory provision seek "Pepper v Hart" statements from the minister. The rule may even lead to the confounding of the presumption of parliamentary respect for certain fundamental constitutional principles where the intention clearly reveals that Parliament wished, say, to oust the court's jurisdiction or to breach the rule of law.[104] It no doubt increases the cost of litigation in certain cases. Perhaps its most troubling aspect has been pointed out extra-judicially by Lord Steyn: "To give the executive, which promotes a Bill, the right to put its own gloss on a Bill is a   **5-034**

2007 a new system for correcting errors in *Hansard* was introduced: see D. Greenberg, "Hansard, the whole Hansard and nothing but the Hansard" (2008) 124 L.Q.R. 181.

[100] *Pepper v Hart* [1993] A.C. 593. It was not foreseen that any statement other than that of the minister or other promoter of the bill was likely to meet those criteria. The Australian Acts Interpretation Act 1901 (Cth) s.15AB(1) permits resort to extrinsic material to ascertain the meaning of a statutory provision where there is ambiguity or obscurity, or where the ordinary meaning of the text leads to a result that is manifestly absurd or unreasonable. A non-exhaustive list of material may be considered which includes the second-reading speech of the minister (s.15AB(2)). Most Australian States have similar legislation. The courts frequently refer to *Hansard*, although Heydon J thought that the exercise is usually "barren and useless": *Momcilovic v R.* (2011) 245 C.L.R. 1 at 154.

[101] *A v HM Treasury (JUSTICE intervening)* [2010] UKSC 2 and [2010] UKSC 5; [2010] 2 A.C. 534 at [15]–[16] ("There was no indication during the debates at Second Reading in either House that it was envisaged that the Security Council would find it necessary under article 41 to require states to impose restraints or take coercive measures against their own citizens"), [43], [152]–[153] ("reference to Hansard demonstrates the enthusiasm in 1946 of all sections of both Houses for the new United Nations and the Security Council, of which the United Kingdom was a permanent member. Parliament should not be presumed to have intended that the measures covered by section 1 of the 1946 Act would be restricted to measures similar to the examples in article 41 of the Charter"), [213].

[102] *R v Forsyth*; R. v Mabey [2011] UKSC 9; [2011] 2 A.C. 69.

[103] See, e.g. *R. (on the application of Innovia Cellophane Ltd and Innovia Films Ltd) v The Infrastructure Planning Commission* [2011] EWHC 2883 (Admin); [2012] P.T.S.R. 1132.

[104] D. Oliver, "Pepper v Hart: A Suitable Case for Reference to Hansard?" [1993] P.L. 5; T. Bates, "Parliamentary Material and Statutory Construction: Aspects of the Practical Application of Pepper v Hart" (1993) 14 Stat.L.R. 46, p.54; F. Bennion, "Executive Estoppel: Pepper v Hart Revisited" [2007] P.L.1; and more broadly R. Ekins, *The Nature of Legislative Intent* (2012).

substantial inroad on a constitutional principle, shifting legislative power from
Parliament to the Executive".[105]

5-035   The House of Lords in *Spath Holme* sought to mitigate some of these negative
effects of *Pepper v Hart* by permitting reference to ministerial statements only to
clarify the meaning of a statutory expression (such as the term "cost of a benefit"
in *Pepper v Hart*), and not to clarify the scope of the ministerial power (such as, in
Spath Holme, whether a statutory power to make delegated legislation to restrict
rent levels could be employed for a purpose other than the control of inflation).[106]
In the latter case, only if a minister were to give a "categorical assurance" to Parliament that a power would be used in a particular way, could the statement be
admissible.[107]

5-036   While *Spath Holme* restricted recourse to statements in Parliament, the House of
Lords in *Wilson v First County Trust Ltd*[108] somewhat extended it in cases where
the courts are, under the Human Rights Act 1998, considering whether a statute may
be incompatible with the ECHR. Since the courts have to consider, in the context
of some Convention rights, whether the legislation pursued a legitimate objective
and did so proportionately, it was necessary to assess the "practical effect" of the
legislation and thus it might occasionally be necessary to consider the words spoken
by a minister in the course of a debate on a Bill. The House of Lords was clear that
such a resort to the parliamentary record was only for the purpose of "background
information". Lord Nicholls said that "the court is called upon to evaluate the
proportionality of the legislation, not the adequacy of the minister's exploration of
the policy options or of his explanations to Parliament. The Latter would contravene
Art. 9 of the Bill of Rights 1689" (which provides that "the freedom of speech and
debates or proceedings in Parliament ought not to be impeached or questioned in
any court or place out of Parliament").[109]

5-037   The European Court of Human Rights has, however, been more willing to have
recourse to the reasoning (or lack of reasoning) of parliamentary debates. In *Hirst
v United Kingdom (No.2)* the Court considered whether the United Kingdom's
blanket ban on convicted prisoners voting in general and local elections breached
ECHR art.3 of Protocol 1. It held that the *failure* by Parliament to give adequate
reasons for the relevant statutes displayed lack of evidence that Parliament had assessed the proportionality of the ban.[110] The absence of the required justification led
the Court to hold that the ban violated the prisoners' Convention rights. This approach is diametrically opposed to that of the House of Lords in *Wilson*, and may

---

[105] Lord Steyn, "Pepper v Hart; A Re-Examination" (2001) 21 O.J.L.S. 59. Lord Nicholls sought in
Jackson v Attorney General [2005] UKHL 56; [2006] 1 A.C. 262 to rescue *Pepper v Hart* from the
"cloud" under which Lord Steyn had placed it; his Lordship sought to invoke the post-enactment
history of the Parliament Acts as an aid in their construction, a course which Lord Steyn "emphatically rejected" (at [99]), as did Lord Cooke in "A Constitutional Retreat" (2006) 122 L.Q.R. 224.
See also Lord Nicholls' dicta in *R. (on the application of Spath Holme Ltd) v Secretary of State for
the Environment, Transport and the Regions* [2001] 2 A.C. 349 at 396 and in *Wilson v First County
Trust Ltd (No.2)* [2003] UKHL 40; [2004] 1 A.C. 816 at 827.
[106] *R. (on the application of Spath Holme Ltd) v Secretary of State for the Environment, Transport and
the Regions* [2001] 2 A.C. 349, Lords Nicholls and Cooke dissenting. Which also held that in
interpreting a consolidated statute, reference could be had to earlier versions of the various
consolidated acts.
[107] *R. (on the application of Spath Holme Ltd) v Secretary of State for the Environment, Transport and
the Regions* [2001] 2 A.C. 349 at 212 (Lord Bingham of Cornhill).
[108] *Wilson v First County Trust Ltd (No.2)* [2003] UKHL 40; [2004] 1 A.C. 816.
[109] *Wilson v First County Trust Ltd (No.2)* [2003] UKHL 40; [2004] 1 A.C. 816.
[110] *Hirst v United Kingdom (No.2)* (2006) 42 E.H.R.R. 41 at [78]–[85]. For Parliament's response to
the European Court of Human Right's judgment, see para.1-053 above.

well violate art.9 of the Bill of Rights 1689 if employed by a domestic court in the future.

Explanatory Notes and other government guidance

The practice, since 1999, of publishing Explanatory Notes, prepared by departmental lawyers to accompany all bills and updated during the course of the bills' passage through Parliament, provide contextual information on the Bill that may be helpful in interpreting its provisions and purpose. The orthodox view is that recourse to Explanatory Notes may only be had if the legislation in question is ambiguous.[111] Where there is ambiguity, the court may also consider statements of government policy.[112]

5-038

Using the parliamentary record for purposes other than interpretation

The parliamentary record may also be used in judicial review claims for purposes other than as an aid to statutory interpretation, subject to relevancy and the constitutional principle of parliamentary privilege.[113]

5-039

Always-speaking statutes

Reference to the parliamentary record and the "original intent" of a statute may be of limited value,[114] especially in cases where its purpose is not defined, or in the case of a "framework Act", which deliberately leaves the definition of purpose to be developed in the course of the statute's implementation. However, even in cases where a term seems at the time of enactment relatively specific, its meaning over time may alter. For example, in *McCartan Turkington Breen v Times Newspapers Ltd*, the question was whether 'public meeting' could include a press conference; Lord Bingham said, in relation to the Defamation Act (Northern Ireland) 1955: "Although the 1955 reference to 'public meeting' derives from 1888, it must be interpreted in a manner which gives effect to the intention of the legislature *in the social and other conditions which obtain today*".[115] And Lord Steyn said that, unless they reveal a contrary intention, statutes are to be interpreted as always speaking.[116] The notion of the "always speaking" statute or constitution has been applied in a number of recent cases considering the interpretation of Com-

5-040

---

[111] *R. (on the application of D) v Secretary of State for Work and Pensions* [2010] EWCA Civ 18; [2010] 1 W.L.R. 1782 at [48]; *Coventry and Solihull Waste Disposal Co. Ltd v Russell* [1999] 1 W.L.R. 2093, 2103.

[112] *Adeboyin v Secretary of State for the Home Department* [2010] EWCA Civ 773; [2011] 1 W.L.R. 564 (ambiguity in Immigration Rules as to whether "false" means "dishonest" or "incorrect").

[113] *R. (on the application of Federation of Tour Operators) v HM Revenue & Customs* [2007] EWHC 2062 (Admin) at [108]–[125] (Stanley Burnton J: "it is necessary to consider whether this material would otherwise be admissible on or relevant to the determination of the Claimants' substantive claims, before deciding whether its origin precludes their adducing it in evidence"); *Toussaint v Attorney General of St Vincent and the Grenadines* [2007] UKPC 48; [2007] 1 W.L.R. 2825 (proper of a claimant to rely on evidence of what was said by a minister in Parliament to show the motivation for the government's actions outside Parliament).

[114] *R. v Clarke (Ronald Augustus)* [2008] UKHL 8; [2008] 1 W.L.R. 338, where the issue was whether a failure to sign an indictment had deprived a trial court of its jurisdiction. Lord Bingham held that in interpreting the Administration of Justice (Miscellaneous Provisions) Act 1933, "The 'always speaking' principle has no application. The answer to the question now is the same as should have been given then. It is inescapable: Parliament intended that the bill should not become an indictment unless and until it was duly signed by the proper officer" (at [18]).

[115] *McCartan Turkington Breen v Times Newspapers Ltd* [2001] 2 A.C. 277 at 292 (emphasis added).

[116] *McCartan Turkington Breen v Times Newspapers Ltd* [2001] 2 A.C. 277 at 296.

monwealth constitutions,[117] but it has relevance to statutory interpretation in different contexts.[118] As we shall soon consider, courts should of course be careful in accepting ministerial or other statements of policy as the best evidence of a change in a statute's meaning.[119] However, especially in cases where the purpose of a statute has never been defined, either generally, or by reference to any particular relevant considerations, its purposes may well change over time. The area of land-use planning provides a vivid example.

5-041 Since 1947, when the systematic control of land use and development was introduced by the Town and Country Planning Act of that year, local authorities and the Secretary of State on appeal, have possessed seemingly unlimited power to grant and refuse planning permission. The governing statute[120] requires "regard to be had" to the development plan as drafted by the local authority, but it has always allowed "other material considerations" also to be considered.[121] Conditions may be imposed upon permissions as the authority "think fit".[122]

5-042 The judicial construction of the Town and Country Planning Acts and related legislation over time shows that the purposes pursued by a statutory scheme may not be static. The Town and Country Planning Act 1947 was concerned largely with what have been called physical criteria: questions such as access to the site, siting of the buildings, their height, bulk, set-back, mass, design and external appearance. It was held unequivocally that the "character of the use of the land, not the particular purposes of a particular occupier"[123] was the concern of planning, and therefore the authority could not seek to pursue social policies through its planning policies, for example, requiring developers to provide housing for the less well-off.[124] Over time, however, policies changed, and the courts accepted that the pursuit of "affordable housing" may be a material planning consideration.[125]

5-043 The experience of the interpretation of planning powers over time provides a sali-

---

[117] See, e.g. *Balkissoon Roodal v The State* [2003] UKPC 78; *Matthew v State of Trinidad and Tobago* [2004] UKPC 33; *R. v Ireland* [1998] A.C. 147; *Robinson v Secretary of State for Northern Ireland* [2002] UKHL 32; [2002] N.I. 390.

[118] *Re McFarland* [2004] UKHL 17; [2004] 1 W.L.R. 1289 at [25] (Lord Steyn: "legislation, whether primary or secondary, must be accorded an always-speaking construction unless the language and structure of the statute reveals an intention to impress on the statute a historic meaning. Exceptions to the general principle are a rarity"). For cases displaying a similar approach in New Zealand, see J. Burrows, *Statute Law in New Zealand*, 3rd edn (2003), pp.177–199. For an example, see *R. (on the application of Blackpool Council) v Howitt and Secretary Of State for Culture Media and Sport* [2008] EWHC 3300 (Admin); [2009] L.L.R. 325 (the term "crime and disorder" in the Licensing Act 2003 s.4 included breaches of the smoking ban introduced by the Health Act 2006).

[119] On interpretation of policies, see 5-058.

[120] Now the Town and Country Planning Act 1990 (a consolidation Act).

[121] Formerly the development plan and other material considerations had equal influence. Since 1991, however, the development plan shall be followed unless other material considerations "indicate otherwise".

[122] Town and Country Planning Act 1990 s.70(1).

[123] *East Barnet UDC v British Transport Commission* [1962] 2 Q.B. 484 (Lord Parker CJ).

[124] *R. v Hillingdon LBC Ex p. Royco Homes Ltd* [1974] Q.B. 720.

[125] *Mitchell v Secretary of State for the Environment* [1994] J.P.L. 916, CA (upheld the refusal of permission to change the use of a house in multiple occupation to self-contained flats in order to meet the need for cheap rental accommodation); *ECC Construction Ltd v Secretary of State for the Environment* (1994) 69 P. & C.R. 51. Since these cases the law has changed to the extent that if a policy (such as to pursue affordable housing) is articulated in the development plan, then if the policy is lawful there is a presumption (under s.54A of the Act) that the development plan should be followed: *Persimmon Homes (North West) Ltd v First Secretary of State and West Lancashire DC* [2006] EWHC 2643 (Admin). In addition, Local Government Act 2000 s.4 requires every local authority to prepare a "community strategy" for "promoting or improving the economic, social and environmental well-being of their area". Under the Planning and Compulsory Purchase Act 2004 s.62(5) local planning authorities must have regard to the "community strategy".

ent reminder of the fluid nature of statutory purposes and the danger of freezing their purpose for all time through undue reliance upon the so-called "original intent" of the legislature (even if such intent is capable of discovery).[126] The goals of a scheme of public regulation can be gauged by a number of sources of public law. In the planning area these include statutory instruments as well as various policy documents issued by the relevant department from time to time on different subjects.[127] Although not having the force of law, they nevertheless are considerations to which the decision-maker must have regard and therefore themselves fall within the scope of the statutory power. Interpretation of the contemporary scope of planning therefore requires some understanding of what planners on the ground actually do. The court will therefore need to be guided by those who keep abreast of changing social and professional expectations and approaches.

Overarching statutory duties

In most contexts, a public authority will be subject to statutory duties of an overarching nature that apply when more specific statutory powers and duties are exercised. These include the Equality Act 2010, which creates a "public sector duty regarding socio-economic inequalities" (applicable when making "decisions of a strategic nature")[128] and a "public sector equality duty".[129] The Human Rights Act 1998 s.6 makes it "unlawful for a public authority to act in a way which is incompatible with a Convention rights".[130]

5-044

Interpretation in relation to constitutional principles and constitutional rights

The Human Rights Act 1998 now incorporates provisions of the European Convention on Human Rights into domestic law.[131] Breach of Convention rights by anyone exercising public functions therefore offends legality. However, what we now explicitly call constitutional rights, based on constitutional principles such as the rule of law, have always been acknowledged in the common law. With continu-

5-045

---

[126] If parliamentary records are resorted to in cases such as these they may well inhibit, if not used sensibly, the kind of incremental development of purpose seen in planning law.

[127] Known variously over time as Planning Policy Statements (PPS), Planning Policy Guidance Notes (PPG) and now the National Planning Policy Framework: see Department for Communities and Local Government, *National Planning Policy Framework* (2012), which "sets out the Government's planning policies for England and how these are expected to be applied. There are also other published policies, e.g. on waste and nationally significant infrastructure projects.

[128] Equality Act 2010 s.1: "An authority ... must, when making decisions of a strategic nature about how to exercise its functions, have due regard to the desirability of exercising them in a way that is designed to reduce the inequalities of outcome which result from socio-economic disadvantage".

[129] Equality Act 2010 s.149: a "public authority must, in the exercise of its functions, have due regard to the need to— (a) eliminate discrimination, harassment, victimisation and any other conduct that is prohibited by or under this Act; (b) advance equality of opportunity between persons who share a relevant protected characteristic; foster good relations between persons who share a relevant protected characteristic and persons who do not share it". See further 11-062; M. Bell, "Judicial enforcement of the duties on public authorities to promote equality" [2010] P.L. 672; S. Fredman, "The Public Sector Equality Duty" (2011) 40 I.L.J. 405. The main question in relation to the PSED is not whether the outcome is justifiable, but whether, in the process leading to the making of the decision, the decision-maker had "due regard" to the relevant considerations. For a summary of the case law on the correct approach, see *R. (on the application of Bracking) v Secretary of State for Work and Pensions* [2013] EWCA Civ 1345; [2014] Eq. L.R. 60 at [25] (McCombe LJ) and see para.5–072 below.

[130] On which bodies and functions fall within the scope of the HRA, see 3-066; on the Convention rights, see Ch.13.

[131] See Ch.13.

ing political debate about the future of the Human Rights Act,[132] it is important not
to lose sight of common law constitutional principles and rights.[133]

5-046   Recognition of common law constitutional principles and rights provides the
court with a tool of interpretation. The courts presume that Parliament does not
intend to deprive the subject of his or her common-law rights and therefore, in the
absence of express words or necessary intendment, statutes are not to be interpreted
so as to authorise their interference. Among other rules of construction, express
words are necessary to empower a public authority to raise money from the
subject,[134] or to warrant the exercise of a statutory power with retroactive effect.[135]
In *Simms*, the common law "principle of legality" was enunciated.[136] It means that,
in the absence of express language or implication to the contrary, the courts will assume that even the most general statutory words were intended to be subject to the
basic rights of the individual (in that case freedom of expression). For example, the
House of Lords considered whether a statute authorised disclosure by the bank of
its instructions to and advice of counsel in relation to a tax avoidance scheme.[137]
Lord Hoffmann considered that the words in the statute could not be read as necessarily implying that the long-established common law right to legal professional
privilege could be overridden. In another example, the Supreme Court held that
delegated legislation seeking to give domestic effect to UN Security Council
measures on asset freezing to counter terrorism was ultra vires because it sought,
on the basis of general wording only, to deprive people of the fundamental right of
access to an effective judicial remedy and made no provision for basic procedural
fairness in decision-making.[138] In other cases applying the principle of legality, it
has been held that the words of the statute were sufficiently clear and precise to

---

[132] 1-021.
[133] See further M. Fordham, "Common Law Rights" [2011] J.R. 14, arguing that common law protection of basic rights has two main advantages: autonomy from the ECHR and opportunities for cross-
fertilisation between the common law and ECHR; W. Sadurski, "Judicial Review of the protection
of constitutional Rights (2002) 22 O.J.L.S. 275. In *Osborn v Parole Board* [2013] UKSC 61; [2014]
A.C. 1115 at [57], Lord Reed stated: "The importance of the [Human Rights] Act is unquestionable.
It does not however supersede the protection of human rights under the common law or statute, or
create a discrete body of law based on the judgments of the European Court. Human rights continue
to be protected by our domestic law, interpreted and developed in accordance with the Act when
appropriate." See also para.1–117 above. In New Zealand, see H. Wilberg "Common Law Rights
Have Justified Limits: Refining The Principle of Legality" in D. Meagher and M. Groves (eds) *The
Principle of Legality in Australia and New Zealand* (2017).
[134] *Attorney General v Wilts United Dairies Ltd* (1921) 37 T.L.R. 884; *Brocklebank (T & J) Ltd v R.*
[1924] 1 K.B. 647 (reversed on other grounds, [1925] 1 K.B. 252); *Liverpool Corp v Maiden (Arthur)
Ltd* [1938] 4 All E.R. 200; *Davey Paxman & Co v Post Office, The Times,* 16 November 1954, which
made it necessary to pass the Wireless Telegraphy (Validation of Charges) Act 1954; *City Brick &
Terra Cotta Co v Belfast Corp* [1958] N.I. 44; *Daymond v Plymouth CC* [1976] A.C. 609 (see Water
Charges Act 1976 ss.1, 2); *Congreve v Home Office* [1976] Q.B. 629; *Clark v University of
Melbourne* [1978] V.R. 457 at 463-465. Unparliamentary taxation for the use of the Crown
contravenes the Bill of Rights 1689; cf. *Cobb & Co v Kropp* [1967] 1 A.C. 141; *Customs and Excise
Commissioners v Thorn Electrical Industries Ltd* [1975] 1 W.L.R. 1661 at 1673 (Kilbrandon LJ: the
presumption may have outlived its usefulness, "A modern Hampden would in many quarters be pil-
loried as a tax-evader"); *McCarthy and Stone (Developments) Ltd v Richmond-upon-Thames LBC*
[1992] 2 A.C. 48; *Revenue and Customs Commissioners v Total Network SL; Total Network SL v
Revenue and Customs Commissioners* [2008] UKHL 19; [2008] 1 A.C. 1174 at [21]-[33] (Lord Hope
of Craighead).
[135] See 5-042.
[136] *R. v Secretary of State for the Home Department Ex p. Simms* [2000] 2 A.C. 115 at 131 (Lord
Hoffmann).
[137] *R. (on the application of Morgan Grenfell & Co Ltd) v Special Commissioners of Income Tax* [2002]
UKHL 21; [2003] 1 A.C. 563.
[138] *Ahmed v Her Majesty's Treasury (JUSTICE intervening) (Nos 1 and 2)* [2010] UKSC 2, [2010]
UKSC 5; [2010] 2 A.C. 534.

infringe the human right.[139] Moreover, the constitutional principle of parliamentary supremacy permits Parliament to legislate to abolish or restrict common law rights[140] (at least insofar as to do so is compatible with analogous Convention rights and subject to several judicial hints that in an extreme case, the courts would seek to protect a fundamental common law right against illegitimate parliamentary incursion).

The rule of law as a fundamental constitutional principle will be considered in more detail in Chapter 11.[141] Of the common-law presumptions, the most influential in modern administrative law is one based on the rule of law, namely, that the courts should have the ultimate jurisdiction to pronounce on matters of law. Accordingly, only in the most exceptional circumstances will the courts construe statutory language so as to endow a public body with exclusive authority to determine the ambit of its own powers.[142] Access of the individual to the courts, another fundamental requirement of the rule of law, is similarly recognized. In *Raymond v Honey* it was held that the Home Secretary had no power to make prison rules to "authorise hindrance or interference with so basic a right" as the citizen's right of access to the court.[143] In *Leech (No.2)*,[144] the Court of Appeal held unlawful a regulation which permitted a prison governor to read and stop correspondence between a prisoner and his legal adviser. Despite a generally worded governing statute,[145] it was held, following *Raymond v Honey* that a prisoner retains all his rights which are not taken away expressly or by necessary implication. It was also held that a prisoner's right of unimpeded access to his solicitor was an inseparable part of the right of access to the courts themselves.[146]

5-047

A vivid case study of how emphasising different constitutional principles can lead

5-048

---

[139] See, e.g. *R. (on the application of Gillan) v Commissioner of Police of the Metropolis* [2006] UKHL 12; [2006] 2 A.C. 307 (stop and search powers of police upheld); and *McE v Prison Service of Northern Ireland and another (Northern Ireland Human Rights Commission and others intervening)* [2009] UKHL 15; [2009] 1 A.C. 908 (powers of covert surveillance of persons in custody with their legal and medical advisers upheld despite the infringement of professional privilege). In *R. (on the application of Richards) v Teeside Magistrates' Court* [2015] EWCA Civ 7; [2015] 1 W.L.R. 1695, the Court of Appeal upheld a requirement in a sexual offences prevention order (SOPO) that the claimant wear an electronic tag, considering that the order had been "imposed pursuant to a specific power" in the Sexual Offences Act 2003 and moreover that there was a "necessary implication" that many standard prohibitions in SOPOs would interfere with fundamental rights of the person subject to them.

[140] See, e.g. *R. v Davis (Iain)* [2008] UKHL 36; [2008] 1 A.C. 1128 (Lord Bingham of Cornhill at [5]: "a long-established principle of the English common law that, subject to certain exceptions and statutory qualifications, the Defendant in a criminal trial should be confronted by his accusers in order that he may cross-examine them and challenge their evidence") and the Criminal Evidence (Witness Anonymity) Act 2008 (introducing witness anonymity orders).

[141] See 11-059.

[142] See Ch.4.

[143] *Leech (No.2)* [1983] 1 A.C. 1 at 11 (Lord Wilberforce).

[144] *R. v Secretary of State for Home Affairs Ex p. Leech (No.2)* [1994] Q.B. 198.

[145] Prison Act 1952 s.47(1), conferring power on the Home Secretary to make rules for the "regulation and management" of prisons and for the "classification, treatment, employment, discipline and control of persons required to be detained therein". The material part of the disputed rr.33(3) and 37A of the Prisons Rules 1964 provided that the prison governor could read every letter to or from a prisoner and stop any letter that was "objectionable or of inordinate length", except for correspondence between a prisoner who was party to proceedings in which a writ had been issued and his legal adviser.

[146] See also *Golder v UK* (1975) 1 E.H.R.R. 524 In *Drew v Attorney General* [2002] 1 N.Z.L.R. 58, the New Zealand CA struck down a prison regulation as ultra vires the Penal Institutions Act 1954. The regulation purported to deny prisoners legal representation in every disciplinary hearing. The empowering provision was in general terms, authorising the making of regulations to ensure "the discipline of inmates" including "prescribing the procedures for the hearing of such complaints". The court reached this result by "applying common law principles of construction guided by the

to different outcomes is provided by the UK Supreme Court in *R. (on the applica-tion of Evans) v Attorney General (Campaign for Freedom of Information intervening).*[147] The court had to consider the circumstances in which it was law-ful for the Attorney General to issue a certificate under s.53(3) of the Freedom of Information Act 2000 that he had "reasonable grounds" for forming the opinion that there had been no breach of the Act, effectively overriding the judgment of the Up-per Tribunal (part of the judiciary under the s.3(5) of the Constitutional Reform Act 2005). The background to the litigation was a request under the 2000 Act by a journalist for copies to the so-called "black spider" letters written to ministers by the Prince of Wales on matters of public policy. Lord Neuberger of Abbotsbury PSC (with whom Lord Kerr of Tonaghmore and Lord Reid JJSC agreed) suggested that a statutory provision that entitled a member of the executive "to overrule a deci-sion of the judiciary merely because he does not agree with it would be unique in the laws of the United Kingdom" and would "cut across two constitutional principles which are also fundamental components of the rule of law" (at [51])—the basic principle that a decision of a court is binding as between the parties and cannot be ignored and that decisions of the executive are reviewable by the court (at [52]). It was not "crystal clear" to Lord Neuberger that Parliament intended these fundamental constitutional principles to be disapplied (at [90]). Against this constitutional background, the expression "reasonable grounds" did not permit the Attorney General to issue a certificate "simply because, on the same facts and admittedly reasonably, he takes a different view from that adopted by" the Upper Tribunal "after a full public hearing" (at [88]). The ambit of s.53(3) was confined to issues that were not before the Tribunal (at [89]). Dissenting, Lord Wilson JSC was critical of the Court of Appeal—and Lord Neuberger—for "rewriting" s.53(3): "It invoked precious constitutional principles but among the most precious is that of parliamentary sovereignty, emblematic of our democracy" (at [169]). Lord Wilson agreed that a power of the executive to override decisions on issues of law "would have been an unlawful encroachment on the principle of separation of pow-ers" but "issues relating to the evaluation of the public interest is entirely differ-ent" (at [171]). Agreeing in large part with Lord Wilson JSC, Lord Hughes JSC said "The rule of law is of the first importance. But it is an integral part of the rule of law that courts give effect to Parliamentary intention" (at [154]) and concluded that Parliament had "plainly shown" an intention to empower a member of the execu-tive to override a decision of a court on where the balance in the public interest lay.

Interpretation of Convention rights

5-049   The Human Rights Act 1998 at s.3(1) places the following interpretive obliga-tion on courts: "So far as it is possible to do so, primary legislation and subordinate

---

principles of natural justice", and did not need to refer to the guarantee of the observance of natural justice in the New Zealand Bill of Rights Act s.27. See also *Pham v Secretary of State for the Home Department (Open Society Justice Initiative intervening)* [2015] UKSC 19; [2015] 1 W.L.R. 1591, [119] (Lord Reed JSC: "… where Parliament authorises significant interferences with important legal rights, the courts may interpret the legislation as requiring that any such interference should be no greater than is objectively established to be necessary to achieve the legitimate aim of the interference: in substance, a requirement of proportionality".) And the recent decision of the Supreme Court in *R. (UNISON) v Lord Chancellor (Equalities and Human Rights Commission intervening) (Nos 1 and 2)* [2017] UKSC 51; [2017] 3 W.L.R. 409.

[147] *R. (on the application of Evans) v Attorney General (Campaign for Freedom of Information interven-ing)* [2015] UKSC 21; [2015] 2 W.L.R. 813. The judgments of Lord Mance JSC (with which Baron-ess Hale of Richmond DPSC agreed) did not expressly emphasise constitutional principles. See further M. Elliott, "A tangled constitutional web: the black-spider memos and the British constitution's relational architecture" [2015] P.L. 539.

legislation must be read and given effect in a way which is compatible with the Convention rights".[148] The courts are also under an obligation, under s.2, to "take into account" the case law of the European Court of Human Rights and the former Commission.[149] What is important to note at this point is that the interpretive obligation created by s.3 of the HRA applies only where a Convention right, as defined by the HRA, exists; legislation may therefore be interpreted differently depending on whether or not a Convention right is involved.[150] These issues are considered in Chapter 13.

Interpretation of European Union law

European Union law requires national courts interpreting national legislation to apply the principle of "conforming interpretation" in those situations in which there is a potential infringement of European Union law, a matter we consider in Chapter 14.[151]

5-050

Interpretation and international law

In considering the approach of the domestic courts to international law,[152] a distinction must be drawn between (a) interpretive questions relating to treaties and similar instruments of international law which have been incorporated into national law—in the United Kingdom's dualist legal system, international treaties are not part of domestic law unless and until they are expressly incorporated by legislation; (b) the use that the domestic courts may make of treaties that have been ratified but not expressly incorporated into national law; and (c) customary international law.[153]

5-051

Incorporated treaties

The constitutional importance and complexity of two bodies of treaties require special consideration-the reception of Convention rights from the ECHR into domestic law by the Human Rights Act 1998[154] and the treaties establishing the European Union.[155] Here we focus on other treaties. It is wrong to think of incorporation as a single phenomenon; a treaty may be received into and given effect in the law of England and Wales in more than one way. The most straightfor-

5-052

---

148 See 13-041.
149 See 13-035.
150 *R. (on the application of Hurst) v HM Coroner for Northern District London* [2007] UKHL 13; [2007] 2 W.L.R. 726 at [10]-[12] (Lord Rodger).
151 See 14-047.
152 We deal with the following aspects of the relationship between judicial review and international law: see 3-019 (the extent to which questions international law falls outside the jurisdiction of the Administrative Court or is non-justiciable); interpretation of international law (see 5-046); whether international law may be a relevant consideration to which a public authority ought to have regard in exercising a public function (see 5-133); and the court's adaptation of the unreasonableness test to "anxious scrutiny" to decisions which affect fundamental rights, some of which may be reflected in unincorporated treaty provisions (See 11-093).
153 See generally: S. Fatima, *Using International Law in Domestic Courts* (2005); D. Feldman, "The internationalization of public law and its impact on the United Kingdom", Ch.5 in J. Jowell and D. Oliver (eds), *The Changing Constitution*, 8th edn (2013); P. Sales and J. Clements, "International law in domestic courts: the developing framework" (2008) 124 L.Q.R. 388; L. Jones, "Is International Law a Part of the Law of England?" [2011] J.R. 192; R. Hopkins, "International Rule of Law After Al-Jedda" [2012] J.R. 77.
154 See Ch.13.
155 See Ch.14.

ward situation is where an Act of Parliament is enacted to bring a treaty into English law, but even here there are various drafting techniques. In some Acts, the text or part of the text, of a treaty has been "copied out"; in others parliamentary counsel have used English statutory language to give general effect to the treaty (but which may, upon proper interpretation, confer rights that are narrower or broader than those contained in the treaty). There are other ways of bringing about incorporation—including what may variously be called "indirect" or "for practical purposes" or an "informal mode" of incorporation. Thus, s.2 of the Asylum and Immigration Act 1993 provides, under the heading "Primacy of the Convention" that "Nothing in the immigration rules [made under the Immigration Act 1971] shall lay down any practice which would be contrary to the Convention"—a reference to the Convention and Protocol relating to the Status of Refugees.[156]

5-053   If a treaty has been incorporated (by whatever technique) into domestic law, the question then is how should the courts approach the task of interpreting the treaty. The language of treaties is often broader and more open-textured than the precise wording that is the earmark of English statutory drafting. The Vienna Convention on the Law of Treaties 1969, especially arts 31-33, provides the basic guidelines.[157] Generally, it can be said that[158]: the starting point is the language and structure of the text in question; words should be given the natural and ordinary meaning, avoiding over-sophisticated analysis and "prolonged debate about the niceties of language"[159]; treaties may contain implied as well as express provisions[160]; where a provision is ambiguous, "the interpretation which is less onerous to the State owing the Treaty obligation is to be preferred"[161] and regard may be had to the traveaux préparatoires; good faith is required in the interpretation and performance of a treaty[162]; the provisions "must be read together as part and parcel of the scheme" of the treaty[163]; relevant reservations and derogations must be considered[164]; and, above all, a broad, purposive interpretation is required.[165] The court must not lose sight of the fact that it is an international legal instrument that is being interpreted, and that its concepts have a meaning that is autonomous of the particularities of a domestic legal system,[166] though in some cases the international instrument as-

---

[156] Cmnd 9171 and Cmnd 3906. See *R. (on the application of European Roma Rights Centre) v Immigration Officer, Prague Airport* [2004] UKHL 55; [2005] 2 A.C. 1.

[157] In force since 27 January 1980 and strictly speaking applying only to treaties in force after that date—but the main provisions concerning interpretation (arts 31 and 32) reflect customary international law: see *R. (on the application of European Roma Rights Centre) v Immigration Officer, Prague Airport* [2004] UKHL 55; [2005] 2 A.C. 1 at [18].

[158] S. Fatima, *Using International Law in Domestic Courts* (2005) Ch.4 and the cases surveyed there.

[159] *Horvath v Secretary of State for the Home Department* [2001] 1 A.C. 489 at 508.

[160] As the ECHR and its interpretation by the European Court of Human Rights amply illustrate: see Ch.13.

[161] *R. (on the application of Marchiori) v Environment Agency* [2002] EWCA Civ 3; [2002] Eu. L.R. 225 at [58].

[162] *R. (on the application of European Roma Rights Centre) v Immigration Officer, Prague Airport* [2004] UKHL 55; [2005] 2 A.C. 1 at [19].

[163] *R. (on the application of Mullen) v Secretary of State for the Home Department* [2004] UKHL 18; [2005] 1 A.C. 1 at [38].

[164] *R. v Secretary of State for the Home Department Ex p. Ahmed (Mohammed Hussain)* [1999] Imm. A.R. 22, 33 (Lord Woolf MR).

[165] See, e.g. *Horvath v Secretary of State for the Home Department* [2001] 1 A.C. 489 at 494-495; *R. (on the application of Adams) v Secretary of State for Justice (JUSTICE and another intervening)* [2011] UKSC 18; [2012] 1 A.C. 48 ("miscarriage of justice" in Criminal Justice Act 1988 s.133 interpreted having regard to International Covenant on Civil and Political Rights 1966 art.14.6).

[166] See, e.g. *R. (on the application of AH (Algeria)) v Secretary of State for the Home Department* [2012] EWCA Civ 395; [2012] 1 W.L.R. 3469 (meaning of "serious non-political crime" to be found in

sumes there to be national meaning to a term.[167] Interpretations reached by courts in other national systems is of persuasive authority[168]; inevitably, however, courts in different legal systems may reach interpretations that are difficult to reconcile.

Unincorporated treaties

The dualist principles that underpin the British constitution—which require a divide between ratifying treaties (an action of the executive branch of government) and law-making (the province of Parliament and the courts)—has the consequence of limiting the scope for utilising unincorporated treaties as part of a judicial review claim.[169] Unincorporated treaties have no direct effect in the courts of England and Wales and the courts accordingly are loathe to enter into questions of interpretation beyond assuring themselves that the public body has adopted a reasonably tenable view of the instrument.[170] That is not to say, however, that they have no effect. First, circumstances may arise in which a minister, by ratifying a treaty, creates a legitimate expectation that government decision-making and policy will follow the terms of that treaty; we consider this possibility in Chapter 12.[171] Secondly, unincorporated treaties may be used as an aid to interpretation of domestic legislation (and in interpreting the treaty, the approach described above in relation to incorporated treaties applies). Where an ambiguity in domestic legislation arises, the English courts will—in the absence of clear statutory words to the contrary—presume that Parliament intended to legislate in conformity with the

5-054

---

international, not national, law); *R. (on the application of Adan (Lul Omar)) v Secretary of State for the Home Department* [2001] 2 A.C. 477 at 515-516; *Mullen* [2004] UKHL 18; [2005] 1 A.C. 1 at [36]. And see *Pham v Secretary of State for the Home Department (Open Society Justice Initiative intervening)* [2015] UKSC 19; [2015] 1 W.L.R. 1591, [38] (Lord Mance JSC, "I would accept that the question arising under art.1(1) of the 1954 Convention [relating to the Status of Stateless Persons] in this case is not necessarily to be decided solely by reference to the text of the nationality legislation of the state in question, and that reference may also be made to the practice of the government, even if not subject to effective challenge in the courts").

[167] See, e.g. *R. (on the application of ST) v Secretary of State for the Home Department* [2012] UKSC 12; [2012] 2 A.C. 135 ("lawfully within their territory" in Convention and Protocol relating to the Status of Refugees meant what was to be treated as lawful according to the national law of the contracting state).

[168] *Forthergill v Monarch Airlines* [1981] A.C. 251 at 284.

[169] Whether this constitutional principle ought to continue to apply to human rights treaties has been questioned: R. Higgins, "The Relationship between International and Regional Human Rights Norms and Domestic Law" (1992) 18 *Commonwealth Law Bulletin* 1268; *Re McKerr's Application for Judicial Review* [2004] UKHL 12; [2004] 1 W.L.R. 807 at [49]–[50] (Lord Steyn). In *R. (on the application of SG) v Secretary of State for Work and Pensions (Child Poverty Action Group intervening)* [2015] UKSC 16; [2015] 1 W.L.R. 1449, Lord Kerr (dissenting at [254]–[257]) argued explicitly for "an exception to the dualist theory in human rights Conventions" and that he considered "that article 3.1 of the [United Nations Convention on the Rights of the Child] is directly enforceable in United Kingdom domestic law." See further para.3-019 above.

[170] See, e.g. *R. (on the application of Corner House Research) v Director of the Serious Fraud Office* [2008] UKHL 60; [2009] 1 A.C. 756 at [43]–[44], [65] (HL considered the OECD Convention on Combating Bribery of Foreign Public Officials in International Business Transactions (1997)); *R. v (on the application of The Badger Trust) v The Welsh Ministers* [2010] EWHC 768 (Admin) at [113]–[128] (Bern Convention on the Conservation of European Wild Animals and Habitats 1979); *R. (on the application of ICO Satellite Ltd) v The Office of Communications* [2010] EWHC 2010 (Admin) at [88]–[96]; *R. v Lyons (Isidore Jack) (No.3)* [2002] UKHL 44; [2003] 1 A.C. 976 at [27]; D. Lloyd Jones, "Is International Law a Part of the Law of England?" [2011] J.R. 192. In *R. (Yam) v Central Criminal Court* [2015] UKSC 76; [2016] A.C. 771, the Supreme Court rejected an argument that a court's discretionary common law power was constrained by the United Kingdom's international obligations, emphasising that while a domestic decision-maker exercising a general discretion may have regard to the United Kingdom's international obligations, he is not bound to do so.

[171] See 12-026.

international law obligations of the United Kingdom on the same subject matter.[172] The courts adopt a similar approach in relation to developing the common law.[173]

Customary international law

5-055 Customary international law is a source of English common law—but "applicable in the English courts only where the constitution permits".[174] Customary international law consists of those norms about which there is clear consensus among States, which are based on general and consistent practice and a sense of legal obligation.[175] *Jus cogens* (peremptory norms) is that body of customary international law comprising of fundamental principles which cannot be derogated from by States.[176] There are a number of references to customary international law in the case law.[177]

5-056 It falls outside the scope of this book to give a comprehensive account of this field, but the following are illustrations of how customary international law may be used. Principles of customary international law were recognised in relation to: the immunity from criminal process of a head of state[178]; the right to admit, exclude and expel aliens[179]; and prohibition of torture.[180] But the courts have held that: there is no right of conscientious objection to military service[181]; no duty on governments

---

[172] A.V. Dicey, *An Introduction to the Study of the Law of the Constitution*, 10th edn (1959), pp.62–63; *R. v Secretary of State for the Home Department Ex p. Brind* [1991] 1 A.C. 696 at 747, 760; *R. v Asfaw (Fregenet)* [2008] UKHL 31; [2008] 1 A.C. 1061 (a criminal appeal raising issues on the UN Convention relating to the Status of Refugees 1951 (United Nations), art.31 and domestic statutes).

[173] J. Laws, "Is the High Court the Guardian of Fundamental Human Rights? [1993] P.L. 59, 66–67; *Lyons* [2002] UKHL 44; [2003] 1 A.C. 976 at [27]; *Reynolds v Times Newspapers Ltd* [2001] 2 A.C. 127 at 223.

[174] See, e.g. *R. v Jones (Margaret)* [2006] UKHL 16; [2007] 1 A.C. 136 at [11] (Lord Bingham, citing "old and high authority") with the caveat quoted (see [23]); *R. (on the application of Al-Haq) v Secretary of State for Foreign and Commonwealth Affairs* [2009] EWHC 1910 (Admin) at [40] (Pill LJ: "The issue of the incorporation of customary international law into domestic law is not susceptible to a simple or general answer ..."); R. O'Keefe, "The Doctrine of Incorporation Revisited" (2008) 78 *British Year Book of International Law* 7.

[175] *R. (on the application of European Roma Rights Centre) v Immigration Officer, Prague Airport* [2004] UKHL 55; [2005] 2 A.C. 1 at [23].

[176] See, e.g. prohibition of torture (*A v Secretary of State for the Home Department* [2005] UKHL 71; [2006] 2 A.C. 221).

[177] See, e.g. *R. (on the application of Al-Saadoon) v Secretary of State for Defence* [2009] EWCA Civ 7; [2009] U.K.H.R.R. 638 at [70] (CA was "in no position whatever to arrive at any overall conclusion as to the effects of hanging for the purpose of making an assessment of its compatibility or otherwise with norms of customary international law"); *MK (Somalia) v Entry Clearance Officer* [2008] EWCA Civ 1453; [2009] 2 F.L.R. 138 (CA rejected an argument that customary international law recognised de facto adoption of children, which the claimants contended was important in relation to a country where formal adoption was unlikely to take place because institutions of the state were depleted and for religious reasons); *BE (Iran) v Secretary of State for the Home Department* [2008] EWCA Civ 540; [2009] I.N.L.R. 1 at [29] (it was right to describe the outlawing of anti-personnel mines "as an emerging norm of international law": accordingly, the claimant, who had deserted from the Iraqi army in order to avoid involvement in the laying of unmarked anti-personnel mines in roads used by civilians, was entitled to asylum).

[178] *R. v Bow Street Metropolitan Stipendiary Magistrate Ex p. Pinochet Ugarte (No.3)* [2000] 1 A.C. 147 at 201, 265, 268. Immunity applies equally to a foreign head of state in his personal capacity as it applies to his public capacity: see *Aziz v Aziz* [2007] EWCA Civ 712; [2008] 2 All E.R. 501.

[179] *R. (on the application of European Roma Rights Centre) v Immigration Officer, Prague Airport* [2004] UKHL 55; [2005] 2 A.C. 1 at [11].

[180] *A v Secretary of State for the Home Department* [2005] UKHL 71; [2006] 2 A.C. 221 at [34].

[181] *R. (on the application of Septet) v Secretary of State for the Home Department* [2003] UKHL 15; [2003] 1 W.L.R. 856.

to provide diplomatic assistance to protect citizens from actions of foreign states[182]; and maintenance of nuclear weapons is not contrary to international law.[183]

MANDATORY AND DIRECTORY DUTIES AND POWERS

When Parliament prescribes the manner or form in which a duty is to be performed or a power exercised, it seldom lays down what will be the legal consequences of failure to observe its prescriptions. The courts have therefore formulated their own criteria for determining whether the prescriptions are to be regarded as mandatory, in which case disobedience will normally render invalid what has been done, or as directory, in which case disobedience may be treated as an irregularity not affecting the validity of what has been done.[184] **5-057**

These terms, like others we have been considering in this chapter, often cause more problems than they solve. The law relating to the effect of failure to comply with statutory requirements thus resembles an inextricable tangle of loose ends and judges have often stressed the impracticability of specifying exact rules for the assignment of a provision to the appropriate category. Nevertheless, it is possible to state the main principles that the courts have generally followed and to illustrate their application in a few settings. In brief, the principles are as follows: **5-058**

(a) A decision or action is in general to be treated as valid until struck down by a court of competent jurisdiction. This issue has been discussed in Chapter 4 and need not be repeated now.[185]

(b) Statutory words requiring things to be done as a condition of making a decision, especially when the form of words requires that something "shall" be done, raise an inference that the requirement is "mandatory" or "imperative" and therefore that failure to do the required act renders the decision unlawful.

(c) The above inference does not arise when the statutory context indicates that the failure to do the required act is of insufficient importance, in the circumstances of the particular decision, to render the decision unlawful.

(d) The courts, in appropriate cases and on accepted grounds may, in their discretion refuse to strike down a decision or action or to award any other remedy. This is discussed in Chapter 18.[186]

One of the causes of the loose ends entangling this area of the law is the failure **5-059**

---

[182] *R. (on the application of Abassi) v Secretary of State for Foreign and Commonwealth Affairs* [2002] EWCA Civ 1598; [2003] U.K.H.R.R. 76.

[183] *R. (on the application of Marchiori) v Environment Agency* [2002] EWCA Civ 3; [2002] Eu. L.R. 225.

[184] In some cases it has been said that there must be "substantial compliance" with the statutory provisions if the deviation is to be excused as a mere irregularity, e.g. *Coney v Choyce* [1975] 1 W.L.R. 422 (where the attempt bona fide to comply and the absence of prejudice from the non-compliance are also emphasised); *Grunwick Processing Laboratories Ltd v ACAS* [1978] A.C. 655 at 691–692 (where mandatory duties in absolute form were contrasted with duties to be performed "as far as reasonably practicable"); *Donnelly v Marrickville Municipal Council* [1973] 2 N.S.W.L.R. 390 at 398. Authorities are reviewed in *Cullimore v Lyme Regis Corp* [1962] 1 Q.B. 718; *Graham v Attorney General* [1966] N.Z.L.R. 937 at 953–961; *Parisienne Basket Shoes Pty Ltd v Whyte* (1938) 59 C.L.R. 369; *Scurr v Brisbane City Council* (1973) 133 C.L.R. 242 (an approach that still applies where the Act specifies that substantial compliance suffices); *Queensland v Queensland Land Council Aboriginal Corp* (2002) 195 A.L.R. 106 at 169.

[185] 4-059.

[186] 18-047.

to distinguish factors that rebut the presumption that a requirement is legally required (proposition (c) above) from factors that justify the court's exercise of discretion to excuse the breach of a legal requirement (proposition (d) above). The first set of factors raises questions about the lawful consequence of the requirement, which is not dependent upon the exercise of judicial discretion. The second set of factors raises questions about the appropriate use of judicial discretion in relation to the grant of a remedy.

5-060   A second reason for the tangle in this area is the use of the terms "mandatory" and "directory"; the latter term is especially misleading. All statutory requirements are prima facie mandatory. However, in some situations the violation of a provision will, in the context of the statute as a whole and the circumstances of the particular decision, not violate the objects and purpose of the statute. Condoning such a breach does not, however, render the statutory provision directory or discretionary. The breach of the particular provision is treated in the circumstances as not involving a breach of the statute taken as a whole. Furthermore, logically, a provision cannot be mandatory if a court has discretion not to enforce it.

5-061   Lord Hailsham expressed this point well in *London and Clydeside Estates v Aberdeen District Council* where he distinguished two ends of a spectrum. At the one end are cases "where a fundamental obligation may have been so outrageously and flagrantly ignored or defied that the subject may safely ignore what has been done and treat it as having no legal consequence". At the other end of the spectrum the defect may be "so nugatory or trivial" that the authority can proceed on the assumption that "if the subject is so misguided as to rely on the fault, the courts will decline to listen to his complaint". Lord Hailsham considered that language like "mandatory", "directory", "void", "voidable" and "nullity" only served to confuse the situation and stretch or cramp the facts of a case into rigid legal categories or "on a bed of Procrustes invented by lawyers for convenient exposition".[187]

5-062   In order to decide whether a presumption that a provision is "mandatory" is in fact rebutted, the whole scope and purpose of the enactment must be considered, and one must assess "the importance of the provision that has been disregarded, and the relation of that provision to the general object intended to be secured by the Act".[188] In Assessing the importance of the provision, particular regard should be given to its significance as a protection of individual rights; the relative value that

---

[187] *London and Clydeside Estates v Aberdeen DC* [1980] 1 W.L.R. 182 at 189–90 (the issue was whether under the Town and Country Planning legislation it was a mandatory requirement that a certificate issued by a local authority include a statement setting out the applicant's right of appeal to the Secretary of State—it was). See also *R. v Tower Hamlets LBC Ex p. Tower Hamlets Combined Traders Association* [1994] C.O.D. 325 (Sedley J analyses the obiter remark of Lord Hailsham in *Clydeside* and concludes that two points were being made: first, that the consequences of non-compliance are variable, and secondly, that the grant of relief is discretionary). On discretion to withhold remedies, see 18-047.

[188] *Howard v Bodington* (1877) 2 P.D. 203 at 211; *Spicer v Holt* [1977] A.C. 987 (compliance with procedure for administering breath-tests, a condition precedent for valid conviction); *Grunwick Processing* [1978] A.C. 655; *Sheffield City Council v Graingers Wines Ltd* [1978] 2 All E.R. 70; *Tower Combined Traders Association* [1994] C.O.D. 325; *Wang v Commissioner of Inland Revenue* [1994] 1 W.L.R. 1286, PC. *R. v Stocker* [2013] EWCA Crim 1993; [2014] 1 Cr. App. R. 18 (appeal against rape conviction on the basis that the defendant had been indicted under the wrong Act dismissed even though the Criminal Procedure Rules 2013 stated that the indictment "must" identify the legislation that created the offence. The clear purpose of the relevant rule was to ensure that an accused had sufficient information to know the case he had to meet. The error was a pure technicality that had caused no prejudice. It was not so fundamental as to render the proceedings a nullity and the draftsman would not have intended such an outcome for such a breach); *Aylesbury Vale DC v Call a Cab Ltd* [2013] EWHC 3765 (Admin); [2014] P.T.S.R. 523 (although the Local Government (Miscellaneous Provisions) Act 1976 s.45(3) clearly made it mandatory for a district council to give notice to each parish council of its intention to pass a resolution to bring the hackney car-

is normally attached to the rights that may be adversely affected by the decision, and the importance of the procedural requirement in the overall administrative scheme established by the statute. Breach of procedural or formal rules is likely to be treated as a mere irregularity if the departure from the terms of the Act is of a trivial nature,[189] or if no substantial prejudice has been suffered by those for whose benefit the requirements were introduced.[190] But the requirement will be treated as "fundamental" and "of central importance" if members of the public might suffer from its breach.[191] Another factor influencing the categorisation is whether there may be another opportunity to rectify the situation; of putting right the failure to observe the requirement.[192]

The principle that the whole scope and purpose of the Act must be looked at is illustrated by a decision of the Court of Appeal in which the validity of a reference to a rent tribunal was challenged on the ground that the tenant had given the name of the wrong landlord. The minister, who had power to make regulations with regard to proceedings before these tribunals, had made regulations requiring (among other things) that the name of the landlord be specified in an application. The court held that the regulations were directory only and that the reference was therefore valid; the minister had no power to impose conditions of validity when Parliament itself had not done so, and it could be assumed to have omitted to do so because it had contemplated that applications would often be made by tenants who had "no lawyers to advise them and no regulations by their side".[193] If, on the other hand, the primary purpose is to promote the public interest rather than the interests of individuals,[194] the courts are likely to take a strict view of minor deviations from a statutory code of procedure on the part of persons seeking to obtain exemption from the prescribed system of regulation.[195]

5-063

Some classes of procedural requirements are so important that they will nearly

5-064

---

riage licensing provisions into force for the whole of its area, reading the statute as a whole and recognising the complete lack of prejudice to the defendants from non-compliance with the statutory requirements beyond the fact that non-compliance might give them an argument whereas validity would deprive them of it, if there was substantial compliance with the statutory provision, the act was not invalid).

[189] *R. v Dacorum Gaming Licensing Committee Ex p. EMI Cinemas and Leisure Ltd* [1971] 3 All E.R. 666 (minor typographical error in notice of application for licence could be disregarded, despite general strictness of statutory requirements); *R. v Inner London Betting Licensing Committee Ex p. Pearcy* [1972] 1 W.L.R. 421 (unimportant additional words added to advertisement and notice of application).

[190] See, e.g. *R. v Liverpool City Council* [1975] 1 W.L.R. 701; *Coney v Choyce* [1975] 1 W.L.R. 222; *George v Secretary of State for the Environment* (1979) 250 E.G. 339; *Main v Swansea City Council* (1985) 49 P. & C.R. 26, CA; cf. *London and Clydeside Estates* [1980] 1 W.L.R. 182 at 195 (Lord Fraser: "The validity of a certificate is not in my opinion dependent on whether the appellants were actually prejudiced by it or not").

[191] *R. v Lambeth LBC Ex p. Sharp* (1988) 55 P. & C.R. 232 (notice published by local authority failed to specify the period within which representation should be made to a planning application. The CA held that these requirements were "fundamental" and "strict").

[192] *Brayhead (Ascot) Ltd v Berkshire CC* [1964] 2 Q.B. 303; *London & Clydeside Estates* [1980] 1 W.L.R. 182.

[193] *Francis Jackson Development Ltd v Hall* [1951] 2 K.B. 488 at 493; distinguished in *Chapman v Earl* [1968] 1 W.L.R. 1315 where, on somewhat similar facts, a different intent was attributed to the provisions of a subsequent Rent Act; cf. *R. v Devon and Cornwall Rent Tribunal Ex p. West* (1975) 29 P. & C.R. 316.

[194] cf. *Kammins Ballrooms Co Ltd v Zenith Investments (Torquay) Ltd* [1971] A.C. 850; *Mercantile and General Reinsurance Co Ltd v Groves* [1974] Q.B. 43 (time limit imposed for the benefit of one party waivable by him); cf. *Meah v Sector Properties Ltd* [1974] 1 W.L.R. 547; *Gyle-Thompson v Wall Street (Properties) Ltd* [1974] 1 W.L.R. 123; *Dedman v British Building etc. Ltd* [1974] 1 W.L.R. 171.

[195] See, e.g. *R. v Pontypool Gaming Licensing Committee Ex p. Risca Cinemas Ltd* [1970] 1 W.L.R.

always be held to be "mandatory". For example, an authority which fails to comply with a statutory duty to give prior notice or hold a hearing or make due inquiry or consider objections in the course of exercising discretionary powers affecting individual rights will seldom find the courts casting an indulgent eye upon its omissions.[196] Non-compliance or inadequate compliance with an express duty to give particulars of rights of appeal may render an administrative determination invalid.[197] A provision requiring consultation with named bodies before a statutory power is exercised is also likely to be construed as mandatory.[198] Similarly, a statutory requirement that a bill of indictment is signed by a proper officer; many errors pertaining to indictments fell into the category of procedural error but the failure to sign the indictment deprived the court of jurisdiction there could be no valid trial on indictment if there was no indictment.[199] In another example, the omission of a claimant to seek the permission of a High Court judge under the Mental Health Act 1983 s.136 before making a damages claim (shortly before the expiry of the limitation period) resulted in the proceedings being a complete nullity.[200]

5-065   The practical effects of the exercise of a power upon the rights of individuals will often determine whether the relevant formal and procedural rules are to be classified as mandatory. Thus, where powers are conferred to issue orders or certificates that affect civil liberties or rights to compensation, the courts have insisted that the decision-maker must closely observe all material requirements as to form.[201] For many years the formalities surrounding the issue, service and content of enforce-

---

1299 (time limit for submitting advertisement of bingo licence application exceeded). cf. *Howard v Secretary of State for the Environment* [1975] Q.B. 235 (only the filing of the notice but not the statement of the grounds of appeal to the minister against an enforcement notice was held to be mandatory); *Button v Jenkins* [1975] 3 All E.R. 585; *R. v Urbanowski* [1976] 1 W.L.R. 455 (time limitations within which magistrates must state a case and accused person be tried only directory: judge of Crown Court may extend time).

[196] *Grunwick* [1978] A.C. 655 (statutory duty was to ascertain the opinions of affected workers; the means by which this was to be done, however, were entrusted to the discretion of the authority); *Donnelly v Marrickville Municipal Council* [1973] 2 N.S.W.L.R. 390. However, substantial compliance with statutory provisions prescribing the method of giving notice may suffice: *Smith v East Sussex CC* (1977) 76 L.G.R. 332. For an illustration of the vitiating effect of failure to give sufficient notice where this entailed a breach of a statutory duty to afford interested parties a genuine opportunity of making representations against a proposed scheme for comprehensive schools, see *Lee v Department of Education and Science* (1967) 66 L.G.R. 211; *Lee v Enfield LBC* (1967) 66 L.G.R. 195; *Legg v ILEA* [1972] 1 W.L.R. 1245; cf. *Coney v Choyce* [1975] 1 W.L.R. 422; *R. v Southwark Juvenile Court Ex p. J* [1973] 1 W.L.R. 1300 (provision for attendance at hearing by a non-party directory, but decision quashed for lacking appearance of fairness).

[197] See, e.g. *London and Clydeside Estates v Aberdeen DC* [1980] 1 W.L.R. 182; *Agricultural, Horticultural and Forestry Industry Training Board v Kent* [1970] 2 Q.B. 19; *Rayner v Stepney Corp* [1911] 2 Ch. 312; cf. *Jones v Lewis* (1973) 25 P. & C.R. 375; *George v Secretary of State for the Environment* (1979) 250 E.G. 339; *Skinner and King v Secretary of State for the Environment* [1978] J.P.L. 842 (statutory duty to serve notice on both joint tenants not discharged by service on one, although relief may not be granted in the absence of substantial prejudice; *R. v Chief Immigration Officer, Manchester Airport Ex p. Insah Begum* [1973] 1 W.L.R. 141 (statutory duty to give notice of refusal of entry to immigrant discharged by delivery to agent); *Re Bowman* [1932] 2 K.B. 621.

[198] *May v Beattie* [1927] 2 K.B. 353; *R. v Minister of Transport Ex p. Skylark Motor Coach Co* (1931) 47 T.L.R. 325; *Agricultural etc. Industry Training Board v Aylesbury Mushrooms Ltd* [1972] 1 W.L.R. 190; *Hamilton City v Electricity Distribution Commission* [1972] N.Z.L.R. 605.

[199] *R. v Clarke (Ronald Augustus)* [2008] UKHL 8; [2008] 1 W.L.R. 338 (Administration of Justice (Miscellaneous Provisions) Act 1933 ss.1–2). Cf. *R. v Stocker* [2013] EWCA Crim 1993; [2014] 1 Cr. App. R. 18.

[200] *Seal v Chief Constable of South Wales* [2007] UKHL 31; [2007] 1 W.L.R. 1910 (Lord Woolf and Baroness Hale of Richmond dissenting).

[201] *Hill v Ladyshore Coal Co (1930) Ltd* [1936] 3 All E.R. 299; *Enraght v Lord Penzance* (1881) 6 Q.B.D. 376 at 461, 463, 471–472; *R. v Secretary of State for the Home Department Ex p. Budd* [1942] 2 K.B. 14.

ment notices (preliminary to taking measures to secure compliance with planning controls) were construed rigorously and literally by the courts; later they tended to consider whether disregard of a formal or procedural requirement by the local planning authority might have substantially prejudiced the developer.[202] The principle that failure to observe formal or procedural rules in the administrative process may be venial if no substantial prejudice has been caused to those immediately affected now appears in a number of statutory contexts.[203]

In *Wang v The Commissioner of Inland Revenue*,[204] the Privy Council held that the breach of a time provision by the Inland Revenue of Hong Kong would not "deprive the decision-maker of jurisdiction and render any decision which he purported to make null and void". It is noteworthy that although the terms "mandatory" and "directory" were used in argument, they were nowhere employed in the judgment. Two principal reasons were given for the Board's decision. The first was that the Inland Revenue's decision resulted in "no real prejudice for the taxpayer in question by reason of the delay". The second reason was that to invalidate the decision "would not only deprive the Government of revenue, it would also be unfair to other taxpayers who need to shoulder the burden of Government expenditure"[205] (a more dubious reason, as we shall presently suggest).

5-066

In a number of more recent cases our highest courts have displayed flexibility in the face of breaches of imperative language. The Court of Appeal considered the consequence of the Secretary of State failing to use a prescribed form for applying for leave from the Special Adjudicator to the Immigration Appeals Tribunal.[206] The only difference between the form used and the prescribed form was the absence of a declaration of truth. Lord Woolf, for the Court, adopted the dictum of Lord

5-067

---

[202] Town and Country Planning Act 1990 s.174(2) empowering the Secretary of State on an appeal against an enforcement notice to correct immaterial informalities, defects and errors. For the scope of this amending power, see *Miller-Mead v Minister of Housing and Local Government* [1963] 2 Q.B. 196; *R. v Endersby Properties Ltd* (1976) 32 P. & C.R. 399 (distinguishing *East Riding CC v Park Estate (Bridlington) Ltd* [1957] A.C. 223); *Graddage v Haringey LBC* [1975] 1 W.L.R. 241 (omission of official's signature invalidated notice demanding payment for work done to make houses fit for human habitation—an example of an application of the strict approach to formal irregularities).

[203] See, e.g. Town and Country Planning Act 1990 s.288(1). For an illustration of non-compliance with minor formal statutory requirements being held not to have caused substantial prejudice, see *Gordondale Investments Ltd v Secretary of State for the Environment* (1971) 70 L.G.R. 15; cf. *McCowan v Secretary of State for Scotland*, 1972 S.L.T. 163 (property-owner deprived of opportunity to object to compulsory purchase order through failure to serve notice on him).

[204] *Wang v The Commissioner of Inland Revenue* [1994] 1 W.L.R. 1286.

[205] cf. *London & Clydeside Estates* [1980] 1 W.L.R. 182 at 195 (Lord Fraser): "the validity of the certificate is not in my opinion dependent on whether the appellants were actually prejudiced by it or not". See also: *Devan Nair v Yong Kuan Teik* [1967] 2 A.C. 31; *James v Minister of Housing and Local Government* [1966] 1 W.L.R. 135, CA; *R. v Inspector of Taxes Ex p. Clarke* [1974] Q.B. 220; cf. *R. v Liverpool City Council Ex p. Liverpool Taxi Fleet Operators' Association* [1975] 1 W.L.R. 701 at 706 (requirement to state reasons directory only, but decision could be set aside if applicant showed that he had been thereby prejudiced); *R. v Fairford Justices Ex p. Brewster* [1976] Q.B. 600 (magistrates may lose jurisdiction by a delay in issuing a summons that prejudices the accused, despite the absence of a statutory time limitation).

[206] *R. v Immigration Appeal Tribunal Ex p. Jeyeanthan* [2000] 1 W.L.R. 354; also *Credit Suisse v Allerdale BC* [1997] Q.B. 306. For an example of the application of *Jeyeanthan*, see *R. (on the application of London Borough of Waltham Forest) v Waltham Forest Magistrates' Court* [2008] EWHC 3579 (Admin): the requirement under the Non Domestic Rating (Collection and Enforcement) (Local Lists) Regulations 1989 (SI 1058/1989) reg.5(1) that a demand for business rates "shall be served as soon as practicable" was a directory rather than a mandatory requirement. It was held that the requirement was satisfied by substantial compliance.

Hailsham in *London & Clydesdale Estates*.[207] Eschewing a rigid adherence to the language of "mandatory" and "directory" (although it was to be regarded as a "first step"),[208] it was held that the matter should be judged upon the overall intent of the legislation, and the interests of justice. In particular, if there had been "substantial compliance" with the requirement, and if the irregularity was capable of being waived, then whether the non-compliance could be justified depended upon the consequences of non-compliance which, in the circumstances of that case, did not materially prejudice the appellants.

5-068   A similar approach was taken by the Privy Council in *Charles*,[209] where the Board upheld a failure to observe time limits laid down by regulations dealing with discipline in the public service in Trinidad and Tobago. In *Attorney General's Reference (No.3 of 1999)*,[210] the House of Lords considered a breach of a duty to destroy the fingerprints and DNA samples of a defendant cleared of an offence. The DNA samples then led to his subsequent conviction for rape. Again the mandatory/directory distinction was ignored in favour of a test based upon the intent of Parliament and the consequence of non-compliance. A unanimous House held that the prosecution was valid[211] and this approach was repeated in *R. v Soneji* where the House of Lords, again unanimously, refused to quash two confiscation orders despite a clear defect in the procedure,[212] Lord Steyn considering that the mandatory/directory distinction had "outlived its usefulness".[213] Many other examples of the approach can be found.[214] Circumstances remain, however, were the courts will insist on compliance with statutory requirements.[215]

5-069   A similar approach has been adopted in the courts of Australia, New Zealand and

---

[207] *London and Clydeside Estates v Aberdeen DC* [1980] 1 W.L.R. 182.

[208] *R. v Immigration Appeal Tribunal Ex p. Jeyeanthan* [2000] 1 W.L.R. 354 at [16].

[209] *Charles v Judicial and Legal Services Commission* [2002] UKPC 34; [2003] 1 L.R.C. 422.

[210] *Attorney General's Reference (No.3 of 1999)* [2000] UKHL 71; [2001] 2 A.C. 91.

[211] *Attorney General's Reference (No.3 of 1999)* [2000] UKHL 71; [2001] 2 A.C. 91, Lord Steyn (at 117–118); Lord Cooke (at 120–121); Lord Clyde (at 121).

[212] *R. v Soneji* [2005] UKHL 49; [2006] 1 A.C. 340 (the statute provided that the orders could be postponed only where there were established exceptional circumstances. Since these had not been established, the CA had held that the postponement rendered the orders invalid). The case was the subject of a judgment of the European Court of Human Rights as *Bullen v United Kingdom* (3383/06) [2009] Lloyd's Rep. F.C. 210 (held that the periods of delay in the proceedings for confiscation of assets were in breach of the reasonable time under EHCR art.6).

[213] At [23].

[214] See, e.g. *R. (on the application of Dulai) v Chelmsford Magistrates' Court* [2012] EWHC 1055 (Admin); [2013] 1 W.L.R. 220 (non-compliance with procedure for issuing notice of good seized by food authority did not necessarily render seizure unlawful); *R. (on the application of Garland) v Secretary of State for Justice* [2011] EWCA Civ 1335; [2012] 1 W.L.R. 1879 (Parliament did not intend non-compliance with Prison Rules on time limit within which disciplinary charges to be laid, however minimal and devoid of prejudicial effect, should render subsequent proceedings invalid); *R. (Herron and another) v Parking Adjudicator* [2011] EWCA Civ 905; [2012] P.T.S.R. 1257 (test for invalidity of controlled parking zone was not whether signage irregularities were trivial but whether there was substantial compliance with the statutory definition); *R. (on the application of JJB Sports Plc) v Telford and Wrekin BC* [2008] EWHC 2870 (Admin); [2009] R.A. 33 (local authority not prevented by reason of serving the demand notice 56 days late from proceeding to seek a liability order enforcing payment of business rates); *R. (on the application of P) v Haringey LBC* [2008] EWHC 2357 (Admin); [2009] E.L.R. 49 (school governors in a decision letter had specified the wrong date for lodging an appeal against their determination that a pupil should be permanently excluded; applying a flexible approach, the court held that the notice was not for that reason invalid but the local authority had acted unlawfully in not recognising that the appeal had indeed been lodged on the due date—an email had arrived after school closing time but before midnight on that day); *R. (on the application of Winchester College) v Hampshire CC* [2008] EWCA Civ 431; [2009] 1 W.L.R. 138.

[215] See, e.g. *R. (on the application of Bhatti) v Croydon Magistrates' Court* [2010] EWHC 522 (Admin); [2011] 1 W.L.R. 948 (non-compliance with Police and Criminal Evidence Act 1984 requirements

Canada. The Australian High Court has criticised the "elusive distinction between directory and mandatory" as well as the division of directory acts into those which have substantially been complied with and those which have not. The Court considers the test for determining the issue of validity is "to ask whether it was a purpose of the legislation that an act done in breach of the provision should be invalid".[216] In New Zealand, Cooke J said that whether non-compliance with a procedural requirement is fatal depends upon "its place in the scheme of the Act or regulations and the degree and seriousness of the non-compliance".[217] In the recent case of *Tannadyce Investments Ltd v Commissioner of Inland Revenue*, the NZ Supreme Court said that "the correct modern approach to procedural requirements is for the courts to focus not on literal classification but rather on what should be the legal consequence of non-compliance with a statutory or regulatory provision".[218] In Canada too, the mandatory/directory distinction has been departed from and the question asked: "would it be seriously inconvenient to regard the performance of some statutory direction as an imperative?"[219] In Ireland, it has been observed that the courts tend to use the traditional language of mandatory/directory but in practice, examine the circumstances of the case to determine whether disregard of procedural requirements in the particular context has caused real prejudice.[220]

The breakdown of inappropriate technical distinctions is obviously to be applauded, as is the need to concentrate upon legislative purpose and the requirements of justice, but there is danger in the courts readily arrogating to themselves the power to dispense with procedural or other duties. In the mind of the public, law-breaking should not be condoned, especially by courts of law. On the other hand, excessive legalism serves no useful purpose. In the result, the circumstances in which a flawed decision should be held valid should be narrowly drawn. The criteria suggested by Tipping J in *Charles* would seem acceptable: endorsing the validity of a breach of a time limit, he noted that "in the present case the delays were in good faith, they were not lengthy and they were entirely understandable. The appellant suffered no material prejudice; no fair trial considerations were or could have been raised, and no fundamental human rights are in issue".[221]

5-070

Comparative perspectives

Evans JA approached the criteria from a different perspective in the Canadian Federal Court of Appeal: "the more serious the public inconvenience and injustice likely to be caused by invalidating the resulting administrative action, including frustrating the purposes of the legislation, public expense and hardship to third parties, the less likely it is that a court will conclude that legislative intent is best implemented by a declaration of invalidity".[222] This statement is helpful except perhaps in the value it places upon "inconvenience" and "expense" as a factor to

5-071

---

in making copies of warrant rendered entry, search and seizure unlawful and material had to be returned); *R. (on the application of E (Russia)) v Secretary of State for the Home Department* [2012] EWCA Civ 357; [2012] 1 W.L.R. 3198 (notice of immigration decision that erroneously stated that right of appeal may be exercised only from outside the UK was invalid).

[216] *Project Blue Sky Inc v Australian Broadcasting Authority* (1998) 194 C.L.R. 355 at 390.
[217] *New Zealand Institute of Agricultural Science Inc v Ellesmere County* [1976] 1 N.Z.L.R. 630 at 636.
[218] *Tannadyce Investments Ltd v Commissioner of Inland Revenue* [2011] NZSC 158; [2012] 2 N.Z.L.R. 153 at [74].
[219] *British Columbia (Attorney General) v Canada (Attorney General): An Act respecting the Vancouver Island Railway (Re)* [1994] 2 S.C.R. 41 (Iacobucci J).
[220] G. Hogan and D.G. Morgan, *Administrative Law in Ireland*, 4th edn (2010) at paras 11–26–11–30.
[221] *Charles v Judicial and Legal Services Commis* [2002] UKPC 34; [2003] 1 L.R.C. 422 at [12].
[222] *Society Promoting Environmental Conservation v Candada (Attorney General)* (2003) 228 D.L.R.

be taken into account on the question of validity. As we noted,[223] these utilitarian considerations were also raised by Lord Slynn in the Privy Council to justify the validity of a breach of a time limit in *Wang*.[224] Is administrative inconvenience a proper reason for rebutting the presumption that a decision which violates a statutory provision is unlawful? Administrative inconvenience is an accepted criterion in relation to remedies provided by the courts in judicial review. For example, where a series of commercial transactions have been undertaken in reliance upon the impugned decision the court may, in its discretion, fail to quash that decision in view of the administrative chaos that would result from such a remedy.[225] Judicial discretion is employed here to balance fairness to the individual against the general public interest. The task, however, of deciding the force of a statutory provision does not involve judicial discretion. It involves the faithful construction of the objects and purposes of an Act of Parliament in the context of the particular decision. Although aspects of public policy may play a part in this exercise,[226] it would be wrong of the courts to impute any general implication that Parliament may intend administrative inconvenience, or indeed expense,[227] to excuse in advance the violation of its statutes. Such an implication invites careless administration and assumes that the legislature would too easily excuse a breach of its statutes.

Marginal failures by individuals to comply with requirements

5-072   So far, discussion has focused on whether a public body has complied with statutory requirements and, if not, what ought to be the consequences of failure to do so. In some disputes, the courts have considered the reverse position, where an individual has marginally failed to meet requirements set out in legislation or published policy but nevertheless seeks the benefit of a decision. In some cases, the failure is appropriately characterised as de minimis: the Court of Appeal has held that "if a departure from a rule is truly de minimis, the rule is considered to have been complied with".[228] A different situation is the "near miss", where the requirement has not been complied with but it is argued, by the individual, that discretion should be exercised in their favour. An example of a "near miss" would be failure to satisfy the requirement of five years' lawful residence as a work permit holder, by two months. The courts have been emphatic in rejecting the idea that there is a "near miss" principle favouring the individual.[229]

(4th) 693 at 710. The Australian High Court took the same approach in *Project Blue Sky Inc v Australian Broadcasting Authority* (1998) 194 C.L.R. 355 at 392. It is a consequence of the same court's refusal to treat all errors of law as having the capacity to invalidate the outcome. Australia maintains a distinction between errors of law that are jurisdictional and those that are not: *Kirk v Industrial Court of New South Wales* (2010) 239 C.L.R. 531 at 571–573.

[223] See 5-061.

[224] *Wang v The Commissioner of Inland Revenue* [1994] 1.W.L.R. 1286. See also the celebrated New Zealand case where the Governor-General had issued his warrant for the holding of a general election later than the date specified by statute. A challenge directed against the validity of the election failed on the ground that a contrary decision would have had the catastrophic effect of nullifying a number of Acts of Parliament, together with all actions already taken under them: *Simpson v Attorney General* [1955] N.Z.L.R. 271. cf. *Transport Ministry v Hamill* [1973] 2 N.Z.L.R. 663.

[225] See 18-047.

[226] See 5-068.

[227] On financial considerations, see 5-134.

[228] *Miah v Secretary of State for the Home Department* [2012] EWCA Civ 261; [2013] Q.B. 35.

[229] See, e.g *Miah v Secretary of State for the Home Department* [2012] EWCA Civ 261; [2013] Q.B. 35 (two months short of five year requirement; not following *Pankina v Secretary of State for the Home Department* [2010] EWCA Civ 719; [2011] Q.B. 376); *Mongoto v Secretary of State for the Home Department* [2005] EWCA Civ 751 (appellant did not meet Home Office "family conces-

Duties owed to the public generally

In some cases where what appears to be a clear (mandatory) duty is imposed upon an authority, the courts have held that is not directly enforceable by any individual.[230] Such a duty seeks to achieve more an aspiration than an obligation. The authority is simply required to "do its best"[231] and failure to achieve the duty does not result in illegality. Examples include:

5-073

- Education Act 1996 s.14 ("A local authority shall secure that sufficient schools for providing—(a) primary education, and (b) education that is secondary education ... are available for their area ...").[232]
- National Assistance Act 1948 s.21 ("a local authority may with the approval of the Secretary of State, and to such extent as he may direct shall, make arrangements for providing—(a) residential accommodation for persons who by reason of age, illness, disability or any other circumstances are in need of care and attention which is not otherwise available to them").
- Children Act 1989 s.17 ("It shall be the general duty of every local authority (in addition to the other duties imposed on them by this Part)—(a) to safeguard and promote the welfare of children within their area who are in need; and (b) so far as is consistent with that duty, to promote the upbringing of such children by their families, by providing a range and level of services appropriate to those children's needs".
- National Health Service Act 2006 s.1 ("The Secretary of State must continue the promotion in England of a comprehensive health service ...").[233]
- Criminal Justice and Court Services Act 2000 s.12 ("(1) In respect of family proceedings in which the welfare of children is or may be in question, it is a function of the [Children and Family Court Advisory and Support] Service to—... (c) make provision for the children to be represented in such proceedings" and "(2) The Service must also make provision for the performance of any functions conferred on officers of the Service by virtue of this Act or any other enactment (whether or not they are exercisable for the purposes of the functions conferred on the Service by subsection (1))").[234]

Courts allow great flexibility to authorities to achieve this kind of duty, as long

5-074

---

sion" policy criteria); *R. (on the application of Hafeez) v Secretary of State for the Home Department* [2014] EWHC 1342 (Admin) (the fact that H's leave to remain in the United Kingdom expired in November 2011 and his university course finished in January 2012 was not a "near miss" justifying the grant of leave; the absence of a near-miss principle in such cases was well established).

[230] C. Callaghan, "What is a Target Duty?" [2000] J.R. 184; L. Clements, *Community Care and the Law* (2004), pp.11–13; J. King, "The Justiciability of Resource Allocation" (2007) 70 M.L.R. 197, 214–216.

[231] *R. v Islington LBC Ex p. Rixon* [1997] E.L.R. 66 at 69; *R. v Radio Authority Ex p. Bull* [1998] Q.B. 294 at 309; *Friends of the Earth v Secretary of State for Business Enterprise and Regulatory Reform* [2009] EWCA Civ 810 at [20] (an obligation to implement a strategy to ensure that "as far as reasonably practicable persons do not live in fuel poverty" was an obligation "correctly described in terms of effort or endeavour").

[232] *R. v Inner London Education Authority Ex p. Ali* (1990) 2 Admin. L.R. 822, such a duty was called a "target duty" by Woolf LJ.

[233] *R. (on the application of YA) v Secretary of State for Health* [2009] EWCA Civ 225 at [69]. See also *R. (A) v Secretary of State for Health (Alliance for Choice and others intervening)* [2017] UKSC 1 at [9]. Note however the dissenting remarks of Lord Kerr, which suggest that the duty in s.1 is capable of being enforced by individuals: [78]–[82].

[234] *R. (on the application of R (Minors) v Children and Family Court Support Service* [2012] EWCA Civ 853; [2013] 1 W.L.R. 163.

as they are not "outside the tolerance" of the statutory provision.[235] And since these duties normally require the decision to allocate scarce resources among competing needs, the courts will not interfere readily,[236] although a target duty may "crystallise" into an enforceable duty in certain circumstances.[237] At the other extreme is what has been called a "proactive duty".[238]

5-075 While it is clear that not all duties phrased in general terms are intended to be readily enforceable, there is a danger that general duties will devalue the notion of a duty and permit Parliament to reassure the public with empty gestures and the executive to sit back and take no further notice.[239] Duties incorporated in a statute ought not to be treated the way some constitutions (such as the Indian and Irish) treat certain rights (normally the socio-economic rights such as the right to "an adequate means of livelihood").[240] Unlike the fundamental rights enumerated in the Constitution, they are not enforceable. They, however, "guide the Court in determining crucial questions on which the validity of an important enactment may be hinged".[241] Where the statutory discretion relates to institutional appointments, failure to give weightage to factors that affect institutional integrity would make the recommendation *non est* and amenable to judicial review.[242]

5-076 There will of course be cases where limited resources might (depending on the scheme) excuse some degree of implementation. However, the courts ought to examine each case in its context and rigorously apply the standards of public law.[243] They ought not therefore permit the decision-maker simply to sleep on the target duty and fail to put his mind to its implementation[244]; or fail to take relevant

---

[235] *R. v Inner London Education Authority Ex p. Ali* (1990) 2 Admin. L.R. 822; *R. (on the application of Ahmad) v Newham LBC* [2009] UKHL 14; (2009) 153(9) S.J.L.B. 29 at [13] (Baroness Hale of Richmond: "there is a fundamental difference in public law between a duty to provide benefits or services for a particular individual and a general or target duty which is owed to a whole population").

[236] On resource allocation see 1-042 and 5-134.

[237] See, e.g. *R. (on the application of G) v Barnet LBC* [2003] UKHL 57; [2004] 2 A.C. 208, where Lord Hope (for the majority) at [80] held that a target duty to promote the welfare of children in need under Children Act 1989 s.17(1) was concerned with general principles and not designed to confer rights upon individuals. Nor could it easily crystallise in into an enforceable duty, [88]. Note however, *R. (on the application of West) v Rhondda Cynon Taff CBC* [2014] EWHC 2134 (Admin); [2015] A.C.D. 9, where a breach of duty was found when a local authority failed to give regard to its duties under s.17(1) and s.18 (provision of day care for children in need) of the 1989 Act; similar breaches were found in respect of the local authority's duties under s.118 of the School Standards and Framework Act 1998 (duty to secure nursery education) and s.22 of the Childcare Act 2006 (duty to secure sufficient childcare for working parents).

[238] Such duty requires an authority under a duty, e.g. to reassess periodically the chronically sick and disabled, even in the absence of a request to do so. *R. v Bexley LBC Ex p. B* (2000) 3 C.C.L.R. 15 at 22; *R. v Gloucester CC Ex p. RADAR* (1998) 1 C.C.L.R. 476 (duty to reassess needs for community care requires more than a letter inviting a request for an assessment).

[239] In this context, note the concluding words of criticism in *R. (on the application of R (Minors)) v Children and Family Court Support Service* [2011] EWHC 1774 (Admin); [2012] 1 W.L.R. 811 at [100] ("It is surely a serious question for government and Parliament whether the state of affairs revealed, and not for the first time, by these cases can continue to be tolerated").

[240] Constitution of India art.39(a).

[241] *Society for Unaided Private Schools of Rajasthan v Union of India* (2012) 6 S.C.C. 1 at 32.

[242] *Centre for PIL v Union of India* (2011) 4 S.C.C. 1 at 16, 21, 24, 25.

[243] See, e.g. the South African case *Minister of Works v Kyalami Ridge Environmental Assoc* 2001 (3) S.A. 1151, CC where it was held that it was a constitutional duty to provide relief to victims of natural disasters even in the absence of authorising legislation. However, the majority decision in the recent case of *Constitutional Court Doctors for Life International v Speaker of the National Assembly* 2006 (6) S.A. 416, CC suggests that the court will defer to the legislature's decision on how to meet a duty.

[244] *R. v Secretary of State for the Home Department Ex p. Fire Brigades Union* [1995] 2 A.C. 513

considerations into account, or to take irrelevant considerations into account.[245] Nor should the courts excuse the pursuit of the purpose of the relevant scheme, or the cogent justification of its non-implementation.[246] However, this approach does not mean that non observance of a requirement will mean that the failure results inevitably in a non-conforming action being necessarily void. This is more likely to be true in circumstances where the consequences of the failure to comply with the requirement does not cause injustice, or where any injustice can be remedied by other means. This approach was followed by the Northern Ireland Court of Appeal in relation to a challenge to the minister for failing to issue advice or guidance to women and clinicians on the availability of termination of pregnancy services (*Family Planning Association of Northern Ireland v The Minister for Health, Social Services and Public Safety*.[247] The relevant Order—the Health and Personal Social Services Order (Northern Ireland) 1972—provided a general duty to provide "integrated health services" and "personal social services designed to promote the social welfare of the people and to secure effective co-ordination of Health and Personal Social Services". At first instance these provisions were held by Kerr J to be mere target duties with which the court could not interfere, but Nicholson LJ in the Court of Appeal held that, although there was a degree of tolerance and elasticity with which the courts should be slow to intervene, the courts would be well within their competence to indicate to the public body that they should consider what steps they should take to fulfil the target duty, even though they would not necessarily order the body concerned to perform a specific act.

Making good unlawfulness

Where a public body has failed in the past to fulfil a statutory duty, the question may arise as to what if any duty it has to make things right. The Court of Appeal has held that "There is no general rule that, wherever it has acted unlawfully, a local authority must undo its past errors to the fullest extent that it can"—rather it was a matter of discretion depending all the circumstances, including countervailing considerations of public interest.[248]   **5-077**

Duties to "have regard to" the desirability of something

Statutes may place on a public body a duty "to have regard" to some desirable goal. For example, local authorities making agreements and orders relating to public footpaths must "have due regard to—(a) the needs of agriculture and forestry, and (b) the desirability of conserving flora, fauna and geological and physiographical   **5-078**

(requiring the minister to implement an ex gratia scheme for compensating victims of crime).

[245] On the notion of relevancy, see 5-120.

[246] For example, the enforcement of the right to housing (South African Constitution s.26) on the basis of familiar public law principles in *Government of South Africa v Grootboom* 2001 (1) S.A. 46, CC. On justification, see 11-098 and following.

[247] *Family Planning Association of Northern Ireland v The Minister for Health, Social Services and Public Safety* [2004] NICA 37.

[248] See *R. (on the application of GE (Eritrea)) v Secretary of State for the Home Department* [2014] EWCA Civ 1490; [2015] 1 W.L.R. 4123: GE, an asylum seeker, claimed to be 16½ years old but the local authority determined her to be an adult and consequently performed none of the duties that would have arisen under the Children Act 1989. A court subsequently held that GE had been a child at the relevant time. The issue before the CA was whether GE should be treated as a "former relevant child" with continuing rights to support. The majority held that it was not open to the court to "deem" accommodation to have been provided to GE so bringing her within the scope of the statutory definition.

features".[249] The Lord Chancellor is to "have regard to the need for the judiciary to have the support necessary for them to exercise their functions".[250] As we have noted, the Equality Act 2010 s.149 frames the public sector equality duty thus: a "public authority must, in the exercise of its functions, have due regard to the need to—(a) eliminate discrimination, harassment, victimisation and any other conduct that is prohibited by or under this Act; (b) advance equality of opportunity between persons who share a relevant protected characteristic; foster good relations between persons who share a relevant protected characteristic and persons who do not share it".[251]

5-079   Duties such as these are described as "mandatory" but not imposing "a duty to achieve results".[252] In challenges to alleged failures to fulfil "to have regard to" duties, the courts have laid down guidelines as to what is expected of a public body.[253] The required approach is contextual: "'Due regard' is the 'regard that is appropriate in all the circumstances'".[254] It is not sufficient for the public body to show merely that it made its decision with "a general awareness of the duty"; a "substantial, rigorous and open-minded approach" is required.[255] The test whether a decision-maker has had due regard is a test of the substance of the matter, not of mere form or box-ticking, and the duty must be performed with "vigour and an open mind".[256] The duty requires a "conscious directing of the mind to the obligations".[257] "Due regard" must be given "before and at the time that a particular policy that will or might affect disabled people is being considered by the public authority in

---

249 Highways Act 1980 s.29.
250 Constitutional Reform Act 2005 s.3.
251 For a summary of the correct approach to be taken to the public sector equality duty, see *R. (on the application of Bracking) v Secretary of State for Work and Pensions* [2013] EWCA Civ 1345; [2014] Eq. L.R. 60 at [25] (McCombe LJ), followed in *R. (on the application of MA) v Secretary of State for Work and Pensions* [2014] EWCA Civ 13; [2014] P.T.S.R. 584. In *R. (on the application of Cushnie) v Secretary of State for Health* [2014] EWHC 3626; [2015] P.T.S.R. 384 at [114] Singh J drew an analogy between the PSED and "the well known principle of administrative law that a public authority must have regard to all relevant considerations. If it fails to do so, it will breach that duty and in principle that failure in its decision-making process will vitiate the resulting decision. The failure may be an 'innocent' one. Nevertheless, the fact that the decision-maker has not had regard to a relevant consideration is a breach of one of the most basic requirements of administrative law". In *R. (West Berkshire DC) v Secretary of State for Communities and Local Government* [2016] EWCA Civ 441; [2016] 1 W.L.R. 3923, the court accepted an equality statement that "takes a relatively broad brush approach" and emphasised that "[t]he requirement to pay due regard to equally impact under s.149 is just that. It does not require a precise mathematical exercise to be carried out in relation to particular affected groups or, for example, urban areas as opposed to rural areas" (at [83]).
252 *R. (on the application of Brown) v Secretary of State for Work and Pensions (Equality and Human Rights Commission intervening)* [2008] EWHC 3158 (Admin); [2009] P.T.S.R. 1506 at [80]–[82].
253 For a helpful summary, see *R. (on the application of JM and NT) v Isle of Wight Council* [2011] EWHC 2911 (Admin) [96]–[107].
254 *R. (on the application of Baker) v Secretary of State for Communities and Local Government (Equality and Human Rights Commission intervening)*[2008] EWCA Civ 141; [2009] P.T.S.R. 809 at [31].
255 *R. (on the application of Boyejo) v Barnet LBC* [2009] EWHC 3261 (Admin); (2010) 13 C.C.L.R. 72 at [58], [59] and [63].
256 *R. (on the application of Domb) v Hammersmith and Fulham LBC* [2009] EWCA Civ 941; [2009] L.G.R. 843. In *R. (Logan) v Havering LBC* [2015] EWHC 3193 (Admin); [2016] P.T.S.R. 603, there was a lack of due regard: "There must be conscientious consideration of the impact of the proposals on relevant groups, whether by diligent reading of the EIA or some other evidence based assessment"; on the facts, there was "insufficient evidence to indicate that the decision-makers [each member of the full council] had accessed the EIA attached to the officers' report or had understood the importance of reading it in order to discharge their statutory obligation. It was not sufficient to assume that they could have done so and therefore would have done so" (at [53]).
257 *R. (on the application of Meany) v Harlow DC* [2009] EWHC 559 (Admin) at [74]; approved in *R. (on the application of Bailey) v Brent LBC* [2011] EWCA Civ 1586.

question".[258] Due regard to the duty must be an "essential preliminary" to any important policy decision, not a "rearguard action following a concluded decision".[259] Consideration of the duty must be an "integral part of the formation of a proposed policy, not justification for its adoption".[260] The weight to be given to the countervailing factors is a matter for the public authority rather than the court unless the assessment is unreasonable or irrational.[261] But "the question of whether 'due regard' has been paid is for the court itself to review—the court should not merely consider whether there was no regard to the duty at all, or whether the decision was *Wednesbury* unreasonable".[262] The concept of "due regard" requires the court to ensure that there has been a proper and conscientious focus on the statutory criteria, "but if that is done, the court cannot interfere with the decision simply because it would have given greater weight to the equality implications of the decision than did the decision maker".[263]

Obligations to "have regard to" may also be created by ministerial guidance: for example, the Secretary of State issued a circular to local authorities under the Local Authority Social Services Act 1970 s.7(1) in which it was said that "councils should have due regard to the actual costs of providing care and other local factors" in setting rates they would pay providers of residential accommodation and care for people for whom the local authorities were responsible. Duties such as this, in a circular or other non-statutory guidance, are not to be equated with statutory duties to "have regard to" and the courts will not "read across" to apply the detailed, structured approach to decision-making developed in relation to the statutory duties.[264]

5-080

Strategic outcome duties

Another sort of duty imposes an obligation to achieve a broad but measurable and very specific strategic outcome in relation to complex problems.[265] The Climate Change Act 2008 s.1(1) describes a "target", providing that "It is the duty of the Secretary of State to ensure that the net UK carbon account for the year 2050 is at least 80% lower than the 1990 baseline".[266] The Child Poverty Act 2010 ss.1–6 provide specific targets for the reduction of child poverty by 1 April 2020.[267]

5-081

Many of the factors contributing to the achievement or failure to achieve the target are likely to be outside the direct control of the minister. These strategic target

5-082

---

[258] R. (on the application of Brown) v Secretary of State for Work and Pensions and another (Equality and Human Rights Commission intervening) [2008] EWHC 3158 (Admin); [2009] P.T.S.R. 1506 at [91].

[259] R. (on the application of BAPIO Action Ltd) v Secretary of State for the Home Department [2007] EWCA Civ 1139 at [3].

[260] R. (on the application of Kaur and others) v Ealing LBC [2008] EWHC 2062 (Admin) at [24].

[261] R. (on the application of Baker) v Secretary of State for Communities and Local Government [2008] EWCA Civ 141; [2009] P.T.S.R. 809 at [31]; R. (on the application of Brown) v Secretary of State for Work and Pensions (Equality and Human Rights Commission intervening) [2008] EWHC 3158 (Admin); [2009] P.T.S.R. 1506 at [82].

[262] R. (on the application of JM and NT) v Isle of Wight Council [2011] EWHC 2911 (Admin) at [104].

[263] R. (on the application of Hurley and Moore) v Secretary of State for Business Innovation & Skills [2012] EWHC 201 (Admin); [2012] H.R.L.R. 13 at [78].

[264] R. (on the application of Members of the Committee of Care North East Northumberland) v Northumberland CC [2013] EWCA Civ 1740; [2014] P.T.S.R. 758.

[265] See further C. Reid, "A new sort of duty? The significance of 'outcome duties' in the Climate Change and Child Poverty Acts" [2012] P.L.

[266] See also Climate Change (Scotland) Act 2009 for a similar duty on the Scottish Ministers.

[267] For a progress report, see Department for Work and Pensions, Department for Education, *Child Poverty in the UK: the report on the 2010 target* (2012).

duties, notably devoid of qualification, differ from others, such as the duty in the Warm Homes and Energy Conservation Act 2000 s.2 (for the Secretary of State to prepare and publish a strategy setting out policies for reducing fuel poverty in England "as far as reasonably practicable"—described by the Court of Appeal as a duty framed in terms of effort or endeavour rather than a guarantee of success).[268] The authors of the Westlaw annotation to the Climate Change Act 2008 s.1 assert that the duty in that section (see above) "must be read as a duty to take reasonable steps".[269] It is not self-evident that this is correct: in construing the scope and content of the duty the court will be driven by what the purpose intended by Parliament is, as revealed in the words of the enactment. Had Parliament wanted to create a duty to take reasonable steps, it could have done so expressly. Had Parliament wanted to exclude or reduce the scope for judicial review challenge, it could have done so expressly.[270] The better view is that a court called upon to review whether a hard-edged strategic outcome duty has been fulfilled should do so on the basis of evidence; the answer is either yes or no.

Public policy considerations

5-083
A related question to that of administrative inconvenience is the extent to which public policy might be employed to rebut the presumption that a statutory provision is mandatory. Public policy is employed here as the public law equivalent of private law equitable principles, such as that which states that no person may benefit from his own wrong. Thus the courts will presume that Parliament did not intend to imperil the welfare of the state or its inhabitants.

5-084
This question arose in the case of *R. v Registrar General Ex p. Smith*.[271] The appellant was detained in a secure mental hospital following his conviction for murder and the manslaughter of a cellmate during a psychotic bout under a belief that he was killing his adoptive mother. He had no knowledge of his natural mother's identity and applied under s.51 of the Adoption Act 1976 to the Registrar General for a copy of his birth certificate. The application was refused on the ground that the Registrar General, after receiving medical advice, believed that Smith's natural mother might be in danger if he were ever released and her identity known to him. Under the statute the duty of the Registrar General to supply the information was in terms absolute.[272] Nevertheless, the Court of Appeal held that this duty may be vitiated by public policy. In this case the public policy involved the prevention of

---

[268] *R. (on the application of Friends of the Earth) v Secretary of State for Energy and Climate Change (formerly Secretary of State for Business, Enterprise and Regulator reform and another)* [2009] EWCA Civ 810; [2010] P.T.S.R. 635 at [20] ("Without proffering authoritative interpretations of legislation which is not in issue in the present case, one can at least observe that sometimes the drafting is more hard-edged than it is in the 2000 Act. It seems to me that it behoves a court to proceed with caution so as to ensure that softer obligations are not construed in a more prescriptive manner than their language and context require").

[269] *http://login.westlaw.co.uk/*.

[270] See, e.g. Fiscal Responsibility Act 2010 s.4 (now repealed), which stipulated that "The only means of securing accountability in relation to" duties created by the Act that the Treasury must ensure that in 2011–16, public sector net borrowing expressed as a percentage of GPD is less than it was for the preceding financial year "is that established by the provision made by or under s.3 for the making of progress reports and reports as to compliance" to Parliament.

[271] *R. v Registrar General Ex p. Smith* [1991] 2 Q.B. 393; A. Le Sueur, "Public Policies and the Adoption Act" [1991] P.L. 326.

[272] "... the Registrar-General shall on an application made in the prescribed manner by an adopted person a record of whose birth is kept by the Registrar-General and who has attained the age of 18 years supply to that person on payment of the prescribed fee (if any) such information as is necessary to enable that person to obtain a certified copy of the record of his birth".

crime. Parliament is thus presumed not to have intended that a statutory duty should be enforced either to reward crime in the past,[273] or to promote serious crime in the future.[274] Nor should the duty be enforced if there is "a significant risk"[275] or "current and justified apprehension" that to do so would facilitate "crime resulting in danger to life".[276]

In *Smith* it was made clear that the decision of the Court of Appeal was "in no way connected with the discretion of the court to refuse relief in judicial review cases".[277] Nor was the language of a directory (as opposed to a mandatory) statutory provision employed. In effect, the court held that a mandatory provision may simply be vitiated by the dictates of public policy[278] and rightly emphasised that such a result is founded upon the interpretation of statutory purpose, rather than upon any strained distinction between mandatory and directory statutory provisions. Today, under the terms of the Human Rights Act 1998, Convention rights might have been specifically invoked in a such a case, as public policy is an "unruly horse"[279] which must be ridden with care, as policy is within the proper realm of the legislature and not the courts. Such care was taken in a subsequent case where the Court of Appeal would not employ public policy to enable the Registrar General to refuse to provide a marriage certificate to a prisoner to enable him to marry his long-term girlfriend on the ground that that girlfriend would no longer be a compellable witness at the prisoner's forthcoming murder trial.[280]

5-085

Discretionary power in the context of law enforcement

When a public officer has discretion to prosecute an unlawful act, should that power be interpreted to be mandatory rather than directory? The rule of law suggests the law ought to be enforced and the power therefore interpreted as mandatory rather than directory. On the other hand, there are many reasons why prosecutors should be able to engage in "selective enforcement", in the public interest. The reasons include the fact that the authority may only possess limited resources and

5-086

---

273 See, e.g. *Welwyin Hatfield BC v Secretary of State for Communities and Local Government* [2011] UKSC 15; [2011] 2 A.C. 304 (dwelling house constructed within a barn on greenbelt land and lived in undetected for four years).

274 *R. v National Insurance Commissioner Ex p. Connor* [1981] Q.B. 758 (applicant unable to recover the widow's allowance under the Social Security Act 1975 because she had unlawfully killed her husband); *R. v Secretary of State for the Home Department Ex p. Puttick* [1981] Q.B. 767 (applicant denied the benefit of registration of the United Kingdom and Colonies under the British Nationality Act 1948 although she was lawfully married to a citizen, because she had committed perjury and forgery in the course of procuring the marriage). For a summary of the private law principle that the courts will not enforce a contract if to do so would enable the plaintiff to benefit from his own crime see *Euro-Diam Ltd v Bathhurst* [1990] 1 Q.B. 1 at 35 (Kerr LJ).

275 Staughton and McCowan LJJ.

276 McCowan LJ.

277 Staughton LJ.

278 For earlier cases where public policy has been engaged, see *Nagle v Feilden* [1966] 2 Q.B. 633 (Jockey Club's refusal of horse trainer's licence to woman held against public policy); *Edwards v SOGAT* [1971] Ch. 354 (unfair discrimination in withdrawal of collective bargaining rights).

279 *Enderby Town Football Club v Football Association* [1971] Ch. 591 (Lord Denning MR: "I know that over 300 years ago Hobart CJ said that "Public policy is an unruly horse". It has often been repeated since. So unruly is the horse, it is said [Burrough J in *Richardson v Mellish* (1824) 2 Bing 229 at 252], that no judge should ever try to mount it lest it run away with him. I disagree. With a good man in the saddle, the unruly horse can be kept in control. It can jump over obstacles. It can leap the fences put up by fictions and come down on the side of justice, as indeed was done in *Nagle v Feilden* [1966] 2 Q.B. 633. It can hold a rule to be invalid even though it is contained in a contract").

280 *R. (on the application of the Crown Prosecution Service) v Registrar General of Births, Deaths and Marriages* [2002] EWCA Civ 1661; [2003] Q.B. 1222.

therefore need to concentrate on prosecutions of strategic importance.[281] There are also questions of public interest which the prosecutor is uniquely qualified to judge; such as the need to avoid defendants espousing unpopular causes having a hearing in the court, with the resultant elevation of the defendant to the status of a martyr.[282] Furthermore, full enforcement of a law may not fulfil its ultimate purpose (for example, the purpose of road safety will not be served by requiring the prosecution of a doctor who narrowly exceeded the speed limit while driving to the scene of an accident in the early hours of the morning). Political, rather than legal accountability is therefore generally thought to be the better method of controlling discretion in these cases, and the courts have generally refrained from intervening to require the discretion of a prosecutor[283] or other law enforcement officer to be exercised, outside of cases of bad faith or manifest unreasonableness.[284]

5-087   Enforcement decisions are not, however, entirely immune from attack on the ground of illegality. If enforcement of a particular law were simply abandoned, the rule of law could be offended.[285] And where guidelines as to prosecution have been made, it has been held that judicial review may lie where the guidelines themselves are based upon an unlawful policy, or where the prosecutor fails to follow his own guidelines.[286] A prosecutor may be under a legal duty to publish a policy as to how the public interest element of prosecutorial decisions in relation to a specific offence will be approached.[287]

---

[281] *R. v Chief Constable of Sussex Ex p. International Traders' Ferry Ltd* [1999] 2 A.C. 418 (decision partially to withdraw police protection from protestors against the export of animals upheld as lawful and not disproportionate or irrational). On limited resources, see 5-134; on justiciability, see 1-032.

[282] *Gouriet v Union of Post Office Workers* [1978] A.C. 435 (refusal of the Attorney General to support a private action to restrain breach of the law by the Union held not justiciable on that ground).

[283] *R. v Director of Public Prosecutions Ex p. Kebilene* [2000] 2 A.C. 326 (in the absence of "dishonesty or mala fide or an exceptional circumstance" decisions by the DPP to consent to a prosecution are not amenable to judicial review").

[284] 3-017.

[285] *F Hoffmann La Roche & Co AG v Secretary of State for Trade and Industry* [1975] A.C. 295 at 364 (Lord Diplock: "The Crown does owe a duty to the public at large to initiate proceedings to secure that the law is not flouted"); *R. v Coventry Airport Ex p. Phoenix Aviation* [1995] 3 All E.R. 37 (failure to provide any police protection to secure safety of exporters affected by animal rights protests a breach of the rule of law); *R. (on the application of Corner House Research) v Director of the Serious Fraud Office* [2008] UKHL 60; [2008] 3 W.L.R. 568 (HL declined to hold that a decision to stop investigations into allegedly corrupt payments, following threats from the Saudi officials to cease co-operation on counter-terrorism, was unlawful. *Phoenix Aviation* was distinguished on the ground that the DSFO had given careful thought to the implications for the rule of law in stopping the investigation whereas the council in *Phoenix* had not (see Lord Brown of Eaton-Under-Heywood at [58]); R. Hopkins and C. Yeginsu, "Storm in a Teacup: Domestic and International Conservatism from the Corner House Case" [2008] J.R. 267; J. Jowell, "Caving In: Threats and the Rule of Law" [2008] J.R. 273.

[286] *R. v Chief Constable of Kent Ex p. L* [1993] 1 All E.R. 756; *R. v DPP Ex p. C* [1995] 1 Cr. App. R. 136 at 141 (Kennedy LJ). It appears too that a decision to prosecute an accused for an offence in circumstances in which an alternative and more serious offence could have been charged is also susceptible to judicial review: G. Dingwall, "Judicial Review of Public Prosecutions" [1995] C.L.J. 265.

[287] *R. (on the application of Purdy) v DPP* [2009] UKHL 45; [2010] 1 A.C. 345 (the DPP was required to promulgate an offence-specific policy identifying the facts and circumstances that he would take into account in deciding whether to consent to a prosecution under s.2(1) of the Suicide Act 1961). Cf. *Nicklinson v Ministry of Justice* [2014] UKSC 38; [2015] A.C. 657 (the court should not involve itself with the terms of the DPP's policy; it was one thing for the court to decide that the DPP must publish a policy, but quite another for it to dictate what should be in that policy, reversing the Court of Appeal [2013] EWCA Civ 961; [2014] 2 All E.R. 32 on this point).

THE INTERPRETATION OF POLICIES

We shall below consider to what extent policies or guidance, lawfully **5-088** promulgated by ministers, departments and other public authorities must or may be taken into account as "relevant considerations".[288] What should the approach of the courts be to the interpretation of policy? Clearly the policy must not fall outside the terms and purpose of the relevant power. Nor will policies be subjected to the fine analysis of a statute.[289] But to whom does it fall to interpret the meaning of the policy? Is it for the courts to pronounce upon the natural meaning of the language used, or for the decision-maker, subject only to the constraints of rationality?[290] In other words, should the courts defer to the decision-maker's own interpretation of his policy or should the court apply its plain meaning?

In *R. (on the application of Springhall) v Richmond on Thames LBC*, it was said **5-089** that the decision-maker's "approach to policy will only be interfered with by the court if it goes beyond the range of reasonable meanings that can be given to the language used".[291] The opposite view was expressed in *R. v Derbyshire CC Ex p. Woods* where it was said that it is for the court, as a matter of law, to determine a policy's meaning and that if the decision-maker failed properly to understand that meaning then it will have made an error of law.[292] The approach of *Woods* was accepted in *First Secretary of State v Sainsbury's Supermarkets Ltd* where Sedley LJ made clear that "the interpretation of policy is not a matter for the Secretary of State. What a policy says, it is".[293] This approach is surely correct. Although, as Sedley LJ said, a policy is "a rule not a guide" and thus may be balanced against countervailing principles, policies do have legal consequences. Decision-makers take them into account as "relevant considerations".[294] And, as we shall later see, they may not lightly abandon policies that have created legitimate expectations or that breach the principle of consistency.[295] For that reason, when they fall to be interpreted in the courts, their ordinary meaning should prevail.[296] In *R. (on the application of Raissi) v Secretary of State for the Home Department*, the Court of Appeal had to consider whether the Home Secretary's ex gratia compensation scheme—set out in a policy statement—for those imprisoned following a wrongful conviction also applied to a person detained pursuant to extradition proceedings. The court, acknowledging that in different contexts different approaches had been

---

[288] See 5-120.

[289] *R. v Secretary of State for the Home Department Ex p. Urmaza* [1996] C.O.D. 479.

[290] On policy see 12-023, 031, 037 and following; and 9-008–013. N. Blake, "Judicial Interpretation of Policies Promulgated by the Executive" [2006] J.R. 298.

[291] *R. (on the application of Springhall) v Richmond on Thames LBC* [2006] EWCA Civ 19; [2006] B.L.G.R. 419 at [7] (Auld LJ).

[292] *R. v Derbyshire CC Ex p. Woods* [1997] J.P.L. 958 at 967–968 (Brooke LJ).

[293] *First Secretary of State v Sainsbury's Supermarkets Ltd* [2005] EWCA Civ 520; [2005] N.P.C. 60. cf. *R. v Director of Passenger Rail Franchising Ex p. Save Our Railways* (1996) C.L.C. 589 at 610 (Sir Thomas Bingham MR said of the Secretary of State's directions: "the Court cannot … abdicate its responsibility to give the document its proper meaning. It means what it means, not what anyone would like it to mean"); *R. (on the application of Vale of White Horse DC) v Secretary of State for Communities and Local Government* [2009] EWHC 1847 (Admin) at [23] (there was nothing in *R. (on the application of Raissi) v Secretary of State for the Home Department* [2008] EWCA Civ 72; [2008] Q.B. 836 "which purports to overrule the general approach to planning policies in planning cases to which I have referred above and in my judgment the proper approach should remain as set out in *Woods*").

[294] See 5-130.

[295] See Ch.12 and 11-059.

[296] On policies as "relevant considerations", see 5-130.

adopted, held that they had[297]:

> "some difficulty with the reasonable meaning approach. One presumes that, if the minister has applied a meaning to some part of the policy, then the minister, without announcing any change in the policy, could not in a later case adopt another meaning, arguing that both meanings are reasonable and it is up to him or her to choose which meaning to use in any particular case. If that is right, then the reasonable meaning approach would only benefit the minister when interpreting the meaning of a particular part of the policy for the first time".

Nothing said in *Re McFarland*[298] prevented the Court of Appeal from deciding what the policy means.

EXERCISE OF A DISCRETIONARY POWER FOR EXTRANEOUS PURPOSE

5-090   If a power granted for one purpose is exercised for a different purpose, that power has not been validly exercised. In administrative law[299] this elementary proposition was first laid down in cases concerning the exercise of powers of compulsory acquisition. These cases held that when persons were authorised by Parliament to take compulsorily the lands of others, paying to the latter proper compensation, they cannot be allowed to exercise the powers conferred on them for any collateral object; that is, for any purposes except those for which the legislature has invested them with extraordinary powers.[300]

5-091   An expression of judicial solicitude for private property rights[301] was thus enlarged into a fundamental principle of English administrative law, possibly even based upon an implied constitutional principle. Most of the reported cases deal with the misapplication of powers by local authorities, though the same general principle governed the exercise of delegated legislative power by the executive.[302]

5-092   When a decision-maker pursues a purpose outside of the four corners of his powers, he may do so by taking an "irrelevant consideration" into account (the term "relevant" referring to the purpose of the legislation). The interpretation of purpose, and the relevance of considerations taken into account in pursuing that purpose, are therefore often inextricably linked. However, in some cases neither the motive for the decision, nor the considerations taken into account in reaching that decision, are apparent. In such a case the purpose pursued is judged alone, without reference to the considerations by which it was influenced. The definition of purpose and the

---

[297] *R. (on the application of Raissi) v Secretary of State for the Home Department* [2008] EWCA Civ 72; [2008] Q.B. 836 at [122].

[298] *Re McFarland* [2004] UKHL 17; [2004] 1 W.L.R. 1289.

[299] The doctrine of a fraud upon a power is well known in equity.

[300] *Galloway v London Corp* (1866) L.R. 1 HL 34 at 43.

[301] For other early dicta, see *Webb v Manchester & Leeds Ry* (1839) 4 Myl. & Cr. 116 at 118; *Dodd v Salisbury & Yeovil Ry* (1859) 1 Giff. 158; *Stockton & Darlington Ry v Brown* (1860) 9 H.L.C. 246 at 254, 256; *Biddulph v St George's, Hanover Square, Vestry* (1863) 33 L.J.Ch. 411 at 417; *Hawley v Steele* (1877) 6 Ch.D. 521 at 527–529. See also *Marshall Shipping Co v R.* (1925) 41 T.L.R. 285: "You can never beat into the heads of people exercising bureaucratic authority that they must exercise their powers singly, and not for collateral objects".

[302] For byelaws, see e.g. *Scott v Glasgow Corp* [1899] A.C. 470 at 492; *Baird (Robert) Ltd v Glasgow Corp* [1936] A.C. 32, 42; *Boyd Builders Ltd v City of Ottawa* (1964) 45 D.L.R. (2nd) 211; *Re Burns and Township of Haldimand* (1965) 52 D.L.R. (2nd) 101; *Prince George (City of) v Payne* [1978] S.C.R. 458; *R. v Toohey Ex p. Northern Land Council* (1981) I.S.I. C.L.R. 170, where the majority of the court regarded legislative and administrative powers as equally susceptible to judicial review.

relevance of considerations must therefore be considered as separate aspects of the illegal decision.[303]

The abandonment of purpose has been expressed in different ways. Sometimes it is said that decision-makers should not pursue "collateral objects", or that they should not pursue ends which are outside the "objects and purposes of the statute". On other occasions it is said that power should not be "exceeded" or that the purposes pursued by the decision-maker should not be "improper", "ulterior", or "extraneous" to those required by the statute in question. It is also said that "irrelevant considerations" should not be taken into account in reaching a decision. All these terms of course "run into each other" and "overlap".[304]

5-093

However, the designation of a purpose as "improper" is distinct because of its connotation of *moral* impropriety. In most cases where the term "improper" has been employed the decision-maker either knowingly pursues a purpose that is different from the one that is ostensibly being pursued, or the motive behind the decision is illicit (based for example on personal factors such as financial gain, revenge or prejudice). Because, therefore, of its adverse moral imputation, the notion of improper purposes is more akin to that of bad faith, which will now be considered separately.

5-094

Bad faith and improper motive

Fundamental to the legitimacy of public decision-making is the principle that official decisions should not be infected with improper motives such as fraud or dishonesty, malice or personal self-interest. These motives, which have the effect of distorting or unfairly biasing the decision-maker's approach to the subject of the decision, automatically cause the decision to be taken for an improper purpose and thus take it outside the permissible parameters of the power.

5-095

A power is exercised *fraudulently* if its repository intends for an improper purpose, for example dishonestly, to achieve an object other than that which he claims to be seeking. The intention may be to promote another public interest or private interests. A power is exercised *maliciously* if its repository is motivated by personal animosity towards those who are directly affected by its exercise.

5-096

Bad faith[305] is a serious allegation which attracts a heavy burden of proof.[306] Examples of cases involving fraudulent or dishonest motives include those where a local authority acquired property for the ostensible purpose of widening a street or redeveloping an urban area but in reality for the purpose of reselling it at a profit[307]; or preventing the owner from reaping the benefit of the expected incre-

5-097

---

[303] On irrelevant considerations, see 5-120.

[304] *Associated Provincial Picture Houses v Wednesbury Corp* [1948] 1 K.B. 223 at 228 (Lord Greene MR).

[305] Bad faith has been defined rarely, but an Australian case defined it as "a lack of an honest or genuine attempt to undertake the task and involves a personal attack on the honesty of the decision-maker": *SCAS v Minister of Immigration* [2002] FCAFC 397 at [19]. Objectively recklessness decision-making was held not to involve bad faith (*NAFK v Minister of Immigration* (2003) 130 F.L.R. 210 at 219]).

[306] *Daihatsu Australia Pty Ltd v Federal Commission of Australia* (2001) 184 A.L.R. 576 (Finn J at 587).

[307] *Gard v Commissioners of Sewers for the City of London* (1885) L.R. 28 Ch.D. 486; *Donaldson v South Shields Corp* [1899] W.N. 6; *Fernley v Limehouse Board of Works* (1899) 68 L.J. Ch. 344; *Denman & Co v Westminster Corp* [1906] 1 Ch. 464 at 475; *R. v Minister of Health Ex p. Davis* [1929] 1 K.B. 619 at 624. Contrast *CC Auto Port Pty Ltd v Minister for Works* (1966) 113 C.L.R. 365. But see the puzzling decision, *Robins (E) & Son Ltd v Minister of Health* [1939] 1 K.B. 520 (CA held the local authority had an unfettered discretion in its choice of method (clearance or demoli-

ment in land values[308]; or giving an advantage to a third party.[309] Licensing powers cannot be used to augment public funds.[310] An authority, purporting to exercise powers of compulsory acquisition for the purpose of widening streets, proposed to widen a street only to a minute extent, its true purpose being to alter the street level.[311] A local authority empowered to acquire unfit houses purported to do so in order to provide temporary accommodation pending their demolition, but in reality intended to render them fit for habitation and add them to its permanent housing stock.[312] An authority purporting to dismiss school teachers on educational grounds, in reality dismissed them for reasons of economy.[313] An authority claiming to raise the salaries of its employees to reflect an increase in their duties, in reality did so in order to grant an employee a salary increase unrelated to the changes in his duties.[314] A police authority which called its former chief constable, who was living abroad, ostensibly for medical examination (and cancelled his pension when he failed to appear) in reality called him so as to facilitate the execution of a warrant of arrest issued against him by the Bankruptcy Court.[315] A local authority sought to acquire land for its benefit, when its true motive was to remove gypsies from the

---

tion) of dealing with compulsorily acquired land. Mackinnon LJ (at 537–538) also observed that, even had the property owners succeeded in establishing that the local authority had adopted the method of compulsory purchase in order to be able to resell the land to the owners (who wished to develop it) at a high price, that would not have affected the validity of the decision). cf. *Merrick v Liverpool Corp* [1910] 2 Ch. 449 at 463.

[308] *Sydney Municipal Council v Campbell* [1925] A.C. 338; *Grice v Dudley Corp* [1958] Ch. 329 and other authorities there cited at 341–342.

[309] *Bartrum v Manurewa Borough* [1962] N.Z.L.R. 21.

[310] *R. v Bowman* [1898] 1 Q.B. 663; *R. v Birmingham Licensing Planning Committee Ex p. Kennedy* [1972] 2 Q.B. 140: *R. v Shann* [1910] 2 K.B. 418 at 434.

[311] *Lynch v Commissioners of Sewers for the City of London* (1886) 32 Ch.D. 72. Attempts to impugn compulsory purchase orders in the English courts for improper purpose were successful in *Grice v Dudley Corp* [1958] Ch.329, *London & Westcliff Properties Ltd v Minister of Housing and Local Government* [1961] 1 W.L.R. 519, *Webb v Minister of Housing and Local Government* [1965] 1 W.L.R. 755, *Meravale Builders Ltd v Secretary of the Environment* (1978) 36 P. & C.R. 87; *Victoria Square Property Co Ltd v Southwark LBC* [1978] 1 W.L.R. 463; and unsuccessful in *Hanks v Minister of Housing and Local Government* [1963] 1 Q.B. 999; *Simpsons Motor Sales (London) Ltd v Hendon Corp* [1964] A.C. 1088; *Moore v Minister of Housing and Local Government* [1966] 2 Q.B. 602. See also *Birmingham & Midland Motor Omnibus Co v Worcestershire CC* [1967] 1 W.L.R. 409 (diversion of traffic for unauthorised purpose).

[312] *Victoria Square Property Co Ltd v Southwark LBC* [1972] 1 W.L.R. 463; *R. v Birmingham City Council Ex p. Sale* (1983) 9 H.L.R. 33.

[313] *Hanson v Radcliffe UDC* [1922] 2 Ch. 490; *Sadler v Sheffield Corp* [1924] 1 Ch. 483. See also *Smith v McNally* [1912] 1 Ch. 816 at 825–826; *Martin v Eccles Corp* [1919] 1 Ch. 387 at 400 ("grounds connected with the giving of religious instruction"). Contrast *Price v Rhondda UDC* [1923] 2 Ch. 372; *Short v Poole Corp* [1926] Ch. 66.

[314] *R. (Wexford CC) v Local Government Board* [1902] 2 I.R. 349. See also the leading Australian case *Brownells Ltd v Ironmongers' Wages Board* (1950) 81 C.L.R. 108 at 120, 130 (wages board fixed high overtime rates in reality to bring about closure of shops at hours different from those required by statute).

[315] *R. v Leigh (Lord)* [1897] 1 Q.B. 582; *R. v Brixton Prison Governor Ex p. Soblen* [1963] 2 Q.B. 243 (where it was unsuccessfully alleged that the true purpose of deportation was to comply with a request for extradition); *R. v Secretary of State for the Environment Ex p. Ostler* [1977] Q.B. 122 (applicant was issued with false information which misled him not to appear at a public inquiry. But judicial review was excluded by an ouster clause. In other cases it has been said that where bad faith is established, the courts will be prepared to set aside a decision procured or made fraudulently, despite the existence of a formula purporting to exclude judicial review); *Lazarus Estates Ltd v Beasley* [1956] 1 Q.B. 702 at 712, 713 (Denning LJ), 722 (Parker LJ: fraud "vitiates all transactions known to the law of however high a degree of solemnity"); cases cited by counsel in *Smith v East Elloe RDC* [1956] A.C. 736 at 740 where it was held that the statutory language was sufficiently clear to exclude challenge for bad faith to a compulsory purchase order outside the short statutory limitation period. See further 4-025.

land.[316] In a case concerning the refusal to accept advertisements from a Christian campaign group stating "Not gay! Ex-gay, post-gay and proud. Get over it!", the Court of Appeal held that there was uncertainty as to who had made the refusal decisions—Transport for London (the defendant) or the Mayor of London (not a party); the court ordered further inquiry by the Administrative Court to be conducted as to whether the decision was instructed by the Mayor and whether it was made for the improper purpose of advancing his election campaign.[317]

A decision based on *malice* is usually one that is directed to the person, e.g. where **5-098** a byelaw or order has been made especially to thwart an individual application for a permit.[318] The malice may arise out of personal or political animosity built up over a series of past dealings.[319] For instance, in a Canadian case the cancellation of a liquor licence was held to be an abuse of power where the decision was prompted by the proprietor's support of a religious sect which was considered a nuisance by the police.[320] In another Canadian case the court inferred mala fides from the fact that a byelaw was made for the compulsory purchase of land which was the subject of pending litigation between the owner and the local authority.[321] And in a third it was held that a local authority cannot use its licensing power to prohibit lawful businesses of which it disapproves.[322] In an English case the decision of Derbyshire County Council to cease advertising in journals controlled by Times Newspapers which had written articles critical of its councillors was explicitly held to have been motivated by bad faith and therefore declared invalid for that reason alone.[323] In a case concerning hijackers from Afghanistan, the Home Secretary refused any form of leave to enter to the claimants (to which they were entitled) but had instead granted them "temporary admission". Since his motive was, according to Sullivan J, to thwart a decision of the Immigration Appellate Authority by giving himself time "in the hope that something would turn up", his decision was void and an abuse of power.[324]

---

[316] *Costello v Dacorum DC* (1980) 79 L.G.R. 133.

[317] *R. (Core Issues Trust) v Transport for London (Secretary of State for Culture, Media and Sport and Minister for Women and Equalities intervening)* [2014] EWCA Civ 34; [2014] P.T.S.R. 785.

[318] *Lubrizol Corp Pty Ltd v Leichhardt Municipal Council* [1961] N.S.W.R. 111; *Boyd Builders Ltd v City of Ottawa* (1964) 45 D.L.R. (2nd) 211.

[319] The allegation by Mrs Smith in *Smith v East Elloe RDC* [1986] A.C. 736. Personal animosity towards a party may also disqualify an adjudicator: *R. (Donoghue) v Cork County Justices* [1910] 2 I.R. 271; *R. (Kingston) v Cork County Justices* [1910] 2 I.R. 658; *R. (Harrington) v Clare County Justices* [1918] 2 I.R. 116; *Law v Chartered Institute of Patent Agents* [1919] 2 Ch. 276; *R. v Handley* (1921) 61 D.L.R. 656; *Re "Catalina" and "Norma"* (1938) 61 Ll. Rep. 360.

[320] *Roncarelli v Duplessis* (1959) 16 D.L.R. (2nd) 689 at 705. For further proceedings see [1959] S.C.R. 121.

[321] *Re Burns and Township of Haldimand* (1966) 52 D.L.R. (2nd) 101.

[322] *Prince George (City of) v Payne* [1978] 1 S.C.R. 458. In any event a power to regulate will not normally be constructed to allow total prohibition: *Tarr v Tarr* [1973] A.C. 254 at 265–268. For another interesting Canadian case, see *Re Doctors Hospital and Minister of Health* (1976) 68 D.L.R. (3rd) 220 (power to revoke approval as public hospital wrongly exercised in the interests of economy). More recently, see *Canadian Union of Public Employees v Ontario (Minister of Labour)* [2003] 1 S.C.R. 539 (the use of a ministerial appointment power for an improper purpose).

[323] *R. v Derbyshire CC Ex p. The Times Supplement Ltd* [1991] C.O.D. 129. In *R. v Ealing LBC Ex p. Times Newspaper Ltd* (1986) 85 L.G.R. 316, councils imposed a ban on purchasing the publications of the Times Newspapers in their libraries. Watkins LJ, without going so far as to label the "shadowy" reasons for imposing the ban (to punish a "tyrannical employer") as bad faith—he called them "a transparent piece of camouflage"—did hold the decision both irrational and an abuse of power (as well as illegal, as discussed at 5-111). cf. *R. v Lewisham LBC Ex p. Shell UK Ltd* [1988] 1 All E.R. 938 (ban on purchasing Shell's products to pressure parent company to sever links with South African subsidiary illegal but not unreasonable, although "very near the line").

[324] *R. (on the application of S) v Secretary of State for the Home Department* [2006] EWCA Civ 1157;

Specified purposes

5-099   Even when purposes are specified in legislation, it is often difficult to determine
their scope, as the following examples show. The case of *Spath Holme* typifies the
search for purpose and also demonstrates how difficult it is to draw general rules
from individual statutory powers.[325] In 1999 the Secretary of State made Orders to
cap the rents of regulated tenants who, as a result of judicial decisions, faced
increases in their rents. The Order was made under a consolidated statute which had
originally conferred temporary powers on the Secretary of State directed to preventing inflation in the economy. The landlord challenged the Order on the ground that
it was outwith the power of the statute which had at its purpose the countering of
general inflation in the economy and not the alleviation of hardship. Having first
decided (by majority) that it was not appropriate to seek the general purpose of the
statute by reference to the parliamentary record,[326] the House of Lords held that the
earlier legislation was not confined to the specific anti-inflationary purpose.

5-100   Where a statute conferred power upon local authorities to incur expenditure for
the "publication within their area of information on matters relating to local government", an expensive media and poster campaign mounted by the Inner London
Education Authority was invalidated on the ground that it was made with the dual
purpose both of informing the public of the detail of the education service and also
of persuading the public to support the authority's opposition to the government's
"rate-capping" policy. The first objective of the campaign (information) was lawful, but the second objective (persuasion) was held to be an unlawful purpose, which
materially influenced the decision.[327]

5-101   The legality of sanctions imposed by local authorities for various motives has
arisen in a number of cases. Where a statute imposed a duty upon every Library
authority to provide a comprehensive and efficient library service",[328] the action of
three London local authorities in banning from their libraries all publications of the
Times Newspaper Group was held unlawful.[329] The ban was imposed to demonstrate support for the trade unions involved in a long and bitter dispute with the
newspaper's proprietors. It was held that the ban pursued an "ulterior purpose"
which was "set by a political attitude to a so-called workers' struggle against a
tyrannical employer with the object of punishing the employer".[330] In an earlier case
Lord Denning indicated that the closure of schools during a prolonged labour
dispute could, if influenced by trade union pressure, amount to an unlawful extraneous purpose.[331]

5-102   Where local authorities have sought to impose conditions upon the use of their
land, the courts have required them to further the purposes authorised by the statutes
under which the land was acquired—though all such cases now need to be read in
the light of the Localism Act 2011 Pt 1, which creates a general power of
competence for local authorities.[332] A London authority attached a condition to

---

[2006] I.N.L.R. 575 at [102].

[325] *R. (on the application of Spath Holme Ltd) v Secretary of State for the Environment, Transport and the Regions* [2001] 2 A.C. 349.

[326] See 5-030.

[327] *R. v ILEA Ex p. Westminster CC* [1986] 1 W.L.R. 28. On plurality purposes, see 5-109.

[328] Public Libraries and Museums Act 1964 s.7(1).

[329] *R. v Ealing LBC Ex p. Times Newspapers Ltd* (1986) 85 L.G.R. 316.

[330] The ban was also held to be unreasonable: see 11-072.

[331] *Meade v Haringey LBC* [1979] 1 W.L.R. 637.

[332] 5-100.

permission for the holding of a community festival in a park.[333] The condition required the banning at the festival of "any political party or organisation seeking to promote or oppose any political party or cause". It was held that those restrictions were extraneous to the purpose of the statute under which the authority had purchased the park, namely "for the purpose of being used as public walks or a pleasure ground".[334]

Prior to the Hunting Act 2004, which banned the hunting of various mammals **5-103** with dogs, and before the existence of a general power of competence for local authorities,[335] the Somerset County Council had passed a resolution to ban hunting on their (council-owned) land on the Quantock Hills. The ban was motivated by the "moral repugnance" of the majority of the council towards hunting. The land had been acquired under a statute generally authorising acquisition of land for "the benefit, improvement or development of their area".[336] That purpose was interpreted as permitting the council to pursue objects which would "conduce to the better management of the estate". Had the ban been introduced to protect rare flora damaged by the hunt, or to eliminate physical interference with the enjoyment of others of the amenities offered on the land, it might have been lawful. However, since the ban was fuelled by the "ethical perceptions of the councillors about the rights and wrongs of hunting", the purposes it sought were outwith that of the governing statute.[337]

The power of the Foreign Secretary to grant assistance to overseas countries was **5-104** subjected to judicial scrutiny in relation to the funding of the Pergau dam hydroelectric project in Malaysia. The Overseas Development and Co-operation Act 1980 conferred such power on the Secretary of State "for the purpose of promoting the economy of a country or territory outside the United Kingdom, or the welfare of its people".[338] It was clear that the Pergau project was not economically "sound" and was a "very bad buy". However, it was contended for the Secretary of State that wider political and economic interest were and could have been taken into account, including an alleged undertaking by the Prime Minister to provide the assistance (perhaps, as alleged in the press—although not directly alluded to in the judgments—as part of a wider arrangement involving an agreement to purchase defence items in the United Kingdom). The court, however, held that these wider purposes were not sufficient in themselves to qualify as a project for assistance under the statute. Although the statute did not specifically require an assisted project to be economically "sound", so much had to be implied. Had there been a "developmental promotion purpose" within s.1 of the Act, only then would it have been proper to take into account the wider political and economic considerations, including the impact which withdrawing from the offer would have had on commercial relations with Malaysia. In the circumstances, however, there was, at the time when assistance was provided, "no such purpose within the section".[339]

In a number of South African cases, the courts have impugned decisions because **5-105**

---

[333] *R. v Barnet LBC Ex p. Johnson* [1989] C.O.D. 538.

[334] Public Health Act 1875 s.164. The ban was also held to be an unreasonable infringement of the right of association.

[335] Localism Act 2011 Pt 1; see 5-100.

[336] Local Government Act 1972 s.120(1).

[337] *R. v Somerset CC Ex p. Fewings* [1995] 1 All E.R. 513 (Laws J). The CA upheld this decision, although on different grounds [1995] 1 W.L.R. 1037. See D. Cooper, "For the Sake of the Deer: Land, Local Government and the Hunt" (1997) 45 *Sociological Review* 668.

[338] Overseas Development and Co-operation Act 1980 s.1(1); repealed by the International Development Act 2002.

[339] *R. v Secretary of State for Foreign Affairs Ex p. World Development Movement Ltd* [1995] 1 W.L.R. 386.

they pursued extraneous purposes. For example, the Premier of a province was found to have appointed a commission of inquiry in order to embarrass his political opponents and without honestly believing that such an inquiry was necessary for a lawful purpose[340]; and police in the same province were found to have been arresting prostitutes as a form of harassment rather than for the lawful purpose of having them prosecuted.[341] It should be noted that these judgments relied on the general principle of legality, an aspect of the rule of law, rather than on the specific ground of review in the Promotion of Administrative Justice Act 2000 (PAJA) s.6(2)(e)(ii). The rule of law covers precisely the same terrain when it comes to illegality and it obviates the need to establish that the offending decision is "administrative action".

5-106   In *Gauteng Gambling Board v MEC for Economic Development. Gauteng*[342] a unanimous Supreme Court of Appeal confirmed that "acting with an ulterior motive of purpose is subsumed under the principle of legality". In this remarkable instance the administrator went so far as to dissolve a statutory board that had thwarted her by refusing to comply with an unlawful instruction from her. A more worthy but still ulterior aim was pursued in *Minister of Justice v SA Restructuring and Insolvency Practitioners Association*[343] which dealt with a policy governing the appointment of insolvency practitioners. While the policy attempted to address past race and gender discrimination, the court found that it failed to recognise or serve the fundamental purpose of the insolvency legislation: the interests of creditors.

Incidental powers

5-107   Even when purposes are clearly specified in legislation, the common law permits authorities to undertake tasks that are "reasonably incidental" to the achievement of those purposes,[344] provided that they do not contradict any statutory power. We have seen how the common law under the Ram doctrine may apply in respect of the powers of the ministers and the problems associated with this for the rule of law.[345] In respect of the activities of local authorities, statutory recognition is given to the rule of common law, authorising them to do any thing which is "calculated to facilitate, or is conducive or incidental to, the discharge of any of their functions".[346] This phrase has itself been the subject of statutory construction in cases where, for example, local authorities have attempted to raise revenue by charging fees or speculating on the financial markets. When a local education authority decided to charge fees for individual and group music tuition, that decision was held unlawful as the duty under the statute to provide "education" without charge[347] included the duty to provide music tuition.[348] Similarly, a local authority was held not entitled to charge for consultations with developers prior to applica-

---

[340] *City of Cape Town v Premier, Western Cape* 2008 (6) S.A. 345, C.

[341] *Sex Worker Education and Advocacy Task Force v Minister of Safety and Security* 2009 (6) S.A. 513, WCC.

[342] *Gauteng Gambling Board v MEC for Economic Development. Gauteng* 2013 (5) S.A. 24, SCA, at [47].

[343] *Minister of Justice v SA Restructuring and Insolvency Practitioners Association* 2017 (3) S.A. 95, SCA.

[344] *Ashbury Railway Carriage and Iron Co Ltd v Riche* (1875) L.R. 7 HL 653; *Attorney General v Great Eastern Railway Company* (1880) 5 App. Cas. 473; *Attorney General v Fulham Corp* [1921] 1 Ch. 440.

[345] See 5-022.

[346] Local Government Act 1972 s.111; Local Government Act 2003 s.93(7); see also Local Government Act 2003 s.92 (charges for provision of services for local authorities' powers, though not duties); Police Act 1996 ss.18, 25, 26 (powers to police to charge for services and goods).

[347] Education Act 1944 s.61.

tions for planning permission being lodged. The House of Lords held that, although pre-application advice was not a duty or a discretionary power, but an incidental power authorised by the statute, the power to charge for that incidental power was not authorised.[349] (The effect of the judgment was reversed by the Local Government Act 2003 s.93, which permitted charging for discretionary services). The courts also struck down the power of a local authority to enter into interest rate swap transaction, which involved speculation as to future interest trends, with the object of making a profit to increase the available resources of the authority. That activity was held inconsistent with the borrowing powers of local authorities and not "conducive or incidental' to the discharge of those limited powers.[350] In *R. (on the application of the National Secular Society) v Bideford Town Council* a parish council's practice of saying prayers as part of the formal business of full meetings of the council was not authorised by s.111 of the 1972 Act.[351] In many situations after February 2012, local authorities have legal powers under the general power of competence created by the Localism Act 2011 Pt 1, to achieve things that previously would have been ultra vires.

In *Stennett*[352] the question before the House of Lords was whether a duty to **5-108** provide after-care services for those discharged from compulsory detention under the Mental Health Act 1983 also authorised the authority to charge for those services. Despite the huge cost to local authorities of providing this service free of charge (estimated at between 30 million and 80 million), the House of Lords agreed with the Court of Appeal[353] that that a public authority could not charge for services unless it was explicitly authorised to do so and it was held that s.117 of the 1983 Act did not so authorise any charge as it was a "free-standing" section, and did not act as a "gateway" to the incorporation of provisions of other legislation which did authorise charging.[354]

General power of competence for local authorities

Statutory provisions have attempted to widen local authorities' powers. As we **5-109** have noted, the Local Government Act 1972 s.111 enables councils to do any thing which is "calculated to facilitate, or is conducive or incidental to, the discharge of any of their functions".[355] The Local Government Act 2000 s.2 tried to provide greater latitude for councils through a "power to do anything which they consider is likely to achieve" the promotion or improvement of economic, social or

---

[348] *R. v Hereford and Worcester Local Education Authority Ex p. Jones* [1981] 1 W.L.R. 768. In general authorities require specific authorisation to raise revenue. *Attorney General v Wilts United Dairies Ltd* (1921) 37 T.L.R. 884.

[349] *McCarthy and Stone (Developments) Ltd v Richmond-upon-Thames LBC* [1992] 2 A.C. 48.

[350] *Hazell v Hammersmith & Fulham LBC* [1992] 2 A.C. 1. See also: *Credit Suisse v Allerdale BC* [1997] Q.B. 306; *Credit Suisse v Waltham Forest LBC* [1997] Q.B. 362; *Sutton London LBC v Morgan Grenfell and Co Ltd* (1997) 9 Admin. L.R. 145. cf. *R. v Greater Manchester Police Authority Ex p. Century Motors (Farnworth) Ltd, The Times* 31 May 1996 (necessary implication that power to levy charges for vehicle recovery operation); *R. v Powys CC Ex p. Hambidge, The Times,* 5 November 1997 (Local authority may charge for services under Chronically Sick and Disabled Persons Act 1970 s.2).

[351] [2012] EWHC 175 (Admin); [2012] 2 All E.R. 1175. See para.5–100 below.

[352] *R. (on the application of Stennett) v Manchester City Council* [2002] UKHL 34; [2002] 2 A.C. 1127.

[353] *R. (on the application of Stennett) v Manchester City Council* [2001] Q.B. 370.

[354] National Assistance Act 1948 s.21; see A. Scully, "Scarce Resources Again" [2003] C.L.J. 1, 2 who makes the point that the result of charging could mean delay in releasing a person from detention, as if no after-care has been arranged detention may be continued under the authority of *R. (on the application of J) v Ashworth Hospital Authority* [2002] EWCA Civ 923.

[355] See 5-098.

environmental "well-being of their area"; but this was little used by councils and interpreted narrowly.[356]

5-110   The Localism Act 2011 Pt 1 endeavours to enlarge significantly the powers of local authorities from 18 February 2012.[357] Section 1 of the Localism Act 2011 creates a "general power of competence" (GPoC): "A local authority has power to do anything that individuals generally may do", "anywhere in the United Kingdom or elsewhere", "for a commercial purposes or otherwise for a charge, or without charge", and "to do it for, or otherwise for, the benefit of the authority, its area or persons resident in its area"; the GPoC "is not limited by the existence of any other power of the authority which (to any extent) overlaps with the general power" and "any such other power is not limited by the existence of the general power". Section 2 provides for "boundaries": in short, local authorities remain subject to any statutory limitations in legislation which overlap with the GPoC or which expressly limit it. Section 3 prevents local authorities from charging for services provided under statutory duties but does allow charges to cover costs of discretionary services. Section 4 covers activities done for a commercial purpose and requires them to be exercised through the vehicle of a company or cooperative.

5-111   During the second reading debate on the bill that became the 2011 Act, the Secretary of State said in the House of Commons that the GPoC "turns the determination requirements on their head. All those fun-loving guys who are involved in offering legal advice to local authorities, who are basically conservative, will now have to err on the side of permissiveness".[358] In the Public Bill Committee, a minister said that s.1 "sets out very clearly the Government's intention to take power out of Whitehall and Westminster and to take it back to town halls and communities".[359] The minister boasted that the "courts will find it difficult—we have been advised that they will find it impossible—to unpick" the breadth of the GPoC.[360] Whether the obscure drafting of s.1(1) will indeed achieve the Government's stated aims remains to be seen; the GPoC appears to fall well short of the political rhetoric emphasising limitless powers.

5-112   First, the idea that an entity which is (a) a public authority and (b) a corporation has the powers of "an individual" is legally puzzling. The plain meaning of "powers of individuals generally" extends activities permitted under s.1 only to nongovernment functions, such as powers to purchase and manage land and enter into contracts. Individuals do not generally have powers to regulate, inspect, legislate, create criminal offences or demand taxes. Second, councils remain obliged to carry out all existing statutory duties which apply because of their status as public bodies, including those under the Human Rights Act 1998, the public sector equality

---

[356] *Brent LBC v Risk Management Partners Ltd* [2009] EWCA Civ 490; [2010] P.T.S.R. 349 (well-being power did not permit councils to set up and fund a mutual insurance company). Under the Localism Act 2011, the well-being power will no longer apply to England but continues in Wales.

[357] It was brought into force earlier than expected, in response to the government's disagreement with the outcome of a successful judicial review challenge to Bideford Town Council's practice of opening formal council meetings with prayers: *R. (on the application of National Secular Society) v Bideford Town Council* [2012] EWHC 174 (Admin); [2012] 2 All E.R. 1175 at [33] ("the Council has no power to hold prayers as part of a formal Council meeting, or to summon Councillors to a meeting at which such prayers are on the agenda").

[358] *Hansard*, HC Vol.521, col.562 (17 January 2011) (Eric Pickles MP, Secretary of State for Communities and Local Government).

[359] PBC (Bill 126) 2010–11, 5th Sitting, Tuesday February 1, 2011 (morning), col.175 (Andrew Stunell MP).

[360] PBC (Bill 126) 2010–11, 5th Sitting, Tuesday February 1, 2011 (morning), col.181 (Andrew Stunell MP).

duty[361] and those regulating public procurement. Moreover, councils remain bound in exercising the GPoC to meet the common law standards required of public bodies to make lawful, rational and procedural fair decisions. The plain meaning of s.1(1) does not absolve councils from meeting these standards even though they do not generally apply to individuals acting in a private capacity. Third, the GPoC does not operate retrospectively to cure any unlawfulness arising from actions taken before 18 February 2012.[362]

Unspecified purposes

If a discretionary power is conferred without express reference to purpose, it must still be exercised in accordance with such implied purposes as the courts attribute to the legislation.[363] We have seen that the minister who, in reliance upon an ostensibly unfettered discretionary power, refused to refer a complaint by milk producers to a committee of investigation because this might lead him into economic and political difficulties, was held to have violated the unexpressed purpose, or the "policy and objects" of the Act, for which the power of reference had been conferred[364] and (according to a somewhat hyperbolical interpretation of their Lordships' comments) was "roundly rebuked by the House of Lords for his impudence".[365] In order to avoid paying an announced (but not yet enacted) increase in the fee for a television licence, some licence-holders obtained another licence at the old rate before their existing licence expired. The Court of Appeal held that the minister could not use his power to revoke the licences, despite the lack of apparent limits on that power, in order to deprive licensees of the advantage that they had secured from the gap between the Government's announcement and parliamentary authorisation of the change in fees.[366] In *R. (on the application of Ben Hoare Bell Solicitors) v Lord Chancellor* a regulation introducing a "no permission, no fee" arrangement for making a legally aided judicial review application was held to be incompatible with the purposes of the enabling legislation, as it did not further the Act's purpose of incentivising legal aid providers to reflect on the merits of a case before applying for judicial review.[367] In *R. (on the application of Rights of Women) v Lord Chancellor and Secretary of State for Justice*, a regulation provided that legal aid would only be available to victims of domestic violence where documentary evidence of domestic violence was available in the 24-month period before the application for legal aid. The Court of Appeal held that this regulation frustrated the

5-113

---

[361] 5-072.

[362] *Manydown Company Ltd v Basingstoke and Dean BC* [2012] EWHC 977 (Admin) at [145].

[363] See, e.g. *Liversidge v Anderson* [1942] A.C. 206 at 220, 248, 261, 278; *Barber v Manchester Regional Hospital Board* [1958] 1 W.L.R. 181 at 193; *Potato Marketing Board v Merricks* [1958] 2 Q.B. 316 at 331; *Smith v East Elloe RDC* [1956] A.C. 736 at 740. The proposition stated in the text has nevertheless been doubted or contradicted (see *Yates (Arthur) & Co Pty Ltd v Vegetable Seeds Committee* (1945) 72 C.L.R. 37 at 68 (Latham CJ) by some authorities. The decision in *R. v Paddington & St Marylebone Rent Tribunal Ex p. Bell London & Provincial Properties Ltd* [1949] 1 K.B. 666 (block reference of 555 tenancies by local authority to rent tribunal without considering wishes of tenants or circumstances of particular cases; reference held invalid in that council was using tribunal as a general rent-fixing agency) has generally been regarded as a good illustration of the proposition in the text, but the case has now been explained as an example of a merely capricious reference: *R. v Barnet & Camden Rent Tribunal Ex p. Frey Investments Ltd* [1972] 2 Q.B. 342, CA. See also *Rowling v Takaro Properties Ltd* [1975] 2 N.Z.L.R. 62, NZCA; and [1988] A.C. 473, PC where the NZCA and PC took different views as to the implied purposes of the regulations.

[364] *Padfield v Minister of Agriculture, Fisheries and Food* [1968] A.C. 997; see 5-009.

[365] *Breen v Amalgamated Engineering Union* [1971] 2 Q.B. 175 at 191 (Lord Denning MR).

[366] *Congreve v Home Office* [1976] Q.B. 629.

[367] *R. (on the application of Ben Hoare Bell Solicitors) v Lord Chancellor* [2015] EWHC 523 (Admin); [2015] 1 W.L.R. 4175

purpose of the relevant provision of the Legal Aid, Sentencing and Punishment of Offenders Act 2012, which was to save money through withdrawal of civil legal services from certain categories of case, while continuing to provide civil legal services to the most deserving cases. The 24-month requirement rendered legal aid unavailable to many victims of domestic violence who were in need of it.[368]

5-114   In the case of *Magill v Porter*,[369] the Conservative leaders of Westminster City Council had used their powers to increase the number of owner-occupiers in marginal wards for the purpose of encouraging them to vote for the Conservative Party in future elections. The District Auditor held that this was an unlawful purpose and, through wilful conduct, had lost the Council money which the leaders of the Council should pay by way of surcharge. The House of Lords upheld the District Auditor's decision. It was held that although the powers under which the Council could dispose of the land was very broad,[370] and although elected politicians were entitled to act in a manner which would earn the gratitude and support of their electorate,[371] they could only act to pursue a "public purpose for which the power was conferred". The purpose of securing electoral advantage for the Conservative Party was, it was held, no such "public purpose".[372]

5-115   When an authority which is clothed with powers to regulate an activity and accompanies its regulations with a sanction or penalty, the courts look carefully at the restrictions and penalties to ensure that they are within the policy and objects of the empowering statute. This is true even where the power permits conditions to be attached to the regulations or licences. Thus where conditions in an ice-cream vendors' licence restricted their right to open shops at times of their choosing, the conditions were held to be unlawful.[373] A local authority was not entitled to lay down conditions relating to the customers of a licensee of a caravan site as it interfered with the licensee's freedom to contract with his customers and to matters that did not relate to the manner of the use of the site.[374] A similar approach was taken in a case where the House of Lords held that a Scottish local authority which had power to regulate second-hand car dealing acted unlawfully when it failed to renew a licence to a dealer who had failed to provide pre-sales information and inspection reports to his customers. Lord Hope held that the principal mischief to which the power was directed was the handling of stolen property and that the conditions imposed pursued a policy of consumer protection, which was not one of the objects and purposes of the statute.[375] In *R. (on the application of Gordon-Jones) v Secretary of State for Justice*, the High Court considered that the effect of

---

[368] *R. (on the application of Rights of Women) v Lord Chancellor* [2016] EWCA Civ 91; [2016] 1 W.L.R. 2543.

[369] *Magill v Porter* [2001] UKHL 67; [2002] 2 A.C. 357.

[370] Housing Act 1985 s.32.

[371] *Porter v Magill* [2001] UKHL 67; [2002] 2 A.C. 357 at [20] (Lord Bingham).

[372] See, e.g. *R. v Tower Hamlets LBC Ex p. Chetnick Developments Ltd* [1988] A.C. 858 at 872 (Lord Bridge: "Statutory power conferred for public purposes is conferred ... upon trust, not absolutely-that is to say, it can validly be used only in the right and proper way which Parliament when conferring it is presumed to have intended"); *Credit Suisse v Allerdale BC* [1997] Q.B. 306 at 333 (Neill LJ described that principle as "a general principle of public law").

[373] *Rossi v Magistrates of Edinburgh* (1904) 7 F 85, HL; *Spook Erection Ltd v City of Edinburgh DC*, 1995 S.L.T. 107, Sh Ct.

[374] *Mixnam's Properties Ltd v Chertsey UDC* [1965] A.C. 735 at 763 (Lord Upjohn), 755 (Lord Reid).

[375] *Stewart v Perth and Kinross Council* [2004] UKHL 16; 2004 S.C. 71, HL. It was held too that the conditions were not intended to interfere with the relationship between the dealer and his contractors, and that consumer legislation of this could kind should preferably be introduced through national legislation, in order to be consistently applied.

a Prison Service Instruction in restricting prisoners' access to books in pursuance of an incentive scheme was to undercut the rehabilitative purpose of that scheme.[376]

Another case concerned Afghans fleeing from the Taliban regime by means of a **5-116** hijacked plane which landed in England and where they requested asylum. Criminal convictions against them for hijacking were quashed because of misdirection by the judge. The Home Secretary had rejected their claim for asylum and this was upheld by a panel of adjudicators. The Home Secretary was unable to deport them as their lives would be at risk on their return to Afghanistan. The Home Secretary then decided not to allow the claimants discretionary leave, which he was entitled to do under his policy on "humanitarian grounds" and granted them instead "temporary admission". The Court of Appeal held that the purpose of temporary admission had not been sanctioned by Parliament. There had been ample time for the Home Secretary to obtain parliamentary authority for this new measure, but he had not done so and therefore his policy was unlawful.[377] In another immigration case, the claimants were the wife and adult children of a person assessed by the Home Secretary to be an Islamist extremist. They sought naturalisation as British citizens and though they met the statutory requirements, the Home Secretary refused their application.[378]

Other cases made it clear that the imposition of a penalty in the absence of a legal **5-117** wrong pursues an extraneous purpose. Purporting to be acting under the general duty under s.61 of the Race Relations Act 1976 to "promote good race relations", and also purporting to act under its broad powers to manage its own land, Leicester City Council withdrew the licence of a local rugby club to use the council-owned recreation ground. The council did this as a mark of their disapproval that the club had been unable to persuade some of its members to withdraw from the English rugby footballers' tour of South Africa, at the time of apartheid and as a demonstration of their effort to promote good relations between persons of different racial or ethnic groups. The House of Lords held the council's action unlawful, Lord Templeman considering it to be a "misuse of power ... punishing the club where it had done no wrong".[379] Similar reasons (the opposition to apartheid and the promotion of good race relations) motivated the London Borough of Lewisham which decided to boycott the products of Shell UK Ltd so as to put pressure on the parent companies of the group to withdraw their interests from South Africa. It was held that the dominant purpose of the boycott was to penalise the applicant for the fact that the group to which it belonged had trading links with South Africa. These links were not unlawful and the council's decision had therefore been influenced by an

---

[376] *R. (on the application of Gordon-Jones) v Secretary of State for Justice* [2014] EWHC 3997 (Admin); [2015] A.C.D. 42.

[377] *R. (on the application of S) v Secretary of State for the Home Department* [2006] EWCA Civ 1157; [2006] I.N.L.R. 575.

[378] *R. (MM) v Secretary of State for the Home Department* [2015] EWHC 3513 (Admin); [2016] 1 W.L.R. 2858.

[379] *Wheeler v Leicester City Council* [1985] A.C. 1054. cf. the approach of Lord Browne-Wilkinson in his dissenting judgment in the CA (at 1064–1065), where he raised the conflict between "two basic principles of a democratic society", one that allowed a "democratically elected body to conduct its affairs in accordance with its own views" and the other "the right to freedom of speech and conscience enjoyed by each individual". Basing his decision on illegality rather than on unreasonableness (the council having taken a "legally irrelevant factor" into account), he came close to deciding the matter on the ground of the council's acting inconsistently with "fundamental freedoms of speech and conscience". cf. the New Zealand decision of *Ashby v Minister of Immigration* [1981] 1 N.Z.L.R. 222 (refusal of Minister to bar the entry of the South African rugby football team into New Zealand upheld on the ground that the public interest, a relevant consideration in the context of the Minister's power, allowed the decision—although it was not the role of the court to second-guess the minister on that question in the context of foreign relation).

"extraneous and impermissible purpose".[380] Another boycott was considered by the courts when Liverpool City Council threatened to withdraw grant aid from organisations which might consider joining a (voluntary) employment training scheme introduced by the Government. The Court of Appeal held the purpose (punishment or coercion) to be unlawful.[381]

5-118   When two school governors were removed by an education authority because they had opposed the authority's educational policy, the House of Lords considered whether the broad discretion conferred on the authority permitted this action. The statute simply provided that a governor "shall be removable by the authority by whom he was appointed". It was held that the power could not be exercised in a way that usurped the governor's independent function and that such a usurpation was in effect extraneous to the power conferred.[382] But when eight recalcitrant councillors were removed from a local authority housing committee ostensibly to reduce the size of that committee (and not to punish their behaviour), the decision was not held unlawful.[383]

Plurality of purposes

5-119   We now take hold of a legal porcupine which bristles with difficulties as soon as it is touched. In a case where the actor has sought to achieve unauthorised as well as authorised purposes, what test should be applied to determine the validity of his act? At least six separate tests have been applied where plural purposes or motives are present. The choice of one test in preference to another can materially affect the decision. Despite this, it is not uncommon to find two or more of the tests applied in the course of a single judgment.[384] The following tests, none of which is entirely satisfactory, have been formulated.

Test 1: What was the true purpose for which the power was exercised?

5-120   If the actor has in truth used his power for the purpose for which it was conferred, it is immaterial that he achieved as well a subsidiary object. Thus, if a power to construct an underground public convenience is exercised in such a way as to provide a subway leading to the convenience that can also be used by pedestrians who do not wish to take advantage of its facilities, the power has been validly exercised. The position would have been different if the construction of the conveniences was a colourable device adopted in order to enable a subway to be built.[385] A local authority empowered to spend money upon altering and repairing streets "as and when required" acts lawfully in resurfacing a road that is in fact in need of repair, although the immediate occasion for carrying out the work is the hope of at-

---

[380] *R. v Lewisham LBC Ex p. Shell UK Ltd* [1988] 1 All E.R. 938.

[381] *R. v Liverpool CC Ex p. Secretary of State for Employment* [1989] C.O.D. 404.

[382] *Brunyate v Inner London Education Authority* [1989] 1 W.L.R. 542.

[383] *R. v Greenwich LBC Ex p. Lovelace* [1990] 1 W.L.R. 18; affirmed [1991] 1 W.L.R. 506. See also *Champion v Chief Constable of the Gwent Constabulary* [1990] 1 W.L.R. 1 (refusal of membership of school appointments committee to police constable governor held unlawful as it was not "likely" to give the appearance of partiality); *R. v Warwickshire CC Ex p. Dill-Russell* (1991) 3 Admin. L.R. 1, QBD; affirmed (1991) 3 Admin. L.R. 415, CA (lawful for all governors of school to resign simultaneously so as to achieve proportionality with political representation on reappointment).

[384] See, e.g. *Webb v Minister of Housing and Local Government* [1965] 1 W.L.R. 755 at 773–774, 777H (test (5)), 778G (test (2)); *Grieve v Douglas-Home* 1965 S.C. 313 (tests (1) and (2)); *R. v Inner London Education Authority Ex p. Westminster CC* [1986] 1 W.L.R. 28 (tests (1) and (5)).

[385] *Westminster Corp v L & NW Ry* [1905] A.C. 426.

tracting an automobile club to use it for racing trials.[386] If the Home Secretary is honestly satisfied that the deportation of an alien is conducive to the public good and there is some basis for his belief, his deportation order is valid although the practical effect (and perhaps a secondary desired effect) of the order is to secure the extradition of the alien to another country seeking his rendition for a non-extraditable offence.[387]

Test 2: What was the dominant purpose for which the power was exercised?

If the actor pursues two or more purposes where only one is expressly or impliedly permitted, the legality of the act is determined by reference to the dominant purpose. This test, based on an analogy with the law of tortious conspiracy,[388] has been applied in several cases.[389] In substance it may often prove to be nothing more than a different verbal formulation of the "true purpose" test. Where several purposes coexist, attempts to single out the "true" purpose have an air of unreality. If, of course, the avowed purpose is shown to be a mere sham, the "true purpose" test can readily be applied. It is of some interest that in *Soblen* the courts concentrated their analysis on the question of whether the deportation order was a sham, or a pretext for procuring an unlawful extradition; they abstained from asking themselves what was the Home Secretary's dominant purpose in making the order, though this would not appear to have been an irrelevant question.[390]   **5-121**

In the Pergau dam case[391] it was held that the minister's dominant purpose in funding the uneconomic project was not the authorised one of furthering the "economy" or "welfare" of the people of Malaysia. In the stag hunting ban case[392] it was held that the dominant purpose of fulfilling the "ethical perceptions" of the councillors did not fulfil the statute's authorised purpose that of improvement of the amenity of the area. Perhaps in both these cases the sole purpose was unauthorised.   **5-122**

The House of Lords adopted a combination of the "true" and "dominant" purpose tests in a case where an accountant challenged an application by the police to produce documents relating to her dealings with a client. The statute under which the police made the application provided that it could be made for purposes of investigation into whether a person has "benefited from any criminal conduct".[393] However, the accountant submitted that the predominant reason for seeking the documents was to investigate, under a power provided in different legislation,[394] whether "the conduct from which the person had benefited was criminal". It was held that since "true and dominant purpose" of the application was to investigate the proceeds of criminal conduct in order to obtain evidence for the prosecution, the application should therefore be granted. Furthermore, the application should be   **5-123**

---

[386] *R. v Brighton Corp Ex p. Shoosmith* (1907) 96 L.T. 762.

[387] *R. v Brixton Prison Governor Ex p. Soblen* [1963] 2 Q.B. 243. It is to be noted that the Home Secretary's discretion was couched in subjective terms and was exercisable on "policy" grounds.

[388] *Crofter Hand Woven Harris Tweed Co v Veitch* [1942] A.C. 435.

[389] *Earl Fitzwilliam's Wentworth Estates Co v Minister of Town and Country Planning* [1951] 2 K.B. 284 at 307 (Denning LJ, dissenting). The HL did not give any ruling on this point on appeal ([1952] A.C. 362). For subsequent formulations of a similar test, *Webb* [1965] 1 W.L.R.755 at 778; *Grieve v Douglas-Home* 1965 S.C. 313 *R. v Immigration Appeals Adjudicator Ex p. Khan* [1972] 1 W.L.R. 1058 (whether primary purpose of entering UK as full-time student was to take up permanent residence; *R. v Ealing LBC Ex p. Times Newspapers Ltd* (1986) 85 L.G.R. 316 (dominant purpose in imposing ban on purchase of publications for library was to interfere in industrial dispute).

[390] *R. v Brixton Prison Governor Ex p. Soblen* [1963] 2 Q.B. 243.

[391] *R. v Secretary of State for Foreign Affairs Ex p. World Development Movement* [1995] 1 W.L.R. 386.

[392] *R. v Somerset CC Ex p. Fewings* [1995] 1 W.L.R. 1037.

[393] Criminal Justice Act 1988 s.93H.

[394] Police and Criminal Evidence Act 1984 s.9(1).

granted even if an incidental consequence might be that the police would obtain evidence relating to the commission of an offence.[395]

5-124   In the New Zealand case *Attorney General v Ireland*[396] it was held that when a power was exercised for two purposes, one of which was authorised and the other not, the exercise of the one purpose is valid if the statute does not limit the power to "only" the explicitly authorised purpose and the additional purpose does not thwart or frustrate the purpose of the Act. However, in South Africa it was held that a minister's exercise of a power to regulate the granting of asylum did not extend to preventing asylum seekers from taking up employment or studying.[397]

Test 3: Would the power still have been exercised if the actor had not desired concurrently to achieve an unauthorised purpose?

5-125   This test was applied by the High Court of Australia.[398]

Test 4: Was any of the purposes pursued an authorised purpose?

5-126   If so, the presence of concurrent illicit purposes does not affect the validity of the act. This test appears to have been applied in only one English case, and even then somewhat equivocally.[399] It is submitted that in English law the existence of one legitimate purpose among illegitimate purposes will only save the validity of an act if the purpose for which the power was granted has been substantially fulfilled.

Test 5: Were any of the purposes pursued an unauthorised purpose?

5-127   If so, and if the unauthorised purpose has materially influenced the actor's conduct, the power has been invalidly exercised because irrelevant considerations have been taken into account. The effect of applying such a test may be directly opposed to that produced by the preceding test.[400] This is a curious state of affairs, for the concepts of improper purpose and irrelevancy are intimately related and are

---

[395] *R. v Southwark Crown Court Ex p. Bowles* [1998] A.C. 641.

[396] [2002] 2 N.Z.L.R. 220, CA—citing this paragraph in the 5th edition of this work, at [38]. Affd *Unison Networks Ltd v Commerce Commission* [2007] NZSC 74 and on the same point, *PF Sugrue Ltd v Attorney General* [2005] UKPC 44. And see *Hawke's Bay Regional Investment Company Ltd v Royal Forest and Bird Protection Society of New Zealand Inc* [2017] NZSC 106. See also H. Wilberg, "The Ireland Principle on Unauthorised but not Improper Purposes: An Exploration and a Defence" [2016] N.Z.L. Rev. 95; P.A. Joseph, *Constitutional and Administrative Law in New Zealand*, 4th edn (2014), pp.944–946..

[397] *Minister of Home Affairs v Watchenuka* 2004 (4) S.A. 326, SCA.

[398] *Thompson v Randwick Municipal Council* (1950) 81 C.L.R. 87 at 106. It may have the disadvantage of requiring the courts to speculate about motives for which it is usually ill-equipped, but it is not very different from test (6) below. The leading Australian text suggests that Australian cases now suggest a "substantial purpose" test, "in the sense that the decision would not have been made without the illegitimate purpose". However, the same text is also critical of tests that hinge upon the weight (in the decision-maker's reasoning) of the forbidden purpose, and suggests that a better test would be "whether the challenger missed a real chance because one of the decision-maker's purposes was unlawful": M. Aronson, M. Groves and G. Weeks, *Judicial Review of Administrative Action and Government Liability*, 6th edn (2017) para.5.570.

[399] *Earl Fitzwilliam* [1951] 1 K.B. 203 at 217–219 (Birkett J); see also Lord MacDermott's observations in the HL [1952] A.C. 362 at 385.

[400] Thus, in *Sadler v Sheffield Corp* [1924] 1 Ch. 483, where notices of dismissal served on teachers were held to be invalid because they have been served not on "educational grounds" (as was required by the Act) but in reality on financial grounds, Lawrence J said obiter (at 504–505) that even if bona fide educational grounds for dismissal had coexisted with the financial grounds, it would have been wrong to try to separate them, and that mixed educational and financial grounds were not educational

often analytically indistinguishable.[401] That the possibility of a sharp conflict between them exists has seldom been recognised. The question was considered in a case where the validity of a compulsory purchase order was impugned and the court preferred the test of irrelevancy: had the making of the order been significantly or substantially influenced by irrelevant considerations.[402]

Cases have affirmed this approach. When irrelevant considerations have been taken into account, the courts have invalidated the decision if those considerations have had a substantial" or "material" influence upon the decision.[403]   **5-128**

Test 6: Would the decision-maker have reached the same decision if regard had only been had to the relevant considerations or to the authorised purposes?

This is a subtle variation of the previous (material influence) test. It was applied when the Broadcasting Complaints Commission refused to investigate a complaint for a number of reasons, only one of which was bad (that the investigation would impose too great a burden on the Commission's limited staff). It was held that where the bad reason was not mixed and could be disentangled from the good, then the decision could stand if the Commission would have reached precisely the same decision on the other valid reasons".[404]   **5-129**

DECISIONS BASED UPON IRRELEVANT CONSIDERATIONS OR FAILURE TO TAKE ACCOUNT OF RELEVANT CONSIDERATIONS

When exercising a discretionary power a decision-maker may take into account a range of lawful considerations. Some of these are specified in the statute as matters to which regard may be had. Others are specified as matters to which regard may not be had. There are other considerations which are not specified but which the decision-maker may or may not lawfully take into account.[405] If the exercise of a discretionary power has been influenced by considerations that cannot lawfully be taken into account, or by the disregard of relevant considerations required to be taken into account (expressly or impliedly), a court will normally hold that the power has not been validly exercised.   **5-130**

It may be immaterial that an authority has considered irrelevant matters in arriv-   **5-131**

---

grounds within the meaning of the Act, which were the only grounds that could lawfully be taken into account (applying dictum in *R. v St Pancras Vestry* (1890) L.R. 24 Q.B.D. 371.

[401] *Padfield v Minister of Agriculture, Fisheries and Food* [1968] A.C. 997.

[402] *Hanks v Minister of Housing and Local Government* [1963] 1 Q.B. 999 at 1018–1020 (Megaw J); cf. *Meravale Builders Ltd v Secretary of State for the Environment* (1978) 36 P. & C.R. 87. In practice the result of analysing a situation by reference to the effect of irrelevant considerations will often be the same as that produced by applying the "dominant purpose" test; cf. *Fawcett Properties Ltd v Buckingham CC* [1958] 1 W.L.R. 1161 at 1167–1168.

[403] See, e.g. *R. v Inner London Education Authority Ex p. Westminster CC* [1986] 1 W.L.R. 28 (advertising campaign for the purposes of: (a) information about rate-capping and (b) persuasion against it. Persuasion held an extraneous purpose which materially influenced the decision); *R. v Lewisham LBC Ex p. Shell UK Ltd* [1988] 1 All E.R. 938 (boycott in order to induce Shell to sever its trading links with South Africa held "substantial influence" on decision); and *R. v Ealing LBC Ex p. Times Newspapers Ltd* (1986) 85 L.G.R. 316.

[404] *R. v Broadcasting Complaints Commission Ex p. Owen* [1985] Q.B. 1153; *R. v Rochdale MBC Ex p. Cromer Ring Mill Ltd* [1982] 3 All E.R. 761 (misconceived guidelines "substantially influenced" decision not to refund rates, despite good reasons which could not be disentangled).

[405] These three considerations were set out by Simon Brown LJ in *R. v Somerset CC Ex p. Fewings* [1995] 1 W.L.R. 1037 at 1049.

ing at its decision if it has not allowed itself to be influenced by those matters[406] and it may be right to overlook a minor error of this kind even if it has affected an aspect of the decision.[407] However, if the influence of irrelevant factors is established, it does not appear to be necessary to prove that they were the sole or even the dominant influence. As a general rule it is enough to prove that their influence was material or substantial. For this reason there may be a practical advantage in founding a challenge to the validity of a discretionary act on the basis of irrelevant considerations rather than extraneous purpose, though the line of demarcation between the two grounds of invalidity is often imperceptible.[408]

5-132   In cases where the reasons for the decision are not available, and there is no material either way to show by what considerations the authority was influenced, the court may determine whether their influence is to be inferred from the surrounding circumstances. In such cases the courts may infer that an extraneous purpose was being pursued.[409] In some circumstances, a decision-maker may be required to promulgate a policy explaining what factors are regarded by him as relevant to the exercise of discretion.[410] In some contexts, written statements of reasons for a decision may be "set out in brief form and their brevity does not indicate a failure to take account of any material considerations".[411] Where the question is whether due regard was had to all material facts in making delegated legislation, the court may consider parliamentary material: there was no objection to referring to parliamentary debates in *Hansard* and select committee reports simply in relation to any relevant information contained in them, so long as there was no attempt to analyse or criticise anything contained in the material contrary to art.9 of the Bill of Rights 1689.[412]

5-133   If the ground of challenge is that relevant considerations have not been taken into account, the court will normally try to assess the actual or potential importance of the factor that was overlooked,[413] even though this may entail a degree of speculation. The question is whether the validity of the decision is contingent on

---

[406] *R. v London (Bishop)* (1890) 24 Q.B.D. 213 at 226–227 (affd. on grounds not identical, sub nom. *Allcroft v Bishop of London* [1891] A.C. 666); *Ex p. Rice; Re Hawkins* (1957) 74 W.N. - (N.S.W) 7, 14; *Hanks v Minister of Housing and Local Government* [1963] 1 Q.B. 999 at 1018–1020; *Re Hurle-Hobbs' Decision* [1944] 1 All E.R. 249.

[407] *Hounslow LBC v Twickenham Garden Developments Ltd* [1971] Ch. 233, 271; *R. v Barnet & Camden Rent Tribunal Ex p. Frey Investments Ltd* [1972] 2 Q.B. 342; *Bristol DC v Clark* [1975] 1 W.L.R. 1443 at 1449–1450 (Lawton LJ); *Asher v Secretary of State for the Environment* [1974] Ch. 208 at 221, 227.

[408] *Marshall v Blackpool Corp* [1935] A.C. 16; *Padfield v Minister of Agriculture, Fisheries and Food* [1968] A.C. 997; *R. v Rochdale MBC Ex p. Cromer Ring Mill Ltd* [1982] 2 All E.R. 761.

[409] Or that the exercise of discretion was unreasonable: *Lonrho Plc v Secretary of State for Trade and Industry* [1989] 1 W.L.R. 525 at 539 (Lord Keith said that where reasons for a decision were absent "and if all other known facts and circumstances appear to point overwhelmingly in favour of a different decision, the decision-maker ... cannot complain if the court draws the inference that he had no rational reason for his decision"); *R. v Civil Service Appeal Board Ex p. Cunningham* [1991] 4 All E.R. 310 (absence of reasons for low compensation award and no reasons given inference made that decision irrational); *Padfield* [1968] A.C. 997 at 1032–1033, 1049, 1053–1054, 1061–1062 (Lords Reid, Hodson, Pearce and Upjohn).

[410] See, e.g. *R. (on the application of Purdy) v DPP (SPUC intervening)* [2009] UKHL 45; [2010] 1 A.C. 345 (factors for and against decisions to prosecute for offence of assisted suicide).

[411] *R. (on the application of Evans) v Cornwall Council* [2013] EWHC 4109 (Admin); [2014] P.T.S.R. 556.

[412] *R. (Hurley) v Secretary of State for Work and Pensions (Equality and Human Rights Commission intervening)* [2015] EWHC 3382 (Admin); [2016] P.T.S.R. 636 at [15]–[27], Collins J noting that "I should not make my view prevail over the informed view of both Houses of Parliament as expressed in the democratic process".

[413] *R. v London (Bishop)* (1890) 24 Q.B.D. at 266–227, 237, 244; *Baldwin & Francis Ltd v Patents Appeal Tribunal* [1959] A.C. 663 at 693 (Lord Denning); *R. v Paddington Valuation Officer Ex p.*

strict observance of antecedent requirements. In determining what factors may or must be taken into account by the authority, the courts are again faced with problems of statutory interpretation. If relevant factors are specified in the enabling Act it is for the courts to determine whether they are factors to which the authority is compelled to have regard.[414] If so, may other, non-specified considerations be taken into account or are the specified, considerations to be construed as being exhaustive?

This question arose in a case where members of the Labour Party challenged the recommendations of the Boundary Commission.[415] The Commission was under a duty to make recommendations to the Home Secretary about the boundaries of parliamentary constituencies (though the final decision rested with Parliament). The statute set out a series of rules to which the Commission were required to give effect. These included the requirements (a) that "so far as practicable" the constituencies are not to cross London borough boundaries and (b) that "the electorate shall be as near to the electoral quota" as possible.[416] If it appeared, however, that it was desirable to avoid an "excessive disparity" between the electoral quota and the actual electorate of any constituency, the Commission had a discretion to take (c) "geographical considerations" into account. The Commission were also permitted to take account, in so far as they reasonably could, of (d) "inconvenience attendant on alterations of constituencies and of any local ties broken by such alterations". The applicants considered that the Commission had laid undue emphasis on the requirement of not crossing local boundaries and insufficient emphasis on the requirement of achieving equality of numbers in the electorates of their constituents. It was held that although the Acts set out requirements to which the Commission had to have regard, the burden on the applicants of showing that the commission had exercised their powers wrongly was heavy as the rules themselves were no more than guidelines. Despite the wide disparity in some constituency boundaries, there was no evidence that the Commission had misunderstood or ignored Parliament's instructions.

If the relevant factors are not specified (e.g. if the power is merely to grant or refuse a licence, or to attach such conditions as the competent authority thinks fit), it is for the courts to determine whether the permissible considerations are impliedly restricted, and, if so, to what extent,[417] although when the courts conclude that a wide range of factors may properly be considered, they will be reluctant to lay down a list with which the authority will be required to comply in every case.[418] In *R. v Secretary of State for Transport Ex p. Richmond LBC*,[419] Laws J said that where relevant considerations are not specified in a statute the decision-maker's consideration of what is a relevant consideration can only be subject to review on the ground of unreasonableness. With respect, this ignores the fact that the (non-specified) considerations adopted by the decision-maker may be matters that are extraneous to the purpose of the statute, and therefore reviewable for illegality.

5-134

5-135

Peachey Property Corp Ltd [1966] 1 Q.B. 380.

[414] On mandatory and directory considerations, see 5-049; e.g. *Yorkshire Copper Works Ltd v Registrar of Trade Marks* [1954] 1 W.L.R. 554 (HL held that the Registrar was bound to have regard to specific factors to which he was prima facie empowered to have regard); *R. v Shadow Education Committee of Greenwich BC Ex p. Governors of John Ball Primary School* (1989) 88 L.G.R. 589 (failure to have regard to parental preferences).

[415] *R. v Boundary Commission for England Ex p. Foot* [1983] 1 Q.B. 600, CA.

[416] House of Commons (Redistribution of Seats) Act 1949 s.2(1)(a) Sch.2, rr.4, 5.

[417] 5-120.

[418] See, e.g. *Elliott v Southwark LBC* [1976] 1 W.L.R. 499 at 507; *Bristol DC v Clark* [1975] 1 W.L.R. 1443 (the court looked for guidance on the factors relevant to the exercise of a statutory discretion to a departmental circular issued after the enactment of the legislation).

[419] *R. v Secretary of State for Transport Ex p. Richmond LBC* [1994] 1 W.L.R. 74 at 95.

5-136   The question of relevancy may relate not to specified factors that need to be taken into account by the decision-maker, but to the decision-maker's approach to the evidence before him. In *R. (on the application of National Association of Health Stores) v Department of Health*[420] the minister decided to accept the view of the Medicines Commission that a herbal remedy ought to be banned. The Commission, unusually, informed the minister that one of its members was opposed to the ban, but failed to inform him that that member was especially qualified in psychopharmacology and had recently completed a meta-analysis of the scientific evidence of the remedy. Nor was the minister informed of the conclusions of the review. Were these factors "relevant considerations" which the minister had ignored? In the circumstances of this case it was held that the minister must know, or be told "enough" to ensure that no relevant considerations are ignored, but need not know "everything that is relevant". The court followed Lord Cooke's distinction in *CREEDNZ Inc v Governor General*[421] between "matters which are so relevant that they must be taken into account" (which included the Commission's report and the matters about which he was informed) and "matters which are not irrelevant and therefore may legitimately be taken into account" (which included the matters about which he was not informed). Sedley LJ held that "only a failure to take into account something in the former class would vitiate a public law decision",[422] and the minister had sufficient information to make a decision. The second category surely begs the question of whether the "not irrelevant" matter ought to have been taken into account so as to give the minister a complete picture of the weight he ought to have accorded to the dissenting expert's view.[423]

5-137   Examples of discretionary powers having been unlawfully exercised on legally irrelevant grounds are multitudinous. Many of the earlier cases are concerned with magistrates refusing to issue summonses for extraneous reasons,[424] or failing to consider relevant factors before ordering a surety to forfeit a recognisance,[425] or with tribunals improperly refusing or agreeing to adjourn proceedings before them,[426] and

---

[420] [2005] EWCA Civ 154; *The Times,* 9 March 2005; I. Steele, "Note on R. (National Association of Health Stores) v Department of Health" [2005] J.R. 232.

[421] *CREEDNZ Inc v Governor General* [1981] 1 N.Z.L.R. 172. *CREEDNZ* was endorsed by Lord Scarman in *Re Findlay* [1985] A.C. 318. See also *Minister of Aboriginal Affairs v Peko-Wallsend* (1986) 162 C.L.R. 24.

[422] *National Association of Health Stores* [2005] EWCA Civ 154; *The Times,* 9 March 2005 at [63] and [75] (Keene LJ); and see the approach of Gibbs CJ in *Minister of Aboriginal Affairs v Peko-Wallsend* (1986) 162 C.L.R. 24 at 31 (distinction made between "insignificant or insubstantial matters" which are not brought to the attention of the minister, and "material facts which he is bound to consider") and Brennan J at 61 (makes the distinction between "minutiae", which the minister need not consider, and "salient facts which give shape and substance to the matter"). For a discussion of the *weight* to be attached to relevant considerations, see 11-033.

[423] On mandatory and discretionary requirements, see 5-052.

[424] *R. v Adamson* (1875) 1 Q.B.D. 201; *R. v Boteler* (1864) 33 L.J.M.C. 101; *R. v Mead Ex p. National Health Insurance Commrs* (1916) 85 W.K.B. 1065 (refusals based on disapproval of conduct of complainants or of the policy or application of the legislation concerned); *R. v Bennett and Bond* (1908) 72 J.P 362; *R. v Nuneaton Borough Justices* [1954] 1 W.L.R. 1318 (refusal on ground that other proceedings more appropriate).

[425] See, e.g. *R. v Southampton Justices Ex p. Green* [1976] Q.B. 11; *R. v Horseferry Road Stipendiary Magistrate Ex p. Pearson* [1976] 1 W.L.R. 511.

[426] On the question whether a tribunal is entitled to adjourn a matter because a change in the law is pending, see *R. v Whiteway Ex p. Stephenson* [1961] V.R. 168, 171; *Boyd Builders Ltd v Ottawa* (1964–45 D.L.R. (2nd) 211 (adjournment improper); but the position may be different if the change in the law is imminent and reasonably certain; cf. *Clifford Sabey (Contractors) Ltd v Long* [1959] 2 Q.B. 290 at 298–300. For non-judicial exercise of discretion to postpone operation of demolition order, see *Pocklington v Melksham UDC* [1964] 2 Q.B. 673. See also *Royal v Prescott-Clarke* [1966] 1 W.L.R. 788; *Walker v Walker* [1967] 1 W.L.R. 327.

with licensing justices refusing applications,[427] granting them subject to irrelevant conditions,[428] or even granting them unconditionally on irrelevant grounds.[429] There are decisions on the unlawful expenditure of public funds by local authorities,[430] and a miscellany of decisions which illustrate the general rule in a wide range of contexts.[431]

As we have seen, the interpretation of statutory purpose and that of the relevancy of considerations are closely related, since the question in regard to the considerations taken into account in reaching a decision is normally whether that consideration is relevant to the statutory purpose. This is seen in respect of the considerations taken into account by planning authorities as a basis of a refusal of planning permission. Is it relevant to refuse an application for permission to change the use on the site from use A to use B on the ground that the authority wishes to preserve the use of site as A (and have no inherent objection to use B)? It has been held that the preservation of an existing use may be a material planning consideration, but only if, on the balance of probabilities, there is a fair chance of use A being continued.[432] Where, however, the authority wished to retain the existing use so that it could be kept in their own occupation, it was held that that consideration was not a legitimate planning consideration.[433] Other disputed considerations in the area of planning law involve the regard that has been had to factors such as precedent (it has been held that permission may be refused because it would be difficult to resist similar applications in the future)[434]; to the fact that alternative sites would be more appropriate for the development, or to the personal circumstances of the applicant.

5-138

Where a university, after consultation with the police, refused to permit a meeting on its premises addressed by members of the South African Embassy during the apartheid regime, it did so in the belief that the meeting would provoke public violence in the neighbouring area. The statute required universities to ensure that freedom of speech was secured and that the use of university premises was not denied to any individual body on the ground of their beliefs, policy or objectives. It was held that in taking into account the likelihood of violence outside of their premises the decision had been influenced by an irrelevant consideration and was therefore ultra vires.[435] The action of a local trading standards officer was held to have been unlawful when, three days after a children's toy was found to have been

5-139

---

[427] See, e.g. *R. v de Rutzen* (1875) 1 Q.B.D. 55.

[428] See, e.g. *R. v Bowman* [1898] 1 Q.B. 663; *R. v Birmingham Licensing Planning Committee Ex p. Kennedy* [1972] 2 Q.B. 140 (refusal to allow application to proceed unless irrelevant condition complied with); see too *Fletcher v London (Metropolis) Licensing Committee* [1976] A.C. 150.

[429] See, e.g. *R. v Cotham* [1898] 1 Q.B. 802.

[430] *Attorney General v Tynemouth Poor Law Union Guardians* [1930] 1 Ch. 616; *Roberts v Hopwood* [1925] A.C. 578; *Prescott v Birmingham Corp* [1955] Ch. 210; *Taylor v Munrow* [1960] 1 W.L.R. 151.

[431] See, e.g. *Padfield v Minister of Agriculture, Fisheries and Food* [1968] A.C. 997; *R. (on the application of Sainsbury's Supermarkets Ltd) v Wolverhampton City Council* [2010] UKSC 20; [2011] 1 A.C. 437 (whether in compulsory purchase it is permissible to take into account "off site" benefits of a proposed development related to the development for which the CPO was made); and many of the cases on improper purpose.

[432] *Westminster CC v British Waterways Board* [1985] A.C. 676: *London Residuary Body v Lambeth LBC* [1990] 1 W.L.R. 744; *Clyde & Co v Secretary of State for the Environment* [1977] 1 W.L.R. 926 (desirability of maintaining the possibility that land would be used to relieve housing shortage a material consideration); cf. *Granada Theatres Ltd v Secretary of State for the Environment* [1976] J.P.L. 96.

[433] *Westminster CC v British Waterways Board* [1985] A.C. 676 (Lord Bridge).

[434] *Collis Radio Ltd v Secretary of State for the Environment* (1975) 29 P. & C.R. 390.

[435] *R. v Liverpool University Ex p. Caesar Gordon* [1991] 1 Q.B. 124; *R. v Coventry Airport Ex p. Phoenix Aviation* [1995] 3 All E.R. 37, DC (unlawful surrender to the dictates of pressure groups opposed to the export of live animals). cf. *R. v Chief Constable of Sussex Ex p. International Trad-*

dangerous, he suspended the manufacturer from supplying the toy for six months. He claimed to have had regard to a regulation which would have permitted the suspension, but which was not yet in force. The court held that consideration to be irrelevant.[436] Where a statute gave the power to the minister to licence medicines for importation into the United Kingdom when it was "expedient" to do so, it was held that his taking into account of trade mark (private) rights was a consideration irrelevant to the public law powers in the circumstances of that case.[437] In *R. (on the application of Gulliver) v Parole Board* the claimant challenged a decision by the Parole Board not to direct his re-release from prison, following his recall to prison by the Secretary of State for Justice. The claimant was required to wear a satellite tracking unit to monitor his whereabouts and the reason for his recall was that he failed to recharge the battery. The question for the Court of Appeal was whether the Parole Board, having held that there was in fact no breach of the appellant's licence conditions, was entitled to consider all the evidence available at the date of the oral hearing, and to hold that the appellant's risk to the public was such that he should not have been released. The court held that the Parole Board:

"is to have regard to all the circumstances of the case, including, of course, the circumstances of the recall, but in the end to decide whether to recommend the release of the prisoner having made an assessment of risk to the public, on the basis of all the material available to it when it makes its decision. One of those considerations will, of course, be whether appropriate licence conditions could be devised. The Parole Board considered the available licence conditions in this case and plainly decided that, in all the circumstances, they could not".[438]

Government policy as a relevant consideration

5-140   As we examine elsewhere, a public body may have several different standards of legality in relation to the policies it adopts.[439] Policies must be rational[440] and not contrary to Convention rights.[441] The adoption of a policy may create a legitimate expectation, which should not be resiled from without justification.[442] The adoption of a rigid policy about how a discretion will be exercised may unlawfully fetter that discretion.[443] There may be a duty to promulgate a policy.[444] The question has also arisen as to whether or not a circular may amount to an authoritative account of the law at all, and thus be subject to judicial review.[445] Normally policy will be expressed through a government circular or a code of practice which lacks binding effect.[446] A policy need not normally have been promulgated in any

---

ers Ferry [1999] 2 A.C. 418.
[436] *R. v Birmingham CC Ex p. Ferrero Ltd* (1991) 3 Admin. L.R. 613.
[437] *R. v Secretary of State for Social Services Ex p. Wellcome Foundation* [1987] 2 All E.R. 1025.
[438] *R. (on the application of Gulliver) v Parole Board* [2007] EWCA Civ 1386; [2008] 1 W.L.R. 1116 at [35] (Sir Anthony Clarke MR).
[439] On what constitutes "policy", see 5-080.
[440] See Ch.11.
[441] See Ch.13.
[442] See Ch.12.
[443] See Ch.9.
[444] See, e.g. *R. (on the application of Purdy) v DPP* [2009] UKHL 45; [2010] 1 A.C. 345.
[445] See 3-025.
[446] R. Baldwin and J. Houghton, "Circular Arguments: The Status and Legitimacy of Administrative Rules" [1986] P.L. 239; G. Ganz, *Quasi-legislation* (1986). For the distinction between direction and guidance see *Laker Airways v Department of Trade* [1977] Q.B. 643, 714. See also *R. v Secretary of State for Social Services and the Social Fund Inspector Ex p. Stilt* (1992) 4 Admin. L.R. 713.

particular way, but after-dinner speeches do not qualify.[447] Draft policy statements may or may not qualify.[448]

In a number of cases the question has arisen of whether regard may or must be had to various forms of government advice or indication of government policy— or, indeed, whether a policy is an irrelevant consideration.[449] The House of Lords considered the status of a code of practice which the Secretary of State was required to prepare under the terms of the Mental Health Act 1983 in order to guide the treatment of patients in hospitals dealing with mental disorders.[450] The code then required hospitals to produce their own codes, and the question was whether a local hospital trust's code was unlawful because it was not in conformity with the Secretary of State's code.[451] The House of Lords held that although the Secretary of State's code did not have the binding effect of a statutory provision, and purported to be "guidance", not "instruction", it was guidance which should be given "great weight" from which the hospital could only depart with "great care".[452] Similarly, formal statements of planning policy issued by the responsible central government Department, although only advisory in nature, have been held to be material planning considerations to which regard must be had by both local authorities and the Secretary of State in making decisions about development control.[453]

5-141

To what extent can a failure to have regard to a government non-statutory policy invalidate a decision for disregard of a material consideration? An authority is entitled to ignore or act contrary to a policy circular which misstates the law.[454] A policy cannot make a matter that is an irrelevant consideration, or outside the purpose of the statute, relevant or lawful. If the decision-maker attaches a meaning to the words of the policy which they are not capable of bearing, he will have made an error of law.[455] If there has been a change in the policy, it has been held that the decision must relate to the new policy, even if it has not been published and

5-142

---

[447] *Dinsdale Developments Ltd v Secretary of State for the Environment* [1986] J.P.L. 276.

[448] *Richmond-upon-Thames LBC v Secretary of State for the Environment* [1984] J.P.L. 24; but may not: *Pye JA (Oxford) Estates Ltd v Secretary of State for the Environment* [1982] J.P.L. 577.

[449] See, e.g. *R. (on the application of Clue) v Birmingham City Council (Shelter intervening)* [2010] EWCA Civ 460; [2011] 1 W.L.R. 99 (local authority deciding whether to exercise powers under Children Act 1989 s.17 to provide support for mother and children pending their application for indefinite leave to remain in the UK was wrong to take into account Home Secretary's published immigration policies on circumstances in which children may be removed from the UK).

[450] *R. (on the application of Munjaz) v Mersey Care NHS Trust* [2005] UKHL 58; [2006] 2 A.C. 148.

[451] See 9-120-122.

[452] *R. (on the application of Munjaz) v Mersey Care NHS Trust* [2005] UKHL 58; [2006] 2 A.C. 148 at [21] (Lord Bingham); and see *R. (on the application of Khatun) v Newham LBC* [2004] EWCA Civ 55; [2005] Q.B. 37 at [47] (Laws LJ). In *R. (on the application of Winder) v Sandwell Metropolitan Borough Council (Equality and Human Rights Commission intervening)* [2014] EWHC 2617 (Admin); [2015] P.T.S.R. 34 the defendant council was considered to have acted unlawfully, when, in designing a council tax reduction scheme, it failed to take into account stated government policy objectives relating to the localisation of support for council tax.

[453] See 5-039.

[454] *R. v Secretary of State for the Environment Ex p. Tower Hamlets LBC* [1993] Q.B. 632 (Code of Guidance to Local Authorities on Homelessness by Department of the Environment held to misstate the law); *R. v Secretary of State for the Environment Ex p. Lancashire CC* [1994] 4 All E.R. 165 (policy guidance issued to local government Commissioners to replace their authorities with unitary authorities held more in the nature of directions than guidance and therefore unlawful).

[455] See, e.g. *Horsham DC v Secretary of State for the Environment* [1992] 1 P.L.R. 81; *Virgin Cinema Properties Ltd v Secretary of State for the Environment* [1998] 2 P.L.R. 24; and *R. (on the application of Howard League for Penal Reform) v Secretary of State for the Home Department (No.2)* [2002] EWHC 2497 (Admin); [2003] 1 F.L.R. 484; *R. (on the application of Burke) v General Medical Council* [2005] EWCA Civ 1003; [2006] Q.B. 273 at [21] (review of guidance on the withdrawal of artificial feeding. Noting that "the court should not be used as a general advice centre"); Cf. *R. (on the application of Lambeth LBC) v Secretary of State for Work and Pensions* [2005] EWHC 637

is not known to the parties.[456] However, this proposition may be subject to any legitimate expectation on their part.[457] If the decision-maker departs from the policy, clear reasons for doing so must be provided, in order that the recipient of the decision will know why the decision is made as an exception to the policy and the grounds upon which the decision is taken.[458] In *Munjaz*, the House of Lords held that the hospital could only depart from the Secretary of State's code if it had provided "cogent reasoned justification" for so doing, which the court "should scrutinize with the intensity which the importance and sensitivity of the subject matter requires".[459]

International law and relevancy

5-143   We have already drawn a distinction between (a) incorporated treaty provisions, (b) unincorporated treaty provisions and (c) customary international law.[460] The question whether a public authority has acted unlawfully in the exercise of its discretion by failing to take into account international law relates to (b). The concern of the courts has often been that if such an argument is accepted, it is tantamount to incorporation of the treaty "through the back door"—in other words, it would in practice be giving effect to a treaty provision (the making of which is an executive action) which Parliament has not expressly provided should be part of domestic law. The high water mark for such an approach is the House of Lords' decision in *Brind*,[461] in which—before the Human Rights Act 1998—their Lordships rejected an argument that a minister should exercise his discretion within the limitations imposed by the ECHR. Lord Bridge said that the contrary conclusion "would be a judicial usurpation of the legislative function".[462] This approach has been softened in recent years. While it still remains the case that a decision will not be held unlawful just because a public authority has failed to take into account an unincorporated treaty provision, in such situations the courts will now subject the decision to "anxious scrutiny" in testing its reasoning and calling for a justification from the public authority.[463]

(Admin); [2005] B.L.G.R. 764 (change in government policy will not in general justify treating a refusal to alter a previous decision).

[456] *Newham LBC v Secretary of State for the Environment* (1987) 53 P. & C.R. 98.

[457] On legitimate expectations, see Ch.12.

[458] *EC Gransden & Co Ltd v Secretary of State for the Environment* (1987) 54 P. & C.R. 86; *Carpets of Worth Ltd v Wyre Forest DC* (1991) 62 P. & C.R. 334. For application of these principles outside of planning law, in relation to police negotiating machinery, see *R. v Secretary of State for the Home Department Ex p. Lancashire Police Authority* [1992] C.O.D. 161.

[459] *R. (on the application of Munjaz) v Mersey Care NHS Trust* [2005] UKHL 58; [2006] 2 A.C. 148 at [21] (Lord Bingham); see also *Argos Ltd v Office of Fair Trading* [2006] EWCA Civ 1318; [2006] U.K.C.L.R. 1135 (Competition Act 1998 s.38(1) required the OFT to prepare and publish guidance and s.38(8) required it to "have regard" to the guidance in setting penalties. It was held that the OFT must give reasons for departing from the guidance); *Royal Mail Group Plc v The Postal Services Commission* [2007] EWHC 1205 (Admin) (PSC unlawfully departed from its policy on penalties).

[460] See 5-046.

[461] *R. v Secretary of State for the Home Department Ex p. Brind* [1991] A.C. 696; and *R. (on the application of Hurst) v HM Coroner for Northern District London* [2007] UKHL 13; [2007] 2 W.L.R. 726 at [53]–[59] (Lord Browne); P. Sales and J. Clements, "International law in domestic courts: the developing framework" (2008) 124 L.Q.R. 388.

[462] *Brind* [1991] A.C. 696 at 748; also *R. v Ministry of Defence Ex p. Smith* [1996] Q.B. 517 at 558 (Sir Thomas Bingham MR).

[463] See 11-086.

Financial considerations and relevancy

There are three ways in which the relevance of financial considerations may be engaged: (a) whether the cost of a project may be taken into account as a factor relevant to the decision; (b) whether the expenditure of public funds is simply too extravagant, and (c) whether the authority's lack of resources may justify the non-implementation of a power or duty. Under (b) and (c) particularly, the question of the amenability of the courts to pronounce on the matter of resource allocation comes into sharp focus.[464]

5-144

Cost as a relevant consideration

In the area of planning, the question of cost has been raised in different contexts. It has been held that the likelihood that a development would, because of its excessive cost, never be implemented, may be a material consideration in refusing planning permission.[465] Yet the question of whether a development was a good investment proposition for the developer was held not to be material.[466] The refusal of planning permission because of the absence in the proposal of any "planning gain" (a benefit by means of a voluntary material contribution to the authority) has also been held to be a non-material consideration.[467] Westminster City Council granted planning permission to the Directors of the Covent Garden Opera House for an office development near (but not on) its site, on the ground that the profits from the development would be devoted to improving the facilities of the opera house. Although the office development would not have been given planning permission on its own, the fact that it enabled an otherwise unaffordable development was held by the Court of Appeal to be a material consideration which justified the permission.[468]

5-145

Excessive expenditure

At the other extreme are cases where an authority's expenditure has been challenged for being excessive.[469] The attempt of the Poplar Borough Council in 1925 to raise the wages and salaries of its employees, and to pay women employees rates equal to that of men, was held contrary to law. The House of Lords in that case came

5-146

---

[464] On justiciability, see 1-032.

[465] *Sovmots Investments Ltd v Secretary of State for the Environment* [1979] A.C. 144.

[466] *Murphy (J) & Sons Ltd v Secretary of State for the Environment* [1973] 1 W.L.R. 560; *Walters v Secretary of State for Wales* [1979] J.P.L. 172 (cost of development not a material planning consideration); cf. *Sovmots Investments Ltd v Secretary of State for the Environment* [1977] Q.B. 411 at 422–425; *Hambledon and Chiddingfold PC v Secretary of State for the Environment* [1976] J.P.L. 502; *Niarchos (London) Ltd v Secretary of State for the Environment* (1978) 35 P. & C.R. 259).

[467] *Westminster Renslade Ltd v Secretary of State for the Environment* [1983] J.P.L. 454.

[468] *R. v Westminster City Council Ex p. Monahan* [1990] 1 Q.B. 87, although it was doubted whether such a consideration would be material or relevant if the benefit was not in physical proximity to the development (e.g. if the benefit was in the form of a swimming pool at the other end of the town). On the use of planning obligations (formerly planning agreements) to achieve this kind of benefit, see 5-039. cf. *R. v Camden LBC Ex p. Cran, The Times,* 25 January 1995 (relevant for Council to seek to make a profit from a car parking scheme).

[469] See, e.g. *R v. Secretary of State for the Environment Ex p. Hammersmith and Fulham LBC* [1991] 1 A.C. 521 at 593, 597 (Lord Bridge: local authorities' claim that the Secretary of State's determination of their expenditure as "excessive" was not capable of resolution by the courts as it admitted of no objective justification); *R. v Secretary of State for Health Ex p. Keen* (1991) 3 Admin. L.R. 180 (lawful for resources to be allocated in anticipation of a new scheme proposed in a parliamentary Bill, provided the authority's discretion was not fettered).

close to holding that expenditure unreasonable,[470] but the ratio of the case was based upon the view that the amounts paid were at a time of falling cost of living, more in the nature of a gratuity than the wages and salaries which the authority was authorised to pay.[471] In 1983 the question of local authority expenditure arose again in respect of the decision of the Greater London Council to reduce transport fares by 25 per cent.[472] The fare cuts would have lost the council approximately 50 million of the rate support grant which they would otherwise have been entitled to receive from the central government sources. Although the governing statute gave wide discretion to promote the provision of "integrated, efficient and economic transport facilities",[473] it also required the authorities to make up any deficit incurred in one accounting period in the next such period.[474] This provision was held to limit the authorities' discretion and subject them to a duty to run the system on ordinary business principles, which the drastic reductions in the fares contravened.[475]

5-147   The courts have, from time to time, invoked the principle that local authorities owe an implied "fiduciary duty" to their ratepayers. The breach of such a duty has rarely formed the ratio of a decision to strike down the expenditure concerned.[476] The fiduciary duty could be interpreted in two ways: first, it could imply a duty to act on ordinary business principles and not to be "thriftless"[477] with ratepayers" money. Such a meaning of the fiduciary duty comes close to permitting the courts themselves to decide the levels of expenditure which meet those standards. As the House of Lords has reminded us in a different context, courts are not, in judicial review, equipped to make such decisions.[478] A second interpretation views the fiduciary duty as a duty to take into account, in reaching a decision on expenditure, the interests of the ratepayers.[479] Since the ratepayers' interests are likely to be adversely affected by a decision to increase expenditure, it is surely right that those interests should be considered by the local authority (although not necessarily slavishly followed). This second meaning of the fiduciary duty does not involve the courts in a function to which, in judicial review, they are unsuited. It merely involves them in requiring that considerations which are relevant to the local authority's powers, namely, the interests of the local taxpayers, be taken into account. This function is perfectly suited to judicial review. It is noteworthy that in *Magill v Porter*,[480] a case in which members of Westminster Council were held to have incurred unlawful expenditure on behalf of the Council, the fiduciary concept was not employed and the House of Lords were content to find simply that

---

[470] *Roberts v Hopwood* [1925] A.C. 578.

[471] A point made by Ormrod LJ in *Pickwell v Camden LBC* [1983] Q.B. 962. See also Sir David Williams, "Law and Administrative Discretion" (1994) Indiana J. of Global Legal Studies 191. For a consideration of the "fiduciary principle" raised in *Roberts v Hopwood* and other cases, see 11-069; *Prescott v Birmingham Corp* [1955] Ch. 210; *Taylor v Monrow* [1960] 1 W.L.R. 151.

[472] *Bromley LBC v Greater London Council* [1983] 1 A.C. 768.

[473] Transport (London) Act 1969 s.1.

[474] Transport (London) Act 1969 s.7(3)(b).

[475] A subsequent scheme, known as the "balanced fare scheme", was held to be lawful: *R. v London Transport Executive Ex p. Greater London Council* [1983] Q.B. 484.

[476] See, e.g. *Roberts v Hopwood* [1925] A.C. 578; *Bromley LBC v GLC* [1983] 1 A.C. 768. Both these cases were decided on the basis of "illegality". See also *Re Westminster City Council* [1986] A.C. 668 (grants by GLC unlawful but not unreasonable). cf. *Prescott v Birmingham Corp* [1955] Ch. 210.

[477] *Bromley LBC v GLC* [1983] 1 A.C. 768 at 899 (Lord Diplock); cf. *Hazell v Hammersmith and Fulham LBC* [1992] 2 A.C. 1 at 37 (Lord Templeman referred to the duty of the local authority to be "prudent" with ratepayers' money.

[478] *R. v Secretary of State for the Environment Ex p. Hammersmith and Fulham LBC* [1991] 1 A.C. 521 at 593, 597 (Lord Bridge), at least in relation to unreasonableness. On justiciability, see 1-032.

[479] Today, commercial ratepayers and domestic council taxpayers.

[480] *Magill v Porter* [2001] UKHL 67; [2002] 2 A.C. 357.

the councillors' actions failed to pursue a "public purpose" in seeking to obtain party-political gain at the expense of the ratepayers.[481] In *Charles Terence Estates Ltd v Cornwall CC* a local authority raised its own alleged breach of fiduciary duty to its local taxpayers as a defence to an action in private law proceedings for recovery of rent due under lease agreements. The Court of Appeal held that there had been no breach of fiduciary duty but, in any case, such a breach would only render an act ultra vires and void and so provide a defence to a claim in private law if it went to legal capacity.[482]

Limited resources

Even before the unprecedented cuts in public spending imposed by government policy following the financial crisis of 2007, public authorities have frequently pleaded lack of resources as an excuse for cutting services, not fulfilling their duties or exercising discretionary powers. Whether this limited resources is lawful, as we have seen, is highly contextual and depends in the first instance on whether the duty merely a general duty (unenforceable by any individual), or whether it is, or has crystallised into, an enforceable duty.[483] In *Barnett*,[484] considering whether a local authority owed a duty to provide resources to children "in need", the majority of the House of Lords held that the duty was a mere "target duty" and therefore the Lords could not require the expenditure of additional resources. A similar view was taken in *R. v Gloucestershire CC Ex p. Barry*, where the House of Lords held that the authority was entitled to take into account its limited resources when it considered whether it could fulfil the "needs" of disabled persons.[485] Later, the House of Lords refused to interfere in a decision of a chief constable to deploy his resources by withdrawing full-time protection from animal exporters threatened by demonstrations by animal welfare groups.[486] However, in *R. v Sussex CC Ex p.*

5-148

---

[481] In *Bromley LBC v GLC* [1983] 1 A.C. 768 a further question concerned the relevance to the decision of the council's so-called "mandate". It was argued that the promise to reduce transport fares was the major part of the manifesto on which the new ruling party had fought the recent election. The House of Lords clearly held, however, that a so-called mandate from the electorate can have no influence on the *legality* of a decision, which must fulfil the purposes authorised by the statute which governs the power in question. Compare the influence of the mandate upon the reasonableness of a decision, discussed at 11-017; cf. *R. v Merseyside CC Ex p. Great Universal Stores Ltd* (1982) 80 L.G.R. 639. In New Zealand there is a line of cases in which the fiduciary concept has been applied: *Lovelock v Waitakere CC* [1996] 3 N.Z.L.R. 310; *Waitakere CC v Lovelock* [1997] 2 N.Z.L.R. 385, CA.

[482] *Charles Terence Estates Ltd v Cornwall CC* [2012] EWCA Civ 1439; [2013] 1 W.L.R. 466, reversing [2011] EWHC 2542 (QB); [2012] 1 P. & C.R. 2. If the decision of Cranston J in the High Court was correct then, in the words of Maurice Kay LJ in the Court of Appeal, Cornwall had succeeded "in ridding itself of what it considered to be bad bargains".

[483] See 5-068.

[484] *R. (on the application of G) v Barnet LBC* [2003] UKHL 57; [2004] 2 A.C. 208.

[485] [1997] A.C. 206; see E. Palmer, "Resource Allocation, Welfare Rights—Mapping the Boundaries of Resource Allocation in Public Administrative Law" (2000) O.J.L.S. 63; *R. v Southwark LBC Ex p. Udu* (1996) 8 Admin. L.R. 25 (policy of refusing grants to courses at private colleges, including the College of Law; held, local authority was a political body with limited funds, and it was entitled to have policies and to decide how to allocate those funds).

[486] *R. v Chief Constable of Sussex Ex p. International Traders Ferry Ltd* [1999] 2 A.C. 418; also *R. (on the application of Pfizer Ltd) v Secretary of State for Health* [2002] EWCA Civ 1566; [2003] 1 C.M.L.R. 19 (CA upheld decision to provide the drug Viagra to a limited category of patients); K. Syrett, "Impotence or Importance?" Judicial Review in an Era of Explicit NHS Rationing" (2004) 67 M.L.R. 289. cf. *R. (on the application of Rogers) v Swindon NHS Primary Care Trust* [2006] EWCA Civ 392; [2006] 1 W.L.R. 2649 (policy on funding breast cancer treatment with an unlicensed drug called Herceptin was irrational); K. Syrett, "Opening Eyes to the Reality of Scarce Health Care

Tandy[487] the House of Lords took the opposite view in holding that the authority could not take its limited resources into account in considering whether it could provide "suitable education" to children in need. In that case the council did have the resources to perform the duty but preferred to expend it in different ways. Lord Browne-Wilkinson said that permitting the authority to follow that preference would, wrongly, "downgrade a statutory duty to a discretionary power ... over which the court would have very little control".[488] Similarly, in *R. (Kebede) v Newcastle City Council*, the Court of Appeal held that a local authority is not permitted to take into account restrictions on its own resources in decision-making under the Children Act 1989 s.23C(4)(b) to give assistance to relevant children "to the extent that his welfare and his educational needs require it".[489] More recent cases under the Human Rights Act, where "positive duties" are increasingly recognised, have also held irrelevant the excuse of lack of resources.[490]

5-149   The statement of Lord Nicholls in *Barnet*,[491] that the existence of an "absolute duty" (as opposed to a "target duty") always "precludes the ... authority from ordering its expenditure priorities for itself"[492] is, however, only a starting point, for three further factors need to be considered:

(a)   Even if the duty is strictly enforceable, it is not always clear whether, or to what extent, the courts may disallow, amend or reorder the allocation of the authority's budgetary decisions and allocation of resources.

(b)   Even if the authority possesses a discretionary power, there is a question as to

---

Resources? R. (on the application of Rogers) v Swindon PCT and Secretary of State for Health" [2006] P.L. 664. Cf. *R. (on the application of Rose) v Thanet Clinical Commissioning Group* [2014] EWHC 1182 (Admin). A 25-year-old woman suffering from Crohn's disease was refused funding for oocyte cryopreservation before undergoing chemotherapy with the probable consequence of infertility and early onset of menopause. R was not considered by T to be clinically exceptional. Jay J, at [113], refused to accept that the policy was a blanket policy that permitted of no exceptions: "In the present case the wording of the exceptionality policy ... cannot be regarded as potentially discriminatory; the issue is the more limited one of whether it could ever be fulfilled by someone in the claimant's position, and if not whether that matters." An argument based on ECHR arts 8, 12 and 14 also failed.

[487]   *R. v Gloucestershire CC Ex p. Barry* [1997] A.C. 714; *R. (McDonald) v Kensington and Chelsea RLBC (Age UK intervening)* [2011] UKSC 33; [2011] P.T.S.R. 1266 (Barry applied); *R. (on the application of KM) v Cambridgeshire CC (National Autistic Society and others intervening)* [2012] UKSC 23; [2012] P.T.S.R. 1189 (obiter discussion of Barry); see also *R. v Sefton MBC Ex p. Help the Aged* [1997] 4 All E.R. 532, CA (lack of financial resources does not entitle a local authority to defer compliance with their duty under Chronically Sick and Disabled Persons Act 1970 s.2); *R. v Cheshire CC Ex p. C* [1998] E.L.R. 66 (decision about special educational needs should be made on purely educational grounds without reference to financial considerations); Case C-44/95 *R. v Secretary of State for the Environment Ex p. RSPB* [1997] Q.B. 206 (ECJ held that economic considerations are not relevant to determining wild bird protection areas under Directive 79/409); *R. v Secretary of State for the Environment Ex p. Kingston-Upon-Hull City Council* [1996] Env. L.R. 248 (cost of the treatment of waste water was not a relevant consideration); cf. *R. v National Rivers Authority Ex p. Moreton* [1996] Env. L.R. D17 (investment budget relevant to decision of NRA to allow discharge); *R. v Hillingdon LBC Ex p. Governing Body of Queensmead School* [1997] E.L.R. 331 (budgetary constraints and lack of funds could play no part in the assessment of a child's special educational needs).

[488]   *R. v East Sussex CC Ex p. Tandy* [1998] A.C. 714 at 749.

[489]   *R. (on the application of Kebede) v Newcastle City Council* [2013] EWCA Civ 960; [2014] P.T.S.R. 82.

[490]   J. King, "The Justiciability of Resource Allocation" (2007) 70 M.L.R. 197; S. Fredman, "Positive Rights and Transformed: Positive Duties and Positive Rights" [2006] P.L. 498; see e.g. *R. v Secretary of State for the Home Department Ex p. Limbuela* [2005] UKHL 66; [2006] 1 A.C. 396.

[491]   *R. (on the application of G) v Barnet LBC* [2003] UKHL 57; [2004] 2 A.C. 208. Lord Nicholls and Lord Steyn dissented, regarding the duty as an "absolute" and not "target duty".

[492]   *R. (on the application of G) v Barnet LBC* [2003] UKHL 57; [2004] 2 A.C. 208 at [13].

what extent it possesses the discretion to ignore or neglect the sufficient allocation of its scarce resources in pursuit of that power.

(c) A further (and somewhat separate question) is the extent to which the courts ought to avoid making judgments or imposing remedies which cause the expenditure of public funds.[493]

In Chapter 1, we saw that the allocation of resources is regarded as a matter which is not normally amenable to judicial review for one or more of four reasons.[494] First, the question of expenditure often goes hand in hand with a "policy" question (e.g. whether to devote additional resources to a space or nuclear programme rather than pre-school education), which lies squarely within the constitutional competence of the legislature or executive and not the courts. Secondly, the decision of the court to increase or reduce expenditure may not be able to be made by reference to any objective standards. Thirdly, the courts may not have the expertise to decide the question. Fourthly, the decision may be "polycentric" in character, namely, it will require a series of adjustments in the decision-maker's other budgetary allocations (in the context of finite resources) which the courts are not competent either to set in motion or to decide.[495] Examples of polycentric situations are discussed in Chapter 1, and reflected in the approach in *R. v Cambridge DHA Ex p. B (No.1)*, where the decision of a hospital not to provide expensive treatment to a child with cancer was upheld by the Court of Appeal. Acknowledging that in the "real world ... difficult and agonising judgments have to be made as to how a limited budget is best allocated to the maximum advantage of the maximum number of patients" (for example making decisions as to whether kidney dialysis over a period of months should be sacrificed to the urgent cancer operation in that case), Sir Thomas Bingham MR held "that is not a judgment which a court can make".[496]

5-150

Nevertheless, there are a number of different situations where the courts have required the allocation of resources, even where no particular duty was engaged. Parliament had enacted a statute to implement a new criminal injuries compensation scheme. The statute conferred upon the Home Secretary discretion as to when to bring the new scheme into effect. Before implementing the new scheme, the Home Secretary sought to introduce, under his prerogative powers (by means of which the previous scheme had been administered), a scheme different from that envisaged by the legislation. The House of Lords held that the courts should "hesitate long" before holding the Home Secretary under a duty to implement the scheme contemplated by the statute. However, he did not have absolute and unfettered discretion not to do so. The cost of implementing the statutory scheme was a factor relevant to his decision as to when the new scheme might be implemented. But the cost was not decisive, and would not justify the frustration of the statutory purpose by a scheme inconsistent with that approved by Parliament.[497] Another case where a power rather than duty was in issue involved the Broadcasting Complaints

5-151

---

[493] The first two questions (which he considers as one) are referred to by King as questions of "discretionary allocative decision-making" and the third as a question of "allocative impact": J. King, "The Justiciability of Resource Allocation" (2007) M.L.R. 197.

[494] See 1-042.

[495] See 1-042.

[496] *R. v Cambridge DHA Ex p. B (No.1)* [1995] 1 W.L.R. 898; and see the South African case *T. Soobramoney v Minister of Health KwaZulu Natal* 1997 (1) S.A. 767, CC.

[497] *R. v Secretary of State for the Home Department Ex p. Fire Brigades Union* [1997] 2 A.C. 513. cf. *R. v Blackledge* (1995) 92 L.S.G. 32 (prosecutions made under orders made pursuant to a statute contemplating their existence only for the period of the "emergency", following the declaration of war in 1939, not ultra vires); see also *Willcock v Muckle* [1951] 2 K.B. 844.

Commission, which decided not to investigate a complaint on the ground that to do so would be burdensome and perhaps require the employment of additional staff. These reasons were held not to excuse the failure to investigate the complaint.[498]

5-152   In addition, the issue of allocation of resources presents itself in different guises. It by no means always rests on the distinction between target duties and enforceable duties. General principles of public law may be engaged, as was the case where a company had overpaid rates to a local authority. The local authority claimed unfettered discretion whether or not to refund the rates, which it was reluctant to do because of its own poor financial situation and the adverse effect of the expenditure on the situation of the ratepayers. It was held that, in the circumstances, the authority should, as a prime consideration, have had regard to the unfairness to the company.[499] In some cases the issue may rest upon the interpretation of a particular statutory provision rather than the category of duty (target or enforceable). For example the Court of Appeal considered whether a local authority had given the applicant a "reasonable opportunity" to secure accommodation. It was held that the expression "reasonable opportunity" referred to what was reasonable from the standpoint of the applicant, and did not permit the authority to take into account its own lack of resources.[500] And even when a duty is clearly engaged, such as the duty to award social security benefit, the courts have held that delay in processing claims for the benefit could be excused by the lack of sufficient funds or resources.[501]

5-153   The lack of resources has sometimes been pleaded to excuse a delay particularly (but not confined to) situations concerning the right under art.5(4) of the ECHR to a "speedy" decision in deprivation of liberty cases and under art.6(1) ECHR to a hearing "within a reasonable time" for civil and criminal matters. The court will not "shut their eyes to the practicalities of litigious life",[502] nor to the fact that in general the court is not well equipped to consider the adequacy of resources. However, adequacy of resources or "administrative necessity" will not automatically excuse delay. Therefore, if it has been established that the delays were inconsistent with the standard of "speed" or "reasonable time", then the onus of justifying the delay will be on the authority,[503] and the court will carry out a careful analysis of the reasons underlying the justification,[504] if necessary requiring that "further resources must be found".[505]

5-154   In general, therefore, public authorities are limited in the circumstances in which they can plead lack of resources as an excuse to judicial intervention. However, the

---

[498] *R. v Broadcasting Complaints Commission Ex p. Owen* [1985] Q.B. 1153.

[499] *Tower Hamlets LBC v Chetnik Developments Ltd* [1988] A.C. 858; *R. v Rochdale MBC Ex p. Cromer Ring Mill Ltd* [1982] 3 All E.R. 761.

[500] *R. (on the application of Conville) v Richmond upon Thames LBC* [2006] EWCA Civ 718; [2006] 1 W.L.R. 2808.

[501] *R. v Secretary of State for Social Services Ex p. Child Poverty Action Group* [1990] 2 Q.B. 540, CA.

[502] *Dyer v Watson and another; K v HM Advocate* [2002] UKPC D1; [2004] 1 A.C. 379 at [55] (Lord Bingham). Lord Bingham was there summarising the jurisprudence of the ECtHR on the matter, but also endorsed, at [29], the approach of the PC in *Darmalingum v The State* [2002] 1 W.L.R. 2303.

[503] *Dyer v Watson; K v HM Advocate* [2002] UKPC D1; [2004] 1 A.C. 379 at [55] (Lord Bingham: "a marked lack of expedition, if unjustified, will point towards a breach of the reasonable time requirement, and the authorities make clear that while, for purposes of the reasonable time requirement, time runs from the date when the defendant is charged, the passage of any considerable period of time before charge may call for greater than normal expedition thereafter"); see further S. Lambert and A. Strugo, "Delay as a Ground of Review" [2005] J.R. 253; 11-072.

[504] *R. (on the application of KB) v Mental Health Review Tribunal* [2002] EWHC 639 (Admin); (2002) 5 C.C.L. Rep. 458 at [47] (Stanley Burnton J); and *R. (on the application of Murray) v Parole Board* [2003] EWCA Civ 1561; (2004) 101(1) L.S.G. 21.

[505] *R. (on the application of Noorkoiv) v Secretary of State for the Home Department* [2002] EWCA Civ 770; [2002] 1 W.L.R. 3284 at [58] (Simon Brown LJ).

courts too are limited in the circumstances in which they can order the re-allocation of an authority's finite resources. The issue is fundamental to the separation of powers and the rule of law and requires delicate handling for the following reasons:

- In the real world, limited resources must play a part in the exercise of powers and duties.
- However, in the interest of the rule of law the courts should not hesitate to require public duties to be implemented, even where that requires additional expenditure.[506]
- Courts should, however, be sensitive to their constitutional limitations to make policy decisions involving allocation of resources and to their institutional limitations in themselves deciding how (rather than whether) additional expenditure is required. The courts can order additional expenditure but should be wary of reordering the detail of an authority's budget.
- Even when the authority possesses a mere power, or target duty (rather than an enforceable or crystallised duty), the authority should not be able simply to sit on its hands and ignore the implementation of that power or target duty, whether or not that implementation requires expenditure.

PARTIAL ILLEGALITY AND SEVERANCE

What if an act or decision is partly legal and partly illegal? Suppose that a public body has power to revoke a person's licence. It revokes X's licence, and proceeds to order that he shall be disqualified from applying for a new licence for five years. It has no power to impose such a disqualification. In this case, X will be able to obtain a quashing order in respect of the five-year disqualification, or a declaration that the disqualification is void; but the court can still hold that the revocation of his licence is valid, for the two limbs of the public body's order are severable from one another.   **5-155**

Cases of partial invalidity are often more complicated than this because the good and the bad elements are not clearly distinct. The typical problem in this area of the law arises where a permit or licence has been granted subject to unlawful conditions. Three approaches may be followed by the court, assuming that the jurisdiction of the court (e.g. to enter in an appeal against the conditions alone) has not been demarcated by statute. First, it may set aside the entire decision because the competent authority might well have been unwilling to grant unconditional permission; the applicant must therefore start again.[507] Secondly, it may simply sever the bad from the good. In such a case the effect will be to give unconditional permission if all the conditions are struck down, and this may frustrate the inten-   **5-156**

---

[506] Or, as King rightly points out, courts ought not to refuse to award remedies such as damages or compensation on the ground of expense to the authority (J. King, "The Justiciability of Resource Allocation" (2007) M.L.R. 197). In *R. (on the application of Stennett) v Manchester City Council* [2002] UKHL 34; [2002] 2 A.C. 1127, it was held that, despite a burden of between 30 million and 80 million on local authorities of providing after-care services to those released from detention under the Mental Health Act 1983, charging for those services was not authorised under that Act. The case also underlined the point that the existence of a duty does not inevitably mean that the authority has the (incidental) power to implement that duty by charging for it (see 5-019).

[507] *Hall & Co v Shoreham-by-Sea UDC* [1964] 1 W.L.R. 240; *Pyx Granite Co v Ministry of Housing and Local Government* [1958] 1 Q.B. 554 at 578-579 (Hodson LJ); *R. v Hillingdon LBC Ex p. Royco Homes Ltd* [1974] Q.B. 720.

tions of the competent authority.[508] Thirdly, the court may adopt an intermediate position, and sever the invalid condition only if it is trivial, or if it is quite extraneous to the subject matter of the grant, or perhaps if there are other reasons for supposing that the authority would still have granted permission had it believed that the conditions might be invalid. This approach has recommended itself to the House of Lords in a case involving the validity of planning conditions.[509] But it involves the courts in a speculative attribution of intent to an administrative body.

5-157   It was once difficult to elicit any clear principle from the cases on partly invalid byelaws, though the courts had less compunction about striking out only the invalid words if the character of what remained was unaltered by a decision to sever the bad from the good.[510] In *DPP v Hutchinson*,[511] the House of Lords considered the validity of byelaws prohibiting entry onto the Greenham Common where there were military installations. The enabling legislation permitted such byelaws to be made, provided that rights of common were not interfered with. The appellants claimed that the byelaws did interfere with the rights of common and this contention was upheld. Could the bad parts of the byelaw be severed from the good? The House of Lords considered whether, in order to be severable, the test was that of "textual severability" or "substantial severability" If textual severability was the correct test, then the bad part of the instrument could be disregarded as exceeding the lawmaker's power, provided what remained was still "grammatical and coherent".[512] If, however, the proper test was that of substantial severability, then what remained after severance could survive as lawful provided that is was "essentially unchanged in its legislative purpose, operation and effect".[513] The majority of their Lordships accepted the test of "substantial severability" and it was held that this could be achieved in the following two situations:

> (a) Where the text could be severed so that the valid part could operate independently of the invalid part, then the test of substantial severability

---

[508] Nevertheless, this course has been adopted in a number of cases, e.g. *Ellis v Dubowski* [1921] 3 K.B. 621 (though this was a prosecution for breach of an invalid condition and the question of severability did not directly arise); *Mixnam's Properties Ltd v Chertsey UDC* [1965] A.C. 735; *Hartnell v Minister of Housing and Local Government* [1965] A.C. 1134; *Lowe (David) & Sons Ltd v Provost, etc. of Burgh of Musselburgh* 1974 S.L.T. 5.

[509] *Kingsway Investments (Kent) Ltd v Kent CC* [1971] A.C. 72 at 90–91, 102–103, 112–114; though cf. [1971] A.C. 106–107 (Guest LJ); *Allnatt London Properties Ltd v Middlesex CC* (1964) 62 L.G.R. 304. See also *Transport Ministry v Alexander* [1978] 1 N.Z.L.R. 306 at 311–312 (invalid part severable because it was "not fundamental or part of the structure of the regulation").

[510] *Potato Marketing Board v Merricks* [1958] 2 Q.B. 316 at 333 (Devlin J) (a case of a partly unauthorised demand for information under the threat of a penalty). The cases on byelaws are generally unhelpful, e.g. *R. v Lundie* (1862) 31 L.J.M.C. 157; *Reay v Gateshead Corp* (1886) 55 L.T. 92 at 103; *Strickland v Hayes* [1896] 1 Q.B. 290 at 292; *Rossi v Edinburgh Corp* [1905] A.C. 21.

[511] *DPP v Hutchinson* [1990] 2 A.C. 783; A. Bradley, "Judicial Enforcement of Ultra Vires Byelaws: The Proper Scope of Severance" [1990] P.L. 293.

[512] Sometimes called the "blue pencil test": *R. v Company of Fisherman of Faversham* (1799) 8 Dwrn & E. 352 at 356; *Ahmed v HM Treasury (JUSTICE intervening)(Nos 1 and 2)*[2008] EWCA Civ 1187; [2010] 2 A.C. 534 at [104] (CA applied *DPP v Hutchinson* holding that the words "or may be" were severable in delegated legislation); the question of severability was not considered in the Supreme Court: [2010] UKSC 2; [2010] UKSC 5; [2010] 2 A.C. 534.

[513] See, e.g. *Dunkley v Evans* [1981] 1 W.L.R. 1522; *Daymond v Plymouth CC* [1976] A.C. 609. See also the Australian approach followed in *R. v Commonwealth Court of Conciliation and Arbitration Ex p. Whybrow and Co* (1910) 11 C.L.R. 1; *Owners of SS Kalibav Wilson* (1910) 11 C.L.R. 689. In Australia, severability is governed by legislation: Acts Interpretation Act 1901 (Cth) ss.15(A) and 46(1)(b), which allow for severance in the context of judicial review challenges to the validity of statutes and administrative decisions respectively. Severance is not possible if it would require adjustments to what remains. The leading case is *Re Dingjan; Ex p. Wagner* (1995) 183 C.L.R. 323.

would be satisfied when the valid part is unaffected by, and independent of, the invalid part.

(b) Where severance could only be effected by modifying the text, this can only be done "when the court is satisfied that it is effecting no change in the substantial purpose and effect of the impugned provision".[514]

Omissions

The corollary of severance by "blue pencilling" arises when some required provi-   **5-158**
sion is omitted from a regulation. Is it open to the court to supply that omission? Can the court write in an exemption? The Court of Appeal held that an omission was curable in a case where it "appears to have affected nobody" and therefore, "however cogent the case in legal theory" for striking down the regulation, to do so "would represent a triumph of logic over reason".[515] The omission related to the failure in the regulation (which banned a herbal medicine) to exempt goods in transit. Sedley LJ recognised that there may be occasions where it is simply too late, or simply insufficient, to allow the rule-maker to supply the omission. In such a case, the test would be the same as that in *Hutchinson*, namely, would the new provision be "totally different in character" from the impugned one? However, if the omission can be made good without doing harm, or disrupting the existing, lawful text, then the court could permit the rule-maker to "insert the missing brick", rather than pull down the entire structure.[516] This new doctrine of "innocuous amendment"[517] is a pragmatic response to a difficult situation. However, care must be exercised lest it encourage lax drafting and encourages litigation in order to fill in the gap.

DELEGATION OF POWERS

The rule against delegation

A discretionary power must, in general, be exercised only by the public author-   **5-159**
ity to which it has been committed. It is a well-known principle of law that when a power has been conferred to a person in circumstances indicating that trust is being placed in his individual judgment and discretion, he must exercise that power personally unless he has been expressly empowered to delegate it to another.[518] This principle has been applied in the law of agency, trusts and arbitration as well as in

---

[514] *DPP v Hutchinson* [1990] 2 A.C. 783 at 811 (Lord Bridge); cf. Lord Lowry, dissenting, at 819: "To liberalise the [severance] test would be anarchic, not progressive". For an example of the severance of an invalid part of a statutory instrument (void for unreasonableness) under situation (a) above, *R. v Immigration Appeal. Tribunal Ex p. Begum Manshoora* [1986] Imm. A.R. 385. cf. *R. v Inland Revenue Commissioners Ex p. Woolwich Equitable Building Society* [1990] 1 W.L.R. 1400, HL (alteration of substance by textual severance too great); *R. v North Hertfordshire DC Ex p. Cobbold* [1985] 3 All E.R. 486 (unreasonable conditions attached to license for pop concert. Severance would alter whole character of licence). See also *Mouchell Superannuation Fund Trustees v Oxfordshire CC* [1992] 1 P.L.R. 97, CA.

[515] *R. (on the application of National Association of Health Stores) v Department of Health* [2005] EWCA Civ 154.

[516] At [18]–[20].

[517] I. Steele, "Note on R.(National Association of Health Stores) v Department of Health" [2005] J.R. 232.

[518] Sometimes expressed in the form of the maxim *delegatus non potest delegare* (or *delegata potestas non potest delegari*), a maxim which, it has been suggested, "owes its origin to medieval commentators on the Digest and the Decretals, and its vogue in the common law to the carelessness of a

public law. The former assumption that the principle applies only to the sub-delegation of delegated *legislative* powers and to the sub-delegation of other powers delegated by a superior *administrative* authority, is unfounded. It applies to the delegation of *all* classes of powers, and it was indeed originally invoked in the context of delegation of judicial powers. It is therefore convenient to travel beyond the delegation of discretionary powers in the strict sense and to view the problem as a whole.

5-160   The cases on delegation have arisen in diverse contexts, and many of them turn upon unique points of statutory interpretation. The judgments are not always consistent. The principle does not amount to a rule that knows no exception; it is a rule of construction which makes the presumption that "a discretion conferred by statute is prima facie intended to be exercised by the authority on which the statute has conferred it and by no other authority, but this presumption may be rebutted by any contrary indications found in the language, scope or object of the statute".[519] Courts have sometimes wrongly assumed that the principle lays down a rule of rigid application, so that devolution of power cannot (in the absence of express statutory authority) be valid unless it falls short of delegation. This has resulted in an unreasonably restricted meaning often being given to the concept of delegation.[520]

Delegation of "judicial" powers

5-161   The principle has been applied most rigorously to proceedings of courts,[521] requiring a judge to act personally throughout a case except in so far as he is expressly absolved from this duty by statute.[522] Special tribunals and public bodies exercising functions broadly analogous to the judicial are also precluded from delegating their powers of decision unless there is express authority to that effect.[523] This may be the case where judicial functions are expressly "privatised" or "contracted out".

---

sixteenth-century printer": P. Duff and H. Whiteside, "The Maxim in American Constitutional Law: A Study in Delegation of Legislative Power" (1929) 14 Cornell L.Q. 168, 173. The authors suggest that the maxim, recited by Coke in his Institutes (ii, 597), was probably taken from an incorrect rendering in a passage in an early printed edition of Bracton. But see H. Ehmke, "'Delegata Potestas Non Potest Delegari: A Maxim of American Constitutional Law" (1961) 47 Cornell L.Q. 50, 54–55, pointing out that Bracton was indeed addressing himself to the impropriety of sub-delegating judicial power delegated by the King.

[519] J. Willis, "Delegatus non potest delegare" (1943) 21 Can. B.R. 257, 259.
[520] See cases cited by Willis (1943) 21 Can. B.R. 257, 257-258.
[521] *Caudle v Seymour* (1841) 1 Q.B. 889 (depositions taken by justices' clerk). cf. *Hunt v Allied Bakeries Ltd (No.2)* [1959] 1 W.L.R. 50 at 56; *R. v Brentford Justices Ex p. Catlin* [1975] Q.B. 455; *R. v Majewski* [1977] A.C. 443 at 449–451 (registrar's power to refer criminal appeals for summary dismissal); *R. v Gateshead Justices Ex p. Tesco* [1981] Q.B. 470 (power of single justice or justices' clerk to issue summonses could not be delegated to court official; approved in *Hill v Alderton* (1982) 75 Cr. App. R. 346, HL; *Olympia Press Ltd v Hollis* [1973] 1 W.L.R. 1520 where it was held that each magistrate did not have to read all the books that were the subject of forfeiture proceedings provided that they collectively discussed them before making a decision (*Burke v Copper* [1962] 1 W.L.R. 700 distinguished).
[522] On implied power to sub-delegate ministerial functions: *Allam & Co v Europa Poster Services Ltd* [1968] 1 W.L.R. 638 (where the sub-delegated function, though not the decisions culminating in it, was merely "ministerial").
[523] See, e.g. *GMC v UK Dental Board* [1936] Ch. 41; *Barnard v National Dock Labour Board* [1953] 2 Q.B. 18; *Vine v National Dock Labour Board* [1957] A.C. 488; *Labour Relation Board of Saskatchewan v Speers* [1948] 1 D.L.R. 340; *Turner v Allison* [1971] N.Z.L.R. 833. cf. *Re S. (a Barrister)* [1970] 1 Q.B. 160 (jurisdiction to disbar, though ostensibly delegated, was in truth original); *Re Schabas and Caput of University of Toronto* (1975) 52 D.L.R. (3rd) 495; *Re Bortolotti and Ministry of Housing* (1977) 76 D.L.R. (3rd) 408 (chairman of tribunals has no inherent power to make rulings on points of law that bind the other members). Legislation may be construed to define the tribunal as those members who sit in a particular case. See *Howard v Borneman (No.2)* [1976]

Contracting out of internal complaints handling has not been objected to by the courts.[524] In countries with written constitutions the question has arisen as to whether certain disciplinary or quasi-judicial functions can ever be devolved. For example, is prison discipline involving the imposition of penalties a core state function, or can it be devolved to private companies running prisons?[525] Generally, in spite of the retreat from a rigid conceptual distinction between administrative, judicial, and quasi-judicial functions,[526] it is still the case that the courts will be more ready to find a necessary implication of delegation in respect of a body that does not exercise strictly "judicial" functions.[527]

But, as we shall see in the discussion on procedural propriety,[528] the courts will sometimes concede that a public body has an implied power to entrust a group of its own members with authority to investigate, to hear evidence and submissions and to make recommendations in a report, provided that (a) it retains the power of

5-162

A.C. 301. *Heald v Brent LBC* [2009] EWCA Civ 930, practice adopted by some local authorities of contracting-out the reviews they are required to conduct under s.202 of the Housing Act 1996 where an applicant for housing assistance requests a review held that the Local Authorities (Contracting Out of Allocation of Housing and Homelessness Functions) Order 1996 clearly permits such practices, notwithstanding doubts expressed in several speeches in *Runa Begum v Tower Hamlets LBC* [2003] UKHL 5; [2003] 2 A.C. 430 about the difficulties that would be associated with contracting out such a function *R. (on the application of Gilboy) v Liverpool City Council* [2008] EWCA Civ 751; (not cited in *Heald* concerned a "demoted tenancies" scheme (reference at [47] to the "good sense of non-delegation" of review functions to officers *in another local authority*) *Morina v Secretary of State for Work and Pensions; Borrowdale v Secretary of State for Work and Pensions* [2007] EWCA Civ 749; [2007] 1 W.L.R. 3033 (legally qualified panel members of the Social Security Appeal Tribunal).

524 In the context of housing, see: *De-Winter Heald v Brent LBC* [2009] EWCA Civ 930; [2010] 1 W.L.R. 990 (practice adopted by some local authorities of contracting-out the reviews they are required to conduct under s.202 of the Housing Act 1996 where an applicant for housing assistance requests a review considered; held that the Local Authorities (Contracting Out of Allocation of Housing and Homelessness Functions) Order 1996 clearly permits such practices, notwithstanding doubts expressed in several speeches in *Runa Begum v Tower Hamlets LBC* [2003] UKHL 5; [2003] 2 A.C. 430 about the difficulties that would be associated with contracting out such a function) *R. (on the application of Gilboy) v Liverpool City Council* [2008] EWCA Civ 751; [2009] Q.B. 699 (not cited in *Heald*, concerned a "demoted tenancies" scheme (reference at [47] to the "good sense of non-delegation" of review functions to officers *in another local authority*); *Morina v Secretary of State for Work and Pensions; Borrowdale v Secretary of State for Work and Pensions* [2007] EWCA Civ 749; [2007] 1 W.L.R. 3033 (legally qualified panel members of the Social Security Appeal Tribunal). See also 1-071 on "independent" complaints handlers established by several public bodies.

525 This issue was discussed in the South African Constitutional Court in *AAA Investments Ltd v The Micro Finance Regulatory Council and the Minister of Trade and Industry* [2006] C.C.T. 51/05 (26 July 2006), where it was held that such delegation of governmental functions was not "overbroad" provided that responsibility for the functions lay ultimately with the government.

526 See Appendix B.

527 *Young v Fife Regional Council*, 1986 S.L.T. 331 (Scottish Teachers Salaries Committee and no power to delegate decision regarding teachers' pay to sub-committee, because since functions was "at least" quasi judicial, there was no implied power of delegation); *R. v Gateshead Justices Ex p. Tesco* [1981] Q.B. 470 (court officials could lawfully carry out non-judicial duties of justices' clerk, but no judicial duties). Pre-democratic South African courts allowed implied delegation of "purely administrative" or "ministerial" functions but not of "legislative" or "judicial" functions: see L. Baxter, *Administrative Law* (1984) pp.439–40.

528 cf. *Osgood v Nelson* (1872) L.R. 5 H.L. 636 (council could validly empower one of its committees to investigate charges against an official, the council itself retaining the power of decision); *Devlin v Barnett* [1958] N.Z.L.R. 828 (promotions board entitled to entrust another body with conduct of tests); *Attorney General (ex rel. McWhirter) v Independent Broadcasting Authority* [1973] Q.B. 629 at 651, 657-658 (Authority normally able to rely on staff reports except when credible evidence contradicting a report is received): *R. v Commission for Racial Equality Ex p. Cottrell and Rothon* [1980] 1 W.L.R. 1580 (CRE allowed to delegate formal investigation into alleged discrimination and hence could rely and act on evidence received in reports); *Vine* [1957] A.C. 488, 512; cf. *Re Sarran* (1969) 14 W.L.R. 361.

decision in its own hands and receives a report full enough to enable it to comply with its duty to "hear" before deciding,[529] and (b) the context does not indicate that it must perform the entire "adjudicatory" process itself.[530] Determinations by ministers, however, stand in a special class[531]; not only may the hearing be conducted by a person authorised on their behalf, but the decision may be made by an authorised official in the minister's name.[532]

Delegation of "legislative" powers

5-163   There is a strong presumption against construing a grant of delegated legislative power as empowering the delegate to sub-delegate the whole or any substantial part of the law-making power entrusted to it.[533] In New Zealand cases this presumption was invoked as a ground for holding regulations and orders made by the sub-delegate to be invalid.[534] But the presumption is not irrebuttable, and in a Canadian emergency measures case the power of the Governor General in Council to make such regulations as he might by reason of the existence of war deem necessary or advisable for the defence of Canada was held to be wide enough to enable him to sub-delegate to the Controller of Chemicals power to make regulations.[535] There seems to be no English authority directly in point in constitutional or administra-

---

[529] It seems that if a public authority is required to be satisfied of the existence of certain facts before exercising a power but is not obliged to afford any hearing beforehand, its satisfaction may be sufficiently expressed by formally adopting findings made by its committees even though these findings do not fully record the materials on which they were based: *Goddard v Minister of Housing and Local Government* [1958] 1 W.L.R. 1151; *Savoury v Secretary of State for Wales* (1976) 31 P. & C.R. 344 (also illustrates the difficulty of reviewing the validity of the resolution for lack of evidence when the applicant is unable to discover upon what evidence the council acted); cf. *Electronic Industries Ltd v Oakleigh Corp* [1973] V.R. 177 (court prepared to infer that the council had not considered a particular matter). But in some contexts (e.g. where bodies making decisions significantly affecting individual rights perfunctorily adopt findings by officials) the courts may hold that failure to exercise independent judgment or discretion constitutes an unlawful abdication of authority; *R. v Chester CC Ex p. Quietlynn Ltd* (1984) 83 L.G.R. 308; *R. v Birmingham CC Ex p. Quietlynn Ltd* (1985) 83 L.G.R. 461.

[530] Delegation of purely investigatory or fact-finding functions may therefore be lawfully delegated, e.g. *R. v North Thames RHA Ex p. L (An Infant)* [1996] 7 Med. L.R. 385; *R. v Hertsmere BC Ex p. Woolgar* (1995) 27 H.L.R. 703.

[531] On the *Carltona* principle, see 5-172.

[532] *Doody v Secretary of State for the Home Department* [1994] 1 A.C. 531, HL (a decision required to be taken by the Home Secretary on the period which a life sentence prisoner should serve for the purposes of retribution and deterrence may be taken by a Minister of state at the Home Office on his behalf. However, any advice on that question given by the Lord Chief justice must be given by the holder of that office, as his function cannot be delegated. The Home Secretary no longer has this function but has power not to release prisoners after the minimum term has been served: Criminal Justice Act 2003 ss.224-236).

[533] *King-Emperor v Benoari Lal Sarma* [1945] A.C. 14 at 24; *R. v Lampe Ex p. Maddolozzo* [1966] A.L.R. 144 (dicta); B. Fox and O. Davies, "Sub-Delegated Legislation" (1955) 28 A.L.J. 486.

[534] *Geraghty v Porter* [1917] N.Z.L.R. 554 (distinguished in *Hookings v Director of Civil Aviation* [1957] N.Z.L.R. 929); *Godkin v Newman* [1928] N.Z.L.R. 593; *Jackson (FE) & Co v Collector of Customs* [1939] N.Z.L.R. 682 at 732–734; *Hawke's Bay Raw Milk Producers' Co-operative Co v New Zealand Milk Board* [1961] N.Z.L.R. 218 (distinguished in *Van Gorkom v Attorney General* [1977] 1 N.Z.L.R. 535). See C. Aikman, "Subdelegation of the Legislative Power" (1960) 3 Victoria Uni. of Wellington L. Rev 69 for an authoritative analysis of these still relevant cases. More recently, see *Videbeck v Auckland City Council* [2002] 3 N.Z.L.R. 842 (court would not permit 'rubber stamping' by decision-maker of recommendations by officials, nor de facto delegation contrary to statutory requirements).

[535] *Reference Re Chemicals Regulations* [1943] S.C.R. 1; but see *Attorney General of Canada v Brent* [1956] S.C.R. 318 (powers of Governor-General in Council to make regulations with respect to immigration restrictions not validly exercised by making of regulations which in substance transferred to public officers the effective power to make the necessary rules); with which contrast *Hookings v*

tive law. In the First World War the sweeping legislative powers vested by the Defence of the Realm Acts in the King in Council were extensively sub-delegated to ministers and others; the validity of such sub-delegation was not, apparently, challenged in the courts. In the Second World War the King in Council was expressly empowered by s.1(3) of the Emergency Powers (Defence) Act 1939 to sub-delegate his legislative powers under the Act. It is doubtful whether implied authority to sub-delegate legislative powers would ever be conceded by the English courts save in time of grave emergency.[536] For when Parliament has specifically appointed an authority to discharge a legislative function, a function normally exercised by Parliament itself, it cannot readily be presumed to have intended that its delegate should be free to empower another person or body to act in its place. Nevertheless, one can envisage circumstances in which a carefully delimited sub-delegation of rule-making power could more reasonably be upheld than a sub-delegation of uncontrolled administrative discretion to be exercised in relation to individual cases.[537]

Delegation of "administrative" powers

Most of the practical problems concerned with sub-delegation have been related to the exercise of powers of a discretionary character—to regulate, to grant licences and permits, to requisition, to require the abatement of nuisances and to institute legal proceedings.

5-164

Delegation and agency

In this context, sharp differences of opinion have been expressed on the relationship between the concepts of delegation and agency. They have sometimes been treated as being virtually indistinguishable[538] but in many cases a distinction has been drawn between them, particularly where the court is acting on the assumption that an authority can validly employ an agent but cannot delegate its powers.

5-165

The correct view seems to be that the distinctions drawn between delegation and agency are frequently misconceived in so far as they are based on the erroneous assumption that there is never an implied power to delegate. However, some relationships that are properly included within the concept of delegation are substantially different from those which typify the relationship of principal and agent. There are three main characteristics of agency. First, the agent acts on behalf of his principal, he does so in his name, and the acts done by the agent within the scope of his authority are attributable to the principal. These principles are broadly applicable to delegation in administrative law, and it would generally be held to be unlawful for an authority to invest a delegate with powers exercisable in his own name. But where legislative powers are delegated by Parliament, or validly sub-delegated by

5-166

Director of Civil Aviation [1957] N.Z.L.R. 929 (delegation of dispensing power); and *Arnold v Hunt* (1943) 67 C.L.R. 429; cf. *Croft v Rose* [1957] A.L.R. 148; J. Merralls, "Note" (1957) 1 Melbourne Univ. L.R. 105.

[536] Reference to extrinsic documents in delegated legislation is common, and is not considered to involve sub-delegation unless the document is not in existence when the instrument is approved, and its content is beyond the control of the minister; see criticisms of the Joint Committee on Statutory Instruments. HC Paper No. 21-XI (Session 1974/75); cf. *R. v Secretary of State for Social Services Ex p. Camden LBC* [1987] 1 W.L.R. 819.

[537] C. Aikman, "Subdelegation of the Legislative Power" (1960) 3 Victoria Uni. of Wellington L. Rev. 69, 82–83.

[538] See, e.g. *Huth v Clarke* (1890) 25 Q.B.D. 391; *Lewisham Borough v Roberts* [1949] 2 K.B. 608, 622; *Gordon, Dadds & Co v Morris* [1945] 2 All E.R. 616.

Parliament's delegate, the delegate or sub-delegate exercises his powers in his own name. And in the schemes of administrative delegation drawn up in local government law, the relationships between the local authorities concerned have often been far removed from those connoted by the relationship of principal and agent.[539]

5-167 Secondly, the agent can be—given detailed directions by his principal and does not usually have a wide area of discretion. On the other hand one to whom statutory discretionary powers are delegated often has a substantial measure of freedom from control in exercising them. But the degree of freedom from control with which he is vested may be a decisive factor in determining the validity of the delegation made to him.

5-168 The more significant are the effective powers of control retained by the delegating authority, the more readily will the courts uphold the validity of the delegation; and they may choose to uphold its validity by denying that there has been any delegation at all, on the ground that in substance the authority in which the discretion has been vested by statute continues to address its own mind to the exercise of the powers.[540]

5-169 Thirdly, in agency the principal retains concurrent powers. This principle was generally applicable to delegation by a local authority to its committees. Thus, the local authority retained power to make decisions in relation to matters comprised within the delegation[541]—a rule now expressly restated by statute[542]—and it could (and presumably still can) revoke the authority of a delegate.[543] Nevertheless, it has sometimes been stated that delegation implies a denudation of authority.[544] Such a statement was made by the Employment Appeal Tribunal in *Robertson v Department for the Environment, Food and Rural Affairs*.[545] This cannot be accepted as an accurate general proposition.[546] On the contrary, the general rule is that an authority which delegates its powers does not divest itself of them indeed, if it purports to abdicate it may be imposing a legally ineffective fetter on its own discretion[547]— and can resume them. But if it has validly delegated an executive power to make decisions, it will normally be bound by a particular decision, conferring rights on individuals (and possibly one derogating from those rights), made in pursuance of the delegated power and will be incapable of rescinding or varying it[548]; nor will it be competent to "ratify" with retroactive effect a decision made by the delegate in

---

[539] Inter-delegation between local authorities was considerably diminished by the Local Government Act 1972; but see now Localism Act 2011 Pt 1.

[540] As in *Devlin v Barnett* [1958] N.Z.L.R. 828; cf. *Winder v Cambridgeshire CC* (1978) 76 L.G.R. 549.

[541] *Huth v Clarke* (1890) 25 Q.B.D. 391; *Gordon, Dadds & Co v Morris* [1945] 2 All E.R. 616 at 621; *Winder v Cambridgeshire CC* (1978) 76 L.G.R. 549 (local authority retained residual discretion to exercise a power that it had delegated under a statutorily required instrument of college government, when the refusal of the delegate to act would otherwise frustrate the discharge of the authority's overall educational responsibilities).

[542] Local Government Act 1972 s.101(4) as amended by Local Government Act 2003 s.99.

[543] *Manton v Brighton Corp* [1951] 2 K.B. 393 (power of council to revoke authority of member of sub-committee).

[544] *Blackpool Corp v Locker* [1948] 1 K.B. 349 at 377-378 (Scott and Asquith LJJ).

[545] *Robertson v Department for the Environment, Food and Rural Affairs* [2005] EWCA Civ 138; [2005] I.C.R. 750.

[546] Strong support for the position here, and criticism of *Robertson and Blackpool Corp* is provided by S. Bailey, "Delegation and Concurrent Exercises of Power" [2005] J.R. 84.

[547] On the general rule that a public authority cannot fetter itself in the exercise of discretionary powers, see Ch.9.

[548] *Battelley v Finsbury BC* (1958) 56 L.G.R. 165; *Morris v Shire of Morwell* [1948] V.L.R. 83. cf. the unsettled question of whether the Home Secretary may disregard a decision by an immigration officer to grant leave to enter that is not consistent with the immigration rules: *R. v Secretary of State for the Home Department Ex p. Choudhary* [1978] 1 W.L.R. 1177; *R. v Secretary of State for the Home Department Ex p. Ram* [1979] 1 W.L.R. 148.

excess of the powers so delegated, even though the delegating authority could validly have made the decision itself in the first place.[549]

It must be explained that in local government law there may be delegation either of executive power[550] (in which case the delegating-authority may be bound by the delegate's decisions and the degree of supervision exercisable over the delegate may sometimes be minimal) or of power to make recommendations or decisions subject to the approval of the delegating authority. In the latter class of case (which is not always categorised as true delegation) difficult marginal problems of interpretation have arisen where a delegate or sub-delegate has taken action e.g. to require the execution of works on private property or to institute legal proceedings), without antecedent approval and the authority whose approval is required has purported to ratify the action already taken.[551] Other difficult problems, peripheral to the general question of delegation, have arisen in cases where it has been contended that a local government officer, acting without a formal grant of authority, has imposed legally binding obligations on his employers by virtue of undertakings, assurances or other conduct.[552] Where under s.37 of the Local Government Act 2000 a local authority has adopted and published a constitution detailing its executive arrangements, it acts unlawfully if it departs from the scheme of delegation.[553]

5-170

General principles of delegation

The following are some of the principles elicited from the cases in which delegation of discretion has been considered.

5-171

---

[549] This appears to be the best explanation of the decision in *Blackpool Corp v Locker* [1948] 1 K.B. 349. A minister delegated requisitioning powers, subject to restrictive conditions, to local authorities or their clerks by a departmental circular. A town clerk requisitioned L's house without complying with certain conditions. It was unsuccessfully contended that a subsequent letter from the minister had cured the invalidity by ratification. It was doubtful, moreover, whether the purported ratification was to be construed as anything more than an act of affirmation, or whether the local authority or its clerk was to be regarded as an agent of the minister, who was himself acting "on behalf of His Majesty". But the assertion (at 379) that the minister was incompetent to requisition the house anew because he had not reserved powers to himself in the instrument of delegation cannot be supported. See also *Attorney General Ex rel. Co-operative Retail Services Ltd v Taff-Ely BC* (1980) 39 P. & C.R. 223, CA, affirmed 42 P. & C.R. 1, HL (council could not ratify purported grant of planning permission by district clerk, since ultra vires act could not be ratified; quaere whether in any case council had power to grant planning permission). And see the discussion on estoppel, 12-063 and following.

[550] The power of local authorities to delegate to committees, sub-committees and officers, and of committees to sub-delegate was greatly extended by the Local Government Act 1972 Pt VI, esp. s.101. A scheme of delegation may lawfully provide for dual and concurrent delegation to both a regulatory board and officers—delegation need not be a simple hierarchical structure: see *R. (on the application of Couves) v Gravesham BC* [2015] EWHC 504 (Admin); [2015] J.P.L. 1193 (QBD (Admin).

[551] On the one hand, *Firth v Staines* [1897] 2 Q.B. 70; *R. v Chapman Ex p. Arlidge* [1918] 2 K.B. 298; and *Warwick RDC v Miller-Mead* [1962] Ch. 441 applied by the CA in *Stoke on Trent CC v B & Q Retail Ltd* [1984] Ch. 1; on the other hand, *St Leonard's Vestry v Holmes* (1885) 50 J.P 132 and Bowyer, *Philpott & Payne Ltd v Mather* [1919] 1 K.B. 419. cf. *Attorney General Ex rel. Co-operative Retail Services Ltd v Taff-Ely BC* (1979) 39 P. & C.R. 223.

[552] M. Freedland, "The Rule Against Delegation and the Carltona doctrine in an Agency Context" [1996] P.L. 19.

[553] See *R. (on the application of Bridgerow Ltd) v Cheshire West and Chester Borough Council* [2014] EWHC 1187 (Admin); [2015] P.T.S.R. 91 (power to determine renewal of licences had been sub-delegated to a panel "comprising" three members drawn from the licensing committee; "comprising" was prescriptive rather than permissive so the full licensing committee acted unlawfully when it purported to make the determination).

Vesting authority without supervisory control

5-172   Where an authority vested with discretionary powers empowers one of its committees or subcommittees, members or officers to exercise those powers independently without any supervisory control by the authority itself, the exercise of the
powers is likely to be held invalid. Thus, where the Minister of Agriculture had
validly delegated to a war agricultural executive committee power to give directions with respect to the cultivation, management or use of land, and the committee sub-delegated to its officer power to determine in which fields a specified crop
should be grown and to issue a direction to the farmer without reference to the committee, a direction issued by the officer was held to be invalid.[554] A byelaw by which
a local authority hands over its own regulatory powers to an official by vesting him
with virtually unrestricted discretion may be held to be unlawful.[555] A delegation
of power to review prosecutions to decide whether there was sufficient evidence to
proceed, from the Director of Public Prosecutions to non-lawyers, was held unlawful since the statute by giving the power to the DPP clearly contemplated that it
would only be delegated to a member of the Crown Prosecution Service, who would
be a lawyer.[556] The powers to determine the state of health of a child, in relation to
the question of whether free transport to school should be provided, could not be
delegated to the school medical officer but had to be exercised by the education
committee as a whole.[557]

Degree of control maintained may be material

5-173   The degree of control (before or afterwards) maintained by the delegating authority over the acts of the delegate or sub-delegate may be a material factor in
determining the validity of the delegation. In general the control preserved (e.g. by
a power to refuse to ratify an act or to reject a recommendation) must be close
enough for the decision to be identifiable as that of the delegating authority.[558] That
the decision of the delegate is not final or conclusive because of control exerted by
a third party, in the form of an appeal or review from the decision of the delegating authority and/or delegate, may also be an important factor in determining the
validity of the delegation.[559]

Amplitude, impact and importance

5-174   How far, if at all, delegation of discretionary power is impliedly authorised may
also depend on the amplitude of the power, the impact of its exercise upon

---

[554] *Allingham v Minister of Agriculture and Fisheries* [1948] All E.R. 780; *High v Billings* (1903) 67
J.P 388.

[555] *Madoc Township v Quinlan* (1972) 21 D.L.R. (3rd) 136; *R. v Sandler*, 286.

[556] *R. v DPP Ex p. Association of First Division Civil Servants, The Times,* 24 May 1988. However, the
HL did not hold invalid power exercised by a subordinate officer of a rating authority when the power
was conferred on the authority itself: *Provident Mutual Life Assurance Association v Derby CC*
[1981] 1 W.L.R. 173, HL.

[557] *R. v Devon CC Ex p. G* [1989] A.C. 573. On the *Carltona* principle and whether delegation or
devolution may not be permitted if the function requires particular competence or qualifications, see
5-176.

[558] *Hall v Manchester Corp* (1915) 84 L.J. Ch. 734 at 741 and *Cohen v West Ham Corp* [1933] Ch. 814
at 826-827 on the duty of local authorities to exercise independent discretion before acting on reports
by their officers; *R. v Board of Assessment, etc.* (1965) 49 D.L.R. (2nd) 156 (tax assessment board,
by simply adopting valuations made by official, failed to perform statutory duties).

[559] *Provident Mutual Life Assurance Assn v Derby CC* [1981] 1 W.L.R. 173, 181, HL (principal rating
assistant could serve completion notice without consulting borough treasurer; right of appeal to
county court existed).

individual interests and the importance to be attached to the efficient transaction of public business by informal delegation of responsibility.[560] If authorisation is permitted, the choice of one officer over another for the exercise of the delegated power is a matter for the holder of the power, within the limits of rationality, and the choice of the level of the delegated office-holder will depend not primarily on rank, but on matters such as "resources, availability, skills, contacts, experience, knowledge and so forth".[561]

Generally improper to delegate wide powers

It is improper for an authority to delegate wide discretionary powers to another authority over which it is incapable of exercising direct control, unless it is expressly empowered so to delegate.[562] Thus, the Minister of Works could not allocate to the Minister of Health part of his functions in the system of building licensing.[563] A Canadian provincial marketing board, exercising delegated authority, could not sub-delegate part of it regulatory powers to an inter-provincial authority.[564] Nor could a local authority, empowered to issue cinematograph licences subject to conditions, attach a condition that no film shall be shown which had not been certified for public exhibition by the British Board of Film Censors,[565] unless the authority has expressly reserved to itself power to dispense with that requirement in any individual case.[566] It is doubtful how far a minister would be held to have an implied power to devolve discretionary functions upon local authorities and their officers, over whom he is constitutionally enabled to exercise indirect control. One may surmise that the courts would not readily uphold the validity of a devolution of very wide discretionary powers, but that if the devolution of discretion covered a relatively narrow field they might characterise the relationship as agency rather than delegation and hold that it had been validly created.[567]

5-175

---

[560] *Ex p. Forster, re University of Sydney* (1963) 63 S.R. (N.S.W) 723 at 733-734; Willis; *R. v Monopolies and Mergers Commission Ex p. Argyll Group Plc* [1986] 1 W.L.R. 763, CA held that the Chairman of the MMC did not have authority to act on his own to request the Secretary of State to lay the reference about the company aside. However, a properly constituted group of MMC members would have reached the same conclusion and therefore the act was valid. But where a chairman of a local education committee designated the date for the closure of a school, that was held an unlawful delegation: *R. v Secretary of State for Education and Science Ex p. Birmingham CC* (1984) 83 L.G.R. 79.

[561] *R. (on the application of Chief Constable of the West Midlands Police) v Gonzales* [2002] EWHC 1087 (Admin) at [18] (Sedley LJ).

[562] cf. *Kyle v Barbor* (1888) 58 L.T. 229.

[563] *Jackson, Stansfield & Sons v Butterworth* [1948] 2 All E.R. 558 at 564-566 (dicta); but is it true that the Minister of Works in that case had done anything more than use the Minister of Health as a convenient channel of communication with local authorities? And see *Lavender (H) & Son Ltd v Minister of Housing and Local Government* [1970] 1 W.L.R. 1231 (Minister X determining planning appeal by mechanically applying policy of Minister Y; decision in effect that of Minister Y, and therefore ultra vires). cf. *Kent CC v Secretary of State for the Environment* (1977) 75 L.G.R. 452, where the minister was held to have decided a planning appeal himself although he had had regard to the opinion of another minister on an important issue in the appeal. If a minister delays the making or implementation of a discretionary decision till the matter has been debated in Parliament he is not, of course, delegating his power of decision at all: *R. v Brixton Prison Governor Ex p. Enaharo* [1963] 2 Q.B. 455.

[564] *Prince Edward Island Potato Marketing Board v Willis (HB) Inc* [1952] 2 S.C.R. 391.

[565] *Ellis v Dubowski* [1921] 3 K.B. 621. See also *R. v Burnley Justices* (1916) 85 L.J.K.B. 1565.

[566] *Mills v LCC* [1925] 1 K.B. 213; *R. v Greater London Council Ex p. Blackburn* [1976] 1 W.L.R. 550.

[567] *Jackson, Stansfield & Sons v Butterworth* [1948] 2 All E.R. 558 564-565.

Named officers

5-176   Where the exercise of a discretionary power is entrusted to a named officer—
e.g. a chief officer of police, a medical officer of health or an inspector—another
officer cannot exercise his powers in his stead unless express statutory provision
has been made for the appointment of a deputy or unless in the circumstances the
administrative convenience of allowing a deputy or other subordinate to act as an
authorised agent very clearly outweighs the desirability of maintaining the principle
that the officer designated by statute should act personally.[568] But where statute
permitted discharge of disciplinary functions of the Law Society Council to "an
individual (whether or not a member of the Society's staff)", there was nothing
which required the Council to familiarise itself with the name of the delegatee; the
Council could delegate to the holder from time to time of an office.[569] The presumption of deliberate selection is not an independent normative principle, but is merely
a principle of statutory construction which will readily give way to legislative
indications to the contrary.[570]

Further sub-delegation

5-177   The restrictions on the power to delegate have on the whole been applied more
strictly to the further sub-delegation of sub-delegated powers than to the sub-
delegation of primary delegated powers.[571] This is in accordance with the maxim
that the expression of one excludes the other[572]: where Parliament has expressly
authorised sub-delegation of a specific character, it can generally be presumed to
have intended that no further sub-delegation shall be permissible.

Exercise of deliberate judgment

5-178   Again, it may generally be presumed that express authority to sub-delegate powers is to be construed as impliedly excluding authority to sub-delegate the
performance of duties involving the exercise of deliberate judgment, unless the
performance of the duty is inextricably interwoven with the exercise of the power.[573]

---

[568] *Nelms v Roe* [1970] 1 W.L.R. 4, 8; *Mason v Pearce, The Times*, 7 October 1981; *R. v Majewski*
[1977] A.C. 443 at 449–451. This passage was cited with approval in *R. (on the application of WH
Smith Ltd) v Croydon Justices* [2001] E.H.L.R. 12 at [15] (Elias J); and in *R. v Chief Constable of
Greater Manchester Police Ex p. Lainton, The Times*, April 4, 2000. Sedley LJ in *Chief Constable
of West Midlands Police* [2002] EWHC 1087 (Admin) overruled *Nelms v Roe* insofar as Parker CJ
said in that case that the power in question was not subject to the *Carltona* principle, but had to be
expressly or impliedly delegated. In *R. (on the application of Queen Mary, University of London) v
Higher Education Funding Council for England* [2008] EWHC 1472 (Admin); [2008] E.L.R. 540
at [39] a decision of HEFCE was unlawful "because Chief Executive did not make the decision as
he should have done within the scheme of delegation" made in accordance with the Further and
Higher Education Act 1992 Sch.1 para.10; it had been made by an auditor. And see *R. (on the application of Blow Up Media UK Ltd) v Lambeth LBC* [2008] EWHC 1912 (Admin); [2009] 1 P. &
C.R. 10 (interpretation of local authority's scheme of delegation—court looked at the substance
rather than the form of the matter).
[569] *R. v Solicitors Complaints Bureau Ex p. Curtin* (1994) 6 Admin. L.R. 657.
[570] *R. v Solicitors Complaints Bureau Ex p. Curtin* (1994) 6 Admin L.R. 657 (Steyn LJ).
[571] See, e.g. *Cook v Ward* (1877) 2 C.P.D. 255. Powers of sub-delegation are greatly extended by the
Local Government Act 1972 at s.101.
[572] *Expressio unius est exclusio alterius.*
[573] *Mungoni v Attorney General of Northern Rhodesia* [1960] A.C. 336; *R. v DPP Ex p. Association of
First Division Civil Servants, The Times*, 24 May 1988.

Delegation in accordance with statute

Where power to sub-delegate prescribed functions has been conferred by statute, **5-179**
strict requirements to the form of delegation must normally be observed.[574] Delegation must therefore be conveyed in an authorised form[575] to the designated authority,[576] and must identify sufficiently what are the functions thus delegated instead
of leaving the sub-delegate to decide the ambit of his own authority.[577]

Comparative perspectives on delegation

In Australia it has been held that delegation to an office-holder does not require **5-180**
renewal each time there is a change in the holder of that office; it has also held that
revocation of a delegation does not affect the validity of the delegate's acts until the
moment of revocation.[578] In addition, the delegation by an office holder does not
require renewal each time there is a change in the holder of that office.[579]

Canadian courts have in the past taken a restrictive view of the competence of **5-181**
local authorities to confer a free discretion on their members or officials to dispense
with prohibitions embodied in byelaws. Thus, Montreal could not make a byelaw
providing that nobody was to run a business in the city without an official permit;
this was analysed as an invalid sub-delegation.[580] And in another case,[581] a marketing board (itself a sub-delegate) was empowered to make regulations on certain
matters; the regulations that it made were held invalid on the ground that they
contained no standards, but reserved to the board the power to exercise its discretion case by case. The board was said not to have exercised the legislative function delegated to it but to have sub-delegated to itself an administrative function.[582]

The New Zealand decisions are conflicting; sometimes such provisions have been **5-182**

---

[574] *B (A Solicitor) v Victorian Lawyers RPA Ltd* (2000) 6 V.R. 642.

[575] For the manner of conveying such authorisation within a police force: *Nelms v Roe* [1970] 1 W.L.R.
4; *Pamplin v Gorman* [1980] R.T.R. 54; cf. *Record Tower Cranes Ltd v Gisbey* [1969] 1 W.L.R. 148.

[576] cf. *Esmonds Motors Pty Ltd v Commonwealth* (1970) 120 C.L.R. 463 (minister acted ultra vires by
designating himself); *R. v Secretary of State for the Environment Ex p. Hillingdon LBC* [1986] 1
W.L.R. 192, aff'd [1986] 1 W.L.R. 807 (power under s.101(1) of the Local Government Act 1972
to delegate to a committee does not give the power to delegate to a committee of one); cf. *R. v
Secretary of State for Education and Science Ex p. Birmingham CC* (1984) 83 L.G.R. 79 (no power
to delegate to a member of an authority).

[577] *Ratnagopal v Attorney General* [1970] A.C. 972 (Governor-General, empowered to appoint a commissioner of inquiry, left terms of reference excessively vague). cf. *R. v Law Society Ex p. Curtin*
(1994) 6 Admin. L.R. 657; delegation to a named official may not be required. See also the situations in which the authority may be estopped from denying the authority of an officer to whom power
has not been officially delegated: See 12-063 and following.

[578] *Fyfe v Bordoni* [1998] SACS 6860.

[579] *Johnson v Veteran's Review Board* (2002) 71 A.L.D. 16.

[580] *Vic Restaurant Inc v Montreal* [1959] S.C.R. 58 (distinguished in *Lamoureux v City of Beaconsfield*
[1978] 1 S.C.R. 134).

[581] *Brant Dairy Co Ltd v Milk Commission of Ontario* [1973] S.C.R. 131; *Re Canadian Institute of
Public Real Estate Companies and City of Toronto* (1979) 25 N.R. 108, SCC. cf. however, *Re
Bedesky and Farm Products Marketing Board of Ontario* (1976) 58 D.L.R. (3rd) 484 at 502–504.

[582] This reasoning reflects to a limited degree the argument advanced in K.C. Davis, *Discretionary
Justice: a Preliminary Inquiry* (1969), pp.57–59, that bodies and officials in whom discretion is
vested should be under an obligation to confine and structure it by the promulgation of decisional
criteria so as to strike the best balance in the context between rules and discretion. This is a variation on the non-delegation doctrine at one time used by the Supreme Court of the United States to
render invalid statutes that delegated legislative power without setting sufficiently precise limits upon
its exercise, e.g. *Field v Clark* 143 U.S. 649 (1892). See Jaffe, "An Essay on Delegation of Legislative Power" (1947) 47 Colum. L. Rev. 359, 561. It later reappeared in other contexts, e.g. *Shut-
tlesworth v Birmingham* 394 U.S. 147 (1969) (byelaw requiring that permit be obtained before holding public demonstration, invalid because of the broad discretion entrusted to an official); *Furman*

construed as valid conditional prohibitions, and sometimes as sub-delegations the validity of which may be dependent on the prescription of standards governing the exercise of the dispensing power.[583] Issues such as these have seldom arisen in the English courts.[584] If an absolute prohibition would be valid, then prima facie a conditional prohibition should be upheld[585]; but it may be relevant in some cases to consider the context, the persons to whom the dispensing or regulatory power are delegated and the scope of the authority "delegated" to them.

5-183   In India the principle that plenary or essential legislative functions cannot be delegated has also been upheld,[586] however "due to the enormous rise in the nature of activities to be handled by statutory authorities, the maxim *delegates non potest delegare* is not being applied especially when there is a question of exercise of administrative discretionary power".[587] The legislature may, after laying down the legislative policy, confer discretion on an administrative agency as to execution of the policy and leave it to the agency to work out the details within the framework of the policy.[588] The trend of the judgments of the Supreme Court over the decades show that while the principle of non delegation of essential functions has been reiterated, in its application the court has shown considerable latitude recognising the need for greater flexibility, especially in economic law.[589]

5-184   In South Africa the principle of non-delegation is more strictly applied, although "it is not every delegation of delegated powers that is [prohibited], but only such delegations as are not, either expressly or by necessary implication, authorised by the delegated powers".[590] The important case of *AAA Investments (Pty) Ltd v Micro Finance Regulatory Council*[591] illustrates degrees of willingness to find implied authority for sub-delegation. In her dissenting judgment O'Regan J readily accepted that even in the absence of express authority it would be practically neces-

---

v Georgia 408 U.S. 238 (1972); *Profitt v Florida* 428 U.S. 242(1976), where the constitutionality of capital punishment was attacked in part because of the broad discretion "delegated" to the judge and jury in imposing it. cf. *Francis v Chief of Police* [1973] A.C. 761 at 773, where the PC held that a statutory requirement that the permission of the Chief of Police be obtained before "noisy instruments" could lawfully be used at public meetings did not delegate so much discretion as to infringe the freedom of speech and assembly provisions of a constitution of St Christopher, Nevis and Anguilla.

[583] *Mackay v Adams* [1926] N.Z.L.R. 518; *Jackson (FE) & Co v Collector of Customs* [1939] N.Z.L.R. 682; *Hazeldon v McAra* [1948] N.Z.L.R. 1087; *Ideal Laundry Ltd v Petone Borough* [1957] N.Z.L.R. 1038; *Hookings v Director of Civil Aviation* [1957] N.Z.L.R. 929. See also *Hanna v Auckland City Corp* [1945] N.Z.L.R. 622 (unfettered dispensing power). For a review of these and other Commonwealth decisions, see C. Aikman, "Subdelegation of the Legislative Power" (1960) 3 Victoria Univ of Wellington L. Rev. 69, 85–95; P.H. Thorp, "The Key to the Application of the Maxim "Delegatus non potest delegare" (1972-1975) 2 Akl.U.L.R 85. On delegated and sub-delegated powers more generally, see M. Taggart, "From 'Parliamentary Powers' to Privatization: the chequered history of delegated legislation in the twentieth century" (2005) U. Tor. L.J. 575. See also *Attorney General v Mount Roskill Borough* [1971] N.Z.L.R. 1030. For a penetrating analysis of the New Zealand approach which does not permit delegation of unfettered or overbroad discretion see P. Joseph, *Constitutional and Administrative Law in New Zealand*, 3rd edn (2007), 25.7.1–25.7.4 -and 22.3.6(2)–(3).

[584] *Francis v Chief of Police* [1993] A.C. 761, PC. In England licensing powers are nearly always conferred directly by statute or under explicit statutory authority.

[585] *Williams v Weston-super-Mare UDC* (1907) 98 L.T. 537 at 540.

[586] *SKL Co. v Southern Railways* (2015) 16 S.C.C. 509 at 523.

[587] *Sahni Silk Mills (P) Ltd v ESI Corp* (1994) 5 S.C.C. 346 at 350.

[588] *Sidhartha Sarawgi v Kolkata Port* (2014) 16 S.C.C. 248 at 253, 254, citing with approval *Khambhalia Municipality v State of Gujarat AIR* 1967 SC 1048 at 1051.

[589] *Essar Steel Ltd v Union of India* (2016) 11 S.C.C. 1 at 29; *Lohia Machines Ltd v Union of India* (1985) 2 S.C.C. 197 at 241–244.

[590] *Attorney General, OFS v Cyril Anderson Investments (Pty) Ltd* 1965 (4) SA 628, A at 639D.

[591] *AAA Investments (Pty) Ltd v Micro Finance Regulatory Council* 2007 (1) S.A. 343, CC.

sary for the Minister to sub-delegate his regulatory power to the Council.[592] In another dissenting opinion Langa CJ was more cautious, suggesting that "courts should be slow to infer the delegation of power to bodies that cannot be held directly accountable through ordinary political processes".[593]

The Carltona principle

Special considerations arise where a statutory power vested in a minister or a department of state is exercised by a departmental official. The official is not usually spoken of as a delegate, but rather as the alter ego of the minister or the department[594]; power is devolved rather than delegated.[595] (A different analysis must, of course, be adopted where powers are explicitly conferred upon or delegated to an official by a law-making instrument.[596]) Under the "*Carltona*" principle the courts have recognised that "the duties imposed on ministers and the powers given to ministers are normally exercised under the authority of the ministers by responsible officials of the department. Public business could not be carried on if that were not the case".[597] In general, therefore, a minister is not obliged to bring his own mind to bear upon a matter entrusted to him by statute but may act through a duly authorised officer[598] of his department.[599] The officer's authority need not be conferred upon him by the minister personally[600]; it may be conveyed generally and informally by the officer's hierarchical superiors in accordance with departmental

5-185

---

[592] para.135.

[593] para.88. The majority held that owing to the limited scope of the challenge, the sub-delegation had to be accepted as lawful (paras 47–8).

[594] See, e.g. *Lewisham Borough v Roberts* [1949] 2 K.B. 608, 629 at *R. v Skinner* [1968] 2 Q.B. 700; *Re Golden Chemical Products Ltd* [1976] Ch. 300 at 307; cf. *Woollett v Minister of Agriculture and Fisheries* [1955] 1 Q.B. 103. The harmless fiction of the "alter ego principle" (D. Lanham, "Delegation and the Alter Ego Principle" (1984) 100 L.Q.R. 587) does, however, have its limits. Admissions by a civil servant will not necessarily be treated as admissions by his minister, *Williams v Home Office* [1981] 1 All E.R. 1211. Similarly, evidence of receipt of a letter by a minister's department will not satisfy a requirement that advice be received by a minister of the Crown, although evidence of receipt by an official with responsibility for the matter in question will suffice: *Air 2000 Ltd v Secretary of State for Transport (No.2)* 1990 S.L.T. 335.

[595] *R. v Secretary of State Ex p. Oladehinde* [1991] 1 A.C. 254 at 283–284, CA.

[596] As where power to decide certain classes of planning appeals have been vested in inspectors by legislation. And see *Somerville v Scottish Ministers* [2007] UKHL 44; [2007] 1 W.L.R. 2734, in which one of the issues was whether a prison governor making an order under the Prisons and Young Offenders (Scotland) Rules 1994 r.80(1)—on the removal of association—should be regarded as a member of the Scottish Executive. The HL held the *Carltona* principle did not apply in these circumstances.

[597] *Carltona Ltd v Commissioners of Works* [1943] 2 All E.R. 560 at 563 (Lord Greene MR); *West Riding CC v Wilson* [1941] 2 All E.R. 827 at 831 (Viscount Caldecote CJ); *In re Golden Chemical Products Ltd* [1976] Ch. 300. cf. *R. v Secretary of State for the Home Department Ex p. Phansopkar* [1976] Q.B. 606 where the minister was held to have no power to require applicants for certificates of partiality to obtain them from British Government officials in the applicant's country of origin rather than from the Home Office in London.

[598] cf.*Customs and Excise Commissioners v Cure & Deeley Ltd* [1962] 1 Q.B. 340 (manner of authorisation prescribed by statute held, not complied with).

[599] *West Riding* [1941] 2 All E.R. 827; *Point of Ayr Collieries Ltd v Lloyd-George* [1943] 2 All E.R. 546; *Carltona* [1943]2 All E.R. 560; *Lewisham* [1949] 2 K.B. 608; *Woollett* [1955]1 Q.B. 103. *Castle v Crown Prosecution Service* [2014] EWHC 587 (Admin); (2014) 178 J.P. 285 (one of the questions posed in an appeal by way of case stated against a speeding conviction was whether an order imposing temporary and variable speed limits was ultra vires because it was signed and/or made by an employee of the Highways Agency (which was not part of the Minister's department); it was held that the *Carltona* principle allowed this delegation of power; the Agency was the alter ego of the Secretary of State in the areas for which he accepted responsibility in Parliament just as he did for the actions of civil servants housed under his departmental roof).

[600] *Lewisham* [1949] 2 K.B. 608; *Woollett* [1995] 1 Q.B. 103; *R. v Skinner* [1968] 2 Q.B. 700 cf. *Horton*

practice.[601] Whether it is necessary for the authorised officer explicitly to profess to act on behalf of the minister is not certain, but it is suggested that this will not usually be required.[602]

5-186   In *R. (on the application of National Association of Health Stores) v Department of Health*, the Court of Appeal considered whether the knowledge within the department should in law be imputed to the minister (who made the decision to prohibit the use of a herbal remedy in foodstuffs in ignorance of the special expertise of a particular adviser). Sedley LJ held that to impute the knowledge would be "antithetical to good government",[603] and result in a situation where "the person with knowledge decides nothing and the person without knowledge decides everything". Modern departmental government, he felt, required ministers to be properly briefed about the decisions they must take. He was not willing to accept that the collective knowledge of the civil servants in his department or their collective expertise would necessarily be treated as the minister's own knowledge and expertise.[604]

5-187   It may be that there are, however, some matters of such importance that the minister is legally required to address himself to them personally,[605] despite the fact that many dicta that appear to support the existence of such an obligation are at best equivocal.[606] It is, however, possible that orders drastically affecting the liberty of the person—e.g. deportation orders,[607] detention orders made under wartime

---

v St Thomas Elgin General Hospital (1982) 140 D.L.R. (3rd) 274.

[601] *Lewisham* [1949] 2 K.B. 608; see esp. *Woollett* [1955] 1 Q.B. 103 at 124–126 (Jenkins LJ); *Re Golden Chemical Products Ltd* [1976] Ch. 300, 305.

[602] cf. *Woollett* [1955] 1 Q.B. 103 at 120-121, 132, 134 (Denning and Morris LJJ); *Re Reference Under Section 11 of the Ombudsman Act* (1979) 2 A.L.D. 86, 94. In *Golden Chemical* [1976] Ch. 300 at 311, it was said to be preferable for the departmental officer who had in fact taken the decision to state that he had been satisfied that the statutory criterion for exercising the power had been met. For Australia, it has been suggested that as with any other agent, a *Carltona* agent may act with ostensible authority: E. Campbell, "Ostensible Authority in Public Law" (1999) 27 Fed. L. Rev. 1; and M. Aronson, M. Groves and G Weeks, *Judicial Review of Administrative Action and Government Liability*, 6th edn (2017), para.6.130.

[603] *R. (on the application of National Association of Health Stores) v Secretary of State for Health* [2005] EWCA Civ 154 at [26].

[604] Thus distinguishing Lord Diplock's assertion to the contrary in *Bushell v Secretary of State for the Environment* [1981] A.C. 75 at 95. It was held that the considerations of which the minister had no knowledge were not "relevant". See also M. Freedland, "The Rule Against Delegation and the Carltona Doctrine in an Agency Context" [1996] P.L. 19 (who argues that in conferring a discretionary power on a minister, the parliamentary draftsmen are in effect employing a formula that the discretion is conferred upon the government department). Sedley LJ considered that such a proposition would have the effect that "ministers need to know nothing before reaching a decision so long as those advising them know the facts" at [37]—which he called "the law according to Sir Humphrey Appleby" (an illusion to the permanent secretary in the television comedy "Yes Minister"); I. Steele, "Note on R. (National Association of Health Stores) v Department of Health" [2005] J.R. 232.

[605] *Re Golden Chemical Products Ltd* [1976] Ch. 300 the judge denied that such a category existed. But see *Ramawad v Minister of Manpower and Immigration* [1978] 2 S.C.R. 375 and *R. (on the application of Tamil Information Centre) v Secretary of State for the Home Department* [2002] EWHC 2155 (Admin); (2002) 99 L.S.G. 32 where it was held that ministerial authorisation was an impermissible delegation as the statute required the minister personally to exercise his judgment.

[606] *Re Golden Chemical Products Ltd* [1976] Ch. 300 at 309–310, Brightman J concluded that the dicta in *Liversidge v Anderson* [1942] A.C. 206 should be understood as referring to political expediency and to the minister's personal responsibility to Parliament, rather than to his legal obligation.

[607] *R. v Chiswick Police Station Superintendent Ex p. Sacksteder* [1918] 1 K.B. 578 at 585–586, 591–592 (dicta). The decision has in fact been taken by the Home Secretary personally (Cmnd 3387 (1967), 16). In *Oladehinde v Secretary of State for the Home Department* [1991] 1 A.C. 254, which concerned the provisional decision to deport, the HL appeared to accept that the final decision to deport had to be taken by the Secretary of State personally or by a junior Home Office minister if

security regulations[608] and perhaps discretionary orders for the rendition of fugitive offenders[609] require the personal attention of the minister.[610]

On the other hand, the minister was not required personally to approve breath-testing equipment, despite its importance to the liberty of motorists suspected of driving after consuming alcohol,[611] and a decision on the question of a life sentence prisoner's tariff period may be taken on behalf of the Home Secretary by a Minister of State at the Home Office.[612] Objection to the production of documentary evidence in legal proceedings on the ground that its production would be injurious to the public interest must be taken by the minister or the permanent head of the department, certifying that personal consideration has been given to the documents in question.[613] Statutory instruments are signed by senior officials acting under a general grant of authority from the minister.[614]

5-188

Similarly, it is uncertain whether the courts will examine the suitability of the official who performs the work. The *Carltona* case emphasised that Parliament, not the courts, was the forum for scrutiny of the minister's decision,[615] but more recently it has been accepted that the courts may also examine the devolvement of authority, by way of judicial review.[616] At the very least, it would seem that the official must satisfy the test of *Wednesbury* unreasonableness: he must not be so junior that no reasonable minister would allow him to exercise the power.[617] There may be some tasks which by their nature ought not to allow of delegation or devolution,

5-189

---

he was unavailable. *R. v Secretary of State for the Home Department Ex p. Mensah* [1996] Imm. A.R. 223.

[608] *Liversidge v Anderson* [1942] A.C. 206 at 223–224, 265, 281; *Point of Ayr* [1943] 2 All E.R. 546 at 548 (dicta).

[609] *R. v Brixton Prison Governor Ex p. Enahoro* [1963] 2 Q.B. 455 at 466.

[610] Had he believed that such a category existed, the judge in Re Golden Chemicals might well have included in it the power to present a petition for the compulsory winding up of a company (Companies Act 1967 s.10). See D. Lanham, "Delegation and the Alter Ego Principle" (1984) 100 L.Q.R. 587, 592–594 (who argues that where life or personal liberty are at stake, the *alter ego* principle may not apply).

[611] *R. v Skinner* [1968] 2 Q.B. 700: it might, of course, be argued that the reliability of the equipment raises technical questions to which the minister will normally bring no special expertise.

[612] *Doody v Secretary of State for the Home Department* [1994] 1 A.C. 531.

[613] *Duncan v Cammell, Laird & Co* [1942] A.C. 624, 638.

[614] E.C. Page, *Governing by Numbers: Delegated Legislation and Everyday Policy-Making* (2001). Departmental practice varies; in some departments all or nearly all statutory instruments are signed by the minister personally (Report of the Joint Committee on Delegated Legislation. HC Paper No. 475 (Session 1971/72), Minutes of Evidence, 196-203). In *Lewisham Borough v Roberts* [1949] 2 K.B. 608 at 621–622 Denning LJ indicated that legislative functions had to be performed by the minister personally; but Bucknill and Jenkins LJJ at 619, 629–630) were of the contrary opinion.

[615] *R. v Secretary of State for the Home Department Ex p. Oladehinde* [1991] 1 A.C. 254 at 281–282, CA.

[616] *R. v Secretary of State for the Home Department Ex p. Oladehinde* [1991] 1 A.C. 254, QBD at 260; CA at 282. Although it did not arise for decision in the case, in *DPP v Haw* [2007] EWHC 1931 (Admin); [2008] 1 W.L.R. 379 Lord Phillips CJ suggested (at [29]) that there was scope for further refinement of the *Carltona* principle, and devolution of a minister's powers should be subject to a requirement that the seniority of the official exercising a power should be of an appropriate level having regard to the nature of the power in question. *Haw* was applied by the Divisional Court in *R. (on the application of Hamill) v Chelmsford Justices* [2014] EWHC 2799 (Admin); [2015] 1 W.L.R. 1798, which held that the delegation of the Chief Constable's duty to determine a review under s.91C of the Sexual Offences Act 2003 could properly be delegated to an officer of superintendent rank or above.

[617] *R. v Secretary of State for the Home Department Ex p. Oladehinde* [1991] 1 A.C. 254 at 303 (Lord Griffiths perhaps went further in stating that development of authority to officials under the Carltona principle was permissible "providing ... that the decisions are suitable to their grading and experience"); *R. (on the application of Chief Constable of the West Midlands Police) v Birmingham Magistrate's Court* [2002] EWHC 1087; [2003] Crim. L.R. at 37 [10] (Sedley LJ considered that delegation had to be to "somebody suitable" but that question was for the official subject to the test

such as some disciplinary powers.[618] And different tasks conferred on a decision-maker may be delegable to different levels within the organisation.[619] Moreover, the purpose for which a power is conferred may prevent delegation. In *R. (on the application of Bourgass) v Secretary of State for Justice (Howard League for Penal Reform intervening)* it was held that the purpose of a power to review the continued segregation of prisoners was to act as a safeguard for prisoners; as this safeguard could only be meaningful if exercised by an official independent of the management of the prison, it was not possible to delegate the power from the Secretary of State to the prison governor.[620]

5-190   The *Carltona* principle may be expressly excluded by legislation,[621] but whether it may in addition be excluded by statutory implication remains uncertain. Two situations should be distinguished. Where a power of delegation is expressly conferred by Parliament on a minister, it may compel the inference that Parliament intended to restrict devolution of power to the statutory method, thus impliedly excluding the *Carltona* principle.[622] Commonwealth authority, however, suggests that such an implication will not readily be drawn.[623] It has also been suggested that the principle may be impliedly excluded where it appears inconsistent with the intention of Parliament as evinced by a statutory framework of powers and responsibilities.[624] However, where the Immigration Act 1971 apparently clearly divided responsibilities between immigration officers and the Secretary of State, the Court of Appeal and House of Lords held that the *Carltona* principle enabled powers of the Secretary of State to be exercised by immigration officers. In the Court of Appeal it was said that the *Carltona* principle was not merely an implication which would be read into a statute in the absence of any clear contrary indication, but was a common law constitutional principle, which could not be excluded by implication unless "a challenge could be mounted on the possibly broader basis that the decision to devolve authority was *Wednesbury* unreasonable".[625] The House of Lords allowed the devolution of power on the narrower ground that the implication to exclude could not be drawn; the devolution did "not conflict with or embarrass [the officers] in the discharge of their specific statutory duties under the Act".[626] Although their statu-

---

of irrationality).

[618] *R. v North Thames Regional Health Authority and Chelsea and Westminster NHS Trust Ex p. L* (1996) 7 Med L.R. 385 (Sedley J, although the Trust had no express power to delegate disciplinary powers to the Regional Health Authority, certain stages of the disciplinary process might be delegated, although the Trust alone had the duty to evaluate the findings of the inquiry).

[619] For example, the application task and the consultation task in *Chief Constable of the West Midlands Police* [2002] EWHC 1087 (Admin); [2003] Crim. L.R. 37 and the different tasks involved in the disciplinary functions in *North Thames RHA* [1996] Med. L.R. 385; *E v Hertsmere BC Ex p. Woolgar* [1996] 2 F.C.R. 69 (powers of investigation, but not ultimate decision, may be delegated).

[620] *R. (on the application of King) v Secretary of State for Justice* [2015] UKSC 54; [2016] A.C. 384.

[621] See, e.g. Immigration Act 1971 ss.13(5), 14(3) and 15(4), which referred to action by the minister "and not by a person acting under his authority".

[622] *Customs and Excise Cmrs v Cure and Deeley Ltd* [1962] 1 Q.B. 340 (conferment by Parliament of express power of delegation on Commissioners deprived them of previously existing benefit of Carltona principle): but compare *Carltona* itself.

[623] *O'Reilly v Commissioner of State Bank of Victoria* (1982) 44 A.L.R. 27; (1983) 153 C.L.R. 1.cf *Re Reference Under s.11 of the Ombudsman Act* (1979) 2 A.L.D. 86; cf. D. Lanham, "Delegation and the Alter Ego Principle" (1984) 100 L.Q.R. 587, 600–603.

[624] *Ramawad v Minister of Manpower and Immigration* (1978) 81 D.L.R. (3rd) 687; *Sean Investments v MacKellar* (1981) 38 A.L.R. 363.

[625] *R. v Secretary of State for the Home Department Ex p. Oladehinde* CA, 282 (Lord Donaldson MR).For unreasonableness, see Ch.11.

[626] *R. v Secretary of State for the Home Department Ex p. Oladehinde* HL, 303 (Lord Griffiths). This conclusion was influenced by the fact that the minister retained a personal role in reviewing and sign-

tory analysis may be questioned,[627] the approach of the House of Lords accorded greater weight than the Court of Appeal to Parliament's intent. However, in *R. (on the application of Bourgass) v Secretary of State for Justice (Howard League for Penal Reform intervening)* the Supreme Court held that *Carltona* cannot apply to the holder of a statutory office who is himself constitutionally responsible for the manner in which he discharges his office and is thus constitutionally demarcated from the Secretary of State. As such the principle could not operate to permit the delegation of the power to segregate prisoners from the Secretary of State to a prison governor.[628]

Does the *Carltona* principle apply to public authorities or officers besides ministers?[629] Powers of the Queen or Governor in Council may be exercised by a minister or official in his department, although any formal decision necessarily will be made by the Queen in Council.[630] Powers conferred on senior departmental officers may be devolved to more junior officials in the department.[631] In *Nelms v Roe*[632] the Divisional Court upheld a decision of a police inspector acting on behalf of the Metropolitan Police Commissioner, on whom the power had been conferred. However, Lord Parker did not think that the inspector could be considered the alter ego of the Commissioner and preferred to base the case on implied delegated authority.

5-191

However, the Court of Appeal has held that the *Carltona* principle is transferable to non-ministerial bodies and that applications for antisocial behaviour orders (ASBOs) could be made by junior police officers despite the fact that the power was conferred upon a local council or chief officer of police. Sedley LJ stressed that *Carltona* was based not only on convenience (the alter ego aspect) but also upon the fact that the minister continued to be responsible for the decision taken by the

5-192

---

ing each deportation order.

[627] Weight was placed on several explicit limitations of the minister's powers to him personally, as excluding further implicit limitations; yet it was surely consistent of Parliament to intend some powers to be exercised by the minister personally, some to be exercised by the minister or his civil servants in the department, and others to be exercised by immigration officers as the statutory scheme appeared to require.

[628] *R. (on the application of King) v Secretary of State for Justice* [2015] UKSC 54; [2015] 3 W.L.R. 457.

[629] See e.g. D. Lanham, "Delegation and the Alter Ego Principle" (1984) 100 L.Q.R. 587, 604 and following.

[630] *FAI Insurances Ltd v Winneke* (1982) 151 C.L.R. 342; *South Australia v O'Shea* (1987) 163 C.L.R. 378; cf. *Attorney-General v Brent* [1956] 2 D.L.R. (2nd) 503.

[631] *Commissioners of Customs and Excise v Cure and Deeley* [1962] 1 Q.B. 340; *O'Reilly v Commissioners of State Bank of Victoria* (1982) 44 A.L.R. 27; (1983) 153 C.L.R. 1; *R. v Secretary of State for the Home Department Ex p. Sherwin* (1996) 32 B.M.L.R. 1. (*Carltona* applied to the Benefits Agency which was held to be part of the Department of Social Security and the agency staff belonged to the Civil Service). See also *R. v Greater Manchester Police Authority Ex p. Century Motors (Farnworth) Ltd, The Times,* 31 May 1996; cf. *R. v Oxfordshire CC Ex p. Pittick* [1995] C.O.D. 397 (Education Act 1981 s.7(2)—council had not improperly delegated its duty to provide special needs education to the school); *R. v Harrow LBC Ex p. M* [1997] 3 F.C.R. 761 (obligations on a local education authority under Education Act 1993 s.168 to arrange that special educational provision be made for a child was not delegable); *MFI Furniture Centre Ltd v Hibbert* (1996) 160 J.P. 178 (validity of council's Minutes of Delegation); *Noon v Matthews* [2014] EWHC 4330 (Admin); [2015] A.C.D. 53; (validity of delegation of decision to bring a prosecution to enforce byelaws relating to a river). It is exceptional in Australia for Carltona to be applied to structures other than government departments for which a Minister is responsible in Parliament: *O'Reilly v State Bank of Victoria* (1983) 153 C.L.R. 1; and M. Aronson, M. Groves and G. Weeks, *Judicial Review of Administrative Action and Government Liability,* 6th edn (2017)) para.6.140. In Ireland, the courts assess whether the dominant purpose was proper: *State (Cassidy) v Minister for Industry and Commerce* [1978] I.R. 297.

[632] *Nelms v Roe* [1970] 1 W.L.R. 4 at 8 (Lord Parker CJ).

official in his department. Provided that (a) the power is delegable, and (b) is not required to be performed by a particularly qualified individual (such as a medical officer of health or a statutory inspector), it may be exercised at different levels. The delegation or devolution of powers was, in those circumstances, for the Chief Constable to decide, and the court could not second-guess him unless his choice was irrational or beyond his powers.[633]

Acting under dictation

5-193   An authority entrusted with a discretion must not, in the purported exercise of its discretion, act under the dictation of another body or person. In at least two Commonwealth cases, licensing bodies were found to have taken decisions on the instructions of the heads of government who were prompted by extraneous motives.[634] But, as less colourful cases illustrate, it is enough to show that a decision which ought to have been based on the exercise of independent judgment was dictated by those not entrusted with the power to decide,[635] although it remains a question of fact whether the repository of discretion abdicated it in the face of external pressure.[636] And it is immaterial that the external authority has not sought to impose its policy. For instance, where a local authority, in assessing compensation for loss of office, erroneously made certain deductions because it thought it was obliged to do so, having regard to the practice followed in such cases by the Treasury (to which an appeal lay from its decisions), mandamus issued to compel it to determine the claim according to law.[637] Where a minister entertaining a planning appeal dismissed the appeal purely on the strength of policy objections entered by another minister, it was held that his decision had to be quashed because he had, in effect, surrendered his discretion to the other minister.[638] Authorities directly entrusted with statutory discretions, be they executive officers or members of distinct tribunals, are usually entitled and are often obliged to take into account

---

[633]   *R. (on the application of Chief Constable of the west Midlands) v Birminghan Magistrates Court* [2002] EWHC 1087 (Admin); [2003] Gin L.R. 37 at [16]. But see *DPP v Haw* [2007] EWHC 1931 (Admin); [2008] 1 W.L.R. 379 at [33] (Lord Phillips CJ holding that where a statutory power is conferred on an officer, who is himself a creature of statute, the question of whether that officer has the power to delegate is dependent upon the interpretation of the relevant statute). Where the responsibilities of the office are such that delegation is inevitable, there will be an implied power to delegate unless the statute, expressly or by implication, provides to the contrary. These principles are indistinguishable from the Carltona principle, and thus, whether Sedley LJ was correct to hold in *R. (on the application of Chief Constable of the West Midlands) v Birmingham Justices* [2002] EWHC 1087 (Admin); [2002] Po. L.R. 157 that the *Carltona* principle applied to a Chief Constable's statutory functions, was "of only academic significance".

[634]   *Roncarelli v Duplessis* [1959] S.C.R. 121; *Rowjee v State of Andhra Pradesh, AIR* 1964 S.C. 962; and see *Ellis-Don Ltd v Ontario (Labour Relations Board)* 2001 SCC 4; [2001] 1 S.C.R. 221; *Thamotharem v Canada (Minister of Citizenship and Immigration)* 2007 FCA 198; [2008] 1 F.C.R. 385, (cases involving allegations of the interference with the decision-making independence of adjudicators). For examples of the rule against acting under dictation in Ireland, see: *McLoughlin v Minister for Social Welfare* [1958] I.R. 1 and *State (Rajan) v Minister for Industry and Commerce* [1988] I.L.R.M. 231.

[635]   *McLoughlin v Minister for Social Welfare* [1958] I.R. 1 at 27.

[636]   *Hlookoff v City of Vancouver* (1968) 65 D.L.R. (2nd) 71; 63 W.W.R. 129; *Malloch v Aberdeen Corp (No.2)* 1974 S.L.T. 253 at 264.

[637]   *R. v Stepney Corp* [1902] 1 K.B. 317; *Buttle v Buttle* [1953] 1 W.L.R. 1217.

[638]   *Lavender (H) & Son Ltd v Minister of Housing and Local Government* [1970] 1 W.L.R. 1231 (where the other minister might be said to have imposed his policy); cf. *Kent CC v Secretary of State for the Environment* (1977) 75 L.G.R. 452. See also *R. v Secretary of State for Trade and Industry Ex p. Lonrho Plc* [1989] 1 W.L.R. 525 at 583 (Lord Keith said that "the discretion ... must be exercised by him and not at the dictation of another minister or body"); *Ainooson v Secretary of State for the Home Department* [1973] Imm.A.R. 43.

considerations of public policy, and in some contexts the policy of a minister or of the Government as a whole may be a relevant factor in weighing those considerations[639]; but this will not absolve them from their duty to exercise their personal judgment in individual cases,[640] unless explicit statutory provision has been made for them to be given binding instructions by a superior,[641] or (possibly) unless the cumulative effect of the subject-matter and their hierarchical subordination[642] (in the case of civil servants and local government officers)[643] make it clear that it is constitutionally proper for them to receive and obey instructions conveyed in the proper manner and form.[644]

The rule against acting under dictation—as a "puppet" of another authority does **5-194** not, however, mean that authority X cannot, if it possesses the power, authorise a decision by authority Y, so long as authority X maintains control of the ultimate decision. In *Audit Commission for England and Wales v Ealing LBC*[645] the Audit Commission, in carrying out its performance assessment of local authorities, relied on the Commission for Social Care Inspection to conduct an assessment of performance in the social services. The Court of Appeal held that the Audit Commission had maintained control over the assessment principles and the ultimate decision, to which it had applied its mind, and therefore had not acted under the dictation of the Social Care Commission.[646]

Needless to say, a duty not to comply with executive instructions[647] to decide **5-195** individual cases in a particular way is always strictly cast upon courts.[648]

---

[639] cf. *R. v Mahony Ex p. Johnson* (1931) 46 C.L.R. 131 at 145; *R. v Anderson Ex p. Ipec-Air Pty Ltd* (1965) 113 C.L.R. 177; *Ansett Transport Industries (Operations) Pty Ltd v Commonwealth* (1977) 17 A.L.R. 513; *Re Innisfi (Township of) and Barrie (City of)* (1977) 80 D.L.R. (3rd) 85. See also *Roberts v Dorset CC* (1977) 75 L.G.R. 462 (adoption by local authority of central government circular). cf. *Re Multi-Malls Inc and Minister of Transportation and Communications* (1977) 73 D.L.R. (3rd) 18 (minister's refusal of permit for proposed development invalid because he had regard to general government planning policy, rather than limiting his decision to road traffic matters).

[640] See *Ipec-Air* (1965) 113 C.L.R. 177 for divergent expressions of opinion on the question of how far a decision of the Director-General of Civil Aviation (a public officer) to refuse permission to import aircraft and to refuse a charter licence to operate an inter-state air service could properly be predetermined by current government policy. On government policy as a "relevant consideration", *R. v Parole Board Ex p. Watson* [1996] 1 W.L.R. 906 (Parole Board must make up its own mind and not simply review Secretary of State's reasons for revocation of parole); Cf. *R. (on the application of S (A Child)) v Brent LBC* [2002] EWCA Civ 693; [2002] E.L.R. 556 (a view that statutory guidance re pupil exclusion should "normally" be upheld was not an unlawful exercise of discretion).

[641] *Laker Airways Ltd v Department of Trade* [1977] Q.B. 643 at 698-700, 713, 714, 724-725, considering the Civil Aviation Act 1971 at s.4(3) (power of Secretary of State to give specific directions to licensing authority for certain purposes); and s.3(2) authorising the Secretary of State to issue guidance to the authority on the performance of its statutory functions which it must perform "as it considers is in accordance with the guidance".

[642] I. Zamir, "Administrative Control of Administrative Action" (1969) 57 California L.R. 866.

[643] But in local government, treasurers have been obliged to obey the law and to disobey the council's instructions if contrary to law.

[644] cf. *Simms Motor Units Ltd v Minister of Labour and National Service* [1946] 2 All E.R. 201 (where instructions were communicated to the officers in an unauthorised form).

[645] *Audit Commission for England and Wales v Ealing LBC* [2005] EWCA Civ 556; (2005) 8 C.C.L. Rep. 317.

[646] J. Brair, "When is a Fetter not a Fetter?" [2005] J.R. 217.

[647] Or advice: *Sankey v Whitlam* [1977] 1 N.S.W.L.R. 333.

[648] *Evans v Donaldson* (1909) 9 C.L.R. 140; *Ex p. Duncan* (1904) 4 S.R. (N.S.W) 217; *R. (Courtney) v Emerson* [1913] 2 I.R. 377. See also *Buttle v Buttle* [1953] 1 W.L.R. 1217.

CHAPTER 6

Procedural Fairness: Introduction, History and Comparative Perspectives

TABLE OF CONTENTS

SCOPE

6-001   Chapters 6 to 10 are concerned primarily with the manner in which functions are performed by public authorities, rather than the validity of the decisions themselves. The chapters deal with issues of procedural justice. An important concern of procedural justice is to provide the opportunity for individuals to participate in decisions by public authorities that affect them. Another is to promote the quality, accuracy and rationality of the decision-making process. Both concerns aim at enhancing the legitimacy of that process while at the same time improving the quality of decisions made by public authorities.

6-002   Procedural justice, or procedural fairness, has to be contrasted with substantive justice. The general objective of substantive justice is to ensure that the decisions of public authorities are within the scope of the powers conferred on those authorities. Substantive justice ensures that those powers are not exceeded. Procedural justice aims to provide individuals with a fair opportunity to influence the outcome of a decision and so ensure the decision's integrity. It deals with issues such as the requirement to consult, to hear representations, to hold hearings and to give reasons for decisions. It addresses the nature of those consultations, representations and hearings, so as to ensure that they are appropriate in the circumstances, meaningful, and that they assist and do not hinder the administrative process.

6-003   Chapter 7 examines the circumstances that give rise to *an entitlement* to procedural fairness and *the content* of that entitlement. The entitlement can arise from a statutory duty to follow a particular procedure or from the relationship between the person or body taking the decision and the person or body who could be affected adversely by the decision. It may arise out of a "legitimate expectation" encouraged by the decision-maker, but our main examination of this aspect of procedural fairness is postponed until Chapter 12. Depending upon the situation, the content of the procedural protection may range from the mere right to be consulted, to a full public hearing containing most of the features of a judicial trial.

6-004 Chapter 8 considers the situations in which there would normally be an entitlement to fair procedure, but where the circumstances (such as those involved in a decision concerning questions of national security) may negate or curtail the right.

6-005 Chapters 9 and 10 consider the principal techniques that ensure that the procedures provided are meaningful. These include the rule against the fettering of discretion (Chapter 9) and the entitlement to an unbiased decision-maker (Chapter 10).

6-006 The remainder of this chapter will: first, examine the concept of natural justice or fairness from a theoretical perspective; secondly, describe the different stages in the historical evolution of this concept in this jurisdiction; and thirdly, present a brief comparative overview of procedural fairness.

INTRODUCTION

6-007 A minority of administrative decisions do not permit any participation; those for example that require speed and despatch and cannot be delayed. A hearing may not be able to be held about whether a fire brigade, in the course of a fire, should destroy a building.[1] In cases where participation is appropriate, the content of the procedure will vary in accordance with the nature of the decision to be made: in some circumstances a full public inquiry may be required,[2] whereas in others there will only be a bare entitlement to consultation.[3] Courts, in deciding the scope and limits of procedural fairness, must be alert to the interests of good administration, and therefore sensitive to the subject-matter of the decision. Participation should not however be seen as opposed to the interests of effective administration. On the contrary it can greatly improve the quality of official decisions by providing the decision-makers with information they might not otherwise receive; information about the quality of the decision, as well as its perceived impact upon individuals or groups.

6-008 The interest of individuals in participation in decisions by which they could be affected is obvious: they will wish to influence the outcome of the decision. Fairness requires that, in appropriate circumstances, they should have the opportunity of doing so. Among the reasons for this are; procedural fairness may improve the quality of the decision, serve the purpose of protecting human dignity[4] and assist

---

[1] See 8-026; *R. (on the application of Louis Brehony) v Chief Constable of Greater Manchester Police* [2005] EWHC 640; (2005) 149 S.J.L.B. 393 at [17] (Bean J distinguishing between an "on-the-spot" decision of a police officer not to permit an assembly, and a decision regarding an intention to hold a future assembly).

[2] On public inquiries, see 1-101.

[3] See 7-040.

[4] R. Dworkin, *Taking Rights Seriously* (1977), Ch.4; G. Maher, "Natural Justice as Fairness", Ch.6 in N. MacCormick and P. Birks (eds), *The Legal Mind: Essays for Tony Honoré* (1986); J. Mashaw, *Due Process in the Administrative State* (1985), Chs 4–7. The difference between instrumental and non-instrumental accounts of procedural fairness are discussed in P. Craig, *Administrative Law*, 8th edn (2016), para.12-002; Lord Millett "The Right to Good Administration in European Law" [2002] P.L. 309 (distinguishing between common law and civil law systems); D. Galligan, *Due Process and Fair Procedures: A Study of Administrative Procedures* (1996) (prioritising instrumental rationales); T. Allan, "Procedural Fairness and the Duty of Respect" (1998) 18 O.J.L.S. 497 and *Constitutional Justice: A Liberal Theory of the Rule of Law* (2001) (defending a more dignitarian, non-instrumental rationale). See also P. Cane, *Administrative Law*, 5th edn (2011). For a full account of

in achieving a sense that justice has both been done and seen to be done; it may promote objectivity and impartiality,[5] or, as just noted, increase the likelihood of an accurate substantive outcome.[6] But of course, the exercise of the opportunity to make representations will not automatically result in the representations made being accepted. Nor does the existence of fair procedures guarantee the open mind of the decision-maker. There is always room for "symbolic reassurance",[7] and for the cynical manipulation of procedural forms on the part of a decision-maker who has no intention of being persuaded and whose mind is closed. The procedure that is required to be followed can provide protection against this. The decision must usually be taken by an individual who is free from bias.[8] The fettering of discretion is normally not allowed thus ensuring that the decision-maker keeps an open mind.[9] Most importantly, the duty to give reasons for decisions, where it exists, assists in ensuring the rationality of the decision[10] and that the arguments presented to the decision-maker are seen to be taken into account.

Historically, the principle of natural justice appropriated most of procedural fairness, but, as we shall see, eventually unnecessarily confined itself to situations where a body was acting "judicially", and where "rights" rather than "privileges" were in issue.[11] Although often retained as a general concept, the term natural justice has since been largely replaced and extended by the more general duty to act "fairly".[12] In 1984, Lord Diplock adopted the term "procedural propriety" to

6-009

---

fair procedures in discretionary decisions, see D. Galligan, *Discretionary Powers: a Legal Study of Official Discretion* (1986), Ch.7. See also L. Sossin, "An Intimate Approach to Fairness, Impartiality and Reasonableness in Administrative Law" (2002) 27 Queen's L.J. 809; L. Solum, "Procedural Justice" (2004) 78 S. Cal. L. Rev. 181, for a general theoretical defence of the importance of participation in decision-making procedures. For an example of the influence of instrumental and non-instrumental justifications on judicial reasoning, see *R. v Secretary of State for the Home Department Ex p. Doody* [1994] 1 A.C. 531 at 551 (Lord Mustill noting that a prisoner, given a life sentence for murder, would wish to know the reasons for his imprisonment term, "partly from an obvious human desire to be told the reason for a decision so gravely affecting his future, and partly because he hopes that once the information is obtained he may be able to point out errors of fact or reasoning and thereby persuade the Secretary of State to change his mind, or if he fails in this to challenge the decision in the courts"). See also *Sengupta v Holmes* [2002] EWCA Civ 1104 at [38] (Laws LJ referring to "the central place accorded to oral argument in our common law adversarial system. This I think is important, because oral argument is perhaps the most powerful force there is, in our legal process, to promote a change of mind by the judge. That judges in fact change their minds under the influence of oral argument is not an arcane feature of the system; it is at the centre of it").

[5] J. Rawls, *A Theory of Justice* (1971), p.239 ("the rule of law requires some form of due process ... designed to ascertain the truth ... The precepts of natural justice are to insure that the legal order will be impartially and regularly maintained"). See also H.L.A. Hart, *The Concept of Law* (1961), pp.156, 202.

[6] Rawls, *A Theory of Justice* (1971); J. Resnick, "Due Process and Procedural Justice" in J. Pennock and J. Chapman (eds), *Due Process* (1977), p.217.

[7] M. Edelman, *The Symbolic Uses of Politics* (1974).

[8] See Ch.10.

[9] See Ch.9.

[10] See 7-088. For a theoretical consideration of the duty to give reasons, see D. Dyzenhaus and M. Taggart, "Reasoned Decisions and Legal Theory", Ch.5 in D. Edlin (ed), *Common Law Theory* (2007).

[11] See 6-029.

[12] For an early discussion of the transition from natural justice to procedural fairness, see M. Loughlin, "Procedural Fairness: A Study of the Crisis in Administrative Law Theory" (1978) 28 U. of Toronto L.J. 215; D. Mullan, "Fairness: the New Natural Justice?" (1975) 25 U. of Toronto L.J. 281; R. MacDonald, "Judicial Review and Procedural Fairness in Administrative Law" (1979–1980) 25 McGill L.J. 520 and (1980–1981) 26 McGill L.J. 1. More recently, see Craig, *Administrative Law* (2016), paras 12-009–12-010; and H. Biehler, *Judicial Review of Administrative Action* 3rd edn (2013), pp.239–244.

describe one of the three "grounds" of judicial review.[13] Such a term extends the exclusively common law ambit of natural justice and fair hearings to situations where there are procedures that are provided by statute. His term did not include other aspects of fair procedures, such as the duty not to fetter discretion, a duty which requires a decision-maker, even where a policy has been announced, to consider representations arguing for an exception to be made to the policy (thus ensuring the continuous possibility of effective participation in the decision-making process).

THE CONCEPT OF NATURAL JUSTICE

6-010   The expression "natural justice", which is the source from which procedural fairness now flows, has been described as one "sadly lacking in precision".[14] It has been consigned more than once to the lumber room. Thus, it has been said that in so far as it "means that a result or process should be just, it is harmless though it may be a high-sounding expression; in so far as it attempts to reflect the old *jus naturale*, it is a confused and unwarranted transfer into the ethical sphere of a term employed for other distinctions; and, in so far as it is resorted to for other purposes, it is vacuous".[15] No one who has the slightest acquaintance with the medieval English legal system[16] or with legal systems in other parts of the world[17] will suggest that those elements of judicial procedure which are now regarded as the hallmark of a civilised society have been generally enforced or even generally regarded as proper. But courts and commentators who decline to accept any form of justice as natural may take their choice from among "substantial justice",[18] "the essence of justice",[19] "fundamental Justice",[20] "universal justice",[21] "rational Justice",[22] the "principles of British justice",[23] or simply "justice without any epithet",[24] "fair play in action"[25] or "fairness writ large and juridically"[26] as phrases which express the same

---

[13] *Council of Civil Service Unions v Minister for the Civil Service* [1985] A.C. 374 at 410; and *R. v Oxford Regional Mental Health Review Tribunal Ex p. Secretary of State for the Home Department* [1988] A.C. 120 at 126 (Lord Bridge referring to a "decision ... made in breach of the rules of natural justice, which in a word means unfairly").

[14] *R. v Local Government Board* [1914] 1 K.B. 160; *Norwest Holst Ltd v Secretary of State for Trade* [1978] Ch. 201 at 226 (Ormrod LJ: "natural" adds nothing to justice "except perhaps a hint of nostalgia").

[15] *Local Government Board v Arlidge* [1915] A.C. 120 at 138 (Lord Shaw); and *Maclean v Workers' Union* [1929] 1 Ch. 602 at 624; *McInnes v Onslow-Fane* [1978] 1 W.L.R. 1520 at 1530; and *Norwest Holst* [1978] Ch. 201 at 226 (a "mesmerising" effect is attributed to the phrase "the requirements of natural justice").

[16] D. Gordon, "Observance of Law as a Condition of Jurisdiction" (1931) 47 L.Q.R. 386, 403–404.

[17] J. Wigmore, *A Kaleidoscope of Justice* (1941).

[18] *Smith v R.* (1878) 3 App.Cas. 614 at 623.

[19] *Spackman v Plumstead District Board of Works* (1883) 10 App.Cas. 229 at 240.

[20] *Hopkins v Smethwick Local Board of Health* (1890) 24 Q.B.D. 712 at 716.

[21] *Drew v Drew* (1855) 2 Macq. 1 at 8.

[22] *R. v Russell* (1869) 10 B. & S. 91 at 117.

[23] *Errington v Minister of Health* [1935] 1 K.B. 249 at 280.

[24] *Green v Blake* [1948] I.R. 242 at 248; *Norwest Holst* [1978] Ch. 201 at 226 (Ormrod LJ: "the ordinary principles of justice").

[25] *Ridge v Baldwin* [1963] 1 Q.B. 539 at 578 (Hannan LJ, a much-quoted phrase); and *Fairmount Investments Ltd v Secretary of State for the Environment* [1976] 1 W.L.R. 1255 at 1266 (for another vaguely sporting metaphor, "a fair crack of the whip").

[26] *Furnell v Whangarei High Schools Board* [1973] A.C. 660 at 679 (Lord Morris of Borth-y-Gest, adding that it was not "a leaven to be associated only with judicial or quasi judicial occasions").

idea.[27] And in any event "natural justice" was written into the statute book in 1969.[28] Moreover, "natural justice" is said to express the close relationship between the common law and moral principles.[29] Certainly it has an impressive ancestry. That no man is to be judged unheard was a precept known to the Greeks",[30] inscribed in ancient times upon images in places where justice was administered,[31] proclaimed in Seneca's Medea,[32] enshrined in the scriptures,[33] mentioned by St. Augustine,[34] embodied in Germanic[35] as well as African[36] proverbs, ascribed in the Year Books to the law of nature,[37] asserted by Coke to be a principle of divine justice,[38] and traced by an 18th-century judge to the events in the Garden of Eden.[39] Of course, if the concept of "natural justice" is vulnerable to rational criticism, so too are the "unalienable rights" of the Founding Fathers of the American Constitution or the notion of "due process". The view that "natural justice is so vague as to be practically meaningless" is tainted by "the perennial fallacy that because something cannot be cut and dried or nicely weighed or measured therefore it does not exist".[40]

Certainly, "natural justice" did exist in English law, and it became identified with the two constituents of a fair hearing; (a) that the parties should be given a proper

6-011

---

[27] These expressions are not always regarded as helpful however. See, e.g., *Secretary of State for Communities and Local Government v Hopkins Developments* [2014] EWCA Civ 470 at [49] for concern about use of the expression "fair crack of the whip".

[28] Foreign Compensation Act 1969 s.3(10) (ground for impugning purported determination by Foreign Compensation Commission); and Mental Capacity Act 2005 Sch.3 Pt IV para.19; Anatomy Act 1984 s.7A(3)(c); Licensing (Scotland) Act 2005 s.131. In New Zealand, see s.27(1) of the New Zealand Bill of Rights Act 1990. See also 6-053.

[29] A. Goodhart, *English Law and the Moral Law* (1953), p.65.

[30] J. Kelly, "Audi Alteram Partem" 9 *Natural Law Forum* 103 (1964); he points out, however, that the Greeks tended to regard the principle as a practical aid to making good decisions rather than an abstract principle of justice. But since equal application of the law to similar situations is an important aspect of justice, there is a significant overlap between good decision-making and justice. See also A. Harrison, *The Law of Athens* (1968–71) Vol.2.

[31] G. Del Vecchio, *Justice: An Historical and Philosophical Essay* (1953), pp.172–173.

[32] "Qui statuit aliquid, parte inaudita altera, aequum licet statuerit, haud aequus fuerit", lines 199–200, cited in *Boswell's Case* (1606) 6 Co.Rep. 48b at 52a, *Bagg's Case* (1615) 11 Co.Rep. 93b at 99a, and in several 19th century cases.

[33] "Doth our law judge any man, before it hear him, and know what he doth?" (King James Bible (1611) John 5: 51). But cf. fn.37, below.

[34] *De Duabus Animabus* (1891), Vol. 14, ii.

[35] "Fines Mannes Rede ist Keines Marines Rede, Man soll sie billig horen beede"; "Richter sollen zwei gleiche Ohren haben" (Lotmar, Die Gereclitigkeit, 77, 92).

[36] Thus, it is commended in proverbs and songs of the Lozi tribe in Barotseland (M. Gluckman, *The Judicial Process Among the Barotse of Northern Rhodesia* (1967), p.102). See also the Kiganda proverb referred to by E. Haydon, *Law and Justice in Buganda* (1960), p.333. The Kiganda proverb corresponding to the maxim *nemo judex in causa sua* means literally "a monkey does not decide an affair of the forest" (p.333). Practice did not always conform to precept.

[37] "In lege naturae requiritur ques les parties soient presentes ou que ils soient absentes per contumacie" ((1469) Y.B. 9 Edw. 4, Tin. pl. 9). cf. *R. v Clegg* (1721) 8 Mod. 3 at 4. See also H. Marshall, *Natural Justice* (1959), Ch.2.

[38] E. Coke, *Institutes of the Laws of England* (1817), Vol. 3, p. 35. Rhadamanthus, the cruel judge of Hell, punished before he heard. "But far otherwise doth Almighty God proceed … 1. Vocat 2. Interrogat, 3 Judicat".

[39] *R. v Chancellor of the University of Cambridge* (1723) 1 Str. 557 at 567 (Fortescue J: "even God himself did not pass sentence upon Adam, before he was called upon to make his defence. 'Adam' (says God) 'where art thou? Hast thou not eaten of the tree, whereof I commanded thee that thou shouldst not eat?'"). But the biblical precedents are conflicting: see R.F.V. Heuston, *Essays in Constitutional Law*, 2nd edn (1964), p.185, and J. Kelly, "Audi Alteram Partem" 9 *Natural Law Forum* 103 (1964), p.110.

[40] *Ridge v Baldwin* [1964] A.C. 40 at 64–65 (Lord Reid).

opportunity to be heard and to this end should be given due notice of the hearing[41] and (b) that a person adjudicating should be disinterested and unbiased.[42]

HISTORICAL DEVELOPMENT BEFORE THE FIRST WORLD WAR

Early development of the right to a fair hearing[43]

6-012   In 1850, it was said that "No proposition can be more clearly established than that a man cannot incur the loss of liberty or property for an offence by a judicial proceeding until he has had a fair opportunity of answering the case against him,[44] unless indeed the Legislature has expressly or impliedly given an authority *to act* without that necessary preliminary".[45]

6-013   Most of the earliest reported decisions in which natural justice was applied[46] concerned summary proceedings before justices. Service of a summons upon the party affected was regarded as a condition of the validity of such proceedings[47] not only in criminal matters but also in applications for the issue of distress warrants and orders for the levying of taxes and the charges imposed by public authorities upon the subject.[48] Justices who adjudicated summarily without having issued a summons were at one time punishable in the Court of King's Bench for a misdemeanour.[49] Decisions on the effect of non-service of process were numerous and not always reconcilable,[50] but instances were not wanting of the strict application of the general principle that service is mandatory in civil as well as criminal proceedings before judicial tribunals.[51]

---

[41] *Audi alteram partem*. Fair hearings are considered in Ch.7.

[42] *Nemo judex in causa sua*. Bias is dealt with in Ch.10.

[43] For an overview of the evolution of procedural fairness, see: H.W.R. Wade and C.F. Forsyth, *Administrative Law*, 11th edn (2014), pp.371–377 (natural justice generally), and pp.402–405 (the right to be heard in particular); R. Beloff, "Natural Justice and Fairness: the Audi Alteram Partem Rule" in H. Fenwick (ed), Supperstone, Goudie and Walker (eds), *Judicial Review*, 6th edn (2017), paras 11.1–11.17. For a general historical overview of administrative law, including procedural fairness, see: G. Drewry, "*Judicial Review: the Historical Background*" also in Supperstone, Goudie and Walker, Ch.2.

[44] The rule was said by Hawkins to be implied in the construction of all penal statutes (Pleas of the Crown, i, 420); and *Painter v Liverpool Oil Gas Light Co* (1836) 3 A. & E. 433 at 448–449 ("a party is not to suffer in person or in purse without an opportunity of being heard").

[45] *Bonaker v Evans* (1850) 16 Q.B. 162 at 171 (Parke B). See also Ch.8.

[46] See cases collected in note (a) to 8 Mod. 154.

[47] *R. v Dyer* (1703) 1 Salk. 181; *R. v Benn and Church* (1795) 6 T.R. 198. A more modern example is *R. v Dudley JJ Ex p. Payne* [1979] 1 W.L.R. 891 (no notice of hearing given to a defendant before sentence).

[48] *Benn and Church* (1795) 6 T.R. 198; *Harper v Carr* (1797) 7 T.R. 270; *Gibbs v Stead* (1828) 8 B. & C. 528; *Painter* (1836) 3 A. & E. 433; *R. v Totnes Union* (1854) 14 Q.B. 349; *R. v Cheshire Lines Committee* (1873) L.R. 8 Q.B. 344; see also R.B. Hankins, "The Necessity for Administrative Notice and Hearing" (1940) 25 Iowa L. Rev. 457, pp.460–462.

[49] *R. v Venables* (1724) 2 Ld.Raym. 1405; *R. v Alington* (1726) 2 Str. 678.

[50] Early authorities are reviewed in *Marsh v Marsh* [1945] A.C. 271 and more fully in *Posner v Collector for Inter-State Destitute Persons (Victoria)* (1946) 74 C.L.R. 461. See also Gordon, "Observance of Law as a Condition of Jurisdiction" (1931) 47 L.Q.R. 386, pp.557–563, 579–582.

[51] See, e.g. *R. v North Ex p. Oakey* [1927] 1 K.B. 491; *Craig v Kanssen* [1943] K.B. 256; *Chettiar v Chettiar* [1962] 1 W.L.R. 279; *R. v London County Q.S. Appeals Committee Ex p. Rossi* [1956] 1 Q.B. 682 (appealed in *R. v Industrial Court Ex p. George Green & Thomson Ltd* (1967) 2 K.I.R. 259); *R. v Havering JJ. Ex p. Smith* [1974] 3 All E.R. 484. But statutorily prescribed detail on the manner of service may not be mandatory: *R. v Devon and Cornwall Rent Tribunal Ex p. West* (1975)

A second line of cases relates to the deprivation of offices and other dignities. **6-014**
Here the effective starting-point is 1615, when James Bagg, a chief burgess of
Plymouth, who had been disfranchised for singularly unbecoming conduct,[52] was
reinstated by mandamus because he had been removed without notice or hearing.[53]
In 1723 mandamus was issued to restore Dr Bentley to his academic degrees in the
University of Cambridge, of which he had been deprived without a summons.[54] It
became established with respect to offices that removal had to be preceded by notice
and hearing if the office was a freehold or was to be forfeited only for cause,[55] but
not if there was a discretionary power to remove the holder at pleasure.[56] These
principles, which extended even to dismissals of schoolmasters and parish clerks,
came to be largely forgotten, partly, perhaps, because of the decline of the concept
of a freehold *office*, and partly because the tenure of public office was usually
determinable either at pleasure or in accordance with specific statutory, contractual
or customary procedures. In 1963 they were rescued from oblivion, dressed in
modern garb, by the House of Lords.[57]

Linked with this group of cases are the decisions on the regulation of the clergy. **6-015**
Where a bishop issued an order for the sequestration of the profits of a benefice
without having given the vicar notice of the charges of neglect that had been made
against him or an opportunity to refute them, and where the Archbishop of
Canterbury dismissed an appeal by a curate against the revocation of his licence
without having afforded him an adequate hearing, the courts gave redress for violation of natural justice.[58] One of the most remarkable illustrations of the right to be
heard (*audi alteram partem*) principle in a reported case was *Capel v Child*,[59] where
a bishop, empowered by statute to order a vicar to appoint a curate (to be paid by
the vicar) when satisfied, either of his own knowledge or by affidavit, that the vicar
had neglected his duties, was held to be under an absolute duty to give the vicar
notice and opportunity to be heard before making the order. This was a high-water
mark of, at that time, judicial intervention; in later cases the courts generally showed
themselves disinclined to require investigations conducted by ecclesiastical authorities to conform to judicial standards.[60]

Nineteenth and early twentieth century decisions established that the right to be **6-016**

---

29 P. & C.R. 316. In criminal law: Magistrates' Courts Act 1980 s.1 (issue of summons); s.14
(invalidity of proceedings where accused was unaware of them); Criminal Procedure and Investigations Act 1996 ss.3, 7A (disclosure obligations of the prosecutor).

[52] As by saying to the mayor "You are a cozening knave" and "I will make thy neck crack"; and by
"turning the hinder part of his body in an inhuman and uncivil manner" towards the mayor, saying
"Come and kiss".

[53] *Bagg's Case* (1615) 11 Co.Rep. 93.

[54] *Chancellor of the University of Cambridge* (1723) 1 Str. 557.

[55] *Bagg's Case* (1615) 11 Co.Rep. 93; *Protector v Colchester* (1655) Style 446 at 452; *R. v Wilton
(Mayor)* (1696) 2 Salk. 428; *R. v Ipswich (Bailiffs)* (1705) 2 Ld.Raym. 1233; *R. v Smith* (1844) 5
Q.B. 614; *Re Fremington School* (1846) 10 Jur. (o.s.) 512; *Ex p. Ramshay* (1852) 21 L J.Q.B. 238
at 239; *Osgood v Nelson* (1872) L. R. 5 H.L. 636; *Fisher v Jackson* [1891] 2 Ch. 84.

[56] *R. v Stratford-on-Avon (Mayor)* (1670) 1 Lev. 291; *R. v Andover* (1701) 1 Ld.Raym. 710; *R. v
Darlington Free Grammar School Governors* (1844) 6 Q.B. 682; *Re Poor Law Commissioners*
(1850) 19 L.J.M.C. 70; *Dickson v Viscount Combermere* (1863) 3 F. & F. 527 at 548, note (a).

[57] *Ridge v Baldwin* [1964] A.C. 40 (chief constable, removable only for statutory cause, dismissed
without notice of charges against him or adequate opportunity to be heard; dismissal declared
invalid).

[58] *Bonaker* (1850) 16 Q.B. 163; *R. v Canterbury (Archbishop)* (1859) 1 E.&E. 545.

[59] (1832) 2 Cr. & J. 558; but Cf. *Re Hammersmith Rent Charge* (1849) 4 Ex. 87 at 94, 100.

[60] *Abergavenny (Marquis) v Llandaff (Bishop)* (1888) L.R. 20 Q.B.D. 460; *R. v Canterbury
(Archbishop) Ex p. Morant* [1944] K.B. 282; cf. *Oakey* [1927] 1 K.B. 491.

heard (*audi alteram partem*) rule was to govern the conduct of arbitrators,[61] of professional bodies and voluntary associations in the exercise of their disciplinary functions,[62] and indeed of "every tribunal or body of persons invested with authority to adjudicate upon matters involving civil consequences to individuals".[63] An individual who was expelled from membership of a club[64] or similar association,[65] or from a trade union,[66] was prima facie entitled to have the decision set aside by the courts unless he had been given adequate notice of the allegations made against him and a fair opportunity to reply to them. This principle was subsequently applied with particular vigour where the sanction imposed would deprive a person of his livelihood[67] or where there was a charge of discreditable conduct.[68]

6-017   With the extension of the franchise and the decline of the doctrine of laissez faire in the latter half of the 19th century came a vast increase in the regulatory functions of public authorities, especially in the fields of housing and public health. Where a statute authorising interference with property or civil rights was silent on the question of notice and hearing, the courts, drawing upon the authority of the older cases, invoked "the justice of the common law" to "supply the omission of the legislature".[69] In a long line of cases on demolition orders, beginning with *Cooper v Wandsworth Board of Works*,[70] the rule, said to be "of universal application and founded on the plainest principles of justice",[71] was laid down that public authorities must either give the person concerned "notice that they intend to take

---

[61]   *Re Brook* (1864) 16 C.B. (n.s.) 403; see now D. Sutton and J. Gill, *Russell on Arbitration*, 22nd edn (2003), pp.172–177, paras 5-050–5-064.

[62]   D. Lloyd, "The Discretionary Powers of Professional Bodies" (1950) 13 M.L.R. 281; Z. Chafee, "The Internal Affairs of Associations not for Profit" (1930) 43 Harv. L.Rev. 993; D. Lloyd, *Law Relating to Unincorporated Associations* (1938), pp.127–129.

[63]   *Wood v Woad* (1874) L.R. 9 Ex. 190 at 196.

[64]   *Innes* (1844) 1 Car. & Kir. 257; *Dawkins v Antrobus* (1881) 17 Ch.D. 615; *Fisher v Keane* (1878) 11 Ch.D. 353; *Gray v Allison* (1909) 25 T.L.R. 531; *Lamberton v Thorpe* (1929) 141 L.T. 638.

[65]   *Wood* (1874) L.R. 9 Ex. 190 (mutual insurance society); see also *Lapointe v L'Association de Bienfaisance et de Retraite de la Police de Montreal* [1906] A.C. 535 (denial of pension to member of police friendly society); *John v Rees* [1970] Ch. 345 (suspension or expulsion from political party). This decision was distinguished in *Lewis v Heffer* [1978] 1 W.L.R. 1061 on the ground that the suspension was imposed pending an inquiry and not as a punishment. Nor was the rule applied in *Gaiman v National Association for Mental Health* [1971] Ch. 317 (exclusion from membership of a company).

[66]   *Parr v Lancashire & Cheshire Miners' Federation* [1913] 1 Ch. 366; *Burn v National Amalgamated Labourers' Union* [1920] 2 Ch. 364. See also *Abbott v Sullivan* [1952] 1 K.B. 189 at 199; *Annamunthodo v Oilfield Workers' Trade Union* [1961] A.C. 945; *Lawlor v Union of Post Office Workers* [1965] Ch. 712; *Taylor v National Union of Seamen* [1967] 1 W.L.R. 532; *Hiles v Amalgamated Society of Woodworkers* [1968] Ch. 440; *Leary v National Union of Vehicle Builders* [1971] Ch. 34; *Edwards v SOGAT* [1971] Ch. 354; see also *Roebuck v National Union of Mineworkers* [1977] I.C.R. 573 (bias).

[67]   *Russell v Duke of Norfolk* [1949] 1 All E.R. 109 at 119; *Abbott* [1952] 1 K.B. 189, 199 (Denning LJ); *SOGAT* [1971] Ch. 354. After a number of years of dormancy, this jurisprudence has been revived by the courts: *Bradley v Jockey Club* [2005] EWCA Civ 1056, *The Times,* 14 July 2005 at [13] and [2004] EWHC 2164 and *Mullins v McFarlane* [2006] EWHC 986 at [38].

[68]   *G.M.C. v Spackman* [1943] A. C. 627 at 637–638 (Lord Atkin); *Breen v AEU* [1971] 2 Q.B. 175 (dicta).

[69]   *Cooper v Wandsworth Board of Works* (1863) 14 C.B. (N.S.) 180 at 194.

[70]   *Wandsworth Board of Works* (1863) 14 C.B. (N.S.) 180 at 194; *Brutton v St George's, Hanover Square, Vestry* (1871) L.R. 13 Eq. 339; *Masters v Pontypool Local Governrnent Board* (1878) L.R. 9 Ch.D. 677; *Hopkins v Smethwick Board of Health* (1890) 24 Q.B.D. 712; *Sydney Municipal Council v Harris* (1912) 14 C.L.R. 1. See also *Urban Housing Co v Oxford City Council* [1940] Ch. 70; *Delta Properties Pty Ltd v Brisbane City Council* (1955) 95 C.L.R. 11 at 18; *Police Commissioner v Tanos* (1958) 98 C.L.R. 383 at 395–396.

[71]   *Wandsworth Board of Works* (1863) 14 C.B. (N.S.) 180 at 190.

this matter into their consideration with a view to coming to a decision, or, if they have come to a decision, that they propose to act upon it, and give him an opportunity of showing cause why such steps should not be taken".[72] An authority empowered to postpone the operation of a demolition order on the owner's application had to permit him adequately to present his case for postponement.[73] The general rule, which was applied in a variety of legislative contexts,[74] might be satisfied if an opportunity was available of obtaining a full review of the initial decision[75] or of making other representations[76] before the order became finally operative or was enforced; and it was, of course, displaced by express statutory provisions dispensing with the need to serve notice.[77]

Maitland had pointed out in 1888 that England and Wales was becoming "a much governed nation, governed by all manner of councils and boards and officers, central and local, high and low Exercising the powers which have been committed to them by modern statutes", and that half the reported cases in the Queen's Bench Division had to do with aspects of administrative law such as rating, licensing, public health and education.[78] At this time it was usual to confer new adjudicatory functions upon the existing departments of State and local authorities; special tribunals had been established for the regulation of railway traffic and the determination of income tax appeals, but the proliferation of ad hoc tribunals was to be a 20th-century phenomenon. The courts, while recognising that it would be hopeless to require government departments, making institutional decisions, to follow the procedure of courts of justice, nevertheless superimposed upon their statutory responsibilities the duty to act judicially, in certain situations, in the manner prescribed by the rules of natural justice. The best-known statement of the right to be heard rule in English administrative law was formulated by the House of Lords in relation to the appellate functions of a government department; but it is of broad application:

6-018

"Comparatively recent statutes have extended, if they have not originated, the practice of imposing upon departments or officers of State the duty of deciding or determining questions of various kinds ... In such cases ... they must act in good faith and fairly listen to both sides, for that is a duty lying upon everyone who decides anything. But I do not think they are bound to treat such a question as though it were a trial ... They can obtain information in any way they think best, always giving a fair opportunity to those who are

---

[72] *Urban Housing Co* [1940] Ch. 70 at 85 (Sir Wilfrid Greene MR). For local colour and the aftermath of this case, see R. Heuston, *Essays in Constitutional Law* (1964), pp.186–188.

[73] *Broadbent v Rotherham Corp* [1917] 2 Ch. 31.

[74] For example, closing orders in respect of houses unfit for human habitation (*Hall v Manchester Corp* (1915) 84 L.J.Ch. 732 at 741–742); forfeiture of a lease of Crown land in Australia (*Smith v R.* (1878) 3 App.Cas. 614); transfer of indentures of immigrants from one employer to another in Trinidad (*De Verteuil v Knaggs* [1918] A.C. 557); applications to present a case before a wages board (*R. v Amphlett (Judge)* [1915] 2 K.B. 223); confirmation of grant of liquor licence (*R. v Huntingdon Confirming Authority* [1929] 1 K.B. 698).

[75] *St James and St. John, Clerkenwell, Vestry v Feary* (1890) L.R. 24 Q.B.D. 703 (order to supply sanitary installations); but this exception is untypical.

[76] *Attorney General v Hooper* [1893] 3 Ch. 483 (removal of projection over highway); *Robinson v Sunderland Corp* [1899] 1 Q.B. 751 at 757–758 (supply of sanitary installation); *De Verteuil* [1918] A.C. 557. See also *Knuckey v Peirce* [1964] W.A.R. 200 (notice requiring removal of rubbish from site). In principle however, a duty to give prior notice and opportunity to be heard arises when an individual will suffer direct detriment from the act or decision (*Delta Properies* (1955) 95 C.L.R. 11).

[77] *Cheetham v Mayor of Manchester* (1875) L.R. 10 C.P. 249.

[78] F.W. Maitland, *Constitutional History of England* (1913), pp.501, 505; and H.W. Arthurs, *"Without the Law": Administrative Justice and Legal Pluralism in Nineteenth Century England* (1985).

parties in the controversy for correcting or contradicting any relevant statement prejudicial to their view."[79]

Operation of the rule reviewed

6-019   These dicta by Lord Loreburn in *Board of Education v Rice* must nevertheless be viewed with caution. The Board in that case had been required to determine a dispute between a local education authority and the managers of a school, that is a *lis inter partes*.[80] Had the education authority complied with its statutory duty to maintain the school efficiently when it was discriminating against the teachers in the school by paying them lower salaries than those paid to teachers in other schools doing similar work? The determination of this question involved the ascertainment of questions of law and fact as well as the exercise of judicial discretion. It is doubtless true to say that in such situations the deciding authority is under an implied duty to listen fairly to both sides. It does not follow that "everyone who decides anything" is subject to a similar duty, or that persons involved in a controversy must always be given an opportunity of rebutting statements prejudicial to them. A decision to increase the rate of income tax, to arrest a participant in an armed robbery, to pull down a building to prevent the spread of a fire, may have serious adverse effects on those directly concerned, but there is no duty to give prior notice or opportunity to be heard. Moreover, only four years after the decision in *Board of Education v Rice*,[81] the House of Lords held in *Arlidge*[82] that a government department determining a housing appeal was not obliged to divulge one of its inspector's reports to the appellant, even though the report might well have contained relevant statements prejudicial to his case which he might have wished to controvert. This decision marked the beginning of a partial retreat by the English courts from their earlier position—a retreat which was not halted till the 1960s. For nearly half a century they were to show a marked reluctance to hold that an implied duty to give prior notice and opportunity to be heard was imposed on persons and authorities empowered to make decisions in the general field of administrative law.

HISTORICAL DEVELOPMENT AFTER THE FIRST WORLD WAR

The path of deviation

6-020   The state of the law at the outbreak of the First World War can be briefly restated. Judicial tribunals empowered to deprive persons of their liberty, impose financial burdens on them and ascertain their legal rights had to observe the requirements of a fair hearing, or the *audi alteram partem* rule. So did arbitrators and government departments when called upon to decide questions of law and fact in situations resembling a legal action between two parties. The rule would also normally be held to apply where the trappings of adjudication were present although the decision involved the exercise of wide discretion. It was prima facie applicable in various

---

[79]   *Board of Education v Rice* [1911] A.C. 179 at 182 (Lord Loreburn LC) See also *Local Government Board v Arlidge* [1915] A.C. 120 at 132–134; *Spackman* (1885) 10 App.Cas. 229 at 240; *Parsons v Lakenheath School Board* (1889) 58 L.J.Q.B. 371 at 372.

[80]   See 6-037.

[81]   *Board of Education v Rice* [1911] A.C. 179.

[82]   *Local Government Board v Arlidge* [1915] A.C. 120.

other situations where there was nothing resembling a dispute determinable by a third party: removal from an office not tenable merely at pleasure, the disciplining of the clergy, the exercise of disciplinary powers by professional authorities and voluntary organisations, and administrative intrusions (e.g. by demolition, destruction and compulsory execution of works) upon private property rights. In the aftermath of the First World War, however, the principles of natural justice experienced a notable demise.[83]

Venicoff's Case

The first leading case in which the courts refused to apply the rule at all in a situation where it clearly ought to have been applied was *Venicoff's* case.[84] The Home Secretary had been empowered by legislation to deport an alien whenever he deemed this to be "conducive to the public good".[85] When a deportation order was impugned, it was held that he was exercising purely executive functions, importing no duty to act judicially.[86] The court laid emphasis on the amplitude of the Secretary of State's discretion, the context of an emergency[87] and the impracticability of giving prior notice in such a case; the impact of a deportation order on personal liberty was treated as an irrelevant consideration,[88] and the feasibility of requiring a hearing after the order had been made but before it had been executed was not canvassed in the judgments.[89] In 1962 the Court of Appeal reaffirmed the rule established in *Venicoff's* case that an alien deportee has no implied legal right to any hearing,[90] but this rule has now been modified by statute.[91]

6-021

---

[83] Of the impact of the First World War on civil liberties more generally, Gearty and Ewing note the following: "The First World War offers a fascinating study of a state in crisis and of the ease with which liberal values may be surrendered in times of emergency. It also offers a valuable insight into the role of the different institutions of government, tending to reveal a largely unaccountable executive restrained only be a sometimes quiescent legislature and a compliant judiciary" (C. Gearty and K. Ewing, *The Struggle for Civil Liberties. Political Freedom and the Rule of Law in Britain 1914-1945* (2001)).

[84] *R. v Leman Street Police Station Inspector Ex p. Venicoff* [1920] 3 K.B. 72.

[85] Article 12(1) of the Aliens Order 1919, made under the Aliens Restriction Act 1914 (passed immediately after the outbreak of war).

[86] On the distinctions between "administrative", "judicial" and "ministerial" and "legislative", see 6-031.

[87] *Venicoff* [1920] 3 K.B. 72 at 80 (Earl of Reading CJ),

[88] It was observed that the validity of a still more drastic curtailment of personal freedom, the summary preventive detention of British subjects by administrative order, had been upheld only three years earlier: *R. v Halliday* [1917] A.C. 260. For discussion of *Halliday*, see D. Foxton, "R. v Halliday Ex parte Zadig in Retrospect" (2003) 119 L.Q.R. 455.

[89] Though the Home Secretary had offered to entertain representations informally: [1920] 3 K.B. 72 at 78.

[90] *R. v Brixton Prison Governor Ex p. Soblen* [1963] 2 Q.B. 243 (interpreting art.20(2)(b) of the Aliens Order 1953 (SI 1953/1671), which reproduced the words construed in *Venicoff's* case). See Lord Denning MR (at 298-299) reserved his opinion on the question whether the deportee might have a legal right to be heard after the order had been made but before it had been executed. See also, for dicta to the same effect, *Schmidt v Home Secretary* [1969] 2 Ch. 149 at 171, where it was held that an alien had no right to a hearing before a refusal of either initial entry or renewal of leave to remain.

[91] Pursuant to s.82 of the Nationality, Immigration and Asylum Act 2002, where an "immigration decision" is made in respect of a person, he may appeal to the Asylum and Immigration Tribunal. An "immigration decision" includes refusal of leave to enter the UK (s.82(2)(a)), refusal of entry clearance (s.82(2)(b)), refusal to vary a person's leave to enter or remain if the result of the refusal is that the person has no leave to enter or remain in the UK (s.82(2)(d)) and a decision to remove a person who is unlawfully in the UK (s.82(2)(g)). Limitations and exceptions to the right of appeal, for example, where an immigration decision is made on grounds of national security, are found in ss.88, 88A, 89, 92, and 94-99.

6-022   The tenor of the judgments in *Venicoff's* Case foreshadowed the debilitation of the *audi alteram partem* rule as a common-law standard applied by the court to administrative decision-making. In the first place, there were the references to emergency situations. During wartime, enormous powers over persons and property were vested in the Government, and the courts showed an understandable reluctance to scrutinise the exercise of essential powers in such a way as to make it more difficult for the Government to govern. Not surprisingly, it was hard to persuade the courts that war emergency powers were subject to an implied qualification that persons adversely affected by their exercise were entitled to prior notification and an opportunity to be heard.[92] But the climate of judicial opinion engendered by the exigencies of war tended to persist long after hostilities had ended.[93]

6-023   Secondly, the existence of a wide policy discretion vested in a minister responsible to Parliament was thought to dictate not only abstention from judicial review of the merits of particular decisions but also (and with less justification) the impropriety of setting minimum procedural standards to be observed in the course of reaching or before executing such decisions.

6-024   Thirdly, there was the implicit assumption that the role of the courts in relation to the administrative process should be one of rigorous self-restraint; the administration ought not to be embarrassed by well-meaning judicial intruders. Such an assumption had already been clearly articulated in *Arlidge*.[94] It was to be revealed in other contexts.

6-025   Fourthly, the characterisation of the Secretary of State's functions as executive and non-judicial was understood to exclude any implied obligation on his part to act in accordance with natural justice, despite the impact of his decisions on individual rights. The importance of analytical labels in restricting the scope of the obligation to act judicially was to be underlined in the years that followed, perhaps most notably by Atkin LJ's much-quoted judgment in the *Electricity Commissioners* case, defining the circumstances in which the writ of certiorari would issue to quash the decisions of public authorities. Certiorari (and prohibition) would issue to "any body of persons having legal authority to determine questions affecting the rights of subjects, and having the duty to act judicially".[95] In natural justice cases this dictum was generally understood to mean that a duty to act judicially was not to be inferred merely from the impact of a decision on the "rights of subjects"; such a duty would arise only if there were "superadded" an express obligation to follow a judicial-type procedure in arriving at the decision.[96] In pursuit of a circuitous (and sometimes circular) line of reasoning the courts lost sight of the older cases[97]; in which a duty to act judicially in accordance with natural justice had been held to arise by implication from the nature and effect of the powers exercised.[98]

---

[92] In the following cases persons aggrieved by the exercise of executive powers were held to be unprotected by the *audi alteram partem* rule: *Irving v Patterson* [1943] Ch. 180; *Howell v Addison* [1943] 1 All E.R. 29, 32 (consent by Minister to determination of agricultural tenancy (though cf. *West Riding CC v Wilson* [1941] 2 All E.R. 827 at 832)); *Carltona Ltd v Commissioners of Works* [1943] 2 All E.R. 560 at 562 (requisitioning of factory).

[93] On the legality of discretionary powers, see Ch.5.

[94] *Local Government Board v Arlidge* [1915] A.C. 120.

[95] *R. v Electricity Commissioners* [1924] 1 K.B. 171 at 204-205 (where the contention was not that natural justice had been contravened, but that the impugned order was ultra vires).

[96] *Nakkuda Ali v Jayaratne* [1951] A.C. 66, another decision which gave extremely influential support for this approach.

[97] See 6-012; though the ratio of *Wandsworth Board of Works* was momentarily glimpsed in 1939: *Urban Housing Co* [1940] Ch. 70.

[98] A point emphasised by H.W.R. Wade, "The Twilight of Natural justice?" (1951) 67 L.Q.R. 103 and

The rise of statutory procedures and the demise of the audi alteram partem principle

Paradoxically, the decline of the *audi alteram partem* principle as an implied common-law requirement of administrative procedure was hastened by its embodiment in statutory forms. Twentieth-century statute law reflected the disfavour with which the common law viewed administrative claims to be entitled to take direct action against private property without giving prior notice or opportunity to be heard. Public health, housing, highways and town planning legislation in particular spell out the procedural conditions under which enforcement powers are exercisable.[99] Where no statutory provision is made for prior notice to be given, it may sometimes be assumed that the omission is deliberate; so, too, where statutory provision is made for a hearing that falls short of the requirements of natural justice, the statutory procedure can often be assumed to be exhaustive. In Victorian times detailed codes were exceptional, and the courts supplied the omissions, in the interests of justice to individuals, by importing common-law principles.

6-026

Of more general significance in the reshaping of judicial attitudes was the fact that in the 1930s and 1940s the typical administrative law controversy in the superior courts was a challenge directed against the validity of a slum clearance or compulsory purchase order. The procedure for the compulsory acquisition of land by public authorities almost invariably provides for prior notice and opportunity to be heard. It was largely standardised by the Acquisition of Land (Authorisation Procedure) Act 1946 (which substantially reproduced earlier legislation on the matter), supplemented by statutory rules.[100] The acquiring authority (normally a local authority) must give public notice of its intentions, and must also notify owners, lessees and occupiers individually. Objections to the order may be lodged within a prescribed period by the persons individually served. If an objection so made is not withdrawn, the Minister who will have to decide whether or not to confirm the order must (unless the objection relates only to compensation) either cause a public local inquiry to be held or afford the objector an opportunity of being heard before a person appointed for the purpose, and must consider the objections and the report on the inquiry or hearing. Broadly similar rules govern clearance orders to secure the demolition of slum property in an area.[101]

6-027

Persons who had not expressly been given the right to prior notice or opportunity to be heard found difficulty in persuading the courts that implications affording them such a right ought to be read into the enabling Acts.[102] As far as the courts were concerned, the obligations of the acquiring authority had been codified by statute. To be sure, the inspector conducting the public local inquiry or private hearing had to act in conformity with natural justice even though he had no

6-028

---

later elaborated by Lord Reid in *Ridge v Baldwin* [1964] A.C. 40 at 74-76.

[99] See 7-011.

[100] Now see the Acquisition of Land Act 1981. See also Compulsory Purchase (Inquiries Procedure) Rules 2007 (SI 2007/3617); Compulsory Purchase of Land (Written Representations Procedure) (Ministers) Regulations 2004 (SI 2004/2594); Compulsory Purchase of Land (Vesting Declarations) Regulations 1990 (SI 1990/497); and Compulsory Purchase of Land (Prescribed Forms) (Ministers) Regulations 2004 (SI 2004/2595).

[101] Housing Act 1985 ss.269, 269A, 272, 317, 318; and Housing Act 2004 Pt I.

[102] *Fredman v Minister of Health* (1935) 154 L.T. 240 (owner not entitled to be heard by the local authority before it declared a building to be included in a clearance area); *Cohen v West Hain Corp* [1933] Ch. 814 at 827 (a somewhat anomalous decision; no right to be heard before issue of notice to execute works). For the position today in which natural justice may supplement a statutory code, see 7-013 and 7-042.

power to make an initial decision[103] but for the rest, judicial review was to be interstitial; and to the courts the interstices seemed very narrow. Decisions in the 1940s and 1950s showed a persistent tendency to substitute for the presumption that the *audi alteram partem* principle conditioned the exercise of powers in relation to persons and property a still stronger presumption that unless a procedural duty was expressed (e.g. to consider objections,[104] or to decide "after due inquiry"[105]), none was to be implied.[106] Power to obtain information from any source was assumed to be inconsistent with the existence of any duty to notify the person affected by the information obtained.[107]

The rise of analytical distinctions and the demise of the audi alteram partem principle

The distinctions adopted

6-029   More significant to the demise of natural justice than the increase in statutory procedures, however, was the distinction drawn in *Venicoff's* case, as noted above, between "executive" and "non-judicial"[108]; and this case heralded an era of increased focus on analytical distinctions in determining the applicability of natural justice. A sharp distinction was drawn between the deprivation of a right and the deprivation of a mere privilege, the latter function importing no duty to act fairly.[109] Distinctions were also drawn between "judicial" and "quasi-judicial" functions, which attracted the duty to act in accordance with the requirements of natural justice, and "administrative" and "legislative" decisions, which did not attract such a duty. The impact of the distinctions is well-illustrated by the decision in the 1951 case of *Nakkuda Ali v Jayaratne*.[110] The Controller of Textiles in Ceylon had

---

[103] *Marriott v Minister of Health* (1935) 154 L.T. 47 at 50; *Denby (William) & Sons Ltd v Minister of Health* [1936] 1 K.B. 337 at 342-343. Where the holding of a hearing or a local inquiry was provided for by statute, it was always open to the courts to hold that the proceedings were too defective to constitute a hearing (see *Ealing Borough Council v Minister of Housing and Local Government* [1952] Ch. 856) or an inquiry within the meaning of the Act, even though the functions of the Minister under the Act in question were characterised as purely administrative (*Franklin v Minister of Town and Country Planning* [1948] A.C. 87 at 102, 105-106; *Wednesbury Corp v Ministry of Housing and Local Government (No.2)* [1966] 2 Q.B. 275 at 302-303 (dicta)).

[104] cf. *R. v British Columbia Pollution Control Board* (1967) 61 D.L.R. (2nd) 221.

[105] This is generally understood to mean an inquiry conducted in accordance with natural justice: *Leeson v General Medical Council* (1890) 43 Ch.D. 366 at 383; *General Medical Council v Spackman* [1943] A.C. 627; *Memudu Lagunju v Olubadan-in-Council* [1952] A.C. 387 at 399; cf. *Patterson v District Commissioner of Accra* [1948] A.C. 341 ("after inquiry, if necessary"); *Beetham v Trinidad Cement Co* [1960] A.C. 132 (government's power to "inquire" into facts of trade dispute and then appoint a board of inquiry, held purely administrative); *Abergavenny (Marquis) v Llandaff (Bishop)* (1880) 20 Q.B.D. 460 at 472; *R. v Staines Union* (1893) 69 L. 714. And cf. *Ross-Clunis v Papadopoullos* [1958] 1 W.L.R. 546 at 560-562 (power of Commissioner to conduct inquiry as he thinks fit, subject to his being satisfied as to its fairness; limited scope of judicial review).

[106] See wartime cases cited at fn.91; *Patterson* [1948] A.C. 341 (levying of differential charges on inhabitants for extra police protection); *Nakkuda Ali* [1951] A.C. 66 (revocation of trader's licence); *Musson v Rodriguez* [1953] A.C. 530 (deportation of prohibited immigrant); *R. v Metropolitan Police Commissioner Ex p. Parker* [1953] 1 W.L.R. 1150 (revocation of taxi-cab driver's licence); *R. v St Lawrence's Hospital, Caterham, Statutory Visitors Ex p. Pritchard* [1953] 1 W.L.R. 1158 at 1162.

[107] *R. v Central Professional Committee for Opticians Ex p. Brown* [1949] 2 All E.R. 519 at 521; *Musson* [1993] A.C. 530; *Ex p. Parker* [1953] 1 W.L.R. 1150. Contrast *Capel v Child* (1832) 2 Cr. & J. 558.

[108] See 6-021.

[109] *Nakkuda Ali* [1951] A.C. 66; and *Ex p. Parker* [1953] 1 W.L.R. 1150.

[110] *Nakkuda Ali* [1951] A.C. 66.

cancelled a textile dealer's licence in pursuance of a power to revoke a licence when he had "reasonable grounds" for believing its holder to be unfit to continue as a dealer. The dealer applied for certiorari to quash the order, contending that the Controller had not held an inquiry conducted in conformity with natural justice. The Judicial Committee of the Privy Council dismissed his appeal, holding that the Controller, although obliged to act on reasonable grounds,[111] was under no duty to act judicially, so that certiorari could not issue and compliance with natural justice was unnecessary. Two reasons were given for the decision: first, that certiorari would issue only to an authority that was required to follow a procedure analogous to the "judicial" procedure in arriving at its decision; and second, that the Controller was not determining a question affecting the rights of subjects but was merely "taking executive action to withdraw a privilege".[112] Yet the first assertion was contradicted in many cases on the scope of certiorari[113]; and the second served only to demonstrate the limitations of a conceptualistic approach to administrative law. Demolition of a property owner's uninhabitable house might be for him a supportable misfortune; deprivation of a licence to trade might mean a calamitous loss of livelihood; but the judicial flavour detected in the former function was held to be absent from the latter. The decision, whilst not unique,[114] was inconsistent with the previously-adopted attitude of the English courts towards the licensing and regulation of trades and occupations[115] and in general towards the right to earn one's living.[116]

Servitude to the classifications between "right" and "privilege" and "judicial" and "administrative" has now been abandoned, and the notion that a fair hearing is reserved to a "judicial" or "quasi-judicial" situation has been firmly "scotched" as a "heresy".[117] Nonetheless, these distinctions are worth examining briefly,[118] since they had a significant impact on the evolution of natural justice, and are relevant to aspects of the discussion in the subsequent chapters.

6-030

Understanding the distinctions

It is fair to say that the meanings attributed by the courts to the terms "judicial", "quasi-judicial", "administrative", "legislative" and "ministerial" for administrative law purposes were often inconsistent. Terms were used loosely and without

6-031

---

[111] Distinguishing *Liversidge v Anderson* [1942] A.C. 206 on this point.

[112] *Nakkuda Ali* [1951] A.C. 66 at 78. The Judicial Committee also held that the dealer had in fact been given an adequate opportunity to put his case against revocation; but this finding clearly did not reduce the other grounds for the decision to the status of obiter dicta. The reasons for holding that there was no duty to observe natural justice have been almost universally criticised by academic writers. They were trenchantly criticised by Lord Reid in *Ridge v Baldwin* [1964] A.C. 40 at 77-79; his Lordship was prepared, however, to explain the decision as one resting on the wording of defence regulations (at 73, 78). The decision was restrictively distinguished by Lord Parker CJ in *Re HK (An Infant)* [1967] 2 Q.B. 617 at 630, 631, and disapproved by Lord Denning MR in *R. v Gaming Board for Great Britain Ex p. Benaim and Khaida* [1970] 2 Q.B. 417 at 430; though in *Durayappah v Fernando* [1967] 2 A.C. 337 at 349, the PC observed, rather opaquely, that it did not "necessarily agree" with Lord Reid's comments.

[113] See, e.g. *R. v Manchester Area Legal Aid Committee Ex p. Brand (RA) & Co* [1952] 2 Q.B. 413 and cases there cited at 427-428.

[114] *Ex p. Parker* [1953] 1 W.L.R. 1150; and cf. *Ex p. Fry* [1954] 1 W.L.R. 730.

[115] See 6-016.

[116] See, e.g. *Abbott* [1952] 1 K.B. 189.

[117] Words used by Lord Denning in *R. v Gaming Board Ex p. Benaim and Khaida* [1970] 2 Q.B. 417 at 430 in respect of the decision of the HL in *Ridge v Baldwin* [1964] A.C. 40. See also Lord Diplock in [1983] 2 A.C. 237, 279. And see 7-003.

[118] For a detailed discussion of the distinctions, see the Appendix to the 5th edition of this work.

deliberation; sometimes the method of characterisation could be seen as a contrivance to support a conclusion reached on non-conceptual grounds; and it was sometimes impossible to discern why a court characterised a given function as "judicial" or "administrative". Broadly speaking, though, the characterisations described in the following paragraphs applied.

6-032   The term "ministerial" was used to describe any duty, the discharge of which involved no element of discretion or independent judgment; to describe the issue of a formal instruction, in consequence of a prior determination which may or may not be of a judicial character, that direct action be taken in relation to another's person or property[119]; or to describe the execution of such an instruction by an inferior officer (sometimes called a ministerial officer). Alternatively, the term was sometimes used loosely to describe any act that was neither "judicial" nor "legislative", and in this sense the term was used interchangeably with "executive" or "administrative".[120]

6-033   A wide range of meanings was capable of being attached to the term "administrative". A distinction often made between "legislative" and "administrative" acts was that between the general and the particular: while a legislative act entails the creation and promulgation of a general rule of conduct without reference to particular cases; an administrative act cannot be exactly defined, but it includes the adoption of a policy, the making and issue of a specific direction, and the application of a general rule to a particular case in accordance with the requirements of policy or expediency or administrative practice. For example, every measure duly enacted by Parliament is regarded as legislation, so if land was compulsorily acquired by means of a Private Act of Parliament or a Provisional Order Confirmation Act, the acquisition was deemed to be a legislative act; though if the acquisition was effected by means of a compulsory purchase order made under enabling legislation, it would usually be classified as an administrative act. Similarly, departmental instruments or announcements which, although general in application, normally neither create legally enforceable rights nor impose legally enforceable obligations were usually referred to as examples of "administrative action".[121]

6-034   The term "quasi-judicial" could have any one of three meanings. It could describe a function that was partly judicial and partly administrative—e.g. the making of a compulsory purchase order (a discretionary or administrative act) preceded by the holding of a judicial-type local inquiry and the consideration of objections. It could, alternatively, describe the "judicial" element in a composite function; holding an inquiry and considering objections in respect of a compulsory purchase order are thus "quasi judicial" acts. Or it could describe the nature of a discretionary act itself where the actor's discretion is not unfettered.

---

[119] D.M. Gordon, "'Administrative' Tribunals and the Courts" (1933) 49 L.Q.R. 94 at 98 and following. Thus the duty of an official to notify an applicant for planning permission of the decision made by the local planning authority might aptly be described as ministerial: see *R. v Yeovil Corp Ex p. Elim Pentecostal Church Trustees* (1971) 70 L.G.R. 142. On whether an estoppel may arise if the official errs in the performance of his duty, see *Norfolk CC v Secretary of State for the Environment* [1973] 1 W.L.R. 1400.

[120] *Haridas v Khan* [1971] 1 W.L.R. 507 at 512; *Dean v District Auditor for Ashton-in-Makerfield* [1960] 1 Q.B. 149 at 156.

[121] See, e.g. *Bizony v Secretary of State for the Environment* [1976] 239 E.G. 281 at 283; *Birdi v Home Secretary, The Times*, 12 February 1975; *Purewal v Entry Clearance Officer* [1977] Imm. A.R. 93 (Immigration Appeal Tribunal: amnesty provisions not within jurisdiction of immigration appellate authorities). cf. *Salemi v MacKellar (No.2)* (1977) 137 C.L.R. 396.

In determining whether a function was 'judicial', a number of factors were considered, albeit that none of these factors was determinative in itself. The first test that was applied turned upon whether the performance of the function terminated in an order that had conclusive effect[122]; and a body exercising powers which were of a merely advisory,[123] deliberative,[124] investigatory[125] or conciliatory[126] character, or which did not have legal effect until confirmed by another body,[127] or involved only the making of a preliminary decision,[128] as not normally held to have judicial capacity.

6-035

A second test turned primarily on the presence or absence of certain formal and procedural attributes. The manner in which courts proceed is distinguished by a number of special characteristics. They determine matters in cases initiated by parties; they must normally sit in public[129]; they are empowered to compel the attendance of witnesses, who may be examined on oath; they are required to follow the rules of evidence; they are entitled to impose sanctions by way of imprisonment, fine, damages or mandatory or prohibitory orders, and to enforce obedience to their own commands. The fact that a body has been endowed with many of the "trappings of a court" may not always be sufficient to establish conclusively that it has been invested with judicial power[130]; but the presence of such trappings tended to support that conclusion. Thus, in seeking to establish that the proceedings (or the functions) of a body are to be classified as judicial for any given purpose, it may be material to show that the body is called a "tribunal" which holds "sittings" and makes "decisions" in relation to "cases" before it,[131] that it is empowered to summon witnesses and administer oaths,[132] that it is normally required to sit in public,[133] that its members are debarred from sitting if personally interested in a matter before

6-036

---

[122] See, e.g. *Stow v Mineral Holdings (Australia) Pty Ltd* (1977) 51 A.L.J.R. 672.

[123] *Re Clifford and O'Sullivan* [1921] 2 A.C. 570; *R. v MacFarlane Ex p. O'Flanagan and O'Kelly* (1923) 32 C.L.R. 518; *Ex p. Pritchard* [1953] 1 W.L.R. 1158.

[124] *R. v Legislative Committee of the Church Assembly Ex p. Haynes-Smith* [1928] 1 K.B. 411.

[125] See, e.g. *Re Grosvenor & West-End Railway Terminus Hotel Co* (1897) 76 L.T. 337; *Hearts of Oak Assurance Co v Attorney General* [1932] A.C. 392; *O'Conner v Waldron* [1935] A.C. 76; *St John v Fraser* [1935] S.C.R. 441; *Lockwood v Commonwealth* (1954) 90 C.L.R. 177; *Ex p. Mineral Deposits Pty Ltd; re Claye and Lynch* (1959) S.R. (N.S.W.) 167; *R. v Fowler Ex p. McArthur* [1958] Qd.R 41; *R. v Coppel Ex p. Viney Industries Pty Ltd* [1962] V.R. 630; *Testro Bros Pty Ltd v Tait* (1963) 109 C.L.R. 353; *Guay v Lafleur* [1965] S.C.R. 12; *R. v Collins Ex p. ACTU-Solo Enterprises Pty Ltd* (1976) 8 A.L.R. 691. Contrast *Re Pergamon Press Ltd* [1971] Ch. 388; cf. however, the subsequent decision in *Maxwell v Department of Trade and Industry* [1974] Q.B. 523.

[126] *Ayriss (FF) & Co v Alberta Labour Relations Board* (1960) 23 D.L.R. (2nd) 584 at [9]; *R. v Clipsham Ex p. Basken* (1965) 49 D.L.R. (2nd) 747; *R. v Race Relations Board Ex p. Selvarajan* [1975] 1 W.L.R. 1686.

[127] *R. v Hastings Local Board of Health* (1865) 6 B. & S. 401; *Re Local Government Board Ex p. Kingstown Commissioners* (1885) 16 L.R.Ir. 150; (1886) 18 L.R.Ir. 509; *Re Zadrevec and Town of Brampton* (1973) 37 D.L.R. (3rd) 326.

[128] *Jayawardane v Silva* [1970] 1 W.L.R. 1365; *Pearlberg v Varty* [1972] 1 W.L.R. 534 (cf. however, *Wiseman v Borneman* [1971] A.C. 297).

[129] *Scott v Scott* [1913] A.C. 417; *McPherson v McPherson* [1936] A.C. 177; *Stone v Stone* [1949] P. 165; *Re Agricultural Industries* [1952] 1 All E.R. 1188; *B (otherwise P) v Attorney-General* [1967] P. 119. cf. *Hearts of Oak* [1932] A.C. 392.

[130] cf. *Shell Co of Australia Ltd v Federal Commission of Taxation* [1931] A.C. 275 at 296-297 (dealing with judicial power under the Australian Constitution).

[131] *Jackson (FE) & Co v Price Tribunal (No.2)* [1950] N.Z.L.R 433 at 448-449; *New Zealand United Licensed Victuallers' Association of Employers v Price Tribunal* [1957] N.Z.L.R. 167 at 204, 207.

[132] *Jackson (FE) & Co v Price Tribunal (No.2)* [1950] N.Z.L.R 433 at 448-449. And see *Attorney General v BBC* [1978] 1 W.L.R. 477 at 481.

[133] *Copartnership Farms v Harvey-Smith* [1918] 2 K.B. 405 at 411.

them,[134] or that it has power to award costs[135] or to impose sanctions to enforce compliance with its orders.[136]

6-037 Perhaps the most obvious characteristic of ordinary courts though is that they determine, on the basis of evidence and arguments submitted to them, disputes between two or more parties about their respective legal rights and duties, powers and liabilities, privileges and immunities.[137] If, then, the functions of a body include the determination of issues that closely resemble *lis inter partes*, it could be expected that those functions would be classified as judicial. Of course, in administrative law many of the issues that arise between contending parties are different in character from those typically determined by courts. An applicant may appear before a licensing tribunal to seek a legal privilege; a member of the public may appear to oppose the application. Superficially the tribunal seems to be deciding a *lis inter partes*; but if it decides to refuse the application it is not deciding only in favour of the objector; it is deciding that it is not in the public interest to grant the licence, and the decision may in effect be in favour of the public at large, who are not directly represented at the hearing.[138] Nevertheless, functions may become reviewable as "judicial" because of statutory interpolation of a procedure bearing a superficial resemblance to a *lis inter partes*. Thus, the proceedings of licensing authorities that were required to conduct hearings were sufficiently judicial to be amenable to review by certiorari and prohibition and must be conducted in conformity with natural justice. A tribunal or other deciding body was therefore likely to be held to be acting in a judicial capacity when, after investigation and deliberation, it determined an issue conclusively by the application of a pre-existing legal rule or another objective legal standard to the facts found by it. Likewise, where the decision-maker was interpreting, declaring and applying the law.[139]

Applying the distinctions

6-038 The application of these distinctions often created significant complications. To illustrate in the context of the statutory schemes regarding housing and planning, described above. Between 1935 and 1947, a number of property owners endeavoured, with scant success, to impugn compulsory purchase orders and clearance orders on the ground that the Minister as confirming authority had failed to observe the rules of natural justice. The courts held that the Minister's functions were essentially administrative, but that once objections were lodged he assumed a quasi judicial role which imposed upon him the duty to follow the rules of natural justice when considering the objections and the report on the inquiry.[140] Before objec-

---

[134] *Copartnership Farms* [1918] 2 K.B. 405.

[135] *R. v Manchester JJ* [1899] 1 Q.B. 571; *R. v Sunderland JJ* [1901] 2 K.B. 357 at 369.

[136] The power of the Commonwealth Court of Conciliation and Arbitration to impose penalties for breaches or non-observance of its orders and awards was held by the PC in the *Boilermakers'* case to be "plainly judicial": *Attorney General of Australia v R.* [1957] A.C. 288 at 322.

[137] *Labour Relations Board of Saskatchewan v John East Iron Works Ltd* [1949] A. C. 134 at 149. See also *Boulter v Kent JJ.* [1897] A.C. 556 at 569; *Huddart Parker & Co Pty Ltd v Commonwealth* (1908) 8 C.L.R. 330 at 357 (Griffith CJ). cf. *Re Rubber Plastic and Cable Making Industry Award* 8 F.L.R. 396 (Commonwealth Industrial Court exercising judicial power of the Commonwealth in interpreting award although no dispute between parties bound by the award).

[138] *Boulter* [1897] A.C. 556 at 569 (Lord Herschell); *R. v Howard* [1902] 2 K.B. 363; *Tynemouth Corp v Attorney General* [1899] A.C. 293 at 307; *R. v Ashton Ex p. Walker* (1915) 85 L.J.K.B. 27 at 30.

[139] *Moses v Parker* [1896] A.C. 245; *United Engineering Workers; Union v Devanayagam* [1968] A.C. 356 for acknowledgements of this principle.

[140] *Stafford v Minister of Health* [1946] K.B. 621 (where under a temporary Act the Minister was empowered to dispense with a local inquiry, he was still obliged in considering objections to act in

tions were lodged he could offer advice to the local authority on housing mat-ters[141] and even express tentative approval of the proposed order.[142] He could obtain information from other departments[143] or from the local authority,[144] which he was not obliged to disclose to the objector although it might be prejudicial to the lat-ter's case.[145] To this extent the objector was denied part of the protection afforded by the *audi alteram partem* rule.[146] After objections had been lodged the Minister had to hold himself aloof from the parties, in so far as he was not to receive ex parte statements from the local authority relating to the subject matter of objections examined at the inquiry.[147] But he was not precluded from discussing with the lo-cal authority matters not related to the order,[148] or (possibly) matters related to the order but not made the subject of objections at the inquiry. He was apparently entitled after the inquiry to consult with other departments on matters relevant to his decision whether or not to confirm the order, but–the point was never cleared up by the courts–the character of the information thus obtained might be such as to impose on him an obligation to disclose it to the objector to enable him to chal-lenge its accuracy.[149] He was under no implied legal duty to disclose the contents of the inspector's report to the parties[150]; here again the courts diluted the *audi alteram partem* rule. His decision whether or not to confirm the order was "administrative," inasmuch as it could not be impeached for lack of evidence to sup-port it.[151] If no objections were lodged his function was said to be administrative throughout.[152]

Where the Minister was both confirming authority and initiator of the order the courts showed an even stronger disinclination to review the discharge of his statu-tory duties in terms of judicial standards. Under the New Towns Act 1946 the

6-039

---

conformity with natural justice).

[141] *Frost v Minister of Health* [1935] 1 K.B. 286; *Offer v Minister of Health* [1936] 1 K.B. 40.

[142] *Re Manchester (Ringway Airport) Compulsory Purchase Order* (1935) 153 L.T. 219.

[143] *Miller v Minister of Health* [1946] K.B. 626; *Summers v Minister of Health* [1947] 1 All E.R. 184.

[144] *Price v Minister of Health* [1947] 1 All E.R. 47; *Summers* [1947] 1 All E.R. 184; *Johnson (B) & Co (Builders) Ltd v Minister of Health* [1947] 2 All E.R. 395.

[145] *Johnson* [1947] 2 All E.R. 395; *Bushell v Secretary of State for the Environment* [1981] A.C. 75 (Minister both proposing and affirming authority for compulsory purchase order under the Highways Act 1959).

[146] cf. *Rice* [1911] A.C. 179 at 182; *R. v City of Westminster Assessment Committee* [1941] 1 K.B. 53.

[147] *Errington* [1935] 1 K.B. 249.

[148] *Horn v Minister of Health* [1937] 1 K.B. 164.

[149] *Darlassis v Minister of Education* (1954) 118 J.P. 452 at 466 (dictum). This issue was directly raised in *Buxton v Minister of Housing and Local Government* [1961] 1 Q.B. 278 (arising out of a plan-ning appeal, but the application was dismissed on a preliminary point of law because the applicant lacked locus standi). The circumstances in which information obtained by the Minister after the inquiry must be disclosed, and the consequences of disclosure, are now specified by regulations, e.g. Town and Country Planning (Major Infrastructure Project Inquiries Procedure) (England) Rules 2005 (SI 2005/2115). The Secretary of State is required to go back to the parties where he (a) differs from the inspector or on any matter of fact mentioned in, or appearing to him to be material to, a conclu-sion reached by the inspector, or (b) takes into consideration any new evidence or new matter of fact (not being a matter of government policy): (SI 2005/2115) r.21. See also Town and Country Plan-ning Appeals (Determination by Inspectors) (Inquiry Procedures) (England) Rules 2000 (SI 2000/1625) r.18.

[150] *Denby (William) & Sons Ltd* [1936] 1 K.B. 337; *Steele v Minister of Housing and Local Govern-ment* (1956) 6 P. & C.R. 386, following *Arlidge* [1915] A.C. 120. Disclosure or inspection of the report is now required: Town and Country Planning (Major Infrastructure Project Inquiries Procedure) (England) Rules 2005 (SI 2005/2115) r.22.

[151] *Johnson* [1947] 2 All E.R. 395; *Re Falmouth Clearance Order* 1936 [1937] 3 All E.R. 308; *Re LCC Order* 1938 [1945] 2 All E.R. 484.

[152] *Errington* [1935] 1 K.B. 249 at 259; *Johnson* [1947] 2 All E.R. 395.

Minister was empowered to make orders designating areas as the sites of satellite towns. If objections were lodged against a draft order, he had to cause a public local inquiry to be held with respect thereto and to consider the inspector's report before finally making the order.[153] Before the New Towns Bill had been introduced into Parliament, the Government had expressed its intention of designating Stevenage as the first of the new towns. In *Franklin v Minister of Town and Country Planning*[154] an attempt was made to impugn an order relating to Stevenage inthat the Minister had not called evidence at the inquiry in support of the draft order and had been biased in favour of the order when he had finally made it. The House of Lords rejected these contentions; the inquiry, it held, was directed to the objections, not to the order itself, and was prescribed for the further information of the Minister[155] and the criterion of bias, appropriate to measure the conduct of a quasi-judicial officer, had no relevance to the functions of the Minister which were "purely administrative". Provided that a properly conducted inquiry had been held, the only grounds of challenge could be that the Minister had not in fact considered the report or the objections or "that his mind was so foreclosed that he gave no genuine consideration to them".[156] Whilst it was undoubtedly proper to conclude from the nature of the legislative scheme that the Minister was entitled to approach his statutory duty to consider objections with a strong inclination to implement his own policy, the House of Lords used terminology which could be regarded as lending countenance to the view that a public authority did not act in a judicial capacity, in the sense of being required to observe the rules of natural justice, unless it occupied the role of an adjudicator determining something approximating to a *lis inter partes*, in which case a duty to observe natural justice might be superimposed upon the procedural requirements already prescribed by statute.[157]

The impact of the distinctions

6-040   These lines of cases profoundly influenced the attitude of English courts towards the procedural duties of public authorities invested with statutory powers in relation to individual rights. As was considered above, the courts tended to assume that a duty to observe the rules of natural justice arose only where the authority was already under a statutory duty to consider objections or conduct an inquiry in a "triangular" situation with two other contending parties before it; and that where no such statutory duty was imposed the functions of the authority could not be characterised as judicial for this purpose.[158] They overlooked the reasons that lay behind the somewhat artificial system of characterisation adopted in the Housing

---

[153] Sch.1; now New Towns Act 1981 Sch.1.

[154] *Franklin v Minister of Town and Country Planning* [1948] A.C. 87.

[155] Following *Re Trunk Roads Act 1936* [1939] 2 K.B. 515; distinguished in *Magistrates of Ayr v Lord Advocate* 1950 S.C. 102. See also *Wednesbury (No.2)* [1966] 2 Q.B. 275 (inquiries in connection with objections to proposals for review of local government).

[156] *Franklin v Minister of Town and Country Planning* [1948] A.C. 87 at 102, 103. See, to like effect, *Robinson v Minister of Town and Country Planning* [1947] K.B. 702; cf. *Magistrates of Ayr* 1950 S.C. 102.

[157] cf. H.W.R. Wade, *Towards Administrative Justice* (1963), p.67: "the right result was reached by the wrong road." cf. K.C. Davis, "English Administrative Law—An American View" [1962] P.L. 139, 154–155, approving the terminology used.

[158] Statutory rules impose upon Ministers who initiate compulsory purchase orders almost exactly the same procedural duties as are prescribed in connection with orders initiated by local authorities: Compulsory Purchase (Inquiries Procedure) Rules 2007 (SI 2007/3617). Analogous rules now also apply to the confirmation of highway schemes initiated by the Minister: Highways (Inquiries Procedure) Rules 1994 (SI 1994/3263).

Act cases. There the courts had a threefold purpose in stressing the "essentially administrative" nature of the Minister's functions: to emphasise that the Minister had an overriding political responsibility for matters of housing policy, for which he was answerable to Parliament, so that in reviewing his functions in confirming individual orders it would be inappropriate to impose upon him standards appropriate to a judge determining *lites inter partes*; to protect from disclosure departmental files and communications made to and by him in his political capacity; and to resist the contention that his final decision upon an order involved the exercise of a "quasi judicial" discretion that might be reviewed on its merits. The housing and town planning cases achieved so much prominence that older cases establishing a right to notice and hearing despite the absence of a *lis inter partes* or express procedural requirements lurked, neglected and half-forgotten, in the shadows of the past.

HISTORICAL DEVELOPMENT SINCE THE 1960S

Revisionism revised

By this stage, valedictory addresses to the *audi alteram partem* rule in English   **6-041**
administrative law were becoming almost commonplace. It was nevertheless suggested in the first edition of this work that the time had "not yet arrived to think of pronouncing obsequies or writing obituary notices", and that "the comatose must not be assumed to be moribund"[159]; and in the 1960s, the rule recovered much of its former vitality as an implied common-law requirement of fair administrative procedure. Perhaps the state of its debility had been slightly exaggerated. Its revival was indirectly stimulated by a growing awareness among practitioners and judges of old forsaken paths, of more imaginative judicial achievements in other English-speaking countries, and of academic legal literature. Undoubtedly the enactment of the Tribunals and Inquiries Act 1958, which extended the scope of judicial review in other directions, modified the general climate of judicial opinion. Above all, there had been a growth of informed interest in problems of administrative adjudication and judicialised administration generated by the publication of the Franks Report (1957), the establishment of the Council on Tribunals, the proliferation of statutory procedural rules in administrative law and the controversies aroused by the decision-making process in town and country planning. Judges do not inhabit an intellectual vacuum, and they were impelled to do some hard thinking about their own role in administrative law.

There were some indications in the first years of the 1960s, both from English   **6-042**
courts[160] and the Privy Council, that considerations of the need for fairness in the administrative process had not been entirely eliminated from judicial thinking.

---

[159] (1959), p.136.

[160] *R. v Registrar of Building Societies* [1960] 1 W.L.R. 669; *Hoggard v Worsbrough UDC* [1962] 2 Q.B. 93. In a number of other cases, proceedings before courts and regularly constituted tribunals were set aside for non-compliance with the *audi alteram partem* rule: *Chettiar* [1962] 1 W.L.R. 279; *R. v Birkenhead JJ. Ex p. Fisher* [1962] 1 W.L.R. 1410; *Brinkley v Brinkley* [1965] P. 75; *Fowler v Fowler* [1963] P. 311; *Abraham v Jutsun* [1963] 1 W.L.R. 658; *Disher v Disher* [1965] P. 31; *Appuhamy v R.* [1963] A.C. 474; *Sheldon v Bromfield JJ.* [1964] 2 Q.B. 573; *S v S (1964)* [1965] 1 W.L.R. 21; *Hodgkins v Hodgkins* [1965] 1 W.L.R. 1448; *R. v Aylesbury JJ. Ex p. Wisbey* [1965] 1 W.L.R. 339 (courts); *The Seistan* [1960] 1 W.L.R. 186; *R. v Deputy Industrial Injuries Commissioner Ex p. Jones* [1962] 2 Q.B. 677; *R. v Industrial Tribunal Ex p. George Green & Thomson Ltd* (1967) 2 K.I.R. 259 (other statutory tribunals). Decisions on non-statutory arbitrations and domestic tribunals have been omitted.

Particular mention should be made of Lord Denning who, in a series of cases involving the powers of voluntary associations was concerned to ensure that these powers were tempered by corresponding responsibilities, of which the duty to hold fair inquiries was one.[161] Characteristically, Lord Denning was not concerned with the formal nature of the decision but with the fact that voluntary associations have monopoly powers and that their decisions in effect deprived individuals of their livelihoods.

6-043   Then in 1963 the House of Lords restored the law to the path from which it had deviated. For in *Ridge v Baldwin*,[162] it was held by a majority that a chief constable, dismissible only for cause prescribed by statute,[163] was impliedly entitled to prior notice of the charge against him and a proper opportunity of meeting it before being removed by the local police authority for misconduct.[164] In an illuminating review of the authorities,[165] Lord Reid repudiated the notions that the rules of natural justice applied only to the exercise of those functions which were analytically judicial, and that a "superadded" duty to act judicially had to be visible before an obligation to observe natural justice could arise in the exercise of a statutory function affecting the rights of an individual. He emphasised that the duty to act in conformity with natural justice could, in some situations, simply be inferred from a duty to decide "what the rights of an individual should be".[166]

6-044   This decision gave a powerful impetus to the emergent trend,[167] an impetus which is not yet spent in administrative law. It opened an era of activism in which the courts have subjected the working of government to a degree of judicial scrutiny, on substantive as well as procedural grounds, which shows little sign yet of diminishing; and which has received renewed impetus with the advent of the Human Rights Act 1998.[168]

---

[161] See, e.g. *Duke of Norfolk* (1949) 65 T.L.R. 225 (withdrawal of horse trainer's licence by jockey Club); *Abbott* [1952] 1 K.B. 189 (dockworker struck off Union's register and therefore could no longer be employed); *Lee v Showmen's Guild* [1952] 2 Q.B. 329 (expulsion from a trade association). See generally, J. Jowell, "Administrative Law" in J. Jowell and P. McAuslan (eds), *Lord Denning: The Judge and The Law* (1984).

[162] *Ridge v Baldwin* [1964] A.C. 40.

[163] Negligence or other unfitness (Municipal Corporations Act 1882 s.191(4)), repealed by Police Act 1964 s.64(3) and Sch.10. See now Police Act 1996 s.11 (chief constable may be called upon to retire or resign in the interests of efficiency and effectiveness; before seeking approval of Secretary of State for retirement or resignation, the chief constable is entitled to reasons and an opportunity to make representations).

[164] The implications of the decision were much discussed, e.g. A. Bradley, "Failure of Justice and Defect of Police" [1964] Cam. L.J. 83; A. Goodhart, "Ridge v Baldwin: Administrative and Natural Justice" (1964) 80 L.Q.R. 105. The decision was criticised by some New Zealand writers because of the omission of a "superadded" requirement to act judicially: J. Northey, "The Electricity Commissioners and the Chief Constable" [1963] N.Z.L.J. 448; D. Patterson, "Natural justice and licensing applications: Hohfeld and the Writ of Certiorari" [1966] N.Z.L.J. 107; but see J. Farmer, "Natural justice and licensing applications: Hohfeld and the Writ of Certiorari" (1967) 2 N.Z.U.L.Rev. 282.

[165] *Ridge v Baldwin* [1964] A.C. 40 at 71–79.

[166] *Ridge v Baldwin* [1964] A.C. 40 at 75–76.

[167] PC decisions in the 1960s applying the *audi alteram partem* rule to set aside administrative action included: *Kanda v Government of Malaya* [1962] A.C. 322; *Shareef v Commissioner for Registration of Indian and Pakistani Residents* [1966] A.C. 47; *Alaradana Mosque Trustees v Mahmud* [1967] 1 A.C. 13; *Jeffs v New Zealand Dairy Production and Marketing Board* [1967] 1 A.C. 551. See also *Durayappah* [1967] 2 A.C. 337 (implied duty to observe natural justice, but appeal dismissed on a technical point. cf. *Vidyodaya University Council v Silva* [1965] 1 W.L.R. 77; *Pillai v Singapore City Council* [1968] 1 W.L.R. 1278.

[168] See Ch.13 and 7-032, 7-037 and 7-120.

The duty to act fairly

In the case law since the late 1960s, the courts have demonstrated considerable **6-045** flexibility in their manipulation of the principal criteria used for determining the circumstances in which a duty to observe the rules of natural justice would be implied. As long as it was remembered that the degree of procedural formality required by the rules was capable of considerable variation according to the context,[169] an extension of the range of situations to which they were applied did not attract the criticism that the courts were "over judicialising" administrative procedures. Since 1967 the courts began to employ the term "duty to act fairly" to denote an implied procedural obligation—the content of which may fall considerably short of the essential elements of a trial or a formal inquiry—accompanying the performance of a function that could not readily be characterised as judicial in nature.[170]

Thus, before refusing leave to enter, immigration officers were not required to **6-046** hold a judicial hearing at which the individual could produce witnesses and evidence to support his claim: this would unduly burden the administration of the system of immigration control in which officers at the ports are required, within a relatively short period of time, to make a large number of decisions.[171] However, they were under a legal obligation to exercise their powers fairly, and this meant that they must inform a person who claims a legal right to enter why they are disposed to refuse and allow him an opportunity to allay their suspicions.[172] Similar obligations were imposed upon inspectors conducting inquiries into allegations of improprieties committed against companies by their officers.[173] While the damage to reputations that might be suffered as a result of the publication of a report containing adverse criticisms required that affected individuals have a prior opportunity to be informed of and to comment upon any serious allegations made against them, to insist on an adjudicative hearing would be inconsistent with the

---

[169] Dicta to this effect in *Duke of Norfolk* [1949] 1 All E.R. 109 at 118 were cited with predictable regularity. See *R. (on the application of Lewis) v Redcar and Cleveland BC* [2008] EWCA Civ 746; [2009] 1 W.L.R. 83 and *R. (on the application of Fraser) v National Institute for Health and Clinical Excellence* [2009] EWHC 452 (Admin); (2009) 107 B.M.L.R. 178, for examples of the application, post-*Ridge v Baldwin*, of the duty to act fairly to bodies that are not judicial or quasi-judicial, with a modification of content of the duty to suit the context.

[170] See P. Craig, "Perspectives on process: common law, statutory and political" [2010] P.L. 275. On similar developments in other jurisdictions, see 6-051.

[171] Immigration Act 1971 Sch. 2.

[172] *Re HK (An Infant)* [1967] 2 Q.B. 617: applicant had a legal right to enter if he could establish his claim to be the son, under the age of 16, of a Commonwealth citizen settled in the UK. The reason for Lord Parker CJ's doubt over the proper characterisation of the immigration officer's function arose from the exigencies of the administration of immigration control at the ports of entry, rather than from the nature of the decision to be made. Those without a legal entitlement (or, it should now be added, a legitimate expectation) to enter or remain in the UK may be refused without the benefit of any implied procedural rights: *Schmidt v Home Office* [1969] 2 Ch. 149. Since 1969, there has been a right to a hearing on an appeal against many immigration decisions to independent tribunals. This is one context in which statutory justice has, to an extent at least, supplied the omission of the common law. However, the statutory duty to give reasons for refusal, before a notice of appeal is given, has been construed narrowly: *R. v Secretary of State for the Home Department Ex p. Swati* [1986] 1 W.L.R. 477; *R. (on the application of Hicks) v Secretary of State for the Home Department* [2005] EWHC 2818 (Admin); [2006] A.C.D. 47.

[173] Companies Act 1985 Pt.14 and Companies Act 2006 Pt.10; *Re Pergamon Press Ltd* [1971] Ch. 388; *Maxwell* [1974] Q.B. 523. cf. *Norwest Holst Ltd* [1978] Ch. 201 (appointment of inspectors), and *R. v Secretary of State for Trade Ex p. Perestrello* [1981] Q.B. 19 (exercise of power under Companies Act 1967 s.109 (now Companies Act 1985 s.447) to require the production of corporate documents), where the duty to act fairly was given hardly any independent content.

public interest in protecting the confidentiality of evidence given to the inspector, and in ensuring that the inquiry is conducted with reasonable expedition. Moreover, an adverse report does not directly deprive a person of any legal rights in the strict sense. The duty to act fairly also extended the scope of the hearing to situations where a "privilege" rather than a "right" was in issue. For example, an applicant for a renewal of gaming licence cannot be refused on grounds of personal unacceptability unless the board has first intimated to him its concerns in such a way that allows the applicant to respond, but without prejudicing the confidentiality of the board's sources of information.[174]

6-047 The principal benefit of the introduction of the duty to act fairly into the court's vocabulary was to extend the benefit of basic procedural protections to situations which it would be inappropriate to describe the decision-makers functions as judicial, or even quasi-judicial, and inappropriate to insist on a procedure analogous to a trial.[175]

European influences

The ECHR

6-048 The incorporation of the ECHR into English law in 2000 as a result of the Human Rights Act 1998 has proved to be an important stimulus to the evolution of

---

[174] *R. v Gaming Board of Great Britain Ex p. Benaim and Khaida* [1970] 2 Q.B. 417.

[175] See 6-029. As will be seen in Ch.7, courts now tend to reason in terms of a general duty to act fairly. See also *Ahmed v Her Majesty's Treasury (Justice intervening) (Nos 1 and 2)* [2010] UKSC 5; [2010] 2 A.C. 534 at [80] (Lord Hope); *Bank Mellat v Her Majesty's Treasury (No.2)* [2011] EWCA Civ 1; [2012] Q.B. 101 at [99] (Elias LJ dissenting in the case and referring to a hearing as "this most basic principle of fairness"). However, for earlier cases on the relationship between classification of a function as administrative and importation of a duty to act "fairly" rather than "judicially," e.g. *Pearlberg* [1972] 1 W.L.R. 534 at 547 (Lord Pearson); *Bates v Lord Hailsham of St Marylebone* [1972] 1 W.L.R. 1373 at 1378 (Megarry J); *R. v Liverpool Corp Ex p. Liverpool Taxi Fleet Operators' Association* [1972] 2 Q.B. 299 at 307–308, 310 (Lord Denning MR and Roskill LJ); *Herring v Templeman* [1973] 3 All E.R. 569 at 584 (no duty to disclose academic assessments to student liable to expulsion); *Ex p. Selvarajan* [1975] 1 W.L.R. 1686 at 1693–1696, 1700 (delegation of decision-making by a body whose functions were largely investigative and conciliatory). While judges often adopted different characterisations of the same power, and used different terms to describe the applicable procedural duty, they could still agree on whether the authority was obliged to afford to the applicant the procedural right in question, e.g. *Re H.K.* [1967] 2 Q.B. 617 at 630–631 (Lord Parker CJ, "fairly") 632–633 (Salmon LJ, "natural justice"), (Blain J, neutral); *Re Pergamon Press Ltd* [1971] Ch. 388 at 399–400 (Lord Denning MR, "fairly"), 402–403 (Sachs LJ, "natural justice"), 407 (Buckley LJ "not a judicial function"); *Breen* [1971] 2 Q.B. 175 at 190 (Lord Denning MR, "fairly"), 195 (Edmund Davies LJ, "natural justice"), 200 (Megaw LJ, neutral); and *Grunwick Processing Laboratories Ltd v ACAS* [1978] A.C. 655 at 660, 667 (Lord Denning MR: "judicial", "natural justice"), 677 (Geoffrey Lane LJ: "unfair or contrary to the rules of natural justice"); but on appeal Lord Diplock, speaking for the majority in the HL, disposed of the questions of statutory interpretation in issue without reference to either term. For an example, see: *Manning v Ramjohn* [2011] UKPC 20 (proposing to "put aside consideration of the principles of natural justice (if, indeed, in this context they are materially different from the demands of fairness) and … to address simply the question whether, in the exercise of the power in question, the Prime Minister acted in a fair manner"); see also *R. (on the application of L) v West London Mental Health NHS Trust* [2014] EWCA Civ 47; (2014) 158(6) S.J.L.B. 37 at [68], [69] (Beatson LJ expressing concern that the emphasis on flexibility could lead to an inappropriate drawing together of the concepts of procedural and substantive fairness and undue uncertainty). See also *Secretary of State for Communities and Local Government v Hopkins Developments* [2014] EWCA Civ 470 at [85] ("it does not generally matter whether what is at issue is characterised as 'natural justice' or 'procedural fairness'"). See also *R. (on the application of Moseley) v Haringey LBC* [2014] UKSC 56; [2014] 1 W.L.R. 3947 at [24]: "[f]airness is a protean concept, not susceptible of much generalised enlargement."

procedural fairness, in particular due to articles 2 and 6 ECHR.[176] In summary, art.6 requires a "fair and public hearing within a reasonable time" by an "independent and impartial tribunal established by law" for the determination of an individual's "civil rights and obligations".[177] As is evident from the wording of the provision and, as is discussed in Chapter 7, the entitlement to art.6 protection only arises where "civil rights and obligations" are in issue.[178] The term "civil rights and obligations" is clearly "rooted in a paradigm of private law rights",[179] and the Strasbourg Court has experienced considerable difficulty in determining its scope.[180] Initially interpreted very restrictively,[181] over time art.6 has been given a more generous application. For example, it has been applied to the determination of welfare benefits[182] and the withdrawal of a banking licence.[183] It is certainly not as restricted in its scope as the *Nakkuda Ali* formulation considered above but the article is clearly not of unrestricted scope.[184] In this respect, it lacks the flexibility of application of the common law duty to act fairly.[185] The content of the protection provided by art.6 will be considered in detail in Chapters 7, 8 and 10, but for present

---

[176] For the impact of art.6 ECHR on common law procedural fairness, see 7-032 and 7-120 and for art.2 ECHR see 7-037 and 7-130; S. Juss, "Constitutionalising Rights without a Constitution: The British Experience under Article 6 of the Human Rights Act 1998" (2006) 27 Statute L. Rev. 29. On art.6 specifically, see Lord Lester, D. Pannick and J. Herberg, *Human Rights Law and Practice*, 3rd edn (2009) and R.C. White and C. Ovey, *Jacobs, White & Ovey: The European Convention on Human Rights*, 7th edn (2017). See also *R. (on the application of TH (Bangladesh) v Secretary of State for the Home Department* [2016] EWCA Civ 815 at [22] (Beatson LJ observing that his "starting point is that the history of procedural fairness shows it to be the result of implying into broadly-phrased powers and procedures the requirements of procedural fairness reflected in the principles of natural justice and, since the enactment of the Human Rights Act 1998, the duty of the court where possible to construe such powers, if necessary by reading them down, as compatible with the Convention rights. It is in that context and in that sense that it can be said that procedural fairness is … a well-established principle ingrained in public administration").

[177] See 7-032, 7-120 and 10-088.

[178] See 7-033; P. Craig, "The Human Rights Act, Article 6 and Procedural Rights" [2003] P.L. 753; J. Herberg, A. Le Sueur and J. Mulcahy, "Determining Civil Rights and Obligations" in J. Jowell and J. Cooper (eds), *Understanding Human Rights Principles* (2001), p.91, at pp.112 and 114–121.

[179] Craig, "The Human Rights Act, Article 6 and Procedural Rights" [2003] P.L. 753, 754.

[180] Craig, "The Human Rights Act, Article 6 and Procedural Rights" [2003] P.L. 753; Lester, Pannick and Herberg (2009). The jurisprudence relating to the applicability of art.6 to civil service disputes has been particularly protracted: *Massa v Italy* (1994) 18 E.H.R.R. 266; *De Santa v Italy* (App. No.25574/94); *Lapalorcia v Italy* (App. No.25586/94); *Abenavoli v Italy* (App. No.25587/94), Judgments of 2 September 1997; *Neigel v France* (2000) 30 E.H.R.R. 310; *Pellegrin v France* (2001) 31 E.H.R.R. 26.

[181] See 7-033; *Ringeisen v Austria* (1979–80) 1 E.H.R.R. 455.

[182] See 7-035 and, e.g. *Salesi v Italy* (1998) 26 E.H.R.R. 187; *Tsfayo v UK* App. No.60860/00, [2007] H.L.R. 19.

[183] *Capital Bank AD v Bulgaria* (2007) 44 E.H.R.R. 48 at [88].

[184] See 7-033 and, e.g. *Charalambos v France* App. No.49210/99, admissibility decision of 8 February 2000 (determination of tax liability); *Maaouia v France* (2001) 33 E.H.R.R. 1037 (proceedings to challenge an exclusion order). For domestic case law in which art.6 has not been regarded as engaged, see: *R. (on the application of G) v X School Governors* [2011] UKSC 30; [2012] 1 A.C. 167 (school disciplinary hearing where right to practice profession would be determined by a separate authority); *R. (on the application of A) v Croydon LBC* [2009] UKSC 8; [2009] 1 W.L.R. 2557 (duty to provide accommodation for a "child"); *R. (on the application of BB (Algeria)) v Special Immigration Appeals Commission* [2011] EWHC 2129 (Admin); [2012] 1 All E.R. 229 (bail proceedings before the Special Immigration Appeals Commission); *R. v Richmond upon Thames LBC Ex p. JC* [2001] E.L.R. 21 (school admission decision). See also *Ali v Birmingham City Council* [2010] UKSC 8; [2010] 2 A.C. 39 (accommodation for a homeless applicant did not engage ECHR art.6); *Ali v United Kingdom* (2016) 63 E.H.R.R. 20 (finding ECHR art.6 engaged); *Poshteh v Kensington and Chelsea RLBC* [2017] UKSC 36; [2017] A.C. 624 (not following *Ali*).

[185] On occasion, English courts have deliberately avoided the issue altogether, and decided cases on alternative grounds: *Begum v Tower Hamlets LBC* [2003] UKHL 5; [2003] 2 A.C. 430.

purposes, it is worth noting that the provision's most notable impact has been due to its requirement of an "independent" tribunal, to accompany the common law principle that no one should be a judge in his own cause or "*nemo judex in causa sua*".[186] The influence of art.6 has resulted in an "independent" tribunal being declared to be a requirement of common law procedural fairness[187]; an important jurisprudence has also evolved regarding the extent to which judicial review can remedy the absence of institutional or structural independence on the part of the decision-maker.[188] Meanwhile, art.2 ECHR imposes an obligation to ensure effective judicial review and to conduct an investigation in circumstances in which the State have breached its substantive art.2 duty to protect life.[189]

European Union law

6-049   European Union law has undoubtedly had a very important impact on English administrative law, which is explored in detail in Chapter 14. However, its impact has been more notable in the context of substantive review and legitimate expectations, than it has been in the context of procedural fairness. Aside from the example of a duty to give reasons, which applies both in respect of acts of the Union and in respect of national measures which interfere with Union law rights,[190] there is a stronger case for asserting that European Union law on procedural fairness has been inspired more by, and borrowed more from, English common law, than vice versa.[191]

The national security challenge

6-050   By way of final comment in this short overview of the evolution of the duty to act fairly, it is important to mention the most significant recent challenge to application of the duty, namely, national security. This is a matter which is discussed in detail in Chapter 8.[192] Very briefly, while, as was discussed above,[193] courts have long-grappled with national security qualifications to the duty to act fairly, the invocation of national security by way of qualifier of the duty to act fairly has become significantly more commonplace following 11 September 2001. As such, in its most recent phase of evolution, the most pressing issue arising in the context of the duty to act fairly is the extent to which the duty can be limited by national security concerns. In particular, the entitlement of an individual to know the case against him or her has come under intense strain due to increasing Governmental reliance on the doctrine public interest immunity, closed material procedures and

---

[186] See 10-088.

[187] *R. (on the application of Bewry) v Norwich City Council* [2001] EWHC Admin 657; [2002] H.R.L.R. 2.

[188] See 10-089.

[189] See 7-037 and 7-130. Where other rights of the Convention are engaged, there may also be procedural requirements specific to the engagement of that particular right. For example, a discussion of the influence of ECHR art.5(4) on procedural requirements in the context of parole board hearings can be found in *Re Reilly's Application for Judicial Review* [2013] UKSC 61; [2013] 3 W.L.R. 1020 at [54]–[63] (noting that Convention law permeates the domestic legal system and that domestic law is interpreted and developed in accordance with the Convention as appropriate).

[190] See 14-145 and 14-156.

[191] *Transocean Marine Paint Association v Commission* (17/74) [1974] E.C.R. 1063 at 1088–1090 (AG Warner noting that in English law, the right to be heard was a "rule of natural justice", regardless of whether there was a written obligation to provide a hearing). On process rights in the EU, see further P. Craig, *EU Administrative Law* 2nd edn (2012), Ch.12.

[192] See 8-006.

[193] See 6-021.

special advocates in such contexts as deportation, employment recruitment and measures targeted specifically at counter-terrorism.[194] Moreover, although the Supreme Court has held that closed material procedures—pursuant to which material may be presented to the court but withheld entirely from the affected person—may only be used where statutorily-established,[195] the Justice and Security Act 2013 now extends the possibility of using a CMP to all civil proceedings.[196] At present, the duty to act fairly—and in particular the *audi alteram partem* element of the duty—is under significant strain.[197]

COMPARATIVE PERSPECTIVES

Historical comparisons

When reviewing the evolution of procedural fairness in comparative historical context, the debt owed in England and Wales, and the Commonwealth more generally, to the large body of American case-law and the sophisticated writings of American commentators[198] on the right to a hearing is worthy of note. While the impact of American experience and thought on English courts was neither immediate nor obvious, its influence on English academics was marked. That said, the *audi alteram partem* principle did find vibrancy in courts across the Commonwealth from the 1950s onwards. The High Court of Australia reaffirmed the presumption in favour of the maxim in two cases where summary action derogating from private property rights had been taken in reliance on legislation which afforded no procedural safeguard.[199] The Supreme Court of Ceylon, although bound by *Nakkuda Ali v Jayaratne*,[200] contrived to give effect to the maxim in a range of situations extending from the disqualification of a university student for misconduct to the removal of local councillors.[201] The vitality of the maxim had survived in Canada as well. The Supreme Court applied the *audi alteram partem* rule to a deci-

6-051

---

[194] See, e.g. *RB (on the application of Algeria) v Secretary of State for the Home Department* [2009] UKHL 10; [2010] 2 A.C. 110 (use of special advocate in deportation context); *Tariq v Home Office* [2011] UKSC 35; [2012] 1 A.C. 452 (employment); *MB v Secretary of State for the Home Department: AF v Secretary of the Home Department* [2007] UKHL 46; [2008] 1 A.C. 440 at [34]–[35] (Lord Bingham) (control orders); *Secretary of State for the Home Department v F (No.3)* [2009] UKHL 28; [2010] 2 A.C. 269 at [59].

[195] *Al-Rawi v The Security Service* [2011] UKSC 34; [2012] 1 A.C. 452. The power may be necessarily implied into the statutory framework: *Bank Mellat v HM Treasury (No.1)* [2013] UKSC 38; [2014] A.C. 700 at [37]–[43] (since s.40(2) of the 2005 Act provides that an appeal lies to the Supreme Court against "any" judgment of the Court of Appeal, that must extend to parts of a closed judgment as justice will not be able to be done in some cases if the appellate court cannot consider the closed material). For comment, see C. Sargeant, "Two Steps Backward, One Step Forward—the Cautionary Tale of Bank Mellat (No.1)" [2014] 3(1) C.J.I.C.L. 111.

[196] See discussion at 8-009.

[197] For commentary on the bill as it passed through Parliament, see T. Hickman, '*Justice and Security Bill: Defeat or Not a Defeat: That is the Question*' UK Const. L. Blog (27 November 2012).

[198] See, e.g. K.C. Davis, *Administrative Law Treatise* (1994), and R. Pierce, 5th edn (2010); P.L. Strauss, T. Rakoff, C.R. Farina and G.E. Metzger, *Gellhorn and Byse's Administrative Law: Cases and Comments*, 11th edn (2011) Chs 3–7; R. Stewart, "The Reformation of American Law" (1974–5) 88 Harv. L.Rev. 1667; J. Mashaw, *Due Process in the Administrative State* (1985).

[199] *Delta Properties Pty Ltd* (1956) 95 C.L.R. 11 at 18 (resolution prohibiting erection of dwellings on land); *Tanos* (1958) 98 C.L.R. 383 at 385–386 (judge declaring restaurant a disorderly house on an ex parte application).

[200] *Nakkuda Ali* [1951] A.C. 66.

[201] *Fernando v Ceylan University* (1957) 59 NLR 265 (reversed on the merits [1960] 1 W.L.R. 223).

sion of a Labour Relations Board to decertify a trade union as the bargaining agent for employees.[202] And in a striking decision the Appellate Division of the South African Supreme Court demonstrated its independence by invalidating a restriction order served by a minister under the Suppression of Communism Act, the person affected not having been given the opportunity of making representations against it in accordance with the "sacred maxim," *audi alteram partem*.[203] Finally, the New Zealand courts, whilst regarding themselves bound by *Nakkuda Ali*, were nonetheless prepared to apply the rule to situations far removed from that of a judge deciding a *lis inter partes*, by finding statutory indications of a duty to act judicially, albeit that the legislation did not expressly require notice or hearing.[204] Beyond the Commonwealth, in Ireland, the principle of natural justice had been promoted by the courts before the 1950s[205] and took on a constitutional dimension in 1965.[206]

---

[202] *Alliance des Professeurs Catholiques de Montreal v Labour Relations Board of Quebec* [1953] 2 S.C.R. 140. See also *Saltfleet Board of Health v Knapman* [1956] S.C.R. 877; *Wisell v Metropolitan Corp of Greater Winnipeg* [1965] S.C.R. 512; *Re Nicholson and Haldimand-Norfolk Police Commissioners* (1979) 88 D.L.R. (3rd) 671. But the line has not always been firmly held, e.g. *Calgary Power Ltd Copitliorne* [1959] S.C.R. 24; *Howarth v National Parole Board* [1976] 1 S.C.R. 453; *Martineau and Butters v Matsqui Institution Inmate Disciplinary Board* [1978] 1 S.C.R. 118 (although the latter two cases turn specifically on the interpretation of the Federal Court Act 1970 s.28(1)). For a discussion of the evolution of procedural fairness in Canadian law, see *Dunsmuir v New Brunswick (Board of Management)* 2008 SCC 9; [2008] 1 S.C.R. 1 at [85]–[90] ("procedural fairness has grown to become a central principle of Canadian administrative law. Its overarching purpose is not difficult to discern: administrative decision-makers, in the exercise of public powers, should act fairly in coming to decisions that affect the interests of individuals": at [90]). In terms of entitlement to judicial review, the *Dunsmuir* case also establishes that, in the public employment context, if there is a contract of employment, the public law duty of fairness will not apply: at [102]–[103].

[203] *R. v Ngwevela* 1954 (1) S.A. 123 (rule not excluded by Parliament expressly or by necessary implication, and no exceptional circumstances, such as paramount need for swift preventive action, present). See also *Saliwa v Minister of Native Affairs*, 1956 (2) S.A. 310; contrast, however, *South African Defence and Aid Fund v Minister of Justice*, 1967 (1) S.A. 263, indicating a retreat by the judges from their bold attitude towards executive encroachments on individual freedom. The duty to act fairly has been described as "a requirement of the rule of law which requires that the exercise of public power should not be arbitrary": *Masetlha v President of South Africa*, 2008 (1) S.A. 566 at [189].

[204] *New Zealand Dairy Board v Okitu Co-operative Dairy Co Ltd* [1953] N.Z.L.R. 366 at 403–405, 417, 422; *New Zealand United Licensed Victuallers* [1957] N.Z.L.R. 167 at 203–205, 207; *Low v Earthquake Commission* [1959] N.Z.L.R. 1198.

[205] See, e.g. *Maunsell v Minister for Education* [1940] I.R. 213 at 234 (Gavan Duffy J, observing that natural justice is "elementary justice; it applies even where the person affected has no merits; it applies though the enactment does not seem to have contemplated notice; and it applies to every body having authority to adjudicate upon matters involving civil consequences to individuals ... The principle cannot be more tersely expressed than in the lines of Seneca: 'Quicunque aliquid statuerit, parte inaudita altera, aequum licet statuerit, haud aequus fuerit'".

[206] G. Hogan and D.G. Morgan, *Administrative Law in Ireland*, 4th edn (2010) at para.12-47 (citing *McDonald v Bord nag Con* [1965] I.R. 217 at 242). Although there was some uncertainty as to whether the terms "natural justice" and "constitutional justice" were co-terminous, the uncertainty appeared to have been resolved in favour of the proposition that natural justice had been fully subsumed into constitutional justice and that constitutional justice "must be understood to import more than the two well-established principles that no man shall be judge in his own cause, and *audi alteram partem*": *McDonald* [1965] I.R. 217 at 242; *State (Furey) v Minister for Defence* [1988] I.L.R.M. 89 at 99. See also M. de Blacam, *Judicial Review*, 3rd edn (2017), para.14.22. Some doubt has been cast on this position by obiter comments of the Supreme Court, however, it is suggested here that those comments should be treated with caution: see 6-055.

Contemporary comparisons

Generally, across common law jurisdictions, recognition of the importance of **6-052** observing the requirements of procedural fairness continues apace. Perhaps the most definitive statement that can be made though is that, while similar procedural fairness questions appear to have occupied courts across jurisdictions, the precise solutions reached by those courts have not always been uniform.

As in England and Wales, elsewhere, the common law duty to act in accordance **6-053** with natural justice has generally been overtaken by a duty to act fairly.[207] Just as in England and Wales, procedural fairness has been affected by the incorporation of Convention rights into domestic law,[208] across the common law world principles of procedural fairness continue to be influenced by constitutional and statutory developments. Well-established examples include:

- s.7 of the Canadian Charter of Rights and Freedoms 1990, which states that the right to life, liberty and security of the person may only be deprived "in accordance with the principles of fundamental justice"[209];
- s.27(1) of the New Zealand Bill of Rights Act 1990, which states that "[e]very person has the right to the observance of the principles of natural justice by any tribunal or other public authority which has the power to make a determination in respect of that person's rights, obligations, or interests protected or recognised by law";
- s.18.1(4)(b) of the Canadian Federal Courts Act RSC 1985, c.F-7, which, like the New Zealand Bill of Rights Act, refers expressly to "natural justice";
- in South Africa, the Promotion of Administrative Justice Act 2000 ("the PAJA") implements the call in s.33(3) of the South African Constitution for national legislation to give effect to the rights to administrative justice listed in s.33(1) and s.33(2). The Act provides the default pathway for judicial review, and, like the s.33 rights in the Constitution, applies to "administrative action". However, a distinction is drawn between "administrative action" affecting an individual[210] and "administrative action" that affects "the rights of the public".[211] Procedural fairness in the former context is broad

---

[207] See, e.g. in New Zealand: *Chandra v Minister of Immigration* [1978] 2 N.Z.L.R. 559 at 564 reviewing authorities on the relationship between fairness and natural justice. In Australia the term "procedural fairness" has normally been invoked in preference to "natural justice": *Kioa v West* (1985) 159 C.L.R. 550 at 583, although the Australian Administrative Decisions (Judicial Review) Act 1977 ss.5(1)(a) and 6(1)(a) prescribe natural justice as a ground of review. The applicability and content of natural justice under the Act are, however, the same as at common law. *Kioa* (1985) 159 C.L.R. 550 at 576 and 583–584.

[208] See *Woolcock v The Secretary of State for Communities and Local Government* [2018] EWHC 17 (Admin) at [50] ("[i]n making a decision, the relevant public body must adopt the minimum standards of procedural fairness imposed by the common law, as now reinforced by the procedural guarantees deriving from the European Convention on Human Rights".

[209] *Singh v Minister of Employment and Immigration* [1985] 1 S.C.R. 177. For a general discussion, see D. Mullan and D. Harrington, "The Charter and Administrative Decision-Making" (2002) 27 Queen's L.J. 879. Section 7 has, for example, had a particular influence on the question of a right to legal representation: *Howard v Presiding Officer of Inmate Disciplinary Court of Stony Mountain Institution* (1985) 19 D.L.R. (4th) 502. Where s.7 of the Charter or some other constitutional protection is not engaged, the common law duty to provide procedural fairness in Canada may still be overridden by statute: *Ocean Port Hotel Ltd v British Columbia (General Manager, Liquor and Control Licensing Branch)* [2001] 2 S.C.R. 781.

[210] PAJA s.3.

[211] PAJA s.4; see *Earthlife Africa (Cape Town v Director-General: Department of Environmental Affairs and Tourism and Another* 2005 (3) S.A. 156, C; *Chairpersons' Association v Minister of Arts*

in nature and involves notice and an opportunity to be heard. In the latter context it may entail recourse to (essentially voluntary) public inquiries or notice and comment procedures.

Apart from the PAJA, the principle of legality (an aspect of the rule of law) imposes a basic requirement of rationality on every exercise of public power. That requirement of rationality has, in turn, been held to demand procedural fairness in appropriate cases.[212] As a result of these important developments, some non-administrative action (or action not shown to be administrative action) may nevertheless be held to standards of procedural fairness ordinarily associated with the PAJA. Furthermore, in *Minister of Defence and Military Veterans v Motau*, the Constitutional Court seemed to acknowledge that procedural fairness could also be a "stand-alone requirement under the principle of legality", namely, an independent of rationality.[213]

- In Ireland, as already noted, reference is made to natural and constitutional justice. It is not usually necessary to draw sharp distinctions between the two concepts, although the former remains a common law rebuttable doctrine, while the latter is regarded as implicit in the Constitution.[214] Although references to natural and constitutional justice are still predominant, the courts also refer to "the requirement that there be due fairness of procedures".[215]

6-054   In terms of entitlement to procedural fairness, different trends are to be noted. Generally, the former distinction between quasi-judicial and administrative acts has now been abandoned,[216] and in India, for example, the distinction has been "gradu-

---

and Culture and Others 2006 (2) S.A. 32 T; *Minister of Health v New Clicks South Africa (Pty) Ltd* 2006 (2) S.A. 311, CC.

[212] *Albutt v Centre for the Study of Violence and Reconciliation* 2010 (3) S.A. 293, CC, and see also for instance *Minister of Home Affairs v Somali Association of South Africa* 2015 (3) S.A. 545, SCA, as well as the giving of reasons (in *Judicial Service Commission v Cape Bar Council* 2013 (1) S.A. 170, SCA.

[213] *Minister of Defence and Military Veterans v Motau* 2014 (5) S.A. 69, CC at [81].

[214] Hogan and Morgan, *Administrative Law in Ireland* (2010) para.12-52, citing *Re Haughey* [1971] I.R. 217; *Glover v BLN Ltd* [1973] I.R. 388; *Kiely v Minister for Social Welfare (No.2)* [1977] I.R. 267; *Garvey v Ireland* [1981] I.R. 75.

[215] See, e.g. *BFO v The Governor of Dóchas Centre* [2003] IEHC 622; [2005] 2 I.R. 1 at 26.

[216] *Canada Nicholson v Haldimand-Norfolk Regional Board of Commissioners of Police* [1979] 1 S.C.R. 311 (probationary constable entitled to procedural fairness before being let go, even though the statutory rules prescribing a hearing before dismissal did not apply to a power to dispense with services of a probationer); and *Elliott v Burin Peninsula School Board District 7* (1998) 161 D.L.R. (4th) 112, 119. But see *Dunsmuir* [2008] 1 S.C.R. 190 at [102]–[103] (holding that a civil servant, holding office "at pleasure" but also pursuant to contract, was not entitled to public law procedural fairness and commenting that dismissing an office holder and contractual employee both involved the private employer "merely exercising its private law rights as an employer"). But on the continuing survival of a category of "legislative" decisions, see *Cardinal v Kent Institution* (1985) 24 D.L.R. (4th) 44 at [14] (Le Dain J): "There is as a general common law principle a duty of procedural fairness lying on every public authority making an administrative decision which is not of a legislative nature and affects the rights, privileges or interests of an individual". In Australia, the old common law restriction of the duty to observe the requirements of procedural fairness to decisions of a judicial character was discarded in *Banks v Transport Regulation Board* (1968) 119 C.L.R. 222. The full force of this shift was not realised until much later when the High Court cast the requirements of fairness over a widening range of administrative decisions. In the key case of *Kioa v West* (1985) 159 C.L.R. 550 at 616–617, Brennan J stressed that the degree to which a decision might affect a person was much more important than the status of the decision-maker or any label (such as right, benefit, or privilege) that might attach to the interest claimed. This approach signalled the inevitable abolition of distinctions between rights and privileges and also between application and deprivation cases. The High Court unanimously rejected an attempt to revive the application/deprivation

ally obliterated".[217] Even an administrative order with what have been described as "civil consequences"[218] must be consistent with the requirements of natural justice[219]; and the phrase "civil consequences" "encompasses infraction of not merely property or personal rights but of civil liberties, material deprivations and non pecuniary damages. In its wide umbrella comes everything that affects a citizen in his civil life".[220] However, the applicability of these principles would also depend on the express language and the basic scheme of the provision conferring the power, the nature of the power conferred, the purpose for which the power is conferred and the effect of that power.[221]

Meanwhile, in New Zealand, s.27(1) of the New Zealand Bill of Rights Act 1990, states that natural justice applies to determinations in respect of rights, obligations and interests. While this clearly rejects the "right"-"privilege" distinction discussed above,[222] the courts have generally followed the intent of the drafters that the requirements of natural justice should only be applied by courts in the individuated decision-making paradigm.[223] Moreover, courts have often regarded "legislative" decisions,[224] or to use the term used more frequently now, "decisions affecting many"[225] as not being subject to the requirements of procedural fairness. In Ireland, the issue of what triggers an entitlement to procedural fairness has received little judicial attention, although the law has generally moved towards abolishing arbitrary categorisations such as the quasi-judicial/judicial distinction.[226] The Supreme Court has observed that:

6-055

---

distinction, holding that any possible difference between the conferral or revocation of rights *"proceeds from too narrow a conception of the circumstances in which an obligation to afford procedural fairness might arise"*: *Plaintiff M61E/2010 v Commonwealth* (the "Offshore Processing case") (2010) 243 C.L.R. 319, 353. See also *Plaintiff S10/2011Kaur v Minister for Immigration and Citizenship* (2012) 246 C.L.R. 636 at 658–659. In New Zealand, see *Fowler & Roderique Ltd v A-G* [1987] 2 N.Z.L.R. 56; *Lower Hutt City Council v Bank* [1974] 1 N.Z.L.R.; and *Daganayasi v Minister of Immigration* [1980] N.Z.L.R. 130 at 141 (Cooke J noting that "the requirements of natural justice vary with the power that is exercised and the circumstances. In their broadest sense, they are not limited to occasions which might be labelled judicial or quasi-judicial").

[217] *A.K. Kraipak v Union of India* (1969) 2 S.C.C. 262 at 268, 269.

[218] *SL Kapoor v Jagmohan A.I.R.* 1981 A.C. 136 at 140.

[219] *Rajesh Kumar v Dy CIT* 2007 (2) S.C.C. 181 at 192, 193, [96].

[220] *Canara Bank v V.K. Awasthy* (2005) 6 S.C.C. 321 Pa. 14 (cited with approval in *Sahara India (firm) v CIT* (2008) 14 SCC 151 at 163).

[221] *Canara Bank* (2005) 6 S.C.C 321 at [14] (cited with approval in *Sahara India (firm) v CIT* (2008) 14 S.C.C. 151 at 163).

[222] See 6-029.

[223] *Chisholm v Auckland City Council* [2005] N.Z.A.R. 661 at [32] (Tipping J, CA); *Henderson v Director, Land Transport Safety Authority* [2006] N.Z.A.R. 629 at [70]–[71]; *Air Nelson Ltd v Minister of Transport* [2007] N.Z.A.R. 266, HC. At common law, the courts had rejected the judicial-administrative distinctions: see fn.200. There has, however, been some discussion in the courts as to whether s.27 is narrower in its scope than the common law. This has arisen from comments of the Supreme Court in the case of *Taunoa v Attorney General* [2007] NZSC 70; [2008] 1 N.Z.L.R. 429 at [221] (to the effect that visits by a superintendent and medical officer to prisoners did not engage s.27(1) because they did not involve "an adjudicative function"). The comments have subsequently been interpreted by the Court of Appeal not to indicate that s.27(1) is narrower than the common law: *Combined Beneficiaries Union Incorporated v Auckland City COGS Committee* [2009] 2 N.Z.L.R. 56 at [38] (see also [15], where it is noted that the term "determination" in s.27(1) is "open-ended" and [50] where it is held that the content of s.27(1) is "coincident with that at common law").

[224] *Attorney General of Canada v Inuit Tapirisat of Canada* [1980] 2 S.C.R. 735; G. Carter, "Procedural Fairness in Legislative Functions: The End of Judicial Abstinence?" (2003) 53 U.T.L.J. 217.

[225] PAJA s.4.

[226] See generally the discussion in Hogan and Morgan, *Administrative Law in Ireland* (2010) at paras 14-171–14-179; de Blacam, *Judicial Review* (2017) at para.4.08 (noting that the "courts nowadays tend to say that judicial review is available as a remedy where the decision in question has a 'public

"The overarching principle is that persons affected by administrative decisions should have access to justice, that they should have the right to seek the protection of the courts in order to see that the rule of law has been observed, that fair procedures have been applied and that their rights are not unfairly infringed".[227]

6-056   As for the content of procedural fairness, as a general observation, the importance of flexibility in this context has been widely recognised[228]; and this flexibility has even survived statutory codification—albeit that any given statutory scheme will provide the most important starting point in determining the procedure to be followed.[229] In South Africa, s.3(2) of the PAJA even stipulates that a "fair administrative procedure depends on the circumstances of each case". Section 3 of the PAJA divides the demands of fairness in individual cases into five minimum requirements and three discretionary cases. However, the Constitutional Court has held that in appropriate cases even the minimum requirements may not be enforced—and that this is so even when the "departures" provision, s.3(4), is not explicitly invoked.[230] This approach allows for even greater flexibility, though it obviously detracts from the certainty promised by a statutory list of mandatory

---

element'").

[227] *Mallak v Minister for Justice, Equality and Law Reform* [2012] IESC 59 at [52]. It seems from the context that Fennelly J was referring here both to the application of natural justice and to that of constitutional justice. In an earlier case, certain obiter comments of the Supreme Court had suggested that for constitutional justice to be engaged, it may be necessary to demonstrate that the decision had an effect on a constitutional right: *Dellway Investments v NAMA* [2011] IESC 13; [2012] 4 I.R. 1. Opposing views are expressed by different judges in the case and the precise implications of the comments are unclear. It is suggested here that comments made suggesting a necessity to demonstrate an effect on a constitutional right before an entitlement to constitutional justice is engaged should be treated with caution. Not only were the relevant comments obiter, but the view expressed by Hardiman J, in favour of a freestanding entitlement to constitutional justice is preferable; it is more compatible with this statement of Fennelly J in the *Mallak* case and more consistent with developments elsewhere.

[228] In Australia see, e.g. *Kioa v West* (1985) 159 C.L.R. 550, 612 (where Brennan J stated that natural justice had a flexible "chameleon-like quality"); and *RCB v Forrest* (2012) 247 C.L.R. 304 at 32 where five members of the High Court stated that the content of fairness "is dependent upon the nature of the proceedings and the person claiming its benefit." The High Court has also stressed that, unless there is sufficient attention to the statutory context in which decisions are made, consideration of the content of natural justice "proceeds at too high a level of abstraction": *SZBEL v Minister for Immigration and Multicultural and Indigenous Affairs* (2006) 228 C.L.R. 152 at 161. Likewise, in Ireland, see *Ó Ceallaigh v An Bord Altranais* [2000] 4 I.R. 54 at 92 (Barron J noting that "[w]hat is fair is dependent upon a number of factors"); *International Fishing Vessels Ltd v Minister for the Marine (No 2)* [1991] 2 I.R. 93 at 102 (McCarthy J stating that "[n]either natural justice nor constitutional justice requires perfect or the best possible justice; it requires reasonable fairness in all the circumstances"). In Canada see *Knight v Indian Head School Division No.19* (1990) 69 D.L.R. (4th) 489 at 510 (L'Heureux-Dubé J noting that the concept of procedural fairness is "eminently variable"); *Baker v Canada (Minister of Citizenship and Immigration)* [1999] 2 S.C.R. 817 (L'Heureux-Dubé J noting that "the more important the decision is to the lives of those affected and the greater its impact is on that person or persons the more stringent the procedural protections that will be mandated"); and *Martineau v Matsqui Institution Disciplinary Board* [1980] 1 S.C.R. 602 at [61]–[63].

[229] *Waitemata County v Local Government Commission* [1964] N.Z.L.R. 689; *French v Law Society of Upper Canada* [1975] 2 S.C.R. 767 at 783–786; *Salemi v McKellar (No.2)* (1977) 137 C.L.R. 396; *Bourke v State Services Commission* [1978] 1 N.Z.L.R. 633 at 644–646; *CREEDNZ Inc v Governor General* [1981] 1 N.Z.L.R. 172 at 177–178. cf., however, *Re Cardinal and Board of Commissioners of Police of the City of Cornwall* (1974) 42 D.L.R. (3rd) 323. In the United States the Supreme Court, in a landmark case, *Vermont Yankee Nuclear Power Corp v Natural Resources Defense Council, Inc* 435 U.S. (1978) 519 at 543 it was held that absent constitutional constraints or extremely compelling circumstances, courts may not force agencies to utilise rulemaking procedures beyond those prescribed in the Administrative Procedure Act 1946 or other statutory or constitutional provisions.

[230] *Joseph v City of Johannesburg* 2010 (4) S.A. 55, CC at [57]–[59]. PAJA s.3(4) provides that an

requirements. As to the requirements themselves, the courts have drawn freely on the common law in developing their jurisprudence on the meaning and content of the various ingredients of fairness.[231]

In India, given the courts' presumption that Parliament did not intend to contravene fundamental rights,[232] the principle of *audi alteram partem* has regularly been implied into statutory schemes.[233] The principles of procedural fairness generally and natural justice in particular are now recognised as dimensions of the constitutional right to equality.[234] Thus, the Supreme Court read a requirement to comply with the principles of natural justice into a rule providing for recovery of a penalty and interest for an alleged violation of an indemnity bond, so as to render the rule compliant with the principles of equality and non-arbitrariness under art.14 of the Constitution.[235]   **6-057**

Likewise, in India, it has been held that a delegated legislative function may require consideration of the viewpoint of those affected by the exercise of power,[236] while if a ban order is to be introduced, those affected should have the opportunity of meeting the facts.[237] More generally, in the absence of a statutory requirement, pre-existing practice or policy, or a representation creating a legitimate expectation that consultation will be conducted, the circumstances in which a common law duty to consult will arise are likely to remain limited.   **6-058**

The Australian High Court has engaged in a long running battle with the legislature in attempts to codify the requirements of procedural fairness, and therefore preclude the implication of further hearing requirements at common law. The High Court has long accepted that the statutory context of any decision is a crucial source of influence to determine the requirements of fairness.[238] The court initially read down procedural codes for the hearings conducted by migration tribunals despite the clear implication that the code was intended to be exhaustive.[239] The court then interpreted specific procedural requirements within those schemes rigidly, sometimes requiring literal compliance on pain of invalidity.[240] The High Court eventually accepted that if drafted with sufficient clarity, exhaustive codes   **6-059**

---

administrator may depart from any of the minimum requirements if it is reasonable and justifiable in the circumstances, having regard to a list of factors.

[231] See, e.g. *Minister of Health v New Clicks South Africa (Pty) Ltd* 2006 (2) S.A. 311, CC at [147]; *Bato Star Fishing (Pty) Ltd v Minister of Environmental Affairs* 2004 (4) S.A. 490, CC at [45]; *Premier, Mpumalanga v Executive Committee, Association of State-Aided Schools, Eastern Transvaal* 1999 (2) S.A. 91, CC at [39]; *President of the Republic of South Africa v South African Rugby Football Union* 2000 (1) S.A. 1, CC at [219].

[232] *IR Coelho v State of TN* 2006 (8) S.C.C. 212 at 240, 241; *Sahara India (firm)* (2008) 14 S.C.C. 151.

[233] See, e.g. See, for e.g. *Manohar v State of Maharashtra* (2012) 13 S.C.C. 14 at 23, *Gorkha Security Services v Government (NCT of Delhi)* (2014) 9 S.C.C. 105 at 120–122.

[234] *Anita Kushwaha v Pushap Sudan* (2016) 8 S.C.C. 509 at 529, 530.

[235] *Kesar Enterprises v Uttar Pradesh* (2011) 13 S.C.C. 733 at [32]–[36].

[236] *Cellular Operators Association of India v Union of India* (2016) 7 S.C.C. 703 at 751, 759 (where the court encouraged Parliament to frame legislation "by which all subordinate legislation is subject to a transparent process by which due consultations with all stakeholders are held, and the rule or regulation making power is exercised after due consideration of all stakeholders' submissions, together with an explanatory memorandum which broadly takes into account what they have said and the reasons for agreeing or disagreeing with them.")

[237] *Godawat Pan Masala Products IP Ltd v Union of India* (2004) 7 S.C.C. 68 at 105. For an example of consultation of the judiciary in matters relating to the policies that impinge on the administration of justice, see: *Brij Mohan Lal v Union of India* (2012) 6 S.C.C. 502 at 572.

[238] *National Companies and Securities Commission v News Corp Ltd* (1984) 156 C.L.R. 313–314, 326; *SZBEL v Minister for Immigration and Multicultural and Indigenous Affairs* (2006) 228 C.L.R. 152, 161.

[239] *Re Minister for Immigration and Multicultural Affairs; Ex p. Miah* (2001) 206 C.L.R. 57.

[240] *SAAP v Minister for Immigration and Multicultural and Indigenous Affairs* (2005) 228 C.L.R. 294 at 321–322, 345–356, 353–354; *SZFDE v Minister for Immigration and Citizenship* (2007) 232

could and did displace common law hearing requirements.[241] Beyond migration decision making, the flexibility of the common law remains. In the US, the extent of due process protection required is usually determined by a number of factors: first, the private interest that will be affected by the official action; second, the risk of an erroneous deprivation of such interest through the procedures used, and the probable value, if any, of additional or substitute procedural safeguards; and finally, the government's interest, including the function involved and the fiscal and administrative burdens that the additional or substantive procedural requirement would entail.[242] However, US federal courts also frequently apply a more general test of assessing what is "reasonable" in the circumstances.[243] In Canada, five non-exhaustive factors have been identified as relevant to determining the content of procedural fairness: the nature of the decision being made and the process followed in making that decision; the nature of the statutory scheme and the terms of the statute pursuant to which the body operates; the importance of the decision to the individual affected (the more important the decision is to the lives of those affected and the greater its impact on that person or persons, the more stringent the procedural protections that will be mandated); the legitimate expectation of the person challenging the decision; and the choice of procedure made by the decision-maker itself when the statute leaves to the decision-maker the ability to choose its own procedures.[244]

6-060
More specifically, the importance of prior notice has been universally accepted.[245] It has been equally widely accepted that an oral hearing will not always be required to comply with a duty to act fairly,[246] and various factors have been identified regarding when an oral hearing will be necessary.[247] The importance in certain circumstances of being able to call and cross-examine witnesses and to legal

---

C.L.R. 189 at 201, 205–206. Some requirements were not interpreted rigidly: *Minister for Immigration and Citizenship v SZIZO* (2009) 238 C.L.R. 627.

[241] *Saeed v Minister for Immigration and Citizenship* (2010) 214 C.L.R. 252, though this case also made clear that the limits of such codes will be enforced strictly by the courts.

[242] *Mathews v Eldridge* 424 U.S. 319 (1976) at 335.

[243] *Mullane v Central Hanover Bank & Trust Co* 339 U.S. 306 (1950) at 339 (stating that notice must be "reasonably calculated, under all the circumstances, to apprise interested parties of the pendency of the action and afford them an opportunity to present their objections"). See also *Dusenbery v United States*, 534 U.S. 161 (2002) at 167–168.

[244] *Baker* [1999] 2 S.C.R. 817 (L'Heureux-Dubé J); see also *The Board of Education of the Indian Head School Division No.19 of Saskatchewan v Knight* [1990] 1 S.C.R. 653 at [28].

[245] See 7-044 and e.g. *Murdoch v New Zealand Milk Board* [1982] N.Z.L.R. 108; *Birss v Secretary of State for Justice* [1984] 1 N.Z.L.R. 513 (notice required where suspension under consideration); *Gage v Attorney General for Ontario* (1992) 90 D.L.R. (4th) 537 at 552 (stating that "notice is an essential component of natural justice" and that it will be a mixed question of fact and law in each case whether the notice given is adequate); *TV3 v Independent Radio and television Commission* [1994] 2 I.R. 439. Australian courts increasingly judge the adequacy of notice at common law by a contextual assessment of the issues, including the complexity of the applicable law and relevant facts, the ability of the person affected to prepare for any hearing, and whether any earlier opportunities for participation have been provided: *Ogawa v Minister for Immigration and Citizenship* (2011) 199 F.C.R. 51 at 58; *Dunghutti Elders Council (Aboriginal Corporation) RNTBC v Registrar of Aboriginal and Torres Strait Islander Corporations* (2011) 195 F.C.R. 318 at 367–368.

[246] See Ch.7. In Canada, even where the word "hearing" is used in statute, which "almost always" indicates an oral hearing, written representations may suffice on occasion: *Re Attorney General of Manitoba and National Energy Board* (1974) 48 D.L.R. 73 at 89; see also *US v Florida East Coat Rly Co* 410 U.S. 224 (1973); *Zhang de Yong v Minister for Immigration* (1993) 118 A.L.R. 165, 187. In Australia, an oral hearing is only one of many procedural benefits that may be required in the circumstances of each case. As the point depends heavily on context, there is no fixed rule that fairness will always require an oral hearing: *Minister for Immigration and Border Protection v WZARH* (2015) 256 C.L.R. 326 at 336, 343.

[247] See 7-062. It has been suggested in Canada that an oral hearing is required where there is threat to

representation at oral hearings has been recognised; but these rights are certainly not absolute and whether they are necessary to ensure procedural fairness depends on the circumstances.[248]

While the duty to consult has been established in the United States since the introduction of notice and comment rule-making procedures in the Administrative Procedure Act 1946,[249] it has been increasing in importance across other jurisdictions.[250] In Australia several jurisdictions have included a requirement for public notice and comment for the making of delegated legislation. Most of the statutes that require such public participation in rule making also expressly provide that a failure to do so does not affect the validity of those rules.[251] These limited legislative schemes for public notice and comment might explain the cautious approach of Australian courts, which have not adopted any wide ranging common law duty of consultation.[252] **6-061**

Meanwhile, in South Africa, as noted above, s.4 of the PAJA makes provision for public inquiries, notice and comment proceedings and other forms of public participation. Likewise, in India, it has been held that a delegated legislative function may require consideration of the viewpoint of those affected by the exercise of power,[253] while if a ban order is to be introduced, those affected should have the opportunity of meeting the facts.[254] More generally, in the absence of a statutory requirement, pre-existing practice or policy, or a representation creating a legitimate expectation that consultation will be conducted, the circumstances in which a common law duty to consult will arise are likely to remain limited. **6-062**

The absence of an over-arching common law duty on administrative decision- **6-063**

---

life or liberty (*Singh* [1985] 1 S.C.R. 177; where there is a loss of an existing right or privilege (*Maple Ridge (District) v Thornhill Aggregates Ltd* (1998) 162 D.L.R. 203 at 217); or where there is a "serious issue of credibility" (*Khan v University of Ottawa* (1997) 148 D.L.R. (4th) 577. The variable content of fairness in Australia means the question of whether the common law requires an oral hearing depends on the "practical requirements" of fairness in the case at hand: *Minister for Immigration and Border Protection v WZARH* (2015) 256 C.L.R. 326 at 336. Oral hearings are usually required when the issues cannot be fully and fairly decided in writing, such as a dispute about the credibility or personal characteristics of a party: *Hill v Green* (1999) 48 N.S.W.L.R. 161 at 171 and 193. In India, where issues are complex or technical, fairness may demand a hearing: *Travancore Rayons v India A.I.R.* 1971 S.C. 862.

[248] See, e.g. *Innisfil v Township of Vespra* [1981] 2 S.C.R. 145 at 166; *Minister for Immigration and Border Protection v WZARH* (2015) 256 C.L.R. 326 at 336, 343; *Badger v Whangarei Commission of Inquiry* [1985] 2 N.Z.L.R. 688 at 697. In Canada, the right to legal representation has been considered important where a penalty is at stake (*Re Husted and Ridley* (1981) 58 C.C.C. (2nd) 156; *Howard v Presiding Office of Inmate Disciplinary Court of Stony Mountain Institution* (1985) 19 D.L.R. 502) and in "factual situations which are closer or analogous to criminal proceeding" (*Dehghani v Canada* (1993) 101 D.L.R. (4th) 654).

[249] 5 U.S.C. §553. For discussion, see M. Shapiro "Trans-Atlantic: Harlow Revisited" in P. Craig and R. Rawlings (eds) *Law and Administration in Europe: Essays in Honour of Carol Harlow* (2003), Ch.12. See also T. Ziamou "Alternative Modes of Administrative Action: Negotiated Rule-Making in the United States, Germany and Britain" (2000) 6 Eur. P. L. 45; P. Cane *Administrative Law*, 4th edn (2011).

[250] See 7-054 for the position in this jurisdiction.

[251] Subordinate Legislation Act 1989 (NSW) s.9; Statutory Instruments Act 1992 (Qld) s.41; Subordinate Legislation Act 1992 (Tas) s.10; Legislation Act 2003 (Cth) s.19.

[252] M. Aronson, M. Groves and G. Weeks, *Judicial Review of Administrative Action and Government Liability*, 6th edn (2017) at paras 7.220–7.230.

[253] *State of Tamil Nadu v K Sabanayagam* [1998] (1) S.C.C. 318.

[254] *Godawat Pan Masala Products IP Ltd v Union of India* [2004] (7) S.C.C. 68 at 105 at [76]. For an example of consultation of the judiciary in matters relating to the policies that impinge on the administration of justice, see: *Brij Mohan Lal v Union of India* (2012) 6 S.C.C. 502 at [192].

makers to give reasons[255] continues to cause strain, and the absence of a duty is increasingly superseded by a growing number of statutory requirements of reason-giving, of greater or less generality.[256] For example, in South Africa, the omission of the common law has largely been overtaken by s.33(2) of the 1996 Constitution, which confers a right to written reasons for administrative action, and by s.5 of the PAJA, which gives effect to this right by means of a mechanism for request-ing reasons.[257] However, more limited statutory interventions can have the consequence of unevenness in coverage. As for the case law, individual judges from

---

[255] Although see *Baker* [1999] 2 S.C.R. 817; *Suresh v Canada (Minister of Citizenship and Immigration* (2002) 208 D.L.R. (4th) 1; *R. v Sheppard* (2002) 210 D.L.R. (4th) 608; M. Liston, "'Alert, alive and sensitive': Baker, the Duty to Give Reasons, and the Ethos of Justification in Canadian Public Law" in D. Dyzenhaus (ed), *The Unity of Public Law* (2004), p.113; D. Dyzenhaus and E. Fox-Decent, "Rethinking the Process/Substance Distinction: Baker v Canada" (2001) 51 U.T.L.J. 193. See also *R. v Sheppard* [2002] 1 S.C.R. 869 (trial judges); *R. v M* [2008] 3 S.C.R. 3 at [14], [19]–[20] (criminal trial judges, although the trial judge need not expound on matters that are well-settled, uncontroversial, understood and accepted by the parties, nor detail his or her finding on each piece of evidence, so long as the findings linking the evidence to the verdict can be logically discerned). For a discussion of the rationale for a duty to give reasons and the sufficiency of reasons, see 7-088. See also *Dunsmuir* 2008 SCC 9; [2008] 1 S.C.R. 190 at [47] (the Supreme Court noting that reasonableness is concerned mostly with the existence of "justification, transparency and intel-ligibility within the decision-making process"). In Ireland, it appears the law is extremely close to recognising a general duty to provide reasons, with reasons seemingly only not required where they are obvious and the lack of them does not preclude effective judicial review: *Mallak* [2012] IESC 59 at [66]. It has also been observed that in the developing jurisprudence of the Irish courts, it must be unusual for a decision-maker to be permitted to refuse and at the very least, the decision-maker must be able to justify the refusal: [74]. Courts had already imposed a duty to provide reasons, at least where the relevant decision was subject to appeal or review: see, e.g. *State (Daly) v Minister for Agriculture* [1987] I.R. 165 at 172; *International Fishing Vessels Ltd v Minister for the Marine* [1989] I.R. 149 at 155–156. In the *Mallak* judgment, the Supreme Court quashed a naturalisation decision—which pursuant to the statutory regime fell within the "absolute discretion" of the Minister—on the basis of a failure to provide reasons: *Mallak* [2012] IESC 59 (Fennelly J observ-ing at [67] "[s]everal converging legal sources strongly suggest an emerging commonly held view that persons affected by administrative decisions have a right to know the reasons on which they are based, in short to understand them"; see also [66]). Where rights are affected, the courts have gone further and it has been held that it can no longer be seriously doubted that administrative bodies have a duty to give reasons: *Deehan v State Examinations Commission* [2016] IEHC 213 at [15].

[256] See, e.g. s.23 of the Official Information Act 1982 (NZ) (although s.2(6) excludes from the cover-age of the Act "[a] Court" and "[i]n relation to its judicial functions, a Tribunal"); and in Australia, Administrative Decisions (Judicial Review) Act 1977 (Cth) s.13 and Administrative Appeals Tribunal Act 1975 s.28. The Australian provisions create rights to gain reasons for decisions subject to tribunal or statutory judicial review. Information other than reasons can be obtained through the Freedom of Information Act 1982 (Cth), which creates a general right of access, subject to many exceptions, to information held by government agencies. On the requirement to give reasons, see 7-085. See also D Dyzenhaus and M. Taggart, "Reasoned Decisions and Legal Theory" in Ch.5 in D.E. Edlin (ed), *Common Law Theory* (2007). The Freedom of Information Act 1997 in Ireland has been described as causing a "transformation" in this context: Biehler, *Judicial Review of Administra-tive Action*, (2013), p.354. Section 18(1) of the Act imposes a general obligation on every head of a public body, on application of any person affected by any of its acts and with a material interest, to provide a written statement of reasons for the act.

[257] In South Africa, the request-driven mechanism in s.5 of the PAJA is the main source of the duty to give reasons for administrative action. However, it has also been held that reasons may have to be given for non-administrative action (or action not shown to be administrative action) by virtue of the principle of legality, precisely because it requires all exercises of public power to observe a basic requirement of rationality. In *Judicial Service Commission v Cape Bar Council* 2013 (1) S.A. 170, SCA at [45], the court held that the Judicial Service Commission was generally bound to give reasons for its decision not to recommend a candidate for judicial office (a piece of non-administrative action). If it were otherwise, the JSC would otherwise effectively be immune from a challenge based on rationality—for as Brand JA said, "it is difficult to think of a way to account for one's decisions other than to give reasons" (at [44]).

many jurisdictions have reviewed a requirement to give reasons favourably.[258] In New Zealand, although not imposing an enforceable general common law obligation to give reasons,[259] courts have indicated an openness to hearing argument on the issue,[260] and have imposed a duty to give reasons in particular contexts.[261] Recently, in *Ririnui v Landcorp Ltd*, a majority of the Supreme Court addressed the point from another angle, saying that a "duty of candour"[262] applying to those whose decisions are challenged by judicial review meant that a failure to explain the process may result in a court drawing an adverse inference from that stance.[263] In Australia, the High Court affirmed in *Osmond*[264] that there is no general common law requirement for administrative decision-makers to provide reasons for their decisions. *Osmond*'s survival owes much to the subsequent legislative developments which have greatly narrowed the need for change via the common law.[265] Most jurisdictions have schemes for tribunal review and statutory judicial review which include a right to reasons for the decisions to which those schemes apply. The most recent decision of the High Court about a statutory duty to give reasons stressed that the distinct nature of each such duty requires close attention to the relevant statute.[266] The broad scope of these statutory rights has limited the ability of the courts to explore the possibility raised in *Osmond*, that reasons might be required at common law in exceptional circumstances.[267] The occasional murmurings of lower courts have not tempted the High Court to revisit the issue at common law.[268]

In India, there has been significant judicial support for imposing a requirement   **6-064**

---

[258] See, e.g. *Re Northwestern Utilities and the City of Edmonton* (1978) 89 D.L.R. (3rd) 161 at 175 (Estey J); *Potter v New Zealand Milk Board* [1983] N.Z.L.R. 620 at 624.

[259] See, e.g. *Manakau Golf Club Inc v Shoye Venture Ltd* [2012] NZSC 109; *Lewis v Wilson & Horton Ltd* [2000] 3 N.Z.L.R. 546, CA (upholding the position taken in *R. v Awatere* [1982] 1 N.Z.L.R. 644, CA and *R. v MacPherson* [1982] N.Z.L.R. 650, CA (cases which had refused to establish a legally enforceable obligation on the part of inferior courts to give reasoned decisions).

[260] *Lewis* [2000] 3 N.Z.L.R. 546 at 567 (Elias CJ: "Whether it is time to say that as a general rule Judges must give reasons, is a matter this court would wish to consider at an early opportunity").

[261] *FT v JML* [2012] NZHC 1388 at [20] (Keane J observing: "Even when a decision is given and is then deemed to be valid, it will always be open to challenge if it unsupported by reasons").

[262] On the duty of candour, see *New Zealand Fishing Industry Association v Minister of Agriculture and Fisheries* [1988] 1 N.Z.L.R 544 (CA) and *Fiordland Venison Ltd v Minister of Agriculture and Fisheries* [1978] 2 N.Z.L.R. 341 (CA).

[263] *Ririnui v Landcorp Ltd* [2016] NZSC 62 at [105].

[264] *Public Service Board of New South Wales v Osmond* (1986) 159 C.L.R. 656. The law on judicial reasons is stricter but there is no unyielding constitutional rule that judges must always provide reasons. In *Wainohu v New South Wales* (2011) 243 C.L.R. 181 at 215, 227, 238 the High Court held that State legislation enabling courts to make orders without providing grounds or reasons for those orders was invalid because it was repugnant to the institutional integrity required of courts. The court also accepted that reasons were not required for all judicial decisions but gave little real guidance on such cases.

[265] See, e.g. Administrative Decisions (Judicial Review) Act 1977 (Cth) s.13; Administrative Appeals Tribunal Act 1975 (Cth) s.28. These and the similar statutes that exist in most states and territories enable reasons to be obtained without commencement of a substantive application.

[266] *Wingfoot Australia Partners Pty Ltd v Kocak* (2013) 252 C.L.R. 480 at 497–498.

[267] *Osmond* (1986) 159 C.L.R. 656 at 666–670.

[268] See, e.g. *L & B Linings Pty Ltd v WorkCover Authority of NSW* [2011] NSWSC 474 at [108] where the court stated that that there is "a growing expectation that persons affected by administrative conduct will know why it is they have been so affected". However, the High Court made a passing, perhaps approving, reference to the continued standing of *Osmond* in *Wingfoot Australia Partners Pty Ltd v Kocak* (2013) 252 C.L.R. 480 at 497-498.

to provide reasons[269] and the duty to give reasons has regularly been implied into statutory schemes.[270]

6-065   In cases where an order has an impact on the rights of parties, the insistence upon reasons being provided has been based upon the right of the affected party to know "why the decision has gone against him",[271] instil openness in government and in judicial administration, as well as facilitate judicial review.[272] On account of the constitutional status accorded to the principles of procedural fairness, giving reasons was held to be the "antithesis of arbitrariness" and the violation of this rule requiring reasons would be violate of art.14 of the Constitution.[273]

6-066   Finally, on the issue of exceptions to the availability of procedural fairness,[274] if the common law requirements of procedural fairness are to be excluded by statute, it is settled that legislatures must state that they are doing so explicitly.[275] In Australia, the duty to observe the requirements of procedural fairness can be excluded or limited by statute but the possibility of legislative exclusion remains much more one of theory than practice. The Australian High Court has held that the requirements of fairness are a "fundamental principle" that can only be removed by legislation expressed with "irresistible clearness."[276] That approach echoes the principle of legality and makes clear that common law requirements of fairness cannot be excluded by indirect means, such as the enactment of a procedural code,[277] or the inclusion of only limited statutory procedural rights.[278] Other interpretive principles adopted by the High Court can make statutory procedural codes counterproductive. The requirements of fairness have been accepted as a restraint or an implied precondition for the valid exercise of a statutory power.[279] Those principles enable legal error to be found where legislative procedures are not strictly

---

[269] *J. Ashoka v University of Agricultural Sciences* (2017) 2 S.C.C. 609 at 620, 621.

[270] See e.g. *Sham Lal v State of Punjab* (2013) 14 S.C.C. 393 at 404.

[271] *Ravi Yashwant Bhoir v Collector* (2012) 4 S.C.C. 407 at 431.

[272] *Kranti Associates v Masood Ahmed Khan* (2010) 9 S.C.C. 496 at 509–510.

[273] *B.A. Linga Reddy v Karnataka State Transport Authority* (2015) 4 S.C.C. 515. Although the case relates to the road transport schemes, in relation to which the power of the authority was considered to be quasi judicial, the judgment cites an earlier judgment which held that "… in a parliamentary democracy governed by the rule of law, any action, decision, or order of any statutory/public authority/functionary must be founded upon reasons stated in the order of staring from the record": *Krishnaswami v Union of India* (1992) 4 S.C.C. 605 at [47].

[274] See Ch.8.

[275] In Australia the rules of procedural fairness are regarded as fundamental requirements of the common law and therefore their exclusion by statute will normally require a clear expression of legislative intent. See *Kioa* (1985) 159 C.L.R. 550 at 585; *South Australia v O'Shea* (1987) 163 C.L.R. 378 at 415; *Re Minister for Multicultural Affairs; Ex p. Miah* (2001) 206 C.L.R. 57 (McHugh J), 102 (Kirby J) 114 (it was held that the Codes of Procedure relating to fair and efficient administrative decision making under the Migration Act 1958 (Cth) did not exclude common law natural justice). In response to the decision, the government amended the Act to the effect that the Codes of Procedure contained in the Act did constitute an exhaustive statement of the requirements of the natural justice rules. Even that formulation failed to exclude common law procedural fairness: *Saeed v Minister for Immigration and Citizenship* (2010) 241 C.L.R. 252. And see *Fraser v State Services Commission* [1984] 1 N.Z.L.R. 116 at 121 where Cooke J questioned whether the legislature could exclude the common law rules of natural justice even by express enactment. It must be noted of course that in Ireland, constitutional justice cannot be excluded by legislation (which is subordinate to it): see, e.g. *O'Brien v Bord na Mona* [1983] I.R. 255 at 270–271; *McCann v Monaghan District Court* [2009] IEHC 276; [2009] 4 I.R. 200 at 255–256.

[276] *Saeed v Minister for Immigration and Citizenship* (2010) 241 C.L.R. 252 at 259.

[277] *Re Minister for Immigration and Multicultural Affairs; Ex p. Miah* (2001) 206 C.L.R. 57. McHugh J held that the incorporation of words such as "code" in the legislation was insufficient to find a clear legislative intention to exclude the common law requirements of fairness".

[278] *Annetts v McCann* (1990) 170 C.L.R. 595.

[279] *Saeed v Minister for Immigration and Citizenship* (2010) 241 C.L.R. 252 at 258; *Plaintiff S10/ 2011 v Minister for Immigration and Citizenship* (2012) 246 C.L.R. 636 at 666.

observed, but do not prevent the implication of additional requirements of fairness at common law. The High Court has also accepted that natural justice may not be capable of application to discretionary powers that are exercised in circumstances where there is no real ability to accord the trappings of fairness.[280]

It has also been increasingly accepted that a procedurally fair appeal can cure an initial procedurally unfair procedure; although again, everything depends on the circumstances.[281]

6-067

---

[280] *CPCF v Minister for Immigration and Border Protection* (2015) 255 C.L.R. 514 at 558, 653. The powers in that case were ones that allowed naval and other officials to detain and transfer asylum seekers who were intercepted at sea to other locations. The unique regime within which the powers were exercised may have led to an equally unique finding by the High Court.

[281] *Slipper Island Resort Ltd v Number One Town and Country Planning Appeal Board* [1981] 1 N.Z.L.R. 143 at 145; *Twist* (1976) 136 C.L.R. 106; *Ainsworth v Criminal Justice Commission* (1992) 175 C.L.R.; *McNamara v Ontario Racing Commission* (1998) 164 D.L.R. (4th) 99.

CHAPTER 7

Procedural Fairness: Entitlement And Content

TABLE OF CONTENTS

SCOPE

This chapter examines, first, entitlement to procedural fairness. There are three **7-001** broad bases on which a public authority may owe a duty to exercise its functions in accordance with fair procedures: (a) where legislation imposes a duty to follow fair procedures[1]; (b) where the common law requires fair procedures to be followed in order to safeguard rights and interests[2]; and (c) since the Human Rights Act 1998, to meet the procedural requirements of Convention rights, most notably ECHR art.6 (in relation to determination of "civil rights and obligations" and "criminal charges")[3] and ECHR art.2 (right to life, in respect of investigations of deaths).[4] Entitlement may also arise from a legitimate expectation created by a

---

[1] See 7-011.
[2] See 7-017.
[3] See 7-032.
[4] See 7-037. Where other rights of the Convention are engaged, there may also be procedural requirements specific to the engagement of that particular right. For example, a discussion of the influence of ECHR art.5(4) on procedural requirements in the context of parole board hearings can be found

public authority's assurances or conduct, a possibility that we consider in Chapter 12.

7-002   Secondly, this chapter considers the *content* of fair procedures. There is a broad range of requirements, which vary according to the context in which the public function is exercised, including: (a) to give notice of a proposed decision before making it[5]; (b) to consult and receive written representations[6]; (c) to disclose information before a final decision is reached[7]; (d) to provide oral hearings,[8] at which (e) the person is offered legal representations or other assistance,[9] and (f) has the right to cross examine witnesses[10]; and (g) a right to be given reasons explaining why a decision or action was taken.[11] Public inquiries raise additional considerations,[12] while ECHR art.6 and art.2, in the situations to which they apply, impose further requirements.[13]

ENTITLEMENT TO PROCEDURAL FAIRNESS: OVERVIEW

From "natural justice" to "the duty to act fairly"

7-003   Procedural fairness, as we have seen, is no longer restricted by distinctions between "judicial" and "administrative" functions or between "rights" and "privileges".[14] This "heresy was scotched"[15] in *Ridge v Baldwin*.[16] The term "natural justice" has largely been replaced by a general duty to act fairly, which is a key element of procedural propriety.[17] On occasion, the term "due process" has also been invoked.[18] Whichever term is used, the entitlement to fair procedures no longer depends upon the adjudicative analogy, nor whether the authority is required or

---

in *Re Reilly's Application for Judicial Review* [2013] UKSC 61; [2013] 3 W.L.R. 1020 at [54]–[63].

5   See 7-044.
6   See 7-054.
7   See 7-060.
8   See 7-065.
9   See 7-076.
10   See 7-084.
11   See 7-088.
12   See 7-117.
13   See 7-120 and 7-130.
14   See 6-029.
15   *R. v Gaming Board for Great Britain Ex p. Benaim and Khaida* [1970] 2 Q.B. 417 at 430 (Denning MR).
16   *Ridge v Baldwin* [1964] A.C. 40.
17   See 6-045. In *O'Reilly v Mackman* [1983] 2 A.C. 237 at 275 (Lord Diplock: the rules of natural justice "mean no more than the duty to act fairly ... and I prefer so to put it"). See also *Odelola v Secretary of State for the Home Department* [2009] UKHL 25; [2009] 1 W.L.R. 1230 at [33] ("simple fairness"). *Re Reilly's Application* [2013] UKSC 61; [2013] 3 W.L.R. 1020 at [2], [65]–[71] (reference to "the common law duty to act fairly"); *R. (on the application of L) v West London Mental Health NHS* [2014] EWCA Civ 47; (2014) 158(6) S.J.L.B. 37 at [67] ("the common-law principles of natural justice or fairness"). See also *Secretary of State for Communities and Local Government v Hopkins Developments* [2014] EWCA Civ 470 at [85] ("it does not generally matter whether what is at issue is characterised as 'natural justice' or 'procedural fairness'").
18   *R. v Secretary of State for the Home Department Ex p. Hindley* [2000] Q.B. 152 at 163-164 (Lord Woolf MR); *R. v Camden LBC Ex p. Paddock* [1995] C.O.D. 130; *Flannery v Halifax Estate Agencies Ltd* [2000] 1 W.L.R. 377 at 381; *R. (on the application of Murungaru) v Secretary of State for the Home Department* [2008] EWCA Civ 1015; [2009] I.N.L.R. 180 at [39] ("a common law due process claim").

empowered to decide matters analogous to a legal action between two parties.[19] The law has moved on; the courts are now able to insist upon some degree of participation in reaching most official decisions by those whom the decisions will affect in widely different situations, subject only to well-established exceptions.[20] Procedural fairness is therefore not these days rationed at its source, blocked at the outset on the ground of a decision being administrative rather than judicial, or governing a privilege rather than a right. It may, in exceptional situations, be diverted during the course of its flow where special circumstances, such as national security excuse a right to a fair hearing.[21] And the breadth of the flow will depend upon the circumstances surrounding the decision. As we will see, some decisions require full adjudicative-type hearings, others only narrowly permit the mere right to make representations.[22] Increasing resort to the open-textured standard of fairness is not, though, without its drawbacks. There is a point at which the benefits of its flexible application may be outweighed by the costs of uncertainty.[23] The courts are perhaps creating "a surrogate political process to ensure the fair representation of a wide range of affected interests in the administrative process".[24] Doubts have been expressed as to whether the courts are institutionally equipped for such tasks,[25] and whether the unconstrained expansion of participation might paralyse effective administration.[26]

Attempts to categorise boundaries of procedural fairness

In response to these doubts, various attempts have been made to devise categories or criteria of relative precision to determine the bounds of procedural fairness. In

7-004

---

[19] See 6-045.

[20] *R. v Secretary of State for the Environment Ex p. Kirkstall Valley Campaign Ltd* [1996] 3 All E.R. 304 at 324 (Sedley J noting: "Since *Ridge v Baldwin*, although not without occasional deviations, public law has returned to the broad highway of due process across the full range of justiciable decision-making"). See also *R. (on the application of LH) v Shropshire Council* [2014] EWCA Civ 404; [2014] P.T.S.R. 1052 at [28] ("the duty to consult will arise when a person has an interest which the law decides is one which is to be protected by procedural fairness").

[21] See 8-006.

[22] See 7-040.

[23] See, e.g. *L* [2014] EWCA Civ 47; (2014) 158(6) S.J.L.B. 37 at [68], [69], [72] (Beatson LJ expressing concern that the emphasis on flexibility could lead to an inappropriate drawing together of the concepts of procedural and substantive fairness and undue uncertainty).

[24] R. Stewart, "The Reformation of American Administrative Law" (1975) 88 Harv. L.R. 1669, 1670. See also *L* [2014] EWCA Civ 47; (2014) 158(6) S.J.L.B. 37 (in which the Court of Appeal overturned the procedural requirements specified by the lower court for the decisions of managers of a medium security hospital contemplating referring a detainee to high security conditions as the requirements turned what was largely a clinical decision into an inappropriately adversarial process which went beyond what fairness required).

[25] M. Loughlin "Procedural Fairness: A Study of the Crisis in Administrative Law Theory" (1978) 28 U.T.L.J. 215; R. A. MacDonald "Judicial Review and Procedural Fairness in Administrative Law" (1980) 25 McGill L.J. 520 and (1980) 26 McGill L.J. 1 where the development of the duty to act fairly is regarded as a major theoretical departure in the law of procedural review. Contrast P. Craig, *Administrative Law*, 8th edn (2016), paras 12-009–12-010. And for a judicial recognition of the limited nature of the courts' role, see *R. v Brent LBC Ex p. Gunning* (1985) 84 L.G.R. 168 at 180.

[26] See, e.g. Sir R. Scott, "Procedures at Inquiries: The Duty to be Fair" (1995) 111 L.Q.R. 596; B. Hadfield, "R. v Lord Saville of Newdigate Ex p. Anonymous Soldiers: What is the Purpose of a Tribunal of Inquiry?" [2003] P.L. 663; Blom-Cooper, "Tribunals under Inquiry" [2000] P.L. 1; L. Blom-Cooper, "Public Interest in Public Inquiries" [2003] P.L. 578; C Bourne "Public Inquiries and Parallel Proceedings" [2012] *Encyclopedia of Local Government Law*: Bulletin, Nov, 1; L. Blom-Cooper, "What went wrong on Bloody Sunday: a critique of the Saville Inquiry" [2010] P.L. 61.

Ridge v Baldwin[27] it was stated that the duty to observe the rules of natural justice should be inferred from the nature of the power conferred upon the public authority. It has been suggested[28] that whether the nature of the power requires such an inference to be drawn may be determined by considering the following three factors: first, the nature of the complainant's interest; secondly, the conditions under which the public authority is entitled to encroach on those interests; and thirdly, the severity of the sanction that can be imposed. These factors offer some guidance as to which interests should be protected by fair procedures, but leave a great deal open to speculation.

7-005   A more precise classification was provided in *McInnes v Onslow Fane*,[29] where the following three situations were distinguished: (a) "forfeiture" or "deprivation" cases, where a vested interest (such as a licence to trade) has been withdrawn; (b) "application" cases, where no interest yet exists, but is merely being sought (such as an application for a licence, passport or a council house); and (c) "expectation" cases, where there is a reasonable expectation of a continuation of an existing benefit which falls short of a right. A fair hearing, it was suggested, should be granted in cases involving "forfeiture" and (normally) "expectation", but not in those involving a mere "application". In general there are practical reasons why a hearing cannot be given to every applicant for a licence, for the same reason that the hearing cannot be given to all applicants for scarce resources (such as hospital beds, or university places). The task of allocation in these circumstances requires despatch, and the class of applicant may be entirely open-ended.[30] However, the *McInnes* analysis would, if strictly applied, result in anomalies and injustice for there are situations where the refusal of an application could adversely affect an interest deserving of protection by means of a fair hearing. For example, the refusal of an application for a passport not only prevents the exercise of a basic liberty to travel, but may also cast aspersions on a person's character.[31] It would seem unfair to deny an applicant for planning permission procedural protection (as is provided by statute)[32] so that he may argue in favour of his interest in developing his land. It would also seem unfair to deny an applicant for a licence to export goods the op-

---

[27]   *Ridge v Baldwin* [1964] A.C. 40 at 76.

[28]   *Durayappah v Fernando* [1967] 2 A.C. 337 at 349; *Lloyd v McMahon* [1987] A.C. 625 at 702-703 (Lord Bridge). For comparative perspectives, see 6-052.

[29]   *McInnes v Onslow Fane* [1978] 1 W.L.R. 1520.

[30]   On non-justiciability, see 1-034.

[31]   *R. v Secretary of State for Foreign and Commonwealth Affairs Ex p. Everett* [1989] Q.B. 811 at 820 (Taylor LJ: a passport was a "normal expectation of every citizen"). In *R. v Secretary of State for the Home Department Ex p. Fayed (No. 1)* [1998] 1 W.L.R. 763 at the CA held (Woolf MR, Phillips LJ, Kennedy LJ dissenting), that the applicants for British citizenship were wrongly deprived of an opportunity to make representations in advance of the refusal of their applications. The statute itself precluded a requirement for reasons. The ratio appears to be (Lord Woolf at 237-238; Phillips LJ at 251) that, although the applicants had no vested rights to citizenship (as in *Attorney General v Ryan* [1980] A.C. 718, PC, constitutional entitlement to citizenship of the Bahamas), the refusal of the application would in the circumstances of this case lead to adverse inferences being drawn about the applicants' characters. For a similar case where an applicant was afforded the right to a fair hearing see *R. v Secretary of State for the Home Department Ex p. Moon* [1997] I.N.L.R. 165. See also *R. (on the application of Thamby) v Secretary of State for the Home Department* [2011] EWHC 1763 (Admin) at [68]–[71] (an applicant for naturalisation was entitled to be informed of the nature of matters adverse to his application so as to be afforded a reasonable opportunity to address them, although the obligation of fairness would not require the Secretary of State to interview an applicant as to his good character other than in truly exceptional cases).

[32]   Town and Country Planning Act 1990 s.78.

portunity to make representations in support of his application (again, such an opportunity is presently provided by statute[33]).

In addition, some decisions deserving of a fair hearing do not fall into any of the three categories set out in *McInnes*. For example, it has been held that in some circumstances an interested person such as a neighbour is entitled to object to a proposed development of land despite the absence of a statutory right to make representations and the absence of any legitimate expectation of so doing.[34] That kind of situation fits none of the categories in *McInnes*, as the interested person is neither in the position of an applicant, nor someone deprived of an existing right, interest or legitimate expectation.

7-006

Moreover, on occasion, the unfairness of the summary refusal of a licence or the summary award of a licence to a competitor will be so manifest (e.g. because the worthiness of the applicant rather than the availability of resources is the dominant factor shaping a decision),[35] that it will be right for a court to hold that the deciding body is under a duty to give the applicant an opportunity to make representations (whether in writing or orally) and of being apprised of all information on which the decision may be founded.[36] In express reliance on these considerations, it was held in *R. (on the application of Quark Fishing Ltd) v Secretary of State for Foreign and Commonwealth Affairs* that the applicant for an extremely valuable licence to fish for Patagonian Toothfish was entitled not to be left in any doubt about the criteria upon which the licence would be granted.[37]

7-007

Other situations where applicants may be accorded the benefits of a fair hearing include those where the licensing authority is constituted as a distinct tribunal, or is expressly required to entertain representations or objections or appeals, or to conduct hearings or inquiries, when deciding whether or not to grant a licence.[38] A duty to act fairly may also be imposed upon "application" cases when policy guidelines have been established (especially if published) within which discretion will normally be exercised. They may raise an expectation of benefit in those who believe that they fall within the guidelines.[39] In addition, an opportunity to be heard, both on the application and the merits of the policy, may be required in order to prevent a fettering of discretion.[40]

7-008

---

[33]   Export Control Order 2008 (SI 2008/3231) art.33.

[34]   *R. v Great Yarmouth BC Ex p. Botton Bros* (1988) 56 P. & C.R. 99.

[35]   See, e.g. *R. v Aston University Senate Ex p. Roffey* [1969] 2 Q.B. 538 at 554 (university places); and *Stininato v Auckland Boxing Assocation* [1978] 1 N.Z.L.R. 1; *Trivett v Nivison* [1976] 1 N.S.WL.R. 312; and H. Friendly, "Some Kind of Hearing" (1975) 123 U. Penn.L.Rev. 1267.

[36]   In *R v Huntingdon DC Ex p. Cowan* [1984] 1 W.L.R. 501 it was held that an applicant for an entertainments licence was entitled to know the substance of objections and to have an opportunity of responding to those objections in writing.

[37]   *R. (on the application of Quark Fishing Ltd) v Secretary of State for Foreign and Commonwealth Affairs* [2001] EWHC Admin 1174; [2002] A.C.D. 197 at [67]-[68] and [2002] EWCA Civ 1409.

[38]   Though the obligation may be qualified by a right to refrain from disclosing the source and precise content of highly confidential information: *Benaim and Khaida* [1970] 2 Q.B. 417 at 431. See also *Abbey Mine Ltd v Coal Authority* [2008] EWCA Civ 353; (2008) 152(16) S.J.L.B. 28 at [27]-[35] (where there were rival applications for a licence to undertake a commercial venture, fairness required that the applicant be told of the decision-maker's concerns about one's own case and that each applicant be treated alike, but fairness did not require a right to know the details of the rival's case).

[39]   See Ch.12. See also See also *Manning v Ramjohn* [2011] UKPC 20 at [48] (Lord Brown noting that the *McInnes* classification was of "limited assistance in the present context"; an applicant for senior public office who had been successful in a competitive selection process had an expectation of being fairly treated: at [45]-[48]).

[40]   See Ch.9; *British Oxygen Co Ltd v Board of Trade* [1971] A.C. 610 at 625; *R. v Criminal Injuries Compensation Board Ex p. Ince* [1973] 1 W.L.R. 1334 at 1345.

The recognition of a general duty of fairness

7-009   While a starting point, the *McInnes* approach, like other attempts at classification, has its shortcomings. It is therefore preferable to adopt a more comprehensive approach, recognising that the duty of fairness cannot and should not be restricted by artificial barriers or confined by inflexible categories. The duty is a general one, governed by the following propositions:

- Whenever a public function is being performed there is an inference, in the absence of an express requirement to the contrary, that the function is required to be performed fairly.[41]

- The inference will be more compelling in the case of any decision which may adversely affect a person's rights or interests or when a person has a legitimate expectation of being fairly treated.

- The requirement of a fair hearing will not apply to all situations of perceived or actual detriment. There are clearly some situations where the interest affected will be too insignificant, or too speculative, or too remote to qualify for a fair hearing.[42] Whether this is so will depend on all the circumstances but a fair hearing ought no longer to be rejected out of hand, for example, simply because the decision-maker is acting in a "legislative" capacity.[43]

- Special circumstances may create an exception which vitiates the inference of a duty to act fairly. The inference can be rebutted by the needs of national security, or because of other characteristics of the particular function. For example, a decision to allocate scarce resources amongst a large number of contenders which needs to be made with despatch may be inconsistent with an obligation to hold a fair hearing.[44] The inference may also not be drawn if the protection is to be achieved another way. For example, in the case of a "legislative" decision, at least where participa-

---

[41]   English law must comply with ECHR art.6, which requires a fair hearing in the "determination" of "civil rights and obligations" or of "criminal charges" (on which see 7-033).

[42]   In such cases where there has been a claim for judicial review the claimant may not qualify for standing on the ground of not possessing a "sufficient interest" in the matter to which the application relates. Alternatively, the applicant may have failed to suffer any "substantial prejudice" from any lack of procedural propriety where the statute requires it, see, e.g. *Save Britain's Heritage v Number One Poultry Ltd* [1991] 1 W.L.R. 153, HL. cf. *R. v Swansea City Council Ex p. Elitestone Ltd* [1993] 2 P.L.R. 65 at 70; *R. v Westminster City Council Ex p. Ermakov* [1996] 2 All E.R. 302; and see below on the extent to which it is necessary to show prejudice.

[43]   *Leech v Parkhurst Prison Deputy Governor* [1988] A.C. 533 at 538 (Lord Oliver); *R. v Secretary of State for Health Ex p. United States Tobacco International Inc* [1992] Q.B. 353. cf. *R. v Lord Chancellor Ex p. The Law Society* (1994) 6 Admin L.R. 833. For discussion of the principle against imposing natural justice requirements in "legislative" contexts see G. Craven, "Legislative Action by Subordinate Authorities and the Requirements of a Fair Hearing" (1988) 16 M.U.L.Rev. 596 and G. Cartier, "Procedural Fairness in Legislative Functions: The End of Judicial Abstinence?" (2003) 53 U.T.L.J. 217. For comparative perspectives, see 6-052. "Legislative" decisions, or "decisions affecting many" (see 6-031), continue to be subject to different treatment and the full rigours of procedural fairness may not apply, although this situation is changing: contrast *Bates v Lord Hailsham of St Marylebone* [1972] 1 W.L.R. 1373 with *R. (on the application of BAPIO Action Ltd) v Secretary of State for the Home Department* [2008] UKHL 27; [2008] 1 A.C. 1003). In Canada, see *Cardinal v Kent Institution* (1985) 24 D.L.R. (4th) 44 at [14] (Le Dain J).

[44]   On the other hand, local authorities are now statutorily required to maintain for public inspection their rules for determining priority among applicants for council housing and their procedural rules for allocating it: Housing Act 1985 s.106. A local authority that has made and published its rules of procedure may well be held to have acted unlawfully if, in some material respect, it does not apply them fairly (e.g. by an officer's failing to disclose some unfavourable impression gained as a result of a home visit or from the third party and to allow the applicant an opportunity to respond).

tion is built into the decision-making process elsewhere, the safeguard which would be provided by a fair hearing can be achieved by other means; as in cases where the decision is taken by democratically elected representatives accountable to Parliament or to the electorate for the exercise of the relevant power.[45]

- What fairness requires will vary according to the circumstances.[46] We shall see that some decisions, while attracting the duty to be fair, will permit no more to the affected person than a bare right to submit representations.[47] In other cases, however, there will be a right to an oral hearing with the essential elements of a trial.[48] In between these extremes are a large variety of decisions which, because of the nature of the issues to be determined or the seriousness of their impact upon important interests, require some kind of a hearing (which may not even involve oral representations), but not anything that has all the characteristics of a full trial.[49]

- Whether fairness is required and what is involved in order to achieve fairness is for the decision of the courts as a matter of law. The issue is not one for the discretion of the decision-maker. The test is not whether no reasonable body would have thought it proper to dispense with a fair hearing.[50] The *Wednesbury*[51] reserve has no place in relation to procedural propriety.

---

[45] The exceptions to the requirement of fair hearing are considered fully in Ch.8.

[46] See 7-040.

[47] For a minimalist view of fairness, as involving no more than a duty to act without bias, see, e.g. *R. v Secretary of State for Trade Ex p. Perestrello* [1981] Q.B. 19.

[48] Decision-making that formerly would have been characterised as "judicial" fall into this category (see 6-035); e.g. *R. v Immigration Tribunal Ex p. Mehmet* [1977] 1 W.L.R. 795. In the US case of *Mathews v Eldridge* 424 U.S. 319 (1976), it was held that whether the constitutional guarantee of due process requires an evidentiary hearing depends on the individual interest at stake, the extent to which a trial procedure was more likely than the procedure actually used to avoid an erroneous decision, and the government's interest, including the extra cost of the procedure requested. It has been argued that this kind of utilitarian approach fails adequately to take account of the moral harm or sense of injustice suffered by a person who is wrongly deprived of a right without a hearing, as opposed, for example, to the reaction engendered by a contested policy decision such as the siting of a motorway: see R. Dworkin, "Principle, policy, procedure" in C. Tapper (ed), *Crime, Proof and Punishment: Essays in Memory of Sir Rupert Cross* (1981), pp.193 and 221 and following; and 6-008, fn.4.

[49] *Lloyd* [1987] A.C. 625 at 702 (Lord Bridge: "the so-called rules of national justice are not engraved on tablets of stone."; *R. (on the application of H) v Secretary of State for Justice* [2008] EWHC 2590 (Admin); [2009] Prison L.R. 205 at [1] ("It is clear that procedural fairness does not impose the straightjacket of a quasi-judicial process and more informal procedures than what one expects before the courts or even tribunals may be acceptable. An oral hearing does not necessarily imply the adversarial process"). A similar approach has been adopted in other jurisdictions: see 6-056 and in Canada: *Martineau v Matsqui Institution Disciplinary Board* [1980] 1 S.C.R. 602 at [61]–[63]. In Ireland, see *Ó Ceallaigh v An Bord Altranais* [2000] 4 I.R. 54 at 92-93; *International Fishing Vessels v Minister for the Marine (No.2)* [1991] 2 I.R. 93 at 102; *Flanagan v University College Dublin* [1988] I.R. 724 at 730-731.

[50] *R. v Panel on Takeovers and Mergers Ex p. Guinness Plc* [1990] 1 Q.B. 146 (Woolf and Lloyd LJJ who said that "the court is the arbiter of what is fair"); *Re Reilly's Application* [2013] UKSC 61; [2013] 3 W.L.R. 1020 at [65] (the court's function is "not merely to review the reasonableness of the decision-makers judgment of what fairness required"); *LH* [2014] EWCA Civ 404 at [29] ("[f]airness is a matter for the Court not the Council to decide"); *R. (on the application of Flatley) v Hywel Dda University Local Health Board* [2014] EWHC 2258 (Admin) at [88] ("[i]t is a matter for the court to decide whether a fair procedure was followed"); see also *R. (on the application of Woolcock) v Secretary of State for Communities and Local Government* [2018] EWHC 17 (Admin) at [50]. However, in limited circumstances, the court may give great weight to the decision-maker's view of what is fair, see, e.g. *R. v Monopolies and Mergers Commission Ex p. Stagecoach Holdings Ltd, The Times,* 23 July 1996 ("The court is the arbiter of what is fair", although the court would give great weight to the MMC's own view of fairness); *Interbrew SA and Interbrew UK Holdings Ltd v*

7-010   The significance of this approach is that at first sight it imposes on all administrators an obligation to act fairly. Without acknowledging this expressly, the majority of the recent decisions of the courts are in practice no more than conscious or unconscious illustrations of the approach. They can be conveniently examined under the following four headings.

- Where the terms of a statute confirm the inference of a fair hearing.
- Where the inference of a fair hearing is confirmed by the need to safeguard a right or interest.
- Where the inference of a fair hearing is confirmed by the need to safeguard an expectation induced by the decision-maker.
- ECHR art.6.
- ECHR art.2.

STATUTORY REQUIREMENTS OF FAIR PROCEDURES

Express statutory requirements

7-011   When a mandatory procedure is set out in a statute, it must be followed.[52] Many areas of public administration provide elaborate procedural codes. Town and country planning legislation, for example, requires notification of applications for planning permission,[53] requires consultation with given bodies[54] and provides the opportunity for applicants to appeal a refusal of a planning application or a condition attached to an application.[55] The appeal may be by way of written representations or a full structured inquiry.[56] In the context of health care provision, health authorities, Primary Care Trusts and NHS Trusts have duties to involve and consult, either directly or through representatives, those who use their services.[57]

Supplementing statutory procedures

7-012   Even where the procedural code is comprehensive in its scope, the courts are called upon to adjudicate on the extent to which the statutory procedure has been fulfilled. For example, are the reasons, required of the Secretary of State on a plan-

---

The Competition Commission and the Secretary of State for Trade and Industry [2001] EWHC Admin 367; [2001] E.C.C. 40 at [70]-[72].

[51]   See 11-012 for discussion of the *Wednesbury* case and the margin of discretion accorded the decision-maker in cases involving abuse of discretion.

[52]   For the distinction between requirements which are "mandatory" and "directory" see 5-057.

[53]   Town and Country Planning (Development Management Procedure) (England) Order (SI 2015/595) art.13; Town and Country Planning Act 1990 s.71; Planning (Listed Buildings and Conservation Areas) Act 1990 s.73.

[54]   Town and Country Planning (Development Management Procedure) (England) Order (SI 2015/595) arts 18–26.

[55]   Town and Country Planning Act 1990 ss.78, 78A, 79. On inquiries, see 7-117.

[56]   Town and Country Planning (Appeals) (Written Representations Procedure) (England) Regulations 2009 (SI 2009/452); Town and Country Planning (Hearings Procedure) (England) Rules 2000 (SI 2000/1626); Town and Country Planning Appeals (Determination by Inspectors) (Inquiries Procedure) (England) Rules 2000 (SI 2000/1625).

[57]   *R. (on the application of Morris) v Trafford Healthcare NHS Trust* [2006] EWHC 2334; (2006) 9 C.C.L. Rep. 648; *R. (on the application of Smith) v North Eastern Derbyshire Primary Care Trust* [2006] EWCA Civ 1291; [2006] 1 W.L.R. 3315; *Flatley* [2014] EWHC 2258 (Admin) (limiting the extent of the duty of consultation to that provided for in Community Health Councils (Constitution, Membership and Procedures) (Wales) Regulations 2010 reg.27(7)). See also Local Government and Public Involvement in Health Act 2007 s.221.

ning appeal, "proper, adequate and intelligible"?[58] Has the consultation required been "genuine"?[59] In these cases there are no express statutory requirements in relation to the adequacy, intelligibility or genuineness of the reasons or consultations, but the courts employ these criteria so as to ensure the correct standards of fairness. In doing so, the courts are not imposing additional requirements but are instead ensuring the effectiveness of existing requirements.

Can the courts supplement the statutory procedures with requirements over and above those specified? For example, can the courts impose a requirement upon a local planning authority to consult on a planning application with neighbours where no such requirement is provided in the statute? There have been cases where the courts have supplemented a statutory scheme.[60] Indeed, recently, a majority of the Supreme Court expressed the following view:

7-013

"The duty of fairness governing the exercise of a statutory power is a limitation on the discretion of the decision-maker which is implied into the statute. But the fact that the statute makes some provision for the procedure to be followed before or after the exercise of a statutory power does not of itself impliedly exclude either the duty of fairness in general or the duty of prior consultation in particular, where they would otherwise arise."[61]

---

58   *Save Britain's Heritage* [1991] 1 W.L.R. 153 at 166; *Westminster City Council v Great Portland Estates Plc* [1985] A.C. 661 at 663; *Vicarage Gate Ltd v First Secretary of State, Royal Borough of Kensington and Chelsea* [2007] EWHC 768 (Admin); [2007] N.P.C. 50 at [8]; *George Wimpey UK Ltd v Tewkesbury Borough Council* [2007] EWHC 628 (Admin); (2007) 151 S.J.L.B. 506 at [69]; *Chris Jaram Developments Ltd v First Secretary of State* [2004] EWHC 1220; *Uprichard v Scottish Ministers* [2013] UKSC 21; [2013] P.T.S.R. D37 at [47]; *Garlick v Secretary of State for Communities and Local Government* [2013] EWHC 1126 (Admin); *Farah v Hillingdon LBC* [2014] EWCA Civ 359; [2014] H.L.R. 24. In a different context, see *Nzolameso v Westminster City Council* [2015] UKSC 22; [2015] 2 All E.R. 942 (a decision on a temporary accommodation offer must clearly show that "proper" or "serious" consideration was given to the local authority's obligations under the statutory framework).
59   *R. v Secretary of State for Social Services Ex p. Association of Metropolitan Authorities* [1986] 1 W.L.R. 1; *R. v North and East Devon Health Authority Ex p. Coughlan* [2001] Q.B. 213 at [108]; see 7-052. See also *R. (on the application of Moseley) v Haringey LBC* [2014] UKSC 56; [2014] 1 W.L.R. 3947 at [25]; *R. (on the application of United Company Rusal Plc) v London Metal Exchange* [2014] EWCA Civ 1271; [2015] 1 W.L.R. 1375.
60   See 7-015 and 7-042; *R. (on the application of S) v Brent LBC* [2002] EWCA Civ 693; [2002] E.L.R. 556 at [14]; *Raji v General Medical Council* [2003] UKPC 24; [2003] 1 W.L.R. 1052 (even though Medical Act 1983 s.41(1) and (6) permitted consideration of suspension and restoration together, the two issues should have been considered separately); *Belfast City Council v Miss Behavin' Ltd* [2007] UKHL 19; [2007] 1 W.L.R. 1420 at [8] (discretion to consider late objections supplementary to the statutory scheme to ensure its fair and workable operation); *Bank Mellat v HM Treasury* [2013] UKSC 39; [2014] A.C. 700 at [32] (unless the Act expressly or impliedly excluded any relevant duty of consultation, fairness required an opportunity to make representations before a direction was made); *Fairmount Investments Ltd v Secretary of State for the Environment* [1976] 1 W.L.R. 1255; *Lake District Special Planning Board v Secretary of State for the Environment* [1975] J.P.L. 220; and elsewhere: *Rich v Christchurch Girls' High School Board of Governors (No.1)* [1974] 1 N.Z.L.R. 1 at 9, 18-20; *Birss v Secretary of State for Justice* [1984] 1 N.Z.L.R. 513; *Heatley v Tasmanian Racing and Gaming Commission* (1977) 137 C.L.R. 487. In *R. (on the application of Breckland District Council) v Electoral Commission Boundary Committee for England* [2009] EWCA Civ 239; [2009] P.T.S.R. 1611 at [44], it was held that while s.6(4)(b) of the Local Government and Public Involvement in Health Act 2007 required publication of an alternative proposal and "such steps as [the authority considers] sufficient to secure that persons who may be interested" were informed of the draft proposal, it was also necessary to publish a summary of the reasons why a change was proposed and why the proposed change was considered to meet the Secretary of State's criteria. See also *R. (on the application of Chief Constable of Nottinghamshire) v Nottingham Magistrates' Court* [2009] EWHC 3182 (Admin); [2010] 2 All E.R. 342 at [30]-[39]; *R. (on the application of Andersson) v Parole Board* [2011] EWHC 1049 (Admin) (exclusion of a power to adjourn would require clear statutory provision).
61   *Bank Mellat* [2013] UKSC 39; [2014] A.C. 700 at [35].

7-014   However, in others the maxim *expressio unius exclusio alterius* (the express mention of one thing excludes all others) has been invoked to avoid doing so.[62] Lord Reid unusually expressed an inclination in favour of judicial restraint when he warned against the use by the courts of "this unusual kind of power" (extending statutory procedures) which he felt should be exercised only when it is "clear that the statutory procedure is insufficient to achieve justice and that to require additional steps would not frustrate the apparent purpose of the legislation".[63] But the maxim *expressio unius*, like other aids to interpretation, may be "a valuable servant, but a dangerous master to follow ... [and] ought not to be applied when it leads to inconsistency or injustice.[64] A bolder approach has been suggested by Lord Bridge, who said that "the courts will not only require the procedure prescribed by the statute to be followed, but will readily imply so much and no more to be introduced by way of additional procedural safeguards as will ensure the attainment of fairness".[65] Similarly, in *Bank Mellat v HM Treasury*, Lord Sumption observed that he found it hard to envisage cases in which the maximum *expres-*

---

[62]   See, e.g. *Pearlberg v Varty* [1972] 1 W.L.R. 534; *Furnell v Whangarei High Schools Board* [1973] A.C. 660 at 679; *Wiseman v Borneman* [1971] A.C. 297; *R. (on the application of Venture Projects Ltd) v Secretary of State for the Home Department* unreported 20 October 2000 CA (although the maxim was not invoked, a duty to give reasons was held not to arise where an EU Directive required reasons for certain decisions, but not this type of decision); see likewise *R. (on the application of Edwards) v Environment Agency (No.2)* [2008] UKHL 22; [2008] 1 W.L.R. 1587. See also *R. (on the application of Hillingdon LBC, Leeds City Council, Liverpool City Council, Norfolk City Council) v Lord Chancellor, Secretary of State for Communities and Local Government* [2008] EWHC 2683 (Admin); [2009] C.P. Rep. 13 (where Parliament had prescribed the nature and extent of consultation which the Lord Chancellor was required to undertake before exercising his power to prescribe court fees no wider duty of consultation existed at common law (in the absence of a clear promise to consult more widely or any clear established practice of wider consultation by the decision-maker) (at [38]); the courts should not add a burden of consultation which the democratically elected body decided not to impose (at [39])). See also *Re Findlay* [1985] A.C. 318; *Bird v St Mary Abbotts Vestry* (1895) 72 L.T. 599; *Hutton v Attorney General* [1927] 1 Ch. 427 at 437-438; *R. (on the application of Buckinghamshire CC) v Kingston Upon Thames RLBC* [2011] EWCA Civ 457; [2012] P.T.S.R. 854 at [55] (although the inclusion of an express duty to consult specified persons is not, of necessity, a complete bar to any wider duty, it will usually be a powerful starting point which is likely to trump anything but the strongest contextual considerations which might point the other way); *R. (on the application of Heather Moor & Edgecomb Ltd) v Financial Service Ombudsman* [2008] EWCA Civ 642; [2008] Bus. L.R. 1486. See, 6-026 and, see, e.g. *Waitemata County v Local Government Commission* [1964] N.Z.L.R. 689; *Brettingham-Moore v St. Leonards Municipality* (1969) 121 C.L.R. 509; *French v Law Society of Upper Canada* [1975] 2 S.C.R. 767 at 783-786; *Salemi v McKellar (No.2)* (1977) 137 C.L.R. 396; *Bourke v State Services Commission* [1978] 1 N.Z.L.R. 633 at 644-646; *CREEDNZ Inc v Governor General* [1981] 1 N.Z.L.R. 172 at 177-178. In the USA, the Supreme Court, in a landmark case, *Vermont Yankee Nuclear Power Corp v Natural Resources Defense Council, Inc* 435 U.S. 519 (1978) at 543 it was held that absent constitutional constraints or extremely compelling circumstances, courts may not force agencies to utilise rulemaking procedures beyond those prescribed in the Administrative Procedure Act 1946 or other statutory or constitutional provisions. In Ireland, statutory scrutiny will not end the matter because if the statute is deficient, the principle of constitutional justice will apply and override the statutory shortcomings: see 6-066, fn.260 and see, e.g. *McCann v Monaghan District Court* [2009] IEHC 276; [2009] 4 I.R. 200 at 250-255.

[63]   *Wiseman* [1971] A.C. 297 at 308.

[64]   *Colquhoun v Brooks* (1887) 19 Q.B.D. 400 at 406; on appeal (1888) 21 Q.B.D. 52.

[65]   *Lloyd* [1987] A.C. 625 at 702-703; *R. (on the application of BAPIO Action Ltd) v Secretary of State for the Home Department* [2007] EWCA Civ 1139; [2008] A.C.D. 7 at [35] ("where there is a want of fairness in procedures laid down by Parliament, the common law will supply it"); *R. (on the application of Lumba) v Secretary of State for the Home Department* [2011] UKSC 12; [2012] 1 A.C. 245 at [201] ("the law has ... imposed procedural requirements upon apparently open-ended statutory powers"); *Hopkins Developments* [2014] EWCA Civ 470 at [62] (observing that the Town and Country Planning Appeals (Determination by Inspectors) (Inquiries Procedure) (England) Rules 2000 were "not a complete code for achieving procedural fairness"); *LH* [2014] EWCA Civ 404.

sion unius exclusion alterius could suffice to exclude so basic a right as that of fairness.[66]

Thus, the test today of whether to supplement statutory procedures is no longer whether the statutory procedure alone could result in manifest unfairness.[67] The preferable view is that fairness must, without qualification, be attained, and that the "justice of the common law" may supplement that of the statute unless by necessary implication the procedural code must be regarded as exclusive.[68] Under either test, similar factors are likely to be relevant: the comprehensiveness of the code, the degree of deviation from the statutory procedure required, and the overall fairness of the procedures to the individual concerned.[69]   **7-015**

Where legislation, instead of placing a duty on a body to hold a hearing, merely gives a *discretion* to do so, the inference must normally be that no duty to hear exists in that context, particularly if the legislation explicitly requires that body to conduct hearings or inquiries in the performance of other functions.[70] Similarly, where a statutory provision conferred a degree of flexibility as to how consultation should be conducted in framing the obligation as an obligation to "take such steps as [the decision-makers] consider sufficient", "the court should not place them in a rigid straightjacket beyond that which the statute necessitates".[71] However, even where there is discretion, it may be held that a refusal to hold a hearing is an improper exercise of discretion.[72]   **7-016**

Statutory requirements and legitimate expectations

The existence of a statutory scheme will also have an impact on whether a particular legitimate expectation as to procedure can arise, and may have the effect of preventing the expectation from arising.[73]   **7-017**

---

66 *Bank Mellat v HM Treasury* [2013] UKSC 39; [2014] A.C. 700 at [35].
67 *Furnell* [1973] A.C. 660 at 679.
68 *Furnell* [1973] A.C. 660 at 686 (Viscount Dilhorne and Lord Reid, dissenting); *Wiseman* [1971] A.C. 297 at 308, 317; *R. (on the application of Khatun) v Newham LBC* [2004] EWCA Civ 55; [2005] Q.B. 37 at [30] (Laws LJ: "a right to be heard [can] be inserted or implied into the statutory scheme not by virtue of the statute's words, but by force of our public law standards of procedural fairness"); *R. v Parole Board Ex p. Wilson* [1992] Q.B. 740; see 7-041; *Re Hamilton; Forrest v Brighton Justices* [1981] A.C. 1038; *Re Northern Ireland Housing Executive's Application for Judicial Review* [2006] N.I. 234, Q.B.D (NI).
69 Examples of cases where the courts considered that it would have frustrated the statutory purpose to supplement the statutory procedures include: *R. v Birmingham City Council Ex p. Ferrero Ltd* [1993] 1 All E.R. 530; *R. (on the application of McIntyre) v Gentoo Group Ltd* [2010] EWHC 5 (Admin); (2010) 154(2) S.J.L.B. 29 (relief not granted because a private law remedy for breach of contract and statutory proceedings were available).
70 cf. *Ronaki v Number One Town and Country Planning Appeal Board* [1977] 2 N.Z.L.R. 174.
71 *Breckland DC* [2009] EWCA Civ 239; [2009] P.T.S.R. 1611 at [43].
72 *Binney v Secretary of State for the Environment* [1984] J.P.L. 871.
73 See 12-010; *R. v DPP Ex p. Kebilene* [2000] 2 A.C. 326, HL; *R. v Secretary of State for Education Ex p. Begbie* [2000] 1 W.L.R. 1115, CA; *Flasz v Havering Primary Care Trust* [2011] EWHC 1487 (Admin) at [36] and [42]. On the interaction between legitimate expectation and statutory provision, see also *R. (on the application of Majed) v Camden LBC* [2009] EWCA Civ 1029; [2010] J.P.L. 621 at [14] (Sullivan LJ observing that "reference to the statutory requirements is of no real assistance. Legitimate expectation comes into play when there is no statutory requirement ... when there is a promise or a practice to do more than that which is required by statute").

FAIRNESS NEEDED TO SAFEGUARD RIGHTS AND INTERESTS

7-018   There is a presumption that procedural fairness is required whenever the exercise of a power adversely affects an individual's rights protected by common law or created by statute. These include rights in property, personal liberty, status and immunity from penalties or other fiscal impositions. The right or immunity may be enjoyed by either a private person (including a corporation) or a public authority.[74]

7-019   As is already apparent however, the duty to afford procedural fairness is not limited to the protection of legal rights in the strict sense: it also applies to more general interests, of which the interest in pursuing a livelihood and in personal reputation have received particular recognition.[75] The interests also extend to personal freedom (of a prisoner seeking parole)[76] and other benefits and advantages the conferral of which are in the discretion of the decision-maker (and were formerly regarded as "privileges",[77] and thus not meriting procedural protection).

---

[74] See, e.g. *Durayappah* [1967] 2 A.C. 337; *R. v Secretary of State for the Environment Ex p. Norwich City Council* [1982] Q.B. 808 at 824 (dicta); *R. v Secretary of State for the Environment Ex p. Brent LBC* [1982] Q.B. 593 at 642-643; *R. v Secretary of State for Transport Ex p. Greater London Council* [1986] Q.B. 556.

[75] *Ridge v Baldwin* [1964] A.C. 40; *McInnes v Onslow Fane* [1978] 1 W.L.R. 1520 at 1527-1528; *R. v Barnsley MBC Ex p. Hook* [1976] 1 W.L.R. 1052; *Re Pergamon Press Ltd* [1971] Ch. 388 at 399; *Rees v Crane* [1994] 2 A.C. 173, PC. cf. *Lloyd* [1987] A.C. 625 at 702-703 (Lord Bridge, where fairness appears confined to decisions which "affect the rights of individuals"); cf. *Leech* [1988] A.C. 533 at 578; see also *R. (on the application of Hodgson) v South Wales Police Authority* [2008] EWHC 1183 (Admin); [2008] A.C.D. 78; *Abbey Mine Ltd* [2008] EWCA Civ 353; (2008) 152(16) S.J.L.B. 28 (procedural fairness applied where the applicant was applying for an underground coal mining licence and demise of coal).

[76] See, e.g. *R. v Secretary for the Home Department Ex p. Doody* [1994] 1 A.C. 531; *R. (on the application of Ali) v Director of High Security Prisons* [2009] EWHC 1732 (Admin); [2010] 2 All E.R. 82 at [18]–[26] (high security prisoner had to be given reasons for his escape classification in sufficient detail to enable him to decide whether a worthwhile challenge could be made and had to be given an opportunity of making representations with a view to modifying the decision); *R. v Secretary of State for the Home Department Ex p. Duggan* [1994] 3 All E.R. 277 (a classification of a prisoner directly affected his liberty and thus a fair hearing was required). *R. (on the application of West) v Parole Board* [2005] UKHL 1; [2005] 1 W.L.R. 350 (on revocation of release on licence). ECHR art.5(4) has been found to be engaged where the decision at issue was whether to transfer a life prisoner to open prison conditions: *Roose v Parole Board* [2010] EWHC 1780 (Admin); *The Times*, 1 September 2010 at [35] (concluding that given the importance of the decision for an individual who had been in prison 17 years beyond the date of expiration of his minimum term and the views of a consultant psychologist, a decision refusing an oral hearing should be quashed); see also *R. (on the application of Hopkins) v Parole Board* [2008] EWHC 2312 (Admin); [2009] Prison L.R. 223; *Re Reilly's Application* [2013] UKSC 61; [2013] 3 W.L.R. 1020 at [54]– [63], [80]–[96] (noting that a parole board's common law duty to act fairly was influenced by the requirements of ECHR art.5(4) and outlining the circumstances in which oral hearings would be required).

[77] See 6-029; *Nakkuda Ali v Jayarante* [1951] A.C. 66; *R. v Metropolitan Police Commissioner Ex p. Parker* [1953] 1 W.L.R. 1150. For the limits of the obligation of common law fairness, see *EK (Ivory Coast) v Secretary of State for the Home Department* [2014] EWCA Civ 1517 (the Secretary of State for the Home Department was not responsible for a college's administrative error in withdrawing a letter of confirmation of acceptance for studies before an application for leave to remain had been determined and where the Secretary of State saw that the letter had been withdrawn, the general public law duty of fairness had not obliged her to adjourn any decision to give the applicant notice of the problem and an opportunity to rectify it).

Licences and similar benefits

Because the interest of the claimant, rather than the discretionary power of the decision-maker, now founds a right to a fair hearing, a hearing is required in most situations where licences or other similar benefits are revoked, varied, suspended or refused; even where the decision-making power affords wide discretion to the decision-maker. Thus a strong presumption exists that a person whose licence is threatened with revocation should receive prior notice of that fact and an opportunity to be heard.[78] The presumption should be especially strong where revocation causes deprivation of livelihood or serious pecuniary loss, or carries an implication of misconduct. Variation of the terms of an existing licence to the licensee's detriment will also prima facie attract the duty to act fairly.[79] A decision to increase the number of licences, with the effect of diminishing the value of existing licences, may in some situations also attract the duty.[80]

7-020

Whether a suspension of a licence should be preceded by notice and opportunity to be heard may depend on various factors, for example, the degree of urgency involved, the duration of the suspension, whether suspension implies a finding of guilt, whether it entails material financial loss and whether it is a purely temporary measure pending full review.[81]

7-021

Non-renewal of an existing licence is usually a more serious matter than refusal to grant a licence in the first place. Unless the licensee has already been given to understand when he was granted the licence that renewal is not to be expected, non-renewal may seriously upset his plans, cause him economic loss and perhaps cast a slur on his reputation. It may therefore be right to imply a duty to hear before a decision not to renew irrespective of whether there is a legitimate expectation of renewal,[82] even though no such duty is implied in the making of the original decision to grant or refuse the licence.[83]

7-022

Applicants for new licences are in a different position from those whose existing licences are revoked, suspended, varied or not renewed.[84] The reason why applicants for new licences or other permissions may be denied a hearing is because in many cases there is no vested interest involved to defend. The applicant will be adversely affected by a refusal of something which he does not yet have only to the extent that he is disappointed and may have suffered some "transaction costs" in

7-023

---

[78] R. (on the application of London Reading College Ltd) v Secretary of State for the Home Department [2010] EWHC 2561 (Admin); [2010] E.L.R. 809 at [42]-[48].

[79] Re CTV Television Network Ltd (1980) 116 D.L.R. (3rd) 741.

[80] R. v Liverpool Corp Ex p. Liverpool Taxi Fleet Operators' Association [1972] 2 Q.B. 299 (Lord Denning, whose view was not expressed by the other members of the CA).

[81] See, e.g. Hlookoff v City of Vancouver (1968) 67 D.L.R. (2nd) 119 (summary suspension of licence of premises for publishing newspaper on account of gross misconduct; suspension invalid); see also R. (on the application of New London College) v Secretary of State for the Home Department [2011] EWHC 856 (Admin) at [57]-[59] (overturned although not this ground at [2012] EWCA Civ 51; [2012] Imm. A.R. 563). cf. Furnell [1973] A.C. 660; on preliminary hearings, see 8-040.

[82] See 12-005.

[83] This paragraph was cited with approval in Hook [1976] 1 W.L.R. 1052 at 1058 (Scarman LJ). Supporting this distinction: Schmidt v Secretary of State for Home Affairs [1969] 2 Ch. 149 at 171, 173; Breen v AEU [1971] 2 Q.B. 175 at 191; Liverpool Taxi [1972] 2 Q.B. 299 (reduction in value of existing licences); Hook [1976] 1 W.L.R. 1052 at 1057; McInnes [1978] 1 W.L.R. 1520. cf. Salemi (1977) 137 C.L.R. 396. Generally, in the US, a benefit is not a protected entitlement if officials have discretion to grant or deny it: Kentucky Department of Corrections v Thompson 490 U.S. 454 (1989) at 462-463; Town of Castle Rock Colorado v Gonzales 545 U.S. 748 (2005).

[84] McInnes [1978] 1 W.L.R. 1520; FAI Insurances Ltd v Winneke (1982) 151 C.L.R. 342.

the process of the application.[85] Nevertheless, as has been discussed,[86] there may be a number of situations in which the decision to grant or refuse an application for a licence may attract a fair hearing.[87]

The scope of interests protected by fair procedures

7-024   The right to a fair procedure is not confined to those who are direct parties to a decision.[88] However, the right does not extend to every vested right or interest. Some may be too remote or too speculative to justify their having an opportunity of being heard.[89] However, care should be exercised that decision-makers do not prejudge the impact of the decision which is in issue.[90] To what extent should a fair procedure be provided to individuals whose interests in library use are threatened by a local authority's proposal to close a local public library?[91] Does a local authority, having consulted widely on the need to close a certain number of day care

---

[85]   That the considerations applicable to the revocation of licences may be different from those applicable to the refusal of licences has been recognised in a number of cases, e.g. *McInnes* [1978] 1 W.L.R. 1520, and particularly in Canadian provincial cases, holding that licensees have an implied right to be heard before revocation, e.g. *Re Watt and Registrar of Motor Vehicles* (1958) 13 D.L.R. (2nd) 124 (driving licences); *Klymchuk v Cowan* (1964) 45 D.L.R. (2nd) 587 (used car dealer's permit); *R. v Calgary Ex p. Sanderson* (1966) 53 D.L.R. (2nd) 477 (store licence); *Re Halliwell and Welfare Institutions Board* (1966) 56 D.L.R. (2nd) 754 (rest home licence); though cf. *Re Foremost Construction Co and Registrar of Companies* (1967) 61 D.L.R. (2nd) 528. And see *Re North Coast Air Services Ltd* [1972] E.C. 390 at 404. Earlier Australian decisions distinguished between applicants for new licences and existing licence holders on the basis that the latter had a different and stronger interest: *Stollery v Greyhound Racing Control Board* (1972) 128 C.L.R. 509; *Winneke* (1982) 151 C.L.R. 342. The Australian conception of interests to which procedural fairness now attaches is so broad that distinctions between application/revocation cases are clearly obsolete: *Plaintiff M61E/2010 v Commonwealth (the "Offshore Processing Case")* (2010) 243 C.L.R. 319 at 353. The universal inquiry is now about the content of fairness, which depends on the manner and degree to which an interest is affected: *Kioa v West* (1985) 159 C.L.R. 550, 616-617; quoted in *Plaintiff S10/2011 v Minister for Immigration and Citizenship* (2012) 86 A.L.J.R. 1019 at [66]; and *Hecht v Monaghan* 121 N.E.2d 421 (1954), where, on facts almost identical to those in *Parker* [1953] 1 W.L.R. 1150 the court reached the opposite conclusion.

[86]   See 7-007; *Fayed (No.1)* [1998] 1 W.L.R. 763.

[87]   *Doody* [1994] 1 A.C. 531 at 565-566 (Lord Mustill: where the applicant is treated differently from other similarly placed applicants it has been suggested that the applicant has a right to be given reasons for the refusal of a licence, in order to defend his interest in equal treatment); *R. (on the application of Quark Fishing Ltd) v Secretary of State for Foreign and Commonwealth Affairs* [2001] EWHC Admin 1174 at [67]-[68]. See also *Manning* [2011] UKPC 20 at [48] (noting that there the *McInnes* classifications were of little assistance when considering the exercise of a veto against the proposed appointment of a candidate successful in a competitive selection process; such a person must surely have an expectation of being fairly treated).

[88]   See, e.g. *R. v LAUTRO Ex p. Ross* [1993] Q.B. 17 (self-regulatory body was required to consult a non-member who was not a party to the decision but whose reputation could have been adversely affected by the decision); cf. *Cheall v Association of Professional Executive and Computer Staff* [1983] 2 A.C. 180. A. Lidbetter, "Financial Services: The Right to Make Representations" [1992] P.L. 533.

[89]   See, e.g. *R. (on the application of Niazi) v Secretary of State for the Home Department* [2008] EWCA Civ 755; (2008) 152(29) S.J.L.B. 29, DC (applicants for ex gratia payments, paid to victims of miscarriages of justice pursuant to a discretionary scheme, which was withdrawn before they made their claim, were not entitled to be consulted before the scheme was withdrawn).

[90]   *R. v Ealing Justices Ex p. Fanneran* (1996) 8 Admin. L.R. 351 (applicant not informed of a hearing before justices at which they made a destruction order in relation to her pit bull terrier following her nephew's conviction of having the dog in a public place without a muzzle. Held that even though the applicant's presence at a hearing may not have made any difference to the outcome, it was important that justices acted in accordance with the rules of natural justice. The destruction order was quashed).

[91]   See *R. (on the application of L) v Warwickshire County Council* [2015] EWHC 203 (Admin); [2015] B.L.G.R. 81 at [42] (government would not be possible if every decision-maker were required in

centres, owe a specific duty to then consult with users of individual centres?[92] Or to shopkeepers whose business interests may be threatened by a proposed car parking scheme?[93] Before a decision is taken to increase the number of taxi licences, should a local authority hear representations from the existing licensees, who have a private interest in preserving the commercial value of their licences?[94] Should the authority also be required to hear from those concerned that any increase in traffic may add to congestion and levels of pollution, and adversely affect public transport?[95]

Resource allocation decisions

In the past exemption from the duty of fairness has been accorded to decisions **7-025** regarded as essentially allocative,[96] or inherently non-justiciable[97] because of their substantial policy content or "managerial" qualities.[98] However, the courts are increasingly insisting that even decisions of this kind ought to provide those whose interests are affected the opportunity to participate at least in some degree. For example, decisions of prison governors, formerly considered as falling outside the ambit of judicial review, are now within its ambit.[99] A consultation on the future development of air transport was quashed as unfair because the Secretary of State excluded any options relating to the possibility of expansion of Gatwick airport.[100] A minister's decision to support building nuclear power stations as part of the national future "electricity generating mix" was quashed on the ground that the consultation process leading to the decision was procedurally flawed.[101] It has also been held that where a local authority decided to close a day care centre as a result of budgetary constraints, even though there was no express or implied statutory duty

---

every case to consult everyone who might be affected by his decision, and a duty to consult was not imposed on a local authority before it made the political decision in a meeting of its full council to approve a budget which cut funding to certain services supplied to vulnerable members of the community; this was an example of democratic power being properly, lawfully and constitutionally exercised).

[92] *LH* [2014] EWCA Civ 404 (finding that a local authority had breached its common law duty in failing to consult with the users of a particular day care centre).

[93] *R. v Camden LBC Ex p. Cran* [1995] R.T.R. 346 (failure adequately to consult residents on proposed car parking zone).

[94] *Liverpool Taxi* [1972] 2 Q.B. 299 (corporation's assurance created what was in essence a legitimate expectation of a hearing. Lord Denning MR, alone in the CA, further suggested that even in the absence of any legitimate expectation, the taxi drivers would have a sufficient interest by virtue of their existing licences to be entitled to consultation before a decision to increase the number of licences was taken). On the distinction between interests and legitimate expectations, see 7-005 and 12-003.

[95] Of course, those motivated by self-interest to make representations may bring to the attention of the decision-maker whatever considerations support their position, including matters relevant to the wider public interest that might otherwise have been overlooked: *R. v Bromley Licensing Justices Ex p. Bromley Licensed Victuallers' Association* [1984] 1 W.L.R. 585 at 589.

[96] A term used by L. Fuller, *The Morality of Law* (1969), pp.46-47, 170-177.

[97] On justiciability, see 1-034.

[98] *R v Secretary of State for the Environment Ex p. Hammersmith and Fulham LBC* [1991] 1 A.C. 521 at 585 (Lord Bridge).

[99] *West* [2005] UKHL 1; [2005] 1 W.L.R. 350; *Leech* [1988] A.C. 533. See also *R. (on the application of Gulliver) v Parole Board* [2007] EWCA Civ 1386; [2008] 1 W.L.R. 1116; *Roose* [2010] EWHC 1780 (Admin); [2010] E.L.R. 809; *Re Reilly's Application* [2013] UKSC 61; [2013] 3 W.L.R. 1020. See also *R. (on the application of Foster) v Secretary of State for Justice* [2015] EWCA Civ 281.

[100] *R. (on the application of Medway Council) v Secretary of State for Transport, Local Government and the Regions* [2002] EWHC 2516; [2003] J.P.L. 583.

[101] *R. (on the application of Greenpeace Ltd) v Secretary of State for Trade and Industry* [2007] EWHC 311; [2007] N.P.C. 21.

to consult, the obligation stemmed from the expectation that a public body, making decisions affecting the public, would act fairly.[102]

Legislative decisions

7-026   In the 4th edition of this work in 1979 it was contended that the decision of a minister to close a coal pit would, because government economic policy was involved, not attract the duty to act fairly.[103] In a later case, however, it has been held that just such a decision was void for failure to consult the unions and others who had a legitimate expectation of being consulted prior to the pit closures.[104] Nevertheless, aside from situations where a legitimate expectation exists, decisions such as these, and others categorised as "legislative", have remained relatively immune from the assault that has been made upon the distinction between duties that are analytically "judicial" and those that are "purely administrative".[105] English courts have been reluctant to impose the duty to consult on ministers exercising powers delegated under legislation to issue orders or directions.[106] Nor is such a duty imposed upon the procedures for making policy of a less formal kind,[107] although where consultation is required by statute the courts will police its implementation and insist that it is adequate and genuine.[108] By contrast, in the United States full opportunity for notice and comment for most administrative rule-making is provided by statute.[109]

---

[102] *LH* [2014] EWCA Civ 404; [2014] P.T.S.R. 1052 at 21 (Longmore LJ observing that "[i]f … a local authority withdraws a benefit previously afforded to the public, it will usually be under an obligation to consult with the beneficiaries of that service before withdrawing it"; see also [26] (describing the closure as "undoubtedly a serious step")).

[103] G. Evans (ed), *De Smith: Judicial Review of Administrative Action*, 4th edn (1980), p.180.

[104] *R. v British Coal Corporation and Secretary of State for Trade and Industry Ex p. Vardy* [1993] I.C.R. 720, DC. See Ch.12.

[105] See 6-029.

[106] See, e.g. *Bates* [1972] 1 W.L.R. 1373; *BAPIO* [2007] EWCA Civ 1139; [2008] A.C.D. 7 at [47] (there was no obligation to consult those affected or their representatives before introducing the material changes to the Immigration Rules, but Sedley LJ did not want to "elevate this to a general rule that fairness can never require consultation as a condition of the exercise of a statutory function"; see also *Moseley* [2014] UKSC 56; [2014] 1 W.L.R. 3947, in which Lord Reed JSC referred at [35] to the fact that there is no "general common law duty to consult persons who may be affected by a measure before it is adopted" save where "there is a legitimate expectation of such consultation"). The point was not considered in the House of Lords: ([2008] UKHL 27; [2008] 1 A.C. 1003).

[107] G. Ganz, *Quasi Legislation: Recent Developments in Secondary Legislation* (1987).

[108] See 7-054, for a detailed discussion of consultation rights. See also *R. (on the application of C (A Minor)) v Secretary of State for Justice* [2008] EWCA Civ 882; [2009] Q.B. 657 at [45] ("The legal obligation to take certain steps before laying legislation before Parliament is that of the executive. It is not Parliament's role to control that obligation: that is the function of the courts").

[109] S.G. Breyer, R.B. Stewart, C.R. Sunstein, A. Vermeule and M. Herz, *Administrative Law and Regulatory Policy: Problems, Text and Cases*, 7th edn (2011), Ch.6. A distinction has been drawn between trial-type hearings which are appropriate for the determination of "adjudicative facts" (facts about particular parties) and argument-type hearings to help a tribunal determine "legislative facts" (matters pertaining to questions of law, policy or discretion): R.J. Pierce, *Administrative Law Treatise* 5th edn (2009), Ch.7. This distinction is broadly acceptable in an English context, and although it has not fully been adopted by the law its effect can be seen, for example, in the inquiry procedure followed in the making of planning, compulsory purchase and highway decisions, e.g. *Bushell v Secretary of State for the Environment* [1981] A.C. 75. A duty to consult specified or other interested bodies before a regulation-making power is exercised is not an uncommon feature of British legislation, see e.g. Companies Act 2006 s.789; Anti-terrorism Crime and Security Act 2001 s.103. See generally, M. Asimov, "Delegated Legislation: United States and United Kingdom" (1983) 3 O.J.L.S. 253; B. Bracha, "The Right to be Heard in Rule Making Proceedings in England and Israel: Judicial Policy Reconsidered" (1987) Fordham International L.J. 613; C. Donnelly, "Participation and

There are two reasons why "legislative" decisions[110] have been held exempt from **7-027** the duty to provide a fair hearing: first, where the decision is taken by a minister or other elected official who is accountable to Parliament or a local authority, the courts will be chary of adding an additional forum of participation where one is already in place as part of the process of political accountability. The second reason is a practical one: bodies may be exempt from the duty to provide a hearing where the potential of adversely affected interests is too diverse or too numerous to permit each individual to participate.

The participation of both public interest groups and individuals asserting general **7-028** interests, for example, in the environment, is accepted in areas such as planning and education.[111] The planning legislation allows interested parties the opportunity to participate in planning appeals.[112] Where, however, discretion exists to deny a hearing the courts have intervened, for example to require the Secretary of State for the Environment not to dispense with an inquiry as unnecessary, when the merits of the proposal were the subject of acute local controversy among the champions of conflicting facets of the public interest.[113] It has also been held that a prominent objector to a proposed development had a right to be positively consulted prior to the holding of an appeal.[114]

When it is appropriate for the courts, rather than the legislature or the administra- **7-029** tion, to extend rights of participation to these kinds of situations is an issue of some difficulty. Undoubtedly, increasing public participation in decision-making causes delay, hinders the conferral of the intended benefits of a particular programme and imposes burdens upon governmental resources. The preparation and presentation of effective representations also takes time and money, commodities that are not evenly spread among all segments of society. Whether, and how, procedural arrangements should be made to enable broader ranges of interest to be represented raises fundamental issues about the adequacy of existing institutional arrangements for ensuring that government hears the concerns of the governed, and is sufficiently responsive and accountable to them.

While taking care not to hamper unduly effective administration, the common **7-030** law duty of fairness surely has a useful role in opening new channels of public participation, while leaving their precise contours to be defined by legislative or administrative action. As the *British Coal* case shows,[115] a legislative-type decision,[116] and one involving issues of national economic policy, is not ipso facto exempt from the duty to act fairly. Even in the absence of a legitimate expectation of a hearing, it would seem fair to allow representations by at least some of those objecting to the decisions whose interests are substantially threatened by an adverse outcome.

Expertise" in S. Rose-Ackerman, P.L. Lindseth and B. Emerson, *Comparative Administrative Law*, 2nd edn (2017), p.370.

[110] See 6-031.

[111] See 7-011.

[112] See 7-011.

[113] *Binney* [1984] J.P.L. 871; cf. *R. v Secretary of State for the Environment Ex p. Greenpeace Ltd* [1994] 4 All E.R. 352.

[114] *Wilson v Secretary of State for the Environment* [1988] J.P.L. 540; *Mancetter Developments Ltd v Secretary of State for the Environment* [1993] J.P.L. 439. Interested parties have a right to be consulted when a decision to hold a new inquiry is made: *R. v Secretary of State for the Environment Ex p. Fielder Estates (Canvey) Ltd* (1989) 57 P. & C.R. 424.

[115] [1993] I.C.R. 720.

[116] See 6-029.

Legitimate expectations

7-031   Finally, in broad terms, the existence of a legitimate expectation can affect procedural fairness in two ways: first, a representation or practice or policy indicating that a particular procedure will be followed can give rise to an entitlement that the procedure be followed[117]; and second, if there is a legitimate expectation of a substantive benefit, this may give rise to an entitlement to a fair procedure before the benefit can be withheld.[118] The impact of legitimate expectations on procedural fairness is discussed in detail in Chapter 12.[119]

FAIR PROCEDURES UNDER ECHR ART.6: THRESHOLD ISSUES

7-032   ECHR art.6 provides that:

> "In the determination of his civil rights and obligations or of any criminal charge against him, everyone is entitled to a fair and public hearing within a reasonable time by an independent and impartial tribunal established by law. Judgement shall be pronounced publicly but the press and public may be excluded from all or part of the trial in the interest of morals, public order or national security in a democratic society, where the interests of juveniles or the protection of the private life of the parties so require, or the extent strictly necessary in the opinion of the court in special circumstances where publicity would prejudice the interests of justice."[120]

7-033   Thus, the procedural fairness protection conferred by art.6 applies only to the

---

[117] *Liverpool Taxi* [1972] 2 Q.B. 299 (representation); *Attorney General of Hong Kong v Ng Yuen Shiu* [1983] 2 A.C. 629 (representation); *Nichol v Gateshead Metropolitan Borough Council* (1988) 87 L.G.R. 435 (past practice); *Vardy* [1993] I.C.R. 720 (past practice). See also *Niazi* [2008] EWCA Civ 755; (2008) 152(29) S.J.L.B. 29 at [50] (if an authority has distinctly promised to consult those affected or potentially affected, then ordinarily it must consult); *R. (on the application of Actis SA) v Secretary of State for Communities and Local Government* [2007] EWHC 2417 (Admin) at [136], [155]; *R. (on the application of Luton BC) v Secretary of State for Education* [2011] EWHC 217 (Admin); [2011] Eq. L.R. 481 at [93]-[94]; *R. (on the application of Kelly) v Hounslow LBC* [2010] EWHC 1256 (Admin) at [25]; *R. (on the application of East Midlands Care) v Leicestershire CC* [2011] EWHC 3096 (Admin) at [59]. Contrast *Niazi* [2008] EWCA Civ 755; (2008) 152(29) S.J.L.B. 29, (no legitimate expectation or exceptional circumstance to require consultation regarding changes to scheme for compensation); see also *R. (on the application of Badger Trust) v Secretary of State for the Environment, Food and Rural Affairs* [2014] EWCA Civ 1405. See further the dictum of Lord Wilson JSC in *Moseley* [2014] UKSC 56; [2014] 1 W.L.R. 3947 at [23] on the duty of consultation: "[t]he search for the demands of fairness in this context is often illumined by the doctrine of legitimate expectation."). See also *R. (on the application of Plantagenet Alliance Ltd) v Secretary of State for Justice* [2014] EWHC 1662 (Admin) at [98]; *British Dental Association v General Dental Council* [2014] EWHC 4311 (Admin) at [36] (specific public announcements can give rise to a legitimate expectation that a consultation would be conducted); *R. (on the application of Telefonica Europe Plc) v Revenue and Customs Commissioners* [2016] UKUT 173 (TCC) (even where there is no legitimate expectation, a duty to consult may arise where an abrupt change of policy would be so unfair as to amount to an abuse of power). However, a statement made in Parliament as to an intention to consult has been held not to ground a legitimate expectation of consultation: *R. (on the application of Scott H-S) v Secretary of State for Justice* [2017] EWHC 1948 (Admin).

[118] *McInnes* [1978] 1 W.L.R. 1520.

[119] See P. Craig, *Administrative Law*, 8th edn (2016), para.12-017 for a discussion of the different ways in which legitimate expectations affect the entitlement to procedural fairness.

[120] Lord Lester, D. Pannick and J. Herberg, *Human Rights Law and Practice*, 3rd edn (2009), paras 4.6.8-4.6.12; R.C.A. White and C. Ovey, *Jacobs and White The European Convention on Human Rights*, 7th edn (2017), Ch.12; P. Craig, "The Human Rights Act, Article 6 and Procedural Rights" [2003] P.L. 753; J. Herberg, A. Le Sueur and J. Mulcahy, "Determining Civil Rights and Obligations" in J. Jowell and J. Cooper (eds), *Understanding Human Rights Principles* (2001), pp.91-

determination of "civil rights or obligations" or of a criminal charge; and as was noted in Chapter 6, the boundaries of these terms have required much judicial consideration, at both the Strasbourg and the domestic level.[121] The terms have autonomous meanings, and domestic interpretations of the terms are not determinative.[122] Moreover, to engage art.6, there should be a dispute,[123] although, generally, this requirement is not interpreted too restrictively.[124]

The result of the proceedings must be decisive of the "civil rights or obligations".[125] The mere fact that an official investigation makes findings detrimental to the applicant, where it is not dispositive of a civil right or obligation, will not bring the investigation within the scope of art.6.[126] It had previously been considered that interim proceedings, such as injunction proceedings, would not usually engage art.6,[127] however, this position has now changed.[128] In general, the assessment of whether initial or interim proceedings engage art.6 is to be ap-

7-034

138; P. Van Dijk, "The interpretation of 'civil rights and obligations' by the ECtHR—One more Step to Take" in F. Matscher and H. Petzold (eds), Protecting Human Rights: The European Dimension: Studies in Honour of Gérard J. Wiarda (1990) (considering the legislative history of the provision); see also J. Varuhas, "The Reformation of English Administrative Law? Rights, Rhetoric and Reality" [2013] 72(2) C.L.J. 369.

[121] See 6-048; Lester, Pannick and Herberg, *Human Rights Law and Practice*, 3rd edn (2009), paras 4.6.8-4.6.12; T. Cross, "Is there a 'Civil Right' under Article 6? Ten Principles for Public Lawyers" [2010] J.R. 366.

[122] *König v Federal Republic of Germany* (1979-80) 2 E.H.R.R. 170 at [88]-[89]; *Baraona v Portugal* (1991) 13 E.H.R.R. 329 at [42]; *Malige v France* (1999) 28 E.H.R.R. 578 at [34]; *Maaouia v France* (2001) 33 E.H.R.R. 42 at [34]. See also *R. (on the application of MK (Iran)) v Secretary of State for the Home Department* [2010] EWCA Civ 115; [2010] 1 W.L.R. 2059 (that assessment of refugee status did not amount to art.6 civil proceedings has not been changed by the implementation of Council Directive 2004/83/EC of 29 April 2004 on minimum standards for the qualification and status of third country nationals or stateless persons as refugees or as persons who otherwise need international protection and the content of the protection granted); *R. (on the application of Mdlovu) v Secretary of State for the Home Department* [2008] EWHC 2089 (Admin) at [13].

[123] This requirement appears to derive from the French version of art.6.1, which reads "contestations sur ses droits et obligations de caracter civil"; J. Herberg, A. Le Sueur and J. Mulcahy, "Determining Civil Rights and Obligations" in J. Jowell and J. Cooper (eds), *Understanding Human Rights Principles* (2001), p.93.

[124] *Moreira de Azevedo v Portugal* (1991) 13 E.H.R.R. 721 at [66].

[125] *Le Compte, Van Leuven and De Meyere v Belgium* (1982) 4 E.H.R.R. 1; *Obermeier v Austria* (1991) 13 E.H.R.R. 290. See also *R. (on the application of Gallastegui) v Westminster CC* [2013] EWCA Civ 28 at [54]-[59] (removal direction did not engage art.6).

[126] *Fayed v UK* (1994) 18 E.H.R.R. 393; *Saunders v UK* (1997) 23 E.H.R.R. 313; *R. v Secretary of State for Health Ex p. C* [2000] 1 F.L.R. 627 (inclusion in a list of people about whom there were doubts as to their suitability to work with children was not determinative of civil rights and obligations); *Philips v News Group Newspapers* [2012] EWCA Civ 48; [2012] 2 W.L.R. 848 at [72]-[74] (if information provided by an individual in the course of a civil investigation were to be used in a criminal trial against the individual, an art.6 argument would come into play in the criminal proceedings, but the article would not be engaged in the civil investigation) (not considered in [2012] UKSC 28; [2013] 1 A.C. 1).

[127] See, e.g. *R. (on the application of Kenny) v Leeds Magistrates Court* [2003] EWHC 2963 (Owen J dismissed a challenge to an interim anti-social behaviour order made without notice); *R. (on the application of Wright) v Secretary of State for Health* [2009] UKHL 3; [2009] 1 A.C. 739 at [20]; *R. (on the application of M) v Secretary of State for Constitutional Affairs* [2004] EWCA Civ 312; [2004] 1 W.L.R. 2298 at [39(5)] (interim anti-social behaviour orders were not a determination of a civil right or obligation, since they were merely interim and short-term); *Elanay Constructs Ltd v The Vestry* [2001] B.L.R. 33 (adjudicator dealing with construction contract disputes was not subject to art.6 because he was not making a "final determination").

[128] *Markass v Cyprus* [2002] E.H.R.L.R. 387; *App No 17056/06 Micallef v Mortar GC*, 15 October 2009 at [75] (holding that art.6 would be engaged where the interim measure was drastic, disposed of the main action to a considerable degree, and unless reversed on appeal would affect the legal rights of parties for a substantial period of time); *Secretary of State for the Home Department v AF* [2010] EWHC 42 (Admin); [2010] A.C.D. 47 at [59] (the interim nature of control order applications did

proached on a pragmatic, context-sensitive basis; it is a sufficient reason, but not a necessary prerequisite, for art.6 to be engaged that the initial proceedings would be truly dispositive of the civil right which is the subject of determination in the later proceedings, or would at least cause irreversible prejudice in those later proceedings; the court, in reaching its decision, should follow the practice of the European court of asking how close the link was between the two sets of proceedings, whether their object was the same, and whether there were any policy reasons for holding that art.6(1) should not apply in the initial proceedings.[129] Determinations of preliminary points on liability, costs or quantum of damages[130] and proceedings to enforce a settlement agreement are also considered to engage art.6.[131]

7-035　　The rights and obligations of private persons in their relations as between themselves are civil rights and obligations, such as in tort,[132] family law,[133] employment law[134] and the law of real property.[135] With regard to relations between the individual and the state, it appears that art.6 applies to the determination of all rights of a pecuniary nature, including for example, rights to real[136] and personal[137] property, the right to engage in a commercial activity,[138] the right to practise a

---

not mean that art.6 was not engaged as they had a clear and decisive impact on the exercise of a civil right); *Perry v Nursing and Midwifery Council* [2013] EWCA Civ 145; [2013] 1 W.L.R. 3423 at [15]–[16] (assumed though not determined that ECHR art.6 rights were engaged by an interim investigation and suspension decision taken by the Nursing and Midwifery Council).

[129] *R. (on the application of G) v Governors of X School* [2011] UKSC 30; [2012] 1 A.C. 167 at [35], [64]–[69], [90]. See also *R. (on the application of Aggregate Industries UK Ltd) v English Nature* [2002] EWHC 908; [2003] Env. L.R. 3 at [56] (decision-making process should be "directly decisive" of the civil rights or obligation in question); see also *Wright* [2009] UKHL 3; [2009] 1 A.C. 739 (a provisional listing of a care worker as unsuitable to work with vulnerable adults could result in possibly irreparable damage to a person's employment or prospects of employment in the care sector and engaged ECHR art.6(1) notwithstanding that it was only an interim measure); *BM v Secretary of State for the Home Department* [2009] EWHC 1572 (Admin); [2010] 1 All E.R. 847 at [8] (ECHR art.6 was engaged by an appeal against the modification of a control order as the interference with the civil right would be for an "uncertain, but finite, period").

[130] *Obermeier* (1991) 13 E.H.R.R. 290 at [66]-[67]; *Robins v UK* (1998) 26 E.H.R.R. 527 at [28]-[29]; *Silva Pontes v Portugal* (1994) 18 E.H.R.R. 156 at [30]-[36].

[131] *Pérez de Rada Cavanilles v Spain* (2000) 29 E.H.R.R. 109 at [39]; *R. (on the application of Mitchell) v Horsham District Council* [2003] EWHC 234 Admin at [32]–[33].

[132] *Axen v Germany* (1984) 6 E.H.R.R. 195.

[133] *Airey v Ireland* (1979) 2 E.H.R.R. 305.

[134] *Bucholz v Germany* (1980) E.H.R.R. 597; *Wright* [2009] UKHL 3; [2009] 1 A.C. 739.

[135] *Langborger v Sweden* (1989) 12 E.H.R.R. 416.

[136] *Holy Monasteries v Greece* (1994) 20 E.H.R.R. 1 at [85]; *Bryan v UK* (1995) 21 E.H.R.R. 342 at [31]; *Friends Provident Life and Pensions Ltd v Secretary of State for Transport, Local Government and Regions* [2001] EWHC Admin 820; [2002] 1 W.L.R. 1450 at [70] (planning decision a determination of civil rights and obligations of corporate objector, given the latter's property interests). cf. *Bovis Homes Ltd v New Forest DC* [2002] EWHC 483 (Admin) at [300] (decision to make a local plan so that development of the claimant's land was less likely, was not a determination of a civil right or obligation).

[137] *Anca v Belgium* App. No.10259/83, 40 D.R. 170 (1984) (bankruptcy proceedings); *X v Austria* App. No.7830/77, 14 D.R. 200 (1978) (patent rights).

[138] *The Tre Traktörer Aktiebolag v Sweden* (1989) 13 E.H.R.R. 309 (withdrawal of an alcohol licence from a restaurant); *Pudas v Sweden* (1988) 18 E.H.R.R. 188 (licence to operate a taxi); *R. (on the application of Chief Constable of Lancashire) v Preston Crown Court* [2001] EWHC Admin 928; [2002] 1 W.L.R. 1332 at [17] (liquor licensing decision a determination of a civil right or obligation because it goes to the right to make a living or economic activity); *R. (on the application of Thompson) v Law Society* [2004] EWCA Civ 167; [2004] 1 W.L.R. 2522 at [80] (art.6 applies to disciplinary proceedings where the right to exercise a profession is at stake); *L v Law Society* [2008] EWCA Civ 811; see also *Re Solicitor No.13 of 2007* [2008] EWCA Civ 411 (assumed although not determined that imposing conditions on a practising certificate determines a civil right).

profession,[139] and the right to compensation for illegal state acts.[140] Disciplinary proceedings resulting in professional suspension,[141] questions relating to children taken into care[142]; decisions relating to planning and the environment[143]; inclusion in a list barring an individual from working with children and vulnerable adults[144]; conditions of detention[145]; extradition of a UK citizen[146]; an application for release from detention in a prison psychiatric wing[147]; and use of individuals as covert human intelligence sources[148] also engage art.6. Even a first-time applicant for a licence may be entitled to art.6 protection.[149] In addition, art.6 applies in the field of social insurance, not only to assistance linked to private employment contracts,[150] but also where the benefit is non-contributory, provided it is not entirely discretionary.[151] While previously, prisoner disciplinary decisions have been

---

[139] *König* (1979-80) 2 E.H.R.R. 469. See also *Crompton v UK* (2010) 50 E.H.R.R. 36 (redundancy from the Territorial Army).

[140] *Editions Périscope v France* (1992) 14 E.H.R.R. 597 at [35]-[40].

[141] *Fredin v Sweden* (1991) 13 E.H.R.R. 784 (medical profession); *Le Compte* (1982) 4 E.H.R.R. 1; *Paluda v Slovakia* App. 33392/12, 23 May 2017; see also *McCarthy v Visitors to the Inns of Court* [2015] EWCA Civ 12. In this context, it has been held that the relevant consideration is whether the decision of the disciplinary body *could* result in a determination of civil rights and obligations, such as through suspension, rather than considering whether the outcome of the disciplinary hearing may be admonishment: *Tehrani v UK Central Council for Nursing, Midwifery & Health Visiting* [2001] I.R.L.R. 208 at [33]; *Thompson* [2004] 1 W.L.R. 2522 at [83]; *Threlfall v General Optical Council* [2004] EWHC 2683 (Admin); [2005] Lloyd's Rep. Med. 250 at [33]-[35]; *Perry* [2013] EWCA Civ 145; [2013] 1 W.L.R. 3423. ECHR art.6 would not be engaged, however, in ordinary disciplinary proceedings where all that could be at stake is the loss of a specific job: *R. (on the application of Puri) v Bradford Teaching Hospitals NHS Foundation Trust* [2011] EWHC 970 (Admin); [2011] I.R.L.R. 582; *Kulkarni v Milton Keynes Hospital NHS Trust* [2009] EWCA Civ 789; [2010] I.C.R. 101 at [65]; *R. (on the application of Mattu) v University Hospitals of Coventry and Warwickshire NHS Trust* [2012] EWCA Civ 641; [2012] 4 All E.R. 359; *Christou v Haringey London Borough Council* [2013] EWCA Civ 178.

[142] *McMichael v UK* (1995) 20 E.H.R.R. 205.

[143] *Mats Jacobsson v Sweden* (1991) 13 E.H.R.R. 79; *Taskin v Turkey* (2006) 42 E.H.R.R. 50.

[144] *R. (on the application of Royal College of Nursing) v Secretary of State for the Home Department* [2010] EWHC 2761 (Admin); [2011] P.T.S.R. 1193. See also *Wright* [2009] UKHL 3; [2009] 1 A.C. 739 (interim listing as unsuitable care worker).

[145] *Ganci v Italy* (2005) 41 E.H.R.R. 16; *Musumeci v Italy* App. No.33695/96 (11 January 2005). However, decisions on segregation and cellular confinement of prisoners taken by prison governors or segregation review boards have not been regarded as engaging art.6: *R. (on the application of King) v Secretary of State for Justice* [2012] EWCA Civ 376; [2012] 1 W.L.R. 3602 at [36]-[41]; overruled although not on this ground (*R. (on the application of Bourgass) v Secretary of State for Justice* [2015] UKSC 54 at [123]).

[146] *Pomiechowski v District Court of Legnica* [2012] UKSC 20; [2012] 1 W.L.R. 1604 at [31]-[33].

[147] *Aerts v Belgium* (2000) 29 E.H.R.R. 50.

[148] *R. (on the application of K) v Secretary of State for Defence* [2016] EWCA Civ 1149; [2017] 1 W.L.R. 1671.

[149] *Benthem v Netherlands* (1985) 8 E.H.R.R. 1 (an application for a grant of a statutory licence to operate an installation for the supply of liquefied petroleum gas was rejected, and this was found to constitute a "civil right" given that it was a pre-condition for the exercise of business activity: [36]); *McInnes* [1978] 1 W.L.R. 1520. But see *Ladbrokes Worldwide Betting v Sweden* (2008) 47 E.H.R.R. SE10 (application for a permit to provide betting and gaming services in Sweden did not engage art.6 where the grant of the permit was entirely within the discretion of the government and there were no clear criteria).

[150] See, e.g. *Lombardo v Italy* (1992) 21 E.H.R.R. 188 at [14]-[17] (pension linked to employment).

[151] *Salesi v Italy* (1993) 26 E.H.R.R. 187; *Tsfayo v UK* App. No.60860/00; [2007] B.L.G.R. 1 (discussed further at 10-089); *R. (on the application of Husain) v Asylum Support Adjudicator* [2001] EWHC Admin 852 [2002] A.C.D. 61 at [25] (termination of asylum support engaged art.6); see also *Primary Health Investment Properties Ltd v Secretary of State for Health* [2009] EWHC 519 (Admin); [2009] P.T.S.R. 1586 (where a trust had discretion to deny financial assistance a civil right for the purpose of art.6 did not arise); *R. (on the application of Ali) v Secretary of State for Justice* [2013] EWHC

excluded from the scope of ECHR art.6,[152] the ECtHR has itself identified a "shift" in its own case law.[153] By contrast, however, it appears that the Strasbourg Court is generally reluctant to extend the protection of art.6 to certain non-pecuniary benefits[154]; and school exclusions and disciplinary proceedings,[155] asylum or citizenship applications,[156] deportation,[157] and questions regarding tax liability,[158] generally do not engage art.6. In a tendering process, where a contracting committee was obliged to recommend tenders which ensured the best value for money at the lowest possible cost, this did not mean that the least expensive bid had to be chosen, and there was no expectation, even less so a right, that the lowest offer would be

---

72 (Admin); [2013] 1 W.L.R. 3536 at [65]–[72] (doubting if a statutory scheme for compensation for reversal of a conviction engaged ECHR art.6).

[152] See, e.g., *R. (on the application of King) v Secretary of State for Justice* [2012] EWCA Civ 376; [2012] 1 W.L.R. 3602 at [36]–[41]; overruled although not on this ground (*R. (on the application of Bourgass) v Secretary of State for Justice* [2015] UKSC 54 at [123]).

[153] *De Tommaso v Italy* (2017) 65 E.H.R.R. 19 at [151] (imposition of a preventative order engaged art.6);

[154] See, e.g. *Pierre-Bloch v France* (1997) 26 E.H.R.R. 202 at [50]–[55] (holding that the right to stand for election to the National Assembly in France was a "political" and not a "civil" right); *Adams and Benn v UK* (1997) 23 E.H.R.R. C.D. 160 (Commission) (holding that the right to move within the EU pursuant to art.18 of the EC Treaty did not engage art.6); See also *R. (on the application of R) v Children and Family Court Advisory and Support Service* [2012] EWCA Civ 853; [2013] 1 W.L.R. 163 (CAFCASS obligation to provide scheme for representation of children in care proceedings was a target duty and did not amount to an actionable duty or engage ECHR art.6).

[155] *R. (on the application of B) v Head Teacher of Alperton Community School* [2001] EWHC Admin 229; [2002] B.L.G.R. 132; (no private right to education, therefore art.6 not engaged); *R. (on the application of M-P) v Barking LBC* [2002] EWHC 2483; [2003] E.L.R. 144 at [28] (the decision to remove a pupil from a school register was not a determination of a civil right or obligation) *R. v Richmond upon Thames LBC Ex p. JC* [2001] E.L.R. 21 at [59] (primary school admissions decision was not a determination of "civil rights"). cf. *S* [2002] EWCA Civ 693; [2002] E.L.R. 556 at [30] (considering and assuming that a school exclusion does engage art.6); *R. (on the application of V) v Independent Appeal Panel for Tom Hood School* [2010] EWCA Civ 142; [2010] P.T.S.R. 1462 at [12]–[15]; *Governors of X School* [2011] UKSC 30; [2012] 1 A.C. 167.

[156] *Maaouia* (2001) 33 E.H.R.R. 42 (proceedings to challenge an exclusion order); *R. (on the application of Harrison) v Secretary of State for the Home Department* [2003] EWCA Civ 432, [2003] I.N.L.R. 294 (where it was doubted whether citizenship decisions were capable of constituting determinations of civil rights or obligations); *MK (Iran)* [2010] EWCA Civ 115; [2010] 1 W.L.R. 2059 at [70]-[76] (claim to refugee status under art.13 of Council Directive 2004/83/EC was not a "civil right" for the purposes of art.6, however, Sedley LJ observed that he reached this conclusion with "considerable reluctance" on the basis that it was not appropriate for the domestic court to move ahead of Strasbourg's jurisprudence); *Murungaru* [2008] EWCA Civ 1015; [2009] I.N.L.R. 180 at [33] (a challenge to the withdrawal of a visa was a challenge to immigration controls and could not be disguised as an assertion of property rights); *R (YA) v Secretary of State for the Home Department* [2013] EWHC 3229 (Admin) at [103] (refusal of leave to an alien to enter and conditions on leave to stay did not engage art.6); *R. (on the application of Rahman) v Secretary of State for the Home Department* [2015] EWHC 1146 (Admin) at [32]. But see *R. (on the application of Gudanaviciene) v Director of Legal Aid Casework* [2014] EWCA Civ 1622; [2015] 1 W.L.R. 2247 at [181] (the Lord Chancellor's guidance on exceptional civil legal aid funding pursuant to s.10(3)(a) of the Legal Aid, Sentencing and Punishment of Offenders Act 2012 impermissibly stated that only in rare and extreme cases, and in no immigration cases, would a refusal of legal aid amount to a breach of ECHR art.6(1), and hence the guidance itself was incompatible with ECHR art.6(1) and ECHR art.8). See also *R. (on the application of S) v Director of legal Aid Casework* [2016] EWCA Civ 464; [2016] 3 Costs L.R. 569.

[157] *RB (Algeria) v Secretary of State for the Home Department* [2009] UKHL 10; [2010] 2 A.C. 110; see also *BB v Secretary of State for the Home Department* [2015] EWCA Civ 9 (ECHR art.6 was not used in quashing a subsequent deportation decision in respect of the same appellant as in *RB*).

[158] *Charalambos v France* App. No.49210/99, Admissibility Decision of 8 February 2000 (determination of tax liability). See also *Hargreaves v Revenue and Customs Commissioners* [2016] EWCA Civ 174; [2016] 1 W.L.R. 2981; *Walapu v Revenue and Customs Commissioners* [2016] EWHC 658 (Admin); [2016] S.T.C. 1682.

awarded the tender.[159] There has also been a complicated and unsatisfactory series of cases regarding civil service employment. Initially, the ECtHR held that "disputes relating to the recruitment, careers and termination of service of civil servants are as a general rule outside the scope of art.6(1)".[160] However, after a number of cases,[161] the position that has now emerged is that in order to prevent civil servants relying on ECHR art.6, the state must show (a) that national law had expressly excluded access to a court for the post or category of staff in question; and (b) that the exclusion was justified on objective grounds in the state's interest.[162] There has been some uncertainty regarding whether art.6 is engaged by the regime in the Terrorist Asset-Freezing etc Act 2010, which provides, inter alia, for the inclusion of an individual on a list of persons suspected of connections with terrorism and consequent freezing of assets. The better view of the case law is that art.6 is engaged by this regime[163]; this position is also appropriate, given the obviously detrimental impact of such a designation on the individual involved.[164] There has also been a divergence of view between the domestic courts and the Strasbourg court on whether a determination by a local housing authority that it had discharged its duty to a homeless housing applicant engages art.6.[165]

In determining whether the proceedings are determinative of a criminal charge, it is necessary to consider: the classification of the proceedings in domestic law; the nature of the offence itself; and the severity of the penalty which may be imposed.[166] If the proceedings are categorised as "criminal" in domestic law, this will be decisive. If, however, the proceedings are categorised as "civil", the ECtHR will conduct an independent examination of the nature of the proceedings. The sever-

7-036

---

[159] *ITC Ltd v Malta* (2008) 46 E.H.R.R. SE13 at [41].

[160] *Massa v Italy* (1994) 18 E.H.R.R. 266 at [26].

[161] See, e.g. *De Santa v Italy* App. No.25574/94; *Lapalorcia v Italy* App. No.25586/94; *Abenavoli v Italy* App. No.25587/94 (2 September 1997); *Neigel v France* (2000) 30 E.H.R.R. 310.

[162] *Vilho Eskelinen v Finland* (2007) 45 E.H.R.R. 43 at [62]; *Pellegrin v France* (2001) 31 E.H.R.R. 26 at [66]. For a comparative perspective on this question, see *Dunsmuir v New Brunswick (Board of Management)* 2008 S.C.C. 9; [2008] 1 S.C.R. 190; *Société de l'assurance automobile du Québec v Cyr* [2008] S.C.C. 13; see also *Klausecker v Germany* (2015) 60 E.H.R.R. SE9; *Boyraz v Turkey* (2015) 60 E.H.R.R. 30.

[163] Sedley LJ reached an obiter view that it was not engaged in *R. (on the application of Maftah) v Secretary of State for Foreign and Commonwealth Affairs* [2011] EWCA Civ 350; [2012] Q.B. 477 (also rejecting (at [25]) an argument that there was an overriding class of exempted acts representing the exercise of the state's sovereign power). See also: *R. (on the application of Bhutta) v HM Treasury* [2011] EWHC 1789 (Admin); [2011] A.C.D. 106. However, in *Bank Mellat v HM Treasury* [2010] EWCA Civ 483; [2012] Q.B. 91, the Court of Appeal upheld the conclusion of Mitting J that art.6 applied in the context of financial restrictions (overturned though not on this ground in *Bank Mellat* [2013] UKSC 39; [2014] A.C. 700). Lord Kerr proceeded on the assumption (at [129]) that art.6 applies, albeit that this was not decided; see also *Mastafa v HM Treasury* [2012] EWHC 3578 (Admin) (Collins J concluding at [15] that it was "inevitable" that art.6 applied).

[164] *Mastafa* [2012] EWHC 3578 (Admin) at [4] (Collins J observing that a designation produces "serious constraints on the person's ability to live his life as he would normally expect and so interferes with his human rights"); see also *Bank Mellat* [2013] UKSC 39; [2014] A.C. 700 at [157] per Lord Hope (dissenting) ("it is not disputed that the Bank's right to carry on its business was a civil right and that the effect of the direction was to greatly impede the exercise of that right").

[165] *Ali v Birmingham CC* [2010] UKSC 8; [2010] 2 A.C. 39 (duty to secure that accommodation was available for occupation by a homeless applicant did not engage art.6(1)). In this case, Lord Collins criticised (at [60]) the Strasbourg court's "apparent reluctance to enunciate principles which will enable a line to be drawn between those rights in public law which are to be regarded as 'civil rights' and those which are not to be so regarded". When the case was considered by the ECtHR in *Ali v United Kingdom* (2016) 63 E.H.R.R. 20, it was held that art.6 was engaged. However, in *Poshteh v Kensington and Chelsea RLBC* [2017] UKSC 36; [2017] 2 W.L.R. 1417, the Supreme Court followed its own ruling in *Ali*, noting that the Strasbourg court had not engaged sufficiently with the reasoning of the Supreme Court in *Ali*.

[166] *Engel v Netherlands* (1976) 1 E.H.R.R. 647 at [82].

ity of the penalty will often be decisive[167] and in particular, if there is a power to impose imprisonment, this will generally suffice to categorise the proceedings as "criminal", unless the "nature, duration or manner of execution of the imprisonment" is not "appreciably detrimental".[168] Certain prison disciplinary proceedings may engage art.6, if they are sufficiently serious.[169] Even in cases where the penalty is in the nature of a fine rather than imprisonment,[170] if a punitive and deterrent penalty is attached, it is likely that the proceedings will be regarded as criminal in character, rather than disciplinary. However, where the offence is limited to a restricted group, as is generally the case in relation to disciplinary offences, a court would be unlikely to characterise the charge under the applicable disciplinary or regulatory code as criminal, at least unless it involves or may lead to loss of liberty.[171]

FAIR PROCEDURES UNDER ECHR ART.2: THRESHOLD ISSUES

7-037   The obligation to protect the right to life under art.2, in conjunction with the State's general duty under art.1 to "secure to everyone within [its] jurisdiction the rights and freedoms defined in [the] Convention" also requires by implication that there should be some form of effective official investigation when individuals have been killed as a result of the use of force, either by State officials or private individuals.[172] This includes where there has been a breach of the right to life through the use of lethal force,[173] but also arises in a range of other circumstances.[174] For example, it has been held that the art.2 obligation to conduct an investigation

---

[167] *Brown v UK* (1998) 28 E.H.R.R. CD 233. See also *British-American Tobacco (Holdings) Ltd v Revenue and Customs Commissioners* [2017] UKFTT 167 (TC); [2017] S.F.T.D. 550 at [479]–[485]

[168] *Engel* (1976) 1 E.H.R.R. 647 at [82]; *R. (on the application of Napier) v Secretary of State for the Home Department* [2004] EWHC 936; [2004] 1 W.L.R. 3056 (the decision to impose additional days on a prisoner was "criminal" for the purposes of art.6); *R. v H* [2003] UKHL 1; [2003] 1 W.L.R. 41 (jury procedure for dealing with a defendant unfit to stand trial was not the determination of a criminal charge because it could not culminate in a penal sanction); *West* [2005] UKHL 1; [2005] 1 W.L.R. 350 (the decision to recall a determinative sentence prisoner, released on licence, not the determination of a criminal charge so as to render an oral hearing for that reason necessary); *R. (on the application of Manjit Singh Sunder) v Secretary of State for the Home Department* [2001] EWHC Admin 252 at [22] (reclassification of a prisoner did not engage art.6, there being no determination of a criminal charge); *Galstyan v Armenia*, App.No.26986/03 (15 November 2007) at [56]–[60]; *Secretary of State for the Home Department v MB* [2007] UKHL 46; [2008] 1 A.C. 440 (control orders civil and not criminal); *Pomiechowski* [2012] UKSC 20; [2012] 1 W.L.R. 1604 (extradition does not involve a criminal charge but determination of a civil right to remain in the United Kingdom).

[169] *Campbell and Fell v UK* (1984) 7 E.H.R.R. 165; *Ezeh and Connors v UK* (2002) 35 E.H.R.R. 691.

[170] *Han (t/a Murdishaw Supper Bar) v Customs and Excise Commissioners* [2001] EWCA Civ 1048; [2001] 1 W.L.R. 2253 at [66].

[171] *Han* [2001] EWCA Civ 1048; [2001] 1 W.L.R. 2253; see also *Flaxmode Ltd v Revenue and Customs Commissioners* [2010] UKFTT 28 at [39] (daily penalty pursuant to tax legislation was not a criminal charge).

[172] *Huseynova v Azerbaijan*, App. No. 10653/10 13 April 2017, at [105].

[173] *McCann v UK* (1995) 21 E.H.R.R. 97; *R. (on the application of Middleton) v West Somerset Coroner* [2004] UKHL 10; [2004] 2 A.C. 182 at [3]; *R. (on the application of A) v Lord Saville of Newdigate* [2001] EWCA Civ 2048; [2002] 1 W.L.R. 1249 at [10]–[11]; *R. (on the application of Green) v Police Complaints Authority* [2004] UKHL 6; [2004] 1 W.L.R. 725 at [11].

[174] *Rabone v Pennine Care Trust* [2012] UKSC 2; [2012] 2 A.C. 72 at [15]–[16] (giving the examples of prisoners, immigrants in administrative detention, psychiatric patients detained in public hospitals and military conscripts). See also *Öneryildiz v Turkey* (2005) 41 E.H.R.R. 325 (endorsed recently

can be triggered in the context of a near-suicide of a prisoner. This is because prisoners as a class present a particular risk of suicide, and art.2 requires prison authorities to put in place systemic precautions to prevent suicide and to take operational measures when they know or ought to know of a real and immediate risk that a prisoner might commit suicide.[175] Likewise, where the death of a mental health patient who had been detained by the state raised issues as to whether the medical authorities had failed in their obligation to take general measures to save her from dying.[176] The art.2 duty will not just arise where individuals are in the custody of the state. It applies to the death of patients in the care of the medical profession, whether in the public or the private sector.[177] It also extends to those under the authority or control of the state and its agents, as well as those affected a state's agents when exercising authority and control on the state's behalf.[178] Article 2 does not, however, apply to questions about the legality of resort to war.[179] While it had previously been held that art.2 did not apply to the investigation of any death occurring before the entry into force of the HRA,[180] it is now the case that the procedural obligation under art.2 is independent and may arise at the time of the investigation, irrespective of whether any substantive obligation under art.2 applied to the death.[181] However, this obligation arises in relation to the applicable standards for an ongoing investigation, rather than to the question of whether there

---

in *Sinim v Turkey* App. No. 9441/10, 6 June 2017).

[175] *R. (on the application of L (A Patient)) v Secretary of State for Justice (Equality and Human Rights Commission intervening)* [2008] UKHL 68; [2009] 1 A.C. 588 at [39], [57]. Contrast *R. (on the application of P) v Secretary of State for Justice* [2009] EWCA Civ 701; [2010] Q.B. 317 at [40]–[42].

[176] *R. (on the application of Allen) v HM Coroner for Inner North London* [2009] EWCA Civ 623; [2009] LS Law Medical 430. However, where a person detained had committed suicide while in hospital, the State was not required, in fulfilling its procedural obligation under art.2, to perform an immediate and independent investigation into the circumstances of the death prior to an inquest: *R. (on the application of Antoniu) v Central and North West London NHS Foundation Trust* [2013] EWHC 3055; [2014] A.C.D. 44.

[177] *Iwanowicz v Poland* (2017) 64 E.H.R.R. SE2 at [53].

[178] *R. (on the application of Al Skeini) v United Kingdom* (2011) 53 E.H.R.R. 18; *Smith v Ministry of Defence* [2013] UKSC 41; [2014] A.C. 52. In this case, the Supreme Court took the step of departing from its earlier decision in *R. (on the application of Smith) v Oxfordshire Assistant Deputy Coroner (Equality and Human Rights)* [2010] UKSC 29; [2011] 1 A.C. 1. In the earlier case, it had been held that unless they were on a UK military base, British troops on active service overseas were not within the jurisdiction of the United Kingdom. However, in light of the ruling in *Al-Skeini*, the State could be held to exercise jurisdiction extraterritorially wherever the State through its agents exercised control and authority over an individual. See also G. Junor, "A Soldier's (Human) Rights when Fighting Abroad: The Supreme Court Decides" [2013] 37 S.L.T. 251. The jurisdiction test in *Al-Skeini* has also been applied in *Jaloud v Netherlands* (2015) 60 E.H.R.R. 29 (see [154]); see also *R. (on the application of Al Saadoon) v Secretary of State for Defence* [2016] EWCA Civ 811; [2017] 2 W.L.R. 219.

[179] *R. (on the application of Gentle) v Prime Minister* [2008] UKHL 20; [2008] 1 A.C. 1356 at [8]–[9], [22], [58], [70] (refusing review of the Government's decision to hold an independent inquiry into the circumstances leading to the invasion of Iraq). See also *Ministry of Defence* [2013] UKSC 41; [2014] A.C. 52 at [65], [75]–[76], [81] in which the Supreme Court held that the extent to which the application of the substantive obligation under art.2 could be held impossible or inappropriate would vary according to context and that procurement decisions, although remote from the battlefield, would not always be appropriate for review. The court had to avoid imposing unrealistic positive obligations on the state regarding the planning and conduct of military operations, but it had to give effect to obligations where it was reasonable to expect the protection of ECHR art.2.

[180] *Re McKerr's Application for Judicial Review* [2004] 1 W.L.R. 807; *Keyu v Secretary of State for Foreign and Commonwealth Affairs* [2015] UKSC 69; [2015] 3 W.L.R. 1665 (declining to decide whether *Re McKerr* remains good law in circumstances in which the Supreme Court had not reached a clear and unanimous view).

[181] *Re McCaughey's Application for Judicial Review* [2011] UKSC 20; [2012] 1 A.C. 725; *McCaughey v United Kingdom* (2014) 58 E.H.R.R. 13; *Šilih v Slovenia* (2009) 49 E.H.R.R. 996 at

is an obligation to commence an investigation into an historic death.[182] For the obligation to be engaged, there must exist a genuine connection between the death and the entry into force of the Convention in respect of the respondent state for the procedural obligations; a significant proportion of the procedural steps required by this provision—which include not only an effective investigation into the death of the person concerned but also the institution of appropriate proceedings for the purpose of determining the cause of the death and holding those responsible to account—will have been or ought to have been carried out after the date of entry into force.[183] However, the Strasbourg Court has not excluded the possibility that in certain circumstances the connection could also be based on the need to ensure that the guarantees and the underlying values of the Convention are protected in a real and effective manner.[184]

7-038   Lack of state protection, rather than just direct state involvement, will trigger the art.2 procedural duty,[185] and where authorities are informed of a death, this in itself can give rise to an obligation to carry out an effective investigation into the circumstances surrounding the death.[186] This is because the object of an art.2 investigation is not limited to securing the accountability of state agents, but extends to opening up the circumstances, correcting mistakes, identifying good practice and learning lessons for the future.[187] The fact that a security situation exists in the country will not relieve the state of its obligation.[188]

CONTENT OF PROCEDURAL FAIRNESS: OVERVIEW

7-039   The content of procedural fairness in any given context may be determined by statute, the common law, the ECHR and European Union law. As a general observation, the general position of the English courts is that the requirements of art.6 and

---

[159]–[163]; *Janowiec v Russia* (2014) 58 E.H.R.R. 30 at [132]–[133], [145]–[148]. See also *Keyu* [2015] UKSC 69; [2015] 3 W.L.R. 1665; *Varnava v Turkey* (2010) 50 E.H.R.R. 21.

[182]   *Keyu* [2015] UKSC 69; [2015] 3 W.L.R. 1665.

[183]   While both criteria were satisfied in *Finucane v Secretary of State for Northern Ireland* [2017] NICA 7, a review rather than a public inquiry was not incompatible with the State's procedural obligation.

[184]   *Šilih* (2009) 49 E.H.R.R. 996 at [163]; *Janowiec* (2014) 58 E.H.R.R. 30 at [132]–[133]. In *Re McCaughey's Application* [2011] UKSC 20; [2012] 1 A.C. 725, it was significant that an inquest was to be held in to the deaths at issue, which meant that art.2 was engaged. The criteria were held not to have been satisfied in *Keyu* [2015] UKSC 69; [2015] 3 W.L.R. 1665 in respect of the deaths of 24 unarmed civilians killed by British soldiers in colonial Malaya in 1948. Baroness Hale dissented on the issue of identifying the "critical date" for the operation of the requirement for a genuine connection between the death and the entry into force of the Convention, with the majority regarding the relevant date as being the date of recognition of the right of individual petition to the Strasbourg court (for the United Kingdom, 1966), and Baroness Hale regarding the date as being the date of entry into force of the Convention (for the United Kingdom, 1953).

[185]   *R. (on the application of Challender) v Legal Services Commission* [2004] EWHC 925; [2004] A.C.D. 57 at [49]; *R. (on the application of Letts) v Lord Chancellor* [2015] EWHC 402 (Admin); [2015] 1 W.L.R. 4497 at [95] (case law identified a variety of circumstances and types of case of real public importance and significance where the duty arose independently of the existence of such evidence).

[186]   *Tanrikulu v Turkey* (2000) 30 E.H.R.R. 950; *Menson v UK* (2003) 37 E.H.R.R. C.D. 220; *Ergi v Turkey* (2001) 32 E.H.R.R. 388; *Yasa v Turkey* (1998) 28 E.H.R.R. 408 at [100]; *R. (on the application of Litvinenko) v Secretary of State for the Home Department* [2014] EWHC 194 (Admin); [2014] H.R.L.R. 6 at [50]–[52] (here the ECHR art.2 obligation was discharged by an "extremely thorough" and "exceptionally detailed" police investigation into the death of a man in a London restaurant from radiation poisoning and the attempted extradition of two named suspects).

[187]   *Gentle* [2008] 1 A.C. 1356 at [5]–[7]; *L (A Patient)* [2008] UKHL 68; [2009] 1 A.C. 588 at [24], [29], [40].

[188]   *Tanrikulu* (2000) 30 E.H.R.R. 950.

the common law are equivalent,[189] albeit that, as was noted in Chapter 6 and just discussed, common law procedural fairness is broader in its scope of application.[190] ECHR art.2 has a very specific impact on the content of procedural fairness: it requires an effective official investigation where an individual is killed as a result of the use of force and identifies the elements which must be satisfied in order for an investigation to be deemed "effective".[191] Meanwhile, as was also noted in Chapter 6, the most notable contribution of European Union law to the content of procedural fairness is the requirement to give reasons where the decision of a national authority has the effect of denying a fundamental European Union right, and this requirement is discussed in Chapter 14.[192]

A flexible and evolving concept

The content of procedural fairness is infinitely flexible.[193] It is not possible to lay down rigid rules and everything depends on the subject-matter.[194] The requirements necessary to achieve fairness range from mere consultation at the lower end,

7-040

---

[189] See, e.g. *R. (on the application of Bright) v Central Criminal Court* [2001] 1 W.L.R. 662 at 679 (Judge LJ noting that "by now we surely fully appreciate that the principles to be found in ECHR arts 6 and 10 are bred in the bone of the common law"); *Guardian News and Media Ltd v Incedal* [2014] EWCA Crim 1861; [2015] 1 Cr. App. R. 4 at [11] (no difference in substance between common law and ECHR art.6 in relation to the principle that "[t]he Court does not require a party to destroy the right it is seeking to assert or protect as the price of its vindication"). See also *R. (on the application of B) v Westminster Magistrates' Court* [2014] UKSC 59; [2015] A.C. 1195 at [28] and [34] (ECHR art.6 did not require in the determination of extradition proceedings a further exception, to the ordinary principles of open inter partes justice, beyond those identified by Lord Dyson JSC in *Al Rawi v Security Service* [2011] UKSC 34; [2012] 1 A.C. 531); *R. (on the application of O'Connor) v Aldershot Magistrates' Court* [2016] EWHC 2792 (Admin); [2017] 1 W.L.R. 2833 at [52] (noting that that "this is a case where, without recourse to the Convention, the common law has all the resources needed to protect the rights concerned"); *McCarthy* [2015] EWCA Civ 12 (a material non-disclosure of a witness statement in disciplinary proceedings against a barrister was procedurally unfair, and it was immaterial in this context whether the question was answered using the common law or ECHR art.6). But see *Al Rawi* [2011] UKSC 34; [2012] 1 A.C. 531 at [68] (although a closed material procedure was lawful pursuant to ECHR art.6 it was a distinct question whether it was lawful under the common law as it was open to the courts to provide greater protection through the common law than that which was guaranteed by the Convention).

[190] See 6-009 and 7-017; *R. (on the application Wooder) v Feggetter* [2002] EWCA Civ 554; [2003] Q.B. 219 at [46] ("the common law sets high standards of due process in non-judicial settings to which the European Court of Human Rights at Strasbourg declines to apply art.6").

[191] See 7-130.

[192] See 6-049, 14-145 and 14-156.

[193] *Pergamon* [1971] Ch. 388 at 403 (Sachs LJ noting the need for "real flexibility"); *Russell v Duke of Norfolk* [1949] 1 All E.R. 109 at 1188 (Tucker LJ noting "There are, in my view, no words which are of universal application to every kind of inquiry and every kind of domestic tribunal. The requirements of natural justice must depend on the circumstances of the case, the nature of the inquiry, the rules under which the tribunal is acting, the subject-matter under consideration and so on"). *Hopkins Developments* [2014] EWCA Civ 470 (Jackson LJ noting at [85] that "[f]airness is thus a flexible concept"). However, caution was expressed in respect of an emphasis on procedural fairness being "flexible" in *L* [2014] EWCA Civ 47; (2014) 158(6) S.J.L.B. 37 at [68]–[69]. Beatson LJ was concerned that the emphasis could lead to an inappropriate drawing together of the concepts of procedural and substantive fairness and undue uncertainty. For comparative perspectives, see 6-056.

[194] *Benaim and Khaida* [1970] 2 Q.B. 417 at 439 (Lord Denning MR); *Sheridan v Stanley Cole (Wainfleet) Ltd* [2003] EWCA Civ 1046; [2003] 4 All E.R. 1181 at [33] (Ward LJ noting that "[e]verything depends on the subject matter and the facts and circumstances of each case"); *R. (on the application of Hoffmann) v Commissioner of Inquiry* [2012] UKPC 17 at [38] ("the requirements of fairness must be tailored in a manner that has regard to all the circumstances"); *Manning* [2011] UKPC 20 at [39] ("the requirements of fairness in any given case depend crucially upon the particular circumstances"); *R. (on the application of Shoesmith) v Ofsted* [2011] EWCA Civ 642; [2011] P.T.S.R. 1459 at [52] ("the requirement of procedural fairness varies according to the context"); *Principal Reporter v K* [2010] UKSC 56; [2011] 1 W.L.R. 18 at [17].

upwards through an entitlement to make written representations, to make oral representations, to a fully-fledged hearing with most of the characteristics of a judicial trial at the other extreme. What is required in any particular case is incapable of definition in abstract terms. As Lord Bridge has put it:

> "the so-called rules of natural justice are not engraved on tablets of stone. To use the phrase which better expresses the underlying concept, what the requirements of fairness demand when any body, domestic, administrative or judicial, has to make a decision which will affect the rights of individuals depends on the character of the decision-making body, the kind of decision it has to make and the statutory or other framework in which it operates."[195]

Procedural fairness is also a "constantly evolving concept".[196] However, although the extent of fair procedures required is context-based, it appears that there is a core minimum of process rights required, involving notice and some form of hearing.[197]

7-041   The content of a hearing is easier to determine in cases where it is based upon a legitimate expectation of a hearing[198]—but even in such a case the scope of the expected hearing may not be easy to define. Where the right to procedural fairness has a statutory source[199] then substantial guidance as to what should be provided can be obtained, usually by construction of the legislation in question.[200] Even in such a case, however, terms such as "consultation" need elaboration[201] and degrees of disclosure or candour will differ in different circumstances. Furthermore, as was discussed above, the courts may be prepared to supplement the statutory code.[202] In the case of *Doody*,[203] Lord Mustill in summarising the effect of the authorities said:

> "The principles of fairness are not to be applied by rote identically in every situation. What fairness demands is dependent on the context of the decision, and this is to be taken into

---

[195] *Lloyd* [1987] A.C. 625 at 702; *Doody* [1994] 1 A.C. 531 at 560 (Lord Mustill noting that what fairness requires is "essentially an intuitive judgment"); *R. (on the application of X) v Secretary of State for the Home Department, Governor of HMP Drake Hall, Governor of HMP East Sutton Park* [2005] EWHC 1616 at [31]. But for the dangers of excessive informality, see *Dyason v Secretary of State for the Environment, Transport and the Regions* (1998) 75 P. & C.R. 506. See also *Brockwell's Application for Judicial Review* [2017] NIQB 53 at [79] (the concept of procedural fairness must "have some irreducible minimum if it is to be meaningful").

[196] *R. v H* [2004] UKHL 3; [2004] 2 A.C. 134 at [11] (Lord Bingham).

[197] P. Craig, *Administrative Law*, 8th edn (2016), para.12-025, citing *Kanda v Government of Malaya* [1962] A.C. 322 at 337 (Lord Denning observing, if "the right to be heard is to be a real right which is worth anything, it must carry with it a right in the accused man to know the case which is made against him"); *R. (on the application of Anufrijeva) v Secretary of State for the Home Department* [2003] UKHL 36; [2004] 1 A.C. 604; *Hopkins Developments* [2014] EWCA Civ 470 at [85]; but see *Secretary of State for the Home Department v F* [2009] UKHL 28; [2010] 2 A.C. 269; see also *Bank Mellat* [2013] UKSC 39; [2014] A.C. 700. See, e.g., *Re S-W (Children) (Care Proceedings: Summary Disposal at Case Management Hearing)* [2015] EWCA Civ 27; [2015] 2 F.L.R. 136 (while family law reforms were intended to resolve children's cases without delay, this was not at the expense of fairness and the right to a fair trial; interim care orders ought not therefore normally be made final at case management hearings).

[198] See 12-003.

[199] See 7-011.

[200] See, e.g. *Kioa v Minister for Immigration and Ethnic Affairs* (1985) 62 A.L.R. 321 at 369 ("to ascertain what must be done to comply with the principles of natural justice in a particular case, the starting point is the statute creating the power"); *Buckinghamshire CC* [2011] EWCA Civ 457; [2012] P.T.S.R. 854 at [55] (inclusion of an express duty to consult specific persons not a complete bar to a wider duty but a powerful starting point).

[201] See, e.g. *Association of Metropolitan Authorities* [1986] 1 W.L.R. 1.

[202] See 7-013.

[203] *Doody* [1994] 1 A.C. 531 at 560. See also *Foster* [2015] EWCA Civ 281 at [30].

account in all its aspects. An essential factor of the context is the statute which creates the discretion, as regards both its language and the shape of the legal and administrative system within which the decision is taken."

While the statute is an essential factor it is not the only feature and where the statutory procedure is "insufficient to achieve justice", the courts will supplement the statutory code to the extent necessary to ensure that it operates fairly,[204] or if the statute is silent, add or imply a code.[205] Rules and regulations may also be supplemented with fair procedures.[206] In all cases though, any implied or inserted procedures must not frustrate the statutory scheme.[207]

7-042

Consequences of following flawed procedures

The consequence of non-compliance with a statutory requirement for fair procedure should be derived from the legislator's intention, which should be assessed on a consideration of the language of the legislation against the factual circumstances of the non-compliance.[208] Where the procedure followed by the decision-maker is found to be flawed it will usually, but not always, be appropriate to quash the decision. If a decision-maker can demonstrate to the court that the same decision would have been reached even if consultation had been carried out properly, the court may exercise its discretion to withhold a remedy.[209]

7-043

---

[204] *Wiseman* [1971] A.C. 297 at 298; *S* [2002] EWCA Civ 693; [2002] E.L.R. 556 at [14]; *Raji* [2003] UKPC 24; [2003] 1 W.L.R. 1052, PC (even though Medical Act 1983 ss.41(1) and (6) permitted consideration of suspension and restoration together, the two issues should have been considered separately); *R. (on the application of Cheltenham Builders Ltd) v South Gloucestershire DC* [2003] EWHC 2803; [2003] 4 P.L.R. 95 at [34]-[36]; *Hopkins Developments* [2014] EWCA Civ 470 at [62] (the Town and Country Planning Appeals (Determination by Inspectors) (Inquiries Procedure) Rules 2000 "are not a complete code for achieving procedural fairness").

[205] *Doody* [1994] 1 A.C. 531 at 562; *Khatun* [2004] EWCA Civ 55; [2005] Q.B. 37 at [30] (Laws LJ noting that "a right to be heard [can] be inserted or implied into the statutory scheme not by virtue of the statute's words, but by force of our public law standards of procedural fairness"). *Wiseman* [1971] A.C. 297 at 308, 311, 312, 317G and 320; *Lloyd* [1987] A.C. 625 at 702H-703A (Lord Bridge); *Pearlberg* [1972] 1 W.L.R. 534 at 551A-B (Lord Salmon—but cf. Lord Hailsham 540C-D); *Feggetter* [2003] Q.B. 219 at [44] (Sedley LJ noting that "[t]he process is not one of discerning implied terms but of adding necessary ones").

[206] *R. (on the application of Bentley) v HM Coroner for Avon* [2001] EWHC Admin 170; (2002) 166 J.P. 297 (held that the refusal of the Coroner to give advance disclosure of documents to the family of the deceased was unlawful, even though the relevant rules made no provision for such disclosure); and fn.176 above.

[207] *Ferrero* [1993] 1 All E.R. 530, 542 (Taylor LJ); *Wiseman* [1971] A.C. 297 at 308; and fn.60 above.

[208] See 5-052. See also *R. (on the application of E (Russia)) v Secretary of State for the Home Department* [2012] EWCA Civ 357; [2012] 1 W.L.R. 3198 at [41]–[45] (see in particular at [41] "Parliament would have intended that a failure in a notice of decision to comply with the requirement to advise an appellant that he was entitled to an in-country right of appeal would render the notice invalid"); *R. (on the application of Kilroy) v Governing Body Parrs Wood High School* [2011] EWHC 3489 (Admin); [2012] E.L.R. 146 at [24]; *R (on the application of Child Poverty Action Group) v Secretary of State for Work and Pensions* [2012] EWHC 2579 (Admin); [2012] A.C.D. 109 at [37]; *R. (on the application of Garland) v Secretary of State for Justice* [2011] EWCA Civ 1335; [2012] 1 W.L.R. 1879 at [20]; *Natt v Osman* [2014] EWCA Civ 1520; [2015] 1 W.L.R. 1536 at [25] and [33] ("[t]he modern approach is to determine the consequence of non-compliance as an ordinary issue of statutory interpretation, applying all the usual principles of statutory interpretation" and, in cases involving the acquisition of property rights by private persons pursuant to statute, the intention of the legislature is to be ascertained in the light of the statutory scheme as a whole").

[209] See 18-047. See also *R. (on the application of Wainwright) v Richmond upon Thames LBC* [2001] EWCA Civ 2062 at [55].

PRIOR NOTICE OF THE DECISION

The importance of prior notice

7-044   Procedural fairness generally requires that persons liable to be directly affected by proposed administrative acts, decisions or proceedings be given adequate notice of what is proposed, so that they may be in a position:

- to make representations on their own behalf[210]; or
- to appear at a hearing or inquiry (if one is to be held); and
- effectively to prepare their own case and to answer the case (if any) they have to meet.[211]

7-045   The Court of Appeal has characterised the principle of natural justice or procedural fairness as requiring that any participant in adversarial proceedings is entitled to know the case which he has to meet and to have a reasonable op-

---

[210] See, e.g. *Hoggard v Worsbrough UDC* [1962] 2 Q.B. 93; *Doody* [1994] 1 A.C. 531 at 563 where Lord Mustill described it as a proposition of common sense; *R. v (Banks) v Secretary of State for the Environment, Food and Rural Affairs* [2004] EWHC 416; [2004] N.P.C. 43 at [95]; *Fayed (No.1)* [1998] 1 W.L.R. 763 (applicant for British citizenship entitled to be told of Secretary of State's concerns, notwithstanding statutory provision excluding duty to give reasons); *Lewis v Attorney-General of Jamaica* [2001] 2 A.C. 50 (a prisoner sentenced to death had a right to information and documents regarding the prerogative of mercy); *R. v Governors of Dunraven School Ex p. B* [2000] E.L.R. 156; *Lumba* [2012] 1 A.C. 245 at [35]; *R. (on the application of Reilly) v Secretary of State for Work and Pensions* [2013] UKSC 68; [2014] A.C. 453 at [65] (invocation of a statutory power in a way which will or may impose a requirement to perform work on a jobseeker allowance claimant and which may have serious consequences on the claimant's ability to meet his or her living needs required the claimant to have access to such information as needed to make an informed and meaningful representation before the decision). See also *Ware Homes Ltd v Secretary of State for Communities and Local Government* [2016] EWHC 103 (Admin) (fairness required that parties to a planning inquiry should be aware of the points to be addressed and have a reasonable opportunity to deal with them).

[211] *Re D (Minors) (Adoption Reports: Confidentiality)* [1996] A.C. 593 at 603–604 (Lord Mustill, describing it as the "first principle of fairness"). See, e.g. *R. (on the application of Elliott) v First Secretary of State* [2007] EWHC 3492 (Admin); *Re T (A Child)* [2012] EWCA Civ 191; [2012] Fam. Law 506; *Re P (Children) (Care Proceedings)* [2012] EWCA Civ 401; [2012] 2 F.L.R. 1184 at [18]-[19]; *Thamby* [2011] EWHC 1763 (Admin) at [61]-[69]; *R. (on the application of Lunn) v Revenue & Customs Commissioners* [2011] EWHC 240 (Admin); [2011] S.T.C. 1028 at [39]-[43]; *Al Rawi* [2011] UKSC 34; [2012] 1 A.C. 531 at [89] ("the right to know and effectively challenge the opposing case has long been recognised by the common law as a fundamental feature of the judicial process"); *R. (on the application of British Sky Broadcasting Ltd) v Central Criminal Court* [2011] EWHC 3451 (Admin); [2012] Q.B. 785 at [28] ("It is a fundamental principle of fairness at common law that a party should have access to the evidence on which the case against him is based and thus an opportunity to comment on it and, if appropriate, challenge it") (the holding in this case was affirmed in [2014] UKSC 17; [2014] 2 W.L.R. 558 at [28]-[31] on the basis of an interpretation of the relevant statutory provision); *Re Application for Judicial Review by JR17* [2010] UKSC 27; [2010] N.I. 105 at [50] (a person's right to have afforded to him a reasonable opportunity of learning what is alleged against him and of putting forward his own case in answer to it is "one of the fundamental rights accorded by the common law rules of natural justice"); *Shoesmith* [2011] EWCA Civ 642; [2011] P.T.S.R. 1459 at [66]; *Sayce v TNT (UK) Ltd* [2011] EWCA Civ 1583; [2012] 1 W.L.R. 1261 at [15] (unfair for court to decide a case on a basis contrary to that on which it had been argued without allowing an opportunity for representations); *F* [2009] UKHL 28; [2010] 2 A.C. 269 at [63]; *B* [2014] UKSC 59; [2015] A.C. 1195 (an appeal of a refusal of judicial review of a decision not to order a closed material procedure was dismissed, on the basis that the sought exception to the principles of open inter partes justice would deny the ability of the Rwandan Government, which was involved in extradition proceedings against the appellant, to hear evidence in relation to these proceedings).

portunity to adduce evidence and make submissions in relation to that opposing case.[212]

Individuals should not be taken unfairly by surprise.[213] In disciplinary and analogous situations, there will often be a further reason why adequate prior notice should be given to the party to be charged—to give him the opportunity of offering to resign[214] or (for example) surrender his licence, rather than face the prospect of formal condemnation. The duty to notify also includes the duty to take into consideration any representations made in response to notification.[215]

7-046

In a large number of the reported cases where breach of the requirements of fairness has been alleged, no notice whatsoever of the action taken or proposed to be taken was given to the person claiming to be aggrieved,[216] and failure to give him prior notice was tantamount to a denial of an opportunity to be heard.[217] The requirement that prior notice be given, therefore, usually follows automatically from a right to be consulted or heard (whether in writing or orally). However, as the knowledge of the basic requirements of fairness has increased, the proportion of cases involving a complete failure to give notice has fallen, as compared to those cases involving a challenge to the extent or nature of the notice.

7-047

---

[212] *Hopkins Developments* [2014] EWCA Civ 470 at [47] (holding that it was not a breach of natural justice for a planning inspector to base her decision on issues which emerged in evidence during the course of a planning inquiry but which she had not previously identified as issues in statements produced pursuant to the relevant rules).

[213] *Anufrijeva* [2004] 1 A.C. 604 at [30] (Lord Steyn noting that "[i]n our system of law surprise is regarded as the enemy of justice"); *MacDonald v Western Isles Licensing Board* 2001 S.C. 628; *R. (on the application of Ashley) v Secretary of State for Communities and Local Government* [2012] EWCA Civ 559; [2012] J.P.L. 1235 at [42]–[53] (where an interested party to an appeal against the refusal of planning permission by way of written representations had been denied the opportunity to respond to expert evidence because it had been submitted by the developer on the last day of the six-week period in which representations could be made, that amounted to unfairness and a breach of natural justice); *R. (on the application of Longato) v Camberwell Green Magistrates' Court* [2009] EWHC 691 (Admin) at [16]; *R. (on the application of Harrison) v Birmingham Magistrates' Court* [2011] EWCA Civ 332; (2011) 108(14) L.S.G. 21 at [44] and [54] (unfair for forfeiture order to be made without notice); *R. (on the application of S) v Secretary of State for the Home Department* [2011] EWHC 2120 (Admin); (2011) 108(35) L.S.G. 20 at [152]–[161] (notice had to be given before a deportation order could be regarded as being in force); *Lumba* [2011] UKSC 12; [2012] 1 A.C. 245 at [34] (immigration detention powers need to be transparently identified through formulated policy statements).

[214] See, e.g. Comment, "Judicial Control of Acts of Private Associations" (1963) 76 Harv. L.R. 983, p.1028. Of course, it does not necessarily follow that the competent authority is obliged to accept such a resignation or withdrawal.

[215] *Wainwright* [2001] EWCA Civ 2062; (2002) 99(9) L.S.G. 29 at [6]; *R. v North Yorkshire CC Ex p. M* [1989] Q.B. 411 (there was a "duty on the part of the local authority, not only to disclose proposals for change in relation to the child, but also to listen to the views of the guardian ad litem").

[216] See, e.g. *Bagg's Case* (1615) 11 Co.Rep. 93b; *Cooper v Wandsworth Board of Works* (1863) 14 C.B.(N.S.) 180; *Ridge* [1964] A.C. 40; *Glynn v Keele University* [1971] 1 W.L.R. 487; *R. v Havering Justices Ex p. Smith* [1974] 3 All E.R. 484.

[217] *Annamunthodo v Oilfield Workers' Trade Union* [1961] A.C. 945; *Fairmount Investments* [1976] 1 W.L.R. 1255; and *Hadmor Productions v Hamilton* [1983] 1 A.C. 191 at 233B-C; *Manning* [2011] UKSC 20; [2012] 1 A.C. 725; *Shoesmith* [2011] EWCA Civ 642; [2011] P.T.S.R. 1459 at [61]–[62]; *R. (on the application of L) v Commissioner of Police of the Metropolis* [2009] UKSC 3; [2010] 1 A.C. 410 at [46] (if there were any doubt as to whether sensitive information contained in central records ought to be disclosed in an enhanced criminal record certificate, the chief officer of police should, before disclosing it, give the person concerned the opportunity of making representations as to why the information should not be disclosed). cf. *United States Tobacco International Inc* [1992] Q.B. 353 at 370F-G; *Chief Constable of North Wales Police v Evans* [1982] 1 W.L.R. 1155.

The degree of notice required

7-048   If there is a duty to give prior notice, it does not invariably follow that notice must actually be served and received[218]; it is not uncommon for legislation to provide that it is sufficient if reasonable steps are taken to give notice.[219] If the number of persons affected is indeterminate,[220] to give public notice in a manner fairly and reasonably calculated to alert those likely to be interested in the subject matter may be enough to satisfy the rule.[221] But where a person is likely to suffer particular loss from the decision, the duty of "candour" is much higher.[222] If a person upon whom notice ought to be served, or his representative, obstructs service[223] or negligently fails to notify a change of address,[224] non-service of notice may be excused.[225] If the matter is one of special urgency, non-service of notice may also be excused.[226] Other possible exceptions to the general rule—where the person claiming to be aggrieved must be assumed to have known or did in fact know what was being al-

---

[218] But the general rule is that it must be: see, e.g. *Re Wykeham Terrace, Brighton* [1971] Ch. 204; cf. *R. v Kensington and Chelsea Rent Tribunal Ex p. MacFarlane* [1974] 1 W.L.R. 1486 (notice served but not received: proceedings valid, but tribunal has discretion to reconsider its decision in light of representations subsequently made by absent party).

[219] For example, under the Town and Country Planning Act 1990 s.65, and art.13 of the Town and Country Planning (Development Management Procedure) Order 2010 (SI 2015/595), a local planning authority shall not entertain an application for planning permission unless the applicant has certified that he is the sole owner of all the land to which the application relates, or has notified the owner of the land or any tenant of the land. Where, however, the applicant has been unable to identify the owner or tenant, he must show that he has taken reasonable steps to do so and has advertised the notice locally. It may still be wrong to proceed if it is known that notice has not in fact been received, at least where the statute makes the time at which notice is received important: *R. v London County QS Appeals Committee Ex p. Rossi* [1956] 1 Q.B. 682. cf. *R. v Devon and Cornwall Rent Tribunal Ex p. West* (1975) 29 P. & C.R. 316; *Willowgreen Ltd v Smithers* [1994] 1 W.L.R. 832. Contrast *Gidden v Chief Constable of Humberside* [2009] EWHC 2924 (Admin); [2010] 2 All E.R. 75.

[220] And not merely large; cf. *Young v Ladies Imperial Club Ltd* [1920] 2 K.B. 523 (irregularly constituted meeting; fact that a committee member was known to wish not to attend did not justify failure to summon her).

[221] See, e.g. *Wilson v Secretary of State for the Environment* [1973] 1 W.L.R. 1083; *Waitemata* [1964] N.Z.L.R. 689 at 698-699.

[222] *United States Tobacco International Inc* [1992] Q.B. 353, DC; *Fanneran* (1996) 8 Admin. L.R. 351 (dog owner entitled to be heard before destruction order is made).

[223] *De Verteuil v Knaggs* [1918] A.C. 557 at 560-561.

[224] *James v Institute of Chartered Accountants* (1907) 98 L.T. 225; *Glynn* [1971] 1 W.L.R. 487; *Al-Mehdawi v Secretary of State for the Home Department* [1990] 1 A.C. 876 (no unfairness where the negligence was that of the appellant's solicitor); *R. (on the application of Mathialagan) v Southwark LBC* [2004] EWCA Civ 1689; *R. (on the application of R) v Secretary of State for the Home Department* [2005] EWHC 520.

[225] cf. *R. v the Criminal Injuries Compensation Board Ex p. A* [1999] 2 A.C. 330 at 345 ("[i]t does not seem to me to be necessary to find that anyone was at fault"); *Haile v Immigration Appeal Tribunal* [2001] EWCA Civ 663; [2002] Imm. A.R. 170 at [26] (Simon Brown LJ noting that aspects of *Al-Mehdawi* [1990] 1 A.C. 876 "may in any event now need to be reconsidered"); *FP (Iran) v Secretary of State for the Home Department* [2007] EWCA Civ 13; [2007] Imm. A.R. 450 at [45] (suggesting that *Al-Mehdawi* does not apply to asylum cases and not applying it given potentially serious consequences for the applicants caused by legal representative's error); *Pomiechowski* [2012] UKSC 20; [2012] 1 W.L.R. 1604 at [36]-[37] (Lord Mance seemingly doubtful that the interests of finality and certainty pursued by the *Al-Mehdawi* surrogacy principle outweighed the interests of ensuring proper access to justice by appeal in the limited number of extradition cases). However, see *R. (on the application of Nori) v Secretary of State for the Home Department* [2011] EWHC 1604 (Admin) at [48] ("as a general proposition the failure of a solicitor is to be equated with a failure of the individual"); 7-053.

[226] *De Verteuil* [1918] A.C. 557.

leged or what was likely to happen to him,[227] or that he suffered no real detriment by the omission[228] or impliedly waived the defect by appearing at a subsequent hearing[229]—must be viewed with some reserve.[230] Seldom will the absence of prior notice leave a person with an adequate opportunity of preparing his own case or his answers.

As the reason for imposing an obligation to give prior notice is usually to afford those who will be affected an opportunity to make representations, the notice must be served in sufficient time to enable representations to be made effectively.[231] Where a decision-maker's exercise of its power to adjourn is reviewed, there is no margin of appreciation for the decision-maker and the court itself will decide whether fairness required an adjournment.[232] If an oral hearing is to be held, the time and place must be properly notified.[233] If charges are to be brought, they should be specified with particularity,[234] and in any event an interested party ought not to be taken by surprise by being expected to give an immediate answer to an important point raised for the first time at the hearing.[235]

7-049

A breach of fairness will also be found where an individual has been informed of only one charge, although there are two[236]; or where the person is found guilty of a different offence from the one with which she was actually charged.[237] A breach

7-050

---

[227] cf. *Robinson v Sunderland Corp* [1899] 1 Q.B. 751 at 757, 758; *Russell* [1949] 1 All E.R. 109 at 117-118; *Byrne v Kinematograph Renters Society Ltd* [1958] 1 W.L.R. 762 at 785.

[228] cf. *Davis v Carew-Pole* [1956] 1 W.L.R. 833 at 838-840. See generally on this point, *John v Rees* [1970] Ch. 345 at 402.

[229] *Noakes v Smith* (1942) 107 J.P 101.

[230] See, e.g. *Hibernian Property Co Ltd v Secretary of State for the Environment* (1974) 27 P. & C.R. 197 at 213; *Fairmount Investments* [1976] 1 W.L.R. 1255 at 1266; and *Rees* [1994] 2 A.C. 173, PC.

[231] *R. v Thames Magistrates Court Ex p. Polemis* [1974] 1 W.L.R. 1371 (refusal of an adjournment); *R. v Guildford Justices Ex p. Rich* [1997] 1 Cr. App. R. (S) 49; *R. v Devon CC Ex p. Baker* [1995] 1 All E.R. 73; *Moon* (1996) 8 Admin. L.R. 477; *R. v Northern & Yorks Regional Health Authority Ex p. Trivedi* [1995] 1 W.L.R. 961 at 975; *Kelly* [2010] EWHC 1256 (Admin) at [19]-[20] (receipt of notification of planning meeting on the day the meeting took place did not give objector sufficient notice). See also *R. (on the application of Joicey) v Northumberland CC* [2014] EWHC 3657 (Admin); [2015] P.T.S.R. 622 (where information which was statutorily required to be accessible to members of the public is not available in a timely fashion to enable them to participate effectively in democratic decision-making, a claimant is entitled to have the decision quashed unless the decision-maker can demonstrate that it would inevitably have come to the same conclusion even if the information had been available).

[232] *R. v Cheshire CC Ex p. C* [1998] E.L.R. 66 at 73 (Sedley J); see 7-066. See also *R. (on the application of Cameroon) v Asylum and Immigration Tribunal* [2008] EWCA Civ 100; [2008] 1 W.L.R. 2062 at [10]; *Powell v Secretary of State for Environment, Food and Rural Affairs* [2009] EWHC 643 (Admin); [2009] J.P.L. 1513 at [31]; *H* [2008] EWHC 2590 (Admin); [2009] Prison L.R. 205 at [20].

[233] *Hopkins v Smethwick Board of Health* (1890) 24 Q.B.D. 712 at 715; *Wilson v Secretary of State for the Environment* [1988] 3 P.L. 520; cf. *Ostreicher v Secretary of State for the Environment* [1978] 1 W.L.R. 810 (date of hearing inconvenient for religious reasons).

[234] *Ex p. Daisy Hopkins* (1891) 61 L.J.Q.B. 240; *R. v LAUTRO Ex p. Tee* (1995) 7 Admin. L.R. 289; *McDonald v Lanarkshire Fire Brigade Joint Committee* 1959 S.C. 141. On duty of adequate disclosure, see 7-060.

[235] *R. v Chance Ex p. Coopers & Lybrand* (1995) 7 Admin. L.R. 821 at 835 (surprise as the enemy of justice); *R. v Rodney and Minister of Manpower and Immigration* (1972) 27 D.L.R. (3rd) 756.

[236] *Board of Trustees of the Marandana Mosque v Mahmud* [1967] 1 A.C. 13 at 24-25. See further *Singleton v The Law Society* [2005] EWHC 2915 at [12]–[13] (where it was unfair not to give a solicitor timely notice that the allegation of "conduct unbefitting a solicitor" was being made on the basis of dishonesty). Similarly, unfairness was found where a planning inspector relied on noise and disturbance, without raising this at the hearing, when experts had agreed these factors were not in issue: *R. (on the application of Gates Hydraulics Ltd) v Secretary of State for Communities and Local Government* [2009] EWHC 2187 (Admin) at [30].

[237] *Lau Liat Meng v Disciplinary Committee* [1968] A.C. 391 (notice given of proposed action on

of fairness will not be found where there has been a failure to give notice of the legal quality of a particular executive act.[238]

Statutory requirements for notice

7-051   Statutory rules may set out in varying detail the requirements for the giving of notice and for consultation. There is no set form, and procedures will differ for different decisions. Under current regulations on proposals for development plans[239] the local planning authority is required to carry out consultations with a list of named consultees.[240] This duty carries with it a duty to "take into account any representations received from any consultee".[241] Planning applications must be publicised by the local planning authority, including by way of site notice, notification of neighbours or newspaper advertisements, depending on the nature of the application.[242]

7-052   Statutory notice requirements are also imposed in the education context.[243] If a local education authority wishes to invite proposals for a new school, it must notify interested parties that the local authority thinks appropriate.[244] The notice inviting proposals for the new school must be published on the website of the local authority as well as in both a national and local newspaper,[245] and the proposals received sent to a number of parties including the Secretary of State.[246] Notice and consultation obligations also exist in the context of re-organisation of the NHS[247] and aspects of health strategy.[248]

Consequences of inadequate notice

7-053   Although the non-issue or the inadequacy of the notice can invalidate the subsequent proceedings,[249] exceptions to the general rule have been introduced by statute. For example, under a number of statutes procedural defects will only be a ground for setting aside an order if a defect has resulted in the applicant being substantially prejudiced thereby.[250] In the absence of such express provision, however, the courts will not normally imply a requirement that prejudice be shown

---

ground X but action taken on ground Y of which no notice, or inadequate notice, had been given).

[238] *R. (on the application of Children's Rights Alliance for England) v Secretary of State for Justice* [2013] EWCA Civ 34; [2013] 1 W.L.R. 3667.

[239] Town and Country Planning (Development Management Procedure) (England) Order (SI 2015/595).

[240] SI 2015/595 art.18.

[241] SI 2015/595 art.18(7).

[242] SI 2015/595 art.15.

[243] School Organisation (Establishment and Discontinuance of Schools) Regulations 2013 (SI 2013/3109).

[244] SI 2013/3109 reg.5(4)(d).

[245] SI 2013/3109 reg.5(2).

[246] SI 2013/3109 reg.10(4).

[247] See, e.g. Primary Care Trusts (Consultation on Establishment, Dissolution and Transfer of Staff) 1999 (SI 1999/2337).

[248] Health and Social Care Act 2012 s 118.

[249] See, e.g. *London Reading College* [2010] EWHC 2561 (Admin); [2010] E.L.R. 809 at [54]. See 7-043; the consequences of failing to comply with a statutory requirement to give prior notice should be determined from a consideration of the legislation.

[250] See, e.g. Town and Country Planning Act 1990 ss.176(5) and 288. For an application of s.288, see *Powys County Council v Welsh Ministers* [2015] EWHC 3284 (Admin). See also non-disclosure in the context of parole board hearings: *R. (on the application of Roberts) v Parole Board* [2005] UKHL 45; [2005] 2 A.C. 738 at [43], [52]-[56], [60]-[62]; note Lord Steyn's strong dissent. See also *Hopkins Developments* [2014] EWCA Civ 470 at [62] (noting that if there is procedural unfairness which materially prejudices a party to a planning inquiry that may be a good ground for quashing the

and non-service or inadequacy of a notice depriving the applicant of a proper opportunity to put his case will normally constitute substantial prejudice.[251]

CONSULTATION AND WRITTEN REPRESENTATIONS

In some situations, it is sufficient if written representations are considered.[252]   **7-054**
Where a duty of "consultation" is placed upon the decision-maker, this is almost always interpreted by the courts to require merely an opportunity to make written representations, or comments upon announced proposals. However, where the words "hearing" or "opportunity to be heard" are used in legislation, they usually[253] require a hearing[254] at which oral submissions and evidence can be tendered.

Standards of consultation

When a duty to entertain written representations is imposed by statute, by way   **7-055**
of a duty to consult, what is required of the decision-maker in each case to comply with the duty will depend upon the statutory context.[255] It has been observed that for a non-statutory consultation process, the question of whether there has been a breach of procedural fairness is fact and context sensitive, with the test being whether the process has been so unfair as to be unlawful.[256] Indeed, whether the duty to consult has been satisfied depends in all cases on an intensely case-sensitive

---

Inspector's decision).

[251] But see *McCarthy* [2015] EWCA Civ 12 (a judge had erred in concluding that, although the Bar Standards Board's failure to disclose a witness statement in disciplinary proceedings against a barrister had breached the rules governing tribunal proceedings and had been procedurally unfair, the outcome of the proceedings had not been affected by the non-disclosure). The courts will also not insist on compliance with statutory procedures which produce absurd results: *Oldham MBC v Tanna* [2017] EWCA Civ 50; [2017] 1 W.L.R. 1970; see also *R. (on the application of Plant) v Lambeth LBC* [2016] EWHC 3324 (Admin); [2017] P.T.S.R. 453 (consultation document failed to explain that local authority's inability to service its debt was the real constraint on the provision of housing revenue account funding, but this did not justify quashing the decision unless a substantial prejudice had been caused).

[252] See, e.g. *Naraynsingh v Commissioner of Police* [2004] UKPC 20; (2004) 148 S.J.L.B. 510 (no obligation to hold an oral hearing in relation to revocation of a firearms certificate although on the facts, a more extensive written procedure should have taken place); *R. (on the application of Jemchi) v Visitor of Brunel University* [2003] E.L.R. 125 (not unfair for University Visitor to proceed without an oral hearing). For an example of an oral hearing being required, see *Mehmet* [1977] 1 W.L.R. 795; *Foster* [2015] EWCA Civ 281 (no oral hearing required in the context of a home detention curfew decision).

[253] cf. *R. v Housing Appeal Tribunal* [1920] 3 K.B. 334; and *Lloyd* [1987] A.C. 625; *R. v Army Board of the Defence Council Ex p. Anderson* [1992] Q.B. 169; cf. *R. v Hull Prison Board of Visitors Ex p. St Germain (No.2)* [1979] 1 W.L.R. 1401.

[254] Not merely an informal meeting: *Ealing BC v Minister of Housing and Local Government* [1952] Ch. 856.

[255] See, e.g. *Moseley* [2014] UKSC 56; [2014] 1 W.L.R. 3947 per Lord Reed JSC. For a comprehensive analysis of the duty to consult, both of when it arises and of what it entails, see: *Plantagenet Alliance* [2014] EWHC 1662 (Admin) at [84]-[86] and [98] (noting in particular that a duty to consult will arise in four circumstances: where there is a statutory duty; where there has been a promise to consult; where there has been an established practice of consultation; and where a failure to consult would lead to conspicuous unfairness). See also *R. (on the application of Forest Heath DC) v Electoral Commission* [2009] EWCA Civ 1296; [2010] P.T.S.R. 1205 at [31]-[36] (a requirement to have "dialogue" with local authorities with a view to formulating proposals did not require the committee to consult the local authorities at the pre-publication formulation stage).

[256] *R. (on the application of West Berkshire DC) v Secretary of State for Communities and Local Government* [2016] EWCA Civ 441; [2016] P.T.S.R. 982.

analysis.[257] Overall, the consultation has to be fair, but it does not have to be perfect, since with the benefit of hindsight, it will no doubt often be possible to show that a consultation could have been carried out rather better.[258] But the fundamental requirements of the duty of consultation have been summarised by Lord Woolf:

> "To be proper, consultation must be undertaken at a time when proposals are still at a formative stage; it must include sufficient reasons for particular proposals to allow those consulted to give intelligent consideration and an intelligent response; adequate time must be given for this purpose; and the product of consultation must be conscientiously taken into account when the ultimate decision is taken."[259]

7-056   Essentially, in developing standards of consultation, and applying those standards to particular statutory contexts, the courts are using the general principles of fairness to ensure that the consulted party is able properly to address the concerns of the decision-maker.[260] Although consultation must take place at the formative stage, it does not require consultation on every possible option[261] and while the decision-maker is entitled to narrow the options prior to consultation, provided the proposed

---

[257]   *R. (on the application of Steven Sumpter) v Secretary of State for Works and Pensions* [2015] EWCA Civ 1033 at [50] (citing from *London Metal Exchange* [2014] EWCA Civ 1271 at [28]).

[258]   *Sumpter* [2015] EWCA Civ 1033 at [50] (citing from *London Metal Exchange* [2014] EWCA Civ 1271 at [28]).

[259]   *Coughlan* [2001] Q.B. 213 at [108]; and *Gunning* (1985) 84 L.G.R. 168 the Supreme Court affirmed these requirements in *Moseley* [2014] UKSC 56; [2014] 1 W.L.R. 3947 at [25]; *Association of Metropolitan Authorities* [1986] 1 W.L.R. 1 at 4 (Webster J noting that consultation requires that "sufficient information must be supplied by the consulting to the consulted party to enable it to tender helpful advice. Sufficient time must be given by the consulting to the consulted party"); *R. v Gwent CC and Secretary of State for Wales Ex p. Bryant* [1988] C.O.D. 19 (consultation arising from legitimate expectation), where Hodgson J considered the requirements of fair consultation, and stressed that the process must take place at a sufficiently early stage in the decision-making process for the exercise to be meaningful. Note, where an authority gives an assurance that it will conduct a lawful consultation, it is "hopeless" to seek judicial review on the basis that the assurance will not be upheld: *R. (on the application of Hide) v Staffordshire CC* [2007] EWCA Civ 860; (2008) 11 C.C.L. Rep. 28 at [8]. See also *LH* [2014] EWCA Civ 404 at [21] (the obligation to consult "requires that there be a proposal, that the consultation takes place before a decision is reached and that responses be conscientiously considered"); *Flatley* [2014] EWHC 2258 (Admin) at [88]; *Rusal* [2014] EWCA Civ 1271; [2015] 1 W.L.R. 1375 at [25].

[260]   See, e.g. *Medway Council* [2002] EWHC 2516; [2003] J.P.L. 583 at [28] (Maurice Kay J rejecting the submission that fairness had ceased to be an aspect of consultation: "It is an aspect of what is 'proper'; the word used in *Coughlan* [108] … it is axiomatic that consultation, whether it is a matter of obligation or undertaken voluntarily, requires fairness."); *R (on the application of Edwards) v Environment Agency (No.2)* [2007] Env. L.R. 9 at [90]-[94], [102]-[106] (affirmed [2008] UKHL 22; [2008] 1 W.L.R. 1587); *Greenpeace* [2007] EWHC 311; [2007] N.P.C. 21 at [61] (Sullivan J noting that "the overriding requirement that any consultation must be fair is not in doubt"). See also *Rusal* [2014] EWCA Civ 1271; [2015] 1 W.L.R. 1375 at [26].

[261]   *The Vale of Glamorgan Council v The Lord Chancellor and Secretary of State for Justice* [2011] EWHC 1532 (Admin) at [24]. See also *R. (on the application of EasyJet Airline Co Ltd) v Civil Aviation Authority* [2009] EWCA Civ 1361; [2010] A.C.D. 19 at [53]-[57]; *Flatley* [2014] EWHC 2258 (Admin) at [88] (there is no need for a "pre-consultation consultation"); but see *Moseley* [2014] UKSC 56; [2014] 1 W.L.R. 3947 at [40]-[41] (the question is generally whether the provision of information on alternative options is required by the statutory duty to consult in the context of the statute concerned, in other words whether such information is necessary in order for the particular consultees to whom that statutory duty is owed to be able to express meaningful views on the proposal, but the duty does not require a detailed discussion of the alternatives or of the reasons for their rejection); *Vale of Glamorgan* distinguished on the basis that such information was not considered necessary there, having regard to the nature and purpose of the particular consultation exercise at issue in that case (Lord Reed JSC); "[s]ometimes, particularly when statute does not limit the subject of the requisite consultation to the preferred option, fairness will require that interested persons be consulted not only upon the preferred option but also upon arguable yet discarded alternative options" (Lord Wilson JSC at [27])). See also *R. (on the application of Rose) v Secretary of State*

course can still be altered as a result of the consultation, there may be a necessity to deal with alternative options where it would be unfair not to do so.[262] Consultation may be phased,[263] but if it is phased, the full package has to be sufficiently identified as part of the final stage of publication, and there has to be adequate time after the publication of the final part of the package for the package to be considered as a whole and for representations to be made.[264] It is clearly necessary to consult sufficiently widely[265]; and to give adequate time to those consulted to respond.[266] Proper consultation requires the "candid disclosure of the reasons for what is proposed"[267] and that consulted parties are aware of the criteria to be adopted and any factors considered to be decisive or of substantial importance.[268] Consultation

---

[for Justice [2017] EWHC 1826 (Admin).

[262] *Rusal* [2014] EWCA Civ 1271 [2015] 1 W.L.R. 1375 (a public body is not required to consult on proposals which it had discarded unless there were very specific reasons for doing so); but see now *Moseley* [2014] UKSC 56; [2014] 1 W.L.R. 3947 at [29] and [39] (consultation inevitably involves inviting and considering views about possible alternatives; those consulted were the most economically disadvantaged residents in the borough to whom real hardship would in all likelihood be caused by the proposed scheme and fairness demanded brief reference in the consultation document to other ways of absorbing the shortfall and the reasons why (Lord Wilson JSC); outline of reasonable alternatives required (Lord Reed JSC)). See also *Medway Council* [2002] EWHC 2516 (Admin); [2003] J.P.L. 583 (irrational to exclude Gatwick from consultation exercise over future development of air transport in south-east England); *Greenpeace* [2007] EWHC 311 (Admin); [2007] Env. L.R. 29 (necessary to consult on new nuclear build where the Government had created a legitimate expectation that it would not consider this option).

[263] *R. (on the application of Parents for Legal Action Ltd) v Northumberland CC* [2006] EWHC 1081 (Admin); [2006] B.L.G.R. 646.

[264] *Breckland DC* [2009] EWCA Civ 239; [2009] P.T.S.R. 1611 at [49].

[265] See, e.g. *Wainwright* [2001] EWCA Civ 2062 (criticising, although not invalidating due to other circumstances, a consultation in respect of a toucan crossing in which the council had not ensured that one letter per flat was mailed). There had been no breach of the duty to consult where there had been consultation of representative organisations that had expertise and representatives of affected junior doctors: *R. (on the application of Legal Remedy UK Ltd) v Secretary of State for Health* [2007] EWHC 1252 (Admin); (2007) 96 B.M.L.R. 191 at [135]. See also *R. (on the application of Milton Keynes Council) v Secretary of State for Communities and Local Government* [2011] EWCA Civ 1575; [2012] J.P.L. 728 at [32] (there must be fairness in deciding whom to consult).

[266] *R. v Secretary of State for Education and Employment Ex p. National Union of Teachers* [2000] Ed. C.R. 603 (four days was an insufficient period for consultation in respect of imposing an obligation on teachers to engage in assessment of their peers); *R. (on the application of Anvac Chemical UK Ltd) v Secretary of State for Environment, Food and Rural Affairs* [2001] EWHC Admin 1011; [2002] A.C.D 219 at [63] (noting that a period of notification of two days was too short, even taking into account the urgent situation prior to suspension of use of a pesticide).

[267] *R. (on the application of L) v Barking and Dagenham LBC* [2001] EWCA Civ 533 at [13] (Schiemann LJ); and *R. (on the application of Madden) v Bury MBC* [2002] EWHC 1882 at [58]; *R. v Secretary of State for Transport Ex p. Richmond Upon Thames LBC* [1995] Env L.R. 390 at 405 (misleading consultation paper rendering the consultation process flawed); *R. (on the application of Westminster City Council) v Mayor of London* [2002] EWHC 2440 (Admin); [2003] L.G.R. 611 at [27] (noting that adequate information had been provided in a consultation as to the Congestion Charging Scheme for London as to enable consultees to make an "intelligent response"); *London Metal Exchange* [2014] EWCA Civ 1271; [2015] 1 W.L.R. 1375 at [85] ("the explanation provided by a consultant body in its consultation document is not unfair unless something material has been omitted or something has been materially misstated").

[268] *R. (on the application of Capenhurst) v Leicester City Council* [2004] EWHC 2124 at [46]; *R. (on the application of JL & AT Baird) v Environment Agency* [2011] EWHC 939 (Admin) at [41] ("[t]he *Coughlan* principles do not require as their starting point an omniscient decision maker who will have correctly identified each and every relevant factor at the outset"); *Devon CC v Secretary of State for Communities and Local Government* [2010] EWHC 1456 (Admin); [2011] B.L.G.R. 64; *R. (on the application of Save our Surgery Limited v Joint Committee of Primary Care Trusts* [2013] EWHC 439 (Admin); [2013] P.T.S.R. D16 at [27], [109] (sub-scores in assessments of cardiac centres were not "underlying workings" which did not need to be disclosed).

documents "should be clear as to their purpose".[269] The consultation must also be in respect of proposals, rather than merely a bland generality.[270] There may be cases where consultation on alternatives is required in order to ensure fairness, for example, where there is a legitimate expectation that consultation will include alternatives,[271] but there is no duty to consult on non-viable options.[272] Where the decision-maker has access to important documents which are material to its determination whose contents the public would have a legitimate interest in knowing, these documents should be disclosed as part of the consultation process.[273] However, the mere fact that information is "significant" does not mean that fairness necessarily requires its disclosure, although the degree of significance of the undisclosed material is a "highly material factor".[274] Where there is doubt over whether a document is a consultation paper or merely an issues paper, the court should resolve this by asking whether those consultees who took the document at face value could reasonably foresee that following consideration of their responses, the issue of principle would be decided.[275] While consultation requires that sufficient reasons be given for the particular proposals to enable those consulted to give intelligent consideration and an intelligent response to the proposals, it does not usually require that sufficient information be given about any objections to the proposals to enable those consulted to give intelligent consideration and an intelligent response to the objections.[276] Moreover, in general, there is no duty to re-consult unless there is a "fundamental difference" between the proposals consulted on and

---

[269] *Greenpeace* [2007] EWHC 311 (Admin); [2007] N.P.C. at [74] (Sullivan J distinguishing between putting an "issues paper" to the public and putting "policy proposals" to the public).

[270] See, e.g. *R. (on the application of Peat) v Hyndburn PC* [2011] EWHC 1739 (Admin) at [50]-[52] (consultation as to general principles insufficient and precision required regarding designation of an area as subject to selective licensing, including, licence conditions and fee structures); *R. (on the application of the Law Society) v Legal Services Commission* [2010] EWHC 2550 (Admin); [2011] Costs L.R. Online 57 at [83] (neither the consultation document nor the subsequent history of consultation made the importance of accreditation clear); *R. (on the application of O'Callaghan) v The Charity Commission for England and Wales* [2007] EWHC 2491 (Admin); [2008] W.T.L.R. 117 at [26] (it was a "nonsense" to hold a consultation on a lease without disclosing the terms of the lease).

[271] *The Bard Campaign v Secretary of State for Communities and Local Government* [2009] EWHC 308 (Admin) at [90].

[272] *R. (on the application of Enfield BC) v Secretary of State for Health* [2009] EWHC 743 (Admin) at [17]. It has also been held that explaining why three units were not used instead of 10 units in the context of a consultation on affordable housing involved descending into a level of particularity and a detailed analysis of options that was not necessary: *West Berkshire DC* [2016] EWCA Civ 441; [2016] P.T.S.R. 982 at [63].

[273] *Edwards* [2006] EWCA Civ 877; [2007] Env L.R. 9 at [94] (affirmed [2008] UKHL 22; [2008] 1 W.L.R. 1587). See also *Save our Surgery Ltd* [2013] EWHC 439 (Admin).

[274] *R. (on the application of Eisai Ltd) v National Institute for Health and Clinical Excellence* [2008] EWCA Civ 438; (2008) 11 C.C.L. Rep. 385 at [26].

[275] *Greenpeace* [2007] EWHC 311 (Admin); [2007] N.P.C. 21; *The Bard Campaign* [2009] EWHC 308 (Admin) at [74]-[75].

[276] *R. (on the application of Beale) v Camden LBC* [2004] EWHC 6 at [19] (Munby J). See further *R. (on the application of Ramda) v Secretary of State for the Home Department* [2002] EWHC 1278 (Admin) at [25] ("the Home Secretary is not required to be drawn into a never-ending dialogue"); *R. v Secretary of State for Wales Ex p. Williams* [1997] E.L.R. 100 (no duty to prolong consultation to allow everybody to comment on everybody else's comments); *R. (on the application of Robin Murray & Co) v Lord Chancellor* [2011] EWHC 1528 (Admin); [2011] A.C.D. 103 at [46]-[47]; *Moseley* [2014] UKSC 56; [2014] 1 W.L.R. 3947 at [40] per Lord Reed (the content of a statutory duty to consult in circumstances in which meaningful public participation was required depended, in the context of providing information on rejected options, on whether the provision of such information was necessary in order for the consultees to express meaningful views on the proposal).

those which the consulting party subsequently wishes to adopt,[277] or if, after consultation has concluded, the decision-maker becomes aware of some internal material or a factor of potential significance to the decision to be made.[278] A consultation may be vitiated, however, where errors have been made by either the consulted party or the adviser.[279] Whether or not consultation is a legal requirement, if it is embarked upon it must be carried out properly.[280] Furthermore, where an authority is subject to a limited statutory duty of consultation, but embarks on a process of consultation going beyond that required, it may not then take refuge in the limited scope of its statutory duty.[281]

Considering the representations

It is necessary for proper consideration to be given to representations made in the consultation and the government authority must "have embarked on the consultation process prepared to change course, if persuaded by it to do so".[282] This is not, however, a duty not to make a decision without prior agreement of the consulted parties.[283] It is also not a duty to adopt the submissions of respondents to the consultation; the decision-maker is entitled to consider the whole range of responses

7-057

---

[277] *R. (on the application of Smith) v East Kent Hospital NHS Trust* [2002] EWHC 2640 at [45]; *R. (on the application of 007 Stratford Taxis) v Stratford on Avon DC* [2010] EWHC 1344 (Admin) at [41]; see also [2011] EWCA Civ 160. cf. *R. (on the application of Carton) v Coventry City Council* (2001) 4 C.C.L.R. 41 at 44 (further consultation was required where a fundamental change in day-care charging arrangements from those originally proposed); *Re Christian Institute's Application for Judicial Review* [2007] NIQB 66; *Devon CC* [2010] EWHC 1456 (Admin); [2011] B.L.G.R. 64 (consultation process was unfair where decisions made on a different basis from that upon which consultation had taken place and consultees had no opportunity to address his change in stance); *Milton Keynes Council* [2011] EWCA Civ 1575; [2012] J.P.L. 728 at [32]-[38] (no requirement to directly consult local authorities during a limited consultation where a full consultation had taken place the previous year during which the authorities had the opportunity to make representations); *R. (on the application of Elphinstone) v Westminster City Council* [2008] EWHC 1289 (Admin): see also [2008] EWCA Civ 1069; [2009] B.L.G.R. 158.

[278] *Edwards* [2006] EWCA Civ 877; [2007] Env L.R. 9 at [103] (affirmed [2008] UKHL 22; [2008] 1 W.L.R. 1587); *Interbrew* [2001] E.C.C. 40 at [33]-[35]; *United States Tobacco International Inc* [1992] Q.B. 353 at 370-371, 376; *Greenpeace* [2007] EWHC 311 (Admin); [2007] N.P.C. 21 at [116]. cf. *Withers v First Secretary of State* [2005] EWCA Civ 1119 (no additional factual findings made). *R. (on the application of M) v Haringey LBC* [2013] EWCA Civ 116; [2013] P.T.S.R. 1285 (announcement of a transitional grant scheme after a consultation for a council tax reduction scheme did not require further consultation as it was not a change of such significance that the council would have been required to draw it to the attention of what would have been a much broader category of consultees than the 36,000 current council tax benefit claimant households in its area; decision on the transitional grant scheme affirmed on appeal [2014] UKSC 56; [2014] 1 W.L.R. 3947 but Lord Wilson JSC noted at [32] the council's "illuminating concession" that, had it known of the scheme when it commenced its consultation exercise, it would have referred to it; the duty to consult normally requires brief reference to other discarded options).

[279] *R. (on the application of Goldsmith) v Wandsworth LBC* [2004] EWCA Civ 1170; (2004) 7 C.C.L. Rep. 472 at [66]-[77] (decision to terminate residential placement was vitiated by flaws by the Care Panel whose recommendations it adopted, since the Panel had failed to keep minutes, give reasons, take account of a relevant care assessment and allow the claimant's daughter to attend a meeting); *Eisai* [2008] EWCA Civ 438; (2008) 11 C.C.L. Rep. 385. But if the error had no effect on the final outcome, a court may declare the consultation unfair but refuse relief: *Edwards* [2006] EWCA Civ 877; [2007] En. L.R. 9 (affirmed [2008] UKHL 22; [2008] 1 W.L.R. 1587). On refusal of relief, see 18-047.

[280] *Coughlan* [2001] Q.B. 213 at [108]; *Eisai* [2008] EWCA Civ 438; (2008) 11 C.C.L. Rep. 385 at [24]; *Milton Keynes Council* [2011] EWCA Civ 1575; [2012] J.P.L. 728 at [17]; *R. (on the application of Silus Investments SA) v Hounslow LBC* [2015] EWHC 358 (Admin); [2015] B.L.G.R. 291.

[281] *EasyJet* [2009] EWCA Civ 1361; [2010] A.C.D. 19 at [46].

[282] *R. v Barnet LBC Ex p. B* [1994] E.L.R. 357 at 375.

[283] *East Kent Hospital NHS Trust* [2002] EWHC 2640 (Admin); (2003) 6 C.C.L. Rep. 251 at [61].

and to form his own conclusion independently of the view of any particular section of consultees or indeed the views of his own advisers.[284] As is the case where written representations are required, the courts may be in a poor position to ensure that the decision-maker considers those representations. At the lowest, the courts will attempt to ensure that all written representations are before the decision-maker when the decision is made, and will quash a decision made in disregard of representations.[285] Nevertheless, where a large-scale consultation exercise has been carried out, the courts may be effectively powerless to ensure that representations have been read and digested unless the decision-maker is required to address representations received by way of reasons.[286] Furthermore, where consultations are invited upon detailed proposals which have already been arrived at, the duty of the court to ensure that genuine consideration has been given to critical representations is taxed to the utmost.[287] In practice, as has been observed, it will be difficult to show that representations have not been taken into account.[288]

The increasing importance of consultation

7-058   Finally, the importance of an appropriate consultation procedure has been given greater emphasis by the government in recent years. The Cabinet Office Consultation Principles[289] indicate, inter alia, that consultation should be clear and concise, have a purpose, be informative, last for a proportionate amount of time, and be targeted, and responses should be published in a timely fashion. Though the principles do not have legal force, and cannot prevail over statutory or mandatory external requirements,[290] they should otherwise generally be regarded as binding on UK departments and their agencies, unless Ministers conclude that exceptional circumstances require a departure from them.

7-059   Finally, it is important to note that when considering whether or not to impose a duty to re-consult, it is necessary to consider any differences between the proposal and material consulted upon, and the decision that the public body in fact intends to proceed to make.[291]

---

[284] *West Berkshire DC* [2016] EWCA Civ 441; [2016] 1 W.L.R. 3923 at [62].

[285] See e.g. *R. v Manchester Metropolitan University Ex p. Nolan, The Independent,* 15 July 1993; *R. (on the application of Morris) v Newport City Council* [2009] EWHC 3051 (Admin); [2010] B.L.G.R. 234 at [38] (decision flawed where failed to take into account the consultee's "main and biggest point").

[286] See 7-088.

[287] See, e.g. *R. v Hillingdon Health Authority Ex p. Goodwin* [1984] I.C.R. 800 for the extent to which a proposed scheme may be developed in advance of a consultation process; compare *Rollo v Minister of Town and Country Planning* [1948] 1 All E.R. 13. But see *Cran* [1995] R.T.R. 346 (consultation should have taken place before the Council's "mind was made up").

[288] H. Fenwick (ed), *Supperstone, Goudie and Walker: Judicial Review* 6th edn (2017), para.10.45.

[289] Published on 17 July 2012 and updated on 14 January 2016 *https://www.gov.uk/government/publications/consultation-principles-guidance* [Accessed 31 October 2017] .

[290] See, e.g. European Union law (see 14-015); on the binding force of policy, see 12-023 (legitimate expectation).

[291] *Keep Wythenshawe Special Ltd v NHS Central Manchester CCG* [2016] EWHC 17 (Admin) at [75].

DUTY OF ADEQUATE DISCLOSURE BEFORE A DECISION IS TAKEN

The level of disclosure required

If prejudicial allegations are to be made against a person, he must normally, as we have seen, be given particulars of them before the hearing so that he can prepare his answers.[292] The level of detail required must be such as to enable the making of "meaningful and focused representations".[293] In order to protect his interests, the person must also be enabled to controvert, correct or comment on other evidence or information that may be relevant to the decision and influential material on which the decision-maker intends to rely[294]; including, in certain cases, disclosure of representations or information provided by third parties.[295] At least in some circumstances there will also be a duty on the decision-maker to disclose informa-

7-060

---

[292] See 7-044. In *Council of Civil Service Unions v Minister for the Civil Service* [1985] A.C. 374 at 415; *Hadmor Productions* [1983] 1 A.C. 191 at 233 (Lord Diplock: one of the most fundamental rules of natural justice "[is] the right … to be informed of any point adverse … that is going to be relied upon … and to be given an opportunity of stating what his answer to it is"); *Bushell* [1981] A.C. 75 at 96 (Lord Diplock); *R. v Hampshire CC Ex p. K* [1990] 2 Q.B. 71 (duty of local authorities in child abuse cases to be open and to disclose all relevant material); *Ramda* [2002] EWHC 1278 (Admin) at [25] (Sedley LJ noting that in extradition proceedings the Home Secretary "must not rely on potentially influential material which is withheld from the individual affected"); *Independent Education Appeal Panel of Bromley LBC* [2007] EWCA Civ 1010; [2008] B.L.G.R. 267 (parents entitled to be told, case to be met on reinstatement); *R. (on the application of Benson) v Secretary of State for Justice* [2007] EWHC 2055 (Admin); [2008] Prison L.R. 132 (recalled prisoner is entitled to information regarding alleged licence breach such as to know "what the allegations against him are in sufficiently detailed form so that he can make meaningful objections or put forward meaningful representations": at [22]); *R. (on the application of Z) v Croydon LBC* [2011] EWCA Civ 59; [2011] P.T.S.R. 748 at [21]. Reference should also be made to the requirement to give reasons for a decision, 7-088.

[293] *R. v Secretary of State for the Home Department Ex p. Harry* [1998] 1 W.L.R. 1737 at 1748; *Breckland DC* [2009] EWCA Civ 239; [2009] P.T.S.R. 1611 at [44], [46] (important to enable "effective representations" to be made and to publish enough material to enable all those interested to respond intelligently). But see *R. (on the application of O) v Independent Appeal Panel for Tower Hamlets LBC* [2007] EWHC 1455 (Admin); [2007] E.L.R. 468 at [42] (no general duty to draw attention to every provision that might be relevant to the conduct of an appeal).

[294] *Ramda* [2002] EWHC 1278 (Admin) at [25]; *Banks* [2004] EWHC 416; [2004] N.P.C. 43 at [104] (noting that DEFRA deliberately refused to disclose highly material information to the claimants); *Wiseman* [1971] A.C. 297 at 309; *R. (on the application of O'Leary) v Chief Constable of the Merseyside Police* [2001] EWHC Admin 57 at [16] (noting that it was unfair not to disclose and allow comment on departmental report relied on in imposing employment restrictions); *Sheridan* [2003] 4 All E.R. 1181 (unfair for EAT not to allow chance to make representations on new authorities relied on, if central to its decision); *Eisai* [2008] EWCA Civ 438; (2008) 11 C.C.L. Rep. 385 at [59] (even if disclosure were prima facie a breach of confidence, the public authority would have a public interest defence available to it if disclosure were necessary in order to meet the requirements of procedural fairness). Contrast *R. (on the application of Centro) v Secretary of State for Transport, West Midlands Travel* [2007] EWHC 2729 (Admin); [2008] A.C.D. 19 (not unfair not to disclose internal advice received from employees as it was not suggested that the material on which advice was received related to matters that had not been raised or considered by the parties); *R. (on the application of Bedford) v Islington LBC* [2002] EWHC 2044 (Admin); [2003] Env L.R. 463 at [102] (no unfairness in non-disclosure of confidential information relating to planning application).

[295] See, e.g. *R. (on the application of Anglian Water Services Ltd) v Environment Agency* [2003] EWHC 1506 (Admin); [2004] Env. L.R. 15 at [26] (unfair for EA not to disclose residents' representations for sewerage company to comment, where there was a dispute as to whether to impose a requirement to provide a public sewer); *Primary Health Investment Properties Ltd* [2009] EWHC 519 (Admin); [2009] P.T.S.R. 1586 (unfairness where a district valuer, instructed on behalf of a trust, obtained one party's expert file and only disclosed to the other party the fact that he had that file and

tion favourable to the applicant, as well as information prejudicial to his case.[296] If material is available before the hearing, the right course will usually be to give him advance notification; but it cannot be said that there is a hard and fast rule on this matter, and sometimes natural justice will be held to be satisfied if the material is divulged at the hearing, which may have to be adjourned if he cannot fairly be expected to make his reply without time for consideration.[297]

Failure to make adequate disclosure

7-061   If relevant evidential material is not disclosed at all to a party who is potentially prejudiced by this, there is prima facie unfairness, irrespective of whether the material in question arose before, during or after the hearing. This proposition can be illustrated by a large number of cases involving the use of undisclosed reports by decision-makers.[298] If the deciding body receives or appears to receive evidence ex parte which is not fully disclosed, or holds ex parte (without notice to others involved) inspections during the course of or after the conclusion of the hearing, the case for setting the decision aside is obviously very strong; the maxim that justice must be seen to be done can readily be invoked.[299] If an appellate tribunal has communications with a tribunal of first instance with a view to altering the original decision, the parties to the proceedings before that tribunal ought to be notified so that they can make further submissions.[300] A fortiori, it can be a breach of fairness for an appellate authority, or a body receiving the report of the appellate

---

would only disclose any material derived from it if he saw fit). But see *Abbey Mine Ltd* [2008] EWCA Civ 353; (2008) 152(16) S.J.L.B. 28 at [31]–[32] (licence bidder entitled to be told concerns regarding bid, but not details of rival bidder's case).

[296] *Re D (Minors)* [1996] A.C. 593 at 603 (Lord Mustill: "It is a first principle of fairness that each party to a judicial process shall have the opportunity to answer by evidence and argument any adverse material which the tribunal may take into account when forming its opinion"); *Fayed (No.1)* [1998] 1 W.L.R. 763 (duty on Secretary of State to disclose his concerns in application for citizenship). See also *MH v Secretary of State for the Home Department* [2009] EWCA Civ 287; [2009] 1 W.L.R. 2049 at [17].

[297] See 7-069.

[298] See, e.g. *Kanda* [1962] A.C. 322; *R. (on the application of A) v Liverpool City Council* [2007] EWHC 1477 (Admin); (2007) 10 C.C.L. Rep. 716; *R. v Milk Marketing Board Ex p. North* (1934) 50 T.L.R. 559; *R. v Westminster (City of) Assessment Committee* [1941] 1 K.B. 53; *R. v Architects' Registration Tribunal Ex p. Jaggar* [1945] 2 All E.R. 131; *R. v Kent Police Authority Ex p. Godden* [1971] 2 Q.B. 662; *Fairmount Investments* [1976] 1 W.L.R. 1255; *Evans* [1982] 1 W.L.R. 1155; *K* [1990] 2 Q.B. 71; *R. v Enfield LBC Ex p. TF Unwin (Roydon)* (1989) 46 B.L.R. 1, DC. For the general rule, see *Board of Education v Rice* [1911] A.C. 179 at 182; *Shareef v Commissioner for Registration of Indian and Pakistani Residents* [1966] A.C. 47.

[299] See, e.g. *R. v Bodmin Justices Ex p. McEwen* [1947] K.B. 321; *Fowler v Fowler* [1963] P. 311; *R. v Birmingham City Magistrate Ex p. Chris Foreign foods (Wholesalers) Ltd* [1970] 1 W.L.R. 1428; *R. v Newmarket Assessment Committee* [1945] 2 All E.R. 371; *R. v Deputy Industrial Injuries Commissioner Ex p. Jones* [1962] 2 Q.B. 677; *Taylor v National Union of Seamen* [1967] 1 W.L.R. 532; *R. v Home Secretary Ex p. Georghiades* (1992) 5 Admin L.R. 457; and *Re Gregson and Armstrong* (1894) 70 L.T. 106 and *Goold v Evans* [1951] 2 T.L.R. 1189; *Errington v Minister of Health* [1935] 1 K.B. 249; *Highlands and Islands Airports Ltd v Shetlands Islands Council* [2012] CSOH 12 (an adjudicator who in the course of an adjudication in relation to a contractual dispute sought informal legal advice from senior counsel in respect of a clause in the contract without advising either of the contracting parties, was in material breach of natural justice). See also *R. (on the application of Tait) v Secretary of State for Communities and Local Government* [2012] EWHC 643 (Admin) (it was unlawful for a planning inspector, conducting an appeal of an enforcement notice issued by a local planning authority, to have carried out a site visit of a property in the presence of a local planning authority representative where the property owner was absent since there was a real risk of prejudice to the owner); see similarly *R. (on the application of Broxbourne Borough Council) v North & East Hertfordshire Magistrates' Court* [2009] EWHC 695 (Admin); [2009] N.P.C. 60.

[300] *R. v Huntingdon Confirming Authority* [1929] 1 K.B. 698. cf. *The Corchester* [1957] P. 84.

authority, to hold private interviews with witnesses.[301] In relation to central government decision-making, especially on issues of policy, the duty of disclosure may be lessened in respect of information originating within the government department. When a minister considers whether to grant a planning application following a local inquiry and consequent report by the inspector, he is under no obligation to disclose to objectors or to give them an opportunity of commenting on advice, expert or otherwise, which he receives from the department in the course of making up his mind.[302] And where the Parliamentary Commissioner for Administration has produced a draft report pursuant to an individual's complaint passed to him by the complainant's Member of Parliament, the Ombudsman does not act unfairly or contrarily to natural justice in sending a copy of the draft report to the government department involved but not to the complainant, since it is the department rather than the complainant which is being investigated and which may have to justify its conduct before a parliamentary select committee and face public criticism.[303]

Exceptions

To the general rule there are various exceptions, some of which have already been indicated, and which will be discussed in detail in Chapter 8. Briefly, there are cases where disclosure of evidential material might inflict serious harm on the person directly concerned (e.g. disclosure of a distressing medical report to a claimant for a social security benefit)[304] or other persons[305]; where disclosure would be a breach of confidence or might be injurious to the public interest (e.g. because it would involve the revelation of official secrets, inhibit frankness of comment and the detection of crime, and might make it impossible to obtain certain classes of essential information at all in the future)[306]; or where disclosure is sought of sensi-

7-062

---

[301] *Palmer v Inverness Hospitals Committee* 1963 S.C. 311; *Wilcox v H.G.S* [1976] I.C.R. 306; *Fairmount Investments* [1976] 1 W.L.R. 1255 at 1266.

[302] *Bushell* [1981] A.C. 75 at 102, HL (Lord Diplock); *R. v Secretary of State for the Environment, Transport and the Regions Ex p. Holdings & Barnes Plc* [2001] UKHL 23; [2003] 2 A.C. 295. Further, the HL held in *Bushell* that even where the post-inquiry evidence contradicts or modifies evidence given at the inquiry, the Secretary of State is not obliged to reopen the inquiry. However, if the new evidence is on a matter of central importance rather than (as in *Bushell*) on a matter held to be tangential or irrelevant to the inquiry, there would be a duty to reopen the inquiry, or to afford individuals the right to make further written representations; *United States Tobacco International Inc* [1992] Q.B. 353, DC; *Edwards* [2006] EWCA Civ 877; [2007] Env. L.R. 9 at [92]–[94].

[303] *R. v Parliamentary Commissioner for Administration Ex p. Dyer* [1994] 1 W.L.R. 621 (applied in *R. (on the application of Cavanagh) v Health Service Commissioner* [2004] EWHC 1847, overturned on other grounds in [2005] EWCA Civ 1578; [2006] 1 W.L.R. 1229 (but consider whether in some circumstances the complainant's interest in receiving fair consideration of his or her complaint might not in fairness demand that the draft report be disclosed to him or her)).

[304] *Godden* [1971] 2 Q.B. 662 (undisclosed official psychiatric report on police officer; court ordered disclosure to officer's own medical adviser but not to the officer himself). cf. *Re WLW* [1972] Ch. 456.

[305] *R. v Harrow Borough Ex p. D* [1990] 2 All E.R. 12 (mother not told that she was suspected child abuser justified by need to protect interests of the child).

[306] *R. v Lewes Justices Ex p. Gaming Board of Great Britain* [1973] A.C. 388; *R. v Secretary of State for the Home Department Ex p. Hickey* [1995] Q.B. 43, CA; cf. *R. v Poole BC Ex p. Cooper* (1995) 27 H.L.R. 605 (information received by local authority during statutory inquiries about homelessness of housing applicant could not be protected from disclosure on ground of confidentiality); *R. v Joint Higher Committee on Surgical Training Ex p. Milner* (1995) 7 Admin L.R. 454 (Committee not obliged to disclose references to applicant for accreditation as surgeon; interests of confidentiality outweighed applicant's interest in disclosure).

tive intelligence information.[307] Where a committee is entitled to sit in private session, it is not obliged to disclose legal advice of its officers to persons with a right to be heard, or to invite representations on the advice.[308] In such situations the person claiming to be aggrieved should nevertheless be adequately apprised of the case he has to answer, subject to the need for withholding details in order to protect other overriding interests.[309] An argument relying upon mere administrative inconvenience—for example, in having to prepare and disclose summaries of evidence which cannot itself be disclosed—is unlikely to succeed.[310]

JUDICIAL AND OFFICIAL NOTICE

7-063   Against this background one must consider the concept of judicial notice, which in administrative law shades off into what is known in the United States as "official notice".[311] Courts, which are required to decide cases on the basis of the rules of evidence, are also allowed to take judicial notice of matters of common knowledge, and these need not be put to the parties before them. How far judicial notice can properly extend is not altogether clear. The general principle is "that a person exercising judicial functions is not justified in noticing directly or indirectly by statement or otherwise facts within his private knowledge. He ought to be sworn and state them as a witness".[312] Exceptionally (if, for example, magistrates propose to take into account their impressions of a party before them, derived from earlier proceedings in which he was involved),[313] an adjudicator may be permitted to use his personal knowledge, provided that there is no real danger of bias and the matter to be taken into account is clearly disclosed to the party concerned.[314] In one case,[315] an appeal was lodged against an acquittal by lay magistrates, on the ground that one of them had used his medical expertise during their retirement to consider their verdict, to persuade them to reject the only evidence given on a particular issue. The appeal was dismissed; such expertise may properly be used to evaluate evidence given, but not to contradict evidence or introduce new evidence that

---

[307] For detailed discussion of the circumstances in which non-disclosure may be appropriate where sensitive intelligence is at issue, see 8-009.

[308] *Stoop v Kensington and Chelsea LBC* [1992] 1 P.L.R. 58 (local authority planning and conservation committee).

[309] *Benaim and Khaida* [1970] 2 Q.B. 417 (how much information ought to be disclosed to applicants for consents to run gaming clubs); *R. v Secretary of State for the Home Department Ex p. Hosenball* [1977] 1 W.L.R. 766 (intelligence information and deportation); *Duggan* [1994] 3 All E.R. 277. See also *Evans v Royal Wolverhampton Hospitals NHS Foundation Trust* [2014] EWHC 3185 (QB); [2015] 1 All E.R. 1091; [2014] 6 Costs L.O. 899 at [29] (Leggatt J noting that "… adherence to the principle of natural justice is not an optional feature of litigation from which a court has power to derogate because it considers that in the particular circumstances the need to follow a fair procedure is outweighed by a conflicting public or private interest. Subject only to certain established and tightly defined exceptions, the right to participate in proceedings in accordance with the principle of natural justice is absolute").

[310] *Duggan* [1994] 3 All E.R. 277.

[311] For a critical survey of the American doctrine, see R.J. Pierce, *Administrative Law Treatise*, 5th edn (2009); J Smillie, "The Problem of 'Official Notice'" [1975] P.L. 64.

[312] *R. (on the application of Giant's Causeway, etc., Tramway Co) v Antrim Justices* [1895] 2 I.R. 603. 649; and *Re Frank Bros Ltd and Hamilton Board of Police Cmrs* (1967) 63 D.L.R. (2nd) 309.

[313] *Thomas v Thomas* [1961] 1 W.L.R. 1; *Brinkley v Brinkley* [1965] P. 75; cf. *Munday v Munday* [1954] 1 W.L.R. 1078; *Dugdale v Kraft Foods Ltd* [1977] I.C.R. 487 at 54–55.

[314] See Ch.10.

[315] *Wetherall v Harrison* [1976] Q.B. 773. The court did warn, however, against the expert's unduly pressing his opinion upon his non-expert colleagues.

should be made available to the parties.[316] Characteristic of the standards appropriate for administrative adjudication was the attitude adopted towards arbitrators deciding workmen's compensation cases, who were permitted to draw on their own accumulated knowledge of general and local labour conditions to supplement evidence, but were obliged to disclose their thoughts to the claimant if nondisclosure would unfairly deprive him of his right to lead evidence or tender submissions on specific facts in issue.[317]

Public authorities may be set up because they already have or can be expected to acquire specialised expertise. Clearly they are entitled to use their expertise to draw inferences from evidence. If a decision-maker is under an obligation to observe the rules of evidence it cannot use its own expert opinion as a substitute for evidence,[318] though it may still be able to rely on an extended concept of judicial notice to supplement evidence. But a number of special tribunals are not bound by the strict rules of evidence. They are charged with the task of actively finding the material facts by any appropriate means; they may be permitted to adopt inquisitorial procedures,[319] undertake unaccompanied inspections,[320] consult experts[321] and use their own technical and local knowledge[322] and their past experience which may be based on evidence given in previous cases[323]; their final decision may, in some cases, be based on broad considerations of public policy. They are nevertheless obliged to act fairly. And this means that, in the absence of contrary intendment, they must not place a party at a disadvantage by depriving him of an adequate opportunity of commenting on material relevant to their decision if it is gleaned from

7-064

---

[316] For a stricter approach to the problem see *R. v Prosser* (1836) 7 C. & P 648; and *R. v Field Ex p. White* (1895) 64 L.J.M.C. 158. cf. Minister's duty to disclose evidence upon which he relies when disagreeing with a finding of fact by an inspector in a planning or compulsory purchase appeal.

[317] See, e.g. *Peart v Bolckow, Vaughan & Co* [1925] 1 K.B. 399; *Reynolds v Llanelly Associated Tinplate Co* [1948] 1 All E.R. 140; and generally, *Learmonth Property Investment Co v Aitken* 1971 S.L.T. 349 at 356; *Norbrook Laboratories (GB) Ltd v Health and Safety Executive, The Times,* 23 February 1998 (justices proposing to rely upon local knowledge should let both prosecution and defence know to give them opportunity to comment); and see *Mullen v Hackney LBC* [1997] 2 All E.R. 906 (CA held judge entitled to take judicial notice of matters which were notorious, or clearly established, or susceptible of demonstration by reference to a readily obtainable and authoritative source. He could rely on his local knowledge provided he did so properly and within reasonable limits).

[318] *Moxon v Minister of Pensions* [1945] K.B. 490.

[319] cf. *R. v Medical Appeal Tribunal (North Midland Region) Ex p. Hubble* [1958] 2 Q.B. 228 at 240–241; affirmed [1959] 2 Q.B. 408.

[320] cf. *R. v Brighton & Area Rent Tribunal Ex p. Marine Parade Estates (936) Ltd* [1950] 2 K.B. 410. cf. *Halsey v Esso Petroleum Co* [1961] 1 W.L.R. 683 at 689; *Salsbury v Woodland* [1970] 1 Q.B. 324 (unaccompanied view by judge). For recognition of the greater flexibility given in this respect to inspectors conducting public local inquiries, see *Fairmount Investments Ltd* [1976] 1 W.L.R. 1255 at 1264; *Hickmott v Dorset CC* (1977) 35 P. & C.R. 195.

[321] *R. (on the application of Ferguson) v Secretary of State for Justice* [2011] EWHC 5 (Admin) at [34]–[37] (although "inconceivable" that those representing the claimant would have gained anything from sight of an internal prison psychologist's report); and *Wislang v Medical Practitioners Disciplinary Committee* [1974] 1 N.Z.L.R. 29 (no duty to disclose legal advice obtained from outside the tribunal on a point of law upon which the individual had addressed the tribunal). Contrast *Jones* [1962] 2 Q.B. 677.

[322] *Croft on Investment Trust Ltd v Greater London Rent Assessment Committee* [1967] 2 Q.B. 955; *Kalil v Bray* [1977] 1 N.S.W.L.R. 256 (specialist tribunal may rely on its own expertise to reject otherwise uncontradicted lay evidence).

[323] cf. *R. v Deputy Industrial Injuries Commissioner Ex p. Moore* [1965] 1 Q.B. 456; *Bristol City Council v Aldford Two LLP* [2011] UKUT 130 (LC) at [55] (residential property tribunals should make their own assessments of the hazard of housing conditions and should not treat figures given for national averages as compelling, bringing their knowledge, experience and common sense to bear).

an outside source[324] or in the course of their own investigations,[325] or from evidence given in earlier cases.[326] An important consideration is whether the person who is affected by the decision could or could not be expected to anticipate what happened. That person should be mindful of his own interests. Accordingly, the doctrine of "official notice" is more readily applicable where the information relied upon is drawn from the general, accumulated experience of the decision-maker, rather than from an identifiable source upon which he has relied, whether it be another person, particular documents or specific prior events. As yet the case law gives no clear indication of the extent to which decision-makers will be permitted to abstain from disclosing during the hearing their own expert opinions, or information relevant to the exercise of their discretion.[327] The courts will lean in favour of imposing judicial standards as far as practicable,[328] so that if a person is misled as to the basis on which the decision-maker is likely to decide and is thus placed at a material disadvantage in putting his case, he may be held to have been denied procedural fairness.[329]

HEARINGS

7-065   A fair "hearing" does not necessarily mean that there must be an opportunity to be heard orally: "one is entitled to an oral hearing where fairness requires that there should be such a hearing, but fairness does not require that there should be an oral hearing in every case".[330] It has been observed that where an oral hearing is required, "[t]he interests at stake are such as to trump other factors in the balance

---

[324] As in *Jones* [1962] 2 Q.B. 677; *Hibernian Property Co* (1974) 27 P. & C.R. 197 (views of occupiers favouring demolition of unfit houses); *Kiely v Minister for Social Welfare (No.2)* [1977] I.R. 267.

[325] *R. v Paddington & St Marylebone Rent Tribunal Ex p. Bell, London & Provincial Properties Ltd* [1949] 1 K.B. 666 at 682; *Croft* [1967] 2 Q.B. 955 at 968 (dictum); *Fairmount Investments* [1976] 1 W.L.R. 1255 1265; and *Hickmott* (1977) 35 P. & C.R. 195; *Edward Ware New Homes Ltd v Secretary of State for Transport, Local Government and the Regions* [2003] EWCA Civ 566; [2004] 1 P. & C.R. 6 at [22]–[23]; *Wigan MBC v Secretary of State for the Environment* [2001] EWHC Admin 587; [2002] J.P.L. 417, 425; *Castleford Homes v Secretary of State for the Environment* [2001] P. L.C.R. 470 at [65]; *Killiney and Ballybrack v Minister for Local Government (No 1)* (1978) 112 I.L.T.R. 69.

[326] *Moore* [1965] 1 Q.B. 456 at 466–468, 489–490 (dicta); *Re Martin (John) & Co Ltd* (1974) 8 S.A.S.R. 237, where on the facts an opportunity to rebut the evidence was found to have been given.

[327] cf. R.J. Pierce, *Administrative Law Treatise*, 5th edn (2009): matters of policy and material affecting the exercise of discretion should, as far as is practicable, be disclosed but be controvertible by argument rather than by adducing evidence.

[328] See, e.g. *Learmonth* 1971 S.L.T. 349. cf. however, *Wetherall* [1976] Q.B. 773.

[329] *Shareef* [1966] A.C. 47 (applicant's advocate misled as to importance attached by tribunal to specific item of evidence; decision quashed); *Societe Franco-Tunisienne d'Ammement-Tunis v Government of Ceylon* [1959] 1 W.L.R. 787 (arbitration; giving the decision on basis of point of law not raised at the hearing is misconduct); *Re Chien Sign-Shou* [1967] 1 W.L.R. 1155; *Re Simeon* [1935] 2 K.B. 183; and *Ince* [1973] 1 W.L.R. 1334 at 1344–1345; cf. *British Oxygen* [1971] A.C. 610; [2005] EWCA Civ 1119; [2002] 4 P.L.R. 102 at [27] (noting that this was not a case where the inspector had made factual findings without permitting the parties to comment). cf. *Drewitt v Price Tribunal* [1959] N.Z.L.R. 21 (parties inadequately aware of basis of decision, but no fault attributable).

[330] *R. (on the application of Ewing) v Department of Constitutional Affairs* [2006] 2 All E.R. 993 at [27]; *West* [2005] UKHL 1; [2005] 1 W.L.R. 350 (where a Parole Board is resolving challenges to licence revocations, whether an oral hearing is necessary depends on the circumstances of each case; and it is likely to be necessary where facts are in issue that could affect the outcome or where it might otherwise contribute to achieving a just decision); see also *Foster* [2015] EWCA Civ 281 at [38] (the requirements of procedural fairness are flexible and context-dependent and in this case did not require the flexibility of oral presentation or evidence to determine the truth of the appellant's account; the

such as cost and perhaps efficiency".[331] Whether an oral hearing is necessary in any given case will depend on the facts of the particular case and it will be preferable to have an oral hearing where, for instance, on the evidence, there are facts which are in dispute,[332] (although a dispute of fact alone will not automatically necessitate an oral hearing[333]) or if there is doubt as to whether an oral hearing may be of assistance, the presumption should be in favour of it.[334] In any case, if there is a

---

context of home detention curfew meant the appellant had been under detention by other means and had been released on the discretion of the Secretary of State subject to compulsory curfew). On the importance of an oral hearing though, see: *Sengupta v Holmes* [2002] EWCA Civ 1104 at [38] (Laws LJ referring to "the central place accorded to oral argument in our common law adversarial system. This I think is important, because oral argument is perhaps the most powerful force there is, in our legal process, to promote a change of mind by the judge. That judges in fact change their minds under the influence of oral argument is not an arcane feature of the system; it is at the centre of it"); *Heather Moor and Edgecomb Ltd* [2008] EWCA Civ 642; [2008] Bus. L.R. 1486 (a fair determination of the dispute required that there should be an oral hearing but one that was limited to those officers of the applicant and the complainant who had been directly involved); *R. (on the application of Deeds) v Parking Adjudicator* [2011] EWHC 1921 (Admin) at [15] ("[a] party is only entitled to an oral hearing if the relevant procedural rules give him that entitlement; or, if they do not, where a failure to hold an oral hearing would in any event be a breach of the rules of natural justice or Article 6"); *R. (on the application of Sandhar) v Office of the Independent Adjudicator for Higher Education* [2011] EWCA Civ 1614; [2012] E.L.R. 160 at [45].

[331] *H* [2008] EWHC 2590 (Admin); [2009] Prison L.R. 205 at [1].

[332] *Hopkins* [2008] EWHC 2312 (Admin); [2009] Prison L.R. 223 at [33]. See also *H* [2008] EWHC 2590 (Admin); [2009] Prison L.R. 205 (inconsistency between the approach of local prison and the Director of High Security Prisons was a factor which favoured an oral hearing). But see *Heather Moor & Edgecomb Ltd* [2008] EWCA Civ 642; [2008] Bus. L.R. 1486 at [65] (oral hearing sought for purposes of cross-examination which was unnecessary especially given that the Ombudsman was intended to provide a system of resolving disputes quickly); *R. (on the application of Storm) v Secretary of State for Justice* [2009] EWHC 2168 (Admin); *Thompson* [2004] EWCA Civ 167; [2004] 1 W.L.R. 2522 at [51] (asking whether any "disputed issue of fact which was central to the Adjudication Panel's assessment in [the claimant's] case and which could not fairly be resolved without hearing oral evidence and without an oral hearing"); *R. v Criminal Injuries Compensation Board Ex p. Dickson* [1997] 1 W.L.R. 58 (applicant not entitled to oral hearing because no dispute as to primary facts); *R. v Criminal Injuries Compensation Board Ex p. Cook* [1996] 1 W.L.R. 1037; *R. v Secretary of State for Wales Ex p. Emery* [1996] 4 All E.R. 1 (conflict of documentary evidence as to footpath should have been tested at public inquiry; Secretary of State acted unfairly in deciding without convening inquiry); *Heather Moor & Edgecomb Ltd* [2008] EWCA Civ 642; [2008] Bus. L.R. 1486 at [58]. *Re Reilly's Application* [2013] UKSC 61; [2013] 3 W.L.R. 1020 generally at [80]–[96] and in particular at [85]–[86] (guidance on the necessity for oral hearings before parole boards, which are required in particular where facts which appear to be important are in dispute or where a significant explanation or mitigation is advanced which needs to be heard orally to be accepted, including where an assessment may depend on the view formed by the board of the characteristics of a prisoner which can best be judged by seeing or questioning him in person, where a psychological assessment is disputed or where the board may be materially assisted by hearing evidence, for example, from a psychologist or psychiatrist). For comment, see P. Murray, "Procedural Fairness, Human Rights and the Parole Board" [2014] 73(1) C.L.J. 5. It has been held that oral hearings for categorisation reviews will be "comparatively rare": *Hassett v Secretary of State for Justice* [2017] EWCA Civ 331 at [61]; see also *R. (on the application of Cummings) v Secretary of State for Justice* [2017] EWHC 266 (Admin). However, an oral hearing was required in *Rose* [2017] EWHC 1826 (Admin) at [62].

[333] The existence of a disputed issue of fact does not in itself mean that there must be an oral hearing: *R. (on the application of Calland) v The Financial Services Ombudsman Service Ltd* [2013] EWHC 1327 (Admin) at [110]. In Ireland, see *Coleman v The Financial Services Ombudsman* [2016] IEHC 169 at [23].

[334] *R. (on the application of Philip Riley) v Governor of Frankland Prison* [2009] EWHC 3598 (Admin) at [17] (no test of exceptionality as to whether to conduct an oral hearing; the correct approach was to balance the interests at stake and the extent to which better decision-making would be achieved against cost and administrative efficiency); *H* [2008] EWHC 2590 (Admin); [2009] Prison L.R. 205. See also *R. (on the application of McLuckie) v Secretary of State for Justice* [2011] EWCA Civ 522. For comprehensive guidelines on when oral hearings will be required in respect of decisions affect-

failure to request an oral hearing, it may be fatal to a judicial review challenge on this ground.[335]

Requirements at an oral hearing

7-066   A person who is entitled to be heard orally, or who is given an oral hearing as a matter of discretion under a power conferred by statutory or other formal rules,[336] must be allowed an adequate opportunity of putting his own case. As noted above, he will normally be entitled to that opportunity, particularly where there is some dispute as to material facts or other matter on which oral argument will be of assistance to the decision-maker.[337] If he has a right to appear, it will, of course, be a breach of that right, in addition to being unfair, for the decision-maker to refuse, deliberately or through inadvertence, to hear him[338] or even to allow him to be present.[339] His right to be heard must not be stultified by constant interruptions. Nevertheless, the right to an oral hearing does not in all cases confer the right to be personally present at the hearing, if the case is being conducted by a representative. Thus the Secretary of State was entitled to require a prisoner to meet

---

ing the prospective liberty of prisoners or the conditions in which they are detained, see: *Re Reilly's Application* [2013] UKSC 61; [2014] A.C. 1115 at [2]; *Foster* [2015] EWCA Civ 281 at [25] and *R. (on the application of Whiston) v Secretary of State for Justice* [2014] UKSC 39; [2015] A.C. 176. See also *R. (on the application of King) v Secretary of State for Justice* [2015] UKSC 54; [2015] 3 W.L.R. 457 at [93] (fairness at common law required that prisoners should usually have a meaningful opportunity to make representations before a decision was made to impose further segregation of 14 days). For application of *Re Reilly's Application* in the context of a hearing involving a disabled person before an employment tribunal, see *Galo v Bombardier Aerospace UK* [2016] NICA 25.

[335] *Re Solicitor* [2008] EWCA Civ 411 at [27]. Similarly, if the defendant or his duly authorised advocate agrees (in a voluntary, informed and unequivocal way) that a member of the tribunal can be absent for a part of the hearing and read a transcript of evidence and contribute to the decision, there is no breach of the rules of natural justice: *R. (on the application of Hill) v Chartered Accountants in England and Wales* [2013] EWCA Civ 555; [2014] 1 W.L.R. 86 at [23].

[336] On "voluntary" hearings, see 7-072, and for situations where there is no right to an oral hearing, see *Lloyd* [1987] A.C. 625 and 7-065.

[337] See 7-065, above.

[338] *R. v Birkenhead Justices Ex p. Fisher* [1962] 1 W.L.R. 1410; *R. v Gravesend Justices Ex p. Sheldon* [1968] 1 W.L.R. 1699; *R. v Kingston-upon-Hull Rent Tribunal Ex p. Black* (1949) 65 T.L.R. 209; *Chettiar v Chettiar* [1962] 1 W.L.R. 279; *Malloch v Aberdeen Corp* [1971] 1 W.L.R. 1578; similarly where the tribunal will not hear a party on an essential issue: *Sheldon v Bromfield Justices* [1964] 2 Q.B. 573; *R. v Worcester Justices Ex p. Daniels* (1997) 161 J.P 121 (magistrate appearing not to pay attention); *Jones v Welsh Rugby Football Union, The Times,* 6 March 1997 (noted [1997] P.L. 340) (arguable that failure by RFU to let applicant challenge by question or evidence the factual basis of the evidence against him, or to vary procedure for viewing video evidence, was unfair); *R. v Clerkenwell Metropolitan Stipendiary Magistrate Ex p. Hooper* [1998] 1 W.L.R. 800 (oral hearing before bindover and/or order for surety). *Hill* [2013] EWCA Civ 555; [2014] 1 W.L.R. 86 at [15] (if it is decided that a defendant or a witness will give oral evidence, that evidence will be "heard" and it is important that each member of the tribunal should if at all possible "hear" all the evidence; reading the transcript is normally no substitute for hearing evidence from a live witness given orally and for a tribunal member, juror or judge to absent himself without consent while oral evidence is given is usually a breach of the *audi alteram partem* rule).

[339] *R. v Dewsbury Magistrates Court Ex p. K, The Times,* 16 March 1994; *R. v Ely Justices Ex p. Burgess* [1972] Crim. L.R. 888 (Div Ct held that a view was part of a criminal trial, and that the absence of the accused, unless there were special circumstances, was a fatal matter. The fact that the justices travelled to the view in the same car as the prosecutor, even though there was no evidence that they discussed the issue, meant a fair trial was not possible, applying Ackner LJ in *R. v Liverpool City Justices Ex p. Topping* [1983] 1 W.L.R. 119); *R. (on the application of Drinkwater) v Solihull Magistrates' Court* [2012] EWHC 765 (Admin); (2012) 176 J.P. 401; *R. (on the application of Raheem) v Nursing and Midwifery Council* [2010] EWHC 2549 (Admin) at [42]–[43].

the costs of his production at court for an application for judicial review, since there was no fundamental right to be present.[340]

The fact that there is a right to an oral hearing usually indicates that the hearing is to be in public.[341] This enables the public to see that justice is done and plays a significant part in the maintenance of proper standards. In the case of judicial-type bodies the circumstances in which the public can be excluded from the substantive hearing are strictly circumscribed. This does not however apply to preliminary hearings, which are frequently held in private. When a hearing should normally be heard in public there is usually a discretion to exclude the public for good reason, such as national security, but the public should not be excluded to any greater extent than is necessary in the interests of justice.[342]

7-067

An oral hearing will not necessarily be conducted as though it was a hearing in court.[343] In some cases, it will merely involve the right to deliver oral representations, untrammelled by rules of evidence or rights to produce or cross-examine witnesses. In other cases, an oral hearing will be afforded in the context of a fully judicialised procedure. Unless the proceedings are criminal it is unlikely the decision-maker will be bound by strict rules of evidence. Today, in civil proceedings, as result of the Civil Procedure Rules (Pts 1, 32 and 33) a judge, as long as no injustice is caused, has considerable discretion to control evidence, determine what evidence is called and decide how matters are to be proved. In the past, the rejection of relevant and admissible evidence was considered a mere "error of law", but nowadays it may constitute denial of a fair hearing according to the requirements of procedural fairness.[344] Again, procedural fairness may be violated by a refusal to allow a party (or his legal representative) to address the decision-maker on the law or the facts[345] or, after a finding of guilt, on the penalty to be imposed.[346]

7-068

---

[340] *R. v Secretary of State for the Home Department Ex p. Wynne* [1992] 1 Q.B. 406, CA; also *R. v Morley* [1988] Q.B. 601. For the right to be present at an oral hearing pursuant to ECHR art.6(1), see 7-125 below.

[341] See, e.g. *Storer v British Gas Plc* [2000] 1 W.L.R. 1237 (decision of industrial tribunal quashed and remitted because not conducted in public). cf. *Meerabux v Attorney-General of Belize* [2005] UKPC 12; [2005] 2 A.C. 513 at [39]–[41].

[342] *Scott v S* [1913] A.C. 417; *Attorney General v Leveller Magazine Ltd* [1979] A.C. 440; *R. v Malvern Justices Ex p. Evans* [1988] Q.B. 540 (unruly persons may be excluded from an inquiry); *Lovelock v Minister of Transport* (1980) 39 P. & C.R. 468; *Morley* [1988] Q.B. 601 (even a defendant who is disruptive and is appearing in person can be removed during his trial for a criminal offence). Where there is a general rule that a hearing is conducted in public, even if the applicant requests a hearing in private, the general rule should not be departed from unless there is "good reason": *Re A Solicitor No. 18 of 2008* [2008] EWCA Civ 1358 at [3]; *Law Society* [2008] EWCA Civ 811; *Bank Mellat* [2013] UKSC 39; [2014] A.C. 700 at [67]–[74]; *Incedal* [2014] EWCA Crim 1861; [2015] 1 Cr. App. R. 4 at [31]. On the right to a public hearing under ECHR art.6, see 7-125.

[343] See, e.g. *Mahon v Air New Zealand Ltd* [1984] A.C. 808 at 821 (Lord Diplock: "[t]he technical rules of evidence applicable to civil or criminal litigation form no part of the rules of natural justice"); *R. (on the application of B) v Merton LBC* [2003] EWHC 1689 (Admin); [2003] 4 All E.R. 280 at [50] ("[j]udicialisation of relatively straightforward decisions is to be avoided"). See also *R. (on the application of Maxwell) v Office of the Independent Adjudicator for Higher Education* [2011] EWCA Civ 1236; [2012] P.T.S.R. 884 at [38] (OIA "not intended to be fully judicial, or to be operated in accordance with civil trial procedures").

[344] *General Medical Council v Spackman* [1943] A.C. 627; *Bond v Bond* [1967] P. 39.

[345] *Disher v Disher* [1965] P 31; *Mayes v Mayes* [1971] 1 W.L.R. 679.

[346] *Ex p. Kelly, re Teece* [1966] 2 N.S.WR. 674; *Ex p. Kent, re Callaghan* [1969] 2 N.S.W.R. 84; see also *Fullbrook v Berkshire Magistrates' Courts Committee* (1970) 69 L.G.R. 75 (clerk dismissed for misconduct, entitled to opportunity to be heard on question whether pension should be forfeited).

Adjournments

7-069   Wrongful refusal of an adjournment to a party unable to attend the hearing[347] or denying time to produce a witness or other important evidence may be tantamount to a denial of justice.[348] It may also be contrary to the rules of procedural fairness for a decision-maker to refuse to grant an adjournment where the continuation of the proceedings may prejudice the fairness of the trial of other proceedings, at least if there is a real risk of injustice.[349] In deciding whether fairness does or does not require an adjournment in order to allow further time to consider such material and to prepare representations, a court or other decision-maker should take into account the importance of the proceedings and the likely adverse consequences on the party seeking the adjournment; the risk that the applicant would be prejudiced; the risk of prejudice to any opponent if the adjournment were granted; the convenience of the Court and the interests of justice in ensuring the efficient despatch of business; and the extent to which the applicant has been responsible for the circumstances leading to the request for an adjournment.[350] It has been emphasised that the power to adjourn is one "which has to be exercised with great care and only when there is a real risk of serious prejudice which may lead to injustice".[351] It would appear that, in practice, the test is difficult to satisfy.[352]

7-070   The language of "consultation" usually finds no place in the vocabulary of procedural protection where the entitlement derives from the common law duty of natural justice or fairness (except where the source of the entitlement is a legitimate expectation).[353] Nevertheless, in this situation too, the opportunity to make written representations may on occasion be held to be all that fairness requires.[354] For example, when considering a first application for an entertainments licence a local

---

[347] *Re M (an Infant)* [1968] 1 W.L.R. 1897; *Rose v Humbles* [1972] 1 W.L.R. 33; and *R. v Llandrindod Wells Justices Ex p. Gibson* [1968] 1 W.L.R. 598; *Priddle v Fisher & Sons* 1478 (tribunal should have granted adjournment though not expressly requested); *R. v Kingston-upon-Thames Justices Ex p. Martin*, *The Times,* 25 March 1993. Contrast *R. (on the application of Montgomery) v Police Appeals Tribunal* [2012] EWHC 936 (Admin) at [19] (not wrong on the facts of the case not to await criminal proceedings, but dangerous to refuse to adjourn a disciplinary process if there is a real issue as to whether a particular offence which is relied on has been committed).

[348] *R. v Medical Appeal Tribunal (Midland Region) Ex p. Carrarini* [1966] 1 W.L.R. 883; *Polemis* [1974] 1 W.L.R. 1371; *Guinness Plc* [1990] 1 Q.B. 146; *Re P (Children)* [2012] EWCA Civ 401; [2012] 2 F.L.R. 1184; *CP v M Technology School* [2010] UKUT 314 (AAC). *R. (on the application of Gatawa) v Nursing and Midwifery Council* [2013] EWHC 3435 (Admin) at [18]–[19] (decision not to adjourn a Nursing and Midwifery Council disciplinary hearing to allow more time for a lay representative to prepare on behalf of a nurse, who was suffering from mental illness and was absent, had not been procedurally unfair, where her representative had been given many opportunities to ask for more time).

[349] *R. v Panel on Takeovers and Mergers Ex p. Fayed* [1992] B.C.C. 524 at 531; *R. v Institute of Chartered Accountants Ex p. Brindle* [1994] B.C.C. 297, CA; *R. (on the application of Agogo) v North Somerset Magistrates' Court* [2011] EWHC 518 (Admin); [2011] A.C.D. 47 at [15].

[350] *R v Kingston Upon Thames Justices Ex p. Martin* [1994] Imm. A.R. 172; *R. (on the application of Turner) v Highbury Corner Magistrates' Court* [2005] EWHC 2568; [2006] 1 W.L.R. 220 at [35]–[38]. See also *Cameroon* [2008] 1 W.L.R. 2062.

[351] *Fayed* [1992] B.C.C. 524 at 531 (Neill LJ).

[352] In addition to the above cases: *Abbas v General Medical Council* [2017] EWHC 51 (Admin); *Harrold v Nursing and Midwifery Council* [2016] EWHC 3027 (Admin); *Simon v Salliss* [2017] EWCA Civ 312; *Turner* [2005] EWHC 2568 (Admin); [2006] 1 W.L.R. 220 at [35]–[38] (exceptional circumstances justifying adjournment existed where the claimant, against whom a closure order under s.1 of the Anti-social Behaviour Act 2003 had been sought, had mental health problems and was not legally represented).

[353] For example, in *Council of Civil Service Unions* [1985] A.C. 374; see Ch.12.

[354] *R. v Amphlett (J)* [1915] 2 K.B. 223; *R. v Central Tribunal Ex p. Parton* (1916) 32 T.L.R. 476; *Housing Appeal Tribunal* [1920] 3 K.B. 334; *Stuart v Haughley Parochial Church Council* [1935] Ch. 452 affirmed [1936] Ch. 32); *Fairmount Investments* [1976] 1 W.L.R. 1255 at 1266. See generally

authority was held to be under no duty to give the applicant an oral hearing, although it was necessary to inform him of objections made and to give him an opportunity to reply.[355] The true question in every case is whether the decision-maker acted fairly in all the circumstances, and therefore written representations may be sufficient in a particular case although the nature of the right or interest affected would normally indicate that an oral hearing was necessary.[356] In many cases, it is the impracticality of requiring the decision-maker to hold oral hearings which leads the courts to hold that written representations are sufficient. Thus, in the case of the first-time applicant for an entertainment licence, the court could not but take account of the danger of requiring that oral hearings be held for a completely open-ended category of applicants.[357]

Failure to appear at an oral hearing

It should not be assumed that entitlement to an oral hearing means that the applicant can choose to make written representations instead. A litigant has no basic right to conduct his case in writing without attending the hearing, and a decision-maker may therefore be justified in disregarding written submissions where an applicant has failed to appear.[358] Although this may be thought surprising, it should not be forgotten that an oral hearing may not be helpful. The decision-maker may form an adverse impression of the applicant.

7-071

Statutory tribunals and inquiries may be required to conduct oral hearings.[359] Sometimes an appellant may be able to waive his right to an oral hearing in favour of a hearing by means of written representations.[360] If a tribunal has a general discretion to proceed by way of written representations, it should not have an inflexible policy of declining requests for oral hearings, but must consider whether there are circumstances—for example substantial disputes on questions of fact—which

7-072

Local Government Board v Arlidge [1915] A.C. 120. If, however, the deciding body conveys the impression that it will accord an oral hearing but then determines the issue on the basis of preliminary written submissions, it may be held to have contravened natural justice: *R. v Secretary of State for Wales Ex p. Green* (1969) 67 L.G.R. 560; and *Liverpool Taxi* [1972] 2 Q.B. 299 (no proper opportunity to make any submissions); *Lloyd* [1987] A.C. 625 (proceedings for surcharging councillors only given an opportunity to make written representations upheld).

[355] *Cowan* [1984] 1 W.L.R. 501 (decision quashed because of failure to give the applicant an opportunity to reply to the objections).

[356] See, e.g. *Lloyd* [1987] A.C. 625, HL (a district auditor had not acted unfairly in not offering oral hearings to councillors before certifying that financial losses of the council were the result of their wilful misconduct, since the councillors had made extensive written representations. However, for at least some of their Lordships, the determining factor was that the applicants had not requested an oral hearing. "If any had asked to be heard orally and the auditor had refused, there would have been clear ground for a complaint of unfairness" (Lord Bridge at 706); see also Lord Templeman at 714D).

[357] *Cowan* [1984] 1 W.L.R. 501.

[358] *Banin v MacKinlay* [1985] 1 All E.R. 842, CA (taxpayer who did not attend hearing of Special Commissioners but merely sent materials marked "Pleadings and Affidavit" could not complain when the Commissioners dismissed his appeal solely on the evidence and arguments put forward by the Crown. There was no breach of natural justice, and a statutory privilege for barristers and solicitors (s.50(5) Taxes Management Act 1970) entitling them to plead in writing did not extend to litigants in person). Per contra, it may be unfair to require written evidence when the individual is not at liberty to provide it: *R. v South Western Magistrates Ex p. Doyle* [1996] C.O.D. 309.

[359] See, e.g. Town and Country Planning Act 1990 ss.78 and 79(2).

[360] See, e.g. Town and Country Planning (Appeals) (Written Representations Procedure) (England) Regulations 2009 (SI 2009/452) as amended by the Town and Country Planning (Appeals) (Written Representations Procedure and Advertisements) (England) (Amendment) Regulations 2013 (SI 2013/2114).

should lead it to depart from its usual course of action.[361] Administrative convenience must not be allowed to override the exigencies of a particular case.[362] If there are contending parties before a tribunal and one is permitted to give oral evidence, the same facility must, of course, be afforded to the others.[363]

7-073   If a person who is entitled to request an oral hearing abstains from so doing, how far does he waive entitlement to other procedural protection—such as the opportunity to make written representations—which fairness would have afforded him? In one case it was indicated that he impliedly abandons his right to be apprised of and comment on evidential material obtained by the decision-maker.[364] This may be a reasonable interpretation in special situations where the proceedings are essentially inquisitorial; but it should not be accepted as a general principle of law.[365]

Right to call witnesses

7-074   Where a party is entitled to an oral hearing before a decision is taken which materially affects his rights or interests, he may be entitled to call witnesses to support his case.[366] A decision-maker will normally have a discretion whether or not to grant such a request, but the discretion must be exercised reasonably and in good faith, so that, for example, the decision of a prison board of visitors at a disciplinary hearing not to allow a prisoner to call witnesses because of administrative inconvenience was held to be contrary to procedural fairness.[367] The failure of prosecution authorities to inform the defendant of potential witnesses may also invalidate a decision,[368] although such cases have been explained (at least in the criminal context) as resting not upon a breach of procedural fairness but upon a breach of duty owed by the prosecution to the court and defence.[369] Where magistrates declined to issue warrants for the arrest of reluctant defence witnesses whose evidence was plainly material, a defendant succeeded in establishing a

---

[361] *Anderson* [1992] Q.B. 169. The Secretary of State for the Environment has a discretion not to hold a public inquiry under the Highways Act 1980, instead merely entertaining written representations. But he may not refuse to hold a hearing simply because he considers that all the necessary information is before him and that the issues raised are clear to him; he must also be satisfied that he can properly weigh any two or more conflicting issues, and that those with the right to make representations can have their representations properly taken into account: see *Binney* [1984] J.P.L. 871 where it was held that the minister in question had misdirected himself as to the factors to take into account; and, *Shorman v Secretary of State for the Environment* [1977] J.P.L. 98.

[362] *R. v Department of Health Ex p. Gandhi* [1991] 1 W.L.R. 1053 at 1063 (Taylor LJ).

[363] *Black* (1949) 65 T.L.R. 209.

[364] *Moore* [1965] 1 Q.B. 456, CA, 476 at 490.

[365] And see *Lloyd* [1987] A.C. 625 where there was no suggestion that the fact that the applicants had failed to request oral hearings meant that the district auditor was not under a duty to consider their written representations.

[366] *Vye v Vye* [1969] 1 W.L.R. 588. Natural justice does not require that witnesses be excluded while other witnesses are giving evidence; *Moore v Lambeth County Court Registrar* [1969] 1 W.L.R. 141.

[367] *St Germain (No.2)* [1979] 1 W.L.R. 1401. Similarly, it was held that the attendance of witnesses could not be refused because the tribunal thought there was ample evidence against the prisoner. *R. v Gartree Prison Visitors Ex p. Mealy, The Times,* 14 November 1981 (decision of prison board of visitors quashed where prisoner not allowed to question his own witness or to comment on the evidence presented); *Cheung v Minister of Employment and Immigration* [1981] 2 F.C. 764 (1981); 122 D.L.R. (3rd) 41 (immigration adjudicator wrong to refuse to allow applicant to call for purposes of cross-examination an immigration officer who had made a damaging statutory statement about the applicant).

[368] *R. v Leyland Magistrates Ex p. Hawthorn* [1979] Q.B. 283; *R. v Blundeston Prison Board of Visitors Ex p. Fox-Taylor* [1982] 1 All E.R. 646.

[369] *Al-Mehdawi* [1990] 1 A.C. 876, HL.

breach of procedural fairness.[370] In child care cases, a local authority has a duty to weigh fairly and objectively its discretion to authorise or refuse a medical examination of a child requested by parents in the hope of obtaining expert evidence in their favour,[371] and the authority must also allow evidence to be brought and witnesses to be called at a hearing for an interim care order where the order is opposed.[372]

Finally, it may be a breach of procedural fairness for a decision-maker to refuse to allow a person to call his witnesses in the order that he thinks best, if there is a real possibility of prejudice to the effective presentation of the case.[373]   **7-075**

RIGHT TO LEGAL REPRESENTATION AND OTHER ASSISTANCE

Fairness may require that a person be permitted to be legally represented at a hearing, have an interpreter or the assistance of a non-legally qualified person. Such a person was formerly described as a "McKenzie friend", although it has been observed that the term "applicant's friend" or "applicant's helper" may be more appropriate.[374]   **7-076**

Legal representation

There is some authority for the proposition that a person who is entitled to appear before an adjudicatory body is also usually entitled, in the absence of express or implied provision to the contrary,[375] to be represented by a lawyer or by any other appropriate spokesman of his choice.[376] However this puts the case too high, and it is more accurate to say that the decision-maker possesses a discretion whether to allow legal representation and everything depends on the circumstances of the particular case,[377] in particular, the legal or factual complexity of the issue, the consequences for the individual and whether the individual has the capacity to present his or her own case.[378]   **7-077**

Thus in a series of cases concerning the right of prisoners to be represented at disciplinary hearings before Boards of Visitors (the former adjudicatory body within   **7-078**

---

[370] *R. v Bradford Justices Ex p. Wilkinson* [1990] 1 W.L.R. 692.

[371] *K* [1990] 2 Q.B. 71; *R. v Hereford Magistrates Court Ex p. Rowlands* [1998] Q.B. 110.

[372] *R. v Birmingham City Juvenile Court Ex p. Birmingham CC* [1988] 1 W.L.R. 337 (this result was reached both, it would seem, on construction, and on natural justice grounds).

[373] *Briscoe v Briscoe* [1968] P. 501; *Barnes v BPC (Business Forms) Ltd* [1975] 1 W.L.R. 1565.

[374] *R v Conaghan* [2017] EWCA Crim 597; [2017] 2 Cr. App. R. 19. In Ireland, see *Knowles v Governor of Limerick Prison* [2016] IEHC 33; *Coffey v Environmental Protection Agency* [2013] IESC 11; [2014] 2 I.R. 125 at [17].

[375] *Maynard v Osmond* [1977] Q.B. 240 (disciplinary proceedings against police officer). On the right to legal representation where ECHR art.6 applies, see 7-121.

[376] *R. v St Mary Abbotts Assessment Committee* [1891] 1 Q.B. 378; *R. v Board of Appeal Ex p. Kay* (1916) 22 C.L.R. 183; and *R. v Birmingham Justices Ex p. Wyatt* [1976] 1 W.L.R. 260. The scope of the rule is not, however, clear either in England or in some other jurisdictions. See *Fraser v Mudge* [1975] 1 W.L.R. 1132 (disciplinary proceedings against a prison inmate); *Maynard* [1977] Q.B. 240 at 253 (dicta); cf. *Robinson v R.* [1985] A.C. 956 and *R. v Board of Visitors Maze Prison Ex p. Hone* [1988] A.C. 379.

[377] *Hone* [1988] A.C. 379 at 392 (Lord Goff). See also *Re BP's Application for Judicial Review* [2015] NICA 20 (there was no overriding principle that everyone giving evidence to an inquiry was entitled to legal representation; procedural fairness may often not require it, as it would increase the inquiry's costs and duration, and encourage the proliferation of side issues).

[378] *Regina (Howard League for Penal Reform) v Lord Chancellor (Equality and Human Rights Commission intervening)* [2017] EWCA Civ 244; [2017] 4 W.L.R. 92 at [43].

prisons),[379] the courts quashed decisions where there was a refusal to allow representation where the charge and potential penalty were particularly grave, or where relevant factors such as the ability of the prisoner to present his case, the availability of witnesses, the complexity of the case in fact and law, and the necessity for even-handedness between prisoners and prison officers had not been properly considered.[380] Where the charge had a straightforward factual and legal basis,[381] and where the prisoner was intelligent, articulate and had a clear appreciation of the proceedings,[382] courts declined to interfere with decisions not to allow representation. It is now clear, however, that art.6 is presumed to apply to any prison disciplinary proceedings which may result in the award of additional days of detention for a prisoner.[383] Such an award constitutes a fresh deprivation of liberty imposed for punitive reasons after a finding of culpability and should be categorised as "criminal" rather than disciplinary within the meaning of art.6.[384] This presumption of the applicability of art.6 can only be rebutted entirely exceptionally, and only if the deprivation of liberty cannot be considered appreciably detrimental given its nature, duration or manner of execution.[385] The Prison Rules were amended in 2002 to comply with art.6, and where the governor of a prison determines that the charge against a prisoner is sufficiently serious to warrant the award of additional days of detention, he must refer it to an adjudicator, who is to inquire into the offence.[386] At the relevant inquiry, the prisoner who has been charged is given the opportunity to be legally represented.[387]

7-079   As regards informal proceedings before a decision-maker, it is similarly the case that decision-makers possess a discretion as to whether to allow representation, although the courts will be less willing to intervene where representation is refused.[388] However, it may be that where the allegation is an "infamous" one, the decision-maker can only reasonably exercise its discretion in one way, and there is therefore a duty to allow legal representation.[389] Furthermore, where the case before the disciplinary committee is legally complex, again, legal representation may be

---

[379] Prison Boards of Visitors have had their name changed to Independent Monitoring Boards and since 1992, have not had responsibilities for adjudicating on prison discipline: Prison (Amendment) Rules 1992 (SI 1992/514) (since repealed) and Prison Rules 1999 (SI 1999/728) rr.75–78.

[380] See, e.g. *R. v Secretary of State for the Home Department Ex p. Tarrant* [1985] Q.B. 251; approved in *Hone* [1988] A.C. 379, HL.

[381] *R. v Board of Visitors of HM Remand Centre Risley Ex p. Draper, The Times,* 24 May 1988.

[382] *R. v Board of Visitors of Parkhurst Prison Ex p. Norney* [1990] C.O.D. 133.

[383] See 7-036.

[384] *Ezeh v United Kingdom* (2004) 39 E.H.R.R. 1 at [124]; see 7-036.

[385] *Ezeh* (2004) 39 E.H.R.R. 1 at [125].

[386] Prison Rules 1999 (SI 1999/728) r.53A, as inserted by para.3 of the Sch. to Prison (Amendment) Rules 2002 (SI 2002/2116).

[387] Prison Rules 1991 (SI 1999/728) r.54(3), as inserted by para.4 of the Sch. to Prison (Amendment) Rules 2002 (SI 2002/2116).

[388] *Re Macqueen and Nottingham Caledonian Society* (1861) 9 C.B. (N.S.) 793; *Enderby Town Football Club Ltd v Football Association Ltd* [1971] Ch. 591; *Pett v Greyhound Racing Association Ltd (No.2)* [1970] 1 Q.B. 46; *Ex p. Death* (1852) 18 Q.B. 647. There is some authority for the proposition that when a body has made no formal rule on the matter, it cannot refuse to exercise its discretion to consider allowing legal representation to a person whose ability to pursue his livelihood is in jeopardy: *Pett v Greyhound Racing Association Ltd (No.1)* [1969] 1 Q.B. 125 (as explained by Lord Denning MR in *Enderby Town* [1971] Ch. 591 at 605–606). However, it would appear possible for legal representation to be excluded altogether, whether as of right or in the discretion of the tribunal, by the exercise of an express rule-making power (e.g. *Enderby Town* [1971] Ch. 591 at 609 (Cairns LJ); *Maynard* [1977] Q.B. 240 at 252, 256, where it was held that legal representation had effectively been excluded by a rule made under a statutory power).

[389] *Manchanda v Medical Eye Centre Assn* (1987) 131 S.J. 47 (natural justice required that doctor be represented before Medical Eye Centre Association committee hearing allegation of unbecoming conduct); *Kulkarni* [2009] EWCA Civ 789; [2010] I.C.R. 101 at [68] (held, obiter, that a doctor fac-

required.[390] There may be no requirement to allow legal representation at professional disciplinary hearings which lead to temporary suspension without financial penalty.[391]

No matter what the status or functions of the decision-maker, it would be contrary to the requirements of procedural fairness to allow one side to be legally represented but to refuse the same right to the other. It has also been held to be inappropriate for a tribunal to proceed with an appeal as a country guidance determination in the absence of legal representation for the appellant, as a "proper contradictor" to the submissions of the Secretary of State.[392] And where legal representation is permitted or granted, a party may be entitled to confer with non-legally qualified advisers, although such persons would be barred from fully representing the party.[393] Further, the right to legal representation will where appropriate extend beyond the courtroom or hearing venue, and will be subsumed into the general principle that every citizen has a right of unimpeded access to a court and to legal advice. Thus, prison rules which authorised a prison governor or officer designated by him, to open and read any communication to a prisoner, and to intercept any communication of objectionable content or inordinate length, were held to be ultra vires the Prison Act 1952 to the extent that they authorised intrusion beyond the minimum necessary to ensure that correspondence was bona fide legal correspondence.[394] It may also be procedurally unfair not to facilitate an opportunity to seek legal advice.[395]

7-080

In considering whether procedural fairness implies a right to legal representation (if a party is able to obtain it), it should be borne in mind that only reasonable standards of fair adjudication, and not ideal standards, are required. Whether, and if so when, legal representation ought to be permitted before a decision-maker, can raise difficult questions of policy. The reasons for excluding legal representatives (or permitting them to appear only with the decision-maker's consent) are various. It is said that they tend to introduce too much formality and an inappropriate adversarial element into the proceedings, which are apt to become unnecessarily prolonged[396]; they disturb witnesses and inexpert members of the decision-making body by asking awkward questions and making "technical" points; their

7-081

---

ing what was effectively a criminal charge although dealt with by disciplinary proceedings had implied right to legal representation pursuant to ECHR art.6).

[390] *R. (on the application of S) v Knowsley NHS Primary Care Trust* [2006] EWHC 26; [2006] Lloyd's Rep. Med. 123.

[391] *R. (on the application of Malik) v Waltham Forest Primary Care Trust* [2006] EWHC 487; [2006] 3 All E.R. 71 (overturned on other grounds: [2007] EWCA Civ 265).

[392] *HM (Iraq) v Secretary of State for the Home Department* [2011] EWCA Civ 1536 at [43]–[51].

[393] *R. v Leicester City Justices Ex p. Barrow* [1991] 2 Q.B. 260 (poll tax protestors allowed to have non-legally qualified assistants in magistrates' court). See also [1985] Q.B. 251 at 282–283, 298; *R. v London Borough of Newham Ex p. Ajayi* (1996) 28 H.L.R. 25 at 29 (absence of anyone present at interview underlined unfairness).

[394] *R. v Secretary of State for the Home Department Ex p. Leech (No.2)* [1994] Q.B. 198, CA; see now the Prison Rules 1999 (SI 1999/728) r.39 which permits a prisoner to correspond with his legal adviser and any court (including the European Commission and Court of Human Rights) without the correspondence being read, whether or not legal proceedings have commenced subject to restrictions where the governor has reason to believe the communication may contain an illicit enclosure, or may endanger prison security, the safety of others, etc. cf. *Murray v UK* (1996) 22 E.H.R.R. 29.

[395] *R. (on the application of Medical Justice) v Secretary of State for the Home Department* [2011] EWCA Civ 1710 (no error of law by a judge who had concluded that a policy of allowing the removal, without providing the standard 72 hours' notice, of certain categories of persons who had made unsuccessful claims to enter or remain in the United Kingdom, constituted an abrogation of access to justice).

[396] An argument used in connection with the imposition of punishment on members of disciplined organisations, see, e.g. *Fraser* [1975] 1 W.L.R. 1132.

presence increases the likelihood of subsequent proceedings in the courts to impugn the decision. Notwithstanding these points, in general, legal representation of the right quality before statutory tribunals is desirable, and a person threatened with social or financial ruin by disciplinary proceedings in a purely domestic forum may be gravely prejudiced if he is denied legal representation.

Interpreter

7-082   In asylum proceedings, although an asylum claimant has no right to be accompanied by an interpreter at an interview, a refusal to permit an interpreter has been quashed for irrationality.[397] Generally, a party who is unable to understand the English language should be allowed to engage (and in serious cases ought to be provided with) an interpreter.[398] Where neither a legal representative nor an interpreter is present at the asylum interview, the interviewee must be permitted to tape record the interview in order to provide the applicant with an adequate means of ensuring that the record is adequate and reliable.[399]

Litigation friend

7-083   Although the relevant decision-maker has the discretion to permit the individual to be assisted by an adviser, an individual does not have a right to have a friend or adviser attend a hearing.[400] However, a party to proceedings has the right to present his own case and should be afforded all reasonable facilities to do so, including the assistance of a friend to give advice and take notes unless, in the interests of justice and in order to maintain order and regulate proceedings.[401] It has also been held in the context of family law proceedings that if a litigant in person applies to use the services of an unpaid adviser, the application should only be refused for compelling reasons.[402]

RIGHT TO CROSS-EXAMINATION

7-084   Refusal to permit cross-examination of witnesses may amount to procedural unfairness,[403] especially if a witness has testified orally and a party requests leave to confront and cross-examine him[404] or if the evidence is fundamental or highly

---

[397] *R. v Secretary of State for the Home Department Ex p. Bostanci* [1999] Imm. A.R. 411.

[398] cf. *Re Fuld's Estate (No.2)* [1965] 1 W.L.R. 1336; *R. v Merthyr Tydfil Justices Ex p. Jenkins* [1967] 2 Q.B. 21 at 23 (dictum) (see now Welsh Language Act 1993 ss.22, 24).

[399] *R. (on the application of Dirshe) v Secretary of State for the Home Department* [2005] EWCA Civ 421; [2005] 1 W.L.R. 2685.

[400] *Tarrant* [1985] Q.B. 251 at 282–283, 298.

[401] *Barrow* [1991] 2 Q.B. 260 at 289; *R. (on the application of AS) v Great Yarmouth Youth Court* [2011] EWHC 2059 (Admin); [2012] Crim. L.R. 478 at [8]–[9].

[402] *Re O (Children)* [2005] EWCA Civ 759; [2006] Fam. 1.

[403] *Re Fremington School* (1846) 10 Jur. (O.S.) 512; *Osgood v Nelson* (1872) L.R. 5 HL 636 at 646, 660; *Marriott v Minister of Health* (1936) 154 L.T. 47 at 50; *Newmarket Assessment Committee* [1945] 2 All E.R. 371 at 373; *Magistrates of Ayr v Lord Advocate* 1950 S.C. 102 at 109. Refusal to permit cross-examination of a witness in proceedings in a court will be a denial of justice; see *R. v Edmonton Justices Ex p. Brooks* [1960] 1 W.L.R. 697; *Blaise v Blaise* [1969] P. 54; *Loutfi v General Medical Council* [2010] EWHC 1762 (Admin). Procedural codes for statutory tribunals and inquiries normally give an express right of cross-examination.

[404] *Knowsley* [2006] EWHC 26; [2006] Lloyd's Rep. Med. 123 (where there was a serious dispute of fact between a witness and the doctor, questioning of the witness by the chair was unlikely to be an

contested.[405] The fact that the proceedings may be inquisitorial and informal is inconclusive.[406] As with the question of entitlement to legal representation, the matter is one for the discretion of the decision-maker. However, where a "judicialised" procedure has been adopted and witnesses are called to give evidence, the courts will be very ready in the absence of strong reasons to the contrary to find unfairness where a decision-maker declines to allow the evidence of those witnesses to be tested in cross-examination, and indeed it may be unfair for the decision-maker not to grant an adjournment to allow witnesses to attend for the purpose of being cross-examined.[407] As Lord Edmund-Davies has pointed out, "there is a massive body of accepted decisions establishing that procedural fairness requires that a party be given an opportunity of challenging by cross-examination witnesses called by other parties on relevant issues".[408] The true question in every case is whether the absence of cross-examination renders the decision unfair in all the circumstances. If no useful purpose is likely to be served by allowing cross-examination then the courts will be slow to disturb that decision.[409] Thus in *Bushell v Secretary of State for the Environment*, the majority of the House of Lords held that an inspector at a motorway planning inquiry had not acted unfairly in refusing to allow cross-examination of witnesses from the Department of Transport in relation to traffic flow forecasts, because such evidence "was Government policy in the relevant sense of being a topic unsuitable for investigation by individual inspectors upon whatever material happens to be presented to them at local inquiries held throughout the country".[410] It is submitted that there is no conflict of principle between such reasoning and the dicta of Lord Edmund-Davies, who dissented in the case. The differ-

---

effective way of probing the witness's evidence, compared with cross examination).
[405] *R. (on the application of Sim) v Parole Board* [2003] EWCA Civ 1845; [2004] Q.B. 1288 at [59] (parole board recall decision). cf. *Head Teacher of Alperton Community School* [2001] EWHC Admin 229; [2002] A.C.D. 15 (school expulsion hearing); *R. (on the application of Bonhoeffer) v General Medical Council* [2011] EWHC 1585 (Admin); [2012] I.R.L.R. 37 at [44] and [109] (Stadlen J also noting at [40] that there was "no absolute rule whether under art.6 or in common law entitling a person facing disciplinary proceedings to cross-examine witnesses on whose evidence the allegations against him are based"); *R. (on the application of Evans) v Chief Constable of Sussex* [2011] EWHC 2329 (Admin); *R. (on the application of Headley) v Parole Board* [2009] EWHC 663 (Admin); [2010] 1 Prison L.R. 135 at [22]; *R. (on the application of Bancoult) v Secretary of State for Foreign and Commonwealth Affairs* [2012] EWHC 2115 (Admin).
[406] *Brighton & Area Rent Tribunal* [1950] 2 K.B. 410 at 419; *Ceylon University v Fernando* [1960] 1 W.L.R. 223 at 235 (dicta). In the *Fernando* case (involving disciplinary charges) it was held that a fair hearing had been given although witnesses had been heard in Fernando's absence; he had been given a sufficient account of what they had said and he had not asked to confront or cross-examine them. But quaere whether it was reasonable in the circumstances to make Fernando's right to cross-examine contingent on his taking the initiative in making such a request; he was not legally represented. Nor, indeed, was he represented at the hearing of the appeal before the PC. In *R. v Commission for Racial Equality Ex p. Cottrell & Rothon* [1980] 1 W.L.R. 1580, it was held that a hearing held pursuant to s.58(5) of the Race Relations Act 1976 (where the CRE was minded to issue a non-discrimination notice) was more investigative than judicial in character, and consequently fairness did not require that the applicants should have the opportunity to cross-examine witnesses.
[407] *R. v Criminal Injuries Compensation Board Ex p. Cobb* [1995] C.O.D. 126.
[408] *Bushell* [1981] A.C. 75 at 116; *Errington* [1935] 1 K.B. 249 at 272; *Moore* [1965] 1 Q.B. 465 at 488, 490; *Wednesbury Corp v Ministry of Housing and Local Government (No.2)* [1966] 2 Q.B. 275 at 302; *Errington v Wilson* 1995 S.C. 550 (Outer House of the Court of Session, justices' food destruction order where conflicting scientific evidence).
[409] *Bushell* [1981] A.C. 75 at 108 (Viscount Dilhome); *Johnson Brothers v Secretary of State for Communities and Local Government* [2009] EWHC 580 (Admin) at [29] (nothing to suggest that the claimant was not given an opportunity to ventilate issues freely).
[410] *Bushell* [1981] A.C. 75 at 100H-101A; 123 (Lord Lane). It might be asked why, this being the case, it was that the inspector permitted evidence to be led at the inquiry in relation to the traffic forecasts. It is submitted that in an ordinary case, if a tribunal allows a witness to lead evidence which is not strictly relevant, it ought also to allow cross-examination on such evidence. *Bushell* is perhaps

ence between their Lordships simply concerned whether such evidence was indeed a "relevant issue" for the inquiry.

7-085   Even if cross-examination of some witnesses is permitted, the decision-maker is not necessarily obliged to allow cross-examination of every other witness by every party,[411] and there may exceptionally be valid grounds for disallowing questions to a witness on a particular matter.[412] It has been suggested that the proper approach of the courts to all these questions is to ask whether the decision-maker's exercise of its discretion can be faulted on normal judicial review grounds, for example, has it, in considering whether to allow cross-examination, had regard to irrelevant considerations, or is its decision unreasonable?[413] However, such an approach is only justifiable in those situations where the decision in all the circumstances complies with the minimum requirements of procedural fairness. In respect of decisions which are subject to the requirements of procedural fairness, the decision-maker has no discretion to adopt a procedure which will not comply with the minimum standards of fairness applicable.

7-086   If a party to proceedings claims that he has suffered an injustice because the non-appearance of a witness has made it impossible to cross-examine him, an attack on the validity of the proceedings may seem to be justified but may well prove to be abortive. A decision-maker may be entitled to base its decision on hearsay, written depositions or medical reports.[414] In these circumstances a person aggrieved will normally be unable to insist on oral testimony by the original source of the information, provided that he has had a genuine opportunity to controvert that information.[415] It is the responsibility of the decision-maker to make due allowance for the lack of an opportunity to cross-examine when assessing the evidence.

7-087   Three final points can be made. First, often a party cannot effectively exercise his right to cross-examine unless he is represented by a lawyer. Secondly, in proceedings culminating in the imposition of a penalty, procedural fairness requires the case has been proved, or even if there is no dispute as to the law and facts in the first place,[416] that there should be a right to address the decision-maker in mitiga-

---

unusual in that the ultimate decision-maker was not the tribunal (the inspector) but the Secretary of State, who had indicated that such evidence was not a matter appropriate for the inquiry. There was therefore no prejudice in allowing the untested evidence to stand, since the decision-maker (the Secretary of State) appreciated that it was not relevant to the decision which he had to make. See also *Johnson Brothers* [2009] EWHC 580 (Admin).

[411] *R. v London Regional Passengers Committee Ex p. Brent LBC, The Times,* 23 May 1985.

[412] As where questions are put to a civil servant on the merits of government policy (*Bushell* [1981] A.C. 75). The immunity from cross-examination conceded to the civil servant witness in *Re Trunk Roads Act 1936* [1939] 2 K.B. 515 seems to have been more extensive than this.

[413] See *Brent LBC, The Times,* 23 May 1985.

[414] *R. v Epping and Harlow Justices Ex p. Massaro* [1973] Q.B. 433 (prosecution not obliged to produce for cross-examination at committal proceedings witnesses who will be called at trial). See also *AM (Afghanistan) v Secretary of State for the Home Department* [2017] EWCA Civ 1123 (civil rules about admission of hearsay did not apply to the Immigration and Asylum Chamber of the First-tier Tribunal and Upper Tribunal).

[415] *Wilson v Esquimait & Nanaimo Ry* [1922] 1 A.C. 202; *R. v War Pensions Entitlement Appeal Tribunal Ex p. Bott* (1933) 50 C.L.R. 228; *Miller (TA) Ltd v Minister of Housing and Local Government* [1968] 1 W.L.R. 992 (enforcement notice appeal). In these cases the relevant evidential material was disclosed in writing; and *Kavanagh v Chief Constable of Devon and Cornwall* [1974] Q.B. 624 (Crown Court, on an appeal from a refusal to register a person under the Firearms Act 1968, may, like the original decision-maker, rely upon hearsay evidence). cf. *WLW* [1972] Ch. 456, where production of the author of a report for cross-examination was held to be a requisite of natural justice in a proceeding in a court of law.

[416] *Ridge* [1964] A.C. 40 at 68; *Burn v National Amalgamated Labourers Union* [1920] 2 Ch. 364 at 374; *Edgar v Meade* (1917) 23 C.L.R. 29 at 43; cf. *Weinberger v Inglis* [1919] A.C. 606 at 632.

tion[417] unless the penalty is automatic. Thirdly, there may well be questions of law or opinion on which a party cannot properly claim any right to lead evidence or to cross-examine witnesses but on which he can fairly claim an implied right to make submissions to the deciding body.

RIGHT TO REASONS

A failure by a public authority to give reasons, or adequate reasons, for a decision may be unlawful in two ways. First, it may be said that such a failure is *procedurally* unfair. Secondly, a failure to give adequate reasons may indicate that a decision is *irrational*.[418] We look at these in turn.

7-088

Reasons as an aspect of procedural fairness

It has long been a commonly recited proposition of English law that there is no general rule of law that reasons should be given for administrative decisions.[419] On this view, a decision-maker is not normally required to consider whether fairness or procedural fairness demands that reasons should be provided to an individual affected by a decision because the giving of reasons has not been considered to be a requirement of the rules of procedural propriety. This situation has changed enormously.[420]

7-089

The absence of a duty to give reasons has sometimes been explained as following from the fact that the courts themselves are not obliged at common law to give reasons for their decisions.[421] However, today not only the higher courts, but all courts, at least in relation to some of their decisions, are under such an obligation, for:

7-090

"It is the function of professional judges to give reasons for their decisions and the decisions to which they are a party. This court would look askance at the refusal by a judge to give reasons for a decision particularly if requested to do so by one of the parties ... it may well be that if such a case should arise this court would find that it had power to order the judge to give his reasons for his decision".[422]

---

[417] *Fullbrook* (1970) 69 L.G.R. 75.

[418] On irrationality generally, see Ch.11.

[419] See, e.g. *Stefan v General Medical Council* [1999] 1 W.L.R. 1293 at 1300 (Lord Clyde: "the established position of the common law [is] that there is no general duty, universally imposed on all decision-makers"); *Benaim and Khaida* [1970] 2 Q.B. 417 at 431 (where, however, the need to keep confidential the sources of the board's information was a paramount consideration); *R. (on the application of Hasan) v Secretary of State for Trade and Industry* [2008] EWCA Civ 1312; [2009] 3 All E.R. 539 at [19] and [21]; *R. (on the application of Lee-Hirons) v Secretary of State for Justice* [2014] EWCA Civ 553; [2015] Q.B. 385 (the Supreme Court judgment did not address the question of a common law duty of care: [2016] UKSC 46; [2016] 3 W.L.R. 590).

[420] See, e.g. *Hasan* [2008] EWCA Civ 1312; [2009] 3 All E.R. 539 at [19] and [21]. For discussion, see M. Elliott "Has the Common Law Duty to Give Reasons Come of Age Yet?" [2011] P.L. 56. For the duty to give reasons under ECHR art.6, see 7-125.

[421] See, e.g. the 4th edition of this book, at p.195 ("Minimum standards [of fairness] cannot be higher than those prescribed by the courts for themselves. Courts are not obliged to give reasons ...").

[422] *R. v Knightsbridge Crown Court Ex p. International Sporting Club* [1982] Q.B. 304 (Griffiths LJ). In relation to decisions of magistrates: *R. v Southend Stipendiary Magistrate Ex p. Rochford DC* [1995] Env L.R. 1 (no general duty on magistrates to give judgments or reasons for decisions); *R. v Haringey Magistrates Ex p. Cragg* [1997] C.O.D. 160 (no general duty to give reasons, even where no appeal from magistrates' decision); *Harrison v Department of Social Security* [1997] C.O.D. 220. See generally, M. Taggart, "Should Canadian Judges Be Legally Required to Give Reasoned Deci-

7-091   Judges are under a general duty to provide reasons,[423] and the number of exceptions to the duty are progressively decreasing[424]; even the formerly well-established exception on a judge's refusal of leave to appeal to the Court of Appeal from his decision to refuse leave to appeal from the decision of an arbitrator[425] has been doubted.[426] ECHR art.6 requires that "adequate and intelligible reasons must be given for judicial decisions".[427] Reasons have been required on costs decisions[428]; decisions refusing an extension of time in respect of leave to appeal[429]; on application for an interim remedy[430]; where the crown court is sitting in an appellate capacity[431]; in respect of applications for citizenship[432]; and when issuing warrants.[433] If a judge does not give reasons, his decision may be quashed and remitted for a rehearing.[434]

7-092   It is firmly established that "the law does not at present recognise a general duty

---

sions in Civil Cases" (1983) 33 U.T.L.J. 1.

[423] *Flannery* [2000] 1 W.L.R. 377 at 381B (Henry LJ noting that "today's professional judge owes a general duty to give reasons is clear"); *Eagil Trust Co v Pigott-Brown* [1985] 3 All E.R. 119 at 122, CA (Griffiths LJ, in application to strike out action for want of prosecution, judge should give sufficient reasons to show the CA the principles on which he has acted and the reasons that have led to his conclusion); *R. (on the application of Nottingham Healthcare NHS Trust) v Mental Health Review Tribunal* [2008] EWHC 2445 (Admin); [2008] M.H.L.R. 326 at [18] (referring to "the general duty in courts to give their reasons"); *EE & Brian Smith (1928) Ltd v Hodson* [2007] EWCA Civ 1210 at [28] (it is sometimes possible to announce a decision at the conclusion of the hearing but to reserve the reasons for it but if that is done, the reasons should follow without undue delay). See also *S-W* [2015] EWCA Civ 27; [2015] 1 W.L.R. 4099; *Weymont v Place* [2015] EWCA Civ 289; [2015] C.P. Rep. 29; *Re V (A Child) (Inadequate Reasons for Findings of Fact)* [2015] EWCA Civ 274. But see the dicta of Lord Phillips MR in *English v Emery Reimbold & Strick Ltd* [2002] EWCA Civ 605; [2002] 1 W.L.R. 2409 at [24] that while judges should not "have a second bite at the cherry", the Court of Appeal was "much less attracted at the prospect of expensive appellate proceedings on the ground of lack of reasons", noting that the successful party would suffer an injustice if a rational judgment were set aside because the judge did not include adequate reasons in the judgment.

[424] See, e.g. *Moran v Director of Public Prosecutions* [2002] EWHC 89 (Admin); (2002) 166 J.P. 467 (magistrates not required to give reasons for rejecting a submission of no case to answer); *R. v Secretary of State for the Home Department Ex p. Berhe* [2000] Imm. A.R. 463 (no duty on the IAT to give reasons for deciding to extend time for giving its decision); *R. (on the application of Birmingham CC) v Birmingham Crown Court* [2009] EWHC 3329 (Admin); [2010] 1 W.L.R. 1287 at [50] (reasons not required for an interlocutory decision akin to a case management decision to extend time).

[425] *Antaios Compania Naviera SA v Salen Rederiema AB (The Antaios)* [1985] A.C. 191, HL (judges ought not to give reasons for such a refusal of leave); *Mousaka Inc v Golden Seagull Maritime Inc* [2002] 1 W.L.R. 395, QBD (Comm).

[426] *North Range Shipping Ltd v Seatrans Shipping Corp* [2002] EWCA Civ 405; [2002] 1 W.L.R. 2397 at [27] (Tuckey LJ).

[427] *Anya v University of Oxford* [2001] EWCA Civ 405; [2001] I.C.R. 847 at [12].

[428] *English* [2002] EWCA Civ 605; [2002] 1 W.L.R. 2409; *R. (on the application of Cunningham) v Exeter Crown Court* [2003] EWHC 184 (Admin); [2003] 2 Cr. App. R. (S.) 64 at [14] (Crown Court should give reasons for costs decisions in criminal cases).

[429] *R. (on the application of Tofik) v Immigration Appeal Tribunal* [2003] EWCA Civ 1138; [2003] I.N.L.R. 623 at [17].

[430] *Douglas v Hello! Ltd (No.1)* [2001] Q.B. 967 at [9].

[431] *R. v Snaresbrook Crown Court Ex p. Lea, The Times,* 5 April 1994.

[432] *MH* [2009] 1 W.L.R. 2049.

[433] *R. v Central Criminal Court Ex p. Propend Finance Property Ltd* [1996] 2 Cr.App.R. 26 (reasons particularly important where the court was "exercising a draconian jurisdiction").

[434] As is now the case in relation to Crown Court decisions (save perhaps for some interlocutory or procedural decisions): *R v Harrow Crown Court Ex p. Dave* [1994] 1 W.L.R. 98; *Lea, The Times,* 5 April 1994; *R. v Stafford Crown Court Ex p. Reid, Independent,* 13 March 1995 (no duty to give reasons for Crown Court refusal to extend time for appealing against conviction before magistrates); *R. v Southwark Crown Court Ex p. Samuel* [1995] C.O.D. 249; *R. v Winchester Crown Court Ex p. Morris* [1996] C.O.D. 104; *R. v Southwark Crown Court Ex p. Brooke* [1997] C.O.D. 7 (following *Dave*); *R. v Bozat* (1997) 9 Admin. L.R. 125 (Crown Court Judge should give reasons for recom-

to give reasons for an administrative decision".[435] However, it may be more accurate to say that "the common law is moving to the position whilst there is no universal obligation to give reasons in all circumstances, in general they should be given unless there is a proper justification for not doing so".[436] The increasing number of so-called "exceptional" circumstances[437] in which fairness or procedural fairness does now require that reasons be afforded to an affected individual means that the proposition that there is no general duty is meaningless apart from demonstrating that the mere fact that a decision-making process is held to be subject to the requirements of fairness does not automatically lead to the further conclusion that reasons must be given. However, it is certainly now the case that a decision-maker subject to the requirements of fairness should consider carefully whether, in the particular circumstances of the case, reasons should be given. Indeed, fairness or procedural fairness usually will require a decision-maker to give reasons for its decision.[438] Overall, "the trend of the law has been towards an

---

mending deportation).

[435] *Doody* [1994] 1 A.C. 531 at 564 (Lord Mustill). This position was confirmed in *Oakley v South Cambridgeshire DC* [2017] EWCA Civ 71; [2017] 2 P. & C.R. 4 at [29] (noting that it was firmly established that there was no obligation to give reasons at common law, however, "the tendency increasingly is to require them rather than not"). See also: J. Bell "Kent and Oakley: a re-examination of the common law duty to give reasons for grants of planning permission and beyond" (2017) 22 *Judicial Review* 105; Sir Patrick Neill QC, "The Duty to Give Reasons: The Openness of Decision-Making" in C. Forsyth and I. Hare (eds), *The Golden Metwand and the Crooked Cord* (1998), p.161; *Stefan* [1999] 1 W.L.R. 1293 at 1300 (Lord Clyde: "the established position of the common law [is] that there is no general duty, universally imposed on all decision-makers"); *Rey v Government of Switzerland* [1999] 1 A.C. 54 at 66 (Lord Steyn). cf. *R. v Lambeth LBC Ex p. Walters* [1994] 2 F.C.R. 336, where Sir Louis Blom-Cooper QC, sitting as a deputy judge, suggested that English law has now arrived at a point where there is at least a general duty to give reasons wherever the statutorily impregnated administrative process is infused with the concept of fair treatment to those potentially affected by administrative action. But see *R. v Kensington and Chelsea LBC Ex p. Grillo* (1996) 28 H.L.R. 94, CA, where Neill LJ doubted the proposition of the judge at first instance (also Sir Louis Blom-Cooper QC) that there was a general duty to give reasons "in every aspect of the homeless persons legislation". Neill LJ did, however, foresee that "there may come a time when English law does impose a general obligation on administrative authorities to give reasons ..." (at 105); Sir Louis Blom-Cooper QC in *R. v Islington LBC Ex p. Hinds* (1995) 27 H.L.R. 65; (1996) 28 H.L.R. 302, CA; and *Public Services Board of New South Wales v Osmond* (1986) 159 C.L.R. 656 held that there is no general common law duty upon administrative tribunals or officials to provide reasons for their decisions. Although the High Court of Australia in *Osmond* did not discount a limited common law duty in "exceptional circumstances": 159 C.L.R. 656, 670, 676, that loophole was somewhat contrary to the rest of the court's reasoning and has not been used in the more than 30 years since *Osmond* was decided. The High Court showed no interest in revisiting or expanding that possible exception when it most examined reasons for decisions in *Wingfoot Australia Partners Pty Ltd v Kocak* (2013) 252 C.L.R. 480. That case concerned the nature and scope of a duty to give reasons arising under statute. The High Court pointedly avoided discussion of common law duties to give reasons and also made clear that any statutory duty depended heavily on the statute at hand.

[436] *Oakley* [2017] EWCA Civ 71; [2017] 2 P. & C.R. 4 at [30]. This reflects the position adopted by the Irish Supreme Court in *Mallak v Minister for Justice, Equality and Law Reform* [2012] IESC 59; [2012] 3 I.R. 297 at [74]. It has also been held in Ireland that where rights are affected it can no longer be seriously doubted that administrative bodies have a duty to give reasons: *Deehan v State Examinations Commission* [2016] IEHC 213 at [15].

[437] *R. v Universities Funding Council Ex p. Institute of Dental Surgery* [1994] 1 W.L.R. 242 (Divisional Court rejected the contention that the duty to give reasons could any longer be described as an "exceptional one").

[438] *R v Ministry for Defence Ex p. Murray* [1998] C.O.D. 134; *R. v Secretary of State for Education Ex p. G* [1995] E.L.R. 58 at 67 (Latham J); *Mubarak v General Medical Council* [2008] EWHC 2830 (Admin) at [36] ("The duty to give reasons is a facet of the obligation to deal fairly with the parties").

increased recognition of the duty to give reasons"[439] and there has been a strong momentum in favour of greater openness and transparency in decision-making.[440]

Advantages of a duty to give reasons

7-093   The absence of a general duty to give reasons has long been condemned as a major defect of our system of administrative law. As the Justice-All Souls Committee concluded, "no single factor has inhibited the development of English administrative law as seriously as the absence of any general obligation upon public authorities to give reasons for their decisions".[441] The beneficial effects of a duty to give reasons are many.[442] To have to provide an explanation of the basis for their decision is a salutary discipline for those who have to decide anything that adversely affects others.[443] The giving of reasons is widely regarded as one of the principles of good administration[444] in that it encourages a careful examination of the relevant issues, the elimination of extraneous considerations, and consistency in decision-making. If published, reasons can provide guidance to others on the body's likely future decisions, and so deter applications which would be unsuccessful. The giving of reasons may protect the body from unjustified challenges, because those adversely affected are more likely to accept a decision if they know why it has been

---

[439] *North Range Shipping Ltd* [2002] 1 W.L.R. 2397 at [15] CA, (Tuckey LJ). But the absence of a general duty to give reasons was affirmed in *Hasan* [2009] 3 All E.R. 539 at [8]; *R. (on the application of Savva) v Kensington & Chelsea RLBC* [2010] EWCA Civ 1209; [2011] P.T.S.R. 761 at [19] (the duty may perhaps be satisfied by a timely offer of the provision of reasons on request: [23]).

[440] See, e.g. *Institute of Dental Surgery* [1994] 1 W.L.R. 242 at 259 (Sedley J in a case where reasons were not required, but Sedley LJ has since suggested that, if decided today, reasons would be required even in that context: see *Feggetter* [2002] EWCA Civ 554; [2003] Q.B. 219 at [40]); *Murray* [1998] C.O.D. 134 (Hooper J referring to the "perceptible trend towards an insistence on greater openness in the making of administrative decisions"); see also *R. v Billington (Jason Leon)* [2017] EWCA Crim 618; [2017] 4 W.L.R. 114 at [32] (reasons for sentencing required as "[t]ransparency in the working of the justice system is integral to the maintenance of public confidence in that system").

[441] Justice-All Souls Committee Report, *Administrative Justice, Some Necessary Reforms* (1988), p.71, quoting the earlier Justice Committee Report, *Administration Under Law* (1971), p.23. See further, H.W.R. Wade and C. Forsyth, *Administrative Law*, 11th edn (2014), pp.440-443; H. Woolf, *Protection of the Public—A New Challenge* (1989), p.92; P. Craig *Administrative Law*, 8th edn (2016), para.12-038; the important survey in *Murray* [1998] C.O.D. 134; P. Craig, "The Common Law, Reasons and Administrative Justice" (1994) 53 C.L.J. 282; F. Schauer, "Giving Reasons" (1995) 47 Standford L.R. 633.

[442] See, e.g. *Osmond v Public Service Board* [1984] 3 N.S.W.L.R. 447 at 463 where Kirby P gives several reasons why giving reasons is desirable: (a) assists in seeing if a reviewable or appeal able error has occurred; (b) giving of reasons adds legitimacy; (c) provides a disincentive for arbitrariness; (d) the discipline of giving reasons will make administrators more careful and rational; and (e) reasons give guidance for future cases.

[443] *Tramountana Annadora SA v Atlantic Shipping Co SA* [1978] 2 All E.R. 870 at 872 (Donaldson J: "Having to give reasons concentrates the mind wonderfully"); *Hinds* (1995) 27 H.L.R. 65 at 75 (noting that "[g]iving reasons is also a self-disciplining exercise"); *Cullen v Chief Constable of the Royal Ulster Constabulary* [2003] UKHL 39; [2003] 1 W.L.R. 1763 at [7] (Lord Steyn noting that the statutory duty to give reasons for deferring access to a solicitor "impose[s] a discipline ... which may contribute to such refusals being considered with care"); *R. (on the application of O'Brien) v Independent Assessor* [2004] EWCA Civ 1035 at [77] (Auld LJ noting that the purpose of the giving of reasons is to focus the Independent Assessor's mind on the relevant statutory criteria, guidance and principles of law on the make-up of his awards before and when considering their totality; appeal dismissed at [2007] UKHL 10; [2007] 2 A.C. 312); *Flannery* [2000] 1 W.L.R. 377 at 381 (Henry LJ noting that "a requirement to give reasons concentrates the mind").

[444] See, e.g. G. Richardson, "The Duty to Give Reasons: Potential and Practice" [1986] P.L. 437; J. Garton, "The Judicial Review of the Decisions of Charity Trustees" (2006) 20 *Trust Law International* 160, 177; A. Le Sueur "Taking the Soft Option? The Duty to Give Reasons in the Draft Freedom of Information Bill" [1999] P.L. 419, 423.

taken.[445] Basic fairness and respect for the individual often requires that those in authority over others should tell them why they are subject to some liability or have been refused some benefit: in short, "justice will not be done if it is not apparent to the parties why one has won and the other has lost".[446] The giving of reasons increases public confidence in the decision-making process.[447]

In addition to helping to ensure the fairness of an initial hearing, a requirement of reasons is of particular importance where decisions are subject to a right of appeal on questions of law.[448] A reasoned decision is necessary to enable the person prejudicially affected by the decision to know whether he has a ground of appeal,[449] or alternatively, a ground of challenge by way of judicial review.[450] Reasons will also assist the appellate or reviewing court to scrutinise effectively the decision for relevant error, without necessarily usurping the function of the decision-maker by itself re-determining the questions of fact and discretion which Parliament entrusted to the decision-maker.[451] Without reasons, it can be extremely difficult to detect errors.[452]   **7-094**

It is because of these very real benefits which result from the giving of reasons   **7-095**

---

[445] See, e.g. *R. v Secretary of State for the Home Department Ex p. Singh, The Times,* 8 June 1987, QBD, where Woolf LJ explained that it was highly undesirable for the Home Office not to give written notification of a decision on an application for asylum, not only because of the potential unfairness to the applicant, but because without notice, an applicant would be likely to receive leave to move for judicial review, whatever the real merits of his case, if he indicated that as far as he was aware no decision had been taken on his case. See also *Oakley* [2017] EWCA Civ 71 at [58] (noting the instrumental justification for reasons to "enable [the person affected] to be satisfied that the decision was lawfully made and to challenge it if they believe that it was not").

[446] *English* [2002] EWCA Civ 605; [2002] 1 W.L.R. 2409 at [16]; *Flannery* [2000] 1 W.L.R. 377 at 381 (Henry LJ noting that "fairness surely requires that the parties—especially the losing party—should be left in no doubt why they have won or lost"); see also *S-W* [2015] EWCA Civ 27; [2015] 1 W.L.R. 4099 at [46]; *Re V (A Child)* [2015] EWCA Civ 274 at [31] (noting that the parties needed to know why the judge preferred the evidence of one against the other, which was important "not simply as a matter of justice and a matter of having a fair trial which comes to a clear and transparent conclusion" but, as this was a family law case, in order to enable the father to undertake counselling or therapy on the basis of the findings made); *Oakley* [2017] EWCA Civ 71; [2017] 2 P.& C.R. 4 at [58] (those affected "have a legitimate interest in knowing how important decisions affecting the quality of their lives have been reached").

[447] *Stefan* [1999] 1 W.L.R. 1293 at 1300; *Secretary of State for the Home Department v CC* [2014] EWCA Civ 559 at [38]–[39] (control orders quashed for material non-disclosure where provision of reasons for rejecting abuse allegations in closed judgment prevented the public from knowing the extent to which their allegations had been accepted or rejected).

[448] See, e.g. Tribunals and Inquiries Act 1992 s.10.

[449] See, e.g. *Hinds* (1995) 27 HLR 65 at 75 (noting that reasons enable the claimant to determine if the decision is "legally challengeable"); see also *Billington* [2017] EWCA Crim 618; [2017] 4 W.L.R. 114.

[450] *O'Brien* [2004] EWCA Civ 1035 at [77] (appeal dismissed at [2007] UKHL 10; [2007] 2 A.C. 312); *Horada v Secretary of State for Communities & Local Government* [2016] EWCA Civ 169 at [34]; *R. (on the application of Dowley) v Secretary of State for Communities and Local Government* [2016] EWHC 2618 (Admin); [2016] A.C.D. 129 at [56]. Of course, whether the reasons provided demonstrate error of fact or law is separate from the question of the adequacy of the reasons: see *R. (on the application of C) v Financial Services Authority* [2013] EWCA Civ 677 at [48].

[451] *Cullen* [2003] 1 W.L.R. 1763 at [7] (Lord Steyn). See, e.g. *Edwards v Bairstow* [1956] A.C. 14 at 36 (reasoning setting out the facts found and the determination revealed irrationality constituting error of law); *R. (on the application of Kelsall) v Secretary of State for the Environment, Food and Rural Affairs (No.1)* [2003] EWHC 459 at [35] ("if [the] reasons do not bear scrutiny they add substance to the argument that the provisions of the Order are so flawed as to be irrational and unfair"); *R. (on the application of Quark Fishing Ltd) v Secretary of State for Foreign and Commonwealth Affairs (No.1)* [2002] EWCA Civ 1409 (unlawful approach became clear from documents disclosed following the court order).

[452] *R. v Nat Bell Liquors Ltd* [1922] 2 A.C. 128 at 159 (Lord Sumner); *O'Reilly* [1983] 2 A.C. 237 at 277 (Lord Diplock noting that judicial review for error of law on the face of the record "was liable

that a legal duty to give reasons has become an integral part of the model of administration that has dominated English administrative law since the publication of the Franks Report.[453] If those entitled to be heard have no right to know how a tribunal resolved the issues in dispute at the hearing, they may well regard as an empty ritual their legally conferred opportunity to be heard and to influence the tribunal by producing witnesses and other evidence to establish the relevant facts, advancing arguments on the proper exercise of any discretion and the resolution of any legal questions, and challenging their opponents' case. Unless the tribunal makes findings on disputes as to fact, explains the exercise of its discretion (by indicating the considerations that it has taken into account and relative weight assigned to them, for example) and gives its answers to any questions of law, there can be no assurance that the tribunal has discharged its obligation to correctly decide issues of law and base its decision upon the material presented at the hearing, rather than on extraneous considerations.[454]

Disadvantages of a duty to give reasons

7-096   There are, however, some significant objections which can be raised to the courts extending a general requirement to provide reasons and findings of fact to all administrative bodies that are in any case obliged by the duty of fairness to inform those whom they may prejudicially affect of the case that they have to meet and to offer them an opportunity to submit representations. These include the possibility that reasons, especially if published, will unduly increase "legalisation" and the formal nature of the decision making process,[455] place burdens upon decision-makers that will occasion administrative delays, and encourage the disappointed to pore over the reasons in the hope of detecting some shortcoming for which to seek redress in the courts.[456] In addition, a reluctance to give reasons perhaps because they may occasion harm (by, for example, causing personal distress,[457] revealing

---

to be defeated by the decision-making body if it gave no reasons for its determination"); *Hinds* (1995) 27 H.L.R. 65 at 75 (noting that reasons facilitate review as "adequate reasons ... expose any errors of law, unsubstantial findings and extraneous considerations").

[453] Cmnd. 218 (1957), para.98; similar recommendations had been made 25 years earlier by the Donoughmore Committee Cmd. 4060 (1932) p.100, but they were not implemented. The US Administrative Procedure Act's requirement of reasons applies principally to formal adjudication, although the courts have imposed a duty to make findings of fact and to state reasons in some other situations: see R. Pierce, *Administrative Law Treatise*, 5th edn. (2009). In contrast, all regulations, decisions and directives of the EU Council and Commission must be supported by reasons.

[454] cf. *R. v Mental Health Review Tribunal Ex p. Clatworthy* [1985] 3 All E.R. 699 at 703–704.

[455] cf. *Varndell v Kearney & Trecker Marwin Ltd* [1983] I.C.R. 683 at 694–695 (warning to tribunals not to reduce questions of facts, degree and discretion to legal propositions by excessively elaborate reasons); *Stefan* [1999] 1 W.L.R. 1293 at 1300 (noting that "there are dangers and disadvantages in a universal requirement for reasons. It may impose an undesirable legalism into areas where a high degree of informality is inappropriate and add to delay and expense").

[456] *McInnes* [1978] 1 W.L.R. 1520 at 1535; *R. v Chief Registrar of Friendly Societies Ex p. New Cross Building Society* [1984] Q.B. 227 at 245 (detailed reasons may tempt a reviewing court erroneously to assume an appellate of de novo jurisdiction); and the disadvantages listed by Hooper J in *Murray* [1998] C.O.D. 134; *Uprichard* [2013] UKSC 21; [2013] P.T.S.R. D37 at [48] (observing that it was important to maintain a sense of proportion when considering the duty to give reasons and not to impose a burden on decision-makers which is unreasonable having regard to the purpose intended to be served and noting that "[i]f the ministers were to be expected to address, line by line, every nuance of every matter raised in every objection, the burden imposed in such circumstances would be unreasonable").

[457] *McInnes* [1978] 1 W.L.R. 1520 at 1533; cf. *Grundy (Teddington) Ltd v Plummer* [1983] I.C.R. 367 at 373–374.

confidences, or endangering national security[458]) could discourage the making of difficult or controversial decisions or result in the production of anodyne, uninformative and standard reasons. In addition, the determination of an issuer may not lend itself to reasoning, being a matter of impression, or taste, or a matter on which no objective justification is possible or useful.[459] Nonetheless, apart from the exceptional case, the advantages of providing reasons so clearly outweigh the disadvantages that fairness requires that the individual be informed of the basis of the decision.

Distinction between duty to give reasons and disclosure

The duty to give reasons for a decision must be distinguished from the **7-097**
fundamental principle of procedural fairness already considered[460] which imposes an obligation to provide information about the case which a party affected may want to answer. Some cases which appear to suggest that reasons are required by natural justice or fairness are in reality examples of this more basic requirement. For example, a local authority must not suspend a contractor from its list of approved contractors without giving detailed reasons immediately (or as soon as is practicable in a case where serious impropriety is suspected).[461] This is not an example of a case where reasons are required, but rather safeguards of the contractor's right to make further representations: the authority must disclose the case against the contractor so that it may be able to answer the allegation as quickly as possible. Thus the right to information protects the right to make representations, but does not by itself automatically entitle the contractor to a reasoned justification of the final decision.[462]

Circumstances in which reasons will be required

The categories of situations where reasons are required are not closed but a **7-098**
failure to provide reasons may give grounds for challenging an administrative decision on the ground that this amounts to procedural impropriety in the following circumstances.[463]

---

[458] cf. Regulation of Investigatory Powers Act 2000 s.69, which enables the Secretary of State to make rules enabling the Tribunal to hear proceedings without the person who has brought the proceedings being given reasons. See *R. v Secretary of State for the Home Department Ex p. Adams* [1995] All E.R. (E.C.) 177 (reasons not required where, to be meaningful, they would have to reveal sensitive intelligence information).

[459] *Institute of Dental Surgery* [1994] 1 W.L.R. 242.

[460] See 7-044.

[461] *TF Unwin (Roydon)* [1989] C.O.D. 466; cf. *Cinnamond v British Airports Authority* [1980] 1 W.L.R. 582 at 591.

[462] See, e.g. *R. v Secretary of State for the Home Office Ex p. Thirukumar* [1989] Imm. A.R. 270, (applicant for asylum should be made aware of reasons why his application is being at least provisionally refused; in reality so that he can make further representations); cf. *Everett* [1989] Q.B. 811, CA (O'Connor LJ, Secretary of State did not have to afford applicant opportunity to be heard before refusing application for a passport, but "was entitled to refuse the passport but to give his reason for so doing" and "tell him that if there were any exceptional grounds which might call for the issue of a passport he would consider them"). An important example of the distinction is *Fayed* [1997] 1 W.L.R. 228, CA (no duty to give reasons because of statutory exclusion, but duty to disclose to applicant the subject matter of the decision-maker's concern to allow meaningful representations).

[463] *R. v University of Cambridge Ex p. Evans (No.1)* [1998] E.515 at 521–523 (Sedley J); *Feggetter* [2002] EWCA Civ 554; [2003] Q.B. 219 at [40] (Sedley LJ).

Required by statute

7-099   Reasons for a decision may be expressly or impliedly required by statute.[464] A duty to supply reasons when requested to do so is imposed by the Tribunals and Inquiries Act 1992 on a large number of statutory tribunals and on Ministers notifying decisions after the holding of a statutory inquiry or in cases where the person concerned could have required the holding of such an inquiry.[465] This duty, which is qualified by a narrow range of exceptions,[466] is enforceable by a mandatory order.[467] A similar duty has been imposed on various other tribunals and public authorities by statute or regulations.[468] There are indications, for example, that in deciding a planning appeal on the basis of written representations, an inspector is obliged to give reasons dealing with the parties' major contentions, even though the statutory duty to give reasons without a request from a party applies only to decisions made after an inquiry.[469]

7-100   Although not strictly speaking obligations to give reasons, public authorities are also subject to qualified statutory obligations to disclose information under the Freedom of Information Act 2000, the Data Protection Act 1998 and regulations on environmental information.[470]

To enable an effective right of appeal

7-101   Where statute or regulation provides a right of appeal from a decision, reasons may be required so as to enable the affected individual to exercise effectively that right. A right to reasons in these circumstances may be explained either by refer-

---

[464] A. Le Sueur, "Legal Duties to Give Reasons" (1999) 52 C.L.P. 150; *Stefan* [1999] 1 W.L.R. 1293 at 1297 (implied statutory duty). In Canada, statutory entitlement to reasons has been a feature of general procedural statutes for many years, starting in 1966 with the Alberta Administrative Procedures Act S.A. 1966, c.1 (now the Administrative Procedures and Jurisdiction Act RSA 2000, c.A.3, s.7), followed in 1971 by the Ontario Statutory Powers Procedure Act SO 1971, c.47 (now RSO 1990, c.S.22(as amended), s.17(1). See also the Quebec An Act respecting Administrative Justice, CQLR, c.J-3, s.8, and the British Columbia Administrative Tribunals Act, SBC 2004, c.45, s.51.

[465] Tribunals and Inquiries Act 1992 s.10, Sch.1.

[466] The duty does not apply to ministerial decisions in connection with orders and schemes of a legislative character: Tribunals and Inquiries Act 1992 s.10(5). Where the duty applies, a statement of reasons may still be refused or restricted by the tribunal or Minister on grounds of national security; and it may also be withheld in the interests of a party to the decision if it is asked for by someone not primarily concerned with the decision. Orders may be made after consultation with the Administrative Justice and Tribunals Council excluding particular classes of decisions from the scope of s.10 (s.10(7)); there have been few such Orders.

[467] *Parrish v Minister of Housing and Local Government* (1961) 59 L.G.R. 411 at 418; *Brayhead (Ascot) Ltd v Berkshire CC* [1964] 2 Q.B. 303 at 313–314; *Mountview Court Properties Ltd v Devlin* (1970) 21 P. & C.R. 689 at 693.

[468] See, e.g. Enterprise Act 2002 s.38(2), (considered in *Somerfield Plc v Competition Commission* [2006] CAT 4; [2006] Comp. A.R. 390 and *IBA Health Ltd v Office of Fair Trading* [2004] EWCA Civ 142; [2004] 4 All E.R. 1103); Animal Welfare Act 2006 s.34(8)(a); Anti-Terrorism, Crime and Security Act 2001 Sch.3 para.11; Criminal Justice Act 2003 s.110; Mental Health Review Tribunal Rules 1983 r.23(2) and *Mental Health Review Tribunal* [2008] EWHC 2445 (Admin); [2008] M.H.L.R. 326.

[469] *Grenfell-Baines v Secretary of State for the Environment* [1985] J.P.L. 256. For another example in the planning context, see *R. (on the application Midcounties Co-operative Ltd) v Forest of Dean DC* [2007] EWHC 1714 (Admin); [2007] 2 P. & C.R. 30, (planning permissions were quashed for failure to give summary reasons as required by (now repealed) the Town and Country Planning (General Development Procedure) Order 1995 (SI 1995/419)).

[470] See 16-028.

ence to the rules of procedural fairness, or, more usually, by a necessary implication from the rules which provide for the appeal.[480]

Required by the common law

Whether the above decisions are explainable on the basis of a statutory implication or not, it is now clear that fairness may itself require, in a wide range of circumstances, that reasons be given. In a landmark decision, the Court of Appeal in *R. v Civil Service Appeal Board Ex p. Cunningham* held that the Civil Service Appeal Board, a "judicialised" tribunal established under the royal prerogative, was under a duty to give outline reasons for its decisions, sufficient to show to what it has directed its mind and to indicate whether its decisions are lawful, and a failure to do so is a breach of procedural fairness.[471] It is preferable not to attempt to separate out the different grounds upon which a duty to give reasons may arise; rather, there is a "unitary test"[492] which rests on familiar considerations of fairness[472]; within such a test, regard may be had, where appropriate, to the multiple grounds which may exist, such as a need for reasons to know whether to challenge the decision (by appeal or judicial review), the importance of the decision on the individual's liberty or livelihood, the advantage of concentrating the decision-maker's mind and ensuring that the issues have been conscientiously addressed, the general nature of the adjudicating process,[473] and so on.[474] Where an authority

7-102

---

[471] *R. v Civil Service Appeal Board Ex p. Cunningham* [1991] 4 All E.R. 310; see J. Herberg, "The Right to Reasons: Palm Trees in Retreat" [1991] P.L. 340; *R. (on the application of Viggers) v Pensions Appeal Tribunal* [2006] EWHC 1066 (QB); [2006] A.C.D. 80. The Australian Administrative Decisions (Judicial Review) Act 1977 (Cth) s.13 entitles applicants for judicial review to a statement of reasons from the decision-maker. This and other statutory rights to obtain reasons have been interpreted to require a level of particularity in reasons not unlike that required by UK cases: M. Groves, "Reviewing Reasons for Administrative Decisions" (2013) 35 *Sydney Law Review* 627, 644–646. In Canada, in 1999, in *Baker v Canada (Minister of Citizenship and Immigration)* [1999] 2 S.C.R. 817 at [35]–[44], the Supreme Court of Canada accepted that the common law principles of procedural fairness could give rise to an obligation on the part of the decision-maker to provide reasons for a decision. While the court did not go so far as hold that this was a universal requirement for decisions-makers subject to the duty of procedural fairness, generally, it has been assumed that this obligation attaches to such decision-making. However, there are exceptions. In *Canada (Attorney General) v Mavi* 2011 SCC 30; [2011] 2 S.C.R. 504 at [45], the Supreme Court held that while a ministerial decision to proceed with recovery of guarantees provided by those sponsoring immigrants attracted a limited level of procedural fairness, that did not include a right to reasons. Reasons may also be required as a component of the Crown's obligation to consult and, where appropriate, accommodate the rights, claims and interests of Indigenous Peoples: see, e.g., *Gitxaala Nation v Canada* 2016 FCA 187; [2016] 4 F.C.R. 418, at [311]–[324].

[472] In *Cunningham* [1991] 4 All E.R. 310 Lord Donaldson MR relied in his judgment upon the general words of guidance offered by Lord Bridge in *Lloyd* [1987] A.C. 625 and cited at the opening of this chapter, that the requirements of fairness in every case must be determined by a consideration of the character of the decision making body and the framework within which it operates (to which may be added, the effect which the decision is likely to have upon the affected individual).

[473] *Grillo* (1996) 28 H.L.R, 94, CA (Neill LJ, where the court, in holding that fairness did not require the provision of reasons, relied on the fact that the appellate procedure in question was voluntary); *Murray* [1998] C.O.D. 134.

[474] See, e.g. the duty to give reasons in the context of disciplinary proceedings: *Brabazon-Drenning v UK Central Council for Nursing Midwifery and Health Visiting* [2001] H.R.L.R. 91 at [24]–[29] (UK Central Council for Nursing Midwifery and Health Visiting). However, it has been held that there is no general duty to give reasons for a disciplinary committee's findings of fact (although on occasion the principle of fairness may require reasons for decisions even on matters of fact). There is a duty to give reasons in respect of the penalty: *Gupta v General Medical Council* [2001] UKPC 61; [2002] 1 W.L.R. 1691.

decides to depart from a legitimate expectation, fairness requires that the authority articulate its reasons so that their propriety may be tested by the court.[475]

7-103   Since the duty to give reasons may now be seen simply as yet another aspect of the requirements of procedural fairness, it would be wrong to imagine that the duty may be artificially confined to situations in which the decision-maker is acting in a "judicial" or "quasi-judicial" capacity. Although in *Cunningham*, some reliance was placed upon the fact that the Civil Service Appeal Board is a fully "judicialised" tribunal, and one that is almost unique among tribunals in not falling under a statutory duty to give reasons, subsequent decisions have made it clear that reasons may be required of a body exercising "quasi-judicial" functions, such as that of the Home Secretary in relation to the tariff period to be served by life sentence prisoners,[476] and "administrative" functions, such as a local authority making decisions regarding an individual's housing application.[477] Fairness may also require that a body explain why it is rejecting or preferring particular evidence[478] or why it is failing to give effect to a legitimate expectation.[479] The distinction between judicial, quasi-judicial and administrative functions may be consigned to history in this context, as well as more generally. As Sedley J has put it, in rejecting such a submission in the context of the duty to give reasons, "[i]n the modern state the decisions of administrative bodies can have a more immediate and profound impact on people's lives than the decisions of courts, and public law has since *Ridge v Baldwin* been alive to that fact".[480]

Brief survey of case law on reason giving

7-104   The following brief survey of the case law demonstrates some of the situations in which reasons have, and have not, been required.

- In the criminal justice context, reasons were required where the DPP had decided not to prosecute despite the fact that an inquest jury had decided that there had been an unlawful killing and that a prima facie case had been established against an identifiable individual.[481] But no reasons were required for the Solicitor-General's decision not to institute contempt proceedings against newspaper editors.[482]
- The Criminal Injuries Compensation Authority should give reasons for its conclusion that an applicant's conduct had "caused or contributed to the incident".[483]

---

[475] *R. (on the application of Bibi) v Newham LBC* [2001] EWCA Civ 607; [2002] 1 W.L.R. 23 at [59].

[476] *Doody* [1994] 1 A.C. 531; since the Criminal Justice Act 2003, the Home Secretary no longer exercises this function.

[477] *R. v Islington LBC Ex p. Trail* [1994] 2 F.C.R. 1261; *Walters* [1994] 2 F.C.R. 336 (both decisions of Sir Louis Blom-Cooper QC); *R. v Kensington and Chelsea RLBC Ex p. Campbell* (1996) 28 H.L.R. 160; *R. v Lambeth LBC Housing Benefit Review Board Ex p. Harrington, The Times,* 20 December 1996 (duty to supply material facts and reasoning); *R. v Housing Benefit Review Board of South Tyneside MBC Ex p. Tooley* [1996] C.O.D. 143.

[478] See, e.g. *R. (on the application of Beeson) v Dorset CC* [2002] H.R.L.R. 368 at [39] (reversed or other grounds [2002] EWCA Civ 1812); *R. (on the application of H) v Ashworth Hospital Authority Council* [2002] EWCA Civ 923; [2003] 1 W.L.R. 127 at [81]; cf. *R. (on the application of Alliss) v Legal Services Commission* [2002] EWHC 2079; [2003] A.C.D. 16 at [65].

[479] *Bibi* [2002] 1 W.L.R. 237 at [59].

[480] *Institute of Dental Surgery* [1994] 1 W.L.R. 242 at 258.

[481] *R. v DPP Ex p. Manning* [2001] Q.B. 330 at [33].

[482] *R. v Solicitor-General Ex p. Taylor and Taylor* [1996] 1 F.C.R. 206. On the jurisdiction of Law Officer's decisions.

[483] *R. v Criminal Injuries Compensation Authority Ex p. Leatherland* [2001] A.C.D 76; *R. (on the ap-*

- A doctor's decision forcibly to administer medication to a competent non-consenting adult should have been accompanied by written reasons.[484]
- A rent officer should give reasons for a determination whereby a local reference rent fell below the contractual rent and affected housing benefit.[485]
- The Court of Aldermen was required to give reasons, in relation to a decision not to confirm the election of an Alderman following victory in a ward vote.[486]
- The Home Secretary's decision not to extend exceptional leave to remain in the United Kingdom,[487] and to refuse exceptional leave to remain, required reasons.[488]
- A local authority's decision as to community care and educational provision for a disabled person, where it was departing from guidelines, required reasons.[489]
- An Admissions Appeal Panel allowing an appeal from a local education authority's decision on the ground that it was unreasonable had to supply reasons.[490]
- A coroner should have given reasons for her conclusion that there was no evidence on which the jury could have returned an unlawful killing verdict.[491]
- Reasons were not required, however, for arms export decisions.[492]

The standard of reasons required

It remains difficult to state precisely the standard of reasoning the court will demand. Much depends upon the particular circumstances[493] and the statutory context[494] in which the duty to give reasons arises. Where the issues dealt with by the tribunal or administrative actor are "extremely important", the duty to give reasons may be equated with the general duty in courts to give their reasons, rather

7-105

---

plication of Mahmood) v Criminal Injuries Compensation Appeal Panel [2005] EWHC 2919 (Admin) (panel failed to give any reasons for its departure from the guidelines).

[484] Feggetter [2002] EWCA Civ 554; [2003] Q.B. 219.

[485] R. (on the application of Cumpsty) v Rent Service [2002] EWHC 2526 (Admin) at [86]–[87]; cf. Friends Provident Life [2001] EWHC Admin 820; [2002] 1 W.L.R. 1450 at [103] (no general duty on the Secretary of State to give reasons for refusing to call-in a planning application).

[486] R. v Mayor, Commonality and Citizens of the City of London Ex p. Matson [1997] 1 W.L.R. 765.

[487] R. v Secretary of State for the Home Department Ex p. Erdogan (Resul) [1995] Imm. A.R. 430.

[488] R. v Secretary of State for the Home Department Ex p. Quaquah (No.2) unreported 1 September 2000.

[489] R. v Islington LBC Ex p. Rixon [1997] E.L.R. 66.

[490] R. (on the application of Reading BC) v Admissions Appeal Panel for Reading BC [2005] EWHC 2378 (Admin); [2006] E.L.R. 186.

[491] R. (on the application of Cash) v Northamptonshire Coroner [2007] EWHC 1354 (Admin); [2007] 4 All E.R. 903 at [45].

[492] R. (on the application of Hasan) v Secretary of State for Trade & Industry [2007] EWHC 2630 (Admin); [2008] A.C.D. 10; affirmed Hasan [2008] EWCA Civ 1312; [2009] 3 All E.R. 539 at [8].

[493] R. (on the application of The Asha Foundation) v The Millennium Commission [2003] EWCA Civ 88 at [27] (Lord Woolf CJ); Flannery [2000] 1 W.L.R. 377 at 382 (Henry LJ noting that "[t]he extent of the duty, or rather the reach of what is required to fulfil it, depends on the subject matter"); Hodson [2007] EWCA Civ 1210 at [30]; Re V (A Child) [2015] EWCA Civ 274 at [15] (in a straightforward fact-finding exercise, there is no need for an elaborate distillation of every point; what is required is a straightforward explanation of the key factors that the judge has taken into account and his or her reasons for preferring one part of the evidence over another).

[494] R. (on the application of Bewley Homes Plc) v Waverley BC [2017] EWHC 1776 (Admin) at [55] (an examiner conducting a statutory inquisitorial process into a neighbourhood plan was not subject to the same duty of reasons as an inspector deciding a contested adversarial appeal; the examiner was subject "to a limited statutory duty to give reasons").

than the "less exacting standard applied to ordinary administrative decision-making".[495] It is clear that the reasons given must be intelligible and must adequately meet the substance of the arguments advanced.[496] It will not suffice to merely recite a general formula or restate a statutorily-prescribed conclusion.[497] It is also preferable if the reasons demonstrate that a systematic analysis has been undertaken by the decision-maker.[498] However, the courts have not attempted to define a uniform standard or threshold which the reasons must satisfy, and on occasion, courts have expressed concern that decision-makers should be granted "a certain latitude in how they express themselves".[499] The reasons must generally state the decision-maker's material findings of fact (and, if the facts were disputed at the hearing, their evidential support[500]), and meet the substance of the principal arguments that the decision-maker was required to consider.[501] If a decision is made on the basis of the evidence of witnesses or experts, reasons for preferring one wit-

---

[495] *Mental Health Review Tribunal* [2008] EWHC 2445 (Admin); [2008] M.H.L.R. 326 at [18].

[496] *Re Poyser and Mills' Arbitration* [1964] 2 Q.B. 467 at 477–478; approved in *Great Portland Estates Plc* [1985] A.C. 661 at 673; cf. *Save Britain's Heritage* [1991] 1 W.L.R. 153 at 165; and *Edwin H. Bradley & Sons Ltd v Secretary of State for the Environment* (1982) 47 P. & C.R. 374 (same standard was applied despite the subjective element in the minister's duty under the Town and Country Planning Act 1971 s.9(8) to give such statement as he considers appropriate of the reasons for his decision); *R. (on the application of Wheeler) v Assistant Commissioner of the Metropolitan Police* [2008] EWHC 439 (Admin); *Financial Services Authority* [2013] EWCA Civ 677 at [44]–[51]; *R. (on the application of Kingston) v Secretary of State for Education* [2017] EWHC 421 (Admin) at [22] (amongst the purposes of reasons was the need to explain the difference between the conclusions of a National College for Teaching conduct panel and those of the Secretary of State).

[497] *R. v Birmingham City Council Ex p. B* [1999] E.L.R. 305 at 311 (Scott Baker J noting that the letter sent did "nothing more than make ritual incantation of the two-stage process that is applicable for deciding these appeals"). However, where the decision involves a clear application of policy, "[t]he reason is the policy": *R. (on the application of Thompson) v Secretary of State for the Home Department* [2003] EWHC 538 (Admin) at [41]; *R. (on the application of London Fire and Emergency Planning Authority) v Secretary of State for Communities and Local Government* [2007] EWHC 1176 (Admin); [2007] B.L.G.R. 591 at [64].

[498] See, e.g. *R. (on the application of Lowe) v Family Health Services Appeal Authority* [2001] EWCA Civ 128 at [18] (reasons inadequate because they did not deal with the question in correct "logical sequence"); *R. v Crown Court at Canterbury Ex p. Howson-Ball* [2001] Env L.R. 36 at [32] (referring to a need for the Crown Court to provide "some analysis" of the relevant matters); *Curtis v London Rent Assessment Committee* [1999] Q.B. 92 at 118–119 (the rent assessment committee's duty to give reasons required some "working through", i.e. an arithmetical explanation, of the assessment); *R. (on the application of Sivanesan) v Secretary of State for the Home Department* [2008] EWHC 1146 (Admin); (2008) 152(23) S.J.L.B. 30; *R. (on the application of S) v Secretary of State for the Home Department* [2009] EWCA Civ 688 at [8] (absence in the decision letter of any indication that the Secretary of State had considered ill-treatment at the hands of Sri Lankan authorities, which constituted a failure to apply anxious scrutiny).

[499] *R. v Brent London LBC Ex p. Baruwa* (1997) 29 H.L.R. 915 at 929, approved in *William v Wandsworth LBC* [2006] EWCA Civ 535; [2006] H.L.R. 42 at [18]; *R. (on the application of London Fire and Emergency Planning Authority) v Board of Medical Referees* [2007] EWHC 2805 (Admin) at [41] (accepting that it was "wrong to be too critical of the reasons given by a board that is not chaired by a lawyer", but nonetheless the reasons given were inadequate as they did not set out the legal test, the standard of proof, why the injury was a qualifying one within the rules, why the board's views differed from a medical opinion); *Nzolameso* [2015] UKSC 22; [2015] 2 All E.R. 942 (a "standard paragraph" would not suffice but the Supreme Court accepted that there are various ways for an authority to ensure that its decisions are properly evidenced and properly explained); see also *Ajilore v Hackney LBC* [2014] EWCA Civ 1273; *SoulCycle Inc v Matalan Ltd* [2017] EWHC 496 (Ch) at [29] ("[t]he duty to give reasons must not be turned into an intolerable burden").

[500] cf. *R. v Secretary of State for the Home Department Ex p. Swati* [1986] 1 W.L.R. 477 (passenger refused entry entitled only to be told the ground for refusal; statement of facts required only after notice of appeal is given).

[501] See *R. (on the application of Campaign to Protect Rural England) v Dover DC* [2016] EWCA Civ 936; [2017] J.P.L. 180 (degree of particularity required of a local planning authority's reasons for the grant of planning permission depended on the nature of the issues to be decided; on an applica-

ness or expert over another should generally be explained.[502] In short, the reasons must show that the decision-maker successfully came to grips with the main contentions advanced by the parties,[503] and must tell the parties in broad terms why they lost or, as the case may be, won.[504] Provided the reasons satisfy these core criteria, they need not be lengthy.[505] Judicial review may be inappropriate where the dispute relates to issues about the precise drafting of a decision.[506] Courts should also not scrutinise reasons with the analytical rigour employed on statutes or trust instruments,[507] and ought to forgive obvious mistakes that were unlikely to have misled anyone.[508]

Some general guidance on the standard of reasons required may also be derived **7-106** from a consideration of the purposes served by a duty to give reasons. Thus, reasons should be sufficiently detailed as to make quite clear to the parties—and especially the losing party—why the decision-maker decided as it did, and to avoid the impression that the decision was based upon extraneous considerations, rather than the matters raised at the hearing.[509] Reasons must be sufficient to reveal whether the

---

tion for permission of a large-scale residential development in an area of outstanding natural beauty, where the planning committee departed from the planning officer's recommendations and where there was a statutory duty to give reasons, the reasons should have dealt with the issue of harm in much more detail).

[502] *H* [2003] 1 W.L.R. 127 at [81]; *Consistent Group Ltd v Kalwak, Welsh Country Foods Ltd* [2008] EWCA Civ 430; [2008] I.R.L.R. 505 at [46] ("it was basic that the Chairman had to provide a proper explanation as to why, given the evidential conflicts, he was preferring one side's evidence to that of the other"); *Hampshire CC v JP* [2009] UKUT 239 (AAC) at [37] and [39].

[503] In addition to *Re Poyser* [1964] 2 Q.B. 467 authority for the proposition in the text can be found, e.g. in: *R. v Immigration Appeal Tribunal Ex p. Khan* [1983] Q.B. 790; *R. v Immigration Appeal Tribunal Ex p. Jebunisha Patel* [1996] Imm. A.R. 161 at 167; *Arulandandam v Secretary of State for the Home Department* [1996] Imm. A.R. 587 at 592; *G* [1995] E.L.R. 58 at 67; *R. v Lancashire CC Ex p. Maycock* (1995) 159 L.G. Rev. 201 ("standard letter" with individual variations sufficient in circumstances).

[504] *UCATT v Brain* [1981] I.R.L.R. 224 at 228. See also *R. (on the application of Bahrami) v Immigration Appeal Tribunal* [2003] EWHC 1453 (Admin) at [8] (Maurice Kay J: "what is essential is not that an adjudicator should deal with every point at length, but that the determination should be sufficiently reasoned to enable a claimant, his advisers, and any appellate or reviewing body, to see why the claimant lost on a particular issue"). Reasons should also be read from the standpoint of an "informed party": *R. (on the application of Roberts) v Secretary of State for Communities and Local Government* [2008] EWHC 677 (Admin); [2009] J.P.L. 81. For useful summary of the standard of reasons required, see *Proctor & Gamble UK v Revenue and Customs Commissioners* [2009] EWCA Civ 407 at [19]; *R. (on the application of Macrae) v Herefordshire DC* [2012] EWCA Civ 457; [2012] J.P.L. 1356 at [14] and [20] (local planning authority's references to officers' reports recommending a refusal of planning permission left the claimant in the dark as to the reasons for granting planning permission); *Uprichard* [2013] UKSC 21; [2013] P.T.S.R. D37 at [48].

[505] *Stefan* [1999] 1 W.L.R. 1293 at 1304 (reasons "need not be elaborate nor lengthy"); *Mubarak* [2008] EWHC 2830 (Admin) at [35] (a "short initial explanation" was "more than adequate" to enable the appellant to know why the Panel had found against the claimant); *Mental Health Review Tribunal* [2008] EWHC 2445 (Admin); [2008] M.H.L.R. 326 at [15] ("the length of reasons ... is not itself necessarily a reflection of their quality. Short reasons can be adequate."); *Re A (Children) (Fact-finding Hearing: Ex tempore Judgment)* [2011] EWCA Civ 1611; [2012] 1 F.L.R. 1243 at [47]–[48] (ex tempore judgments should not be discouraged and "[i]t would be worse than unfortunate if the impression were to gain ground that experienced judges who have the gift of brevity should be deterred from displaying it by an inappropriate readiness on the part of appellate courts to interfere"); *S-W* [2015] EWCA Civ 27; [2015] 1 W.L.R. 4099 at [46] ("[t]he reasons may be brief but they must be explanatory").

[506] *R. (on the application of W) v Acton Youth Court* [2005] EWHC 954 (Admin); (2006) 170 J.P. 31.

[507] *Seddon Properties Ltd v Secretary of State for the Environment* (1978) 42 P. & C.R. 26; *UCATT* [1981] I.R.L.R. 224.

[508] *Elmbridge BC v Secretary of State for the Environment* (1980) 39 P. & C.R. 543 at 547–548.

[509] See, e.g. *Clatworthy* [1985] 3 All E.R. 699; *R. (on the application of Ashworth Hospital Authority)*

tribunal made any error of law.[510] Reasons must also enable the court to which an appeal lies to discharge its appellate function, and when this is limited to questions of law, it will only be necessary to explain the exercise of discretion and to set out the evidence for the findings of fact in enough detail to disclose that the decision-maker has not acted unreasonably.[511] The reasons should refer to the main issues in the dispute, but need not necessarily deal with every material consideration.[512] Brevity is an administrative virtue, and elliptical reasons may be perfectly comprehensible when considered against the background of the arguments at the hearing.[513] Some decisions (such as the refusal of planning permission by an inspector) should be accompanied by reasons that are sufficiently precise to permit the individual to make the modifications necessary to secure a favourable decision in the future, or (where a Secretary of State disagrees with an inspector) to enable an objector to know what, if any, impact the planning considerations taken into account in a grant of planning permission may have in relation to the determination of future applications.[514] Where a decision-maker is disagreeing with a recommendation, such as with a planning inspector's report, there will be a duty to explain why the inspector's view is rejected.[515]

7-107   The standard of reasons required in certain specific contexts has been considered. For example, a mental health review tribunal should explain why one witness is preferred to another; the reasons should sufficiently inform the patient and the

---

v *Mental Health Review Tribunal for West Midlands and North West Region* [2001] EWHC Admin 901 at [77]; *South Bucks DC v Porter (No.2)* [2004] UKHL 33; [2004] 1 W.L.R. 1953 at [36].

[510] *Ashworth Hospital Authority* [2001] EWHC Admin 901 at [77]; *South Bucks* [2004] UKHL 33; [2004] 1 W.L.R. 1953 at [36].

[511] *Varndell* [1983] I.C.R. 683 at 693–694, criticising the possibly more stringent test propounded in *Alexander Machinery (Dudley) Ltd* [1974] I.C.R. 120 at 122; cf. *Thameside MBC v Secretary of State for the Environment* [1984] J.P.L. 180, where the court may have set a high standard to ensure that a peripheral consideration in the determination of a planning appeal had not been given undue importance. And see *New Cross Building Society* [1984] Q.B. 227.

[512] *South Bucks* [2004] UKHL 33; [2004] 1 W.L.R. 1953 at [36]; *Cook* [1996] 1 W.L.R. 1037 at 1043; *Lavis v Nursing and Midwifery Council* [2014] EWHC 4083 (Admin); [2015] A.C.D. 64 at [24] (it is not necessary for a judge to deal with every argument presented by counsel in support of its case); *Chelmsford City Council v Secretary of State or Communities and Local Government* [2016] EWHC 3329 (QB) (not necessary for the inspector to deal with each and every aspect of the case raised by the parties on an economic activity rate dispute where his reasons more than adequately explained his preference for the developer's case).

[513] *Elliot v Southwark LBC* [1976] 1 W.L.R. 499; *R. v Mental Health Tribunal Ex p. Pickering* [1986] 1 All E.R. 99; *Great Portland Estates Plc* [1985] A.C. 661 at 673. In Canada, in the assessment of the adequacy of reasons, prolixity is not a requirement. The decision-maker does not have to address explicitly "all the arguments, statutory provisions, jurisprudence or other details" nor must the decision include an explicit "finding on each constituent element": *Newfoundland and Labrador Nurses' Union v Newfoundland and Labrador (Treasury Board)* 2011 SCC 62; [2011] 3 S.C.R. 708, at [22]. Rather, the reasons should demonstrate that the decision-maker was "alive to the question at issue" and enable the court to effectively exercise its judicial review authority. The former reflects the procedural entitlement of the parties to be heard while the latter focuses on the substantive outcome (at [26]). For further discussion, see *Vancouver International Airport Authority v Public Service Alliance of Canada* 2010 FCA 158; [2011] 4 F.C.R. 425. Reasons should not have to be derived by inference: *EMI Records (Ireland) Ltd v Data Protection Commissioner* [2013] IESC 34; [2013] 2 I.R. 669 at [81].

[514] *Save Britain's Heritage* [1991] 1 W.L.R. 153 at 167. A mental health review tribunal should give sufficiently precise reasons to enable patients and medical advisers to cover the matters on a renewed application.

[515] *Horada* [2016] EWCA Civ 169 at [40] (finding that the Secretary of State had failed to explain why he disagreed with the inspector, beyond merely stating his conclusion that he did). However, there is no obligation on the majority of a tribunal to explain their disagreement with the dissenting majority, any more than there is an obligation on the Court of Appeal or the Supreme Court for the majority to examine and address directly the views of the dissenting minority (*Federation of Independent Practitioner Organisations v Competition and Markets Authority* [2016] EWCA Civ 777).

hospital of the findings of the tribunal; and the court should take into account the fact that the tribunal has a legally qualified chairman and that reasons do not have to be given immediately.[516] As for immigration adjudicators, it has been held that there is no duty on the adjudicator to deal with every argument raised by the advocate in the case,[517] but the critical matters must be explained sufficiently clearly for the "thought processes" of the adjudicator on "material findings" to be understood.[518] While a judge conducting a fact-finding hearing is entitled to explain his thought processes and reasoning in whatever way he deems appropriate, in a case where there is satisfactory proof on some matters but suspicion and specula-tion on others, it would be artificial and potentially misleading for the judge to sup-press all reference to the latter while giving appropriate prominence to the former.[519]

However, whilst concern for the quality of administrative justice does not require **7-108** that all tribunals in all circumstances comply with some universally applicable standard, it is, nonetheless, essential that the courts do not allow the duty to give reasons to atrophy. In principle a remedy ought to lie for failure to give reasons,[520] unless the court is satisfied that no real prejudice has been caused to the claimant.[521]

Whatever standards are applied by judges to the adequacy of reasons given under **7-109** a duty, it seems likely that reasons given voluntarily—where there is no duty—will be reviewed in accordance with the same standards as are applied to compulsory reasons.[522]

The rationality of the reasons given

When reasons are required, either by statute or by the growing common law **7-110** requirements, or where they are provided, even though not strictly required, those reasons must be both "adequate and intelligible". They must therefore both ration-ally relate to the evidence in the case,[523] and be comprehensible in themselves.[524]

---

[516] *Ashworth Hospital Authority* [2001] EWHC Admin 901 at [77].

[517] *Eagil Trust* [1985] 3 All E.R. 119 at 122 (Griffiths LJ).

[518] *English* [2002] 1 W.L.R. 2409 at [19] (Lord Phillips MR).

[519] *Re A (A Child) (Fact Finding: Speculation)* [2011] EWCA Civ 12; [2011] 1 F.L.R. 1817 at [29]. It has been held that where a challenge to a decision notice made by the Financial Services Authority involved a full rehearing, the reasons need to explain why the decision notice was made and not deal with every point made by the recipient of the decision notice: *Financial Services Authority* [2013] EWCA Civ 677 at [49]-[52].

[520] On an appeal from a decision on a question of law the courts may well have an inherent jurisdic-tion to direct the minister or tribunal to give adequate reasons although no formal application for mandamus has been made; see *Iveagh (Earl) v Minister of Housing and Local Government* [1964] 1 Q.B. 395 at 410.

[521] *R. v Liverpool City Council Ex p. Liverpool Taxi Fleet Operators' Association* [1975] 1 W.L.R. 701 at 706; cf. *Preston BC v Secretary of State for the Environment* [1978] J.P.L. 548 (omission of significant part of reasoning normally prejudicial); *Save Britain's Heritage* [1991] 1 W.L.R. 153. Outside the planning field, however (where the requirement to demonstrate substantial prejudice is required by statute), the courts will not readily conclude that an applicant is not prejudiced by an inadequately reasoned decision. The test may be whether any other conclusion than that reached was realistically possible: *Murray* [1998] C.O.D. 134, or whether it is "obvious" that there is no injustice (*Morris* [1996] C.O.D. 104).

[522] *Elmbridge BC* (1980) 39 P. & C.R. 543; *Westminster City Council v Secretary of State for the Environment* [1984] J.P.L. 27 at 29–30; also *Grenfell-Baines* [1985] J.P.L. 256. cf. *Kentucky Fried Chicken Pty Ltd v Gantidis* (1979) 140 C.L.R. 675. See also *R. (on the application of Martin) v Legal Services Commission* [2007] EWHC 1786 (Admin) at [60].

[523] In *Re Poyser* [1964] 2 Q.B. 467 at 478 (Megaw J, speaking of the duty to give reasons imposed by s.12 of the Tribunals and Inquiries Act 1958, said that the required reasons "must be read as mean-ing that proper adequate reasons must be given ... which deal with the substantial points that have been raised"); *Great Portland Estates Plc* [1985] A.C. 661 at 673 (Lord Scarman).

The reasons for a decision must not be "self contradictory".[525] The reasons will not be construed in the same way as courts would construe a statute, but a decision may be struck down where an applicant can show substantial prejudice resulting from a failure on the part of the decision-maker to demonstrate how an issue of law had been resolved or a disputed issue of fact decided, or by "demonstrating some other lack of reasoning which raised substantial doubts over the decision-making process",[526] or by indicating "that the tribunal had never properly considered the matter ... and that the proper thought processes have not been gone through".[527]

The implications which can be drawn from a failure to provide reasons

7-111   Where an applicant seeks to impugn a decision of an administrative authority other than by claiming non-compliance with a duty to give reasons—for example by challenging the legality or rationality of the decision—a failure by that authority to offer any answer to the allegations may justify an inference that its reasons were bad in law or that it had exercised its powers unlawfully. "Absurd" or "perverse" decisions may be presumed to have been decided in that fashion, as may decisions where the given reasons are simply unintelligible.[528] However, the absence of reasons does not automatically give rise to the inference that none exist,[529] and there is a conflict of authorities at the highest level as to the strength of the evidence of collateral unlawfulness which the applicant must adduce in order to benefit from the inference of unlawfulness if no justification of the decision is given. In *Padfield v Minister of Agriculture, Fisheries and Food*, where the challenge was to the purpose to which the Minister had applied the regulations in question, the House of Lords suggested that if a prima facie case of unlawfulness was established by the applicant, then in the absence of reasons the court could infer that the power was exercised outside of the legislative purpose.[530]

7-112   A more restrictive approach was adopted in *R. v Secretary of State for Trade and Industry Ex p. Lonrho*, where, upon a challenge for irrationality, it was held that the absence of reasons could provide no support for the suggested irrationality of the

[524] *Hope v Secretary of State for the Environment* (1975) 31 P. & C.R. 120 at 123 (Phillips J, referring to a decision of a planning inspector which "must be such that it enables the appellant to understand on what grounds the appeal has been decided and be in sufficient detail to enable him to know what conclusions the inspector has reached on the principal important issues"); *Ward v Secretary of State for the Environment* (1989) 59 P. & C.R. 486 at 487 (Woolf LJ: "With regard to the requirement to give reasons it suffices to say that the reasons must be ones which are understandable to those who will receive those reasons"), cited with approval in *Save Britain's Heritage* [1991] 1 W.L.R. 153 at 165 (Lord Bridge), *Bolton MDC v Secretary of State for the Environment* (1996) 71 P. & C.R. 309; *R. v Hammersmith & Fulham LBC Ex p. Earls Court Ltd, The Times,* 7 September 1993 (a condition imposed upon an entertainment licence which was so obscure that it necessitated the issue of a construction summons was "unreasonable in the *Wednesbury* sense" (Kennedy LJ)).

[525] *Mahon* [1984] A.C. 808 at 835 (Lord Diplock required the finding to be based on some material that tends logically to show the existence of facts consistent with the finding).

[526] *Save Britain's Heritage* [1991] 1 W.L.R. 153 at 168 (Lord Bridge, emphasising, however, that the adequacy of reasons depended upon the legislative context and could not be answered in vacuo. It used to be said that it was a requirement of natural justice that the material logically relates to the finding); *Lord Diplock in Mahon* [1984] A.C. 808.

[527] *Crake v Supplementary Benefits Commission* [1982] 1 All E.R. 498 at 508.

[528] *Institute of Dental Surgery* [1994] 1 W.L.R. 242 at 258 (referring to "an apparently inexplicable decision") and 261 (noting that a decision may be "so aberrant as in itself to call for an explanation").

[529] *R. (on the application of Farrakhan) v Secretary of State for the Home Department* [2002] EWCA Civ 606; [2002] Q.B. 1391 at [7].

[530] *Padfield v Minister of Agriculture, Fisheries and Food* [1968] A.C. 997 at 1053, 1061, 1032–1033, 1049 (Lords Pearce, Upjohn, Reid and Hodson; *R. v Brixton Prison Governor Ex p. Soblen (No.2)* [1963] 2 Q.B. 243 at 302, 307–308 (Lord Denning MR and Donovan LJ).

decision unless, "if all other known facts and the circumstances appear to point overwhelmingly in favour of a different decision, the decision-maker cannot complain if the court draws the inference that he has had no rational reason for his Decision".[531] Although there is some support for the restrictive *Lonrho* test, at least where an authority has a specific exemption from a statutory duty to give reasons (in which case the courts ought not to force the authority to choose between waiving the exemption and risking an adverse inference[532]) in general, the *Padfield* approach has been favoured, even in cases where the ground of review is irrationality (as in *Lonrho*) rather than illegality.[533]

Thus where a local authority made a very meagre disclosure of reasons in response to an application for judicial review of a decision not to award a student grant, the Court of Appeal suggested that if the applicant could merely show that the facts were sufficient to obtain leave to apply for judicial review then, even though there was no obligation on the decision-maker to give reasons to the applicant, the authority would be under a duty to make full and fair disclosure to the court.[534] And where the Civil Service Appeal Board had awarded an inexplicably low sum in compensation for unfair dismissal, the failure of the Board to provide reasons to the court to dispel the "arguable" case of the applicant led the court to presume that the prima facie irrational decision was in fact irrational.[535] The *Padfield* approach can also be supported by reference to more general principles of the law of evidence. As Lord Lowry has pointed out, in another case concerning a challenge for irrationality in the absence of justification by the decision-maker:

7-113

"In our legal system generally, the silence of one party in face of the other party's evidence may convert that evidence into proof in relation to matters which are, or are likely to be, within the knowledge of the silent party and about which that party could be expected to

---

[531] *R. v Secretary of State for Trade and Industry Ex p. Lonrho* [1989] 1 W.L.R. 525 at 539; *Eagil Trust* [1985] 3 All E.R. 119 (tribunal presumed to have acted properly when court can see how a point could have been answered, despite failure of reasons to deal with it expressly).

[532] *R. v Secretary of State for Social Services Ex p. Connolly* [1986] 1 W.L.R. 421, CA; cf. *R. v Inland Revenue Commissioners Ex p. TC Coombs & Co* [1991] 2 A.C. 283.

[533] In Canada, the Supreme Court has also acknowledged that a finding of inadequate reasons does not lead automatically to a quashing of that decision for unreasonableness. In situations where the reasons are inadequate, the court will still have to determine whether the decision is otherwise unreasonable and should be quashed without more, or whether a quashing and remission back for reconsideration in the form of an opportunity to provide adequate reasons is appropriate: *Alberta (Information and Privacy Commissioner) v Alberta Teachers' Association*, 2011 SCC 61; [2011] 3 S.C.R. 654, at [55].

[534] *R. v Lancashire CC Ex p. Huddleston* [1986] 2 All E.R. 941 (court did not on the facts infer that the authority had erred in exercising its discretion or that it had acted irrationally; Parker LJ and Sir George Waller did not share Lord Donaldson's unease about the lack of disclosure in the case, but "I do not understand them to have disagreed with the principle" (Lord Donaldson MR in *Cunningham* [1991] 4 All E.R. 310). cf. *New Zealand Fishing Industry Assn v Minister of Agriculture and Fisheries* [1988] 1 N.Z.L.R. 544, CA (minister's failure to file affidavit giving reasons for decision could serve to strengthen misgivings as to lawfulness of action).

[535] *Cunningham* [1991] 4 All E.R. 310; *R. v Criminal Injuries Compensation Board Ex p. Cummins* [1992] C.O.D. 297 (although the CICB is not under statutory duty to give reasons, failure to show basis of fact on which it relied in making award to victim of crime rendered the award perverse); *R. v Secretary of State for the Home Department Ex p. Sinclair* [1992] Imm. A.R. 293 (decision of Home Secretary to sign extradition warrant *Wednesbury* unreasonable); *R. v Secretary of State for Education Ex p. Standish, The Times*, 15 November 1993 (ground upon which teacher debarred from his employment was not identified by the Secretary of State by reasons or by his affidavit, and hence the decision quashed for irrationality); cf. *R. v Criminal Injuries Compensation Board Ex p. Gambles* [1994] P.I.Q.R. 314 (reasoning which omitted one important step was defective and hence decision must be quashed).

give evidence. Thus, depending on the circumstances, a prima facie case may become a strong or even an overwhelming case."[536]

7-114   It should be noted, however, that in the absence of reasons it will often be difficult to establish a prima facie case that a wide discretionary power has been improperly exercised,[537] so a claimant may not be able to obtain permission and thereby pressure the decision-maker to justify the decision to the court. The readiness of the courts to infer unlawfulness is therefore no substitute for a duty on public bodies to give reasons for their decisions to affected individuals.

Remedy for lack or insufficiency of reasons

7-115   Usually, the remedy given in a case of breach of duty to give reasons or adequate reasons is an order quashing the unreasoned decision,[538] rather than an order to require provision of the reasons. The former remedy is usually deemed preferable as it reflects the purpose of reasons to encourage focused decision-making and avoids the risk of reconstruction of reasons after the decision.[539] Given that there is a lapse of time between the original decision and the judicial review proceedings, it may also be impractical to order a remedy requiring reasons to be provided.[540]

7-116   It is only in limited circumstances that the absence or inadequacy of reasons can be remedied by provision of further fresh reasons in evidence when the decision is challenged,[541] as "[i]t is well-established that the court should exercise caution before accepting reasons for a decision which were not articulated at the time of the

---

[536] *Coombs* [1991] 2 A.C. 283 at 300 (sparseness of evidence provided by the Revenue to justify a notice compelling the disclosure of documents should not lead to the conclusion that the Revenue had acted irrationally); it is suggested that the decision turned on special circumstances which justified the failure to provide reasons: the fact that the notice had been scrutinised by a Commissioner and hence the presumption of regularity *omnia praesumuntur rite et solenniter esse acta donec probelur in contrarium* applied; the fact that there was a general duty of confidentiality on the Revenue; and that on the facts there had been an express promise of anonymity and confidentiality.

[537] See, e.g. *Cannock Chase DC v Kelly* [1978] 1 W.L.R. 1. cf. *Secretary of State for Employment v ASLEF (No.2)* [1972] 2 Q.B. 455; also *British Airways Board v Laker Airways Ltd* [1985] A.C. 58, 92 (ultra vires difficult to establish in decision concerning international relations).

[538] See, e.g. *Flannery* [2000] 1 W.L.R. 377 at 383; *Cedeno v Logan* [2001] 1 W.L.R. 86; *R. (on the application of Nash) v Chelsea College of Art and Design* [2001] EWHC Admin 538 at [27]. cf. *English* [2002] EWCA Civ 605; [2002] 1 W.L.R. 2409 at [25]; *Hodson* [2007] EWCA Civ 1210 at [38]; *R. (on the application of Bancoult) v Secretary of State for Foreign & Commonwealth Affairs* [2007] EWCA Civ 498; [2008] Q.B. 365 at [70]: reversed on other grounds [2008] UKHL 61; [2009] 1 A.C. 453. See also *London Fire and Emergency Planning Authority* [2007] EWHC 1176 (Admin); [2007] L.G.R. 591 at [66]; *C* [2008] EWCA Civ 882; [2009] Q.B. 657 at [49]; *Re V (A Child)* [2015] EWCA Civ 274.

[539] M. Fordham, *Judicial Review Handbook*, 6th edn (2012) para.62.5. In Canada, the Supreme Court of Canada has also, for review characterisation purposes, drawn a distinction between a failure to give reasons and inadequate reasons. A failure to provide reasons gives rise to review on the basis of a denial of procedural fairness. In contrast, any argument based on inadequate reasons must be subsumed within a challenge to the substantive reasonableness of the decision under review: *Newfoundland and Labrador Nurses' Union v Newfoundland and Labrador (Treasury Board)* 2011 SCC 62; [2011] 3 S.C.R. 708 at [22].

[540] See, e.g. *Flannery* [2000] 1 W.L.R. 377 at 383 (Henry LJ: since "more than a year had passed since the hearing. It would not have been realistic for the judge to reconstitute his reasons").

[541] See, e.g. *R. (on the application of Young) v Oxford City Council* [2002] EWCA Civ 990; [2002] 3 P.L.R. 86 at [20] (Pill LJ noting the dangers in permitting a planning authority to provide an explanatory statement); cf. *Hijazi v Kensington and Chelsea LBC* [2003] EWCA Civ 692; [2003] H.L.R. 1113 at [32] ("nothing objectionable in a decision-maker making a subsequent statement in which he identifies the material that he took into account in the course of the decision-making process"); *R. (on the application of Moore) v Chief Constable of Merseyside* [2015] EWHC 1430 (Admin).

decision but were only expressed later, in particular after the commencement of proceedings".[542] Where there is a statutory duty to provide reasons, such that the adequacy of reasons is central to the legality of the decision itself, this caution also applies.[543] The types of considerations that should be taken into account in deciding whether to accept subsequent evidence of the reasons include[544]: whether the new reasons are consistent with the original reasons[545]; whether it is clear that the new reasons are indeed the original reasons of the original committee or whether there is a real risk that the new reasons have been composed subsequently to support the decision; the delay before the later reasons were put forward; and the circumstances in which the later reasons were put forward. In particular, reasons put forward after the commencement of proceedings should be treated especially carefully. Where the subject matter is less important than human rights for example, the court may be more ready to accept subsequent reasons; the court should also bear in mind the qualifications and experience of the persons involved; it is one thing to require comprehensiveness and clarity from lawyers and from those who regularly sit on administrative tribunals and another to require those qualities of occasional non-lawyer tribunal chairmen and members. Where the later reasons merely elucidate reasons given contemporaneously with the decision, they will normally be considered by the court.[546] The courts have also considered whether the decision-maker would have been expected to state in the decision document the

---

[542] *R. (on the application of D) v Secretary of State for the Home Department* [2003] EWHC 155; [2003] 1 F.L.R. 979 at [18] (Maurice Kay J), [19]; also *Ermakov* [1996] 2 All E.R. 302; *R. (on the application of August) v Criminal Injuries Compensation Appeals Panel* [2001] Q.B. 774 at [86]; *S* [2002] EWCA Civ 693; [2002] E.L.R. 556 at [26]; *R. (on the application of Wandsworth LBC) v Schools Adjudicator* [2003] EWHC 2969; [2004] E.L.R. 274 at [79]; *Wandsworth LBC* [2004] EWCA Civ 1170; (2004) 7 C.C.L. Rep. 472 at [91]; *R. (on the application of Richards) v Pembrokeshire CC* [2004] EWCA Civ 1000; [2005] B.L.G.R. 105; *Bancoult* [2008] Q.B. 365 at [70] ("in principle a decision-maker who gives one set of reasons cannot, when challenged, come up with another set") reversed on other grounds [2008] UKHL 61; [2009] 1 A.C. 453. See also *London Fire and Emergency Planning Authority* [2007] EWHC 1176 (Admin); [2007] L.G.R. 591 at [66]; *R. (on the application of S) v Independent Appeal Panel of St Thomas Catholic Primary School* [2010] EWHC 3785 (Admin); (2009) 106(37) L.S.G. 15 at [34] (noted obiter that even if a first decision letter was inadequate, the matter was rectified by a letter sent just over one month after the appeal and before proceedings commenced). See also *R. (on the application of Jedwell) v Denbighshire County Council* [2015] EWCA Civ 1232; [2016] P.T.S.R. 715 at [42], noting that even if a reasonable time has elapsed for the provision of reasons, the competent authority may still cure the deficiency by supplying reasons or further reasons before the application to the court is actually made. However, a local authority which had issued an inadequately reasoned negative screening opinion could not rectify its breach of duty to give proper reasons by supplying the information in a witness statement made in the course of judicial review proceedings challenging the screening opinion. On the facts of the case, it was held that cross-examination ought to have been conducted to assess whether the contents of a witness statement entailed ex post facto rationalisation of the decision.

[543] *Ermakov* [1996] 2 All E.R. 302 at 312; *Nash* [2001] EWHC Admin 538 at [34].

[544] *Nash* [2001] EWHC Admin 538 at [34]; *London Fire and Emergency Planning Authority* [2007] EWHC 1176 (Admin); [2007] B.L.G.R. 591 at [65]; see also *Caroopen v Secretary of State for the Home Department* [2016] EWCA Civ 1307; [2017] 1 W.L.R. 2339 (Underhill LJ not approving Stanley Burnton J's summary in *Nash* as a comprehensive account of the correct approach, given voluminous case law to which the court had not been referred, but noting that: "In broad terms, however, he recognised that even in a case where there was no explicit statutory duty to give reasons the courts should approach attempts to rely on subsequently-provided reasons with caution; he said that that was particularly so in the case of reasons put forward after the commencement of proceedings and where important human rights are concerned. I would endorse that").

[545] See, e.g. *R. (on the application of T) v Independent Appeal Panel for Devon CC* [2007] EWHC 763 (Admin); [2007] E.L.R. 499 at [42].

[546] *Merton LBC* [2003] EWHC 1689; [2003] 4 All E.R. 280 at [42]; *R. v South Bank University Ex p. Coggeran* [2001] E.L.R. 42 at [36] (evidence rejected because it was used to alter or contract the contemporaneous minutes); *W v The Independent Appeal Panel of Bexley LBC* [2008] EWHC 758 (Admin); [2008] E.L.R. 301 at [36] (clerk's notes did not amount to "contradiction, but simply a

reason that he is seeking to adduce later and whether it would be just in all the circumstances to refuse to admit the subsequent reasons.[547]

PUBLIC INQUIRIES

7-117   As we noted in Chapter 1, public inquiries can take a number of forms and may be established in different contexts.[548] Public inquiries engage a duty to act fairly,[549] and the precise procedures to be followed usually depend on the particular circumstances of the inquiry.[550] The chairman of the inquiry also has discretion to direct the procedure and conduct of the inquiry.[551] The difficulty often lies in "securing an acceptable balance between the thorough investigation of a matter of 'urgent public importance' so as to ascertain the truth, on the one hand, and on the other the need fully to accord implicated individuals a fair procedure".[552]

7-118   Certain public inquiries, over the years illustrate a change of emphasis in the role of the person conducting an inquiry. The traditional approach in the past, much favoured by planning inquiry inspectors, was to let anyone who had an interest appear, call every witness he wished, and be separately represented if he was prepared to meet the expenses involved. Alternatively, a more "hands on" approach is adopted. In the case of the Woolf Inquiry into the Strangeways and other prison riots, only those persons whose actions were at risk of being criticised were allowed to be represented, witnesses were normally only called by counsel to the inquiry, who exercised his discretion as to whom should be called, and cross-examination was strictly limited. Different techniques were used for different classes of evidence, only part was given orally (not all in public), other evidence was written and in the case of the Prison Inquiry even seminars were employed to canvass issues of wide-ranging nature. This departure from the usual common law adversarial nature of resolving issues of fact was used to save both time and resources and to avoid the inquiries being overwhelmed by material. It meant that

---

clarification or supplementation, of the decision letter"); *Swords v Secretary of State for Communities and Local Government* [2007] EWCA Civ 795; [2007] B.L.G.R. 757 at [47]; *Keane v Law Society* [2009] EWHC 783 (Admin) at [27] (account taken of reasons provided after proceedings initiated where the Adjudicator's evidence did not contradict anything in the decision letter; he was a single decision-maker (where problems of post-decision evidence are more acute where the decision-maker is a group of people); the evidence also sought to respond to an issue which was raised for the first time in the judicial review proceedings). In Ireland, the position is not entirely clear: contrast *Mulholland v An Bord Pleanála (No.2)* [2005] IEHC 306; [2006] 1 I.R. 453 and *Deerland Construction v Aquatic Licensing Appeals Board* [2008] IEHC 289; [2009] 1 I.R. 673. It is suggested that the view expressed in *Deerland* is preferable as it was taken having considered the English jurisprudence on the issue and in particular, the judgment in *Nash* [2001] EWHC Admin 538.

[547]   *R. (on the application of Leung) v Imperial College of Science, Technology and Medicine* [2002] EWHC 1358; [2002] E.L.R. 653 at [29]–[30] (Silber J).

[548]   See 1-108. See J. Beer, *Public Inquiries* (2011).

[549]   *Bushell* [1981] A.C. 75 at 95 (Lord Diplock).

[550]   See, e.g. R. Scott, "Procedures at Inquiries: The Duty to be Fair" (1995) 111 L.Q.R. 596; Hadfield, "R. v Lord Saville of Newdigate Ex p. Anonymous Soldiers: What is the Purpose of a Tribunal of Inquiry?" [2003] P.L. 663; Blom-Cooper, "Tribunals under Inquiry" [1999] P.L. 1; Blom-Cooper, "Public Interest in Public Inquiries" [2003] P.L. 578.

[551]   Inquiries Act 2005 s.17.

[552]   B. Hadfield, "R. v Lord Saville of Newdigate Ex p. Anonymous Soldiers: What is the Purpose of a Tribunal of Inquiry?" [2003] P.L. 663, 667. In general also, inquiries should not discuss matters of national policy: *Bushell* [1981] A.C. 75. This is a difficult distinction to maintain in practice: *R. v Secretary of State for Transport Ex p. Gwent CC* [1988] Q.B. 429 at 437 (Woolf LJ).

reports were able to be produced within reasonable time limits, which was very much in the public interest, without any complaints of lack of fairness.[553]

An even more restricted approach to the representation of witnesses was adopted in the case of the inquiry conducted by Scott LJ into the Matrix Churchill, Arms to Iraq affair.[554] Meanwhile, the Budd inquiry into the circumstances surrounding the resignation of David Blunkett, was primarily inquisitorial without formal hearings or the questioning of witnesses by lawyers.[555] In general, there is an emphasis on an inquisitorial approach,[556] however, as just noted, much will depend on the nature of the inquiry. At the Leveson inquiry into the culture, practice and ethics of the press, core participants were legally represented, while in the unique circumstances of the Bloody Sunday inquiry, where the right to life of witnesses may have been at risk, questions regarding anonymity of witnesses and the location in which evidence would be given, were of paramount importance.[557] The Grenfell Tower Inquiry has also issued a Protocol for legal representation.[558]

7-119

ECHR ART.6: CONTENT

A number of rights are contained within ECHR art.6.[559] The right to a fair hearing, the right to a public hearing, and the right to a hearing within a reasonable time are separate and distinct rights from the right to a hearing before an independent and impartial tribunal established by law.[560]

7-120

Fair hearing

The right to a fair hearing in art.6 requires access to "equality of arms", which means that it is necessary to strike a "fair balance" between the parties.[561] Thus, each party must be afforded a reasonable opportunity to present his case, including his evidence, under conditions that do not place him at a substantial disadvantage in

7-121

---

[553] As to techniques used at the Woolf Inquiry, see *Prison Disturbances*, section 2 (Cm. 1456, 1991); R. Morgan, "Woolf: In Retrospect and Prospect" (1991) M.L.R. 713.

[554] L. Blom-Cooper, "Witnesses and the Scott Inquiry" [1994] P.L. 1.

[555] *An Inquiry into an Application for Indefinite Leave to Remain.* HC Paper No.175 (Session 2004/05). cf. the Hutton Inquiry, which combined inquisitorial and adversarial elements in a two-stage process: *Report of the Inquiry into the Circumstances Surrounding the Death of Dr David Kelly CMG.* HC Paper No.247 (Session 2004/05) paras 4-8. For discussion, see N. Bamforth, "Political Accountability in Play: The Budd Inquiry and David Blunkett's Resignation" [2005] P.L. 229.

[556] The Rgt Hon The Lord Thomas of Cwmgiedd "The future of public inquiries" [2015] P.L. 225.

[557] B. Hadfield, "R. v Lord Saville of Newdigate Ex p. Anonymous Soldiers: What is the Purpose of a Tribunal of Inquiry?" [2003] P.L. 663; see also *R. v Lord Saville of Newdigate Ex p. B (No.2)* [2000] 1 W.L.R. 1855, CA; *Saville* [2002] 1 W.L.R. 1249. For the Leveson inquiry, see *http://www.LevesonInquiry.org.uk* [Accessed 31 October 2017].

[558] See Protocol on Legal Representation at Public Expense, 23 August 2017, *https://www.grenfelltowerinquiry.org.uk/news/legal-funding-protocol-released-inquiry/* [Accessed 31 October 2017].

[559] On Convention rights generally, see Ch.13.

[560] *Magill v Porter* [2001] UKHL 67; [2002] 2 A.C. 357 at [87] (Lord Hope of Craighead).

[561] *R. v Secretary of State for the Environment Ex p. Challenger* [2001] Env. L.R. 209 at [48]–[51] (the court was not persuaded that there was "inequality of arms" where the claimant did not have financial resources for representation at a rail public inquiry given that the claimant had applied for and been rejected funding; given that the Inspector at the public inquiry would ensure the proper presentation of Challenger's case; and the local authority had a role in adducing evidence which would support Challenger's case). The concept of "equality of arms" was first mentioned in the case of *Neumeister v Austria* (1979-80) 1 E.H.R.R. 91.

relation to his opponent.[562] Absolute equality of arms is not required however, and there is, for instance, no duty on the State to provide legal aid to an indigent litigant to such a level as to ensure total parity with a wealthy opponent, as long as each side is afforded a reasonable opportunity to present his or her case under conditions that do not place him or her at a substantial disadvantage vis-à-vis the adversary.[563] This may include the right to legal representation, although there is no absolute right to legal representation.[564] The right to a fair hearing will be violated where the defendant, without good cause, prevents an applicant from gaining access to, or falsely denies the existence of, documents in its possession which are of assistance to the applicant's case.[565] The right also means that in certain circumstances, parties to civil proceedings should be entitled to cross-examine witnesses.[566]

7-122   There is no express requirement to provide reasoning in art.6. The ECtHR has, however, regarded this requirement as implicit in the obligation to provide a fair hearing and art.6 includes an obligation to give a reasoned judgment to enable the decision to decide whether to appeal.[567] Whether this requirement adds anything to

---

[562] *Dombo Beheer BV v The Netherlands* (1994) 18 E.H.R.R. 213 at [33]; *Ruiz-Mateos v Spain* (1993) 16 E.H.R.R. 505; *Lilly France v France* App. No. 53892/00 (14 October 2003) (violation of art.6(1) where party had not received a copy of the report submitted by the reporting judge to the Court of Cassation, whereas the advocate-general had); *Williams v Cowell* [2000] 1 W.L.R. 187, CA (no violation of art.6 where Employment Appeal Tribunal sitting in London refused to conduct proceedings in Welsh, given that the appellant could speak and understand English): *MB* [2007] UKHL 46; [2008] 1 A.C. 440 (art.6 meant that defendants in control order proceedings had the right to know the key evidence against them and that defendants were entitled to "such measure of procedural protection as is commensurate with the gravity of the potential consequences": [24]-[90]); *F* [2009] UKHL 28; [2010] 2 A.C. 269. Retrospective legislation affecting the result of pending proceedings may also infringe ECHR art.6(1): *R. (on the application of Reilly) v Secretary of State for Work and Pensions* [2016] EWCA Civ 413.

[563] *Steel and Morris v UK* (2005) 41 E.H.R.R. 403 at [59] and [62] (finding on the facts, given the complexity of the case, that denial of legal aid to defendants in defamation proceedings resulted in an unacceptable inequality of arms). See also *Satambrogio v Italy* (2005) 41 E.H.R.R. 1082; see also *Gudanaviciene* [2014] EWCA Civ 1622; [2015] 1 W.L.R. 2247 (guidance on the Legal Aid, Sentencing and Punishment of Offenders Act 2012 stating that the refusal of legal aid would amount to a breach of ECHR art.6 only in rare and extreme cases was unsupported by case law and incompatible with ECHR art.6); *R. (on the application of Brady) v Lord Chancellor* [2017] EWHC 410 (Admin) at [72] (no absolute right under art.6 to publicly-funded representation but depending on the facts of any particular case, such a right may well arise).

[564] *X v Austria* 42 C.D. 145 (1972) E. Com. H.R. Legal representative includes lawyers from other EU Member States: *R. (on the application of Van Hoogstraten) v Governor of Belmarsh Prison* [2002] EWHC 1965; [2003] 1 W.L.R. 263; and *Ezeh and Connors v UK* (2002) 35 E.H.R.R. 691. See also *Ibrahim v United Kingdom* (2015) 61 E.H.R.R. 9 (holding that the Terrorism Act 2000 struck an appropriate balance between the importance of a suspect's right to legal advice and the need in exceptional cases to enable the police to obtain information necessary to protect the public).

[565] *McGinley and Egan v UK* (1998) 27 E.H.R.R. 1 at [86].

[566] *Buchberger v Austria* (2003) 37 E.H.R.R. 13 at [50]. Contrast *Financial Services Authority v Rourke* [2002] C.P. Rep. 14 (cross-examination not necessary in cases suitable for summary disposal, without breach of art.6(1)). See also *Al Khawaja and Tahery v United Kingdom* (2012) 54 E.H.R.R. 23 at [147] (where a hearsay statement is the sole or decisive evidence against a defendant, its admission as evidence will not automatically result in a breach of art.6(1); the question in each case is whether there are sufficient counterbalancing factors in place, including measures that permit a fair and proper assessment of the reliability of that evidence to take place). In *McKevitt v United Kingdom*, App. 61474/12, 6 September 2016, a complaint that civil proceedings were unfair for reliance on hearsay evidence was found to be manifestly ill-founded and inadmissible.

[567] *Hadjianastassiou v Greece* (1993) 16 E.H.R.R. 219; *Garcia Ruiz v Spain* (1999) 31 E.H.R.R. 589; *Ruiz Jorija v Spain* (1994) 19 E.H.R.R. 553; *Anya* [2001] E.L.R. 711 at [12]; *English* [2002] 1 W.L.R. 2409 at [8]-[14]; *Battista v Bassano* [2007] EWCA Civ 370.

the common law position has been questioned.[568] The ECtHR will hold that art.6(1) has been violated if a judgment leaves it unclear whether the court in question has addressed a contention advanced by a party that is fundamental to the resolution of the litigation.[569] In relation to the standard of reasons, art.6 requires that a decision contains reasons that are sufficient to demonstrate that the core issues raised by the parties have been addressed by the domestic court and how those issues have been resolved. It does not, however, seem to go further and require a judgment to explain why one contention, or piece of evidence, has been preferred to another.[570] Moreover, reasons do not have to be given on every point, but they must enable the party to understand the essence of the decision in order to be able to exercise appeal rights.[571] In certain situations, fairness does not require that the parties should be informed of the reasoning: interlocutory decisions in the course of case management provide an obvious example.[572] By contrast, a failure to give reasons on costs decisions can only comply with art.6 if the reason for the decision in respect of costs is clearly implicit from the circumstances in which the award is made.[573]

Public hearing and public pronouncement of judgment

ECHR art.6 confers a general right to an oral hearing, deriving from the right to   **7-123**
a public hearing and the public pronouncement of judgment.[574] The failure to provide an oral hearing before an administrative or other tribunal determining "civil rights and obligation" may not however constitute a violation of art.6, if the case is considered on appeal or reviewed by a court sitting in public.[575] An oral hearing is not required if an accused or a party has waived his right to such a hearing, if the waiver is unequivocal and there is no important public interest consideration that calls for the public to have the opportunity to be present.[576] Similarly, while art.6 normally requires that a criminal sentence is determined at a public hearing,[577] the right is qualified and a hearing in private may be justified in certain circumstances,

---

568 *English* [2002] 1 W.L.R. 2409 at [12].
569 See, e.g. *Ruiz Torija v Spain* 19 E.H.R.R. 553; *Hiro Balani v Spain* (1994) 19 E.H.R.R. 566.
570 *English* [2002] 1 W.L.R. 2409 at [12]. Cf. the application of the common-law principle in *Weymont* [2015] EWCA Civ 289; [2015] C.P. Rep. 29 (a re-trial was ordered on the basis of a judge's unreasoned judgment, in which there had been blanket acceptance of one party's evidence and blanket rejection of the evidence produced by the other party's witnesses, and not one sentence was provided in the judgment on the facts with the judge's specific findings of fact or the reasons for making them).
571 *Helle v Finland* (1998) 26 E.H.R.R. 505.
572 *English* [2002] 1 W.L.R. 2409 at [13].
573 *English v Emery Reimbold & Strick Ltd* [2002] 1 W.L.R. 2409 at [14].
574 The right to a public hearing implies a right to an oral hearing at the trial court level unless there are exceptional circumstances which justify excluding a hearing: *Fischer v Austria* (1995) 20 E.H.R.R. 349 at [44]; *Allan Jacobsson v Sweden (No.2)* (2001) 32 E.H.R.R. 463.
575 *Schuler-Zgraggen v Switzerland* (1993) 16 E.H.R.R. 405 at [5] (court recognised that there were technical areas of decision-making where there are good reasons for avoiding oral hearings); *R. (on the application of Adlard) v Secretary of State for the Environment, Transport and the Regions* [2002] EWCA Civ 735; [2002] 1 W.L.R. 2515 (upholding refusal to grant oral hearing to objectors to a planning application); *Hellborg v Sweden* (2007) 45 E.H.R.R. 3 at [56]. However, see: *Selmani v The Former Yugoslav Republic of Macedonia*, App. No. 67259/14, 9 February 2017 (absence of oral hearing in proceedings before Constitution Court violated ECHR art.6).
576 *Warren v Random House Group Ltd* [2008] EWCA Civ 834; [2009] Q.B. 600.
577 *R. (on the application of Smith) v Secretary of State for the Home Department* [2004] EWCA Civ 99 at [91]; *R. (on the application of Hammond) v Secretary of State for the Home Department* [2005] UKHL 69; [2006] 1 A.C. 603 at [16]-[17], HL (statutory provision which precluded the possibility of an oral hearing to determine the minimum term of a mandatory life prisoner violated art.6).

including in the interests of public order.[578] Thus, it has been considered contrary to public interest, given the public order problems of moving prisoners out of prisons to judges, to require all disciplinary prison matters to be determined in public hearings.[579] Similarly, the interests of justice have necessitated a private hearing where the trustees of a charity applied for the directions of the court in relation to legal proceedings to which the charity was a party,[580] or where the interests of children are at issue.[581] It is also the case that categories of cases may be designated as not requiring an oral hearing, without infringing art.6.[582]

7-124   In criminal cases, art.6 confers a right to a hearing in the presence of the accused.[583] In civil cases, however, the right of a party to be present at the hearing has been held to extend only to certain kinds of cases, such as cases which involve an assessment of a party's personal conduct,[584] including proceedings relating to the exercise of a profession.[585] Where the professional has been given proper notice however, but fails to attend without good reason, the tribunal may proceed in his absence.[586]

7-125   As for public pronouncement of judgment, when deciding whether a judgment in the context of a High Court challenge to arbitration should be public, although the court could start with the parties' wish for confidentiality and privacy, it should hear representations from either party for the hearing to continue in public, or even, if appropriate, raise the possibility itself of having the hearing in public. It is for the court to ensure the hearing is in compliance with art.6 and to determine if the public interest in a public hearing outweighed the parties' wishes for continuing privacy.[587] Even if the hearing has been in private however, the court must take into account that stricter standards have to be imposed in relation to the public pronouncement of the judgment than to the public hearing of the underlying proceedings and that where judgment could be given without disclosing significant confidential information, the public interest in ensuring appropriate standards of fairness in the conduct of arbitrations militated in favour of a public judgment.[588] Generally, it is not necessary for the judgment to be pronounced at a public hearing where it is available to the public.[589]

---

[578] *R. (on the application of Bannatyne) v Secretary of State for the Home Department, The Independent Adjudicator* [2004] EWHC 1921 at [66].

[579] *Bannatyne* [2004] EWHC 1921.

[580] *Re Trusts of X Charity* [2003] EWHC 1462, Ch; [2003] 1 W.L.R. 2751.

[581] *P and B v UK* (2002) 34 E.H.R.R. 529 (hearing to determine the residence of children).

[582] *Ewing* [2006] 2 All E.R. 993 at [42]-[43] (no violation of art.6 where there was no entitlement to an oral hearing for those seeking to have a civil proceedings order set aside, given that the court had an unfettered discretion to order an oral hearing).

[583] *Ekbatini v Sweden* (1988) 13 E.H.R.R. 504 at [25]; *Hermi v Italy* (2008) 46 E.H.R.R. 46 (Grand Chamber) at [58].

[584] *Muyldermans v Belgium* (1993) 15 E.H.R.R. 204 at [64].

[585] *Bakker v Austria* (2004) 39 E.H.R.R. 26.

[586] *Dhirendra Nath Das v General Medical Council* [2003] UKPC 75 at [8]; also *Komanicky v Slovakia*, App. No. 32106/96 (4 June 2002) at [50]-[55] (violation of art.6(1) where adjournment not granted despite applicant's good medical reason for non-attendance and the importance of his presence at the appeal hearing).

[587] *Department for Economics, Policy and Development of City of Moscow v Bankers Trust Co* [2004] EWCA Civ 314; [2005] Q.B. 207; *Aziz v Aziz* [2007] EWCA Civ 712; [2008] 2 All E.R. 501 (redactions should be refused where not strictly necessary and justified and where the judgment could not be understood without the relevant parts sought to be redacted).

[588] *City of Moscow* [2004] EWCA Civ 314; [2005] Q.B. 207 [39].

[589] *Pretto v Italy* (1984) 6 E.H.R.R. 182; *P and B* (2002) 34 E.H.R.R. 529.

Hearing within a reasonable time

ECHR art.6 requires that a hearing take place within a reasonable time. This right **7-126** is not an aspect of overall fairness, but is an independent right which must be considered separately.[590] An accused is not required to show that prejudice has been, or is likely to be, caused, as a result of delay. It is simply necessary to determine whether, having regard to all the circumstances of the case, the time taken to determine the person's rights and obligations was unreasonable.[591] The threshold for proving a breach of the "reasonable time" requirement has been held to be a high one. If the period of delay was one which, on its face and without more, gave grounds for real concern it was almost certainly unnecessary to go further. This was because the concern in such a case was that there were infringements of basic human rights and not departures from the ideal.[592]

Relevant circumstances to be considered include complexity of the factual or **7-127** legal issues raised by the case; the conduct of the applicant and the competent administrative and judicial authorities; and what is "at stake" for the applicant.[593] For example, "special diligence" was required where an applicant dying of AIDS sought compensation from the State for having negligently infected him with HIV.[594] An overall assessment may be made though, without considering each of these specific criteria.[595] In general, the threshold of proving a breach of the reasonable time requirement is high.[596]

The reasonable time requirement applies to all stages of criminal proceedings, **7-128** including sentencing, confiscation orders and appeals.[597] Where there has been an unreasonable delay, the appropriate remedy depends on the nature of the breach and all the circumstances, including particularly the stage of the proceedings at which the breach was established.[598] It would be appropriate to stay or dismiss the proceedings only if either a fair hearing was no longer possible or it would be, for any compelling reason, unfair to try the defendant. The public interest in the final determination of criminal charges require that such a charge should not be stayed

---

[590] *Magill* [2002] 2 A.C. 357 at [108]-[109]. *O'Neill v HM Advocate (No.2)* [2013] UKSC 36; [2013] 1 W.L.R. 1992 at [25] (noting that art.6(1) of the ECHR contains four separate rights that can and should be considered separately and a complaint that one of them has been breached cannot be answered by showing that the other rights were not breached; see also [36]). For an example of "culpable and undue" delay giving rise to "conspicuous unfairness" at common law, see *FH (Bangladesh) v Secretary of State for the Home Department* [2009] EWCA Civ 385; [2010] Imm. A.R. 32 at [15].

[591] *Magill* [2002] 2 A.C. 357 at [108]-[109].

[592] *Dyer v Watson* [2002] UKPC D 1; [2004] 1 A.C. 379 at [52] (Lord Bingham of Cornhill). See also *R. v Kerrigan (David Joseph)* [2014] EWCA Crim 2348 (the delay at issue, while it might not have been ideal, was far from excessive and there was a satisfactory explanation for it).

[593] *Zimmerman and Steiner v Switzerland* (1983) E.H.R.R. 587; *Davies v UK* (2002) 35 E.H.R.R. 720; *Vilho Eskelinen* (2007) 45 E.H.R.R. 43 at [67]; *R. v Duncan Evans* [2016] EWCA Crim 671.

[594] *A v Denmark* (1996) 22 E.H.R.R. 458.

[595] *Ferrantelli and Santangelo v Italy* (1996) 23 E.H.R.R. 288.

[596] *R (on the application of Lloyd) v Bow Street Magistrates Court* (2003) EWHC 2294. For rejection of an attempt to use ECHR art.6 to create a duty on administrative decision-makers to make decisions within a reasonable time, see *R. (on the application of C) v Secretary of State for Work and Pensions* [2015] EWHC 1607 (Admin).

[597] *Bow Street Magistrates Court* [2003] EWHC 2294 (Admin) at [14], [18], [27], [29] (breach of art.6.1 due to delay in having enforcement proceedings in respect of a confiscation order determined within a reasonable time).

[598] See, e.g. *R. (on the application of Sturnham) v Secretary of State for Justice* [2013] UKSC 23; [2013] 2 A.C. 254 (detention beyond a tariff period caused by delay would warrant damages if it could be shown that an earlier hearing would result in earlier release, or had caused sufficiently serious frustration and anxiety).

or dismissed if any lesser remedy would be just and proportionate in all the circumstances. Where the breach is discovered retrospectively, it is only appropriate to quash the conviction where the hearing was unfair or it was unfair to try the defendant at all.[599] Where there has been an unreasonable delay between the conviction and the hearing of an appeal, if the conviction is upheld as sound, it may not be necessary to quash the conviction. Instead it may be sufficient to compensate the individual by reducing his sentence.[600]

7-129   ECHR art.6 does not guarantee a right of appeal. However, where a right of appeal is provided in domestic law, art.6 will apply to the appeal proceedings.[601]

ECHR ART.2: CONTENT

The requirements of art.2

7-130   ECHR art.2 protects the right to life.[602] Where a death has occurred, the State may have a positive obligation to conduct an investigation.[603] To constitute an "effective" investigation, it is generally necessary for the person carrying out the investigation to be independent from those implicated in the events.[604] An investigation may be inadequate and ineffective if "appropriate steps" are not taken to reduce the risk of collusion.[605] This means not only a lack of hierarchical or institutional connection but also a practical independence.[606] The investigation should be capable of leading to the determination of whether the force used in the case was or was not

---

[599] *Attorney General's Reference No.2 of 2001* [2003] UKHL 68; [2004] 2 A.C. 72 at [24]. See further *HM Advocate v R.* [2002] UKPC D 3; [2004] 1 A.C. 462 (unreasonable delay rendered the continuance of a prosecution incompatible with art.6).

[600] *Mills v Her Majesty's Advocate* [2002] UKPC D 2; [2004] 1 A.C. 441 at [52]-[56].

[601] *Delcourt v Belgium* (1970) 1 E.H.R.R. 355 at [25]; *Tolstoy Miloslavsky v United Kingdom* (1995) 20 E.H.R.R. 442; *Pomiechowski* [2012] UKSC 20; [2012] 1 W.L.R. 1604 at [39] (time limits for appeals against an extradition order must be read subject to the qualification that the court must have a discretion in exceptional circumstances to extend time for both filing and service where to prevent an appeal would conflict with the right of access to an appeal process held to exist under art.6(1)); *Fraser v HM Advocate* [2011] UKSC 24; *Beggs v United Kingdom* (2013) 56 E.H.R.R. 26 (violation of ECHR art.6 where appeal proceedings had lasted for over 10 years); see also *Goldtrail Travel Ltd (In Liquidation) v Onur Air Tasimacilik AS* [2017] UKSC 57; [2017] 1 W.L.R. 3014 at [12] (if an appellant had permission to bring an appeal, it was wrong to impose a condition, such as a payment into court, which had the effect of preventing him from bringing it or continuing it, noting that "[t]here will seldom be a 'fair hearing' within article 6 if a court which has permitted a litigant to bring an appeal then, by indirect means, does not permit him to bring it"); *Magomedov v Russia* App. No. 33636/09, 28 March 2017 (violation of art.6 where there was an extension, without valid reason, of time limit for authorities to appeal).

[602] See 13-062.

[603] See 13-063.

[604] *Jordan v UK* (2003) 37 E.H.R.R. 52 at [106]; *Giuliana v Italia* (2011) 52 E.H.R.R. 3 at [300]; *R. (on the application of Mousa) v Secretary of State for Defence* [2013] EWHC 1412 (Admin); [2013] A.C.D. 84 at [108]–[123] and [147].

[605] *R. (on the application of Saunders) v Independent Police Complaint Commissioner* [2008] EWHC 2372 (Admin); [2009] 1 All E.R. 379 at [40]. See also *R. (on the application of Delezuch) v Chief Constable of Leicestershire* [2014] EWCA Civ 1635 (police guidance provisions were not unlawful for failing to require the immediate separation of officers who used force or who witnessed its use; whether such a failure to separate impairs the adequacy of an investigation depends on the circumstances, including the other safeguards in place, and on an overall assessment of relevant factors, of which the risk of collusion is only one).

[606] *Jordan* (2003) 37 E.H.R.R. 52 at [106]; *Finucane v UK* (2003) 37 E.H.R.R. 29; *SP v Secretary of State for Justice* [2009] EWHC 13 (Admin); [2009] A.C.D. 59 (an investigation into the claimant's detention while in young offender institutions was not sufficiently independent to make the report compliant with ECHR art.2 because an investigator for the report had worked for the prison service

justified and to the identification and punishment of those responsible.[607] There is an implicit requirement of promptness and reasonable expedition,[608] and there must be a sufficient element of public scrutiny of the investigation or its results to secure accountability in practice as well as in theory; and the investigation must involve the next of kin in the investigative procedure to the extent necessary to protect their legitimate interests.[609] It has also been held that an art.2 investigation must encompass broader issues such as planning and control of operations and all surrounding circumstances, not just the actions of State agents who directly used lethal force, and must include "lessons learned" from the identification of wider or systemic issues.[610] The types of procedural failures which will violate art.2 include: failing to exercise proper control over the scene of the investigation[611]; failure to seek follow-up information from those present at the scene of the incident[612]; failure to interview military personnel or police officers immediately after the incident[613]; failure to fully explore the facts surrounding the death[614]; and a failure to give reasons for refusing to prosecute police officers for collusion in an incident.[615]

Excessive investigative delay will violate ECHR art.2.[616] Lack of independence has been found where the investigation is conducted by officers who are part of the police force suspected of issuing threats against the victim[617] and where it was proposed that an investigation would be conducted by the Police Service of Northern Ireland into the death of a woman in 1972 which fresh evidence suggested may have been at the hands of a soldier under the control of the Ministry of Defence.[618] The minimum standards for an effective investigation will also not be met where the inquiry is held in private and without participation of the family of the victim[619]; although it may be necessary to grant anonymity to a witness if the

---

for 30 years on issues relevant to the investigation and had a social acquaintance with the governor of one of the institutions investigated); *Mocanu v Romania* (2015) 60 E.H.R.R. 19.

[607] *Jordan* (2003) 37 E.H.R.R. 52 at [107]. Also: *Middleton* [2004] UKHL 10; [2004] 2 A.C. 182 at [20]; *R. (on the application of Hurst) v Commissioner of Police of the Metropolis* [2007] UKHL 13; [2007] 2 A.C. 189 at [19].

[608] *Jordan* (2003) 37 E.H.R.R. 52 at [108]; *Dodov v Bulgaria* (2008) 47 E.H.R.R. 41; *McCaughey* (2014) 58 E.H.R.R. 13.

[609] *Jordan* (2003) 37 E.H.R.R. 52 at [109].

[610] *Mousa* [2013] EWHC 1412 (Admin); [2013] A.C.D. 84 at [147].

[611] *Jordan* (2003) 37 E.H.R.R. 52 at [118] (although on the facts in Jordan, there was no such failure).

[612] *Jordan* (2003) 37 E.H.R.R. 52; *Jaloud* (2015) 60 E.H.R.R. 29 at [197]–[203]; [209]–[211].

[613] *Kelly v UK* App. No.30054/96 (4 May 2001); *McKerr v UK* (2002) 34 E.H.R.R. 20; *Jaloud* (2015) 60 E.H.R.R. 29 at [197]–[203]; [206]–[208].

[614] *R. (on the application of Medihani) v HM Coroner for Inner South District of Greater London* [2012] EWHC 1104 (Admin); [2012] A.C.D. 63 at [48]-[50]; *Jaloud* (2015) 60 E.H.R.R. 29 at [212]–[220].

[615] *Shanaghan v UK* App. No.377115/97 (May 4, 2001), *The Times*, 18 May 2001; *Finucane* (2003) 37 E.H.R.R. 29 at [77]–[78]. See also *Litvinenko* [2014] EWHC 194 (Admin); [2014] H.R.L.R. 6 at [57]–[74] (deficiencies in the reasons "*so substantial*" that a decision for refusing to launch a public inquiry into a death due to radiation poisoning in suspicious circumstances could not stand).

[616] *McCaughey* (2014) 58 E.H.R.R. 13 at [121]–[140] (prompt response by the authorities in investigating the use of lethal force was essential to maintain public confidence in adherence to the rule of law and in preventing any appearance of collusion in or tolerance of unlawful acts; there had been excessive delay where an inquest began over 21 years after the deaths in question).

[617] *Finucane* (2003) 37 E.H.R.R. 29 at [76].

[618] *McQuillan's Application for Judicial Review* [2017] NIQB 28.

[619] *R. (on the application of Amin) v Secretary of State for the Home Department* [2003] UKHL 51; [2004] 1 A.C. 653. However, where the incident results in near-suicide, rather than death, a public inquiry will not necessarily be required, although an "enhanced investigation" (not an internal investigation) will be necessary: *L (A Patient)* [2009] 1 A.C. 588 at [41].

life of that witness is at risk.[620] It is not necessary for the investigator to investigate and state his conclusion in relation to every issue raised; what is required is that the investigation is focused on the central issue or issues in the case.[621] It is not necessary for the investigation to be conducted by way of one unified procedure; the aims of fact-finding and accountability may be carried out by or shared between several authorities, as long as the various procedures provide for the necessary safeguards in an accessible and effective manner.[622] It has been held that there are only two realistic ways in which the State can fulfil its ECHR art.2 obligations in respect of deaths in custody, namely, by setting up an overarching public inquiry or by developing a procedure based on coroner's inquests,[623] which are now discussed.

Inquests

7-131   The mere fact that an inquest has been held will not mean that the requirements of art.2 are satisfied; whether art.2 is satisfied will depend on how the inquest is conducted.[624] There are two types of inquest: the traditional inquest and the art.2 inquest. The essential difference between them is twofold.[625] First, the permissible verdict or verdicts in a traditional inquest is significantly narrower than in an art.2 inquest, which requires an expression, however brief, of the jury's conclusion on the disputed factual issues at the heart of the case.[626] Secondly the scope of the investigation is or is likely to be narrower at a traditional inquest.[627] The inquest should involve participation of the family of the deceased,[628] and art.2 may require that the deceased's family is given funding for legal representation,[629] however, usually this will only be where the case falls into the "exceptional category where legal representation is needed in order to ensure effective participation by the deceased's family and an effective investigation".[630] An inquest must also, at the very least, "culminate in an expression, however brief, of the jury's conclusion on the disputed factual issues at the heart of the case".[631]

---

[620] *R. (on the application of A) v HM Coroner for Inner South London* [2004] EWCA Civ 1439; [2005] U.K.H.R.R. 44 See *Re Officer L* [2007] UKHL 36; [2007] 1 W.L.R. 2135 (the test is whether the risk of injury or death would be materially increased if evidence was given without anonymity).

[621] *Allen* [2009] EWCA Civ 623; [2009] LS Law Medical 430.

[622] *Pearson v United Kingdom* (2012) 54 E.H.R.R. SE11 at [71].

[623] *Mousa* [2013] EWHC 1412 (Admin); [2013] A.C.D. 84 at [197]–[201], [210] (refusing to direct a public inquiry into deaths of Iraqi civilians in the custody of British armed forces).

[624] *R. (on the application of Wright) v Secretary of State for the Home Department* [2001] EWHC Admin 520; [2002] H.R.L.R. 1; *Manning* [2001] Q.B. 330.

[625] *R. (on the application of Smith) v Oxfordshire Assistant Deputy Coroner* [2009] EWCA Civ 441; [2011] 1 A.C. 1 at [64]; on appeal. See [2010] UKSC 29 at [152]-[153]

[626] *Smith* [2009] EWCA Civ 441; [2011] 1 A.C. 1 at [64] and [71]-[76].

[627] *Smith* [2009] EWCA Civ 441; [2011] 1 A.C. 1 at [64].

[628] *R. (on the application of Khan) v Secretary of State for Health* [2003] EWCA Civ 1129; [2004] 1 W.L.R. 971 at [69].

[629] *Khan* [2003] EWCA Civ 1129; [2004] 1 W.L.R. 971 at [74]-[75]; *R. (on the application of D) v Secretary of State for the Home Department* [2006] 3 All E.R. 946 at [47]; *R. (on the application of Humberstone) v Legal Services Commission* [2010] EWCA Civ 1479; [2011] 1 W.L.R. 1460.

[630] *Challender* [2004] EWHC 925; [2004] A.C.D. 57, [68]; *Khan* [2003] EWCA Civ 1129; [2004] 1 W.L.R. 971 at [74]-[75]. There is no obligation in art.2 for the inquest to explore "collateral matters" of earlier lethal force incidents of the soldiers involved: *Re Gribben's Application for Leave to Apply for Judicial Review* [2017] NICA 16 at [19].

[631] *Middleton* [2004] UKHL 10; [2004] 2 A.C. 182.

CHAPTER 8

Procedural Fairness: Exceptions

TABLE OF CONTENTS

SCOPE

We have seen in Chapter 7 that decision-makers performing public functions are **8-001** generally required to adopt fair procedures; and in relation to a variety of different circumstances, we considered the content of the requirements of procedural fairness. As we noted, a person may also have a legitimate expectation of fair treatment, and that will be considered in Chapter 12.

This chapter examines the situations where, although the requirements of **8-002** procedural fairness are on first appearance applicable, the decision-maker may be exempt from all or some of the procedural safeguards that would otherwise be required.[1] Several factors may be identified as capable of excluding the normal procedural fairness requirements: (a) express statutory exclusion[2]; (b) legislation expressly requires fairness in some situations, but is silent about others[3]; (c) disclosure would be prejudicial to the public interest[4]; (d) prompt action is needed[5]; (e) it is impractical to comply with fairness requirements[6]; (f) a procedurally flawed

---

[1] The situations examined in the chapter are where there is no entitlement to procedural fairness. The courts may also hold that there has been a breach of procedural fairness requirements but nonetheless exercise discretion at the conclusion of a claim for judicial review to withhold a remedy: see 18-047. The distinction between these two ways of denying an enforceable right to procedural fairness has not always been articulated with clarity: see 7-043 and 18-047.

[2] See 8-003.

[3] See 8-005.

[4] See 8-009.

[5] See 8-035.

[6] See 8-040.

decision has been followed by a hearing or appeal that is fair[7]; (g) the procedurally flawed decision is merely a preliminary one[8]; (h) the procedural defect would have made no difference to the outcome[9]; and (i) the failure to provide a fair procedure is no fault of the decision-maker.[10] We examine these in turn.

EXPRESS STATUTORY EXCLUSION

8-003   Provided it does so "clearly and expressly",[11] an Act of Parliament may dispense with the requirements of fair procedures where they would otherwise be required.[12] However, of course, any statutory exclusion of fair procedures must be interpreted in accordance with any obligations imposed by the European Convention on Human Rights ("the ECHR").[13] A statute may, for example, permit the exercise of powers without notice.[14] In the interests of administrative efficiency and expedition, the requirements of fairness have been excluded by statutory provisions which, for example, enable decision-makers to decline to conduct an oral hearing,[15] or to entertain particular kinds of representations and objections.[16]

---

[7]   See 8-043.
[8]   See 8-053.
[9]   See 8-065.
[10] See 8-075.
[11] *Wiseman v Borneman* [1971] A.C. 297 at 318.
[12] See 7-013. Australian law abounds with attempts at this, especially in migration legislation where governments seek to limit challenges on the grounds of denial of natural justice by codifying the procedures of migration tribunals (and thus limiting their obligations under the hearing rule). Statutory procedures are apt to be read literally, and often narrowly, by the courts: *Re Minister for Immigration and Multicultural Affairs; Ex p. Miah* (2001) 206 C.L.R. 57. The High Court of Australia has accepted that fairness may be codified and excluded to the extent of its codification but this requires unmistakably clear drafting because natural justice is a fundamental right protected by the principle of legality: *Saeed v Minister for Immigration and Citizenship* (2010) 241 C.L.R. 252.
[13] For instance, in *R.(on the application of X) v Chief Constable of the West Midlands* [2004] EWCA Civ 1068; [2005] 1 W.L.R. 65, that there was no duty on a chief constable to provide an opportunity for representations prior to disclosure of details of discontinued criminal charges to a prospective employer pursuant to a statutory power (since repealed), since disclosure was the "policy of the legislation in order to serve a pressing social need". This position was disapproved in *R. (on the application of L) v Commissioner of Police of the Metropolis* [2009] UKSC 3; [2010] 1 A.C. 410, in which it was held (at [44]-[45]) that the statutory power was not incompatible with ECHR art.8, provided that when exercising his discretion as to what information ought to be included in an enhanced criminal record certificate, the chief police officer gave proper consideration to the individual's right to respect for his private life. The guidance given in *R. (on the application of X)* [2005] 1 W.L.R. 65, that the chief police officer was under a duty to disclose if the information might be relevant, unless there was some good reason for not making such disclosure, did not strike the balance in the right place. See also: *R. (on the application of A) v B* [2010] EWHC 2361 (Admin) and *R. (on the application of C) v Chief Constable of Greater Manchester* [2011] EWCA Civ 175; [2011] 2 F.L.R. 383.
[14] See, e.g. *R. (on the application of M) v Secretary of State for Constitutional Affairs* [2004] EWCA Civ 312; [2004] 1 W.L.R. 2298 at [39].
[15] See, e.g. Criminal Procedure Rules 2015 (SI 2015/1490) r.47.60; see also *Re A* [2006] EWCA Crim 4; [2006] 1 W.L.R. 1361).
[16] See, e.g. *R. (on the application of WB and KA) v Leeds Organisation Committee* [2002] EWHC 1927 (Admin); [2003] E.L.R. 67; Highways Act 1980 s.258 (objections to compulsory purchase order excluded where objections are based on urging alternative route and are not made in accordance with the specified procedure); *Re Berkhamsted Grammar School* [1908] 2 Ch. 25; and for a more equivocal formula which was held to exclude any duty to act judicially, *Patterson v District Commissioner for Accra* [1948] A.C. 341; for a Canadian case, see *British Columbia Wildlife Federation v Debeck* (1976) 1 B.C.L.R. 244 at [17]-[19] (no duty to act in accordance with procedural fairness where there was no requirement to hear objections). On situations in which courts will supplement

Any statutory exclusion of procedural fairness will be construed strictly. Thus, **8-004** where a statutory provision did not expressly or by necessary implication exclude the right to legal professional privilege, the provision was interpreted not to do so.[17] Subordinate legislation purporting to exclude a hearing should also be strictly construed.[18] Indeed, even when a discretion to hold a hearing or conduct an inquiry is conferred by a statute, a refusal to hold the inquiry may constitute a denial of natural justice if fairness plainly demands that a hearing be held.[19] And an express statutory power to proceed without a hearing will not necessarily exclude the right to make informal or written representations.[20] Similarly, an express statutory provision excluding a duty to give reasons has been held not to exclude a duty to disclose the substance of the case so that an applicant for citizenship could make representations.[21] Finally, where the statute purporting to limit or exclude procedural fairness engages a Convention right, the limitation must be compatible with the Convention.[22]

the statutory procedure, see 7-013 and 7-042. See also *Walapu v Revenue and Customs Commissioners* [2016] EWHC 658 (Admin) (ruling that the provisions applicable to a power on the part of HMRC to issue an accelerated payment notice pursuant to the Finance Act 2014 was perfectly fair and adequate).

[17] *R. (on the application of Morgan Grenfell & Co Ltd) v Inland Revenue Commissioners* [2002] UKHL 21; [2003] 1 A.C. 563; and *R. (on the application of Singh) v Chief Constable of the West Midlands Police* [2006] EWCA Civ 1118; [2006] 1 W.L.R. 3374 at [79]-[83]; in Canada see *R. v British Columbia Pollution Control Board* (1967) 61 D.L.R. (2nd) 221 (objector had no right to be "heard", but his right to lodge objections imposed certain implied procedural duties on the deciding body).

[18] *R. v Housing Appeal Tribunal* [1920] 3 K.B. 334; *R. v Local Government Board* [1911] 2 I.R. 331 at 342-343; in New Zealand see *Tauhara Properties Ltd v Mercantile Developments Ltd* [1974] 1 N.Z.L.R. 584 at 590; *Drew v Attorney General* [2002] 1 N.Z.L.R. 58 (prison regulation that would lead to some disciplinary hearings being conducted in breach of the natural justice right contained in s.27 of the New Zealand Bill of Rights Act 1990 held ultra vires). cf. decisions in which procedural rules contained in regulations have been held directory only in the absence of a specific statutory power to impose formal requirements by regulation: *Francis Jackson Developments Ltd v Hall* [1951] 2 K.B. 488; *R. v Devon and Cornwall Rent Tribunal Ex p. West* (1975) 29 P. & C.R. 316. On directory and mandatory requirements, see 5-057.

[19] *Binney v Secretary of State for the Environment* [1984] J.P.L. 871; *R. v Secretary of State for Transport Ex p. Ellison* (1995) 70 P. & C.R. 161, QBD; in New Zealand see *Fraser v State Services Commission* [1984] 1 N.Z.L.R. 116 at 122 (Cooke J) and 124-125 (Richardson J). Fairness will not require a public inquiry where, without an inquiry, the two or more conflicting issues can be properly weighed and those with a right to make representations can have their representations properly taken into account: *R. (on the application of Little) v Secretary of State for Trade and Industry* [2002] EWHC 3001 (Admin) at [25]; and *Decra Plastics Ltd v Waltham Forest LBC* [2002] EWHC 2718 (Admin); *R. (on the application of Persimmon Homes (South East) Ltd) v Secretary of State for Transport* [2005] EWHC 96 (Admin); [2005] 2 P. & C.R. 24.

[20] *Ex p Guardian Newspapers Ltd (Written Submissions), The Times*, 26 October 1993, CA; *Re A* [2006] EWCA Crim 4; [2006] 1 W.L.R. 1361 at [28]; in Canada see *Hundal v Superintendent of Motor Vehicles* (1985) 20 D.L.R. (4th) 592; cf. *Nicholson v Haldimand-Norfolk Regional Board of Commissioners of Police* [1979] 1 S.C.R. 311 at [22]-[27].

[21] *R. v Secretary of State for the Home Department Ex p. Fayed* [1998] 1 W.L.R. 763. See also *R. (on the application of AHK) v Secretary of State for the Home Department* [2012] EWHC 1117 (Admin); [2012] A.C.D. 66 and *R. (on the application of Thamby) v Secretary of State for the Home Department* [2011] EWHC 1763 (Admin).

[22] See, e.g. *R. (on the application of G) v Immigration Appeal Tribunal* [2004] EWCA Civ 1731; [2005] 1 W.L.R. 1445 (even though the Nationality, Immigration and Asylum Act 2002 did not provide for an oral hearing in its statutory review of refusal of permission to appeal against the decision of an immigration officer, the statutory procedure provided adequate and proportionate protection of the rights of asylum seekers and judicial review remained available in respect of errors not susceptible to statutory review); see 8-003, 8-008 and 8-012.

LEGISLATION REQUIRES FAIRNESS FOR SOME BUT NOT OTHER PURPOSES

8-005   There are circumstances in which the requirements of procedural fairness may be invoked to supplement statutory procedures.[23] The obverse circumstances can exist and a statutory procedural framework may impliedly exclude the more extensive protection provided by common law by means of application of the maxim *expressio unius est exclusio alterius* (the expression of one thing implies the exclusion of another), although on occasion, the courts have expressed reservations about the application of this maxim.[24] The common law requirements of fair procedures should not be excluded unless the statute represents a settled legislative intent that the procedural safeguard should be excluded, rather than a case of a "mere omission" which may be filled by the courts.[25] For example, where the statute provides for certain documents to be disclosed, it may exclude an obligation to disclose all relevant documents[26]; or an obligation to communicate may be excluded where other forms of communication are expressly envisaged by the legislation.[27] Similarly, where regulations specifically provide for reasons to be given with respect to certain circumstances and not others, a common law duty to give reasons may not arise in respect of the circumstances not listed in the

---

[23]   See 7-013 and 7-042.

[24]   *R. (on the application of West) v Parole Board* [2005] UKHL 1; [2005] 1 W.L.R. 350 at [29] (Lord Bingham noting that "the maxim *expressio unius exclusio alterius* can rarely, if ever, be enough to exclude the common law rules of natural justice"). See also: *R. (on the application of Downs) v Secretary of State for Justice* [2011] EWCA Civ 1422; [2012] A.C.D. 38; *Veolia ES Nottinghamshire Ltd v Nottinghamshire CC* [2010] EWCA Civ 1214; [2012] P.T.S.R. 185 at [15] (Rix LJ); *R. (on the application of Buckinghamshire CC) v Kingston-upon-Thames RLBC* [2011] EWCA Civ 457; [2012] P.T.S.R. 854 at [54]-[55] ("[a]bsent the express exclusion or modification of the right to be heard, it will usually require strong language to justify the same result by implication"); *Bank Mellat v HM Treasury (No.2)* [2013] UKSC 39; [2014] A.C. 700 at [35] (Lord Sumption observing: "I find it hard to envisage cases in which the maximum expression unius exclusion alterius could suffice to exclude so basic a right as that of fairness"); *EK (Ivory Coast) v Secretary of State for the Home Department* [2014] EWCA Civ 1517 at [26] (the Secretary of State accepting, correctly, that the Immigration Rules do not exclude the general public law duty to act fairly which rests upon the Secretary of State in exercising her functions). A different approach is taken with respect to appeals against refusal of permission to appeal. In *Sarfraz v Disclosure and Barring Service* [2015] EWCA Civ 544, it was held that while there was force in an argument that exceptions on the right of appeal were set out exhaustively in the legislation and there was no room for further exception, the court could not ignore the long-standing principle, established by *Lane v Esdaile* [1891] A.C. 210, that, in the absence of express statutory language to the contrary, a provision giving a court the power to grant or refuse permission to appeal should be construed as not extending to an appeal against a refusal of permission to appeal. See also *R. (on the application of Rowe) v Revenue and Customs Commissioners* [2015] EWHC 2293 (Admin) at [59] (observing that where Parliament has prescribed a set of procedural protections, the courts should generally be slow to impose a further set of obligations as a matter of common law).

[25]   *R. v Secretary of State for the Home Department Ex p. Abdi* [1996] 1 W.L.R. 298; *R. v Secretary of State for Education and Employment Ex p. M* [1996] E.L.R. 162; *R. v Secretary of State for Wales Ex p. Emery* [1996] 4 All E.R. 1; and see 7-013.

[26]   *Abdi* [1996] 1 W.L.R. 298 at 314 (holding that an implied obligation to disclose all relevant documents would be wholly inconsistent with the express obligation to disclose specific documents set out in the (now repealed) Asylum Appeals (Procedure) Rules 1993).

[27]   *Furnell v Whangarei High Schools Board* [1973] A.C. 660 at 681 (Lord Morris concluding that an omission "must have been deliberate since the regulations proceed with great particularity to specify when and how communication should be made to him and when and how he should make response").

regulations.[28] Furthermore, where the recognition of additional fair procedure requirements to those specified in the legislation would frustrate the purpose of the statutory scheme or its practical operation, additional fair procedures will not be implied into the statutory scheme.[29] In practice, the context will determine the scope of the common law duty of fairness in the particular circumstances under consideration and it has been observed that the starting point should not be whether the statute on its proper construction has limited the duty to what it permits, but whether the duty in the context of the statutory process requires anything more.[30]

RISK TO THE PUBLIC INTEREST

Risks to national security

In Chapter 16 we examine the statutory right to disclosure of certain informa-   **8-006**
tion under the Freedom of Information Act 2000, the Data Protection Act 1998 and other legislation and the limits of the rights to access to information.[31] Here we consider the limits to common law rights to disclosure.[32] In the past, the courts of England and Wales readily accepted the argument that to require ministers to reveal to interested parties materials prepared or obtained in the course of departmental duties might unduly interfere with the administrative process by destroying the anonymity of the civil service, discouraging frank comment in official reports and undermining the principle of ministerial responsibility to Parliament.[33] Likewise, in housing and town planning cases, courts often refused to require the disclosure of inspectors' reports on inquiries and other relevant materials, even where the minister's functions were recognised as including a judicial element.[34] In general, the climate of opinion has changed; and the administrative process has become less opaque.[35]

National security and terrorism continue however to be invoked as justifica-   **8-007**

---

28 *R. (on the application of Venture Projects Ltd) v Secretary of State for the Home Department*, unreported 20 October 2000 at [3], [4] and [13] (Schiemann LJ noting that "statutory provisions echoed a choice which had to be made"); and *R. v Birmingham City Council Ex p. Ferrero Ltd* [1993] 1 All E.R. 530.

29 *R. (on the application of Rowe) v Revenue and Customs Commissioners* [2015] EWHC 2293 (Admin) at [70].

30 *Buckinghamshire CC* [2011] EWCA Civ 457; [2012] P.T.S.R. 854 at [57].

31 See 16-028.

32 On the duty to disclose, see 7-060.

33 *R. v Local Government Board Ex p. Arlidge* [1915] A.C. 120; *Laffer v Gillen* [1927] A.C. 886 at 895-896.

34 See 6-038.

35 cf. Town and Country Planning (Inquiries Procedure) Rules 1974 (SI 1974/419) r.10(4), which allowed an inspector of a planning appeal "not to require or permit the giving or production of any evidence ... which would be contrary to the public interest". This provision has been removed from the Rules (now Town and Country Planning (Inquiries Procedure) (England) Rules 2000 (SI 2000/1624). But Town and Country Planning Act 1990 s.321 enables the Secretary of State to give directions limiting public access to information regarding national security, information regarding the measures taken or to be taken to ensure the security of any premises or property, or information the disclosure of which would be contrary to the national interest; also Planning (National Security Directions and Appointed Representatives) (England) Rules 2006 (SI 2006/1284); *R. v Secretary of State for Defence Ex p. Camden LBC* [1995] J.PL. 403; H. McCoubrey, "Security Planning Regulations and Defence Establishments" [1994] J.P.L. 1075; "National Security—Application of Circular 18/94 Pt IV—Car Park Building at Regent's Park Barracks" [1995] J.P.L. 403; "Applying the Planning Acts to the Crown" [2005] J.P.L. B23-24.

tions for limitations on fair procedures. Just as the First and Second World Wars resulted in the detention of individuals in circumstances where their rights were not properly protected,[36] so have terrorist incidents in London and elsewhere created similar situations. In the current era of global terrorism, Parliament has enacted legislation which in various ways excludes the ordinary entitlements to fairness of those suspected of terrorist-related activities.[37] The common law has also for many years recognised the exigencies of national security.[38] In so doing, the courts have often been unwilling to examine the strength of a public authority's defence that national security justifies departure from the entitlement to procedural fairness that would otherwise exist.[39] It has also been "clearly established that, where there are real concerns about national security, the obligations of fairness may have to be modified or excluded".[40] Even the requirements of ECHR art.6 may be qualified where national security interests are at stake, provided that appropriate procedural safeguards remain in place.[41]

---

[36]   See 6-020.

[37]   See, e.g. D. Feldman, "Human Rights, Terrorism and Risk: the Roles of Politicians and Judges" [2006] P.L. 364; D. Dyzenhaus, *The Constitution of Law: Legality in a Time of Emergency* (2006); L. Lustgarten and I. Leigh, *In from the Cold; National Security and Parliamentary Democracy* (1994); J. Strawson, *Law after Ground Zero* (2002); C Walker, *Terrorism and the Law* (2011); C. Gearty, *Liberty and Security* (2013).

[38]   See, e.g. *Council of Civil Service Unions v Minister for the Civil Service* [1985] A.C. 374; *Hutton v Attorney General* [1927] 1 Ch. 427 at 439 (defence policy); *R. v Secretary of State for the Home Department Ex p. Cheblak* [1991] 1 W.L.R. 890 (immigrant not entitled to full particulars of the case against him or legal representation where the deportation was stated to be for reasons of national security); *R. v Secretary of State for the Home Department Ex p. Chahal* [1995] 1 W.L.R. 526 and *Chahal v UK* (1997) 23 E.H.R.R. 413 (violations of ECHR art.13, art.3, and art.5(4)).

[39]   See, e.g. *R. v Secretary of State for Home Affairs Ex p. Hosenball* [1977] 1 W.L.R. 766 at 783-4 (Lord Lane noting in the context of a deportation order that, if disclosure of information to an alien might have an adverse effect on national security, "[t]he choice is regrettably clear: the alien must suffer, if suffering there be, and this is so on whichever basis of argument one chooses"); *Cheblak* [1991] 1 W.L.R. 890 at 902 (Lord Donaldson describing national security as "the exclusive responsibility of the executive"); *Council of Civil Service Unions* [1985] A.C. 374 at 410 (Lord Diplock describing national security as "par excellence a non justiciable question").

[40]   *R. (on the application of Tucker) v Director General of the National Crime Squad* [2003] EWCA Civ 57 at [43] (Scott Baker LJ citing *R. v Secretary of State for the Home Department Ex p. Hosenball* [1977] 1 W.L.R. 766 at 773, 786); and e.g. *R. v Secretary of State for the Home Department Ex p. B*, Divisional Court, 25 January 1991, *The Independent,* 29 January 1991 (deportation); *R. v Secretary of State for the Home Department Ex p. Al-Harbi* (Otton J, 21 March 1991) (asylum); *Balfour v Foreign and Commonwealth Office* [1994] 1 W.L.R. 681 at 688 (dismissal of employee); *R. v Secretary of State for the Home Department Ex p. Gallagher* [1994] 3 C.M.L.R. 295, CA, at [12]-[18] (when making an exclusion order on the grounds of national security, the Secretary of State was permitted to withhold allegations and the identity of the statutory adviser); *R. v Secretary of State for the Home Department Ex p. McQuillan* [1995] 4 All E.R. 400 (Sedley J) (exclusion order). For discussion see T. Poole, "Courts and Conditions of Uncertainty in 'Times of Crisis'" [2008] P.L. 234.

[41]   The House of Lords has held that although a judge in control order proceedings could, pursuant to statutory power, refuse to disclose evidence to the defendant the power of non-disclosure did not apply "where to do so would be incompatible with the right of the controlled person to a fair trial": *MB(FC) v Secretary of State for the Home Department: AF v Secretary of State for the Home Department* [2007] UKHL 46; [2008] 1 A.C. 440 at [72]: see also [84]. On the modification of procedural fairness requirements in the interests of national security, see [32], [63], [80] and [91] ; *Re T (Wardship: Impact of Police Intelligence)* [2009] EWHC 2440; [2010] 1 F.L.R. 1048 (in cases where public interest immunity has been established and the court considers that some material evidence cannot be disclosed to all the parties, rights under the ECHR fall to be adapted in a proportionate manner to accommodate the priority that has to be given to that material) at [87]; *Bank Mellat v HM Treasury (No.1)* [2013] UKSC 38; [2014] A.C. 700 at [52] (ECHR art.6 is the principled control mechanism on what the legislature can prescribe, and it is for the courts to decide, within parameters set down by the legislature, how the tension between the need for natural justice and confidentiality is to be resolved in the natural interest). See also 8-012.

The challenges to procedural fairness created by national security concerns can **8-008** be particularly difficult for courts and tribunals. On the one hand, it is of critical importance that the courts and tribunals are vigilant in protecting individuals who are detained or subjected to other restrictions on their activities in connection with suspected terrorist activities who have not been charged with any offence. On the other hand, the courts have to be sensitive to the responsibility of security services to protect the public at large from what can be deadly incidents. In general, while it is "self-evidently right that national courts must give great weight to the views of the executive on matters of national security", nonetheless, issues of national security "do not fall beyond the competence of the courts",[42] and "judges have a duty, also entrusted by Parliament, to examine Ministerial decisions or actions in accordance with the ordinary tests of rationality, legality, and procedural regularity, and, where Convention rights are in play, proportionality."[43] In the Belmarsh detainees case,[44] a majority of the House of Lords made it clear that although the response necessary to protect national security was a matter of political judgement for the executive and Parliament, where Convention rights were in issue, national courts were required to afford them effective protection by adopting an intensive review of whether such a right had been impugned, and the courts were not precluded by any doctrine of deference from examining the proportionality of a measure taken to restrict such a right.[45] As has been observed: "It is no answer that terrorism is horrendous ... However grave the case, there can come a point where 'the court's sense of justice and propriety is offended'".[46]

Disclosure

In particular, it may be necessary to restrict the disclosure of information. There **8-009** are currently two processes pursuant to which evidence may be withheld. The first, public interest immunity is a common law process, derived from Crown privilege and enables the court to consider whether the evidence should be withheld.[47] It requires a balance between the need for confidentiality and the need for disclosure and, as Simon Brown LJ has summarised it, the question to be asked is:

"Does the public interest in making the limited further disclosure now sought outweigh the remaining confidentiality in the report? That in turn seems to me to depend upon whether disclosure to the requesting states is required in the interests of fairness. If fairness demands disclosure, then to my mind disclosure clearly becomes the overriding public interest."[48]

---

[42] *Secretary of State for the Home Department v Rehman* [2001] UKHL 47; [2003] 1 A.C. 153 at [31] (Lord Steyn).

[43] *R. (on the application of Naik) v Secretary of State for the Home Department* [2011] EWCA Civ 1546; [2012] Imm. A.R. 381 at [48] (Carnwath LJ); see also *R. (on the application of Mohamed) v Secretary of State for Foreign and Commonwealth Affairs* [2010] EWCA Civ 65; [2011] Q.B. 218 (confidentiality of working arrangements between US and UK intelligence services not absolute).

[44] *X v Secretary of State for the Home Department* [2004] UKHL 56; [2005] 2 A.C. 68.

[45] See, e.g. *Secretary of State for the Home Department v MB* [2006] EWCA Civ 1140; [2007] Q.B. 415 (for HL, see [2007] UKHL 46; [2008] 1 A.C. 440 and 8-013); *Fitt v UK* (2000) 30 E.H.R.R. 480. On proportionality and deference, see 11-091.

[46] *Secretary of State for the Home Department v CC and CF* [2014] EWCA Civ 559 at [16] (Kay LJ).

[47] See P. Craig, *Administrative Law*, 8th edn (2016), paras 13-002–13-014.

[48] *R. v Secretary of State for the Home Department Ex p. King of Belgium*, unreported 15 February 2000; *R. (on the application of Gunn-Russo) v Nugent Care Society* [2001] EWHC Admin 566; [2002] 1 F.L.R. 1 (holding that the care society should have considered each document to balance confidentiality against disclosure). It seems that a public interest immunity procedure, although not usually, may also involve the participation of a special advocate: *AHK* [2012] EWHC 1117 (Admin);

It has been observed that the effect of public interest immunity is to exclude material, such that the court and the parties are deprived of relevant material.[49]

8-010   The second process, known as a closed material procedure, has been enacted by Parliament originally in certain specific contexts, such as employment[50] and in cases involving allegations of terrorism,[51] and subsequently through the Justice and Security Act 2013, extended to all civil proceedings.[52] According to this process, the litigant is entitled to submit evidence without disclosing it to the other party and there is no balancing of the competing interests; the closed material is withheld from the person and a special advocate may be appointed to represent the party to whom the evidence is not disclosed.[53] As has been observed, the difference between the two processes is that, with public interest immunity, undisclosed evidence cannot be adduced during the proceedings, whereas with a closed material procedure, the party can rely upon evidence that has not been disclosed to the other side.[54] It has been observed that the process of considering an application to withhold information from disclosure on the grounds of public interest, and the closed material procedure are very different, and in their essence may be thought of as conflicting.[55] It has also been held that only Parliament can replace public interest immunity with a closed material procedure,[56] although it is not clear whether the parties could agree

---

[2012] A.C.D. 66 at [97]-[98]. See also *Kiani v Secretary of State for the Home Department* [2015] EWCA Civ 776; [2016] Q.B. 595 at [39]–[40].

[49]   *Belhaj v Straw* [2017] EWHC 1861 (QB) at [28].

[50]   Employment Tribunals (Constitutional and Rule of Procedure) Regulations 2004 (SI 2004/1861) Sch.1, para.54; see now Employment Tribunals (Constitution and Rule of Procedure) Regulations 2013 (2013/1237) Sch.1, reg.94.

[51]   Counter-Terrorism Act 2008 s.67 and Sch.7; CPR Pt 79; Terrorist Asset-Freezing etc Act 2010 s.28; Terrorism Prevention and Investigation Measures Act 2011 s.18 and Sch.4; and CPR Pt 80. Justice and Security Act 2013.

[52]   For discussion of the Bill as it passed through Parliament, see J. Jackson, "Justice, Security and the Right to a Fair Trial: Is the Use of Secret Evidence Ever Fair?" (2013) P.L. 720; A. Tomkins, "Justice and Security in the United Kingdom" (2014) 47 Israel L. Rev. 305. The central provision in the legislation is s.6, which sets out the conditions in which the court may make a declaration that the proceedings are proceedings in which the closed material application may be made to the court. For application of the legislation, see *CF v Security Service and Mohamed v Foreign and Commonwealth office* [2013] EWHC 3402 (QB); [2014] 1 W.L.R. 1699; *R. (on the application of Sarkandi) v Secretary of State for Foreign and Commonwealth Affairs* [2014] EWHC 2359 (Admin) at [30] (in deciding whether an application for public interest immunity rather than a closed material procedure was the more appropriate course, it was necessary to consider whether the claim could fairly be tried without the sensitive material; see now [2015] EWCA Civ 687).

[53]   J. Ip, "Al Rawi, Tariq, and the future of closed material procedures and special advocates" (2012) 75 M.L.R. 606, 608. For a comparative perspective, see A. Gray, "A Comparison and Critique of Closed Court Hearings" [2014] E. & P. 230.

[54]   For a useful summary, see K. Hughes, "The right to know the case against you in civil claims" (2012) 71 C.L.J. 21. See also K Clubb, "'Secret Justice': a critical review of closed material proceedings and the Justice and Security Act 2013" (2014) 2 *Covert Policing, Terrorism and Intelligence Law Review* 75.

[55]   *F v Security Service* [2013] EWHC 3402 (QB); [2014] 1 W.L.R. 1699 at [15] (Irwin J also referring to *Al Rawi v Security Service* [2012] 1 A.C. 531, in which Lord Dyson JSC described (at [41]) a closed procedure as "the very antithesis of PII").

[56]   *Al-Rawi v The Security Service* [2011] UKSC 34; [2012] 1 A.C. 452 (four of the justices in the majority concluded that there was no power at common law for a court to introduce a closed material procedure either as a substitute for or supplement to public interest immunity ([40]-[49] per Lord Dyson, [73] per Lord Hope, [81]-[82] per Lord Brown and [95] per Lord Kerr). In particular, Lord Phillips agreed that a court could not order a closed material procedure as a substitute for public interest immunity ([192]); *R. (on the application of British Sky Broadcasting Ltd) v Central Criminal Court* [2014] UKSC 17; [2014] A.C. 885 at [30]–[31]. See also: *AHK* [2012] EWHC 1117 (Admin); [2012] A.C.D. 66; *R. (on the application of Youssef) v Secretary of State for Foreign & Commonwealth Affairs* [2012] EWHC 2091 (Admin); [2012] Lloyd's Rep. F.C. 702. For discussion of

to conduct a closed material procedure,[57] The power to conduct a closed material procedure is necessarily implied into the statutory right to appeal decisions where a closed material procedure has been used.[58] It is not necessary that a public immunity process be concluded before a closed material procedure could be adopted.[59]

In general, when considering public interest immunity, the courts require that a balancing exercise be undertaken between, on the one hand the requirements of national security (or other public objective), and on the other hand, the interests of the individual in the fairness of the decision.[60] In a civil law context, in which the

8-011

Al-Rawi, see M Chamberlain, "Al-Rawi v Security Service and Home Office v Tariq" [2011] C.J.Q. 360; J Ip, "Al Rawi, Tariq, and the future of closed material procedures and special advocates" (2012) 75 M.L.R. 606. For useful discussion of the use of the closed material procedure, see M Fordham, "Secrecy, Security and Fair Trials: The UK Constitution in Transition" [2012] J.R. 187. For examples of the use (and attempted use) of the closed material procedure in practice, see also: *AHK* [2012] EWHC 1117 (Admin); [2012] A.C.D. 66; *R. (on the application of Youssef) v Secretary of State for Foreign & Commonwealth Affairs* [2012] EWHC 2091 (Admin); [2013] 2 W.L.R. 904; *R. (on the application Omar) v Foreign Secretary* [2012] EWHC 1737 (Admin); [2013] 1 All E.R. 161; see also [2013] EWCA Civ 118; *Secretary of State for the Home Department v CC and CF* [2014] EWCA Civ 559; *R. (on the application of Evans) v Secretary of State for Defence* [2010] EWHC 1445 (Admin); [2011] A.C.D. 11; *R. (on the application of B) v Westminster Magistrates' Court* [2014] UKSC 59; [2015] A.C. 1195 at [28]–[34] (holding that extradition proceedings did not fall within the special category of cases which justified or called for a further qualification of the principle of open justice). For comment, see T Garner, "Behind closed doors?" (2014) 164 *New Law Journal* 164, and Lord Kerr "'Only Parliament can do that'? The reliance of British jurisprudence on the common law in the national security context" (2015) 34 C.J.Q. 244. See also *R. (on the application of Immigration Law Practitioners' Association) v Tribunal Procedure Committee* [2016] EWHC 218 (Admin); [2016] 1 W.L.R. 3519 at [14] (finding statutory power to introduce a rule which permitted the First-tier Tribunal to give a direction prohibiting the disclosure of a document or information to a person, if satisfied that such disclosure would be likely to cause that person or some other person serious harm and having regard to the interests of justice that it was proportionate to give such a direction). It has also been held in *Da Costa v Sargaco* [2016] EWCA Civ 764; [2016] C.P. Rep. 40 at [59] that the decision in *Al-Rawi v Security Service* [2011] UKSC 34; [2012] 1 A.C. 531 was not authority for the proposition that, in order for a party to have a fair trial, there was an absolute requirement that he or she had to have the opportunity to be present throughout the hearing.

57 Contrast *AHK* [2012] EWHC 1117 (Admin); [2012] A.C.D. 66 at [97] (Ouseley J holding that there could be no such procedure on consent in naturalisation cases, save as in inherent in the public interest immunity process) and *Youssef* [2012] EWHC 2091 (Admin); [2013] 2 W.L.R. 904 at [67] (leaving the question open in a judicial review challenging a decision of the Foreign Secretary to list the claimant on a list of individuals designated as associated with Al-Qaida).

58 *Bank Mellat v HM Treasury (No.1)* [2013] UKSC 38; [2014] A.C. 700 at [37]–[43] (since s.40(2) of the 2005 Act provides that an appeal lies to the Supreme Court against "any" judgment of the Court of Appeal, that must extend to parts of a closed judgment as justice will not be able to be done in some cases if the appellate court cannot consider the closed material). For comment, see C. Sargeant, "Two Steps Backward, One Step Forward—the Cautionary Tale of Bank Mellat (No 1)" [2014] 3(1) C.J.I.C.L. 111.

59 In *CF v Security Service and Mohamed v Foreign and Commonwealth office* [2013] EWHC 3402 (QB); [2014] 1 W.L.R. 1699 the court made its first ruling on the use of the Justice and Security Act 2013, accepting that the government could make a closed material application to the court in a civil claim for damages. It was unnecessary that a public immunity process should be concluded before the court accepted a closed material application. The courts have criticised the uneasy coexistence of the closed material and public interest immunity procedures (see [2014] 1 W.L.R. 1699 at [56]). See also *R. (on the application of Sarkandi) v Secretary of State for Foreign and Commonwealth Affairs* [2014] EWHC 2359 (Admin) at [9] (it was agreed that CPR 82.23(4), which gives effect to s.6 of the legislation and which allows for a hearing in the absence of the specially represented party and the specially represented party's legal representative, ought to be interpreted as allowing such a hearing "so far as necessary"); see now [2015] EWCA Civ 687.

60 *R. v Chief Constable West Midlands, Ex p. Wiley* [1995] 1 A.C. 274, 281; *R. (on the application of Mohamed) v Secretary of State for Foreign and Commonwealth Affairs* [2009] EWHC 152 (Admin); [2009] 1 W.L.R. 2653 at [18] (referring to the balancing of the public interest in national security and the public interest in open justice, the rule of law and democratic accountability; see on appeal

liberty of the subject is not at stake, where a prima facie case of public interest immunity is established, a person who wishes to invite the court to inspect the material must show that it is likely to provide substantial support to his or her case.[61] Relevant factors in the balancing include the following: the seriousness of the claim for which disclosure is sought, whether or not the government is itself a party or alleged to have acted unconscionably, the relevance of the particular evidence to the dispute, taking account of other possible sources of evidence, the significance of the evidence to the case, the importance of the public interest claimed, the nature and degree of the risk that disclosure presents and the nature of the litigation.[62] The approach to be taken by the court is to decide whether the material over which public interest immunity is claimed is relevant and significant to the issues, and if so, whether it is covered by a public interest which would make it immune from disclosure in the absence of an overriding interest in its disclosure in the interests of justice.[63] Once the court has decided that it is relevant, and that it is properly covered by public interest immunity, it has to consider whether there are ways in which the salient points can be disclosed without any harm being done, for example by sharing the essence of the case or "gisting" or concession.[64] In short, any denial of disclosure or inspection must be limited to circumstances where such denial is strictly necessary, and where some restriction is necessary, consideration should be given to the use of redaction, confidentiality rings, anonymity orders and other steps to respect protected interests.[65]

8-012   Where an individual's fundamental rights are in issue, such as the right to life, to freedom,[66] or other rights protected by the ECHR,[67] the balancing exercise will

---

[2010] EWCA Civ 65; [2011] Q.B. 218). See also: *AHK* [2012] EWHC 1117 (Admin); [2012] A.C.D. 66 at [34]-[38]; and the guidance given by the court in *Commissioner of Policy of the Metropolis v Bangs* [2014] EWHC 546 (Admin); (2014) 178 J.P. 158 at [30]–[51], [59] (Beatson J noting at [40] that "[i]n all cases where the issue of PII is raised, what has to be balanced are the public interest which demands the material be withheld as against the public interest in the administration of justice that the individual and the court should have the fullest possible access to all relevant material"). See also *R. (on the application of X) v Chief Constable of Y* [2015] EWHC 484 (Admin) at [23]; *Worcestershire CC v HM Coroner for Worcestershire* [2013] EWHC 1711 (QB) at [65].

[61] *Al-Rawi* [2011] UKSC 34; [2012] 1 A.C. 531 at [102].

[62] *Al-Rawi* [2011] UKSC 34; [2012] 1 A.C. 531 at [102]; *AHK* [2012] EWHC 1117 (Admin); [2012] A.C.D. 66, in which it was held (at [34]-[38]); *Commissioner of Policy of the Metropolis v Bangs* [2014] EWHC 546 (Admin); (2014) 178 J.P. 158 at [58]. See also *R. v Ryan (Veronica)* [2014] NICA 72 at [16] (where convictions had been found to be unsafe on account of the prosecution having failed at trial to disclose certain confidential information, the setting aside of those convictions was all that was required to satisfy the public interest and it was not in the interests of fairness and justice for the court to provide a fully reasoned judgment on what material had been withheld, why it had been withheld, and by whom; the public interest would be undermined not advanced by the disclosure of material covered by the PII certificate which the court had found to be properly issued).

[63] However, it has been held that the appropriate question is not whether disclosure "would" result in the harm identified but rather whether there is a real risk of the harm occurring: *Commissioner of Policy of the Metropolis v Bangs* [2014] EWHC 546 (Admin) at [50].

[64] *AHK* [2012] EWHC 1117 (Admin); [2012] A.C.D. 66 at [33]; *Bank Mellat* [2013] 4 All E.R. 495 at [68]–[69]; *Bangs* [2014] EWHC 546 (Admin) at [34]–[35], [50]–[51]; *CF v Security Service* [2013] EWHC 3402 (QB); [2014] 1 W.L.R. 1699 at [45]; *Secretary of State for the Home Department v CC and CF* [2014] EWCA Civ 559 (withholding of Secretary of State's case on a potentially dispositive issue and total confinement of reasons for rejecting applicant's case on those issues to the closed judgment invalid).

[65] *R. (on the application of X) v Chief Constable of Y* [2015] EWHC 484 (Admin) at [40].

[66] *Chahal v Secretary of State for the Home Department* [1995] 1 W.L.R. 526; *Chahal* (1997) 23 E.H.R.R. 413.

[67] *Johnston v Constable of the Royal Ulster Constabulary* [1986] 3 C.M.L.R. 240 at 262 (decision of CJEU that provision of Northern Ireland Sex Discrimination Order requiring Tribunals to treat a

be especially important.[68] If Convention rights are engaged, the ECtHR has observed that:

"The concepts of lawfulness and the rule of law in a democratic society also require that measures affecting fundamental human rights must be subject to some form of adversarial proceedings before an independent body competent to review the reasons for the decision and relevant evidence, if need be with appropriate procedural limitations on the use of classified information."[69]

The procedural protection must be practical and effective.[70] In *Chahal v United Kingdom*,[71] the ECtHR held unanimously that the failure of the English courts to carry out or supervise effectively a balancing test (weighing national security considerations) was a breach of ECHR art.5(4), since Mr Chahal's deprivation of liberty had not been subject to any effective judicial control. The court considered that it must be possible to employ techniques which both accommodate legitimate security concerns about the nature and sources of intelligence information and yet accord the individual a substantial measure of procedural justice.[72]

Where the government certifies that information cannot be disclosed in the interests of national security, the complete integrity of any public interest immunity certificates and the schedules attached to them, signed by Ministers of the Crown, is absolutely essential as the courts must be able to have complete confidence in the credibility and reliability of such certificates and schedules.[73]   **8-013**

There has been extensive case law on the use of closed material procedures in recent years.[74] In sum, the proceedings involve an "open" and "closed" element. All of the material is presented to the court and the special advocate, while the individual and his representative are only present at the open hearings and only have access to the open hearings.[75] It is accepted that the closed material procedure is a serious departure from the fundamental principles of open justice and natural justice, but that it is a departure authorised by Parliament in defined circumstances for the protection of national security.[76] It has been described as "certainly an   **8-014**

---

national security certificate as conclusive evidence that conditions for derogating from the principle of equal treatment were fulfilled were contrary to the provision of effective judicial control laid down in art.6 of the Equal Treatment Directive; the court relying upon principles of the ECHR); *IR (Sri Lanka) v SSHD* [2011] EWCA Civ 704; [2012] 1 W.L.R. 232 (ECHR art.8); *Naik* [2011] EWCA Civ 1546; [2012] Imm. A.R. 381 (ECHR art.10).

[68] For discussion of the difference in the balancing in the civil and criminal context, see *Commissioner of Policy of the Metropolis v Bangs* [2014] EWHC 546 at [39]–[40].

[69] *Al-Nashif v Bulgaria* (2003) 36 E.H.R.R. 37 at [123]. See also D Heaton, "Carnduff, Al Rawi, the 'unfairness' of public interest immunity and sharp procedure" (2015) 34 Civil Justice Quarterly 191.

[70] *Turek v Slovakia* (2007) 44 E.H.R.R. 43 at [113]. See also: *Lupsa v Romania* (2008) 46 E.H.R.R. 36 at [34]-[38]; *Liu v Russia* (2008) 47 E.H.R.R. 33 at [59]-[62] and *CG v Bulgaria* (2008) 47 E.H.R.R. 51 at [40].

[71] *Chahal* (1997) 23 E.H.R.R. 413.

[72] *Chahal* (1997) 23 E.H.R.R. 413 at [131].

[73] *R. (on the application of Al-Sweady) v Secretary of State for Defence* [2009] EWHC 1687 (Admin) at [14], [45] (also deploring the "lamentable history" of systemic and individual failures underpinning the certificates and schedules under consideration).

[74] For an interesting discussion of the difference between closed material procedures and in camera proceedings, see *Guardian News and Media Ltd v Incedal* [2014] EWCA Crim 1861 at [11]–[12] (the former involving a departure from natural justice and the latter a departure from open justice).

[75] For a useful description of the procedure, see P. Craig, *Administrative Law*, 8th edn (2016), para.13-015.

[76] *R. (on the application of Sarkandi) v Secretary of State for Foreign and Commonwealth Affairs* [2015] EWCA Civ 687 at [57]. See also *McGartland v Attorney General* [2015] EWCA Civ 686 at [34]; *Guardian News and Media Ltd v Incedal* [2014] EWCA Crim 1861. It has been observed that

exceptional procedure", which "in the nature of things one would expect ... to be used only rarely".[77] However, the relevant statutory provisions are not to be given a narrow or restrictive construction, save for any reading down that may be required, in accordance with the terms of the statute itself, for compliance with art.6 ECHR.[78]

8-015   It is also important to be clear that, where a closed material procedure is at issue, there is no question of the court ordering disclosure. Rather, the court should ensure first that there remains no material which can be disclosed without harm to national security. It must then identify what material needs to be disclosed for the purpose of ECHR art.6. It then refuses permission to withhold that material, reading the clear obligations to the contrary as subject to the requirement that they do not apply if disclosure is necessary for the purposes of art.6. This does not alter the right of the Secretary of State to refuse to disclose the material. Rather, the Secretary of State is entitled to decide not to disclose that material, but he cannot then rely on it, whether the case is continued in closed material procedure or not.[79]

8-016   Where a declaration is sought pursuant to s.6 of the Justice and Security Act 2013 for use of a closed material procedure, the court cannot consider an application unless satisfied that, before making it, the Secretary of State had considered whether to make a claim for public interest immunity in relation to the material on which the application was based.[80] The court has to be satisfied that a party to the proceedings would be required to disclose sensitive, or national security, material to another person, and that it is in the interests of the fair and effective administration of justice in the proceedings to make the declaration. It is also necessary for the court to consider other possible ways of proceeding apart from making a s.6 declaration.[81] For example, sharing the essence of the case or "gisting" may not be appropriate where the detail contained in documentation is important or where use of a confidentiality ring is not likely to be a satisfactory method of dealing with sensitive information.[82] There is no requirement for a court to decide the application by reference to the sensitive material relating to issues of central relevance or to find that the material is highly relevant.[83] It has also been held that a s.6 application is not an appropriate situation in which to consider to the rationality of a decision of the Secretary of State not to pursue a public interest immunity application; a s.6 ap-

---

open justice "is an important principle of the common law" but it is not absolute and must "sometimes bow to other rights such as the right to life, or other elements of the public interest such as national security": *R. (on the application of Yam) v Central Criminal Court* [2014] EWHC 3558 (Admin); [2015] 3 W.L.R. 1050 (affirmed on appeal in [2015] UKSC 76; [2016] A.C. 771).

[77]   *R. (on the application of Sarkandi) v Secretary of State for Foreign and Commonwealth Affairs* [2015] EWCA Civ 687 at [58]. See also *McGartland v Attorney General* [2015] EWCA Civ 686 at [35].

[78]   *R. (on the application of Sarkandi) v Secretary of State for Foreign and Commonwealth Affairs* [2015] EWCA Civ 687 at [58]. See also *McGartland v Attorney General* [2015] EWCA Civ 686 at [35].

[79]   *K, A and B v Secretary of State for Defence, Secretary of State for Foreign and Commonwealth Affairs* [2017] EWHC 830 (Admin) at [11].

[80]   See *R. (on the application of Sarkandi) v Secretary of State for Foreign and Commonwealth Affairs* [2014] EWHC 2359 (Admin) at [30] (in deciding whether an application for public interest immunity rather than a closed material procedure was the more appropriate course, it was necessary to consider whether the claim could fairly be tried without the sensitive material; see now [2015] EWCA Civ 687). For an example in the immigration context, see: *BB, PP, W, U v Secretary of State for the Home Department* [2015] EWCA Civ 9.

[81]   *Re Gallagher's Application for Judicial Review* [2016] NIQB 95 at [33]-[59].

[82]   *Re Gallagher's Application* [2016] NIQB 95 at [46], [52]–[57].

[83]   *Belhaj v Straw* [2017] EWHC 1861 (QB) at [37].

plication is not the occasion for a judicial review of the decision of the Secretary of State.[84]

The extent of disclosure required will be linked to the requirements of the specific right at issue.[85] It has been observed that there is a spectrum of cases and a spectrum of disclosure rather than a hierarchy.[86] Where liberty is at stake, and an individual is at risk of consequences as severe as those normally imposed under a control order, for example, it has been held that non-disclosure in the context of a closed material procedure cannot go so far as to deny a party knowledge of the essence of the case against him. In particular, as was held in *Secretary of State for the Home Department v F (No.3)*,[87] disclosure must be such as to enable the individual to give effective instructions in relation to any allegations. Thus, there is a minimum degree of fairness that must exist if the whole process is not to be regarded as so fundamentally flawed that it contravenes the rule of law. In *F*, Lord Phillips noted that there were strong policy considerations that supported a rule that a trial procedure could never be considered fair if a party to it was kept in ignorance of the case against him. The first was that there would be many cases where it was impossible for the court to be confident that disclosure would make no difference. Further, there would be feelings of resentment if a party to legal proceedings was placed in a position where it was impossible for him to influence the result. Indeed, if the wider public were to have confidence in the justice system, they needed to be able to see that justice was done rather than being asked to take it on trust.[88]

Even if no Convention right is engaged, an individual is entitled to expect consistency between the closed and open cases before the court.[89] However, ECHR art.6 does not require "gisting" in all cases without exception.[90] In summary, the

8-017

8-018

---

[84] *Belhaj* [2017] EWHC 1861 (QB) at [52].

[85] See, e.g. *IR (Sri Lanka)* [2011] EWCA Civ 704; [2012] 1 W.L.R. 232 at [20] (the procedural protection required by ECHR art.8 was limited and did not equiparate with the procedural protections guaranteed pursuant to ECHR arts 5 or 6).

[86] *K, A and B v Secretary of State for Defence, Secretary of State for Foreign and Commonwealth Affairs* [2017] EWHC 830 (Admin) at [12].

[87] *F (No.3)* [2009] UKHL 28; [2010] 2 A.C. 269 at [59]. See also: *Secretary of State for the Home Department v AT* [2012] EWCA Civ 42 at [50]-[51]; *AH v Secretary of State for the Home Department* [2011] EWCA Civ 787; *Bank Mellat v HM Treasury (No.1)* [2013] UKSC 38; [2013] 4 All E.R. 495; *Secretary of State for the Home Department v CC and CF* [2014] EWCA Civ 559 at [16] (use of closed material procedure in abuse of process proceedings against the Secretary of State which would have led to quashing of control orders involved "a radical departure from procedural and constitutional normality" as the closed material procedure limited the obligation of disclosure and permitted much of the detail to be dealt with only in a closed judgment). See also *R. (on the application of the Immigration Law Practitioners' Association) v Tribunal Procedure Committee* [2016] EWHC 218 (Admin); [2016] 1 W.L.R. 3519 (use of a closed material procedure in the context of the First-tier Tribunal was lawful as it could only be ordered where the judge considered it to be proportionate and it was improbable that a judge would not properly direct himself as to the requirements of fairness in making this assessment. Nonetheless, the court suggested that the very existence of the power was troubling, and that this was an issue that the Chamber President or the Senior President of Tribunals would wish to consider issuing guidance on).

[88] *F* [2009] UKHL 28; [2010] 2 A.C. 269 at [63]-[64]. See also: *Secretary of State for the Home Department v CD* [2011] EWHC 2087 (Admin) (sufficient disclosure to enable effective instructions to be given). For discussion generally on the risks of secret evidence, see G. Van Harten, "Weaknesses of Adjudication in the Face of Secret Evidence" (2009) 13 E. & P. 1.

[89] *SS (Libya) v Secretary of State for the Home Department* [2011] EWCA Civ 1547 (asylum) at [58].

[90] *Tariq v Home Office* [2011] UKSC 35; [2012] 1 A.C. 452 at [138]. See also: *AM v Secretary of State for the Home Department* [2011] EWHC 2486 (Admin) (no breach of ECHR art.6 where the court had kept ECHR art.6 rights under constant review, the Secretary of State and the special advocate agreed that there had been sufficient disclosure to enable instructions to be given and at issue were refusals to modify a non-derogating control order regulating, inter alia, internet access); *R. (on the*

requirements of art.6 depend on context and all the circumstances of the case, such as: whether the case involves the liberty of the subject; whether the claimant has been provided with a degree of information as to the basis for the decision; whether there is real scope for the special advocate to test the issues without obtaining instructions on the facts, and the extent of ECHR art.6 rights applicable.

8-019   In terms of specific examples of what is required, it has been held that the standard in *F (No.3)*, rather than any lower standard, applies where financial restrictions had been imposed which had an utterly damaging effect on an Iranian bank's ability to function.[91] In a security vetting case, the Strasbourg jurisprudence indicates that an individual is not entitled to full ECHR art.6 rights if to accord him such rights would jeopardise the efficacy of the vetting regime itself.[92] It has also been confirmed that, in a case not directly affecting the liberty of the subject, there is no irreducible minimum of disclosure or necessary minimum revelation by summary or gist of the defendant's case, which the court would require despite the consequences for national security.[93] Refusal by the English courts to permit disclosure to the ECtHR of material heard in camera during a murder trial does not breach the courts' obligations under ECHR art.6.[94] Meanwhile, where Afghan nationals brought claims for protection, relocation and compensation related to their alleged roles as covert human intelligence sources for the UK in Afghanistan, it was held that the claims were based on public law obligations in relation to the risk of harm to life and limb. While this was not at the level of control orders of asset freezing, and *F* disclosure did not therefore apply, it was at the higher end of the spectrum when it came to procedural fairness. It was not the case that there could be no disclosure which might harm national security; rather a balance would have to be struck. For example, where there was a complaint about the existence of a policy or a duty to have a policy, that could be handled by a special advocate; the claimants could themselves give evidence about the risks they faced; meanwhile, a claimant could not receive disclosure of the essence of the case if it would jeopardise the efficacy of the particular regime itself.[95]

8-020   In principle, a protective costs order may be made where an individual who brought a claim had been accused of terrorism and reliance was placed on closed evidence, rendering it impossible for him to determine the merits of his claim.[96] The

application of A) v Director of Establishments of Security Service [2009] UKSC 12; [2010] 2 A.C. 1 at [30]; *Bank Mellat (No.1)* [2013] UKSC 38; [2014] A.C. 700 at [5]–[6]; *Secretary of State for the Home Department v CC and CF* [2014] EWCA Civ 559 at [43]; *R. (on the application of X) v Chief Constable of Y Police* [2015] EWHC 484 (Admin) at [35] (while the art.6 right to a fair trial is a powerful factor in the balancing exercise the court is to undertake when determining a claim for public interest immunity, that factor is not decisive of the question of whether a party is entitled to disclosure of the gist of allegations against him, being capable of being overridden by other compelling factors). Contrast *R. (on the application of Wright) v Secretary of State for Health)* [2009] UKHL 3; [2009] 1 A.C. 739 (art.6 required the right to make representations prior to being listed as unsuitable to work with children). D Kelman, "Closed trials and secret allegations: an analysis of the 'gisting' requirement" (2016) (80) J of Criminal L 264.

91   *Bank Mellat v HM Treasury* [2015] EWCA Civ 1052; [2016] 1 W.L.R. 1187.
92   *Kiani v The Secretary of State for the Home Department* [2015] EWCA Civ 776; [2016] Q.B. 595 at [23].
93   *CF v Ministry of Defence* [2014] EWHC 3171 at [23] (noting that as the case before the court was a claim for compensation, it was in a category where the court must conduct a balancing exercise, bearing in mind the competing principles of maximising the fairness of the trial and protecting the public through the preservation of national security). *Khaled v Secretary of State for Foreign and Commonwealth Affairs* [2017] EWHC 1422 (Admin).
94   *R. (on the application of Yam) v Central Criminal Court* [2015] UKSC 76; [2016] A.C. 771.
95   *K v Secretary of State for Defence* [2017] EWHC 830 (Admin) at [24]-[27].
96   *Begg v HM Treasury* [2016] EWCA Civ 568; [2016] C.P. Rep. 39 at [19].

granting of such an order is dependent on satisfaction of four conditions: first, the case has to be of real benefit to the individual bringing it; secondly, the applicant has to be able to assess the prospects of success in the ordinary way; thirdly, having regard to the individual's financial resources and the amount of likely costs, it has to be fair and just to make the order; and fourthly, it has to be shown that if the order is not made, the applicant would probably discontinue the proceedings and would be acting reasonably in doing so. To avoid unfairness, the second condition must be considered prior to the making of disclosure, since otherwise, an individual would be required to embark on an appeal without the protection of a protective costs order, at least until the Treasury had served its evidence, including any gisting of the closed material.[97]

Consideration has also been given recently to the use of a closed material **8-021** procedure in the appeal context. In *Bank Mellat v HM Treasury (No.2)*, the Supreme Court concluded that, while the Supreme Court rules contained no express power to conduct a closed material procedure, it nonetheless had the power to adopt such a procedure in an appeal under the Counter Terrorism Act 2008 if justice required it.[98] The principles governing an appeal against an open and closed judgment have also been considered.[99] An appellate court should only be asked to conduct a closed hearing if it is strictly necessary for fairly determining the appeal, so that any party who is proposing to invite the appellate court to take such a course should consider very carefully whether it really is necessary to go outside the open material in order for the appeal to be fairly heard.[100] If the appellate court decides that it should look at closed material, careful consideration should be given by the advocates and the court to the question whether it would nonetheless be possible to avoid a closed substantive hearing.[101]

It has also been held that where there has been an open and a closed hearing and **8-022** a judge gives an open and a closed judgment, it is highly desirable in the open judgment to identify every conclusion in that judgment which has been reached in whole or in part in the light of points made in evidence referred to in the closed judgment and state that this is what has been done.[102] In addition, where closed material has been relied on, the judge should, in the open judgment, say as much as can properly be said about that closed material.[103]

Overall, if a court decides that a closed material procedure appears to be neces- **8-023** sary, the parties should try and agree a way of avoiding or minimising the extent of a closed hearing.[104] If there is a closed hearing, the lawyers representing the party who is relying on the closed material, as well as that party itself, should ensure that, well in advance of the hearing of the appeal: (i) the excluded party is given as much information as possible about any closed documents (including any closed judgment) relied on; and (ii) the special advocates are given as full information as possible as to the nature of the passages relied on in such closed documents and the arguments which will be advanced in relation thereto.[105] Appellate courts should be robust about acceding to applications to go into closed session or even to look at

---

97 *Begg v HM Treasury* [2016] EWCA Civ 568; [2016] C.P. Rep. 39 at [27].
98 *Bank Mellat v HM Treasury (No.2)* [2013] UKSC 39; [2014] A.C. 700 at [62].
99 *Bank Mellat (No.1)* [2013] UKSC 38; [2014] A.C. 700.
100 *Bank Mellat (No.1)* [2013] UKSC 38; [2014] A.C. 700 at [70].
101 *Bank Mellat (No.1)* [2013] UKSC 38; [2014] A.C. 700 at [71].
102 *Bank Mellat (No.1)* [2013] UKSC 38; [2014] A.C. 700 at [68].
103 *Bank Mellat (No.1)* [2013] UKSC 38; [2014] A.C. 700 at [69].
104 *Bank Mellat (No.1)* [2013] UKSC 38; [2014] A.C. 700 at [72].
105 *Bank Mellat (No.1)* [2013] UKSC 38; [2014] A.C. 700 at [73].

closed material. Given that the issues will have already been debated and adjudicated upon, there must be very few appeals where any sort of closed material procedure is likely to be necessary. And, in those few cases where it may be necessary, it is hard to believe that an advocate seeking to rely on closed material or seeking a closed hearing, could be unable to articulate convincing reasons in open court for taking such a course.[106]

8-024   Meanwhile, in ZZ, the CJEU has suggested that art.47 of the Charter of Fundamental Rights of the European Union imposes an obligation to inform the person precisely and in full of the grounds on which a decision is based, and to disclose related evidence limited to that which is strictly necessary; in any event, the person must be informed of the essence of the grounds which takes due account of the necessary confidentiality of the evidence.[107] It has been observed that the distinctions drawn in ZZ may on occasion be difficult to apply in practice, not least because the effectiveness of disclosure may depend on the level of generality with which the grounds are stated. It is also the case that the grounds are highly fact-specific.[108]

The role of special advocates in closed material procedures

8-025   In a closed material procedure, an individual is often allocated a special advocate to appear on his behalf who would know what was relied on by the security services but could not take instructions from the suspect in relation to the matters of which he was aware.[109] The special advocate could, however, cross examine the witnesses relied on by the security services. The courts have endorsed the sufficiency of the safeguards provided by special advocates as follows: (1) there is no conflict of interest arising out the appointment of special advocates by the Attorney General as this is purely formal as special advocates are appointed from the independent bar or solicitor advocates on the basis of open competition[110]; (2) there is also no conflict

---

[106] *Bank Mellat (No.1)* [2013] UKSC 38; [2014] A.C. 700 at [74].

[107] *ZZ (France) v Secretary of State for the Home Department* (C–300/11) EU:C:2013:363 at [68] (see generally also [53]–[69] for discussion on the EU position). See also *Bank Mellat v HM Treasury* [2014] EWHC 3631 (Admin); [2015] H.R.L.R. 6 at [19] (describing ZZ as a "bad decision") (judgment affirmed without considering EU law in [2015] EWCA Civ 1052; [2016] 1 W.L.R. 1187). See also *S1 v Secretary of State for the Home Department* [2016] EWCA Civ 560 (finding that the disclosure made satisfied the "essence of the grounds" obligations, albeit that EU law did not apply). It has also been observed that, while the right in art.41 of the Charter of Fundamental Rights of the European Union reflects a general principle of Union law, Member States are entitled to withhold disclosure, and hence restrict the right to make representations, on grounds of national security: *R. (AZ) v Secretary of State for the Home Department* [2015] EWHC 3695 (Admin) (involving refusal of a travel document which was not as serious as interference with the free movement of EU nationals or refoulement).

[108] *ZZ (France) v Secretary of State for the Home Department (No.2)* [2014] EWCA Civ 7; [2014] Q.B. 820 at [24]–[26] (appeal dismissed as being academic: [2017] EWCA Civ 133); see also *R. (on the application of XH) v Secretary of State for the Home Department* [2017] EWCA Civ 41; [2017] 2 W.L.R. 1437 at [131].

[109] The role of special advocate was created by the Special Immigration Appeals Commission Act 1997, which established SIAC (a superior court of record). See *A v Secretary of State for the Home Department* [2005] UKHL 71; [2006] 2 A.C. 221 and House of Commons Constitutional Affairs Committee, *The Operation of the Special Immigration Appeals Commission (SIAC) and the use of Special Advocates*. HC Paper No. 323-I (Session 2004/05). See generally M. Chamberlain, "Special Advocates and Procedural Fairness in Closed Proceedings" (2009) 28 C.J.Q. 314; J. Ip, "The Rise and Spread of the Special Advocate" [2008] P.L. 717; "Al Rawi, Tariq, and the Future of Closed Material Procedures and Special Advocates" (2012) 75 M.L.R. 606; C. Murphy, "Counter-Terrorism and the Culture of Legality: The Case of Special Advocates" (2013) 24 K.L.J 19.

[110] *Tariq* [2011] UKSC 35; [2012] 1 A.C. 452 at [47].

of interest arising from the support given to special advocates by the Special Advocates Support Office ("SASO") given that SASO "operates for all practical purposes as a separate unit, with an established Chinese wall arrangement dividing it from the rest of the Treasury Solicitor's Department"[111]; and (3) there is no insufficiency in the safeguards due to the lack of supervision and guidance for special advocates, given that special advocates are experienced independent practitioners, accustomed to taking difficult decisions.[112] However, although the availability of a special advocate is certainly better than no protection and there have been cases where they have secured the release of those who are detained, they clearly act under a significant disadvantage. So great is the disadvantage, the question arises whether that process is so flawed that it cannot amount even to the restricted form of hearing that Parliament intended in providing for the special advocate procedure.

The use of special advocates will also vary according to context.[113] In control **8-026** order proceedings (now replaced by terrorism prevention and investigation measures, in respect of which the procedural fairness requirements are similar), the House of Lords has held that the special advocate procedure will not in all cases constitute a sufficient safeguard against the unfairness which results from the non-disclosure of key evidence; and consequently, the judge's powers of non-disclosure do not extend "to withholding particulars of reasons or evidence where to do so would deprive the [subject] of a fair trial".[114] In the case of *A v United Kingdom*,[115] the Grand Chamber of the European Court of Human Rights made it clear that non-disclosure could not go so far as to deny a party knowledge of the essence of the case against him, at least where he is at risk of consequences as severe as those normally imposed under a control order. That decision established that the subject has to be given sufficient information about the allegations against him to enable him to give effective instructions in relation to those allegations. Provided that this requirement is satisfied, there could be a fair trial notwithstanding that the subject is not provided with the detail or the sources of the evidence forming the basis of the allegations. Where, however, the open material consists purely of general assertions and the case against the subject is based solely or to a decisive degree on closed materials, the requirements of a fair trial will not be satisfied, however cogent the case based on the closed materials might be. The Strasbourg Court accepted that the judge is in the best position to form a judgment about the extent to which the subject is disadvantaged by the lack of disclosure or to put it the other way, the proceedings over which he is presiding afford a sufficient measure of procedural protection.[116] Overall, the circumstances of an

---

[111] *Tariq* [2011] UKSC 35; [2012] 1 A.C. 452 at [50]-[54].

[112] *Tariq* [2011] UKSC 35; [2012] 1 A.C. 452 at [55].

[113] *MH v Secretary of State for the Home Department* [2009] EWCA Civ 287; [2009] 1 W.L.R. 2049 at [45]-[47]; *ZZ v Secretary of State for the Home Department* [2014] EWCA Civ 7; [2014] 2 W.L.R. 791 at [37], [39].

[114] *MB v Secretary of State for the Home Department: AF v Secretary of the Home Department* [2007] UKHL 46; [2008] 1 A.C. 440 at [34]-[35] (Lord Bingham); [65]-[67], [72] (Baroness Hale); [81]-[85] (Lord Carswell); [90] (Lord Brown). The reading down of the (now repealed) Prevention of Terrorism Act 2005 in *MB* was upheld in *F (No.3)* [2009] UKHL 28; [2010] 2 A.C. 269 at [67]. See also: Terrorism Prevention and Investigation Measures Act 2011 and on the application of ECHR art.6: *Secretary of State for the Home Department v BM* [2012] EWHC 714 (Admin); [2012] 1 W.L.R. 2734 at [2] and [21].

[115] *A v United Kingdom (3455/05)* (2009) 49 E.H.R.R. 29.

[116] *A v United Kingdom (3455/05)* (2009) 49 E.H.R.R. 29; 26 B.H.R.C. 1 at [220]. See also *F (No.3)* [2009] UKHL 28; [2010] 2 A.C. 269 (Lord Phillips noting that "with the assistance of the dedicated special advocates that are available and the input of judges with the ability and experience of those

individual case will be closely scrutinised and the tribunal will want to be satisfied that there are no circumstances which would justify greater protection being provided to the suspect; the balance is a fine one.

8-027   In the context of financial restrictions, the relationship between the position under Union law and the standard applied pursuant to the Convention has also been explored.[117] It has been suggested that there is difficulty in discerning that there was any practical difference between the requirement under Union law, as identified in the ZZ case,[118] that the essence of the grounds be disclosed, and the Convention position. However, it has been observed that it may be that the requirement under Union law to inform the person concerned of the essence of the grounds, limited to that which was strictly necessary, required only limited disclosure and set a standard which might be below that set by the Convention, as applied in *F (No.3)*.[119]

8-028   In citizenship cases, where an individual is refused citizenship on the ground that he is not of "good character" and the Secretary of State refuses to give full reasons or to disclose relevant material which he took into account in reaching his decision, it is not the case that a special advocate must always be appointed. Rather, a special advocate should be appointed where it is just to do so, having regard to the requirement that proceedings must be fair to the claimant and to the Secretary of State.[120] In such cases the Secretary of State should consider with counsel, who should consider the issue dispassionately, whether it is appropriate for the trial judge to have the assistance of a special advocate. A special advocate should be appointed where it is just, and therefore necessary, to do so in order for the issues to be determined fairly. Where the material is not to be disclosed, or full reasons are not to be given to the claimant, there are only two possibilities, namely that the judge will determine the issues by looking at the documents himself, or that he will do so with the assistance of a special advocate. The appointment of a special advocate is likely to be just where there might be significant issues or a significant number of documents. Everything depends on the circumstances of the particular case, but it is important to have in mind the importance of the decision from the claimant's point of view, the difficulties facing the claimant in effectively challenging the case against him in open court and whether the assistance of a special advocate would or might assist him in meeting the case against him and assist the court in arriving at a fair conclusion. If the judge decides to read the documents, in order to consider whether or not a special advocate should be appointed, the Secretary of State should not make oral or written submissions but should include a short note merely identifying the key pages or documents in order to direct the

---

who hear these cases, the approach approved by this House in *MB*, including the 'makes no difference' principle, could have been applied without significant risk of producing unjust results": at [62]); *Secretary of State for the Home Department v N* [2009] EWHC 1966 (Admin) at [3] (art.6 was violated where non-disclosure went so far as to deny N of the "essence" of the case against him); *Secretary of State v AF* [2010] EWHC 42 (Admin); [2010] A.C.D. 47 (control orders quashed where the controlee did not have the possibility to challenge the allegations against him). See also *CC and CF* [2014] EWCA Civ 559; *ZZ (France)* (C–300/11) EU:C:2013:363; *ZZ (France) (No 2)* [2014] 2 W.L.R. 791.

[117] *Bank Mellat v HM Treasury* [2014] EWHC 3631 (Admin); [2015] H.R.L.R. 6 (judgment affirmed without considering Union law in [2015] EWCA Civ 1052; [2016] 1 W.L.R. 1187).

[118] *ZZ (France) (No.2)* [2014] Q.B. 820 at [24]-[26] (appeal dismissed as being academic: [2017] EWCA Civ 133); see also *R. (on the application of XH) v Secretary of State for the Home Department* [2017] EWCA Civ 41; [2017] 2 W.L.R. 1437 at [131].

[119] *Bank Mellat v HM Treasury* [2014] EWHC 3631 (Admin); [2015] H.R.L.R. 6 at [16]. See also [19] (observing that *ZZ* was "*a bad decision*") (judgment affirmed without considering Union law in [2015] EWCA Civ 1052; [2016] 1 W.L.R. 1187).

[120] *MH* [2009] EWCA Civ 287; [2009] 1 W.L.R. 2049 at [35].

judge to the relevant material and briefly stating the grounds upon which it was said that the material should not be disclosed. The judge should then decide how to proceed in the light of all the circumstances of the case and after hearing oral open submissions.[121]

In the deportation context, it has been held that where safety on return is in is-   **8-029**
sue, it is not likely to be critically important for the special advocate advancing the case of the deportee to obtain input from him in relation to the evidence which the receiving state wishes to remain closed. It is not the case that the deportee does not know the case against him; rather the deportee will normally be aware of the facts which create the risk of a violation of his human rights on return to his own country, and indeed he will be relying on them to establish the risk that he faces on his return. His situation is not that of an individual who is unaware of the case that is made against him.[122]

In the employment context, it has been held that a closed material procedure is   **8-030**
necessary where there is a manifest need to preserve secrecy in security vetting and that special advocates provide sufficient safeguards to an individual challenging a decision to revoke his security clearance in proceedings in the Employment Tribunal.[123]

In the context of parole, in *Roberts v Parole Board*, the House of Lords decided   **8-031**
by a majority that the special advocate provided just sufficient protection to avoid it being necessary to prevent the Parole Board relying on closed material when determining whether a murderer who had served his tariff should be refused parole.[124]

Detailed consideration has also been given to the extent to which the Secretary   **8-032**
of State had to provide disclosure of closed material to special advocates appointed to represent the interests of claimants in proceedings before the Special Immigration Appeals Commission.[125] It was held that a complete understanding of the issues involved was required by the commission and a recognition that the inability of the special advocates to take instructions from the interested parties on the closed-procedure material heightened the obligation to review that material with care.[126] That limitation on the ability to have a complete understanding of the position from the interested parties' perspective, to contrast with the Secretary of State's arguments, was regarded as equally important in respect of the issue of the material which should be available.[127] The court held, however, that to require disclosure

---

[121] *MH* [2009] EWCA Civ 287; [2009] 1 W.L.R. 2049 at [37].

[122] *RB (Algeria) v Secretary of State for the Home Department* [2009] UKHL 10; [2010] 2 A.C. 110; *Re CM (EM Country Guidance: Disclosure: Zimbabwe)* [2013] EWCA Civ 1303; [2014] Imm. A.R. 326.

[123] *Tariq* [2011] UKSC 35; [2012] 1 A.C. 452 at [47]-[55] and [72]-[83].

[124] *Roberts v Parole Board* [2005] UKHL 45; [2005] 2 A.C. 738. See also *Gregson v Parole Board* [2009] EWHC 3639 (Admin) at [29] (the Parole Board erred in not directly addressing the crucial issue of whether it was fair for it to have had regard to closed material in the probation officer's report without giving the applicant an opportunity to answer it); *R. (on the application of Rowe) v Parole Board* [2012] EWHC 1272 (Admin); *Sher v Chief Constable of Greater Manchester* [2010] EWHC 1859 (Admin); [2011] 2 All E.R. 364. See also *R. (on the application of the Immigration Law Practitioners'Association) v Tribunal Procedure Committee* [2016] EWHC 218 (Admin); [2016] 1 W.L.R. 3519 (referring to the *Roberts* guidance on the minimum requirement of a fair hearing in the context of rules of the First-tier Tribunal).

[125] *Secretary of State for the Home Department v Special Immigration Appeals Commission* [2015] EWHC 681 (Admin).

[126] *Secretary of State for the Home Department v Special Immigration Appeals Commission* [2015] EWHC 681 (Admin) at [28].

[127] *Secretary of State for the Home Department v Special Immigration Appeals Commission* [2015]

of all the material the summary writer could have accessed, took the investigation far beyond a review. The disclosure had to be sufficient to permit challenge, if appropriate, to the underlying rationality of any part of the decision and its reasoning. Therefore, the Secretary of State should disclose the underlying material relied on by the summary writer in identifying facts or reaching a conclusion. That was consistent with the obligation to ensure that the material enabled a proper determination of the proceedings as required under r.4(3).[128] It was also observed that this level of disclosure was in addition to, and had to be distinguished from, the Secretary of State's duty of candour, and as a matter of practice the Secretary of State should require the material used to establish the facts to be annexed to, or identified by, the summary so that appropriate disclosure to the special advocates could proceed without difficulty.[129]

Other public interests

8-033   Modifications of the disclosure requirements of procedural fairness have been deemed acceptable for the protection of other facets of the public interest, including: the internal workings of the decision-maker[130]; the sources of information leading to the detection of crime or other wrongdoing[131]; sensitive intelligence information[132]; and other information supplied in confidence for the purposes of government,[133] or the discharge of certain public functions.[134] The conception that secrecy

---

EWHC 681 (Admin) at [29].

[128] *Secretary of State for the Home Department v Special Immigration Appeals Commission* [2015] EWHC 681 (Admin) at [34].

[129] *Secretary of State for the Home Department v Special Immigration Appeals Commission* [2015] EWHC 681 (Admin) at [34].

[130] *R. (on the application of Edwards) v Environment Agency (No.2)* [2006] EWCA Civ 877; [2007] Env. L.R. 9 at [91]; *Bushell v Secretary of State for the Environment* [1981] A.C. 75. See *R. (on the application of Bonhoeffer) v General Medical Council* [2011] EWHC 1585 (Admin); [2012] I.R.L.R. 37 at [59] (holding that there was nothing in *Bushell* which supported the proposition that there may not be circumstances in which fairness requires that a person facing serious charges which amount to criminal offences in disciplinary proceedings should be afforded the opportunity to cross-examine the witness or witnesses upon whose evidence the charges depended).

[131] *R. v Gaming Board for Great Britain Ex p. Benaim and Khaida* [1970] 2 Q.B. 417; *R. v Lewes Justices Ex p. Home Secretary* [1973] A.C. 388 (names of informants, details of information supplied to police and content of police reports in respect of applicants for gaming club consents); *R. (on the application of X) v Chief Constable of Y* [2015] EWHC 484 (Admin) at [24] (referring to the "well established public interest in protecting the identity of policy informants"). See also *Shah v HSBC Private Bank (UK) Ltd* [2011] EWCA Civ 1154; [2012] Lloyd's Rep. F.C. 105 at [49]-[51] (the issue of public interest immunity did not arise as a request for the names of employees who had reported suspicions of money laundering was based on speculation). cf. *R. v Chief Constable of the West Midland Police Ex p. Wiley* [1995] 1 A.C. 274, HL (no justification for imposing general class public interest immunity on all documents generated by police complaints procedure). For an example in the context of a forced marriage or "honour violence" case, see: *Re A (Forced Marriage: Special Advocates)* [2010] EWHC 2438 (Fam); [2012] Fam. 102.

[132] *R. (on the application of Tucker) v Director General of the National Crime Squad* [2003] EWCA Civ 57; [2003] I.C.R. 599; (although the decision to terminate the appellant's secondment to the NCS did not involve sufficient public law elements to justify susceptibility to judicial review (see 3-066), the CA added that fairness did not require that reasons should be given for the termination given the sensitivity of the work of the NSC); and *Ex p. Hosenball* [1977] 1 W.L.R. 766 (intelligence information). It has been held however that the holding in *Tucker* cannot be invoked to dilute a statutory obligation to act fairly: see *Manning v Ramjohn* [2011] UKPC 20 at [34] (on the facts in this case, however, no possible damage to national security could have arisen from disclosure of the allegations against the appellant).

[133] *Collymore v Attorney General* [1970] A.C. 538 (confidential information about industrial disputes and relations); *Crompton (Alfred) Amusement Machines Ltd v Customs and Excise Commissioners*

may be in the public interest has not been confined to matters of administration, and for example, the welfare of children[135] and of psychiatric patients[136] has arisen in a number of cases. In one child custody case, the House of Lords refused disclosure of confidential reports made to the court by the Official Solicitor because their disclosure to the parents concerned might damage children whose welfare it was the paramount duty of the court to protect. It was reasoned that common-law duties to abide by the rules of natural justice were not ends in themselves, and where they did not serve the ends of justice, they could not be allowed to "become the master instead of the servant of justice".[137]

Overall though, it is important to remember that disclosure is the rule, not the exception.[138]

8-034

(*No.2*) [1974] A.C. 405 (non-disclosure of documents which would have disclosed the commissioners' methods and information obtained from third parties both voluntarily and under statute); Cf. *Norwich Pharmacal Co v Customs and Excise Commissioners* [1974] A.C. 133 (confidential information supplied by traders to commissioners making inquiries). Confidential particulars relating to an informant's commercial or financial affairs supplied in connection with air transport licences must normally be withheld by the Civil Aviation Authority: Civil Aviation Act 1982 ss.23, 64-72; and *R. v Board of Visitors of Wandsworth Prison Ex p. Raymond, The Times,* 17 June 1987, DC (circumstances which could justify withholding a welfare report made on prisoner for disciplinary hearing, although normally to ensure that "justice ... be seen to be done", it should be disclosed); *R. v Secretary of State for Health Ex p. US Tobacco International Ltd* [1992] Q.B. 353 at 371 (Taylor LJ: disclosure of scientific advice given to Secretary of State by independent experts in relation to proposed ban on oral snuff).

[134] cf. *D v NSPCC* [1978] A.C. 171; *Science Research Council v Nasse* [1980] A.C. 1028. See *Mears Ltd v Leeds City Council* [2011] EWHC 40 (QB); [2011] B.L.R. 155 at [49]-[50] (disclosure of model answers in a procurement process ordered to legal advisers only given that broader disclosure would render it impossible for the contracting authority to re-tender). See also *R. (on the application of Bourgass) v Secretary of State for Justice* [2015] UKSC 54; [2015] 3 W.L.R. 457 at [103] (in the context of prison segregation decisions, fairness does not require the disclosure of information which could compromise the safety of an informant, the integrity of prison security or other overriding interests. It will be sufficient to inform the prisoner in more or less general terms of the gist of the reasons for seeking the authority of the Secretary of State); *Da Costa v Sargaco* [2016] EWCA Civ 764; [2016] C.P. Rep. 40 at [59] (the decision in *Al-Rawi v Security Service* [2011] UKSC 34; [2012] 1 A.C. 531 was not authority for the proposition that, in order for a party to have a fair trial, there was an absolute requirement that he or she had to have the opportunity to be present throughout the hearing).

[135] *Re K (Infants)* [1965] A.C. 201.; *Re D (Infants)* [1970] 1 W.L.R. 599 (local authority case records on children under care); *Re B (Disclosure to Others)* [2001] 2 F.L.R. 1017 (father of child had art.6 rights, but not entitled to see police and psychiatric reports on other children of same mother where that would interfere with art.8 rights of children); *C v C* [2005] EWHC 2741 at [20]-[21]. See also *H v H* [1974] 1 W.L.R. 595 (information supplied to judge in confidence by a child during custody proceedings); cf. *B v W* [1979] 1 W.L.R. 1041 (breach of natural justice not to disclose social workers report used by court to assess character of party in wardship proceedings); *SB* [2010] EWHC 2528 (Fam); [2011] 1 F.L.R. 651 at [33] (an expert involved in Children Act cases could not receive information in confidence as all relevant information had to be shared with other parties and the court).

[136] *Re W.L.W.* [1972] Ch. 456 (report on condition of psychiatric patient); *R. v Kent Police Authority Ex p. Godden* [1971] 2 Q.B. 662 (disclosure of medical report to be restricted to applicant's own doctor). Outside the context of cases involving children and psychiatric patients, see: *Re Murjani (A Bankrupt)* [1996] 1 W.L.R. 1498 (non-adversarial bankruptcy proceedings); *R. v Canterbury (Archbishop) Ex p. Morant* [1944] K.B. 282 at 292 (non-disclosure in the interests of the "peace of the parish").

[137] *Re K* [1965] A.C. 201 at 238 (Lord Devlin).

[138] *A County Council* [2010] EWHC 2528 (Fam); [2011] 1 F.L.R. 651 at [29].

FAIR PROCEDURES WOULD HINDER PROMPT ACTION

Statutory relaxation of procedural propriety

8-035　　Desirable though it may be to allow a hearing or an opportunity to make representations, or simply to give prior notice, before a decision is taken, summary action may be alleged to be justifiable when an urgent need for protecting the interests of other persons arises.[139] There are in fact remarkably few situations in which the enforcement powers of public authorities are exercisable without notice[140]; but examples exist. For example, interim anti-social behaviour orders made without notice are not unlawful where it is necessary for the court to act urgently to protect the interests of a third party or to ensure that the order of the court is effective.[141] Similarly, where investors had participated in tax avoidance measures which were subsequently disputed in the First-tier Tribunal, HMRC was entitled to issue notices to those investors requiring accelerated payment of tax which it considered would be due after the resolution of that substantive dispute.[142]

8-036　　There are numerous illustrations of statutory provisions which for reasons of public safety or public health permit public authorities to interfere with property or other rights. For example: the destruction of infected crops[143]; the cancellation of a residential care or nursing home's registration[144]; the prevention of the business of a bank being carried on in a manner detrimental to the interests of the public or of depositors or other creditors[145]; prohibition on entry to an airport[146]; suspension of the licence of a public service vehicle[147]; seizure of obscene works[148]; seizure of food suspected of not complying with food safety requirements.[149] Public health officers may also destroy or disinfest verminous articles offered for sale.[150] A differ-

---

[139] See 7-048 and 7-065; *Kioa v West* (1985) 159 C.L.R. 550 at 586 (Mason J), 626 (Brennan J), 633 (Deane J).

[140] See, e.g. the notices required for planning enforcement: Town and Country Planning Act 1990 s.172; and the relatively recent "Planning Contravention Notice", Town and Country Planning Act 1990 s.171C.

[141] *R. (on the application of M) v Secretary of State for Constitutional Affairs* [2004] EWCA Civ 312; [2004] 1 W.L.R. 2298 at [24]. Contrast *R. (on the application of Medical Justice) v Secretary of State for the Home Department* [2010] EWHC 1925 (Admin) (a policy allowing the removal of individuals who had made unsuccessful claims to enter or remain in the United Kingdom without giving the standard minimum 72 hours' notice in certain circumstances was declared unlawful as it failed to adequately safeguard the right of proper access to legal advice and to the courts). See also *R. (on the application of the Howard League for Penal Reform, Prisoners' Advice Service) v Lord Chancellor* [2015] EWCA Civ 819 at [20] (applying the *Medical Justice* test of whether a system, removing certain categories of decisions affecting prisoners from the scope of criminal legal aid, considered in the round carried an unacceptable risk of unfairness).

[142] *R. (on the application of Rowe) v Revenue and Customs Commissioners* [2015] EWHC 2293 (Admin) at [62] (the accelerated payment required did not involve any determination of final liability, but rather addressed where the tax should be held pending resolution of the dispute and any hardship suffered by the taxpayer was always a risk that might materialise when entering a tax avoidance scheme without making provision for payment of tax if the scheme failed).

[143] Plant Health Act 1967 ss.3, 4 (as amended).

[144] Care Standards Act 2000 s.14.

[145] *Suisse Security Bank & Trust Ltd v Governor of the Central Bank of the Bahamas* [2006] UKPC 11; [2006] 1 W.L.R. 1660 at [35]-[36].

[146] *R. (on the application of Scott) v Heathrow Airport Ltd* [2005] EWHC 2669 (Admin).

[147] Road Traffic Act 1988 ss.69, 70, 72.

[148] Customs Consolidation Act 1876 s.42; Customs and Excise Management Act 1979 s.139 Sch.3; Obscene Publications Act 1959 s.3(3).

[149] Food Safety Act 1990 s.9.

[150] Public Health Act 1961 37; see also, e.g. Health and Social Care Act 2008 s.30. Other direct enforce-

ent kind of public interest is protected when the owner of a building is not entitled to prior notice of its intended listing as being of architectural or historic interest,[151] but should he wish to alter the building, he is entitled to a hearing against a refusal of listed building consent.[152]

In some of these examples in which summary action needs to be taken without prior notice, a range of safeguards after the action is provided by statute law. For example, although interim anti-social behaviour orders can be made without notice, they are subject to the safeguards of early review or discharge hearings, which are compliant with procedural fairness.[153] Moreover, the application to be made without notice and the order can only be made for a limited period when the court considered it just to make it.[154]   **8-037**

Even where a statutory power to give prior notice exists, legislation may permit prior notice to be dispensed with if it is impracticable to give it, for example where direct action has to be taken to make a dangerous building safe.[155] Alternatively, powers of direct enforcement may become exercisable only by virtue of an order made by a magistrate upon an application made by a competent authority.   **8-038**

Common law exclusion of procedural propriety for urgency

Urgency may warrant relaxing the requirements of fairness even where there is no legislation under which this is expressly permitted.[156] Thus a local authority could, without any consultation, withdraw children from a special school after allegations of persistent cruelty and abuse without this involving any procedural impropriety. In such circumstances there exists an emergency in which the primary concern is as to the safety and welfare of the children.[157] The suspension without first affording an opportunity to be heard, of a Romanian Airline's flight permit, following the failure by five of its pilots of Civil Aviation Authority examinations in aviation law, flight rules, and procedures, was not unfair where an immediate threat to air safety was apprehended.[158] Similarly where a self-regulatory organisation acted urgently to protect investors, it was not required to consider whether there was   **8-039**

---

ment powers conferred by public health legislation are exercisable only when notice has been served on the persons affected, e.g. powers to cleanse and disinfect premises and articles in order to prevent the spread of infectious disease, and to destroy rodents which are overrunning premises: Health Protection (Notification) Regulations 2010; Prevention of Damage by Pests Act 1949 s.6.

[151] Planning (Listed Buildings and Conservation Areas) Act 1990 ss.1-2.
[152] Planning (Listed Buildings and Conservation Areas) Act 1990 s.20.
[153] *M* [2004] EWCA Civ 312; [2004] 1 W.L.R. 2298 at [39].
[154] *M* [2004] EWCA Civ 312; [2004] 1 W.L.R. 2298 at [39].
[155] Building Act 1984 ss.77, 78(1) and (2). The question whether it would have been more reasonable to apply to a magistrates' court for an order to be made against the owners can be determined in proceedings in which the recovery of expenses for the work executed is claimed (Building Act 1984 s.78(3) and (5)).
[156] *De Verteuil v Knaggs* [1918] A.C. 557 at 560-561. Thus a magistrate is under no obligation to hear a person other than the informant before issuing a search warrant: *R. v Peterborough Justices Ex p. Hicks* [1977] 1 W.L.R. 1371. For a broad statement, restricting the application of the requirements of procedural fairness in the interests of public health, see *R. v Davey* [1899] 2 Q.B. 301 305-306. In Ireland, see *O'Callaghan v Commissioners of Public Works* [1985] I.L.R.M. 364, 373-374; *Dellway Investments v NAMA* [2011] IESC 14; [2011] 4 I.R. 1 at [116]-[118] (Denham J) (finding that the exception was not borne out on the facts).
[157] *R. v Powys CC Ex p. Horner* [1989] Fam. Law 320.
[158] *R. v Secretary of State for Transport Ex p. Pegasus Holdings (London) Ltd* [1988] 1 W.L.R. 990. cf. in Australia, *Coutts v Commonwealth* (1985) 157 C.L.R. 91 (no requirement of natural justice where air force pilot, whose appointment was held at the pleasure of the Crown, was compulsorily retired on medical grounds).

sufficient time to receive representations.[159] Likewise, a local authority was entitled to prohibit allegedly dangerous toys as an "emergency holding operation".[160] There may also be circumstances where an injunction has to be granted as a matter of urgency without it being possible to give full reasons on the same day.[161] In general, whether the need for urgent action outweighs the importance of following fair procedures depends on an assessment of the circumstances of each case on which opinions can differ.

IMPRACTICABLE TO PROVIDE FAIR PROCEDURE

8-040   In the past the duty to act fairly did not normally apply to decisions containing a substantial "policy" content or regarded as essentially "allocative".[162] Even after the demise of the old distinction between "judicial" and "administrative" decisions, the category of "legislative" decision has tended to survive in other jurisdictions[163]; and has also been affirmed in this jurisdiction on occasion, at least in respect of the making of delegated legislation.[164] As we have contended, however,[165] "policy" or "legislative" decisions should not on the ground of being classified as such be excused from the duty to act fairly. Indeed, in a number of cases that duty has been imposed in a policy setting,[166] although the content of the duty may be relaxed.[167]

---

[159] *R. v Life Assurance Unit Trust Regulatory Organisation Ex p. Ross* [1993] Q.B. 17, CA; also *Ferrero* [1993] 1 All E.R. 530, CA. The rules of natural justice do not apply to the making a Notice of Intervention in a solicitor's practice on the ground of suspected dishonesty under the Solicitors Act 1974, so that there is no requirement to give particulars of the reasons for intervention in the Notice: *Giles v Law Society* (1996) 8 Admin. L.R. 105, CA. However, the Act does afford a right of judicial consideration after the event. However, see now Legal Services Act 2007 Sch.14 (requiring a minimum of eight days' notice).

[160] *Ferrero* [1991] 3 Admin. L.R. 613.

[161] *EE & Brian Smith (1928) Ltd v Hodson* [2007] EWCA Civ 1210 at [30] (although not relevant in this case as judgment had been reserved for almost four weeks).

[162] See 6-029.

[163] For example, in Canada *Inuit Tapirisat of Canada v Attorney General of Canada* [1980] 2 S.C.R. 735; *Cardinal v Kent Institution* [1985] 2 S.C.R. 643 at [14]; cf. in New Zealand *Fowler & Roderique Ltd v Attorney General* [1987] 2 N.Z.L.R. 56. In Ireland, the position is unclear: see *Gorman v Minister for the Environment* [2001] 2 I.R. 414 at 437 and *Garda Representative Association v Minister for Public Expenditure and Reform* [2016] IECA 18, but contrast *Burke v Minister for Labour* [1979] I.R. 354 at 361-362; see also G. Hogan and D.G. Morgan, *Administrative Law in Ireland*, 4th edn (2010) at paras 14-216–14-221.

[164] *Bates v Lord Hailsham* [1972] 1 W.L.R. 1373 (affirmed in *BAPIO Action Ltd v the Secretary of State for the Home Department* [2007] EWHC 199 at [47] (point not considered in the House of Lords: [2008] UKHL 27; [2008] 1 A.C. 1003). See also *Plaintiff S10/2011 v Minister for Immigration and Citizenship* (2012) 246 C.L.R. 636 at 656, 667 (Australian High Court).

[165] See 7-030.

[166] See, e.g. *R. v Secretary of State for Health Ex p. United States Tobacco International Inc* [1992] Q.B. 353 (although a statutory duty to consult applied here); *R. (on the application of Capenhurst) v Leicester City Council* [2004] EWHC 2124; (2004) 7 C.C.L. Rep. 557 (since the local authority had accepted that voluntary organisations should be consulted, the consultation should be fair); *R. (on the application of Newsum) v Welsh Assembly (No.2)* [2005] EWHC 538 (Admin); [2006] Env. L.R. 1; *R. v Secretary of State for the Environment Ex p. Brent LBC* [1982] Q.B. 593, DC. The existence of a legitimate expectation may also result in requirements of procedural fairness even in a policy or legislative context: see 12-003; *R. v British Coal Corp & Secretary of State for Trade & Industry Ex p. Vardy* [1993] I.C.R. 720, DC; *R. v Lord Chancellor Ex p. The Law Society* (1994) 6 Admin L.R. 833.

[167] See, e.g. in respect of the right to cross examination *Bushell* [1981] A.C. 75; *Walton v Scottish Ministers* [2012] CSIH 19 (even had the view been reached that the Scottish Ministers had acted in

There may however, in a particular case, be good reasons why the duty to act **8-041** fairly should not apply where the decision involves policy formulation or rule-making. The most convincing reason will be that the number of persons affected by a particular order, act or decision is so great as to make it manifestly impracticable for them all to be given an opportunity of being heard by the competent authority beforehand.[168] This is the reason why representations may not be required for the making of regulations of a legislative character.[169] But a statute may impliedly require an opportunity to be given for representations to be made against local authority byelaws before they are confirmed by a minister,[170] and an Act can provide for notice and opportunity to be heard prior to statutory instruments being made.[171] We noted in Chapters 6 and 7, the contrast with the well-established American experience, where extensive "rulemaking" procedures are required for all subordinate law-making, and also with the more recent similar South

---

such a way that certain legal requirements had been breached, the court should not exercise its discretion to grant the remedy of quashing the schemes and orders, as it would be inappropriate to allow an individual to prevent the proposed peripheral route from proceeding where its genesis had come about approximately 30 years previously, there had been a huge amount of public discussion and debate thereon, and the interests of the unrepresented general members of the public, who were in favour of the route and clearly argued against the quashing of the schemes and orders, had to be treated as paramount). See also: [2012] UKSC 44; [2013] P.T.S.R. 51.

[168] cf. *BAPIO Action Ltd* [2007] EWHC 199 at [47] (Stanley Burnton J noting that "the remedy is political rather than judicial"); *R. v Secretary of State for Social Services Ex p. Child Poverty Action Group, The Times*, 8 August 1985, CA; in New Zealand see *Waitemata County v Local Government Commission* [1964] N.Z.L.R. 689 at 698-699. The Australian High Court has held that categorisation of a decision as legislative rather than administrative is not itself a coherent reason to preclude the rules of fairness: *Bread Manufacturers of New South Wales v Evans* (1981) 180 C.L.R. 404 at 415-416, 432-433. Some Australian cases have sought to exclude any duty to observe the requirements of fairness for decisions of a legislative or political character because such decisions normally have a general effect, which precludes an individual claiming the required affectation: *Kioa* (1985) 159 C.L.R. 550 at 584. Other Australian cases have adopted a more functional approach and accepted that fairness may be difficult to apply to decisions affecting a large class of people (as legislative or political decisions typically do) because the class of people affected, or the nature of the impact, may be difficult to identify: *Castle v Director General, State Emergency Service* [2008] NSWCA 231 at [6]. Another obstacle to judicial review of legislative decisions is the coverage of the Administrative Decisions (Judicial Review) Act 1977 (Cth) (ADJR), which applies only to decisions of "an administrative character". This formula does not preclude review of legislative decisions at common law, but the simpler statutory avenue of review is not available in respect of legislative decisions at the Commonwealth level and in Queensland, Tasmania and the Australian Capital Territory where ADJR has been replicated. In Ireland, the argument regarding the unworkability of according fair procedures has been considered in circumstances other than legislative: *Dellway Investments* [2011] IESC 14; [2011] 4 I.R. 1 at [119] (Denham J) (although rejected on the facts). In *Garda Representative Association v Minister for Public Expenditure and Reform* [2016] IECA 18, it was held that there was no duty to consult prior to the enactment of regulations.

[169] For Australia, see *Pharmacy Restructuring Authority v Martin* (1994) 53 F.C.R. 589 (claim for a right of notice and hearing by existing pharmacy owners for decisions to grant new pharmacy licences rejected due to cost and difficulty of identifying those who might claim right). In Canada, the fact that a decision is contained in an instrument normally associated with legislative powers (e.g. a byelaw or regulation) is not determinative of the characterisation of the power as being exempt from a fair hearing: *Homex Realty and Development Co Ltd v Wyoming (Village)* [1980] 1 S.C.R. 1011. The legislative nature of a board's powers was however given as reason for keeping to a minimum the procedural content of an express statutory duty to conduct a hearing: *Manitoba League of the Physically Handicapped Inc v Manitoba (Taxicab Board)* (1988) 56 D.L.R. (4th) 191.

[170] Local Government Act 1972 s.236 (as amended).

[171] See 7-028.

African experience.[172] Another reason for excluding the fair hearing in such cases may be that the decision-maker is responsible to Parliament for the decision.[173]

8-042   The large number of applicants competing for scarce resources may make it impracticable to offer each applicant a hearing. If, for example, there are 1,000 applicants for 100 places available in a university law department (or a corresponding ratio of applicants to available licences, permits or grants) it may be impossible to afford interviews (or hearings) to many of those who, from the particulars supplied with their written applications, appear sufficiently meritorious or suitable to warrant fuller personal consideration.[174] Criteria for selection should, however, be evolved and applied in an attempt to do justice as far as this is possible; but there will inevitably be persons who will reasonably feel aggrieved at having been denied an adequate opportunity of presenting their case. Where a hearing can be provided, considerations of administrative practicality may influence or determine the content of the procedure which is capable of being adopted.[175] Even if the court finds that a breach of procedural fairness has occurred, administrative impracticability may still be relied upon as a reason for refusing a remedy in its discretion.[176]

SUBSEQUENT FAIR HEARING OR APPEAL

8-043   The common law and the ECHR both permit a public authority to make decisions which do not comply fully with procedural fairness requirements if the person affected has recourse to a further hearing or appeal which itself provides fairness.

Common law and subsequent hearings

8-044   There are situations where the absence of procedural fairness before a decision is made can subsequently be adequately "cured", for example on appeal.[177] A prior

---

[172] See 6-053, 6-061 and 7-025.

[173] See, e.g. *Essex CC v Ministry of Housing & Local Government* (1967) 66 L.G.R. 23. cf. *CREEDNZ v Governor General* [1981] 1 N.Z.L.R. 172 at 189.

[174] *R. v Aston University Senate Ex p. Roffey* [1969] 2 Q.B. 538 at 554; and *Central Council for Education and Training in Social Work v Edwards, The Times,* 5 May 1978 (supports the propositions contained in the text, but where a refusal to admit was declared invalid on the ground that the interview was conducted unfairly; in the context of licences); *McInnes v Onslow Fane* [1978] 1 W.L.R. 1520 (Megarry VC's distinction between "application" and "revocation" cases may be explained as resting upon this basis; see 7-005).

[175] See, e.g. *R. v Birmingham CC Ex p. Darshan Kaur* [1991] C.O.D. 21, DC (lack of translator at public meeting not improper because it was administratively impossible to provide translators for every language spoken at the meeting); *R. v Secretary of State for Wales Ex p. Williams* [1996] C.O.D. 127 (Secretary of State, having consulted in relation to a proposal to close special schools, was not required to consult further in relation to representations of local authority made during consultation process; it was undesirable so to prolong the consultation process); *R. (on the application of Robin Murray & Co) v Lord Chancellor* [2011] EWHC 1528 (Admin); [2011] A.C.D. 103 (it was not necessary for a public body engaged in a consultation process to circulate the submissions of those who responded to the consultation to all others who had responded to it. Furthermore, there was no obligation on a minister to communicate advice received from officials or internal material or information to consultees); *WWF UK Ltd v Scottish Natural Heritage* [1999] 1 C.M.L.R. 1021 (when consulting the public on prevention of adverse environmental effects, a planning authority was not in principle obliged to submit the final terms of proposed measures for such consultation, since that would make the process unduly protracted).

[176] See 18-047.

[177] On a claim for judicial review under CPR Pt 54, the person will in any event normally be expected to use such an alternative method of challenging the legality of the initial decision: see 16-014.

hearing may be better than a subsequent hearing, but a subsequent hearing is better than no hearing at all[178]; and in some cases the courts have held that statutory provisions for an administrative appeal[179] or even full judicial review on the merits[180] are sufficient to negative the existence of any implied duty to have a hearing before the original decision is made.[181] This approach may be acceptable where the original decision does not cause significant detriment to the person affected,[182] or where there is also a paramount need for prompt action, or where it is otherwise impracticable to afford antecedent hearings.[183]

The question of whether a decision vitiated by a breach of the rules of fairness **8-045** can be made good by a subsequent hearing does not admit of a single answer applicable to all situations in which the issue may arise. Whilst it is difficult to reconcile all the relevant cases, case law indicates that the courts are increasingly favouring an approach based in large part upon an assessment of whether, in all the circumstances of the hearing and appeal, the procedure as a whole satisfied the requirements of fairness. Of particular importance are (a) the gravity of the error committed at first instance,[184] (b) the likelihood that the prejudicial effects of the error may also have permeated the rehearing,[185] (c) the seriousness of the consequences for the individual, (iv) the width of the powers of the appellate body (d) whether the appellate decision is reached only on the basis of the material before the original tribunal or by way of fresh hearing, or rehearing *de novo*,[186] and (e) if applicable, the purpose of the statutory scheme.[187] In India it has been held that a

---

[178] *NBMW v Minister for Immigration and Citizenship* (2013) 213 FCR 309. But cf. *Cinnamond v British Airports Authority* [1980] 1 W.L.R. 582.

[179] *Calvin v Carr* [1980] A.C. 574 at 593-593; *Pearlberg v Varty* [1972] 1 W.L.R. 534 (tax assessments); *Furnell* [1973] A.C. 660 (suspension of teacher pending full hearing); *Maynard v Osmond* [1977] Q.B. 240 at 253 (right of legal representation on appeal a reason for not implying the same right in original proceedings). In Australia see *Twist v Randwick MC* (1976) 136 C.L.R. 106 at 116; *Marine Hull & Liability Insurance Co v Hurford* (1985) 67 A.L.R. 77.

[180] In Australia see *Literature Board of Review v HMH Publishing Co Inc* [1964] Qd.R. 261; *Twist* (1976) 136 C.L.R. 106; and on enforcement powers 8-035.

[181] Similarly, a fair hearing may not be required at the second hearing of a two-stage process where the person affected had an adequate hearing at the first stage, in Australia see: *South Australia v O'Shea* (1987) 163 C.L.R. 378. cf. *Haoucher* (1990) 169 C.L.R. 648.

[182] Although detriment may not be immediately obvious; it may be less easy to convince a decision-maker that a decision already taken is wrong than to persuade the body initially of the merits of one's case. cf. *R. v Portsmouth CC Ex p. Gregory* (1990) 89 L.G.R. 478, DC, where the determinations of a special council committee set up to investigate two councillors were irremediably flawed by the earlier investigations of a council subcommittee. In Ireland, see *Dunnes Stores Ireland Company v Maloney* [1999] 3 I.R. 542; *Scariff v Taylor* [1996] 1 I.R. 242 (distinguished in *Ó Ceallaigh v An Bord Altranais* [2000] 4 I.R. 54).

[183] But such logic cannot extend to appeals that would repeat the original problem, such as one that does not allow a claimant to gain access to crucial material not available in the first hearing: *Gould v ISIS Club Inc* [2015] QSC 253, [75]-[76].

[184] Thus an original decision vitiated by bias will normally not be allowed to stand: in New Zealand, see *Anderton v Auckland CC* [1978] 1 N.Z.L.R. 657 at 700.

[185] Similarly, it was held in *R. (on the application of Patmore) v Brentwood Borough Council* [2012] EWHC 1244 (Admin) at [50]-[51] that any reconsideration pending judicial review proceedings was potentially tainted by a desire to avoid the consequences of judicial review.

[186] See, e.g. *Pillai v Singapore CC* [1968] 1 W.L.R. 1278 at 1286; *Calvin* [1980] A.C. 574; *Lloyd v McMahon* [1987] A.C. 625; *Twist* (1976) 136 C.L.R. 106; *R. v LAUTRO Ex p. Tee* (1995) 7 Admin. L.R. 289; *R. v Legal Aid Board Ex p. Donn & Co (A Firm)* [1996] 3 All E.R. 1 (Area Committee's unfairness in failing to consider full representations of solicitors seeking legal aid contract not cured by chairman subsequently confirming individually with six of seven members of committee that full representations made no difference to their decision).

[187] *R. (on the application of Brown) v Carlisle City Council* [2010] EWCA Civ 523; [2011] Env. L.R. 71 at [40] (since the object of the regulatory scheme was to ensure that environmental effects were

post-decisional hearing cannot normally cure an act that is a nullity for want of natural justice.[188] On occasion, the United States courts have also upheld the principle of a "post-decisional hearing".[189]

8-046 In general, it is increasingly the case that the courts will not intervene on grounds of procedural unfairness where the procedurally unfair decision is subject to correction by a procedure which has proper procedural safeguards.[190] In *Calvin v Carr*[191] the Privy Council doubted that there was a general rule[192] that a failure of fairness at the initial hearing is not to be cured by procedurally correct appeal; in particular, it was suggested, a more latitudinarian attitude should be taken towards the proceedings of domestic tribunals whose authority is derived from the consensual rules of a voluntary association. Thus, in that case, an appeal to the Committee of the Australian Jockey Club was held, for this reason, to cure a defective decision of race stewards who had disqualified the owner of a horse alleged to have been raced improperly. In *Lloyd v McMahon*,[193] the House of Lords confirmed this trend outside the context of domestic tribunals. It was held that the decision of a district auditor to surcharge councillors for failure to set a valid rate, without according them oral hearings would, had it been procedurally defective, have been cured by the statutory appeal from the auditor's decision to the High Court. It should be noted, however, with reference to the criteria set out above, that the scope of the appeal was very wide, all the evidence being susceptible of re-examination, including the merits of the decision.[194]

8-047 Where there is an option for rapidly seeking annulment or amendment of the order made, the initial procedurally unfair proceeding will not be reviewed.[195] Thus, where interim anti-social behaviour orders were made without notice, there was no breach of procedural fairness since the orders were subject to the safeguards of early review or discharge hearings, which were compliant with procedural fairness.[196]

---

considered before any planning decision was taken, giving an assurance to consider such effects at a later stage would only exceptionally justify not quashing a permission granted in breach). On occasion, the United States courts have also upheld the principle of a "post-decisional hearing": see, e.g. *Philips v Commissioner of Internal Revenue* 283 U.S. 589 (1931). However, in general, due process requires that individuals must receive notice and an opportunity to be heard before the government deprives them of property: *US v James Daniel Good Real Property* 510 U.S. 43 (1993). The legislation at issue in *Phillips* has since been amended to provide a pre-deprivation hearing: see *Kindred v Commissioner of Internal Revenue* 454 F.3d 688 at 695 (7th Cir. 2006).

[188] *Canara Bank v V K Awasthy* (2005) 6 S.C.C. 321 at [5], [6], [7] and [18]; *Sahara v CIT* (2008) 14 S.C.C. 151 at [31]; *Shekhar Ghosh v UOI* (2007) 1 S.C.C. 331 at [14].

[189] See, e.g. *Philips* 283 U.S. 589 (1931). However, in general, due process requires that individuals must receive notice and an opportunity to be heard *before* the government deprives them of property: *James Daniel Good Real Property* 510 U.S. 43 (1993). The legislation at issue in *Phillips* has since been amended to provide a pre-deprivation hearing: see *Kindred* 454 F.3d 688 at 695 (7th Cir. 2006).

[190] If a claimant commences judicial review before the completion of a hearing, or fails to use an appeal route or other alternative remedy, permission may be refused: see 16-014.

[191] *Calvin v Carr* [1980] A.C. 574; cf. *Rees v Crane* [1994] 2 A.C. 173 at 192, where Lord Slynn, having referred to the 4th edition of this book, went on to say "the courts should not be bound by rigid rules" and to stress in that case the respondent could not rely on urgency or administrative inconvenience.

[192] As proposed by Megarry J in *Leary v National Union of Vehicle Builders* [1971] Ch. 34 (trade union expulsion case).

[193] *Lloyd v McMahon* [1987] A.C. 625.

[194] It was expressly suggested that the situation might be different if the appellate body was bound by findings of fact, or restricted to questions of law (Lord Templeman at 891); this suggests that a rehearing by way of judicial review would not be sufficient (Lord Bridge at 884).

[195] *Wiseman* [1971] A.C. 297 at 318F-G.

[196] *M* [2004] EWCA Civ 312; [2004] 1 W.L.R. 2298 at [39]. See also *R. (on the application of Rowe) v Revenue and Customs Commissioners* [2015] EWHC 2293 (Admin) (no breach of procedural fair-

Similarly, where a re-categorisation decision is being made in respect of a determinate sentence prisoner, there is no need to permit the prisoner to make representations in advance of the re-categorisation decision; all that fairness requires is that the prisoner have an opportunity to appeal the re-categorisation decision.[197] It has also been held that unfairness in the context of school exclusion decisions are capable of being cured by means of statutory appeal, provided that the independent appeal body is entrusted with the task of dealing with the merits of the case fully and *de novo*, and that it does so in a way that is not open to challenge on normal judicial review grounds and the appeal process is not contaminated in some real sense by the defect in the earlier decision-making process.[198] The curative principle also applies in the immigration context[199] and in the context of care proceedings.[200] It is not just appeal procedures which can cure an initial defective decision and defective decisions have been cured by a minister's lawful approval[201] and later fair and open-minded reconsideration of the decision.[202]

Limits

There are, however, limits to the extent to which procedural unfairness can be "cured". There may be situations in which, although the provision of a right of appeal is not required, a court will be satisfied that nothing short of compliance with the requirements of procedural fairness at both stages will afford to the individual the standards of fairness demanded in the particular context.[203] For example, trial **8-048**

---

ness where accelerated payment notices where tax avoidance measures were in dispute did not give rise to determination of final liability).

[197] *R. (on the application of Palmer) v Secretary of State for the Home Department* [2004] EWHC 1817 at [27]-[28].

[198] *R. (on the application of DR) v Head Teacher of St George's Catholic School* [2002] EWCA Civ 1822 at [55] (Keene LJ); and *R. v Visitors of the Inns of Court Ex p. Calder & Persaud* [1994] Q.B. 1 at 59C (noting that an appeal to visitors, entailing a full re-hearing on the merits, should cure any procedural defect on the part of the initial tribunal); *R. (on the application of A) v Enfield LBC* [2002] EWHC 395 at [18] (Mitchell J, even at the first level, decision-makers must "act in the knowledge that their decisions are amenable to judicial review", although it will be "rare" that recourse to judicial review will be appropriate).

[199] *Ex p. Sesay* [1995] Imm AR 521 at 522-523 (Sedley J).

[200] *Re C (Care Proceedings: disclosure of local authority's decision-making process)* [2002] EWHC 1379 (Fam) [2002] 2 F.C.R. 673 at [240] (although there had been unfairness and incompatibility with the ECHR art.6 in the earlier stages of the care proceedings, nevertheless the trial had been fair overall).

[201] *R. v Secretary of State for Education Ex p. Cumbria CC* [1994] E.L.R. 220 at 228.

[202] *R. (on the application of Martin) v Secretary of State for the Home Department* [2003] EWHC 1512 (Admin); *The Times,* 15 May 2003. cf. *R. (on the application of Banks) v Secretary of State for the Environment, Food and Rural Affairs* [2004] EWHC 416 (Admin); [2004] N.P.C. 43 at [107] where there was no evidence of a "fair, open-minded and comprehensive" reconsideration); *R. (on the application of Q) v Secretary of State for the Home Department* [2003] EWCA Civ 364; [2004] Q.B. 36 at [91] (fact that Secretary of State willing to reconsider an adverse decision as to welfare benefits for asylum-seekers "not a substitute for proper and fair primary decision making"); *R. v Commissioners of Customs and Excise Ex p. Mortimer* [1999] 1 W.L.R. 17 at 23 (remedy refused where there was availability of full hearing on appeal to magistrates of procedural defective customs decision); *R. v Secretary of State for the Home Department Ex p. Pierson* [1998] A.C. 539 (refusal to grant leave for judicial review where Secretary of State willing to consider further representations); *R. (on the application of Shields) v Crown Court at Liverpool* [2001] EWHC Admin 90; [2001] U.K.H.R.R. 610 (the issue of whether there had been a fair trial in compliance with ECHR art.6 could be addressed on appeal to the CA).

[203] *Leary* [1971] Ch. 34; in New Zealand, see *Denton v Auckland City* [1969] N.Z.L.R. 256 at 269; *Chalmers v Disciplinary Committee of the Pharmaceutical Society of New Zealand* (1991) 9 N.Z.A.R. 529 (provision for full appeal on the merits did not cure the defects because what was said

on indictment is not an adequate alternative to judicial review for committal on inadmissible evidence given the importance of providing a right to cross-examine at a preliminary stage.[204] Similarly, inadequate consultation was not corrected by appeal where a budgetary decision was easier to overturn before it was firmly made[205]; while a procedurally defective decision will not be cured by the decision-maker communicating with the aggrieved party after the decision, in defence of the decision.[206] A right of individual petition to the ECtHR is also not a right of appeal to an appeal court capable of curing the national authorities' failure to provide a fair trial.[207]

ECHR art.6 and subsequent hearings

8-049   It is well-established in the case law of the ECtHR that the requirements of art.6 are satisfied if either (a) the initial decision-maker is independent and impartial or (b) there is control by a judicial body with full jurisdiction, which does satisfy the art.6 requirements.[208] In other words, the question is whether the composite procedure satisfies art.6.[209] The expression "full jurisdiction" does not mean full decision-making power. It means "full jurisdiction to deal with the case as the nature of the decision requires".[210] In assessing compatibility with art.6, it is necessary to have regard to matters such as the subject matter of the decision appealed against, the manner in which that decision was arrived at, and the content of the dispute, including the desired and actual grounds of appeal.[211]

8-050   Given that judicial review does not involve a fresh hearing on the merits and has traditionally involved limited review of factual errors,[212] the question has often arisen as to whether judicial review is sufficient to remedy any shortcomings in an initial decision-making procedure. In most cases, courts in England and Wales have been satisfied that the availability of judicial review can remedy an initial decision-making process which has not been compliant with art.6.[213] Generally, the more

---

at the initial stages had permeated the proceedings and influenced the appellate body). These cases should not now be regarded as authority for the wider proposition that defects may never be cured by a fair hearing at an appeal: *Calvin* [1980] A.C. 574.

[204] *R. v Bedwellty Justices Ex p. Williams* [1997] A.C. 225 at 235-236.

[205] *R. (on the application of Haringey Consortium of Disabled People and Carers Association) v Haringey LBC* (2002) 5 C.C.L. Rep. 422 at [49].

[206] *R. v P Borough Council Ex p. S* [1999] Fam 188 at 221-222.

[207] *R. (on the application of Ramda) v Secretary of State for the Home Department* [2002] EWHC 1278 at [27].

[208] *Albert and Le Compte v Belgium* (1983) 5 E.H.R.R. 533. See also *Re CS's Application for Judicial Review* [2015] NIQB 36 at [14] (holding that the art.6 compliance of a decision by a university's review panel required considering the hearing before the Board of Visitors and the right to such a hearing being reviewed by the High Court on certain limited, but defined grounds).

[209] See, e.g. *Magill v Porter* [2001] UKHL 67; [2002] 2 A.C. 357 (no breach of art.6 when the procedure of district auditor and the Divisional Court on appeal were considered as a whole); see 10-088.

[210] *R. v Secretary of State for the Environment, Transport and the Regions Ex p. Holdings & Barnes Plc* (the Alconbury case) [2001] UKHL 23; [2003] 2 A.C. 295 at [87]; *Rooney v Secretary of State for Communities and Local Government* [2011] EWCA Civ 1556; [2012] J.P.L. 684 at [23] (any perceived lack of independence in the inspectorate was remedied by the right of appeal on judicial review grounds which could examine any allegation that an inspector had acted unfairly); *R. (on the application of Derrin Bros Properties Ltd) v First-tier Tribunal* [2016] EWCA Civ 15; [2016] 1 W.L.R. 2423 (judicial review was an adequate remedy to ensure that third party information notices had been validly issued).

[211] *Bryan v UK* (1996) 21 E.H.R.R. 342; *Tower Hamlets LBC v Begum (Runa)* [2003] UKHL 5; [2003] 2 A.C. 430 at [51]; *Flynn v Basildon BC* [2011] EWHC 2569 (QB).

[212] See 11-036.

[213] See, e.g. *R. (on the application of MA) v National Probation Service* [2011] EWHC 1332 (Admin);

administrative and less judicial the decision-making process established by Parliament, the less intensive will be the judicial review required to ensure compliance with art.6[214]; but the overriding requirement is that the overall procedure must be lawful and fair.[215] In the planning context, judicial review sufficed where the minister has power to call in applications for planning permission or to hear a recovered appeal against a refusal of planning permission.[216] In relation to the latter, the House of Lords concluded that the procedural rules applying to the minister's decision[217] combined with the rules on judicial review meant that the procedure as a whole complied with art.6.[218] Judicial review has also been deemed adequate in relation to decisions on compensation for miscarriages of justice[219];

[2011] A.C.D. 86; *R. (on the application of Ali) v Secretary of State for Justice* [2013] EWHC 72 (Admin); [2013] 1 W.L.R. 3536 at [66]–[72]; *R. (on the application of King) v Secretary of State for Justice* [2015] UKSC 54; [2015] 3 W.L.R. 457 at [123] (while a decision to authorise continued segregation does not fall within the ambit of art.6.1, in any event, the availability of judicial review would meet the requirements of art.6.1, in particular, given that such a decision is unlikely to turn on the determination of disputed questions of fact); *Ali v Birmingham City Council* [2010] UKSC 8; [2010] 2 A.C. 39 at [53]-[55] (upheld: *Ali v United Kingdom* [2015] H.L.R. 46). The ECtHR has also been satisfied of ECHR art.6 compliance in most cases, see, e.g. *Crompton v United Kingdom* (2010) 50 E.H.R.R. 36 (judicial review adequate to remedy any lack of independence of the Army Board in determining whether the applicant compensation for redundancy from the army) (for a different conclusion reached by the ECtHR, see 8-038 below). cf. *R. (on the application of Chief Constable of Lancashire) v Preston Crown Court* [2001] EWHC Admin 928; [2002] 1 W.L.R. 1332 at [40] (since Crown Court's "appreciation of local conditions is not something which, on its merits, can sensibly be second guessed in judicial review proceedings", the lack of independence and impartiality "is, in reality, beyond the scope of judicial review securely to cure or amend") and *R. (on the application of Kehoe) v Secretary of State for Work and Pensions* [2004] EWCA Civ 225; [2004] Q.B. 1378 (judicial review could not overcome the shortcomings in the system for taking enforcement proceedings for child maintenance payments against the absent parent, as established by the Child Support Act 1991). See also App No 47315/13 *Adorisio v Netherlands* (2015) 61 E.H.R.R. SE1.

[214] See, e.g. *Begum* [2003] UKHL 5; [2003] 2 A.C. 430 at [5] (Lord Bingham, noting the intensity of review required to cure non-compliance at first instance that "the narrower the interpretation given to 'civil rights', the greater the need to insist upon review by a judicial tribunal exercising full powers. Conversely, the more elastic the interpretation given to 'civil right', the more flexible must be the approach to the requirement of independent and impartial review if the emasculation (by over judicialisation) of administrative welfare schemes is to be avoided."); *R. (on the application of Beeson) v Dorset CC* [2002] EWCA Civ 1812; [2003] H.R.L.R. 11 at [22] (in general a statutory scheme involving administrative-type decisions albeit by a non-independent decision-maker will satisfy art.6 where judicial review is available); *R. (on the application of Ali) v Secretary of State for Justice* [2013] EWHC 72 (Admin); [2013] 1 W.L.R. 3536 at [66]–[72].

[215] *Begum* [2003] UKHL 5; [2003] 2 A.C. 430.

[216] *Holding & Barnes Plc* [2001] UKHL 23; [2003] 2 A.C. 295. See also *Rooney* [2011] EWCA Civ 1556; [2012] J.P.L. 684.

[217] The rules included where the minister differed from the inspector on a matter of fact, or took into account new evidence or was disposed to disagree with the inspector, notifying persons entitled to appear at the inquiry, allowing written representation and giving reasons for any difference with the inspector: Town and Country Planning (Inquiries Procedure) (England) Rules 2000 r.17(5).

[218] *Holding & Barnes Plc* [2001] UKHL 23; [2003] 2 A.C. 295 at [16]-[19], [49]-[56] (Lord Slynn); [155]-[160] (Lord Clyde); [188]-[189] (Lord Hutton); in the planning context, *R. (on the application of Adlard) v Secretary of State for the Environment, Transport and the Regions* [2002] EWCA Civ 735; [2002] 1 W.L.R. 2515; *Adan v Newham LBC* [2001] EWCA Civ 1916; [2002] 1 W.L.R. 2120 (although council's internal review not "independent and impartial" appeal to the county court ensured compatibility with art.6); *Q* [2003] EWCA Civ 364; [2004] Q.B. 36 at [116]-[117] (provided that fair system of questioning of asylum-seekers in relation to welfare benefits, availability of judicial review would ensure compliance with art.6); *Friends Provident Life and Pensions Ltd v Secretary of State for Transport, Local Government and the Regions* [2001] EWHC Admin 820; [2002] 1 W.L.R. 1450 (planning authority not independent and impartial but judicial review Court having full jurisdiction in relation to a matter of planning judgment).

[219] *R. (on the application of Mullen) v Secretary of State for the Home Department* [2002] EWHC 230 (Admin); [2002] 1 W.L.R. 1857 (although Secretary of State not an independent and impartial

decision-making on welfare benefits,[220] including benefits for asylum-seekers[221]; decisions within prisons and in respect of release from prison[222]; and in disciplinary proceedings,[223] although if the disciplinary proceedings are determining a civil right or obligation, it will be necessary to provide an appeal on the merits, rather than merely an appeal on point of law.[224] It is also open to a court in judicial review to adopt a more intensive scrutiny of the rationality of the initial decision, by considering whether it had been made on a misunderstanding or ignorance of an established and relevant fact, or where rights are at stake, by using proportionality.[225] It has also been held that judicial review is sufficient where the decision under review entails the exercise of judgment and a particular expertise, and that conventional judicial review is a flexible remedy which can extend to investigation of the factual basis of a decision, where appropriate, without assuming an independent fact-finding role.[226]

Limits of curative effect

8-051   However, every decision-making procedure must be reviewed in its entirety, and judicial review will not always be considered to have curative effect. This point was emphasised in the decision of the ECtHR in *Tsfayo v United Kingdom*,[227] in which it was held that judicial review could not provide sufficient remedy for a decision taken on the basis of "a simple question of fact", and without the need for professional knowledge or experience and exercise of administrative discretion.[228] The applicant in *Tsfayo*, an Ethiopian national seeking asylum in the United Kingdom, had been successful in her application to Hammersmith and Fulham LBC (the council) for housing and council tax benefit, but had failed to renew her application the following year, as was required by law.[229] On realising that her benefits had ceased,

---

tribunal in relation to compensation for miscarriages of justice, art.6 compliance because of supervisory jurisdiction of the court, if necessary including questions of fact) (this issue did not arise on appeal: [2004] UKHL 18; [2005] 1 A.C. 1].

[220] *R. (on the application of Bono) v Harlow DC* [2002] EWHC 423 (Admin); [2002] 1 W.L.R. 2475 (council's housing benefit decision not independent and impartial but judicial review remedying the deficiency where sufficient control in respect of issues of primary fact).

[221] *Q* [2003] EWCA Civ 364; [2004] Q.B. 36 at [116]-[117] (provided that fair system of questioning of asylum-seekers in relation to welfare benefits, availability of judicial review would ensure compliance with art.6).

[222] *R. (on the application of Bourgass) v Secretary of State for Justice* [2015] UKSC 54; [2016] A.C. 384 at [126]; *MA* [2011] EWHC 1332 (Admin); [2011] A.C.D. 86.

[223] *R. (on the application of Thompson) v Law Society* [2004] EWCA Civ 167; [2004] 1 W.L.R. 2522 at [100] (if Office for Supervision of Solicitors had been determining a civil right or obligation, availability of judicial review would have secured art.6 compatibility).

[224] *Albert and Le Compte* (1983) 5 E.H.R.R. 533 at [36] (in a case involving disciplinary decisions relating to doctors taken by professional associations not complying with art.6(1), an appeal to a Belgian Court of Cassation only on a point of law was a violation of art.6); *Ghosh v General Medical Council* [2001] UKPC 29; [2001] 1 W.L.R. 1915 (GMC proceedings as a whole complying with art.6 given availability of rehearing on appeal to PC).

[225] *Holding & Barnes* [2001] UKHL 23; [2003] 2 A.C. 295 at [49]-[54] (Lord Slynn); see 11-073.

[226] *R. (on the application of XH and AL) v Secretary of State for the Home Department* [2017] EWCA Civ 41 at [147].

[227] *Tsfayo v United Kingdom* [2007] H.L.R. 19.

[228] *Tsfayo* [2007] H.L.R. 19 at [45]. For a similar approach in Ireland, see *Donegan and Gallagher v Dublin City Council* [2012] IESC 18, 27 February 2012 at [124]; see also *O'Driscoll v Limerick City Council, Ireland and Attorney General* [2012] IEHC 594 (distinguishing between the adequacy of judicial review for review of a fact and review of an opinion).

[229] *Tsfayo* [2007] H.L.R. 19 at [9]-[10].

she applied to the council for both prospective and backdated benefits.[230] Although her application for prospective benefits was successful, her application for backdated benefits was rejected on the basis that she did not have "good cause" for failing to renew her claim for benefits earlier.[231] The council upheld its decision,[232] and on appeal, the council's decision was upheld by Hammersmith and Fulham LBC Housing Benefit and Council Tax Benefit Review Board (the HBRB), on the basis that the applicant did not have "good cause" for failing to renew earlier and was not a credible witness.[233] With three councillors from the council in its membership and advised by a barrister from the council's legal department, the HBRB clearly did not satisfy the "independence" requirement of art.6, and the issue arose as to whether judicial review could provide curative effect in this situation.[234] The ECtHR reasoned that, while the Administrative Court had the power to quash the decision if it considered, inter alia, that there was no evidence to support the HBRB's factual findings, that its findings were plainly untenable, or that the HBRB had misunderstood or been ignorant of an established and relevant fact,[235] it did not have jurisdiction to rehear the evidence or substitute its own views as to the applicant's credibility.[236] This meant that there was never a possibility that the central issue would be determined by a tribunal that was independent of one of the parties to the dispute, and consequently, a violation of art.6 was found.[237]

Thus, in deciding whether a breach of art.6 at the first stage of the process can be cured by a later stage of the process, it is necessary to have regard to the nature of the first stage breach.[238] The more serious the breach in the first stage of the process, the more likely it is that a breach in the first stage of the process cannot be cured at the second stage; where the breach involves "denial of one of the fundamental elements of the right to a fair determination of a person's civil rights, namely the right to be heard", judicial review does not afford full jurisdiction, since it cannot make good the consequences of the denial of the opportunity to make representations at the earlier stage.[239]

8-052

PRELIMINARY DECISIONS

In what circumstances must the rules of procedural fairness be observed by persons entrusted with the conduct of an investigation but having no power to give a binding decision? This is one of the most troublesome problems in relation to procedural fairness. The authorities often appear to be, and sometimes are, in

8-053

---

230 *Tsfayo* [2007] H.L.R. 19 at [10].
231 *Tsfayo* [2007] H.L.R. 19 at [11].
232 *Tsfayo* [2007] H.L.R. 19 at [13].
233 *Tsfayo* [2007] H.L.R. 19 at [14], [47].
234 *Tsfayo* [2007] H.L.R. 19 at [35], [40], [46].
235 See 11-036.
236 *Tsfayo* [2007] H.L.R. 19 at [47].
237 *Tsfayo* [2007] H.L.R. 19 at [48].
238 *Wright* [2007] EWCA Civ 999; [2008] Q.B. 422 at [105]) (upheld [2009] UKHL 3; [2009] 1 A.C. 739; *R. (on the application of Royal College of Nursing) v Secretary of State for the Home Department* [2010] EWHC 2761 (Admin); [2011] P.T.S.R. 1193 at [67].
239 *Wright* [2007] EWCA Civ 999; [2008] Q.B. 422 at [106] (holding that a failure to afford a worker the opportunity to make representations before being included in a list of those deemed unsuitable to work with vulnerable adults could not be cured by judicial review) (upheld [2009] UKHL 3; [2009] 1 A.C. 739); *AF* [2010] EWHC 42 (Admin); [2010] A.C.D. 47; *Royal College of Nursing* [2010] EWHC 2761 (Admin); [2011] P.T.S.R. 1193; *BX v Secretary of State for the Home Department* [2010] EWCA Civ 481; [2010] 1 W.L.R. 2463.

conflict with one another. When one comes across a judicial formulation of general legal principle it is not infrequently misleading because the court has in mind only a limited range of contexts in which the problem arises. Again, some of the best-known dicta have been uttered in cases where no allegation of unfairness was made, and one can never be certain that the same words would have been used if that issue had been before the court. Nor is it always possible to assess how far the form of the proceedings has influenced the approach adopted by the court. If a quashing order is sought in relation to a non-binding report, the court may well look askance[240]; although this will not be the case if the report has "potentially wide implications"[241] and it is in the public interest to withdraw it.[242] If a prohibiting order is sought to prevent an investigation from going further, the court is also likely to be more easily persuaded.[243] Many of the considerations relevant in this context are also in play where the court is invited to refuse permission to apply for judicial review because an applicant has failed to pursue an alternative remedy.[244] However, the case law considered here is distinctive because the courts are considering a prior question; namely, are the procedural framework and effects of the preliminary decision such that it would be unfair to the affected person to hold that his entitlement to be heard at a later stage, or his entitlement to challenge the preliminary decision, means that no hearing or other procedural protection is required in respect of the preliminary decision?

8-054   Even if we ignored the existing authorities altogether, and the problem is examined entirely in the light of the need for fairness to be shown to individuals and for efficiency to be displayed in the conduct of public affairs, it is unlikely that any neat set of answers will emerge. It may not be very difficult to give the best available answer to a problem set in a given legislative and factual context; it is very difficult to supply satisfactory answers couched in general terms. However, the following tentative observations, based on principle as well as authority, are offered.

Proximity between investigation and act or decision

8-055   The degree of proximity between the investigation in question and an act or decision directly adverse to the interests of the claimant may be important. Thus, a person conducting a preliminary investigation with a view to recommending or deciding whether a formal inquiry or hearing (which may lead to a binding and adverse decision) should take place is not normally under any obligation to comply with the rules of fairness.[245] But such a person may be placed under such an obligation if the investigation is an integral and necessary part of a process which may

---

[240] See, e.g. *R. v St Lawrence's Hospital, Caterham, Statutory Visitors Ex p. Pritchard* [1953] 1 W.L.R. 1158; *R. (on the application of United Cooperatives Ltd) v Manchester City Council* [2005] EWHC 364 at [21] (Elias J noting that. "the courts are in principle reluctant to permit mere advice to be the subject of review"). cf. 3-026.

[241] *United Cooperatives Ltd* [2005] EWHC 364 (Admin) at [22].

[242] See, e.g. *Gillick v West Norfolk and Wisbech Area Health Authority* [1986] A.C. 112; *R. (on the application of Association of British Travel Agents Ltd (ABTA)) v Civil Aviation Authority* [2006] EWCA Civ 1356 at [65].

[243] See 8-047, 8-055 and 7-034.

[244] See 16-014.

[245] See, e.g. *Beetham v Trinidad Cement Co* [1960] A.C. 132, PC; *Parry-Jones v Law Society* [1969] 1 Ch. 1; in Australia, see *Medical Board of Queensland v Byrne* (1958) 100 C.L.R. 582; *Apache Northwest Pty Ltd v Agostini (No.2)* [2009] WASCA 231 (placing weight on whether the relevant report may be published).

terminate in action adverse to the interests of a person claiming to be heard before him.[246]

For instance, the principles of fairness must be observed by magistrates conducting a preliminary investigation in respect of a charge of an indictable offence.[247] A further reason for requiring observance of natural justice in a preliminary investigation by magistrates is that the investigation may end with a remand in custody or a requirement that bail be furnished; but because of the limited purpose of the hearing the accused is not entitled to confront and cross-examine all the witnesses who may be called by the prosecution at trial.[248] Although "prosecuting" decisions, whether in the criminal or disciplinary sphere, may be reviewable,[249] it would only be in a wholly exceptional case that the prosecutor might come under a duty to hear or consult the prospective accused, the complainant, or any other party, before coming to a decision as to whether or not to prosecute.[250] The exercise of the court's power of judicial review is less rare in the case of a decision not to prosecute than

8-056

---

[246] *Wiseman* [1971] A.C. 297 at 317 (Lord Wilberforce) (preliminary steps towards tax assessment; requirements of fairness satisfied by statutory procedure); *R. (on the application of Rowe) v Revenue and Customs Commissioners* [2015] EWHC 2293 (Admin) (no breach of fair procedures where an accelerated payment notice was issued prior to determination of dispute regarding tax avoidance measures); cf. *Pearlberg* [1972] 1 W.L.R. 534 (no duty to observe natural justice). In Canada, see *Re Attorney General Canada and Canadian Tobacco Manufacturers' Council* (1986) 26 D.L.R. (4th) 677 (duty of fairness applied to a power to recommend if, as a result of the recommendation, adverse consequences for the applicant are "probable or close to probable"). In Ireland suspensions may not require a fair hearing when made not as a way of punishment but by way of a holding operation pending full investigation of the complaint: *Morgan v The Provost Fellows and Scholars of the College of the Most Holy and Undivided Trinity of Queen Elizabeth near Dublin* [2003] IEHC 167; [2003] 3 I.R. 157 (although a person who is being suspended pending a full inquiry must be informed of the reason for his suspension and the full hearing must be heard within a reasonable time). However, in *Shatter v Guerin* [2016] IECA 318, doubt was cast on the distinction drawn between preliminary and final decisions for the purpose of the application of fair procedures. The issue was also considered in *Crayden Fishing Company Ltd v Sea Fisheries Protection Authority* [2017] IESC 74. See also *State (Shannon Atlantic Fisheries Limited) v McPolin* [1976] I.R. 93.

[247] *R. v Coleshill Justices Ex p. Davies* [1971] 1 W.L.R. 1684; cf. in Australia *Sankey v Whitlam* (1978) 142 C.L.R. 1 at 83-84 (Mason J).

[248] *R. v Epping and Harlow Justices Ex p. Massaro* [1973] Q.B. 433; cf. the duty of fairness imposed upon the prosecution in a trial to call or to reveal to the accused beforehand the identity of material witnesses: *R. v Leyland Justices Ex p. Hawthorn* [1979] Q.B. 283 (although quaere whether this decision should properly be seen as resting upon a duty of fairness: *Ex p. Al-Mehdawi* [1990] 1 A.C. 876). However, the defendant has the right to give evidence after the magistrates have rejected his submission of no case to answer: *R. v Horseferry Road Stipendiary Magistrate Ex p. Adams* [1977] 1 W.L.R. 1197, DC. Courts may also be reluctant to intervene in the conduct of preliminary examinations before their conclusion: *R. v Wells Street Stipendiary Magistrate Ex p. Seillon* [1978] 1 W.L.R. 1002 (refusal of cross-examination).

[249] See 3-006; *R. v Metropolitan Police Commissioner Ex p. Blackburn* [1968] 2 Q.B. 118; *R. v General Council of the Bar Ex p. Percival* [1991] 1 Q.B. 212. In the Canadian case of *Re Peel Board of Education and B* (1987) 59 O.R. (2nd) 654, it was held that a school principal must give a pupil an opportunity to be heard before suspending for misconduct; *Knight v Indian Head School Division No.19* (1990) 69 D.L.R. (4th) 489 (education director entitled to notice and fair opportunity to respond before being dismissed, even though dismissible without cause and the opportunity of subsequent review by a board).

[250] *Wiseman* [1971] A.C. 297. In *Selvarajan v Race Relations Board* [1975] 1 W.L.R. 1686 at 1696, Lawton LJ suggested that the courts might be entitled to interfere with the DPP's discretion to initiate a prosecution if he acted "unfairly" but there was no suggestion that fairness might require consultation: *Blackburn* [1968] 2 Q.B. 118; *R. v Police Complaints Board Ex p. Madden* [1983] 1 W.L.R. 447 (where it was accepted that the Board was under a duty to act "fairly" in considering complaints); *Percival* [1991] 1 Q.B. 212; *Brooks v DPP of Jamaica* [1994] 1 A.C. 568 (decision of DPP to prefer indictment, or of judge to consent to preferral, was a purely procedural step and neither principles of fairness nor Jamaican Constitution entitled person indicted to be given prior notice of DPP's decision, or to attend before Judge).

a decision to prosecute because the former is final whereas the latter leaves the defendant free to challenge the prosecution's case in the usual way through the criminal court.[251]

Preliminary investigations subject to procedural fairness

8-057   Principles of procedural fairness may also apply to the conduct of an inquiry or investigation, the holding of which is not a prerequisite of further proceedings or action.

Public inquiries

8-058   For instance, since the hearings and report of an inquiry set up to investigate an alleged public scandal attract a great deal of publicity, it may be unfair to deny a person against whom damaging allegations may be made before the tribunal the procedural protection accorded to a defendant in legal proceedings.[252] But even where the report of such an inquiry may be expected to contain criticism of particular persons, it may be that the efficient conduct of the inquiry requires that rights to legal representation and particularly cross-examination be dispensed with.[253] It may also be the case that confidentiality is required in the conduct of the inquiry and such confidentiality will not mean that the right to fair procedures have been violated.[254] It has been held in respect of an inquiry that while ultimately the question of fairness is one of law for the court, nonetheless, the court would give great weight to the tribunal's own view of what was fair and would not lightly decide that the tribunal had adopted an unfair procedure.[255]

---

[251] *R. (on the application of FB) v Director of Public Prosecutions* [2009] EWHC 106 (Admin); [2009] 1 W.L.R. 2072 at [52]. See also *NXB v Crown Prosecution Service* [2015] EWHC 631 (QB).

[252] See Inquiries Act 2005 s.9 (requirement of impartiality), s.17 (evidence and procedure). Procedural irregularities in a report may be raised collaterally in proceedings to declare invalid an instrument for the making of which a valid report was a prerequisite: *Hoffmann-La Roche (F) & Co AG v Secretary of State for Trade and Industry* [1975] A.C. 295 at 354, 365. In Canada, in *Syndicat des employés de production du Québec et de l'Acadie v Canada (Canadian Human Rights Commission)* [1989] 52 S.C.R. 879, the Supreme Court stated, obiter, that complainants are entitled to know the substance of evidence contained in the investigative report and to comment on it before their complaint of discrimination is dismissed. And in *Federation of Women's Teachers' Association of Ontario v Ontario (Human Rights Commission)* (1988) 67 O.R. (2d) 492 it was held that the Commission, before deciding whether to refer a complaint of discrimination for adjudication, was required to inform those under investigation of the substance of the case against them.

[253] See Sir Louis Blom-Cooper, "Witnesses and the Scott Inquiry" [1994] P.L. 1 (on the Arms to Iraq inquiry); and 7-114. In New Zealand natural justice has been held to apply to preliminary decisions: *Birss v Secretary for Justice* [1984] 1 N.Z.L.R. 513; *Fraser* [1984] 1 N.Z.L.R. 116; and when reporting and making recommendations affecting private interests Royal Commissions and Commissions of Inquiry in New Zealand must observe natural justice principles: *Re Erebus Royal Commission; Air New Zealand Ltd v Mahon* [1984] A.C. 808, PC; *Peters v Davison* [1999] 3 N.Z.L.R. 164.

[254] *Re LP's Application for Judicial Review* [2014] NICA 67 (holding that the Historical Institutional Abuse Inquiry was entitled to refuse to give a witness who had given evidence a recording of her statement; the forum was intended as a confidential service where victims and survivors could recount their experience with total confidence in the confidentiality of that stage of the inquiry, and witnesses had been informed at the outset that no recordings would be made available).

[255] *Re LP's Application for Judicial Review* [2014] NICA 67 at [31].

Investigations under the Companies Act

The case for requiring a Department of Trade inspector conducting a formal **8-059**
investigation into a company's affairs[256] to observe the detailed rules of fairness has
been thought to be perhaps less strong: here again the report may lead to judicial
proceedings, but is not a prerequisite of the institution of such proceedings; the
inspector's report may at the discretion of the Secretary of State be published,[257] but
the investigation is carried out in private. The balance is still a fine one: the
investigation (to which officers or agents of the company, or any other person whom
the inspectors believe may be in possession of information relating to any matter
which they believe is relevant to the investigation may be compelled to attend and
to answer questions and produce documents)[258] and the report expose persons to a
legal hazard[259] as well as potentially damaging publicity. It has accordingly been
held that the rudiments of procedural fairness must be observed. The inspector must,
before publishing a report containing serious criticisms and allegations against a
person, put to that person the substance of them and give him an opportunity of
rebutting them.[260]

However, it has been held that the inspector is not required to allow the cross-   **8-060**
examination of witnesses, nor is he required to recall the person to rebut allegations subsequently made by other witnesses, nor to submit his tentative conclusions to the "accused" before sending his report to the minister (although it is in fact
the usual practice of inspectors to submit draft conclusions to affected
individuals).[261] The minister is under no implied procedural duty to entertain
representations or to disclose the information that he has acquired before exercising his discretion to appoint inspectors to conduct an inquiry.[262] Judicial authority
on investigations of the kind conducted under the Companies Act has often laid
emphasis on their non-judicial character, the importance of an expeditious conclusion and the difficulty of the investigative task.[263] This view has also been taken by
the ECtHR, on a challenge to an inspectors' report on the ground that it violated the
applicants' rights to honour and reputation under art.6(1) of the Convention, and
denied them effective court access.[264] The ECtHR held that the functions performed
by the inspectors were essentially investigative, in that they did not adjudicate either

---

[256] Companies Act 1985 ss.431-434; 436-437, 439, 441, 442-445, 446A-E.

[257] Companies Act 1985 s.437(3)(c).

[258] Companies Act 1985 s.434.

[259] cf. *Testro Bros Pty Ltd v Tait* (1963) 109 C.L.R. 353 at 370 (Kitto J, concurring with the proposition in the text); *Wiseman* [1971] A.C. 297 at 317. As to the effect of the privilege against self-
incrimination, see *McClelland, Pope & Langley Ltd v Howard* [1968] 1 All E.R. 569, HL. *In Re
London United Investments Plc* [1992] Ch. 578 (privilege is impliedly excluded by 1985 Act); see
now *Saunders v UK* (1997) 23 E.H.R.R. 313.

[260] *Re Pergamon Press Ltd* [1971] Ch. 388.

[261] *Maxwell v Department of Trade and Industry* [1974] Q.B. 523; *R. v Cheltenham Justices Ex p.
Secretary of State for Trade* [1977] 1 W.L.R. 95, DC (witness summons, issued to inspector to reveal
evidence given in confidence at an inquiry, quashed); but below for the position under the European
Convention. As was done by the Scott Inquiry (n. 166); *R. (on the application of Clegg) v Secretary
of State for Trade and Industry* [2002] EWCA Civ 519; [2003] B.C.C. 128.

[262] *Norwest Holst Ltd v Department of Trade* [1978] Ch. 201.

[263] See, e.g. *Re Grosvenor & West-End Ry. Terminus Hotel Co* (1897) 76 L.T. 337; *Hearts of Oak Assurance Co v Attorney General* [1932] A.C. 392; *O'Connor v Waldron* [1935] A.C. 76. See also s.236
of the Insolvency Act 1986, under which a person may be compelled to answer questions without
the benefit of the privilege against self-incrimination: In *British & Commonwealth Holdings Plc
(Joint Administrators) v Spicer and Oppenheim* [1993] A.C. 426; *Bishopsgate Investment Management v Maxwell* [1993] Ch. 1.

[264] *Fayed v UK* (1994) 18 E.H.R.R. 393.

in form or in substance, nor make a civil or criminal adjudication concerning the applicants' rights. Even though the report may have led to uncompensated damage to the applicants' reputations, it was held that the potential remedy of judicial review, while limited, provided sufficient guarantees for the persons affected.[265]

8-061   In another context, the seeking of information from a private investigator in proceedings arising from phone hacking, it has been held that where a defendant's right to claim privilege against self-incrimination in the context of an investigation is removed by statute, the statute will not be regarded as breaching art.6, provided that it contains a provision preventing the evidence from being used against the individual in criminal proceedings.[266]

Binding nature of preliminary decision

8-062   In a number of cases in which the proceedings of investigating bodies have been impugned (mainly on grounds other than non-compliance with the principles of fairness), the courts have refused to intervene unless the investigation does or can culminate in a determination or order which has binding force or will itself acquire binding force upon confirmation or promulgation by another body or which otherwise controls the decision of that other body.[267] To put the matter in another way, an investigating body is under no duty to act fairly if it cannot do more than recommend or advise on action which another body may take in its own name and in its own discretion.[268] This proposition cannot be accepted without qualification. Whilst it would be absurd to impose judicial standards on every body who advises a government department as to the exercise of its executive functions, justice will sometimes demand, as the courts are increasingly recognising, that an investigation preceding a discretionary administrative decision be conducted in accordance with the requirements of procedural fairness.[269]

Illustrations

8-063   •   Inspectors holding inquiries in respect of compulsory purchase orders are undoubtedly obliged to act fairly,[270] although their findings and recommendations are in no way binding on the minister when he decides whether or not to confirm the order.

   •   If express procedural duties are cast upon an investigating authority this in

---

[265] *R. (on the application of Harrison) v Secretary of State for the Home Department* [2003] EWCA Civ 432; [2003] I.N.L.R. 284 (Minister of State's letter refusing Harrison's claim for citizenship and inviting him to make a fresh application for naturalisation was at its highest a provisional determination of the claimant's application); *R. v Secretary of State for Health Ex p. C* [2000] 1 F.L.R. 627.

[266] *Phillips v News Group Newspapers Ltd* [2012] EWCA Civ 48; [2012] 2 W.L.R. 848 at [74] (dealing with s.72 of the Senior Courts Act 1981). See also: [2012] UKSC 28; [2013] 1 A.C. 1.

[267] See 3-026.

[268] For example, in Canada: *R. v Macfarlane Ex p. O'Flanagan and O'Kelly* (1923) 32 C.L.R. 518 (not a natural justice case); *Ex p. Pritchard* [1953] 1 W.L.R. 1158; *Guay v Lafleur* [1965] S.C.R. 12; *de Freitas v Benny* [1976] A.C. 239. cf. *Rees* [1994] 2 A.C. 173; *R v Wokingham DC Ex p. J* [1999] 2 F.L.R. 1136, QBD.

[269] Whether or not the function may be characterised as "judicial": *Re Pergamon Press Ltd* [1971] Ch. 388; *R. v Race Relations Board Ex p. Selvarajan* [1975] 1 W.L.R. 1686; *R. v Commission for Racial Equality Ex p. Cottrell and Rothon* [1980] 1 W.L.R. 1580 at 1587; *Ex p. Hosenball* [1977] 1 W.L.R. 766 (hearing before advisory committee pending deportation on national security grounds); *Ex p. Cheblak* [1991] 1 W.L.R. 890.

[270] See 7-025, fn.103.

itself may support the view that a common-law duty to observe the requirements of fairness attaches to the investigations.[271]

- Even where statute expressly accords a great degree of procedural latitude to the Parliamentary Ombudsman, the courts recognise that a report containing criticisms of a government department should be sent in draft to the department for comments.[272] However, it has been held that a person whose complaint initiated the Ombudsman's investigation—and who may be offered financial recompense as a consequence of his report—is not entitled to a copy of the draft report, because although the complainant's rights are affected by the decision, it is the department and not the complainant who is being investigated and who is liable to face public criticism for its acts.[273]

- A duty of procedural fairness is imposed upon the proceedings of the Parole Board both by statute and by the common law, inasmuch as a decision by the Home Secretary to revoke the licence of a released prisoner and recall him to jail may be contingent upon the receipt of a recommendation by the Board to that effect.[274]

Duty to observe principles of fairness

In special situations, persons conducting an inquiry limited to the purpose of collecting information may be obliged to observe the principles of procedural fairness, although they are not even entitled to make recommendations to the deciding body.[275] Such a situation can arise because the type of inquiry conducted is one in which members of the public have come to expect certain minimum procedural standards to be maintained. In this situation, as in some of the others reviewed in this chapter, the observance of the *audi alteram partem* principle (hear both sides) may be called for because non-observance would give the appearance of injustice. This was the position with the preliminary investigation into the conduct of a judge:

8-064

---

[271] For example, in Canada: *Saulnier v Quebec Police Commission* [1976] 1 S.C.R. 572; and *Moumdjian v Canada (Security Intelligence Review Committee)* (1999) 177 D.L.R. (4th) 192.

[272] The obligation to give the official against whom a complaint is made and his departmental head an opportunity of commenting on the allegations may be regarded as importing a more general duty to act fairly with respect to those officials; but, this apart, the ombudsmen enjoy the widest freedom of action in relation to matters within his competence (Parliamentary Commissioner Act 1967 s.7; Health Service Commissioner Act 1993 s.11; Local Government Act 1974 ss.28, 29); *Grunwick Processing Laboratories Ltd v ACAS* [1978] A.C. 655 where an express statutory duty to ascertain workers' opinions was construed as mandatory; although it is virtually inconceivable that this would ever require a formal hearing to be held, some of the judgments referred to the body's function as judicial and to its procedural duty to comply with the rules of natural justice. On Ombudsmen generally, see 1-077.

[273] *R. v Parliamentary Commissioner for Administration Ex p. Dyer* [1994] 1 W.L.R. 621, DC; cf. *R. v Commissioner for Local Administration Ex p. Eastleigh BC* [1988] Q.B. 855; *R. v Commissioner for Local Administration Ex p. Croydon LBC* [1989] 1 All E.R. 1033. See also *Traveller Movement v Ofcom* [2015] EWHC 406 (Admin).

[274] Crime (Sentences) Act 1997 ss.28, 32; *Thynne, Wilson and Gunnell v UK* (1991) 13 E.H.R.R. 666; *R. v Parole Board Ex p. Wilson* [1992] Q.B. 740. However, where the Parole Board merely reviewed (as an extra-statutory practice) and confirmed the decision of the Secretary of State to recall to prison a discretionary life sentence prisoner who had been released on licence, prior to a full statutory review, the CA held that the requirements of full hearing do not apply, because that review was only intended to be "tentative and provisional": *R. v Parole Board Ex p. Watson* [1996] 1 W.L.R. 906 (Sir Thomas Bingham MR); cf. *R. v Secretary of State for the Home Department Ex p. Seton* unreported 25 April 1996. Moreover, in an emergency situation, the Secretary of State has the power pursuant to s.32(2) to revoke the licence without consulting the Board: *Re Cummings* [2001] EWCA Civ 45; [2001] 1 W.L.R. 822.

[275] *Wednesbury Corp v Ministry of Housing and Local Government (No.2)* [1966] 2 Q.B. 275 at 302-303 (Diplock LJ).

the suspension of a judge, even temporarily, was a matter of such significance that he should be given the opportunity of making representations before it happened.[276]

LACK OF FAIR PROCEDURE MADE NO DIFFERENCE OR CAUSED NO HARM

8-065   The contention that a procedural flaw "made no difference", in so far as the defendant public authority would have made the same decision even if different procedures had been followed, can be made in two distinct ways: (a) the court may hold that there is no *entitlement* to fair procedure; (b) the court may accept that there is an entitlement to fair procedure but exercise *discretion to withhold a remedy*.[277] In each situation, the court is in some measure invited to look beyond the narrow question of whether the decision was taken in a procedurally improper manner, to the wider question of whether a decision properly taken would or could have benefited the applicant.

8-066   This chapter is concerned with situation (a), though a sharp distinction is not always drawn in the judgments. The response of the courts to this argument, in its many forms, is still uncertain.[278] In some cases the courts have refused to grant relief when satisfied that the outcome could not have been different had natural justice been fully observed.[279] These decisions have been sought to be explained on the

---

[276] *Rees* [1994] 2 A.C. 173. cf. the majority decision in *Furnell v Whangerei High School Board* [1973] A.C. 660 (suspension of school teacher). On suspension of a judge, see now Constitutional Reform Act 2005 ss.108-121 and Sch.14.

[277] See 18-047.

[278] For comparative perspectives, see the Australian case *Re Refugee Review Tribunal; Ex p. Aala* (2000) 204 C.L.R. 802 (where constitutional writs are sought, refusal of relief on basis that breach of procedural fairness made no difference approached very strictly) and *Minister for Immigration and Border Protection v WZARH* (2015) 256 C.L.R. 326 at 342 (holding that proof of harm not required when the procedure itself was inherently unfair). Australian cases hesitate to deny relief on discretionary grounds, unless either a legal requirement or an incontrovertible fact would almost certainly compel the same result: *Ucar v Nylex Industrial Products Pty Ltd* (2007) 17 V.R. 492 at 519. In Canada, see *Mobil Oil Canada Ltd v Canada Newfoundland Offshore Petroleum Board* (1994) 111 D.L.R. (4th) 1. See also A. Mills, "The 'Makes no Difference' Controversy" [2013] J.R. 124; D. Feldman, "Error of Law and Flawed Administrative Acts" [2014] C.L.J. 275.

[279] *R. v Monopolies and Mergers Commission Ex p. Argyll* [1986] 1 W.L.R. 763; *Durayappah v Fernando* [1967] 2 A.C. 337 at 350; *Fulop (Imre) v Secretary of State for the Home Department* [1995] Imm. A.R. 323, CA ("no possibility" of a different decision since missing documents unhelpful to applicant); *R. v Camden LBC Ex p. Paddock* [1995] C.O.D. 130 (case "falls within the narrow margin of cases in which the court can say with confidence that the [unfairness] has caused no actual injustice"; *R. v Islington LBC, Ex p. Degnan* [1998] C.O.D. 46, CA ("exceptional case"; judge "near to certainty" that the flawed decision made no difference to the result); *R. (on the application of Ghadami) v Harlow DC* [2004] EWHC 1883 (Admin) at [73]; *Aston v Nursing & Midwifery Council* [2004] EWHC 2368 (Admin) at [73]; *R. (on the application of Varma) v Duke of Kent* [2004] EWHC 1705 (Admin) at [27]; *R. (on the application of Wainwright) v Richmond upon Thames LBC* [2001] EWCA Civ 2062; *Mousaka Inc v Golden Seagull Maritime Inc* [2002] 1 W.L.R. 395 at [35]; *W v The Independent Appeal Panel of Bexley LBC* [2008] EWHC 758 (Admin); [2008] E.L.R. 301 at [38]; *Edwards* [2008] 1 W.L.R. 158 at [65] (pointless to quash a permit simply to enable the public to be consulted on out-of-date data) (distinguished in *R. (on the application of Corus UK Ltd (t/a Orb Electrical Steels)) v Newport City Council* [2010] EWCA Civ 1626 at [14]-[15], in which the court allowed an appeal against an order of the trial judge refusing to quash a planning permission; the trial judge had erred in treating the matter as a planning dispute which could be resolved by balancing the prejudice of one against the other and had ignored the important consideration that a planning permission was a public act and if unlawful, the normal result was that it should be quashed); *SH (Afghanistan) v Secretary of State for the Home Department* [2011] EWCA Civ 1284

ground that the relief sought was discretionary,[280] or on the ground that breach makes an order voidable rather than void.[281] It is submitted that neither explanation is sufficient. As to the former, it is right to note that a refusal of relief on the ground that it would make "no difference" may be explained either as an exercise of the courts' discretion as to the grant of relief,[282] or as a part of the consideration of whether the principles of fairness have in fact been infringed at all. However, this in itself goes no way towards an identification of those cases in which the courts are prepared to refuse relief, as a matter of discretion or otherwise. As to the latter, it is clear that the court may still have discretion to refuse the statutory remedy even though the decision is void.[283] There are also cases, arising in various contexts, in which it has been assumed that the inadequacy of the hearing is in itself sufficient for the decision to be set aside: in those instances the courts have declined to embark upon a speculative inquiry about the possible impact of the procedural irregularity upon the decision.[284] It is however clear that it is not necessary for the claimant to show that the decision would inevitably have been different.[285]

Statutory applications to quash

Whether a person who has been denied an adequate hearing must also establish that this affected the ultimate decision is particularly relevant when proceedings are brought for the statutory remedy to quash, for example, a planning appeal or a compulsory purchase order.[286] Relief may be granted either, if there has been a failure to comply with statutory requirements and the applicant has been substantially prejudiced thereby, or if the decision or order in question was not one that the authority was empowered to make.[287]   **8-067**

In some cases where it has been assumed that a breach of the rules of natural justice falls under the first limb, the claimant has been granted relief upon show-   **8-068**

---

at [15] (tribunals like courts, had to set aside a determination reached by the adoption of an unfair procedure unless satisfied that it would be pointless to do so because the result would be the same); *Regina (on the application of Bruton) v Secretary of State for Justice* [2017] EWHC 1967 (Admin); [2017] 4 W.L.R. 152.

[280] *Glynn* [1971] 1 W.L.R. 487; *Ex p. Roffey* [1969] 2 Q.B. 538 (certiorari; undue delay); *Fullbrook v Berkshire Magistrates' Courts Committee* (1970) 69 L.G.R. 75 (declaration; unreasonable conduct of plaintiff). See also *R. (on the application of English Speaking Board (International) Ltd v Secretary of State for the Home Department* [2011] EWHC 1788 (Admin) at [59]-[63] (declaration granted instead of a quashing order as even though it was procedurally flawed to make changes to the Immigration Rules without consultation, there was insufficient evidence that they had impacted adversely on those genuinely wishing to take courses in support of their applications). See 18-047.

[281] In *Stevenson v United Road Transport Union* [1977] I.C.R. 893, the characterisation of the decision as void or voidable was stated to be relevant only to the court's approach to its exercise of discretion to grant relief, in that case a declaration. On the void/voidable distinction, see 4-058.

[282] See 18-047.

[283] *Miller v Weymouth and Melcombe Regis Corp* (1974) 27 P. & C.R. 468 at 480-481 (not a natural justice case, but where the court declined to quash a void decision for lack of prejudice to the applicant); cf. *Goddard v Minister of Housing and Local Government* [1958] 1 W.L.R. 1151 at 1153; *Savoury v Secretary of State for Wales* (1976) 31 P. & C.R. 344 at 347.

[284] *John v Rees* [1970] Ch. 345, 402; *R. v Thames Magistrates' Court Ex p. Polemis* [1974] 1 W.L.R. 1371 at 1375-1376; *West* (1975) 29 P. & C.R. 316 at 320-332 and the cautionary dicta of Lord Hailsham in *London & Clydeside Estates Ltd v Aberdeen DC* [1980] 1 W.L.R. 182 at 189.

[285] *R. (on the application of Gopikrishna) v Office of the Independent Adjudicator for Higher Education* [2015] EWHC 207 (Admin) at [209].

[286] See 17-024.

[287] See, e.g. Town and Country Planning Act 1990 s.288. There may also be cases where the statutory provisions clearly identify the consequences of non-compliance with any statutory procedural requirements: *R. (on the application of Kilroy) v Parrs Wood High School Governing Body* [2011] EWHC 3489 (Admin); [2012] E.L.R. 146 at [22].

ing that had he been afforded the hearing to which he was entitled, the decision might have been different.[288] In other cases, however, the courts have treated the defect as falling under the second limb, but have defined a breach of natural justice to include the risk that the irregularity might have affected the outcome, although no clear guidance has emerged on the closeness with which a court should scrutinise the facts.[289] Once again, it may be questioned, however, whether such categorisation does more than mask the principles upon which the courts act. It appears clear that in planning cases, where a failure to comply with a statutory procedural requirement is alleged, substantial prejudice must be shown.[290] In other circumstances, however, the position is less clear although courts are unlikely to interfere with decisions where the results, however irregular, are of trivial importance, or wholly speculative,[291] or remote.

Caution required in relation to the "no difference" argument

8-069   The courts have rightly cautioned against the suggestion that no prejudice has been caused to the applicant because the flawed decision would inevitably have been the same and as a general principle, a court will be slow to rule that no harm has been done.[292] It is not for the courts to substitute their opinion for that of the authority constituted by law to decide the matters in question.[293] As it has been put, in a case involving a destruction order under the Dangerous Dogs Act 1991,[294]

"the notion that when the rules of natural justice have not been observed, one can still

---

[288] See, e.g. *Wilson v Secretary of State for the Environment* [1973] 1 W.L.R. 1083 at 1095-1096 (if adequate notice had been given, representations might have been made and an inquiry might have been held); *Davies v Secretary of State for Wales* [1977] J.P.L. 102; and *George v Secretary of State for the Environment* (1979) 250 E.G. 339 (relief denied). Where statutory requirements were a matter of reasonable judgment, and sufficient notice had been provided to tenants regarding the consequences of a failure to pay water charges, substantial compliance with the statutory requirements would suffice: *Rochdale BC v Dixon* [2011] EWCA Civ 1173; [2012] P.T.S.R. 1336 at [56]. See also *R. (on the application of Tait) v Secretary of State for Communities and Local Government* [2012] EWHC 643 (Admin) at [70]-[71] (there was no need to identify any actual prejudice as it was important that justice was seen to be done; in any case, if an inspector had a conversation in the absence of a representative there was a real risk that justice would not be seen to be done); *R. v Mayor of Greenwich LBC Ex p. Patel* (1985) 51 P. & C.R. 282 (real as opposed to remote or fanciful loss or prejudice must be shown) *R. v Canterbury City Council Ex p. Springimage Ltd* (1994) 68 P. & C.R. 171 (relief denied because "no real possibility" of different decision).

[289] *Hibernian Property Co Ltd v Secretary of State for the Environment* (1974) 27 P. & C.R. 197 at 212, 214; *Lake District Special Planning Board v Secretary of State for the Environment* [1975] J.P.L. 220; *Performance Cars Ltd v Secretary of State for the Environment* (1977) 34 P. & C.R. 92; *General Accident Fire & Life Assurance Corp Ltd v Secretary of State for the Environment* (1977) 241 E.G. 842; *R. v Visiting Justice at Her Majesty's Prison, Pentridge Ex p. Walker* [1975] V.R. 883 (magistrate's failure to realise that he had a discretion to allow legal representation did not prejudice applicant); *George* (1979) 250 E.G. 339.

[290] *Ex p. Patel* (1985) 51 P. & C.R. 282; *R. (on the application of Midcounties Co-operative Ltd) v Wyre Forest DC* [2009] EWHC 964 (Admin) at [96]. See also *Rochdale BC* [2011] EWCA Civ 1173; [2012] P.T.S.R. 1336 at [56] (substantial compliance with the statutory provisions was sufficient to avoid quashing). Contrast *R. (on the application of Warley) v Wealden DC* [2011] EWHC 2083 (Admin); [2012] Env. L.R. 4 (a tailpiece in a planning permission offended against the rule of law as the public were entitled to know in public documents what planning permission had been granted).

[291] Although in such cases the claimant for judicial review is unlikely to be regarded as having "sufficient interest" for the grant of permission (see Ch.2). In India, it has been held that a prior hearing is required when an administrative action is "prejudicial to the citizen": *The Scheduled Caste and Weaker Sections Welfare Assoc v State of Karnataka A.I.R.* 1991 S.C. 1117.

[292] *R. v Tandridge District Council Ex p. Al-Fayed* [2000] 1 P.L.R 58.

[293] *Chief Constable of the North Wales Police v Evans* [1982] 1 W.L.R., 1160 (Lord Hailsham), 1173 (Lord Brightman); *John v Rees* [1970] Ch. 345, 582; *Brent* [1982] Q.B. 593 at 734.

[294] *R. v Ealing Magistrates Court Ex p. Fanneran* (1996) 160 J.P. 409 (Staughton LJ).

uphold the result because it would not have made any difference, is to be treated with great caution. Down that slippery slope lies the way to dictatorship. On the other hand, if it is a case where it is demonstrable beyond doubt that it would have made no difference, the court may, if it thinks fit, uphold a conviction even if natural justice had not been done."

Further, "natural justice is not always or entirely about the fact or substance of   **8-070**
fairness. It has also something to do with the appearance of fairness. In the hallowed phrase, 'Justice must not only be done, it must also be seen to be done'".[295]
These cases support the view that the fundamental principle at stake is that public confidence in the fairness of adjudication or hearing procedures may be undermined if decisions are allowed to stand despite the absence of what a reasonable observer might regard as an adequate hearing, rather than that injustice lies only in holding an individual bound by a decision whose substantive reliability is cast in doubt by the existence of procedural irregularities.[296]

But on the whole judges have declined to commit themselves unequivocally to   **8-071**
the proposition that intervention will never be withheld when they are satisfied that no amount of procedural propriety would have affected the outcome.[297]

Illustrations

*   A decision by school governors refusing to correct an inaccurate statement in   **8-072**
    a consultation paper, and refusing to extend the consultation period was not

---

[295] *Ex p. Fanneran* (1996) 8 Admin. L.R. 351, 358 (Staughton LJ). A possibly more extreme formulation was set out by Rougier J in the same case (at 359): "... no one can ever say for certain what must have happened in the circumstances which have not, in fact, arisen. The robing rooms up and down this land are full of strange tales of seemingly impregnable cases foundering on some unforeseen forensic reef. It is not, in my opinion, for this court to employ its imagination to postulate facts which might or might not have occurred or arguments which might or might not have succeeded had the rules of natural justice been followed". See also *R. (on the application of C) v Secretary of State for Justice* [2008] EWCA Civ 882; [2009] Q.B. 657 at [49] (regulations were quashed where a race equality impact assessment had been carried out subsequently even though it validated the decision as refusing relief would have sent the "wrong message" to public authorities). See also: *Tait* [2012] EWHC 643 (Admin) at [70]-[71]; *San Vicente v Secretary of State for Communities and Local Government* [2013] EWHC 2713 (Admin); [2014] J.P.L. 217 at [29]–[31] (although overruled on whether or not there had actually been unfairness on appeal, [2014] EWCA Civ 1555; [2015] J.P.L. 562).

[296] *Cheall v Association of Professional Executive, Clerical and Computer Staff* [1983] Q.B. 126 (Donaldson LJ). On the facts, relief was refused on the ground that although the applicant had been denied a fair hearing, the court held that he could not "feel unfairly treated", effectively because the decision-maker did not have a discretion to decide in his favour (on appeal it was found that there had been no denial of natural justice: [1983] 2 A.C. 180). cf. *R. v Inner West London Coroner Ex p. Dallaglio* [1994] 4 All E.R. 139; *Harada Ltd (t/a Chequepoint UK Ltd) v Turner (No.1)* [2001] EWCA Civ 599; *R. (on the application of Takoushis) v HM Coroner for Inner North London* [2005] EWCA Civ 1440; [2006] 1 W.L.R. 461; *Jones v HM Coroner for the Southern District of Greater London* [2010] EWHC 931 (Admin); [2010] Inquest L.R. 80 (new inquest ordered where there had been insufficient inquiry into the means by which a deceased came to die from fentanyl toxicity and where there was a wider public interest in a full inquiry given that there had been a considerable number of deaths in the United States and the United Kingdom linked to unintended overdoses of fentanyl).

[297] See, e.g. *Ridge v Baldwin* [1964] A.C. 40 at 68; *Wislang v Medical Practitioners Disciplinary Committee* [1974] 1 N.Z.L.R. 29 at 42, 45; *R. v Hull Prison Board of Visitors Ex p. St Germain* [1979] Q.B. 425 at 450-451; *Stininato v Auckland Boxing Association (Inc)* [1978] 1 N.Z.L.R. 1 at 29 (but see the dissenting view of Woodhouse J at 15-16). cf. *Bhardwaj v Post Office* [1978] I.C.R. 144 (appeal from industrial tribunal dismissed because no real likelihood that chairman's overly strict attitude towards the appellant would have affected the result: but the tribunal's order of costs against appellant was allowed).

unfair because the error in question could not have led a person reading the pamphlet to have reached a different conclusion.[298]

- A decision by the chairman of the Monopolies and Mergers Commission to recommend to the Secretary of State that a take-over reference be laid aside, while beyond his powers, should not, in the discretion of the court, be quashed because there was little doubt that a properly constituted committee would have reached the same decision.[299]
- Moreover, it has been held that there was no procedural unfairness caused by refusing to permit a prisoner to make further submissions on the basis of a report and the failure to do so had not been procedurally unfair as the report did not contain any new information and was based entirely on evidence placed before the parole board.[300]
- There was no procedural unfairness where notices of a planning application were served by post and one person had not been served notice as that person clearly knew of the planning application and was not denied the opportunity to make representations.[301]
- Although the claimant should have seen the evidence put to the university visitor in respect of a decision to terminate his registration as a student, he could not have made any representations which would have affected the result and consequently, leave for judicial review was refused.[302]
- Similarly, although a local authority had breached its statutory duty to consult by failing sufficiently to notify individual local residents of plans to construct a toucan crossing, the decision to approve the crossing could stand because there was no real possibility that the local authority would have reached a different decision had it complied with the duty to consult.[303]

---

[298] *R. v Haberdashers' Ashe's Hatcham School Governors Ex p. ILEA, The Times,* 9 March 1989; *R. (on the application of Siborurema) v Office of the Independent Adjudicator* [2007] EWCA Civ 1365; [2008] E.L.R. 209 at [66] (there was "no real possibility" that disclosure of the information for comment would have affected the decision). In *R. (on the application of Gopikrishna) v Office of the Independent Adjudicator for Higher Education* [2015] EWHC 207 (Admin) at [209], it was held that there was no real possibility that a letter from the university confirming that it did not have formal procedures for re-opening appeals and a response from the claimant would have materially affected the decision: [217].

[299] *Ex p. Argyll* [1985] 1 W.L.R. 763 (the CA also took into account the needs of good public administration); cf. *R. v Secretary of State for Education and Science Ex p. ILEA* [1990] C.O.D. 319; *R. v Bristol CC Ex p. Pearce* (1984) 83 L.G.R. 711 (food hawkers not shown objections; but those objections could not possibly have motivated decision).

[300] *R. (on the application of Faulkner) v Secretary of State for the Home Department* [2006] EWHC 563 (Admin).

[301] *Ghadami* [2004] EWHC 1883 (Admin) at [73] (although the notice was defective for want of a closing date for representations, the court would refuse relief as the defect had not frustrated the relevant object of giving the public an opportunity to make representations about the proposed development and neither the applicant nor the public had suffered any prejudice).

[302] *Varma* [2004] EWHC 1705 (Admin); [2004] E.L.R. 616 at [27]. See also *Burger v Office of the Independent Adjudicator for Higher Education* [2013] EWHC 172 (Admin); [2013] E.L.R. 331 (assessment criteria should have been disclosed to students in advance of an examination; however, non-publication would not have made any difference to complainant's examination performance and would not gain from decision being quashed).

[303] *Wainwright* [2001] EWCA Civ 2062 at [55]; *Mousaka* [2002] 1 W.L.R. 395 at [35] (since there was no effective right of appeal from the decision of the High Court on an application for appeal of an arbitrator's award, a requirement on the judge to provide reasons in full for refusing the application would be "completely worthless"); *Aston* [2004] EWHC 2368 (Admin) at [73] (although a defendant's legal representative had been incompetent during the conduct of a trial, the legal adviser and, save for one exception, the solicitor appearing for the Council were astute to prevent the representative from damaging the presentation of the claimant's case: he did have a full op-

A decision of a tribunal was not found to be invalid where a tribunal had obtained information through its own research, where, in particular, the information was almost identical to that already in evidence and given that the claimant had ultimately been able to respond to the information during the hearing, such that the breach of procedural propriety had been remedied.[304]

Whether the requisite flexibility is to be found in the definition of a breach of the **8-073** *audi alteram partem* (hear both sides) principle, in the statutory requirement of substantial prejudice" or in the court's discretion over the remedy will generally be immaterial (except where the relief sought is non-discretionary, for example, an appeal[305] or a claim for damages).

Undeserving claimants

In some cases it has been suggested that a claimant who is for some reason **8-074** undeserving may forfeit the right to procedural fairness.[306] The forfeiture may be based upon a prejudgement of their merit as claimants, or a prejudgment of the likelihood of their wining the sympathy of the decision-maker. We suggest below[307] that a legitimate expectation which is derived from the representation of the decision-maker should not be forfeited by the conduct of the claimant, however unmeritorious. It is also wrong for a hearing to be conditional upon the good behaviour of the claimant, and risky to prejudge the merits of the claimant's present case upon his previous wrongdoing.

DECISION-MAKER NOT AT FAULT

Where alleged procedural unfairness is not the fault of the tribunal or other **8-075** decision-maker, is a claimant still entitled to have the decision quashed on the basis that he has not been accorded procedural fairness? Where, at a hearing on notice, the absence of procedural fairness is due to the conduct of, or a failure by, the other party to the hearing, it was at one time thought that the courts had discretion to quash the decision.[308] Thus, where prison authorities failed to make known to a prisoner charged with an offence against discipline the existence of a witness to the alleged offence, the determination of the prison board of visitors was quashed on the grounds of unfairness, albeit that this was not caused by the tribunal itself.[309] Where an important prosecution witness on a charge of shoplifting deceived the court as to his reason for resigning from the Metropolitan Police (being in fact

---

portunity to put his side, his version of the facts, and there was a full opportunity for the committee to judge the Council's witnesses when tested in cross-examination).

[304] *Re Crawford's Application for Judicial Review* [2016] NIQB 97 at [60]–[62].

[305] cf. *Ottley v Morris* [1979] 1 All E.R. 65 (whether refusal of adjournment constituted ground of appeal on point of law depended on whether appellant might thereby have suffered a substantial injustice). *Hickmott v Dorset CC* (1977) 35 P. & C.R. 195 (evidence improperly received in breach of audi alteram partem rule could not have affected the result: appeal dismissed in absence of miscarriage of justice).

[306] See, e.g. *Cinnamond* [1980] 1 W.L.R. 582 (minicab drivers at Heathrow Airport previously prosecuted frequently for breach of byelaw thus not entitled to fair hearing because no legitimate expectation (Lord Denning) or because it would have "availed them nothing" (Lord Brandon); *Scott* [2005] EWHC 2669 at [25]-[28].

[307] See 12-045, fn.140.

[308] *R. v Blundeston Prison Board of Visitors Ex p. Fox-Taylor* [1982] 1 All E.R. 646; *R. v Leyland J. Ex p. Hawthorn* [1979] Q.B. 283; *R. v Bolton Justices Ex p. Scally* [1991] 1 Q.B. 537; *Al-Mehdawi* [1990] 1 A.C. 876.

[309] *Ex p. Fox-Taylor* [1982] 1 All E.R. 646.

required to resign following disgraceful conduct including a conviction), it was held that his deliberate concealment constituted unfairness, so that the conviction should be quashed.[310]

8-076   It has been suggested, however, that these decisions should be viewed not as resting on principles of fairness, but as based upon the alternative principle that "fraud unravels everything", or because the "process leading to conviction" has been distorted and vitiated as a result of a breach of duty owed to the court and to the defence by a prosecutor.[311] The principles of fairness, in contrast, are "concerned solely with the propriety of the procedure adopted by the decision-maker".[312] But this approach, it is submitted, risks leaving uncorrected procedural errors which are the responsibility of the prosecution or respondent, but which cannot be characterised as fraud or breach of duty. As Bingham LJ has said, "If a procedural mishap occurs as a result of misunderstanding, confusion, failure of communication, or perhaps even inefficiency, and the result is to deny justice to the applicant, I should be very sorry to hold that the remedy of judicial review was not available".[313] Moreover, recent cases have found decisions of authorities to be unfair notwithstanding lack of fault by the decision-maker[314]; and where there has been blameless unfairness, not caused by unfairness or malpractice by any party, a conviction will be quashed in judicial review.[315]

8-077   As a general rule, a person who has himself impeded or frustrated the service of notice of impending action cannot afterwards be heard to complain that he did not receive actual notice.[316] But where the mistake is due to the conduct of the applicant's legal representatives, the position is not entirely clear. The question was expressly left open in *R. v Immigration Appeal Tribunal, Ex p. Enwia*.[317] In *R. v Im-*

---

[310] *R. v Knightsbridge Crown Court Ex p. Goonatilleke* [1986] Q.B. 1 (since the witness in question had presented the defendant for prosecution, and had ensured that he was prosecuted, it is suggested that he was effectively in the position of a prosecutor or respondent rather than a true third party).

[311] Lord Bridge in *Al-Mehdawi* [1990] 1 A.C. 876 at 895-896; Lord Bridge's reinterpretation of the earlier decisions is not entirely satisfactory, because it is not clear that in all such cases there has been anything approaching a breach of duty owed to the court or to the defence, let alone fraud. For example, in *Ex p. Scally* [1991] 1 Q.B. 537, evidence led by the Crown Prosecution Service of blood alcohol levels in a drink-driving case was held to be unreliable due to "an ordinary lack of care". The court held that certiorari would lie, because the prosecution's error had "corrupted the process leading to conviction in a manner which was unfair" (Watkins LJ), but it would not appear that anything approaching fraud or breach of duty was established. See J. Herberg, "The Right to a Hearing: Breach without Fault" [1990] P.L. 467.

[312] *Al-Mehdawi* [1990] 1 A.C. 876 at 894.

[313] *Bagga Khan v Secretary of State for the Home Department* [1987] Imm. A.R. 543 at 555.

[314] *R. (on the application of Maqsood) v Special Adjudicator* [2001] EWHC Admin 1003; [2002] Imm. A.R. 268; *R. (on the application of Harrison) v Birmingham Magistrates Court* [2011] EWCA Civ 332; (2011) 108(14) L.S.G. 21 (the claimant had not had notice of forfeiture proceedings and the order would therefore be quashed).

[315] *R. (on the application of Pownall) v Flintshire Magistrates Court* [2004] EWHC 1289 (QB) at [13]-[14].

[316] *De Verteuil* [1918] A.C. 557 at 560-561; *James v Institute of Chartered Accountants* (1907) 98 L.T. 225; *Glynn v Keele University* [1971] 1 W.L.R. 487 at 495 (failure to notify change of address); *R. v Newport Justices Ex p. Carey* (1996) 160 J.P 613, DC (applicant's absence from hearing his own fault); *R. v Secretary of State for the Home Department Ex p. Kikaka* [1996] Imm. A.R. 340 (applicant had chosen to represent herself); *Pine v Law Society* [2001] EWCA Civ 1574; [2002] U.K.H.R.R. 81 at [42]-[43] (when the claimant could not afford the fare to attend a hearing he could have sought an adjournment, sought admission of evidence by affidavit or some more informal means, sought a hearing closer to where he lived, or asked the tribunal to re-open the hearing).

[317] *R. v Immigration Appeal Tribunal, Ex p. Enwia* [1984] 1 W.L.R. 117, CA. At first instance, Comyn J held that the court could grant relief in such circumstances, although his judgment was reversed

migration Appeal Tribunal, Ex p. Rahmani,[318] the Court of Appeal held that where an immigrant applicant's solicitors had negligently failed to proceed with an appeal from a refusal of an application for an extension of stay, the applicant was entitled to judicial review of the dismissal of her appeal, since she had been denied a basic opportunity to be heard, and the applicant herself was wholly innocent of responsibility for this. Although the House of Lords in *Rahmani* upheld the decision of the Court of Appeal, it did so on different grounds and did not approve or reject the Court of Appeal's view.[319]

However, in *R. v Secretary of State for the Home Department Ex p. Al-Mehdawi*,[320] the House of Lords did directly consider the Court of Appeal's decision in *Rahmani*, and came to a very different conclusion. In *Al-Mehdawi*, the applicant had lodged an appeal against the Home Secretary's decision to make a deportation order against him. Notice of the appeal was sent to his solicitors, who misaddressed the letter when sending it on to the applicant, who consequently never received notice of the appeal. The appeal was therefore dismissed in his absence. On an application for judicial review of the decision to dismiss the appeal, on the ground that the applicant had been denied a fair (or any) hearing, the House of Lords held that a party cannot complain of a denial of a fair hearing where he has failed to make use of an opportunity to be heard through the fault of his own advisers, even if he himself is not responsible in any way for that failure. Lord Bridge drew an analogy with the position in private law, where a party who lost the opportunity to have his case heard through the negligence of his legal advisers would be left with no remedy except against those advisers. Their Lordships were clearly influenced by the fear that to allow review in such circumstances could open the way for manipulation of hearings, and would hinder the dismissal of abandoned appeals by administrative bodies.[321] However, the *Al-Mehdawi* rule is not absolute. In the case of *R. v The Criminal Injuries Compensation Board Ex p. A*, Lord Slynn, noting that the failure of the board and the police to acquire and consider a medical report of which they were aware constituted procedural unfairness, added that it did not seem to be "necessary to find that anyone was at fault in order to arrive at this result. It is sufficient if objectively there is unfairness".[322] It has also been

8-078

---

on the facts by the CA.

[318] *R. v Immigration Appeal Tribunal, Ex p. Rahmani* [1985] Q.B. 1109, CA; [1986] A.C. 475, HL (sub nom. *Rahmani v Diggines*).

[319] cf. *Rahmani* holding on claimant's lack of fault has been applied in other cases: *R. (on the application of Tataw) v Immigration Appeal Tribunal* [2003] EWCA Civ 925; [2003] I.N.L.R. 585 at [20].

[320] [1990] 1 A.C. 876; *Hassan v Secretary of State for the Home Department* [1994] Imm. A.R. 482, CA: *Secretary of State for the Home Department v Mohammed Yasin* [1995] Imm. A.R. 118 at 121-122 (failure of applicant's advisers to draw Tribunal's attention to brother's case); *Samuel Dele Adeniyi v Secretary of State for the Home Department* [1995] Imm. A.R. 101 (failure of solicitors to send notice of appeal to correct address); *R. v Governors of Sheffield Hallam University Ex p. R* [1995] E.L.R. 267; [1994] C.O.D. 470 (failure of applicant's solicitor to seek sufficient adjournment to consider new material); *R. v Secretary of State for the Home Department Ex p. Osei Yaw Yeboah* [1995] Imm. A.R. 393 (applicant not represented at appeal through fault of solicitor); *R. v Monopolies and Mergers Commission Ex p. Stagecoach Holdings Plc, The Times,* 23 July 1996.

[321] *R. (on the application of Mathialagan) v Southwark LBC* [2004] EWCA Civ 1689; [2005] R.A. 43; *R. (on the application of R) v Secretary of State for the Home Department* [2005] EWHC 520 (Admin); *Maqsood v the Special Adjudicator and the Secretary of State* [2001] EWHC Admin 1003; *Parmar (t/a Ace Knitwear) v Woods (Inspector of Taxes) (No.1)* [2002] EWHC 1085 (Ch). On the other hand, fault by an applicant's legal advisers may be a "good reason" for delay in bringing an application for judicial review; *R. v Secretary of State for the Home Department Ex p. Oyeleye* [1994] Imm. A.R. 268; *R. v Newham LBC Ex p. Gentle* (1994) 26 H.L.R. 466.

[322] [1999] 2 A.C. 330 at 345. See also: *R. (on the application of Connolly) v Havering LBC* [2009] EWCA Civ 1059; [2010] 2 P. & C.R. 1 (there was unfairness arising from a local authority's failure

suggested in *Haile v Immigration Appeal Tribunal* that *Al-Mehdawi* did not preclude a court from considering "the wider interests of justice".[323]

---

to provide an inspector with the full and material planning history of the site such that the inspector's decision should be quashed).

[323] *Haile v Immigration Appeal Tribunal* [2001] EWCA Civ 663; [2002] Imm. A.R. 170 at [26] (Simon Brown LJ). See also *FP (Iran) v Secretary of State for the Home Department* [2007] EWCA Civ 13; [2007] Imm. A.R. 450 at [45] (distinguishing *Al-Mehdawi*); *SL (Vietnam) v Secretary of State for the Home Department* [2010] EWCA Civ 225; [2010] I.N.L.R. 651.

CHAPTER 9

Procedural Fairness: Fettering of Discretion

TABLE OF CONTENTS

SCOPE

This chapter examines two ways in which a discretion conferred on a public **9-001** authority may be "fettered" unlawfully: (a) by the over-rigid application of a self-created rule or policy; and (b) by giving an undertaking to exercise its discretion in a particular manner.

FETTERING OF DISCRETION BY SELF-CREATED RULES OR POLICY

A decision-making body exercising public functions which is entrusted with **9-002** discretion must not disable itself from exercising its discretion in individual cases. It may not "fetter" its discretion. A public authority that does fetter its discretion in that way may offend against either or both of two grounds of judicial review: the ground of legality and the ground of procedural propriety. The public authority offends against legality by failing to use its powers in the way they were intended, namely, to employ and to utilise the discretion conferred upon it.[1] It offends against procedural propriety by failing to permit affected persons to influence the use of that discretion. By failing to "keep its mind ajar", by "shutting its ears" to an application, the body in question effectively forecloses participation in the decision-making process.

Because the "no fettering" principle is mostly employed as a means of keeping **9-003** open the possibility of meaningful participation in the decision-making process, we deal with it in this section of the book as a species of the genus procedural fairness. Other treatments of the no-fettering doctrine see it as part of a more general head of review, namely, the "retention of discretion".[2] This includes the requirement that the exercise of discretion should not be delegated to another—a matter we consider

---

[1] See Ch.5.
[2] See, e.g. H.W.R. Wade and C. Forsyth, *Administrative Law*, 11th edn (2014), Ch.10.

under the ground of "illegality" in Chapter 5.[3] The non-fettering principle has also been described as a "general principle of the common law", which is critical to lawful public decision-making, since without it, decisions would be liable to be unfair, through failing to have regard to what affected persons had to say or unreasonable, through failing to have regard to relevant factors, or both.[4] As we have said, the so-called grounds of review are by no means entirely self-contained and aspects of the no-fettering doctrine could also fit within the ground of "irrationality".[5]

9-004   The principle against fettering discretion does not prevent public authorities upon which a discretionary power has been conferred guiding the implementation of that discretion by means of a policy or a rule that is within the scope of its conferred powers.[6] The principle directs attention to the *attitude* of the decision-maker, preventing him from rigidly excluding the possibility of any exception to that rule or policy in a deserving case.[7] Nor does the principle focus upon the content of the hearing or other means of communication which must be afforded to persons interested in changing the decision-maker's mind. The decision-maker must allow interested individuals the opportunity to persuade him to amend or deviate from the rule or policy, but, unlike the principle of natural justice or fair hearing, the principle against fettering is not concerned with any particular form of hearing or with any particular technique of making or receiving representations.[8] Thus, while the issue of fettering often arises where an authority has adopted a fixed rule or policy, complaints of fettering may also arise in the context of "one-off" decisions.[9] In

---

3   See 5-159.
4   *R. (on the application of West Berkshire District Council) v Secretary of State for Communities and Local Government* [2016] EWCA Civ 441; [2016] P.T.S.R. 982 at [19] (adding that in the law of planning, the principle is reflected in the description of planning policy not as a rule, but a guide).
5   See Ch.11.
6   See, e.g. *R. (on the application of Milner) v South Central Strategic Health Authority* [2011] EWHC 218 (Admin); [2011] P.T.S.R. D27 at [45] ("a public body must have regard to relevant published government policy insofar as it is not inconsistent with statute or regulations, and if it is going to depart from the policy (which it may do) it must give its reasons for doing so").
7   *R. (on the application of Lumba) v Secretary of State for the Home Department* [2011] UKSC 12; [2012] 1 A.C. 245 at [21] (Lord Dyson: "it is a well established principle of public law that a policy should not be so rigid as to amount to a fetter on the discretion of decision-makers").
8   *R. v Secretary of State for the Environment Ex p. Brent LBC* [1982] Q.B. 593 (decision of the Secretary of State was held unlawful both for fettering of discretion and for failing to provide a fair hearing). See also *British Telecommunications Plc, Everything Everywhere Ltd v Office of Communications* [2011] CAT 24 (no policy can be comprehensive and seek to deal with every future case, which is why policies cannot and should not act as fetters on discretion: there will always be individual circumstances not anticipated by the policy (at [209]); [2014] UKSC 42 (CAT decision upheld, although the fettering point was not discussed).
9   *R. (on the application of Luton BC) v Secretary of State for Education* [2011] EWHC 217 (Admin); [2011] Eq. L.R. 481 at [54] and [60] (Holman J observing that "even if the Secretary of State was making a 'one-off' decision, he did so in circumstances in which the essential duty not to fetter discretion so as to preclude individual consideration of individual cases was in play" and finding that effectively rules had been applied in a single, short period of time which determined, without more, the outcome). See also *R. (on the application of St Mary Magdalene Academy) v Secretary of State for the Home Department* [2015] EWHC 725 (Admin) at [48] and [52] (finding that a policy of not granting sponsor licences to state schools seeking to admit foreign students, while lawful itself, had been applied too rigidly and that no consideration had been given to the individual circumstances with the "flexibility, fairness and good sense that the law requires"). A similar result was reached in *R. (on the application of Robson) v Crown Prosecution Service* [2016] EWHC 2191 (Admin) at [45] (a guidance on conditional cautions for offences was not unlawful, but the decision-maker had interpreted the guidance as possessing no flexibility at all and as permitting no exceptions). By contrast, in *R. (on the application of Project Management Institute) v Minister for the Cabinet Office* [2016] EWCA Civ 21; [2016] 1 W.L.R. 1737, the policy was found to allow a considerable degree of flexibility in its application (at [42]).

short, the no-fettering principle means that a person must know what the relevant policy of a public authority entails and must be able to make submissions about its application in their individual case. The public authority must then consider that case on its merits.[10] It may also be the case that an appearance of fettering, as opposed to a finding of fettering in fact, could give rise to unlawfulness; the object is to ascertain whether there was such a real risk that the decision was taken with a closed mind that it is not in the public interest for it to be upheld.[11] It is important to add that the non-fettering principle will not render mandatory rules unlawful in every statutory context, and a distinction has been drawn between statutes which expressly permit rules to be made and those which do not.[12]

Underlying rationale

The underlying rationale of the principle against fettering discretion is to ensure   **9-005**
that two perfectly legitimate values of public law, those of legal certainty and consistency (qualities at the heart of the principle of the rule of law), may be balanced by another equally legitimate public law value, namely, that of responsiveness.[13] While allowing rules and policies to promote the former values, it insists that the full rigour of certainty and consistency be tempered by the willingness to make exceptions, to respond flexibly to unusual situations, and to apply justice in the individual case.[14] As has been observed, there is a tension in public law decision-making between flexibility in the decision-making process and predictability of its outcome. The more there is of one, the less room there is for

---

[10] *Lumba* [2011] UKSC 12; [2012] 1 A.C. 245 at [34]–[38]. See also: *Odelola v Secretary of State for the Home Department* [2009] UKHL 25; [2009] 1 W.L.R. 1230. It has also been observed that "the exercise of public discretionary power requires the decision-maker to bring his mind to bear on the very case; he cannot blindly follow a pre-existing policy without considering anything said to persuade him that the case in hand is an exception": *West Berkshire District Council* [2016] EWCA Civ 441; [2016] P.T.S.R. 982.

[11] *R. (on the application of Hewitson) v Guildford BC* [2011] EWHC 3440 (Admin); [2012] B.L.G.R. 637 at [33]–[34]. See Case Comment "R. (on the application of Hewitson) v Guildford BC: fettering discretion—appearance of fetter—casting vote—procedural irregularity" (2012) 8 J.P.L. 951.

[12] *R. (on the application of Sayaniya) v Upper Tribunal* [2016] EWCA Civ 85; [2016] 4 W.L.R. 58 at [15]. Here, it was held that the Immigration Rules were not statements of policy subject to all the public law constraints on policies and discretionary powers including the non-fettering principle, since they were expressly contemplated by the Immigration Act 1971. The court reasoned that, to the extent that the non-fettering principle applied to Immigration Rules, a rule expressed in mandatory terms did not fall foul of it since the Secretary of State had discretion outside the rules which he could exercise in favour of those who did not qualify under them: *Sayaniya* [2016] EWCA Civ 85; [2016] 4 W.L.R. 58 at [21] and [36].

[13] *R. v Ministry for Agriculture, Fisheries and Food Ex p. Hamble Fisheries (Offshore) Ltd* [1995] 2 All E.R. 714 at 722 (Sedley J described the "two conflicting imperatives of public law", rigidity and certainty, as against individual consideration); see also *R. (on the application of Alvi) v Secretary of State for the Home Department* [2012] UKSC 33; [2012] 1 W.L.R. 2208 at [111].

[14] C. Hilson, "Judicial Review, Policies and the Fettering of Discretion" [2002] P.L. 111; D. Galligan, "The Nature and Functions of Policy Within Discretionary Power" [1976] P.L. 332. For an analysis of the advantages and disadvantages of creation by various administrative techniques, criteria to regulate the exercise of discretion, see J. Jowell, "The Legal Control of Administrative Discretion" [1973] P.L. 178; *Law and Bureaucracy* (1975); D. Galligan, *Discretionary Powers, A Legal Study of Official Discretion* (1986); K.C. Davis, *Discretionary Justice* (1969). On the distinction between rules and objectives, see *Oddy v Transport Salaried Staff's Association* [1973] I.C.R. 524; H. Molot, "The Self-Created Rule of Policy and Other Ways of Exercising Administrative Discretion" (1972) 18 McGill L.J. 310; *R. v Secretary of State for the Home Department Ex p. Venables* [1998] A.C. 407 at 494 (Lord Browne-Wilkinson restated the distinction between a proper policy and an over-rigid or inflexible one, and referred to the passage in the text).

the other, and getting the balance right is often difficult.[15] Moreover, it must be remembered that an inflexible policy could prioritise consistency at the expense of equal treatment in fact.[16] In this regard, the duty to follow policy has been described as subordinate to the duty to exercise statutory power lawfully, and it has been held to be wrong to allow policy to fetter discretion if there was good reason not to follow it.[17] There are also other background values in play, namely, accountability (public bodies could be held to account (politically if not legally) if they do not fulfil their announced policies) and efficiency; it is clearly more efficient for a housing authority to set out its criteria for admission through a "points system" than to assess each application afresh. For similar reasons, university departments normally publish their admissions criteria which not only assist the admissions tutor to make decisions with despatch, but also help prospective applicants by discouraging applications that, in the absence of exceptional circumstances, are unlikely to succeed. It has also been observed that the principle against fettering ensures that decisions taken represent "a true and proper exercise of the discretion conferred by Parliament".[18]

Application of the no-fettering principle

9-006   The no-fettering principle does not necessarily frown on the articulation of policies (provided, as we shall see, that they are lawful and rational) but it does not permit them to be rigidly applied.

Illustrations

9-007
- In the planning context, the Secretary of State for the Environment was held to have fettered his discretion in adopting a policy of disallowing all purely local objections to the allocation of land for gypsy sites.[19]
- In the award of costs, a tribunal which has power to award costs fails to exercise its discretion if it fixes specific amounts to be applied indiscriminately to all cases before it.[20] However, a tribunal's statutory discretion may be wide enough to justify the adoption of a rule not to award any costs save in exceptional circumstances,[21] as distinct from a rule never to award any costs at all.

---

15   *Sayaniya* [2016] EWCA Civ 85; [2016] 4 W.L.R. 58 at [16] (citing from Lord Walker in *Alvi* [2012] UKSC 33; [2012] 1 W.L.R. 2208 at [111]).
16   *R. (on the application of Singh) v Cardiff City Council* [2012] EWHC 1852 (Admin) at [80] (fettering "can lead to the risk of arbitrary and unequal treatment").
17   *Gage v Scottish Ministers* [2015] CSOH 174 at [20]; see also *Mandalia* [2015] UKSC 59; [2015] 1 W.L.R. 4546. A failure to follow a policy may however provide a ground for judicial review: *Lumba* [2011] UKSC 12; [2012] 1 A.C. 245 at [35]; *R. (on the application of O) v Secretary of State for the Home Department* [2016] UKSC 19; *Onos v Secretary of State for the Home Department* [2016] EWHC 59 (Admin) at [62] (requiring good reason to depart from policy); *R. (on the application of FK) v Secretary of State for the Home Department* [2016] EWHC 56 (Admin); *Mandalia v Secretary of State for the Home Department* [2015] UKSC 59; [2015] 1 W.L.R. 4546.
18   *R. (on the application of Hillsden) v Epping Forest* [2015] EWHC 98 (Admin) at [29].
19   *R. v Secretary of State for the Environment Ex p. Halton DC* (1983) 82 L.G.R. 662. By contrast, in *St Albans City and District Council v Secretary of State for Communities and Local Government* [2015] EWHC 655 (Admin), the Secretary of State had not fettered his discretion when determining a second planning appeal by requiring a very good reason to be shown for departing from the conclusion reached in the first appeal, where the "very good reason" has been applied as a matter of judgment rather than as a legal test.
20   *R. v Merioneth Justices* (1844) 6 Q.B. 153; *R. v Glamorganshire Justices* (1850) 19 L.J.M.C. 172.
21   *Re Wood's Application* (1952) 3 P. & C.R. 238; *R. v Secretary of State for the Environment Ex p.*

- The Law Society was entitled to have policies governing claims against the Compensation Fund (including a policy excluding compensation for consequential loss) provided that such policy admitted of exceptions in appropriate cases, and that any special reasons put forward were considered.[22]
- The House of Lords has even applied the non-fettering principles to the discretionary award of investment allowances to industrialists by a government department.[23]
- There have also been many cases where local authorities' policies prohibiting discretionary grants to students have in practice amounted to an unlawful fetter on their discretion, despite an apparent willingness to consider exceptional cases.[24]
- In the context of appointments, in a Scottish case it was assumed that the Secretary of State, in deciding whether to approve an appointment to the office of chief constable, was not entitled to adopt a rigid rule never to approve the appointment of an officer who was already a member of the local police force in question.[25]
- Educational policies should be flexible; and local authorities must be prepared, at least when an objection is expressly raised,[26] to make exceptions, after considering the merits of individual cases, to their general rules about, inter alia, allocating children to denominational schools,[27] abolishing secondary schools that admit children on the basis of ability,[28] or refusing applications for requests for assessments of a child's special educational needs.[29]
- Housing policies of local authorities should be open to flexible application, as has been held in respect of policies on eviction of tenants of council houses who are in arrears with their rent,[30] on payment for the provision of temporary housing accommodation,[31] on refusal of applications for housing by children of those "intentionally homeless",[32] on requiring a homeless individual who

---

Reinisch (1971) 70 L.G.R. 126. Indeed, when a tribunal departs from its normal rule it may be required to give clear reasons for its decision: *Pepys v London Transport Executive* [1975] 1 W.L.R. 234; *R. v Wreck Commissioner Ex p. Knight* [1976] 3 All E.R. 8.

[22] *R. v Law Society Ex p. Reigate Projects Ltd* [1993] 1 W.L.R. 1531.

[23] *British Oxygen Co Ltd v Board of Trade* [1971] A.C. 610; compare *R. v Secretary of State for Transport Ex p. Sheriff & Sons Ltd, The Times,* 18 December 1986.

[24] See, e.g. *R. v Warwickshire CC Ex p. Collymore* [1995] E.L.R. 217; *R. v Warwickshire CC Ex p. Williams* [1995] E.L.R. 326; *R. v Bexley LBC Ex p. Jones* [1995] E.L.R. 42. See also *R. v Secretary of State for the Home Department Ex p. Bennett, The Times,* 18 August 1986 (Home Secretary's criteria for approval of police rent allowance was over-rigid); *R. v Barnsley Supplementary Benefits Appeal Tribunal Ex p. Atkinson* [1977] 1 W.L.R. 917. Blanket policies may also create human rights concerns, see, e.g., *R. (on the application of Tigere) v Secretary of State for Business, Innovation and Skills* [2015] UKSC 57; [2015] 1 W.L.R. 3820; *R. (on the application of T) v Chief Constable of Greater Manchester Police* [2014] UKSC 35; [2015] A.C. 49.

[25] *Kilmarnock Magistrates v Secretary of State for Scotland,* 1961 S.C. 350 (entitled to adopt a general policy to that effect, subject to willingness to make exceptions in special cases).

[26] *Smith v Inner London Education Authority* [1978] 1 All E.R. 411.

[27] *Cummings v Birkenhead Corp* [1972] Ch. 12.

[28] *Smith* [1978] 1 All E.R. 411.

[29] *R. v Hampshire CC Ex p. W* [1994] E.L.R. 460; *P v Hackney LBC* [2007] EWHC 1365 (Admin).

[30] *Bristol DC v Clark* [1975] 1 W.L.R. 1443 at 1448 (dicta); *R. v Tower Hamlets LBC Ex p. Khalique* (1994) 26 H.L.R. 517 (rule that cases where rent arrears greater than £500 would be rendered "non-active" went well beyond the bounds of a lawful policy since it permitted no flexibility whatsoever); *R. v Lambeth LBC Ex p. Njomo* (1996) 28 H.L.R. 737; compare *Elliott v Brighton BC* (1980) 79 L.G.R. 506 (fettering of discretion to recondition substandard houses after failure to comply with improvement notice).

[31] *Roberts v Dorset CC* (1977) 75 L.G.R. 462.

[32] *Attorney General ex rel. Tilley v Wandsworth LBC* [1981] 1 W.L.R. 854 at 858 (Templeman LJ went

had rejected accommodation as unsuitable to first move into the accommodation before being permitted to appeal,[33] on suspending a person who had
unreasonably refused accommodation from the housing register for two
years,[34] and on referral of tenancies to a rent tribunal.[35]

- In the context of prosecutions and disciplinary decisions, a chief constable
  ought not to adopt a rigid rule not to institute any prosecution at all for an anti-
  social class of criminal offence[36] nor should he fetter his discretion by treating the decision of the Director of Public Prosecutions that there was insufficient evidence to justify the prosecution of an officer, as determinative of the
  question of whether to dismiss for unfairness disciplinary charges against that
  officer based on substantially the same facts.[37]

- In the conduct of hearings, domestic tribunals have been said to act improperly
  in refusing to allow a party to appear at a disciplinary hearing with a legal
  representative solely because it has never been their practice to permit it.[38] It
  has also been held that the Army Board of the Defence Council cannot have
  an inflexible policy not to hold an oral hearing where allegations of race
  discrimination are made.[39]

- Policies on the imposition of penalties or sentences should not be so rigid as
  to exclude consideration of the proportionality of the penalty in particular
  circumstances.[40] For example, in *R. v Secretary of State for the Home Department Ex p. Venables*,[41] the Secretary of State for the Home Office was held to
  have fettered his discretion in setting a "tariff" period of 15 years for a person
  sentenced to be detained at Her Majesty's Pleasure, because the "tariff" period
  did not permit review on grounds other than those relating to the circumstances
  of the commission of the crime and the applicant's state of mind, contrary to
  the Secretary of State's statutory power which was not fettered in this way.[42]

- In the realm of politics, the courts have required that a manifesto commit-

---

further in suggesting that even a policy resolution hedged around with exceptions might not be
entirely free from attack).

[33] *R. v Newham LBC Ex p. Dada* [1996] Q.B. 507 at 516A.

[34] *R. v Westminster City Council, Ex p Hussain* (1999) 31 H.L.R. 645.

[35] *R. v Barnet & Camden Rent Tribunal Ex p. Frey Investments Ltd* [1972] 2 Q.B. 342 (explaining *R.
v Paddington & St Marylebone Rent Tribunal Ex p. Bell London & Provincial Properties Ltd* [1949]
1 K.B. 666 as a case of a capricious reference made without consideration of relevant matters). See
also, *R. (on the application of Hardy) v Sandwell Metropolitan Borough Council* [2015] EWHC 890
(Admin) at [43] (a council's policy of always taking into account the care component of disability
living allowance when assessing the amount of a discretionary housing payment was an unlawful
fetter).

[36] *R. v Metropolitan Police Commissioner Ex p. Blackburn* [1968] 2 Q.B. 118 (gaming offences in
clubs).

[37] *R. v Chief Constable Thames Valley Police Ex p. Police Complaints Authority* [1996] C.O.D. 324.

[38] See, e.g. *Pett v Greyhound Racing Association (Ltd) (No.1)* [1969] 1 Q.B. 125; *Enderby Town
Football Club Ltd v Football Association Ltd* [1971] Ch. 591 at 605–606.

[39] *R. v Army Board of the Defence Council, Ex p. Anderson* [1992] Q.B. 169 at 188.

[40] *Lindsay v Commissioners of Customs and Excise* [2002] EWCA Civ 267; [2002] 1 W.L.R. 1766;
Gascoyne v Commissioners of Customs and Excise [2003] EWCA Civ 892 at [19].

[41] *Ex p. Venables* [1998] A.C. 407.

[42] *Ex p. Venables* [1998] A.C. 407 at 494–498 (Lord Browne-Wilkinson), 522–524 (Lord Steyn,
although his Lordship did not use the language of fettering of discretion) and 532–536 (Lord Hope);
compare CA [1997] 2 W.L.R. 67 at 90 (Lord Woolf MR); the Home Secretary no longer has a role
in setting tariff periods; and *R. v Secretary of State for the Home Department, Ex p. Hindley* [2001]
1 A.C. 410; *R. (on the application of Smith) v Secretary of State for the Home Department* [2005]
UKHL 51; [2006] 1 A.C. 159 (no unlawfulness where regular review of sentence in place). See also
R. (on the application of Shutt) v Secretary of State for Justice [2012] EWHC 851 (Admin) at [25].

ment is not blindly implemented following an election victory.[43] It has also been held that a local council's resolution could be quashed if councillors voted for it on orders from their political party, although not if they conscientiously decided to prefer the party's policy to their own opinions.[44]

- In the operation of prisons, policies should usually be applied flexibly and a policy of the Prison Service requiring incarcerated mothers to be separated from their children after 18 months was held to be applied too inflexibly and therefore unlawful.[45] It has also been held that the Secretary of State for Justice had erred in restricting childcare resettlement leave to prisoners who were within two years of their release date and had been allocated to open conditions.[46] Likewise, where a prisoner had received a consecutive sentence in default of payment of a confiscation order and applied for temporary release while serving her first sentence, to refuse her pursuant to a blanket policy which provided that release could only be considered during the second period of imprisonment amounted to an unlawful fettering of discretion.[47]
- A local authority could not fetter its discretion by a term in a secure tenancy agreement to the effect that it would not use its statutory power to vary tenancy agreements by notice without approval of the tenants' representatives.[48]
- In the context of asylum applications, it was unlawful for the Secretary of State to defer dealing with a whole class of applications, older applications, in order to meet targets set for consideration of more recent applications; this amounted to "a textbook case" of unlawful fettering of discretion.[49] The court noted that although the principle is normally applied to substantive decisions on applications, there was no reason why it should not apply equally to "a procedural decision to defer a whole class of applications without good reasons and without consideration of the effects on the applicants".[50] Similarly, an exclusion policy which barred the Secretary of State from considering applications for indefinite leave to remain from those who were in various exclusion

---

[43] *R. v GLC Ex p. Bromley LBC* [1983] 1 A.C. 768 (the "Fares Fair" case). Lords Diplock and Brandon, in particular, criticised the G.L.C. for implementing its manifesto commitment to introduce a subsidy policy automatically after the election. Compare *R. v Merseyside CC Ex p. Great Universal Stores Limited* (1982) 80 L.G.R. 639, where the Fares Fair case was distinguished on the ground, inter alia, that the Merseyside had considered its manifesto commitment afresh after the election, before implementing the policy; compare *R. v Waltham Forest LBC Ex p. Baxter* [1988] Q.B. 419 (councillors entitled to regard manifesto as very important factor in reaching decision).

[44] *Ex p. Baxter* [1988] Q.B. 419 (on the evidence, the councillors had exercised their discretion).

[45] *R. v Secretary of State for the Home Department Ex p. Q* [2001] EWCA Civ 1151; [2001] 1 W.L.R. 2002; and *R. (on the application of P) v Secretary of State for the Home Department*, unreported 17 May 2002; *R. v Secretary of State for the Home Department Ex p. Simms* [2000] 2 A.C. 115. Compare *R. v Secretary of State for the Home Department Ex p. Zulfikar* [1996] C.O.D. 256 (blanket policy of strip-searching prisoners after every visit not unlawful).

[46] *R. (on the application of MP) v Secretary of State for Justice* [2012] EWHC 214 (Admin); [2012] A.C.D. 58 at [186].

[47] *AA v Governor of HMP Downview* [2008] EWHC 2612 (Admin); [2009] Prison L.R. 254 at [43]–[51]. See also *Shutt* [2012] EWHC 851 (Admin) at [25]; *R. (on the application of Guittard) v Secretary of State for Justice* [2009] EWHC 2951 at [23]–[24].

[48] *R. (on the application of Kilby) v Basildon DC* [2007] EWCA Civ 479; [2007] H.L.R. 39 at [32]–[35].

[49] *R. (on the application of S) v Secretary of State for the Home Department* [2007] EWCA Civ 546; [2007] Imm. A.R. 781 at [50].

[50] *S* [2007] EWCA Civ 546. See also *R. (on the application of AK) v Secretary of State for Foreign and Commonwealth Affairs* [2008] EWHC 2227 (Admin) at [32] (Blake J observing obiter that it would "probably be unlawful for a Secretary of State to fetter her statutory discretion about the admission of people who are subject to immigration control").

categories before ten years had elapsed gave rise to a failure to exercise discretion.[51]

- By contrast, there was no fettering where a policy guidance explained that a regulatory discretion to waive fees for applicants seeking a visa to enter the United Kingdom would only be exercised where there were the most exceptional, compelling and compassionate circumstances, as the policy was consistent with expectations underlying the statutory scheme, relevant to the exercise of the relevant powers, consistent with the purpose of the enabling legislation and not arbitrary, capricious or unjust.[52]

- In the context of an application for citizenship, it was held that the Secretary of State had fettered her discretion in adopting a blanket policy that treated 16 and 17 year olds as adults for the purpose of determining the "good character" requirements of the British Nationality Act 1981.[53]

- An unpublished blanket policy which admitted of no exceptions of detention for all foreign national prisoners on completion of their sentences of imprisonment for criminal offences pending the making of deportation orders against them was unlawful.[54]

- Where a statute granted to the courts a wide discretion to consider what is equitable having regard to all the circumstances, it was not desirable to fetter that discretion by rules.[55]

- Finally, non-fettering principles have also been applied to the disclosure of information by voluntary adoption agencies.[56]

Power to articulate rules or policy

9-008   It is obvious that a rule or policy must not be based on considerations extraneous to those contemplated by the enabling Act; otherwise the body will have exercised its discretion invalidly by taking irrelevant considerations into account or exceeding the statutory purpose.[57] Even a factor that may properly be taken into account in exercising a discretion may become an unlawful fetter upon discretion if it is elevated to the status of a general rule that distorts the purpose of the statutory scheme by pursuing that one factor in preference to others or by creating rigidity when flexibility was intended.[58] Thus the policy of the Prison Service to remove children over the age of 18 months from mother and baby units in prison, although

---

[51]   *R (on the application of Mayaya) v Secretary of State for the Home Department* [2011] EWHC 3088 (Admin); [2012] 1 All E.R. 1491 at [53] (although no such fettering arose in respect of a 12-month sentence threshold for identifying a serious offence in circumstances in which such a threshold was a reliable and rational measure of seriousness: at [45]–[46]). See also *R. (on the application of SA) v Secretary of State for the Home Department* [2015] EWHC 1611 at [36] and [42] (holding that the defendant was entitled to adopt a policy on the way in which criminal convictions will normally be considered by her caseworkers, but it should not be applied mechanistically and inflexibly; there had to be a comprehensive assessment of each applicant's character, as an individual, which involves an exercise of judgment, not just ticking boxes on a form; the official did not properly weigh in the balance the strong countervailing evidence of the claimant's good character against the fact of his conviction).

[52]   *Re Salad's Application for Leave to Apply for Judicial Review* [2015] NIQB 32 at [22].

[53]   *SA* [2015] EWHC 1611 (Admin).

[54]   *Lumba* [2012] 1 A.C. 245 at [34]–[39].

[55]   *Dunn v Parole Board* [2008] EWCA Civ 374; [2009] 1 W.L.R. 728 at [31], [43].

[56]   *R. (on the application of Gunn-Russo) v Nugent Care Society* [2001] EWHC Admin 566; [2001] U.K.H.R.R. 1320 at [39]–[43].

[57]   See 5-119 and 5-130.

[58]   *R. v Flintshire CC County Licensing (Stage Plays) Committee Ex p. Barrett* [1957] 1 Q.B. 350 (committee adopted general rule that no alcoholic liquor or tobacco be sold in a theatre if adequate drinking facilities were available nearby, irrespective of the past record of the theatre, and having imposed

permitting the occasional exception, nevertheless contradicted the aim of the relevant provision, which was to further the welfare of the child.[59]

A public authority to which discretion has been entrusted may also, of course, **9-009** have been expressly authorised to make regulations or issue a code of practice etc. in order to confine its discretion and to provide guidance about how it is likely to be exercised. For example, licensing authorities are required by statute to determine and publish three-year policies.[60] Planning authorities possess the power to make plans to guide their decisions on development and the Department of Communities and Local Government has power to issue regulations about the scope of those plans.[61] As we have discussed above,[62] regulations must of course be within the scope of the powers conferred.[63] However, when the purpose of the function is not expressly defined in the statute (and nowhere in the Planning Acts is "planning" defined) it may be elaborated in the process of regulation-making, within limits that are not always easy to discover.

Even, however, where there is no specific power to make regulations or issue **9-010** guidelines, the courts have recognised such a power as implicit. Lord Clyde has said that the provision of guidance of a discretion is "perfectly proper" and that policies are "an essential element in securing the coherent and consistent performance of administrative functions".[64] It is obviously desirable that a public authority should openly state any general principles by which it intends to be guided in the exercise of its discretion and the courts have encouraged licensing decision-makers to fol-

---

this condition on one theatre imposed it on the applicants in the interests of consistency).

[59] *Ex p. Q* [2001] EWCA Civ 1151; [2001] 1 W.L.R. 2002: the principal argument was based upon Convention rights and the restriction was held to be disproportionate, but the same result is achieved under fettering principles in domestic law; for further examples, see C. Hilson, "Judicial Review, Policies and the Fettering of Discretion" [2002] P.L. 111. Compare *Tilley* [1981] 1 W.L.R. 854 (a policy not to house families with children whose parents had become "intentionally homeless" was declared both an unlawful fetter on the authority's discretion and contrary to the purpose of the legislation).

[60] Licensing Act 2003 s.5(1). The policy must, however, be kept under review during the five-year period and revisions made as appropriate: s.5(4).

[61] Planning and Compulsory Purchase Act 2004 ss.36, 38 (note that s.38(6) states that if "regard is to be had to the development plan for the purpose of any determination to be made under the planning Acts the determination must be made in accordance with the plan unless material considerations indicate otherwise").

[62] See 5-002.

[63] As must a code of practice: *R. (on the application of Munjaz) v Mersey Care NHS Trust* [2005] UKHL 58; [2006] 2 A.C. 148.

[64] *R. v Secretary of State for the Environment, Transport and the Regions Ex p. Holdings & Barnes Plc (the Alconbury case)* [2001] UKHL 23; [2003] 2 A.C. 295 at [143]; *Ex p. Venables* [1998] A.C. 407 at 432 (the area of prisoner release "calls out" for the development of policy to provide consistency, certainty and fairness); *A v Croydon LBC, Secretary of State for the Home Department* [2009] EWHC 939 (Admin); [2010] 1 F.L.R. 193 at [70] (a policy of giving prominence to a particular assessment in determining whether an immigrant was a child did not constitute an unlawful fetter provided that the Home Office was satisfied that there had been a proper assessment and that the reasons given and observations made had been satisfactory; not considered on appeal [2009] UKSC 8; [2009] 1 W.L.R. 2557); *R. (on the application of Banks) v The Mayor and Burgess of Tower Hamlets LBC* [2009] EWHC 242 (Admin) at [48]–[55] (a local authority had not abdicated the exercise of its discretion by adopting a policy generally not to prosecute for over-sized market stalls as it had brought a small number of prosecutions); *R. (on the application of Siborurema) v Office of the Independent Adjudicator* [2007] EWCA Civ 1365; [2008] E.L.R. 209 at [77] (where there was nothing in the facts of the case to require the Adjudicator to carry out a review otherwise than in accordance with its standard practice, it would not be a fetter of its discretion to do so). See also *SA* [2015] EWHC 1611 (Admin) at [31] (observing that the defendant was entitled to adopt a policy "provided that she exercised her statutory function lawfully").

low this practice.[65] When a decision-maker is required to give an individual an opportunity to be heard, it may be a denial of natural justice not to disclose the principles upon which the decision-maker proposes to exercise its discretion.[66] In some cases the courts have come close to saying that there is not only a power but a duty to articulate policies and that the lack of a policy to guide the public may amount to irrationality.[67]

9-011   Yet in other cases where specific statutory criteria are provided, it has been held that the power to supplement those criteria by others may be limited.[68] Overall, therefore, whether the policy itself constitutes a fetter on the exercise of discretion will largely depend on the function performed and on how the policy is phrased. In a case involving an application for a discretionary grant for the Legal Practice Course, the policy was expressed in terms that first, provided that no discretionary awards would be provided, then went on to admit applications in exceptional circumstances and, finally, provided a list of criteria that would count as exceptional circumstances. The court made it clear that, had there not been a category of "other" criteria in the list, the effect of the policy would have been to provide exhaustive criteria which would have fettered the discretion.[69] Some policies have the effect of predetermining the issue, as by resolving to refuse all applications,[70] or all applications of a certain class,[71] or all applications except those of a certain class.[72] A policy that permits applications to depart from it only in circumstances that are "most extraordinary" may also fall foul of the no-fetter principle as amounting in practice to a blanket policy.[73]

9-012   It will, however, be a rare case where a policy is not permitted, as policies and guidance are normally advisory rather than mandatory (as opposed to statutory instruments which do have the force of law).[74] That is not to say, however, as we

---

[65]   See, e.g. *R. (on the application of Quark Fishing Ltd) v Secretary of State for Foreign and Commonwealth Affairs* [2001] EWHC Admin 1174; [2002] A.C.D. 197 at [67]–[68] and [2002] EWCA Civ 1409; *R. v Holborn Licensing Justices Ex p. Stratford Catering Co* (1926) 136 L.T. 278 at 281; *R. v Torquay Licensing Justices Ex p. Brockman* [1951] 2 K.B. 784 at 788.

[66]   *R. v Criminal Injuries Compensation Board Ex p. Ince* [1973] 1 W.L.R. 1334 at 1345. In Canada, it has been held that precise standards may be required: see *Re Garden Gulf Court & Motel Inc v Island Telephone Co* (1981) 126 D.L.R. (3d) 281; *Re Irving Oil Ltd v Public Utilities Commission* (1986) 34 D.L.R. (4th) 448.

[67]   *R. v North West Lancashire Health Authority Ex p. A* [2000] 1 W.L.R. 977 at 991 (Auld LJ).

[68]   In Australia, see *Green v Daniels* (1977) 13 A.L.R. 1, which held that a statutory welfare entitlement could not validly be withheld by reference to non-statutory criteria laid down in a departmental guideline.

[69]   *Ex p. Williams* [1995] E.L.R. 326.

[70]   *R. v Walsall Justices* (1854) 3 W.R. 69.

[71]   *R. v LCC Ex p. Corrie* [1918] 1 K.B. 68 (local authority resolved to refuse all further permits, without exception, to distribute literature in public parks); compare *Sharp v Hughes* (1893) 57 J.P 104; and *Sagnata Investments Ltd v Norwich Corp* [1971] 2 Q.B. 614; *R. v Tower Hamlets LBC Ex p. Kayne-Levenson* [1975] Q.B. 431; *R. v Wakefield Crown Court Ex p. Oldfield* [1978] Crim.L.R. 164; *R. v Rochdale MBC Ex p. Cromer Ring Mill Ltd* [1982] 3 All E.R. 761.

[72]   Also *R. v Sylvester* (1862) 31 L.J.M.C. 93 (refusal to issue any beer house licences except to applicants who agreed to take out an excise licence for sale of spirits also); *R. v Barry DC Ex p. Jones* (1900) 16 T.L.R. 556 (refusal to issue any new taxicab licences except to two proprietors and their drivers).

[73]   *Ex p. Collymore* [1995] E.L.R. 217 (Judge J); compare *Ex p. Williams* [1995] E.L.R. 326 (Schiemann J, the council was entitled to have a policy to make no discretionary education grants save in "exceptional circumstances").

[74]   For comparative perspectives on the acceptability of a flexible policy, see in Canada, *Halfway River First Nation v British Columbia* (1999) 178 D.L.R. (4th) 666; in Australia, see: M. Aronson, M. Groves and G. Weeks, *Judicial Review of Administrative Action and Government Liability* 6th edn (2017) at paras 3.270–3.290 and 5.240–5.290. In Ireland, see *McCarron v Superintendent Peadar*

have seen,[75] that guidance is wholly without legal effect. Depending upon the statutory scheme it will normally be a relevant consideration that must be taken into account. In one case[76] this issue was complicated by the fact that the scheme allowed two sets of guidance to be issued which were not compatible. Under the terms of the Mental Health Act 1983 the Secretary of State for Health was required to prepare a code of practice for the guidance of mental health practitioners and hospitals in relation to "the admission and medical treatment of patients suffering from mental disorder". The Secretary of State published the code, which included a chapter on the procedures to be adopted for the confinement of patients. The chapter provided that hospitals should themselves have clear written guidelines on the subject. The Mersey Care Trust drew up such guidelines which provided for less frequent reviews of patients than the Secretary of State's code and one of the questions was which code should prevail. By majority, the House of Lords held that the Secretary of State's code did not have the binding effect of a statute or statutory instrument and was "guidance" rather than "instruction". As such, the hospital was at liberty to depart from it, but only if such a departure was supported by "cogent reasoned justification".[77]

Do exceptions have to be specified in the rule or policy?

It is clear that a policy will usually be valid if it provides, for example, that unless "exceptional circumstances" are present, it will not grant any further licences to enable residential hotels to serve liquor to non-residents.[78] Another permitted formulation is that the body will "normally" give priority to those applicants for licences, for which demand exceeds supply, who do not already have one.[79] However, as just discussed, a general rule or policy that does not on its face admit of exceptions will be permitted in most circumstances.[80] There may be a number of circumstances where the authority will want to emphasise its policy, such as that "no discretionary awards [for student grants] will be made"[81] but the proof of the fettering will be in the willingness to entertain exceptions to the policy, rather than in the words of the policy itself.[82] It has also been held that this principle-and indeed the rule against fettering discretion-apply whether or not the policy-maker and the decision-maker are the same or different persons, since, if it were otherwise, neither

9-013

Kearney [2010] IESC 30; [2010] 3 I.R. 302 at [66]–[69]; *Carrigaline Community Television Broadcasting Company Ltd v Minister for Transport, Energy and Communications (No.2)* [1997] 1 I.L.R.M. 241 at 284: *Mishra v Minister for Justice* [1996] 1 I.R. 189 at 205; *CSB v Minister for Social Protection* [2016] IECA 116 (statistics alone did not prove fettering).

[75] See 5-088 and 5-140.

[76] *Munjaz* [2006] 2 A.C. 148.

[77] *Munjaz* [2006] 2 A.C. 148 at [24]. But see the dissents of Lords Steyn and Brown.

[78] *Brockman* [1951] 2 K.B. 784; *Stratford Catering Co* (1926) 136 L.T. 278. Contrast *Ex p. Simms* [2000] 2 A.C. 115 (a blanket policy that forbade prisoners access to the press, apart from "exceptionally", was held to be unlawful). See also *R. (on the application of London School of Science and Technology) v Secretary of State for the Home Department* [2017] EWHC 423 (Admin) (no fettering where there was a residual discretion which was on occasion exercised).

[79] *Ex p. Kayne-Levenson* [1975] Q.B. 431 at 446, 452; *Perilly v Tower Hamlets LBC* [1973] Q.B. 9 (rule that licences granted in order of application upheld).

[80] But see *Tilley* [1981] 1 W.L.R. 854 (a policy which stated that the council would not house families with young children where the parents of those children had become intentionally homeless was held to be unlawful).

[81] *Collymore* [1995] E.L.R. 217; and see the examples of the regulation of taxis provided by C. Hilson, "Judicial Review, Policies and the Fettering of Discretion" [2002] P.L. 111, 117–120.

[82] This statement of principle was recently endorsed by the Court of Appeal in *West Berkshire District Council* [2016] EWCA Civ 441; [2016] P.T.S.R. 982 at [17] (overturning the ruling of the lower court on the basis that it had conflated what the policy said with how it could lawfully be deployed).

would have any integrity as a principle.[83] It was also observed that a policy-maker is entitled to express his policy in qualified terms, as it would be idle, and most likely confusing, to require every policy statement to include a health warning in the shape of a reminder that the policy must be applied consistently with the rule against fettering.[84] Thus, where a policy not to fund a particular medical treatment listed unspecified "exceptional personal or clinical circumstances" as an exception to the policy, it was necessary for the decision-maker to be able to envisage what such exceptional circumstances might be: if it was not possible to envisage any such circumstances, the policy would be in practice a complete refusal of assistance, and unlawful.[85] Moreover, how the exceptions are defined is important: a trust which required an application for funding to be refused where a patient was "representative of a group of patients" did not in fact allow for exceptional cases, but actually required patients to demonstrate uniqueness rather than exceptionality to qualify for funding.[86]

Tribunals

9-014   The role of precedent in tribunal decisions requires special mention.[87] Formerly, the courts have expressed strong disapproval of the use of precedent in tribunal decision-making, and in the past, the Court of Appeal has warned the Transport Tribunal (in its capacity as a transport licensing appellate authority) against developing a body of rigidly binding precedent.[88] Courts now, however, place greater emphasis on fairness and consistency.[89] For example, in immigration decisions, while immigration judges must examine the facts of individual cases, it has been held that there is no public interest in multiple examinations of the political backdrop of a particular state and that a system of "factual precedent",[90] or "judicial policy (with the flexibility that the word implies) needs to be adopted on the effect of the in-country data in recurrent classes of case".[91] Thus, failure by an adjudicator without good reason, to follow such a "country guidance" decision of the Asylum and Immigration Tribunal, which is intended to be authoritative as to the situation for the time being in the country in question, may give rise to error of law.[92] Of course, this is all subject to the proviso that "each case, whether or not such guidance is available, must depend on an objective and fair assessment of its own facts".[93]

9-015   Similarly, in the employment context, the Employment Appeal Tribunal has also

---

[83]   *West Berkshire District Council* [2016] EWCA Civ 441; [2016] P.T.S.R. 982 at [18].

[84]   *West Berkshire District Council* [2016] EWCA Civ 441; [2016] P.T.S.R. 982 at [21].

[85]   *R. (on the application of Rogers) v Swindon NHS Primary Care Trust* [2006] EWCA Civ 392; [2006] 1 W.L.R. 2649.

[86]   *R. (on the application of Ross) v West Sussex Primary Care Trust* [2008] EWHC 2252 (Admin); (2008) 11 C.C.L. Rep. 787 at [78]–[79].

[87]   T. Buck "Precedent in Tribunals and the Development of Principles" (2006) 25 C.J.Q. 458.

[88]   *Merchandise Transport Ltd v British Transport Commission* [1962] 2 Q.B. 173 at 186, 192–193.

[89]   See, e.g. *Shirazi v Secretary of State for the Home Department* [2003] EWCA Civ 1562; [2004] 2 All E.R. 602 at [29]; *Januzi v Secretary of State for the Home Department* [2006] 2 A.C. 426 ; [2006] UKHL 5 at [50].

[90]   *S v Secretary of State for the Home Department* [2002] EWCA Civ 539; [2002] I.N.L.R. 416 at [28].

[91]   *Shirazi* [2003] EWCA Civ 1562; [2004] 2 All E.R. 602 at [29].

[92]   *R. (on the application of Iran) v Secretary of State for the Home Department* [2005] EWCA Civ 982; [2005] Imm. A.R. 535 at [90].

[93]   *Januzi* [2006] 2 A.C. 426 at [50].

considered, as part of its function, the development of guidance as to the general approach to what constitutes reasonable conduct by an employer.[94]

Evidence of a fetter on discretion

How do the courts ensure that the authority is genuine in its professed willing-ness to depart from a fixed rule or policy? It should be remembered here that the authority is not obliged to consider every application before it afresh, but must at least keep its mind ajar in the interest of fairness and the achievement of its statu-tory purpose. In *British Oxygen*, Lord Reid upheld the claim of a fetter on the Department's discretion, but emphasised that the principle did not require the Department to listen to "a multitude of similar applications" but simply be prepared to listen to someone with "something new to say".[95] The relevant principles were well stated by Bankes LJ in a case in which the Port of London Authority had refused an application for a licence to construct certain works, on the ground that it had itself been charged with the provision of accommodation of that character.

9-016

> "There are on the one hand cases where a tribunal in the honest exercise of its discretion has adopted a policy, and, without refusing to hear an applicant, intimates to him what its policy is, and that after hearing him it will in accordance with its policy decide against him, *unless there is something exceptional in his case* ... if the policy has been adopted for reasons which the tribunal may legitimately entertain, no objection could be taken to such a course. On the other hand there are cases where a tribunal has passed a rule, or come to a determination, not to hear any application of a particular character by whosoever made. There is a wide distinction to be drawn between these two classes."[96]

Conduct of the decision-maker

The courts will therefore scrutinise closely the conduct of a decision-maker in assessing whether or not he has unlawfully fettered his discretion. A course of conduct involving the consistent rejection of applications belonging to a particular class may justify an inference that the competent authority has adopted an unavowed rule to refuse all.[97] In cases involving discretionary grants for students it was held that although the policy admitted of exceptions, in practice there was no evidence of any procedures to allow applications in exceptional circumstances.[98] Where a departmental handbook on its face fettered the discretion of the Ministry, the courts were prepared to go behind a claim that the handbook was not in fact relied upon in reaching the impugned decision, and held that the handbook was so much a "part of the Department's thinking" that its influence could not be

9-017

---

[94] *Grundy (Teddington) Ltd v Plummer and Salt* [1983] I.C.R. 367 at 375; and T. Buck, "Precedent in Tribunals and the Development of Principles" (2006) 25 C.J.Q. 458, 481.

[95] *British Oxygen* [1971] A.C. 610 at 625; adopted in *Ex p. Brent* [1982] Q.B. 593.

[96] *R. v PLA Ex p. Kynoch Ltd* [1919] 1 K.B. 176 at 184 (Bankes LJ's emphasis). The vital words here italicised (by the author of the first edition of this work) are omitted from the report of Bankes LJ's judgment in other series of reports: 88 L.J.K.B. 559; 120 L.T. 179; 83 J.P 43. The judgment appears to have been substantially rewritten for the purpose of publication in the *Law Reports*.

[97] cf. *Macbeth v Ashley* (1874) L.R. 2 H.L.Sc. 352 at 357. This passage was expressly approved in *Collymore* [1995] E.L.R. 217 where Judge J held that where, over a period of three years, 300 appeals from decisions of the council to refuse discretionary student grants had all failed, it could be inferred that the policy to refuse to award discretionary grants save in "most extraordinary" circumstances had been applied far too rigidly. See also *Ex p. Dada* [1996] Q.B. 507; *R. (on the application of Kelly) v Liverpool Crown Court* [2006] EWCA Civ 11 (taxi licence applications).

[98] *Ex p. Jones* [1995] E.L.R. 42.

dismissed.[99] On the other hand, where a policy to ban taxi drivers who had been found guilty of plying for hire without a licence was enforced with very few exceptions, it was held that to hold the line on the policy in that way was necessary in order to provide an effective deterrent.[100]

9-018   A blanket policy may also be acceptable where it is "unrealistic and impractical" to consider each case individually.[101] The courts should, however, be sufficiently alert to spot a charade. Where a health authority's policy was to refuse surgical treatment of transsexualism, and the policy on its face provided for an exception in cases of "overriding clinical need", it was held that the authority was in practice operating a "blanket policy" of refusing surgery under any circumstance.[102] In addition, it should be noted that the duty not to fetter a discretion continues after representations have been entertained, up to the time that the final decision is taken, and accordingly, it may well be an unlawful fetter for a decision-maker to refuse to entertain a delegation who have already been heard, if the decision-maker does not ascertain whether they have any new representations to make.[103]

Prior opportunity to make representations

9-019   In determining the validity of the exercise of discretion particular importance may be attached to the fact that before the agency applied its rules or policy an opportunity was afforded the individual affected to make representations. It will be rare that the repository of discretion will be held to have fettered its exercise unlawfully if it has been addressed on the applicability of the non-statutory criterion to the particular case, on whether an exception to the rules or policy should be made in that instance and on the soundness of the standard that has been adopted.[104] One reason why the courts have rarely impugned decisions for fettering ministerial dispositions of planning appeals, proposals for compulsory acquisition of land and other matters that are decided after a public inquiry has been held, is that individuals affected by these decisions will have had an opportunity to bring to the Minister's attention considerations that may mitigate against a mechanical application of some rule of thumb.[105] Another reason for judicial reluctance to intervene is the wide range of policy considerations relevant to the exercise of the statutory

---

[99] *Sheriff, The Times,* 18 December 1986. compare *R. v Southwark LBC Ex p. Udu* (1996) 8 Admin. L.R. 25 (local authority entitled to have general policy of not funding courses at private colleges and postgraduate courses, subject to "exceptional cases").

[100] *R. v Nottingham CC Ex p. Howitt* [1999] C.O.D. 530.

[101] *R. (on the application of S) v Chief Constable of South Yorkshire* [2004] UKHL 39; [2004] 1 W.L.R. 2196 at [60] (blanket policy to retain DNA and fingerprint samples; was considered "unrealistic and impracticable" to consider each case individually); *R. v Secretary of State for the Home Department Ex p. Hepworth* [1998] C.O.D. 146 (Laws J regarded a system of incentives in prisons as no fetter as "in a mileu such as this there cannot be black-and-white rules"); *R. (on the application of Sandiford) v The Secretary of State for Foreign and Commonwealth Affairs* [2014] UKSC 44; [2014] 1 W.L.R. 2697 at [65] (blanket policy under prerogative powers to refuse funding of foreign litigation due to domestic policy and funding considerations not unacceptable).

[102] *Ex p. A* [2000] 1 W.L.R. 977.

[103] *Ex p. Brent* [1982] Q.B. 593 (Secretary of State fettered discretion in refusing to entertain new representations from affected local authorities).

[104] See, e.g. *Walsh v Wilson* [1907] A.C. 45; *British Oxygen* [1971] A.C. 610 at 625, 631; *Malloch v Aberdeen Corp (No.2)* 1974 S.L.T. 253.

[105] *Stringer v Minister of Housing and Local Government* [1970] 1 W.L.R. 1281.

powers in question. It will require a decision letter worded with particular infelicity or the adoption by the court of an unduly narrow construction of it.[106]

Duty to hear the applicant?

In order to ensure that the authority genuinely takes into account representations to apply its policy flexibly, the courts may require the applicant to have a hearing, although there is little authority on the point. A hearing of some sort might be thought to be appropriate in these circumstances to guard against any improper fettering of discretion,[107] and because the adoption of more specific criteria may give rise to disputes for the resolution of which a hearing would be appropriate.[108] Normally, however, the courts seek a system or procedure for making representations, rather than any specific form of hearing.[109] An inflexible policy *not* to hold an oral hearing may, itself constitute an unlawfully fettering of its discretion.[110]

9-020

Policies engendering legitimate expectations

When a public authority openly prescribes the criteria upon which it proposes to decide may thereby create a legitimate expectation create an interest that in fairness should be given some procedural, or even substantive, protection. Thus there are circumstances in which an authority will not be permitted to depart from its previously announced policy without affording a hearing to those adversely affected by it. This question is examined in Chapter 12, but here we should note a subtle change in the argument and in the interests and values advanced. Up to now we have seen the public authority seeking, in the interest of legal certainty (and perhaps also of efficiency) to operate a known and certain rule or policy. The claimant wishes to persuade the authority to depart from the rule or policy in the interest of responsive administration, so as to provide justice in the individual case. Where a legitimate expectation is claimed, it is the claimant who, in the interest of legal certainty, wishes the public body to abide by its policy and to fulfil expectations engendered by its representations. And it can be the public authority that

9-021

---

[106] See, e.g. *Lavender (H) & Son Ltd v Minister of Housing and Local Government* [1970] 1 W.L.R. 1231 to lead the court to the conclusion that the Minister, in effect, viewed the inquiry and the inspector's report with the utmost cynicism. It may also be noted that there are dicta in the majority judgments in *Sagnata Investments Ltd* [1971] 2 Q.B. 614 at 632, 633, 639 that lend support to the view that even after a hearing, an administrative discretion may not be exercised solely on the basis of a policy decision to grant no more licences of specified types. However, in that case the court was primarily considering the legality of a decision of Quarter Sessions, to which an appeal lay by way of rehearing from the licensing authority, rather than whether the original decision to refuse the licence was ultra vires the local authority. Moreover, an unimpeachable finding of fact by the Recorder was treated as virtually amounting to an assertion that the hearing had been treated by the council as a mere formality.

[107] See e.g. *British Oxygen* [1971] A.C. 610.

[108] See, e.g. *Stratford Catering Co Ltd* (1926) 42 T.L.R. 778 at 781; *Ex p. Ince* [1973] 1 W.L.R. 1334 at 1345 (tribunals that are in any event required to conduct a hearing should disclose the principles upon which they propose to make their decision). See also *Salemi v MacKellar (No.2)* (1977) 137 C.L.R. 396, for conflicting dicta on whether, before deciding to deport an alien on the ground that he did not fall within the terms of an amnesty for certain classes of prohibited immigrants, the Minister must allow representation to be made. Compare *Birdi v Home Secretary* (1975) 119 S.J. 322. In *Ex p. Brent* [1982] Q.B. 593 it was held that the failure of the Secretary of State to hear London councils which were pleading against a reduction in their grants for overspending amounted both to an unlawful fetter on the Secretary of State's discretion and a breach of the duty to provide a fair hearing.

[109] *Ex p. Jones* [1995] E.L.R. 42 (Leggatt LJ required "an exceptions procedure worthy of the name" and which would provide evidence of "genuine willingness" to hear the case).

[110] *Ex p. Anderson* [1992] Q.B. 169 at 188.

wishes to be free to depart from its previous announcements in the interest of responsive administration and in order to fulfil its public duties.

UNDERTAKING NOT TO EXERCISE A DISCRETION

9-022   A public authority cannot effectively bind itself not to exercise a discretion if to do so would be to disable itself from fulfilling the primary purposes for which it was created. It has been said that

> "if a person or public body is entrusted by the Legislature with certain powers and duties expressly or impliedly for public purposes, those persons or bodies cannot divest themselves of these powers and duties. They cannot enter into any contract or take any action incompatible with the due exercise of their powers or duties".[111]

So to act would be "to renounce a part of their statutory birthright".[112] Clearly this cannot be understood to mean that a public authority is never competent to limit its discretion by entering into commercial contracts[113] or restrictive covenants[114]; the principle must be stated more conservatively. Breaking it down into a series of neat propositions presents problems: formulations are not uniform, the decided cases have arisen in a variety of contexts and not all are reconcilable with one another. However, some generalisations are possible.

General principle

9-023   A public authority cannot effectively disable itself by contractual or other undertakings from making[115] or enforcing[116] a byelaw, refusing or revoking a grant of planning permission,[117] or exercising any other statutory power of primary

---

[111] *Birkdale District Electricity Supply Co v Southport Corp* [1926] A.C. 355 at 364.

[112] *Birkdale* [1926] A.C. 355 at 371; and *Ayr Harbour Trustees v Oswald* (1883) 8 App.Cas. 623 at 634. For discussion, see P. Hogg, Patrick J. Monahan, Wade K. Wright, *Liability of the Crown*, 4th edn (2011) Ch.9; A. C. L Davies, "Ultra Vires Problems in Government Contracts" (2006) 122 L.Q.R. 98; A.C.L. Davies, *The Public Law of Government Contracts* (2008); M. Freedland, "Government by Contract and Public Law" [1994] P.L. 86; C. Turpin, *Government Procurement Contracts* (1989); P. Vincent-Jones, *The New Public Contracting: Regulation, Responsiveness, Relationality* (2006); C. Donnelly, *Delegation of Governmental Power to Private Parties: A Comparative Perspective* (2007), pp.357–358; R. Noguellou and U. Stelkens (eds), *Comparative Law on Public Contracts* (2010).

[113] See, e.g. *Birkdale* [1926] A.C. 355. Compare *York Corp v Henry Leetham & Son* [1924] 1 Ch. 557; *R. v GLC Ex p. Burgess* [1978] I.C.R. 991 (Local Government Act 1972 s.111 wide enough to enable local authority to enter into a closed shop agreement).

[114] See, e.g. *Stourcliffe Estates Co v Bournemouth Corp* [1910] 2 Ch. 12.

[115] *Cory (William) & Son Ltd v City of London Corp* [1951] 2 K.B. 475; compare *Commission v Council* (81/72) [1973] E.C.R. 575.

[116] *Bean (William) & Sons Ltd v Flaxton RDC* [1929] 1 K.B. 450.

[117] *Ransom & Luck Ltd v Surbiton BC* [1949] Ch. 180 at 195, 198; *Stringer* [1970] 1 W.L.R. 1281 (though in this case the planning authority did not purport to fetter itself absolutely); *Windsor and Maidenhead RBC v Brandrose Investments Ltd* [1983] 1 W.L.R. 509 (planning authority cannot bind itself by contract to grant planning permission; relief refused in court's discretion). compare *R. v Sevenoaks DC Ex p. Terry* [1985] 3 All E.R. 226 (council which granted planning permission to developer did not act unlawfully in resolving previously to sell site to developers, since formal sale agreement not entered into until after grant of planning permission, *Steeples v Derbyshire CC* [1985] 1 W.L.R. 256 not followed). Decisions such as *Terry* are susceptible to an analysis in terms of bias. See, *R. v St Edmundsbury BC Ex p. Investors in Industry Commercial Properties Ltd* [1985] 1 W.L.R. 1168.

importance,[118] such as a power of compulsory purchase,[119] nor can it effectively bind itself to exercise such a power in any particular way. Similarly, it cannot be estopped by its inertia or acquiescence from fulfilling a duty to exercise a power when the occasion arises for it to be exercised.[120] These principles apply a fortiori to fettering the effective discharge of public duties.[121]

Discretion in relation to land

More specifically, a public authority endowed with statutory powers and duties exercisable for public purposes in relation to land cannot disable itself from fulfilling those purposes by dedicating or granting the land or interests therein in a manner or for a purpose incompatible with the fulfilment of the primary purposes.[122] Whether a proposed new purpose is compatible with the primary purposes may

9-024

---

[118] *Ayr* (1883) 8 App.Cas. 623; in New Zealand, *Ski Enterprises Ltd v Tongariro National Park Board* [1964] N.Z.L.R. 884. Compare *Stourcliffe* [1910] 2 Ch.12 where the power restricted was of a subsidiary nature; and *R. v Secretary of State for the Home Department Ex p. Fire Brigades Union* [1995] 2 A.C. 513 (Home Secretary could not disable himself from ability to bring statutory scheme into effect by adopting alternative scheme having consequence that statutory scheme "will not now be implemented"); *R. (on the application of Newhaven Port and Properties) v East Sussex CC* [2015] UKSC 7; [2015] 2 W.L.R. 601 (SC) (public not entitled to acquire by user rights which were incompatible with the continuing use of the land for statutory purposes). In Ireland, see G. Hogan and D.G. Morgan, *Administrative Law in Ireland*, 4th edn (2010), para.19-13 (discussing *Kenny v Cosgrave* [1926] I.R. 517; *Clinton v Minister for Justice, Equality and Law Reform*, unreported, 21 June 2010 High Court; and *Gilheaney v Revenue Commissioners* [1998] 4 I.R. 150 at 165).

[119] *Triggs v Staines UDC* [1969] 1 Ch. 10; compare *Sovmots Investments Ltd v Secretary of State for the Environment* [1977] Q.B. 411 at 420–421, 479–480; [1979] A.C. 144 at 185–186 (local authority did not unlawfully fetter its discretion when, on its compulsory acquisition of leasehold interest, it undertook to obey the covenants and not to seek unilaterally to acquire the freehold).

[120] *Yabbicom v R* [1899] 1 Q.B. 444 (power to prosecute for breach of byelaw). For the circumstances in which assurances (including assurances given by officials) may possibly operate as an estoppel, see Ch.12.

[121] *Sunderland Corp v Priestman* [1927] 2 Ch. 107 at 116; *Maritime Electric Co v General Dairies Ltd* [1937] A.C. 610; *Customs and Excise Commissioners v Hebson Ltd* [1953] 2 Lloyd's Rep. 382; *Society of Medical Officers of Health v Hope* [1960] A.C. 551 at 568, 569; in New Zealand see *Union Steam Ship Company of New Zealand Ltd v Commissioner of Inland Revenue* [1962] N.Z.L.R. 656; *Smith v Attorney General* [1973] 2 N.Z.L.R. 393 at 397. The position has been modified somewhat by the Privy Council decision in *Butcher v Petrocorp Exploration Ltd* [1991] 1 N.Z.L.R. 641 where the Privy Council distinguished between the Crown as a regulator from the Crown as a commercial partner or contractor. In this instance, where the regulatory power does not engage with the contract, the Crown's obligations as a commercial entity do not affect its powers as a regulator. In two cases following *Petrocorp*, the courts considered situations where the functions of a public authority were commercial in nature: in *The Power Co Ltd v Gore District Council* [1997] 1 N.Z.L.R. 537, the Court of Appeal upheld a contract that provided that the power board was bound by a contractual term to supply the Council (which owned the board's generating plant) power at a set rate in perpetuity; and in *Shotover Jet (Queenstown) Ltd v Kauwerau Jet Services Ltd* unreported 26 July 1996 High Court, Christchurch, Pankhurst J in the High Court said that whether there was an unlawful fetter depended on a consideration of both the regulatory power and the terms of the contract. Meanwhile, the Australian High Court has held that a government contract would be unenforceable if it were to seek to bind the government not to seek a certain legislative change to the law. However, the government can validly contract to adjust the contract price it must pay if the relevant law is indeed changed: *Port of Portland Pty Ltd v Victoria* (2010) 242 C.L.R. 348.

[122] *Ayr* (1883) 8 App.Cas. 623; *Patterson v Provost of St Andrews* (1881) 6 App.Cas. 833; *R. v Leake (Inhabitants)* (1833) 5 B. & Ad. 469 at 478; *Kilby* [2007] EWCA Civ 479; [2007] H.L.R. 39; *British Transport Commission v Westmorland CC* [1958] A.C. 126; *Dowty Boulton Paul Ltd v Wolverhampton Corp (No.2)* [1976] Ch. 13 (com cf. *Dowty Boulton Paul Ltd v Wolverhampton Corp* [1971] 1 W.L.R. 204); *R. v Hammersmith and Fulham LBC Ex p. Beddowes* [1987] Q.B. 1050; *Stourcliffe* [1910] 2 Ch.12 restriction upon discretion to use land for a subordinate purpose held binding where there were two conflicting statutory provisions); *Blake v Hendon Corp* [1962] 1 Q.B. 283 at 301–303 (statutory power to let was subordinate to primary power to make land available as a

raise questions of interpretation, fact and reasonably foreseeable probability; incompatibility cannot be established by mere conjecture.[123] Contracts for the sale of council houses have been specifically enforced even after the local authority has changed its policy on this matter[124]; similarly, a resolution by a Conservative-dominated local authority authorising the sale of a council-owned block of flats on terms including a restrictive covenant preventing the authority from letting vacant flats in council-retained neighbouring blocks was held (by a majority of the Court of Appeal) to be a lawful resolution not fettering the exercise by the council of its housing powers, because the policy was consistent with the purposes of the housing legislation.[125]

Discretion and contract

9-025   Contracts and covenants entered into by the Crown are not to be construed as being subject to implied terms that would exclude the exercise of general discretionary powers for the public good; on the contrary, they are to be construed as incorporating an implied term that such powers remain exercisable.[126] This is broadly true of other public authorities also, but the status and functions of the Crown in this regard are of a higher order. Indeed, the principle that the Crown's general power to dismiss its servants cannot be ousted even by the express terms of a contract has never been over-ruled[127] albeit that it has been significantly eroded by statute, the civil service disciplinary scheme and the courts' acceptance that civil servants may be engaged under contract of employment.[128]

9-026   Assertions such as that the Crown is incapable of so contracting as to fetter its

---

public park and would not therefore be lawfully exercisable unless compatible with that power). *Kilby* [2007] EWCA Civ 479; [2007] H.L.R. 39 at [32] (where a statute specifically stated that the local authority's contractual tenancies could be varied by unilateral notice, a system which circumscribed that power by giving to tenants' representatives an absolute veto was incompatible with the statute).

[123] *Westmorland* [1958] A.C. 126; compare *British Railways Board v Glass* [1965] Ch. 538 (a curious case in which CA held BRB to be bound by a right of way across the lines conferred by a predecessor in title, although there was evidence that the right of way gave rise to danger and inconvenience); P. Rogerson, "On the Fettering of Public Powers" [1971] P.L. 288.

[124] *Storer v Manchester CC* [1974] 1 W.L.R. 1403; *Gibson v Manchester CC* [1978] 1 W.L.R. 520 (reversed [1979] 1 W.L.R. 294 on other grounds).

[125] *Ex p. Beddowes* [1987] Q.B. 1050. However, as the dissent of Kerr LJ suggests, it should not of itself be sufficient answer to a charge of unlawful fettering to establish that the policy implemented is within the four corners of the empowering legislation; where the legislation leaves open a choice of policy alternatives it may, it is submitted, be an unlawful fetter to resolve in advance of the decision to adopt a particular policy approach, e.g. *R. v Legal Aid Board Ex p. RM Broudie & Co (A Firm)* [1994] C.O.D. 435 (guidance to taxing officer as to choice of circumstances which could be regarded as "exceptional" in determining uplift to solicitor's costs was unlawful as restricting taxing officer's discretion where words of legislation—"all the relevant circumstances" were unlimited).

[126] *Crown Lands Commissioners v Page* [1960] 2 Q.B. 274 (no covenant for quiet enjoyment to be implied in Crown lease so as to preclude Crown from exercising statutory requisitioning powers); *Molton Builders Ltd v City of Westminster* (1975) 30 P. & C.R. 182 at 188 (applicability of the doctrine of derogation from grant to exercise by Crown Estate Commissioners of their statutory power to consent to enforcement notice left open); *Cudgen Rutile (No.2) Ltd v Chalk* [1975] A.C. 520 (contract to lease Crown land other than in accordance with statutory provisions invalid). On contracts and judicial review generally, see 3-053. See also *Kilby* [2007] EWCA Civ 479; [2007] H.L.R. 39. For an example of a case in which no fettering was found where there was an express term in the contract that the authority would not be constrained in acting in any other capacity as a result of being a contracting party, see *R. (on the application of Khan) v Sutton* [2014] EWHC 3663 (Admin).

[127] *Riordan v War Office* [1959] 1 W.L.R. 1046 at 1053–1054.

[128] Employment Rights Act 1996 ss.191 and 192 (protection against unfair dismissal); Civil Service Order in Council 1992 on civil service discipline; on civil servant contracts, see *R. v Lord Chancel-*

future executive action in any way, or that in all contracts entered into by the Crown there is an implied term that the Crown may repudiate its obligations whenever in its opinion executive necessity so demands, must be viewed with reserve today.[129] The Crown cannot be allowed to tie its hands completely by prior undertakings, but the courts will not allow the Crown to evade compliance with ostensibly binding obligations whenever it thinks fit.[130] How and where the line is to be drawn is anything but clear.

As noted above in the context of the exercise of discretion in relation to land, the court will consider statutory interpretation, fact and reasonably foreseeable probability: and where it is contended that a contract is incompatible with a statutory discretion, the relevant factors will not only be whether the contract is incompatible with the public body's statutory purpose, but also whether the public body is likely to exercise the relevant statutory discretion and whether there are good reasons to preserve its ability to do so.[131] Where a public authority, rather than the Crown, wishes to exercise a statutory discretion which is incompatible with a contract which it has entered into, the statutory discretion will almost always be prioritised with the result that the contract will be found to be ultra vires.[132] However, this will not always be the case[133] and again, the line is difficult to draw.[134]

9-027

If a public authority lawfully repudiates or departs from the terms of a binding contract in order to exercise its overriding discretionary powers, or if it is held never to have been bound in law by an ostensibly binding contract because the undertakings would improperly fetter its general discretionary powers, at common law, the other party to the agreement has no right whatsoever to damages or compensation under the general law, no matter how serious the damage that party may have suffered.[135] There is a case for providing an appropriate remedy by way of an award of compensation determinable by a judicial body.[136] In the case of the local authority certified private finance contracts, the Local Government (Contracts) Act 1997

9-028

---

lor's Department Ex p. Nangle [1992] 1 All E.R. 897; A. Suterwalla, "Discretion and Duty: the Limits of Legality" in M. Supperstone, J. Goudie and P. Walker (eds), *Judicial Review*, 6th edn (2017), para.7.24.5.

[129] The rule ambiguously formulated in *Rederiaktiebolaget Amphitrite v R.* [1921] 3 K.B. 500 is one of open texture. For a critical discussion, see *Ansett Transport Industries (Operations) Pty Ltd v Commonwealth* (1977) 17 A.L.R. 513. Specific relief in civil proceedings is in any event not available directly against the Crown.

[130] *Page* [1960] 2 Q.B. 274 at 291–294 (Devlin LJ); *HTV Ltd v Price Commission* [1976] I.C.R. 170 at 185G–H (Lord Denning MR); *R. v IRC Ex p. Preston* [1985] A.C. 835 at 865 (Lord Templeman) and *R. v Secretary of State for Home Department Ex p. Doody* [1994] 1 A.C. 531.

[131] Davies, "Ultra Vires Problems in Government Contracts" [2006] 122 L.Q.R. 98 at 106; and *Leake* (1833) 5 B. & Ad. 469; *Westmoreland* [1958] A.C. 126 at 144; *Blake* [1962] 1 Q.B. 283.

[132] *Cory* [1951] 2 K.B. 475.

[133] *Dowty Boulton Paul Ltd* [1971] 1 W.L.R. 204.

[134] Davies "Ultra Vires Problems in Government Contracts" (2006) 122 L.Q.R. 98.

[135] For two well-known examples of the common law position on ultra vires government contracts, see: *Crédit Suisse v Allerdale BC* [1997] Q.B. 306; *Hazell v Hammersmith and Fulham LBC* [1992] 2 A.C. 1. See also *National Transport Co-operative Society Ltd v Attorney General of Jamaica* [2009] UKPC 48. See also *Credit Suisse International v Stichting Vestia Groep* [2014] EWHC 3103 (Comm); [2015] Bus. L.R. D5.

[136] Such provisions exist in French administrative law: Davies (2006) 122 L.Q.R. 98, 112, citing the "*fait du prince*" remedy, which applies where the public authority upsets the economic equilibrium of the contract by exercising its public powers, and enables the contractor to either seek an indemnity from the public authority or, where appropriate, increase its charges to consumers. The only exception is for changes in the law "affecting all citizens equally". See L. Brown and J. Bell, *French Administrative Law*, 5th edn (1998), pp.207–208; Davies (2008) pp.176–183; P. Craig, *Administrative Law*, 8th edn (2016), para.5-048. Reliance by a public body on the ultra vires principle could also constitute a breach of the right to property: *Stretch v United Kingdom* (2004) 38 E.H.R.R. 12. We suspect that today a court faced with this problem would find a method of awarding compensa-

modifies the common law position and provides protection for private contractors in the event of a finding of ultra vires[137]: the contract may be continued,[138] discharged on terms set out in the contract,[139] or discharged on the basis that the private contractor is entitled to whatever payments would have been due up to the date of the court's order and in addition to damages as for a repudiatory breach by the local authority.[140]

Common law discretionary powers

9-029   More generally, the non-fettering doctrine does not apply to common law discretionary powers of central government. In *R. (on the application of Elias) v Secretary of State for Defence*, it was held that the non-fettering principle did not apply to a policy on ex gratia payment.[141] Similarly, the doctrine does not apply to prerogative powers.[142]

---

tion, as justice so clearly requires this.

[137] Local Government (Contracts) Act 1997 ss.2 and 4.
[138] Local Government (Contracts) Act 1997 s.5(3).
[139] Local Government (Contracts) Act 1997 s.6(2)(b).
[140] Local Government (Contracts) Act 1997 s.7(2).
[141] [2006] EWCA Civ 1293; [2006] 1 W.L.R. 3213 at [191]. See also 5-030 on common law powers and the Ram doctrine.
[142] *Sandiford* [2014] UKSC 44 at [54], [62] (referring to the reasoning in *R. (on the application of Elias) v Secretary of State for Defence* [2006] EWCA Civ 1293; [2006] 1 W.L.R. 3213, in which it had been held that it is within the power of the decision-maker to decide on the extent to which to exercise a power such as setting up a scheme, it was held that prerogative powers have to be approached on a different basis from statutory powers as there is no necessary implication, from their mere existence, that the State as their holder must keep open the possibility of their exercise in more than one sense). For comment, see K Costello "The scope of application of the rule against fettering in administrative law" (2015) 131 L.Q.R. 354.

CHAPTER 10

Procedural Fairness: Bias and Conflict of Interest

TABLE OF CONTENTS

SCOPE

This chapter considers: **10-001**

- The history of the concept of bias in judicial and administrative settings.
- The test of bias.
- Situations which will normally disqualify a decision-maker for bias.
- Situations which will not normally disqualify a decision-maker for bias.
- The requirements of ECHR art.6.
- Comparative perspectives.

Introduction

Procedural fairness demands not only that those whose interests may be af-   **10-002**
fected by an act or decision should be given prior notice and an adequate opportunity to be heard, but also requires that the decision-maker should not be biased
or prejudiced in a way that precludes fair and genuine consideration being given
to the arguments advanced by the parties.[1] Although perfect objectivity may be an
unrealisable objective, the rule against bias thus aims at preventing a hearing from
being a sham or a ritual or a mere exercise in "symbolic reassurance",[2] due to the
fact that the decision-maker was not in practice persuadable. An adjudicator may

---

[1] Bias has been defined as "an operative prejudice, whether conscious or unconscious": *R. v Queen's County Justices* [1908] 1 I.R. 285 at 294 (Lord O'Brien CJ); and see *Flaherty v National Greyhound Racing Club Ltd* [2005] EWCA Civ 1117; (2005) 102(37) L.S.G. 31 at [28] (Scott-Baker LJ: "a predisposition or prejudice against one party's case or evidence on an issue for reasons unconcerned with the merits of the issue). See also *R. (on the application of DM Digital Television Ltd) v Office of Communications* [2014] EWHC 961 (Admin) at [36].

[2] M. Edelman, *The Symbolic Uses of Politics* (1974).

indeed seldom achieve "the icy impartiality of a Rhadamanthus",[3] and the idea that "by taking the oath of office as a judge, a man ceases to be human and strips himself of all predilections, becomes a passionless thinking machine",[4] is doubtless beyond achievement.

10-003 Nevertheless, the common law (and sometimes statute) disqualifies a decision-maker from adjudicating whenever circumstances point to a real possibility that his decision may be predetermined in favour of one of the parties. This may arise from: (a) personal connections or predispositions which raise real doubts about the decision-maker's *impartiality*; or (b) the institutional setting of the decision-making process which throws doubt upon its *independence*.[5]

10-004 ECHR art.6 is also of course relevant here and states (with emphasis added):

> "In the determination of his civil rights and obligations or of any criminal charge against him, everyone is entitled to a fair and public hearing within a reasonable time *by an independent and impartial tribunal* established by law".

10-005 Insofar as the common law test of bias previously differed from the ECHR test, necessary adjustments have in most respects been made and it has been claimed that nowadays there is "no difference between the common law test of bias and the requirement under art.6 of the Convention of an independent and impartial tribunal".[6]

10-006 The principle expressed in the maxim *nemo iudex in sua causa* (no one should be a judge in his own cause) refers not only to the fact that no one shall adjudicate his own case; it also refers to the fact that no one should adjudicate a matter in which he has a conflicting interest.[7] In order to give effect to those two aspects of the principle, the concern is not only to prevent the distorting influence of *actual bias*, but also to protect the integrity of the decision-making process by ensuring that, however disinterested the decision-maker is in fact, the circumstances should not give rise to the *appearance of bias*. As has been famously said: "justice should not only be done, but should manifestly and undoubtedly be seen to be done".[8]

10-007 In defining the scope of the rule against bias and its content, at least two requirements of public law are in play. The first seeks accuracy in public decision-making. If a person is influenced in a decision by his private interests or personal

---

[3]   E. Coke, *Institutes of the Laws of England* (1817), Vol.3, p.35: Rhadamanthus, the cruel judge of Hell, punished before he heard; cf. *Jackson v Barry Railway Company* [1893] 1 Ch. 238 at 248 (Bowen J).

[4]   *Re JP Linahan* 138 F 2d 650 (1942) (Jerome Frank J); and *R. v Barnsley Licensing Justices Ex p. Barnsley and District Licensed Victuallers Association* [1960] 2 Q.B. 167 (Devlin LJ) on unconscious bias; and see generally, for a sophisticated analysis with special reference to international adjudication.

[5]   *Gillies v Secretary of State for Work and Pensions* [2006] UKHL 2; [2006] 1 W.L.R. 781 at [38] (Baroness Hale of Richmond draws a distinction between impartiality which she defines as "the tribunal's approach to deciding the cases before it" and independence, which she defines as the "structural or institutional framework which secures this impartiality", a structure which should be viewed as unbiased not only by members of the tribunal but also by members of the public, now referred to as "the fair-minded and informed observer").

[6]   *Lawal v Northern Spirit Ltd* [2003] UKHL 35; [2004] 1 All E.R. 187 at [14] (Lord Steyn). On the extent to which the requirement of an unbiased decision applies in a situation outside of a judicial setting or when interests are being considered which fall short of what art.6 calls "civil rights and obligations", see 10-012. See also *R. v Abdroikov* [2007] UKHL 37; [2007] 1 W.L.R. 2679 at [17]; *Thames Water Utilities Ltd v Newbound* [2015] EWCA Civ 677 at [91] (Lady Justice King observing that "[u]nderlying both of them is the fundamental consideration that justice should not only be done but should manifestly and undoubtedly be seen to be done").

[7]   In Israel, the test of bias is named "conflict of interest": I. Zamir and A. Zysblat, *Public Law in Israel* (1997), p.96.

[8]   *R. v Sussex Justices Ex p. McCarthy* [1924] 1 K.B. 256 at 259 (Lord Hewart CJ).

predilections, he will not follow, or may be tempted not to follow, the required standards and considerations which ought to guide the decision.[9] An accurate decision is more likely to be achieved by a decision-maker who is in fact impartial or disinterested in the outcome of the decision and who puts aside any personal prejudices. The second requirement is for public confidence in the decision-making process.[10] Even though the decision-maker may in fact be scrupulously impartial, the appearance of bias can itself call into question the legitimacy of the courts and other decision-making bodies.[11]

HISTORICAL DEVELOPMENT

Early background

Bracton wrote that a judge was not to hear a case if he was suspected of partial- **10-008** ity because of consanguinity, affinity, friendship or enmity with a party or because of his subordinate status towards a party or because he was or had been a party's advocate.[12] These principles, which Bracton set out as if they were already part of the common law, were in fact the canon law rules for recusation of suspected judges,[13] which were applied in the English ecclesiastical courts[14] and also, it seems, in medieval Scottish courts.[15] They bear a close resemblance to the grounds for disqualification of judges for likelihood of bias in modern English law. It might well be supposed, therefore, that they were imported into the common law in its early formative period by Bracton himself, or by his contemporaries or predecessors. Indirect support for an opinion that they were received into the common law might be derived from the fact that the grounds of exception for interest and bias to the competency of witnesses in courts Christian had been applied from the earliest times to the challenge of jurors of the grand assize[16] and the possessory assizes.[17] Moreover, at least as early as the 14th century, common law judges were held to

---

9   D. Galligan, Due Process and Fair Procedures (1996). Lord Steyn has stated that procedural fairness "plays an instrumental role in promoting just decisions": *Rajiv General Medical Council* [2003] UKPC 24; [2003] 1 W.L.R. 1052 at [13].

10   *Belilos v Switzerland* (1998) 10 E.H.R.R. 466 at [67] (ECtHR based the rule against bias under art.6 on the need for "the confidence which must be inspired by the courts in a democratic society"). *Resolution Chemicals Limited v H Lundbeck A/S* [2013] EWCA Civ 1515; [2014] 1 W.L.R. 1943 at [35] ("underlying both article 6 of the Convention and the common law principles is the fundamental consideration that justice should not only be done but should manifestly and undoubtedly be seen to be done").

11   In this respect, it is important to emphasise that if the fair-minded and informed observer would conclude that there is a real possibility that the tribunal will be biased, the judge is automatically disqualified from hearing the case. The decision to recuse in those circumstances is not a discretionary case management decision reached by weighing various relevant factors in the balance. Considerations of inconvenience, cost and delay are irrelevant: *Resolution Chemicals* [2013] EWCA Civ 1515; [2014] 1 W.L.R. 1943 at [35]. A "pragmatic precautionary approach" is required: [40].

12   Bracton, De Legibus, Clark, NJ: Lawbook Exchange Ltd (2009), p.412.

13   For the grounds of exception to the suspectus judex in canon law (pecuniary interest, advocacy, kinship, friendship, great enmity), see *Codex Juris Canonici*, canons 1613–1614. There is a legend that a Pope (subsequently canonised) once condemned himself to be burned to death for his sins ((1430) YB. 8 Hen. 6, Hill. pl. 6).

14   F.W. Maitland, *Roman Canon Law in the Church of England* (1898), p.114.

15   Lord Cooper (ed), *Regiam Majestatem and Quoniam Attachiamenta* (1947), pp.324–325.

16   Glanvill, *De Legibus*, (1932) Bk. 11, c.12 (transl. Pound and Plucknett, *Readings on the History and System of the Common Law*, 3rd edn (1927) p.143. For the canon law rules, see *Wigmore on Evidence*, 3rd edn (1940), Vol.2, p.678, fn.14; *Dictionaire de droit Canonique* (1935–65), Vol.4, pp.483–484.

be incompetent to hear cases in which they were themselves parties.[18] Yet there seems to be no evidence that Bracton's broad statement of canon law doctrine as common law was accepted and acted upon by his successors. On the contrary, it was laid down that favour was not to be presumed in a judge.[19]

10-009   The principle that a judge was disqualified from adjudicating whenever there was a real likelihood that he might be biased was not unequivocally established until the 1860s.[20] Bracton is not cited in any of the leading English cases on the matter. One must conclude that the balance of probability is tilted against the view that the canon law rules were ever directly incorporated in the common law. The common law judges came to adopt principles substantially the same as those of the canon lawyers, not by way of conscious imitation, but by moving independently towards a just and reasonable solution.

10-010   The reluctance of the common lawyers to recognise the concept of disqualification of judges for interest or bias is illustrated by Coke's bald assertion[21] that judges and justices, unlike jurors, could not be challenged, an assertion reiterated by Blackstone, who thought it a salutary rule of public *policy*.[22] Long before Blackstone's day, however, Sir Nicholas Bacon,[23] the Earl of Derby[24] and the Mayor of Hereford (who was laid by the heels by the Court of King's Bench)[25] had discovered that the common law did not permit a judge to determine a matter in which he had a direct pecuniary or proprietary interest.[26] And it was Coke himself who had elevated to a fundamental principle of the common law the proposition that no man should be a judge in his own cause. In *Dr Bonham's case*, when examining the claim of the College of Physicians to fine its members for malpractice, he said that the censors of the College "cannot be judges, ministers, and parties ... *quia aliquis non debet esse judex in propria causa* ... and one cannot be judge and attorney for any of the parties". Moreover, "when an Act of Parliament is against common right or reason, or repugnant, or impossible to be performed, the common law will controul it, and adjudge such Act to be void". So "if any Act of Parliament gives to any to hold, or to have conusans of all manner of pleas arising before

---

17   Bracton, *De Legibus* (1640), pp.143b, 185. See (1354) 28 Lib.Ass. 18 (juror challengeable because member of commonalty that was party to suit); (1481) YB. 21 Edw. 4, Mich. pl. 3 (juror challengeable in assize brought by dean and chapter of Lincoln, because he was brother of a prebendary of the chapter). The King could judge his own causes, with the exception that he could not be both actor and judex in cases of high treason: Bracton, *De Legibus* (1640), p.119; L. Ehrlich, *Proceedings Against the Crown* 1216–1377 (1921), pp.47–49.

18   See, e.g. (1371) 45 Lib.Ass. 3, where a party in a case at assizes that had to be heard before two judges was himself appointed judge upon the death of one of the two justices of assize: held, he could not judge his own cause. References to early Yearbook cases are collected by S. Thorne (ed), *Egerton's Discourse upon the Statutes* (1942), 73n. See also 2 Roll Abr. 92–93.

19   *Brooks v Earl of Rivers* (1668) Hardres 503 (Chamberlain of Chester not disqualified from hearing an action in which his brother-in-law was a party).

20   Blackburn J's judgment in *R. v Rand* (1866) L.R. 1 Q.B. 230 is regarded as the *locus classicus*.

21   Co.Litt. 294a.

22   W. Blackstone *Commentaries on the Laws of England* (printed for J. Exshaw, H. Saunders, B. Grierson, J. Williams, and J. Milliken (1769)), Vol.3, p.361 ("For the law will not suppose the possibility of bias or favour in a judge, who is already sworn to administer impartial justice, and whose authority greatly depends upon that presumption and idea").

23   *Sir Nicholas Bacon's case* (1563) 2 Dyer 220b.

24   *Earl of Derby's case* (1613) 12 Co.Rep. 114.

25   *Anon.* (1697) 1 Salk, 396 (facts given in *Wright v Crump* (1702) 2 Ld.Raym. 766).

26   For other early reported cases, see the *Foxham Tithing case* (1704) 2 Salk. 607 (surveyor adjudicated as justice in matter concerning his office); *Company of Mercers and Ironmongers of Chester v Bowker* (1725) 1 Str. 639 (member of company became mayor and member of court before judgment). cf. *Markwick v City of London* (1707) 2 Bro. PC. 409: *Great Charte v Kennington* (1742) 2 Str. 1173 (justices in removal case interested as local ratepayers).

him within his manor ... yet he shall have no plea, to which he himself is party; for, as hath been said, *iniquum est aliquem suae rei esse judicem*".[27] Similar views were expressed by Hobart[28] and Holt.[29] It is doubtful whether a court ever held a statute to be void solely because it made a man a judge in his own cause[30] and it has been argued that Coke was merely laying down that statutes framed in such terms were to be strictly construed to avoid what would appear to be an obvious absurdity.[31] While Parliament may be competent to make a person a judge in his own cause[32] but the courts continue to uphold the common law tradition by declining to adopt such a construction of a statute if its wording is open to another construction.[33]

Later developments

In developing the modern law relating to disqualification of judicial officers for interest and bias, the superior courts have striven to apply the principle enumerated by Lord Hewart CJ that it "is of fundamental importance that justice should not only be done, but should manifestly and undoubtedly be seen to be done",[34] without giving currency to "the erroneous impression that it is more important that justice should appear to be done than that it should in fact be done".[35] The emphasis thus shifted from the simple precepts of the law of nature to the need to maintain public confidence in the administration of justice.[36] In some cases, such as when the person was a party to proceedings or who had any direct pecuniary or proprietary interest in the result it was held that the person was automatically disqualified at common law to adjudicate in those proceedings. If, however, it was alleged that the adjudicator has made himself partisan, by reason of his words or deeds or his association with a party who was instituting or defending the proceedings before him, the courts would not hold him automatically to be disqualified.

10-011

---

[27] (1610) 8 Co.Rep. 113b, 118. See also Co.Litt. 141a.

[28] *Day v Savadge* (1614) Hob. 85 at 86, 87.

[29] *London (City of) v Wood* (1701) 12 Mod. 669 at 686–688.

[30] T. Plucknett, "Bonham's Case and Judicial Review" (1926) 40 Harv.L.Rev. 30.

[31] R. MacKay, "Coke: Parliamentary Sovereignty or the Supremacy of Law" (1924) 22 Mich. L.Rev. 215; S. Thorne, "Dr Bonham's Case" (1938) 54 L.Q.R. 543; J. Gough, *Fundamental Law in English Constitutional History* (1955), pp.31–39.

[32] *Great Charte* [1742] 2 Str. 1173 (dictum); *Lee v Bude & Torrington Junction Ry.* (1871) L.R. 6 C.P 576 at 582 (Willes J describes Hobart CJ's dicta in *Day* (1614) Hob. 85 as "a warning, rather than an authority to be followed"); *Rich v Christchurch Girls' High School Board of Governors (No.1)* [1974] 1 N.Z.L.R. 1 at 9, 18–20. This power is of course subject to the requirements of European Union law (Ch.14) and the Human Rights Act 1998 (see 10-083 and Ch.13), as well as, potentially, to the requirements of the rule of law: see *R. (on the application of Jackson) v Attorney General* [2005] UKHL 56; [2006] 1 A.C. 262 at [107] and [159].

[33] Bl.Comm. i, 91; *Mersey Docks & Harbour Board Trustees v Gibbs* (1866) L.R. 1 H.L 93 at 110; *Wingrove v Morgan* [1934] Ch. 423 at 430; *Rice v Commissioner of Stamp Duties* [1954] A.C. 216 at 234; *University of Edinburgh v Craik* [1954] S.C. 190 at 195; cf. *R. v Minister of Agriculture & Fisheries Ex p. Graham* [1955] 2 Q.B. 140; *Wilkinson v Barking Corp* [1948] 1 K.B. 721; and *Jeffs v New Zealand Dairy Production and Marketing Board* [1967] 1 A.C. 551. See the discussion of the "principle of legality" at 5-040.

[34] *Ex p. McCarthy* [1924] 1 K.B. 256 at 259; *R. v Essex Justices Ex p. Perkins* [1927] 2 K.B. 475 at 488 (Avory J suggests that "be seen" must be a misprint for "seem").

[35] *R. v Camborne Justices Ex p. Pearce* [1955] 1 Q.B. 41 at 52. cf. *R. v Byles* (1912) 77 J.P. 40 (Avory J: "It is as important (if not more important) that justice should seem to be done, as that it should be done"); cf. *Shrager v Basil Dighton Ltd* [1924] 1 K.B. 274 at 284 (Atkin LJ: "Next to the tribunal being in fact impartial is the importance of its appearing so"); cf. *R. v Atkinson* [1978] 1 W.L.R. 425 at 428 (Lord Scarman: "in this sensitive area, the appearance of justice is part of the substance of justice").

[36] *Serjeant v Dale* (1876–1877) L.R. 2 Q.B.D. 558 at 567.

THE TEST OF BIAS

10-012   A decision may always be invalidated if actual bias on the part of a decision-maker is proved.[37] However, courts will often not be concerned to investigate evidence of actual bias and there is authority to the effect that submissions of actual bias should not be made.[38] There are a number of reasons why the courts have seldom embarked on such inquiries. Actual bias has been described as rare and difficult to prove.[39] It is no doubt desirable that all adjudicators, like Caesar's wife, should be above suspicion,[40] but it would not be desirable to inquire into the mental state of a judge, a member of a jury or justices or their clerk because of the confidential nature of the judicial decision-making process. Nor would it be useful to do so because in many cases bias may be unconscious (subconscious may be a more accurate description) in its effect.[41] There are also obvious difficulties in exploring the actual state of mind of a judge (for example, a judge is not compellable as a witness in relation to his own decision) and it may be very difficult to establish.[42] For those reasons, the courts look at the circumstances of the particular case to see if there is an appearance of bias.[43] Of course, even an allegation of apparent bias should only be made on a proper basis; it is open to submit that certain findings of a panel may be characterised as wrong or lacking any proper basis, or even perverse, but that is quite a different thing from making a serious allegation of bias against a panel of this sort, whether actual or apparent.[44]

Various tests developed

10-013   Various tests have been applied to establish the limits of apparent bias. At the one extreme, the courts have disallowed any decision where there has been a "reasonable suspicion of bias".[45] At the other extreme, it has been suggested that a decision-

---

37   See, e.g. *R. v Burton Ex p. Young* [1897] 2 Q.B. 468 at 471; *R. v Tempest* (1902) 86 L.T. 585 at 587.
38   *Jackson v Thompsons Solicitors* [2015] EWHC 218 (QB) at [16].
39   *Broadview Energy Developments Ltd v Secretary of State for Communities and Local Government* [2015] EWHC 1743 (Admin) at [47].
40   *Lesson v General Medical Council* (1889) 43 Ch.D 366 at 385.
41   The courts have frequently emphasised that they are not concerned with the question whether an adjudicator was in fact biased. *Allinson v General Medical Council* [1894] 1 Q.B. 750 at 758; *Queen's County Justices* [1908] 2 I.R. 285 at 306; *R. v Halifax Justices Ex p. Robinson* (1912) 76 J.P 233 at 234–235; *R. v Caernarvon Licensing Justices Ex p. Benson* (1949) 113 J.P 23 at 24; *Barnsley Licensing Justices* [1960] 2 Q.B. 167 at 187; *Jackson v Thompsons Solicitors* [2015] EWHC 218 (QB) at [16].
42   *Jackson* [2015] EWHC 218 (QB) at [16].
43   For discussion, see J. Goudkamp, "The Rule against Bias and the Doctrine of Waiver" (2007) 26 C.J.Q. 310; H. Stout, "Bias" [2011] J.R. 458. See also *Jackson v Thompsons Solicitors* [2015] EWHC 218 (QB) at [17].
44   *R. (on the application of Allen) v Parole Board of England and Wales* [2015] EWHC 2069 (Admin) at [43].
45   *Ex p. McCarthy* [1924] 1 K.B. 256 at 259 (Hewart CJ: "Nothing is to be done which creates even a suspicion that there has been an improper interference with the course of justice"); *R. v Huggins* [1895] 1 Q.B. 563; *Cottle* [1939] 2 All E.R. 535. *Metropolitan Properties Co (FGC) Ltd v Lannon* [1969] 1 Q.B. 577 at 599 (Lord Denning: "The court does not look to see if there was a real likelihood that he would, or did, in fact favour one side at the expense of the other. The court looks at the impression which would be given to other people"), 606 (Edmund Davies LJ: it was enough if there is "reasonable suspicion of bias"), 601–602 (Danckwerts LJ). After Lannon, the reasonable suspicion test was applied by Lord Widgery CJ in *R. v Uxbridge Justices Ex p. Burbridge, The Times,* 21 June 1972, and *R. v McLean Ex p. Aikens* (1974) 139 J.P. 261. But he was more uncertain in *R. v Altrincham Justices Ex p. N. Pennington* [1975] Q.B. 549. See also *R. v Liverpool City Justices Ex*

maker should only be disqualified where there is a "real likelihood of bias".[46] "Real likelihood" can refer to either the possibility or the probability of bias. In respect of either test, there are two variants. Under the first, the suspicion or likelihood of bias is derived in the circumstances of the case from the point of view of the "reasonable man".[47] Under the second variant, the courts themselves decide the matter, based upon the impression they have of bias in the light of their own knowledge of the circumstances of the case.

The various tests of bias thus range along a spectrum (see Figure 1). At the one end, a court will require that, before a decision is invalidated, bias must be shown to have been present. At the other end of the spectrum, the court will strike at the decision where a reasonable person would have a reasonable suspicion from the circumstances of the case that bias might have infected the decision. In between these extremes is the "probability of bias" (this being closer to the "actual bias" test), and the "possibility of bias" (this test being closer to that of reasonable suspicion).

10-014

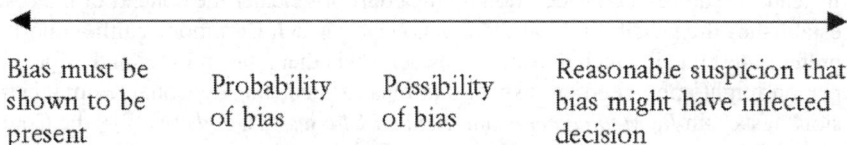

| Bias must be shown to be present | Probability of bias | Possibility of bias | Reasonable suspicion that bias might have infected decision |

Figure 1

Gough: "real danger" of bias

In *R. v Gough*, the House of Lords considered these various tests in relation to an allegation of bias on the part of a juror in a criminal trial.[48] Having carefully considered the authorities, it was held that direct pecuniary or proprietary interest always disqualified the decision-maker.[49] Outside that category, it was held that the correct test was whether, in the circumstances of the case, the court considered that there appeared to be a "real danger of bias". In such a case, the decision should not stand. This test is similar to that of the "real likelihood of bias" and it was made clear that it refers to the *possibility*—not probability—of bias.[50] The "reasonable suspicion test" was thus rejected. It was also held that the same test should be applied in all cases of apparent bias (whether concerning justices, members of tribunals, arbitrators, justices' clerks or jurors). It was held too that the "real danger"

10-015

---

p. *Topping* [1983] 1 W.L.R. 119; *R. v Morris* (1991) 93 Cr. App. R. 102.

[46] *Barnsley Licensing Justices Ex p. Barnsley & District Licensed Victuallers' Association* [1960] 2 Q.B. 167 at 187 (Devlin LJ); and *Rand* (1866) L.R. 1 Q.B. 230 (Blackburn J); *Frome United Breweries Co Ltd v Bath Justices* [1926] A.C. 586 at 591; *Ex p. Pearce* [1955] 1 Q.B. 41.

[47] Lord Denning MR in *Metropolitan Properties Co v Lannon* [1969] 1 Q.B. 577; and *R. v Sunderland Justices* [1901] 2 K.B. 357 at 373; *Hannam v Bradford Corp* [1970] 1 W.L.R. 937 at 942 (Sachs LJ), 949 (Cross LJ). See also *Ardahalian v Unifert International SA (The Elissar)* [1984] 2 Lloyd's Rep. 84; *Bremer Handelsgesellschaft mbH v Ets. Soules et Cie* [1985] 1 Lloyd's Rep. 160; [1985] 2 Lloyd's Rep. 199.

[48] *R. v Gough* [1993] A.C. 646. The appellant was indicted on a single count of conspiring with his brother to commit robbery. The brother had been discharged, but after conviction it was discovered that the brother's neighbour had served on the jury.

[49] See 10-019.

[50] The expression "real danger" of bias had been adopted by Lord Ackner in *R. v Spencer* [1987] A.C. 128, approving *R. v Sawyer* (1980) 71 Cr. App. R. 283 at 285. See also *R. v Putnam* (1991) 93 Cr. App. R. 281. The Gough test was followed in *R. v Secretary of State for the Environment Ex p. Kirkstall Valley Campaign* [1996] 3 All E.R. 304.

test should be applied from the point of view of the court, not from that of the "reasonable man", however slim the difference between the two points of view in practice. As Lord Goff said:

"Since however the court investigates the actual circumstances, knowledge of such circumstances as are found by the court must be imputed to the reasonable man; and in the results it is difficult to see what difference there is between the impression derived by a reasonable man to whom such knowledge has been imputed, and the impression derived by the court, here personifying the reasonable man".[51]

Gough reconsidered

10-016   In *Pinochet*,[52] Lord Browne-Wilkinson indicated that the test in *Gough* may need to be reconsidered, and it was then questioned, on the ground that it does not evaluate the interest of the decision-maker by the standard of the perception of appearance of bias on the part of the public (whose confidence is necessary in such cases). Instead, it requires a consideration by the court of whether the context of the case establishes the possibility that there was bias.[53] Much Commonwealth authority prefers a test under which the court considers "whether a fair-minded and informed person might apprehend or suspect that bias existed (the "reasonable apprehension" test).[54] In *Re Medicaments and Related Classes of Goods (No.2)*[55] the Court of Appeal considered the test of bias under ECHR art.6 where the European Court of Human Rights asks whether there is a risk of bias "objectively" in the light of the circumstances which the court has identified.[56] Lord Phillips of Worth Matravers MR felt that both because the test in *Gough* did not command universal approval and because it was at odds with the test under art.6, it should be modified[57] and that, in order to fulfil the confidence of the public, the court should consider the question of bias through the eyes of an "objective onlooker".[58]

---

[51]   *Gough* [1993] A.C. 646 at 667–668. In *Auckland Casino Ltd v Casino Control Authority* [1995] 1 N.Z.L.R. 142, the New Zealand Court of Appeal noted that since *R. v Gough and Webb v R.* (1994) 122 A.L.R. 41 there was, as to the test for apparent bias, a conflict of approach between the HL and the High Court of Australia, but said that once it is accepted that the hypothetical reasonable observer must be informed, the distinction between the real danger and reasonable suspicion tests becomes very thin. In *R. v Bow Street Metropolitan Stipendiary Magistrate Ex p. Pinochet Ugarte (No.2)* [2000] 1 A.C. 119 the majority of the HL seemed to prefer the Australian approach to *Gough*, although that matter was not directly decided.

[52]   *Pinochet (No.2)* [2000] 1 A.C. 119, discussed at 10-023.

[53]   See, e.g. *Locabail (UK) Ltd v Bayfield Properties Ltd* [2000] Q.B. 451 at [16] (Lord Bingham MR and Simon Brown LJ).

[54]   See e.g. the Australian case of *Webb v The Queen* (1994) 181 C.L.R. 41 referred to in *R. v Central Criminal Court Ex p. Bright* [2001] 1 W.L.R. 662. See *Law v Chartered Institute of Patent Agents* [1919] 2 Ch. 276; *Doherty v McGlennan* 1997 S.L.T. 444; *Bradford v McLeod* 1986 S.L.T. 244; *Millar v Dickson* 2001 S.L.T. 988 at 1002–1003; for comparative perspectives, see 10-099.

[55]   *Re Medicaments and Related Classes of Goods (No.2)* [2001] 1 W.L.R. 700.

[56]   See, e.g. *Piersack v Belgium* (1983) 5 E.H.R.R. 169 at 179–80; *De Cubber v Belgium* (1985) 7 E.H.R.R. 236 at 246; *Pullar v United Kingdom* (1996) 22 E.H.R.R. 391 at 402–403; *Farhi v France* (2009) 48 E.H.R.R. 34 at [23]. In *Hauschildt v Denmark* (1990) 12 E.H.R.R. 266 at 279, the ECtHR observed that in considering whether a judge was biased the standpoint of the accused is important, but not decisive: "what is decisive is whether this fear can be held objectively justified".

[57]   *Re Medicaments and Related Classes of Goods (No.2)* [2001] 1 W.L.R. 700 at [67].

[58]   *Re Medicaments and Related Classes of Goods (No.2)* [2001] 1 W.L.R. 700 at [87] ("the court must first ascertain all the circumstances which have a bearing on the suggestion that the judge was biased. It must then ask whether those circumstances would lead a fair-minded and informed observer to conclude that there was a real possibility ... that the tribunal was biased").

Gough adjusted: "real possibility"

The matter was then resolved by the House of Lords in *Porter v Magill*,[59] where **10-017**
Lord Hope suggested a "modest adjustment" to the test in *Gough*. The reference to
"real danger" was deleted and the test was held to be whether "the fair-minded and
informed observer, having considered the facts, would conclude that there was a real
possibility of bias".[60] The emphasis thus shifts from the view of the court to that
of an objective and informed observer.[61] This point was emphasised when the Court
of Appeal observed that "the opinion of the notional informed and fair-minded
observer is not to be confused with the opinion of the litigant".[62] Indeed, the litigant
has been noted to not be the fair-minded observer, lacking the objectivity which is
the hallmark of the fair-minded observer, being "far from dispassionate"; since
litigation is a stressful and expensive business, most litigants "are likely to oppose
anything that they perceive might imperil their prospects of success, even if, when
viewed objectively, their perception is not well-founded".[63]

Despite the alteration in the test of bias, it will not always be clear whether the **10-018**
perspective of the judge or that of the "fair-minded observer" will differ and much
judicial attention has been directed to the identification of the attributes of the "fair-
minded and informed observer". The concept has been described as "hypothetical", posited to assist the court in deciding whether the proceedings in question were
seen to be fair.[64] However, it has been observed frequently that there are conceptual
difficulties in creating a fictional character, investing that character with an ever-
growing list of qualities and then speculating about how such a person would
answer the question before the court. The notional observer has been described as
"something of a paragon. Not only is he fair-minded and impartial, but he has
diligently educated himself about the circumstances of the case".[65] The obvious
danger is that the judge will simply project on to that fictional character his or her
personal opinions.[66] As Lord Kerr has noted, there is a danger of characterising the
observer as "someone who, by dint of his engagement in the system that has generated the challenge, has acquired something of an insider's status".[67] Thus, the
observer should not be regarded as unduly neurotic or, as put by Kirby J in an

---

[59] *Porter v Magill* [2001] UKHL 67; [2002] 2 A.C. 357; see S. Atrill, "Who is the 'Fair-Minded Observer'? Bias after Magill" [2003] C.L.J. 279.

[60] *Porter v Magill* [2001] UKHL 67; [2002] 2 A.C. 357 at [103].

[61] This approach was endorsed by the HL in *Lawal* [2003] UKHL 35; [2004] 1 All E.R. 187 at [19] (Lord Steyn), citing in support *Belilos* (1988) 10 E.H.R.R. 466 at [67]. See also *Davidson v Scottish Ministers* [2004] UKHL 34; 2005 1 S.C. (H.L.) 7 where it was held that a former Lord Advocate (the Law Officer of the Scottish Executive) was disqualified from sitting in the Court of Session when he was called upon to interpret legislation the meaning of which he had previously advised. Lord Bingham at [17] said that the fair-minded and informed observer "would conclude that there was a real possibility that [the judge] ... would subconsciously strive to avoid reaching a conclusion which would undermine the very clear assurances he had given to Parliament".

[62] *Harb v Aziz* [2016] EWCA Civ 556 at [69] (adding that the test "ensures that there is a measure of detachment in the assessment of whether there is a real possibility of bias"). For comment, see C. Hollander "Apparent bias against an entire barristers' chambers? Harb v HRH Prince Abdul Aziz [2016] EWCA Civ 556" (2016) 35 C.J.Q. 287; K. Anderson, "Lost luggage and judicial baggage: Harb v HRH Prince Abdul Aziz [2016] EWCA Civ 556" (2016) 35 C.J.Q. 290.

[63] *Harb* [2016] EWCA Civ 556 at [69].

[64] *Virdi v Law Society* [2010] EWCA Civ 100; [2010] 1 W.L.R. 2840 at [37].

[65] *Dar Al Arkan Real Estate Development Company v Majid Al-Sayed Bader Hashim Refai* [2014] EWHC 1055 (Comm) at [37].

[66] *Lanes Group Plc v Galliford Try Infrastructure Ltd (t/a Galliford Try Rail)* [2011] EWCA Civ 1617; [2012] Bus. L.R. 1184 at [52].

[67] *Belize Bank Ltd v Attorney General of Belize* [2011] UKPC 36 at [38]. Elliott has observed that, "if legal doctrine in this sphere is to reflect that policy that underpins it", namely, to preserve public

Australian case, "neither complacent nor unduly sensitive or suspicious".[68] The observer is also often envisaged by the courts as being particularly well-informed and in possession of quite extensive knowledge.[69]

For example, apparent bias was not found where an advisory steering group to a medical body had included in its composition two consultants from medical centres which were being considered by the medical body as the objective observer would know the following: that the decision to be taken was with respect to which questions to put to public consultation and would not be final; the actual decision was comprised of representatives of all but one of the 152 English primary care trusts; the steering group was a clinically expert body with no decision-making role; the group was chaired by a distinguished neo-natal paediatrician, consisted of 29 experts all of whom knew that they had been appointed to represent their disciplines and professional bodies, not their hospitals; and all the issues would also remain at large in the consultation process.[70] Similarly, although the Office of the Independ-

---

confidence, "reviewing judges should certainly make greater efforts to avoid ... 'holding up a mirror' to themselves": M. Elliott, "The appearance of bias, the fair-minded and informed observer, and the 'ordinary person in Queen Square market'" (2012) 71 C.L.J. 247, 250. See also A.A. Olowofoyeku "Bias and the informed observer: a call for a return to Gough" [2009] 68 C.L.J. 388.

[68] *Johnson v Johnson* (2000) 20 C.L.R. 488; cited with approval in *Gillies* [2006] UKHL 2; [2006] 1 W.L.R. 781 at [17] (Lord Hope), [39] (Baroness Hale); *R. v Oldfield (Ryan Alexander)* [2011] EWCA Crim 2910; [2012] 1 Cr.App.R. 17. For discussion, see "Bias—application to change plea of guilty— conflict of evidence between applicant and former counsel" (2012) 1 Arch. Rev. 1; see *Helow v Secretary of State for the Home Department* [2008] UKHL 62; [2008] 1 W.L.R. 2416 at [1]–[3] for further consideration of the attributes of the objective observer; see also *Congregation of the Poor Sisters of Nazareth v Scottish Ministers* [2015] CSOH 87; 2015 S.L.T. 445 at [31] (applied in *Beggs, Petitioner* [2016] CSOH 61); *R. (on the application of Forge Field Society v Sevenoaks DC* [2014] EWHC 1895 (Admin) at [25] ("[t]he fair-minded observer is neither complacent nor unduly sensitive or suspicious. He views the relevant facts in an objective and dispassionate way"); *Ecovision Systems Limited v Vinci Construction UK Limited* [2015] EWHC 587 (TCC) at [95]. For reliance on *Helow* for the proposition that it could be assumed that a judge would be able to discount material which he or she had read and reach an impartial decision according to the law, see: *Rasool v General Pharmaceutical Council* [2015] EWHC 217 (Admin).

[69] See, e.g. *Belize Bank Ltd* [2011] UKPC 36 (no appearance of bias where the Minister for Finance of Belize had made public comments about perceived financial irregularities on the part of a bank but had also exercised his statutory obligation to appoint members of an administrative appeal board to determine an appeal concerning those perceived irregularities as the fair-minded and informed observer would be aware: that the Minister was statutorily authorised to appoint members of the appeal board; that there was a limited pool of candidates; that the appointees were required to take the oath of office; and would take into account that the Minister's appointees could not outvote the chairman, whose appointment had nothing to do with the Minister; and that those performing the important task of serving on the appeal board were professional people against whom no criticism had been levelled (at [34], [37]–[41])). For discussion of the qualities of the fair-minded observer, see also: Elliott (2012) 71 C.L.J. 247; *O'Neill v HM Advocate (No.2)* [2013] UKSC 36; [2013] 1 W.L.R. 1992 at [53] (the fair-minded and informed observer would be aware that a judge who had made negative comments about two convicted defendants in the context of trial for sexual offences was a professional judge who had taken the judicial oath and had years of relevant training and experience and who would hear and understand the context in which the remarks had been made— namely, in open court, from the bench, while performing his duty as judge and would also appreciate that when the judge was presiding over a second trial against the defendants for murder, he would be doing so in the performance of his duty to preside over that case). For the attributes of the fair-minded observer in the planning context, see: *Turner v Secretary of State for Communities and Local Government* [2015] EWCA Civ 582 at [18]. For further examples of the detailed knowledge attributed to the fair-minded and informed observer, see: *Broadview Energy Developments Ltd v Secretary of State for Communities and Local Government* [2015] EWHC 1743 (Admin) at [45]; *Broadview Energy Developments Limited v Secretary of State for Communities and Local Government* [2016] EWCA Civ 562 at [36]; *Somerford PC v Cheshire East BC* [2016] EWHC 619 (Admin); *Beggs, Petitioner* [2016] CSOH 61, at [141]–[142].

[70] *R. (on the application of Royal Brompton and Harefield NHS Foundation Trust) v Joint Committee*

ent Adjudicator for Higher Education was funded by the higher education institutions against whom complaints on which the Adjudicator was adjudicating were made, apparent bias did not arise as the fair-minded observer would be aware the Adjudicator had to act independently of the board of directors of the office, the higher education institutions and complainants; the board of directors was responsible for preserving the independence of the scheme and there was no evidence that the board had ever failed to live up to that responsibility. A well-informed and fair-minded observer would also have particular regard to the fact that Parliament had envisaged that the office was to be funded by the universities and would be aware that the wages of individual case-handlers were not paid by the university against whom the complaint was levelled but came from funds generally available to the office from all higher education institutions.[71]

While it had previously been held that the fair-minded and informed observer can be assumed to have access to all the facts that are capable of being known by members of the public generally,[72] it has also been held that the facts known to the fair-minded and informed observer are not limited to those in the public domain.[73] In addition, it has been held that the court must look at all the circumstances as they appear from the material before it, not just at the facts known to the objectors or available to the hypothetical observer at the time of the decision[74]; what is required is an examination of all the relevant facts.[75] In other words, the position is to be judged at the time the matter comes before the court.[76] In a similar vein, the courts will also have regard to admissible evidence about what actually happened in the course of the deliberations of the tribunal against which apparent bias is alleged,[77] and it has been observed that it is important to consider "all of the facts when considering whether apparent bias is established".[78] Overall, the courts will not readily make assumptions from the facts that indicate bias,[79] and have been keen to emphasise that "[t]he test is not one of 'any possibility' but of a 'real' possibility of bias" and that each case turns on an intense focus on the essential facts of the

---

of Primary Care Trusts [2012] EWCA Civ 472; (2012) 126 B.M.L.R. 134 at [127]–[132].

[71] R. (on the application of Sandhar) v Office of the Independent Adjudicator for Higher Education [2011] EWCA Civ 1614; [2012] E.L.R. 160 at [30]–[36].

[72] Gillies [2006] UKHL 2; [2006] 1 W.L.R. 781 at [17]. In India, although there are some inconsistencies in the judgments, the Supreme Court laid down the test in P.D. Dinakaran (1) v Judges Inquiry Committee (2011) 8 S.C.C. 380 at 427 as "whether a reasonably intelligent man fully apprised of all the facts would have a serious apprehension of bias ... real likelihood of bias should appear not only from the materials ascertained by the complaining party, but also from such other facts which it could have readily ascertained and easily verified by making reasonable inquiries".

[73] Virdi [2010] EWCA Civ 100; [2010] 1 W.L.R. 2840 at [37]–[44]. This was confirmed in Harb [2016] EWCA Civ 556 at [72].

[74] Paice v Harding (t/a MJ Harding Contractors) [2016] EWHC 2945 (TCC) at [41].

[75] Harb [2016] EWCA Civ 556 at [75].

[76] Sisk & Son Ltd v Duro Felguera UK Ltd [2016] EWHC 81 (TCC) at [37] (and will include consideration of the manner in which a decision or judgment has been reached).

[77] DM Digital Television [2014] EWHC 961 (Admin) at [38], [45]–[47] (observing that, where it is available, it would be wrong in principle to reach a conclusion that there has been apparent bias without having regard to such admissible evidence and holding that the conclusion of a disciplinary panel was supported by the thoroughness of the final decision letters and the notes of the deliberations, which showed that the panel was at pains to address all relevant matters and that no new matters had been introduced in deliberations which the claimant had not had every opportunity to address).

[78] DM Digital Television [2014] EWHC 961 (Admin) at [37].

[79] W Ltd v M Sdn Bhd [2016] EWHC 422 (Comm) at [23] (where a conflict check did not alert an arbitrator to the relationship between the respondent and the parent company of his firm, or to the fact that the latter was the firm's client, the fair-minded observer would therefore conclude that the arbitrator did not know the relationship between the two companies, rather than being someone who "must have known" and whose credibility was therefore to be doubted).

case.[80] As has been observed, assuming such extensive knowledge on the part of the objective observer may undermine the purpose of apparent bias of ensuring public confidence in the administration of justice.[81]

AUTOMATIC DISQUALIFICATION FOR BIAS

10-019   There are some interests which have been held to be so clearly indicative of bias that the courts have automatically disqualified the decision-maker from taking part in the decision on the ground that public confidence would inevitably be shaken if the decision were allowed to stand. However, it has been queried whether the doctrines of automatic disqualification and apparent bias are actually separate doctrines. In *R. (on the application of Kaur) v Institute of Legal Executives Appeal Tribunal*,[82] Lord Justice Rix observed that he was "somewhat sceptical" that the doctrines of automatic disqualification and apparent bias "remain to this day separate doctrines". He was of the view that it may be possible to view the two doctrines as "two strands of a single over-arching requirement: that judges should not sit or should face recusal or disqualification where there is a real possibility on the objective appearance of things assessed by the fair-minded and informed observer" that the tribunal could be biased.[83]

Direct pecuniary or proprietary interest

10-020   The category of automatic disqualification has not, however, been overruled and applies where the decision-maker has a direct pecuniary or proprietary interest in the outcome of the proceedings.[84] These cases clearly breach the maxim that nobody may be judge in his own cause[85] and "attract the full force [of the requirement that] justice must not only be done but manifestly be seen to be done".[86] The rule of automatic disqualification was held to apply in the case of *Dimes v Grand Junc-*

---

[80]   *Resolution Chemicals* [2013] EWCA Civ 1515; [2014] 1 W.L.R. 1943 at [35]–[36] (also noting that a "pragmatic precautionary approach" should guide the approach of the court to applications for recusal: [40]). For commentary on recusals generally, see A.A. Olowofoyeku, "Inappropriate recusals" (2016) 132 L.Q.R. 318.

[81]   Elliott has observed that, "if legal doctrine in this sphere is to reflect that policy that underpins it", namely, to preserve public confidence, "reviewing judges should certainly make greater efforts to avoid … 'holding up a mirror' to themselves": Elliott 71 C.L.J. 247, 250. See also Olowofoyeku [2009] 68 C.L.J. 388. For a less onerous, albeit obiter, statement of the position, see *Thames Water Utilities Ltd v Newbound* [2015] EWCA Civ 677 at [91]–[94].

[82]   *R. (on the application of Kaur) v Institute of Legal Executives Appeal Tribunal* [2011] EWCA Civ 1168; [2012] 1 All E.R. 1435 at [44] (Vice President of the Institute of Legal Executives, due to her leading role in the body and her interest in its policy of disciplinary regulation, was disqualified from sitting on its disciplinary or appeal tribunal).

[83]   *R. (on the application of Kaur) v Institute of Legal Executives Appeal Tribunal* [2011] EWCA Civ 1168; [2012] 1 All E.R. 1435 at [45].

[84]   See, e.g., *Kelton v Wiltshire Council* [2015] EWHC 2853 (Admin) at [41].

[85]   See, e.g. *Rand* (1866) L.R. 1 Q.B. 230 at 232 (Blackburn J: "Any pecuniary interest, however small, in the subject matter of the inquiry, does disqualify a person from acting as a judge in the matter"); *Dimes v Proprietors of Grand Junction Canal* (1852) 3 H.L. Cas. 759 at 793 (Lord Campbell).

[86]   *R. v Gough* [1993] A.C. 646 at 661 (Lord Goff). The above passage was approved in *Pinochet (No.2)* [2000] 1 A.C. 119 where it was held by the HL that a Law Lords was automatically disqualified from hearing a matter in a case where his decision could lead to the promotion of a cause in which the judge was involved with one of the parties (in this case the Law Lord was a director of a charity closely associated to a party and sharing its objectives).

tion Canal Co Proprietors[87] where the decision-maker was no less exalted than the Lord Chancellor with respect to a company in which he was a shareholder. The application of this rule has been strictly applied, whether or not the judge could reasonably be suspected of having allowed himself to be influenced by his pecuniary interest.[88] In other words, the interest is regarded as so obviously requiring disclosure that it is not even necessary to conduct an investigation into whether there was any likelihood or suspicion of bias. The mere fact of the interest is sufficient to suggest disqualification, unless sufficient disclosure has been made. The rule applies to members of magistrates' courts[89] and arbitrators.[90] The application of the rule extends beyond judicial appointments and was well brought out by a case in which the unanimous decision of a local authority to grant permission for the development of land as a roadhouse in the face of objections by other ratepayers was quashed because one of the councillors was acting as agent for the existing owner of the land in negotiations for sale to the prospective developer.[91]

In a number of cases, reaching into the second half of the 19th century, justices **10-021** who were ratepayers were held to be disqualified from making orders for the removal of paupers from their own parishes,[92] and from performing other duties in which they had had pecuniary interests by virtue of their membership of a local community.[93] If the pecuniary interest of a justice was in no way personal but arose solely from his capacity as a trustee for the general body of ratepayers, he was not disqualified.[94] With the disappearance of the conditions that had called for its adoption, the ratepayers' disqualification was abolished by statute.[95] Where a councillor retired with a subcommittee for part of the decision-making process about whether to renew the licence to operate a sex establishment, it was held that the councillor should have been disqualified, even though he did not take part in the debate, because he was a director of the co-operative society which owned the premises next to the shop.[96] Where members of a tribunal are disqualified for pecuniary interest but the invalidating effect of that interest upon their decisions is removed by statute, the nature and effect of their pecuniary interest may still have

---

[87] *Dimes v Grand Junction Canal Co Proprietors* (1852) 3 H.L. Cas. 759. cf. *Sir Nicholas Bacon's case* (1563) 2 Dyer 220b; *Earl of Derby's case* (1613) 12 Co.Rep. 114. There can be no real doubt that interest as a creditor will normally disqualify: *Jeffs* [1967] 1 A.C. 551; *Barker v Westmorland CC* (1958) 56 L.G.R. 267 (dicta).

[88] *Dimes* (1852) 3 H.L. Cas. 759; *R. v Cambridge Recorder* (1857) 120 E.R. 238.

[89] *R. v Cheltenham Commissioners* (1841) 1 Q.B. 467; *Ex p. Steeple Morden Overseers* (1855) 19 J.P. 292 (justices hearing rating appeals concerning premises in which they had a proprietary interest); and *R. v O'Grady* (1857) 7 Cox C.C. 247 for presence of proprietary interest in another context.

[90] *Blanchard v Sun Fire Office* (1890) 6 T.L.R. 365; cf. *Re Elliott and South Devon Ry* (1848) 12 Jur. (O.S.) 445 and *Ranger v Great Western Ry* (1854) 5 H.L.C. 72.

[91] *R. v Hendon RDC Ex p. Chorley* [1933] 2 K.B. 696; cf. *R. v Holderness DC Ex p. James Roberts Developments Ltd* (1993) 157 L.G.R. 643 (rival developer not disqualified from sitting on local authority planning committee).

[92] *Great Charte* (1742) 2 Str. 1173; *R. v Yarpole Inhabitants* (1790) 4 T.R. 71; *R. v Rishton* (1813) 1 Q.B. 479; *R. v Suffolk Justices* (1852) 18 Q.B. 416; *R. v Breconshire Justices* (1873) 37 J.P. 404. On the changing role of Justices of the Peace, see Ch.15.

[93] *R. v Gudridge* (1826) 5 B. & C. 459; *Cambridge Recorder* (1857) 8 E. & B. 637 (where the rule was applied extremely strictly); *R. v Gaisford* [1892] 1 Q.B. 381.

[94] *R. v Middlesex Justices* (1908) 72 J.P. 251. A similar principle was applied in another context in *Rand* (1866) L.R. 1 Q.B. 230. Such an interest may still give rise to a likelihood of bias.

[95] Effect was given to statutes removing disqualifications in *R. v Essex Justices* (1816) 5 M. & S. 513; *R. v Bolingbroke* [1893] 2 Q.B. 347; *Ex p. Workington Overseers* [1894] 1 Q.B. 416.

[96] *R. v Chesterfield BC Ex p. Darker Enterprises Ltd* [1992] C.O.D. 466. Contrast *Kelton* [2015] EWHC 2853 (Admin) (apparent rather than actual bias found). For comment, see "Kelton v Wiltshire Council: disclosable pecuniary interests—apparent bias" [2016] *Journal of Planning & Environment Law* 273.

to be examined in order to determine whether it gives rise to a real possibility of bias on their part.[97]

10-022　　Statutory disqualifications for pecuniary interest may add to those of the common law. For example, officers and members of local authorities in Wales are generally disqualified from participating in any question in which they have a personal interest that could be regarded by a member of the public as so significant that it is likely to prejudice his or her judgment of the public interest.[98]

Pinochet: extension of automatic disqualification to "promotion of a cause"

10-023　　The events surrounding the arrest in London of the former Chilean dictator Augusto Pinochet led the House of Lords to clarify and then to extend the rule of automatic disqualification.[99] The Lords had held that Pinochet was not immune from arrest and extradition proceedings in respect of his conduct during the time he was in office. At the hearing Amnesty International, a charitable organisation which promotes human rights, was granted permission to appear as an intervener. After the decision was handed down it was revealed that one of the Law Lords in the majority in the case was a director and chairman of Amnesty International Charity Ltd, a charity which was closely linked to Amnesty International. It should be stressed that he was unpaid and that there was never any suggestion that he was in any way actually biased. However, his interest was not declared to the parties during the hearing and it was therefore held, on petition of the matter to the House of Lords, that the decision was vitiated by bias.[100] Lord Browne-Wilkinson made the following distinction between two ways in which a person could judge in their "own cause":

> "First, it may be applied literally: if a judge is in fact a party to the litigation or has a financial or proprietary interest in its outcome then he is indeed sitting as a judge in his own cause ... and that ... is sufficient to cause his automatic disqualification. The second application of the principle is where a judge is not a party to the suit and does not have a financial interest in its outcome, but in some other way his conduct or behaviour may give rise to a suspicion that he is not impartial, for example because of his friendship with a party. This second type of case is not strictly speaking an application of the principle that a man must not be a judge in his own cause, since the judge will not normally be himself benefiting, put providing a benefit to another by failing to be impartial."[101]

10-024　　Lord Brown-Wilkinson in the above passage appears to confine the rule of automatic disqualification to cases of financial or proprietary interest alone, but it was unanimously held that, despite the fact that interest in this case was not pecuniary or proprietary—since the Law Lord would have had nothing financially to gain by the decision—automatic disqualification extends, particularly in a case involving criminal litigation, to the "promotion of a cause".[102]

---

[97]　*Barnsley Licensing Justices Ex p. Barnsley & District Licensed Victuallers' Association* [1960] 2 Q.B. 167; *Tempest* (1902) 86 L.T. 585.

[98]　Local Authorities (Model Code of Conduct) (Wales) Order 2008 (SI 2008/788), Schedule at paras 10 and 12.

[99]　D. Woodhouse (ed), *The Pinochet Case: A Legal and Constitutional Analysis* (2000).

[100]　*Pinochet (No.2)* [2000] 1 A.C. 119.

[101]　*Pinochet (No.2)* [2000] 1 A.C. 119 at 132–133.

[102]　*Pinochet (No.2)* [2000] 1 A.C. 119 at 132–133 (Lord Browne-Wilkinson: "If the absolute impartiality of the judiciary is to be maintained, there must be a rule which automatically disqualifies a judge who is involved, whether personally or as a director of a company, in promoting the same causes in the same organisation as is a party to the suit. There is no room for fine distinctions"). Following

Further extension of automatic disqualification

In some cases, it has seemed that the automatic disqualification test is being **10-025** extended even beyond *Pinochet*. In *AWG Group Ltd (formerly Anglian Water Plc) v Morrison*,[103] the judge designated to hear the trial informed the parties that a witness the claimants proposed to call was a long-standing family acquaintance. The defendants sought the judge's recusal but the judge instead accepted the claimant's suggestion that they would call other witnesses instead, as the case was complex and postponement would not be in the interest of the parties. Mummery LJ stressed that the prejudicial effect that the judge's withdrawal from the trial would have had on the parties and the administration of justice was irrelevant as "efficiency and convenience" were not the "determinative values" in this situation,[104] and it was held that because of the depth of the connection between the judge and the witness, and the fact that the withdrawal of the witness would not practically remove him from the events, the judge ought to have recused himself under the rule of automatic disqualification.

The automatic disqualification rule was also invoked to invalidate the composi- **10-026** tion of a disciplinary tribunal of the Council of the Inns of Court since one of the members of the tribunal had been a member of the Professional Conduct and Complaints Committee of the Bar Council (PCCC) which was the body responsible for the decision to prosecute the member of the Bar. It was held by the Visitors to the Inns of Court that each member of the PCCC had a common interest in the prosecution and therefore was acting as a judge in his or her own cause.[105]

Exceptions to automatic disqualification

The automatic disqualification rule has always been subject to a number of **10-027** exceptions.

Trivial interests

Although some cases have held that the rule of automatic disqualification ap- **10-028** plies however trivial the interest,[106] disqualification will not attach if the connection between the pecuniary interests of the decision-makers and the issue before

---

the *Pinochet* case the Lord Chancellor, Lord Irvine, suggested that future decisions on potential bias in the House of Lords should be a collectively taken, with the panel of judges addressing the issue of bias before the hearing, with the Law Lord in the chair taking the final decision: K. Malleson, "Judicial Bias and Disqualification after Pinochet (No.2)" (2000) 63 M.L.R. 119.

[103] *AWG Group Ltd (formerly Anglian Water Plc) v Morrison* [2006] EWCA Civ 6; [2006] 1 W.L.R. 1163.

[104] *AWG Group Ltd (formerly Anglian Water Plc) v Morrison* [2006] EWCA Civ 6; [2006] 1 W.L.R. 1163 at [29].

[105] *P (A Barrister) v General Council of the Bar* [2005] 1 W.L.R. 3019; cf. *Preiss v General Dental Council* [2001] UKPC 36; [2001] 1 W.L.R. 1926 (lack of independence and impartiality but no automatic disqualification); *R. (on the application of Kaur) v Institute of Legal Executives Appeal Tribunal* [2011] EWCA Civ 1168; [2012] 1 All E.R. 1435 (decided on the basis of apparent bias rather than automatic disqualification).

[106] Justices who were shareholders in a railway company were held to be disqualified from hearing charges against persons accused of travelling on the railway without a proper ticket: *Re Hopkins* (1858) E.B. & E. 100; *R. v Hammond* (1863) 9 L.T. (N.S.) 423 (Blackburn J: "The interest to each shareholder may be less than 1/4d but it is still an interest"); cf. *Auckland Casino Ltd* [1995] 1 N.Z.L.R. 142 at 148 (New Zealand Court of Appeal was prepared to accept that the de minimis rule could apply).

them is very tenuous,[107] or if their pecuniary interest will arise only upon the occurrence of an improbable sequence of events.[108] A judge who had a shareholding in a bank robbed by the appellant was not disqualified from trying his case.[109]

Interests of spouses

10-029   In Australian cases, it has been held that the pecuniary interest of a judge's spouse in an issue does not automatically disqualify the judge from adjudicating, though it will be a different matter if the circumstances give rise to a real likelihood of bias.[110] In *Pinochet*, Lord Browne-Wilkinson said, obiter, that the fact that the Law Lord's wife was employed by Amnesty International would not lead to automatic disqualification. And the Court of Appeal has held that the fact that the husband of the judge was a barrister in chambers that undertook work for one of the parties neither led to automatic disqualification nor, in the circumstances, to any implication of bias.[111]

Great degree of flexibility in application of automatic disqualification

10-030   There have been indications of flexibility in the application of automatic disqualification. In *Locabail (UK) Ltd v Bayfield Properties Ltd*,[112] the deputy judge in the case became aware that the law firm in which he was a senior partner was acting against one of the parties to the litigation before him on another matter. It was held that automatic disqualification would not be necessary as the connection between the firm's success in the case and its profits was "tenuous".[113] It was also held that the complaining party had effectively waived her right to challenge an adverse decision.[114] In a joined appeal, a challenge was mounted to the judge who, as was revealed by a newspaper, was a director of a family property company whose tenants included the defendant in the case. It was held that the judge's "nominal and indirect interest" did not establish a bar to the judge sitting in the case.[115]

10-031   In an appeal from New Zealand, the Privy Council held that an association between a judge and a witness as solicitor and client eight years previously did not

---

[107] *R. v McKenzie* [1892] 2 Q.B. 519 (shipping official prosecuted union leader for disorderly picketing held, justices not disqualified because of shareholdings in shipping companies); cf. *Auten v Rayner* [1958] 1 W.L.R. 1300. See also *Kelton* [2015] EWHC 2853 (Admin) at [42] (no automatic disqualification where one of the councillors who had voted in favour of a grant of planning permission for a residential development including affordable housing was a director of the housing association likely to be awarded the contract to provide the affordable housing, since the decision of the committee did not lead to the councillor obtaining any benefit) (although apparent bias was found)).

[108] *Ex p. Young* [1897] 2 Q.B. 468 (X, a justice who was a member of the Incorporated Law Society, held qualified to hear charge brought by Society against Y for falsely pretending to be a solicitor; no pecuniary interest could arise unless costs were awarded against the Society and the society was dissolved, making X personally liable).

[109] *R. v Mulvihill* [1990] 1 W.L.R. 438.

[110] *R. v Industrial Court* [1966] Qd.R. 245 (citing unreported passage in *Bank of New South Wales v Commonwealth* (1948) 76 C.L.R. 1).

[111] *Jones v Das Legal Expenses Insurance Co Ltd* [2003] EWCA Civ 1071; [2004] I.R.L.R. 218.

[112] *Locabail (UK) Ltd v Bayfield Properties Ltd* [2000] Q.B. 451, CA (constituted by the Lord Chief Justice, Master of the Rolls and Vice Chancellor).

[113] Note Lord Bingham CJ's warning at [14] that an extension of the automatic disqualification rule could lead to cost and delay.

[114] On waiver, see 10-066.

[115] *R v Bristol Betting and Gaming Licensing Committee Ex p. O'Callaghan* [2000] Q.B. 451 (CA).

amount to bias.[116] Similarly, the fact that the judge was a client of the claimant's solicitor was held not to constitute bias, even though the solicitor had not charged for amending the judge's will. Lord Woolf felt that the "fair-minded and informed observer" could be expected to understand the legal traditions and culture of this jurisdiction. He regarded these to be sufficient safeguards of high standards of integrity and not to require the judiciary to isolate itself from contact with the legal profession.[117] This is a good example of the concern expressed above regarding the degree of knowledge the judiciary is prepared to attribute to the "fair-minded and informed observer"; Atrill warns that to impute this kind of specialised knowledge of the cultural traditions of the legal profession risks divorcing the test of bias from the interests it is meant to advance, namely, the confidence of the non-specialised public.[118] When the issue is complex the view of the "fair-minded observer" is bound to become the view of the court.[119]

Can automatic disqualification be justified?

In some respects the rule of automatic disqualification for pecuniary or proprietary interests is a misnomer, and might be more accurately considered a rule of automatic disclosure.[120] This is because the parties may waive the offer of the decision-maker to recuse himself.[121] In addition, some financial or proprietary interests have been held to be subject to the de minimis rule and not to invoke automatic disqualification where the interest is "so small as to be incapable of affecting the decision one way or another".[122] The *Pinochet* case was in any event held to be exceptional on its facts.

10-032

However, should the automatic disqualification rule extend beyond financial and proprietary interests, and should the rule apply irrespective of the context of the decision? Do the circumstances of financial interest in themselves indicate an impression of bias without even the need to carry out an evaluation as to whether there is any "danger", or "likelihood", or "apprehension" of bias? Some commentators believe that automatic disqualification is "mechanistic", "smacks of abdication", and is "draconian, disproportionate and unnecessary".[123] It has also been argued that in *Pinochet* the same result could have been reached by assessing the context of the decision by the standards of the appropriate test, and that the result will deter judges from involving themselves with the activities of the growing list of parties who may become interveners in cases before them.[124] It may also be that if automatic disqualification is applied without discrimination the "public

10-033

---

[116] *Man O'War Station Ltd v Oakland City Council (No.1)* [2002] UKPC 28.

[117] *Taylor v Lawrence (Appeal: Jurisdiction to Reopen)* [2002] EWCA Civ 90; [2003] Q.B. 528; see also *Baker v Quantum Clothing Group* [2009] EWCA Civ 566 (tenuous connection between a judge and a firm of solicitors could not give rise to apparent bias); *Resolution Chemicals* [2013] EWCA Civ 1515; [2014] 1 W.L.R. 1943 at [46] (the fair-minded and informed observer would not discount the matters of judicial training, experience and ethos).

[118] S. Atrill, "Who is the 'Fair-Minded and Informed Observer'? Bias after Magill" [2003] P.L. 279.

[119] As in relation to the technicalities of trade mark law in *Hart v Relentless Records* [2002] EWHC 1984; [2003] F.S.R. 36; a point made by S. Hanif, "The Use of the Bystander Test for Apparent Bias" [2005] J.R. 78, 81.

[120] T. Jones, "Judical Bias and disqualification in the Pinochet case" [1999] P.L. 391, 399; *Resolution Chemicals* [2013] EWCA Civ 1515; [2014] 1 W.L.R. 1943 at [42].

[121] On waiver, see 10-061. In addition, a situation of "necessity" may exist (where there is no other qualified decision-maker), see 10-070.

[122] See 10-028; *Locabail (UK) Ltd v Bayfield Properties Ltd* [2000] Q.B. 451 at [10].

[123] A. Olowofoyeku, "The Nemo Judex Rule: The Case Against Automatic Disqualification" [2000] P.L. 456. P. Havers and O. Thomas, "Bias Post-Pinochet and Under the ECHR" [1999] J.R. 111.

[124] K. Malleson, "Judicial Bias and Disqualification after Pinochet (No.2)" (2000) 63 M.L.R. 119;

confidence"[125] that the rule seeks to inspire will be compromised by an appearance of technicality,[126] exacerbated by the additional cost and delay that a change of judge may entail.[127]

10-034   The state of the law on automatic disqualification is uncertain and as noted above at paragraph 10-019, it may be preferable to regard it as part of an over-arching doctrine against bias where there is a real possibility on the objective appearance of things assessed by the fair-minded and informed observer that the tribunal may be biased. The doctrine of automatic disqualification is not always applied to purely financial or proprietary interests and it is not clear how far beyond that it may extend. Perhaps the most sensible approach is to require in each case a realistic assessment of the possibility of bias on the part of the "fair-minded observer". Some situations will then raise a presumption of bias and others not; the presumptions in either case would be open to rebuttal. In *Locabail*, Lord Bingham CJ suggested some of the factors which would and would not raise the presumption of bias. In most cases, he thought, "the answer, one way or the other, will be obvious. But if in any case there is real ground for doubt, that doubt should be removed in favour of recusal".[128]

10-035   Factors which *will*, on their face, raise a presumption of bias include: personal friendship or animosity; close acquaintance and other "real ground for doubting the ability of the judge to ignore extraneous considerations, prejudices and predilections and bring an objective judgment to bear on the issues before him".[129] Thus, where a deputy coroner of the Queen's household determined that she had jurisdiction to conduct an inquest into the death of Princess Diana without a jury, there was a risk of an impression that the coroner was on the side of the royal family.[130]

10-036   Factors which *will not* give rise to a real danger of bias include: religion; ethnic

---

"Safeguarding Judicial Impartiality" (2002) 22 L.S. 53; D. Williams, "Bias, the Judges and the Separation of Powers" [2000] P.L. 45.

[125] *Metropolitan Properties Ltd v Lannon* [1969] 1 Q.B. 577 at 599 (Lord Denning justified the *nemo iudex* rule by the fact that "justice is rooted in confidence").

[126] Olowofoyeku [2000] P.L. 456; and M. Elliott (ed), *Beatson, Matthews, and Elliott's Administrative Law: Text and Materials* 4th edn (2011), Ch.9.

[127] *Ebner v Official Trustee in Bankruptcy* [1999] F.C.A. 110 at [37] (Finn, Kenny and Sackville JJ): criticism of the automatic disqualification rule has been voiced by the Australian Federal Court of Appeal in a case where it was held that a judge's shareholding in a corporate party to litigation should not lead to automatic disqualification where the shares were worth so little that no reasonable person could suggest any suspicion of bias (the test of bias applied in Australia). It was doubted whether the "confidence of fair-minded people in the administration of justice would be shaken by the existence of a direct pecuniary interest of no tangible value" and suggested that confidence was more likely to be shaken "by the waste of resources and the delays brought about by setting aside a judgment on the ground that the judge is disqualified for having such an interest".

[128] *Locabail* [2000] Q.B. 451 at [25].

[129] *Locabail* [2000] Q.B. 451 at [25]. However, see *R. (on the application of Shaw) v HM Coroner for Leicester City and South Leicestershire* [2013] EWHC 386 (Admin) (the fully informed independent observer would not have been troubled by a friendship between an assistant deputy coroner and a member of the management of the hospital in which the deceased had died, where the member of management had left the hospital before the deceased's procedure and death).

[130] *R. (on the application of Paul) v Coroner of the Queen's Household* [2007] EWHC 408 (Admin); [2008] Q.B. 172 at [60]. Contrast *R. (on the application of Shaw) v HM Coroner for Leicester City and South Leicestershire* [2013] EWHC 386 (Admin) (no bias arose from the personal friendship between an assistant deputy coroner and the former chief executive of an NHS trust involved in an inquest where the executive had left the post before the incident giving rise to the inquest). In *Shaw*, guidance was provided (at [105]) to coroners where they have an interest which could create apparent bias: disclosure of the interest should be put in writing or otherwise recorded in a permanent record. The coroner should then usually advise any interested person affected of the options: (i) consent to the hearing going ahead and losing the right to object later (waiver); (ii) apply to the coroner to recuse himself (which the coroner will not take amiss), and, if he recuses himself, what

or national origin; gender; class; means; or sexual orientation of the judge. Nor "at any rate ordinarily" will the following factors indicate bias:

"social or educational or service or employment background or history, nor that of any member of the judge's family; or previous political associations; or membership of social or sporting or charitable bodies; or Masonic associations; or previous judicial decisions; or extra-curricular utterances (whether in text books, lectures, speeches, articles, interviews, reports or responses to consultation papers); or previous receipt of instructions to act for or against any party, solicitor or advocate engaged in a case before him; or membership of the same Inn, circuit, local Law Society or chambers".[131]

OTHER SITUATIONS IN WHICH BIAS MAY OCCUR

The existence of bias depends entirely on the context of the relevant relation-   **10-037**
ships between the decision-maker and a party with an interest in, or influence upon, the decision. We now examine: (a) situations where a decision-maker participates in a subsequent decision (for example, an appeal against his original decision); (b) relationships; and (c) attitudes towards an issue.

Participation in subsequent decisions

Normally a decision will be invalid for bias if the decision-maker takes part in a   **10-038**
determination or appeal against one of his own decisions, or one in which he has participated.[132] Of course, in almost every case, the judge who heard the substantial application will be the right judge to deal with consequential issues as to costs:

---

effect recusal would have on the timing of the inquest. Any person affected should have adequate time to reflect and, if necessary, take legal or other advice before making a free and informed decision.

[131] *Locabail (UK) Ltd v Bayfield Properties Ltd (Leave to Appeal)* [2000] Q.B. 451 at [25]; *R. (B) v Wolverhampton Youth Court* [2009] EWHC 2706 (Admin); (2010) 174 J.P. 90 at [11] (no bar to magistrate hearing a case that she had taught at the school where a person appearing before her had formerly been a pupil, particularly where she had never taught him and had had no personal dealings with him). See also *Resolution Chemicals* [2013] EWCA Civ 1515; [2014] 1 W.L.R. 1943 at [45]–[49] (fact that a judge was a former pupil of an expert witness who had supervised his university thesis some 30 years previously was not enough to constitute bias in the absence of a continuing link). But see *Re Duffy (FC) (Northern Ireland)* [2008] UKHL 4; [2008] N.I. 152.

[132] See, e.g. *R. (on the application of AB) v X* [2009] EWHC 1149 (Admin); [2009] P.N.L.R. 30, (a Crown Court judge who had presided over the discharge of a jury in a fraud trial, should have recused himself from hearing a wasted costs order against the claimant barrister who had made misleading closing remarks, where the claimant intended to directly challenge the reasonableness of the judge's decision to discharge the jury). But see *Bolkiah v Brunei Darussalam* [2007] UKPC 63 PC (Bru) (fanciful that the Chief Justice of Brunei would break his judicial oath and jeopardise his reputation in order to please the Sultan). See also: *Holmes v Royal College of Veterinary Surgeons* [2011] UKPC 48 (disciplinary procedures of the Royal College of Veterinary Surgeons did not give rise to any appearance of bias arising out of fact that the membership of the committee dealing with the prosecution of charges and that dealing with the determination of charges was statutorily-required to be drawn from the College's governing body, in whose name charges were brought). For examples of the application of this principle in the ECHR art.6 context see *Kyprianou v Cyprus* (2007) 44 E.H.R.R. 27 (a want of impartiality where the same judges of the court in respect of which the applicant had allegedly committed contempt had tried, convicted and sentenced him for that contempt); *Ekeberg v Norway*, App.No.11106/04 31 July 2007, ECtHR at [42]; *Chmelir v The Czech Republic* (2007) 44 E.H.R.R. 20 where separate proceeding had previously been brought by the applicant against the judge personally). cf. *Lindon v France* (2008) 46 E.H.R.R. 35 (Grand Chamber) (no lack of impartiality where two out of the three judges had previously ruled against two of the applicants in closely-related matters where the facts were different in material respects and the "accused" was not the same: at [78]–[79]); *Elezi v Germany* (2008) 47 E.H.R.R. 53; Case

Mengiste v Endowment Fund for the Rehabilitation of Tigray.[133] At best he is likely to incline towards affirming his earlier decision; at worst, he can be depicted as a judge in his own cause. In general, a decision-maker must not participate or indeed give the impression of participating in such an appeal.[134]

Illustrations

10-039
- A clerk to a statutory tribunal ought not to act as clerk to a tribunal hearing an appeal against that decision if he takes part in the appellate tribunal's deliberations.[135]
- Similarly, a lay representative who served on a disciplinary panel conducting a hearing into a disciplinary matter concerning a barrister, was held to be disqualified by reason of the fact that she had attended a meeting of the Professional Conduct Committee which had decided to prosecute the barrister.[136]
- A magistrate who had convicted a defendant of threatening to kill his wife was disqualified from sitting on the bench which a month later tried the defendant for a separate offence.[137]
- The president of a mental health review tribunal who had previously sat on the case of an applicant seeking discharge from an institution was not disqualified from sitting on a later application by the same patient.[138]
- But a licensing justice was not disqualified from sitting on an appeal against a refusal of a wine bar licence when he had sat on the decision to refuse a

---

C-341/06 P *Chronopost SA v Union Francaise de l'Express (UFEX)* [2008] ECR I-4777 (no lack of impartiality where the judge-rapporteur for the Chamber delivering the judgment had been the president and judge-rapporteur of the Chamber delivering an interim ruling in the same case).

[133] [2013] EWCA Civ 1003; [2014] P.N.L.R. 4 at [58].

[134] An appeal process must be contrasted with the taking of multiple decisions by the same decision-maker in a process, where there is review and second opinion but not an actual appeal: *R. (on the application of Hofstetter) v Barnet London Borough Council* [2009] EWHC 3282 (Admin); [2010] P.T.S.R. 1527; *O'Neill v HM Advocate (No.2)* [2013] UKSC 36; [2013] 1 W.L.R. 1992 at [53] (the fair-minded observer would appreciate that a judge's comments, although condemning, were made separately in each context, and did not carry over to new decisions. It would only be where the judge had expressed entirely gratuitous opinions that expression of a prior opinion in the judicial context could demonstrate bias). Contrast *R v S* [2009] EWCA Crim 2377; [2010] 1 W.L.R. 2511 (CA (Crim Div)) at [43] (judge who had heard nine previous trials involving fraud in which S had been alleged to have been the central figure should not have conducted S's trial on a judge-only basis); *Dar Al Arkan Real Estate Development Company v Majid Al-Sayed Bader Hashim Refai* [2014] EWHC 1055 (Comm) [37] (recusal appropriate where the facts informing an earlier and separate decision remained similar).

[135] *R. v Salford Assessment Committee Ex p. Ogden* [1937] 2 K.B. 1 (where a strict rule was applied). cf. *Re Lawson* (1941) 57 T.L.R. 315; *R. v Architects' Registration Tribunal Ex p. Jaggar* [1945] 2 All E.R. 131. In *R. v South Worcestershire Magistrates Ex p. Lilley* [1995] 1 W.L.R. 1595 (lay justices heard and rejected public interest immunity application and then went on to hear prosecution. The procedure was such that "a reasonable and fair-minded person could reasonably have suspected the applicant could not have a fair trial").

[136] *P (A Barrister)* [2005] 1 W.L.R. 3019; and see also *Preiss* [2001] 1 W.L.R. 1926 and *Tehrani v UK Central Council for Nursing, Midwifery and Health Visiting* [2001] I.R.L.R. 208.

[137] *R. v Downham Market Magistrates' Court Ex p. Nudd* [1989] R.T.R. 169 (it was made clear, however, that in such a case the mere knowledge of the defendant's previous convictions did not necessarily preclude a fair trial); cf. *Huchard v DPP* [1994] C.O.D. 459 show the bench details of a previous conviction of the same offence (drink driving) but application refused as the applicant had pleaded guilty and the previous conviction was only relevant to sentence and in addition the bench had itself concluded the knowledge was not prejudicial.

[138] *R. v Oxford Regional Mental Health Review Tribunal Ex p. Mackman, The Times,* 2 June 1986.

previous application by the applicant; licensing justices were bound to and entitled to bring to bear their local knowledge on licensing matters.[139]

- In *Gillies*,[140] the House of Lords held that the fact that a member of a tribunal has in the past been employed as an expert by the defendant authority does not in itself raise an implication that she would lean in favour of accepting reports of other doctors in that class. In that and other cases, the local experience of tribunal members has been favoured and not regarded as tainting the integrity of the tribunal.[141]

- A traffic commissioner who had made very robust and critical findings against the claimant and who was overturned on appeal should not have been involved in making a decision that a fresh public inquiry was required to determine if the claimant should continue to hold an operator's licence.[142]

- The fact that a trial judge made adverse comments about defendants at the conclusion of a sexual offences trial would not lead the fair-minded observer to doubt the professional judge's ability to preside over the defendant's subsequent murder trial, unless those comments consisted of entirely gratuitous opinions.[143]

- A judge who had made two orders against a father for failing to cause the return of his son to the jurisdiction, and had made adverse comments about him and his likely imprisonment, should have recused herself from a committal application.[144]

- The making of an error of law or wrong decision on the facts by a decision-maker in a previous determination in the same case will not, without more, give rise to apparent bias.[145]

Superior courts

However, it has been held that the superior judges may not apply an objection **10-040** to participation in subsequent decisions to the exercise of their own appellate func-

---

[139] *R. v Crown Court at Bristol Ex p. Cooper* [1990] 1 W.L.R. 1031, CA; and *R. v Secretary of State for Trade Ex p. Perestrello* [1981] Q.B.19; *R. v Board of Visitors of Frankland Prison Ex p. Lewis* [1986] 1 W.L.R. 130. On the doctrine of necessity, see 10-070.

[140] *Gillies* [2006] UKHL 2; [2006] 1 W.L.R. 781.

[141] See, e.g. *R v Hereford and Worcester Council Ex p. Wellington DC* [1996] J.P.L. 573; *M and J Gleeson and Co v Competition Authority* [1999] 1 I.L.R.M. 401.

[142] *R. (on the application of Al-Le Logistics Ltd) v Traffic Commissioner for the South Eastern and Metropolitan Traffic Area* [2010] EWHC 134 (Admin).

[143] *O'Neill v HM Advocate (No.2)* [2013] UKSC 36; [2013] 1 W.L.R. 1992 at [53]. Contrast *Dar Al Arkan Real Estate Development Co v Majid Al-Sayed Bader Hashim Al Refa* [2014] EWHC 1055 (Comm) at [36]–[37]. The judge decided to recuse himself from subsequent application where initial decision contained detailed and specific views about the credibility of the witnesses and other crucial issues likely to arise on hearing of the subsequent application, observing as follows: "But it is one thing for the fair-minded and impartial observer to have faith that a judge will reassess his views with an open mind when presented with new evidence and argument. It is asking more of the observer's faith when similar evidence and arguments are presented to assess the same issues. There comes a point when he is entitled to think that, though 'o' independent mind', a judge is 'a man for a' that'. In this case the claimants and Sheikh Abdullatif are entitled to have another judge decide the contempt application." This case has been distinguished in *Butt v Commissioners for Her Majesty's Revenue and Customs* [2015] UKFTT 0510 (TC) at [563]. While in *Dar*, evidence had been called and robust findings of fact made, here, in an application for summary judgment, no evidence had been called, no findings of fact made and the judge had been cautious not to pre-judge the issues which fell to be determined in the context of the substantive appeal.

[144] *K (A Child)* [2014] EWCA Civ 905 at [56]–[57].

[145] *Re Jordan's Application for Judicial Review* [2009] NIQB 76 at [56].

tions,[146] and judges who, in the Administrative Court have refused permission to a claimant on a paper hearing, have heard the oral application for permission to appeal.[147] It has also been held that the general rule is that a judge hearing an application which relies on his own previous findings should not recuse himself, unless he either considers that he genuinely cannot give one or other party a fair hearing, or that a fair-minded and informed observer would conclude that there was a real possibility that he would not do so.[148] Furthermore, it has been held that judges ought not to recuse themselves too readily in long and complex cases.[149] It is obviously convenient in a case of any complexity that a single judge should deal with all relevant matters, actual bias or a real possibility of bias must conclude the matter in favour of the applicant; nevertheless there must be substantial evidence of actual or imputed bias before the general rule can be overcome. All the cases, moreover, emphasise that the issue of recusal is extremely fact-sensitive.[150] The mere fact that allegations of actual bias are made does not alter the approach that ought to be adopted.[151] This approach may, however, be less important in less complex cases.[152] However, it may be that a judge will be concerned that an informed observer could not have the necessary confidence in the proceedings where a judge had already considered the essential evidence that would be deployed on the committal application and had come to the conclusion that the witnesses giving it were lying.[153] Moreover, strident and concluded comments in the interim report of a Commission of Inquiry about an individual's criminal conduct created a perception that the Commissioner's mind was closed to further evidence[154]; a judge's conduct and comments during a case management hearing created the impression that he had formed a final and adverse view of one of the parties,[155] while a judge's threats of imprisonment with a heavy sentence for failure to comply with court orders created a similar apprehension of bias.[156]

10-041   Overall, the decision for a judge whether or not to recuse himself involves a "delicate jurisdiction", and in summary, if the judge himself feels embarrassed to continue, he should not do so, and if he does not so feel, he should.[157] In general, it seems that the stronger the terms in which an interim or provisional finding is expressed, the stronger the likelihood of there being apparent bias. Conversely, where interim findings are expressed with greater caution or expressly said to be

---

[146] *R. v Lovegrove* [1951] 1 All E.R. 804.
[147] See, e.g. *R. (on the application of Holmes) v General Medical Council* [2002] EWCA Civ 1838. See *Shaw (Personal Representative of the Estate of Ewan (Deceased) v Kovac* [2017] EWCA Civ 1028. Here, one judge criticised a schedule used by the plaintiff in judicial review proceedings, while the second judge agreed with comments that the judicial review proceedings had been based on speculation and assertion. These comments did not however demonstrate a predilection against the plaintiff when viewed from the perspective of a fair-minded and informed observer.
[148] *Otkritie International Investment Management Ltd v Urumov* [2014] EWCA Civ 1315; [2015] C.P. Rep. 6 at [13] and [22]. See also A.A. Olowofoyeku, "Inappropriate recusals" (2016) 132 L.Q.R. 318. See also *H v L* [2017] EWHC 137 (Comm); [2017] 1 W.L.R. 2280 (there were no grounds for removing an arbitrator even where he would be acting in more than one arbitration with overlapping facts and parties).
[149] *Otkritie* [2014] EWCA Civ 1315; [2015] C.P. Rep. 6 at [32] (holding that a judge who had conducted a trial had been wrong to recuse himself from hearing a subsequent committal application).
[150] *Otkritie* [2014] EWCA Civ 1315; [2015] C.P. Rep. 6 at [13].
[151] *Otkritie* [2014] EWCA Civ 1315; [2015] C.P. Rep. 6 at [23] ("the mere fact that a litigant decides to raise the stakes in that way cannot give rise to any difference of legal principle").
[152] *Otkritie* [2014] EWCA Civ 1315; [2015] C.P. Rep. 6 at [33]. See also *Re K* [2014] EWCA Civ 905.
[153] *Dar Al Arkan Real Estate Development Company v Al Refai* [2014] EWHC 1055.
[154] *Mitchell v Georges* [2014] UKPC 43.
[155] *Re Q (Children)* [2014] EWCA Civ 918; [2014] 3 F.C.R. 517 (CA (Civ Div)).
[156] *Re K* [2014] EWCA Civ 905.
[157] *Otkritie* [2014] EWCA Civ 1315; [2015] C.P. Rep. 6 at [32].

provisional and subject to further evidence at the time they are made, it is unlikely that apparent bias will arise. The centrality of the issue arising for determination at the interim stage for the subsequent decision will also be of relevance.[158]

Local authorities

It has also been held that the "practical realities" in a London council housing department permit a housing officer to sit twice on a determination of whether a person is homeless (at least when the matter is thereafter open to appeal in the county court).[159]   **10-042**

Sub-committees

Practical problems are liable to arise where a body exercising licensing or disciplinary functions refers a particular case to a committee or sub-committee of its members for hearing and report, and the report is then considered and the issue decided by the parent body. Are the members who made the report disqualified from sitting on the parent body when it makes its decision?[160] Disqualification normally attaches if members of the sub-committee show active partisanship as members of the parent body.[161] However, in one such case it was held that a president of a mental health review tribunal, who had sat on the case of a patient seeking discharge from a mental health institution, was not disqualified by statute from sitting on a later application by the same patient.[162] In general, the mere fact that a tribunal has previously decided an issue would not in itself be sufficient to justify a conclusion of apparent bias if there were to be a second adjudication.[163]   **10-043**

A similar issue has arisen where persons other than the decision-makers are present during the decision-making process.[164] In this context, a finding of bias can arise where the identity or status of the outsider either does influence the tribunal or would lead a fair-minded person who knows the facts to conclude that there is a real possibility that the tribunal will be influenced.[165] It seems, however, that a pragmatic approach may be taken to the assistance of outsiders. In *R. (on the application of DM Digital Television Ltd) v Office of Communications*, it was held that it was inevitable that the Board of Ofcom should be assisted by others in the discharge of its regulatory function, as otherwise, the sheer volume of work could not be managed.[166]   **10-044**

---

[158] D. Heaton, "Bias and previous determinations: four recent decisions in the Court of Appeal and Privy Council" (2015) 34 C.J.Q. 138, 149.

[159] *Feld v Barnet LBC* [2004] EWCA Civ 1307; [2005] H.L.R. 9 at [49] (Ward LJ); see 1-071.

[160] *Osgood v Nelson* (1872) L.R. 5 H.L. 636 was decided on the assumption that participation in the final decision by the members concerned was unexceptionable; and *Jeffs* [1967] 1 A.C. 551.

[161] *R. v LCC Ex p. Akkersdyk* [1892] 1 Q.B. 190.

[162] *Ex p. Mackman, The Times,* 2 June 1986.

[163] *Ecovision Systems Limited v Vinci Construction UK Limited* [2015] EWHC 587 (TCC) at [99].

[164] *DM Digital Television* [2014] EWHC 961 (Admin) at [32]–[36].

[165] *DM Digital Television* [2014] EWHC 961 (Admin) at [36].

[166] *DM Digital Television* [2014] EWHC 961 (Admin) at [44].

Relationships

Friendship[167]

10-045   Normally close personal friendship will give rise to a real possibility of bias.[168] The Court of Appeal has held that a judge was wrong not to recuse himself from a trial when he discovered that one of the potential witnesses in the case was a longstanding friend whose role in the trial was not predictable. The agreement not to call the witness was not held relevant as substitute witness would not remove him from the case.[169] In Australia, the decision of a tribunal was set aside because a member of the tribunal was a personal friend of an applicant's husband.[170]

10-046   Members of local tribunals are, of course, often acquainted with the parties who appear before them. A member who is a close friend of a party will normally think it proper not to sit if a quorum can be formed without him. In *Gough*,[171] the fact that a juror was a neighbour of the defendant's brother was held, on the facts of that case, not to have been indicative of bias. Similarly, the friendship of an assistant deputy coroner with the former chief executive of an NHS trust involved in an inquest was not indicative of bias where the executive had left the post before the matter giving rise to the inquest arose, and the inquest concerned the hospital's specialist medical team, rather than management.[172]

Family and kinship

10-047   Kinship has always been recognised as a ground for challenging a juror, and in 1572 a court went so far as to uphold an objection to proceedings in which the sheriff who had summoned the jury was related in the ninth degree to one of the parties.[173] Despite a 17th century decision that kinship did not operate as a disqualification for a judge,[174] it was later well established that it does disqualify wherever it is close enough to cause a likelihood of bias.[175] Family relationship between judge and counsel does not appear to be exceptionable, but it has been suggested that judges are disqualified from sitting in cases where near relatives are witnesses.[176] There is no reason for differentiating between the courts and administrative tribunals in these matters. In a Canadian case, the decision of a tribunal was set aside because the chairman was the husband of an executive officer of a body which was a party to proceedings before the tribunal.[177] As we have

---

[167]   See A. Olwofoyeku, "Subjective Objectivity, Judicial Impartiality and Social Intercourse in the US Supreme Court" [2006] P.L.15.

[168]   Personal friendship is listed in Lord Bingham's list of matters likely to give rise to a real possibility of bias in *Locabail*: see 10-035.

[169]   *Feld* [2004] EWCA Civ 1307.

[170]   *Ex p. Blume, re Osborn* (1958) 58 S.R. (N.S.W.) 334.

[171]   *Gough* [1993] A.C. 646.

[172]   *R. (on the application of Shaw) v HM Coroner for Leicester City and South Leicestershire* [2013] EWHC 386 (Admin).

[173]   *Vernon v Manners* (1572) 2 Plowd. 425.

[174]   *Brookes v Earl of Rivers* (1668) Hardres 503. cf. *Bridgman v Holt* (1693) 1 ShowPC. 111, where Holt CJ withdrew from a case in which his brother was a party.

[175]   *Rand* (1866) L.R. 1 Q.B. 230 at 232–233; *R. (Murray and Wortley) v Armagh County Justices* (1915) 49 I.L.T. 56; and *Becquet v Lempriere* (1830) 1 Knapp 376 (Jurat of Royal Court of Jersey held by PC to be disqualified from hearing case in which deceased wife's nephew a party); cf. *Auten* [1958] 1 W.L.R. 1300.

[176]   Sir Alfred Denning, "The Independence and Impartiality of the Judges" (1954) 71 S.A.L.J. 345, 355.

[177]   *Ladies of the Sacred Heart of Jesus v Armstrong's Point Association* (1961) 29 D.L.R. (2d) 373. R.

discussed, in *Pinochet*,[178] Lord Browne-Wilkinson said, obiter, that the fact that the Law Lord's wife was employed by Amnesty International could have led to the implication of appearance of bias. However, the Court of Appeal has held that the fact that the husband of the judge was a barrister in chambers that undertook work for one of the parties did not, in the circumstances of that case, lead to any implication of bias.[179] The fact that a lay member of a professional conduct committee had worked in Wales was not held to disqualify her from considering cases from Wales.[180]

Professional and vocational relationships

Possibility of bias may arise because of the professional,[181] business,[182] or other **10-048**
vocational relationship of an adjudicator with a party before him. For example, an arbitrator was removed on the ground of apparent bias where 18 per cent of his appointments and 25 per cent of his arbitrator income over the previous three years derived from cases involving the defendant.[183] In general, it is unlikely that proceedings could be successfully impugned on this ground unless the community of inter-

---

v Wilson and Sprason (1996) 8 Admin. L.R. 1 (wife of prison officer on jury); *R. v Salt* (1996) 8 Admin. L.R. 429 (son of usher on jury).

[178] *Pinochet* [2000] 1 A.C. 119.

[179] *Jones* [2003] EWCA Civ 1071; [2004] I.R.L.R. 218. See also *R. (on the application of Compton) v Wiltshire Primary Care Trust* [2009] EWHC 1824 (Admin); [2010] P.T.S.R. (C.S.) 5.

[180] *Nwabueze v General Medical Council* [2000] 1 W.L.R. 1760. Considered in *Emmanual v South Gloucestershire PCT* [2009] EWHC 3260; [2010] Med. L.R. 32; and *Modahl v British Athletic Federation Ltd (No.2)* [2001] EWCA Civ 1447; [2002] 1 W.L.R. 1192.

[181] On the competence of a barrister to rule as arbitrator on the misconduct of solicitors with whom he had had close professional relations, see *Bright v River Plate Construction Co* [1900] 2 Ch. 835; *Abdroikov* [2007] UKHL 37; [2007] 1 W.L.R. 2679. See also *Oldfield* [2011] EWCA Crim 2910; [2012] 1 Cr. App. R. 17 (although a complaint of apparent bias was not accepted, it was observed that if an application to change a plea of guilty was likely to involve a conflict of evidence between the defendant and his former counsel, it would be sensible to have the application heard by a judge from outside the area who had no personal knowledge of counsel); *R. (on the application of Primary Health Investment Properties Ltd) v Secretary of State for Health* [2009] EWHC 519 (Admin); [2009] P.T.S.R. 1563. See also *R. (on the application of Project Management Institute) v Minister for the Cabinet Office* [2016] EWCA Civ 21; [2016] 1 W.L.R. 1737 (a decision of the Privy Council to recommend the grant of a Royal Charter to a professional project management association was not invalidated on the basis of apparent bias where steps had been taken to subject the application to an independent assessment by the Cabinet Office and an opportunity had been given to the claimant to make representations); *McCarthy v Bar Standards Board* [2017] EWHC 969 (Admin) (relationship between chairman of the Bar Standards Board tribunal and predecessor chairman (former pupil master and head of chambers) did not create an appearance of bias).

[182] *Veritas Shipping Co v Anglo-Canadian Cement Ltd* [1966] 1 Lloyd's Rep. 76. See *BAA Ltd v Competition Commission* [2010] EWCA Civ 1097; [2011] U.K.C.L.R. 1 (the Competition Appeal Tribunal had erred in finding apparent bias in a report published by the Competition Commission regarding ownership of airports on the basis that a member of the Commission was an adviser to a fund which owned an airport operating company that played a role in the Commission's investigation and which later made a bid to purchase an airport which the report had recommended be divested; for most of the duration of the investigation, the interest was too remote and any apparent bias in the final few months had not contaminated the remaining members of the Commission); S. Holmes and G. Christian, "The tricky problem of Professor Moizer and apparent bias" (2010) 9 *Competition Law Insight* 3. See also *Peter Sanders, Brian Ross v Airports Commission, Secretary of State for Transport* [2013] EWHC 3754 (Admin) at [121], [138], [150], [164], [165] (no real possibility of bias where a Commissioner was appointed to a Commission set up to report on airport expansion)). For a further example of the extent of the knowledge of the fair-minded and informed observer, see: *Hussain v Sandwell Metropolitan BC* [2017] EWHC 1641 (Admin).

[183] *Cofely Ltd v Bingham* [2016] EWHC 240 (Comm).

est between decision-maker and party (or the conflict of interest between them)[184] was directly related to the subject matter of the proceedings.[185] The courts have refused to hold that a person is disqualified from sitting to hear a case merely on the ground that he is a member of the public authority, or a member of or subscriber to the voluntary association, that is a party to the proceedings.[186] However, all the surrounding circumstances should be considered in evaluating the relevance of the relationship in question.[187]

10-049   Professional relationships between magistrates' clerks (who may still be solicitors in private practice) and parties before the magistrates' court may render the proceedings vulnerable. Just as it is improper for the one person to act as judge and advocate,[188] so is it improper for the clerk of the court to act as solicitor for a party.[189] In one case, the clerk was a member of a firm of solicitors which was acting for a party in civil proceedings arising out of a motoring accident in connection with

---

[184] *Huggins* [1895] 1 Q.B. 563 (one member of bench belonged to small class of licensed river pilots; defendant charged with infringement of their privileges; conviction of defendant quashed, despite no finding that there had been real likelihood of bias); cf. *Ex p. Young* [1897] 2 Q.B. 468. In the ECHR art.6 context, see *Eggertsdottir v Iceland* (2009) 48 E.H.R.R. 32 at [53]–[54] (violations of impartiality where certain members of the special expert body which advised the Supreme Court on medical matters were closely associated with one of the parties).

[185] *Stevens v Stevens* (1929) 93 J.P. 120 (validity of matrimonial proceedings unaffected by fact that one of the justices was member of husband's trade union); *Resolution Chemicals* [2013] EWCA Civ 1515; [2014] 1 W.L.R. 1943 at [46]–[47] (the fact that an expert witness in the trial of a complex patent action had supervised the doctoral thesis of the specialist High Court judge 30 years previously, where there was no continuing link, did not give rise to apparent bias); cf. *Barnsley Licensing Justices* [1960] 2 Q.B. 167 (decision to grant an off-licence to a co-operative society was upheld although all but one of the justices were members of the society); cf. *Lannon* [1969] 1 Q.B. 577; *Man O'War Station Ltd (No.1)* [2002] UKPC 28 (professional association between witness and judge as solicitor and client eight years ago gave no rise to danger of partiality); and M. Taggart, "Judicial Review in the Grove of Academe" [1999] N.Z.L.J. 171.

[186] *R. v Handsley* (1881) 8 Q.B.D. 383 (member of local authority not disqualified for likelihood of bias from adjudicating in proceedings brought by the authority); *Allinson* [1894] 1 Q.B. 750 (members of GMC hearing charges of professional misconduct against doctors were members of the Medical Defence Union which had initiated the proceedings, but they had themselves taken no part in initiating them); *R. v Pwllheli Justices Ex p. Soane* [1948] 2 All E.R. 815 (justice member of fishery board who were prosecutors; he had taken no part in resolution to prosecute); *R. v Altrincham Justices Ex p. Pennington* [1975] Q.B. 549 (magistrate not disqualified by her membership of local authority from hearing case in which an officer of the authority was the prosecutor); *Hanson v Church Commissioners for England* [1978] Q.B. 823 (Lord Chief Justice and Master of the Rolls not disqualified from hearing appeal from rent assessment committee by virtue of their ex officio status as Commissioners, the landlords of the appellant). See also *Virdi* [2010] EWCA Civ 100; [2010] 1 W.L.R. 2840 at [36]–[44] (there was no apparent bias where a Law Society clerk, who had been seconded to the Solicitors Disciplinary Tribunal, retired with the Tribunal while they considered their decision); *Colman v General Medical Council* [2010] EWHC 1608 (QB); [2011] A.C.D. 38; *Holmes* [2011] UKPC 48. See also *R. (on the application of Leathley) v Visitors to the Inns of Court* [2014] EWCA Civ 1630 (no apparent bias where a member of the Tribunal Appointments Board was one of four individuals who selected the pool of members of the Inns of Court Council).

[187] *R. (on the application of Lewis) v Redcar and Cleveland BC* [2008] EWCA Civ 746; [2009] 1 W.L.R. 83 at [62] (elected members of a planning committee would be entitled, and indeed expected, to have, and to have expressed, views on planning issues and the test to be applied was very different from that which applied in a judicial or quasi-judicial position). See also *R. (on the application of Gardner) v Harrogate BC* [2008] EWHC 2942 (Admin); [2009] J.P.L. 872 (it was held that the number of complaints made about the relationship between the chair of a planning committee and a fellow Conservative councillor who was granted planning permission by the committee was relevant to the question of bias); *R. (on the application of Siraj) v Kirklees MC* [2010] EWHC 444 (Admin); [2010] N.P.C. 28 at [35]–[37] (not pursued on appeal: [2010] EWCA Civ 1286).

[188] Though conceptions of judicial propriety were still fluid in the 19th century: *Thellusson v Rendlesham* (1859) 7 H.L.C. 429.

[189] *R. v Brekenridge* (1884) 48 J.P. 293.

which the other party was convicted of a criminal offence by the justices[190]; in another case the clerk's own firm had (unknown to him) given advice on matrimonial matters to a party, who, some years later, instituted matrimonial proceedings before the justices.[191] Although in each case the clerk had retired with the justices while they considered their decision but he had not actually influenced the decision, the decisions of the magistrates were quashed by the Divisional Court for apparent bias.[192]

We have seen above that the relationships between barristers, judges and their clients must be seen in the context of the facts of each case and also of the prevailing culture.[193] In a case from Belize, the Privy Council held that mere membership of a professional organisation such as the Bar Association did not automatically disqualify the chairman of a body considering whether a judge had misbehaved while in office. The situation might have been otherwise if the chairman has actively participated in the decision to take proceedings against the judge.[194] Similarly, the argument that a scheme pursuant to which judges assessed barristers' competence would affect the independence of the judge in his conduct of the trial, due to the possibility of the judge being sued for giving an unfavourable assessment, was rejected. While a concern about being sued might cause the judge to refuse to complete the assessment, or to give a more favourable assessment than he otherwise would have done, it would not have an impact on the conduct of the proceedings.[195] It has also been held that a barrister sitting as a deputy High Court judge had been correct in not recusing herself from a probate action on the ground of appearance of bias where she was leading the claimant's barrister in another unrelated matter.[196] Apparent bias also did not arise where a judge presiding over the trial of a wildlife campaigner for offences committed against a terrierman because the judge had previously represented the terrierman when acting as a solicitor.[197] **10-050**

There has been quite extensive case law addressing the issue of apparent bias on the part of members of juries. In the context of jury selection, it is important to distinguish between partiality towards the case of one of the parties and partiality **10-051**

---

[190] *Ex p. McCarthy* [1924] 1 K.B. 256.

[191] *Ex p. Perkins* [1927] 2 K.B. 475; cf. *R. v Lower Munslow Justices Ex p. Pudge* [1950] 2 All E.R. 756 (clerk had acted for previous owner of property that was subject of proceedings).

[192] See also *R. v Legal Aid Board Ex p. Donn and Co (A Firm)* [1996] 3 All E.R. 1 (presence of territorial officer at application to Legal Aid Board for action arising out of claim for Gulf War Syndrome). Contrast *Virdi* [2010] EWCA Civ 100; [2010] 1 W.L.R. 2840 and *Colman* [2010] EWHC 1608 (QB); [2011] A.C.D. 38.

[193] See 10-031.

[194] *Meerabux v Attorney General of Belize* [2005] UKPC 12; [2005] 2 A.C. 513; see also *A v B* [2011] EWHC 2345 (Comm); [2011] 2 Lloyd's Rep. 591 (no real possibility of bias merely because an arbitrator had acted as counsel whether in the past or simultaneously with the arbitration for one of the solicitors firms acting in the arbitration) discussed in "Removal of arbitrator: unconscious bias" [2012] *Arbitration Law Monthly* 4. See S. Shetreet, *Judges on Trial* (1976) p.310; S.H. Bailey, "Grounds for Judicial Review: Due Process, Natural Justice and Fairness" in D. Feldman (ed), *English Public Law* 2nd edn (2009), para.15.77, citing *Leeson v General Council of Medical Education and Registration* (1889) 43 Ch. D. 366 and *Allison v General Council of Medical Education and Registration* [1894] 1 Q.B. 750. See also *Congregation of the Poor Sisters of Nazareth v Scottish Ministers* [2015] CSOH 87; 2015 S.L.T. 445 at [23] (advocate did not have close relationship with an interested party to an inquiry and had no involvement "away from the ordinary receipt of instructions"). In the ECHR art.6 context, see *Chmelir* (2007) 44 E.H.R.R. 20 (breach of art.6 where separate proceeding had previously been brought by the applicant against the judge personally).

[195] *R. (on the application of Lumsdon) v Legal Services Board* [2014] EWCA Civ 1276; [2014] H.R.L.R. 29 at [63].

[196] *Watts v Watts* [2015] EWCA Civ 1297.

[197] *R. (on the application of Hewitt) v Denbighshire Magistrates' Court* [2015] EWHC 2956 (Admin). For comment, see "Judge: R. (on the application of Hewitt) v Denbighshire Magistrates' Court" [2016] Crim. L.R. 209.

towards a witness; association with or partiality towards a witness will not necessarily result in the appearance of bias. It is necessary to consider two issues: first,
whether the fair-minded observer would consider that partiality of the juror to the
witness may have caused the jury to accept the evidence of that witness and if so,
whether the fair-minded observer would consider that this may have affected the
outcome of the trial.[198] In considering the first question, it is necessary to have
regard to the possibility that the individual juror may have influenced his or her fellow jurors when evaluating the evidence of the witness in question, although the
fact that jurors are selected at random provides some safeguard against the disposition of one of them to accept the evidence of a particular witness.[199] Where a jury
or juror knows or learns of a matter prejudicial to the defendant, that does not
constitute partiality to the case of one of the parties and does not therefore have the
automatic effect that the jury or the juror is considered to be biased against the
defendant.[200] It has also been held that the fact that a juror may have a strong and
well-publicised view on issues such as law and order did not mean that his service
as a foreman on a jury rendered a conviction unsafe.[201] However, where an allegation of improper communication between a prosecutor and members of a jury is
made, such an allegation is sufficiently serious to warrant an investigation in order
to satisfy the requirements of ECHR art.6.[202] In cases where there has been pre-
trial publicity which may have influenced the jury or members of the tribunal, the
test is "whether the risk of prejudice is so grave that no direction by a trial judge,
however careful, could reasonably be expected to remove it".[203]

10-052   With respect to participation of police officers on juries, this is a practice which
may require revision in light of the general disapproval expressed by the Strasbourg
court in the *Hanif and Khan* case, in which the Court engaged in an extensive
review of comparative experience.[204] At present however, the position appears to
be that where there is no conflict between the evidence of the police and the
evidence of the defendant, and there is no particular link between the trial court and
the station where the police officer on the jury served or between the police witnesses and the juror, it would not appear to the fair-minded and informed observer
that there was a possibility that the jury was biased due to the inclusion of the police
officer on the jury. However, where there is a crucial dispute on the evidence
between the defendant and a police sergeant who, although not known to the police
officer on the jury, shared the same local service background, justice may not be

---

[198] *R v Khan (Bakish Alla)* [2008] EWCA Crim 531; [2008] 3 All E.R. 502 at [9]–[10] (this is a statement of general principle taken from *Khan*; in that case, on the facts, the complaint of bias was
dismissed by the Court of Appeal but upheld by the ECtHR: see *Hanif and Khan v United Kingdom*
(2012) 55 E.H.R.R. 16). See also *R. v Connors (Josie)* [2013] EWCA Crim 368; [2013] Crim. L.R.
854.
[199] *Khan* [2008] EWCA Crim 531; [2008] 3 All E.R. 502 at [11].
[200] *Khan* [2008] EWCA Crim 531; [2008] 3 All E.R. 502 at [12]; cf. *R. v Puladian-Kari (Ramin)* [2013]
EWCA Crim 158; [2013] Crim. L.R. 510 at [80]–[85] (a fair-minded and informed observer would
have concluded that there was a real possibility of bias where a juror passed a note to the judge stating that, in his professional experience, the alleged transaction of the defendant would entail
automatic rejection at his institution, and found it difficult to forget details of the case which would
be "red signals" in his professional environment).
[201] *R v C* [2009] EWCA Crim 2458; [2010] Crim. L.R. 504.
[202] *Farhi* (2009) 48 EHRR 34.
[203] *Montgomery v HM Advocate* [2003] 1 A.C. 641 at 667 (Lord Hope); *R. (on the application of
Mahfouz) v General Medical Council* [2004] EWCA Civ 233; [2004] Lloyd's Rep. Med. 377 at [33]
(Carnwath LJ: "knowledge of prejudicial material need not be fatal: its effects must be considered
in the context of the proceedings as a whole, including the likely impact of the oral evidence and
the legal advice available").
[204] *Hanif* (2012) 55 E.H.R.R. 16.

seen to be done; likewise, where a member of the jury was a full-time, salaried employee of the prosecuting authority.[205]

Membership of particular organisations which adopt well-known attitudes towards particular issues may or may not disqualify a decision-maker for bias. In *R. (on the application of Port Regis School Ltd) v North Dorset DC*[206] it was held that members of the Society of Freemasons were not barred on the ground of bias from participating in local government decisions whenever another Freemason had an interest in the decision's outcome.[207]   **10-053**

Similarly, in *Helow v Secretary of State for the Home Department*,[208] the fact that Lady Cosgrove was a member of the International Association of Jewish Lawyers and Jurists was insufficient to establish bias in her hearing an appeal by a Palestinian woman in an asylum case. It was argued that there was a real possibility of bias either by virtue of Lady Cosgrove's membership of the association or because she might have been influenced by the views expressed in its publications. While certain statements in the association's publications would, if they had been made by the judge herself, have led to a conclusion of bias, there was no basis on which it could be concluded that there was a real possibility of bias. It was "possible to conceive of circumstances involving words or conduct so extreme that members might be expected to become aware of them and dissociate themselves by resignation if they did not approve or wish to be thought to approve of them"[209] but the material at issue fell far short of this. The suggestion that "mere membership" would give rise in the eyes of a fair-minded observer to "a real possibility of unconscious influence, through some form of osmosis,"[210] was easily rejected. However, in *Re Duffy's Application for Judicial Review*,[211] the appointment of two members of the Orange Order to the Northern Ireland Parades Commission was held to be unlawful. The appointees had both been prominent and committed proponents of the loyalist parade along the Garvaghy Road to Portadown and, when appointed, neither had resigned from the bodies to which they belonged.   **10-054**

---

[205] *Abdroikov* [2007] UKHL 37; [2007] 1 W.L.R. 2679 (the requirement for impartiality had been breached where a police officer sat as a juror in a case which turned on a dispute on the evidence between the defendant and a police sergeant with the same local policing background as the juror and where a Crown prosecutor sat as a juror). See also *Hanif* (2012) 55 E.H.R.R. 16 (breach of art.6 where police officer juror had known the police officer witness for 10 years and, although not from the same police station, had on three occasions worked with him in the investigation of the same incident) *R. v L* [2011] EWCA Crim 65; [2011] 1 Cr. App. R. 27 (while not every CPS employee should be disqualified from jury service in a trial prosecuted by the CPS, in this case, the service of the CPS employee was long enough and of sufficient importance (nine years full time, including as a Director for one CPS sector) to fall within the ambit of the prohibition identified in *Abdroikov*).

[206] *R. (on the application of Port Regis School Ltd) v North Dorset DC* [2006] EWHC 742 (Admin); [2006] B.L.G.R. 696.

[207] See also *R. (on the application of L) v Secretary of State for Justice* [2009] EWHC 2416 (Admin); [2010] H.R.L.R. 4 (chartered forensic psychologist had no hierarchical or institutional connection with any individual potentially implicated in the circumstances of an attempted suicide in prison and her membership of a working group promoted her independence such that her investigation was not incompatible with ECHR art.2).

[208] *Helow v Secretary of State for the Home Department* [2008] UKHL 62; [2008] 1 W.L.R. 2416. For comment on *Helow* see J. Goudkamp, "Apparent Bias: Helow v Secretary of State for the Home Department" (2009) 28 C.J.Q. 183.

[209] *Helow v Secretary of State for the Home Department* [2008] UKHL 62; [2008] 1 W.L.R. 2416 at [55] (Lord Mance).

[210] *Helow v Secretary of State for the Home Department* [2008] 1 W.L.R. 2416 at [56] (Lord Mance).

[211] *Re Duffy's Application for Judicial Review* [2008] UKHL 4; [2008] N.I. 152.

Employer and employee

10-055   Possibility of bias may arise from the fact that an adjudicator is the employer or employee of one of the parties, if their personal relationship is a close one or if their respective interests are directly involved in the subject matter of the proceedings.[212]

10-056   In a number of cases it has been held that a former employee of an authority is not necessarily infected with bias in favour of that organisation when making subsequent decisions on a contractual basis. The Court of Appeal held that a consultant psychiatrist member of a review tribunal to which the appellant had applied for his discharge from detention under s.3 of the Mental Health Act 1983 was not disqualified from considering the appellant's case because he was employed by the Mersey Care National Health Service Trust.[213] In *Gillies*,[214] it was held that a doctor who had previously been employed by the Benefits Agency was not necessarily to be seen by a fair-minded observer as a "Benefits Agency doctor" and thereby partial in his assessments in the role of independent adviser. The distinction should be made of the decision-maker's knowledge or the particular facts of the relevant case, and his knowledge of the subject matter in general.[215]

Judicial tenure

10-057   Useful consideration has also been given to the impact of judicial tenure on independence. In *Misick v The Queen*,[216] at issue was whether a retired judge, appointed ad hoc to preside over a high profile criminal trial, had sufficient security of tenure to demonstrate judicial independence. The Privy Council observed that temporary or ad hoc appointments are not uncommon and need not necessarily involve any lack of independence.[217] If the judge has genuinely accepted appointment for a specific task, at least in the absence of some special factor, he will have no expectation of renewal or of further appointment. No objective observer would therefore fear that he would be unable independently to discharge his duty as a

---

[212]   cf. *R. v Hoseason* (1811) 14 East 605; and *Ex p. Pennington* [1975] Q.B. 549 at 556; *Abdroikov* [2007] UKHL 37; [2007] 1 W.L.R. 2679 (jury member was a full-time, salaried employee of the prosecuting authority); *R. (on the application of Primary Health Investment Properties Ltd) v Secretary of State for Health* [2009] EWHC 519 (Admin); [2009] P.T.S.R. 1563 (assistance given by CEO of a valuation office to a body determining a rent dispute led to apparent bias where an employee of the same valuation office had assisted one of the parties to the dispute); *Amritpal Singh Virdi v The Law Society* [2010] EWCA Civ 100 (the fact that the clerk to the Solicitors Disciplinary Tribunal was an employee of the Law Society, which was a party to proceedings against a suspended solicitor, did not result in bias as the clerk's employment was technical employment for remuneration purposes and she was not the decision-maker); *SP v Secretary of State for Justice* [2009] EWHC 13 (Admin); [2009] A.C.D. 59; and *R. (on the application of Reynolds) v Chief Constable of Sussex* [2008] EWHC 1240 (Admin). See also *Galojan v Estonia* [2014] EWHC 3942 (Admin), in which an interesting argument was made unsuccessfully that because of the relationship between the appellant and two individuals who held the office of Minister of Justice in Estonia, from whose Ministry a European Arrest Warrant issued, the Ministry was precluded from being a judicial authority for the purpose of s.2 of the Extradition Act 2003.
[213]   *R. (on the application of PD) v West Midlands and North West Mental Health Review Tribunal* [2004] EWCA Civ 311; (2004) 148 S.J.L.B. 384.
[214]   *Gillies* [2006] UKHL 2; [2006] 1 W.L.R. 781. Contrast *R v L* [2011] EWCA Crim 65; [2011] 1 Cr. App. R. 27.
[215]   Baroness Hale at [45]. See also *R v Spear* [2002] UKHL 31; [2003] 1 A.C. 734.
[216]   *Misick v The Queen* [2015] UKPC 31; [2015] 1 W.L.R. 3215.
[217]   *Misick* [2015] UKPC 31; [2015] 1 W.L.R. 3215 at [25].

judge because he was in place for a limited period; indeed, his ad hoc position often strengthens his independence.[218]

Communications between the decision-maker and one of the parties

Decision-makers are required to be very open regarding communications with parties. A deliberate failure to disclose communications between the decision-maker and one of the parties may in itself give rise to apparent bias. Thus, where the adjudicator determining a contract dispute failed to disclose a lengthy telephone conversation between one of the parties and his office manager (who was his wife) about the dispute, this failure to disclose, in itself, gave rise to apparent bias.[219] A denial by the adjudicator that any contact took place was misleading, where no contact had taken place with the adjudicator personally, but it had taken place with his office manager and also gave rise to apparent bias.[220] The explanations provided for any communications will also be relevant, and where the adjudicator's explanations were aggressive and unapologetic, this too gave rise to apparent bias.[221]

10-058

Personal hostility

Personal animosity towards a party disqualifies a judge from adjudicating on the ground of bias. Thus, a conviction by an Irish magistrate was quashed when it was shown, by an uncontradicted affidavit, that very bad feeling (originating in a trespass by a fowl) existed between him and the defendant's family, and that shortly after the conviction he had used words indicative of enmity towards the defendant.[222] In Canada, a magistrate was held to be disqualified from hearing a charge against a person with whom he had recently come to blows.[223] Where a judge had been involved in unsuccessful negotiations to join a firm and had indicated that he was very unimpressed with the firm, he should have recused himself from a case in which the partners of the firm were involved.[224] But the evidence must be compelling; the courts are reluctant to conclude that any judicial officer's judgment is likely to be warped by personal feeling.[225] General expressions of hostility towards a group

10-059

---

[218] *Misick* [2015] UKPC 31; [2015] 1 W.L.R. 3215 at [26] (it was also relevant that the judge had been asked to take on his appointment outside his home territory and in his retirement, such that his temporary appointment, far from carrying a danger of lack of independence had very clearly been made in order to bring to locally highly controversial cases an independent outsider).

[219] *Paice* [2015] EWHC 661 (TCC); [2015] B.L.R. 345 at [38].

[220] *Paice* [2015] EWHC 661 (TCC); [2015] B.L.R. 345 at [45].

[221] *Paice* [2015] EWHC 661 (TCC); [2015] B.L.R. 345 at [51].

[222] *R. (Donoghue) v Cork County Justices* [1910] 2 I.R. 271; and *R. (Kingston) v Cork County Justices* [1910] 2 I.R. 658; *R. (Harrington) v Clare County Justices* [1918] 2 I.R. 116 (X, a participant in a political procession, charged Y, a police officer, with assault arising out of a clash with the procession; Z, also a participant in the procession, held disqualified from hearing the summons against Y).

[223] *R. v Handley* (1921) 61 D.L.R. 656.

[224] *Howell v Lees Millais* [2007] EWCA Civ 720; (2007) 104(29) L.S.G. 24.

[225] *O'Neill v HM Advocate (No.2)* [2013] UKSC 36; [2013] 1 W.L.R. 1992 at [53] (the fair-minded observer would understand the context in which judicial comments were made, and would appreciate that the judge could differentiate his decision in one case from his duty to be impartial in another). See also *Shaw (Personal Representative of the Estate of Ewan (Deceased)) v Kovac* [2017] EWCA Civ 1028; *Miley v Friends Life Ltd* [2017] EWHC 1583 (QB) (email from a judge to parties in an insurance case, identifying issues on which further submissions may be helpful, did not raise an appearance of bias). See, however, *R. v Abingdon Justices Ex p. Cousins* (1964) 108 S.J. 840, where the court, applying a test of suspicion of bias, set aside the conviction of an unsatisfactory former pupil of the chairman of the Bench (who was a headmaster); *Howell* [2007] EWCA Civ 720; (2007) 104(29) L.S.G. 24 at [26] (the Court of Appeal describing the judge's contribution to the exchange

to which a party belongs (e.g. poachers or motorists[226] or indeed, judges in general[227]) very rarely justify disqualification.[228] A teetotaller was competent to sit as a licensing justice; the courts declined to accept the view that his principles were likely to prevent him from dealing fairly with applications before him.[229] Where, however, an adjudicator expressed his general sentiments so vehemently as to make it likely that he would be incapable of dealing with an individual case in a judicial spirit (as where a licensing justice who was a proselytising teetotaller wrote that he would have been a traitor to his principles if he had voted for the granting of a particular licence,[230] or where an arbitrator said that in his experience all persons of the nationality of one of the parties before him were untruthful witnesses),[231] the courts have held him to be disqualified. Again, where an adjudicator manifested open hostility to a party or his advocate[232] at the hearing, the only reasonable conclusion may be that a fair hearing has not been granted. When the chair of the bench of magistrates produced a note to be used as a basis for passing sentence of the defendants before all the evidence had been called, it was held that the note had promoted the appearance of bias.[233] In one case it was held that when a coroner used the terms "unhinged" and "mentally unwell" to describe relatives of the deceased,

---

between the judge and counsel for the firm as "intemperate").

[226] *Ex p. Wilder* (1902) 66 J.P. 761.

[227] *Triodos Bank NV v Dobbs (Application for Stay of Appeal)* [2005] EWCA Civ 468; [2006] C.P. Rep. 1 (Neuberger LJ held that he and others on the bench need not recuse themselves on the ground of prejudice towards one of the parties who had previously made trenchant criticism of the judges in general, and Neuberger LJ in particular).

[228] See also *C v Crown Prosecution Service* [2008] EWHC 148 (Admin) (the appellant had been convicted of harassment and it was considered whether a reference by the Crown Court to "generously" taking into account the appellant's culture amounted to subconsciously stereotyping him, but this "subconscious bias" argument could not withstand scrutiny in the light of the finding that the appellant had acted completely out of character, a character that the Crown Court had found to be impeccable); *R. v C* [2009] EWCA Crim 2458; [2010] Crim. L.R. 504. Contrast *Peninsula Business Services Ltd v Rees*, EAT, 23 July 2009.

[229] *R. v Dublin Justices* [1904] 2 I.R. 75; *Goodall v Bilsland* 1909 S.C. 1152; *McGeehen v Knox* 1913 S.C. 688 (members of and subscribers to bodies that include opposition to grant of new licences among their objects are not disqualified); *R. v Nailsworth Licensing Justices Ex p. Bird* [1953] 1 W.L.R. 1046 at 1048.

[230] *Ex p. Robinson* (1912) 76 J.P. 233. See also *Rand* (1913) 15 D.L.R. 69 for prejudgment of a case.

[231] *Re "Catalina" v "Norma"* (1938) 61 Ll.Rep. 360 (actual bias shown); and *Ex p. Schofield, re Austin* (1953) 53 S.R. (N.S.W) 163 (magistrate, in convicting X and Y for obstructing Z in the course of his duty, called X and Y perjurers; he immediately heard and dismissed summonses brought by X and Y against Z for assault; held, disqualified from adjudicating in second case). *R. v Horseferry Magistrates' Court Ex p. Bilhar Chima* [1995] C.O.D. 317 (clerk made racist remark).

[232] *R. v Magistrate Taylor Ex p. Ruud* (1965) 50 D.L.R. (2nd) 444; *Re Elliott* (1959) 29 W.W.R. (N.S.) 579; *Re Golomb and College of Physicians and Surgeons of Ontario* (1976) 68 D.L.R. (3rd) 25; *R. v Watson Ex p. Armstrong* (1976) 136 C.L.R. 248 (statement by judge in the course of proceedings that he did not believe the evidence of either party held to be vitiating bias); *Mengiste v Endowment Fund for the Rehabilitation of Tigray* [2013] EWCA Civ 1003; [2014] P.N.L.R. 4 at [58]–[64] (judge who had made trenchant criticisms of the appellant's solicitors should have recused himself as he had expressed his criticisms in absolute terms, failing to leave room for any explanation and had made criticisms at a time when there had been no need to make them to anticipate an application for wasted costs that had not been made); cf. *Re College of Physicians and Surgeons of Ontario and Casullo* [1977] 2 S.C.R. 2 (vigorous questioning of an evasive witness justifiable); and see *Stanley Muscat v Health Professions Council* [2008] EWHC 2798 (QB) (suggestion by a member of the tribunal that the appellant had been misleading did not give rise to bias; criminal cases argued by analogy, in which the judge had asked too many questions and was taking over role of prosecutor, distinguished; *Ross v Micro Focus Ltd, Employment Appeal Tribunal*, EAT, 18 November 2009 (hostile body language and discourteous conduct of a lay member of an employment tribunal fell short of basic rules but did not evidence bias, rather, it was a rational reaction to what she saw as unmeritorious arguments).

[233] *R. v Romsey Justices Ex p. Gale* [1992] Crim. L.R. 451; and *Ellis v Ministry of Defence* [1985] I.C.R.

these expressions indicated a real possibility that he had unconsciously allowed himself to be influenced against the applicant's argument that the inquest should be reopened.[234] A judge who joked about whether respondent who was an Arab Sheikh would disappear on his flying carpet, that an affidavit was "a bit like Turkish delight", and about a "relatively fast-free time of the year", was found to have used language which was mocking and disparaging of the respondent for his status as a Sheikh and/or his Saudi nationality and/or his ethnic origins and/or his Muslim faith. It was concluded therefore that there was an appearance to the fair-minded and informed observer that there was a real possibility that the judge would carry into his judgment the scorn and contempt his words conveyed.[235]

On the other hand, robust questioning of a party at a hearing of a domestic tribunal has been held not to amount to an indication of either actual or apparent bias, particularly where an inquisitorial approach to the testing of evidence is adopted.[236] The House of Lords held that the fair-minded and informed observer would not consider that there was an appearance of bias arising out of a press conference attended by an auditor who gave his provisional views as to the culpability of the respondents.[237] Furthermore, it is important to distinguish between hostility to an advocate, and hostility to the parties. It has been observed that even if a judge is irritated by or shows hostility towards an advocate, it does not follow that there is a real possibility that it will affect his approach to the parties and jeopardise the fairness of the proceedings, since, "[f]rom time to time, the patience of judges can be sorely tested by the behaviour of advocates".[238] Thus, where a barrister had written to Heads of Chambers, complaining about an article written about a member of that Chambers, it could not be concluded without more that bias would affect a determination of case in which other members of the Chambers were appearing, in particular, given that the judge had given an indication of his conclusions before reading the article.[239]

If members of a tribunal have formed an unfavourable impression of a party in previous proceedings before them, it may be unrealistic to insist that they should not sit in judgment on that party again.[240] Thus a number of cases have held that the appearance of bias did not exist when there had been previous exposure to one

10-060

---

257 (a preliminary or tentative indication of the decision-maker's view is permissible, provided that it does not give the impression of being a concluded decision at a stage when evidence is still to be received and arguments heard).

[234] *R. v Inner West London Coroner Ex p. Dallaglio* [1994] 4 All E.R. 139. *Dallaglio* was applied in *R. v Highgate Magistrate's Court Ex p. Riley* [1996] C.O.D. 12.

[235] *El-Farargy v El-Farargy* [2007] EWCA Civ 1149; [2007] 3 F.C.R. 711 at [30]–[31].

[236] *Flaherty* [2005] EWCA Civ 1117; (2005) 102(37) L.S.G. 31; and *Connor v Chief Constable of Merseyside Police* [2006] EWCA Civ 1549; [2007] H.R.L.R. 6 ("inappropriate" or "inavisable" comments in a lengthy trial not prejudicial in the circumstances). See also *R. (on the application of Bates) v Parole Board* [2008] EWHC 2653 (Admin); [2009] Prison L.R. 234, where remarks by the chairman of the parole board expressing scepticism that the claimant would be honest with his supervisors may have meant that the chair had been somewhat brisk in his manner of dealing with the claimant but that was a long way short of being able to establish a claim of potential bias.

[237] *Porter v Magill* [2002] 2 A.C. 357.

[238] *Harb v Aziz* [2016] EWCA Civ 556 at [71].

[239] *Harb* [2016] EWCA Civ 556 at [76] (in this situation, it was regarded as "fanciful" to suppose that the judge made major changes to the judgment as a reaction to the article).

[240] *Re B (TA) (an Infant)* [1971] Ch. 270 at 277–278; *Ewert v Lonie* [1972] V.R. 308; *Ex p. Lewis* [1986] 1 W.L.R. 130 (no bias where Chairman of Board of Visitors trying prisoner for drug offence had previously been a member of the local review committee considering his application for release on licence). But extreme cases may arise, creating a likelihood of bias or prejudice: *Munday v Munday* [1954] 1 W.L.R. 1078 at 1082. See also *R v S* [2009] EWCA Crim 2377; [2010] 1 W.L.R. 2511.

of the parties in the role of company inspector,[241] member of a board of prison visitors,[242] member of a health tribunal,[243] and a licensing justice.[244]

10-061   Knowledge of prejudicial material about a party may disqualify a decision-maker, depending on the circumstances. The test is the same as the common law test when applied to pre-trial publicity, namely, "whether the risk of prejudice is so grave that no direction by a trial judge however careful could reasonably be expected to remove it".[245] In disciplinary hearings what will be relevant to the issue of prejudice is the directions received on the matter by the judge or chair or independent legal adviser, the length of time since the publication of the material, and the impact of any witnesses on the proceedings.[246]

Partisan views on a particular issue

10-062   Another situation in which attitudes may amount to bias concerns the expression of partisan views on a particular issue. Thus, a judge's comments on the ECHR may disqualify him from hearing a case on that subject again.[247] Extra-judicial writings, depending of course on how expressed, may also raise an implication of bias.[248] However, directing questions to counsel with scepticism will not be demonstrative of apparent bias or predetermination.[249] Consultation processes may also be vitiated by bias where advisers to the decision-maker have expressed a view on what the outcome of any consultation should be; such views may taint the consultation process.[250]

---

[241] *Ex p. Perestrello* [1981] Q.B. 19. This and the following cases are considered in greater detail under the doctrine of necessity in Ch.11.

[242] *Ex p. Lewis* [1986] 1 W.L.R. 130.

[243] *Ex p. Mackman, The Times,* 2 June 1986.

[244] *Ex p. Cooper* [1990] 2 All E.R. 193, CA; and *CREEDNZ v Governor-General (NZ)* (1981) N.Z.L.R. 172 (no "predetermination" when decision taken by Executive Council).

[245] *Montgomery* [2003] 1 A.C. 641 at 667 (Lord Hope).

[246] *Subramanian v General Medical Council* [2002] UKPC 64; [2003] Lloyd's Rep. Med. 69 (appellant's conduct 20 years ago unlikely to affect credibility); *Mahfouz* [2004] EWCA Civ 233; [2004] Lloyd's Rep. Med. 377.

[247] *Hoekstra v HM Advocate (No.3)* 2000 J.C. 391.

[248] *Timmins v Gormley* (one of the Locabail appeals) [2000] Q.B. 451; *Peninsula Business Services Ltd,* EAT, 23 July 2009. Contrast *R v C* [2009] EWCA Crim 2458; [2010] Crim. L.R. 504.

[249] *Worldspreads v Foley* [2015] EWCA Civ 697 at [11]-[15]. See also *Willmott v Rotherham NHS Foundation Trust* [2017] EWCA Civ 181; (2017) 155 B.M.L.R. 58 (no apparent bias arising from judge's comments about knee surgery during a clinical negligence trial).

[250] *R. (on the application of Evans) v Lord Chancellor* [2011] EWHC 1146 (Admin); [2012] 1 W.L.R. 838 at [29] and [33] (consultation vitiated as letter of the Secretary of State for Defence to Parliamentary Under-Secretary of State for Justice recommending amendment to the funding code as adverse judgments in public interest judicial review claims could have serious consequences for the United Kingdom's defence interests was not disclosed in consultation and exerted influence); *R. (on the application of Royal Brompton and Harefield NHS Foundation Trust) v Joint Committee of Primary Care Trusts* [2012] EWCA Civ 472; (2012) 126 B.M.L.R. 134 at [123] (although bias was not found on the facts, it was possible that a decision-maker could receive "tainted advice" if there was apparent bias on the part of an advisory steering group); *R. (on the application of Compton) v Wiltshire Primary Care Trust* [2009] EWHC 1824 (Admin); [2010] P.T.S.R. (C.S.) 5 at [91]. On the role of advisers, contrast *Dr Kofi Adu v General Medical Council* [2014] EWHC 4080 (Admin) (an unrelated experience nine years earlier had no real or apparent bearing upon any advice given to the Panel).

Pre-determination

Although apparent bias and pre-determination are sometimes considered **10-063** together,[251] it seems that they should be regarded as distinct concepts.[252] Pre-determination can be regarded as the surrender by a decision-maker of its judgment by having a closed mind and failing to apply it to the task, while in a case of apparent bias, the decision-maker may have in fact applied its mind properly to the matter but a reasonable observer would consider that there was a real danger of bias on its part. In summary, "[b]ias is concerned with appearances whereas predetermination is concerned with what has in fact happened".[253] The importance of observing the distinction has been confirmed, given that administrative decision-makers, unlike judicial decision-makers, are often quite properly influenced by policy considerations and may, in some cases, slip silently from predisposition to predetermination.[254] There is, however, a distinction between a predisposition and a predetermination.[255] For example, a decision-maker may consult upon an issue that he has a firm view about. Indeed, if the decision-maker's cards are laid squarely upon the table consultees are fully informed as to that predisposition and have the clearest possible target at which to aim their submissions. A strong predisposition is not, therefore, inimical to a fair consultation assuming, of course, that the decision-maker is prepared to keep an open mind and be willing to change his or her views if the evidence and submissions tendered are properly persuasive.

Where the context is the decision of a body whose members may be expected to **10-064** have prior views, such as a planning decision by a local authority, the requirement is that the members approach the issue fairly and on the merits:

"So the test would be whether there is an appearance of predetermination, in the sense of a mind closed to the planning decision in question … [what needs to be shown is] something which goes to the appearance of a predetermined, closed mind in the decision-making itself."[256]

A showing of prior views is insufficient.[257] This is because it has been observed that it is a human characteristic that people have predilections, beliefs and sympathies,

---

[251] *National Assembly of Wales v Condron* [2006] EWCA Civ 1573; [2007] B.L.G.R. 87; *Lewis* [2008] EWCA Civ 746; [2009] 1 W.L.R. 83.

[252] *R. (on the application of Persimmon Homes Ltd) v Vale of Glamorgan Council* [2010] EWHC 535 at [116]-[117].

[253] *Persimmon Homes* [2010] EWHC 535 at [116]-[117].

[254] *Michael v Official Receiver* [2014] EWCA Civ 1590 at [15].

[255] *R. (on the application of British Academy of Songwriters, Composers and Authors) v Secretary of State for Business, Innovation and Skills* [2015] EWHC 1723 (Admin) at [277]; *Re JR 65's Application for Judicial Review* [2016] NICA 20 at [82].

[256] *Lewis* [2008] EWCA Civ 746; [2009] 1 W.L.R. 83 at [96] (Rix LJ); *Chandler v Camden LBC* [2009] EWHC 219 (Admin); [2009] Eu. L.R. 615; *Forge* [2014] EWHC 1895 (Admin). In *R. (on the application of T) v West Berkshire Council* [2016] EWHC 1876 (Admin), predetermination arose where a local authority's initial decision to cut funding to voluntary sector organisations which provided short breaks for disabled children was unlawful, as the authority had failed to take into account mandatory relevant considerations and a subsequent decision affirming the initial decision was vitiated by apparent predetermination. See also *Secretary of State for the Home Department v AF* [2008] EWCA Civ 117; [2008] 1 W.L.R. 2528 to the effect that in a hearing under s.3(1) of the Prevention of Terrorism Act 2005, findings made by the court in a previous hearing under the same subsection were not binding or even the starting point for second or subsequent control orders, but that the judge was to have such regard to those findings, as a factor to be taken into account, as was appropriate in all the circumstances of the particular case. See also *Gardner* [2008] EWHC 2942 (Admin); [2009] J.P.L. 872; *Siraj* [2010] EWHC 444 (Admin); [2010] N.P.C. 28 at [35]-[37].

[257] See, e.g. *Lanes Group Plc* [2011] EWCA Civ 1617; [2012] Bus. L.R. 1184 (an adjudicator's provisional decision based on submissions of one party, disclosed for the assistance of the parties,

and judges and tribunals are no exception. The fact that a judge or tribunal may hold certain pre-conceived views does not by itself constitute actual bias unless it is such as to render them immune to contrary argument; "the crucial distinction is between a predisposition towards a particular outcome and a predetermination of the outcome".[258] Furthermore, it has been held that disclosure by a judge of his current thinking may positively assist the advocate or litigant in knowing where particular efforts may need to be pointed, so that, in general terms, there need be no bar on robust expression by a judge, so long as it is not indicative of a closed mind.[259] It is also necessary to consider the proceedings as a whole in engaging in the objective assessment of whether there was a real possibility that the tribunal was biased.[260] In addition, a lengthy period of deliberations has no bearing on the issue of bias.[261] Similarly, the provision of an incomplete draft judgment, although unusual, was intended to help the parties and did not indicate any real possibility of bias.[262] There must at least be a pre-determination, a closed mind at an early stage and this is a difficult test to satisfy.[263] This test was not satisfied in *R. (on the ap-*

---

had not amounted to apparent bias or apparent pre-determination); *CD (Democratic Republic of Congo) v Secretary of State for the Home Department* [2011] EWCA Civ 1425; *Ross*, Employment Appeal Tribunal, 18 November 2009 (hostile body language and discourteous conduct of a lay member of an employment tribunal did not evidence a closed mind or bias). Neither the fact that an ombudsman expressed views in an initial assessment, nor her unwillingness to accept that the doctors discharged certain duties as a matter of practice without recording that they had done them, were evidence of predetermination: *Miller v Parliamentary and Health Service Ombudsman* [2015] EWHC 2981 (Admin).

[258] *Jackson* [2015] EWHC 218 (QB) at [15]. For the distinction between predisposition and predetermination, see *British Academy of Songwriters, Composers and Authors* [2015] EWHC 1723 (Admin) at [277]. See also *R. (on the application of Mackaill) v Independent Police Complaints Commission* [2014] EWHC 3170 (Admin) (the decision of the Independent Police Complaints Commission to redetermine the mode of an investigation into police officers' conduct had vitiated by apparent bias, since it had been taken by the Commission's deputy chair, who had publicly and repeatedly made plain her disagreement with the conclusions of the investigation).

[259] *Singh v Secretary of State for the Home Department* [2016] EWCA Civ 492; [2016] 4 W.L.R. 183 at [35]. See also *Gulf Agencies Ltd v Ahmed* [2016] EWCA Civ 44 at [47]-[60] (the fact that a judge had challenged whether a landlord was in fact a solicitor at the start of a trial, and subsequently explained that his experience in other cases prompted the question, did not provide a legitimate ground for suggesting that the judge had formed an adverse view of the landlord and his credibility). See similarly *R. v Bush* [2015] EWCA Crim 2313; see also *R. v Uddin* [2015] EWCA Crim 1918; [2016] 4 W.L.R. 24.

[260] *Singh v Secretary of State for the Home Department* [2016] EWCA Civ 492; [2016] 4 W.L.R. 183 at [36]. The court in this case also set out general guidance as to the approach to be taken by the Upper Tribunal in cases where allegations of bias or misconduct had been made: (a) any intended appeal should be closely scrutinised at the permission stage and allegations meriting the grant of permission to appeal should be properly particularised and appropriately evidenced; (b) if an allegation of bias or misconduct was deemed sufficient to merit the grant of permission to appeal, the Upper Tribunal should normally obtain the written comments of the judge concerned; (c) any such written comments should be provided to the parties for the purposes of the appeal hearing in the Upper Tribunal and retained on file pending any further appeal to the Court of Appeal; (d) since proceedings in the First-tier Tribunal were not ordinarily recorded, it might be necessary to obtain the tribunal judge's own notes of the hearing; (e) it would normally assist the Upper Tribunal to obtain a statement from the respondent's advocate as to his recollection of the events before the First-tier Tribunal; (f) consideration should be given to whether oral evidence was needed at the appeal hearing; (g) the file should be reviewed and any directions given by the Upper Tribunal in good time before the substantive appeal hearing ([53]-[54]).

[261] *R. (on the application of Gopalakrishnan) v General Medical Council* [2016] EWHC 1247 (Admin) at [110].

[262] *Marsh v Ministry of Justice* [2015] EWHC 3767 (QB) at [33].

[263] See *R. (on the application of Lewis v Redcar and Cleveland BC* [2008] EWCA Civ 746; [2009] 1 W.L.R. 83 at [109] (Longmore LJ). The test was satisfied in *R. (on the application of Pounder) v*

plication of Fraser) v National Institute for Health and Clinical Excellence,[264] involving a challenge that the constitution and membership of an expert body proposing guidelines for treatment of a medical condition gave rise to an appearance of pre-determination because of the alleged prior preference of members of the body in favour of a particular treatment. As well as the lack of sufficient evidence to make out a case, the recommendation was a decision of a large group and the public interest in the need for clinical guidance also had to be considered. A distinction must be drawn between reaching a provisional view disclosed for the assistance of the parties, and reaching a final decision prematurely.[265]

The position taken in the case law is now largely reflected in the Localism Act   **10-065** 2011 s.25. This provision applies (according to s.25(1)) where, as a result of an allegation of bias or predetermination or otherwise, there is an issue about the validity of a decision of a relevant authority and it is relevant to that issue whether the decision-maker or any of the decision-makers had or appeared to have had a closed mind when making the decision. The crucial provision is s. 25(2) which provides as follows:

> "A decision-maker is not to be taken to have had, or to have appeared to have had, a closed mind when making the decision just because—
>
> (a)   the decision-maker had previously done anything that directly or indirectly indicated what view the decision-maker took, or would or might take, in relation to a matter, and
> (b)   the matter was relevant to the decision."

It has been observed that the use of "just because" in s.25 indicates that a former history of a fixed position or a close mind will be irrelevant unless there also evidence of a closed mind at the actual time of the decision.[266] This suggests that bias may arise where there is evidence of a former view accompanied by actions taken at the decision-making meeting indicating that the relevant decision-maker continues to have a closed mind. An example given is where a councillor had supported an application before the meeting and appears to try to push through the application at the meeting; by contrast, comments made before the meeting would have limited significance if it could be shown that there was open-minded consideration at the meeting.[267]

HM Coroner for North & South Districts of Durham & Darlington [2010] EWHC 328 (Admin); [2010] Inquest L.R. 38 (coroner could not conduct a fresh inquest having previously expressed decided views on matters which would be important in the later inquest).

[264] *R. (on the application of Fraser) v National Institute for Health and Clinical Excellence* [2009] EWHC 452 (Admin); (2009) 107 B.M.L.R. 178.

[265] *Lanes Group Plc* [2011] EWCA Civ 1617; [2012] Bus. L.R. 1184 at [56]. See also *Michael* [2014] EWCA Civ 1590 at [22]–[26] (the test was also not satisfied where the Chief Registrar had frequently interrupted a litigant who had produced prolix written submissions and who would not focus on the real issues in either evidence or oral submissions and who had commented that the litigant's answers were not always regarded as honest).

[266] Editorial, "Current Topics" (2012) 6 J of Planning & Environment L 641, 642.

[267] "Current Topics" (2012) 6 J of Planning & Environment L 641, 642.

SITUATIONS WHERE BIAS WILL NOT APPLY

Waiver

10-066   A party may waive his objections to a decision-maker who would otherwise be disqualified on the ground of bias.[268] Objection is generally deemed to have been waived if the party or his legal representative knew of the disqualification and acquiesced in the proceedings by failing to take objection at the earliest practicable opportunity.[269] But there is no presumption of waiver if the disqualified adjudicator failed to make a complete disclosure of his interest,[270] or if the party affected was prevented by surprise from taking the objection at the appropriate time[271] or if he was unrepresented by counsel and did not know of his right to object at the time.[272] Where an explanation for the circumstances that may give rise to apparent bias is accepted by the applicant, it may be treated as accurate. Where the explanation is not treated as accurate by the applicant, it becomes one further matter to be considered from the viewpoint of a fair-minded observer, and the court does not have to rule on whether the explanation should be accepted or rejected.[273] In order for waiver to arise, there must be both awareness of the right to challenge the adjudicator's decision and a clear and unequivocal act, which, with the required knowledge, amounts to waiver of the right.[274]

10-067   Since one of the objectives of the principle against bias is that public confidence should be preserved in the administration of justice, caution must be exercised in

---

[268] *R. (Giant's Causeway, etc. Tramway Co) v Antrim Justices* [1895] 2 I.R. 603. For discussion, see J. Goudkamp, "The Rule against Bias and the Doctrine of Waiver" (2007) 26 C.J.Q. 310.

[269] *Byles* (1912) 77 J.P 40. In *R. v Richmond Justices* (1860) 24 J.P 422 and *Ex p. Ilchester Parish* (1861) 25 J.P 56 it was held that an applicant for certiorari had to specify in his affidavits that neither he nor his advocate knew of the objection at the time of the hearing or acquiesced in it; cf. *R. v Essex Justices* [1927] 2 K.B. 475. See also *RR. (on the application of B) v South Region Mental Health Review Tribunal, Broadmoor Special Hospital, The Secretary of State for the Home Department* [2008] EWHC 2356 (Admin); [2008] M.H.L.R. 312 at [19] (the High Court suggested that if a tribunal was so obviously biased as had been asserted, one would have expected some submissions to that effect to have been made to the tribunal at the time of the hearing); *Steadman-Byrne v Amjad* [2007] EWCA Civ 625; [2007] 1 W.L.R. 2484 at [17] (appellate and reviewing courts tend not to look favourably on complaints of vitiating bias made only after the complainant has taken his chance on the outcome and found it unwelcome); *Re Jordan's Application for Judicial Review* [2009] NIQB 76; *O'Neill* [2013] UKSC 36; [2013] 1 W.L.R. 1992 at [55]–[56] (failure to object may also indicate to the fair-minded observer that the parties did not consider that there was indeed an existence of bias); *R. DM Digital Television* [2014] EWHC 961 (Admin) at [41]. It was also held in this case that waiver can be inferred from conduct or even silence, provided that the conduct or silence is voluntary, informed and unequivocal: at [43]. See also *R. (on the application of Shaw) v HM Coroner for Leicester City and South Leicestershire* [2013] EWHC 386 (Admin) at [101]. See also *Bhardwaj v FDA* [2016] EWCA Civ 800 at [75] (employment tribunal had informed the applicant during the hearing that one of the respondents was a lay member in the same region as the panel such that her waiver of her right to object to the tribunal continuing was valid and irrevocable).

[270] *R. v Cumberland Justices* (1882) 52 J.P 502; *Paice* [2015] EWHC 661 (TCC); [2015] B.L.R. 345 at [54]–[57] (where a defendant was aware that calls had taken place between the adjudicator and the claimant, but not the content of the calls or between whom exactly the calls had taken place, the defendant could not have waived his right to allege apparent bias).

[271] *R. (Harrington) v Clare County Justices* [1918] 2 I.R. 116.

[272] *Ex p. Perkins* [1927] 2 K.B. 475.

[273] *Paice* [2015] EWHC 661 (TCC); [2015] B.L.R. 345 at [17] (endorsing the comments of Lord Phillips in *Re Medicaments and Related Classes of Goods (No.2)* [2001] 1 W.L.R. 700).

[274] *Paice* [2015] EWHC 661 (TCC); [2015] B.L.R. 345 at [55] (endorsing *Farrelly (M&E) Building Services Ltd v Byrne Brothers (Formwork) Ltd* [2013] EWHC 1186 (TCC)).

resting the decision in one of the parties, especially if the case affects the broader public.[275]

Sometimes the declaration of interest by the decision-maker is done in an **10-068** informal way at the beginning of the hearing and counsel to the claimant may put informal pressure on him not to seek a replacement. The question in such a case is whether the claimant acted freely and in full knowledge of the facts relevant to the decision whether or not to waive. In *Jones v Das Legal Expenses* Ward LJ, for the Court of Appeal, laid down a five-point check list for the guidance of the court in such situations,[276] the "vital requirements" of which were summarised in a subsequent case by Lord Phillips of Matravers CJ as "that the party waiving should be aware of all material facts, of the consequences of the choice open to him, and given a fair opportunity to reach an un-pressured decision".[277] In *Jones* it was held that, in all the circumstances, the claimant had waived his right but in *Smith*[278] it was held that the appellant had not waived his rights as he was not told when the trial could take place before another judge (and was wrongly urged by his counsel not to object on the ground of costs).

Cases have raised the question of the proper behaviour expected of an inspector **10-069** following a planning inquiry.[279] There is little doubt that an inspector who accepts hospitality or a lift to the site visit from one party in the absence of the other would be disqualified for bias, but this would not be the case where the inspector had asked sought and obtained the consent of the parties.[280] A distinction has also been drawn between an objection to the judge based on facts discovered during the course of, or only at the end of, the hearing and a situation where the objection is taken before the hearing has begun. In the latter situation, there is scope for the sensible application of the precautionary principle, and prudence naturally leans on the side of being safe rather than sorry.[281]

---

[275] *Auckland Casino Ltd* [1995] 1 N.Z.L.R. 142 (although confronted with an agonising choice, the party ultimately complaining in that case had waived the objection by delaying until the decision was known. It was accepted, however, that displays of blatant bias, likely to undermine public confidence in the justice system, should not necessarily be capable of private waiver; while in criminal cases private waiver should not normally be possible at all); B. Toy-Cronin, "Waiver of the Rule Against Bias" (2002) 9 Auckland U. L. Rev. 850.

[276] *Jones* [2003] EWCA Civ 1071; [2004] I.R.L.R. 218 at [35]: (i) the first step involves the judge seeking a replacement if possible. If this is not possible then (ii) time should be taken to prepare a full explanation of the extent of bias that will be explained to the parties; (iii) to avoid controversy and the matter becoming a "festering sore" the explanation should be carefully recorded; (iv) a full explanation should be given to the parties as to matters which might give rise to possible conflict of interest and the possibilities of moving the case; (v) the options should be explained to the parties, including seeking the judge's recusal; (vi) the time for reflection should be established, if necessary providing help to the claimant to seek advice.

[277] *Smith v Kvaerner Cementation Foundations Ltd* [2006] EWCA Civ 242; [2007] 1 W.L.R. 370 at [29]. See also *BAA Ltd* [2010] EWCA Civ 1097 (finding that BAA had produced sufficient evidence of its lack of awareness of cause for disqualification and that it would be inappropriate to, for example, require individual witness statements from every employee who had had any involvement with the investigation: [59]).

[278] *Smith* [2006] EWCA Civ 242; [2007] 1 W.L.R. 370 at [35]-[38].

[279] *Fox v Secretary of State for the Environment and Dover DC* [1993] J.P.L. 448; *Halifax Building Society v Secretary of State for the Environment* [1983] J.P.L. 816.

[280] *Fox* [1993] J.P.L. 448.

[281] *Thames Water Utilities Ltd v Newbound* [2015] EWCA Civ 677 at [92].

Necessity

10-070   There are two ways in which the doctrine of "necessity" has been held to apply. First, if the person who makes the decision is biased, but cannot effectively be replaced, e.g. if a quorum cannot be formed without him.[282] Secondly, where the administrative structure makes it inevitable that there is an appearance of bias.

Illustrations

10-071 • If proceedings were brought against all the superior judges, they would have to sit as judges in their own cause.[283] In such a situation, a judge may even, in theory, be obliged to hear a case in which he has a pecuniary interest.[284]
   • Similarly, a colonial governor could validly assent in the Queen's name to a Bill indemnifying him against the legal consequences of his own conduct, since there was no other officer who could have done so.[285] In such cases it is not possible for the matter to be delegated to another or others, or the tribunal to be reconstituted. The doctrine of necessity therefore applies to prevent a failure of justice overall.
   • What if a minister were called upon to decide whether or not to confirm an order made by a local authority affecting his own property? As we have seen in Ch.5, he could not lawfully transfer or delegate to another minister his duty to decide.[286] He might depute one of his own officials to make the decision, but the decision would nevertheless be made in the minister's name. If it were possible to show that the minister had taken into account his own interests, the decision could be challenged for the taking into account of an irrelevant consideration, or for bad faith,[287] but otherwise it might be difficult to assert that the minister was judge in his own cause; for the legal duty to decide the matter had been cast upon him, and upon him alone.[288]
   • The doctrine of necessity was applied in a case where inspectors authorised by the Secretary of State for Trade investigated the affairs of a company of which the applicant was chairman, and some of the same inspectors had previously investigated another company of which he was chairman. It was held that the terms of the inspectors' powers inevitably permitted them to have "suspicions" about the applicant's conduct.[289]

---

[282] cf. Lamond, "Of Interest as a Disqualification in Judges" (1907) 23 S.L.R. 152-153, citing a Scottish case of 1744 where withdrawal of the interested judges would have left the court without a quorum; and R. Tracey, "Disqualified Adjudicators: The Doctrine of Necessity in Public Law" [1982] P.L. 628.

[283] 2 Roll.Abr. 93, pl.6; and 16 Vin.Abr. (2nd edn), 573, citing 15th-century cases.

[284] *Great Charte* (1742) 2 Str. 1173; *Essex Justices* (1816) 5 M. & S. 513; *Grand Junction Canal Co v Dimes* (1849) 12 Beav. 63; *Dimes v Grand Junction Canal Proprietors* (1852) 3 H.L.C. 759 at 778-779, *Ranger* (1854) 5 H.L.C. 72 at 88.

[285] *Phillips v Eyre* (1870) L.R. 6 Q.B. 1; and *The Judges v Attorney General for Saskatchewan* (1937) 53 T.L.R. 464 (judges required to rule on the constitutionality of legislation rendering them liable to pay more income tax); *Willing v Hollobone (No.2)* (1975) 11 S.A.S.R. 118 (magistrates not disqualified for bias, inter alia, because the ground applied to all magistrates); *Re Caccamo and Minister of Manpower and Immigration* (1977) 75 D.L.R. (3rd) 720 (disqualification applicable to all immigration officers).

[286] See 5-159. But most legislation nowadays avoids specifying which minister should exercise powers, referring instead to the "Secretary of State", which is a single office (see 3-003); presumably in such circumstances another Secretary of State could exercise the power for his colleague.

[287] See 5-130 (irrelevant considerations); 5-095 (bad faith).

[288] cf. *Auten* [1958] 1 W.L.R. 1300.

[289] *Ex p. Perestrello* [1981] Q.B. 19.

- On the other hand, where a board of prison visitors found a prisoner guilty of having a controlled drug in his cell, and the prisoner alleged the presence of bias because the chairman of the board had been a member of a local review committee which had earlier considered the prisoner's release on licence under the parole system, the application was dismissed because the functions of the board of visitors were such that they would inevitably have considerable knowledge of a prisoner charged with a disciplinary offence.[290]
- Evidence of political affiliation or of the adoption of policies towards a planning proposal will not for these purposes by itself amount to an appearance of the real possibility of predetermination or what counts as bias for these purposes on the part of councillors on a planning committee.[291]

The doctrine of necessity has been sparingly employed, and if possible, the decision-making body should remove that part of it which is infected with bias (for example, by the recusal of those members of a disciplinary committee who had been a part of a previous sub-committee which decided to institute proceedings against the claimant).[292] Alternatively, where possible the body should be reconstituted (e.g. by constituting a separate panel). However, as we have seen, this is not always possible.   **10-072**

Since the Human Rights Act 1998, the doctrine of necessity may be more difficult to assert in the face of a *right* to an independent and impartial tribunal under ECHR art.6(1).[293] However, the issue does not appear to have generated as much difficulty as might have been expected. In *Kingsley v United Kingdom*[294] it was argued that the Gaming Board could not be impartial in its decision to revoke the applicant's certificate of approval for a management position, having already previously taken the view that the claimant was not a "fit and proper person" to be director of a casino company. Although it was held that there was not unconscious bias in that case, it was stated that had there been such bias the doctrine of necessity would apply as the decision could only be taken by the Gaming Board and delegation to any other body would be unlawful.   **10-073**

When *Kingsley* was argued before the ECtHR[295] it is noteworthy that counsel for the government argued that the doctrine of necessity was not applicable to a case where the allegation was one of actual bias. The argument that the doctrine did apply to cases of apparent bias, however, failed. The court was critical of the fact that English courts did not have the power ("full jurisdiction")[296] either to remit the matter for a fresh decision by a differently composed decision-making tribunal, or to decide the matter themselves.   **10-074**

Since the government has already conceded, in *Kingsley*, that necessity should not excuse actual bias, it would not be a far step to concede that apparent bias should similarly not be condoned. In order to do this, they would have to employ radical means to avoid apparent bias, at least where an individual's right to an independent and impartial tribunal is in issue.[297] Where there is no possibility of removing the bias by lawfully constituting another tribunal under the relevant statu-   **10-075**

---

[290] *Ex p. Lewis* [1986] 1 W.L.R. 130.
[291] *Lewis* [2008] EWCA Civ 746; [2009] 1 W.L.R. 83.
[292] As in *P (A Barrister)* [2005] 1 W.L.R. 3019.
[293] See 10-088.
[294] *Kingsley v United Kingdom* [1996] C.O.D. 178.
[295] Kingsley (2001) 33 E.H.R.R. 288.
[296] For the ECtHR's position to the procedures of judicial review, see 10-094.
[297] This may not apply to some of the examples mentioned above, e.g. where judicial salaries are the subject of litigation.

tory scheme, the courts may have to declare the scheme itself incompatible[298] with ECHR art.6(1).[299]

Policy and bias

10-076 Closely related to the doctrine of necessity is that which permits decision-makers to exhibit certain kinds of bias in the exercise of their judgment or discretion on matters of public policy. Ordinary members of legislative bodies are entitled, and sometimes expected, to show political bias. They ought not to show personal bias, or to participate in deliberations on a matter in respect of which they have a private pecuniary or a proprietary interest, but their participation in such circumstances may not in itself affect the validity of a legislative instrument.[300]

10-077 Where a councillor had previously indicated his opposition in general to the existence of sex establishments, he was not disqualified from sitting on a panel to license sex establishments,[301] provided he gave genuine consideration to the decision.[302] Nor was a minister disqualified from determining a planning application on a site where he had previously (as a Member of Parliament) supported an opponent of planning permission.[303] Councillors were entitled to be predisposed to determine a planning application in accordance with their political views and policies provided that they had regard to all material considerations and gave fair consideration to relevant points raised with them.[304]

10-078 However, if the personal interests of members participating in a decision affecting individual rights or interests (such as a decision to grant planning permission) preclude them from acting fairly, the decision can be declared to be invalid.[305] It has been held, however, that a builder was not disqualified from sitting on a local authority planning committee on the ground of his being a commercial rival of the applicant for planning permission.[306]

10-079 When an authority is expressly empowered to make a provisional decision, and is then empowered to entertain representations or consider objections against it with a view to deciding whether or not to give it final effect, it is absurd to expect that authority to be totally impartial between itself and the objectors; the authority is naturally likely to be biased in favour of the proposal that it has initiated.[307]

10-080 Members of tribunals exercising discretionary regulatory powers, such as planning inspectors, will normally be entitled, indeed expected, to adopt and follow

---

[298] HRA s.4; see 13-047.

[299] Under the CPR r.54.19(2), discussed at 18-032 (suggested by I. Leigh, "Bias, Necessity and Convention Rights" [2002] P.L. 407). Such an innovation may now be more difficult since the amendment of Supreme Court Act (Senior Court Act) 1981 s.31(5).

[300] If a member of the House of Commons votes on a matter on which he has a private pecuniary interest, his vote may be disallowed: E. May, *Parliamentary Practice*, 24th edn (2011), pp.83-85. For the duties of local authority members and officers to declare pecuniary interests, see 10-022.

[301] *R. v Reading BC Ex p. Quietlynn Ltd* 85 L.G.R. 387; *R. v Tower Hamlets LBC Ex p. Khatun* (1995) 27 H.L.R. 465, CA (an interview regarding intentional homelessness not flawed as conducted by council employee aware of local housing conditions).

[302] See also *Ex p. Darker Enterprises Ltd* [1992] C.O.D. 466.

[303] *London and Clydeside Estates Ltd v Secretary of State for Scotland* (1987) S.L.T. 459; see also *CREEDNZ* (1981) N.Z.L.R. 172.

[304] *Lewis* [2008] EWCA Civ 746; [2009] 1 W.L.R. 83. See also *Gardner* [2008] EWHC 2942 (Admin); [2009] J.P.L. 872. *Siraj* [2010] EWHC 444 (Admin); [2010] N.P.C. 28 at [35]-[37].

[305] *Ex p. Chorley* [1933] 2 K.B. 696 (certiorari issued to quash a grant of planning permission vitiated by a councillor's pecuniary interest).

[306] *Ex p. James Roberts Developments Ltd* (1993) 157 L.G.R. 643 (Butler-Sloss LJ considered that architects or surveyors would also not be disqualified in these circumstances).

[307] As in *Franklin v Minister of Town and Country Planning* [1948] A.C. 87.

general policy guidelines. These guidelines will influence their decisions in individual cases. But by announcing their intention to follow those guidelines they ought not, in general, to be regarded as disqualified for bias unless they have committed themselves so firmly to the implementation of those policies as to make it impracticable for them to deal fairly with subsequent cases on their merits.[308]

In some situations, those who have to make decisions can hardly insulate   **10-081**
themselves from the general ethos of their organisation or institution; they are likely to have firm views about the proper regulation of its affairs, and they will often be familiar with the issues and the conduct of the parties before they assume their role as adjudicators. Licensing justices have been held entitled to bring their local knowledge to bear on their decisions, including information they may have obtained about an applicant during a previous hearing.[309] Applications of the rules against interest and bias must be tempered with realism; educational institutions, trades unions, clubs and even professional associations are apt to present special problems.[310]

The normal standards of impartiality applied in an adjudicative setting cannot   **10-082**
automatically be applied to a body entitled to initiate a proposal and then to decide whether to proceed with it in the face of objections. For example, it may be necessary to modify the standards expected where the Secretary of State for the Environment when he has to decide whether or not to confirm a compulsory purchase order or clearance order made by a local authority or to approve a local planning authority's structure plan or to allow an appeal against refusal of planning permission. It would arguably be inappropriate for the courts to insist on his maintaining the lofty detachment required of a judicial officer determining a dispute between the parties. Nonetheless, the courts have held that planning inspectors, employed by the Secretary of State, have independence akin to that provided for judges, and should adopt the same approach that judges would adopt in deciding whether they should recuse themselves.[311]

In some situations, it will even be perfectly proper for a public body to make a   **10-083**
particular decision for its own pecuniary advantage (as distinct from the pecuniary advantage of individual members or officers). It has been held to be a "material" planning consideration that the developer will contribute some of the profits of the development to a benefit or advantage for the local community.[312] However, in *Steeples v Derbyshire CC*[313] a local planning authority had entered into an agreement with a developer which provided that the authority would be liable for liquidated damages if it failed to use its "best endeavours" to procure planning permissions. The decision was invalidated on the ground of bias.[314] Later cases, however, have made it clear that the courts will not lightly interfere with a plan-

---

[308] On fettering of discretion, see Ch.9; on government policy as a material or relevant consideration, see 5-140.

[309] *Ex p. Cooper* [1990] 1 W.L.R. 1031.

[310] But see a case where latitudinariasm was carried too far: *Ward v Bradford Corp* (1971) 70 L.G.R. 27. cf. *Hannam* [1970] 1 W.L.R. 937, CA (three out of 10 members of Education Authority Committee governors of school from which applicant dismissed. Held: disqualification because of real likelihood of bias); *Rees v Crane* [1994] 2 A.C. 173 (PC thought it right to take into account the distinguished nature of the members of the Judicial and Legal Service Commission and say of them that "their professional backgrounds are such that an assumption of bias should not be lightly made").

[311] *R. (on the application of Ortona Ltd) v Secretary of State for Communities and Local Government* [2008] EWHC 3207 (Admin); [2009] J.P.L. 1033 at [55].

[312] See, e.g. *R. v Westminster City Council Ex p. Monahan* [1990] 1 Q.B. 87; *R (on the application of Derwent Holdings Ltd) v Trafford BC* [2011] EWCA Civ 832; [2011] N.P.C. 78, see 5-135 on the limits of "planning gain".

[313] *Steeples v Derbyshire CC* [1984] 3 All E.R. 468.

[314] cf. *Lower Hutt City Council v Bank* [1974] 1 N.Z.L.R. 545 (council had precluded itself from fairly

ning decision made on the basis of a predetermined policy so long as the authority gives genuine consideration to the application. Thus, where the majority party group had met and decided in advance to support an application for a development, it was held that the members of the group were not disqualified from subsequently sitting on the committee which determined the application. Politics was held to play so large a part in local government that, if disqualification was to be avoided, the planning committee would have had to adopt impractical standards.[315] Other cases have held that a local authority was not disqualified from granting a planning permission on a site in which the authority had an interest where the decision was properly considered, was by no means a foregone conclusion[316] and the council had not acted in such a way that it "could not exercise proper discretion".[317]

10-084   Despite the latitude given to policy decisions, it should be remembered that four other principles of public law remain in play. First, the person or tribunal holding an inquiry into the matter may not ignore the other part of procedural fairness, namely, the granting of a fair hearing. Thus the procedural protections considered above[318] would still apply in an appropriate case. Secondly, the "no fettering doctrine" would apply.[319] The policy could therefore not be applied rigidly, and the decision-maker will still be required not to shut his ears to someone with something new to say. Any inquiry must genuinely take into account the argument presented.[320]

10-085   Thirdly, the body will not be able to pursue powers outside of the statutory purposes conferred upon it. In *Magill v Porter*,[321] the Conservative party leaders of Westminster City Council pursued a policy of increasing the number of owner-occupiers. The policy was directed to marginal wards and its purpose was to encourage votes for the Conservative Party in future elections—a purpose which was held to be unlawful.

10-086   Fourthly, it is no longer the case that the full rigours of procedural safeguards are

---

considering objections to its own proposed scheme by entering into a contract to carry out the work contemplated by the scheme).

315 *R. v Amber Valley DC Ex p. Jackson* [1985] 1 W.L.R. 298; and *R. v Waltham Forest LBC Ex p. Baxter* [1988] Q.B. 419 (local authority councillor entitled to give weight to views of party colleagues and party whip but could not abdicate responsibility by voting blindly in support of party policy. On the evidence, discretion not fettered by party whip). In *Ex p. Kirkstall Valley Campaign Ltd* [1996] 3 All E.R. 304 Sedley J carefully considered to what extent participation in proceedings would amount to bias. He concluded that the person need not necessarily withdraw from discussion, but it would be "wise advice" to do so. See also *R. v Buckinghamshire CC Ex p. Milton Keynes BC* (1997) 9 Admin. L.R. 159 (Conservative party members had not been "instructed" to vote, on proposals for the establishment of a grammar school, in a manner inconsistent with what was lawfully allowed in the interest of party unity as set out in *Baxter*); and *R. (on the application of Island Farm Development Ltd) v Bridgend CBC* [2006] EWHC 2189; [2007] B.L.G.R. 60. See also *Lewis* [2008] EWCA Civ 746; [2009] 1 W.L.R. 83.

316 *R. v Sevenoaks DC Ex p. Terry* [1985] 3 All E.R. 226; *R. v Merton LBC Ex p. Burnett* [1990] 1 P.L.R. 72; [1990] J.P.L. 354; *R. v Canterbury CC Ex p. Springimage Ltd* [1995] J.P.L. 20.

317 *Terry* [1985] 3 All E.R. 226 at 233 (Glidewell J). This test was followed in *R. v City of Wakefield MDC and British Coal Corp Ex p. Warmfield Co Ltd* [1994] J.P.L. 341.

318 See Chs 7-8.

319 See Ch.9.

320 Cases where the matter was held unlawfully predetermined by closed minds include: *Bovis Homes Ltd v New Forest Plc* [2002] EWHC 483 (Admin); *R. (on the application of Partingdale Residents Association) v Barnet LBC* [2003] EWHC 947 (Admin), citing *Lower Hutt* [1974] 1 N.Z.L.R. 545; *Georgoiu v Enfield LBC* [2004] EWHC 779 (Admin) (Richards J's statements in *Georgiou* on bias at [35]-[36] doubted by Collins J at [30]). On the other hand, where a previous commitment to a development was reversed when a new party gained control of the council, their previous opposition to the proposal was held to be a legitimate "predisposition" rather than an unlawful "predetermination": *Island Farm Development Ltd* [2006] EWHC 2189 (Admin); [2007] B.L.G.R. 60.

321 *Magill v Porter* [2001] UKHL 67; [2002] 2 A.C. 357.

reserved only for decisions that are "judicial". Although this distinction was firmly scotched in the 1960s[322] in relation to the *audi alteram partem* (hear both sides) principle, it rears its head from time to time in relation to bias.[323] However, as Sedley J has pointed out, "in the modern state the interests of individuals or of the public may be more radically affected by administrative decisions than by the decisions of courts of law and judicial tribunals".[324] The fact that the body is "administrative" rather than judicial or quasi-judicial has therefore been rejected in favour of one that looks at the "particular nature and function of the body whose decision is impugned".[325] Even in a situation, therefore, where the application of policy is being decided in a non-judicial setting, the decision will be struck down if, in the circumstances of the case, its outcome has been "predetermined whether by adoption of an inflexible policy or by the effective surrender of the body's independent judgment".[326]

Finally, it should be noted that many decisions require a consideration of fact, judgement and policy. For example, a decision whether to enforce against a breach of planning law may require the decision-maker to determine whether a building's use has been changed to another (a question of fact); whether that use is suitable to be carried out in that area (a question of planning judgment) and whether wider questions of public policy dictate the need to enforce the law against the change of use (a question of policy). As we shall see in the section below, it has been an article of faith in this country that ministers accountable to Parliament should ultimately be charged with deciding matters of policy, despite the fact that they are predisposed in favour of their policies. A wholly independent and judicialised tribunal would therefore be wanting in terms both of expertise and democratic accountability. To what extent that approach can be sustained under ECHR art.6 will now be considered.

10-087

ECHR ART.6

We have seen that fair procedures in the United Kingdom are now governed not only by the common law but also by the provisions of ECHR art.6 under the Human Rights Act 1998. It is necessary to consider the way that ECHR art.6 requirements relate to the common law and, in turn, how the common law has been, and may in the future be influenced by art.6.[327] Article 6(1) requires "a fair and public hearing" only in circumstances where there has been "determination of [a person's] civil rights and obligations, or any criminal charge", a matter considered in Ch.7.[328] Questions arise therefore of what is meant by "civil rights and obligations", and in particular, to what extent decisions of a policy nature (the issue discussed in the previous section) come within that definition. If so, what are the ingredients of

10-088

---

[322] *Ridge v Baldwin* [1964] A.C. 40.

[323] See, e.g. *Ex p. Quietlynn Ltd* (1986) 85 L.G.R. 387.

[324] *Kirkstall Valley Campaign Ltd* [1996] 3 All E.R. 304 at 323.

[325] *Kirkstall Valley Campaign* [1996] 3 All E.R. 304 at 320.

[326] *Kirkstall Valley Campaign* [1996] 3 All E.R. 304 at 321.

[327] P. Craig, "The Human Rights Act, Art.6 and Procedural Rights" [2003] P.L. 753. It should also be noted that there is a requirement for independence in investigations required pursuant to other provisions of the Convention, such as ECHR art.2: see, e.g., *Re McQuillan's Application for Judicial Review* [2017] NIQB 28 (proposed investigation by the Police Service of Northern Ireland into death that may have been at the hands of a soldier under the control of the Ministry of Defence not sufficiently independent).

[328] On which, see 7-032.

independence and impartiality required by the ECHR? If the requirement is a judicial-style tribunal,[329] this causes problems for the many decision-making bodies to make decisions involving policy, from the Minister deciding whether to grant or refuse planning permission to other decisions taken by committees of local authority politicians, discussed above.[330]

10-089   This issue has been considered by the courts on a number of occasions. It came before the House of Lords in the *Alconbury* litigation.[331] The decision in question was that of the minister, considering an appeal against a decision of a local authority to enforce a breach of planning law. The Minister would act on the advice of a planning inspector (an official), who had heard the appeal in accordance with fair procedures, but two local groups objected to the Minister deciding the matter as he was not considered by them to be "independent or impartial" because of his prior commitment to policies which were predisposed to enforcement in that case.

10-090   It was held that since this decision involved substantial considerations of "policy" and "public interest" (or, in the words of the ECtHR, "expediency") it did not need to be taken by a judicial-style tribunal, indeed it was desirable that the decision be made by a public official responsible to Parliament. As Lord Nolan put it, to hand over those policy functions to an "independent and impartial body with no central electoral accountability would not only be a recipe for chaos: it would be profoundly undemocratic".[332] However, in accordance both with common law principles about bias, and ECHR art.6, the overall decision-making process (including the prior investigation of the facts by a departmental Inspector) had provided adequate procedural safeguards (particularly as the facts found by the Inspector must be accepted by the Minister unless he had notified the objectors and given them an opportunity to make representations[333]). In addition, it was held that, as had been accepted by the ECtHR in the *Bryan* case,[334] the fact-finding procedures of any subsequent judicial review of the Minister's decision provided a "sufficiency of

---

[329] There is no requirement under art.6 that prosecutors in criminal cases be independent and impartial: *R. (on the application of Haase) v Independent Adjudicator* [2008] EWCA Civ 1089; [2009] Q.B. 550. However, it has been held that a court martial tribunal for the trial of a civilian lacked the independence and impartiality necessary to comply with ECHR art.6 and that the trial of a civilian by military court martial would, in the absence of special circumstances, always be contrary to ECHR art.6: *Martin v United Kingdom* (2007) 44 E.H.R.R. 31.

[330] While this is perhaps the primary issue that has arisen in the case law regarding the ECHR art.6 requirements for impartiality and independence, ECHR art.6 has obviously also been invoked in many other contexts: *R. v Dunn* [2010] EWCA Crim 1823; [2011] 1 W.L.R. 958 (the self-certification by the Court of Appeal that a point of law was of general public importance for the purposes of appeal to the Supreme Court was not incompatible with ECHR art.6); *Starrs and Chalmers v Procurator Fiscal, Linlithgow* [2000] H.R.L.R. 191 (temporary sheriffs were not compatible with ECHR art.6, in particular, due to their lack of security of tenure and the responsibility of the Lord Advocate to recall appointments, where the prosecution constituted an act of the Lord Advocate); *Hoekstra* 2000 J.C. 291 (where judge had written newspaper articles criticising the ECHR gave rise to apparent bias where the judge was adjudicating upon an appeal including ECHR issues). A decision-maker who exercises legislative as well as judicial functions may not meet the ECHR art.6 test. In *R. (on the application of Barclay) v Lord Chancellor and Secretary of State for Justice* [2008] EWCA Civ 1319; [2009] 2 W.L.R. 1205, it was held that the combination in Sark of the judicial with the other functions of the Seneschal was inconsistent with the art.6 requirement to establish by law an independent and impartial tribunal.

[331] *R. v Secretary of State for the Environment, Transport and the Regions Ex p. Holdings & Barnes Plc* [2001] UKHL 23; [2003] 2 A.C. 295.

[332] At [60]; see also Lord Hoffmann at [128]: "The Human Rights Act 1998 no doubt intended to strengthen the rule of law but not to inaugurate the rule of lawyers."

[333] Town and Country Planning (Inquiries Procedure) (England) Rules 2000 r.17(5).

[334] In *Bryan v UK* (1996) 21 E.H.R.R. 342 holding that judicial review provides "full jurisdiction" and thus has a curative effect on any procedural defects of the primary decision.

review", especially as they permitted review for lack of evidence or ignorance of an established and relevant fact.[335]

In a subsequent case, *Tower Hamlets LBC v Begum (Runa)*[336] the House of Lords **10-091** considered a decision by a local authority as to whether accommodation offered to the appellant was "suitable". The decision was reviewed by a rehousing officer in the same local authority. This issue was held to involve a determination of "civil rights and obligations" but it was also held that the reviewing officer need not be an independent tribunal exercising full judicial powers.[337] This was because questions of fact were only part of broader considerations concerning local conditions and requiring specialist knowledge and experience. In addition, the review process contained adequate procedural safeguards that the applicant's representations would be taken into account. Finally, it was held that an appeal to a county court of the reviewing officer's decision would provide sufficiency of review, as accepted in *Bryan*. Lord Hoffmann also considered that in schemes of social welfare the values of "efficient administration and the sovereignty of Parliament" entitled Parliament to take the view "that it is not in the public interest that an excessive proportion of the funds available for a welfare scheme should be consumed in administration and legal disputes". That "full jurisdiction" requires "sufficient jurisdiction" has also been confirmed by the ECtHR.[338]

Assertions of breaches of the ECHR art.6 requirements of impartiality and **10-092** independence have also been made where the review decision has been contracted out to a third party. The issue arose for consideration in the case of *De-Winter Heald v Brent London Borough Council*[339] where a local housing authority had contracted out to a third party the carrying out of reviews of the suitability of temporary accommodation provided by the local authority or of the refusal of homelessness applications. The court reasoned, on the assumption that ECHR art.6 was engaged, that given that in *Begum*, it had been held that a review carried out by an employee of a local housing authority did not infringe ECHR art.6, even though that employee was not independent, a third party would not necessarily be any less impartial than an employee.[340] Whether he could be so regarded may depend on the particular facts, and in particular the terms of the contract between the authority and the third party. In this case, the third party's decision on review was adopted by the authority and it was therefore irrelevant that the third party was not democratically elected or directly democratically accountable.[341]

Neither the utilitarian considerations raised by Lord Hoffmann in *Begum*, nor the **10-093** arguments accepted there and in *Alconbury* in favour of the non-judicialisation of the respective decision-making schemes was held by the High Court to apply to a scheme to review challenges to decisions by a local authority on the entitlement of

---

[335] See 11-036.

[336] [2003] UKHL 5; [2003] 2 A.C. 430.

[337] Lord Bingham, at [5] considered that a flexible approach ought to be taken in such a case "if emasculation (by over-judicialisation) of administrative welfare schemes is to be avoided" (a view supported in *R. (on the application of A) v Croydon LBC* [2009] UKSC 8; [2009] 1 W.L.R. 2557 at [44]).

[338] *Ali v United Kingdom* (2016) 63 E.H.R.R. 20 at [76] (requirement of a fair hearing before an impartial tribunal was satisfied by the local authority's internal review process and the availability of a subsequent appeal to the county court, even though such an appeal was by way of review rather than rehearing).

[339] *De-Winter Heald v Brent London Borough Council* [2009] EWCA Civ 930; [2010] 1 W.L.R. 990.

[340] *De-Winter* [2009] EWCA Civ 930; [2010] 1 W.L.R. 990 at [51].

[341] *De-Winter* [2009] EWCA Civ 930; [2010] 1 W.L.R. 990 at [52]-[53] (Stanley Burnton LJ observed that there may be a tension between building a high degree of independence into the contract— such as for example prescribing a long contractual term terminable only for serious breach—which could be met with the objection that the third party is not democratically accountable).

housing and other benefit.[342] The decision in question was reviewed by a Board known as the Housing Benefit and Council Tax Benefit Review Board consisting of three councillors from the same council which had made the initial decision, advised by a lawyer from the council's legal department.[343] Moses J held that the situation was different from that of *Alconbury*, as the judgment was not largely based upon matters of policy but upon a finding of fact.[344] In addition, in such a case the court on judicial review exercised "only limited control" as it could not substitute its views as to the weight of evidence. The "curative" effect of judicial review was thus inadequate and could not "replenish the want of independence in the Review Board, caused by its connection to a party in the dispute".[345]

10-094   In *Tsfayo v United Kingdom*,[346] the ECtHR considered the proceedings of the same Board's decision as to whether the appellant had "good cause" for delay in submitting an application for benefit. It was held that the Board's lack of structural independence (on the ground that it was directly connected to one of the parties to the dispute) amounted to a violation of art.6(1). *Bryan* was distinguished both by the fact that it did not involve a determination of civil rights and by the fact that, although it did involve some fact-finding, the Inspector was called upon "to exercise his discretion on a wide range of policy matters"[347] and it was those policy judgments, rather than the findings of primary fact, that were challenged in that case. In contrast, in *Tsfayo* the Board "was deciding a simple question of fact", unlike both *Bryan* and *Begum* where "the issues to be determined required a measure of professional knowledge or experience and the exercise of administrative discretion pursuant to wider policy aims".[348] It was also held that the central issue of fact was not open to a "sufficiency of review" because, despite the power of the High Court to quash the decision if its findings were plainly untenable, or if it had misunderstood or been ignorant of an established and relevant fact, "it did not have jurisdiction to rehear the evidence or substitute its own views as to the applicant's credibility".[349]

10-095   As we have seen, it has been suggested that our common law standards relating

---

[342] *R. (on the application of Bewry) v Norwich CC* [2001] EWHC Admin 657; [2002] H.R.L.R. 2.

[343] The Board, criticised by the Council on Tribunals, has now been replaced. *Bewry* was followed, even after the HL judgment in *Begum* in *R. (on the application of Bono) v Harlow DC* [2002] EWHC 423; [2002] 1 W.L.R. 2475.

[344] In *Begum* [2003] UKHL 5; [2003] 2 A.C. 430, Lord Bingham at [7]-[8] similarly said that although judicial review allows review for lack of evidence or for a misunderstanding or ignorance of an established fact, the "judge may not make fresh findings of fact and must accept apparently tenable conclusions on credibility made on behalf of the authority". Lord Hoffmann, however, suggested that a full appeal is no different from review in that respect, as "it is not easy for an appellate tribunal which has not itself seen the witnesses to differ from the decision-maker on questions of primary fact, and more especially ... on questions of credibility" (at 47).

[345] On curative effect, see also 8-043.

[346] *Tsfayo v United Kingdom* (2009) 48 E.H.R.R. 18; see 8-051.

[347] At [42].

[348] At [44].

[349] At [47]. Contrast *Crompton v UK* (2010) 50 E.H.R.R. 36 at [77]-[80] (dispute was not one of fact but rather about the approach of the Army Board in assessing the level of compensation, which had been examined on judicial review and accordingly, no violation of ECHR art.6 arose); see also *Ali v Birmingham City Council* [2010] UKSC 8; [2010] 2 A.C. 39 (obiter comments at [53]-[56]). Lord Kerr observed as follows at [78]: "Where the decision involves an evaluative judgment one can quite see that a judicial review challenge would be appropriate but where a conclusion on a simple factual issue is at stake, judicial review does not commend itself as an obviously suitable means by which to rid the original decision of its appearance of bias. In particular, judicial review might be said to be a singularly inapt means of examining issues of credibility which lie at the heart of the present appeals"; *R. (on the application of MA) v National Probation Service* [2011] EWHC 1332 (Admin); [2011] A.C.D. 86; *King v Secretary of State for Justice* [2012] EWCA Civ 376; [2012] 1 W.L.R. 3602. *R. (on the application of A) v Croydon London Borough Council* [2009] UKSC 8; [2009] 1

to bias and those under ECHR art.6 are the same.[350] There certainly is no significant difference between them and they are likely in any event to converge. In situations where what is being decided is an entitlement or right[351] or matter of factual determination,[352] it is clear that both standards require the absence of apparent bias. In the area of policy-making,[353] or decisions which require special expertise or professional knowledge, it seems that the lack of structural independence will still be tolerated in English law for reasons that these qualities are necessary to determine questions of the public interest, provided of course that other public law principles are observed.

After *Tsfayo*, however, we can be less sure that utilitarian arguments (e.g. about **10-096** the cost of providing appeal mechanisms)[354] against the establishment of judicial-style tribunals will, or ought any longer to prevail in respect of many decisions so far regarded as involving at least a substantial element of policy-making. Similar doubts apply to the doctrine of necessity.[355] Clearly the greater the element of fact-finding, the more judicialised should be the tribunal be. Moreover, when the relevant decision depends for its outcome upon a finding of fact or a finding of credibility, the availability of judicial review may no longer prove sufficient to "cure" any defects in the structure of the primary decision-making process, at least so long as our judicial review does not permit the rehearing of evidence or the substitution of its own view of the facts.[356]

The ECtHR has stressed that it is not the function of ECHR art.6 to ensure review **10-097** by a body that could substitute its opinion for that of the administrative authority, since respect has to be accorded to decisions taken by administrative authorities. Thus, in assessing the sufficiency of a judicial review, it is necessary to consider: the powers of the judicial body; whether the decision concerned a specialist issue requiring professional knowledge; the extent to which the decision involved the exercise of administrative discretion; the manner in which the decision had been

---

W.L.R. 2557 at [45] (the determination of whether a person was a "child" for whom the local authority was obliged to provide accommodation was ultimately a question for the court, which meant that the procedures coupled with judicial review on conventional grounds satisfied ECHR art.6). See also *R. (on the application of XH) v Secretary of State for the Home Department* [2016] EWHC 1898 (Admin) at [106] (while the Secretary of State's decision would involve a consideration of facts, it essentially involved a risk assessment being made in the light of a policy set out in a written ministerial statement; the court added (at [107]) that "judicial review is a flexible process and the court can examine facts in an appropriate case"); *R. (on the application of Derrin Brother Properties Ltd) v Revenue and Customs Commissioners* [2016] EWCA Civ 15; [2016] 1 W.L.R. 2423 at [112] (judicial review was adequate to ensure compliance with statutory pre-conditions for judicial approval of third party information notices).

[350] *Kataria v Essex Strategic Health Authority* [2004] EWHC 641; [2004] 3 All E.R. 572 at [46] (Stanley Burnton J). See also the position under ECHR art.5(4). In *R. (on the application of Brooke) v Parole Board* [2008] EWCA Civ 29; [2008] 1 W.L.R. 1950 it was held that the Parole Board did not meet the requirements of the common law and of ECHR art.5(4) for a court to have demonstrated objective independence of the executive and the parties, with the funding of the Parole Board (by the Ministry of Justice and previously by the Home Office) creating the impression that the Board was either part of the Home Office or the Prison Service; see also *Resolution Chemicals* [2013] EWCA Civ 1515; [2014] 1 W.L.R. 1943 at [35] ("underlying both article 6 of the Convention and the common law principles is the fundamental consideration that justice should not only be done but should manifestly and undoubtedly be seen to be done").

[351] See 10-088 and 10-089.

[352] As in *Tsfayo* (2009) 48 E.H.R.R. 18.

[353] As in *R. (on the application of Cummins) v Camden LBC* [2001] EWHC (Admin) 1116.

[354] As suggested by Lord Hoffmann in *Begum* [2003] UKHL 5; [2003] 2 A.C. 430.

[355] J. Howell, "Alconbury Crumbles" [2007] J.R. 9.

[356] See *Crompton* (2010) 50 EHRR 36 at [77]-[80]; *Ali* [2010] UKSC 8; [2010] 2 A.C. 39 at [78]. For a further discussion of inadequate factual basis of decisions see 11-036.

reached; the procedural guarantees available before the adjudicatory body; and the content of the dispute; and the legislative scheme as a whole.[357]

10-098 The obligation in ECHR art.6 to ensure access to independent and impartial courts for the resolution of "civil rights and obligations" imposes an obligation on states to respect the court process and to comply with judgments delivered by the courts. This means that contracting states cannot legislate in a manner which affects the judicial determination of a dispute involving the State or private parties. Thus, in *R. (on the application of Reilly) (No.2) v Secretary of State for Work and Pensions*,[358] the Jobseekers (Back to Work Scheme) Act 2013 was declared incompatible with ECHR art.6 insofar as it purported to validate sanctions retrospectively for those claimants who had already appealed against their sanctions.

COMPARATIVE PERSPECTIVES

Australia

10-099 The bias test in Australian law deals with both actual and apprehended bias, but the lesser evidence required for an apprehension of bias has seen virtually all bias claims pursued under that category. The year after automatic disqualification was affirmed and extended by the House of Lords in *Pinochet (No.2)*, it was entirely rejected by the Australian High Court in *Ebner v Official Trustee*.[359] *Ebner* held that all interests, financial or otherwise, should be assessed according to a single two-fold process. The first step is to identify that which might lead a judge or other decision-maker to decide a case other than on its merits. The second step is to articulate how the relevant interest or influence might lead the judge to decide a case other than according to its merits.[360] Courts still sometimes lose sight of the simplicity of this two-fold test, as happened in *Michael Wilson*,[361] when a lower court found apprehension of bias against a trial judge who had decided many preliminary applications against one party. The High Court held that even a large number of adverse rulings did not create an apprehension of bias,[362] and also cautioned against using the reasons of a judge to decide the existence of an apprehension of bias.[363] The true vice in this case was that use of the reasons presumed the existence of the very apprehension that was in dispute. Courts should not "invert the proper order of inquiry by first assuming the existence of the reasonable apprehension" and then inspect any reasons for confirmation of that presumption.[364]

Automatic disqualification

10-100 Until the decision in *Ebner*, an automatic disqualification rule applied, irrespective of an appearance of bias, if the decision-maker was a member of the judiciary

---

[357] *Ali* (2016) 63 E.H.R.R. 20 at [78]–[79].

[358] *R. (on the application of Reilly) (No.2) v Secretary of State for Work and Pensions* [2016] EWCA Civ 413.

[359] *Ebner v Official Trustee* (2000) 205 C.L.R. 337. Strictly speaking the case did not reject automatic disqualification. Instead the majority held that the *Dimes* case has been wrongly interpreted to support such a rule: 355-357. Kirby J rejected this as "a historical approach": 378.

[360] Gageler J has suggested a third step of considering "the reasonableness of the apprehension of that deviation [from neutrality] being caused by that factor in that way": *Isbester v Knox City Council* (2015) 255 C.L.R. 135 at 155–156. This added step has not yet gained traction in Australian law.

[361] *Michael Wilson & Partners Ltd v Nicholls* (2011) 244 C.L.R. 427.

[362] *Michael Wilson* (2011) 244 C.L.R. 427 at 448.

[363] *Michael Wilson* (2011) 244 C.L.R. 427 at 446.

[364] *MZAEU v Minister for Immigration and Border Protection* [2016] FCAFC 100 at [45].

with a direct *pecuniary interest* in the outcome of the decision. However, *Ebner* held that there is no free-standing automatic disqualification rule and each case will depend upon the application of the fair-minded lay observer test.[365] The rejection of automatic disqualification has not simplified the bias test as much as might have been expected. *Ebner*'s second step is a regular source of difficulty, because the test for apprehended bias involves two "mights"—in the form of a requirement to articulate how an interest *might* influence a decision-maker, who *might* not be sufficiently impartial.[366] Another difficulty with the *Ebner* test is that its outcome will always depend heavily on the facts of each case. Past cases provide limited guidance because it is always difficult for judges who apply the test to "know what a lay observer might think about a particular issue."[367] The apparent flexibility of the test is also a two edged sword. The determination of the second step of the *Ebner* test will take account of the character and functions of the decision-maker. That enables, for example, the courts to accept a level of intervention and forthright behaviour from an inquisitorial tribunal that would surely create an apprehension of bias on the part of a judge.[368] Similarly, government ministers may state their views and predispositions to an extent that would cause a finding of prejudgment in other decision-makers.[369] Most of these problems are not due to the *Ebner* test, but are instead a consequence of the assessment of bias claims through the eyes of the fictional fair-minded and informed observer. Kirby J long cautioned that judges should strive to separate their subjective views from that of the more objective observer, lest the court "hold up a mirror to itself."[370] The courts now seem more alert to the fact that the fair-minded observer invariably contains a clear element of subjective judicial assessment. When the use of the fictional observer was most recently challenged in the High Court, French CJ agreed that the fictional observer was a necessarily limited concept, but remained useful to remind "the judges making such decisions of the need to view the circumstances of claimed apparent bias, as best they can, through the eyes of non-judicial observers.[371]

Canada

The standard test in Canada for bias remains that articulated by de Grandpré J **10-101** in his dissenting judgment in *Committee for Justice and Liberty v National Energy Board*[372]:

"[T]he apprehension must be a reasonable one, held by reasonable and right-minded

---

[365] *Ebner* (2000) 205 C.L.R. 337 at 351. Kirby J dissented and has reaffirmed his position in *Hot Holdings Pty Ltd v Creasy* (2002) 210 C.L.R. 438 at 474.

[366] The test is "one of possibility (real and not remote), not probability": *Ebner v Official Trustee* (2000) 205 C.L.R. 337 at 345.

[367] *Kirby v Centro Properties Ltd (No.2)* (2008) 172 F.C.R. 376 at 382.

[368] *Minister for Immigration and Multicultural Affairs v Jia* (2001) 205 C.L.R. 507 (rejecting a bias claim against a minister who stated his general views in a radio interview about the character of people whose deportation he might or might not order. The High Court held that the minister's remarks did not create an apprehension of bias in the form of prejudgment because the remarks were general and media interviews on such issues were an inevitable task for ministers).

[369] *Re Refugee Review Tribunal; Ex p. H* (2001) 179 A.L.R. 425 (upholding a bias claim against a tribunal member who constantly interjected and belittled an applicant. The High Court accepted that inquisitorial tribunals could engage in more active conduct in a hearing but held the tribunal member had gone too far in this case).

[370] *Johnson v Johnson* (2000) 201 C.L.R. 488 at 506. Kirby J made sharper criticisms in *Smits v Roach* (2006) 227 C.L.R. 423 at 457.

[371] *British American Tobacco Australia Services Ltd v Laurie* (2011) 242 C.L.R. 283 at 306-307.

[372] *Committee for Justice and Liberty v National Energy Board* [1978] 1 S.C.R. 369 at 394-395; and *Canadian Pacific Ltd v Matsqui Indian Band* [1995] 1 S.C.R. 3; *Wewaykum Indian Band v Canada*

people, applying themselves to the question and obtaining thereon the required information. In the words of the Court of Appeal, that test is "what would an informed person, viewing the matter realistically and practically—and having thought the matter through—conclude."

10-102   Lower courts in Canada continue to be divided on whether the "closed mind" test for bias is a free-standing and more forgiving alternative to the standard reasonable apprehension of bias test[373] or is descriptive of what is required to establish a reasonable apprehension of bias at the "legislative" end of the spectrum on which the principles of procedural fairness operate.[374] Irrespective of the merits of that disagreement, Canadian courts continue to apply the more difficult to establish closed mind test to a range of decision-making to which the principles of procedural fairness apply less intensively. Within the realm of decision-making with a high policy content, the Federal Court of Appeal has recently used the closed mind test in a challenge to a Governor in Council decision on whether to adopt a National Energy Board report recommending approval of a pipeline.[375] Similarly, the Ontario Divisional Court has deployed that test in the context of an application to review a decision on the closing of a school.[376] As illustrated by another judgment of the Federal Court of Appeal, the test may also reach decisions involving the rights and interests of an individual, in that instance the removal by the Governor in Council on the recommendation of the responsible Minister of the holder of an office held at pleasure.[377]

Lack of independence

10-103   In *McKenzie v British Columbia (Minister of Public Safety and Solicitor General)*,[378] a single judge of the British Columbia Supreme Court, restrictively distinguishing the Supreme Court's judgment in *Ocean Port*, held that, by reference to underlying constitutional principles, Residential Tenancy Arbitrators had a constitutional guarantee of independence which could not be overridden by primary legislation. However, subsequently, the Courts of Appeal of both Saskatchewan[379] and Alberta[380] held that *Ocean Port* precluded the extension of a general constitutional guarantee of independence to adjudicative tribunals. Therefore, it now seems clear that unless a right guaranteed by either s.7 or s.11(d) of the Canadian Charter of Rights and Freedoms—or possibly ss.1(a), 2(e)[381] or 2(f) of the "quasi-constitutional" Canadian Bill of Rights—is at stake in tribunal proceedings, the

---

[2003] 2 S.C.R. 259 (involving an allegation of bias against a judge of the Supreme Court). It remains unclear whether pecuniary bias has been subsumed within the general test or remains an automatic basis for disqualification provided the interest is non-trivial.

[373] *Pelletier v Canada (Attorney General)*, 2008 FCA 1; [2008] 3 F.C.R. 40, at [56]–[58].

[374] *Citizens for Accountable and Responsible Education Niagara Inc v District School Board of Niagara*, 2016 ONSC 2058, at [111].

[375] *Gitxaala Nation v Canada*, 2016 FCA 187; [2016] 4 F.C.R. 418, at [195]–[200].

[376] *Citizens for Accountable and Responsible Education Niagara Inc*, 2016 ONSC 2058.

[377] *Pelletier v Canada (Attorney General)*, 2008 FCA 1; [2008] 3 F.C.R. 40.

[378] *McKenzie v British Columbia (Minister of Public Safety and Solicitor General)* 2006 BCSC 1372; 272 D.L.R. (4th) 455.

[379] *Saskatchewan (Federation of Labour) v Saskatchewan (Attorney General)*, 2013 SKCA 61; 363 D.L.R. (4th) 263, at [47]–[64], leave to appeal to the Supreme Court of Canada refused [2013] SCCA No. 351 (QL).

[380] *Altus Group Ltd v Calgary (City)*, 2015 ABCA 86; 382 D.L.R. (4th) 455, affirming 2013 ABQB 617.

[381] For a restriction of the reach of s.2(e), see *Kazemi Estate v Islamic Republic of Iran*, 2014 SCC 62; [2014] 3 S.C.R. 176, at [116]–[120] (per Rothstein J).

principle of adjudicative independence does not trump primary legislation establishing the terms and conditions of tribunal appointments.

Automatic disqualification

In *Newfoundland Telephone Co* the Supreme Court accepted that bias was automatically disqualifying and could not be cured by the tribunal's subsequent decision.[382] The hearing and any subsequent decision is void. Whether there are any kinds of interest that are automatically disqualifying without more is unclear.[383]

10-104

New Zealand

In *Muir v Commissioner of Inland Revenue*,[384] the Court of Appeal adopted the *Porter v Magill* test, overruling *Auckland Casino Ltd v Casino Control Authority*[385] (which had imported the test formulated by the House of Lords in *R. v Gough*[386]). This brings the law on apparent bias into line with that in England and Australia. The decision in *Muir* was approved by the Supreme Court in *Saxmere Company Ltd Wool Board Disestablishment Company Ltd (No.1)*.[387]

10-105

Automatic disqualification

While New Zealand law is now the same as Australian law on the test for apparent bias, on the separate aspect of automatic disqualification for pecuniary interest the two jurisdictions now are poles apart. The dissent of Kirby J in the High Court of Australia's decision in *Ebner*[388]—supporting continuation of automatic disqualification for financial interest where it is "direct" and not saved by the de minimis principle is in line with the New Zealand position.[389] Although doubt was cast on the New Zealand approach in *Muir v Commissioner of Inland Revenue*,[390] and also by Tipping J in *Saxmere Company Ltd Wool Board Disestablishment Company Ltd (No.1)* who said "there should no longer be any distinction between cases in which the allegation of apparent bias rests on financial interest as against those involving other matters. The same test should apply generally",[391] the position in *Auckland Casino* remains undisturbed.

10-106

---

[382] *Telephone Co v Newfoundland (Board of Commissioners of Public Utilities)* [1992] 1 S.C.R. 623.

[383] In *Wewaykum* [2003] 2 S.C.R. 259 at [70]-[71], the court discusses *Locobail* and *Pinochet* but does not come to any definite conclusion.

[384] *Muir v Commissioner of Inland Revenue* [2007] 3 N.Z.L.R. 495.

[385] *Auckland Casino Ltd v Casino Control Authority* [1995] 1 N.Z.L.R. 142, CA.

[386] *R. v Gough* [1993] A.C. 646.

[387] *Saxmere Company Ltd Wool Board Disestablishment Company Ltd (No.1)* [2010] 1 N.Z.L.R. 35. Although this decision was recalled and its orders rescinded in *Saxmere Company Ltd Wool Board Disestablishment Company Ltd (No.2)* [2010] 1 N.Z.L.R. 76, this did not affect the statements as to the law on apparent bias.

[388] *Ebner* (2000) 205 C.L.R. 337.

[389] *Auckland Casino Ltd* [1995] 1 N.Z.L.R. 142, CA.

[390] *Muir v Commissioner of Inland Revenue* [2007] 3 N.Z.L.R. 495 at [37]-[43].

[391] *Saxmere Company Ltd Wool Board Disestablishment Company Ltd (No.1)* [2010] 1 N.Z.L.R. 76 at [42].

South Africa

10-107   The test for bias in South African law has authoritatively been set as a "reasonable suspicion" of bias.[392] The confusion at common law prior to this decision was whether the appropriate test was "a real likelihood" or a "reasonable suspicion" of bias.[393] The Promotion of Administrative Justice Act 3 of 2000 (PAJA) subsumes both of these approaches, however. Section 6(2)(a)(iii) allows review of administrative decisions if the administrator taking the decision "was biased or reasonably suspected of bias". The Constitutional Court has formulated the reasonable suspicion test as follows:

> "(1)   There must be a suspicion that the administrator might—not would—be biased.
> (2)   The suspicion must be that of a reasonable person in the position of the person affected.
> (3)   The suspicion must be based on reasonable grounds. ...
> (4)   The suspicion must be one which the reasonable person referred to would—not might—have".[394]

10-108   Hoexter considers that the preference of the Constitutional Court for the term "apprehension" of bias over "suspicion" is not significant.[395] There does not seem, therefore, to be any basis for "automatic disqualification" in South African law. Whatever interests or connections an adjudicator has to a particular case will be relevant to the crucial inquiry as to whether the administrator is in fact biased, or can be said to be reasonably suspected of bias. The inquiry will have to be performed whatever the circumstances and whatever the allegation of bias, and it will have to be established in each case that the administrator was in fact biased or that a reasonable person would have had a reasonable suspicion of bias. South African courts have held, though, that the "smallest pecuniary interest" may be enough to raise a reasonable suspicion of bias;[396] and in the context of judicial bias and recusal, that "disclosure should still be made, no matter how small the interest may be".[397]

10-109   In *Turnbull-Jackson v Hibiscus Coast Municipality*,[398] the Constitutional Court was moved to caution against "wanton, gratuitous allegations of bias" against public officials. The applicant in this case had alleged "reactive bias", i.e. bias resulting from repeated insults hurled at the administrator by the applicant himself. This novel

---

[392]   *BTR Industries South Africa (Pty) Ltd v Metal and Allied Workers' Union* 1992 (3) S.A. 673, A. This has since been confirmed by the Constitutional Court in *President of the Republic of South Africa v South African Rugby Football Union* 1999 (4) S.A. 147, CC and *S v Basson* 2005 (12) B.C.L.R. 1192, CC. Although this later case law deals with recusal of judges, the courts have noted that the factors relevant to the determination of bias in an administrative-law setting are the same. See *Gold Fields Ltd v Connellan NO* [2005] 3 All S.A. 142, W. However, the burden will be heavier on the litigant who alleges judicial bias: see *Bernert v Absa Bank Ltd* 2011 (3) S.A. 92, CC.

[393]   *City and Suburban Transport (Pty) Ltd v Local Board Road Transportation, Johannesburg* 1932 W.L.D. 100.

[394]   *Turnbull-Jackson v Hibiscus Coast Municipality* 2014 (6) S.A. 592, CC at [30], borrowing from *S v Roberts* 1999 (4) S.A. 915, S.C.A. at [32]-[34]. While the test in *Roberts* was formulated for complaints against judges, the Constitutional Court confirmed that it is suitable for administrators as well (at [30] fn.54).

[395]   C. Hoexter, *Administrative Law in South Africa* 2nd edn (2012), p.453. As the court explained in *President of the Republic of South Africa v South African Rugby Football Union* 1999 (4) S.A. 147, CC at [38], "inappropriate connotations" may be attached to the word "suspicion".

[396]   *Rose v Johannesburg Local Road Transportation Board* 1947 (4) S.A. 272, W; *Barnard v Jockey Club of South Africa* 1984 (2) S.A. 35, W; and see Hoexter (2012), pp.454-5.

[397]   *Bernert v Absa Bank Ltd* 2011 (3) S.A. 92, CC at [56].

[398]   2014 (6) S.A. 592, CC at [35].

stratagem failed, however, for the applicant was unable to discharge the evidential onus.

Ireland

In Ireland, it has been suggested that there are three situations in which bias may **10-110** arise: first, actual bias; second, apparent bias where the decision-maker has a proprietary or other definite personal interest in the outcome of the proceedings, where a presumption of bias without further proof arises; and, third, other cases of apparent bias where a reasonable person may apprehend bias.[399] Although the second category broadly equates with the concept of "automatic disqualification" found in other jurisdictions, Irish courts have not formally adopted a category of "automatic disqualification" as such, and the second and third categories are generally regarded as forms of apparent bias.[400]

There have been various articulations of the test for apparent bias, including **10-111** whether "there is a reasonable apprehension or suspicion that the decision-maker might have been biased",[401] and "whether a reasonable person in the circumstances would have a reasonable apprehension that the applicant ... would not receive a fair trial of the issues."[402] What is clear, however, is that the courts have rejected the requirement that an applicant demonstrate a "real likelihood" of bias.[403] However, there is a lack of clarity in the law regarding whether a distinction is drawn between the test for apparent bias with respect to judicial or quasi-judicial functions on the one hand and administrative functions on the other.[404] Apparent bias can arise from a variety of sources, including material interest,[405] personal animosity,[406] association with the issue,[407] family relationship,[408] professional relationship,[409] and prior

---

[399] *Orange Communications Ltd v Director of Telecommunications Regulation (No.1)* [2000] IESC 79; [2000] 4 I.R. 159 at 252. See generally, G. Hogan and D.G. Morgan, *Administrative Law* 4th edn (2010), Ch.13; H. Biehler, *Judicial Review of Administrative Action* 3rd edn (2013), pp.255-269; M. de Blacam, *Judicial Review*, 3rd edn (2017), Ch.15; D.G. Morgan, *Hogan and Morgan's Administrative Law*, 4th edn (2012), Ch.13.

[400] Morgan, *Hogan and Morgan's Administrative Law* (2012), para.13-03. See also *Goode Concrete v CRH Plc* [2015] IESC 70; [2015] 3 I.R. 493 at [24]-[30].

[401] *Orange Communications Ltd v Director of Telecommunications Regulation (No.1)* [2000] IESC 79; [2000] 4 I.R. 159 at 186 (Keane CJ).

[402] *Bula Ltd v Tara Mines Ltd (No.6)* [2000] 4 I.R. 412 at 439 (Denham J). See also at 485 (McGuinness J observing that the test is "that of the reasonable person's reasonable apprehension of bias"). The articulation of Denham J was endorsed by the Supreme Court in *Ó Ceallaigh v An Bord Altranais* [2011] IESC 50 (also endorsing the formulation in *Orange Communications Ltd v Director of Telecommunications Regulation (No.1)* [2000] IESC 79; [2000] 4 I.R. 159 at 186); *Goode Concrete v CRH Plc* [2015] IESC 70; [2015] 3 I.R. 493 at [66]; *Reid v Industrial Development Agency* [2015] IESC 82; [2015] 4 I.R. 494.

[403] Hogan and Morgan, *Administrative Law* (2010), para.13-58. In practice of course, the extent to which the different formulations produce different results may be debatable: see Morgan, *Hogan and Morgan's Administrative Law* (2012), para.13-41.

[404] The following cases suggest a less stringent standard may be applied to administrative decision-making: *O'Brien v Bord na Móna* [1983] I.R. 255; *Huntsgrove Developments Ltd v Meath County Council* [1994] 2 I.L.R.M. 36 at 49-50; *Radio Limerick One Ltd v Independent Radio and Television Commission* [1997] 2 I.R. 291. Contrast *Carroll v Law Society* [2000] 1 I.L.R.M. 161 at 182-183 (applying the reasonable apprehension test to disciplinary proceedings); *North Wall v Dublin Docklands Development Authority* [2008] IEHC 305 (holding that the same test applies to judicial and administrative bodies).

[405] *People (Attorney General) v Singer* [1975] I.R. 408; *Connolly v McConnell* [1983] I.R. 172.

[406] *R. (Donoghue) v Cork County Justices* [1910] 2 I.R. 271.

[407] *Dublin Wellwoman Centre Ltd v Ireland* [1995] 1 I.L.R.M. 408.

[408] *O'Reilly v Cassidy (No.2)* [1995] 1 I.L.R.M. 311; *Kenny v Trinity College Dublin* [2007] IESC 42;

involvement in the decision-making process.[410] On the issue of the degree of knowledge assumed of the "reasonable person", the Irish courts have perhaps not gone quite as far as their English counterparts in their attribution of knowledge.[411] Nonetheless, it has been held that the "hypothetical reasonable person is an independent observer, who is not over-sensitive and who has knowledge of the facts".[412]

10-112   The Irish courts also recognise that bias can arise as a result of prejudgment on the part of the adjudicator, where the adjudicator reaches a conclusion on the question in controversy between the parties at a time prior to it being proper for such adjudicator to reach such a decision.[413] Prejudgment applies also to decisions relating to the decision-maker's own proposal, although arguably with less rigour.[414] Prejudgment is unlikely to arise where prior involvement in the decision-making process takes the form of co-ordination, and not consideration of the substantive issues.[415]

10-113   The Court may take into account whether the apparent bias can be excused by necessity;[416] waiver is also recognised,[417] but a "high level of knowledge on the part of a litigant is required before he can be held to have elected to waive his right to object".[418]

[2008] 2 I.R. 40.

[409]   See, e.g. *Bula Ltd (No.6)* [2000] 4 I.R. 412 and *Ó Ceallaigh* [2011] IESC 50 (not established on facts). See also: *O'Driscoll v Hurley* [2016] IESC 32 ("the administration of justice would grind to a halt if judges regularly recused themselves by responding in an over scrupulous way to an invitation to recuse").

[410]   *O'Neill v Irish Hereford Breed Society Ltd* [1992] 1 I.R. 431; *Heneghan v Western Regional Fisheries Board* [1986] I.L.R.M. 225 at 229; *O'Donoghue v Veterinary Council* [1975] I.R. 398. Contrast *O'Callaghan v Disciplinary Tribunal* [2002] 1 I.R. 1. In *Ryanair Ltd v Terravision London Finance Ltd* [2011] IEHC 244; [2011] 3 I.R. 192 (no apparent bias where a judge had earlier presided over proceedings in which untruths in affidavits filed by Ryanair and in which he had observed that "the truth and Ryanair are uncomfortable bedfellows", although the judge decided to recuse himself in any case). In *Commissioner of An Garda Síochána v Penfield Enterprises* [2016] IECA 141, it was held that a reasonable person would reasonably apprehend that a High Court judge had pre-judged an upcoming contempt motion based on his statements that the publication of an article related to ongoing litigation was "reckless and irresponsible".

[411]   See, e.g. *Bula Ltd v Tara Mines Ltd (No.6)* [2000] 4 I.R. 412 at 444; *Ryan v Law Society of Ireland* [2002] IEHC 161; [2002] 4 I.R. 21 at 42. In addition, it has been held that pragmatically, the views of the parties will have to be taken into account: *Nurendale Ltd t/a Panda Waste Services v Dublin City Council* [2009] IEHC 588; [2013] 3 I.R. 417.

[412]   *Kenny* [2007] IESC 42; [2008] 2 I.R. 40 at 45 (Fennelly J). Other cases have suggested that the "reasonable person" should have as much information as the applicant: *Dublin Wellwoman Centre Ltd* [1995] 1 I.L.R.M. 408 at 420; *Ryan v Law Society of Ireland* [2002] 4 I.R. 21 at 38.

[413]   *AP v McDonagh* [2009] IEHC 316.

[414]   *Greenstar Ltd v Dublin City Council* [2009] IEHC 589; [2013] 3 I.R. 510 at [45].

[415]   *North East Pylon Pressure Campaign Limited v An Bord Pleanála* [2017] IEHC 338 at [87]. See also *Callaghan v An Bord Pleanála* [2015] IEHC 357 (no prejudgment found where Board had adopted a preliminary ex parte view on matters relevant to the grant or refusal of permission).

[416]   *O'Neill v Beaumont Hospital* [1990] I.L.R.M. 419 at 440 (Finlay CJ). See also *Toal v The Honourable Society of the King's Inns Barristers Disciplinary Tribunal* [2015] IEHC 512 (citing the 7th edn of this book at [21]).

[417]   See, e.g. *Corrigan v Irish Land Commission* [1977] I.R. 317.

[418]   *Bula Ltd* [2000] 4 I.R. 412 at 504 (McGuinness J); *O'Neill v Irish Hereford Breed Society Ltd* [1992] I.R. 431. See also *Goode Concrete* [2015] IESC 70; [2015] 3 I.R. 493 (knowledge was insufficient to establish waiver).

CHAPTER 11

Substantive Review and Justification

TABLE OF CONTENTS

SCOPE

This chapter considers the following matters.   **11-001**

- The constitutional context in which the courts carry out judicial review of the substance of decisions and the origin and development of the *Wednesbury* formulation of unreasonable decision-making.[1]
- Judicial intervention in a decision where the reasoning process underlying the decision has been defective (including failures properly to balance relevant considerations, flaws in logic and reasoning, and decisions which rest on inadequate evidence of mistake of fact).[2]
- Judicial intervention in a decision the outcome of which is regarded as constitutionally unacceptable (including violation of a common law right, violation of the common law constitutional principles of the rule of law or equality).[3]
- Judicial intervention in a decision the impact of which is regarded as unacceptable such as it is unduly uncertain or oppressive or disproportionate.[4]
- The intensity of substantive review by the court, which ranges from "correctness review" for abuse of power, to "structured proportionality", and a variable intensity of unreasonableness review.[5]

---

[1] See 11-015.
[2] See 11-028.
[3] See 11-052.
[4] See 11–069.
[5] See 11-087.

- Comparative perspectives.[6]

INTRODUCTION

11-002   We now turn to the ground of review normally referred to as "unreasonableness" under the tautological formulation of the *Wednesbury* case[7] or, under Lord Diplock's redefinition, as "irrationality".[8] This chapter is called "substantive review and justification" for a number of reasons. First, there are a number of well-documented difficulties with the terms "unreasonableness" and "irrationality".[9] Secondly, the increasing adoption of "proportionality" as a test for review, particularly for review of European Union law[10] and Convention rights (under the Human Rights Act 1998)[11] renders unreasonableness an inapt description of the range of review that courts engage in under this heading. Thirdly, even in respect of purely domestic law, the deeper *justification* required of decision-makers under the test of proportionality has infiltrated all public decision-making. Finally, "unreasonableness" obscures a distinction which must be made in relation to substantive review between three distinct sets of grounds. The first set of grounds concern the question whether there was a *defect in the reasoning process* through which the decision was made, such as that the decision maker has failed properly to balance relevant considerations, or the decision rests on an error of fact. The second set of grounds concern decisions which contain constitutionally *unacceptable outcomes*, such as decisions which violate fundamental common law rights, the rule of law or the principle of equal treatment. The third set of grounds include decisions where the impact of the decision is unacceptable, on the grounds that it is unduly uncertain or oppressive.

11-003   The issue under this ground of review is not whether the decision-maker strayed outside the terms or authorised purposes of the governing statute (the test of "illegality", considered in Chapter 5 above). It is whether the power under which the decision-maker acts, a power normally conferring a broad discretion, has been insufficiently justified or improperly exercised.

11-004   The question of the appropriate measure of deference, respect, restraint, latitude or discretionary area of judgment[12] (to use some of the terms variously employed) which the courts should grant the primary decision-maker under this head of review is one of the most complex in all of public law and goes to the heart of the principle of the separation of powers. This is because there is often a fine line between assessment of the *merits* of the decision (evaluation of fact and policy) and the assessment of whether the principles of "just administrative action"[13] have been met. The former questions are normally matters for the primary decision-maker, but the latter are within the appropriate capacity of the courts to decide. As we shall see, however, this does not mean that the courts may not consider whether the facts or

---

6   See 11-104.
7   *Associated Provincial Picture Houses v Wednesbury Corporation* [1948] 1 K.B. 223.
8   *Council of Civil Service Unions v Minister for the Civil Service* [1985] A.C. 374 at 410–411.
9   See the essays on this subject in H.Wilberg and M. Elliott, *The Scope and Intensity of Substantive Review: Traversing Taggart's Rainbow* (2015).
10   See Ch.14.
11   See Ch.13.
12   On intensity of review, see 11-087.
13   The term used in s.33 of the Constitution of South Africa and includes the right to administrative action that is "lawful, reasonable and procedurally fair"; cf. Charter of Fundamental Rights of the European Union art.41, which establishes a right to "good administration".

judgment of the authority are properly determined. As public law develops, we are increasingly adopting a "culture of justification"[14] and accountability in English public decision-making, permitting the courts to assess the decisions or actions by reference to increasingly accepted standards of reasoning on the one hand, and impact on the other.

THE CONSTITUTIONAL CONTEXT OF SUBSTANTIVE REVIEW

The constitutional context of judicial review in general has already been considered in Chapter 1. What follows here is consideration of the implications of constitutional context for substantive review more specifically. Questions of the constitutional justification of judicial review are particularly acute in relation to substantive review, where the court, particularly when reviewing for legally unacceptable outcomes or impact, may sometimes appear to be skirting close to the forbidden territory of merits review. There is a need for careful consideration of the constitutional propriety of judicial intervention in the substance of decisions, particularly the relative institutional capacity of the courts and the original decision maker, and the impact of any democratic mandate for a decision.

11-005

Asserting the constitutional capacity of the courts in these situations does not, however, mean that the courts should not recognise both their own constitutional and relative institutional limitations. As we have already discussed in relation to the question of "justiciability",[15] decisions involving "policy"—the utilitarian calculation of the public good—such as decisions about the levels of taxation or public expenditure are, constitutionally, in the realm of the legislature.[16] In respect of other decisions, the relative institutional capacity of courts and the legislature, executive and other bodies will be relevant to the extent and degree of judicial intervention. Decisions that are polycentric, involving the allocation of scarce resources[17] (for example, whether a hospital should provide very expensive treat-

11-006

---

[14] The late Professor Etienne Mureinik wrote about the shift in South Africa after the end of apartheid in 1994 from "a culture of authority" to a "culture of justification": E. Mureinik, "A Bridge to Where? Introducing the Interim Bill of Rights" (1994) S.A.J.H.R. 31, 32. See further D. Dyzenhaus, "Law as Justification: Etienne Mureinik's Conception of Legal Culture" (1998) 13 S.A.J.H.R. 11; M. Taggart, "Reinventing Administrative Law" in N. Bamforth and P. Leyland (ed), *Public Law in a Multi-Layered Constitution* (2004), p.311.

[15] See 1-034–1-049.

[16] *Wilson v First County Trust Ltd* [2003] UKHL 40; [2004] 1 A.C. 816 at [70] (Lord Nicholls: "The more the legislation concerns matters of broad social policy the less ready will be a court to intervene"); *R. (on the application of Hooper) v Secretary of State for Work and Pensions* [2003] EWCA Civ 813; [2003] 1 W.L.R. 2623 at [63]–[64] (Laws LJ: "A very considerable margin of discretion must be accorded to the Secretary of State. Difficult questions of economic and social policy were involved, the resolution of which fell within the province of the executive and the legislature rather than the courts"; appeal allowed by the HL in *Hooper v Secretary of State for Work and Pensions* [2005] UKHL 29; [2005] 1 W.L.R. 1681); *R. (Hurley) v Secretary of State for Work and Pensions (Equality and Human Rights Commission intervening)* [2015] EWHC 3382 (Admin); [2016] P.T.S.R. 636 (Collins J: "public finance is a particularly … inapt subject for judicial scrutiny, albeit such scrutiny is not ruled out.").

[17] See 1-044; and see, e.g. *Michalak v Wandsworth LBC* [2002] EWCA Civ 271; [2003] 1 W.L.R. 617 at [41] (Brooke LJ: "this is pre-eminently a field in which the courts should defer to the decisions taken by a democratically elected Parliament, which has determined the manner in which public resources should be allocated for local authority housing"). And see *R. (on the application of Bancoult) v Secretary of State for Foreign and Commonwealth Affairs (No.2)* [2008] UKHL 61;

ments) are similarly not normally suited to decision by courts.[18] Decisions taken by experts,[19] and those best able to calculate risk, indicate some measure of institutional respect.

11-007   However, even where the courts recognise their lack of relative capacity or expertise to make the primary decision,[20] they should nevertheless not easily relinquish their secondary function of probing the quality of the reasoning and ensuring that assertions are properly justified[21] or unnecessarily onerous or oppressive. And even policy decisions may contain within them a legal or constitutional principle (the decision of the hospital might, for example, engage a Convention right or fundamental right recognised by the common law) which is the court's to safeguard (for example, where the policy was applied in a discriminatory fashion or offended the right to life). As Lord Nicholls said in *Ghaidan v*

[2009] 1 A.C. 453 at [132] (Lord Carswell: "Decisions about how far to accommodate such concerns and wishes are very much a matter for ministers, who have access to a range of information not available to the courts and are accountable to Parliament for their actions. I think that courts should be more than a little slow to pin that butterfly to the wheel"—about the possibility of a policy for resettlement of the Chagos Islands).

[18]   This point has been made most forcefully by Lord Hoffmann, "Separation of Powers" [2002] J.R. 137 and his statement in *R. v Secretary of State for the Environment, Transport and the Regions Ex p. Holdings & Barnes Plc* (the Alconbury case) [2001] UKHL 23; [2003] 2 A.C. 295 at [75]–[76], where he distinguished "policy decisions" from a "determination of right". Policy decisions should be made not by the courts, he said, but, in a democracy by "democratically elected bodies or persons accountable to them". In *Grape Bay Ltd v Attorney General of Bermuda* [2000] 1 W.L.R. 574 at 585 (Lord Hoffmann, for the PC, held that a restriction on the expansion of a US restaurant chain in Bermuda was a "pure question of policy, raising no issue of human rights or fundamental principle" and the matter was therefore "pre-eminently one for democratic decision by the elected branch of government").

[19]   See, e.g. *R. v Secretary of State for the Home Department Ex p. Swati* [1986] 1 W.L.R. 477; *R. v Chief Constable of the Merseyside Police Ex p. Calveley* [1986] 1 Q.B. 424; *Pulhofer v Hillingdon LBC* [1986] A.C. 484; *R. v Secretary of State for Social Services Ex p. Stitt* [1990] C.O.D. 288; *R. (on the application of W) v Thetford Youth Justices* [2002] EWHC 1252 (Admin); [2003] 1 Cr. App. R. (S.) 67 at [40] (Sedley LJ: "A youth court has expertise which a higher court lacks"); *R. (on the application of Legal Remedy UK Ltd) v Secretary of State for Health* [2007] EWHC 1252 (Admin); (2007) 96 B.M.L.R. 191 (court wary of "donning the garb of policy maker" in challenge to restructuring of postgraduate medical training).

[20]   See, e.g. *R. (on the application of Farrakhan) v Secretary of State for the Home Department* [2002] EWCA Civ 606; [2002] Q.B. 1391; *R. v Secretary of State for the Home Department Ex p. Turgut* [2001] 1 All E.R. 719 at 729 (Simon Brown LJ: "The court is hardly less well placed than the Secretary of State himself to evaluate the risk once the relevant material is placed before it"). *R. (on the application of Lord Carlile of Berriew) v Secretary of State for the Home Department* [2014] UKSC 60; [2015] A.C. 945 (refusal to allow the entry of a dissident Iranian politician into the United Kingdom) at [105] per Baroness Hale DPSC: "The court has a particular expertise in assessing the importance of fundamental rights and protecting individuals against the over-mighty power of the state or the majority. The Government has much greater expertise in assessing risks to national security or the safety of people for whom we are responsible." In *Bank Mellat v HM Treasury* [2013] UKSC 39; [2014] A.C. 700 (Order in Council prohibiting transactions or business relationships with Iranian Bank to prevent development of nuclear weapons in Iran) at [21] Lord Sumption cautioned against the court taking over the functions of the executive, least of all in the area of foreign policy and national security "which would once have been regarded as unsuitable for judicial scrutiny"; the question whether a measure was apt to limit the risk posed for the national interest by nuclear proliferation was "pre-eminently a matter for the executive". He endorsed the view of Lord Reed JSC that "the making of government and legislative policy cannot be turned into a judicial process". Lord Sumption JSC, in a majority of five to four, nevertheless allowed the Bank's appeal on the ground, inter alia, that the Order in Council was not a rational or proportionate response to the aim of hindering Iran's nuclear ambitions.

[21]   T.R.S. Allan, "Human Rights and Judicial Review: a Critique of 'Due Deference'" [2006] C.L.J. 671 at 693.

Godin-Mendoza[22] in respect of national housing policy:

"Parliament has to hold a fair balance between the competing interests of tenants and landlords, taking into account broad issues of social and economic policy. But, even in such a field, where the alleged violation comprises differential treatment based upon grounds such as race or sex or sexual orientation the court will scrutinize with intensity any reasons said to constitute justification".

In addition, as was reflected in *Huang*,[23] there are some matters in which the **11-008** determination of policy by the legislative or executive branch is deficient. Lord Bingham distinguished between a case which concerns established housing policy[24]—where the result represented "a considered democratic compromise", and where all parties were represented in the debate and where the issue involved the allocation of finite resources—and with the situation in immigration policy where those elements were not present.[25] In cases, therefore, where relevant interests have not been well represented, and where there are other reasons for confidence in the relative institutional capacity of the courts to decide the matter, courts can quite properly review the substance or justification of the matter in question.

Political mandate and respect for the view of Parliament and the executive

The courts have on occasion regarded it as relevant to the reasonableness of a **11-009** decision of a Minister that the decision had by resolution been approved by one or both Houses of Parliament.[26] While these resolutions of course fall short of statutory authority, they may constitute strong evidence of the reasonableness of a decision. But such evidence should not be regarded by the courts as conclusive proof of unreasonableness.[27] The resolutions cannot make what is unreasonable, reasonable. The resolutions do not have the imprimatur of statutes and so do not excuse the courts from performing their proper role. Subordinate legislation has been held unreasonable despite the fact it was approved in Parliament and supported by ministerial statements. As Lord Phillips of Matravers MR put it,

"the 'wider principle' of common law must accommodate the right and the duty of the Court to review the legality of subordinate legislation. The fact that, in the course of debate, the Secretary of State or others make statements of fact that support the legitimacy

---

[22] *Ghaidan v Godin-Mendoza* [2004] UKHL 30; [2004] 2 A.C. 557 at [19]. A similar view was taken in respect of fair trial rights at [36]. But compare *R. (on the application of Carson) v Secretary of State for Work and Pensions* [2005] UKHL 37; [2006] 1 A.C. 17 at [57]; *R. (on the application of Williamson) v Secretary of State for Education and Employment* [2005] UKHL 15; [2005] 2 A.C. 246 at [57]; *Leeds Group Plc v Leeds City Council (No.2)* [2011] EWCA Civ 1447; [2012] 1 W.L.R. 1561 at [49].

[23] *Huang v Secretary of State for the Home Department* [2007] UKHL 11; [2007] 2 A.C. 167.

[24] As in *Kay v Lambeth LBC* [2006] UKHL 10; [2006] 2 A.C. 465.

[25] But see *R. (on the application of MM (Lebanon)) v Secretary of State for the Home Department* [2014] EWCA Civ 985 (where the Court of Appeal was persuaded as to the Secretary of State's proposed "Minimum Income Requirement" for a UK partner to sponsor the entry of a non EEA partner) at [148] per Aikens LJ: "… appropriate weight has to be given to the judgment of the Secretary of State, particularly where, as here, she has acted on the results of independent research and wide consultations".

[26] *R. v Secretary of State for the Environment Ex p. Nottinghamshire CC* [1986] A.C. 240 at 247 (Lord Scarman); *R. v Secretary of State for the Environment Ex p. Hammersmith & Fulham LBC* [1991] 1 A.C. 521 at 597 (Lord Bridge).

[27] In *R. v Secretary of State for the Home Department Ex p. Brind* [1991] 2 A.C. 696, the Home Secretary's directions were also approved by both Houses of Parliament. Yet the directives that were held partially invalid in *R. v Immigration Appeal Tribunal Ex p. Begum Manshoora* [1986] Imm. A.R. 385 had also been laid before Parliament.

of the subordinate legislation, and that the House thereafter approves the subordinate legislation, cannot render it unconstitutional for the Court to review the material facts and form its own judgment, even if the result is discordant with statements made in parliamentary debate".[28]

11-010   In *Huang v Secretary of State for the Home Department*, the House of Lords found unpersuasive the submission of the Secretary of State that the decision-maker and the court should assume that the immigration rules adopted by the responsible Minister and laid before Parliament "had the imprimatur of democratic approval and should be taken to strike the right balance between the interests of the individual and those of the community".[29] In other cases the courts have deferred to the judgement of public authorities on the ground that they were elected and are politically accountable for their actions.[30] However, political and legal authority should be distinguished, and the courts should not automatically defer to the legislature as they would thus be abdicating their own fundamental responsibility to determine whether the matter in question is lawful.[31]

11-011   Sometimes local authorities have asserted that their mandate from the electorate permits them to implement a policy without legal restraint. In *Bromley*[32] the Greater London Council justified a 25 per cent reduction in transport fares partly on the basis that the recent election had given them a "mandate" to lower the fares in the way the successful majority party had promised in its electoral manifesto. The House of Lords disagreed; those elected had to consider the interests of all the inhabitants of the area, in the light of their legal duties.[33] In the *Tameside* case[34] the local authority introduced a scheme, promised at a recent local election, to abolish

---

28   R. (on the application of Javed) v Secretary of State for the Home Department [2001] EWCA Civ 789; [2002] Q.B. 129 at [37] (holding a statutory instrument, approved by resolution of both Houses of Parliament, was unreasonable).

29   *Huang v Secretary of State for the Home Department* [2007] UKHL 11; [2007] 2 W.L.R. 581 at [17]; cf. *Kay v Lambeth LBC* [2006] UKHL 10; [2006] 2 A.C. 465, where such an assumption was made in relation to housing policy.

30   *Secretary of State for Home Affairs v Rehman* [2001] UKHL 47; [2003] 1 A.C. 153 at [62] (Lord Hoffmann); *International Transport Roth GmbH v Secretary of State for the Home Department* [2002] EWCA Civ 158; [2003] Q.B. 728 at [27] (Laws LJ).

31   D. Dyzenhaus, "The Politics of Deference: Judicial Review and Democracy" in M. Taggart (ed), *The Province of Administrative Law* (1997); J. Jowell, "Judicial Deference and Human Rights: A Question of Competence" in P. Craig and R. Rawlings (ed), *Law and Administration in Europe; Essays in Honour of Carol Harlow* (2003), p.67; J. Jowell, "Judicial Deference: Servility, Civility or Institutional Capacity?" [2003] P.L. 592; R. Clayton, "Judicial Deference and the Democratic Dialogue: The Legitimacy of Judicial Intervention Under the HRA 1998" [2004] P.L. 33; R. Clayton, "Principles for Due Deference" [2006] J.R. 109; Lord Justice Dyson, "Some Thoughts on Judicial Deference" [2006] J.R. 103; R. Edwards, "Judicial Deference under the HRA" (2002) 65 M.L.R. 859; Lord Steyn, "Deference: a Tangled Story" [2005] P.L. 346 and "2000–2005: Laying the Foundations of Human Rights Law in the United Kingdom" [2005] E.H.R.L.R. 349, 359. M. Hunt, "Why Public Law Needs 'Due Deference'", in N. Bamforth and P. Leyland (eds), *Public Law in a Multi-Layered Constitution* (2003), p.351; T.R.S. Allan, "Human Rights and Judicial Review: A Critique of 'Due Deference'" [2006] C.L.J. 671; A. Barak, *The Judge in a Democracy* (2006), pp.251–252. And see J. Jowell, "What Decisions Should Judges Not Take?" in M. Andenas and D. Fairgrieve (eds), *Tom Bingham and the Transformation of the Law* (2009), Ch.9; A. Kavanagh, "Judging Judges under the Human Rights Act: Deference, Disillusionment and the 'War on Terror'" [2009] P.L. 287. For justiciability in the area of foreign affairs and international law, see D. Goldrick, "The Boundaries of Justiciability" (2010) 59 I.C.L.Q. 981. For deference approached from the perspective of administrative decision makers, see M. Lewans, *Administrative Law and Judicial Deference* (2016).

32   *Bromley LBC v GLC* [1983] 1 A.C. 768.

33   Cited with approval in *R. (on the application of Island Farm Developments Ltd) v Bridgend County BC* [2006] EWHC 2189; [2007] B.L.G.R. 60 at [23] (Collins J); and *R. v Secretary of State for Employment Ex p. Begbie* [2001] 1 W.L.R. 1115 (pre-election promise does not create a legitimate expectation).

34   *Secretary of State for Education and Science v Tameside MBC* [1977] A.C. 1014.

certain recently established comprehensive schools and to reintroduce grammar schools by a process of selection, all in a period of four months. The Secretary of State sought to intervene under s.68 of the Education Act 1944 which permitted him to do so when "he was satisfied" that a local authority were acting "unreasonably". The House of Lords held that the Secretary of State did not in those circumstances have the power to intervene because the council had not acted unreasonably in the *Wednesbury* sense. This decision was considerably influenced by the fact that the local authority was recently elected, with a mandate to reintroduce grammar schools. While superficially contradictory, these two cases were decided on different grounds. The *Bromley* case was decided on the basis of the council exceeding the particular powers established in the governing statute. It is therefore authority for the correct proposition that no "mandate" from the electorate can serve as a justification for an illegal act.[35] In *Tameside*, although the scope of the governing statute was in issue, the case turned on the unreasonableness of the local authority's behaviour. A manifesto commitment may be relevant evidence of the reasonableness of a decision which permits a range of lawful courses of action. It should never, however, be taken as conclusive proof of reasonableness, as other factors may be weighed against it.[36]

THE WEDNESBURY FORMULATION AND ITS SUBSEQUENT DEVELOPMENT

Substantive review in English law has been dominated by the concept of unreasonableness closely identified with the famous formulation by Lord Greene MR in the *Wednesbury* case,[37] that the courts can only interfere if a decision "is so unreasonable that no reasonable authority could ever come to it".[38] Our law is filled with examples of phrases that set general standards of behaviour so there is nothing intrinsically unacceptable about the notion of "reasonableness" as a guide to ac-

11-012

---

[35] In *Bromley*, Lord Denning, in the CA, [1982] 2 W.L.R. 62 said that a manifesto should "not be taken as gospel ... When a party gets into power, it should consider any proposal or promise afresh, and on its merits". And see his reservations about the doctrine of the mandate in *The Changing Law* (1953) where he wrote: "Some people vote for [a member] because they approve of some of the proposals in his party's manifesto, others because they approve of others of the proposals. Yet others because, while they do not really approve of the proposals, they disapprove still more of the counter-proposals of the rival party, and so forth. It is impossible to say therefore that the majority of the people approve of any particular proposal, let alone every proposal in the manifesto" (at pp.8–10).

[36] See also *R. v Somerset CC Ex p. Fewings* [1995] 1 All E.R. 513 where (in relation to the council's ban on stag-hunting over its own land) Laws J held that the fact that the council were an elected body would not influence the court to interpret "benevolently" whether the decision was within the permissible scope of the statute, "as may be the approach in the case of an assessment of the reasonableness of the exercise of a discretionary power". But see *R. (on the application of Al-Haq) v Secretary of State for Foreign and Commonwealth Affairs* [2009] EWHC 1910 (Admin); [2009] A.C.D. 76 at [59] where Cranston J said that the overall conduct of foreign policy is entrusted to those with a democratic mandate. For examples of where foreign affairs and international relations have been reviewed, see D. McGooldrick, "The Boundaries of Justiciability" (2010) 59 I.C.L.Q. 981 at 1001.

[37] *Associated Provincial Picture Houses Ltd v Wednesbury Corp* [1948] 1 K.B. 223. For a history of that case see M. Taggart, "Reinventing Administrative Law", in N. Bamforth and P. Leyland (eds), *Public Law in a Multi-Layered Constitution* (2004) at 312; for discussion of scope of *Wednesbury* review see: Lord Irvine, "Judges and Decision-Makers: the theory and practice of Wednesbury review" [1996] P.L. 59; P. Walker, "What's Wrong with Irrationality?" [1995] P.L. 556; A. Le Sueur, "The Rise and Ruin of Unreasonableness" [2005] J.R. 32; J. Goodwin, "The Last Defence of Wednesbury" [2012] P.L. 445.

[38] *Wednesbury* [1948] 1 K.B. 223 at 229–230.

ceptable administrative behaviour. As has been pointed out recently, standards in private law are often referred to by reference to those of a fictional person such as "the reasonable man" (aboard the famous Clapham omnibus). In *Healthcare at Home v Common Services Agency* Lord Reed identified other such fictional persons, such as[39]:

> "the right-thinking member of society, familiar from the law of defamation, the officious bystander, the reasonable parent, the reasonable landlord, and the fair-minded and informed observer, all of whom have had season tickets [on the Clapham Omnibus] for many years ...".

11-013   As Lord Radcliffe observed in *Davis Contractors Ltd v Fareham Urban District Council*[40]:

> "The spokesman of the fair and reasonable man, who represents after all no more than the anthropomorphic conception of justice, is and must be the court itself."

11-014   Lord Reed continued:

> "It follows from the nature of the reasonable man, as a means of describing a standard applied by the court, that it would be misconceived for a party to seek to lead evidence from actual passengers on the Clapham omnibus as to how they would have acted in a given situation or what they would have foreseen, in order to establish how the reasonable man would have acted or what he would have foreseen. Even if the party offered to prove that his witnesses were reasonable men, the evidence would be beside the point. The behaviour of the reasonable man is not established by the evidence of witnesses, but by the application of a legal standard by the court."

11-015   The standard of unreasonableness in public law provides no reference to the mind-set of a hypothetical public official. Yet, as Lords Radcliffe and Reed observed, it is the judge who is required to assess the decision. Under the *Wednesbury* test there is the added barrier that the decision must be not only unreasonable in itself but also *manifestly* unreasonable.

11-016   That formulation attempts, albeit imperfectly, to convey the point that judges should not lightly interfere with official decisions on this ground. In exercising their powers of review, judges ought not to imagine themselves as being in the position of the competent authority when the decision was taken and then test the reasonableness of the decision against the decision they would have taken. To do that would involve the courts in a review of the merits of the decision, as if they were themselves the recipients of the power. For that reason Lord Greene in *Wednesbury*[41] thought that an unreasonable decision under his definition "would require something overwhelming" (such as a teacher being dismissed on the ground of her red hair).[42] More recently, the epithets devised by judges to describe unreasonable behaviour have included decisions which are "perverse",[43] or "absurd"—implying that the decision-maker has "taken leave of his senses".[44]

11-017   In contrast, in 1898 a relatively specific account of unreasonableness in the context of a review of local authority byelaws was provided in the case of *Kruse v*

---

[39] *Healthcare at Home v Common Services Agency* [2014] UKSC 49, at [1]–[3]. The case concerned the European Union concept of the 'well-informed and normally diligent tenderer'.

[40] *Davis Contractors Ltd v Fareham Urban District Council* [1956] A.C. 696, 728.

[41] *Wednesbury* [1948] 1 K.B. 223.

[42] *Wednesbury* [1948] 1 K.B. 223 at 229. The illustration is from *Short v Poole Corp* [1926] Ch. 66.

[43] *Pulhofer v Hillingdon LBC* [1986] A.C. 484 at 518 (Lord Brightman).

[44] *R. v Secretary of State for the Environment Ex p. Notts CC* [1986] A.C. 240 at 247–248 (Lord Scarman).

Johnson.[45] Lord Russell of Killowen CJ expressed the view there that byelaws should be benevolently interpreted by the courts, but could be struck down for unreasonableness:

> "If, for instance, they were found to be partial and unequal in their operation between different classes; if they were manifestly unjust; if they disclosed bad faith; if they involved such oppressive or gratuitous interference with the rights of those subject to them such as could find no justification in the minds of reasonable men".[46]

Although this formulation includes the indeterminate notion of "manifest   **11-018**
injustice", it has the advantage of specifying aspects of unreasonableness such as unequal treatment, bad faith and decisions which constitute an unjustified interference with rights. In the *GCHQ* case,[47] in the famous passage where he formulated the "grounds" of judicial review, Lord Diplock preferred to use the term "irrational", rather than "unreasonable", which he described as applying to "a decision which is so outrageous in its defiance of logic or accepted moral standards that no sensible person who had applied his mind to the question to be decided could have arrived at it".[48] This definition is at least candid in its acknowledgement that courts can employ both logic and accepted moral standards as criteria by which to assess official decisions, but it does not assist in elucidating any more specific categories of legally unacceptable substantive decisions. In addition, as has been pointed out, the term irrationality has the drawback that it casts doubt on the mental capacity of the decision-maker,[49] whereas many decisions which fall foul of this ground of review have been coldly rational. In addition, Lord Diplock's precondition of decisions which are "outrageous" denotes a very low level of judicial scrutiny.[50] Lord Bingham has noted that the threshold of irrationality is "notoriously high", and that a claimant making a challenge under that head has "a mountain to climb".[51]

Combined with its high but uncertain threshold, the *Wednesbury* test adds   **11-019**
uncertainty to the law because of its tautological definition, defining the term "unreasonableness" in the negative by reference to the positive "reasonableness"

---

45   *Kruse v Johnson* [1889] 2 Q.B. 291.
46   Lord Russell's formulation was approved by Aikens LJ in the context of a challenge to immigration rules in *R. (on the application of MM (Lebanon)) v Secretary of State for the Home Department* [2014] EWCA Civ 985 at [94]–[95].
47   *Council of Civil Service Unions v Minister for the Civil Service* [1985] A.C. 374.
48   *Council of Civil Service Unions v Minister for the Civil Service* [1985] A.C. 374 at 410; cf. *Luby v Newcastle-under-Lyme Corp* [1964] 2 Q.B. 64 at 72. See *HMB Holdings Ltd v Antigua and Barbuda* [2007] UKPC 37 at [31], where the test of irrationality was held to apply to a decision "where no sensible person who had applied his mind to the question to be decided could have arrived at".
49   *R. v Devon CC Ex p. George* [1988] 3 W.L.R. 49 at 51 (Lord Donaldson MR: "I eschew the synonym of 'irrational', because, although it is attractive as being shorter than Wednesbury unreasonable, and has the imprimatur of Lord Diplock … it is widely misunderstood by politicians, both local and national, and even more by their constituents, as casting doubt on the mental capacity of the decision-maker, a matter which in practice is seldom, if ever, in issue"); reversed in HL [1989] A.C. 573.
50   Lord Diplock's other attempts at definitions of unreasonableness were based on the notion of "justifiabity": *Bromley LBC v Greater London Council* [1983] A.C. 768 at 821 ("decisions that, looked at objectively, are so devoid of any plausible justification that no reasonable body of persons could have reached them"); *Luby v Newcastle-under-Lyme Corp* [1964] 2 Q.B. 64 at 72 (whether the decision was "exercised in a manner which no reasonable man could consider justifiable"). Under the 1994 Interim Constitution of South Africa where "just administrative action" was enshrined as a fundamental right, it was provided that every person shall have the right to "administrative action which is justifiable in relation to the reasons given for it where any of his or her rights is affected or threatened". Compare s.33 of the current South African Constitution.
51   *R. v Lord Chancellor Ex p. Maxwell* [1997] 1 W.L.R. 104 at 109.

by which a lawful body should act.[52] Lord Greene did attempt to provide a list of administrative sins which he thought were covered by his notion of unreasonableness, all of which he considered to "overlap to a very great extent" and "run into one another".[53] These included: bad faith, dishonesty, attention given to extraneous circumstances, disregard of public policy, wrong attention given to irrelevant considerations, and failure to take into account matters which are bound to be considered. Some of these instances, particularly those referring to the taking into account of irrelevant considerations (or failing to take them into account) we have seen in Chapter 5 are today more appropriately considered as instances of illegality rather than unreasonableness, because they are extraneous to the objects or purposes of the statute under which the power is being exercised, thus taking the decision outside the "four corners" of the governing statute.

Attempts to reformulate Wednesbury

11-020   Lord Cooke opined that *Wednesbury* was

"an unfortunately retrogressive decision in English administrative law, insofar as it suggested that there are degrees of unreasonableness and that only a very extreme degree can bring an administrative decision within the legitimate scope of judicial invalidation".[54]

11-021   For that reason, there have been various attempts to reformulate the *Wednesbury* test, such as: "a decision so unreasonable that no person acting reasonably could have come to it",[55] or a decision which elicits the exclamation: "My goodness, that is certainly wrong!"[56]

These tests perhaps help to give an indication of the flavour of the conduct which qualifies as being within the concept of unreasonableness, but are no more helpful as guides to its precise parameters. Lord Cooke regretted the fact that the *Wednesbury* formula had become "established incantations in the courts of the United Kingdom and beyond".[57] He thought that judges had no need for "admonitory circumlocutions", and preferred the simple test of "whether the decision in question was one which a reasonable authority could reach".[58] He considered that such an "unexaggerated" criterion would "give the administrator ample and rightful rein, consistently with the constitutional separation of powers".[59] Under criticisms such as these, the test is being increasingly rephrased to a decision which is "within the range of reasonable responses".[60]

---

[52] *R. v IRC Ex p. Taylor (No.2)* [1989] 3 All E.R. 353 at 357 (Glidewell LJ: "... we still adhere to [the *Wednesbury* definition of unreasonableness] out of usage if not affection"); for a criticism of *Wednesbury* see J. Jowell and A. Lester, "Beyond Wednesbury: Towards Substantive Standards of Judicial Review" [1987] P.L. 368.

[53] *Wednesbury* [1948] 1 K.B. 223 at 229.

[54] *R. v Secretary of State for the Home Department Ex p. Daly* [2001] UKHL 26; [2001] 2 A.C. 532 at [32].

[55] *Champion v Chief Constable of the Gwent Constabulary* [1990] 1 W.L.R. 1 at 16 (Lord Lowry).

[56] *Neale v Hereford & Worcester CC* [1986] I.C.R. 471 at 483 (May LJ, not in the context of judicial review, but employed by the Lord Donaldson MR in *R. v Devon CC Ex p. George* [1998] 3 W.L.R. 49 and in *Piggott Brothers & Co Ltd v Jackson* [1992] I.C.R. 85).

[57] *R. v Chief Constable of Sussex Ex p. International Trader's Ferry Ltd* [1999] 2 A.C. 418.

[58] cf. *Boddington v British Transport Police* [1999] 2 A.C. 143 at 175 (Lord Steyn, asking whether the decision is "within the range of reasonable decisions open to the decision maker").

[59] *International Trader's Ferry* [1999] 2 A.C. 418 at 452.

[60] See, e.g. *Ala v Secretary of State for the Home Department* [2003] EWHC 521 at [44]–[45] (Moses J); *Edore v Secretary of State for the Home Department* [2003] EWCA Civ 716; [2003] 1 W.L.R. 2979 at [20] (Simon Brown LJ); *R. (on the application of Razgar) v Secretary of State for the Home*

Identifying Categories of Substantive Review

Given the variety of unacceptable decisions, there is probably merit in retaining   **11-022**
a residual pigeon-hole of decisions which are simply not reasonable. However, there
is also merit in the articulation of more certain standards, principles and criteria in
order to guide the behaviour of officials, affected persons and their advisors. Legal
certainty and integrity are important administrative values too, as well as being
central to the principle of the rule of law.

In the early editions of this work, unreasonableness was presented as an unusual   **11-023**
ground of review which required something "overwhelming" and was therefore
rather rare. In preparing the 5th edition, and trawling through the case law that had
developed by the 1990s, we found that there were a large number of cases where
the decision was held to be unreasonable. Deeper analysis revealed that in virtually every instance the decision could have been held unlawful on the ground of a
much more specific tenet or principle of substantive judicial review (occasionally,
but not often, then articulated independently). Of these, some require very light
scrutiny, but others do not (e.g. where the decision is simply inconsistent with previous decisions). We believe that both the accessibility of the principles of judicial
review and its coherence are best served by extrapolating those distinct tenets and
principles rather than hiding them under the general but much more vague concept
of unreasonableness, however defined.[61] Such accessibility and coherence is best
provided by recognising that these different administrative requirements fall under
very different categories, as follows.

Unreasonable process

This first category involves a material defect in the decision-making *process*.[62]   **11-024**
The assessment here focuses upon the quality of reasoning underlying or supporting the decision; upon the weight placed upon the factors taken into account on the
way to reaching the decision; upon the way the decision is justified. We shall
examine here: (a) decisions based on considerations which have been accorded
manifestly inappropriate weight; (b) strictly "irrational" decisions, namely, decisions which are apparently illogical or arbitrary; (c) decisions supported by
inadequate or incomprehensible reasons or (e) by inadequate evidence or which are
made on the basis of a material mistake or material disregard of fact.

Department (No.2) [2003] EWCA Civ 840; [2003] Imm. A.R. 529 at [40]–[41] (Dyson LJ); *Huang
v Secretary of State for the Home Department* [2005] EWCA Civ 105 (Laws LJ). See also *Anwar v
Secretary of State for the Home Department* [2010] EWCA Civ 1275; [2011] 1 W.L.R. 2552 (Sedley
LJ considering Lord Diplock's definition in the context of a "serious misuse of power"); *Gokool v
Permanent Secretary for the Ministry of Health and Quality of Life* [2008] UKPC 54 at [18] (a "decision ... within the range of reasonable responses which a reasonable decision-maker might have
made in the circumstances").

[61]   This approach received judicial endorsement from Lord Mance JSC in *Kennedy v Charity Commission (Secretary of State for Justice intervening)* [2014] UKSC 20; [2015] A.C. 455 at [55]: "But the
right approach is now surely to recognise, as *de Smith's Judicial Review*, 7th ed (2013), para.11-
028 suggests, that it is inappropriate to treat all cases of judicial review together under a general but
vague principle of reasonableness, and preferable to look for the underlying tenet or principle which
indicates the basis on which the court should approach any administrative law challenge in a
particular situation. Among the categories of situation identified in de Smith are those where a common law right or constitutional principle is in issue". See also J. Jowell, ("Proportionality and
Unreasonableness: Neither Merger Nor Takeover") in M. Elliott and H. Wiberg (eds), *The Scope and
Intensity of Substantive Review* (2015), Ch.4.

[62]   See 11-028–11-031.

Violations of common law rights or constitutional principles

11-025   Secondly, there are situations in which it is alleged that decisions taken violate common law rights or constitutional principles governing the exercise of official power.[63] These principles include the rule of law (under which a number of different values are protected, such as access to justice). Legal certainty is also an ingredient of the rule of law and therefore decisions violating certainty also infringe the rule of law. Another facet of legal certainty requires the protection of a person's legitimate expectations, which is considered in the next chapter (only because it has developed so many different requirements over the past few years, and thus merits separate treatment).[64]

11-026   Another constitutional principle is equality, which requires decisions to be consistently applied and prohibits measures which make unjustifiable or unfair distinctions between individuals.

Oppressive decisions

11-027   A third category contains what might be called oppressive decisions.[65] The focus here is upon the end-product of the decision; upon its effect on individuals (and not upon the process by which the decision was reached). Decisions may be impugned under this head because of the unnecessarily onerous impact they impose on the rights or interest of persons affected by them. While this category is more pragmatically grounded, it too is not unaffected by the fundamentally British constitutional principle which requires a person's liberties not to be unreasonably infringed.

     We now examine each of these categories in turn.

DEFECTIVE DECISION-MAKING PROCESS

11-028   This first category of grounds involves some defect in the process of arriving at the decision; in the way the decision was reached or in the manner by which it has been justified. The focus here is thus upon the factors taken into account by the decision-maker on the way to making the decision; the evidence by which the decision was influenced or the quality of it justification. We shall first look at decisions where the considerations taken into account are wrongly balanced; then at strictly "irrational" decisions, for instance those that are based upon the lack of ostensible logic; and finally at those which depend upon an error of fact.

Balance of relevant considerations

11-029   As we have seen in Chapter 5, the question of what is a relevant or material consideration is a question of law, whereas the question of what weight to be given to it is a matter for the decision-maker. However, where undue weight is given to any particular consideration, this may result in the decision being held to be unreasonable, and therefore unlawful, because manifestly excessive or manifestly inadequate weight has been accorded to a relevant consideration.[66] As we shall see below, English law may stand at the brink of a development that would allow a

---

[63] See 11-052–11-068.
[64] See Ch.12.
[65] See 11-069–11-072.
[66] This passage was approved by Silber J in *Secretary of State for Trade and Industry Ex p. BT3G Ltd* [2001] Eu.L.R. 325 at [187] (see subsequently [2001] EWCA Civ 1448). See also *R. (on the ap-*

more direct question to be asked in this situation, namely whether a decision is unlawful because it is disproportionate (without needing to have regard to the concept of unreasonableness).[67]

The law reports contain countless examples of the unreasonableness approach to balance. In the context of town and country planning, for instance, a local authority, or the Secretary of State on appeal, may, in considering whether to grant a permission for the change of use of a building, have regard not only to the proposed new use but also to the existing use of the building and weigh the one against the other. The courts are concerned normally to leave the balancing of these considerations to the planning authority.[68] However, where the refusal of planning permission is based on the preference for the preservation of the building's existing use, the refusal may be struck down in the extreme case where there is in practice "no reasonable prospect" of that use being preserved.[69] In effect, in such a case the courts are holding that the existing use is being accorded excessive weight in the balancing exercise involved. Although planning authorities are required, in deciding whether to grant or refuse planning permission, to have regard to government circulars, or to development plans,[70] a "slavish" adherence to those (relevant and material) considerations may render a decision invalid.[71] The courts have also interfered with the balancing of "material" planning considerations, by holding that excessive weight had been accorded to a planning permission that had long since expired.[72] Although these are all matters of "planning judgment" which is normally for the authority to decide, courts are not "shy in an appropriate case of concluding that it would have been irrational of a decision-maker to have had regard to an alternative proposal as a material consideration or that, even if possibly he should have done so, to have given it any or any sufficient weight".[73]

11-030

In licensing cases it has also been held that too much weight had been placed by an authority upon recent precedent refusing refreshment licences and too little on the 50-year previous enjoyment of the licence by the claimant.[74] Similarly, an adjudicator on an asylum appeal, who had reversed the Secretary of State's decision to deport an asylum seeker who had served a prison sentence in the United Kingdom, had placed excessive weight upon the risk of the appellant re-offending,

11-031

---

plication of Sainsbury's Supermarkets Ltd) v Wolverhampton City Council [2010] UKSC 20; [2011] 1 A.C. 437; Secretary of State for the Home Department v AP (No.1) [2010] UKSC 24; [2011] 2 A.C. 1 (Lord Brown said that "The *weight* to be given to a relevant consideration is, of course, always a … matter for the decision-maker—subject only to the challenge for irrationality").

[67] See 11-073—11-085. And see R. (on the application of Gallagher) v Basildon DC [2010] EWHC 2824 (Admin); [2011] P.T.S.R. 731 at [41] (Parker J said that "the challenged decision has given manifestly disproportionate weight to certain considerations").

[68] Tesco Stores v Secretary of State for the Environment [1995] 1 W.L.R. 759, HL.

[69] London Residuary Body v Lambeth LBC [1990] 1 W.L.R. 744; Westminster City Council v British Waterways Board [1985] A.C. 676 at 683 (Bridge LJ: "In a contest between the planning merits of two competing uses, to justify refusal of permission for use B on the sole ground that use A ought to be preserved, it must, in my view, be necessary at least to show a balance of probability that, if permission is refused for use B, the land in dispute will be effectively put to use A"); Nottinghamshire CC v Secretary of State for the Environment, Transport and the Regions [2001] EWHC Admin 293; [2002] 1 P. & C.R. 30.

[70] See 5-088–5-089.

[71] Simpson v Edinburgh Corp 1960 S.C. 313; Niarchos (London) Ltd v Secretary of State for the Environment (1977) 35 P. & C.R. 259; R. v Derbyshire CC Ex p. Woods [1997] J.P.L. 958.

[72] South Oxfordshire DC v Secretary of State for the Environment [1981] 1 W.L.R. 1092.

[73] R. (on the application of Mount Cook Land Ltd) v Westminster CC [2003] EWCA Civ 1346; [2004] C.P. Rep. 12 at [33] (Auld LJ).

[74] R. v Flintshire County Licensing Committee Ex p. Barrett [1957] 1 Q.B. 350.

and insufficient weight upon the character of the offence.[75] And where the police, in the face of disruptive demonstrations by animal welfare groups, withdrew protection from the exporters of animals for certain days of the week, it was held by the House of Lords that the considerations taken into account (e.g. pressures on police protection elsewhere in the county) had been fairly balanced against the danger to the rule of law that the withdrawal of protection would entail.[76]

Rationality: logic and reasoning

11-032   Although the terms irrationality and unreasonableness are these days often used interchangeably, irrationality is only one facet of unreasonableness.[77] A decision is irrational in the strict sense of that term if it is unreasoned; if it is lacking ostensible logic or comprehensible justification. Instances of irrational decisions include those made in an arbitrary fashion, perhaps "by spinning a coin or consulting an astrologer".[78] In such cases claimant does not have to prove that the decision was "so bizarre that its author must have been temporarily unhinged", but merely that the decision simply fails to "add up—in which, in other words, there is an error of reasoning which robs the decision of logic".[79]

11-033   "Absurd" or "perverse" decisions may be presumed to have been decided in that fashion, as may decisions where the given reasons are simply unintelligible. Less extreme examples of the irrational decision include those in which there is an absence of logical connection between the evidence and the ostensible reasons for the decision, where the reasons display no adequate justification for the decision, or where there is absence of evidence in support of the decision. Mistake of material fact may also, according to recent cases, render a decision unlawful.

11-034   We have seen that the absence of reasons for a decision may constitute a breach

---

75   R. (Kenya) v Secretary of State for the Home Department [2004] EWCA Civ 1094; The Times, 13 September 2004 (May and Judge LJJ, Sedley LJ dissenting); also R. (on the application of Harris) v Secretary of State for the Home Department [2001] EWHC Admin 225; [2001] I.N.L.R. 584 (unreasonable to refuse leave to re-enter the UK to a person who had made a brief visit to a dying relative abroad, on the ground of a previous conviction which itself would not have been a ground for deportation); R. (on the application of Rahman) v Secretary of State for the Home Department [2015] EWHC 1146 (Admin); [2015] A.C.D. 107 (irrational for the Home Secretary to ignore findings of fact made by the Asylum and Immigration Tribunal when refusing to renew a passport).

76   R. v Chief Constable of Sussex Ex p. International Trader's Ferry Ltd [1999] 2 A.C. 418; Lord Hoffmann, "A Sense of Proportion" (1997) The Irish Jurist 49. But substantial withdrawal of police protection was held to be unlawful and a violation of the rule of law: R. v Coventry City Council Ex p. Phoenix Aviation [1995] 3 All E.R. 37.

77   R. v Secretary of State for the Home Department Ex p. Omibiyo [1996] 2 All E.R. 901 at 912 (Sir Thomas Bingham MR: "I would accordingly incline to accept the Secretary of State's argument on this point, while observing that decisions reached by him are susceptible to challenge on any Wednesbury ground, of which irrationality is only one").

78   R. v Deputy Industrial Injuries Commissioner Ex p. Moore [1965] 1 Q.B. 456 at 488 (Diplock LJ); R. v Lambeth LBC Ex p. Ashley (1997) 29 H.L.R. 385 (points scheme for the allocation of housing was plainly "illogical and irrational"); R. v Islington LBC Ex p. Hassan (1995) 27 H.L.R. 485 (finding of intentional homelessness illogical).

79   R. v Parliamentary Commissioner for Administration Ex p. Balchin [1998] 1 P.L.R. 1, 13, cited in R. (on the application of Norwich and Peterborough Building Society) v Financial Ombudsman Service Ltd [2002] EWHC 2379 (Admin); [2003] 1 All E.R. (Comm) 65 at [59]. See also R. (on the application of A) v Liverpool Council [2007] EWHC 1477(Admin); (2007) 10 C.C.L. Rep. 716 at [39] (the decision "lacks logic to such a degree as is unreasonable"). Also, R. (on the application of Demetrio) v Independent Police Complaints Commission [2015] EWHC 593 (Admin); [2015] A.C.D. 98 at [65]: "Whether the lack of ostensible logic is sufficient to render the decision irrational …".

of a fair hearing.[80] Irrationality may also sometimes be inferred from the absence of reasons.[81] When reasons are required, either by statute or by the growing common law requirements, or where they are provided, even though not strictly required, those reasons must be both "adequate and intelligible".[82] They must therefore both rationally relate to the evidence in the case,[83] and be comprehensible in themselves.[84] The reasons for a decision must not be "self-contradictory".[85]

As we shall see, one of the ingredients of proportionality as applied under European Union law, and under the HRA when applying Convention rights, is that the objectives of a decision or policy must bear a "rational connection" to the measures designed to further the objectives.[86] A similar approach is taken to the notion of unreasonableness or irrationality in domestic law, as shown in a case where a non-statutory scheme was introduced to provide compensation for British civilians interned during World War II by the Japanese. The scheme excluded individuals whose parents or grandparents were not born in the United Kingdom. The Court of Appeal examined carefully whether the exclusion bore a rational connection to the "foundation" and "essential character" of the scheme, but held in the circumstances that the scheme did not fail the *Wednesbury* test.[87] The House of Lords had adopted a similar approach in a case where, under an ex-gratia compensation scheme, British soldiers injured in Bosnia were accorded treatment different from those injured in Northern Ireland.[88] **11-035**

Inadequate evidence and mistake of fact

Since courts in judicial review are concerned with the law and not the merits of a case, they will not normally interfere with a public authority's assessment of the evidence or the facts.[89] Sometimes there is a double limitation on review for fact, for the courts may be reviewing the decision of an appeal tribunal which itself had **11-036**

---

[80] See Ch.7.

[81] *Padfield v Minister of Agriculture Fisheries and Food* [1968] A.C. 997 at 1032, 1049, 1053, 1054, 1061–1062; *Lonrho Plc v Secretary of State for Trade and Industry* [1989] 1 W.L.R. 525 at 539; *R. v Civil Service Appeal Board Ex p. Cunningham* [1991] 4 All E.R. 310. But it may not be possible for the court to infer unreasonableness from the lack of reasons, see e.g. *R. v Secretary of State for the Home Department Ex p. Adams* [1995] E.C.R. 177 (Steyn LJ and Kay J).

[82] See Ch.7.

[83] *Re Poyser and Mills' Arbitration* [1964] 2 Q.B. 467 at 478 (Megaw J, speaking of the duty to give reasons imposed by the Tribunals and Inquiries Act 1958 s.12 said that the required reasons "must be read as meaning that proper adequate reasons must be given ... which deal with the substantial points that have been raised").

[84] In *R. v Hammersmith and Fulham LBC Ex p. Earls Court Ltd, The Times,* 7 September 1993, it was held that a condition imposed upon an entertainment licence which was so obscure that it necessitated the issue of a construction summons was "unreasonable in the Wednesbury sense" (Kennedy LJ).

[85] *Mahon v Air New Zealand Ltd* [1984] A.C. 808 at 835 PC (Lord Diplock required the finding to be based on some material that tends logically to show the existence of facts consistent with the finding).

[86] See 11-080 for the test propounded in *De Freitas v Permanent Secretary of the Ministry of Agriculture, Fisheries, Land and Housing* [1999] 1 A.C. 69, 80 (Lord Clyde), applied by Lord Steyn in *R. (on the application of Daly) v Secretary of State for the Home Department* [2001] UKHL 26; [2001] 2 A.C. 532 at [27].

[87] *R. (on the application of Association of British Civilian Internees (Far East Region)) v Secretary of State for Defence* [2003] EWCA Civ 473; [2003] Q.B. 1397 at [40].

[88] *R. v Ministry of Defence Ex p. Walker* [2000] 1 W.L.R. 806 at 812 (Lord Slynn: "It is not for the courts to consider whether the scheme ... is a good scheme or a bad scheme, unless it can be said that the exclusion is irrational or unreasonable that no reasonable Minister could have adopted it"); Lord Hoffmann considered the distinction to be "fine" but not irrational: "That is too high a hurdle to surmount".

[89] See generally: I. Yeats, "Findings of Fact: The Role of the Courts", in G. Richardson and H. Genn

jurisdiction only to review the primary decision for errors of "law".[90] The complexity intensifies in the light of the notorious difficulty of making a clear distinction between law and fact.[91] These days the prohibition on the court's assessment of fact is being blurred by the requirement that the decision-maker justify all aspects of a decision—be it law, fact, judgement or policy. In addition, when the principle of proportionality is engaged, a closer assessment of fact may be required. Authorities acting on behalf of the public ought to be accountable for the overall quality of the decision-making process. Nevertheless, in general courts in judicial review, which is not appeal, should leave assessment of evidence and fact to the primary decision-maker, who is in any event often in a better position than the court accurately to evaluate the facts of a case and to decide their merits. We should therefore briefly consider the difference between law and fact and then go on to consider under what circumstances the courts may interfere on the ground of inadequate evidence or mistake of fact.

Fact and law distinguished

11-037   There is often no difficulty in distinguishing a question of law from one of fact. A finding of fact may be defined as an assertion that a phenomenon exists, has existed or will exist, independently of any assertion as to its legal effect.[92] The meaning that a lawyer should attribute to the terms of a policy of insurance is a question of law; the question whether the holder of a policy has renewed the policy before its expiry is one of fact.

11-038   Perplexing problems may, however, arise in analysing the nature of the process by which a public authority determines whether a factual situation falls within or without the limits of standard prescribed by a statute or other legal instrument. Every finding by a public authority postulates a process of abstraction and inference. At what point does an inference drawn from facts become an inference of law?

(eds), *Administrative Law and Government Action* (1994), Ch.6; T. Jones, "Mistake of Fact in Administrative Law" [1990] P.L. 507; M. Kent, "Widening the Scope of Review for Error of Fact" [1999] J.R. 239; M. Demetriou and S. Houseman, "Review for Error of Fact: a Brief Guide" [1997] J.R. 27 (comparison of mistake of fact with the notion of "manifest error" as applied by the ECJ). It should not be assumed—as it has been on occasion in the past—that the judicial review procedure is inherently unsuited to dealing with disputes of fact. In *Birmingham City Council v Doherty* [2008] UKHL 57; [2009] 1 A.C. 367 (an appeal in relation to an eviction from a caravan site after 17 years), Lord Scott of Foscote observed that permission for judicial review "is not usually given where the challenge raises and depends upon disputed issues of fact." See also *E (A Child) v Chief Constable of Ulster* [2008] UKHL 66; [2009] 1 A.C. 536 at [31] (in judicial review challenge to the way the police had handled incidents of loyalist violence in 2001, acknowledging that factual disputes about what was said at meetings "cannot readily be resolved in judicial review proceedings"). However, this view seems to be altering. See e.g. *Manchester City Council v Pinnock* [2010] UKSC 45, where Lord Neuberger at [74] said: "Where it is required in order to give effect to an occupier's Article 8 Convention rights, the court's powers of review can, in an appropriate case, extend to reconsidering for the itself the facts found by the local authority, or indeed to considering facts which have arisen since the issue of proceedings by hearing evidence and forming its own view".

[90] See, e.g. Tribunals, Courts and Enforcement Act 2007 s.11 (right of appeal "on any point of law" from First-tier Tribunal to Upper Tribunal); an appeal on point of law lies from decisions of housing authorities to the county courts. See further Ch.17.

[91] *Moyna v Secretary of State for Work and Pensions* [2003] UKHL 44; [2003] 1 W.L.R. 1929 at [22] (test set out in the Social Security Contributions and Benefits Act 1972 s.72 is a notional test to be construed in a general sense, and a person's ability to cook a meal is not to be assessed on a day-to-day basis but rather with regard to a whole period). In *Gillies v Secretary of State for Work and Pensions* [2006] UKHL 2; [2006] 1 W.L.R. 781 at [4]–[7] (Lord Hope: question of whether a person was biased was a question of law); on bias, see Ch.10.

[92] The 5th edition of this work contained a fuller account of the distinction between law and fact in Ch.5 ("Jurisdiction, Law and Fact"), most of which was written by de Smith.

Scrutton LJ suggested that if a judge agrees with a decision of the primary decision-maker he calls it one of fact, but "if he disagrees with them then that is one of law, in order that he may express his own opinion the opposite way".[93] Although this statement may appear cynical, it expresses the view that the purpose of distinguishing law and fact is to delineate a limit on the autonomy of the primary decision-maker.[94]

Matters of degree

What has been called a question of a matter of degree, is a matter of fact but one on which reasonable persons may arrive at different conclusions on the evidence before them.[95] Examples of such questions are: whether a house is "unfit for human habitation" or whether a "substantial part" of premises is to be reconstructed[96]; whether a house has changed its character because of structural alteration[97]; whether operations on land involve a "material change of use" constituting development for which planning permission is required.[98]

11-039

Questions of "mixed law and fact"

A further concept concerns questions of "mixed law and fact". Thus, whether the facts in issue are capable of falling within a category prescribed by statute may be treated as a question of law, since it entails a determination of the legal ambit of that category; whether they do fall within that category may be treated as a ques-

11-040

---

93   *Currie v Commissioners of Inland Revenue* [1921] 2 K.B. 332 at 339.

94   T. Endicott, "Questions of Law" (1998) 114 L.Q.R. 292 (in a subtle analysis, Endicott employs the example of *Couzens v Brutus* [1973] A.C. 854 on disruption of Wimbledon tennis court held not to be "insulting" behaviour, and supports the approach of *Edwards (Inspector of Taxes) v Bairstow* [1956] A.C. 14, concluding that a question of application of fact to law is a question of law when the law requires one answer to the question of application). For an example of rival submissions as to whether a step in a decision-making process involves a question of law or of fact, see *RB (Algeria) v Secretary of State for the Home Department* [2009] UKHL 10; [2010] 2 A.C. 110 at [62]. An appeal lay from a tribunal (the Special Immigration Appeals Commission) to the Court of Appeal on questions of law only. The tribunal's determination involved the following steps in relation to the issue whether the appellants would face a real risk of ill-treatment, contrary to art.3 ECHR, if they were returned to their home nations: (1) the tribunal had to direct themselves as to the appropriate test for a breach of the relevant article—a question of law; (2) the tribunal had to determine the relevant primary facts—obviously, a question of fact; (3) the tribunal had to determine whether those facts satisfied the appropriate test—was this law or fact? The House of Lords held that the assessment carried out at step (3) is a question of fact (see Lord Phillips of Worth Matravers at [73], Lord Hoffmann at [187], and Lord Hope of Craighead (at [214]). SIAC's conclusions that the facts it had found did not amount to a real risk of a flagrant breach of the relevant Convention rights could only be attacked if they were conclusions that no reasonable tribunal, properly directed, could have reached. It is however "now recognised that questions of proportionality which necessarily arise when striking the balance between private and public interests in cases involving qualified Convention rights cannot be regarded as pure questions of fact"; but the "most critical question raised in each appeal was whether the proposed deportees would face a real risk of art.3 ill-treatment on return. *Par excellence* this is a question of fact calling for an evaluation of all the evidence and ultimately a single factual judgment" (Lord Brown at [253]–[254]).

95   W. Wilson, "Questions of Degree" (1969) 32 M.L.R. 361. T. Endicott "Questions of Law" (1998) 114 L.Q.R. 292 does not approve of this distinction.

96   *Re Bowman* [1932] 2 K.B. 621; *Daly v Elstree RDC* [1949] 2 All E.R. 13; *Hall v Manchester Corp* (1915) 84 L.J.Ch. 732; *Atkinson v Bettinson* [1955] 1 W.L.R. 1127; *Bewlay (Tobacconists) Ltd v British Bata Shoe Co* [1959] 1 W.L.R. 45; and *Scurlock v Secretary of State for Wales* (1977) 33 P. & C.R. 202 (whether a building is a "dwelling-house" is a question of fact).

97   *Mitchell v Barnes* [1950] 1 K.B. 448; *Solle v Butcher* [1950] 1 K.B. 671; cf. *Pearlman v Keepers and Governors of Harrow School* [1979] Q.B. 56.

98   Town and Country Planning Act 1990 s.70.

tion of fact.[99] But the latter question can also be treated as a question of law; the factual part of a question of "mixed law and fact" is then confined to the ascertainment of the primary facts and perhaps the drawing of certain inferences from the facts.[100]

Distinction between fact, judgment and policy

11-041   Finally, mention might be made of the distinction between fact, judgment and policy. In English planning law there is a distinction between facts (which are suitable for rigorous examination at public inquiries—such as whether a building will obscure a particular view), planning judgment (the question whether the tall building will nevertheless overall improve the environment) and policy (the question whether buildings over a certain height should be allowed at all).[101]

Situations where review of fact permitted

11-042   Despite dicta attempting to restrict judicial review on questions of fact to situations where the public authority is acting "perversely",[102] review of fact has been permitted in the following situations: (a) where the existence of a set of facts is a condition precedent to the exercise of a power—a matter dealt with in Chapter 4[103]; (b) where there has been a misdirection, disregard or mistake of material fact; and (c) where the decision is unsupported by substantial evidence

Misdirection or mistake of material fact

11-043   Lord Denning contended on at least three occasions that a misdirection of fact or law could form the basis of review.[104] In the *Tameside* case,[105] judgments in both the Court of Appeal[106] and the House of Lords made similar suggestions. In particular, Lord Wilberforce said:

---

[99]   See, e.g. *White v St Marylebone BC* [1915] 3 K.B. 249; *Re Butler* [1939] 1 K.B. 570 at 579; *R. v Supplementary Benefits Commission Ex p. Singer* [1973] 1 W.L.R. 713; *Brooks and Burton Ltd v Secretary of State for the Environment* [1977] 1 W.L.R. 1294; *Clarks of Hove Ltd v Bakers' Union* [1978] 1 W.L.R. 1207 at 1217; *Bocking v Roberts* [1974] Q.B. 307; *Burton v Field & Sons Ltd* [1977] I.C.R. 106; *R. v West London Supplementary Benefits Appeal Tribunal Ex p. Wyatt* [1978] 1 W.L.R. 240.

[100]   See, e.g. *Felix v General Dental Council* [1960] A.C. 704 at 717; *Bhattacharya v General Medical Council* [1967] 2 A.C. 259 at 265; *Faridian v General Medical Council* [1971] A.C. 995.

[101]   See in particular Lord Diplock's attempt to draw that distinction in *Bushell v Secretary of State for the Environment* [1981] A.C. 75 (Lord Edmund-Davies dissenting); *R. v Secretary of State for the Environment, Transport and the Regions Ex p. Holdings & Barnes Plc* (the Alconbury case) [2001] UKHL 23; [2003] 2 A.C. 295 (distinction made between "policy decisions" and "determinations of rights").

[102]   *Pulhofer v Hillingdon LBC* [1986] A.C. 484 at 518 (Lord Brightman: "it is the duty of the court to leave the decision [of the existence or non-existence] of a fact to the public body to whom Parliament has entrusted the decision-making power save in a case where it is obvious that the public body, consciously or unconsciously, are acting perversely").

[103]   See 4-055 and following; see, e.g. *R. v Secretary of State for the Home Department Ex p. Khawajah* [1984] A.C. 74.

[104]   *Secretary of State for Employment v ASLEF (No.2)* [1972] 2 Q.B. 455 at 493; *Laker Airways v Department of Trade* [1977] 1 Q.B. 643 at 705–706; *Smith v Inner London Education Authority* [1978] 1 All E.R. 411 at 415 ("It is clear that, if the education authority or the Secretary of State have exceeded their powers or misused them, the courts can say: 'Stop'. Likewise, if they have misdirected themselves in fact or in law. I go further. If they have exercised their discretion wrongly, or for no good reason, then too the courts can interfere").

[105]   *Secretary of State for Education and Science v Tameside MBC* [1977] A.C. 1014.

[106]   See, e.g. *Tameside* [1977] A.C. 1014 at 1047 (Lord Scarman: "misunderstanding or ignorance of an

"In many statutes a minister or other authority is given a discretionary power and in these cases the court's power to review any exercise of the discretion, though still real is limited. In these cases it is said that the courts cannot substitute their opinion for that of the minister: they can interfere on such grounds as that the minister has acted right outside his powers or outside the purpose of the Act, or unfairly, or upon an incorrect basis of fact."

A number of English planning decisions have assumed that a material mistake of fact is a proper ground for the courts to quash the decision of a planning inspector.[107] Where the decision-maker has taken into account as a fact something which is wrong or where he has misunderstood the facts upon which the decision depends, such a decision is clearly an affront to justice on the ground, we would argue, that it is strictly "irrational". However, the courts have been slow to recognise mistake of material fact as a ground of judicial review, because it appears to involve the judges in assessing the merits of a decision and turns judicial review into appeal. However, there have been instances where the courts have intervened on that basis.[108]

11-044

In *R. v Criminal Injuries Compensation Board Ex p. A* Lord Slynn considered that a decision could be quashed on the basis of a mistake (in relation to material which was or ought to have been within the knowledge of the decision-maker).[109] In *Alconbury* Lord Slynn again confirmed that view, in support of the view that the jurisdiction of the courts in the United Kingdom meet the requirements of the ECHR[110] in that respect.[111] Lord Nolan considered that the matter was settled in *Edwards v Bairstow*,[112] where the House of Lords had upheld the right and duty of an appellate court to reverse a finding which had "no justifiable basis".[113] Lord

11-045

---

established and relevant fact" was within the "scope of judicial review").

[107] See, e.g. *Mason v Secretary of State for the Environment and Bromsgrove DC* [1984] J.P.L. 332 (inspector based decision on miscalculation of distance between two properties; but not material); *Jagendorf v Secretary of State* [1985] J.P.L. 771 (material error that extension would not obstruct premises when clearly would do so); *Hollis v Secretary of State for the Environment* (1984) 47 P. & C.R. 351 (Glidewell J assumes incorrect conclusion by inspector that land never had green belt status a ground for quashing the decision); and T. Jones, "Mistake of fact in Administrative Law" [1990] P.L. 507. cf. *R. v Independent Television Commission Ex p. TSW Broadcasting Ltd* [1996] E.M.L.R. 291, HL (Lord Templeman: "Judicial review does not issue merely because a decision-maker has made a mistake").

[108] See, e.g. *Hollis v Secretary of State for the Environment* (1984) 47 P. & C.R. 351 (incorrect conclusion by inspector that land never had green belt status a ground for quashing the decision); *Simplex GE Holdings Ltd v Secretary of State for the Environment* (1989) 57 P. & C.R. 306 (decision quashed because the Minister mistaken in a "material" or "significant" fact—that council had carried out a study); *Secretary of State for Education and Science v Tameside MBC* [1977] A.C. 1014 at 1030 (Lord Scarman: "misunderstanding of ignorance of an established and relevant fact" could ground a claim in judicial review), 1047 (Lord Wilberforce: need for "proper self-direction on the facts"); *Pulhofer v Hillingdon LBC* [1986] A.C. 484 at 518 (Lord Brightman: duty of a court to leave the decision as to the existence of a fact "to the public body to whom Parliament has entrusted the decision-making power, save in a case where it is obvious that the public body, consciously or unconsciously, are acting perversely"); *Wandsworth LBC v A* [2000] 1 W.L.R. 1246; *R. v Legal Aid Committee No.10 (E. Midlands) Ex p. McKenna* (1990) 2 Admin. L.R. 585 (refusal of legal aid quashed where the decision was based upon a "demonstrably mistaken view of the facts").

[109] *R. v Criminal Injuries Compensation Board Ex p. A* [1999] 2 A.C. 330 at 344–445 (citing in support of that proposition the 5th edition of this work, at p.288 and H.W.R. Wade and C. Forsyth, *Administrative Law*, 7th edn (1994), pp.316–318).

[110] ECHR art.6(1).

[111] *R. (on the application of Holding & Barnes Plc) v Secretary of State for the Environment, Transport and the Regions* [2001] UKHL 23; [2003] 2 A.C. 295 at [54].

[112] *Edwards v Bairstow* [1956] A.C. 14.

[113] *Edwards v Bairstow* [1956] A.C. 14 at [61].

Clyde held that a reviewing court could penetrate the factual areas of a decision which "are irrelevant or even mistaken".[114]

11-046   The matter of mistake or ignorance of fact was considered by the Court of Appeal in *E v Secretary of State for the Home Department*.[115] The issue concerned two asylum seekers, both of whom resisted deportation on the ground that they would risk persecution in the country to which they would be deported. The Home Secretary based his decision to deport them on the ground they would not be subject to persecution, in ignorance of other "objective evidence" to the contrary. On appeal, the Immigration Appeal Tribunal acknowledged the mistake, but refused to reopen the matter in the interest of finality. Faced with conflicting authority as to whether "misunderstanding or ignorance of an established and relevant fact"[116] could be a cause of legal invalidity, Carnwath LJ, for the court, held that mistake of fact "giving rise to unfairness" was indeed a ground on which to quash a decision on judicial review, provided that, first, there was a mistake as to an existing fact (including as to the availability of evidence on the matter). Secondly, the fact must be "established" (and thus "objective" and not "contentious"). Thirdly, the applicant or his advisers must not have been responsible for the mistake and fourthly, the mistake must have played a material (although not necessarily a decisive) part in the decision-maker's reasoning.[117] In so deciding, the Court of Appeal held that mistake of fact under those circumstances could not be absorbed into the traditional grounds of review but that it was a separate and new such ground.[118]

---

[114] *Edwards v Bairstow* [1956] A.C. 14 at [62].

[115] *E v Secretary of State for the Home Department* [2004] EWCA Civ 49; [2004] Q.B. 1044 (discussed by P. Craig, "Judicial Review, Appeal and Factual Error" [2004] P.L. 788).

[116] The words used by Lord Scarman in *Tameside* [1977] A.C. 1014.

[117] The reasoning in the *E* case has been endorsed in *R. (Iran) v Secretary of State for the Home Department* [2005] EWCA Civ 982; [2005] Imm. A.R. 535; and *MT (Algeria) v Secretary of State for the Home Department* [2007] EWCA Civ 808 at [112]. The approach adopted in the *E* case has also been followed in the following cases: *R. (on the application of Lunt) v Liverpool City Council* [2009] EWHC 2356 (Admin); [2009] All E.R. (D) 07 (Aug) (Blake J held authority responsible for approving design of taxis had fundamentally misunderstood documentary evidence about accessibility for wheelchair users); *R. (on the application of McDougal) v Liverpool City Council* [2009] EWHC 1821 (Admin) (officers of the council had made the proper inquiries of central government and they had received answers and the understanding of them was duly communicated to the members of the council who were the decision-makers. In other words, this was not a case of "unfairness resulting from misunderstanding or ignorance of established and relevant fact"); *Phelps v First Secretary of State* [2009] EWHC 1676 (Admin) at [17] (*E* described as "the leading authority on the law as it currently stands in relation to errors of fact amounting to errors of law"—but the case did not fall within the principles articulated in *E*); *VH (Malawi) v Secretary of State for the Home Department* [2009] EWCA Civ 645 at [48] (Longmore LJ: "It may well be that mistake as to an established fact which was uncontentious and objectively verifiable can constitute an error of law as stated in *E v SSHD* ... But the weight which is to be accorded to evidence properly before a tribunal cannot, to my mind, fall within that category"); *Eley v Secretary of State for Communities and Local Government* [2009] EWHC 660 (QB); [2009] All E.R. (D) 28 (Apr), [51] ("a mistake of fact by an inspector who is determining a planning appeal which gives rise to unfairness is now established as a head of challenge in an appeal" under Town and Country Planning Act 1990 s.288); *Bubbs v Wandsworth LBC* [2011] EWCA Civ 1285; [2012] P.T.S.R. 1011 at [7] (Lord Neuberger MR); *R. (on the application of Conolly) v Secretary of State for Communities and Local Government* [2009] EWCA Civ 1059; [2010] 2 P. & C.R. 1 at [37] (Rix LJ); *XX (Ethopia) v Secretary of State for Home Department* [2012] EWCA Civ 742 at [58] (no "unfairness"); *R. (March) v Secretary of State for Health* [2010] EWCA 765 (Admin.); [2012] 4 All E.R. 69 at [53]; *R. (Watt) v Hackney LBC* [2016] EWHC 1978 (Admin); [2016] A.C.D. 115 at [55]. And see generally, M. Fordham, *Judicial Review*, 6th edn (2012), paras 49.22 and 23.

[118] At [62], [63] and [66]. Thus siding with Wade and Forsyth, *Administrative Law*, 7th edn (1994), and not with Lord Slynn who in *R. v Criminal Injuries Compensation Board Ex p. A* [2007] 1 W.L.R. 977 rooted mistake of fact in a breach of natural justice. Carnwath LJ also disagreed with the 5th

Decisions unsupported by substantial evidence

This encompasses situations where there is "no evidence" for a finding upon **11-047** which a decision depends[119] or where the evidence, taken as a whole, is not reasonably capable of supporting a finding of fact. Such decisions may be impugned[120] as "irrational"[121] or "perverse", providing that this was a finding as to a material matter.[122] Should we now go further and adopt a general rule empowering the courts to set aside findings of fact by public authorities if "unsupported by substantial evidence"?[123] If such a rule were to become meaningful, it would require bodies

---

edition of this work (at p.288) that mistake of fact could be absorbed into other traditional grounds of review, such as taking into account an irrelevant consideration.

[119] *Ashbridge Investments Ltd v Minister of Housing and Local Government* [1965] 1 W.L.R. 1320; *Coleen Properties Ltd v Minister of Housing and Local Government* [1971] 1 W.L.R. 433; *Archer and Thompson v Secretary of State for the Environment and Penwith DC* [1991] J.P.L. 1027; *Hertsmere BC v Secretary of State for the Environment and Percy* [1991] J.P.L. 552; *R. v Secretary of State for Home Affairs Ex p. Zakrocki* [1996] C.O.D. 304; *R. v Newbury DC Ex p. Blackwell* [1988] C.O.D. 155 (planning committee's failure to obtain evidence of likely increase in road use on safety "unreasonable in the *Wednesbury* sense"); *R. (on the application of Trafford) v Blackpool BC* [2014] EWHC 85; [2014] 2 All E.R. 947 (see n.259 below) (no evidence that the nature of a solicitor's business whose lease the defendant council refused to renew was "wholly contrary to the stated aims and objectives" of the council).

[120] See, e.g. *Allinson v General Council of Medical Education and Registration* [1894] 1 Q.B. 750 at 760, 763; *American Thread Co v Joyce* (1913) 108 L.T. 353; *Smith v General Motor Cab Co* [1911] A.C. 188; *Doggett v Waterloo Taxi Cab Co* [1910] 2 K.B. 336; *Jones v Minister of Health* (1950) 84 Ll. L.Rep. 416; *Cababe v Walton-on-Thames UDC* [1914] A.C. 102 at 114; *Rowell v Minister of Pensions* [1946] 1 All E.R. 664 at 666; *Davies v Price* [1958] 1 W.L.R. 434 at 441-442; *R. v Birmingham Compensation Appeal Tribunal Ex p. Road Haulage Executive* [1952] 2 All E.R. 100; *Maradana Mosque Trustees v Mahmud* [1967] 1 A.C. 13; *Global Plant Ltd v Secretary of State for Social Services* [1972] 1 Q.B. 139 at 155. In India it has been held that facts may be reviewed in judicial review: *Bombay Dying v Bombay Environment Action Group* 2006 (3) S.C.C. 434 at 490 (Sinha J).

[121] Decisions unsupported by evidence have been held to be unreasonable in: *Osgood v Nelson* (1872) L.R. 5 H.L. 636; *R. v Attorney General Ex p. Imperial Chemical Industries Plc* (1986) 60 Tax Cas. 1; *R. v Birmingham City Council Ex p. Sheptonhurst Ltd* [1990] 1 All E.R. 1026 (no evidence in licensing decision on sex establishment "irrational"); *R. v Housing Benefit Review Board of Sutton LBC Ex p. Keegan* (1995) 27 H.L.R. 92 (lack of evidence of failure to pay rent rendered decision "unreasonable"); *Piggott Bros and Co Ltd v Jackson* [1992] I.C.R. 85 (Lord Donaldson MR, in the context of employment law, held that, to find a decision "perverse", the appeal tribunal had to be able to identify a finding of fact unsupported by any evidence); *Peak Park Joint Planning Board v Secretary of State for the Environment* [1991] J.P.L. 744 (a conclusion which "flew in the face of the evidence" and was "based on a view of the facts which could not reasonably be entertained" was held to be "perverse"). Sometimes such decisions have been held to involve excess of jurisdiction, e.g. *Ashbridge Investments* [1965] 1 W.L.R. 1320. Lord Diplock occasionally held that the principles of natural justice required a decision to be based on "evidential material of probative value", e.g. *Attorney General v Ryan* [1980] A.C. 718; *R. v Deputy Industrial Injuries Commissioner Ex p. Moore* [1965] 1 Q.B. 456 (reached a verdict that "no reasonable coroner could have reached"). In *R. (on the application of Mott) v Environment Agency* [2015] EWHC 314 (Admin); [2015] Env.L.R. 27 the imposition of conditions upon a licence to fish was held irrational where the decision-maker had failed to consider whether the evidence upon which it based its decision was credible and capable of supporting the conclusions drawn from it. The threshold for intervention is high: in *R. (Justice for Health) v Secretary of State for Health* [2016] EWHC 2338 (Admin); [2016] A.C.D. 119, Green J rejected an argument that mixed evidence as to the impact of a new contract for junior doctors rendered the Secretary of State's imposition of said contract irrational for being unsupported by substantial evidence, concluding, at [185] that a decision will not be irrational merely because there is "a respectable body of evidence on the other side of the argument".

[122] *Miftari v Secretary of State for the Home Department* [2005] EWCA Civ 481.

[123] As in the federal administrative law of the USA (Administrative Procedure Act of 1946 s.10(e)) and Canada (Federal Court Act 1970 s.28)). See *R. (on the application of British Sky Broadcasting Ltd) v Central Criminal Court* [2011] EWHC 3451 (Admin); [2012] Q.B. 785 at [35] ("not sufficient

which at present conduct their proceedings informally to have verbatim transcripts or to keep detailed notes of evidence.[124] In some contexts the substantive evidence rule has much to commend it; and, as we have noted, some judges have already asserted jurisdiction to set aside decisions based on clearly erroneous inferences of fact either by classifying this type of error as an error of law or merely by proceeding on the assumption that manifest error of fact makes a decision unlawful.

Evidence not before the decision-maker

11-048   One of the difficulties for the courts in permitting mistake of fact in judicial review proceedings is the extent to which they should permit evidence to be submitted which was not before the primary decision-maker. The principles for new evidence were set out clearly by Denning LJ in *Ladd v Marshall*[125] as follows: (a) when the new evidence could not with reasonable diligence have been obtained for use at the trial (or hearing); (b) the new evidence should probably have had an important (though not necessarily decisive) influence on the result of the case; and (c) the new evidence was apparently credible although it need not be incontrovertible.

11-049   In the *E* case, Carnwath LJ said that the admission of new evidence in a case where mistake of material fact was pleaded was subject to the *Marshall* principles, which might be departed from "in exceptional circumstances where the interests of justice required".[126] It should not, however, be assumed that in the English legal system the failure of a party to adduce evidence will lead the court necessarily to infer that the silence should be converted into proof against that party. As was said by Lord Lowry, "if the silent party's failure to give evidence ... can be explained ... the effect of his silence in favour of the other party may be either reduced or nullified".[127]

11-050   The wrongful rejection of evidence by a decision-maker may also amount either

---

evidence ... to enable [the judge] to reach his decision); *R. (on the application of MD (Gambia)) v Secretary of State for Home Department* [2011] EWCA Civ 121.

[124] See, e.g. *Savoury v Secretary of State for Wales* (1976) 31 P. & C.R. 344 (challenge to a clearance order failed in because of the difficulty in establishing upon what evidence, if any, the local authority decided that there was "suitable accommodation available" for those displaced); cf. *Sabey (H) & Co Ltd v Secretary of State for the Environment* [1978] 1 All E.R. 586 (written evidence admissible to show that there was no evidence upon which the inspector or the Minister could base a finding of fact). For more recent cases where new evidence has been submitted: *R. v Secretary of State for the Home Department Ex p. Turgut* [2001] 1 All E.R. 719; *A v Secretary of State for the Home Department* [2003] EWCA Civ 175; [2003] I.N.L.R. 249; *Khan v Secretary of State for the Home Department* [2003] EWCA Civ 530; *Polat v Secretary of State for the Home Department* [2003] EWCA Civ 1059.

[125] *Ladd v Marshall* [1954] 1 W.L.R. 1489 at 1491. It was not necessary to imply the *Ladd v Marshall* test, designed to place restrictions on the admission of fresh evidence in the Court of Appeal, into the disciplinary procedure of an academic institution: see *R. (on the application of Peng Hu Shi) v King's College London* [2008] EWHC 857 (Admin); [2008] E.L.R. 414 at [33] ("All that is necessary is that there should have been new evidence which was not put before or heard by the Committee, and which was for good reason not made available at the time of the hearing").

[126] *E* [2004] EWCA Civ 49 at [91]; *Iran* [2005] EWCA Civ 982; [2005] Imm. A.R. 535 (Brooke LJ carefully considers under what circumstances new evidence may be admitted by the reviewing court where there has been a change of circumstances since the original decision).

[127] *R. v Inland Revenue Commissioners Ex p. TC Coombs and Co* [1991] 2 A.C. 283 at 300; and *Gouriet v Union of Post Office Workers* [1978] A.C. 435 at 486 (Lord Dilhorne). Expert evidence may be rejected without evidence to contradict it where the matter is within the professional experience of a planning inspector: see *Kentucky Fried Chicken (GB) Ltd v Secretary of State for the Environment* (1978) 245 E.G. 839; *Ainley v Secretary of State for the Environment* [1987] J.P.L. 33. Lack of reasons may, however, permit an interference of irrationality: see the cases cited at n.99 above.

to a failure to take into account a relevant consideration[128] and or to a failure to afford procedural propriety[129] and thus render the decision unlawful.

General principles summarised

Our view is that a material mistake or disregard of a material fact in and of itself **11-051** renders a decision irrational or unreasonable.[130] In general it is right that courts do leave the assessment of fact to public authorities which are primarily suited to gathering and assessing the evidence. Review must not become appeal. On the other hand it should be presumed that Parliament intended public authorities rationally to relate the evidence and their reasoning to the decision which they are charged with making. The taking into account of a mistaken fact can just as easily be absorbed into a traditional legal ground of review by referring to the taking into account of an irrelevant consideration; or the failure to provide reasons that are adequate or intelligible, or the failure to base the decision upon any or adequate evidence. In this limited context material error of fact has always been a recognised ground for judicial intervention. Since *E*, however, the circumstances in which a decision of the primary decision-maker may be impugned on fact has been somewhat curtailed. In *Shaheen v Secretary of State for the Home Department*,[131] Brooke LJ, for the Court of Appeal, was unwilling to reopen the decision of the primary decision-maker taken on a mistaken belief that there was no evidence to refute a material fact. He suggested the following possible summary of the situation to date:

"(i)   Proof or admission that the tribunal of fact misapprehended a potentially decisive element of the evidence before it discloses an error of law (as held in the *E case*)[132]

(ii)   Proof or admission of a subsequently discovered fact permits an appellate court to set aside a decision for fraud, provided that it was potentially decisive and it can be shown that the defendant was responsible for its concealment.

(iii)   The emergence of any other class of new fact, whether contested or not, has either to be processed (within the Immigration Rules in that case) or simply lived with, as Lord Wilberforce explained in the *Ampthill Peerage* case[133] ... In any other case, finality prevails"."

---

[128]   See 5-130.
[129]   See Ch.7. See e.g. *R. v Wood* (1855) 5 E. & B. 49 (conviction after refusal to hear submission that byelaw contravened was ultra vires); *GMC v Spackman* [1943] A.C. 627 (doctor struck off register after GMC had refused to receive evidence by him to disprove adultery with patient); *R. v Kingston-upon-Hull Rent Tribunal Ex p. Black* (1949) 65 T.L.R. 209 (tribunal reduced rent after failing to give landlady opportunity to be heard on the substantial issue); *R. v Birkenhead Justices Ex p. Fisher* [1962] 1 W.L.R. 1410; *Bond v Bond* [1967] P. 39.
[130]   See, e.g. *R. (on the application of March) v Secretary of State for Health* [2010] EWHC 765 (Admin); [2010] Med. L.R. 271 at [53] (Holman J said that a decision may be quashed for "material error of fact in the reasoning process"); *R. (on the application of MD (Gambia)) v Secretary of State for the Home Department* [2011] EWCA Civ 121 at [25] (Elias LJ said that the question was whether the "conclusion [is one] which no Secretary of State on the evidence could properly reach").
[131]   *Shaheen v Secretary of State for the Home Department* [2005] EWCA Civ 1294; [2006] Imm. A.R. 57; and *Verde v Secretary of State for the Home Department* [2004] EWCA Civ 1726.
[132]   *E* [2004] EWCA Civ 49; [2004] Q.B. 1044.
[133]   *The Ampthill Peerage* [1977] A.C. 547 at 569.

VIOLATION OF COMMON LAW RIGHTS AND CONSTITUTIONAL PRINCIPLES

11-052   We turn now to consider the second category of grounds within substantive review, based upon violation of common law rights or constitutional principles. We have seen in a number of situations how the scope of an official power cannot be interpreted in isolation from general principles governing the exercise of power in a constitutional democracy.[134] The English courts have relatively recently explicitly referred to the notion of constitutional rights and principles, even in the absence of any written constitution. In the mid-1990s, even before the Human Rights Act 1998 incorporated Convention rights into domestic law, the courts adopted an approach which, instead of seeking to apply the ungrounded unreasonableness standard, based their assessment upon the rule of law and other necessary condition of a constitutional democracy. Thus the absence of a prisoner's access to a lawyer,[135] or to the press[136] was struck down not on the ground of unreasonableness (however strictly scrutinised), but on the ground that a fundamental constitutional principle (access to justice and free expression respectively) had been infringed. These principles were implied from the fact that public officials ought to maintain the standards of a modern European democracy.[137] An orthogonal principle of "legality" provided that the courts would apply the rule of law and any other constitutional principles (such as free expression) unless Parliament expressly and clearly excluded them. Ambiguity was not enough to exclude those principles. In practice, any departure from these "home grown" constitutional principles was assessed under the structured proportionality test that we shall consider below[138] under which these rights may be curtailed only to the extent necessary to meet the ends which justify their curtailment.

11-053   Judicial emphasis upon common law protection of rights has been particularly strong in recent years, especially in the Supreme Court.[139] Judges have been keen to emphasise the common ground between the common law and human rights instruments,[140] and of the continuing importance of the development of the common law.[141] The extent to which this trend is a response to uncertainty concerning the future of the Human Rights Act 1998 and the possibility of future withdrawal from the European Convention on Human Rights is a matter of debate.[142]

11-054   In Chapter 1 we outlined the constitutional justification for recognising and

---

[134] See 1-019; 5-045.

[135] *R. v Secretary of State for the Home Department Ex p. Leech (No.2)* [1994] Q.B. 198.

[136] *R. v Secretary of State for the Home Department Ex p. Simms* [2000] 2 A.C. 115.

[137] *R. v Secretary of State for the Home Department Ex p. Pierson* [1998] A.C. 539.

[138] See 11-077–11-084.

[139] See, for example: *Osborne v Parole Board* [2013] UKSC 61; [2014] A.C. 1115; *Kennedy v Information Commissioner* [2014] UKSC 20; [2015] 2 A.C. 445; *Re BBC* [2014] UKSC 25; [2015] A.C. 588; *R. (Unison) v Lord Chancellor* [2017] UKSC 51; [2017] 3 W.L.R. 409.

[140] *R. (West) v Parole Board* [2005] UKHL 1; [2005] 1 W. L.R. 350 at [44], [51]. And [63]; *A v Secretary of State for the Home Department* [2005] UKHL 71; [2006] 2 A.C. 221 at [52], [97] and [115]; *Kennedy v Information Commissioner* [2014] UKSC 20; [2015] A.C. 455 at [133]; *Re BBC* [2014] UKSC 25; [2015] A.C. 588 at [55]–[57]; *R. (Osborne) v Parole Board* [2013] UKSC 61; [2014] A.C. 1115 at [57]–[63].

[141] *R. (Guardian News and Media Ltd) v City of Westminster Magistrates' Court (Article 19 intervening)* [2012] EWCA Civ 420; [2013] Q.B. 618 at [88]; *Osborne v Parole Board* [2013] UKSC 61; [2014] A.C. 1115 at [61]; *Kennedy v Information Commissioner* [2014] UKSC 20; [2015] A.C. 455 at [46] and [133] *Re BBC* [2014] UKSC 25; [2015] A.C. 588 at [40] and [56].

[142] Lady Hale, *"UK Constitutionalism on the March?"* (Constitutional and Administrative Law Bar Association Conference, 12 July 2014); R. Clayton, "The empire strikes back: common law rights and the Human Rights Act" [2015] P.L. 3; P. Bowen "Does the renaissance of common law rights mean

protecting rights in this way which, in the absence of a codified constitution or a domestic bill of rights, might otherwise seem perplexing.[143] In Chapter 5 we considered the impact of constitutional rights upon statutory interpretation. We now examine "the common law's emphatic reassertion in recent years of the importance of constitutional rights",[144] in the context of substantive review. Among the rights acknowledged by the common law are the following.[145]

- Access to a judicial remedy.[146]
- The right to life.[147]
- The liberty of the person.[148]

---

that the Human Rights Act 1998 is now unnecessary?" [2016] E.H.R.L.R. 361. For further academic consideration of common law rights see W. Sadurski, "Judicial review of the Protection of Constitutional Rights" (2002) 22 O.J.L.S 275; M.Fordham, "Common Law Rights" [2011] J.R. 14; R. Masterman and S. Wheatle, "A common law resurgence in rights protection?" [2015] E.H.R.L.R. 57; P. Sales, "Rights and fundamental rights in English law" [2016] C.L.J. 86.

[143] *Watkins v Home Office* [2006] UKHL 17; [2006] 2 A.C. 395 at [47]–[64] (Lord Rogers).

[144] *D v Secretary of State for the Home Department* [2005] EWCA Civ 38; [2006] 1 W.L.R. 1003 at [130] (Brooke LJ).

[145] For a somewhat different attempt to catalogue the rights, see Lord Lester of Herne Hill and D. Oliver (eds), *Constitutional Law and Human Rights* (1997). For an account of judicial review that reject rights, and promotes legitimacy, as the basis for judicial review, see T. Poole, "Legitimacy, Rights and Judicial Review" (2005) 25 O.J.L.S. 697.

[146] See, e.g. *Re Boaler* [1915] 1 K.B. 21 at 36 (Scrutton J: "One of the valuable rights of every subject of the King is to appeal to the King in his Courts if he alleges that a civil wrong has been done to him, or if he alleges that a wrong punishable criminally has been done to him, or has been committed by another subject of the King"); *Raymond v Honey* [1983] 1 A.C. 1 at 11 (Lord Wilberforce—Home Secretary had no power to make prison rules to "authorise hindrance or interference with so basic a right" as the citizen's right of access to the court); *R. v Secretary of State for the Home Department Ex p. Leech* [1994] Q.B. 198, 210; *R. v Lord Chancellor Ex p. Witham* [1998] Q.B. 575 at [13] (Laws LJ: "the common law has clearly given special weight to the citizens' right of access to the courts"). Witham distinguished in *R. v Lord Chancellor Ex p. Lightfoot* [2000] Q.B. 597 and *R. (on the application of Ewing) v Department for Constitutional Affairs* [2006] EWHC 504 (Admin); [2006] 2 All E.R. 993; *A v B (Investigatory Powers Tribunal: jurisdiction)* [2008] EWHC 1512 (Admin); [2008] 4 All E.R. 511 at [12] (Collins J: "The courts of this country have always recognised that the right of a citizen to access a court is a right of the highest constitutional importance and that legislation removing that right is prima facie contrary to the rule of law"); *Seal v Chief Constable of South Wales* [2007] UKHL 31; [2007] 1 W.L.R. 1910; *Ahmed v Her Majesty's Treasury (JUSTICE intervening) (Nos 1 and 2)* [2010] UKSC 2 and [2010] UKSC 5; [2010] 2 A.C. 534 (the Al-Qaida and Taliban (United Nations Measures) Order 2006 (SI 2006/2952) was ultra vires the United Nations Act 1946 as there was a denial of fundamental rights of access to a judicial remedy. The Terrorist Asset-Freezing (Temporary Provisions) Act 2010 and subsequently the Terrorist Asset-Freezing etc Act 2010 were enacted to provide the necessary powers to implement the UN Security Council measures); see also ECHR art.6 on fair trails (See 7-117) and art.13 on effective remedies (See 13-010). *R. (on the application of the Public Law Project) v Lord Chancellor* [2016] UKSC 39; [2016] 3 W.L.R. 387 (an amendment by secondary legislation to the Legal Aid, Sentencing and Punishment of Offenders Act 2012 introducing a residence test for eligibility to legal aid was ultra vires. The power to make delegated legislation had to be construed in the context of the statutory policy and aims. The primary objective of the Act was based on funding those with a priority need. The residence test was focused entirely on reducing cost); *R. (Unison) v Lord Chancellor* [2017] UKSC 51 (fees imposed by the Lord Chancellor in respect of proceedings in employment tribunals and the employment appeal tribunal were xxx).

[147] See, e.g. *R. v Secretary of State for the Home Department Ex p. Bugdaycay* [1987] A.C. 514 at 531 (Lord Bridge, in a deportation case "The most fundamental of human rights is the individual's right to life and when an administrative decision under challenge is said to be one which may put the applicant's life at risk, the basis of the decision must surely call for the most anxious scrutiny"); *R. v Secretary of State for the Home Department Ex p. Khawaja* [1984] A.C. 74 at 110–111 (Lord Scarman). See also ECHR art.2, discussed at 7-127. For 'anxious scrutiny' see 11-093.

[148] See, e.g. *Bowditch v Balchin* (1850) 5 Exch. 378 (Pollock C.B.: "In a case in which the liberty of the subject is concerned, we cannot go beyond the natural construction of the statute"); *R. v Thames*

- The doing of justice in public.[149]
- The right to a fair hearing.[150]
- The prohibition on the retrospective imposition of criminal penalty.[151]

Magistrate Ex p. Brindle [1975] 1 W.L.R. 1400, CA (Roskill LJ: "When [a court] has to consider a matter involving the liberty of the individual, it must look at the matter carefully and strictly, and it must ensure that the curtailment of liberty sought is entirely justified by the Act relied on by those who seek that curtailment"); *Liversidge v Anderson* [1942] A.C. 206 (Lord Atkin, in his courageous dissent: "It has always been one of the pillars of freedom, one of the principles of liberty for which on recent authority we are now fighting, that the judges are no respecters of persons and stand between the subject and any attempted encroachments on his liberty by the executive, alert to see that any coercive action is justified in law"; *Raymond v Honey* [1983] 1 A.C. 1 at 13 (Lord Wilberforce: "a basic right" of prisoners to enjoy liberty not necessary for their custody)); *R. (on the application of Juncal) v Secretary of State for the Home Department* [2007] EWHC 3024 (Admin) at [47] (Wyn Williams J held that "the citizens of this country do enjoy a fundamental or constitutional right not to be detained arbitrarily at common law. That conclusion is not capable of much elaboration"); *Secretary of State for the Home Department v GG (proceedings under the Prevention of Terrorism Act 2005)* [2009] EWCA Civ 786 at [12] (Sedley LJ: "It is in my judgment axiomatic that the common law rights of personal security and personal liberty prevent any official search of an individual's clothing or person without explicit statutory authority. That these are rights customarily defined by correlative wrongs rather than by affirmative declarations is an artefact of our constitutional history; but it makes them no less real and the courts' vigilance in defence of them no less necessary"; *R. (on the application of Lumba) v Secretary of State for the Home Department (JUSTICE and another intervening)* [2011] UKSC 12; [2012] 1 A.C. 245 at [341] (Lord Brown, quoting Lord Bingham in his 2002 Romanes Lecture: "Freedom from executive detention is arguably the most fundamental right of all"). See also ECHR art.5, discussed at 13-072.

149 See, e.g. *Scott v Scott* [1913] A.C. 417 at 477 (Lord Shaw of Dunfermline: "To remit the maintenance of constitutional right to the region of judicial discretion is to shift the foundations of freedom from the rock to the sand"); *R. (on the application of Malik) v Central Criminal Court* [2006] EWHC 1539 (Admin); [2006] 4 All E.R. 1141 at [30]; *Al Rawi v Security Service (JUSTICE and other intervening)* [2011] UKSC 34; [2012] 1 A.C. 531 at [11] ("The open justice principle is not a mere procedural rule. It is a fundamental common law principle"); *R. (Guardian News and Media Ltd) v City of Westminster Magistrates' Court* [2012] EWCA Civ 420; [2013] Q.B. 618 at [69] (Lord Neuberger of Abbotsbury MR: "The open justice principle is a constitutional principle to be found not in a written text but in the common law. It is for the courts to determine its requirements, subject to any statutory provision. It follows that the courts have an inherent jurisdiction to determine how the principle should be applied"); *Kennedy v Charity Commission (Secretary of State for Justice Intervening)* [2014] UKSC 20; [2015] A.C. 455 at [110] (Lord Toulson: "It has long been recognised that judicial processes should be open to public scrutiny unless and to the extent that there are valid countervailing reasons. This is the open justice principle. The reasons for it have been stated on many occasions. Letting in the light is the best way of keeping those responsible for exercising the judicial power of the state up to the mark and for maintaining public confidence"). But see *Guardian News and Media Ltd v AB, Court of Appeal (Criminal Division)*, 12 June 2014; *The Times,* 18 June 2014, where Gross LJ stated at [2]: "Open justice is both a fundamental principle of the common law and a means of ensuring public confidence in our legal system: exceptions are rare and must be justified on the facts. Any such exceptions must be necessary and proportionate. No more than the minimum departure from open justice will be countenanced." However, open justice must give way to "the yet more fundamental principle that the paramount object of the Court is to *do* justice" (at [5]). This case was "exceptional" and, as a matter of necessity, the *core* (emphasis supplied) of the trial must be heard *in camera*. See also paras 8-009 to 8-014. See also ECHR art.6 (see 7-117).

150 See, e.g. *R. (on the application of McCann) v Manchester Crown Court* [2002] UKHL 39; [2003] 1 A.C. 787 at [29] (Lord Steyn: "Moreover, under domestic English law they undoubtedly have a constitutional right to a fair hearing in respect of such proceedings"—for a breach of an anti-social behaviour order); *Al Rawi v Security Service (JUSTICE and other intervening)* [2011] UKSC 34; [2012] 1 A.C. 531 (refusing to allow "closed material procedure" to be used in a tort claim); see now Justice and Security Act 2013; cf. *Tariq v Home Office* [2011] UKSC 35; [2012] 1 A.C. 452 (Employment Tribunal Rules of Procedure 2004 did permit closed material procedure to be used in that tribunal).

151 See, e.g. *Pierson v Secretary of State for the Home Department* [1998] A.C. 539 (Lord Steyn: "It is a general principle of the common law that a lawful sentence pronounced by a judge may not retrospectively be increased").

- Freedom of expression.[152]
- The rights of access to legal advice and to communicate confidentially with a legal adviser under the seal of legal professional privilege.[153]
- Limitations on searches of premises and seizure of documents.[154]
- Prohibition on the use of evidence obtained by torture.[155]
- That a British citizen has a fundamental right to live in, or return to, that part of the Queen's territory of which he is a citizen.[156]
- The deprivation of property rights without compensation.[157]
- The privilege against self-incrimination.[158]

---

[152] See, e.g. *Attorney-General v Guardian Newspapers Ltd (No.2) (the "Spycatcher case")* [1990] 1 A.C. 109 at 283–284 (Lord Goff, remarking that in the field of freedom of speech there is no difference in principle between English law on the subject and ECHR art.10); *Derbyshire CC v Times Newspapers Ltd* [1993] A.C. 534 at 547 (Lord Keith, in a case in which a local authority sought to sue for defamation: "it is of the highest public importance that a democratically elected body should be open to uninhibited criticism. The threat of a civil action for defamation must inevitably have an inhibiting effect on free Speech"); *R. v Secretary of State for the Home Department Ex p. Simms* [2000] 2 A.C. 115 (Lord Steyn, in a case concerning restrictions on prisoners communicating with journalists: "The starting point is the right of freedom of expression. In a democracy it is the primary right: without it an effective rule of law is not possible. Nevertheless, freedom of expression is not an absolute right. Sometimes it must yield to other cogent social interests"). See also ECHR art.10, discussed at 13-090.

[153] See, e.g. *R. v Secretary of State for the Home Department Ex p. Daly* [2001] UKHL 26; [2001] 2 A.C. 532 at [5] (Lord Bingham of Cornhill); *Colley v Council for Licensed Conveyancers (Right of Appeal)* [2001] EWCA Civ 1137; [2002] 1 W.L.R. 160 at [26] ("The right of access to a court is of fundamental constitutional importance. It is scarcely necessary to refer to authority for that obvious proposition"). See also ECHR art.8 (discussed at 13-085).

[154] See, e.g. *Marcel v Commissioner of Police* [1992] Ch. 225, CA, approving the words of Sir Nicholas Browne-Wilkinson VC reported at [1991] 2 W.L.R. 1118 ("Search and seizure under statutory powers constitute fundamental infringements of the individual's immunity from interference by the state with his property and privacy—fundamental human rights"). See also ECHR art.8 (discussed at 13-084).

[155] *A v Secretary of State for the Home Department* [2005] UKHL 71; [2006] 2 A.C. 221 at [11]–[12] (Lord Bingham of Cornhill, holding the prohibition of evidence received through torture "more aptly categorized as a constitutional principle than as a rule of evidence" and "In rejecting the use of torture, whether applied to potential defendants or potential witnesses, the common law was moved by the cruelty of the practice as applied to those not convicted of crime, by the inherent unreliability of confessions or evidence so procured and by the belief that it degraded all those who lent themselves to the practice").

[156] See, e.g. *R. v Secretary of State for the Foreign and Commonwealth Office Ex p. Bancoult* [2001] Q.B. 1067; *R. (on the application of Bancoult) v Secretary of State for Foreign and Commonwealth Affairs (No.2)* [2008] UKHL 61; [2009] 1 A.C. 453 at [44] (Lord Hoffmann "At common law, any subject of the Crown has the right to enter and remain in the United Kingdom whenever and for as long as he pleases: see *R. v Bhagwan* [1972] A.C. 60. The Crown cannot remove this right by an exercise of the prerogative. That is because since the 17th century the prerogative has not empowered the Crown to change English common or statute law. In a ceded colony, however, the Crown has plenary legislative authority. It can make or unmake the law of the land").

[157] See, e.g. *Central Control Board v Cannon Brewery Co* [1919] A.C. 744 at 752; *Bournemouth-Swanage Motor Road & Ferry Co v Harvey & Sons* [1929] 1 Ch. 686, 697; *Colonial Sugar Refining Co v Melbourne Harbour Trust Commrs* [1927] A.C. 343; *Consett Iron Co v Clavering Trustees* [1935] 2 K.B. 42, 65; *Foster Wheeler Ltd v Green (E) & Son Ltd* [1946] Ch. 101, 108; *Hall v Shoreham-by-Sea UDC* [1964] 1 W.L.R. 240; *Hartnell v Minister of Housing and Local Government* [1965] A.C. 1134; *Langham v City of London Corp* [1949] 1 K.B. 208 at 212, 213; *Burmah Oil Co v Lord-Advocate* [1965] A.C. 75 (prerogative powers; cf. War Damage Act 1965). The presumption is still stronger where powers conferred by delegated legislation are in question: *Newcastle Breweries Ltd v R.* [1920] 1 K.B. 854. But the force of the presumption is weak in the context of modern planning legislation: *Westminster Bank Ltd v Beverley BC* [1971] A.C. 508; *Hoveringham Gravels Ltd v Secretary of State for the Environment* [1975] Q.B. 754; *R. v Hillingdon LBC Ex p. Royco Homes Ltd* [1974] Q.B. 720. See also ECHR Protocol 1, art.1.

[158] See, e.g. *W v P* [2006] EWHC 1226, Ch; [2006] Ch. 549 (principle extends not only to the right to

- A duty on the State to provide subsistence to asylum-seekers.[159]
- Freedom of movement within the United Kingdom.[160]

Note however the Supreme Court's denial of a common law right to vote in *Moohan v Lord Advocate (Advocate General for Scotland intervening)*.[161]

11-055   The foundation in precedent for the presumption against the infringement of human rights in English domestic law is therefore solid. The foundation in theory is less apparent in the absence of a written constitution or enumerated bill of rights. However, fundamental rights can be properly viewed as integral features of a democratic state.[162] Freedom of speech is an obvious component of any democratic society, as are other rights, both those which address democratic procedures and those which address the treatment of individuals in a democracy.[163] Courts in other countries have recognised this explicitly.[164]

Violation of Common Law Principles

11-056   To the rights of the individual which have been recognised by the common law, we must add the common law *principles* of respect for the rule of law and equality.[165] The courts presume that these principles apply to the exercise of all public functions. Even where the decision-maker is invested with wide discretion, that discretion is to be exercised in accordance with those principles. However, as

---

refuse to answer questions but also to incriminating material); *Master Ladies Tailors Organisation v Minister of Labour and National Service* [1950] 2 All E.R. 525 at 528; *Howell v Falmouth Boat Construction Co* [1951] A.C. 837. cf. *Sabally and Njie v Attorney General* [1965] 1 Q.B. 273; *R. v Pentonville Prison Governor Ex p. Azam* [1974] A.C. 18; *Scott v Aberdeen Corp* 1976 S.L.T. 141; *Re O* [1991] 2 W.L.R. 475 at 480.

[159] *R. v Secretary of State for Social Security Ex p. Joint Council for the Welfare of Immigrants* [1997] 1 W.L.R. 275, CA (Simon Brown LJ, citing Lord Ellenborough, CJ in *R v Inhabitants of Eastbourne* (1803) 4 East 103: "As to there being no obligation for maintaining poor foreigners before the statutes ascertaining the different methods of acquiring settlements, the law of humanity, which is anterior to all positive laws, obliges us to afford them relief, to save them from starving").

[160] *R. v Secretary of State for the Home Department Ex p. McQuillan* [1995] 4 All E.R. 400 (Sedley J).

[161] *Moohan v Lord Advocate (Advocate General for Scotland intervening)* [2014] UKSC 67; [2015] A.C. 901.

[162] See, e.g. R. Dworkin, "Equality, Democracy and the Constitution" (1990) Alberta L.R. 324 This view was enunciated in the UK By Lord Browne-Wilkinson, "The Infiltration of a Bill of Rights" [1992] P.L. 406, 406 ("Can it really be suggested that Parliament intended to authorise, for example a directive prohibiting broadcasts which are critical of the government for the time being in power, or of the Home Secretary himself?"); R. Cooke, "Fundamentals" [1988] N.Z.L.J. 158; Sir John Laws, "Is the Constitution the Guardian of Fundamental Rights?" [1993] P.L. 59; "Law and Democracy" [1995] P.L. 72; Sir Stephen Sedley, "The Sound of Silence: Constitutional Law without a Constitution" (1994) 110 L.Q.R. 270; M. Kirby, "Lord Cooke and Fundamental Rights", in P. Rishworth (ed), *The Struggle for Simplicity in Law: Essays in Honour of Lord Cooke of Thorndon* (1998), p.331; M. Elliott, *The Constitutional Foundations of Judicial Review* (2001); M. Hunt, *Using Human Rights Law in English Courts* (1997), Ch.6; T. Allan, *Constitutional Justice: A Liberal Theory of the Rule of Law* (2001); M. Kirby, "Deep-Lying Rights—A Constitutional Conversion Continues" (2004) 3 N.Z.J. of International and Public Law 195; D. Dyzenhaus, *The Constitution of Law* (2006). cf. T. Poole, "Legitimacy, Rights and Judicial Review" (2005) O.J.L.S. 697.

[163] T. Allan, *Law, Liberty and Justice* (1993).

[164] See, e.g. Israel—D. Kretzmer, "The New Basic Laws and Human Rights: A Mini-Revolution in Israeli Constitutional Law?" (1992) *Israel Law Review* 238; S. Goldstein, "Protection of Human Rights by Judges: The Israeli Experience" (1994) St Louis U.L.J. 605; A. Barak, *The Judge in a Democracy* (2006). Australia—H.P. Lee, "The Australian High Court and Implied Fundamental Guarantees" [1993] P.L. 606. South Africa—C. Hoexter, "The Principle of Legality in South African Administrative Law" (2004) Macquarie L.J. 165. See the endorsement of this approach in New Zealand in *R. v Pora* [2001] 2 N.Z.L.R. 37 at [53], [157], CA (Elias CJ, Tipping and Thomas JJ); *Ngati Apa Ki Te Waipounama Trust v R* [2000] 2 N.Z.L.R. 659 at [82].

[165] See 1-019–1-020 and the citations in fn.41 there.

long as parliamentary sovereignty endures as the prime constitutional principle (subject to European Union law), other constitutional principles will ultimately give way to Parliament's clear expression of intent to override them.

The rule of law

The rule of law has proved itself to be elastic enough to be able, particularly in recent years, to act as a significant constraint upon the exercise of administrative discretion in different circumstances. It received statutory recognition in s.1 of the Constitutional Reform Act 2005.[166] The rule of law has been a resilient and effective force behind the general development of judicial review.[167] Dicey's view of the rule of law[168] has been contested,[169] but as a general principle it has provided the major justification for constraining the exercise of official power, promoting the core institutional values of legality, certainty, consistency, due process and access to justice. Being a principle and not a clear rule, the precise content of the rule of law has been articulated on a case-by-case basis, particularly in recent years.

11-057

In practice, many of the decisions held unreasonable are so held because they offend the values of the rule of law. The concept of "unreasonableness", or "irrationality" in itself imputes the arbitrariness that Dicey considered was the antithesis of the rule of law. A disproportionate decision may also violate the rule of law.[170] A local authority which withdrew the licence of a rugby club whose members had visited South Africa during the apartheid regime fell foul of the rule of law on the ground that there should be no punishment where there was no law (since sporting contacts with South Africa were not then prohibited).[171] A Minister's rules allowing a prison governor to prevent a prisoner corresponding with his lawyer, even when no litigation was contemplated, was held to violate the prisoner's "constitutional right" of access to justice.[172] Access to Justice as a value of the rule of law was again held to have been violated by the imposition of court fees which an

11-058

---

[166] "This Act does not adversely affect—(a) the existing constitutional principle of the rule of law, or (b) the Lord Chancellor's existing constitutional role in relation to that principle".

[167] Lord Bingham, *The Rule of Law*, (2010); J. Jowell, "The Rule of Law and its Underlying Values" Ch.1 in J. Jowell and D. Oliver (eds), *The Changing Constitution*, 8th edn (2013); Lord Bingham, "The Rule of Law" [2007] C.L.J. 67; P. Craig, Appendix 6 to the House of Lords Select Committee on the Constitution, *Relations between the executive, the judiciary and Parliament* HL Paper No.151 (Session 2006/07); European Commission for Democracy Through Law ("The Venice Commission"), *Report on the Rule of Law*, March 2011, CDL-AD (2011) 003-rev.

[168] A.V. Dicey, *The Law of the Constitution*, 10th edn (1959).

[169] See, e.g. Sir Ivor Jennings, *The Law and the Constitution* (1933).

[170] See G. Huscroft, M. Miller and G. Webber (eds), *Proportionality and the Rule of Law* (2014), especially the chapters by TRS Allen, D Dyzenhaus, S. Gardbaum and T. Endicott.

[171] *Wheeler v Leicester City Council* [1985] A.C. 1054.

[172] *Ex p. Leech (No.2)* [1994] Q.B. 198.

impecunious litigant was unable to afford.[173] The courts will not lightly sanction the withdrawal of policing in the face of protesters if to do so offends the rule of law.[174]

11-059 The richness of the rule of law's underlying values was demonstrated when a decision had not been communicated to the person affected.[175] The appellant could not easily invoke the normal requirements of the rule of law in her favour as the decision did not take effect retrospectively; ignorance of the law does not normally excuse its application, and the doctrine of prior notice normally applies only to permit the appellant to make representations on the case to the primary decision-maker (here the Home Secretary). Nevertheless, the House of Lords, by majority, held that the decision violated "the constitutional principle requiring the rule of law to be observed".[176] Lord Steyn, with whom the majority of their Lordships concurred, based his argument both upon legal certainty ("surprise is the enemy of justice") and upon accountability: the individual must be informed of the outcome of her case so "she can decide what to do" and "be in a position to challenge the decision in the courts" (this being an aspect of the principle of the right of access to justice).[177] Similarly, the Court of Appeal held that the Home Secretary could not follow unpublished guidelines on detention of asylum seekers, and that in the case of interference with the liberty of the subject, publication of the policy was neces-

---

[173] *R. v Lord Chancellor Ex p. Witham* [1997] 1 W.L.R. 104. The Tribunal of the Southern African Development Community (SADC) held that the lack of opportunity of Zimbabwe farmers to challenge the taking of their land violated the rule of law: *Mike Campbell (Pvt) Ltd et al v The Republic of Zimbabwe* [2008] SADC (T) 02/2007 (28 November 2008). See also *Ahmed v Her Majesty's Treasury (Nos.1 and 2)* [2010] UKSC 2; [2010] 2 A.C. 534 (anti-terrorist measures ultra vires the United Nations Act 1946 as denial of fundamental rights of access to a judicial remedy). See the recent judgment of Lord Reed, citing a number of authorities and cases on that point and holding invalid an Order imposing excessive court fees for access to employment tribunals as violating access to justice as a key ingredient of the rule of law. *R. (UNISON) v Lord Chancellor* [2017] UKSC 51.

[174] *R. v Coventry City Council Ex p. Phoenix Aviation Ltd* [1995] 3 All E.R. 37; cf. *R. v Chief Constable of Sussex Ex p. International Trader's Ferry Ltd* [1999] 2 A.C. 418. But the withdrawal of a prosecution in the face of threats from a foreign country to withdraw intelligence-sharing was not held to violate the rule of law: *R. (on the application of Corner House Research) v Director of the Serious Fraud Office* [2008] UKHL 60; [2009] 1 A.C. 756 (on which, see R. Hopkins and C. Yengistu, "Storm in a Teacup: Domestic and International Conservatism from the Corner House Case" [2008] J.R. 267 and J. Jowell, "Caving In: Threats and the Rule of Law" [2008] J.R. 273).

[175] *R. (on the application of Anufrijeva) v Secretary of State for the Home Department* [2003] UKHL 36; [2004] 1 A.C. 604 (legislation permitted asylum-seekers' right to income support to be terminated once their application for asylum had been refused by a "determination" of the Home Secretary. The refusal in this case was recorded only in an internal file note in the Home Office and communicated to the Benefits Agency, which promptly denied the appellant future income support. The determination was not, however, communicated to the appellant).

[176] *R. (on the application of Anufrijeva) v Secretary of State for the Home Department Lord Steyn* at [28].

[177] *R. (on the application of Anufrijeva) v Secretary of State for the Home Department Lord Steyn* at [26]–[38] (who had no truck with the notion that the Home Secretary's determination had formally and strictly been made. This was "legalism and conceptualism run riot", which is reminiscent of the state described by Kafka "where the rights of an individual are overridden by hole in the corner decisions or knocks on the doors in the early hours"). See also *R. (on the application of Medical Justice) v Secretary of State for the Home Department* [2011] EWCA Civ 1710 (quashing an immigration removal policy as contrary to access to justice); *Ahmed v HM Treasury* [2010] UKSC 2; [2010] 2 A.C. 534. The extent to which common law rights survive Convention rights under the Human Rights Act 1998 is controversial. For a view that they may not, see Lord Rodger in *Watkins v Secretary of State for the Home Department* [2006] UKHL 17; [2006] 2 A.C. 395 at [61]–[62]. For the view that common law rights may go further than Convention rights see Lord Brown in *Rabone v Pennine Care NHS Trust* [2012] UKSC 2; [2012] 2 A.C. 72 at [113]; and Toulson LJ in *R. (on the application of Guardian News and Media Ltd) v City of Westminster Magistrates' Court* [2012] EWCA Civ 420; [2012] 3 W.L.R. 1343 at [88].

sary to afford it legality.[178] Retrospective legislation also violates the rule of law in the absence of very strong justification.[179]

One of the essential ingredients of the rule of law is that decisions should be certain and predictable. Substantial doubt over what is intended may result in a decision being held invalid for uncertainty. A byelaw or statutory instrument may be pronounced invalid for uncertainty where it fails to indicate adequately what it is prohibiting.[180] However, a byelaw will be treated as valid unless it was so uncertain in its language as to have no ascertainable meaning or was so unclear in its effect as to be incapable of certain application.[181] Mere "ambiguity" would not suffice.[182] Uncertainty is a ground for invalidating conditions annexed to grants of planning permission and site licences. Such conditions may be void for uncertainty if they can be given no meaning at all, or no sensible or ascertainable meaning.[183] An uncertain decision could also be described as arbitrary, in the sense that "it is incapable of providing any meaningful answer",[184] or indeed as failing to comply with the rule of law.[185] In 2011 the Supreme Court pronounced in a case where the release date of a prisoner was not accurately calculated by the Home Office. This

11-060

---

[178] *R. (on the application of Nadarajah) v Secretary of State for the Home Department* [2003] EWCA Civ 1768; [2004] I.N.L.R. 139 at [68]; and *R. v North West Lancashire Health Authority Ex p. A* [2000] 1 W.L.R. 977 (suggested that it might be irrational for a health authority not to draft a policy for the allocation of different medical treatments); on legitimate expectations, see Ch.12.

[179] *R. (on the application of Reilly (No.2) and Hewstone) v Secretary of State for Work and Pensions* [2014] EWHC 2182 (Admin); [2015] Q.B. 573(the Jobseeker's (Back to Work Schemes) Act 2013 sought to retrospectively validate the 2011 Jobseeker's Allowance (Employment, Skills and Enterprise Scheme) Regulations, notification letters that had failed to comply with those regulations and sanctions which had been imposed pursuant to the regulations; the court granted a declaration of incompatibility) at [82] per Lang J: "The constitutional principle of the rule of law was expressly recognised in section 1, Constitutional Reform Act 2005. It requires, inter alia, that Parliament and the Executive recognise and respect the separation of powers and abide by the principle of legality. Although the Crown in Parliament is the sovereign legislative power, the Courts have the constitutional role of determining and enforcing legality. Thus, Parliament's undoubted power to legislate to overrule the effect of court judgments generally ought not to take the form of retrospective legislation designed to favour the Executive in ongoing litigation in the courts brought against it by one of its citizens, unless there are compelling reasons to do so. Otherwise it is likely to offend a citizen's sense of fair play." See also para.1-033 nn.94 and 105.

[180] *Staden v Tarjanyi* (1980) 78 L.G.R. 614 at 623 at 624; D. Williams, "Criminal Law and Administrative Law: Problems of Procedure and Reasonableness", in P. Smith (ed), *Criminal Law: Essays in Honour of J.C. Smith* (1987), p.170. In *McEldowney v Forde* [1971] A.C. 632, the majority of their Lordships assumed that the test of uncertainty applied to statutory instruments as well as byelaws.

[181] *Percy v Hall* [1997] Q.B. 924 at 941 (Simon Brown LJ).

[182] cf. *Kruse v Johnson* [1898] 2 Q.B. 473.

[183] cf. *Fawcett Properties Ltd v Buckingham CC* [1961] A.C. 636; *Hall v Shoreham-by-Sea UDC* [1964] 1 W.L.R. 240; *Mixnam's Properties Ltd v Chertsey UDC* [1964] 1 Q.B. 214; [1965] A.C. 735; *David Lowe and Sons Ltd v Musselburgh Corp* 1974 S.L.T. 5 (condition incapable of any certain or intelligible interpretation); *Bizony v Secretary of State for the Environment* (1976) 239 E.G. 281 at 284 (test of uncertainty applied to a planning condition was limited to linguistic ambiguity or uncertainty in meaning: mere difficulty in determining whether the condition had been breached on particular facts was not enough); *Shanley M.J. Ltd (In liquidation) v Secretary of State for the Environment* [1982] J.P.L. 380 (condition favouring local people was void for uncertainty); cf. *Alderson v Secretary of State for the Environment* [1984] J.P.L. 429, CA (condition limiting occupation of premises to persons "employed locally in agriculture" was not uncertain); *Bromsgrove DC v Secretary of State for the Environment* [1988] J.P.L. 257 (difficulty of enforcement does not invalidate for uncertainty); *R. v Barnett LBC Ex p. Johnson* [1989] C.O.D. 538 (conditions attached to grant-aid for a community festival prohibiting "political activity" were held "meaningless"). See also *R. v Blackpool BC Ex p. Red Cab Taxis Ltd* [1994] C.O.D. 513 (vague condition held to be *Wednesbury* unreasonable).

[184] *R. v Bradford Metropolitan Council Ex p. Sikander Ali* [1994] E.L.R. 299 at 308.

[185] *R. v Hammersmith and Fulham LBC Ex p. Earls Court Ltd, The Times*, 15 July 1993; *R. (on the application of Z L) v Secretary of State for the Home Department* [2003] EWCA 25 at [17]. See also

was perhaps not unsurprising since there had been no fewer than 55 Acts of Parliament since 1967 altering the rules of criminal justice in England and Wales. Lord Judge remarked that

"it is simply unacceptable in a society governed by the rule of law for it to be well nigh impossible to discern from statutory provisions what a sentence means in practice".[186]

The principle of equality

11-061   Baroness Hale has observed that:

"Democracy is founded on the principle that each individual has equal value. Treating some as automatically having less value than others not only causes pain and distress to that person but also violates his or her dignity as a human being."[187]

There are two senses of equality: formal equality and substantive equality.

Formal equality (consistency)

11-062   Formal equality requires officials to apply or enforce the law consistently and even-handedly, without bias. Dicey considered this to be fundamental to his notion of the rule of law: "With us, every official, from the Prime Minister down to a constable or collector of taxes, is under the same responsibility for every act done without legal justification".[188] This kind of consistency was fundamental to Dicey primarily because of its value in furthering the central feature for him of the rule of law, namely, legal certainty and predictability.[189] Consistent application of the law also, however, possesses another value in its own right—that of ensuring that all persons similarly situated will be treated equally by those who apply the law. It is this notion of the equal (rather than the certain or predictable) application of the law which is the central aim of formal equality.

11-063   A number of cases have considered the question as to whether selective enforcement or selective concessions (e.g. concessions to individuals or groups of taxpayers by the HM Revenue and Customs) violates equal treatment, or whether to cease a previously unfair practice is unfair to those who were previously unfairly treated. In general, selective enforcement of the law has been held not to breach the principle of equal treatment in view of the limited resources available to the prosecuting officials and the legitimacy of exemplary prosecutions.[190] As Lord Hoffmann has said, although "it would be unfair of the Secretary of State not to treat

---

R. (on the application of Limbu) v Secretary of State for the Home Department [2008] EWHC 2261 (Admin); [2008] H.R.L.R. 48 at [70] (a policy "so ambiguous as to the expression of its scope as to mislead").

[186] *R. (on the application of Noone) v Governor of Drake Hall* [2010] UKSC 30; [2010] 1 W.L.R. 1743. And see the cases about the uncertain state of the immigration rules, discussed in M. Elliott, "The Immigration Rules, The Rule of Law and the Separation of Powers" [2012] C.L.J.486.

[187] *Ghaidan v Godin-Mendoza* [2004] UKHL 30; [2004] 2 A.C. 557 at [132].

[188] A.V. Dicey, *The Law of the Constitution*, 10th edn (1959), p.193.

[189] This aim is connected with Dicey's view that discretionary power inevitably leads to its arbitrary exercise. Equal application of the law also formed the basis of Dicey's dubious claim that, unlike what he saw as the French position, in "England" officials were subject to the same law as ordinary individuals.

[190] On prosecutorial discretion, see 5-078—5-079 and Y. Dotan, "Should Prosecutorial Discretion Enjoy Special Treatment in Judicial Review? A Comparative Analysis of the Law in England and Israel" [1997] P.L. 513; e.g. *Vestey v IRC* [1980] A.C. 1148; *R. v IRC Ex p. National Federation of Self-Employed and Small Businesses Ltd* [1982] A.C. 617; *R. v IRC Ex p. Mead* [1993] 1 All E.R. 772; *Woods v Secretary of State for Scotland* 1991 S.L.T. 197; cf. dicta indicating equality of treatment may be applied in the tax field: *J Rothschild Holdings v IRC* [1988] S.T.C. 435; *R. v IRC Ex p.*

like cases alike ... it would unduly restrict his discretion if he could not make an ex gratia concession on the ground of a general public interest in the fair and efficient administration of the immigration law".[191] However, the principle of consistency has been applied in a number of cases.[192] In holding that the test of whether an applicant for a student grant was "ordinarily resident in the United Kingdom" should be consistently applied, the Master of the Rolls said that "it is a cardinal principle of good public administration that all persons in a similar position should be treated similarly".[193] Where mushroom pickers were excluded from a reduced minimum wage for harvesters, the decision was held to be unreasonable and unlawful.[194] It is well established that planning permission may be refused on the ground that a grant of permission would create a precedent from which, as a practical matter, it would be difficult for the authority to depart without creating an impression of unfairness,[195] thus upholding the notion of consistency and equality of treatment as a "material consideration" in planning. And it is material to the grant of planning permission that permission was granted in other similarly situated cases.[196]

Although in the past the decisions of planning inspectors were not considered "material considerations" which should be followed in like cases, they have now been accorded the status of precedent in the interest of consistency and equality of treatment.[197] Where there is apparent inconsistency between a grant of planning permission in one case and a refusal in an earlier case, there is need for an explanation.[198] Where a London council devolved its powers to allocate housing to the homeless to seven neighbourhoods, and where this arrangement resulted in the application of variable standards for letting housing to the homeless, this was held to be "unfair and irrational".[199] The preferential allocation of council housing to a councillor, in order to put her in a better position to fight a local election in her own constituency, was held to be an "abuse of power" because it was unfair to others

11-064

Warburg [1994] S.T.C. 518 at 541.

[191] *R. (on the application of Zequiri) v Secretary of State for the Home Department* [2002] UKHL 3; [2002] Imm. A.R. 296 at [56].

[192] K. Steyn, "Consistency—A Principle of Public Law?" [1997] J.R. 22; *R. (on the application of Munjaz) v Mersey Care NHS Trust* [2005] UKHL 58; [2006] 2 A.C. 148 at [122] (Lord Brown of Eaton-under-Heywood: requirement of the ECtHR that the "quality of the law"—in the context of the expression "in accordance with the law"—requires compatibility with the rule of law (*Hewitt v UK* (1992) 14 E.H.R.R. 657) and regarded the "quality of the law" "to encompass notions of transparency, accessibility, predictability and consistency, features of a legal regime designed to guard against the arbitrary use of power and to afford sufficient legal protection to those at risk of its abuse").

[193] *R. v Hertfordshire CC Ex p. Cheung, The Times*, 4 April 1986 (Lord Donaldson MR). See *R. (on the application of O'Brien) v Independent Assessor* [2007] UKHL 10; [2007] 2 A.C. 312; at [30] (Lord Bingham said "it is generally desirable that decision-makers, whether administrative or judicial, should act in a broadly consistent manner" unless the previous decision was erroneous).

[194] *R. (on the application of Middlebrook Mushrooms Ltd) v Agricultural Wages Board of England and Wales* [2004] EWHC (Admin) 1635 at [74] (citing the 5th edition of this work with approval).

[195] See, e.g. *Collis Radio v Secretary of State for the Environment* (1975) P. & C.R. 390; *Tempo Discount v Secretary of State for the Environment* [1979] J.P.L. 97; *Poundstretcher Ltd v Secretary of State for the Environment & Liverpool Council* [1989] J.P.L. 90. *Rumsey v Secretary of State for the Environment, Transport and the Regions* (2001) 81 P.& C.R. 32.

[196] *Ynys Mon Isle of Anglesey BC v Secretary of State for Wales and Parry Bros* [1984] J.P.L. 646.

[197] *North Wiltshire DC v Secretary of State for the Environment* [1992] J.P.L. 955, CA; *Aylesbury Vale DC v Secretary of State for the Environment and Woodruff* [1995] J.P.L. 26.

[198] *JJ Gallagher v Secretary of State for Transport, Local Government and the Regions* [2002] EWHC 1812 (Admin); [2002] 4 P.L.R. 32.

[199] *R. v Tower Hamlets LBC Ex p. Ali* (1992) 25 H.L.R. 158 at 314.

on the housing list.[200] It has been held that a decision to renew a licence should not disregard the fact that licences were recently granted in other like cases.[201] The Home Secretary was bound to apply an existing policy to the claimant (where no good reason had been advanced for not doing so) in the interest of consistency and fairness.[202]

11-065　　The principle of consistency is linked to other aspects of the rule of law, such as that law should be predictable and known in advance so that people are not in ignorance of the way that the law is applied. For that reason, in cases where a policy is insufficiently specified, there may be a legal obligation to provide precise rules to affected parties so that they can be reasonably certain how to plan their actions.[203] An "overbroad" policy may also be held incompatible with the requirement in a number of Convention rights that interference with a right, to be lawful, must be "prescribed by law" (ECHR arts 10 and 11) or "in accordance with the law" (ECHR art.8). In *R. (on the application of S) v Secretary of State for the Home Department*[204] it was held that a policy document conferring very wide discretion on a Minister to depart from its terms was incompatible with the Convention requirements because it failed to "give any protection against arbitrary interference by Ministers" and because its open-ended nature was not "foreseeable".[205]

Substantive equality

11-066　　The second type of equality, substantive equality, does not refer to the enforcement of law but to its content. It seeks equal laws—laws which themselves do not discriminate between individuals on invidious grounds. There are a number of different philosophical theories of substantive equality[206] which obviously have not formed the basis for any judicial application of the principle in English law.

---

[200] *R. v Port Talbot BC Ex p. Jones* [1988] 2 All E.R. 207, QBD.

[201] *R. v Birmingham City Council Ex p. Steptonhurst Ltd* [1990] 1 All E.R. 1026.

[202] *R (on the application of Rashid) v Secretary of State for the Home Department* [2005] EWCA Civ 744; [2005] Imm. A.R. 608 at [34] (Pill LJ). See N. Blake, "Judicial Interpretation of Policies Promulgated by the Executive" [2006] J.R. 298; R. Clayton, "Legitimate Expectations, Policy and the Principle of Consistency" [2003] C.L.J. 93 (emphasising that the rationale of the case was not legitimate expectation but the free-standing principle of consistency); M. Elliott, "Legitimate Expectations, Consistency and Abuse of Power: The Rashid case" [2005] J.R. 281. *R. (on the application of O'Brien) v Independent Assessor* [2007] UKHL 10; [2007] 2 W.L.R. 544 at [30] (concerning the calculation of compensation for miscarriages of justice, "It is generally desirable that decision-makers, whether administrative or judicial, should act in a broadly consistent manner. If they do, reasonable hopes will not be disappointed").

[203] See, e.g. *R. (on the application of Quark Fishing Ltd) v Secretary of State for Foreign and Commonwealth Affairs* [2001] EWHC 1174; [2002] EWCA Civ 1409 (applicants for valuable fishing licence entitled to be in no doubt about circumstances in which it would be granted); cf. rule against fettering of discretion discussed in Ch.9. See also *R. (on the application of Lumba) v Secretary of State for the Home Department* [2011] UKSC 12; [2012] 1 A.C. 245 at [35] (Lord Dyson said that "the rule of law calls for a transparent statement by the executive of the circumstances in which the broad statutory criteria will be exercised, describing "the right to know" the relevant policy so as to be able to make representations about it; see also Lord Phillips at [302]).

[204] *R. (on the application of S) v Secretary of State for the Home Department* [2006] EWCA Civ 1157; [2006] I.N.L.R. 575.

[205] At [113].

[206] J. Jowell, "Is Equality a Constitutional Principle?" (1994) C.L.P Pt 2, 1; R. Singh, "Equality: The Neglected Virtue" [2004] E.H.R.L.R. 141; D. Feldman, *Civil Liberties and Human Rights in England and Wales*, 2nd edn (2002), Ch.3; T.R.S. Allan, *Law, Liberty and Justice* (1993); C. McCrudden, "Equality and Non-Discrimination", Ch.11 in D. Feldman (ed), *English Public Law* (2004); Baroness Hale of Richmond, "The Quest for Equality and Non-Discrimination" [2005] P.L. 571; S. Fredman, "From Deference to Democracy: the Role of Equality under the Human Rights Act 1998" (2006) 112 L.Q.R. 53.

However, a particular restricted formulation of substantive equality is applied as a "general principle of law" in European Union law[207] and in the law relating to the ECHR, in particular in relation to art.14.[208] Principles of substantive equality are given effect in several provisions of domestic legislation.[209]

The requirement of substantive equality has also justified a number of decisions in English administrative law sometimes expressly, but mostly under the guise of unreasonableness. We have already seen that in the 19th century Lord Russell considered that byelaws could be held unreasonable because of "partial and unequal treatment in their operation as between different classes".[210] Although subsequent cases did not articulate the principle with equivalent clarity, unequal treatment has justified a number of instances where the courts have struck down a decision or provision which infringes equality in either its formal or its substantive sense. English common law has traditionally placed ancient duties, requiring equality of treatment, upon common carriers, inn-keepers and some monopoly enterprises such as ports and harbours, obliging them to accept all travellers.[211] In addition the courts have occasionally invoked notions of "public policy" to strike down discriminatory provisions. In *Nagle v Fielden*[212] the Jockey Club's refusal of a horse trainer's licence to a woman was held to be against public policy, and in *Edwards v SOGAT*,[213] a case involving a challenge to the withdrawal of collective bargaining rights, Lord Denning said that our courts "will not allow a power to be exercised arbitrarily or capriciously or with unfair discrimination, neither in the making of rules or in the enforcement of them" (a statement which addresses itself to both substantive and formal equality). In *Ghaidan v Godin Mendoza* (a case under the HRA), holding that unmarried same sex partners were entitled to same inheritance rights to tenancies as unmarried heterosexual partners, Baroness Hale of Richmond said that unequal treatment

11-067

"is the reverse of the rational behaviour we now expect from government and the state. Power must not be exercised arbitrarily. If distinctions are to be drawn, particularly upon

---

[207] See Ch.14. See, e.g. *Patmalniece v Secretary of State for Work and Pensions* [2011] UKSC 11; [2011] 1 W.L.R. 783 (unjustified indirect discrimination in pensions on ground of nationality).

[208] See Ch.13. See, e.g. *AL (Serbia) v Secretary of State for the Home Department* [2008] UKHL 42; [2008] 1 W.L.R. 1434. The UK government has not signed ECHR Protocol 12, which contains a freestanding prohibition of discrimination.

[209] Formerly the Sex Discrimination Act 1975; Race Relations Act 1976; Disability Discrimination Act 1995; Employment Equality (Religion or Belief) Regulations 2003 (SI 2003/1660); Employment Equality (Sexual Orientation) Regulations 2003 (SI 2003/1661); Employment Equality (Age) Regulations 2006 (SI 2006/1031). See now the Equality Act 2010, which codifies the provisions and under which public authorities owe a general duty not to discriminate on protected grounds. These include the duty not to discriminate, directly or indirectly, on those grounds and also to have "due regard" in the promotion of equality. For illustrations see M. Fordham, *Judicial Review Handbook*, 6th edn (2012), para.55.3; M. Bell, "Judicial Enforcement of the Duties on Public Authorities to Promote Equality" [2010] P.L. 672; S. Fredman, "The Public Sector Equality Duty" (2011) 40 I.L.J 405. The Equality and Human Rights Commission, set up in 2006, has the function of promoting and enforcing both equality and human rights legislation. See 5-044.

[210] *Kruse v Johnson* [1889] 2 Q.B. 291.

[211] *Rothfield v NB Railway* 1920 S.C. 805 ("and others who are in a reasonable fit condition to be received"); *Pidgeon v Legge* (1857) 21 J.P. 743. Similar principles have applied to the providers of some utilities, e.g. *South of Scotland Electricity Board v British Oxygen Ltd* [1959] 1 W.L.R. 587.

[212] *Nagle v Fielden* [1966] 2 Q.B. 633.

[213] *Edwards v SOGAT* [1971] Ch. 354. The reach of public policy was not sufficient to prohibit certain forms of discrimination which were thus made unlawful through legislation first passed in the 1960s and now consolidated in the Equality Act 2006.

a group basis, it is an important discipline to look for a rational basis for those distinctions."[214]

Illustrations of application of substantive inequality principle in common law

11-068   Independently of European Union law and the ECHR, equality of treatment has shown itself to be a principle of lawful administration in English law.

- *Religion.* In *Board of Education v Rice*, a case noted for its application of natural justice, the substantive issue was the authority's power to fund church schools less favourably than other schools. Lord Halsbury, who felt that the differential treatment was based upon hostility to the church schools said: "it is clear that the local education authority ought to be as impartial as the rate collector who demands the rate without reference to the peculiar views of the ratepayer".[215]

- *Age.* In *Prescott v Birmingham Corp*[216] the corporation, which had power to charge "such fares as they may think fit" on their public transport services introduced a scheme for free bus travel for the elderly. The decision was declared to be an improper exercise of discretion because it conferred out of rates "a special benefit on some particular class of inhabitants [and] would amount simply to the making of a gift or present in money's worth to a particular section of the local community at the expense of the general body of ratepayers".[217] The House of Lords has held (in advance of statutory or European Union law requirements on the matter) that the adoption by a local authority of the statutory criterion of pensionable age (65 for men and 60 for women) as the qualification for free admittance to a leisure centre is a breach of the statutory prohibition against sex discrimination.[218]

- *Location-related factors.* Conditions in planning policies that favour "locals only" in the allocation of housing or office space have been held unlawful, although if the provision is placed in a development plan, it may thus be considered a material consideration.[219] Questions of place of residence have also arisen in relation to the admissions criteria for schools.[220] The courts have held that admissions policies must treat children both within and

---

[214] *Ghaidan v Godin Mendoza* [2004] UKHL 30; [2004] 2 A.C. 557, [132]; see also *R. (on the application of E) v Nottinghamshire Healthcare NHS Trust* [2009] EWCA Civ 795; [2010] P.T.S.R. 674 at [90] (Lord Clarke and Moses LJ accepted that the common law "principle of equality ... simply means that distinctions between different groups must be drawn on a rational basis. It is thus no more than an example of the application of *Wednesbury* rationality").

[215] *Board of Education v Rice* [1911] A.C. 179, 186.

[216] *Prescott v Birmingham Corp* [1955] 1 Ch. 210.

[217] Clearly the notion of equality applied in *Prescott* would not suit all theories of equality. Local authorities were given power ultimately to allow certain classes of free travel by the Travel Concessions Act 1964. In *Roberts v Hopwood* [1925] A.C. 578 the HL confirmed the view of the district auditor that the attempt of Poplar BC to raise the level of wages of both men and women employees to an equal level was unlawful. Lord Atkinson considered that the council was guided by "eccentric principles of socialistic philanthropy, or feminist ambition to secure the equality of the sexes". Despite its headnote, the case was not decided on unreasonableness but on the ground of illegality, there being no "rational proportion" between the rates paid to women employees and the going market rate; *Pickwell v Camden LBC* [1993] Q.B. 962 at 999–1000 (Ormrod LJ).

[218] *James v Eastleigh BC* [1990] 2 A.C. 751.

[219] *Slough Industrial Estates Ltd v Secretary of State for the Environment* [1987] J.P.L. 353; *Kember v Secretary of State for the Environment* [1982] J.P.L. 383. Such conditions may be void for uncertainty, see 11-040. For unreasonably discriminatory taxi licence conditions (giving advantages to Hackney cabs) see *R. v Blackpool BC Ex p. Red Cab Taxis, The Times,* 13 May 1995.

[220] See now Department for Education and Skills, *School Admissions Code* (2007).

outside a local authority boundary in the same way,[221] though proximity to a school may be a valid consideration in determining a school admissions policy,[222] as may religious affiliation even where the school in question was not a church school.[223] The Court of Appeal considered whether the policy to exclude from compensation to former internees (of British nationality) by the Japanese in the Second World War those whose parents or grandparents were not born in the United Kingdom offended the principle of equality. While subscribing to the general acceptance of equality as a constitutional principle, Dyson LJ held that the birth-related criteria in that case were "not unreasonable in the *Wednesbury* sense".[224] A similar conclusion was reached by the House of Lords in rejecting an argument that differential treatment under an ex gratia compensation scheme of British soldiers injured in Bosnia as compared with those injured in Northern Ireland should be regarded as an irrational distinction.[225]

A common law principle of equality was accepted in a case in which Gurkhas challenged a change of policy in relation to the grant of indefinite leave to remain in the United Kingdom at the conclusion of military service; different policies applied according to whether discharge took place before or after July 1997.[226]

- *Financial circumstances.* Regulations which restricted the admission of dependent relatives to those having a standard of living "substantially below [their] own country", which would benefit immigrants from affluent countries, were held to be "manifestly unjust and unreasonable".[227] But the court refused to intervene in arrangements under which prisoners, granted legal aid for legal representation, could represent themselves in civil proceedings or judicial review claims only if able to meet the costs of travel and a security escort, or make a formal request to the Home Secretary for a direction (which the claimant in this case refused to do).[228]

- *Sexual orientation.* Prior to the HRA, the Court of Appeal accepted the principle of equality as being applicable to the question of the exclusion of homosexual men and women from the armed forces; the policy was not, however, held to be irrational.[229]

---

[221] *R. v Greenwich LBC Ex p. Governors of the John Ball Primary School* (1989) 88 L.G.R. 589; *R. v Kingston-on-Thames LBC Ex p. Kingwell* [1992] 1 F.L.R. 182; *R. v Bromley LBC Ex p. C* [1992] 1 F.L.R. 174; *R. v Rochdale MBC Ex p. Schemet* (1993) 91 L.G.R. 425; *R. v Devon CC Ex p. George* [1989] A.C. 573.

[222] *R. v Rotherham MBC Ex p. LT* [2000] B.L.G.R. 338, CA.

[223] *R. v Governors of Bishop Challoner Roman Catholic School Ex p. Choudhury* [1992] 2 A.C. 182.

[224] *R. (on the application of Association of British Civilian Internees (Far East Region)) v Secretary of State for Defence* [2003] EWCA Civ 473; [2003] Q.B. 1397.

[225] *R. v Ministry of Defence Ex p. Walker* [2000] 1 W.L.R. 806 at 812 (Lord Slynn: "It is not for the courts to consider whether the scheme with its exclusion is a good scheme or a bad scheme, unless it can be said that the exclusion is irrational or so unreasonable that no reasonable Minister could have adopted it").

[226] *R. (on the application of Limbu) v Secretary of State for the Home Department* [2008] EWHC 2261 (Admin); [2008] H.R.L.R. 48.

[227] *R. v Immigration Appeal Tribunal Ex p. Manshoora Bugum* [1986] Imm.A.R. 385 (the offending provision was severed from the rest of the regulations).

[228] *R. v Secretary of State for the Home Department Ex p. Wynne* [1993] 1 W.L.R. 115, HL.

[229] *R. v Ministry of Defence Ex p. Smith* [1996] Q.B. 517, CA: *Smith and Grady v UK* (1999) 29 E.H.R.R. 493 (ECtHR held that the exclusion offended Convention rights under arts 8 and 13, but did not base their decision upon equality).

- *Nationality.* Rules excluding from employment at GCHQ people whose parents were foreign nationals were held to be made in the interests of national security and non-justiciable.[230]
- *Language.* In a Privy Council appeal, where a challenge was made to a new policy which added Oriental languages to the list of subjects be taken as part of the school-leaving curriculum, the appellants claimed that the policy favoured children from homes where those languages were spoken. Lord Hoffmann did not doubt that equality before the law was a principle which is "one of the building blocks of democracy and necessarily permeates any democratic constitution", as well as "a general axiom of rational behaviour".[231] However, he also acknowledged that the reason for different treatment may involve "questions of social policy, on which views may differ".

OPPRESSIVE DECISIONS

11-069   The third category of substantive review contains decisions which are unduly oppressive because they subject the complainant to an excessive hardship or an unnecessarily onerous infringement of his rights or interests. As we shall see, the principle of proportionality directs itself to the evaluation of the permitted degree of infringement of rights or interests.[232] However, whether or not proportionality is expressly applied, this aspect of substantive review is well known to English law. As Laws LJ has said:

> "Clearly a public body may choose to deploy powers it enjoys under statute in so draconian a fashion that the hardship suffered by affected individuals in consequence will justify the court in condemning the exercise as irrational and perverse".[233]

11-070   The focus of attention in these cases will be principally the *impact* of the decision upon the affected person. The outcome or end-product of the decision-making process will thus be assessed, rather than the way the decision was reached (although the factors taken into account in reaching the decision may also be—or may be assumed to be—incorrectly weighed). Since the claim is essentially abuse of power, in the sense of excessive use of power, each case must be considered in the context of the nature of the decision, the function of the particular power and the nature of the interests or rights affected.

11-071
- *Imposing an uneven burden.* A very early case involved the Commissioner of Sewers imposing on one landowner alone charges for repairs to a river bank from which other riparian owners had also benefited. This decision was held to be contrary to the law and reason.[234] The actions of a local authority were held *Wednesbury* unreasonable when, in order to avoid rais-

---

[230] *R. v Secretary of State for Foreign and Commonwealth Affairs Ex p. Manelfi* [1996] 12 C.L. 65.

[231] *Matadeen v Pointu* [1999] A.C. 98 at 109, citing paras 13-036 to 13-045 of the 5th edn of this work with approval. In *Matadeen*, the appellants failed in their claim that the new policy offended the limited prohibition of unequal treatment under the constitution of Mauritius.

[232] See 11-073 and following.

[233] *R. (on the application of Khatun) v Newham LBC* [2004] EWCA Civ 55; [2005] Q.B. 37 at [41] (neither oppressive, perverse or disproportionate for the council to require a claimant who had not viewed an offered property to accept it on pain of his existing accommodation being cancelled if he did not); see also *R. v Governor of Frankland Prison Ex p. Russell* [2000] 1 W.L.R. 2027 (policy restricting prisoners to one meal a day was held to be "arbitrary and unjustified").

[234] *Rooke's case* (1598) 5 Co.Rep. 99b.

ing rents generally as required by legislation, they charged the whole of required rent increases upon a single unoccupied and unfit property.[235]

- *When implementation is impossible.* A byelaw requiring the annual cleaning of lodging houses when access was not always possible.[236] A hooding exception in guidance for intelligence officers was held "unworkable".[237]
- Where delegated legislation deviates materially from the general law of the land in imposing "burdensome prohibitions".[238]
- Regulations have been held unreasonable where their effect is to prevent access to the courts.[239] In *AXA General Insturance Ltd v HM Advocate* the question was whether the insurance industry was being called upon to bear a "disproportionate and excessive burden".[240]
- Town and country planning provides countless examples where planning conditions have been held unreasonable because of their unnecessarily onerous impact. Although the legislation permitted the local authority, or the Secretary of State on appeal, to attach conditions to planning permissions as they "think fit",[241] conditions have been held unreasonable which, in effect, require the developer to dedicate part of his land for public use[242] or otherwise require the developer to provide the off-site physical infrastructure necessary to unlock the development.[243] Similarly, a planning condition was held unreasonable which, in effect, required the developer to construct housing to local authority standards and rents, and to take tenants from the council's waiting list.[244] Conditions attached to similar broad powers to license caravan sites were held by the House of Lords to be unreasonable because they were "a gratuitous interference with the rights of the occupier".[245] A condition attached to the reopening of a public inquiry

---

[235] *Backhouse v Lambeth LBC, The Times,* 14 October 1972.

[236] *Arlidge v Mayor etc. of Islington* [1909] 2 K.B. 127. Cf. *Dr Bonham's case* (1610) 8 Co.Rep. 107(a) (Coke CJ said that an Act of Parliament could be controlled by the common law if the Act "is against common right or reason, or repugnant, or impossible to be performed"); in Germany a provision which is impossible of implementation falls foul of the principle of proportionality.

[237] *R. (on the application of Equality and Human Rights Commission) v Prime Minister* [2011] EWHC 2401 (Admin); [2012] 1 W.L.R. 1389.

[238] See, e.g. *London Passenger Transport Board v Sumner* (1935) 154 L.T. 108; *Powell v May* [1946] K.B. 330; *R. v Brighton Corp. Ex p. Tilling (Thomas) Ltd* (1916) 85 L.J.K.B. 1552; *R. v Customs and Excise Commissioners Ex p. Hedges & Butler Ltd* [1986] 2 All E.R. 164 (regulation unlawful because it gave power to officials to inspect all the records of a business, and not only those records pertaining to dutiable goods).

[239] *Commissioner of Customs and Excise v Cure and Deeley Ltd* [1962] 1 Q.B. 340; *R. v Secretary of State for the Home Department Ex p. Leech (No.2)* [1994] Q.B. 198.

[240] *AXA General Insurance Ltd v HM Advocate* [2011] UKSC 46; [2012] 1 A.C. 868 at [36].

[241] Town & Country Planning Act 1990 s.70(1).

[242] *Hall & Co Ltd v Shoreham-by-Sea UDC* [1964] 1 W.L.R. 240. The purpose of the condition was to ensure safe access to the site—a purpose well within the "four corners" of the legislation.

[243] *City of Bradford MC v Secretary of State for the Environment* [1986] J.P.L. 598. But such a condition may survive if framed in negative terms: *Grampian RC v Aberdeen CC* 1984 S.C. (H.L.) 58. A negative condition may survive even if there is no "reasonable prospect" of the development being carried out: *British Railways Board v Secretary of State for the Environment* [1993] 3 P.L.R. 125, HL.

[244] *R. v Hillingdon LBC Ex p. Royco Homes Ltd* [1974] 1 Q.B. 720. For an older case holding it unlawful to seek developers' contributions, see *R. v Bowman* [1898] 1 Q.B. 663. But where these contributions are provided by means of what are now called "planning obligations" (and used to be called "planning agreements" or "planning gain") under s.106 of the Town and Country Planning Act 1990, developers' contributions may be upheld.

[245] *Mixnam's Properties Ltd v Chertsey UDC* [1965] A.C. 735 (the conditions provided, inter alia, for security of tenure, no premium charged, and no restrictions on commercial or political activity); *R.*

by the Secretary of State was held to be unreasonable because it resulted in "considerable expense, inconvenience and risk to the applicant".[246] The Secretary of State's refusal to renew a temporary planning permission was struck down because it would be "unreasonably burdensome" on the applicant.[247]

- The exercise of compulsory purchase powers has similarly been held unreasonable when the authority already possessed, or was able to acquire voluntarily, other equally suitable land.[248] Where a local authority acquired land for one purpose (such as a wall to protect the coast), it was held unreasonable for it to acquire more land than it needed.[249]

- A long delay before the Home Secretary's review of a life prisoner's sentence (a power now abolished) was held to be unreasonable and "excessive beyond belief".[250] Excessive delay in giving notice of pending police disciplinary proceedings has invalidated those proceedings[251] and the courts ordered an end to delay in admitting a British "patrial" into the country.[252] When the primary decision-maker seeks to excuse delay on the ground of inadequate resources in the past the courts have not readily intervened, as has been discussed in previous chapters.[253] However, it should be noted that the ECHR now requires a "speedy" trial under art.5(4)[254] and a hearing

---

v North Hertfordshire DC Ex p. Cobbold [1985] 3 All E.R. 486 (oppressive condition attached to licence for pop concert); R. v Barnett LBC Johnson (1989) 89 L.G.R. 581 (condition prohibiting political parties and activities at community festival held unreasonable).

[246] R. v Secretary of State for the Environment Ex p. Fielder Estates (Canvey) Ltd (1989) 57 P. & C.R. 424; Niarchos (London) Ltd v Secretary of State for the Environment (1980) 79 L.G.R. 264.

[247] Niarchos Ltd v Secretary of State for the Environment (1977) 35 P. & C.R. 259.

[248] Brown v Secretary of State for the Environment (1978) 40 P. & C.R. 285; Prest v Secretary of State for Wales (1982) 81 L.G.R. 193; cf. R. v Secretary of State for Transport Ex p. de Rothschild [1989] 1 All E.R. 933; R. v Rochdale MBC Ex p. Tew [1999] 3 P.L.R. 74; R. v Bristol City Council Ex p. Anderson (1999) 79 P. & C.R. 358.

[249] Webb v Minister of Housing and Local Government [1965] 1 W.L.R. 755. See also Gard v Commissioners of Sewers of City of London (1885) 28 Ch.D. 486; Leader v Moxon (1773) 3 Wils.K.B. 461 (Paving Commissioners empowered to execute street works in such a manner "as they shall think fit". Held, action for trespass lay where they had exercised their discretion "oppressively"); and cases where byelaws were invalidated for imposing burdensome prohibitions: Munro v Watson (1887) 57 L.T. 366; Johnson v Croydon Corp (1886) 16 Q.B.D. 708 (prohibition of musical instruments). But see R. v Powell (1884) 51 L.T. 92; Slee v Meadows (1911) 75 J.P. 246; cf. Williams, "Criminal Law and Administrative Law: Problems of Procedure and Reasonableness"; London Passenger Transport Board v Summer (1935) 154 L.T. 108; R. v Brighton Corp Ex p. Tilling (Thomas) Ltd (1916) 85 L.J.K.B. 1552 at 1555 (Sankey J).

[250] R. v Secretary of State for the Home Department Ex p. Handscombe (1987) 86 Cr.App.R. 59; Doody v Secretary of State for the Home Department [1994] 1 A.C. 531 (Lord Mustill). The Home Secretary no longer has a role in setting tariffs for life prisoners. R. v Secretary of State for the Home Department Ex p. Zulfikar [1996] C.O.D. 256 (policy of strip-searching prisoners not unreasonable).

[251] R. v Merseyside Chief Constable Ex p. Calvaley [1986] Q.B. 424.

[252] R. v Home Secretary Ex p. Phansopokar [1976] Q.B. 606; citing the Magna Carta 1215, c.29: "to no one will we delay right or justice." See also Re Preston [1985] A.C. 835 at 870 (Lord Templeman); R. v Glamorgan CC Ex p. Gheissary, The Times, 18 December 1985 (decisions to refuse student grants irrational when the delay in the students' applications was caused by misleading advice from the authority's officials); R. (on the application of M) v Criminal Injuries Compensation Authority [2002] EWHC 2646 (Admin); (2003) 100(2) L.S.G. 31 (delay in dealing with compensation claim held unreasonable); R. v Secretary of State for the Home Department Ex p. Mersin [2000] Imm. A.R. 645 (unreasonable delay in granting refugee status following asylum claim); R. (on the application of J) v Newham LBC [2001] EWHC Admin 992; (2002) 5 C.C.L. Rep. 302 (irrational to postpone assessments under Children Act).

[253] On justiciability, see 1-034; on implementation of duties, see 5-134—5-145.

[254] See Ch.13.

within a "reasonable time" under art.6(1).[255] It has recently been held that it was "manifestly unreasonable" to delay the transfer of an immigration detainee to hospital.[256] In *Noorkoiv* the Court of Appeal considered the parole board's decision to postpone the claimant's review at the end of the quarter following the end of his tariff period. It was held that the delays were unacceptable because they treated every case alike, and Burnton J held that if the delay is inconsistent with a speedy hearing then the onus was on the authority to justify its excuse of lack of resources and the court would assess carefully whether it had taken sufficient measures to rectify the problem.[257]

- It was perverse for magistrates to have imposed the same sanction on a poll tax defaulter who could not afford to pay because destitute as one who simply refused to pay.[258] The award of excessively low compensation was held, in the absence of justifying reasons, to be irrational,[259] as had been the award to a retiring civil servant of a derisory gratuity.[260] The initiation of an investigation by the Commission for Racial Equality has also been struck down as being oppressive.[261]

- In the 1980s, some local authorities were held unlawfully to have imposed excessive penalties on bodies with associations with South Africa during the apartheid regime. In *Wheeler v Leicester City Council*[262] the council withdrew the licence of a local rugby club to use the council-owned recreation ground. The reason was that the club had refused sufficiently to press four of its members, who had been selected for the English rugby footballers' tour of South Africa, to withdraw from that tour. Although it was not unlawful for the members to travel to South Africa, the council acted under its broad statutory power (to grant licences on their own land) and also in pursuance of its general statutory duty under the Race Relations Act 1976 s.61 to "promote good relations between persons of different racial or ethnic groups". The House of Lords held the council's action unlawful, Lord Templeman considering it to be a "misuse of power", "punishing the club where it had done no wrong". Lord Roskill referred to the "unfair manner in which the council set about attaining its objective".[263] The reasoning in *Wheeler* was supported by reference to the earlier case of *Congreve v Home*

---

[255] See Chs 7 and 13.

[256] *R. (on the application of HA (Nigeria)) v Secretary of State for the Home Department* [2012] EWHC 979 (Admin); [2012] Med. L.R. 353.

[257] *R. (on the application of Noorkoiv) v Secretary of State for the Home Department (No.2)* [2002] EWCA Civ 770; [2002] 1 W.L.R. 3284 at [47]; and *R. (on the application of C) v Mental Health Review Tribunal* [2001] EWCA Civ 1110; [2002] 1 W.L.R. 176; *R. (on the application of Murray) v Parole Board* [2003] EWCA Civ 1561; (2004) 101(1) L.S.G. 21; S. Lambert and A. Strugo, "Delay as a Ground of Review" [2005] J.R. 253.

[258] *R. v Mid-Hertfordshire Justices Ex p. Cox* (1996) Admin. L.R. 409.

[259] *R. v Civil Service Appeal Board Ex p. Cunningham* [1991] 4 All E.R. 310, CA; cf. *R. v Investors Compensation Scheme Ltd Ex p. Bowden* [1996] 1 A.C. 261, HL (refusal to provide full compensation not unreasonable).

[260] *Williams v Giddy* [1911] A.C. 381.

[261] *R. v Commission for Racial Equality Ex p. Hillingdon LBC* [1982] Q.B. 276; *R. v Hackney LBC Ex p. Evenbray Ltd* (1987) 19 H.L.R. 557 (unreasonable for authority to seek to invoke statutory powers or to complain about standards in hotels in which the authority had housed homeless families as an interim measure).

[262] *Wheeler v Leicester City Council* [1985] 1 A.C. 1054.

[263] None of their Lordships expressly considered the ban unreasonable, although Lord Roskill would have been prepared so to hold, but instead, unusually, used the term "procedural impropriety" to describe the lack of relation between the penalty and the council's legitimate objectives.

Office,[264] where the Home Secretary's decision to withdraw television licences from those who had failed to pay a higher fee (but were nevertheless within their rights so to do) was held by the Court of Appeal to be unlawful because it imposed a punishment which related to no wrong. In both cases, the courts refused to countenance the achievement of a legitimate end (the raising of revenue in *Congreve* and the promotion of good race relations in *Wheeler*) by means which were excessive (punishing, in each case, where the individual had done no legal wrong).[265]

- Similar reasoning was employed in a case where some London local authorities decided to withdraw their subscriptions to all publications in their public libraries published by the Times Newspapers group. Following an acrimonious labour dispute, the action was taken in an attempt to impose sanctions on the newspaper proprietors. This consideration was held to be extraneous to the statutory duty of providing a comprehensive and efficient library service".[266] The imposition of the sanctions was also held to be unreasonable and an abuse of the councils' powers.[267]

- When the Secretary of State for Social Security made a regulation which sought to discourage asylum claims by economic migrants by effectively excluded a large class of such migrants from income support, the Court of Appeal invalidated the regulations on the ground that they were so draconian that they rendered the rights of the migrants to remain in the country nugatory. Simon Brown LJ held that the regulations contemplated

---

[264] *Congreve v Home Office* [1976] 1 Q.B. 629.

[265] There may be different explanations of the grounds on which both *Congreve* and *Wheeler* were decided. One ground may be the infringement of the principle of legal certainty (see 11-040). Another may be that the decisions were "illegal" in that both the council in *Wheeler* and the Home Secretary in *Congreve* acted for an improper purpose (namely, the imposition of a punishment): see Ch.5; cf. Browne-Wilkinson LJ in his dissenting judgment in the CA (see n.246) at 1064–1065, where he raised the conflict between "two basic principles of a democratic society", one that allowed a "democratically elected body to conduct its affairs in accordance with its own views" and the other "the right to freedom of speech and conscience enjoyed by each individual". Basing his decision on illegality rather than on unreasonableness (the council having taken a "legally irrelevant factor" into account), he came close to deciding the matter on the ground of the council's acting inconsistently with "fundamental freedoms of speech and conscience". *R. v Lewisham LBC Ex p. Shell UK Ltd* [1988] 1 All E.R. 938 (boycott of the products of the Shell company in order to bring pressure on one of its subsidiary companies to withdraw its (lawful) business from South Africa held illegal). See also *R. (on the application of Trafford) v Blackpool BC* [2014] EWHC 85 (Admin); [2014] 2 All E.R. 947 (decision not to renew solicitor's business tenancy because the solicitor had acted for a number of clients who had brought personal injury claims against the council held to be unlawful) at [71] per HH Judge Stephen Davies: "The exercise of a power with the sole or the dominant intention of punishing the claimant ... in circumstances where there was no evidence that the claimant was actually doing anything at all unlawful or improper, was ... the intentionally improper exercise of the power ... and the exercise of that power for unauthorised purposes."

[266] Public Libraries and Museums Act 1964 s.7(1).

[267] *R. v Ealing LBC Ex p. Times Newspapers* (1986) 85 L.G.R. 316 (not explicitly stated that the decision amounted to an excessive and unnecessary infringement on freedom of expression). The case raises interesting questions as to the reasonableness of decisions to cease subscriptions to, or remove books from the library of "politically incorrect" material. In *R. v Liverpool CC Ex p. Secretary of State for Employment* (1988) 154 L.G.R. 118, the council sought to boycott the Government's Employment Training Scheme, despite the fact that it was voluntary. The council did this outside of any statutory framework, by imposing a standard condition on all grant aid that the organisation to be aided took no part in the scheme. The purpose, punishment of the organisations, was held to be unlawful.

for some migrants "a life so destitute that, to my mind no civilisation can tolerate it".[268]

Systemic unfairness

Recently, the fact that a rule, an administrative system or a policy gives rise to an unacceptable risk of "systemic unfairness" may result in that rule, system or policy being impugned.[269] The key test here is whether the system is "inherently unfair" and "the risk inheres in the policy itself, as opposed to the ever-present risk of aberrant decisions".[270] In considering whether a system is inherently or systemically unfair it is important for the court to examine "the full run of cases which go through the system" in order to assess whether the unfairness is truly systemic: unfairness will not be inherent where only particular cases are affected.[271] Thus where a system is capable of being operated fairly, unfairness will not be systemic.[272] As such, systemic failure cannot necessarily be equated with proof of a series of individual failures.[273]

11-072

---

[268] *R. v Secretary of State for Social Security Ex p. Joint Council for the Welfare of Immigrants* [1997] 1 W.L.R. 275, 292 (Simon Brown LJ, duty to maintain foreigners was held to emanate from the common law, citing Lord Ellenborough CJ in *R v Eastbourne (Inhabitants)* 1803 4 (East) 103 at 107, who said "As to there being no obligation for maintaining poor foreigners ... the law of humanity, which is anterior to all positive laws, obliges us to afford them relief, to save them from starving"); *R. v Secretary of State for Social Security Ex p. Tamenene* [1997] C.O.D. 480 (judicial response to legislation that sought to reinstate provisions held unlawful in the *JCWI* case). See also *R. (on the application of MM (Lebanon)) v Secretary of State for the Home Department* [2014] EWCA Civ 985, [150] (reversing [2013] EWHC 1900 (Admin); [2014] 1 W.L.R 2306) (challenge to a "Minimum Income Requirement" for a UK partner to sponsor the entry of a non-EEA partner) at [147]–[148] per Aikens LJ: "Essentially the debate is about figures and what should be the minimum necessary income figure and what other possible sources of income should or should not be taken into account to see if that minimum can be reached ... the key question is: to what extent should the court substitute its own view of what, as a matter of general policy, is the appropriate level of income for that rationally chosen as a matter of policy by the executive, which is headed by ministers who are democratically accountable? ... Individuals will have different views on what constitutes the minimum income requirements needed to accomplish the stated policy aims ... it is not the court's job to impose its own views unless, objectively judged, the levels chosen are ... irrational, or inherently unjust or inherently unfair."

[269] *R. (Howard League for Penal Reform) v Lord Chancellor* [2017] EWCA Civ 244; [2017] 4 W.L.R. 92 at [48] (the removal of funding for a number of areas of decision-making concerning prisoners from the scope of the criminal legal aid scheme gave rise to a risk of systemic unfairness); see also *R. (Detention Action) v First Tier Tribunal (Immigration and Asylum Chamber)* [2015] EWCA Civ 840; 1 W.L.R. 5341 (although Fast Track Rules for asylum appeals contained safeguards, these did not overcome the inherent difficulties in the scheme and the timescales for lodging appeals such that the system was rendered structurally unfair).

[270] *R. (Refugee Legal Centre) v Secretary of State for the Home Department* [2004] EWCA Civ 1481; [2005] 1 W.L.R. 2219 at [7]. Though the fast track adjudication of asylum claims was not found to be so flawed, Sedley LJ's formulation was cited with approval by the Court of Appeal in *R. (Howard League for Penal Reform) v Lord Chancellor* [2017] EWCA Civ 244; [2017] 4 W.L.R. 92 at [48].

[271] *R. (Detention Action) v First Tier Tribunal (Immigration and Asylum Chamber)* [2015] EWCA Civ 840; 1 W.L.R. 5341 at [27].

[272] *R. (Tabbakh) v Staffordshire and West Midlands Probation Trust* [2014] EWCA Civ 827; [2014] 1 W.L.R. 4620 at [49], concluding that the Multi Agency Public Protection Arrangements were capable of operating fairly in reaching decisions about the imposition of licence conditions on offenders following their release from prison.

[273] *R. (S) v Director of Legal Aid Casework* [2016] EWCA Civ 464; [2016] 1 W.L.R. 4733 at [18] (a series of individual failings did not render the exceptional case funding scheme was not systemically and inherently unfair).

THE PLACE OF PROPORTIONALITY

11-073   Proportionality was suggested by Lord Diplock in the *GCHQ* case in the mid-1980s as a possible fourth ground of judicial review in English law.[274] Yet it has been said that the adoption of proportionality into domestic law would lower the threshold of judicial intervention and involve the courts in considering the merits and facts of administrative decisions.[275] This understanding has, however, come more recently to be questioned.[276] Originating in Prussia[277] in the 19th century, proportionality has assumed a specific form under the case law of the European Court of Justice, where it is regarded as a "general principle of law"[278] and it is similarly employed by the European Court of Human Rights as a standard by which to assess a State's compliance with aspects of the ECHR.[279] British courts now explicitly apply proportionality in respect of directly effective European Union

---

[274] *Council for Civil Service Unions v Minister of State for the Civil Service* [1985]1 A.C. 374, 410.

[275] *R. v Secretary of State for the Home Department Ex p. Brind* [1991] A.C. 696 at 766-767 (Lord Lowry), 762 (Lord Ackner)—argument on proportionality. See also S. Boyron, "Proportionality in English Administrative Law: A Faulty Translation?" (1992) 12 O.J.L.S. 237; R. Thomas, *Legitimate Expectations and Proportionality in Administrative Law* (2000), pp.77ff; G. Wong, "Towards the Nutcracker Principle: reconsidering the Objections to Proportionality" [2000] P.L. 92.

[276] See, e.g. *Kennedy v Charity Commission (Secretary of State for Justice intervening)* [2014] UKSC 20; [2015] A.C. 455, [54] (Lord Mance JSC: "As Professor Paul Craig has shown (see e.g. "The Nature of Reasonableness" (2013) 66 C.L.P. 131), both reasonableness review and proportionality involve considerations of weight and balance, with the intensity of the scrutiny and the weight to be given to any primary decision maker's view depending on the context. The advantage of the terminology of proportionality is that it introduces an element of structure into the exercise, by directing attention to factors such as suitability or appropriateness, necessity and the balance or imbalance of benefits and disadvantages. There seems no reason why such factors should not be relevant in judicial review even outside the scope of Convention and EU law. Whatever the context, the court deploying them must be aware that they overlap potentially and that the intensity with which they are applied is heavily dependent on the context"). See further, R. Williams, "Structuring Substantive Review" [2017] P.L. 99.

[277] The principle of Verhaltnismassigkeit was invoked by the Prussian Supreme Administrative Court to check the discretionary powers of police authorities. See M. Singh, *German Administrative Law: A Common Lawyer's View* (1985), pp.88-101; J. Jowell and A. Lester, "Proportionality: Neither Novel nor Dangerous" in J. Jowell and D. Oliver (eds), *New Directions in Judicial Review* (1989), p.5; J. Schwartze, *European Administrative Law* (revised edn. 2006), Ch.5. For a recent magisterial account of proportionality by a scholar and judge, see Aharon Barak, *Proportionality* (2012); see also the excellent account of proportionality and its relationship to other principles of substantive review, Tom Hickman, *Public Law after the Human Rights Act* (2010); and G. Huscroft, B. Miller and G. Webber, *Proportionality and the Rule of Law* (2017). For recent critique of proportionality as an approach see F. Urbina, *A Critique of Proportionality and Balancing* (2017). See also: G. Lubbe-Wolff, "The principle of Proportionality in the Case Law of the German Federal Constitutional Court" (2014) 34 H.R.L.J. 12.

[278] See Ch.14.

[279] See Ch.13. See D. Feldman, "Proportionality and the Human Rights Act 1998" in E. Ellis (ed), *The Principle of Proportionality in the Laws of Europe* (1999); P. Craig, *Administrative Law*, 5th edn (2003), pp.617 ff.; P. Sales and B. Hooper, "Proportionality and the Form of Law" (2003) 119 L.Q.R. 426; M. Fordham and T. de la Mare, "Proportionality and the Margin of Appreciation" in J. Jowell and J. Cooper (eds), *Understanding Human Rights Principles* (2000). And see T. Hickman, "The substance and structure of proportionality" [2008] P.L. 694 (concluding "[w]e are at a crossroads, and there is a choice: proportionality can either become the fig leaf for unstructured judicial decision-making or it can become a powerful normative and predictive tool in public law"). For articles for and against proportionality as a free-standing public law principle, see P. Craig, "Proportionality, Rationality and Review" [2010] N.Z.L.Rev. 265; compare M. Taggart, "Proportionality, Deference, Wednesbury" [2008] N.Z.L.Rev. 423; T. Hickman, "Problems and Proportionality" [2010] N.Z.L.Rev. 303; P. Sales, "Rationality, proportionality and the development of the law" (2013) 129 L.Q.R. 223; for a middle view see J. King, "Proportionality: A Halfway House", [2010] N.Z.L.Rev. 327. For an account of the Canadian approach see D. Mullan, "Proportionality—A Proportionate Response to an Emerging Crisis in Canadian Judicial Review law" [2010] N.Z.L.Rev. 233. And see

law[280] and, under the HRA 1998, as a structured test to evaluate compatibility with Convention rights, particularly the qualified rights under arts 8-11.[281] Proportionality is also applied in the domestic law of some European countries, and was recommended for adoption in all the Contracting States of the Council of Europe by its Committee of Ministers.[282] It was defined there as requiring an administrative authority, when exercising a discretionary power, to "maintain a proper balance between any adverse effects which its decision may have on the rights, liberties, or interests of persons and the purpose which it pursues".

English law is faced with the decision whether proportionality should now become a separate ground of review, or whether it should supplant unreasonableness as a ground of review. In *British Civilian Internees* Dyson LJ said that "the result that follows will often be the same whether the test that is applied is proportionality or *Wednesbury* unreasonableness". However, he felt that he was unable, without the sanction of the House of Lords, yet "to perform its [unreasonableness'] burial rights".[283] Since then, in the UK Supreme Court, Lord Mance JSC has expressed clear preference for the advantages of proportionality over the vagueness of irrationality.[284] Nonetheless, the prevailing orthodoxy is that (in the words of Lord Sumption JSC) "although English law has not adopted the principle of proportionality generally, it has stumbled towards a concept which is in significant respects similar"—namely, variable intensity rationality review."[285] As we have set out above, there are in fact two different ways in which proportionality is applied:

11-074

---

the essays in H.Wilberg and M. Elliott, *The Scope and Intensity of Substantive Review: Traversing Taggart's Rainbow* (2015).

[280] See 11-077.

[281] See 11-079. I. Leigh, "Taking Rights Proportionately: Judicial Review, the Human Rights Act and Strasbourg" [2002] P.L.265; R. Clayton and H. Tomlinson, *The Law of Human Rights* (2009), para.6-78.

[282] Adopted 11 March 1980.

[283] *R. (on the application of the Association of British Civilian Internees (Far East Region)) v Secretary of State for Defence* [2003] EWCA Civ 473; [2003] Q.B. 1397 at [33]-[35]; *R. v Secretary of State for the Environment, Transport and the Regions Ex p. Holdings & Barnes Plc (the Alconbury case)* [2001] UKHL 23; [2003] 2 A.C. 295 at [50]-[51] (Lord Slynn); *R. (on the application of Daly) v Secretary of State for the Home Department* [2001] UKHL 26; [2001] 2 A.C. 532 at [32] (Lord Cooke). In *Somerville v Scottish Ministers* [2007] UKHL 44; [2007] 1 W.L.R. 2734, the House of Lords left open whether proportionality is an independent ground of judicial review. See Lord Neuberger PSC, "*The Role of Judges in Human Rights Jurisprudence: A Comparison of the Australian and UK Experience*" (conference speech given at the Supreme Court of Victoria, Melbourne, 8 August 2014, available at *http://www.supremecourt.uk/docs/speech-140808.pdf* para.31): "... we now have new ideas to grapple with and to apply to our domestic law, such as the concept of proportionality. But we are also wondering whether ... it makes sense to have such different approaches between a traditional JR challenge to an executive decision on the merits, and a Convention challenge to an administrative decision. On that issue, the judgment in Kennedy (*Kennedy v Charity Commission* [2014] UKSC 20; [2015] A.C. UKSC 455) has something to offer."

[284] See *Kennedy v Charity Commission (Secretary of State for Justice intervening)* [2014] UKSC 20; [2015] A.C. 455 at [54] (Lord Mance JSC, with whom Lord Neuberger of Abbotsbury PSC And Lord Clarke Of Stone-Cum-Ebony JSC agreed), discussed above at para.11-073; *Pham v Secretary of State for the Home Department (Open Society Justice Initiative intervening)* [2015] UKSC 19; [2015] 1 W.L.R. 1591, [98] ("Removal of British citizenship under a power by provided by s.40(2) of the British Nationality Act 1981 is, on any view, a radical step ... A correspondingly strict standard of judicial review must apply to any exercise of the power contained in s.40(2), and the tool of proportionality is one which would, in my view and for the reasons explained in [Kennedy], be both available and valuable for the purposes of such a review"); R. (Keyu) v Secretary of State for Foreign and Commonwealth Affairs [2015] UKSC 69; [2015] 3 W.L.R. 1665 (in which Lord Neuberger, Lord Mance and Lord Hughes indicated that the move from irrationality to proportionality was a decision which ought to be taken by a panel of nine justices rather than the five in the instant case).

[285] *Pham v Secretary of State for the Home Department (Open Society Justice Initiative intervening)* [2015] UKSC 19; [2015] 1 W.L.R. 1591, [105] (Lord Neuberger of Abbotsbury PSC, Baroness Hale

(a) a test of fair balance; and (b) a structured test to examine whether interference by a public authority with a fundamental norm can be justified.

Proportionality as a test of fair balance

11-075   Insofar as the general concept of proportionality is a test requiring the decision-maker to achieve a fair balance, it provides an implicit explanation for some of the existing judicial interventions on the ground of unreasonableness, particularly under two of the categories of unreasonableness we have identified above, namely, those held invalid because they manifestly failed to balance one or more (relevant) consideration,[286] and those where the decision was held to be unreasonably onerous or oppressive.[287] Under the first of these, the courts evaluate whether manifestly disproportionate *weight* has been attached to one or other considerations relevant to the decision. Under the second, the courts consider whether there has been a disproportionate *interference* with the claimant's rights or interests. There will of course always be an examination of rationality in its narrow sense of logical connection between ends and means. In these instances, it makes little difference whether the term employed to describe the administrative wrong is "unreasonable" or "disproportionate" although the latter describes more accurately why the decision is unacceptable. The principal difference between this kind of proportionality and the structured test is that the burden of asserting the disproportion is normally on the claimant rather than the decision-maker.

11-076   As a mere test of "fair balance", proportionality is not therefore alien to English law. Article 20 of Magna Carta provides that "For a trivial offence, a free man will be fined only in proportion to the degree of his offence, and for a serious offence correspondingly, but not so heavily as to deprive him of his livelihood". Proportionality therefore fits well within the ambit of unreasonableness as fair balance, despite dicta almost suggests that proportionality might found the basis of all judicial review,[288] On occasions its name has been specifically invoked, even before it became familiar in the context of the interpretation of EU and ECHR law. For example, Lord Denning would have struck down a decision suspending a stallholder's licence on the ground that "the punishment is altogether excessive and out of proportion to the occasion".[289] A resolution of a local authority banning a member of the public from local authority property was held to be "out of propor-

---

of Richmond DPSC and Lord Wilson JSC agreed). In *R. (Youssef) v Secretary of State for Foreign and Commonwealth Affairs* [2016] UKSC 3; [2016] 2 W.L.R. 509, the Supreme Court considered the standard of review applicable to a challenge to the Foreign Secretary's decision to no longer to support the removal of the claimant from an official list of people associated with Islamic terrorism. Counsel for the Foreign Secretary accepted "that the court is likely to take the approach signalled in *Kennedy* and *Pham* as its starting point, and that the facts of the case make it one in which the review to be conducted will be towards 'the intense end of the scale', conducted 'in accordance with common law principles, incorporating notions of proportionality'" (at [54]). Lord Carnwath JSC (with whom the other Justices agreed) noted the need for the consideration by the Supreme Court of "a general move from the traditional judicial review tests to one of proportionality" and "[s]uch a review might aim for rather more structured guidance for the lower courts than such imprecise concepts as 'anxious scrutiny' and 'sliding scales'" (at [55]).

[286] See 11-033—11-036.

[287] See 11-070—11-072.

[288] *R. v Secretary of State for Education and Employment Ex p. Begbie* [2001] 1 W.L.R. 1115 at [68]; *Nadarajah and Abdi v Secretary of State for the Home Department* [2005] EWCA Civ 1363; *The Times,* 14 December 2005, [68]-[69] (Laws LJ).

[289] *R. v Barnsley MBC Ex p. Hook* [1976] 1 W.L.R. 1052 at 1057 (offence was urinating in the street and using offensive language; CA struck down the suspension on the ground of the lack of a fair hearing); *R. v Secretary of State for the Home Department Ex p. Benwell* [1984] I.C.R. 723 at 736 (Hodson J.: "in an extreme case an administrative or quasi-administrative penalty can be attacked

tion to what the applicant had done",[290] and proportionality was expressly used to test the government's suspension of the permits of Romanian pilots.[291] Laws J held that when justices were determining what sentence to impose upon a person who had failed to pay his non-domestic rates, sufficient regard should be had to the principle of proportionality".[292] He also refused to prohibit the publication of a report critical of the claimant by the Advertising Standards Authority pending a judicial review unless there was a "pressing ground (in the language of the ECtHR, a "pressing social need") to restrain the public body from carrying out its functions in the ordinary way".[293]

Proportionality as a structured test of justifiability in European Union Law

A more sophisticated version of proportionality provides a structured test—a series of questions for the court to address in assessing whether the impugned decision is justifiable. **11-077**

Proportionality is applied by the European Court of Justice and the Court of First Instance to test the lawfulness of Union action or the action of Member States where Union law applies.[294] It applies in domestic courts where European Union law is engaged.[295] Here the courts ask first whether the measure which is being challenged is suitable to attaining the identified ends (the test of *suitability*). Suitability here includes the notion of 'rational connection' between the means and ends. The next step asks whether the measure is necessary and whether a less restrictive or onerous method could have been adopted (the test of *necessity*, requiring *minimum impairment* of the right or interest in question). If the measure passes both tests the court may then go on to ask whether it attains a *fair balance* of means and ends.[296] It is important to note here that the burden of justification in such cases falls on the public authority which has apparently infringed the rights of the claimant or offended a norm of European Union law. **11-078**

Structured proportionality in Convention rights

Although the ECHR does not specify proportionality as a standard of review, proportionality is employed in a similar way to European Union law as a structured test, in particular to assess the conformity of a measure with one of the rights which **11-079**

---

on the ground that it was so disproportionate to the offence as to be perverse"); J. Beatson, "Proportionality" (1988) 104 L.Q.R. 180.

[290] *R. v Brent LBC Ex p. Assegai* (1987) 151 L.G.R. 891 (reason for the ban was the claimant's unruly behaviour at previous meetings).

[291] *R. v Secretary of State for Transport Pegasus Holidays (London) Ltd and Airbro (UK) Ltd* [1988] 1 W.L.R. 990.

[292] *R. v Highbury Corner Justices Ex p. Uchendu* [1994] R.A. 51; *Commissioner of Customs and Excise v Peninsular & Oriental Steam Navigation Company* [1994] S.T.C. 259 (in relation to a penalty imposed for a serious misdeclaration of VAT, only in the most limited circumstances will the doctrine of proportionality be applied to penalties provided for by national law).

[293] *R. v Advertising Standards Authority Ltd Ex p. Vernon Organisation* [1992] 1 W.L.R. 1289.

[294] See Ch.14; proportionality is now expressly recognised in art.5 of the EC Treaty and fundamental rights recognised in art.6 of the Treaty on European Union; P. Craig, *EU Administrative Law* (2006), Chs 17 and 18; J. Schwartze, *European Administrative Law* (2006), Pt II.

[295] See 11–058. See e.g. *Zalewska v Department of Social Security* [2008] UKHL 67; [2008] 1 W.L.R. 2602; *R. (on the application of Sinclair Collis Ltd) v Secretary of State for Health* [2011] EWCA Civ 437; [2012] Q.B. 394. For detailed consideration of proportionality in domestic courts where European Union law is engaged see the decision of the Supreme Court in *R.(on the application of Lumsdon) v Legal Services Board* [2015] UKSC 41; [2015] 3 W.L.R. 121.

[296] Referred to by Craig as "proportionality strictu senso" (2006), p.657.

may be limited—the "qualified rights" under arts 8-12.[297] Here too the burden is on the public authority to justify the departure from the right in question. The authority will normally be required to demonstrate that the measures are "prescribed by the law"; that they pursue a legitimate end or an end specified in the relevant article (ends such as national security or public safety); that they are rationally connected to that end; that no less restrictive alternative could have been adopted, and that they are necessary (and not merely desirable). Some of the articles specify the concept of necessity as being "necessary in a democratic society". This requirement engages the courts in an exercise of constitutional review. This is because it seeks not merely a 'fair balance' between the measure and the social end, but because it requires the court to assess the measures by the standards of a constitutional democracy.[298] This point is well illustrated by the difference of approach between the Court of Appeal and the ECtHR in *Smith*,[299] where, despite applying the test of "anxious scrutiny",[300] the Court of Appeal upheld the ban on homosexuals in the armed forces. The ECtHR not only required more convincing justification for the ban, but also tested it by the democratic requirements of "pluralism, tolerance and broadmindedness".[301]

Structured proportionality in English law

11-080   In *Daly*,[302] a case which came to be decided before the HRA came into force, the House of Lords adopted the test of proportionality adopted by the Privy Council in *de Freitas v Permanent Secretary of Ministry of Agriculture, Fisheries, Land and Housing*.[303] Drawing on South African, Canadian and Zimbabwean authority, it was said that:

> "When determining whether a limitation (by an act, rule or decision) is arbitrary or excessive the court should ask itself: whether: (i) the legislative objective is sufficiently important to justify limiting a fundamental right; (ii) the measures designed to meet the legislative objective are rationally connected to it; and (iii) the means used to impair the right or freedom are no more than is necessary to accomplish the objective".

11-081   Clearly this test is, as Lord Steyn said in *Daly*, "more sophisticated than the traditional (i.e. unreasonableness) ground of judicial review".[304] It is much more

---

[297] See Ch.13; I. Leigh, "Taking Rights Proportionately: Judicial Review, the Human Rights Act and Judicial Review" [2002] P.L. 265; P. Craig, "The Courts, the Human Rights Act and Judicial Review" (2001) 117 L.Q.R. 589; M.Elliott, "The HRA 1998 and the Standard of Substantive Review" (2001) 60 C.L.J. 301.

[298] J. Jowell, "Beyond the Rule of Law: Towards Constitutional Judicial Review" [2000] P.L. 671.

[299] *R. v Ministry of Defence Ex p. Smith* [1996] Q.B. 517.

[300] See 11-086 and following.

[301] *Smith and Grady v United Kingdom* (1999) 29 E.H.R.R. 493, [138]-[139]. In *Bank Mellat v HM Treasury* [2013] UKSC 39; [2014] A.C. 700 at [70], [72] Lord Reed commented that the European Court of Human Rights often approached striking a fair balance "in a relatively broad-brush way … The intensity of review varies considerably according to the right in issue and the context in which the question arises. Unsurprisingly … its approach to proportionality does not correspond precisely to the various approaches adopted in contracting states". Further, on the approach to proportionality adopted in the UK domestic courts under the Human Rights Act, he continued: "In accordance with the analytical approach to legal reasoning characteristic of the common law, a more clearly structured approach has generally been adopted."

[302] *R. v Secretary of State for the Home Department Ex p. Daly* [2001] UKHL 26; [2001] 2 A.C. 532.

[303] *de Freitas v Permanent Secretary of Ministry of Agriculture, Fisheries, Land and Housing* [1999] 1 A.C. 69, 80 (Lord Clyde).

[304] At [27]. See also Aharon Barak, *Proportionality: Constitutional Rights and their Limitations* (2012), who sees proportionality as a "legal construction" or "methodological tool" to justify the limitation of constitutional rights. He regards it as made of four components: Proper purpose; rational connec-

than the "fair balance" test.[305] It requires the court to seek first whether the action pursues a legitimate aim (i.e. one of the designated reasons to depart from a Convention right, such as national security). It then asks whether the measure employed is capable of achieving that aim, namely, whether there is a "rational connection" between the measures and the aim. Thirdly it asks whether a less restrictive alternative could have been employed. Even if these three hurdles are achieved, however (and the tripartite *de Frietas* test ignores this) there is a fourth step which the decision-maker has to climb, namely, to demonstrate that the measure must be "necessary" which requires the courts to insist that the measure genuinely addresses a "pressing social need", and is not just desirable or reasonable, by the standards of a democratic society.[306] In *Huang*, Lord Bingham acknowledged that that fourth step, which featured in the judgment of Dickson CJ in the Canadian case *R. v Oakes*,[307] "should never be overlooked or discounted" and the failure to consider that final step "should be made good".[308]

---

tion; necessary means, and a proper relation between the benefit gained by realising the proper purpose and the harm caused to the constitutional right (the last component—the 'balancing' element—called "proportionality *stricto sensu*" (at 131)).

[305] *Brown v Stott* [2003] 1 A.C. 681, 728 (Lord Hope alluded to it as a "fair balance" test).

[306] *Sunday Times v UK* (1979) 2 E.H.R.R. 245 at 275, 277-278; *R. v Secretary of State for the Home Department Ex p. Daly* [2001] UKHL 26; [2001] 2 A.C. 532 at [28] (a point elaborated by Lord Steyn in *Daly* when dealing with the intensity of review, which he said was determined by "the twin requirements that the limitation of the right was necessary in a democratic society, in the sense of meeting a pressing social need, and the question whether the interference was really proportionate to the legitimate aim being pursued").

[307] *R. v Oakes* [1986] 1 S.C.R. 103 at 139.

[308] *Huang v Secretary of State for the Home Department* [2007] UKHL 11; [2007] 2 W.L.R. 581 at [19]—as it had been overlooked in *R. (on the application of Razgar) v Secretary of State for the Home Department (No.2)* [2004] UKHL 27; [2004] 2 A.C. 368 at [20]. Lord Bingham described the *Oakes* test as requiring "the striking of a fair balance between the rights of the individual and the interests of the community". This is indeed described in *Oakes* as a general objective of the proportionality test, however the actual words used in Oakes require a proportionality between "the effects of a measure [responsible for limiting the Canadian Charter's rights]" and the "objective which has been identified as of 'sufficient importance'". This in effect imports the 'necessity' test in the context of the Canadian Charter of Rights and Freedoms, s.1 which requires the rights and freedoms set out in it to be subject only to "such reasonable limits prescribed by law as can be demonstrably justified in a free and democratic society". In *Bank Mellat v HM Treasury* [2013] UKSC 39; [2014] A.C. 700 at [74] Lord Reed, in a statement approved by the whole court, said that the approach in Oakes could be summarised by saying that it is necessary to determine: "(1) whether the objective of the measure is sufficiently important to justify the limitation of a protected right, (2) whether the measure is rationally connected to the objective, (3) whether a less intrusive measure could have been used without unacceptably compromising the achievement of the objective, and (4) whether, balancing the severity of the measure's effects on the rights of the persons to whom it applies against the importance of the objective, to the extent that the measure will contribute to its achievement, the former outweighs the latter." Further, "... there is a meaningful distinction to be drawn ... between the question whether a particular objective is in principle sufficiently important to justify limiting a particular right (step one), and the question whether, having determined that no less drastic means of achieving the objective are available, the impact of the rights infringement is disproportionate to the likely benefits of the impugned measure (step four)" (at [76]). Lord Sumption also acknowledged the fourth step in his leading judgment as requiring "a fair balance ... between the rights of the individual and the interests of the community" (at [20]). In *R. (on the application of Miranda) v Secretary of State for the Home Department* [2014] EWHC 255 (Admin); [2014] 1 W.L.R. 3140 at [40] Laws LJ said of the Oakes fourth step: "I think it needs to be approached with some care. It requires the court ... to decide whether the measure, though it has a justified purpose and is no more intrusive than necessary, is nevertheless offensive because it fails to strike the right balance between private right and public interest; and the court is the judge of where that balance should lie ... there is real difficulty in distinguishing this from a political question to be decided by the elected arm of government. If it is properly within the judicial sphere, it must be on the footing that there is a plain case." On the facts of that case, however, the balance was to be

11-082   In 1991, proportionality was pleaded in *Brind*, and, although not there applied, future application was not ruled out.[309] However, in *Attorney General v Guardian Newspapers Ltd (No.2)*, Lord Goff had said that

> "It is established in the jurisprudence of the European Court of Human Rights that ... interference with freedom of expression should be no more than is proportionate to the legitimate aim pursued. I have no reason to believe that English law, as applied in the courts, leads to any different conclusion."[310]

11-083   The reserve expressed towards proportionality in *Brind* was not shared in *Leech*, in which the Court of Appeal upheld the constitutional right of a prisoner to access to the courts.[311] The question was whether the interference with a prisoner's mail permitted by the regulations was broad enough to infringe that right. The test adopted by Steyn LJ to decide that question was whether there was a "self-evident and pressing need" for such a power.[312] None was demonstrated. The language of proportionality was thus explicit and the Court of Appeal even went so far as to consider the case law of ECtHR on the matter which, although not directly applicable in this pre-HRA case, "reinforces a conclusion that we have arrived at in the light of the principles of our domestic jurisprudence".[313] In *Daly*,[314] although Lord Steyn held that proportionality is "applicable in respect of review where Convention rights are at stake",[315] Lord Bingham made it clear that proportionality was also the test under common law constitutional rights. He said that

> "the policy provides for a degree of intrusion into the privileged legal correspondence of prisoners which is greater than is justified by the objectives the policy is intended to serve, and so violates the common law rights of prisoners".[316]

11-084   The application of a common law test of proportionality was considered by the Supreme Court in *Pham v Secretary of State for the Home Department*.[317] While the case did not turn upon proportionality, all seven justices gave support to the "flexible approach to principles of judicial review" (per Lord Carnworth at [60]) endorsed by the Supreme Court in *Kennedy v Information a Commissioner (Secretary of State for Justice intervening)*.[318] Moreover, the majority of the court explicitly endorsed the possibility of a common law standard of proportionality review. As Lord Mance observed at [98]:

> "Removal of British citizenship under the power provided by section 40(2) of the British Nationality Act 1981 is, on any view, a radical step, particularly if the person affected has little real attachment to the country of any other nationality that he possesses and is

---

struck between two aspects of the public interest—press freedom and national security—and, on the facts, the balance clearly favoured national security.

[309] *R. v Secretary of State for the Home Department Ex p. Brind* [1991] 1 A.C. 696 (Lords Bridge, Roskill and Templeman); *R. v Independent Television Commission TSW Broadcasting Ltd* [1996] E.M.L.R. 291 (Lord Templeman was willing to apply proportionality if appropriate, which it was not).

[310] *Attorney General v Observer Ltd* [1990] 1 A.C. 109 at 283; Lord Griffiths at 273.

[311] *R. v Secretary of State for the Home Department Ex p. Leech* [1994] Q.B. 198.

[312] At 211; also referred to as "objective need" (at 212) or "demonstrable need" (at 213).

[313] At 212 (Steyn L.J); the case referred to was *Campbell v UK* (1993) 15 E.H.R.R. 137.

[314] *R. (on the application of Daly) v Secretary of State for the Home Department* [2001] UKHL 26; [2001] 2 A.C. 532 (where the approach in *Leech* ([1994] Q.B. 198)) was confirmed.

[315] At [24].

[316] At [21].

[317] *Pham v Secretary of State for the Home Department* [2015] UKSC 19; [2015] 1 W.L.R. 1591.

[318] *Kennedy v Information a Commissioner (Secretary of State for Justice intervening)* [2014] UKSC 20; [2015] A.C. 455.

unlikely to be able to return there. A correspondingly strict standard of judicial review must apply to any exercise of the power contained in section 40(2), and the tool of proportionality is one which would, in my view and for the reasons explained in *Kennedy v Information Comr* ... be both available and valuable for the purposes of such a review."

Similarly, Lord Sumption at [105]:

"...although English law has not adopted the principle of proportionality generally, it has for many years stumbled towards a concept which is in significant respects similar, and over the last three decades has been influenced by European jurisprudence even in areas of law lying beyond the domains of EU and international human rights law. Starting with the decision of the House of Lords in *R v Secretary of State for the Home Department, Ex p Bugdaycay* [1987] A.C. 514 it has recognised the need, even in the context of rights arising wholly from domestic law, to differentiate between rights of greater or lesser importance and interference with them of greater or lesser degree. This is essentially the same problem as the one to which proportionality analysis is directed. The solution adopted, albeit sometimes without acknowledgment, was to expand the scope of rationality review so as to incorporate at common law significant elements of the principle of proportionality."[319]

The overlap between proportionality and unreasonableness

We have seen that the standards of proportionality—in both its senses—and unreasonableness are inextricably intertwined. Unreasonableness contains two elements of proportionality when it requires the weight of relevant considerations to be fairly balanced, and when it forbids unduly oppressive decisions.[320] The notion of "rational connection" between means and ends is another. As we have noted above, such a test was applied, for example in a case where a non-statutory scheme was introduced to provide compensation for British civilians interned during World War II by the Japanese. The scheme excluded individuals whose parents or grandparents were not born in the United Kingdom. The Court of Appeal examined carefully whether the exclusion bore a rational connection to the "foundation" and "essential character" of the scheme, but held in the circumstances that the scheme did not fail the *Wednesbury* test.[321] The House of Lords had adopted a similar approach in a case where, under an ex gratia compensation scheme, British soldiers injured in Bosnia were accorded treatment different from those injured in Northern Ireland.[322] The Canadian Supreme Court defined the notion of "rational connection" under their test of structured proportionality in terms which show strikingly how the notion of reasonableness lies deep within proportionality: "The measures

11-085

---

[319] See also *R. (Keyu) v Secretary of State for Foreign and Commonwealth Affairs* [2015] UKSC 69; [2015] 3 W.L.R. 1665, in which the majority in the Supreme Court emphasised the close relationship between rationality and proportionality, indicating that they would produce identical outcomes in the instant case; *R. (Youssef) v Secretary of State for Foreign and Commonwealth Affairs* [2016] UKSC 3; [2016] 2 W.L.R. 509, to similar effect.

[320] Some cases hold that proportionality refers to outcome alone, and not the reasoning process: see, e.g. *Belfast City Council v Miss Behavin'* [2007] UKHL 19; [2007] 1 W.L.R. 1420.

[321] *R. (on the application of Association of British Civilian Internees (Far East Region)) v Secretary of State for Defence* [2003] EWCA Civ 473; [2003] Q.B. 1397 at [40]; see *Ganga v Commissioner of Police* [2011] UKPC 28 at [21], [28] ("The measures designed to further the objective must be rationally connected to it").

[322] *R. v Ministry of Defence Ex p. Walker* [2000] 1 W.L.R. 806 at 812 (Lord Slynn: "It is not for the courts to consider whether the scheme ... is a good scheme or a bad scheme, unless it can be said that the exclusion is so irrational or unreasonable that no reasonable Minister could have adopted it"), 816 (Lord Hoffmann: the distinction was "fine" but not irrational: "That is too high a hurdle to surmount").

must be carefully designed to meet the objective in question. They must not be arbitrary, unfair or based on irrational considerations".[323]

11-086   In addition, the notion in proportionality of "minimal impairment" (that a less restrictive alternative be pursued) has been applied in a number of cases based overtly on unreasonableness. As we have seen, planning conditions have been struck down because a less restrictive or less onerous alternative could be provided—such as would permit compensation to be paid to the owner of the land.[324] Compulsory purchase of land has been invalidated because the authority was able voluntarily to acquire other equally suitable land.[325] It has been held that the decision to delist a company, as opposed to "lesser measures" (such as the continuation of the suspension of the shares) was, in the circumstances, and having taken into account the interests of the shareholders, "not disproportionate to the damage which it was designed to prevent either at common law or under Community law".[326] However, there seems some reluctance to adopt the full rigour of the minimum impairment requirement of proportionality.[327]

---

[323] *R. v Chaulk* [1990] 3 S.C.R. 1303 at 1335-1336 (Lamer CJ). The test was first established in *R. v Oakes* [1988] 1 S.C.R. 103 at 137-138.

[324] *Hall and Co v Shoreham-by-Sea UDC* [1964] 1 W.L.R. 240. See Tom Hickman, *Public Law After the Human Rights Act* (2010) who, at 190, prefers to identify the minimum impairment (or less injurious) component of proportionality as "relative", as opposed to "overall" proportionality.

[325] *Brown v Secretary of State for the Environment* (1978) 40 P. & C.R. 285.

[326] *R. v International Stock Exchange of the United Kingdom and the Republic of Ireland Ex p. Else (1982) Ltd* [1993] Q.B. 534 (proportionality was applied here as an aspect of rationality); *R. v Tamworth Justices Ex p. Walsh* [1994] C.O.D. 277 (justices acted unreasonably in committing to custody a solicitor who criticised the listing system in court. Three alternative measures were available: ordering his removal; reporting him to the Law Society, or adjourning the matter. They had used "a sledgehammer to crack a nut"); *R. v Camden LBC Ex p. Cran* [1995] R.T.R. 346 (consultation with residents about car-parking scheme deficient because "there had been no recognition of the possibility let alone the fact that a number of the beneficial results of introducing full controls might have been well achieved by other means").

[327] See, e.g. *Bank Mellat v Her Majesty's Treasury (No.2)* [2011] EWCA Civ 1; [2012] Q.B. 101 (Maurice Kay LJ, although not requiring the wholesale rejection of the minimum interference test, counselled its "cautious deployment"). The Court of Appeal's decision was reversed by the Supreme Court [2013] UKSC 39; [2014] A.C. 700. In his leading judgment, however, Lord Sumption stated at [20] that he agreed with the view expressed in the court below by Maurice Kay LJ that "this debate [on minimum interference] is sterile in the normal case where the effectiveness of the measure and the degree of interference are not absolute values but a question of degree, inversely related to each other. The question is whether a less intrusive measure could have been used without unacceptably compromising the objective". Lord Reed commented at [75]: "In relation to (the minimum interference test) Dickson CJ made clear in *R v Edwards Books and Art Ltd* [1986] ... that the limitation of the protected right must be one that 'it was reasonable for the legislature to impose', and that the courts were 'not called on to substitute judicial opinions for legislative ones as to the place at which to draw a precise line.' This approach is unavoidable, if there is to be any real prospect of a limitation on rights being justified: as Blackmun J once observed, 'a judge would be unimaginative indeed if he could not come up with something a little less drastic or a little less restrictive in almost any situation, and thereby enable himself to vote to strike legislation down'". *R. (on the application of Sinclair Collis Ltd) v Secretary of State for Health* [2011] EWCA Civ 437; [2012] Q.B. 394 (CA, Laws LJ dissenting, asked whether the conclusion that a less intrusive measure was "manifestly inappropriate"); cf. *R. (on the application of E) v Governing Body of JFS* [2009] UKSC 15; [2010] 2 A.C. 728. See T. Hickman, "Proportionality: Comparative Law Lessons" [2007] J.R. 31. Minimum impairment has been applied in Israeli law: I. Zamir and Z. Zysblat, *Public Law in Israel* (1996), Pts 2, 3 and 11, see e.g. *Laor v Board of Censorship for Films and Plays* (1987) 41(1) P.D. 421 (total ban on a film causing "near certainty of substantial damage" to public order was held disproportionate where less restrictive measures, such as the cutting out of certain scenes, could have dealt with the problem); I. Zamir, "Unreasonableness, Balance of Interests and Proportionality" (1993) *Tel-Aviv Studies in Law* 131; A. Barak, *The Judge in a Democracy* (2006), pp.254-260. For an application of the least restrictive alternative approach (under a test of unreasonableness) in Hong Kong, see *Society for the Protection of the Harbour Ltd v Town Planning Board* (Ct of First Instance No.19

INTENSITY OF REVIEW

Whether a court carries out substantive review of a decision by reference to the concept of unreasonableness or proportionality, two questions arise: To what extent should the courts allow a degree of latitude or leeway to the decision-maker?[328] And to what extent should it be uniform?[329] The answers to these questions depend in large part on the respective constitutional roles of the court and the primary decision-maker (the impugned public authority),[330] but also on practical considerations. The willingness of the courts to invalidate a decision on the ground of its substance will be influenced in part by the administrative scheme under review; the subject matter of the decision; the importance of the countervailing rights or interests and the extent of the interference with the right or interest. Indeed the intensity of review will differ, for the reason that "in public law, context is all".[331] The threshold of intervention is particularly influenced by the respective institutional competence of the decision-maker and the court. Figure 1 below illustrates the range of intensity of review employed in different contexts.

11-087

---

of 2003, Chu J (upheld for different reasons by the Court of Final Appeal of the Hong Kong Special Administrative Region No.14 of 2003 (Civil)).

[328] On the "discretionary area of judgement", see D. Pannick, "Principles of Interpretation of Convention Rights Under the HRA and the Discretionary Area of Judgment" [1998] P.L. 545; A. Lester and D. Pannick, *Human Rights Law and Practice*, 2nd edn (2004), paras 3.18-3.21.

[329] J. Rivers, "Proportionality and variable intensity of review" [2006] C.L.J. 174; Y. Arai-Takahashi, *The Margin of Appreciation Doctrine and the Principle of Proportionality in the Jurisprudence of the ECHR* (2000); M. Elliott, "The Human Rights Act and the Standard of Substantive Review" [2001] C.L.J. 301; A. Le Sueur, "The Rise and Ruin of Unreasonableness" [2005] J.R.32. See various chapters in H. Wilberg and M. Elliott, *The Scope and Intensity of Substantive Review: Traversing Taggart's Rainbow* (2015).

[330] See 11-014.

[331] *Daly* [2001] UKHL 26; [2001] 2 A.C. 532 at [28] (Lord Steyn). In other words, the court is required to carry out a careful exercise of weighing the legitimate aim to be pursued, the importance of the right which is the subject of the interference and the extent of the interference. Thus an interference whose object is to protect the community from the danger of terrorism is more readily justified as proportionate than an interference whose object is to protect the community from the risk of low level crime and disorder. See *R. (on the application of Gillan) v Commissioner of Police of the Metropolis* [2006] UKHL 12; [2006] 2 A.C. 307; *Wood v Commissioner of Police of the Metropolis* [2009] EWCA Civ 414; [2010] 1 W.L.R. 123 at [83]–[86] (Dyson LJ). See also *SS (Nigeria) v Secretary of State for the Home Department* [2013] EWCA Civ 550; [2014] 1 W.L.R. 998 at [41]–[42] per Laws LJ: "But the principle [of minimal interference] does not tell us that ... the court must always be the primary judge of the principle's fulfilment or otherwise. The court insists that the decisionmaker respect the principle; but this is perfectly consonant with the decisionmaker's enjoyment of a margin of discretion as to what constitutes minimal interference ... the breadth of this margin is conditioned by context, and in particular driven by two factors: (1) the nature of the public decision, and (2) its source ... The principle ... can never ... be treated as a token or ritual. But the margin of discretionary judgment enjoyed by the primary decisionmaker, though variable, means that the court's role is kept in balance with that of the elected arms of government." See A. Vaughan, "Minimum Interference Versus Rationality: The New Battleground in HRA Proportionality?" [2013] J.R. 416. In *Pham v Secretary of State for the Home Department (Open Society Justice Initiative intervening)* [2015] UKSC 19; [2015] 1 W.L.R. 1591, [107] Lord Sumption JSC questioned whether the distinctions drawn by Lord Steyn in *Daly* between proportionality and rationality review were "as simple as this", stating that "It is for the court to assess how broad the range of rational decisions is in the circumstances of any given case. That must necessarily depend on the significance of the right interfered with, the degree of interference involved, and notably the extent to which, even on a statutory appeal, the court is competent to reassess the balance which the decision-maker was called on to make given the subject-matter. The differences pointed out by Lord Steyn may in practice be more or less significant depending on the answers to these questions. In some cases, the range of rational decisions is so narrow as to determine the outcome".)

FULL INTESITY REVIEW	STRUCTURED PROPORTIONALITY REVIEW	VARIABLE INTENSITY UNREASONABLENESS REVIEW Depending on the nature of the subject matter			NON-JUSTICIABLE
Court decides "correctness" and whether power abused	Intensity of review may vary according to the context Burden of justification on public authority	←		→	But adequacy of justification still required
		Anxious scrutiny unreasonableness review Burden on public authority	Standard *Wednesbury* unreasonableness review Burden on claimant	"Light touch" unreasonableness review Burden on claimant	

Figure 1

Full intensity "correctness" review for abuse of power

11-088   There are situations in which there is no constitutional reason, or reason based upon institutional capacity,[332] for the court to allow any margin of discretion to the public authority. The court is in as good a position as the primary decision-maker to assess the relevant factors and may indeed have a duty to do so. When the court intervenes in this way it sometimes refers to the ground of review as "abuse of power" rather than unreasonableness or proportionality. Three main fields may be identified.

- First, as we have seen above there are cases where no evidence for the decision exists, or where a decision is taken in ignorance of an established or relevant fact.[333]
- Secondly, are decisions offending against consistency.[334]
- Thirdly, are some (but not all) decisions where the decision-maker seeks to disappoint a legitimate expectation, which will be discussed in Chapter 12.

11-089   In many cases of legitimate expectation the courts will show deference to the decision-maker who wishes to alter his policy in the public interest, but when the class of promisee is limited and the promise is in the "nature of a contract", the court itself will determine whether the breach of promise is unlawful.

Structured proportionality review

11-090   As we have seen, structured proportionality requires the public authority to justify its actions by satisfying the court that it fulfils a series of stepped standards.[335] It is more searching than unreasonableness review because the burden is on the public authority to justify a departure from a fundamental norm.[336] This involves a more sophisticated scrutiny than mere unreasonableness review because it erects more barriers for the decision-maker to hurdle (some of which overlap with ordinary unreasonableness review, such as those which require a "rational connection" and "fair balance" between ends and means). As Lord Hope said in *R. v Shayler*,

---

[332] See 11-005.

[333] See 11-036.

[334] See 11-062.

[335] *R. (on the application of HH) v Deputy Prosecutor of the Italian Republic, Genoa* [2012] UKSC 25; [2012] 3 W.L.R. 90 (Baroness Hale described the "structured approach" to a case under ECHR art.8).

[336] *R. (on the application of Quila) v Secretary of State for the Home Department* [2011] UKSC 45; [2012] 1 A.C. 621 at [44] (Lord Wilson); *R. (on the application of Sinclair Collis Ltd) v Secretary of State for Health* [2011] EWCA Civ 437; [2012] Q.B. 394 at [48].

proportionality (under the HRA) requires "a close and penetrating examination of the factual justification of the restriction"[337] and Lord Bingham said the "the court will now conduct a much more rigorous review than was once thought to be permissible".[338] The requirement under proportionality of "minimum impairment" of rights, requires decision-makers to consider less onerous means to achieve their ends. Although, as we have seen,[339] the English courts have sometimes required the decision-maker to have considered less onerous alternatives, they have not generally gone that far.[340] This process of justification will therefore require more attention from the courts to the process of reasoning of the decision-maker, and the relationship between the facts and the inferences drawn from them, than the default position of unreasonableness review normally concedes. In *Tweed v Parades Commission for Northern Ireland* it was held that "the proportionality of a public authority's interference with a protected Convention right is likely to call for a careful and accurate evaluation of the facts"[341] and therefore in order to assess the issues of proportionality the court should have access to documents from which the Commission received information and advice.

However, structured proportionality does not herald the end of deference. In European Union law, even in the context of structured proportionality, the ECJ requires "manifest" disproportionality before interfering with certain decisions.[342] Varying levels of the intensity of review will be appropriate in different categories of case. For example, in respect of measures involving the European Commission in "complex economic assessment", such as in the implementation of anti-dumping measures, the ECJ will display "extreme self restraint"[343] and only substitute its own discretion for that of the Commission if it can be shown that the conclusions of the Commission were "manifestly" or "patently" wrong.[344]   **11-091**

Similarly, in relation to Convention rights, the courts tend to defer to the legislature or administration in decisions involving "broad social policy"[345] or the   **11-092**

---

[337] *R. v Shayler* [2003] 1 A.C. 247 at [61].

[338] *R. v Shayler* [2003] 1 A.C. 247 at [33].

[339] See 11-086.

[340] See *R. (on the application of Sinclair Collis Ltd) v Secretary of State for Health* [2011] EWCA Civ 437; [2012] Q.B. 394.

[341] *Tweed v Parades Commission for Northern Ireland* [2006] UKHL 53; [2007] 1 A.C. 650 at 655 (Lord Bingham). See the discussion on evidence and fact, above, summarised at 11-056.

[342] See Ch.14; e.g. *R. v Ministry of Agriculture, Fisheries and Food Ex p. Astonquest* [2000] Eu L.R. 371 (Robert Walker LJ) using the test of "manifest inappropriateness". See *R. (on the application of Sinclair Collis Ltd) v Secretary of State for Health* [2011] EWCA Civ 437; [2012] Q.B. 394.

[343] A. Egger, "The Principle of Proportionality in Community Anti-dumping Law" (1993) 18 E.L. Rev. 367.

[344] See Case 57/72 *Westzucker v EVS Zucher* [1973] E.C.R. 321; Case 136/77 *Rache v HZA Mainz* [1978] E.C.R. 1245.

[345] This point has been made most forcefully by Lord Hoffmann: "Separation of Powers" [2002] J.R. 137 and his statement in *R. v Secretary of State for the Environment, Transport and the Regions Ex p. Holdings & Barnes Plc (the Alconbury case)* [2001] UKHL 23; [2003] 2 A.C. 295 at [75]-[76], where he distinguished a "policy decisions" from a "determination of right". Policy decisions should be made not by the courts, he said, but, in a democracy by "democratically elected bodies or persons accountable to them". *Wilson v Secretary of State for Trade and Industry* [2003] UKHL 40; [2004] 1 A.C. 816 at [70] (Lord Nicholls: "The more the legislation concerns matters of broad social policy the less ready will be a court to intervene"); *Hooper v Secretary of State for Work and Pensions* [2003] EWCA Civ 813; [2003] 1 W.L.R. 2623 at [63]-[64] (Laws LJ: "A very considerable margin of discretion must be accorded to the Secretary of State. Difficult questions of economic and social policy were involved, the resolution of which fell within the province of the executive and the legislature rather than the courts"); *R. v Secretary of State for Education and Employment Ex p. Begbie* [2000] 1 W.L.R. 1115 at 1131 (Laws LJ: less intrusive judicial review should apply to decisions in the "macro-political field"). And see the decision of the UK Supreme Court holding that there

allocation of finite financial resources[346] (although, as we shall consider below,[347] these categories do not wholly relieve the authority from judicial scrutiny, particularly in order to determine whether the decision was otherwise properly justified).[348]

Variable intensity unreasonableness review

11-093   It has been suggested in a number of cases that we now have a "sliding scale of review".[349] Over the past 20 years or so, the courts carrying out substantive review under the head of unreasonableness have sought to develop a series of categories to explain the intensity or lack of intensity of review that should be used in particular contexts.

Heightened scrutiny unreasonableness review

11-094   There was a growing realisation that the traditional *Wednesbury* standard was inappropriate where a decision interfered with a fundamental right or important interest. Such decisions should be subject to the "most anxious scrutiny of the courts".[350] In *Brind*, the majority indicated that a decision-maker who exercises broad discretion must show that an infringement of the right to expression can only be justified by an "important competing public interest".[351] Perhaps the clearest indication of this approach is to be found in the Court of Appeal's decision in *R. v Ministry of Defence Ex p. Smith*. In this challenge to the exclusion of homosexuals from the armed forces, Sir Thomas Bingham MR accepted that "the more substantial the interference with human rights, the more the court will require by

---

should be a wide margin of discretion to decisions involving broad social policy: *R (Tigere) v Secretary of State for Busniness, Innovation and Skills* [2015] UKSC 57; [2015] 1 W.L.R. 3820.

[346] *Michaelek v Wandsworth LBC* [2002] EWCA Civ 271; [2003] 1 W.L.R. 617 at [41] (Brooke LJ: "this is pre-eminently a field in which the courts should defer to the decisions taken by a democratically elected Parliament, which has determined the manner in which public resources should be allocated for local authority housing").

[347] See 11-100–11-101.

[348] A point well made by T.R.S. Allan, "Human Rights and Judicial Review: A Critique of Due Deference" [2006] C.L.J. 671.

[349] *Begbie* [2000] 1 W.L.R. 1115 at 1130. And see *Kennedy v Information Commissioner (Secretary of State for Justice intervening)* [2014] UKSC 20; [2015] A.C. 455, [51] (Lord Mance: "The common law no longer insists on the uniform application of a rigid test of irrationality once thought applicable under the so-called Wednesbury principle ... The nature of judicial review in every case depends on the context"). See, however, Lord Carnwath's disapprobation of the "imprecise concepts" of "anxious scrutiny" and "sliding scales" in *Youseff v Secretary of State for Foreign and Commonwealth Affairs* [2016] UKSC 3; [2016] A.C. 1457.

[350] *Bugdaycay v Secretary of State for the Home Department* [1987] A.C. 514 at 531 (Lord Bridge, speaking of the right to life in a deportation case); and *National and Local Government Officers Association v Secretary of State for the Environment* (1993) Admin. L.R. 785 (applying the test to the restriction on the political activities on local government officers); In *Prest v Secretary of State for Wales* (1982) 81 L.G.R. 193 (Watkins LJ said that compulsory purchase decisions must be "carefully scrutinised", and Lord Denning MR said the Secretary of State must in such cases show that the public interest "decisively demands" the compulsory purchase order); *R. v Secretary of State for the Home Department Ex p. Launder* [1997] 1 W.L.R. 839 (it was normally open to the court to review the exercise of the Home Secretary's discretion under the Extradition Act 1989 s.12. The fact that a decision was taken on policy grounds of an important or sensitive nature and involving delicate relations between foreign states did not affect the court's duty to ensure the claimant was afforded proper protection, although the court would be mindful of both the limitations of its constitutional role and the need in such a case for "anxious scrutiny"). For recent detailed consideration of anxious scrutiny see P Craig, "Judicial review and anxious scrutiny: foundations, evolution and application" [2015] P.L. 60.

[351] *R. v Secretary of State for the Home Department Ex p. Brind* [1991] A.C. 696 at 749-751.

justification before it is satisfied that the decision is reasonable"[352]—a formulation which goes some way towards asking not the claimant to demonstrate unreasonableness, but the decision-maker to justify that the decision was "reasonable".[353] In *Saville*, the Court of Appeal said that "it is not open to the decision-maker to risk interfering with fundamental rights in the absence of compelling justification".[354]

This notion of "anxious" or "heightened" scrutiny is difficult to define with any precision, but it does indicate that the full rigour of *Wednesbury* is softened. Two fundamentals govern the court's role. First, the court's function remains one of review for error of law.[355] The court is not a fact-finder (though, as we have seen,[356] it may evaluate the fact-finding process of the primary decision-maker).[357] Secondly, the burden of argument shifts from the claimant to the defendant public authority, which needs to produce a justification for the decision. The court will be less inclined to accept ex post facto justifications from the public authority, compared to traditional unreasonableness review.[358]   **11-095**

That is not to say that there should be no deference. Heightened scrutiny is not merits or "correctness" review[359] any more than is structured proportionality and the courts have urged a "common sense" approach. Anxious scrutiny "does not mean that the court should strive by tortuous mental gymnastics to find error in the decision under review when in truth there has been none".[360] Moreover, "the concern of the court ought to be substance not semantics", so it is inappropriate to focus "on particular sentences" in a decision-maker's determination "and to subject them to the kind of legalistic scrutiny that might perhaps be appropriate in the case of a statutory instrument, charter party or trust deed".[361] But while it would be wrong to interpret the decision of a decision-maker "in a minute textual fashion ... it must be right in every case to see whether substantial and proper reasons are given".[362]   **11-096**

The scope for application of anxious scrutiny approaches to unreasonableness has changed since the coming into force of the HRA. Many of the leading statements   **11-097**

---

[352] A similar approach has been taken in India towards interference with fundamental rights: *Om Kumar v Union of India* 2001 (2) S.C.C. 386 at 399, 405 (Rao J).

[353] *R. v Ministry of Defence Ex p. Smith* [1996] Q.B. 517.

[354] *R. v Lord Saville of Newdigate Ex p. A* [2000] 1 W.L.R. 1855 at [37]. See also *R. (on the application of Bancoult) v Secretary of State for Foreign and Commonwealth Affairs (No.2)* [2008] UKHL 61; [2009] 1 A.C. 453 at [53]: Lord Hoffmann rejected the proposition that the court should adopt a "light touch" approach to review (as submitted by the Crown on the basis that it was "acting in the interests of the defence of the realm, diplomatic relations with the United States and the use of public funds in supporting any settlement on the islands") and preferred the view that the court should adopt an "anxious degree of scrutiny" adding that the right in issue "should be seen for what it is, as a right to protest in a particular way and not as a right to the security of one's home or to live in one's homeland". See also Lord Mance, dissenting, at [172] and Lord Carswell, at [131].

[355] *R. (on the application of Davila-Puga) v Immigration Appeal Tribunal* [2001] EWCA Civ 931 at [31] (Laws LJ: "As is well known, in 1987 Lord Bridge said in the case of *Musisi* [1987] 1 A.C. 514 that these cases need to be approached with anxious scrutiny, given what may be involved. And so they must. But as a reading of his Lordship's speech in that case readily demonstrates, the court's role remains one of review for error of law. There is no error of law here").

[356] See 11-042.

[357] See 11-051.

[358] *R. (on the application of Leung) v Imperial College of Science, Technology and Medicine* [2002] EWHC 1358 (Admin); [2002] E.L.R. 653.

[359] *Daly* [2001] UKHL 26; [2001] 2 A.C. 532 at [27]-[28] (Lord Slynn). See generally P. Craig, "Judicial Review and Anxious Scrutiny: Foundations, Evolution and Application" [2015] P.L. 60.

[360] *R. (on the application of Sarkisian) v Immigration Appeal Tribunal* [2001] EWHC Admin 486 (Mumby J).

[361] *R. (on the application of Puspalatha) v Immigration Appeal Tribunal* [2001] EWHC Admin 333, [43] (Sullivan J).

[362] *R. (on the application of Kurecaj) v Secretary of State for the Home Department* [2002] EWHC 1199 (Gibbs J).

explaining the need for anxious scrutiny were made before English courts could directly apply Convention rights. Today, assessment of the lawfulness of decisions in many of these cases would fall to be determined by the structured proportionality test. Nevertheless, some role for anxious scrutiny remains. The Court of Appeal approved the use of a heightened form of *Wednesbury* when reviewing the Quality Assurance Scheme for Advocates, citing the court's "high level of institutional competence and constitutional legitimacy when addressing challenges to the criminal justice process."[363] "Rigorous" scrutiny was also adopted when the challenge was to a decision whether a child was a victim of human trafficking for the purposes of the Convention on Action against Trafficking in Human Beings, with the Administrative Court emphasising both that a fundamental right was engaged and that the claim arose in an area "in which a court has the requisite knowledge."[364] Different intensities of review may apply to a chain of decisions: the Home Secretary's determination that a person had been trafficked involved fundamental rights to which anxious scrutiny review should be applied; whereas a consequential decision about the person's eligibility for a residence permit would be subject to the ordinary standard.[365]

11-098   By contrast, an attempt to apply a heightened scrutiny approach in reviewing the Lord Chancellor's proposals to make significant changes to the provision of criminal legal aid services by solicitors was rejected, despite the criminal justice dimension to the case.[366]

Wednesbury, light-touch review and non-justiciability[367]

11-099   The default position is still, at the time of writing, that of the *Wednesbury* formulation,[368] although it has been reformulated to a standard that requires the decision-maker to act within the "range of reasonable responses".[369] Beyond that, however, recent cases, even those where human rights are engaged, have sometimes reverted to what we have called light-touch review, allowing considerable latitude to public authorities and interfering only when the decision is "outrageous",[370] or "arbitrary".[371] Beyond that there may be cases which are not easily amenable to judicial review (sometimes called non-justiciable decisions). These decisions

---

[363] *R. (on the application of Lumsdon) v Legal Services Board* [2014] EWCA Civ 1276; [2014] H.R.L.R. 29.

[364] *R. (SF (St Lucia)) v Secretary of State for the Home Department* [2015] EWHC 2705 (Admin); [2016] 1 W.L.R. 1439.

[365] *R. (K) v Secretary of State for the Home Department* [2015] EWHC 3668 (Admin); [2016] 4 W.L.R. 25.

[366] *R. (on the application of London Criminal Courts Solicitors' Association) v Lord Chancellor* [2015] EWHC 295 (Admin); [2015] A.C.D. 95.

[367] On justiciability, see 1-034–1-049. But see *R. (UNISON) v Lord Chancellor* [2017] UKSC 51.

[368] See T. Hickman, "The Reasonableness Principle" [2004] C.L.J. 166.

[369] The late Michael Taggart (our former New Zealand correspondent scholar of international note, in his last article argued that "in the absence of 'rights' there is no compelling normative justification for more searching or intensive review than provided by the usual grounds of review and traditional (*Wednesbury*) unreasonableness as residual safety net". M. Taggart, "Proportionality, Deference, Wednesbury" [2008] N.Z.L.R. 423 at 477. And see the essays in H.Wilberg and M. Elliott, *The Scope and Intensity of Substantive Review: Traversing Taggart's Rainbow* (2015), and P. Craig, "Judicial Review and Anxious Scrutiny: Foundations, Evolution and Application" [2015] P.L. 60.

[370] *CCSU v Minister for the Civil Service* [1985] A.C. 374 at 410 (Lord Diplock).

[371] See, e.g. *Pro-Life Alliance v BBC* [2003] UKHL 23; [2004] 1 A.C. 185, where the HL held that the prohibition of the showing of aborted foetuses in a party election broadcast could not be interfered with unless the decision was "arbitrary". Lord Scott, dissenting, held that since free expression was engaged a structured proportionality test ought to be employed. See E. Barendt, "Free Speech and Abortion" [2003] P.L. 580; J. Jowell, "Judicial Deference: Servility, Civility or Institutional Capac-

include those in which the court is constitutionally disabled from entering on review, because the matter concerns policy—such as setting the level of taxation, undertaking a space programme, or generally involving the allocation of scarce resources.[372] Other decisions are not justiciable, or require due deference from the court because of their lack of relative institutional capacity to enter into a review of the decision. This issue is discussed in Chapter 1[373] and need not be repeated now.

A culture of justification

A sensitive appreciation of relative institutional capacity must however be qualified in two respects. First, as has been discussed above,[374] institutional deference does not mean constitutional deference. The courts ought not automatically to kowtow to Parliament (when legislation is being reviewed under the Human Rights Act or European Union law) or to the executive or other officials, on the ground that they are accountable to the electorate and the courts are not. **11-100**

Secondly, the acceptance of institutional imperfection on the part of the courts, or of a superior institutional capacity on the part of the primary decision-maker (for example, on the ground that he had access to "special sources of knowledge and advice")[375] should not inevitably signal a low level of scrutiny of the decision. As was said in *Huang*,[376] although the public authority may be better placed to investigate the facts and test the evidence, the court cannot abdicate its responsibility of ensuring that the facts are properly "explored and summarized in the decision, with care".[377] Even where the courts recognise their lack of relative capacity or expertise to make the primary decision, they should nevertheless not easily relinquish their secondary function of probing the quality of the reasoning and ensuring that assertions are properly justified. The proper approach to this issue was taken by O'Regan J. in *Bato Star Fishing Ltd v The Chief Director: Marine and Coastal Management*[378] that a decision on the allocation of fishing quotas and requiring "an equilibrium to be struck between a range of competing interests or considerations and which is to be taken by a person or institution with special expertise in that area must be shown respect by the Courts". Nevertheless, she said **11-101**

---

ity?" [2003] P.L. 592. In *R. (on the application of Woods) v Chief Constable of Merseyside* [2014] EWHC 2784 (Admin); [2015] 1 W.L.R. 539 the Administrative Court considered the appropriate approach to *Wednesbury* review where the reason for a decision had been subject to a successful public interest immunity claim such that a reasoned justification for the decision could not be provided. In such circumstances, it was held at [36] per Stewart J "there would have to be clear evidence of dishonesty or bias or caprice" to justify intervention; that threshold was not reached on the facts.

[372] See 1-035; See e.g: *R. (on the application of Gentle) v Prime Minister* [2006] EWCA Civ 1690 (invasion of Iraq); *R. (on the application of Marchiori) v Environment Agency* [2002] EWCA Civ 3; [2002] Eu. L.R. 225 (national defence policy). On the imposition of recent cuts on social programmes see Thom Dyke, "Judicial Review in an Age of Austerity" [2011] J.R. 202. And see the squabble in the Supreme Court on the subject of community care and needs assessment: *R. (on the application of McDonald) v Royal Borough of Kensington and Chelsea* UKSC 33. But see *R. (on the application of A) v Croydon London Borough Council* [2009] UKSC 8, [2009] 1 W.L.R. 2557 (whether a child is "in need" is an evaluative question which could not be determined "[w]ithin the limits of fair process and *Wednesbury* reasonableness" (at [26] per Baroness Hale. See also Lord Hope's comments at [53].

[373] See 1-034–1-049.

[374] See 11-034–11-049.

[375] *Huang* [2007] UKHL 11; [2007] 2 W.L.R. 581.

[376] *Huang* [2007] UKHL 11; [2007] 2 W.L.R. 581 at [16].

[377] *Huang* [2007] UKHL 11; [2007] 2 W.L.R. 581 at [15].

[378] *Bato Star Fishing Ltd v The Chief Director: Marine and Coastal Management* (2004) (4) S.A. 490 at [48], CC.

that:

> "this does not mean, however, that where the decision is one which will not reasonably result in the achievement of the goal, or which is not reasonably supported on the facts, or is not reasonable in the light of the reasons given for it, a Court may not review that decision ... a court should not rubber-stamp an unreasonable decision simply because of the complexity of the decision or the identity of the decision-maker".

The Chief Justice of Canada made a similar point when she warned against judicial deference "simply on the basis that the problem is serious and the solution difficult".[379]

11-102   Although it is too early to pronounce the demise of unreasonableness, the increased use of structured proportionality has changed our expectations of how decision-makers ought to behave. It has introduced what has been called a "culture of justification",[380] which requires decision-makers not only to act in accordance with bare rationality, but also to consider carefully the relationship between the means of a decision and its ends, to insist upon the consideration of less oppressive alternatives in appropriate cases and to ask for more cogent justification than bare *Wednesbury* permits when decisions interfere with established rights and significant interests. Despite not officially adopting proportionality in place of *Wednesbury*, and despite still sometimes requiring the disproportionate decision to contain an element of "manifest" proportionality, the courts were willing to probe the evidence of various restrictions on rights and interests and were not shy of holding that the lack of "robust" evidence justifying the measure rendered the restriction disproportionate.[381]

11-103   If these expectations are confirmed in the case law of the future, the abandonment of the test of unreasonableness will not have breached the line between judicial review and appeal. We shall still not have adopted merits review. The courts will simply require more fulsome justification of a decision, the merits of which still lie within the scope of the primary decision-maker. However, instead of getting away with simply stating that he has carried out a proper balancing exercise, a decision-maker will be required positively to "identify the factors he has weighed

---

[379]   *RJR-MacDonald v Canada (Attorney General)* [1995] 3 S.C.R. 119 (McLauglan CJ). The former President of Israel's Supreme Court, Aharon Barak, considers that the term "deference" does not serve a useful purpose because if a court does not invalidate a decision as unreasonable it is lawful and if it exceeds the zone of unreasonableness then it must be invalidated and there is no room for deference: The Judge in a Democracy (2006), pp.251-252.

[380]   See the works of E. Mureinik, "A Bridge to Where? Introducing the Interim Bill of Rights" (1994) S.A.J.H.R. 31.

[381]   See, e.g. *R. (on the application of Quila) v Secretary of State for the Home Department* [2011] UKSC 45; [2012] 1 A.C. 621 (disproportionate to raise from 18 to 21 years the age at which a foreign national married to a British citizen could apply for a marriage visa (for the purpose of deterring forced marriages) was disproportionate as the Secretary of State had no "robust evidence" that it would have that effect.); *R. (on the application of F) v Secretary of State for the Home Department* [2010] UKSC 17; [2011] 1 A.C. 331 (sexual offenders of sufficient gravity to notify personal information to police indefinitely a disproportionate interference with their ECHR art.8 rights as "no evidence adduced that some offenders posed significant risk of reoffending [at 56]; but see Lord Brown's dissent at [90] and [91]. See also *Manchester City Council v Pinnock* [2010] UKSC 45; [2010] 3 W.L.R. 1441 (possession order does not violate ECHR art.8 rights and weight should be given to the discretionary area of judgment of the local authority); and *R. (on the application of Sinclair Collis Ltd) v Secretary of State for Health* [2011] EWCA Civ 437; [2012] Q.B. 394 (ban by means of secondary legislation on tobacco vending machines was held not to be a [manifestly] disproportionate interference with economic rights). Compare the approach taken in the Scottish context in *Sinclair Lewis v The Lord Advocate* [2012] CSIH 80 P576/10, reaching the same conclusion but not requiring that the disproportionality be "manifest".

and explain why he has given weight to some factors and not to others".[382] The function of the courts in ensuring adequate justification of decisions is always within their institutional capacity and is indeed the task they are best qualified to perform.[383]

COMPARATIVE PERSPECTIVES[384]

Australia

Australian judicial review operates within the context of a constitutionally entrenched separation of the judicial power of the Commonwealth from the Commonwealth's legislative and executive powers. The separation of the judicial power is seen as constitutionally entrenching a distinction between the merits of an administrative decision and its legality. Judicial and non-judicial powers can (and frequently do) overlap, but the separation of powers prevents a judicial review court from judging an administrative decision to have been unlawful simply because it was unfair, or resulted in an injustice, or appeared to the court to be in disconformity with the principles of good administration.[385] According to Brennan J:

11-104

> "The consequence is that the scope of judicial review must be defined not in terms of the protection of individual interests but in terms of the extent of power and the legality of its exercise".[386]

These protestations of unconcern with substantive injustice should not, however, be taken literally. Whilst it is true that Australian courts will not grant judicial review simply because a decision was unfair, unjust, or a violation of rule of law principles, it is also accepted that such normative concerns inform the development and application of the grounds of judicial review.[387] Aside from migration decisions, most Commonwealth administrative action is amenable to judicial review under the Administrative Decisions (Judicial Review) Act 1977 (Cth) (ADJR Act). Judicial review according to common law principles is constitutionally entrenched, and therefore operates as the safety net where schemes such as ADJR do not apply. ADJR's review grounds are largely a re-statement of the review grounds at common law, and both have been criticised for their absence of directly applicable overarching statements of normative principle.[388] The Administrative Review Council (ARC) considered those criticisms, and unanimously rejected the option of supplementing (or even replacing) ADJR's existing grounds with a higher-level statement of governing standards or principles. The ARC did accept that such a state-

11-105

---

[382] *R. (on the application of X) v Chief Constable of the West Midlands* [2004] EWCA Civ 1068; [2005] 1 W.L.R. 65 at [101].

[383] Account will also have to be taken of the possible need to engage in a more intensive fact-finding review following the decision of the ECtHR in *Tsfayo v United Kingdom* (2009) 48 E.H.R.R. 18. But see the discussion in 11-044 above and *Manchester City Council v Pinnock* [2010] UKSC 45.

[384] See also T. Hickman, "Proportionality: Comparative Law Lessons" [2007] J.R. 31.

[385] *Attorney General (NSW) v Quin* (1990) 170 C.L.R. 1 at 35–36; and *Re Minister for Immigration and Multicultural and Indigenous Affairs; Ex p. Lam* (2003) 214 C.L.R. 1 at 12 and 23.

[386] *Attorney General (NSW) v Quin* (1990) 170 C.L.R. 1 at 36.

[387] *Plaintiff S157/2002 v Commonwealth* (2003) 211 C.L.R. 476 at 482–483 and 492 (Gleeson CJ), and 513–514 (Gaudron, McHugh, Gummow, Kirby and Hayne JJ).

[388] See: *Re Minister for Immigration and Multicultural Affairs; Ex p. Applicant S20/2002* (2003) 198 A.L.R. 59 at [157] and [166] (Kirby J); and M. Taggart, "Australian Exceptionalism in Judicial Review" (2008) 36 Fed. L. Rev. 1. cf. M. Aronson, "Is the ADJR Act Hampering the Development of Australian Administrative Law?" (2004) 15 P.L.R. 202 at 214–216.

ment might occasionally assist in the articulation of new review grounds and in the application of existing grounds. It concluded, however, that any attempt to develop and articulate a binding set of meta-principles would open up a set of new debates, and end up generating more complexity and dispute, rather than less.[389]

11-106   The separation of the judicial power entrenches not just a limitation upon the development of substantive grounds of judicial review. It also entrenches a limitation upon substantive remedies being granted upon judicial review. It is fundamental to Australian judicial review that the court will neither directly nor indirectly substitute its own decision for that made by the government official. Mason J said in *Minister for Aboriginal Affairs v Peko-Wallsend Ltd*[390]:

> "The limited role of a court reviewing the exercise of an administrative discretion must constantly be borne in mind. It is not the function of the court to substitute its own decision for that of the administrator by exercising a discretion which the legislature has vested in the administrator. Its role is to set limits on the exercise of that discretion, and a decision made within those boundaries cannot be impugned."

11-107   The overall result of these constitutional concerns with the separation of powers is that Australian courts acknowledge *Wednesbury* unreasonableness as a ground of review, but apply it with considerable (although no longer virtually insurmountable) caution.[391] Similarly, administrative decisions are reviewable for serious irrationality, but only where that irrationality is both material and virtually indefensible.[392]

11-108   A number of factors affect the extent of justification required for an administrative decision. There is no generalised duty to give reasons at common law,[393] but statutory duties to supply reasonably detailed reasons apply (generally upon timely request) to most administrative decision-making that is either appealable to a merits appeal tribunal[394] or reviewable under statutory judicial review schemes such as ADJR.[395]

11-109   There is no common law presumption that administrative decision-makers have a duty to seek out further facts in addition to those supplied by the parties, although an undemanding duty might apply to tribunals in limited circumstances.[396]

11-110   At common law, review for error of fact is available if the fact is jurisdictional in the sense that its objective existence is a condition precedent to the valid exercise of power.[397] Common law review is also available for seriously irrational findings or inferences of material facts.[398]

11-111   The UK Human Rights Act has only two analogues in Australia. Human rights

---

[389] Administrative Review Council, *Federal Judicial Review in Australia* (Report No 50) (Canberra, 2012) pp.126–132.

[390] *Minister for Aboriginal Affairs v Peko-Wallsend Ltd* (1986) 162 C.L.R. 24 at 40–41.

[391] *Minister for Immigration and Citizenship v Li* (2013) 249 C.L.R. 332 at 364 [68], per Hayne, Kiefel and Bell JJ: "The legal standard of unreasonableness should not be considered as limited to what is in effect an irrational, if not bizarre, decision—which is to say one that is so unreasonable that no reasonable person could have arrived at it—nor should Lord Greene MR be taken to have limited unreasonableness in this way in his judgment in *Wednesbury*".

[392] *Minister for Immigration and Citizenship v SZMDS* (2010) 240 C.L.R. 611.

[393] *Public Service Board (NSW) v Osmond* (1986) 159 C.L.R. 656.

[394] Administrative Appeals Tribunal Act 1975 (Cth) s.28.

[395] Administrative Decisions (Judicial Review) Act 1977 (Cth) s.13.

[396] M Aronson, M Groves and G Weeks, *Judicial Review of Administrative Action and Government Liability*, 6th edn (2017) para.5.4. The issue has not been conclusively decided: *Minister for Immigration and Citizenship v SZIAI* (2009) 259 A.L.R. 429.

[397] *Enfield City Corp v Development Assessment Commission* (2000) 199 C.L.R. 135; and *Gedeon v Crime Commission (NSW)* (2008) 236 C.L.R. 120.

[398] *Re Minister for Immigration and Multicultural Affairs; Ex p. Applicant S20/2002* (2003) 198 A.L.R.

legislation in the Australian Capital Territory and Victoria requires the production of statements of compatibility with the chartered rights for all bills introduced to the Parliament.[399] Queensland law requires justification for newly introduced bills that infringe upon individual rights and liberties.[400] Similarly, a New South Wales Act empowers the Legislative Review Committee to report to Parliament on all bills that trespass on personal rights and liberties.[401] At the federal level, the Parliamentary Joint Committee on Human Rights examines all bills and legislative instruments for compatibility with "human rights", a term which embraces all those rights or freedoms recognised or declared in seven major international treaties.[402]

Canada

The Supreme Court of Canada has pioneered the principle of proportionality as a tool for assessing Charter rights.[403] Proportionality is not only an essential component in the assessment of whether a legislative violation of a Charter right or freedom can be justified under s.1 of the Charter,[404] but, in a less structured way, in the judicial review of the exercise of statutory authority that engages Charter rights, freedoms and values.[405]   **11-112**

In *Loyola High School v Quebec (Attorney General)*,[406] a majority of the Supreme Court of Canada reaffirmed its commitment to the *Doré* approach to review of discretionary decision-making engaging the rights, freedoms, and underlying values of the Canadian Charter of Rights and Freedoms. That approach is one that generally requires deferential reasonableness assessment of the exercise of discretionary powers implicating Charter rights, freedoms and underlying values. However, reasonableness review in this context differs from the administrative law norm in that it is characterised as an inquiry into whether the decision "reflects a proportionate balance between the Charter protections at stake and the relevant statutory mandate."[407] In contrast, proportionality assessment is still not otherwise an explicit component of the assessment of the reasonableness of the exercise of discretionary powers. Moreover, this form of deferential reasonableness review to the exercise of discretionary power does not extend to the prior determination as to whether, as a matter of law, the decision under review engages a Charter right, freedom or underlying value.   **11-113**

The Supreme Court of Canada has held that, in the absence of statutory specification of the standard of review, for every case of substantive (though not procedural)   **11-114**

---

59 at [53]–[54]; and *Minister for Immigration and Citizenship v SZMDS* (2010) 240 C.L.R. 611. See See M. Aronson, M. Groves and G. Weeks, *Judicial Review of Administrative Action and Government Liability*, 6th edn (2017) para.4.16.

399 Human Rights Act 2004 (ACT) s.37; and Charter of Human Rights and Responsibilities Act 2006 (Vic) s.28. Each statute makes clear that a failure to comply with the requirements of these statements does not affect the validity of any relevant bill when enacted: Human Rights Act 2004 (ACT) s.39; and Charter of Human Rights and Responsibilities Act 2006 (Vic) s.29.

400 Legislative Standards Act 1992 (Qld) Pt 2.

401 Legislation Review Act 1987 (NSW) s8A.

402 Human Rights (Parliamentary Scrutiny) Act 2011 (Cth) s.3 lists treaties relating to racial discrimination; economic, social and cultural rights; civil and political rights; the elimination of discrimination against women; the prohibition of torture and other cruel, inhuman or degrading treatment; the rights of the child; and the rights of persons with disabilities.

403 D. Beattie, *The Ultimate Rule of Law* (2003), Ch.5; D. Mullan, "Proportionality—A Proportionate Response to an Emerging Crisis in Canadian Judicial Review law" [2010] N.Z.L.Rev. 233.

404 *R. v Oakes* [1986] 1 S.C.R. 103.

405 *Doré v Barreau du Québec* [2012] 1 S.C.R. 395.

406 *Loyola High School v Quebec (Attorney General)* 2015 SCC 12; [2015] 1 S.C.R. 613.

407 *Loyola High School v Quebec (Attorney General)* 2015 SCC 12; [2015] 1 S.C.R. 613 at [37].

review and appeal from statutory authorities, including challenges for abuse of discretion, the first step is to establish a standard of review by reference to various "standard of review" factors.[408]

11-115   The issue of whether there is any room for deferential reasonableness review on issues of procedural fairness remains contentious in Canada. The majority position to this point has been that on procedural issues either standard of review has no relevance[409] or that review for procedural unfairness is conducted on a non-deferential correctness basis.[410] However, there are several authorities that call into question the universality of that proposition. For example, in *Mission Institution v Khela*,[411] the Supreme Court, after holding that correctness is the standard of review for issues of procedural fairness,[412] went on to recognise that there should be deference in the form of a margin of appreciation for the decision-maker when weighing whether or not to allow the release of sensitive material for the purposes of a hearing: balancing considerations of confidentiality against procedural fairness based claims to access to all relevant material.[413] More generally, some courts have accepted that reasonableness review applies when a decision-maker has discretion with respect to procedural questions[414] or, particularly in the Quebec Court of Appeal, where the procedural right asserted depends on the interpretation of a specific provision in the decision-maker's constitutive or "home" statute.[415] As is implicit in *Khela*, a margin of appreciation is more generally appropriate where a decision-maker is applying correctly identified principles of procedural fairness to particular fact situations such as whether on the facts the criteria for a right to representation by counsel have been met.[416] Indeed, this margin of appreciation may extend not just to procedural rulings but to the validity of procedural rules developed by the tribunal.[417]

11-116   In *Dunsmuir v New Brunswick*, the Supreme Court of Canada revisited its approach to determining whether courts should show deference to the decisions or actions of a statutory or prerogative authority.[418] It determined that there should no longer be three possible standards of review at common law but just two, correctness and unreasonableness. It jettisoned the previously most deferential standard, that of "patent unreasonableness." The court also abandoned the language of "pragmatic and functional" used to describe the approach that courts should adopt in determining the appropriate standard of review. Rather, the process is now called simply "standard of review analysis." However, despite the reduction in the number of standards and the name change, the four factors that form part of this inquiry

---

[408] *Dunsmuir v New Brunswick* [2008] 1 S.C.R. 190.

[409] *Moreau-Bérubé v New Brunswick Judicial Council* 2002 SCC 11; [2002] 1 S.C.R. 249 at [74].

[410] *Canada (Citizenship and Immigration) v Khosa*, 2009 SCC 12; [2009] 1 S.C.R. 339 at [43].

[411] *Mission Institution v Khela* 2014 SCC 24; [2014] 1 S.C.R. 502.

[412] *Mission Institution v Khela* 2014 SCC 24; [2014] 1 S.C.R. 502 at [79].

[413] *Mission Institution v Khela* 2014 SCC 24; [2014] 1 S.C.R. 502 at [89].

[414] Including the Supreme Court in *Council of Canadians with Disabilities v VIA Rail Canada*, 2007 SCC 15; [2007] 1 S.C.R. 650 at [230]-[231]. See also the somewhat contrasting discussions of this issue in *Re Sound v Fitness Industry of Canada* 2014 FCA 48; [2015] 2 F.C.R. 170 at [34]-[42], and *Maritime Broadcasting System Ltd v Canadian Media Guild*, 2014 FCA 59; 373 DLR (4th) 59 at [46]-[64].

[415] *Syndicat des travailleuses et travailleurs de ADF-CSN c. Syndicat des employees de Au Dragon Forgo*, 2013 QCCA 793; [2013] R.J.Q. 831 and *Travailleuses et travailleurs unit d'alimentation et du commerce, local 503 c. Systems' Techno-pumps Inc*, 2017 QCCA 997 at [19]-[29].

[416] *Maritime Broadcasting System Ltd v Canadian Media Guild* 2014 FCA 59; 373 DLR (4th) 59 and *Forest Ethics Association v Canada (National Energy Board)* 2014 FCA 245; [2015] 4 F.C.R. 75 at [82].

[417] *Forest Ethics* 2014 FCA 245; [2015] 4 F.C.R. 75 at [70]-[77].

[418] *Dunsmuir v New Brunswick* 2008 SCC 9; [2008] 1 S.C.R. 190.

remain the same: the presence or absence of a privative or preclusive clause, the purpose of the tribunal as indicated by its constitutive legislation, the nature of the question at issue, and the tribunal's expertise.

In an endeavour to minimise the attention paid in applications for judicial review **11-117** and statutory appeals to the determination of an appropriate standard of review, the court also identified a number of presumptions intended to serve as signposts as to whether the standard in any particular case should be that of correctness or unreasonableness. Aside from an admonition to courts to accept precedents where the standard of review has already been determined satisfactorily and a continuing emphasis that a privative or preclusive clause provides a strong indicator of the need for deference, the court identified two situations where unreasonableness review is generally required: (i) issues of fact, discretion or policy; and (ii) interpretations of the statutory authority's "own statute or statutes closely connected to its function, with which it will have particular familiarity".[419]

Deference might also be justified with respect to the application of common and **11-118** civil law rules with which the statutory authority has developed a particular expertise or familiarity.

In contrast, correctness should be the standard where issues of jurisdiction or **11-119** vires arise, as, for example, pure questions of constitutional law,[420] the jurisdictional lines between competing tribunals, and the limits of the authority of municipalities to enact byelaws. The courts should also assess on a correctness basis determinations of questions of general law that are "both of central importance to the legal system as a whole and outside the adjudicator's special area of expertise".

Given the comprehensive framework within which the court articulated the new **11-120** approach in *Dunsmuir*, it seemed clear that it would apply not just to judicial review of tribunals but all forms of statutory or prerogative authority as well as statutory appeals. Thereafter, in *Canada (Citizenship and Immigration) v Khosa*, the court not only reiterated the application of the standard of review methodology to statutory appeals but also held that it constituted an overlay on the codified grounds of review in the Federal Courts Act.[421] Thus, for example, an unqualified statutory specification of error of law review did not amount to a direction that the Federal Court and Court of Appeal should review all questions of law on a correctness basis.

However, this judgment does not affect those statutory provisions (such as found **11-121** in the British Columbia Administrative Tribunals Act (SBC) 2004 c.45 ss.58–59) that actually specify a standard of review, and now most relevantly, patent unreasonableness. In *Manz v British Columbia (Workers' Compensation Appeal Tribunal)*,[422] the British Columbia Court of Appeal rejected a challenge to the constitutionality of those provisions. The constitutional guarantee of access to judicial review did not extend to a proscription on legislative designation of the standard of review.

The Supreme Court of Canada has made it clear that the presumption of **11-122** deferential reasonableness review applicable when a tribunal is interpreting its home statute extends to situations where the setting for judicial review is a statutory ap-

---

[419] para.54.
[420] However, it is now clear that, where the challenge is to the exercise of a discretionary power that engages Charter rights, freedoms and values and also probably to findings of fact and mixed law and fact where such rights, freedoms and values are engaged, a standard of review analysis will be required with the standard of review frequently being the deferential standard of reasonableness: *Doré v Barreau du Québec* [2012] 1 S.C.R. 395.
[421] *Canada (Citizenship and Immigration) v Khosa* [2009] 1 S.C.R. 339.
[422] *Manz v British Columbia (Workers' Compensation Appeal Tribunal)* (2009) 91 B.C.L.R. (4th) 92.

peal on questions of law with leave of the court[423] as well as the determination of questions of law certified to the reviewing court as of general importance.[424]

11-123 At present, the deferential standard of review (unreasonableness) is most clearly indicated in the case of expert adjudicative tribunals, decisions of which are protected by a strong privative clause, and also in the case of broad discretion with polycentric dimensions typically involving a Cabinet Minister or specialised administrative agencies. In contrast, aside from true jurisdictional questions, including competing jurisdictional claims and pure questions of constitutional law, correctness is most clearly indicated in the case of a tribunal determining questions of general importance to the legal system as a whole and outside the realm of its expected area of expertise. It is also probably the standard for review of the vires of subordinate legislation,[425] and generally the determination of pure questions of law by Ministers of the Crown and other non-adjudicative decision-makers.[426]

11-124 In an effort to forestall litigation over the standard of review and perhaps as an implicit criticism of the courts' standard of review jurisprudence, British Columbia in its 2005 Administrative Tribunals Act (SBC) 2004 has attempted both to specify the standard of review applicable to tribunals coming within the reach of that Act and to define what each of the standards embraces. While there is legislation in other jurisdictions, such as the Federal Courts Act, specifying the grounds of judicial review, British Columbia is the only jurisdiction to attempt a partial legislative codification of the actual standards of review.

11-125 What constitutes for the purposes of correctness review a "question of general importance to the legal system as a whole and outside the realm of [the decision-maker's] expected area of expertise" remains controversial. The Supreme Court has, however, identified the resolution of issues of solicitor/client privilege by a freedom of information and privacy commissioner as coming within that category.[427] The issue transcended the particular adjudicative setting. The court has also accepted that correctness review may be justified where there is overlapping jurisdiction as between a tribunal and a court as a matter of first impression with respect to an issue of interpretation.[428] In contrast, however, the court rejected an argument that the presumption of reasonableness review for the interpretation of home statutes may be rebutted where there is conflicting tribunal jurisprudence on an issue of statutory interpretation.[429]

11-126 The Supreme Court has now accepted that deferential or unreasonableness review of determinations of law may extend to domains other than adjudicative tribunals and, in particular, members of the executive branch. Thus, in *Canadian National Railway Co v Canada (Attorney General)*,[430] the court adopted the reasonableness

---

[423] *Edmonton (City) v Edmonton East (Capilano) Shopping Centres Ltd* 2016 SCC 47; [2016] 2 S.C.R. 293 at [27]-[35].

[424] *Kanthasamy v Canada (Citizenship and Immigration)* 2015 SCC 61; [2015] 3 S.C.R. 909 at [42]-[45].

[425] *United Taxi Drivers Fellowship of Southern Alberta v Calgary (City)* [2004] 1 S.C.R. 485.

[426] *Georgia Strait Alliance v Canada (Minister of Fisheries and Oceans)* 2010 FC 1233.

[427] *Alberta (Information and Privacy Commissioner) v University of Calgary* 2016 SCC 53; [2016] 2 S.C.R. 555 at [19]-[27].

[428] *Rogers Communications Inc v Society of Composers, Authors and Music Publishers of Canada* 2012 SCC 35; [2012] 2 S.C.R. 283 at [16]-[19].

[429] *Wilson v Atomic Energy of Canada Ltd* 2016 SCC 29; [2016] 1 S.C.R. 770.

[430] *Canadian National Railway Co v Canada (Attorney General)* 2014 SCC 40; [2014] 2 S.C.R. 135. See also *Gitxaala Nation v Canada* 2016 FCA 187; [2016] 4 F.C.R. 418. With respect to the determination of questions of law by Ministers, see *Kandola v Canada (Minister of Citizenship and Immigration)* 2014 FCA 85; [2014] 1 F.C.R. 549, where the conflicting authorities are discussed as a prelude to a holding that the presumption of deference applied.

standard in the context of a review of a decision made on an appeal to the Governor in Council from a decision of the Canadian Transportation Commission. However, the court did take care[431] to distinguish this case from the review of subordinate legislation made by the Governor in Council. There, challenges to validity were still to be dealt with by reference to the principles of ultra vires and whether the regulation in issue came within the scope of the empowering statutory provision. Lower courts have respected this distinction and reviewed regulations on the basis of an ultra vires analysis.[432] As a matter of statutory interpretation, does the regulation come within the scope of the authorising provision? In contrast, especially in the case of municipal by-laws and other legislatively based rules, the court has emphasised the universality of the Dunsmuir principles and applied the presumption of reasonableness review to the interpretation of home statutes.[433] In this context, reasonableness review takes the form of an inquiry into whether the by-law or rule "is one that no reasonable body informed by [the relevant] factors could have [enacted]."[434] How these two approaches can or will be reconciled remains to be seen.

In Canada, the common law grounds of judicial review and much of the legislative codification of the grounds of review and conferral of a right of appeal continue to be expressed in terms of the traditional common law grounds: jurisdiction, error of law (though not requiring the error to appear on the face of the record), a decision based on a complete lack of evidence, and the usual abuse of discretion grounds: bad faith, taking account of irrelevant factors, failure to take account of relevant factors, acting for an improper purpose, unlawful fettering of discretion, acting under dictation, and, occasionally, *Wednesbury* unreasonableness. However, the standard of review jurisprudence has had a significant impact on the grounds of review. Error of fact review is now more commonly considered in terms of whether there has been an "unreasonable finding of fact".[435] Similarly, *Wednesbury* unreasonableness has been subsumed within unreasonableness when that is the chosen standard of review.[436] Also, in cases where the chosen standard is that of unreasonableness, exercises of discretionary power will often be subject to a more searching review than was the case under *Wednesbury*. It is, however, the case that the courts have yet to come to terms with the detail of the impact of applying a standard of review to abuse of discretion challenges not only in this context but also in relation to the discrete grounds of abuse of discretion.[437] In *Dunsmuir*, the court provided a template for the conduct of reasonableness review and linked it with the common law or statutory duty to provide reasons to which most statutory authorities are now subject.[438] In conducting reasonableness review, the courts are to have regard "both to the process of articulating the reasons and to outcomes." For the most part, reasonableness review should focus on the presence of "justification,

11-127

---

[431] *Canadian National Railway Co v Canada (Attorney General)* 2014 SCC 40; [2014] 2 S.C.R. 135 at [51] (referencing *Katz Group Canada Inc v Ontario (Health and Long-Term Care)* 2013 SCC 64; [2013] 3 S.C.R. 810).

[432] See e.g. *Wildlands League and Federation of Ontario Naturalists v Lieutenant Governor in Council* 2016 ONCA 741; 134 O.R. (3d) 450.

[433] *Green v Law Society of Manitoba* 2017 SCC 20 at [20]-[25].

[434] *Green v Law Society of Manitoba* 2017 SCC 20 at [20], citing *Catalyst Paper Corp v North Cowichan (District)* 2012 SCC 2: [2012] 1 S.C.R. 5 at [24].

[435] See, e.g. *Alberta (Education) v Canadian Copyright Licensing Agency (Access Copyright)* 2012 S.C.C. 37.

[436] See, e.g. *Catalyst Paper Corp v North Cowichan (District)* [2012] 1 S.C.R. 5.

[437] See the difference of judicial opinion in *Kane v Canada (Attorney General)* 2011 F.C.A. 19, currently on reserve in the Supreme Court of Canada.

[438] para.47.

transparency and intelligibility within the decision-making process." However, the decision reached is also relevant in the sense that it must fall "within a range of possible, acceptable outcomes which are defensible in respect of the facts and the law." Where reasons are inadequate or not required, reasonableness review will depend on the court's assessment of the broader evidential context against which the decision under review has been taken.[439]

11-128   Where there are no reasons or no adequate reasons for a decision, the conduct of judicial review on substantive grounds may be impeded. However, in such circumstances, reviewing courts may respond in a number of ways to effectuate the applicant's right to seek judicial review. If, for example, the decision-maker has implicitly relied on past rulings on the issue, the court may allow as part of an expanded record, the introduction of the decisions incorporating those rulings. Indeed, in those rare cases where the argument for judicial review depends on an issue not raised before the decision-maker and immediate remission to the decision-maker is not justified, the court may go so far as to allow full submissions on those issues with the record supplemented to the extent necessary to support the resolution of those issues. More generally, in the instance of decision-makers who do not have a common law or statutory obligation of procedural fairness and therefore no obligations to provide reasons, the traditional conception of a record does not have much purchase. As a consequence, reviewing courts will have to adopt an expanded conception of the record or allow other forms of evidence to enable the effective conduct of judicial review.[440]

11-129   To this point, the Supreme Court has shown no disposition to move with the courts of England and Wales and to adopt or adapt other grounds of review such as proportionality (save in reviewing the exercise of powers that engage Charter rights, freedoms and values), substantive legitimate expectation, and inconsistency. Indeed, the court has explicitly rejected a doctrine of legitimate expectation with substantive consequences and review for inconsistency.[441]

11-130   As noted above, in *Wilson v Atomic Energy of Canada Ltd*, the Supreme Court reaffirmed its traditional position on review for inconsistency: the presence of inconsistent tribunal jurisprudence did not justify moving from a reasonableness to a correctness standard of review.[442]

India

11-131   The approach of the Indian courts, including the breadth and depth of review has been influenced by the primacy accorded to the Fundamental Rights in the Constitution, and on account of which even plenary legislation is subject to judicial review. The right to equality has been interpreted expansively to include procedural fairness as a dimension of this right, and thus the violation of principles of natural justice or arbitrariness (including opacity) in the decision-making process is viewed as a violation of a constitutional right. While the principles of judicial deference in matters of economic policy have generally been adhered to, the trend of decisions,

---

[439] *Newfoundland and Labrador Nurses' Union v Newfoundland and Labrador (Treasury Board)* [2011] 3 S.C.R. 708 and *Catalyst Paper v North Cowichan (District)* [2012] 1 S.C.R. 5.

[440] For discussion, see *Edmonton (City) v Edmonton East (Capilano) Shopping Centres Ltd* 2016 SCC 47; [2016] 2 S.C.R. 293 at [36]-[40], referencing, at [38], *Alberta (Information and Privacy Commissioner) v Alberta Teachers' Association* 2011 SCC 61; [2011] 3 S.C.R. 654 at [56], and *McLean v British Columbia (Securities Commission)* 2013 SCC 67; [2013] 3 S.C.R. 895 at [72].

[441] *Domtar Inc v Québec (Commission d'appel en matière de lesions professionnelles)* [1993] 2 S.C.R. 756; *National Steel Car Ltd v United Steelworkers of America, Local 7135* (2006) 218 O.A.C. 207 (CA).

[442] *Wilson v Atomic Energy of Canada Ltd* 2016 SCC 29; [2016] 1 S.C.R. 770.

especially in cases involving violation of human rights, have shown considerable expansion in the role of the courts in exercising the power of judicial review.[443]

In some cases, the Supreme Court has also noted that the doctrine of reasonableness has "given way" to the doctrine of proportionality.[444] In the context of constitutional rights **11-132**

"... Jurisprudentially, "proportionality" can be defined as the set of rules determining the necessary and sufficient conditions for limitation of a constitutionally protected right by a law to be constitutionally permissible".[445]

In a surprising cross fertilisation of jurisprudence in two different fields, the *Wednesbury* Standard was referred to in relation to a review by the courts of commercial arbitration awards, as a test of whether the order violated the *fundamental policy of Indian law*.[446] The state of law, after the amendments to the statute made in 2016,[447] remains uncertain.

Ireland

In Ireland, until 2010, the two leading cases on review of administrative discretion were *The State (Keegan) v Stardust Victims' Compensation*[448] and *O'Keeffe v An Bord Pleanála*,[449] both of which had given formulations to the *Wednesbury* unreasonableness test. In *Keegan*, Henchy J held that "the test of unreasonableness or irrationality in judicial review lies in considering whether the impugned decision plainly and unambiguously flies in the face of fundamental reason and common sense".[450] In *O'Keeffe*—which involved a challenge to planning permission—Finlay CJ repeated the *Keegan* formulation and added to it that a decision could only be impugned if the decision-maker "had before it no relevant material which would support its decision".[451] Clearly therefore, while following the rubric of *Wednesbury* unreasonableness, the Irish courts have generally set the threshold for judicial intervention quite high. **11-133**

For a long period of time, there was uncertainty as to whether these tests should also apply where fundamental rights were affected by the decision under challenge[452]: some courts adopted an anxious scrutiny standard in such cases,[453] while other courts simply applied the *Keegan* and *O'Keeffe* standards of review.[454] By a 3–2 majority, in the case of *Meadows v Minister for Justice, Equality and Law* **11-134**

---

[443] *Centre for Public Interest Litigation v Union of India* (2012) 13 S.C.C. 1 at 62.

[444] *Maharashtra Land Development Corp v State of Maharashtra* (2011) 15 SCC 616 citing Lord Diplock in *Council of Civil Service Unions v Minister for Civil Service* [1985] A.C. 374 (410), and also *Moni Shankar v Union of India* (2008) 3 SCC 484 at [17].

[445] *Modern Dental College & Research Centre v State of MP* (2016) 7 SCC 353 at [60]).

[446] *Oil & Natural Gas Corporation Limited v Western Geco International Limited* (2014) 9 S.C.C. 263 at [280].

[447] Arbitration and Conciliation Act 1996.

[448] *The State (Keegan) v Stardust Victims' Compensation* [1986] I.R. 642. See generally D.G. Morgan, *Hogan and Morgan's Administrative Law*, 4th edn (2010) at paras 15-47–15-205; H. Biehler, *Judicial Review of Administrative Action*, 3rd edn (2013) at pp.114-154; G. Hogan and D.G. Morgan, *Administrative Law in Ireland*, 4th edn (2012) at paras 15-22–15-135; M. de Blacam, *Administrative Law*, 3rd edn (2017) at Chs 20-25.

[449] *O'Keeffe v An Bord Pleanála* [1993] 1 I.R. 39.

[450] *The State (Keegan) v Stardust Victims' Compensation* [1986] I.R. 642 at 658.

[451] *O'Keeffe v An Bord Pleanála* [1993] 1 I.R. 39 at 72.

[452] See, e.g. *Z v Minister for Justice, Equality and Law Reform* [2002] IESC 14; [2002] 2 I.R. 135 at 158; *AO v Minister for Justice, Equality and Law Reform* [2003] 1 I.R. 1 at 61 and 126.

[453] See, e.g. *Bailey v Flood* [2000] IEHC 169.

[454] See, e.g. *Green Party v RTÉ* [2003] 1 I.R. 558; *Camara v Minister for Justice*, High Court (Kelly

Reform,[455] the Supreme Court concluded that proportionality could be applied as part of the *Keegan* test where decisions affected fundamental rights. The judgment is not straightforward and many different viewpoints are expressed in it, including by the different members of the majority.[456] In theory, the position following *Meadows* is that proportionality is considered in cases involving fundamental rights.[457] In practice, one of the difficulties created by the differing positions adopted in *Meadows* is that there is a lack of clarity regarding the meaning of the concept of proportionality. The consequence has been that, while in subsequent cases, lower courts have purported to follow *Meadows* in applying proportionality, the actual test applied is not a proportionality test, as generally understood, but rather a test that is closer in its formulation to anxious scrutiny, or indeed, to the former *Keegan* test.[458] As such, while the endorsement of proportionality in *Meadows* is to be welcomed, a more whole-hearted adoption of proportionality in cases involving fundamental rights would have been preferred. Notwithstanding this, it has been confirmed that the principle of proportionality is part of Irish law,[459] and there have also been a number of successful invocations of it in practice.[460]

11-135   On the question of error of fact, it has been suggested that the cases where the court can intervene by way of judicial review to correct errors of fact will be rare.[461] Moreover, previously, if intervening to correct an error of fact, Irish courts sought to characterise the error as an element of another well-established ground of review, such as breach of the principle of procedural fairness.[462] However, in general, now, it appears that Irish courts will quash a decision which is vitiated by *material* error of fact.[463]

J) 26 July 2000.

[455] *Meadows v Minister for Justice, Equality and Law Reform* [2010] IESC 3; [2010] 2 I.R. 701.

[456] For an analysis, see H. Delany and C. Donnelly, "The Supreme Court Inches Towards Proportionality Review" [2011] P.L. 9; H. Biehler and C. Donnelly "Proportionality in the Irish Courts: the Need for Guidance" (2014) 3 E.H.R.L.R. 272.

[457] See, e.g. *Efe v Minister of Justice, Equality and Law Reform* [2011] IEHC 214; [2011] 2 I.R. 798 at [28]–[29].

[458] The test as applied is often applied differently from the formulation, for example, in *Huang v Secretary of State for the Home Department* [2007] UKHL 11; [2007] 2 A.C. 167. For example, see *F v Minister for Justice, Equality and Law Reform* [2010] IEHC 457 at [10] (an applicant must demonstrate that a decision "is disproportionate in the sense of being irrational or unreasonable according to the Keegan/O'Keeffe test"); *U v Minister for Justice, Equality and Law Reform* [2010] IEHC 371 at [35] ("Both sides must be viewed and balanced"); *O v Minister for Justice, Equality and Law Reform* [2010] IEHC 343 at [53] ("unless the balance struck as proportional by the Minister is fundamentally at variance with reason and common sense, his decision cannot be struck down as unlawful"). See also *Afolabi v Minister for Justice and Equality* [2012] IEHC 192 at [19].

[459] *Efe* [2011] IEHC 214; [2011] 2 I.R. 798.

[460] See, e.g., *PS v Minister for Justice, Equality and Law Reform* [2011] IEHC 92 at [31] (decision was both disproportionate and unreasonable); *McSorley v Minister for Education and Skills* [2012] IEHC 201 (although here there was a "manifest disproportionality"); *Gorry v Minister for Justice and Equality* [2014] IEHC 29 (applying a structured proportionality test); *AMS v Minister for Justice and Equality* [2014] IESC 65; [2015] 1 I.LR.M. 170 (Clarke J noting in the Supreme Court at [7.15] that "the Minister's balancing exercise in this case was clearly wrong").

[461] *Ryanair Ltd v Flynn* [2000] IEHC 36; [2000] 3 I.R. 240 at 264 (Kearns J). For discussion, see de Blacam (2017) at para.13.05 and Hogan and Morgan (2010) at paras 10.132—10.137.

[462] *AMT v Refugee Appeals Tribunal* [2004] 2 I.R. 607. See also *Hill v Criminal Injuries Compensation Tribunal* [1990] I.L.R.M. 36 (taking into account an irrelevant consideration).

[463] *Efe* [2011] IEHC 214; [2011] 2 I.R. 798 at [33]. Most of the case law has arisen in the asylum and refugee context (see, e.g. *R v Refugee Appeals Tribunal* [2011] IEHC 151; *Keagnene v Minister for Justice, Equality and Law Reform* [2007] IEHC 17; *KK v Minister for Justice* [2007] IEHC 148 at [12]; *AD (Afghanistan) v Refugee Appeals Tribunal* [2015] IEHC 30 (reference to "fundamental er-

New Zealand

Proportionality and unreasonableness

Proportionality is a central element in deciding the reasonable limits of right **11-136** under the New Zealand Bill of Rights Act 1990 (NZBORA). The doctrine requires that the legislative measures designed to give effect to certain objectives must be rationally connected to those objectives and impair rights no more than is necessary to accomplish the objectives. In New Zealand proportionality is known as the *Oakes* test,[464] having been having imported from Canada[465] and modified subsequently.[466] It is assumed that any challenge to the exercise of administrative power on the ground that it unreasonably limits rights in the NZBORA will go through the three or four steps in this proportionality analysis.[467] Since 2007, a growing consensus has emerged among commentators that the structured proportionality test should be adopted in New Zealand. Taggart has observed that the methodology is already applied where NZBORA rights are at stake, and he opines that proportionality methodology is more or less the same methodology as is used in variable reasonableness review where "rights" are at stake.[468]

The main debate in New Zealand now concerns whether proportionality should **11-137** be limited to cases involving NZBORA rights, or also be applied in cases involving fundamental common law rights thus subsuming variable reasonableness review where "rights" are at stake (favoured by Taggart), or be applied more generally and beyond the area of fundamental rights, potentially supplanting reasonableness review altogether, favoured by Joseph[469] and Chief Justice Dame Sian Elias speaking extra-judicially,[470] supporting the argument made by Craig that the proportionality methodology is appropriate to administrative law more generally.[471]

This difference of academic opinion was discussed in *Mihos v Attorney* **11-138** *General*[472] where Baragwanath J considered the possibility of proportionality applying outside the NZBORA context. In the process he discussed the distinction made in the 6th edition of *De Smith* between the structured proportionality test and proportionality as a test of fair balance[473] while also noting the discussion in *De*

---

ror of fact": [25]), but not all of it has: *Hill* [1990] I.L.R.M. 36; *West Cork Bar Association v Courts Service* [2016] IEHC 389 at [22]-[27].

[464] See 11-111.

[465] *Ministry of Transport v Noort* [1992] 3 N.Z.L.R. 260 at 283, CA (Richardson J).

[466] See *Taylor v Chief Executive of the Department of Corrections* [2015] NZCA 477; *Hansen v R* [2007] 3 N.Z.L.R. 1, SC.

[467] *Commerce Commission v Air New Zealand* [2011] NZCA 64; *Schubert v Wanganui District Council* [2011] N.Z.A.R 233; *Drew v Attorney General* [2002] 2 N.Z.L.R. 58; see also C Geiringer "Sources of Resistance to Proportionality Review of Administrative Power under the Bill of Rights Act" (2013) 11(1) N.Z.J.P.I.L. 123; P. Rishworth, G. Huscroft, S. Optican and R. Mahoney, *The New Zealand Bill of Rights* (2003), pp.176–186.

[468] M. Taggart, "Proportionality, Deference, Wednesbury" [2008] N.Z. L. Rev. at 423, 448-449. See also D. Knight, "Mapping the Rainbow of Review: Recognising Variable Intensity" [2010] N.Z.L.Rev. 393 and P.A. Joseph, "Extraordinary Questions in Administrative Law" (2012) 25 N.Z.U.L.R. 73, 81-87.

[469] See P.A. Joseph, *Constitutional and Administrative Law in New Zealand* 3rd edn (2007), 21.7.5 and 23.5.2.

[470] S. Elias, "Righting Administrative Law" in D. Dyzenhaus, M. Hunt and G. Huscroft (eds), *A Simple Common Lawyer: Essays in Honour of Michael Taggart* (2009), pp.55, 72.

[471] Craig, *Administrative Law*, 5th edn (2003) p.630.

[472] *Mihos v Attorney General* [2008] N.Z.A.R. 177, [87]-[98] (HC).

[473] *Mihos* [2008] N.Z.A.R. 177 [11-074].

Smith of the historical origins of proportionality.[474] On the facts he did not feel it necessary to resolve this issue and preferred to opt for "the familiar tool" of variable intensity review. Two decisions of the Court of Appeal discussed whether proportionality should be applied in the context of decisions not to cancel orders for the removal of individuals unlawfully in New Zealand, where their children had been born in New Zealand and granted New Zealand citizenship. The statutory context examined in both cases was identical. Glazebrook J in a separate judgment in *Ye v Minister of Immigration*[475] noted the academic commentary on proportionality, showing some sympathy for Taggart's argument that proportionality should be applied outside the NZBORA context where fundamental rights are at stake. She did not need to resolve this question as the case could be decided on established administrative law grounds. However, she did opine that a case involving the fundamental rights of the child and the potential break-up of a family unit should attract anxious scrutiny, and she doubted whether upholding immigration policy could ever be proportionate to breaking up a family without there being some other public interest factors. In *Huang v Minister of Immigration*[476] the Court of Appeal considered Glazebrook J's dicta, and were firm in their rejection of the proportionality methodology, grounding this conclusion in the statutory context and established precedent. Although proportionality was applied to immigration decisions in the United Kingdom, the court observed the UK courts operate in a "legislative and human rights environment which is very much influenced by s.6 of the Human Rights Act 1998 (UK) and the European Convention on Human Rights" and that New Zealand courts operate in a different environment. Furthermore, the court thought it would be difficult to apply an "undiluted" proportionality test given the weighting to be apportioned to various considerations was implicit in the words of the relevant statutory provision, which set out the circumstances in which a person illegally in New Zealand may be able to avoid removal on humanitarian grounds. The court further said that engaging in a balancing approach would be inconsistent with precedent which provided for an approach based on orthodox administrative law grounds in the relevant statutory context. Also, the interests of the family and the children had already been subject to consideration by the Removal Review Authority, and there had been no appeal from or timely application for review of the Authority's decision. The court thus fell back on previous precedent which held that a court should ensure that the children's interests are genuinely taken into account as a primary consideration, but that how the final balance is struck between competing relevant considerations is for the decision-maker and not the court, unless the decision is so unreasonable that no reasonable decision-maker could have come to it. Both of these decisions, *Ye* and *Huang*, were appealed to the Supreme Court. However in neither case did the court consider the proportionality issue. It found that the cases turned on "relatively straightforward principles of judicial review", namely error of law.[477]

11-139   Taggart draws a distinction between administrative law cases involving "rights" (NZBORA and common law) and those involving "public wrongs").[478] He argues that proportionality should only be applied in rights cases since the presence of

---

[474] *Mihos* [2008] N.Z.A.R. 177 [11-073].

[475] *Ye v Minister of Immigration* [2009] 2 N.Z.L.R. 596 (CA).

[476] *Huang v Minister of Immigration* [2009] 2 N.Z.L.R. 700 (CA).

[477] *Ye v Minister of Immigration* [2010] 1 N.Z.L.R. 104, [11], *Huang v Minister for Immigration* [2009] NZSC 77.

[478] "Proportionality, Deference, Wednesbury" [2008] N.Z. L. Rev. 423. cf. M. Hunt, "Against Bifurcation" in D. Dyzenhaus, M. Hunt and G. Huscroft (eds), *A Simple Common Lawyer: Essays in Honour of Michael Taggart* (2009) p.99.

rights is crucial to the workability of the proportionality methodology and to its normative justification. Taggart expresses the concern that application of proportionality outside the rights area could tempt greater judicial intervention in administrative decision making. Furthermore, New Zealand, not being subject to the same European imperatives as the United Kingdom, should feel free to chart its own indigenous public law path. In cases not involving rights he believes a traditional *Wednesbury* standard should be used as a safety-net to catch those cases of administrative unlawfulness not covered by the other heads of review. He does not consider variable intensity of reasonableness review to be necessary given the expansion and refinement of existing substantive grounds that has occurred, and he argues that the general application of proportionality would subvert the doctrinal approach of carefully going through the established grounds of review. He therefore opposes variable intensity reasonableness review in cases of public wrongs, and supports a "bifurcated" public law; he believed that this approach will in the end lead to greater clarity and certainty in the law.

Intensity of review

In the last decade the New Zealand courts, following UK developments, overtly **11-140** have adopted a variable approach to the intensity of review: that is, the graver the impact of the decision upon the individual affected by it, the more substantial the justification that will be required to assure the court of its legality.[479] The emphasis on justification is all-important, and it is not coincidental that the common law is increasingly requiring reasons and putting greater emphasis on transparency. It is now generally recognised that judicial review of discretionary decision-making involves a sliding scale, with non-justiciability at one end and close scrutiny at the other.[480] This recognition of the need to intensify review when fundamental human rights and interests are threatened is of a piece with the principle of legality.[481]

Outside the "human rights" arena of administrative law (either affirmed in the **11-141** NZBORA or fundamental common law rights), New Zealand has yet to embrace the doctrine of proportionality and so far have stuck with *Wednesbury* unreasonableness[482] (albeit of variable intensity). New Zealand courts remain wary of a stand-alone doctrine of proportionality in the "non-rights" part of administrative law.[483]

---

[479] See generally, D.R. Knight, "Modulating the Depth of Scrutiny in Judicial Review: Scope, grounds, Intensity, Context" [2016] N.Z. Law Rev. 63 and D.R. Knight, "Mapping the Rainbow of Review: Recognising Variable Intensity" [2010] N.Z. Law Rev. 393.

[480] *Pharmaceutical Management Agency Ltd v RousselUclaf Australia Pty Ltd* [1998] N.Z.A.R. 58 at 66, CA; *Ports of Auckland Ltd v Auckland City Council* [1999] 1 N.Z.L.R. 601, HC; *Wolf v Minister of Immigration* [2004] N.Z.A.R. 414, HC; *Progressive Enterprises Ltd v North Shore City Council* [2006] N.Z.R.M.A. 72, HC; *Hamilton City Council v Fairweather* [2002] N.Z.A.R. 477, [45], HC.

[481] M. Taggart, "Proportionality, Deference, Wednesbury" [2008] N.Z. L. Rev. 423; P.A. Joseph, *Constitutional and Administrative Law in New Zealand*, 3rd edn (2007) at paras 21.7.4-21.7.5, 23.1-23.4; D.R. Knight, "A Murky Methodology: Standards of Review in Administrative Law" (2008) 6 N.Z.J.P.I.L. 117.

[482] *McGuire v Wellington Standards Committee (No.1)* [2014] NZHC 3042; *Carroll v The Coroner's Court at Auckland* [2013] NZHC 906; *C v Medical Council of New Zealand* [2013] NZHC 825.

[483] In 2002, the CA held a professional disciplinary sanction "altogether excessive and out of proportion" and quashed the orders made: *The Institute of Chartered Accountants of New Zealand v Bevan* [2003] 1 N.Z.L.R.154. This is the principle described by Tipping J as "[a] sledgehammer should not be used to crack a nut" (*Moonen v Film & Literature Board of Review* [2000] 2 N.Z.L.R.9, [16]). The CA in *Bevan's* case stressed that it was not entering into the "broader question ... whether proportionality is a distinct head of review", noting that the disproportionate penalty case it was following (*R. v Barnsley MBC Ex p. Hook* [1976] 1 W.L.R. 1052) was accepted by commentators as well established (at [55]). That left the law as laid down by Tipping J in *Isaac v Minister of Consumer*

This was confirmed in *Wolf v Minister of Immigration*,[484] where Wild J refused to accept proportionality as a stand-alone principle in the absence of any infringement of NZBORA rights, and opted instead to apply *Wednesbury* unreasonableness. Wild J accepted, however, the view that *Wednesbury* was not a monolithic test and that the intensity of review varied depending on the context, and that the most important factor pointing in the direction of the most intense scrutiny was the presence of human or fundamental rights. He applied a more intensive or searching scrutiny in that case because the decision "involve[d] the deportation of the appellant, and the consequent break up of a New Zealand family unit" and implicated New Zealand's international obligations under the ICCPR and the Convention on the Rights of the Child (although the rights of the child or the right to family life do not find expression in the NZBORA, but the NZBORA only affirms existing rights, and is not intended to affect other existing but unenumerated rights).[485] Wild J was wary of the "Europeanisation" of UK public law which rendered its importation in New Zealand inapt. He held that proportionality should remain within the traditional fold of (*Wednesbury*) unreasonableness, and not standalone.

11-142   New Zealand's constitutional and administrative law is evolving in ways quite different to that of the United Kingdom.[486] Now that appeal to the Privy Council has been abolished, New Zealand courts may chart an indigenous course, although the Court of Appeal has noted in *R. v Chilton* that it considered itself still bound by Privy Council decisions in relation to New Zealand until those decisions are overruled by the New Zealand Supreme Court.[487] The Supreme Court has made it clear in *Hansen v The Queen*[488] that parliamentary sovereignty holds greater sway in New Zealand than amongst many of the higher judiciary in the United Kingdom.

11-143   There are voices advocating adoption of proportionality in New Zealand.[489] However, where NZBORA rights are engaged, proportionality applies; in all other case variable intensity (*Wednesbury*) unreasonableness applies, with the possibility of a grey area of fundamental common law rights or interests somewhere in the middle.

11-144   However, on occasion, some New Zealand judges on review have invoked the American terminology of "hard look" to describe a more intensive scrutiny of the reasonableness of administrative action. In the Court of Appeal in *Pharmaceutical Management Agency Ltd v Roussel Uclaf Australia Pty Ltd* it was said "in some cases, such as those involving human rights, a less restricted approach, even perhaps, to use the expression commonly adopted in the United States, a 'hard look' may be required".[490] In *Thompson v Treaty of Waitangi Fisheries Commission*,[491] one of the prime judicial movers behind the introduction of this terminology Ham-

---

Affairs [1990] 2 N.Z.L.R. 606, 636, HC that disproportionality goes to *Wednesbury* unreasonableness. See also *Waitakere City Council v Lovelock* [1997] 2 N.Z.L.R. 385, 408, CA (Thomas J).

[484] *Wolf v Minister of Immigration* [2004] N.Z.A.R. 414, [32], HC. See also *Mihos v Attorney General* [2008] N.Z.A.R 177 (HC).

[485] NZBORA s.28.

[486] G. Beresford, "The Processes of Constitutionalism in New Zealand and the UK" (2005) 2 N. Z. Postgraduate L. e-Journal.

[487] *R. v Chilton* [2006] 2 N.Z.L.R. 341 at [11].

[488] *Hansen v The Queen* [2007] 3 N.Z.L.R. 1 But see the extra-judicial comments of Chief Justice Dame Sian Elias in "Sovereignty in the 21st Century: Another Spin on the Merry-go-round" (2003) 14 P.L.R. 148.

[489] J. Varuhas, "Keeping Things in Proportion: The Judiciary, Executive Action and Human Rights" (2006) 22 N.Z.U.L.R. 300.

[490] *Pharmaceutical Management Agency Ltd v Roussel Uclaf Australia Pty Ltd* [1998] N.Z.A.R. 58, 66; and see, e.g. Dame Sian Elias, "'Hard Look' and the Judicial Function" (1996) 4 Waikato L. Rev. 1; P. Joseph, *Constitutional and Administrative Law in New Zealand*, 3rd edn (2007), p.933.

mond J attempted to rebadge the "hard look" doctrine as an "adequate consideration doctrine". This doctrine, he said, would go further than taking into account, or
failing to take into account, relevant considerations. Presumably it would go further,
too, than reasonableness review for giving manifestly too much or too little weight
to relevant factors.[492] The notion of adequate consideration, said Hammond J, would
"check poor public administration and inadequate, cursory and ill-considered
decisions". Professor Taggart has argued that in the New Zealand context "hard
look" is an unnecessary transplant and should be rejected[493] as it is no more precise
than unreasonableness and does not tell a judge how hard to look in any particular
case.[494]

In recent years, it would appear that New Zealand courts are moving away from   **11-145**
the "hard look" approach: in *Singh v Minister of Immigration*, the Court of Appeal
preferred to proceed according to "relatively straightforward principles of judicial
review" as articulated by the Supreme Court in *Ye v Minister of Immigration*.[495] In
the High Court case of *O'Brien v Immigration and Protection Tribunal*, Simon
France J stated that he found "'orthodox review', based on *Puli'uvea*, *Huang* and
Singh v Minister of Immigration [2011] N.Z.C.A. 532 more convincing", adding:
"It is also an available inference from *Ye* that the Court does not consider the answer
to these cases will normally be found in debates about the intensity of review".[496]

Consistency

The New Zealand courts have yet to firmly establish this as a ground of review   **11-146**
for essentially the same reasons they are hesitant about substantive legitimate
expectations (indeed expectations based on past practice or decisions often support the claim of inconsistency): it may unduly fetter discretion and hence be
contrary to the public interest. The strongest statement in New Zealand law for
review for inconsistency is in the dissenting judgment of Thomas J in *Pharmaceutical Management Agency Ltd v RousselUclaf Australia Pty Ltd*,[497] where he was of
the view that the agency "failed to act even-handedly between two companies in
direct competition".[498] But more recently, the High Court in *Westpac Banking
Corporation v Commissioner of Inland Revenue* raised doubts as to the "extent to
which inconsistency survives today as a stand-alone ground of judicial review",[499]
adding:

---

[491] *Thompson v Treaty of Waitangi Fisheries Commission* [2005] 2 N.Z.L.R. 9 at [214]-[219], CA.
[492] *New Zealand Fishing Industry Association Inc v Minister of Agriculture and Fisheries* [1988] 1
N.Z.L.R. 546, 552, CA (Cooke P); and *Minister for Aboriginal Affairs v Peko-Wallsend Ltd* (1986)
66 A.L.R. 229, 309-310, H.C.A. (Mason J).
[493] M. Taggart, "Review of Developments in Administrative Law" [2006] N.Z. L. Rev. 75, 85-87.
[494] *New Zealand Public Service Association Inc v Hamilton City Council* [1997] 1 N.Z.L.R. 30, 34-35
HC. See also *Watson v Chief Executive of Corrections* [2015] NZHC 1227.
[495] *Ye v Minister of Immigration* [2011] NZCA 532, [35]-[36], Wild J.
[496] *O'Brien v Immigration and Protection Tribunal* [2012] NZHC 2599, [fn.11].
[497] *Pharmaceutical Management Agency Ltd v RousselUclaf Australia Pty Ltd* [1998] N.Z.A.R. 58, CA.
[498] Citing the 5th edition of this work at pp.576–582, Thomas J invoked the principles of equality, and
of equal and consistent treatment (at 72). The majority decision was upheld on further appeal to the
Privy Council: *Roussel claf Australia Pty Ltd v Pharmaceutical Management Agency Ltd* [2001]
N.Z.A.R. 476 for substantially the reasons given by the majority below.
[499] *Westpac Banking Corporation v Commissioner of Inland Revenue* (2008) N.Z.T.C. 21, 694, [73],
Harrison J.

"The reason, I think, for its failure to evolve is its conceptual difference from orthodox grounds of administrative or public law review which focus on the process and logic of decision making".[500]

11-147   In 2016, the Supreme Court appeared to take a step back from this stance in *Ririnui v Lancorp Ltd* where it said that "consistency of treatment has a role to play in judicial review when issues of arbitrariness or unreasonableness are raised."[501] However, the particular facts of the case counsel against seeing this as a wholesale affirmation of a ground of consistent treatment.[502]

Review for mistake of fact

11-148   It was a New Zealand appeal to the Privy Council[503] that gave Lord Diplock (as he had by then become) the opportunity to confirm at the highest Commonwealth level what he had said as a puisne judge 20 years earlier in *R. v Deputy Industrial Injuries Commissioner, Ex p. Moore*[504]; namely, it is a breach of natural justice to base a finding of fact upon material which does not logically support it. Despite the formerly binding nature of Privy Council decisions in New Zealand law[505] this procedural approach to "no evidence" review has not really taken hold.

11-149   The courts have preferred to see error of fact as an error going to substance or outcome. In a series of dicta, emanating in the beginning from Sir Robin Cooke when on the New Zealand Court of Appeal, and for some time not decided by other members of the court, review was permitted if decision-makers proceeded upon an incorrect basis of fact or misunderstood an established and relevant fact or decided on no evidence.[506] In *S&D v M & Board of Trustees of Auckland Grammar School*,[507] Smellie J noted the continuing division of view at the Court of Appeal level but pointed out that there are "numerous [High Court] decisions where mistake of fact has been held to be a ground of review", naming nine High Court judges who had done so between 1987-97. Smellie J went on to invalidate a school's suspension of a student as based on a "significantly incorrect factual basis". By the mid-1990s, mistake of fact had become accepted as a ground of review at High Court level and is now orthodoxy in New Zealand administrative law. To succeed on this ground, however, the "fact" must be clearly established or "an established and recognised opinion" and "it cannot be said to be a mistake to adopt one of two different points of view of the facts, each of which may be reasonably held".[508] In *Zafirov v Minister of Immigration*[509] Mallon J considered the question "whether evidence of fact that was not before the decision maker can be relevant to an ap-

---

[500] *Westpac* (2008) N.Z.T.C. 21, 694, at [73].
[501] *Ririnui v Lancorp Ltd* [2016] NZSC 62 at [95].
[502] H. Wilberg "Administrative Law" [2016] N.Z. Law Rev. 571, 577.
[503] *Re Erebus Royal Commission; Air New Zealand v Mahon* [1983] N.Z.L.R. 662, 671.
[504] *R. v Deputy Industrial Injuries Commissioner, Ex p. Moore* [1965] 1 Q.B. 456, 488.
[505] Although see *R. v Chilton* [2006] 2 N.Z.L.R. 341 for discussion on this point.
[506] *Daganayasi v Minister of Immigration* [1980] 2 N.Z.L.R. 130, 145-148 (note reservations of other judges, [1980] 2 N.Z.L.R. 130, 132, 149); *New Zealand Fisheries Association Inc v Minister of Agriculture & Fisheries* [1988] 1 N.Z.L.R. 544, 552 CA (Cooke P) (note reservation of Richardson J, [1988] 1 N.Z.L.R. 544, 564); *Devonport v Local Government Commission* [1989] 2 N.Z.L.R. 203 at 208 CA; *Auckland City Council v Minister of Transport* [1990] 1 N.Z.L.R. 264, 293, CA (Cooke P); *Southern Ocean Trawlers v Director-General of Agriculture & Fisheries* [1993] 2 N.Z.L.R. 53 61, CA (Cooke P).
[507] *S&D v M & Board of Trustees of Auckland Grammar School* unreported 11 June 1998 (High Court, Auckland,).
[508] *New Zealand Fisheries Association Inc v Minister of Agriculture & Fisheries* [1988] 1 N.Z.L.R. 544, 552, CA (Cooke P).
[509] *Zafirov v Minister of Immigration* [2009] N.Z.A.R. 457, HC.

peal confined to questions of law".[510] She answered this question in the affirmative and adopted the approach of the English Court of Appeal in *E v Secretary of State for the Home Department*[511] that "mistake of fact giving rise to unfairness" should be accepted as "a separate head of challenge in an appeal on a point of law". Mallon J also adopted the English Court of Appeal's four requirements for a finding of unfairness. On the facts of the case she held that the Deportation Review Tribunal's failure to consider certain available evidence as to the applicant's future risk of criminal offending gave rise to unfairness based on her application of the four-point test set down in *E*. She opined that she could have alternatively decided the case on the basis of more traditional review grounds including failure to take into account relevant considerations and general unreasonableness.

How Mallon J's decision marries up with the previous decision of the Supreme **11-150** Court in *Bryson v Three Foot Six Ltd*[512] is an open question. In that case the Supreme Court examined the circumstances in which an error of fact can constitute an "error of law" in the context of an appeal on a point of law. The court held that,

> "provided that the [Employment] Court has not overlooked any relevant matter or taken account of some matter which is irrelevant to the proper application of the law, the conclusion is a matter for the fact-finding Court, unless it is clearly unsupportable".[513]

As to what was "unsupportable" the court adopted the test set out by Lord **11-151** Radcliffe in *Edwards v Bairstow*: that there exists a state of affairs "in which there is no evidence to support the determination" or "one in which the evidence is inconsistent with and contradictory of the determination" or "one in which the true and only reasonable conclusion contradicts the determination".[514] Mallon J took the view that the Supreme Court had not considered the specific point whether uncontentious or material facts which ought to have been before the decision-maker but were not could constitute an error of law, thus leaving the door open for her to adopt the approach in *E*. However, the Supreme Court's dicta that decision-making authorities not overlook relevant matters would appear directly relevant to the facts of *Zafirov*, especially given Mallon J took the view that the case could have been resolved on the basis of failure to take into account relevant considerations. Most recently, the Supreme Court briefly addressed mistake of fact in the context of a sale of land that was potentially the subject of a Treaty of Waitangi claim, saying that in that case, there "may be scope for argument" as to whether the relevant mistake was one of fact or law. *E* was cited with apparent approval but not discussed or applied.[515] However, it then went on to say that the distinction was not material in that case.

South Africa

The South African Constitution 1996 enshrines the notion of "just administra- **11-152** tive action", which is described in s.33(1) as administrative action which is "lawful, reasonable and procedurally fair"; and s.33(2) imposes a duty to give written reasons for administrative action in certain circumstances. Section 33(3) requires a statute to fill in the detail of those requirements, and in 2000 Parliament enacted

---

[510] *Zafirov v Minister of Immigration* [2009] N.Z.A.R. 457, HC at [76].
[511] *E v Secretary of State for the Home Department* [2004] Q.B. 1044 at [66].
[512] *Bryson v Three Foot Six Ltd* [2005] 3 N.Z.L.R. 721.
[513] *Bryson v Three Foot Six Ltd* [2005] 3 N.Z.L.R. 721 at [25].
[514] *Edwards v Bairstow* [1956] A.C. 14 at 36.
[515] *Ririnui v Landcorp Ltd* [2016] NZSC 62; on mistake of fact generally, see H Wilberg, "Mistakes About Mistake of Fact: The New Zealand Story" (2017) 28 *Public Law Review* 248.

the Promotion of Administrative Justice Act (PAJA). While the statute, too, applies only to "administrative action" as defined in s.1, *every* exercise of public power is today required to be at least lawful and rational in accordance with the rule of law—a value on which the state is founded in terms of s.1(c) of the Constitution. In *Pharmaceutical Manufacturers Association* the Constitutional Court held:

> "It is a requirement of the rule of law that the exercise of public power by the Executive and other functionaries should not be arbitrary. Decisions must be rationally related to the purpose for which the power was given, otherwise they are in effect arbitrary and inconsistent with this requirement."[516]

11-153   This momentous statement paved the way for more recent judgments intensifying the courts' scrutiny under rule-of-law rationality[517] and holding that rationality may, in appropriate cases, also, demand procedural fairness and the giving of reasons.[518] These developments make review under the rule of law (or an aspect of it, the principle of legality) more attractive than ever to litigants as well as the courts, and thus tend to subvert the doctrine of subsidiarity and threaten the status of the PAJA as the primary pathway to judicial review.[519]

Standard of review

11-154   The Constitution thus envisages two standards of review, or two standards of judicial scrutiny of exercises of public power. First, "administrative action" must be lawful, reasonable and procedurally fair, and reasons must be given for it on request. Secondly, all acts entailing the use of public power must be lawful and rational (or non-arbitrary); and rationality may in turn impose further requirements of fairness and reason-giving in appropriate cases. The Constitutional Court has on a number of occasions since *Pharmaceutical Manufacturers* used this second, supposedly less exacting standard of scrutiny to review decisions without considering whether the action in question amounts to "administrative action".[520] Indeed, encouraged by the bold approach of the highest court in *Albutt v Centre for the Study of Violence and Reconciliation*,[521] litigants and courts alike have in recent years tended to bypass the entire "administrative action" inquiry and simply rely on the rule of law and its principle of legality. It is hoped that the Constitutional

---

[516] *Pharmaceutical Manufacturers Association of SA: Re Ex p. President of the Republic of South Africa* 2000 (2) S.A. 674, CC at [85] (footnotes, including to the 5th edition of this work, excluded).

[517] See especially *Democratic Alliance v President of the Republic of South Africa* 2013 (1) S.A. 248, CC and its recognition of procedural as well as substantive rationality; and for comment see L. Kohn, "The Burgeoning Constitutional Requirement of Rationality and the Separation of Powers: Has Rationality Review Gone Too Far?" (2013) 130 South African Law Journal 810. The more recent case of *Electronic Media Network Ltd v e.tv (Pty) Ltd* [2017] ZACC 17 (8 June 2017) illustrates a notably more deferential application of rationality by the majority, but cf. the minority opinion of Cameron and Froneman JJ.

[518] As to procedural fairness, see *Albutt v Centre for the Study of Violence and Reconciliation* 2010 (3) S.A. 293, CC; and for a more recent example, see *Minister of Home Affairs v Somali Association of South Africa* 2015 (3) S.A. 545, SCA. As to the giving of reasons, see *Judicial Service Commission v Cape Bar Council* 2012 (11) B.C.L.R. 1239, SCA.

[519] See further C. Hoexter, *Administrative Law in South Africa*, 2nd edn (2012), pp.131-7.

[520] See, e.g. *Head of Department, Mpumalanga Department of Education v Hoërskool Ermelo* 2010 (2) S.A. 415, CC; *AAA Investments (Pty) Ltd v Micro Finance Regulatory Council* 2006 (11) B.C.L.R. 1255, CC; *Affordable Medicines Trust v Minister of Health* 2006 (3) S.A. 247, CC.

[521] *Albutt v Centre for the Study of Violence and Reconciliation* 2010 (3) S.A. 293, CC at [79]-[84], where the court found that because the matter could be resolved on the rule of law, the application of the PAJA was an "ancillary" question that sound judicial policy did not require the court to "reach". For full discussion and criticism see Hoexter, (2012) pp.133-7.

Court will reconsider the permissibility of this approach, which seems to subvert the PAJA.[522]

Statutory unreasonableness

The PAJA sets out a comprehensive list of grounds of judicial review, one of which is the *Wednesbury* formulation. PAJA s.6(2)(h) reads: **11-155**

"A court or tribunal has the power to judicially review an administrative action if the exercise of the power or the performance of the function authorised by the empowering provision, in pursuance of which the administrative action was purportedly taken, is so unreasonable that no reasonable person could have so exercised the power or performed the function".

As has been discussed above,[523] in *Bato Star Fishing (Pty) Ltd v Minister of Environmental Affairs*, O'Regan J held for a unanimous Constitutional Court that this formulation was not consistent with the right enshrined in the South African Constitution to administrative action which is "reasonable".[524] Reading the PAJA provision down, she held[525]:   **11-156**

"Even if it may be thought that the language of s.6(2)(h), if taken literally, might set a standard such that a decision would rarely if ever be found unreasonable, that is not the proper constitutional meaning which should be attached to the subsection. The subsection must be construed consistently with the Constitution and in particular s 33 which requires administrative action to be "reasonable". Section 6(2)(h) should then be understood to require a simple test, namely that an administrative decision will be reviewable if, in Lord Cooke's words, it is one that a reasonable decision-maker could not reach".

As to the substance of reasonableness review, the court in *Bato Star* adopted an approach based on "reasonable equilibrium". Where an administrator is enjoined by legislation to have regard to a range of considerations in making a decision, and has to strike a balance between competing considerations, the court's role "is merely to determine whether the decision made is one which achieves a reasonable equilibrium in the circumstances". This is consistent with the view of the leading work, where Hoexter suggests that reasonableness as a standard of review connotes "an area of 'legitimate diversity', a space within which 'various reasonable choices may be made'.[526] O'Regan J set out a range of factors that courts must consider when investigating whether the administrative action concerned is reasonable or not. These include: **11-157**

"the nature of the decision, the identity and expertise of the decision-maker, the range of

---

[522] In *Minister of Defence and Military Veterans v Motau* 2014 (5) S.A. 69, CC [27] at fn.28 the court acknowledged that "the correct order of enquiry is to consider, first, whether PAJA applies, and only if it does not, what is demanded by general constitutional principles such as the rule of law". However, this pronouncement was made unobtrusively in a footnote and without reference to the court's contrary approach in Albutt, and it seems to have had no discernible effect on the behaviour of litigants or courts. In *State Information Technology Agency Soc Ltd v Gijima Holdings (Pty) Ltd* 2017 (2) S.A. 63, SCA, the primacy of the PAJA was asserted by the majority of the court but questioned by a minority. At the time of writing, the Constitutional Court was due to hand down its judgment on appeal in this matter.

[523] See 11-099.

[524] *Bato Star Fishing (Pty) Ltd v Minister of Environmental Affairs* 2004 (4) S.A. 490, CC.

[525] para.44 (footnotes omitted). The reference to Lord Cooke is to *R. v Chief Constable of Sussex, Ex p. International Trader's Ferry Ltd* [1999] 2 A.C. 418.

[526] C. Hoexter, *Administrative Law in South Africa*, 2nd edn (2012), p.347; see also "The Future of Judicial Review in South African Administrative Law" (2000) 117 *South African Law Journal* 484, 509-10.

factors relevant to the decision, the reasons given for the decision, the nature of the competing interests involved and the impact of the decision on the lives and well-being of those affected".[527]

11-158   Like the concept of "reasonable equilibrium" itself, some of these factors clearly lend themselves to a proportionality inquiry, and in the case law on s.6(2)(h) there has been some explicit engagement with proportionality as well as other aspects of unreasonableness.[528]

11-159   In *Bato-Star* O'Regan J also considered the notion of deference, and although willing to concede to the expertise of the primary decision-maker in a complex case of resource allocation, was not willing to "rubber-stamp" such a decision. She was anxious to emphasise that:

"The use of the word 'deference' may give rise to misunderstanding as to the true function of a review Court. This can be avoided if it is realised that the need for courts to treat decision-makers with appropriate deference or respect flows not from judicial courtesy or etiquette but from the fundamental constitutional principle of the separation of powers itself".[529]

Mistake of fact

11-160   At common law, mistakes of (non-jurisdictional) fact were not reviewable in themselves but only on certain grounds: *mala fides*, ulterior motive, failure to apply the mind and breach of an express statutory provision. However, the position is quite different now as a result of the important decision of *Pepcor Retirement Fund v Financial Services Board*.[530] The Promotion of Administrative Justice Act 3 of 2000 (PAJA) does not expressly include mistake of fact as a ground of review, but the Supreme Court of Appeal held in *Pepcor* that s.33(1) of the Constitution and the constitutional principle of legality (an aspect of the rule of law) demanded the recognition of mistake of fact as such a ground. While the PAJA was not of application in this case, the court also suggested that the ground of mistake of fact could be read into s.6(2)(e)(iii) of the statute, which allows for review where "irrelevant considerations were taken into account or relevant considerations were not considered".[531]

11-161   In the *Pepcor* case, certificates had been issued by the Registrar of Pension Funds on the basis of what turned out to be incorrect actuarial information supplied to him, and a significant sum of money had in turn been transferred to a retirement fund. The court a quo reasoned that the Registrar had been precluded from applying his mind properly to the matter. The Supreme Court of Appeal, however, took inspiration from the *Tameside* case and approached the problem more directly. In the words of Cloete JA:

"[a] material mistake of fact should be a basis on which a Court can review an administrative action. If legislation has empowered a functionary to make a decision, in the public interest, the decision should be made on the material facts which should have been available for the decision properly to have been made. And if a decision has been made in ignorance of facts material to the decision and which therefore should have been before the functionary, the decision should ... be reviewable ... The doctrine of legality ... requires that the power conferred on a functionary to make decisions in the public inter-

---

[527] *Bato Star Fishing (Pty) Ltd v Minister of Environmental Affairs* 2004 (4) S.A. 490, CC at [45].
[528] See, e.g., *Ehrlich v Minister of Correctional Services* 2009 (2) S.A. 373, E.
[529] para.46.
[530] *Pepcor Retirement Fund v Financial Services Board* 2003 (6) S.A. 38, SCA.
[531] para.46.

est, should be exercised properly, ie on the basis of the true facts; it should not be confined to cases where the common law would categorise the decision as ultra vires."[532]

The *Pepcor* principle has been applied several times since then and has become **11-162** fully established both under the principle of legality and under the PAJA.[533] Important qualifications were added in *Dumani v Nair*,[534] where Cloete JA emphasised that the ground of review should not be confused with an appeal: the court is not entitled to reconsider the matter afresh, and the ground is confined to facts that are established in the sense of being "uncontentious and objectively verifiable".[535]

---

[532] para.47.
[533] In relation to the principle of legality, see, e.g., *Government Employees Pension Fund v Buitendag* 2007 (4) S.A. 2, SCA; and in relation to the PAJA, see *Chairpersons' Association v Minister of Arts and Culture* 2007 (5) S.A. 236, SCA, where s.6(2)(e)(iii) was relied on.
[534] *Dumani v Nair* 2013 (2) S.A. 274, SCA.
[535] para.32, with reference to *E v Secretary of State for the Home Department* [2004] EWCA Civ 49; [2004] Q.B. 1044 at [66]. See e.g. *Gorhan v Minister of Home Affairs* [2016] ZAECPEHC 70 (20 October 2016), concerning an application for asylum, where the High Court observed that "facts relating to the current situation in Somalia do not fall within this narrow band" and that the ground was thus not applicable.

CHAPTER 12

Legitimate Expectations

TABLE OF CONTENTS

INTRODUCTION

Since the early 1970s one of the principles justifying the imposition of both **12-001** procedural and substantive protection has been the legitimate expectation. Such an expectation arises where a decision-maker has led someone affected by the decision to believe that he will receive or retain a benefit or advantage (including that a hearing will be held before a decision is taken). It is a basic principle of fairness that legitimate expectations ought not to be thwarted.[1] The protection of legitimate expectations is at the root of the constitutional principle of the rule of law, which requires regularity, predictability, and certainty in government's dealings with the public.[2] "Legal certainty" is also a basic principle of European Community law.[3] For these reasons the existence of a legitimate expectation may, even in the absence of a right in private law, justify recognition in public law.[4]

---

[1] J. Rawls, *A Theory of Justice* (1972), pp.235–243; Blackstone, *Commentaries of the Laws of England* (1765) Vol.1, p.44; F. Maitland, *Collected Papers*, Vol.1 (1911), p.81 ("Known general laws, however bad, interfere less with freedom than decisions based on no previous known rule"; Maitland equated arbitrary power with power that is "uncertain" or "incalculable"); note the Roman Law principle that the Praetor could not depart from the published terms of his edict (Asconius, in Cornelianum, 52 and Dio Cassius 36.40; A. Watson, *Law Making in the Later Roman Republic* (1974), pp.93–94; and Bentham's "disappointment-prevention principle" as an element of his greatest happiness principle. This requires more than "regret", but the loss of an "expectation". See P. Schofield (ed), *Official Aptitude Maximised; Expense Minimised* (1993), Appendix B "On Retrenchment". For a recent account of the philosophical underpinnings of the legitimate expectation see A. Brown, "Justifying Compensation for Frustrated Legitimate Expectations" 30 Law & Phil. 699.

[2] See generally J. Raz, *The Authority of Law* (1979), Ch.11.

[3] See Ch.14; J. Schwarze, *European Administrative Law* (2006). The European law is based upon the concept of "vertrauensschutz" (the honouring of a trust or confidence).

[4] The phrase "legitimate expectation" has been described as being "much in vogue": *EB (Kosovo)) v Secretary of State for the Home Department* [2008] UKHL 41; [2009] 1 A.C. 1159 at [31] (Lord Scott).

12-002   Initially, the legitimate expectation was employed to found a fair hearing: a person's legitimate expectations (to a benefit or advantage, including the expectation of a hearing) could not be terminated without giving the person the opportunity to advocate its retention. In Chapter 7 we merely noted the extension of the scope of the fair hearing so as to encompass the legitimate expectation. We now return to consider that aspect of the legitimate expectation in more detail, together with a consideration of the more recent expansion of the legitimate expectation to the protection of what have been described as secondary procedural legitimate expectations and of substantive rights (thus adding to the armoury of substantive principles considered in Chapter 11).

Legitimate expectations of procedural fairness

12-003   The term "legitimate expectation" first made an appearance in the context of procedural fairness in *Schmidt v Secretary of State for Home Affairs.*[5] A foreign student sought review of the Home Secretary's decision to refuse an extension of his temporary permit to stay in the United Kingdom. In rejecting the student's contention that he ought to have been afforded a hearing, Lord Denning M.R. said obiter that the question of a hearing "all depends on whether he has some right or interest, or, I would add, some *legitimate expectation*, of which it would not be fair to deprive him without hearing what he has to say".[6]

12-004   *Schmidt* and the cases which followed it referred to the legitimate expectation without analysing its scope or basis, and in particular without distinguishing it from the right to a hearing arising from the existence of a protectable interest.[7] The distinction between the legitimate expectation and protectable interest may not always be clear, particularly if the two overlap.[8] However, the underlying principles justifying one or the other are distinct. The legitimate expectation derives its justification from the principle of allowing the individual to rely on assurances

---

[5] *Schmidt v Secretary of State for Home Affairs* [1969] 2 Ch. 149. A legitimate expectation that a particular procedure will be followed has recently been described as the "paradigm case" of procedural expectation: *R. (on the application of Niazi) v Secretary of State for the Home Department; R. (on the application of Bhatt Murphy (A Firm)) v Independent Assessor* [2008] EWCA Civ 755; *The Times,* 21 July 2008 at [29].

[6] *Schmidt v Secretary of State for Home Affairs* [1969] 2 Ch. 149 at 170 (emphasis added). Lord Denning's dicta were not supported by the other members of the CA. Russell LJ, dissenting, simply thought that the case was not sufficiently clear to warrant an order to strike out the action; Widgery J classified a situation where the renewal of a licence might "reasonably be expected" as being "tantamount to the withdrawal of a right" (at 353).

[7] In *Schmidt v Secretary of State for Home Affairs* [1969] 2 Ch. 149 Lord Denning suggested that a revocation of an existing permit would have given the applicant "an opportunity of making representations: for he would have a legitimate expectation of being allowed to stay for the permitted time". See also *Breen v Amalgamated Engineering Union* [1971] 2 Q.B. 175; *McInnes v Onslow Fane* [1978] 1 W.L.R. 1520; *O'Reilly v Mackman* [1983] 2 A.C. 237 (Lord Diplock).

[8] See, e.g. *R. v Assistant Commissioner of Police of the Metropolis Ex p. Howell* [1985] R.T.R. 52, CA: Assistant Commissioner refused to renew the taxi licence of H, a cab driver, without first having given him an indication of the objections to renewal and without having given him a fair chance to meet the objections. In holding that the action of the Assistant Commissioner was unfair, and that the decision should be set aside, the CA used both strands of reasoning. On the one hand, a protectable interest was taken away without consultation: "I think natural justice required that the Assistant Commissioner, before reaching a final decision on a matter of such momentous importance to [H], should at the very least have given him the opportunity to comment..." (Slade LJ at 61); on the other hand, "given the doctor's view [that] he was fit to drive taxi cabs, and having been told [in the regulations] by the Assistant Commissioner that before he could grant him a further licence he would need a certificate to that effect, [H] had a reasonable expectation that the licence would be granted to him on the provision by his doctor of that certificate" (Ackner LJ at 60).

given, and to promote certainty and consistent administration. Such a justification is distinct from that which permits a person to participate in the process of reaching a decision which may threaten his rights or interests.

In *R. v Liverpool Corporation Ex p. Liverpool Taxi Fleet Operators' Association* it was held that the Corporation's decision to increase the number of taxi licences without consulting the Operator's Association was unfair because the decision was in breach of an assurance to the contrary.[9] Although the duty to hear was not expressly justified by the doctrine of legitimate expectation in that case, later cases adopted and explained the decision on that basis.[10] In 1983 the Privy Council quashed an order of the Hong Kong government to deport an immigrant in breach of a promise to give immigrants a fair opportunity to present their case in advance of deportation. The failure to implement the promise was held not to be in the "interest of good administration".[11]

12-005

GCHQ case defines legitimate expectation

The first attempt at a comprehensive definition of the principle of legitimate expectation was provided by the House of Lords in *Council of Civil Service Unions v Minister for the Civil Service* ("the GCHQ case").[12] A bare majority of their Lordships rested their conclusion on the fact that, but for national security, there would have been a duty on the Minister to consult with the Union, on the ground that the civil servants had a legitimate expectation that they would be consulted before their trade union rights were taken away.[13] Lord Diplock stated that, for a legitimate expectation to arise, the decision:

12-006

> "must affect [the] other person ... by depriving him of some benefit or advantage which either (i) he had in the past been permitted by the decision-maker to enjoy and which he can legitimately expect to be permitted to continue to do until there has been communicated to him some rational grounds for withdrawing it on which he has been given an opportunity to comment; or (ii) he has received assurance from the decision-maker will not be withdrawn without giving him first an opportunity of advancing reasons for contending that they should not be withdrawn."[14]

---

[9] *R. v Liverpool Corporation Ex p. Liverpool Taxi Fleet Operators' Association* [1972] 2 Q.B. 299.

[10] Lord Denning M.R. did not refer to the nascent doctrine, but to the "private law" principle of equitable estoppel. For other cases which adopted the doctrine of legitimate expectation as the basis for a duty to be heard, see the Australian case of *Salemi v MacKellar (No.2)* (1977) 137 C.L.R. 396 (Stephen J, dissenting) and *R. v Secretary of State for the Home Department Ex p. Asif Mahmood Khan* [1984] 1 W.L.R. 1337.

[11] *Attorney General of Hong Kong v Ng Yuen Shiu* [1983] 2 A.C. 629.

[12] *Council of Civil Service Unions v Minister for the Civil Service* [1985] A.C. 374. This was not the first time that the HL had considered the doctrine; see *O'Reilly v Mackman* [1983] 2 A.C. 237 at 275 (Lord Diplock, obiter), a prisoner has a legitimate expectation that he will not be awarded a forfeiture of remission by board of visitors without being heard in accordance with the procedures of natural justice; *Re Findlay* [1985] A.C. 318 (prisoner has no legitimate expectation that he will be granted parole under policy which has been superseded by a more restrictive one).

[13] *Council of Civil Service Unions v Minister for the Civil Service* [1985] A.C. 374, Lords Diplock (at 408–409), Fraser (at 401B) and Roskill (at 1204H) all expressed a preference for the term "legitimate" over the term "reasonable" expectation. Lords Scarman and Brightman affirmed the duty to consult without resting on the doctrine of legitimate expectation ([1985] A.C. 374 at 1193G and 1208E).

[14] *Council of Civil Service Unions v Minister for the Civil Service* [1985] A.C. 374 at 408–409; contrast *R. (on the application of British Medical Association) v General Medical Council* [2008] EWHC 2602 (Admin); *The Times, 19 January 2009* at [83] (factor in deciding against legitimate expectation that the GMC had never consulted before when changing fee exemptions).

12-007   This definition indicates the two ways in which the expectation may found the right to a hearing. First, the expectation may be based upon an assurance that a past benefit (such as the right to trade union membership in GCHQ) will continue. In such a case the benefit may not be denied without a hearing. However, the reference by Lord Diplock to *past* advantage or benefit is unduly restrictive. The expectation may also surely extend to a benefit in the future which has not yet been enjoyed but which has been promised.

12-008   Second, the expectation may be based upon an assurance of a hearing itself, which should not be denied. In the GCHQ case Lord Fraser held that the civil servants enjoyed a legitimate expectation that they would be consulted before their trade union membership was withdrawn. The expectation was in his view grounded on the fact that prior consultation had in the past been the standard practice when conditions of service were significantly altered.[15]

Voluntary compliance with fair procedures

12-009   If a body which is entitled to reach a decision without any prior hearing elects to give a hearing before coming to its decision, can that decision be impugned on the ground that the hearing did not conform to the standards of fairness? Some older authority suggests that it cannot.[16] In other areas of the law the volunteer is at times burdened with the same duties as the conscript. I am under no obligation to give a hitchhiker a lift in my car, but if I choose to give him a lift I owe him the same duty of care as I would if he were a fare-paying passenger and I were a common carrier or bound by contract to convey him. Whatever the position may have been in the past,[17] it seems clear today that by providing a voluntary hearing the decision-maker will have induced a legitimate expectation of fairness and the hearing will therefore have to conform to the standards appropriate to the decision being made.

Statutory fair procedure requirements

12-010   A statutory scheme requiring a hearing or specifying particular procedures may have the effect of preventing a legitimate expectation from arising.[18]

Secondary procedural legitimate expectation

12-011   Laws LJ has suggested a third category of legitimate expectation, namely "a secondary case of procedural expectation". Such an expectation is that an obligation to consult will arise if, without any promise, a public authority has established a policy distinctly and substantially affecting a specific person or group who in the circumstances was in reason entitled to rely on its continuance and did so. A secondary case of legitimate expectation will not often be established since, where there has been no assurance either of consultation (the paradigm case of procedural

---

[15] *Council of Civil Service Unions v Minister for the Civil Service* [1985] A.C. 374 at 401–403.

[16] *Ex p. Death* (1852) 18 Q.B. 647 at 659; *Green v Blake* [1948] I.R. 242 at 267; *Russell v Duke of Norfolk* [1948] 1 All E.R. 488 at 491; [1949] 1 All E.R. 109 at 115; *Nakkuda Ali v Jayaratne* [1951] A.C. 66 at 77; in Canada, *R. v Bird* (1963) 38 D.L.R. (2nd) 354. cf. *R. v Minister of Labour Ex p. General Supplies Ltd* (1965) 47 D.L.R. (2nd) 189, applying a dictum in *R. v Metropolitan Police Commissioner Ex p. Parker* [1953] 1 W.L.R. 1150 at 1157.

[17] See J. Evans (ed), *De Smith's Judicial Review of Administrative Action*, 4th edn (1980), pp.237–238 (a previous edition of this work).

[18] *R. v DPP Ex p. Kebiline* [2000] 2 A.C. 326; *R. (on the application of Breckland DC) v Electoral Commission Boundary Committee for England* [2009] EWCA Civ 239; [2009] P.T.S.R. 1611 at [43].

expectation) or as to the continuance of the policy (substantive expectation), there will generally be nothing in the case save a decision by the authority in question to effect a change in its approach to one or more of its functions.[19] Thus, the assurance required to found such a secondary procedural legitimate expectation must be "pressing and focussed".[20]

Legitimate expectations of substantive benefit

When considering the procedural, as opposed to substantive aspects of the legitimate expectation, the promise or representation or conduct which creates the expectation will only require that the person receive a fair hearing. The expectation therefore extends only to the opportunity to make representations or to any other component of a fair hearing, for example, the duty to give reasons.[21] Once the duty to give the hearing has been fulfilled there is not necessarily any further duty to provide the actual substance of the expectation. From the mid-1980s the English courts began to uphold the protection of substantive expectations under limited conditions.[22] In what circumstances may a decision which disappoints an expectation of a substantive benefit or advantage be held invalid on that account? **12-012**

The answer to this question engages a number of public law values.[23] In particular, the relative virtues and defects of certainty and flexibility must be kept in mind. A stubborn concern for internal consistency[24] may fetter an authority's discretion.[25] Yet flexibility can lead to inconsistency and unequal treatment. Fairness to the disappointed individual (who might also have suffered financial loss in reliance upon the expectation) may conflict with the authority's duty to the public. And what will be the practical effect of the principle? Will the assiduous fulfilment of legitimate expectations deter public bodies from articulating their policies?[26] Policies must not be treated as a set of rules, yet, as Sedley LJ put it: "a **12-013**

---

[19] R. (on the application of Niazi) v Secretary of State for the Home Department; R. (on the application of Bhatt Murphy (A Firm)) v Independent Assessor [2008] EWCA Civ 755; The Times, 21 July 2008 at [39].

[20] R. (on the application of Niazi) v Secretary of State for the Home Department; R. (on the application of Bhatt Murphy (A Firm)) v Independent Assessor [2008] EWCA Civ 755; (2008) 152(29) S.J.L.B. 29; The Times, 21 July 2008 at [46].

[21] R. v Secretary of State for the Home Department Ex p. Duggan [1994] 3 All E.R. 277.

[22] See, e.g. R. v Secretary of State for the Home Department Ex p. Ruddock [1987] 1 W.L.R. 1482 (legitimate expectation that circular establishing procedures for telephone tapping should be fulfilled but held that it was); R. v IRC Ex p. MFK Underwriting Agencies Ltd [1990] 1 W.L.R. 1545 (ruling on tax consequences of scheme could create expectation of fulfilment, but not on the facts of this case); R. v Secretary of State for Health Ex p. U.S. Tobacco International Inc [1992] 1 Q.B. 353 (change of policy led to manufacture of "oral snuff" being banned. Held no substantive-but only procedural-legitimate expectation in the circumstances); Olonilvyi v Secretary of State for Home Affairs [1989] Imm. A.R. 135 (representation that applicant would be able to re-enter UK must be fulfilled). But see R. v Secretary of State for Home Affairs Ex p. Patel [1990] 3 Imm. A.R. 89; R. v Croydon Justices Ex p. Dean [1993] Q.B. 769 (expectation that would not be prosecuted); R. v Lord Chancellor Ex p. Hibbit and Saunders [1993] C.O.D. 326 (unfair to fulfil a legitimate expectation where applicants who had previous long-standing contracts as court shorthand writers not given opportunity to submit lower tender in new tender procedure. But not amenable to judicial review as "private law"); R. v Walsall MBC Ex p. Yapp [1994] I.C.R. 528 (council able to seek fresh tenders for building works and no legitimate expectation that own workforce would be favoured).

[23] P. Craig, Administrative Law, 7th edn (2012) at para.22-005.

[24] Decisions of public authorities "may not be internally inconsistent": R. v IRC Ex p. MFK Underwriting Agencies Ltd [1990] 1 W.L.R. 1545 at 1569, DC (Bingham LJ). On consistency and equality, see 11-062–11-065.

[25] On fettering of discretion, see Ch.9.

[26] On tort liability for erroneous statements, see Ch.19.

policy has virtues of flexibility which rules lack and virtues of consistency which discretion lacks".[27] Underlying these questions is the fundamental issue of the degree of scrutiny (*Wednesbury* or more intrusive) which the courts should employ when judging whether the non-application or alteration of a policy in the public interest outweighs the unfairness to the individual who legitimately expected the policy to be applied.

12-014 The complexity of weighing these often contradictory values may be the reason why a number of common law jurisdictions have avoided or rejected at least the substantive legitimate expectation, preferring to allow public decision-makers to keep their options open and to retain the freedom to change their minds.[28] The liberty of a public body to change its policies is an important constitutional principle. Yet in this country we have not only endorsed the legitimate expectation as a value worth protecting, but have even sometimes flirted with its application even when the expectation is induced by a representation that the authority has no legal power to fulfil. Of course the protection of the legitimate expectation is hedged with qualifications and is contingent upon a number of different factors, to which we shall shortly turn, after first considering the essential features of the legitimate expectation (which are common to expectations which induce both procedural and substantive rights).

Illustrations

12-015
- British Coal and the Secretary of State were held in breach of their duty to consult with the unions on the question of pit closures. The expectation was in that case based upon an agreement establishing review procedures (known as the Modified Colliery Review Procedure) and procedures to refer pit closures to an independent tribunal.[29]
- Gypsies have had a legitimate expectation that a council would not evict them without finding an alternative site.[30]
- Contractors on a council's list of approved contractors had a legitimate expectation that they would not be removed from the list without a hearing.[31]
- An applicant submitting a tender for council land enjoyed a legitimate expectation that he would be given a further opportunity to tender following the failure of the favoured bid, since he had been "left with that impression".[32]
- A prisoner serving his sentence in Scotland where remission was one half of the sentence had a legitimate expectation when transferred to England, where remission was only one third of sentence, that the earlier release date would be applied.[33]
- The Commission for the New Towns had a legitimate expectation (based on

---

[27] *R. v Department of Education and Employment Ex p. Begbie* [2000] 1 W.L.R. 1115.
[28] On fettering of discretion, see Ch.9.
[29] *R. v British Coal Corp and Secretary of State for Trade and Industry Ex p. Vardy* (1994) 6 Admin. L.R. 1 (considered in *United States v Nolan* [2010] EWCA Civ 1223; [2011] I.R.L.R. 40).
[30] *R. v Brent LBC Ex p. MacDonagh* (1990) 21 H.L.R. 494. The legitimate expectation arose both from an express promise of the council, and because of a past practice of letting the gypsies stay on the land, providing services, etc. Today, ECHR art.8 may be relevant.
[31] *R. v Enfield LBC Ex p. T.F. Unwin (Roydon) Ltd* (1989) 1 Admin. L.R. 51. The legitimate expectation would seem to be as a result of past practice: the contractors had been on the council's list "for many years". But see *R. v Lord Chancellor Ex p. Hibbit and Saunders* [1993] C.O.D. 326 (shorthand writers on list of Lord Chancellor's Department). On judicial review of contracting decisions, see Ch.3.
[32] *R. v Barnet LBC Ex p. Pardes House School* [1989] C.O.D. 512.
[33] *Walsh v Secretary of State for Scotland* 1990 S.L.T. 526.

a representation more than 15 years earlier) that if a local council constructed a highway, it would do so without charge.[34]

- Residents in a home for the elderly had a legitimate expectation to be consulted about its closure.[35]
- Detainees had a legitimate expectation that the Secretary of State would consider a British National's request that representations be made on his behalf.[36]
- Yet when the Secretary of State decided to abolish a discretionary ex gratia scheme under which compensation was paid to those who had suffered a miscarriage of justice, and did so without consultation, it was held that there had been no representation or promise that the scheme would continue indefinitely, or that the Secretary of State would consult or give notice before withdrawing it.[37]
- Those admitted to the Highly Skilled Migrant Programme had a legitimate expectation that they would enjoy the benefits of the programme as they were at the time they joined it.[38]
- A decision-maker had to follow his own policy, absent good reasons, and could not rely on his unpublished policy to render lawful something inconsistent with his published policy.[39]
- A farmer's bull could not be slaughtered after blood tests contrary to the Department's policy.[40]
- A person qualifying as a doctor could rely on clear, unequivocal and unqualified assurances from the GMC that if he completed his proposed distance learning course of study in a reasonable time his qualification would be

---

[34] *R. v Northamptonshire CC Ex p. Commission for the New Towns* [1992] C.O.D. 123.

[35] *R. v Devon CC Ex p. Baker* [1995] 1 All E.R. 73; *R. v Wandsworth LBC Ex p. Beckith* (1995) 159 L.G.Rev. 929 (duty to consult extends to residents of other homes only indirectly affected by closure). In *R. (on the application of LH) v Shropshire Council* [2014] EWCA Civ 404; (2014) 17 C.C.L. Rep. 216, the *Baker* principle was applied in the context of the closure of adult day care centres. In *LH* the council had engaged in a general consultation process on reorganisation of day centres across the county but the issue was whether there should have been specific consultation about the closure of Hartleys Day Centre, used by LH. Informed by that general consultation, the council then decided which particular day centres to close. The Court of Appeal, reversing the Administrative Court decision [2013] EWHC 4222 (Admin), concluded that the fairness of the procedure was for the court to decide and although the council had initially undertaken widerranging consultation it should have mounted a fresh consultation in relation to any individual day centre it then sought to close; *R. (on the application of Save our Surgery Ltd)* [2013] EWHC 439 (Admin); [2013] Med. L.R. 150 (consultation process for identification of seven specialist centres in England for the future performance of paediatric cardiac surgery declared unfair; in the subsequent determination of what relief to grant the claimant, the court granted a quashing order but declined to dictate what steps should be taken because it had neither the requisite knowledge or expertise: [2013] EWHC 1011 (Admin); [2013] Med. L.R. 172).

[36] *R. (on the application of Al Rawi) v Secretary of State for Foreign and Commonwealth Affairs* [2006] EWCA Civ 1279; [2008] Q.B. 289.

[37] *R. (on the application of Niazi) v Secretary of State for the Home Department; R. (on the application of Bhatt Murphy (A Firm)) v Independent Assessor* [2008] EWCA Civ 755; *The Times*, 21 July 2008.

[38] *R. (on the application of HSMP Forum (UK) Ltd) v Secretary of State for the Home Department* [2009] EWHC 711 (Admin).

[39] *R. (on the application of Lumba) v Secretary of State for the Home Department* [2011] UKSC 12; [2012] 1 A.C. 245.

[40] *R. (on the application of K and AC Jackson and Son) v Department of Environment, Food and Rural Affairs* [2011] EWHC 956 (Admin).

recognised even though the registration criteria had been changed before completion.[41]

THE SOURCE OF A LEGITIMATE EXPECTATION

12-016   In *GCHQ*, Lord Fraser indicated the two ways in which a legitimate expectation may arise: "either from an express promise given on behalf of a public authority or from the existence of a regular practice which the claimant can reasonably expect to continue".[42] The representations which induce a legitimate expectation can thus be express or implied.[43]

Express representation

12-017   An obvious example is where an express undertaking is given which induces an expectation of a specific benefit or advantage. The form of the express representation is unimportant as long as it appears to be a considered assurance, undertaking or promise of a benefit, advantage or course of action which the authority will follow.[44] The express representation can include a promise made by a junior minister in Parliament,[45] although not if consideration of the expectation would involve questioning proceedings in Parliament and undermining parliamentary privilege.[46]

12-018   The promise may relate to an existing situation which will continue, or to a future benefit. In the case an expectation inducing a right to procedural fairness, rather than the substance of the expectation, the promise, as we have seen, may be either to the benefit itself or to a fair hearing (or any aspect of a fair hearing).

12-019   The representation may be directed at a single individual, or a number of individuals,[47] or a class.[48] An example of a personally-directed representation occurred in one of the earliest cases on the substantive expectation (although those

---

[41]   *R. (on the application of Patel) v General Medical Council* [2013] EWCA Civ 327; [2013] 1 W.L.R. 2801, reversing [2012] EWHC 2120 (Admin); (2012) 128 B.M.L.R. 146.

[42]   *Council of Civil Service Unions v Minister for the Civil Service* [1985] A.C. 374 at 401B.

[43]   See F. Ahmed and A. Perry, "The Coherence of the Doctrine of Legitimate Expectations" [2014] C.L.J. 61 for a rule-based account of why certain promises, practices and policies give rise to legitimate expectations whereas others do not.

[44]   Where the Revenue have entered into an agreement under Taxes Management Act 1970 s.54(1) with a taxpayer in relation to a scheme, it has been held that they are precluded from litigating the subject-matter of the agreement, even if it is based upon an error of law. *Cenlon Finance Co Ltd v Elwood* [1962] A.C. 782; *Olin Energy Systems Ltd v Scorer* [1985] A.C. 645 at 658 (Lord Keith); for an unusual example, see *R. (on the application of Kinsley) v Barnet Magistrates' Court* [2009] EWHC 464 (Admin); [2009] R.V.R. 133 at [27] and [30] (where a local authority alleged that a taxpayer was liable for council tax on the basis of Local Government Finance Act 1992 s.6(2)(a), the taxpayer had a legitimate expectation that he would win his case if the local authority failed to make its case and a valuation tribunal could not proceed to find the taxpayer liable under a different statutory provision).

[45]   *R. (on the application of O'Callaghan) v Charity Commission for England and Wales* [2007] EWHC 2491 (Admin) at [23] ("it is of particular importance that a promise of that kind, given in Parliament, is honoured"). Although see *R. v Director of Public Prosecutions Ex p. Kebilene* [2000] 2 A.C. 326 (DC) at 399F (court was "hesitant to hold that a legitimate expectation could be founded on answers given in Parliament to often general questions. To do so is to invest assertions by the executive with a quasi-legal authority, which could involve an undesirable blurring of the distinct features of the legislature and the executive").

[46]   *R. (on the application of Wheeler) v Office of the Prime Minister* [2008] EWHC 1409 (Admin) at [49] (alleged expectations in respect of statements on the holding of a referendum on the Constitutional Treaty). And see *R. (on the application of UNISON) v Secretary of State for Health* [2010] EWHC 2655 (Admin); [2011] A.C.D. 10.

[47]   As in *R. v North and East Devon HA Ex p. Coughlan* [2001] Q.B. 213, where residents of a home

words were not used). In *Preston v Inland Revenue Commissioners*,[49] the applicant taxpayer claimed that the Revenue should honour an agreement with him not to pursue certain tax claims. It was held on the facts that the agreement did not bind the Revenue, but Lord Templeman made it clear that, in principle, conduct equivalent to a breach of contract or breach of representation could amount to an "abuse of power" on the part of the tax authorities.[50] Later, the House of Lords unanimously accepted that it may be an abuse of power for the Revenue to seek to extract tax contrary to an advance clearance given to the taxpayer by the Revenue.[51]

The analogy of the express representation giving rise to a legitimate expectation with the law of contract and the private law principle of estoppel is obvious and probably encouraged the acceptance by the courts that creating a legitimate expectation can have consequences in public law. However, the House of Lords indicated that to have effect a substantive legitimate expectation does not depend upon being able to identify a private law analogy. In *R. (on the application of Reprotech Ltd) v East Sussex CC*, Lord Hoffmann said that "... in this area, public law has already absorbed whatever is useful from the moral values which underlie the private law concept of estoppel and the time has come for it to stand on its own two feet".[52]

12-020

---

for severely disabled people had been promised a "home for life".

[48] Racehorse owners in *R. v Jockey Club Ex p. RAM Racecourses Ltd* [1993] All E.R. 225; and *R. v IRC Ex p. Camcq Corp* [1990] 1 W.L.R. 191.

[49] *Preston v Inland Revenue Commissioners* [1985] A.C. 835. For discussion of the substantive legitimate expectation: G. Ganz, "Legitimate Expectation: A Confusion of Concepts" in C. Harlow (ed), *Public Law and Politics* (1986), Ch.8; R. Baldwin and D. Home, "Expectations in a Joyless Landscape" (1986) 49 M.L.R. 685; P. Elias, "Legitimate Expectation and Judicial Review" in J. Jowell and D. Oliver (eds), *New Directions in Judicial Review* (1988), pp.37–50; C. Forsyth, "The Provenance and Protection of Legitimate Expectations" [1988] C.L.J. 238; B. Hadfield, "Judicial Review and the Concept of Legitimate Expectation" (1988) 39 N.I.L.Q. 103; P. Craig, "Legitimate Expectations: a Conceptual Analysis" (1992) 108 L.Q.R. 79; P. Craig, "Substantive Legitimate Expectations in Domestic and Community Law" [1996] C.L.J. 289; A. Lester, "Government Compliance with International Human Rights Law: A New Year's Legitimate Expectation" [1996] P.L. 187; R. Singh and K. Steyn, "Legitimate Expectation in 1996: Where Now?" [1996] J.R. 17; C. Himsworth, "Legitimately Expecting Proportionality?" [1996] P.L. 46; Y. Dotan, "Why Administrators should be Bound by Their Policies" (1997) 17 O.J.L.S. 23; S. Schonberg, *Legitimate Expectations in Administrative Law* (2000); P. Craig and S. Schonberg, "Substantive Legitimate Expectations after Coughlan" [2000] P.L. 684; S. Schonberg, *Legitimate Expectations in Administrative Law* (2000); R. Clayton, "Legitimate Expectations, Policy, and the Principle of Consistency" [2003] C.L.J. 93; P. Sales and K. Steyn, "Legitimate Expectations in English Public Law: An Analysis" [2004] P.L. 564; I. Steele, "Substantive Legitimate Expectations: Striking the Right Balance?" (2005) 121 L.Q.R. 300; M. Elliott, "Legitimate Expectations and the Search for Principle: Reflections on Abdi and Nadarajah" [2006] J.R. 281; M. Elliott, "British Jobs for British Bodies: Legitimate Expectations and Interdepartmental Decision-making" (2008) 67(3) C.L.J. 453; C. Forsyth, Legitimate Expectations Revisited" [2011] J.R. 429; D. Kolinsky "A Legitimate Expectation of a Successful Challenge?" [2012] J.R. 161; C. Knight, "Expectations in Transition: Recent Development in Legitimate Expectations [2009] P.L. 15; P. Reynolds, "Legitimate Expectations and the Protection of Trust in Public Officials" [2011] P.L.330; R. Williams, "The multiple doctrines of legitimate expectations (2016) 132 L.Q.R. 639; J. Bell "The doctrine of legitimate expectations: power-constraining or right-conferring legal standard?" [2016] P.L. 437; Y, Vanderman, "Substantive legitimate expectation (2016) 21 J.R. 174; M. Groves and G. Weeks (eds) *Legitimate Expectations in the Common Law World* (2017) And see R. Moules, *Actions Against Public Officials: Legitimate Expectations, Mistatements and Misconduct* (2009).

[50] *Preston v Inland Revenue Commissioners* [1985] A.C. 835 at 867. See also Lord Scarman at 851–852 and his speech extolling the virtues of consistency in *HTV Ltd v Price Commission* [1976] I.C.R. 170.

[51] *R. v Inland Revenue Commissioners Ex p. Matrix Securities* [1994] 1 W.L.R. 334 (Lord Browne-Wilkinson).

[52] *R. (on the application of Reprotech Ltd) v East Sussex CC* [2002] UKHL 8; [2003] 1 W.L.R. 348 at

Implied representation

12-021   The promise or representation on which the expectation is based may be implied, e.g. from past conduct or a practice which the claimant may reasonably expect will be continued—as in another tax case where the Court of Appeal held that the Revenue could not resile from a long practice of accepting a claim for a tax refund despite the fact that the statutory time limit had expired.[53]

12-022   Not all past practice, however, may justify a legitimate expectation that the practice will continue. For example, a general, though informal, practice of notification of applications for planning permission to neighbours on adjacent sites was held not to create a legitimate expectation of consultation in a case where an individual had not been notified because of the council's oversight.[54] No legitimate expectation that the council would refuse a planning application could be "spelled out" of previous refusals where those schemes were "materially different" from the present scheme.[55] A representation did not arise from the fact that a property company had become the local authority's biggest supplier of temporary accommodation to the effect that the arrangements between the property company and the local authority would not be terminated without adequate notice.[56] An alien with leave to remain in the United Kingdom for a limited period who, within that period, temporarily left the country in reliance upon first, the leave and a stamp stating that the holder was exempt from having to obtain a visa[57] and secondly, an oral assurance by a Home Office official that she would have "no trouble returning", had a legitimate expectation that she would be allowed to re-enter the United Kingdom.[58] However, another alien who relied on the effect of the stamp alone could not establish a legitimate expectation that he was allowed to re-enter even though the use of the stamp appeared "almost calculated to mislead".[59] However, a legitimate expectation was held to arise from government practice that consideration would be given to diplomatic intervention,[60] and to regular and consistent private use of a stretch of water on the river Thames.[61]

To whom directed—personal or general?

12-023   As the examples above make clear, where the legitimate expectation derives from an express representation, that representation need not be made to the applicant

---

[35], with which Lord Mackay agreed (at [6]); S. Atrill, "The End of Estoppel in Public Law?" [2003] C.L.J. 3.

53   *R. v Inland Revenue Commissioners Ex p. Unilever* [1996] S.T.C. 681.

54   *R. v Secretary of State for the Environment Ex p. Kent* [1988] J.P.L. 706: affirmed [1990] J.P.L. 124, CA (individual affected by planning application who was not notified either of council hearing of application, or of appeal to Secretary of State, could not challenge the decision since jurisdiction was ousted by a six-week limitation clause and there was no legitimate expectation of notification, nor a protectable interest in consultation).

55   *R. (on the application of Loader) v Poole BC* [2009] EWHC 1288 (Admin) at [28].

56   *First Real Estates (UK) Ltd v Birmingham City Council* [2009] EWHC 817 (Admin).

57   And a stamp imposed pursuant to Immigration Act 1971 s.3(3)(b), stating that the leave granted would apply unless superseded by any subsequent leave obtained by the holder.

58   *R. v Secretary of State for the Home Department Ex p. Oloniluyi* [1989] Imm. A.R. 135.

59   *R. v Secretary of State for the Home Department Ex p. Islam* [1990] Imm. A.R. 220; and *R. v Secretary of State for the Home Department Ex p. Patel* (1990) 3 Admin. L.R. 89.

60   *R. (on the application of Abbasi) v Secretary of State for Foreign and Commonwealth Affairs* [2002] EWCA Civ 1598; [2003] U.K.H.R.R. 7; applied in *Rahmatullah v Secretary of State for Foreign and Commonwealth Affairs* [2011] EWHC 2008 (Admin); [2011] 4 All E.R. 926 (for subsequent litigation, in which the legitimate expectation issue was not relevant, see [2011] EWCA Civ 1540, [2012] EWCA Civ 182;[2012] 1 W.L.R. 1462 and [2012] UKSC 48; [2012] 3 W.L.R. 1087). And see *Paponette v Attorney General of Trinidad and Tobago* [2010] UKPC 32; [2012] 1 A.C. 1.

61   *Rowland v Environment Agency* [2002] EWHC 2785 (Ch); [2003] Ch. 1 (see below at 12-071).

personally or directly; a general policy which affects the applicant as a member of a class is sufficient.[62] Similarly, a regular past practice not previously affecting the applicant and not directed at him personally could provide the basis for a legitimate expectation. It is of course necessary that the applicant is a member of the class of persons who are the subject of the representation while that representation is operative.[63]

If a representation is made generally, directed to the world at large, this normally means that a public body has adopted a *policy*.[64] However, policies can also be directed at a class, for example, those who chose to read published decisions of the Revenue about extra-statutory concessions.[65] However, to benefit from an extra-statutory concession, it is necessary for the claimant to have a case "falling clearly within" the terms of the concession.[66] In a recent case, the Supreme Court held, by majority, that there was no "settled practice" on the part of HM Revenue and Customs to adopt a more generous interpretation of the law relating to a taxpayer's period of "ordinary residence" in the United Kingdom.[67]

12-024

When the expectation arises from a policy, its assertion may have different consequences reflecting different (albeit overlapping) values. First, the claimant may require the policy to be *implemented* and not departed from in his particular case. In one of the earliest cases where a substantive legitimate expectation was recognised, the Court of Appeal held that the Home Office could not disappoint an expectation raised by the terms of a Home Office circular, setting out the conditions for the adoption of children from abroad.[68] In such a situation the claim is based less on the principle of legal certainty than that of *consistency*, which is an

12-025

---

[62] See *Attorney General for Hong Kong v Ng Yuen Shiu* [1983] 2 A.C. 629 and *R. v Secretary of State for the Home Department Ex p. Asif Mahmood Khan* [1984] 1 W.L.R. 1337. See also *R. (on the application of S) v the Secretary of State* [2009] EWHC 1315 (Admin) [44] (where the Secretary of State had elected to adopt a policy on how to deal with applications pursuant to a statutory discretion, "there must be a procedural legitimate expectation that he will comply with it"). Of course, an individual personally in receipt of a representation may be in a better position factually to establish a legitimate expectation than a member of a class: this explains the decision in *R. v Secretary of State for the Home Department Ex p. Islam* [1990] Imm. A.R. 220, DC (lack of a personal assurance from the Home Office led to the conclusion that no legitimate expectation could arise, distinguishing *R. v Secretary of State for the Home Department Ex p. Oloniluyi* [1989] Imm. A.R. 135).

[63] *R. v IRC Ex p. Camacq Corp* [1990] 1 W.L.R. 191, CA (where the revenue operates a practice to benefit one class of taxpayer, only someone within that class may have a legitimate expectation that it will continue). See also *R. v Jockey Club Ex p. RAM Racecourses* [1993] 2 All E.R. 225 at 238–39.

[64] On policies, see 5-130, 9-008 and following, and 12-043.

[65] The Revenue may give advice through official published statements and unofficial private "rulings" and advance clearances. They also have discretion to disapply the law by means of extra-statutory concessions under its powers of "wide managerial discretion". See e.g. *R. v IRC Ex p. National Federation of Self-Employed and Small Businesses Ltd* [1982] A.C. 617; *Vestey v IRC (Nos 1 & 2)* [1980] A.C. 1148; *R. v Inspector of Taxes Ex p. Fulford Dobson* [1987] 1 Q.B. 978 at 988.

[66] *Accenture Services Ltd v Commissioners of HM Revenue and Customs* [2009] EWHC 857 (Admin) at [35], [53] (Sales J).

[67] *R. (on the application of Davies and Gaines-Cooper) v Revenue and Customs Commissioners* [2011] UKSC 47; [2011] 1 W.L.R. 2625.

[68] *R. v Secretary of State for the Home Department Ex p. Asif Mahmood Khan* [1984] 1 W.L.R. 1337. Parker LJ considered, following *Attorney General of Hong Kong v Ng Yuen Shiu* [1983] 2 A.C. 629, PC, that the Secretary of State having induced a reasonable expectation that the circular advice would be followed, could not "resile from that undertaking without affording interested persons a hearing and then only if the overriding public interest demanded it". Dunn LJ held that, although the circular letter did not create an estoppel, the Home Secretary reached his decision on irrelevant considerations, having failed to take into account his own rules, and had therefore acted unreasonably. But see *R. (on the application of Lumba) v Secretary of State for the Home Department* [2011] UKSC 12; [2012] 1 A.C. 245 (decision-maker had to follow his published policy absent good reason and could not rely on an aspect of his unpublished policy).

element of the rational decision that we have discussed in the previous chapter.[69] This claim is of course subject to the policy fitting the claim—a matter of interpretation, discussed above.[70] The claim will also be subject to the fact that policies may differ in their determinacy. Some are regarded as mere guidance for the exercise of an authority's discretion, while others are intended to apply unless exceptional circumstances indicate otherwise.

12-026   In a second case of a legitimate expectation arising from a policy the consequences of the claim is more radical: it seeks not only that the policy be implemented, but that the recipient of the expectation should *not be subject to a new policy*. The claimant here asserts that that the expectation carries such weight that it cannot be altered or replaced where to do so would unfairly disappoint the expectation that is raised. Such a claim engages the principles of certainty and fairness but also raises a fundamental constitutional question about the freedom of public bodies to alter their policies in the public interest, which will be discussed below.[71]

International treaties

12-027   In some cases a legitimate expectation has arisen in relation to an international treaty which has not been incorporated in domestic law.[72] In *Minister for Immigration and Ethnic Affairs v Teoh*,[73] the High Court of Australia held in relation to the International Covenant on the Rights of the Child, that[74]:

> "… ratification of a convention is a positive statement by the executive government of this country to the world and to the Australian people that the executive government and its agencies will act in accordance with the Convention. That positive statement is an adequate foundation for a legitimate expectation, absent statutory or executive indications to the contrary, that administrative decision-makers will act in conformity with the Convention".

12-028   Recognition that legitimate expectations may arise in this way is not (as some critics have suggested) tantamount to incorporating a treaty into domestic law "by the back door"—that is, without parliamentary legislation—because there is no suggestion that the courts are enforcing the provisions of a treaty directly or treating them as binding legal rules. If the government makes it clear that the action of ratification is not intended to create a legitimate expectation, then none will be created. *Teoh* has been followed in England and Wales in *R. v Secretary of State for the Home Department Ex p. Ahmed*[75] and in *R. v Uxbridge Magistrates' Court Ex*

---

[69]   See 11-062; *R. v Secretary of State for the Home Department Ex p. Gangadeen* [1998] 1 F.L.R. 762; *R. v Secretary of State for the Home Department Ex p. Urmaza* [1996] C.O.D. 479; *R. (on the application of Rashid) v Secretary of State for the Home Department* [2005] EWCA Civ 744; [2005] Imm. A.R. 608.

[70]   See 5-019 and following.

[71]   See 12-047.

[72]   See also 5-049 for a discussion on unincorporated treaties as an aid to statutory interpretation.

[73]   *Minister for Immigration and Ethnic Affairs v Teoh* (1995) 183 C.L.R. 273; M. Groves, "Unincorporated Treaties and Expectations: The Rise and Fall of Teoh in Australia" [2010] J.R. 323.

[74]   *Minister for Immigration and Ethnic Affairs v Teoh* (1995) 183 C.L.R. 273 at [34] (Mason CJ and Deane J).

[75]   *R. v Secretary of State for the Home Department Ex p. Ahmed* [1999] Imm. A.R. 22, CA (Lord Woolf describing *Teoh* as "wholly convincing"). On the facts, the UK Government had not created a legitimate expectation because policy statements has been lawfully adopted which made clear how officials should take into account the international convention in question.

p. Adimi[76]; in Scotland[77]; and in Northern Ireland.[78] The majority and minority judgments in the Privy Council death penalty case *Thomas v Baptiste* accepted that, in principle, a legitimate expectation may arise in relation to a government's acceptance of treaty obligations.[79] However, it has been held that where a public officer asserts that his decision accords with an unincorporated treaty obligation, the courts will not entertain a challenge to the decision based upon his arguable misunderstanding of that obligation and then itself decide the point of international law at issue.[80]

While the Australian High Court has effectively disapproved (though not formally overruled) *Teoh*[81] and the Canadian Supreme Court has held that no legitimate expectation arose from the ratification of the UN Convention on the Rights of the Child,[82] there is now little doubt in the United Kingdom that as a matter of general principle, ratification of a treaty may be regarded as part of the conduct of government. Things said and done by government in relation to the nation's treaty obligations should not—by reason only of the action being on the international plane—be excluded from the wide range of governmental assurances and practices that may from time to time give rise to a legitimate expectation. A court will need to assess the whole context; it is a matter of evidence.[83] In seeking to identify what if any express or implied representations the government may have made in relation to an unincorporated treaty, account may be had of (among other factors) the fact of ratification, things said[84] or done by the government in relation to ratification, the nature of the treaty rights in issue—particularly whether they are of such a nature as to define individual rights[85]—and any steps that the government may have made in giving practical effect to the treaty. If a statutory provi-

12-029

---

[76] *R. v Uxbridge Magistrates' Court Ex p. Adimi* [2001] Q.B. 667 at [56] (Simon Brown LJ), DC. The applicants argued that they were entitled to be protected from prosecution for travelling on false papers by art.31(1) of the UN Convention relating to the Status of Refugees 1951. cf. *R. (on the application of European Roma Rights Centre) v Immigration Officer, Prague Airport* [2003] EWCA Civ 666; [2004] Q.B. 811 at [101] (Laws LJ, expressing "some unease in relation to [this] particular line of authority").

[77] *Musaj v Secretary of State for the Home Department* 2004 S.L.T. 623 at [23] (Court of Session (Outer House), Lady Smith: "the nature of the Dublin Convention is not such that ratification would of itself give rise to any legitimate expectation on the part of the individual applicant for asylum. Nor was there anything about the circumstances of its ratification which did so. It is clear that its purpose was not that of affording benefit to such individuals"). See also *Khairandish v Secretary of State for the Home Department* 2003 S.L.T. 1358.

[78] *Re Phillips (A Minor)* [2000] NIQB 38 (Carswell LJ, obiter); *Re T* [2000] N.I. 516.

[79] *Thomas v Baptiste* [1999] UKPC 13; [2000] 2 A.C. 1 at [34]–[37] (Lord Browne-Wilkinson, Lord Steyn and Lord Millett; at [58] (Lord Goff of Chieveley and Lord Hobhouse of Woodborough, dissenting on other points: "We accept that treaty obligations assumed by the Executive are capable of giving rise to legitimate expectations which the Executive will not under the municipal law be at liberty to disregard"); cf. *Higgs v Minister of National Security* [2000] A.C. 228.

[80] *R. (on the application of Corner House Research) v Director of the Serious Fraud Office (Justice intervening)* [2008] UKHL 60; [2009] 1 A.C. 756 at [67]. For recent discussion of the domestic effect of international law, see P. Sales and J. Clement, "International Law in Domestic Courts: The Developing Framework" (2008) 124 L.Q.R. 388.

[81] *R. v Minister for Immigration Ex p. Lam* (2003) 214 C.L.R. 1; see further 12-081 below.

[82] *Baker v Minister of Citizenship and Immigration* [1999] 2 S.C.R. 817.

[83] *Musaj v Secretary of State for the Home Department* 2004 S.L.T. 623 at [21]–[22].

[84] *R. v Secretary of State for the Home Department Ex p. Behluli* [1998] Imm. A.R. 407 CA (Beldam LJ: "The extent to which statements can found such an expectation must depend upon the circumstances in which they are made, whether reasonably construed they can be taken as propounding a policy or are merely statements applicable to particular cases or classes of case").

[85] See, e.g. *R. v Secretary of State for the Home Department Ex p. Senkoy* [2001] EWCA Civ 328; [2001] Imm. A.R. 399.

sion is part of the background to the claim, that must be taken into account as well.[86] Each case must be judged in the round.

12-030
There is some uncertainty as to whether the expectation is limited to procedural fairness or whether it may extend to substantive benefit. In *Ex p. Ahmed*, the Court of Appeal implied that it extended to substantive benefit,[87] something accepted in *Musaj*,[88] but in *Thomas v Baptiste* the Privy Council appears to take the view that only procedural protection is available.[89]

LEGITIMACY

12-031
It has been said that the term "legitimate expectation" is a "legal term of art"; it has a "normative element", and "a public authority that is the object of a legitimate expectation is under a legal duty, albeit qualified, in relation to the fulfilment of that expectation".[90] To qualify as "legitimate" the expectation must possess the following qualities.[91]

---

[86] *R. v Secretary of State for the Home Department Ex p. Behluli* [1998] Imm. A.R. 407.

[87] *R. v Secretary of State for the Home Department Ex p. Ahmed* [1999] Imm. A.R. 22 (Lord Woolf MR: "This legitimate expectation could give rise to a right to relief, as well as additional obligations of fairness, if the Secretary of State, without reason, acted inconsistently with the obligations which this country had undertaken").

[88] *Musaj v Secretary of State for the Home Department* 2004 S.L.T. 623 at [21] ("it is simply a matter of assessing whether, in the whole circumstances, the act of ratification gives rise to an inference that the government thereafter intends to afford to individuals, the benefit of its terms").

[89] *Thomas v Baptiste* [2000] 2 A.C. 1 at [37] ("Even if a legitimate expectation founded on the provisions of an unincorporated treaty may give procedural protection, it cannot by itself, that is to say unsupported by other constitutional safeguards, give substantive protection, for this would be tantamount to the indirect enforcement of the treaty").

[90] *R. (on the application of SRM Global Master Fund LP) v Commissioners of HM Treasury* [2009] EWHC 227 (Admin); [2009] B.C.C. 251 at [129] (Stanley Burnton LJ, commenting also on the contrast with a "reasonable expectation" which denotes "a purely factual expectation, with no normative content"; [135]); and see *R. (on the application of C) v Stratford Magistrates' Court* [2012] EWHC 154 (Admin) at [20] (a representation not legitimate if "perverse").

[91] In *United Kingdom Association of Fish Producer Organisations v Secretary of State for the Environment, Food and Rural Affairs* [2013] EWHC 1959 (Admin) at [92] Cranston J said: "[T]he threads of the English doctrine of substantive legitimate expectation can be drawn together in the following propositions: 1. The undertaking must be clear, unambiguous and without relevant qualification: *Bancoult*, [60]. 2. On ordinary principles an undertaking can derive from a representation or a course of conduct. However, the mere existence of a scheme is inadequate in itself to generate a substantive legitimate expectation: *Bhatt Murphy*, [63]. 3. Whether there is such an undertaking is ascertained by asking how, on a fair reading, the representation or course of conduct would reasonably have been understood by those to whom it was made: *Patel*, [44]–[45], applying *Paponette*, [30]. 4. Although in theory the defined class being large is no bar to their having a substantive legitimate expectation, in reality it is likely to be small if the expectation is to be made good: *Bhatt Murphy*, [46]. In *Paponette* the successful class to whom a collective promise had been made was some 2,000. 5. Detrimental reliance is not an essential requirement. However, it may be necessary where the issue is in the macropolitical field or a personspecific undertaking is alleged: *Bancoult*, [60]; *Begbie*, 1124 BC, 1133 DF. 6. To justify frustration of a substantive legitimate expectation, the decision maker must have taken into account as a relevant consideration the undertaking and the fact that it will be frustrated: *Paponette*, [45]–[46]. 7. Legitimate expectation is concerned with exceptional situations: *Bhatt Murphy*, [41]. 8. Justification turns on issues of fairness and good administration, whether frustrating the substantive legitimate expectation can be objectively justified in the public interest and as a proportionate response. Abuse of power is not an adequate guide: *Nadarajah*, [70]. 9. The intensity of review depends on the character of the decision. There will be a more rigorous standard than *Wednesbury* review, with a decision being judged by the court's own view of fairness. A public body will not often be held bound to maintain a policy which on reasonable grounds it has chosen to change. There will be less intrusive review in the macropolitical field.

Clear, unambiguous and devoid of relevant qualification

The representation must be "clear, unambiguous and devoid of relevant **12-032** qualification".[92] Whether or not the representation fulfils these qualities is a matter

---

As well, respect will be accorded to the relative expertise of a decisionmaker: *Bhatt Murphy*, [35], [41]; *Patel*, [60]–[62], [83]. 10. Transitional arrangements, and whether there has been a warning of possible change, are not essential but may be relevant to the court's assessment of justification: *Bhatt Murphy* [18]–[20], [56]–[57], [60]–[61], [65]–[70]; *Patel*, [77], [83]."

[92] *R. v IRC Ex p. MFK Underwriting Agencies Ltd* [1990] 1 W.L.R. 1545 at 1570 (Bingham LJ); and *R. v Shropshire County Council Ex p. Jones* (1997) 9 Admin. L.R. 625 (applicant for student grant given to understand he has a very good chance of securing an award does not acquire a legitimate expectation); *R. v IRC Ex p. Unilever Plc* [1996] S.T.C. 681, CA; *R. v Gaming Board of Great Britain Ex p. Kingsley (No.2)* [1996] C.O.D. 241. See also *R. (on the application of Bancoult) v Secretary of State for Foreign and Commonwealth Affairs* [2008] UKHL 61; [2009] 1 A.C. 453 at [60] and [134] (an undertaking to work "on the feasibility of resettling the Ilois" on the Chagos Island and of change to the law to permit resettlement did not amount to an "unequivocal assurance" that the Ilois could return); *R. (on the application of Misick) v Secretary of State for Foreign and Commonwealth Affairs* [2009] EWHC 1039 (Admin) at [36] (no legitimate expectation that there would be a trial by jury had been created by the establishment of a commission to investigate allegations of corruption on the part of elected members of the legislature); *R. (on the application of Khan-Udtha) v Secretary of State for the Home Department* [2009] EWHC 1287 (Admin) at [41] (where a published guidance made it clear that a review of a decision could result in a new ground for refusing an application for a work permit transfer, the argument that the earlier decision gave rise to a legitimate expectation that no new ground of refusal would be raised was "unsustainable"); *R. (on the application of Stamford Chamber of Trade and Commerce) v Secretary of State for Communities and Local Government* [2009] EWHC 719 (Admin) at [87] (where parties have to "lever" an implied promise out of passages from a range of different documents published at different times, an expectation could not be founded); *NA and AA v Secretary of State for the Home Department* [2009] EWHC 420 (Admin); *R. (on the application of Al-Saadoon) v Secretary of State for Defence* [2008] EWHC 3098 (Admin) at [202] (a policy of strong opposition to the death penalty and a policy to seek assurances that the death penalty will not be imposed did not go so far as to constitute a policy not to transfer a person to another state in the absence of such assurances); *R. (on the application of Domb) v Hammersmith LBC and Fulham LBC* [2008] EWHC 3277 (Admin) (a council minute of "noted and adopted" in relation to a manifesto promise did not give rise to a legitimate expectation); *R. (on the application of SRM Global Master Fund LP) v Commissioners of HM Treasury* [2009] EWHC 227 (Admin): not discussed at [2009] EWCA Civ 788 (no reasonable expectation prior to nationalisation that the Bank of England would provide or continue to provide financial assistance to any bank); *Odelola v Secretary of State for the Home Department* [2009] UKHL 25; [2009] 1 W.L.R. 1230 at [29] (the applicant accepted that there was "no question her being able to invoke the principle of legitimate expectation" in respect of immigration rules which could be changed at any time in such a way as to deprive a current applicant of any entitlement to the leave being sought) (followed in *R. (on the application of Elmi) v Secretary of State for the Home Department* [2010] EWHC 2775 (Admin); *R. (on the application of Coke-Wallis) v Institute of Chartered Accountants of England and Wales* [2008] EWHC 2690 (Admin) at [37] (representation by professional institute that dismissal of a case would bring the matter to an end did not give rise to a legitimate expectation, as it was not a specific representation that a second disciplinary complaint would not be laid but was merely general advice about the disciplinary process. Legitimate expectation argument not considered on appeal: [2009] EWCA Civ 730; reversed by Supreme Court [2011] UKSC 1; [2011] 2 A.C. 146). *R. (on the application of Lewisham LBC v Assessment and Qualifications Alliance (AQA)* [2013] EWHC 211 (Admin); [2013] E.L.R. 281 (assurance relied upon not sufficiently unequivocal to create a legitimate expectation that GCSE grade boundaries would not change from one assessment point to the next); *United Kingdom Association of Fish Producer Organisations v Secretary of State for the Environment, Food and Rural Affairs* [2013] EWHC 1959 (Admin) (no clear, unambiguous and without qualification undertaking by the Secretary of State that the fishing fixed quota allocation system adopted for the past 13 years would continue in its existing form; the representations amounted to no more than an explanation as to how the system operated); *R. (on the application of Enfield LBC) v Secretary of State for Transport* [2016] EWCA Civ 480 (while emails stating that train service tender would require a four train per hour service were clear and unambiguous, they had not been sent to the local authority directly and moreover, the local authority knew that a four train per hour service was "inherently unlikely").

of construction as to which the intention of the promissor and the understanding of the promisee may be relevant but not determinative.[93] However, a public authority is not entitled to "thwart legitimate expectations by putting a strained or unconventional meaning" on a policy.[94]

12-033　　The context of the representation is therefore important.[95] As was said in *Zeqiri*,[96] "while it might be appropriate in the case of dealings between the Revenue and sophisticated tax advisers to insist upon a high degree of clarity in the alleged representation, this need not necessarily be required in other cases".[97] The Secretary of State had not acted in breach of a legitimate expectation in deciding to abolish a discretionary ex gratia scheme under which compensation was paid to those who had suffered a miscarriage of justice. There was nothing that amounted to a representation or promise that the scheme would continue indefinitely.[98] In the context of prosecutions it, has been suggested that it is not likely to constitute an abuse of process to proceed with a prosecution unless (i) there has been an unequivocal representation by those with the conduct of the investigation or prosecution of a case that the defendant will not be prosecuted and (ii) that the defendant has acted on that representation to his detriment. Even then, if facts come to light which were not known when the representation was made, these may justify proceeding with the prosecution despite the representation.

12-034　　The expected benefit or advantage must be more than a "mere hope".[99] For example, a departmental circular letter setting out the criteria for the adoption of children from abroad may induce a legitimate expectation that its details will be followed.[100] But other circulars, as we have just noted, may be more in the nature

---

[93] *R. v Ministry of Agriculture Fisheries and Food Ex p. Hamble Fisheries (Offshore) Ltd* [1995] 2 All E.R. 714 (Sedley J); *R. v Secretary of State for the Home Department Ex p. Ahmed* [1999] Imm. A.R. 22 at 40 (Hobhouse LJ: the principle of legitimate expectation was a "wholly objective concept and not based on any actual state of knowledge of individual immigrants"). See also *R. (on the application of A) v Coventry City Council* [2009] EWHC 34 (Admin); [2009] 1 F.L.R. 1202; *Paponette v Attorney General of Trinidad and Tobago* [2010] UKPC 32; [2012] 1 A.C. 1 (legitimate expectation must be "understood by the people to whom it is addressed").

[94] *Johnson Brothers v Secretary of State for Communities and Local Government* [2009] EWHC 580 (Admin) at [12]. See J. Watson, "Clarity and Ambiguity: A New Approach to the Test of Legitimacy in the Law of Legitimate Expectations" (2010) 30 L.S. 633, who argues that the better test is whether the regulation is "clear enough" in the light of individual expectations and administrative intent.

[95] See, e.g. *R. (on the application of Ishtiaq Ahmed) v The Parole Board for England and Wales* [2008] EWHC 3111 (Admin) (a representation did not arise in the context of a prisoner seeking parole, as the Parole Board must always address the question as to whether or not release would be too dangerous on a particular day in question). See also *R. (on the application of Roberts) v Secretary of State for Communities and Local Government* [2008] EWHC 677 (Admin); [2009] J.P.L. 81 at [80] (discussion of the role of legitimate expectations in the planning context where "the most formally expressed planning policies are always susceptible to change"); *R. (on the application of Stamford Chamber of Trade and Commerce) v Secretary of State for Communities and Local Government* [2009] EWHC 719 (Admin) at [92].

[96] *R. v Secretary of State for the Home Department Ex p. Zeqiri* [2002] UKHL 3; [2002] Imm. A.R. 296.

[97] *R. v Secretary of State for the Home Department Ex p. Zeqiri* [2002] UKHL 3; [2002] Imm. A.R. 296 at [44] (Lord Hoffmann).

[98] *R. (on the application of Niazi) v Secretary of State for the Home Department; R. (on the application of Bhatt Murphy (A Firm)) v Independent Assessor* [2008] EWCA Civ 755; *The Times*, 21 July 2008.

[99] See Sedley LJ in *R. v Secretary of State for Education and Employment Ex p. Begbie* [2000] 1 W.L.R. 1115.

[100] *R. v Secretary of State for the Home Department Ex p. Asif Mahmood Khan* [1984] 1 W.L.R. 1337; and *R. v Secretary of State for Defence Ex p. Camden LBC* [1995] J.P.L. 403; *R. (on the application of Midcounties Co-Operative Ltd) v Wyre Forest DC* [2009] EWHC 964 (Admin) (a circular gave rise to a legitimate expectation).

of advisory documents, purporting to interpret the law[101] or the likely implementation of government policy and therefore not intended or understood as inducing binding expectations (for example, Planning Policy Guidance notes issued by the Department for Communities and Local Government on diverse matters, including policy in relation to affordable housing, or to permissible conditions attached to planning permissions). Answers or representations made in Parliament, however, have been held not to give rise to legitimate expectations.[102] Nor have after-dinner speeches given by government Ministers.[103] Nevertheless, it is often difficult to determine the precise source of a policy. They emerge from ministerial statements, White Papers, appeal decisions, and draft circulars or codes. A genuinely consultative document cannot be regarded as a policy from which any obligations flow.[104]

Induced by the conduct of the decision-maker

A legitimate expectation must be induced by the conduct of the decision-maker. **12-035** The representation by a different person or authority will therefore not found the expectation. Thus representations by the police will not create a legitimate expectation about the actions of the prison service.[105] However, the representation of one minister may bind another minister, as both ministers are "formulating and implementing the policies of a single entity, Her Majesty's Government".[106]

It is important to note that we are not here dealing with an expectation of fair- **12-036** ness in general, or to the reasonable exercise of the decision-maker's discretion.[107] The legitimate expectation does not flow from any generalised anticipation of be-

---

[101] *R. (on the application of Beale) v Camden LBC* [2004] EWHC 6 (Admin); [2004] H.L.R. 48 at [22] (Munby J: "Statements by ministers as to what the law are no more determinative of the citizen's rights than similar statements by anyone else ... if correct it adds nothing: if it is incorrect, it is for present purposes irrelevant").

[102] *R. v Secretary of State for the Home Department Ex p. Sakala* [1994] Imm. A.R. 227; *R. v DPP Ex p. Kebilene* [2000] 2 A.C. 326 at 329 (Lord Bingham was "hesitant to hold that a legitimate expectation could be founded on answers given in Parliament to often very general questions; to do so is to invest assertions by the executive with a quasi-legislative authority, which could involve an undesirable blurring of the distinct functions of the legislature and the executive").

[103] *Dinsdale Developers Ltd v Secretary of State for the Environment* [1986] J.P.L. 276.

[104] *Pye (JA) (Oxford) Estates Ltd v Secretary of State for the Environment and West Oxford DC* [1982] J.P.L. 577; cf. *Richmond upon Thames LBC v Secretary of State for the Environment* [1984] J.P.L. 24 and *Westminster City Council v Secretary of State for the Environment* [1984] J.P.L. 27 (account may be taken of advice to Secretary of State, although not yet formally policy).

[105] *R. (on the application of Bloggs 61) v Secretary of State for the Home Department* [2003] EWCA Civ 686; [2003] 1 W.L.R. 2724; *R. v Secretary of State for the Home Department Ex p. Mapere* [2001] Imm. A.R. 89 at [36] ("wrong in principle for courts to rule that a decision-maker's discretion should be limited by an assurance given by another person").

[106] *R. (on the application of BAPIO Action Ltd) v Home Secretary* [2008] UKHL 27; [2008] 1 A.C. 1003; M. Elliott, "British Jobs for British Doctors: Legitimate Expectations and Inter-Departmental Decision-making" (2008) 67 C.L.J. 453.

[107] In *R. (on the application of Rashid) v Secretary of State for the Home Department* [2005] EWCA Civ 744; [2005] Imm. A.R. 608 it was suggested that the expectation was that public officials will implement their own policies on asylum—see the criticism of I. Steele, "Substantive Legitimate Expectations: Striking the Right Balance?" (2005) 121 L.Q.R. 300, who regards such an approach as "denuding the concept of any utility". See also *R. (on the application of S, H and Q) v Secretary of State for the Home Department* [2009] EWCA Civ 142 at [46] ("[t]here can moreover be no question of intervention by the court on the basis of a generalised and unfocussed idea of fairness; or by consideration of what subsequently may have happened to the individual in question and categorised in broad terms such as prejudice, loss and detriment"). But see *Manning v Ramjohn* [2011] UKPC 20, referring to "the expectation to be treated fairly" (at [48]). See also *R. (on the application of Grimsby Institute for Further and Higher Education) v Chief Executive of Skills and Funding* [2010] EWHC 2134 (Admin); [2010] 3 E.G.L.R. 125 at [89]; *R. (on the application of Dudley Metropolitan*

ing treated justly, based upon the scale or context of the decision.[108] In the context of the legitimate expectation which induces a procedural right, this distinction marks the difference between an entitlement to a hearing based upon the legitimate expectation and that based upon other interests.[109] It is therefore misleading to classify under the head of legitimate expectation interests which may require procedural protection irrespective of the conduct of the decision-maker.[110] For example, while the Court of Appeal in *R. v Liverpool Corporation Ex p. Liverpool Taxi Fleet Operators'Association*[111] rightly held that the express assurance of consultation by the Corporation created a legitimate expectation, the obiter view of Lord Denning MR that even in the absence of an assurance the applicants' interest in maintaining the value of their licences would have entitled them to a hearing before the number of licences was increased, identifies a protectable interest quite separate from that derived from the legitimate expectation.[112] It has also been held that objectors to an application for planning permission had no legitimate expectation of be-

---

Borough Council v Secretary of State for Communities and Local Government [2012] EWHC 1729 (Admin) at [47]; *Hanover Company Services Ltd v Revenue and Customs Commission* [2010] UKFTT 256 (TC); [2010] S.F.T.D. 1047 (Commission's assessment which was inconsistent with the guidance was held not to be "outrageously unfair").

[108] As was insisted by Lords Diplock and Fraser in *Council of Civil Service Unions v Minister for the Civil Service* [1985] A.C. 374, thus indorsing *Attorney General of Hong Kong v Ng Yuen Shiu* [1983] 2 A.C. 629 (PC) and impliedly rejecting, insofar as it conflicted, the approach of earlier cases such as *Schmidt v Secretary of State for Home Affairs* [1969] 2 Ch. 149; *Breen v Amalgamated Engineering Union* [1971] 2 Q.B. 175 and *McInnes v Onslow Fane* [1978] 1 W.L.R. 1520. G. Ganz, "Legitimate Expectation: A Confusion of Concepts" in C. Harlow (ed), *Public Law and Politics* (1986), Ch.8 criticises the "confusion" which *Council of Civil Service Unions v Minister for the Civil Service* [1985] A.C. 374 imports into the law, but it is contended that it in fact resolves the confusion which previously existed. For criticism of the analysis of the legitimate expectation as resting on the conduct of the decision-maker, see the Australian cases of *Kioa v Minister for Immigration and Ethnic Affairs* (1986) 62 A.L.R. 321 at 370–375 (Brennan J, arguing that since the principles of judicial review have their basis in the presumed intentions of Parliament, therefore "legitimate expectation" could not be based on expectations engendered by decision-makers, which would be irrelevant to the construction of the statutory framework); cf. *Salemi v Mackellar (No.2)* (1977) 137 C.L.R. 396, 404 (Barwick CJ). But for criticism of this view see P. Elias, "Legitimate Expectation and Judicial Review" in J. Jowell and D. Oliver (eds), *New Directions in Judicial Review* (1988), pp.37–50.

[109] e.g. the view of Lord Bridge in *Re Westminster CC* [1986] A.C. 668. Rejecting an argument that "the scale of [the] decisions [in respect of which natural justice was sought] and the context in which they were taken were such that the [affected] bodies would clearly have a legitimate expectation to be consulted", he warned that "if the courts were to extend the doctrine of legitimate expectation [beyond the foundation of "either a promise or a practice of consultation"] to embrace expectations arising from the "scale" or "context" of particular decisions, the duty of consultation would be entirely open-ended and no public authority could tell with any confidence in what circumstances a duty of consultation was cast upon them [and] the suggested development of the law would, in my opinion, be wholly lamentable". Lord Bridge clearly sought to limit the doctrine to situations arising out of representations of the decision-maker and argues against its expansion to take in a class of interests (of a certain "scale" or "context") independent of this basis. See also the clear distinction between legitimate expectations and protectable interests made by Taylor J in *R. v Secretary of State for the Environment Ex p. GLC* [1985] J.P.L. 543 (Secretary of State's exercise of discretion to delay consideration of the GLC's proposed amendments to the Greater London Development Plan not vitiated by lack of natural justice: not requirement to consult either on basis of a legitimate expectation, or under the audi altarem partem rule or because of a duty to act fairly, considering *Durayappah v Fernando* [1967] 2 A.C. 337).

[110] A view taken by commentators such as G. Ganz, "Legitimate Expectation: A Confusion of Concepts" in C. Harlow (ed), *Public Law and Politics* (1986), Ch.8; but see P. Elias, "Legitimate Expectation and Judicial Review" in J. Jowell and D. Oliver (eds), *New Directions in Judicial Review* (1988), pp.37–50.

[111] *R. v Liverpool Corporation Ex p. Liverpool Taxi Fleet Operators'Association* [1972] 2 Q.B. 299.

[112] Of course, it is possible that a requirement of procedural fairness may flow from both causes, e.g. the revocation of a licence without a hearing may well infringe the interest protectable in itself and

ing able to make representations because no conduct of the planning authority had induced such an expectation. Nevertheless, the objectors were entitled to be heard in order to defend their interests[113] as the proposed action would affect them adversely.[114] Further, in *R. v Secretary of State for Health Ex p. US Tobacco International Inc*,[115] while it was held that the applicants could have no (substantive) legitimate expectation that the Minister would not change his policy regarding the production and sale of oral snuff, it was held that the Minister was in breach of his (statutory) duty to consult by refusing to reveal the contents of an independent report. The "high degree of fairness and candour" to the applicants was based upon the "catastrophic" effect of the ban on the applicants' financial interests.

Made by a person with actual or ostensible authority

The representation must be made by a person with actual or ostensible author-   **12-037**
ity to make the representation.[116] The authority will not be bound if the promisee knew, or ought to have known, that the person making the representation had no power to bind the authority.[117] A manifesto commitment made by a political party or a pre-election promise by a politician seeking election, would therefore not qualify as an enforceable representation, as that party or person had no right at that point to speak on behalf of the government of which it or he was not yet part.[118] When a Minister piloting a bill through Parliament makes a statement about its intended implementation, that statement, as we have seen, may be relevant to the subsequent interpretation of the statute's purpose.[119] Being relevant to the manner in which the way discretion under the statute will be exercised, the statement could be said to give rise to a legitimate expectation, but such an expectation should always be subject to the overall statutory scheme and purpose. In *Sakala*[120] the claimant contended that the Home Secretary should be bound by a statement made in Parliament during the passage of the Immigration Bill 1988—that he would, in a decision about political asylum, "invariably accept the recommendations of a special adjudicator", unless the decision was perverse or unlawful. It was held that he was not so bound.

One of the class to whom it may reasonably be expected to apply

A person who seeks to rely upon a representation must be one of the class to   **12-038**
whom it may reasonably be expected to apply. Thus a report from the Jockey Club announcing the intended availability of new licensed racecourses, which was sent

---

disappoint a legitimate expectation derived from the past conduct of the body which granted the licence.

[113] *R. v Great Yarmouth BC Ex p. Botton Brothers Arcades Ltd* [1988] J.P.L. 18.

[114] It was held that the circumstances of this case were, however, unique because the council had reversed its previously declared policy as to the amusement arcades in coming to the decision complained of. There was at that time no general duty on councils to consult or notify those affected by a grant of planning permission; see also *R. v Secretary of State for the Environment Ex p. Kent* [1968] J.P.L. 706; [1990] J.P.L. 124.

[115] *R. v Secretary of State for Health Ex p. US Tobacco International Inc* [1992] 1 All E.R. 212.

[116] *South Buckinghamshire DC v Flanagan* [2002] EWCA Civ 690; [2002] 1 W.L.R. 2601 (Keene LJ).

[117] See, e.g. *R. v Inland Revenue Commissioners Ex p. Matrix Securities* [1994] 1 W.L.R. 334 where the assurance was given by a local inspector of taxes, but should have been given by the Financial Division of the Revenue.

[118] *R. v Secretary of State for Education and Employment Ex p. Begbie* [2000] 1 W.L.R. 1115. On the question of the mandate, see 11-017.

[119] In the case of an ambiguity under *Pepper v Hart* [1993] A.C. 593; see 5-026–31.

[120] *R. v Secretary of State for the Home Department Ex p. Sakala* [1994] Imm. A.R. 227.

to existing racecourse owners, was held not to apply to prospective new racecourse owners who spent money on a new site in reliance upon the report.[121]

Full disclosure

12-039   The representation must be preceded by full disclosure. Thus where a person is seeking advance clearance for a scheme from the tax authorities he must be frank about what is being sought and put "all his cards face up on the table", giving full details of the specific transaction on which a ruling is required, the ruling that is sought, and the use intended to be made of it.[122] It has been suggested that where there is no written request for a tax ruling, then in anything other than very exceptional circumstances a tax official will not have been put on proper notice of the desire of the taxpayer to have a fully considered ruling on the point at issue and will not have been put on proper notice of the importance and significance of the ruling which he is being asked to provide.[123]

Is knowledge of the representation necessary?

12-040   Is knowledge of the representation necessary to found a legitimate expectation? How can an expectation be claimed when the claimant has been unaware of the representation upon which it is supposedly based? Yet should a person in the class to which the representation is directed be deprived of the benefits of that representation simply because they were ignorant of it?

12-041   As Lord Hoffmann has said, "Kosavar refugees cannot be expected to check the small print".[124] There is surely merit in encouraging good administration which requires decision-makers to bear the normal consequences of their representations.[125] But is this rationale based less upon the existence of a legitimate expectation than upon a general expectation of fairness, good governance, or consistency in public administration? In *Rashid* the claimant asylum seeker was denied asylum in the United Kingdom contrary to a settled policy: the claimant was ignorant of the policy, yet it was held that the Secretary of State had breached the claimant's legitimate expectation "that the Secretary of State will apply his policy on asylum to the claim".[126] Knowledge on the part of the claimant of the policy was held not to be "relevant" or "material" to that expectation.[127]

12-042   Clearly there should be an expectation that public officials will implement their own policies, but the use of the term "expectation" in that context may not add

---

[121] *R. v Jockey Club Ex p. RAM Racecourses Ltd* [1993] 2 All E.R. 225; and *R. v IRC Ex p. Camacq Corp* [1990] 1 W.L.R. 191 (applicant not within the class of intended beneficiaries of tax clearance).

[122] *R. v IRC Ex p. MFK Underwriting Agencies Ltd* [1990] 1 W.L.R. 1545 1569-1570 (Bingham LJ). Lack of full disclosure also vitiated the expectation in *R. v Inland Revenue Commissioners Ex p. Matrix Securities* [1994] 1 W.L.R. 334.

[123] *Corkteck Ltd v HM Revenue and Customs* [2009] EWHC 785 (Admin) (absence of full disclosure).

[124] *R. v Secretary of State for the Home Department Ex p. Zeqiri* [2002] UKHL 3; [2002] Imm. A.R. 296 at [44].

[125] *R. (on the application of Bancoult) v Secretary of State for Foreign and Commonwealth Affairs (No.2)* [2008] UKHL 61; [2009] 1 A.C. 453 at [182] (Lord Mance noting that he had "no difficulty in accepting as the underlying principle a requirement of good administration, by which public bodies ought to deal straightforwardly and consistently with the public").

[126] *R. (on the application of Rashid) v Secretary of State for the Home Department* [2005] EWCA Civ 744; [2005] Imm. A.R. 608 at [25] (Pill LJ).

[127] *R. (on the application of Rashid) v Secretary of State for the Home Department* [2005] EWCA Civ 744; [2005] Imm. A.R. 608 at [25] (Pill LJ) and see [47] (Dyson LJ). But see *R. (on the application of Weaver) v London and Quadrant Housing Trust* [2008] EWHC 1377 (Admin); [2009] 1 All E.R. 17 (lack of knowledge fatal to legitimate expectation).

anything to these general public law duties and indeed may dilute their essence. In any event, as has been discussed in Chapter 11, there is an independent duty of consistent application of policies,[128] which is based on the principle of equal implementation of laws, non-discrimination and the lack of arbitrariness. Although in some cases lack of knowledge of an assurance or practice has defeated a legitimate expectation,[129] it is surely right that knowledge should not be a "necessary precondition" of a legitimate expectation "where statements are made to the public at large".[130]

Detrimental reliance not essential

Despite dicta to the contrary,[131] it is not normally necessary for a person to have **12-043** changed his position or to have acted to his detriment in order to qualify as the holder of a legitimate expectation.[132] In a number of leading cases it has been held that a legitimate expectation should have been fulfilled in a situation where detrimental reliance had not taken place or was not appropriate or required in the circumstances.[133] For example, the applicant may legitimately seek the promised benefits of a tax scheme without having expended funds on promoting the scheme,[134] and individuals might legitimately seek the enforcement of a policy about the tapping of telephones[135] or the criteria for the adoption of children from abroad,[136] without incurring expenditure or otherwise acting to their detriment. Private law analogies from the field of estoppel are, we have seen, of limited relevance where a public law principle requires public officials to honour their undertakings and respect legal certainty, irrespective of whether the loss has been

---

[128] See R. Clayton, "Legitimate Expectations, Policy and the Principle of Consistency" [2003] C.L.J. 93.

[129] See, e.g. *R. v Secretary of State for the Home Department Ex p. Hindley* [2001] 1 A.C. 410 (Myra Hindley's lack of knowledge of a 30-year tariff which was not communicated to her defeated a legitimate expectation); *R. v Minister of Defence Ex p. Walker* [2000] 1 W.L.R. 806; *R. (on the application of Niazi) v Secretary of State for the Home Department; R. (on the application of Bhatt Murphy (A Firm)) v Independent Assessor* [2008] EWCA Civ 755; *The Times,* 21 July 2008 at [46] (substantive expectation likely to be based on representations to small groups). And see 12-049 below.

[130] *R. v Department for Education and Employment Ex p. Begbie* [2000] 1 W.L.R. 1115 at 1133 (Sedley LJ). But see *R. (on the application of Midcounties Co-Operative Ltd) v Wyre Forest DC* [2009] EWHC 964 (Admin) at [94]-[97]; *R. (on the application of Dwr Cymru Cyfyngedig (Welsh Water)) v The Environment Agency* [2009] EWHC 435 (Admin); [2009] 2 All E.R. 919 at [53] (the doctrine of legitimate expectation could not be argued because parties who had relied on an initial decision which had subsequently been withdrawn were not involved in the action).

[131] *Rootkin v Kent CC* [1981] W.L.R. 1186; *R. v Jockey Club Ex p. RAM Racecourses Ltd* [1993] 1 All E.R. 225; *R. v IRC Ex p. Camacq Corp* [1990] 1 W.L.R. 191.

[132] This statement does not apply to the legitimate expectation in European Community law: see *Milk Marketing Board of England and Wales v Tom Parker Farms Ltd* [1998] 2 C.M.L.R. 721.

[133] *R. v Ministry for Agriculture, Fisheries and Foods Ex p. Hamble Fisheries (Offshore) Ltd* [1995] 2 All E.R. 714 at 725 (Sedley J: "the decision-maker's knowledge or ignorance of the extent of reliance placed by the applicant upon the factors upon which the expectation is founded has no bearing upon the existence or legitimacy of the expectation"); and *R. (on the application of Bibi) v Newham LBC (No.1)* [2001] EWCA Civ 607; [2002] 1 W.L.R. 237 at [31] (Schiemann LJ).

[134] *R. v IRC Ex p. MFK Underwriting Agencies Ltd* [1990] 1 W.L.R. 1545 at 1569-1570 (Bingham LJ did not require detrimental reliance but said that "if a public authority so conducts itself so as to create a legitimate expectation that a certain course will be followed it would often be unfair if the authority were permitted to follow a different course to the detriment of one who entertained the expectation *particularly if he relied on it*").

[135] *R. v Secretary of State for the Home Department Ex p. Ruddock* [1987] 1 W.L.R. 1482.

[136] *R. v Secretary of State for the Home Department Ex p. Asif Mahmood Khan* [1984] 1 W.L.R. 1337.

incurred by the individual concerned.[137] In addition, as pointed out by Schiemann LJ, "to disregard the legitimate expectation because no concrete detriment can be shown would be to place the weakest in society at a particular disadvantage. It would mean that those who have a choice and the means to exercise it in reliance on some official practice or promise would gain a legal toehold inaccessible to those who, lacking any means of escape, are compelled simply to place their trust in what has been represented to them".[138] More recently, Lord Hoffmann has said that "it is not necessary that an applicant should have relied upon the promise to his detriment, although this is a relevant consideration in deciding whether the adoption of a policy in conflict with the promise would be an abuse of power".[139]

12-044   Although detrimental reliance should not therefore be a condition precedent to the protection of a substantive legitimate expectation, it may be relevant particularly in two situations: first, it might provide *evidence* of the existence or extent of an expectation. In that sense it can be a consideration to be taken into account in deciding whether a person was in fact led to believe that the authority would be bound by the representations. Secondly, detrimental reliance may affect the *weight of the expectation* and the issue of the fairness of disappointing the expectation.[140] This is particularly relevant to the decision of the authority whether to disappoint a legitimate expectation—an issue which we now consider.

WHEN IS THE DISAPPOINTMENT OF A SUBSTANTIVE LEGITIMATE EXPECTATION UNLAWFUL?

12-045   Given the duty of a public body not to fetter its discretion,[141] and to act in the public interest, under what circumstances will the courts require a body not to deviate from a representation or policy? Clearly the deviation must involve a lawful exercise of discretion,[142] taking into account relevant considerations, ignoring the irrelevant and pursuing authorised and not extraneous purposes.[143] These considerations and purposes can include matters such as the need to maintain national security[144] and matters of public policy.[145] However, although it may be free to depart from its representation or policy, the authority is by no means free to ignore the existence of a legitimate expectation. Now that the legitimate expectation has been accepted in law as an interest worthy of protection, its existence itself becomes

---

[137] S. Atrill, "The End of Estoppel in Public Law?" [2003] C.L.J. 3.

[138] *R. v Newham LBC Ex p. Bibi* [2001] EWCA Civ 607; [2002] 1 W.L.R. 237 at [31].

[139] *R. (on the application of Bancoult) v Secretary of State for Foreign and Commonwealth Affairs (No.2)* [2008] UKHL 61; [2009] 1 A.C. 453 at [60].

[140] See 12-059.

[141] See Ch.9.

[142] Scarman LJ in *Re Findlay* [1985] A.C. 318; *R. v Criminal Injuries Compensation Board Ex p. M (A Minor)* [1988] P.I.Q.R. P107; [1998] C.O.D. 128, affirmed by CA [2000] R.T.R. 21; [1999] P.I.Q.R. Q195 (suggestions that the prerogative power cannot be extended by the representation of an authority in ways which might create a legitimate expectation). On prerogative powers, see 3-032. We doubt whether, these days, the prerogative should be treated any differently in this respect from any other power.

[143] The conduct of the person to whom the representation was made should not be regarded as a relevant consideration to disappointing the expectation, as it was held to be in *Cinnamond v British Airport Authority* [1980] 1 W.L.R. 582 (Lord Denning MR). However, appropriate conduct could be implied as a condition of the fulfilment of the expectation. The conduct could of course be taken into account in the decision of the court as to whether, in its discretion, to award the applicant a remedy.

[144] As in *Council of Civil Service Unions v Minister for the Civil Service* [1985] A.C. 374.

[145] As in *R. v Secretary of State for Health Ex p US Tobacco International Inc* [1992] 1 Q.B. 353 where the expectation was disappointed in the interest of protecting public health.

a relevant consideration which must be taken into account in the exercise of discretion. It is placed upon the scale and must therefore be properly weighed.

In this exercise, on the one side of the scale is the unfairness to an individual of **12-046** the disappointment of the expectation induced by the decision-maker. Other things being equal, fairness dictates that a public authority ought to abide by the important principle of legal certainty which is, as we have seen, a cornerstone of the rule of law. On the other side of the scale, however, is the duty of the authority to pursue the public interest which is never static and may conflict with the interest of the recipient of the legitimate expectation. In the days when judicial review was driven by the need to fulfil the public interest, rather than to respect private rights and interests, the courts would have been inclined to permit the authority wide freedom to override an individual's expectation in favour of its public duty. These days, however, as we have seen, public power must be exercised with due respect for those for whose benefit the power exists. Therefore there is still a balancing exercise to be performed, both by the authority and then by the courts, who have to decide what discretionary leeway to permit the authority on the matter.

A number of cases have emphasised that, by declaring a policy, a decision- **12-047** maker "cannot preclude any possible need to change it".[146] In one such case two life-sentence prisoners claimed that they should have been released under the terms of a policy in relation to parole announced by the Home Secretary but which had since been suddenly changed. Lord Scarman, with whom the other members of the House of Lords agreed, said that:

"Given the substance and purpose of the legislative provisions governing parole, the most that a convicted prisoner can legitimately expect is that his case will be examined individually in the light of whatever policy the Secretary of State sees fit to adopt provided always that the adopted policy is a lawful exercise of discretion conferred upon him by statute. Any other view would entail the conclusions that the unfettered discretion conferred by the statute on the minister can in some cases be restricted so as to hamper, or even prevent, changes of policy."[147]

A similar view was expressed in a case where the applicants had been encour- **12-048** aged through a government grant to manufacture their product, "oral snuff", in the United Kingdom. Shortly after their factory opened the Minister was advised to ban the product on the ground of its danger to health. The applicants claimed that the decision infringed their legitimate expectation to continue to manufacture their product. It was held, however, that the Minister's "moral obligations" to the applicants could not fetter his discretion and could not therefore "prevail over the public interest".[148]

However, in *Pierson*, Lord Steyn made it clear that a decision of the Home **12-049**

---

[146] *R. v Secretary of State for the Home Department Ex p. Ruddock* [1987] 1 W.L.R. 1482 at 1497 (Taylor LJ). Although a hearing may have to be provided before changing it.

[147] *Re Findlay* [1985] A.C. 318 at 338; and *Hughes v Department of Health and Social Security* [1985] A.C. 776 at 788 (Lord Diplock: "The liberty to make such change [of administrative policy] is something which is inherent in our form of constitutional government", in relation to compulsory retirement of civil servants at 65 changed to 60).

[148] *R. v Secretary of State for Health Ex p. US Tobacco International Inc* [1992] 1 Q.B. 353 at 369 (Taylor LJ); and 372 (Moreland J). The legitimate expectation did, however, found a right on the part of the applicants to a fair hearing. *R. (on the application of Alansi) v Newham LBC* [2013] EWHC 3722; [2014] B.L.G.R. 138 (a change of housing policy resulting in A losing her status as a priority home seeker was a proportionate response to a pressing and widespread social problem despite a prior clear and unequivocal assurance that A would retain her priority status if she took up a private rented tenancy which the new policy then excluded from priority status); *R. (on the application of Birks) v Commissioner of Police of the Metropolis* [2014] EWHC 3041 (Admin); [2015] I.C.R 204 (rescinding acceptance of the claimant's resignation from the police was proportionate,

Secretary to raise the minimum "tariff" period after which a life prisoner could expect parole offended the rule of law because it breached the prisoners' substantive legitimate expectation[149] and, as we have seen, the unfairness of disappointing a legitimate expectation has succeeded in a number of other cases in recent years. In *Coughlan*, the Court of Appeal held that the authority was not free to disappoint its promise of a "home for life" to the appellant, who was seriously ill and disabled, in a residential care home providing specialist care.[150] In *Patel*, the Court of Appeal held that the GMC had to honour a clear, unequivocal and unqualified assurance given to P that if he completed his distance learning course of study in a reasonable time, his qualification would be recognised. This was not outweighed by any prevailing public interest; transitional arrangements should have been put in place.[151]

THE STANDARD OF JUDICIAL REVIEW

12-050   We now come to one of the liveliest questions about the legitimate expectation— the standard by which the courts, on judicial review, should scrutinise the authority's decision to disappoint a legitimate expectation. Ought it to be on a mere *Wednesbury* basis,[152] or a more intrusive standard? Two contrasting views on this matter were put forward in the High Court in the 1990s. Laws J. proposed that the courts should only second-guess the authority's view of the overriding public interest under the *Wednesbury* standard of review.[153] Sedley J, in line with his interpretation of the approach to the issue under European Community law, preferred the standard of full review, under which it is for the courts to judge the fairness of the disappointment of the legitimate expectation.[154] Sedley J's view was then held to be a "heresy"[155] and "wrong in principle"[156] by the Court of Appeal. A few years later, however, in *Coughlan*, the Court of Appeal was asked to decide whether the authority could disappoint its promise to the appellant (who was seriously ill and disabled) of a "home for life" in a residential care home providing specialist care.[157] Lord Woolf, for the court (which included Sedley LJ), posed three ways in which

---

despite clear prior representations to the contrary, due to the public interest in facilitating the investigation of a death in custody); *R. (Project Management Institute) v Minister for the Cabinet Office*; [2016] 1 W.L.R. 1737 (the policy of the Privy Council in deciding whether or not to grant a Royal Charter was to be given a broad construction and to allow for a degree of flexibility, such that a compelling public interest in favour of the grant outweighed any failure to meet the main criteria of the policy in full).

[149] *R. v Secretary of State for the Home Department Ex p. Pierson* [1998] A.C. 539.
[150] *R. v North and East Devon HA Ex p. Coughlan* [2001] Q.B. 213. For a recent appraisal of the *Coughlan* case and its impact see K. Hughes, "R. v North and East Devon Health Authority [2001]: Coughlan and the Development of Public Law" in S. Juss and M. Sunkin (eds) *Landmark Cases in Public Law* (2017).
[151] *R. (on the application of Patel) v General Medical Council* [2013] EWCA Civ 327; [2013] 1 W.L.R. 2801.
[152] See Ch.11.
[153] *R. v Secretary of State for Transport Ex p. Richmond-upon-Thames LBC* [1994] 1 W.L.R. 74.
[154] *R. v Minister of Agriculture, Fisheries and Food Ex p. Hamble (Offshore) Fisheries Ltd* [1995] 2 All E.R. 714 at 731-35.
[155] *R. v Secretary of State for the Home Department Ex p. Hargreaves* [1997] 1 W.L.R. 906 at 921, with whom Peter Gibson LJ agreed.
[156] *R. v Secretary of State for the Home Department Ex p. Hargreaves* 1997 1 W.L.R. 906 at 924 (Pill LJ).
[157] *R. v North and East Devon Health Authority Ex p. Coughlan* [2001] Q.B. 213.

the matter could be decided[158]:

"(a)   the court may decide that the public authority is only required to bear in mind its previous policy or other representation, giving it the weight it thinks right, but no more, before deciding whether to change course. Here the court is confined to reviewing the decision on *Wednesbury* grounds ...

(b)   ... the court may decide that the promise or practice induces a legitimate expectation of ... being consulted before a particular decision is taken. Here, it is uncontentious that the court will require the *opportunity for consultation* to be given unless there is an overriding reason to resile from it, in which case the court itself will judge the adequacy of the reason advanced for the change in policy, taking into account what fairness requires.

(c)   Where the court considers that a lawful promise or practice has induced a legitimate expectation of a *benefit which is substantive*, not simply procedural, authority now establishes that here too the court will in a proper case decide whether to frustrate the expectation is so unfair that to take a new and different course will amount to an abuse of power. Here, once the legitimacy of the expectation is established, the court will have the task of weighing the requirements of fairness against any overriding interest relied upon for the change in policy".

It was held that, in the circumstances of that case, the question whether the disappointment of the expectation was unfair or an abuse of power should be decided under the third of the above approaches. As would be the case in the second approach, where purely procedural matters were in issue, the court would weigh the various issues relevant to the question as to whether the expectation was unfairly disappointed and whether the authority's power was abused. In other words, the courts would decide the "correctness" of the matter themselves.[159]

12-051

Coughlan, however, by no means requires that the deference associated with the *Wednesbury* standard is to be abandoned in all cases involving the disappointment of a legitimate expectation in the future. In particular, as the court was careful to point out, this is a developing area of law, and the representation in that case had "the character of a contract" (in the sense that it was expressly made to a small group of people on more than one occasion in unambiguous terms). In addition, this case was driven by (i) the importance of the promise (the fact that the appellant's human right to respect for her home were in issue—as we have seen, the *Wednesbury* approach is softened where human rights are engaged), (ii) the fact that the promise was limited to a few individuals, and not to the world at large, and (iii) the fact that the consequences to the authority of requiring it to honour its promise were likely to be financial only (and not of very great financial consequence at that).

12-052

Subsequent cases have emphasised both that the three approaches set out in *Coughlan* are not "hermetically sealed",[160] and that the judicial reserve associated with the *Wednesbury* test has by no means been abandoned in all cases involving a legitimate expectation. In *Begbie*, even Sedley LJ, who was a member of the unanimous Court of Appeal in *Coughlan*, felt that the distinctions between the first and third approaches in *Coughlan* "deserves further examination" and that a policy

12-053

---

[158] *R. v North and East Devon Health Authority Ex p. Coughlan* [2001] Q.B. 213 at [57].

[159] *Corkteck Ltd v HM Revenue and Customs* [2009] EWHC 785 (Admin) (a substantive legitimate expectation claim depended on the true underlying facts as found by the court and did not proceed by reference to a test whether the person said to have given the assurance had acted irrationally in refusing to acknowledge it).

[160] *R. v Secretary of State for Education and Employment Ex p. Begbie* [2001] 1 W.L.R. 1115 (Laws J).

"must not be treated by its custodians as a set of rules".[161] In *Mullen*,[162] the House of Lords considered whether the Home Secretary needed to apply his policy to provide compensation to persons wrongfully convicted. The claimant was given a fair opportunity to make representations on the matter but was refused compensation on the ground that he had been involved in terrorist activity. The House applied a test of rationality in upholding the Home Secretary's decision.[163]

12-054   It seems therefore as if there will now be a "sliding scale of review, more or less intrusive according to the nature and gravity of what is at stake".[164] Such an approach would be in accord with the tendency of the courts to provide stricter scrutiny to decisions engaging human rights[165] (as in Coughlan, which involved the right to a home). In *Begbie* the newly-elected Labour government had passed legislation which was at variance with various undertakings (issued both before and after the election of 1997) to honour a commitment to provide assisted places at certain schools to pupils who had already been offered them.[166] In that case the expectation yielded to the contrary terms of an amending statute. However, it was also made clear that the *Coughlan* approach, under which the court is the judge of whether the overriding public interest justifies disappointing a legitimate expectation, was not necessarily appropriate in cases involving "wide-ranging issues of social policy".[167] In such cases the courts should respect the fact that the decision-maker is obliged to take into account a number of different interests in addition to those of the disappointed claimant, including, as Laws LJ put it "interests not represented before the court".[168]

12-055   In *Begbie*, Laws LJ considered that the test of "abuse of power" was not sufficiently precise to act as a standard of review to guide the issue of whether a legitimate expectation ought to be protected. Instead he offered the test of proportionality.[169] Laws LJ also proposed the test of proportionality in the *Niazi* case on the basis that: "the doctrine of legitimate expectation, should be treated as a legal standard which, although not found in terms in the European Convention on Hu-

---

[161] *R. v Secretary of State for Education and Employment Ex p. Begbie* [2001] 1 W.L.R. 1115.

[162] *R. (on the application of Mullen) v Secretary of State for the Home Department* [2004] UKHL 18; [2005] 1 A.C. 1.

[163] *R. (on the application of Mullen) v Secretary of State for the Home Department* [2004] UKHL 18, [2005] 1 A.C. 1 [58]-[62] (Lord Steyn).

[164] *R. v Secretary of State for Education and Employment Ex p. Begbie* [2001] 1 W.L.R. 1115 at [66]-[68] (Laws LJ). In *R. (on the application of Patel) v General Medical Council* [2013] EWCA Civ 327; [2013] 1 W.L.R. 2801 at [83], Lloyd Jones LJ held: "When the court considers the fairness of overriding a substantive legitimate expectation, the standard of review is a sliding scale ... Normally, the court would accord a considerable degree of respect to a specialist body such as the GMC which is required by Parliament to decide what qualifications should be recognised." But: (i) there was no reason to conclude that distance learning was such a problem as to demand immediate withdrawal of recognition without any steps to mitigate the impact of such a decision; (ii) the expectation was founded upon an express statement rather than a former policy or course of conduct; (iii) the representation was made to an individual personally; (iv) the expectation was of high importance to P; (v) detrimental reliance was present in abundance; and (vi) the decision of the GMC was not in the macropolitical field.

[165] See 11-093–11-094.

[166] *Begbie* [2001] 1 W.L.R. 1115 at [65].

[167] *Begbie* [2001] 1 W.L.R. 1115 at [69].

[168] *Begbie* [2001] 1 W.L.R. 1115 at [69].

[169] *Begbie* [2001] 1 W.L.R. 1115 [68], requiring any disappointed expectation to be "objectively justified as a proportionate response in the circumstances". See also *R (W) v Secretary of State for Education* [2011] EWHC 3256 (Admin).

man Rights", takes its place alongside such rights as fair trial, and no punishment without law".[170]

In some ways the approach of proportionality is apposite as a standard in these cases. This is because the disappointment of the legitimate expectation requires positive justification. As we saw in the last chapter, the standard of structured proportionality differs from that of domestic rationality in that it places the burden on the authority to justify its decision, which involves a departure from a fundamental norm.[171] The breach of legal certainty as an integral requirement of the rule of law similarly requires such justification. Proportionality is not however a complete answer to the difficult balancing issues involved in these questions.[172] For a start, as we have just noted, and as Laws LJ asserted in *Begbie*, in decisions involving what he called "macro-political" issues of policy,[173] the rationality test was considered more appropriate.[174] In other cases, the courts have simply required the authority to take the legitimate expectation into account as a relevant consideration.[175] Finally, in some instances the courts have only permitted the substantive expectation to ground a fair hearing, rather than the benefit itself.[176]

12-056

On the whole, however, where a legitimate expectation has been disappointed the onus should be on the authority to justify its frustration. No magic formula can reach the right answer as to whether the expectation should be honoured, but in considering whether the disappointment of an expectation is deserving of protection, the following factors may be relevant:

12-057

The subject matter of the representation

The distinction between a mere "hope" and an expectation has already been made. However, some expectations are more secure than others. Most secure will be those where the claimant already possesses a benefit or advantage, such as a home,[177] or a tax advantage,[178] which the alteration of policy is seeking to take away. In these "forfeiture", or "deprivation" cases the authority will be seeking to deprive the claimant of a right or interest which is already vested and therefore may be more deserving of protection[179] than a promise of some benefit in the future (such as an assisted place at a school[180]). In addition, more weight might be placed on expectations of a fundamental human right, such as, in *Coughlan*, the right to a home or,

12-058

---

[170] *R. (on the application of Niazi) v Secretary of State for the Home Department; R. (on the application of Bhatt Murphy (A Firm)) v Independent Assessor* [2008] EWCA Civ 755; *The Times,* 21 July 2008 at [51].

[171] See 11-077.

[172] M. Elliott, "Legitimate Expectations and the Search for Principle: reflections on Abdi and Nadarajah" [2006] J.R. 281.

[173] *Begbie* [2001] 1 W.L.R. 1115 at [69].

[174] See *Hanover Company Services Ltd v HM Revenue and Customs Commission* [2010] UKFTT 256 (TC), where the Commissioners' assessment, which was inconsistent with guidance, was held not to be "outrageously unfair".

[175] See, e.g. *R. (on the application of Ibrahim) v Redbridge LBC* [2002] EWHC 2756; [2003] A.C.D. 25 at [12] (proper account had been taken of the expectation of permanent accommodation and therefore it was for the authority to "balance the legitimate aspirations of those on the housing waiting list and the legitimate expectations of the Claimant and others in like position"). See D. Pievsky, "Legitimate Expectations as a Relevancy" [2003] J.R. 147.

[176] As in *R. v Secretary of State for Health Ex p US Tobacco International Inc* [1992] 1 Q.B. 353.

[177] *Coughlan* [2001] Q.B. 213.

[178] *Unilever* [1996] S.T.C. 681.

[179] Compare *McInnes v Onslow Fane* [1978] 1 W.L.R. 1520.

[180] *Begbie* [2001] 1 W.L.R. 1115. Cf. *R. (on the application of Patel) v General Medical Council* [2013] EWCA Civ 327; [2013] 1 W.L.R. 2801 (expectation that undertaking an existing distance learning course would lead to recognition of the qualification awarded in the future).

as in cases involving deportation, the right to life. On the other hand, as Lord Hoffmann pointed out in *Reprotech*, some rights are entitled to greater protection than others.[181] He contrasted the right to a home (as engaged in *Coughlan*), with property rights which "are in general far more limited by considerations of public interest".

Particular or general

12-059   It is more likely that the legitimate expectation should be respected where it arises from a representation to an individual or a class rather than the world at large. The numbers in the class may not be relevant. In one case the Hong Kong Court of Final Appeal protected a legitimate expectation made by over 1,000 claimants who had been led to believe that they could postpone their own claims in deference to a particular test case.[182] However, as was shown in *Coughlan*, representations which have "the character of a contract" (and therefore not likely to affect a broader section of the public) are specially deserving of protection. This is because the impact of the case in such cases is likely to be "discrete and limited".[183]

Degree of reassurance

12-060   Another factor which affects the strength or weight of the expectation is the extent to which the promisee has been reassured by the promissor that the expectation will not be dashed. Clearly a representation which is implied (e.g. from repeated past conduct) is unlikely to carry as much weight as an express oral or written representation.[184] Few cases of implied representations founding legitimate expectations exist.[185] In some cases it has been suggested that the weight of a representation is diminished where the claimant had the opportunity to seek reassurance about the expectation (e.g. where he was legally represented), but failed to do so.[186]

Nature of the decision

12-061   A body should be less willing to yield to a legitimate expectation where it is duty bound to make policies which lie in what has been described as "the macro-political field".[187] In these cases the authority might rightly give priority to decisions that affect the public at large, or a significant section of it. On the other hand,

---

[181] *R. (on the application of Reprotech (Pebsham) Ltd v East Sussex CC* [2002] UKHL 8; [2003] 1 W.L.R. 348 at [34]; followed in *Flattery v Secretary of State for Communities and Local Government* [2010] EWHC 2868 (Admin).

[182] *Ng Siu Tung v Director of Immigration* [2002] 1 HKLRD 561.

[183] *Begbie* [2001] 1 W.L.R. 1115.

[184] *R. (on the application of Patel) v General Medical Council* [2013] EWCA Civ 327; [2013] 1 W.L.R. 2801.

[185] *Unilever* [1996] S.T.C. 681.

[186] See, e.g. *Henry Boot Homes Ltd v Bassetlaw DC* [2002] EWCA Civ 983; [2003] 1 P. & C.R. 23 at [58] (Keene LJ: "it is relevant that the appellant ... had access to legal advice ... It was as capable as the Local Planning Authority of informing itself as to the legal consequences of commencing development in breach of a condition"); and *Rowland v Environment Agency* [2003] EWCA Civ 1885, [2005] Ch 1 at [157]-[159] (Mance LJ).

[187] *Begbie* [2001] 1 W.L.R. 1115 (Laws LJ). See also *R. (on the application of Patel) v General Medical Council* [2013] EWCA Civ 327; [2013] 1 W.L.R. 2801; *Re Finucane's Application for Judicial Review* [2015] NIQB 57; and *United Policyholders Group v Attorney General of Trinidad and Tobago* [2016] UKPC 17; [2016] 1 W.L.R. 3383 in which the Privy Council took the same approach to macro-economic decisions.

the fact that the authority would need to engage in expenditure in order to meet a legitimate expectation may not be decisive. For example, in *Coughlan*, the local authority would be inconvenienced and caused expense in relation to its plans to close a nursing home if it was decided that the representation was binding. However, the court in that case preferred the claim of the occupants' health which could be very adversely affected by an enforced move.

Detrimental reliance

We have seen that in *Reprotech*, Lord Hoffmann stated that the legitimate expectation should separate itself from private law estoppel and "stand on its own two feet".[188] That statement strongly suggests that to the extent that detrimental reliance may be a condition precedent to estoppel in private law, it need not be a condition precedent to the existence of a legitimate expectation in public law. Nevertheless, detrimental reliance is a factor to be placed on the scales of the fairness and will add to the weight of the legitimate expectation.[189] It may be overridden by a competing public interest, but the greater the evident detriment to the promisee, the greater the countervailing weight of the public interest must be in order to override an expectation that is held to be legitimate.[190]

12-062

Mitigation of the effects of a disappointed expectation

Short of implementing the legitimate expectation, a body may instead mitigate the effects of its disappointment. In *Matrix Securities*, Lord Griffiths said that if the person relying on a clearance from the Inland Revenue were entitled to do so, and spent money promoting a scheme before the clearance was withdrawn, then "fairness demands that the applicant should be reimbursed for out-of-pocket expense and it could be regarded as an abuse for the Revenue to refuse to do so".[191] This statement makes the valuable point that a change of policy resulting in a disappointed expectation is more likely to be held unlawful where it is within the capacity of the authority to compensate the claimant but failed to do so. In so far, however, as the dictum may suggest that compensation will *always* release the authority from the duty to satisfy the full expectation (in *Matrix Securities*, the expectation of the tax-free benefit for the scheme), then it is of more doubtful validity.[192] In *Rowland v Environment Agency*, a case involving an unlawful representation which nevertheless created a legitimate expectation, Mance LJ said that where it would be unfair

12-063

---

[188]   *R. (on the application of Reprotech Ltd) v East Sussex CC* [2002] UKHL 8; [2003] 1 W.L.R. 348 at [35], with which Lord Mackay agreed (at [6]); S. Atrill, "The End of Estoppel in Public Law?" [2003] C.L.J. 3; see 12-018.

[189]   See 12-040-41.

[190]   See C. Forsyth (ed), Wade and Forsyth: Administrative Law, 10th edn (2009); P. Sales and K. Steyn, "Legitimate Expectations in English Administrative Law" [2004] P.L. 564, 72; *R. (on the application of Bancoult) v Secretary of State for Foreign and Commonwealth Affairs* [2008] UKHL 61; [2009] 1 A.C. 453 at [60] and [135]; *Gokool v Permanent Secretary of the Ministry of Health and Quality of Life* [2008] UKPC 54 at [21]; *Oxfam v Revenue and Customs Commission* [2009] EWHC 3078 (Ch); [2010] S.T.C. 686 (in the circumstances of that case, the absence of detrimental reliance was fatal to the argument that to modify the assurance would involve an abuse of power). *R. (on the application of Patel) v General Medical Council* [2013] EWCA Civ 327; [2013] 1 W.L.R. 2801 (course undertaken in expectation that it would lead to a recognised qualification was extremely demanding in terms of time and effort with a total financial cost of some US$40,000).

[191]   *R. v Inland Revenue Commissioners Ex p. Matrix Securities* [1994] 1 W.L.R. 334 at 346H.

[192]   In *R. (on the application of Bibi) v Newham LBC (No.1)* [2001] EWCA Civ 607; [2002] 1 W.L.R. 237 the matter was remitted to the body for consideration of whether the effect of the (unlawful) disappointment of the expectation might be reconsidered.

to disappoint such an expectation, the unfairness could be mitigated by compensation, or by smoothing the position as far possible consistently with [the authority's other duties.[193] Sedley LJ has also said that

> "the unfairness which a change of policy may work on those who have relied on the earlier policy can often be adequately mitigated by ... compensating them in money. The point, however, is that such a payment of money is not an anticipatory payment of damages: it is a practical means of eliminating unfairness".[194]

12-064   There may also be other ways than monetary compensation of mitigating the effect of the frustrated expectation, for example, in *Jones v Environment Agency*, it was held that an expectation that a licence would not be required could be disappointed, but only if the claimant was given at least a year's notice of that fact.[195]

CAN UNLAWFUL REPRESENTATIONS CREATE LEGITIMATE EXPECTATIONS?

12-065   To what extent can a public body with limited powers bind itself by an undertaking to act outside of its authorised powers? And if it purports to repudiate that undertaking can it be bound to it by the person to whom it was made? There is a great deal of authority that answers both those questions in the negative,[196] and goes further to assert that a body entrusted with duties or with discretionary powers for the public benefit may not avoid its duties or fetter itself in the discharge of its powers (including duties to exercise its powers free from extraneous impediments).[197] In *R. v Ministry of Agriculture, Fisheries and Food Ex p. Hamble (Offshore) Fisher-*

---

[193] *Rowland v Environment Agency* [2003] EWCA Civ 1885; [2005] Ch. 1 at [153].

[194] *R. v Commissioners of Customs and Excise Ex p. F&I Services Ltd* [2001] EWCA Civ 762; [2001] S.T.C. 939, [72]; see also *R. (on the application of Bibi) v Newham LBC (No.1)* [2001] EWCA Civ 607; [2002] 1 W.L.R. 237 at [56] where it was suggested that monetary compensation or assistance could mitigate the breach of a legitimate expectation. For monetary compensation see Ch.19. An official's statement, if untrue and given in response to a specific request could also found a tort claim for damages for negligent misstatement; see e.g. *Davy v Spelthorne DC* [1984] A.C. 262. cf. In *R. (on the application of Nurse Prescribers Ltd) v Secretary of State for Health* [2004] EWHC 403 (claimant sought damages for expenditure wasted as result of the Department of Health's change of policy on prescribing saline solution, which had not been communicated to the claimant. The court found that a legitimate expectation had been disappointed but considered there was no basis to award damages). See C. Forsyth, above, note 178; A. Brown, "Justifying Compensation for Frustrated Legitimate Expectations" (2010) 30 Law & Phil.699; Y. Vanderman, "Ultra Vires Legitimate Expectations: An Argument for Compensation" [2012] P.L.85.

[195] *Jones v Environment Agency* [2005] EWHC 2270 (Admin).

[196] *Fairtitle v Gilbert* (1787) 2 T.R. 169 (invalid mortgage); *Rhyl UDC v Rhyl Amusements Ltd* [1959] 1 W.L.R. 465 (invalid lease); *Cudgen Rutile (No.2) Pty Ltd v Chalk* [1975] A.C. 520, PC (invalid contract to lease); *Co-operative Retail Services Ltd v Taff-Ely BC* (1980) 39 P. & C.R. 223 (unauthorised communication of void planning permission cannot estop local authority from denying the permission); *Rootkin v Kent CC* [1981] 1 W.L.R. 1186 (council not estopped from denying factual error which would have prevented it from exercising its statutory discretion); *R. v West Oxfordshire DC Ex p. Pearce Homes Ltd* [1986] J.P.L. 522 (council not estopped from resiling from previous resolution granting permission because notification of that permission had been qualified by a condition not yet accepted); *R. v Yeovil BC Ex p. Trustees of Elim Pentacostal Church* (1972) 23 P. & C.R. 39.

[197] *Customs and Excise Commissioners v Hebson Ltd* [1953] 2 Lloyd's Rep. 382 at 396-397; *Sovmots Investments Ltd v Secretary of State for the Environment* [1977] Q.B. 411 at 437, 479-480, reversed on other grounds [1979] A.C. 144; *Laker Airways Ltd v Department of Trade* [1977] Q.B. 643 at 708, 728 (cf. the somewhat ambiguous formulation on Lord Denning MR at 707); *Turner v DPP* (1978) 68 Cr.App.R. 70; *Hughes v Department of Health and Social Security* [1985] A.C. 776 at 788 (Lord Diplock: "The liberty to make such changes [in policy] is inherent in our constitutional form

ies Ltd, Sedley J said that to bind public bodies to an unlawful representation would have the "dual effect of unlawfully extending the[ir] statutory power and destroying the ultra vires doctrine by permitting public bodies arbitrarily to extend their powers".[198] On the other hand, to bind bodies to a promise to act outside their powers would in effect endorse an unlawful act. It must, on this view, be doubtful whether the expectation that a body will exceed its powers can be legitimate.[199]

There may, however, be situations where fairness requires an expectation to be fulfilled, even where the public body exceeds its authority. In such a situation should the principle of legality yield to those of legal certainty and fairness, especially where there has been no significant harm to third parties? To what extent should the law permit this to happen without posing a real threat to the rule of law's fundamental requirement that public bodies should always act within the scope of their conferred powers?   **12-066**

Principles of agency

In the law of agency an agent (a) cannot bind his principal to do what is ultra vires and probably (b) cannot bind his principal by exceeding his own authority if that authority is circumscribed by statute.[200] Nor do purported authorisation, waiver, acquiescence and delay preclude a public body from reasserting its legal rights or powers against another party if it has no power to sanction the conduct in question or to endow that party with the legal right or immunity that he claims.[201]   **12-067**

There are, however, dicta to the effect that planning authorities may waive certain defects in formal procedural requirements,[202] at least so long as third parties are not adversely affected. And in respect of unauthorised and erroneous assurances or advice given by officials upon whom members of the public rely to their detriment, there have been two approaches.   **12-068**

At one time it could be safely said that such assurances were simply nugatory (unless they fell within the scope of agency in contract), although a negligent mis-   **12-069**

---

[198] of government"); *Re Findlay* [1985] A.C. 318, 338 (Lord Scarman); *R. v Secretary of State for Health Ex p. US Tobacco International Inc* [1992] 1 Q.B. 353 at 369 (Taylor LJ).

[198] *R. v Ministry of Agriculture, Fisheries and Food Ex p. Hamble (Offshore) Fisheries Ltd* [1995] 2 All E.R. 714 at 731; and M. Elliott, "Legitimate Representations and Unlawful Representations" [2004] C.L.J. 261.

[199] *Re Findlay* [1985] A.C. 318 at 338 (Lord Scarman, emphasis supplied: "It is said that the refusal to except [the appellants] from the new policy was an unlawful act on the part of the Secretary of State in that his decision frustrated their expectation. But what was their *legitimate* expectation?"); *Flanagan and Flanagan v South Bucks DC* [2002] J.P.L. 1465 (no legitimate expectation arose from the a representation from the council's solicitor that planning enforcement notices would be withdrawn as the solicitor lacked the authority to withdraw the notices; Keene LJ (at [18]) held that unless the representor had actual or ostensible authority to make the representation, although the representee might have "subjectively acquired the expectation", it was not "legitimate"); see also *Brown v Government of Rwanda* [2009] EWHC 770 (Admin) at [29] (Laws LJ noting: "It is elementary that a concrete statutory duty of this kind cannot be overridden by any claim based on legitimate expectation"); *R. (on the application of Sovio Wines Ltd) v The Food Standards Agency (Wine Standards Branch)* [2009] EWHC 382 (Admin); *The Times*, 9 April 2009 at [95] (any legitimate expectation must yield to the agency's statutory duties); *R. v Connolly* [2008] EWCA Crim 2643 at [10] (where a prisoner was wrongly informed as to the effect of his sentence, no legitimate expectation arose from the judge's erroneous explanation).

[200] See, e.g. G. Ganz, "Estoppel and Res Judicata in Administrative Law" [1965] P.L. 321; P. Craig, "Representations by Public Bodies" (1977) 73 L.Q.R. 398.

[201] A. Bradley, "Administrative Justice and the Binding Effect of Official Acts" (1981) 34 C.L.P. 1.

[202] *Wells v Minister of Housing and Local Government* [1967] 1 W.L.R. 1000 at 1007 (Lord Denning); *Lever Finance Ltd v Westminster CC* [1971] 1 Q.B. 222. This aspect of *Lever Finance* was approved in *Western Fish Products Ltd v Penwith DC* [1981] 2 All E.R. 204, CA.

statement or course of conduct causing economic loss might give rise to liability in tort.²⁰³ Thus if a local government officer to whom the necessary powers have not been delegated assures a builder that planning permission is not required for what he proposes to do, this assertion, though acted upon by the builder, does not affect the power of the local authority to arrive at and act on an opposite decision.²⁰⁴

12-070   Another line of cases, attributable in large part to the efforts of Lord Denning, held that in some circumstances when public bodies and officers, in their dealings with a citizen, take it upon themselves to assume authority on a matter concerning him, the citizen is entitled to rely on their having the authority that they have asserted if he cannot reasonably be expected to know the limits of that authority; and he should not be required to suffer for his reliance if they lack the necessary authority.²⁰⁵ Thus, public authorities have been held bound by assurances given in disregard of a formal statutory requirement, upon which an individual relied to his detriment.²⁰⁶ The Court of Appeal in *Lever Finance* applied this principle to a determination by a planning official, even though the power to decide had not been delegated to him in proper form.²⁰⁷

12-071   The general principle remains, however, that a public authority may not vary the scope of its statutory powers and duties as a result of its own errors or the conduct of others. Judicial resort to estoppel in these circumstances may prejudice the interests of third parties.²⁰⁸ For example, the neighbouring property owners in *Lever Finance*, who found that houses had been built closer to their boundary line than had been allowed under the original planning permission, might well feel aggrieved that they had had no opportunity to object to the form of the permission that

---

²⁰³ See 19-046.
²⁰⁴ *Southend-on-Sea Corp v Hodgson (Wickford) Ltd* [1962]1 Q.B. 416; *Western Fish Products Ltd v Penwith DC* [1981] 2 All E.R. 204, CA.
²⁰⁵ *Robertson v Minister of Pensions* [1949] 1 K.B. 227 at 223 (Denning J); *Falmouth Boat Construction Co Ltd v Howell* [1950] 2 K.B. 16 at 26 (Lord Denning); *Re L (AC) (an Infant)* [1971] 3 All E.R. 743 (local authority, having misled mother into believing that she need not lodge a second formal objection to the authority's application for parental rights, not entitled to rely on her failure to lodge the second objection in due time); cf. *Hanson v Church Commissioners for England* [1978] Q.B. 823 (tenant denied a hearing before rent assessment committee as a result, in part, of misleading advice given to him by the clerk to the committee); and *R. v Tower Hamlets LBC Ex p. Kayne-Levenson* [1975] Q.B. 431 at 441 (Lord Denning: local authority misled licensee into thinking that she could not nominate the applicant to be her successor; Lord Denning appeared to think that the local authority was not bound to treat the applicant as though he had been nominated). cf. *Suthendran v Immigration Appeal Tribunal* [1977] A.C. 359 (erroneous intimation by Home Office that appellant had a right of appeal caused no prejudice); *R. v Melton and Belvoir Justices Ex p. Tynan* (1977) 75 L.G.R. 544. For an example of the estoppel where no question of vires was raised, see *Crabb v Arun DC* [1976] Ch. 179.
²⁰⁶ *Wells v Minister of Housing and Local Government* [1967] 1 W.L.R. 1000 (informal determination that planning permission not required); cf. *Western Fish Products Ltd v Penwith DC* [1981] 2 All E.R. 204, CA where *Wells* was narrowly distinguished; *Re L (AC) (an Infant)* [1971] 3 All E.R. 743 (*Wells* followed in different context); *English-Speaking Union of the Commonwealth v Westminster (City) LBC* (1973) 26 P. & C.R. 575.
²⁰⁷ *Lever Finance Ltd v Westminster CC* [1971] 1 Q.B. 222 (oral assurance by borough architect that planning permission not required). This decision, applying *Robertson v Minister of Pensions* [1949] 1 K.B. 227 and *Re L (AC) (An Infant)* [1971] 3 All E.R. 743 cannot be reconciled with *Southend on Sea Corp v Hodgson (Wickford)* [1962] 1 Q.B. 416, or with the observations in *Falmouth Boat Construction Co Ltd v Howell* [1950] 2 K.B. 16. Delegation to officials by local authority members was authorised by the Local Government Act 1972 as amended.
²⁰⁸ And may curtail the willingness of public officials to give informal advice: *Brooks and Burton Ltd v Secretary of State for the Environment* (1976) 75 L.G.R. 285 at 296 (*Lever Finance Ltd v Westminster CC* [1971] 1 Q.B. 222 was described as "the most advanced case of the application of the estoppel doctrine, and one not to be repeated"); on appeal, the CA stated that an estoppel could not be established on the facts: [1977] 1 W.L.R. 1294 at 1300.

ultimately bound the planning authority.[209] Despite the cases to the contrary, it seems today that, in general, authority that is unlawfully assumed will not bind a public authority. Even Lord Denning appeared to have relented when he said in respect of a purported grant of a planning permission by a town clerk unauthorised to grant the permission, that:

> "The protection of the public interest is entrusted to the representative bodies and to the ministers. It would be quite wrong that it should be pre-empted by a mistaken issue by a clerk of a printed form—without any authority in that behalf ... when the result would be to damage the interests of the public at large".[210]

The two lines of authority are not easily reconciled. However, in general, both authority and principle assert that a public authority cannot be estopped from denying its lawful duties and powers.[211] Nor can estoppel be pleaded by a public authority against an individual who has apparently accepted the benefits of an unlawful act or provision.[212]   **12-072**

There have, however, been two exceptions to these rules. The first exception has arisen when the authority has power to delegate authority to an official and there are special circumstances justifying the applicant in believing that the officer concerned had power to bind the authority (e.g. where there was evidence of a widespread practice of delegation of powers to officers, to authorise immaterial modifications of approved plans).[213] The second exception has arisen where the authority has waived a formal procedural requirement. In such a case it has been estopped from relying on its absence.[214]   **12-073**

The courts have become reluctant to permit a public official or body to extend   **12-074**

---

[209] Could they have recovered damages from the local authority by establishing that the officer was careless and that the permission would not have been granted had it been originally applied for in its subsequently amended form? See 19-046.

[210] *Co-operative Retail Services Ltd v Taff-Ely BC* (1980) 39 P. & C.R. 223 at 239-240; and *R. v Yeovil BC Ex p. Trustees of Elim Pentacostal Church; R. v W. Oxfordshire DC Ex p. Pearce Homes Ltd* [1986] J.P.L. 523 (formal notification of a decision has no effect if the notification is contrary to the terms of the decision); *R. v Secretary of State for Education & Science Ex p. Hardy* [1989] C.O.D. 186 (decision to approve scheme could be revoked because it was not a "formal precise and published" decision). cf. *Costain Homes Ltd v Secretary of State for the Environment* [1988] J.P.L. 701; *R. v Southwark LBC Ex p. Bannerman* (1990) 2 Admin. L.R. 381 (despite lack of formal delegation to official it is "to be assumed that those who write letters on behalf of their superiors have the authority to do so").

[211] *Western Fish Products Ltd v Penwith DC* [1981] 2 All E.R. 204, CA and *Tandridge DC v Telecom Securicor Cellular Radio* [1996] J.P.L. 128 (refusal to grant planning permission to erect a multi-antenna mast for mobile telephone service); *Lever Finance Ltd v Westminster CC* [1971] 1 Q.B. 222; *Camden LBC v Secretary of State for the Environment and Barker* (1994) 67 P. & C.R. 59 (considered on question of whether estoppel arose; no evidence of detrimental reliance); *R. v Criminal Injury Compensation Board Ex p. Keane & Marsden* [1988] C.O.D. 128.

[212] *City of Bradford MC v Secretary of State for the Environment* [1986] J.P.L. 598, CA. cf. *Hidenborough Village Preservation Society v Secretary of State for the Environment* [1978] J.P.L. 708.

[213] *Lever Finance Ltd v Westminster CC* [1971] 1 Q.B. 222 was followed, despite the qualifications of *Western Fish Products Ltd v Penwith DC* [1981] 2 All E.R. 204, CA, presumably under this exception, in *Camden LBC v Secretary of State for the Environment and Barker* (1994) 67 P. & C.R. 59 (authority held to the terms of a letter written by officer representing that a proposed roof extension did not require planning permission; officer had actual or ostensible authority); *Gowa v Attorney General* [1985] 1 W.L.R. 1003 (Crown estopped, by letter from colonial governor 30 years earlier, from denying registration of British citizenship).

[214] *Camden LBC v Secretary of State for the Environment and Barker* (1994) 67 P. & C.R. 59; A. Bradley, "Administrative Justice and the Binding Effects of Official Acts" (1981) 34 C.L.P 1; M. Akehurst, "Revocation of Administrative Decisions" [1982] P.L. 613; N. Bamforth, "Legitimate Expectation and Estoppel" [1998] J.R. 196.

their authority by way of an unlawful representation, especially in areas where the interests of third parties or the public might be compromised. In *Henry Boot Homes Ltd v Bassetlaw DC*, the Court of Appeal considered whether a developer possessed a legitimate expectation that works carried out in breach of the conditions under a planning permission would be treated as a "commencement" of the works within five years (thus preserving the permission).[215] The council had indicated that the works would be treated in that way, having misinterpreted the law.[216] Keene LJ said that "the interests of third parties and the public ... greatly reduce the potential for a legitimate expectation ... to arise".[217] Although not prepared to adopt an absolute position that the legitimate expectation could never arise in similar circumstances, he agreed with the court below, that "the public nature of Town and Country Planning ... is not a matter for private agreement between developers and Local Planning Authorities".[218] The House of Lords took a similar view in *R. v East Sussex CC Ex p. Reprotech (Pebsham) Ltd*, where Lord Hoffmann held that a determination by a planning sub-committee did not amount to a binding representation with juridical effect. He said that[219]:

> "[A] determination is not simply a matter between the applicant and the planning authority in which they are free to agree on whatever procedure they please. It is also a matter which concerns the general public interest and which requires other planning authorities, the Secretary of State on behalf of the national public interest and the public itself to be able to participate."

A changing approach?

12-075   The decision of the Court of Appeal in *Rowland v Environment Agency* does contain suggestions, albeit obiter, that an unlawful promise may give rise to a legitimate expectation.[220] The case concerned the ancient public rights of navigation on the river Thames. The agency had made a cut in the river in order to bypass a stretch of water difficult to navigate and put up signs to the effect that there was no thoroughfare on that part of the river and that it was private. The claimant owned land abutting on that part of the river, including the river bed, which she had always treated as private, and objected when the authority sought to reopen it to public navigation. She claimed that the initial representation had given rise to a legitimate expectation,[221] the disappointment of which was an abuse of power. The Court of Appeal held that the authority's representation to the appellant was beyond their statutory power and that they were not bound by it in the circumstances of the case.

12-076   In *Rowland* the principle of lawfulness prevailed over that of fairness and certainty, but interest was taken in the proposition of Professor Craig that in some

---

215 *Henry Boot Homes Ltd v Bassetlaw DC* [2002] EWCA Civ 983; [2003] 1 P. & C.R. 23.
216 Under the *Whitley* principle (*Whitley and Sons v Secretary of State for the Environment* (1992) 64 P. & C.R. 296), where Woolf J held that operations carried out in breach of a condition to a planning permission cannot be relied on as a material consideration capable of "commencing" the development.
217 *Henry Boot Homes Ltd v Bassetlaw DC* [2002] EWCA Civ 983; [2003] 1 P. & C.R. 23 at [55].
218 *Henry Boot Homes Ltd v Bassetlaw DC* [2002] EWCA Civ 983; [2003] 1 P. & C.R. 23 at [52] (Sullivan J); *R. v Leicester CC Ex p. Powergen United Kingdom Plc* [1994] 4 P.L.R. 91 at 101G-H (Dyson J).
219 *R. v East Sussex CC Ex p. Reprotech (Pebsham) Ltd* [2002] UKHL 8; [2003] 1 W.L.R. 348 at [29]. *Reprotech* was followed in *South Bucks DC v Flanagan* [2002] EWCA Civ 690; [2002] 1 W.L.R. 2601. See S. Atrill, "The End of Estoppel in Public Law" [2003] C.L.J. 3.
220 *Rowland v Environment Agency* [2003] EWCA Civ 1885; [2005] Ch. 1; S. Hannett and L. Busch, "Ultra Vires Representations and Illegitimate Expectations" [2005] P.L. 729.
221 As well as a possession under ECHR art. 8 and ECHR Protocol 1, art.1.

circumstances fairness should prevail, even in the case of an ultra vires representation.[222] Craig's argument had to some extent been endorsed in two cases of the European Court of Human Rights, *Pine Valley Developments v Ireland*,[223] and *Stretch v UK*.[224] In *Pine Valley* it was held that a legitimate expectation may constitute a "possession" under article 1 of Protocol 1 of the Convention and may be protected "notwithstanding the fact that it was beyond the powers of the public body which fostered the expectation to realize the expectation". In such circumstances, however, the expectation did not automatically entitle the person to a "realisation" of the ultra vires expectation, but may entitle him to other discretionary relief, such as compensation, "which it is within the powers of the public body to afford".[225]

The Court in *Pine Valley*, while allowing an unlawful representation to give rise to a legitimate expectation, limited the circumstances in which the expectation was required to be fulfilled. The Court went on to say that the fact that that the representation was unlawful "may be a reason, and indeed a strong reason, going to the justification for the interference [with the person's "possession"] and its proportionality".[226]   **12-077**

In *Stretch* the Court considered whether a representation, that the authority had power to grant an option to renew a lease, which was mistakenly thought to be lawful, could bind the authority. It was held that the unlawful representation could give rise to a legitimate expectation and a "possession" under ECHR First Protocol art.1. In this case the authority was held to be bound by the expectation as the transaction was essentially of a private law nature and not against any "public interest or prejudicial to third party interests.[227]   **12-078**

As a result of those two cases, as Mance LJ said in *Rowlands*: "Whatever the previous position ... [the lack of the Agency's power] can no longer be an automatic answer under English law to a case of legitimate expectation".[228] In *Rowland* itself, it was unanimously held that, despite the fact that the representation of the kind contended for by the appellant would have been unlawful, it nevertheless gave rise to a "legitimate" expectation. This much was new. However, despite the fact that the expectation was legitimate, it was held that the authority was not required to fulfil its substance, for different reasons. May LJ considered that the unfairness in this case "illustrates a defect in the law", but nevertheless held that the Court of Appeal was "obliged to uphold an unjust outcome". Mance LJ noted the distinction between the *existence* of a legitimate expectation and its *strength*, as discussed above.[229] He held that, despite the legitimacy of an expectation (albeit based upon an unlawful expectation), it lacked the weight to justify its protection. As opposed to *Pine Valley* and *Stretch*, the representation in *Rowlands* was not based upon any "direct commercial relationship" between the parties, nor did they obtain any as-   **12-079**

---

[222] P. Craig, *Administrative Law*, 7th edn (2012), para.22-037. For a different view, see Y. Vanderman, "Ultra vires legitimate expectations: an argument for compensation" [2012] P.L. 85.

[223] *Pine Valley Developments v Ireland* (1992) 14 E.H.R.R. 319.

[224] *Stretch v UK* (2004) 38 E.H.R.R. 12.

[225] *Pine Valley Developments v Ireland* (1992) 14 E.H.R.R. 319 at [80].

[226] However, since other developers in a similar position had been granted relief, there was held to be a violation of ECHR art.14 for which substantial compensation was later awarded against the Irish State: (1993) 16 E.C.H.R. 379.

[227] *Rowland v Environment Agency* [2003] EWCA Civ 1885; [2005] Ch. 1 at [38] and [39].

[228] *Rowland v Environment Agency* [2003] EWCA Civ 1885; [2005] Ch. 1 at [152].

[229] *Rowland v Environment Agency* [2003] EWCA Civ 1885; [2005] Ch. 1 at [156].

surances as to the nature of the interest. In the circumstances, therefore, it was right that the appellant should bear the risk of the transaction.[230]

12-080 What is the point of calling an expectation "legitimate" if it can be overridden for lack of "strength" or cannot be upheld in law? Mance LJ considered that even though an unlawful legitimate expectation need not bind the authority, the expectation which it created was legitimate at least to the extent that it could "still survive and require recognition".[231] In his view the expectation is a factor that must be taken into account by the decision-maker although it will not, at least in the present state of the law, bind the authority. In cases where it would be unfair to disappoint such an expectation, the unfairness could be mitigated by compensation, or by "smoothing the position as far possible, consistent with the authority's other duties".[232] However, the court will not reserve jurisdiction over the performance of the authority by continuous supervision of any assurances that may have been offered.[233]

12-081 Clear principles do not obviously or easily emerge from the present state of the case law on unlawful expectations. In our view the law should be slow to weaken the principle of legality, which is the fundamental ingredient of the rule of law. Yet there is growing authority to suggest that an unlawful expectation can at least be "legitimate". If that is so, its legitimacy is conferred under the principles of legal certainty (which is, after all, another important ingredient of the rule of law) and fairness.

12-082 If an authority is to be held to the terms of its unlawful representation (and we are not convinced that it should),[234] then the balance of fairness in favour of the claimant should be overwhelming and the following conditions at least should apply:

(a) Although, as we have seen,[235] both knowledge of the representation and detrimental reliance are not always required to support an expectation based upon an intra vires representation, both those requirements are surely necessary to bind an ultra vires representation. In the absence of those requirements, unfairness is unlikely to weigh very much, especially if the claimant has had access to legal advice on the lawfulness of the representation.

(b) As in *Pine Valley* and *Stretch*,[236] where the breach of the expectation would lead to the recipient being deprived of a human right (such as a "possession" under art.1 of the First Protocol) the deprivation of the right needs to be balanced against the public interest.

(c) An unlawful representation should not prevail where third party interests were or might have been compromised.

12-083 In general the courts, as suggested in *Rowland*, should prefer to require compensation to be given to the claimant, rather than permitting the expectation to be upheld and thereby sanctioning an unlawful act by a public body with limited powers. However, administrative redress will in any event often be a more appropri-

---

[230] *Rowland v Environment Agency* [2003] EWCA Civ 1885; [2005] Ch. 1 at [157] and [162].

[231] *Rowland v Environment Agency* [2003] EWCA Civ 1885; [2005] Ch. 1 at [155].

[232] *Rowland v Environment Agency* [2003] EWCA Civ 1885; [2005] Ch. 1 at [153].

[233] *Rowland v Environment Agency* [2003] EWCA Civ 1885; [2005] Ch. 1 at [155] (Peter Gibson LJ and Mance LJ); cf. *R. (on the application of Bibi) v Newham LBC* [2001] EWCA Civ 607; [2002] 1 W.L.R. 23 at [42]. But the claimant may be able to raise the matter by way of separate claim.

[234] See, e.g. *R. (on the application of Albert Court Residents Association) v Westminster City Council* [2011] EWCA Civ 430; [2012] P.T.S.R. 604 at [35] ("an otherwise legitimate expectation cannot require a public authority to act contrary to statute"); and see further M. Fordham, *Judicial Review Handbook*, 6th edn (2012), para.41.1.2.

[235] See 12-038–12-041.

[236] See 12-073.

ate remedy than judicial review, and complaints may be investigated by the appropriate Ombudsman as allegations of injustice caused by maladministration.[237]

COMPARATIVE PERSPECTIVES

Australia

The High Court of Australia regularly referred to the legitimate expectation as one of the various interests that the requirements of procedural fairness served to protect,[238] although some of its members found the term unhelpful.[239] The doctrine appeared useful in the evolution and expansion of the scope of procedural fairness because compendious references to the "rights, interests and legitimate expectations" of those seeking the benefit of procedural fairness allowed that doctrine to cover the widest possible range of affectation. While some argued that it remains a necessary aspect of the threshold test for whether procedural fairness is owed,[240] the increasing doubts expressed by the High Court about the legitimate expectation slowly pushed the concept to the margins of Australian law.[241] The turning point was *Re Minister for Immigration and Multicultural Affairs Ex p. Lam*,[242] where the High Court rejected the more substantive variant of the legitimate expectation adopted in England in *Coughlan*, and also strongly doubted the continued value of the more procedural variety of the doctrine that had long been acknowledged in Australian law. The newer English doctrine was rejected (without either party having relied on it in argument) on the constitutional ground that it would draw the judicial arm of government too close to the enforcement of normative assumptions about good government,[243] though one might question whether this judicial discomfort was also about the unsettled principles upon which relief was ultimately founded in many English cases. Strong doubt was also expressed in *Lam* about the traditional approach in which a legitimate expectation could assist in the application or content of fairness. Several members of the court suggested that this function of the legitimate expectation had been overtaken by the strong presumption that procedural fairness applied to a wide range of interests and could be moulded to the context of each case.[244] The influential judgment of Gleeson CJ in *Lam* stressed the "practical" nature of fairness, which led to the question of "whether there has been

12-084

---

[237] See 1-071.

[238] *Kioa v West* (1985) 159 C.L.R. 550, 582-584, 632; *Annetts v McCann* (1990) 170 C.L.R. 596, 598; *Ainsworth v Criminal Justice Commission* (1992) 175 C.L.R. 564, 576.

[239] e.g. *Salemi v Mackellar (No.2)* (1977) 137 C.L.R. 396 at 404–407 (Barwick CJ); *Kioa v West* (1985) 159 C.L.R. 550 at 617–627 (Brennan J).

[240] Sir Anthony Mason, "Procedural Fairness: its Development and Continuing Role of Legitimate Expectation" (2005) 12 *Australian Journal of Administrative Law* 103, 106.

[241] *Haoucher v Minister for Immigration and Ethnic Affairs* (1990) 169 C.L.R. 648, 651-652; *Minister of State for Immigration and Ethnic Affairs* (1995) 183 C.L.R. 273, 311; *Sanders v Snell* (1998) 196 C.L.R. 329, 348. These views arguably represent the fruition of longstanding doubts about the legitimate expectation expressed by Brennan J: *Kioa v West* (1985) 159 C.L.R. 55, 611, 617-618; *South Australia v O'Shea* (1987) 163 C.L.R. 378, 411; *Annetts v McCann* (1990) 170 C.L.R. 596, 604-607; *Ainsworth v Criminal Justice Commission* (1992) 175 C.L.R. 564, 591-592.

[242] *Re Minister for Immigration and Multicultural Affairs Ex p. Lam* (2003) 214 C.L.R. 1.

[243] *Re Minister for Immigration and Multicultural Affairs Ex p. Lam* (2003) 214 C.L.R. 1, 12, 23. On this rejection of substantive unfairness, see M. Groves, "Substantive Legitimate Expectations in Australian Administrative Law" (2008) 32 *Melbourne University Law Review* 470.

[244] *Re Minister for Immigration and Multicultural Affairs Ex p. Lam* (2003) 214 C.L.R. 1, 16, 38, 45-48. That reasoning was essentially confirmed in later cases that have held that the duty to observe the requirements of fairness attaches a very wide range of rights and interest, but made no refer-

unfairness, not whether an expectation has been disappointed."[245] An emphasis on practical injustice inevitably shifts the focus from what was expected (and whether it was actually expected by a claimant, or imputed by the court via the terminology of legitimate expectation), to the questions of what an official had actually done and whether that had been procedurally fair in the circumstances. The High Court has now made this change of emphasis explicit.[246] While Australian courts take a more restricted approach than their UK counterparts to what citizens might expect from the state and how such expectations might be met,[247] this is in large part due to their different constitutional arrangements. Lord Sumption has indicated that in countries with written constitutions, "[a]ny expectation based on statute is by its nature defeasible. What Parliament gives, Parliament may take away provided that it does so consistently with the Constitution."[248]

12-085   In *Minister for Immigration and Ethnic Affairs v Ah Hin Teoh*,[249] the High Court of Australia held that a legitimate expectation arose from the ratification of an international treaty. Ratification was a positive statement that the executive would act in accordance with the Convention on the Rights of the Child. Absent any contrary indication from the executive,[250] the legitimate expectation operated to require officials whose decisions might not be in accordance with the convention to notify people affected of that possibility and provide a chance to argue against that course. Successive federal governments issued executive statements designed to overcome *any* legitimate expectation that might arise from *all* international treaties ratified by Australia, but none enacted the several bills designed to overcome the effect of *Teoh*.[251] The case appeared intact but it slowly waned. The guidelines devised by migration officials were eventually accepted to be so detailed that they displaced any legitimate expectation.[252] It is now generally the case in Australia, but not elsewhere, that the doctrine of legitimate expectations does not avail a person who has relied on guidelines or other soft law.[253] A close inspection of the guidelines suggests that they implemented, rather than displaced, the expectation constructed in *Teoh* for cases involving similar facts. A more wide ranging obstacle arose in *Re*

---

ence to legitimate expectations. See *Plaintiff M61E/2010 v Commonwealth (the "Offshore Processing case")* (2010) 243 C.L.R. 319, 353; *Plaintiff S10/2011 v Minister for Immigration and Citizenship* (2012) 246 C.L.R. 636 at 658–659.

[245] *Re Minister for Immigration and Multicultural Affairs Ex p. Lam* (2003) 214 C.L.R. 1, 13.

[246] *Minister for Immigration and Border Protection v WZARH* (2015) 256 C.L.R. 326; M. Groves, 'Legitimate Expectations in Australia: Overtaken by Formalism and Pragmatism' in M. Groves and G. Weeks (eds), *Legitimate Expectations in the Common Law World* (2017) p.319.

[247] Australian courts have also consistently rejected a doctrine of public law estoppel; see G. Weeks, 'What Can We Legitimately Expect from the State?' in M. Groves and G. Weeks (eds), *Legitimate Expectations in the Common Law World* (2017) pp.147, 156.

[248] *Ferguson, Maritime Life (Caribbean) Ltd v Attorney General of Trinidad and Tobago* [2016] UKPC 2, at [36].

[249] *Minister for Immigration and Ethnic Affairs v Ah Hin Teoh* (1995) 183 C.L.R. 273. The case was widely criticised; see M Groves, "Unincorporated Treaties and Expectations: The Rise and Fall of Teoh in Australia" [2010] J.R. 323.

[250] The possibility of "statutory or executive indications" contrary to a legitimate expectation arising from ratification was expressly acknowledged by the majority in *Teoh*: (1995) 183 C.L.R. 273, 291.

[251] An equivalent version was passed in South Australia: Administrative Decisions (Effect of International Instruments) Act 1995 (SA). The Supreme Court of that jurisdiction held the statute to be effective in *Collins v State of South Australia* (1999) 74 S.A.S.R. 200 at 213; *O'Shea v DPP* (1998) 71 S.A.S.R. 109.

[252] *Baldini v Minister for and Multicultural Affairs* [2000] F.C.A. 173 at [30]; *Lam v Minister for Immigration and Multicultural Affairs* (2006) 157 F.C.R. 215 at [32]. Such findings about the effect of detailed guidelines which govern the same situation that arose in *Teoh* imply that earlier executive statements which sought to eradicate all legitimate expectations that might arise from any treaty were ineffective, though the issue has not been directly confronted by the courts.

[253] G. Weeks, *Soft Law and Public Authorities: Remedies and Reform* (2016) at pp.157–178.

Minister for Immigration and Multicultural Affairs; Ex p. Lam,[254] where the High Court revisited *Teoh* even though it was not central to the case of either party. Several members of the High Court strongly questioned whether ratification of a treaty without more could constitute a positive statement to the general public capable of supporting a legitimate expectation.[255] The suggestion by several judges that an expectation should be either subjectively held, or be a reasonable inference in the circumstances, further undercut *Teoh* by subtly precluding the protean expectation in the general public that might arise from ratification of a treaty.[256] The ratification of treaties nonetheless has consequences in judicial review proceedings. For example, the *United Nations Convention on the Rights of the Child*, which opened for signature 20 November 1989, is frequently treated as a mandatory relevant consideration in child protection cases.[257]

Canada

The Supreme Court of Canada has still not accepted on its merits a legitimate expectation argument. Most recently, in *Quebec (Attorney General) v Canada (Attorney General)*,[258] the court reaffirmed that the doctrine does not apply to the introduction and passage of primary legislation even if that action frustrates the expectation of a province or provinces. Earlier in *Agraira v Canada (Public Safety and Emergency Preparedness)*,[259] the court also reiterated that the doctrine does not give rise to substantive rights but only an entitlement to some form of procedural fairness when the applicant for judicial review establishes sufficiently an expectation of a substantive outcome. The court was also guarded on the issue of whether the doctrine was engaged by an expectation arising out of Guidelines and through representations that certain factors would be considered.[260] In contrast, however, *Canada (Attorney General) v Mavi*[261] accepted that procedural obligations could be generated by a sufficiently established expectation that a decision-maker would take into account in exercising a discretion various substantive considerations. *Mavi* also reaffirmed that the doctrine's application did not depend on proof of reliance.[262] However, the court specified that, at least with respect to undertakings, the doctrine requires no more than that the decision-maker live up to the undertaking in a "substantial way."[263]

12-086

---

[254] *Re Minister for Immigration and Multicultural Affairs Ex p. Lam* (2003) 214 C.L.R. 1.

[255] *Re Minister for Immigration and Multicultural Affairs Ex p. Lam* (2003) 214 C.L.R. 1, 31-34 (McHugh and Gummow JJ), 48 (Callinan J). The High Court may not have flatly disclaimed the possibility that ratification of a treaty might generate legitimate expectations or other rights in administrative decision making, but lower courts now seem unwilling to take the chance. See, e.g. *Australian Crime Commission v NTD8* (2009) 177 F.C.R. 263, 277.

[256] *Re Minister for Immigration and Multicultural Affairs Ex p. Lam* (2003) 214 C.L.R. 1, 31 (McHugh and Gummow JJ), 47 (Callinan J).

[257] *Re Tracey* (2011) 80 NSWLR 261; *JL v Secretary, Department of Family and Community Services* [2015] NSWCA 88; *Re Henry; JL v Secretary, Department of Family and Community Services* [2015] NSWCA 89; G. Weeks, *Soft Law and Public Authorities: Remedies and Reform* (2016) at pp.133–136.

[258] *Quebec (Attorney General) v Canada (Attorney General)* 2015 SCC 14; [2015] 1 S.C.R. 693 at [25].

[259] *Quebec (Attorney General) v Canada (Attorney General)* 2013 SCC 36; [2013] 2 S.C.R. 559 at [97].

[260] *Quebec (Attorney General) v Canada (Attorney General)* 2013 SCC 36; [2013] 2 S.C.R. 559 at [101].

[261] *Canada (Attorney General) v Mavi* 2011 SCC 30; [2011] 2 S.C.R. 504 at [72].

[262] *Canada (Attorney General) v Mavi* 2011 SCC 30; [2011] 2 S.C.R. 504 at [68].

[263] *Canada (Attorney General) v Mavi* 2011 SCC 30; [2011] 2 S.C.R. 504.

12-087   In relation to international agreements, in *Baker*,[264] on the facts of that case, the court held that a ratified but unincorporated treaty did not give rise to a legitimate expectation of enhanced procedural protections but explicitly left open the question whether in other circumstances that could be the case. Thereafter, however, the court held that, in any event, the provisions of the ratified but unincorporated treaty were, nonetheless, relevant considerations that the decision-maker was obliged to take into account.

India

12-088   In India, the principle of legitimate expectation is a facet of procedural fairness based on past consistent practice[265] when an administrative body by reason of a representation or by past practice or conduct aroused an expectation which it would be within its powers to fulfil unless some overriding public interest comes in the way.[266] While this principle has "substantive aspects",[267] the expectation must be founded on the sanction of law. The principle of legitimate expectation does not create a jurisprudential basis for substantive rights[268] and "ordinarily" does not have application when the legislature has enacted a statute.[269] The "substantive part" of the principle is limited to representations made in accordance with law that a benefit of a substantive nature will be granted, continued or not substantially varied.[270] Change in policy is not judged on the touchstone of legitimate expectation "when the appropriate authority is empowered to take a decision by an executive policy or under law".[271] But like any discretion exercisable by the Government or public authority, change in policy must be in conformity with *Wednesbury* reasonableness.[272]

Ireland

12-089   The leading summary of the conditions which must be satisfied in order to give rise to a successful claim for breach of legitimate expectations in Ireland can be found in obiter comments of the Supreme Court in the case of *Glencar v Mayo County Council*[273] and are as follows: (1) the public authority must have made a statement or adopted a position amounting to a promise or representation, express or implied as to how it would act in respect of an identifiable area of its activity; (2) the representation must be addressed or conveyed either directly or indirectly

---

[264] *Baker* [1994] 2 S.C.R. 817.
[265] *Navjyoti Co-op Group Housing Society v Union of India* (1992) 4 S.C.C. 477.
[266] *Sethi Auto Service Station v Delhi Development Authority* (2009) 1 S.C.C. 180 at 190; *Reliance Telecom Ltd v Union of India* (2017) 4 S.C.C. 269 at 313.
[267] *Punjab Communications Ltd v Union of India* (1999) 4 S.C.C. 727, reaffirmed in *Union of India v Lt Col PK Choudhary* (2016) 4 S.C.C. 236 at 266 with the qualification that "the legitimate substantive expectation merely permits the Court to find out if the change of policy which is the cause for defeating the legitimate expectation is irrational or perverse or one which no reasonable person could have made".
[268] *Bannari Amman Sugars v CTO* (2005) 1 S.C.C. 625.
[269] *State of UP v United Bank of India* (2016) 2 S.C.C. 757 at 776.
[270] *Punjab Communications Ltd v Union of India* (1999) 4 S.C.C. 727 at 742.
[271] *Union of India v Lt Col PK Choudhary* (2016) 4 S.C.C. 236 at 268; *Bajaj Hindustan Limited v Sir Shadi Lal Enterprises Ltd* (2011) 1 S.C.C. 640 at 655.
[272] *Shimnit UTSCH India Private Limited v West Bengal Transport Infrastructure Development Corp Ltd* (2010) 6 S.C.C. 303 at 325.
[273] [2002] 1 I.R. 84 at 162-163. See generally M. de Blacam, *Administrative Law*, 3rd edn (2017) at Ch.18; H. Biehler, *Judicial Review of Administrative Action*, 3rd edn (2013) at Ch.4; G. Hogan and D.G. Morgan, *Administrative Law in Ireland*, 4th edn (2010) at Ch.19; and D.G. Morgan, *Hogan and Morgan's Administrative Law*, 4th edn (2012) at Ch.19.

to an identifiable person or group of persons, affected actually or potentially, in such a way that it forms part of a transaction definitively entered into or a relationship between that person and the group and the public authority or that the person or group has acted on the faith of the representation; and (3) it must be such as to create an expectation reasonably entertained by the person or group that the public authority will abide by the representation to the extent that it would be unjust to permit the public authority to resile from it. It has also been held that there are negative factors, the presence of which may exclude a legitimate expectation: it may not be legitimate to entertain an expectation that a past error will be continued; there may be a need to preserve the entitlement of a decision-maker to exercise a statutory discretion or to enable legitimate changes in executive policy to take place.[274]

A legitimate expectation can arise from a representation[275] or established **12-090** practice,[276] and it may also be implied;[277] a representation may even arise by inaction.[278] The representation must, however, be reasonable,[279] clear and unambiguous.[280] A representation that a plaintiff may do an unlawful act cannot give rise to a legitimate expectation,[281] and, although it does not appear to have been considered extensively, it seems that ultra vires representations will not be enforced.[282] It is not entirely clear whether detrimental reliance is a necessary precondition to a successful claim of breach of legitimate expectations; the better view is that it is not,[283] although Irish courts are more concerned to retain the link between promissory estoppel and legitimate expectations than their English counterparts.[284] Whether the representation must be communicated to the individual purporting to rely on it is also not settled,[285] although published representations may

---

[274] *Lett & Co Ltd v Wexford Borough Corp* [2007] IEHC 195.

[275] *Webb v Ireland* [1988] I.R. 353 at 384.

[276] *Glenkerrin Homes Ltd v Dun Laoghaire Rathdown Corporation* [2007] IEHC 298 at [5.5]-[5.6]. It appears that the practice must be consistent over a period of time: *Wiley v Revenue Commissioners* [1989] I.R. 350 at 356 ("doing of something on two occasions only could not constitute a practice") (appeal dismissed: [1994] 2 I.R. 160 (SC)).

[277] *Glencar* [2002] 1 I.R. 84 at 162; *Philips v Medical Council* [1991] 2 I.R. 115 at 138.

[278] de Blacam (2017) at para.15-09 citing *Ghneim v Minister for Justice* (1989) Irish *Times*, 2 September 1989 (the applicant's application for permission to stay in Ireland had not been dealt with in a year and a half, there was a reasonable expectation that he could remain in the jurisdiction to complete his studies).

[279] *Farleigh v Temple Bar Renewal Ltd* [1999] 2 I.R. 508 at 517; *McCarthy v Minister for Education and Skills* [2012] IEHC 200 at [6.5].

[280] *Devitt v Minister for Education* [1989] I.L.R.M. 639 at 650-652. For examples of cases where a representation has not been established, see, e.g. *Carbery Fishing Ltd v Minister for Agriculture, Fisheries and Food* [2011] IEHC 427 at [5.7]; *Triatic Ltd v Cork County Council* [2006] IEHC 111; [2007] 3 I.R. 57 at 86; *Devitt* [1989] I.L.R.M. 639 at 650-651; *Maigueside Communications Ltd v Independent Radio and Television Commission* [1998] 4 I.R. 115 at 126-127.

[281] *Bates v Minister for Agriculture, Fisheries and Food* [2011] IEHC 429 (Laffoy J) at [4.7].

[282] *Dublin Corp v McGrath* [1978] I.L.R.M. 208; *Wiley* [1994] 2 I.R. 160; *Abrahamson v Law Society* [1996] 1 I.R. 403.

[283] *Fakih v Minister for Justice* [1993] 2 I.R. 406 at 423 (lack of altering of position in reliance on a representation not an impediment to a successful claim); see also *Daly v Minister for the Marine* [2001] 3 I.R. 513 at 528 ("An expectation may be legitimate and cognisable by the courts even in the absence of the sort of action to the claimant's detriment that forms part of the law of estoppel"). Contrast *MC v Legal Aid Board* [1991] 2 I.R. 43 at 55; *Power v Minister for Social and Family Affairs* [2006] IEHC 170; [2007] 1 I.R. 543 at 559; *Garda Representative Association v Ireland* [1989] I.R. 193 at 205.

[284] *Cromane* at [35] (Charleton J) ("the harmony between legitimate expectation and promissory estoppel, or estoppel by convention, should be maintained").

[285] *Nolan v Minister for Environment* [1989] I.R. 357 at 366; *Re "La Lavia"* [1999] 3 I.R. 413 at 479 (both cases suggesting that evidence of communication of the representation required). Contrast *Fakih* [1993] 2 I.R. 406.

be invoked without demonstrating advance knowledge on the part of the beneficiary.[286]

12-091 There is authority suggesting that substantive legitimate expectations will be protected, at least where a non-statutory power is at issue.[287] Irish courts explain their reluctance to uphold substantive legitimate expectations where a statutory discretion is at issue by reference to the non-fettering doctrine;[288] this position, however, fails to give adequate protection to the legitimate expectation.

12-092 Both procedural and substantive legitimate expectations may be overridden if outweighed by the public interest[289] and it has been held that the public policy requirements that need to be given significant weight are much more likely to be present and to weigh heavily in the case of a substantive rather than a procedural legitimate expectation.[290] The Supreme Court has noted that "once a legitimate expectation ... has been identified [and] it is necessary to make good the equity so found, ... the court can make an order, whether characterised as damages or restitution, in order to make good the breach identified",[291] however, the availability of damages for breach of legitimate expectation has not been definitely determined.[292]

New Zealand

12-093 The concept of legitimate expectation as an aspect of procedural fairness has been well established in New Zealand administrative law since the late 1970s. There is, however, no clear adoption of the doctrine of substantive legitimate expectation by the higher judiciary.

12-094 In *Brierley Investments Ltd v Bouzaid*,[293] the Court of Appeal split over the place of legitimate expectation in the tax context. There a company attempted to stop the Commissioner conducting a broad investigation into its tax affairs on the ground that the Commissioner had agreed previously to the use of the formula employed by the company (and now questioned by the Revenue). It was alleged this action

---

[286] *Fakih* [1993] 2 I.R. 406; *Keogh v Criminal Assets Bureau* [2004] IESC 42; [2004] 2 I.R. 159. See also *Power* [2006] IEHC 170; [2007] 1 I.R. 543 at 556 (suggesting that making an application pursuant to a policy created an individualised promise and representation rather than the mere enunciation of a policy).

[287] *Abrahamson* [1996] 1 I.R. 403 at 423; *Power* [2007] 1 I.R. 543 (non-statutory scheme); *Lett* 2007] IEHC 195 at [4.6] and [4.7] (see also, *Lett* [2012] IESC 14; [2012] 2 I.R. 198, 254); *Curran v Minister for Education and Science* [2009] IEHC 378; [2009] 4 I.R. 300; *VI v Commissioner of An Garda Síochána* [2006] IEHC 30; [2007] 4 I.R. 47 at 58; *Kenny v Kelly* [1988] I.R. 457 at 463. For an example of a substantive legitimate expectation being enforced in the context of statutory discretion, see: *Duff v Minister for Agriculture (No.2)* [1997] 2 I.R. 22 at 74 (although concerns have been expressed by the Supreme Court about the precedential value of *Duff* in *Cromane v Minister for Agriculture, Fisheries and Food* [2016] IESC 6; [2016] 2 I.L.R.M. 81 at 91).

[288] *Tara Prospecting Ltd v Minister for Energy* [1993] I.L.R.M. 771 at 788; *Hempenstall v Minister for the Environment* [1994] 2 I.R. 20 at 32; *Gilheany v The Revenue Commissioners* [1998] 4 I.R. 150 at 169. It has been held that the "executive enjoys a constitutional entitlement to change policy": *Glenkerrin Homes* [2007] IEHC 298 at [5.6].

[289] See, e.g. *Curran* [2009] IEHC 378; [2009] 4 I.R. 300 at 316-319; *McCarthy* [2012] IEHC 200 at [5.6].

[290] *Atlantic Marine Supplies Ltd* [2010] IEHC 104; [2011] 2 I.L.R.M. 12 at 34-35.

[291] *Lett* [2012] IESC 14; [2012] 2 I.R. 298 at [25] (O'Donnell J). See also See *Abrahamson* [1996] 1 I.R. 403 at 423; *Atlantic Marine Supplies Ltd* [2010] IEHC 104; [2011] 2 I.L.R.M. 12 at 35; *Cromane Foods Ltd v Minister for Agriculture, Fisheries and Food* [2016] IESC 6 at [10.13]. Damages may be awarded where enforcing the expectation would be futile: *Hennessy v St Gerard's School Trust*, 17 February 2005 (Haugh J) High Court. Monetary remedies will of course apply where compensation forms part of the expectation: *Lett* [2007] IEHC 195 at [4.15]; but see the more general statement in [2012] IESC 14 at [22]-[23].

[292] *Cromane Foods* [2016] IESC 6 at [10.13] (Clarke J).

[293] *Brierley Investments Ltd v Bouzaid* [1993] 3 N.Z.L.R. 655.

was an abuse of power, and relied on *R. v Inland Revenue Commissioners Ex p. MFK Underwriting Agents Ltd*.[294] The Court of Appeal was unanimous in rejecting the challenge on the ground that no "agreement" had been reached or representation made, but the three judges each took a different position on the law. Richardson J distinguished the English cases on the ground that the New Zealand tax legislation put the Commissioner under a duty to collect all tax due, and there could be no estoppel as it would be incompatible with the Commissioner's statutory duty. "As a public authority," Richardson J said, "the commissioner cannot by contract or conduct abdicate or fetter the future exercise of his audit functions in particular cases". Casey J took the exact opposite view on the law, applying *Re Preston* and the later English legitimate expectation cases. He was disposed to accept that "in an appropriate case a decision by the commissioner to act inconsistently with a taxpayer's legitimate expectation in the process leading up to an assessment could constitute unfairness amounting to an abuse of power, so as to justify intervention by way of judicial review". McKay J disposed of the case on the facts and left the resolution of the difference of opinion for another day.

Shortly after that decision the New Zealand tax legislation was changed, adopting the British legislative model of "care and management".[295] Consequently, the British tax cases that provided the platform for the judiciary to develop the law of substantive legitimate expectation.[296] However, in 1994 a regime was introduced allowing taxpayers to seek and receive rulings that bind the Revenue, even if they later turn out to be incorrect in law.[297] There is an argument that the provision of this statutory avenue for providing certainty and protecting detrimental reliance might be seen as inconsistent with a wider acceptance of legitimate expectation doctrine in the tax area based on less formal advice, practices and representations. Moreover, although there has been significant use of judicial review in tax cases in New Zealand administrative law, the impact of this case law on broader administrative law is less evident. In a 2006 tax case, where the Inland Revenue had proffered a (subsequently held) erroneous interpretation of a statute in publications that misled the claimant initially as to his rights, the Court of Appeal and Supreme Court simply remarked that this could not affect the correct interpretation of the statute.[298]   **12-095**

In other cases appellate courts have often been critical of High Court judges invoking the doctrine of legitimate expectation instead of grappling with the basic issues of statutory interpretation that, if correctly decided, would obviate the need to rely on the doctrine.[299] Early cases were mixed. Some rejected the substantive version out of hand,[300] whereas *Northern Roller Milling Co Ltd v Commerce Commission*[301] was accepting of the concept. More recently, the High Court has been   **12-096**

---

[294] *R. v Inland Revenue Commissioners Ex p. MFK Underwriting Agents Ltd* [1990] 1 W.L.R. 1545.

[295] Tax Administration Act 1994 (NZ) s.6A.

[296] *Miller v Commissioner of Inland Revenue* [1995] 3 N.Z.L.R. 664, CA; *Golden Bay Cement Co Ltd v Commissioner of Inland Revenue* [1996] 3 N.Z.L.R. 665, CA.

[297] Tax Administration Act 1994 Pt VA.

[298] *Allen v Commissioner of Inland Revenue* [2006] 3 N.Z.L.R. 1 at [38], SCNZ; *Westpac Banking Corp v Commissioner of Inland Revenue* [2009] NZCA 24 at [56]-[59] (noting that the introduction of the care and management provisions created a legislative context which was more conducive to following the English cases but that nonetheless it was appropriate to continue to apply the established principles).

[299] *Attorney General v Unitec Institute of Technology* [2007] 1 N.Z.L.R. 750, [54]-[59], CA; *Attorney General v E* [2000] 3 N.Z.L.R. 257, CA.

[300] *Tay v Attorney General* [1992] 2 N.Z.L.R. 693, HC, Hillyer J.

[301] *Northern Roller Milling Co Ltd v Commerce Commission* [1994] 2 N.Z.L.R. 747, HC, Gallen J; strongly criticised by M. Poole, "Legitimate Expectation and Substantive Fairness: Beyond the Limits of Procedural Propriety" [1995] N.Z.L.Rev. 426.

cautious.[302] In *Challis v Destination Marlborough Trust Board Inc*[303] the alleged substantive legitimate expectation was not made out on the facts so it was unnecessary to decide whether New Zealand public law recognised such a doctrine. Wild J denied that estoppel had any part to play in New Zealand public law, in part because it "is analogous to legitimate expectation, overlapping and essentially duplicating it, and adding nothing but confusion". In *GXL Royalties Ltd v Minister of Energy*, Wild J repeated his opinion, saying "New Zealand law still does not entertain a legitimate expectation of substantive outcome".[304] More ambiguous is the stance in *Staunton Ltd v Chief Executive Ministry of Fisheries*,[305] where the contesting views were briefly surveyed and the judge said "abuse of power" had to be the basis of the doctrine of legitimate expectation "as it would be unfair to permit a [p]ublic [a]uthority to depart from its promulgated policy or promise".

Substantive unfairness

12-097   Legitimate expectation language is sometimes mixed with the notion of substantive unfairness.[306] The doctrine of substantive unfairness is part of New Zealand law primarily due to the Court of Appeal decision in *Thames Valley Electric Power Board v NZFP Pulp & Paper Ltd*[307] (one of the last judgments given by Sir Robin Cooke prior to his life peerage). However, in *Air New Zealand Ltd v Wellington International Airport Ltd*, Wild J stated that, due to the development of variable intensity of review in unreasonableness cases, "substantive unfairness has met an end, and is no longer a tenable stand-alone ground for review".[308]

International treaties

12-098   *Teoh*[309] is occasionally relied upon in New Zealand.[310] The current New Zealand approach, stemming from dicta in *Tavita v Minister of Immigration*,[311] is that ratified but unincorporated treaty obligations are mandatory relevant considerations and must be taken into account.[312] Although the Court of Appeal in subsequent cases was slow to endorse *Tavita* enthusiastically[313] more recently, in *Ye v Minister of Immigration*, in separate judgments, Glazebrook J and Chambers and Robertson JJ

---

302 *Lumber Specialties Ltd v Hodgson* [2000] 2 N.Z.L.R. 347, [125]-[139], HC, Hammond J.
303 *Challis v Destination Marlborough Trust Board Inc* [2003] 2 N.Z.L.R. 107, HC, Wild J.
304 *GXL Royalties Ltd v Minister of Energy* [2009] N.Z.A.R. 478, [44]. See also the Wild J's summary of the reception of the doctrine of substantive legitimate expectation in *Air New Zealand Ltd v Wellington International Airport Ltd* [2009] N.Z.A.R. 138, [57]-[62].
305 *Staunton Ltd v Chief Executive Ministry of Fisheries* [2004] N.Z.A.R. 68, HC Gendall J.
306 *Northern Roller Milling Co Ltd v Commerce Commission* [1994] 2 N.Z.L.R. 747, HC, Gallen J.
307 *Thames Valley Electric Power Board v NZFP Pulp & Paper Ltd* [1994] 2 N.Z.L.R. 641, CA.
308 *Air New Zealand Ltd v Wellington International Airport Ltd* [2009] N.Z.A.R.138, [34].
309 *Teoh* (1995) 183 C.L.R. 273.
310 See *New Zealand Maori Council v Attorney General* [1996] 3 N.Z.L.R. 140,184-185, CA, founding an expectation on the Treaty of Waitangi (Thomas J). cf. *Ngai Tahu Maori Trust Board v Director General of Conservation* [1995] 3 N.Z.L.R. 553, CA. See more recently *Ye v Minister of Immigration* [2009] 2 N.Z.L.R. 596, [105]; *Al-Hosan v Minister of Immigration* 3 May 2007 (HC, Auckland,).
311 *Tavita v Minister of Immigration* [1994] 2 N.Z.L.R. 257, CA.
312 *Zaoui (No.2)* [2005] NZSC 38. See C. Geiringer, "Tavita and All That: Confronting the Confusion Surrounding Unincorporated Treaties and Administrative Law" [2004] 21 N.Z.U.L.R 66; P.A. Joseph, "Extraordinary Questions in Administrative Law" (2012) 25 N.Z.U.L.R. 73, 97-100.
313 *Puli'uvea Removal Review Authority* (1996) 2 H.R.N.Z. 510; *Rajan v Minister of Immigration* [1996] 3 N.Z.L.R. 543; Justice Ken Keith, "Sources of Law, Especially Statutory Interpretation, With Suggestions about Distinctiveness" in R. Bigwood (ed), *Legal Method in New Zealand: Essays & Commentaries* (2001), pp.77, 90.

made comments approving the *Tavita* approach).[314] On appeal, a majority of the Supreme Court endorsed the views of Glazebrook J.[315] Numerous High Court judges have also applied ratified but unincorporated human rights treaty obligations as mandatory relevant considerations.[316] Most recently, in *Helu v Immigration and Protection Tribunal*, McGrath J in the Supreme Court outlined the limits of international law in the domestic sphere where the international instrument had not been replicated exactly in the domestic statute: "Resort may still be had to the international instrument to clarify the meaning of the statute under the long-established presumption of statutory interpretation that so far as its wording permits, legislation should be read in a manner consistent with New Zealand's international obligations. But the international text may not be used to contradict or avoid applying the terms of the domestic legislation."[317]

Now that New Zealand is no longer bound by precedents from the Privy Council, there is no longer any danger that the flirtation with *Teoh* in the Caribbean death penalty Privy Council cases will endanger the well-settled mandatory relevant consideration approach in New Zealand. **12-099**

South Africa

The Promotion of Administrative Justice Act 3 of 2000 (PAJA) states that all administrative actions that affect rights *or legitimate expectations* adversely must be procedurally fair (s.3(1)). Administrative action is defined in s.1 of PAJA, however, as a decision that affects "rights" adversely.[318] In *Walele v City of Cape Town*[319] the Constitutional Court resolved this inconsistency by reasoning that for the purposes of PAJA s.3, administrative action has a broader meaning that encompasses legitimate expectations. So although review on the grounds listed in s.6(2) is limited to administrative action, or decisions that affect rights, all decisions that affect legitimate expectations must nevertheless be procedurally fair. **12-100**

The requirements for establishing a legitimate expectation, set out in *National Director of Public Prosecutions v Phillips*[320] and endorsed many times since then,[321] are (i) a reasonable expectation (ii) induced by the decision-maker and based on (iii) a clear, unambiguous representation that was (iv) competent and lawful for the decision-maker to make. As suggested by the last requirement, an unlawful promise or representation is unlikely to found a legitimate expectation in South African **12-101**

---

314 [2008] NZCA 291, [202] ("*Tavita* and *Puli'uvea* still represent the law in New Zealand", Glazebrook J) and [552] ("*Tavita* and *Puli'uvea* ... remain good law" Chambers and Robertson JJ). See also the Court of Appeal decision in *Huang v Minister of Immigration* [2009] 2 N.Z.L.R. 700.

315 *Ye v Minister of Immigration* [2010] 1 N.Z.L.R. 104, [24].

316 See e.g. *Elika v Minister of Immigration* [1996] 1 N.Z.L.R. 741; *Mil Mohammud v Minister of Immigration* [1997] N.Z.A.R. 223; *Patel v Minister of Immigration* [1997] 1 N.Z.L.R. 252; *O'Brien v Immigration Protection Tribunal* [2012] NZHC 2599, [18] (UNCROC held to be a mandatory relevant consideration).

317 *Helu v Immigration and Protection Tribunal* [2015] NZSC 28 at [143].

318 This inconsistency apparently led one court to construe a legitimate expectation as a right for the purposes of s.1 of the PAJA. See *Tirfu Raiders Rugby Club v SA Rugby Union* [2006] 2 All S.A. 549, C, discussed by R. Stacey, "Substantive Protection of Legitimate Expectations in the Promotion of Administrative Justice Act: Tirfu Raiders Rugby Club v SA Rugby Union" (2006) 22 *South African Journal on Human Rights* 664.

319 *Walele v City of Cape Town* 2008 (6) S.A. 129, CC at [37].

320 *National Director of Public Prosecutions v Phillips* 2002 (4) S.A. 60, W, at [28], relying mainly on the 5th edition of this work.

321 See e.g. *South African Veterinary Council v Szymanski* 2003 (4) S.A. 42, SCA at [20] and *Duncan v Minister of Environmental Affairs and Tourism* 2010 (6) S.A. 374, SCA at [15].

law.[322] However, the courts have not been consistent in requiring a "representation" in the form of a promise or a regular practice, and the Constitutional Court has sometimes supported a considerably more flexible approach associated with the duty to act fairly.[323]

12-102   There are isolated instances of courts affording some degree of substantive protection to legitimate expectations.[324] The courts have not yet decided the issue,[325] but they have left the way open for substantive enforcement; and in *Duncan v Minister of Environmental Affairs and Tourism*, the Supreme Court of Appeal predicted that the time would come "in an appropriate case … for our courts to cut the Gordian knot".[326] While *KZN Joint Liaison Committee*[327] proved not to be that case, the majority judgment of the Constitutional Court shows some interesting connections with the English jurisprudence on substantive enforcement.[328]

---

[322] See e.g. *Van Schalkwyk v Mkiva* [2007] ZAFSHC 69 (5 July 2007) and *Gibbs v Minister of Justice and Constitutional Development* [2009] 4 All S.A. 109, SCA at [26].

[323] See e.g. *President of the Republic of South Africa v South African Rugby Football Union* 2000 (1) S.A. 1, CC at [216], and more recently *MEC for Education, Gauteng Province v Governing Body, Rivonia Primary School* 2013 (6) S.A. 582, CC at [60] fn.56; and see further C. Hoexter, "The Unruly Horse and the Gordian Knot: Legitimate Expectations in South Africa" in M Groves and G Weeks (eds), *Legitimate Expectations in the Common Law World* (2017) pp.165, 173–7.

[324] See e.g. *Ampofo v MEC for Education, Arts, Culture, Sports and Recreation, Northern Province* 2002 (2) S.A. 215, T, *Coetzer v Minister of Safety and Security* 2003 (3) S.A. 368, LC and *Quinella Trading (Pty) Ltd v Minister of Rural Development* 2010 (4) S.A. 308, LCC. For academic analysis, see G. Quinot, "The Developing Doctrine of Substantive Legitimate Expectations in South African Administrative Law" (2004) 19 *South African Public Law* 543; J. Campbell, "Legitimate Expectations: the Potential and Limits of Substantive Protection in South Africa" (2003) 12 *South African Law Journal* 292.

[325] *Residents of Joe Slovo Community, Western Cape v Thubelisha Homes* 2010 (3) S.A. 454, CC at [300].

[326] *Duncan v Minister of Environmental Affairs and Tourism* 2010 (6) S.A. 374, SCA at [14].

[327] *KwaZulu-Natal Joint Liaison Committee v MEC for Education, KwaZulu-Natal* 2013 (4) S.A. 262, CC.

[328] See further C. Hoexter, "The Unruly Horse and the Gordian Knot: Legitimate Expectations in South Africa" in M Groves and G Weeks (eds), *Legitimate Expectations in the Common Law World* (2017) pp.165, 177–88.

CHAPTER 13

Convention Rights as Grounds for Judicial Review

TABLE OF CONTENTS

SCOPE

This chapter analyses the use of the rights set out in the European Convention on Human Rights and Fundamental Freedoms (ECHR) as grounds for judicial review. Since Convention rights have been incorporated into United Kingdom law under the Human Rights Act 1998 (HRA), their infringement by public authorities has become a ground of illegality.[1] In addition, the courts may review legislation for conformity with Convention rights.[2] Some of the Convention rights are absolute, but others may be limited and in those circumstances the courts have to decide whether the infringement of the right has been adequately justified under the test of proportionality considered in Chapter 11.[3] We start by setting out the background to the protection of fundamental rights in international law and then consider the approach to the ECHR established by the European Court of Human Rights (ECtHR). The chapter then sets out the provisions of the HRA and the approach of domestic courts to Convention rights, both when reviewing official action and legislation. Finally, the Convention rights themselves are briefly considered in order to give a flavour of the judicial approach in the first two decades to the application of the HRA.

13-001

PROTECTION OF FUNDAMENTAL RIGHTS IN DOMESTIC AND INTERNATIONAL LAW

The protection of fundamental rights recognised by the common law is addressed in Chapter 1.[4] It is sufficient to say here that in the past the concept of

13-002

---

[1] On illegality as a ground of review generally, see Ch.5.
[2] On review of legislation generally, see 3-011.
[3] See 11-077.
[4] See 1-119.

parliamentary sovereignty and the residual nature of common law rights combined to make fundamental rights vulnerable to interference, especially at times of actual or perceived national emergency.[5] In addition, the development of independent common law rights protection was, ironically, hampered by the existence of the ECHR. Since Parliament had decided not to incorporate the ECHR into domestic law, the courts felt constrained not to achieve the same effect through the common law for fear of being accused of circumventing Parliament's decision.[6]

13-003   The development of the notion of binding international human rights took significant hold with the adoption of the Universal Declaration on Human Rights by the then recently-formed General Assembly of the United Nations in 1948. The limits and even dangers of unrestrained popularism, without any protection for fundamental rights, had been highlighted by the tyrannies in Germany, Italy and Spain which had precipitated the Second World War. The Universal Declaration did not have the status of an enforceable international treaty but was, nonetheless, one of the principal signs of a shift in the understanding of the nature of international law which had previously been known as the law of nations.[7] For the first time, individuals (rather than states) were seen as the holders of international legal rights.

The Council of Europe

13-004   The results of two World Wars on European soil and the disregard for human rights in some of its own nations led to the foundation of the Council of Europe in 1949. The 10 founding members of the Council committed themselves to upholding the rule of law and the protection of fundamental freedoms.[8] The greatest monument to the Council is the ECHR which came into force on 3 September 1953.[9]

13-005   However, even within Europe, there were divisions about the content of the ECHR and how it would be enforced. Largely at the insistence of the United Kingdom government, the jurisdiction of the ECtHR and the right of individual petition were initially optional.[10] The ECHR in its present form was substantially drafted in Whitehall by a former senior legal adviser to the Home Office and contained 15 articles.[11] However, three of those (the rights to property, education

---

5   For example habeas corpus was liable to be suspended by Parliament. The last occasion for the then UK was 1866-69 in Ireland, although it was also suspended in British colonies in the 20th century. Executive detention was introduced in 1915 by delegated legislation (not having been mentioned in the parent legislation: the Defence of the Realm Consolidation Act 1914). Such detention was upheld (with only one dissent: Lord Shaw of Dunfermline) in *R. v Halliday Ex p. Zadig* [1917] A.C. 260. See A. Simpson, *In the Highest Degree Odious: Detention Without Trial in Wartime Britain* (1994); K. Ewing and C. Gearty, *The Struggle for Civil Liberties: Political Freedom and the Rule of Law in Britain, 1914-1945* (2000); and D. Foxton, "R. v Halliday ex parte Zadig in Retrospect" (2003) 119 L.Q.R. 455.
6   *R. v Secretary of State for the Home Department Ex p. Brind* [1991] 1 A.C. 690 at 748, 761-762.
7   The Declaration was given legal content by the International Covenant on Civil and Political Rights and the International Covenant on Economic, Social and Cultural Rights (1966) (Cmnd 6702); see Lord Steyn, "Human Rights: The Legacy of Mrs. Roosevelt" [2002] P.L. 473.
8   The founding members were Belgium, Denmark, France, Ireland, Italy, Luxembourg, the Netherlands, Norway, Sweden and the UK.
9   The ECHR required to be ratified by 10 members before it entered into force. The UK was the first State Party to do so in March 1951.
10   Discussed in Simpson, *Human Rights*, pp.655-65 and 523-525.
11   G. Marston, "The United Kingdom's Part in the Preparation of the European Convention on Human Rights, 1950" (1993) 42 I.C.L.Q. 796; Lord Lester, "UK Acceptance of the Strasbourg Jurisdiction: What Really Went on in Whitehall in 1965" [1998] P.L. 237; E. Wicks, "The United Kingdom Government's Perception of the ECHR at the Time of Entry" [2000] P.L. 438; and E. Bates, *The European Convention on Human Rights: From its Inception to the Creation of the Permanent*

and free and secret elections) were not considered compatible with the policy of the UK government at the time which was committed to the widespread nationalisation of industry, the abolition of fee-paying schools and maintenance of often undemocratic forms of government in parts of the Commonwealth (to which the application of the ECHR was to be extended). For this reason, the ECHR initially contained 12 articles and the other three were hived off into the First Protocol.[12]

The institutional structure of the Council of Europe was established at Strasbourg and was threefold: the Committee of Ministers, the European Commission on Human Rights and the ECtHR.[13] However, the increasing popularity of petitioning Strasbourg and the expansion of the Council of Europe (to some 47 members in 2017) created an unacceptable backlog of cases. The response was to streamline the procedure by eliminating the role of the Commission and replacing it with a single full-time court.[14] The ECtHR now comes in four incarnations: the Plenary Court,

13-006

Court of Human Rights (2010).

12 Simpson, *Human Rights*, Ch.15.

13 In 1990 the Council of Europe set up another body, the Commission for Democracy Through Law (the Venice Commission), to assist the countries of the former Soviet Union with their new democratic constitutions, institutions of democracy and the rule of law.

14 The reformed procedure is set out in Protocol 11 to the ECHR which came into force on 1 November 1998. The Commission in fact continued to function until 31 October 1999 to deal with cases which had already been declared admissible. The role of the Committee of Ministers was also limited to supervising the execution of judgments (art.46(2)): P. Leach, "The Effectiveness of the Committee of Ministers in Supervising the Enforcement of Judgments of the European Court of Human Rights" [2006] P.L. 443. In light of the continued backlog of cases, Protocol 14 entered into force on 1 June 2010. Protocol 14 introduces three new mechanisms for limiting the ECtHR's caseload: permitting single judges to determine the admissibility of unmeritorious cases (over 30,000 cases were declared inadmissible under this procedure in 2016); introducing a new admissibility criterion that the applicant has suffered significant disadvantage (*Heather Moor and Edgecomb Ltd v UK (No.2)* (2012) 55 E.H.R.R. SE20 at [24]-[28]); and allowing three-judge committees to decide repetitive cases: S. Greer, "Reforming the European Convention on Human Rights: towards Protocol 14" [2003] P.L. 663; and Lord Woolf, *Review of the Working Methods of the European Court of Human Rights* (2005). The ECtHR has also introduced a Pilot judgment procedure where it selects and decides one case covering systemic or structural issues and can call upon the relevant government to bring domestic law into line with the Convention (*Greens and MT v UK* (2011) 53 E.H.R.R. 21 at [105]-[122] gave the UK limited further time (until 22 November 2012) to change the blanket ban on prisoner voting which was the subject of 2,500 pending cases before the Court at the time). As a result of these reforms, the backlog of cases has started to reduce for the first time in the ECtHR's history, although it still stood at over 75,000 at the end of 2016. The Council of Europe's Brighton Conference in April 2012 was the third attempt in two years to address these problems (following those at Interlaken and Izmir). The Brighton Declaration emphasised the importance of the case management measures introduced by the ECtHR and recommended reducing the time limit for applications to the ECtHR to four months (from six) and requiring applicants to have relied on their Convention rights before the domestic court as further limiting measures. Reform proposals are discussed in J. Christoffersen and M.R. Madsen, *The European Court of Human Rights between Law and Politics* (2011). The ECtHR now has a section of its website (*http://www.echr.coe.int/echr*) dedicated to Court Reform. The Brighton Conference was followed in March 2015 with a further conference in Brussels on the implementation of ECtHR judgments (on which, see the *Ninth Report of the Committee on Legal Affairs and Human Rights of the Parliamentary Assembly* (2017)). Two further Protocols have been adopted but not yet entered into force. Protocol 15 would give effect to the proposed reduction in the time limit for bringing proceedings in art.35 of the ECHR from six months to four and would introduce references in the Preamble to the ECHR to the principles of subsidiarity and the margin of appreciation (on which, see A. Tickell, "More 'efficient' justice at the European Court of Human Rights: but at whose expense?" [2015] P.L. 206). Protocol 16 would permit the highest courts of state parties to request an advisory opinion relating to the interpretation or application of Convention rights (on which, see K. Dzehtsiarou and N. O'Meara, "Advisory Jurisdiction and the European Court of Human Rights: A Magic Bullet for Dialogue and Docket Control?" (2014) 34 L.S. 444). The Joint Committee on Human Rights in Protocol 15 to the European Convention on Human Rights (HL Paper 71); (HC Paper 837) (2014–2015) recommended that the UK should

Committees, Chambers and the Grand Chamber. The Plenary Court does not decide cases, but has overall procedural control in adopting rules of the ECtHR and setting up Chambers and electing their Presidents.[15] To hear cases, the ECtHR may sit in a Committee of three judges, in Chambers of seven or in a Grand Chamber of 17 judges.[16] The judge from the State Party concerned is always a member of the Chamber or Grand Chamber. Upon the introduction of these reforms in 1998, the right of individual petition and the acceptance of the jurisdiction of the ECtHR were made compulsory.

13-007   There are two mechanisms provided by the ECHR for its enforcement: complaints brought by other State Parties and individual petition.[17] Inter-state complaints have been very rare although some of them have proved to be highly significant.[18] Individual petitions are much more common and it is these which have seen the greatest growth: from 138 in 1955 to over 53,000 in 2016.[19] Article 34, in fact, confers standing not just on individuals, but also non-governmental organisations and groups of individuals.[20] The right to freedom of association (art.11) can as easily be violated against a trade union as against an individual. However, certain other Convention rights can only be enforced by natural persons: the rights not to be subject to degrading treatment and punishment (art.3), to freedom of conscience (art.9), and to education (art.2 of the First Protocol).[21] However, unlike in domestic judicial review, there is no concept of the pure public interest application and

---

ratify Protocol 15 after its having been debated in both Houses. The same report noted that the Government has no intention of signing or ratifying Protocol 16, on the basis that it is "unconvinced" of the value of advisory opinions.

15 ECHR art.26.

16 ECHR art.27; A. Mowbray, "An Examination of the Work of the Grand Chamber of the European Court of Human Rights" [2007] P.L. 507. See fn.14 above. Within three months of the delivery of a Chamber judgment, the parties may request that it should be referred to the Grand Chamber. If such a request is received, a panel of five judges shall determine whether the case raises a serious question of interpretation or a serious issue of general importance. In the absence of such a request, the Chamber's judgment becomes final after three months (arts 42-44).

17 ECHR arts 33 and 34 respectively. The UK delayed accepting the right of individual petition until it was thought too late for the Burmah Oil Company to impugn the War Damage Act 1965 (which retrospectively deprived the company of its legal victory in *Burmah Oil Co v Lord Advocate* [1965] A.C. 75).

18 See e.g. the case brought by the Republic of Ireland against the UK relating to alleged violations of art.3 in the treatment of terrorist suspects in Northern Ireland (*Ireland v UK* (1978) 2 E.H.R.R. 25). Cyprus has brought a series of cases against Turkey relating to the situation in Northern Cyprus. The very first case brought under the ECHR in 1956 was by Greece against the UK and concerned action taken to suppress an insurrection in the then Crown Colony of Cyprus (Simpson, *Human Rights*, Chs 18-19).

19 Of the 79,750 applications pending before the ECtHR in 2016, over 18,000 are against Ukraine with (in descending order) Turkey, Hungary, Russia, Romania and Italy having between 6,000 and 12,000. At the end of 2016, there were 231 pending cases against the UK. The number of judgments delivered by the ECtHR has also increased dramatically: from 56 in 1995 to 38,000 in 2016 (of which 1,926 were decided by a judgment, rather than being declared inadmissible or struck out). The ECtHR produces an informative annual survey of its activities which is available on its website *http://www.echr.coe.int/Pages/home.aspx?p=home* [Accessed 31 October 2017]. From the same web address, the ECtHR is now making available "Guides on Case-law" which are prepared by the Registry. 12 such Guides have so far been published: on arts 1 (French only), 4, 5, 6 (civil and criminal), 7, 9 and 15; arts 2 and 3 of the First Protocol; art.4 of the Fourth Protocol; and art.4 of the Seventh Protocol.

20 *Air Canada v UK* (1995) 20 E.H.R.R. 150 involved a non-European based corporate entity complaining of a breach of art.6.

21 P. Van Dijk, F. van Hoof, A. van Rijn and L. Zwaak, *Theory and Practice of the European Convention on Human Rights*, 4th edn (2006), para.1.13.2.

individuals are required to demonstrate that they are (or may be) the victim of any alleged violation.[22]

THE EUROPEAN CONVENTION ON HUMAN RIGHTS

Before we turn to examine how the United Kingdom has given effect to the ECHR by the HRA, it is necessary to understand something of how the ECHR operates as an international legal instrument.[23]   **13-008**

The ECHR protects the following rights: to life (art.2), to be free from inhuman and degrading treatment or punishment (art.3), to be free from slavery and forced labour (art.4), to liberty and security of the person (art.5), to a fair trial (art.6), to be free from retrospective criminal legislation (art.7), to respect for one's private and family life, home and correspondence (art.8), to freedom of thought, conscience and religion (art.9), to freedom of expression (art.10), to freedom of assembly and peaceful association (art.11), to freedom to marry and found a family (art.12), and not to be discriminated against in the exercise of Convention rights (art.14).[24] The First Protocol contains the right to the enjoyment of possessions (art.1), the right to education (art.2) and the right to free elections (art.3). The Sixth Protocol (arts 1 and 2) abolishes the death penalty.   **13-009**

Article 1 of the ECHR requires State Parties to secure to everyone within their jurisdiction the rights and freedoms set out in the Convention. The ECHR also contains the right to an effective remedy before a national authority for breach of the ECHR (art.13). Article 13 is therefore a further illustration (along with art.1) of the general principle that national authorities bear the primary responsibility for implementing and enforcing Convention rights.[25] It is also consistent with the requirement that individuals should exhaust their domestic remedies before petitioning the ECtHR (art.35(1)). Article 13 is not a free-standing right and must be linked to at least an alleged violation of another Convention right.   **13-010**

The relevant national enforcement need not be judicial in nature but it must be sufficiently independent of the body which is challenged and it must be able to provide effective redress. For example, the power of the UK courts to exclude evidence obtained through covert surveillance was held not to be an effective remedy since the court could not address the substance of the complaint that the interference with art.8 was not in accordance with law or provide that the individual could obtain a suitable remedy for a violation of art.8.[26] As with other areas of the   **13-011**

---

[22] See 2-035 and 2-036.
[23] See further Van Dijk et al. (2006); C. Ovey and R. White, *Jacobs and White: The European Convention on Human Rights*, 6th edn (2014); and E. Bates, "British Sovereignty and the European Court of Human Rights" (2012) 128 L.Q.R. 382.
[24] On art.14, see 13-100.
[25] *Kudla v Poland* (2002) 35 E.H.R.R. 11 at [152]-[155]. In *Poghosyan v Armenia* (2015) 61 E.H.R.R. 2 at [43]-[48], the ECtHR held that there had been a breach of art.13 where under domestic law the applicant was unable to apply for compensation for the non-pecuniary damage he had suffered as a result of his ill-treatment in detention. See further A. Lee, "Focus on Article 13 ECHR" [2015] J.R. 33.
[26] *Khan v United Kingdom* (2001) 31 E.H.R.R. 45 at [44]. The power to exclude is contained in s.78 of the Police and Criminal Evidence Act 1984. See also *Nada v Switzerland* (2013) 56 E.H.R.R. 18. Mr Nada was added to the UN Security Council sanctions list as a suspected funder and supporter of al-Qaeda and the Taliban. This required states to impose a travel ban, implemented in Switzerland by way of its domestic "Taliban Ordinance". Although Mr Nada could apply to the national authorities to have his name deleted from the list annexed to the Taliban Ordinance, the national courts held

ECHR, the more serious the interference and the more fundamental the right concerned, the more that is required to comply with art.13.[27] This gives rise to the question of whether pre-HRA judicial review provided an adequate remedy. In some cases, it has been held to. However, in other cases, the inability of the domestic courts to address the substance of the question of justification (i.e. whether the restriction fulfils a pressing social need and is proportionate) has been found to breach art.13.[28] Since 2000, such matters are properly before a domestic court.[29]

13-012   In addition to these express rights, the ECtHR has developed implied rights in certain limited circumstances. The most striking example is the right of access to the courts which the ECtHR found to be inherent in the right to a fair hearing protected by art.6(1).[30]

Absolute, limited and qualified rights

13-013   Convention rights may be grouped in a number of different ways. One distinction is between qualified and unqualified (or absolute) rights.

Absolute rights

13-014   An example of an unqualified right is provided by art.3 which states: "No one shall be subjected to torture or to inhuman or degrading treatment or punishment".[31] If the claimant establishes on the balance of probabilities that his art.3 rights have been interfered with, that is the end of the ECtHR's inquiry and the State is not permitted to seek to justify the interference by reference to overriding State interests. The ECtHR has held that:

> "79.   art.3 enshrines one of the most fundamental values of democratic society …The Court is well aware of the immense difficulties faced by States in modern times in protecting their communities from terrorist violence. However, even in these circumstances, the ECHR prohibits in absolute terms torture or inhuman or degrading treatment or punishment, irrespective of the victim's conduct. Unlike most of the substantive clauses of the ECHR and of Protocols Nos. 1 and 4, art.3 makes no provision for exceptions and no derogation from it is permissible under art.15 even in the event of a public emergency threatening the life of the nation …
>
> 80.   The prohibition provided by art.3 against ill-treatment is equally absolute in expulsion cases. Thus, whenever substantial grounds have been shown for believing that an individual would face a real risk of being subjected to treatment contrary to art.3 if removed to another State, the responsibility of the Contracting State to safeguard him or her against such treatment is engaged in the event of expulsion … In these

---

that Switzerland could not examine the merits of his complaints about breach of the ECHR rights as Switzerland was bound by the UN Security Council resolution. The ECtHR held that Mr Nada had been deprived of an effective remedy, but did not rule determinatively on the question of how to resolve such conflicts between a requirement of a UN Security Resolution and of the ECHR (on which, see S. Hollenberg, "The diverging approaches of the European Court of Human Rights in the cases of Nada and Al-Dulimi" [2015] I.C.L.Q. 445).

[27]   *Z v UK* (2002) 34 E.H.R.R. 3 at [109]-[11] (violations of arts 2 and 3 may require investigation by the state as well as compensation).

[28]   See 11-079.

[29]   See 13-084.

[30]   *Golder v United Kingdom* (1975) 1 E.H.R.R. 524 at [36]. On art.6, see 7-117.

[31]   The other unqualified rights are in arts 2 (right to life), 4 (prohibition on slavery and forced labour), 5 (right to liberty and security), 6 (right to a fair trial), 7 (no punishment without law), 12 (right to marry), 14 (prohibition on discrimination), art.2 of the First Protocol (the right to education), and art.3 of the First Protocol (the right to free elections).

circumstances, the activities of the individual in question, however undesirable or dangerous, cannot be a material consideration ...

82. It follows from the above that it is not necessary for the Court to enter into a consideration of the Government's untested, but no doubt bona fide, allegations about the first applicant's terrorist activities and the threat posed by him to national security."[32]

As this passage indicates, art.3 is an example of an absolute right in the sense that the State cannot derogate from it even in times of emergency.[33] Other examples of absolute rights are the right to life, the prohibition on slavery and the ban on punishment without law.[34]   **13-015**

Limited rights

Some unqualified rights are, however, limited. Limited Convention rights are those which contain express limitations which authorise interferences with the right in certain circumstances. An example is the right to liberty and freedom of the person under art.5.[35] The permitted limitations on this right are described at 13-072.   **13-016**

Qualified rights

By contrast, art.10 provides an example of a qualified right since it makes provision for interferences to be justified by the State: **13-017**

"1. Everyone has the right to freedom of expression. This right shall include freedom to hold opinions and to receive and impart information and ideas without interference by public authority and regardless of frontiers. This Article shall not prevent States from requiring the licensing of broadcasting, television or cinema enterprises.

2. The exercise of these freedoms, since it carries with it duties and responsibilities, may be subject to such formalities, conditions, restrictions or penalties as are prescribed by law and are necessary in a democratic society, in the interests of national security, territorial integrity or public safety, for the prevention of disorder or crime, for the protection of health or morals, for the protection of the reputation or rights of others, for preventing the disclosure of information received in confidence, or for maintaining the authority and impartiality of the judiciary."[36]

Under art.10, therefore, a finding of interference does not exhaust the inquiry and States have frequently successfully argued that an interference is nonetheless justified. In order to justify an interference with a qualified Convention right, a State Party has to demonstrate on the balance of probabilities that it has acted in a manner which is prescribed by law, for one of the reasons identified as legitimate in the relevant article and that the interference was necessary in a democratic society.[37]   **13-018**

---

[32] *Chahal v United Kingdom* (1997) 23 E.H.R.R. 413. The case concerned a challenge to the Home Secretary's decision to deport Mr Chahal on national security grounds even though he faced the risk of ill-treatment if returned to his native India.

[33] The concept of derogation is explained at 13-023.

[34] See 13-061.

[35] Other examples of limited rights are the prohibition on force labour (art.4(2) and (3)), the right to marry (art.12) and to education (art.2 of the First Protocol).

[36] The other qualified rights are in arts 8 (right to private and family life), 9 (right to freedom of thought, conscience and religion), 11 (freedom of assembly and association) and art.1 of the First Protocol (the right to the enjoyment of possessions).

[37] See 13-084.

General limitations on Convention rights

13-019   There are several general limitations on the exercise of Convention rights. Article 16 permits the state to impose restrictions on the political activities of aliens notwithstanding arts 10, 11 and 14.[38] Article 18 limits the restrictions permitted in the ECHR to the purposes for which they have been prescribed.[39] More importantly, art.17 provides that: "Nothing in this Convention may be interpreted as implying for any state, group or person any right to engage in any activity or perform any act aimed at the destruction of any of the rights and freedoms set forth herein or at their limitation to any greater extent than is provided for in the Convention".[40] On occasion, the ECtHR does not make express reference to art.17, but nonetheless qualifies the protection of Convention rights by reference to the principle it enshrines.[41] The scope of this broad and troublesome provision is tempered

---

[38]   This limitation is to be strictly construed (*Piermont v France* (1995) 20 E.H.R.R. 301 at [59]-[64]). This restriction cannot apply to citizens of the EU. The Fourth and Seventh Protocols (neither of which has been ratified by the UK) provide a number of protections for aliens including freedom of movement within a state and freedom to leave it, freedom from collective expulsion and restrictions on individual expulsion. They are described in greater detail in Lord Lester of Herne Hill, Lord Pannick and J. Herberg, *Human Rights Law and Practice*, 3rd edn (2009), para.4.16.

[39]   A potentially lawful detention to answer charges of fraud became a breach of art.18 (read with art.5) when the state offered to drop the charges if the applicant sold his media business to Gazprom at a reduced rate (*Gusinskiy v Russia* (2005) 41 E.H.R.R. 17 at [73]-[78]).

[40]   Under this provision, the ECtHR rejected a challenge based on art.10 (freedom of expression) by a defendant fined for placing a poster in the window of his house depicting the World Trade Centre in flames with a prohibition sign across it and the words "Islam out of Britain" (*Norwood v UK* (2005) 40 E.H.R.R. SE11). The ECtHR relied on art.17 to hold that: "Such a general, vehement attack against a religious group, linking the group as a whole with a grave act of terrorism, is incompatible with the values proclaimed and guaranteed by the ECHR, notably tolerance, social peace and non-discrimination." See also *Jersild v Denmark* (1995) 19 E.H.R.R. 1. In *HADEP v Turkey* (2013) 56 E.H.R.R. 5 at [61], the ECtHR stated that a political party whose leaders incite others to violence or put forward a policy which does not comply with one or more of the rules of democracy or which is aimed at the destruction of democracy and the flouting of the rights and freedoms recognised in a democracy cannot lay claim to the Convention's protection against penalties imposed on those grounds (although the dissolution of HADEP was held to have breached art.11 on the grounds that it was disproportionate). There is some welcome evidence in more recent cases that the ECtHR is moving away from this over-reliance on art.17 and confining it only to truly extreme cases. In *Paksas v Lithuania* (2014) 59 E.H.R.R. 30 at [87]-[88], the ECtHR reiterated that "since the general purpose of art.17 is … to prevent individuals or groups with totalitarian aims from exploiting in their own interests the principles enunciated in the Convention, this article is applicable only on an exceptional basis and in extreme cases". *Perinçek v Switzerland* (2016) 63 E.H.R.R. 6 at [114]-[115] concerned public statements made by the applicant denying the Armenian genocide. The ECtHR held that in cases concerning art.10, art.17 applies to preclude consideration of the substantive right only where it is "immediately clear that the impugned statements sought to deflect [art.10] from its real purpose by employing the right to freedom of expression for ends clearly contrary to the values of the Convention". Absent that clarity, the art.17 question fell to be joined to the merits of the complaint under art.10. See further, A. Buyse, "Dangerous expressions: the ECHR, violence and free speech" [2014] I.C.L.Q. 491.

[41]   See e.g. *Refah Partisi (The Welfare Party) v Turkey* (2003) 37 E.H.R.R. 1 (rejection of art.11 (freedom of association) challenge to the decision of the Turkish Constitutional Court to dissolve the political party, Refah, which was committed to the introduction of Sharia contrary to the express commitment to secularism in the Turkish Constitution. The ECtHR subsumed consideration of art.17 within its analysis of art.11(2) and stated: "In view of the very clear link between the Convention and democracy, no one must be authorised to rely on the Convention's provisions in order to weaken or destroy the ideals and values of a democratic society. Pluralism and democracy are based on a compromise that requires various concessions by individuals or groups of individuals, who must sometimes agree to limit some of the freedoms they enjoy in order to guarantee greater stability of the country as a whole", para.99). See further *United Communist Party of Turkey v Turkey* (1998) 26 E.H.R.R. 121.

somewhat by the requirement that there be a link between the right abused and that which the state seeks to limit.[42]

The ECtHR has accepted that some Convention rights can be waived in certain circumstances. The issue has arisen most often in two contexts: whether an individual can waive his right to a fair hearing under art.6 and whether public authorities can lawfully persuade their employees to waive certain Convention rights such as freedom of expression and privacy. The ECtHR has acknowledged that advantages may flow from a waiver for the individual, but has sought to ensure that the individual is safeguarded by insisting on a clear and unequivocal waiver that has been entered into in circumstances where the individual was not under undue pressure to do so.[43]   **13-020**

The ECtHR has also developed the concept of implied limitations on unquali-fied Convention rights. For example, in relation to the implied right of access to the court: **13-021**

> "The Court considers ... that the right of access to the courts is not absolute. As this is a right which the Convention sets forth ... without, in the narrower sense of the term, defin-ing, there is room, apart from the bounds delimiting the very content of any right, for limitations permitted by implication ... The Government and the Commission have cited examples of regulations, and especially of limitations which are to be found in the national law of states in matters of access to the courts, for instance regulations relating to minors and persons of unsound mind. Although it is of less frequent occurrence and of a very dif-ferent kind, the restriction complained of by *Golder* constitutes a further example of such a limitation."[44]

The ECtHR still requires that the restriction should pursue a legitimate aim and that there is a reasonable relationship of proportionality between that aim and the means used to achieve it.[45]   **13-022**

---

[42] Thus, the Irish government could not rely on art.17 to limit the art.5 and 6 rights of members of the IRA where there was no suggestion that the IRA had abused arts 5 and 6 in the course of its activi-ties (*Lawless v Ireland (No.3)* (1970) 1 E.H.R.R. 15 at [7]). Similarly, in *Ould Dah v France* (2013) 56 E.H.R.R. SE17 at [35]–[36], the ECtHR rejected the argument that an application brought on the basis of a breach of art.7 was an abuse of rights within the meaning of art.17 because the applicant had committed acts in breach of art.3.

[43] *Deweer v Belgium* (1980) 2 E.H.R.R. 439 at [49]. The leading case on restrictions on the activities of public servants is *Vogt v Germany* (1996) 21 E.H.R.R. 205 at [53]–[61] which acknowledges that it may be legitimate to restrict their rights of political expression and activity in order to ensure neutrality. The restrictions were also found to go too far on the facts in *Kudeshkina v Russia* (2011) 52 E.H.R.R. 37 at [86]-[100]. In *Khodorkovskiy v Russia* (2014) 59 E.H.R.R. 7 at [644], the ECtHR affirmed that there was no restriction on an individual waiving his rights under art.6 so long as any such waiver is established in an unequivocal manner and is attended by minimum safeguards com-mensurate with its importance. In addition, it must not run counter to any important public interest. Waiver has also arisen in relation to art.8. In *M v Chief Constable of Hampshire* [2014] EWCA Civ 1651; [2015] 1 W.L.R. 1176 at [18], the CA held that where a sex offender allowed the police to enter his home without objection he would in almost all cases have waived his right, both at common law and under art.8, to refuse entry.

[44] *Golder* (1995) 1 E.H.R.R. 524 at [38]–[39]. Here, the Home Secretary had introduced a require-ment that prisoners should obtain his permission before consulting a solicitor. On the facts, the ECtHR held that this restriction did violate the right of access to the court.

[45] Restrictions have been upheld in a number of cases: e.g. the immunity of police investigations from negligence claims in tort was held to serve the legitimate aim of maintaining an effective police force and thereby preventing disorder and crime, but the blanket nature of the immunity was held to breach ECHR rights in *Osman v United Kingdom* (1998) 29 E.H.R.R. 245 at [150]. The right to vote and stand for election in art.3 of the First Protocol has also been held to be subject to implied limita-tions (*Mathieu-Mohin and Clerfayt v Belgium* (1987) 10 E.H.R.R. 1 at [52]). As to the limitations imposed on the right of access to a court by virtue of an assertion of state immunity, see P. Luckhurst,

Derogations

13-023   Article 15(1) defines the circumstances in which Member States may derogate from certain Convention rights[46]:

"In time of war or national emergency threatening the life of the nation, any High Contracting Party may take measures derogating from its obligations under this Convention to the extent strictly required by the exigencies of the situation, provided that such measures are not inconsistent with its other obligations under international law".[47]

Reservations

13-024   The ECHR also permits reservations to the extent set out in art.57:

"Any State may, when signing this Convention or when depositing its instrument of ratification, make a reservation in respect of any particular provision of the Convention to the extent that any law then in force in its territory is not in conformity with this provision. Reservations of a general character shall not be permitted under this Article."[48]

Positive obligations

13-025   As stated above, art.1 requires the high contracting parties to secure Convention rights to everyone within their jurisdiction. There is no requirement that the victim should be a national of the relevant State or indeed of any Contracting State to the ECHR. The State's responsibilities may also extend to areas of foreign states where it exercises effective control as a consequence of lawful or unlawful military action.[49] By art.56(1) and by declaration, the United Kingdom has extended its

---

"State Immunity in Employment Disputes and the Fundamental Right of Access to a Court" [2015] J.R. 90.

[46]   As stated above, no derogation is permitted from arts 2, 3, 4(1) and 7. For this reason, it is difficult to see the Government's announcement in October 2016 that it intended to derogate from the ECHR in relation to overseas conflict as having much effect, except in relation to art.5.

[47]   The UK derogated from the obligation under art.5(3) to bring arrested or detained persons "promptly before a judge or other officer authorised by law to exercise judicial power" after the detention of terrorist suspects for periods of four to six days in Northern Ireland was found to be in breach of the ECHR (*Brogan v UK* (1988) 11 E.H.R.R. 117 at [58]-[62]). The ECtHR upheld the UK's derogation in *Brannigan and McBride v UK* (1993) 17 E.H.R.R. 539 at [58]-[60]). The UK's more recent derogation in response to the threat of terrorism after the September 11 attacks in the USA was held to violate the ECHR by domestic courts in *X v Secretary of State for the Home Department* [2004] UKHL 56; [2005] 2 A.C. 68. The ECtHR agreed with the House of Lords' conclusions that there had been a situation of emergency at the time and that the measure was disproportionate (*A v United Kingdom* (2009) 26 B.H.R.C. 1 at [181] and [190]). The UK currently has no derogations in force. The "nation" means the nation seeking to derogate and the UK could not therefore rely on a situation of emergency in another state to which it had posted troops (*Mohammed v Secretary of State for Defence (No.2)* [2017] UKSC 2; [2017] 2 W.L.R. 327 at [45]).

[48]   The UK has entered a reservation in relation to the right to education under art.2 of the First Protocol which provides that "the right of parents to ensure teaching and instruction in conformity with their own religious and philosophical convictions" is subject to the extent to which this is compatible with the provision of efficient instruction and the avoidance of unreasonable public expenditure (Pt II of Sch.3 to the HRA).

[49]   Responsibility for acts outside a state's territory is exceptional, but can be made out where the state through its agents exercises control and authority over an individual or where the state, through lawful or unlawful military action, exercises effective control of an area (either directly or through a subordinate local administration) (*Al-Skeini v United Kingdom* (2011) 53 E.H.R.R. 18 at [132]-[150] and *Al-Jedda v United Kingdom* (2011) 53 E.H.R.R 23 at [74]-[86]). On the territorial reach of the HRA, Ch.3. The decision of the ECtHR in *Al-Skeini* was applied in the UK by the SC in *Smith v Ministry of Defence* [2013] UKSC 41; [2014] A.C. 52, in which it was held that the requirement

protection of Convention rights to those non-self-governing territories which belong to the Commonwealth.

In common with most human rights instruments, the Convention's main func- **13-026** tion has been to protect the individual from state action which breaches their rights.[50] However, art.1 has been held to contain positive obligations on the State Parties which can lead to liability even where the act which gave rise to the violation was performed by a private party.[51] Other manifestations of the State's obligation to provide positive protection for Convention rights include the duty to change the law or administrative practice or to provide financial assistance to protect

---

of "exceptionality" does not set an especially high threshold [46] and that the jurisdiction of the United Kingdom extends to securing the protection of art.2 to members of the armed forces when they are serving outside its territory [55]. *Al-Skeini* was also applied in *R. (on the application of Sandiford) v Secretary of State for Foreign and Commonwealth Affairs* [2014] UKSC 44; [2014] 1 W.L.R. 2697, in which it was held that the applicant was not within the jurisdiction of the UK for the purposes of art.1 in relation to the policy of refusing to fund legal representation for those facing capital charges overseas. The decisions in Al-Skeini and Smith are heavily criticised in the context of military operations by the CA in *Mohammed v Secretary of State for Defence* [2015] EWCA Civ 843; [2016] 2 W.L.R. 247 at [93]–[97] on the basis that they involve a substantial extension of the scope of the ECHR to all cases where the state exercises control over an individual as opposed to a territorial area. In *Mohammed v Secretary of State for Defence (No.2)* [2017] UKSC 2; [2017] 2 W.L.R. 327 at [48], Lord Sumption referred to the "serious analytical and practical difficulties" to which Al-Skeini gave rise since it extended the essentially regional scope of the ECHR and potentially brought it into conflict with other sources of international law. See also *Jaloud v Netherlands* (2015) 60 E.H.R.R. 29 at [152], where jurisdiction was established in respect of the Netherlands in circumstances where Mr Jaloud died when a vehicle in which he was a passenger was fired upon while passing through a checkpoint manned by personnel under the command and direct supervision of a Netherlands Royal Army officer. The ECtHR has stated that the matter is heavily fact sensitive (*Chiragov v Armenia* (2016) 63 E.H.R.R. 9 at [168]). In *R. (Keyu) v Secretary of State for Foreign and Commonwealth Affairs & Secretary of State for Defence* [2015] UKSC 69; [2016] A.C. 1355 at [64]–[65], the SC (while rejecting the claim on time grounds) accepted that under the constitutional arrangements then in force, the United Kingdom was in complete control of the State of Malaya and hence the relatives of victims of the 1948 massacre of 24 civilians by members of the British Army in the State of Selangor could potentially rely on art.2.

[50] Certain Convention rights carry express positive obligations, such as the duty to hold free elections (art.3 of the First Protocol (see 13-099 below)) and to inform anyone arrested of the reason for his arrest and bring him promptly before a judge (art.5(2) and (3) (see 13-074 below)).

[51] For example, the State cannot avoid its obligations to protect school pupils from inhuman and degrading treatment and to protect their privacy by arguing that the disciplinary regime in private, fee-paying schools is a matter for the school and does not engage the State's ECHR obligations (*Costello-Roberts v United Kingdom* (1993) 19 E.H.R.R. 112 at [26]–[28]). In fact, there was found to be no violation of arts 3 and 8 in this case by the headmaster's administration of three blows with a slipper on a pupil's clothed buttocks. The limits of the State's liability for private acts is illustrated by *Appleby v United Kingdom* (2003) 37 E.H.R.R. 38 at [41]–[50] in which the ECtHR rejected the claim that a ban on the distribution of leaflets in a privately owned shopping mall engaged the State's obligation to protect art.10. The ECtHR emphasised the need to balance the competing rights of the owners of the mall under art.1 of the First Protocol and the fact that there remained other outlets for the claimant's message. In imposing positive obligations, the ECtHR also relies on the principle of effectiveness (see 13-029 below) and the duty to provide an effective remedy in art.13. See further, A. Mowbray, *The Development of Positive Obligations under the European Convention on Human Rights by the European Court of Human Rights* (2004); E. Bates, *The Evolution of the European Convention on Human Rights* (2010) and D. Xenos, *The Positive Obligations of the State under the European Convention of Human Rights* (2011). In *Michael v Chief Constable of South Wales* [2015] UKSC 2; [2015] A.C. 1732 at [139], the applicant's art.2 claim was permitted to proceed to trial. The case concerned an emergency call handler's failure to prioritise the police response to a call stating that the victim's former partner had threatened to kill her. See also *O'Keeffe v Ireland* (2014) 59 E.H.R.R.15 (Ireland's failure to implement an adequate legal or regulatory framework to protect children in primary education against the risk of sexual abuse by teachers constituted a breach of art.3).

Convention rights.[52] The ECtHR has applied the concept of positive obligations to all Convention rights, although the most developed doctrine is in relations to arts 2 and 8.[53] In determining the existence and extent of positive obligations, the ECtHR must strike an appropriate balance between the competing interests of the individual and those of the community as a whole.[54]

Interpreting the ECHR

13-027   One of the most important characteristics of the application of the ECHR is the doctrine of the margin of appreciation.[55] In essence, this doctrine permits the ECtHR to accord some latitude to the State in how Convention rights are protected. This reflects the fact that the ECtHR's role is subsidiary to that of the States in ensuring the protection of Convention rights. The doctrine is most often invoked in fields where there is no consensus across the Council of Europe about how a matter should be addressed or where a matter lends itself to having local circumstances taken into account. In the context of an obscenity prosecution and freedom of expression, the ECtHR has stated:

> "[I]t is not possible to find in the domestic law of the various Contracting States a uniform European conception of morals. The view taken by their respective laws of the requirements of morals varies from time to time and from place to place, especially in our era which is characterised by a rapid and far-reaching evolution of opinions on the subject. By reason of their direct and continuous contact with the vital forces of their countries, State authorities are in principle in a better position than the international judge to give an opinion on the exact content of these requirements as well as on the 'necessity' of a 'restriction' or 'penalty' intended to meet them".[56]

The doctrine of the margin of appreciation is not confined to cases arising under art.10.[57]

13-028   The ECtHR adopts a number of additional principles when interpreting Convention rights. As an international treaty, it is accepted that the ECHR should be interpreted in accordance with the general principles of international law as set out in the Vienna Convention on the Law of Treaties 1969. The overriding principle established by the Vienna Convention is that treaties should be interpreted in good faith in accordance with the ordinary meaning to be given to the terms of the docu-

---

[52]   *Gaskin v United Kingdom* (1989) 12 E.H.R.R. 36 at [49] (the UK was required to amend the administrative practice which prevented transsexuals from altering their gender on their birth certificates in order to protect the right to private life) and *Steel and Morris v United Kingdom* (2005) 41 E.H.R.R. 22 at [59]–[72] (the UK had failed to ensure equality of arms as required by art.6 between the indigent defendants in libel proceedings and the claimant corporation (Macdonalds)).

[53]   See 13-063 and 13-086 below.

[54]   *Keegan v Ireland* (1994) 18 E.H.R.R. 342 at [49]. This is not a very helpful indication. The ECtHR appears to be more likely to find a positive obligation to exist if it relates to the core of the right in question, if it will not impose unreasonable financial or other burdens on the state and if there is some consistency of application in other states. The ECtHR in *O'Keeffe v Ireland* (2014) 59 E.H.R.R.15 at [144] indicated that more is required by way of positive obligation in relation to children and vulnerable persons.

[55]   Its origins are discussed in Simpson, *Human Rights*, p.1003.

[56]   The doctrine was first set out by the ECtHR in *Handyside v United Kingdom* (1976) 1 E.H.R.R. 737 at [48]. The ECtHR has identified the following factors as relevant to the breadth of the margin of appreciation in relation to art.8: the importance of the individual right at stake, whether there is a consensus across the Council of Europe on how to address the matter, whether the case involves sensitive moral or ethical issues and whether there is a balance between private and public interests (*Evans v United Kingdom* (2008) 49 E.H.R.R. 21 at [77]).

[57]   For the application of a margin of appreciation, more properly described as the discretionary area of judgment, under the HRA see 11-004.

ment in their context and in light of the treaty's object and purpose.[58] The ECtHR may also have regard to other international legal instruments in interpreting the Convention.[59]

An example of the ECtHR's contextual approach is its dynamic interpretation of the ECHR. The ECHR is to be read as a living instrument and its interpretation can therefore change over time to keep pace with changes in the approach to social issues within the Contracting States.[60] A further principle is that of effectiveness. This principle is intended to ensure that practical protection is provided for Convention rights and not safeguards which are merely theoretical or illusory.[61] The final general characteristic of the interpretation of the ECHR is that the Strasbourg court adopts an autonomous definition of the concepts which appear in it.[62]

13-029

The Council of Europe has adopted a total of 16 Protocols. Of these, Protocols 1, 4, 6, 7, 12 and 13 added further rights or liberties to those guaranteed in the main body of the ECHR. The United Kingdom has ratified the First,[63] the Sixth and the

13-030

---

58 Article 31(1) of the Vienna Convention 1980, Cmnd 7964. See 5-053.

59 For example in *T and V v United Kingdom* (2000) 30 E.H.R.R. 121 at [44], the ECtHR relied on the United Nations Convention on the Rights of the Child in determining the scope of the art.6 rights of children accused of murder.

60 The treatment of transsexuals under the ECHR provides an excellent example. The ECtHR held in a series of cases up to 1986 that the state did not breach the right to respect for private life in failing to recognise the individual's change of gender on the birth registration system (*Rees v United Kingdom* (1986) 9 E.H.R.R. 56 at [42]–[3]). However, by 2002, the ECtHR had changed its mind on this issue after taking account of "the clear and uncontested evidence of a continuing international trend in favour not only of increased social acceptance of transsexuals but of legal recognition of the new sexual identity of post-operative transsexuals" (*Goodwin v United Kingdom* (2002) 35 E.H.R.R. 18 at [85]). The HL applied this decision in the domestic context in *Bellinger v Bellinger* [2003] UKHL 21; [2003] 2 A.C. 467 in which it granted a declaration of incompatibility in relation to the Matrimonial Causes Act 1973 which made no provision for the recognition of gender reassignment ([68]–[70], Lord Hope). The violation was remedied by the Gender Recognition Act 2004. The ECtHR has also changed its position on whether denying adoption to a single homosexual person is consistent with art.14 read with art.8 (*EB v France* (2008) 47 E.H.R.R. 21 at [70]–[73] and [91]–[93]). The ECtHR acknowledged that new policing methods may be required to deal with protestors who can use mobile communications to avoid traditional policing tactics in *Austin v United Kingdom* (2012) 55 E.H.R.R. 14 at [53]. In *Vallianatos v Greece* (2014) 59 E.H.R.R. 12 at [91], the ECtHR acknowledged the trend emerging in the legal systems of the Council of Europe (which has yet to reach consensus) to recognise same-sex relationships. A 2008 Greek law which excluded same-sex couples from forming civil unions was a breach of art.8 read with art.14. See further *Oliari v Italy* (2015) 40 B.H.R.C. 549 at [178]. In contrast, in *Jones v United Kingdom* (2014) 59 E.H.R.R. 1 at [213]–[215], the ECtHR held that, despite some emerging support in favour of a special rule or exception in public international law cases concerning civil claims for torture lodged against foreign state officials, it was still the case that a grant of immunity to state officials reflected generally recognised rules of public international law, such that there had been no violation of art.6(1).

61 For example art.6(1) was found to contain a right to civil legal aid in *Airey v Ireland* (1979) 2 E.H.R.R. 305 at [26]–[28]. Mrs Airey could not afford a lawyer and required a judicial decree of separation. The effective protection of her right of access to the courts required that she be provided with public funding in the circumstances. *Steel and Morris* (2005) 41 E.H.R.R. 403. In *Kiarie v Secretary of State for the Home Department* [2017] UKSC 42; [2017] 1 W.L.R. 2380 at [78]–[80], the SC held that requiring a foreign criminal to pursue an arguable challenge to his deportation from abroad did not provide effective protection for his rights under art.8 given the almost insurmountable difficulties likely to be faced in arranging for live evidence to be presented and the necessary weakening of their family bonds which would follow from being required to leave the country.

62 For example the concepts of "civil rights and obligations" or "criminal charge" in art.6 and of "possessions" in art.1 of the First Protocol are entirely independent of the meanings which may be attached to them in domestic law (*Engel v Netherlands* (1976) 1 E.H.R.R. 647 at [82]: domestic classification of proceedings as civil is no more than a starting point for the ECtHR in determining whether the matter relates to a criminal charge). On the autonomous definition of possessions, see *Tre Taktorer Aktiebolag v Sweden* (1989) 13 E.H.R.R. 209 at [53].

63 See 13-078, 096 and 099.

Thirteenth Protocols (which abolish the death penalty). The Fourth Protocol is described above.[64] The Seventh Protocol provides additional rights in criminal cases: to a review of a criminal conviction or sentence and to compensation after a miscarriage of justice. It also prohibits double jeopardy. The UK Government has indicated that it does not intend to sign or ratify the Twelfth Protocol (which prohibits discrimination in the exercise of any right set forth by law, not just Convention rights) on the ground that it is "too general and open-ended".[65]

THE HUMAN RIGHTS ACT 1998[66]

13-031   The campaign for the incorporation of the ECHR into domestic law has a long history.[67] It bore fruit with the election of the Labour government on 1 May 1997 which had committed itself to incorporation. In October of the same year, a White Paper, *Rights Brought Home: The Human Rights Bill*, was produced together with the draft Bill.[68] The HRA was passed in 1998 and entered into force on 2 October 2000.[69] The Long Title to the HRA states that it is designed to "give further effect to" Convention rights.[70] Convention rights for the purposes of the HRA are those set out in arts 2–12 and 14 of the ECHR, arts 1–3 of the First Protocol and art.1 of the Thirteenth Protocol.[71]

Constitutional status of the HRA

13-032   The HRA is not an entrenched provision in the sense that it is not protected substantively or procedurally from express amendment or repeal. Indeed, as explained below, Parliament has provided that its sovereignty is preserved so that it can legislate inconsistently with Convention rights.[72] However, it has also been

---

[64] See fn.38.

[65] *Hansard*, HL Vol.617, col.WA37 (11 October 2000). The ECtHR held that the ineligibility of persons of Roma and Jewish origin to stand for election to the House of Peoples and the Presidency of Bosnia and Herzegovina breached the Twelfth Protocol (*Sejdic v Bosnia and Herzegovina* (2009) 28 B.H.R.C. 201).

[66] On the HRA generally: Lester, Pannick and Herberg, *Human Rights Law and Practice*, 3rd edn (2009), R. Clayton and H. Tomlinson, *Human Rights Law*, 2nd edn (2009); J. Beatson, S. Grosz, T. Hickman, R. Singh and S. Palmer, *Human Rights: Judicial Protection in the United Kingdom* (2008); J. Wadham, H. Mountfield, E. Prochaska and R. Desai, *Blackstone's Guide to the Human Rights Act 1998*, 7th edn (2015).

[67] The campaign is described by one of its principal participants (Lord Lester of Herne Hill) in Lester, Pannick and Herberg, *Human Rights Law and Practice* (2009), paras 1.35–1.46. For many years, the campaign ran with a parallel one for a domestic Bill of Rights as either a free-standing document or as part of a written constitution. This issue has continued to be debated since the HRA: see 13-102.

[68] Cm. 3782.

[69] The delay was substantially in order to ensure that there was sufficient time to train the judges and others who would have to apply the HRA in Convention principles.

[70] Lord Irvine of Lairg LC explained this in Parliament: the HRA "does not create new human rights or take any existing human rights away. It provides better and easier access to rights which already exist" (*Hansard*, HL col.755 (5 February 1998)).

[71] HRA s.1(1). Convention rights take effect subject to any reservation that the UK has made to the Convention or any derogation that it has made or may make from Convention rights (HRA ss.14, 15).

[72] Some have questioned whether the HRA actually incorporates the ECHR at all: G. Marshall, "*Patriating Rights—With Reservations: The Human Rights Act 1998*" in J. Beatson, C. Forsyth and I. Hare (eds), Constitutional Reform in the United Kingdom: Practice and Principles (1998), p.73. The HRA is weaker than an ordinary Act of Parliament in that it does not impliedly repeal earlier

argued that the HRA has a constitutional status.[73] It certainly marks a shift in both practice and expectations by making it possible for courts to adjudicate upon the compatibility of legislation with Convention Rights. In addition, the requirement that all legislation whenever passed must be read and given effect so far as possible in a way consistent with Convention rights does modify the doctrine of implied repeal as far as the HRA is concerned. Thus a later Act of Parliament will not be read as impliedly repealing any Convention rights.[74]

The omission of arts 1 and 13

Parliament did not include arts 1 (obligation to respect human rights) and 13 **13-033** (right to an effective remedy) in the list of incorporated Convention rights. The ostensible justification was that this was unnecessary since the HRA itself was securing Convention rights and providing adequate domestic remedies. Whatever the merits of that argument, the consequences of Parliament's failure have been much mitigated by judicial decision:

"The domestic counterpart to art.13 is sections 7 and 8 of the Human Rights Act, read in conjunction with section 6. This domestic counterpart to art.13 takes a different form from art.13 itself. Unlike art.13, which declares a right ('Everyone whose rights ... are violated shall have an effective remedy'), sections 7 and 8 provide a remedy. art.13 guarantees the availability at the national level of an effective remedy to enforce the substance of Convention rights. Sections 7 and 8 seek to provide that remedy in this country. The object of these sections is to provide in English law the very remedy art.13 declares is the entitlement of everyone whose rights are violated."[75]

As stated above, judicial review will generally provide adequate protection for **13-034** Convention rights since the enactment of the HRA. The ECtHR has also acknowledged that the Home Office's general practice of not seeking to enforce a decision in relation to which permission to seek judicial review has been granted does provide sufficient protection despite the difficulties of obtaining interim relief against the Crown.[76] Further, the discretionary nature of judicial review remedies does not breach art.13.[77]

---

inconsistent legislation. Lord Hoffmann described it as "misleading" to refer to the HRA as incorporating Convention rights: the HRA creates domestic rights in the same terms as those contained in the Convention, but they are domestic rights, not international rights (*Re McKerr* [2004] UKHL 12; [2004] 1 W.L.R. 807 at [63]).

[73] *Thoburn v City of Sunderland* [2002] EWHC 195 (Admin); [2003] 1 Q.B. 151 at [62] (Laws LJ described the HRA as falling into the category of constitutional measures along with, for example, Magna Carta, the Act of Union 1706 and the European Communities Act on the ground that they condition the relationship between the individual and the State in a general, overarching manner or enlarge or diminish the scope of fundamental rights). See also J. Jowell, "Parliamentary Sovereignty under the New Constitutional Hypothesis" [2006] P.L. 562 and T. Hickman, *Public Law after the Human Rights Act* (2010), pp.24–49.

[74] *Thoburn* [2002] EWHC 195 (Admin); [2003] 1 Q.B. 151 at [62].

[75] *Re S (Children) (Care Order: Implementation of Care Plan)* [2002] UKHL 10; [2002] 2 A.C. 291 at [61] (Lord Nicholls of Birkenhead). In *R. (on the application of K) v Camden and Islington Health Authority* [2001] EWCA Civ 240; [2002] Q.B. 198 at [54], Sedley LJ described art.13 as reflecting "the longstanding principle of our law that where there is a right there should be a remedy".

[76] *Soering v United Kingdom* (1989) 11 E.H.R.R. 433 at [123]. Section 6 was held to fulfil the same role in relation to art.1 in *DSD v Commissioner of Police of the Metropolis* [2015] EWCA Civ 646; [2016] Q.B. 161 at [17].

[77] *Vilvarajah v United Kingdom* (1991) 14 E.H.R.R. 248 at [126]. One matter which is not satisfactorily resolved concerns the status of art.13 in relation to primary domestic legislation which violates Convention rights. Article 13 has never been held to require that the Convention itself be

The authority of Strasbourg decisions

13-035   In interpreting Convention rights, domestic courts are required to "take into account" (but not to follow) any relevant decision of the Strasbourg organs.[78] What
this means in practice continues to be subject to judicial elaboration. The starting
point is that domestic courts should follow a "clear and constant line of decisions"
from Strasbourg.[79] The justification for this approach is said to lie in the fact that
the ECHR is an international legal instrument whose correct interpretation should
be decided uniformly across all members of the Council of Europe by the ECtHR.
It is not generally appropriate for the domestic court to dilute or weaken the effect
of Strasbourg case law. Indeed to do so may place the court itself in breach of its
duty to act compatibly with Convention rights under s.6 of the HRA. More
controversially, it was held that, while it is open to the legislature of a member state
to provide greater protection for Convention rights than the Strasbourg court has
determined, domestic courts should not seek to do so.[80] Since the purpose of the
HRA was to give further effect to Convention rights in the UK, it would not be appropriate for domestic courts to provide less protection than the Strasbourg cases
indicate. However, the converse is less plainly correct. In adopting an interpretation of a Convention right which provides greater protection than the current
Strasbourg doctrine, a domestic court is not supplanting the role of the ECtHR as
the authoritative body to determine the meaning of the ECHR throughout the
member states. The domestic court's interpretation will not apply outside the UK.
Moreover, as stated above, Strasbourg jurisprudence evolves in line with the
ECtHR's view of the Convention as a living instrument. If UK courts are to

---

incorporated into domestic law and does not require that primary legislation which requires a
particular result be set aside. The answer is different if the domestic legislation is merely facilita-
tive (*Peck v United Kingdom* (2003) 36 E.H.R.R. 41 at [101].) However, this result appears to be
inconsistent with post-HRA decisions of the ECtHR in which it has been held that the declaration
of incompatibility does not constitute an effective remedy which needs to be exhausted before an
application to Strasbourg could be made (*Hobbs v UK* (App No. 63684/00, 18 June 2002)). The
ECtHR based the decision on the fact that the declaration does not bind the parties to the litigation
and does not require the Minister to introduce amending legislation. The ECtHR has indicated that
over time the consistent practice of giving effect to declarations of incompatibility may crystallise
into a binding obligation and that, at that time, applicants would be required to exhaust this national
remedy before applying to Strasbourg (except where an effective remedy necessarily required the
award of damages) (*Burden and Burden v United Kingdom* (2008) 47 E.H.R.R. 38 at [43]).

[78] HRA s.2(1). As a result of the procedural reforms described at 13-006, this is likely to mean
principally decisions of the ECtHR in future. This is contrast to the obligation to follow relevant decisions of the Court of Justice of the European Communities, see para.14-048. See generally, E. Bjorge,
Domestic Application of the ECHR: Courts as Faithful Trustees (2015).

[79] *Pinnock v Manchester City Council* [2011] UKSC 6; [2011] 2 A.C. 104 at [48] (Lord Neuberger).

[80] *R. v Special Adjudicator Ex p. Ullah* [2004] UKHL 26; [2004] 2 A.C. 323 at [20] (Lord Bingham).
In this case, the HL declined to extend the ECtHR jurisprudence to cover the case where an
individual facing expulsion from the UK sought to rely on potential violations of his art.9 right to
freedom of thought, conscience and religion. The ECtHR has previously held that individuals may
only rely on alleged breaches of rights overseas (other than art.3) in the most exceptional
circumstances. Lord Bingham concluded that the domestic court's duty was to keep pace with the
developing doctrine: "no more, but certainly no less", at [20]. This is consistent with other judicial
statements that the purpose of the HRA was not to enlarge the Convention rights or the remedies
available to those in the UK, but to enable those rights and remedies to be asserted and enforced by
the domestic courts and not only by recourse to Strasbourg (*R. (on the application of SB) v Governors
of Denbigh High School* [2006] UKHL 15; [2007] 1 A.C. 100 at [29] (Lord Bingham)). *SB* concerned
an unsuccessful challenge to the ban on wearing the jilbab on art.9 and art.2 of the First Protocol
grounds. *In R. (on the application of Nicklinson) v Ministry of Justice* [2014] UKSC 38; [2015] A.C.
657 at [70], Lord Kerr suggested that Lord Bingham's dictum was not on point in cases to which a
wide margin of appreciation applied.

contribute to that evolution, their role cannot be confined merely to replicating what the Strasbourg court has done in the past.[81]

In any event, it is clear that there are now three recognised exceptions to the principle that domestic courts should follow Strasbourg jurisprudence. First, the domestic court may be unable to identify a clear and constant line of ECtHR authority.[82] This "exception" may be said to flow directly from the formulation of the principle itself. A related aspect of the absence of clear Strasbourg authority is where the ECtHR has not had the opportunity to address a question at all. In such cases, it must be legitimate for domestic courts to decide the matter, rather than await guidance from the ECtHR.[83] Secondly, the Strasbourg cases may be inconsist-

13-036

---

[81] A majority of the House of Lords in *Re G* [2008] UKHL 38; [2009] 1 A.C. 173 accepted that there would be circumstances where it was legitimate for a domestic court to provide greater protection for fundamental rights than required by the Strasbourg jurisprudence (see below). Examples of our highest court going beyond Strasbourg jurisprudence to provide greater protection for Convention rights include *Limbuela* and *EM (Lebanon)* at 13-065 and 13-087. A number of influential commentators have encouraged UK courts (or at least the Supreme Court) to depart from Strasbourg decisions in appropriate cases: for example, N. Bratza, "The Relationship Between the UK Courts and Strasbourg" (2011) E.H.R.L.R. 505. Lord Irvine has gone further in "A British Interpretation of Convention Rights" [2012] P.L. 237. See further, P. Sales, "Strasbourg jurisprudence and the Human Rights Act: a reply to Lord Irvine" [2012] P.L. 253 and R. Clayton, "Smoke and Mirrors: The Human Rights Act and the Impact of Strasbourg Case Law" [2012] P.L. 639. Sales J expressed his views judicially in *R. (on the application of S) v Secretary of State for Justice* [2012] EWHC 1810 (Admin); [2013] 1 W.L.R. 3079 at [50]–[71]. See also N. Ferreira, "The Supreme Court in a final push to go beyond Strasbourg" [2015] P.L. 367, commenting on the decisions in Ullah and Nicklinson, and P. Mahoney, "The relationship between the Strasbourg court and the national courts" (2014) 130 L.Q.R. 568.

[82] See e.g *N v Secretary of State for the Home Department* [2005] UKHL 31; [2005] 2 A.C. 296 (concerning art.3 and the interpretation of the ECtHR's earlier ruling in *D v United Kingdom* (1997) 24 E.H.R.R. 423). In the very exceptional circumstances of the latter case, it was found to be a breach of art.3 to expel D to St Kitts where the treatment available for his HIV/AIDS was very limited. Since *D*, the ECtHR had sought to limit the effect of this decision but without establishing clear principles distinguishing the case from others. Lord Nicholls described the doctrine as "not in an altogether satisfactory state" (*N*, at [11]), but held that D should not be extended further. Lord Hope of Craighead, at [26]–[50] and Lord Brown, at [78]–[94] carried out extensive reviews of the ECtHR jurisprudence without being able to identify any clear principles. The HL therefore felt constrained to reject the application in *N* on the basis that N's advanced HIV/AIDS did not prevent her compulsory return to Uganda despite the prospect that her life expectancy would be reduced to a year or two in the absence of the treatment she had received since arriving in the UK. The House of Lords' decision in *N* was affirmed by the ECtHR, see 13-066, fn.175 below. Lines of Strasbourg authority may become less clear over time. However, the fact that there may be a "direction of travel" in Strasbourg jurisprudence which appears to depart from a formerly stated principle will not allow for that principle to be replaced with a "new interpretation" without "a clear, high level exegesis of the salient principle and its essential components": *Kennedy v Charity Commission* [2014] UKSC 20; [2015] A.C. 455 at [145]–[148]. In *Kennedy*, the SC held that there was no art.10 right to receive information from public authorities: see para.13-090. In *Moohan v Lord Advocate* [2014] UKSC 67; [2015] A.C. 901 at [104]–[105], Lord Hodge chronicled the SC's substantial modification of the Ullah principle, holding that "where there is no directly relevant decision of the ECtHR with which it would be possible (even if appropriate) to keep pace, we can and must do more. We must determine for ourselves the existence or otherwise of an alleged Convention right." That principle was reflected in the judgment of Lord Kerr in *R. (Keyu) v Secretary of State for Foreign and Commonwealth Affairs & Secretary of State for Defence* [2015] UKSC 69; [2016] A.C. 1355 at [234]–[235]. His Lordship postulated that while a domestic court should exercise "caution" in determining what the ECtHR would decide absent relevant jurisprudence, it should not be deterred from that duty. The SC declined to follow the chamber decision in *Ali v United Kingdom* (2016) 63 E.H.R.R. 20 that housing authorities' duties under Pt VII of the Housing Act 1996 gave rise to duties under art.6. The SC noted the absence of Grand Chamber authority on the point and that the decision in Ali went beyond the previous doctrine (*Poshteh v Kensington and Chelsea LBC* [2017] UKSC 36; [2017] 2 W.L.R. 1417).

[83] *Re (Adoption: Unmarried Couple)* [2008] UKHL 38; [2009] 1 A.C. 173 at [27]–[38] (Lord Hoffmann) and at [120]–[124] (Baroness Hale) concerned a Northern Ireland ban on adoptions by

ent with some fundamental substantive or procedural aspect of domestic law.[84] Thirdly, the ECtHR may have failed to appreciate or misunderstood some argument or point of principle.[85] This can give rise to a form of judicial dialogue between the ECtHR and domestic courts. So far, the ECtHR has tended to accept the reinterpretation of its precedents by UK courts.[86]

13-037   This leaves the further question of whether a domestic court is entitled to depart from otherwise binding UK authority where Strasbourg has taken a different line.

---

unmarried couples. Strasbourg had not directly confronted the question and the HL felt able to go further than existing ECtHR doctrine required in finding that an absolute ban violated art.14 read with art.8. The HL was assisted in this conclusion by the fact that this was an area which fell within the member state's margin of appreciation. There were competing views on whether the SC should decide an issue unresolved by *Strasbourg in Ambrose v Harris* [2011] UKSC 43; [2011] 1 W.L.R. 2435 at [15] (Lord Hope) compared to at [128]–[129] (Lord Kerr): Lord Kerr favoured a more expansive role for the SC. In *Rabone v Pennine Care NHS Trust* [2012] UKSC 2; [2012] 2 A.C. 72 at [112], Lord Brown (agreeing with the leading judgment of Lord Dyson) made clear that the absence of Strasbourg authority does not prevent a domestic court from addressing a question of the interpretation of the ECHR. Rather, Lord Brown stated that a domestic court should not unwillingly decide a case against a public authority (which would have no right to seek to have that decision overturned in Strasbourg) unless the existing authorities compel that result.

[84] *Pinnock* [2011] UKSC 6; [2011] 2 A.C. 104 at [48] (Lord Neuberger).

[85] *Pinnock* [2011] UKSC 6; [2011] 2 A.C. 104 at [48] (Lord Neuberger). In *R. v Horncastle* [2009] UKSC 14; [2010] 2 A.C. 373 at [11], [14] and [95]–[108] (Lord Phillips), the SC declined to follow ECtHR doctrine on the exclusion of hearsay evidence in criminal trials. The SC held that the ECtHR had failed to appreciate the crafted code which Parliament had introduced in the Criminal Justice Act 2003 and that, when looked at in its proper context, there was no breach of art.6. The Grand Chamber of the ECtHR accepted the SC's position on art.6 (reversing the Chamber's position) in *Al-Khawaja and Tahery v United Kingdom* (2012) 54 E.H.R.R. 23 at [129]–[151]. The HL previously felt able to depart from a decision of the ECtHR in *R. v Spear* [2002] UKHL 31; [2003] 1 A.C. 734 (an art.6 challenge to the independence and impartiality of the junior officers who sit on courts-martial). In that case, Lord Bingham suggested that in the earlier case of *Morris v United Kingdom* (2002) 34 E.H.R.R. 52, the ECtHR had "not receive[d] all the help which was needed to form a conclusion" and had therefore reached an erroneous view on a matter particularly within the knowledge of the domestic courts (at [12]). Lord Rodger expressed a similar view (at [92]). The challenge was rejected. The CA has summarised the above authorities and the more recent SC cases of *R. (on the application of Osborn) v Parole Board* [2013] UKSC 61; [2014] A.C. 1115 at [56]–[57] and *R. (on the application of Chester) v Secretary of State for Justice* [2013] UKSC 63; [2014] A.C. 271 at [27], [120]–[124] in the following principles: (1) it is the duty of the national courts to enforce domestically enacted Convention rights; (2) the ECtHR is the court that, ultimately, must interpret the meaning of the Convention; (3) the UK courts will be bound to follow an interpretation of a provision of the Convention if given by the Grand Chamber as authoritative, unless it is apparent that it has misunderstood or overlooked some significant feature of English law or practice which, properly explained, would lead to that interpretation being reviewed by the ECtHR when its interpretation was being applied to English circumstances; (4) the same principle and qualification applies to a "clear and constant" line of decisions of the ECtHR other than one of the Grand Chamber; (5) Convention rights have to be given effect in the light of the domestic law which implements in detail the "high level" rights set out in the Convention; and (6) where there are "mixed messages" in the existing Strasbourg case law, a "real judicial choice" will have to be made about the scope and application of the relevant provision of the Convention (*R. (on the application of Hicks) v Commissioner of Police of the Metropolis* [2014] EWCA Civ 3; [2014] 1 W.L.R. 2152 at [80]). The SC affirmed the decision on slightly different grounds at [2017] UKSC 9; [2017] A.C. 256 at [32]–[40] and declined to follow the majority view in *Ostendorf v Germany* (2013) 34 B.H.R.C. 738. See further fn.170.

[86] A recent example concerns the question of whether or not whole-life tariffs (imposed for the most serious offences) are compatible with art.3. The ECtHR has established a line of authority that domestic law must provide some hope of release on a sufficiently clear basis. In *Hutchinson v UK* (App. No. 57592/08) (17 January 2017), the Grand Chamber accepted that the CA's decision in *Re Attorney General's Reference (No.69 of 2013)* [2014] EWCA Crim 188; [2014] 1 W.L.R. 3964 had addressed the concerns expressed in *Vinter v UK* (2016) 63 E.H.R.R. 1 about the UK position and that there was no violation as long as the Secretary of State exercised his discretion compatibly with art.3.

Save for in limited and exceptional circumstances, the domestic court should follow the domestic precedent and expedite an appeal rather than following the Strasbourg jurisprudence.[87]

Giving effect to Convention rights

The HRA seeks to give further effect to Convention rights through four principal mechanisms which are addressed in turn below.   **13-038**

- Public authorities (which include courts and tribunals) are required to act in a way which is compatible with Convention rights.[88]
- Legislation (whenever passed) is to be interpreted so far as possible in a manner which is consistent with Convention rights.[89]
- Where it is not possible to interpret primary legislation compatibly with a Convention right, the court may make a declaration of incompatibility.[90] The declaration does not affect the result in the individual case or the validity of the primary legislation, but it does trigger a ministerial power to take remedial action to remove the incompatibility through a streamlined legislative process.[91]
- A minister in charge of a Bill before Parliament must make a statement of compatibility to the effect that the Bill is consistent with Convention rights or must explain why he wishes to proceed despite any incompatibility.[92]

Although compatible with the doctrine of parliamentary sovereignty, the HRA is far more than an ordinary Act of Parliament. Lord Hope of Craighead stated: "the incorporation of the European Convention on Human Rights into our domestic law will subject the entire legal system to a fundamental process of review and, where necessary, reform by the judiciary".[93]   **13-039**

---

[87] *Kay v Lambeth LBC* [2006] UKHL 10; [2006] 2 A.C. 465 at [33] (Lord Bingham of Cornhill). This is subject to the most limited exception arising in the circumstances of *D v East Berkshire Community NHS Trust* [2003] EWCA Civ 1151; [2004] Q.B. 558 where the CA held that the decision of the HL in *X (Minors) v Bedfordshire County Council* [1995] 2 A.C. 633 could not survive the introduction of the HRA since its policy basis had been completely removed. The Court of Appeal may depart from one of its own decisions where it concludes that it is inconsistent with a subsequent decision of the ECtHR (*R. (on the application of RJM) v Secretary of State for Work and Pensions* [2008] UKHL 63; [2009] 1 A.C. 311 at [59]–[67] (Lord Neuberger)). The House of Lords departed from its own decision in *Pretty v UK* (2002) 35 E.H.R.R. 1 on whether the right to respect for private life is engaged in cases concerning decisions to terminate one's own life in light of the ECtHR's decision in that case (*R. (on the application of Purdy) v Director of Public Prosecutions* [2009] UKHL 45; [2009] 1 Cr.App.R. 32 at [35]–[39] (Lord Hope)). *Pinnock* provides a further example. The SC in *Brown v Parole Board for Scotland* [2017] UKSC 69; [2017] 3 W.L.R. 1373 departed from its own recent decision in *R. (on the application of Kaiyam) v Secretary of State for Justice* [2014] UKSC 66; [2015] A.C. 1344 to align domestic law with the ECtHR's decision in *James, Wells and Lee v UK* (2013) 56 E.H.R.R. 12 (see fn.193). The SC affirmed that, in line with the Strasbourg jurisprudence, any failure to provide prisoners sentenced to life imprisonment or who were detained for public protection with a real opportunity for rehabilitation had to meet a high threshold before rendering the detention arbitrary and a breach of art.5 (at [38]–[45]).
[88] HRA s.6(1).
[89] HRA s.3(1).
[90] HRA s.4.
[91] HRA s.10.
[92] HRA s.19.
[93] *R. v DPP Ex p. Kebilene* [2000] 2 A.C. 326 at 374–375.

Public authorities

13-040   The definitions of "public authority" and "function of a public nature" are examined in Chapter 3.[94] It is important to note the limits on the duty contained in s.6 of the HRA which relate to the preservation of parliamentary sovereignty. First, just as a national court cannot set aside primary legislation, a public authority is not required to act compatibly with Convention rights where primary legislation requires it to act differently or where the authority is acting to give effect to or enforce primary or secondary legislation which cannot be read compatibly with Convention rights.[95] Secondly, an act is defined to include a failure to act, but does not include a failure to introduce in, or lay before, Parliament a proposal for legislation or a failure to make any primary legislation or remedial order.[96]

The duty to interpret legislation compatibly with Convention rights[97]

13-041   The obligation to read and give effect to all legislation in a way which is compatible with Convention rights so far as it is possible to do so applies to all courts and tribunals and in all proceedings whether or not a public authority is a party to the proceedings. This obligation is deliberately stronger than its equivalent in the New Zealand Bill of Rights Act 1990 which was one of the models for the HRA.[98] The obligation has been described as creating a rebuttable presumption in favour of a meaning which is compatible with Convention rights.[99] Moreover, the obligation does not depend on any finding of ambiguity and is retrospective in operation. Lord Steyn has described s.3 as the HRA's "principal remedial measure".[100] The following illustrations reveal the extent of the obligation.

13-042   In *R. v A (No.2)*,[101] the House of Lords had to consider the provisions of the Youth Justice and Criminal Evidence Act 1999 which were introduced drastically to reduce the use of evidence of a complainant's prior sexual history in rape trials. The plain words of s.41 of the 1999 Act would have led to the exclusion of certain evidence which would prejudice the defendant's right to a fair trial under art.6 of the ECHR. The House held that this section should be read subject to the implied

---

94   See 3-077 and 3-082.

95   *Aston Cantlow and Wilmcote with Billesley Parochial Church Council v Wallbank* [2003] UKHL 37; [2004] 1 A.C. 546 at [19] (Lord Nicholls of Birkenhead).

96   HRA s.6(6). On the balancing of rights protection and parliamentary sovereignty, see F. Klug, "The Human Rights Act—A 'Third Way' or 'Third Wave' Bill of Rights" (2001) 4 E.H.R.L.R. 361 and C. Gearty, *Principles of Human Rights Adjudication* (2004). See also C. Gearty, "On Fantasy Island: British politics, English judges and the European Convention on Human Rights" [2015] E.H.R.L.R. 1.

97   On statutory interpretation generally, see 5-019.

98   M. Taggart, "Tugging on Superman's Cape: Lessons from the Experience with the New Zealand Bill of Rights Act 1990" [1998] P.L. 266. Other comparisons are discussed by S. Kentridge, "Parliamentary Supremacy and the Judiciary under a Bill of Rights: Some Lessons from the Commonwealth" [1997] P.L. 96.

99   Lord Steyn, "Incorporation and Devolution: A Few Reflections on the Changing Scene" [1998] E.H.R.L.R. 153 at 155. Lord Steyn states that, given the inherent ambiguity of language, the presumption is likely to be a strong one.

100   *Ghaidan v Godin-Mendoza* [2004] UKHL 30; [2004] 2 A.C. 557 at [39]. Lords Steyn and Rodger also drew an analogy (at [45] and [122]) between s.3 and the obligation on national courts under EU law, as far as possible, to interpret national legislation in the light of the wording and purpose of directives (on which, see *Marleasing SA v La Comercial Internacional de Alimentación SA* (Case C-106/89) [1990] ECR I-4135 at 4159). See C. Gearty, "Reconciling Parliamentary Democracy and Human Rights" (2002) 118 L.Q.R. 248.

101   *R. v A (No.2)* [2001] UKHL 25; [2002] 1 A.C. 45.

proviso that evidence or questioning which is required to ensure a fair trial under art.6 should be admitted.[102]

Perhaps an even more striking example is provided by the House's decision in **13-043** *Ghaidan v Godin-Mendoza*.[103] This concerned the interpretation of the 1977 Rent Act's provisions on succession to a protected tenancy. The 1977 Act draws a clear distinction between spouses and those living together as husband and wife on the one hand and other members of the tenant's family on the other. In an earlier decision, the House had decided that same sex partners could not be considered as living together as husband and wife.[104] After the HRA entered into force, Mr Godin-Mendoza alleged that the 1977 Act violated his right not to be discriminated against under art.14 when read with art.8. Article 8 creates no right to be provided with a home by the State. However, if the State does provide such resources, it must not do so in a way which discriminates contrary to art.14. The clear distinction on grounds of sexuality in the present case was found not to pursue any legitimate aim: the Rent Act could not be justified as being in support of the traditional family because it extended beyond married couples and to those with no children and no prospect of having any. As such, it could only be based on an assumption that the relationship between heterosexual couples is somehow closer. Lord Nicholls rejected this: "A homosexual couple, as much as a heterosexual couple, share each other's life and make their home together. They have an equivalent relationship. There is no rational or fair ground for distinguishing the one couple from the other in this context".[105] The 1977 Act was therefore read as extending to same sex couples and Mr Godin-Mendoza was entitled to succeed to the tenancy.

---

[102] Lord Steyn accepted that s.3 required the court to adopt on occasion "an interpretation which linguistically may appear strained" (*R. v A* [2001] UKHL 25, [2002] 1 A.C. 45 at [44]). In *Connolly v DPP* [2007] EWHC 237 (Admin); [2008] 1 W.L.R. 276 at [18] (Dyson LJ), the Divisional Court held that the prohibition on sending a communication of an indecent or grossly offensive nature with the purpose of causing distress or anxiety in the Malicious Communications Act 1988 should be read so as not to criminalise communications which fell within art.10 (as in the present case where the material was part of an anti-abortion claim). The SC relied on s.3 to interpret the domestic legislation on the retention of biometric data compatibly with art.8 (as explained by the ECtHR in *S and Marper v UK* (2008) 48 E.H.R.R. 50) in *R. (on the application of GC) v Commissioner of Police of the Metropolis* [2011] UKSC 21; [2011] 1 W.L.R. 1230 at [24]–[35] (Lord Dyson). In *R. (on the application of T) v Chief Constable of Greater Manchester* [2014] UKSC 35; [2015] A.C. 49 at [53], the SC held it was impossible to read and give effect to the domestic provisions on the disclosure of convictions and cautions (however old and minor) of the Police Act 1997 in a way which was compatible with art.8. Recent cases in which it was held not possible to "read down" the relevant legislation in order to give effect to the applicants' Convention rights include *R. (on the application of Tigere) v Secretary of State for Business, Innovation and Skills* [2015] UKSC 57; [2015] 1 W.L.R. 3820 at [48]–[49] (concerning student loans and immigration status); *Lawrence v Fen Tigers Ltd (No.3)* [2015] UKSC 50; [2015] 1 W.L.R. 3485 at [88] (concerning success fee up-lifts in litigation); *Benkharbouche v Embassy of Sudan* [2015] EWCA Civ 33; [2016] Q.B. 347 at [67] (concerning the State Immunity Act 1978 in relation to which a declaration of incompatibility was granted) and *McDonald v McDonald* [2016] UKSC 28; [2017] A.C. 273 at [70] (concerning mandatory possession orders in favour of private landlords, although the court found no incompatibility). In *Re X (A Child) (Parental Order: Time Limit)* [2014] EWHC 3135 (Fam); [2015] Fam. 186 at [68], the court read down s.54 of the Human Fertilisation and Embryology Act 2008 (which imposes a six-month time limit on applications for a parental order) to achieve compatibility with art.8. In *Re Z (A Child) (Surrogate Father: Parental Order)* [2015] EWFC 73; [2017] Fam. 25 at [35]–[40], however, while the court affirmed previous cases in which s.54 was read down, it was not possible to read down that legislative provision in order to bring a single parent within the statutory requirements for the grant of a parental order. The Secretary of State conceded that the legislation was incompatible with art.8 read with art.14 and a declaration of incompatibility was granted ([2016] EWHC 1191 (Fam); [2017] Fam. 25; [2016] 3 W.L.R. 1369).

[103] *Ghaidan v Godin-Mendoza* [2004] UKHL 30; [2004] 2 A.C. 557.

[104] *Fitzpatrick v Sterling Housing Association Ltd* [2001] 1 A.C. 27.

[105] *Godin-Mendoza* [2004] UKHL 30; [2004] 2 A.C. 557 at [17]. Lord Nicholls of Birkenhead also

13-044   More recently, the Supreme Court held that the provisions on the confiscation of assets obtained as a result of crime in the Proceeds of Crime Act 2002 had to be read down to ensure that they did not constitute an interference with the peaceful enjoyment of possessions as protected by art.1 of the First Protocol. The Supreme Court held that a confiscation order should be limited to what was proportionate in order to deprive the criminal of the benefits of their wrong-doing and should not contain an element of deterrence.[106]

13-045   However, the obligation has limits.[107] Parliament expressly preserved the principle of parliamentary sovereignty in the HRA[108] and the procedures for making a declaration of incompatibility and taking remedial action would be otiose unless there were some matters of incompatibility which could not be interpreted away. Two such limits have been established in the cases: where the proposed interpretation is contrary to a fundamental feature of the legislation or where the impact of the interpretation is not predictable within the judicial process. An example of the first limitation is *Re S (Care Order: Implementation of Care Plan)*.[109] The case concerned final care orders made under the Children Act 1989. The Court of Appeal held that the manner in which the care orders were made and implemented breached the parents' Convention rights under arts 6(1) and 8 and therefore introduced a new system whereby stages in the implementation of the care plan would be "starred". The local authority's failure to implement the starred aspects of a care plan would trigger the right to come back to court for further directions. The House of Lords overturned this result on the basis that s.3 of the HRA could not be used to produce a result which departed substantially from a fundamental feature of an Act of Parliament. In this case, it was a cardinal principle of the Children Act that the courts would not intervene in the manner in which local authorities discharged their responsibilities under final care orders. In an important passage, Lord Nicholls acknowledged the importance of s.3 and the forthright and uncompromising language in which it is expressed. However, his Lordship

---

rejected the argument that the interpretation should be subject to the discretionary area of judgment. While accepting that housing policy did involve a balancing of social concerns which required some judicial reticence, distinctions drawn on grounds of race, sex or sexual orientation will be scrutinised "with intensity" (at [19]). Lord Millett disagreed forcefully (at [100]).

[106] *R. v Waya* [2012] UKSC 51; [2013] 1 A.C. 294 at [24]-[29].

[107] For example *Godin-Mendoza* was distinguished in *R. (on the application of Wilkinson) v IRC* [2005] UKHL 30; [2005] 1 W.L.R. 1718 where a widower argued that s.262(1) of the Income and Corporation Taxes Act 1988 which conferred a tax allowance on "his widow [where] a married man whose wife is living with him dies" should be read as entitling him to the allowance to avoid gender discrimination contrary to art.14; the HL rejected the argument and distinguished *Godin-Mendoza* on the basis that the presence of the phrase "as his or her wife or husband" was a general concept which gave the court greater interpretative discretion than the more specific words of the 1988 Act, at [18]). There is an extensive literature on the relationship between s.3 and s.4 of the HRA. Some commentators suggest that these provisions ensure a "democratic dialogue" between the courts and legislature (A.L. Young, *Parliamentary Sovereignty and the Human Rights Act* (2009), Chs 5 and 6, T. Hickman, *Public Law after the Human Rights Act* (2009), Ch 3, A. Kavanagh, *Constitutional Review under the UK Human Rights Act* (2009), Chs 5, 12 and 13 and D. Nicol, "Law and Politics after the Human Rights Act" [2006] P.L. 722). Other commentators suggest that this ignores the fact that the HRA is seeking to give effect to international legal norms which are authoritatively determined by the ECtHR and the doctrine of the discretionary area of judgment is the appropriate mechanism for dealing with questions of the separation of powers (P. Sales and R. Ekins, "Rights-Consistent Interpretation and the Human Rights Act 1998" (2011) 127 L.Q.R. 217).

[108] HRA s.3(2)(b) and (c) provide that s.3 does not affect the validity, continuing operation or enforcement of any incompatible primary legislation or subordinate legislation if primary legislation prevents the removal of the incompatibility. Of course, a legislator will be acting in breach of s.6 and therefore ultra vires if he adopts subordinate legislation in breach of Convention rights (unless required by the parent Act).

[109] *Re S (Care Order: Implementation of Care Plan)* [2002] UKHL 10; [2002] 2 A.C. 291.

emphasised that s.3 is a tool of interpretation and not amendment and the difficulty for the courts lay in determining where the legitimate judicial task of interpretation ended and impermissible amendment began. Lord Nicholls stated that this line is likely to be crossed where the interpretation involves a departure from a fundamental feature of the legislation, especially where, as here, the departure would have practical repercussions which the court is not equipped to evaluate.[110]

The second limitation is illustrated by *Bellinger v Bellinger*.[111] In this case, the question was whether the parties were lawfully married. It was not disputed that the petitioner was born male, but underwent gender re-assignment treatment and had gone through a ceremony of marriage in 1981 with Michael Bellinger. Section 11(c) of the Matrimonial Causes Act 1973, provides that a marriage is void unless the parties are "respectively male and female". The House held that it was unable to resolve this matter through interpretation and so issued a declaration of incompatibility. Lord Nicholls explained the judicial reason for not relying on s.3 of the HRA on the ground that such an interpretation would represent a major change in the law with far-reaching ramifications. His Lordship referred to the extensive research and consultation into the issues which would be required and which went beyond the judicial capacity of enquiry. Such matters were especially suited to determination by Parliament where the legislature had indicated that it intended to introduce comprehensive primary legislation on the subject.[112]

13-046

Declaration of incompatibility[113]

Only the higher courts listed in s.4(5) of the HRA have the power to make a declaration of incompatibility. These are the Supreme Court, the Judicial Committee of the Privy Council, the Courts Martial Appeal Court, the Court of Appeal and the High Court (in England, Wales and Northern Ireland) and the Court of Session and the High Court of Justiciary sitting otherwise than as a trial court (in Scotland). This list indicates the importance of the declaration of incompatibility and the government's reluctance to have criminal trials in the Crown Court or before magistrates disrupted by declarations of incompatibility. These higher courts are under no obligation to make a declaration of incompatibility and have a discretion on the matter. This fits with the general discretionary nature of the declaration as a common law remedy (and, indeed, with all other public law remedies). However, it is difficult to envisage circumstances in which a court would find there to be incompatibility and yet would not issue a declaration to that effect.[114]

Again, Parliament was careful to state that the declaration has no effect on the

13-047

13-048

---

[110] *Re S (Care Order: Implementation of Care Plan)* [2002] UKHL 10; [2001] 2 A.C. 29 at [37]-[40]. See also *Lawrence v Fen Tigers Ltd (No.3)* [2015] UKSC 50; [2015] 1 W.L.R. 3485 at [89]-[94].

[111] *Bellinger v Bellinger* [2003] UKHL 21; [2003] 2 A.C. 467.

[112] *Bellinger v Bellinger* [2003] UKHL 21; [2003] 2 A.C. 467 at [37]. Lord Nicholls gave examples of the breadth of the issues raised at [38]-[49].

[113] See Table 1 at the end of this chapter for a summary of the declarations of incompatibility made up to the end of September 2017. Section 4 of the Joint Committee on Human Rights' *Human Rights Judgments* (HL Paper 130); (HC Paper 1088) (4 March 2015) notes that during the 2010–2015 Parliament, there was a significant downward trend in the numbers of declarations of incompatibility made. There has been a slight increase since then (see Table 1 at the end of this chapter). S. Wilson Stark, "Facing facts: judicial approaches to section 4 of the Human Rights Act 1998" (2017) 133 L.Q.R. 631 argues that the courts should be willing to look beyond the facts of the case before them and consider whether the challenged legislation could have a broader impact which is incompatible with Convention rights.

[114] In Parliament, Lord Irvine LC gave the example of where there was an alternative remedy by way of statutory appeal which could be used rather than the declaration of incompatibility which would place pressure on Parliament to take remedial action (*Hansard*, HL col.546 (18 November 1997)).

validity, continuing operation or enforcement of legislation.[115] The effect of the declaration of incompatibility is therefore to place the onus back on Parliament to decide whether or not to amend the offending provision. Judges have therefore emphasised that in making a declaration of incompatibility, the courts are not in conflict with the will of the legislature, but are simply performing the task which Parliament assigned to them by s.4 of the HRA.[116]

13-049　　Moreover, a declaration of incompatibility is not even binding on the parties to the proceedings in which it is made.[117] A declaration may trigger remedial action under s.10 of the HRA. This is not the only trigger. The other arises where it appears to a Minister or Her Majesty in Council that a provision of UK legislation is incompatible with Convention rights as a result of a decision of the ECtHR involving the UK after the HRA came into force.[118] In either case, or where "he considers that there are compelling reasons" for doing so, the Minister then has a discretion make such amendments by order to the legislation as he considers necessary to remove the incompatibility.[119] As is clear from this, the minister is under no obligation to act on a declaration of incompatibility.[120] Amending legislation has usually been by way of Act of Parliament rather than remedial order.

As David Pannick points out, this explanation does not really make sense since it is only after a declaration has been made that Parliament can take remedial action as envisaged by the Act and such a declaration does not place pressure on Parliament since Parliament has an unreviewable discretion to ignore a declaration (Lester, Pannick and Herberg, *Human Rights Law and Practice* (2009) para.2.4.2, fn.3).

[115] HRA s.4(6)(a).

[116] *R. (on the application of Anderson) v Secretary of State for the Home Department* [2002] UKHL 46; [2003] 1 A.C. 837 at [63] (Lord Hutton). In this case, the HL decided that the Home Secretary's power to set the tariff period for mandatory life prisoners was incompatible with the art.6(1) right to a fair hearing by an independent and impartial tribunal. However, the Minister's power was expressly confirmed by s.29 of the Crime (Sentences) Act 1997 and this could not be read compatibly with the ECHR. Therefore the HL was required to issue a declaration of incompatibility. Similarly, in *R. (on the application of F (A Child)) v Secretary of State for the Home Department* [2010] UKSC 17; [2011] 1 A.C. 331 at [51]-[58] (Lord Phillips), the SC held that the provisions of the Sexual Offences Act 2003 which subjected those convicted of certain sexual offences to indefinite notification requirements were incompatible with art.8 and issued a declaration of incompatibility. The court may express a view in making a declaration as to how the incompatibility can be removed. However, the court will be reluctant to do so where the incompatibility arises from the interaction of different elements of a statutory scheme or where there is likely to be comprehensive legislative reform of the whole area (*R. (on the application of Wright) v Secretary of State for Health* [2009] UKHL 3; [2009] 1 A.C. 739 at [39] (Baroness Hale)). In *R. (on the application of Nicklinson) v Ministry of Justice* [2014] UKSC 38; [2015] A.C. 657, the majority of the nine-member SC held that it would not have been outside the court's institutional power to declare the Suicide Act 1961 s.2 to be incompatible with the ECHR even though the question was one within the UK's margin of appreciation as far as the ECtHR was concerned. However, in a "controversial area raising difficult moral and ethical issues", the court should adopt a "light touch" when reviewing the proportionality of primary legislation (at [112]-[113]). The majority stated that a declaration of incompatibility would not have the effect of forcing Parliament to act, but declined to grant one on the facts. See J. Finnis, "A British 'Convention right' to assistance in suicide?" (2015) 131 L.Q.R. 1. The CA has granted permission for a further judicial review of the position on assisted dying in light of the fact that it is no longer under active consideration by Parliament (*R. (on the application of Conway) v Secretary of State for Justice* [2017] EWCA Civ 275; (2017) 156 B.M.L.R. 169).

[117] HRA s.4(6)(b). This has the effect that damages will not be available against a defendant who has been found to have acted in breach of Convention rights where a declaration has been made.

[118] HRA s.10(1)(b).

[119] HRA s.10(2). Schedule 2 to the HRA makes further provision about remedial orders. Remedial orders are thus a fast-track procedure for removing incompatibilities in legislation by means of the affirmative resolution procedure without having to introduce amending primary legislation.

[120] Lord Irvine LC indicated that where a Minister has made a statement of compatibility under s.19 and a declaration of incompatibility is subsequently granted "it is hard to see how the Minister could withhold remedial action" ("Keynote Address" in Beatson, Forsyth and Hare, *Constitutional Reform*

The HRA gives the Crown the right to intervene in any proceedings where the   **13-050**
court is considering making a declaration of incompatibility.[121] The court will give
notice to the Crown in any case where it is considering whether or not to make a
declaration of incompatibility. In response, the relevant representative of the Crown
is entitled to be joined to the proceedings.[122]

Ministerial statement of compatibility

The requirement that the minister in charge of a Bill in either House of Parlia-   **13-051**
ment shall make a statement of compatibility before the second reading of the Bill
is designed to ensure that adequate consideration is given to the impact the Bill may
have on Convention rights.[123] The statement must be in writing and published in
whatever manner the minister considers appropriate.[124] A court is, of course, not
bound by any such statement.[125] Equally, there can be no liability under the HRA
or otherwise arising out of the nature of such a statement.[126] Parliamentary scrutiny
is further informed by the work of the Joint Committee on Human Rights.[127]

Standing under the HRA

The HRA repeats the formulation of the test for standing under the ECHR itself.   **13-052**
That is, an individual may only rely on the ECHR if he is or would be a victim of
the unlawful act in question.[128] Section 7 of the HRA also makes clear that a victim
so defined may rely on their Convention rights either in proceedings they institute
in the appropriate court or tribunal[129] or in any legal proceedings. This latter formula
covers proceedings which are instituted by a public authority where the defendant
may bring a collateral challenge to the lawfulness of the statute under which he is

---

[121] (1998), p.4).
[121] HRA s.5.
[122] HRA s.5(1) and (2).
[123] HRA s.19. This provision is similar to the requirement under s.7 of the New Zealand Bill of Rights
Act 1990 to bring to the attention of the House of Representatives any provision of a Bill which appears to be inconsistent with the rights and freedoms contained in the Bill of Rights Act. The statement has been referred to as a "strong spur to the courts to find a means of construing statutes
compatibly with the Convention" (Lord Irvine of Lairg, "The Development of Human Rights in
Britain under an Incorporated Convention on Human Rights" [1998] P.L. 221, 228).
[124] The Statement will usually be referred to in the Explanatory Notes which have accompanied all
Government Bills since 1998. They are available at *http://www.parliament.uk* (Bills) and
http://www.legislation.hmso.gov.uk (Acts). Although they do not form part of the Act, the Notes are
admissible in legal proceedings: *Wilson v First County Trust Ltd (No.2)* [2003] UKHL 40; [2004] 1
A.C. 816 at [64] (Lord Nicholls).
[125] *R. v A* [2001] UKHL 25; [2002] 1 A.C. 45 at [69] (Lord Hope). The decision to proceed with legislation and to make a statement under s.19(1)(b) of the HRA that the Government intended to introduce
the legislation while acknowledging the doubt about whether the ban on the broadcasting of political advertising was consistent with art.10 of the ECHR was held to be an additional reason to attach weight to Parliament's view in *R. (Animal Defenders International) v Secretary of State for
Culture, Media and Sport* [2008] UKHL 15; [2008] 1 A.C. 1312 at [33] (Lord Bingham). See fn.257
below.
[126] The making of the statement will fall within the immunity for those "exercising functions in connection with proceedings in Parliament" in s.6(3).
[127] The JCHR was established in 2001 to consider matters relating to human rights generally, proposals for remedial orders and whether attention should be drawn to them. The Committee's reports are
available at *http://www.parliament.uk*. See D. Feldman, "The Impact of Human Rights on the UK
Legislative Process" (2004) 25 Statute L.R. 91.
[128] See 2-048.
[129] CPR r.7.11 states that proceedings under s.7(1)(a) concerning a judicial act must be brought in the
High Court, but that any other claim under this sub-section may be brought in any appropriate court.

charged[130] or where a Convention point is taken on appeal.[131] There is authority from other legal systems that the court may modify the ordinary costs rules in order not to deter individuals from asserting their Convention rights.[132]

Time limits

13-053   Proceedings brought against a public authority under s.7(1)(a) of the HRA must be instituted before the end of the period of one year beginning with the date on which the act complained of took place or such longer period as the court considers equitable having regard to all the circumstances.[133] This provision is subject to any rule imposing a stricter time limit. Given the shorter and less flexible three-month time limit for judicial review generally, there is a risk of inconsistency.[134]

Remedies

13-054   Where the court finds that an act of the public authority is unlawful by virtue of s.6(1) of the HRA, it may grant such relief or remedy (or make such order) within its powers as it considers to be just and appropriate.[135] Only those courts or tribunals which have the power to award damages or order the payment of compensation in civil proceedings may do so.[136] As such, the Crown Court would not be able to award damages for a breach of Convention rights. Further, awards of damages are only to be made where, taking account of all the circumstances, the award is necessary to afford just satisfaction to the person in whose favour it is made.[137] In deciding whether to award damages and the amount of such damages, the court must take into account the principles applied by the ECtHR when deciding whether to award compensation under art.41 ECHR. The principles governing the award of damages under the HRA are considered in Chapter 19.[138]

13-055   Applications for damages in relation to judicial acts must be brought by way of appeal or a claim for judicial review.[139] In any event, no award of damages may be made in relation to a judicial act where the act was done in good faith.[140] The exception is for compensation required by art.5(5) (the right to compensation for arrest

---

[130] On collateral challenge in judicial review proceedings generally, see 3-112.

[131] HRA s.7(6).

[132] See Ch.16.

[133] HRA s.7(5). While not wishing to limit the factors which could be taken into account when exercising the court's discretion to extend time, the Court of Appeal has indicated that the length of, and reasons for, the delay, the impact of such delay on the cogency of evidence, whether the defendant might have contributed to such delay and the duration of any disability under which the claimant may have been labouring when the cause of action accrued will be relevant in certain cases (*Dunn v Parole Board* [2008] EWCA Civ 374; [2009] 1 W.L.R. 728 at [30]-[33] and [39] (Thomas LJ). A claimant cannot circumvent the one-year time limit by combining a claim under the HRA with another claim with a longer limitation period (*Somerville v Scottish Ministers* [2007] UKHL 44; [2008] SC(HL) 45 at [71] (Lord Scott) and at [172]-[175] (Lord Mance)). In *Rabone v Pennine Care NHS Trust* [2012] UKSC 2; [2012] 2 A.C. 72 at [74]-[79] (Lord Dyson), the SC extended time by four months because of the strength of the claim that art.2 had been breached, the absence of any suggestion that the cogency of evidence had been affected by any delay or of any other prejudice to the defendant and because the claimants had acted reasonably in waiting for an internal report into the incident.

[134] See 16-055.

[135] HRA s.8(1).

[136] HRA s.8(2).

[137] HRA s.8(3).

[138] See 19-081.

[139] HRA s.9(1). This does not expand the availability of judicial review in relation to court decisions (s.9(2)). On the availability of judicial review of court decisions, see 3-008.

[140] The purpose of s.9(3) was to preserve the effect of s.2(5) of the Crown Proceedings Act 1947 in rela-

or detention in breach of the ECHR).[141] In relation to compensation under art.5(5), an award can only be made against the Crown and then only if the responsible Minister is joined to the proceedings.[142]

Safeguarding existing rights

Section 11 of the HRA makes clear that reliance on a Convention right does not restrict any other right conferred upon an individual under United Kingdom law or his right to bring any proceedings independently of the terms of the HRA.[143]   **13-056**

Special regard to the freedoms of expression and of thought, conscience and religion

Sections 12 and 13 of the HRA contain provisions which make no significant dif-   **13-057**
ference to the scope of Convention rights and were inserted in the course of the parliamentary debates as a result of lobbying by the Press Complaints Commission and various religious bodies.[144] They require the courts to pay particular regard to the rights contained in arts 10 (freedom of expression) and 9 (freedom of thought, conscience and religion) where the matter before them raises issues under these articles.[145] Section 12 goes further and states that no relief which might affect the Convention right to freedom of expression shall be granted unless the respondent to the application is present in court, the applicant has taken appropriate steps to notify the respondent or there are compelling reasons why he should not be notified. Further, no such relief shall be granted which restrains publication before trial unless the court is satisfied that the applicant is likely to establish that the publication should not be allowed. Finally, in relation to journalistic, literary or artistic material, the court is to have regard to the extent to which the material has, or is about to, become available to the public or it is, or would be, in the public interest for the material to be published.[146] It is doubtful whether these sections confer any special preferred status on those rights.

The domestic effect of derogations and reservations

Section 1(2) of the HRA provides that Convention rights should have effect   **13-058**
subject to any designated derogations or reservations.[147] A designated derogation is defined as any derogation designated for the purposes of the HRA in an order

tion to claims under the HRA (*Begraj v Secretary of State for Justice* [2015] EWHC 250 (QB) at [20]).

[141] HRA s.9(3).
[142] HRA s.9(4) and (5).
[143] The provision fulfils a similar purpose to art.53 ECHR.
[144] *Cream Holdings v Banerjee* [2004] UKHL 44; [2005] 1 A.C. 253.
[145] HRA s.12(4) and 13(1).
[146] HRA s.12(2)–(4). Lord Neuberger MR gave general guidance about cases involving public figures and the national media in *JIH v News Group Newspapers Ltd* [2011] EWCA Civ 42; [2011] 1 W.L.R. 1645 at [19]-[25], emphasising the cardinal importance of open justice and that any order of anonymity must be no more than is strictly necessary to protect art.8 rights. In *PJS v News Group Newspapers Ltd* [2016] UKSC 26; [2016] A.C. 1081 at [33]–[35], the SC granted an injunction and held that the court should have regard to the qualitative difference between the availability of material on the internet and its widespread dissemination in hard copy (and on newspaper websites) by the English media.
[147] See 13-023.

made by the Secretary of State for Justice.[148] A designated reservation means the existing reservation to art.2 of the First Protocol (the right to education) or any other reservation designated by the Secretary of State by order.[149] The aim is to ensure that the liability of public authorities under the HRA reflects that of the United Kingdom before the ECtHR. The HRA expressly reserves the right of the Secretary of State to make a fresh designation or reservation order (which may be done in anticipation of a proposed derogation by the United Kingdom).[150] Derogations are intended to be temporary in nature and a designation order will lapse within five years of it being made unless renewed by order under the affirmative resolution procedure.[151] The Secretary of State shall also review any designated reservation on a five-yearly basis.[152]

Territorial and temporal scope of the HRA

13-059   One matter not addressed in the HRA is its territorial scope.[153] This matter is considered more fully in Chapter 3.[154] Where proceedings are brought against him by a public authority, an individual may rely on Convention rights whenever the act in question took place. Otherwise, an individual may only rely on their Convention rights in relation to an act occurring after 2 October 2000.[155]

---

[148]   HRA s.14(1).

[149]   HRA s.15(1).

[150]   HRA s.14(4) and (6) and 15(4).

[151]   HRA s.16(1) and 20(4).

[152]   HRA s.17.

[153]   HRA s.22(6) provides that the HRA applies to Northern Ireland. It does not apply to Jersey, Guernsey or the Isle of Man (which have adopted legislation broadly similar to the HRA). In *R. (on the application of Barclay) v Secretary of State for Justice* [2014] UKSC 54; [2015] A.C. 276 at [36], the SC held that it was not for a UK court to read down Channel Island legislation to make it compatible with Convention rights. The HRA does not apply to the Channel Islands. An Order in Council made in exercise of the royal prerogative did not fall within the definition of primary legislation in s.2(1) of the HRA.

[154]   See 3-099.

[155]   HRA s.22(4). The most extensive discussion of the (limited) retrospective effect of the HRA is in *Wilson v First County Trust Ltd (No.2)* [2003] UKHL 40; [2004] 1 A.C. 816 at [19]-[21], [98]-[99], [160] and [212]. The HL there held that there was no indication that the HRA was intended to have retrospective effect and so the interpretative obligation under s.3 was not relevant to the application of the Consumer Credit Act 1974 to an agreement entered into before the HRA came into force. The question of retrospective effect was stated to be one of degree: the greater the unfairness or effect on vested rights, the clearer an expression of Parliament's intention which will be required. See further, *R. (on the application of Hurst) v London Northern District Coroner* [2007] UKHL 13; [2007] 2 A.C. 189 at [53]-[59] (Lord Brown of Eaton-under-Heywood), in which the HL declined to require a coroner to exercise his discretion in accordance with art.2 in relation to an inquest into a death occurring before the HRA came into force. See also *Smith v Carillion (JM) Ltd* [2015] EWCA Civ 209; [2015] I.R.L.R. 467 at [43]. There, all the impugned acts occurred prior to the coming into force of the HRA. An argument that the acts were "continuing" was rejected on the facts. In *R (Keyu) v Secretary of State for Foreign and Commonwealth Affairs & Secretary of State for Defence* [2015] UKSC 69; [2016] A.C. 1355 at [246]–[249], the SC considered that *Re McKerr* [2004] UKHL 12; [2004] 1 W.L.R. 807 remained good law, as such the HRA did not have retrospective effect. However, the impact of the ECtHR's decision in *Šilih v Slovenia* (2009) 49 E.H.R.R. 37 on art.2 is significant. In *Re McCaughey* [2011] UKSC 20; [2012] 1 A.C. 725 at [61]–[63], the SC held that *Šilih* had extended the scope of the free-standing and autonomous procedural obligation in art.2 where death occurred before the court's assumption of jurisdiction and if significant procedural steps required by art.2 took place after that date. In *McCaughey*, therefore, although the deaths took place in 1990, an inquest in 2009 was required to comply with the requirements of art.2.

The content of Convention rights under the HRA

As stated above, Convention rights under the HRA fall into three groups: **13-060**
absolute, limited and qualified rights. These are addressed in turn.

Absolute rights

As stated above, absolute rights are those which are not qualified and from which **13-061**
the State cannot derogate. They include the right to life (art.2), the right to be free
from torture, inhuman and degrading treatment or punishment (art.3), the prohibition on slavery (art.4) and the ban on punishment without lawful authority (art.7).

The right to life   Article 2(1) provides that everyone's life shall be protected by **13-062**
law.[156] Despite its status as an absolute right, art.2(2) provides exceptions where the
use of force is strictly necessary in defence of any person from unlawful violence,
in order to effect a lawful arrest or prevent escape from lawful detention or in action taken to quell a riot or insurrection. Recent controversy has arisen in relation
to the beginning and the end of life. For some time, it appeared clear that art.2 could
not be invoked to protect the interests of a foetus.[157] However, as a result of more
recent decisions, it may be that the Strasbourg court will extend some protection
to the unborn in certain circumstances.[158] On the other hand, it is now established
that art.2 does not protect the right to die.[159]

The right to life imposes a number of positive obligations on State Parties which **13-063**

---

[156] Article 2(1) provides an exception for the death penalty which is no longer relevant given the Sixth
and Thirteenth Protocols.

[157] *Paton v United Kingdom* (1981) 3 E.H.R.R. 408 at [22]-[23].

[158] In a much criticised decision, the Grand Chamber refused to decide the matter in *Vo v France* (2005)
40 E.H.R.R. 12 at [82]. The ECtHR has emphasised that the question of when life begins for the
purposes of art.2 is a matter for domestic law (*Evans v UK* (2006) 43 E.H.R.R. 21 at [45]-[46]). In
Evans v UK (2008) 46 E.H.R.R. 34 at [54]-[56]). In Evans, the Grand Chamber held that the provisions of the Human Fertilisation and Embryology Act 1990 which required that embryos should be
destroyed on withdrawal of consent by either potential parent did not violate art.2 since the embryos
did not have the right to life under domestic law.

[159] In *Pretty v UK* (2002) 35 E.H.R.R. 1 at [38]-[40], the ECtHR followed the reasoning of the HL in
rejecting a challenge by the victim of a degenerative disease to the Director of Public Prosecution's
decision not to offer an assurance not to prosecute the victim's husband if he assisted her suicide.
The HL decision is *R. (on the application of Pretty) v DPP* [2001] UKHL 61; [2002] 1 A.C. 800.
The HL subsequently departed from its position in Pretty and required the Director of Public Prosecutions to clarify prosecution policy on assisted suicide on the grounds that the uncertainty in the current policy did not satisfy the requirements of art.8(2) (see *R. (on the application of Purdy) v Director of Public Prosecutions* [2009] UKHL 45; [2009] 1 Cr.App.R. 32 at [54]-[56]). The CPS
published its new policy on assisted suicide in February 2010
(*http://www.cps.gov.uk/publications/prosecution/assisted_suicide_policy.html* [Accessed 31 October
2017]), updated in October 2014. In *R. (on the application of Nicklinson) v Ministry of Justice* [2014]
UKSC 38; [2015] A.C. 657 at [141], [145], [249], [278], the SC declined to go further and tell the
Director of Public Prosecutions what her policy should actually contain. An application to the ECtHR
(*Nicklinson and Lamb v the United Kingdom* (App. nos. 2478/15 and 1787/15) was declared inadmissible on the basis that art.8 did not impose procedural obligations requiring domestic courts to examine
the merits of a challenge brought in respect of primary legislation; to do so would deny the domestic court the opportunity to conclude, as did the SC, that Parliament is best placed to take a decision
on certain issues. In any case, the ECtHR held that the SC had considered the substance of Ms Nicklinson's claim. Lord Falconer's (private members') Assisted Dying Bill [HL] 2014–2015 reached the
second reading stage before running out of time. The second reading of Lord Falconer's re-tabled
Assisted Dying Bill [HL] 2015–2016 is yet to be scheduled. Robert Marris MP's (private members')
Assisted Dying (No.2) Bill 2015–16 was rejected by the House of Commons at the second reading
debate on 11 September 2015 by 330 votes to 112. See also *Lambert v France* (2016) 62 E.H.R.R.
2.

go beyond a requirement to refrain from action which may cause death. These obligations have both substantive and procedural elements. Substantively, the State has a general duty to have in place an effective system of deterrence against threats to life and may further be required to take reasonable steps to protect an individual from the criminal acts of another private individual where there is a real and immediate risk to life.[160] The latter is the so-called operational duty under art.2 and is owed to those over whom the state has assumed responsibility (such as prisoners, military conscripts or psychiatric patients detained in a public hospital) and who are particularly vulnerable (because of their youth or mental state).[161] The operational duty may extend to the prevention of suicide or accidental deaths in some situations.[162] The State may also be required to provide life-sustaining treatment.[163] Procedurally, art.2 requires that there should be an adequate official investigation into deaths which occur as a result of force used by the State or in other cases giving rise to a presumption of breach of the substantive obligation in art.2.[164] The state

---

[160]   *Osman v United Kingdom* (2000) 29 E.H.R.R. 245 at [115]–[116]. The ECtHR held in *Osman* that it is sufficient for an applicant to show that the authorities did not do all that could reasonably be expected of them to avoid a real and immediate risk to life of which they were, or ought to have been, aware. In *Van Colle v Chief Constable of Hertfordshire Police* [2008] UKHL 50; [2009] 1 A.C. 225 at [36] (Lord Bingham), the House of Lords overturned an award of damages to the family of a victim who was a witness against the murderer on the basis that the latter's previous offences were relatively minor and did not give rise to a sufficiently real risk at the relevant time. This result was affirmed by the ECtHR in *Van Colle v United Kingdom* (2013) 56 E.H.R.R. 23 at [98]–[105]. There is no requirement that there should be a risk to the life of an identified or identifiable individual; it is sufficient, for example, that individuals were known to be in the vicinity of the street where disorder was being caused (*Sarjantson v Chief Constable of Humberside Police* [2013] EWCA Civ 1252; [2014] Q.B. 411 at [22]–[36]).

[161]   Lord Dyson summarises the doctrine in *Rabone v Pennine Care NHS Trust* [2012] UKSC 2; [2012] 2 A.C. 72 at [15]–[25].

[162]   The HL provided guidance on the extent of health authorities' duties to protect the lives of patients in hospital (particularly the most vulnerable) in *Savage v South Essex Partnership NHS Foundation Trust* [2008] UKHL 74; [2009] 1 A.C. 681 at [67]–[72] (Lord Rodger), and [97]–[100] (Baroness Hale). The HL distinguished cases of mere negligence where appropriate general measures are in place which would not breach art.2. In *Rabone* [2012] UKSC 2; [2012] 2 A.C. 72 at [25]–[34] (Lord Dyson), the SC held that the operational duty under art.2 to protect life was engaged in relation to the suicide of a voluntary mental health patient while on a home visit. The patient had been particularly vulnerable and the risk of suicide was one which no reasonable psychiatric practitioner would have ignored. The court further held that the family's acceptance of compensation did not prevent a claim under art.2 (which was to deal with non-pecuniary losses) and that family members were victims in their own right for the purposes of the HRA (at [46]–[50] (Lord Dyson)). In relation to accidental deaths, Turkey was held to have breached art.2 in failing to take adequate measures of waste storage or to provide suitable information to slum dwellers about the dangers they faced in inhabiting a rubbish tip when a landslide caused the death of the applicant's relatives (*Oneryildiz v Turkey* (2005) 41 E.H.R.R. 20 at [75] and [101]). In *Budayeva v Russia* (App. No.15339/02) (20 March 2008) at [147]–[165], the ECtHR found substantive and procedural violations of art.2 since the state had been warned of the risk of mud slides (which killed some of the applicants' relatives or destroyed their homes), but had taken no steps to prevent the harm and had dispensed with the criminal investigation too early and prevented the inquest from apportioning responsibility. In *Smith v Ministry of Defence* [2013] UKSC 41; [2014] A.C. 52, the SC permitted claims of a breach of the positive substantive obligation in art.2 to proceed to trial. The claims related to the deaths of British servicemen in Iraq from improvised explosive devices while they were travelling in modified Land Rover vehicles. There was no evidence of systemic failures which led to the high level of suicides at HMP Woodhill (*R. (on the application of Scarfe) v Secretary of State for Justice* [2017] EWHC 1194 (Admin)).

[163]   *NHS Trust A v M* [2001] Fam. 348 at [37] (Dame Elizabeth Butler-Sloss P.), concerning a hospital's obligations towards a patient in a permanent vegetative state. Domestic law on withdrawing life-sustaining treatment to a child against his parents' wishes was found to be compatible with art.2 (and art.8) in *Gard v United Kingdom* (2017) 65 E.H.R.R. SE9.

[164]   *R. (on the application of Gentle) v Prime Minister* [2008] UKHL 20; [2008] 1 A.C. 1356 at [6] (Lord

retains a certain degree of flexibility in the nature of the investigation, but it must be independent, permit some participation by the victim's relatives, identify and allow for the punishment of those found to have caused unlawful death and be prompt.[165]

Bingham). There is no obligation under art.2 to hold an inquiry into the legality of a war in which the lives of British citizens were lost (*Gentle*, at [8]-[10] (Lord Bingham)). For this reason, it is not necessary that there should be an inquiry into the deaths of all servicemen who are on active service. However, on the facts of *Smith*, there was a suggestion that there may have been a systemic failure to take adequate measures to deal with the extreme heat to which servicemen were subject in Iraq (*R. (on the application of Smith) v Oxfordshire Assistant Deputy Coroner* [2010] UKSC 29; [2011] 1 A.C. 1 at [84]-[7] (Lord Phillips)). Examples of where an art.2 investigation was required include: *R. (on the application of Amin) v Secretary of State for the Home Department* [2003] UKHL 51; [2004] 1 A.C. 653 at [30]-[33] (Lord Bingham) (concerning the liability of a prison for a death in custody caused by a fellow prisoner of known racist tendencies); *R. (on the application of Middleton) v HM Coroner for Western District of Somerset* [2004] UKHL 10; [2004] 2 A.C. 182 at [30]-[35] (Lord Bingham) (a prisoner who hanged himself while in custody); and *Opuz v Turkey* (2010) 50 E.H.R.R. 28 at [128]-[153] (concerning the murder of the applicant's mother by her husband after a sustained period of serious violence against her and her mother of which the authorities were aware). See also *Jaloud v Netherlands* (2015) 60 E.H.R.R. 29 (concerning the failure effectively to investigate the shooting of an Iraqi civilian potentially caused by troops from the Netherlands). The Lord Chancellor's Exceptional Funding Guidance (Inquests) was declared unlawful for failing to reflect that the investigatory duty may arise in all cases involving compulsorily detained psychiatric patients who committed suicide even in the absence of evidence of a substantive breach of art.2 in *R. (on the application of Letts) v Lord Chancellor* [2015] EWHC 402 (Admin); [2015] 1 W.L.R. 4497. In *Al-Saadoon v Secretary of State for Defence* [2016] EWCA Civ 811; [2017] 2 W.L.R. 219; [2017] Q.B. 1015 at [69], the CA (overturning the decision at first instance) held that the use of lethal or potentially lethal force was not sufficient to establish extra-territorial jurisdiction in the absence of an element of control over the individual prior to the use of force. Further, the CA held that the investigative duty under art.3 is triggered by an arguable claim that the individual has suffered treatment infringing art.3, not merely a breach of the Soering obligation not to send an individual to another state where there are substantial grounds for believing that he would face a real risk of being subject to torture or other prohibited treatment (at [124]-[125]).

[165] *Edwards v United Kingdom* (2002) 35 E.H.R.R. 19 at [69]-[73]. Lord Phillips identified six essential ingredients for an investigation. To comply with art.2, it must: be initiated by the state itself; be prompt and carried out with reasonable expedition; be effective; be carried out by a person who is independent of those implicated in the events being investigated; there must be a sufficient element of public scrutiny of the investigation or its results; and the next of kin of the victim must be involved in the procedure to the extent necessary to safeguard his or her legitimate interests (*R. (on the application of L (A Patient)) v Secretary of State for Justice* [2008] UKHL 68; [2009] 1 A.C. 588 at [35]). The case concerned an individual who attempted suicide while in custody and was left with a serious injury as a result (which carries a reduced art.2 obligation). See further, *Ramsahai v Netherlands* (2008) 46 E.H.R.R. 43 at [326]-[335], in which the ECtHR found a number of failures in relation to the procedural obligation under art.2, including the fact that the initial 15 hours of the investigation were carried out by the police and the officers involved in the fatal incident were not separated. The procedural obligation is "a detachable obligation" and applies to an inquiry which took place after the entry into force of the HRA even if the death occurred before it (*Re McCaughey* [2011] UKSC 20; [2012] 1 A.C. 725 at [50]-[53] (Lord Phillips)).There was an insufficient connection between the ECHR and the Russian state at the time to justify a finding of a breach of art.2 in relation to the Katyn massacre in 1940 (*Janowiec v Russia* (App. No.55508/07) (16 April 2012) at [129]-[142]). In *R. (Keyu) v Secretary of State for Foreign and Commonwealth Affairs & Secretary of State for Defence* [2015] UKSC 69; [2015] 3 W.L.R. 1665 at [71]-[89], the SC rejected the application for judicial review of the Minister's decision not to order an inquiry into the deaths in 1948 of 24 civilians at the hands of British troops in what was then the State of Malaya. However, the SC held that while the Convention did not generally have retrospective effect, the European court's jurisprudence (in particular, *Janowiec v Russia* (2014) 58 E.H.R.R. 30) obliged a state to investigate a death which had occurred before the critical date, namely the date of entry into force of the Convention with respect to that state, where (i) there existed relevant acts or omissions after the critical date; and (ii) there was a genuine connection between the death, as the triggering event, and the critical date, so long as the period between the two did not exceed 10 years. The first criterion was fulfilled as there had been no full or public investigation prior to 1970 (and the critical date was

13-064   The circumstances in which the State may use lethal force are limited by the requirements of strict necessity. Thus, it will not be justified to use lethal force to effect an arrest just because the individual may otherwise escape apprehension if the fugitive poses no threat to life or limb and is not suspected of committing a violent offence.[166] Article 2 also requires the court to examine the circumstances surrounding the use of force and to enquire whether better intelligence or earlier intervention could have averted the situation in which force had to be used.[167] However, art.2 does not require the court to substitute its judgment for that of the officer on the scene.[168]

The right to be free from torture, inhuman and degrading treatment or punish-
13-065   **ment**   Article 3 provides that no one shall be subjected to torture or to inhuman or degrading treatment or punishment. Article 3 is (like art.2) one of the fundamental provisions of the ECHR. Also like art.2, art.3 contains negative and positive obligations and has a procedural aspect. Treatment must attain a minimum level of severity to fall within art.3 and there is a hierarchy of treatment within the article. Torture is the most severe form and requires deliberate inhuman treatment causing very serious and cruel suffering. Inhuman treatment causes intense physical and mental suffering. Degrading treatment arouses feelings of fear, anguish and inferiority in the victim which are capable to humiliating and debasing the victim and possibly of breaking his physical or moral resistance.[169] Treatment may also be regarded as inhuman or degrading where, to a seriously detrimental extent, it denies

---

1966 when the UK had first recognised the right of individual petition), but more than 10 years had passed between the deaths and 1966. In *R. (on the application of Litvinenko) v Secretary of State for the Home Department* [2014] EWHC 194 (Admin); [2014] H.R.L.R. 6 at [50]–[54], the DC found that the extensive police investigation into Mr Litvinenko's death was sufficient to fulfil art.2. In *Mocanu v Romania* (2015) 60 E.H.R.R. 19, an investigation into civilian deaths following a state crackdown on demonstrations was held to be inadequate where it had been entrusted to military prosecutors, who lacked objectivity and impartiality.

[166] *Nachova v Bulgaria* (2006) 42 E.H.R.R. 43 at [93]–[109].

[167] *McCann v United Kingdom* (1995) 21 E.H.R.R. 97 at [202]–[214] concerning the deaths of three IRA members who were shot by British soldiers on Gibraltar. See now, *Finogenov v Russia* (App. No.18299/03) (20 December 2011) at [243], [266]–[268] and [277]–[282]) concerning the Moscow hostage crisis in 2002 which left more than a hundred hostages dead (the Court held that lethal force was justified, but there was a breach of art.2 in relation to both the poor planning of the rescue operation and the failure to hold an effective official investigation) and *Tagayeva v Russia* (App. No.26562/07) (13 April 2017) concerning the Beslan school hostage crisis. In *Giuliani v Italy* (2011) 52 E.H.R.R. 3 at [174]–[262] and [298]–[326], the ECtHR found no breach of the substantive (in relation to the use of force itself or the prior planning for the demonstration) or procedural aspects of art.2 in relation to the shooting of the applicants' relative by police while he was protesting at the G8 summit in Genoa in 2001.

[168] In *Bubbins v United Kingdom* (2005) 41 E.H.R.R. 24 at [138]–[140], the ECtHR found that there was no violation of art.2 where a police officer shot dead an individual who had pulled a replica gun. See also *Al-Saadoon v Secretary of State for Defence* [2015] EWHC 715 (Admin); [2015] 3 W.L.R. 503 at [111] which holds that a killing may be lawful under art.2 even if it is not strictly necessary for the purposes of art.2(2)(a)–(c) if it is authorised under international humanitarian law. This issue was not addressed by the CA at [2016] EWCA Civ 811; [2017] Q.B. 1015.

[169] *Ireland v United Kingdom* (1979-80) 2 E.H.R.R. 25 at [162]–[181]. Ireland concerned the use of interrogation techniques by the UK security forces against suspected terrorists. The techniques included wall-standing, hooding, subjection to continuous noise and food and sleep deprivation. In the circumstances, these were found to constitute degrading treatment, but not torture. The ECtHR has held that acts previously classified inhuman or degrading treatment may be classified as torture in the future (*Selmouni v France* (2000) 29 E.H.R.R. 403 at [101]). In *Selmouni*, the victim was found to have been tortured where he was severely beaten, threatened with a blowtorch and urinated on by police. Rape can also amount to torture: *Aydin (Sukran) v Turkey* (1998) 25 E.H.R.R. 251. In *Cestaro v Italy* (App. No. 6884/11) (7 April 2015), the ECtHR found that repeated kicks and beatings with a baton, causing multiple fractures and a permanent impediment in the applicant's right

the most basic needs of any human being.[170] The court will also consider the duration of any such treatment and the effect on the particular victim (for example, in relation to their age and health).[171] Conditions of detention may be found to constitute degrading treatment.[172] Because of its particular associations, race discrimination may also constitute degrading treatment in some situations.[173]

---

arm and right leg amounted to torture. In *Bataliny v Russia* (App. No. 10060/07) (23 July 2015), forced psychiatric treatment in the absence of an established medical need and being included in scientific research into a new antipsychotic drug (without consent) amounted to inhuman and degrading treatment. In *NXB v Crown Prosecution Service* [2015] EWHC 631 (QB) at [79], the court entertained the possibility of a breach of art.3 occasioned by a decision to withdraw a prosecution for sexual assault against a minor, although on the facts no breach was found. In *Blokhin v Russia* (App. No. 47152/06) (23 March 2016), inadequacy of medical assessment and treatment in juvenile detention amounted to inhuman and degrading treatment.

[170] *R. (on the application Limbuela) v Secretary of State for the Home Department* [2005] UKHL 66; [2006] 1 A.C. 396 at [7] (Lord Bingham of Cornhill). In that case, the HL held that statutory provisions which prevented the state from providing welfare benefits to asylum seekers in certain circumstances could breach art.3. In cases where the individual is reduced to sleeping in the street, lacks nourishment or is unable to maintain basic requirements of hygiene, there is likely to be a violation of art.3. See S. Fredman, "Human Rights Transformed: Positive Duties and Positive Rights" [2006] P.L. 498. The ECtHR has now adopted a similar position (*MSS v Belgium* (2011) 53 E.H.R.R. 2 at [250]–[264]). It was accepted in *E v Chief Constable of the RUC* [2008] UKHL 66; [2009] 1 A.C. 536 at [43] (Lord Carswell) that sectarian abuse and the throwing of missiles could constitute inhuman or degrading treatment of school children. However, there was no breach of art.3 on the facts as the police had discharged their obligations to take all reasonable steps to avoid it.

[171] *Pretty* [2001] UKHL 61; [2002]1 A.C. 800 at [52]. It was degrading treatment in breach of art.3 to detain a man suffering from severe psychiatric problems in police custody without making any provision for his mental condition (*MS v United Kingdom* (App. No.24527/08) (3 May 2012) at [38]–[46]. In *DD v Secretary of State for the Home Department* [2015] EWHC 1681 (Admin), it was held that the requirement to wear an electronic monitoring tag pursuant to a terrorism prevention and investigation measure had become a violation of the subject's art.3 rights given a deterioration in his mental health and paranoid belief that the tag contained a bomb. The ECtHR has also held that particular importance should be attached to the increased vulnerability of asylum seekers. In *V.M. v Belgium* (2017) 65 E.H.R.R. 14 it was held that conditions of extreme poverty faced by a family of asylum seekers constituted a violation of art.3 (inhuman or degrading treatment). In *Razzakov v Russia* (2017) 65 E.H.R.R. 10 it was held that the applicant's vulnerability had been exacerbated by the fact that he was a foreigner who understood little Russian. In *Korneykova and Korneykov v Ukraine* (2017) 64 E.H.R.R. 24, it was held that unjustified restraint of a prisoner who had just given birth and was therefore "particularly sensitive" amounted to inhuman and degrading treatment, and that having regard to her son's young age, the failure to ensure his medical monitoring also amounted to a breach of art.3 in his case.

[172] For example, the detention of a severely disabled person in extremely cold and insanitary conditions (which carried a risk of physical harm) was held to breach art.3 in *Price v United Kingdom* (2002) 34 E.H.R.R. 53 at [30]. The practice of slopping out in prison when there was no access to lavatory facilities was held not to constitute degrading treatment in *Grant v Ministry of Justice* [2011] EWHC 3379 (QB) at [31]–[79] (Hickinbottom J). The ECtHR took the opportunity in *Mursic v Croatia* (2017) 65 E.H.R.R.1 to clarify its previous doctrine on the minimum personal space permitted to prison detainees in multi-occupancy accommodation: the minimum standard is three square metres. In *Vinter v UK* (2016) 63 E.H.R.R. 1 at [110]–[115], the ECtHR held that it was a breach of art.3 to impose whole life sentences on prisoners which only permitted release on compassionate grounds at the discretion of the Secretary of State. In *Re Attorney General's Reference (No.69 of 2013)* [2014] EWCA Crim 188; [2014] 1 W.L.R. 3964 at [25]–[36], a five-person CA held that, despite Vinter, such sentences were still permitted in exceptional cases and that the circumstances in which continued detention could be reviewed were sufficiently clear and had to be read consistently with art.3. In *Hutchinson v UK* (App. No. 57592/08) (17 January 2017), [71]–[74], the Grand Chamber of the ECtHR accepted the CA's interpretation of national law as definitive and that the UK's system of reviewing whole-life sentences complied with art.3. In *Elashmawy v Italy* [2015] EWHC 28 (Admin), the court set out the principles applicable to an alleged violation of art.3 deriving from prison conditions in another contracting state. In *Murray v the Netherlands* [2017] 64 E.H.R.R. 3 at [125]–[127], the applicant's life sentence was found to be de facto irreducible, and therefore in breach of art.3, where a lack of any kind of treatment or assessment of treatment needs

13-066   The positive obligations to which art.3 gives rise have substantive and procedural elements. The UK has been found in breach of its positive obligations in failing to protect children from sustained abuse and neglect of which the local authority was aware.[174] The risk of treatment in breach of art.3 will also engage the State's responsibility where it may occur abroad if an individual is removed from the United Kingdom.[175] Where the source of harm is a non-state actor, the individual will also be required to demonstrate that the foreign state has failed to provide a reasonable level of protection against such harm.[176] A breach of art.3 may arise from the suffering inherent in certain forms of illness where the treatment afforded by the State exacerbates it.[177] There is also a procedural obligation on the State to carry out an effective official investigation into plausible allegations of a breach of art.3 by State actors.[178] Domestic courts have drawn on art.3 in determining whether

---

for his mental condition rendered his rehabilitation impossible. The ECtHR held that there was no breach of art.3 in extraditing prisoners to the USA where they would face detention in very high security facilities (including periods of solitary confinement) (*Ahmad v United Kingdom* (2013) 56 E.H.R.R. 1 at [181]–[224]). The ECtHR found a breach in the case of the extradition of an individual with severe mental health problems (*Aswat v United Kingdom* (2014) 58 E.H.R.R. 1). The Grand Chamber has decided that the post-Vinter case law does not constitute new information such that it should revisit its earlier decision not to interfere with extradition to the US with the risk of life imprisonment without parole in *Harkins v UK* (App. No. 71537/14) (10 July 2017).

[173] *East African Asians v United Kingdom* (1981) 3 E.H.R.R. 76 at [207]–[208]. In a possible extension of this principle, in *Identoba v Georgia* (2015) 39 B.H.R.C. 510 at [65], the ECtHR held, citing East African Asians in the context of homophobic, rather than racist, remarks, that "Discriminatory remarks and insults must in any event be considered as an aggravating factor when considering a given instance of ill-treatment in the light of Article 3."

[174] *Z v United Kingdom* (2002) 34 E.H.R.R. 3 at [73]-[75].

[175] *Chahal v United Kingdom* (1997) 23 E.H.R.R. 413 at [79]-[80] and *D v UK* (1997) 24 E.H.R.R. 423 at [48]-[54]. In *R. (on the application of Wellington) v Secretary of State for the Home Department* [2008] UKHL 72; [2009] 1 A.C. 335, the HL decided that there was no breach of art.3 in ordering Wellington's extradition to the United States where he would face a mandatory life sentence without the prospect of early release (save in the most exceptional circumstances). The majority also held that the desirability of extradition (as opposed to permitting a suspect to evade justice) could be taken into account when considering whether his treatment overseas would violate art.3, that is, that a relativist approach to art.3 was permissible (at [20]-[28] (Lord Hoffmann)). This latter finding appears to be in conflict with the clear terms of art.3 itself and the decision of the ECtHR in *Saadi v Italy* (2008) 24 B.H.R.C. 123 (see Lord Brown's dissent in *Wellington*, at [85]-[87]). In *N v United Kingdom* (2008) 47 E.H.R.R. 39 at [42]-[51], the ECtHR affirmed that it was only in the most exceptional circumstances (such as in *D v UK*, above) that expulsion of a person with a serious illness to a country where the healthcare system was less effective would constitute a breach of art.3. If the conditions under which an asylum seeker would be required to live if returned to another state under the Dublin II Regulation (in this case Italy) created a real risk that art.3 would be violated (even if not as a result of systemic failings), this would violate the ECHR (*R. (on the application of EM (Eritrea)) v Secretary of State for the Home Department* [2014] UKSC 12; [2014] A.C. 1321 at [58]–[64], [68]–[69]). The case was remitted to the Administrative Court to determine on the facts whether such a risk arose. Such returns were considered by the ECtHR in the recent case of *Tarakhel v Switzerland* (2015) 60 E.H.R.R. 28. It was held that the Swiss authorities would be in breach of art.3 if they returned a family of asylum seekers to Italy without first obtaining assurances that they would be received in facilities and in conditions adapted to the age of the children, and that the family would be kept together. In *FG v Sweden* (2016) 41 B.H.R.C. 595 the ECtHR held that there was a duty on the returning state to assess individual risk factors of which it became aware, even if they were not relied on by the applicant in support of a claim against expulsion on the grounds of arts 2 or 3.

[176] *R. (Bagdanavicius) v Secretary of State for the Home Department* [2005] UKHL 38; [2005] 2 A.C. 668 at [22]-[24] (Lord Brown).

[177] *Pretty* [2001] UKHL 61; [2002] 1 A.C. 800 at [52].

[178] *Assenov v Bulgaria* (1999) 28 E.H.R.R. 652 at [95]. The state had failed to carry out an adequate investigation into ill-treatment during an outbreak of disorder at an immigration detention centre in *R. (AM) v Secretary of State for the Home Department* [2009] EWCA Civ 219; [2009] U.K.H.R.R. 973 at [60]-[69] (Sedley LJ). As to the state's obligations to disclose information about allegations

evidence which may have been obtained by torture should be admissible in legal proceedings.[179]

The prohibition on slavery and forced labour   Article 4 expressly prohibits   **13-067**
slavery and servitude and any requirement to perform forced or compulsory labour. The prohibition on forced labour is more accurately described as a limited right as art.4(3) excludes the following from the definition of forced or compulsory labour: work required to be done in the ordinary course of detention imposed according to art.5 or during conditional release from such detention; military service (or service exacted instead of military service in countries where conscientious objection to military service is recognised); service exacted in case of emergency or calamity threatening the life or well-being of a community; and work which forms part of normal civic obligations.[180] Strictly speaking, only the right to be free from slavery or servitude is non-derogable under art.15.

Perhaps unsurprisingly, there have been very few cases under art.4. Slavery has   **13-068**
been defined as "the status or condition of a person over whom any or all of the powers attaching to the right of ownership are exercised".[181] Servitude carries the obligation to provide one's services to another and to live on the other's property without the chance to alter one's condition, but is regarded as less serious since it does not import the concept of ownership.[182] Forced or compulsory labour arises where work is compelled by the threat of a penalty or is otherwise involuntary.[183] Article 4 carries positive obligations on states to prevent and prosecute offences of

---

of torture, see 16-073. The relevant principles are summarised in *DSD v Commissioner of Police for the Metropolis* [2015] EWCA Civ 646; [2016] Q.B. 161 at [59]–[69], in which the CA held that the police investigations relating to the so-called "Black cab rapist" did not fulfil art.3. Laws LJ rejected the concept that the investigative duty was "ancillary" or "adjectival" to a substantive breach. Rather, at [45] he held that "there is perhaps a sliding scale: from deliberate torture by State officials to the consequences of negligence by non-State agents …. The margin of appreciation enjoyed by the State as to the means of compliance with Article 3 widens at the bottom of the scale but narrows at the top". In *Al-Saadoon v Secretary of State for Defence* [2016] EWCA Civ 811; [2017] Q.B. 1015 at [124]–[125], the CA held that the investigative duty under art.3 is triggered by an arguable claim that the individual has suffered treatment infringing art.3, not merely a breach of the Soering obligation not to send an individual to another state where there are substantial grounds for believing that he would face a real risk of being subject to torture or other prohibited treatment.

[179] In *A v Secretary of State for the Home Department (No.2)* [2005] UKHL 71; [2006] 2 A.C. 221 at [119]–[127] (Lord Hope) the HL decided that the Special Immigration Appeals Commission (which had been established in part to determine appeals of those foreign nationals detained on suspicion of involvement in international terrorism) should exclude evidence where it was established on the balance of probabilities that it had been obtained by torture of a third party in a foreign state.

[180] The last category has been held to cover compulsory fire service (*Schmidt v Germany* (1994) 18 E.H.R.R. 513 at [23]) and, domestically, filling in a balance sheet on a tax return (*Murat v Ornoch (Inspector of Taxes)* [2004] EWHC 3123; [2005] S.T.C. 184 at [20]–[21] (Moses J)). However, the imposition of a civic obligation only on members of one gender may violate art.4 read with art.14 (*Adami v Malta* (2007) 44 E.H.R.R. 3 at [47]).

[181] Article 1 of the Slavery Convention 1926, cited in *Siliadin v France* [2006] 43 E.H.R.R. 16 at [122]. In this case, a child without immigration status was required to work for private individuals without pay. The ECtHR held that this constituted forced labour and servitude, but not slavery. On the application of art.4 to instances of child labour, see S. Egan, "Tackling the rise of child labour in Europe: homework for the European Court of Human Rights" [2015] 64 I.C.L.Q. 601.

[182] *Van Droogenbroeck v Belgium*, Case B 44 (1977) 17 D.R. 59 at 72.

[183] In *Van der Mussele v Belgium* (1983) 6 E.H.R.R. 163, [32]–[34], the ECtHR rejected a claim that the professional requirement on pupil advocates to represent indigent litigants without payment violated the prohibition on forced labour. The ECtHR held that the burden imposed was not disproportionate to the advantages attached to the future exercise of the profession (which the applicant had chosen voluntarily to enter). The HL has rejected the claim that art.4 protects a right to refuse to participate in military operations on grounds of conscience: *Sepet v Secretary of State for the Home Department* [2003] UKHL 15; [2003] 1 W.L.R. 856 at [21]–[23] (Lord Bingham). The

slavery or people trafficking and to carry out adequate investigations into alleged breaches.[184]

13-069   **The ban on punishment without lawful authority**   Article 7 contains two prohibitions: first, no one may be found guilty for any act or omission which did not constitute a criminal offence under national or international law at the time it was committed; and, secondly, no one shall have a heavier penalty imposed than was applicable at the time the offence was committed.[185] Article 7 is subject to the exception in art.7(2) which permits the trial and punishment of an individual for an act or omission which was criminal according to the general principles of law recognised by civilised nations at the time it was committed.[186]

13-070   Article 7 only applies to criminal proceedings. However, the scope of what is

---

CA rejected a challenge to the "back to work" scheme on art.4 grounds in *R. (on the application of Reilly) v Secretary of State for Work and Pensions* [2013] EWCA Civ 66 at [65]–[67]. The SC in *Reilly* affirmed the CA's decision with regard to art.4: "Jobseeker's allowance, as its name suggests, is a benefit designed for a person seeking work, and the purpose of the condition is directly linked to the purpose of the benefit. The provision of a conditional benefit of that kind comes nowhere close to the type of exploitative conduct at which article 4 is aimed" ([2013] UKSC 68; [2014] A.C. 453 at [83]). The provisions were found to be ultra vires on other grounds. The claimant's art.4 submissions were not revisited in *R. (on the application of Reilly (No.2)) v Secretary of State for Work and Pensions* [2014] EWHC 2182 (Admin); [2015] Q.B. 573 which concerned the attempt to retrospectively validate the Regulations.

[184] In *O v The Commissioner of Police for the Metropolis* [2011] EWHC 1246 (QB); [2011] H.R.L.R. 29 at [169]–[179], Wyn Williams J held that the police breached their duty to investigate credible allegations of violations of art.4 in relation to a group of Nigerian women who were brought to the UK and required to work for no pay in households where they were subject to physical and emotional abuse. See *Rantsev v Cyprus* (2010) 51 E.H.R.R. 1 at [296]–[309] on states' positive obligations to halt people trafficking under art.4. In *CN v United Kingdom* (App. No.4239/08) (13 November 2012) at [70]–[82], the ECtHR found that the UK had failed to investigate allegations of domestic servitude adequately. In *R. (on the application of H) v Secretary of State for the Home Department* [2016] EWCA Civ 565 at [35], the Secretary of State was found not to have breached her positive obligation to identify and support victims of trafficking under ECHR art.4. The Competent Authority's failure to follow policy guidance did not amount to a breach of art.4; the application of the guidance not being the mechanism by which the UK satisfied its procedural obligations under the Convention. In *Al-Malki v Reyes* [2015] EWCA Civ 32; [2016] 1 W.L.R. 1785, the appellants, who were victims of trafficking, were domestic workers for Saudi Arabian diplomats. They brought claims against the diplomats for racial discrimination and harassment and failure to pay the national minimum wage. The employers claimed diplomatic immunity. The CA held that granting immunity in such circumstances did not breach arts 4 or 6 ECHR which had to be read in light of general principles of international law, including diplomatic immunity. The Modern Slavery Act 2015 received Royal Assent on 26 March 2015 and entered into force on 31 July 2015. Section 1(1) provides for an offence of slavery, servitude and forced or compulsory labour. It replaces the existing offence in s.71 of the Coroners and Justice Act 2009. Subsection (2) requires subsection (1) to be interpreted in accordance with art.4 of the ECHR. Section 2 provides for a single offence of human trafficking covering sexual and non-sexual exploitation.

[185] The prohibition on retrospective criminalisation is an established principle of English common law, although the exceptions to this principle may offend art.7 (*C v DPP* [1996] 1 A.C. 1). In *Contrada v Italy (No.3)* (App. No. 66655/13) (14 April 2015), a conviction for "aiding and abetting a mafia-type organisation from the outside" was held to breach art.7. The applicant's actions took place in 1979–1988 and the relevant offence had resulted from a development in case law which had begun toward the end of the 1980s and was consolidated in 1994. It was not therefore sufficiently clear and foreseeable at the time of the events in question. In *Vasiliauskas v Lithuania* (2016) 62 E.H.R.R. 31 at [183]–[184], the ECtHR held that the applicant's conviction in 2004 for genocide had no basis in law in 1953. While genocide was a crime in international law in 1953, it was unclear and therefore not foreseeable that political groups came under the definition of protected groups at that point, or that the Lithuanian partisans killed constituted part of the protected groups of "ethnic" Lithuanians or Lithuanian "nationals", rather than a separate group.

[186] The so-called Nuremberg exception. The ECtHR was not satisfied that the applicant's homicide conviction arising from his actions in quelling a riot during the 1956 revolution was in accordance

treated as criminal is an autonomous concept and the ECtHR is not bound by the domestic classification of a norm as civil. In deciding whether a penalty is criminal in nature, the ECtHR has regard to whether it was imposed following conviction for a criminal offence, the classification in domestic law, its nature and purpose, the procedures involved in its creation and implementation and its severity.[187] Article 7 only applies to proceedings which result in a conviction or the imposition of a penalty. As such, it does not apply where a prosecution is abandoned or to extradition, preventative detention or to changes in the parole rules.[188] Most cases involve a challenge to the decision to apply the existing criminal law to a new situation rather than new laws which impose retrospective sanctions. The ECtHR has accepted that the laws of the State in question may be expressed with some uncertainty where a concept is very broad or difficult to define and that the law must be permitted to develop. The ECtHR has also upheld convictions for conduct not previously considered to be criminal where it falls within the original concept of the offence.[189] In such cases, the crucial requirement is that the law must be reasonably foreseeable with the help of legal advice, if necessary.[190] The ECtHR also draws a distinction between the imposition of a retrospective penalty and laws on recidivism which may impose a more serious penalty for a later offence on the ground that the offender has committed a similar offence in the past.[191]

---

with such general principles as it was not clear that the victim had laid down his arms and could therefore properly have been regarded at the time as a non-combatant (*Korbely v Hungary* (2008) 25 B.H.R.C. 382 at [89]–[94]).

[187] *Welch v United Kingdom* (1995) 20 E.H.R.R. 247 at [27]–[36]. In *Welch*, the ECtHR held that the application of a new law (which involved the forfeiture of the proceeds of crime and potential imprisonment for refusal to pay them over) to the applicant who had been convicted of drug dealing the year before did involve the retrospective imposition of a heavier penalty and breached art.7. By contrast, the imposition of a requirement that a convicted sex offender should register with the police was found not to be a penalty (*Adamson v United Kingdom* (App.No.44293/98) (26 January 1999). Domestic courts have held that civil recovery orders and financial reporting orders are not penalties for the purposes of art.7 (on the latter, see *R. v Adams* [2008] EWCA Crim 914; [2009] 1 W.L.R. 301 at [25] (Latham LJ)).

[188] *X v Netherlands* (1976) 6 D.R. 184 (extradition); *De Wilde Ooms and Versyp v Belgium* (1971) 1 E.H.R.R. 373 at [87] (preventative detention); and *Hogben v United Kingdom* (1986) 46 D.R. 231 (parole rules). Nor is art.7 engaged when the Parole Board conducts a review under s.28(6) of the Crime (Sentences) Act 1997 (*Hall, Koselka v Parole Board of England & Wales* [2015] EWHC 252 (Admin) at [46]).

[189] The ECtHR rejected a challenge to the change in the common law (*R. v R* [1992] 1 A.C. 599) which removed the previous exemption of husbands from criminal prosecution for rape of their wives (*SW v United Kingdom* (1995) 21 E.H.R.R. 363). This development of the criminal law was sufficiently foreseeable given the progressive narrowing of the exemption which had occurred over previous years.

[190] *SW* (1995) 21 E.H.R.R. 363 at [33]–[36]. The ECtHR held that it was reasonably foreseeable that the emerging Lithuanian government would be likely to take steps against the applicants for their attempts to overthrow it notwithstanding the fact that Lithuania was not yet an independent state (*Kuolelis v Lithuania* (App. No.74357/01) (19 February 2008) at [116]–[121]). In *Rohlena v Czech Republic* (App. No. 59552/08) (27 January 2015) at [70]–[73], the Grand Chamber found art.7 not to have been breached. The applicant had been convicted for a continuous criminal offence of abusing a person living under the same roof. The applicant complained that his conviction encompassed his conduct before that offence had been introduced into the law on 1 June 2004. The court ruled that the fact of finding the applicant guilty under a later version of the Code in respect of acts committed before, as well as after, that date, did not constitute a retroactive application of the law. The offence had had a basis in national law at the time it was committed and the law had defined the offence sufficiently clearly to meet the requirement of foreseeability.

[191] The ECtHR upheld a 1994 law which doubled the applicant's sentence for a later offence because of his previous conviction for a similar crime some 10 years earlier (*Achour v France* (2007) 45 E.H.R.R. 2 at [51]–[55]). In a departure from previous authority (which was justified by, among other things, the European Union's Charter of Fundamental Rights), the ECtHR held that art.7 entitled a

Limited rights

13-071   Limited rights contain express exceptions and include the right to liberty and security of the person (art.5), the prohibition on forced labour (art.4(2) and (3)), the right to marry (art.12) and to education (art.2 of the First Protocol).

13-072   **The right to liberty and security of the person**   Article 5(1) protects the right to liberty and security of the person and only permits exceptions which are in accordance with a procedure established by law and in the following circumstances.[192]

(a)   The lawful detention after conviction by a competent court. A competent court is one with jurisdiction to determine the case and there must be lawful procedures in place to carry out the detention. However, the court is not concerned with the validity or the fairness of the conviction or the conditions of detention under this article.[193]

(b)   The lawful arrest or detention of a person for non-compliance with the lawful order of a court or in order to secure the fulfilment of any obligation prescribed by law. Under this provision, the obligation or order must be sufficiently clear, the individual must have the opportunity to comply and detention must be the only reasonable way to secure compliance.

(c)   The lawful arrest or detention of a person effected for the purpose of bringing him before the competent legal authority on reasonable suspicion of having committed an offence or when it is reasonably considered necessary to prevent his committing an offence or fleeing after having done so. This clearly

---

defendant to the more lenient penalty in force at the time of his sentence, rather than the more severe one in force at the time of the commission of the offence (*Scoppola v Italy* (2010) 51 E.H.R.R. 12 at [93]-[109]). *Scoppola* did not prevent a judge from imposing a sentence of imprisonment for public protection just before such sentences were abolished as life imprisonment was plainly a sentencing option in light of the nature of the offences (*R. v Docherty (Shaun Kevin)* [2016] UKSC 62 at [45]–[47]; [53]–[55]).

[192]   See further, J. Murdoch, *Article 5 of the European Convention on Human Rights: The Protection of Liberty and Security of Person*, 2nd edn (2002).

[193]   In *R. (on the application of James) v Secretary of State for Justice* [2009] UKHL 22; [2010] 1 A.C. 553 at [14]-[15] (Lord Hope) and [51] (Lord Brown), the HL held that detention after conviction which is lawful under art.5(1)(a) may become arbitrary and unlawful if a prisoner sentenced to an indeterminate sentence for public protection is detained for a long period after the expiry of the tariff without a meaningful opportunity to demonstrate that his continued detention is no longer justified, although there was no breach of art.5(1) on the facts. The ECtHR disagreed in *James, Wells and Lee v United Kingdom* (2013) 56 E.H.R.R. 12 at [201]-[222], holding that, although the strict limits on judicial discretion were lawful, the absence of resources which would permit the prisoners to be rehabilitated was in breach of art.5(1). Indeterminate sentences for public protection are abolished by s.123 of the Legal Aid, Sentencing and Punishment of Offenders Act 2012. In *R. (on the application of Sturnham) v Parole Board* [2013] UKSC 47; [2013] 2 A.C. 254 at [18]–[23], the SC confirmed that a breach of art.5(4) does not necessarily lead to a finding that art.5(1) has been violated, distinguishing *James*. A violation of art.5(1) will only follow if the detention has become arbitrary. In *Bayliss v Parole Board for England and Wales* [2014] EWCA Civ 1631, the applicant had sought to appeal, over six years out of time, against his sentence of imprisonment for public protection. The Court of Appeal allowed his appeal, quashed the order of imprisonment and imposed a determinate sentence of four years, resulting in his immediate release. The applicant argued that the Court of Appeal's decision rendered his detention from April 2008 unlawful; alternatively, his detention was arbitrary for the purposes of ECHR art.5(1). The CA held that an appeal decision quashing a sentence did not render detention pursuant to that sentence unlawful. In *Mozer v Republic of Moldova and Russia* (App. No. 11138/10) (23 February 2016) at [147]–[150], the ECtHR held that detention ordered by the courts of the "Moldavian Republic of Transdniestria" (MRT) could not be considered "lawful" for the purposes of art.5. Russia (which controlled the MRT courts) had failed to demonstrate, and it could not be assumed, that the MRT court system reflected a judicial tradition compatible with the Convention.

requires that there should an objective basis for the suspicion and an honest belief will not suffice.[194]

(d) The detention of a minor by lawful order for the purpose of educational supervision or his lawful detention for the purpose of bringing him before the competent legal authority. A minor is a person under the age of 18.

(e) The lawful detention of persons for the prevention of the spreading of infectious diseases, of persons of unsound mind, alcoholics or drug addicts or vagrants. This provision is potentially very broad and the Court has emphasised that detention must be proportionate. As such, it will not be sufficient that a person is simply, say, of unsound mind. It will also be necessary to demonstrate that their condition justifies compulsory detention.[195]

(f) The lawful arrest or detention of a person to prevent his effecting an unauthorised entry into the country or of a person against whom action is being taken with a view to deportation or extradition. Until a state has authorised entry to the country, detention is in order to prevent unauthorised entry, even where the individual has surrendered himself to the authorities and is openly pursuing the legal process to obtain lawful entry.[196] The court will also not examine the merits of the decision to deport under this provision, but merely require that there be a legal basis for it and a genuine intention to effect deportation.[197]

The aim of these permitted exceptions is to prevent arbitrary detention.[198]   **13-073** Examples of arbitrary detention include where there has been an element of bad faith or deception in securing the detention; where either the order to detain or the execution of the detention do not genuinely conform to the purpose of the restrictions permitted by the relevant part of art.5(1); where there is no relationship between the ground of permitted detention in art.5(1) and the fact and conditions of detention; and where there is no proportionality between the ground of deten-

---

[194] Article 5(1)(c) is disjunctive: if a person is arrested to prevent his committing an offence, the arrest is not rendered unlawful by the fact that the suspect is not subsequently brought before the competent legal authority. Article 5 must be read pragmatically: art.5(1)(c) does not require an individual to be brought before a court if he is released before it is practical to do so (*R. (on the application of Hicks) v Commissioner of Police of the Metropolis* [2017] UKSC 9; [2017] A.C. 256 at [32]-[40]. On the inter-relation of art.5(1)(b) and (c), see *Ostendorf v Germany* (2013) 34 B.H.R.C. 738 at [66]-[68], [82]-[86], [93]-[95] and the SC's criticisms of it in *Hicks*, above.

[195] *Johnson v United Kingdom* (1999) 27 E.H.R.R. 296 at [59]-[60].

[196] *Saadi v United Kingdom* (2008) 47 E.H.R.R. 17 at [65]-[66]. The ECtHR found that the UK had acted in good faith and to ensure a speedy resolution of asylum claims. The conditions of detention were also found to be adequate at [75]-[79]. In order to avoid arbitrariness, art.5 requires that the state must not act in bad faith, and for the purposes of art.5(1)(b), (d) and (e), the detention must be necessary, at [69]-[71]. However, the specific reasons for detaining the applicant were not provided until 76 hours after his detention and then only orally. As such, there was a violation of art.5(2), at [84]-[85]. A period of two and half years detention with a view to deportation was considered lawful in *Ahmed v United Kingdom* (2017) 65 E.H.R.R. 18.

[197] In *Chahal* (1996) 23 E.H.R.R. 413 at [112], the ECtHR held that detention is only justified if deportation proceedings are in progress.

[198] The UK was found to have breached art.5(1) in interning the applicant for three years in Iraq without charge (*Al-Jedda v United Kingdom* (2011) 53 E.H.R.R. 23 at [98]-[110]). The ECtHR rejected the argument that United Nations Security Council Resolution 1546 overrode art.5. See now, *Hassan v UK* (2014) 38 B.H.R.C. 358 in which the ECtHR acknowledged that art.5 must be interpreted and applied in a way which takes account of international humanitarian law and that this may supplement the grounds in art.5(1)(a)-(f). The crucial questions which determine the legality of detention in armed conflict are whether there is a legal basis for the detention and a means of challenging its lawfulness (*Mohammed v Secretary of State for Defence (No.2)* [2017] UKSC 2; [2017] 2 W.L.R. 327 at [63]).

tion relied upon and the detention in question.[199] However, art.5 is only concerned with the deprivation of liberty rather than restrictions on freedom of movement.[200] The dividing line between the two is a question of degree and the court will take into account the type, duration, effects and manner of implementation of the measure in question.[201]

13-074   Article 5 also confers a number of procedural rights on those subject to detention. Article 5(2) provides that everyone who is arrested shall be informed promptly, in a language which he understands, of the reasons for his arrest and of any charge against him. The obvious aim of this right is to permit a challenge to be made to the lawfulness of a detention. Article 5(3) grants everyone arrested or detained in accordance with the provisions of art.5(1)(c) the right to be brought promptly before

---

[199] *James, Wells and Lee* (2013) 56 E.H.R.R. 12 at [192]–[195].

[200] The system of control orders under the Prevention of Terrorism Act 2005 was found (by a majority) to amount to a deprivation of liberty in *Secretary of State for the Home Department v JJ* [2007] UKHL 45 at [20]–[24] (Lord Bingham). The orders confined the claimants to their one-bedroom flats (which were subject to spot searches by the police) for 18 hours a day, required any visitors to be authorised by the Home Office and restricted them in the remaining six hours of the day to a limited urban area. *JJ* was distinguished in *Secretary of State for the Home Department v E* [2007] UKHL 47; [2008] 1 A.C. 499 at [11] (Lord Bingham) and [25] (Baroness Hale) where, analysing the core element of art.5 as confinement, the House of Lords held that the control order in that case (involving a 12-hour curfew and other restrictions) did not involve a deprivation of liberty. The existence of a condition in a control order which interfered with art.8 (in this case, that the claimant had to live 150 miles from London where his family was located) could be sufficient to cause a deprivation of liberty (*R. (on the application of AP) v Secretary of State for the Home Department* [2010] UKSC 24; [2011] 2 A.C. 1 at [13]–[19] (Lord Brown). In *R. (on the application of Gillan) v Commissioner of Police of the Metropolis* [2006] UKHL 12; [2006] 2 A.C. 307, the HL held that the stop and search provisions of the Terrorism Act 2000 did not constitute a deprivation of liberty. The ECtHR in *Gillan and Quinton v UK* (2010) 50 E.H.R.R. 45 at [56]-[7], held that the element of coercion in the use of the powers was indicative of deprivation of liberty, but did not decide the issue as it found for the applicants on art.8. In *Austin v Metropolitan Police Commissioner* [2009] UKHL 5; [2009] 1 A.C. 564 at [22]-[23] and at [34] (Lord Hope), the HL held that although art.5 is expressed in absolute terms, there remains scope to consider the purpose of any restriction and the need to balance individual and collective interests. As such, confining a group of protestors to a small area for a period of hours in order to preserve public order did not infringe art.5. The ECtHR in *Austin v the United Kingdom* (2012) 55 E.H.R.R. 14 at [52]-[60] approved the HL decision where the restriction on public movement was for the collective good, unavoidable as a result of circumstances beyond the control of the authorities, necessary to avert a real risk of serious injury or damage and kept to the minimum required for that purpose. In *Surrey County Council v P* [2014] UKSC 19; [2014] A.C. 896 at [45]-[50], the majority of the SC held that a deprivation of liberty must be assessed objectively: living arrangements that would amount to a deprivation of liberty in the case of a non-disabled person would also be a deprivation of liberty in the case of a disabled person (irrespective of the reasons for the deprivation or whether the person consented). In *R. (on the application of Roberts) v Commissioner of Police of the Metropolis* [2014] EWCA Civ 69; [2014] 1 W.L.R. 3299 at [10]-[13], the CA held that there was no deprivation of liberty under art.5 where the claimant was detained (at one point in handcuffs) in order for a police officer to search her under a stop and search authority granted under the Criminal Justice and Public Order Act 1994 s.60. The appellant unsuccessfully appealed to the SC in *R. (on the application of Roberts) v Commissioner of Police of the Metropolis* [2015] UKSC 79; [2016] 1 W.L.R. 210, not on the basis of art.5. Control orders were replaced with orders under the Terrorism Prevention and Investigation Measures Act 2011; on which, see *Mohamed v Secretary of State for the Home Department* [2014] EWCA Civ 559; [2014] 1 W.L.R. 4240. Further amendments to this regime were made by Part 2 of the Counter-Terrorism and Security Act 2015.

[201] *Guzzardi v Italy* (1980) 3 E.H.R.R. 333 at [91]-[94]. The presence of an informal patient at a mental hospital (*HL v United Kingdom (Bournewood)* (2004) 40 E.H.R.R. 761 at [91]-[94]) was held to be a deprivation of liberty. The ECtHR held that detaining illegal immigrants in the transit zone of an international airport for over 10 days was a deprivation of liberty under art.5 (*Riad and Idiab v Belgium* (App. No.29787/03) (24 January 2008) at [78] (French text)). The court went on to hold that being forced to live in a public place without proper facilities also violated art.3: paras 104-108.

a judge or other officer authorised by law to exercise judicial power. This is designed to prevent prolonged detention before charge.[202] Article 5(3) also requires that an individual once charged shall be entitled to trial within a reasonable time or to release on bail.[203] Release may be conditioned by guarantees to appear for trial.

Article 5(4) provides that everyone who is deprived of his liberty by arrest or detention shall be entitled to take proceedings by which the lawfulness of his detention shall be decided speedily by a court and his release ordered if the detention is not lawful. Although the reference to a court does not necessarily require a traditional judicial body, any decision-maker must be independent of the executive.[204] What constitutes a speedy determination will depend on the circumstances. A prolonged period of detention will require a process to determine the lawfulness of the detention at reasonable intervals.[205] Article 5(5) entitles everyone who has been the victim of arrest or detention in contravention of art.5 to an enforceable right to compensation.[206] Article 5 also contains positive obligations.[207]

13-075

---

[202] *Brogan v United Kingdom* (1998) 11 E.H.R.R. 117.

[203] The refusal of bail must be justified by reasons such as preventing absconding, interference with the course of justice, further offending or a risk to public order.

[204] *Benjamin and Wilson v United Kingdom* (2003) 36 E.H.R.R. 1 at [33]. The Mental Health Review Tribunal has been held to be sufficiently independent for art.5(4) and the Parole Board has not (*R. (on the application of Brooke) v Parole Board* [2008] EWCA Civ 29; [2008] 1 W.L.R. 1950 at [77]–[80] (Lord Phillips CJ)). The ECtHR upheld the use of closed evidence in terrorist cases so long as the open material was sufficiently specific to ensure that the applicant could properly instruct the special advocate appointed to represent him (*A v United Kingdom* (2009) 49 E.H.R.R. 29 at [217]–[224]). See further, *Secretary of State for the Home Department v AF (No.3)* [2009] UKHL 28; [2010] 2 A.C. 269 at [60]–[69] (Lord Phillips). In *R. (on the application of Osborn) v Parole Board* [2013] UKSC 61; [2014] A.C. 1115 at [81]–[96], the SC indicated that an oral hearing before the Parole Board as a matter of common law fairness and compliance with art.5(4) was likely to be necessary where: important facts or issues of mitigation were in dispute; the Board could not otherwise make an independent assessment of risk; face-to-face encounter with the Board was necessary to enable the prisoner's case to be put or tested effectively; or where, in light of the prisoner's representations, it would be unfair for the matter to be determined on paper. In *Sher v UK* (App. No. 5201/11) (20 October 2015), the ECtHR found no breach of art.5 where the applicants, Pakistani nationals, had been arrested and detained for 13 days without charge in connection with an anti-terrorism operation. The applicants complained of failure to disclose evidence in their detention review hearings, some of which were also held in private session. The ECtHR held that the threat of an imminent terrorist attack at the time of their detention justified the restrictions on the applicants' art.5 rights.

[205] See e.g. *T and V v United Kingdom* (1999) 30 E.H.R.R. 121 at [119]–[121] concerning the imprisonment of the juvenile murderers of Jamie Bulger and *R. (on the application of MH) v Secretary of State for Health* [2005] UKHL 60; [2006] 1 A.C. 441 at [17] (Baroness Hale) in which the inherent changeability of mental disorders made it essential that reviews of detention should take place at reasonable intervals. In *James* [2009] UKHL 22; [2010] 1 A.C. 553, at [21] (Lord Hope) and [60] (Lord Brown), the House of Lords held that art.5(4) is concerned exclusively with procedure. The SC has held that routine delays in referring prisoners' cases to the Parole Board may cause a breach of art.5(4) (*R. (on the application of Faulkner) v Secretary of State for Justice* [2013] UKSC 23; [2013] 2 A.C. 254. A majority of the House of Lords upheld the power of the Secretary of State to depart from the Parole Board's recommendation for release at the half-way stage of a determinate sentence against a challenge based on art.5(4) (*R. (on the application of Black) v Secretary of State for Justice* [2009] UKHL 1; [2009] 1 A.C. 949 at [78]–[85] (Lord Brown)). In *Betteridge v UK* (2013) 57 E.H.R.R. 7, the ECtHR held that a delay in the applicant's Parole Board review breached art.5(4) and awarded £750 for nonpecuniary damage arising from feelings of frustration at the delay of just over a year.

[206] HRA s.9(3) makes a limited exception to the principle that damages are not available against the decision of a court to accommodate this requirement.

[207] The positive obligation extends to taking reasonable steps to protect the vulnerable from non-state actors where the authorities are, or ought to be, aware of the risk of a deprivation of liberty (*Storck*

13-076   **The right to a fair hearing**   This right is considered in Chapters 6 and 7[208] and Chapter 10.[209]

13-077   **The right to be free from forced labour**   This right is considered at 13-067.

13-078   **The right to marry and found a family**   Article 12 provides that men and women of marriageable age shall have the right to marry and found a family according to the national laws governing the exercise of this right. Article 12 does not concern interferences with the relations between parent and child which are covered by art.8.[210] Article 12 clearly provides the State with substantial leeway to determine, for example, what is marriageable age and any formalities necessary for a valid marriage.[211] However, restrictions must serve some legitimate State purpose.[212] There is no right to a dissolution of marriage. As regards founding a family, the ECtHR has not accepted that there is a right to adopt or that the failure to provide artificial insemination was a breach of art.12.[213]

13-079   **The right to education**   Article 2 of the First Protocol states that no person shall be deprived of the right to education. This article is unusual in that it protects a social or cultural right, rather than a civil or political right like all the other Convention rights.[214] The right breaks down into the following elements: a right to effective education; a right of effective access to existing educational institutions; a right

---

v Germany (2006) 43 E.H.R.R. 6 at [100]–[108]). The SC in *Brown v Parole Board for Scotland* [2017] UKSC 69; [2017] 3 W.L.R. 1373 departed from its own recent decision in *R. (on the application of Kaiyam) v Secretary of State for Justice* [2014] UKSC 66; [2015] A.C. 1344 to align domestic law with the ECtHR's decision in *James, Wells and Lee v UK* (2013) 56 E.H.R.R. 12 (see fn.193). The SC affirmed that, in line with the Strasbourg jurisprudence, any failure to provide prisoners sentenced to life imprisonment or who were detained for public protection with a real opportunity for rehabilitation had to meet a high threshold before rendering the detention arbitrary and a breach of art.5 (at [38]-[45]). In *R. (on the application of Hussain) v Secretary of State for Justice* [2017] EWCA Civ 1074; [2017] 1 W.L.R. 3748, the CA emphasised that any alleged breach of the duty should be considered in the round and not as a snapshot at a given point in the course of detention. The state has an investigative duty in relation to detainees who have disappeared, but not more generally (*Al-Saadoon v Secretary of State for Defence* [2016] EWCA Civ 811; [2017] Q.B. 1015 at [162]–[170]).

[208] See 6-048, 7-120.
[209] See 10-088.
[210] *P, C and S v UK* (2002) 35 E.H.R.R. 31.
[211] In *X v Y (Overseas Same-Sex Relationship)* [2006] EWHC 2022 (Fam) at [55]–[67], Sir Mark Potter P. found no violation of art.12 in the UK's refusal to recognise a same-sex marriage as a marriage, but to classify it instead as a civil partnership. The ECtHR agreed in *Schalk and Kopf v Austria* (2011) 53 E.H.R.R. 20 at [40]–[64], leaving the matter to the national authorities. See further, *Vallianatos v Greece* (2014) 59 E.H.R.R. 12 (discussed at para.13-029). The position in Schalk was restated in *Hämäläinen v Finland* [2015] 1 F.C.R. 379 at [71] and in *Aldeguer Tomás v Spain (App. No. 35214/09) (14 June* 2016) at [90].
[212] The bans on all prisoners (*Hamer v United Kingdom* (1982) 4 E.H.R.R. 139 at [70]–[74]) and transsexuals (*Goodwin v United Kingdom* (2002) 35 E.H.R.R. 18 at [103]) marrying were found to violate art.12. A requirement for persons subject to immigration control to obtain a certificate of approval if not marrying in accordance with the rites of the Church of England was found to be a disproportionate means of preventing sham marriages and to be in violation of art.12 in *R. (on the application of Baiai) v Secretary of State for the Home Department* [2008] UKHL 53; [2009] 1 A.C. 287 at [28]–[32] (Lord Bingham). The ECtHR found an amended scheme to breach art.12 on the grounds that it did not require evidence of the genuineness of the marriage from all applicants, was a blanket prohibition and required a fee which the poor might find prohibitive (*O'Donoghue v United Kingdom* (2011) 53 E.H.R.R. 1 at [82]–[91]).
[213] See *Dickson v United Kingdom* (2008) 46 E.H.R.R. 41 at [80]-[85], in which the ECtHR found the policy of denying artificial insemination facilities to prisoners to be in violation of art.8 and did not consider art.12 separately.
[214] The UK's reservation to this right is described at 13-024.

to be educated in the (or one of the) national language(s); and a right to obtain official recognition of completed studies.[215] The negative formulation of the right does not require the State to establish or fund education of any particular type.[216] The State also retains its right to insist that children attend school or are adequately taught at home.[217] Although the focus of art.2 is on primary and secondary education, it has been held to extend to higher education.[218]

Article 2 also requires the state to respect the right of parents to ensure that their children's education is in conformity with their own religious and philosophical convictions. This does not prevent the State from teaching religious or philosophical matters so long as the instruction is objective, critical and pluralistic and does not constitute indoctrination.[219] The obligation extends beyond the curriculum to organisation and finance and school discipline.[220]

13-080

---

[215] *The Belgian Linguistics Case (No.2)* (1968) 1 E.H.R.R. 252 at [3]-[7], [21] and [42]. See further fn.286 below on indirect discrimination in assigning Roma children to special schools. As a matter of domestic law, a rule which prevented the child of a convert to Judaism from entering a Jewish faith school was held to be directly discriminatory in breach of the Race Relations Act 1976 (*R. (on the application of E) v The Governing Body of JFS* [2009] UKSC 15; [2010] 2 A.C. 728 at [33]-[46] (Lord Phillips)). In *Mansur Yalçin v Turkey (App. No. 21163/11) (16 September* 2014) the ECtHR held, in response to an application by members of the Alevi faith, that the Turkish education system did not provide adequate means by which the beliefs of parents of children holding a faith other than Sunni Islam might be respected.

[216] In *Ali v United Kingdom* [2011] 53 E.H.R.R. 12 at [55]-[63], the ECtHR upheld the decision to exclude the applicant from school until the conclusion of a police investigation into an offence of arson. The court went on to hold that art.2 of the First Protocol requires the UK to guarantee to every child of compulsory school age access to an educational facility which will provide an education in accordance with the national curriculum. The SC rejected a claim that a local authority breached art.2 of the First Protocol during an 18-month period when the child did not attend school while a residential placement (which was required to deal with his needs and behaviour) was located. A had not been deprived of the essence of the right to education (*A v Essex County Council* [2010] UKSC 33; [2011] 1 A.C. 280 at [20]-[22]] (Lord Clarke)). The SC did find it arguable that the local authority could have done more to provide educational assistance during this period (at [89] (Lord Phillips)).

[217] *Family H v United Kingdom* (1984) 37 D.R. 105.

[218] *Sahin v Turkey* (2007) 44 E.H.R.R. 5 at [134]-[142]. A state which chooses to provide institutions of higher education must also provide effective access to them, but the imposition of tuition fees was a proportionate means of achieving the legitimate aim of expanding participation (given the availability of loans): *R. (on the application of Hurley and Moore) v Secretary of State for Business Innovation and Skills* [2012] EWHC 201 (Admin); [2012] H.L.R. 13 at [42]-[65] (Elias LJ). In *R. (on the application of Tigere) v Secretary of State for Business, Innovation and Skills* [2015] UKSC 57; [2015] 1 W.L.R. 3820 at [47]-[49], the SC found a breach of art.2 of the First Protocol, read with art.14 ECHR, in the context of funding for higher education. The applicant was a Zambian national who had been educated in the UK since her arrival in 2012, and who held discretionary leave. She was unable to obtain a student loan due to the requirement that an applicant for a student loan has to be "settled" in the UK (i.e. having indefinite leave to remain).

[219] *Kjeldsen v Denmark* (1976) 1 E.H.R.R. 711 at [54] where the ECtHR rejected a parental objection to sex education. The state was held to have crossed the line where there was very limited teaching of the Alevi faith although its followers represented a substantial minority (*Zengin v Turkey* (2008) 46 E.H.R.R. 44 at [60]-[70]). The ECtHR has held that the rule which permitted parents to request a partial exemption for their children from predominantly Christian religious and philosophical teaching was in breach of art.2 as it required parents to expose their own philosophical views to scrutiny and was based on an unrealistic distinction between observation of, and participation in, the classes (*Folgero v Norway* (2008) 46 E.H.R.R. 47 at [85]-[102]). The display of the "passive symbol" of the crucifix in state schools classrooms in Italy was held not to violate the right to education (*Lautsi v Italy* (2012) 54 E.H.R.R. 3 at [57]-[78]). In *R. (on the application of Fox) v Secretary of State for Education* [2015] EWHC 3404 (Admin); [2016] P.T.S.R. 405 at [74]-[75], the HC reviewed the ECtHR jurisprudence on religious instruction, acknowledging that the state's duties of impartiality and plurality do not require equal emphasis to be given to all shades of belief or conviction. However, the "complete exclusion of any study of non-religious belief", as mandated by the impugned syl-

Qualified rights

13-081   As stated above, the qualified Convention rights are contained in arts 8 (right to private and family life), 9 (right to freedom of thought, conscience and religion), 10 (freedom of expression), 11 (freedom of assembly and association) and the right to the enjoyment of possessions (art.1 of the First Protocol). Interference with a qualified right may be justified if the public authority can fulfil three conditions. These are: (i) that the limitation is prescribed by (or in accordance with for art.8) the law; (ii) that it is done to secure a legitimate aim under the relevant article; and (iii) that it is necessary in a democratic society, that is, it fulfils a pressing social need and goes no further than is strictly necessary to secure that need. This latter is the principle of proportionality. Since this structure is common to all qualified rights, it is addressed before the individual rights themselves.

13-082   **Prescribed by law**   The requirement that a limitation is prescribed by law is a fundamental aspect of the rule of law or the principle of legality. It has three main elements: that the public authority should be able to point to legal authority for any interference, that the legal authority must be reasonably accessible to the individual and that it must be sufficiently certain that the individual can foresee the likelihood of State intervention.[221] Where there is no legal basis for an interference, the

---

labus, was incompatible with art.2. The state's assertion that such a syllabus would fulfil its religious education duties failed to ensure pluralism and as such amounted to a breach of the right to education.

[220] The ECtHR upheld a parent's objection to corporal punishment in *Campbell and Cosans v United Kingdom* (1982) 4 E.H.R.R. 293 at [37]. The HL has held that the ban on corporal punishment may interfere with a parental belief in its virtues, but the interference is justified (*R. (on the application of Williamson) v Secretary of State for Education and Employment* [2005] UKHL 15; [2005] 2 A.C. 246 at [49]–[52] (Lord Nicholls)). The HL decision in *R. (on the application of SB) v Governors of Denbigh High School* [2006] UKHL 15; [2007] 1 A.C. 100 has been applied to wearing a purity ring (*R. (on the application of Playfoot (A Child)) v Millais School Governing Body* [2007] EWHC 1698 (Admin); [2007] H.R.L.R. 34 at [23] where the wearing of the ring was found not to be intimately linked to a belief in chastity before marriage) and the niqab (*R. (on the application of X) v Head Teachers and Governors of Y School* [2007] EWHC 298 (Admin); [2008] 1 All E.R. 249 at [30]–[36] (Silber J) where an alternative school was available where the niqab was permitted), but not to the kara bangle (*R. (on the application of Watkins-Singh) v Aberdare Girls' High School Governors* [2008] EWHC 1865 (Admin) where the school's refusal to allow a Sikh pupil to wear a religious steel bangle at school was found to be indirect discrimination under the Race Relations Act). In *R. (on the application of Diocese of Menevia) v Swansea City and County Council* [2015] EWHC 1436 (Admin) at [87]–[89], it was held that the obligation to respect a parent's rights did not extend to subsidising or paying for transportation to school. The applicants had challenged the local authority's decision to alter its free transport policy for budgetary reasons, such that children attending faith schools would only be given free transport if there were no other alternative schools, including non-faith schools, located within two or three miles of their homes. Although there was no breach of art.2 of the First Protocol, the effect was indirectly discriminatory against black and minority ethnic children.

[221] *Sunday Times v United Kingdom* (1979) 2 E.H.R.R. 245 at [46]–[53] (where the common law of contempt of court passed the test) and *Malone v United Kingdom* (1984) 7 E.H.R.R. 14 at [68]–[80] (where the informal system for authorising telephone tapping did not). These requirements were satisfied domestically by the law on official secrets: *R. v Shayler* [2002] UKHL 11; [2003] 1 A.C. 247 at [56] (Lord Hope). In *Liberty v United Kingdom* [2009] 48 E.H.R.R. 1 at [64]–[70], the ECtHR held that the provisions (which were neither legislative nor made public) used to justify the interception of communications from a number of groups between 1990 and 1997 were not in accordance with the law and in breach of art.8. See further, *R. (on the application of Purdy) v Director of Public Prosecutions* [2009] UKHL 45; [2009] 1 Cr.App.R. 32. In *Gillan v United Kingdom* (2010) 50 E.H.R.R. 45 at [76]–[87], the police discretion to stop and search was too broad to be in accordance with the law. In *R. (on the application of Catt) v Association of Chief Police Officers of England, Wales and Northern Ireland* [2015] UKSC 9; [2015] A.C. 1065 at [11]–[13], the SC held that retaining information on a "domestic extremism" database maintained by the National Public Order Intel-

claimant will necessarily succeed under the ECHR.[222] However, such challenges are relatively rare since if there is no domestic law justifying the public authority's actions, the individual will normally have a remedy without relying on their Convention rights. Where a public authority relies on guidance which does not itself have the status of law, such guidance must be adequately supported by statutory authority.[223]

The legitimate aim The existence or otherwise of a legitimate aim is determined by the text of the qualified Convention right in question and not all the lists of legitimate interests in the second parts of arts 8–11 are identical. However, they are generally expressed in broad terms and it is rare for challenges to succeed on the basis that a limitation was not in pursuit of a legitimate aim. The reference to the "rights of others" in these articles is not limited to Convention rights.[224]   **13-083**

Necessary in a democratic society: proportionality The ECtHR has held that the term necessary requires something more than reasonable, desirable or useful, but less than indispensable. The best definition is that it requires that the measure should fulfil a "pressing social need" and a powerful justification is required to limit Convention rights.[225] The ECtHR has also emphasised the link between the terms "necessary" and "democratic society". The characteristics of the latter include   **13-084**

---

ligence Unit and supervised by the first defendant was in accordance with the law for the purposes of art.8 although it lacked any statutory basis as it was subject to the provisions of the Data Protection Act 1998 and administrative codes issued under the Police Act 1996. In *R. (on the application of Roberts) v Commissioner of Police of the Metropolis* [2015] UKSC 79; [2016] 1 W.L.R. 210 at [42]–[48], the SC held that the power of stop and search under the Criminal Justice and Public Order Act 1994 s.60, was in accordance with the law for the purposes of art.8. The power had to be exercised lawfully and in accordance with s.6(1) HRA, the Equality Act 2010, the Police and Criminal Evidence Act 1984 and the Force's Standard Operating Procedures, all of which provided safeguards enabling the proportionality of the interference to be adequately examined. In contrast, in *Christian Institute v Lord Advocate* [2016] UKSC 51; 2016 S.L.T. 805 at [79]–[85], the provisions of Pt 4 of the Children and Young People (Scotland) Act 2014 which created the "named person scheme" for all children was not in accordance with the law. In *Cumhuriyet Halk Partisi v Turkey* (App. No. 19920/13) (26 July 2016) at [106]–[107], the ECtHR found that the imposition of financial sanctions on the applicant, the largest opposition party in Turkey, was an interference with its rights under art.11. A lack of foreseeability of the applicable law on political expenditure and absence of guidance on sanctions meant that the interference was not prescribed by law.

[222] *Halford v United Kingdom* (1997) 24 E.H.R.R. 523 at [61]–[63]. In *K v United Kingdom* (2010) 51 E.H.R.R. 14 at [75]–[80], the ECtHR held that a hospital's decision to take blood samples and intimate photographs of a child thought to be the victim of sexual abuse without her parents' consent was not in accordance with the law and breached art.8. The same result was reached in *Elberte v Latvia* (2015) 61 E.H.R.R. 7 (concerning the removal of tissue from the applicant's deceased husband's body without her consent). A violation of art.3 was also found.

[223] See e.g. *R. (on the application of Munjaz) v Mersey Care NHS Trust* [2005] UKHL 58; [2006] 2 A.C. 148 at [127] (the dissent of Lord Brown concerning the use of a code of practice to regulate the seclusion of mental patients).

[224] *VgT Verein Gegen Tierfabriken v Switzerland* (2001) 34 E.H.R.R. 4 at [59]–[62].

[225] *Sunday Times* (1979) 2 E.H.R.R. 245 at [59]. See *Bank Mellat v HM Treasury (No.2)* [2013] UKSC 38; [2014] A.C. 700 at [20]–[21], [68]–[76], [93]. In particular, Lord Reed identified four questions (at [72]) for the court to answer: (1) is the legislative objective sufficiently important to justify limiting a fundamental right; (2) are the measures which have been designed to meet it rationally connected to it; (3) are they no more than are necessary to accomplish it; and (4) do they strike a fair balance between the rights of the individual and the interests of the community? In *R. (Lord Carlile of Berriew) v Secretary of State for the Home Department* [2014] UKSC 60; [2015] A.C. 945 at [34] the SC gave guidance on the quality of the judicial scrutiny called for when considering the proportionality of an interference with a Convention right. The principle of proportionality in EU law is neither expressed nor applied in the same way as the principle of proportionality under the European Convention on Human Rights: see *R. (on the application of Lumsdon) v Legal Services Board* [2015] UKSC 41; [2016] A.C. 697 at [22]–[82], in which Lord Reed comprehensively sum-

pluralism, tolerance and broadmindedness and the test of necessity must be set against this background.[226] The ECtHR then applies the test of proportionality proper.[227] In applying the test of proportionality, the ECtHR will consider whether the interference affects the essence of the right or is more peripheral to it, whether there exist effective safeguards over the interference as a matter of domestic law and whether there is a less restrictive alternative which would achieve the State's legitimate aims but involve less interference with Convention rights. Finally, the ECtHR considers whether the State has advanced relevant and sufficient reasons to justify the interference.[228] We have seen in Chapter 11[229] how our domestic courts apply the concept of proportionality by the standards set out in *R. v Secretary of State for the Home Department Ex p. Daly*[230] and *de Freitas v Permanent Secretary of Ministry of Agriculture, Fisheries, Land and Housing*.[231] In the following paragraphs, we consider the application of this test to the actual scope of qualified Convention rights.

13-085   **The right to respect for private and family life**   Article 8 protects a number of rights which fall within the broad scope of privacy: the rights to respect for one's private life, family life, one's home and one's correspondence. It is therefore potentially of a very broad nature. The ECtHR has adopted an inclusive definition of it:

> "As the Court has had previous occasion to remark, the concept of 'private life' is a broad term not susceptible to exhaustive definition. It covers the physical and psychological integrity of a person.[232] It can sometimes embrace aspects of an individual's physical and social identity. Elements such as, for example, gender identification, name and sexual orientation and sexual life fall within the personal sphere protected by art.8. Article 8 also protects a right to personal development, and the right to establish and develop relationships with other human beings and the outside world. Although no previous case has established as such any right to self-determination as being contained in art.8 of the ECHR, the Court considers that the notion of personal autonomy is an important principle underlying the interpretation of its guarantees."[233]

13-086   Private life has been held to extend to business relationships and environmental

---

marised the principles of proportionality under EU law. On the potential for a proportionality approach to supplant the common law ground of rationality in claims for judicial review, particularly those which engage fundamental rights, see *Youssef v Secretary of State for Foreign and Commonwealth Affairs* [2016] UKSC 3; [2016] A.C. 1457 at [55]–[57].

[226] *Lustig-Prean and Beckett v United Kingdom* (2000) 29 E.H.R.R. 548 at [80].

[227] *Soering v United Kingdom* (1989) 11 E.H.R.R. 439 at [89].

[228] In *Hirst v United Kingdom* (2006) 42 E.H.R.R. 41 at [78]-[79], the ECtHR found that the UK had failed to provide evidence of any considered debate in the legislature before the imposition of the blanket ban on prisoners voting.

[229] See 11-080.

[230] *R. v Secretary of State for the Home Department Ex p. Daly* [2001] UKHL 26; [2001] 2 A.C. 532 at [27] (Lord Steyn).

[231] *de Freitas v Permanent Secretary of Ministry of Agriculture, Fisheries, Land and Housing* [1999] 1 A.C. 69 at 80 (Lord Clyde).

[232] Article 8 includes the protection of reputation (*Guardian News and Media Ltd* [2010] UKSC 1; [2010] 2 A.C. 697 at [37]–[42] (Lord Rodger), explaining the ECtHR's decision in *Karako v Hungary* (2011) 52 E.H.R.R. 36 at [22]-[28], which appeared to distinguish between the right to personal integrity (which is protected by art.8) and the right to reputation. The Defamation Act 2013 came into force on 25 April 2013.

[233] *Pretty v United Kingdom* (2002) 35 E.H.R.R. 1 at [61]. A majority of the SC (Baroness Hale and Lord Kerr dissenting) rejected a challenge to the blanket ban on assisted suicide on the basis of art.8 in *R. (Nicklinson) v Ministry of Justice* [2014] UKSC 38; [2015] A.C. 657. An application to the ECtHR by the same individuals was ruled inadmissible: [2015] ECHR 709 (16 July 2015).

issues such as noise or pollution may give rise to a claim.[234] Article 8 may even provide some protection in what may appear to be public places if the individual has a reasonable expectation of privacy there.[235] Family life is also broadly defined

---

[234] *Niemietz v Germany* (1993) 16 E.H.R.R. 97 at [29]-[33] (a search of a lawyer's offices) and *Hatton v United Kingdom* (2002) 34 E.H.R.R. 1 at [107] (noise pollution from night flights over houses). See also *Dubetska v Ukraine* (2015) 61 E.H.R.R.11 (a factory and mine causing subsidence). The House of Lords rejected a challenge to the hunting ban on the basis that it was fundamentally a public activity (*R. (on the application of Countryside Alliance) v Attorney General* [2008] UKHL 52; [2008] 1 A.C. 719 at [15] (Lord Bingham), [54]-[55] (Lord Hope), [90]-[100] (Lord Rodger), [115]-[116] (Baroness Hale) and [137]-[141] (Lord Brown)). The ECtHR affirmed that the ban did not constitute an interference with art.8 on the basis of its "essentially public nature" in *Countryside Alliance v United Kingdom* (2010) 50 E.H.R.R. SE6 at [40]-[46]. The House of Lords held that art.8 may be engaged by being placed on a provisional list of carers considered unsuitable to work with vulnerable adults given its effect on livelihood (*Wright* [2009] UKHL 3; [2009] 1 A.C. 739). See *R. (on the application of G) v Nottinghamshire Healthcare NHS Trust* [2009] EWCA Civ 795 at [46]-[51] (art.8 was not engaged by a smoking ban inside and outside a high security psychiatric institution given the expectations of privacy in such accommodation and given that smoking was not sufficiently integral to a person's identity to engage art.8). Cellular confinement without association with other prisoners for 10-16 days may interfere with art.8 (*R. (on the application of King) v Secretary of state for Justice* [2010] EWHC 2522 (Admin); [2011] 1 W.L.R. 2667 at [114] (Pitchford LJ). The SC agreed that the latter was unlawful (reversing the CA's decision) but decided the case on the basis that the segregation had not been authorised by the relevant legislation. The SC decision is *R. (on the application of King) v Secretary of State for Justice* [2015] UKSC 54; [2016] A.C. 384. Further examples of situations in which art.8 may be engaged include: long-lasting and severe restrictions on a prisoner's ability to receive prison visits (*Khoroshenko v Russia (App. No. 41418/04) (30 June 2015)* at [148]); the manner in which criminal proceedings are conducted (*Y v Slovenia* (2016) 62 E.H.R.R. 3, in which during criminal proceedings for sexual assault the alleged victim was subjected to lengthy and traumatic cross-examination by the alleged perpetrator); the requirement for an individual wishing to undergo sex reassignment surgery to first obtain a court authorisation which would only be granted where the individual had undergone sterilisation (*YY v Turkey* (App. No. 14793/08) (10 March 2015)); the failure of the state to provide information about the fate of a baby who died in a state-run medical centre (*Jovanovic v Serbia* (2015) 61 EHRR 3 at [74]-[75]); the failure to provide legal aid in certain immigration cases (*R. (on the application of Gudanaviciene) v Director of Legal Aid Casework* [2014] EWCA Civ 1622; [2015] 1 W.L.R. 2247); the failure of the state properly to investigate allegations of racially motivated abuse (*RB v Hungary* (2017) 64 E.H.R.R. 25; and a prison policy implementing an absolute prohibition on growing a beard where the state failed to demonstrate a pressing social need or any justification based on hygiene or the need to identify prisoners (*Biržietis v Lithuania* (App. No. 49304/09) (14 June 2016)). In *R. (on the application of JK) v Registrar General for England and Wales* [2015] EWHC 990 (Admin), it was held that the UK's birth registration scheme did not breach arts 8 or 14 by requiring men who had changed gender from male to female to be listed as the "father" on the birth certificates of their biological children. There is no breach of art.8 in prosecuting someone for possessing an identity card relating to someone else with the intention of passing oneself of as the other person (*SXH v Crown Prosecution Service* [2017] UKSC 30; [2017] 1 W.L.R. 1401). There was no interference with the claimant's art.8 rights in the application of the Prevent Duty Guidance to him since he had entered into public debate on the relevant matters (*R. (on the application of Butt) v Secretary of State for the Home Department* [2017] EWHC 1930 (Admin); [2017] 4 W.L.R. 154 at [219]-[227]).

[235] A public figure may therefore be protected from press intrusion while engaged in everyday activities (such as shopping or fetching their children from school): *Von Hannover v Germany* (2005) 40 E.H.R.R. 1 at [61]-[69]. *Murray v Express Newspapers Plc* [2008] EWCA Civ 446; [2009] Ch. 481 at [45]-[61] (Sir Anthony Clarke MR) involved a domestic application of the *Von Hannover* principle in a claim for damages arising from photographs of Mrs Murray's (the author J.K. Rowling's) two-year old son in the street. See further, M. Warby, N. Moreham and I. Christie, *The Law of Privacy and the Media* (2011) and, for a comparative perspective, M. Colvin (ed), *Developing Key Privacy Rights: The Impact of the Human Rights Act 1998* (2002). Article 8 was breached by the release of CCTV footage taken in the street of a man attempting suicide (*Peck v United Kingdom* (2003) 36 E.H.R.R. 41 at [62]-[87]) and a police search of the person and their belongings in public was a clear interference with art.8 in *Gillan and Quinton* (2010) 50 E.H.R.R. 45 at [61]-[65]. In *Re JR38's Application for Judicial Review* [2015] UKSC 42; [2016] A.C. 1131, the SC found that publication by the police of images of a 14-year-old boy committing public order offences did not violate his art.8

and extends beyond formal relationships and covers de facto couples, illegitimate or adopted children and the extended family.[236] The definition of home is broad, but requires the existence of sufficient and continuous links. There is no right to a choice of a particular home.[237] Correspondence extends beyond more traditional written forms of communication.[238] Article 8 also imposes positive obligations on

rights as he could not have had a reasonable expectation that photographs of him committing the offences would not be published. Opinion was divided as to whether art.8(1) was engaged at all. Participation in politics has been held to be a matter of public life, to which art.8 can have only limited application: *Misick v United Kingdom* (2013) 56 E.H.R.R. SE13 at [29]. There, the applicant claimed his removal as the elected representative of the North Caicos East constituency violated his art.8 right to respect for his private life. The application was declared inadmissible in the absence of any evidence of an encroachment on the applicant's private life or privacy. In *Weller v Associated Newspapers Ltd* [2015] EWCA Civ 1176; [2016] 1 W.L.R. 1541, the CA found that publication of photographs taken in California of the children of a British celebrity by an English newspaper breached the children's art.8 rights, and that the family had a reasonable expectation of privacy notwithstanding that publication of the photographs would have been lawful under Californian law (appeal outstanding).

[236] *Kroon v Netherlands* (1994) 19 E.H.R.R. 263 at [30] (de facto relationships) and *Marckx v Belgium* (1979) 2 E.H.R.R. 330 at [31] (illegitimate children). The ECtHR has traditionally been less willing to acknowledge homosexual relationships as constituting family (as opposed to private) life. This may be changing (see *Goodwin*, (2002) 35 E.H.R.R. 18). See *EB v France* (2008) 47 E.H.R.R. 21. The SC struck down an amendment to the Immigration Rules 2004 which provided that a marriage visa would not usually be granted unless both parties were over 21 years of age (*R. (on the application of Quila) v Secretary of State for the Home Department* [2011] UKSC 45; [2012] 1 A.C. 621 at [44]-[59] (Lord Wilson). See *Vallianatos v Greece* (2014) 59 E.H.R.R. 12 and *Oliari v Italy* (2015) 40 B.H.R.C. 549 at [178] and [185]-[187] on the ECtHR's developing recognition of same-sex relationships. In *R. (on the application of Bright) v Secretary of State for Justice* [2014] EWCA Civ 1628; [2015] 1 W.L.R. 723, the CA held that the decision to separate prisoners who were in long-term, same-sex relationships with fellow prisoners had not breached their art.8 rights. The ECtHR held that there had been no breach of art.8 in a case in which a child was removed from a couple who had entered into an (illegal) commercial surrogacy arrangement. The court held that the couple had no family life with the 9 month old baby and that their rights to a private life were overridden by the need to avoid condoning a breach of the criminal law (*Paradiso and Campanelli v Italy* (2017) 65 E.H.R.R. 2). In *R. (on the application of MM (Lebanon)) v Secretary of State for the Home Department* [2017] UKSC 10; [2017] 1 W.L.R. 771 at [56]-[61], the SC upheld the requirements of the Immigration Rules which imposed minimum income requirements on those with the right to live in the United Kingdom who wished to bring their spouses who were non-EEA citizens to this country against a general challenge (although the interests of children could give rise to a breach). An appeal to the SC has been heard, and judgment reserved. The positive obligations imposed on a state by art.8 are also frequently cited in cases concerning the Hague Convention on the Civil Aspects of International Child Abduction. In an important decision, the HC of Northern Ireland held that the criminal prohibition on abortion violated art.8 in relation to fatal foetal abnormalities at any time and pregnancies resulting from rape and sexual assault up to the date of viability, and issued a declaration of incompatibility (*Re Northern Ireland Human Rights Commission's Application for Judicial Review* [2015] NIQB 96 at [160]-[166]).

[237] *Buckley v United Kingdom* (1996) 23 E.H.R.R. 101 at [84]. The court must be able to consider art.8 issues in a possession case (although art.8 is unlikely to be decisive): *Pinnock v Manchester City Council* [2011] UKSC 6; [2011] 2 A.C. 104 at [61]-[64] (Lord Neuberger) and *LB of Hounslow v Powell* [2011] UKSC 8; [2011] 2 A.C. 186 at [33]-[43]. See also *R. (on the application of N) v Lewisham LBC* [2014] UKSC 62; [2015] A.C. 1259 (eviction from temporary accommodation under the Housing Act 1996 s.188 did not breach art.8) and *R. (on the application of SG) v Secretary of State for Work and Pensions* [2015] UKSC 16; [2015] 1 W.L.R. 1449 at [139] (in which Lord Hughes held that the art.8 rights of children were not infringed by the benefit cap scheme introduced by the Benefit Cap (Housing Benefit) Regulations 2012: "elastic as that article has undoubtedly proved, it does not extend to requiring the state to provide benefits, still less benefits calculated simply according to need, nor does it require the state to provide a home". Nor was there a violation of art.14 read with art.1 of the First Protocol).

[238] A reasonable expectation of privacy may extend to telephone calls, emails and internet usage at work if the employer has given no indication that such usage may be monitored (*Copland v United Kingdom* (2007) 45 E.H.R.R. 37 at [41]-[42]). The ECtHR differed strongly from the House of Lords

the State which may give rise to liability arising from the acts of private individuals.[239]

The breadth of this definition means that most cases are resolved at the second stage of justification. Since domestic law contained no right to privacy before the HRA,[240] art.8 has been a focus of litigation since 2000.[241] Where the right to privacy

13-087

---

in holding that the indeterminate retention of fingerprints, DNA profiles and cellular samples from those arrested (even if subsequently acquitted) and which bore no relation to the gravity of the offence or the individual's age at the time of their arrest was disproportionate (*S and Marper v UK* (2009) E.H.R.R. 50 at [105]-[125]). The issue is now addressed in the Protection of Freedom Act 2012. In ordinary circumstances, merely taking a photograph of an individual in a public place would not engage art.8, but where the police did so and retained it in relation to an individual with no criminal record who was not suspected of committing a criminal offence, art.8 was breached (*R. (on the application of Wood) v Commissioner of Police of the Metropolis* [2009] EWCA Civ 414; [2010] 1 W.L.R. 123 at [82]-[90] (Dyson LJ)). Retention of photographs taken on arrest where there is no subsequent conviction also breaches art.8 (*R. (on the application of RMC and FJ) v Commissioner of Police of the Metropolis* [2012] EWHC 1681 (Admin) at [54]-[5], (Richards LJ)). The provisions of the Regulation of Investigatory Powers Act 2000 which permitted covert surveillance of those arrested in breach of their rights to legal professional privilege violated art.8 and a declaration of incompatibility was made (*McE v Prison Service of Northern Ireland* [2009] UKHL 15; [2009] 1 A.C. 908 at [96]-[105] (Lord Carswell)). In *R. (on the application of T) v Chief Constable of Greater Manchester Police* [2014] UKSC 35; [2015] A.C. 49, the SC held that provisions in Pt V of the Police Act 1997 concerning the disclosure of enhanced criminal record certificates, including records of privately issued police cautions, constitute an aspect of the private life of the recipient and so engage art.8. The SC held that the provisions breached the requirements in art.8(2) since the cumulative effect of the failure to draw distinctions based on: the nature of the offence; the disposal of the case; the time elapsed since the offence took place; the relevance of the offence to the employment sought; and the absence of any independent review of the decision to disclose was that the provisions were not in accordance with the law (at [113]-[114], [119] and [158]). The SC also held that the provisions bore no rational connection to the assessment of the risks posed by those wishing to work with children or the elderly and were therefore not necessary in a democratic society (at [121], [158]). The CA held the amended scheme (which did not generally require the disclosure of spent convictions or cautions) remained in breach of art.8 because, for example, it required the disclosure of multiple offences (however minor) and serious offences (however long ago and whatever the disposal) (*R. (on the application of P) v Secretary of State for the Home Department* [2017] EWCA Civ 321; [2017] 2 Cr. App. R. 12 at [39]-[45]). The SC held that the powers to detain and question those suspected of involvement in terrorism contained in Sch.7 to the Terrorism Act 2000 do not violate art.8 as it contained sufficient safeguards to avoid arbitrary application (*Beghal v Director of Public Prosecutions* [2015] UKSC 49; [2016] A.C. 88 at [52]-[56]). In *Re Gaughran's Application for Judicial Review* [2015] UKSC 29; [2016] A.C. 345 at [44]-[49,] the SC held that the indefinite retention of the DNA profiles (not samples) of those who had been convicted of recordable offences was proportionate and justified under art.8(2). The case was distinguished from *S and Marper v the UK* (2008) 48 E.H.R.R. 50. In *R. (on the application of Catt) v Association of Chief Police Officers of England, Wales and Northern Ireland* [2015] UKSC 9; [2015] A.C. 1065 at [33]-35], the retention of records of an elderly man's non-violent participation in demonstrations organised by an extremist protest group was held to be proportionate. See *Secretary of State for the Home Department v Davis* [2015] EWCA Civ 1185; [2017] 1 All E.R. 62 at [110] for consideration of data retention under EU law and the "more extensive protection" provided by the Charter of Fundamental Rights of European Union arts 7 and 8 compared to art.8 of the Convention.

[239] In *Von Hannover* (2005) 40 E.H.R.R. 1, the state was liable because its law provided insufficient protection from intrusion by the media. The ECtHR held that the state had failed to provide sufficient protection for the applicant's reputation where national proceedings against the editor of a newspaper which had accused the applicant of hounding a pro-Nazi professor to death failed on the basis of fair comment (*Pfeifer v Austria* (2009) 48 E.H.R.R. 8 at [37]-[48]). This decision may require domestic courts to extend the scope of protection for reputation provided by the current law of defamation. Norway's failure to provide information about the damaging effects of decompression on divers amounted to a breach of art.8 (*Vilnes v Norway* (2013) 36 B.H.R.C. 297 at [233]-[245]).

[240] *Wainwright v Home Office* [2003] UKHL 53; [2004] 2 A.C. 406 (a strip search in breach of the Prison Rules on two visitors gave rise to no cause of action in English law). The ECtHR unsurprisingly found a violation of art.8 (*Wainwright v United Kingdom* (2007) 44 E.H.R.R. 40 at [46]-[49]).

comes into potential conflict with the right to freedom of expression (or, more specifically, freedom of the press), the court will engage in a balancing exercise on the facts with no priority accorded to the rights on either side of the balance.[242] It has often been invoked in the context of immigration decisions.[243] Domestic courts

---

[241] It has been invoked in relation to decisions to dismiss employees for sexual activity outside the workplace (*X v Y (Unfair Dismissal)* [2004] EWCA Civ 662; [2004] I.C.R. 1634 at [51] (Mummery LJ, no interference since the activity was found to take place in public)). In *Pay v United Kingdom* (2009) 48 E.H.R.R. SE2, the ECtHR rejected as inadmissible the applicant's claim that his dismissal for taking part in bondage-domination-sado-masochistic floor shows in private clubs was a breach of art.8. The ECtHR did not express a concluded view on whether the activities fell within art.8. In *Mosley v News Group Newspapers Ltd* [2008] EWHC 1777 (QB); [2008] E.M.L.R. 20 at [98]-[109] (Eady J), mild BDSM activities were held to fall within art.8 even when paid for and when they involved a number of participants. Mr Mosley was awarded substantial damages. Dissatisfied with this, Mr Mosley argued in Strasbourg that the UK was required to introduce a rule that newspapers would have to notify an individual that it was proposing to publish private information before doing so. The ECtHR held that art.8 carried no such obligation and that the availability of damages was generally sufficient given the need to balance art.8 against freedom of the press (*Mosley v United Kingdom* (2011) 53 E.H.R.R. 30 at [117]-[132]). Freedom of the press also outweighed the art.8 interests in anonymity of suspected terrorists whose assets had been frozen in *Re Guardian News and Media Ltd* [2010] UKSC 1; [2010] 2 A.C. 697 at [63]-[75] (Lord Rodger). On anonymity more generally, see *JIH*, fn.146 above. *Re A (A Child)* [2012] UKSC 60; [2013] 2 A.C. 66 at [33]-[35] involved a successful claim that a child's rights to be protected from a potentially abusive parent outweighed the other parties' rights to anonymity. In *X (A Child) v Dartford & Gravesham NHS Trust* [2015] EWCA Civ 96; [2015] 1 W.L.R. 3647, the CA gave guidance as to the granting of anonymity orders where the court approves the settlement of personal injury damages. Unless it is judged unnecessary, an order should normally be made without the need for a formal application (though the press should first be permitted to make submissions). In *McDonald v UK* (2015) 60 E.H.R.R. at [53]-[58], the ECtHR found that the decision to reduce the amount allocated for Ms McDonald's care did interfere with her art.8 rights since it required her to wear incontinence pads at night when she was not incontinent and had previously been assisted to use the lavatory by a night-time carer. However, the ECtHR found the interference to be necessary in the field of allocating scarce welfare resources and to have appropriately balanced her needs against the interests of the wider community.

[242] *Khuja v Times Newspapers Ltd* [2017] UKSC 49; [2017] 3 W.L.R. 351 at [23] (Lord Sumption). In that case, as majority of the SC held that Mr Khuja was not entitled to an injunction preventing his name from being reported in relation to child exploitation proceedings in which he had been arrested but never charged. The SC relied on the common law's strong commitment to open reporting of legal proceedings and the public's awareness that arrest did not connote guilt (at [34]-[35]).

[243] Immigration authorities are required to take account of the impact of a proposed removal on the individual concerned and their family (usually a spouse or minor child) (*Beoku-Betts v Secretary of State for the Home Department* [2008] UKHL 39; [2009] 1 A.C. 115 at [41]-[44] (Lord Brown)). Where the deportation of parents will entail the removal of a child, the child's best interests must be a primary consideration (*ZH (Tanzania) v Secretary of State for the Home Department* [2011] UKSC 4; [2011] 2 A.C. 166 at [30]-[33] (Baroness Hale)). In *EM (Lebanon) v Secretary of State for the Home Department* [2008] UKHL 64; [2009] 1 A.C. 1198 at [7]-[18] (Lord Hope), the HL found that there would be flagrant breach of art.8 in the exceptional circumstances of the case if the claimant were returned to Lebanon where, under Sharia law, her son would be handed over to his abusive father who he had never met. Exceptional circumstances are required under art.8 to outweigh the general public interest in extradition: *Norris v Government of the United States of America* [2010] UKSC 9; [2010] 2 A.C. 487 at [56] (Lord Phillips) and *H(H) v Deputy Prosecutor of the Italian Republic, Genoa* [2012] UKSC 25; [2013] 1 A.C. 338 at [67]-[79]. See fn.175 above. In *Jeunesse v Netherlands* (2015) 60 E.H.R.R. 17, the Grand Chamber noted that where family life is created in the knowledge of precarious immigration status, only in exceptional circumstances will removal of a non-national family member violate art.8. However, such exceptional circumstances did, on the facts, exist: all members of the applicant's family with the exception of herself were Netherlands nationals; the applicant had been in the Netherlands for more than 16 years and had no criminal record; although there would apparently be no insurmountable obstacles for the family to settle in Suriname, it was likely that the applicant and her family would experience a degree of hardship if they were forced to do so; and the best interests of the children were of paramount importance and were not served by disrupting their present circumstances. In the UK, "Appendix FM" to the Im-

have used art.8 to develop a right not to be subject to offensive disclosures and to replace the protective jurisdiction of the Family Division over children's right to privacy.[244]

Freedom of thought, conscience and religion   Article 9 protects the right to   **13-088**
freedom of thought, conscience and religion which includes the right to change one's religion or belief and to manifest those beliefs in worship, teaching, practice and observance either alone or with others and in public or private.[245] Freedom of thought, conscience and religion is a fundamental Convention right and may be regarded as absolute, in contrast to the right to manifest such beliefs which may be subject to legitimate interference. There is no qualitative restriction on which beliefs fall within art.9. However, the ECtHR has required that a belief must go beyond mere opinions or ideas and achieve a certain level of cogency, seriousness, cohesion and importance.[246] In order to qualify for protection under art.9, domestic

migration Rules purports to establish a "complete code" for the court's assessment of art.8 claims under the Rules and requires that there should be exceptional circumstances for art.8 to outweigh the public interest in deporting foreign criminals. *Ali v Secretary of State for the Home Department* [2016] UKSC 60; [2016] 1 W.L.R. 4799 decides that the decision-maker should attach considerable weight to the manner in which the Rules had struck the balance between the competing interests. In *R. (MA (Pakistan)) v Upper Tribunal (Immigration and Asylum Chamber)* [2016] EWCA Civ 705; [2016] 1 W.L.R. 5093, the CA held that when assessing the best interests of a child in the context of an art.8 evaluation, the court is not obliged to start by considering the child's best interests, but must nevertheless treat them as a primary consideration. See *Kiarie* [2017] UKSC 42; [2017] 1 W.L.R. 2380 on out of country appeal rights. The SC rejected a challenge to the immigration rule which requires a foreign spouse of a British citizen to produce a certificate of knowledge of English prior to entry, although noting that breaches could occur in individual cases (*R. (on the application of Bibi) v Secretary of State for the Home Department* [2015] UKSC 68; [2015] 1 W.L.R. 5055). It was lawful to deprive the applicant of his British citizenship and deport him on the basis of his activities with Al-Shabaab (*K2 v United Kingdom* (2017) 64 E.H.R.R. SE18).

[244] The model Naomi Campbell's art.8 rights were violated by photographs of her leaving a meeting of Narcotics Anonymous: *Campbell v MGN Ltd* [2004] UKHL 22; [2004] 2 A.C. 457 at [116]-[118] (Lord Hope) and [149]-[157] (Baroness Hale). Domestic relief was founded on the cause of action in breach of confidence based on the misuse of private information. N. Moreham, "Privacy in Public Places" [2006] C.L.J. 606. See further, *Re S (A Child)* [2004] UKHL 47; [2005] 1 A.C. 593 at [15]-[17] (Lord Steyn).

[245] See further, S. Knights, *Freedom of Religion, Minorities and the Law* (2006); C. Evans, *Freedom of Religion Under the European Convention on Human Rights* (2001); R. Sandberg, *Law and Religion* (2011), Ch 5; and I. Leigh and R. Ahdar, "Post-Secularism and the European Court of Human Rights: Or How God Never Really Went Away" (2012) 75 M.L.R. 1064. See further, J. Dingemans, C. Yeginsu, T. Cross and H. Masood, *The Protections for Religious Rights: Law and Practice* (2013).

[246] *Campbell and Cosans* (1982) 4 E.H.R.R. 243 at [36]. This covers beliefs as diverse as pacifism or veganism. In *Lautsi v Italy* (2012) 54 E.H.R.R. 3 at [58], the ECtHR found that the views of secularists who challenged the presence of crucifixes in state schools qualified as philosophical convictions. Domestic courts have applied the same approach (*R. (on the application of Williamson) v Secretary of State for Education and Skills* [2005] UKHL 15; [2005] 2 A.C. 246 at [23]-[24] (Lord Nicholls). The High Court of Australia also adopted a similar approach in *Church of the New Faith v Commissioner of Pay-Roll Tax (Victoria)* (1983) 154 C.L.R. 120 at 129-130 and 174 where it found scientology to be a religion. The belief should also be consistent with Convention values and worthy of respect in a democratic society. The Employment Appeal Tribunal relied on the ECtHR's jurisprudence under art.9 and art.2 of the First Protocol in holding that the opinion that children were better brought up by a heterosexual couples was not a philosophical or religious belief as it was expressly stated to be based on evidence and logic (*McClintock v Department of Constitutional Affairs* [2008] I.R.L.R. 29 at [45] (Elias J)). A belief in the anthropogenic causes of climate change and human responsibility for addressing it can constitute a philosophical belief for the purpose of the Employment Equality (Religion or Belief) Regulations 2003: *Grainger Plc v Nicholson* [2010] I.C.R. 360 at [27]-[31] (Burton J) as can belief in the sanctity of life and opposition to hunting animals for sport (*Hashman v Milton Park (Dorset) Ltd* (ET/3105555/09, 31 January 2011)). In R.

courts have held that a manifestation must be intimately linked to it (rather than merely being associated with it).[247]

13-089   The existence of an established church does not violate art.9, but the State's responsibility is generally to hold the ring and permit a variety of religions to be practised. The State should not impose severe disadvantage on the individual in order to encourage support for a particular belief.[248] Restrictions on this right must fulfil the standard criteria for limiting qualified Convention rights and generally require evidence that the State has sought to strike a fair balance between the competing interests.[249]

(on the application of Hodkin) v Registrar of Births, Deaths and Marriages [2013] UKSC 77; [2014] A.C. 610, the SC held that a chapel of the Church of Scientology was a "place of meeting for religious worship" for the purposes of the Places of Worship Registration Act 1855. In *Izzettin Doğan v Turkey* (2017) 64 E.H.R.R. 5, the GC found a violation of art.9 taken alone and in conjunction with art.14. The Turkish authorities' failure to recognise the Alevi faith amounted to denying its members their right to "effectively enjoy" their religious freedom. The GC reiterated (at [107]) that while states may assess objective elements of a belief (seriousness, cohesion etc.), that role excluded "any discretion on its part to determine whether religious beliefs or the means used to express such beliefs are legitimate".

[247] As such, the distribution of leaflets to soldiers encouraging them not to serve in Northern Ireland was an attempt to challenge British policy in that province rather than an expression of pacifist beliefs (*Arrowsmith v United Kingdom* (1978) 3 E.H.R.R. 218 at [71]). The wearing of a purity ring was held not to be sufficiently intimately connected with Christian belief in *Playfoot* [2007] EWHC 1698 (Admin); [2007] H.R.L.R. 34. In *R. (on the application of Bashir) v Independent Adjudicator* [2011] EWHC 1108 (Admin) at [20]–[21] (HHJ Pelling QC), a prisoner's refusal to break his fast to provide a urine sample for drug testing was held to be a manifestation of his belief even though it was a personal fast and not part of a religious festival. Article 9 also protects the negative right not to manifest one's faith: In *Isik v Turkey* (2015) 61 E.H.R.R. 6 at [42]–[53], it was held, on this basis, that the art.9 rights of the Alevi applicant had been violated by the mandatory requirement to display his faith on an identity card (though it was not violated by the refusal of the authorities to indicate Alevi, rather than Islam).

[248] Requiring a member of parliament to swear on the gospel in order to retain his seat was a breach of art.9 (*Buscarini v San Marino* (2000) 30 E.H.R.R. 208 at [34]–[41]). This level of severity was not reached by requiring lower test scores for Catholics than Protestants in order to enter the Northern Ireland Police Service (*Re Parson's Application for Judicial Review* [2004] N.I. 38). The House of Lords upheld a decision not to exempt certain buildings owned by the Mormon Church from business rates on the ground that they were not open to the public (*Gallagher (Valuation Officer) v Church of Jesus Christ of the Latter-Day Saints* [2008] UKHL 56; [2008] 1 W.L.R. 1852 at [12] (Lord Hoffmann)). The requirement that the building be open to the public was of general application and did not prevent the members of the church from manifesting their religion. The ECtHR found no violation of art.9 in *Church of Jesus Christ of Latter-Day Saints v UK* (2014) 59 E.H.R.R. 18. The SC powerfully emphasised that the right to freedom of thought and opinion must extend to the right not to express support for a particular view in *RT (Zimbabwe) v Secretary of State for the Home Department* [2012] UKSC 38; [2013] 1 A.C. 152 at [25]–[52].

[249] For example, between a Muslim teacher's desire for time off to attend Friday prayers and the state's need to organise the school curriculum efficiently (*Ahmad v United Kingdom* (1981) 4 E.H.R.R. 126 at [11]–[19]). Restrictions on wearing headscarves for university students to support the secular nature of the State have been upheld (*Sahin v Turkey* (2007) 44 E.H.R.R. 5). See further, D. McGoldrick, *Human Rights and Religion: The Islamic Headscarf Debate in Europe* (2006). In *SAS v France* (2015) 60 E.H.R.R. 11 at [106]–[159], the Grand Chamber held that the interference with the art.9 rights of the applicant, who wore a niqab (full face veil) occasioned by Law No.2010–1192, which prohibited concealment of the face in public places, was proportionate to the aim pursued: namely the preservation of the conditions of "living together". A similar ban was upheld as lawful against challenges based on arts 9 and 10 in *Belcacemi and Oussar v Belgium* (App. No.37798/13) (11 July 2017) (French only). The domestic cases of *Williamson* and *SB* are described at fn.218. In *SB*, the majority of the HL decided that the school's prohibition on the jilbab was not an interference with SB's art.9 rights since she could have attended another school in the area which permitted it. Restrictions must, of course, be proportionate and a criminal ban on door-to-door proselytising exceeded the state's margin of appreciation (*Kokkinakis v Greece* (1993) 17 E.H.R.R. 397 at [47]–[50]). The Court of Appeal upheld the decision not to grant an exemption from the policy

Freedom of expression   Article 10 protects the right to freedom of expression and   **13-090**
the right to hold opinions and receive and impart information without interference
by a public authority.²⁵⁰ Freedom of expression is regarded as one of the
cornerstones of any democratic society. Expression is broadly defined and includes
artistic and commercial expression as well as the political and journalistic.²⁵¹ It ap-

on slaughtering cattle with bovine tuberculosis in relation to a Hindu community's temple bullock
(*R. (on the application of Swaami Suryananda) v Welsh Ministers* [2007] EWCA Civ 893 at [51]–
[60] (Pill LJ)). It was held to be a legitimate interference with hotel owners' art.9 beliefs (that unmarried couples (including, by definition, homosexuals) should not share a bed: *Bull and Bull v Hall
and Preddy* [2012] EWCA Civ 83; [2012] 1 W.L.R. 2514 at [50]–[51] (Rafferty LJ)). The SC affirmed the CA's decision in *Preddy v Bull* [2013] UKSC 73; [2013] 1 W.L.R. 3741 at [38]–[39] and
[51]–[55]. For helpful discussion of the relationship between the state's duties under art.9 and art.11,
see *Sindicatul "Păstorul Cel Bun" v Romania* (2014) 58 E.H.R.R. 10, discussed in fn.263 below.
On the interrelation of arts 9 and 11 see also *Karaahmed v Bulgaria* (App. No. 30587/13) (24 February 2015). There was a violation of the art.9 rights of worshippers in a Bulgarian mosque on the basis
that the state had failed to strike a proper balance in the steps they took to ensure the effective and
peaceful exercise of rights of demonstrators from the Ataka political party and the rights of the applicant and the other worshippers to pray together. See also *Church of Scientology of St Petersburg
v Russia* (App. No. 47191/06) (2 October 2014) at [37]–[48], in which the ECtHR held that Russia's refusal to grant legal-entity status to the applicant amounted to a breach of art.9 interpreted in
the light of art.11. In *Eweida v United Kingdom* (2013) 57 E.H.R.R. 8 the ECtHR held that it was a
breach of art.9 to refuse to permit an employee to wear a discrete cross at work, but permissible to
discipline a registrar who refused to carry out civil partnership ceremonies (between couples of the
same gender) on the grounds of her religious beliefs. Departing from earlier authority, the ECtHR
has held that conscientious objection to military service is covered by art.9 and a conviction for refusing to serve (rather than establishing alternative forms of public service) was a breach: *Bayatyan v
Armenia* (2012) 54 E.H.R.R. 15 at [99]–[128]. The CA upheld a requirement that a carer should work
on Sundays despite her Christian faith since there was no other viable and practicable way of running a care home (*Mba v Merton LBC* [2013] EWCA Civ 1562; [2014] 1 W.L.R. 1501 at [34]–
[37]). In *Doogan v Greater Glasgow and Clyde Health Board* [2014] UKSC 68; [2015] A.C. 640,
the "conscience clause" in s.4(1) of the Abortion Act 1967 was held not to exempt the midwife applicants from various managerial and supervisory tasks in a labour ward in which abortions were
carried out. At [23]–[24] Baroness Hale, while describing art.9 as a "distraction", observed: "a state
employer has also to respect his employees' Convention rights ... even if not protected by the
conscience clause in section 4, the petitioners may still claim that, either under the Human Rights
Act 1998 or under the Equality Act 2010, their employers should have made reasonable adjustments to the requirements of the job in order to cater for their religious beliefs". In *Lee v Ashers Bak-
ing Co Ltd* [2016] NICA 39, the refusal of a bakery owned by two Christians to bake a cake which
had printed on it a picture of "Bert and Ernie" and the caption "Support Gay Marriage" was held to
be unlawful direct discrimination on grounds of sexual orientation (which must be wrong in its
analysis of the appropriate comparison). In *Süveges v Hungary* (App. No. 50255/12) (5 January
2016) at [151]–[157], the ECtHR held that the art.9 right of an applicant held under house arrest pre-
trial had not been violated, the interference with his ability to attend Mass being proportionate to
the state's legitimate aim. In *Ebrahimian v France* (App. No. 64846/11) (26 November 2015) the
ECtHR found no violation of art.9 where a public hospital had refused to renew the contract of a
social assistant who refused to remove her headscarf, a symbol of her Muslim faith.

²⁵⁰ See further, E. Barendt, *Freedom of Speech*, 2nd edn (2007).
²⁵¹ *Wingrove v United Kingdom* (1996) 24 E.H.R.R. 1 at [47]–[50] (film) and *Barthold v Germany* (1985)
7 E.H.R.R. 383 at [42]–[43] (advertising). Expression on matters of general public interest is entitled
to the highest level of protection. In *Rubins v Latvia* [2015] I.R.L.R 319 at [80]–[93], the ECtHR
held that the state had violated art.10 by upholding the dismissal of a university professor who had,
in an email, criticised the management of his university following changes to his employment
contract, in part on the basis that the email covered matters of public interest. Further, the termination of the mandate of the President of the Supreme Court in response to criticism by him of the
government's plans to reform the judiciary was a violation of art.10 (*Baka v Hungary* (2017) 64
E.H.R.R. 6). In contrast, in *R. (on the application of Lord Carlile of Berriew QC) v Secretary of State
for the Home Department* [2014] UKSC 60; [2015] A.C. 945, the SC upheld the Secretary of State's
decision to maintain a ban on a dissident Iranian politician entering the United Kingdom to address
the House of Lords (on the basis that Iran would see any lifting of the exclusion as a political move
against it and would be likely to engage in reprisals). In *Karácsony v Hungary* (2017) 64 E.H.R.R.

plies to expressive conduct as well as speech and writing.[252] It also protects speech which shocks, offends or disturbs.[253] However, art.10 provides limited protection

---

10, the GC found a violation of art.10 where opposition members of parliament were subject to disciplinary measures and fined for displaying banners and using a megaphone during a parliamentary session. The ECtHR may be moving towards greater protection for artistic expression. In *Vereinigung Blidender Kunstler v Austria* (2008) 47 E.H.R.R. 5 at [26]-[39], the court found an injunction which was unlimited in time and space preventing the display of a painting depicting a number of public figures engaged in sexual activities to be disproportionate. A ban on tobacco advertising was easily justified on health and economic grounds (*R. (on the application of British American Tobacco UK Ltd) v Secretary of State for Health* [2004] EWHC 2493; [2005] A.C.D. 27 at [38]-[55] (McCombe J)). The ECtHR has acknowledged the fundamental role played by the press in advancing freedom of expression and journalists should be entitled to protect their sources unless there are compelling countervailing arguments (*Financial Times v United Kingdom* (2010) 50 E.H.R.R. 46 at [59]-[62]). The ECtHR distinguished *Financial Times* and similar authorities in a case where the "source" in question was the perpetrator of a bomb attack whose disclosure was "not motivated by the desire to provide information which the public were entitled to know", but rather who "was claiming responsibility for crimes which he had himself committed ... to don the veil of anonymity with a view to evading his own criminal accountability" (*Stichting Ostade Blade v Netherlands* (2014) 59 E.H.R.R. SE9 at [65]). Where the identity of the source is not secret, the issue does not arise as was the case with material appropriated by Edward Snowden: *R. (on the application of Miranda) v Secretary of State for the Home Department* [2016] EWCA Civ 6; [2016] 1 W.L.R. 1505 at [102]. In Miranda, the CA found that the stopping and detention of David Miranda at Heathrow airport for nine hours under Sch.7 of the Terrorism Act 2000 was lawful. However, due to the absence of adequate safeguards against its arbitrary exercise, the CA declared that the stop power conferred by para.2(1) of Sch.7 was incompatible with art.10 in relation to journalistic material (at [113]–[115]). In *Morice v France* (2016) 62 E.H.R.R. 1, the conviction of a lawyer for complicity in defamation following publication of comments in the press was held to be in breach of art.10, those comments comprising value judgments with a sufficient factual basis. The ECtHR acknowledged the special role of lawyers in the administration of justice and held that they may comment in public on the administration of justice, provided that their criticism does not overstep certain bounds (at [132]–[139]). However, lawyers, as protagonists in the justice system, cannot be equated with journalists, who are external witnesses whose task it is to inform the public (at [148]). In *Bédat v Switzerland* (2016) 63 E.H.R.R. 15, the GC considered the art.10 rights of a journalist versus the art.6 rights of a person accused in pending criminal proceedings. The GC determined that the same balancing exercise should be applied as in cases where arts 8 and 10 were engaged (at [52]–[53]). In the present case, there was no art.10 violation by the state where a journalist was convicted and fined for publishing information covered by secrecy of the on-going criminal investigation. In *C (A Child)* [2016] EWCA Civ 798; [2016] 1 W.L.R. 5204 at [24]–[34], the CA considered the balancing of arts 6 and 10, where a judge had refused to allow publication of care proceedings because the child's father, convicted of her murder, had indicated an intention to appeal. The CA held that the risk of art.6 violation was minimal and was outweighed by the principle of open justice and the art.10 rights of the media organisations seeking publication of the judgment.

252   Such as defacing the United States flag at an American airbase (*Percy v DPP* [2001] EWHC Admin 1125 at [27]–[33] (Hallett J) or engaging in sabotage of a fox hunt (*Hashman and Harrup v United Kingdom* (2000) 30 E.H.R.R. 241 at [28]). In *Gough v United Kingdom* (2015) 61 E.H.R.R. 8 at [150], the ECtHR held that the applicant's public nudity, in order to give expression to his opinion as to the inoffensive nature of the human body, fell within the ambit of art.10 (though no breach of art.10 was found).

253   *Lingens v Austria* (1986) 8 E.H.R.R. 407 at [41]-[42]. Some recent decisions of the ECtHR suggest that the protection of reputation and encouraging responsible standards of journalism are being given greater weight than the right to criticise public figures (see, for example, *Lindon, Otczakovsky-Laurnes & July v France* (2008) 46 E.H.R.R. 35 at [57]). Article 10 is frequently balanced against the right to privacy in art.8. For a recent example, where the balance came down in favour of art.10, see *McClaren v News Group Newspapers Ltd* [2012] EWHC 2466; [2012] E.M.L.R. 33 at [26]-[36]. In the GC judgment of *Delfi AS v Estonia* (2016) 62 E.H.R.R. 6, the ECtHR for the first time considered the duties and responsibilities of internet news portals, such as Delfi, under art.10(2). Following Delfi's news articles was a facility for readers to add comments. There was also a facility for readers to mark comments as obscene or insulting (upon which they were removed). Victims of defamatory comments were, in addition, able to notify Delfi directly and Delfi would then immediately remove the comment. Delfi explained this system, along with a statement that the com-

to speech which may be regarded as grossly offensive to groups or individuals.[254] Article 10 imposes positive obligations on the State.[255] Article 10 does not contain a general right to receive information from the state, although the ECtHR is moving towards the recognition such a right where the disclosure of information was

---

ments did not reflect its own opinion and that the authors of comments were responsible for their content, in its "Rules of Comment". Nevertheless, the Grand Chamber found that the domestic courts' imposition of liability on Delfi for certain offensive and threatening comments posted by readers did not constitute a breach of art.10.

[254] In *Jersild v Denmark* (1995) 19 E.H.R.R. 1 at [31]–[37], the ECtHR held that art.10 was breach by prosecuting a journalist for reporting racist insults, but accepted that the speech itself fell outside art.10. In *R. (on the application of Gaunt) v OFCOM* [2011] EWCA Civ 692; [2011] 1 W.L.R. 2355 at [39] (Lord Neuberger), the CA rejected a challenge to the broadcasting regulator's decision to uphold complaints about the offensiveness of an interview carried out with a politician about a local authority's policy on fostering. The CA found that the interview had degenerated into gratuitous abuse. An application to Strasbourg was declared inadmissible in *Gaunt v United Kingdom* (2016) 63 E.H.R.R. SE15. See I. Hare: "Crosses, Crescents and Sacred Cows: Criminalising Incitement to Religious Hatred" [2006] P.L. 521 and "Extreme Speech Under International and Regional Human Rights Standards" in I. Hare and J. Weinstein (eds), *Extreme Speech and Democracy* (2009). Other domestic cases reveal a mixed record. In *Hammond v DPP* [2004] EWHC 69 (Admin) at [32] (May LJ), the court upheld the conviction of an evangelical Christian who carried anti-homosexual signs. On the other hand, the court set aside a conviction for putting up an insulting and abusive poster aimed at the president of a Sikh temple in *Dehal v Crown Prosecution Service* [2005] EWHC 2154 (Admin) at [5]–[11] (Moses J). In *R. (on the application of Core Issues Trust) v Transport for London* [2014] EWCA Civ 34; [2014] P.T.S.R. 785 at [63]–[70], [83]–[89], the CA upheld the defendant's decision to refuse to carry advertisements on its buses on behalf of a Christian organisation ("Not gay! Ex-gay, post-gay and proud. Get over it!"), which responded to a campaign that it had carried by Stonewall ("Some people are gay. Get over it."). Despite this preference for one viewpoint over another, the CA upheld the decision on the grounds that the Christian organisation's message may be offensive to homosexuals. In *Maguire v United Kingdom* (2015) 60 E.H.R.R. SE12, the applicant claimed his art.10 rights had been breached by his sentence and conviction for breach of the peace deriving from his clothing (a black top which, in bright green letters displayed on the front the letters "INLA" (the Irish National Liberation Army), and on the back of which was the slogan "FXCK YOUR POPPY REMEMBER DERRY"). The application was declared inadmissible. In *James Rhodes v OPO* [2015] UKSC 32; [2016] A.C. 219, a mother sought to prevent a father from publishing a book about his life containing descriptions of his subjection to sexual abuse which she considered risked causing psychological harm to their son relying on the tort of intentionally causing physical or psychological harm. The SC held that the tort was not made out. Brief reference was made to art.10 at [120], in stating that the common law should be "generally consistent" with the Convention. In *M'Bala M'Bala v France* (App. No. 25239/13) (20 October 2015) at [34]–[42], the ECtHR considered a well-known comedian's challenge to sanctions imposed by the state following a public performance of an anti-Semitic nature. The ECtHR was "unable to accept that the expression of an ideology which is at odds with the basic values of the Convention, […] can be assimilated to a form of entertainment […] which would be afforded protection" by art.10, and therefore held that the application was inadmissible ratione materiae. In *Perinçek v Switzerland* (see fn.40 above), the GC found a violation of art.10 where the applicant had been convicted of a crime for statements made denying the existence of an Armenian genocide. Russian legislation that banned public activities aimed at the promotion of homosexuality among minors violated art.10 and art.14 (*Bayev v Russia* (App. No. 67667/09) (20 June 2017)). The court would not decide the compatibility of the Prevent Duty Guidance with art.10 in the abstract and would await a concrete case (*R. (on the application of Butt) v Secretary of State for the Home Department* [2017] EWHC 1930 (Admin); [2017] 4 W.L.R. 154 at [152]).

[255] These did not go so far as to require that an individual be given access to a particular forum which was on private property (a shopping centre) where there existed other avenues for such expression (*Appleby v UK* (2003) 37 E.H.R.R. 38 at [47]). However, the state is required to establish an independent procedure for determining whether the public interest requires disclosure of journalists' sources (*Sanoma Uitgevers BV v The Netherlands* [2011] E.M.L.R. 4 at [88]–[100]). In *Centro Europa 7 Srl v Italy* (App. No. 38433/09) (7 June 2012) at [129]-[146], the ECtHR found that Italy had breached its positive obligations under art.10 to guarantee effective pluralism in the audiovisual media in failing to institute an appropriate legal framework to allocate television frequencies to the Europa 7 Channel. The Court awarded just satisfaction of €10m.

necessary to allow meaningful exercise of the right to freedom of expression, especially in relation to the conduct of public affairs.[256]

13-091   As regards limitations, the legitimacy of the licensing of broadcasting, television and cinema is expressly preserved and art.10(2) states that the exercise of the right to freedom of expression carries with it duties and responsibilities.[257] The ECtHR is particularly sceptical of prior restraints and criminal sanctions on expression.[258]

13-092   **Freedom of peaceful assembly and association**   Article 11 confers the right to

---

[256] *Magyar Helsinki Bizottsag v Hungary* (App. No.18030/11) (8 November 2016) at [155]–[168]. The previous position is set in a long line of authorities (and summarised by the Grand Chamber in *Roche v UK* (2005) 42 E.H.R.R. 30 at [172]). More recently, the ECtHR has suggested a broader interpretation of the notion of freedom to receive information (*Tarsasag a Szabadsagjogokert v Hungary* (2009) 53 E.H.R.R. 3 at [36] and *Gillberg v Sweden* (2012) 127 B.M.L.R. 54 at [93]–[94]). Lord Brown expressed strong disapproval of this departure in *BBC v Sugar (No.2)* [2012] UKSC 4; [2012] 1 W.L.R. 439 at [94]. In *Kennedy v Charity Commission* [2014] UKSC 20; [2015] A.C. 455 at [57]–[89], Lord Mance undertook an extensive review of the Strasbourg authorities concerning whether art.10 contained a positive right to receive information from the state. While acknowledging the ECtHR's apparent inconsistency on the point, the SC concluded that no such right could be said to exist on the present state of the authorities (at [93]–[96], [144]–[148], [154]). See further, K. O'Byrne, "Freedom of Information under Article 10 ECHR and the Common Law" (2014) E.H.R.L.R. 284. In *Kalda v Estonia* (2016) 42 B.H.R.C. 145 at [48]–[54], the ECtHR considered restrictions placed by the state on a prisoner's access to certain internet sites. While the court did not assert that states were required to give prisoners access to the internet, where access was available, restrictions and limitations must be lawful and justified. In the present case, restrictions on access to sites containing legal information on fundamental and prisoners' rights were unnecessary in a democratic society and thus a violation of art.10.

[257] The licensing of broadcasting is not therefore subject to art.10(2), but the ECtHR has held that any interference with broadcasting should be minimal and consistent with the broad aims of art.10(2) (*Autotronic AG v Switzerland* (1990) 12 E.H.R.R. 485 at [49]–[52]). In *R. v Dryzner (Ewa)* [2014] EWCA Crim 2438; (2015) 179 J.P. 29, the applicants applied for permission to appeal against convictions for supplying video recordings without classification contrary to the Video Recordings Act 1984 s.9 and a declaration that that provision was incompatible with art.10. The applicant had affixed his own labels to the DVDs choosing their age classification himself. He submitted that the inflexible classification regime was disproportionate when applied to innocuous material and infringed the right to freedom of expression. It was held that the classification requirements that the Act imposed were lawful, necessary and justified for the protection of public health and morals. The House of Lords upheld the total ban on political advertising on the broadcast media (*Animal Defenders*, fn.124 above). It remains unclear whether an absolute prohibition on political advertising is compatible with art.10 (*TV Vest v Norway* (2009) 48 E.H.R.R. 51 at [64]–[78]), particularly in relation to small parties. See T. Lewis and P. Cumper, "Balancing Freedom of Political Expression against Equality of Political Opportunity: the Courts and the UK Broadcasting Ban on Political Advertising" [2009] P.L. 89. By the narrowest majority (of nine votes to eight), the ECtHR upheld the ban as proportionate on the basis of the widespread debate which preceded it and the impact of the broadcast media (*Animal Defenders International v UK* (2013) 57 E.H.R.R. 21 at [106]–[125]). See J. Rowbottom, "Animal Defenders International: Speech, Spending, and a Change of Direction in Strasbourg" (2013) 5 J.M.L. 1. The Divisional Court quashed the application of a policy of refusing permission to a broadcast journalist to interview a terrorism suspect who had been awaiting extradition to the United States for seven years on the ground that it was a disproportionate interference with art.10 in *R. (on the application of the BBC) v Secretary of State for Justice* [2012] EWHC 13; [2013] 1 W.L.R. 964 at [76]–[98] (Singh J).

[258] *Observer v United Kingdom* (1991) 14 E.H.R.R. 153 (the *Spycatcher* case) and *Varh v Turkey* (App. No. 57299/00) (27 April 2006). Domestic courts have upheld criminal restrictions on speech in the Official Secrets Act 1989 (*R. v Shayler* [2002] UKHL 11; [2003] 1 A.C. 247) and a ban on a party political broadcast on grounds of offensiveness (*R. (on the application of ProLife Alliance) v British Broadcasting Corporation* [2003] UKHL 23; [2004] 1 A.C. 185 at [12]–[16] (Lord Nicholls), [78]–[81] (Lord Hoffmann), cf. Lord Scott's dissent, at [94]–[100]). The ECtHR held that conditional fee agreements where the costs awarded to the successful party may be increased by up to 100% to pay the successful party's lawyers did not strike a fair balance between arts 8 and 10 (*MGN v United Kingdom* (2011) 53 E.H.R.R. 5 at [201]–[219]).

freedom of peaceful assembly and to association with others and includes the right to join trade unions for the protection of one's interests. The right to peaceful assembly is often considered along with the right to freedom of expression and is similarly broadly interpreted.[259] As with art.10, the ECtHR will require particularly compelling justifications for restrictions on political assemblies.[260] However, the ECtHR is more willing to accept the imposition of conditions rather than complete bans.[261]

The right to freedom of association does not necessarily mean that an individual can join a particular trade union[262] and does not extend to the regulatory bodies of liberal professions.[263] The right not to associate is also implicitly protected by art.11.[264]   **13-093**

Article 11 also carries positive obligations which may require the State to take   **13-094**

---

[259] A women's peace camp outside Aldermaston was held to be within art.11 in *Tabernacle v Secretary of State for Defence* [2009] EWCA Civ 23.

[260] The ECtHR held a ban on a peaceful demonstration in opposition to a ceremony by surviving members of the SS at a cemetery was in violation of art.11 where there was little evidence of a likelihood of interference with the art.9 rights of other cemetery users: *Ollinger v Austria* (2008) 46 E.H.R.R. 38 at [43]-[51]. The HL held that the decision to escort buses of protestors back to London to prevent them from protesting at an airbase where there was no imminent breach of the peace was a wholly disproportionate interference with art.11 (and art.10): *R. (on the application of Laporte) v Chief Constable of Gloucestershire* [2006] UKHL 55; [2007] 2 A.C. 105. The Court of Appeal rejected the justifications for prohibiting the women's peace camp which had been established for 23 years outside Aldermaston where the form and location of the protest were essential to its effectiveness (*Tabernacle* [2009] EWCA Civ 23 at [40]-[44] (Laws LJ)). In contrast, the court was not persuaded that it was essential to the message of anti-capitalist protestors that they should camp outside St Paul's Cathedral (thereby interfering with the art.9 rights of worshippers) in *The Mayor Commonality and Citizens of London v Samede* [2012] EWCA Civ 160; [2012] 2 All E.R. 1039 at [40]-[50] (Lord Neuberger MR). In *Karpyuk v Ukraine* (2015) 40 B.H.R.C. 74 at [222]-[238], the ECtHR held that in relation to three of the seven applicants, the imposition of long prison sentences for organising an initially peaceful although disruptive protest was a violation of art.11. While a sanction for organising an obstructive gathering and inciting violence might be warranted, the severe sanctions imposed "must have had a chilling effect" on others organising protests and were disproportionate.

[261] In *Bukta v Hungary* (2010) 51 E.H.R.R. 25 at [33]-[39], the ECtHR affirmed that notice requirements for a public demonstration were not necessarily inconsistent with art.11, but that a decision to close down a protest which was a justifiably spontaneous response to a recent event where there was no threat to public order was a disproportionate response. The recent weekly marches against the removal of the Union flag from Belfast City Hall could not be described as spontaneous and should properly have been treated as illegal (*Re DB's Application for Judicial Review* [2017] UKSC 7 at [62]). Domestic courts have upheld the police tactic of containing large crowds (known as "kettling") in order to prevent a breach of the peace in *Moos and McClure v Commissioner of Police of the Metropolis* [2012] EWCA Civ 12 at [77]-[92] (Lord Neuberger MR) in relation to the climate camp in the City of London in 2009 and *R. (on the application of Castle) v Commissioner of Police of the Metropolis* [2011] EWHC 2317 (Admin); [2012] 1 All E.R. 953 at [64]-[73] (Pitchford LJ) in relation to the student protests in Whitehall in November 2010. See *Austin* (2012) 55 E.H.R.R. 14, fn.200 above.

[262] The ECtHR upheld a complaint by the union ASLEF that its art.11 rights had been violated by a UK law which prevented it from excluding a member on the grounds of membership of a political party (in that case, the British National Party) where there was no effect on the individual's livelihood and the union was not a state body (*ASLEF v United Kingdom* (2007) 45 E.H.R.R. 34 at [50]-[53]). Domestic courts upheld the right of the RSPCA to exclude individuals from membership who wished to oppose the Society's position on hunting (*Royal Society for the Prevention of Cruelty to Animals v Attorney General* [2002] 1 W.L.R. 448 at [37] (Lightman J)).

[263] *Le Compte v Belgium* (1981) 4 E.H.R.R. 1 at [64]-[65].

[264] As such, a requirement that all employees should belong to a trade union on pain of dismissal was a breach (*Young, James and Webster v United Kingdom* (1981) 4 E.H.R.R. 38 at [62]-[65]). The ECtHR's decision in *Sorensen v Denmark* (2008) 46 E.H.R.R. 29 at [54]-[71] contains a useful discussion of the positive and negative aspects of freedom of association in the context of union membership.

steps to ensure that other individuals or groups do not interfere with the right of peaceful assembly by violent counter-demonstrations or to prohibit private employers from imposing financial penalties on employees who belong to a trade union.[265] The ECtHR has traditionally held that art.11 does not protect the right to collective bargaining or to call a strike, but these rights are increasingly recognised.[266]

13-095   Limitations must be justified according to the usual requirements. General bans on organisations or on membership of them will rarely be justified.[267] However, art.11(2) expressly legitimises the imposition of lawful restrictions on the exercise of art.11 rights by members of the armed forces, the police or the administration of the state.[268]

13-096   **The right to the enjoyment of possessions**   Article 1 of the First Protocol provides that every natural or legal person is entitled to the peaceful enjoyment of his possessions and that no one shall be deprived of his possessions except in the public interest and subject to the conditions provided for by law and by the general

---

[265] *Plattform "Artze fur das Leben" v Austria* (1988) 13 E.H.R.R. 204 at [32] and *Wilson v United Kingdom* (2002) 35 E.H.R.R. 20 at [47]–[48] respectively. However, it may still be legitimate for the police to intervene against those likely to provoke violence even if they are not themselves engaged in unlawful conduct (*R. (on the application of Hicks) v Commissioner of Police of the Metropolis* [2017] UKSC 9; [2017] A.C. 256 at [32]–[40]. The ECtHR held that the UK had failed to provide adequate protection for the art.11 rights of an elected BNP councillor who was dismissed by his private employer and who could not claim unfair dismissal since he had less than one year's continuity of employment (*Redfearn v United Kingdom* (App. No.47335/06) (6 November 2012) at [42]–[57]). The CA held that the prohibition on having structures such as tents in Parliament Square in the Police Reform and Social Responsibility Act 2011 was not contrary to the UK's positive obligations to facilitate protest in *R. (on the application of Gallastegui) v Westminster CC* [2013] EWCA Civ 28; [2013] 1 W.L.R. 2377 at [40]–[50].

[266] *Schmidt v Sweden* (1976) 1 E.H.R.R. 632, [35]–[36] sets out the traditional view. The earlier case law now needs to be reviewed in light of the ECtHR's judgments in *Demir and Baykara v Turkey* [2009] 48 E.H.R.R 54 at [145]–[154], in which the court held that as a result of international legal developments, the right to bargain collectively had become one of the essential elements of the right to join trade unions under art.11 and *Enerji Yapi-Yol Sen v Turkey* (App. No.68959/01) (21 April 2009 (French text)) in which the ECtHR recognised the right to strike (although it could be subject to conditions and restrictions). In *Unison v Kelly* [2012] I.R.L.R. 442 at [33]–[45] (Supperstone J), restrictions on trade union discipline imposed by the Trade Union and Labour Relations (Consolidation) Act 1992 s.64 were held not to be in breach of art.11. The ECtHR held that a statutory ban on secondary industrial action did not breach art.11 in *National Union of Rail, Maritime and Transport Workers v UK* (2015) 60 E.H.R.R. 10 at [78]–[105]. There was no arguable breach of art.11 in the abolition of the Agricultural wages Board (*Unite the Union v UK* (2016) 63 E.H.R.R. SE7). In *Sindicatul "Păstorul Cel Bun" v Romania* (2014) 58 E.H.R.R. 10 at [143]–[145], [157], [159]– [173], the ECtHR held, by a majority of 11 to six, that a decision of a Romanian Court to revoke registration of a trade union comprised of members of the Orthodox clergy did not amount to a violation of art.11. While the duties performed by the clergy in question did have many of the characteristic features of an employment relationship (which had been denied by the Romanian Government), the ECtHR found that the decision was prescribed by law and not disproportionate (particularly in light of the state's duties under art.9 of the Convention).

[267] A ban on a political party which is committed to the implementation of a manifesto which is contrary to the democratic structure of the state and in conflict with Convention rights was upheld in *Refah Partisi v Turkey* (2003) 37 E.H.R.R. 1 at [93]–[136].

[268] Staff at the UK General Communications Headquarters were held to be covered by this (*Council of Civil Service Unions v United Kingdom* (1987) 50 D.R. 228), but German schoolteachers were not (*Vogt v Germany* (1995) 21 E.H.R.R. 205 at [66]–[67]). Even these general restrictions must be justified by convincing and compelling reasons which were not made out in the case of *Tum Haber Sen and Cinar v Turkey* (2008) 46 E.H.R.R. 19 at [135]–[140]. In *ADEFDROMIL v France* (App. No. 32191/09) (2 October 2014) and *Matelly v France* (App. No. 10609/10) (2 October 2014), the ECtHR held, unanimously, that the blanket ban on trade unions within the French armed forces contravened art.11.

principles of international law.[269] The ECtHR has adopted a broad definition of possessions (which is an autonomous concept under the ECHR) which may include intellectual property rights, shares, licences, rights to compensation and legitimate expectations.[270] After a long period of controversy, it is now also established that there is no need for a statutory benefit to be contributory before it can constitute a possession under the ECHR.[271] The protection of the right may involve positive obligations on the State.[272]

Article 1 has been held to contain three distinct prima facie rights: that the peace-   **13-097**

---

[269] The background to the provision is described in T. Allen, *Property and the Human Rights Act 1998* (2005).

[270] A legitimate expectation must be more than a mere hope, but can arise from an ultra vires act: *Stretch v United Kingdom* (2004) 38 E.H.R.R. 12 at [32]–[41], where the local authority was held to have violated Mr Stretch's legitimate expectation that a lease would be renewed even though the original grant was unlawful. See the domestic case of *Rowland v Environment Agency* [2003] EWCA Civ 1885; [2005] Ch. 1 discussed at 12-075. In cases involving the revocation of a licence, the court must determine whether the licence itself is a possession (as it may be if it has market value and is transferrable) and, if not, whether the revocation has an effect on the good will of the business (which may be a possession) or merely on future unearned income (which is not): *R. (on the application of New London College Ltd) v Secretary of State for the Home Department* [2012] EWCA Civ 51; [2012] Imm. A.R. 563 at [95] (Richards LJ). *New London College Ltd* was decided by the SC on other grounds: [2013] UKSC 51; [2013] 1 W.L.R. 2358. See further on this issue, *R. (on the application of Guildhall College) v Secretary of State for Business, Innovation and Skills* [2014] EWCA Civ 986 at [72]–[75]. *Salvesen v Riddell* [2013] UKSC 22; [2013] H.R.L.R. 23 at [40]–[45] held that provisions of the Agricultural Holdings (Scotland) Act 2003 breached the art.1 rights of landlords. In *Breyer Group Plc v Department of Energy and Climate Change* [2015] EWCA Civ 408; [2015] 1 W.L.R. 4559 at [23] and [47]–[49], the CA held that goodwill was (and loss of future income was not) a possession: a distinction that may require analysing the marketability of the goodwill and the accounting arrangements of the alleged victim. In *R. (on the application of APVCO 19 Ltd) v HM Treasury* [2015] EWCA Civ 648; [2015] S.T.C. 2272 at [46], the CA held that money impressed with an arguable claim by HMRC is not a possession where legislation retrospectively removed loopholes relating to the payment of stamp duty. In *Parrillo v Italy* (2016) 62 E.H.R.R. 8 at [214]–[216], the GC held that human embryos cannot be considered a possession for the purposes of art.1, "[h]aving regard to the economic and pecuniary scope of that Article". In *Bank Mellat v HM Treasury* [2016] EWCA Civ 452; [2017] Q.B. 67 at [28]–[30], the CA held that the general principle is that the company and not its shareholders have the status of victim in relation to claims under art.1. There may be exceptional circumstances where, for example, the sole shareholder is sufficiently linked to the business as to be in effect the owner.

[271] *Stec v United Kingdom* (2006) 43 E.H.R.R. 47 at [53]. This does not mean that the individual can claim a right that a benefit shall continue, but just that their claim to it must be determined in accordance with the law in force at the relevant time. See further, the House of Lords decision in *RJM* (fn.86 above). *Stec* was recently applied by the UK Supreme Court in *Humphreys v Revenue and Customs Commissioners* [2012] UKSC 18; [2012] 1 W.L.R. 1545. See also *AM v Secretary of State for Work and Pensions* [2015] UKSC 47; [2015] 1 W.L.R. 3250 at [24]–[26], in which it was held that the withdrawal of disability living allowance falling within the ambit of art.1 of the First Protocol from a child who was hospitalised for more than 84 days violated his human rights under art.14. In *Béláné Nagy v Hungary* (App. No. 53080/13) (12 December 2016), a bare majority (of 9 votes to 8 votes) found that the applicant's loss of entitlement to a disability pension due to newly introduced eligibility criteria resulted in a violation of art.1 of the First Protocol. The dissenting judges criticised this for going further than existing ECHR jurisprudence.

[272] A failure to take steps to protect the applicants' property from destruction by a landslide at a municipal tip breached art.1 (*Oneryildiz v Turkey* (2005) 41 E.H.R.R. 20 at [134]–[136]). See the domestic case of *Marcic v Thames Water Utilities Ltd* [2003] UKHL 66; [2004] 2 A.C. 42 at [36] (Lord Nicholls) (repeated failure to prevent flooding could violate art.1). The state's positive obligations may be engaged in cases concerning the property and housing rights of persons displaced as a result of international or internal armed conflict. In *Sargsyan v Azerbaijan* (2017) 64 E.H.R.R. 4, the Armenian applicant had been unable to return to his land and home in the disputed territory of Nagorno-Karabakh since 1992. The ECtHR held that the situation concerned a restriction of the applicant's right to the peaceful enjoyment of his possessions (at [218]) and that Azerbaijan's failure to take any alternative measures to restore his property rights or to provide him with compensation resulted in a continuing breach of art.1 of the First Protocol (at [241]–[242]). The case also ad-

ful enjoyment of one's possessions will not be interfered with by the State; that the State will not deprive an individual of his possessions; and that the State will not subject possessions to control.[273] An interference with peaceful enjoyment is generally less intrusive than the exercise of control over it or, of course, a deprivation. The ECtHR will look at the substance of the right in determining whether there has been a deprivation and may find there to be one even if the applicant retains legal ownership.[274] Examples of State control over the use of property include the imposition of taxes, restrictions on evicting tenants and planning controls.[275] The importance of the distinctions is that the ECtHR requires a stronger State justification for deprivations than for control or interferences.

13-098   The limitation clause provides that art.1 is subject to the right of a State to enforce such laws as it deems necessary to control the use of property in accordance with the general interest or to secure the payment of taxes or other contributions or penalties. The interference must be lawful and must strike a fair balance between the public interest and the rights of the individual. The public interest is broadly defined and may be pursued by measures which do not benefit the public as a whole.[276] The requirement that there should be a fair balance essentially requires that the individual should not be excessively prejudiced by the pursuit of the general interest.[277] There is no right to receive the full value of appropriated property under the ECHR, but the level of compensation will plainly be relevant to the fairness of the treatment.[278]

---

dresses jurisdictional issues under art.1 at [121]–[151].

[273] *Sporrong and Lonnroth v Sweden* (1982) 5 E.H.R.R. 35 at [61].

[274] The law on adverse possession was found not to violate art.1 in *JA Pye (Oxford) Ltd v UK* (2008) 46 E.H.R.R. 45 at [64]-[66].

[275] *Mellacher v Austria* (1989) 12 E.H.R.R. 391 at [41]-[44] (rent control). The dividing line between control and a deprivation is not always easy to draw. In *Air Canada v United Kingdom* (1995) 20 E.H.R.R. 150, the airline argued that the state had deprived it of one of its aircraft which was seized after drugs were found onboard and would only be returned on payment of £50,000. The ECtHR found that this amounted to control only (at [33]-[34]). The control of the aircraft by the state was in the public interest and therefore proportionate to the restriction on the enjoyment of possessions.

[276] In *James v United Kingdom* (1986) 8 E.H.R.R. 123 at [45]-[52], the ECtHR rejected a challenge to the leasehold enfranchisement laws by a number of landlords. The interference was justified by the general public interest in property distribution even though only particular leaseholders benefited from it.

[277] For example it was not fair to require small landowners opposed to hunting to transfer their hunting rights to another (*Chassagnou v France* (1999) 29 E.H.R.R. 615 at [74]-[85]). There is no requirement that the State should choose the course of action which involves the least possible impairment of the property owner's rights (e.g. *R. (on the application of Petsafe Ltd) v Welsh Ministers* [2010] EWHC 2908 (Admin) at [65]-[77] (Beatson J) in which a ban on the use of dog collars which could administer an electric shock was upheld on animal welfare grounds.). Nor, when the state seeks to control the use of property, and could do so using different provisions with different consequences in terms of compensation, is there any requirement that it invoke the provision carrying some (or greater) compensation: *Cusack v Harrow LBC* [2013] UKSC 40; [2013] 1 W.L.R. 2022 at [45]–[49], [69]. In *Re. Recovery of Medical Costs for Asbestos Diseases (Wales) Bill* [2015] UKSC 3; [2015] A.C. 1016 at [35]–[69], although decided on other grounds, the SC held that the Recovery of Medical Costs for Asbestos Diseases (Wales) Bill had the potential to deprive both compensators and their liability insurers of their possessions by retrospectively altering their existing legal liabilities. Article 1 of the First Protocol was engaged and special justification was required before the court would accept that a fair balance had been struck between the demands of the general interest of the community and the requirement to protect individual rights. None had been shown.

[278] *Holy Monasteries v Greece* (1994) 20 E.H.R.R. 1 at [71]. The ECtHR found a breach of art.1 of the First Protocol where all of the compensation paid for expropriation of the applicant's property (and more) had to be paid over in court fees incurred as a result of the expropriation (*Perdigao v Portugal* (App No 24768/06) (16 November 2010) at [71]–[79]). The Court of Appeal dismissed a challenge by shareholders of Northern Rock to the basis for the assessment of compensation following its

The right to free elections Article 3 of the First Protocol appears merely to   **13-099**
impose an obligation on the State to hold free elections for the legislature at reasonable intervals.[279] However, the ECtHR has held that art.3 of the First Protocol does
confer individual rights to vote and to stand for election. Although not subject to
express limitation, the State may impose conditions which pursue a legitimate aim,
are not disproportionate and do not frustrate the aim of the article.[280] The legislature
may include some regional bodies, but the term election is not apt to cover
referenda. The State retains a broad discretion concerning the electoral system.[281]

The prohibition on discrimination Article 14 guarantees that the rights and   **13-100**
freedoms set forth in the Convention shall be secured without discrimination on
grounds such as sex, race, colour, language, religion, political or other opinion,
national or social origin, association with a national minority, property birth or other

"nationalisation" in *R. (on the application of SRM Global Master Finance Ltd) v Commissioners of Her Majesty's Treasury* [2009] EWCA Civ 788 at [73]–[77] (Laws LJ). The court summarised the correct approach to the principles of balance, proportionality and the margin of appreciation by ask-ing whether the state measure was manifestly without reasonable foundations. A restriction imposed on a licence holder in relation to salmon fishing was so extensive (reducing his catch by 95%) that he should be entitled to claim damages under A1P1 (*R. (on the application of Mott) v Environment Agency* [2016] EWCA Civ 564; [2016] 1 W.L.R. 4338).

[279] The elections must be by secret ballot and under conditions which will ensure the free expression of the opinion of the people in the choice of the legislature.

[280] *Mathieu-Mohin v Belgium* (1987) 10 E.H.R.R. 1 at [52]–[57]. The ECtHR found the automatic statu-tory bar on convicted prisoners voting to be disproportionate (*Hirst v United Kingdom* (2006) 42 E.H.R.R. 41 at [78]–[85]) and required that the state should define the circumstances were depriva-tion would take place or leave the question of proportionality to the courts (*Scoppola v Italy (No.3)* (2013) 56 E.H.R.R. 19). In *Greens and MT v United Kingdom* (2011) 53 E.H.R.R. 21, the ECtHR (in a pilot judgment) held that the automatic ban on prisoners voting was in breach of art 3. The UK's extended time period to implement this decision expired on 22 November 2012. Age and residence requirements have been upheld. The ECtHR upheld a requirement that candidates for election to the national parliament should provide information about their property and sources of income (*Rus-sian Conservative Party of Entrepreneurs v Russia* (2008) 46 E.H.R.R. 39 at [62]). In the same case, the court rejected a challenge that a voter had not been able to vote for his party of choice as it had been denied registration (at [78]).

[281] A challenge to the UK's electoral system was rejected in *Liberal Party v United Kingdom* (1982) 4 E.H.R.R. 106 at [8]–[9]. Rules requiring the forfeiture of (modest) electoral deposits (*Sukhovetskyy v Ukraine* (2007) 44 E.H.R.R. 57 at [61]–[74]) and an electoral threshold of 10 per cent of the national vote to be represented in Parliament have been upheld (*Yumak and Sadak v Turkey* (2009) 48 E.H.R.R. 4 at [66]–[78]). The traditional (unelected) position of the Seigneur and Seneschal in Sark's unicameral legislature and ban on aliens standing for election were held not to offend art.3 when viewed overall and in the context of the constitutional history of the Crown Dependency (*R. (on the application of Barclay) v Secretary of State for Justice* [2009] UKSC 9; [2010] 1 A.C. 464 at [53]–[64] (Lord Collins). In *Grosaru v Romania* (2015) 61 E.H.R.R. 1 at [54]–[57], there was held to have been a violation of art.3 of the First Protocol read with art.13. The applicant stood as a candidate in parliamentary elections and secured 5,624 votes in 19 constituencies. The parliamentary seat was allocated instead to a candidate who had secured 2,943 votes in a single constituency. The breach was found on the basis of a lack of clarity of the electoral law and a lack of sufficient guarantees of impartiality on the part of those examining the applicant's challenges. That art.3 of the First Protocol is inapplicable to referenda was confirmed in *Moohan, Petitioner* [2014] UKSC 67; [2015] A.C. 901 which at [7]–[18] considered the Strasbourg case law in the context of the Scot-tish referendum on independence. In *Paunović and Milivojević v Serbia* (App. No. 41683/06) (24 May 2016), the ECtHR found a violation of art.3 of the First Protocol read with art.13. The ap-plicants, elected to parliament in 2003, had been required to sign undated resignation letters which were then held by the party. In 2006, following internal trouble, the MPs declared their intention to retain their seats. The party leader nevertheless tendered their resignations, which the parliamentary committee accepted as genuine. The ECtHR reaffirmed that art.3 guarantees not only a right to stand for election, but to sit as MP once elected (at [58]), and held that the impugned measure was not compliant with the domestic framework which required resignations to be submitted in person (at [63]–[66]).

status.[282] Article 14 therefore only applies to discrimination in the enjoyment of other substantive Convention rights and requires that a prohibition at least falls within the ambit of another Convention right before it can be invoked.[283] In effect, art.14 is treated as if it is incorporated in each of the other Convention rights. Article 14 is not, however, limited to the State's acts in fulfilling its other obligations under the ECHR. Thus, if the State provides a benefit, it must comply with art.14 even if it is under no ECHR obligation to provide the benefit in the first place.[284]

13-101   The prohibited grounds of discrimination under art.14 are broadly defined and non-exhaustive.[285] It is for the applicant to prove that he has been treated differently from those who are in an analogous or relevantly similar situation and the burden then shifts to the respondent to justify the difference in treatment.[286] Justification is the familiar two-stage process: does the distinction fulfil a legitimate

---

[282] Equality is also recognised by the common law (see 11-062) and in European Community law (see 14-158). S. Fredman, "From Deference to Democracy: The Role of Equality under the Human Rights Act 1998" (2006) 122 L.Q.R. 53.

[283] Indeed, the ECtHR will not usually proceed to consider the merits of an art.14 complaint at all if it finds the breach of a substantive right to be made out (*Dudgeon v United Kingdom* (1981) 4 E.H.R.R. 149 at [69]). By contrast, the unratified Protocol 12 would provide a general requirement of equal treatment. The narrowness of the court's focus has been criticised: A. Baker, "The Enjoyment of Rights and Freedoms: A New Conception of the 'Ambit' under art.14 ECHR" (2006) 69 M.L.R. 714. See also R. O'Connell, "Cinderella comes to the Ball: Article 14 and the right to non-discrimination in the ECHR" (2009) 29 *Legal Studies* 211.

[284] For example, the State may be under no duty to provide a particular welfare benefit, but will be subject to art.14 scrutiny if the manner in which it does so is discriminatory (*Stec v United Kingdom* (2006) 43 E.H.R.R. 47). See further, *Godin-Mendoza* [2004] UKHL 30; [2004] 2 A.C. 557 discussed at 13-105. Compare *Runkee and White v United Kingdom* [2007] 2 F.C.R. 178 at [45] (violation of art.14 read with art.1 of the First Protocol in relation to widowers' non-entitlement to a widow's payment) to *Burden and Burden*, fn.76 above at [53]–[61] (no violation of the same Convention rights where sisters living together were not entitled to the same inheritance reliefs as married couples or those with civil partnerships). In *R. (on the application of Hardy) v Sandwell MBC* [2015] EWHC 890 (Admin); [2015] B.L.G.R. 283, a local authority's policy of taking into account the care component of disability living allowance when assessing the amount of a discretionary housing payment breached art.14.

[285] The "other status" must relate to a personal characteristic of the person or group by which they are distinguishable from each other (*Kjeldsen, Busk Madsen and Pederen v Denmark* (1976) 1 E.H.R.R. 711 at [56]), but is not otherwise limited and has been applied to marital status (*Sahin v Germany* (2003) 36 E.H.R.R. 43 at [55]–[61]), conscientious objection (*Thlimmenos v Greece* (2000) 31 E.H.R.R. 15 at [42]) or residence (*Darby v Sweden* (1990) 13 E.H.R.R. 774 at [29]-[34]). In *RJM* [2008] UKHL 63; [2009] 1 A.C. 311, the HL held that homelessness counted as a personal characteristic. Lord Walker at [5], referred to certain innate and immutable characteristics which are closely connected with an individual's personality (such as gender, sexual orientation, colour, congenital disabilities, nationality, language, religion and politics) and which are at the core of art.14 and others (such as military status, residence and domicile, past employment in the KGB) which are further outside. Lord Neuberger stated that a personal characteristic was not determined by whether it was voluntary or not (at [47]). Ordinary residence was found to fall within art.14 in *Carson v United Kingdom* (2009) 48 E.H.R.R 41 at [76]. However, the challenge to the UK's rules on drawing state pensions overseas failed as the applicants were not in an analogous situation to UK resident pensioners and the difference in treatment was, in any event, justified at [78]-[81]. Poverty has been held not to constitute "other status": *R. (on the application of Williams) v Secretary of State for the Home Department* [2015] EWHC 1268 (Admin); [2015] A.C.D. 111 at [96] (rejecting the argument that *RJM* supported this wider proposition) (affirmed in [2017] EWCA Civ 98; [2017] 1 W.L.R. 3283 at [75]).

[286] The ECtHR has now held that art.14 prohibits indirect discrimination (*DH v Czech Republic* (2007) 44 E.H.R.R. 37 at [175]-[8] and [184]-[9]). The court accepted that the applicants' statistical evidence gave rise to a presumption that the psychological tests used to determine school allocation had a disparate impact on Roma children and that the state had failed to discharge the burden of demonstrating that they were objectively justified. The court therefore found there to be a violation of art.14 read with art.2 of the First Protocol. This decision has potentially wide-ranging consequences. See Baroness Hale's discussion of justification in *AL (Serbia) v Secretary of State for*

aim and is there a reasonable relationship of proportionality between the means employed and the aim sought to be achieved.[287] The House of Lords has described the correct approach in the following terms:[288]

"Article 14 does not apply unless the alleged discrimination is in connection with a Convention right and on a ground stated in Art.14. If this prerequisite is satisfied, the essential question for the court is whether the alleged discrimination, that is, the difference in treatment of which complaint is made, can withstand scrutiny. Sometimes the answer to this question will be plain. There may be such an obvious, relevant difference between

the Home Department [2008] UKHL 42; [2008] 1 W.L.R. 1434 at [29]-[49]. Article 14 prohibits a third form of discrimination described in the case of *Thlimmenos v Greece* (2001) 31 E.H.R.R. 15 at [44]: where the state fails to treat differently persons whose situations are significantly distinct without objective and reasonable justification.

[287] There is no list of legitimate aims for the purposes of art.14 and a broad range of such interests have been recognised, including, for example, supporting the traditional family (*Marckx v Belgium* (1979) 2 E.H.R.R. 330, para.32). The ECtHR will scrutinise distinctions based on nationality, religion, gender, race, sexual orientation, marital status and birth particularly closely. Nevertheless, gender discrimination of the treatment of the spouses of General Practitioners under the National Health Service pension scheme was held to have an objective and reasonable justification where it had been introduced to combat the disadvantaged position of women and was being gradually phased out (*R. (on the application of Cockburn) v Secretary of State for Health* [2011] EWHC 2095 (Admin) at [64]-[86] (Supperstone J). The SC held (by a slender majority) that the fact that women from Northern Ireland were required to pay for abortion services on travelling to Great Britain was justified by the fact that abortion services were a devolved matter (*R. (on the application of A & B) v Secretary of State for Health* [2017] UKSC 41; [2017] 1 W.L.R. 2492. In *Boyraz v Turkey* (2015) 60 E.H.R.R. 30 at [56], the ECtHR held no legitimate aim had been shown, where the applicant was dismissed from her post as a security guard for not being a man.

[288] *R. (on the application of Carson) v Secretary of State for Work and Pensions* [2005] UKHL 37; [2006] 1 A.C. 173 at [3] (Lord Nicholls). In *Carson*, the HL cast doubt on the more structured series of questions set out by the CA in *Wandsworth LBC v Michalak* [2002] EWCA Civ 271; [2003] 1 W.L.R. 617 at [20] (Brooke LJ) which were: (i) Do the facts fall within the ambit of one or more Convention rights? (ii) Was there a difference in treatment in respect of that right between the complainant and others put forward for comparison? (iii) Were those others in an analogous situation? (iv) Was the difference in treatment objectively justifiable? (v) Was the difference in treatment based on one or more of the grounds proscribed by art.14? These questions are likely still to prove a valuable analytical tool if not applied rigidly. For the ECtHR's approach (which is similar to that of the HL) see *Belgian Linguistics Case (No.2)* (1968) 1 E.H.R.R. 252 at [10]. The benefit cap introduced in the Welfare Reform Act 2012 was held to discriminate indirectly against women, but its discriminatory effect was not manifestly without reasonable foundation and so not unlawful. There was thus no violation of art.14 read with art.1 of the First Protocol: *R. (on the application of JS) v Secretary of State for Work and Pensions* [2015] UKSC 16; [2015] 1 W.L.R. 1449 at [63]-[77]. The reduction in the eligible rent used to calculate housing benefit based on the number of bedrooms in the property discriminated against disabled people in two of the joined appeals (*R. (on the application of Carmichael) v Secretary of State for Work and Pensions* [2016] UKSC 58; [2016] 1 W.L.R. 4550 at [40]-[49]). The "manifestly without reasonable foundation" test was applied (and was not met) in *R. (Cushnie) v Secretary of State for Health* [2014] EWHC 3626 (Admin); [2015] P.T.S.R. 384. This case concerned an unsuccessful asylum seeker who could not be removed from the UK because he was unfit to fly. Being disabled he received support from his local authority under s.21 of the National Assistance Act 1948, rather than from the Home Office. He required non-urgent medical treatment, which he could not pay for, but was not entitled to free NHS treatment, whereas an able-bodied destitute failed asylum seeker receiving Home Office support was so entitled. In *Sanneh v Secretary of State for Work and Pensions* [2015] EWCA Civ 49; [2016] Q.B. 455 at [28]-[29], the CA held that "Zambrano carers" (non-EU citizens responsible for the care of an EU citizen child) were not entitled to social assistance on the same basis as lawfully resident EU citizens. Article 14 was not breached as the Government's policy reasons for differentiating the two categories of carers were not "clearly without foundation". There was no breach of art.14 (read with art.8) in declining to extend the availability of civil partnerships to heterosexual couples for the time being since the Secretary of State was entitled to a limited amount of flexibility in relation to removing the discriminatory impact (*Steinfeld v Secretary of State for Education* [2017] EWCA Civ 81; [2017] 4 All E.R. 47).

the claimant and those with whom he seeks to compare himself that their situations cannot be regarded as analogous. Sometimes, where the position is not so clear, a different approach is called for. Then the court's scrutiny may best be directed at considering whether the differentiation has a legitimate aim and whether the means chosen to achieve the aim is appropriate and not disproportionate in its adverse impact."

The impact of the HRA

13-102   In July 2006 the Department of Constitutional Affairs published its *Review of the Implementation of the Human Rights Act*.[289] This Review concluded that the HRA had no significant impact on the Government's ability to protect the public from crime or on government policy on immigration and asylum. The Review did find that the HRA has had an impact on counter-terrorism legislation which was said to arise principally from the decision in *Chahal v United Kingdom*.[290] Overall, the Review concluded that the HRA had a beneficial impact on UK law by increasing the influence of human rights considerations on policy making and prompting a dialogue between UK judges and those in Strasbourg.[291]

13-103   A more empirical enquiry into the impact of the HRA was carried out by the Public Law Project. Their study provided a detailed breakdown of the civil judicial review claims issued and granted permission in various categories of subject matter in the first half of 2002. The conclusion was that the HRA did not appear to have contributed materially to the number of cases before the Administrative Court. Moreover, although cited in around half of the claims issued, in the majority of cases the HRA made little difference to the claimant's prospects of success.[292]

13-104   The HRA has also reinvigorated the debate about whether the United Kingdom should adopt its own domestically drafted Bill of Rights either to supplement or replace the ECHR. Some commentators have criticised the HRA as out-dated for lacking direct protection for economic social and cultural rights, freedom of information, a right to administrative justice or a free-standing right to equality.[293] This is part of the wider debate about a new constitutional settlement for the United

---

[289] DCA 38/06. The Review was triggered by the reporting of a number of high-profile cases decided (or thought to have been decided) under the HRA, in particular, the cases of the Afghani aircraft hijackers, the unreturned foreign prisoners and that of Anthony Rae.

[290] *Chahal v United Kingdom* (1996) 23 E.H.R.R. 413.

[291] Similar conclusions were reached by the Joint Committee on Human Rights, *The Human Rights Act: the DCA and Home Office Reviews*. HL Paper No.278/AC Paper No.1716 (Session 2006/07).

[292] The Public Law Project, *The Impact of the Human Rights Act on Judicial Review: An Empirical Research Study* (2003). See further, S. Shah and T. Poole, "The Impact of the Human Rights Act on the House of Lords" [2009] P.L. 347.

[293] I. Hare, "Social Rights as Fundamental Rights" in B. Hepple (ed), *Social and Labour Rights in a Global Context: International and Comparative Perspectives* (2002) and P. O'Connell, "The Death of Socio-Economic Rights" (2011) 74 M.L.R. 532. See further, Justice, *A British Bill of Rights: Informing the Debate* (2007) (available from *http://www.justice.org.uk*) and the Joint Committee on Human Rights, *A Bill of Rights for the UK?* (HL Paper 165-1); (HC Paper 150-1) (2007-08). The JCHR recommended supplementing the rights protected by the HRA with additional rights to trial by jury (in England and Wales), to administrative justice, to equality and, to a limited extent, to economic, social and cultural rights. The JCHR was sceptical of the then Government's wish to link rights to responsibilities. The Labour Government responded in *A Bill of Rights for the UK? Government's Response to the Committee's Twenty-ninth Report of Session 2007-08* (HL Paper 15), (HC Paper 145) (2008-09) and its Green Paper, *Rights and Responsibilities: Developing Our Constitutional Framework* (Cm 7577) (2009) in which it proposes a new Bill of Rights and Responsibilities which would bring together Convention rights and fundamental common law and statutory rights (including some welfare entitlements). The 2010 election removed the Labour Government from power before any of these proposals could be implemented. The Commission on a Bill of Rights appointed by the Coalition Government reported in two volumes in 2012: *A UK Bill of Rights? The Choice Before Us*. The majority of the Commission was in favour of a UK Bill of Rights in order to

Kingdom which may include entrenchment of the devolution settlements in Scotland, Wales and Northern Ireland, further reform of the structure and working of Parliament and a re-negotiation of legal relations with the European Union.[294] Since the coalition government came to power in 2010, there have been repeated calls to repeal the HRA and replace it with a domestic Bill of Rights. The coalition Government established the Commission on a Bill of Rights in March 2011. After an interim advice to Government and two consultation exercises,[295] the Commission's report was published in December 2012.[296] The Commission failed to reach a unanimous conclusion, but the majority favoured the adoption of a UK Bill of Rights in order to encourage wider public acceptance for the legal protection of human rights. The majority favoured the addition of some rights to the list contained in the ECHR (especially the right to equality and rights guaranteeing aspects of the civil and criminal justice systems), but not socio-economic or environmental rights. The majority did not favour making rights dependent on responsibilities. The Commission supported the overall structure of the HRA and the remedies it makes available. A minority of the Commission did not feel that it would be appropriate to adopt a Bill of Rights at present, but that the issue should be re-considered as part of a Constitutional Convention after the question of Scottish independence was resolved.

---

promote a sense of "ownership" by the public. The Commission expressed support for the inclusion in such a Bill of a right to equality and non-discrimination, perhaps with additional protections in the administrative and criminal justice fields. The majority opposed including socio-economic and environmental rights. The enforcement mechanisms would remain largely as under the HRA. The proposals are convincingly criticised by F. Klug and A. Williams, "The Choice Before Us? The Report of the Commission on a Bill of Rights" [2013] P.L. 459. The manifesto of the current Conservative government in 2015 pledged that they will repeal the Human Rights Act, curtail the powers of the ECtHR (reducing it to giving advisory opinions) and enact a British Bill of Rights (S. Greer and R. Slowe, "The Conservatives' Proposals for a British Bill of Rights: Mired in Muddle, Misconception and Misrepresentation?" [2015] E.H.R.L.R. 372 and L. Blom-Cooper, "The Road to Rome and Strasbourg via San Francisco: Human Rights in Charters and Declarations" [2015] P.L. 571); see also D. Grieve QC MP "Can a Bill of Rights do better than the Human Rights Act?" [2016] P.L. 223, and A. Williams and G. Williams, "The British Bill of Rights Debate: Lessons from Australia" [2016] P.L. 471. The Equality and Human Rights Commission (established under the Equality Act 2006) published its (broadly supportive) *Human Rights Inquiry Report* in June 2009 (available at *http://www.equalityhumanrights.com*). The debate about the effectiveness of the Human Rights Act continues: compare, K. Ewing, *Bonfire of the Liberties: New Labour, Human Rights, and the Rule of Law* (2010) and A. Kavanagh, "Judging the Judges under the Human Rights Act: Deference, Disillusionment and the 'War on Terror'" [2009] P.L. 287. See also A. Donald "A Bill of Rights for the U.K.? Why the process matters" (2010) E.H.R.L.R. 459.

[294] The Northern Ireland Human Rights Commission has a statutory duty to consult and advise the Secretary of State on the scope of defining fundamental rights beyond those protected by the Convention. Its preliminary report is available at *http://www.nihrc.org*. The Northern Ireland Human Rights Commission gave its final advice to the Secretary of State for Northern Ireland on a possible Bill of Rights for Northern Ireland on 10 December 2008, although there was no unanimity on which rights, in addition to those in the Convention, should be included (available at *http://www.nihrc.org*). See V. Bogdanor, *The New British Constitution* (2009); J. Beatson, "Reforming an Unwritten Constitution" (2010) 126 L.Q.R. 48; and S. Peers, "European Integration and the European Union Act 2011: an irresistible force meets an immovable object" [2013] P.L. 119.

[295] *http://www.justice.gov.uk/about/cbr*.

[296] *A UK Bill of Rights? The Choice Before Us*. See further, the Equality and Human Rights Commission Research report 83: *"The UK and the European Court of Human Rights"* (2012).

Table 1: Declarations of incompatibility under HRA s.4—updated to September 2017

Source: information derived in part from a table prepared by the Ministry of Justice in the Annex to their paper: Responding to Human Rights Judgments, Report to the Joint Committee on Human Rights on the Government's response to human rights judgments 2014-16 (November 2016) (Cm. 9360).

	Judgment	Right	Legislation	Response
1	*R. (on the application of H) v Mental Health Review Tribunal for the North and East London Region* [2001] EWCA Civ 415; [2002] Q.B. 1	Art.5(1), 5(4)	Mental Health Act 1983 s.73: did not require tribunal to discharge a patient where it could not be shown that he suffered from a mental disorder warranting detention	Mental Health Act 1983 (Remedial) Order 2001 (SI 2001/ 3712)
2	*McR's Application for Judicial Review* [2002] NIQB 58; [2003] N.I. 1	Art.8	Offences Against the Person Act 1861 s.62: offence of attempted buggery continued to apply in Northern Ireland to consenting adults	Sexual Offences Act 2003 repealed s.62 of the 1861 Act
3	*International Transport Roth GmbH v Secretary of State for the Home Department* [2002] EWCA Civ 158; [2003] Q.B. 728	Art.6, art.1 of First Protocol	Immigration and Asylum Act 1999 Pt II: penalty system for carriers who unknowingly transported clandestine entrants to the UK	Nationality Immigration and Asylum Act 2002 s.125 modified the system
4	*R. (on the application of Anderson) v Secretary of State for the Home Department* [2002] UKHL 46; [2003] 1 A.C. 837	Art.6	Crime (Sentences) Act 1997 s.29: Home Secretary set minimum period to be served by a mandatory life sentence prisoner before he could be considered for release on licence	Criminal Justice Act 2003 ss.303 and 332 repealed s.29 of the 1997 Act
5	*R. (on the application of D) v Secretary of State for the Home Department* [2002] EWHC 2805 (Admin); [2003] 1 W.L.R. 1315	Art.5(4)	Mental Health Act 1983 s.74 gave discretion to Home Secretary whether or not to refer a discretionary life prisoner's case to Parole Board where a mental health review tribunal concluded that prisoner no longer liable to be detained under 1983 Act	Criminal Justice Act 2003 s.295 amended s.74 of the 1983 Act
6	*Blood v Secretary of State for the*	Art.8, art.14	Human Fertilisation and Embryology Act 1990	Human Fertilisation and

	Judgment	Right	Legislation	Response
	Health (Sullivan J, unreported, 28 February 2003)		s.28(6)(b) prevented deceased father's name being entered on his child's birth certificate	Embryology (Deceased Fathers) Act 2003
7	*Bellinger v Bellinger* [2003] UKHL 21; [2003] 2 A.C. 467	Art.8, art.12	Matrimonial Causes Act 1973 s.11(c): no provision for recognition to valid marriage for a post-operative transsexual	Gender Recognition Act 2004
8	*R. (on the application of M) v Secretary of State for Health* [2003] EWHC 1094 (Admin); [2003] U.K.H.R.R. 746	Art.8	Mental Health Act 1983 ss.26 and 29: patient liable to be detained under the Act had no choice over appointment of "nearest relative" or legal means of challenge where adoptive father appointed even though he had abused M as a child	Mental Health Act 2007
9	*R. (on the application of Hooper) v Secretary of State for Work and Pensions* [2003] EWCA Civ 875 (unaffected by judgment [2005] UKHL 29; [2005] 1 W.L.R. 1681)	Art.14, art.8, art.1 of First Protocol	Social Security Contributions and Benefit Act 1992 ss.36–37: Widowed Mothers Allowance payable to women but not men	Welfare Reform and Pension Act 1999 s.54(1) had already altered law prospectively
10	*R. (on the application of Wilkinson) v Inland Revenue Commissioners* [2003] EWCA Civ 814; [2003] 1 W.L.R. 2683 (unaffected by subsequent House of Lords judgment [2005] UKHL 30; [2005] 1 W.L.R. 1718)	Art.14, art.1 of First Protocol	Income and Corporation Taxes Act 1988 s.262: payment of widows but not widowers	Finance Act 1999 ss.34(1) and 139 had already repealed s.262 prospectively
11	*X v Secretary of State for the Home Department* (Belmarsh detainees case) [2004]	Art.5, art.14	Anti-terrorism, Crime and Security Act 2001 s.23: Home Secretary empowered to order detention of foreign nationals living in	Prevention of Terrorism Act 2005 repealed detention order system (and

	Judgment	Right	Legislation	Response
	UKHL 56; [2005] 2 A.C. 68		the UK suspected of terrorism who could not be deported without breaching art.3	created new system of control orders)
12 & 13	R. (on the application of Morris) v Westminster City Council (No.3) [2005] EWCA Civ 1184; [2006] 1 W.L.R. 505; similar point in R. (on the application of Gabaj) v First Secretary of State (unreported), relating to claimant's pregnant wife who was not a British citizen	Art.14	Housing Act 1996 s.185(4): requiring dependent child who is subject to immigration control to be disregarded when determining whether a British citizen has priority need for accommodation	Schedule 15 to the Housing and Regeneration Act 2008
14	R. (on the application of Baiai and others) v Secretary of State for the Home Department [2008] UKHL 53; [2009] 1 A.C. 287	Art.12, art.14	Asylum and Immigration (Treatment of Claimants, etc.) Act 2004 s.19(3): procedures designed to stop sham marriages must be completed before any persons subject to immigration control may marry in the UK	The Asylum and Immigration (Treatment of Claimants, etc.) Act 2004 (Remedial) Order 2011
15	R. (on the application of Wright) v Secretary of State for Health [2009] UKHL 3; [2009] 1 A.C. 739	Art.6, art.8	Care Standards Act 2000 s.82(4)(b): provisional listing of persons unsuitable to work with vulnerable adults	Safeguarding Vulnerable Groups Act 2006
16	R. (on the application of Clift) v Secretary of State for the Home Department; Hindawi v Secretary of State for the Home Department [2006] UKHL 54; [2007] 1 A.C. 484	Art.14, art.5	Criminal Justice Act 1991 ss.46(1) and 50(2): early release from prison provisions applied differently to British and foreign nationals	Criminal Justice Act 2003 repealed the main provision and the transitional arrangements were terminated by the Criminal Justice and Immigration Act 2008

	Judgment	Right	Legislation	Response
17	*Smith v Scott*, 2007, CSIH 9; 2007 S.L.T. 137	Art.3 of First Protocol	Representation of the People Act 1983 s.3(1): incapacity of convicted prisoners to vote in general elections	Government considering the implications of this ruling in light of ECtHR ruling to similar effect in *Hirst v UK* (2006) 42 E.H.R.R. 41 and other cases
18	*R. (on the application of F and Thompson) v Secretary of State for the Home Department* [2010] UKSC 17; [2011] 1 A.C. 331	Art.8	Sexual Offences Act 2003 s.82: notification requirements applied for an indefinite period without scope for a review	Sexual Offences Act 2003 (Remedial) Order 2012
19	*R. (on the application of Royal College of Nursing) v Secretary of State for the Home Department* [2010] EWHC 2761 (Admin); [2011] 2 F.L.R. 1399	Art.6, art.8	Schedule 3 to the Safeguarding of Vulnerable Adults Act 2006 (see above): failed to provide a method for making representations before listing	Protection of Freedoms Act 2012 s.67(2) and (6)
20	*R. (on the application of Reilly (No. 2)) v Secretary of State for Work and Pensions* [2014] EWHC 2182 (Admin); [2015] Q.B. 573	Art.6.1	Jobseekers (Back to Work Schemes) Act 2013; retroactive effect not justified by compelling grounds of the general interest	The Secretary of State unsuccessfully appealed the grant of a declaration of incompatibility: [2016] EWCA Civ 413. No remedial action has been taken
21	*R. (on the application of T) v Chief Constable of Greater Manchester Police* [2014] UKSC 35; [2015] A.C. 49	Art.8	Police Act 1997	Amended by the Police Act 1997 (Criminal Record Certificates: Relevant Matters) (Amendment) (Eng-

	Judgment	Right	Legislation	Response
				land and Wales) Order 2013
22	*Benkharbouche v Embassy of Sudan* [2015] EWCA Civ 33; [2015] 3 W.L.R. 301	Art.6, art.14	State Immunity Act 1978 s.16(1)(a)	No remedial action has been taken (pending the outcome of an appeal heard on 6-8 June 2017)
23	*R. (on the application of Miranda) v Secretary of State for the Home Department and another* [2016] EWCA Civ 6; [2016] 1 W.L.R. 1505	Art.10	Terrorism Act 2000 Sch.7 para.2(1) insofar as it relates to journalistic material	No remedial action has been taken
24	*Re Z (A Child) (No 2)* [2016] EWHC 1191 (Fam); [2016] H.R.L.R. 15	Art.8 read with art.14	Human Fertilisation and Embryology Act 2008 s.54	No remedial action has been taken
25	*R. (on the application of G) v Chief Constable of Surry Police* [2016] EWHC 295 (Admin); *R. (on the application of P and A) v Secretary of State for Justice* [2016] EWHC 89 (Admin)	Art.8	The 2013 amendments to the Police Act 1977 (see 21 above) were still not sufficient to protect art.8.	No remedial action has been taken

CHAPTER 14

Review under European Union Law

TABLE OF CONTENTS

SCOPE

This chapter examines the principal ways in which European Union (EU/ **14-001**
Union)[1] law may be utilised in claims for judicial review in the Administrative
Court, including:

- the principle of indirect effect[2];
- the requirement of effective protection of Union law rights,[3] including effective judicial review[4] and state liability for breaches of Union law[5];
- and the grounds of review under Union law, including: equal treatment and

---

[1] On the entry into force of the Treaty of Lisbon (which was signed at Lisbon, on 13 December 2007 and entered into force on 1 December 2009), the European Community was replaced by the European Union. In this Chapter, the abbreviation EC or EEC is used where the reference is historic, to particular provisions of the Treaties establishing the European Communities. The majority of references are to the post-Lisbon arrangement: TEU refers to the Treaty on European Union and TFEU refers to the Treaty on the Functioning of the European Union.

[2] See 14-068.

[3] See 14-078.

[4] See 14-089.

[5] See 14-098.

non-discrimination[6]; proportionality[7]; legal certainty and legitimate expectations[8]; fundamental rights[9]; and requirements to state reasons.[10]

INTRODUCTION

14-002   The United Kingdom's membership of the EU brought with it significant changes
to the English legal system and the UK constitution.[11] However, on 23 June 2016,
the United Kingdom voted in the "Brexit" referendum, conducted pursuant to the
European Union Referendum Act 2015, by a margin of 52% to 48%, to leave the
EU. Unsurprisingly, the outcome of this historic vote sent shockwaves across
Europe and worldwide, and has been the subject of much debate, analysis and commentary since.

14-003   As for the timing of the United Kingdom's withdrawal, the United Kingdom
formally notified the European Council of its intention to withdraw pursuant to
art.50 of the Treaty on European Union on 29 March 2017. Article 50 states that
the Treaties shall cease to apply to a Member State which has invoked art.50 from
the date of entry into force of a withdrawal agreement negotiated between that State
and the Union, or failing that, two years after notification of an intention to
withdraw pursuant to art.50. This suggests that, by April 2019, the United Kingdom
will have withdrawn from the Union.

14-004   It has been determined that the UK's constitutional requirements placed the decision and notification to leave the EU upon Parliament, pursuant to the constitutional
principle of parliamentary sovereignty, rather than upon the executive, pursuant to
the prerogative power of the Crown in relation to the conduct of international
relations.[12] The terms on which the United Kingdom will leave the EU are unknown
at present.[13]

14-005   It is clear that the status of all of the legal principles and laws in this Chapter will
be open for question and reconsideration in the coming years, and the relationship
between the United Kingdom and the EU will be entering a new and uncertain
phase. At the time of writing, the EU (Withdrawal) Bill is before Parliament. It has
been described as an "enormously complex piece of legislation which is likely to
bequeath a similarly complex—and uncertain—post-Brexit legal system".[14] In
particular, there will be uncertainty as to which of the UK's myriad of "rights, pow-

---

[6]   See 14-130 and 14-152.
[7]   See 14-133 and 14-173.
[8]   See 14-139 and 14-153.
[9]   See 14-039 and 14-145.
[10] See 14-151 and 14-163.
[11] See generally: D. Chalmers, G. Davies and, G. Monti, *European Union Law*, 3rd edn (2014); S.
      Weatherill, *Cases & Materials on EU Law*, 12th edn (2016); P. Craig and G. de Búrca, *EU Law: Text,
      Cases and Materials*, 6th edn (2015); T.C. Hartley, *The Foundations of European Union Law*, 8th
      edn (2014); A. Dashwood, M. Dougan, B. Rodger, E. Spaventa and D. Wyatt, *Wyatt and Dashwood's
      European Union Law*, 6th edn (2011); A. Arnull, *The European Union and its Court of Justice* 2nd
      edn (2006); P. Craig, *EU Administrative Law*, 2nd edn (2012). For a comprehensive treatment of the
      role of Union law in judicial review: R. Gordon, *EU Law in Judicial Review* 2nd edn (2014).
[12] *R. (on the application of Miller) v Secretary of State for Exiting the European Union* [2017] UKSC
      5; [2017] 2 W.L.R. 583. For comment, see J. Jowell, "Brexit Judicialised: Crown v Parliament
      Again" (2017) 8 *The UK Supreme Court Yearbook* 1.
[13] At the time of writing, negotiations are reported to be proceeding with difficulty: see e.g., D. Bof-
      fey, "'Now they have to pay': Juncker says UK stance on Brexit Bill untenable" *The Guardian*, 13
      October 2017; H. Zeffman, "Jean-Claude Juncker: 'Thanks for the war, but pay up for Brexit talks",
      The Times, 14 October 2017.
[14] M Elliott, "The Devil in the Detail: Twenty Questions about the EU (Withdrawal) Bill", *Public Law*

ers, liabilities, obligations and restrictions from time to time created or arising by under the Treaties" will have legal effect, or the same legal effect, when the savings provision lapses. This is because the rights, powers, and so on, have become part of UK law in so many different ways: through UK regulations implementing EU directives; through directly effective EU regulations; through rulings of the CJEU, or even by way of non-enforcement of a UK statute which has been held to be in breach of EU law.[15] Reciprocal "passporting" arrangements, for products as wide-ranging as electrical appliances and financial instruments, will also require attention. In the area of human rights, the UK will no longer be bound (insofar as it is now) by the requirements of the Charter of Fundamental Rights of the European Union (Charter) or, presumably, the EU's "fundamental principles".[16] New treaty arrangements may or may not also need to be in conformity with the ECHR.[17] For now, Union law continues in full force, but the impact of the "Brexit" vote, which will take time to fully emerge, can be expected to be far-reaching.

Thankfully, this Chapter, which is written on the basis that EU law continues to have full force for the present, has the narrower focus of examining the use of EU law in judicial review claims in England and Wales, though that needs to be set in the general context of the EU legal system. In the Administrative Court: **14-006**

- claimants may challenge actions and omissions by English public authorities, and even provisions of an Act of Parliament, on the ground of breach of Union law[18];
- less commonly, claims for judicial review may also raise questions about the validity of administrative decisions and legislation made by the institutions of the EU.[19]

Union law has also had an impact on the basic methods of work of national courts, including their approach to interpreting legislation,[20] the procedures to be followed by litigants and the nature of the remedies available to protect individuals' rights under Union law.[21]   **14-007**

The two courts of the EU—the Court of Justice of the European Union (CJEU)[22] and the General Court (formerly the Court of First Instance (CFI))[23]—have important roles. When a national court or tribunal requests it to do so, the CJEU   **14-008**

---

for Everyone, 14 August 2017. See also "EU withdrawal bill faces rough ride through parliament" (2017) 510 *Legislative Comment* 10.

[15] See, e.g. *HSBC Holdings Plc and Vidacos Nominees Ltd v Commissioners of Her Majesty's Revenue & Customs* (C-569/07) EU:C:2009:594.

[16] See below 14-045–14-052.

[17] House of Commons Library, "*Brexit: Impact Across Policy Areas*", 26 August 2016.

[18] See 14-061.

[19] See 14-063.

[20] See 14-068.

[21] See 14-078.

[22] The Court of Justice was established in 1952 and its jurisdiction includes jurisdiction to hear actions brought against Member States for failure to fulfil Union obligations (TFEU arts 258 and 259); to hear actions brought by individuals against Union institutions (TFEU art.263); to hear actions against the Parliament, Council or Commission for failure to act (TFEU art.265), and to give rulings on preliminary references (TFEU art.267). The term "CJEU" will be used here to refer to the Court of Justice both before and after the Lisbon Treaty reforms.

[23] The CFI was created in 1988 (TFEU art.256) to determine certain types of case. The name of the CFI was changed to the General Court on the coming into force of the Lisbon Treaty. The General Court hears cases brought by individuals against EU institutions. It does not give preliminary rulings under TFEU art.267 on which see 14-110. For a detailed comment on the jurisdictional divide between the CJEU and the General Court, see P. Craig, *EU Administrative Law* (2012), Ch.10.

gives authoritative rulings on questions of interpretation of Union law.[24] Both courts also have powers to determine actions brought directly to them alleging that Member States or institutions of the Union have breached Union law, though consideration of this last aspect of their work falls outside the scope of this chapter.[25]

OVERVIEW OF THE EU LEGAL SYSTEM

14-009   Following the entry into force of the Lisbon Treaty in 2009, the EU legal system is now based on two treaties, the Treaty on European Union (TEU) and the Treaty on the Functioning of the European Union (TFEU) (together "the EU Treaties"), both of which have the same legal status.[26] This framework resulted from the reordering of the EU Treaties introduced by the Lisbon Treaty, art.1 of which amends the TEU and art.2 of which contains the amendments to the Treaty Establishing the European Community. As is well-known, the Lisbon Treaty followed the Constitutional Treaty, which, signed by heads of state and government in 2004, was a historic step forward in consolidating and revising the treaty framework, but was not ratified following failures to secure affirmative votes in referendums in some Member States. Following the Lisbon Treaty reordering, the TEU is divided into six titles, the first of which, common provisions, outlines the Union's values and objectives. TEU art.6 contains a cross-reference to the Charter,[27] giving it legally binding effect and setting out the scope of its application. The second title contains provisions on democratic principles, including provisions aimed at strengthening the role of national parliaments in the policing of subsidiarity (derived from a proposal originally contained in the Constitutional Treaty).[28] The remaining titles (provisions on institutions; provisions on enhanced co-operation[29]; general provisions on the Union's external action and specific provisions on the common foreign and security policy; and final provisions) also integrate many of the institutional changes proposed in the Constitutional Treaty. Moreover, following the entry into force of the Lisbon Treaty, the Union has replaced the former European Community (EC).[30] In the United Kingdom, the various EU treaties adopted over the years have been incorporated into national law by successive Acts of Parliament.[31]

Policy areas within the field of the European Union

14-010   Some indication of the broad range of policy areas which fall within the ambit of Union law can be seen from its areas of competence, which are categorised and delineated in TFEU arts 2-6. One of the amendments made by the Lisbon Treaty was to clarify the categories of Union competence, which, pursuant to TFEU art.2 are broadly fivefold:

---

[24]   14-110.
[25]   See e.g. A. Ward, *Judicial Review and the Rights of Private Parties in EU Law*, 2nd edn (2007), Chs 6 and 8.
[26]   TEU art.1 para.3. For a helpful discussion of the evolution of the Treaties founding the EU and the impact of the Lisbon Treaty, see P. Craig, *The Lisbon Treaty: Law, Politics, and Treaty Reform* (2010) (in particular, see Ch.1 for a summary).
[27]   Charter of Fundamental Rights of the European Union [2010] OJ C83/2.
[28]   TEU art.12; see also Protocol (No.1) on the Role of National Parliaments in the European Union.
[29]   For consideration, see *Spain and Italy v Council* (Cases C-274/11 and C-295/11) EU:C:2013:240.
[30]   TEU art.1 para.3.
[31]   European Communities Act 1972.

- Exclusive, which means that only the Union may legislate and adopt legally binding acts[32];
- Shared, which means that the Union and the Member States may legislate and adopt legally binding acts in the relevant area, but Member States shall only exercise their competence to the extent that the Union has not exercised its competence[33];
- Competence to provide arrangements within which Member States shall co-ordinate their economic and employment policies[34];
- Competence to define and implement, in accordance with the provisions of the TEU, a common foreign and security policy, including the progressive framing of a common defence policy[35]; and
- Competence to take action to support, coordinate or supplement actions of Member States.[36]

The Union enjoys exclusive competence in five areas: customs union, the functioning of the internal market, monetary policy, conservation of marine biological resources and common commercial policy.[37] **14-011**

TFEU art.4(2) sets out the Union's range of shared competences as follows: **14-012**

"(a) internal market;
(b) social policy, for the aspects defined in this Treaty;
(c) economic, social and territorial cohesion;
(d) agriculture and fisheries, excluding the conservation of marine biological resources;
(e) environment;
(f) consumer protection;
(g) transport;
(h) trans-European networks;
(i) energy;
(j) area of freedom, security and justice;
(k) common safety concerns in public health matters, for the aspects defined in this Treaty."

Pursuant to TFEU art.5(1), Member States are under an obligation to coordinate their economic policies within the Union, to which end the Council shall adopt measures and in particular broad guidelines for these policies. The Union shall take measures to ensure co-ordination of the employment policies of the Member States by defining guidelines for these policies,[38] while it may also take initiatives to ensure co-ordination of Member States' social policies.[39]

The areas in which the Union enjoys the competence to support, co-ordinate or supplement the actions of the Member States are listed in TFEU art.6 as follows: **14-013**

"(a) protection and improvement of human health;
(b) industry;
(c) culture;
(d) tourism;

---

[32] TFEU art.2(1).
[33] TFEU art.2(2).
[34] TFEU art.2(3).
[35] TFEU art.2(4).
[36] TFEU art.2(5).
[37] TFEU art.3. See *Opinion 2/13* EU:C:2014:2454 at [172] (noting that TEU 3 sets out provisions which "are part of the framework of a system that is specific to the EU, are structured in such a way as to contribute—each within its specific field and with its own particular characteristics—to the implementation of the process of integration that is the *raison d'être* of the EU itself").
[38] TFEU art.5(2).
[39] TFEU art.5(3).

(e)   education, vocational training, youth and sport;
(f)   civil protection;
(g)   administrative co-operation."

14-014   Even where the EU has exclusive competence, however, schemes will neverthe-less normally be given practical implementation by national institutions such as HM Customs and Revenue and the Department for Environment, Food and Rural Af-fairs in England and so claimants may challenge the legality of the steps taken to administer EU policy and law. This is known as "shared management"[40]; "direct" or "indirect" management,[41] whereby EU institutions implement programmes either themselves, by outsourcing to a private party or delegating to an executive agency, is less common. Some spheres of governance remain matters wholly internal to Member States and Union law has no application. However, as can be seen from the breadth of the competences enjoyed by the Union, there are few areas of govern-ance that remain entirely unaffected by EU policies, and even in areas of govern-ment where Member States retain competence, they have to respect common EU policies which touch upon that area.[42]

Union law as "a new legal order"

14-015   The EU has given rise to "a new legal order"[43] with distinctive characteristics, including direct effect and primacy over inconsistent national law of Members States. A critical review of the characteristics of this new legal order can be found in *Opinion 2/13*, which considered the draft agreement for accession of the Union to the ECHR.[44] The CJEU observed that Union law was characterised by the fact that it stems from an independent source of law, the EU Treaties, by its primacy over the laws of the Member States, and by the direct effect of a whole series of provi-sions which are applicable to their nationals and to the Member States themselves.[45] These essential characteristics of Union law have given rise to a structured network of principles, rules and mutually interdependent legal relations linking the Union and its Member States, and its Member States with each other, which are now

---

[40]   Regulation (EU, Euratom) No.966/2012 of the European Parliament and of the Council of 25 October 2012 on the financial rules applicable to the general budget of the Union and repealing Council Regulation (EC, Euratom) No.1605/2002 art.58(1)(b); P. Craig, "The Constitutionalisa-tion of Community Administration" (2003) 28 E.L. Rev. 840; P. Craig, *EU Administrative Law* (2012), Ch.4.

[41]   Regulation (EU, EURATOM) No.966/2012 on the financial rules applicable to the general budget of the Union and repealing Council Regulation (EC, Euratom) No.1605/2002 [2012] OJ L298/1 arts 58(1)(a), 58(1)(b), 60-63. See P. Craig, *EU Administrative Law* (2012) Ch.3.

[42]   See, e.g. *R. v HM Treasury Ex p. Centro-Com Sri* (C-124/95) EU:C:1997:8 at [30] (Member States retained competence in the area of foreign and security policy, but had to respect the Union's com-mon commercial policy in whatever foreign and security measures were taken). For consideration of competence, see *Philip Morris Brands SARL v Secretary of State for Health* (C-547/14) EU:C:2016:325; *Commission v Council* (C-137/12) EU:C:2013:675; *Daiichi Sankyo and Sanofi-Aventis Deutschland* (C-414/11) EU:C:2013:520; and *United Kingdom v Council* (C-431/11) EU:C:2013:589.

[43]   *Van Gend en Loos NV v Nederlandse Tariefcommissie* (26/62) EU:C:1963:1 at 12. See also: *Opinion 2/13* EU:C:2014:2454 at [178] holding that the accession of the EU to the ECHR as envisaged by the draft agreement was liable adversely to affect the specific characteristics of EU law and its autonomy).

[44]   *Opinion 2/13* EU:C:2014:2454.

[45]   *Opinion 2/13* EU:C:2014:2454 at [166].

engaged, as is recalled in the second paragraph of TEU art.1, in a "process of creating an ever closer union among the peoples of Europe".[46]

It was also observed that the Union was, under international law, precluded by its very nature from being considered a State.[47] This legal structure is based on the fundamental premise that each Member State shares with all the other Member States, and recognises that they share with it, a set of common values on which the Union is founded, as stated in TEU art.2. Furthermore, the premise of TEU art.2 implies and justifies the existence of mutual trust between the Member States that those values will be recognised and, therefore, that the law of the EU that implements them will be respected.[48]

14-016

The principle of mutual trust between the Member States is also of fundamental importance in EU law, given that it allows an area without internal borders to be created and maintained. That principle requires, particularly with regard to the area of freedom, security and justice, each of those States, save in exceptional circumstances, to consider all the other Member States to be complying with EU law and particularly with the fundamental rights recognised by EU law.[49]

14-017

Rules of Union law have their main sources in the TEU and TFEU, the Charter (which, as will be seen,[50] had an important influential impact on the development of EU law even before it became legally binding in December 2009), in secondary legislation made by the institutions of the EU, and in the general principles of law developed by the CJEU.

14-018

Primacy of Union law

Early on, the CJEU propounded the doctrine that any rule of Union law, whatever its source, prevails over inconsistent rules of national law in Member States,[51] which doctrine was acknowledged in the Declaration concerning primacy Annexed to the Final Act of the Intergovernmental Conference which adopted the Treaty of Lisbon. The Declaration states that it is "well settled" that case law of the CJEU, the Treaties and the law adopted by the Union on the basis of the Treaties "have primacy over the law of Member States." The primacy of Union law is absolute. It applies whether the national rule came into being before or after the rule of Union law; it precludes the adoption of new legislative measures to the extent that they would be incompatible with Union law; it also applies to all forms of national law, including constitutional norms.[52] Where a person before an inferior court or tribunal seeks to rely upon a rule of Union law which is irreconcilable with national law, that court

14-019

---

[46] *Opinion 2/13* EU:C:2014:2454 at [167].

[47] *Opinion 2/13* EU:C:2014:2454 at [156].

[48] *Opinion 2/13* EU:C:2014:2454 at [168].

[49] *Opinion 2/13* EU:C:2014:2454 at [191]-[192]. See also *Council v Liberation Tigers of Tamil Eelan* (C-599/14) EU:C:2016:723 at [62].

[50] See 14-048.

[51] *Costa v ENEL* (6/64) [1964] EU:C:1964:66. See also *Opinion 2/13* EU:C:2014:2454 at [166].

[52] *Amministrazione delle Finanze dello Stato v Simmenthal SpA* (106/77) EU:C:1978:49 at [17]-[22]. There is one narrow exception to the principle of supremacy where the national provision is necessary to give effect to obligations under an international agreement entered into by the Member State *before* it became a party to the relevant Union Treaty. This exception is qualified however. Member States are under an obligation pursuant to TFEU art.351 to take "all appropriate steps" to eliminate any incompatibilities between the international agreement and EU law; see, also, *Martin Luksan* (C-277/10) EU:C:2012:65, at [61]-[63] (where an international agreement allows, but does not require a measure contrary to EU law, the Member State must refrain from adopting such a measure and, if there is a development in EU law which means that a legislative measure adopted by a Member State in accordance with an earlier international agreement appears contrary to EU law, the Member State cannot rely on the earlier agreement to exempt itself from obligations subsequently arising under

or tribunal is obliged immediately to disregard the national law: under Union law, it has "the power to do everything necessary at the moment of its application to set aside national legislative provisions which might prevent [Union] rules from having full force and effect".[53] In England and Wales, primacy therefore means that all courts and tribunals must, in a case where Union rights are in issue, "disapply" any provision in an Act of Parliament or statutory instrument, and depart from any common law precedent, that is irreconcilable with Union law.[54] Thus, while English law generally requires public law issues to be dealt with by the CPR Pt 54 claim for judicial review procedure,[55] Union law requires that questions of compatibility of national laws with Union law be dealt with by the court or tribunal in which they first arise during the ordinary course of legal proceedings. This may result in a bench of lay magistrates or the First-tier Tribunal adjudicating on the applicability of an Act of Parliament. Claims for judicial review are only one of many types of legal proceedings in which the primacy principle operates; civil claims, criminal proceedings and tribunal appeals, for example, may all provide the forum for raising arguments about compatibility of domestic law with Union law.

14-020   There may, however, be limits to the primacy of EU law. In *R. on the application of Buckinghamshire v Secretary of State for Transport*,[56] requirements laid down in Directive 2011/92/EU concerning the way in which Member States take certain decisions were at issue, including the decision in respect of the construction of the proposed "HS2" high-speed rail network. The decision was taken through the enactment of a "hybrid Bill", which was described as effectively a public bill, which affects a particular private interest in a manner different from the private interests of other persons or bodies of the same category or class.[57] The difficulty with scrutinising the decision-making process was that it might impinge "upon long-established constitutional principles governing the relationship between Parliament and the courts, as reflected for example in art.9 of the Bill of Rights 1689".[58] It was decided that the Directive did not require review that was constitutionally problematic, but the court considered briefly what would have happened had the Directive called for such scrutiny and commented that the issue could not be:

> "resolved simply by applying the doctrine developed by the Court of Justice of the supremacy of EU law, since the application of that doctrine in our law itself depends upon the [European Communities Act 1972]. If there is a conflict between a constitutional principle, such as that embodied in article 9 of the Bill of Rights, and EU law, that conflict has to be resolved by our courts as an issue arising under the constitutional law of the United Kingdom."[59]

EU law). See also even in the criminal context, *Criminal Proceedings against Taricco* (C-105/14) EU:C:2015:55.

[53] *Simmenthal* EU:C:1978:49 at [22].
[54] See 14-061.
[55] On procedural exclusivity see Ch.3. The Human Rights Act 1998 restricts declarations of incompatibility of legislation with Convention rights (s.4) to the higher courts, though all courts and tribunals are obliged to read and give effect legislation so far as possible in ways which are compatible (s.3).
[56] *R. on the application of Buckinghamshire v Secretary of State for Transport* [2014] UKSC 3; [2014] 1 W.L.R. 324.
[57] *R. on the application of Buckinghamshire v Secretary of State for Transport* [2014] UKSC 3; [2014] 1 W.L.R. 324 at [57].
[58] *R. on the application of Buckinghamshire v Secretary of State for Transport* [2014] UKSC 3; [2014] 1 W.L.R. 324 at [78].
[59] *R. on the application of Buckinghamshire v Secretary of State for Transport* [2014] UKSC 3; [2014] 1 W.L.R. 324 at [79].

Direct effect of Union law measures

Early on in the development of the Union law, the CJEU held that certain provi- **14-021** sions of the treaties may be relied upon directly by litigants in national courts (the doctrine of "direct effect") even though they may not have been specifically incorporated into a Member State's domestic legal system.[60] It can now be said that direct effect extends to all provisions in the EU Treaties which create rights and obligations which are sufficiently complete, unconditional, clear and precise.[61] A provision will be unconditional where it identifies an obligation which is not quali- fied by any condition or subject in its implementation or effects to the taking of any measure either by the institutions of the Union or by the Member State. It will be sufficiently precise to be relied on by an individual and applied by a court where it sets out an obligation in unequivocal terms.[62] These requirements are not applied strictly[63] and generally, only very open-ended provisions will not be found to be directly effective.[64] A provision can also be found to be partially directly effective, where it is capable of application in certain areas, but where further implementing measures are necessary for the provision to be enforceable over the whole of its range of intended application.[65] The provisions which are directly effective may be relied upon by litigants in national courts and tribunals both "vertically" against state institutions[66] and also "horizontally" against other citizens, trade unions[67] and business enterprises.[68]

---

[60] *Van Gend en Loos* EU:C:1963:1. The relationship between national law and treaty obligations var- ies between the Member States according to the constitution of each. For discussion of the doctrine of direct effect, see: B. De Witte, "Direct Effect, Primacy and the Nature of the Legal Order" in P. Craig and G. de Búrca (eds), *The Evolution of EU Law*, 2nd edn (2011), Ch.12.

[61] *Van Gend en Loos* EU:C:1963:1 at 13 (only those provisions which were clear, negative, unconditional, containing no reservation on the part of the Member State, and not dependent on a national implementing measure can be directly effective); and *Marks & Spencer Plc v Customs and Excise Commissioners* (C-62/00) EU:C:2002:435 at [25]; *Association de médiation sociale v Union locale des syndicats CGT* (C-176/12) EU:C:2014:2 at [31].

[62] *Gassmayr v Bundesminister für Wissenschaft und Forschung* (C-194/08) EU:C:2010:386 at [45].

[63] Through subsequent case law, these criteria have evolved to a looser requirement of justiciability: P. Pescatore, "The Doctrine of 'direct effect': an Infant Disease of Community Law" (1983) 8 E.L. Rev. 155, pp.176-177; A. Ward, *Judicial Review and the Rights of Private Parties in EU Law* (2007) Ch.2; e.g. *Defrenne v Société Anonyme Belge de Navigation Aérienne* (43/75) EU:C:1976:56 at [16] (which found directly effective the obligation in then EC art.119 (slightly re-worded now in TFEU art.157) on States to ensure "the application of the principle that men and women should receive equal pay for equal work", at least in so far as it related to direct discrimination).

[64] See, e.g. *Zaera v Institutio Nacionale de la Seguridad Social* (126/86) EU:C:1987:395 at [10]- [11]; *Petrie v Commission* (T-191/99) EU:T:2001:284 at [34]-[35] (principle of access to docu- ments in TFEU art.15 was not unconditional and required further implementation and so could not be directly effective); *Echirolles Distribution SA v Association du Dauphine* (C-9/99) EU:C:2000:532 at [25]. For examples of provisions in secondary legislation that have not been found to be capable of direct effect, see: *Impact v Minister for Agriculture and Food* (C-268/06) EU:C:2008:223 at [74]- [80]; *AGIM v Belgium* (C-471/07 and C-472/07) EU:C:2010:9 at [25]-[28]; *Association de média- tion sociale v Union locale des syndicats CGT* (C-176/12) EU:C:2014:2 at [44]-[45] (Charter art.27 must be given more specific expression in EU or national law). Contrast *Benkharbouche v Embassy of the Republic of Sudan* [2015] EWCA Civ 33; [2015] 3 W.L.R. 301 at [80] (Charter art.47 is capable of vertical and horizontal direct effect).

[65] C. Lewis, *Judicial Remedies in Public Law*, 5th edn (2014) at para.17-012. In *Defrenne* EU:C:1976:56, then EC art.119 (slightly re-worded now in TFEU art.157) was not found to be directly effective in relation to indirect discrimination.

[66] See, e.g. *Van Gend en Loos* EU:C:1963:1.

[67] *International Transport Workers' Federation and Finnish Seamen's Union v Viking Line ABP and Oü Viking Line Eesti* (C-438/05) EU:C:2007:772 at [61].

[68] *Walrave & Koch v Association Union Cycliste Internationale* (36/74) EU:C:1974:140 at [15]-[17];

SECONDARY LEGISLATION

14-022   An unusual feature of the EU, in contrast from other international organisations, is that legislative powers have been conferred on its institutions by the Treaties. TFEU art.288 provides:

> "To exercise the Union's competences, the institutions shall adopt regulations, directives, decisions, recommendations and opinions
>   A regulation shall have general application. It shall be binding in its entirety and directly applicable in all Member States.
>   A directive shall be binding, as to the result to be achieved, upon each Member State to which it is addressed, but shall leave to the national authorities the choice of form and methods.
>   A decision shall be binding in its entirety. A decision which specifies those to whom it is addressed shall be binding only on them.
>   Recommendations and opinions shall have no binding force."[69]

14-023   These forms of legal instruments were devised at the inception of the Union. The practical distinction between regulations and directives has lost some of its significance. This is in part because of a legislative practice of often drafting regulations and directives with a similar degree of detail; in part because of the development in the case law of the CJEU of the notion of direct effect of directives.[70] Nevertheless, important differences remain.

Regulations

14-024   All regulations are "directly applicable". Regulations thus become part of national law without any need for the Member State to adopt implementing measures. Indeed, it will often be unlawful for Member States to transpose regulations into national law. This is so in particular where such transposition may obscure or distort the Union provisions, or have the effect of concealing their Union character.[71] Moreover, in some fields, the Union will be regarded as having exclusive legislative competence, so that the adoption of EU regulations will preclude Member States from adopting any legislative measures in the field occupied by the regulations.[72]

14-025   Regulations may, however, sometimes be incomplete in that they do not specify,

---

Defrenne EU:C:1976:56 at [39]; *Union Royale Belge des Sociétés de Football Association v Bosman* (C-415/93) EU:C:1995:463 at [82]-[84]; *Angonese v Cassa di Risparmio di Bolzano SpA* (C-281/98) EU:C:2000:296 at [31]; *Raccanelli v Max-Planck-Gesellschaft zur Förderung der Wissenschaften* (C-94/07) EU:C:2008:425 at [41]-[46]; *Fra.bo Spa v Deutsche Vereinigung des Gas-und Wasserfaches eV* (C-171/11) EU:C:2012:453 at [31]-[32] (holding that TFEU art.34 applied to a private standardisation and certification body where the body "in reality [held] the power to regulate the entry into the German market of products such as the copper fittings at issue in the main proceedings"). For discussion, see P. Oliver, *Oliver on Free Movement of Goods in the European Union*, 5th edn (2010), pp.67-77.

69   See further TEU art.25 (enabling the Union to define general guidelines; adopt decisions defining actions to be undertaken by the Union and positions to be taken by the Union as well as arrangements for implementing those decisions; and to strengthen systematic co-operation between Member States in the conduct of common foreign and security policy).

70   See 14-036.

71   *Commission v Italy* (39/72) EU:C:1973:13 at [17]; *Variola* (34/73) EU:C:1973:101 at [991]; cf. *Commission v Italy* (272/83) EU:C:1985:147 at [27].

72   See, e.g. *Hauptzollamt Bremen v Krohn* (74/69) EU:C:1970:58 at 458. cf. *Bollman* (40/69) EU:C:1970:12 at 79. This is reminiscent of the notion of pre-emption in US constitutional law, where the expression "occupying the field" is used of US federal legislation, see, e.g. *Sprietsma v Mercury*

for example, the administrative measures necessary for their application or the penalties to be imposed in the event of non-compliance. Thus, it is settled case law that Member States may adopt rules for the application of a regulation if they do not obstruct its direct applicability, do not conceal its Union nature and specify that a discretion granted by the regulation is being exercised; provided that they adhere to the parameters laid down under it.[73] In such cases, Member States, far from being prohibited from acting, are under a duty to adopt the legislative measures necessary to make the regulations fully effective.[74]

Since regulations are, by virtue of TFEU art.288 directly applicable, it is not usu- **14-026** ally necessary to consider separately the question of their direct effect. But direct effect is distinct from direct applicability. Not all provisions of regulations have direct effect, just as not all provisions of Acts of Parliament create rights and duties. However, the CJEU has ruled that regulations are "capable of creating individual rights which national courts must protect"[75] and where the provisions of regulations are by their nature and wording directly enforceable, they will readily be held to have direct effect.[76] The CJEU has also deemed regulations to be "horizontally" directly effective, and capable of being enforced by one private litigant against another.[77]

Directives

Directives, as has been seen, are binding on Member States as to the result to be **14-027** achieved, but leave to the national authorities the choice of forms and methods. Directives, therefore, in contrast to regulations,[78] require that national measures should be adopted to give effect to them.

Implementation of directives

In principle, a directive must be implemented by legislation, not by mere changes **14-028** in administrative practice or by the adoption of administrative circulars. Implementation must fully satisfy the requirement of legal certainty; Member States must therefore transpose their terms into national law as binding provisions.[79] Moreover it is a general requirement of Union law, following from the principles of legal certainty and legal protection of the individual, that Member States' laws "should be worded unequivocally so as to give the persons concerned a clear and precise understanding of their rights and obligations and enable national courts to ensure that those rights and obligations are observed."[80] Legislative action may not be necessary where the existence of general principles of constitutional or administrative law renders implementation by specific legislation superfluous provided that the principles guarantee that national authorities will in fact apply the

---

Marine 537 U.S. 51 (2002) at 69.

[73] *Commission v Netherlands* (C-113/02) EU:C:2004:616 at [16]; *Danske Svineproducenter v Justitsministeriet* (C-316/10) EU:C:2011:863 at [41].

[74] *Commission v United Kingdom (Tachographs)* (128/78) EU:C:1979:32; *Commission v Netherlands* (72/85) EU:C:1986:144.

[75] *Politi SAS v Italian Ministry for Finance* (43/71) EU:C:1971:122 at [9].

[76] *Leonesio v Ministero dell'Agricoltura e Foreste* (93/71) EU:C:1972:39 at [22].

[77] *Muñoz y Cia SA and Superior Fruiticola SA v Frumar Ltd, Redbridge Produce Marketing Ltd* (C-253/00) EU:C:2002:497; see also *Opinion of AG Geelhoed* EU:C:2001:697 at [41].

[78] See 14-021.

[79] *Commission v Belgium* (239/85) EU:C:1986:457 at [7]; on the limits of the Member State's discretion, see *Commission v Denmark* (143/83) EU:C:1985:34 at [8]-[9]; *Commission v Germany* (C-262/95) EU:C:1996:427.

[80] *Commission v Italy* (257/86) EU:C:1988:324 at [12].

directive fully and that where the directive is intended to create rights for individuals, the legal position is sufficiently clear and precise.[81]

14-029   However, secondary legislation may require specific provision for the implementation of Union law. Thus, where Directive 2003/4 stated that the protection of the confidentiality of public proceedings must be "provided for by law"-a condition which corresponded to the requirement laid down in art.4(4) of the Aarhus Convention that the confidentiality of proceedings must be "provided for under national law"-the CJEU concluded that "the European Union legislature clearly wanted an express provision to exist in national law with a precisely defined scope, and not merely a general legal context".[82]

14-030   The CJEU has frequently held that "a Member State may not plead provisions, practices or circumstances existing in its internal legal system in order to justify a failure to comply with the obligations and time-limits laid down in a directive".[83] Failure to implement a directive may render the Member State liable in damages, giving those affected a Union right to sue in the national courts.[84]

Direct effect of directives

14-031   Although directives are not "directly applicable" (in the sense that they are not intended to have the force of law in the absence of national implementing measures), nevertheless they may-like some treaty provisions[85]-have "direct effect".[86] This means that litigants before national courts and tribunals may rely directly on provisions contained in a directive if certain conditions are satisfied. First, the time limit set for Member States to implement the directive must have expired. Secondly, the Member State must have failed to implement the directive into national law properly or at all. Thirdly, the directive must create justiciable rights or obligations (this criterion is similar to that for the direct effect of treaty provisions): the provision relied upon must be unconditional and sufficiently precise.[87] A directive that has not been properly implemented into national law cannot, however, impose obligations on private individuals.[88] Once a directive has been correctly transposed into national law, an individual is confined to his remedies under the domestic legislation and no longer has an individually enforceable Union right under the directive.[89] However, where a directive has been correctly implemented, but is not being correctly *applied* by national administrative authorities, an individual may still rely on the directive before national courts.[90]

14-032   There is an important difference between the operation of the principle of direct effect in relation to treaty provisions and directives. Treaty provisions which are

---

81 *Commission v Germany* (29/84) EU:C:1985:229 at [23]; and *Commission v Italy* (C-456/03) EU:C:2005:388 at [51].

82 *Flachglas Torgau GmbH v Federal Republic of Germany* (C-204/09) EU:C:2012:71 at [61].

83 *Commission v Germany* (C-298/95) EU:C:1996:501.

84 *Francovich* (C-6/90 and C-9/90) EU:C:1991:428; and see 14-098.

85 On direct effect of treaty provisions, see 14-026.

86 *Van Duyn v Home Office* (41/74) EU:C:1974:133.

87 *Cooperativa Agricola Zootecna S Antonio v Amministrazione delle finanze dello Stato* (C-246/94) EU:C:1996:329 at [17]-[19]; *Marks & Spencer* EU:C:2002:435 at [25]. See also *Hochtief AG and Linde-Kca-Dresden GmbH v Közbeszerzések Tanácsa Közbeszerzési Döntobizottság* (C-138/08) EU:C:2009:627 at [24]-[30] (confirming that a directive cannot have direct effect before the deadline for its implementation has passed).

88 *Accardo* (C-227/09) EU:C:2010:624 at [46]. See also *Association de médiation sociale v Union locale des syndicats CGT* (C-176/12) EU:C:2014:2 at [36].

89 *R. v Hammersmith and Fulham LBC Ex p. CPRE London Branch* [2000] Env. L.R. 565 at [32]-[35].

90 *Marks & Spencer* EU:C:2002:435.

directly effective may be relied upon by a litigant against any other litigant, including fellow citizens and business enterprises. The principle of direct effect allows directives, in contrast, to be relied upon only "vertically" against "emanations of the state".[91]

This limitation on the direct effect of directives is mitigated in arguably five ways, however.[92] First, the notion of the state is broadly defined for this purpose; a body is an emanation of the state, "whatever its legal form", if it is "subject to the authority or control of the state or [has] special powers beyond those which result from the normal rules applicable to relations between individuals".[93] Thus, the obligation to give effect to directives is one incumbent on all authorities of the Member States, including local authorities,[94] public authorities providing health services[95]; the governing body of a profession where "entrusted with a public duty"[96]; and the governing body of a voluntary aided school.[97] Most bodies which are subject to judicial review in the English courts would therefore be regarded as a manifestation of the state for the purpose of permitting an individual to invoke a directive against them. The obligation to comply with a directive applies regardless of the capacity in which the organ of the state is acting.[98] A public corporation will also be deemed to be "an organ of the state" if, whatever its legal form, it has been made responsible pursuant to a measure adopted by the state for providing a public service under the control of the state and has special powers over and above those powers enjoyed by ordinary individuals.[99] Thus, it has been held that, prior to privatisation, British Gas was an organ of the state.[100]

14-033

Secondly, there is a requirement that national legislation must be construed

14-034

---

91   *Tullio Ratti* (148/78) EU:C:1979:110 at [22]; *Marshall v Southampton and South West Hampshire Area Health Authority (Teaching)* (152/84) EU:C:1986:84 at [48]. For detailed criticism of this position, see P. Craig, "The Legal Effect of Directives: Policy, Rules and Exceptions" (2009) 34 E.L. Rev. 349. For confirmation that Directives do not, in themselves, create obligations on the part of individuals and cannot be relied upon against those individuals, see: *Papasavvas v O Fileleftheros Dimosia Etairia Ltd* (C-291/13) EU:C:2014:2209 at [54].

92   See further A. Ward, *Judicial Review and the Rights of Private Parties in EU Law* (2007), pp.31-35.

93   *Foster v British Gas Plc* (C-188/89) EU:C:1990:313 at [18], [22]. See also *Farrell v Whitty (MIBI)* (C-356/05) EU:C:2007:229 at [40]-[41]; *Medipac-Kazantzidis AE v Venizeleio-Pananio (PESY KRITIS)* (C-6/05) EU:C:2007:337 at [43]; *Maribel Dominguez v Centre informatique du Centre Ouest Atlantique* (C-282/10) EU:C:2012:33 [2012] I.R.L.R. 321 at [39]. On "public functions" as a test of amenability to judicial review in England, see 3-038; on "functions of a public nature" in Human Rights Act 1998 s.6, see 3-066. The criteria are disjunctive not conjunctive: *Farrell v Whitty (C-413/15)* EU:C:2017:74; at [24]–[29].

94   *Costanzo v Comune di Milano* (103/88) EU:C:1989:256; see also *Günter Fuß v Stadt Halle* (C-243/09) EU:C:2010:609.

95   *Marshall* EU:C:1986:84.

96   *Rienks* (5/83) EU:C:1983:382.

97   *National Union of Teachers v St Mary's Church of England (Aided) Junior School Governing Body* [1997] 3 C.M.L.R. 630. See also *Vasil Ivanov Georgiev v Tehnicheski universitet-Sofia, filial Plovdiv* (C-250/09 and C-268/09) EU:C:2010:699 at [71] (the CJEU accepting the national court's determination that the University was a public body falling within the *Foster* criteria).

98   Public bodies have had directives relating to equality in employment matters enforced against them, see, e.g. *Johnston v Chief Constable of the Royal Ulster Constabulary* (222/84) EU:C:1986:206.

99   *Foster* EU:C:1990:313 at [20].

100   *Foster* EU:C:1990:313; HL in [1991] 2 A.C. 306; cf. *Doughty v Rolls Royce* [1992] I.C.R. 538; *Griffin v South West Water Services Ltd* [1995] I.R.L.R. 15 (applying *Foster*, a privatised water company is a State authority against which directives can be enforced directly; the material criterion for the purposes of direct effect is not whether the body in question is under the control of the State but whether the public service which it performs is under State control). See also *Fish Legal v Information Commissioner* (C-279/12) EU:C:2013:853 at [64]–[73] (in the context of art.2 of Directive 2003/4/EC of the European Parliament and of the Council of 28 January 2003 on public access to environmental information and repealing Council Directive 90/313/EEC, to determine whether an

wherever possible so as to conform to directives[101]: this is known as the indirect effect of directives and applies in litigation between private parties.[102] Indirect effect will be discussed in further detail below.[103]

14-035   Thirdly, directives may be invoked in so-called "triangular" situations,[104] even if the application of the directive would result in what the CJEU has described as "mere adverse repercussions on the rights of third parties."[105] This is known as the "incidental effect" of directives. Thus, the CJEU has held that directives which require certain actions on the part of the Member State, such as notification to the Commission of technical standards likely to impede the free movement of goods[106] or the undertaking of an environmental impact assessment,[107] may be relied upon by individuals in national courts, even where this may have negative consequences for third parties. In the case of *Wells*, the claimant sought to rely on Directive 85/337 in judicial review proceedings against the Mineral Planning Authority in respect of its grant of permission to the owner of a long dormant quarry to resume mining in the quarry without having conducted an environmental impact assessment. The CJEU approved reliance on the directive, even though its application had the potential to result in the loss of mining permission for the owner of the quarry.[108]

14-036   Fourthly, it appears that where a regulation refers to a directive, this may result in horizontal direct effect for the relevant directive provision. In the case of *Viamex*,[109] payment of export refunds for live animals was dealt with through

---

entity is a legal person which performs "public administrative functions", it is necessary to examine whether those entities are vested, under national law, with special powers beyond those which result from the normal rules applicable in relations between persons governed by private law and a body will be under the "control" of such an entity where it does not determine in a genuinely autonomous manner the way in which it provides those services since a public authority is in a position to exert decisive influence on its action in the environmental field).

[101] *Von Colson and Kamann v Land Nordrhein-Westfalen* (14/83) EU:C:1984:153.
[102] *Administration des Douanes v Gondrand Freres* (169/80) EU:C:1981:171 at [17]; *Salumi* (212-217/80) EU:C:1981:270 at [10]; *Kloppenburg* (70/83) EU:C:1984:71 at [11].
[103] See 14-068.
[104] K. Lackhoff and H. Nyssens, "Direct effect of directives in triangular situations" (1998) 23 E.L. Rev. 397; and S. Weatherill, "Breach of Directives and Breach of Contract" (2001) 26 E.L. Rev. 177; D. Colgan, "Triangular Situations: the Coup de Grâce for the Denial of Horizontal Effect of Community Directives" (2002) 8 E.P.L. 545.
[105] *Wells v Secretary of State for Transport, Local Government and the Regions* (C-201/02) EU:C:2004:12 at [57]; *Arcor AG & Co KG v Germany* (C-152-154/07) EU:C:2008:426 at [36]. See also *R. v Durham CC Ex p. Huddleston* [2000] 1 W.L.R. 1484 at [18] ("enforcement of a Directive by an individual against the state is not rendered inadmissible solely by its consequential effect on other individuals").
[106] Directive 83/189 [1983] OJ L109/8, as amended; see *CIA Security International SA v Signalson SA and Securitel SPRL* (C-194/94) EU:C:1996:172; *Sapod Audic v Eco-Emballages SA* (C-159/00) EU:C:2002:343; *Unilever Italia SpA v Central Food SpA* (C-443/98) EU:C:2000:496; *Adeneler v Ellinikos Organismos Galaktos* (C-212/04) EU:C:2006:443; *Sonia Chacon Navas v Eurest Cole* (C-13/05) EU:C:2006:456; *James Elliott Construction Ltd v Irish Asphalt Ltd* (C-613/14) EU:C:2016:821 at [64]–[65]. The scope of the principle has been limited to those cases where application of national regulations would hinder the use or marketing of a product not in conformity with them: *Lemmens* (C-226/97) EU:C:1998:296.
[107] See, e.g. *Wells* EU:C:2004:12. For a similar example, see *R. v The Medicines Control Agency Ex p. Smith & Nephew Pharmaceuticals Ltd* (C-201/94) EU:C:1996:432 at [39].
[108] *Wells* EU:C:2004:12 at [57]-[58], [69]-[70]. See also: *Arcor AG & Co KG* EU:C:2008:426 at [38] ("removal of benefits cannot be regarded as an obligation falling on a third party pursuant to the directives"). Whether the third parties who are negatively affected may be able to claim the protection of legitimate expectations in this context is unclear: see A. Dashwood, M. Dougan, B. Rodger, E. Spaventa, and D. Wyatt, *Wyatt and Dashwood's European Union Law* (2011), p.264, fn.150.
[109] *Viamex Agrar Handels GmbH and Zuchtvieh-Kontor GmbH (ZVK) v Hauptzollamt Hamburg-Jonas* (C-37 and 58/06) EU:C:2008:18.

Regulation 615/98,[110] which conditioned payment on compliance with rules concerning the welfare of live animals during transit set down in Directive 91/628.[111] The German authorities refused to pay the refunds where the exporter had not complied with the 24-hour rest period for animals prescribed by the Directive.[112] The CJEU stated that a directive cannot of itself impose obligations on an individual,[113] but added that, it could not be:

"precluded, in principle, that the provisions of a directive may be applicable by means of an express reference in a regulation to its provisions, provided that general principles of law and, in particular, the principle of legal certainty, are observed".[114]

Fifthly, where a provision of a directive mirrors a general principle of Union law, **14-037** the obligation imposed will not be regarded as only being triggered at the date for the transposition of the directive and may be capable of horizontal direct effect both prior to and after the implementation date of the directive. For example, in *Mangold v Rüdiger Helm*, it was held that, given that Directive 2000/78 was intended to lay down a general framework for combating discrimination on the grounds of religion or belief, disability, age or sexual orientation, and given that the principle of non-discrimination on grounds of age must be regarded as a general principle of Union law, observance of that general principle could not be conditional upon the expiry of the period allowed to Member States for the transposition of a directive intended to lay down a general framework for combating discrimination on the grounds of age.[115] The principle of horizontal application of the principle of non-discrimination has also been extended to the period following the date for transposition of a directive.[116] This line of jurisprudence has been criticised on the grounds of the potential lack of legal certainty it generates.[117] However, in *Dansk Industri (DI), acting on behalf of Ajos A/S v Estate of Karsten Eigil Rasmussen*, the CJEU rejected an objection to *Mangold* raised on grounds of legal certainty and protection of legitimate expectations.[118]

Decisions

Under provisions of the TFEU and of EU legislation, the Council or the Com- **14-038** mission are empowered to adopt binding decisions, addressed to Member States or

---

[110] Regulation 615/98 of 18 March 1998 laying down specific detailed rules of application for the export refund arrangements as regards the welfare of live bovine animals during transport [1998] OJ L82/19 (no longer in force).

[111] Directive 91/628 EEC of 19 November 1998 on the protection of animals during transport and amending Directives 90/425 and 91/496 [1991] OJ L340/17, as amended by Directive 95/29/EC of 29 June 1995 concerning the protection of animals during transport [1995] OJ L148/52 (and now repealed).

[112] This rule was found in point 48(5) of Ch.VII of the Annex to Directive 91/628 (now repealed).

[113] *Viamex* EU:C:2008:18 at [27].

[114] *Viamex* EU:C:2008:18 at [28].

[115] *Mangold v Rüdiger Helm* (C-144/04) EU:C:2005:709 at [74]-[77]; *Vasil Ivanov Georgiev v Tehnicheski universitet Sofia* (C-250/09) EU:C:2010:699.

[116] *Seda Kücükdeveci v Swedex GmbH & Co KG* (C-555/07) EU:C:2010:21.

[117] P. Craig and G. de Búrca (eds), *EU Law: Texts, Cases and Materials* (2015), pp.195-196. Insofar as the *Mangold* line of cases requires a national court to disapply national legislation in a claim against a private party where the provision of national law is inconsistent with a directive, it has been confined by the English High Court to the "fundamental principle of non-discrimination": see *Alstom Transport v Eurostar International Ltd* [2012] EWHC 28 (Ch); [2012] 3 All E.R. 263 at [47] (Roth J observing: "[w]ere it otherwise, the distinction between vertical and horizontal direct effect would in practical terms be abolished, and the difference between directives and regulations that is expressed in TFEU art.288 would be emasculated").

[118] *Dansk Industri (DI), acting on behalf of Ajos A/S v Estate of Karsten Eigil Rasmussen* (C-441/14) EU:C:2016:278.

to individuals. In accordance with TFEU art.288, decisions are binding in their entirety upon those to whom they are addressed. A decision addressed to a Member State may often impose obligations on it: such a decision might require it, for example, to abolish an unlawful tax or an unlawful state aid. Such decisions may have direct effect where their terms are clear and precise, and so confer rights on individuals enforceable in the national courts.[119]

THE CHARTER OF FUNDAMENTAL RIGHTS OF THE EU

14-039   The Charter was solemnly proclaimed at Nice on 7 December 2000, by the European Parliament, the Council and the Commission. It became legally binding in December 2009 on the coming into force of the Lisbon Treaty and has been published in the Official Journal.[120] In terms of content, it is often said that the Charter does not provide any new rights that were not already protected by Union law, and that its purpose is merely declaratory.[121] However, it is clear that the Charter reformulates existing rights, with potential for different interpretations[122]; while it also recognises as fundamental, rights which would not previously have been described as such.[123] It provides a combination of classic civil and political rights, in addition to economic and social rights, which are found in six chapters: dignity[124]; freedoms[125]; equality[126]; solidarity[127]; citizen's rights[128]; and justice.[129] The rights were derived from a number of sources, including: rights recognised in the TEU, the TFEU, the European Convention on Human Rights (ECHR), the Social Charters adopted by the Union and by the Council of Europe, and the case law of the CJEU and European Court of Human Rights; rights recognised in the constitutions of the Member States; and international human rights treaties concluded by the Member States.[130] A distinction is drawn between rights and principles[131]; although the impact of the distinction and the categorisation of provisions as rights

---

[119] *Grad v Finanzamt* (9/70) EU:C:1970:78.

[120] [2010] OJ C83/389; see P. Craig, *EU Administrative Law* (2012) Ch.16. By way of background, see, e.g. P. Eeckhout, "The EU Charter of Fundamental Rights and the Federal Question" (2002) 39 C.M.L. Rev. 945; C. McCrudden, *The Future of the EU Charter of Fundamental Rights*, Jean Monnet Working Paper 13/01. For a comprehensive consideration of the Charter, see S Peers, J Kenner, A Ward, TK Hervey *The EU Charter of Fundamental Rights: A Commentary* (2014).

[121] Lord Goldsmith, "The Charter of Rights-A Brake not an Accelerator" (2004) 5 E.H.R.L.R. 473. Other commentators have disputed this: P. Eeckhout, "The EU Charter of Fundamental Rights and the Federal Question" (2002) 39 C.M.L. Rev. 945; K. O'Brien and B. Kolterman, "The Charter of Fundamental Rights of the EU in Practice" (2013) 14 *ERA Forum* 457.

[122] For example, while ECHR art.8(1) refers to the right to "respect ... for correspondence"; art.7 of the Charter refers to right to "respect ... for communications" which takes into account the growth of electronic communications.

[123] P. Eeckhout, "The EU Charter of Fundamental Rights and the Federal Question" (2002) 39 C.M.L. Rev. 945, p.951.

[124] Charter arts 1-5.

[125] Charter arts 6-19.

[126] Charter arts 20-26.

[127] Charter arts 27-38.

[128] Charter arts 39-46.

[129] Charter arts 47-50.

[130] Charter Preamble. See also *R. (on the application of AB) v Secretary of State for the Home Department* [2013] EWHC 3453 (Admin); [2014] 2 C.M.L.R. 22 at [12]-[16] (obiter, noting that the Charter "enunciates a host of new rights" not expressly incorporated into EU law under the Human Rights Act 1998).

[131] TEU art.6 states that "The Union recognises the rights, freedoms and principles set out in the Charter of Fundamental Rights of the European Union..."; see also Charter art.52(1) (referring to "rights

or principles is not yet entirely clear.[132] Article 52(5) provides that any provisions of the Charter which contain principles may be implemented by legislative and executive acts taken by institutions, bodies, offices and agencies of the Union, and by acts of Member States when they are implementing Union law, in the exercise of their respective powers; it provides further that principles shall be judicially cognisable only in the interpretation of such acts and in the ruling on their legality. Rights recognised by the Charter for which provision is made in the EU Treaties are to be exercised under the conditions and within the limits defined by the Treaties[133]; and likewise, notwithstanding any difference of language, those Charter provisions which correspond to a provision in the ECHR have the same meaning and scope as the Convention rights.[134] It appears, however, that the interpretation of the Charter provisions will not necessarily be constrained by their correlating ECHR provisions or indeed, the Explanations.[135] It also appears that where Charter provisions and ECHR provisions overlap, it is necessary to refer to the Charter provisions.[136] In this regard, the CJEU has emphasised that the ECHR "does not constitute, as long as the European Union has acceded to it, a legal instrument which has been formally incorporated into EU law".[137] In so far as Charter provisions draw upon the constitutional traditions common to the Member States, they should be interpreted "in harmony" with those constitutional traditions.[138] It is also important to note that the Explanations drawn up to provide guidance on the interpretation of

---

and freedoms"), art.52(5) (delimiting the justiciability of "principles"), art.23, which refers to the "principle" of equality between men and women and art.21 which sets out the right to non-discrimination on grounds of sex.

[132] The word "principle" sometimes appears in the wording of the provision, but frequently its special character must be inferred from other aspects of the drafting method, e.g. the formula "the Union recognises and respects" may signal that a provision is a principle rather than a right. An example of this, in relation to social security benefits and social services, is found in art.34 of the Charter. See C. Hilson, "Rights and Principles in EU Law: A Distinction without Foundation?" (2008) 15 *Maastricht J. of European and Comparative L.* 193. The distinction between rights and principles may have an impact on whether a Charter provision has horizontal direct effect: *Association de médiation sociale v Union locale des syndicats* CGT (C-176/12) EU:C:2014:2 at [47]-[51]; and (C-176/12) EU:C:2014:2 at [43]-[48] (finding that some Charter provisions, such as art.21(1), are capable of horizontal direct effect, but others, such as art.27, are not). See also N. Lazzerini, "(Some of) the Fundamental Rights Granted by the Charter may be a Source of Obligations for Private Parties" [2014] 51(3) C.M.L. Rev. 907; H. Hofmann and B. Mihaescu, "The Relation between the Charter's Fundamental Rights and the Unwritten General Principles of EU Law: Good Administration as the Test Case" [2013] 9(1) E.C.L. Review 73.

[133] Charter art.52(2).

[134] Charter art.52(3).

[135] See, e.g. *Brahim Samba Diouf v Ministre du Travail* (C-69/10) EU:C:2011:102 (Opinion of Advocate General Cruz Villalón at [39] ("the right to effective judicial protection, as expressed in Article 47 of the CFREU, has, through being recognised as part of European Union law by virtue of Article 47, acquired a separate identity and substance under that article which are not the mere sum of the provisions of Articles 6 and 13 of the ECHR"). See also *R. (on the application of EM (Eritrea)) v Secretary of State for the Home Department* [2014] UKSC 12; [2014] 2 W.L.R. 409 at [44]-[62] (the Supreme Court, when faced with an CJEU interpretation of a Charter right which would involve incompatibility with ECHR art.3, considered that the CJEU "did not intend" to alter the meaning of art.3).

[136] *Europese Gemeenschap v Otis NV* (C-199/11) EU:C:2012:684 at [47]; *Radu* (C-396/11) EU:C:2013:39 at [32].

[137] *Inuit Tapiriit Kanatami v Commission, Parliament and Council* (T-526/10) EU:T:2013:215 at [105] (it was appropriate for the General Court to examine the legislation under challenge solely by reference to provisions of the Charter). However, contrast *Deutsche Bahn AG v Commission* (C-583/13 P) EU:C:2015:404 at [32]-[36] and [46]-[48] (reaching a determination by reference to ECHR case law before considering the Charter).

[138] Charter art.52(4). See also Charter art.53 for the relationship between Charter and national constitutional rights and *Melloni* (C-399/11) EU:C:2013:107 at [60] (holding that, while art.53 confirms that national courts remain free to apply national standards of protection of fundamental

the Charter[139] must be "given due regard by the courts of the Union and of the Member States".[140]

14-040 The CJEU, the General Court and various Advocates General began referring to the Charter in its rulings well before the Charter received formal legal status as a result of the Lisbon Treaty revisions.[141]

14-041 Since coming into force, the Charter has been invoked in a significant number of cases, with judgments of the CJEU and the General Court and already, a broad range of the Charter's articles have been subject to interpretation.[142] A number of cases have arisen in the context of private and family life,[143] as well as regarding protection of personal data.[144] There have also been judgments dealing with more

---

rights, this is "provided that the level of protection provided for by the Charter, as interpreted by the Court, and the primacy, unity and effectiveness of EU law are not thereby compromised"). On the facts of the case, this meant that the Spanish courts could not make the surrender, pursuant to Framework Decision 2002/584, of a person convicted in absentia conditional upon the conviction being open to review in the issuing Member State, in order to avoid an adverse effect on the right to a fair trial and the rights of defence guaranteed by the national constitution: [64]. The Spanish Constitutional Court reacted by lowering the degree of protection afforded by the Spanish Constitution in line with Union law: STC 26/2014. See also *Cruciano Siragusa v Regione Sicilia— Soprintendenza Beni Culturali e Ambientali di Palermo* (C-206/13) EU:C:2014:126 at [32]. For discussion of *Melloni*, see, e.g. A. Torres Perez, "Melloni in Three Acts: From Dialogue to Monologue" (2014) 10 E.C.L. Review 308; L.F.M. Besselink, "The Parameters of Constitutional Conflict after Melloni" (2014) 39 E.L. Rev. 531. See also *Opinion 2/13* EU:C:2014:2454 at [188] (noting that in *Melloni*, the CJEU had interpreted Charter art.53 as meaning that the application of national standards of protection of fundamental rights must not compromise the level of protection provided by the Charter or the primary, unity and effectiveness of Union law). In *Opinion 2/13*, the CJEU also observed (at [192]) that when implementing Union law, the Member States may, under Union law, be required to presume that fundamental rights have been observed by the other Member States, so that not only may they not demand a higher level of national protection of fundamental rights from another Member State than that provided by EU law, but, save in exceptional cases, they may not check whether that other Member State has actually, in a specific case, observed the fundamental rights guaranteed by the EU.

139 Explanations Relating to the Charter of Fundamental Rights (2007/C 303/02).
140 Charter art.52(7).
141 See, e.g. *Parliament v Council* (C-540/03) EU:C:2006:429 at [38]. See also; *Unibet (London) Ltd v Justitiekanslern* (C-432/05) EU:C:2007:163 at [37]; *Advocaten voor de Wereld VZW v Leden van de Ministerraad* (C-303/05) EU:C:2007:261 at [46] (noting that the principle of the legality of criminal offences and penalties and the principle of equality and non-discrimination are "reaffirmed" in the Charter); *Varec v Belgium* (C-450/06) EU:C:2008:91 at [48] (referring to the right to respect for private life which is "restated" in art.7 of the Charter); *Kadi and Al Barakaat International Foundation v Council* (C-415/05) EU:C:2008:461 at [335]; *Jégo-Quéré* (T-177/01) EU:T:2002:112 at [42].
142 There have been too many cases decided to list here. Notable cases however include: *N. S. v Secretary of State for the Home Department and M. E. and Others v Refugee Applications Commissioner and Minister for Justice, Equality and Law Reform* (C-411/10 and C-493/10) EU:C:2011:865 (Grand Chamber) (arts 4 and 51(1)); *Agrofert Holding v Commission* (T-111/07) EU:T:2010:285 (access to documents) (art.7); *Rhimou Chakroun v Minister van Buitenlandse Zaken* (C-578/08) EU:C:2010:806 (art.7).
143 See, e.g. *Agrofert Holding* (T-111/07) EU:T:2010:285; *Rhimou Chakroun* (C-578/08) EU:C:2010:117; *Ilonka Sayn-Wittgenstein v Landeshauptmann von Wien* (C-208/09) EU:C:2010:117; *Malgožata Runevič-Vardyn and Łukasz Paweł Wardyn v Vilniaus miesto savivaldybės administracija* (C-391/09) EU:C:2011:291; *Murat Dereci and Others v Bundesministerium für Inneres* (C-256/11) EU:C:2011:734; *PPU J. McB. v L. E.* (C-400/10) EU:C:2010:582; *Natthaya Dülger v Wetteraukreis* (C-451/11) EU:C:2012:504; *Land Baden-Württemberg v Panagiotis Tsakouridis* (C-145/09) EU:C:2010:708.
144 See, e.g. *Scarlet Extended SA v Société belge des auteurs, compositeurs et éditeurs SCRL (SABAM)* (C-70/10) EU:C:2011:771; *Kelly v National University of Ireland (University College, Dublin)* (C-104/10) EU:C:2011:506; *Sophie in 't Veld v Council* (T-529/09) EU:T:2012:215. For a relatively unusual example of case in which the CJEU found a violation of human rights in EU legislation, see *Volker und Markus Schecke and Eifert* (C-92/09 and C-93/09) EU:C:2010:662 at [85]-[86]. See

novel aspects of the Charter, such as workers' rights to information and consultation in art.27,[145] the entitlement to social security and social assistance in art.34[146] and art.35 regarding health care.[147] However, to date, the most heavily cited provision appears to have been art.47 regarding the right to an effective remedy and fair trial,[148] many of which cases have arisen in the competition law context.[149]

The Charter is binding on EU institutions and on Member States "when they are   **14-042**

---

also *Digital Rights Ireland v Minister for Communications, Marine and Natural Resources* (C-293, 594/12) EU:C:2014:238 at [45]–[70] (holding that the Data Retention Directive violated art.7 of the Charter due to a lack of proportionality); *Google Inc v Agencia Española de Protección de Datos (AEPD)* (C-131/12) EU:C:2014:317 at [97]–[99]; *Schrems v Data Protection Commissioner* (C-362/14) EU:C:2015:650 (finding invalid the Safe Harbour arrangement for data transfers to the US); *Tele2 Sverige AB v Post-och telestyrelsen* (C-203/15) EU:C:2015:650. For an example in the national context, see *Vidal-Hall v Google Inc* [2015] EWCA Civ 311; [2015] 3 W.L.R. 409 at [70]–[79]); *R. (on the application of Davis) v Secretary of State for the Home Department* [2015] EWCA Civ 1185; [2016] 1 C.M.L.R. 48 (reference sought on the implications of the *Digital Rights Ireland* case); *Privacy International v Secretary of State for Foreign and Commonwealth Affairs* IP/15/110/ CH.

[145] *Association de médiation sociale* (C-176/12) EU:C:2014:2.

[146] *Servet Kamberaj v Istituto per l'Edilizia sociale della Provincia autonoma di Bolzano (IPES)* (C-571/10) EU:C:2012:233, (Grand Chamber).

[147] *Deutsches Weintor v Land Rheinland-Pfalz* (C-544/10) EU:C:2012:526; *José Manuel Blanco Pérez and María del Pilar Chao Gómez v Consejería de Salud y Servicios Sanitarios and Principado de Asturias* (C-570/07 and C-571/07) (Grand Chamber) EU:C:2010:300.

[148] Examples include: *DEB Deutsche Energiehandels- und Beratungsgesellschaft mbH v Bundesrepublik Deutschland* (C-279/09) EU:C:2010:811 (the right to legal aid under art.47 applies to both natural and legal persons); *Orizzonte Salute-Studio Infermieristico Associato v Azienda Pubblica di Servizi alla persona San Valentino-Citta di Levico Terme* (C-61/14) EU:C:2015:655; *G v Cornelius de Visser* (C-292/10) EU:C:2012:142 (art.47 does not preclude judgment being entered against a defendant in default of appearance given that it was impossible to locate him, the document instituting proceedings had been served by a public notice under national law and the court seised of the matter had first satisfied itself that all investigations required by the principles of diligence and good faith had been undertaken to trace the defendant); *Užsienio reikalų ministerija v Vladimir Peftiev* (C-314/13) EU:C:2014:1645 (freezing of funds should not prevent access to legal representation); *Inuit Tapiriit Kanatami v Parliament and Council* (C-583/11) EU:C:2013:625 at [105] (art.47 does not require an unconditional entitlement to bring a direct action for annulment of Union legislative acts); *Commission v Kadi* (C-584/10P, C-593/10P, C-595/10P) EU:C:2013:518; *ZZ v Secretary of State for the Home Department* (C-300/11) EU:C:2013:363 at [57] (disclosure in national security contexts); *R. (on the application of Edwards and Pallikaropoulos) v Environment Agency* (C-260/11) EU:C:2013:221 at [35] (environmental context); *Commission v United Kingdom of Great Britain and Northern Ireland* (C-530/11) EU:C:2014:67. For comment see J. Krommendijk, "Is there a light on the horizon? The distinction between 'Rewe effectiveness' and the principle of effective judicial protection in Article 47 of the Charter after Orizzonte" (2016) 53 C.M.L. Rev. 1395. In *Berlioz Investment Fund SA v Directeur de l'adminisration des contributions directes* (C-682/15) EU:C:2017:373, it was held that art.47 may be invoked in respect of a measure "adversely affecting" a person (at [51]-[52]). For interpretation of art.47 in the domestic courts, see *R. (on the application of AZ) v Secretary of State for the Home Department* [2017] EWCA Civ 35; [2017] 4 W.L.R. 94; *R. (on the application of XH) v Secretary of State for the Home Department* [2017] EWCA Civ 41 at [136] (regard can be had to the ECHR art.6 case law in interpreting art.47); *S1, T1, U1, V1 v Secretary of State for the Home Department* [2016] EWCA Civ 560 at [34]; and *Yanukovych v Council* (Case T-346/14) EU:T:2016:497 (duty to give reasons).

[149] *Mindo Srl v Commission* (T-19/06) EU:T:2011:561; *Areva Société anonyme v Commission* (T-117/07 and T-121/07) EU:T:2011:69 (imposition of joint and several liability); *KME Germany AG, KME France SAS and KME Italy SpA v Commission* (C-272/09 P) EU:C:2011:810; *Chalkor AE Epexergasias Metallon v Commission* (C-386/10 P) EU:C:2011:815 (it was not necessary for the General Court to engage in full review of the Commission's decision in the competition law sphere in order to satisfy the requirements of art.47); see also *Schindler Holding v Commission* (C-501/11) EU:C:2013:522 at [33]-[34]. For a particularly important case on the role of the Commission in competition proceedings, see *Europese Gemeenschap v Otis NV* (C-199/11) EU:C:2012:684.

implementing Union law".[150] The application of the Charter to the institutions appears to be straightforward,[151] but not so with respect to the Member States. The position of the CJEU has long been that Member States must abide by the fundamental rights jurisprudence of the CJEU when acting "within the scope of Community [now Union] law".[152] After some uncertainty, it was clarified that the provisions of the Charter will not be interpreted more narrowly than the CJEU's current formulation.[153] There had been indications from the CJEU that the term "implementing EU law" would not be interpreted narrowly and that the Charter would be applicable where Member States "act within the scope of EU law".[154] Indeed, in the case of *Dereci*,[155] referring to the scope of application of the Charter, the CJEU observed briefly that if the matter was "covered by European Union law", it was necessary for the national court to assess the question vis-à-vis art.7 of the Charter, and if the matter was "not covered by European Union law", the national court should assess the question pursuant to the equivalent ECHR art.8.[156] An even broader proposal for the scope of application of fundamental rights jurisprudence-being dependent upon the existence and scope of material Union competence-was suggested by Advocate General Sharpston in the well-known *Zambrano* case, but has not yet been adopted by the CJEU.[157] Finally, in *Åklagaren v Hans Åkerberg Fransson*, the CJEU ruled that:

> "[s]ince the fundamental rights guaranteed by the Charter must therefore be complied with where national legislation falls within the scope of European Union law, situations cannot exist which are covered in that way by European Union law without those fundamental rights being applicable. The applicability of European Union law entails applicability of the fundamental rights guaranteed by the Charter."[158]

14-043   Following *Åklagaren*, the CJEU has also explained, in *Cruciano Siragusa*, that

---

[150] Charter art.51(1).

[151] See, e.g. *Parliament v Council* (C-130/10) EU:C:2012:472 (Grand Chamber); *Ministero dell'Interno v Fastweb SpA* (C-19/13) EU:C:2014:2194. See also *Ledra Advertising v Commission and European Central Bank* (C-8/15 P to C-10/15 P) EU:C:2016:701, where it was held that, even where the Commission is acting outside the scope of Union law and in the context of a Memorandum of Understanding within the framework of the European Stability Mechanism, it is bound by the Charter. It was added that the Commission, in "its role of guardian of the Treaties", should "refrain from signing a memorandum of understanding whose consistency with EU law it doubts" (including consistency with the Charter) (see [59]). The CJEU also held that the Charter is addressed to EU institutions when they act outside the EU legal framework (see [67]).

[152] *ERT v DEP & Sotirious Kouvelas* (C-260/89) EU:C:1991:254 and 14-135. For an application of the Charter to national measures, see *R. (on the application of British American Tobacco Ltd) v Secretary of State for Health* [2016] EWCA Civ 1182; [2017] 3 W.L.R. 225.

[153] Charter art.52(7) provides that "the explanations drawn up as a way of providing guidance in the interpretation of this Charter shall be given due regard by the courts of the Union and of the Member States". The Declaration concerning the Explanations relating to the Charter of Fundamental Rights interprets art.51(1) to mean that the Charter is binding on Member States when they "act in the context of Community [now Union] law" and refers specifically to the existing CJEU case law, see, e.g. *Wachauf v Germany* (5/88) EU:C:1989:321; *ERT* EU:C:1991:254. See further 14-135.

[154] *Scattolon v Ministero dell'Istruzione, dell'Università e della Ricerca* (C-108/10) EU:C:2011:211 (Opinion of Advocate General Bot at [119]); *Anton Vinkov v Nachalnik Administrativno-nakazatelna deynost* (C-27/11) EU:C:2012:326 at [58].

[155] *Murat Dereci and Others v Bundesministerium für Inneres* (C-256/11) EU:C:2011:734 (Grand Chamber) at [72].

[156] See also *Pringle v Government of Ireland, Ireland and the Attorney General* (C-370/12) EU:C:2012:756 (Grand Chamber) at [180].

[157] Opinion of AG Sharpston, *Gerardo Ruiz Zambrano v Office national de l'emploi* (C-34/09) EU:C:2010:560 at [163]-[170].

[158] *Åklagaren v Hans Åkerberg Fransson* (C-617/10) EU:C:2013:105 at [21]; see also [29] for an interesting comment on the relationship between Charter rights and national standards.

the concept of "implementing Union law" requires a certain degree of connection with Union law above and beyond the matters covered being closely related or one of those matters having an indirect impact on the other. When determining whether national legislation involves the implementation of Union law, some of the points to be considered are: whether that legislation is intended to implement a provision of Union law; the nature of that legislation and whether it pursues objectives other than those covered by Union law, even if it is capable of indirectly affecting Union law; and also whether there are specific rules of EU law on the matter or capable of affecting it. Furthermore, the fact that national legislation could have an indirect effect on a system established by Union law could not constitute a sufficient connection to bring such legislation within the scope of Union law. This meant that an order requiring a property owner to restore property within a landscape conservation area to its original state did not engage art.17 of the Charter where EU law did not impose any obligations to protect the specific landscape; there was only an indirect connection between the facts and Union law which was not sufficient to attract the application of the Charter.[159] It is also apparent that the Charter is not unlimited in its scope of application, and, for example, where a Member State stores and uses fingerprint data, originally collected in compliance with a Union Regulation, but which the Member State then uses for purposes other than those stipulated in the Regulation, the Member State is not acting within the scope of Union law and therefore is not bound by the Charter.[160]

It has been held that certain provisions of the Charter are capable of horizontal direct effect, although there is a lack of clarity on which provisions are capable of such effect.[161]   **14-044**

Any limitation on the exercise of the rights and freedoms recognised by the Charter must be provided for by law and respect the essence of those rights and freedoms. Subject to the principle of proportionality, limitations may be made only if they necessarily and genuinely meet objectives of general interest recognised by the Union or the need to protect the rights and freedoms of others.[162]   **14-045**

As is well-known, the United Kingdom and Poland entered into a Protocol with respect to the Charter, which has two substantive provisions. Article 1 provides: **14-046**

---

[159] *Cruciano Siragusa v Region Sicilia-Soprintendenza Beni Culturali e Ambientali di Palermo* (C-206/13) EU:C:2014:126 at [24]-[27]. The CJEU also observed (at [22]) that Member States were only bound by EU fundamental rights in respect of matters "covered by EU law". See also *Érsekcsanádi Mezogazdasági Zrt v Bács-Kiskun Megyei Kormányhivatal* (C-56/13) EU:C:2014:352 (parts of a national implementing measure providing for compensation to affected parties could not be challenged under the Charter); *Pelckmans Turnhout NV v Walter Van Gastel Balen NV* (C-483/12) EU:C:2014:304 at [20] (prohibition on seven-day trading outside the scope of Union law). See also *Opinion 2/13* EU:C:2014:2454 (18 December 2014) at [171]; *Paoletti* (C-218/15) EU:C:2016:748 at [14]-[15]; *Milkova v Izpalnitelen director na Agentsiata za privatizatsia I sledprivatzatssionen control* (C-406/15) EU:C:2017:198 at [50]-[54].

[160] *Willems v Burgemeester van Nuth* (C-446/12) EU:C:2015:238. See also *Fag og Arbejde v Kommunernes Landsforening (KL)* (C-354/13) EU:C:2014:2463 (holding that the Charter was inapplicable to a complaint of discrimination on grounds of obesity because obesity discrimination does not fall within the scope of Union law (albeit that the CJEU proceeded to rule that in certain circumstances, obesity may give rise to a disability engaging the duty not to discriminate on grounds of disability)).

[161] *Association de médiation sociale v Union locale des syndicats CGT* (C-176/12) EU:C:2014:2 at [43]-[48] (see also *Dansk Industri* EU:C:2016:278 at [36]).

[162] Charter art.52(1). See *Digital Rights Ireland v Minister for Communications, Marine and Natural Resources* (C-293, 594/12) EU:C:2014:238 at [45]-[71] for an example of a case in which legislation, the Data Retention Directive, was found incompatible with the Charter due to a lack of proportionality. See also *British American Tobacco* [2016] EWCA Civ 1182; [2017] 3 W.L.R. 225 at [121]-[124] (rejecting the argument that the "essence" of the right is a separate test from the proportionality test).

"1.   The Charter does not extend the ability of the Court of Justice of the European Union, or any court or tribunal of Poland or of the United Kingdom, to find that the laws, regulations or administrative provisions, practices or action of Poland or of the United Kingdom are inconsistent with the fundamental rights, freedoms and principles that it reaffirms.

2.   In particular, and for the avoidance of doubt, nothing in Title IV of the Charter creates justiciable rights applicable to Poland or the United Kingdom except in so far as Poland or the United Kingdom has provided for such rights in its national law."

Article 2 provides as follows:

"To the extent that a provision of the Charter refers to national laws and practices, it shall only apply to Poland or the United Kingdom to the extent that the rights or principles that it contains are recognised in the law or practices of Poland or of the United Kingdom."

14-047   The Protocol has had a limited impact on the effect of the Charter in this jurisdiction. A holding of the High Court to the effect that the Charter could not be relied upon directly against the United Kingdom (and only as an indirect influence by way of an aid to interpretation) was abandoned by the Secretary of State in its submissions to the Court of Appeal.[163] The CJEU itself has also held that the Protocol does not call into question the applicability of the Charter in the United Kingdom; nor does it intend to exempt the United Kingdom from the obligation to comply with the provisions of the Charter or to prevent a court of one of those Member States from ensuring compliance with those provisions.[164] The CJEU's approach was considered in *R. (on the application of AB) v Secretary of State for the Home Department* by Mostyn J, who regarded it as "absolutely clear that the contracting parties agreed that the Charter did not create one single further justiciable right in our domestic courts" but that this view was not shared by the CJEU.[165] The Supreme Court has also observed that the UK, as an EU Member State, is obliged to observe and promote the application of the Charter whenever implementing an instrument of EU law.[166]

GENERAL PRINCIPLES OF LAW

14-048   An important source of Union law is the general principles of law applied by the CJEU.[167] These principles stem from the legal systems of the Member States and have been used by the CJEU. In order for the CJEU to apply a general principle, it is not necessary that it is recognised in the domestic law of all Member States; and

---

163   *R. (on the application of Saeedi) v Secretary of State for the Home Department* [2010] EWHC 705 (Admin) at [155] and [2010] EWCA Civ 990 at [6]-[7]; see also *R. (on the application of Zagorski and Baze) v Secretary of State for Business, Innovation and Skills* [2010] EWHC 3110 (Admin); [2011] Eu. L.R. 315 (in which it was not in dispute that a challenge could be taken against a decision of the Secretary of State for non-compliance with the Charter).

164   *NS v Secretary of State for the Home Department* (C-411/10) EU:C:2011:865 at [119]–[120]. See also *R. (on the application of Medhanye) v Secretary of State for the Home Department* [2012] EWHC 1799 (Admin); *R. (on the application of HH) v Deputy Prosecutor of the Italian Republic, Genoa* [2012] UKSC 25; [2013] 1 A.C. 338.

165   *R. (on the application of AB) v Secretary of State for the Home Department* [2013] EWHC 3453 (Admin); [2014] 2 C.M.L.R. 22.

166   *R. (on the application of EM (Eritrea)) v Secretary of State for the Home Department* [2014] UKSC 12; [2014] 2 W.L.R. 409 at [62].

167   See U. Bernitz, J. Nergelius and C. Cardner, *General Principles of EC Law in a Process of Development* (2008); Editorial, "The Scope of Application of the General Principles of Union Law: An Ever Expanding Union?" (2010) 47 C.M.L. Rev. 1589.

even where it is so recognised, its scope in Union law may be different from its scope in national law. Where a Union measure infringes a general principle, such as the principle of non-discrimination (or equality), it may be annulled by the CJEU[168]; it may also give rise to an action in the CJEU for damages against the EU under TFEU art.340(2).[169] The CJEU has also held that an action in restitution can lie against Union institutions even though such an action is not expressly provided for in the TFEU, because unjust enrichment is a source of non-contractual obligation common to the legal systems of the Member States, and the Union could not be excused from the application to itself of the same principles.[170] Further, the CJEU uses the general principles as an aid for the interpretation of EU acts. The general principles of law are binding not only on the EU institutions but also, within the scope of Union law, on the Member States and a national measure may be held invalid on the ground that it is incompatible with a general principle.[171] General principles may also be capable of creating obligations for private parties.[172]

EUROPEAN COMMUNITIES ACT 1972 AND THE EUROPEAN UNION ACT 2011

So far as the courts and tribunals of England and Wales are concerned, the **14-049** sources of Union law are incorporated into English law by virtue of the European Communities Act 1972 and its subsequent amendments. The Act has been described as a "constitutional" statute.[173] Of course, also of note is the European Union Act 2011.

---

[168] See 14-129.

[169] See, e.g. *Commission v Systran and Systran Luxembourg* (C-103/11) EU:C:2013:245.

[170] *Masdar (UK) Ltd v Commission* (C-47/07 P) EU:C:2008:726 (Grand Chamber) at [44]-[48]; see also *Agrana Zucker GmbH* (C-309/10) EU:C:2011:531.

[171] See 14-160.

[172] *Mangold* EU:C:2005:709 at [75]-[77] (reliance on the principle of non-discrimination before the time period for transposition of a directive had expired); *Kücükdeveci* EU:C:2010:21 (reliance on the principle of non-discrimination after the time period for transposition of a directive had expired). The *Mangold* jurisprudence has been criticised by Advocates General: see, e.g. *Palacios de la Villa v Cortefiel Servicios SA* (C-411/05) EU:C:2007:106 at [79]-[100], per A.G. Mazák; *Michaeler v Amt für sozialen Arbeitsschutz and Autonome Provinz Bozen* (C-55-56/07) EU:C:2008:42 at [14]-[29] (AG Ruiz-Jarabo Colomer). The *Mangold* ruling had been distinguished by the CJEU in *Bartsch* (C-427/06) EU:C:2008:517, on the basis that there was no link to EU law in this latter case. However, the principle was reaffirmed in *Kücükdeveci*. Likewise, in *Association de médiation sociale v Union locale des syndicats CGT* (C-176/12) EU:C:2014:2 at [41], the CJEU endorsed *Kücükdeveci*, albeit in passing and albeit distinguishing it from the circumstances at issue. Both cases were applied in *Dansk Industri* EU:C:2016:278 at [32]-[36], in which the CJEU held that if national legislation cannot be interpreted compatibly with a Directive due to constraints of legal certainty, the court should proceed to interpret the general principle of law which the provision of secondary law is intended to put into specific terms; in the event of a conflict between the principle and national law, the general principle can be invoked in a dispute between individuals in order to preclude the application of the national provision which is contrary to EU law. It is not clear how far or when the principles of *Kücükdeveci* apply in cases not involving age discrimination: see *United States v Nolan* [2015] UKSC 63; [2016] A.C. 463 at [43]. This case law has provoked considerable discussion, see: K. Lenaerts, J.A. Gutierrez-Fons, "The constitutional allocation of powers and general principles of EU law." (2010) 47 C.M.L. Rev. 1629; M. Dougan, "In Defence of Mangold?" in A. Arnull, C. Barnard, M. Dougan and E. Spaventa (eds) *A Constitutional Order of States? Essays in EU Law in Honour of Alan Dashwood* (2011), p.219; C. Murphy, "Using the EU Charter of Fundamental Rights against Private Parties after Association de Mediation Sociale" [2014] E.H.R.L.R. 170.

[173] *Thoburn v Sunderland City Council* [2002] EWHC 195 (Admin); [2003] Q.B. 151 at [62]-[64], [69]; *R. (on the application of Buckinghamshire County Council) v Secretary of State for Transport* [2014] UKSC 3; [2014] 1 W.L.R. 324 at [207] (describing it as a "constitutional instrument"); see also *Miller*

14-050   The European Communities Act 1972 (ECA) seeks to give legal effect in the United Kingdom to the principles of primacy and direct effect. The scheme of the Act is straightforward; apart from limited amendments to the law, it contains in s.2, two principal provisions, s.2(1) and s.2(2), which enable the entire corpus of Union law to be given effect in the United Kingdom. Section 2(1) provides in substance that all directly effective Union law should have such effect in the United Kingdom:

> "All such rights, powers, liabilities, obligations and restrictions from time to time created or arising by or under the Treaties, and all such remedies and procedures from time to time provided for by or under the Treaties, as in accordance with the Treaties are without further enactment to be given legal effect or used in the United Kingdom shall be recognised and available in law, and be enforced, allowed and followed accordingly; and the expression 'enforceable EU right' and similar expressions shall be read as referring to one to which this subsection applies."

The wording makes it clear that the question whether a particular provision has direct effect[174] is determined by Union law.

14-051   Section 2(2) makes provision for the implementation of Union law in the United Kingdom by means of subordinate legislation.[175] This part of the Act has been amended by Pt III of the Legislative and Regulatory Reform Act 2006. Implementation of Union law may be by Order in Council or by order, rules, regulations or schemes made by a minister or department designated for the purpose by Order in Council.[176] Implementing measures will take the form of a statutory instrument.[177] If not approved by each House, they will be subject to annulment by negative resolution of either House.[178] Paragraph 1A of Sch.2 to the 1972 Act, as inserted by s.28 of the Legislative and Regulatory Reform Act 2006, provides for ambulatory references to be made to Union legislation in the implementing statutory instrument. Detailed provision is also made for statutory instruments containing provisions made in exercise of the power conferred by s.2(2) of the 1972 Act to be laid before Parliament for approval by resolution of each House of Parliament and the instrument also contains provision made in exercise of a power conferred by any other enactment and various conditions apply.[179]

14-052   Section 2(4) of the Act provides that implementing measures made under s.2(2) may include "any such provision (of any such extent) as might be made by Act of Parliament". It would seem therefore that such measures are not subject to the limitations normally applicable to delegated legislation and that they may override Acts of Parliament.[180]

14-053   Section 3(1) of the Act provides as follows:

[2017] UKSC 5; [2017] 2 W.L.R. 583 at [67]).

[174] Elegantly rendered by s.2(1) as: to be given legal effect, etc. without further enactment.

[175] For the interpretation of s.2(2), see *R. v Secretary of State for Trade and Industry Ex p. Unison* [1996] I.C.R. 1003; *Oakley Inc v Animal Ltd* [2005] EWCA Civ 1191; [2006] Ch. 337 at [28] and [39]. See also *Department of the Environment, Food and Rural Affairs v Asda Ltd* [2003] UKHL 71; [2004] 1 W.L.R. 105 at [26] (subordinate legislation may implement not only existing EU obligations, but also embrace future amendments to the obligations).

[176] ECA s.2(2) as amended by Legislative and Regulatory Reform Act 2006 s.27(1)(a).

[177] ECA Sch.2, para.2(1) and s.1(1) of the Statutory Instruments Act 1946.

[178] ECA Sch.2, para.2(2).

[179] ECA Sch.2 paras 2A-2C as inserted by the Legislative and Regulatory Reform Act 2006 s.29.

[180] *R. v Secretary of State for Transport Ex p. Factortame Ltd (No.1)* [1990] A.C. 85 at 140 (Lord Bridge); P. Craig, "Sovereignty of the UK Parliament after Factortame" (1991) Y.E.L. 221. Implementing measures made under s.2(2) may not, however, by Sch.2: (a) impose or increase taxation; (b) enact retroactive legislation; (c) sub-delegate legislative power (except to make rules of procedure for any court or tribunal); (d) create any new criminal offence punishable with imprisonment for more than two years or punishable on summary conviction with imprisonment for more

"For the purposes of all legal proceedings any question as to the meaning or effect of any of the Treaties, or as to the validity, meaning or effect of any EU instrument, shall be treated as a question of law (and, if not referred to the European Court, be for determination as such in accordance with the principles laid down by and any relevant decision of the European Court)."

Thus the case law of the CJEU is expressed to be binding on United Kingdom courts and tribunals.

Turning to the European Union Act 2011 (EUA), this is a complex statute, which imposes certain parliamentary and referendum constraints on EU Treaty amendments and a range of other EU decisions. The Act appears to have little relevance following the outcome of the Brexit referendum. However, s.4 specifies a broad range of circumstances in which a referendum is required, including for example, the extension of the objectives of the EU as set out in TEU art.3 and the conferral of a new exclusive or shared competence or the extension of various categories of competence.[181] Approval of certain EU decisions by statute, or another form of parliamentary approval, before they can have the force of law for the UK is required by ss.7–10 of the Act. Decisions requiring approval of an Act of Parliament are identified in s.7(2) and include: a decision pursuant to TFEU art.25 permitting adoption of provisions to strengthen or add to the rights of EU citizens in TFEU art.20(2)[182]; a decision under TFEU art.223(1) permitting the laying down of provisions necessary for the election of Members of the European Parliament in accordance with that article[183]; a decision under TFEU art.262 permitting conferral of jurisdiction on the CJEU in disputes relating to the application of acts adopted on the basis of the EU Treaties which create European intellectual property rights[184]; and a decision under TFEU art.311(3) to adopt a decision laying down provisions relating to the system of EU own resources.[185]

The EUA also contains a so-called "sovereignty clause", which purports to identify the status of Union law in this jurisdiction as deriving entirely from statute and s.18 of the Act.[186]

14-054

14-055

CHALLENGING A NATIONAL MEASURE IN A NATIONAL COURT

In judicial review, as in other types of litigation, national courts and the CJEU and General Court have separate and different roles in adjudicating on issues of Union law. In England and Wales, a claimant for judicial review in the Administrative Court may seek to utilise rules of Union law in various ways. A claimant for judicial review may argue that an act or omission by a public authority in England

14-056

---

than the prescribed term (see Sch.2, para.3) or with a fine of more than level 5 on the standard scale or statutory maximum or with a fine of more than £100 per day.

[181] EUA s.4(1).
[182] EUA s.7(2)(a).
[183] EUA s.7(2)(b).
[184] EUA s.7(2)(c).
[185] EUA s.7(2)(d).
[186] For discussion of the 2011 Act, see M. Gordon and M. Dougan, "The United Kingdom's European Union Act 2011: Who won the bloody war anyway?" (2012) 37 E.L. Rev. 3; P. Craig, "The European Union Act 2011: locks, limits and legality" (2011) 48 C.M.L. Rev. 1915; S. Peers, "European Integration and the European Union Act 2011: An Irresistible Force Meets an Immovable Object" [2013] P.L. 119.

and Wales is in breach of Union law.[187] By virtue of the principle of supremacy, all national measures, including Acts of Parliament, may be challenged as being contrary to any rule of Union law.[188] Union law is thus a broad "chapter head" of judicial review in addition to those of illegality, procedural impropriety and irrationality propounded by Lord Diplock.[189] Alternatively, like a breach of Convention rights, a breach of Union law may be held to offend the ground of illegality. The constituent parts of this chapter head will be considered in more detail below.[190] Where a Member State makes delegated legislation or takes administrative action to implement EU provisions, such national measures may also be open to challenge on the ground that the EU provisions are themselves invalid.[191] Even the "intention or obligation" of the government to implement a directive, without further implementing measures, is open to challenge on the ground that the directive is invalid.[192] A statutory instrument made pursuant to s.2(2) of the European Communities Act 1972 may also be challenged on the ground that it is contrary to *English* law if it goes beyond the enabling provision by purporting to do more than is required to implement the Union measure.[193]

14-057   Arguments based on Union law cannot be used in all cases. A claimant for judicial review needs to show that the act or omission of the public authority which is complained about falls within the scope of Union law. If the impugned decision is authorised solely by national law, that is, it is wholly internal to a Member State, then Union law has no application.[194] The question of the scope of application of EU law is, as was noted above in the context of the reach of EU fundamental rights

---

[187] On what constitutes a public authority (or a body exercising public functions), see Ch.3 above. Note that the Union law concept of "emanation of the state", used to determine against whom directives may be directly effective, is formulated in different terms: see 14-155.

[188] See 14-012; *R. v Secretary of State for Transport Ex p. Factortame Ltd (No.2)* [1991] 1 A.C. 603; *R. v Secretary of State for Employment Ex p. Equal Opportunities Commission* [1995] 1 A.C. 1 at 28; *A v Chief Constable of West Yorkshire* [2004] UKHL 21; [2005] 1 A.C. 51; *Fleming (t/a Bodycraft) v Customs and Excise Commissioners* [2008] UKHL 2; [2008] 1 W.L.R. 195 at [24] (as noted by Lord Walker, "[t]he provision is not made void but it must be treated as being (as Lord Bridge of Harwich put it in *Factortame (No.1)* [1990] 2 A.C. 85, 140) 'without prejudice to the directly enforceable Community rights of nationals of any member state of the EEC'"). Lord Walker also commented that disapplication is different from the obligation of conforming interpretation and "[t]he process of disapplication does not involve reading words into the national legislation (that would be … to confuse it with conforming interpretation": *Fleming* at [49]. See also *Test Claimants in the FII Group Litigation v Revenue and Customs Commissioners* [2008] EWHC 2893 (Ch) at [142]–[146]; [2009] S.T.C. 254 (for Supreme Court, see: [2012] UKSC 19; [2012] 2 A.C. 337); *R. (on the application of British Telecommunications Plc) v Secretary of State for Culture, Olympics, Media and Sport* [2012] EWCA Civ 232 (challenge to the Digital Economy Act 2010 unsuccessful); *Vidal-Hall v Google Inc* [2015] EWCA Civ 311 [2015] 3 W.L.R. 409.

[189] *Council of Civil Service Unions v Minister for the Civil Service* [1985] A.C. 374 at 410.

[190] See 14-156.

[191] See, e.g. *R. v Minister of Agriculture, Fisheries and Food Ex p. FEDESA* [1988] 3 C.M.L.R. 661. This ground of challenge presumably does not apply to Acts of Parliament. Note that a national court has no power to determine that a Union measure is invalid (though it may declare that it is valid): see 14-065.

[192] *R. v Secretary of State Ex p. British American Tobacco (Investments) Ltd and Imperial Tobacco Ltd* (C-491/01) EU:C:2002:741 at [2], [24]–[25], [28]–[41] (this challenge was also permitted although the time limit for implementing the directive had not expired).

[193] *Hayward v Cammell Laird Shipbuilders (No.2)* [1988] A.C. 894.

[194] See, e.g. *R. v Ministry of Agriculture, Fisheries and Food Ex p. First City Trading Ltd* [1997] 1 C.M.L.R. 250 (general principles of Union law could not be used as ground of review of UK's Beef Transfer Scheme, which granted emergency aid to slaughterhouses in the wake of the BSE crisis, because the Scheme was not adopted pursuant to Union law and the UK government did not have to rely upon any Union law permission in order to implement it). However, the number of areas untouched by Union law is shrinking: see 14-010.

jurisprudence, a difficult issue.[195] It is difficult to describe succinctly what fields of government decision-making will be open to challenge on Union grounds but the range of government actions which can be deemed to be purely internal is constantly decreasing.[196]

CHALLENGING A UNION MEASURE IN A NATIONAL COURT

Most claims for judicial review in which issues of Union law arise are concerned with attempts to argue that a public authority in the United Kingdom has acted contrary to Union law, as outlined in the previous sections. Occasionally, however, the intent is different and the claimant seeks to argue that a Union regulation,[197] directive[198] or a decision,[199] or a rule contained within it, is itself invalid. This may be a necessary step in an attempt to challenge a national measure (e.g. an argument that a statutory instrument is ineffective because the directive which it purports to transpose into English law is, as a matter of Union law, invalid) or the aim may bluntly be the Union measure in and of itself.[200] The grounds for arguing that Union measures are invalid are considered below.   **14-058**

There are obvious problems in allowing national courts to adjudicate upon the efficacy of rules of Union law not least the practical ones that courts in Member States may reach different conclusions and the judgments of the courts in one Member State have no binding precedent in others. To avoid these difficulties, the following arrangements have been devised. National courts are allowed to examine the validity of a Union measure and, if they decide that the arguments advanced to challenge its validity are unfounded, they may conclude that the Union measure is valid.[201]   **14-059**

National courts are not, however, permitted to declare measures adopted by EU institutions invalid: if the national court is minded to do this, it must refer the question to the CJEU for a preliminary ruling on the correct interpretation of Union law.[202] The CJEU has sole jurisdiction to rule definitively on the validity of ac-   **14-060**

---

[195] See 14-042.
[196] See, e.g. *Carpenter v Secretary of State for the Home Department* (C-60/00) EU:C:2002:434 (upholding a challenge to a UK deportation order in respect of a third country national on the ground that it violated the third country national's husband's freedom to provide services pursuant to TFEU art.56, as read in the light of ECHR art.8). This case is discussed in further detail at 14-141. cf. *W (China) v Secretary of State for the Home Department* [2006] EWCA Civ 1494 (distinguishing *Carpenter*). See further *Dory v Germany* (C-186/01) EU:C:2003:146 at [35] (CJEU considered Germany's practice of reserving compulsory military service to men to be outside the scope of Union law but commented that "decisions of the Member States concerning the organisation of their armed forces cannot be completely excluded from the application of Union law, particularly where observance of the principle of equal treatment of men and women in connection with employment, access to military posts, is concerned").
[197] See 14-024.
[198] See 14-027.
[199] See 14-038.
[200] See, e.g. *British American Tobacco* EU:C:2002:741.
[201] *Firma Foto-Frost v Hauptzollamt Lübeck-Ost* (314/85) EU:C:1987:452 at [14]; *R. (on the application of SPCM SA) v Secretary of State for the Environment, Food and Rural Affairs* [2007] EWHC 2610 (Admin), [38] and [39]: [2008] Eu. L.R. 250 (the claimant's challenge to arts 5 and 6.1 of Regulation 1907/2006 was "unfounded" and not "arguable" and so a reference would not be made).
[202] *Firma Foto-Frost* EU:C:1987:452 at [20]. See, e.g. *SPCM SA* [2007] EWHC 2610 (Admin) at [23]. On the procedure by which national courts obtain preliminary rulings, see 14-085. See also: *R.*

tions and omissions of the EU institutions.[203] Pending the CJEU's ruling, a national court may grant interim remedies. Where the contested Union measure has been incorporated into national law by national legislation, for example, measures implementing a directive or furthering the implementation of a regulation,[204] the national court may grant interim remedies to suspend the operation of the national measure.[205] National courts are not, however, permitted to grant interim relief where the Union fails to act since in such cases, they cannot make a reference to the CJEU.[206]

INTERPRETATION BY NATIONAL COURTS

14-061   In the course of a claim for judicial review, as in other forms of legal proceedings, national courts may have the task of interpreting national legislation which deals with the same subject matter as Union law. They have an obligation to interpret national legislation in a manner which is consistent with and gives effect to the rules of Union law.[207] This "principle of conforming interpretation"[208] or "indirect effect", is an incident of the general duty placed on Member States by TEU art.4(3) which provides as follows:

> "Pursuant to the principle of sincere cooperation, the Union and the Member States shall, in full mutual respect, assist each other in carrying out tasks which flow from the Treaties.
>
> The Member States shall take any appropriate measure, general or particular, to ensure fulfilment of the obligations arising out of the Treaties or resulting from the acts of the institutions of the Union.

(*International Air Transport Association*) v *Department of Transport* (C-344/04) EU:C:2006:10; *Ministero dell'Industria, del Commercio e dell'Artigianato* v *Lucchini SpA* (C-119/05) EU:C:2007:434 at [53]. It has been held that harmonised technical standards can be the subject of a preliminary reference: *James Elliott Construction Ltd* (C-613/14) EU:C:2016:821 at [32]–[47]. For comment see A Volpato, "The harmonised standards before the ECJ: *James Elliott Construction Ltd* v *Irish Asphalt Ltd (C-613/14)*" (2017) 54 C.M.L. Rev. 591.

[203] *Firma Foto-Frost* EU:C:1987:452 at [17].

[204] *Zuckerfabrik Süderdithmarschen AG* v *Hauptzollant Itzehoc* (143/88) EU:C:1991:65 at [23]-[31].

[205] Three conditions were set out in *Zuckerfabrik Süderdithmarschen AG* EU:C:1991:65 at [33] and a fourth was added in *Atlanta Fruchthandelsgesellschaft mbH v Bundesamt fur Ernahrung and Forstwirtschaft* (C-465/93) EU:C:1995:369 at [51]. Interim relief can only be granted (i) if the national court entertains serious doubts as to the validity of the Union measure and, should the question of the validity of the contested measure not already have been brought before the CJEU, itself refers that question to the CJEU; (ii) if there is urgency and a threat of serious and irreparable damage to the applicant; (iii) if the national court takes due account of the Union interests; and (iv) in its assessment of all those conditions, the national court respects any decisions of the CJEU or the General Court ruling on the lawfulness of the regulation or on an application for interim measures seeking similar interim relief at Union level. For an example of interim relief being granted, see *R. (on the application of ABNA) v Secretary of State for Health* [2003] EWHC 2420 (Admin).

[206] *T Port GmbH v Bundesanstalt für Landwirtschaft und Ernährung* (C-68/95) EU:C:1996:452 at [53].

[207] This obligation is sometimes referred to as the obligation of "conform-interpretation": S. Weatherill, *Cases and Materials on EU Law* (2016). For discussion of the duty, see, e.g. G. Betlem, "The Principle of Indirect Effect of Community Law" (1995) 3 *European Review of Private Law* 1; M. Amstutz, "In-Between Worlds: Marleasing and the Emergence of Interlegality in Legal Reasoning" (2005) 11 *European Law Journal* 766; M. Klamert, "Judicial Implementation of Directives and Anticipatory Indirect Effect: Connecting the Dots" (2006) 43 C.M.L. Rev. 1251.

[208] *Criminal Proceedings against Pupino* (C-105/03) EU:C:2005:386 at [43]; and *Dabas v High Court of Justice in Madrid* [2007] UKHL 6; [2007] 2 A.C. 31 at [76].

The Member States shall facilitate the achievement of the Union's tasks and refrain from any measure which could jeopardise the attainment of the Union's objectives."[209]

The CJEU has stated that the obligation is "inherent in the system of the Treaty" since it permits the national courts to ensure the full effectiveness of Union law when it determines the dispute before it.[210] Thus, national legislation must be construed in the light of the wording and aims of any relevant Union measures, including provisions of the TFEU[211]; directives[212]; and recommendations of institutions, although they have no binding force.[213] **14-062**

Most of the case law in this area has focused on the obligation to interpret national law in the light of the wording and purpose of any pertinent directives and indirect effect is the primary method of ensuring the effectiveness of directives.[214] It is worth noting that when interpreting the provision of Union law itself, account should be taken not only of the wording of that provision and the objectives which it pursues, but also of its context and the provisions of Union law as a whole,[215] as well as its origins.[216] The obligation of conforming interpretation applies even if a Member State has failed to transpose a directive into national law by the due date, or it has failed to do so fully.[217] The interpretative obligation also applies whether the national legislation was passed before or after the directive in question and whether or not the national legislation was passed specifically to implement the directive.[218] After some uncertainty,[219] it has been settled that the date on which the interpretative obligation arises is the date on which the period for transposition of the directive has expired,[220] albeit that, from the date upon which a directive has entered into force, the courts of the Member State must refrain as far as possible **14-063**

---

[209] See, e.g. *Von Colson* EU:C:1984:153 at [26].

[210] *Pfeiffer v Deutsches Rotes Kreuz* (C-397/01) EU:C:2004:584 at [114]; *Impact v Ministry of Agriculture and Food* (C-268/06) EU:C:2008:223 at [99].

[211] See, e.g. *Van Munster v Rijksdienst voor Pensioenen* (C-165/91) EU:C:1994:359. For a useful discussion of the use of recitals in interpretation of EU secondary legislation, see *Recall Support Services Ltd v Secretary of State for Culture, Media and Sport* [2013] EWHC 3091 (Ch) at [50] (not overturned on appeal: [2014] EWCA Civ 1370.

[212] *Von Colson* EU:C:1984:153 at [26]; *Marleasing SA v La Comercial Internacional de Alimentacion SA* (C-106/89) EU:C:1990:395 (Spanish Civil Code had to be interpreted in the light of Directive 68/151). Leading House of Lords cases involving interpretation of directives include *Litster v Forth Dry Dock & Engineering Co Ltd* [1990] 1 A.C. 546; *Pickstone v Freemans* [1989] A.C. 66. See further *Ghaidan v Godin-Mendoza* [2004] UKHL 30; [2004] 2 A.C. 557 at [45]–[48] (Lord Steyn, discussing the principle in *Marleasing, Litster, Pickstone*); *Hashwani v Jivraj* [2011] UKSC 40; [2011] 1 W.L.R. 1872.

[213] *Grimaldi* (322/88) EU:C:1989:646 at [18].

[214] G. Betlem, "The Doctrine of Consistent Interpretation: Managing Legal Uncertainty" (2002) 22 O.J.L.S. 397, p.399.

[215] See, Advocate General Opinion, *Council of the European Union v Vereniging Milieudefensie* (C-401/12 P) EU:C:2014:310 at [116] (adding that the context to a provision of Union law may also contain elements relevant to its interpretation: see *Pringle v Ireland* (C-370/12) EU:C:2012:756 at [135]).

[216] *Commission v Germany* (C-220/15) EU:C:2016:815 at [39] (referring to wording, context, aims and origins). See also *Inuit Tapiriit Kanatami* EU:C:2013:625 at [50], where the CJEU placed particular emphasis on the travaux préparatoires: [59], [60], [70].

[217] *Von Colson* EU:C:1984:153.

[218] *Marleasing* EU:C:1990:395; *Mangold* EU:C:2005:709 at [68]. See also *R. (on the application of Nutricia Ltd) v The Secretary of State for Health* [2015] EWHC 2285 (Admin) at [115].

[219] See *Officier van Justitie v Kolpinghuis Nijmegen* (80/86) EU:C:1987:431 at [15] and *Centrosteel v Adipol* (C-456/98) EU:C:2000:402 at [17] (interpretative duty arose in relation to "facts postdating the expiry of the period for transposing the Directive"); and cf. *Adeneler* EU:C:2005:654 at [47]–[54] (AG Kokott indicated a preference for the duty of interpretation to begin from the moment of publication).

[220] *Adeneler* EU:C:2006:443 at [115]; see also *Hochtief AG* (C-138/08) EU:C:2009:627 at [25].

from interpreting domestic law in a manner which might seriously compromise, after the period for transposition has expired, attainment of the objective pursued by that directive.[221]

14-064 In so far as the extent of the interpretative obligation is concerned, the CJEU has articulated the duty as follows[222]:

> "in applying national law, whether the provisions were adopted before or after the directive, the national court is called upon to interpret it is required to do so, as far as possible, in the light of the wording and purpose of the directive in order to achieve the result pursued by the latter and thereby comply with the third paragraph of art.189 [now art.288] of the Treaty".[223]

14-065 Since then questions have arisen as to what this requires: does "as far as possible" require a national court to distort the clear meaning of national legislation? It is clear that no ambiguity in the national legislation is required and the court must first establish the meaning of the EU obligation and conclude whether it is possible to achieve the necessary reconciliation with national law.[224] The interpretative obligation, which the court has described as enabling a national court to ensure the full effectiveness of EU law, applies not only to the national law that implements the directive but requires the national court to consider national law as a whole in order to assess to what extent it may be applied so as not to produce a result contrary to that sought by EU law.[225]

14-066 English courts have stated that although a construction which departs boldly from the ordinary meaning of the language can be adopted, "the exercise must still be one of construction and it should not exceed the limits of what is reasonable".[226] The obligation has been described as not dissimilar to that found in s.3 of the Human Rights Act 1998[227] and it has been suggested that interpretation should not create "a new and different scheme", offend the legislation's "cardinal principles", remove the "core and essence" of the legislation,[228] or "alter a fundamental feature" of the legislation.[229] As it has also been put, "it is not possible to construe a national measure to mean 'black' (the requirement in the Directive) when it explicitly states

---

[221] EU:C:2006:443 at [123]; *Stichting Natuur en Milieu* (C-165/09) EU:C:2011:348 at [78]; *PPU Civil proceedings concerning Kadzoev (Huchbarov)* (C-357/09) EU:C:2009:741; [2010] All E.R. (EC) at [32]–[39]. See also *Milev* (C-439/16) EU:C:2016:818 at [32] (the obligation does not however seem to apply to a measure which neither implements a Directive nor is capable of ensuring that national law is consistent with it: Opinion of Advocate General Bobek EU:C:2016:760, [51]).

[222] *Marleasing* EU:C:1990:395 at [8]. See also *Dori v Recreb Srl* (C-91/02) EU:C:1994:292 at [26].

[223] See also *Centrosteel* EU:C:2000:402 at [19].

[224] *Pickstone* [1989] A.C. 66; *Litster* [1990] 1 A.C. 546; *Murphy* [2007] EWHC 3091 (Admin) at [26]; [2008] 1 W.L.R. 1869 (the obligation is to "construe the provisions so nearly as possible as to achieve the result required by the relevant directive, once the time for the implementation of the latter has passed"). See also *Swift (trading as A Swift Move) v Robertson* [2014] UKSC 50; [2014] 1 W.L.R. 3438 at [22] (the court must not only keep faith with the wording of Union law but "must have closely in mind its purpose").

[225] *Seydaland* (C-239/09) EU:C:2010:778 at [50]; *Hessen v Franz Mucksch OHG* (C-53/10) EU:C:2011:585 [2011] All E.R. (D) 86 at [33].

[226] *Clarke v Kato* [1998] 1 W.L.R. 1647 at 1656 (Lord Clyde); and *Ex p. Huddleston* [2000] 1 W.L.R. 1484 at [10] (primary legislation incompatible with directive and "convergent construction" solution not possible); *R. (on the application of Equal Opportunities Commission) v Secretary of State for Communities and Local Government* [2007] EWHC 483 (Admin) at [61].

[227] See 13-041. See, for example, *Vidal-Hall v Google Inc (Information Commissioner intervening)* [2015] EWCA Civ 311; [2015] 3 W.L.R. 409 at [87] (Lord Dyson MR observing that "our courts have noticed a close parallel between the Marleasing principle and section 3 of the Human Rights Act 1998").

[228] *Vodafone 2 v Revenue and Customs Commissioners* [2009] EWCA Civ 446; [2010] Ch. 77 at [71].

[229] *Vidal-Hall v Google Inc (Information Commissioner intervening)* [2015] EWCA Civ 311; [2015] 3

that it means 'blue'".[230] There are number of techniques of which courts may avail themselves in order to comply with the principle of conforming interpretation, including reading words into a national measure (to expand its potential field of application) or by reading the national provision down (to narrow its potential field of application), and even by disapplying or striking down part of it in order to make it compatible with a Directive; in short, "[v]arious interpretative techniques may be deployed in order to eliminate an incompatibility".[231]

The CJEU has also indicated that a *contra legem* interpretation is not required; **14-067** and that, where it is not possible to interpret national legislation in conformity with the directive, a damages remedy against the relevant Member State is the only option.[232]

On occasion, however, the CJEU has articulated the obligation on the national **14-068** court in extremely robust terms, as being "to do whatever lies within its jurisdiction, having regard to the whole body of national law, to ensure" that the directive is fully effective.[233] In the *Pfeiffer* case, the CJEU considered the appropriate interpretation of the German implementation of Directive 93/104, the Working Time Directive, which permitted derogation from the 48-hour weekly limit found in the Directive. The CJEU described the interpretative obligation as requiring the national court to do whatever lay within its jurisdiction to ensure that the maximum period of weekly working time, which is set at 48 hours by art.6(2) of Directive 93/104, was not exceeded.[234] This effectively required the national court to search for interpretative methods which would enable it to interpret national legislation permitting derogation from the 48-hour limit, to preclude derogation from the 48-hour limit.[235] The CJEU has indicated subsequently to *Pfeiffer* that the interpretative obligation is limited by the general principles of legal certainty and non-

---

W.L.R. 409 at [91]–[92] (holding that s.13(2) of the Data Protection Act 1998 enacted limits on the right to compensation for breaches of the right to privacy of individuals with respect to the processing of their personal data which were a fundamental feature of the legislation, such that s.13(2) could not be interpreted compatibly with art.23 of Parliament and Council Directive 95/46/EC and had to be disapplied). It was also observed in *Vidal-Hall* (at [86]) that if a national court is unable to rely on the *Marleasing* principle to interpret the national legislation so as to conform with the Directive, the appropriate remedy for an aggrieved person is to claim Francovich damages against the state). See also *R. (on the application of Chester) v Secretary of State for Justice* [2013] UKSC 63; [2014] A.C. 271 at [74]–[75].

[230] *Nutricia* [2015] EWHC 2285 (Admin) at [120] (adding that "[t]he principle of purposive [construction] is not therefore, a rule which requires national courts to do permanent and irrevocable damage to the language of domestic implementing legislation, or other legislation existing within the field and scope of the directive, in order to achieve the object of the Directive").

[231] *Vidal-Hall v Google Inc (Information Commissioner intervening)* [2015] EWCA Civ 311; [2015] 3 W.L.R. 409 at [89]–[90].

[232] *Wagner-Miret v Fondo de Garantia Salarial* (C-334/92) EU:C:1993:945 at [22]; *Impact* EU:C:2008:223 at [100]–[103] (a national court was not required to interpret national legislation with retrospective effect where, as a matter of national law, legislation was not to be given retrospective effect unless there was a clear and unambiguous indication to the contrary). For examples of cases in which the English courts have concluded that a conforming interpretation was not possible, see: *ITV Broadcasting Ltd v TV Catchup Ltd* [2011] EWHC 1874 (Pat); [2012] Eu. L.R. 187 at [134]; *Football Association Premier League Ltd v QC Leisure (a trading name)* [2012] EWHC 108 (Ch); [2012] 2 C.M.L.R. 16 at [72]–[77]; *Alstom Transport* [2012] EWHC 28 (Ch) at [34]–[48] and [93]; [2012] 3 All E.R. 263 (UK Regulations were applicable to domestic bodies and to interpret the provision in the Regulations to cover bodies in all other 26 Member States would go against the grain of the Regulations). *Association de médiation sociale v Union locale des syndicats CGT* (C-176/12) EU:C:2014:2 at [39]; *Dansk Industri* EU:C:2016:278 at [32], [43]; *Klausner Holz Niedersachsen GmbH v Land Nordrhein-Westfalen (C-505/14)* at [32].

[233] *Pfeiffer* EU:C:2004:584 at [118]; *Impact* EU:C:2008:223 at [101].

[234] *Pfeiffer* EU:C:2004:584 at [119].

[235] See further *Coote v Granada Hospitality* (C-185/97) EU:C:1998:424; *Quelle AG v Bundesverband*

retroactivity and the obligation not to adopt an interpretation *contra legem*[236]; however, it is clear that the interpretative obligation is "forceful".[237]

14-069 The CJEU has stated repeatedly that the interpretative duty should not result in an imposition on an individual of an obligation laid down in a directive which has not been transposed.[238] This statement must also be qualified however. It is clear that a directive cannot, of itself and independently of a national law adopted by a Member State for its implementation, have the effect of determining or aggravating the liability in criminal law of persons who act in contravention of the provisions of that directive.[239] However, outside of the criminal law context, the obligation of conforming interpretation may result in civil law obligations for private individuals.[240]

14-070 Overall, it is apparent that the CJEU places significant emphasis on indirect effect as a means of ensuring the application of EU law and it has indicated that its preference is for a conforming interpretation to be adopted, rather than for the disapplication of national law which is incompatible with EU law.[241]

EFFECTIVE PROCEDURES AND REMEDIES[242]

14-071 While occasionally Union law provides procedural rules for the enforcement of Union rights,[243] Union law more often than not vests rights in individuals without

---

der Verbraucherzentralen und Verbraucherverbande (C-404/06) EU:C:2008:231. *Océano Grupo Editorial v Rocio Murciano Quintero* (C-240-244/98) EU:C:2000:346; S. Drake, "Twenty Years after Von Colson: the Impact of 'Indirect Effect' on the Protection of the Individual's Community Rights" (2005) 30 E.L. Rev. 329.

[236] See, e.g. *Impact* (C-268/06) EU:C:2008:223 at [99]–[100]; *Maribel Dominguez* (C-282/10) EU:C:2012:33; [2012] I.R.L.R. 321 at [25]; *Association de médiation sociale v Union locale des syndicats CGT* (C-176/12) EU:C:2014:2 at [39]. See also *Dansk Industri* EU:C:2016:278 at [30]–[33] (where interpretation in conformity with EU law proves impossible, the national court has the obligation to give EU law its full effect, if need be by setting aside any incompatible provisions of national law).

[237] P. Craig, "The Legal Effect of Directives: Policy, Rules and Exceptions" (2009) 34 E.L. Rev. 349, 359. See also *Uniplex* (C-406/08) EU:C:2010:45 at [45]–[48]; *Prudential Assurance Co Ltd v Revenue and Customs Commissioners* [2013] EWHC 3249 (Ch); [2014] 2 C.M.L.R 10 at [102], [105] (*Marleasing* implies a "highly muscular" approach to conforming interpretation).

[238] *Criminal Proceedings against Arcaro* (C-168/95) EU:C:1996:363 at [42].

[239] *Kolpinghuis Nijmegen* EU:C:1987:431 at [13]; *Criminal Proceedings against X* (C-60/02) EU:C:2004:10 at [64]; and *Silvio Berlusconi* (C-387/02) EU:C:2005:270 at [74].

[240] In *Centrosteel* EU:C:2000:137, AG Jacobs (at [33]–[34]) expressly rejected the proposition that the *Arcaro* case (EU:C:1996:363) placed a limit on the interpretative obligation outside the criminal law context. Even in the criminal law context, although, as already noted, criminal liability cannot be exacerbated by a conforming interpretation; the procedure by which the criminal trial is conducted can be affected, provided it does not render the trial unfair: *Pupino* EU:C:2005:386 (Italian law, which did not provide for special procedures for cross-examining vulnerable witnesses, had to be interpreted in light of the Framework Decision which did provide such special procedures). But see *QDQ Media SA v Omedas Lecha* (C-235/03) EU:C:2005:147 at [14]–[16] (where it was clear from the explanation given by the national court that national law could not be interpreted in conformity with the directive, the directive could not of itself impose obligations on an individual).

[241] See, e.g. *Sorge v Poste Italiane SpA* (C-98/09) EU:C:2010:369 at [55].

[242] For a more detailed account, see T. Tridimas, *The General Principles of EU Law*, 2nd edn (2006) Ch.9; M. Dougan, *National Remedies before the Court of Justice* (2004); C. Kilpatrick, T. Novitz and P. Skidmore (eds), *The Future of Remedies in Europe* (2000); M Dougan "The Vicissitudes of Life at the Coalface: Remedies and Procedures for Enforcing Union Law before the National Courts" in P. Craig and G. de Búrca (eds), *The Evolution of EU Law* (2011) 407; A. Arnull, "The principle of effective judicial protection in EU law: an unruly horse?" (2011) 36 E.L. Rev. 51; P.V. Cleynenbreugel, "Judge-made standards of national procedure in the post-Lisbon constitutional

prescribing explicitly the procedural rules applicable in national courts or tribunals or the remedies for the infringement of the rights. The question then arises to what extent Union law governs the procedural rules applicable and the remedies available. The issue has frequently been put before the CJEU in references from national courts themselves; and a number of different phases in the CJEU's approach can be detected.[244] The cases are often difficult to reconcile and the outcome seems to depend on the particular facts and the rule at issue.[245] National courts and tribunals and the CJEU must ensure the full application of Union law in all Member States and ensure judicial protection of an individual's rights under that law.[246] The overarching requirement is, as made clear by a new provision, introduced by the Lisbon Treaty, TEU art.19(1) that "Member States shall provide remedies sufficient to ensure effective legal protection in the fields covered by Union law". The right to effective judicial protection is also protected by art.47 of the Charter, and as was observed above,[247] is one of the most heavily litigated provisions of the Charter.

Principle of national procedural autonomy

In principle, it is the national law which applies to procedures and remedies, for **14-072** Union law and national law are independent systems of law, each operating autonomously in its own sphere. This is known as the principle of national procedural autonomy and provides that "it is for the domestic legal system of each Member State to designate the courts having jurisdiction and to determine the procedural conditions governing actions at law intended to ensure the protection of the rights which citizens have from the direct effect of Community [now Union] law".[248] The principle has always been subject to two conditions, namely, equivalence and practical possibility or effectiveness. The condition of equivalence requires that national rules governing the exercise of Union law rights must not be less favourable than those governing the same right of action on an internal matter; while the condition of effectiveness requires that the rules must not make it impossible or excessively difficult in practice to exercise the Union law rights.[249] The criteria of effective protection of Union law rights and equivalence are cumulative.[250]

---

framework" (2012) 37 E.L. Rev. 90.

[243] See, e.g. Directive 2007/66/EC of the European Parliament and of the Council of 11 December 2007 amending Council Directives 89/665/EEC and 92/13/EEC with regard to improving the effectiveness of review procedures concerning the award of public contracts [2007] OJ L335/31.

[244] See in particular P. Craig and G. de Búrca, *EU Law Text, Cases and Materials* (2015), pp.231-250.

[245] See D. Chalmers, G. Davies, and G. Monti, *European Union Law* (2014), pp.276, 283.

[246] *Opinion 2/13* EU:C:2014:2454 at [175].

[247] See 14-040.

[248] *Comet BV v Produktschap voor Siergewassen* (45/76) EU:C:1976:191 at [13]. See also *Unibet (London) Ltd* (C-432/05) EU:C:2007:163 at [39].

[249] See, e.g. *Rewe-Handelsgesllschaft Nord mbH v Hauptzollamt Kiel* (158/80) EU:C:1981:163 at [5]; *Cofidis SA v Jean Louis Fredout* (C-473/00) EU:C:2002:705 at [36]–[37]; *Ecotrade SpA v Agenzia delle Entrate-Ufficio di Genova 3* (C-95/07 and C-96/07) EU:C:2008:267 at [46]; *Willy Kempter KG v Hauptzollamt Hamburg-Jonas* (C-2/06) EU:C:2008:78 at [57]; *Danske Slagterier v Bundesrepublik Deutschland* (C-445/06) EU:C:2009:178 at [48]. For consideration of the principle of effectiveness, in the context of the fee regime for bringing and continuing claims in employment tribunals and the Employment Appeal Tribunal, see *R. (on the application of Unison) v Lord Chancellor* [2017] UKSC 51; [2017] 3 W.L.R. 409.

[250] *Amministrazione delle finanze dello Stato v San Giorgio* (199/82) EU:C:1983:318.

Principle of effective judicial protection

14-073   Initially, the CJEU emphasised the principle of national procedural autonomy and indicated, in strong terms, that the EU Treaties were not intended to create new remedies in the national courts.[251] On other occasions, however, the principle of effective protection has been given precedence[252] and the CJEU has required the displacement of all procedural and other obstacles to the protection of Union law rights, with the result that national courts have been required not to apply any rule of national law whose effect is to preclude immediate enforcement of a Union law right.[253] One of the most striking examples of the application of the effectiveness requirement is found in the *Factortame* case, in which the CJEU did not even refer to its case law on national procedural autonomy, but required that national courts have "the power to do everything necessary" at the moment of application of Union law "to set aside national legislative provisions which might prevent, even temporarily Community [now Union] rules from having full force and effect".[254] This resulted in the novel grant of interim relief to suspend the operation of a Westminster statute. The principle of effectiveness has also led the CJEU to hold that a party to a contract which violates EU competition law can nonetheless receive damages, provided that the party seeking the damages did not bear significant responsibility for the distortion of competition caused by the contract.[255] The CJEU has also held that it is not necessary for a national legal order to create a free-

---

[251] *Rewe-Handelsgesllschaft Nord* EU:C:1981:163 at [44]; and *Humblet v Belgium* (6/60) EU:C:1960:48; *Société Roquette Fréres v Commission* (26/74) EU:C:1976:69 (it was for Member States to decide whether to award interest on the reimbursement of sums wrongly levied under Union law). See D.J. Rhee, "The principle of effective judicial protection: reaching those parts other (principles) cannot reach" [2011] 16 J.R. 440.

[252] See, e.g. *Autologic Holdings Plc v Inland Revenue Commissioners* [2004] EWCA Civ 690; [2005] 1 W.L.R. 52 at [25] (Peter Gibson LJ noting that "[t]he importance of the principle of effectiveness in Community [now Union] law cannot be overstated").

[253] The first clear statement of this principle was in *Simmenthal* EU:C:1978:49; see para.14-042. In *Emmott v Minister for Social Welfare* (C-208/90) EU:C:1991:333 at [23] it was held that until such time as a directive has been properly transposed, a defaulting Member State could not rely on an individual's delay in initiating the proceedings against it in order to protect rights conferred upon him by the provisions of the directive and that a period laid down by national law within which proceedings must be initiated could not begin to run before that time. In a number of cases, the ruling in *Emmott* has been described by the CJEU as "justified by the particular circumstances of that case": see, e.g. *Danske Slagterier* EU:C:2009:178 at [54]; *Tonina Enza Iaia v Ministero dell'Istruzione* (C-452/09) EU:C:2011:323 [2011] All E.R. (D) 213 at [19]. The *Emmott* approach should therefore be treated with caution, having been effectively "sidelined": A. Arnull "The principle of effective judicial protection in EU law: an unruly horse?" (2011) E.L.R. 51, 53. See also *Marshall v Southampton and South West Area Health Authority II* (C-271/91) EU:C:1993:335 (two national rules governing remedies, one imposing a ceiling on damages and the other removing the power to award interest, had to be overridden or disapplied by the national court). See also *The Trustees of the BT Pension Scheme v The Commissioners for Her Majesty's Revenue and Customs* [2015] EWCA Civ 713 at [117] (describing the decision in Emmott as "highly fact-specific").

[254] *R. v Secretary of State for Transport Ex p. Factortame Ltd* (C-213/89) EU:C:1990:257 at [20]. Another striking example is found in the CJEU's case law on state liability in damages, as to which see 14-092.

[255] *Courage v Crehan* (C-453/99) EU:C:2001:465 at [30]-[31]. See further G. Cumming, "Courage Ltd v Crehan" (2002) 23 European Competition L. Rev. 199; G. Monti "Anticompetitive Agreements: The innocent party's right to damages" (2002) 27 E.L. Rev. 282; O. Odudu and J. Edelman, "Compensatory Damages for Breach of Article 81" (2002) 27 E.L. Rev. 327. See also *Communication from the Commission on quantifying harm in actions for damages based on breaches of Article 101 or 102 [TFEU]* [2012] OJ C167/07; and see now Directive 2014/104/EU of the European Parliament and of the Council of 26 November 2014 on certain rules governing actions for damages under national law for infringements of the competition law provisions of the Member States and of the European Union. For discussion of the principle of national procedural autonomy in the competi-

standing action to examine the compatibility of national provisions with the TFEU, provided that other effective legal remedies, no less favourable than those governing domestic actions, make it possible to determine the question of compatibility.[256] However, the requirements for effective judicial protection may result in the imposition of positive obligations on Member States.[257] For example, interim relief should be available until compatibility is determined, if necessary to ensure effectiveness of the judgment[258]; and even if it is uncertain under national law whether an action to safeguard respect for an individual's rights under Union law is admissible, the principle of effective judicial protection still requires the national court to be able, at that stage, to grant the interim relief necessary to ensure those rights are respected.[259] The principle of effective judicial protection may require annulment of a decision with retroactive effect.[260] Moreover, it has been held that specialised national courts should extend their jurisdiction to hear and determine an applicant's claims arising directly from a directive, in respect of the period between the deadline for transposing the directive and the date on which the transposing legislation entered into force, if it is established that the obligation on that applicant to bring, at the same time, a separate claim based directly on the directive before an ordinary court would involve "procedural disadvantages" liable to render excessively difficult the exercise of the rights conferred on him by EU law.[261] It has also been held that the "piggyback argument"—that wherever a domestic statutory provision infringes the EU rights of one person, then anyone else who is a national of a Member State may claim relief for the adverse consequence for him of the existence or enforcement of that provision—is assessed by reference to the principle of effectiveness. In short, if the protection intended to be conferred by a particular EU right or freedom upon nationals of EU Member States will not be effective if only those whose rights are thereby infringed can take proceedings in rela-

---

tion law context, see: SB Volcker, "Ignorantia legis non excusat and the demise of national procedural autonomy in the application of the EU competition rules" (2014) 51 C.M.L. Rev. 1497; N Dunne, "Courage and compromise: the Directive on Antitrust Damages" (2015) 40 E.L.Rev. 581.

[256] *Unibet* EU:C:2007:163 at [47]. For comment, see G. Anagnostaras, "The Incomplete State of Community Harmonisation in the Provision of Interim Protection by the National Courts" (2008) 33 E.L. Rev. 586; A. Arnull, "Case C-432/05, Unibet (London) Ltd and Unibet (International) Ltd v Justitiekanslern, judgment of the Grand Chamber of 13 March 2007" (2007) 44 C.M.L. Rev. 1763; K. Lenaerts, "The Rule of Law and the Coherence of the Judicial System of the European Union" (2007) 44 C.M.L. Rev. 1625.

[257] *VEBIC v Raad voor de Mededinging* (C-439/08) EU:C:2010:739 at [57]–[58] (the principle of effectiveness of EU law required Belgium to adapt national procedural rules to allow the national competition authority to participate in national proceedings as to do otherwise would jeopardise the attainment of objectives of EU law, including the effective enforcement of its competition rules); M. Frese, "Case Note Case C-439/08, Vlaamse federatie van verenigingen van Brood- en Banketbakkers, Ijsbereiders en Chocoladebewerkers (VEBIC); Judgment of the European Court of Justice (Grand Chamber) December 7, 2010" (2011) 48 C.M.L. Rev. 893.

[258] *Unibet* EU:C:2007:163 at [67]. See also *Centre public d'action sociale d'Ottignies-Louvain-la-Neuve v Abdida* (C-562/13) EU:C:2014:2453 [2015] 1 W.L.R. 3109 (holding that Directive 2008/115, arts 5 and 13, taken in conjunction with Charter arts 19(2) and 47, must be interpreted as precluding national legislation which does not make provision for a remedy with suspensive effect in respect of a return decision whose enforcement may expose a third country national to a serious risk of grave and irreversible deterioration in his state of health).

[259] *Unibet* EU:C:2007:163 at [73]. If the application is inadmissible in national law, and Union law does not call into question that inadmissibility, interim relief need not be available: [73]. The criteria governing the grant of interim relief are those applicable to equivalent domestic actions, provided they comply with the principles of equivalence and effectiveness: [82].

[260] *Prezes Urzędu Komunakcji Elektroniczne and Petrotel* (C-231/15) EU:C:2016:769 at [24]–[25].

[261] *Impact* EU:C:2008:223 at [55]. For reference to the "procedural disadvantage" standard, see also: *Florentina Martínez Andrés v Servicio Vasco de Salud* (C-184/15) EU:C:2016:680.

tion to that infringement, the right of action may be extended to a wider class of persons adversely affected by the infringement.[262]

Balancing procedural autonomy and effective protection

14-074 At present, the CJEU tends to apply what has been described as requirement for national courts "to strike an appropriate, proportionality-based, case-by-case balance between the requirement of effective judicial protection for EU law rights and the application of legitimate national procedural and remedial rules".[263] The balancing must be conducted:

> "by reference to the role of that provision in the procedure, its progress and its special features, viewed as a whole, before the various national instances. In the light of that analysis the basic principles of the domestic judicial system, such as protection of the rights of the defence, the principle of legal certainty and the proper conduct of procedure, must, where appropriate, be taken into consideration."[264]

14-075 The national rule must be examined not in the abstract, but in the specific circumstances of each case,[265] on a case-by-case basis, taking account of each case's own factual and legal context as a whole, which cannot be applied mechanically in fields other than those in which they were made.[266] Thus, the CJEU has found that a Dutch rule preventing a party from raising a new point of law involving questions of fact on appeal did not render the exercise of the Union right impossible or excessively difficult since "it safeguards the right of the defence; and it ensures proper conduct of proceedings".[267] By contrast, a rule preventing a taxpayer from raising a new point of law on appeal to the Court of Appeal from the decision of an administrative tax official, after the lapse of a period of 60 days, where the Court of Appeal could not raise the issue of its own motion, was found to violate the requirement of effective protection, given that the administrative official could not himself make a reference to the CJEU.[268] Furthermore, in the context of consumer protection, the CJEU has explained that what exists is not a "mere power" on the part of national courts to raise the EU consumer protection point, but an obligation,[269] as effective consumer protection would not be achieved if the consumer were himself obliged to raise the point.[270] In the absence of a problem of

---

[262] *The Trustees of the BT Pension Scheme* [2015] EWCA Civ 713 at [51].

[263] P. Craig and G. de Búrca, *EU Law: Text, Cases and Materials* (2015), p.239.

[264] *Peterbroeck, Van Campenhout & Cie v Belgian State* (C-312/93) EU:C:1995:437 at [14]; *Van Schijndel & Van Veen v Stichting Pensioenfonds voor Fysiotherapeuten* (C-430–431/93) EU:C:1995:441 at [19]; *Santex SpA v Unita Socio Sanitaria Locale No.42 di Pavia* (C-327/00) EU:C:2003:109 at [56].

[265] P. Craig and G. de Búrca, *EU Law: Text, Cases and Materials* (2015), p.240.

[266] *Cofidis* EU:C:2002:705 at [37].

[267] *Van Schijndel* EU:C:1995:441 at [21]. See also *Heemskerk BV, Firma Schaap v Productschap Vee en Vlees* (C-455/06) EU:C:2008:650 at [44]-[48] (a Dutch court was not obliged to raise points of EU law of its own motion where examining EU law would result in denial of the principle of Dutch law that an individual bringing an action must not be placed in a less favourable position than if he had not brought that action (the principle of the prohibition of *reformatio in pejus*): such would undermine the rights of the defence, legal certainty and protection of legitimate expectations); *Van der Weerd v Minister van Landbouw, Natuur en Voedselkwaliteit* (C-222/05) EU:C:2007:318 at [28]–[38].

[268] *Peterbroeck* EU:C:1995:437.

[269] *Pannon GSM Zrt v Erzsébet Sustikné Gyrfi* (C-243/08) EU:C:2009:350 at [32] and [35]; *Océano Grupo* EU:C:2000:346 at [29]–[32]; *Cofidis* EU:C:2000:346 at [33]; and *Mostaza Claro v Centro Movil Milenium SL* (C-168/05) EU:C:2006:675 at [28].

[270] *Océano Grupo* EU:C:2000:346 at [26]; *Cofidis* EU:C:2002:705 at [33]; *Mostaza Claro*

equivalence, which is discussed below,[271] this duty has not been extended beyond the consumer protection context as yet,[272] although it has been articulated as applying more generally "in exceptional cases where the public interest requires" the court's intervention.[273]

Requirement of equivalence

In essence, the condition of equivalence requires that the national rule at issue **14-076** be applied without distinction, whether the infringement alleged is of Union law or national law, where the purpose and cause of action are similar.[274] It is not a straightforward concept. In assessing equivalence, both the CJEU and the domestic courts have applied different tests at different times. Tests applied by the CJEU have included: whether the purpose and essential characteristics of the two measures are the same[275]; whether the role played by the provision in the procedure as a whole, as well as the operation and any special features of that procedure before different national courts, sustain or detract from the claim to equivalence[276]; and whether the purpose and cause of action of the two measures should be similar.[277] It is, however, unclear if any or all of these criteria are indispensable requirements. At domestic level also, different approaches have been applied: a quite restrictive approach has involved considering whether the domestic law claim is "in juristic structure very close to the [Union] law claim"[278]; a less stringent test has considered two "sub-questions": (i) Is there a "similar domestic action"? (ii) Are the rules applicable to the Union right "not less favourable"?[279] The relationship between the two tests is not entirely clear, however, and both may have a role depending on the context.[280]

While there is a lack of certainty regarding the standard applied, in terms of the **14-077** process of assessing equivalence, in determining whether the requirement of equivalence has been satisfied, it is necessary to take into account the role played by the relevant provision in the procedure as a whole, as well as the operation and any special features of that procedure before the different national courts.[281] This analysis must not be carried out subjectively by reference to circumstances of fact,

---

EU:C:2006:675 at [28]; *Asturcom Telecomunicaciones* (C-40/08) EU:C:2009:615 at [59]; *Eva Martín Martín v EDP Editores SL* (C-227/08) EU:C:2009:792 at [36].

[271] 14-076. See, e.g., *Farkas* (C-564/15) EU:C:2017:302 at [35].

[272] *Van der Weerd v Minister van Landouw, Natuur en Voedselkwaliteit* (C-225/05) EU:C:2007:318 at [41].

[273] *Eva Martín Martín* EU:C:2009:792 at [20].

[274] *BS Levez v TH Jennings (Harlow Pools) Ltd* (C-326/96) EU:C:1998:577 at [39]. See also *i-21 Germany GmbH and Arcor AG & Co KG (formerly, ISIS Multimedia Net GmbH & Co KG) v Germany* (C-392/04 and C-422/04) EU:C:2006:586 at [69]. The principle of equivalence has been described as irrelevant where the comparator "domestic" cause of action included substantive national rules implementing EU law: *Danqua* (C-429/15) EU:C:2016:789 at [33]-[35].

[275] *Rosalba Palmisani v Istituto nazionale della previdenza sociale* (C-261/95) EU:C:1997:351 at [34]–[38].

[276] *Levez* EU:C:1998:577 at [44].

[277] *Levez* EU:C:1998:577 at [41].

[278] *Matra Communications SA v Home Office* [1999] 1 W.L.R. 1646 (doubted on a different point of the relevance of Francovich criteria to damages in procurement actions in *Energy Solutions EU Ltd v Nuclear Decommissioning Authority* [2017] UKSC 34; [2017] 1 W.L.R. 1373). See also: *Preston v Wolverhampton Healthcare NHS Trust (No.2)* [2001] 2 A.C. 455 at [21] (in which Lord Slynn accepted that "superficial similarity" should not be sufficient).

[279] *Byrne v Motor Insurers' Bureau* [2008] EWCA Civ 574; [2009] Q.B. 66 at [22].

[280] *FA (Iraq) v Secretary of State for the Home Department* [2011] UKSC 22 at [35] (reference needed on the requirements of "equivalence" in order to determine whether a humanitarian protection claim pursuant to Directive 2004/83 was equivalent to an asylum claim).

[281] *Levez* EU:C:1998:577 at [43]–[44]; *Danske Slagterier* EU:C:2009:178 at [40]–[41].

but must involve an objective comparison in the abstract, of the procedural rules at issue.[282] The national court must also scrutinise the domestic procedures to determine not only whether they are comparable but also whether there is any inherent discrimination in their application in favour of domestic claims.[283] The principle does not mean that a Member State must extend its most favourable national rule to the Union action,[284] but the national court must consider both the purpose and the essential characteristics of allegedly similar domestic actions in order to reach its conclusions.[285] It has also been held that there must be a latitude in the application of the equivalence principle, and that the "no most favourable treatment" proviso—namely, that the equivalence principle is satisfied if there is equivalence with domestic rules applying to other similar actions which are not in the most favourable category—is an established feature of the equivalence principle.[286]

Limitation periods

14-078   In numerous cases, national courts in Member States have had to consider the criteria of equivalence and effectiveness in relation to limitation periods for bringing a legal action, and there have been references to the CJEU for preliminary rulings. As a general principle, reasonable national time limits are consistent with the principle of effective judicial protection since such time limits are an application of the principle of legal certainty protecting both individuals and administration. In general, the adequacy of the time limit is to be determined by reference to the principles of effectiveness and legitimate expectation, to ensure that the period is not so short as to render it practically impossible or excessively difficult for a person with an accrued right to make his claim.[287] The decision as to whether a limitation period is reasonable is one for the national court, following the guidance of the CJEU.[288] Similarly, it is for the national court to determine whether the time limit complies with the requirement of equivalence, although it may receive extensive guidance as to the outcome from the CJEU.[289]

14-079   The principle of legal certainty has been very important in assessing limitation

---

[282] *Wolverhampton Healthcare NHS Trust* EU:C:2000:247.

[283] *Douanias v Ypourgio Oikonomikon* (C-228/98) EU:C:2000:65 at [65].

[284] See *Ministero delle Finanze v Spac* (C-260/96) EU:C:1998:402; *Aprile v Amminstrazione delle Finanze dello Stato* (C-228/96) EU:C:1998:544; *Dilexport v Amministrazione delle Finanze dello Stato* (C-343/96) EU:C:1999:59; *Roquette Fréres v Direction des Services Fiscaux du Pas-de-Calais* (C-88/99) EU:C:2000:652. cf. *Emmott* EU:C:1991:333; and *Pontin v T-Comalux SA* (C-63/08) EU:C:2009:666 at [45].

[285] *Levez* EU:C:1998:577 at [43]. See further Case *Edis v Ministero delle Finanze* (C-231/96) EU:C:1998:401 at [36] (time limits). See *Transportes Urbanos y Servicios Generales SAL v Administración del Estado* (C-118/08) EU:C:2010:39 at [48] (the CJEU ruling that a requirement of exhaustion of all domestic remedies could not be applied to an action for damages alleging a breach of EU law where such a rule was not applicable to an action for damages against the State alleging a breach of the Constitution); *Club Hotel Loutraki AE v Ethniko Simvoulio Radiotileorasis* (C-145 and C-149/08) EU:C:2010:247 at [75]–[77], [80].

[286] *Totel Ltd v Revenue and Customs Commissioners* [2016] EWCA Civ 1310; [2017] 1 W.L.R. 2313.

[287] *Fleming (t/a Bodycraft)* [2008] UKHL 2; [2008] 1 W.L.R. 195 at [79(f)]. In *Pontin* EU:C:2009:666 at [67] the CJEU observed that a 15-day limitation period did not appear to satisfy the principle of effectiveness, but that this was a matter for the referring court to determine. See *Danqua v Minister for Justice and Equality* (C-429/15) EU:C:2016:789 (finding ineffective a time limit for an application for subsidiary status of 15 working days of notification that such an application could be made).

[288] *Comet* EU:C:1976:191 (CJEU expressed no view as to whether a 30-day time limit constituted a reasonable period of limitation, leaving the issue to be decided by the national court). However, sometimes the CJEU will give its view on how the question of equivalence should be answered: *Bulicke* (C-246/09) EU:C:2010:418 at [30]–[34].

[289] *Levez* EU:C:1998:577 at [29]–[53]; *Danske Slagterier* EU:C:2009:178 at [35].

periods. Where a Member State imposes a time limit within which a claim has to be made, either by introducing a new time limit or shortening an existing one, the time limit has to be fixed in advance so as to provide legal certainty.[290] A situation marked by significant legal uncertainty might involve a breach of the principle of effectiveness, because reparation of the loss or damage caused to individuals by breaches of Union law for which a Member State could be held responsible might be rendered excessively difficult in practice if the individuals were unable to determine the applicable limitation period with a reasonable degree of certainty.[291] Formulations of time limits such as "at the earliest opportunity"[292] and "promptly"[293] have been regarded as not sufficiently clear and precise.[294] It has been held that what is required is that the true effect or interpretation of the limitation period should be reasonably foreseeable or clear; the existence of an arguable doubt or of a need for interpretation will not, of itself, render national law insufficiently foreseeable.[295] In the situation where a retrospective time limit is introduced, the legislation has to include an adequate transitional period, so that those with accrued rights have a reasonable time limit within which to make their claims before the new retrospective time limit applies.[296] Any application "by analogy" of a limitation period must also be sufficiently foreseeable.[297] However, there is no general principle that ignorance or uncertainty about the state of the law is sufficient to prevent time running on grounds of effectiveness.[298]

The CJEU has also emphasised that time limits must run from the date of knowledge of an infringement, rather than the date upon which the infringement arose.[299] Where there is a frailty in a limitation period, whether because it is triggered otherwise than by knowledge of the applicant or because there is uncertainty in its formulation or otherwise, it appears that the availability of judicial discretion to extend the time limit in favour of the applicant will not suffice to remedy the problem.[300]

14-080

In the context of limitation periods for *Francovich* damages actions, the fact that institution of infringement proceedings by the Commission does not have the effect of interrupting or suspending the limitation period does not make it impossible or excessively difficult for individuals to exercise their Union rights or breach the principle of equivalence, since an individual may bring a *Francovich* action without having to wait until a judgment finding that the Member State has infringed

14-081

---

[290] *Fleming (t/a Bodycraft)* [2008] UKHL 2; [2008] 1 W.L.R. 195 at [79(c)].

[291] *Danske Slagterier* EU:C:2009:178 at [33]-[34].

[292] *Commission v Ireland* (C-456/08) EU:C:2010:46 at [73]-[81].

[293] *Uniplex v NHS Business Services Authority* (C-406/08) EU:C:2010:45 at [41]-[43].

[294] See further below 14-083.

[295] *BCL Old Co Ltd v BASF SE (formerly BASF AG) (No.2)* [2012] UKSC 45; [2012] 1 W.L.R. 2922.

[296] *Fleming (t/a Bodycraft)* [2008] UKHL 2; [2008] 1 W.L.R. 195 at [79(d)]. See also: *The Commissioners for Her Majesty's Revenue and Customs v The Investment Trust Companies (in liquidation)* [2017] UKSC 29; [2017] 2 W.L.R. 1200; *Commission v United Kingdom* (C-640/13) EU:C:2014:2457; [2015] Ch. 476; [2015] 2 W.L.R. 1555 (the United Kingdom failed to comply with its obligations under TEU art.4(3) given that s.107 of the Finance Act 2007 curtailed retroactively and without notice or transitional arrangements, the right of taxpayers to recover taxes levied in breach of Union law).

[297] *Ze Fu Fleischhandel GmbH v v Hauptzollamt Hamburg-Jonas* (C-201/10) EU:C:2011:282; *Vion Trading GmbH v v Hauptzollamt Hamburg-Jonas* (C-202/10) EU:C:2010:323 at [32].

[298] *The Trustees of the BT Pension Scheme* [2015] EWCA Civ 713 at [117].

[299] *Uniplex* (C-406/08) EU:C:2010:45 at [48]; see also *Bulicke* EU:C:2010:418 at [39]-[41] (time limit could not run from the date of rejection of a job application but "the point at which the worker has knowledge of the alleged discrimination").

[300] *Commission v Ireland* (C-456/08) EU:C:2010:46 at [75]-[81].

Union law has been delivered.[301] Where the complaint is that a directive has not been transposed or incorrectly transposed, EU law does not preclude the limitation from beginning to run on the date on which the first injurious effects of the incorrect transposition have been produced and further effects are foreseeable, even if that date is prior to the correct transposition of the directive.[302] Where a temporal restriction is imposed on the right to obtain a refund of charges levied in breach of Union law, the general rule regarding reasonable time limits is subject to the additional principles, first, that the time limit not be specifically intended to limit the consequences of a judgment of the court and second, that the time set for the application of the time limit must be sufficient to ensure that the right to repayment is effective.[303]

14-082   On occasion, the requirements of Union law have been applied very strictly, with the result that national provisions may have to be applied *more* favourably to a claimant where a Union law right is in issue than in a case of a purely internal character[304]: this principle has been limited, however, to the situation where a time bar has the result of depriving the applicant of any opportunity whatever to rely on her Union right[305]; or where the delay in exercising the remedy is due in some way to the conduct of the national authorities.[306] Moreover, an otherwise reasonable time limit may be displaced by the particular circumstances. The CJEU has held that a national rule applicable in an equal pay claim under which entitlement to arrears of remuneration is restricted to the two years preceding the date on which the proceedings were instituted was not in itself open to criticism. However, given that the claimant in the national proceedings was late in bringing her claim because of inaccurate information provided by her employer, to allow the employer to rely on the time limit in such circumstances would be "manifestly incompatible with the principle of effectiveness".[307]

14-083   As observed above, the CJEU has held that a time limit which requires legal proceedings to be initiated "promptly" is incompatible with the principle of legal certainty and also that time limits should be triggered by the date of knowledge of an infringement, rather than the date upon which the grounds of the infringement arose.[308] This jurisprudence has had implications for the requirement in CPR Pt 54.5 that applications for permission to apply for judicial review be made "promptly and in any event within three months from the date when grounds for the application

---

[301] *Danske Slagterier* EU:C:2009:178 at [39]–[45].

[302] *Danske Slagterier* EU:C:2009:178 at [53]–[58].

[303] *Marks & Spencer* EU:C:2002:435 at [36].

[304] See, e.g. *Emmott* EU:C:1991:333.

[305] *Fantask A/S v Indus triministeriet (Erhvervsministeriet)* (C-188/95) EU:C:1997:580; *Danske Slagterier* EU:C:2009:178 at [54]; *Tonina Enza Iaia* [2011] All E.R. (D) 213 at [19].

[306] *Edis* EU:C:1998:401 at [48]; *Ansaldo Energia SpA v Amministrazione delle Stato* (C-279/96, C-280/96 and C-281/96) EU:C:1998:403 at [22]; *Spac SpA* EU:C:1998:402 at [31]; *Santex* EU:C:2003:109 at [62]; *Tonina Enza Iaia* [2011] All E.R. (D) 213 at [20]–[21] (a Member State is not precluded from relying on the expiry of a reasonable limitation period even though the Member State did not transpose the directive correctly, on condition that by its conduct, the Member State was not responsible for the delay in bringing the action).

[307] *Levez* EU:C:1998:577 at [20], [27]–[34]. See also *Birmingham Hippodrome Theatre Trust Ltd v Commissioners for HM Revenue and Customs* [2014] EWCA Civ 684; [2014] B.V.C. 27 at [46]–[49] (noting that "certainty is not a trump card" such that it did not breach the principles of effectiveness, equality or legal certainty for Revenue and Customs to be entitled to set off a repayment of input tax which should not have been made against a taxpayer's claim for repayment of output tax, despite being out of time to claim repayment of the wrongly repaid input tax). Contrast *Ecotrade SpA* EU:C:2008:267 at [48] (two year time limit did not render the exercise of a right to deduct tax virtually impossible or excessively difficult).

[308] See 14-079; *Uniplex* (C-406/08) EU:C:2010:45; *Bulicke* (C-246/09) EU:C:2010:418 at [39]–[41].

first arose".[309] It is now the case that for judicial review applications involving questions of Union law, the time limit in CPR Pt 54.5 must be construed in accordance with court's jurisprudence, in other words, three months from the date upon which the claimant knew or ought to have known of the alleged infringement.[310] Union law does not however require that a time limit in the field of environmental law should be subject to the court's discretionary power to extend it.[311]

Effective judicial review

The CJEU lays considerable stress on the requirement that Member States provide effective means of judicial review and it has been described as a basic principle of EU law that national law should provide effective legal protection.[312] In *Les Verts*,[313] it emphasised that the EU "is a Union based on the rule of law, inasmuch as neither its Member States nor its institutions can avoid a review of the question whether the measures adopted by them are in conformity with the basic constitutional charter, the Treaty".[314] The national courts may be required to ensure the effective protection of rights created by the Treaty or by secondary legislation. In *Johnston v Chief Constable of the Royal Ulster Constabulary*[315] in 1986, the CJEU ruled that the principle of effective judicial review laid down in art.6 of the directive reflected a general principle of law which underlay the constitutional traditions common to the Member States and was also laid down in ECHR arts 6 and 13 (right to a fair trial of civil rights and obligations and effective remedies for breach of Convention rights).[316] The CJEU has also held that review for arbitrariness will not suffice in the context of EU procurement rules.[317] Similarly, in *UNECTEF v Heylens*, the CJEU ruled that a decision by a national authority rejecting a claim under Union law must be reasoned and subject to judicial review in the national courts even if this is not normally the case under the relevant national legal system.[318] Furthermore, where the decision of a national authority not to recommend granting aid from an EU fund is binding on the Commission, the national court must review the national authority's decision for lawfulness, and regard an

14-084

---

[309] See 16-009. The issue was raised although not decided in *R. (on the application of Macrae) v Herefordshire DC* [2012] EWCA Civ 457; [2012] J.P.L. 1356 at [10]–[11] (the appeal turned on its own particular facts).

[310] *R. (on the application of Buglife Invertebrate Conservation Trust) v Medway Council* [2011] EWHC 746 (Admin); *R. (on the application of U & Partners (East Anglia) Ltd) v Broads Authority* [2011] EWHC 1824 (Admin); *R. (Berky) v Newport City Council* [2012] EWCA Civ 378. The CPR Pt 54.5 requirement still applies, however, to domestic judicial review actions: *Macrae* [2011] EWHC 2810 (Admin) (issue not necessary to decide on appeal [2011] EWCA Civ 1475).

[311] *R. (on the application of Williams) v Secretary of State for Energy and Climate Change* [2015] EWHC 1202 (Admin).

[312] *Tariq v Home Office* [2011] UKSC 35; [2012] 1 A.C. 452 at [15]; see also *FA (Iraq) v Secretary of State for the Home Department* [2011] UKSC 22; [2011] 4 All E.R. 503 at [12].

[313] *Partie Ecologiste (Les Verts) v European Parliament* (294/83) EU:C:1986:166 at [23]. For consideration of the rule of law and institutional balance, see: *Council v Commission* (C-409/13) EU:C:2015:217 (Commission's power to withdraw legislative proposals).

[314] See also *Advocate General Opinion, Vereniging Milieudefensie* EU:C:2015:4 at [70].

[315] *Johnston v Chief Constable of the Royal Ulster Constabulary (222/84)* [1987] Q.B. 129.

[316] See also *Opinion 2/13* (18 December 2014) at [175].

[317] *Hospital Ingenieure Krankenhaustechnik Planungs GmbH (HI) v Stadt Wien* (C-92/00) EU:C:2002:379 at [63]: holding that review of a local authority's withdrawal of its invitation to tender for a public service contract, limited to whether the decision was arbitrary, did not satisfy the requirement in Directive 89/665 to ensure effective review of contracting authorities to ensure compliance with the Union public procurement rules.

[318] *UNECTEF v Heylens* (222/86) EU:C:1987:442. See further *Irène Vlassopoulou v Ministerium für Justiz, Bundes-und Europaangelegenheiten Baden-Württemberg* (C-340/89) EU:C:1991:193.

action brought for that purpose as admissible even if domestic rules of procedure do not provide for this.[319]

14-085   However, where a directive required that individuals be able to pursue their claims under it "by judicial process", it was sufficient that a general claim before civil courts for compensation against the State was available.[320] The principle of effective judicial protection will also not require a national court to substitute its own judgment for that of a national authority where the national authority applying Union law is called upon to make complex assessments or has a wide measure of discretion. In such a case, judicial review may be restricted to verifying that the action taken by the national authority is not vitiated by manifest error or a misuse of powers and that the authority has not clearly exceeded the bounds of its discretion.[321] The CJEU has also ruled that it is permissible to provide only a remedy by way of judicial review to an EU national who has been refused entry on grounds of public policy, even where there was a more substantial remedy by way of appeal for nationals whose immigration status was in question, because it considered that the two situations were not comparable.[322]

Exhaustion of remedies

14-086   The question of whether a requirement to exhaust domestic remedies would infringe the principle of effectiveness has been raised with the CJEU but not decided.[323]

Repayment

14-087   Where a charge is imposed contrary to Union law, the question arises of the extent to which an action for recovery is governed by national law or Union law.[324] The CJEU has insisted that entitlement to repayment of charges levied contrary to Union law is a consequence of and an adjunct to the rights conferred on individuals by the Union provisions prohibiting such charges.[325] Provided that the conditions of equivalence and effective protection are satisfied, recovery may be made conditional on the claimant's proving that the charges had not been passed on to third parties.[326] However, this defence must be narrowly construed since it entails

---

[319] *Oleificio Borelli SpA v Commission* (C-97/91) EU:C:1992:491 at [12]–[13].

[320] *Schneider v Bundesminister der Justiz* (C-380/01) EU:C:2004:73 at [26]–[28].

[321] *Upjohn Ltd v The Licensing Authority established by the Medicines Act 1968* (C-120/97) EU:C:1999:14 (noting that there is no need for national courts to engage in more extensive review than that in which the CJEU engages in similar circumstances).

[322] *R. v Secretary of State for the Home Department Ex p. Shingara and Ex p. Radiom (C-65/95 and C-111/95)* EU:C:1997:300.

[323] *Transportes Urbanos* EU:C:2010:39 at [47].

[324] On rights to restitution under English law, see 19-075.

[325] *San Giorgio* EU:C:1983:318; *Comateb v Directeur Général des Douanes et Droits Indirects* (C-192/95) EU:C:1997:12. See further M. Dougan, "Cutting your Losses in the Enforcement Deficit: A Community Right to the Recovery of Unlawfully Levied Charges" (1998) 1 C.Y.E.L.S. 233. For further consideration of *San Giorgio*, see *The Commissioners for Her Majesty's Revenue and Customs v The Investment Trust Companies (in liquidation)* [2017] UKSC 29; [2017] 2 W.L.R. 1200. See also *Test Claimants in the FII Group Litigation v Revenue and Customs Commissioners* [2014] EWHC 4302; [2015] S.T.C. 1471 (holding that the remedy in Union law in respect of tax unlawfully levied based on *San Giorgio* was wider than the recovery which would be provided for unjust enrichment in English law). See also *Coin-a-Drink Ltd v Revenue and Customs Commissioners* [2015] UKFTT 495 (TC); *Littlewoods Ltd v Revenue and Customs Commissioners* [2017] UKSC 70; [2017] 3 W.L.R. 1401.

[326] *San Giorgio* EU:C:1983:318; *Commission v Italy* EU:C:1988:171. It has been observed that the only

placing a limitation on a subjective right derived from the EU legal order,[327] and the Member State can only plead the defence, where "it is established that the charge has been borne in its entirety by another person and that reimbursement of the trader would constitute unjust enrichment".[328] The CJEU has dismissed an argument that an excusable error by the authorities, such as imposing charges over a long period of time while unaware that the charges were in breach of Union law, could constitute a defence to a claim for repayment.[329] It is not necessary for interest to be paid on arrears of social security benefits; however, interest payments are required on compensation for loss or damage caused by national authorities.[330] Limits on damages, even in respect of compensation, may be permissible.[331]

No general obligation to reopen final judicial and administrative decisions

The CJEU held in *Kapferer v Schlank & Schick* that EC art.10 (now effectively TEU art.4(3))[332] does not require a national court to disapply its internal rules of procedure in order to re-open and set aside a judicial decision which has become final, even if that decision should be contrary to Union law.[333] This is because of the importance, both for the Union legal order and national legal systems, of the principle of res judicata, and because it is important, in order to ensure both stability of the law and legal relations and the sound administration of justice, that judicial decisions which have become definitive after all rights of appeal have been exhausted or after expiry of the time limits provided for in that connection can no longer be called into question.[334] The duty of res judicata in respect of a decision which is contrary to Union law does not, however, extend to preventing recovery of state aid granted in breach of Union law which has been found to be incompatible with the internal market in a decision of the Commission which has become final.[335] This ruling appears to be limited in its application, and thus far, has only been extended to the VAT context where there was a risk of continuous misapplication of EU law.[336]   **14-088**

Similarly, in principle, administrative bodies are not under an obligation to reopen   **14-089**

---

exception to the right of repayment of taxes levied in breach of EU law is where a charge that was not due has been directly passed on by the taxable person to another person: *SECIL* (C-464/14) EU:C:2016:896 at [165].

[327] *Ministre du Budget, des Comptes publics et de la Fonction publique v Accor SA* (C-310/09) EU:C:2011:581 [2012] S.T.C. 438 at [73]; *Lady & Kid* (C-398/09) EU:C:2011:540 [2012] All E.R. (EC) 410 at [20].

[328] *Comateb* EU:C:1997:12; *Ministre du Budget* [2012] S.T.C. 438 at [74]; *Lady & Kid* (C-398/09) EU:C:2011:540 at [26].

[329] *Fantask* EU:C:1997:580.

[330] *R. v Secretary of State for Social Security Ex p. Eunice Sutton* (C-66/95) EU:C:1997:207 at [23]-[24].

[331] *Draehmpaehl v Urania Immobilienservice* (C-180/95) EU:C:1997:208.

[332] The text of TEU art.4(3) is set out at 14-047, above.

[333] *Kapferer v Schlank & Schick* (C-234/04) EU:C:2006:178 at [21], [24].

[334] *Kapferer v Schlank & Schick* (C-234/04) EU:C:2006:178 at [21].

[335] *Lucchini SpA* EU:C:2007:434 at [63].

[336] In *Amministrazione dell'Economia e delle Finanze, Agenzia delle Entrate, v Fallimento Olimpiclub Srl* (C-2/08) EU:C:2009:506 at [25]-[32], the CJEU suggested that *Lucchini* was in effect a special case because of the nature of the state aid regime and should not in itself be seen to undermine *Kapferer* and the principle of res judicata. However, the Court proceeded to state that there may be situations (here where there was a risk of continuous misapplication of EU VAT rules without it being possible to rectify the interpretation) that may mean a State cannot rely on res judicata). In *Ufficio IVA di Piacenza v Belvedere Costruzioni Srl* (C-500/10) EU:C:2011:754 [2012] B.V.C. 202, 17 November 2011 at [45], Advocate General Sharpston stressed that the approach taken in *Fallimento Olimpiclub* was specific to a VAT context.

an administrative decision which has become final.[337] In relation to administrative decisions, the principle is subject to an exception. This is where under national law the administrative body (a) has the power to re-open the relevant decision, (b) the administrative decision in question has become final as a result of the judgment of a national court ruling at final instance, (c) that judgment is, in the light of a decision given by the CJEU subsequent to it, based on a misinterpretation of Union law which was adopted without a question being referred to the CJEU for a preliminary ruling under TFEU art.267(3) and (d) the person concerned complained to the administrative body concerned immediately after becoming aware of that decision of the CJEU.[338] The CJEU has subsequently clarified that the fourth requirement to seek review immediately cannot be interpreted as an obligation to make the application for review within a certain specified period and Member States remain free to set reasonable time limits for seeking remedies, in a manner consistent with the Union principles of effectiveness and equivalence.[339] It has also been held that the duty to re-open administrative decisions is not dependent upon the litigant involved having relied upon Union law in the initial decision-making process.[340] The CJEU has located this duty in the duty of fidelity now found in TEU art.4(3).[341]

14-090　In *Kapferer*, the CJEU did not decide the question of whether a similar exception applied in respect of final judicial decisions, but noted that, even assuming that the principles laid down in that judgment could be transposed into a context which, like that of the main proceedings, relates to a final judicial decision, the obligation of the body concerned to review a final decision, is subject to the condition, among other things, that that body should be empowered under national law to reopen that decision.[342]

14-091　In sum, the principle of res judicata may often be required to yield to the requirement to take a binding ruling of EU law into consideration.[343]

State liability in damages for breach of Union law

14-092　The requirement to provide effective remedies for the protection of Union law rights may also include the obligation to provide adequate compensation.[344] It is a principle of Union law that Member States are obliged to pay compensation for harm caused to individuals by breaches of Union law for which they are held responsible.[345] Where there is a dispute over payment of such compensation, it is national courts which adjudicate on the issues.[346] The harm in question may be caused in many ways, for instance by the failure to transpose a directive into

---

[337] *Kühne & Heitz NV v Productschap voor Pluimvee en Eieren* (C-453/00) EU:C:2004:17 at [24]; *i-21 Germany GmbH and Arcor AG & Co KG* EU:C:2006:586 at [51].

[338] *Kühne & Heitz* EU:C:2004:17 at [28]; *i-21* [2007] 1 C.M.L.R. 10 at [52].

[339] *Willy Kempter KG* EU:C:2008:78 at [56], [60].

[340] *Willy Kempter KG* EU:C:2008:78 at [45]. See A. Ward, "Do unto Others as You Would have them do unto you: Willy Kempter and the Duty to Raise EC Law in National Litigation" (2008) 33 E.L. Rev. 739.

[341] *Willy Kempter KG* EU:C:2008:78 at [38]. See 14-047.

[342] *Kapferer* EU:C:2006:178 at [23].

[343] P. Craig and G. de Búrca, *EU Law: Text, Cases and Materials* (2015), p.242.

[344] On rights to damages under English law, see 19-025; on the approach to damages under Human Rights Act 1998 s.8, see 19-081.

[345] The High Court has affirmed that a person adversely affected by a breach of EU law is not required to challenge the legality of the measure in proceedings before the national court before bringing a claim for *Francovich* damages: see *Recall Support Services* [2013] EWHC 3091 (Ch); [2014] 2 C.M.L.R. 2 at [220] (following *Metallgesellschaft Ltd v Inland Revenue Commissioners* (C-397/98) EU:C:2001:134 (see now: [2014] EWCA Civ 1370; [2015] 1 C.M.L.R. 38)).

[346] Only those courts in the UK which have power to award damages generally may grant damages for

national law within the required period[347]; by incorrectly transposing a directive[348]; by enacting primary legislation contrary to the provisions of the TFEU[349]; or by officials taking administrative action such as refusing an export licence in breach of Union law.[350] In *Francovich v Italy*, the CJEU (giving a preliminary ruling to an Italian court) held that the full effectiveness of Union rules would be impaired and the protection of rights which they granted would be weakened if individuals were unable to obtain compensation when their rights were infringed by breach of Union law for which a Member State was responsible.[351] The possibility of compensation by the Member State was particularly indispensable where (as on the facts of the case) the full effectiveness of Union rules was subject to prior action on the part of the state and, consequently, individuals could not, in the absence of such action, enforce the rights granted to them before the national courts.[352] Further foundation for the Member States' obligation to pay compensation for such harm was to be found in TEU art.4(3), which requires Member States to take all appropriate measures, whether general or particular, to ensure fulfilment of their obligations under Union law.[353]

In *Francovich* and subsequent cases in which national courts have requested preliminary rulings, the CJEU has laid down the broad principles for liability, although in the absence of Union legislation, it is a matter for the internal legal order of each Member State to develop more specific conditions.[354] It is also for the internal legal order of each Member State to designate the competent courts and lay down the detailed procedural rules governing the new damages remedy.[355] **14-093**

---

breach of Union law; where a statutory tribunal, such as an employment tribunal, lacks that power, a claimant will have to pursue a claim in the county courts or the High Court in the ordinary way: *Potter v Secretary of State for Employment* [1998] Eu L.R. 388. A claim for judicial review made under CPR Pt 54 may include a claim for damages: see 19-005.

[347] *Francovich v Italy* EU:C:1991:428. Italy had failed to transpose Directive 80/987, guaranteeing employees a minimum level of protection in the event of an employer's insolvency, into national law. Member States were required to set up institutions which would provide specific guarantees of payment of unpaid wage claims. The CJEU held that provisions in the Directive were not sufficiently precise and unconditional to be directly effective: see 14-031.

[348] See, e.g. *R. v HM Treasury, Ex p. British Telecommunications Plc* (C-392/93) EU:C:1996:131 [1996] Q.B. 615.

[349] See, e.g. *R. v Secretary of State for Transport Ex p. Factortame Ltd* (C-48/93) EU:C:1996:79 (enactment by UK Parliament of Merchant Shipping Act 1988, Pt II contrary to provisions in the EC Treaty). See also *Danske Slagterier* EU:C:2009:178.

[350] See, e.g. *R. v Ministry of Agriculture, Fisheries and Food Ex p. Hedley Lomas (Ireland) Ltd* (C-5/94) EU:C:1996:205 (refusal, contrary to TFEU, of export licence for live sheep destined for Spanish slaughterhouse).

[351] *Francovich* EU:C:1991:428 at [33].

[352] *Francovich* EU:C:1991:428 at [34].

[353] *Francovich* EU:C:1991:428 at [36]; see 14-061. For a discussion of the absorption of *Francovich* into national law, see M. Künnecke, "Divergence and the Francovich Remedy in German and English Courts" in S. Prechal and B. van Roermund (eds), *The Coherence of EU Law: The Search for Unity in Divergent Concepts* (2008), p.233.

[354] *Francovich* EU:C:1991:428 at [42]. TEU art.4(3), which replaced EC art.10, provides: " ... The Member States shall take any appropriate measure, general or particular, to ensure fulfilment of the obligations arising out of theTreaties or resulting from the acts of the institutions of the Union. The Member States shall facilitate the achievement of the Union's tasks and refrain from any measure which could jeopardise the attainment of the Union's objectives". It has recently been held that the *Francovich* criteria apply to claims for damages for breaches of public procurement rules: *Energy Solutions* [2017] UKSC 34; [2017] 1 W.L.R. 1373.

[355] *Francovich* EU:C:1991:428 at [42].

Synthesising the pronouncements of the CJEU, it may now be said that there is an entitlement to compensation where three conditions are met by the claimant.[356]

Right-conferring provision

14-094   First, the rule of Union law which has been infringed (i) must be intended to confer rights on individuals and (ii) where the complaint is that a directive has not been transposed, the content of those rights must be able to be identified on the basis of the provisions of the directive itself.[357] The right conferred by Union law may or may not be directly effective.[358]

Sufficiently serious breach

14-095   Secondly, the breach of Union law must be "sufficiently serious", which means that the Member State had "manifestly and gravely disregarded the limits on its discretion".[359] As already noted, in principle it is for the national court to determine whether the conditions for state liability are met, although the CJEU "may indicate certain circumstances which the national courts may take into account in their evaluation".[360] The "sufficiently serious" test is "not a hard-edged test" and "it requires a value judgment by the national court".[361]

14-096   As a general matter, the following factors will be material in determining whether an infringement passes the threshold of seriousness[362]: (i) the clarity and precision of the rule breached[363]; (ii) the measure of discretion left by that rule to the national

---

356 See further A. Biondi and M. Farley, *The Right to Damages in European Law* (2010); P. Giliker, *The Europeanisation of English Tort Law* (2014), Ch.4; T. Lock, "Is private enforcement of EU law through State liability a myth? An assessment 20 years after Francovich" (2012) 49 C.M.L.Rev. 1675.

357 These conditions were specified in *Francovich* EU:C:1991:428. In *Bowden v South West Water Services Ltd* [1998] Env. L.R. 445 there was a failure to demonstrate that the Directive involved the grant of rights to individuals; see also *Paul v Germany* (C-222/02) EU:C:2004:606 at [51]; *Three Rivers DC v Governor and Company of the Bank of England* [2000] 2 A.C. 1 at 196, 219.

358 In *R. v Secretary of State for Transport Ex p. Factortame (No.4)* (C-48/93) EU:C:1996:79 [1996] Q.B. 404 the successful claim against the United Kingdom was that the Merchant Shipping Act 1988 breached a directly effective provision in the TFEU prohibiting discrimination on the ground of nationality. The CJEU rejected an argument that *Francovich* was concerned only "to fill a lacuna in the system for safeguarding the rights of individuals" and was limited to situations where the Union law right was not directly effective.

359 *Brasserie du Pêcheur SA v Germany* (C-46/93) EU:C:1996:79 at [55]. See further A. Cygan, "Defining a Sufficiently Serious Breach of Community Law: The House of Lords casts its nets into the Waters" (2000) 25 E.L. Rev. 452 (discussing the *Factortame* litigation).

360 *Sweden v Stockholm Lindöpark Aktiebolag* (C-150/99) EU:C:2001:34 at [38].

361 *Byrne* [2009] Q.B. 66 at [45].

362 *Brasserie du Pêcheur* EU:C:1996:79 at [56]; *R. v Secretary of State for Transport, Ex p. Factortame Ltd (No.4)* [1996] Q.B. 404; *Recall Support Services* [2013] EWHC 3091 (Ch) at [165] (see now: [2014] EWCA Civ 1370).

363 *British Telecommunications* [1996] Q.B. 615 (no serious breach where article in Directive imprecisely worded, reasonably capable of bearing the United Kingdom's good faith interpretation, which was shared by other Member States) cf. *Rechberger v Austria* (C-140/97) EU:C:1999:306 at [50]-[51] (where art.7 of Directive 90/314 on package travel, package holidays and package tours gave no discretion to the Member State and as such, the attempt of Austria to limit its application constituted a sufficiently serious breach of Union law to give rise to a damages action) *Synthon BV v Licensing Authority of the Department of Health* (C-452/06) EU:C:2008:565 at [42]-[43] (a sufficiently serious breach arose where the Licensing Authority refused an application for mutual recognition of a product pursuant to Directive 2001/83, the relevant provision of which had been "clearly and precisely" worded); *Specht v Land Berlin* (C-501/12–C-506/12) EU:C:2014:2005 at [105] (legislation which is not clear and precise may become so from the date upon which the court

authorities³⁶⁴; (iii) whether the infringement and damage caused was intentional or involuntary; (iv) whether any error of law was excusable or inexcusable³⁶⁵; (v) the fact that the position taken by a EU institution may have contributed towards the omission; and (vi) the adoption or retention of national measures or practices contrary to Union law.³⁶⁶ More specifically, a failure by a Member State to transpose a directive within the prescribed period is per se a serious breach of Union law and the circumstances of the failure are not relevant to determining liability,³⁶⁷ although this principle is subject to slight modification where an administrative authority has attempted to give the provisions of the directive immediate effect despite its non-implementation by the national legislature.³⁶⁸ Where the Member State concerned is not in a position to make any legislative choices and has only a considerably reduced, or even no, discretion, the mere infringement of Union law may be sufficient to establish the existence of a sufficiently serious breach.³⁶⁹ Where the breach, whether intentional or otherwise, is of a fundamental principle of the TFEU, such as the prohibition on discrimination on the grounds of nationality, this will almost invariably give rise to liability in damages.³⁷⁰ Furthermore, "on any view", a breach of Union law will be sufficiently serious if it has persisted despite a judgment finding the infringement in question to be established or a preliminary ruling or settled case law of the CJEU on the matter from which it is clear that the conduct in question constituted an infringement.³⁷¹ Failing to adopt measures necessary to comply with an interim order of the CJEU will also constitute a sufficiently seri-

gives clarity and definition to a rule of EU law); *R. (on the application of Chester) v Secretary of State for Justice* [2013] UKSC 63; [2014] A.C. 271 at [79].
³⁶⁴ For example, in *Hedley Lomas* [1997] Q.B. 139 the United Kingdom imposed a general ban on the export of live animals to Spain for slaughter, contrary to TFEU art.34 on the free movement of goods. The CJEU held that here the national authorities had not been called upon to make any legislative choices and had only reduced discretion, or even no discretion. In such a situation the mere infringement of Union law may be sufficient to establish the existence of a sufficiently serious breach. See also *Synthon BV* EU:C:2008:565 at [41]-[43] (a sufficiently serious breach arose where the Licensing Authority refused an application for mutual recognition of a product pursuant to Directive 2001/83 which granted "only a very limited discretion" in relation to refusal). *R. (on the application of Chester) v Secretary of State for Justice* [2013] UKSC 63; [2014] A.C. 271 at [76]. See also *Delaney v Secretary of State for Transport* [2015] EWCA Civ 172; [2015] 3 All E.R. 329 (where the natural reading of an article of a Directive only permitted exclusions which were set out in the article itself; a reference in the recitals to the Directive to "certain limited exclusions" was not a sound basis for adding additional exclusions and there was no discretion to adopt additional exclusions, resulting in a sufficiently serious breach in *Francovich* damages). See also *Angus Growers Ltd v Scottish Ministers* [2016] CSOH 26 at [40] (confirming that where there is a lack of discretion, it may not be sufficient to merely prove that there has been a breach of EU law—more may be required).
³⁶⁵ For example, in *R. v Secretary of State for Transport Ex p. Factortame Ltd (No.5)* [1998] 1 All E.R. 736 (Note), the High Court held that the damage caused by the enactment of the Merchant Shipping Act 1988 Pt II was sufficiently serious because: (1) discrimination on the ground of nationality contrary to the TFEU was the intended effect of the criteria; (2) the government was aware that those criteria would necessarily injure the applicants who would be unable to fish against the British quota; (3) the Act was constructed to ensure it would not be delayed by legal challenges and this made it impossible for the applicants to obtain interim relief without the CJEU's intervention; and (4) the Commission had been consistently hostile to the proposed legislation. See also *Angus Growers Ltd v Scottish Ministers* [2016] CSOH 26 at [43]-[45].
³⁶⁶ These factors were endorsed in *Delaney v Secretary of State for Transport* [2015] EWCA Civ 172; [2015] 3 All E.R. 329 at [36].
³⁶⁷ See *Dillenkofer v Germany* (C-178, C-179, C-188-190/94) EU:C:1996:375 [1997] Q.B. 259 at [26].
³⁶⁸ See 14-100.
³⁶⁹ *Hedley Lomas* [1997] Q.B. 139 at [28]; *Dillenkofer* EU:C:1996:375 [1997] Q.B. 259 at [25].
³⁷⁰ *Factortame (No.5)* [1998] C.O.D. 381.
³⁷¹ *Brasserie du Pêcheur* EU:C:1996:79 at [56]; *Byrne* [2009] Q.B. 66 at [44] (the fact that the CJEU had given an "unambiguous statement" regarding the meaning of the Directive contributed to a find-

ous breach.[372] By contrast, if a decision by an official would have been the same even if no breach of Union law had occurred, this may be insufficiently serious to warrant compensation.[373] Where there has been a bona fide misinterpretation of an unclear provision that is also unlikely to constitute a "sufficiently serious breach".[374] The obligation to make reparation for loss or damage caused to individuals cannot depend upon a condition based on any concept of fault going beyond a sufficiently serious breach of EU law.[375] If the breach has "serious consequences", the national courts will also include this as a relevant factor to consider in determining whether there has been a "sufficiently serious breach".[376] While a finding of breach by the CJEU is an important factor, it is not indispensable for establishing that the breach of Union law was sufficiently serious; an individual can bring an action for damages, without having to wait for a prior judgment by the CJEU that the Member State has breached Union law.[377] Similarly, an individual's ability to take an action for damages cannot be dependent on the Commission's assessment of the expediency of taking action against a Member State pursuant to TFEU art.258. However, where the Commission considers whether to bring an infringement and decides against it, that will be a "pointer" against a finding of sufficiently serious breach.[378]

14-097   A "manifest breach" of EU law is required before a damages action will be available in respect of the judgment of a court.[379] The CJEU has in the past been reluctant

---

ing of a sufficiently serious breach). *Hogan v Minister for Social and Family Affairs* (C-398/11) EU:C:2013:272 at [51]–[52] (the requirements of art.8 of Directive 80/987 as amended were clear and specific from the date of a prior judgment, as such, Ireland's failure to transpose the Directive correctly gave rise to a sufficiently serious breach of Union law); *Specht v Land Berlin* (C-501/12–C-506/12) EU:C:2014:2005 at [105] (legislation which is not clear and precise may become so from the date upon which the court gives clarity and definition to a rule of EU law).

[372] EU:C:1996:79 at [64].

[373] *R. v Secretary of State for the Home Department Ex p. Gallagher* [1996] 2 C.M.L.R. 951, CA (order excluding applicant from entering Great Britain was made under the Prevention of Terrorism (Temporary Provisions) Act 1989 without following the rules of procedural fairness set out in Directive 64/221, but the breach was not sufficiently serious to merit an award of compensation as there was no evidence to suggest that the Secretary of State would have reached a different conclusion had he received the applicant's representations at an earlier stage).

[374] *R. v Ministry of Agriculture, Fisheries and Food Ex p. Lay and Gage* [1998] C.O.D. 387.

[375] *Fuß* (C-243/09) EU:C:2010:609 at [67] (holding that imposing a requirement on a worker to make a prior application to an employer in order to be entitled to reparation for loss or damage would be contrary to the principle of effectiveness); *Traghetti del Mediterraneo SpA (In Liquidation) v Italy* (C-173/03) EU:C:2006:391 at [46].

[376] *Byrne* [2009] Q.B. 66 at [45].

[377] *Danske Slagterier* EU:C:2009:178 at [37] and [39].

[378] *Recall Support Services* [2014] EWCA Civ 1370 at [87]. It has also been held that excessively lengthy General Court proceedings (three years) are not a sufficiently serious breach of the duty to adjudicate within a reasonable period: *Aloys F Dornbracht GmbH & Co KG v Commission (Re Bathroom Fittings Cartel)* (C-604/13 P) EU:C:2017:45; see also *Trafilerie Mediionali SpA v Commission (Re Prestressing Steel Cartel Appeal)* (C-519/15P) EU:C:2016:682.

[379] In *Köbler v Republik Österreich* (C-224/01) EU:C:2003:513 at [53] (*Francovich* reparation is available in principle where there has been default by a domestic court, although this will be "only in the exceptional case where the court has manifestly infringed the applicable law"). Furthermore, *Köbler* suggested that liability could only arise in respect of national courts of last instance rather than more generally. In *Köbler* itself, the CJEU found that the Austrian court had interpreted CJEU case law incorrectly and had wrongfully withdrawn a preliminary reference, but found neither act to constitute a manifest infringement since the CJEU considered that Union law did not provide an obvious answer to the question: [120]-[126]. See H. Scott and N. Barber, "State Liability under Francovich for Decisions of National Courts" (2004) 120 L.Q.R. 403; B. Beutler, "State Liability for breaches of Community Law by National Courts: Is the Requirement of a Manifest Infringement of the Applicable Law an Insurmountable Obstacle? (2009) 46 C.M.L. Rev. 773; P. Wattel, "Köbler, CILFIT

to find that the "manifest breach" test has been satisfied,[380] although there is evidence that its approach in this respect is changing.[381] At the domestic level, the Court of Appeal has found itself in the "anomalous position"[382] of adjudicating upon the question of whether an earlier Court of Appeal had erred in EU law in its disposal of judicial review proceedings challenging the grant of outline planning permission in the absence of an Environmental Impact Assessment.[383] Arden LJ's reasons for refusing to find a "manifest breach" of Union law included the difficulty and specialist concept of "development consent" in Directive 85/337, the nature of the judicial function, and the fact that breach would not be regarded as "manifest" if the answer to the question before the court was not evident.[384]

Causal link

Thirdly, a causal link must exist between the breach of the Member State's obligation and the harm sustained by the injured party.[385] This condition is to be decided in accordance with national rules on liability, provided that national law is not less favourable than those relating to a similar purely domestic claim and they are not such, as in practice to make it impossible or excessively difficult to obtain effective reparation for loss or damage resulting from breach of Union law.

14-098

Quantum

Where liability is established, Member States must compensate for the loss or damage caused by the breach, in accordance with national laws on liability, provided that national laws do not treat the Union law claim less favourably than a similar domestic claim and do not make it impossible or excessively difficult in practice to obtain compensation.[386] The quantum awarded must be "commensurate with the loss or damage sustained".[387] Thus, in the absence of Union provisions, it is for the domestic legal system of each Member State to set the criteria for determining the extent of reparation, subject to the Union principles of equivalence and effectiveness. Thus, for example, the CJEU has held that English rules, which restrict liability to cases where the tort of misfeasance in public office is established, make it impossible in practice to enforce liability where the national legislature is responsible for the breach.[388] A national court may not totally exclude loss of profit

14-099

---

and Welthgrove: We Can't Go on Meeting Like This" (2004) 42 C.M.L. Rev. 177; T. de la Mare and C. Donnelly, "Preliminary Rulings and EU Legal Integration: Evolution and Stasis" in P. Craig and G. de Búrca, *The Evolution of EU Law* (2011), Ch.13, pp.374-377.

[380] See, e.g. *Commission v Italy* (C-129/00) EU:C:2003:656 (while the Commission placed stress on the fault of the Corte suprema di cassazeione, the CJEU was careful to reason the case in such a way to find that the ultimate fault was with the legislature); B. Beutler, "State Liability for breaches of Community Law by National Courts: Is the Requirement of a Manifest Infringement of the Applicable Law an Insurmountable Obstacle? (2009) 46 C.M.L. Rev. 773.

[381] In *Commission v Spain* (C-154/08) EU:C:2009:695 (available in French and Spanish), the breach by Spain of Union law was established in enforcement proceedings (for the first time based on TFEU art.258) and related to a judgment delivered by its national Supreme Court.

[382] *Cooper v Attorney General* [2010] EWCA Civ 464; [2011] Q.B. 976.

[383] *Cooper* [2010] EWCA Civ 464; [2011] Q.B. 976 at [61].

[384] *Cooper* [2010] EWCA Civ 464; [2011] Q.B. 976 at [59]-[81].

[385] See further G. Anagnostaras, "Not as Unproblematic as You Might Think: The Establishment of Causation in Governmental Liability Actions" (2002) 27 E.L. Rev. 663.

[386] C. Lewis, *Judicial Remedies in Public Law* (2014) at para.17-072; *Factortame* [1996] Q.B. 404 at [67]-[74].

[387] *Brasserie du Pêcheur* EU:C:1996:79 at [82].

[388] *Factortame* [1996] Q.B. 404 at [73]; see C. Lewis, *Judicial Remedies in Public Law* (2014) at

as a head of damage.[389] If exemplary damages are available in domestic claims, these may be awarded in similar situations for breach of Union law.[390] A national court may, however, enquire whether the injured person showed reasonable diligence in order to avoid the loss or damage or limit its extent and whether "he availed himself in time of all the legal remedies available to him".[391]

Identifying the defendant

14-100 In identifying the defendant to a damages action, a "unitary" or indivisible concept of the state has been adopted by the CJEU and the obligation to pay compensation arises without the state being allowed to "plead the distribution of powers and responsibilities between the bodies that exist in its national legal order to free itself from liability on this basis".[392] Thus damages actions can be brought in respect of the actions of administrative authorities,[393] the legislature[394] and, as already discussed, even against the highest court for a "manifest breach" of Union law.[395] Moreover, damages actions can be brought against territorial bodies and public law entities enjoying a degree of institutional and functional autonomy from the central government.[396] In short,

> "[i]t is for each Member State to ensure that individuals obtain reparation for damage caused to them by non-compliance with Community [now Union] law, whichever public authority is responsible for the breach and whichever public authority is in principle, under the law of the Member State concerned, responsible for making reparation".[397]

14-101 That said, it is possible for the named defendant to be the autonomous public body, and the named defendant will not always be "the state".[398] Indeed, the choice of defendant may be of crucial importance in determining liability. Thus, in *Brinkmann*,[399] the autonomous actions of a Danish tax authority, given administrative effect to the Second Tax Directive as if the Directive had actually been

---

para.17-072. On misfeasance in public office, see 19-048.

[389] C. Lewis, *Judicial Remedies in Public Law* (2014) at para.17-073; *Factortame* [1996] Q.B. 404 at [87]-[88]. Contrast, however, *Evropaïki Dynamiki-Proigmena Systimata Tilepikoinonion Pliroforikis kai Tilematikis AE* (T-39/08) at [46]-[49]; *Evropaïki Dynamiki* (T- 461/08) at [209]-[212].

[390] In *Factortame Ltd (No.5)* (1998) 10 Admin. L.R. 107, the High Court held that liability for a breach of Union law could best be compared with breach of statutory duty (on which see para.16-054), as it was not possible to compare the UK's actions with the tort of misfeasance in public office (see para.16-048). Under English law, a breach of statutory duty only gave rise to exemplary damages if there was express statutory provision for them and no such provision existed in this case.

[391] *Brasserie du Pêcheur* EU:C:1996:79 at [84]. See also *Energy Solutions* [2017] UKSC 34; [2017] 1 W.L.R. 1373 at [43]-[45].

[392] *Konle v Austria* (C-302/97) EU:C:1999:271 at [62]. See further *Gervais Larsy v Institut national d'assurances sociales pour travailleurs independents ("INASTI") (No.2)* (C-118/00) EU:C:2001:368 at [35]; *Haim v Kassenzahnärztliche Vereinigung Nordrhein* (C-424/97) EU:C:2000:357 at [27]. See further R.W. Davis, "Liability in Damages for a Breach of Community Law: Some Reflections on the Question of Who to Sue and the Concept of 'the State'" (2006) 31 E.L. Rev. 69.

[393] See, e.g. *Hedley Lomas* [1997] Q.B. 139; *Norbrook Laboratories Ltd v Ministry of Agriculture, Fisheries and Food* (C-127/95) EU:C:1998:151; *Brinkmann Tabakfabriken GmbH v Skatteministeriet* (C-319/96) EU:C:1998:429.

[394] *Francovich* EU:C:1991:428; *Brasserie du Pêcheur* EU:C:1996:79; *British Telecommunications* [1996] Q.B. 615; *Dillenkofer* [1997] Q.B. 259; *Denkavit Internationaal BVs v Bundesampt für Finanzen* (C-283, 291 and 292/94) EU:C:1996:387; *Konle* EU:C:1999:271; *Rechberger* EU:C:1999:306.

[395] See above at 14-079.

[396] *Haim* EU:C:2000:357; *Brinkmann* EU:C:1998:429; *Konle* EU:C:1999:271.

[397] *Larsy II* EU:C:2001:368.

[398] *Larsy II* EU:C:2001:368.

[399] *Brinkmann* EU:C:1998:429 above.

implemented, were held to have severed the necessary link between the government's clear failure to implement the Directive by executive order and the harm suffered by the claimant. While the failure of the Danish Government to implement the Directive would have constituted a sufficiently serious breach of Union law, the tax authority's failure to correctly interpret the Directive was not a sufficiently serious breach, since its interpretation of the Directive was reasonable.

Mitigating loss

Given that it is a general principle common to the legal systems of the Member States that an injured party must show reasonable diligence in limiting the extent of loss or damage incurred, or risk having to bear the loss or damage himself, in relation to the damages liability of a Member State for breach of EU law, the CJEU has held that a national court may inquire whether the injured person showed reasonable diligence in seeking to avoid the loss or damage, or to limit its extent, and whether he availed himself in time of all the legal remedies available to him.[400] However, it is contrary to the principle of effectiveness to oblige an injured party to have recourse systematically to all the legal remedies available to it if that would give rise to excessive difficulties or could not be reasonably required.[401] The CJEU has held that the fact that an alternative remedy may give rise to an art.267 preliminary reference is not a reason for concluding that the remedy is not reasonable, given that the art.267 procedure is "an instrument of cooperation between the Court of Justice and the national courts".[402]

14-102

The reach of the Francovich principles

The *Francovich* principles are also relevant where the right to seek damages is provided in an EU legal instrument, unless the CJEU has provided guidance which is particular to the specific action.[403]

14-103

PRELIMINARY RULINGS

Evolution of the preliminary ruling procedure

Any national court or tribunal is empowered to refer questions on the interpretation of Union law to the CJEU. In relation to claims for judicial review in England and Wales, this means the Administrative Court, Court of Appeal and Supreme Court may, and in some situations must, refer questions of law to the CJEU. Prior to the Lisbon Treaty, the preliminary ruling procedure had three different forms: EC

14-104

---

[400] *Danske Slagterier* EU:C:2009:178 at [60]-[61].
[401] *Danske Slagterier* EU:C:2009:178 at [62].
[402] *Danske Slagterier* EU:C:2009:178 at [65]-[66]. See also *Energy Solutions* [2017] UKSC 34; [2017] 1 W.L.R. 1373 (on the principle of mitigation and alternative available remedies).
[403] See the position for public procurement law in *Combinatie Spijker Infrabouw-De Jonge Konstruktie and others* (C-568/08) EU:C:2010:751 9 December 2010 at [92]. The CJEU's statement in this case regarding the precise role of the *Francovich* principles is somewhat unclear: the *Francovich* principles must be complied with, but once this requirement is satisfied, it appears to be for the national legal order, subject to equivalence and effectiveness, to determine the criteria on the basis of which damage arising from an infringement of EU law must be determined and estimated. For recent consideration, see *Energy Solutions* [2017] UKSC 34; [2017] 1 W.L.R. 1373.

art.234 (now TFEU art.267), the "gold standard" procedure[404]; the restricted procedures of EC art.68 (repealed) applying to Visas, Asylum, Immigration and Other Policies Concerning the Free Movement of Persons; and TEU art.35 (repealed), applying in the context of Police and Judicial Co-operation in Criminal Matters. Pursuant to TEU art.35, the CJEU only had jurisdiction to give preliminary rulings if the Member State accepted the court's jurisdiction by making a declaration and only in relation to framework decisions, decisions and conventions. In accepting jurisdiction, the Member State could also limit the availability of preliminary rulings to final instance courts. Meanwhile, EC art.68 stated that a preliminary ruling could only be sought by a national court or tribunal against whose decisions there was no judicial remedy in national law.

14-105 Following the Lisbon Treaty, however, TFEU art.267 applies the preliminary ruling procedure to all questions of Union law, with the only restriction being preclusion of the CJEU from reviewing the validity or proportionality of operations carried out by the police or other law-enforcement services of a Member State, or the exercise of the responsibilities incumbent upon Member States with regard to the maintenance of law and order and the safeguarding of internal security.[405] Moreover, by way of response to concerns about the efficiency of preliminary ruling procedures,[406] TFEU art.267 also provides that if the question raised by the national court relates to a person in custody, the CJEU must act with the minimum of delay.[407] Overall though, the most important aspect of the Lisbon Treaty reform of the preliminary ruling procedure is that the availability of the procedure has been significantly extended.

Limitations to the jurisdiction of the court in a preliminary reference

14-106 The CJEU cannot, however, rule on the applicability or interpretation of provisions of purely national or international law[408]: this applies even where the national

---

[404] A. Arnull, "Me and My Shadow: The European Court of Justice and the Disintegration of European Union Law" (2008) 31 Fordham Intl L. J. 1174 at 1197.

[405] TFEU art.276. See also Note for Guidance on References by National Courts for Preliminary Rulings [2011] OJ C160/1 (issued by the CJEU) and *Practice Direction (Supreme Court: References to the Court of Justice of the European Communities)* [1999] 1 W.L.R. 260 (issued in England and Wales). See further D. Anderson and M. Demetriou, *References to the European Court*, 2nd edn (2002); M. Broberg and N. Fenger, *Preliminary References to the European Court of Justice*, 2nd edn (2014); B. Lang (ed), *Administrative Court: Practice and Procedure* (2006), Ch.14; A. Arnull, "The Law Lords and the European Union: Swimming with the Incoming Tide" (2010) 35 EL Rev 57; T. De la Mare and C. Donnelly, "Preliminary Rulings and EU Legal Integration: Evolution and Stasis" in P. Craig and G. de Búrca (eds), *The Evolution of EU Law* (2011), Ch.13; B. Broberg and N. Fenger, "Preliminary references as a right—but for whom? The extent to which preliminary references decisions can be subject to appeal" (2011) E.L. Rev. 276.

[406] See, e.g. *R. v Minister of Agriculture, Fisheries and Food, Ex p. Portman Agrochemicals Limited* [1994] 3 C.M.L.R. 18, where the delay was an explicit factor that both parties agreed was material in persuading the domestic court not to refer. The average length of time for a preliminary ruling to be heard in 2016 was 15 months and was the shortest for more than 30 years. The CJEU also received 460 requests for a preliminary ruling in 2016, a record in its history: see Court of Justice of the European Union, Press Release No.17/17, 17 February 2017.

[407] Such references are addressed by the urgent preliminary ruling procedure (PPU). There are 9 such references in 2016: *Annual Report of the Court of Justice of the European Union* (2016).

[408] *R. v Secretary of State for the Home Department Ex p. Abdulnasir Savas* (C-37/98) EU:C:2000:224 at [71]. This includes "mixed agreements" where both the EU and the Member States are parties: *Demirel* (12/86) EU:C:1987:400; *Dior* (C-300/98 and C-392/98) EU:C:2000:688; *Irène Bogiatzi* (C-301/08) EU:C:2009:649 (CJEU does not have jurisdiction to interpret the Warsaw Convention) at [24].

law has been introduced to implement EU obligations,[409] although the CJEU may accept a preliminary reference in a purely internal situation where domestic legislation adopts a solution which is consistent with Union law on the basis that accepting the reference will promote uniformity in the interpretation of Union law.[410] The preliminary ruling procedure has been described by the Grand Chamber as "keystone", which, by setting up dialogue between one court and another, specifically between the CJEU and the courts and tribunals of the Member States, has the object of securing uniform interpretation of EU law, which thereby serves "to ensure its consistency, its full effect and its autonomy as well as ultimately, the particular nature of the law established by the Treaties".[411] The initiation of this dialogue between the national court and the CJEU is not dependent on there being raised an issue of EU law before the national court.[412] The CJEU will also provide the national court with all the elements of interpretation of Union law which may be of use for deciding the case before it, whether or not that court has referred to them in the wording of its question,[413] and to this end, may reformulate the question referred.[414]

The CJEU does however have jurisdiction to interpret an international agreement concluded by the Union itself, which forms an integral part of the EU legal order.[415] The CJEU has no jurisdiction to apply Union law to particular facts in the main proceedings,[416] although it may rule on the legal consequences of given primary facts.[417] In this regard, it has been observed that, where a preliminary reference is made on a question of proportionality, for example, the CJEU often effectively determines the proportionality of the national measure in issue, by reformulating the question referred so as to ask whether the relevant provision of EU legislation, or general principles of EU law, preclude a measure of that kind, or alternatively whether the measure in question is compatible with the relevant provision of EU legislation or general principles. As the Supreme Court has noted, that practice reflects the fact that it can be difficult to draw a clear dividing line between the interpretation of the law and its application in concrete circumstances, and an answer which explains how the law applies in the circumstances of the case

14-107

---

[409] *Rey Soda v Cassa Conguaglio Zucchero* (23/75) EU:C:1975:142 at [50]-[51]; see also *Érsekcsanádi Mezogazdasági Zrt v Bács–Kiskun Megyei Kormányhivatal* (C-56/13) EU:C:2014:352 at [48]–[57] (a national requirement to pay compensation subject to an exclusion of compensation for loss of profits in an implementing measure where the EU measure did not provide for any compensation could not be challenged under the Charter and the CJEU did not have jurisdiction to rule on it).

[410] *Dzodzi* (297/88 and 197/89) EU:C:1990:360 at [37]; *Salzmann* (C-300/01) EU:C:2003:283 at [34]; *British American Tobacco Manufacturing BV v Hauptzollamt Krefeld* (C-222/01) EU:C:2004:250 at [40]-[41]. Indeed, the CJEU has on occasion justified providing a preliminary ruling in a seemingly internal situation on a tenuous basis: see, e.g. *Attanasio Group Srl v Comune di Cabognano* (C-384/08) EU:C:2010:133 at [24] ("it is far from inconceivable that companies established in Member States other than the Republic of Italy have been or are interested in selling motor fuel in the Republic of Italy").

[411] *Opinion 2/13* EU:C:2014:2454 at [176].

[412] *Secretary of State for Work and Pensions v Tolley* (C-430/15) EU:C:2017:74 at [30].

[413] *Productores de Música de España (Promusicae) v Telefónica de España SAU* (C-275/06) EU:C:2008:54 at [42].

[414] *Danqua* (C-429/15) EU:C:2016:789 at [36]-[37].

[415] *TNT Express Nederland BV v AXA Versicherung AG* (C-533/08) EU:C:2010:243 at [60]-[61] (the CJEU has jurisdiction to interpret international agreements concluded by the EU but does not have jurisdiction to interpret international agreements concluded between Member States and non-member countries. See also: *Raad van Bestuur van de Sociale Verzekeringsbank v Evans* (C-179/13) EU:C:2015:12 at [35].

[416] European Communities Act 1972 s.3(1); *Traunfellner* (C-421/01) EU:C:2003:549 at [21]-[24]; *British Horseracing Board Ltd v William Hill Organisation Ltd* [2005] EWCA Civ 863; [2006] E.C.C. 16 at [22] (Jacobs LJ).

[417] *Arsenal Football Club Plc v Reed* (C-206/01) EU:C:2002:651; [2003] Ch. 454.

before the referring court is likely to be helpful to it; this practice also avoids the risk that Member States may apply EU law differently in similar situations, or may be insufficiently stringent in their scrutiny of national measures.[418] It is also worth noting that preliminary rulings apply *ex tunc*.[419]

The referral discretion of the lower national courts

14-108   The enabling of national courts to refer is evidently a modulating factor heavily in the control of Member States and as the CJEU has observed repeatedly, this aspect of referral is "*solely* for the national court"[420] and "depends *entirely* on the national court's assessment as to whether a reference is appropriate and necessary".[421] The CJEU will not accept preliminary references where there is no legal dispute,[422] the factual and legal context has not been provided in sufficient detail for the CJEU to be able to give an answer,[423] or the question is not relevant to the dispute,[424] although any question referred will enjoy a presumption of relevance.[425] The fact that, following annulment of a decision, the EU institution may make a second decision with the same outcome for the applicant, does not, in itself, mean that a ruling will not be relevant for the main proceedings before the national court.[426] Whether the doctrine of precedent applies to rulings of the CJEU for preliminary references was unresolved for some time[427]; but it is now clear that rulings given by the CJEU bind all courts and administrative authorities in the

---

[418] *R. (on the application of Lumsdon) v Legal Services Board* [2015] UKSC 41; [2016] A.C. 697 (it was added that this may give rise to difficulties if the CJEU's understanding of the measure, or of the relevant facts, is different from that of the referring court and reference was made to *Revenue and Customs Commissioners v Aimia Coalition Loyalty UK Ltd* [2013] UKSC 15) at [30]).

[419] *Commission v Ireland* (C-455/08) EU:C:2009:809 at [39].

[420] *Pedro IV Servicios SL v Total España SA* (C-260/07) EU:C:2009:215 at [28] (emphasis added).

[421] *Kempter* EU:C:2008:78 at [42] (emphasis added). The CJEU has also emphasised that a national procedural rule pursuant to which legal rulings of a higher court bind the lower courts cannot call into question the discretion of the latter courts to request the court for a preliminary ruling where they have doubts as to the interpretation of EU law: *Križan v Slovenská inšpekcia životného prostredia* (C-416/10) EU:C:2013:8 at [67].

[422] The CJEU does not provide advisory opinions in the context of a preliminary reference: *Foglia v Novello* (244/80) EU:C:1981:302 at [18], [20]-[31] (it does of course provide "Advisory Opinions" pursuant to its jurisdiction under TFEU art.218(11)).

[423] *Telemarsicabruzzo SpA v Circostel* (C-320/90) EU:C:1993:26 at [5]; *United Pan-Europe Communications Belgium SA v Belgium* (C-250/06) EU:C:2007:783 at [19]-[21].

[424] *PreussenElektra v Schleswag* (C-379/98) EU:C:2001:160; *Mangold* EU:C:2005:709 at [36]-[38]; *Canal Satélite Digital* (C-390/99) EU:C:2002:34 at [18] and [19]; *Adolf Truley* (C-373/00) EU:C:2003:110 at [21] and [22]; *Schneider* EU:C:2004:73 at [21] and [22]; *Meilicke v ADV/ORGA FA Meyer AG* (C-83/91) EU:C:1992:332; *Société Régie Networks v Direction de Contrôle Fiscal Rhône-Alpes Bourgogne* (C-333/07) EU:C:2008:764 (Grand Chamber) at [46]-[52]. See also *Eckelkamp v Belgium* (C-11/07) EU:C:2008:489 at [28] (the court should only refuse to rule where it is "quite obvious" that the question is irrelevant to the main proceedings). Opinion of AG Kokott, *Rosa Garcia Blanco* (C-225/02) EU:C:2004:669 at [28]; *Lucchini SpA* EU:C:2007:434 at [44]; *Filipiak* (C-314/08) EU:C:2009:719 at [42]-[43]; *Caja de Ahorros y Monte de Piedad de Madrid* (C-484/08) EU:C:2010:309 at [19]. For an example of case in which the CJEU has found a reference inadmissible due to lack of relevance, see: *Minister voor Wonen, Wijken en Integratie v Woningstichting Sint Servatius* (C-567/07) EU:C:2009:593 at [42]-[47]. See also *Fish Legal v Information Commissioner* (C-279/12) EU:C:2013:853 at [30].

[425] *Société Régie Networks* EU:C:2008:764 (Grand Chamber) at [46]-[52] (irrelevance should be "obviously" apparent); *Fish Legal* EU:C:2013:853 at [30]; *Maatschap T van Oosterom en A van Oosterom-Boelhouwer v Staatssecretaris van Economische Zaken* (C-485/12) EU:C:2014:250 at [31]-[32] (presumption cannot be rebutted by fact that the facts remain contested).

[426] *Société Régie Networks* EU:C:2008:764 (Grand Chamber) at [53]-[61].

[427] D. Chalmers, G. Davies, and G. Monti, *European Union Law* (2014), p.170.

EU,[428] unless the national court seeks to obtain a fresh ruling from the CJEU in which the question can be reconsidered. Where a court, not under an obligation to make a preliminary reference, is faced with a TFEU art.267 issue the determination of which is critical to the court's final decision, the appropriate course is ordinarily to refer the issue to the CJEU unless the national court can with complete confidence resolve the issue itself.[429] In addition, however, when deciding whether to make a reference, "the court must observe some measure of self-restraint; lest the Court of Justice become overwhelmed".[430] A further justification for the exercise of caution can be found in the increasing familiarity of English courts with Union law.[431] In particular, the court should be cautious when asked to make a reference for a preliminary ruling in a case where it may turn out, after the facts have been established, that the point does not, in the event, arise.[432] Caution should also be exercised where there is an established body of case law; or where the question turns on a narrow point considered in the light of a very specific set of facts and the ruling is unlikely to have any application beyond the instant case.[433] By contrast, it will be appropriate to make a reference "where the question is one of general importance and where the ruling is likely to promote the uniform application of the law throughout the European Union".[434] Although it is unusual for a reference for a preliminary ruling to be made at the permission stage in judicial review proceedings, and before a fully reasoned judgment of an English court, such a reference may be made where it is both convenient and necessary to do so.[435] A second reference in the same case on the same issue has also been sought where the meaning of the CJEU's first preliminary ruling was "not beyond reasonable argument".[436]

Referral obligation of national courts of last instance

Pursuant to TFEU art.267 it would normally be compulsory for the Supreme Court as the final court of appeal on the judicial review claim to make a reference **14-109**

---

[428] *Kühne & Heitz* EU:C:2004:17 at [21]-[27].

[429] *R. v International Stock Exchange of the United Kingdom and the Republic of Ireland Ltd Ex p. Else Ltd* [1993] Q.B. 534 at 545 (Sir Thomas Bingham MR).

[430] *Prudential Assurance Co Ltd v Prudential Insurance Co of America (No.1)* [2003] EWCA Civ 327; [2003] 1 W.L.R. 2295 at [50] (Chadwick LJ, declining to make a reference where determination of the point would not have been decisive); *Trinity Mirror Plc (formerly Mirror Group Newspapers Ltd) v Customs and Excise Commissioners* [2001] EWCA Civ 65; [2001] S.T.C. 192 at [51]–[55]; *Professional Contractors Group v Commissioners for Inland Revenue* [2001] EWCA Civ 1945; [2002] S.T.C. 165 at [91] (Walker LJ).

[431] *Professional Contractors' Group* [2001] EWCA Civ 1945; [2002] S.T.C. 165 at [91]; *Aimia Coalition Loyalty UK* [2013] UKSC 15 (declining to follow the CJEU's ruling in a preliminary reference, or make a further preliminary reference, where the CJEU had ruled on arguments not made by the parties, and due to the UK court's understanding of the established EU principle and greater understanding of the facts and arguments made).

[432] *Prudential Assurance* [2003] 1 W.L.R. 2295 at [50].

[433] *Wiener v SI GmbH v Hauptzollamt Emmerich* (C-338/95) EU:C:1997:352, Opinion of AG Jacobs at [20]; *Trinity Mirror* [2001] EWCA Civ 65; [2001] S.T.C. 192 at [52].

[434] *Wiener* EU:C:1997:352 at [20].

[435] *R. (on the application of Mellor) v Secretary of State for Communities and Local Government* [2008] EWCA Civ 213; [2009] Env. L.R. D1 (the unusual circumstances of the case justified making a reference at the permission stage).

[436] *O'Byrne v Aventis Pasteur MSD Ltd* [2008] UKHL 34; [2008] 4 All E.R. 881 at [24]. See also *Test Claimants* [2010] EWCA Civ 103; [2010] S.T.C. 1251 at [43]. There has been some gentle criticism of the CJEU by the Supreme Court. In *Aimia Coalition Loyalty UK* [2013] UKSC 15 at [87], Lord Hope observed that a judgment, in respect of which the CJEU had not sought an opinion from the Advocate General before it proceeded to judgment, lacked the depth of reasoning which a judgment informed by an opinion would have provided, albeit that his Lordship noted that this was quite rare.

for a preliminary ruling. The fact that leave must be sought to bring an appeal before the Supreme Court means that if a question arises as to the interpretation or validity of a rule of Union law, TFEU art.267 imposes an obligation on the House to refer the question to the CJEU either at the stage of the examination of the admissibility of the appeal or at a later stage.[437] However, where the question of Union law is "so obvious as to leave no scope for any reasonable doubt as to the manner in which the question raised is to be resolved",[438] a reference will not be necessary. This doctrine is referred to as the acte clair doctrine and it only applies to courts of last instance, within the meaning of TFEU art.267(3). The conditions to satisfy the doctrine are extremely stringent,[439] although the practice of national courts has often been to misapply or even disregard them.[440] The CJEU has been invited to relax the requirements of the acte clair doctrine, but has declined to do so.[441] Indeed, given that a failure to refer a question which is not acte clair may give rise to a damages action, the CJEU clearly intends the referral obligation to regarded as strict by national supreme courts.[442] The Supreme Court has emphasised that the role of the CJEU is one of interpretation and the national court's is one of application.[443]

14-110   It will always be compulsory for a national court to seek a preliminary ruling where it is intending to question the validity of an EU act (for example a regula-

---

[437] *Lyckeskog* (C-99/00) EU:C:2002:329 at [18]. This confirmed the "concrete" understanding of TFEU art.267 which understood a reference to be obligatory for the highest court in the case; as opposed to the "abstract" understanding of TFEU art.267 which considered a reference obligatory for only the highest court in the land. See also *Križan* EU:C:2013:8 at [62] (a national court is a court against whose decisions there is no judicial remedy under national law, within the meaning of TFEU art.267(3) and which is thus required to request a preliminary ruling, even where national law provides for the possibility of bringing before the constitutional court of the Member State concerned an action against its decisions limited to an examination of a potential infringement of the rights and freedoms guaranteed by the national constitution or by an international agreement).

[438] *CILFIT Srl v Ministry of Health* (283/81) EU:C:1982:335 at [16].

[439] In determining whether the Union law point is so obvious as to leave no scope for reasonable doubt, it is also necessary for the national court to consider "the characteristic features of [Union] law and the particular difficulties to which its interpretation gives rise", including (a) the need to compare the different language versions of [Union] legislation, each of which is equally authentic; (b) the use of terminology which is peculiar to Union law, or which has a different meaning in Union law from its meaning in the law of the various Member States; and (c) the need to place every provision of Union law in its context and to interpret it in the light of the provisions of Union law as a whole, regard being had to the objectives of Union law and to its state of evolution at the date on which the provision in question is to be applied: see *CILFIT* EU:C:1982:335 at [17]-[20]; M. Broberg, "Acte Clair Revisited: Adapting the Acte Clair Criteria to the Demands of the Times" (2008) 45 C.M.L. Rev. 1383.

[440] D. Chalmers, G. Davies, and G. Monti, *European Union Law* (2014), p.177; Anderson and Demetriou, *References to the European Court* (2002) at paras 6-051–6-058; the Supreme Court does not generally consider each of the *CILFIT* criteria but asks if the answer is "clear beyond the bounds of reasonable argument": *R. (on the application of Countryside Alliance) v Attorney General* [2007] UKHL 52 at [32]; [2009] 1 A.C. 719 at [31]; *O'Byrne* [2008] UKHL 34; [2008] 4 All E.R. 881 at [23]-[24]. See also *Buckinghamshire* [2014] UKSC 3; [2014] P.T.S.R. 182 at [53], [117], [128]; *Aimia Coalition Loyalty UK* [2013] UKSC 15.

[441] *Lyckeskog* (C-99/00) EU:C:2002:329 at [9], [20]-[21].

[442] *Köbler* EU:C:2003:513. For a strict application of the *CILFIT* criteria, in which it was held that where a question of Union law had given rise to conflicting decisions in the lower courts of that Member State and the issue was one which frequently gave rise to issues of interpretation in Member States, the court of final instance had an obligation to make a reference, see *João Filipe Ferreira da Silva e Brito v Portugal* (C-160/14) EU:C:2015:565. However, it does not necessarily suffice to trigger the obligation to make a reference if a lower court has made a reference to the CJEU in a similar case with the same legal issue, if the court of last instance regards the issue as acte clair: *X v Inspecteur van Rijksbelastingdienst* (C-72/14) EU:C:2015:564.

[443] *Bloomsbury International Ltd v Department for Environment, Food and Rural Affairs* [2011] UKSC 25; [2011] 1 W.L.R. 1546 at [51].

tion or directive).[444] Indeed, the CJEU has stated that "[a]ll national courts or tribunals *must* therefore refer a question to the court when they have doubts about the validity of a such an act, stating the reasons for which they consider that that act may be invalid".[445] In such cases, the caution of self-restraint noted above does not apply.[446]

DIRECT ACTIONS IN THE CJEU AND GENERAL COURT

The CJEU and General Court have their own powers to adjudicate directly on challenges to the legal validity of legal instruments, acts and omissions of the EU institutions, but not national measures.[447] Detailed consideration of the work of the CJEU and General Court in determining actions made directly to them fall outside the scope of this book, except insofar as it has an impact on the manner in which the Administrative Court in England and Wales exercises its own function of judicial review. Two main types of proceedings are relevant.   **14-111**

Enforcement actions

The Commission, or under certain conditions a Member State, may bring an action directly before the CJEU against a Member State for failure of the latter to fulfil an obligation under the EU Treaties.[448] The CJEU has no power to adjudicate on complaints from individuals against Member States.[449] If the CJEU finds that the defendant Member State has infringed Union law, it must take the necessary measures to comply with the judgment of the CJEU. The CJEU may impose a financial penalty on a Member State. Claims for judicial review by a person against a public authority, alleging breach of Union law, are sometimes conducted at the same time as the Commission brings an enforcement action before the CJEU. Thus, in relation to provisions of the Merchant Shipping Act 1988, Spanish trawler owners commenced judicial review against the Secretary of State for Transport in the High Court and the Commission brought proceedings against the United Kingdom in the CJEU.[450] Attempts of the United Kingdom Government to comply with a ruling of the CJEU in enforcement proceedings may themselves be subject to judicial review[451] though the Commission also monitors compliance by Member States.   **14-112**

---

[444] See 14-059.
[445] CJEU emphasis in Recommendations to national courts and tribunals in relation to the initiation of preliminary ruling proceedings [2012] OJ C 338/1 para.16.
[446] *Wiener* EU:C:1997:352, Opinion of AG Jacobs at [25]; *R. (on the application of Unitymark Ltd) v Secretary of State for the Environment, Food and Rural Affairs* [2003] EWHC 2748 (Admin); [2004] Eu. L.R. 338 at [28]-[31] (Evans-Lombe J).
[447] TEU art.19 provides that the CJEU shall rule on all matters for which it has been given jurisdiction under the Treaties. Notable matters that are outside its jurisdiction include (with some exceptions) provisions relating to common foreign and security policy (TFEU art.275) and certain police and law-enforcement activities (TFEU art.276).
[448] TFEU arts 258–260.
[449] It is, however, open to an aggrieved person to lodge a complaint with the Commission inviting the Commission to institute proceedings under TFEU art.258; but the individual cannot compel the Commission to institute such proceedings and cannot challenge any failure or refusal by the Commission.
[450] *Commission v United Kingdom* (C-246/89) EU:C:1991:375.
[451] *R. v Secretary of State for the Environment Ex p. Friends of the Earth Ltd* (1995) 7 Admin. L.R. 793.

Review of legality

14-113   One of the main functions of the CJEU and General Court is to review the legality of secondary legislation and actions[452] and failures to act[453] of the EU institutions. The courts may annul a measure adopted by an EU institution or require an EU institution to adopt a measure and acts open to challenge are any measures adopted by the institutions, whatever their form, which are intended to have legal effects.[454] Where the applicant in such an action is an institution of the EU or a Member State, the action is dealt with by the CJEU. The CJEU and General Court do not, however, have jurisdiction, when exercising judicial review of legality under TFEU art.263, to issue declaratory judgments or directions, even where they concern the manner in which their judgments are to be complied with.[455]

14-114   Where the applicant is an individual, business enterprise or pressure group (known as non-privileged applicants) the General Court also has jurisdiction.[456] As is well-known, pursuant to EC art.230, non-privileged applicants were entitled to bring annulment proceedings provided they were "directly and individually concerned" by the relevant EU measure. The CJEU persisted with a restrictive test for the requirement of "individual concern"—requiring a non-addressee to demonstrate membership of a "closed category", i.e. a fixed group that could be identified before the measure entered into force[457]—in spite of calls to relax the requirements from both the General Court and Advocates General.[458]

14-115   The standing requirements for a non-privileged applicant were relaxed slightly by the Lisbon Treaty but are still strict[459]: TFEU art.263 provides that a non-privileged applicant can challenge the validity of decisions addressed to that person[460]; and where the decision is not addressed directly to the particular applicant, the applicant will have standing against an act that is "of direct and individual concern" to that person and against a regulatory act which is "of direct concern" to that person and which "does not entail implementing measures".[461] Aside from the question of standing, TFEU art.263 also widened the range of

---

[452] TFEU art.263.

[453] TFEU art.265. See also *Commission v Germany* (C-95/12) EU:C:2013:676 (dismissal of an action brought by the Commission for a failure to comply with a previous judgment of the CJEU finding a failure to fulfil obligations).

[454] *Commission v Council (CITES)* (C-370/07) EU:C:2009:590 at [42]. For examples of annulment actions, see *Inuit Tapiriit Kanatami* EU:C:2013:625 and *Telefónica v Commission* (C-274/12 P) EU:C:2013:852. See also *Mallis and Malli v Commission and ECB* (C-105/15 P to C-109/15P) EU:C:2016:702 (a statement of the Eurogroup, which remains a forum for discussion between ministers of the Member States whose currency is the euro, cannot be regarded as a measure intended to produce legal effects with respect to third parties, and can therefore not be annulled under TFEU art.263).

[455] *Omya AG v Commission* (T-145/06) EU:T:2009:27 at [23].

[456] TFEU art.256(1).

[457] *Plaumann v Commission* (25/62) EU:C:1963:17.

[458] *Jégo-Quéré v Commission* (T-177/01) EU:T:2002:112 (CFI proposed that the "individual concern" requirement would be satisfied by an individual if the measure "affects his legal position, in a manner which is both definite and immediate, by restricting his rights or by imposing obligations on him"); cf. response of CJEU in *Commission v Jégo-Quéré* (C-263/02 P) EU:C:2004:210 at [45]; and *Unión de Pequeños Agricultores v Council* (C-50/00 P) EU:C:2002:462.

[459] For discussion, see, S. Peers and M. Costa, "Judicial review of EU acts after the Treaty of Lisbon" (2012) 8 E.C.L. Rev. 82; A. Kornezov, "Locus standi of Private Parties in Actions for Annulment: Has the Gap been Closed?" [2014] 73(1) C.L.J. 25.

[460] For the definition of a "decision", see 14-038.

[461] TFEU art.263. It was held in *Telefónica v Commission* (C-274/12 P) EU:C:2013:852 at [30]–[31] that the question of whether a regulatory act entails "implementing measures" must be assessed by reference to the position of the person pleading the right to bring proceedings and that it is irrelevant whether the act in question entails implementing measures with regard to other persons.

institutions susceptible to judicial review from that found in EC art.230, adding the European Council and "bodies, offices or agencies of the Union" and added that "legislative acts" to the list of instruments which could be reviewed.

The impact of the revised test has been explored.[462] It has been held that, given that the purpose of the redrafting of TFEU art.263 was "opening up the conditions for bringing direct actions", the concept of "direct concern" could not be subject to a more restrictive interpretation than the notion of direct concern as it appeared in EC art.230.[463] In terms of the new aspects of TFEU art.263, the concept of a "regulatory act" has been interpreted to refer to all acts of general application apart from legislative acts, with the latter of course only being capable of challenge if they are of direct and individual concern.[464] The CJEU also held that the term "regulatory act" does not extend to legislative acts.[465] It has been observed that this categorisation is potentially fraught, particularly if consideration is given to whether, in substance, an individual measure is of "general application".[466] It has also been held that art.47 of the Charter is not intended to change the system of judicial review set down by the EU Treaties, and particularly, the rules relating to the admissibility of direct actions.[467]

14-116

The time limit for bringing actions is only two months. The grounds upon which actions may be brought are "lack of competence, infringement of an essential procedural requirement, infringement of the Treaties or of any rule of law relating to their application, or misuse of powers".[468] A person with standing to challenge the legality of a decision or regulation, but who fails to do so within the two-month time limit, is precluded from questioning the validity of that decision before a national court.[469]

14-117

Furthermore, reference should be made exclusively to the subject matter of the action, and where the applicant seeks only the partial annulment of an act, it is solely the implementing measures which that part of the act entails that must, as the case may be, be taken into consideration. For an example of the CJEU being quick to conclude that a measure entailed "implementing measures" which ought to be challenged at national level, see: *T&L Sugars Ltd v Sidul Açúcares, Unipessoal Lda* (C-456/13 P), EU:C:2015:284 (the court disagreeing with the Advocate General and observing that the "allegedly mechanical nature of the measures taken at national level" did not undermine the conclusion that they were implementing measures: at [41]). Thus, even non-substantive, administrative implementing measures appear to be capable of falling within the scope of the concept of "implementing measure", a conclusion which the Advocate General in *T&L Sugars* argued against "if the objective of relaxing the admissibility conditions for natural and legal persons in connection with non-legislative regulatory acts is not to be wholly frustrated" (at [31]). The CJEU's application of the "direct concern" test was challenged unsuccessfully by reference to art.47 in *Ackermann Saatzucht v Parliament* (C-408/15 P and C-409/15P) EU:C:2016:893.

[462] *Inuit Tapiriit Kanatami* EU:C:2013:625; *Telefónica v Commission* (C-274/12 P) EU:C:2013:852.

[463] *Microban International Limited* (T-262/10) EU:T:2011:623 [2012] All E.R. (EC) 595 at [32].

[464] *Inuit Tapiriit Kanatami* EU:C:2013:625 at [58]–[60].

[465] *Inuit Tapiriit Kanatami* EU:C:2013:625 at [60]. The CJEU rejected an argument made in the case for the requirement for "direct and individual concern" to be replaced with a criterion of "substantial adverse effect": [69]–[71]. The case is also notable for its heavy reliance on the *travaux preparatoires* relating to Article III-365(4) of the proposed Treaty establishing a Constitution for Europe, the content of which was reproduced in identical terms in TFEU art.263(4).

[466] A. Albors-Llorens, "Sealing the fate of private parties in annulment proceedings? The General Court and the new standing test in article 263(4) TFEU" (2012) 71 C.L.J. 52. See also A. Kornezov, "Shaping the new architecture of the EU system of judicial remedies: comment on Inuit" (2014) 39 E.L. Rev. 251.

[467] *Ackermann Saatzucht* EU:C:2016:893 at [49].

[468] TFEU art.263.

[469] *TWD Textilwerke Deggendorf GmbH v Germany* (C-188/92) EU:C:1994:90; *Wiljo NV v Belgium* (C-178/95) EU:C:1997:46 [1997] All E.R. (E.C.) 226; *Lucchini SpA* EU:C:2007:434 at [54]-[56]; *A v Minister van Buitenlandse Zaken* (C-158/14) EU:C:2017:202 at [63] and [70]. However, where a person would not "undoubtedly" have satisfied the "individual concern" requirement, it will be pos-

14-118   Union measures, even though irregular, are in principle presumed to be lawful and to produce legal effects until they are declared void.[470] By way of exception to that principle, measures tainted by an irregularity the gravity of which is so obvious that it cannot be tolerated by the Union legal order must be treated as having no legal effect, even provisional, and must be regarded as legally non-existent.[471] The CJEU has explained that the purpose of this exception is to maintain a balance between two fundamental, but sometimes conflicting, requirements with which a legal order must comply, namely, stability of legal relations and respect for legality. The gravity of the consequences attaching to a finding that a measure of a Union institution is non-existent means that, for reasons of legal certainty, such a finding may be reserved for quite extreme situations.[472] Where a measure has been annulled for formal or procedural defects, the institution is entitled to adopt an identical measure afresh, having observed the formal and procedural requirements, and to give the new measure retroactive effect, if that is essential to the attainment of the public-interest objective pursued and if the legitimate expectations of the persons concerned are protected.[473]

GROUNDS OF JUDICIAL REVIEW AGAINST UNION MEASURES: OVERVIEW

14-119   Union law provides grounds for challenging both the legality of Union measures and of national measures. The next two sections of the Chapter consider each of these situations in turn. As we have already noted, Union measures may be challenged either directly in the CJEU and General Court[474] or (with restrictions) in proceedings before a national court.[475] The grounds of review are broadly the same in each situation and include the following:

(i)   manifest error of assessment
(ii)   lack of adequate reasoning;
(iii) failure to state, or state correctly, the provisions of the treaty under which the measure was adopted;
(iv)   failure to hear a person affected before adopting the measure;
(v)   failure to consult other bodies where consultation is required;
(vi)   breach of the general principles of law developed by the European Court including proportionality, non-discrimination, respect for fundamental rights, legal certainty, and protection of legitimate expectations.

14-120   The CJEU has also held that even where a Union institution possesses broad

---

sible for that person to plead the illegality of the Union provisions in proceedings in national courts and seek a reference for a preliminary ruling under TFEU art.267: *Textilwerke* EU:C:1994:90; see also *Roquette Frères v Ministre de l'Agriculture, de l'Alimentation, de la Pêche et de la Ruralité* (C-441/05) EU:C:2007:150 at [48] and *Afton Chemical Ltd v Secretary of State for Transport* (C-343/09) EU:C:2010:419 at [25]; *Pringle* (C-370/12) (Grand Chamber) at [38]-[43].

[470] *People's Mojahedin Organization of Iran v Council* (T-256/07) EU:T:2008:461 at [55].

[471] *People's Mojahedin Organization of Iran* EU:T:2008:461 at [56]; *Commission v Kadi* EU:C:2013:518.

[472] *People's Mojahedin Organization of Iran* EU:T:2008:461 at [57]. See, e.g. *Commission v Kadi* EU:C:2013:518 at [130] (finding that if the application of a contested asset-freezing measure has grounding in at least one valid reason, the decision will not be annulled, notwithstanding that the same cannot be said of other reasons).

[473] *People's Mojahedin Organization of Iran* EU:T:2008:461 at [65].

[474] See 14-111.

[475] See 14-110.

discretion, the court is able to review the institution's interpretation of the relevant facts, and must not only establish whether the evidence relied on is factually accurate, reliable and consistent, but must also ascertain whether the evidence contains all the relevant information to be taken into account to assess the situation and whether it is capable of substantiating the conclusions drawn from it.[476]

The provisions of an international agreement to which the Union is a party may **14-121** be relied upon in support of an action for annulment of an act of secondary Union legislation or an exception based on the illegality of such an act. However, this is only where the nature and the broad logic of that agreement do not preclude it and where the provisions appear, as to their content, to be unconditional and sufficiently precise.[477] There are two very specific exceptions to this position: first, where the Union intended to implement a particular obligation assumed in the context of agreements concluded in the context of the World Trade Organisation, and second, where the Union act sought to be annulled explicitly refers to the specific provisions of the international agreements.[478]

The CJEU has also made it clear that, for example, measures adopted by the **14-122** Union for national security or anti-terrorism objectives will not be considered non-justiciable and they will not escape all review by the Union judicature.[479] Likewise, Union measures adopted to give effect to UN measures will not be considered, for that reason, to be non-reviewable by the CJEU or General Court.[480]

The grounds of review are thus wider than those under English law. A ground of **14-123** challenge recognised under English law will probably be available under Union law; while some grounds available in Union law, for example lack of adequate reasoning, are not yet generally available under English law.[481] In any case in which the validity of a Union measure is in issue in the English courts, the court may have to consider whether the question of validity should be referred to the CJEU under TFEU art.267. The English court will thus have to give preliminary consideration to a challenge based on any of the grounds indicated above, in order to decide whether a reference is justified.

---

[476] *People's Mojahedin Organization of Iran* EU:T:2008:461 at [138]; *Spain v Commission* (C-525/04 P) EU:C:2007:698 at [57]; see also *Chalkor AE Epexergasias Metallon v Commission* (C-386/10 P) EU:C:2011:815 at [54].

[477] *Vereniging Milieudefensie* EU:C:2015:4 at [55] (holding that art.9(3) of the Aarhus Convention did not contain any unconstitutional and sufficiently precise obligation capable of directly regulating the legal position of individuals); see also *Council of the European Union v Stichting Natuur en Milieu* (C-404/12 P) EU:C:2015:5.

[478] *Vereniging Milieudefensie* EU:C:2015:4 at [56]–[57] (Regulation 1367/2006, art.10(1) did not implement specific obligations of art.9(3) of the Aarhus Convention).

[479] *Kadi* EU:C:2008:461 (Grand Chamber) at [343]; *Commission v Kadi* EU:C:2013:518 at [97].

[480] *Kadi* EU:C:2008:461 (Grand Chamber) at [281]-[292] (see the Opinion of AG Maduro, noting, at [28], that there was no basis in the TFEU from which it "could logically follow that measures taken for the implementation of Security Council resolutions have supraconstitutional status and are hence accorded immunity from judicial review").

[481] See 7-089.

General principles of law[482]

14-124   The general principles of Union law constitute a considerable limitation on the policy-making powers of the EU institutions.[483] They also govern the interpretation of provisions of Union law and on occasion the CJEU may adopt a strained interpretation of a measure in order to avoid conflict with one of the general principles.[484] Most of the principles are wholly or mainly the product of judicial development, although the principle of proportionality is expressly recognised in the TEU as a constitutional principle of the Union legal order in TEU art.5. Similarly, fundamental rights were first recognised by the CJEU's case law, then endorsed by declarations of the institutions and finally written into the fundamental law of the EU.[485] As will be seen, the CJEU's jurisprudence on general principles is constantly evolving, with new principles over time acquiring the status of a "general principle".[486]

Equal treatment and non-discrimination

14-125   Although certain provisions of the TFEU provide for the principle of equal treatment with regard to specific matters,[487] the CJEU has held that the principle of equality is a general principle of law of which those provisions are merely specific expressions and which precludes comparable situations from being treated differently unless the difference in treatment is objectively justified.[488] It also prohibits different situations from being treated in the same way unless such treatment is

---

[482] See T. Tridimas, *The General Principles of EU Law* (2006); J. Usher, *General Principles of EC Law in a Process of Development* (1998); H. Nehl, *Principles of Administrative Procedure in EC Law* (1999); K. Lenaerts and J. Gittierez-Fons, "The Constitutional Allocation of Powers and General Principles of EU Law" (2010) 47 C.M.L. Rev. 1629.

[483] See, e.g. *Cousin* (162/82) EU:C:1983:93 (CJEU invalidated a Regulation which provided substantially more severe criteria for the determination of the origin of cotton yarn than for the determination of the origin of cloth and fabrics).

[484] *Deuka v EVGF* (78/74) EU:C:1975:44 (legitimate expectations); *Rechnungshof v österreichischer Rundfunk* (C-465/00, C-138/01 & C-139/01) EU:C:2003:294 at [68]-[72], [91] (fundamental rights); *Vlaams Gewest v Commission* (T-214/95) EU:T:1998:77 (General Court held that guidelines adopted by the Commission had to be applied in accordance with the principle of equal treatment with the implication that like cases, as defined in the guidelines, had to be treated alike).

[485] TEU art.6.

[486] See 14-048. Contrast *Audiolux SA v Groupe Bruxelles Lambert SA (GBL)* (C-101/08) EU:C:2009:626 (CJEU refusal to accept that there is a general principle of equal treatment of minority shareholders).

[487] See, e.g. TFEU art.18 (prohibition of discrimination on the grounds of nationality); TFEU art.40(2) (prohibition of discrimination between producers and consumers in the common agricultural policy); TFEU art.157 (equal pay for equal work for men and women); TFEU art.19 (conferring positive competence on the Union to take action to combat discrimination based on sex, racial or ethnic origin, religion or belief, disability, age or sexual orientation). For a case on equality in the context of sexual orientation (in which TFEU art.19 was ignored), see *Leger v Ministre des Affaires sociales, de la Sante et des Droits des femmes* (C-528/13) EU:C:2015:288 [2015] All E.R. (EC) 755. For an interesting holding that obesity may, where it hinders the full and effective participation of some persons in professional life on a long-term basis, constitute a disability, see: *Fag og Arbejde v Kommunernes Landsforening (KL)* (C-354/13) EU:C:2014:2463.

[488] See, e.g. *Uberschar v Bundesversichorungsanstalt fur Angestellte* (810/79) EU:C:1980:228 at [16]; *Ruckdeschel v Hauptzollamt Hamburg St Annen* (117/76 and 16/77) EU:C:1977:160 at [7]; *Sotgiu v Deutsche Bundespost* EU:C:1974:13 at [11]; *Bela-Mühle Josef Bergman v Grows-Farm* (114/76) EU:C:1977:116 (the effect of a policy making animal feed producers use skimmed-milk powder was to increase the price of animal feed and this harmed all livestock breeders and the benefits of the policy were felt only by dairy farmers; thus the policy operated in a discriminatory manner between different categories of farmers); and *Mangold* EU:C:2005:709 at [75] (CJEU asserted that the principle of non-discrimination on grounds of age must be regarded as a general principle of Union

objectively justified.[489] Whether objective justification exists depends on the particular circumstances of each case, account being taken of the objectives of the measure in question. In general, the CJEU has interpreted the notion of "objective justification" broadly.[490]

In order to determine whether two products or two undertakings are in a comparable situation, the CJEU may have recourse to the criterion of competition. Thus, in the case of products, the CJEU will consider whether the one can be substituted for the other in the specific use to which the latter is traditionally put. Where two products are interchangeable they are in a comparable competitive position and, in principle, should be treated in the same manner.[491] By contrast, products which have different applications are not in a comparable situation and a difference in their treatment will not normally amount to prohibited discrimination.[492] In the case of undertakings, the CJEU may have regard to their production or to their legal structure[493] with a view to determining whether their competitive positions are comparable. The CJEU has held that differences in treatment which are based on objective differences arising from the underlying economic situations of Member States cannot be considered discriminatory.[494]

14-126

Proportionality

Action taken by the EU must be proportionate to its objectives.[495] It requires, in particular, that "the individual should not have his freedom of action limited beyond

14-127

---

law). On age discrimination, see also *R. (on the application of The Incorporated Trustees of the National Council on Ageing (Age Concern England)) v Secretary of State for Business, Enterprise and Regulatory Reform* (C-388/07) EU:C:2009:128; *Palacios* EU:C:2007:106; *Seldon v Clarkson Wright, Jakes (A Partnership)* [2012] UKSC 16; [2012] 3 All E.R. 1301 at [32] et seq. See also *Römer* (C-147/08) EU:C:2010:425 [2011] All E.R. (D) 212 [60]-[61] (Advocate General Jääskinen urged the CJEU to make the prohibition of discrimination on grounds of sexual orientation a general principle of EU Law. The court held, however, that the complaint relating to discrimination on grounds of sexual orientation did not fall within the scope of Union law: [63]-[64]).

[489] *Sermide v Cassa Conguaglio Zucchero* (106/83) EU:C:1984:394 at [28]; *R. (on the application of Novartis Pharmaceuticals UK Ltd) v Licensing Authority* (C-106/01) EU:C:2004:245 at [69]; *Poland v Council* (C-273/04) EU:C:2007:622 (Grand Chamber) at [87]-[89] (Poland's complaint about discrimination because of difference in treatment between old and new Member States in the context of the Common Agricultural Policy was rejected on the basis that the agricultural situation in the new Member States was "radically different" from that in the old Member States).

[490] For example, it has been held that the discrimination which arises from the fact that a Council Regulation grants aid for sugar in transit between two approved warehouses situated in a single Member State but refuses such aid for sugar in transit between two approved warehouses situated in different Member States is objectively justified on the ground of the difference in the supervisory measures required: *Wagner* (8/82) EU:C:1983:41.

[491] See, e.g. *Ruckdesche* EU:C:1977:160; *Moulins Pont-a-Mousson v Office Interprofessionnel des Cereales* (124/76 and 20/77) EU:C:1977:161.

[492] See, e.g. *Koninklijke Scholten-Honig v Hoofdproduktschap voor Akkerbouwprodukten* (125/77) EU:C:1978:187 at [30]-[31]; *Maizena GmbH v Hauptzollamt Krefeld* (C-18/89) EU:C:1990:264.

[493] *Klockner v High Authority* (17 and 20/61) EU:C:1962:30 at 345; *Moccia Irme SpA v Commission* (C-280/99) EU:C:2001:348 at [189]-[210].

[494] *Eridania v Minister for Agriculture and Forestry* (230/78) EU:C:1979:216 at [19]; *Deschamps v Ofival* (C-181, C-182 and C-218/88) EU:C:1989:642.

[495] The principle was initiated in 19th-century Prussia and developed in German law as *Verhältnismäs- sigkeit*, a principle which in the case law of the *Bundesverfassungsgericht* (Federal Constitutional Court) has been held to underlie certain provisions of the German Grundgesetz (Basic Law). cf. the scope of the principle in areas of English law where Union law does not apply; J. Schwarze, *European Administrative Law* (2006), Ch.5; J. Jowell and A. Lester, "Proportionality: Neither Novel nor Dangerous" in J. Jowell and D. Oliver (eds), *New Directions in Judicial Review* (1988), p.51; G. de Búrca, "The Principle of Proportionality and its Application in EC Law" (1993) 13 Y.E.L. 105; T. Harbo, "The function of the proportionality principle in EU law" (2010) 16 E.L.J. 158-185.

the degree necessary in the public interest to attain the purpose of the measure".[496] The assessment of proportionality is carried out by what we have described in Chapter 11 as a structured test, involving a series of stepped questions. Thus, in order to establish whether a provision of Union law is consonant with the principle of proportionality, it is necessary to establish, first, whether the means it employs to achieve the aim correspond to the importance of the aim and, secondly, whether they are necessary for its achievement.[497] In other words, there is a test of suitability and a test of necessity.[498] Where there is a choice between several appropriate measures, recourse must be had to the least onerous, and the disadvantages caused must not be disproportionate to the aims pursued.[499] It has been observed, in the context of review of national measures for compliance with the principle of proportionality, that:

---

[496] *Internationale Handelsgesellschaft v Einfuhr-und Vorratsstelle Getreide* (11/70) EU:C:1970:100 at 1147 (AG de Lamothe); *Omya* EU:T:2009:27 at [34] (a power of the Commission to request information from an undertaking should not constitute a burden on that undertaking which was disproportionate to the requirements of the inquiry). See also: *Federation internationale de football association (FIFA) v Commission* (T-68/08) EU:T:2011:44 at [143].

[497] See *R. v Ministry of Agriculture, Fisheries and Food* (C-331/88) EU:C:1990:391 at [13]; *Fromancais v Forma* (66/82) EU:C:1983:42 at [8]; *Man (Sugar) v IBAP* (181/84) EU:C:1985:359; *Atalanta v Produktschap voor Vee en Vless* (240/78) EU:C:1979:160; cf. *Cereol Italia v Azienda Agricola Castello* (C-104/94) EU:C:1995:313. In domestic case law, the test to be applied has been that identified in *Tesco Plc v Competition Commission* [2009] CAT 6 at [137] (holding that the measure: "(1) must be effective to achieve the legitimate aim in question (appropriate), (2) must be no more onerous than is required to achieve that aim (necessary), (3) must be the least onerous, if there is a choice of equally effective measures, and (4) in any event must not produce adverse effects which are disproportionate to the aim pursued"); see also *R. (on the application of Mabanaft) v Secretary of State for Energy and Climate Change* [2009] EWCA Civ 224 at [47]. Contrast *R. (on the application of Sinclair Collis Limited) v Secretary of State for Health* [2011] EWCA Civ 437; [2012] Q.B. 394, in which the majority considered whether the measures challenged were "manifestly inappropriate". The approach of the majority does not appear to be in accordance with the test for proportionality as generally applied in EU jurisprudence, a point made by Laws LJ in the minority, and has been described by the Supreme Court as "open to criticism" and as not providing "reliable guidance" where at issue is a derogation from a Union right (see *Lumsdon* [2015] UKSC 41; [2016] A.C. 697 at [82] and [103]).

[498] T. Tridimas, *The General Principles of EU Law* (2006), p.139. This has been debated: de Búrca has suggested that there is a three part test, namely: (1) is the measure suitable to achieve a legitimate aim; (2) is the measure necessary to achieve that aim and (3) does the measure have an excessive effect on the applicant's interests: G. de Búrca, "The Principle of Proportionality and its Application in EC Law" (1993) Y.E.L. 105, 113. Tridimas notes, however, that, while the tripartite test has received "some judicial support", "in practice the Court does not distinguish in its analysis between the second and third test": p.139. In *Herbert Schaible v Land Baden-Württemberg* (C-101/12), Advocate General Wahl (EU:C:2013:334) expressed the view at [40] that the court's jurisdiction also extends to evaluating whether the measure strikes a fair balance between the interests of those affected, i.e. proportionality *stricto sensu*). See also EU:C:2013:661 at [29]; P. Craig, *EU Administrative Law* (2012), Chs 19 and 20. For an example of the CJEU applying a structured proportionality analysis, see: *Sky Österreich GmbH v Österreichischer Rundfunk* (C-283/11) EU:C:2013:28 at [48]–[50]; *Digital Rights Ireland v Minister for Communications, Marine and Natural Resources* (C-293, 594/12) EU:C:2014:238 at [45]–[70]. That proportionality usually entails a two-part test has been endorsed by the Supreme Court: *Lumsdon* [2015] UKSC 41; [2016] A.C. 697 at [33] (adding that there is some debate as to whether there is a third question, sometimes referred to as proportionality *stricto sensu*: namely, whether the burden imposed by the measure is disproportionate to the benefits secured. In practice, the court usually omits this question from its formulation of the proportionality principle. It was added that where the question has been argued, however, the court has often included it in its formulation and addressed it separately, as in *R. v Minister for Agriculture, Fisheries and Food, Ex p Fedesa* (C-331/88) EU:C:1990:391; [1990] E.C.R. I–4023).

[499] *R. v Minister of Agriculture, Fisheries and Food Ex p National Farmers' Union* (C-157/96) EU:C:1998:191 at [60]; *Galileo Zaninotto v Ispettorato Central Repressione Frodi-Ufficio di Conegliano—Ministero delle Risorse Agricole, Alimentari e Forestali* (C-375/96) EU:C:1998:517 at [63].

"[p]roportionality is a test for assessing the lawfulness of a decision-maker's choice between some legal norm and a competing public interest. Baldly stated, the principle is that where the act of a public authority derogates from some legal standard in pursuit of a recognised but inconsistent public interest, the question arises whether the derogation is worth it."[500]

The principle of proportionality enables the CJEU to review not only the legality but, to some extent, also the merits of legislative and administrative measures taken by the EU institutions.[501] However, the intensity with which the principle is applied will range from extremely deferential to rigorous and searching depending on such factors as the interest of the individual at stake, the importance of the objective alleged to be served by the measure and by the expertise and competence of the CJEU as against the decision-making authority.[502] In the field of economic law, the principle is particularly important and often applied rigorously, since this field "frequently involves imposing taxes, levies, charges or duties on businessmen in the hope of achieving economic objectives".[503] In this context, the CJEU has also held that although, in exercising their powers, the EU institutions must ensure that the amounts which commercial operators are charged are no greater than is required to achieve the aim which the authorities seek to accomplish,[504] it does not necessarily follow that that obligation must be measured in relation to the individual situation of any one particular group of operators since, given the multiplicity and complexity of economic circumstances, such an evaluation would not only be impossible to achieve but would also create perpetual uncertainty in the law.[505]   **14-128**

The CJEU applies the principle of proportionality less stringently in cases where the institution has a wide margin of appraisal or where it must make political, economic and social policy choices which require complex assessments. In such cases, which include the common agricultural policy,[506] distribution of European Structural Funds among regions of the United Kingdom,[507] health,[508] state aid,[509] technology,[510] judicial review of the exercise of discretion is usually limited to "examining whether it has been vitiated by manifest error or misuse of powers, or whether the institution concerned has manifestly exceeded the limits of its discretion".[511] It has also been emphasised that the criterion to be applied is not whether the measure adopted "was the only or best possible measure, since its legal-   **14-129**

---

[500] R. (on the application of Rotherham Metropolitan Borough Council) v Secretary of State for Business, Innovation and Skills [2015] UKSC 6 at [47].

[501] T. Tridimas, The General Principles of EU Law (2006), p.140; UK v Council (C-84/94) EU:C:1996:431 at [58]; British American Tobacco EU:C:2002:741 at [123].

[502] G. de Búrca, "The Principle of Proportionality and its Application in EC Law" (1993) Y.E.L. 105, 111–112.

[503] T.C. Hartley, The Foundations of European Union Law (2014), p.168; e.g. Atalanta EU:C:1979:160 at 2151; Man Sugar (181/84) EU:C:1985:359; see 14-068.

[504] See, e.g. Hauptzollamt Hamburg-Jonas v Wunscher (C-26/90) EU:C:1991:389.

[505] See, e.g. Balkan-Import-Export v Hauptzollamt Berlin-Packhof (5/73) EU:C:1973:109 at [22]; Jippes v Minister van Landbouw, Natuurbeheer en Visserij (C-189/01) EU:C:2001:420 at [99].

[506] FEDESA EU:C:1990:391 at [14]; Denka International v Commission (T-334/07) EU:T:2009:453 at [139].

[507] R. (on the application of Rotherham Metropolitan Borough Council) v Secretary of State for Business, Innovation and Skills [2015] UKSC 6 at [167] (Lord Mance noting that he agreed with the Court of Appeal that the decisions "were concerned with matters of broad economic, social and political judgment, for which the objectives were widely defined").

[508] Ex p. British American Tobacco EU:C:2002:741; and R. v Secretary of State for Health Ex p. Swedish Match AB (C-210/03) EU:C:2004:802 at [58].

[509] Société Régie Networks EU:C:2008:764 (Grand Chamber) at [77]–[78]; Hotel Cipriani SpA v Commission (T-254/00) EU:T:2008:537 at [280]–[290].

[510] Afton Chemical EU:C:2010:419.

[511] UK v Council EU:C:1996:431 at [58]; Omya EU:T:2009:27 at [32]; R. (on the application of

ity can be affected only if the measure is manifestly inappropriate having regard to the objective".[512] The CJEU has explained that misuse of powers refers to cases where an authority has used its powers for a purpose other than that for which those powers had been conferred on it. Where more than one aim was pursued—even if the grounds of a decision include, in addition to proper grounds, an improper aim— that would not make the decision invalid for misuse of powers, since it does not nullify the main aim.[513]

14-130   Even where the Union institutions are granted wide discretion by the court— such as in the context of anti-terrorism measures or economic assessments—the role of the Union judicature is not only to establish whether the evidence relied on is factually accurate, reliable and consistent, but to ascertain whether that evidence contains all the relevant information to be taken into account in order to assess the situation and whether it is capable of substantiating the conclusions drawn from it. When conducting such a review, the Union court must not, however, substitute its own assessment of what is appropriate.[514]

14-131   As a general matter, proportionality as a ground of review of EU measures is concerned with the balancing of private interests adversely affected by such measures against the public interests which the measures are intended to promote. Proportionality functions in that context as a check on the exercise of public power of a kind traditionally found in public law, although cases in which measures adopted by the EU legislator or administration in the public interest are held by the EU judicature to be disproportionate interferences with private interests are likely to be relatively infrequent.[515]

14-132   In summary, although the principle of proportionality permits the CJEU to substitute its own evaluation of the exercise of discretion there are cases where the margin of appraisal allowed to the decision-making institution is wider than others.

Legal certainty and legitimate expectations

14-133   The principles of legal certainty and of the protection of legitimate expectations require that the effect of Union legislation must be clear and predictable for those who are subject to it.[516] One of the most important manifestations of the principle of legal certainty is the principle of non-retroactivity. According to the established

---

Vodafone Ltd) v Secretary of State for Business, Enterprise and Regulatory Reform (C-58/08) 8 June 2010 at [51]–[53]. Alternatively, the CJEU has stated that the legality of a measure in such a sphere "can be affected only if the measure is manifestly inappropriate having regard to the objective which the competent institution is seeking to pursue": *FEDESA* EU:C:1990:391. See further *Schrader v Hazptzollamt Gonau* (265/87) EU:C:1989:303 at [21] and [22]; *Ex p. British American Tobacco* EU:C:2002:741 at [123]. Even in this context, however, the CJEU has on occasion engaged in quite considered review: *Jippes* EU:C:2001:420 at [85]–[100] (a proportionality challenge to the Union policy to tackle foot-and-mouth disease was found unsuccessful but only after careful scrutiny by the CJEU).

[512] *R. (on the application of Vodafone Ltd and others) v Secretary of State for Business, Enterprise and Regulatory Reform* (C-58/08) EU:C:2010:321 at [52].

[513] *Omya* EU:T:2009:27 at [99].

[514] *People's Mojahedin Organization of Iran* EU:T:2008:550 at [55]; *Spain v Commission* (C-525/04 P) EU:C:2007:698 at [57].

[515] *Lumsdon* [2015] UKSC 41; [2016] A.C. 697 at [36]. See also *British American Tobacco Ltd* [2016] EWCA Civ 1182; [2017] 3 W.L.R. 225.

[516] Opinion of AG Jacobs in *Konstantinidis* (C-168/91) EU:C:1992:504; and *Kingdom of Denmark v Commission* (C-233/96) EU:C:1998:126 at [38] (Union rules must enable those concerned to know precisely the extent of the obligations imposed on them); *Grondrand Frères* (169/80) EU:C:1981:171 at 1942; *Germany v Commission* (C-245/97) EU:C:2000:687 at [72]; *ThyssenKrupp Stainless AG v Commission* (T-24/07) EU:T:2009:236 at [79]–[90] (the principles of legal certainty and legitimate expectations required application of the ECSC Treaty, rather than the EC Treaty, even though the

case law of the CJEU, a Union measure, other than a criminal measure, may "exceptionally" take effect from a point in time before its publication provided that two conditions are fulfilled: the purpose to be achieved by the measure so demands and the legitimate expectations of those concerned are duly respected.[517] With regard to criminal provisions, however, the prohibition of retroactive application is absolute.[518] The principle of legal certainty also requires that sufficient information is made public to enable parties to know clearly what the law is so that they may comply with it; it is applied particularly strictly in the case of measures liable to have financial consequences in order that those concerned may know precisely the extent of the obligations which are imposed on them.[519] It also means that the Commission cannot depart from the ordinary meaning of words used in secondary legislation when it implements the legislation.[520] The principle also requires that penalties must have a proper legal basis, which requirement is not breached if the precise level of fine that might be imposed in respect of certain conduct is not known in advance.[521]

The concept of legitimate expectation has been described as "the corollary of the principle of legal certainty".[522] The CJEU has emphasised that three conditions are required to be satisfied in order to claim entitlement to the protection of legitimate expectations: first, precise, unconditional and consistent assurances originating from authorised and reliable sources are required to have been given to the person concerned by the Union authorities; secondly, those assurances are required to be such as to give rise to a legitimate expectation on the part of the person to whom they were addressed; and thirdly, the assurances given are required to comply with the applicable rules.[523] Legitimate expectations may arise out of conduct of the EU institutions[524] or out of previous legislation.[525] A legitimate expectation can arise in respect of representations of EU institutions, such as in guidelines, notices and so

14-134

ECSC Treaty had expired (upheld on appeal: C-352/09)). See further S. Schonberg, *Legitimate Expectations in Administrative Law* (2000).

[517] See, e.g. *Racke* (98/78) EU:C:1979:14 at [20]; *Decker* (99/78) EU:C:1979:15 at [8]; *Amylum v Council* (108/81) EU:C:1982:322 at [4]–[17]; *Crispoltoni* (C-368/89) EU:C:1991:307 at [17]. See also *AC-Treuhand AG v Commission* (T-99/04) EU:T:2008:256 at [113] (the general principles of Union law, including the principle of *nullum crimen, nulla poena sine lege*, as applicable to Union competition law, need not necessarily have the same scope as when they apply to a situation covered by criminal law in the strict sense).

[518] *R. v Kirk* (63/83) EU:C:1984:255 at [21]–[22]. See also 14-053.

[519] *Opel Austria v Council* (T-115/94) EU:T:1997:3 at [124].

[520] *Germany v Commission* EU:C:2000:687 at [72].

[521] *Schunk GmbH v Commission* (T-69/04) EU:T:2008:415 at [27]–[29], [45]–[46]. See also *Ori Martin SA and SLM SpA v Commission* (Cases C-490/15 P and C-505/15 P) (given that it was reasonably foreseeable that the Commission could at any time decide to increase the level of the fine, the fact that guidelines were applied to conduct preceding their introduction did not violate the principle of legal certainty); *Dornbracht v Commission* EU:C:2017:45 (C-604/13 P).

[522] *Duff v Minister for Agriculture and Food, Ireland and the Attorney General* (C-63/93) EU:C:1996:51 at [20]; *Commission v Spain* (C-83/99) EU:C:2001:31 at [24].

[523] *Omya* EU:T:2009:27 at [117]; *Masdar* EU:C:2008:726 (Grand Chamber) at [84], [86] (no legitimate expectation arose as to receipt of financial assistance where a contractor had not implemented a project in accordance with the conditions to which the grant of assistance was made subject and the contractor could not rely on "vague indications").

[524] See, e.g. *Commission v Council* (81/72) EU:C:1973:60; *Grogan v Commission* (127/80) EU:C:1982:86; *Embassy Limousines & Services v European Parliament* (T-203/96) EU:T:1998:302 (there could be a breach of legitimate expectations where a company submitting a tender was encouraged to make irreversible investments in advance of the contract being awarded and thereby to go beyond the risks inherent in making a bid).

[525] See, e.g. *Sofrimport v Commission* (C-152/88) EU:C:1990:259.

on, as opposed to just formal decisions.[526] One of the most notable examples of the application of the principle is provided by the milk quota cases. With a view to curbing excess milk production, the Council enacted Regulation No.1078/77 offering a premium to producers who undertook not to market milk products for a period of five years and those who undertook to convert their dairy farms to meat production for a period of four years. Subsequently, Council Regulation 857/84 introduced a levy payable on quantities of milk delivered beyond a guaranteed threshold known as reference quantity. It did not provide, however, for the allocation of a reference quantity to producers who, pursuant to an undertaking under Regulation 1078/77, had not delivered milk and who, upon the termination of their undertaking, were willing to resume milk production. The court held that the total exclusion of those producers from the allocation of a reference quantity ran counter to the principle of legitimate expectations.[527] Regulation 857/84 was subsequently amended so as to provide that those producers were entitled to a reference quantity equal to 60 per cent of the quantity of milk delivered by the producer during the 12 calendar months preceding the month in which his application for the non-marketing or conversion premium under Regulation 1078/77 was made. The court held, however, that the ceiling of 60 per cent was also contrary to the principle of legitimate expectations and therefore invalid.[528]

14-135   A legitimate expectation will not be protected unless it is reasonable: the question is whether a "prudent and discriminating" person would have had the expectation.[529] Thus, the CJEU has emphasised that traders cannot have an expectation that an existing situation which is capable of being altered by the EU institutions in the exercise of their discretionary power will be maintained.[530] In particular, if a prudent and alert economic operator could have foreseen the adoption of a Union measure likely to affect his interests, he cannot plead that principle if the measure is adopted.[531] A trader cannot have a legitimate expectation to derive an advantage from a particular measure if that measure was never intended to bestow that advantage[532]; similarly, an undertaking to which aid is granted cannot entertain a legitimate expectation that the aid is lawful unless it has been granted in accordance with proper procedure, and a diligent businessman should be able to determine whether the procedure has been followed.[533] In addition, a legitimate expectation cannot be relied upon against "a *precise* provision of Union law, or an *unambigu-*

---

[526] *CIRFS v Commission* (C-313/90) EU:C:1993:111 at [34]–[36] (CJEU accepted that the Commission was bound by the terms of a policy framework); and *Louwage v Commission* (148/73) EU:C:1974:7 at [12].

[527] *Mulder v Minister van Landbouw en Visserij* (120/86) EU:C:1988:213; *Von Deetzen v Hauptzollamt Hamburg-Jonas* (170/86) EU:C:1988:214.

[528] *Spagl* (C-189/89) EU:C:1990:450 at [22]; *Pastatter* (C-217/89) EU:C:1990:451 at [13].

[529] *Irish Farmers Association v Minister for Agriculture, Food and Forestry* (C-22/94) EU:C:1997:187 at [25]; *RENV DEI v Commission*(T-169/08) EU:T:2016:733.

[530] *Delacre v Commission* (C-350/88) EU:C:1990:71; *Galileo Zaninotto* EU:C:1998:517 at [50] (CAP); *Kingdom of Spain v Council* (C-284/94) EU:C:1998:548 at [43].

[531] *P v Koninklijke FrieslandCampina NV* EU:C:2009:556 at [84].

[532] *Mackprang v Commission* (2/75) EU:C:1975:66.

[533] *Daewoo Electronics Manufacturing Espana SA (DEMESA) v Commission* (C-183/02 P) EU:C:2004:701 at [44]; *Hotel Cipriani* EU:T:2008:537 at [392]–[393] (the beneficiary of unlawful aid might not entertain a legitimate expectation that the aid was lawful where the aid scheme had not been notified and recovery of the aid was therefore a foreseeable risk) (appeal unsuccessful: C-71/09 P, C-73/09 P and C-76/09 P); *Commission v Salzgitter (Germany, intervening)* (C-408/04) EU:C:2008:236 (Grand Chamber) at [98]–[105]; *Centre d'Exportation du Livre Français (CELF) v Société Internationale de Diffusion et d'Édition (SIDE)* (C-199/06) EU:C:2008:79 at [65]–[68].

ous provision of Union law", or against an overriding public interest.[534] A legitimate expectation may not be relied upon by an undertaking which has committed a manifest infringement of the rules in force.[535] Furthermore, even if the Union had first created a situation capable of giving rise to legitimate expectations, an overriding public interest may preclude transitional measures from being adopted in respect of situations which arose before the new rules came into force but which are still subject to change.[536]

Human rights[537]

Although references to human rights did not feature in the founding Treaties, as observed above, the EU now has a catalogue of fundamental rights in the form of the Charter. The current position under the Treaties as amended by the Lisbon Treaty is that human rights values are specified in a number of Treaty provisions, including TEU art.2 which provides that, among the values upon which the Union is founded, is "respect for human rights".[538] Notably, TEU art.7 and TFEU art.354 provide for a mechanism for the suspension of Member State's rights in the event of breach of any of the values (including human rights) mentioned in TEU art.2. In addition, TEU art.6 provides for the accession of the Union to the ECHR; accession negotiations are ongoing. Even though, ultimately, the CJEU is likely to rely increasingly on the Charter as a source of human rights obligations,[539] the general fundamental rights principles remain relevant. As was discussed above,[540] the scope of application of the Charter appears to have now been clarified as being the same as that of the general fundamental rights principles. If the court had adopted a narrower perspective on the Charter's scope of application—in reliance on the language of art.51(1) of the Charter ("implementing Union law")—the general fundamental rights principles would have had a separate relevance for those cases falling "within the scope of Union law", but not entailing the implemention of Union law.[541] That is not now the case. Nonetheless, the general fundamental rights principles will continue to provide guidance on the interpretation of the Charter.[542]

14-136

After initially refusing to countenance arguments that EU institutions had violated human rights,[543] the CJEU acknowledged the importance of human rights[544] and then in its seminal judgment in *Internationale Handelsgesellschaft*, went further

14-137

---

[534] *Firma P Krücken* (316/86) EU:C:1988:201 at 2239; *SpA Lois Lageder and others v Amministrazione delle Finanze dello Stato* (C-31/91 to C-44/91) EU:C:1993:132 at [34]; *Emsland-Starke GmbH v Landwirtschaftskammer Hannover* (C-94/05) EU:C:2006:185. On overriding public interest, see *CNTA v Commission* (74/74) EU:C:1975:59 at [43] and *Dieckmann & Hansen GmbH v Commission* (T-155/99) EU:T:2001:256 at [80].

[535] *Sideradria v Commission* (67/84) EU:C:1985:506 at [21]; *Industrias Pesqueras Campos v Commission* (T-551/93, 231/94 233-234/94) EU:T:1996:54 at [76]; *José Martí Peix SA v Commission* (T-125/01) EU:T:2003:72 at [107].

[536] *P v Koninklijke FrieslandCampina NV* (C-519/07) EU:C:2009:556 at [85].

[537] L. Betten and N. Grief, *EU Law and Human Rights* (1998); P. Alston (ed), *The EU and Human Rights* (1999). For human rights as a ground of challenge to national measures in the scope of application of Union law, see 14-158.

[538] See also: TEU art.3(5) (noting, inter alia, that the Union, in its relations with the wider world, shall contribute to "the protection of human rights"; TEU art.6(1) (the "Union recognises the rights, freedoms and principles set out in the Charter") and TEU art.21.

[539] See *Otis NV* (C-199/11) EU:C:2012:684 at [47]; *Radu* (C-396/11) EU:C:2013:39 at [32].

[540] See 14-159.

[541] P. Craig, *The Lisbon Treaty: Law, Politics, and Treaty Reform* (2010), pp.212–213. For discussion of human rights post-Lisbon Treaty, see also, e.g. S. Douglas-Scott, "The European Union and human rights after the Treaty of Lisbon" (2011) 11 *Human Rights Law Review* 645.

[542] See the references to the general principles throughout the Explanations to the Charter.

[543] *Stork v High Authority* (1/58) EU:C:1959:4; *Geitling v High Authority* (36, 37, 38 and 40/59)

with the pronouncement that[545]:

> "respect for fundamental rights forms an integral part of the general principles of law protected by the CJEU. The protection of such rights, whilst inspired by the constitutional traditions common to the Member States, must be ensured within the framework of the structure and objectives of the Community [now Union]".

14-138   In *Nold*[546] the CJEU stated that it could not uphold measures which are incompatible with fundamental rights recognised and protected by the Constitutions of the Member States.[547] It also identified as a source of human rights international treaties for the protection of human rights on which the Member States have collaborated or of which they are signatories. In subsequent cases, the CJEU has indicated that the ECHR has special significance in this respect.[548] However, even though the ECHR is a special source for the CJEU's jurisprudence, if a right does not form part of the ECHR jurisprudence, the CJEU can deem it to be a right.[549] The CJEU has also referred regularly to a variety of international instruments, including the International Covenant on Civil and Political Rights of the United Nations,[550] the Community Charter of Fundamental Social Rights of Workers, the European Social Charter[551] the Geneva Convention relating to the Status of Refugees,[552] and the International Covenant on Economic, Social and Cultural Rights.[553]

14-139   The rights which were recognised by the CJEU prior to the coming into force of the Charter (and which are now enshrined in the Charter) can be broadly categorised[554] as civil, economic and rights of the defence (in French, *droits de la défense*).[555] Civil rights include freedom of trade union activity,[556] which includes the right to strike,[557] prohibition of discrimination based on sex,[558] protection from

---

EU:C:1960:36; *Sgarlata v Commission* (40/64) EU:C:1965:36.

[544] *Stauder v City of Ulm* (29/69) EU:C:1969:57 (referring to the "fundamental rights enshrined in the general principles of Community [now Union] law and protected by the Court").

[545] *Internationale Handelsgesellschaft* EU:C:1970:100 at [4].

[546] *Nold v Commission* (4/73) EU:C:1974:51.

[547] See also *Hauer v Land Rheinland-Pfalz* (44/79) EU:C:1979:290 (CJEU reviewed the property provisions in the constitutions of Germany, Italy and Ireland and also analysed in some detail the relevant provisions of the ECHR).

[548] *Johnston* EU:C:1986:206; *ERT* EU:C:1991:254, *Roquette Frères* EU:C:2002:603 at [23]; *Kremzow v Austria* (C-299/95) EU:C:1997:254; *AC-Treuhand AG v Commission* [2009] Bus. L.R. 677 at [45]; *Kadi* EU:C:2008:461 (Grand Chamber) at [283].

[549] In *AM&S v Commission* (155/79) EU:C:1982:157, AG Warner noted that the ECHR made no mention of a principle of lawyer/client confidentiality, yet the CJEU held that it was part of Union law, at [290]–[291].

[550] *Orkem v Commission* (374/87) EU:C:1989:387.

[551] *Blaizot v Belgium* (24/86) EU:C:1988:43; *Viking Line ABP and Oü Viking Line Eesti* EU:C:2007:772 at [43]; *Laval v Svenska Byggnadsarbetareförbundet* (C-341/05) EU:C:2007:809 at [90]; *Istituto nazionale della previdenza sociale (INPS) v Tiziana Bruno* (C-395/08 and C-396/08) EU:C:2010:329 at [30].

[552] *Aydin Salahadin Abdulla et al v Germany* (C-175–179/08) EU:C:2010:105 at [53].

[553] *Bressol v Gouvernement de la Communauté française* (C-73/08) EU:C:2010:181 at [86] (observing that art.13(2)(c) of the Covenant pursued the same objective as TFEU arts 18 and 21).

[554] D. Chalmers, G. Davies and G. Monti, *European Union Law* (2014), pp.235–236.

[555] O. Due, "Le respect des droits de la défense dans le droit administratif communautaire" in *Cahiers de Droit Européen* (1987), p.383. For an extensive treatment, see Schwarze, *European Administrative Law* (2006), pp.1243–1371; *Hoechst AG v Commission* (46/87 and 227/88) EU:C:1989:337 at [14] (referring to "the rights of the defence").

[556] *Union Syndicate v Council* (175/73) EU:C:1974:95.

[557] *Viking Line ABP and Oü Viking Line Eesti* EU:C:2007:772 at [43]–[44]; *Laval* EU:C:2007:809 at [90]–[91].

discrimination on grounds of sexual orientation,[559] religious equality,[560] freedom of expression,[561] freedom to receive information,[562] the right to respect for private life and medical secrecy,[563] the protection of the privacy of business premises,[564] the right to fair legal process within a reasonable period,[565] the right to effective judicial protection,[566] protection of personal data,[567] the right to free and informed consent before any medical procedure,[568] and human dignity.[569] The economic rights include the right to property,[570] the right freely to choose and practise a trade or profession,[571] and freedom of trade,[572] and freedom to conduct business.[573] The rights of the defence include, in particular, the right to an effective legal remedy before the national courts,[574] the right to be heard,[575] the right in certain circumstances to be assisted by a lawyer,[576] legal professional privilege,[577] the right not to be compelled to provide the Commission with answers which might involve an admission on the

---

[558] *Defrenne* EU:C:1978:130.

[559] *KB v National Health Service Pensions Agency* (C-117/01) EU:C:2004:7; *Coleman v Attridge Law* (C-303/06) EU:C:2008:415; [2008] All E.R. (EC) 1105;*Tadao Maruko v Versorgungsanstalt der Deutschen Bühnen* (C-267/06) EU:C:2008:179 at [66]–[73].

[560] *Prais v Council* (130/75) EU:C:1976:142.

[561] *ERT* EU:C:1991:254; *Ter Voon* (C-219/91) EU:C:1992:414; *Kabel Deutschland Vertrieb und Service GmbH & Co KG v Niedersächsische Landesmedienanstalt für privaten Rundfunk* (C-336/07) EU:C:2008:765 at [37] (noting that the maintenance of pluralism which national legislation sought to guarantee was "connected with freedom of expression", which is protected by ECHR art.10, and one of the "fundamental rights guaranteed by the Community [now Union] legal order"); *United Pan-Europe Communications* EU:C:2007:783 at [41]; *Tietosuojavaltuutettu v Satakunnan Markkinapörssi Oy and Satamedia Oy* (C-73/07) EU:C:2008:727 (Grand Chamber) at [52]–[57].

[562] *Kabel* EU:C:2008:765 at [33].

[563] *National Panasonic v Commission* (136/79) EU:C:1980:169; *Commission v Germany* (C-62/90) EU:C:1992:169; *X v Commission* (C-404/92 P) EU:C:1994:361;*Tietosuojavaltuutettu* EU:C:2008:727 (Grand Chamber) at [52]–[57] (right to privacy with respect to the processing of personal data); *Productores de Música* EU:C:2008:54 at [64] (for discussion see: I. Davies and S. Helmer, "Case Comment: Productores de Música de España ("Promusicae") v Telefónica de España SAU ("Telefonica")" (2008) 30 European Intellectual Property Rev. 307; L. Hetherington, "Peer-to-Peer File Sharing—ISPS and Disclosure of User Identities" (2008) 19 Entertainment L. Rev. 81).

[564] *Roquette Frères* EU:C:2002:603 at [29]; *Varec* EU:C:2008:91 at [48].

[565] *Baustahlgewebe GmbH v Commission* (C-185/95 P) EU:C:1998:608 at [20]–[22]. See now *Gascogne Sack Deutschland GmbH v Commission* (C-40/12) EU:C:2013:768; *Kendrion NV v Commission* (C-50/12) EU:C:2013:771; *Groupe Gascogne SA v Commission* (C-58/12) EU:C:2013:770.

[566] *Unibet* EU:C:2007:163 at [37]; *Kadi* EU:C:2008:461 (Grand Chamber) at [335]; *Masdar* EU:C:2008:726 (Grand Chamber) at [50]–[51]; *Inuit Tapiriit Kanatami v Parliament and Council* (C-583/11) EU:C:2013:625 [2014] Q.B. 648; at [105] (art.47 does not require that an individual should have an unconditional entitlement to bring an action for annulment of Union legislative acts directly before the Courts of the EU); *Abdulraihim v Council of the European Union and European Commission* (C-239/12 P) EU:C:2013:331 at [67]–[70] (effective judicial protection meant that an appellant still had an interest in annulling legislation which had already been repealed, since annulment was retrospective and not merely *ex nunc*).

[567] *Lindqvist* (C-101/01) EU:C:2003:596; *Rechnungshof* EU:C:2003:294; *Commission v Bavarian Lager* (C-28/08) EU:C:2010:378.

[568] *Netherlands v Parliament and Council* (C-377/98) EU:C:2001:523.

[569] *Omega Spielhallen-und-Automatenaufstellungs v Oberbügermeisterin der Bundesstadt Bonn* (C-36/02) EU:C:2004:614.

[570] *Hauer* EU:C:1979:290; *Kadì* [2008] E.CR. I-6351 at [359]–[371]; *Productores de Música* EU:C:2008:54 at [62].

[571] *Nold* EU:C:1974:51; *Hauer* EU:C:1979:290.

[572] *Kraus v Land Baden-Wurttemberg* (C-19/92) EU:C:1993:125.

[573] See, e.g. *Herbert Schaible v Land Baden-Württemberg* (C-101/12) EU:C:2013:661.

[574] *Johnston* EU:C:1986:206.

[575] *Transocean Marine Paint v Commission* (17/74) EU:C:1974:106; *Kadi* EU:C:2008:461 (Grand Chamber) at [333]–[353].

[576] See, e.g. *Demont v Commission* (115/80) EU:C:1981:308.

[577] *AM & S v Commission* (155/79) EU:C:1982:157 (the exchange with the lawyer must be connected

undertaking's part of the existence of an infringement which it is incumbent upon the Commission to prove and the right of access to the file.[578] The principle of nullum crimen, nulla poena sine lege is also protected in Union law.[579]

14-140   It is not easy to identify in the abstract the exact content of a right recognised by the CJEU as forming part of the EU legal order. The court has held, for example, that the right to property and the individual's right freely to choose and practise a trade or profession do not constitute unfettered rights but must be viewed in the light of their social function.[580] On this basis, the CJEU has held that those rights may be restricted, for example, in the context of a common organisation of the market, provided that those restrictions correspond to objectives of general interest pursued by the EU and that they do not constitute a disproportionate and intolerable interference which infringes upon the very substance of the rights guaranteed.[581] In general, therefore, provided that the substance of a right is respected, certain aspects of it may have to give way to the attainment of EU objectives or may be sacrificed in order to safeguard an overriding interest.[582] The CJEU has held, however, that fundamental rights, such as freedom of expression, may take precedence over the TFEU free movement rights, provided the interference with free movement is proportionate.[583]

Emerging principles

14-141   As was observed above, the general principles are always evolving, and three emerging principles warrant brief mention, namely: the principle of transparency, the principle against abuse of rights, and the precautionary principle.

14-142   Whether transparency has yet acquired the status of a "general principle" of Union law and the content of any such principle are not entirely clear.[584] The importance of transparency pervades the Treaties, for example, with transparency appearing as a general objective of the Union in TEU art.1,[585] Union institutions being placed under an obligation to maintain "open, transparent and regular dialogue" with representative associations and civil society[586] and obligations of public law-

---

with "the client's rights of defence" and must emanate from "independent lawyers", namely, "lawyers who are not bound to the client by a relationship of employment"). See also: *Akzo Nobel Chemicals and Akcros Chemicals v Commission* (C-550/07) EU:C:2010:512 (confirming that privilege does not apply to communications with in-house lawyers).

[578] *Aalborg Portland v Commission ("Cement")* (C-219/00 P) EU:C:2002:337 at [65] and [68]. However, the CJEU has held that the Commission is not prevented from taking account, when settling the amount of the fine, of the assistance given by the undertaking of its own volition: *Timav Industries and CFPR v Commission* (C411/15P) EU:C:2017:11.

[579] *Amann & Sohne GmbH v Commission* (T-446/05) EU:T:2010:165.

[580] *Nold* EU:C:1974:51; *Hauer* EU:C:1979:290.

[581] T.C. Hartley, *The Foundations of European Union Law* (2014), Ch.5.

[582] See, e.g. *Procureur de la Republique v ADBHU* (204/86) EU:C:1988:450 at [12] (freedom of trade); *Ter Voort* (C-219/91) EU:C:1992:414 at [38] (freedom of expression); L. Besselink, "Entrapped by the Maximum Standard: On Fundamental Rights, Pluralism and Subsidiarity in the European Union" (1998) 35 C.M.L. Rev. 629; J. Weiler, "Fundamental Rights and Fundamental Boundaries: On Standards and Values in the Protection of Human Rights" in N. Neuwahl and A. Rosas (eds), *The European Union and Human Rights* (1995).

[583] This was in the context of review of national rather than Union measures, but is an indication of the growing importance of fundamental rights in the EU legal order: *Schmidberger v Austria* (C-112/00) EU:C:2003:333.

[584] For discussion, see P. Craig, *EU Administrative Law* (2012), Ch.13; K. Lenaerts, "'In the Union We Trust': Trust Enhancing Principles of Community Law" (2004) 41 C.M.L. Rev. 317, 321.

[585] See also TEU art.10(3).

[586] TEU art.11(2); see also TEU art.11(3) and TFEU art.15(1).

making[587] and access to documentation.[588] Access to documentation is also protected by Regulation 1049/2001[589] and art.42 of the Charter. The principle is well-established in the context of public procurement[590]; it derived initially from the necessity to verify compliance with the principle of equal treatment, but it now appears to be regarded as necessary for verifying compliance with the principle of non-discrimination in the context of the free movement provisions more generally.[591] Significantly, the CJEU and General Court have also demonstrated a willingness to read EU legislation as subject to transparency, even where there is no explicit mention of this principle in the relevant articles of the legislation.[592]

Turning to the principle against abuse of EU rights, there have been a large number of cases applying this principle and in brief, EU law cannot be relied on for abusive or fraudulent ends.[593] The principle has been applied in a broad range of contexts.[594]   **14-143**

Finally, there is significant support for the proposition that the precautionary principle has also emerged as a general principle of EU law.[595] The meaning and scope of the precautionary principle are contested, although it can broadly be defined as a general principle that requires competent authorities to take appropriate measures to prevent specific potential risks to public health, safety and the environment, by giving precedence to the requirement related to the protection of those interests over economic interests.[596]   **14-144**

---

[587] TFEU art.16(8) and TFEU art.15(2).

[588] TEU art.15(3).

[589] Regulation (EC) No.1049/2001 of the European Parliament and of the Council of 30 May 2001 regarding public access to European Parliament, Council and Commission documents. In the environmental context, see *Križan v Slovenská inšpekcia životného prostredia* (C-416/10) EU:C:2013:8.

[590] *Unitron Scandinavia et al v Ministeret for Fodvarer* (C-275/98) EU:C:1999:567; *Telaustria and Telefonadress v Telekom Austria* (C-324/98) EU:C:2000:669 at [60]–[61]; *Commission v Ireland* (C-226/09) EU:C:2010:697.

[591] *Commission v Italy* (C-260/04) EU:C:2007:508; *Sporting Exchange Ltd v Minister van Justitie* (C-203/08) EU:C:2010:307; *Carmen Media Group v Land Schleswig-Holstein* (C-46/08) EU:C:2010:505 at [86]–[87]; see also at [90]. See also *R (ABPI) v Medicines and Healthcare Products Regulatory Agency* (C-62/09) EU:C:2010:219; *Altmark Transport GmbH v Nahverkehrsgesellschaft Altmark GmbH* (C-280/00) EU:C:2003:415 at [90] and [95].

[592] *The Queen on the application of Alliance for Natural Health and Nutri-Link Ltd v Secretary of State for Health* (C-154 and 155/04) EU:C:2005:449 at [81]–[82]; *Melli Bank Plc v Council* (T-246 and 332/08) EU:T:2009:266 at [146] (appeal dismissed: C-380/09).

[593] See generally R. de la Feria and S. Vogenauer (eds), *Prohibition of Abuse of Law: A New General Principle of EU Law* (2011); see e.g. *Kefalas and others* (C-367/96) EU:C:1998:222 at [20]; *Diamantis* (C-373/97) EU:C:2000:150 at [33]; *Fini H* (C-32/03) EU:C:2005:128 at [32]; *Halifax Plc, Leeds Permanent Development Services Ltd and County Wide Property Investments Ltd v Commissioners of Customs & Excise* (C-255/02) EU:C:2006:121 at [68].

[594] See, e.g. free movement of services (*Johannes Henricus Maria van Binsbergen v Bestiiur van de Bedrijfsvereniging voor de Metaalnijverheid* (33/74) EU:C:1974:131; freedom of establishment and company law (*Centras Ltd v Erhvervs- ogSelskabsstyrelsen* (C-212/97) EU:C:1999:126); free movement of workers and citizenship (*Franca Ninni-Orasche v Bundesminister fur Wissenschaft, Verkehr und Kunst* (C-413/01) EU:C:2003:600; *Secretary of State for the Home Department v Hacene Akrich* (C-109/01) EU:C:2003:491); broadcasting (*Commission v Belgium* (C-211/91) EU:C:1992:526; direct taxation *Cadbury Schweppes Plc, Cadbury Schweppes Overseas Ltd v Commissioners of Inland Revenue* (C-196/04) EU:C:2006:544.

[595] P. Craig and G. de Búrca, *EU Law: Text, Cases and Materials* (2015), p.575-576; see also P. Craig, *EU Administrative Law* (2012), Ch.21.

[596] *Artegodan GmbH v Commission* (T-74, 76, 83-85, 132, 137 and 141/00) EU:T:2002:283 at [184]. See also *Pfizer Animal Health SA v Council* (T-13/99) EU:T:2002:209. In *Recall Support Services* [2013] EWHC 3091 (Ch), the principle was described (at [112]) as meaning that a Member State did not have to wait until some harm arose to the public before adopting measures to prevent a recur-

The requirement to state reasons[597]

14-145   TFEU art.296 requires "legal acts" to state the reasons on which they are based and to refer to any proposals, initiatives, recommendations, requests or opinions required by the Treaties. Insufficient reasoning constitutes a breach of an essential procedural requirement and can be raised by the CJEU and the General Court of their own motion.[598] The requirement of reasoning has a threefold objective[599]: it seeks to give an opportunity to the parties involved of defending their rights, to the CJEU of exercising its supervisory functions and to the Member States and third persons of ascertaining the circumstances in which the enacting institution has applied the TFEU.

14-146   As a general rule, the statement of reasons must disclose in a clear and unequivocal fashion the reasoning of the authority which adopted the measure in such a way as to enable the persons concerned to ascertain the reasons for the measure and to enable the competent Union Court to exercise its power of review.[600] The reasons must be appropriate to the nature of the contested act and to the context in which it was adopted.[601] For example, where provision of the reasons preclude the disclosure to the person concerned of information or evidence produced before the courts of the EU due to security concerns, it is necessary to strike an appropriate balance between the requirements attached to the right to effective judicial protection and those flowing from the security of the EU or its Member States or the conduct of their international relations.[602] A distinction is drawn between acts of general application and decisions.[603] With regard to general acts, especially regulations, it is sufficient if the reasons given explain in essence the measures taken without need for a specific statement of reasons in support of all the details which might be contained in such a measure, provided that such details fall within the general scheme of the measure as a whole.[604] In principle, an act must state in its preamble the legal basis on which it was adopted. Failure to refer to a precise provision of the Treaty need not constitute an infringement of an essential procedural

---

rence of that harm and which required authorities to take appropriate measures to prevent potential risks to public health, safety and the environment, by giving precedence to the requirements related to the protection of those interests over economic interests. Whether to have recourse to the precautionary principle depends on the level of protection chosen by the competent authority in the exercise of its discretion, taking account of the priorities that it defined in the light of the objectives it pursued in accordance with the relevant rules of the Treaty and of secondary law (see now [2014] EWCA Civ 1370).

[597] For reasons as a ground of challenge to national measures in Union law, see 14-145; and in purely domestic situations, see 7-088.

[598] *Commission v Ireland* (C-89/08 P) EU:C:2009:742 at [34]–[36].

[599] *Germany v Commission* (24/62) EU:C:1963:14 at 69; *Control Data v Commission* (294/81) EU:C:1983:84 at [14].

[600] *Amylum* EU:C:1982:322 at [37]; *Société Régie Networks* EU:C:2008:764 (Grand Chamber) at [62]–[63]; *Mediaset SpA v Commission* (T-177/07) EU:T:2010:233 at [141] (appeal unsuccessful: Case C-403/10 P); *Commission v Kadi* EU:C:2013:518 at [116] (for the requirements for reasons where the reasons represent reasons stated by an international body where the Union is implementing international measures).

[601] *Yanukovych v Council* (T-346/14) EU:T:2016:497 at [77]; *Ben Ali v Council* (T-200/14) EU:T:2016:216 at [94].

[602] *Commission v Kadi* EU:C:2013:518 at [128]; but see *R. (on the application of AZ) v Secretary of State for the Home Department* [2015] EWHC 3695 (Admin).

[603] Opinion of AG Van Gerven in *Commission v BASF* (C-137/92) EU:C:1993:268 at 2571.

[604] *Italy v Commission* (166/78) EU:C:1979:195 at [8].

requirement, however, when the legal basis of the measure can be determined from other parts of that measure.[605]

With regard to individual decisions, the CJEU has stated that the purpose of the **14-147** requirement of reasoning is to enable the CJEU to review the legality of the decision and to provide the person concerned with details sufficient to allow him to ascertain whether the decision is well founded or is vitiated by a defect which will allow its legality to be contested.[606] A decision must therefore refer to the matters of fact and law on which the legal justification for the measure is based.[607] The extent of reasoning required depends on the content of the measure, the nature of the reasons given and the interest which the addressees of the measure or other parties to whom it is of direct and individual concern may have in obtaining explanations.[608] It is not necessary for the reasoning to go into all the relevant facts and points of law, since the question whether the statement or reasons meets the requirements of TFEU art.296 must be assessed with regard not only to its wording but also to its context and to all the legal rules governing the matter in question.[609] However, it is necessary to set out the facts and the legal considerations having decisive importance in the context of the decision.[610] The degree of precision of the statement of the reasons must also be weighed against practical realities and the time and technical facilities available for making the decision.[611]

A few concrete examples are illustrative. When a decision is addressed to a **14-148** Member State and that State has been closely involved in the process by which the decision was made and is therefore aware of the reasons which led the enacting institution to adopt the decision, there is no need for extensive reasoning.[612] When the Commission issues a decision rejecting an application for assistance from the European Social Fund for a vocational training course it is sufficient for that decision to contain a concise statement of reasons. That is an unavoidable consequence of the processing of a large number of applications for assistance upon which the Commission must adjudicate within a short period.[613] By contrast, where an application for assistance from the European Social Fund has been accepted, a decision of the Commission which reduces the amount of the assistance initially granted has more grave adverse consequences for the person concerned and must state

---

[605] *Commission v Council* (45/86) EU:C:1987:163 at [9].

[606] See, e.g. *Sisina v Commission* (32/86) EU:C:1987:187 at [8]; *Mediaset* EU:T:2010:233 at [141] (appeal unsuccessful: C-403/10 P).

[607] See, e.g. *Michelin v Commission* (322/81) EU:C:1983:313 at [14]; *Sytraval and Brink's France SARL v Commission* (T-95/94) EU:T:1995:172.

[608] *Mediaset SpA v Commission* (C-403/10) EU:C:2011:533 at [113].

[609] *Eurocoton v Council* (C-76/01) EU:C:2003:511 at [87]; *Paul Reber GmbH & Co KG v Office for Harmonisation in the Internal Market (Trade Marks and Designs)* (T-304/06) EU:T:2008:268 [2008] E.T.M.R. 68 at [55] (the Boards of Appeal of the OHIM could not be required to provide an account that followed exhaustively and individually each element of the reasoning articulated by the parties before them). See also *Lafarge v Commission* (C-413/08) EU:C:2010:346 at [41]. The reasoning may be "implicit, on condition it enables the persons concerned to know why the measures in question were taken and provides the competent court with sufficient material for it to exercise its power of review": *Inuit Tapiriit Kanatami* EU:C:2013:625 at [82]; *R. (on the application of PJSC Rosneft Oil Co v Treasury* (C-72/15) EU:C:2017:236 at [122].

[610] *Bundesverband deutscher Banken v Commission* (T-36/06) EU:T:2010:61 at [45]; see also *Ellinikos Chrysos AE Metalleion kai Viomichanias Chrysou* (C-100/16 P) EU:C:2017:194.

[611] *Schwarze v Einfuhr- und Vorratsstelle Getreide* (16/65) EU:C:1965:117 at 888; *Delacre* EU:C:1990:71 at [16].

[612] *Netherlands v Commission* (13/72) EU:C:1973:4 at [11]; *Germany v Commission* (819/72) [1981] E.C.R. 31 at [19].

[613] *Gemeente Amsterdam and VIA v Commission* (C-213/87) EU:C:1989:634.

clearly the reasons which justify that reduction.[614] In the competition context, a decision adopted pursuant to TFEU art.102, must mention facts forming the basis of the legal grounds of the measure and the considerations which have led to the adoption of the decision.[615]

14-149 The question whether the grounds of a judgment of the General Court are contradictory or inadequate is a question of law which is amenable to review on appeal by the CJEU.[616] However, the General Court is not obliged to respond in detail to every single argument advanced, particularly if the argument was not sufficiently clear and precise. The General Court is also not obliged to provide an account which follows exhaustively and one by one all the arguments put forward by the parties to the case; the General Court's reasoning may be implicit provided that it enables the persons concerned to know why the General Court has not upheld their arguments and provides the CJEU with sufficient material for it to exercise its power of review.[617]

14-150 Where the Council takes a decision to freeze an individual's funds because of suspected engagement in terrorist activity, there is a requirement to refer not only to the legal conditions of application of the relevant regulation,[618] but also to the actual and specific reasons why the Council considers that the person concerned must be made the subject of a measure freezing funds.[619]

GROUNDS FOR JUDICIAL REVIEW OF NATIONAL MEASURES

14-151 Since in most fields EU measures are implemented by the authorities of the Member States, issues of legality will usually arise between the individual and those authorities, rather than between the individual and the EU institutions themselves. The standard case is that in which the individual claims a right under Union law, contending that the national measures fail to give effect to that right. The failure alleged may be either non-implementation or implementation which purports to give effect to Union law rights but does so incorrectly. Because of the direct effect of many provisions of Union law, the individual will often be able to rely on EU provisions notwithstanding the absence of implementing measures and indeed even in the presence of conflicting national provisions.[620] Such cases will be brought in the national court, and although the national court has no jurisdiction to declare EU measures invalid[621] it can of course declare a national measure unlawful and grant appropriate remedies.[622] It may do so, if the Union law is clear, without a reference to the CJEU.[623]

14-152 By relying upon the direct effect of Union law, the individual may be able to chal-

---

[614] *Consorgan v Commission* (C-181/90) EU:C:1992:244.
[615] *Compagnie Maritime Belge SA v Commission* (T-276/04) EU:T:2008:237 at [82].
[616] *Fabbrica Italiana Accumulatori Motocarri Montecchio SpA (FIAMM) v Council* (C-120/06 P) EU:C:2008:476 at [90].
[617] *Fabbrica Italiana* EU:C:2008:476 at [91], [96]; *Commission v Schneider Electric SA* (C-440/07 P) EU:C:2009:459 (Grand Chamber) at [135].
[618] Council Regulation (EC) 2580/2001 24 December 2001 on specific restrictive measures directed against certain persons and entities with a view to combating terrorism [2001] OJ L-344/70.
[619] *People's Mojahedin Organization of Iran* EU:T:2008:461 at [81]; *Commission v Kadi* EU:C:2013:518 at [116]–[117].
[620] See 14-056.
[621] See 14-059.
[622] On remedies, see Ch.18.
[623] See 14-059.

lenge national measures and have them declared unlawful.[624] All national measures can be subject to review on grounds of compatibility with Union law: primary legislation[625]; secondary regulations[626]; administrative decisions[627]; and the failure to enact primary legislation.[628] Even the "intention or obligation" of the Government to implement a directive, without further implementing measures, is open to challenge on the ground that the directive is invalid.[629] Cases may arise whether or not the individual has a directly enforceable right under Union law.[630] In other cases, an individual may not rely on the direct effect of Union law provisions, but simply contend that the national authorities have acted unlawfully, independently of the question whether the Union law provisions have direct effect.[631]

In terms of the intensity of review, it has been doubted whether **14-153**

"distinctions between primary and secondary legislation ... are of much assistance in determining the margin of appreciation available to a national decision-maker. To give weight to the formal distinction between primary and secondary legislation would be inap-

---

[624] On direct effect of treaty provisions, see 14-021; on direct effect of directives, see 14-027.

[625] *Equal Opportunities Commission* [1995] 1 A.C. 1; *R. v Secretary of State for Transport Ex p. Factortame* [1990] 2 A.C. 85; *Stoke-on-Trent City Council v B&Q Plc* [1991] Ch. 48 at 69 (Hoffmann J); *R. v Secretary of State for the Home Department Ex p. Hoverspeed* [1999] Eu. L.R. 596, QBD; *Gough v Chief Constable of Derbyshire* [2002] EWCA Civ 351; [2002] Q.B. 1213; *R. (on the application of British Telecommunications Plc) v BPI (British Recorded Music Industry) Ltd* [2012] EWCA Civ 232: [2012] Bus. L.R. 1766. For an argument that the English courts have shown excessive deference when reviewing legislative acts, see R. Thompson, "Community Law and the Limits of Deference" (2005) 3 E.H.R.L.R. 243.

[626] *R. v Secretary of State for Social Services Ex p. Urbanek* (1995) 7 Admin. L.R. 781; *R. (on the application of Compassion in World Farming Ltd) v Secretary of State for the Environment, Food and Rural Affairs* [2003] EWHC 2850; [2004] Eu. L.R. 382 (CA at [2004] EWCA Civ 1009; [2004] Eu. L.R. 1021); *Equal Opportunities Commission* [2007] EWHC 483 (Admin) (the Employment Equality (Sex Discrimination) Regulations 2005 were found not to have properly implemented Directive 2002/73/EC of the European Parliament and of the Council of 23 September 2002 amending Council Directive 76/207/EEC on the implementation of the principle of equal treatment for men and women as regards access to employment, vocational training and promotion, and working conditions [2002] OJ L269/15); *R. (British Telecommunications Plc & TalkTalk Telecom Group Plc v Secretary of State for Culture, Olympics, Media and Sport* [2011] EWHC 1021 (Admin) (this aspect of the judgment was not appealed: [2012] EWCA Civ 232); *R. (Sinclair Collis Ltd) v Secretary of State for Health* [2011] EWCA Civ 437; [2012] Q.B. 394 (Protection from Tobacco (Sales from Vending Machines) (England) Regulations 2010 constituted a prima facie derogation from TFEU art.34 but was proportionate). But see now: *Lumsdon* [2015] UKSC 41; [2016] A.C. 697 at [82] and [103]).

[627] *Hedley Lomas* [1997] Q.B. 139 (refusal of licence for live exports based on belief that Spain would not comply with directive was an unjustified restriction on exports); *R. v Chief Constable of Sussex Ex p. International Trader's Ferry Ltd* [1999] 2 A.C. 418; *R. (on the application of Watts) v Secretary of State for Health* [2003] EWHC 2228 at [110]; *Buckinghamshire* [2014] UKSC 3; [2014] 1 W.L.R. 324 (unsuccessful challenge to a Government Command Paper setting out parameters for a high speed rail project).

[628] *R. v Ministry of Agriculture Fisheries & Food Ex p. Bostock* EU:C:1994:116 (application for declaration that failure to enact primary legislation incompatible with EU law); *R. v Commissioners of Customs and Excise Ex p. Lunn Poly Ltd* [1999] Eu.L.R. 653 at 660 (declaration granted that Finance Act 1987 s.21 incompatible with EU law and not capable of being lawfully applied); *R. (on the application of International Transport Roth GmbH) v Secretary of State for the Home Department* [2003] Q.B. 728, CA (immigration carrier penalty scheme not interfering with art.34 rights).

[629] *British American Tobacco* (C-491/01) EU:C:2002:741 at [2], [24]–[25], [28]–[41] (this challenge was also permitted although the time limit for implementing the directive had not expired).

[630] Measures for withdrawal from the Union pursuant to TEU art.50 do not fall within the scope of EU law: *Schindler v Chancellor of the Duchy of Lancaster* [2016] EWCA Civ 469.

[631] See, e.g. *Twyford Parish Council v Secretary of State for the Environment* [1993] Env. L.R. 37; *R. v H.M. Treasury Ex p. Smedley* [1985] Q.B. 657.

propriate, particularly in view of the very wide power to amend primary legislation by order in council conferred by s.2 of the European Communities Act 1972."[632]

14-154   As a result of developments in the case law of the CJEU, the grounds on which national measures may be challenged as being unlawful under Union law correspond closely (although not exactly) with the grounds on which EU measures may be challenged.[633] Thus national measures may be challenged not only as infringing the EU Treaties or EU legislation, but also, where giving effect to Union law provisions, as infringing the general principles of law recognised in Union law: for example the principle of proportionality, the principle of non-discrimination, the principle of respect for fundamental rights, and the principle of protection of legitimate expectations. It is now clearly established that where Union law is applicable, the grounds on which national measures may be challenged in the national courts are not the same as those on which national measures may be challenged in English law. The situations in which Union law may arise are so varied that no definitive general statement is possible; the following points should be treated as illustrative only.

Review of discretion

14-155   Where there is an apparent breach of Union law, the courts will require the decision-maker to justify the breach.[634] This will require a more intrusive scrutiny and closer investigation of the facts of the case than the traditional *Wednesbury* approach would follow.[635]

The requirement to state reasons

14-156   Where a decision of the national authorities has the effect of denying a fundamental Union law right, such a decision must be open to challenge by judicial proceedings so that its legality under Union law can be reviewed; accordingly the person concerned must be able to ascertain the reasons for the decision so that he can decide whether to take proceedings with full knowledge of the relevant facts.[636] It is therefore not sufficient for him to be informed of the reasons for a decision only after legal proceedings have been commenced. The CJEU has explained that the duty to state reasons is linked to the principle of effective judicial review.[637]

14-157   The subsequent communication may take the form, not only of an express statement of the reasons, but also of information and relevant documents being made

---

[632] *R. v Ministry of Agriculture Fisheries and Food, Ex p. Astonquest* [2000] Eu.L.R. 371 at 384. See, however, by contrast: *Sinclair Collis Ltd* [2012] Q.B. 394. But see now: *Lumsdon* [2015] UKSC 41; [2016] A.C. 697 at [82] and [103].

[633] See 14-119.

[634] *R. v Minister of Agriculture, Fisheries and Food Ex p. Bell Lines* [1984] 2 C.M.L.R. 502 at 509–511.

[635] *R. v Secretary of State for Social Services Ex p. Schering Chemicals Ltd* [1987] 1 C.M.L.R. 277; *R. v Minister of Agriculture, Fisheries and Food Ex p. Roberts* [1991] C.O.D. 172.

[636] *Heylens* EU:C:1987:442; *Vlassopoulou* EU:C:1991:193; *Colegio Oficial de agentes de la Propiedad Inmobiliaria v Aguirre Borrell* (C-104/91) EU:C:1992:202; *Kraus* EU:C:1993:125. The obligation on national authorities to state reasons in the field of application of Union law arises from the general principle of good administration (which is reflected in art.41 of the Charter): *LS Customs Services* (C-46/16) at [77].

[637] *Mellor* (C-75/08) EU:C:2009:279 at [59]. See also: *Marie-Noëlle Solvay and others* (C-182/10) EU:C:2012:82 at [59].

available in response to the request made.[638] The obligation to state reasons, however, applies only to individual decisions of national authorities which have adverse legal effects on individuals and not to national rules of general application.[639]

General principles of law

A national measure may be struck down on the ground that it runs counter to a general principle of law. Examples will be given here by reference to the principle of protection of fundamental rights, the principle of proportionality, the principle of equality, and the principle of protection of legitimate expectations.

14-158

Fundamental rights

One of the central questions that has arisen in the context of case law on the review of national measures for compatibility with fundamental rights has been their scope of application. The case law is also relevant in the context of the scope of application of the Charter and is referenced in the Explanations to the Charter.[640]

14-159

Implementation of Union law

The first category may be illustrated by cases in the field of agriculture, where the Member States implement EU legislation. Since the EU institutions are bound by the principle of respect for fundamental rights and their legislation must be interpreted accordingly, it follows that the national authorities, in implementing that legislation, are also so bound.[641] Thus, in *Wachauf*,[642]. Mr Wachauf was a tenant farmer who had received a milk quota under the applicable EU rules. Upon the expiry of his tenancy, he requested compensation for the definite discontinuance of milk production but his request was refused on the ground that the lessor had not given his consent as required by Union law. It was argued that if the EU rules in question were interpreted as meaning that, upon the expiry of the lease, the lessee's milk quota must be returned to the lessor, they could have the effect of precluding the lessee from benefiting from the system of compensation for discontinuance of milk production if the lessor were opposed to it. That is because in so far as the milk quota corresponding to the farm in question returns to the lessor, it cannot be taken into account for the purposes of granting compensation. It was argued that such a consequence would be unacceptable if the lessor had never engaged in milk production since the lessee, who would have acquired the milk quota by his own labour, would then be deprived, without compensation, of the fruits of that labour. After recalling its judgment in *Hauer*, the CJEU stated[643]:

14-160

> "Community [now Union] rules which, upon the expiry of the lease, had the effect of depriving the lessee, without compensation, of the fruits of his labour and of his investments in the tenanted holding would be incompatible with the requirements of the protection of fundamental rights in the Community [now Union] legal order. Since those require-

---

[638] *Mellor* (C-75/08) EU:C:2009:279 at [60]; *Marie-Noëlle Solvay* (C-182/10) EU:C:2012:82 at [60]; see also *Kadi* EU:C:2013:518 at [111].

[639] *Sodemare SA v Fédération de Maisons de Repos Privés de Belgique (Femarbel) ASBL and Regione Lombardia* (C-70/95) EU:C:1997:301.

[640] See 14-042 and 14-057; Explanations, p.32.

[641] *Klensch v Secretaire d'Etat d l'Agriculture et a la Viticulture* (201 and 202/85) EU:C:1986:439.

[642] *Wachauf* EU:C:1989:321; cf. *Bostock* (C-2/92) EU:C:1994:116

[643] *Wachauf* EU:C:1989:321 at [19].

ments are also binding on the Member States when they implement Community [now Union] rules, the Member States must, as far as possible, apply those rules in accordance with those requirements."

In the circumstances of the case, the CJEU found that the EU rules left the competent national authorities a sufficiently wide margin of discretion to enable them to apply those rules in a manner consistent with the requirements of the protection of fundamental rights.

14-161   The CJEU has stressed also that when transposing directives which leave discretion to them, Member States must interpret the directives in a manner which allows a fair balance to be struck between the various fundamental rights protected by the Union legal order. Further, when implementing the measures transposing those directives, the authorities and courts of the Member States must not only interpret their national law in a manner consistent with those directives but also make sure that they do not rely on an interpretation of them which would be in conflict with those fundamental rights or with the other general principles of Union law, such as the principle of proportionality.[644]

Where the Member State is not directly implementing EU measures

14-162   Even where Member States are not implementing EU measures, similar principles may apply. The effect of the ECHR on the review of national measures is demonstrated by the CJEU's judgment in *ERT*, which concerned certain exclusive television rights under Greek law. The court considered the issue of restrictions on the freedom to provide services and the justification for such restrictions under TFEU arts 52 and 62 and devoted a section of its judgment to the issue raised under ECHR art.10 (freedom of expression). It stated that where national legislation falls within the scope of Union law, the CJEU must supply all the elements of interpretation necessary for the national court to assess the conformity of that legislation with the fundamental rights protected by the CJEU, as they derive, in particular, from the ECHR. Where a Member State invokes the combined provisions of TFEU arts 52 and 62 to justify legislation liable to impede the exercise of the freedom to provide services, that justification, provided for by Union law, must be interpreted in the light of the general principles of law and in particular of fundamental rights; thus the national legislation in question may only benefit from the exceptions provided for by the combined provisions of TFEU arts 52 and 62 if it is in conformity with fundamental rights.[645] It followed, the CJEU concluded, that in such a case it was the duty of the national court and, where appropriate, the CJEU to assess the application of those provisions having regard to all the rules of Union law, including the freedom of expression enshrined in ECHR art.10, as a general principle of law protected by the CJEU.[646]

14-163   The CJEU has reviewed for compliance with ECHR art.8 (right to respect for family and private life), a UK deportation order in respect of a Filipino national, Mrs Carpenter, who had violated UK immigration laws by not leaving the country prior to the expiry of her leave to remain as a visitor.[647] Mr Carpenter was a UK national, living in the UK and running a business selling advertising space, which was established in the UK. A significant proportion of the business, however, was conducted with advertisers established in other Member States and Mr Carpenter

---

[644] *Ordre des barreaux francophones et germanophone* (C-305/05) EU:C:2007:383 at [28].
[645] *ERT v Pliroflorisis* EU:C:1991:254 at [42]–[43]; and *SPUC v Grogan* (C-159/90) EU:C:1991:378.
[646] *ERT* EU:C:1991:254 at [44].
[647] See *Carpenter v Secretary of State for the Home Department* EU:C:2002:434.

travelled to other Member States to pursue his business. It was argued that the deportation order would interfere with his TFEU art.56 freedom to provide services. The court accepted that the separation of Mr and Mrs Carpenter would be detrimental to their family life and, therefore, to the conditions under which Mr Carpenter exercised a fundamental freedom.[648] As such, the deportation order could only be upheld if the measure was compatible with the fundamental rights.[649] The court, however, considered that the deportation order was a disproportionate interference with ECHR art.8.[650]

Thus, the court's case law has developed from a review of EU measures adopted   **14-164**
by the EU institutions themselves, to a review of measures adopted by Member States in implementing EU measures, and to a review of measures adopted by Member States which, in one way or another and, even if tenuously, fall within the scope of Union law.[651]

Proportionality

The principle of proportionality[652] can be used as the basis for challenging   **14-165**
national measures and for claiming rights in the national courts. It applies across the whole field of Union law, but its precise effect will depend upon the context. The assessment of proportionality will again here be of a structured kind,[653] asking a series of questions starting with the requirement of a legitimate aim, and proceeding to ask whether the obligation is strictly necessary to attain the aim. The measure must apply the least restrictive alternative and there must be a rational connection between the ends and means.[654]

In the *Lumsdon* case, the Supreme Court clarified the principle of proportional-   **14-166**
ity as it applies in the context of Union law, while emphasising that the way in which the principle of proportionality is applied in Union law depends to a significant extent upon the context.[655] The Supreme Court began by observing that the principle of proportionality is a general principle of Union law, enshrined in TFEU art.5(4),[656] and reflected elsewhere in the Treaties, such as in TEU art.3(6),[657]

---

[648] *Carpenter v Secretary of State for the Home Department* EU:C:2002:434 at [39].

[649] *Carpenter v Secretary of State for the Home Department* EU:C:2002:434 at [40].

[650] *Carpenter v Secretary of State for the Home Department* EU:C:2002:434 at [41]–[45].

[651] Opinion of Advocate General Jacobs *Konstantinidis* EU:C:1992:504. For parallel developments in the context of the Charter, see para.14-042.

[652] In relation to Union measures, see 14-127; for proportionality as a ground in English law, see 11-073; and in relation to Convention rights, see 11-077.

[653] See 11-077.

[654] To comply with the principle of proportionality, Member States must employ means which, whilst enabling them effectively to attain the objectives pursued by their domestic laws, cause the least possible detriment to the objectives and principles laid down by the relevant Union legislation: *Netto Supermarkt GmbH & Co OHG v Finanzamt Malchin* (C-271/06) EU:C:2008:105 at [19]; *R. (on the application of Teleos Plc) v Customs and Excise Commissioners* (C-409/04) EU:C:2007:548 at [52]; *Vlaamse Oliemaatschappij NV* (C-499/10) EU:C:2011:871 at 20–21. Note the contrast in views on proportionality in *Sinclair Collis Ltd* [2012] Q.B. 394 at 437 (but see now *Lumsdon* [2015] UKSC 41; [2015] 3 W.L.R. 121 at [82] and [103]); *Bogusław Juliusz Dankowski v Dyrektor Izby Skarbowej w Łodzi* (C-438/09) EU:C:2010:818 at [37].

[655] *Lumsdon* [2015] UKSC 41; [2016] A.C. 697. See also *Scotch Whiskey Association v Lord Advocate* (C-333/14) EU:C:2015:845; *Scotch Whiskey Association v The Lord Advocate* [2017] UKSC 76; and *British American Tobacco* [2016] EWCA Civ 1182; [2017] 3 W.L.R. 225.

[656] TFEU art.5(4) provides as follows: "Under the principle of proportionality, the content and form of Union action shall not exceed what is necessary to achieve the objectives of the Treaties."

[657] TEU art.3(6) provides as follows: "The Union shall pursue its objectives by appropriate means commensurate with the competences which are conferred upon it in the Treaties."

but that it had been most obviously developed by the CJEU in its jurisprudence.[658] The principle applies generally to legislative and administrative measures adopted by EU institutions. It also applies to national measures falling within the scope of EU law.[659] The principle only applies to measures interfering with protected interest, and is neither expressed nor applied in the same way as the principle of proportionality under the ECHR.[660] Where the proportionality principle is applied by a national court, it must, as a principle of EU law, be applied in a manner which is consistent with the jurisprudence of the court: "as is sometimes said, the national judge is also a European judge".[661] The court endorsed the concept of proportionality as entailing two questions: first, whether the measure in question is suitable or appropriate to achieve the objective pursued; and secondly, whether the measure is necessary to achieve that objective, or whether it could be attained by a less onerous method.[662] The court observed that the other critical aspect of the principle of proportionality is the intensity with which it is applied, and it drew a distinction between review of national measures relying upon derogations from general EU rights, and the review of national measures implementing Union law.[663]

14-167   As a ground of review of national measures, proportionality has been applied most frequently to measures interfering with the fundamental freedoms guaranteed by the EU Treaties. Although private interests may be engaged, the court is concerned first and foremost with the question of whether a Member State can justify an interference with a freedom guaranteed in the interests of promoting the integration of the internal market, and the related social values, which lie at the heart of the EU project. In circumstances of that kind, the principle of proportionality generally functions as a means of preventing disguised discrimination and unnecessary barriers to market integration. In that context, the court, seeing itself as the guardian of the Treaties and of the uniform application of EU law, generally applies the principle more strictly.[664] By contrast, where Member States adopt measures implementing EU legislation, they are generally contributing towards the integration of the internal market, rather than seeking to limit it in their national interests. In general, therefore, proportionality functions in that context as a conventional public law principle. On the other hand, where Member States rely on reservations or derogations in EU legislation in order to introduce measures restricting fundamental freedoms, proportionality is generally applied more strictly, subject to the qualifications which we have mentioned.[665]

14-168   As just noted, many of the applications of the principle to national measures concern the scope of exceptions to the basic freedoms of movement of goods and persons under the EU Treaties. For example, restrictions on the free movement of goods are permitted on such grounds as public health under TFEU art.36, but such grounds must not result in restrictions. Where the national measure is tested against a basic Treaty freedom, such as the free movement of goods, strict scrutiny will be applied to the national restriction. Thus the CJEU has struck down measures which enable pharmaceutical companies to limit imports from other Member States to their own main distributors and to exclude "parallel imports" from other Member

---

[658] *Lumsdon* [2015] UKSC 41; [2016] A.C. 697 at [24].
[659] *Lumsdon* [2015] UKSC 41; [2016] A.C. 697 at [25].
[660] *Lumsdon* [2015] UKSC 41; [2016] A.C. 697 at [26].
[661] *Lumsdon* [2015] UKSC 41; [2016] A.C. 697 at [31].
[662] *Lumsdon* [2015] UKSC 41; [2016] A.C. 697 at [33] (see also fn.447 above).
[663] *Lumsdon* [2015] UKSC 41; [2016] A.C. 697 at [34]–[35] (a third category, review of EU measures, has already been set out above at text to fn.461a).
[664] *Lumsdon* [2015] UKSC 41; [2016] A.C. 697 at [37] (for further detail see [51]–[72]).
[665] *Lumsdon* [2015] UKSC 41; [2016] A.C. 697 at [38] (for further detail see [73]–[74]).

States, in the absence of a compelling public health justification.[666] The court has also held that a Member State may not impose on nationals of other Member States, exercising their right to freedom of movement, the obligation to make a declaration of residence within three days of entering the State's territory, subject to a penal sanction for failure to comply, since the time limit of three days cannot be regarded as reasonable.[667] Where fundamental rights, such as freedom of association, are asserted by Member States to justify interference with Treaty free movement rights, they may take precedence, but again, only if the interference with free movement is proportionate.[668]

In the citizenship context, the principle of proportionality has had a particularly interesting effect. Given the direct effect of TFEU art.21, limitations placed on the right to reside and move of non-economically active Union citizens are scrutinised for proportionality, and in the *Baumbast* case, it was held that national rules may be questioned—even if they are consistent with secondary Union legislation if they produce results which are disproportionate to the objective pursued.[669] Thus, in *Baumbast*, depriving a Union citizen, who had resided for several years in another Member State of his right to reside, because he lacked emergency health insurance, was disproportionate to the aim of preventing him from becoming an "unreasonable burden" on that State's welfare system.[670]

14-169

Criminal penalties imposed by national law are also strictly subject to the test of proportionality.[671] Thus, the CJEU has held that national legislation which penalises offences concerning the payment of VAT on importation from another Member State more severely than those concerning the payment of VAT on domestic transactions is incompatible with TFEU art.110 in so far as that difference is disproportionate to the dissimilarity between the two categories of offences.[672] The court has also held that seizure or confiscation of a product imported illegally could be considered disproportionate, and therefore incompatible with TFEU art.34, to the extent to which the return of the product to the Member State of origin would be sufficient.[673] Similarly, while the objective of preventing tax evasion justifies stringent requirements as regards the obligations of persons liable to payment of VAT, the principle of proportionality requires that the taxable person not be held liable for the entire

14-170

---

[666] *De Peijper v The Netherlands (Ministere Public)* (104/75) EU:C:1976:67; *Ker-Optika bt v ÀNTSZ Dél-dunántúli Regionális Intézete* (C-108/09) EU:C:2010:725 at [65]–[76] (failure of public health justification on grounds of lack of proportionality).

[667] *Criminal Proceedings against Messner* (C-265/88) EU:C:1989:632. For an example of a careful factual analysis resulting in the upholding of the proportionality of restrictions on non-resident nationals accessing Maastricht coffee houses, see: *Josemans v Burgemeester van Maastricht* (C-137/09) EU:C:2010:774 at [71]–[84].

[668] *Schmidberger* EU:C:2003:333.

[669] *Baumbast and R. v Secretary of State for the Home Department* (C-413/99) EU:C:2002:493.

[670] See A. Dashwood, M. Dougan, B. Rodger, E. Spaventa and D. Wyatt, *Wyatt and Dashwood's European Union Law* (2011), Ch.10, p.327 (describing the principle in this context as operating "as an hermeneutic principle"). See also M. Dougan, "The Constitutional Dimension to the Case Law on Union Citizenship" (2006) 31 E.L. Rev. 613. See also *Rhiannon Morgan v Bezirksregierung Köln* (C-11/06 and C-12/06) EU:C:2007:626 at [46].

[671] *Re Casati* (203/80) EU:C:1981:261 at [27].

[672] *Drexl* (299/86) EU:C:1988:103.

[673] *Aime Richardt* (C-367/89) EU:C:1991:376; see further *Donckvnwolcke v Procureur de la Republique* (41/76) EU:C:1976:182; *Procureur de la Republique v Rivoira* (179/78) EU:C:1979:89. On confiscation, see also *Leifer* (C-83/94) EU:C:1995:329; *Bosphorus Hava Yollari Turizm ve Ticaret AS v Minister for Transport and the Attorney General* (C-84/95) EU:C:1996:312; *Ebony Maritime SA v Prefetto della Provincia di Brindisi* (C-177/95) EU:C:1997:89.

shortfall in tax caused by fraudulent acts of third parties over which he has no influence.[674]

14-171   The test of proportionality is clearly a stringent one, especially when the need for the national measure falls to be weighed against a fundamental Treaty freedom, and it has been suggested that there will be circumstances in which a higher standard of justification will be required for interference with EU law than with an ECHR right.[675] However, the application of the principle is far from straightforward, and on occasion, the CJEU has been willing to interpret the principle flexibly, in light of particular values applicable within Member States.[676] Moreover, the fact that a Member State introduces measures which are more restrictive of a particular freedom than subsequent Union measures will not in itself justify the conclusion that the Member State legislation is disproportionate.[677]

14-172   In areas where the Union's competence is weaker, the test of proportionality will be applied flexibly. For example, states have a "wide discretion" to determine what constitutes a service of general economic interest, for the purposes of TFEU arts 14 and 106.[678]

14-173   In conclusion, the application of proportionality can go beyond the English ground of unreasonableness or irrationality and is most strictly applied when the need for a national measure falls to be weighed against a Treaty freedom. However, its application and the margin of appraisal permitted to the decision making authority may vary, in accordance with different situations.

Equality[679]

14-174   The principle of equality, like the principle of proportionality, is binding not only on the EU institutions but also, within the field of Union law, on the Member States. Thus where EU rules leave Member States free to choose between various methods of implementation, a Member State may not choose an option whose implementation in its territory would be liable to create, directly or indirectly, discrimination prohibited by Union law.[680] One of the most fundamental principles of the Treaty

---

[674] *Netto Supermarkt* EU:C:2008:105 at [23].

[675] *Countryside Alliance* [2007] Q.B. 305 at [158]–[159]. On the standard of proportionality review for Convention rights, see Ch.13.

[676] See, e.g. *Omega Spielhallen* EU:C:2004:614: it was held that the public policy justification of the Bonn police for forbidding laser games involving simulated killing, on the basis that it infringed the right to dignity in the German Constitution, was proportionate; and it was not necessary for the restrictive measure to be chosen by all Member States. See also *Läärä, Cotswold Microsystems Ltd and Oy Transatlantic Software Ltd v Finland* (C-124/97) EU:C:1999:435 (granting a public body the exclusive right to operate slot machines in infringement of the freedom to provide services could potentially be justified on grounds of consumer protection). See also P. Craig, *EU Administrative Law* (2012), pp.631–634.

[677] *Tridon* (C-510/99) EU:C:2001:559 at [59].

[678] *British United Provident Association Ltd (BUPA) v Commission* (T-289/03) EU:T:2008:29 at [166].

[679] On equality as a ground of challenge in relation to Union measures, see 14-125; see also arts 20 and 21 of the Charter. As a principle of English law, see Ch.11; on ECHR art.14, see Ch.13.

[680] *Klensch* EU:C:1986:439. See also *R. (on the application of Partridge Farms Limited) v Secretary of State for Environment, Food and Rural Affairs* [2009] EWCA Civ 284; [2009] Eu. L.R. 816 at [58] and [79] (accepting that the principle of equality was one of the "fundamental principles of Community [now Union] law", but that the claimant had not succeeded in persuading the court that the Compensation (England) Order 2006 (SI2006/168) breached the principle of equality by not making provision for high pedigree cattle in setting compensation for cattle slaughtered on account of tuberculosis: "As the European Court has emphasised, the principle of equality does not preclude legislation of general application from affecting different persons in different ways provided it is determined on the basis of objective criteria formulated to meet the relevant objective" (Collins LJ)).

is the prohibition of discrimination on the grounds of nationality.[681] That prohibition covers indirect discrimination, that is to say, discrimination which although it is ostensibly made by the application of other criteria leads effectively to the same result.[682] Thus, depending on the circumstances, discrimination on the ground of residence may result in indirect discrimination.[683]

Legal certainty and legitimate expectations[684]

National authorities responsible for applying Union law are bound to observe the principle of protection of legitimate expectations. The principle is best illustrated in the context of the recovery by national authorities of aid paid by Member States in breach of EU rules. Where for example the Commission finds that aid which has been granted by a state to an undertaking is incompatible with the internal market, and thus unlawful under TFEU art.107, it may require the national authorities to recover that aid.[685] In general, the CJEU has been reluctant to accept that the principle provides a good defence against an order to recover unlawfully paid state aid. In one case,[686] the undertaking concerned claimed that the Commission's order to the national authorities to recover the aid was incompatible with the principle of protection of legitimate expectations on the ground that it had received the aid on the basis of definitive decisions and on the ground that it had used it in relation to a product which was not subject to the guidelines notified to the Member States by the Commission. The court rejected those arguments stating that failure to include that specific product in the guidelines could not justify a legitimate expectation on the part of the undertaking, since the guidelines could not derogate from TFEU arts 107 and 108 of the Treaty which prohibited the granting of the aid. In another case, however, the CJEU accepted that the Commission's unreasonable delay in requiring the recovery of state aid gave rise to a legitimate expectation on the part of the undertaking which prevented the Commission from requiring the national authorities to order the refund of the aid.[687]

14-175

In the context of agricultural aids, the CJEU has held that Union law does not prevent national law from having regard, in excluding recovery of unduly paid aids, to the need to protect legitimate expectations, provided that the same procedural rules are applied to the recovery of purely national financial benefits and that the

14-176

For an interesting example of anomalies in funding between different regions being such as to require explanation, which had not been given, thereby rendering the decisions manifestly inappropriate under EU (and domestic law), see: *R. (on the application of Rotherham MBC) v Secretary of State for Business, Innovation and Skills* [2015] UKSC 6; [2015] 3 All E.R. 1 (Lord Carnwath noting at [174] that issues of equal or unequal treatment and proportionality may play a part in the assessment of whether reasoning was affected by legal error or otherwise manifestly inappropriate).

[681] The general prohibition is contained in TFEU art.18. It is implemented in relation to specific domains by other provisions of the Treaty, e.g. TFEU art.45 (free movement of workers), TFEU art.49 (freedom of establishment) and TFEU art.56 (freedom of services). TFEU art.18 applies independently only to situations with regard to which there is no specific prohibition: *Schluter* (9/73) EU:C:1973:110; *Raulin* (C-357/89) EU:C:1992:87; *European Parliament v Council* (C-295/90) EU:C:1992:398; *Phil Collins v Imtrat Handelsgesellschaft* (C-92/92) EU:C:1993:847.

[682] *Sotgiu* EU:C:1974:13; *Thieffry* (71/76) EU:C:1977:65; *Sudmilch v Ugliola* (15/69) EU:C:1969:46.

[683] *Commission v Belgium* (52/84) EU:C:1986:3.

[684] *Hauptzollamt Krefeld v Maizena* (5/82) EU:C:1982:439 at [22]. For legitimate expectations as a ground for challenging Union measures, see 14-133; as a ground in English law, see Ch.12.

[685] See, e.g. *Commission v Germany* (C-5/89) EU:C:1990:320.

[686] *Deufil v Commission* (310/85) EU:C:1987:96.

[687] *RSV v Commission* (223/85) EU:C:1987:502; cf. *France v Commission* (C-301/87) EU:C:1990:67.

interests of the EU are taken fully into account.[688] In the tax context, the CJEU has held that it would be contrary to the principle of legal certainty if a Member State, which had laid down the conditions for the application of the exemption from VAT by prescribing a list of the documents to be presented to the competent authorities and which had accepted the documents presented by a supplier as establishing entitlement to the exemption, could subsequently require that supplier to account for the VAT, where it emerged that because of a third party's fraud, of which the supplier had and could have had no knowledge, the conditions for the exemption were in fact not met.[689]

14-177   A practice of a Member State which infringes Union law may never give rise to legitimate expectations on the part of an economic operator[690]; and that is so even where a EU institution has failed to take the necessary action to ensure that the state in question correctly applies the EU rules.[691] It should also be noted that, the concept of legitimate expectations in Union law requires detrimental reliance,[692] unlike, it appears, the domestic equivalent.[693]

---

[688] *Deutsche Milchkontor v Germany* (205-215/82) EU:C:1983:233 at [33].

[689] *Netto Supermarkt* EU:C:2008:105 at [26].

[690] *Hauptzollarnt Hamburg-Jonas v Krucken* (316/86) EU:C:1988:201 at [23].

[691] *Hauptzollarnt Krefeld v Maizena* (5/82) EU:C:1982:439 at [22].

[692] *Milk Marketing Board of England and Wales v Tom Parker Farms Ltd* [1999] Eu. L.R. 154 at [39], QBD (Comm) ("In approaching the issue of Union law in this case it is necessary to remember that the purpose of the principle of protection of legitimate expectations is the avoidance of prejudice to a party who has justifiably changed that anterior position to the detriment of the other. The protection afforded by the principle is only to those who, because of their circumstances and their reliance, have been prejudiced. Its conceptual function is not the furtherance of consistency of conduct by public bodies but avoidance of prejudice by inconsistency of conduct.").

[693] See 12-043.

PART III PROCEDURES AND REMEDIES

CHAPTER 15

The Historical Development of Judicial Review Remedies and Procedures

TABLE OF CONTENTS

SCOPE

Professor S.A. de Smith was acutely conscious of the importance of history, yet **15-001** aware that no more than a brief survey could be given in a book of this kind when he prepared the first three editions of this work.[1] This chapter is a synthesis of the historical accounts which, up to the 4th edition of this book, were distributed throughout the text. These have been brought together, and brought up to date, in an attempt to provide a more accessible narrative.

INTRODUCTION

The importance of an historical perspective

An understanding of the historical development of the remedies and procedures **15-002** of judicial review[2] is necessary for several reasons. First, it is impossible to

---

[1] For reasons of space, it has been necessary to abridge the account of the historical origins of the prerogative writs given in Appendix 1 of the 3rd and 4th editions, and to omit some of the footnotes to de Smith's sources. Readers with a special interest will continue to find that appendix a useful point of reference; so too de Smith's journal publications, especially "The Prerogative Writs" (1951) 11 C.L.P. 40 and "Wrongs and Remedies in Administrative Law" (1952) 15 M.L.R. 189.

[2] The distinction between the terms "procedures" and "remedies" is often blurred; some, for example, speak of the "remedy of judicial review". Here, procedure is used to refer to those steps—stipulated in the Civil Procedure Rules and formerly in the Rules of the Supreme Court—which must be followed in order to bring a matter before the court. Remedies refer to the formal orders, both interlocutory and final, which may be granted by the court. The study of such adjectival aspects of administrative law is often as-or more-revealing of the underlying values of the legal system as is the study of the rules of substantive law. cf. Sir Henry Maine's well-known remark that "... substan-

understand many of the early cases on what we now call judicial review without some knowledge of the procedures and remedies in place at the time. Secondly, whilst many Commonwealth countries have undertaken root and branch reform to the supervisory jurisdiction of their courts, modernisation of the judicial review procedures and remedies in England and Wales has been more piecemeal.[3] The Supreme Court Act 1981 (renamed the Senior Courts Act 1981 by the Constitutional Reform Act 2005), which puts the High Court's general power of judicial review on a statutory footing, originally did so by reference to the pre-existing common law powers of the court: s.29(1), before its amendment in 2004,[4] provided that "The High Court shall have jurisdiction to make orders of mandamus, prohibition and certiorari in those classes of cases in which it had power to do so immediately before the commencement of this Act".[5] The jurisdiction exercised by the Queen's Bench Division today is thus directly linked to that of the Court of King's Bench in the 17th century and earlier.

15-003   Thirdly, a further consequence of piecemeal reform is that the High Court continues to exercise its review powers through a hotchpotch of procedures.[6] In addition to judicial review under CPR 54 (formerly RSC Ord.53), aggrieved citizens may make, where appropriate, an application for the writ of habeas corpus (RSC Ord.54) or make a statutory application to quash a decision or order under a variety of specific enactments (governed by RSC Ord.94). There is also a diverse range of appeals to the High Court, some of which resemble judicial review in the role that they perform. The lack of system can only be satisfactorily explained by reference to the historical development of the separate procedures.

15-004   Fourthly, the historical sketch that follows is a salutary reminder that many of the central preoccupations of today, for example, the questions of which bodies are susceptible to judicial review and who has standing to make such challenges, are not new.[7]

The writ system

15-005   One of the central characteristics of the English common law is the writ. In the earliest times, the royal writs were sealed governmental documents, drafted in a crisp, business-like manner, by which the King conveyed notifications or orders.[8]

---

tive law has at first the look of being gradually secreted in the interstices of procedure" (*Early Law and Custom* (1891), p.389).

3   Previous editions of this work described the reforms to judicial review procedures and remedies as "superficial". This description is no longer sustainable given the cumulative extent of the reforms explained in the final section of this chapter.

4   See 3-015.

5   This is a re-enactment of the Administration of Justice (Miscellaneous Provisions) Act 1938 s.7 which turned the prerogative "writs" of mandamus, certiorari and prohibition into "Orders".

6   See 16-001.

7   Other useful work includes: L.J. Jaffe and E.G. Henderson, "Judicial Review and the Rule of Law: Historical Origins" (1956) 72 L.Q.R. 345; E.G.Henderson, *Foundations of English Administrative Law* (1963); H.W. Arthurs, *"Without the Law": Administrative Justice and Legal Pluralism in 19th Century England* (1985); G. Drewry, Ch.2, in M. Supperstone, J. Goudie and P. Walker (eds), *Judicial Review*, 5th edn (2014); M. Loughlin, *Public Law and Political Theory* (1992); S. Anderson, Ch.VI, in W. Cornish, S. Anderson, R. Cocks, M. Lobban, P. Polden and K. Smith, *The Oxford History of the Laws of England*, Vol.XI (2012); and P. Craig, UK, *EU and Global Administrative Law: Foundations and Challenges* (2015), pp.13–95. Two outstanding judicial contributions are J. Laws, *The Common Law Constitution* (2014) and S. Sedley, *Lions Under the Throne: Essays on the History of English Public Law* (2015).

8   R.C. Van Caenegem, *Royal Writs in England from the Conquest to Glanville: Studies in the Early History of the Common Law* (Seldon Society, 1959), p.v and Pt 2.

Certiorari[9] was essentially a royal demand for information; the King, wishing to be certified of some matter, orders that the necessary information be provided for him. Thus, the King wishes to be more fully informed of allegations of extortion made by his subjects in Lincoln, and therefore appoints commissioners to inquire into them.[10] The *Calendar of Inquisitions* mentions numerous writs of certiorari, addressed to the escheator[11] or the sheriff, to make inquisitions; the earliest are for the year 1260.[12] When Parliament grants Edward II one foot-soldier for every township, the writ addressed to the sheriffs to send in returns of their townships to the Exchequer is a writ of certiorari.[13] It was, in fact, one of the King's own writs, used for general governmental purposes.

In early times, the King also issued countless innominate writs that included the word "mandamus—the autocratic head of a vast administrative system will have occasion to 'mandamus' his subjects many times in the course of a day"[14]—but it seems probable that the connection between most of these royal mandates and the modern judicial writ was verbal only. Moreover, the writs called mandamus that appear in the early law books are concerned not with private grievances at all, but with steps to be taken by the escheator or the sheriff in connection with possible accretions to the royal revenues. **15-006**

Subjects unattracted to the justice dispensed by the "antiquated and archaic process" of the local courts came in increasing numbers to seek a remedy from the King himself, in the form of a royal writ. In this way, it has been noted, "arbitrary, even irresponsible interventions in law suits" took place.[15] By the middle of the 12th century, such royal interventions became judicialised and redress was obtained through the King's Court rather than from the King himself. Eventually, writs came to be issued in certain standard forms, collected in the Register of Writs. Each was designed to deal with a particular type of grievance. New forms of writs were capable of creation only by the Chancellor. By the time of Bracton,[16] it could be said that a remedy from the King's Courts could be obtained only if an appropriate writ existed. The development of the writ system, therefore, has about it a hint of paradox for modern administrative law: what began as executive commands aimed at avoiding judicial proceedings became in turn the central mechanism for the judicial control of executive action. **15-007**

The term "prerogative writs"

When and why did some of these judicialised writs come to be called, individually and then later collectively, "prerogative" writs? Although this term for the writs of certiorari, mandamus, prohibition and habeas corpus is well known wherever the language of the common law is spoken, there is no entirely satisfactory answer to these questions. The use of the phrase prerogative writs to refer collectively to these four writs emerges only surprisingly late in the history of writs generally, in the time **15-008**

---

9   The word is not, apparently, of classical origin: Du Cange, *Glossarium Mediae et Infimae Latinitatis*, Vol.2.

10 Placitorum Abbreviatio 155 (49 Hen. 3).

11 cf. Register of Original Writs, and following, 293, 296; for history of the escheator, see W.A. Morris and J.R. Strayer, *The English Government at Work, 1327-36* (1947), Vol.ii, pp.109-167.

12 *Calendar of Inquisitions*, Vol.I, pp.30, 131.

13 *Inquisitions and Assessments Relating to Feudal Aids*, Vol.I, p.16; see also Introduction, p.xxiii.

14 E. Jenks, "The Prerogative Writs in English law" (1923) 32 Yale L.J. 523.

15 See, generally, R.C. Van Caenegem, *The Birth of the English Common Law*, 2nd edn (1988), p.30.

16 Henry de Bracton (d. 1268). His *De Legibus et Consuetudinibus Angliae* (hereinafter De Legibus) was the first systematic treatise on English law.

of Blackstone and Mansfield in the mid-18th century. The origins of the term can, however, be traced to the political inclinations of certain Royalist judges in the 17th century who were keen to associate the beneficent remedy of habeas corpus with the King's personal solicitude for the welfare of his subjects.[17]

15-009   Few judges were more ardently Royalist than Montagu, who succeeded Coke[18] as Chief Justice of the King's Bench after Coke had been removed by the King in 1617. It is in a case decided by Montagu and three brethren not noted for their independence of the Crown that habeas corpus is for the first time reported as being called a prerogative writ. In Montagu's words it is "a prerogative writ, which concerns the King's justice to be administered to his subjects; for the King ought to have an account why any of his subjects are imprisoned".[19] His primary purpose was to emphasise that the writ would run to the Cinque Ports in spite of the fact that they were an exempt jurisdiction to which writs relating to ordinary suits between subjects would not run. Even so, it is reasonable to ascribe his use of the word "prerogative" to his political inclinations. Habeas corpus was a beneficent remedy, and it was sound politics to associate its award with the King's concern for his subjects. Its value became enhanced during the constitutional struggles of the 17th century—albeit, paradoxically, as a safeguard of the liberty of the King's political opponents and it came to be regarded, with Magna Carta,[20] as the greatest bastion of individual liberty.

15-010   Though the four writs had acquired their "prerogative" characteristics by the middle of the 17th century, strangely it was not until a century later, in 1759, that anybody (Mansfield) seems to have thought of classifying the writs as a group.[21] Those shared characteristics included the following:

- They were not writs of course which could be purchased by or on behalf of any applicant[22] from the Royal Chancery; they could not be had for the asking, but proper cause had to be shown to the satisfaction of the court why they should issue.
- The award of the prerogative writs usually lay within the discretion of the court. The court was entitled to refuse certiorari and mandamus to applicants if they had been guilty of unreasonable delay or misconduct or if an adequate alternative remedy existed, notwithstanding that they have proved a usurpation of jurisdiction by the inferior tribunal or an omission

---

[17]   The theory that the prerogative writs were in origin peculiar to the King himself is valid only with respect to certain obsolete and obsolescent writs. The earliest appearances of certiorari and mandamus in judicial proceedings were often as the result of applications made by subjects.

[18]   Sir Edward Coke (1552-1634). He was successively Solicitor General, Speaker of the House of Commons, Attorney General, Chief Justice of Common Pleas and Chief Justice of the King's Bench. He was removed from the last named post by the King in 1617. To the displeasure of the King, he asserted the jurisdiction of the common law courts over royal power: he held that a royal proclamation could not change the law and doubted the King's prerogative to control the conduct of litigation which involved royal interests. His *Institutes* (hereinafter "Co. Inst.") were the first treatise on the modern common law.

[19]   *Richard Bourn's Case* (1620) Cro. Jac. 543. See also the judgments of his brethren reported in Palm. 54 for like language. Similar reasoning was used in two slightly earlier cases in 2 Roll.Abr. 69; but the word "prerogative" is not mentioned there.

[20]   Habeas Corpus was often said to be founded on Magna Carta: Holdsworth, *The History of English Law*, Vol.I, p.228; J. Hudson, "Magna Carta and the Common Law" in *The Oxford History of the Laws of England*, Vol.II (2012). So, too, was mandamus: *R. v Heathcote* (1712) 10 Mod. 48, 53; *Tapping on Mandamus* (1848) pp.2, 5.

[21]   *R. v Cowle* (1759) 2 Burr. 834 at 855-856, per Mansfield. This seems to be the first reference to certiorari as a prerogative writ.

[22]   G.O. Sayles, *Introduction to Vol.57*, Selden Soc., p.lxxvii.

to perform a public duty. But although none of the prerogative writs was a writ of course, not all were discretionary. Prohibition, for example, issued as of right in certain cases; and habeas corpus ad subjiciendum, the most famous of them all, was a writ of right which issued ex debito justitiae when the applicant had satisfied the court that his detention was unlawful. These two writs, therefore, were not in the fullest sense writs of grace.

- The prerogative writs were awarded pre-eminently by the Court of King's Bench.[23] Bracton described the emergent court as "aula regia where the King's justices proprias causas regis terminant."[24] This jurisdiction belonged peculiarly to the King's Bench; the court held—at one time in reality, later only in theory[25]—coram rege ipso.[26] It comprised the hearing of pleas of the Crown and the examination and correction of the errors of other courts.
- At common law they would go to exempt jurisdictions (e.g. the Counties Palatine, the Cinque Ports), to which the King's writs did not normally run.

Today, the prerogative remedies remain at the centre of judicial review and they continue to manifest their early characteristics. Aggrieved citizens still cannot initiate judicial review proceedings as of right; they must first seek the permission of the court. The grant or refusal of a remedy is still in the discretion of the courts. And judicial review remains principally within the jurisdiction of the Queen's Bench Division, of which the Administrative Court is part.[27] **15-011**

The late recognition that the prerogative writs formed a group distinct from other writs is perhaps the oddest feature of their history. Although a relationship between the writs was assumed to exist, its nature was not defined; there was no Bracton to undertake the task of systematic analysis and rationalisation. After Coke and until Mansfield and Blackstone no common lawyer except Hale[28] was able to survey the whole field of the law with scholarship and insight. And by the time that Mansfield had perceived the close relationship between the writs and had chosen to link them verbally with the rights of the Crown, each writ had developed piecemeal its own special characteristics, so that to define the class with precision in terms of characteristics common to all its members had become virtually impossible. But it is easy enough to explain why Mansfield[29] and Blackstone,[30] who were good King's men, should have insisted on the prerogative character of habeas corpus. And if these were the qualities which in their eyes entitled habeas corpus to classification as a prerogative writ, they were shared in large measure by mandamus, "a command issuing in the King's name from the court of King's Bench" and "a writ of a most extensively remedial nature".[31] The writ of mandamus, moreover, expressly alleged a contempt of the Crown[32] consisting in the neglect of a public duty; and it was a writ of grace. The "prerogative" characteristics of prohibition and certiorari **15-012**

---

[23] Proceedings upon the writ ne exeat regno were confined to the Court of Chancery.

[24] De Legibus, f.150b. That is, a Royal hall where the King's justices decide the King's own causes.

[25] Prohibitions del Roy (1607) 12 Co.Rep. 63. That is, before the King himself.

[26] Holdsworth, *History of English Law*, Vol. i, pp.204-206.

[27] See Chs 16 and 17. The Upper Tribunal has also been granted its own "judicial review" jurisdiction in certain areas.

[28] Sir Matthew Hale (1609-76) wrote prolifically. Perhaps most important is his *History of the Common Law* (1713). See A. Cromartie, *Sir Matthew Hale: law, religion, and natural philosophy* (1995).

[29] Earl Mansfield (William Murray), 1705-93 was Chief Justice of the King's Bench from 1756.

[30] Sir William Blackstone, 1723-80, first Vinerian Professor of English law in the University of Oxford. His *Commentaries on the Law of England* (hereinafter Commentaries) were published between 1756-69.

[31] Blackstone, Commentaries, Vol. iii, p.110.

[32] See the form of the writ in *Bagg's Case* (1615) 11 Co. Rep. 93b. The phrase also appeared in some modern forms of the writ: F.H. Short and F.H. Mellor, *Practice on the Crown Side*, 2nd edn (1908),

were still more obvious. Prohibition had always been associated with the maintenance of the rights of the Crown. Certiorari was historically linked with the King's person as well as with the King's Bench; it was of high importance for the control of inferior tribunals, particularly with respect to the administration of criminal justice; it was a writ of course for the King but not for the subject.

15-013　　Mansfield and Blackstone, then, were responsible, if not for the invention of the term "prerogative writ", at least for its acceptance as part of the lawyer's vocabulary. We may now turn to examine in more detail the separate development of each of the prerogative writs.

CERTIORARI AND PROHIBITION[33]

The origins of the writ of certiorari

15-014　　From about 1280, the judicial forms of the writ of certiorari were in common use, issuing on the application of ordinary litigants. Sometimes it was in the nature of a writ of error;[34] sometimes the proceedings at Westminster were in effect general appellate proceedings. The breadth of the issues that could be thus raised is amply illustrated in the edited volumes of King's Bench cases for the reigns of Edward I and his six successors.[35] The conception then prevailing was well expressed in a Canadian case:

> "The theory is that the Sovereign has been appealed to by some one of his subjects who complains of an injustice done him by an inferior court; whereupon the Sovereign, saying that he wishes to be certified—certiorari—of the matter, orders that the record, etc., be transmitted into a court in which he is sitting."[36]

15-015　　Much of this very broad remedial jurisdiction passed from the courts of common law to the Court of Chancery, and in the Tudor and early Stuart periods the writ of certiorari frequently issued to bring the proceedings of inferior courts of common law before the Chancellor.[37] Later, however, the Chancery confined its supervisory functions to inferior courts of equity.

15-016　　From the 14th century until the middle of the 17th century the following seem to have been the main purposes served by certiorari:

(a)　To supervise the proceedings of inferior courts of specialised jurisdiction–for example, the Commissioners of Sewers, the Courts Merchant, the Court of Admiralty, the Courts of the Forests-by bringing up cases to Westminster for trial or, if necessary, retrial or review.

(b)　To obtain information for administrative purposes; for example, the sheriff is told to find out whether one who has been granted the King's protection is tarrying in the city instead of journeying forth in the King's service; the escheator must certify into the Chancery the value of knights' fees (quantity of land deemed sufficient to support a knight) and advowsons (right to

---

pp.518, 591 et passim.

[33]　The writs of certiorari and prohibition shared so many characteristics that they can well be discussed together.

[34]　See S.F.C. Milsom, *Historical Foundations of the Common Law*, 2nd edn (1981) pp.55-58, on certiorari as the progenitor of the writ of error.

[35]　Seldon Soc., Vols 55, 57, 58, 74, 76, 82, 88, edited by G.O. Sayles.

[36]　*R. v Titchmarsh* (1915) 22 D.L.R. 272 at 277-278.

[37]　Cowell, *Interpreter*, M2; Spence, Equitable Jurisdiction, Vol.i, pp.686, 687.

nominate clergy to livings) which have escheated (reverted for want of lawful successor) to the King.

(c) To bring into the Chancery or before the common law courts judicial records and other formal documents for a wide diversity of purposes. The Register of Writs gives many examples.

(d) To remove coroners' inquisitions and indictments into the King's Bench.

The origins of the writ of prohibition

Prohibition is one of the oldest writs known to the law. From the first its primary function seems to have been to limit the jurisdiction of the ecclesiastical courts.[38] The examples given by Glanvill show that it would issue at the suggestion of a subject, and the prohibitory clause recites that the suits in question "ad coronam et dignitatem meam pertinent".[39] It later came to be used as a weapon by the common law courts in their conflicts with the Courts of Chancery and Admiralty. The early history of the writ and its verbal identification with the rights of the Crown help to explain the extravagant language in which later lawyers were wont to describe its qualities. Thus, in *Warner v Suckerman*[40] Coke J, holding that it would issue to the courts of the County Palatine of Lancaster, said: "It is breve regium and jus coronae, and if this writ shall be denied in such cases, this would be in laesionem, exheredationem, et derogationem coronae."[41] The matter was expressed more soberly in another case: "The King is the indifferent arbitrator in all jurisdictions, as well spiritual and temporal, and [it] is a right of his Crown to ... declare their bounds" by prohibitions.[42]   **15-017**

Disobedience to a prohibition was conceived of as a contempt of the Crown. Since it was "the proper power and honour of the King's Bench to limit the jurisdiction of all other courts"[43] the writ usually issued out of that court; but it could also be awarded by the Chancery and the Common Pleas.   **15-018**

The "prerogative" character of the writ has been repeatedly stressed. Fitzherbert says that "the King for himself may sue forth this writ, although the plea in the spiritual court be betwixt two common persons, because the suit is in derogation of his Crown".[44] That the protection of private interests is only a secondary function of the writ is brought out in the comparatively modern case of *Worthington v Jeffries*, where it was said that: **15-019**

"the ground of decision in considering whether prohibition is or is not to be granted, is not whether the individual suitor has or has not suffered damage, but is whether the royal prerogative has been encroached upon by reason of the prescribed order of the administration of justice having been disobeyed."[45]

Hence it has been said that even a complete stranger to the proceeding in the other court could have the writ.[46]

---

[38] N. Adams, "The Writ of Prohibition to Court Christian" (1936) 20 Minn.L.R. 272.
[39] That is, they belong to the Crown and the King's dignity.
[40] *Warner v Suckerman* (1615) 3 Bulst. 119; see also Skin. 626.
[41] That is, it is a royal writ and the law of the Crown if denied, it would be an injury to, and a disinheritance and derogation of, the Crown.
[42] *Doctor James's Case* (1621) Hobart 17; 80 E.R. 168.
[43] *Case of the Company of Homers in London* (1642) 2 Roll.R. 471.
[44] Fitzherbert, Natura Brevium, p.40 E.
[45] *Worthington v Jeffries* (1875) L.R. 10 C.P. 379, 382; see also R.T. Walker, "Is the Writ of Prohibition a Prerogative Writ?" (1939) 37 Mich. L.R. 789; and Note (1923) 36 Harv.L.R. 863.
[46] *Worthington v Jeffries* (1875) L.R. 10 C.P. 379.

The expansion of government

15-020   Before elected borough and county councils were established by the Municipal Corporations Acts 1835 and 1882, local government functions were carried out by the Justices of the Peace. JPs were drawn almost exclusively from the ranks of the landed gentry and their duties included the regulation of wages and prices, the implementation of the Poor Law as well as the administration of petty justice. With the vast increase in the non-judicial duties of the JPs after 1660, certiorari acquired a new importance. By whom and by what means were the decisions of JPs to be subjected to judicial review? The conciliar courts had gone, and no new governmental organ had arisen to take their place. The Court of King's Bench, which had always been associated with the work of government and which had retained a supervisory jurisdiction over the work of the justices in sessions and of other local bodies during the heyday of the Council and the Star Chamber, was manifestly the proper superintending authority. But it could not exercise its authority by means of the writ of error, for although error lay to impeach the record of a judgment given on an indictment it would not lie to quash convictions and orders made in summary proceedings. Persons aggrieved by summary convictions and orders might bring applications for habeas corpus or civil actions for trespass or replevin in order to obtain redress; but these modes of proceeding were not always appropriate, and in any event collateral attack was available only for acts done without jurisdiction.[47] After a period of doubt and vacillation, the court ultimately committed itself to the proposition that the appropriate remedy in all cases where an inferior statutory tribunal had exceeded its jurisdiction or drawn up a conviction or order that was bad on its face was a writ of certiorari to quash the conviction or order. The process by which this proposition came to be established is still not free from obscurity; but by 1700 it was possible for Holt CJ, in the famous case of *Groenvelt v Burwell*,[48] to proclaim the grand generalisation that: "It is a consequence of all jurisdictions to have their proceedings returned here by certiorari to be examined here ... Where any court is erected by statute, a certiorari lies to it".

15-021   Thereafter the King's Bench became inundated with motions for certiorari to quash rates and orders made by justices and other bodies exercising administrative functions under semi-judicial forms. It became what Gneist has called an Oberverwaltungsgericht,[49] a superior administrative court, supervising much of the business of local government by keeping subordinate bodies within their legal limitations by writs of certiorari and prohibition, and ordering them to perform their duties by writs of mandamus. The modern High Court has succeeded to much of this jurisdiction, and there can be no doubt that the absence in the common law systems of a distinct body of public law, whereby proceedings against public authorities are instituted only before special administrative courts and are governed by a special body of rules, is directly traceable to the extensive use of prerogative writs by the Court of King's Bench.

15-022   Certiorari and prohibition established themselves as the most important remedies in administrative law because in the latter part of the 17th century local administration was free from effective supervision by the central government. The role of supervisor was assumed by the Court of King's Bench, which had declared that it would "examine the proceedings of all jurisdictions erected by Act of Parliament

---

47   A. Rubinstein, "On the Origins of Judicial Review" (1964) 1 U. of B.C.Law Rev 1, 3-7.
48   *Groenvelt v Burwell* (1700) 1 Ld.Raym. 454 at 459 (certiorari to review disciplinary decisions of the censors of the College of Physicians).
49   R. von Greist, *Englishe Verfassungsgeschichte* (1882) p.574.

... to the end that ... they keep themselves within their jurisdictions".[50] Apart from their formal ministerial duties, whatever the justices had to do was "the exercise of a jurisdiction".[51] It was assumed that the writs of certiorari and prohibition, by which they were controlled in their capacity as courts of summary jurisdiction, were equally appropriate devices for superintending the exercise of their multifarious governmental functions. All those functions of the justices which were not purely ministerial were regarded for this purpose as being judicial: no separate category of discretionary "administrative" acts, immune from the reach of certiorari and prohibition, was yet recognised.[52] A no less broad conception of "judicial" functions governed review of orders made by the Commissioners of Sewers, who presided over a court of record which performed administrative duties under judicial forms.

Thus, whilst certiorari would not lie to bring up a warrant in issuing which a justice had no statutory discretion,[53] it would lie to bring up and quash discretionary orders for fixing rates for the repair of bridges[54] for the production of poor rate books,[55] and for prohibiting the clerk of the peace from taking certain court fees,[56] and an order by Commissioners of Sewers for the removal of their clerk.[57] The general rule that the discretionary acts of justices were to be treated as judicial was unaffected by a few isolated decisions that went the other way.[58] It was not seriously challenged until it was held in a group of cases in the 1890s that the functions of licensing justices in deciding upon the granting and renewal of licences were not judicial but "administrative" and were not controllable by certiorari.[59] After 1906, however, they were regarded as judicial for this purpose.[60] The distinction is no longer very important in modern law.

15-023

With the coming of industrialisation, urbanisation and democratic reform, the JPs shed many of their general local government functions.[61] A new phase opened in the history of certiorari and prohibition during the 1830s. Two legal issues (still a source of controversy in judicial review proceedings today) engaged the courts during this period. The first was the question of which of the newly created government bodies were amenable to certiorari and prohibition. Ad hoc bodies and elected local government authorities, clothed with extensive regulatory powers over persons and property, were set up to administer the expanding functions of government. Auditors were invested with statutory powers to disallow illegal payments made out of public funds.[62] Parliament not infrequently provided a statutory method of chal-

15-024

---

50   R. v Glamorganshire Inhabitants (Cardiff Bridge Case) (1700) 1 Ld.Raym. 580.

51   F.W. Maitland, "The Shallows and Silences of Real Life," Collected Papers, Vol.i, p.478.

52   See Ferguson v Earl of Kinnoul (1842) 9 Cl. & F. 251 at 290 for an early recognition of a third category of function.

53   R. v Lediard (1751) Say. 6; Ex p. Taunton (1831) 1 Dowl. 55.

54   Cardiff Bridge Case (1700) 1 Ld.Raym. 580.

55   Case of the Borough of Warwick (1734) 2 Str. 991.

56   R. v Coles (1845) 8 Q.B. 75.

57   Arthur v Commissioners of Sewers for Yorkshire (1724) 8 Mod. 331.

58   R. v Lloyd (1783) Cald. 309; R. v Hatfield Peverel (Inhabitants) (1849) 14 Q.B. 298 (order for removal of pauper lunatic to asylum), with which contrast R. v Boycott Ex p. Keasley [1939] 2 K.B. 651; R. v Drummond Ex p. Saunders (1903) 88 L.T. 833 (appointment of justices' clerk), with which contrast dictum in Re Constables of Hipperholme (1847) 5 D. & L. 79 at 81.

59   See, e.g. R. v Sharman [1898] 1 Q.B. 578.

60   R. v Woodhouse [1906] 2 K.B. 501.

61   See W.R. Cornish and G. de N. Clark, Law and Society in England 1750-1950 (1989), p.21.

62   See W.A. Robson, The Development of Local Government (1954) for an account of the development of the office of District Auditor.

lenging the decisions of these authorities by way of certiorari.[63] It was natural that the courts should take the view that common law certiorari and prohibition could properly issue to other authorities discharging similar functions where Parliament had made no express provision for a method of challenge.[64]

15-025   With the accumulation of precedents, the courts took a step further and held (after some vacillation) that the orders of central government departments and ministers[65] (but not of the Crown as such) were amenable to certiorari and prohibition. No longer was the availability of the writs limited to courts stricto sensu, or even to bodies that closely resembled the courts.

15-026   The question whether the writs would issue in any particular case had come to be determined by reference to the character of the act or decision that was impugned and not merely by reference to the general character of the body that had acted or decided. If the act or decision was of a judicial character, its validity could be challenged by certiorari or prohibition. Doubts about the propriety of issuing the writs to administrative bodies had been so far dispelled by 1882 that it could be said, in a case where a local authority sought a prohibition against a central government department, that wherever the legislature entrusts to any body of persons other than to the superior courts the power of imposing an obligation upon individuals, the courts ought to exercise as widely as they can the power of controlling those bodies if they attempted to exceed their statutory powers.[66]

15-027   By the early 1900s, it was well settled that certiorari would issue to a body which "would not ordinarily be called a court, nor would its act ordinarily be termed 'judicial acts'"; that in this context "the term 'judicial act' is used in contrast with purely ministerial acts"; and that in general a judicial act was one which involved "the exercise of some right or duty to decide" a question affecting individual rights.[67] It did not follow, however, that every act affecting individual rights was necessarily "judicial" because it was not ministerial.

Certiorari, prohibition and the problem of locus standi

15-028   Apart from these difficulties over which decisions were amenable to challenge by way of certiorari and prohibition, the courts came to be beset with another problem: who could apply for these prerogative writs?[68] The courts developed a restrictive and highly technical approach to locus standi. As we shall see later, the problem was not confined to the writs of certiorari and prohibition, but also afflicted applications for mandamus and, later, the declaration. The old law in relation to the standing of an applicant for certiorari and prohibition must be stated

---

63   See, e.g. Poor Law Amendment Act 1834 ss.105, 106; Municipal Corporations (General) Act 1837 s.44; Tithe Act 1837 s.3; Poor Law Amendment Act 1844 s.35. In some instances statutory certiorari was apparently intended to take the place of an appeal to the courts and to enable the courts to review the merits of the order impugned: *Re Dent Tithe Commutation* (1845) 8 Q.B. 43 at 59; *R. v Roberts* [1908] 1 K.B. 407. See also *The State (Raftis and Dowling) v Leonard* [1960] I.R. 381. cf. statutory applications to quash, below, Ch.17.

64   See, e.g. *R. v Arkwright* (1848) 12 Q.B. 960 (certiorari to church building commissioners for order stopping up churchyard paths); *R. v Aberdare Canal Co* (1850) 14 Q.B. 854 (certiorari to ad hoc commissioners for sanction given to building of a bridge); *Re Crosby-upon-Eden Tithes* (1849) 13 Q.B. 761 (prohibition to tithe commissioners); *Church v Inclosure Commissioners* (1862) 11 C.B. (N.S.) 664 (prohibition to inclosure commissioners).

65   For a useful judicial survey of the development of remedies against Ministers, see *M v Home Office* [1994] 1 A.C. 377.

66   *R. v Local Government Board* (1882) 10 Q.B.D. 309 at 321 (Brett LJ) a much-quoted dictum.

67   *R. v Woodhouse* [1906] 2 K.B. 501 at 535 (Fletcher Moulton LJ) See also *R. v Dublin Corp* (1878) 2 L.R.Ir. 371 at 376.

68   For an account of the modern law on standing, see Ch.2.

tentatively. This is because of a series of conflicting 19th century decisions,[69] in which the expressions "clear want of jurisdiction", "discretionary", "as of right" and "ex debito justitiae" were used with a singular disregard for consistency. They enveloped the right of access to the courts in a fog that is not easily penetrated. The perplexity of the 19th century author who doubted "whether any legal question has ever given rise to so great a conflict of judicial opinion"[70] is more readily understandable than the confident assertion by another authority that the question "has now been set at rest".[71]

Prohibition and locus standi

The rules that governed locus standi in relation to prohibition may be stated as follows. If a defect of jurisdiction was apparent on the face of the proceedings, in other words was patent, the application for prohibition might be brought not only by a party aggrieved but also by a "stranger" to the proceedings,[72] and the court was obliged to allow the application and was not entitled to have regard to the conduct of the applicant.[73] If the defect of jurisdiction was not patent,[74] the court had a discretion to refuse to award prohibition to the applicant, but whereas it would incline towards exercising its discretion in favour of a party aggrieved,[75] it would refuse an application made by a "stranger" unless he made out a very strong case.[76] **15-029**

The rule that a stranger[77] had locus standi to apply for prohibition was explained by the old idea that a usurpation of jurisdiction was a contempt of the Crown and an encroachment upon the royal prerogative. Consequently it was immaterial by what means and by whom the court was informed of the usurpation.[78] But this was a shaky foundation for such a rule, and it seems unlikely that in administrative law **15-030**

---

[69] See, on the one side, *Worthington v Jeffries* (1875) L.R. 10 C.P. 379 and *Ellis v Fleming* (1876) 1 C.P.D. 237; on the other side, *Forster v Forster and Berridge* (1863) 32 L.J.Q.B. 312; *R. v Twiss* (1869) L.R. 4 Q.B. 407 at 413-414 and *Chambers v Green* (1875) L.R. 20 Eq. 552. The judgment of Willes J in *London Corp v Cox* is authoritative but contains elements of ambiguity. The law is most clearly stated in *Farquharson v Morgan* [1894] 1 Q.B. 552, CA.

[70] J. Shortt, *Informations, Mandamus and Prohibition* (1887), p.441.

[71] F.H. Short and F.H. Mellor, *The Practices on the Crown Side of the Kings Bench Division*, 2nd edn (1908), p.254.

[72] Co.Inst., ii, 607; *De Haber v Queen of Portugal* (1851) 17 Q.B. 171 at 214; *London Corp v Cox* (1867) L.R. 2 H.L. 239 at 279; *Worthington v Jeffries* (1875) L.R. 10 C.P. 379.

[73] *Buggin v Bennett* (1767) 4 Burr. 2035; *Farquharson v Morgan* [1894] 1 Q.B. 552; *R. v Comptroller General of Patents and Designs Ex p. Parke, Davis & Co* [1953] 2 W.L.R. 760 at 764.

[74] The rule concerning latent defects of jurisdiction doubtless applied where breach of the rules of natural justice was alleged.

[75] *Farquharson v Morgan* [1894] 1 Q.B. 552. In *Forster v Forster and Berridge* (1863) 32 L.J.Q.B. 312, 314, *London Corp v Cox* (1867) L.R. 2 H.L. 239 at 283, and *Broad v Perkins* (1888) 21 Q.B.D. 533, prohibition is spoken of as issuing as of right or ex debito justitiae on the application of a party aggrieved, but in each case the court recognised its discretion to refuse the writ if the circumstances so warranted. Sedley J relied on *Broad v Perkins* and other 19th century authorities in his much-cited decision on standing in *R. v Somerset CC Ex p. Dixon* [1998] Env. L.R. 111, 119-120.

[76] *Forster v Forster and Berridge* (1863) 32 L.J.Q.B. 312 at 314; Short & Mellor (1908), p.265.

[77] In the various assertions that a "stranger" had locus standi it is not always clear who is understood to be a stranger. Sometimes the term seemed to mean merely a person who was not a party to the proceedings sought to be prohibited; it did not necessarily follow that the court would have been prepared to accord standing to someone who had no personal interest whatsoever to protect in moving for a prohibition. See S. Thio, *Locus Standi and Judicial Review* (1971), Ch.4. And compare the judgments of Lord Denning MR and Bridge LJ in *R. v GLC Ex p. Blackburn* [1976] 1 W.L.R. 550 at 559, 567.

[78] *Worthington v Jeffries* (1875) L.R. 10 C.P. 379, 382; *Farquharson v Morgan* (1894) 1 Q.B. 552 at 556.

a court would ever award prohibition to an applicant (other than the Crown) who lacked any personal interest at all in the proceedings impugned.[79]

15-031   Still more anomalous was the sharp distinction drawn between patent defects of jurisdiction and the other grounds for prohibition. Two reasons were put forward to support the rule that the court had no discretion if want of jurisdiction appeared on the face of the proceedings: "that the case might become a precedent if allowed to stand without impeachment"[80] and that the defect was one of which the court itself ought to take notice.[81] The first proposition applied with almost equal force to cases where the defect of jurisdiction was not patent; the second meant no more than that it would often be unseemly for the court to refuse to interfere.

Certiorari and locus standi

15-032   Whereas most of the cases on prohibition resulted from proceedings originally instituted before courts stricto sensu,[82] the locus standi required of an applicant for certiorari often arose in the general field of administrative law. But most of the decisions failed to provide a full exposition of the relevant principles and many of the dicta were ambiguous. It was not even clear how far the rules relating to prohibition were applicable to certiorari. There were numerous dicta to the effect that a "stranger" might be awarded certiorari.[83] On the other hand, Lord Denning observed that the court "would not listen, of course, to a mere busybody who was interfering in things which did not concern him"[84] and in no reported English case was an application brought by such a person successful. Certiorari is a discretionary remedy, and the discretion of the court extended to permitting an application to be made by any member of the public. A person aggrieved, i.e. one whose legal rights had been infringed or who had any other substantial interest in impugning an order, might be awarded a certiorari ex debito justitiae[85] if he could establish any of the recognised grounds for quashing; but the court retained a discretion to refuse his application if his conduct was such as to disentitle him to relief.[86] Only in highly exceptional circumstances did the court exercise its discretion in favour of an applicant who was not a person aggrieved. It may be assumed that it would hardly ever exercise its discretion in favour of an applicant who had himself instituted the proceedings[87] or benefited from the order[88] that he impugned. Whether the court retained any discretion where want of jurisdiction appeared on the face of the

---

[79]   It may be remarked that the public interest in securing the release of persons from unlawful detention is more obvious than in preventing the usurpation of jurisdiction by administrative tribunals; yet a stranger cannot bring an application for habeas corpus without the authority of the prisoner, unless access to the prisoner is denied so that no instructions can be received from him.

[80]   *Ricketts v Bodenham* (1836) 4 Ad. & E. 433 at 441; *Marsden v Wardle* (1854) 5 E. & B. 695, 701.

[81]   *Farquharson v Morgan* (1894) 1 Q.B. 552 at 559.

[82]   *R. v Minister of Health Ex p. Villiers* [1936] 2 K.B. 29; *R. v Liverpool Corp* [1972] 2 Q.B. 299 and *R. v GLC Ex p. Blackburn* [1976] 1 W.L.R. 550 are among the more notable exceptions.

[83]   See, e.g. *R. v Surrey JJ* (1870) L.R. 5 Q.B. 466 at 472-473 (where Blackburn J mentions the "very analogous case of prohibition").

[84]   *R. v Paddington Valuation Officer Ex p. Peachey Property Corp Ltd* [1966] 1 Q.B. 380 at 401.

[85]   Understood by Denning LJ in *R. v Thames Magistrates' Court Ex p. Greenbaum* (1957) 55 L.G.R. 129 to mean "injustice to the applicant".

[86]   See, generally, *Greenbaum* (1957) 55 L.G.R. 129 and *R. v Stafford JJ Ex p. Stafford Corp* [1940] 2 K.B. 33 at 43-44 (Lord Greene MR) explaining the judgment of the court in *R. v Surrey JJ* (1870) L.R. 5 Q.B. 466.

[87]   See *Permanent Trustee Co of NSW v Campbelltown Corp* (1960) 105 C.L.R. 401 at 413 (Menzies J).

[88]   See *R. v Denbighshire JJ* (1853) 17 J.P. 312. But see *R. v Assessment Appeal Board Ex p. Cornwall* (1965) 49 D.L.R. (2nd) 769 (certiorari lay to quash severable part of an order although the applicant had benefited from another part).

proceedings was never clearly settled. Since the primary purpose of both certiorari and prohibition was to prevent the usurpation of jurisdiction, it was argued that the same rule ought to apply as for prohibition; on the other hand, there was something to be said against the extension of anomalous doctrines by analogy.

As has been indicated, a court was in practice unlikely to allow an application **15-033** for certiorari unless it had been made by someone whom it regarded as a person aggrieved. For this purpose, persons aggrieved were defined as those who "have a peculiar grievance of their own beyond some grievance suffered by them in common with the rest of the public".[89] Persons who had been deprived of their offices or proprietary rights, or who had been denied or deprived of an occupational licence, clearly fell within this category. But the category was drawn very widely, and included trade rivals objecting to the grant or renewal of a liquor licence,[90] an adjoining landowner objecting (under now repealed planning legislation) to a grant of interim development permission,[91] a local user of a highway that justices had ordered to be stopped up,[92] a prospective defendant in proceedings to be brought by a party to whom a civil legal aid certificate had been granted by a legal aid committee,[93] newspaper proprietors affected by a magistrates' order to restrict reporting of committal proceedings,[94] local ratepayers objecting to the validity of a valuation list[95] and to decisions by a minister,[96] a local authority[97] and a district auditor[98] that would potentially have increased their fiscal liability. It could not be said that the additional burdens, actual or contingent, that were to be borne by the ratepayers who applied for certiorari fell more heavily on them than on other members of the local community; yet they were treated as persons aggrieved. To this extent the definition of "persons aggrieved" quoted above was therefore too narrow, and should be broadened to include members of a local community who have a special grievance of their own by virtue of their membership of that community.[99] Indeed, by the 1960s, the courts were still more liberal, according locus standi to the Crown and the Gaming Board who objected to the production of a police report for the purpose of a private prosecution for libel,[100] and to trades unions applying for certiorari on behalf of members.[101]

A narrower view of locus standi was, however, taken by the courts when the **15-034** ground upon which the decision was challenged was that some person other than

---

[89] *R. v Nicholson* [1899] 2 Q.B. 455 at 471. See also *Greenbaum* (1957) 55 L.G.R. 129, 134 (Parker LJ).

[90] *R. v Groom Ex p. Cobbold* [1901] 2 K.B. 157.

[91] *R. v Hendon R.D.C. Ex p. Chorley* [1933] 2 K.B. 696.

[92] *R. v Surrey JJ* (1870) L.R. 5 Q.B. 466.

[93] *R. v Manchester Legal Aid Committee Ex p. Brand (RA) & Co* [1952] 2 Q.B. 413.

[94] *R. v Russell Ex p. Beaverbrook Newspapers Ltd* [1969] 1 Q.B. 342; *R. v Blackpool JJ Ex p. Beaverbrook Newspapers Ltd* [1972] 1 W.L.R. 95.

[95] *R. v Paddington Valuation Officer Ex p. Peachey Property Corp Ltd* [1966] 1 Q.B. 380. The application was dismissed on the merits.

[96] *R. v Minister of Health Ex p. Dore* [1927] 1 K.B. 765 (remission of surcharge imposed by district auditor on borough councillors for unlawful expenditure).

[97] *R. v Hendon RDC Ex p. Chorley* [1933] 2 K.B. 696 (grant of development permission gave applicant a contingent right to compensation that would be payable by ratepayers).

[98] *R. (Bridgeman) v Drury* [1894] 2 I.R. 489 (unlawful expenditure allowed by auditor). Certiorari is not now the appropriate means of challenging an auditor's decision.

[99] cf. *R. v Taunton St Mary* (1815) 3 M. & S. 465 at 472. And see *R. v GLC Ex p. Blackburn* [1976] 1 W.L.R. 550.

[100] *R. v Lewes JJ Ex p. Home Secretary* [1973] A.C. 388; see also *R. v Cheltenham JJ Ex p. Secretary of State for Trade* [1977] 1 W.L.R. 95 (witness summons issued to department inspector quashed on application of Minister and the inspector).

[101] *R. v Deputy Industrial Injuries Commissioner Ex p. Amalgamated Engineering Union* [1967] 1 A.C. 725.

the applicant was denied a fair opportunity to be heard.[102] To this extent the rules of natural justice seem to confer rights that are personal to those entitled to be heard by the decision-maker. But it may be possible to satisfy a court that an applicant's interests have been prejudiced by a failure on the part of the authority to give proper notice to others who would have lent weight to the representations of the applicant.[103] A person who had a right to be heard before an administrative tribunal had locus standi to challenge a decision of the tribunal on the ground that the hearing that he was afforded was inadequate, and, frequently, on other grounds as well.

THE WRIT OF MANDAMUS

Origins: restoration to office

15-035   Today the main role of the order of mandamus, now obtainable only in CPR Pt 54 judicial review proceedings (and called a mandatory order), is to compel inferior tribunals to exercise jurisdiction that they have wrongfully declined, and to enforce the exercise of statutory duties and discretion in accordance with the law. The origins of the writ are rather later than those of certiorari and prohibition. Although the history and qualities of certiorari and prohibition well qualified them for inclusion in a "prerogative" group of writs, the claims of mandamus were less obvious. Not until 1573 do we find a reported case that centres around a judicial writ of mandamus serving purposes substantially similar to those of the modern writ[104]—it was issued to restore a citizen of London to his franchise of which he had been illegally deprived. The modern writ of mandamus did not, however, begin to emerge till the early years of the 17th century; and for practical purposes its history can be said to have begun with *Bagg's case*.[105] The writ in this case is shown to have issued out of the King's Bench and to have been attested by Coke as Chief Justice; it recited that Bagg, a capital burgess of Plymouth, had been unjustly removed from his office by the mayor and commonalty, and commanded them to restore him unless they showed to the court good cause for their conduct. They failed to satisfy the court and a peremptory mandamus was issued to restore Bagg. From then onward many such writs issued to compel restitution[106] to offices and liberties. By the early years of the 18th century it had become—thanks largely to the work of Holt—something more comprehensive than a writ of restitution. It would go, on the application of a party aggrieved, to compel the performance of a wide range of public or quasi-public duties, performance of which had been wrongfully refused.

---

[102] This would seem to be the explanation of a curious decision of the Privy Council in *Durayappah v Fernando* [1967] 2 A.C. 337. Relief was denied to the mayor of a municipal council which had been dissolved by a Minister without first according the council a hearing. The Board may have proceeded on the assumption that the restrictive rules governing locus standi for injunctions—the appellant was seeking a multiplicity of remedies—were also applicable to certiorari. The mayor was held to have no independent right to be heard. The case may be criticised for taking too restrictive a view of the interests deserving procedural safeguards.

[103] *Wilson v Secretary of State for the Environment* [1973] 1 W.L.R. 1083.

[104] *Middleton's case*, 3 Dyer 332b. The writ in this case was modelled after one issued in an earlier unreported case of a similar character: *Anable's case*, temp. Henry VI. Henderson has observed (*Foundations of English Administrative Law*, pp.49, 53-54) that the writ in Middleton's case was analogous to a writ of privilege. In the 17th century mandamus lost its connection with privilege (*Foundations of English Administrative Law*, pp.75-76).

[105] *Re Bagg's Case* (1615) 11 Co. Rep. 93b.

[106] In the 17th century the writ was often called a writ of restitution: see e.g. 1 Bulst. 174; Poph. 133 at 176; Style 32; 3 Salk. 231; Hale, *Analysis of the Law*, p.60.

It would issue, for example, to compel the admission (as well as the restoration) of a duly qualified alderman to a corporation,[107] or to compel the holding of an election to the office,[108] and it became a valuable device to prevent the unlawful packing of corporations.[109] More important still, it would issue to inferior tribunals that wrongfully declined jurisdiction.[110] Through the writ of mandamus, the King's Bench compelled the carrying-out of ministerial duties incumbent upon both administrative and judicial bodies.

Lord Mansfield's contribution

The rules governing the issue of the writ gradually took shape until they were fully stated by Lord Mansfield in a series of cases.[111] What is particularly interesting about Mansfield's judgments is that he persistently refers to mandamus as a "prerogative" writ.[112] Thus, in a typical passage, he calls it "a prerogative writ flowing from the King himself, sitting in his court, superintending the police and preserving the peace of this country".[113] Speaking in 1762, Mansfield observed that within the past century mandamus had been: **15-036**

> "liberally interposed for the benefit of the subject and advancement of justice … It was introduced, to prevent disorder from a failure of justice, and defect of police. Therefore it ought to be used upon all occasions where the law has established no specific remedy, and where in justice and good government there ought to be one."[114]

Already by that time the primary function of the writ was to compel inferior tribunals to exercise jurisdiction and discretion according to law. But it issued also for what Blackstone called "an infinite variety of other purposes"[115] large and small: to compel the town of Derby to fulfil its obligations under the Militia Acts,[116] to order the election, admission or restoration of a party aggrieved "to any office or franchise of a public nature whether spiritual or temporal",[117] to secure the use of a meeting-house, to obtain production, delivery and inspection of public documents, to compel local officials to pay over sums due and to perform a variety of other public duties, to compel justices of the peace to issue warrants, make rates, appoint overseers and pass accounts, and to compel a body corporate to surrender its regalia or to affix its common seal.   **15-037**

By the middle of the 19th century the body of case law had swollen to grotesque proportions. In 1848 Thomas Tapping incorporated in his exhaustive and unreadable treatise on the writ,[118] an analysis of all the cases, arranged alphabetically according to subject matter. The list, which ranged from Abbot through Bastards,   **15-038**

---

[107] *R. v Norwich* (Mayor) 2 Ld.Raym. 1244.
[108] *R. v Evesham* (Mayor) 7 Mod. 166.
[109] It was regularly used after 1688 by the Whigs to secure admission to the Tory-packed borough corporations.
[110] See, e.g. *Groenvelt v Burwell*, 1 Ld.Raym. 454; *R. v Montague*, Sess.Cas. 106.
[111] See, esp. *R. v Blooer* (1760) 2 Burr. 1043; *R. v Barker* (1762) 3 Burr. 1265; *R. v Askew* (1768) 4 Burr. 2186.
[112] For example, in *R. v Cowle* (1759) 2 Burr. 834, 855; *R. v Barker* (1762) 1 Wm.B1. 352; *R. v Vice-Chancellor (of Cambridge University)* (1765) 3 Burr. 1647 at 1659. For a similar early reference to mandamus, see *Knipe v Edwin* (1694) 4 Mod. 281; cf. *R. v Patrick*, 1 Keb. 610.
[113] *R. v Barker* (1762) 3 Burr. 1265.
[114] *R. v Barker* (1762) 3 Burr. 1265 at 1267.
[115] Blackstone, Commentaries, Vol.iii, p.110.
[116] Holdsworth, *The History of English Law*, Vol.x, p.156.
[117] Blackstone, Commentaries, Vol.iii, p.110.
[118] Entitled "The Law and Practice of the High Prerogative Writ of Mandamus, as it obtains both in England, and in Ireland".

Corpse, Scavenger and Swordbearer down to Yeoman of Wood Wharf, ran to 252 pages. But the heyday of mandamus was by then nearly over, and its significance was to dwindle almost as swiftly as it had risen.

The decline of mandamus

15-039   After 1835, the corrupt oligarchies which had controlled the boroughs were superseded by local councils elected on broad franchise. Half a century later the broom of reform swept through the counties, and for most administrative purposes elected local authorities replaced the county justices and the parish vestries. The new regime made for a more orderly system of local government, in which the delays and irregularities which had evoked so many applications for mandamus were less likely to occur. Central administrative control, exercised by means of district audit of accounts, inspection of services, powers to act in default, and a host of other regulatory devices, became the normal agency for securing the proper discharge of local duties. In respect of acts and decisions by local authorities affecting individual rights, Parliament adopted the practice of providing persons aggrieved with a right of complaint, objection or appeal to a central government department; and by supplying these efficacious alternative remedies it indirectly took away the right of the individual to obtain a mandamus. The decline of mandamus was also expedited by such factors as reform in the administration of other classes of corporations, and the gradual disappearance of the concept of freehold office in which the holder was quasi-proprietary rights enforceable by mandamus.[119] For these and other reasons[120] the area of public activity and inactivity within which mandamus can play an effective part has diminished. So, while reform of local government leads to an increasing role for certiorari and prohibition, it spelt a diminishing importance for mandamus.

Mandamus and locus standi

15-040   As with certiorari and prohibition, the nature of the interest required to support an application for mandamus was always difficult to state with any degree of confidence. It was often said that the applicant had to have a specific legal right to enforce, or a specific legal right to the enforcement of the duty, and in one case a court applied this principle when refusing an application by a local sanitary authority for an order to compel the responsible officers to implement the provisions of the Vaccination Acts in their district.[121] Again, in cases where the courts refused applications for mandamus against Crown servants the decisions were sometimes explained on the ground that the respondent owed no legal duty to the applicant.[122] But in these cases the references to the absence of any legal duty owed towards the

---

[119] The holder of a freehold office was removable only for misbehaviour, and had the right to be heard in his own defence before removal.

[120] Some of which are referred to in J. Shortt, *Informations, Mandamus and Prohibitions* (1887), pp.271-272.

[121] *R. v Lewisham Union Guardians* [1897] 1 Q.B. 498 (one of two reasons for the decision). cf., however, *R. v Keighley Union Guardians* (1876) 40 J.P. 70; and see *R. v Leicester Guardians* [1899] 2 Q.B. 632 (Local Government Board has locus standi to enforce such a duty). The test formulated in the *Lewisham Union* case has been adopted to some more recent decisions: see, e.g. *R. v Customs and Excise Commissioners Ex p. Cook* [1970] 1 W.L.R. 450 at 455; *Environmental Defence Society Inc v Agricultural Chemicals Board* [1973] 2 N.Z.L.R. 758.

[122] See *R. v Lords Commissioners of the Treasury* (1872) L.R. 7 Q.B. 387 at 395, 398-400, 402; *R. v Inland Revenue Commissioners, re Nathan* (1884) 12 Q.B.D. 461; *R. v Secretary of State for War* [1891] 2 Q.B. 326; *R. v Arndel* (1906) 3 C.L.R. 557; *R. v Governor of South Australia* (1907) 4 C.L.R. 1497 at 1512; *Kariapper v Wijesinha* [1968] A.C. 717 at 745.

applicants were designed to bring out the point that the duties cast upon the respondents were owed by them to the Crown alone; they are not to be understood as purporting to lay down propositions about the nature of the legal interest needed for applications for mandamus in general.

What meaning, then, can be attributed to the broader assertions that a legal right-duty relationship had to be present between the applicant and the respondent? Sometimes, one suspects, they were nothing but tautologies: mandamus would be to secure the enforcement of a legal duty on the application of one who was recognised by law as being entitled to apply for its enforcement by this method. In some contexts they may be understood to mean merely that the "duty" imposed on the respondent must be one recognised by law if it is to be enforceable in the courts[123] or that it is not enough for the applicant to rely upon a private equitable right.[124] If they are to be understood to mean that no application for mandamus for the enforcement of a legal duty may be brought except by one who has a right to bring an action for damages for breach of duty, they are manifestly wrong.[125]   **15-041**

Perhaps the most reasonable construction to place on the proposition that the applicant had to show a legal right to the performance of the duty is that he had to have a substantial personal interest in its performance. There is, indeed, a good deal of judicial support for the view that a mere stranger had no locus standi, and that an applicant had to establish that he was specially aggrieved by the non-performance of the duty or had an immediate interest[126] in its performance greater than that of members of the public generally.[127]   **15-042**

It is possible to explain some of these decisions on the basis that the court was not disclaiming jurisdiction because of the insufficiency of the applicant's locus standi but was merely exercising its discretion not to award him the relief he sought. The view has in fact been advanced that in applications for mandamus, as in applications for certiorari, locus standi was not restricted by any rule of common law and that the courts could in their discretion grant an application made by any member of the public.[128] Certainly the courts on occasion showed the utmost liberality in granting applications made by persons whose interest in the performance of   **15-043**

---

[123] cf. *Ex p. Napier* (1852) 18 Q.B. 692; *R. v Secretary of State for War* [1891] 2 Q.B. 326.

[124] *R. v Stafford (Marquis)* (1790) 3 T.R. 646. See, however, *R. v Registrar of Titles Ex p. Moss* [1928] V.L.R. 411; Thio, pp.114-115; Stafford's case was overtaken by the Judicature Acts.

[125] In *R. v Inland Revenue Commissioners, re Nathan* (1884) 12 Q.B.D. 461 Brett MR confused the issue still further by assuming that no duty was owed to the applicant unless he could bring an action and that if an action would lie, mandamus would not.

[126] For a case where mandamus was refused because the applicant's interest was only indirect, see *R. v Frost* (1838) 8 A. & E. 822. See also *R. v Orton Vicarage Trustees* (1849) 14 Q.B. 139; and cf. *R. v Industrial Court Ex p. ASSET* [1965] 1 Q.B. 377 at 389-390 (dictum). The authorities are reviewed in *R. v Whiteway Ex p. Stephenson* [1961] V.R. 168.

[127] Thus, a rating authority was held not to have a sufficient legal interest to obtain a mandamus to compel an assessment committee to perform its statutory duties properly: *R. v City of London Union Assessment Committee* [1907] 2 K.B. 764. In cases in which writs of mandamus were awarded against local authorities to carry out duties to make a byelaw and prepare a town planning scheme in conformity with statute, the courts examined the interests of the applicants at some length on the assumption that unless they were substantial the court would have no jurisdiction to grant the relief sought. In the one case the applicants had a financial interest in the making of the byelaw and had, moreover, secured the insertion of the clause in the Private Bill requiring the byelaw to be made: *R. v Manchester Corp* [1911] 1 K.B. 560. In the other, a modern Irish case in which the English authorities were considered, the applicants were builders who had suffered financial and other detriment because of the corporation's failure to adopt a scheme: *The State (Modern Homes (Ireland) Ltd) v Dublin Corp* [1953] I.R. 202.

[128] See D.C.M. Yardley, "Prohibition and Mandamus and the Problem of Locus Standi" (1957) 73 L.Q.R. 534, 539.

the duty in question was tenuous.[129] Although the preponderance of authority is opposed to the view that the courts were entitled to exercise a free discretion in determining questions of locus standi in applications for mandamus, and indicates that an applicant had to have a direct interest of his own in the performance of the duty, the courts did in practice exercise a wide discretion in deciding the degree of interest required for the purpose of a particular application.

THE WRIT OF HABEAS CORPUS[130]

15-044   Finally, we turn to the prerogative writ of habeas corpus ad subjiciendum.[131] Though it is the most renowned contribution of the English common law to the protection of human liberty, its origins were modest.[132] The earliest writs of habeas corpus were used in mesne process; they were commands addressed to royal officials to bring before one of the King's courts the body of a person whose presence was required for the purpose of a judicial proceeding. In this form habeas corpus preceded Magna Carta. The connection, readily discerned by 17th century writers, between the text of the Charter and the development of the writ owes less to historical fact than to partisan imagination and wishful legend.

15-045   In the 14th century there emerged the writ of habeas corpus cum causa, requiring the person who already had custody of a prisoner to produce him before the court, together with the ground for the detention. A means of testing the legality of the detention, this was the immediate ancestor of the modern writ.[133] It was used by the common law courts at Westminster to protect, assert and extend their own jurisdiction against their various rivals by securing the release of litigants and others from custody.[134] It was also used by private litigants to procure an order for release from wrongful imprisonment; and in this way it came to assume high constitutional importance as a device for impugning the validity of arbitrary imprisonment by the Executive. The decision in *Darnel's case*,[135] that a warrant certifying a committal to be "by the special command of the King" disclosed a sufficient ground for imprisonment, was overruled by the Petition of Right in the following year. But the machinery for removing the abuse of lengthy imprisonment without trial was still defective. Reforms were introduced by the Habeas Corpus Act 1679: if a person was held on a serious criminal charge, he was to be given release on bail or a speedy trial in pursuance of an application for habeas corpus.[136] Severe financial penalties (which are still in force) were imposed on judges wrongfully refusing to issue the writ, on gaolers evading service of or compliance with the writ

---

[129] Thus, in one case a local vicar, who had unsuccessfully objected to the transfer of a liquor licence obtained a mandamus to order the justices to hear and determine the application for transfer according to law: *R. v Cotham* [1898] 1 Q.B. 802 (the court did not discuss the applicant's locus standi).

[130] See 17-008.

[131] Other forms of habeas corpus are now practically obsolete.

[132] M. Cohen, "The Immigration Act and Limitations upon Judicial Power: Bail" (1938) 16 Can.B.R. 92; J. Farbey and R.J. Sharpe, *The Law of Habeas Corpus*, 3rd edn (2011), Ch.1. The US Supreme Court gives an account of its development and reception in that jurisdiction in *Boumediene v Bush*, 476 F. 3d 981 (2008).

[133] M. Cohen, "Some Considerations on the Origins of Habeas Corpus" (1940) 18 Can.B.R. 10, 172. See also Holdsworth, *The History of English Law*, Vol.ix, pp.24-51; E. Jenks, "The Story of Habeas Corpus" (1902) 18 L.Q.R. 64.

[134] In some situations its effect was analogous to that of a writ of prohibition.

[135] *Re Darnel* (1627) 3 St.Tr. 1.

[136] Habeas Corpus Act 1679 s.6. This section was repealed by the Courts Act 1971 s.56(4) Sch.11 Pt iv.

and on persons recommitting a prisoner who had already been discharged on a habeas corpus.

In 1816, the Act was extended to cases of civil detention and the judges were **15-046** empowered to inquire into the truth of the facts set out in the gaoler's return to the writ in such cases.[137] Given a relatively temperate political climate, with an alert body of informed opinion and an independent judiciary, habeas corpus flourished while liberty in many lands languished. Efficiency was its virtue: habeas corpus really worked. "When Dicey declared that the Habeas Corpus Acts were 'for practical purposes worth a hundred constitutional articles guaranteeing individual liberty'[138] he spoke for the mass of English constitutional lawyers".[139] Substantive guarantees unaccompanied by any effective procedural technique for enforcing them are, indeed, often worthless. But a number of modern constitutional bills of rights incorporate not only entrenched substantive guarantees (which Britain lacks) but also entrenched procedures for enforcement in the courts.[140] This new emphasis on the importance of judicial remedies can be regarded as an indirect recognition of English experience.[141] It has, however, been doubted whether habeas corpus serves any useful purpose today, given the expansion in the scope of judicial review.[142]

EQUITABLE REMEDIES: INJUNCTIONS[143]

After the labyrinthine by-ways of the common law prerogative writs one has a **15-047** sense of greater freedom in the fields of equity. The injunction and the declaratory order were more flexible and adaptable instruments of judicial control than the common law remedies. They were less burdened by precedent. They were comparatively free from the abstruse technicalities and hair-splitting distinctions besetting certiorari, prohibition and mandamus. They could be awarded against bodies whose functions contained no judicial element. However, historically the intrusions of equity upon the domain of public law were desultory and selective. The injunction, still pre-eminently a private law remedy, did not come to play a significant part in public law until the 19th century. And although declarations have equitable roots, the remedy is better seen as a statutory one. By the time the equitable remedies had begun to extend their reach, the prerogative writs were recognised as the principle methods of obtaining judicial review of administrative action, and they were too securely entrenched to be readily ousted by newcomers. The expectations of those who looked for a dramatic increase in the part played by equitable remedies in administrative law have not been fulfilled.

Nevertheless, the equitable sector, which until recently was little more than a **15-048** miscellany of loosely connected topics, has acquired cohesion and substance

---

[137] K. Costello, "The Habeas Corpus Act 1816 at two hundred" [2016] P.L. 183.

[138] *Introduction to the Study of the Law of the Constitution*, 10th edn (1959), p.199.

[139] S.A. de Smith, *The New Commonwealth and its Constitutions* (1964), p.167.

[140] See, e.g. Constitution of India, arts 19, 21, 22, 32, 226; Constitution of Jamaica (SI 1962/1550 Sch.2) ss.15, 20, 25, 49, 50.

[141] England was not the only country to devise an effective judicial remedy for obtaining release from wrongful imprisonment. Thus, similar remedies were evolved in Scots law, Roman-Dutch law and some Latin American systems. But habeas corpus has attracted special attention overseas. See, e.g. L. Kutner, *World Habeas Corpus; and Seminar on Amparo, Habeas Corpus and other Similar Remedies* (United Nations, 1962).

[142] A. Le Sueur, "Should we Abolish the Writ of Habeas Corpus" [1992] P.L. 13; cf. M. Shrimpton, "In Defence of Habeas Corpus" [1993] P.L. 24 and Law Com No.226, Pt XI.

[143] On modern law and practice see 18-033.

through the creative activity of individual judges; and the creative impulse is by no means spent.[144] Moreover, a consequence of the procedural reforms of 1977 that enable an applicant for judicial review to request a declaration or an injunction (or both), alone or combined with one or more of the prerogative orders, is that these remedies have moved closer to the mainstream of administrative law.

15-049 The origins of equitable intervention and much of the subsequent course of its evolution are shrouded in obscurity. Three topics in particular are important: the constant interplay between matters of public right and matters of private right; the influence of the Crown's prerogative capacity as parens patriae; and the significant role of the Court of Exchequer.

The Court of Exchequer

15-050 The Court of Exchequer assumed a general equitable jurisdiction during the course of the 16th century.[145] In addition, it exercised equitable powers incidentally to its capacity as a court of revenue.[146] In the exercise of this ancillary jurisdiction it entertained English information filed by the Attorney-General to secure the protection and enforcement of the proprietary and fiscal rights of the Crown against subjects.[147] The relief awarded included injunctions and declaratory orders. The English information may well have been the earliest form of equitable proceeding lying predominantly within the field of public law. Its procedural rules were unwarrantably favourable to the Crown, and a belated recognition of this injustice was one reason why it had fallen into desuetude some years before it was abolished by Parliament in 1947.[148]

15-051 A more beneficent and important contribution made by the Court of Exchequer to public law was its practice of awarding equitable relief against the Crown, represented by the Attorney General.[149] For this purpose it does not seem that the court differentiated between cases where the interests of the Crown were indirectly affected and cases where the interests of the Crown were directly affected.[150] Judgment in favour of the subject usually took the form of a declaratory order. After 1841, the practice of suing the Attorney General in an action for a declaration (except under special statutory provisions or upon a petition of right) fell temporarily into abeyance.[151] But this dormant jurisdiction of the Court of Exchequer passed to the High Court of Justice of 1873; and, as we shall see, it was revived in 1911 in a notable case[152] which gave a new impetus to the action for a declaration in public law.

---

[144] See Lord Denning's own dicta in *Lee v Showmen's Guild of Great Britain* [1952] 2 Q.B. 329 at 346; *Barnard v National Dock Labour Board* [1953] 2 Q.B. 18 at 41-44; *Taylor v National Assistance Board* [1957] P. 101 at 111, and *Pyx Granite Co v Ministry of Housing and Local Government* [1958] 1 Q.B. 554 at 571.

[145] Holdsworth, *History of the Laws of England*, Vol.i, p.241. It was described as "an ancient though originally usurped jurisdiction" in *Attorney General v Halling* (1846) 15 M. & W. 687 at 694, where the history of the several sides to the court's equitable jurisdiction is traced. See also Holdsworth, *History of the Laws of England*, Vol.xii, pp.456-458.

[146] See *Attorney General v Halling* (1846) 15 M. & W. 687 at 694.

[147] G. Robertson, *Civil Proceedings by and against the Crown* (1908), pp.234 and following.

[148] Crown Proceedings Act 1947 s.13 and Sch.1 para.1.

[149] Preceding the award of such relief by the Court of Chancery: Holdsworth, "History of Remedies against the Crown" (1922) 38 L.Q.R., 280-281. See also H.G. Hanbury, *Essays in Equity* (1934), pp.114-120.

[150] G. E. Robinson, *Public Authorities and Legal Liability* (1925), pp.xxxvii-xxxix (introductory chapter on remedies against the Crown by J.H. Morgan).

[151] See Court of Chancery Act 1841.

[152] *Dyson v Attorney General* [1911] 1 K.B. 410.

The Court of Chancery

In its early days the Court of Chancery appears to have had little concern with matters of public law, save in so far as its jurisdiction to issue common injunctions to restrain persons from proceeding in the courts of common law and enforcing judgments obtained at common law[153] incidentally raised questions of constitutional importance. The chronology of its interventions in the field of public law cannot be traced with assurance. One can say that the blurred outlines of its jurisdiction were taking shape soon after the Restoration, that they had become more distinct by the middle of the 18th century and that the process of clarification did not end with the Judicature Acts; but much must be left to conjecture. Blackstone's account of equitable jurisdiction was inadequate, but it would appear that by his time the Court of Chancery was entertaining at least four classes of proceedings that have a bearing on our inquiry. First, the Crown could sue in Chancery as an alternative to bringing an English information in the Exchequer.[154] **15-052**

Secondly, a Crown grantee or other person claiming rights under the Crown was permitted to sue in the King's name in order to take advantage of the prerogative. If he sued in his own name in a proceeding that touched the rights of the Crown, he had to join the Attorney General as co-plaintiff.[155] From these beginnings there emerged a general principle that in matters of equitable jurisdiction in which the King's interests were involved, the Attorney General was competent to sue at the relation of a private plaintiff, the relator bearing the costs and receiving the benefit of the court's award.[156] **15-053**

Thirdly, the court would issue injunctions to restrain the commission or continuance of public nuisances,[157] though this was a power more frequently exercised by the Court of Exchequer.[158] Such an injunction could be addressed even to the members of an inferior court whose order had been responsible for creating the nuisance.[159] In Hardwicke's time it was established that an information by the Attorney General was the proper mode of proceeding,[160] unless an individual had suffered particular damage by reason of the nuisance, in which case the intervention of the Attorney General was unnecessary. **15-054**

Fourthly, during the 17th century the Attorney General was bringing information in the Court of Chancery to secure the establishment and due administration of charitable or public trusts.[161] This class of proceeding was of major historical importance; it was the commonest, and possibly the first, of the early forms of rela- **15-055**

---

[153] Substantially abolished with respect to proceedings in the superior courts by the Supreme Court of Judicature Act 1873 s.24(5). See Supreme Court of Judicature (Consolidation) Act 1925 s.41.

[154] Robertson, *Civil Proceedings by and against the Crown* (1908) pp.237, 238.

[155] Robertson, *Civil Proceedings by and against the Crown* (1908) p.464.

[156] *Attorney General of Duchy of Lancaster v Heath* (1690) Prec.Ch. 13; *Attorney General v Oglender* (1740) 1 Ves Jun. 246, 1 Ves.Jun.Supp. 105.

[157] The general jurisdiction of the Court of Chancery to restrain nuisances goes back to Elizabethan times; *Attorney General v Richards* (1788) 2 Anst. 608; *Story on Equity* (2nd English edn), para.921. See generally W.J. Jones, *The Elizabethan Court of Chancery* (1967).

[158] *Attorney General v Cleaver* (1811) 18 Ves. Jr. 211, 217.

[159] *Box v Allen* (1727) Dick. 49 (injunction to Commissioners of Sewers); *Attorney General v Forbes* (1836) 2 My. & Cr. 123 (injunction to magistrates at quarter sessions).

[160] *Baines v Baker* (1752) Amb. 158 at 159.

[161] The view that the Attorney General's intervention preceded the Statute 43 Eliz. c.4 seems to be erroneous. His intervention is traceable to the time of Charles I and became common in the second half of Charles II's reign: G. Jones, *History of the Law of Charity*, 1532-1827, pp.21-22, 34 and following.

tor actions in equity.[162] It was founded on the status of the Crown as parens patriae; and it was the progenitor of new types of proceedings brought by the Attorney General as the Crown's representative in matters especially appertaining to the public welfare.

15-056 The Sovereign, as parens patriae, is responsible for the superintendence of "infants, idiots, lunatics and charities".[163] The Chancellor, as the keeper of the King's conscience, was the appropriate officer to dispense this prerogative jurisdiction, and the Attorney General, as the King's forensic representative, was the appropriate officer to appear for the Crown in the Chancellor's court. If the funds of a public body were deemed to be impressed with a charitable trust, it was clearly appropriate for the Attorney General to go to the Court of Chancery to seek an injunction against their misapplication. Thus the Attorney General came to bring information to restrain unlawful expenditure of borough funds.[164]

15-057 The concept of a parens patriae had still larger implications. The Crown, as parens patriae, had a visitatorial authority over those charitable and ecclesiastical corporations which lacked founders or visitors. A municipal corporation had no visitor; then let the Crown be its visitor and supervisor.[165] At common law the visitatorial power was exercised by bringing quo warranto informations and applications for writs of mandamus and scire facias in the King's Bench. Most of these proceedings arose out of defaults other than the misuse of corporate funds. Since the Crown was empowered, in a proper case, to sue in such of its courts as it thought fit, it could and did elect to take proceedings in equity generally to secure the observance of the law by municipal corporations.[166] This trend of development could well end with a broad proposition that the Attorney General, representing the Crown, could properly apply to the Court of Chancery to restrain the execution of illegal acts committed not merely by corporations which held property on trust for public purposes but also by other bodies, of statutory as well as of non-statutory origin, where such illegalities tended to injure the public welfare. So, indeed, it did end, but not without a long period of judicial hesitation.[167]

15-058 Gradually, during the course of the 19th century, a group of general principles crystallised. The Attorney General could proceed ex proprio motu (of his own motion) in any action in which he might appear at the instance of a relator[168]; the relator need not show any personal interest in the subject-matter of the suit, for the

---

[162] It was the only form of equitable relator action mentioned by Blackstone, *Commentaries*, Vol.iii, p.427. An early example of a proceeding by way of Attorney General's information and private bill with respect to a charity was *Attorney General v Newman* (1670) 1 Ch.Cas. 157, where the appropriateness of the bill was doubted. For early examples of the settled form of relator action, see *Attorney General v Hart* (1703) Prec.Ch. 225; *Attorney General v Bains* (1708) Prec.Ch. 270. For the limits of the court's intervention, see J. Fonblanque, *Treatise of Equity*, 3rd edn, Vol.ii, pp.205-206; *Attorney General v Smart* (1748) 1 Ves.Sen. 72. At common law the informer who was permitted to bring a civil action upon a penal statute (see Holdsworth, *The History of English Law*, Vol.ii, pp.453-454; Vol.iv, pp.355-359), or a qui tam information for a penalty to be shared by himself and the Crown, was also called a relator (see 21 Jac. 1, c.4). In the 18th century a criminal information could be exhibited either by the Attorney General ex officio or by the Master of the Crown Office at the relation of an informer (*The History of English Law*, Vol.ix, pp.237-246). In civil proceedings at common law the only class of relator action corresponding with the relator action in equity was the information in the nature of a quo warranto; see, e.g. 9 Anne c.20 s.4.

[163] *Chitty on Prerogative*, Ch.IX. Lord Nottingham referred to the King as pater patriae: Reports of Cases by Lord Nottingham, Vol.1 (Selden Soc., Vol.73, edn D.E.C. Yale), 209. The prerogative jurisdiction has been partly superseded by statute.

[164] *Attorney General v Aspinall* (1837) 2 My. & Cr. 613.

[165] cf. Roscoe Pound, "Visitatorial Jurisdiction over Corporations in Equity" (1936) 49 Harv.L.R. 369.

[166] As in *Attorney General v Galway Corp* (1828) 1 Molloy 95.

[167] See H.A. Street and S. Brice, *Ultra Vires* (1930), pp.265-266.

[168] *Attorney General v Dublin Corp* (1827) 1 Bli.(N.S.) 312 at 337-338.

proceedings were the Attorney General's[169]; the right of the Attorney General to intervene depended upon the public consequences of the act complained of, not on the intrinsic characteristics of the defendant body[170]; the right of an individual to sue without joining the Attorney General depended on whether his own legal interests were more particularly affected than those of the public in general. In essence, the general right of the Attorney General to seek the repression of ultra vires acts tending to injure the public grew out of a broad conception of the prerogative of protection, and the details of the rules governing locus standi were substantially borrowed from the law of public nuisance.

There was then only the most tentative relaxation of the rules governing locus standi in relation to injunctions,[171] and the function of the Attorney General as protector of the public interest, enabling him to obtain an injunction to restrain breaches of the criminal law, was extended.[172] But the main factor conducive to an expansion of the role of the injunction in public law has been its close association with the declaratory judgment. It is quite common for injunctive and declaratory relief to be claimed in the same proceedings, and in such cases the courts tend to refrain from drawing fine distinctions between the permissible scope of the two remedies.

15-059

DECLARATIONS[173]

The potential of the declaration in public law have been realised only during the 20th century. But a great authority on the action for a declaration has said that "All that is new about declaratory judgments is the name-the phenomenon itself is as ancient as the administration of justice by courts" and that "Anglo-American statutes have from time immemorial authorised and courts have rendered judgments purely declaratory in form and effect".[174] To question these assertions with reference to English law may be presumptuous, yet it would seem that in England the purely declaratory judgment is a comparatively modern institution.[175]

15-060

---

[169] *Attorney General v Vivian* (1825) 1 Russ. 236.

[170] See, e.g. *Attorney General v Oxford, Worcester & Wolverhampton Ry* (1854) 2 W.R. 330; *Attorney General v Cockermouth Local Board* (1874) L.R. 18 Eq. 172.

[171] In *Gouriet v Union of Post Office Workers* [1978] A.C. 435, the House of Lords reaffirmed the requirements that an injunction to restrain a breach of the criminal law will only be granted to an individual who can establish that the defendant's conduct either endangers a private legal right or may occasion him special loss not suffered by members of the public at large.

[172] In a number of recent cases local authorities have been accorded a similar role as guardians of the public interest in their locality by virtue of the Local Government Act 1972 s.222 (for example, *Stoke-on-Trent CC v B & Q (Retail) Ltd* [1984] A.C. 929 in relation to Sunday trading). In *Gouriet* [1978] A.C. 435, however, a warning was sounded about the dangers of a regular resort to injunctions for this purpose.

[173] On the modern law and practice relating to declarations in judicial review proceedings, see 18-037.

[174] E.M. Borchard, *Declaratory Judgments*, 1st edn (1934), pp.62, 73. The author fails to cite any relevant English authority in support of his assertions. In the second edition the former passage is reworded to read: "All that is new about the declaratory judgment is its name and its broad scope-the phenomenon itself is as old as judicial history" (p.137).

[175] S. Anderson, *The Oxford History of the Laws of England*, Vol. XI (2012), 504-506. The history of the remedy is described in detail in Rt. Hon. The Lord Woolf and J. Woolf, *Zamir and Woolf: The Declaratory Judgment*, 4th edn (2011), Ch.2.

Judicial resistance to declaratory relief

15-061   From its earliest days the Court of Chancery did indeed issue declaratory orders.[176] But the books on Chancery practice are silent on the matter of purely declaratory judgments. And if a general practice of rendering purely declaratory judgments had ever existed, it had certainly been abandoned by the 1840s. Thus, Bruce VC observed in 1847[177]: "Nakedly to declare a right, without doing or directing anything else relating to the right, does not, I conceive, belong to the functions of this Court." This view is supported by many other judicial dicta[178] and the contrary view would make nonsense of Lord Brougham's prolonged agitation for importing the main features of the Scots action of declarator into English law.[179]

15-062   The practice of the Court of Chancery not to make declaratory orders unaccompanied by other relief was subject to a limited exception introduced after 1830. The court would permit a suppliant to bring a petition of right to obtain the consent of the Crown to permit itself to be sued through the Attorney General for equitable relief including a declaration,[180] and in one such case the court awarded the suppliant a pure declaration against the Attorney General.[181]

15-063   After the Petitions of Right Act 1860 (under which the judgment of the court was always declaratory in form,[182] although it would normally declare that the suppliant was entitled to damages or other specific relief), a number of petitions claiming equitable relief were directed against the Crown and in some cases the judgment of the court was purely declaratory in substance as well as in form.[183]

15-064   More significant for the development of the action for a declaration in public law was the practice of the Court of Exchequer, which, uninhibited by the restraints that the Court of Chancery had imposed upon itself, had long awarded equitable relief against the Crown, represented by the Attorney General, on bills filed by subjects.[184] Its jurisdiction to grant relief against the Crown was derived from a statute of 1841,[185] its judgments were usually declaratory in form. Whether its jurisdiction extended to declaring that the Crown was under an obligation (e.g. to pay money) to the plaintiff is very dubious.[186] In 1841 its general equitable jurisdiction passed

---

[176] G. Spence, *Equitable Jurisdiction of the Court of Chancery* (1846), Vol.i, p.390. See also Comment, "Developments in the Law Declaratory judgments, 1941-1949" (1949) 62 Harv.L.R. 787.

[177] *Clough v Ratcliffe* (1847) 1 De G. & S. 164 at 178-179.

[178] See, e.g. *Elliotson v Knowles* (1842) 11 L.J. Ch. 399 at 400.

[179] See Borchard (1941), pp.125-128, for an account of the rules of Scots law and Brougham's campaign.

[180] *Clayton v Attorney General* (1834) 1 Coop.t.Cott. 97.

[181] *Taylor v Attorney General* (1837) 8 Sim. 413.

[182] Petitions of Right Act 1860 s.9; W.B. Clode, *Petition of Right* (1887), p.183.

[183] As in *P&O Steam Navigation Co v R.* [1901] 2 K.B. 686 (declaration as to the amount of crewspace shipowners were required by statute to provide for Lascars); but all the relevant decisions appear to have been given after the introduction of RSC, Ord.25 r.5, in 1883.

[184] The view taken by the Chancery has been that since equity acts in personam it would be indecent to command the Crown and, moreover, the court's command would be nugatory, since it could not be enforced by attachment or sequestration (Clode (1887), pp.142-143). This does not sufficiently explain the refusal to make purely declaratory orders against the Crown. The explanation is to be found in the general practice of the court not to make such orders against any person.

[185] Crown Debts Act 1541 (33 Hen. 8, c.39); see esp. s.79 (repealed). The leading cases on equitable relief against the Crown in the Exchequer include *Sir Thomas Cecil's Case* (1598) 7 Co.Rep. 18b; *Pawlett v Attorney General* (1668) Hardres 465; *Casberd v Attorney General* (1819) 6 Price 411; *Deare v Attorney General* (1835) 1 Y. & C.Ex. 197; *Hodge v Attorney General* (1839) 3 Y. & C.Ex. 342.

[186] See *Tito v Waddell (No.2)* [1977] Ch. 106 at 256-259, where the plaintiffs were unable to proceed under the Crown Proceedings Act 1947 in so far as their claim against the Crown was held not to

to the Court of Chancery,[187] but it seems probable that its jurisdiction to give equitable relief against the Crown was incidental to its capacity as a court of revenue and did not, therefore, pass to the Court of Chancery.[188] But whatever may be the correct view, it appears to have ceased to exercise this jurisdiction after 1841 and the Court of Chancery was never called upon to determine whether it had succeeded to it. Not until 1911 was its jurisdiction to award declaratory judgments in ordinary civil actions against the Crown, represented by the Attorney General, rediscovered and revived[189] and all the precedents cited on that occasion were Exchequer precedents.

Legislative reforms

The aversion of the Court of Chancery to awarding purely declaratory judgments could be cured only by legislative action. Parliament, however, was to find its prescriptions received without enthusiasm. An Act of 1850 empowered persons interested in the construction of written instruments to state a special case for the opinion of the court, which was authorised to declare its opinion thereon without proceeding to administer consequential relief.[190] In 1852, a further step was taken, and it was enacted that no suit should be open to objection on the ground that a merely declaratory decree or order was sought thereby, and that it would be lawful for the court to make binding declarations of right without granting consequential relief.[191] These valuable accessions of authority (which were especially useful for the determination of disputed points arising in the administration of estates and trusts) were construed more restrictively than had seemed possible. The court not only maintained its traditional reluctance to declare future rights, but held that the classes of cases in respect of which declarations could be made had not been enlarged[192]; a declaration could now be made unaccompanied by any consequential relief, but only in cases where the plaintiff would have been entitled to other relief had he but chosen to ask for it.[193] More explicit directions were needed to bestir the court from the torpor of unimaginative conservatism.

15-065

The Judicature Acts of 1873-75 transferred the jurisdiction of the superior courts of common law and equity to the High Court, and empowered the Rule Committee to make rules regulating the practice and procedure of the court. RSC, Ord.25 r.5, made in 1853 provided:

15-066

"No action or proceeding shall be open to objection, on the ground that a merely declara-

---

arise "in respect of His Majesty's Government in the United Kingdom" (s.40(2)(b)). It was further stated that even if jurisdiction to grant declaratory relief in such circumstances did exist, this statutory exemption of the Crown from liability should normally lead the court in its discretion to refuse relief.

[187] Court of Chancery Act 1841.

[188] See *Attorney General v Halling* (1846) 15 M. & W. 687 at 698-699. No clear finding on this point was made in *Dyson v Attorney General* [1911] 1 K.B. 410. If the revenue jurisdiction passed to the High Court under s.10 of the Judicature Act 1873 and was exercised by the Queen's Bench Division after 1881, the point is an academic one.

[189] *Dyson v Attorney General* [1911] 1 K.B. 410.

[190] Court of Chancery, England, Act 1850 ss.1, 14.

[191] Court of Chancery Procedure Act 1852 s.50. See also the Legitimacy Declaration Act 1858, enabling a person to obtain a declaration of legitimacy in an action in which the Attorney General would appear as respondent.

[192] *Langdale (Lady) v Briggs* (1856) 8 De G.M. & G. 391 at 427-428. See also *Garlick v Lawson* (1853) 10 Hare App.xiv; *Bright v Tyndall* (1876) 4 Ch.D. 189 at 196; *Hampton v Holman* (1877) 5 Ch.D. 183. cf. *Jenner v Jenner* (1866) L.R. 1 Eq. 361 for an illustration of judicial conservatism in making declarations of right in another context.

[193] *Jackson v Turnley* (1853) 1 Dr. 617 at 628; *Rooke v Lord Kensington* (1856) 2 K & J 753 at 760-762. See also *Dyson v Attorney General* [1911] 1 K.B. 410, 422.

tory judgment or order is sought thereby, and the Court may make binding declarations of right whether any consequential relief is or could be claimed, or not."

15-067   The concluding words of the rule were designed to rectify the unsatisfactory state of affairs that had arisen through the restrictive interpretation given to the 1852 Act. But the courts, while recognising that RSC Ord.25 r.5, had introduced "an innovation of a very important kind",[194] still showed a curious reluctance to award declarations save in cases where other relief might have been claimed for a legal wrong, and they insisted that the jurisdiction should be exercised with great caution.

The turning point

15-068   The turning-point came in 1911. The Inland Revenue Commissioners issued to Dyson, a taxpayer, a form and notice requiring him under penalty to submit certain particulars. Relying on the pre-1842 Exchequer precedents and RSC Ord.25 r.5, he sued the Attorney General for declarations that the requisition was unauthorised and that he was under no obligation to comply with it inasmuch as it was ultra vires the Finance Act. The Court of Appeal held that this form of proceeding was a proper one,[195] and subsequently granted the declarations sought.[196] The judgments in the first *Dyson* case were founded partly on a misreading of legal history[197]; the court failed, moreover, to consider the question whether RSC Ord.25 r.5, bound the Crown[198] and the decision raised the difficult problem whether, and if so, how far, the action for a declaration against the Attorney General could be employed, when a petition of right against the Crown would have been an appropriate remedy.[199] But the decision was of the highest importance in the development of the action for a declaration. In the first place, the members of the court not merely upheld the propriety of the form of proceeding adopted but gave it their warm approval.[200]

15-069   Secondly, this was a case in which the plaintiff had no "cause of action" that would have entitled him to any other form of judicial relief, the threat to his interests created by the unlawful demand that had been made upon him could be directly averted only by the award of a binding declaration.[201]

15-070   Thirdly, the plaintiff could have waited until he was sued for penalties for non-

---

[194] *Ellis v Duke of Bedford* [1899] 1 Ch. 494 at 515; *Chapman v Michaelson* [1909] 1 Ch. 238 at 243.

[195] *Dyson v Attorney General* [1911] 1 K.B. 410 and [1912] 1 Ch. 158.

[196] *Dyson v Attorney General* [1912] 1 Ch. 158. The *Dyson* principle was applied in *Burghes v Attorney General* [1911] 2 Ch. 139 (affirmed [1912] 1 Ch. 173).

[197] The court erroneously assumed (see also *Esquimalt & Nanaimo Railway Co v Wilson* [1920] A.C. 358 at 365-368) that the Exchequer precedents were equally applicable to the Court of Chancery. For an attempt to explain away this aberration, see *Bombay & Persia Steam Navigation Co v Maclay* [1920] 3 K.B. 402 at 407. But Cozens-Hardy MR observed ([1911] 1 K.B. 410 at 417): "The absence of any precedent does not trouble me".

[198] See H. Street, *Governmental Liability* (1953), p.134, pointing out that as the rule was not expressed to bind the Crown the decision can be defended only on the assumption that the Exchequer precedents alone were being relied on; the Chancery practice had been to refuse to award declarations against the Crown except on a petition of right.

[199] Semble, where the rights of the Crown were directly affected and a petition of right was a proper remedy, an action for a declaration against the Attorney General as the representative of the Crown would not lie: *Attorney General for Ontario v MacLean Gold Mines Ltd* [1927] A.C. 185. The controversy surrounding this question (for which see Street pp.132-133; Glanville Williams, *Crown Proceedings* (1948), p.90) has become largely irrelevant since the Crown Proceedings Act 1947, which abolished the petition of right procedure for almost all purposes; though cf. Colonial Stock Act 1877 s.20; *Franklin v Attorney General* [1974] Q.B. 185. And see *Tito v Waddell (No.2)* [1977] Ch. 106 at 259, 260 (declaratory relief should not be granted when an action under the Crown Proceedings Act 1947 could be instituted).

[200] See Farwell LJ [1911] 1 K.B. 410 at 420; Fletcher Moulton LJ [1912] 1 Ch. 158 at 168.

[201] It would seem that the legal right asserted by Dyson was his privilege to decide what information

compliance with the requisition and then set up its invalidity by way of defence; nevertheless, the court declined to regard that procedure as the only permissible method of determining the issue.

In 1915, the principle laid down in Dyson's case was buttressed by a further deci- **15-071** sion of the Court of Appeal in which it affirmed its power to make a declaration that plaintiffs were not under a legal obligation (to repay money paid to them in respect of certain bills of exchange) to which the defendants (who had instituted proceedings against the plaintiffs in the United States) claimed them to be subject.[202] In this case the defendant had contended that RSC Ord.25 r.5, was not ultra vires. The Rule Committee had statutory power to make rules for practice and procedure with respect to all matters over which the Supreme Court had jurisdiction[203]; it had admittedly no power to extend the jurisdiction of the court. The Court of Appeal held, however, that the rule had not conferred any new jurisdiction upon the court and was, therefore, ultra vires. Jurisdiction to give purely declaratory judgments, even in cases where there was no independent cause of action and no possibility of granting consequential relief, had (so the court held) always resided in the Court of Chancery although the court had adopted a settled practice of refusing to render such judgments.[204] Seldom has the elastic concept of jurisdiction been more judiciously stretched. And Bankes LJ expressed the view that the rule "should receive as liberal a construction as possible".[205]

The growth in use of the declaration

During the 20th century, the declaration has become one of the most popular **15-072** forms of proceedings in the High Court. As early as 1917 an American authority was able to write that the practice of making declarations of right had completely revolutionised English remedial law.[206] Most of the declaratory judgments to which he referred were given in proceedings instituted by originating summons in the Chancery Division for the determination of questions arising out of the administration of estates and trusts or for the construction of various classes of written instruments. Proceedings instituted by writ under RSC Ord.25 r.5, were not frequent until after the *Dyson* case. In those areas of administrative law where statutory tribunals and inquiries do not operate, it has come to be more widely used against public authorities than the older and less flexible non-statutory remedies. Flexibility is, indeed, the greatest merit of the declaratory judgment.

---

to supply to the Commissioners in the absence of any legally enforceable duty of the kind alleged by them. In *Gouriet v Union of Post Office Workers* [1978] A.C. 435 at 502, Lord Diplock suggested that the relevant interest of Dyson was that an unlawful demand had been made for a penalty payable for non-compliance, which, had the plaintiff succumbed, he could have sued to recover; cf. his Lordship's analysis of the applicant's rights affected in *R. v Criminal Injuries Compensation Board Ex p. Lain* [1967] 2 Q.B. 864 at 888-889. See now *Woolwich Equitable Building Society v Inland Revenue Commissioners* [1993] A.C. 70.

[202] *Guaranty Trust Co of New York v Hannay & Co* [1915] 2 K.B. 536 (Pickford and Bankes LJJ Buckley LJ dissenting). The plaintiffs were eventually successful in obtaining the declarations they had sought: see [1918] 2 K.B. 623. See also *Russian Commercial & Industrial Bank v British Bank for Foreign Trade Ltd* [1921] 2 A.C. 438.

[203] Judicature Act 1873 ss.16, 23; Judicature Act 1925 s.17.

[204] [1915] 2 K.B. 563-564. This interpretation of the effect of r.5 is not easily reconcilable with the observations on its effect referred to above, fn.191.

[205] At 572.

[206] E.R. Sunderland, "Modern Education in Remedial Rights; the Declaratory Judgment" (1917) 16 Mich. L.R. 69, 77.

Locus standi and declarations

15-073 Prior to the reforms of 1978, the rules of locus standi in relation to declaratory relief were as difficult to formulate as those relating to the prerogative orders. The plaintiff in an action for a declaration had to establish that he had an immediate personal interest in the subject matter of the proceedings. In a matter affecting the public at large, a plaintiff had normally to show that his own interests were in some way "peculiarly affected"[207] by the defendant's conduct, but in determining whether the plaintiff's interests were sufficiently affected to give him title to sue, the courts exercised a wide and not always consistent discretion. There were decisions founded on the assumption that a plaintiff had title to sue although he was threatened with no greater injury than other members of the section of the community to which he belonged.[208] On the other hand, a plaintiff whose interests were directly and substantially impaired by an invalid grant of planning permission to a third party was held to be lacking in locus standi to impugn the decision because it did not encroach on any legal "right" vested in him.[209] But it was clearly sufficient that the plaintiff had a direct and substantial interest in the proceedings, even though he had no independent cause of action.

LEGISLATIVE REFORM OF PROCEDURES

15-074 So far this historical survey has focused on the development of remedies rather than procedures.[210] As we have seen, the fundamental characteristics of the remedies available to challenge governmental action in the High Court were largely settled by the early years of the 20th century; the major concerns since then have been with the search for effective, efficient and flexible procedures.

Procedural goals in public law proceedings

15-075 In the context of public law, the procedural rules and practices of the Administrative Court and its forerunners can be seen as attempting to achieve a number of goals.[211] As a matter of principle, the underlying test for all reforms to judicial review procedures is that they should maintain or enhance the ability of the courts to review the legality of the exercise of public power. This is fundamental to upholding the rule of law and protecting individual rights. There are further procedural elements to the normative assessment of any proposed reforms: that they should be based on adequate and objective evidence and should be preceded by an appropriate period of consultation. This is not to deny that practical and resource considerations are relevant. Such considerations arise in a number of ways. First, reform proposals may seek to assist the court in achieving the efficient flow of cases

---

[207] The phrase used by Porter J in *Stockwell v Southgate Corp* [1936] 2 All E.R. 1343 at 1351.

[208] See, e.g. *Nicholls v Tavistock UDC* [1923] 2 Ch. 18; *Prescott v Birmingham Corp* [1955] Ch. 210; and see *R. v GLC Ex p. Blackburn* [1976] 1 W.L.R. 550, 559, weakened by *Gouriet v Union of Post Office Workers* [1978] A.C. 435.

[209] *Gregory v Camden LBC* [1966] 1 W.L.R. 899. This case may be contrasted with *Prescott v Birmingham Corp* [1955] Ch. 210 as illustrating the two extreme positions adopted by the court.

[210] For the distinction between procedures and remedies, see 15-002, fn.2.

[211] For a more detailed analysis of these procedural goals in relation to the requirement of leave (now called permission), see A.P. Le Sueur and M. Sunkin "Applications for Judicial Review: the Requirement of Leave" [1992] P.L. 102, 104-107 and I. Hare, "The Law of Standing in Public Interest Adjudication", Ch.22 in M. Andenas (ed), *Liber Amicorum in Honour of Lord Slynn of Hadley: Vol.II Judicial Review in International Perspective* (2000).

through what is today called the Administrative Court (formerly the Crown Office List).[212] The concerns about how best to cope with growing numbers of applications are not new, but stretch back at least as far as the 1930s.[213] There is nothing objectionable about this as a matter of principle: some forms of challenge may be better decided in an alternative forum to the Administrative Court and judicial review loses much of its power if cases cannot be decided promptly. Secondly, the reform of procedures may seek to protect the interests of the defendants (usually, of course, governmental bodies) and third parties from unmeritorious or tardy challenges. Thirdly, the procedures may seek to promote access for claimants, for example, by having relatively relaxed rules as to who has standing to apply for judicial review, by restricting the ability of defendants to recover all of their costs and by ensuring that the procedural regime is as simple as possible. There remains a strong impression that some of the most recent reforms to the judicial review procedure were not based on sufficient evidence and failed to strike an appropriate balance between the competing interests identified above.

The complex array of public law procedures that exist today can be seen as an attempt to accommodate all these goals in differing degrees.[214]

Statutory applications to quash[215]

Statutory review clauses in legislation provide that within a strict time limit, usually six weeks, any person aggrieved by a specified administrative order, notice, scheme, action or other decision made may challenge its legality in the High Court. The procedural regime for so doing is entirely distinct from that of CPR Pt 54; for example, in addition to the different time limits, there is no general requirement that the applicant obtain the permission of the court.[216]

15-076

The first statutory review clause was enacted by s.11 of the Housing Act 1930 which dealt with challenges to slum clearance orders. The innovatory new procedure was prompted by a series of cases during the preceding years in which successful applications for certiorari had been made to quash orders of local authorities when the schemes had been almost brought into operation and after great expense had been incurred. The clause was presented by the government during its passage through Parliament as "a most important and valuable provision. It is the greatest safeguard you can afford to the individual and at the same time provides a

15-077

---

212 On the Administrative Court, see Ch.17.

213 See, e.g. the review by The Business of the Courts Committee chaired by Viscount Hanworth MR established in 1933. See further, A.P. Le Sueur and M. Sunkin, "Applications for Judicial Review: the Requirement of Leave" [1992] P.L.102, 103, fn.5 and pp.107-109; A.P. Le Sueur, "Should we Abolish the Writ of Habeas Corpus?" [1992] P.L. 13. P. Craig, *UK, EU and Global Administrative Law: Foundations and Challenges* (2015), at pp.26–29 demonstrates that there is nothing new about very substantial numbers of applications for public law remedies.

214 Some have argued that the third goal at facilitating access to the courts has been given insufficient weight: see Lord Scarman, "The Development of Administrative law: Obstacles and Opportunities" [1990] P.L. 490, 492; Le Sueur and Sunkin, "Applications for Judicial Review: the Requirement of Leave" [1992] P.L. 102, 127.

215 For an account of the modern practice and procedure, see Ch.17. These paragraphs are provided to give historical context to the following sections on judicial review. Most statutory applications to quash in the field of planning, development, compulsory purchase and rights of way are now considered by the Planning Court, a specialist list of the Administrative Court governed by CPR 54.21–22 and Practice Direction 54E (considered further below at 17–031).

216 But s.289 of the Town and Country Planning Act 1990 provides an appeal to the High Court against an enforcement notice upheld by the Secretary of State for the Environment on appeal. The Planning and Compensation Act 1991 introduced a requirement (now the new s.289(6)) that an appeal may only be brought under that section with the leave of the court. This limitation was proposed by Robert Carnwath QC (as he then was) in his report, *Enforcing Planning Control* (1989).

method by which questions of right can be determined at the earliest possible moment".[217]

15-078   There has been an expansion in the subject areas in which statutory review is used. At first confined to compulsory purchase and land use planning,[218] clauses came to be used increasingly in the field of regulation of industry.[219] The introduction of the statutory review procedure can clearly be seen as instigated by dissatisfaction with the operation of the common law prerogative orders. From the perspective of the respondents—particularly local authorities—the prerogative writs and procedures had failed to provide sufficient safeguards, particularly from tardy challenges.[220] Typically, however, the reforms implemented were piecemeal and designed to deal with one particular context only, namely slum clearance orders. It was to be another three years before the general inadequacies of the prerogative writ procedures were tackled.

Procedures for applying for prerogative writs[221]

15-079   Throughout the 1930s, the courts and government continued to be concerned that the procedures for obtaining the prerogative writs were unacceptably inefficient; they were wasteful of court time and the delays that ensued had a capacity to frustrate administrative action.

Introduction of the leave requirement[222]

15-080   Until 1933, an applicant for any of the prerogative writs applied first for an order (or rule) nisi. At this hearing, before a Divisional Court of three judges, the court considered the applicant's case in full and determined whether the writ sought should issue. If the applicant satisfied the court that his case had merit, the order nisi was granted. The onus then lay on the respondent to show cause, at a second hearing before a Divisional Court, why the order should not be made absolute. Both government and the courts became dissatisfied with this procedure. From the Government's perspective, it was seen as inappropriate that at the second hearing applicants could "sit back" and watch the respondent try to get the order nisi discharged. The court's dissatisfaction lay in what was seen as a duplication of efforts at the nisi and absolute hearings; at both stages a Divisional Court considered the merits of the application.

15-081   Following recommendations of the Hanworth Business of the Court Committee,[223] legislation was introduced to modernise procedures on the Crown Side of the King's Bench Division, though leaving the writ of habeas corpus, and the procedure for obtaining it, untouched. It was apparently thought that to meddle with it might

---

[217] *Hansard*, HL cols 461-463 (July 15, 1930). See also *Hansard*, HL cols 582-583 (21 July 1930).

[218] See, e.g. the provisions in the Town and Country Planning Act 1990 ss.287, 288; Local Government and Planning Act 1980 Sch.32, Pt.I (designation of Enterprise Zones); Ancient Monuments and Archaeological Areas Act 1979 s.55; Highways Act 1980 Sch.2.

[219] See, e.g. Medicines Act 1968 s.107. Other examples (now repealed) included the Petroleum Act 1987 s.4; Airports Act 1986 s.49; and Telecommunications Act 1984 s.18.

[220] The Association of Municipal Councils played an important role in advocating introduction of the new review procedure.

[221] For an account of the modern practice and procedure, see Ch.16.

[222] For a more detailed account of the history of the leave requirement, see Le Sueur and Sunkin, "Applications for Judicial Review: the Requirement of Leave" [1992] P.L. 102.

[223] *The Business of the Courts Committee: Interim Report*, Cmnd 4265 (1933).

be construed as subversive activity.[224] The Administration of Justice (Miscellaneous Provisions) Act 1933 abolished the two stage nisi and absolute procedure and introduced a requirement that an applicant first obtain the leave of the court before an application for a prerogative writ be made. The leave hearing continued to be an ex parte (without notice) hearing before a Divisional Court. The real significance of the reform was that, leave having been granted, the burden remained on the applicant at the second hearing to prove his case. The 1938 Act of the same name replaced the writs of certiorari, prohibition and mandamus by orders of the same names. The change of designation reflected only a simplification of procedure.

Reform agendas

Thirty years later, dissatisfaction with the public law procedures and remedies of the High Court persisted. During the intervening period, branches of administrative law other than judicial review had undergone important reforms: the Crown Proceedings Act 1947 had more or less put the Crown in the same position as that of the ordinary defendant in private law litigation; the Tribunals and Inquiries Act 1958 had implemented many of the recommendations of the landmark Franks Committee Report[225]; and the office of Parliamentary Commissioner for Administration had been created. In contrast, High Court procedures for judicial review—despite the limited reforms of the 1930s—were little different to those that had operated a century before.   **15-082**

In 1966, the Law Commission[226] began to take soundings on administrative law reform, with special reference to the role of the courts. In 1967, it published an exploratory working paper, and after extensive consultations it formally recommended to the Lord Chancellor in May 1969 that a wide-ranging inquiry be conducted by a Royal Commission or a body of similar status into the following questions: (1) whether the form and procedure of existing judicial remedies in administrative law needed to be altered; (2) whether changes in the scope of judicial review were required; (3) how far remedies in respect of administrative acts and omissions should include the right to damages; (4) whether special principles should govern administrative contracts and torts; and (5) how far changes should be made in the organisation and personnel of the courts for the purposes of administrative law.[227]   **15-083**

At this time the civil service was beginning to receive the impact of the Parliamentary Commissioner for Administration and was also about to undergo reconstruction in the light of the recommendations of the Fulton Committee.[228] Many prominent civil servants, moreover, were uneasy at the spontaneous revival of judicial activism. And some lawyers thought that procedural reform was too urgent to be deferred until the conclusion of a large-scale inquiry.   **15-084**

In December 1969, the Lord Chancellor rejected the Law Commission's recommendations and requested it to undertake its own inquiry into question (1), the form   **15-085**

---

[224] See R.M. Jackson, *Machinery of Justice in England*, 6th edn (1972), pp.45-46.
[225] Professor de Smith had highlighted the unsatisfactory state of the existing procedures in his evidence to the Franks Committee: *Report of the Committee on Administrative Tribunals and Enquiries* Cmnd 218 (1957), Minutes of Evidence, Appendix I, p.10.
[226] Constituted as a permanent advisory body on law reform in pursuance of the Law Commissions Act 1965.
[227] Cmnd 4059 (1969).
[228] *Report of the Committee on the Civil Service*, Cmnd 3638 (1968).

and procedure of judicial remedies; changes in the scope of review were to be outside the Commission's terms of reference.[229]

15-086　　In 1971, whilst the Law Commission was carrying out its investigation, the organisation Justice (the British Section of the International Commission of Jurists) published its own report entitled *Administration under Law*, in which it examined some of the basic issues shelved by the Government. Among its proposals were the extension of duties to provide official information and reasons for decisions, the creation of new machinery to enable a court to ascertain the facts on which administrative decisions were based, and the conferment of power to award damages to persons aggrieved by decisions tainted with procedural or substantive irregularity in circumstances where there is no cause of action for damages under the law as it now stands. The detailed recommendations were criticised on various grounds,[230] particularly the burden they would impose on the public service, but can now be seen as prescient. The duty to give reasons and the duty of candour have been developed by the courts over subsequent years to remedy some of the failings identified in the Justice report.[231] The suggestions for compensation and damages highlighted an important weakness in the scope and effect of judicial review which has still not been satisfactorily addressed. However, since this was a report by an unofficial body, it could be and was conveniently ignored by the Government.

The creation of the RSC, Ord.53 application for judicial review

15-087　　The Law Commission, impeded by the unfortunately restrictive nature of its brief, produced its final report in 1976,[232] some four and a half years after the publication of a detailed working paper.[233] The principal proposal of the Commission was that all the existing non-statutory administrative law remedies should be capable of being claimed in a unified application for judicial review. Again, as in the reforms of the 1930s, no consideration was given to the status of the writ of habeas corpus. The Commission's main recommendation was implemented, with an expedition which was previously absent, by amendments to the Rules of the Supreme Court that took effect in January 1978.[234] The new RSC Ord.53 provided for a single procedure for obtaining the prerogative orders, injunctions, declarations and damages in public law proceedings. The leave requirement was retained. The Divisional Court of the Queen's Bench continued to hear both applications for leave[235] and substantive hearings. The limited nature of the reforms is revealed by the fact that they were implemented by means of a series of amendments to the Rules of Court. Only several years later, after questions were raised as to the vires under which the Rule Committee had acted, was the application for judicial review put on a statutory footing.[236] The aspects of the Commission's proposals (in

---

[229] *Hansard*, HL Vol.306, cols 189-190 (4 December 1969).

[230] See, e.g. (1972) 12 J.S.P.T.L. (N.S.) 72.

[231] See 7–088 and 16–027.

[232] Cmnd 6407 (1976).

[233] *Remedies in Administrative Law* (Law Com No.40). A similar working paper on the corresponding remedies in Scots law was issued by the Scottish Law Commission (Memorandum No.14). The working paper's modest proposals evoked a surprising amount of criticism both on technical grounds and because they would indirectly expand the scope of judicial review, which would be undesirable.

[234] RSC (Amendment No.3) 1977 SI 1977/1955) (L.30). cf. Judicature (Northern Ireland) Act 1978 ss.18-25.

[235] Except during Vacation, when the application was to a judge in chambers.

[236] Supreme Court Act 1981 s.31. C. Harlow, "Comment" [1978] P.L. 1 and Lord Denning MR in *O'Reilly v Mackman* [1983] 2 AC 237, 256. Lord Bridge stated in *Cocks v Thanet DC* [1983] 2 A.C.

particular that interim declaratory relief be available against the Crown) which clearly required to be introduced by statute remained unimplemented.[237]

Problems with the new RSC, Ord.53

The new RSC Ord.53 was to some extent a victim of its own success: the avail-   **15-088** ability of a streamlined procedure was one reason for the rapid growth in the number of applications for judicial review. Soon there were considerable delays in determining cases on the Crown Office List. In 1980, two years after the major reform, a number of further extensive and fundamental changes were made to RSC Ord.53. Provision was made for both leave and substantive applications to be heard by single judges rather than the Divisional Court[238] and applications for leave could now be made "on paper" without the need for any hearing.

In 1985, the Government attempted to take a further step to make RSC Ord.53   **15-089** more efficient. By cl.43 of the Administration of Justice Bill, it sought to abolish the applicant's right to renew a leave application to the Court of Appeal. Judges of the Court of Appeal took the unprecedented step of speaking against this proposal while giving judgment[239] and during the committee stage of the Bill in the House of Lords, Lord Denning described the proposal as a "constitutional monstrosity". The clause was defeated, reintroduced in an amended form (allowing renewal to a Divisional Court including a Lord Justice of Appeal), but that too was defeated. For a period, the modified RSC Ord.53 enabled applications for judicial review to be determined with acceptable dispatch. By the close of the 1980s, however, the Crown Court List was again beset with delays.

Justice/All Souls review

Undeterred by the lack of government interest in its earlier report, Justice again   **15-090** picked up the gauntlet of administrative law reform. In 1978, a committee was established in conjunction with All Souls College, Oxford charged with devising practical proposals for reform with the aim of giving administrative law clarity, coherence, comprehensibility and accessibility.[240] Ten years later, it published its report.[241] It made several recommendations in relation to judicial review remedies and procedures. First, that the leave requirement in RSC Ord.53 proceedings should be abandoned. In its place there should be a procedure for striking out hopeless or bogus applications or, alternatively, a two-stage procedure similar to that in Scotland should be introduced.[242] Secondly, the three-month limitation period should be repealed and undue delay should be a barrier only in so far as it causes substantial

---

286, 295 that s.31 "removes any doubt there may have been as to the vires of the 1977 amendment of RSC, Ord 53".

[237] For comments, see H.W.R. Wade, "Reform of Remedies in Administration Law" (1978) 94 L.Q.R. 179; C. Harlow, "Comment" [1978] P.L. 1; J. Beatson and M.H. Matthews, "Reform of Administrative Law Remedies: The First Step" (1978) 41 M.L.R. 437.

[238] A Divisional Court continues to hear applications for leave (permission) and substantive applications in "criminal causes or matters": see 16-079.

[239] *R. v Income Tax Special Commissioner Ex p. Stipplechoice Ltd* [1985] 2 All E.R. 465 at 467 (Ackner LJ). See also A.W. Bradley, "Comment" [1986] P.L. 361.

[240] For a critique of the Committee's methodology, see D.Oliver and R. Austin [1991] P.L. 441; C. Harlow (1990) 10 J.L.S. 85.

[241] Report of the Committee of the Justice/All Souls Review of Administrative Law in the United Kingdom, *Administrative Justice—Some Necessary Reforms*, 1988.

[242] Justice/All Souls Review, Ch.6.

prejudice or hardship to others or would be detrimental to good administration.[243] Thirdly, discovery and cross-examination should be permitted more liberally; the general rule should be that documents which are relevant to contested issues between the parties should be disclosed. Fourthly, the Committee supported the increasingly liberal grant of locus standi.[244]

15-091   The Committee's report attracted considerable interest and no less criticism. Given its commitment to promoting access to justice rather than the safeguarding of respondents or to efficiency, it never looked likely to find favour with government.

Reconsideration by the Law Commission

15-092   During the early 1990s the Law Commission once again turned its attention to judicial review procedures and remedies.[245] Its recommendations were cautious. The liberal interpretation of *O'Reilly v Mackman*[246] and its principle of procedural exclusivity, already accepted by the House of Lords,[247] was approved. The report recommended that the leave stage in RSC Ord.53 proceedings ought to be retained, though renamed the "preliminary consideration" and that the test be whether the application discloses a serious issue which ought to be determined. The Law Commission endorsed the continued existence of a requirement of standing, but argued that the court should have a discretion to allow applications where the applicant was not directly affected by the impugned decision but it was nevertheless in the public interest that the application proceed.[248] In relation to the forms of relief, the report recommended that the Latin names for the prerogative writs (certiorari, prohibition and mandamus) be replaced with plain English ones (quashing, prohibiting and mandatory orders). Interim and advisory declarations should be available to the court which should also have the power to make orders in restitution and debt.[249] The Law Commission also recommended that, in limited circumstances, the Administrative Court should be able to substitute its own decision for that subject to review. The report recommended that there be no reform of habeas corpus as a distinct remedy with its own procedural route, though it argued against the narrow approach to the scope of review adopted by the Court of Appeal in recent applications for habeas corpus.[250]

Recent reforms

15-093   The Law Commission's 1994 recommendations were soon eclipsed by initiatives on two other fronts: the fundamental reforms to the whole civil litigation system in England and Wales; and preparations for implementing the Human Rights Act 1998.

15-094   The Civil Procedure Rules (CPR) sought to create a new approach to litigation,

---

[243] Justice/All Souls Review, Ch.6.

[244] Justice/All Souls Review, para.8-050.

[245] See: *Law Commission Fifth Programme of Law Reform*, Law Com. No.200 (1991); Law Commission Consultation Paper No.126 (1993); *Administrative Law: Judicial Review and Statutory Appeals*, Law Com No.226 (October 1994); I. Hare, "The Law Commission and judicial review: principle versus pragmatism" [1995] C.L.J. 268; R. Gordon [1995] P.L. 11.

[246] See further Ch.3.

[247] *Roy v Kensington and Chelsea and Westminster Family Practitioner Committee* [1992] 1 A.C. 624.

[248] The continuing liberalisation of the standing rules by the court has in effect achieved this without the need for any change to the procedural rules: see Ch.2.

[249] See now 18-042.

[250] See 17-008.

to ensure that the civil justice system is "accessible, fair and efficient".[251] The CPR provided, for the first time, a unified procedural code for the county courts, High Court and Court of Appeal (replacing the Rules of the Supreme Court 1965 and County Court Rules 1981). The reforms put in place the approach recommended by Lord Woolf's inquiry into Access to Justice, commissioned by the Lord Chancellor in 1994 amidst growing concerns that court processes were disproportionately costly and unduly slow.[252] Among the overarching recommendations was that court-based litigation should be a last resort, with aggrieved parties encouraged to use alternative dispute resolution whenever possible. Where there was no alternative to litigation, judges were to assume far greater powers to manage the conduct of the litigation to ensure timeliness and costs in proportion to the importance of the issues at stake. In relation to judicial review, the Access to Justice report endorsed most, though not all of the Law Commission's 1994 proposals.[253] At the time, one of the largest categories in the judicial review caseload was challenges to the lawfulness of decisions by local housing authorities in relation to rights and duties and the homelessness legislation. The report recommended that an appeal on point of law to the county court should replace judicial review; local courts were more accessible and less costly than the High Court. This recommendation was speedily implemented.[254]

The CPR came into force in April 1999. There was not, however, time to revise **15-095** the judicial review procedures and integrate them into the CPR. So for some 18 months the RSC Ord.53 judicial review procedure continued in force, re-enacted as a schedule to the CPR. As it happened, the delay was fortunate because it enabled thought to be given to the impact of the Human Rights Act 1998, which was due to come into force in October 2000. A small committee, chaired by a distinguished accountant Sir Jeffery Bowman, was commissioned by the Lord Chancellor to review the Crown Office list—looking at the pressures thought likely to result from the Human Rights Act, as well as the backlog of immigration and asylum cases and the relationship between the Access to Justice report and the Law Commission's 1994 recommendations.[255] The task of the committee was "to put forward costed recommendations for improving the efficiency of the Crown Office List" that did not "compromise the fairness or probity of the proceedings, the quality of decisions, or the independence of the judiciary".[256]

The Bowman committee concluded that there was a continuing need for a **15-096** specialised court as part of the High Court to deal with public and administrative law cases and recommended that the Crown Office List should be renamed "The Administrative Court" and given additional judicial and administrative resources. Greater specialism among the judiciary was also urged, with judges sitting in the new court for longer periods. In relation to immigration and asylum cases, the committee said that they should remain in the Administrative Court, arguing that it was

---

[251] Civil Procedure Act 1997 s.1(3). The CPR is subordinate legislation made under powers conferred by that Act.

[252] *Access to Justice: a final report to the Lord Chancellor* (1996).

[253] Access to Justice did not support the suggestion that the remedies of mandamus, prohibition and certiorari be renamed; it also proposed including habeas corpus as one of the remedial orders available in a claim for judicial review, while also retaining it as a separate procedure.

[254] Housing Act 1996 ss.202, 204; and see 17-040.

[255] Other members of the committee were Lord Justice Simon Brown, Alan Cogbill (Director of Civil Justice and Legal Aid Reform in the Lord Chancellor's Department), Professor Jeffrey Jowell QC, Mr Justice Keene, Bernadette Kenny (Director of Operational Policy, LCD) and Anne Owers (Director of the organisation Justice). Sir Jefferey Bowman had in 1996-97 conducted an efficiency review of the Court of Appeal Civil Division.

[256] *Review of the Crown Office List* (LCD, London, 2000), p.ii.

not possible to "fast track" them when they represented such a large proportion of the overall judicial review caseload. The committee pointed out that without longer term reforms in the immigration and asylum tribunal system as a whole there was little opportunity to reduce recourse to judicial review in this area.[257] Moreover, there needed to be a comprehensive study of the structure, jurisdiction, procedures, remedies and routes of appeal of tribunals.[258]

15-097　　The committee concluded that special procedures, in addition to the standard ways of initiating and conducting civil proceedings set out in the CPR, were needed.[259] The committee agreed with the conclusions of the Law Commission and Access to Justice report that leave stage requirement (to be called "permission") should be retained in the new procedure, but recommended that in future the application for permission should be served on defendant public authorities, which should have the opportunity at that point to set out their objections to the grant of permission in summary grounds of defence. One aim of defendant involvement at this stage was to encourage the earlier settlement of disputes. The permission procedure should initially be carried out on paper, whereas previously applicants had the choice of whether to make an oral or written application. Significantly, the committee recommended that the criteria for obtaining permission should be made explicit in the new rules and that there should be a presumption in favour of permission being granted. The permission requirement was regarded by the committee as an important tool of case management, allowing the Administrative Court to dispose of cases efficiently.[260] The committee urged a "blitz" on the backlog of cases, in preparation for the coming into force of the Human Rights Act.

15-098　　With considerable speed, the Lord Chancellor's Department drafted the new judicial review rules (which were to become CPR Pt 54) and a practice direction. Following a short period of consultation, they came into force on 2 October 2000, the same day as the Human Rights Act.[261] In most respects, the new rules reflected the recommendations of the Bowman committee (though the rules did not set out any express criteria for the permission stage and nor was there a presumption in favour of its grant). A pre-action protocol on judicial review followed in 2001.[262] Some recommendations of the Law Commission report and the Bowman committee required amendments to primary legislation. Although consultees have overwhelming supported reform of habeas corpus, the Government decided not to proceed with this due to the declining recourse to the remedy.[263] Changes to the Latin names of mandamus, prohibition and certiorari were made in 2004.[264] Several

---

[257] Wide-ranging reforms were eventually introduced by the Asylum and Immigration (Treatment of Claimants etc) Act 2004, which created the Asylum and Immigration Tribunal as the successor to the previous two-tier system (the Immigration Appellate Authority and the Immigration Appeals Tribunal). Government proposals to oust the jurisdiction of the courts in relation to the new tribunal were withdrawn following sustained criticism of them as a threat to the rule of law: see R. Rawlings, "Review, Revenge and Retreat" (2005) 68 M.L.R. 378.

[258] Something achieved in 2001 with the publication of the Report of the Review of Tribunals by Sir Andrew Leggatt: *Tribunals for Users—One System, One Service*, discussed at 1-084; substantially implemented by the Tribunals, Courts and Enforcement Act 2007.

[259] cf. D. Oliver, "Public Law Remedies and Procedures-Do We Need Them?" [2002] P.L. 91.

[260] For a critique of the committee's assumptions, see T. Cornford and M. Sunkin, "The Bowman Report, Access and the Recent Reforms of the Judicial Review Procedure" [2001] P.L. 11.

[261] For further commentary, see M. Fordham, "Judicial Review: The New Rules" [2001] P.L. 4.

[262] Available on the Ministry of Justice website:
https://www.justice.gov.uk/courts/procedure-rules/civil/protocol/prot_jrv [Accessed 6 November 2017].

[263] DCA, CP(R) 10/01 (October 2003).

[264] Civil Procedure (Modification of the Supreme Court Act 1981) Order 2004 (SI 2004/1033), amending Supreme Court Act 1981 ss.29, 31.

procedural routes, including that for statutory applications to quash certain decisions, still require integration into the CPR.[265]

As a result of these reforms, it is no longer accurate to describe the current application for judicial review as simply a codification of the old common law remedies. Some of the reforms may be regarded as superficial. For example, changing the names of the prerogative orders from Latin to English was really no more than giving delayed effect to the general impetus to modernise the vocabulary of civil procedure. Other reforms can properly be described as unpicking some of the procedural patchwork of the common law to produce a simpler and more coherent adjectival landscape. The best example of this is the Supreme Court Act 1981 (as originally enacted) which made all the prerogative remedies available in the same application and unified the rules on permission, standing and promptness. Other reforms have been more substantive: adding new remedies (such as the right to obtain injunctions, declarations and damages and, more recently, restitution or a sum due) and the court's power to substitute its own decision for that of the reviewed body. Taken together, these reforms mean that although judicial review remains recognisable as the progeny of the common law, it is so far amended and augmented that it can only sensibly be regarded as a statutory remedy.[266] **15-099**

There have been two recent bouts of further reform to the procedures for seeking judicial review; the first of them welcome and the other questionable. The first and welcome reform was the introduction of regionalisation of the Administrative Court which has permitted hearings to take place closer to the area with which the parties have connection.[267] The second and questionable set of reforms were prefigured in a Ministry of Justice consultation paper in 2012 and substantially enacted in the Criminal Justice and Courts Act 2015.[268] These reforms include requiring the court to refuse permission where it appears likely that the outcome would not have been substantially different and permitting it to certify applications for permission as totally without merit (with the effect of preventing the claimant from seeking to renew the application orally) along with new limitations on the availability of protective costs orders (renamed costs capping orders). The substance of these reforms is considered in the next chapter. However, they possess two striking features. First, they were not based on the kind of objective and rigorous evidential foundation which preceded most of the reforms described above. In particular, they did not take account of the major reduction in the work of the Administrative Court which was bound to follow the transfer of most asylum and immigration cases to the Upper Tribunal.[269] Secondly, they were championed by a Government which had repeatedly and publicly expressed hostility towards the use of judicial review. **15-100**

---

[265] See 17-003.

[266] In *Michalak v General Medical Council* [2016] EWCA Civ 172; [2016] I.C.R. 628, the CA accepted that "there are aspects of the modern procedure [for judicial review] that can be said to have been changed substantively rather than just procedurally in and after 1982" (at [39]) (Ryder LJ). The CA went on to acknowledge that "one could characterise judicial review after January 1982 as being 'by virtue of an enactment'" for the purposes of s.53 of the Equality Act 2010 (at [40]) (Ryder LJ) and that judicial review has since 1981 "been put on a statutory footing" (at [53]) (Moore-Bick LJ). The SC did not go so far: judicial review remains a common law remedy although "regulated" by statute (*General Medical Council v Michalak* [2017] UKSC 71; [2017] 1 W.L.R. 4193 at [33]).

[267] See 16-003.

[268] See Ministry of Justice, *Judicial Review: proposals for reform* (CP25/2012). See also Ministry of Justice, Command Paper 8703, September 2013, in which proposals for further reform were put forward. Some of these have now been enacted and are discussed at para.16-002, fn.9.

[269] See 17-006. The effect of this reform on the Administrative Court's caseload was predictably dramatic: the total number of judicial review applications in the Administrative Court declined from its peak of just under 16,000 before the transfer, to around 4,000 in the following year (Ministry of Justice, *Civil Justice Statistics Quarterly, England and Wales, January to March 2017 (provisional)*

15-101   The current rules are merely the latest episode in the long history of the remedies and procedures which provide the practical processes for the often small scale, day-to-day vindication of the rule of law. The current rules form the subject matter of the next chapter of this work.

CHAPTER 16

CPR Pt 54 Claims for Judicial Review

TABLE OF CONTENTS

SCOPE

There are several procedures by which the lawfulness of a public authority's decision may be challenged in the Administrative Court.

16-001

- A claim for judicial review under CPR Pt 54.[1]
- An application for the writ of habeas corpus.[2]
- A statutory application to quash specific orders and decisions of Ministers, tribunals and other bodies made under particular statutes and statutory instruments.[3]
- By a complex array of appeals from magistrates, tribunals, Ministers and other decision-making bodies.[4]
- In addition, bodies other than the Administrative Court apply judicial review principles in determining cases including the county courts dealing with appeals against homelessness decisions of local authorities,[5] and the Upper Tribunal in supervising the determinations of the First-tier Tribunal.[6]
- The Upper Tribunal also exercises its own judicial review jurisdiction in certain areas.

This chapter describes and evaluates the first of these procedures.[7] The procedural regime is set out in a "somewhat cumbrous and confusing ... hierarchy of rules and

16-002

---

[1] Introduced in October 2000 to replace RSC Ord.53, dealt with in this Chapter. The Administrative Court has produced its own *Judicial Review Guide* 2017 (July 2017). One aim of the guide is to end what it identifies in the Preface as "bad practices", including: "applications claiming unnecessary urgency, over-long written arguments, and bundles of documents, authorities and skeleton arguments being filed late".

[2] See 17-008.

[3] See 17-024.

[4] See 17-036.

[5] See 17-040.

[6] See 1-084 and 17-006, under Senior Courts Act 1981 s.31A.

[7] For practical guidance, see also: B. Lang (ed), *Administrative Court: Practice and Procedure* (2006); C. Lewis, *Judicial Remedies in Public Law*, 5th edn (2014) Ch.9; M. Supperstone and L. Knapman (eds), *Administrative Court Practice*, (2008); J. Halford, "Strategy in Judicial Review: Using the Procedure to the Claimant's Advantage" [2006] J.R. 153; A. Lidbetter, "Strategy in Judicial Review for Defendants" [2007] J.R. 99.

guidance",[8] comprising: statutory provisions[9]; the Civil Procedure Rules (which are statutory instruments made pursuant to ss.1 and 2 of the Civil Procedure Act 1997)[10]; Practice Directions made by the Lord Chief Justice in exercise of his inherent jurisdiction[11]; various Practice Statements; a Pre-Action Protocol on Judicial Review[12]; and Administrative Court Office Notes for Guidance on Applying for Judicial Review.[13] The Practice Directions provide general guidance, but do not have binding effect, and yield to the CPR in the event of a clear conflict between them.[14]

---

[8] *Mount Cook Ltd v Westminster City Council* [2003] EWCA Civ 1346; [2004] 1 P.L.R. 29 at [67] (Auld LJ).

[9] Senior Courts Act 1981 ss.29, 31, 31A and 43. These provisions were amended on 1 May 2004 by the Civil Procedure (Modification of the Supreme Court Act 1981) Order 2004 (SI 2004/1033), renaming the remedies of mandamus, prohibition and certiorari as mandatory, prohibition and quashing orders respectively. See Appendix C. The Government's most recent reforms to the judicial review procedure are described at paras 1–005 and 15–100. Many of the proposals have now been enacted in the Criminal Justice and Courts Act 2015 (although not all have yet entered into force). They are set out at paras 16–050 (permission) and 16–085 (leapfrog appeals to the SC); and fnn.289 (information on claimant's funding); 301 (intervener's costs); and 307 (costs capping orders). See further, A. Samuels, "Judicial review: the new law: the Criminal Justice and Courts Act 2015 Chapter 2" [2015] J.P.L. 754–758 and A. Mills, "Reforms to Judicial Review in the Criminal Justice and Courts Act 2015: Promoting Efficiency or Weakening the Rule of Law?" [2015] P.L. 583.

[10] See Appendix F.

[11] See Appendices G and H. *R. (on the application of Ewing) v Department for Constitutional Affairs* [2006] EWHC 504 (Admin); [2006] 2 All E.R. 993 at [13]. There are limits to the court's inherent rule-making power and, for example, the court has no power to introduce a new procedure (such as a closed material procedure) which departs from fundamental features of the common law trial (*Al-Rawi v Security Service* [2011] UKSC 34; [2012] 1 A.C. 531 at [10]-[14], [18]-[22] and [67]-[69]). Section 6(4) of the Justice and Security Act 2013 (which came into force on 25 June 2013) sets out the conditions under which the court (on the application of either of the parties or the Secretary of State, or of its own motion) may declare that a closed material application may be made; see para.8–009. The Bill which led to the 2013 Act was convincingly criticised by A. Peto and A. Tyrie, *Neither Just nor Secure* (2012).

[12] See Appendix I. This sets out "a code of good practice and contains the steps which parties should generally follow before making a claim for judicial review" (para.2). Failure to comply with the Pre-Action Protocol may result in a successful party's order for costs being reduced, see e.g. *Aegis Group Plc v Inland Revenue Commissioners* [2005] EWHC 1468 (Ch); [2005] S.T.C. 989. The Pre-action Protocol is reissued from time to time; the version in force at the time of writing is from January 2017.

[13] Available from the Ministry of Justice website (*http://www.justice.gov.uk/courts/rcj-rolls-building/administrative-court/applying-for-judicial-review* [Accessed 8 November 2017]). Her Majesty's Courts and Tribunals Service is an agency of the Ministry of Justice which was established on 1 April 2011.

[14] *Mount Cook Ltd* [2003] EWCA Civ 1346; [2004] 1 P.L.R. 29 at [68]; *Godwin v Swindon BC* [2001] EWCA Civ 1478; [2002] 1 W.L.R. 997 at [11] (May LJ: "They are, in my view, at best a weak aid to the interpretation of the rules themselves"); *Re C (Legal Aid: Preparation of a Bill of Costs)* [2001] 1 F.L.R. 602 at [21] (Hale LJ: "the Practice Directions are not made by Statutory Instrument. They are not laid before Parliament or subject to either the negative or positive resolution procedures in Parliament. They go through no democratic process at all, although if approved by the Lord Chancellor he will bear ministerial responsibility for them to Parliament. But there is a difference in principle between delegated legislation which may be scrutinised by Parliament and ministerial executive action. There is no ministerial responsibility for Practice Directions made for the Supreme Court by the Heads of Division. As Professor Jolowicz says ['Practice directions and the CPR' [2000] C.L.J. 53] 'It is right that the court should retain its power to regulate its own procedure within the limits set by statutory rules, and to fill in gaps left by those rules; it is wrong that it should have power actually to legislate'"). A judge has no power to issue general guidance which departs from or varies a relevant Practice Directions while retaining the power to depart from a Practice Direction in the particular circumstances of the case before him in the exercise of general case management powers (*Bovale Ltd v Secretary of State for Communities and Local Government* [2009] EWCA Civ 171; [2009] 1 W.L.R. 2274 at [28]-[29]).

THE ADMINISTRATIVE COURT

The Administrative Court, created in October 2000 to replace the Crown Office List, is part of the Queen's Bench Division of the High Court. It has jurisdiction over a wide range of matters, several of which fall outside the scope of this book.[15] The Administrative Court sits mainly in the Royal Courts of Justice in London and, since 2009, in the areas covered by the District Registries of the High Court in Cardiff, Birmingham, Manchester and Leeds.[16] The general expectation is that proceedings will be administered and determined in the region with which the claimant has the closest connection, subject to the following considerations: the reason expressed by any party for preferring a particular venue; where the defendant is based; where the claimant's legal representative is based; the ease and cost of travelling to a venue; the availability of suitable alternative means of attending a hearing (such as by video-link); media interest in a particular area; the time within which it is appropriate for the proceedings to be determined; the volume of cases at a particular venue; whether there are similar claims already outstanding at a particular venue; and whether there are devolution issues which would render Cardiff the appropriate venue.[17]

16-003

Most claims for judicial review are now heard by a single judge, though some

16-004

---

[15] Including vexatious litigant proceedings, applications relating to contempt of court, extradition matters, the Proceeds of Crime Act 2002, appeals (formerly made to the Privy Council) relating to the striking off of health care professionals under the National Health Service Reform and Health Care Professions Act 2002; appeals from the Solicitors Disciplinary Tribunal and Medical Practitioners Tribunal; and applications relating to parliamentary and local government elections under the Representation of the People Acts. See further Lang, *Administrative Court: Practice and Procedure* (2006), sections B-J. Applications under s.13 of the Coroners Act 1988 are addressed at 17–034–17–036.

[16] The court may also sit in Bristol (although papers cannot be issued there). Regionalisation of the Administrative Court began on 21 April 2009 when offices of the court were established in the District Registries of the High Court in Birmingham, Cardiff, Leeds and Manchester. The court also sits in Bristol. Regionalisation was foreshadowed in *Justice Outside London: Report of the Judicial Working Group* (led by May LJ) in January 2007. The regional offices do not just deal with the administrative side of the court's business (issuing proceedings and so on), but also hear cases in the region with which the claimant has the closest connection. See S. Nason, D. Hardy and M. Sunkin, "Regionalisation of the Administrative Court and Access to Justice" [2010] J.R. 220 and D.C. Gardiner, "Public law challenges in Wales: the past and the present" [2013] P.L. 1. See now S. Nason, "Justice Outside London? Five Years of 'Regional' Administrative Courts" [2014] J.R. 188.

[17] Practice Direction 54D—Administrative Court (Venue) para.5.2. The standard forms for issuing and defending judicial review proceedings (Forms N461 and N462) now have a section in which the parties may indicate their preference and new forms N464 (application for directions as to venue) and N465 (response to applications for directions as to venue) have been produced; Appendices J-K and M-N. S. Nason, "Regionalisation of the Administrative Court" [2009] J.R. 1. The decision as to venue is a judicial one. Certain matters will remain in London. These include proceedings relating to: control orders (under CPR Pt 76); financial restrictions (CPR Pt 79) and the Proceeds of Crime Act 2002; confiscation and forfeiture (RSC Order 115); terrorism; extradition; and the discipline of solicitors. Proceedings before the Divisional Court and where a special advocate is appointed will also continue to be heard in London (PD 54D para.3.1). For an example of the impact of hearing a case out of London, see *R. (on the application of McDougal) v Liverpool City Council* [2009] EWHC 1821 (Admin); [2009] E.L.R. 510 at [4] (Silber J: "I heard this case in Liverpool and a large number of people connected with the School came to listen to the case. Their presence in such large numbers and the dignified way in which they all listened to the legal submissions was very impressive. I was left in no doubt that many people in the Croxteth area were very troubled by the plans of the Council to close the School."). Specific provision is made for the Administrative Court to sit in Wales where a claim for judicial review relates to a devolution issue arising out of the Government of Wales Act 2006 or an issue concerning the National Assembly for Wales, the Welsh Assembly Government, or any Welsh public body (including a Welsh local authority) whether or not it involves a devolution issue. Proceedings in Wales may take place in Welsh under the Welsh Language Act 1993 s.22.

(notably those in a "criminal cause or matter") continue to be heard by a Divisional Court of two or occasionally three judges.[18] The judges of the Administrative Court are those Justices of the High Court nominated by the Lord Chief Justice to deal with Administrative Court business.[19] Their number has grown from four in 1981 to 50 in 2012. They are mainly judges of the Queen's Bench Division, but also include judges of the Family Division and the Chancery Division. Deputy High Court judges (experienced circuit judges and practitioners appointed to sit on a part-time basis) may also be authorised to deal with Administrative Court matters, though by convention they do not hear cases relating to central government and they have limited powers to hear cases involving the Human Rights Act 1998.[20] The Master of the Administrative Court[21] has no general jurisdiction to make orders in claims for judicial review, except for interim applications (such as orders for expedition or orders and stand out of the list pending determination of a test case).[22] The Master may also consider written submissions on costs following withdrawal of an application for judicial review before a judge has considered the application for permission to apply. Recent amendments permit officers of the Administrative Court office who are also barristers or solicitors to exercise the court's jurisdiction in relation to matters incidental to proceedings or where there is no dispute between the parties. These now include the power to make case management directions, decisions on whether a matter should be listed before a Divisional Court and certain applications for relief from sanctions. They may also dismiss an application where a party has failed to comply with an order, rule or practice direction. Court officers are prohibited from deciding applications for permission, granting injunctions or (except in limited circumstances) issuing a stay of proceedings.[23]

16-005   A Lead Judge of the Administrative Court is appointed by the Lord Chief Justice. The nominated judges spend only some of their time on Administrative Court business (typically there are eight single judges and one Divisional Court sitting in London, the constitutions changing after periods of three weeks); like other High Court judges they also hear other civil and criminal cases on circuit and in London.[24] These arrangements reflect a compromise: while recognising the need for expert judges in the field of public law, it maintains the English tradition that everyone, including public bodies and office-holders, ought to be subject to justice in the ordinary courts.[25]

16-006   The work of the Administrative Court is supported by the legal and administrative staff of the Administrative Court Office[26] (part of Her Majesty's Courts and Tribunals Service), under the direction of the Master of the Administrative Court (formally still the Master of the Crown Office) and the Head of the Administrative Court Office. A team of lawyers assist in the management of cases, each one

---

[18]   Senior Courts Act 1981 ss.19, 66 and 151(4). See Lang, *Administrative Court: Practice and Procedure* (2006), para.1-04. On devolution issues, see 1-126.

[19]   Hence the term "nominated judges" to refer to the judges who determine judicial review claims.

[20]   Practice Direction 2B para.7A: they may not hear a "claim made in respect of a judicial act" or where there is a claim for a declaration of incompatibility under the HRA.

[21]   An office combined with that of Registrar of Criminal Appeals: Courts and Legal Services Act 1990 s.78.

[22]   Practice Direction 2B, para.3.1(c).

[23]   CPR Part 54.1A.

[24]   The Bowman committee reviewing judicial review procedures before the coming into force of the Human Rights Act recommended that it should become a more specialised court with the nominated judges spending a greater proportion of their time on its work (para.23).

[25]   A.V Dicey, *Introduction to the Study of the Law of the Constitution*, 10th edn (1959), p.193: a second meaning of the "rule of law" was that "every man, whatever his rank or condition, is subject to the ordinary law of the realm and amenable to the jurisdiction of the ordinary tribunals".

[26]   Known as the Crown Office until 2000.

specialising in a range of subject areas. Claims for judicial review received by the Administrative Court Office are examined by one of the lawyers. The lawyer to whom the case is assigned produces a note, summarising the issues (without expressing an opinion on the merits of the claim), drawing the court's attention to relevant authorities (especially unreported ones) and alerting the court to any similar cases that may be pending.[27]

The Administrative Court provides commendable transparency and account-   **16-007**
ability for its work though the existence of a "court users' group" which meets at least three times a year "for those who wish to voice their opinions on the running of or issues relating to the Administrative Court and the Administrative Court Office", a Charter for users, a clear system for dealing with complaints by court users about administrative failures and regular newsletters.[28]

CPR PT 54

Of the various procedures for review,[29] it is the claim for judicial review under   **16-008**
CPR Pt 54 that is of prime importance both in terms of the number of claims made and the effect it has had as a stimulus to the development of the principles of administrative law.[30] Although some flexibility now exists, where public law issues are at the heart of a claim, claimants are expected to use the CPR Pt 54 claim form and procedure (a significantly modified variant of the CPR Pt 8 arrangements for litigation) rather than the general procedure and form for commencing civil proceedings laid down by CPR Pt 7, or the alternative procedure in CPR Pt 8.[31]

Two main features distinguish the judicial review procedure from these other   **16-009**
types of civil claims. First, a claimant may not pursue a claim for judicial review to a full hearing without obtaining the permission (formerly "leave") of the Administrative Court to do so.[32] Secondly, there is a requirement that permission be sought promptly, and in any event within three months from the date when grounds for the claim first arose.[33] The time periods for commencing civil claims in tort and breach of contract, laid down in the Limitation Act 1980, are typically six years from the date on which the cause of action arose.

Between 1978 (when judicial review procedures were modernised) and October   **16-010**
2000 (when CPR Pt 54 came into force) judicial review litigation was regulated by Order 53 of the Rules of the Supreme Court. Today, reference to cases about the

---

[27] *R. v Lord Chancellor's Department Ex p. O'Toole* [1998] C.O.D. 269 (claimants have no right at common law to disclosure of such notes, though any unreported judgment mentioned in the note should be disclosed to the claimant to avoid apparent unfairness).

[28] See *http://www.justice.gov.uk* [Accessed 8 November 2017].

[29] See 1-050.

[30] See 3-113.

[32] Since the coming into force of the CPR, the differences between CPR Pt 54 and other proceedings are less pronounced as judges in all cases now have responsibility to manage the conduct of the litigation more closely than once was the case. See 15-094 and see M. Fordham, "Judicial review: the new rules" [2001] P.L. 4 and T. Cornford and M. Sunkin, "The Bowman Report, Access and the Recent Reforms of the Judicial Review Procedure" [2001] P.L. 11. The courts are generally keen that the overall approach to the application of the CPR should apply equally to public law claims (*R. (on the application of Hysaj) v Secretary of State for the Home Department* [2014] EWCA Civ 1633; [2015] 1 W.L.R. 2472 at [40]-[48]).

[33] See 16-055.

RSC Ord.53 procedure must therefore be made with caution.[34] The importance now attached to the "overriding objective" of the CPR may require re-evaluation of practices and principles adopted in the past. So too with the Human Rights Act 1998: it should not be assumed that approaches adopted to the judicial review process prior to October 2000 are always compliant with Convention rights. As a public authority, the Administrative Court must itself avoid acting in a way which is inconsistent with Convention rights.[35] The CPR must be read and given effect in a manner which is compatible with Convention rights so far as it is possible to do so.[36] The law of the European Union is also having a significant impact on areas of judicial review procedure, such as the rules on time limits.[37]

The overriding objective

16-011   CPR Pt 54 must be interpreted and applied in the light of the CPR's "overriding objective of enabling the court to deal with cases justly" and at proportionate cost.[38] This "provides a compass to guide courts and litigants and legal advisers as to their general course".[39] More particularly[40]:

"Dealing with a case justly includes, so far as practicable—

(a)   ensuring that the parties are on an equal footing;
(b)   saving expense;
(c)   dealing with the case in ways which are proportionate—
       (i)   to the amount of money involved;
       (ii)   to the importance of the case;
       (iii) to the complexity of the issues; and
       (iv)   to the financial position of each party;
(d)   ensuring that it is dealt with expeditiously and fairly;
(e)   allotting to it an appropriate share of the court's resources, while taking into account the need to allot the resources to other cases; and
(f)   enforcing compliance with rules, practice directions and orders."

16-012   CPR Pt 3 confers on the court general powers of case management. Except where the CPR provide otherwise, the court may (among other things) "extend or shorten the time for compliance with any rule, practice direction or court order (even if an

---

[34] *Biguzzi v Rank Leisure Plc* [1999] 1 W.L.R. 1926 at 1934 (Lord Woolf MR: "The whole purpose of making the CPR a self-contained code was to send the message that it now generally applies. Earlier authorities are no longer generally of any relevance once the CPR applies"); this does not mean that in all cases the old authorities "should be completely thrown overboard" (*UCB Corporate Services Ltd (formerly UCB Bank Plc) v Halifax (SW) Ltd (Striking Out: Breach of Rules and Orders)* [1999] C.P.L.R. 691 at [24] (Ward LJ)) but it does mean that pre-CPR authorities must always be re-evaluated in the light of the overriding objective.
[35] Human Rights Act 1998 s.6.
[36] Human Rights Act 1998 s.3. If it is impossible to give the CPR a compatible interpretation they will be ultra vires unless the incompatibility is specifically required by the Civil Procedure Act 1997 (*General Mediterranean Holdings SA v Patel* [2000] 1 W.L.R. 272). See generally, J. Jacob, *Civil Justice in the Age of Human Rights* (2007).
[37] See 16-056 and 14-083.
[38] CPR r.1.1(1). CPR r.1.1(2)(f) was added on 1 April 2013 to emphasise the continued importance of compliance with procedural rules to ensure that the civil legal system can function in the interests of all litigants and signal a move away from what some had perceived as a willingness to waive compliance (*Henry v News Group Newspapers Ltd* [2013] EWCA Civ 19; [2013] 2 All E.R. 849).
[39] *Access to Justice: Final Report*, p.275.
[40] CPR r.1.1(2).

application for extension is made after the time for compliance has expired)",[41] "exclude an issue from consideration" and "take any other step or make any other order for the purpose of managing the case and furthering the overriding objective". Generally, purely technical breaches of the rules should not hinder access to the court,[42] though other sanctions (such as costs) may be imposed. The overriding objective requires that parties be dealt with "on an even footing".[43] Equality of arms is also an aspect of ECHR art.6(1).[44]

---

[41] CPR Rule 3.10 provides that an error of procedure (such as a failure to comply with a rule or direction) does not invalidate any step taken in the proceedings unless the court so orders and that the court may make an order to remedy the error. In *R. v Vale of Glamorgan Council Ex p. Clements, The Times,* 22 August 2000, the CA allowed a renewed application for permission for judicial review in exceptional circumstances, even though the application for permission to appeal had not been made within the prescribed seven day period and the documents normally expected to accompany the application had not been lodged with the court.

[42] See, e.g. *Cala Homes (South) Ltd v Chichester DC (Time Limits)* [2000] C.P. Rep. 28 (claimant mistakenly filed a claim form in the wrong court office and used the wrong claim form, but the court declined to strike out the claim), considered in *Islam v Secretary of State for Communities and Local Government* [2012] EWHC 1314 (Admin) at [25], [29]; *R. v Secretary of State for the Environment, Transport and the Regions Ex p. National Farmers Union,* 24 November 1999 (unreported, Keene J) (NFU applied for judicial review rather than made a statutory application to quash but the court allowed the claim to be amended and to proceed). See also *San Vicente v Secretary of State for Communities and Local Government* [2013] EWCA Civ 817; [2014] 1 W.L.R. 966 at [52] on applications to amend claims under s.288 of the Town and Country Planning Act 1990. In relation to applying the new provisions on relief from sanctions in CPR r.3.9, see *Mitchell v News Group Newspapers Ltd* [2013] EWCA Civ 1537; [2014] 1 W.L.R. 795 at [40]–[41] and *Denton v TH White Ltd* [2014] EWCA Civ 906; [2014] 1 W.L.R. 3926 at [24]–[38]. In *Denton,* the CA restated the *Mitchell* principles and set out the three stages which should be addressed: to identify and assess the seriousness and significance of the failure to comply with any rule, practice direction or court order; then to consider why the default occurred; and finally to evaluate all the circumstances of the case in order to deal with the application justly. *Denton* (rather than *Mitchell*) was followed in *Michael Wilson & Partners, Ltd v Thomas Ian Sinclair* [2015] EWCA Civ 774; [2015] C.P. Rep. 45. Both were followed by the SC in *Thevarajah v Riordan* [2015] UKSC 78; [2016] 1 W.L.R. 76 at [13]–[15], in which Lord Neuberger described the CA in *Denton* as having "clarified some of the reasoning" in *Mitchell.*

[43] See, e.g. *Maltez v Lewis* (1999) 96(21) L.S.G. 39 (the overriding objective could not interfere with a party's right to choose a legal representative, but: "if it were to transpire, for instance, that one party could afford very experienced, large and expensive solicitors, whereas the other party could only afford a small and relatively inexperienced firm, then the court can—indeed, I suggest the court should—make orders to ensure that the level playing field envisaged by r.1(2)(a) is, so far as possible, achieved. It might be appropriate, for instance, when ordering disclosure, to give the party with the smaller firm of solicitors more time than the party with the larger firm. On preparing bundles, it might be right to direct the party instructing the larger firm to take on the duty of preparing and copying bundles" (Neuberger J).

[44] See, 6-048, 7-117, 10-083; see, e.g. *Dombo Beheer BV v Netherlands* (1994) 18 E.H.R.R. 213 (each party in a civil proceeding must have a reasonable opportunity to present his case under conditions which do not disadvantage him in relation to his opponent). National security considerations may render a "closed material" procedure (where a party is not provided with all the material before the tribunal) appropriate if sufficient safeguards (such as the appointment of a special advocate) are provided where such a procedure was provided for in the statutory provisions which establish the Employment Tribunal (*Tariq v Home Office* [2011] UKSC 35; [2012] 1 A.C. 452 at [76]-[79]; cf. *Al-Rawi v Security Service* [2011] UKSC 34; [2012] 1 A.C. 531 at [10]-[14] (the courts could not introduce such a procedure in relation to the common law jurisdiction to deal with claims of public interest immunity). *Tariq* was followed in *Kiani v Secretary of State for the Home Department* [2015] EWCA Civ 776; *The Times,* 19 August 2015. *Al-Rawi* was distinguished in *R. (on the application of B) v Westminster Magistrates' Court* [2014] UKSC 59; [2015] A.C. 1195 (extradition proceedings do not justify or call for a further qualification of the principle of open justice, beyond any recognised in *Al Rawi*).

THE PROCEDURAL STAGES

16-013   A claim for judicial review may encompass several stages, each of which will be examined below. Appendix O contains a procedural checklist.

- The exhaustion of other remedies and use of ADR.
- The exchange of letters between the would-be claimant and defendant before starting the claim.
- Gathering of information, including use of the Freedom of Information Act 2000 and Data Protection Act 1998.
- The preparation of the statement of case.
- The application for permission to make a claim for judicial review and any appeal against the refusal of permission.
- An interlocutory stage.
- The hearing of the substantive claim;
- Finally, any appeal against the substantive claim.

Exhaustion of other remedies and ADR

16-014   In numerous cases in recent decades, the Administrative Court and its precursor have made plain that (in the absence of exceptional circumstances) permission to proceed with a judicial review claim will be refused where a claimant has failed to exhaust other possible remedies.[45] A claimant will not be required to resort to some other procedure if that other procedure is "less satisfactory" or otherwise inappropriate.[46] In each case the question is whether the court should exercise its discretion; "it would be both foolish and impossible to seek to anticipate" all the factors that may properly influence the court's discretion.[47]

16-015   Added impetus to the older case law on the need to exhaust alternative remedies has been given by the growing recognition of the importance of alternative dispute resolution (ADR) in civil litigation generally and, more recently, the Ministry of Justice's policy on "proportionate dispute resolution".[48]

---

[45] Pre-Action Protocol for Judicial Review (January2017), para.5 ("Judicial review should only be used where no adequate alternative remedy, such as a right of appeal, is available"); *R. (on the application of Sivasubramaniam) v Wandsworth County Court* [2002] EWCA Civ 1738; [2003] 1 W.L.R. 475. For surveys of the voluminous case law, see M. Fordham, *Judicial Review Handbook*, 6th edn (2012), pp.411-426 and C. Lewis, *Judicial Remedies in Public Law*, 5th edn (2014), paras 12–042–12–076. See also R. Moules, "The exhaustion of alternative remedies: re-emphasising the courts' discretion" [2005] J.R. 350. See also *R. (on the application of Willford) v Financial Services Authority* [2013] EWCA Civ 677 at [36]–[38] (Upper Tribunal "can reconsider the whole matter afresh" and therefore provides a more appropriate alternative remedy).

[46] *R. v Hillingdon LBC Ex p. Royco Homes Ltd* [1974] Q.B. 720; *R. v Chief Immigration Officer Ex p. Kharrazi* [1980] 1 W.L.R. 1396 (not practicable to use the machinery under s.13 Immigration Act 1971 as claimant would have to return to Iran to exercise his right of appeal and would be caught in a war); cf. *R. (on the application of George) v General Medical Council* [2003] EWHC 1124 (Admin); [2004] Lloyd's Rep. Med. 33. A remedy will not be considered to be ineffective just because it is not legally binding if in practice the body against whom it is ordered undertakes to comply with it: *R. (on the application of Carnell) v Regent's Park College* [2008] EWHC 739 (Admin); [2008] E.L.R. 268 at [24]. It was also held in *Carnell* that where a claimant seeks judicial review without exhausting an alternative remedy, and the time limit for pursuing the alternative remedy expires while seeking judicial review, that will not justify allowing the judicial review proceedings to proceed: at [31]-[33]. See also *R. (on the application of Willford) v Financial Services Authority* [2013] EWCA Civ 677 at [36].

[47] *R. v Hereford Magistrates Court Ex p. Rowlands* [1998] Q.B. 110 at 125F.

[48] See 1-054.

Alternative (or substitute) remedies

Claimants are refused permission to proceed with judicial review where the court **16-016** forms the view that some other form of legal proceedings or avenue of challenge is available and should be used. Questions as to whether a claimant should have used another type of redress process should arise on the application for permission and not at or after the substantive hearing of the judicial review claim. Once the court has heard arguments on the grounds of review, there is little purpose in requiring the parties to resort to some other remedy[49]; indeed, to do so may be contrary to the overriding objective of the CPR. But a failure to pursue other remedies may influence how the court exercises its discretion to award costs.[50]

The most obvious type of substitute remedy is an avenue of appeal or review created by statute.[51] A range of other forms of challenge have also been held to be acceptable substitutes for judicial review.[52] There are various reasons why legislation may create an avenue of redress into which the Administrative Court may seek to divert challenges, including: a desire to make access to justice available more locally (although this is less powerful since regionalisation of the Administrative Court); a wish to prevent the Administrative Court becoming overburdened with cases; the fact that a tribunal or other specialist body may have more expertise in the subject of the claim than the Administrative Court; and that substitutes for judicial review may be provided at lesser cost. **16-017**

Avenues of appeal or review created by statute

The most straightforward substitute remedy is where legislation provides an **16-018** appeal. Judicial review is essentially a mechanism to be used where there is no statutory right of appeal. In almost all cases, the Administrative Court will regard a statutory appeal, whether to a court or a tribunal, as a proper substitute for judicial review,[53] though exceptional circumstances may dictate otherwise.[54]

There are numerous examples of appeal and review systems other than judicial **16-019**

---

[49] *R. v Chief Constable of Merseyside Police Ex p. Calveley* [1989] A.C. 1228 and *R. v Secretary of State for the Home Department, Ex p. Swati* [1986] 1 W.L.R. 477 at 485.

[50] See 16-092.

[51] See 16-018.

[52] See 16-021.

[53] *R. v Birmingham City Council Ex p. Ferrero Ltd* [1993] 1 All E.R. 530; *Farley v Secretary of State for Work and Pensions (No.2)* [2006] UKHL 31; [2006] 1 W.L.R. 1817. *Ferrero* was distinguished in a case involving a pure bias challenge where the public interest considerations did not favour resort to the specialist appeal body (*R. (on the application of Al-Le Logistics Ltd) v Traffic Commissioner for the South Eastern and Metropolitan Traffic Area* [2010] EWHC 134 (Admin) at [106]).

[54] *R. v Secretary of State for the Home Department Ex p. Capti-Mehmet* [1997] C.O.D. 61 (error or incompetence of the claimant's legal representatives will not of itself constitute an exceptional circumstance); "gross procedural unfairness" at an appeal hearing may do: *R. (on the application of AM (Cameroon)) v Asylum and Immigration Tribunal* [2007] EWCA Civ 131 at [89]-[91]. See further *R. (on the application of Watch Tower Bible & Tract Society of Britain) v Charity Commission* [2016] EWCA Civ 154; [2016] 1 W.L.R. 2625 at [19] (Lord Dyson MR): "It is only in a most exceptional case that a court will entertain an application for judicial review if other means of redress are conveniently and effectively available. This principle applies with particular force where Parliament has enacted a statutory scheme that enables persons against whom decisions are made and actions taken to refer the matter to a specialist tribunal". In *Watch Tower*, an appeal to the First-tier Tribunal provided an effective remedy in relation to the Charity Commission's decision to initiate the inquiry, but not the challenge to its production order which could proceed by way of judicial review. The principle has little relevance "where the alternative remedy which it is said that the claimant must pursue is a profoundly different claim from the judicial review claim which they seek to advance": *R. (on the application of Veolia ES Landfill Ltd) v Revenue and Customs Commissioners* [2015] EWCA Civ 747; [2015] B.T.C. 23 at [29]. In *Glencore Energy UK Ltd v Commissioners*

review.[55] The new tribunal system created by the Tribunals, Courts and Enforcement Act 2007 creates one such appeal route: first to the First-tier Tribunal, from there to the Upper Tribunal, and then to the Court of Appeal.[56] There is an appeal from decisions of local authorities relating to homelessness to the county courts.[57] In many circumstances, an appeal lies from decisions of magistrates' courts either to the Crown Court or ("by way of case stated") to the Administrative Court.[58] Some appeals may enable the appellate tribunal or court to reconsider the merits of the case, but often appeals are limited to "points of law", which encompasses all the grounds of judicial review.

16-020   The powers of a tribunal or court hearing an appeal will often be at least as extensive as those in judicial review (and perhaps greater). In most situations there can be no constitutional or practical objection to the Administrative Court routinely refusing permission to proceed with a judicial review claim where there is a statutory appeal to a tribunal[59] or a court.[60] To hold otherwise would risk subverting Parliament's intention in creating such appeals.[61] The one appeal system the Administrative Court was called upon to supervise frequently was refusals of permission to appeal from Immigration Adjudicators to the Immigration Appeal Tribunal; this appellate system has now been superseded.[62] The desirability of an authoritative ruling on a point of law may point towards judicial review being the appropriate remedy in some contexts, if the appeal or review procedure is incapable of making such a ruling.[63]

---

of HM Revenue and Customs [2017] EWHC 1476 (Admin); [2017] S.T.C. 1824 at [66]–[73], Green J held that the procedure created by ss.1–1 and 102 of the Finance Act 2015 was an appropriate alternative and that permission to seek judicial review should therefore be refused. Under the statutory procedure, HMRC had to review a charging notice issued to a tax-payer and, if the tax-payer remained dissatisfied with the outcome of the review, he was entitled to appeal to the FTT. Green J considered that the review (although not independent) would refine the issues.

[55] It is arguable that in some contexts appeals (or indeed, judicial review) limited to issues of law are insufficient: this has been the subject of criticisms over several years by the House of Lords Constitution Committee, which has taken the view that "appeals should provide an opportunity for the regulated to have their objections reviewed on the merits of the case": *The Regulatory State: Ensuring its Accountability*. HL Paper No.68 (Session 2004/05) Ch.11.

[56] See 1-098. Section 64 of the Criminal Justice and Courts Act 2015 (in force from 8 August 2016) inserts new ss.14A–14C into the Tribunals, Courts and Enforcement Act 2007, allowing leapfrog appeals from the Upper Tribunal to the SC in certain circumstances: see paras 16–085, 17–005 and fn.17 thereto.

[57] Housing Act 1996; see 17–040.

[58] See 17-036.

[59] *R. v Secretary of State for the Home Department Ex p. Swati* [1986] 1 W.L.R. 477; *R. v Ministry of Defence Ex p. Sweeney* [1999] C.O.D. 122; *R. (on the application of M) v Bromley LBC* [2002] EWCA Civ 1113; [2002] 2 F.L.R. 802 (Care Standards Tribunal established under the Protection of Children Act 1999).

[60] *R. v Mansfield DC Ex p. Ashfield Nominees Ltd* [1999] E.H.L.R. 290 (appeal to county court against repairs notices issued under the Housing Act 1985); *R. v Merton LBC Ex p. Sembi* (2000) 32 H.L.R. 439 (appeal to county court under Housing Act 1996); *R. v Blackpool BC Ex p. Red Cab Taxis Ltd* [1994] R.T.R. 402 (private hire vehicles licensing, appeal to justices). cf. *R. v Hereford Magistrates Court Ex p. Rowlands* [1998] Q.B. 110 (stressing that it was always a question of discretion whether to allow judicial review where a defendant in criminal proceedings had not pursued an appeal to the Crown Court). In *Balogun v DPP* [2010] EWHC 799 (Admin); [2010] 1 W.L.R. 1915 at [31], it was held that challenges to magistrates' decisions to adjourn criminal proceedings (where justified) are better brought by judicial review than by case stated.

[61] See, e.g. *R. (on the application of Sivasubramaniam) v Wandsworth County Court* [2002] EWCA Civ 1738; [2003] 1 W.L.R. 475; and *R. (on the application of Watch Tower Bible & Tract Society of Britain) v Charity Commission* [2016] EWCA Civ 154; [2016] 1 W.L.R. 2625 at [19].

[62] See 1-098; on the new system, see 17-004.

[63] *Falmouth and Truro Port HA v South West Water Ltd* [2001] Q.B. 445.

Other avenues of legal challenge

In addition to statutory appeals, the Administrative Court has regarded a range **16-021** of other grievance redressing mechanisms as substitutes for judicial review. These include: a statutory complaints procedure[64]; an express right to give notice of objection to a government Minister proposing to impose a penalty[65]; the possibility of bringing a private prosecution[66]; remedies under the Public Contracts Regulations 2015[67]; proceedings in the Chancery Division questioning the compatibility of a statutory provision with European Community law[68]; and a request to a Secretary of State to exercise default powers (conferred under various Acts of Parliament) to intervene to prevent the unreasonable exercise of power by a public authority.[69] In this category of case, a more searching inquiry may be needed than in the case of a straightforward statutory appeal; the question ought to be whether the substitute for judicial review adequately protects the rights and interests of the claimant. The other body may for example lack the power to deal with the issue.[70] If the claimant is seeking to raise questions about the lawfulness of a broad question of policy, the Administrative Court may be a more appropriate forum than a criminal court.[71] The other procedure may be less expeditious and if a matter is urgent the court may allow the application to proceed.[72] Among the factors to be considered are "the comparative speed, expense and finality of the alternative processes, the need and scope for fact finding, the desirability of an authoritative ruling on any point of law

---

[64] *R. v East Sussex CC Ex p. W (A Minor)* [1998] 2 F.L.R. 1082 (care order and Children Act 1989).

[65] *R. (on the application of Balbo B&C Auto Transporti Internazionali) v Secretary of State for the Home Department* [2001] EWHC Admin 195; [2001] 1 W.L.R. 1556 (relating to a civil penalty issued under the Immigration and Asylum Act 1999 s.35 on lorry owner), considered in *International Transport Roth GmbH v Secretary of State for the Home Department* [2002] EWCA Civ 158; [2003] Q.B. 728.

[66] *R. v DPP Ex p. Camelot Group Plc* (1998) 10 Admin. L.R. 93; cf. *R. v Commissioner of Police for the Metropolis Ex p. Blackburn* [1968] 2 Q.B. 118.

[67] *Cookson & Clegg Ltd v Ministry of Defence* [2005] EWCA Civ 811; [2006] Eu. L.R. 1092 concerning earlier versions of the Regulations; S.H. Bailey, "Judicial Review and the Public Procurement Regulations" (2005) 6 P.P.L.R. 291.

[68] *Aegis Group Plc v Inland Revenue Commissioners* [2005] EWHC 1468 (Ch); [2006] S.T.C. 23. In *R. (on the application of Roche Registration Ltd) v Secretary of State for Health* [2015] EWCA Civ 1311; [2016] 4 W.L.R. 46 at [60]–[64], it was inappropriate for the domestic courts to grant relief in judicial review proceedings where the claimant would have the opportunity to challenge any penalty imposed pursuant to the EC Penalties Regulation in the appropriate EU courts "which will be able to give a determinative answer".

[69] See, e.g. *R (on the application of Baker) v Devon County Council* [1995] 1 All E.R. 73 at [92], cf. *R. v Inner London Education Authority Ex p. Ali* (1990) 2 Admin. L.R. 822 (the fact that the Secretary of State had power to give directions under the Education Act 1944 s.99, and can do so on complaint, creates no inference that the ordinary jurisdiction of the court is ousted, though it is very relevant to the exercise of the court's discretion). For examples of default powers, see Education Act 1996 Pt 9.

[70] See, e.g. *Leech v Deputy Governor of Parkhurst Prison* [1988] A.C. 533 (at that time the Home Secretary lacked the power to remove a disciplinary finding in relation to a prisoner from his record); *Smith v North Eastern Derbyshire Primary Care Trust* [2006] EWCA Civ 1291; [2006] 1 W.L.R. 3315 (a patients' forum, a body established under the National Health Service Reform and Health Care Professions Act 2002 s.15 lacked the power to require a primary care trust to reverse a decision).

[71] *R. (on the application of A) v South Yorkshire Police* [2007] EWHC 1261 (Admin) (judicial review preferable to raising issues on an application to the Youth Court to dismiss or stay the criminal proceedings on the ground that they are an abuse of the process). In *R. (on the application of MM) v Secretary of State for Work and Pensions* [2012] EWHC 2106 (Admin) at [57]–[58], it was appropriate to issue judicial review proceedings because the claimants sought remedies on behalf of a class of those affected.

[72] *Ex p. Royco Homes Ltd* [1974] Q.B. 720. Judicial review should not be sought where it is "not likely" to be quicker than the alternative remedy: *R. (on the application of Carnell) v Regent's Park College* [2008] EWHC 739 (Admin); [2008] E.L.R. 268 at [25].

arising, and (perhaps) the apparent strength of the claimant's substantive challenge".[73] Recourse to one of the ombudsmen[74] may also, in some cases, provide a substitute for judicial review. As discussed in Chapter 1, the potential problem here is that the ombudsmen may also regard judicial review as appropriate and refuse to conduct an inquiry into what otherwise might be maladministration causing injustice.[75]

Alternative Dispute Resolution (ADR)[76]

16-022   An important aspect of the new approach to civil litigation embraced by the CPR is that all courts must further the overriding objective by "actively managing cases". This includes "encouraging the parties to use an alternative dispute resolution procedure if the court considers that appropriate and facilitating the use of such procedure".[77] The requirement for practitioners to use, or at least consider, the use of ADR instead of resorting too early to judicial review claims was set down by the Court of Appeal in *Cowl v Plymouth CC*.[78] The Court of Appeal spoke of "the paramount importance of avoiding litigation wherever possible" in disputes with public authorities and said that the LSC (now the Legal Aid Agency) should cooperate with the Administrative Court "to scrutinise extremely carefully" judicial review claims so as to ensure that parties tried "to resolve the dispute with the minimum involvement of the courts". The Pre-action Protocol on Judicial Review identifies "some of the options" as: discussion and negotiation; ombudsmen; using relevant public authority complaints or review procedures; and mediation.[79] All of these techniques are encouraged by the Ministry of Justice's policy of "proportionate dispute resolution" (which extends beyond ADR to include, among other things, steps to avoid disputes arising in the first place).[80] In encouraging ADR, it needs to be "recognised that no party can or should be forced to mediate

---

[73] *Falmouth and Truro Port HA v South West Water Ltd* [2001] Q.B. 445.
[74] The Parliamentary and Health Service Ombudsman, the Prisons and Probation Ombudsman, the Local Government Ombudsman and (in Wales) Public Services Ombudsman for Wales: see 1-077. See A. Abraham, "The ombudsman and 'paths to justice': a just alternative or just an alternative?" [2008] P.L. 1.
[75] See 1-096.
[76] See also 1-076.
[77] CPR r.1.4(2)(e).
[78] *Cowl v Plymouth CC* [2001] EWCA Civ 1935; [2002] 1 W.L.R. 803, *R. (on the application of C) v Nottingham City Council* [2010] EWCA Civ 790; [2011] 1 F.C.R. 127 at [31]-[38] (where the proceedings served no useful purposes as the authority offered to provide all the services sought in the proceedings); and *MD v Secretary of State for the Home Department* [2011] EWCA Civ 453 at [5], [8] (where the relief sought had been granted as a result of the issuing of the proceedings); see A. Le Sueur, "How to Resolve Disputes with Public Authorities" [2002] P.L. 203; S. Boyron, "The Rise of Mediation in Administrative Law Disputes: Experiences from England, France and Germany" [2006] P.L. 320.
[79] Paras 9–12 (January 2017 issue). Paragraph 11 refers to S. Blake, J. Browne and S. Sime, *The Jackson ADR Handbook* (2013); the Citizens Advice Bureaux website: *https://www.citizensadvice.org.uk/consumer/alternative-dispute-resolution/settling-out-of-court/using-alternative-dispute-resolution-adr/* [Accessed 8 November 2017] (for information on ADR); and *http://civilmediation.justice.gov.uk/* [Accessed 8 November 2017] (to find a mediation provider). See further, V. Bondy and L. Mulcahy, *Mediation and Judicial Review: An empirical research study* (Public Law Project, 2009) and M. Doyle, *Mediation in Judicial Review: A practical handbook for lawyers* (PLP, 2011) (both available at *http://www.publiclawproject.org.uk* [Accessed 8 November 2017]). The 2009 PLP research project concluded that mediation does not offer a cheaper or faster route than judicial review in most cases, but can offer more innovative remedies.
[80] See 1-054.

or enter into any form of ADR"[81] an important respect in which ADR differs from the court's approach to insisting upon the use of formal rights of appeal in place of judicial review.

In the years following *Cowl*, there has been relatively slow progress towards establishing a principled basis on which ADR can be used in public law disputes (clearly not all disputes are suitable for ADR),[82] establishing a suitable funding regime to pay for ADR and making practical arrangements for its delivery. A particular problem relates to timing. The fact that a claimant has been pursuing alternative remedies or using ADR does not, as the rules now stand, operate to suspend the requirement that claims for judicial review are to be made promptly and in any event within three months. It may therefore be prudent to commence a claim and then stay proceedings pending the outcome of the other remedy: a precaution that somewhat undermines the policy goal of saving cost.

16-023

ECHR arts 6(1) and 13

In deciding whether to steer a would-be claimant away from judicial review, the court needs now to consider ECHR art.6(1) which, in relation to "civil rights and obligations or ... any criminal charge", guarantees a right to "a fair and public hearing within a reasonable time by an independent and impartial tribunal established by law" and which implicitly protects the right of access to a court.[83] Not all claims for judicial review raise "civil rights or obligations" or a criminal charge, but where they do weight needs to be given to protecting access to a court. Where other Convention rights are in issue, the court should attach important to the need for an "effective remedy".[84]

16-024

---

[81] The Pre-action Protocol for Judicial Review (January 2017) states only that "parties should consider whether some form of alternative dispute resolution ... or complaints procedure would be more suitable than litigation, and if so, endeavour to agree which to adopt"; indeed, exploring ADR does not excuse non-compliance with the time limit and so it may be appropriate to issue a claim without having done so (para.9). If, however, a party unreasonably refuses to engage in mediation, the court may subsequently refuse to make a costs order in its favour, see e.g. *Dunnett v Railtrack Plc* [2002] EWCA Civ 303; [2002] 1 W.L.R. 2434 at [12]-[18] (in which the successful party was deprived of any costs award for rejecting out of hand the court's suggestion of ADR). In *PGF II SA v OMFS Co.1 Ltd* [2013] EWCA Civ 1288; [2014] 1 W.L.R. 1386 at [34]–[40], the CA extended the guidance given by the CA in *Halsey v Milton Keynes General NHS Trust* [2004] EWCA Civ 576; [2004] 1 W.L.R. 3002 to the effect that, in general, a party's silence in the face of an invitation to participate in ADR was itself unreasonable regardless of whether or not refusal to engage in ADR might have been reasonable. See also *Laporte v Commissioner of Police of the Metropolis* [2015] EWHC 371 (QB); [2015] 3 Costs L.R. 471at [9]–[14]; and the Pre-Action Protocol for Judicial Review (May 2015) at paras 9 and 12.

[82] For example, where important legal principles are at stake or it is necessary to establish a precedent; cf. M. Supperstone, D. Stilitz and C. Sheldon, "ADR in Public Law" [2006] P.L. 299. In *R. (on the application of Wood) v Leeds City Council* [2014] EWHC 2598 (Admin) at [105]-[110], a case which involved issues of statutory construction, an application to the Local Government Ombudsman was held not to provide a suitable alternative remedy. See however, *R. (on the application of David Soar) v Secretary of State for Justice* [2015] EWHC 392 (Admin) at [47]-[49]: a case involving "fundamental points of procedure relating to natural justice" was granted permission on the basis that judicial review was arguably more suitable than the ombudsman procedure. The HC held that the ombudsman procedure may have been equally effective and appropriate; however, as proceedings had been commenced, the court granted the relief sought rather than remitting the claim to the ombudsman in light of the overriding objective.

[83] See 6-048, 7-120.

[84] See 13-010.

Exchange of letters before claim

16-025   As in other types of litigation, a claimant who proposes to seek permission to make a judicial review claim is generally expected to give full notice in writing to the defendant before doing so.[85] The purpose of the letter is "is to identify the issues in dispute and establish whether they can be narrowed or litigation can be avoided".[86] The public authority is expected to respond in writing within 14 days of a letter before claim, using a standard format letter. Interested parties should be sent copies of both letters.[87] Compliance with the good practices set out in the Pre-Action Protocol for Judicial Review does not affect the requirement that permission be sought promptly and in any event within three months.[88]

Gathering evidence and information

16-026   Although it is often said that claims for judicial review do not (or should not) deal with matters of fact, information in the hands of a public authority is often vital to establishing whether a decision is wrong in law, for instance: that an irrelevant consideration was taken into account or a relevant consideration was not taken into account[89]; or that reasoning processes were so illogical as to amount to irrationality.[90] Where breach of a Convention right is in issue, the court's engagement with the factual background of the case will often be even more intensive than under ordinary domestic review and the court may be required to make findings of fact (not merely assess whether the public authority made reasonable findings of fact).[91] Review on the basis of proportionality requires the court to assess evidence of impact and alternative ways of achieving the public authority's policy goals.[92]

The duty of candour

16-027   The absence in English law of a general duty under common law to give reasons for decisions does not assist the claimant.[93] However, once a claim for judicial review is afoot, the defendant public authority is subject to the "duty of candour". The duty of candour requires that the process of judicial review be "conducted with all the cards face upwards on the table" and acknowledges that "the vast majority of the cards will start in the authority's hands".[94] The duty derives from the relationship between the courts and those who obtain their power from public law. The

---

[85]   Except in urgent cases: see Pre-action Protocol, para.6.
[86]   Pre-action Protocol, para.14. A standard form letter is provided, which claimants "should normally use": Pre-action Protocol.
[87]   See 2-072.
[88]   See 16-058. *R. (on the application of McCallion) v Kennet DC* [2001] EWHC Admin 575; [2002] P.L.C.R. 9.
[89]   See 5-120.
[90]   See 11-032.
[91]   See 11-087. In *HK (Bulgaria) v Secretary of State for the Home Department* [2016] EWHC 857 (Admin); [2016] A.C.D. 86 at [13]–[18], the court reluctantly agreed to admit an expert report by Amnesty International on conditions for returned asylum seekers in Bulgaria, but emphasised that strict compliance with the conditions in CPR Pt 35 was essential in relation to expert reports in judicial review proceedings.
[92]   See 11-087.
[93]   See 7-088.
[94]   *R. v Lancashire CC Ex p. Huddleston* [1986] 2 All E.R. 941 at 945. The Government Legal Department has produced a very helpful document entitled "Guidance on discharging the duty of candour and disclosure in judicial review proceedings" (January 2010) which is available at *https://www.gov.uk/government/organisations/government-legal-department* [Accessed 8 November 2017]. The duty of candour also applies to claimants (*R. (on the application of I) v Secretary of*

relationship is described as a "partnership based on a common aim, namely the maintenance of the highest standards of public administration".[95] The duty has been described as a very high one to assist the court with full and accurate explanations of all the facts relevant to the issues which the court must decide.[96] The duty extends to documents and other information which will assist the claimant's case and/or which may give rise to further grounds of challenge which might not otherwise occur to the claimant. The duty arises as soon as the public authority becomes aware that someone is likely to challenge a decision affecting them and continues until the proceedings are resolved. It is important to emphasise that the duty of candour also applies to claimants.[97] The principle that the ordinary process of disclosure is not required in judicial review proceedings unless the court orders otherwise must be seen against this background.[98] Before they reach the point of issuing proceedings or sending a letter before claim, claimants may consider exercising statutory rights of access to information, an overview of which we provide in the following paragraphs.

Freedom of Information Act 2000

The Freedom of Information Act 2000 (which came into force in 2005) introduced a statutory regime for obtaining information from public authorities.[99] Section 1 provides that:

16-028

State for the Home Department [2007] EWHC 3103 (Admin) at [8]) and third parties (*Belize Alliance of Conservation Non-Governmental Organisations v Department of the Environment* [2004] UKPC 6; [2004] Env. L.R. 38 at [87]). In *R. (on the application of Midcounties Co-operative Ltd) v Forest of Dean DC* [2015] EWHC 1251 (Admin); [2015] P.T.S.R. D32 at [148]–[151], the defendant had taken no active part in proceedings for financial reasons, leaving the interested third party to defend its decision. It was observed that although a third party may be subject to the duty of candour, such an arrangement may not necessarily meet all the practical difficulties which may arise so as to properly discharge the defendant's own duty in this regard. In *Abraha v Secretary of State for the Home Department* [2015] EWHC 1980 (Admin) at [111] and [114], the duty was described as an aspect of, and essential to, the rule of law. One aspect of the duty of candour is that the reviewing court has to be given a sufficient explanation by a statutory regulator operating in a technical or scientific area of how the science related to its decision, so that the court could consider whether it embodied an abuse of discretion or an error of law (*R. (on the application of Mott) v Environment Agency* [2016] EWCA Civ 564; [2016] 1 W.L.R. 4338). It may not be sufficient to provide a "pile of undigested documents" in a document heavy claim without identifying the significant documents (*R. (on the application of Khan) v Secretary of State for the Home Department* [2016] EWCA Civ 416 at [46]).

[95] *Ex p. Huddleston* [1986] 2 All E.R. 941 at 945.

[96] *R (on the application of Al-Sweady) v Secretary of State for Defence* [2009] EWHC 2387 (Admin); [2010] H.R.L.R. 2 at [22]. *Al-Sweady* concerned the alleged killing or ill-treatment of Iraqis detained by members of the British Army in Iraq in 2004. The gravity of the alleged human rights violations and fact that cross-examination would be necessary to resolve disputed factual issues heightened the need to ensure full disclosure. In *R. (on the application of Bancoult) v Secretary of State for Foreign and Commonwealth Affairs (No.4)* [2016] UKSC 35; [2017] A.C. 300 at [24], an omission to disclose documents casting into doubt the independence and reliability of a resettlement report relied on by the government amounted to a "highly regrettable" breach of the Secretary of State's duty of candour (which he accepted). Lord Kerr, dissenting on a slightly different issue, considered the breach "wholly unacceptable when such a fundamental right was at stake" ([183]–[187]). However, that failure was on its own insufficient to justify setting aside the decision of the HL in prior proceedings.

[97] In *R. (on the application of Mohammad Shahzad Khan) v Secretary of State for the Home Department)* [2016] EWCA Civ 416 at [42]–[47], the claimant's duty of candour was held to extend beyond the furnishing of relevant documents and to include drawing to the attention of the court the significance of particular documents adverse to the claim. At the time of writing, the Lord Chief Justice is undertaking a consultation into the defendant's duty of candour and disclosure in judicial review proceedings.

[98] PD 54A, para.12. The ordinary process of disclosure is that set out in CPR Part 31 for standard claims. On disclosure, see 16-072.

[99] For an assessment, see P. Birkinshaw, "Regulating Information", Ch.14 in J. Jowell and D. Oliver,

"Any person making a request for information to a public authority is entitled—(a) to be informed in writing by the public authority whether it holds information of the description specified in the request, and (b) if that is the case, to have that information communicated to him."

Public authorities have a duty "to provide advice and assistance, so far as it would be reasonable to expect the authority to do so, to persons who propose to make, or have made, requests for information to it".[100]

16-029   "Public authority" for the purposes of the 2000 Act has a somewhat different meaning than it does in relation to claims for judicial review and the Human Rights Act 1998.[101] Rather than stipulate a test, the 2000 Act simply lists those office-holders and bodies that constitute a "public authority".[102] Public authorities are required to comply with requests for information "promptly and in any event not later than the twentieth working day following the date of receipt".[103] A public authority may refuse to comply if the cost of obtaining the information would exceed a stipulated limit (at the time of writing, £600 for central government and Parliament; £450 for other public authorities).[104] If a request under the 2000 Act is not complied with, an application may be made to the Information Commissioner who will adjudicate on the matter. An appeal from the Information Commissioner lies to the First-tier Tribunal (Information Rights). An appeal from the First-tier Tribunal lies on a point of law to the Upper Tribunal and, on the same ground, to the Court of Appeal.

16-030   The right to obtain information is subject to three main kinds of exemptions. First, where a public authority is not listed in Sch.1 to the Act (such as the Security Service and the Secret Intelligence Service), any information kept by that body is wholly outside the statutory right to request information. Secondly, the 2000 Act bars access to information by exempting from disclosure whole categories of information or record, such as: information accessible to the applicant by other means; information intended for future publication; information supplied by, or relating to, bodies dealing with security matters; other information required for the purpose of safeguarding national security. Thirdly, the Act creates "contents-based" qualified exemptions in relation to which the public authority must assess each item of information requested and apply a public interest test by assessing whether disclosure "would, or would be likely to, prejudice" the specified interests in question, which include: defence; international relations; relations between any administration in the United Kingdom and any other such administration; the economy; information relating to criminal investigations and proceedings conducted

---

The Changing Constitution, 8th edn (2015); P. Coppel (ed), *Information Rights: Law and Practice*, 4rd edn (2014); and P. Birkinshaw and M. Varney, *Government and Information: The Law Relating to Access, Disclosure and their Regulation*, 4th edn (2011). A helpful and authoritative account of the Act is set out in *R. (on the application of Evans) v Attorney General* [2015] UKSC 21; [2015] A.C. 1787 at [8]–[18]. Lord Sumption described the Act as "a landmark enactment of great constitutional significance for the United Kingdom" in *Kennedy v Information Commissioner* [2014] UKSC 20; [2015] A.C. 455 at [153].

100   Freedom of Information Act 2000 s.16.
101   See Ch.3. See further, *BBC v Sugar* [2009] UKHL 9; [2009] 1 W.L.R. 430 at [24]-[27] (Lord Phillips).
102   Freedom of Information Act 2000 s.3 and Sch.1 (as amended by Order from time to time).
103   Freedom of Information Act 2000 s.10. If reliance is placed on a qualified exemption, the public authority has 40 days. Promptness is the requirement and the time limit in days is intended to be "a long stop" (*APPGER v Information Commissioner and Ministry of Defence* [2011] UKUT 153 (AAC) (15 April 2011) at [41].
104   Freedom of Information Act 2000 s.12. The limit is calculated on the basis of an hourly rate of £25. The estimate must be realistic and supported by cogent evidence (*Roberts v Information Commissioner* (EA/2008/0500) (4 December 2008) at [10]).

by public authorities, law enforcement, formulation of government policy, the effective conduct of public affairs, the health and safety of the public, or personal information.[105]

Environmental Information Regulations 2004

European Union Council Directive 2003/4/EC on public access to environmental information required Member States to legislate to provide rights of access in this field. In England and Wales, the relevant legislation is the Environmental Information Regulations 2004 (SI 2004/3391) (EIR). Public authorities covered by the Freedom of Information Act 2000 are subject to the EIR, but regulations also extend further to cover "any other body or other person, that carries out functions of public administration" and any other body or other person, "that is under the control" of a public authority and "(i) has public responsibilities relating to the environment; (ii) exercises functions of a public nature relating to the environment; or (iii) provides public services relating to the environment".[106] There are a number of exemptions and limits on the right to information under the EIR.

16-031

---

[105] Given the limited rights of appeal, there is relatively little binding authority on the interpretation of the exemptions. Some significant recent cases include: *Department for Work and Pensions v Information Commissioner* [2016] EWCA Civ 758; [2017] 1 W.L.R. 1 (identities of organisations hosting placements under mandatory "workfare" schemes for unemployed people); *Information Commissioner v Colenso-Dunne* [2015] UKUT 471 (AAC) (list of 305 journalists' names seized by the ICO during a raid on the home of a private investigator); *Independent Parliamentary Standards Authority v Information Commissioner* [2015] EWCA Civ 388; [2015] 1 W.L.R. 2879 (on receipts for expense claims made by Members of Parliament); *Ranger v The House of Lords Appointments Commission* [2015] EWHC 45 (QB) (information relating to the conferring by the Crown of any honour or dignity); *Kennedy v Information Commissioner* [2014] UKSC 20; [2015] A.C. 455 (on documents created by, or provided to, a public body relating to an inquiry conducted by that body); *British Broadcasting Corporation v Sugar (No.2)* [2012] UKSC 4; [2012] 1 W.L.R. 439 (on journalistic material); *Department of Health v Information Commissioner* (2012) B.M.L.R. 110 (concerning policy making and risk registers relating to reforms of the National Health Service); *Common Services Agency v Scottish Information Commissioner* [2008] UKHL 47; [2008] 1 W.L.R. 1550 (personal information); *Department of Health v Information Commissioner* [2011] EWHC 1430 (Admin); [2011] A.C.D. 97 (statistics on late-term abortions); *Department of Health v Information Commissioner* [2017] EWCA Civ 374; [2017] 1 W.L.R. 3330 (Ministerial diaries). The Information Commissioner's Office website contains useful guidance (*http://www.ico.org.uk* /[Accessed 8 November 2017]). Over 37,000 information requests were made to central Government offices in the first three quarters of 2012. In the first quarter of 2017, this figure was 12,339 (Freedom of Information Statistics: Implementation in Central Government, January–March 2017, 22 June 2017). The SC overturned the exercise of the Attorney General's veto in relation to correspondence between the Prince of Wales and government departments on the ground that mere disagreement with the conclusions of the Upper Tribunal was not a sufficient basis for the exercise of the veto (*R. (on the application of Evans) v Attorney General* [2015] UKSC 21; [2015] A.C. 1787). On the use of a closed material procedure under the 2000 Act, see *Browning v Information Commissioner* [2014] EWCA Civ 1050; [2014] 1 W.L.R. 3848 at [31]–[36].

[106] SI 2004/3391 reg.2(2). See *R. (Office of Communications) v Information Commissioner* [2009] EWCA Civ 90; [2009] Info. T.L.R. 13 at [34]-[66] (Richards LJ); *Department for the Environment, Food and Rural Affairs v Information Commissioner* [2011] EWCA Civ 1606; [2012] 2 C.M.L.R. 5 (reports on air pollution in London); and *Office of Communications v Information Commissioner* (Case C-71/10) [2012] 1 C.M.L.R. 7; [2012] Env. L.R. 7 (concerning information about the risks associated with mobile telephones). The power to veto a decision to disclose information under the 2000 Act must be exercised compatibly with EU law (see the discussion in *R. (on the application of Evans) v Attorney General* [2015] UKSC 21; [2015] A.C. 1787 at [98]–[108]).

Access requests under the Data Protection Act 1998

16-032   The Data Protection Act 1998 (which came into force in March 2000) regulates the processing of information about individuals.[107] Sections 7-9 create a right for a "data subject" (or his authorised agent) to request a copy of certain kinds of data held by any "data controller" (which may be a public or private sector body or person); the 1998 Act binds the Crown. This is known as a "data subject access request". A data controller may charge a fee of up to £10. A response must be made promptly and in any event within 40 calendar days, describing the personal data held, the purposes for which they are being processed, and those to whom they are or may be disclosed. The data subject is entitled to have communicated to him in an intelligible form the information constituting any personal data of which he is the data subject (generally as a copy of the information in permanent form) and any information available to the data controller as to the source of those data.

16-033   The data in respect of which a subject access request may be made can be a computerised record or manual data in a paper-based filing system. "Data" means information "being processed by means of equipment operating automatically in response to instructions given for that purpose" or which "is recorded with the intention that it should be processed by means of such equipment" or "is recorded as part of a relevant filing system or with the intention that it should form part of a relevant filing system"[108] or "forms part of an accessible record"[109] (which means a "health record",[110] an "educational record",[111] or an "an accessible public record as defined by Schedule 12", in relation to which the general rules governing subject access requests are modified).[112] Expressions of opinion and intention fall within the definition of data.

16-034   Certain data are partly or wholly exempt from subject access requests by Pt 4 of the Act, including data processed in relation to: national security; crime and taxation; information as to the physical or mental health or condition of the data subject; certain regulatory activities; literature, journalism and art; research, history and statistics; information available to the public by or under any enactment; domestic purposes; and miscellaneous matters set out in Sch.7 to the Act.

16-035   If a data controller unlawfully fails to comply with a data subject access request, a court may make an order requiring compliance.[113] County courts and the High Court have jurisdiction.[114] Where the data controller is a public authority and the issue arises in a public law context, a claim for judicial review will normally be appropriate.[115]

---

[107] The 1998 Act gives effect to EC Directive 95/46/EC; it repeals the Data Protection Act 1984. The relevant background is described in *Ittihadieh v 5-11 Cheyne Gardens RTM Co Ltd; Deer v University of Oxford* [2017] EWCA Civ 121 at [35-44]. See also Access to Medical Reports Act 1988. The General Data Protection Regulation (2016/679/EU) will enter into force on 25 May 2018.

[108] Data Protection Act 1998 s.1(1).

[109] Data Protection Act 1998 s.68.

[110] Data Protection Act 1998 s.68(2); and Data Protection (Subject Access Modification) (Health) Order 2000 (SI 2000/413).

[111] Data Protection Act 1998 Sch.11; Data Protection (Subject Access Modification) (Education) Order 2000 (SI 2000/414).

[112] Sch.12 (which deals with housing and social services records); Data Protection (Subject Access Modification) (Social Work) Order 2000 (SI 2000/415).

[113] Data Protection Act 1998 s.7(9). See *Quinton v Peirce* [2009] EWHC 912 (QB); [2009] F.S.R. 17 at [87]-[94] for an unsuccessful attempt to enforce the data protection principles in the context of a local election dispute.

[114] Data Protection Act 1998 s.15(1).

[115] In *R. (on the application of Lord) v Secretary of State for the Home Department* [2003] EWHC 2073

Preparing the claim form

A claim for judicial review is commenced by serving claim form N461 on the defendant and any interested parties and filing it at the Administrative Court Office,[116] along with notice of issue of a civil legal aid certificate (if appropriate), witness statements[117] and the prescribed fee. The claim form acts as both the basis for seeking permission to proceed[118] and, if permission is granted, the basis on which the claimant's case will be put at the full hearing of the claim.[119] Clearly the claim form is a document of great importance in the conduct of the litigation. **16-036**

The claim form must identify and give details[120] of the parties, the decision which is challenged, set out a detailed statement of the grounds for bringing the review, and a statement of the facts relied upon. There is an obligation on the claimant to set out fully and fairly all material facts as he knows them or ought to have known them following inquiries.[121] If relevant, an application to extend the time limit for filing the claim form may be made.[122] The claim form must also set out the remedies sought including any interim remedies. It should also indicate that the pre-action protocol has been complied with or reasons for non-compliance.[123] The claim must be verified by a statement of truth.[124] If a costs capping order (formerly a protective costs order) is sought (limiting liability to pay the defendant's legal costs in the **16-037**

(Admin); [2004] Prison L.R. 65 Munby J ordered disclosure, in full and without redactions, of reports prepared by the Prison Service in relation to a decision to refuse to reclassify the claimant from Category A to B.

[116] CPR rr.8.2, 54.6, PD 54A, paras 5.1 and 5.6-5.7. See Appendix J. On filing a document electronically, see CPR PD 5B. The postal address is for London is The Administrative Court Office, Room C315, Royal Courts of Justice, Strand, London WC2A 2LL. The fee is £154: Civil Proceedings Fees Order 2008 (as amended, most recently in 2016) (2008/1053), Sch.1. If not accompanied by the relevant fee, the Claim Form will be returned. The sealed Claim Form and accompanying documents must be served on the defendant and any interested parties within seven days of being issued (CPR 54.7). Service must be confirmed to the Administrative Court Office within 21 days of serving the Claim Form (CPR 6.17(2)(a)).

[117] Witness statements must comply with CPR Pts 22 and 32. Generally the claimant and the claimant's solicitor will both make witness statements. The claimant may explain the importance and impact of the defendant's action or inaction. The solicitor's statement may explain what steps have been taken to resolve the dispute.

[118] See 16-044.

[119] See 16-078.

[120] "There is good reason why all this information is required and why, although no doubt prolixity is to be discouraged, it is important that the claimant does actually provide, properly particularised, the 'detail' called for by Form N461": *R (on the application of W) v Essex CC* [2004] EWHC 2027 (Admin) at [35] (Munby J). Any application for anonymity should be made at the permission stage, but will only be made where strictly necessary (*Khuja v Times Newspapers Ltd* [2017] UKSC 49; [2017] 3 W.L.R. 351). Children, those detained under the Mental Health Act 1983 and other vulnerable individuals will have a strong claim to anonymity (*R. (on the application of C) v Secretary of State for Justice* [2016] UKSC 2; [2016] 1 W.L.R. 444).

[121] *R. v Lloyd's of London Ex p. Briggs* [1993] 1 Lloyd's Rep. 176. There the obligation was said to arise because (following the practice of the time) applications for leave were made ex parte. Under the CPR, defendants and interested parties now have the right through their acknowledgment of service to put to the court a summary of their reasons for opposing the grant of permission. In *R. (on the application of Gul) v Secretary of State for Justice* [2014] EWHC 373 (Admin); [2014] A.C.D. 106 at [41]-[44], the DC made two important observations on the obligations of claimants: to give full and frank disclosure of matters which may undermine their case (failure to do so may lead to relief being refused); and to reconsider the merits of the claim on receipt of the defendant's evidence (which may have costs consequences). See *R. (on the application of Mohammad Shazad Khan) v Secretary of State for the Home Department)* [2016] EWCA Civ 416 at [42]-[47], fn.97 above.

[122] See 16-061.

[123] Practice Statement (Administrative Court: Listing and Urgent Cases) [2002] 1 W.L.R. 810.

[124] CPR r.22.1. The statement of truth is "not an irrelevant mantra or mere verbiage": *R. (on the application of Akram) v Secretary of State for the Home Department* [2015] EWHC 1359 (Admin) at

event of the claim failing),[125] the claimant should normally do so at the permission stage.[126]

16-038   The claim form must be accompanied by: all relevant written evidence in support of the claim (and any extension of time that is sought); a copy of the order that the claimant challenges; where the decision being challenged is that of a court or tribunal, an approved copy of their reasons; copies of any documents on which the claimant proposes to rely; copies of any relevant legislation; and a list of essential documents for advance reading by the court (with page reference to the passages relied on).[127].

16-039   If a claimant seeks to raise an issue or claim a remedy under the Human Rights Act 1998,[128] the claim form must additionally[129]: give precise details of the Convention right which it is alleged has been infringed and details of the alleged infringement; specify the relief sought; state if the relief includes a claim for a declaration of incompatibility under s.4 or damages under s.9(3) of the HRA; and provide precise details of the legislative provision alleged to be incompatible and details of the alleged incompatibility.

16-040   If a "devolution issue" is at stake,[130] the claim form must specify that the claimant wishes to raise such an issue and identify the relevant provisions of the Government of Wales Act 2006, the Scotland Act 1998 or the Northern Ireland Act 1998 and contain a summary of the facts, circumstances and points of law on the basis of which it is alleged that the devolution issue arises. In any event, the claimant should indicate that he has issued the proceedings in the region with which he has the closest connection (or explain why not).

16-041   If circumstances change or the basic legal arguments are reconsidered, between the time permission is granted and the full hearing, in order to avoid "litigation creep", the claim form should be amended "promptly and properly ... to keep pace with what may be the rapidly changing dynamics of a case".[131] The guiding principle is that the "court will normally permit such amendments as may be required to ensure that the real dispute between the parties can be adjudicated upon".[132] Permission is required to amend the claim form, and such an application should normally be accompanied by a draft of the proposed amendment. The decision, etc. under challenge must be identified with precision and if in the light of

---

[25].

[125] On costs capping orders, see 16-094.

[126] *R. (on the application of Corner House Research) v Secretary of State for Trade and Industry* [2005] EWCA Civ 192; [2005] 1 W.L.R. 2600. See 16-094.

[127] *Judicial Review Guide 2017*, para.6.3.4

[128] See Ch.13.

[129] PD 54A, para.5.3 and PD 16, para.15.

[130] See 1-126. PD 54A, para.5.4.

[131] *R (on the application of W) v Essex CC* [2004] EWHC 2027 (Admin); [2004] All E.R. (D) 103 (Aug) at [39]. Where there have been later decisions which supersede the original decision challenged, permission is likely to be granted to challenge the current decision (*R. v Secretary of State for the Home Department Ex P. Turgut* [2001] 1 All E.R. 719). Where a completely fresh decision has been made, permission to amend may well be refused and the claimant may be expected to issue a fresh claim (*R. (on the application of Bhatti) v Bury MBC* [2013] EWHC 3093 (Admin); (2014) 17 C.C.L. Rep. 64). The court indicated that it is often not appropriate to stay a judicial review claim while the matter is reconsidered and that a fresh claim should be issued (*R. (on the application of Yousuf) v Secretary of State for the Home Department* [2016] EWHC 663 (Admin)). There is an exception to this principle where there will be a predictable series of decisions, following a set timetable, each of which will supersede the previous one (as in relation to the security classification of prisoners) (*R. (on the application of Hussain) v Secretary of State for Justice* [2016] EWCA Civ 1111; [2017] 1 W.L.R. 761 at [22]–[24]).

[132] *W* [2004] EWHC 2027 (Admin); [2004] All E.R. (D) 103 (Aug) at [35].

changing circumstance or evidence it changes, the claim form should reflect this.[133] The same is true of changes to the legal basis of the challenge. While minor changes may be permitted by the court exercising its inherent jurisdiction, a claimant seeking to rely at the full hearing on a ground other than those for which he was initially given permission must seek permission to do so in advance of the hearing.[134]

Urgent cases

There is a specific form for requesting urgent consideration.[135] The form requires the claimant to set out: the reasons for urgency; the timetable in which the matter should be heard; the justification for immediate consideration; and the date and time when it was first appreciated that an immediate application might be necessary and the reason for any delay, if relevant. The claimant must also indicate the efforts that have been made to place the defendant and any interested party on notice of the application. The Divisional Court has made it clear that if these details are not provided, the court will require the attendance of the solicitor responsible in open court together with their senior partner and will list the name of the firm concerned along with the names of the parties. The court may refer the solicitor to the Solicitors Regulatory Authority.[136] The court may also simply refuse to consider the application or may refuse urgent consideration if the form is not correctly and fully completed.[137]

16-042

The acknowledgment of service

Any person (including an interested party) who wishes to take part in the judicial review must file an acknowledgment of service not more than 21 days after service of the claim form and must serve it on the claimant as soon as is practicable and, in any event, within seven days of filing it.[138] The parties may not agree to extend this time limit. The defendant may also request suitable directions (for example, if he seeks expedition). The acknowledgement of service must set out the summary grounds for contesting the claim and should focus on any "knock-out" points upon

16-043

---

[133] *W* [2004] EWHC 2027 (Admin); [2004] All E.R. (D) 103 (Aug) at [35].

[134] CPR r.54.15; PD 54A, para.11 (notice of seven clear days before the full hearing must be given to the court and all parties). In exceptional circumstances, the court may permit a claimant to rely on additional grounds at the substantive hearing without such an application (*R. (on the application of Smith) v Parole Board* [2003] EWCA Civ 1014; [2003] 1 W.L.R. 2548 at [16]).

[135] Form N463 (Appendix L). There is also an "out of hours application" form for Queen's Bench Division cases on the Ministry of Justice website (*http://www.justice.gov.uk/courts/rcj-rolls-building/administrative-court/applying-for-judicial-review* [Accessed 8 November 2017]). Unless made when lodging the application, there is an urgent consideration fee of £255 (Civil Proceedings Fees Order 2008 (as amended, most recently in 2016) (2008/1053), Sch.1).

[136] Wasted costs orders have also been made in cases where the solicitors had exaggerated their client's medical condition or failed to mention his history of criminality (*R. (on the application of Okondu) v Secretary of State for the Home Department* [2014] UKUT 377 (IAC); [2015] Imm. A.R. 155.

[137] *R. (on the application of Hamid) v Secretary of State for the Home Department* [2012] EWHC 3070 (Admin); [2013] C.P. Rep. 6 at [5]–[11]. The court went further and named the solicitors who had failed to provide the information required by the form in *R. (on the application of Awuku) v Secretary of State for the Home Department* [2012] EWHC 3298 (Admin). See further *R. (on the application of Butt) v Secretary of State for the Home Department* [2014] EWHC 264 (Admin), citing *Hamid* in speaking of the "vigorous action" taken by the courts against legal representatives who fail to comply with the rules (not specifically relating to urgent cases), in turn cited in *R. (on the application of Akram) v Secretary of State for the Home Department* [2015] EWHC 1359 (Admin) (see fn.124).

[138] CPR r.54.8. The appropriate form is N462 (Appendix K).

which the defendant relies in order to demonstrate that permission should be refused. Such points may include that the claim is out of time, that there has been a failure to exhaust alternative remedies, that the outcome would not have been any different had the conduct complained of not occurred,[139] or that it is plainly unarguable on the merits. The defendant may, in suitable cases, also seek to demonstrate why the claim is totally without merit and invite the court so to certify it since this will mean that claimant has no right to renew the application at a hearing.[140] The "summary" required is different from the "detailed grounds for contesting the claim" and the supporting "written evidence" which are required following the grant of permission.[141] If the defendant intends to seek its costs of filing the acknowledgement of service, it should request them (in a specified sum and supported by a schedule of costs) in the document. Failure to file an acknowledgment of service means that the defendant may not participate in any permission hearing. However, he may still take part in the substantive hearing if he complies with the rules on submitting detailed grounds for contesting the claim and evidence.[142] The introduction of the acknowledgement of service was a major innovation of the Civil Procedure Rules and has led to permission being refused upon paper consideration in a greater proportion of cases than under the old ex parte procedure.

Permission

16-044 A requirement that a would-be litigant, wishing to challenge the legality of a public authority's decision, first obtain the permission (formerly called "leave") of the court has been a feature of judicial review since 1933.[143] Permission must be sought even if a claim is transferred to the Administrative Court having been commenced elsewhere.[144] Permission must also be sought subsequently if a claimant seeks to rely on grounds other than those for which he has been given permission to proceed.[145]

16-045 The permission stage procedure was modified in significant ways in 2000. Previously permission (leave) was determined in most cases solely on the basis of the claimant's case whereas now the defendant (and any interested parties) are able to provide the court with an acknowledgment of service setting out in summary their reasons for contesting the claim before permission is granted or refused.[146]

---

[139] CPR 54.8(4)(a)(ai) and Senior Courts Act 1981 s.31(3C)–(3F).

[140] CPR 54.12(7) and 23.12.

[141] CPR r.54.14. *Ewing v Office of the Deputy Prime Minister* [2005] EWCA Civ 1583; [2006] 1 W.L.R. 1260 at [43] (Carnwath LJ, offering guidance about the "summary": "The purpose of the 'summary grounds' is not to provide the basis for full argument of the substantive merits ... If a party's position is sufficiently apparent from the Protocol response, it may be appropriate simply to refer to that letter in the Acknowledgement of Service. In other cases it will be helpful to draw attention to any 'knock-out points' or procedural bars, or the practical or financial consequences for other parties (which may, for example, be relevant to directions for expedition). As the Bowman report advised, it should be possible to do what is required without incurring 'substantial expense at this stage'").

[142] CPR r.54.9.

[143] Now Senior Courts Act 1981 s.31(3). See M. Fordham, "Permission Principles" [2006] J.R. 176 and V. Bondy and M. Sunkin, "Accessing Judicial Review" [2008] P.L. 647, for a study regarding the results of the permission stage of judicial review proceedings.

[144] CPR r.54.4.

[145] CPR r.54.15. For an example of a refusal of permission late in the day, see *R. (on the application of RP) v Brent LBC* [2011] EWHC 3251 (Admin) at [299]-[306].

[146] Within 21 days of service on them of the claim form. CPR r.54.8; if permission is granted, the defendant has an opportunity to provide more detailed grounds for resisting the claim: CPR r.54.14.

In almost all cases permission is initially determined without a hearing.[147] Brief **16-046** written reasons for granting or refusing permission are given.[148] Where a claim is certified as totally without merit, the judge should provide fuller reasons.[149] Where an oral hearing takes place, a written judgment may be produced but there is a general prohibition on the citation of such judgments in later cases if the reported point is relates merely to whether the claim is arguable. A judge may decide to order that an application for permission be considered at an oral hearing or that there should be a "rolled-up hearing" where the merits of the claim will be argued immediately afterwards if permission is granted.

An application for permission is a "proceeding" for the purpose of Senior Courts **16-047** Act 1981 s.42 regulating the access to the courts by vexatious litigants, and so a person subject to a civil proceedings order under s.42 must make a separate prior application for permission to institute the proceedings.[150]

The purpose of the permission stage

The permission stage serves a number of purposes. First, it may safeguard public **16-048** authorities by deterring or eliminating clearly ill-founded claims without the need for a full hearing of the matter. The requirement may also prevent administrative action being paralysed by a pending, but possibly spurious, legal challenge.[151] Secondly, for the Administrative Court, the permission procedure provides a mechanism for the efficient management of the ever growing judicial review caseload. A large proportion of claims can be disposed of at the permission stage with the minimum use of the court's limited resources.[152] By granting permission to proceed on some but not all grounds of a claim, the court is able to stop hopeless aspects of a case in their tracks. Thirdly, for the claimant the permission stage, far from being an impediment to access to justice, may actually be advantageous

---

[147] In urgent cases outside of office hours, claimants may contact the duty High Court Judge by telephone (020 7947 6000). The claimant should use the "out of hours application" form (fn.134 above). Urgent cases include decisions of a Crown Court judge to withdraw bail (*R. (on the application of Allwin) v Snaresbrook Crown Court* [2005] EWHC 742 (Admin); [2005] All E.R. (D) 40 (Apr)). Especially where Convention rights are in issue, such as a person's liberty (art.5), judicial authorities must ensure that appropriate provision is made for speedy applications regardless of vacation times (*E v Norway* (1994) 17 E.H.R.R. 30). An application for urgent consideration is referred to a judge within the timeframe set out in the urgency application form: form N463 (Appendix L).

[148] CPR r.54.12(2).

[149] *R. (on the application of Wasif) v Secretary of State for the Home Department (Practice Note)* [2016] EWCA Civ 82; [2016] 1 W.L.R. 2793 at [13]–[21],

[150] *Ex p. Ewing (No.2)* [1994] 1 W.L.R. 1553; CPR rr.3.3(7), 3.11; *Ewing v Office of the Deputy Prime Minister* [2005] EWCA Civ 1583 at [33]-[42]; *Bhamjee v Forsdick* [2003] EWCA Civ 1113; [2004] 1 W.L.R. 88 at [38]-[53].

[151] *Inland Revenue Commissioners v National Federation of Self-Employed and Small Businesses* [1982] A.C. 617 at 643 (Lord Diplock).

[152] The proportion of cases in which permission is refused has varied considerably over the years. There are a number of explanations for this. Levels of refusal of permission were much higher in immigration and asylum cases which made up a very substantial part of the court's docket up to 2013 (when most were transferred to Upper Tribunal (Immigration and Asylum Chamber) (UTIAC)). Permission was granted in more cases before the defendant was required to submit an Acknowledgement of Service (V. Bondy and M. Sunkin, "Accessing Judicial Review" [2008] P.L. 647 and V. Bondy and M. Sunkin, *"The Dynamics of Judicial Review Litigation: The resolution of public law challenges before final hearing"* (Public Law Project, 2009)). The most recent figures (for the first half of 2017) demonstrate that permission has been granted on paper in around 18% of cases. Permission was granted on oral renewal in 27% of cases. The last full year's figures (2016) show that 4,302 cases were lodged. For the first half of 2017, 2,169 have been lodged. See Ministry of Justice, *Civil Justice Statistics Quarterly: April to June 2017.*

since it enables the litigant expeditiously and cheaply to obtain the views of a High Court judge on the merits of his application.[153]

Criteria on which permission is granted or refused

16-049   No comprehensive statement of the criteria for determining applications for permission exists. During the mid-1990s, concerns were expressed that the arrangements then in place led to unacceptable disparities of approach in the ways different nominated judges dealt with applications for leave (now "permission") to commence judicial review claims.[154] In 2000, the Bowman committee recommended that there be a statutory presumption that permission should be given if the claim discloses an arguable case,[155] but this was not implemented. The Senior Courts Act 1981 s.31 and CPR Pt 54 refer expressly to only two grounds on which permission should be refused: where there has been delay in applying to the court[156]; or where the claimant does not have a sufficient interest in the matter to which the claim relates.[157] However, the standing requirement is of limited importance at the permission stage and is designed merely to weed out cranks, mischief-makers and busybodies.[158] The issue of delay is a more substantial hurdle and it is not unusual for permission to be refused on this ground. Delay and standing may be reconsidered at the full hearing.[159] What is tolerably clear is that the test for permission is whether the application is "arguable" or has a "realistic prospect of success". What that means in a given case will depend on all the circumstances and the nature and gravity of the issue to be argued. To be arguable means more than to be potentially arguable on a purely speculative basis and in the hope that the case may strengthen when more documents are obtained.[160]

16-050   The Criminal Justice and Courts Act 2015 has introduced a new criterion at the permission stage. If the court considers it "highly likely" that "the outcome for the applicant" would not "have been substantially different if the conduct complained of had not occurred" then it must refuse permission.[161] The court may consider this question of its own motion, but it must do so if the defendant requests that it does.[162] The court has a limited discretion to grant permission even if the "no difference" test is made out where it "considers that it is appropriate to do so for reasons of exceptional public interest".[163]. If the court grants permission on grounds of

---

153 H. Woolf, *Protection of the Public—A New Challenge* (1990), p.21.
154 L. Bridges et al., *Judicial Review in Perspective*, 2nd edn (1995) and *Law Com. 226*, p.163 (which called the then arrangements "too much of a lottery").
155 Bowman, recommendation 33.
156 Senior Courts Act 1981 s.31(6),(7) and CPR r.54.5. See 16-055.
157 Senior Courts Act 1981 s.31(3). See 2-008.
158 *Inland Revenue Commissioners v National Federation of Self-Employed and Small Businesses* [1982] A.C. 617; *R. v Somerset County Council Ex p. Dixon* (1998) 75 P. & C.R. 175.
159 *Caswell v Dairy Produce Quota Tribunal for England and Wales* [1990] 2 A.C. 738, 747G-H; cf. *R. v Secretary of State for Trade and Industry Ex p. Greenpeace Ltd* [1998] Env. L.R. 415. Le Sueur and Sunkin [1992] P.L. 102, 120-121.
160 These propositions are derived from *Sharma v Brown-Antoine* [2006] UKPC 57; [2007] 1 W.L.R. 780 at [14(4)]. Sharma was described as the locus classicus on permission in *R. (on the application of Wasif) v Secretary of State for the Home Department* [2016] EWCA Civ 82; [2016] 1 W.L.R. 2793 at [13].
161 Criminal Justice and Courts Act 2015 s.84(1)-(3), in force from 13 April 2015, inserting new subss.(3C)-(3F) into Senior Courts Act 1981 s.31. See para.18-050.
162 Senior Courts Act 1981 s.31(3C).
163 Senior Courts Act 1981 s.31(3E). CPR Pt 54.8(4)(a)(ia) requires a defendant to include in their Acknowledgement of Service a summary of their case for inviting the court to refuse permission on the "no difference" basis

exceptional public interest, it must certify that this condition is satisfied.[164] The court may direct a hearing on the issue of "no difference" and the exception to it on at least two days' notice to those who have filed an Acknowledgement of Service.[165] The senior judiciary's response to the Government's consultation warned of "Dress rehearsal permission hearings" involving "detailed consideration of the facts".[166]

Amendments to the Senior Courts Act 1981 (not yet in force) will also prevent **16-051** the court from granting permission unless the claimant has provided the court with such information about the financing of the claim as is specified in rules of court.[167]

As previously discussed, the failure to use a substitute remedy (especially to **16-052** exercise a right of appeal) will normally lead to the refusal of permission.[168] The most commonly given reason for refusing permission is that the claim is unarguable. The test ought to be broadly similar to that governing applications for summary judgment in other types of claim, namely that there is "no real prospect of succeeding on the claim or issue".[169] If permission is granted, it may be subject to conditions or on some grounds only.[170] As stated above, if a claimant at the substantive hearing seeks to rely on grounds not previously granted permission, permission must be sought from the trial judge.[171]

Permission has previously been refused on grounds of policy, notably that to **16-053** subject certain sorts of decision to judicial review challenge would hamper decision-making in some contexts.[172] It is wrong for such a broad discretion to be exercised at this preliminary stage of the litigation process, if only because important issues of principle may often emerge only late in the litigation process.[173]

Permission may be granted on only some of a claimant's grounds, and refused **16-054** on the others.[174] At the subsequent full hearing of the claim the judge would require a "significant justification before taking a different view", but does have discretion to allow submissions on the grounds refused permission if there is a good reason to do so.[175] Permission may also be refused to pursue a particular remedy, while granting it in relation to other remedies.[176] Permission may be granted in relation to one impugned decision and refused in relation to others.[177]

---

[164] Senior Courts Act 1981 s.31(3F).

[165] CPR Pt 54.11A.

[166] *"Response of the Senior Judiciary to the Ministry of Justice's Consultation entitled 'Judicial Review: Proposals for Further Reform'"* (1 November 2013) at [22].

[167] Senior Courts Act 1981 s.31(3)(b) and (3A) inserted by the Criminal Justice and Courts Act 2015 s.85. For the information required, see fn.289. Equivalent provisions will apply to the Upper Tribunal (Tribunals, Courts and Enforcement Act 2007 s.16(3) and (3A)).

[168] See 16-016.

[169] CPR r.24.2. In *R. (on the application of Z) v Croydon LBC* [2011] EWCA Civ 59; [2011] P.T.S.R. 748 at [6], the CA described the test as "a realistic prospect or arguable case".

[170] CPR r.54.12.

[171] CPR r.54.15.

[172] See e.g. *R. v Hillingdon LBC Ex p. Puhlhofer* [1986] A.C. 484 (homeless persons); *R. v Secretary of State for the Home Department Ex p. Swati* [1986] 1 W.L.R. 477 (genuine visitor cases); *R. v Harrow LBC Ex p. D* [1990] Fam. 133 (child protection register). See 3-025.

[173] See Le Sueur and Sunkin [1992] P.L. 102, 125.

[174] CPR r.54.12(1)(ii).

[175] *Smith v Parole Board* [2003] EWCA Civ 1014; [2003] 1 W.L.R. 2548.

[176] *R. (on the application of Anufrijeva) v Southwark LBC* [2003] EWCA Civ 1406; [2004] Q.B. 1124 at [81] the CA held in relation to claims for judicial review seeking damages under the Human Rights Act 1998: "… (iii) Before giving permission to apply for judicial review, the Admin Ct judge should require the claimant to explain why it would not be more appropriate to use any available internal complaint procedure or proceed by making a claim to the [Ombudsmen] at least in the first instance. The complaint procedures of the [Ombudsmen] are designed to deal economically (the claimant pays no costs and does not require a lawyer) and expeditiously with claims for compensation for

The timing of the application for permission

16-055   An application for permission may be refused if it is made tardily or if it is premature.[178] The claim form must be filed (a) "promptly" and (b) in any event not later than three months after the grounds to make the claim first arose.[179] The time limit cannot be extended by agreement between the parties,[180] but the court has a discretion to extend the time limit if there is a good reason to do so.[181] There are shorter time limits in relation to planning cases, public contracts, judicial review of the Upper Tribunal and certain decisions made in relation to public inquiries.[182]

16-056   It is unclear whether the test of promptness is sufficiently certain to meet the requirements of EU law and the ECHR.[183] The CJEU has held that in the context of public procurement a time limit such as promptness which is subject to discretionary assessment by the court is in breach of EU law on grounds of effectiveness and legal certainty.[184] This raises difficult questions which have yet to be conclusively resolved where a claimant relies on some grounds in EU law and others in "pure" domestic law.[185] While the objection based on effectiveness is understandable in relation to an excessively short time limit, it is not clear why the

---

maladministration. (From inquiries the court has made it is apparent that the time scale of resolving complaints compares favourably with that of litigation.) (iv) If there is a legitimate claim for other relief, permission should if appropriate be limited to that relief and consideration given to deferring permission for the damages claim, adjourning or staying that claim until use has been made of ADR, whether by a reference to a mediator or an ombudsman or otherwise, or remitting that claim to a district judge or master if it cannot be dismissed summarily on grounds that in any event an award of damages is not required to achieve just satisfaction".

[177] *R. v Hammersmith and Fulham LBC Ex p. CPRE* [2000] Env. L.R. 532.

[178] Senior Courts Act 1981 s.31(6)–(7); CPR r.54.5; PD 54A, para.4.1. Questions of delay may also be relevant to withholding a remedy after the full hearing: see Ch.18.

[179] CPR r.2.8 stipulates that "(2) A period of time expressed as a number of days shall be computed as clear days. (3) In this rule 'clear days' means that in computing the number of days— (a) the day on which the period begins; and (b) if the end of the period is defined by reference to an event, the day on which that event occurs are not included"—but this probably does not apply to the three *month* limit for judicial review: see *Crichton v Wellingborough BC* [2002] EWHC 2988 (Admin); [2004] Env. L.R. 11 at [56]. "Where 'month' occurs in any judgment, order, direction or other document, it means a calendar month": CPR r.2.10. The Human Rights Act 1998 s.7(5) allows a year for claims in relation to s.6, "but that is subject to any rule imposing a stricter time limit in relation to the procedure in question".

[180] CPR r.54.5(2).

[181] CPR r.3.1; PD 54A, para.5.6(3); see, e.g. *R. (on the application of Harrison) v Flintshire Magistrates Court* [2004] EWHC 2456 (Admin); (2004) 168 J.P. 653 (permission granted 17 months after conviction when it came to light that the speed limit on a road was 60 mph, not 30 mph, as the police, claimant and magistrates had believed).

[182] 16-064.

[183] Doubt was expressed in *R. v Hammersmith and Fulham LBC Ex p. Burkett* [2002] UKHL 23; [2002] 1 W.L.R. 1593 at [53] (Lord Steyn) and [59] (Lord Hope).

[184] *Uniplex (UK) Ltd v NHS Business Services Authority* (C-406/08) [2010] 2 C.M.L.R. 47 at [40]-[41]. *R. (on the application of Buglife) v Medway Council* [2011] EWHC 746 (Admin); [2011] 3 C.M.L.R. 39 at [62]-[63] applied *Uniplex* to a case involving EU law outside the field of public procurement (environmental law). See J. Maurici, "Delay and Promptness Update" [2012] J.R. 87.

[185] In *R. (on the application of Berky) v Newport City Council* [2012] EWCA Civ 378; [2012] 2 C.M.L.R. 44, the CA (obiter) did not agree on the ramifications of *Uniplex*. Carnwath LJ took the view that Uniplex would only apply to an EU law ground and that promptness could continue to apply to domestic grounds of challenge such as bias and irrationality (at [34]-[35]). Sir Richard Buxton thought that *Uniplex* would apply to all the grounds (at [66]-[70]). The CA was also divided on whether *Uniplex* applied to prevent the court from declining to grant a remedy on the grounds of a lack of promptness (Carnwath LJ (at [38]-[41]) and Moore-Bick LJ and Sir Richard Buxton (at [50], [71]-[72])). The United Nations Economic Commission for Europe (Aarhus) Convention on Access to Information, Public Participation in Decision-making and Access to Justice in Environmental Matters (ratified by the UK in 2005), art.9 includes the requirement that court procedures must be

promptness test is objectionable on this ground in the absence of evidence that parties are deterred from challenging a decision because of the uncertainty it creates. Equally, it is not clear why a requirement of promptness is any more objectionable on grounds of certainty than a specific time-limit (such a three months), but with a broad discretion to extend time where appropriate. In any event, on present authority, the requirement of promptness does not offend the certainty requirements of the ECHR.[186]

Generally "grounds to make the claim" arise when the public authority does an act with legal effect, rather than something preliminary to such an act. So in the context of town and country planning, time runs from when planning permission is actually granted rather than from when a local authority adopts a resolution to grant consent.[187] Where a quashing order is sought in respect of any judgment, order, conviction or other proceedings, time begins to run from the date of that judgment, etc.[188] The subjective experience and state of knowledge of the claimant are not relevant in determining the start date,[189] though those facts may be relevant to whether time should be extended. However, the running of time is also subject to EU law principles and, where relevant, time will only be taken to have started running from the time when the claimant became aware or could reasonably have become aware of EU law grounds for the claim.[190]

16-057

The primary requirement is always one of promptness and permission may be refused on the ground of delay even if the claim form is filed within three months.[191] The fact that a breach of a public law duty is a continuing one does not necessarily

16-058

---

fair, equitable, timely and not prohibitively expensive. The Aarhus Compliance Committee found that the United Kingdom failed adequately to implement the requirement that environmental proceedings should be fair and timely in the *Port of Tyne* case because the time limits failed to set a minimum time within which proceedings could be brought and did not count time as running from when the claimant knew, or ought to have known, of the decision (ACCC/C/2008/33, September 2010, paras 138-9). The views of the Compliance Committee have no direct legal consequences in domestic law *(R. (on the application of Evans) v Secretary of State for Communities and Local Government* [2013] EWCA Civ 114; [2013] J.P.L. 1027 at [37]–[38]).

[186] *Lam v United Kingdom* (App No.41671/89) (8 November 2016). In *Hardy v Pembrokeshire CC (Permission to Appeal)* [2006] EWCA Civ 240; [2006] Env. L.R. 28, the CA dismissed the idea that there was any conflict between a requirement of promptness (a term used in the ECHR itself) and the requirements of legal certainty.

[187] *R. v Hammersmith and Fulham LBC Ex p. Burkett* [2002] UKHL 23; [2002] 1 W.L.R. 1593 at [36]–[51]: "In law the resolution is not a juristic act giving rise to rights and obligations. It is not inevitable that it will ripen into an actual grant of planning permission" at [42] (Lord Steyn). This is not to say that a planning resolution cannot be the subject of a judicial review claim. In *R. (on the application of Nash) v Barnet LBC* [2013] EWCA Civ 1004; [2013] P.T.S.R. 1457 at [54]–[65], the CA distinguished *Burkett* and held that the crucial question was not when the decision was finally or irrevocably made, but when the relevant duty (in this case to consult) properly arose. The decisions in the present case were not provisional and each stage might have significant consequences.

[188] PD 54A, para.4.1.

[189] *R. v Department of Transport Ex p. Presvac Engineering Ltd* (1992) 4 Admin. L.R. 121.

[190] *Uniplex (UK) Ltd v NHS Business Services Authority* (C-406/08) [2010] 2 C.M.L.R. 47 at [40]–[41]. *Uniplex* was distinguished in *R. (on the application of Williams) v Secretary of State for Energy and Climate Change* [2015] EWHC 1202 (Admin); [2015] J.P.L. 1257 in which the court held it had no jurisdiction to hear a claim for judicial review of a development consent order where the claim had been issued one day after the expiry of the time limit in the Planning Act 2008 s.118: "The court has no discretion to vary a time limit of this kind. And the judgment of the Court of Justice of the European Union in *Uniplex* does not decide that it should" (at [59]).

[191] See, e.g. *R. v Secretary of State for Health Ex p. Alcohol Recovery Project* [1993] C.O.D. 344; *R. v Swale BC Ex p. Royal Society for the Protection of Birds* (1990) 2 Admin. L.R. 790. The courts have warned of the need for especial promptness in the context of challenges to planning permission; in evaluating this, regard will be had to the fact that in statutory applications to quash the time limit is fixed at six weeks: *R. (on the application of McCallion) v Kennet DC* [2001] EWHC Admin 575; [2002] P.L.C.R. 9 at [26]-[28]. In *Mulvenna v Secretary of State for Communities and Local Govern-*

make it irrelevant to take into account the date at which the breach began in considering any question of delay.[192]

16-059 There is no general legislative formula to guide the court on issues of delay. Factors taken into account include: whether the claimant had prior warning of the decision complained of[193]; and whether there has been a period of time between the taking of the decision impugned and its communication to the claimant.[194]

16-060 The following have been held to be good reasons for delay: time taken to obtain legal aid[195]; the importance of the point of law at stake[196]; the pursuit of alternative legal remedies[197]; or awaiting the outcome of consultation.[198] The following have been held not to be good reasons: tardiness on the part of a claimant's non-legal advisor[199]; time taken pursuing avenues of political redress, such as organising a lobby of Parliament, before applying for permission.[200]

16-061 The mere fact that permission is granted does not mean that an extension of time for making the application is given; an express application for extension of time must be made.[201] If at the permission stage the court extends time under CPR r.3.1(2)(a), the correctness of granting that extension cannot be raised subsequently at the full hearing.[202]

16-062 Section 31(6) SCA 1981 requires the court to consider whether the granting of relief would "be likely to cause substantial hardship to, or substantially prejudice the rights of, any person or would be detrimental to good administration".[203] In all but the clearest cases, the court will, however, normally postpone consideration of hardship, prejudice and detriment to good administration until the full hearing,[204] though only if the judge granting permission has indicated that this should be so, or if fresh and relevant material relating to delay has arisen in the meantime.[205]

16-063 Seeking permission prematurely is almost as common a ground for refusing

---

ment [2015] EWHC 3494 (Admin); [2016] J.P.L. 487 at [46]–[49], the HC refused to extend time for judicial review where the claimants failed to challenge a planning decision until judgment was given in a similar claim, at which point they became aware that the Secretary of State had acted unlawfully. An existing claim may be stayed pending a test case, but claimants "cannot wait until others show that the way is clear". The HC also held that the time limit did not deny the claimants, an Irish Traveller and a Roma Gypsy, an effective remedy regarding their EU right not to be discriminated against (at [52]–[56]) (appeal pending). See paras 16-064 and 17-031, and Appendix HA, on the new Planning Court.

[192] *R. v Essex CC Ex p. C* [1993] C.O.D. 398; and on renewed decisions, see 3-026.

[193] *R. v Secretary of State for Transport Ex p. Presvac Engineering Ltd* (1992) 4 Admin. L.R. 121.

[194] *R. v Redbridge Justices Ex p. Gurmit Ram* [1992] Q.B. 384.

[195] *R. v Stratford on Avon DC Ex p. Jackson* [1985] 1 W.L.R. 1319.

[196] *R. v Secretary of State for the Home Office Ex p. Ruddock* [1987] 1 W.L.R. 1482; *R. (on the application of the Law Society) v Legal Services Commission* [2010] EWHC 2550 (Admin); [2011] Costs L.R. Online 57 at [126]–[127].

[197] See e.g. *R. v Stratford on Avon DC Ex p. Jackson* [1985] 1 W.L.R. 1319; *R. v Rochdale MBC Ex p. Cromer Ring Mill Ltd* [1982] 3 All E. R. 761; *R. v Secretary of State for the Environment Ex p. West Oxfordshire DC* [1994] C.O.D. 134.

[198] *R. (on the application of Royal Brompton and Harefield NHS Foundation Trust) v Joint Committee of Primary Care Trusts* [2012] EWCA Civ 472 at [87]–[95].

[199] *R. v Tavistock General Commissioners Ex p. Worth* [1985] S.T.C. 564.

[200] See, e.g. *R. v Secretary of State for Health Ex p. Alcohol Recovery Project* [1993] C.O.D. 344; *R. v Redbridge LBC Ex p. G* [1991] C.O.D. 398.

[201] *R. v Lloyd's of London Ex p. Briggs* [1993] 1 Lloyd's Rep. 176. This should be included in the claim form.

[202] *R. v Criminal Injuries Compensation Board Ex p. A* [1999] 2 A.C. 330 (overruling *R. v Tavistock General Commissioners Ex p. Worth* [1985] S.T.C. 564 (see 16-060, fn.199) on different grounds).

[203] See 18-051.

[204] *Caswell v Dairy Produce Quota Tribunal for England and Wales* [1990] 2 A.C. 738. On remedies and discretion to withhold remedies, see Ch.18.

[205] *R. v Lichfield DC Ex p. Lichfield Securities Ltd* [2001] EWCA Civ 304; (2001) 3 L.G.L.R. 35.

permission as delay.[206] Judicial review may be premature for several reasons: the decision-taker may not yet have determined the facts[207]; or completed assessment of relevant factors[208] (though in cases involving deprivation of liberty the court will be cautious in rejecting a claim as precipitate)[209]; or the impugned decision may be merely preliminary to a final decision.[210] The court's general approach is to reject challenges made before the conclusion of a hearing in formal proceedings.[211] Importance must also be attached to the fact that judicial review is intended to be an expeditious process and that some decisions taken by public authorities need to be taken quickly.

As stated earlier, there are shorter time limits in relation to planning cases, public **16-064** contracts, judicial review of the Upper Tribunal and certain decisions made in relation to public inquiries. Under the Inquiries Act 2005, judicial review challenges to decisions of a Minster or member of an inquiry panel must be brought within 14 days after the day on which the applicant became aware of the decisions unless that time limit is extended by the court.[212] In claims for judicial review where the grounds arose after 1 July 2013: (1) a claim for judicial review of a planning decision by the Secretary of State or the local planning authority under the planning Acts (as defined) must be brought within six weeks of the date when the application first arose; and (2) a claim for judicial review of a decision to award a contract to which the Public Contracts Regulations 2015 (SI 2015/102) apply must be brought within 30 days beginning on the date when the claimant first knew or ought to have known that grounds for challenging the decision had arisen.[213] Judicial reviews of decisions of the Upper Tribunal must be commenced within 16 days of the date on which the decision was sent to the applicant.[214]

---

[206] Le Sueur and Sunkin [1992] P.L. 102, 123; J. Beatson, "Prematurity and Ripeness for Review", in C. Forsyth and I. Hare (eds), *The Golden Metwand and the Crooked Cord* (1998), D. Elvin QC "Hypothetical, Academic and Premature Challenges" [2006] J.R. 307. On situations where the matter is "hypothetical" or "academic", see 3-026 and 18-042. *R. (on the application of De Whalley) v Norfolk CC* [2011] EWHC 3739 (Admin); [2012] B.L.G.R. 478 at [35], cf. *Sports Direct International Plc v Competition Commission* [2009] CAT 32; [2010] A.C.D. 32 at [50]-[60] (claimant entitled to seek judicial review of a preliminary decision to withhold information, where such preliminary decision may have had an impact on the claimant's rights in the future).

[207] See, e.g. *R. (on the application of Paul Rackham Ltd) v Swaffham Magistrates Court* [2004] EWHC 1417 (Admin); [2005] J.P.L. 224; *Draper v British Optical Association* [1938] 1 All E.R 115; *R. (Lower Mill Estate Limited) v Commissioners of Her Majesty's Revenue and Customs* [2008] EWHC 2409 (Admin); [2008] B.T.C. 5743.

[208] See, e.g. *R. (on the application of A) v East Sussex CC (No.2)* [2003] EWHC 167 (Admin); (2003) 6 C.C.L. Rep. 194.

[209] See, e.g. *R. (on the application of Secretary of State for the Home Department) v Mental Health Review Tribunal* [2004] EWHC 2194 (Admin); [2004] M.H.L.R. 273.

[210] See, e.g. *R. (on the application of St John) v Governor of Brixton Prison* [2001] EWHC Admin 543; [2002] Q.B. 613; *R. (on the application of The Garden and Leisure Group Ltd) v North Somerset Council* [2003] EWHC 1605 (Admin); [2004] 1 P. & C.R. 39.

[211] See, e.g. *R. v Association of Futures Brokers and Dealers Ltd Ex p Mordens Ltd* (1991) 3 Admin. L.R. 254 at [263]; *R. (Hoar-Stevens) v Richmond-upon-Thames Magistrates' Court* [2003] EWHC 2660 (Admin); [2004] Crim. L.R. 474 at [18]; cf. *R. (on the application of Widgery Soldiers) v Lord Saville of Newdigate* [2001] EWCA Civ 2048; [2002] 1 W.L.R. 1249 at [43] (CA stresses that "the concern of the courts is whether what has happened has resulted in real injustice", giving as examples the unfair refusal of an interpreter or an adjournment).

[212] Inquiries Act 2005 s.38.

[213] CPR r.54.5 (as amended by Public Contracts Regulations 2015/102 Sch.6(2) para.11(3)). Schedule 16 to the Criminal Justice and Courts Act 2015 makes a number of amendments to planning legislation concerning permission to bring challenges and costs. R. Harwood, "The Planning Court comes into being" [2014] J.P.L. 699. See PD 54E for timescales and designation in Planning Court claims.

[214] CPR r.54.7A(3).

Challenging the grant of permission

16-065   It is generally no longer possible for a defendant or interested party to seek to overturn the grant of permission to proceed with a claim for judicial review.[215] The rationale for the change is that defendants and interested parties are now routinely able to provide the court with a summary of their reasons for contesting the claim before permission is determined.[216] If through error a defendant has not been served with the claim, or the court wrongly grants permission before the time for serving the acknowledgement of service has elapsed, the court still retains jurisdiction to set aside the grant of permission.[217]

Challenging the refusal of permission

16-066   A claimant who is refused permission without an oral hearing has at that point no right of appeal, but "may request the decision to be reconsidered at a hearing".[218] A claimant who wishes to renew their application at a hearing should request renewal within seven days of receiving the order refusing permission.[219] The claimant should address the judge's reasons for refusing permission on the papers. The standard listing for a renewed hearing is 30 minutes and there is likely to be a significant number of permission applications in the judge's list for that day. The defendant may, but is not required to, attend. Where a claim is filed on or after July 2013 and the court refuses permission to proceed and records the fact that the application is totally without merit in accordance with CPR r.23.12, the claimant cannot request that the decision be reconsidered at an oral hearing (CPR r.54.12(7)). In *R. (on the application of Wasif) v Secretary of State for the Home Department (Practice Note)*,[220] the CA stated that an application is totally without merit where it is bound to fail in the sense that the judge can see no rational basis upon which it could succeed. In such cases, judges should feel no inhibition in so certifying. However, if the judge considers that the claimant has a rational argument, but the judge is confident that the argument is wrong, the proper course is simply to refuse permission. Where a judge does certify a claim as totally without merit, it is particularly important that the reasons for so doing are fully recorded. Studies in the past suggest that a significant proportion of renewed applications for permission are successful.[221]

16-067   The options open to a claimant whose application for permission has been refused after renewal of an oral hearing depends on whether the claim for judicial review is "in a criminal cause or matter". The category of criminal judicial review—typically but not exclusively against magistrates' courts—consists of those proceedings "the outcome of which may be the trial of the applicant and his punishment

---

[215] CPR r.54.13.

[216] See 16-043.

[217] *R. (on the application of Webb) v Bristol City Council* [2001] EWHC Admin 696, applied by *R. (on the application of Enfield BC) v Secretary of State for Health* [2009] EWHC 743 (Admin) at [3]-[11].

[218] CPR r.54.12(3)–(5) and (7); *R. (on the application of MD (Afghanistan) v Secretary of State for the Home Department* [2012] EWCA Civ 194; [2012] 1 W.L.R. 2422 at [19]-[23]. The fee for a request for reconsideration is £350. On the meaning of "totally without merit" see J. Maurici, "'Totally Without Merit' and Judicial Review" [2014] J.R. 258 and *R. (Wasif) v Secretary of State for the Home Department* [2016] EWCA Civ 82; [2016] 1 W.L.R. 2793 at [17].

[219] CPR 54.12(4).

[220] *R. (on the application of Wasif) v Secretary of State for the Home Department (Practice Note)* [2016] EWCA Civ 82; [2016] 1 W.L.R. 2793 at [13]–[21]

[221] M. Sunkin, "What is happening to judicial review?" (1987) 50 M.L.R. 432, 456. In 2005, approximately 18% of renewed applications were granted.

for an alleged offence by a court claiming jurisdiction to do so".[222] The Court of Appeal has no jurisdiction to hear appeals in criminal judicial review, so for practical purposes the refusal of permission by the Administrative Court is final and conclusive.[223]

In other, non-criminal, cases a claimant who is unsuccessful following the **16-068** renewed application has three main options. First, to give up. Secondly, to seek permission to appeal to the Court of Appeal against the refusal of permission to proceed. Permission to appeal should be sought from the Court of Appeal within seven days.[224] In order to prevent unnecessary hearings, the Court of Appeal has jurisdiction to grant permission to proceed with the judicial review not merely permission to appeal.[225] The Court of Appeal may deal with an application for permission to appeal without a hearing. If refused on the papers, "the person seeking permission may request that the decision be reconsidered at a hearing".[226] If it seems likely that the claimant will be able to demonstrate that the claim for judicial review should proceed to a full hearing, the Court of Appeal may hold the hearing on notice, allow the defendant to be represented, and then grant permission to proceed with the claim for judicial review rather than merely permission to appeal.[227] (The full hearing of the claim will normally be directed to be heard by the Administrative Court, or the Court of Appeal itself may hear the claim).[228] The possibility of further appeals to the Supreme against the Court of Appeal's determination depends on the order that was made. If the Court of Appeal refuses only permission *to appeal* against the Administrative Court's refusal to grant permission for judicial review, there is no possibility of an appeal to the Supreme Court. Such a decision of the Court of Appeal is final and conclusive.[229] If, however, the Court of Appeal grants permission to appeal, hears the appeal, and goes on to refuse the application for permission *to proceed* with the judicial review, the Supreme Court does have jurisdiction to consider an application for permission to appeal against that decision.[230]

Thirdly, but only in exceptional cases, a claimant may make a fresh application **16-069** to the Administrative Court for permission to proceed if there has been a significant

---

[222] Senior Courts Act 1981 s.18(1)(a); "matters relating to trial on indictment" are not amenable to judicial review: Senior Courts Act 1981 s.29(3); see 3-010.

[223] The SC may have jurisdiction to receive a petition for leave to appeal from the Admin Ct's refusal of permission, but the Admin Ct would first have to certify that the case involves a point of law of general public importance Supreme Court, PD1, 1.2.10; it is difficult to imagine circumstances in which the Admin Ct would refuse permission to proceed with a judicial review claim when such a point of law is raised.

[224] CPR 52.8(1) and *Glencore Energy UK Ltd v Commissioners of HM Revenue and Customs* [2017] EWHC 1587 (Admin).

[225] CPR r.52.15(3). There is little point in determining permission to appeal, then hearing the substantive appeal and then remitting the claim back to the Admin Ct for it to be granted permission to proceed with the judicial review claim.

[226] CPR r.52.3(4); PD 52C, para.15(2).

[227] *R. (on the application of Werner) v Inland Revenue Commissioners* [2002] EWCA Civ 979; [2002] S.T.C. 1213.

[228] CPR r.52.15(4). This will be the preferable course of events where an appeal to the CA seems inevitable, for example because the Admin Ct is bound by a CA precedent that has been called into question.

[229] *R. v Secretary of State for Trade and Industry Ex p. Eastaway* [2000] 1 W.L.R. 2222. Note that Eastaway "is only authority for the proposition that when the Court of Appeal has refused permission to appeal in the face of a first instance refusal of permission to seek judicial review the House [of Lords] has no jurisdiction to give leave to appeal" (*R. v Hammersmith and Fulham LBC Ex p. Burkett* [2002] UKHL 23; [2002] 1 W.L.R. 1593 at [12] (Lord Steyn)).

[230] *R. v Hammersmith and Fulham LBC Ex p. Burkett* [2002] UKHL 23; [2002] 1 W.L.R. 1593; Supreme Court, PD1, para.1.2.21.

change of circumstances, or if the claimant has become aware of significant new facts, or if a proposition of law is now maintainable which was not previously open to the claimant.[231] As the refusal of permission is an interlocutory judgment, the doctrine of res judicata does not preclude a fresh application, though that may constitute an abuse of process in the absence of new material or circumstances.

Interlocutory Stage

16-070   The court on granting permission may give directions to ensure the case is ready for the substantive hearing. If the court makes no directions, the standard directions will apply. According to the standard directions, the claimant must pay the court fee within seven days of receiving permission to proceed.[232] The defendant and any interested parties who wish to contest the claim must file and serve detailed grounds and any relevant written evidence within 35 days.[233] The claimant must file and serve his skeleton argument no fewer than 21 working days before the hearing along with an indexed and paginated bundle of documents to be used at the hearing. The defendant (and any other party) has a further seven working days in which to file their skeleton argument.

Applications by interveners

16-071   There is a growing incidence of interventions in judicial review claims, by campaign groups, public authorities and other bodies concerned about the outcome of a claim.[234] A person wishing to intervene by making written submissions or being represented at the hearing must seek permission to do so at "at the earliest reasonable opportunity".[235]

Disclosure

16-072   Until the 1978 judicial review reforms,[236] the court had no power to order disclosure of documents (formerly "discovery"). RSC Ord.53 did not introduce an automatic right to disclosure but did allow a party to apply to the court for orders for disclosure of documents. The court was sparing in its use of disclosure orders. One rationale for limiting rights to disclosure is that defendant public authorities are expected, and generally do, approach judicial review litigation in an open-handed manner.[237] This general arrangement continued under CPR Pt 54, with any

---

[231] *R. (on the application of Opoku) v Southwark College Principal* [2002] EWHC 2092 (Admin); [2003] 1 W.L.R. 234. Note that in *Smith v Parole Board* [2003] EWCA Civ 1014; [2003] 1 W.L.R. 2548, the CA doubted the limitations set out by Lightman J in relation to opening up grounds, previously refused permission, at the full hearing; but those are not doubts about the jurisdiction of the court to hear fresh applications for permission when the previously the claimant has been refused permission in toto.

[232] £770 (from July 2016), Civil Proceedings, First-tier Tribunal, Upper Tribunal and Employment Tribunals Fees (Amendment) Order 2016 Sch.1. If the claimant has already paid the fee of £385 for an oral hearing, the fee is a further £385.

[233] For details of the other steps to be taken, reference should be made to Appendix K below.

[234] See 2-073.

[235] PD 54A, para.13.5. The application is made by a letter to the Admin Ct Office (rather than filing an application notice) "identifying the claim, explaining who the applicant is and indicating why and in what form the applicant wants to participate in the hearing"; see 16-087. Section 87 of the Criminal Justice and Courts Act 2015 now provides that interveners may not seek their costs from the parties and should pay any costs caused by their intervention (see fn.301).

[236] See Ch.15.

[237] *Huddleston* [1986] 2 All E.R. 941 (see 16-027 above); this general approach is reflected today in

application for specific disclosure determined in accordance with CPR 31.[238] The court may order pre-action disclosure in judicial review proceedings pursuant to CPR r.31.16(3), although such applications will "rarely" be successful.[239]

Opinion has been divided as to whether disclosure should become more routinely available in judicial review proceedings or whether a strict (or stricter) approach should be maintained.[240] A new, "more flexible and less prescriptive principle, which judges the need for disclosure in accordance with the requirements of the particular case, taking into account the facts and circumstances", and having regard to the overriding objective of the CPR, was signalled by the House of Lords in December 2006.[241] Many claims for judicial review based on Convention rights will require a "careful and accurate evaluation of the facts" in order for the court to make a judgement on the proportionality of a public authority's interference with the right in question. In such cases, disclosure will be ordered where it is necessary to resolve the issues fairly and accurately.[242] Similarly, a reviewing court may be required to consider whether the social aims advanced by domestic legislation conform to the requirements of EU law. In such cases, the court will inevitably receive evidence relating to the parliamentary process which might previously have been thought to

16-073

---

the CPR requirement that parties co-operate with each other in the conduct of the proceedings (CPR r.1.4(2)(a)).

[238] *R. v Secretary of State for Foreign and Commonwealth affairs Ex p. World Development Movement Ltd* [2995] 1 W.L.R. 386 at 396-397.

[239] See *British Union for the Abolition of Vivisection (BUAV) v Secretary of State for the Home Department* [2014] EWHC 43 (Admin); [2014] A.C.D. 69 at [32]–[34], [54]–[67]. Applications for further information under CPR Pt 18 in judicial review cases were discouraged in *R. (on the application of Bredenkamp) v Secretary of State for Foreign and Commonwealth Affairs* [2013] EWHC 2480 (Admin); [2013] Lloyd's Rep. F.C. 690 at [20].

[240] See Law Commission Consultation Paper No.126, *Administrative Law: Judicial Review and Statutory Appeals*, para.8.10. In its 1994 report, the Law Commission made no recommendations for amendments of the Rules dealing with discovery: see *Law Com. No.226*, para.7.12. At the time of writing, the Lord Chief Justice is undertaking a consultation exercise into disclosure in judicial review (see fn.97), and has suggested a procedure be adopted by which a party could apply for specific directions for disclosure. Such a procedure would apply only to the "small minority" of cases in which such directions are required.

[241] *Tweed v Parades Commission for Northern Ireland* [2006] UKHL 53; [2007] 1 A.C. 650 at [32]–[33] (Lord Carswell), applied in *R. (on the application of Al-Sweady) v Secretary of State for Defence* [2009] EWHC 2387 (Admin); [2010] H.R.L.R. 2 at [23]–[29] and *R. (on the application of Mohamed) v Secretary of State for Foreign and Commonwealth Affairs* [2008] EWHC 2048 (Admin); [2009] 1 W.L.R. 2579 at [98]–[108] (where disclosure was ordered under *Norwich Pharmacal* principles in relation to allegations that the claimant had been tortured while in custody of the Pakistani authorities with the knowledge or involvement of the British authorities). The CA has since refused to grant disclosure under *Norwich Pharmacal* principles where evidence is sought for use in overseas proceedings outside the scope of the Crime (International Cooperation) Act 2003 (*R. (on the application of Omar) v Secretary of State for Foreign and Commonwealth Affairs* [2013] EWCA Civ 118; [2014] Q.B. 112 at [25]–[27]). Section 17 of the Justice and Security Act 2013 provides that the court may not exercise its *Norwich Pharmacal* jurisdiction in relation to "sensitive information", which is information: (a) held by an intelligence service; (b) obtained from, or held on behalf of, an intelligence service; (c) derived in whole or part from information obtained from, or held on behalf of, an intelligence service; (d) relating to an intelligence service; or (e) specified or described in a certificate issued by the Secretary of State in relation to the proceedings as information which the disclosing party should not be ordered to disclose. The Secretary of State may issue such a certificate if she considers that it would be contrary to the public interest to disclose: (i) the information; (ii) whether the information exists; or (iii) whether the disclosing party has the information. A disclosure is contrary to the public interest if it would cause damage to the interests of national security or to the interests of the international relations of the United Kingdom.

[242] *Tweed* [2006] UKHL 53; [2007] 1 A.C. 650 at [3] (Lord Bingham). Previously, a claimant was required to show that the defendant's evidence was materially inaccurate or misleading before disclosure would be ordered.

infringe parliamentary privilege.[243] Even where Convention rights and proportionality are in issue, disclosure should be limited to the issues which require it in the interests of justice and, where possible, claimants should specify particular documents or classes of documents rather than seeking an order for general disclosure. Parties should exhibit documents referred to in their witness statements.[244]

16-074   In practice, unless the claimant can show a prima facie breach of public duty, disclosure will not usually be granted.[245] Where the challenge is on the ground of *Wednesbury* irrationality,[246] standard disclosure of the type which is a matter of routine in private law proceedings will seldom be ordered.[247] Applications for disclosure "in the hope that something might turn up" are regarded as an illegitimate exercise, at least in the absence of a prima facie reason to suppose that the deponent's evidence is untruthful.[248] Outside the realm of Convention rights or other matters of factual dispute, disclosure to go behind the contents of a statement of truth will be ordered only if there is some material before the court which suggests that the claim form is not accurate.[249] Even reports referred to in a claim, routinely inspected in private law proceedings, will not be the subject of disclosure in judicial review unless the claimant shows that the production of the documents is necessary for fairly disposing of the matter before the court.[250]

Interim remedies

16-075   Pending the full hearing of the claim, the claimant may apply to the court for one or more interim remedies.[251] These include an interim injunction, interim declaration and stay of proceedings.[252] The term "stay of proceedings" is not confined to proceedings of a judicial nature, but encompasses the process by which any deci-

---

[243] An example is *R (on the application of Age UK) v Secretary of State for Business, Innovation and Skills* [2009] EWHC 2336 (Admin); [2010] 1 C.M.L.R. 21 at [42]-[59]. See further 5-039, above.

[244] *Tweed* [2006] UKHL 53; [2007] 1 A.C. 650 at [33] (Lord Carswell).

[245] *R. v Inland Revenue Commissioners Ex p. National Federation of Self Employed and Small Business Ltd* [1982] A.C. 617 at [654E] (Lord Scarman).

[246] Ch.11.

[247] *R. v Secretary of State for the Environment Ex p. Smith* [1988] C.O.D. 3; cf. *R. v Secretary of State for Transport Ex p. APH Road Safety Ltd* [1993] C.O.D. 150. The Court will not normally stay its own decision unless there is uncertainty as to the law which is likely to be resolved by a forthcoming decision and the outcome of that decision is likely to resolve or substantially affect the outcome of the present case (*R. (on the application of Rama) v Immigration Appeal Tribunal* [2003] EWHC 27 (Admin) at [7] in relation to adjournment).

[248] See, e.g. *R. v Secretary of State for the Environment Ex p. Doncaster BC* [1990] C.O.D. 441; *R. v Secretary of State for the Environment Ex p. Islington LBC and London Lesbian and Gay Centre* [1992] C.O.D. 67; *R. v Secretary of State for Foreign and Commonwealth Affairs Ex p. World Development Movement Ltd* [1995] 1 W.L.R. 386.

[249] *R. v Secretary of State for the Home Department Ex p. BH* [1990] C.O.D. 445; *Brien v Secretary of State for the Environment and Bromley LBC* [1995] J.P.L. 528; *World Development Movement Ltd* [1996] 1 W.L.R. 386. In its 1994 report, the Law Commission considered that this approach was unduly restrictive and undermined the basic test of relevance and necessity laid down in *O'Reilly v Mackman*: see *Law Com. No.226*, para.7.12.

[250] *R. v Inland Revenue Commissioners Ex p. Taylor* [1989] 1 All E.R. 906.

[251] CPR r.25.1; see further Ch.18. The interim application fee is £255 (Civil Proceedings Fees Order 2008 (as amended, most recently in 2016) (2008/1053), Sch.1).

[252] The Admin Ct discharged an interim injunction in *R (Birmingham and Solihull Taxi Association) v Birmingham International Airport Ltd* [2009] EWHC 1462 (Admin) at [31]-[38] on grounds of delay, weak merits and the absence of an undertaking in damages. Unsurprisingly, the Admin Ct will not issue injunctive relief against a private third party (*R. (on the application of HSE) v Wolverhampton CC* [2009] EWHC 2688 (Admin) at [43] (overturned on other grounds in *HSE v Wolverhampton CC* [2012] UKSC 34; [2012] 1 W.L.R. 2264)).

sion challenged has been reached, including the decision itself.[253] Although a stay of proceedings and an interim injunction perform the same function of preserving the status quo until the full hearing, there are conceptual and practical differences between the two forms of relief. While the injunction protects the interest of the litigant in dispute with another, the stay is not addressed to an "opposing" party but rather is directed at suspending the operation of a particular decision. The Administrative Court and Court of Appeal may order that a claimant be temporarily released.[254]

Preparation of skeleton arguments

As stated above, the claimant must submit the skeleton argument 21 working **16-076** days before the date of the hearing; the defendant and interested parties must do so 14 working days before the hearing.[255] Practice Direction 54A sets out the minimum requirements for a skeleton argument. It should contain a time estimate for the complete hearing (including judgment), a list of issues, a list of legal points to be taken, a chronology, a list of essential documents for advanced reading (with a time estimate for doing so) and a list of persons referred to. Judges of the Administrative Court repeatedly remind counsel of the importance of providing a realistic estimate of time required for pre-reading since this is relied on by their staff in allocating cases.

Discontinuing and orders by consent

A significant proportion of claims, given permission to proceed, are withdrawn **16-077** before the full hearing.[256] If the parties agree about the final order to be made, the court may make the order without a hearing if it is satisfied that the order should be made. Because of the public interest involved in many judicial review claims, the parties cannot determine for themselves what order should be made. The court will not make an order if it is not in the public interest to do so. In addition, if a decision of a court or tribunal is the subject of the claim, it would be wrong for that decision to be altered merely by agreement of the parties. The court must be satisfied that this is appropriate.[257]

---

[253] *R. v Secretary of State for Education and Science Ex p. Avon CC (No.2)* [1991] 1 Q.B. 558 at [561F]–[562E].

[254] For an instance of a decision where release of an indefinitely detained prisoner was not ordered on an interim basis, because the court could not make a full assessment of the risk of release, see *R. (on the application of Khan) v Parole Board* [2009] EWHC 756 (Admin); [2010] 1 Prison L.R. 142 at [13].

[255] PD 54A, para.15. Parties are now encouraged to submit their skeleton arguments by email. The address for London is: *Administrativecourtofficelondon.skeletonarguments@hmcts.x.gsi.gov.uk*. The addresses for the Regional Offices are available at:
http://www.justice.gov.uk/courts/rcj-rolls-building/administrative-court [Accessed 8 November 2017]. This site also provides a template for skeleton arguments. It is extremely important that the parties ensure that their skeleton arguments are received by the Admin Ct in good time and counsel can expect to be criticised in court if they fail to do so. The CA criticised overly long and complex skeleton arguments in *Tombstone Ltd v Raja* [2008] EWCA Civ 1444; [2009] 1 W.L.R. 1143 at [122]-[128]. See also *Standard Bank v Via Mat International* [2013] EWCA Civ 490; [2013] 2 All E.R. (Comm) 1222 at [26]–[27] and in *Inplayer Limited v Thorogood* [2014] EWCA Civ 1511 at [52]–[57], where a successful appellant was refused costs for preparation of a skeleton argument which failed to comply with Practice Direction 52.

[256] CPR 38.2. M. Sunkin, "Withdrawing: A Problem in Judicial Review" in P. Leyland and T. Wood (eds), *Administrative Law Facing the Future* (1997), pp.221–241.

[257] PD 54A, para.17 and *Practice Direction (Administrative Court: Uncontested Proceedings)* [2008]

The full hearing

16-078   Where an application for permission has been granted on the papers (or on renewal), a full hearing of the claim for judicial review will take place some weeks or months later (unless there is urgency and an order for expedition is made).[258] In practice, the grant of permission often acts as a spur to negotiations between the parties and in many cases where permission is granted the claimant does not set the claim down for full hearing.[259] Where an application for permission is to be decided at an oral hearing, the court may direct that the permission application and the full hearing be "rolled up" into a single hearing.

16-079   In a criminal cause or matter,[260] the full hearing of the claim normally takes place before a Divisional Court (of two or three judges) rather than a single judge. The rationale for this is that it is the last effective appeal.[261] In other claims, the hearing is normally before a single judge, though a claim may be listed for hearing by a Divisional Court for other reasons (for example, if it raises a new point of law of wide application).

16-080   CPR r.8.6(2)–(3), which applies to claims for judicial review, provides that the court may require or permit a party to give oral evidence at the hearing, and cross examination may be permitted. In practice oral testimony and cross examination remain relatively rare. Cross examination should take place only when justice so demands,[262] for example where there is a conflict of evidence, where the claimant alleges that a precedent fact to the making of a decision did not exist, or where the court must reach its own view on the merits.[263] As with disclosure, cross examination is more likely to be ordered where Convention rights are in issue.

---

1 W.L.R. 1377.

[258] Where a case is ready for a substantive hearing, it enters a warned list and the parties are informed of this by letter. Where counsel are on the record, the listing office will contact chambers to agree a convenient date. The relevant website also lists provision for the short warned list and the factors to be considered in vacating listed hearings (*http://www.justice.gov.uk/courts/rcj-rolls-building/administrative-court/listing-policy* [Accessed 8 November 2017]).

[259] In 2015, 4,679 applications were lodged: of these, 16% were granted permission. Only 198 have reached a decision: Ministry of Justice, Civil Justice Statistics Quarterly, England and Wales (Incorporating The Royal Courts of Justice 2015) January to March 2016 (2 June 2015).

[260] See 3-009.

[261] See 16-085; the only appeal lies to the SC.

[262] The orthodox approach is set out in *R. v Secretary of State for the Home Department Ex p. Khawaja* [1984] A.C. 74 at [125] (Lord Bridge: "oral evidence and discovery, although catered for by the rules, are not part of the ordinary stock in trade of the prerogative jurisdiction") and *Roy v Kensington and Chelsea and Westminster FPC* [1992] 1 A.C. 624 (Lord Lowry). The CA affirmed the traditional reasons for not permitting oral evidence (the risk that the judge will be tempted to decide the merits of the dispute rather than the grounds of review and the additional court time and costs which would result) in *Bubb v Wandsworth LBC* [2011] EWCA Civ 1285; [2012] P.T.S.R. 1011 at [24].

[263] *R. (on the application of Al-Sweady) v Secretary of State for Defence* [2009] EWHC 2387 (Admin); [2010] H.R.L.R. 2 at [19] (cross-examination permitted where there are "hard-edged" questions of fact to be resolved); *R. (on the application of Bancoult) v Secretary of State for Foreign and Commonwealth Affairs* [2012] EWHC 2115 (Admin) at [14]–[17] (cross-examination permitted in relation to leaked documents as the claims could not be fairly determined without determining the allegations). Cross-examination was refused, applying these principles, in *R. v Criminal Injuries Compensation Board Ex p. A* [1999] 2 A.C. 330; [1999] 2 W.L.R. 974, but permitted in *Jedwell v Denbighshire CC* [2015] EWCA Civ 1232; [2016] P.T.S.R. 715 (to determine whether the reasons given for a decision were genuine or part of an attempt to justify the decision retrospectively). In *R. (on the application of Bourgass) v Secretary of State for Justice* [2015] UKSC 54; [2016] A.C. 384 at [126], Lord Reed emphasised the flexibility of the judicial review procedure to resolve disputed questions of fact and to allow cross-examination where appropriate. In *R. (on the application of Radha Naran Patel) v Secretary of State for the Home Department* [2015] EWCA Civ 645 at [64], Underhill LJ strongly encouraged the parties to give careful consideration to whether a case

Written evidence is regulated by CPR r.54.16, and may be relied upon only if it **16-081**
has been served in accordance with any rule in Pt 54, or a direction of the court, or
the court gives permission. The court is generally wary of allowing the claimant to
introduce fresh evidence which the defendant was unable to address before the
claim was commenced.[264] Where the claimant's ground of challenge is that the
defendant failed to give adequate reasons the court will be cautious about allowing the defendant to explain or amplify the reasons originally given to the
claimant.[265]

An innovation introduced by the CPR is that the court may decide a claim for **16-082**
judicial review on the basis of the papers without a hearing where all the parties
agree,[266] though there has not been extensive use of this provision in practice. Where
a claim turns on a discrete point of law, especially one going to the jurisdiction of
the court to deal with the claim, the court may order that that be tried as a
preliminary issue.[267]

Appeals after the full hearing

As *Access to Justice: Final Report* noted: "Appeals serve two purposes: the **16-083**
private purpose, which is to do justice in particular cases by correcting wrong decisions, and the public purpose, which is to ensure public confidence in the
administration of justice by making such corrections and to clarify and develop the
law and to set precedents".[268] The appeal routes from judgments in judicial review
claims vary according to whether or not the claim is in a criminal cause or matter.[269]
The Court of Appeal may entertain what is, in effect, a new challenge to a public
authority's decision where the authority has re-determined the question after successful judicial review proceedings at first instance.[270]

---

started under CPR Part 54 which "throws up substantial issues of primary fact" should be resolved
on the papers or whether it requires oral evidence to be given. The CA repeated the general reluctance
to permit cross-examination and to allow the court to be drawn into the resolution of technical
disputes between experts in judicial review proceedings in *R. (British American Tobacco UK Ltd)
v Secretary of State for Health* [2016] EWCA Civ 1182; [2017] 3 W.L.R. 225 at [250]–[253].

[264] *R. v Secretary of State for the Environment Ex p. Powis* [1981] 1 W.L.R. 584; *R. (on the application of Dwr Cymru Cyfyngedig) v Environment Agency of Wales* [2003] EWHC 336 (Admin); (2003)
100(16) L.S.G. 27. See further *HCA International Ltd v Competition and Markets Authority* [2014]
CAT 10; [2015] Comp. A.R. 9 at [2]–[4] (in relation to expert evidence); and J. Tomlinson, "Adducing Fresh Expert Evidence in Section 179 Review Proceedings in the CAT" [2014] J.R. 253. See
HK (Bulgaria) v Secretary of State for the Home Department [2016] EWHC 857 (Admin); [2016]
A.C.D. 86 at [13]–[18], fn.91 above.
[265] *R. v Westminster City Council Ex p. Ermakov* [1996] 2 All E.R. 302. *Ermakov* was followed and
treated as an important statement of principle by the CA in *R. (on the application of Lanner Parish
Council) v Cornwall Council* [2013] EWCA Civ 1290; [2013] 45 E.G. 75 (C.S.) at [59]–[66].
[266] CPR r.54.18. Once permission is granted the claimant is entitled to an oral hearing even if the claim
has become academic unless the parties agree to dispense with such a hearing (*R. (on the application of Parsipoor) v Secretary of State for the Home Department* [2011] EWCA Civ 276; [2011] 1
W.L.R. 3187 at [25]–[29]). The CA encouraged parties to make greater use of this procedure in *R.
(on the application of Bahta) v Secretary of State for the Home Department* [2011] EWCA Civ 895;
[2011] C.P. Rep. 43 at [69].
[267] See, e.g. *R. (on the application of Heather) v Leonard Cheshire Foundation* [2001] EWHC Admin
429; (2001) 4 C.C.L. Rep. 211 at [9].
[268] Lord Woolf, *Access to Justice: Final Report* (1996), Ch.14, para.2.
[269] On which see 3-009.
[270] *R. (on the application of O) v Hammersmith and Fulham LBC* [2011] EWCA Civ 925; [2012] 1
W.L.R. 1057.

Appeals in a criminal cause or matter

16-084   If the claim for judicial review constitutes a "criminal cause or matter", the appeal route is directly to the Supreme Court (the Court of Appeal having no jurisdiction).[271] The Administrative Court must first certify that the proposed appeal involves a point of law of general public importance.[272]

Appeals in civil judicial review claims

16-085   In non-criminal claims, appeal lies to the Court of Appeal and is governed by CPR Pt 52.[273] Permission to appeal is required. Permission should first be sought orally at the hearing at which the decision to be appealed against is handed down. If permission is refused, permission may be sought from the Court of Appeal in writing. In exceptional cases, an appeal may "leapfrog" directly from the Administrative Court to the Supreme Court, bypassing the Court of Appeal. The Criminal Justice and Courts Act 2015 has expanded the circumstances in which an appeal may "leapfrog" to the SC (Supreme Court) by removing the requirement that all parties should consent to it (s.63(2)(b)) and setting out alternative conditions. These are that there is a point of law of general public importance which either relates to a fully-argued matter of statutory construction or is one in respect of which the judge is bound by a decision of the Court of Appeal, the House of Lords or the SC, or that there is a point of law of general public importance and either the proceedings relate to a matter of national importance; or the proceedings are so significant that the judge considers a hearing by the SC is justified; or the judge considers that the benefit of the matter being considered by the SC outweighs those of it being heard by the Court of Appeal.[274]

Funding judicial review

16-086   The cost of bringing a claim for judicial review, the limited availability of legal aid, and the practice that "costs follow the event"[275] are all serious barriers to access to justice. In 2005, the typical cost of making a claim for judicial review was

---

[271] Senior Courts Act 1981 s.18(1)(a); e.g. *R. (on the application of South West Yorkshire Mental Health NHS Trust) v Bradford Crown Court* [2003] EWCA Civ 1857; [2004] 1 W.L.R. 1664.

[272] Administration of Justice Act 1960 s.1(1)(a).

[273] Senior Courts Act 1981 s.16(1); CPR r.52.3. In 2015, there were 240 appeals from the Admin Ct to the CA (Ministry of Justice, *"Civil Justice Statistics Quarterly, England and Wales (Incorporating The Royal Courts of Justice 2015) January to March 2016"* (2 June 2015)). The fee for an appeal is £240 (Civil Proceedings Fees Order 2008 (as amended, most recently in 2016) (2008/1053), Sch.1).

[274] Administration of Justice Act 1969 s.12(3) and (3A), Supreme Court, PD1, para.1.2.18 One such appeal was *R. v Secretary of State for the Environment, Transport and the Regions Ex p. Holdings & Barnes Plc (the Alconbury case)* [2001] UKHL 23; [2003] 2 A.C. 295, which decided issues of major importance about the compatibility of the planning system in England and Wales with Convention rights; see also *R. (on the application of Jones) v Ceredigion CC (Permission to Appeal)* [2005] EWCA Civ 986; [2005] 1 W.L.R. 3626 (refusal of the HL to entertain an appeal on a particular issue from the High Court under the leapfrog procedure did not preclude an appellant from appealing to the CA on that particular issue where the High Court judge had granted the appellant contingent permission to appeal to the CA in relation to that issue). Section 64 of the Criminal Justice and Courts Act 2015 (in force from 8 August 2016) permits appeals to "leapfrog" to the SC from the Upper Tribunal in similar circumstances.

[275] CPR r.44.2(2): a successful claimant will normally recover his legal costs from the defendant public authority; an unsuccessful claimant will normally be ordered to pay the legal costs of the public authority.

in the region of £9,600.[276] Court fees in a typical claim for judicial review amount to around £900.[277] In October 2004, the Court of Appeal gave the following figures as illustrative of the legal costs (excluding VAT) in one case in which there were appeals to the Court of Appeal and House of Lords.[278]

	Party	Solicitors' bill	Counsel's fees	Other disbursements	Total
High Court (Four days)	Claimant	£9,482	£17,275	£969	£27,726
	Defendant	£8–10,000	£24,300		£32–34,300
Court of Appeal (One day)	Claimant	£18,487	£5,100	£1,247	£25,834
	Defendant	£3,000	£4,000		£7,000
House of Lords (Leave hearing & two days)	Claimant	£39,946	£83,450	£11,945	£135,341
	Defendant	£5,500	£23,800		£29,300

For most claimants, this expense is prohibitive and judicial review litigation cannot be pursued without some form of public funding. The provision of public funding for judicial review has undergone profound change. The old system was based on the Community Legal Service (CLS) Fund administered by the Legal Services Commission (LSC).[279] Since 1 April 2013, the new system has operated under the Legal Aid, Sentencing and Punishment of Offenders Act 2012.[280]   **16-087**

The functions previously discharged by the LSC are now within the remit of the Lord Chancellor, and individual decisions to award legal aid are taken by the Director of Legal Aid Casework as part of the Legal Aid Agency (an executive agency of the Ministry of Justice).[281] Civil legal aid is available for legal services which fall   **16-088**

---

[276] This is the average summary assessment of costs in claims where there was a full hearing lasting half a day.

[277] As of 25 July 2016, the application fee for permission to apply for judicial review is £154. There is a fee of £385 for a request for oral renewal of an application for permission. For judicial review after permission is granted, the fee is £770, or £385 if permission was granted after oral renewal of the application (Civil Proceedings Fees Order 2008/1053 (as amended)). Guidance on obtaining remission of fees is set out on form EX160A (Civil Proceedings Fees Order 2008 (as amended, most recently in 2016) (2008/1053), Sch.1).

[278] *R. (on the application of Burkett) v Hammersmith and Fulham LBC (Costs)* [2004] EWCA Civ 1342; [2005] C.P. Rep. 11 at [10]. Multiplying these figures by 1.5 would provide the 2017 values.

[279] The LSC was established by the Access to Justice Act 1999 to replace the civil legal aid system.

[280] The documents which discussed changes to the system of public funding include: Department of Constitutional Affairs, *A Fairer Deal for Legal Aid*, Cm. 6993 (2005); Lord Carter of Coles, *Legal Aid: a market-based approach to reform* (2006); Department for Constitutional Affairs/Legal Services Commission, *Legal Aid Reform: the Way Ahead*, Cm. 6993 (2006); House of Commons Constitutional Affairs Committee *Implementation of the Carter Review of Legal Aid*. HC Paper No.223-I (Session 2006/07); Lord Justice Jackson, *Review of Civil Litigation Costs: Final Report* (December 2009); Ministry of Justice, *Proposals for the Reform of Legal Aid in England and Wales* (November 2010) (Cm 7967); and *Reforming Civil Litigation Funding and Costs in England and Wales—Implementation of Lord Justice Jackson's Recommendations: The Government Response* (March 2011) (Cm 8401). As of 1 April 2013 new rules have been introduced to ensure costs management in most civil proceedings (section II of CPR Pt 3 and PD 3E). The impact, if any, of these reforms on judicial review is not yet clear. The Public Law Project has produced a useful guide, *How to Apply for Legal Aid Funding for Judicial Review* (Short Guide 05, 2016).

[281] Legal Aid, Sentencing and Punishment of Offenders Act 2012 s.4.

within Pt 1 of Sch.1 to the 2012 Act and where the Director has determined that the individual qualifies for the relevant services: s.9 of the 2012 Act.

16-089   Schedule 1 includes "judicial review of an enactment, decision, act or omission", habeas corpus, deliberate or dishonest abuse by a public authority of its position or powers which results in reasonably foreseeable harm to a person or property and a significant breach of Convention rights.[282] However, this is subject to the specific exclusion of services provided to an individual which do not have the potential to produce a benefit for the individual, a member of his family or the environment.[283] The requirement of benefit has the obvious potential to reduce the availability of legal aid for public interest challenges. It is also questionable whether a claimant whose only remedy would be a declaration of incompatibility under the HRA is likely to qualify. If a claimant falls outside of these provisions, he must rely on the Director's discretion to make an exceptional case determination where the legal services are necessary to avoid a breach of the individual's Convention rights or enforceable EU law rights.[284]

16-090   Section 11 of the 2012 Act provides that the Director's determination that an individual qualifies for the legal services described above is governed by (a) the financial resources of the individual and (b) criteria set out by the Lord Chancellor in regulations to reflect: the likely cost of providing the services and the benefit which may be thus obtained; the availability of resources; the appropriateness of applying those resources, having regard to present and likely future demands; the importance of the matter for the individual; the nature and seriousness of the act, omission, circumstances or other matter in question; other means of resolving the dispute; the individual's prospects of success; the conduct of the individual; and the public interest.[285] Regulations now provide for appeals to an adjudicator against the Director's Determinations.[286]

---

[282] Sch.1, paras 19(1), 20, 21 and 22.

[283] Sch.1, para.19(3). There are further specific exclusions for immigration cases (paras 19(5)-(8) and 24-32).

[284] Legal Aid, Sentencing and Punishment of Offenders Act 2012 s.10(3). A further exception (called a wider public interest determination) applies to inquests under the Coroners Act 1988 into the death of a family member (Legal Aid, Sentencing and Punishment of Offenders Act 2012 s.10(4)). In *Gudanaviciene v Director of Legal Aid* [2014] EWCA Civ 1622; [2015] 1 W.L.R. 2247, the court overturned a number of decisions of the Director in cases involving art.8 of the ECHR on the basis that they were too restrictive. The Lord Chancellor's guidance on exceptional funding was held to be incompatible with the requirements of art.6 ECHR and art.47 of the EU Charter of Fundamental Rights because it sent a signal that refusal of legal aid would breach these provisions only in rare and extreme cases (at [45] and [59]). Appeal to SC outstanding. Amended guidance can be found at *https://www.gov.uk/government/publications/legal-aid-exceptional-case-funding-form-and-guidance* [Accessed 8 November 2017]. Further resources relating to exceptional funding are available at *http://www.publiclawproject.org.uk/exceptional-funding-project* [Accessed 8 November 2017]. The CA in *IS v Director of Legal Aid Casework* [2016] EWCA Civ 464; [2016] 1 W.L.R. 4733 overturned declarations made by the HC in *IS v Director of Legal Aid Casework* [2015] EWHC 1965 (Admin); [2015] 1 W.L.R. 5283. The HC had found that the Defendants' guidance on Exceptional Case Funding was too restrictive and too unclear (especially in light of those to whom they were addressed) to be compatible with ECHR arts 6 and 8 and required substantial change. While acknowledging the "many difficulties" with the regime, the CA found that it fell within the range of lawful choices in the administration of the Legal Aid, Sentencing and Punishment of Offenders Act 2012. See also H. Mountfield QC, "Judicial Review and Human Rights: Challenges to Court Fees and Legal Aid Changes which Limit or Effectively Exclude Right of Access to Court" [2014] J.R. 217.

[285] The criteria reflecting the above factors are contained in the Civil Legal Aid (Merits Criteria) Regulations 2013/104 as amended. The "general merits criteria", set out in reg.39, are that the applicant does not have access to other potential sources of funding other than a conditional fee agreement; the case is unsuitable for a CFA; there is no person other than the individual who can reasonably be expected to bring the proceedings; all reasonable alternatives have been exhausted (including any

Costs

For claimants who are not publicly funded, a significant disincentive to starting **16-091**
litigation is the prospect that if they fail in their claim, they are likely to have to pay
the public authority's legal costs in defending the claim, as well as their own. Court
fees are payable at various points in a claim for judicial review, unless the claimant makes an application for exemption or remission of those fees.[287] The costs of
litigation are substantial and can pose a threat to the constitutional right of access
to the courts.[288]

---

complaints system, ombudsman scheme or other form of ADR); there is a need for representation
in all the circumstances of the case (including the nature and complexity of the issues; the existence of other proceedings; and the interests of other parties to the proceedings); and the proceedings are not likely to be allocated to the small claims track. In addition, regs 53–56 make special
provision for public law cases. Regulation 53 (standard criteria for determinations for legal
representation) requires that reg.39 is met; that the relevant act, omission or other matter is
susceptible to challenge; and that no alternative proceedings before a court or tribunal are available
(unless they are considered to be ineffective). Regulations 54 and 55 relate to investigative
representation. Regulation 56 (criteria for determinations for full representation) provides that as well
as satisfying the general criteria in reg.39, and the standard criteria in reg.53, the proportionality test
set out in reg.8 must be met (the likely benefits of the proceedings to the individual and others must
justify the likely costs, having regard to the prospects of success and all the other circumstances of
the case) and the prospects of success are above 50%, or, if they are either above 45% ("marginal")
or "unclear", only if the case is of significant wider public interest; one with overwhelming
importance to the individual; or if the substance of the case relates to a breach of Convention rights.
The attempt to introduce a residence test for legal aid by delegated legislation was found to be unlawful in *R. (on the application of the Public Law Project) v Secretary of State for Justice* [2016] UKSC
39; [2016] A.C. 1531. It was found to be unlawful to remove legal aid for decisions about prisoner
categorisation, moves to open conditions and placements in close supervision centres in *R. (on the
application of the Howard League for Penal Reform) v Lord Chancellor* [2017] EWCA Civ 244;
[2017] 4 W.L.R. 92. The Civil Legal Aid (Remuneration) Regulations 2013 govern remuneration.
Amendments to the provisions relating to judicial review were made by the Civil Legal Aid
(Remuneration) (Amendment) (No.3) Regulations 2014, restricting payment for work conducted to
cases in which permission was granted. This was successfully challenged in *R. (on the application
of Ben Hoare Bell) v the Lord Chancellor* [2015] EWHC 523 (Admin); [2015] 1 W.L.R. 4175, following which the 2014 Amendment Regulations were quashed. The restrictions on legal aid are
subject to close scrutiny in E. Palmer, T. Cornford, A. Guinchard and Y. Marique (eds), *Access to
Justice: Beyond the Policies and Politics of Austerity* (2016). The current position under reg.2 of the
Civil Legal Aid (Remuneration) (Amendment) Regulations 2015, in force from 27 March 2015,
inserting new reg.5A into the 2013 Regulations, is as follows. Public funding for work conducted
is available in five situations where: (i) the court gives permission to bring judicial review proceedings; (ii) the court neither gives nor refuses permission and the Legal Aid Agency considers payment is reasonable in the circumstances; (iii) the defendant withdraws the decision to which the application for judicial review relates and the withdrawal results in the court (a) refusing permission
to bring judicial review proceedings, or (b) neither refusing nor giving permission; (iv) the court
orders an oral hearing to consider whether to give permission to bring judicial review proceedings;
or (v) the court orders a rolled-up hearing. For a useful summary of the legislative changes in this
area see *R. (on the application of Ben Hoare Bell)* at [8]–[16], above.

[286] Civil Legal Aid (Procedure) Regulations (2012/3098) regs 28, 45–48, 53, 59.
[287] See fn.277.
[288] See, e.g. *R. v Lord Chancellor Ex p. Witham* [1998] Q.B. 575. As stated above (see fn.185 above),
the Aarhus Convention requires that court procedures must not be prohibitively expensive. The
Aarhus Compliance Committee found that the United Kingdom failed adequately to implement the
requirement that environmental proceedings should not be prohibitively expensive in the *Port of Tyne*
case (ACCC/C/2008/33, September 2010, at [128]–[136]). The Aarhus Convention is implemented
in EU law by the Environment Impact Assessment ("EIA") Directive (85/337/EEC) and the
Integrated Pollution Prevention and Control ("IPPC") Directive (96/61/EC). The EIA Directive is
now consolidated in Directive 2011/92/EU and has been subsequently amended by Directive 2014/
52/EU. The IPPC Directive, consolidated as Directive 2008/1/EC, has now been recast as the
Industrial Emissions Directive 2010/75/EU. The SC referred the question of whether costs in

16-092   The court has a broad discretion in making orders as to costs.[289] The general rule

environmental judicial review claims are prohibitively expensive to the CJEU in *R. (on the application of Edwards) v Environment Agency* [2010] UKSC 57; [2011] 1 W.L.R. 79 at [31]-[36]. See R. Turney, "Costs in Planning and Environmental Cases" [2011] Env. Law 20. The CJEU delivered its response in Case C-260/11 on 11 April 2013. The CJEU decided that the court assessing costs at any stage of the proceedings must take account of both the particular situation of this claimant and whether the costs are objectively justified and of the merits of the case and the importance of what is at stake in the proceedings (at [46]-[48]). The SC considered the CJEU's response and decided that the following factors were relevant to the ultimate level of recovery by the defendant: (i) whether the claim had a reasonable prospect of success; (ii) the importance of what is at stake for the claimant; (iii) the importance of what is at stake for the protection of the environment; (iv) the complexity of the relevant law and procedure (in that greater complexity is likely to require higher expenditure by the defendants); and the potentially frivolous nature of the claim at its various stages: *R. (on the application of Edwards) v Environment Agency (No.2)* [2013] UKSC 78; [2014] 1 W.L.R. 55 at [28]. The Civil Procedure Rules Committee has introduced a fixed costs regime for Aarhus Convention claims at first instance with effect from April 2013. Under CPR r.45.41-44, there is an automatic Protective Costs Order of £5,000 for individuals and £10,000 for businesses and legal persons and a reciprocal costs cap of £35,000 on the defendant's liability. The claimant should state in the claim form that the case is covered by the Aarhus Convention. In *Venn v Secretary of State for Communities and Local Government* [2014] EWCA Civ 1539; [2015] 1 W.L.R. 2328 at [34], Sullivan LJ stated: "it is now clear that the costs protection regime introduced by CPR r.45.41 is not Aarhus-compliant in so far as it is confined to applications for judicial review, and excludes statutory appeals and applications. A costs regime … under which costs protection depends not on the nature of the environmental decision or the legal principles on which it may be challenged, but on the identity of the decision-taker, is systemically flawed in terms of Aarhus compliance". In *R. (HS2 AA Ltd) v Transport Secretary (Nos 1&2)* [2014] EWCA Civ 1578 and [2015] EWCA Civ 203; [2015] P.T.S.R. 1025 at [12], the CA held that once it had been determined that a claim for judicial review was an "Aarhus Convention claim", costs liability was dealt with in CPR r.45.43 and PD 45, no further reference to the Aarhus Convention being necessary. From 28 February 2017, the Aarhus rules were amended: those wishing to benefit from them must now submit a statement of means and the court then has the power to vary up or down the figures for capped costs. CPR 52.19A contains new rules on appeals in Aarhus cases.

[289]   Senior Courts Act 1981 s.51; CPR r.44.2. Although the discretion is broad, it is "by no means untrammelled" and "must be exercised in accordance with the rules of court and established principles": *R. (on the application of Corner House Research) v Secretary of State for Trade and Industry* [2005] EWCA Civ 192; [2005] 1 W.L.R. 2600 at [8] (Lord Philips MR). CPR Pt 48 sets out some of the General Principles which guide costs assessments in the Administrative Court. The Criminal Justice and Courts Act 2015 ss.85 and 86 (not in force at the time of writing) will require an applicant to provide information as to the source, nature and extent of the financial resources available. Section 85 amends s.31(3) of the Senior Courts Act 1981 and s.16(3) of the Tribunals, Courts and Enforcement Act 2007, both of which deal with the grant of permission. By s.86, when the High Court, the Upper Tribunal or the Court of Appeal is determining by whom and to what extent costs of or incidental to judicial review proceedings are to be paid, it must have regard to the information required by s.85. The Government's stated purpose in legislating is to obtain greater transparency about how judicial reviews are funded and to limit the potential for third-party funders to avoid their appropriate liability for litigation costs. These concerns were partly based on the judicial review surrounding the burial of the remains of Richard III in which the Government incurred £90,000 of costs in successfully defending proceedings in which the claimant had the benefit of a protective costs order (*R. (on the application of the Plantagenet Alliance) v Secretary of State for Justice* [2014] EWHC 1662 (QB); [2015] 3 All E.R. 261). A consultation as to the implementation of these provisions was undertaken in 2015. At the time of writing, the Government is seeking further views on one aspect of the proposals: the provision to other parties of financial information provided under s.85 (see Ministry of Justice Command Paper 9303, *"Reform of Judicial Review: Proposals for the provision and use of financial information"*). Following the main consultation, the Government remains committed to implementing the planned reforms, with some amendments to the information certain claimant corporate bodies must provide, the suggested threshold amount and the court's ability to make a costs capping order in the absence of full financial information. On the limits to the court's discretion to pay the costs of legal representation, see *Re K (Children) (Unrepresented Father: Cross-Examination of Child)* [2015] EWCA Civ 543; [2015] 1 W.L.R. 3801, in which it was held that the Family Court had no power, outside the legal aid scheme established by the Legal Aid, Sentencing and Punishment of Offenders Act 2012, to order that the court service pay the costs of

guiding the exercise of that discretion is that "the unsuccessful party will be ordered to pay the costs of the successful party".[290] The court will decide whether to apply the general rule that costs follow the event, or award costs on an issue by issue basis.[291] In making costs awards, the court must have regard to the CPR's overriding objective[292] though, in several respects, a different costs regime is required in the context of public law proceedings compared to other civil claims.[293] The court will have regard to the parties' conduct before, as well as during, the proceedings and in particular the extent to which they followed the Practice Directions and Pre-action Protocol.[294] Costs ordered against a legally-aided individual must not exceed the amount it is reasonable for that individual to pay having regard to the financial resources of the parties.[295] In exceptional circumstances, a costs order may be made against a person who is not a party to the proceedings.[296] In many judicial review claims, the defendant is an inferior court, tribunal or coroner which (though making the decision that is challenged) has no real interest in resisting the claim. Where such a party does not participate in the proceedings, or only "in order to assist the court neutrally on questions of jurisdiction, procedure, specialist case law and such like", the court's general approach will be to make no order for costs; costs may, however, be ordered if they appear and actively resist the claim or if there was "a flagrant instance of improper behaviour or when the inferior court or tribunal unreasonably declined or neglected to sign a consent order disposing of the proceedings".[297] In its discretion, the court may decide to make no costs order against an unsuccessful claimant if the defendant unreasonably refuses to consider the alternative remedy of mediation following a suggestion of the judge.[298] The High Court, the Court of Appeal and the Supreme Court (when dealing with civil appeals) have the power to make a pro bono costs order where the successful party has been represented pro bono.[299] Conditional fee agreements remain rare in judicial review proceedings. Since April 2013, the success fee under such an agreement is

---

legal representation for a father for the cross-examination of a child (declining to follow *Q v Q* [2014] EWFC 31; [2015] 1 W.L.R. 2040). There were other means available to avoid a breach of ECHR arts 6 or 8. However, at [62] it was held that this might not always be the case and that consideration should be given to legislating for the payment from central funds for legal representation to conduct such cross-examination.

[290] CPR r.44.2(2). *Boxall v Waltham Forest LBC* (2001) 4 C.C.L. Rep. 258 (Scott Baker J), cited with approval in *R. (on the application of Kuzeva) v Southwark LBC* [2002] EWCA Civ 781.

[291] Z. Leventhal, "Costs Principles on Taking Judgment in a Judicial Review Case" [2005] J.R. 139. In *R. (on the application of Sino) v Secretary of State for the Home Department* [2016] EWHC 803 (Admin); [2016] 4 W.L.R. 80, Hayden J took account of the fact that lawyers taking on publicly-funded work may not be able to recover remuneration at inter partes rates where the claim is successful and this gave rise to a real risk that such practices would become unsustainable which would pose a threat to access to justice.

[292] See 16-011.

[293] *Mount Cook Ltd* [2003] EWCA Civ 1346 at [76].

[294] CPR r.44.2(5).

[295] Legal Aid, Sentencing and Punishment of Offenders Act 2012 s.26.

[296] *Dymocks Franchise Systems (NSW) Pty Ltd v Todd (Costs)* [2004] UKPC 39; [2004] 1 W.L.R. 2807. See also CPR r.46.2 and, for a survey of the authorities, *Weatherford Global Products Ltd v Hydropath Holdings Ltd* [2014] EWHC 3243 (TCC) at [4]–[12] and *Deutsche Bank AG v Sebastian Holdings Inc* [2016] EWCA Civ 23; [2016] 4 W.L.R. 17 at [41]–[21] and [62].

[297] *R. (on the application of Davies) v Birmingham Deputy Coroner (Costs)* [2004] EWCA Civ 207; [2004] 1 W.L.R. 2739.

[298] *Dunnett v Railtrack Plc* [2002] EWHC 9020 (Costs) (not a judicial review claim).

[299] Legal Services Act 2007 s.194. Awards go to the Access to Justice Foundation which distributes them to organisations which provide free legal assistance. T. Jones, "Pro Bono Costs Orders" [2012] J.R. 120.

no longer recoverable from the losing party.[300] Since 2015, there have also been new rules on interveners' costs.[301]

16-093   In his review of civil litigation costs, Lord Justice Jackson originally proposed a form of "qualified one-way costs shifting" (QOCS) in judicial review cases.[302] By this, he meant that any costs order would be limited to an amount which it would be reasonable for the claimant to pay having regard to the financial resources of the parties and the manner in which the litigation had been conducted. The Government has not taken up this proposal, although it was never formally rejected either.[303] On revisiting the issue in 2017, Lord Justice Jackson found the current position unsatisfactory: different rules apply depending on whether the case is an environmental judicial review or not and costs capping orders "are of little practical value" because the procedure for obtaining them is "too cumbersome and expensive".[304] As an alternative to QOCS, Lord Justice Jackson recommended that the Aarhus regime[305] be extended to all judicial review cases and that there should be judicial costs management in cases where the costs were likely to exceed £100,000.[306]

Costs capping order (protective costs orders) in public interest cases

16-094   A costs capping order (CCO)[307] fixes in advance the maximum sum in costs that may be awarded to a party, or determines that whatever the outcome of the claim there should be no order as to costs (with the consequence that the claimant bears only its own costs).[308] The court's power to make such an order has now been placed on an exclusive statutory footing by the s.88 of the Criminal Justice and Courts Act 2015.[309] CCOs were originally developed by the courts (and known as protective costs orders (PCOs)) to facilitate access to justice in "pure public interest" cases.

---

[300] Legal Aid, Sentencing and Punishment of Offenders Act 2012 ss.44 and 46. The reform, is said to be necessary, in part, to implement the judgment of the ECtHR in *MGN Ltd v United Kingdom* (2011) 53 E.H.R.R. 5 at [192]–[220] where the success fees payable by the newspaper were so high that they breached art.10 of the ECHR.

[301] By s.87 of the Criminal Justice and Courts Act 2015, a party to judicial review proceedings may not be required to pay an intervener's costs unless there are exceptional circumstances (so far undefined). The court must order an intervener to pay a party's costs if they have been incurred as a result of the intervener's involvement in the proceedings, and one of four further conditions is made out (s.87(5)). The conditions are (s.87(6)): (a) the intervener has acted, in substance, as the sole or principal applicant, defendant, appellant or respondent; (b) the intervener's evidence and representations, taken as a whole, have not been of significant assistance to the court; (c) a significant part of the intervener's evidence and representations relates to matters that it is not necessary for the court to consider in order to resolve the issues that are the subject of the stage in the proceedings; or (d) the intervener has behaved unreasonably (in both cases unless there are exceptional circumstances that make it inappropriate to do so).

[302] *Review of Civil Litigation Costs: Final Report* (December 2009), Ch. 30, paras 4.1–4.11.

[303] para.1.6.

[304] *Review of Civil Litigation Costs: Supplemental Report Fixed Recoverable Costs* (July 2017), Ch.10, para.2.7.

[305] See fn.288 above.

[306] *Review of Civil Litigation Costs: Supplemental Report Fixed Recoverable Costs*, Ch.10, paras 3–4.

[307] *R. v Lord Chancellor Ex p. Child Poverty Action Group* [1999] 1 W.L.R. 347 (Dyson J: "I think that the adjective 'pre-emptive' is more apt").

[308] R. Clayton, "Public Interest Litigation, Costs and the Role of Legal Aid" [2006] P.L. 429; B. Jaffey, "Protective Costs Orders in Judicial Review" [2006] J.R. 171; G. Opperman, M. Gullick and C. Stone, "Corner House Revisited: The Law Governing Protective Orders" [2009] J.R. 43; J. Maurici, "PCOs in public law cases" [2009] J.R. 245.

[309] Claims for judicial review where the claim form was filed in the High Court before 8 August 2016 continue to be governed by the protective costs orders (PCO) mechanism developed by the courts.

Claimants were typically pressure groups or public spirited individuals.[310] The overriding purpose of a PCO was to enable a claimant

> "to present its case to the court with a reasonably competent advocate without being exposed to such serious financial risks that would deter it from advancing a case of general public importance at all, where the court considers that it is in the public interest that an order should be made".[311]

There are now a number of limitations on the availability of a CCO. First, the **16-095** court may only make a CCO where permission to apply for judicial review has been granted.[312] The criteria for making a CCO are: (a) the proceedings are public interest proceedings; (b) in the absence of the order, the applicant for judicial review would withdraw the application for judicial review or cease to participate in the proceedings; and (c) it would be reasonable for the applicant to do so.[313] In deciding whether or not to make a CCO, the court is required to have regard to: the financial resources of the parties; any benefit which the applicant for the order (or anyone supporting the applicant financially) is likely to obtain; whether the applicant's legal representatives are acting free of charge; and whether the applicant is an appropriate person to represent the interests of other persons or the public interest generally.[314] Proceedings will only be treated as public interest proceedings if: an issue in the proceedings is of general public importance; the public interest requires the issue to be resolved; and these proceedings are likely to provide an appropriate means of resolving the issue.[315] In deciding whether or not the proceedings are public interest proceedings, the court is required to have regard to (among other factors): the number of people likely to be directly affected if relief is granted; how significant that effect is likely to be; and whether the proceedings involve a point of public importance.[316]

The statutory test for CCOs substantially reflects the common law, but is nar- **16-096** rower in that one of the elements of the test for a PCO was that the claimant would probably withdraw the claim if an order was not made.[317] However, limiting CCOs to cases in which permission has been granted is a substantial new limitation since

---

[310] On standing, see 2-007.
[311] *Corner House Research* [2005] EWCA Civ 192; [2005] 1 W.L.R. 2600 at [74]. See also Lord Justice Kay, "*Litigating the Public Interest*" (July 2006).
[312] Criminal Justice and Courts Act 2015 s.88(3) and CPR 46.
[313] Criminal Justice and Courts Act 2015 s88(6).
[314] Criminal Justice and Courts Act 2015 s.89(1). The Lord Chancellor has power to amend the list of relevant factors by regulation (s.89(3)–(5)).
[315] Criminal Justice and Courts Act 2015 s.88(7).
[316] Criminal Justice and Courts Act 2015 s.88(8).
[317] *Corner House Research* [2005] EWCA Civ 192; [2005] 1 W.L.R. 2600 at [74]. Later courts emphasised that all aspects of the guidance in *Corner House* were to be applied flexibly: *Morgan v Hinton Organics (Wessex) Ltd* [2009] EWCA Civ 107; [2009] C.P. Rep. 26 at [38]–[40]. Important guidance on the application of the *Corner House* principles has been provided by the Court of Appeal in *R. (on the application of Compton) v Wiltshire Primary Care Trust* [2008] EWCA Civ 749; [2009] 1 W.L.R. 1436 at [10]–[24] (Waller LJ) and *R. (on the application of Buglife-The Invertebrate Conservation Trust) v Thurrock Thames Gateway Development Corporation* [2008] EWCA Civ 1209 at [18]–[28] (Sir Anthony Clarke MR). PCOs were available to defendants in exceptional cases and to respondents to appeals where they would not otherwise be able to attend and the court would require the assistance of an amicus curiae (*Weaver v London Quadrant Housing Trust* [2009] EWCA Civ 235; [2009] 6 Costs L.R. 875 at [7]–[15]). Other significant cases under the old regime include: *R. (on the application of Young) v Oxford City Council* [2012] EWCA Civ 46 at [11]–[12] (protective costs order refused in circumstance where planning permission was of local community interest rather than general public importance); *Eweida v British Airways Plc* [2009] EWCA Civ 1025; [2010] C.P. Rep. 6 at [38]–[39] (an essentially private dispute between an individual and their employer about whether the former could wear a cross at work); *R. (on the application of Campaign*

substantial costs can be incurred before a decision on permission is made. This is likely to inhibit public interest litigation.

Costs before and at the permission stage

16-097   Where a claim for judicial review is withdrawn because the defendant concedes the merits before the court considers whether or not to grant permission,[318] the court may award costs to the successful party. The traditional position was that the court would only award costs in an exceptional case in order not to discourage defendants from conceding at an early stage.[319] An exceptional case might be made out where the claimant had set out his case with "admirable clarity" in pre-action correspondence, where the claim was on a simple point and the merits are strong.[320] This position must now be revised in light of the increased emphasis on compliance with the Pre-action Protocol and later decisions which have made costs more readily available to claimants where the proceedings are withdrawn after permission to seek judicial review has been granted.[321] Where the response of the defendant to an unanswerable claim has been tardy, costs may be awarded to the claimant on an indemnity basis.[322]

16-098   A defendant is entitled (but not obliged) to respond to a claim for judicial review at the permission stage by filing an acknowledgement of service *summarising* the grounds on which the claim is contested.[323] The general approach is that a successful defendant who does prepare and file such an acknowledgement of service is entitled to recover the costs of doing so from the unsuccessful claimant.[324] Where, however, permission is refused after a hearing at which the defendant chose to be

---

for Nuclear Disarmament) v Prime Minister (Costs) [2002] EWHC 2712 (Admin); [2003] C.P. Rep. 28, CND's liability for adverse costs was capped at £25,000 in respect of its attempt to obtain declarations as to UN Security Council Resolution 1441 and the war in Iraq; and *R. (on the application of the British Union for the Abolition of Vivisection) v Secretary of State for the Home Department* [2006] EWHC 250 (Admin) a cap of £40,000 was imposed; in *Wilkinson* [2006] EWHC 835 (Fam); [2006] 2 F.L.R. 397, the cap was £25,000 (inclusive of VAT).

318 On permission, see 16-044.
319 *R. v RB of Kensington and Chelsea Ex p. Ghebregiogis* (1995) 27 H.L.R. 602; *R. v Liverpool City Council Ex p. Newman* (1993) 5 Admin. L.R. 669 at [617D-672A].
320 *Ex p. Ghebregiogis* (1995) 27 H.L.R. 602 and *R. v Bassetlaw DC Ex p. Aldergate Estates Ltd* 2000 WL 664500 at [11]-[13].
321 See 16-101, below.
322 *R. (on the application of Taha) v Lambeth LBC* [2002] C.L.Y. 348.
323 See 16-043.
324 *R. (on the application of Leach) v Commissioner for Local Administration* [2001] EWHC Admin 455, as explained in *Mount Cook Land Ltd v Westminster City Council* [2003] EWCA Civ 1346; [2004] C.P. Rep. 12. As to the amount of such costs, see the guidance in *R. (Roudham & Larling Parish Council) v Breckland Council* [2008] EWCA Civ 714 at [25]-[31] (Buxton LJ) See also *R. (on the application of Davey) v Aylesbury Vale District Council* [2007] EWCA Civ 1166; [2008] 1 W.L.R. 878 which adds further guidance on the amount of costs at the permission stage. If awarding costs against the claimant, the judge should consider whether they are to include preparation costs in addition to acknowledgment costs. Acknowledgement costs are those costs incurred in preparing and serving an acknowledgement of service with grounds of opposition. Preparation costs refer to other pre-permission costs, such as pre-issue costs. It will be for the defendant to justify the latter costs by showing that it was reasonable and proportionate to incur such cost. There may be no sufficient reason why such costs, if incurred, should be recoverable: at [21]. If the claimant wishes to submit that any or all the costs which would be otherwise recoverable should not be recovered, however reasonable and proportionate they were, it is for him to persuade the court to that effect: at [30]. It is highly desirable that these questions should be dealt with by the trial judge and left to the costs judge only in relation to the reasonableness of individual items: at [21]. If, at the conclusion of such proceedings, the judge makes an undifferentiated order for costs in a defendant's favour (a) the order has to be regarded as including any reasonably incurred preparation costs; but (b) *Practice Statement (Judicial Review: Costs)* [2004] 1 W.L.R. 1760 should be read so as to exclude

represented, PD 54A discourages the court from making a costs order against the unsuccessful claimant in relation to attendance at the hearing, except in exceptional circumstances.[325] The court should make a summary assessment of costs at the conclusion of the permission hearing.[326] The rationale for this approach is that to require claimants who fail at a hearing to bear the entire defendant's cost would risk discouraging claimants from seeking justice.

Where the claimant is granted permission, the costs will be costs in the case unless the judge granting permission makes a different order.[327]   **16-099**

The Court of Appeal has at least three times urged the Rules Committee to provide a specific rule or practice direction governing the procedure for applications for costs at the permission stage, and the principles to be applied—and in the meantime suggested a practice to be followed.[328]   **16-100**

Costs when a claim is discontinued after permission

A significant number of claims are withdrawn between the grant of permission and the full hearing.[329] Where a claim for judicial review is withdrawn because the defendant concedes the merits after the grant of permission,[330] the claimant is   **16-101**

---

any costs of opposing the grant of permission in open court, which should be dealt with on the *Mount Cook* principles: at [21]. In *R. (on the application of Smoke Club Ltd) v Network Rail Infrastructure Ltd* [2013] EWHC 3830 (Admin); [2014] 2 Costs L.O. 123, the Administrative Court declined to follow the usual rules on costs after discontinuance in CPR r.38.6(1) on the basis that special considerations apply to judicial review cases. The court awarded the defendant a proportion of their costs after the Acknowledgement of Service to reflect the fact that the claimant had renewed a hopeless claim and produced fresh evidence which put the defendant to additional expense before the claim was withdrawn.

[325] PD 54A, para.8.6; in *Mount Cook Ltd* [2003] EWCA Civ 1346; [2004] C.P. Rep. 12 a "non-exhaustive list" of exceptional circumstances was provided at [76]: (a) the hopelessness of the claim; (b) the persistence in it by the claimant after having been alerted to facts and/or of the law demonstrating its hopelessness; (c) the extent to which the court considers that the claimant, in the pursuit of his application, has sought to abuse the process of judicial review for collateral ends—a relevant consideration as to costs at the permission stage, as well as when considering discretionary refusal of relief at the stage of substantive hearing, if there is one; and (d) whether, as a result of the deployment of full argument and documentary evidence by both sides at the hearing of a contested application [for permission], the unsuccessful claimant has had, in effect, the advantage of an early substantive hearing of the claim. The defendant was not entitled to the costs of the Acknowledgement of Service where it had been submitted late (*Riniker v Employment Tribunals and Regional Chairmen* [2009] EWCA Civ 1450 at [29]). The Government proposes to invite the Civil Procedure Rule Committee to introduce a principle that the defendant's costs of attending an oral permission hearing should usually be recoverable from the claimant (see para.1-006).

[326] *Payne v Caerphilly CBC (Costs)* [2004] EWCA Civ 433.

[327] *Practice Statement (QBD (Admin Ct): Judicial Review: Costs)* [2004] 1 W.L.R. 1760.

[328] In *Mount Cook* [2003] EWCA Civ 1346; [2004] C.P. Rep. 12 and *R. (on the application of Ewing) v Office of the Deputy Prime Minister* [2005] EWCA Civ 1583; [2006] 1 W.L.R. 1260 at [47] (Carnwath LJ): "(i) Where a proposed defendant or interested party wishes to seek costs at the permission stage, the Acknowledgement of Service should include an application for costs and should be accompanied by a Schedule setting out the amount claimed; (ii) The judge refusing permission should include in the refusal a decision whether to award costs in principle, and (if so) an indication of the amount which he proposes to assess summarily; (iii) The claimant should be given 14 days to respond in writing and should serve a copy on the defendant. (iv) The defendant will have 7 days to reply in writing to any such response, and to the amount proposed by the judge; (v) The judge will then decide and make an award on the papers". See also *Morgan v Hinton Organics (Wessex) Ltd* [2009] EWCA Civ 107; [2009] C.P. Rep. 26 at [36] (where a more "flexible" approach was favoured).

[329] See 16-048.

[330] On permission, see 16-044.

entitled to his costs in the usual way unless there is a good reason to the contrary.[331] The outcome will be different if the claimant does not obtain all of the relief sought on settlement. In such cases, it may be appropriate to make no order as to costs unless it is tolerably clear who would have won if the matter had proceeded to a hearing. If it is reasonably clear who would have won, that party may be entitled to some of their costs.[332]

Costs after the full hearing

16-102   Costs following a full hearing of a claim for judicial review will generally be awarded to the successful party. In some circumstances, however, it may be inappropriate for the unsuccessful claimant to be ordered to meet the defendant's costs, where the claim was brought not with view to personal gain and there was a wider public interest involved.[333] Costs of the successful party may be limited to some of the issues argued. In claims where there is more than one defendant or interested

---

[331] *R. (on the application of Bahta) v Secretary of State for the Home Department* [2011] EWCA Civ 895; [2001] C.P. Rep. 43 at [59], [64]–[68]. The CA there considered it necessary, in light of the importance of the Pre-action Protocol, to modify the less generous approach to awarding costs set out in *R. (on the application of Boxall) v Waltham Forest LBC* (2001) 4 C.C.L. Rep. 258 at [22] where it was suggested that the default position was that no order should be made. In *R (on the application of M) v Croydon LBC* [2012] EWCA Civ 595; [2012] 1 W.L.R. 2607 at [52]–[61], the CA demolished a number of the arguments often relied on to refuse to award costs against a public authority which concedes a judicial review claim (that it might discourage public authorities from settling, that the short time limit for judicial review does not give public authorities sufficient time to consider their position and that defendants sometimes concede claims for pragmatic reasons). The CA was also keen to encourage parties to agree an order as to costs as part of the settlement rather than requiring the court to decide the issue. *R. (on the application of M)* was applied in *R. (on the application of E) v Croydon LBC* [2015] EWHC 2016 (Admin) (a compromise agreement was reached at the substantive hearing; the LBC was ordered to pay half the claimant's costs, taking into account that the claimant had a "very strong moral claim but a much less strong legal claim") and in *R. (on the application of Baxter) v Lincolnshire County Council* [2015] EWCA Civ 1290; [2016] 1 Costs L.O. 37 at [40]–[45] (a claimant failed to establish a clear enough link between the relief sought in the claim and the consent order to be treated as the successful party for the purpose of costs, the claim falling within the third type of case identified by Lord Neuberger MR in *M* at [7], i.e. "a case where there has been some compromise which does not actually reflect the claimant's claims"). *R. (on the application of Bahta)* and *R. (on the application of M)* were distinguished in *R. (on the application of Abraha) v Secretary of State for the Home Department (Costs)* [2014] EWHC 3372 (Admin) (judicial review of allegedly unlawful detention in which the claimant was released on the day of his substantive hearing; costs were refused on the basis that there had been no trial or similar substantive determination by a court of law, nor a consent order or settlement). In *R. (on the application of Tesfay) v Secretary of State for the Home Department* [2016] EWCA Civ 415; [2016] 1 W.L.R. 4853 at [56]–[64] (a case regarding the Secretary of State's withdrawal of human rights certification decisions and settlement of related claims), the CA held that the judge below should have approached the matter by asking two questions: (a) whether the effect of the settlement was that the appellants should be regarded as having succeeded so that they should normally receive their costs; and (b) if so, whether there was a good reason for making a different order. It was appropriate to consider why the Secretary of State withdrew the decisions. The claimant is unlikely to recover his costs if he has failed to comply with the Pre-action Protocol (*R. (on the application of Kemp) v Denbighshire Local Health Board* [2006] EWHC 181 (Admin); [2007] 1 W.L.R. 639 at [75]).

[332] *M* [2012] EWCA Civ 595; [2012] 1 W.L.R. 2607 at [62]-[65]. In M's case, the court awarded the claimant all of his costs from the date of issue of the proceedings, but only half of those before permission was granted as the law was changed as a result of a decision of the SC. See further *R. (on the application of E) v Croydon LBC* [2015] EWHC 2016 (Admin) (fn.310). There is new Guidance for judicial review cases in which the parties have agreed to settle the claim but are unable to agree liability for costs and have submitted that issue for determination by the court: *https://www.justice.gov.uk/downloads/courts/administrative-court/aco-costs-guidance-dec-13.pdf* [XXXLINK not valid].

[333] See, e.g. *R. v Secretary of State for the Environment, Transport and the Regions Ex p. Challenger* [2001] Env. L.R. 12; cf. *R. (on the application of Smeaton) v Secretary of State for Health (Costs)*

party, an unsuccessful claimant will normally be ordered to pay only one set of costs.[334] Neither the Administrative Court nor the Court of Appeal has jurisdiction to award costs out of public funds to the successful party.[335]

[2002] EWHC 886 (Admin); [2002] 2 F.L.R. 146 at [11] (Society for the Protection of Unborn Children, represented by Smeaton, ordered to pay costs of challenge to legality of the "morning after pill"—this was not a matter of public concern until the proceedings were commenced by the Society).

[334] *Corner House Research* [2005] EWCA Civ 192; [2005] 1 W.L.R. 2600 at [24].

[335] *Holden & Co v Crown Prosecution Service (No.2)* [1994] 1 A.C. 22. See also *R. (on the application of Henderson) v Secretary of State for Justice* [2015] EWHC 130 (Admin); [2015] 1 Cr. App. R. 29 at [35]–[38].

CHAPTER 17

Other Judicial Review Proceedings

TABLE OF CONTENTS

SCOPE

In addition to claims for judicial review under CPR Pt 54,[1] several other **17-001** procedures exist through which the Administrative Court exercises its supervisory jurisdiction and the Upper Tribunal may now hear judicial reviews in certain circumstances. This chapter addresses the following[2]:

- Judicial review and tribunals;
- Judicial reviews under the Public Contract Regulations 2015;
- Applications for the writ of habeas corpus for release under CPR Pt 87[3];
- Applications under CPR Pt 8 to quash certain orders, etc. of ministers, tribunals and other bodies made under particular statutes and statutory instruments[4];
- Appeals to the High Court from criminal courts[5];

---

[1] See Ch.16.

[2] See also C. Lewis, *Judicial Remedies in Public Law*, 5th edn (2014), Ch.13 (habeas corpus) (although published prior to the introduction of CPR Pt 87) and Ch.14 (appeals and statutory applications).

[3] See 17-008. CPR Pt 87 replaces RSC Ord.54, part of the old Rules of the Supreme Court which had been preserved in Sch.1 to the CPR (revoked by the Civil Procedure (Amendment No.8) Rules 2014/ 3299). Although the term "habeas corpus" is retained, its three forms are renamed "for release", "to give evidence", and "to answer a charge" (formerly ad subjiciendum, ad testificandum and ad respondendum respectively). Applications for habeas corpus heard since the introduction of Pt 87 include *Tague v Governor of HM Prison Full Sutton and National Crime Agency* [2015] EWHC 3576 (Admin); [2016] 1 Cr. App. R. 15; *Harkins v United States* [2015] EWHC 2336 (Admin) and *R. (on the application of Freeman) v Director of Thameside Prison* [2015] EWHC 1569 (Admin).

[4] See 17-024.

[5] See 17-036.

- Applications to quash certain decisions of coroners, under the Coroners Act 1988 s.13.[6]

17-002 Beyond the Administrative Court, a number of other courts apply judicial review principles, including county courts in relation to decisions of local authorities relating to homelessness under the Housing Act 1996[7] and the Upper Tribunal (which is a superior court of record).[8] Except for a much-criticised anomaly in relation to habeas corpus,[9] the grounds of review or appeal in each of these proceedings are essentially the same as those available in CPR Pt 54 judicial review claims.[10] Where one of these procedures is relevant to an aggrieved person's circumstances, he is expected to use that procedure rather than make a CPR Pt 54 judicial review claim. This is so even if the governing legislation does not expressly oust the jurisdiction of the court to hear a CPR Pt 54 claim because the court is likely to exercise its discretion and apply the general principle that judicial review is a matter of last resort and cannot be used where a reasonably satisfactory alternative remedy exists.[11]

17-003 The justifications for having a range of judicial review and appeal procedures in addition to CPR Pt 54 is explained in two main ways. First, by the forces of inertia. There is no doubt that several of the procedures could usefully be assimilated into CPR Pt 54 and indeed this has been proposed in relation to some of them. As things stand, several of the procedures languish in the backwaters of Sch.1 to the CPR, where a handful of former Rules of the Supreme Court (RSC)[12] still remain awaiting attention. However, the list is now somewhat vestigial. Habeas corpus was removed in 2014 and has now found its place in the CPR. A second explanation is a functional one. The standard judicial review procedure has been found to be inadequate for dealing with the needs of claimants and defendants in some contexts or the pure number of applications has created pressure to remove certain jurisdictions from the already heavily-burdened Administrative Court. In relation to immigration and asylum matters, the perceived need for expedition and finality of litigation has been given priority by modifications to the standard procedure. In relation to some planning, compulsory purchase and regulatory decisions, the need for a speedy resolution to doubts about legality has been accommodated in a special procedure. In relation to homelessness decisions, the need for cheaper, more accessible local justice has prevailed over preserving the High Court's monopoly over the grounds and remedies of judicial review.

---

6 See 17-037.
7 See 17-040.
8 See 17-006 and 1-101.
9 See 17-015.
10 On the assimilation of the grounds of review irrespective of the procedure by which they reach the High Court, see *E v Secretary of State for the Home Department* [2004] EWCA Civ 49; [2004] Q.B. 1044 at [42] (Carnwath LJ: "… in spite of the differences in history and wording, the various procedures have evolved to the point where it has become a generally safe working rule that the substantive grounds for intervention are identical"); *R. v Inland Revenue Commissioners Ex p. Preston* [1985] A.C. 835; *Chief Adjudication Officer v Foster* [1993] A.C. 754.
11 See 16-014.
12 The procedural code that governed practice in the High Court and the Court of Appeal before the introduction of the CPR in 1998.

JUDICIAL REVIEW AND TRIBUNALS[13]

The Tribunals, Courts and Enforcement Act 2007 establishes the First-tier **17-004**
Tribunal and the Upper Tribunal, each organised in "chambers", to which the
jurisdiction of most (but not all) previously existing tribunals will be transferred.[14]
In order to avoid the need for an appeal when it seems clear something has gone
wrong, both the First-tier Tribunal and Upper Tribunal have discretion to review
their own decisions (either on their own motion or on the application of a party),
subject to the Tribunal Procedure Rules.[15] There are two additional ways of challenging a decision: appeal and judicial review.

The new regime provides a uniform system for appeals, all subject to a permis- **17-005**
sion requirement. An appellant may appeal on a point of law from the First-tier
Tribunal to the Upper Tribunal (which is a superior court of record) except from
an "excluded decision".[16] If an appeal is successful, the Upper Tribunal may set
aside the decision of the First-tier Tribunal and either remit the matter back for
reconsideration or re-make the decision itself. From the Upper Tribunal (except in
relation to "excluded decisions"), an appeal on point of law will lie, with permission from either body, to the Court of Appeal.[17]

---

[13] On tribunals, see 1-098.

[14] See 1-101. The Asylum and Immigration Tribunal has now been abolished and its functions
transferred to the First-tier Tribunal (Transfer of Functions of the Asylum and Immigration Tribunal
Order 2010/21, art.2). In 2012, 85% of applications for permission to apply for judicial review
concerned immigration or asylum matters: over 10,000 applications were received, 31% of which
were found to be totally without merit (Ministry of Justice, *Court Statistics Quarterly July to
September 2013*, pp.29–34). In November 2013, the Upper Tribunal (Immigration and Asylum
Chamber) took responsibility for the majority of civil asylum and immigration judicial reviews. The
effect was dramatic: reducing the number of applications from 16,000 before the transfer to around
4,000 in the following year (Ministry of Justice, *Civil Justice Statistics Quarterly, England and
Wales, January to March 2017 (provisional) and Royal Courts of Justice 2016* (1 June 2017)). R.
Thomas, "Mapping Immigration Judicial Review Litigation: An Empirical Legal Analysis" [2015]
P.L. 652. For a more detailed account of the law and practice in this field, see I. Macdonald and R.
Toal (eds), *Macdonald's Immigration Law and Practice*, 9th edn (2014). See A. Le Sueur, "Three
strikes and it's out? The UK government's strategy to oust judicial review from immigration and
asylum decision-making" [2004] P.L. 225. An enlightening account of the development of tribunals
is provided in S. Sedley, *Lions Under The Throne: Essays on the History of English Public Law*
(2015), Ch.13.

[15] Tribunal, Courts and Enforcement Act 2007 ss.9-10.

[16] Tribunal, Courts and Enforcement Act 2007 s.11(5). The Lord Chancellor may by Order add to the
list of excluded decisions and has done in the Appeals (Excluded Decisions) Order 2009/275. The
list of "excluded decisions" has also been expanded by s.48(4), Sch.2, para.5 of the Crime and
Security Act 2010, and s.116 of the Tax Collection and Management (Wales) Act 2016 (not yet in
force).

[17] Tribunal, Courts and Enforcement Act 2007 s.13. Permission will only granted where the proposed
appeal raises some important point of principle or practice or where there is some other compelling
reason for the Court of Appeal to hear the case (Appeals from the Upper Tribunal to the Court of
Appeal Order 2008. *FA (Iraq) v Secretary of State for the Home Department* [2010] EWCA Civ 827
at [1]). The Upper Tribunal cannot review its own decision to refuse permission to appeal and the
only remedy in such cases is for the party aggrieved to seek judicial review of the Upper Tribunal's
refusal (*Samuda v Secretary of State for Work and Pensions* [2014] EWCA Civ 1; [2014] 3 All E.R.
201 at [13]). Section 64 of the Criminal Justice and Courts Act 2015 (in force from 8 August 2016)
inserts new ss.14A–14C into the Tribunals, Courts and Enforcement Act 2007, with the effect of allowing leapfrog appeals to the SC to be initiated in the Upper Tribunal under the same conditions
as appeals from the High Court. See the Explanatory Note to the Criminal Justice and Courts Act
2015 paras 520–524.

Judicial review in the Upper Tribunal

17-006   The Upper Tribunal has limited jurisdiction to deal with claims for "judicial review" (the inverted commas are used in the Act).[18] In these cases, the Upper Tribunal may grant the same judicial review remedies as the High Court.[19] Section 31A of the Senior Courts Act 1981 sets out the circumstances in which judicial review claims can be transferred to the Upper Tribunal.[20] The procedure governing such challenges in terms of permission, standing and time limits is substantially

---

[18]   Tribunal, Courts and Enforcement Act 2007 ss.15–18. For Scotland, see ss.20-21 and *Eba v Advocate General for Scotland* [2011] UKSC 29; [2012] 1 A.C. 710. On appeal from decisions of the Upper Tribunal in cases involving judicial review of First-tier Tribunal decisions, the appellate court should exercise restraint and permit flexibility to the Upper Tribunal to develop guidance on the specialised area of law concerned in order to promote consistency (*R. (on the application of Jones) v First-tier Tribunal* [2013] UKSC 19; [2013] 2 A.C. 48 at [26], [41]–[43], followed in *Criminal Injuries Compensation Authority v First-tier Tribunal (Social Entitlement Chamber)* [2014] EWCA Civ 1554; [2015] Q.B. 459; *BPP Holdings Ltd v Revenue and Customs Commissioners* [2017] UKSC 55; [2017] 1 W.L.R. 2945 at [33]–[34]; and *Criminal Injuries Compensation Authority v Hutton* [2016] EWCA Civ 1305 at [57]–[58]. See also the comments of Lord Carnwath in *Pendragon Plc v Revenue and Customs Commissioners* [2015] UKSC 37; [2015] 1 W.L.R. 2838 at [44]–[51], a case in which the First-tier Tribunal had failed to ask itself the critical question (which was whether certain of the steps in a series of transactions had any purpose save to produce a tax advantage) and hence had made an error of law which should be corrected on appeal.

[19]   Tribunal, Courts and Enforcement Act 2007 ss.15(1) and 16(6). In deciding whether to grant relief, the Upper Tribunal must apply the same principles as the High Court. Where permission to bring judicial review proceedings has been refused by the Upper Tribunal and permission to appeal has been refused by the Upper Tribunal, an application for permission to appeal may be made to the Court of Appeal. The appellant's notice must be filed within 28 days of the date on which notice of the Upper Tribunal's decision on permission to appeal is sent to the appellant: CPR r.52.15A, added by Civil Procedure (Amendment No.6) Rules 2014 (SI 2014/2044) with effect from 1 October 2014, and PD 52D para.3.3. In considering out of time applications for reconsideration of a refusal of permission to seek judicial review by the Upper Tribunal, the court should adopt the approach in relief from sanctions cases and consider: (i) the seriousness and significance of the failure; (ii) why the default occurred; and (iii) all the circumstances of the case (*R. (on the application of Kigen) v Secretary of State for the Home Department (Practice Note)* [2015] EWCA Civ 1286; [2016] 1 W.L.R.723 at [20]). The Upper Tribunal has produced its own Judicial Review standard forms for statements of case (and guidance on them), which are available at http://www.justice.gov.uk/ tribunals/immigration-asylum-upper/application-for-judicial-review [Accessed 9 November 2017]. The Upper Tribunal has also produced guideline judgments on, for example, how it will deal with immigration judicial reviews where the Secretary of State has failed to submit an Acknowledgement of Service within the time limit required by the Tribunal Procedure (Upper Tribunal) Rules 2008 (*R. (on the application of Kumar) v Secretary of State for the Home Department* [2014] UKUT 104 (IAC)). See the additional guideline judgments on the claimant's continuing duty to re-assess the claim in light of developments (*R. (on the application of Mahmood) v Secretary of State for the Home Department* [2014] UKUT 439 (IAC); [2015] Imm. A.R. 193), on the generally unjustifiable incorporation of a claim for costs in an Acknowledgment of Service which contains a concession (*Muwonge v Secretary of State for the Home Department* [2014] UKUT 514 (IAC); [2015] Imm. A.R. 341), and on appealing costs orders of the Upper Tribunal made in immigration judicial review proceedings (*R. (on the application of Soreefan and others) v Secretary of State for the Home Department* [2015] UKUT 594 (IAC)).

[20]   In outline, they are: the application does not seek relief beyond the ordinary judicial review remedies; does not question anything done by the Crown Court; and falls within a class specified by the Lord Chief Justice. Section 31A of the Senior Courts Act 1981 provides for mandatory transfer if all three conditions are met. The Lord Chief Justice has so far identified the following such classes of case: decisions of the First-tier Tribunal on an appeal under the Criminal Injuries Compensation Scheme; where the First-tier Tribunal has declined to review one of its decisions and there is no right of appeal (Practice Direction (Upper Tribunal: Judicial Review Jurisdiction) [2009] 1 W.L.R. 327); and, as of 1 November 2013, any decision made under the Immigration Acts or otherwise relating to leave to enter or remain in the UK outside the immigration rules and a decision of the Immigration and Asylum Chamber of the First-tier Tribunal from which no appeal lies to the Upper Tribunal (except where the application includes: a challenge to the validity of primary or subordinate legislation; a

the same as the High Court.[21] The Upper Tribunal is a superior court of record and so will not be amenable to judicial review in cases where there is no appeal unless there is arguably an error of law in the decisions of both Tribunals and the above criteria for a second-tier appeal are made out.[22]

PUBLIC CONTRACT JUDICIAL REVIEWS

In some cases where a decision under the Public Contract Regulations 2015 is challenged, claimants may issue a claim for judicial review in the Administrative Court along with proceedings in the Technology and Construction Court (TCC). Such should generally proceed before the TCC before a judge who is also designated to sit in the Administrative Court.[23] Claimants should request transfer to the TCC by letter to the Administrative Court Office at the time of issuing the claim. **17-007**

HABEAS CORPUS

The unlawful deprivation or significant curtailment[24] of a person's liberty by a public authority have long been recognised as a constitutional as well as a legal wrong. In modern times, this fundamental right is given expression in ECHR art.5 **17-008**

---

challenge to the lawfulness of detention; a challenge to a decision on citizenship; a challenge to a decision of the Upper Tribunal; an application for a declaration of incompatibility under the HRA (and certain other matters specified in the Direction) (Direction given in accordance with Pt 1 of Sch.2 to the Constitutional Reform Act 2005 and s.18 of the Tribunals, Courts and Enforcement Act 2007, 21 August 2013). In *Ashraf v Secretary of State for the Home Department* [2013] EWHC 4028 (Admin) at [2], the court indicated that it may well be treated as an abuse of process to issue judicial review proceedings challenging removal in the Administrative Court on the basis of an unmeritorious claim of unlawful detention. The most recent statistics (for April to June 2017) show that 2,600 immigration and judicial review applications were issued. In the same period, the UT disposed of 3,182 applications: 7% of which were granted permission on paper; a further 197 were granted permission on oral reconsideration; and 78 reached a substantive hearing (in which the claimant succeeded in 38% of cases) (Ministry of Justice, *Tribunal and Gender Recognition Statistics Quarterly, April to June 2017* (Provisional) (14 September 2017)).

[21] Tribunal, Courts and Enforcement Act 2007 s.16. In relation to "fresh claims", the Upper Tribunal has produced its own Practice Directions (http://judiciary.gov.uk/publications [Accessed 9 November 2017]).

[22] *R. (on the application of Cart) v Upper Tribunal* [2011] UKSC 28; [2012] 1 A.C. 663 at [51]-[57]. In *Cart* itself, there was felt to be nothing exceptional which would justify permitting a judicial review to proceed. A new CPR rule 54.7A was introduced with effect from 1 October 2012 in relation to applications for judicial review of decisions of the Upper Tribunal to refuse permission to appeal. The new rule requires that a claim form and the supporting documents (essentially the First Tier Tribunal's and Upper Tribunal's decision refusing permission and the grounds of appeal to the Upper Tribunal) be filed within 16 days of the decision refusing permission to appeal and be served seven days thereafter. If permission to apply for judicial review is refused on the papers, there is no power to apply for reconsideration at a hearing. E. Laurie, "Assessing the Upper Tribunal's Potential to Deliver Administrative Justice" [2012] P.L. 288 and M. Elliott and R. Thomas, "Tribunal Justice, Cart, and Proportionate Dispute Resolution" [2012] C.L.J. 297.

[23] The Administrative Court, *Judicial Review Guide 2017* (July 2017) at [5.7].

[24] Total incarceration is not necessary: *Re SA (Vulnerable Adult with Capacity: Marriage)* [2005] EWHC 2942 (Fam), [2006] 1 F.L.R. 867 at [54] and [71] (Munby J: "a means of ascertaining whether someone is in fact being kept confined, controlled, coerced or under restraint"). The habeas corpus jurisdiction exists in parallel to the court's inherent jurisdiction to deal with those who are vulnerable but fall outside the Mental Capacity Act 2005: *Re L (Vulnerable Adults with Capacity (No.2))* [2012] EWCA Civ 253; [2013] Fam. 1 at [52]-[68].

which guarantees the right to liberty and security of the person.[25] In the past in England and Wales the prerogative writ of habeas corpus *ad subjiciendum* was one of the principal means for securing the release of a person unlawfully detained.[26] Indeed, earlier editions of this book described habeas corpus as "the most renowned contribution of the English common law to the protection of human liberty".[27] Until the recent introduction of new Pt 87 into the CPR in April 2015, the procedure for obtaining habeas corpus had been left to languish in the backwater of Sch.1 to the CPR. Perhaps in part because of this, the number of applications for habeas corpus has declined.[28] There is doubt about the scope of review.[29] Moreover, habeas corpus has more than once been found by the European Court of Human Rights to be an inadequate remedy because it fails to provide the court with sufficiently intensive powers to review the factual basis or judgments upon which detention has been ordered.[30]

17-009   There are, however, still situations where habeas corpus provides an appropriate procedure for dealing with unlawful confinement[31] (though in most circumstances comparable relief could be obtained by means of a claim for judicial review

---

[25]   See 13-072. There was a violation of art.5(4) in a case where the detained individual lacked capacity to instruct a lawyer to seek a remedy and where her nearest relative was barred from doing so (*MH v UK* (2014) 58 E.H.R.R. 35).

[26]   D. Clark and G. McCoy, *The Most Fundamental Legal Right: Habeas Corpus in the Commonwealth* (2000); R.J. Sharpe, J. Farbey and S. Atrill, *The Law of Habeas Corpus*, 3rd edn (2011); A.P. Le Sueur, "Should the Writ of Habeas Corpus be Abolished?" [1992] P.L. 13; M. Shrimpton, "In Defence of Habeas Corpus" [1993] P.L. 24; Law Com. No.226 (1994), Part XI. P.D. Halliday, *Habeas Corpus: From England to Empire* (2010) (reviewed by T. Bingham, "Habeas Corpus" in T. Bingham, *Lives of the Law: Selected Essays and Speeches 2000-2010* (2011)). The US Supreme Court analysed the history of habeas corpus in *Boumediene et al v Bush*, 476 F. 3d 981 and noted that it was one of the few guarantees of liberty included in the Constitution before the Bill of Rights was adopted.

[27]   J. Evans, *De Smith: Judicial Review of Administrative Action*, 4th edn (1980), p.596. And see *A v Secretary of State for the Home Department* [2005] UKHL 71; [2006] 2 A.C. 221 at [83] (Lord Hoffmann: "the writ of habeas corpus is not only a special (and nowadays infrequent) remedy for challenging unlawful detention but also carries a symbolic significance as a touchstone of English liberty which influences the rest of our law").

[28]   In 2011 the Administrative Court received 29 applications for habeas corpus, of which only one was determined, (Ministry of Justice, *Judicial and Court Statistics* 2011, Table 7.14). In 1998 there were 66 applications, of which 54 were determined. This may, at least in part, have been the result of the introduction of the new appeal procedures in the Extradition Act 2003.

[29]   See 17-015.

[30]   *X v United Kingdom* (1982) 4 E.H.R.R. 188 at [58] (Home Secretary released X, sent him to Broadmoor Hospital following an act of violence on conditional discharge and later recalled him. Habeas corpus did not enable "a court to examine whether the patient's disorder still persisted and whether the Home Secretary was entitled to think that a continuation of the compulsory confinement was necessary in the interest of public safety"); *HL v United Kingdom* (2005) 40 E.H.R.R. 32 (L, an autistic man incapable of consenting to medical treatment, was detained in hospital outside the statutory powers of compulsory detention; held that habeas corpus was not an adequate remedy as it did not allow for the resolution of complaints on the basis of incorrect diagnoses and judgments). See also *R. (on the application of CA (Nigeria)) v Secretary of State for the Home Department* [2011] EWCA Civ 1144 at [18]–[20] (applicant was not granted a stay of the order removing him from the United Kingdom pending determination of his habeas corpus petition because the lawfulness of his removal was a technical point, and if oral evidence were required it could be given by video link).

[31]   An example of the modern relevance of the writ is *Rahmatullah v Secretary of State for Foreign and Commonwealth Affairs* [2012] UKSC 48; [2013] 1 A.C. 614: the fact that the defendant does not have physical custody of the detainee is not fatal. Habeas corpus could be granted to require the Secretary of State to request the return of the claimant to his custody from detention by the United States, but the Secretary of State's response (that the United States asserted that the claimant's detention was lawful) was sufficient. The case concerned a Pakistani national who was captured by British forces in Iraq and handed over the United States who detained him at the Bagram airbase in Afghanistan.

under CPR Pt 54). Among the strengths of the remedy is that it is available as of right and, in contrast to the remedies available in judicial review, a remedy may not be withheld on grounds of public policy.[32] The Extradition Act 2003 provides for an appeal from decisions of district judges to the High Court and this ousts the jurisdiction of the Administrative Court to hear habeas corpus applications except for in exceptional cases.[33] The other main areas are immigration, asylum and mental health.[34]

It is not appropriate to apply for habeas corpus: in relation to children placed into **17-010** the care of a local authority[35]; to challenge a committal order in contempt of court proceedings, whether civil or criminal[36]; or as a way of appealing against conviction or sentence passed by a court of competent jurisdiction.[37] The general rule is that habeas corpus does not issue as a penalty for unlawful detention which has been discontinued.[38]

The need, now as in the past, is for a fast and effective method for challenging **17-011** cases of alleged unlawful detention. Applications for habeas corpus are sometimes said to have the advantage that they take priority over all other court business— though there is provision for handling urgent claims for judicial review under CPR Pt 54.[39] There have been calls for habeas corpus to be incorporated into the standard judicial review procedure, so that it would become a remedy at the disposal of the court on CPR Pt 54 judicial review claim without the need for a separate set of court

---

[32] *Rahmatullah* [2012] UKSC 48; [2013] 1 A.C. 614 at [41]. The SC rejected the argument that because judicial review would not be available of the Secretary of State's conduct of the foreign relations power, habeas corpus should equally be unavailable (*Rahmatullah* at [71]–[74]).

[33] *Hilali v Governor of Whitemoor Prison* [2008] UKHL 3; [2008] 1 A.C. 805 at [40]. An exceptional case may arise where there has been a fundamental change of circumstances in the course of the extradition process and the detention has become unlawful. Habeas corpus may also be available in relation to preliminary aspects of the extradition process which are not covered by the statutory right of appeal: *Nikonovs v Governor of Brixton Prison* [2005] EWHC 2405 (Admin); [2006] 1 W.L.R. 1518.

[34] See, e.g. *R. (on the application of T-T) v Royal Park Centre Hospital Managers* [2003] EWCA Civ 330; [2003] 1 W.L.R. 1272. See also *K v Kingswood Centre Hospital Manager* [2014] EWCA Civ 1332; [2015] P.T.S.R. 287.

[35] *S v Haringey LBC (Habeas Corpus)* [2003] EWHC 2734 (Admin); [2004] 1 F.L.R. 590. Note that where an application is made involving a child in custody it should be made to the Family Division not the Administrative Court: SCA 1981, Sch.1, para.3.

[36] See *Linnett v Coles* [1987] Q.B. 555; *Re Scriven* [2004] EWCA Civ 543; (2004) 148 S.J.L.B. 511. The person should instead appeal against the finding of contempt.

[37] *Re Wring* [1960] 1 W.L.R. 138; *Re Corke* [1954] 1 W.L.R. 899. And see *Wells v Parole Board; Walker v Secretary of State for the Home Department* [2009] UKHL 22; [2010] 1 A.C. 553 at [5] (Lord Hope of Craighead: "As Simon Brown LJ said in *R. v Oldham Justices Ex p. Cawley* [1997] Q.B. 1, 13, where there has been a criminal conviction the courts have firmly excluded collateral attack by habeas corpus, holding that the only proper remedy lies by way of appeal. Sentences of imprisonment for public protection are sentences for an indefinite period, subject to the provisions of Ch II of Pt II of the Crime (Sentences) Act 1997 as to the release of prisoners and duration of licences: Criminal Justice Act 2003 s.225(4). There is no entitlement to release until release has been directed by the Parole Board, and a direction to that effect cannot be given until the Board is satisfied that detention is no longer necessary for the protection of the public. Mandatory orders may be obtained to ensure that the system works properly. But it is not open to the courts to set that system aside by directing release contrary to the provisions of the statute"). This outcome is unaffected by the decision of the ECtHR in *James, Lee and Wells v UK* (2013) 56 E.H.R.R. 12. In *Thomas v Secretary of State for Justice* [2016] EWCA Civ 1389, the CA upheld the HC's refusal of an application for habeas corpus by an individual detained and refused bail pending his trial, holding that the magistrates' decision to detain should be challenged by way of judicial review.

[38] *Barnardo v Ford* [1892] A.C. 326 (where a writ was nevertheless issued so that further inquiries could be pursued).

[39] See 16-042; alternatively the claimant may seek an order for release in habeas corpus proceedings and then seek damages for unlawful detention in judicial review proceedings under CPR Part 54, see *TTM v Hackney LBC* [2011] EWCA Civ 4; [2011] 1 W.L.R. 2873.

procedures.[40] The Law Commission rejected this idea in 1994[41] and following consultation in 2003 the Lord Chancellor decided reform was not needed,[42] partly because of the dwindling number of applications. However, although habeas corpus still forms no part of CPR Pt 54, it has now been incorporated into the CPR proper. CPR Pt 87 was inserted by the Civil Procedure (Amendment No.8) Rules 2014 (SI 2014/3299), in force 6 April 2015, replacing RSC Ord.54, as "part of the ongoing work of the CPR Committee to transfer the remaining Rules of the Supreme Court into the CPR."[43]

Standing and capacity

17-012 The application must be made by or with the concurrence of the detainee, unless he is held incommunicado[44] or is incapable in law or in fact of consenting to the institution of the proceedings. In child custody cases, the claimant may be a parent, guardian, next friend, local authority or possibly the Official Solicitor. Habeas corpus is not limited to British nationals; every person within the jurisdiction is entitled to equal protection.[45] In the past, prisoners of war and enemy aliens were thought to be unable to make applications for habeas corpus,[46] but this was not because of any lack of standing to do so but because the legality of their detention could not be challenged as they were detained under the royal prerogative; this will no longer give rise to difficulties as prerogative actions are now reviewable.[47] It can be expected that the court will usually be much more concerned with the merits of the application than technical questions of standing. It is suggested that the approach should be at least as flexible and liberal as the current approach to standing in claims for judicial review.[48]

Defendants

17-013 The defendant will normally be the person having actual custody of the person detained, for example, a prison governor. In special cases the person who had custody of the detainee but has lost it temporarily in circumstances where he may

---

[40] Le Sueur [1992] P.L. 13; Sir Simon Brown, "Habeas Corpus: a New Chapter" [2000] P.L. 31; *B v Barking, Havering and Brentwood Community Healthcare NHS Trust* [1999] 1 F.L.R. 106 at 117 (Lord Woolf MR).

[41] Law Com. No.126, paras 11.5–11.9.

[42] LCD, "Response to the Consultation Paper 'The Administrative Court: Proposed Changes to the Primary Legislation following Sir Jeffrey Bowman's *Review of the Crown Office List*" (October 2003).

[43] Explanatory Memorandum to the Civil Procedure (Amendment No.8) Rules 2014/3299 (L.36)). The associated Practice Direction—RSC 54 (Application for Writ of Habeas Corpus) was not replicated; there is presently no Practice Direction supplementing CPR Pt 87. Since, according to CPR Update 78 (25 April 2015, accessible at: https://www.justice.gov.uk/courts/procedure-rules/civil [Accessed 9 November 2017]), the intention in modifying the rules was "to update the language and to reflect the process in the Administrative Court which deals with such applications"; it is suggested that the existing authorities will still apply in the context of the new rules.

[44] *Ex p. Child* (1854) 15 C.B. 238; *Re SA (Vulnerable Adult with Capacity: Marriage)* [2005] EWHC 2942 (Fam); [2006] 1 F.L.R. 867 at [46]. The CA has explained that the purpose of the requirement that the application be made at the instance of the person detained is to keep within bounds the right of a stranger to apply for habeas corpus (*Justice for Families Ltd v Secretary of State for Justice* [2014] EWCA Civ 1477).

[45] *R. v Secretary of State for the Home Department Ex p. Khawaja* [1984] A.C. 74 at 111.

[46] *R. v Vine Street Police Station Supt Ex p. Liebmann* [1916] 1 K.B. 268; *R. v Knockaloe Camp Commandant Ex p. Foreman* (1917) 87 L J.K.B. 43; *R. v Bottrill Ex p. Kuechenmeister* [1947] K.B. 41.

[47] See 3-038.

[48] See Ch.2.

be able to resume control may be the only proper defendant.[49] Although, if possible, notice should always be served on the custodian there is no reason of principle why it should not also be served on a minister who has ordered the detention and is competent to countermand it.[50] Nor is there any rule of law precluding the award of the writ against a minister acting in his capacity as a Crown servant.[51] Though in practice rarely issued, there is no reason of principle why the writ cannot lie against detention based upon a decision of a superior court of record.[52] The writ may lie against private individuals as well as public authorities.[53]

Territorial ambit

Habeas corpus will not issue to a custodian on foreign soil nor, traditionally, in respect of detention on foreign soil.[54] Nor will it issue from the High Court to Scotland[55] or Northern Ireland[56]; but it may issue to the Isle of Man.[57] Before 1862 it could issue from London to any dependent territory within Her Majesty's dominions. The Habeas Corpus Act of that year provided that no such writ was to issue into any colony or "foreign dominion of the Crown", where there was a court having authority to issue and enforce the execution of the writ.

17-014

Scope of review

It is very difficult to present a coherent and concise account of the extent of judicial review in habeas corpus applications, for the case law is riddled with contradictions. In particular, it is not clear whether the scope is more limited than in CPR Pt 54 claims for judicial review—and confined to "jurisdictional errors" in the narrow sense.[58] There is high judicial and academic authority for the proposition that the approach of the courts in both forms of judicial review proceedings should be the same.[59] In both habeas corpus and judicial review, the extent of review

17-015

---

[49] As in *R. v Home Secretary Ex p. O'Brien* [1923] 2 K.B. 361; affirmed sub nom. *Home Secretary v O'Brien* [1923] A.C. 603. See now *Rahmatullah v Secretary of State for Foreign and Commonwealth Affairs* [2012] UKSC 48; [2013] 1 A.C. 614, fn.31 above.

[50] *O'Brien* [1923] 2 K.B. 361 or competent to make relevant requests or inquiries to return the individual *Rahmatullah v Secretary of State for Foreign and Commonwealth Affairs* [2012] UKSC 48; [2013] 1 A.C. 614.

[51] *O'Brien* [1923] 2 K.B. 361; *R. v Secretary of State for the Home Department Ex p. Muboyayi* [1992] Q.B. 244; *Rahmatullah v Secretary of State for Foreign and Commonwealth Affairs* [2012] UKSC 48; [2013] 1 A.C. 614.

[52] See, e.g. *Linnett v Coles* [1987] Q.B. 555 and *R v Governor of Spring Hill Prison Ex p. Sohi* [1988] 1 W.L.R. 596.

[53] *Re L (Vulnerable Adults with Capacity) (No.2)* [2012] EWCA Civ 253; [2013] Fam. 1 at [54].

[54] *R. v Pinckney* [1904] 2 K.B. 84 (private detention in France); *Re Ning Yi-Chin* (1939) 56 T.L.R. 3 (imprisonment of Chinese nationals in British leased territory in China). But exceptional cases may warrant deviations from the general rule (cf. *O'Brien* [1923] 2 K.B. 361 and *Rahmatullah v Secretary of State for Foreign and Commonwealth Affairs* [2012] UKSC 48; [2013] 1 A.C. 614 where it was no bar to the issuing of the writ that the detainee was in the custody of United States authorities overseas).

[55] *R. v Cowle* (1759) 2 Burr. 834.

[56] *Re Keenan* [1972] 1 Q.B. 533.

[57] *Ex p. Brown* (1864) 5 B. & S. 280.

[58] See 4-041 for further discussion of this point.

[59] *R. v Secretary of State for the Home Department Ex p. Khawaja* [1984] A.C. 74 at 111 (Lord Scarman): "There are of course procedural differences between habeas corpus and modern ... judicial review ... But the nature of the remedy sought cannot affect the principle of the law." And, per Lord Wilberforce, at 99: "In practice many claimants seek both remedies. The court considers both any detention which may be in force and the order for removal: the one is normally ancillary

of questions of fact is the same[60]—and since the coming into force of the Human Rights Act 1998, more extensive than in the past if the nature of the case requires it.[61] Not only errors of law and defects of form but also erroneous findings of material facts (which may be controverted by affidavit[62]) may be grounds for the award of habeas corpus if the existence of those facts affects the legality of the restraint. The onus of proving that the factual conditions precedent to a lawful detention existed rests on the administrative authority.[63]

Procedure: CPR Pt 87

17-016   Applications for habeas corpus for release are made under CPR Pt 87. This is quite separate from the procedure for claims for judicial review made under CPR Pt 54, although, where no claim for judicial review is made, the High Court judge considering the application for habeas corpus may order it to continue as an application for permission to apply for judicial review.[64] In principle, claimants may commence both forms of proceedings simultaneously though there will normally be no practical need to do so and this should be avoided if it will increase costs unnecessarily. Where a CPR Pt 54 claim and an application for habeas corpus are commenced, "every effort should be made to harmonise the proceedings".[65] In practice this means that the same affidavit and witness statement should be used for both proceedings, both cases should come before a court for interlocutory and full hearings, and in the event of an appeal, the same notice of appeal should suffice. Applications for habeas corpus involve a two-stage procedure: an application which may be made without notice to the other party (formerly called "ex parte"); and a hearing on notice.

Application without notice

17-017   Applications must be made by filing a Pt 8 claim form in the Administrative Court, supported by a witness statement or affidavit.[66] The witness statement or affidavit must: state that the application is made "at the instance of the person being detained"; must set out the nature of the detention; and must be made by the detained person. If the detained person is unable to make the witness statement or affidavit, it may be made by another on his or her behalf, stating the reasons why

---

to the other. I do not think that it would be appropriate unless unavoidable to make a distinction between the two remedies …" Beldam LJ in *R. v Secretary of State for the Home Department Ex p. Cheblak* [1991] 1 W.L.R. 890 at 910 adopted a similar view.

60   *R. v Secretary of State for the Home Department Ex p. Khawaja* [1984] A.C. 74.

61   See 1-123 and Ch.13.

62   Habeas Corpus Act 1816 ss.3, 4. See, however, *Re Shahid Iqbal* [1979] Q.B. 264, affirmed [1979] 1 W.L.R. 425, where habeas corpus was refused even though affidavit evidence established that the ground given for the detention had no support in fact: it was held that the existence of another valid ground for detention and the absence of any prejudice to the claimant from the error justified refusal of the writ. While it might be thought that this reasoning obliquely introduces a discretionary element to the grant of habeas corpus, it does not do so since, if there is another ground for the restraint, it is not unlawful.

63   *Khawaja* [1984] A.C. 74.

64   CPR r.87.4(1)(d) (where the application is considered under r.87.2 on paper) and r.87.5(d) (where the application is considered at a hearing).

65   *R. v BHB Community Healthcare NHS Trust Ex p. B* [1999] 1 F.L.R. 106 at 117 (Lord Woolf MR).

66   CPR r.87.2(1). Forms 87 (Claim form for writ of habeas corpus ad subjiciendum), 88 and 90 have now been deleted. Applications made on behalf of a minor must be made to the Family Court; see fn.35 above and the High Court (Distribution of Business) Order 2014 (SI 2014/3257).

the detainee is unable to do so.[67] The application may be made without notice.[68] If the case is urgent, the judge may dispense with the requirement that a claim form be filed and must give directions for the conduct of the application.[69] Applications for habeas corpus have priority over all other court business.

A single judge of the High Court may give initial consideration to an applica-   **17-018**
tion on paper. Where this is not done, initial consideration must be by a judge sitting in court, or otherwise than in court.[70] Where consideration is given on the papers, the judge has power to make an order for the issue of the writ; to adjourn the application to a hearing (in which case two days' notice must be given to both parties); to direct that the application be considered by a Divisional Court of the Queen's Bench Division; to direct that the application continues as an application for judicial review; to give other directions; or to dismiss the application.[71] Where the application is dismissed on the papers, the applicant may request the decision to be reconsidered at a hearing; this must be filed within seven days after service of the order.[72] Modern practice to date has almost invariably dictated an adjournment, except perhaps in cases where there is no possible defence to the application.

There is no statutory or common law statement of the criteria to be applied by   **17-019**
the court at the without notice stage in deciding whether the application should proceed (or indeed whether the writ should be issued then). The court will generally adopt an approach similar to that at the permission stage of CPR Pt 54 claims for judicial review,[73] though questions of delay will not usually be relevant and there is no statutory time limit within which the writ must be sought. The claimant may be granted bail pending the full hearing, subject now to s.17 of the Criminal Justice Act 2003.[74]

On notice hearing

Where the application is considered at a hearing (including where, following   **17-020**
initial consideration on the papers, the application is adjourned to a hearing or where a reconsideration hearing is requested following the dismissal of the application on the papers), the judge has the same powers as are available at the paper stage with the additional power to "order that the detained person be released". This is sufficient authorisation for the detainee's release.[75] At the hearing, oral argument takes place, although disputed questions of fact are normally dealt with on the basis of witness statements or affidavits upon which deponents are only exceptionally subject to cross-examination.[76] Occasionally, as a formality, the court will order the writ to issue—somewhat incongruously after the release of the claimant. CPR rr.87.8–87.11 apply where the court makes an order for the issue of a writ.

In contrast to the other prerogative remedies available on a claim for judicial   **17-021**

---

67 CPR r.87.2(2)–(3). On third party applications see also *Justice for Families Ltd v Secretary of State for Justice* [2014] EWCA Civ 1477; [2015] 2 F.L.R. 321 at [19]–[23].
68 CPR r.87.2(5).
69 CPR r.87.2(6).
70 CPR r.87.3. Any application made on behalf of a protected party must initially be considered by a judge otherwise than in court: CPR r.87.7.
71 CPR r.87.4(1).
72 CPR r.87.4(2)–(3). There is no statement that the applicant may not appeal this decision; nor that where applications dismissed on the papers are certified as "totally without merit" pursuant to CPR r.23.12, reconsideration is unavailable, as appear in the comparable provisions relating to judicial review, CPR r.54.12.
73 See 16-049.
74 See 18-022.
75 CPR rr.87.5, 87.6.
76 *R. v Secretary of State for the Home Department ex p. Khawaja* [1984] A.C. 74, 124–125.

review,[77] habeas corpus is a writ of right. If the claimant establishes that his detention is unlawful, the court has no discretion to refuse the writ.[78] The court may, however, have power to refuse the writ where the error is merely a technical flaw in the process leading to the claimant's detention.[79] An application may also be struck out as an abuse of the process of the court where it was apparent, looking at the application in the context of a series of other applications, that the machinery of the court was not being used for its proper purposes.[80]

Repeat applications and appeals

17-022   For many years it was thought that an unsuccessful claimant for habeas corpus could renew his application before each superior court and each superior judge in turn.[81] Section 14(2) of the Administration of Justice Act 1960 now provides that no application for habeas corpus shall be made on the same grounds to the same court or judge or any other court or judge, unless fresh evidence is adduced. To come within the exception, the fresh evidence must be relevant and admissible.[82] A claimant who is unsuccessful obtaining permission to proceed with a CPR Pt 54 claim for judicial review can expect to have a subsequent application for habeas corpus, in relation to the same matter, refused as an abuse of process.[83]

17-023   Appeal routes from a refusal or grant of an application for habeas corpus depend on whether it is a criminal matter[84] or a non-criminal matter. In criminal applications the appeal is to the Supreme Court, with permission of either the High Court or the Supreme Court.[85] The court below must certify "that a point of law of general public importance is involved in the decision and it appears to that court or to the Supreme Court, as the case may be, that the point is one which ought to be considered by the Supreme Court."[86] In non-criminal applications, appeal lies to the Court of Appeal. Where the appeal is against the refusal to grant habeas corpus the appeal to the Court of Appeal is as of right: the claimant does not require permission.[87]

---

[77] See Ch.18.
[78] *Greene v Secretary of State for Home Affairs* [1942] A.C. 284 at 302.
[79] *R. v Governor of Pentonville Prison Ex p. Osman (No.3)* [1990] 1 W.L.R. 878.
[80] *Re Osman* [1992] 1 W.L.R. 36.
[81] See, e.g. *Re Hastings (No.1)* [1958] 1 W.L.R. 372; *Re Hastings (No.2)* [1959] 1 Q.B. 358; *Re Hastings (No.3)* [1959] Ch. 368; [1959] 2 W.L.R. 454.
[82] *Ex p. Schtraks* [1964] 1 Q.B. 191. Evidence is only "fresh" for this purpose if the claimant could not, or could not reasonably have been expected to produce it on the first application: *R. v Governor of Pentonville Prison Ex p. Tarling* [1979] 1 W.L.R. 1417. The Administration of Justice Act 1960 s.14(2) has not stopped the phenomenon of successive applications for habeas corpus. During the late 1980s and early 1990s, Mr Lorrain Osman, committed into custody under the Fugitive Offenders Act 1967 s.7(5) awaiting return to Hong Kong, made nine unsuccessful applications for the writ: see, e.g. *R. v Governor of Pentonville Prison Ex p. Osman* [1990] 1 W.L.R. 277 and *Re Osman* [1992] 1 W.L.R. 36.
[83] *Sheikh v Secretary of State for the Home Department* [2001] Imm. A.R. 219; [2001] A.C.D. 33.
[84] On the distinction see Ch.16; and see Administration of Justice Act 1960 s.14(3).
[85] Administration of Justice Act 1960 ss.1, 15; Senior Courts Act 1981 s.18(1). For the position of the detainer at common law, see *Superintendent of Her Majesty's Foxhill Prison v Kozeny* [2012] UKPC 10 at [20]-[27].
[86] See 16-084. Administration of Justice Act 1960 s.1(2).
[87] CPR r.52.3.

APPLICATIONS TO QUASH CERTAIN ORDERS, ETC.

A significant number of statutes and statutory instruments make provision for **17-024** persons aggrieved by certain specified orders, decisions, etc. to make applications to the High Court to quash them. The term "appeal" is sometimes used in relation to these applications but they are more akin to judicial review. They are most commonly found in the context of town and country planning, compulsory land acquisition and regulation of commercial activity (especially of former state-owned enterprises).[88] The grounds of review are broadly comparable to those used in CPR Pt 54 claims for judicial review. There are two main features to applications to quash. First, they must be sought using a procedure distinct and different from the standard judicial review regime under CPR Pt 54. Secondly, applications to quash almost invariably contain a preclusive clause, ousting the jurisdiction of the court to hear challenges to the lawfulness of the order in question except by means of the application to quash procedure.[89]

Where the claimant's challenge is directed not at the order, etc. itself, but a mat- **17-025** ter antecedent or collateral to it, standard proceedings under CPR Pt 54 may be appropriate.[90] In cases where the claimant is not a person aggrieved by the order, etc. or he does not seek actually to quash the order, CPR Pt 54 proceedings may also be used.[91]

Procedure

In non-planning cases, the procedure for applications to quash is now governed **17-026** principally by CPR Pt 8. For cases now dealt with by the Planning Court, see 17-031.

The time period within which proceedings must be made is in most cases six **17-027** weeks (or 42 days). Often the Act in question states that time begins to run from some specific occurrence (such as the publication of an order) and so creates a "window" rather than just an end date. Accordingly, a claimant who commences an application before the start date does so prematurely and is as much out of time as one who is late.[92] In contrast to the requirement of promptness and in any event three months on a claim for judicial review under CPR Pt 54, this limitation period

---

[88] Examples include: Town and County Planning Act 1990 ss.287-288 (formerly, ss.245 and 246 of the 1971 Act); Planning and Compulsory Purchase Act 2004 s.113 (spatial strategies and development plans); Water Industry Act 1991 ss.21, 22E (enforcement orders and financial penalties on water companies); Electricity Act 1989 s.27E (penalties on electricity providers); Gas Act 1986 s.30E; Transport Act 2000 s.23; New Roads and Street Works Act 1991 Sch.2 para.10; Wildlife and Countryside Act 1981 Sch.15 (footpath modification); Highways Act 1980 Sch.2 (orders concerning classification, construction and stopping up of roads); Road Traffic Regulation Act 1984 Sch.9. For an account of the historical development of statutory applications to quash, see 15-076.

[89] On ouster clauses, see 4-017.

[90] For example, in *R. v Camden LBC Ex p. Comyn Ching and Co (London) Ltd* (1984) 47 P. & C.R. 417; [1984] J.P.L. 661 it was held that a resolution by the local authority to make a compulsory purchase order could properly be challenged under the standard judicial review procedure (then RSC Ord.53); but once the order had been made, the Acquisition of Land Act 1981 s.25 required any challenge to be made by statutory review.

[91] In *Greater London Council v Secretary of State for the Environment* [1985] J.P.L. 868, Woolf J held RSC Ord.53 proceedings were appropriate where a claimant sought to challenge the reasoning of a planning inspector who had found in its favour. The statutory review provisions of the Town and Country Planning Act were inapplicable because the claimant was not a person aggrieved and they did not provide an appropriate remedy (i.e. a declaration).

[92] *Enterprise Inns Plc v Secretary of State for the Environment, Transport and the Regions* (2001) 81 P. & C.R. 18.

gives the court no discretion to extend the time for lodging the application,[93] as the court's jurisdiction is defined by the window of time allowed.

17-028   A different form of words ("any person aggrieved") usually defines the standing of potential claimants for statutory review in contrast to the requirement of "a sufficient interest in the matter to which the application relates" for CPR Pt 54 claims. There is, however, a tendency for the courts to equate the forms of standing.[94]

17-029   The remedial powers of the court on an application to quash are normally more limited in scope than CPR Pt 54. In each instance the precise powers are derived from the Act under which the application is made. The court is invariably given power to quash the order generally or in so far as it affects the claimant and is usually given power to make an interim order suspending the operation of the decision challenged until the court determines the application.[95] There are, for example, no powers to make declarations or orders equivalent to the remedy of prohibition or mandamus. In some instances, the court has express powers to remit the decision back to the decision-maker for reconsideration[96]; though even in the absence of such a provision reconsideration will be the normal course of events. Where the application relates to the imposition of the penalty, the court may have a power to substitute a penalty of a lesser amount.[97]

17-030   Proceedings are commenced by claim form, which must be filed in the Administrative Court Office and served on the defendant minister and other parties within the time limit specified by the legislation under which the application is made.[98] In contrast to CPR Pt 54 claims for judicial review, there is no permission stage though it has been suggested that there ought to be.[99] Evidence at the

---

[93]   *Smith v East Elloe RDC* [1956] A.C. 736; *R. v Secretary of State for the Environment Ex p. Ostler* [1977] Q.B. 122; *R. v Cornwall CC Ex p. Huntingdon* [1994] 1 All E.R. 694. The requirement of "promptness" may now be inapplicable even in some CPR Part 54 proceedings, see 16-056. See further *R. (on the application of Blue Green London Plan) v Secretary of State for the Environment, Food and Rural Affairs* [2015] EWHC 495 (Admin) at [43] (no discretion to extend time limit imposed by Planning Act 2008 s.118), *Nottingham CC v Calverton Parish Council* [2015] EWHC 503 (Admin); [2015] A.C.D. 97 at [33]–[34], [46] (relating to the Planning and Compulsory Purchase Act 2004 s.113, where a statutory provision provides that proceedings must be brought no later than the end of a specified period, the bringing of proceedings requires that the court office be functioning and the last day of the prescribed period falls on a day when the court office is closed, then proceedings may be brought on the next day when the court office is open), and *R. (on the application of Williams) v Secretary of State for Energy and Climate Change* [2015] EWHC 1202 (Admin); [2015] J.P.L. 1257 at [44]–[45] (the date on which an order was published online and a link was emailed to the claimant started the time period under s.118 Planning Act 2008, notwithstanding that the order was later published in a different way). Time began to run regardless of the claimant's actual knowledge (at [58–60]), and the fact that decision letters gave misleading guidance on the time limit in s.118 had no effect (at [63])).

[94]   See 2-064.

[95]   See, e.g. Town and Country Planning Act 1990 s.288(5).

[96]   *Botton v Secretary of State for the Environment* (1991) 3 Admin. L.R. 848; [1992] 1 P.L.R. 1.

[97]   See, e.g. Water Industry Act 1991 s.22E. The power to make or vary a substantive decision is unusual in a court with principally supervisory jurisdiction; cf. the little-used power of the court in CPR Pt 54 claims for judicial review: 18-031.

[98]   PD 8A, para.22.3.

[99]   *Enforcing Planning Control*, Report by R. Carnwath QC for the Secretary of State for the Environment (1989), para.6. cf. Town and Country Planning Act 1990 s.289(6), which in relation to appeals on point of law and case stated against enforcement notices requires permission to be obtained. This is an area of recent development: Criminal Justice and Courts Act 2015 s.91 (in force from 26 October 2015) "introduces Sch.16, which contains amendments to provide that challenges to a range of planning related decisions and actions may only be brought with the leave of the High Court", within a six-week time limit: see the Explanatory Memorandum to the 2015 Act at 674–675. The amendments affect ss.287 and 288 of the Town and Country Planning Act 1990; s.63 of the Plan-

hearing is by witness statement.[100] The hearing is before a single judge. Given the rationale for the procedure—expedition in the disposal of legal challenges—time is of the essence in prosecuting applications.

The Administrative Court now has a specialist list called the Planning Court governed by CPR Pt 54.21–24 and Practice Direction 54E.[101] The Planning Court hears all claims lodged after 6 April 2014 (or transferred to it after that date) which involve a judicial review or statutory challenge to planning and some environmental decisions.[102] Significant Planning Court claims are dealt with according to the target time scales set out in the Practice Direction.[103]   **17-031**

Grounds of review

The various Acts usually provide for the validity of an order, decision, action, etc. to be questioned on two alternative grounds, that[104]: (a) it is not within the powers conferred by the statute; or (b) any of the requirements of the statute[105] have not been complied with. The first challenge is based upon the criteria laid down by the Court of Appeal in *Ashbridge Investments Ltd v Minister of Housing and Local Government* where Lord Denning MR said that the court could interfere if the minister[106]:   **17-032**

> "… has acted on no evidence; or if he has come to a conclusion to which on the evidence he could not reasonably come; or if he has given a wrong interpretation to the words of the statute; or if he has taken into consideration matters which he ought not to have taken into account, or vice versa; or has otherwise gone wrong in law. It is identical with the

---

ning (Listed Buildings and Conservation Areas) Act 1990; s.22 of the Planning (Hazardous Substances) Act 1990; and s.113 of the Planning and Compulsory Purchase Act 2004. The amendments do not apply to proceedings where the publication date of the relevant document is earlier than 26 October 2015.

[100] PD 8A, para.22.7.

[101] The proposal to establish the Planning Court appeared in Ch.3 of Ministry of Justice, *Judicial Review: Proposals for Further Reform*, Cm 8703 (September 2013). The Government's aim was stated to be to streamline the legal process for determining challenges in order to reduce the extent to which such challenges unduly hinder economic development and regeneration. Section 91 of the Criminal Justice and Courts Act 2015 (not in force at the time of writing) contains Sch.16, which introduces a permission stage for certain planning challenges. When s.91 enters into force, a new PD 8C—Alternative Procedure for Statutory Review of Certain Planning Matters will also be introduced to support its implementation, along with related amendments to Pt 52, PD 8A—Alternative Procedure for Claims, and PD 54E—Judicial and Statutory Review. See fn.95.

[102] A Planning Court claim includes a judicial review or statutory challenge to: planning permission or other development consents; the enforcement of planning control and the enforcement of other statutory schemes; applications under the Transport and Works Act 1992; wayleaves; highways and other rights of way; compulsory purchase orders; village greens; European Union environmental legislation and domestic transpositions, including assessments for development consents, habitats, waste and pollution control; national, regional or other planning policy documents; and any other matter which the Planning Liaison Judge considers appropriate. The Planning Liaison Judge will be nominated by the President of the Queen's Bench Division who will also nominate specialist planning judges to deal with significant Planning Court claims.

[103] Significant Planning Court claims are defined in Practice Direction 54EPD3.2 as those: relating to developments with significant economic impact either locally or more broadly; which raise important points of law; which generate significant public interest; or, by virtue of the volume or nature of the technical material, are best dealt with by judges with significant experience of handling such matters. It is for the Planning Liaison Judge to designate claims as significant. See further I. Dove and F. Patterson, "The Planning Court: future directions" [2015] J.P.L. 1118.

[104] See, e.g. Town and Country Planning Act 1990 ss.287-288. An unreasonable decision will not be "within the powers conferred by the Act". On unreasonableness generally, see Ch.11.

[105] Or other relevant requirements, e.g. of the Tribunals and Inquiries Act 1992.

[106] *Ashbridge Investments Ltd v Minister of Housing and Local Government* [1965] 1 W.L.R. 1320.

position where the court has power to interfere with the decision of a lower tribunal which has erred in point of law."[107]

17-033 These criteria cannot today be distinguished from the grounds of judicial review known as illegality and unreasonableness.[108] Indeed, the language of judicial review is sometimes employed to assess the validity of decisions challenged under applications to quash. For example, the House of Lords in *Newbury District Council v Secretary of State for the Environment*[109] held that planning conditions may be quashed if they exceed the scope of the Town and Country Planning Act or if they are unreasonable in the *Wednesbury* sense.[110] Yet tests of the validity of individual statutes may be peculiar to their own contexts. Planning conditions, for example, may also be quashed, if they do not "fairly and reasonably relate" to the development.[111]

17-034 The second ground of challenge above relates to procedural requirements. This ground is close to the ground of judicial review of "procedural propriety", which was defined by Lord Diplock in *GCHQ* as including both the common law rules of natural justice and the breach of statutorily required procedures.[112] In applications to quash, the procedural requirements specified in the statute may be supplemented by common law principles of natural justice.[113]

17-035 Normally in applications to quash, for the claimant to succeed in quashing the decision he must have been "substantially prejudiced" by the failure to comply with the statute's procedural conditions.[114] Under both substantive and procedural grounds of review the courts possess a residual discretion not to quash a decision where there has been no prejudice or detriment to the claimant[115] and to refuse relief in exceptional circumstances.[116]

---

[107] *Ashbridge Investments Ltd v Minister of Housing and Local Government* [1965] 1 W.L.R. 1320 at 1326. This formula was adopted in, e.g. *Seddon Properties Ltd v Secretary of State for the Environment* [1978] J.P.L. 835; *Eckersley v Secretary of State for the Environment* (1977) 34 P. & C.R. 124; *Bridgewood Rochester Ltd v Secretary of State for Communities and Local Government* [2008] EWHC 405 (Admin). For similar tests in relation to compulsory purchase orders see *De Rothschild v Secretary of State for Transport* [1989] 1 All E.R. 933. See further *Holywell Property (St Albans) Ltd v Dacorum BC* [2014] EWHC 32 (Admin) at [14]–[15] and *R. (on the application of Brown) v Welsh Ministers* [2016] EWHC 750 (Admin) at [24]–[25].

[108] See Ch.5 (illegality) and Ch.11 (unreasonableness).

[109] *Newbury District Council v Secretary of State for the Environment* [1981] A.C. 578.

[110] See Ch.11.

[111] The condition in *Newbury DC v Secretary of State for the Environment* [1981] A.C. 578 that the buildings be demolished after a period of time was held invalid on this ground as that condition did not fairly and reasonably relate to the application for a mere change of use. The "fairly and reasonably relate" test was applied to the context of compulsory acquisition for development purposes (to be strictly applied given the context) in *R. (on the application of Sainsbury's Supermarkets Ltd) v Wolverhampton CC* [2010] UKSC 20; [2011] 1 A.C. 437 at [70]–[72]. The language of the "fairly and reasonably" requirement has been adopted in the Community Infrastructure Levy Regulations 2010 (SI 2010/948), reg.122. See *Smyth v Secretary of State for Communities and Local Government* [2015] EWCA Civ 174; [2015] P.T.S.R 1417 at [19] (the Regulations require that conservation contributions fairly and reasonably relate to the scale and kind of a proposed development).

[112] *Council of Civil Service Unions v Minister for the Civil Service* [1985] A.C. 374; see Ch.6.

[113] See Chs 7-9.

[114] Town and Country Planning Act 1990 s.288(5)(b).

[115] *Miller v Weymouth & Melcombe Regis Corp* (1974) 27 P. & C.R. 468; *Kent CC v Secretary of State for the Environment* (1977) 33 P. & C.R. 70; *Peak Park Joint Planning Board v Secretary of State for the Environment* (1980) 39 P. & C.R. 361 at 385; *Richmond-upon-Thames LBC v Secretary of State for the Environment* [1984] J.P.L. 24; *Tameside MBC v Secretary of State for the Environment* [1984] J.P.L. 180.

[116] *Bolton MBC v Secretary of State for the Environment* (1991) 61 P. & C.R. 343 (Glidewell LJ, obiter), applied in *O'Donnell v Welsh Ministers* [2011] EWHC 3921 (Admin) at [22]-[26]. The Bolton

APPEALS FROM THE MAGISTRATES' COURTS AND THE CROWN COURT

Detailed consideration of criminal appeals falls outside the scope of a book on **17-036** judicial review.[117] The High Court does, however, continue to carry out its historical role of overseeing the work of magistrates' courts and the Crown Court in relation to summary criminal cases, by means of appeals by way of case stated (as well as judicial review in some situations).[118] In 2001 Sir Robin Auld's review of the criminal courts of England and Wales recommended that the Administrative Court's supervisory jurisdiction over criminal courts be replaced with new routes of appeal to the Court of Appeal (Criminal Division).[119] The Government accepted this and the Law Commission has produced a report recommending how this should be achieved which currently awaits a Government response.[120]

CORONERS

The Coroners Act 1988 s.13(1) currently provides that an application may be **17-037** made by or under the authority of the Attorney General where a coroner refuses or neglects to hold an inquest or investigation which ought to be held, or

> "where an inquest or an investigation has been held by him, that (whether by reason of fraud, rejection of evidence, irregularity of proceedings, insufficiency of inquiry, the discovery of new facts or evidence or otherwise) it is necessary or desirable in the interests of justice that an investigation (or, as the case may be, another investigation) should be held".[121]

The conduct of inquests must, following the Human Rights Act 1998, take into account the requirements of ECHR art.2 (right to life).[122] The grounds of review under s.13(1) are in effect the same as those that may be deployed on a CPR Pt 54 claim for judicial review,[123] though a wider range of remedial orders will be available on a Pt 54 claim. Before commencing the application in the High Court under s.13, a claimant must obtain the consent of the Attorney General.[124] The criterion applied

---

principles were recently approved in e.g. *R. (on the application of Watson) v Richmond upon Thames LBC* [2013] EWCA Civ 513 at [26]; *Hiam v Secretary of State for Communities and Local Government* [2014] EWHC 4112 (Admin) at [40]; and *R. (on the application of Manchester City Council) v Secretary of State for Local Government* [2016] EWHC 4209 (Admin) at [11].

[117] P. Taylor, *Taylor on Criminal Appeals*, 2nd edn (2012).

[118] See 3-009.

[119] Review of the Criminal Courts of England and Wales, Ch.12.

[120] Law Commission, *The High Court's Jurisdiction in Relation to Criminal Proceedings* (2010).

[121] A further inquest will be necessary in the interests of justice where fresh evidence has emerged which may reasonably lead to the conclusion that the substantial truth about how an individual met his death was not revealed at the first inquest (*Attorney General v HM Coroner for South Yorkshire (West)* [2012] EWHC 3783 (Admin); [2012] Inquest L.R. 143 in relation to the Hillsborough disaster).

[122] See 7-130; 13-062. *R (on the application of Humberstone) v Legal Services Commission* [2010] EWCA Civ 1479; [2011] 1 W.L.R. 1460 at [67]-[72].

[123] *Terry v East Sussex Coroner* [2001] EWCA Civ 1094; [2002] Q.B. 312 at [21] (Simon Brown LJ: "the self-same test should apply under s.13(1)(a) as applies on a judicial review challenge. The court cannot conclude that 'an inquest ... ought to be held' unless the coroner has misdirected himself in law or his factual conclusion is irrational").

[124] There is no prescribed procedure for obtaining such consent. It should be sufficient to set out a properly reasoned letter supported by a copy of the Record of Inquest, notes of evidence given by

in each instance is whether there is a reasonable prospect of establishing that it is necessary or desirable in the interests of justice for a fresh inquest to be held.[125]

17-038   The procedure on such applications is governed by the CPR (PD 8A, para.19) and applications are heard by a Divisional Court. Claimants sometimes commence a CPR Pt 54 claim for judicial review at the same time as making an application under s.13 of the 1988 Act. The general principle that the court will exercise its discretion to refuse permission to proceed with a CPR Pt 54 claim where there is an alternative remedy available[126] ought to deter claimants whose case could be made under s.13 from using the standard judicial review procedure.[127] Section 13(2) stipulates the remedies available. The High Court may order another inquest to be held or, where an inquest has been held, quash the Record of Inquest on that inquest. There is also an express power to order the coroner to pay "such costs of and incidental to the application as to the court may appear just".[128]

17-039   With effect from 25 July 2013 (and subject to the exception described below), the Coroners Act 1988 has been repealed by the Coroners and Justices Act 2009. Under the 2009 Act, a new post of Chief Coroner of England and Wales has been created.[129] The main responsibilities of the Chief Coroner include: to set national standards for all coroners (including new inquest rules); to oversee the implementation of the 2009 Act; to maintain a register of coroner investigations which last more than 12 months; to take steps to reduce unnecessary delays; and monitor investigations into the death of service personnel. As originally enacted in the 2009 Act, s.13 of the 1988 Act was to be replaced by a statutory right of appeal to the new post of Chief Coroner. However, the provisions of the 2009 Act creating the new right of

---

witnesses and any material the applicant seeks to rely upon as fresh evidence. The relevant address is: Attorney General's Chambers, 20 Victoria Street, London, SW1H 0NF, telephone 020 7271 2492.

[125] *Hansard*, HC col.WA67 (May 20, 1996) and col.39WA (May 2, 1989) (adding that "it is not my practice to give a more particular reason"); *R. v Attorney General Ex p. Ferrante, Independent*, 3 April 1995 (CA). See also e.g. *HM Coroner for Isle of Wight v Prison Service* [2015] EWHC 1360 (Admin) at [5]. In *HM Coroner for the District of Avon v Elam* [2014] EWHC 3013 (Admin), a further inquest was ordered in the interests of justice as a result of new facts and evidence as to the identity of a previously unidentified person in respect of whom an inquest had already been conducted.

[126] See 16-016.

[127] *R. v HM Coroner for West Berkshire Ex p. Thomas* [1991] C.O.D. 437 (Bingham LJ said that he found it "hard to imagine circumstances in which the court would grant relief by way of judicial review if relief is refused under s.13. Where the Attorney General's leave is given, therefore, it seems clear that s.13 is the preferred route for those to challenge a coroner's inquisition". Judicial review will remain available for those decisions which cannot be challenged under s.13 of the 1998 Act such as those made in advance of the hearing and those relating to the actual conduct of the proceedings.

[128] A protective costs order (now a costs capping order, see 16-094) may be ordered: see *R. (on the application of Ministry of Defence) v Wiltshire and Swindon Coroner* [2005] EWHC 889 (Admin); [2006] 1 W.L.R. 134. On the relevant costs principles, see *R. (on the application of Davies) v Birmingham Deputy Coroner* [2004] EWCA Civ 207; [2004] 1 W.L.R. 2739 at [47]; *R. (on the application of Medihani) v HM Coroner for Inner South District of Greater London* [2012] EWHC 1104 (Admin); [2012] A.C.D. 63 at [59]–[64]; and *R. (on the application of Joseph) v Director of Legal Aid Casework* [2015] EWHC 2749 (Admin). In *R. (on the application of Letts) v Lord Chancellor* [2015] EWHC 402 (Admin); [2015] 1 W.L.R. 4497, the criteria applied by the Legal Aid Agency to the grant of legal aid for representation at an inquest to the relatives of a deceased where the death may engage art.2 of the ECHR were found to be materially in error in lacking detail and creating a misleading impression as to what the law was. In *R. (on the application of RJ) v Director of Legal Aid Casework* [2016] EWHC 645 (Admin); [2016] A.C.D. 90 at [24]–[29], the refusal of legal aid for representation at an inquest to an "interested person" as designated by the Coroners and Justice Act 2009 s.47(2)(f) (a person who might by any act or omission have caused or contributed to a death), was not a breach of art.6 as the individual was not a person "charged with a criminal offence" and the inquest was not a criminal proceeding.

[129] The first holder of the post of Chief Coroner is HHJ Peter Thornton QC who took up his office in September 2012.

appeal have now themselves been repealed on grounds of cost and s.13 of the 1988 Act and judicial review remain the mechanisms for challenge.

HOMELESS APPEALS

Also relevant, though not a matter for the Administrative Court, is the right of appeal on point of law to county courts to challenge local housing authorities' decisions relating to homelessness.[130] By the mid-1990s, a third of all judicial review applications to the High Court concerned homelessness decisions; often the dispute was essentially one of fact and primary judgment (was the person intentionally homeless? was the accommodation offered suitable?) rather than of law. The High Court was encouraged to adopt a restrictive stance towards the grant of leave (now called permission) to proceed with such claims.[131] In Access to Justice, Lord Woolf recommended that the supervisory jurisdiction over the lawfulness of homelessness decision-making should be transferred to the county courts[132] and this was swiftly implemented by Pt 7 of the Housing Act 1996. On appeal, the County Court has the power to make an order confirming, quashing or varying the decision.[133] The grounds of appeal are essentially the same as the grounds for judicial review.[134] The right of appeal does not extend to decisions about the provision of temporary ac-

17-040

---

[130] Housing Act 1996 ss.204 and 204A. The appellant must first seek a review of his request for assistance by the authority (s.202). If he is "dissatisfied with the decision on the review" or the review is not done within the prescribed time limit, he has 21 days to appeal to the county court. Review under s.204 is compliant with art.6: *Tower Hamlets LBC v Begum (Runa)* [2003] UKHL 5; [2003] 2 A.C. 430.

[131] *Puhlhofer v Hillingdon London BC* [1986] A.C. 484 at 518 (Lord Brightman said that it was "not appropriate that ... judicial review should be made use of to monitor the action of local authorities [in this context] save in the exceptional case". *Puhlhofer* was cited in *Sharif v Camden London Borough Council* [2013] UKSC 10; [2013] 2 All E.R. 309 in which, on appeal (rather than an application for judicial review), a similarly restrictive approach was adopted (the word "accommodation" did not equate to "unit of accommodation", such that the duty imposed by s.193(2) of the Housing Act 1996 could be discharged by housing members of the same family in separate units).

[132] *Access to Justice: Final Report* (1996), para.16.76. See also *R. v Brighton & Hove Council Ex p. Nacion* (1999) 31 H.L.R. 1095 at 1100-1101 (Lord Woolf MR: judicial review not an appropriate method of challenge because the need for relief often arose at very short notice; applicants often lived far from London; and High Court proceedings were not regarded as the most appropriate forum for resolving the often delicate issues that arose out of local authorities' responsibilities for providing accommodation).

[133] County courts do not have any *general* powers to make quashing orders, prohibiting orders and mandatory orders: County Courts Act 1984 38(3)(a). See s.204 of the Housing Act 1996 and *Johnston v City of Westminster* [2015] EWCA Civ 554 at [38].

[134] *Tower Hamlets LBC v Begum (Runa)* [2003] UKHL 5; [2003] 2 A.C. 430 at [17] (Lord Hoffmann: "Section 204 provides that an applicant who is dissatisfied with a decision on review may appeal to the county court on 'any point of law arising from the decision'. This enables the applicant to complain not only that the council misinterpreted the law but also of any illegality, procedural impropriety or irrationality which could be relied upon in proceedings for judicial review". While it is important to retain procedural flexibility, it is not generally appropriate for the County Court to embark upon a fact-finding exercise when entertaining an appeal under s.204 (*Bubb v Wandsworth LBC* [2011] EWCA Civ 1285; [2012] P.T.S.R. 1011 at [21]-[22]). See also *Hines v Lambeth LBC* [2014] EWCA Civ 660; [2014] 1 W.L.R. 4112 at [13]-[15], at which Tower Hamlets was cited as authority for the proposition that an appeal under s.204 of the 1996 Act is to be scrutinised on judicial review principles; no greater intensity of review is to be applied. In *Nzolameso v Westminster City Council* [2015] UKSC 22; [2015] 2 All E.R. 942 at [38]-[41], guidance was provided as to the desirability of the local authority maintaining a procurement policy for "out of borough" housing. If publicly available, this would "enable a general challenge to those policies to be brought by way of judicial review. In some ways this might be preferable to a challenge by way of an individual appeal to a county court. But it may not always be practicable to mount a judicial review of an

commodation pending final determination by the local authority or review by the county court; here judicial review continues to be an important method of challenge.[135] The courts have, however, indicated that they will intervene in challenges relating to temporary accommodation only in exceptional circumstances.[136] The existence of a review procedure in the county courts has not taken away the Administrative Court's jurisdiction to exercise its judicial review jurisdiction in the context of decisions relating to homelessness, but that jurisdiction will now be used only in exceptional circumstances.[137]

EVALUATION OF JUDICIAL REVIEW PROCEDURES

17-041   Any evaluation of the procedural arrangements for the conduct of public law litigation has to take place in the context of the broad objectives which judicial review is intended to serve. Apart from the constitutional role of judicial review which has already been considered,[138] two perspectives can be used to highlight the competing demands that are made on the public law procedural regimes in England and Wales. The first focuses on the adjudicatory role performed by the court. The

---

authority's policy, and an individual must be able to rely on any point of law arising from the decision under appeal, including the legality of the policy which has been applied in her case". However, despite the "substantial overlap" between judicial review claims and appeals on points of law, it does not follow that every judicial body with jurisdiction limited to points of law is required to apply judicial review principles in every case: *Bhatia Best Ltd v Lord Chancellor* [2014] EWHC 746 (QB); [2014] 1 W.L.R. 3487 at [30]–[33], [40] and [43]. There, the question before the court was whether s.204 was an enactment which required the county court "to make a decision applying the principles that are applied by the court on an application for judicial review". If so, then s.204 appeals would, for the purposes of legal aid funding, fall within the "public law" category created by para.19(10) of Sch.1 of the Legal Aid, Sentencing and Punishment of Offenders Act 2012. It was held that the absence of reference to judicial review principles in s.204 showed that it was not intended that judicial review principles would be applied, and that this conclusion was unaffected by *Tower Hamlets*: the latter did not develop the jurisprudence beyond *Nipa Begum v Tower Hamlets London Borough Council* [2000] 1 W.L.R. 306, which simply established that s.204 gives rise to a right "akin to" judicial review. In *Ali v United Kingdom* (2016) 63 E.H.R.R. 20 at [82]–[86], the ECtHR held that the legislative scheme for challenging homelessness decision-making pursuant to the Housing Act 1996, including the County Court's powers under s.204, was compatible with art.6. The ECtHR stated at [13] (without reference to the decision of the HC in *Bhatia Best*) that the "jurisdiction exercised by the county court under s.204 was that of judicial review." The SC in *Poshteh v Kensington & Chelsea RLBC* [2017] UKSC 36; [2017] 2 W.L.R. 1417 declined to follow *Ali* and affirmed that the duties of local housing authorities under Pt VII of the Housing Act 1996 did not give rise to civil rights or obligations under art.6 of the ECHR.

[135] M. Sunkin et al., "Mapping the Use of Judicial Review to Challenge Local Authorities in England and Wales" [2007] P.L. 545 at 555. In May 2008, the Law Commission report *Housing Disputes: Proportionate Dispute Resolution* (Law Com No.309/Cm 7377) made several recommendations for reform, including that the county court should have powers to grant interim relief pending the outcome of a local authority's internal review of homelessness cases. The Government rejected this proposal on the ground that there was "a significant risk that any changes in this area would be exploited to circumvent these procedures to the detriment of those who are genuinely homeless and in priority need" (Ministry of Justice statement, 16 July 2009).

[136] *R v Brighton and Hove BC Ex p. Nacion* (1999) 31 H.L.R. 1095 at 1101 (Lord Woolf MR: "If an authority refuses even to consider exercising its discretion under s.204(4) then I can understand that judicial review may be an appropriate remedy. Apart from that situation, I have difficulty in envisaging cases where application for judicial review will be appropriate").

[137] *R. (on the application of Lynch) v Lambeth LBC* [2006] EWHC 2737 (Admin); [2007] H.L.R. 15 (defective decision letter could be dealt with by county court procedure). Decisions of the county court on s 204 reviews may be appealed to the Court of Appeal, subject to the grant of permission under CPR52.3 e.g. *Bury MBC v Gibbons* [2010] EWCA Civ 327; [2010] H.L.R. 33.

[138] See 1-018.

second views the procedures from the standpoints of the different participants in the judicial review process. To these may be added a third: the principle of proportionate dispute resolution—advocated by the courts as well as government—to ensure so far as possible that when disputes arise between the citizen and the State they are resolved in a manner that is timely and cost effective.

The role of the court in judicial review

On a claim for judicial review and the other forms of judicial review proceedings the court may have to deal with questions of (a) law, (b) fact and (c) policy. CPR Pt 54 claims for judicial review provide an adequate framework for determining questions of law, but provide a less effective mechanism for dealing with factual and possibly policy issues.   **17-042**

Questions of law

While questions of law are still decided on the basis of oral argument in court,[139]   **17-043**
written arguments now play an increasingly important role in comparison to other types of claims, both for parties[140] and interveners.[141] But whereas in other types of claims, at least at first instance, points of law do not have to be included in the statement of claim, the claimant in judicial review is required to set out both the factual and legal grounds of challenge (supported by authorities) to the decision in question from the very outset. This is a sensible practice since it enables the defendant and the court to make a preliminary assessment of the merits of the claim and if the grounds need amending permission to amend is normally readily granted. So whether the issue of law is statutory or common law, little complaint can be made of the present arrangements. Arrangements introduced by the Tribunals, Courts and Enforcement Act 2007 for "judicial review" to be carried out by the Upper Tribunal,[142] which is a superior court of record, should prove to be useful in ensuring that points of law relating to fields of administration falling within the ambit of tribunals are determined by judges with expertise in particular statutory regimes (which are often of great complexity) as well as general principles of administrative law.

Questions of fact

The facts upon which a claim is made are frequently agreed; the court will gener-   **17-044**
ally only be concerned with the legal consequences or inferences to be drawn from them. Although it is not generally for the courts on judicial review to alter a public authority's evaluation of issues of fact, a court will often have to satisfy itself, for example, that inferences were reasonably drawn or that conclusions rationally relate

---

[139] Though provision now exists for determinations without a hearing: see 16-082.
[140] See 16-076.
[141] See 2-073.
[142] See 1-101. The courts have adopted a functional, rather than principled, approach to defining what constitutes a question of law for the purposes of the powers of the Upper Tribunal; with the aims of allowing the Upper Tribunal scope to provide guidance in the interests of consistency while retaining a sufficient level of scrutiny by the ordinary courts to protect the rule of law (*R. (on the application of Cart) v Upper Tribunal* [2011] UKSC 28; [2012] 1 A.C. 663; and *R. (on the application of Jones) v First-tier Tribunal* [2013] UKSC 19; [2013] 2 A.C. 48 at [41]–[46], in which Lord Carnwath describes the distinction between law and fact as a matter of policy or expediency). See D. Feldman, "Error of Law and Flawed Administrative Acts" [2014] C.L.J. 275.

to evidence available to a decision-maker.[143] In this situation the existing procedure also works satisfactorily.

17-045   Issues of fact are usually decided on written evidence. While cross-examination of people who have given written evidence can be ordered, permission is not often sought to do so.[144] In addition, formal disclosure of documents is seldom ordered; claimants must rely on the defendant public authority to make full disclosure.[145] In the past, any conflict between a claimant's and defendant's evidence normally had to be resolved in the public authority's favour, on the grounds that the claimant has failed to discharge the onus which he is required to satisfy to show that the defendant has acted unlawfully. There is, however, a growing "culture of justification" in which public authorities are expected to explain the factual as well as the legal basis for their decisions.[146] Especially where Convention rights are in issue, this may entail a greater scrutiny of the underlying evidence to consider whether the defendant public authority has acted proportionately,[147] or the factual basis necessary to justify action (such as detention or compulsory treatment) exists,[148] or the court is required to have "full jurisdiction" in order to satisfy the requirements of ECHR art.6.[149]

17-046   Unfortunately, there are many situations in which there can be disputes as to the assessment of facts between the individual citizen and public authority where there is no or no adequate alternative fact-finding mechanism to the court, such as an appeal body or ombudsman. A written procedure is unsuited to resolve "disguised" appeals as to the merits of the decisions of this nature and the court on judicial review can do no more than decide whether, on the evidence which the public authority contends was available, it was entitled to come to the decision which it did. Reforms to the judicial review procedure over recent years have ensured that certain areas in which disputed questions of fact are likely to arise are transferred to other judicial fora which are better suited to their resolution. The transfer of homelessness cases to the County Court in 1996 and most asylum and immigration claims to the Upper Tribunal in 2013 is likely to ensure greater specialisation and more suitable procedures. For other cases, the Administrative Court has demonstrated flexibility in dealing with evidence where the resolution of factual disputes is fundamental to determining the legal challenge before it.[150]

Questions of policy

17-047   The most acute problems arise where judges are required to make decisions which involve their evaluating public policy considerations. Although it is usually accepted by judges that policy-making is for the administration and should be eschewed by the courts,[151] the courts sometimes need to justify their decisions simply in terms of what is socially desirable rather than on any legal principle. This is perhaps most apparent when a court exercises discretion as to whether to grant a remedy for unlawful action. In judicial review under CPR Pt 54 and applications to quash, a remedy does not follow as of right and relief can be refused even if the

---

[143] See 11-042.
[144] See 16-080.
[145] See 16-072.
[146] See 11-004.
[147] See 11-079.
[148] See 13-072.
[149] See 7-120. *R. (on the application of Wright) v Secretary of State for Health* [2009] UKHL 3; [2009] 1 A.C. 739 at [23] and *Ali v United Kingdom* (2016) 63 E.H.R.R. 20 at [75]–[76].
[150] *Doherty v Birmingham City Council* [2008] UKHL 57; [2009] 1 A.C. 367 at [68] and [138].
[151] See 1-040.

court finds the action or decision tainted by unlawfulness. Relief has been refused on the ground, for example, that to grant the order sought would result in unacceptable administrative disruption[152] or on the absence of prejudice to a claimant. The court, therefore, takes cognisance of the practical impact of its decisions, yet it may not necessarily be fully informed of what this is likely to be.

It is, therefore, not surprising that it has been argued that at the present time we **17-048** have the worst of both worlds: a judiciary which is becoming increasingly interventionist which is confined by procedures and practices which exclude from their consideration certain information and factual investigation which would enable them to make more appropriate decisions as to when and how to intervene. A possible solution which has been proposed is the creation of an Advocate General or Director of Civil Proceedings whose duty would be to present evidence of the public interest to the court,[153] and a movement from adversarial towards inquisitorial procedures. A partial solution which is within the courts' own powers is to permit interventions from bodies which are likely to be able to give the court the benefit of their experience and expertise on a particular area of law and policy.[154] The courts frequently grant permission for such interventions. The courts can convincingly point out that their greater involvement in the review of policy-making in relation to the ECHR and EU law has been expressly willed by Parliament in the HRA and the ECA. However, any extension of review into other areas of policy-making inevitably gives rise to questions about the democratic legitimacy of judicial involvement.

The different interests of those affected by judicial review

The different participants involved in proceedings for judicial review may well **17-049** attach importance to different aspects of the present procedures. The claimant will not be interested in the safeguards which are built into the procedure which are justified by the need to avoid abuse. However, the defendant public authority will attach the greatest importance to their retention since otherwise its activities may be unnecessarily disrupted which would not be in the interests of good administration. The courts are also attaching greater importance to the existence of the safeguards to help them alleviate the problems created by their increasing case load which is subjecting the court system to unwelcome strain.

Neither the claimant nor the defendant will necessarily welcome the involve- **17-050** ment of third parties since their presence may complicate the proceedings and lead to additional expense and delay. However, the presence of the intervener may be of the greatest assistance to the court since otherwise the court may be totally unaware of a consequence of its decision which would be prejudicial to the public at large.[155]

While the interests of the court, the parties and other interested bodies may ap- **17-051** pear to be in conflict, closer examination may indicate that their interests are much closer than they realise. A claimant who has a meritorious case usually will have no difficulty in surmounting the hurdle of obtaining permission, but he could be seriously prejudiced if his case is substantially delayed because of the court having to deal with unmeritorious claims which should have been dealt with at the

---

[152] See, e.g. *R. v Gateshead BC Ex p. Nichol* [1988] C.O.D. 97.
[153] J.A.G. Griffith, "Judicial Decision-Making in Public Law" [1985] P.L. 564; H. Woolf, *Protection of the Public: A New Challenge* (1990), pp.109-113; Sir Jack Jacob, "Safeguarding the Public Interest in English Civil Proceedings" [1982] C.J.Q. 312, 316-319.
[154] 2-073–2-075.
[155] See 2-070.

outset by a refusal of permission. The third party who can be affected by the proceedings may have no desire to incur the expense of being involved in the proceedings. His sole concern could well be that the proceedings should be completed as soon as possible so that, for example, a property which is subject to planning blight may be sold.

17-052   What is required is a procedure which reconciles these interests to the greatest extent possible. A procedure which allows the citizen ready access to a system of justice that he can afford and provides, where he has been unfairly or unreasonably or unlawfully treated, an effective remedy; a system which, while protecting the public from abuse of power is not so interventionist that it is inconsistent with good administration because it is over-intrusive. Devising a system which reconciles these objectives is by no means easy. It requires a careful balancing of the respective interests involved. We have described above the mechanisms whereby parts of the judicial review caseload (for example homelessness appeals and aspects of immigration and asylum) which were imposing extreme demands on the resources of the Administrative Court have been re-directed to other courts and tribunals. Where such judicial bodies are sufficiently independent and their decision-making procedures are at least as well-suited to the resolution of the relevant disputes, there can be little objection to this as a matter of principle. A more worrying development for the rule of law is the Government's intention to amend the judicial review procedures with the express aim of reducing the judicial review caseload.[156]

---

[156] On 19 November 2012, the Justice Secretary announced that the time limits for certain judicial reviews would be further shortened, that the number of potential challenges to a refusal of permission would be reduced and that court fees would be increased to cover the real cost of proceedings. The announcement was based on a mis-reading of the judicial statistics for the Admin Ct. See now, the Ministry of Justice's "Judicial Review: proposals for reform" (CP25/2012). See para.1-005 and Ch.16 for the latest Government initiatives.

CHAPTER 18

Judicial Review Remedies

TABLE OF CONTENTS

SCOPE

This chapter examines the public law remedies—interim and final—that may be **18-001** awarded on a claim for judicial review and the extent of the court's discretion to withhold them. The Administrative Court has at its disposal a range of powers to grant remedial orders in relation to a claim for judicial review, stemming from statutory and common law sources.

- Senior Courts Act 1981 s.37 and CPR Pts 25 and 54 govern interim remedies. These include interim injunctions, stays of proceedings and interim declarations.
- Senior Courts Act 1981 ss.29 and 31[1] and CPR Pt 54 regulate the main types of final remedy in judicial review claims. The various remedies—prohibiting, mandatory and quashing orders, injunctions and declarations—may be granted either singly or in combination.[2]
- The common law may provide a right to damages, restitution or recovery of a sum due where there has been an unlawful administrative act—but only if the elements of a recognised tort (typically negligence, breach of statutory duty and misfeasance of public office) or other cause of action can also be established.[3] In practice, claims for damages and other monetary remedies may be determined at a separate hearing after the public law issues have been decided although this has become less common as more litigants now add a claim for damages under the Human Rights Act to their grounds for judicial review.
- The Human Rights Act 1998 s.4 (declarations of incompatibility) and s.8

---

[1] As amended on 1 May 2004 by The Civil Procedure (Modification of Supreme Court Act 1981) Order 2004 (SI 2004/1033) (which altered the names of the remedies).

[2] Senior Courts Act 1981 s.31(2).

[3] See Ch.19.

(damages for actions breaching Convention rights)[4] provide specific remedies in judicial review and other claims in this context.[5]

- European Community law requires additional and modified remedies to be available in order to ensure the full protection of Community law rights.[6]

FUNCTION OF REMEDIES

18-002   The modern era of English judicial review is marked by two changes in the way remedial orders are made and thought about. First, prior to the reforms to the judicial review system in 1978,[7] a plethora of technical rules restricted the circumstances in which claimants could be granted remedies in public law. Now the courts are reluctant to let the former intricacies and obscurities hamper the provision of effective redress. The courts adopt a flexible approach—though the willingness to innovate has not extended as far as accepting the radical suggestion that there is no longer any need for remedial orders specific to judicial review.[8]

18-003   Secondly, before the modern era of judicial review, the limits of the High Court's supervisory jurisdiction were defined by placing restrictions on the situations in which the particular remedies of certiorari, prohibition and mandamus could be granted. As we have seen, the approach today is a much broader one: the boundaries of the court's supervisory powers are determined by focusing on the source of legal authority and the character of the function,[9] and whether the subject-matter of the claim is justiciable.[10] Little of the old case law on the reach of each remedy is of much practical relevance.[11] The question to be addressed is therefore no longer, "does certiorari lie against such a decision?" but rather whether the impugned decision is one made by a public authority in the exercise of a public function and is justiciable. Today it can be said that the remedial orders at the disposal of the court perform the subsidiary role of giving practical effect to the judgment of the court.

18-004   The importance of remedies should not, however, be underestimated. In the first of the Hamlyn lectures, published as *Freedom under the Law*, Denning J (as he then was) saw the biggest challenge facing the judiciary as the fashioning of new remedies to protect our freedoms. As this and the next Chapters will make clear, this is one challenge that the judiciary, with the help of Parliament and academics and practitioners, have to a considerable extent successfully met. However, there has been a more worrying recent trend towards restricting the availability of judicial review on the basis of apparent hostility to the ordinary operation of the rule of law.

---

[4]   See 19-081.
[5]   See 13-054 The text is set out in Appendix E.
[6]   See 14-056.
[7]   See 15-087.
[8]   D. Oliver, "Public Law Remedies and Procedures—Do We Need Them?" [2002] P.L. 91.
[9]   Ch.3.
[10]   See 1-034; 11-014.
[11]   There is no need, for example, to inquire whether the decision was a "judicial one": see Appendix B on the classification of functions.

REMEDIES AGAINST THE CROWN AND MINISTERS

No coercive remedies against the Crown directly

The prerogative orders (mandatory, prohibiting and quashing orders) and injunc- **18-005**
tions cannot be granted against the Crown directly.[12] Declaratory relief is however
available. The justification given for this restriction is "both because there would
be an incongruity in the Queen commanding herself to do an act, and also because
disobedience to a writ of mandamus is to be enforced by attachment".[13]

Ministers are officers of the Crown

The restriction on coercive remedies against the Crown presents few practical **18-006**
problems as legislation rarely places duties or confers powers on the Crown as such.
Most statutory and prerogative powers of central government are exercised by
Secretaries of State (who are *officers of the* Crown as distinct from the Crown itself)
and coercive judicial review remedies may be granted against ministers in their official capacity.[14]

Interim relief against ministers

The one difficulty that used to face claimants seeking a remedy against a minister **18-007**
was that, until relatively recently, Pt II of the Crown Proceedings Act 1947, which
restricts the circumstances in which injunctions may be granted against ministers,
was held to apply not only to private law proceedings against central government
but also to restrict the court's powers to grant injunctions on applications for judicial
review. In other words, the 1947 Act, which had been passed to make litigation
against central government less hampered by outdated technical protections against
"the Crown", was believed to qualify the plain words in s.31 of the Senior Courts
Act 1981 giving power to the court to grant injunctive relief during a claim for
judicial review. At the time, the bar on injunctive relief against ministers could pose
significant practical difficulties for claimants as injunctions were the only form of
remedial order which, on an application for judicial review, the court was able to
grant on an interim basis pending the full hearing of the case.[15]

Since the 1990s it is clear, however, that the court does indeed have jurisdiction **18-008**
to grant injunctions against ministers on claims for judicial review. First, the House
of Lords held, following the European Court of Justice, that the court had power
to grant interim injunctions against ministers where this was necessary in order to

---

[12] On the nature of the Crown, see 3-033.

[13] *R. v Powell* (1841) 1 Q.B. 352 at 361 (Lord Denman CJ), cited with approval in *M v Home Office* [1994] 1 A.C. 377 at 415, HL (Lord Woolf); cf. *Page v Hull University Visitor* [1993] A.C. 682 where the HL appears to have accepted without argument that certiorari could lie against the Queen "as visitor" to a University. See further 3-032.

[14] *R. v Commissioners of Customs and Excise Ex p Cook* [1970] 1 W.L.R. 450 at 455 (Lord Parker CJ). On the nature of the office of Secretary of State, see 3-003. The Secretary of State would have no immunity from a prohibiting order (or any other judicial review remedy) to prevent him from lay-ing draft Orders in Council before Her Majesty if such draft Orders constituted an abuse of power (*R. (on the application of Bancoult) v Secretary of State for Foreign and Commonwealth Affairs (No.2)* [2007] EWCA Civ 498; [2008] Q.B. 365 at [34]-[36] (Sedley LJ) (overturned on other grounds in *Bancoult* [2008] UKHL 61; [2009] 1 A.C. 453). The Admin Ct made a mandatory order requiring the return of a family to the United Kingdom in *R. (on the application of M) v Secretary of State for the Home Department* [2011] EWHC 3667 (Admin); [2012] A.C.D. 34 at [26]-[28].

[15] Since 1998 the court may grant interim declarations: see 18-021.

protect rights under European Community law.[16] Secondly, the House of Lords held that Pt II of the 1947 Act applies only to "civil proceedings," as defined by s.38(2), not to claims for judicial review.[17] Even though it is now clear that the courts possess jurisdiction to grant injunctions against ministers and other officers of the Crown, this power is exercised only in the most limited of circumstances. A declaration—in interim or final form—will continue to be regarded as the most appropriate remedy on a claim for judicial review involving officers of the Crown.[18]

INTERIM REMEDIES

18-009   Interim remedies "hold the ring".[19] As in most other types of claim, there may be a need in claims for judicial review for the court to grant an interim remedy to preserve the position of the parties until a final resolution of the legal dispute between the claimant and defendant.[20] Interim relief may be sought at *any* point, including (in urgent cases) before the claimant has obtained permission to proceed with the claim and even after the final judgment has been given.[21] Most typically, however, interim remedies are sought at the permission stage.[22] In practice the form of interim remedy most commonly granted in judicial review claims is an interim injunction and stay of proceedings. Interim declarations are also available, along with a variety of other orders listed in CPR 25.1(1). The defendant public authority may be willing to give an undertaking to the court, so avoiding the need for a formal interim order to be sought and made. For this reason, it is important that in most cases, the application for an interim remedy is made on notice to the defendant.[23]

Urgency

18-010   Interim relief will typically be requested by the claimant at the point of applying for permission to proceed with the claim. The determination of an application for permission typically takes in excess of six weeks, not least because the defendant has 21 days to provide an acknowledgment of service. In some cases this length of time would leave a claimant vulnerable, so it is possible to obtain interim remedies before the point at which the court grants permission. CPR Pt 54 and the main Practice Direction (54A) are silent on how to make urgent applications. Following lobbying from practitioners, a Practice Statement and form for "Request of Urgent Consideration" do however now exist.[24] It is essential that the Practice Direction is followed and that the urgent procedure is not abused if it is to func-

---

[16]   See 14-042.

[17]   *M v Home Office* [1994] 1 A.C. 377; in relation to the Scottish Executive, see *Davidson v Scottish Ministers* [2005] UKHL 74; 2006 S.C. (H.L.) 41.

[18]   *M v Home Office* [1994] 1 A.C. 377 at 412. A declaration was sought and granted in *R. (on the application of Miller) v Secretary of State for Exiting the European Union* [2017] UKSC 5; [2017] W.L.R. 583 concerning the power to exercise art.50 TEU without a vote in Parliament.

[19]   An expression used in *R. v Cardiff City Council Ex p. Barry* [1990] C.O.D. 94 and *M v Home Office* [1992] Q.B. 270 at 306G.

[20]   CPR Pt 25 and PD25 govern claims for judicial review as they do other types of claim.

[21]   CPR r.25.2(1).

[22]   On permission, see 16-044.

[23]   *R. v Kensington and Chelsea RLBC Ex p Hammell* [1989] Q.B. 518 at 539B-D.

[24]   Form N463 is available from the Ministry of Justice website, and reproduced in this work in Appendix L; see also *Practice Statement (Administrative Court: Listings and Urgent Cases)* [2002] 1 W.L.R. 810.

tion effectively.[25] In exceptionally urgent cases, application may be made to the out-of-hours judge.[26] Where a request for an interim remedy is refused on the papers, a practice has developed of allowing the application to be renewed at an oral hearing.[27]

Interim injunctions

An interim injunction is one granted before trial, for the purpose of preventing any change in the status quo from taking place until the final determination of the merits of the case and to ensure that any final order that may be made at the full hearing of the claim should not be rendered nugatory. Interim injunctions may be mandatory[28] or prohibitory.

18-011

General approach

The general approach to the grant of interim relief in civil claims was established in 1975, when the House of Lords held that a claimant need no longer establish a prima facie case, but instead demonstrate that there is a serious issue to be tried, i.e. a claim that is not frivolous or vexatious and discloses a reasonable prospect of success.[29] The claimant having shown that there is, at the least, a serious issue to be tried, the court will then consider whether it is just and convenient to grant an interim injunction. This involves the court assessing the relative risks of injustice by deciding whether there is an adequate alternative remedy in damages, either to the claimant seeking the injunction[30] or the defendant in the event that an injunction is granted against him.[31] The availability of a remedy in damages to the claimant will normally preclude the grant to him of an injunction. Even if damages are available, they may not be an adequate remedy.[32] If there is doubt about either or both the claimant's and/or the defendant's remedy in damages, the court will proceed to consider what has become known as the "balance of convenience". The factors to be taken into consideration will vary from case to case. The aim of this approach is to avoid the court having to consider difficult questions of law or fact at the interim stage.

18-012

---

25 *R. (on the application of Hamid) v Secretary of State for the Home Department* [2012] EWHC 3070 (Admin).
26 The telephone number for the duty judge is 020 7947 6000. PD 54D.4 provides that urgent applications are to be made to the relevant Admin Ct District Registry outside London during court opening hours for the attention of the designated judge. Applications out of hours should be made to the duty judge in London. For a practitioner's view, see K. Marcus, "Urgent Applications, Interim Relief and Costs" [2004] J.R. 256.
27 *R. (on the application of Q) v Secretary of State for the Home Department* [2003] EWHC 2507 (Admin) at [10].
28 See, e.g. *R. (on the application of S) v Norfolk CC* [2004] EWHC 404 (Admin); [2004] E.L.R. 259 (local education authority ordered to continue funding child's place at a residential college).
29 *American Cyanamid Co v Ethicon Ltd* [1975] A.C. 396. Since the coming into force of the CPR the context in which interim remedies are sought has changed, not least because there is now encouragement for the early resolution of issues, and at some point the HL's approach may need to be reconsidered.
30 For example, in the event of the interim injunction being refused, but the claimant succeeding at trial.
31 For example, if the interim injunction is granted but the claimant fails at trial. The grant of an interim injunction is usually conditional on the claimant giving an undertaking to pay damages in these circumstances.
32 See, e.g. *R. v Kensington and Chelsea RLBC Ex p. Hammell* [1989] Q.B. 518.

Approach in judicial review claims

18-013   The old prima facie case test continues to apply, in effect, in many judicial review cases[33] because a prerequisite to the grant of an interim injunction is normally the grant of permission, where the threshold often approximates more to the need to show a prima facie case than merely a potentially arguable one.[34] Moreover, questions as to the adequacy of damages as an alternative remedy will usually be less, or not at all, relevant because of the absence of any general right to damages for loss caused by unlawful administrative action per se.[35] Conversely, the defendant does not usually suffer financial loss from the inability to implement its policies for a period.[36] It follows that in cases involving the public interest, for example where a party is a public authority performing public duties, the decision to grant or withhold interim injunctive relief will usually be made not on the basis of the adequacy of damages but on the balance of convenience test.[37] In such cases, the balance of convenience must be looked at widely, taking into account the interests of the general public to whom the duties are owed.[38] The courts will be vigilant to prevent a claimant from seeking an injunction against an interested party in judicial review proceedings when the dispute is really one suitable for a private law claim.[39]

18-014   Another difference from private law proceedings is that in judicial review, there is less likely to be a dispute of issues of fact. Where the only dispute is as to law, the court may have to make the best prediction it can of the final outcome and give that prediction decisive weight in resolving the interlocutory issue.[40]

18-015   Others factors that may be taken into account in determining the balance of convenience include the importance of upholding the law of the land and the duty placed on certain authorities to enforce the law in the public interest.[41] In the case of a challenge to the validity of a law, the court should not exercise its discretion to restrain a public authority by interim injunction from enforcing apparently authentic law unless it is satisfied, having regard to all the circumstances, that the challenge to the validity of the law is, prima facie, so firmly based as to justify so exceptional a course being taken.[42] The general principle that expression of opinion or the expression and the dissemination of information will not be restrained by the courts except on pressing grounds applies as much to a public authority which is under a duty to express an opinion as to a private individual.[43]

---

33   But not all: see, e.g. *R. v Secretary of State for the Home Department Ex p. Doorga* [1990] C.O.D. 109; *Scotia Pharmaceuticals International Ltd v Secretary of State for Health (No.2)* [1994] C.O.D. 241.

34   See 16-049.

35   See Ch.19.

36   *R. (on the application of Medical Justice) v Secretary of State for the Home Department* [2010] EWHC 1425 (Admin); [2010] A.C.D. 70 at [12]. Appealed on other grounds [2011] EWCA Civ 269; [2011] 1 W.L.R. 2852.

37   *R. v Secretary of State for Transport Ex p. Factortame Ltd (No.2)* [1991] 1 A.C. 603 at 672-673.

38   *Factortame (No.2)* [1991] 1 A.C. 603; and *R. v HM Treasury Ex p. British Telecommunications Plc* [1995] C.O.D. 56; cf. *R. v Secretary of State for Health Ex p. Generics (UK) Ltd* [1997] C.O.D. 294.

39   *Eaton v Natural England* [2012] EWHC 2401 (Admin); [2013] 1 C.M.L.R. 10 at [35]-[38].

40   *Factortame (No.2)* [1991] 1 A.C. 603 at 660 (Lord Bridge).

41   *Factortame (No.2)* [1991] 1 A.C. 603 at 672.

42   *Factortame (No.2)* [1991] 1 A.C. 603 at 673 (Lord Goff).

43   *R. v Advertising Standards Authority Ltd Ex p. Vernons Organisation Ltd* [1992] 1 W.L.R. 1289; cf. *R. v Advertising Standards Authority Ex p. Direct Line Financial Services Ltd* [1998] C.O.D. 20 (interim injunction granted restraining ASA from publishing adjudication). *R. (Debt Free Direct Ltd) v Advertising Standards Authority Ltd* [2007] EWHC 1337 (Admin).

The discretionary bars to the award of an injunction[44] are applied with particular **18-016** stringency to the claimant for interim relief, and he is in any event usually required to give an undertaking in damages lest at the trial the interim injunction is shown to have been wrongly granted and the defendant has suffered loss as a result. Many claimants are legally aided and have insufficient means to give an effective undertaking in damages. This is not a bar to the grant of interim relief,[45] for the requirement of a cross-undertaking is a matter of discretion for the court. Neither ministers nor local authorities have any special exemption from giving cross-undertakings in damages, but a court is unlikely to exercise its discretion to require one where an injunction is sought in a law enforcement action.[46]

Stay of proceedings

Under CPR r.54.10(2), the court may grant a stay of proceedings when the claim- **18-017** ant is granted permission to proceed with a judicial review claim. Authorities are divided as to the scope and effect of such a "stay".[47] The Court of Appeal has held that the term is apt to include executive decisions and the process by which the decision was reached and may be granted to prevent a minister from implementing a decision.[48] The Privy Council has however held, obiter, that a stay of proceedings is merely an order which puts a stop to the further conduct of proceedings in court or before a tribunal at the stage which they have reached, the object being to avoid the hearing or trial taking place; and that it could have no possible application to an executive decision which has already been made.[49] The position still awaits clarification by the Supreme Court,[50] but the prevailing view is that a stay of proceedings should be available widely (including in relation to administrative deci-

---

44 See 18-047.
45 *Ex p. Hammell* [1989] Q.B. 518; *Allen v Jambo Holdings Ltd* [1980] 1 W.L.R. 1252 (but note *Belize Alliance of Conservation Non-Governmental Organisations v Department of the Environment (Interim Injunction)* [2003] UKPC 63; [2003] 1 W.L.R. 2839 at [35]-[47], where the PC held that *Allen* "should not be taken too far" as "[t]he court is never exempted from the duty to do its best, on interlocutory applications with far-reaching financial implications, to minimise the risk of injustice". In that case, the risk of prejudice to the developer of a major dam project was too great in the absence of a cross-undertaking in damages. In *R. v Secretary of State for the Environment Ex p. Rose Theatre Trust Company* [1990] 1 Q.B. 504 Schiemann J held the court should be extremely slow to grant an injunction without a cross-undertaking in damages; see also *R. (on the application of Greenpeace Ltd) v Inspectorate of Pollution* [1994] 1 W.L.R. 570 at 574.
46 *F. Hoffmann-La Roche & Co AG v Secretary of State for Trade and Industry* [1975] A.C. 295; *Director General of Fair Trading v Tobyward Ltd* [1989] 1 W.L.R. 517; *Kirklees MBC v Wickes Building Supplies Ltd* [1993] A.C. 227; *Coventry City Council v Finnie* (1997) 29 H.L.R. 658; and *Financial Services Authority v Sinaloa Gold Plc* [2013] UKSC 11; [2013] 2 A.C. 28 at [31]-[35] (Lord Mance).
47 The glossary to the CPR states "A stay imposes a halt on proceedings, apart from taking any steps allowed by the Rules or the terms of the stay. Proceedings can be continued if a stay is lifted".
48 *R. v Secretary of State for Education and Science Ex p. Avon CC (No. 2)* [1991] 1 Q.B. 558 at 561, 563 (Glidewell and Taylor LJJ) (decision of minister to make order giving school grant maintained status); *R. v Secretary of State for the Home Department Ex p. Muboyayi* [1992] Q.B. 244 at 258 (Lord Donaldson MR declines to express opinion on whether *Avon* will survive an appeal to the HL); *R. v Advertising Standards Authority Ltd Ex p. Vernons Organisation Ltd* [1993] 1 W.L.R. 1289 (application for stay "in truth" a claim for an injunction) and *R. (on the application of Yousuf) v Secretary of State for Foreign and Commonwealth Affairs* [2016] EWHC 663 (Admin) (stay of a judicial review claim inappropriate where the decision-maker had agreed to reconsider the decision with a fresh and open mind).
49 *Minister of Foreign Affairs, Trade and Industry v Vehicles and Supplies Ltd* [1991] 1 W.L.R. 550 at 556 (Lord Oliver). The Board was considering s.564B(4) of the Jamaican Civil Procedure Code which was in similar terms to RSC Ord.53 r.3(10)(a) (now CPR r.54.10(2)). *Ex p. Avon* [1991] 1 Q.B. 558 was neither referred to nor cited in argument.
50 The Law Commission has recommended that "proceedings" in this context ought to be given a nar-

sions) where it can add to the effective remedies available on judicial review by ensuring that the successful party obtains the full benefit of his success.[51]

18-018   Unlike an injunction, a stay of proceedings is an order directed not at a party to the litigation but at the decision-making process of the court, tribunal or other decision-maker. It may not, therefore, be an order capable of being breached by a party to the proceedings, or anyone else, and may not be enforceable by contempt proceedings.[52] A decision made by an officer or minister of the Crown can be stayed by an order of the court.[53] Now that it is clear that interim injunctive relief can be ordered against officers and Ministers of the Crown,[54] and the court has power to make interim declarations, this characteristic of the stay is of less importance than it once was. There is much to be said as a matter of logic for the view that, in the light of these developments, stays of proceedings may be confined to use in relation to judicial proceedings.[55] It does however, as we point out below, act as an effective brake on administrative action and it is not only the judicial proceedings which are brought to a halt while the stay is in operation.

18-019   Although the court has a general discretion to grant a stay of proceedings subject to any conditions it considers appropriate, cross-undertakings in damages will not normally be required.

18-020   The practical effect of a stay varies depending on the context.[56] Where the public authority has yet to make a final decision, the grant of a stay prohibits them from taking further steps to make that decision. Where a final decision has been made but not yet implemented, a stay will prevent implementation of the decision, which is suspended for the time being and any formal order is treated as temporarily being of no effect. The more difficult question is whether a stay may be granted where a decision has been both made and implemented. The Court of Appeal has answered this in the affirmative, on the basis that if a final quashing order is eventually made, the decision will be treated as never having had any legal effect and therefore the court should have jurisdiction to say that a decision is without legal effect on a temporary basis.[57]

---

row meaning. This is in light of the fact that injunctions are now available against ministers on a claim for judicial review and the suggestion that the court ought to be empowered to grant interim declarations: see Law Com. No.226, para.6.26.

51   *R. (on the application of H) v Ashworth Special Hospital Authority* [2002] EWCA Civ 923; [2003] 1 W.L.R. 127 at [42] regarding the Privy Council's approach as too narrow. See further, *Cala Homes (South) Ltd v Secretary of State for Communities and Local Government* [2010] EWHC 3278 (Admin); [2011] J.P.L. 553 at [26] (appeal dismissed at [2011] EWCA Civ 639; [2011] J.P.L. 1458).

52   *Vehicles and Supplies Ltd* [1991] 1 W.L.R. 550 at [71] (Lord Oliver).

53   *Ex p. Avon CC* [1991] 1 Q.B. 558 at 558, 562 (Glidewell LJ). cf. *R. v Secretary of State for the Home Department Ex p. Kirkwood* [1984] 1 W.L.R. 913; *R. v Secretary of State for the Home Department Ex p. Mohammed Yacoob* [1984] 1 W.L.R. 920. In the two House of Lords' decisions in the *Factortame cases ((No.1))* [1990] 2 A.C. 85; *(No.2)* [1991] 1 A.C. 603), no mention was made of the question whether the court had power to grant a stay of proceedings against Ministers; it has been suggested that this omission was no accident: see Woolf, *Protection of the Public—a New Challenge* (1990), p.65.

54   *M v Home Office* [1994] 1 A.C. 377.

55   C. Lewis, *Judicial Remedies in Public Law*, 5th edn (2014), para.6–028.

56   *R. (on the application of H) v Ashworth Hospital Authority* [2002] EWCA Civ 923; [2003] 1 W.L.R. 127 at [45]-[48].

57   *Ashworth Hospital Authority* [2002] EWCA Civ 923; [2003] 1 W.L.R. 127 at [46].

Interim declarations

Interim declarations were once "unknown to law" and even said to be "a **18-021** contradiction in terms".[58] Following recommendations by the Law Commission and in Lord Woolf's *Access to Justice* report, an express power to grant interim declarations was included in the CPR when they were enacted in April 1999.[59] The courts are gradually making greater use of interim declarations in judicial review proceedings.[60]

Bail

Until April 2004, the High Court exercised a general inherent power (usually **18-022** heard by a judge in chambers) to grant bail to a person who had been refused bail by a magistrates' court or the Crown Court pending trial or appeal.[61] That general power to grant bail was abolished by s.17 of the Criminal Justice Act 2003.[62] With the abolition of this alternative remedy,[63] now the appropriate course for a person aggrieved by the refusal of bail by a magistrates' court or the Crown Court will often be to apply for judicial review of that refusal, though the court has warned that it will exercise its jurisdiction sparingly.[64]

FINAL REMEDIAL ORDERS

At the conclusion of the full hearing, a successful claimant may request the court **18-023** to grant a mandatory order (formerly called mandamus),[65] a quashing order

---

[58] *International General Electric Co of New York Ltd v Customs and Excise Comrs* [1962] Ch. 784 at 790 (Diplock LJ).

[59] CPR r.25.1(1)(b).

[60] *R. (on the application of AM) v Director of Public Prosecutions* [2012] EWHC 470 (Admin) was an exceptional case where solicitors for an individual who had expressed a wish to end his life after suffering a massive stroke were granted an interim declaration that it would be lawful for them to obtain information relating to his challenge to the DPP's policy on assisted suicide without themselves acting in breach of the Suicide Act 1961. A further example is *G v E* [2010] EWCA Civ 822; [2012] Fam. 78 at [65]-[70], in which the CA upheld an interim declaration that it was in the claimant's best interests to remain in a local authority unit.

[61] *Sezek v Secretary of State for the Home Department (Bail Application)* [2001] EWCA Civ 795; [2002] 1 W.L.R. 348 at [16].

[62] As part of the implementation of Sir Robin Auld's review of the criminal court system; note that s.17(6) provides "Nothing in this section affects any right of a person to apply for a writ of habeas corpus or any other prerogative remedy".

[63] cf. the position in contempt proceedings where there is a right of appeal to the Court of Appeal Criminal Division which must be exercised in preference to making a claim for judicial review: *R. v Serumaga* [2005] EWCA Crim 370; [2005] 2 All E.R. 160.

[64] *R. (on the application of M) v Isleworth Crown Court* [2005] EWHC 263 (Admin); [2005] All E.R. (D) 42 (Mar); *R. (on the application of Allwin) v Snaresbrook Crown Court* [2005] EWHC 742 (Admin) (guidance on bringing a claim). *R. (on the application of Mongan) v Isleworth Crown Court* [2007] EWHC 1087 (Admin) at [10] was one of the rare cases where it was appropriate to permit judicial review as it is concerned whether a material change of circumstance should have led to a re-consideration of the bail application. The court may also permit judicial review where the decision-maker took into account a legally irrelevant factor: *R. (on the application of U) v Northampton Crown Court* [2013] EWHC 4519 (Admin) at [12]. A defendant on trial on indictment in the Crown Court may not challenge a decision to revoke bail made in the midst of a trial: *R. (on the application of Uddin) v Crown Court at Leeds* [2013] EWHC 2752 (Admin); [2014] 1 W.L.R. 1742 at [35].

[65] See 18-024.

(certiorari) or a prohibiting order (prohibition)[66]—a group of remedies for historical reasons known collectively as "prerogative orders".[67] The court may also grant injunctions[68] and declarations.[69] For almost all purposes, the mandatory and prohibiting orders can now be regarded as indistinguishable in their effect from final injunctions[70]: all three remedies "direct any of the parties to do, or refrain from doing, any act in relation to the particular matter".[71] A distinctive feature of all these remedies is that the court has discretion to withhold them from a claimant even if the defendant public authority is held to have acted unlawfully.[72] Remedies may be granted in combination with one another. However, CPR 54.2 provides that the prerogative remedies and an injunction under s.30 of the Senior Courts Act 1981 must be sought by judicial review.

Mandatory orders

18-024   The modern approach to remedies—in which the function of remedial orders is simply to give effect to the judgment of the court on the substance of a claim—means that it is no longer necessary at this stage to describe the kinds of decision in which mandatory orders may be granted.[73] If the court has found there to be breach of a duty, a mandatory order may be granted if in all the circumstances that appears to the court to be the appropriate form of relief.[74] Mandatory orders will

---

[66] See 18-026.

[67] Ch.15. In its 1994 report *Administrative Law: Judicial Review and Statutory Appeals*, the Law Commission argued that the Latin names for the prerogative orders obscured their functions to nonlawyers; it recommended that the Supreme Court Act 1981 be amended to rename them (Law Com. No.226, para.8.3). This suggestion was not supported by Lord Woolf in *Access to Justice*, para.13-065, but did find favour with the Bowman committee (see 15-097) and ss.29 and 31 of the 1981 Act were amended in 2004; see 3-013.

[68] See 18-033.

[69] See 18-037.

[70] *M v Home Office* [1994] 1 A.C. 377 at 415E.

[71] Words used in the Australian Administrative Decisions (Judicial Review) Act 1977 s.30 which introduced a flexible range of remedies to replace prerogative writs with a view to freeing "judicial review from its emphasis on the character of the remedy sought, instead allowing the court to consider the substance of the applicant's grievance" (*Electoral and Administrative Review Commission*, Issues Paper No.4, 1990).

[72] See 18-047. Amendments introduced by the Criminal Justice and Courts Act 2015 to the Senior Courts Act 1981 s.31(2A) (which entered into force on 13 April 2015) require the Administrative Court to refuse to grant relief where "it appears to the court to be highly likely that the outcome for the applicant would not have been substantially different if the conduct complained of had not occurred". The court has a limited discretion to award a remedy even if the "no difference" test is made out where it "considers that it is appropriate to do so for reasons of exceptional public interest". If the court awards a remedy on grounds of exceptional public interest, it must certify that this condition is satisfied. This introduces a lower threshold than the previous law which required that the same result would almost inevitably have been reached and very much reduces the court's discretion (see para.18-050).

[73] On issues to do with substance, see e.g. the distinction between mandatory and "directory" duties and powers (see 5-057); whether lack of resources may excuse failure to perform what otherwise would be a duty (see 5-148).

[74] Striking recent examples of mandatory orders include that the Director of Public Prosecutions should promulgate a specific policy in relation to assisted suicide (*R. (on the application of Purdy) v Director of Public Prosecutions* [2009] UKHL 45; [2010] 1 A.C. 345 at [56] (Lord Hope)) and that the claimant's son should be admitted to the faith school which had excluded him on racial grounds (*R. (on the application of E) v The Governing Body of JFS* [2009] UKSC 15; [2010] 2 A.C. 728). In *R. (on the application of ClientEarth) v Secretary of State for the Environment, Food and Rural Affairs* [2015] UKSC 28; [2015] 4 All E.R. 724 at [30]–[31] and [35], the SC made a mandatory order requiring the Secretary of State to prepare new air quality plans for London and to deliver the plans to the European Commission by the end of the year. ClientEarth has returned to court repeatedly to

not lie to compel the performance of a mere moral duty,[75] or to order anything to be done that is contrary to law.

Many of the narrow technicalities which once applied to the grant of mandamus, for example, that it would not lie for the purpose of undoing that which has already been done in contravention of statute,[76] no longer restrict the remedy. It has long been held to be preferable for the claimant to be able to show that he has demanded performance of the duty and that performance has been refused by the authority obliged to discharge it.[77] A claimant, before applying for judicial review, should address a distinct and specific demand or request to the defendant that he perform the duty imposed upon him.[78] Today this learning is encapsulated in the general obligation on claimants to follow the steps set out in the Pre-Action Protocol for Judicial Review, which includes writing a letter before claim.[79]

18-025

Quashing and prohibiting orders

Historically, the orders of certiorari and prohibition had so many characteristics in common that they may, in their modern forms, be discussed together. The one significant difference between them is that a prohibiting order may, and usually must, be invoked at an earlier stage than a quashing order. A prohibiting order will not be granted unless something remains to be done that a court can prohibit. A quashing order will not lie unless something has been done that a court can quash. But it is sometimes appropriate to apply for both orders simultaneously—a quashing order to quash an order made by a tribunal in excess of its jurisdiction, and a prohibiting order to prevent the tribunal from continuing to exceed its jurisdiction.

18-026

It has been held that the orders will not issue to persons who take it upon themselves to exercise a jurisdiction without any colour of legal authority; the acts of usurpers are to be regarded as nugatory. Where a tribunal which had power to grant cinematograph licences adopted a practice of approving building plans before the application for a licence was made, on the understanding that it would later grant the licence if it approved the plans, the courts held that certiorari and mandamus would not go to the tribunal for a refusal to approve plans, since the tribunal had no legal authority whatsoever to make provisional decisions.[80] However, today, in order to remove uncertainty, a court would issue the orders to public authorities that purport to be acting in pursuance of lawful authority. In relation to a void deci-

18-027

---

police the enforcement of the SC's order: see *R. (on the application of ClientEarth) v Secretary of State for the Environment, Food and Rural Affairs* [2016] EWHC 2740 (Admin); [2016] EWHC 3613 (Admin); [2017] EWHC 1618 (Admin); and [2017] EWHC 1966 (Admin). The difficulties in obtaining a mandatory order in relation to the investigation of criminality was emphasised in *R. (on the application of Soma Oil & Gas Ltd) v Director of the Serious Fraud Office* [2016] EWHC 2471 (Admin).

[75] For example, to make good a military officer's pay: *Ex p. Napier* (1852) 18 Q.B. 692.
[76] See the 4th edition of this work, p.542.
[77] T. Tapping, *On Mandamus* (1853), pp.282-286.
[78] cf. *R. v Bristol & Exeter Ry* (1843) 4 Q.B. 162, where the only demand made was premature.
[79] See Appendix I.
[80] *R. v Barnstaple Justices Ex p. Carder* [1938] 1 K.B. 385. See also *Re Daws* (1838) 8 Ad. & El. 936; *R. v Maguire and O'Sheil* [1923] 2 I.R. 58; and *Re Clifford and O'Sullivan* [1921] 2 A.C. 570 (no prohibition to court martial in state of martial law, for it is not a body exercising legal jurisdiction but an instrument for executing the will of the military commander). But for a more satisfactory result, see *Steve Dart Co v Board of Arbitration* [1974] 2 F.C. 215 (prohibition issued to a tribunal purporting to act under legislation that did not empower its creation).

sion, a quashing order *in effect* declares that it was ineffective ab initio; in the case of a voidable decision, a quashing order will deprive the decision of legal effect.[81]

18-028   It is still not altogether clear what is the earliest stage at which a claim for a prohibiting order may be made. If want of jurisdiction is apparent, a prohibiting order may be applied for at once. If want of jurisdiction is not apparent, the claim must wait until the tribunal has actually stepped outside its jurisdiction (as by continuing the hearing after an incorrect determination of a jurisdictional fact) or is undoubtedly about to step outside its jurisdiction (as where it has announced its intention to entertain matters into which it has no power to inquire).[82] This is the generally accepted doctrine; but doubts have sometimes been expressed about the power to grant prohibiting orders for an anticipatory excess of jurisdiction.[83] On the other hand, there have been more modern decisions in which applications for prohibiting orders have been considered even before the inferior tribunal has had the opportunity to address itself to the disputed question of its jurisdiction.[84] In any event, a doubt as to whether a request for a prohibiting order is premature is likely to be resolved in the claimant's favour if the final order of the tribunal may be protected by statute from challenge.[85]

Remitting the matter back to the decision-maker

18-029   Section 31(5) of the Senior Courts Act 1981 provides that

> "If, on an application for judicial review, the High Court quashes the decision to which the application relates, it may in addition—(a) remit the matter to the court, tribunal or authority which made the decision, with a direction to reconsider the matter and reach a decision in accordance with the findings of the High Court, or (b) substitute its own decision for the decision in question."

18-030   This power to remit is useful in two main circumstances. First, where otherwise—following the quashing of a decision—the claimant would be inconvenienced by having to reapply to the public authority for a decision to be made. Secondly, where a quashing order alone might risk administrative inconvenience if a public authority had to start proceedings against the claimant afresh. In cases involving administrative bodies or tribunals, the matter will generally be remitted to the same decision-maker unless that would cause reasonably perceived unfairness to the affected parties, or would damage public confidence in the decision-making process. There is no set list of factors relevant to this assessment, but the presence of actual or apparent bias will make remission inappropriate. The reviewing court should consider all the circumstances and apply the usual meaning of fairness which is understood in judicial review proceedings. The posi-

---

[81]   On the distinction between void and voidable, see 4-054.

[82]   *Re Zohrab v Smith* (1848) 17 L.J.Q.B. 174 at 176; *London Corp v Cox* (1867) L.R. 2 HL 239; *R. v Electricity Commissioners* [1924] 1 K.B. 171; *R. v Minister of Health Ex p. Villiers* [1936] 2 K.B. 29. See also *R. v Local Commissioner for Administration for North and East Area of England Ex p. Bradford MCC* [1979] Q.B. 287 (reversed in CA), where on a claim to prohibit a local commissioner from investigating certain matters, a declaration was granted that the Commissioner should not investigate complaints that did not prima facie amount to allegations of maladministration.

[83]   *Re Ashby* [1934] O.R. 421 at [431].

[84]   *R. v Tottenham & District Rent Tribunal Ex p. Northfield (Highgate) Ltd* [1957] 1 Q.B. 103 at 107-108 (Lord Goddard CJ); but a court may decline to exercise its discretion to issue prohibition before the tribunal has had an opportunity to explore the factual issues upon which its jurisdiction may depend: *Maritime Telegraph and Telephone Co Ltd v Canada Labour Relations Board* [1976] 2 E.C. 343.

[85]   *R. v Minister of Health Ex p. Davis* [1929] 1 K.B. 619, DC.

tion of political bodies such as local authorities may be different given their policy-making functions.[86]

Substituting a decision

The general principle that a court hearing a judicial review claim does not substitute its decision for the original decision-maker's is subject to two specific and limited exceptions, which extend the jurisdiction of the court when quashing orders are sought. **18-031**

First, where a claimant seeks a quashing order to quash a sentence of a magistrates' court or the Crown Court on the grounds that the court had no power to pass the sentence, the Administrative Court may, instead of quashing the sentence and remitting the matter back, pass any sentence which the former courts could have passed.[87] Secondly, the court may, in certain circumstances, substitute its decision for that of the inferior decision-maker. The power to substitute is confined to cases where three conditions are made out: that the decision in question was made by a court or tribunal; that the decision is quashed on the ground of error of law; and that, without the error, there would only have been one decision which the court or tribunal could have reached.[88] Unless the court directs otherwise, a substituted decision under CPR r.19(2)(b) has effect as if it were a decision of the relevant court or tribunal.[89] **18-032**

Final injunctions[90]

The jurisdiction of the High Court to grant injunctions on a claim for judicial review rests on s.31(2) of the Senior Courts Act 1981[91] which gives the court power to grant an injunction in any case where it appears just and convenient to do so having regard to: (a) the nature of the matters in respect of which relief may be granted by mandatory, prohibiting or quashing orders; (b) the nature of the persons and bodies against whom relief may be granted by such orders; and (c) all the circumstances of the case. **18-033**

An injunction is an order of a court addressed to a party requiring that party to do or to refrain from doing a particular act. Hence an injunction may be prohibi- **18-034**

---

86 These principles are derived from *HCA International Ltd v Competition and Markets Authority* [2015] EWCA Civ 492; [2015] 1 W.L.R. 4341 at [65]–[72].

87 Senior Courts Act 1981 s.43; *R. v St Helens Justices Ex p. Jones* [1999] 2 All E.R. 73; *R. v Nuneaton Justices Ex p. Bingham* [1991] C.O.D. 56; *R. (on the application of Corner) v Southend Crown Court* [2005] EWHC 2334 (Admin); (2006) 170 J.P. 6 at [13].

88 Senior Courts Act 1981 s.31(5A); CPR 54.19(2)(b). cf. *R. (on the application of Y) v Aylesbury Crown Court* [2012] EWHC 1140 (Admin); [2012] E.M.L.R. 26 at [50]–[55] (where there was only one decision which could have been reached) and *R. (on the application of O'Connor) v Avon Coroner* [2009] EWHC 854 (Admin); [2011] Q.B. 106 at [31]-[33] (where the DC could not be sure that there was only one decision to which the Coroner could lawfully come and so remitted the matter). In *R. (on the application of the Governing Body of the London Oratory School) v Schools Adjudicator* [2015] EWHC 1155 (Admin); [2015] E.L.R. 335 at [9], the HC remitted the impugned decision to the School's Adjudicator, being "far from sure that there is only one outcome to any fresh determination" and having regard to the fact that the Adjudicator, unlike the HC, could make a fresh decision on material available to her at the time of the new decision. The court considered that substitution was appropriate in the exceptional circumstances of the case in *Blast 106 Limited's Application* [2015] NICA 16 at [37].

89 Senior Courts Act 1981 s.31(5B).

90 Detailed references to authorities for basic propositions of law relating to injunctions are omitted: see generally, D. Bean, I. Parry and A. Burns, *Injunctions*, 12th edn (2015).

91 See s.30 in relation to injunctions restraining a person not entitled to do so from acting in a public office. On the High Court's general jurisdiction to grant injunctions, see s.37.

tory or mandatory. Until late in the 19th century all injunctions were worded in a prohibitory form (e.g. not to allow an obstruction to continue to interfere with the plaintiff's rights), but the direct mandatory form (e.g. to remove the obstruction) may now be used. A final injunction granted on a claim for judicial review is normally indistinguishable in its effect from a prohibiting or mandatory order[92]: injunctions may be granted to prevent ultra vires acts by public bodies[93] and to enforce public law duties.[94] The court may grant an injunction on such terms and conditions as it thinks fit. Although the discretion conferred is very broad, it will be exercised in accordance with recognised principles.

18-035   A final injunction is granted at the conclusion of the proceedings and is determinative of the rights of the parties, but it need not be expressed to have perpetual effect; it may be awarded for a fixed period, or for a fixed period with permission to apply for an extension, or for an indefinite period terminable when conditions imposed on the defendant have been complied with; or its operation may be suspended for a period during which the defendant is given the opportunity to comply with the conditions imposed on him, the plaintiff being given leave to reapply at the end of that time. The elasticity of form and content that characterises the injunction is, indeed, one of its main advantages over mandatory and prohibitory orders.

18-036   In general, a mandatory injunction will not issue to compel the performance of a continuing series of acts—for example, the execution of building or repair works[95] or the operation of a ferry service[96] or the delivery of mail that has been interrupted by an industrial dispute[97]—which the court is incapable of superintending. This rule cannot be expressed without qualification, for the court has jurisdiction to order the abatement of a nuisance although compliance with its order may entail the execution of extensive works over which the court would not be capable of maintaining effective superintendence[98] and it can award a prohibitory injunction to restrain the discontinuance of a public service.[99] It is doubtful whether a mandatory injunction will issue at the suit of a private plaintiff to compel a public authority to carry out its positive statutory duties, unless the statute is to be interpreted as giving the plaintiff a private right of action for breach of those duties; the more appropriate judicial remedy (if any) will be a mandatory order.[100]

---

[92]   *M v Home Office* [1994] 1 A.C. 377 at 415E.

[93]   See, e.g. *R. v North Yorkshire CC Ex p. M* [1989] Q.B. 411.

[94]   See, e.g. *R. v Kensington and Chelsea RLBC Ex p. Hammell* [1989] Q.B. 518.

[95]   *Attorney General v Staffordshire CC* [1905] 1 Ch. 336 at 342 (a case where a declaration was sought in respect of liability to maintain and repair a highway).

[96]   *Attorney General v Colchester Corp* [1955] 2 Q.B. 207; cf. *Gravesham BC v British Railways Board* [1978] Ch. 379 at 403-405. See also *Attorney General v Ripon Cathedral (Dean & Chapter)* [1945] Ch. 239; *Dowty Boulton Paul Ltd v Wolverhampton Corp* [1971] 1 W.L.R. 204 at 211-212 (maintenance of airfield; injunction prohibitory in form but mandatory in substance).

[97]   *Stephen (Harold) & Co Ltd v Post Office* [1977] 1 W.L.R. 1172.

[98]   See, e.g. *Pride of Derby & Derbyshire Angling Association Ltd v British Celanese Ltd* [1953] Ch. 149. Other limited exceptions to the general rule are mentioned in *Attorney General v Colchester Corp* [1955] 2 Q.B. 207 at 216.

[99]   *Warwickshire CC v British Railways Board* [1969] 1 W.L.R. 1117.

[100] *Glossop v Heston & Isleworth Local Board* (1879) 12 Ch. D. 102; and *Attorney General v Clerkenwell Vestry* [1891] 3 Ch. 527 at 537 (alleged breach of duty in failing to provide proper drainage system). It appears even a claim for mandamus would have been inappropriate because Parliament had provided another specific remedy: *Pasmore v Oswaldtwistle UBC* [1898] A.C. 387. See also *Attorney General v Pontypridd Waterworks Co* [1908] 1 Ch. 388; *Holland v Dickson* (1888) 37 Ch. D. 669 (illustration of a mandatory injunction issuing to compel the performance of a semi-private nature; statutory duty of company to permit stockholder or shareholder to inspect its books); *Meade v Haringey LBC* [1979] 1 W.L.R. 637 (right to sue for damages does not appear to have been

Declarations

A declaration is a formal statement by the court pronouncing upon the exist-   **18-037**
ence or non-existence of a legal state of affairs.[101] It declares what the legal position is and what are the rights of the parties. A declaration is to be contrasted with
an executory, in other words, coercive judgment which can be enforced by the
courts. In the case of an executory judgment, the courts determine the respective
rights of the parties and then order the defendant to act in a certain way, for
example, to pay damages or to refrain from interfering with the claimant's rights.
If the order is disregarded, it can be enforced by official action, usually by levying
execution against the defendant's property or by imprisoning him for contempt of
court. A declaration, on the other hand, pronounces upon the existence of a legal
relationship but does not contain any order which can be enforced against the
defendant.[102] The court may, for example, declare that the claimant is a British
subject or that a notice served upon him by a public authority is invalid and of no
effect. The declaration pronounces on what is the legal position.

The fact that a declaration is not coercive is one of its advantages as a public law   **18-038**
remedy. Because it merely pronounces upon the legal position, it is well suited to
the supervisory role of administrative law in England. In addition, by careful
draftsmanship the declaration can be tailored so as not to interfere with the activities of public authorities more than is necessary to ensure that they comply with the
law. In many situations all that is required is for the legal position to be clearly set
out in a declaration for a dispute of considerable public importance to be resolved.
It usually relates to events which have already occurred. However, as will be seen,
it is increasingly being used to pronounce upon the legality of a future situation and
in that way the occurrence of illegal action is avoided. The courts have jurisdiction to grant an anticipatory injunction, quia timet, where this is the only way to
avoid imminent danger to the plaintiff, but the courts are extremely cautious about
granting such relief and the necessity for it can be avoided by granting a declaration instead.

During the 1970s litigants applied with increasing frequency for declarations in   **18-039**
order to obtain relief against the activities of ministers and other public authorities.
Many of the landmark decisions which Lord Diplock regarded as constituting the
"progress towards a comprehensive system of administrative law [which was] the
greatest achievement of the English courts in [his] judicial lifetime"[103] were decided
in civil proceedings in which the plaintiff sought a declaration. For example, in
perhaps the most important decision of all, *Ridge v Baldwin*,[104] Lord Reid concluded
his historic speech by announcing: "I do not think that this House should do more
than declare that the dismissal of the appellant is null and void and remit the case

---

regarded as a condition precedent to the award of a mandatory injunction).
[101] The power is the same as in relation to injunctions, 18-033 above. A declaration can be sought
without any other remedy (CPR 40.20). On the declaration generally, see J. Woolf, *Zamir and Woolf:
The Declaratory Judgment*, 4th edn (2011).
[102] *Webster v Southwark LBC* [1983] Q.B. 698 (Forbes J, although there had been only a declaration
and no injunction granted and although a declaration was not a coercive order, the court had an inherent power to make an order of sequestration where the interests of justice demanded compliance.
If, for example, the courts have declared that an individual has the right to remain in this country, it
could be contempt for the Home Office to remove him after having had notice of the declaration).
It will only be appropriate to do so in exceptional circumstances: *St George's NHS Trust v S* [1999]
Fam 26 at 60.
[103] *R. v Inland Revenue Commissioners Ex p. National Federation of Self-Employed and Small Businesses Ltd* [1982] A.C. 617 at 641.
[104] *Ridge v Baldwin* [1964] A.C. 40.

to the Queen's Bench Division for further procedure". Similarly, in the almost equally important decision of *Anisminic v Foreign Compensation Commission*,[105] in restoring the decision of Browne J which had been reversed by the Court of Appeal, the House of Lords granted a declaration that a provisional determination by the Commission was made without, or in excess of, jurisdiction and was a nullity.[106]

Negative declarations

18-040   The courts can be unwilling to grant a negative declaration. By a negative declaration is meant a declaration of no right or no liability. It can also be a declaration as to the absence of any right or power in a defendant or defendants. In order to decide whether a declaration is a negative declaration, it is necessary not merely to examine the terms of the declaration, but also its substance since by a careful use of language, what is in fact a negative declaration can be drafted in positive terms.

18-041   There are probably two reasons which explain the reluctance of the court to grant negative declarations.[107] The first is very similar to the reason that explains the opposition to granting declarations as to theoretical issues, if the objective is to anticipate possible proceedings, those proceedings may never occur. The second reason is that they can be used for the purposes of forum shopping.[108] Where there are no existing proceedings, the court will usually want to be satisfied that there is some bona fide reason for commencing them, but if there is such a reason, the court will then be prepared to decide on the merits whether declaratory relief should be granted.[109]

Theoretical issues and advisory declarations

18-042   If an issue is theoretical, then in ordinary civil proceedings that is a compelling factor against the grant of relief and that remains the situation even if one of the parties has a perfectly legitimate reason for seeking clarification of the legal situation.[110] In claims for judicial review, however, there have now been a number of cases in which the courts have given advisory opinions, in the form of a declaration, where it was clearly desirable that they should do so. The declaratory opinions are given in circumstances where no other remedy would be appropriate. Sir John Laws categorises these situations where it is appropriate for the courts to grant declara-

---

[105] *Anisminic v Foreign Compensation Commission* [1969] 2 A.C. 147.

[106] The declaration continues to be an important remedy: *R. (on the application of Walker) v Secretary of State for Justice* [2009] UKHL 22; [2010] 1 A.C. 553 at [5]-[6] and [37] (in relation to the failure to provide rehabilitative courses to prisoners).

[107] *Guaranty Trust Co of New York v Hannay & Co* [1915] 2 K.B. 536 at 564-565 (Pickford LJ: "I think that a declaration that a person is not liable in an existing or possible action is one that will hardly ever be made, but that in practically every case the person asking it will be left to set up his defence in the action when it is brought"); *Dyson v Attorney General* [1911] 1 K.B. 410 at 417.

[108] *Camilla Cotton Oil Co v Granadex SA* [1976] 2 Lloyd's Rep. 10 and the speech of Lord Wilberforce.

[109] *Rediffusion (Hong Kong) Ltd v Attorney General of Hong Kong* [1970] A.C. 1136 at 1156; *British Airways v Laker Airways* [1985] A.C. 58; *Staffordshire Moorlands DC v Cartwright* (1992) 63 P. & C.R. 285, CA (granted declarations that planning permission had not been implemented by the defendants, but Mustill LJ indicated that it was an exceptional case and normally resort should be had to enforcement proceedings).

[110] *Sun Life Assurance v Jervis* [1944] A.C. 111 at 114 (Viscount Simon LC: "the appellants are concerned to obtain, if they can, a favourable decision from this House because they fear that other cases may arise under similar documents in which others who have taken out policies of endowment assurance with them will rely on the decision of the Court of Appeal, but if the appellants desire to have the view of the House of Lords on the issue on which the Court of Appeal has pronounced, their proper and more convenient course is to await a further claim and to bring that claim, if necessary, up to the House of Lords with a party on the record whose interest it is to resist the appeal").

tions as being "hypothetical". They can equally appropriately be described as raising *theoretical* issues. A hypothetical question is a question which needs to be answered for a real practical purpose, although there may not be an immediate situation on which the decision will have practical affect.[111] A "hypothetical" question has to be distinguished from an "academic" question. An academic question is one which need not be answered for any visible practical purpose, although an answer would satisfy academic curiosity, for example, by clarifying a difficult area of the law. Sir John considers that it would be wrong for the court to grant relief in order to answer academic questions.[112]

The court has jurisdiction to make advisory declarations.[113] Advisory declarations have two main functions: first, to reduce the danger of administrative activities being declared illegal retrospectively, and, secondly, to guide public authorities by giving advice on legal questions which is then binding on everyone.[114]   **18-043**

Declarations of incompatibility

By s.4 of the Human Rights Act 1998, the court has jurisdiction to grant declarations of incompatibility; these are considered in Chapter 13.[115]   **18-044**

CONTEMPT

Failure to comply with a mandatory or prohibiting order or injunction, or an undertaking given to the court, is punishable as contempt of court. In theory all the normal sanctions are at the disposal of the court—imprisonment, sequestration, fine—however, in a case where a public authority fails to comply with a court order in judicial review, a mere finding of contempt rather than a penalty may suffice to mark the gravity of the situation.[116]   **18-045**

In relation to central government, a court contemplating making a finding of contempt must consider the difference in constitutional law between ministers (who are responsible to Parliament for the failings of their departments and cannot delegate their functions to officials) and officials (who are servants of the Crown,   **18-046**

---

[111] See, e.g. *R. (on the application of Sacupima) v Newham LBC* [2001] 1 W.L.R. 563 (because of the "considerable practical importance" of the legal issues, the Admin Ct and CA dealt with a challenge to the lawfulness of provision of temporary accommodation even though the claimant had by the time of the hearings been provided with satisfactory long-term housing).

[112] J. Laws, "Judicial Remedies and the Constitution" (1994) 57 M.L.R. 213, 214-219. As cited and discussed by the HC in *R. (on the application of Williams) v Secretary of State for the Home Department* [2015] EWHC 1268 (Admin); [2015] A.C.D. 111 at [55]. The appeal against the decision was dismissed (without discussing the issue) at [2017] EWCA Civ 98; [2017] 1 W.L.R. 3283. Compare J. Beatson, "Prematurity and Ripeness for Review in C. Forsyth and I. Hare, *The Golden Metwand and the Crooked Cord* (1998), pp.243-251.

[113] *Equal Opportunities Commission v Secretary of State for Employment* [1995] 1 A.C. 1 at [27], [36].

[114] J. Woolf, *Zamir and Woolf: The Declaratory Judgment*, 4th edn (2011), p.143, cited with approval in *R. (on the application of Campaign for Nuclear Disarmament) v Prime Minister* [2002] EWHC 2777 (Admin); [2003] A.C.D. 36 at [46]. However, the courts remain reluctant to do so: *R. (on the application of Burke) v General Medical Council* [2005] EWCA Civ 1003; [2006] Q.B. 273 at [21], except in exceptional cases: *R. (on the application of Smith) v Oxfordshire Assistant Deputy Coroner* [2010] UKSC 29; [2011] 1 A.C. 1 at [129].

[115] See 13-047.

[116] *M v Home Office* [1994] 1 A.C. 377. The Admin Ct made a finding of contempt (but imposed no further penalty save in costs) against the Home Secretary in relation to the "wholly remarkable and unacceptable" decision to reconsider the merits of ordering the claimant's release from detention after a clear undertaking had been given to the court to do so (*R. (on the application of Lamari) v Secretary of State for the Home Department* [2012] EWHC 1895 (Admin) at [18]–[20] and [33]–[41]).

not servants or agents of ministers—though they work under the direction of ministers).[117] It is a minister in his official capacity who is a party to the judicial review claim, not officials. It is a minister who is primarily responsible to the court for any failure; but if an official is wilful in his disobedience to a court order, his own conduct may expose him to the risk of being held in contempt.[118] The court may order a senior civil servant to attend court to represent a minister when it is delivering its judgment in contempt proceedings, but a compulsory order to appear should not be made against a civil servant unless there is a good reason for doing so.[119]

DISCRETION IN GRANTING AND WITHHOLDING REMEDIES

Presumption in favour of relief

18-047   The general approach ought to be that a claimant who succeeds in establishing the unlawfulness of administrative action is entitled to be granted a remedial order. The court does, however, have discretion—in the sense of assessing "what it is fair and just to do in the particular case"[120]—to withhold a remedy altogether[121] or to grant a declaration (rather than a more coercive quashing, prohibiting or mandatory order or injunction which may have been sought by the claimant)[122] or to grant relief in respect of one aspect of the impugned decision, but not others.[123] But the requirements of the rule of law mean that "the discretion of the court to do other than quash the relevant order or action where such excessive exercise of power is shown is very narrow".[124] The presumption has now been substantially modified by Parliament (see 18-050 below).

18-048   The discretion is narrower still—or in some circumstances non-existent— where the claimant has succeeded in demonstrating a directly effective right under European Union law, given the general obligation on the court to provide effec-

---

117 *Carltona Ltd v Commissioners of Works* [1943] 2 All E.R. 560; *Beggs v Scottish Ministers* [2007] UKHL 3; [2007] 1 W.L.R. 455 at [8] (letters to a prisoner from his legal advisers continued to be opened by prison officers despite an undertaking that this unlawful action would cease).

118 *Beggs* [2007] UKHL 3; [2007] 1 W.L.R. 455 at [11].

119 *Beggs* [2007] UKHL 3; [2007] 1 W.L.R. 455 at [13], [40].

120 See generally: Lord Justice Bingham, "Should Public Law Remedies be Discretionary?" [1991] P.L. 64, 66.

121 *R. v Lincolnshire CC and Wealden DC Ex p. Atkinson, Wales and Stratford* (1996) 8 Admin. L.R. 529 at 550 (Sedley J: "To refuse relief where an error of law by a public authority has been demonstrated is an unusual and strong thing; but there is no doubt that it can be done").

122 See, e.g. *Great North Eastern Railway Ltd v Office of Rail Regulation* [2006] EWHC 1942 (Admin); [2007] A.C.D. 13 at [96] (challenge to charging regime for track access).

123 Discretion is an inherent characteristic of the remedies of quashing, mandatory and prohibiting orders, declarations and injunctions. Senior Courts Act 1981, s.31(6) makes express provision for delay to be considered by the court (see Appendix C). Quashing orders under various enactments (see 17-022) are expressed in terms of that the court "may quash", see e.g. Town and Country Planning Act 1990 ss.287–288.

124 *Berkeley v Secretary of State for the Environment, Transport and the Regions (No.1)* [2001] 2 A.C. 603 (Lord Bingham). cf. *Crédit Suisse v Allerdale* [1997] Q.B. 306 at 355 (Hobhouse LJ: "The discretion of the court in deciding whether to grant any remedy is a wide one"); *R. v HM Coroner for Inner London South District Ex p. Douglas-Williams* [1999] 1 All E.R. 344 at 347 (Lord Woolf MR: "When it comes to exercising this discretion I cannot suggest a better test for a court to apply when deciding whether it should give relief than that it should be 'necessary or desirable to do so in the interest of justice", in a case relating to an inquest, this must be read in context of the use of that expression in Coroners Act 1988 s.13, which provides an alternative remedy to judicial review).

tive protection.[125] Similarly, where Convention rights are in issue, the court will need to consider the relevance of ECHR art.13 which, while not incorporated into national law by the HRA, has a pervasive influence in requiring effective remedies for breaches of Convention rights.[126] The writ of habeas corpus, examined in Chapter 17, is not discretionary but should issue if unlawful detention is established.[127] As with other aspects of the judicial review process, the court must give effect to the "overriding objective" of the CPR in its decision-making about remedies.[128]

Where the exercise of discretion by a judge at first instance is challenged on appeal, the Court of Appeal will normally intervene only if the judge below proceeded on the basis of the wrong principles.[129]

18-049

Substantially different outcome

The Criminal Justice and Courts Act 2015 (which has effect from 13 April 2015) defines the circumstances in which the High Court *must* refuse relief. Section 84 of the Act provides that the High Court must refuse to grant relief on an application for judicial review, and may not make any award under the Senior Courts Act 1981 s.31(4), if "it appears to the court to be highly likely that the outcome for the applicant would not have been substantially different if the conduct complained of had not occurred".[130] The court has a limited discretion to award a remedy even if the "no difference" test is made out where it "considers that it is appropriate to do so for reasons of exceptional public interest".[131] If the court awards a remedy on grounds of exceptional public interest, it must certify that this condition is satisfied. The concept of "highly likely" is novel, and marks a significant departure from the test of inevitability previously applied at common law as a basis for refusing a remedy.[132] It appears that the judge will be required to consider the significance of the alleged legal defect to the decision in question and speculate as to what the

18-050

---

[125] See 14-073; and *Berkeley* [2001] 2 A.C. 603 where the HL rejected the argument that relief should be refused since all the environmental information that would have been part of an environmental impact assessment (which had not been conducted at all) was already in the public domain; but later cases make clear that the mere existence of a European Community law right is not necessarily a bar on the exercise of the court's discretion: *Bown v Secretary of State for Transport, Local Government and the Regions* [2003] EWCA Civ 1170; [2004] Env. L.R. 26; *R. (on the application of Rockware Glass Ltd) v Chester City Council* [2006] EWCA Civ 99 (operation of quashing order suspended); *R. (on the application of Gavin) v Harringey LBC* [2003] EWHC 2591 (Admin); [2004] 2 P. & C.R. 13 at [40]-[41] (provisions in SCA 1981 s.31(6) on delay not inconsistent with principles relating to Environmental Impact Assessments).

[126] See 13-033.

[127] See 17-008.

[128] See 16-011.

[129] *R. v Islington LBC Ex p. Dignan* (1998) 30 H.L.R. 723, CA.

[130] Criminal Justice and Courts Bill 2014 cl.70, inserting a new subs.2A into s.31 of the Senior Courts Act 1981. In *R. (on the application of Bokrosova) v Lambeth London Borough Council* [2015] EWHC 3386 (Admin); [2016] P.T.S.R. 355 at [88], recognising that s.31(2A) does not expressly impose a burden of proof on a defendant, the HC held that "in accordance with general principle … he who asserts must prove". In that instance, s.31(2A) did not require the HC to refuse relief. Whether a witness statement is required from the defendant to make out the test will depend on all the circumstances (*R. (on the application of DAT) v West Berkshire Council* [2016] EWHC 1876 (Admin); (2016) 19 C.C.L. Rep. 362 at [73]).

[131] The circumstances were not sufficiently exceptional in *R. (on the application of Mrs JH, Mr JH) v Secretary of State for Justice* [2015] EWHC 4093 (Admin); [2016] A.C.D. 56 at [319]–[327].

[132] See para.18-057. In *R. (on the application of Williams) v Powys County Council* [2017] EWCA Civ 427 at [72], the CA declined to withhold a remedy on the basis that "the interests of a lawfully taken decision must prevail, as normally they should" especially where the exercise of discretion involved questions of fact and judgment on planning and aesthetics.

outcome would have been if the defect had not occurred.[133] The courts have historically sought to avoid engaging in such questions.[134] The constitutional implications of this aspect of the Act have been strongly criticised.[135]

Delay

18-051   Delay as a ground on which the court may withhold a remedy is expressly recognised in s.31(6) of the Senior Courts Act 1981 which provides that where there has been undue delay in making a claim for judicial review:

> "the court may refuse to grant (a) leave [i.e. permission] for making the application [i.e. claim], or (b) any relief sought on the application if it considers that the grant of the relief sought would be likely to cause substantial hardship to, or substantial prejudice to the rights of, any person or would be detrimental to good administration."[136]

18-052   CPR r.54.5(1) states that the judicial review claim form must be filed promptly and in any event within three months from the date when grounds for the claim first arose.[137] Delay is thus relevant both at the permission stage and in relation to the grant of relief after the court has determined the merits of the claimant's case. The court regards these as distinct stages and in relation to the latter, delay is a factor to be considered in deciding whether or not to withhold a remedy *only* if to grant relief would be likely to cause hardship, prejudice or detriment to the defendant or a third party within the meaning of s.31(6)(b). At the full hearing the court is not concerned with the question whether there was good reason to extend time for filing the claim form and seeking permission.[138]

18-053   The courts have tended to avoid formulating any precise description of what constitutes detriment to good administration. This is because claims for judicial review arise in many different situations and the need for finality may be greater in one context than another. It has, however, been observed that "there is an interest in good administration independently of hardship, or prejudice to the rights of third parties".[139] In relation to the permission stage, a court may take the view that it is self-evident that a delay has caused detriment to good administration without

---

[133]   This is a difficult task for the court as noted in *R. (on the application of Cooper) v Ashford BC* [2016] EWHC 1525 (Admin); [2016] P.T.S.R. 1455 at [86].

[134]   See fn.148. In *R. (on the application of Logan) v Havering London Borough Council* [2015] EWHC 3193 (Admin); [2016] P.T.S.R. 603 at [55], the HC held per curiam that any consideration of whether s.31(2A) applied "should normally be based on material in existence at the time of the decision and not simply post-decision speculation by an individual decision-maker. Any other course runs the risk of reducing the importance of compliance with duties of procedural fairness and statutory or other requirements that certain matters be taken into account and others disregarded." The HC was concerned that the efficacy of judicial review could be undermined by a "draconian" modification of constitutional principles: if a decision-maker's declaration that obedience of the law would have made no difference led to the court refusing permission or to claimants being deterred from bringing proceedings. The court speculated that the provision may have been intended to apply only to "somewhat trivial procedural failings", suggesting that the legislative history be reviewed to determine its scope.

[135]   See, e.g. B. Jaffey and T. Hickman, *"Loading the Dice in Judicial Review: The Criminal Justice and Courts Bill 2014"*, UK Const L. Blog (6 February 2014), *https://ukconstitutionallaw.org/2014/02/06/ben-jaffey-and-tom-hickman-loading-the-dice-in-judicial-review-the-criminal-justice-and-courts-bill-2014/* [Accessed 9 November 2017].

[136]   *R. (on the application of Parkyn) v Restormel BC* [2001] EWCA Civ 330; [2001] 1 P.L.R. 108 at [32] (Sedley LJ, describing the provision as "distracting and unhelpful").

[137]   See 16-055.

[138]   *R. v Criminal Injuries Compensation Board Ex p. A* [1999] 2 A.C. 330; on good reasons to extend time, see 16-060.

[139]   *R. v Dairy Produce Quota Tribunal Ex p. Caswell* [1990] 2 A.C. 738; *R. v Monopolies and Merg-*

requiring specific evidence that this has in fact occurred,[140] but in relation to withholding relief evidence may be required.[141] Courts should be unwilling to excuse a breach of the standards required by administrative law merely upon the ground that to quash the decision would cause the decision-maker administrative inconvenience: "even if chaos should result, still the law must be obeyed".[142] In *R. v Secretary of State for Social Services Ex p. Association of Metropolitan Authorities*[143] Webster J held that, although the Secretary of State had not complied with his statutory duty to consult, the housing benefit regulations under challenge should not be quashed, as delegated legislation is not normally revoked unless there are exceptional circumstances, and to revoke the existing regulations would result in confusion.[144] Fortunately, however, courts traditionally receive arguments based upon administrative impracticability with scepticism. Except where the difficulty caused to the decision-maker is more than inconvenience, and approaches impracticability or where there is an overriding need for finality and certainty,[145] a remedy should not be refused solely upon this basis. Even if, contrary to Lord Atkin's dictum, convenience and justice are on speaking terms,[146] conversation between the two should be strictly limited.[147]

Standing

The extent of the "sufficient interest" of the claimant is a factor to be considered when deciding what, if any, relief to grant.[148] As we have noted, when it comes to deciding in its discretion whether to grant relief—a court is going to be more **18-054**

---

ers Commission Ex p. Argyll [1986] 1 W.L.R. 763 at 774; *Coney v Choyce* [1975] 1 W.L.R. 422 at 436; *R. v Panel on Takeovers and Mergers Ex p. Guinness Plc* [1990] 1 Q.B. 146 at 177; *R. (on the application of 007 Taxis Limited) v Stratford on Avon DC* [2011] EWCA Civ 160; [2011] A.C.D. 61.

[140] *R. v Newbury DC Ex p. Chieveley Parish Council* (1998) 10 Admin. L.R. 676 (unexplained delay in applying out of time for judicial review of major planning proposal).

[141] *R. v Secretary of State for the Home Department Ex p. Oyeleye (Florence Jumoke)* [1994] Imm. A.R. 268 (no evidence of detriment to good administration had been put before the court and accordingly the court could not be satisfied that there was any such detriment).

[142] *R. v Governors of Small Heath School Ex p. Birmingham CC* [1990] C.O.D. 23, CA; *Bradbury v Enfield LBC* [1967] 1 W.L.R. 1311 at 1324 (Lord Denning MR).

[143] *R. v Secretary of State for Social Services Ex p. Association of Metropolitan Authorities* [1986] 1 W.L.R. 1, HC; *R. v Gateshead MBC Ex p. Nichol* (1988) 87 L.G.R. 435 (CA refused to quash part-implemented school reorganisation scheme); and *Walton v Scottish Ministers* [2012] UKSC 44; [2013] P.T.S.R. 51 at [103] (Lord Carnwath).

[144] Since a large number of local authorities had acted upon the regulations as promulgated by determining claims in accordance with their terms; *R. v Secretary of State for Employment Ex p. Seymour-Smith* [1994] I.R.L.R. 448; *R. v Brent LBC Ex p. O'Malley*; R. v Secretary of State for the Environment Ex p. Walters [1998] C.O.D. 121 (CA upheld decision of Schiemann J that notwithstanding that the extensive consultation process (relating to the redevelopment of council housing estates) carried out by the respondents was flawed, no relief should be granted since there was overwhelming evidence that the granting of review would damage the interests of a large number of other individuals, and it would be "absurd" to ignore such disadvantages); the courts' discretion to refuse relief was said to be a broad one to be exercised in the light of the particular circumstances (see 18-047).

[145] See, e.g. *R. v Monopolies and Mergers Commission Ex p. Argyll Group* [1986] 1 W.L.R. 763 (CA refused to grant a remedy for what was held to be an unlawful delegation of discretion because, among other reasons, commercial considerations dictated that decisions of the MMC should be speedy and final. The CA was influenced, however, by the fact that the unlawful decision had been approved by the minister); cf. *R. v Panel on Takeovers and Mergers Ex p. Datafin* [1987] Q.B. 815, CA.

[146] *General Medical Council v Spackman* [1943] A.C. 627 at 638.

[147] The same principle may be seen in the case law of the ECJ.

[148] See 2-024; see, e.g. *R. v Felixstowe Justices Ex p. Leigh* [1987] Q.B. 582.

hesitant in some situations in granting, for example, a mandatory order or an injunction than a declaration.

Remedy would serve no practical purpose

18-055   The court may exercise discretion not to provide a remedy if to make an order would serve no practical purpose. For example, events can overtake proceedings. So a licence, the validity of which is challenged in the proceedings, may have expired by the time the claim is determined by the Administrative Court. Similarly an activity under challenge may have ceased before a remedy has been granted.[149] It may, for instance, be pointless to quash a decision to enable the public to be consulted on data that has become out of date[150]; or to quash a decision to disclose a report which had, by the date of judgment, already been disclosed.[151] Even a declaration may serve little practical purpose in such circumstances.

18-056   The modern purpose of remedies is simply to give effect to the judgment of the court on the substance of the law.[152] In relation to the procedural fairness, however, the courts have in the past sometimes failed to make a clear distinction between (a) holding that a decision is *not unlawful* because the procedural defect is subsequently cured, for example, by an appeal—in which case the claimant has no grounds of complaint, and (b) situations where a ground of review is established but the court nonetheless withholds relief.[153]

Claimant has suffered no harm

18-057   In some cases the court has withheld a remedy from a claimant on the basis that he has been caused no harm (the term "prejudice" is often used) by the unlawful act of the public authority.[154] Under this head, a minor technical breach of a statutory requirement may be too insignificant to justify relief. The court has also taken into account the fact that the public authority would have made the same decision even if the legal flaw had not occurred.[155] The Criminal Justice and Courts Act 2015 has replaced this discretion with a requirement to refuse relief if "it appears to the court to be highly likely that the outcome for the applicant would not have been substantially different if the conduct complained of had not occurred".[156] In the past, the Law Commission, academic commentators and the courts have all warned of

---

[149] In *Williams v Home Office (No.2)* [1981] 1 All E.R. 1211 and [1982] 2 All E.R. 564, a prison unit had closed.

[150] *R. (on the application of Edwards) v Environment Agency (No.2)* [2008] UKHL 22; [2008] 1 W.L.R. 1587 at [62]-[65] (Lord Hoffmann). K. Yates, "Appealing the Discretionary Grant or Refusal of Relief in Judicial Review Proceedings" [2009] J.R. 129.

[151] *R. v Sunderland Juvenile Court Ex p. G* [1988] 1 W.L.R. 398; cf. *R. v NW Thames Regional Health Authority Ex p. Daniels* [1993] 4 Med. L.R. 364.

[152] See 18-002.

[153] See Ch.8.

[154] See, e.g. *R. v Dairy Produce Quota Tribunal Ex p. Davies* [1987] 2 C.M.L.R. 399; *R. v Lambeth LBC Ex p. Sharp* (1988) 55 P. & C.R. 232; *R. v Governors of Small Heath School Ex p. Birmingham City Council* [1990] C.O.D. 23; *R. v Governors of Bacon's School Ex p. ILEA* [1990] C.O.D. 414; *R. (on the application of Laporte) v Newham LBC* [2004] EWHC 227 (Admin).

[155] See, e.g. *Cinnamond v British Airports Authority* [1980] 1 W.L.R. 582; *R. (on the application of Jones) v Swansea City and CC* [2007] EWHC 213 (Admin); [2007] All E.R. (D) 191 (Feb) at [31] ("virtually inconceivable that the defendant would do other than grant planning permission").

[156] See para.18-050.

the difficulties and risks in prejudging decisions, including overstepping the bounds of the court's reviewing functions.[157]

Financial ramifications of a remedy

As we have seen in earlier chapters, the courts have in some cases considered the impact that their judgments may have on resource allocation in deciding whether or not a public authority has acted unlawfully in the circumstances.[158] At the stage we are concerned with in this chapter—the grant of remedies—it is submitted that financial considerations ought not to feature in the calculation of a court deciding whether to grant a remedial order to a claimant who has demonstrated to the court's satisfaction that a public authority has acted unlawfully. An award of damages will have obvious financial implications for a public authority, but the courts do not have regard to the resources available to the defendant in a particular case if tort liability has been established.[159] The same approach should be applied to other remedies available in judicial review claims.

18-058

Nullity and ultra vires and discretion

The result of a decision being unlawful is considered fully elsewhere.[160] However, if (which is doubtful) for the purposes of public law a decision can ever be categorised as being a nullity, then that will be relevant to the exercise of discretion to grant or withhold relief. There can be no purpose in purporting to keep alive a decision which is devoid of all content. Subject to there being some purpose in obtaining the decision of a court, if the court comes to the conclusion that a decision is totally invalid and of no effect, it will normally readily be prepared to grant a declaration to this effect. Strictly speaking there is nothing to be achieved in the case of a decision which is a nullity in making a quashing order. You cannot quash something which is already a nullity. However, in practice adopting a pragmatic approach and so avoiding becoming involved in issues as to the quality and status of an invalid administrative decision, the court will be prepared to make a quashing order without resolving the complex issue as to whether or not this is strictly necessary. This is subject to the case being one in which the court would in any event have granted relief, if this were necessary, in the form of a quashing order.

18-059

---

[157] Law Com No.226, *Administrative Law: Judicial Review and Statutory Appeals*, para.8.18. See also D. Clark, "Natural Justice: Substance and Shadow" [1975] P.L. 27; *John v Rees* [1970] Ch. 345 at 402 (Megarry J)

[158] See 5-144 (relevance of financial considerations).

[159] See Ch.19.

[160] See 4-067; *Anisminic Ltd v Foreign Compensation Commission* [1969] 2 A.C. 147 at 171; *London and Clydeside Estates Ltd v Aberdeen DC* [1980] 1 W.L.R. 182 at 189, 203; *Chief Constable of North Wales Police v Evans* [1982] 1 W.L.R. 1155 at 1163; *Hoffmann-LaRoche & Co v Secretary of State for Trade and Industry* [1975] A.C. 295. See further, D. Feldman, "Error of Law and Flawed Administrative Acts" [2014] C.L.J. 275; V.S. Nadhamuni, "Suspending Invalidity While Keeping Faith with Nullity: An analysis of the Suspension Order Cases and their Impact on our Understanding of the Doctrine of Nullity" [2015] P.L. 596; and T. Adams, "The Standard Theory of Administrative Unlawfulness" [2017] C.L.J. 289.

Claimant's motive

18-060 The claimant's motive in making a claim for judicial review—whether it is commercial or otherwise—is not a relevant consideration in the court's decision to grant or withhold a remedy.[161]

---

[161] *R. (on the application of Mount Cook Land Ltd) v Westminster City Council* [2003] EWCA Civ 1346; [2004] C.P. Rep. 12 at [45]-[46] (unless the motive raises questions as to abuse of process, on which, see *Land Securities Plc v Fladgate Fielder (a firm)* [2009] EWCA Civ 1402; [2010] Ch. 467 at [67]).

CHAPTER 19

Monetary Remedies in Judicial Review

TABLE OF CONTENTS

SCOPE

This chapter examines the circumstances in which a claimant for judicial review **19-001**
(or a claimant in civil proceedings alleging that a public authority has acted unlawfully in a public law sense) may be awarded a monetary remedy.[1] These are
principally where the public authority:

- has committed a tort during the course of exercising its public functions[2];
- is under an obligation to make restitution of money paid by the claimant[3];
- has breached a Convention right, contrary to the duty in s.6 of the HRA, and

---

[1] See generally D. Fairgrieve, *State Liability in Tort: A Comparative Law Study* (2003); K. Stanton,
    P. Skidmore, M. Harris and J. Wright, *Statutory Torts* (2003); D. Nolan, "Suing the State:
    Governmental Liability in Comparative Perspective" (2004) 67 M.L.R. 844; C. Harlow, *State
    Liability: Tort Law and Beyond* (2004); and T. Cornford, *Towards a Public Law of Tort* (2008).
[2] See 19-025.
[3] See 19-075.

the court considers it is just and appropriate to award damages under s.8 of the HRA[4];

- has committed an actionable breach of European Union law. Damages under European Union law are considered in Chapter 14.[5]

The award of damages serves to compensate but may also act as a sanction to discourage careless or intentional wrongdoing.[6]

OTHER SOURCES OF COMPENSATION

19-002　　The sums of money recoverable for wrongs done by public authorities in the exercise of their public functions are often relatively modest. In contrast, the costs of litigation, particularly in the High Court, may be considerable. One of the overriding objectives of the CPR is to ensure that cases are dealt with in a manner that is proportionate to the amounts of money involved, the complexity and importance of the case.[7] In relation to cases where there is an overlap between maladministration (for example delay or muddle) and breach of a Convention right, the Court of Appeal has emphasised the need for would-be claimants to consider making a complaint to one of the ombudsmen,[8] who have powers to recommend that compensation be paid to a person who has suffered injustice as a result of maladministration. This approach has much to commend it in all situations in which the real gist of the complaint is maladministration.

19-003　　Where there is no statutory or common law right to compensation or restitution for unlawful action, public authorities have discretion in many contexts to make ex gratia payments. Decisions as to whether to make payments of statutory or discretionary compensation, in practice an important source of compensation, may themselves be susceptible to judicial review.[9]

---

[4]　See 19-081.

[5]　See 14-099.

[6]　The role of exemplary (or punitive) damages is considered below at 19-062. Linden argues that "Tort law is an ombudsman. It can be used to apply pressure on those who wield political, economic or intellectual power. This is rarely the expressed aim of a tort suit, but it can be an important side effect" (A. Linden, "Tort Law as Ombudsman" (1973) 51 Can. B.R. 155). In England and Wales, many of the tort claims made against the police and prison services need to be viewed in this light. The impact of tort liability on the behaviour of officials and public bodies is considered at 19-064.

[7]　See 16-011.

[8]　On which, see 1-077; *R. (on the application of Anufrijeva) v Southwark LBC* [2003] EWCA Civ 1406; [2004] Q.B. 1124 at [81].

[9]　See, e.g. *Tower Hamlets LBC v Chetnik Developments Ltd* [1988] A.C. 858; *R. (on the application of Elias) v Secretary of State for Defence* [2005] EWHC 1435 (Admin); [2005] I.R.L.R. 788; *R. (on the application of Association of British Civilian Internees (Far East Region)) v Secretary of State for Defence* [2003] EWCA Civ 473; [2003] Q.B. 1397; *Hooper v Secretary of State for Work and Pensions* [2005] UKHL 29; [2005] 1 W.L.R. 1681, HL; [2003] EWCA Civ 813; [2003] 1 W.L.R. 2623, CA; *R. (on the application of O'Brien) v Independent Assessor* [2007] UKHL 10; [2007] 2 W.L.R. 544. On the withdrawal of the common law ex gratia scheme for compensating victims of miscarriages of justice, see *R. (on the application of Niazi) v Secretary of State for the Home Department* [2007] EWHC 1495 (Admin); [2007] A.C.D. 75 (held: no procedural or substantive legitimate expectation). The statutory scheme under the Criminal Justice Act 1988 s.133 continues (for a challenges to decisions under which, see *R. (on the application of Miller) v Independent Assessor* [2009] EWCA Civ 609) and *R. (on the application of Adams) v Secretary of State for Justice* [2011] UKSC 18; [2012] 1 A.C. 48.

PROCEDURAL ISSUES

Public authorities, like individual citizens and business enterprises, may be **19-004** subject to civil liability to compensate or make restitution as a result of their wrongful acts or omissions in different contexts, many of which are unconnected to issues of public law. This chapter deals with one aspect of this broad field: monetary claims that are related or ancillary to a claim for judicial review.

On a CPR Pt 54 claim for judicial review, the Administrative Court may award **19-005** the claimant "damages, restitution or the recovery of a sum due" if "(a) the application includes a claim for such an award arising from any matter to which the application relates; and (b) the court is satisfied that such an award would have been made if the claim had been made in an action begun by the applicant at the time of making the application".[10] This provision is a procedural one designed to prevent multiplicity of proceedings and does not affect the general rule of substantive law that there is no right to damages for unlawful administrative action per se. A claimant must identify a tortious liability (typically negligence, breach of statutory duty, misfeasance in public office or trespass) or a right to restitution or recovery of a sum due. The Human Rights Act 1998, s.8 provides the court with power to award damages for breach of Convention rights[11] and damages may also be awarded for a serious breach of European Union law.[12]

Civil claim or judicial review?

Prior to the CPR, the relationship between civil actions and applications for **19-006** judicial review was often unhappily the subject of dispute in the courts.[13] Now the case management powers of CPR provide a flexible regime for allocating claims to the most appropriate court and judge.[14] CPR 54.3(2) prohibits a claimant seeking only a monetary remedy in judicial review proceedings: the claim must also include a request for a mandatory, prohibiting or quashing order or a declaration or injunction.[15] Thus where the claimant's sole purpose in resorting to litigation is to obtain damages the appropriate procedure is a CPR Pt 7 civil claim rather than judicial review. Beyond this, a spectrum of different scenarios may arise in which legal advisers and the court need to consider whether a monetary remedy should be sought by way of a claim for judicial review or by a civil claim under CPR Pt 7. The most obvious situations where this may arise are described below.

No public law issues

Where there is no public law content to the dispute (for example, if the claim **19-007** concerns the negligent driving of a vehicle), a claim for judicial review is obviously inappropriate. The claim should be determined by the county court or High Court under CPR Pt 7.

---

[10] Senior Courts Act1981 s.31(4), as substituted by the Civil Procedure (Modification of the Supreme Court Act 1981) Order 2004 (SI 2004/1033). Before 2004, the relevant provisions referred only to damages.

[11] See 19-081.

[12] See 14-099.

[13] See 3-113.

[14] See, e.g. *R. (on the application of Wilkinson) v Broadmoor Special Hospital Authority* [2001] EWCA Civ 1545; [2002] 1 W.L.R. 419 at [62].

[15] Ch.18.

Public law issues a background to the dispute

19-008   Where public functions provide the background to a dispute (for example allegations of failure by a local education authority to provide adequate schooling), a claim for judicial review will be inappropriate where the remedy sought is solely damages[16] and the main issues at stake are whether there has been a tortious wrong. Here again the claim should be determined under CPR Pt 7 in the county court or High Court.

Public law issues must be decided to determine damages claim

19-009   Where questions relating to the unlawfulness of the exercise of a public function (that is, whether the public authority has acted contrary to one of the grounds of judicial review—illegality, irrationality and procedural impropriety) will substantially determine whether the claimant is entitled to a monetary remedy in tort or restitution, the claimant's advisers and the court need to decide how to proceed. Recent decisions relating to procedural exclusivity have emphasised the need to consider whether the procedure adopted by the claimant is well-suited to determine the issues rather than rigid conceptual distinctions between public and private law issues.[17] If the sole or main purpose of a CPR Pt 54 claim is merely to "prime the pump" for a damages claim, it has been indicated that the court should refuse permission for a claim for judicial review and transfer the matter to continue as an ordinary civil claim,[18] but this may not always be the case and the court should adopt a pragmatic approach and determine the most advantageous course for the proceedings it is considering—always bearing in mind that "judicial review was not intended to be used for debt collecting".[19] The CPR Pt 54 judicial review procedure is not well suited to determining those monetary claims which turn on factual disputes which are more appropriately dealt with by a detailed statement of claim and oral evidence from witnesses subject to cross-examination.[20] In such cases, it may be more convenient for the Administrative Court first to determine the public law issues, and then make an order transferring the issues relating to tortious or other private law liability to proceed as if begun under CPR Pt 7.[21] Among other possible ways of determining issues are: the court may award damages at the judicial review hearing, but leave quantum to be assessed by a Master; where a claim is started in the county court but it is thought that expertise in public law issues is needed, the case may be transferred to the High Court to be heard by a judge with Administrative Court experience; or a High Court judge with Administrative

---

16   CPR r.54.3(2).
17   See 3-119.
18   *R. v Blandford JJ Ex p. Pamment* [1990] 1 W.L.R. 1490 (certiorari to quash order of magistrates refused); *R. v Gloucestershire CC Ex p. P* [1993] C.O.D. 303 (declaration that respondent has delayed unreasonably in providing statement of special educational needs refused). *R. v Ministry of Agriculture, Fisheries and Food Ex p. Live Sheep Traders Ltd* [1995] C.O.D. 297.
19   *Trustees of the Dennis Rye Pension Fund v Sheffield CC* [1998] 1 W.L.R. 840, 846 (Lord Woolf MR). Conversely, a claim which in substance involves the examination of a public law issue and which incidentally involves the determination of a private law claim should not be brought as a civil action, see for example *Jones v Powys Local Health Board* [2008] EWHC 2562 (Admin); (2009) 12 C.C.L. Rep. 68 (which concerned a claim for reimbursement of nursing fees where the real challenge was to the review panel's decision).
20   *D v Home Office* [2005] EWCA Civ 38; [2006] 1 W.L.R. 1003 at [105].
21   CPR r.54.20 and Pt 30.

Court expertise may sit as a judge in the county court pursuant to s.5(3) of the County Courts Act 1984.[22]

Claim for damages under s.8 of the HRA

Where a claim for damages under s.8 of the HRA is made separately from a **19-010** judicial review claim, and turns on what is in essence a complaint of "maladministration", the Court of Appeal has indicated that this should be made to the Administrative Court by an ordinary claim under CPR Pt 7.[23] But this ought not to be regarded as an invariable rule, and attention must always be paid to the overriding objective of the CPR.[24] Where, for example, a claim for damages under s.8 arises in the context of a local authority's duties in relation to children, a claim for damages under s.8 may be more appropriately dealt with by the Family Division.

Interest

In the past there has been uncertainty over whether the court has power to award **19-011** interest in relation to a monetary remedy awarded in CPR Pt 54 judicial review proceedings, though the better view is that interest may be awarded.[25]

---

[22] See, e.g. *D v Home Office* [2005] EWCA Civ 38; [2006] 1 W.L.R. 1003 at [129]. There may be good reasons for instituting a private law claim for unlawful detention after (and separately from) a refusal of permission to seek judicial review of a removal decision (*BA v Home Office* [2012] EWCA Civ 944 at [28]-[36]). This paragraph and para.19-025 were found to be "fully justified by authority" in *Tchenguiz v Director of the Serious Fraud Office* [2014] EWCA Civ 472 at [14]. The case concerned the question whether a concession that search orders had been unlawful in public law proceedings prevented the defendant from relying on defences to a private law claim. The CA found that the defendant was entitled to resist the private law claim.

[23] *R. (on the application of Anufrijeva) v Southwark LBC* [2003] EWCA Civ 1406; [2004] Q.B. 1124 at [81]. The CPR do not make clear the presumption that claims for HRA damages should be made to the Administrative Court. See also Practice Direction to Pt 16, para.15 on the requirements of a statement of case for claims arising under the Human Rights Act.

[24] See 16-011.

[25] The court's general power to award interest rests on Senior Courts Act 1981 s.35A. In *R. v Secretary of State for Transport Ex p. Sherriff and Sons Ltd, Independent,* 12 January 1988 it was held that s.35A did not apply to judicial review proceedings in relation to non-payment of a grant under the Railways Act 1974 (Taylor J: "In my judgment, the whole tenor of the language used in section 35A confines its application to civil actions in the private law field. Only by the loosest and most stretched use of language could these proceedings be said to be 'for the recovery of a debt'"). This issue was canvassed, but not resolved, in *R. v Newham LBC Ex p. Barking and Dagenham LBC* [1994] R.A. 13 in relation to a restitutionary award. Late payments of grants made under statutory schemes may, in many contexts, be regarded as giving rise to claims in debt: see, e.g. *Trustees of the Dennis Rye Pension Fund v Sheffield CC* [1998] 1 W.L.R. 840 (landlord could bring ordinary civil proceedings to recover unpaid grant as an ordinary debt, notwithstanding statutory code); *R. v Ministry of Agriculture Fisheries and Food Ex p Lower Burytown Farms Ltd,* CO/956/96, unreported 10 February 1998, Laws J (interest awarded following late payment of "set aside" grant to farmer); cf. *Jones v Department of Employment* [1989] Q.B. 1. The view that interest is not recoverable is surely misconceived since, if it were not, all a claimant would need to do would be to request the court to direct that the claim should be continued as if started under CPR Pt 7 (see CPR r.54.20 and 30) and then the court would have power to grant interest. The Law Commission recommended in its 1994 report that the court should have the same power to award interest as in ordinary civil proceedings: see Law Com. No.226, para.8.8. In *R. (on the application of Kemp) v Denbighshire Local Health Board* [2006] EWHC 181 (Admin); [2007] 1 W.L.R. 639 the Admin Ct accepted it had jurisdiction to award interest on a sum of money reimbursed because a local authority ought to have paid for the claimant's care in a nursing home.

DEFENDANTS IN MONETARY CLAIMS RELATING TO JUDICIAL REVIEW

19-012   In the context with which we are concerned, the person against whom the claim for a monetary remedy is made will usually be the defendant in a judicial review claim or other public law proceeding. However, direct and vicarious liability in tort may make it necessary for some other person to be joined as a party where a monetary remedy is sought. The principle espoused by Dicey and Maitland,[26] that an individual official is personally liable for torts committed in the course of his official duties, remains good today.[27] Usually the official's employer will be vicariously, and so jointly and severally, liable[28]; but an employer of an official will not be vicariously liable for a person who is a public officer given independent statutory powers or duties in his or her own right.[29] After some hesitation, it is now clear that a public authority may be vicariously liable for its officers who commit misfeasance in public office providing that the employee is engaged in a misguided and unauthorised method of performing his or her duties rather than an unauthorised act so unconnected with his or her authorised duties as to be quite independent of and outside those duties.[30] Police officers are neither Crown servants nor employees of the local police authority; the Chief Constable of each police force in the United Kingdom is, however, made by statute vicariously liable for the acts and omissions of his officers and any damages awarded against an officer will be paid out

---

[26]   See 19-026.

[27]   See, e.g. *Lonrho Plc v Tebbit* [1992] 4 All E.R. 280 (minister and officials alleged to have negligently failed to release claimant company from undertakings not to acquire more than 30% of another company following investigation by Monopolies and Mergers Commission). Mr Tebbitt was the Secretary of State for Trade and Industry at the time. In practice, the Crown will pay any damages awarded against a minister or official. *D v Home Office* [2005] EWCA Civ 38; [2006] 1 W.L.R. 1003 at [56] ("there is on the face of it nothing in the slightest bit peculiar about an individual bringing a private law claim for damages against an executive official who has unlawfully infringed his private rights").

[28]   See, e.g. *Phelps v Hillingdon LBC* [2001] 2 A.C. 619 (local education authority vicariously liable for educational professionals); *Home Office v Dorset Yacht Co Ltd* [1970] A.C. 1004 (Borstal officers, for whom the Home Office was vicariously liable, owed a duty to take such care as is reasonable in all the circumstances with a view to preventing the boys under their control from causing damage to private property). cf. the position of a minister who is not vicariously liable for acts or omissions for civil servants in his department; they are not his employees or agents, but the Crown's.

[29]   For example, the council would not have been responsible for their employee, Mr Sharp, the local land charges registrar in *Ministry of Housing and Local Government v Sharp and Hemel Hempstead RDC* [1970] 2 Q.B. 223, Lord Denning MR: "In keeping the register and issuing the certificates, [Mr Sharp] is not acting for the council. He is carrying out his own statutory duties [as the 'proper officer' under the Land Charges Act 1925] on his own behalf. So he himself is responsible for breach of those duties and not the council: see *Stanbury v Exeter Corp* [1905] 2 K.B. 838". The council was, however, vicariously liable for the subordinate clerk employed by them who actually carried out the negligent search. The council did not seek to rely on the fact that the minor clerk, although their employee, was seconded to the registrar and so part of his staff. On vicarious liability for child abuse carried out by a priest (and hence not an employee), see *Various claimants v Catholic Child Welfare Society* [2012] UKSC 56; [2013] 2 A.C. 1 at [34]-[37] and [83]-[87]. This decision was applied to render the Ministry of Justice vicariously liable for injury caused to an employee by a prisoner working in a prison kitchen in *Cox v Ministry of Justice* [2016] UKSC 10; [2016] A.C. 660 at [20]-[29]. In contrast, the Chief Constable was not vicariously liable for acts of personal harassment carried out by one of his officers in relation to the officer's former partner in *Allen v Chief Constable of Hampshire* [2013] EWCA Civ 967 at [28]-[35]. In *Adams v Law Society* [2012] EWHC 980 (QB) at [161], Foskett J criticised a self-represented applicant, who was a solicitor, for naming as personal defendants officers of the Law Society in an action for misfeasance in public office in circumstances where the conduct was within the normal scope of duties of the personal defendants.

[30]   *Racz v Home Office* [1994] 2 A.C. 45 at 53F-H (ill-treatment at the hands of prison officers); see 19-049.

of the police fund.[31] Generally, it has been argued that the imposition of personal liability on individual decision-makers, or vicarious liability on their employer, may have a detrimental impact on their behaviour and that direct governmental liability is to be preferred in an ideal scheme of remedies.[32]

It has been said that "if a man is required in the discharge of a public duty to make a decision which affects, by its legal consequences, the liberty or property of others, and he performs that duty and makes that decision honestly and in good faith, it is ... a fundamental principle of our law that he is protected"[33] against civil liability in respect of the consequences of that decision. Clearly, however, this proposition is inapplicable to many statutory functions involving the exercise of discretion. The donee of a power may often be held liable in tort for the consequences of an erroneous or negligent exercise of his discretion although he has acted in perfectly good faith.[34] Even where a statute has exempted public officers from liability for acts done "bona fide for the purpose of executing this Act", the courts have held that a negligent act causing damage is nonetheless actionable.[35] Nonetheless the passage quoted may be a correct statement of the rules applicable to the exercise of certain classes of statutory functions. Thus, election officers who had wrongfully refused to accept votes of legally qualified voters were held immune from civil liability unless they had acted in bad faith.[36] The General Council of Medical Education and Registration was held not to be liable for having removed

19-013

---

[31] Police Act 1996 s.88. This rule does not apply to a Chief Constable himself who, in theory at least, remains personally liable for damages arising from his own tortious acts. For a detailed treatment of police liability, see R. Clayton et al., *Civil Actions Against the Police*, 3rd edn (2005).

[32] D. Cohen and J. Smith, "Entitlement and the Body Politic: Rethinking Negligence in Public Law" (1986) 64 Can.B.R. 1, 9, 16; P. Schuck, *Suing Government: Citizen Remedies for Official Wrongs* (1983).

[33] *Everett v Griffiths* [1921] 1 A. C. 631 at 695 (Lord Moulton); *Percy v Hall* [1997] Q.B. 924 (the fact that byelaws were later declared void for uncertainty did not render tortious the actions of police officers who, at the relevant time, reasonably believed that byelaw offences were being committed), see further *Secretary of State for the Home Department v Arben Draga* [2012] EWCA Civ 842.

[34] See, e.g. *Evans v Governor of Brockhill Prison (No.2)* [2001] 2 A.C. 19 (tort of false imprisonment was one of strict liability and the fact that the prison governor had acted in good faith was no defence); applied in *AN v Secretary of State for the Home Department* [2010] EWCA Civ 869 at [33] (unlawful control orders). However, until an order of a court was set aside it justified detention so imprisonment pursuant to that order was not tortious (*Quinland v Governor of Belmarsh Prison* [2002] EWCA Civ 174; [2003] Q.B. 306 at [14]-[18]). In respect of statutory schemes which divide responsibility for the exercise of a public power between two or more state agencies, see *TTM v London Borough of Hackney* [2011] EWCA Civ 4; [2011] 1 W.L.R. 2873 at [64].

[35] *Bullard v Croydon Hospital Group Management Committee* [1953] 1 Q.B. 511 construing National Health Service Act 1946 s.72 (now NHS Act 2006 s.69); cf. *Capital & Counties Plc v Hampshire CC* [1997] Q.B. 1004 (CA held that Fire Services Act 1947 s.30 was not apt to establish an implied immunity from proceedings for negligence or breach of statutory duty for fire fighters involved in extinguishing a fire. However, by turning off the sprinkler system, the fire service had contributed directly to the damage suffered.). In *Michael v Chief Constable of South Wales* [2015] UKSC 2; [2015] A.C. 1732, the SC granted summary judgment to two chief constables in respect of claims for negligence in connection with failure to respond to an emergency call, observing that police action in the course of investigating crime is not generally capable of forming the basis of an action in negligence. M. Burton, "Failing to Protect: victims' rights and police liability" (2009) 72 M.L.R. 283. The SC allowed the claim under art.2 of the ECHR to proceed on the basis that it raised questions of fact (precisely what the call-handler had heard) which could not be determined by way of summary judgment.

[36] *Tozer v Child* (1857) 7 E. & B. 377; *Drewe v Coulton* (1787) 1 East 563n., applying Holt CJ's judgment in *Ashby v White* (1703) 2 Ld. Raym. 938; mentioned in *Three Rivers DC v Bank of England (No.3)* [2001] UKHL 16; [2003] 2 A.C. 1 at [191] and 220. No civil liability is now incurred by election officers for breach of official duty (Representation of the People Act 1983 s.63, as amended by s.24 of the Representation of the People Act 1985). For discussion of bad faith in the context of judicial review, see 5-086.

a dentist from the register by an improper procedure but in good faith.[37] The common thread running through these cases is the erroneous exercise of judgment on matters immediately affecting the legal rights of individuals.[38] It would appear to be justifiable to infer that members of administrative bodies which exercise functions of a broadly judicial character are not liable in tort for the consequences of erroneous or unreasonable decisions or procedural irregularities within the scope of their jurisdiction, provided that they have not acted in bad faith. Bad faith is here understood to mean intentional usurpation of power, wilful partiality, or discrimination motivated by considerations which are incompatible with the discharge of public responsibilities.

19-014   Local authorities are statutory corporations given specific powers to institute and defend any legal proceedings.[39] The now routine use of "contracting out" and other market based mechanisms for the delivery of public services has not yet been followed by the development of any new general principles of civil liability. So on normal principles,[40] where service delivery has truly been contracted out to an independent contractor, the public authority will not be vicariously liable for the tortious acts of that contractor (unless statute provides otherwise).[41] The public authority may, however, owe some non-delegable duty to the claimant in these circumstances. But many "bodies" delivering services, such as executive agencies in central government and direct service organisations (DSOs) in local government, have no separate legal personality apart from that of their parent organisation which will remain directly liable for tortious acts.

The Crown as a defendant[42]

19-015   As with amenability to judicial review[43] and judicial review remedies,[44] the Crown—as distinct from its servants and agents—needs special consideration in relation to monetary remedies. Following the enactment of the Crown Proceedings Act 1947, many though not all of the Crown's former immunities from suit for damages in contract and tort enjoyed by central government have been removed and to a large extent it now stands in a broadly (but not wholly) similar position to a

---

[37] *Partridge v General Council of Medical Education and Registration* (1890) L.R. 25 Q.B.D. 90. The authority for this decision is not beyond question, for the General Council's procedural error amounted to a denial of natural justice. Various causes of action (including defamation, misfeasance in public office and negligent misstatement) were struck out in *Vaidya v GMC* [2010] EWHC 984 (QB). Cf. *McGillivray v Kimber* (1915) 52 S.C.R. 142. See also *AB v Home Office* [2012] EWHC 226 (QB), where delay in the exercise of a public duty without bad faith did not constitute misfeasance in public office. However, bad faith is not required in unlawful detention cases: *SK (Zimbabwe) v Secretary of State for the Home Department* at [2011] UKSC 23; [2011] 1 W.L.R. 1299 at [63].

[38] But the categories of those consensually appointed by the parties who enjoy immunity from liability save for bad faith are more narrowly drawn: *Sutcliffe v Thackrah* [1974] A.C. 727; *Arenson v Arenson* [1977] A.C. 405 (distinguishing arbitrators from valuers). See also *Campbell v Edwards* [1976] 1 W.L.R. 403.

[39] Local Government Act 1972 s.222.

[40] Criticised by E. McKendrick, "Vicarious Liability and Independent Contractors: A Re-Examination" (1990) 53 M.L.R. 770.

[41] Under Criminal Justice Act 1991 s.85, any contracted-out remand prison must have a "controller", a Crown Servant appointed by the Secretary of State; presumably the Crown will be vicariously liable for the tort of this officer under Crown Proceedings Act 1947 s.2(1).

[42] P. Hogg, P. Monahan and W. Wright, *Liability of the Crown*, 4th edn (2011).

[43] See 3-030.

[44] See 18-005; *M v Home Office* [1994] 1 A.C. 377; *Davidson v Scottish Ministers* [2005] UKHL 74; 2006 S.C. (HL) 41.

private person of full age and capacity in relation to its liabilities.[45] The constitutional principle of the rule of law requires that "the Crown (that is the executive government in its various emanations) is in general subject to the same common law obligations as ordinary citizens",[46] unless there is a clear exception established by law.

The 1947 Act "does not work by making the state a potential tortfeasor: it works **19-016** by making the Crown vicariously liable for the torts of its servants".[47] In relation to tort, s.2 of the 1947 Act places the Crown in the same position as other defendants for certain categories of liability, namely: (i) vicarious liability in respect of torts committed by its servants or agents; (ii) direct liability to its employees and agents; (iii) direct liability arising from breaches of duties attaching to the ownership, occupation, possession and control of property; and (iv) direct liability for breach of a statutory duty.[48] This approach has been criticised as it may leave the Crown with unintended immunity where no individual Crown servant is negligent (so the Crown is not vicariously liable), yet the duty owed by the Crown directly does not fall within one of the specified categories.[49] For reasons of policy, not all of them convincing, the Crown continues to benefit from a number of specific immunities by reason of its status[50]:

(a) The 1947 Act makes no alteration to the rule that the Crown is not bound by a statute unless such an intention is express or necessarily implied.[51]

(b) The Crown is not directly or vicariously liable for its servants and agents who are discharging or purporting to discharge "any responsibilities of a judicial nature".[52]

(c) Crown immunity under s.10 of the 1947 Act in relation to the armed

---

[45] Crown Proceedings Act 1947 s.2(1).

[46] *Deutsche Morgan Grenfell Group Plc v Inland Revenue Commissioners* [2006] UKHL 49; [2007] 1 A.C. 558 at [133] (Lord Hoffmann). The Secretary of State is not treated as an ordinary citizen when he seeks to act as a claimant and where statute makes express provision for the recovery of over-paid benefits (*R. (on the application of Child Action Poverty Group) v Secretary of State for Work and Pensions* [2010] UKSC 54, [2011] 2 A.C. 15 at [12]-[15]).

[47] *Chagos Islanders v Attorney General* [2004] EWCA Civ 997; *The Times*, 21 September 2004, at [20] (Sedley LJ).

[48] This does not make the Crown liable for damages for breach of public law statutory duties possessed by it alone; there is liability only in respect of statutory duties "binding also upon persons other than the Crown and its officers": see s.2(2). For this reason, the Crown cannot be the sole "public authority" for the purposes of a claim under the HRA (*Morgan v Ministry of Justice* [2010] EWHC 2248 (QB) at [52]).

[49] P. Hogg et al., *Liability of the Crown* 4th edn (2011), pp.184-187.

[50] The 1947 Act made no attempt to separate the governmental from the commercial functions of the Crown.

[51] *BBC v Johns* [1965] Ch.D. 32 at 79; *Lord Advocate v Dumbarton DC* [1990] 2 A.C. 580. cf. P. Hogg et al., *Liability of the Crown* 4th edn (2011), Ch.6, where it is argued that there is no good reason for this rule. In *R. (on the application of Black) v Secretary of State for Justice* [2017] UKSC 81; [2018] 2 W.L.R. 123, the SC held that relevant provisions of the Health Act 2006 which prohibited smoking in many public places were not intended to apply to the Crown to give a prisoner a cause of action for failure to provide access to a confidential help-line to report infringements. The SC emphasised that it was not sufficient that the statute was passed for the benefit of the public, but that it was not necessary to show that the Act would be wholly frustrated if it did not apply to the Crown (at [35]-[36]). In the present case, the Act could still achieve important purposes and the Crown could take voluntary action to achieve the legislative objectives. The SC considered that Parliament shoud consider reversing the presumption (at [35]). H. Street, "The Effect of Statutes upon the Rights and Liabilities of the Crown" (1948) 7 U.T.L.J. 357 has demonstrated that in earlier centuries the Crown was generally bound except in relation to affecting the prerogative rights of the King (*Williams v Berkley* (1561) 1 Plowden 223).

[52] 1947 Act s.2(5); see 19-018.

services has now been suspended[53]; the Secretary of State may by delegated legislation reinstate it in emergency situations.

(d) The monarch in her personal capacity continues to be immune from suit.[54]

(e) In relation to governmental acts performed outside the jurisdiction on the orders of the Crown, the defence of act of state may be available to the Crown (and its servants) in limited circumstances.[55]

(f) Although bad faith can be imputed to ministers of the Crown, it seems that it cannot be imputed to the Crown itself; but an act done by the Crown may be impugned on the ground that it was done in good faith but for an unauthorised purpose.[56]

19-017   Those who carry on the activities of government in the various bodies which collectively constitute the Crown are servants or agents of the Crown. For the purposes of civil proceedings, the 1947 Act states that, unless the context otherwise requires, "agents" includes an independent contractor employed by the Crown and "officer" in relation to the Crown includes any servant of Her Majesty and accordingly includes a minister of the Crown and a Member of the Scottish Government.[57] In relation to liability of the Crown for tort, the Act provides that an "officer" is someone who has been directly or indirectly appointed by the Crown and who is, at the material time, being paid in respect of his duties as an officer of the Crown solely out of the consolidated fund, the Scottish consolidated fund, monies provided by Parliament, or any other fund certified by the Treasury.[58] In accordance with s.17, the Cabinet Office from time to time publishes a list of authorised government departments for the purpose of identifying the department by and against which civil proceedings may be brought.[59] The list is not exhaustive and where a body, which is part of the Crown, is not identified on the list or where there is doubt as to which of the authorised departments on the list is the appropriate one, the proceedings can be brought against the Attorney General.

Judicial immunity from civil liability[60]

19-018   Many judicial review challenges are against the decisions of judges, magistrates, coroners, tribunals or others taking decisions of a judicial nature. In an important

---

[53] Crown Proceedings (Armed Forces) Act 1987; *Mulcahy v Ministry of Defence* [1996] Q.B. 732 (no duty of care existed between soldiers on active service and MoD was not obliged to maintain a safe system of work in battle situations). The so-called "combat immunity" should be narrowly construed and does not insulate decisions relating to the provision of suitable equipment or training (*Smith v Ministry of Defence* [2013] UKSC 41; [2014] A.C. 52 at [89]-[96]). The state may still be liable under art.2 of the HRA in relation to the activities of its armed forces overseas where they exercise sufficient control over the relevant area (*Al-Skeini v UK* (2011) 53 E.H.R.R. 18 at [130]-[150] and *Mohammed (Serdar) v Ministry of Defence* [2015] EWCA Civ 843; [2016] 2 W.L.R. 247 at [64]-[68]). Section 10 is a substantive limitation rather than a procedural bar to civil liability: *Matthews v Ministry of Defence* [2003] UKHL 4; [2003] 1 A.C. 1163.

[54] 1947 Act s.40(1).

[55] *Nissan v Attorney General* [1970] A.C. 179. In the context of the HRA, see 13-064.

[56] *R. v Halliday* [1917] A.C. 260; *Hudson's Bay Co v Maclay* (1920) 36 T.L.R. 469.

[57] 1947 Act s.38(2).

[58] 1947 Act s.2(6).

[59] Sedley LJ laments that practitioners tend to overlook the fact that the list names the "Home Office", not the "Secretary of State for the Home Department", as the relevant name: *Akenzua v Secretary of State for the Home Department* [sic.] [2002] EWCA Civ 1470; [2003] 1 W.L.R. 741 at [1].

[60] See A. Olowofoyeku, *Suing Judges: A Study of Judicial Immunity* (1993); M. Brazier, "Judicial Immunity and the Independence of the judiciary" [1976] P.L. 397; A. Nicol, "Judicial immunity and

exception to the general principle of treating public officials similarly to private persons, the common law confers an extremely high degree of immunity from tortious liability on those exercising judicial functions.[61] First, as already noted, the Crown enjoys complete immunity and is neither primarily nor vicariously liable for any wrongful exercise of power by its judicial officers.[62] Secondly, words spoken in the course of judicial proceedings (including those before some tribunals)[63] are

---

human rights" [2006] E.H.R.L.R. 558 (arguing in favour of qualified, rather than absolute, judicial immunity on human rights grounds). See further, J. Murphy, "Rethinking Tortious Immunity for Judicial Acts" (2013) 33 L.S. 455 (arguing that the same test for liability should apply to superior court judges as in the tort of misfeasance in public office).

[61] The case law relating to ECHR art.6 recognises that judicial immunity is a legitimate means of ensuring the proper administration of justice: see, e.g. *Mond v United Kingdom (Admissibility)* (2003) 37 E.H.R.R. CD129 (immunity from suit afforded to the Official Receiver was proportionate to the legitimate aim of enabling him to discharge his public duties without fear of litigation); cf. in European Union law, Case C-224/01 *Kobler v Austria* [2004] Q.B. 848 (subject to conditions, the principle that Member States were obliged to make reparations for the State's breaches of Community law applied to reparations stemming from decisions by a national court of final instance); see 14-075. See also *Arthur JS Hall & Co v Simons* [2002] 1 A.C. 615 (regarding the abolition of advocate's immunity from suit) and *Jones v Kaney* [2011] UKSC 13; [2011] 2 A.C. 398; (regarding the abolition of expert witnesses' immunity of suit). Judicial officers also have immunity from suit in Human Rights Act cases under s.9 of that Act, see *Forrester Ketley v Brent* [2012] EWCA Civ 324. In *Webster v Ministry of Justice* [2015] EWCA Civ 742; [2016] Q.B. 676 at [31]–[35] and [47], the CA upheld the strike out of proceedings under the HRA relating to the conduct of a criminal trial on the basis that although the trial judge's conduct was open to criticism, it did not constitute bad faith as required by s.9 and did not contain "gross and obvious irregularity" in a way which could give rise to claim under art.5 of the ECHR.

[62] Crown Proceedings Act 1947 s.2(5) ("No proceedings shall lie against the Crown ... in respect of anything done or omitted to be done by any person while discharging or purporting to discharge any responsibilities of a judicial nature vested in him, or any responsibilities which he has in connection with the execution of judicial process.").

[63] A narrow conception of "judicial" has prevailed in cases where it has been sought to establish the proceedings of administrative tribunals are judicial proceedings for the purpose of attracting absolute privilege in respect of defamatory statements and reports made to or by them. "The question ... in every case," it has been said, "is whether the tribunal in question has similar attributes to a court of justice or acts in a manner similar to that in which such courts act": *O'Connor v Waldron* [1935] A.C. 76 at 81 (Lord Atkin). It has often been difficult to persuade the courts that administrative tribunals possess judicial characteristics, even when they are determining questions of legal right. In *Heath v Commissioner of Police of the Metropolis* [2004] EWCA Civ 943; [2005] I.C.R. 329 at [26]-[45], the CA found that proceedings before a police disciplinary board were entitled to absolute immunity: the board was a tribunal recognised by law, dealing with issues very similar to those dealt with by courts, using a judicial procedure and with the power to make binding decisions. In *Singh v Reading BC* [2013] EWCA Civ 909; [2013] 1 W.L.R. 3052 at [43]-[46] and [70]-[72], the CA declined to follow *Heath* and held that the immunity did not apply to a claim for constructive dismissal by a former employee where the allegation was that the employer had placed undue pressure on another employee to produce an untrue witness statement and in *Daniels v Chief Constable of South Wales* [2015] EWCA Civ 680 at [40]-[48], the CA held that absolute immunity did not extend to failures to make proper disclosure of documents in the course of prosecutions against police officers. Singh and Daniels emphasise that absolute immunity is confined to protecting witnesses in the course of giving evidence and should only be extended where necessary to ensure that the protection of witnesses is not lost. In *P v Commissioner of Police for the Metropolis* [2017] UKSC 65, the SC held that the reasoning in *Heath* in relation to EU law was unsound and that acts at a misconduct hearing could give rise to liability under the Framework Directive. As such, P's claim of disability discrimination could be brought in the Employment Tribunal. In Australia, however, absolute immunity from defamation has been extended to proceedings of a board of inquiry, even though its functions were to investigate and make recommendations to the Governor in Council: *Tampion v Anderson* [1973] V.R. 321 at 715. There is undoubtedly much to be said in favour of denying absolute privilege from defamation actions to parties and witnesses appearing before administrative tribunals, for the proceedings are usually lacking the traditional formality that may tend to deter irresponsible persons from making maliciously untrue statements. This factor does not necessarily apply with equal force to the members of the tribunals themselves, and it is arguable that where

absolutely privileged in the law of defamation which means no action lies even if a statement is made maliciously.[64] Thirdly, those carrying out judicial functions enjoy wide immunity from actions for damages generally.[65] This general immunity from actions for damages attaches to judicial functions, not the person or tribunal as such, and so a judge is not protected when exercising administrative or ministerial powers[66] nor when he is functus officio (i.e. having completed his duties in relation to a matter). It is not possible to provide an exhaustive definition of what constitutes a judicial act (as distinct from "administrative" or "ministerial" ones), though they usually involve the evaluation of facts and/or law, resolving disputes between opposed parties and will be determinative of the rights and liabilities of the parties.[67]

19-019   Despite legislation which seeks to place magistrates in the same position as other judges with regard to immunity,[68] the distinction between superior courts and inferior courts of limited jurisdiction is so deep rooted in English law,[69] that it is still prudent to deal separately with the position of different types of courts; otherwise it is difficult to make sense of the case law.

Judges of superior courts

19-020   The position of judges in the Court of Appeal and the High Court is not particularly pertinent to the subject matter of this Chapter (liability to provide compensation for loss caused by acts contrary to the principles of judicial review) because judicial review does not lie against these courts. Superior courts have unlimited jurisdiction in that the court constitutes the sole arbiter as to what matters fall within its jurisdiction.[70] When an order of the High Court is set aside on appeal this is merely the correction of an erroneous exercise of that court's inherent jurisdiction in assuming jurisdiction of the matter; it is a valid order unless and until it is so corrected. The Crown Court, though a superior court, is subject to judicial review (though not for matters relating to trial on indictment)[71] and it is conceivable that an aggrieved person might seek damages following the quashing

---

membership of a tribunal is deemed to require a degree of judicial detachment that is incompatible with membership of the House of Commons (see House of Commons Disqualification Act 1975 s.1 and Sch.1), it ought to carry with it the same immunity from liability for words spoken in the course of proceedings and statements made in orders or judgments as is enjoyed by members of courts stricto sensu.

[64] *Scott v Stansfield* (1868) L.R. 3 Exch. 220. See generally R. Parkes and A. Mullis et al, *Gatley on Libel and Slander*, 12th edn (2013). Absolute privilege against defamation has also been conferred by statute upon reports made by the Parliamentary Commissioner for Administration and other ombudsmen and certain other communications made in connection with the performance of their functions: see Parliamentary Commissioner Act 1967 s.10(5); Local Government Act 1974 s.32(1).

[65] The old common law "action on the case as for a tort" against magistrates acting within their jurisdiction maliciously and without reasonable and probable cause is obsolete and no longer lies: *Re McC* [1985] 1 A.C. 528.

[66] Thus it was recognised from early times that JPs had ministerial duties and that their immunity from civil liability in respect of the erroneous performance of their judicial functions did not extend to their ministerial functions: *Green v Hundred of Bucclechurches* (1589) 1 Leon. 323 at 324.

[67] On the "classification of functions" see Olowofoyeku, *Suing Judges: A Study of Judicial Immunity* (1993), Ch.2.

[68] Now the Courts Act 2003 s.31 (formerly Courts and Legal Services Act 1990, s.108, and from 1997, Justices of the Peace Act 1997s.51); see below.

[69] *Re McC* [1985] 1 A.C. 528 at 550 (Lord Bridge). But see Olowofoyeku, *Suing Judges: A Study of Judicial Immunity* (1993), p.19.

[70] *Sirros v Moore* [1975] Q.B. 118, 139 (Buckley LJ), approved in *Re McC* [1985] 1 A.C. 528 at 559 (Lord Templeman).

[71] Senior Courts Act 1981 s.29(3).

of such a decision. Such a claimant is extremely unlikely to succeed. Judicial review is only available against the County Court where there is no appeal and where the court has fundamentally departed from the correct path in a manner which means that the judicial process has been frustrated or corrupted.[72] At common law, immunity extends to all decisions taken within the judge's very wide jurisdiction (in the sense previously defined) even if actuated by malice or corruption.[73] Only if a judge of a superior court acts deliberately or recklessly without any colour of right can an action in tort lie. Thus, "if the Lord Chief Justice himself, on the acquittal of a defendant charged before him with a criminal offence were to say: 'That is a perverse verdict', and thereupon proceed to pass a sentence of imprisonment, he could be sued for trespass".[74]

Magistrates

Magistrates' courts and justices of the peace are inferior courts with limited jurisdiction and judicial review may lie.[75] With respect to any matter within their jurisdiction, justices of the peace (and justices' clerks exercising the functions of a single justice by virtue of any statutory provision) enjoy immunity from any action for damages in respect to acts or omissions in the execution of their duties and in relation to a matter within his jurisdiction.[76] For acts or omissions with respect to a matter which is not within a magistrate's jurisdiction an action may lie only if it is proved that he acted in bad faith.[77] **19-021**

The question of what is within a magistrate's "jurisdiction" for the purposes of immunity is difficult to answer.[78] Clearly, as with judges of a superior court, where a magistrate acts entirely without any colour of authority, he will act outside his jurisdiction. Jurisdiction will also be absent where there is no "jurisdiction of the cause[79] i.e. the court has no power to entertain the proceedings at all.[80] A magistrate would certainly also be acting outside his jurisdiction were he guilty of some gross and obvious irregularity of procedure or the rules of natural justice.[81] Where, however, a justice has merely misconstrued a statute (a type of error considered by **19-022**

---

[72] *R. (on the application of Strickson) v Preston County Court* [2007] EWCA Civ 1132 at [32]. It is not enough that the judge gets the law or the facts wrong, "even extremely wrong"; it must be shown that the judge has embarked on an enquiry which he lacks all power to deal with or has failed to address a matter where he has an unequivocal duty to do so.

[73] *Anderson v Gorrie* [1895] 1 Q.B. 668; Olowofoyeku, *Suing Judges: A Study of Judicial Immunity* (1993), p.20.

[74] *Re McC* [1985] 1 A.C. 528 at 540 (Lord Bridge).

[75] Judicial review is often excluded in practice, though not expressly, by reason of the existence of a specific alternative remedy such as an appeal to the High Court by way of case stated or appeal to the Crown Court: see 3-009.

[76] Formerly Justice of the Peace Act 1997 ss.51-53, now Courts Act 2003 s.31. See *R. (on the application of Aldous) v Dartford Magistrates' Court* [2011] EWHC 1919 (Admin) at [20].

[77] Formerly Justice of the Peace Act 1997 s.52, now Courts Act 2003 s.32.

[78] Formerly Justices of the Peace Act 1979, now Courts Act 2003 s.31; *R. v Manchester City Magistrates' Court Ex p. Davies (Barry)* [1989] 1 Q.B. 631.

[79] *Marshalsea Case* (1613) 10 Co. Rep. 68b at 76a (court with jurisdiction limited to members of the King's household had no jurisdiction to entertain a suit between two citizen's neither of whom was a member of the King's household. An action lay for false imprisonment).

[80] *Re McC* [1985] 1 A.C. 528 at 536.

[81] *Re McC* [1985] 1 A.C. 528 at 546-547. Lord Bridge was dealing with the statutory formula "without jurisdiction or excess of jurisdiction" in relation to justices of the peace in Northern Ireland. Illustrations offered by Lord Bridge include where one justice absents himself for part of the hearing and relied on another to tell him what happened during his absence or if a justice refused to allow the defendant to give evidence. On the facts of *Re McC*, justices were held to have acted outside their jurisdiction when they failed to inform the defendant of his right to apply for legal aid, as required by legislation, before ordering him to be sent to a training school.

the majority in *Anisminic Ltd v Foreign Compensation Commission* to be "jurisdictional"[82]) this is probably insufficient to take him outside his jurisdiction for the purposes of losing immunity from civil actions.[83] Justices and justices' clerks may be indemnified out of local funds for costs, damages or sums payable in reasonable settlement of any proceedings or claim unless, in the opinion of the Lord Chancellor, the magistrate acted in bad faith.[84]

Tribunals

19-023   As a matter of common law, no claim of damages will lie against bodies such as professional disciplinary tribunals[85] and statutory tribunals where a judicial decision was within the jurisdiction of the body (in the narrow sense described above). In respect to decisions outside their jurisdiction, it is probable that such tribunals stand in a similar position to magistrates and an action may be brought if there is bad faith.[86]

The reason for immunity

19-024   Judicial immunity has been justified on the utilitarian basis that "if one judge in a thousand acts dishonestly within his jurisdiction to the detriment of a party before him, it is less harmful to the health of society to leave that party without a remedy than that nine hundred and ninety nine honest judges should be harassed by vexatious litigation alleging malice in the exercise of their proper jurisdiction".[87] Judicial immunity in this context has been said to stem from the constitutional independence of the judiciary from the executive: "if they are independent no one else can be vicariously answerable for any wrong that they may do".[88] The desirability of finality of legal proceedings and the avoidance of relitigation may also explain the current law. It has, however, been argued that there is no compelling need for a rule of absolute immunity for wrongful acts and omissions within jurisdiction.[89]

NO RIGHT TO DAMAGES FOR UNLAWFUL ADMINISTRATIVE ACTION AS SUCH

19-025   A finding by a court that a public authority, in performing a public function, has breached a ground of judicial review does not of itself provide a basis for entitlement at common law to compensation.[90] Nor does the careless performance of a statutory duty in itself give rise to any cause of action in tort in the absence of a

---

[82]   *Anisminic Ltd v Foreign Compensation Commission* [1969] 2 A.C. 147. On the concept of jurisdiction, see 4-009.

[83]   *Re McC* [1985] 1 A.C. 528 at 546 (Lord Bridge).

[84]   Courts Act 2003 s.35.

[85]   See, e.g. *Partridge v General Council* [1890] L.R. 25 Q.B.D. 90; *Heath v Commissioner of Police of the Metropolis* [2004] EWCA Civ 943; [2005] I.C.R. 329. *Heath* was not followed in *Singh v Reading BC* [2013] EWCA Civ 909; [2013] 1 W.L.R. 3052 at [43]–[46], and was found to be unsound as far as EU rights are concerned in *P v Commissioner of Police for the Metropolis* [2017] UKSC 65.

[86]   Olowofoyeku, *Suing Judges: A Study of Judicial Immunity* (1993), p.85.

[87]   *Re McC* [1985] 1 A.C. 528 at 541 (Lord Bridge).

[88]   H.W.R. Wade and C. Forsyth, *Administrative Law*, 11th edn (2014), p.697. See, however, *Maharaj v Attorney General of Trinidad and Tobago* [1979] A.C. 385.

[89]   Olowofoyeku, *Suing Judges: A Study of Judicial Immunity* (1993), Chs 6-7.

[90]   "Illegality without more does not give a cause of action": *Three Rivers DC v Bank of England (No.3)*

common law duty of care in negligence or a right of action for breach of statutory duty.[91] To recover damages, a recognised cause of action in tort must be pleaded and proved-such as negligence, the tort of breach of statutory duty, misfeasance in public office, false imprisonment or trespass. So while in some cases it may be a necessary[92] condition, it is never a sufficient one for the award of damages that the act or omission complained of be "unlawful" in a public law sense.

The English common law has generally set its face against the development of **19-026** a distinct body of rules for the tortious liabilities of officials and government bodies (though until the enactment of the Crown Proceedings Act 1947, certain procedural difficulties stood in the way of a person wishing to sue the Crown).[93] Where the common law does acknowledge the public status of a defendant in a private law action, this recognition tends merely to be in the form of adaptations to the general framework of the ordinary rules of liability. Professors F.W. Maitland[94] and A.V. Dicey, writing near the start the 20th century, both elevated this characteristic of English law to the status of an aspect of the constitutional principle the rule of law. In Dicey's words, "every man, whatever be his rank or condition, is subject to the ordinary law of the realm and amenable to the jurisdiction of the ordinary tribunals".[95] Dicey then explains that the law reports of his time abounded with cases in which officials were brought before the courts and made, in their personal capacity, liable to the payment of damages for acts done in their official capacity.[96] For Dicey, the function of tortious liability here was principally to provide a mechanism for controlling governmental power.

In modern administrative law in England and Wales, actions for damages and **19-027** restitutionary claims have been eclipsed by the development of principles of judicial review as the main way of controlling executive action within the confines of the law.[97] Today the major question is whether a system of remedies in administrative law can be complete without the provision of rights to compensation and restitution to people harmed by ultra vires acts or omissions of public bodies. If compensation and restitution are to be provided for at least some of the losses caused by such actions of government, the question arises as to how best this can be achieved. The orthodox common law approach, described by Dicey, is still applied with vigour in the courts and enjoys some support among academic writers.[98] Others, however,

---

[2001] UKHL 16; [2003] 2 A.C. 1 at [229] (Lord Hobhouse, citing *Lonrho Ltd v Shell Petroleum Co Ltd (No.2)* [1982] A.C. 173, 189); *X v Bedfordshire CC* [1995] 2 A.C. 633 at 732 and 734-735; *Percy v Hall* [1997] Q.B. 924 at 947.

91 *Geddis v Proprietors of Bann Reservoir* (1878) 3 App. Cas. 430 as explained by the HL in *X (Minors) v Bedfordshire CC* [1995] 2 A.C. 633 at 729.

92 See 19-054.

93 See 19-015. For an account of the civil liability of the Crown prior to 1947, see J. Jacob, "The Debates behind an Act: Crown Proceedings Reform, 1920-1947" [1992] P.L. 452.

94 *The Constitutional History of England* (1908), p.484: "We can hardly lay too much stress on the principle that though the King cannot be prosecuted or sued, his ministers can both be prosecuted and sued, even for what they do by the King's express command. Law, especially modern statute law, has endowed [ministers] with a great many powers, but the question whether they have overstepped those powers can be brought before a court of law, and the plea 'this is an official act, an act of state', will not serve them. A great deal of what we mean when we talk of English liberty lies in this".

95 A.V. Dicey, *Introduction to the Study of the Law of the Constitution*, 10th edn (1959), p.193.

96 A.V. Dicey, *Introduction to the Study of the Law of the Constitution*, 10th edn (1959), p.193. In his exposition, Dicey chose to ignore the special position of the Crown and also the existence of judicial immunity.

97 But see fn.6 above.

98 See, e.g. P. Hogg et al., *Liability of the Crown* (2011), pp.2-4 and 218-219; C. Harlow, *Compensation and Government Torts* (1982), p.80 and *State Liability: Tort Law and Beyond* (2004); H.W.R.

now question whether this model is appropriate for handling losses caused by governmental action and there have been calls for a distinctively public law of tort.[99]

RELATIONSHIPS BETWEEN THE GROUNDS OF JUDICIAL REVIEW AND RIGHTS TO A MONETARY REMEDY

19-028   The correlation between a finding that a decision of a public authority is, as a matter of public law, flawed and a person's right in private law to damages is not straightforward.

19-029   It is generally neither helpful nor necessary to introduce public law concepts as to the validity of a decision into the question of a public authority's liability at common law for negligence.[100] Nonetheless, issues as to the lawful scope of a public authority's discretion do remain important to questions of tortious liability in relation to negligence, breach of statutory duty, misfeasance in public office and other torts. A duty of care in negligence will not be imposed which will be inconsistent with, or fetter, a statutory duty.[101] In recent years, however, the courts have become markedly more sceptical of claims that imposing a duty of care will have an adverse impact on public authorities' work: the defendant will have to establish this (the court should not presume it be so) and this is likely to be demonstrated only in exceptional circumstances.[102]

19-030   The English common law has long drawn a distinction between negligently performed actions and alleged negligence in relation to omissions to act. Where a statute confers a discretion on a public authority as to the extent to which, and the methods by which, a statutory duty is to be performed, only if the decision complained of is outside the ambit of the lawful discretion may a duty of care be imposed; in relation to "policy" decisions[103] of a public authority, a finding that the act or omission was unlawful is normally viewed as a precondition for common law liability in tort.[104]

19-031   Holding a decision to be unlawful does not involve a finding that it was taken negligently; a decision without legal authority may nevertheless have been the

---

Wade, *Constitutional Fundamentals*, rev ed (1989), pp.93-94.

99   See, e.g. D. Cohen and J. Smith, "Entitlement and the Body Politic: Rethinking Negligence in Public Law" (1986) 64 Can. B.R. 1 and B. Hepple, Ch.6 in P. Birks (ed), *Frontiers of Liability*, Vol.II (1994). See also T. Cornford, *Towards a Public Law of Tort* (2008) and N. Foster "The Merits of the Civil Action of Breach of Statutory Duty" 33 Sydney L. Rev. 67 (2011).

100   *Phelps v Hillingdon LBC* [2001] 2 A.C. 619 at 653 (Lord Slynn approves approach in *Barrett v Enfield LBC* [2001] 2 A.C. 550 that "the fact that acts which are claimed to be negligent are carried out within the ambit of a statutory discretion is not in itself a reason why it should be held that no claim for negligence can be brought in respect of them). In *Barrett*, the HL held that a local authority might owe a duty of care in relation to psychiatric problems caused by allegedly negligent foster placements to a child in its care. *X (Minors) v Bedfordshire CC* [1995] 2 A.C. 633; D. Fairgrieve, "Pushing back the Boundaries of Public Authority Liability: Tort Law Enters the Classroom" [2002] P.L. 288, 297-299.

101   On fetters to discretion, see Ch.9. See also *Jain v Trent SHA* [2009] UKHL 4; [2009] 1 A.C. 853.

102   See, e.g. *Phelps v Hillingdon LBC* [2001] 2 A.C. 619 at 653 (no justification for a blanket immunity policy in respect of education officers performing a local authority's functions with regard to children with special educational needs, in particular the failure of an educational psychologist to diagnose dyslexia leading to reduced development doubting the approach in *X (Minors) v Bedfordshire CC* [1995] 2 A.C. 633).

103   The distinction between policy decisions and operational activities of public bodies is considered at 19-041. "Operational" activities are not normally the subject of claims for judicial review.

104   See 19-031.

product of very careful consideration by a decision-maker.[105] Unlawfulness (in the judicial review sense) and negligence are conceptually distinct[106] and so negligence cannot be inferred by a process of "relating back" from a finding of invalidity.[107]

There is no special affinity between any particular grounds of judicial review and the causes of action for damages; whether there is a cause of action will depend on the particular facts. This may be illustrated in the following ways: **19-032**

(a) Where a decision-maker takes into account an irrelevant consideration, as well as providing grounds for quashing the decision, this may create a right to damages for misfeasance in public office if it can be proved that the action complained of was done knowingly or maliciously.[108] But the fact that a consideration was taken into account which is irrelevant says nothing about whether the decision-making process which led to the error involved any failure to take reasonable care-a necessary element for recovery in the tort of negligence.[109]

(b) An official's statement, in addition to creating a legitimate expectation[110] according to the principles of judicial review, may possibly, if untrue and given in response to a specific request, also give an action in damages for negligent misstatement.[111]

(c) The failure of a public authority, contrary to the principles of natural justice, to give a person a proper hearing before making a decision does not, of itself, give rise to a cause of action for damages.[112] In order to recover damages in the public law arena, the aggrieved person will need to show that the procedural impropriety or other unlawful administrative action also constituted an actionable breach of statutory duty, misfeasance in public office or other recognised civil wrong.

(d) Delay in making a decision may result in a mandatory order in a claim for judicial review[113] and, possibly, a claim for damages-though delay of itself

---

[105] P. Craig, "Negligence in the Exercise of a Statutory Power" (1978) 94 L.Q.R. 428, 448.

[106] *Dunlop v Woollahra Municipal Council* [1982] A.C. 158 at 171-172 (Lord Diplock).

[107] P. Craig, "Compensation in Public Law" (1980) 96 L.Q.R. 413, 425.

[108] See 19-049.

[109] Craig (1978) 94 L.Q.R. 428, 448.

[110] See Ch.12.

[111] See, e.g. *Davy v Spelthorne BC* [1984] A.C. 262. In the past an assurance by a government official addressed to an individual may have been treated as contractual (see *The Amphitrite* [1921] 3 K.B. 500), but today this would almost certainly be approached as a matter of public law and consequently there would be no scope for any claim for damages for breach of contract. In *R. (on the application of Nurse Prescribers Ltd) v Secretary of State for Health* [2004] EWHC 403 (Admin) the court found that a legitimate expectation had been disappointed but held that there was no basis on which to award damages for expenditure wasted as a result of the Department of Health's change of policy on prescribing of saline solution, which had not been communicated to the claimant.

[112] *Dunlop v Woollahra Municipal Council* [1982] A.C. 158 at 171-172; *PC and Welbridge Holdings Ltd v Metropolitan Corp of Greater Winnipeg* [1971] S.C.R. 957 (no duty of care owed to person damnified through reliance on validity of council byelaw later held invalid for breach of natural justice). Quaere whether damages might be awarded under Lord Cairn's Act in lieu of an injunction. cf. *Maharaj v Attorney General for Trinidad and Tobago (No.2)* [1979] A.C. 385 at 398F-400E PC (constitutional provision for the redress for breach of fundamental rights under the Trinidad and Tobago (Constitution) Order in Council 1962 held to include award of damages for committal for contempt without complying with the requirements of natural justice). Where a contract exists between the parties, such as a contract of employment, contravention of a principle such as audi alterem partem may amount to a breach of an express or implied term of the contract; but where there is a contractual relationship of this sort, judicial review will not normally lie (see 3-056).

[113] See, e.g. *Wang v Commissioner of Inland Revenue* [1994] 1 W.L.R. 1286, 1296F-G (the Commissioner could be compelled by a mandatory order to make an assessment within a reasonable time).

does not found a cause of action.[114] Negligence or actionable breach of statutory duty will have to be argued.

(e) Although the term "reasonableness" may be used to define both the standard of care imposed by the tort of negligence and as a ground of judicial review, the terminology does not always bear a consistent meaning between the two branches of law. It does not follow that because a decision is held unlawful as *Wednesbury* unreasonable,[115] the decision taker was negligent, i.e. he failed to take reasonable care coming to the decision; it may have been reached after careful deliberation and therefore not contain the arbitrary characteristics normally associated with the irrational or *Wednesbury* unreasonable decision. A court may, however, infer that a decision was so unreasonable that it could only be explained by the presence of malice.[116]

GENERAL DIFFICULTIES

19-033   This section outlines possible grounds for seeking damages in tort against a public authority in circumstances where judicial review may also lie. Many of the difficulties which face any claimant pursuing an action in tort are exacerbated where what is being claimed is compensation for loss due to the activities associated with the public functions of public authorities. This is especially the case where the decisions relate to the allocation of resources, licensing, inspection and other forms of regulation.

19-034   First, the loss suffered by the claimant as a result of a public authority's negligent acts or omissions[117] will often be economic loss, which is not consequential on any damage to property or personal injury, a kind of loss in respect of which the courts are reluctant to provide a remedy in the absence of a contract.[118] Secondly, in many cases, the complaint will be that a public authority failed to prevent a third party inflicting loss on the complainant, for instance by approving plans or inspecting

---

[114] See, e.g. *AB v Home Office* [2012] EWHC 226 (QB) at [105]-[119] and [124]-[143], where delay in the exercise of a public duty (to issue an EEA residence card) did not give rise to a cause of action for breach of statutory duty and, without bad faith, did not constitute misfeasance in public office. cf. *R. v HM Treasury Ex p. Petch* [1990] C.O.D. 19 (Popplewell J held that there was an implied duty owed to a civil servant under the Superannuation Act 1972 to consider his claim for a pension timeously and failure to do so could give rise to damages for breach of statutory duty and in common law negligence—though on the facts there had been no breach. In an unreported decision on 15 January 1990, the CA dismissed the claimant's appeal on the facts without hearing argument on the law.) In *Calveley v Chief Constable of Merseyside Police* [1989] A.C. 1228, police officers were suspended on full pay pending investigation of complaints made against them. They alleged the disciplinary proceedings were conducted improperly and there had been undue delay. It was held that there was no actionable breach of statutory duty because Parliament did not intend to confer on police officers subject to disciplinary proceedings under the Police (Discipline) Regulations 1977 any right to damages; nor was there a common law duty of care as no loss was foreseeable.

[115] See Ch.12.

[116] See, e.g. *Jones v Swansea City Council* [1990] 1 W.L.R. 1453 at 1461 and following (misfeasance in public office).

[117] The position in relation to negligent misstatements and economic loss is rather different: since *Hedley Byrne & Co Ltd v Heller & Partners Ltd* [1964] A.C. 465 pure economic loss arising from negligent information and advice has, in some circumstances, been recoverable. This cause of action is considered separately, see 19-046.

[118] On economic loss generally, see M. Dugdale and M. Jones, *Clerk and Lindsell on Torts*, 20th edn (2010), paras 2-170-174, *Jain v Trent SHA* [2009] UKHL 4; [2009] 1 A.C. 853 at [26]-[27] and *An Informer v A Chief Constable* [2012] EWCA Civ 197; [2013] Q.B. 579 at [57]-[81] (no duty to protect a police informer from economic loss).

buildings[119] (where the breach of duty can be characterised as the failure of a public authority to control the acts or omissions of builders or architects), licensing of financial services (supervision of deposit takers)[120] or in the context of the criminal justice system, failing to detect and prevent the acts of criminals.[121] English tort law is generally unreceptive to the idea of imposing a duty of care for acts of independent third parties.[122]

In addition, it is rare for the common law to impose a duty to take positive action, in the absence of a special relationship and without the defendant having himself created or contributed to the danger,[123] to protect a stranger from being harmed. In the perennial illustration of this principle, a man may stand by and watch a child drown in a shallow pool without committing any tort. The main policy justifications for distinguishing between failing to act (nonfeasance) and acting wrongfully (misfeasance) are, first, that the imposition of affirmative duties is normally more burdensome on an individual in terms of time, trouble, risk and money than are negative duties and, secondly, the difficulty in some cases of identifying the person to be sued.[124] Over the years, the courts have found it difficult to develop satisfactorily the law in the case of nonfeasance by public bodies. The current state of the law rests on the assumption that it will be unusual (though not impossible) for a public authority to owe a duty of care for foreseeable loss cause by a statutory discretion not being performed.[125] The rationale for this restrictive approach is that the fact that Parliament has conferred a discretion must be

19-035

---

[119] *Anns v Merton LBC* [1978] A.C. 728 (now largely overruled); *Curran v Northern Ireland Co-ownership Housing Association Ltd* [1987] A.C. 718; *Murphy v Brentwood DC* [1991] 1 A.C. 398.

[120] *Yuen Kun-yeu v Attorney General of Hong Kong* [1988] A.C. 175.

[121] *Hill v Chief Constable of West Yorkshire* [1989] A.C. 53 (no duty owed by police to victim for alleged failure promptly to apprehend unknown perpetrator of a crime). The approach in *Hill* was found to be in violation of ECHR art.6(1) in *Osman v United Kingdom* (2000) 29 E.H.R.R. 245, where the policy factors which led to a denial of a duty of care, along with the practice of striking out claims at a summary hearing as disclosing no triable issue, were held to constitute an "exclusionary rule". The ECtHR retreated somewhat from this position in *Z v United Kingdom* [2001] 2 F.L.R. 612; (2002) 34 E.H.R.R. 3. See further, *Brooks v Commissioner of Police of the Metropolis* [2005] UKHL 24; [2005] 1 W.L.R. 1495 at [27]-[32] (with hindsight, not every principle in *Hill* could now be supported and a more sceptical approach to the carrying out of all public functions was necessary. However, the core principle of *Hill* had remained unchallenged in domestic and European law for many years and it had to stand) and *Van Colle v Chief Constable of Hertfordshire* [2008] UKHL 50; [2009] 1 A.C. 225 at [73]. In *Michael v Chief Constable of South Wales Police* [2015] UKSC 2; [2015] A.C. 1732 at [113]-[122], Hill was affirmed and applied to strike out a claim of negligence about the mishandling of an emergency call. The art.2 claim was permitted to proceed to trial.

[122] *Clerk and Lindsell on Torts*, 21st edn (2014), paras 14-54-14-64; *X (Minors) v Bedfordshire CC* [1995] 2 A.C. 633 at 751G (Lord Browne-Wilkinson: "In my judgment, the courts should proceed with great care before holding liable in negligence those who have been charged by Parliament with the task of protecting society from the wrongdoings of others"); *JD v East Berkshire Community Health NHS Trust* [2005] UKHL 23; [2005] 2 A.C. 373 at [105] (Lord Rodgers of Earlsferry: "For the most part, then, the settled policy of the law is opposed to granting remedies to third parties for the effects of injuries to other people").

[123] *Mitchell v Glasgow City Council* [2009] UKHL 11; [2009] 1 A.C. 874 at [18]-[25] and [37]-[44]. cf. e.g. *Kane v New Forest DC (No.1)* [2001] EWCA Civ 878; [2002] 1 W.L.R. 312 at [25]-[28] (local authority created source of danger by requiring a footpath with restricted lines of vision to be built, so distinguishing the situation from *Stovin v Wise* [1996] A.C. 923). See further, *Furnell v Flaherty* [2013] EWHC 377 (QB); [2013] P.T.S.R. D20.

[124] P. Cane (ed), *Atiyah's Accidents, Compensation and the Law*, 8th edn (2013), pp.70-83, who goes on to argue that there is no really satisfactory reason for distinguishing between misfeasance and nonfeasance. D. Nolan, "The Liability of Public Authorities for Failing to Confer Benefits" (2012) 127 L.Q.R. 260.

[125] *Stovin v Wise* [1996] A.C. 923 (HL, by a 3:2 majority, held that failure to exercise discretionary powers to remove obstructions conferred by Highways Act 1980 s.79 did not give rise to a duty of care); *Calderdale MBC v Gorringe* [2004] UKHL 15; [2004] 1 W.L.R. 1057 (local authority's statutory

some indication that the policy of the Act conferring the power was not to create a common law right to compensation.[126] There is a two-stage approach. To establish a duty of care it must first be shown that it would have been irrational for the public authority not to have exercised its power "so that there was in effect a public law duty to act".[127] Secondly, some exceptional reason must be demonstrated to show that the statute in question requires compensation to be paid to a person who suffers loss because the power was not exercised.[128]

19-036   The causation of damage also creates particular problems in respect of the imposition of tortious liability on public authorities for unlawful administrative action.[129] It is trite law that judicial review is not concerned with the merits of administrative decisions and the court should ordinarily avoid substituting its own opinion for that of the public authority as to how precisely a discretion should be exercised. How, then, is a court to approach a case where, for example, a claimant alleges that a breach of natural justice activated by malice has caused him loss (such as the refusal of a licence to trade) or the decision-maker negligently failed to take into account a relevant consideration? The court may avoid second-guessing what decision the public authority would have reached had the decision not been tainted by illegality by saying that the claimant has at most lost an opportunity to obtain a benefit. Probability will be defined by, among other facts, the degree of discretion possessed by the decision-maker. Whilst in most cases a court may attempt to place a value on a lost chance,[130] special difficulties arise in relation to damages claims associated with judicial review because this exercise would necessarily involve the court substituting its own discretion for that of the decision-maker.[131] A solution is to defer the claim for damages until after the outcome of the claim for judicial review is known and the public authority has complied with the decision. However, even if the court considering the damages claim waits for the decision-maker to reconsider the decision in accordance with law, conceptual problems may still arise if a decision is characterised as void (rather than voidable)[132]; in these circumstances what will have caused the claimant's loss? One answer, arguably, is the act of taking a void, or the omission to take a valid, decision. If practical steps have been taken to implement a void decision, e.g. by entering onto the claimant's land or seizing his goods, then that physical act may of itself constitute the tort rather than the underlying invalid decision.[133] But often there will be no such steps to execute a decision, e.g. as when a licence to carry on a trade is revoked negligently or in a manner which amounts to misfeasance in public office. In a number of cases, it has

---

duty to promote road safety under Road Traffic Act 1988 s.39 did not create common law duty of care; it would be unusual for a duty of care to arise simply from a failure, however irrational, to provide some benefit which a public authority had a duty or power to provide), applied in *Ali v Bradford MDC* [2010] EWCA Civ 1282; [2012] 1 W.L.R. 161 at [29]-[33].

[126] *Stovin* [1996] A.C. 923 at 953 (Lord Hoffmann).

[127] *Stovin* [1996] A.C. 923 at 953.

[128] *Stovin* [1996] A.C. 923 at 953.

[129] See generally *Clerk and Lindsell on Torts*, 21st edn (2014), paras 1-08-1-09 and Ch.14. In the context of damages in the public law context, see C. Harlow, *Compensation and Government Torts* (1982), p.93. cf. Report of the Committee of the Justice/All Souls Review of Administrative Law in the United Kingdom, *Administrative Justice-Some Necessary Reforms* (1988) para.11.86, which did not see causation as a major problem.

[130] See *Chaplin v Hicks* [1911] 2 K.B. 786 (a case in contract); in relation to tort claims, see *Hotson v East Berkshire AHA* [1987] A.C. 750; *Gregg v Scott* [2005] UKHL 2; [2005] 2 A.C. 176.

[131] Again, the Justice/All Souls review saw no problem in the court considering whether an authority might validly have refused the benefit and taking that into account in determining damages (1988, para.11.86). cf. Craig, (1980) 96 L.Q.R. 413, 438-439.

[132] See 4-058.

[133] See, e.g. *Cooper v Wandsworth Board of Works* (1883) 14 C.B. (N. S.) 180.

been held that a claimant ought to have ignored an invalid decision,[134] with the result that damage has been held to have arisen not from the unlawful administrative decision, but the claimant's own voluntary compliance with it. This approach has rightly been criticised as unrealistic,[135] and the courts have on occasion explicitly or implicitly accepted that a person's act in obeying an invalid order was a reasonable response.[136]

A final difficulty with tort liability for unlawful administrative action lies in the application of the rules as to remoteness of damage,[137] particularly in relation to economic damage.[138] Given the fact that governmental actions will often, of their very nature, foreseeably affect a great many people, it is not clear that the applications of ordinary principles on remoteness will adequately protect public authorities from being subject to crushing liability **19-037**

NEGLIGENCE[139]

In general, liability for negligent acts and omissions will be imposed by a court where: **19-038**

    (a)   the defendant owes the claimant a duty of care. This will exist if (i) the harm suffered by the claimant was reasonably foreseeable; (ii) the relationship between the defendant and claimant was sufficiently "proximate"; and (iii) the imposition of a duty of care would be fair, just and reasonable[140];

---

[134] See e.g. *Dunlop v Woollahra Municipal Council* [1982] A.C. 158 at 172D-E; *Scott v Gamble* [1916] 2 K.B. 504; *O'Connor v Isaacs* [1956] 2 Q.B. 288.

[135] P. Hogg et al., *Liability of the Crown* (2011), p.196, fn.217, citing *McClintock v Commonwealth* (1947) 75 C.L.R. 1. See further A. Rubenstein, *Jurisdiction and Illegality* (1965), p.322.

[136] See, e.g. *Farrington v Thomson* [1959] V.R. 286; *Roncarelli v Duplessis* (1959) 16 D.L.R. (2nd) 689 at 708. See further J. McBride, "Damages as a Remedy for Unlawful Administrative Action" [1979] C.L.J. 323.

[137] *Clerk and Lindsell on Torts*, 21st edn (2014) Ch.2.

[138] *Clerk and Lindsell on Torts*, 21st edn (2014) para.2-173.

[139] *Charlesworth and Percy on Negligence*, 13th edn (2014); C. Booth and D. Squires, *The Negligence Liability of Public Authorities* (2006); B. Markesinis and J. Fedtke, "Damages for the Negligence of Statutory Bodies: The Empirical and Comparative Dimension to an Unending Debate" [2007] P.L. 299.

[140] *Clerk and Lindsell on Torts*, 21st edn (2014) para.8-04. The three-fold classification derives from *Caparo Industries Plc v Dickman* [1990] 2 A.C. 605 at 617-8. See A. Robertson, "Justice, Community Welfare and the Duty of Care" (2011) 127 L.Q.R. 370. Applying *Caparo*, it was not fair, just and reasonable to impose a duty of care on officers engaged in apprehending a suspected drug dealer on the street in relation to a bystander who suffered physical injury as a result of negligence by the officers (*Robinson v Chief Constable of West Yorkshire* [2014] EWCA Civ 15; [2014] P.I.Q.R. P14 at [44]-[51]). Similarly, there was no duty of care owed by a police force to a member of the public who made an emergency call which was mishandled leading to a delayed police response during which time the victim was murdered (*Michael v Chief Constable of South Wales Police* [2015] UKSC 2; [2015] A.C. 1732 at [113]-[122]); and there was no voluntary assumption of responsibility by the police towards witnesses in the course of obtaining and preserving evidence which could lead to the imposition of a duty of care not to disclose their addresses (*CLG v Chief Constable of Merseyside* [2015] EWCA Civ 836 at [22]-[24]). The SC decided that the question of whether it was fair, just and reasonable to impose a duty of care in relation to the deaths of British troops in Iraq arising from a failure to provide suitable equipment should be determined on the evidence at trial, but indicated that the defence of combat immunity should be narrowly construed (*Smith v Ministry of Defence* [2013] UKSC 41; [2014] A.C. 52 at [89]-[101]). The SC held it was fair, just and reasonable to impose a non-delegable duty of care on a school in relation to severe brain damage suffered by a pupil during a school swimming lesson (*Woodland v Swimming Teachers Association* [2013] UKSC 66; [2014] A.C. 537 at [25]). In contrast, a local authority does not owe a non-delegable duty of care

(b) the defendant was in breach of the standard of care required in the circumstances;

(c) the claimant suffered damage as a result of the breach. The damage in question must normally include physical damage to property[141] or the personal or economic loss arising from such damage.[142] (The position in relation to economic loss caused by negligent statements is considered separately below.)

19-039 English law has turned its back on the search for general principles of negligence liability, and instead the law is set to develop incrementally, on a case by case basis. In novel situations, arguments based on analogies to previously decided cases, rather than appeals to principle, are likely to find more favour in the courts.[143]

19-040 In many instances, the application of such general rules of liability to public bodies presents little difficulty: when a pedestrian is struck down by a negligently driven bus it is of no importance whether the driver is on the business of a commercial enterprise or a public authority.[144] Where, however, allegations of negligence are made in relation to the way in which a public authority has performed some public function—such as the state regulation of financial services, social work or the investigation of crime—greater difficulties may arise. Ultimately any judicial decision on whether to impose a duty of care in a novel situation is one of policy. Because of the nature of public functions which give special powers and impose responsibilities on administrators, some factors not usually relevant, or less important, where the defendant is a private person come into play. Regrettably, much effort has been spent deliberating how such considerations are to be taken into account by the common law, rather than in the examination of what they are and when they are to apply. This has led to the extremely unsatisfactory state of the present law which fails to provide clarity for claimants or defendants.

19-041 Much of the debate in the case law and academic literature has been over whether there needs to be a special framework for determining the existence of a duty of care in respect of governmental activities or whether the general test (described above) is sufficiently flexible to be used in this context. In many cases in which the courts have had to decide whether a public authority owes a claimant a duty of care in respect of its public functions, the courts have proceeded simply by the applica-

---

to children it has responsibly placed in foster care in relation to assaults on the children by foster carers. In placing the children with foster parents, the local authority was discharging, not delegating, its duty (*Armes v Nottinghamshire CC* [2015] EWCA Civ 1139; [2016] Q.B. 739 at [24]-[25]). The registrar of companies owes a duty of care to companies to take reasonable care to ensure that when entering a winding-up order it is entered against the correct company's name: *Sebry v Companies House* [2015] EWHC 115 (QB); [2016] 1 W.L.R. 2499. In that case, the registrar's error had catastrophic consequences for the company.

[141] On the need to show damage to property other than to the negligently constructed building or manufactured chattel itself, see *Murphy v Brentwood DC* [1991] 1 A.C. 398. *Phelps v Hillingdon LBC* [2001] 2 A.C. 619 (failure to diagnose a congenital condition such as dyslexia and to take the necessary action, resulting in a child's level of academic achievement being reduced and a consequential loss of wages, could constitute damage for a personal injuries claim),

[142] *Clerk and Lindsell on Torts*, 21st edn (2014), para.1-043.

[143] See, e.g. *Murphy v Brentwood DC* [1991] 1 A.C. 398 at 461 (Lord Keith) *X (Minors) v Bedfordshire CC* [1995] 2 A.C. 633 at 735D (Lord Browne-Wilkinson). "From time to time the courts have looked for some universal formula or yardstick, but the quest has been elusive" (*Michael v Chief Constable of South Wales Police* [2015] UKSC 2; [2015] A.C. 1732 at [103]).

[144] An example given in *Connor v Surrey CC* [2010] EWCA Civ 286; [2011] Q.B. 429 at [79]. A school and its teaching staff owe the same duty to a pupil whether it is a state maintained school or a private school (*Woodland v Swimming Teachers Association* [2013] UKSC 66; [2014] A.C. 537).

tion of the general legal framework.[145] In other cases, the courts have adopted a different and more elaborate approach[146] to determining whether a duty arises in respect of functions which contain an element of "planning" or "policy", as opposed to merely "operational" activities.[147] Those who advocate the need for a special framework suggest it is needed for two broad types of reason. First, the general test is inadequate to accommodate the special policy factors that need to be taken into account in relation to certain public functions. Secondly, application of the general test will, it is thought by some, result in liability being imposed in too many cases,[148] or alternatively that it will result in too large an area of immunity for public bodies.

In *Anns v Merton LBC*,[149] Lord Wilberforce distinguished policy aspects of a local authority's functions from its operational ones and said that a duty of care was more likely to be imposed in respect of the latter. The terms "policy" and "operational" are misleading in that they may suggest a distinction between making a decision and carrying out a decision. It is clear that some stages of the implementation process involve a policy aspect, and so are unlikely to give rise to a duty of care situation.[150] Various synonyms are used: "administrative" or "business powers"[151] instead of operational; "planning" decisions instead of "policy". **19-042**

Where the policy/operational dichotomy has been used, the following have been held to be "operational" decisions[152]: a decision by a local authority to place a boy with known pyromaniac tendencies in an insecure home[153]; the decision of a highway authority not to put up temporary signs warning of the absence of road markings[154]; and a decision of a minister not to release a company promptly from certain undertakings it had been required to give during an investigation by the Monopolies and Mergers Commission.[155] Policy decisions typically involve **19-043**

---

[145] See, e.g. *Phelps v Hillingdon LBC* [2001] 2 A.C. 619; *Jones v Department of Employment* [1989] 1 Q.B. 1 (claim that Adjudication Officer negligently determined entitlement to unemployment benefit); *Welsh v Chief Constable of the Merseyside Police and the Crown Prosecution Service* [1993] 1 All E.R. 692 (claim that Crown Prosecution Service failed to ensure that a magistrates' court was informed that offences for which claimant had been bailed were subsequently taken into consideration by the Crown Court).

[146] Harlow (2004), p.55, describes it as "incredibly complex".

[147] For a critical survey of decisions which have applied, ignored or distinguished the policy/operational test between 1978 and 1985, see S.H. Bailey and M.J. Bowan, "The Policy/Operational Dichotomy-A Cuckoo in the Nest" (1986) 45 C.L.J. 430. See further, H. Wilberg, "Defensive Practice or Conflict of Duties? Policy Concerns in Public Authority Negligence Claims" (2010) 126 L.Q.R. 420.

[148] See, e.g. H. Woolf, *Protection of the Public* (1990), p.60 See further, D. Nolan, "Varying the Standard of Care in Negligence" [2013] C.L.J. 651.

[149] *Anns v Merton LBC* [1978] A.C. 728, 753H-754F; Lord Salmon (at 767-768) drew no such distinction in *Anns*, holding more straightforwardly that every person whether discharging a public duty or not, is under a common law obligation to some persons in some circumstances to conduct himself with reasonable care so as not to injure those persons likely to be injured by his lack of care. So far as English law is concerned, the origins of the policy/operational dichotomy lie in Lord Diplock's speech in *Home Office v Dorset Yacht Co Ltd* [1970] A.C. 1004.

[150] For example, decisions as to the staffing levels at a regulatory agency.

[151] *Rowling v Takaro Properties Ltd* [1988] A.C. 473 at 500.

[152] For further illustrations of the application of the distinction, see: *Clerk and Lindsell on Torts*, 21st edn (2014) paras 14-05-14-08.

[153] *Vicar of Writtle v Essex CC* (1979) L.G.R. 656.

[154] *Bird v Pearce* [1979] R.T.R. 369 (distinguished in *MacDonald v Aberdeenshire Council* [2013] CSIH 83; 2014 S.C. 114 at [42]).

[155] *Lonrho Plc v Tebbit* [1991] 4 All E.R. 973 (Browne-Wilkinson VC); [1992] 4 All E.R. 280, CA.

discretionary decisions on the allocation of scarce resources and the distribution of risks.[156]

19-044 The general status of the House of Lords' decision in *Anns* is now greatly diminished, it now having been overruled by *Murphy* in so far as it was authority for imposing a duty of care in respect of defects in work which has not caused damage to the property or person of the claimant.[157] In *Murphy* nothing was said, however, about the policy/operational approach, and it can be assumed that this aspect of the decision was not intended to be overruled.[158] Since then the usefulness of the distinction has been doubted by the Privy Council[159] and various views have been expressed about its cogency in the House of Lords.[160] It has also been suggested that "there are two areas of potential inquiry": whether the decision is justiciable at all; and "the classic three stage test enunciated in Caparo".[161]

19-045 Wrangling over the dichotomy risks deflecting attention from the heart of the matter: what, if any, factors are uniquely or commonly determinative of public bodies' liability in negligence in respect of their public law functions? An exhaustive list of considerations is, of course, impossible, as all the relevant circumstances of a case will need to be considered.[162] Some of the following may be relevant.

(a) The statutory context within which the public authority exercises its powers must be considered to ensure that a common law duty of care will not be imposed which will be inconsistent with the statutory framework.[163] Where the defendant is performing a specific statutory function the purpose

---

[156] See P. Craig, *Administrative Law*, 7th edn (2012), pp.906-921 for a discussion of justiciability in relation to duties of care in tort law.

[157] *Murphy v Brentwood DC* [1991] 1 A.C. 398. See D. Howarth, "Negligence after Murphy: Time to Re-think" [1991] 50 C.L.J. 58.

[158] *X (Minors) v Bedfordshire CC* [1995] 2 A.C. 633 at 736C (Lord Browne-Wilkinson acknowledges that this part of the decision in *Anns* has largely escaped criticism in later cases).

[159] In determining the question whether a minister who had allegedly misconstrued regulations so as to cause loss to the claimant was liable, the PC in *Rowling v Takaro Properties Ltd* [1988] A.C. 473 at 501A-C inclined to the views, expressed in the academic literature, that the distinction did not provide a touchstone for liability but rather was expressive of the need to exclude altogether those cases in which the decision under attack is of such a kind that a question whether it had been made negligently was not justiciable. Of course, establishing that a decision is an "operational" one is only a precondition to recovering damages for tort—a duty, breach and damage will have to be proved.

[160] *Phelps v Hillingdon LBC* [2001] 2 A.C. 619 at 658 ("Over-use of the distinction between policy and operational matters so as respectively to limit or create liability has been criticised, but there is some validity in the distinction", Lord Slynn); 673-674 ("the classification may provide some guide towards identifying some kinds of case where a duty of care may be thought to be inappropriate", Lord Clyde); 665 ("I have reservations about any attempt to draw a sharp-edged distinction between 'policy' decisions and 'operational' decisions, for the reasons I stated in *Stovin v Wise* [1996] AC 923, 938d-939b", Lord Nicholls); *Stovin v Wise* [1996] A.C. 923 (Lord Hoffmann describes the distinction between policy and operation as "inadequate"; it was often elusive-and even if the distinction were clear cut, so leaving no element of discretion in the sense that it would be irrational, in the public law meaning of that word, for a public authority not to exercise its powers, it did not follow that the law should superimpose a common law duty of care). cf. *X Minors v Bedfordshire CC* [1995] 2 A.C. 633 where the policy/operation distinction received support.

[161] *Carty v Croydon LBC* [2005] EWCA Civ 19; [2005] 1 W.L.R. 2312 at [28] (Dyson LJ), [82] (Mummery LJ) (education officers owed duty of care to child (but had not breached that duty) in relation to decisions about his schooling).

[162] *Rowling v Takaro Properties Ltd* [1988] A.C. 473 at 501-503 (Lord Keith).

[163] In *Jain v Trent SHA* [2009] UKHL 4; [2009] 1 A.C. 853 at [19]-[28], the HL held that the public authority owed no duty of care to the owners of care home when applying for cancellation of their registration as the statutory powers were granted for the protection of the residents of the home. This was despite the careless manner in which the application was made and the devastating effect the cancellation had on the owners' business. See, further *A v Essex CC* [2003] EWCA Civ 1848; [2004] 1 W.L.R. 1881 (adoptive parents claimed local authority negligently failed to convey to them "all relevant information" about a child, but such a duty of care would have been inconsistent with the

for which the power or duty was conferred is regarded as being relevant in determining the existence and extent of any common law duty of care.[164] Thus where the purpose of the duty is to protect health and safety this is seen as impliedly excluding any greater common law duty (e.g. to prevent economic loss arising from a defective building).[165] Arguably this confuses and blurs the boundaries between the tort of negligence and the tort of breach of statutory duty[166] and unduly restricts the development of negligence liability. Since the duty of care in negligence arises from a relationship between the parties, not by virtue of a statute, as in breach of statutory duty, the purpose for which the public authority was given certain powers by statute should at most be no more than a matter to be considered as part of the relationship. In any event the pursuit of identifying a precise implicit legislative purpose is often a fruitless exercise as it is relatively easy to ascribe a variety of objects or purposes to statutes conferring powers.

(b) Many powers and duties of a governmental nature must necessarily contain a large "policy" element and it is for the public authority, not the courts, to decide what policy to pursue.[167] This may apply both to the question of

---

statutory framework under which adoption agencies were entitled to have policies in place about what information should be disclosed to potential adopters); *Desmond v Chief Constable of Nottinghamshire Police* [2011] EWCA Civ 3; [2011] 1 F.L.R. 1361 at [47]-[51] (the existence of a common law duty of care to an individual about whom information is provided to the Criminal Records Bureau would conflict with and inhibit the performance of the statutory purpose in the Police Act 1997 of protecting vulnerable young people). A pre-existing duty of care (owed to an employee) could require a public authority to exercise its statutory powers in a particular case where to do so would be consistent with the full performance of its public law obligations (*Connor v Surrey CC* [2011] EWCA Civ 286; [2011] Q.B. 429 at [104]-[109]). *Murdoch v Department of Work and Pensions* [2010] EWHC 1988 (QB), [79]-[86] (it was inconsistent with the finality expressed in the statutory scheme to provide a remedy for a failure to provide incapacity benefit and income support). Statements by Lords Hoffmann and Scott in *Gorringe v Calderdale MBC* [2004] UKHL 15; [2004] 1 W.L.R. 1057, [38]-[44] and [71] go considerably further and suggest that the existence of a statutory duty is incapable to giving rise to a duty of care and that such a duty will only exist where it would have been imposed anyway, irrespective of the existence of the statute. The effect of the decision may be limited by the fact that it concerned an omission to act. Thus, it did not bar recovery where a highway authority had taken the positive act of planting shrubs in a central reservation which obscured a pedestrian's view of the road (*Yetkin v Mahmodd* [2010] EWCA Civ 776; [2011] Q.B. 827, [25]-[35]).

164 Governors of the *Peabody Donation Fund v Sir Lindsay Parkinson and Co Ltd* [1985] A.C. 210, 242 at 245; *X Minors v Bedfordshire CC* [1995] 2 A.C. 633 at 739C; *Stovin v Wise and Norfolk CC* [1996] A.C. 923 at 952 (Lord Hoffmann: "Whether a statutory duty gives rise to a private cause of action is a question of construction. It requires an examination of the policy of the statute to decide whether it is intended to confer a right to compensation for the breach").

165 *Jain v Trent SHA* [2009] UKHL 4; [2009] 1 A.C. 853. For comment, see L. Blom-Cooper, "When the private lawyer should go public" [2009] P.L. 195.

166 See 19-051. See further K. Stanton et al., *Statutory Torts* (2003), para.14-117.

167 For an illustration of a situation in which a duty of care was denied because the claimant public bodies were carrying out a public duty involving balancing the public interest, see *Bennett v Commissioner of Police of the Metropolis* [1995] 1 W.L.R. 488 (Secretary of State signing public interest immunity certificate). For a very helpful summary, see *Connor v Surrey CC* [2010] EWCA Civ 286; [2011] Q.B. 429 at [103]. It is difficult for the courts to foresee whether the imposition of a duty of care would improve performance in a particular area (such as police responses to domestic violence) or distort the allocation of limited resources which should be governed by public interest considerations (*Michael v Chief Constable of South Wales Police* [2015] UKSC 2; [2015] A.C. 1732 at [121]). Four arguments are identified in the cases as being relied upon to justify restricting the liability of public authorities: it may lead to the diversion of resources or defensive practices; inhibit freedom of action; require the courts to dictate policy to elected bodies; victims often have alternative remedies (B. Markesinis, J.-B. Auby, D. Coester-Waltjen and S. Deakin, *The Tortious Liability of Public Authorities: A Comparative and Economic Analysis of Five Cases* (1999)).

whether a duty of care is imposed and the setting of the standard of care required.

(c) It may be desirable for the law of tort and the grounds of judicial review to set broadly consistent standards as to the conduct required of public authorities.[168] For instance, if a decision which is amenable to judicial review is "reasonable" in the *Wednesbury* sense, it may be undesirable to categorise it as negligent. As Harlow has put it, many judges believe that there must be an exact correspondence between negligence liability and "unlawful" exercise of discretionary power in public law.[169] It is unfortunate that the term "unreasonable" is used both in judicial review and negligence; it usually means different things in each context.[170] The House of Lords has now expressed a clear view that the common law concept of negligence should be applied directly to the exercise of statutory powers without first deciding whether the decision was *Wednesbury* unreasonable.[171]

(d) Often the damage caused by unlawful administrative action will be pure economic loss not consequential on any physical damage. For a variety of policy reasons the law of negligence in general denies recovery for such loss[172]; many of these are as applicable to determining the liability of public authorities for their public functions as elsewhere.

(e) The concern that exists that the imposition of liability may have a chilling effect on the quality of administrators' actions.[173] In more recent cases, however, there has been a growing scepticism about the likelihood that this will occur.[174] Nonetheless, at least in cases where it is claimed that a public authority has negligently failed to exercise a statutory discretion, it is legitimate for the court to have regard to the distorting impact that imposing liability would have on the authority's resource allocation decisions.[175]

(f) The existence or absence of an alternative method of redress for the claimant is often regarded as relevant to determining whether or not a common

---

[168] See 19-029.

[169] C. Harlow, *Compensation and Government Torts* (1982), p.53.

[170] *X (Minors) v Bedfordshire CC* [1995] 2 A.C. 633 at 736F (Lord Browne-Wilkinson: "I do not believe that it is either helpful or necessary to introduce pubic law concepts as to the validity of a decision into the question of liability at common law for negligence. In public law a decision can be ultra vires for reasons other than *Wednesbury* unreasonableness (e.g. breach of the rules of natural justice) which have no relevance to the question of negligence"). As Cane points out, it is unclear why *Wednesbury* unreasonableness has been singled out as the only form of ultra vires which can give rise to liability in tort for negligence (P. Cane, "Suing Public Authorities in Tort" (1996) 113 L.Q.R. 13).

[171] *Barrett v Enfield LBC* [2001] 2 A.C. 550 at 572 and 586 (Lords Slynn and Hutton).

[172] *Clerk and Lindsell on Torts*, 21st edn (2014) para.1-42; *Davis v Radcliffe* [1990] 1 W.L.R. 821 (action by depositors against the Finance Board and Treasury of the Isle of Man) but cf. *Allen v Bloomsbury Health Authority* [1993] 1 All E.R. 651 (action against health authority for economic loss due to failure to sterilise). See further, J. Hartshorne, "Contemporary Approaches Towards Pure Economic Loss in the Law of Negligence" [2014] J.B.L. 425.

[173] See 19-072; e.g. *X (Minors) v Bedfordshire CC* [1995] 2 A.C. 633 at 739D-E, 749H (Lord Browne-Wilkinson).

[174] *Phelps v Hillingdon LBC* [2001] 2 A.C. 619 at 667 (Lord Nicholls): "Denial of the existence of a cause of action is seldom, if ever, the appropriate response to fear of its abuse".

[175] *Stovin v Wise* [1996] A.C. 923 at 958 (Lord Hoffmann); *JD v East Berkshire Community Health NHS Trust* [2005] UKHL 23; [2005] 2 A.C. 373 (health professionals responsible for investigating suspected child abuse did not owe the person suspected of having committed the abuse a duty sounding in damages if they carried out that investigation in good faith but carelessly; Lord Nicholls of Birkenhead at [85]: "But when considering whether something does not feel 'quite right', a doctor must be able to act single-mindedly in the interests of the child. He ought not to have at the back of his mind an awareness that if his doubts about intentional injury or sexual abuse prove unfounded he may be exposed to claims by a distressed parent").

law duty of care exists. Thus, where the claimant may appeal to a tribunal or official against a decision, and the appellate body has power to order compensation, that will indicate that the court ought not impose a tortious liability on the original decision-maker.[176] There are comments in the case law justifying the same inference being drawn because of the existence of the right to apply for judicial review.[177] However, judicial review is available in respect of almost all administrative action and accordingly no special significance can be attached to its availability.

(g)   The courts will be slow to regard the misinterpretation of legislation as indicating negligence on the part of the decision-maker.[178] There is often room for more than one construction of a statutory provision and only a court can give a conclusive interpretation.

NEGLIGENT MISSTATEMENT

Liability for careless false statements of fact and opinion which cause a claim-   **19-046**
ant economic loss is based on somewhat different principles than liability for types of loss caused by careless acts and omissions.[179] In this area of law, no material distinction appears to have been drawn between the liability of public authorities and other persons.[180] It is clear that not every false statement made by a public official will attract liability. A duty of care will be owed only where the following elements are present in the relationship between the maker of the statement or provider

---

[176] See, e.g. *Jones v Department of Employment* [1989] 1 Q.B. 1 (claimant had no cause of action in negligence against an officer who underestimated his entitlement to a welfare benefit. The claimant had successfully appealed against the determination and had received back-payments, though no interest); *X Minors v Bedfordshire CC* [1995] 2 A.C. 633 at 751A-B (in relation to social workers investigating child abuse, a statutory complaints procedure under Children Act 1989 provided means to have grievances investigated (though no compensation) and the Local Government Ombusdman would have power to investigate); *Home Office v Mohammed* [2011] EWCA Civ 351; [2011] 1 W.L.R. 2862 at [18] (failure to grant permanent leave to remain fell within the remit of the Parliamentary Ombudsman); *Desmond v Chief Constable of Nottinghamshire Police* [2011] EWCA Civ 3; [2011] 1 F.L.R. 1361 at [51]. For doubt about the relevance of alternative remedies, see *Phelps v Hillingdon LBC* [2001] 2 A.C. 619 at 672 (Lord Clyde). The absence of adequate safeguards for the rights of care home owners under the existing procedures did not persuade the HL to impose a duty of care in *Jain v Trent SHA* [2009] UKHL 4; [2009] 1 A.C. 853 at [39]-[41]. The HL held that the answer was for safeguards to be introduced by legislation.

[177] See, e.g. *Rowling v Takaro Properties Ltd* [1988] A.C. 473 at 501-502 (Lord Keith) where it was held that the only effect of the allegedly negligent decision by the minister (in misconstruing legislation and so refusing consent) was delay: "This is because the processes of judicial review are available to the aggrieved party; and assuming that the alleged error of law is so serious that it can properly be described as negligent, the decision will assuredly be quashed by a process which, in New Zealand as in the United Kingdom, will normally be carried out with promptitude." See also *Calveley v Chief Constable of the Merseyside Police* [1989] A.C. 1228 at 1237 ff where, in relation to a claim for breach of statutory duty, Lord Bridge refers to judicial review as an alternative remedy justifying the refusal of tortious liability and *Curran v Northern Ireland Co-Ownership Housing Association Ltd* [1987] A.C. 718.

[178] See, e.g. *Rowling v Takaro Properties Ltd* [1988] A.C. 473 and *Dunlop v Woollahra MC* [1982] A.C. 158.

[179] *Hedley Byrne & Co v Heller* [1964] A.C. 465 and *Caparo Industries Plc v Dickman* [1990] 2 A.C. 605. cf. *James McNaughton Paper v Hicks Anderson* [1991] 2 Q.B. 113 at 124 (Neill LJ: in the light of later decisions, detailed reference to *Hedley Byrne* serves little purpose).

[180] See, e.g. *Ministry of Housing and Local Government v Sharp* [1970] 2 Q.B. 223, 268-9. But probably no action will he against the Crown in respect of a negligent statement by one of its servants unless that servant also owed a duty of care (Crown Proceedings Act 1947 s.2(1)(a), proviso).

of advice (the adviser) and the recipient who acts in reliance on it (the advisee)[181]:

(a) the advice must be required for a purpose, whether particularly specified or generally described, which was made known, either actually or inferentially, to the adviser at the time when the advice is given;

(b) the adviser must know, either actually or inferentially, that his advice will be communicated to the advisee, either specifically or as a member of an ascertainable class, in order that it should be used by the advisee for that purpose;

(c) it is known either actually or inferentially, that the advice so communicated is likely to be acted upon by the advisee for that purpose without independent inquiry; and

(d) it is so acted upon by the advisee to his detriment.

Even as between private persons, the courts are very slow to superimpose a common law duty of care on a defendant who is disseminating information in order to comply with a statutory requirement[182]; a similar approach will certainly be adopted in the public law context. In the public law context, liability is most likely to lie against officials giving answers to specific questions.[183] There is unlikely to be a duty of care in relation to the giving of general advice.[184]

19-047 Both in the case of negligent misstatement and other forms of negligence, it must be accepted that as a result of the decisions of the House of Lords and the Privy Council already cited, the circumstances in which liability for negligence for administrative default will be made out are limited to special situations. Unless and until there is legislative intervention or a change of heart on the part of the House of Lords, little progress in developing additional situations where damages will be payable can be expected.[185]

MISFEASANCE IN PUBLIC OFFICE[186]

19-048 As a general rule, in determining questions of tortious liability the motives of the defendant are immaterial, though proof of improper motive may be fatal to a

---

[181] *Caparo Industries Plc v Dickman* [1990] 2 A.C. 605 at 638 (Lord Oliver). Lord Oliver stated that his summary of *Heldey Byrne* was neither conclusive nor exclusive. See further, *Yuen Kun-Yeu v Attorney General of Hong Kong* [1988] A.C. 175 at 194 (Lord Keith).

[182] See, e.g. *Caparo v Dickman* [1990] 2 A.C. 605 (accounts audited pursuant to Companies Act); *Deloitte Haskins & Sells v National Mutual Life Nominees Ltd* [1993] 2 All E.R. 1015 (duty to report under Securities Act 1978).

[183] *Davy v Spelthorne BC* [1984] A.C. 262 (planning officers gave erroneous assurances that the operation of an enforcement notice would be suspended for three years); *Welton v North Cornwall DC* [1997] 1 W.L.R. 570 (special relationship between claimant guesthouse owner and environmental health officers which gave rise to a duty to take reasonable care in statements made about extent of alterations needed to comply with law).

[184] See, e.g. *Tidman v Reading BC* [1994] 3 P.L.R. 72 (although local authority had published a document encouraging persons involved in planning matters to seek guidance and advice from planning officers, a person who sought such guidance or advice did not thereby necessarily place the authority in a position where it owed a *Hedley Byrne* duty); *Commissioner of Police of the Metropolis v Lennon* [2004] EWCA Civ 130; [2004] 1 W.L.R. 2594 (liability imposed for failure to give proper advice to an employee where expressly sought and relied on).

[185] See 19-064 below.

[186] Lord Bingham provides a history of the tort in *Watkins v Secretary of State for the Home Department* [2006] UKHL 17; [2006] 2 A.C. 395 at [11]-[23]. See M. Andenas and D. Fairgrieve, "Misfeasance in Public Office, Governmental Liability and European Influences" (2002) 51 I.C.L.Q.

defence of statutory authority to commit an act that is prima facie tortious.[187] Improper motive (malice and bad faith are often used as synonyms) is, however, an essential ingredient in the tort of misfeasance in public office.

The tort appears to have its genesis in election corruption actions starting in the **19-049** late 17th century,[188] but it fell into disuse.[189] It is now clear that the tort contains the following elements[190]:

(a) an unlawful act or omission done or made in the exercise of power by a public officer. A public officer includes a public authority[191] or person holding a public office.[192] The tort is not confined to those actions or decisions which are capable of being characterised as the exercise of "public" power

---

757; S. Hannett, "Misfeasance in public office: the principles" [2005] J.R. 227; J. Murphy, "Misfeasance in Public Office: a tort law misfit?" (2012) 32 O.J.L.S. 51; C.J.S. Knight, "Constitutionality and misfeasance in public office: contorting the tort?" [2011] J.R. 2011 49. Note also the tort of malicious prosecution and the crime of misconduct in public office (*R. v Bowden (Terence)* [1996] 1 W.L.R. 98; *R v Belton (Alice Tara)* [2010] EWCA Crim 2857; [2011] Q.B. 934 at [29]-[30] (a member of the Independent Monitoring Board held public office although not remunerated and could be convicted of the offence for pursuing inappropriate relationships with prisoners); and the Bribery Act 2010. In *Crawford Adjusters (Cayman) Ltd v Sagicor General Insurance (Cayman) Ltd* [2013] UKPC 17; [2014] A.C. 366, the PC held that there continued to be a tort of the malicious prosecution of civil proceedings where malice and the absence of reasonable cause could be shown. The HL had previously indicated that the tort does not apply to disciplinary proceedings: *Gregory v Portsmouth City Council* [2000] 1 A.C. 419. The SC preferred and followed *Crawford* in *Willers v Joyce* [2016] UKSC 43; [2016] 3 W.L.R. 477. At the time of writing, the Law Commission has consulted on a new criminal offence of misconduct in public office based either on a breach of duty or corruption-based model and with a clear definition of public office and is considering the responses (*Reforming Misconduct in Public Office: A Consultation Paper* (Consultation Paper No 229, 5 September 2016)).

[187] cf. *Westminster Corp v L & NW Ry* [1905] A.C. 426 (where the allegations of improper motives were not, however, made out).

[188] For a useful account of the historical development of the tort, see R. Evans, "Damages for Unlawful Administrative Action: The Remedy for Misfeasance in Public Office" (1982) 31 I.C.L.Q. 640. Revival of interest in the tort dates from a series of Commonwealth decisions: *Farrington v Thomson and Bridgland* [1959] V.C. 286 (wrongful order to close hotel); *Roncarelli v Duplessis* [1959] S.C.R. 121 (Can.); and *David v Abdul Cader* [1963] 1 W.L.R. 834, PC, Ceylon.

[189] The leading authority is now *Three Rivers DC v Bank of England (No.3)* [2001] UKHL 16; [2003] 2 A.C. 1 (a claim brought by depositors in a bank licensed by the Bank of England which went into liquidation). *Society of Lloyd's v Henderson* [2007] EWCA Civ 930; [2008] 1 W.L.R. 2255 at [20], [22], [23], [41], [43], [44], [46].

[190] *Three Rivers* [2001] UKHL 16; [2003] 2 A.C. 1 at [42]-[44].

[191] *Three Rivers* [2001] UKHL 16; [2003] 2 A.C. 1. After some initial hesitation as to whether a public authority could be vicariously liable for the misfeasance of its servants, the HL confirmed that they may be: *Racz v Home Office* [1994] 2 A.C. 45.

[192] A person who is paid out of public funds and who "owes duties to members of the public as to how the office shall be exercised": see *Tampion v Anderson* [1973] V.R. 715 at 720. Also *Henley v Mayor of Lyme* (1828) 5 Bing. 91 at 107. Quaere whether the officer has to be paid out of public funds. The term office is to be understood "in a relatively wide sense" (*Cornelius v Hackney LBC* [2002] EWCA Civ 1073; [2003] B.L.G.R. 178 at [13]) and includes e.g. a local authority's exercise of functions as a landlord (*Jones v Swansea City Council* [1990] 1 W.L.R. 1453). But the Society of Lloyd's is not a public officer: *Society of Lloyd's v Henderson* [2007] EWCA Civ 930; [2008] 1 W.L.R. 2255. A police officer investigating suspected disciplinary offences alleged to have been committed by another officer who makes a written report to his superior officer was, however, held not to have done an "act" amounting to an exercise of power or authority for the purposes of this tort (*Calveley v Chief Constable of the Merseyside Police* [1989] A.C. 1228 at 1240). Such a report may however give rise to a cause of action for defamation. In *R. v Cosford (Karen)* [2013] EWCA Crim 466; [2014] Q.B. 81 at [34]-[39], the CA held that nurses working in a prison were public officers for the purposes of the tort whether or not they were also prison officers and whether employed directly by the state or through a private company since they were responsible in part for the proper, safe and secure running of the prison.

and extends to decisions taken by a public authority in capacities such as being the claimant's landlord or in the exercise of contractual powers.[193] However, there must be a connection between the misconduct complained of and the office of which the misconduct is an alleged abuse (so actions done in an officer's own time may not create liability)[194];

(b) the act or omission must have been done or made in bad faith. There are two forms of bad faith. First, bad faith includes where the public officer acted for an ulterior purpose, specifically intending to injure the claimant.[195] A power is exercised maliciously if its repository is motivated by personal animosity towards those who are directly affected by its exercise.[196] Bad faith is demonstrated by knowledge of probable loss on the part of the public officer.[197] Secondly, however, it also covers "untargeted malice". This is the situation where a decision-maker acting unlawfully does so "with a state of mind of reckless indifference"[198] or "blind disregard" to the legality of his act,[199] and an awareness that the act will in the ordinary and probable course of events cause injury to a person or a class of persons (who need not be identifiable at the time the tort is committed).[200] There is no need to establish any greater proximity, link or relationship between defendant and claimant than this.[201] Bad faith or dishonesty (synonyms in this context) is required on the part of the defendant public officer[202] and is demonstrated by recklessness on his part in disregarding the risk of loss.[203] In both forms, it is necessary "to prove the requisite subjective state of mind of the defendant in relation not only to his own conduct but also its effect on others".[204] In both, the tort concerns deliberate acts—it cannot be committed negligently or inadvertently.[205] In both, the defendant has exercised a power

---

[193] *Three Rivers* [2001] UKHL 16; [2003] 2 A.C. 1 at [191] (Lord Steyn) and *Jones v Swansea City Council* [1990] 1 W.L.R. 1453 at 1458 (Lord Lowry, obiter) (the claimant needed both planning permission and the council's permission as her landlord for the change of use of premises).

[194] *Cornelius v Hackney LBC* [2002] EWCA Civ 1073; [2003] B.L.G.R. 178 at [16].

[195] That is, an intent to injure the claimant: see *Bennett v Commissioner of Police of the Metropolis* [1995] 1 W.L.R. 488 at 501; *Three Rivers* [2001] UKHL 16; [2003] 2 A.C. 1 at [137]. On intention in tort see *Douglas v Hello! Ltd (Trial Action: Breach of Confidence) (No.3)* [2005] EWCA Civ 595; [2006] Q.B. 125 at [159]. In *Weir v Secretary of State for Transport* [2004] EWHC 2772 (Ch); [2005] U.K.H.R.R. 154, a former minister was cross-examined for over two days in an unsuccessful claim in which it was said that he had deliberately impaired the value of their shareholding in the Railtrack Group, leading to the making of an administration order on 7 October 2001, without paying compensation or seeking the prior approval of Parliament.

[196] In *Roncarelli v Duplessis* [1959] S.C.R. 121 at 141, Rand J defined malice more widely, as "acting for a reason and purposed knowingly foreign to the administration".

[197] *Three Rivers* [2001] UKHL 16; [2003] 2 A.C. 1 at [44] (Lord Hope).

[198] *Three Rivers* [2001] UKHL 16; [2003] 2 A.C. 1 at [192].

[199] *Three Rivers* [2001] UKHL 16; [2003] 2 A.C. 1 at [231] (Lord Hobhouse).

[200] *Three Rivers* [2001] UKHL 16; [2003] 2 A.C. 1 at [191] (Lord Steyn), 228 (Lord Hutton), 230 (Lord Hobhouse), 235 (Lord Millett). And see *Three Rivers* [2001] UKHL 16; [2003] 2 A.C. 1 at [46] (Lord Hope). The reckless indifference must be shown in relation to both illegality and the claimant's loss (misfeasance was not made out where the judge had not expressly considered it in relation to legality (*Muuse v Secretary of State for the Home Department* [2010] EWCA Civ 453 at [57]-[60])).

[201] *Akenzua v Secretary of State for the Home Department* [2002] EWCA Civ 1470; [2003] 1 W.L.R. 741.

[202] *Three Rivers* [2001] UKHL 16; [2003] 2 A.C. 1 at [228] (Lord Hutton, who prefers the term "bad faith"), 191 (Lord Steyn: it "involves bad faith inasmuch as the public officer does not have an honest belief that his act is lawful").

[203] *Three Rivers* [2001] UKHL 16; [2003] 2 A.C. 1 at [228] (Lord Hutton), [231] (Lord Hobhouse).

[204] *Three Rivers* [2001] UKHL 16; [2003] 2 A.C. 1 at [164] (Lord Hobhouse).

[205] *Three Rivers* [2001] UKHL 16; [2003] 2 A.C. 1 at [230] (Lord Hobhouse), [235] (Lord Millett); see,

which is unlawful-in the sense of that term similar to that used in judicial review;

(c) the claimant must demonstrate that he has a sufficient interest to sue the defendant; and

(d) the act or omission must have caused the claimants' loss.

Where misfeasance is alleged against a decision-making body, it is sufficient to show that a majority of its members present had made the decision with the object of damaging the claimant.[206] A court will not entertain allegations of bad faith or malice made against the repository of a power unless it has been expressly pleaded and properly particularised.[207] Often there may be no direct evidence of the existence of malice, and in these circumstances the court may make adverse inferences, e.g. from the fact that a decision was so unreasonable that it could only be explained by the presence of such a motive.[208] The claimant must prove that the exercise of power caused loss (financial loss or physical or mental injury). Distress (as opposed to a recognised psychiatric condition), injured feelings, indignation or annoyance are insufficient; it is not a tort actionable per se.[209] Exemplary damages may be awarded in addition to compensatory damages.[210]

19-050

BREACH OF STATUTORY DUTY[211]

English law has witnessed "the painful emergence of a nominate tort" of breach of statutory duty,[212] where in a limited range of circumstances a breach of a statu-

19-051

---

e.g. *Ashley v Chief Constable of Sussex* [2005] EWHC 415 (QB).

[206] *Jones v Swansea City Council* [1990] 1 W.L.R. 1453 at 1458-1459, HL.

[207] *Demetriades v Glasgow Corp* [1951] 1 All E.R. 457 at 460, 461, 463; *Three Rivers* [2001] UKHL 16; [2003] 2 A.C. 1 at [49] (Lord Hope: "In my judgment a balance must be struck between the need for fair notice to be given on the one hand and excessive demands for detail on the other"). The defendant could not rely on a "neither confirm nor deny" policy to avoid pleading a defence to a claim that undercover police officers had, as part of their work, engaged in long-term sexual relationships with those whose activities the police wished to observe (*DIL v Commissioner of Police of the Metropolis* [2014] EWHC 2184 (QB) at [40]–[43]).

[208] *Three Rivers* [2001] UKHL 16; [2003] 2 A.C. 1 at [235]-[263] (Lord Millett: "The question is: why did the official act as he did if he knew or suspected that he had no power to do so and that his conduct would injure the plaintiff?").

[209] *Watkins v Secretary of State for the Home Department* [2006] UKHL 17; [2006] 2 A.C. 395 (prison officers deliberately and in bad faith opened and read legal correspondence to a prisoner, contrary to Prison Rules. However, the HL would not extend the tort to protect constitutional rights where the Human Rights Act could provide a remedy (at [64])). For a broad interpretation, see *Karagozlu v Commissioner of Police of the Metropolis* [2006] EWCA Civ 1691; [2007] 1 W.L.R. 1881 (loss of liberty, if not a form of physical of physical injury, is at least akin to or analogous to physical injury).

[210] *Kuddus v Chief Constable of Leicestershire* [2001] UKHL 29; [2002] 2 A.C 122. "Notwithstanding the fact that the House has ruled in *Kuddus* ... that exemplary damages may in principle be awarded in cases of misfeasance in public office, I should myself prefer to confine the award of such damages very closely indeed" (*Watkins v Secretary of State for the Home Department* [2006] UKHL 17 at [81] (Lord Carswell)).

[211] See further K. Stanton et al., *Statutory Torts* (2003); *Clerk and Lindsell on Torts*, 21st edn, (2014) Ch.9.

[212] *The Queen in Right of Canada v Saskatchewan Wheat Pool* (1983) 143 D.L.R. (3rd) 9, Dixon J (Sup. Ct. of Canada). For the purposes of awards of exemplary damages, breaches of different statutory duties are to be regarded as sui generis torts rather than there being a single nominate tort of branch of statutory duty: see *AB v South West Water Services Ltd* [1993] Q.B. 507 at 620 (overruled in other respects by *Kuddus v Chief Constable of Leicestershire* [2001] UKHL 29; [2002] 2 A.C. 122). See E. Russell, "Breach of statutory duty-time to jettison the 'guesswork puzzle'" (2011) 3 Jur. Rev 227,

tory duty, in and of itself and without proof of negligence, or malice, may give rise to an action in damages.

19-052   Some statutory provisions expressly create rights of action for damages in tort against public bodies in breach of a statutory duty[213] and here few problems arise. Added difficulty arises in the more common situation where the legislation is silent on the issue whether breach entitles a person who suffers loss due to non-compliance with the statutory duty to commence an action for damages. The question is always approached as one of statutory construction to ascertain whether the legislature intended to provide for such private law claims for monetary compensation and for this reason it is difficult to discuss the tort in terms of generally applicable principles.[214] This judicial technique has rightly been criticised: "The failure of the judges to develop a governing attitude means that it is almost impossible to predict, outside the decided authorities, when the courts will regard a civil duty as impliedly created. In effect the judge can do what he likes, and then select one of the conflicting principles stated by his predecessors in order to justify his decision".[215]

19-053   Most statutory duties in the public law context are owed to the public at large rather than to private individuals.[216] Where the legislation in question establishes an administrative system to promote the social welfare of the community, exceptionally clear statutory language will be needed to show a parliamentary intention to create a right to damages for breach of statutory duty.[217] Categorising a duty as being in broad and general terms in this way is fatal to a claim for damages, even on judicial review. On this basis, a breach of s.8 of the Education Act 1944 was held to give no right of action.[218]

19-054   It is therefore a necessary, but not sufficient, precondition to liability to establish that the particular statutory duty was intended to protect a certain class of person (rather than the public at large) from a particular type of damage.[219] Factors which may raise a presumption of no legislative intention to create private rights to compensation include: the existence of a penalty or other remedy (including judicial

---

for a discussion of the extent to which the tort of breach of statutory duty remains incoherent, uncertain and in need of reform.

[213] See, e.g. Highways Act 1980 s.57.

[214] *R. v Deputy Governor of Parkhurst Prison Ex p. Hague* [1992] 1 A.C. 58 at 159 (Lord Bridge).

[215] Glanville Williams, "The Effect of Penal Legislation in Tort" (1960) 23 M.L.R. 233, 246.

[216] On "target" duties, see 5-074.

[217] *X (Minors) v Bedfordshire CC* [1995] 2 A.C. 633 at 731-2, where Lord Browne-Wilkinson sets out the basic test; *Phelps v Hillingdon LBC* [2001] 2 A.C. 619 at 652.

[218] *R. v Inner London Education Authority Ex p. Ali* (1990) 2 Admin. L.R. 822 (local education authority had failed to provide school places for a large number of children in the Stepney area of London). In *Sebry v Companies House* [2015] EWHC 115 (QB); [2016] 1 W.L.R. 2499 at [106], Edis J considered that to create liability for breach of statutory duty by the Registrar of companies in relation to his functions under the Companies Act 2006 would be too wide in relation to the register (which was available to the whole world). To similar effect, see *Human Fertilisation and Embryology Authority v ARGC Ltd* [2016] EWHC 460 (QB).

[219] *Hague* [1992] 1 A.C. 58 at 170 (Lord Jauncey). For example, *Francis v Southwark LBC* [2011] EWCA Civ 1418 at [22]-[23] (no personal remedy for breach of "right-to-buy" obligations under the Housing Act 1985 s.181). *Morrison Sports Ltd v Scottish Power Plc* [2010] UKSC 37; [2010] 1 W.L.R. 1934 at [38] (difficult to identify limited class of public for whom electricity safety regulations were passed). In *Greenway v Johnson Matthey Plc* [2014] EWHC 3957 (QB); [2015] P.I.Q.R. P10 at [34], the concept of welfare in the Health and Safety at Work etc Act 1974 was held not to include interests of a purely economic nature (affirmed without reference to this point at [2016] EWCA Civ 408; [2016] 1 W.L.R. 4487). Section 69 of the Enterprise and Regulatory Reform Act 2013 removes the common law cause of action for breach of statutory duty in relation to the Health and Safety at Work Act 1974 and associated legislation.

review) for non-compliance[220]; the fact that the aggrieved person had opportunities to participate in the decision-making process and had appeal rights[221]; by whom the duty is owed[222]; and the anticipated policy consequences of imposing liability.[223] Where the duty in question arises from a statutory instrument, the court will examine the enabling Act to see whether it gives power to the minister to create private rights.[224] By way of illustration, breach of the Prison Rules has been held to give no right of action in damages to a prisoner[225]; nor the Police (Discipline) Regulations to an officer facing disciplinary action[226]; nor duties under the homeless persons legislation.[227]

DEPRIVATION OF LIBERTY: FALSE IMPRISONMENT[228]

Claims for damages arising from unlawful actions which lead to the unlawful confinement of the claimant are most likely to arise in connection with government functions such as the criminal justice system, immigration control and the treatment of the mentally ill. The tort of false imprisonment has two elements[229]: (a) the fact of complete deprivation of liberty for any time, however short[230]; and (b) the absence of lawful authority to justify it for its full duration.[231] It is not necessary to prove physical incarceration; rather the gist of the tort is restraint (over and above that imposed by the general law or a binding contract) so that a person has

19-055

---

[220] See, e.g. *Lonrho Plc v Shell Petroleum Co (No.2)* [1982] A.C. 173; *Hague* [1992] 1 A.C. 58; *Calveley v Chief Constable of the Merseyside Police* [1989] A.C. 1228; *AB v Home Office* [2012] EWHC 226 (QB) at [113]-[114]. The absence of an alternative remedy does not create a presumption in favour of tortious liability (*St Poulton's Trustee in Bankruptcy v Ministry of Justice* [2010] EWCA Civ 392; [2011] Ch. 1 at [84]-[85] (failure of County Court to notify Chief Land Registrar of a bankruptcy petition)).

[221] *X (Minors) v Bedfordshire CC* [1995] 2 A.C. 633.

[222] So, if the duty is imposed only on a public authority, rather than also on private persons, there may be a presumption against an intention to create liability in damages; see T. Weir, "Compensation in Public Law" [1989] P.L. 40, 53.

[223] *Clegg Parkinson & Co Ltd v Earby Gas* [1896] 1 Q.B. 592.

[224] *Hague* [1992] 1 A.C. 58 at 170 (Lord Jauncey).

[225] *Hague* [1992] 1 A.C. 58.

[226] *Calveley v Chief Constable of the Merseyside Police* [1989] A.C. 1228.

[227] *O'Rourke v Camden LBC* [1998] A.C. 188, HL, overruling *Thornton v Kirklees MBC* [1979] Q.B. 626, CA. Housing Act 1985 Pt III was a social welfare programme intended to confer benefits at public expense pursuant to public policy, which suggested that Parliament did not intend to confer private law rights in relation to it.

[228] *Clerk and Lindsell on Torts*, 21st edn, (2014) paras 15–023–15–048. See also 17-010 on the writ of habeas corpus.

[229] *Hague* [1992] 1 A.C. 58 at 162 (Lord Bridge).

[230] On deprivation of liberty, see *Re L (R. v Bournewood Community and Mental Health NHS Trust Ex p. L)* [1999] 1 A.C. 458 (L's re-admission to hospital under s.131(1) Mental Health Act 1983 did not amount to the tort of false imprisonment as he had not been deprived of his liberty, since he was not kept on a locked ward and had not made any attempt to leave); L successfully challenged this decision in the ECtHR: *L v United Kingdom* (2005) 40 E.H.R.R. 32 as breaching art.5(1) and art.5(4). In *P v Cheshire West and Cheshire Council* [2014] UKSC 19; [2014] A.C. 896 at [45]-[50], the SC held that deprivation of liberty in relation to a mentally incapacitated person was to be given the same meaning as under art.5 of the ECHR.

[231] *Clerk and Lindsell on Torts*, 20th edn, (2010) in what is now para.15-23, quoted with approval by Lord Jauncey in *Hague* [1992] 1 A.C. 58 at 173. A breach of public law (to comply with a published policy) could lead to liability where it had a bearing on the decision to detain (*R. (on the application of Lumba) v Secretary of State for the Home Department* [2011] UKSC 12; [2012] 1 A.C. 245 at [64]-[70]).

no liberty to go at all times to all places where he wishes.[232] The tort is one of strict liability.[233] Bad faith is not an ingredient of the tort of false imprisonment, so it is no defence for the official authorising or carrying out the detention to say that he acted in good faith.[234] A claim may also lie for trespass to the person.

19-056   Where a person has been deprived of liberty, a claim for damages for breach of ECHR art.5 under s.8 of the HRA may also be made.[235]

Lawful authority

19-057   Questions as to whether a person has lawful authority to detain another must, since the coming into force of the HRA, be read subject to the overriding requirements of art.5; some earlier cases must therefore be read with caution and may not be a reliable guide to what constitutes lawful detention.[236] It is unnecessary for a claimant to obtain a quashing order or declaration in relation to the unlawfulness of the detention; that is a matter that may be determined by the court hearing the tort claim.[237]

19-058   As we have noted, judges of the higher courts have absolute immunity from suit[238] and magistrates may be subject to liability only if it can be proved that he acted both in bad faith and in excess of jurisdiction.[239] A police constable in exercising his discretion to arrest under s.24(6) of the Police and Criminal Evidence Act 1984 is subject to judicial control on *Wednesbury* principles.[240] Immunity may also

---

[232] *Hague* [1992] 1 A.C. 58 at 173 (Lord Jauncey). A person may be deprived of their liberty without being aware of it: whether because they are asleep or lack mental capacity (*P v Cheshire West and Cheshire Council* [2014] UKSC 19; [2014] A.C. 896 at [35]). Confining an individual to a doorway (even if only for a few seconds) without lawful authority was a false imprisonment on the basis that "a fundamental constitutional principle is at stake" (*Walker v Commissioner of Police of the Metropolis* [2014] EWCA Civ 897; [2015] 1 W.L.R. 312 at [46]). Damages were awarded in the sum of £5.

[233] It is no defence to the action that the person could certainly have been detained lawfully if the power had been exercised properly (*Lumba* [2011] UKSC 12; [2012] 1 A.C. 245 at [71]); *Evans v Governor of Brockhill Prison* [2001] 2 A.C. 19 (the fact that the prison governor had acted in good faith was no defence).

[234] *Evans* [2001] 2 A.C. 19 at [42].

[235] See 13-072 and 19-081. As a matter of common law, damages should not be merely nominal (*Iqbal v Prison Officers Association* [2009] EWCA Civ 1312; [2010] Q.B. 732 at [44]-[49]) unless the claimant would inevitably have been detained had a lawful decision been made in which case he has suffered no loss (*Lumba* [2011] UKSC 12; [2012] 1 A.C. 245 at [95]). The detention of a prisoner beyond the period when he would have been released had his case been considered speedily in accordance with art.5(4) of the ECHR does not constitute false imprisonment as his detention continues to be lawful as a matter of domestic law (*R. (on the application of Sturnham) v Parole Board* [2013] UKSC 23; [2013] 2 A.C. 254 at [15]–[16]). Similarly, the failure to provide a reasonable opportunity for a prisoner to rehabilitate himself did not directly impact on the lawfulness of his detention, but could give rise to right to compensation for frustration and anxiety under art.5(4) of the ECHR (*R. (on the application of Kaiyam) v Secretary of State for Justice* [2014] UKSC 66; [2015] A.C. 1344 at [35]–[39]). The distinction between the tortious claim for false imprisonment and a claim for breach of art.5 of the ECHR is illustrated by *Zenati v Commissioner of Police of the Metropolis* [2015] EWCA Civ 80; [2015] Q.B. 758 at [47]–[56]. In *Zenati*, the false imprisonment claim failed because his detention was authorised by a judicial authority, but the art.5 claim was allowed to proceed on the basis that the police were responsible for a delay in informing the court that the prisoner's passport was genuine.

[236] *D v Home Office* [2005] EWCA Civ 38; [2006] 1 W.L.R. 1003 at [67]. On art.5, see 13-072.

[237] *D v Home Office* [2005] EWCA Civ 38; [2006] 1 W.L.R. 1003 at [120].

[238] See 19-020.

[239] See 19-021.

[240] *Mohammed-Holgate v Duke* [1984] A.C. 437 at 443; *Cumming v Chief Constable of Northumbria Police* [2003] EWCA Civ 1844; [2004] A.C.D. 42 at [43]-[44]; *Paul v Chief Constable of*

be conferred by statute on those carrying out detention functions in various contexts, such as caring for the mentally ill.[241]

Section 12(1) of the Prison Act 1952 provides lawful authority for the restraint **19-059** of prisoners within the defined bounds of the prison by the governor of the prison. A prisoner has no cause of action for false imprisonment if he is confined for a particular time within a particular part of the prison, for example, he is segregated and held in solitary confinement, even if the restraint was not in accordance with the Prison Rules.[242] Where, however, a prison officer acts in bad faith by deliberately subjecting a prisoner to restraint which he knows he has no authority to impose he may render himself personally liable to an action for false imprisonment.[243] An otherwise lawful imprisonment is not rendered unlawful by reason only of the conditions of detention, however intolerable they may be.[244] Immigration Officers who act unlawfully have no special immunity under Sch.2 to the Immigration Act 1971; the burden of establishing a defence therefore lies upon them.[245]

Procedural considerations

Where a person is allegedly unlawfully detained by a public authority, a chal- **19-060** lenge may be made either in a CPR Pt 54 claim for judicial review or by way of an application for a writ of habeas corpus.[246] In the former proceedings, a claim for damages for false imprisonment may be included; if habeas corpus is sought, a separate claim for damages will have to be commenced. Claims for false imprisonment may be tried by judge and jury.[247]

MEASURE OF DAMAGES IN TORT[248]

Generally, the aim of damages is to compensate the claimant for loss caused by **19-061** the defendant's conduct. In tort, damages put the claimant as nearly as possible into the position he would have been in had the tortious act not occurred. In addition to ordinary damages, exemplary and aggravated may be awarded. Guidelines have

---

[Humberside] [2004] EWCA Civ 308 at [30]; *Hayes v Chief Constable of Merseyside* [2011] EWCA Civ 911; [2012] 1 W.L.R. 517 at [35]-[40].

[241] Mental Health Act 1983 s.139. However, the local authority was not able to rely on s.139 where a breach of art.5 of the ECHR arose as a result of bad faith or lack of reasonable care by a mental health professional in *R. (on the application of M) v Hackney LBC* [2011] EWCA Civ 4; [2011] 1 W.L.R. 2873 at [66]-[69].

[242] *Hague* [1992] 1 A.C. 58. In *Iqbal v Prison Officers Association* [2009] EWCA Civ 1312; [2010] Q.B. 732 at [22]-[27], a prisoner failed to make out liability for false imprisonment in relation to an unlawful strike which led indirectly to loss of time out of his cell on the grounds that the defendant's conduct was an omission and was superseded by the Governor's decision not to permit prisoners to leave their cells.

[243] *Hague* [1992] 1 A.C. 58.

[244] *Hague* [1992] 1 A.C. 58. However, there may be a remedy under art.3 of the ECHR, see 13-065.

[245] *D v Home Office* [2005] EWCA Civ 38; [2006] 1 W.L.R. 1003 (asylum seekers held in detention centre).

[246] See 17-010.

[247] County Courts Act 1984 s.66(3)(b); Senior Courts Act 1981 s.69. The CA provided guidance on where such proceedings should be issued in *BA v Home Office* [2012] EWCA Civ 944 at [27]. In general, claims for unlawful detention should be included in judicial review proceedings where they have been issued.

[248] For a more detailed account of damages generally, see *McGregor on Damages*, 19th edn (2014).

been laid down by the Court of Appeal on the quantum of damages, in the context of claims against the police.[249]

Exemplary damages

19-062   Exceptionally, the court may award exemplary damages in tort to deter and condemn the defendant's conduct rather than merely to compensate the claimant. Such damages are generally viewed as anomalous and courts take a restrictive approach, awarding exemplary damages only if the case falls within one of three categories (based on nature of the defendant's tortious conduct) set out by Lord Devlin in *Rookes v Barnard*.[250] The first is "oppressive, arbitrary or unconstitutional action by the servants of the government". In this context, government servants includes all those who by common law or statute are exercising functions of a governmental character such as local authorities and the police as well as Crown servants. Torts committed in the course of carrying out commercial operations, such as the supply of water, fall outside this category.[251] The meanings of oppressive, arbitrary and unconstitutional are not settled, though it is clear that the three elements are to be read disjunctively.[252] Doubt has been expressed in the Court of Appeal as to whether every ultra vires act is unconstitutional and the absence of aggravating features is something which ought to be taken into account in deciding whether to award exemplary damages.[253] Conduct which is merely negligent is probably insufficient.[254] The real question is whether simple compensation for the harm suffered is adequate to punish the public official for his outrageous conduct and deter him from repeating it.[255] The second category of case is where the defendant committed the tortious act having calculated that the economic benefits to him flowing from the action would be greater than any damages he might be liable to pay. The third category contemplated by Lord Devlin is where the award of exemplary damages was expressly authorised by statute, none of which is particularly relevant in the public law context. Exemplary damages may be awarded against a chief constable of police variously liable for actions of his officers under s.88 of the Police Act 1996.[256]

Aggravated damages

19-063   Aggravated damages "compensate the victim of a wrong for mental distress (or 'injury to feelings') in circumstances in which that injury has been caused or

---

[249] *Thompson v Commissioner of Police of the Metropolis* [1998] Q.B. 498.

[250] *Rookes v Barnard (No.1)* [1964] A.C. 1129 at 1226-1227 (Lord Devlin) applied in *Lumba* [2011] UKSC 12; [2012] 1 A.C. 245 at [150]. In *Lumba*, at [97]-[101], a majority of the SC doubted whether it was ever appropriate to award "vindicatory damages" in tort (in this case for false imprisonment), rather than for the vindication of a constitutional right under a written constitution.

[251] *AB v South West Water Services Ltd* [1993] Q.B. 507 (overruled in other respects by *Kuddus* [2001] UKHL 29; [2002] 2 A.C. 122).

[252] *Holden v Chief Constable of Lancashire* [1987] Q.B. 380 at 388B-E; *Muuse v Secretary of State for the Home Department* [2010] EWCA Civ 453; (2010) 107(19) L.S.G. 24 at [69]-[71].

[253] *Holden* [1987] Q.B. 380.

[254] *Barbara v Home Office* (1984) 134 N.LJ. 888.

[255] *Rookes v Barnard (No.1)* [1964] A.C. 1129 at 1228 (Lord Devlin). There is no additional requirement of "malice, fraud, insolence, cruelty or similar specific conduct" (*Muuse v Secretary of State for the Home Department* [2010] EWCA Civ 453; (2010) 107(19) L.S.G. 24 at [71]).

[256] *Rowlands v Chief Constable of Merseyside* [2006] EWCA Civ 1773; [2007] 1 W.L.R. 1065 at [48]. But "While it is possible that a Chief Constable could bear a responsibility for what has happened, due to his failure to exercise proper control, the instances when this is alleged to have occurred should not be frequent": *Thompson v Commissioner of Police of the Metropolis* [1998] Q.B. 498 at 512 CA.

increased by the manner in which the defendant committed the wrong, or by the defendant's conduct subsequent to the wrong".[257] Although there may be a penal element in the award of aggravated damages, their main purpose, in distinction to exemplary damages, is not punitive.[258] An award of aggravated damages requires "exceptional or contumelious conduct or motive on the part of a defendant in committing the wrong" and "mental distress sustained by the plaintiff as a result".[259]

REFORM FOR TORT LIABILITY

For many years the law and policy relating to civil liability of public authorities has been regarded as unsatisfactory.[260] Some commentators doubt whether the courts are best placed to provide monetary recompense[261]; certainly it needs to be borne in mind that the ombudsmen have powers to recommend compensation for injustice caused by maladministration.[262] There are also concerns about the alleged growth of a "compensation culture" and increased risk aversion,[263] and in this context the deep pockets of public authorities have at times been seen as easy targets.[264] Against this backdrop, s.1 of the Compensation Act 2006 restates in statutory terms the long-standing approach of the common law that

19-064

> "A court considering a claim in negligence or breach of statutory duty may, in determining whether the defendant should have taken particular steps to meet a standard of care (whether by taking precautions against a risk or otherwise), have regard to whether a requirement to take those steps might—(a) prevent a desirable activity from being undertaken at all, to a particular extent or in a particular way, or (b) discourage persons from undertaking functions in connection with a desirable activity."[265]

Public authorities are in a different position compared to private-sector businesses and individuals who choose to carry on activities; a statutory duty may lock the public authority into providing services regardless of the risks of litigation. The 2006 Act also provides that "An apology, an offer of treatment or other redress, shall not of itself amount to an admission of negligence or breach of statutory duty".[266]

19-065

Some people take as their starting-point a belief that public authorities and officials should provide compensation for damage caused by their unlawful administrative conduct. Certainly, it can seem unfair that an aggrieved person is left

19-066

---

[257] Law Commission, *Aggravated, Exemplary and Restitutionary Damages* (Law Com. No.247). The purpose of aggravated damages is to reflect the dignitary (not reputational) interests of the individual affected (J. Murphy, "The Nature and Domain of Aggravated Damages" [2010] C.L.J. 353).

[258] *Thompson v Commissioner of the Police for the Metropolis* [1998] QB 498.

[259] *Appleton v Garrett* [1996] P.I.Q.R. P1.

[260] In 2004 the Law Commission began a project on monetary remedies in public law, later widened to encompass a broader range of remedies: see *Monetary Remedies in Public Law* (October 2004); *Remedies against Public Bodies: a Scoping Report* (October 2006). For a trenchant critique, see R. Bagshaw, "Monetary Remedies in Public Law-Misdiagnosis and Misprescription" (2006) 26 L.S. 4. The Law Commission subsequently withdrew its proposals, 19-071 below.

[261] C. Harlow, *State Liability: Tort Law and Beyond* (2004).

[262] See 19-085.

[263] See House of Commons Constitutional Affairs Committee, *Compensation Culture*. HC Paper No.754-I (Session 2205/06).

[264] A high-water mark is *Anns v Merton LBC* [1978] A.C. 728 (now largely overruled) dealing with local authority liability in respect of a homeowner's repair costs following the failure of foundations which had been laid in the absence of adequate inspection.

[265] The CA has confirmed that s.1 adds nothing to the common law (*Uren v Corporate Leisure (UK) Ltd* [2011] EWCA Civ 66; (2011) 108(7) L.S.G. 16 at [13]).

[266] Compensation Act 2006 s.2.

to shoulder loss where a court finds the administrative action which caused it unlawful and grants judicial review. This is especially so where the public authority erred while carrying out a regulatory function (e.g. by means of licensing) designed to benefit the community as a whole and where it was not practicable for the adversely affected person to insure against the risk of damage.[267] In such circumstances why should it not be the community qua taxpayers—rather than the individual who suffers damage as a result of unlawful administration—which bares the loss? The imperfect interface in English law between notions of unlawful acts in judicial review proceedings and rights to damages in tort means that some victims of bureaucratic error currently go uncompensated,[268] though in the absence of empirical data it is unclear how extensive the problem really is.

19-067   Other concerns point in the opposite direction, to a perceived injustice that there is no common law right to damages for loss caused by unlawful administration action in English law: the regulatory functions of government, improperly carried out, may result in loss of profit; other unlawful action or inaction may result in personal inconvenience or the deprivation of a benefit. The standard judicial review remedies—quashing, prohibiting and mandatory orders—are not necessarily adequate cures.[269]

19-068   Judges, pressure groups and political parties in England have attempted or called for reform but none has yet been successful. In 1966, three members of the High Court of Australia, in a case where the defendant council unlawfully[270] extracted gravel from a river bed thereby preventing the claimant using his right under licence to pump water to irrigate his farmland, asserted the proposition that "by an action for damages upon the case, a person who suffers harm or loss as the inevitable consequence of the unlawful, intentional and positive acts of another, is entitled to recover damages from that other".[271] But this principle has since been rejected by the House of Lords[272] and doubted by the Privy Council,[273] and subsequently overruled by the High Court of Australia.[274]

19-069   In 1988, the Justice/All Souls Review recommended that even in the absence of an actionable tort or other ground for claiming damages in private law, there should be a right to damages for unlawful administrative action or omission which causes a person loss.[275] Four years earlier, the Committee of Ministers of the Council of Europe had also adopted a principle of rights to compensation: "Reparation should

---

[267] Many tort actions against central and local government are, in reality, brought by insurance companies exercising their rights of subrogation under policies. Tony Weir has argued that claims in respect of damage covered by a solvent insurer should be barred absolutely: see "Governmental Liability" [1989] P.L. 40, 59.

[268] See, e.g. *R. (on the application of Quark Fishing ltd) v Secretary of State for Foreign and Commonwealth Affairs* [2003] EWHC 1743 (Admin) at [14].

[269] One often cited illustration of the low-water mark of English law is *R. v Knowsley MBC Ex p. Maguire* (1992) 90 L.G.R. 653, where the court held that there was no remedy in damages for loss suffered as a result of an unlawfully refused hackney carriage licence.

[270] It had failed to obtain the necessary permit or certificate of authority, contrary to regulations.

[271] *Beaudesert District Shire Council v Smith* (1966) 120 C.L.R. 145 at 156. In line of early English cases, damages were awarded on the basis of the unlawfulness of an act in itself, see, e.g. *Ashby v White* (1704) 1 Brown 62 (returning officers liable for rejecting vote of qualified elector without proof of malice).

[272] *Lonrho Ltd v Shell Petroleum (No.2)* [1982] A.C. 173 at 188.

[273] *Dunlop v Woollahra Municipal Council* [1982] A.C. 158.

[274] *Northern Territory of Australia v Mengel* (1995) 60 A.L.J.R. 527.

[275] Report of the Committee of the JUSTICE/All Souls Review of Administrative Law in the United Kingdom, *Administrative Justice—Some Necessary Reforms* (1988), para.11.83: "compensation shall be recoverable by any person who sustains loss as a result of ... (a) any act, decision, determination, instrument or order of a public authority which materially affects him and which is for any reason wrongful or contrary to law; or (b) unreasonable or excessive delay on the part of any public

be ensured for damage caused by an act due to a failure of a public authority to conduct itself in a way which can reasonably be expected from it in relation to the injured person. Such a failure is presumed in case of transgression of an established legal rule".[276]

Neither of the major political parties in the UK has made commitments to enact-   **19-070** ing legislation for compensation in this context. What was previously regarded as most likely to prompt such legislative reform was the growing divergence between rights to compensation for ultra vires acts under European Community law[277] and those in the purely domestic law sphere. As the UK prepares to leave the EU, this divergence will decrease and may disappear altogether. However, for as long as the Human Rights Act remains part of domestic law, there will remain a distinction between those who can bring their claim under one of the Convention rights (which may attract compensation) and those who cannot.[278]

In July 2008, the Law Commission published a consultation paper containing   **19-071** proposals for wide ranging reform.[279] The paper suggested that the torts of breach of statutory duty and misfeasance in public office might be abolished. A new regime, in place of the common law of negligence, was outlined for "truly public" activities, based on what is called "the principles of modified corrective justice". Claimants would have to show "serious fault" by the public authority and that the statutory regime under which the decision was made was designed to confer a benefit on the relevant class of individuals. Under the proposed regime, damages would, in common with other public law remedies, be discretionary.[280] Outside the sphere of "truly public" activities, ordinary tort principles would apply. The Law Commission has now withdrawn its proposals for the reform of state liability.[281] In

---

authority in taking any action, reaching any decision or determination, making any order or carry-ing out any duty". An earlier report by JUSTICE, *Administration under Law* (1971) had also advocated the power to award damages to persons aggrieved by decisions tainted with procedural or substantive irregularity in circumstances where there is no cause of action for damages under the law as it now stands. cf. the criticisms of H. Woolf, *Protection of the Public—A New Challenge* (1990), p.58. In 1991, the Institute for Public Policy Research in its draft constitution for the UK included provision for an Act of Parliament to provide for "effective remedies (including the pay-ment of compensation) in cases where applications for judicial review are upheld" (*The Constitu-tion of the United Kingdom*, art.118.1.3), though this stops short of requiring the creation of a right of action for damages of unlawful administrative action as such.

[276] Principle I contained in Recommendation No.R (84) 15 Relating to Public Liability (adopted by the Committee of Ministers on 18 September 1984 at the 375th meeting of the Ministers' Deputies). The aim of the recommendation, which of course is non-binding, is to encourage uniformity among the Member States of the Council of Europe. The JUSTICE/All Souls Report (1988), para.11.63 argued that this formula probably adds little to the existing heads of liability in English law.

[277] See 14-056.

[278] See 19-081–19-102. The Law Commission regarded this divergence as "unjust" (Law Com. No.322 (2010), *Administrative Redress: Public Bodies and the Citizen*, at [1.17]).

[279] *Administrative Redress: Public Bodies and the Citizen* (Consultation Paper No.187).

[280] For academic commentary see: T. Cornford, "Administrative Redress: the Law Commission's Consultation Paper" [2009] P.L.70; M. Fordham, "Monetary Awards in Judicial Review" [2009] P.L. 1; C. Brasted and J. Potter, "Damages in Judicial Review: The Commercial Context" [2009] J.R. 53; J. Morgan, "Policy reasoning in tort law: the courts, the Law Commission and the critics" (2009) 125 L.Q.R. 215; R. Mullender, "Negligence, Public Bodies, and Ruthlessness" (2009) 72 M.L.R. 961. One criticism of the Law Commission's proposals was that the requirement to show "serious fault" would not increase certainty or reduce likely litigation. This criticism may be over-stated since the requirement to show a sufficiently serious breach is an established element of the recovery of damages from the state for breaches of EU law (see 14-072 and following).

[281] Law Com. No.322 (2010), *Administrative Redress: Public Bodies and the Citizen*. The Law Com-mission noted that the Government's formal response to its consultation "was a single document agreed across Government. This is extremely unusual, if not unique, in recent times" (at [1.3]). The withdrawal was lamented by Sedley LJ in *Home Office v Mohammed* [2011] EWCA Civ 351; [2011]

doing so, the Law Commission relied on the widespread opposition to its proposals (including from Government) and recommended that greater research be carried out into the costs imposed on the state by compensation claims.[282]

19-072   In the absence of new legislation, reform through the courts will be difficult: the general principle of "no damage in the absence of a recognised tort" is now probably too entrenched in domestic case law to permit any far-reaching change of direction by the judges. The dominant judicial attitude during the 1980s and early 1990s was one of hostility towards attempts to extend any further the liability of public authorities, even within the confines of the current framework of tort law. The main fear appears to be that to do so would inhibit effective decision taking by public bodies. Thus, duties of care have been denied in relation to the work of a financial services regulatory agency,[283] social workers[284] and in respect of investigations by the police[285] in part in concern that liability would lead to "detrimentally defensive" administration. In *Rowling v Takaro Properties Ltd*, Lord Keith spoke of the danger of "overkill"[286] and suggested that following the House of Lord's decision in *Anns v Merton LBC*[287] (where council inspectors carrying out statutory functions of inspection of the safety of new building were held to be negligent in approving defective foundations), the cure had been worse than the disease. Building inspectors of some local authorities had reacted by simply increasing, unnecessarily, the requisite depth of foundations, thereby imposing a substantial and unnecessary financial burden on members of the community.[288] A similar danger, Lord Keith believed, arose in relation to the imposition of a duty of care on a minister (as in *Rowling*) not to misconstrue legislation. Similar concerns have been expressed extra-judicially.[289] The judicial view is not, however, monolithic.[290] In *Home Office v Dorset Yacht Co Ltd*,[291] Lord Reid had no hesitation in dismissing a policy argument that imposing vicarious liability on the Home Office for dam-

---

1 W.L.R. 2862 at [20]-[24].

[282] The Law Commission stated that it had been unable to obtain current information about the "current compensation position of public bodies" (Law Com. No.322 (2010), *Administrative Redress: Public Bodies and the Citizen* at [1.5]).

[283] *Yuen Kun-yeu v Attorney General of Hong Kong* [1988] A.C. 175 at 196 In England, partial statutory immunity has in some circumstances been given to those exercising regulatory functions, e.g. under s.222 of the Financial Services and Markets Act 2000 and s.14 of the Lloyd's Act 1982.

[284] *X (Minors) v Bedfordshire CC* [1995] 2 A.C. 633.

[285] *Hill v Chief Constable of West Yorkshire* [1988] 1 A.C. 53 (Lord Keith: "The general sense of public duty which motivates police forces is unlikely to be appreciably reinforced by the imposition of such liability so far as concerns their function in the investigation and suppression of crime … In some instances the imposition of liability may lead to the exercise of a function being carried out with a detrimentally defensive frame of mind"; Although the immunity of the police was found to breach art.6 ECHR in *Osman v United Kingdom* (2000) 29 E.H.R.R. 245 at [150], the policy arguments against the widespread imposition of liability identified in *Hill* continue to be relied upon (*Van Colle v Chief Constable of Hertfordshire* [2008] UKHL 50; [2009] 1 A.C. 225 at [132]-[133]). C. McIvor, "Getting defensive about police negligence: the Hill principle, the Human Rights Act 1998 and the House of Lords" [2010] C.L.J. 133. See now *Michael v Chief Constable of South Wales Police* [2015] UKSC 2; [2015] A.C. 1732, fn.140 above.

[286] *Rowling v Takaro Properties Ltd* [1988] A.C. 473 at 502.

[287] *Anns v Merton LBC* [1978] A.C. 728, (now largely overruled).

[288] See also G. Ganz, "Public Law and the Duty of Care" [1977] P.L. 306; H. Willberg, "Defensive practice or conflict of duties? Policy concerns in public authority negligence claims" (2010) 126 L.Q.R. 420. *Michael v Chief Constable of South Wales Police* [2015] UKSC 2; [2015] A.C. 1732 at [121].

[289] H. Woolf, *Protection of the Public—A New Challenge* (1990), p.58.

[290] On the contradictory "academic and judicial musing … regarding the instrumental effect of state liability", see further D. Cohen and J.C. Smith, "Entitlement and the Body Politic: Rethinking Negligence in Public Law" (1986) 64 Can.B.R. 1.

[291] *Home Office v Dorset Yacht Co Ltd* [1970] A.C. 1004.

age caused as a result of prison officers negligently allowing borstal boys to escape from custody would curtail continued experimentation with minimum security regimes which were an important aspect of rehabilitation schemes. His experience led him to believe that "Her Majesty's servants were made of sterner stuff" than the public servants of New York who had been granted immunity in *Williams v New York State*.[292]

A number of questions emerge from the assertion that the further imposition of **19-073** liability to pay damages for invalid administrative action would have a detrimentally chilling effect on decision-makers. First, the arguments often fail to identify who will be liable and in what sense: is the liability directly that of the public authority, its vicarious liability for the acts of employees, or the personal liability of individual administrators? It has been argued that vicarious and personal liability is undesirable and may indeed have a detrimental impact on decision-making; and that direct state liability is the least disadvantageous.[293] But in practice, even if an individual civil servant or minister is a named defendant in a successful action for damages, the award will be paid out of public funds. Any impact on an administrator's behaviour therefore comes not from anxiety of personal financial inconvenience or ruin flowing directly from the damages award as such.

Why then is the problem of self-protection by administrators more significant in **19-074** relation to damages awards than public law remedies? A sharp distinction has sometimes been drawn between remedies such as prohibiting and quashing orders, which are said to have a beneficial impact on administrative behaviour, and liability for damages which has an undesirable effect.[294] In its broadest sense, however, "judicial review of administrative action" is not confined to the public law grounds of illegality, procedural propriety and unreasonableness. The present function of tort law is not confined to retrospective compensation for harm inflicted; the substantive rules of tort also set standards of acceptable administrative behaviour and so too would any expanded liability for damages. In the absence of more cogent empirical evidence on the effects of imposing (or not imposing) a more extensive liability to pay damages on public officials than currently exists,[295] it would be rash to oppose damages for unlawful acts on this ground alone. But equally, even if greater compensation for invalid administrative acts is desirable, it does not inevitably follow that creating a new action for damages is the most appropriate mechanism for providing it. Alternatives include greater use of the Ombudsmen to recommend, or require, compensation to be paid or the creation of a fund analogous

---

[292] *Williams v New York State* (1955) 127 NE (2nd) 545. See also *Osman v Ferguson* [1993] 4 All E.R. 344.

[293] See D. Cohen and J. Smith (1986) 64 Can.B.R. 1, pp.9, 16; P. Schuck, *Suing Government: Citizen Remedies for Official Wrongs* (1980). These authors point out that the assumptions about rational economic behaviour of private individuals and firms in reaction to tort liability often cannot be applied to government bodies. As Cohen and Smith state succinctly at p.8: "To the extent that private tort law doctrines are premised on deterrent objectives they may be singularly ineffective when applied to the state".

[294] See, e.g. the speech of Lord Bridge in *Hague v Deputy Governor of Parkhurst Prison* [1992] 1 A.C. 58 where it was said that "the availability of judicial review as a means of questioning the legality of action purportedly taken in pursuance of the Prison Rules is a beneficial and necessary jurisdiction which cannot properly be circumscribed by considerations of policy or expediency in relation to prison administration"—in contrast to the "wholly different question" of the availability of damages.

[295] A handful of small-scale empirical studies have been carried out in England, see: G. Ganz, "Public Law and the Duty of Care" [1977] P.L. 306; T. Weir, "Government Liability and the Duty of Care" [1989] P.L. 40, 60.

to that administered by the Criminal Injuries Compensation Authority to which the victim of unlawful administrative action causing loss may apply.

RESTITUTIONARY AND OTHER CLAIMS FOR RETURN OF MONEY

Statutory rights for return of money paid

19-075   Legislation makes express provision for return of money erroneously paid to public authorities in some situations, e.g. overpayments of tax.[296] If a statutory provision for the return of money paid gives a discretion to the public authority as to what sum, if any, to repay, the exercise of that discretion will be subject to judicial review.[297] It is a question of construction in each case as to whether the existence of a statutory right to repayment precludes a claimant making a restitutionary claim.[298]

Procedure

19-076   As with damages claims in tort, a claim under CPR Pt 7 may be a more appropriate route for bringing a dispute about the recovery of money in restitution than a claim for judicial review under CPR Pt 54.[299] It is not appropriate to use a mandatory order in judicial review proceedings to enforce a civil obligation to make restitution to a third party.[300]

Rights for return of money in restitution

19-077   There are four general elements to a claim for restitution[301]: (a) a benefit must have been gained by the defendant; (b) the benefit must have been obtained at the claimant's expense; it is not necessary for a claimant to have requested a service—this element is satisfied if the defendant has freely accepted or acquiesced in the supply for consideration of the services rendered or in exceptional circumstances the defendant has been incontrovertibly benefited from their receipt; (c) there must exist a factor recognised in law rendering it unjust for the defendant to retain the benefit; and (d) there must be no defence available to extinguish or reduce the defendant's liability to make restitution. There are various situations in the public law context in which restitutionary claims may arise.

19-078   First, where tax is purportedly charged without lawful parliamentary authority,

---

[296] Taxes Management Act 1970 s.33.

[297] See 19-003.

[298] *Deutsche Morgan Grenfell Group Plc v Inland Revenue Commissioners* [2006] UKHL 49; [2007] 1 A.C. 558 at [19]. In *R. (on the application of Child Poverty Action Group) v Secretary of State for Work and Pensions* [2010] UKSC 54; [2011] 2 A.C. 15 at [12]-[15], the SC held that the state's right to reclaim overpayments of benefits was confined to the circumstances set out in the Social Security Administration Act 1992 and the state could not maintain a common law restitutionary claim.

[299] See, e.g. *R. (on the application of Rowe) v Vale of White Horse DC* [2003] EWHC 388 (Admin); [2003] 1 Lloyd's Rep. 418 (recovery of payments for sewerage charges).

[300] *R. v Barnet Magistrates Court Ex p. Cantor* [1999] 1 W.L.R. 334 (claimant sought mandamus to compel clerk to the justices to repay money paid by claimant's mother to settle a £30,000 fine held to have been unlawfully imposed).

[301] See generally C. Mitchell, P. Mitchell and S. Watterson, *Goff and Jones: The Law of Unjust Enrichment*, 9th edn, (2016), Chs 22 and 23; R. Williams, *Unjust Enrichment and Public Law* (2010); and G. Virgo, "Restitution from Public Authorities: Past, Present and Future" [2006] J.R. 370.

a claim to repayment arises.[302] In relation to payment of taxes, this ground of restitution also reflects the constitutional prohibition under the Bill of Rights 1689 against taxation without Parliamentary approval.

Secondly, following the House of Lords' landmark decision in *Kleinwort Benson Ltd v Lincoln City Council*,[303] the long-standing rule that money paid under a mistake of law was not recoverable in restitution no longer applies. There is now a general right of recovery in cases of unjust enrichment, subject to relevant defences.[304] The concept of mistake of law is interpreted broadly and extends to overpayments payments of tax made under a mistake of law.[305]   **19-079**

A third possible ground for seeking restitution unique to the public law context arises from a group of decisions sometimes referred to as the colore oficii cases.[306] In these cases, money paid to a person in a public or quasi-public position to obtain performance by him of a duty which he was bound to perform for nothing, or for less than the sum demanded, was recoverable to the extent that the official was not entitled to it.[307] It is not clear whether these cases are to be explained on the basis that refusal to perform a public duty is a special category of duress[308] or whether they were precursors to the now recognised right to recover unlawfully demanded payments per se.[309] In any event, they are probably of no practical importance after the *Woolwich* decision.   **19-080**

COMPENSATION UNDER THE HUMAN RIGHTS ACT

Section 8 of the Human Rights Act 1998 provides[310]:   **19-081**

"**8.**—(1)   In relation to any act (or proposed act) of a public authority which the court finds is (or would be) unlawful, it may grant such relief or remedy, or make such order, within its powers as it considers just and appropriate.

(2)   But damages may be awarded only by a court which has power to award damages, or to order the payment of compensation, in civil proceedings.

(3)   No award of damages is to be made unless, taking account of all the circumstances of the case, including—

---

[302] *Test Claimants in the FII Group Litigation v Revenue and Customs Commissioners* [2012] UKSC 19; [2012] 2 A.C. 337 at [79]. *Woolwich Equitable Building Society v Inland Revenue Commissioners (No.2)* [1993] A.C. 70; [1992] 3 W.L.R. 366 formerly required that there should have been a demand for payment.

[303] *Kleinwort Benson Ltd v Lincoln City Council* [1999] 2 A.C. 349 (the case concerned interest rate swaps, not tax).

[304] The Law Commission gave a full account of current and proposed defences in relation to its model scheme for recovery in Part X of *Restitution: Mistakes of Law and Ultra Vires Public Authority Receipts and Payments* (Law Com No 227).

[305] *Deutsche Morgan Grenfell Group Plc* [2006] UKHL 49; [2007] 1 A.C. 558: ECJ held that an aspect of advance corporation tax was contrary to European Community law because it discriminated between national and multi-national groups of companies.

[306] See: *Piggott's* case (cited in *Cartwright v Rowley* (1799) 2 Esp. 723); *Dew v Parsons* (1819) 2 B. & Ald. 562; *Morgan v Palmer* (1824) 2 B. & C. 729; *Steele v Williams* (1853) 8 Exch. 625.

[307] *Woolwich Equitable Building Society v Inland Revenue Commissioners (No.2)* [1993] A.C. 70; [1992] 3 W.L.R. 366 at [164] (Lord Goff).

[308] C. Mitchell et al., *Goff and Jones: The Law of Unjust Enrichment*, (2016), pp.395-399.

[309] P. Birks, *An Introduction to the Law of Restitution* (1989 rev. edn), pp.175-176. And see J. Steele, "Damages in tort and under the Human Rights Act: remedial or functional separation?" (2008) 67 C.L.J. 606 and D. Nolan, "Negligence and Human Rights: The Case for Separate Development" (2013) 76 M.L.R. 286.

[310] For an early exposition of relevant principles, see Law Commission, *Damages under the Human Rights Act 1998* (October 2000).

> (a)   any other relief or remedy granted, or order made, in relation to the act in ques-
>   tion (by that or any other court), and
>
> (b)   (b) the consequences of any decision (of that or any other court) in respect of
>   that act, the court is satisfied that the award is necessary to afford just satisfac-
>   tion to the person in whose favour it is made.
>
> (4) In determining—
>
> (a)   whether to award damages, or
>
> (b)   the amount of an award, the court must take into account the principles ap-
>   plied by the European Court of Human Rights in relation to the award of
>   compensation under Article 41 of the Convention.
>
> (5) A public authority against which damages are awarded is to be treated—
>
> (a)   in Scotland, for the purposes of section 3 of the Law Reform (Miscellaneous
>   Provisions) (Scotland) Act 1940 as if the award were made in an action of dam-
>   ages in which the authority has been found liable in respect of loss or damage
>   to the person to whom the award is made;
>
> (b)   for the purposes of the Civil Liability (Contribution) Act 1978 as liable in
>   respect of damage suffered by the person to whom the award is made.
>
> (6) In this section—
>
> 'court' includes a tribunal;
> 'damages' means damages for an unlawful act of a public authority; and
> 'unlawful' means unlawful under section 6(1)."

19-082   Section 9(3) provides: "In proceedings under this Act in respect of a judicial act done in good faith, damages may not be awarded otherwise than to compensate a person to the extent required by Article 5(5) of the Convention." This excludes the award of exemplary damages.

19-083   Two provisions in the ECHR are of particular relevance to s.8. First, art.13 requires everyone whose rights and freedoms are violated "to have an effective remedy". This article has not expressly been incorporated into national law by the HRA, but has an influence through the requirement for national courts, under s.2 of the HRA, to take account of Strasbourg case law.[311] Secondly, art.41, referred to in s.8, requires the ECtHR to afford "just satisfaction" to an injured party if this is not provided by a national court.

Principles

19-084   The following principles have emerged about the availability of damages under the HRA.[312]

---

[311] See 13-035.

[312] Many of them were predicted by Lord Woolf in "The Human Rights Act 1998 and Remedies", Ch.30 in M. Andenas (ed), *Liber Amicorum in Honour of Lord Slynn of Hadley: Vol.II Judicial Review in International Perspective* (2000). The principles were cited in *R. (on the application of KB) v South London and South and West Region Mental Health Review Tribunal* [2003] EWHC 193 (Admin); [2004] Q.B. 936 at [20]. The SC has given important guidance on citing ECtHR authorities on art.41 in *R. (on the application of Sturnham) v Parole Board for England and Wales* [2013] UKSC 23; [2013] 2 A.C. 254 at [99]-[103]. The court should be provided with an agreed schedule of the relevant authorities: stating the violations of the ECHR which were established and the sum awarded; summarising the parties' submissions on them; listing the authorities in chronological order; and explaining the principles which are said to derive from them. In *Sturnham* [2013] UKSC 23; [2013] 2 A.C. 254 at [29], the SC indicated that reference to the ECtHR case law is likely to diminish as the award of damages under s.8 of the HRA becomes "naturalised". The ECtHR has produced a Practice Direction on Just satisfaction claims dated 19 September 2016 (available at *http://www.echr.coe.int/Documents/PD_satisfaction_claims_ENG.pdf* [Accessed 12 November 2017]). See generally, J.N.E. Varuhas, *Damages and Human Rights* (2016). Useful guidance may be sought

(a) Damages may only be awarded by a court which has the power to do so in civil proceedings.[313]

(b) The award of damages must be necessary to afford just satisfaction to the claimant.[314] In determining whether an award is necessary, the court will have regard to the availability of alternative remedies.[315] Domestic courts have also taken account of the fact that the ECtHR does not regard providing compensation as the main aim of proceedings before it.[316] Rather they are directed at bringing the violation to an end. As such, the ECtHR routinely treats the finding of a violation as sufficient to provide just satisfaction.

(c) The court is required to take into account the principles applied by the ECtHR in awarding compensation under art.41. It is notoriously difficult to identify any principles which are applied by the Strasbourg court or, at least, any principles which are applied consistently. One principle frequently expressed by the ECtHR is that the purpose of an award is to place the applicant so far as possible in the position he would have been in had the violation not occurred.[317] Damages will only be awarded for losses which are caused by the violation and will take account of any conduct of the applicant which may have contributed to his injury or damage.[318]

(d) The court should not award exemplary or punitive damages.[319] The court may

---

from other legal systems: L. Tortell, *Monetary Remedies for Breach of Human Rights: A Comparative Study* (2006).

[313] HRA s.8(2). The Family Court was held to have the power to award damages under s.8(2) in *Re H (A Child: Breach of Convention Rights: Damages)* [2014] EWFC 38 at [62]-[64].

[314] HRA s.8(3).

[315] HRA s.8(3)(a). *Dobson v Thames Water Utilities* [2009] EWCA Civ 28; [2009] 3 All E.R. 319 at [52] (unlikely that damages under art.8 would exceed those awarded at common law for nuisance caused by a sewage works).

[316] *R. (on the application of Anufrijeva) v Southwark LBC* [2003] EWCA Civ 1406; [2004] Q.B. 1124 at [53] (asylum seekers claimed that local authorities had failed to discharge duties under the National Assistance Act 1948 to arrange for suitable accommodation, contrary to ECHR art.8). Further, awards of damages are not required to encourage compliance by member states since they are under international legal obligations to comply with the ECHR in any event (*R. (on the application of Greenfield) v Secretary of State for the Home Department* [2005] UKHL 14; [2005] 1 W.L.R. 673 at [19]). In *Greenfield*, the denial of legal representation to a prisoner in breach of art.6 did not give rise to an award of damages. In contrast, in *Cyprus v Turkey* (2014) 59 E.H.R.R. 16 at [58], the ECtHR awarded £30bn for non-pecuniary damage suffered by the surviving relatives of the missing persons and £60bn for non-pecuniary damage suffered by the enclaved residents of the Karpas peninsula following its 2001 judgment which found violations of the ECHR in relation to Turkey's military operations in Northern Cyprus. This was the first time that just satisfaction had been awarded in an inter-state case (at [41]-[43]). The ECtHR made clear that the payment was for the benefit of the individual victims and not the Cypriot Government (at [45]-[47]).

[317] *Kingsley v UK* (2002) 35 E.H.R.R. 177 at [40]. The ECtHR set out some guidance on its approach to awarding just satisfaction in *Agrokompleks v Ukraine* (App. No.23465/03) (25 July 2013) at [76]-[81]. In *Al-Jedda v UK* (2011) 53 E.H.R.R. 23 at [114], the ECtHR stated that its function was not "akin to a domestic tort mechanism court in apportioning fault and compensatory damages ... [i]ts guiding principle is equity, which above all involves flexibility". The focus of the domestic court should be on the practice of the ECtHR, which tends not to provide "articulated statements of principle" in relation to awards (*R. (on the application of Sturnham) v Parole Board* [2013] UKSC 23; [2013] 2 A.C. 254 at [13], [31]-[32]). The domestic court should focus on ECtHR cases involving applicants from the UK or countries with a comparable cost of living (*Sturnham* [2013] UKSC 23; [2013] 2 A.C. 254 at [38]-[39]). It is questionable whether this should apply to the nonpecuniary elements of loss.

[318] *R. (on the application of KB) v South London and South and West Region Mental Health Review Tribunal* [2003] EWHC 193 (Admin); [2004] Q.B. 936 at [23]-[24]. See, e.g. *Johnson v United Kingdom* (1999) 27 E.H.R.R. 296 at [77] (applicant's negative attitude and lack of co-operation).

[319] It is not the practice of the ECtHR to do so and, as far as art.5(5) is concerned, HRA s.9(3) limits the court to an award by way of compensation (*R. (on the application of KB) v South London and*

award damages for psychological damages, anxiety and distress.[320] The ECtHR will award damages for proven pecuniary losses, but will generally make no award for the loss of an opportunity. The ECtHR's case law on awards for loss of opportunity is inconsistent.[321]

(e) The quantum of awards is generally low in Strasbourg and domestic courts should follow this doctrine rather than comparable awards in, say, tort.[322] Nonetheless, "the developing domestic jurisprudence under the Act may lead to modest (but more than nominal) awards of damages in cases of deliberate official wrongdoing, even if it does not occasion monetary loss".[323]

19-085 The Court of Appeal in *Anufrijeva* was concerned to ensure that there should be proportionality between the costs of obtaining a remedy and the quantum of damages at stake. To this end, the court suggested:

"i) The courts should look critically at any attempt to recover damages under the HRA for maladministration by any procedure other than judicial review in the Administrative Court.

ii) A claim for damages alone cannot be brought by judicial review (Pt 54.3(2)) but in this case the proceedings should still be brought in the Administrative Court by an ordinary claim.

iii) Before giving permission to apply for judicial review, the Administrative Court judge should require the claimant to explain why it would not be more appropriate to use any available internal complaint procedure or proceed by making a claim to the PCA [Parliamentary Ombudsmen] or LGO [Local Government Ombudsmen] at least in the first instance. The complaint procedures of the PCA and the LGO are designed to deal economically (the claimant pays no costs and does not require a lawyer) and expeditiously with claims for compensation for maladministration ...

iv) If there is a legitimate claim for other relief, permission should if appropriate be limited to that relief and consideration given to deferring permission for the damages claim, adjourning or staying that claim until use has been made of ADR, whether by a reference to a mediator or an ombudsman or otherwise, or remitting that claim to a district judge or master if it cannot be dismissed summarily on grounds that in any event an award of damages is not required to achieve just satisfaction.

v) It is hoped that with the assistance of this judgment, in future claims that have to be determined by the courts can be determined by the appropriate level of judge in a summary manner by the judge reading the relevant evidence. The citing of more than three authorities should be justified and the hearing should be limited to half a day except in exceptional circumstances.

vi) There are no doubt other ways in which the proportionate resolution of this type of claim for damages can be achieved. We encourage their use and do not intend to be prescriptive. What we want to avoid is any repetition of what has happened in the court below in relation to each of these appeals and before us, when we have

---

South and West Region Mental Health Review Tribunal [2003] EWHC 193 (Admin); [2004] Q.B. 936 at [60]). In reality, the ECtHR does appear to be influenced by the gravity of the violation.

[320] *Aksoy v Turkey* (1996) 23 E.H.R.R. 553 at [113].

[321] *McGregor on Damages*, 19th edn (2014) paras 48-057 to 48-064. In *Sturnham* [2013] UKSC 23; [2013] 2 A.C. 254 at [13], the SC held that damages should be awarded where it is established on the balance of probabilities that a violation of art.5(4) has resulted in the detention of a prisoner beyond the date when he would otherwise have been released.

[322] *Greenfield* [2005] UKHL 14; [2005] 1 W.L.R. 673 at [19]; *Anufrijeva* [2003] EWCA Civ 1406; [2004] Q.B. 1124 at [53]-[68].

[323] *Watkins v Home Office* [2006] UKHL 17; [2006] 2 A.C. 395 at [73] (Lord Walker of Gestingthorpe). *R. (Sturnham) v the Parole Board* [2013] UKSC 23; [2013] 2 A.C. 254 at [41], [53]-[54]. *McGregor on Damages*, 19th edn (2014) para.48-055 has a useful table of ECtHR awards for nonpecuniary losses.

been deluged with extensive written and oral arguments and citation from numerous lever arch files crammed to overflowing with authorities. The exercise that has taken place may be justifiable on one occasion but it will be difficult to justify again."[324]

Individual Convention rights

Different considerations apply to different Convention rights.[325] It is not possible here to provide a comprehensive account of the relevant case law, but illustrations in relation to several Convention rights provide some insight into the courts' approach. In having regard to quantum of damages awarded by the ECtHR in particular cases, the English courts should bear in mind that standards of living vary across Europe and should therefore ensure that any compensation that is awarded in an English court is adequate for a person living in the United Kingdom.[326] The English courts "should not aim to be significantly more or less generous than the [ECtHR] might be expected to be, in a case where it was willing to make an award at all".[327]

19-086

Article 2 (right to life)

In *Rabone v Pennine Care NHS Trust*,[328] the Supreme Court awarded £5,000 each to the parents of a mental health patient who had been allowed home and then committed suicide. The court found there was a serious breach of art.2 where family ties were strong and the circumstances of the breach exacerbated the parents' anxiety and distress.

19-087

Article 3 (prohibition of torture, inhumane and degrading treatment)

In *Napier v Scottish Ministers*[329] a prisoner was held on remand for 40 days in an overcrowded and inadequately ventilated cell without access to toilet facilities

19-088

[324] *Anufrijeva* [2003] EWCA Civ 1406; [2004] Q.B. 1124 at [81]. See J.N.E. Varuhas, "A tort-based approach to damages under the Human Rights Act 1998" (2009) 72 M.L.R. 750; J. Steele, "Damages in tort and under the Human Rights Act: remedial or functional separation?" [2008] C.L.J. 606; and G. McLay, "Tort and Constitutional Damages: Towards a Framework" [2012] P.L. 45. Claims for damages under arts 3 and 8 of the ECHR brought under s.7 of the HRA relating to the conduct of undercover police officers in entering into intimate physical relationships with the claimants had to be brought before the Investigatory Powers Tribunal established by the Regulation of Investigatory Powers Act 2000 and not in the High Court (*AKJ v Commissioner of Police of the Metropolis* [2013] EWCA Civ 1342; [2014] 1 W.L.R. 285 at [37]-[43]). The common law claims for deceit, assault, misfeasance in public office and negligence were permitted to proceed before the High Court and the stay granted below was lifted (at [65]).

[325] *R. (Greenfield) v SSHD* [2005] UKHL 14; [2005] 1 W.L.R. 673 at [7] (Lord Bingham: "There is a risk of error if Strasbourg decisions given in relation to one article of the Convention are read across as applicable to another").

[326] *R. (on the application of KB) v South London and South and West Region Mental Health Review Tribunal* [2003] EWHC 193 (Admin); [2004] Q.B. 936 at [47]; *R. (on the application of Bernard) v Enfield LBC* [2002] EWHC 2282 (Admin); [2003] H.R.L.R. 4 at [43].

[327] *R. (Greenfield) v SSHD* [2005] UKHL 14; [2005] 1 W.L.R. 673 at [19].

[328] *Rabone v Pennine Care NHS Trust* [2012] UKSC 2; [2012] 2 A.C. 72 at [80]-[88]. See further, the ECtHR decision in *Reynolds v United Kingdom* (2012) 55 E.H.R.R. 35 which found that the existing rules (at the time) prevented the mother of a young man who committed suicide while compulsorily detained in a mental health unit from establishing civil liability for his death and this breached art.13 read with art.2, at [60]-[69]. She was awarded €7,000 for non-pecuniary damages.

[329] *Napier v Scottish Ministers* 2005 1 S.C. 229 at [94] (Lord Bonomy: "It would in any event be extremely difficult to quantify compensation for any element of the petitioner's experience of his conditions which would not be adequately compensated in this way, bearing in mind the role of stress

at weekends and at night. His eczema flared up during his detention. Having regard to the relatively short period of time, the finding of a breach of art.3 and the award of £2,000 solatium (for breach of a common law duty), the court made no further award under s.8 of the HRA. In *OOO v Commissioner of Police for the Metropolis*,[330] the court awarded £5,000 each to victims of human trafficking who had been required to work for no pay and subject to physical and emotional abuse where the police had failed to act on credible allegations.

Article 5 (right to liberty and security)

19-089   Article 5(5) expressly states that "Everyone who has been the victim of arrest or detention in contravention of the provisions of this article shall have an enforceable right to compensation". This does not, however, mean that damages must be awarded by the ECtHR in all cases in which a breach of art.5 occurs as art.5(5) must be read in the broader context of art.41, under which the ECtHR has a discretion.[331] The practice of the ECtHR is that awards for non-pecuniary loss of any kind are likely to be the exception, not the rule-though the case law does not speak with one voice on this.[332]

19-090   In *R. (on the application of KB) v South London and South and West Region Mental Health Review Tribunal*[333] there were delays in hearings of the claimants' applications for reviews of their detention under the Mental Health Act 1983 by a tribunal, contrary to art.5(4).[334] The Administrative Court accepted that awards under art.5 should be broadly comparable to those that may be obtained for the tort of false imprisonment. In this case, the claimants' loss was in essence the loss of an opportunity to present their case to the tribunal at an earlier date and the chance to secure earlier release. The court held that a "claimant who seeks damages on the basis of an allegation that he would have had a favourable decision at an earlier date if his Convention right had been respected must prove his allegation on the balance of probabilities" with convincing evidence.[335] Damages should relate to the period of time between the date when the tribunal should have determined the claimant's case (which may not always be clear) and when it did so; and the court should avoid calculating damages on a rate per day—the task is necessarily

---

in causing the petitioner's eczema to flare up, the significance that I have already attributed to the conditions of detention in causing that stress, and the account I have taken of his psychological symptoms in assessing solatium"). S. Foster, "Prison Conditions, Human Rights and Art.3 ECHR" [2005] P.L. 35. See generally 13-065.

[330] *OOO v Commissioner of Police for the Metropolis* [2011] EWHC 1246 (QB); [2011] H.R.L.R. 29 at [190]. In *DSD v Commissioner of Police of the Metropolis* [2014] EWHC 2493 (QB); [2015] 1 W.L.R. 1833, awards of £22,500 and £19,000 in damages were made to two rape victims for violations of art.3 on the basis of serious systemic failings and operational failures by the police in relation to their investigative duty. The quantum was not challenged in the unsuccessful appeal in *DSD v Commissioner of Police of the Metropolis* [2015] EWCA Civ 646; [2016] Q.B. 161.

[331] *R. (KB) v Mental Health Review Tribunal* [2003] EWHC 193 (Admin); [2004] Q.B. 936 at [28], citing *Wassink v The Netherlands* (1253/86). The breach of the claimant's rights under art.5(2) to receive a full explanation for his recall to a secure hospital within the time limits set in the Secretary of State's policy was not sufficiently grave to require an award of damages (*R. (on the application of Lee-Hirons) v Secretary of State for Justice* [2016] UKSC 46; [2017] A.C. 52).

[332] *R. (KB) v Mental Health Review Tribunal* [2003] EWHC 193 (Admin); [2004] Q.B. 936 at [36].

[333] *R. (on the application of KB) v South London and South and West Region Mental Health Review Tribunal* [2003] EWHC 193 (Admin); [2004] Q.B. 936. See generally 13-072.

[334] "Everyone who is deprived of his liberty by arrest or detention shall be entitled to take proceedings by which the lawfulness of his detention shall be decided speedily by a court and his release ordered if the detention is not lawful".

[335] *R. (on the application of KB) v South London and South and West Region Mental Health Review Tribunal* [2003] EWHC 193 (Admin); [2004] Q.B. 936 at [64].

impressionistic.[336] Non-pecuniary damages to compensate for frustration and distress may be awarded if that distress is of significant intensity (for example, prompting a note to be made in the claimants' clinical records).[337] Having considered the evidence, the court awarded one of the claimants £4,000, four received £1,000, one £750 and in relation to two of them the finding of a breach was considered to be just satisfaction.

In *R. (on the application of Sturnham) v Parole Board*,[338] the Supreme Court held that where it was demonstrated on a balance of probabilities that a violation of art.5(4) has resulted in the detention of a prisoner beyond the date when he would otherwise have been released, damages should be awarded with pecuniary losses being compensated in full. Nonpecuniary losses for frustration and anxiety should be awarded if sufficiently severe and this will usually be the case where the delay was of three months or more.

19-091

In *Austin v Commissioner of Police of the Metropolis*,[339] the police responded to a surprise political procession on May Day by detaining thousands of people in a cordon for several hours at Oxford Circus in London in order to prevent a breakdown in law and order. The court held that the claimant's detention was a deprivation of liberty within art.5(1) but was justified under art.5(1)(c). The court held, obiter, that if there had been a breach of art.5, no award of damages would have been made under s.8 of the HRA in the light of the guidance laid down in *Anufrijeva*.

19-092

In *R. (on the application of Faulkner) v Secretary of State for Justice*,[340] the Court of Appeal held that once it is found that the Parole Board would have granted release earlier, there arose a compensatable loss of prospective liberty for delay in breach of art.5 for which the appropriate award was £10,000 in the present case. The Supreme Court reduced this sum on appeal to £6,500.

19-093

Article 6 (right to a fair trial)

The first consideration of s.8 of the HRA by the House of Lords took place in *Greenfield*,[341] in which the claimant prisoner had been found guilty of drugs offences in prison by the deputy controller of the prison and ordered to serve an additional 21 days (which he had served by the time his judicial review claim was heard). The defendant conceded that the disciplinary arrangements breached art.6(1) as the deputy controller was not an independent and impartial tribunal and art.6(3) because the claimant had been denied legal representation.[342] Their Lordships held that "In the great majority of cases in which the European Court has found a viola-

19-094

---

[336] *R. (on the application of KB) v South London and South and West Region Mental Health Review Tribunal* [2003] EWHC 193 (Admin); [2004] Q.B. 936 at [65].

[337] *R. (on the application of KB) v South London and South and West Region Mental Health Review Tribunal* [2003] EWHC 193 (Admin); [2004] Q.B. 936 at [72]-[73].

[338] *R. (on the application of Sturnham) v Parole Board* [2013] UKSC 23; [2013] 2 A.C. 254 at [67]-[76]. The SC applied *Sturnham* to hold that prison authorities had a duty to afford prisoners sentenced to imprisonment for public protection a reasonable opportunity to rehabilitate themselves which may include the provision of courses and facilities (*R. (on the application of Kaiyam) v Secretary of State for Justice* [2014] UKSC 66; [2015] A.C. 1344 at [35]-[39]). This duty is ancillary to the scheme of art.5 and a breach of it did not render the detention unlawful, but may entitle a prisoner to compensation for frustration and anxiety.

[339] *Austin v Commissioner of Police of the Metropolis* [2005] EWHC 480 (QB); [2005] H.R.L.R. 20 at [597].

[340] *R. (on the application of Faulkner) v Secretary of State for Justice* [2011] EWCA Civ 349; [2011] H.R.L.R. 23 at [6]-[22] (CA) and [2013] UKSC 23; [2013] 2 A.C. 254 at [87] (SC).

[341] *Greenfield* [2005] UKHL 14; [2005] 1 W.L.R. 673.

[342] In *Ezeh v United Kingdom* (2004) 39 E.H.R.R. 1 the ECtHR held that disciplinary proceedings in

tion of art.6 it has treated the finding of the violation as, in itself, just satisfaction under Art.41".[343] Where damages have been awarded by the ECtHR, this has generally been either to compensate for the loss of an opportunity to put a case and secure a benefit, or for anxiety and frustration. In relation to the former, in conceptualising the loss caused by a breach of art.6, the courts have similar problems as in relation to art.5(4): "A claim ... may be put on the straightforward basis that but for the Convention violation found the outcome of the proceedings would probably have been different and more favourable to the applicant, or on the more problematical basis that the violation deprived the applicant of an opportunity to achieve a different result which was not in all the circumstances of the case a valueless opportunity".[344] To succeed, the claimant must establish a clear causal connection.[345] In relation to feelings of distress, anxiety and frustration, the ECtHR has been sparing in its awards and awards are not generally made in cases of "structural bias". But "To gain an award under this head it is not necessary for the applicant to show that but for the violation the outcome of the proceedings would, or would probably, or even might, have been different, and in cases of delay the outcome may not be significant at all".[346] The House of Lords held that there were no special features in Greenfield's case which warranted the award of damages.

Article 8 (right to respect for private and family life)

19-095   In *R. (on the application of Bernard) v Enfield LBC*[347] the claimants were a severely disabled women and her husband, who lived with their six children in unsatisfactory accommodation. The local authority was held to be in breach of its statutory duties under the National Assistance Act 1948 and the Housing Act 1996; and to be in breach of art.8. The court held that it was necessary to award damages having regard to the deplorable conditions, "wholly inimical to any normal family life, and to ... physical and psychological integrity", which they had endured as a consequence of failures by the local authority over 20 months despite repeated letters urging action from the claimants' solicitor. The court considered awards made by the ombudsmen, which were of "great assistance". The court held that damages should be "at the top of the range" and awarded a total of £10,000.[348]

19-096   In *Anufrijeva*[349] the Court of Appeal heard three appeals from asylum seekers and their families who claimed that their respective local authorities had failed to ar-

---

prison were "criminal proceedings" for the purposes of art.6, so engaging the range of additional rights set out in art.6(3)(a)-(e), where the led to the imposition of additional days as punishment. See further *R. (on the application of Napier) v Secretary of State for the Home Department* [2004] EWHC 936 (Admin); [2004] 1 W.L.R. 3056 and the general discussion of the civil/criminal distinction in Ch.7.

[343] *Greenfield* [2005] UKHL 14; [2005] 1 W.L.R. 673 at [8].

[344] *Greenfield* [2005] UKHL 14; [2005] 1 W.L.R. 673 at [12].

[345] *Greenfield* [2005] UKHL 14; [2005] 1 W.L.R. 673 at [15].

[346] *Greenfield* [2005] UKHL 14; [2005] 1 W.L.R. 673 at [16].

[347] *R. (on the application of Bernard) v Enfield LBC* [2002] EWHC 2282 (Admin); [2003] H.R.L.R. 4. See generally 13-085.

[348] *R. (on the application of Bernard) v Enfield LBC* [2002] EWHC 2282 (Admin); [2003] H.R.L.R. 4 at [62] (Sullivan J: "Although there are two claimants it is important to avoid double counting, and since these damages are intended to give them just satisfaction for a breach of their Art.8 rights, it is sensible to start off with an overall figure to reflect the impact of the breach on their family life together, and then to apportion that figure between the two claimants having regard to the relative effects on their private lives. Bearing all these factors in mind, I conclude that the appropriate figure is £10,000, and I apportion that £8,000 to the second claimant and £2,000 to the first claimant"). Significant awards were made (and general guidance given) in relation to telephone hacking in *Gulati v MGN Ltd* [2015] EWCA Civ 1291; [2017] QB 149).

[349] *Anufrijeva* [2003] EWCA Civ 1406; [2004] Q.B. 1124.

range accommodation and provide benefits to which they were legally entitled and accordingly had failed in their positive obligations under art.8. The court characterised the failings of the local authorities, in particular their delay, as "maladministration". The court held that in cases concerning positive obligations under art.8, in a context in which public funds were limited, it was important to avoid a situation in which "the impression is created that asylum seekers whether genuine or not are profiting from their status, this could bring the Human Rights Act into disrepute".[350] Because the nature of the administrative failings in these cases were akin to maladministration, the court suggested that an appropriate point of comparison for quantum of damages would be the (relatively modest) levels of compensation awarded by the ombudsmen.[351] In relation to one of the claimants, the court held that

"Where a public authority commits acts which it knows are likely to cause psychiatric harm to an individual, those acts are capable of constituting an infringement of Article 8. Maladministration will not, however, infringe Article 8 simply because it causes stress that leads a particularly susceptible individual to suffer such harm in circumstances where this was not reasonably to be anticipated. No lack of respect for private life is manifested in such circumstances. The egg-shell skull principle forms no part of the test of breach of duty under the HRA or the Convention."[352]

In all three appeals, the court held that the local authorities' failings did not constitute a breach of art.8.[353]

Article 14 (prohibition of discrimination)

The House of Lords in *R. (on the application of Wilkinson) v Inland Revenue Commissioners*[354] held the Revenue—even though conceding that their decision was contrary to art.1 of the First Protocol (peaceful enjoyment of possessions) and art.14—had not acted contrary to their duty under s.6 of the HRA in refusing a widow a tax allowance equivalent to the widow's bereavement allowance because (in the words of s.6(2)) they "could not have acted differently" under provisions contained in primary legislation. Although not necessary to do so, the House considered what award would have been made to ensure "just satisfaction". In the context of art.14, what is it necessary for the court to do in order to put the claimant in the position he would have been in had the breach of a Convention right not occurred? Lord Hoffmann explained: "In a discrimination case, in which the wrongful act is treating A better than B, this involves forming a view about whether the state should have complied by treating A worse or B better. Normally one would conclude that A's treatment represented the norm and that B should have been treated better. In some cases, however, it will be clear that A's treatment was an unjustifiable anomaly".[355] His Lordship held that had Parliament paid proper regard to art.14 in this context, it would (as indeed it did) remove the different treatment of widows and widowers by abolishing widow's allowance rather than by extend-

19-097

350 *Anufrijeva* [2003] EWCA Civ 1406; [2004] Q.B. 1124 at [75].

351 *Anufrijeva* [2003] EWCA Civ 1406; [2004] Q.B. 1124 at [74].

352 *Anufrijeva* [2003] EWCA Civ 1406; [2004] Q.B. 1124 at [143].

353 See further, *R. (on the application of G) v Lambeth LBC* [2011] EWCA Civ 526; [2011] 4 All E.R. 453 at [40]-[46].

354 *R. (on the application of Wilkinson) v Inland Revenue Commissioners* [2005] UKHL 30; [2005] 1 W.L.R. 1718. Widow's allowance was abolished by the Finance Act 1999 with effect from April 2000. See generally 13-100.

355 *R. (on the application of Wilkinson) v Inland Revenue Commissioners* [2005] UKHL 30; [2005] 1 W.L.R. 1718 at [26].

ing the allowance to widowers.[356] Lord Browne of Eaton-under-Heywood agreed that art.14 presents particular difficulties in relation to the award of "just satisfaction": "In any claim against a public authority for financial compensation in respect of past discrimination it must be remembered that the general public (often the general body of taxpayers) will be footing the bill. In determining the requirements of just satisfaction, just as in the application of the Convention as a whole, regard should be had not only to the victim's rights but also to the interests of the public generally".[357]

19-098   In *R. (on the application of Baiai) v Secretary of State for the Home Department*[358] the court considered damages claims following findings that arrangements under which a "certificate of approval" was required (at a cost of £135) before immigrants could marry, unless they planned to do so in an Anglican church ceremony, were incompatible with art.12 (right to marry) and art.14. In relation to art.12, the court rejected the defendant's argument that (in the words of s.6(2) of the HRA) he "could not have acted differently" because he had a discretion whether or not to impose fees. The defendant could have established a system for scrutinising marriages, and charged a fee, which was Convention compliant. The claimants were therefore not entitled to recover the fees as the purpose of compensation was to place the claimants in the same position as if their Convention rights had not been infringed. Moreover, the declaration of incompatibility under s.4 of the HRA did not affect the validity of the provision, so the fee was not unlawful as a matter of domestic law.[359] The court also considered and rejected damages claims for "distress and humiliation". On the evidence, the claimants' reaction had not reached the required level of intensity; there was no evidence of the claimants needing medical treatment for their distress; and in any event the claimants must have been extremely worried about the general immigration status of their partners. In relation to art.14, the court held that the defendant "could not have acted differently" as the provision excluding Anglican marriage ceremonies was contained in primary legislation.

First Protocol, art.1 (right to property)

19-099   The CA upheld a very substantial award of damages in relation to the regulator's failure to understand properly the complex provisions governing the availability of certain subsidies in relation to renewable energy sources. Since the losses suffered by the claimant as a result of no longer being able to claim the subsidies were clearly quantifiable, it was appropriate to award them in full.[360]

---

[356] *R. (on the application of Wilkinson) v Inland Revenue Commissioners* [2005] UKHL 30; [2005] 1 W.L.R. 1718 at [28].

[357] *R. (on the application of Wilkinson) v Inland Revenue Commissioners* [2005] UKHL 30; [2005] 1 W.L.R. 1718 at [48].

[358] *R. (on the application of Baiai) v Secretary of State for the Home Department* [2006] EWHC 1035 (Admin) (following on from the judicial review claim in *R. (on the application of Baiai) v Secretary of State for the Home Department* [2006] EWHC 1454 (Admin); [2007] 1 W.L.R. 735).

[359] [2006] EWHC 1454 (Admin); [2007] 1 W.L.R. 735 at [29].

[360] *Gas and Electricity Markets Authority v Infinis Plc* [2013] EWCA Civ 70 at [26]-[27]). In *OAO Neftyanaya Kompaniya Yukos v Russia (Just Satisfaction)* (2014) 59 E.H.R.R. SE12, the ECtHR made its highest award of just satisfaction in the sum of £1.9bn in a First Protocol, art.1 case.

First Protocol, art.2 (right to education)

In *A v Headteacher and Governors of Lord Grey School*[361] the claimant had been **19-100** excluded from school pending a police investigation into an allegation that he had been involved in arson. The majority of the Lordships held that there was no breach of the claimant's right to education. Baroness Hale of Richmond, allowing the appeal against the claimant on different grounds to their other Lordships, held that it was unnecessary to award damages to afford just satisfaction.[362]

First Protocol, art.3 (right to free elections)

In *Firth v United Kingdom*,[363] the ECtHR confirmed that a declaration that the **19-101** automatic ban on voting by prisoners violated the right to free elections constituted just satisfaction and declined to award any compensation.

LIABILITY UNDER EUROPEAN COMMUNITY LAW

The liability of public authorities for breaches of European Community law is **19-102** examined in Chapter 14.[364]

---

[361] *A v Headteacher and Governors of Lord Grey School* [2006] UKHL 14; [2006] 2 A.C. 363.
[362] *A v Headteacher and Governors of Lord Grey School* [2006] UKHL 14; [2006] 2 A.C. 363 at [83].
[363] *Firth v United Kingdom* (2016) 63 E.H.R.R. 25. Following *Firth*, the ECtHR rejected further claims for legal costs and non-pecuniary losses arising out of the same issues in *McHugh v UK* (App. No.51987/08) (10 February 2015) at [17]: the judgment in *Firth* was clear and the applicants did not require legal assistance to submit their applications which were dealt with under a simplified procedure.
[364] See 14-076.

LIABILITY UNDER EUROPEAN COMMUNITY LAW

TABLE OF CONTENTS

APPENDIX A

Note on Citation of Authorities

LAW REPORTS

In written and oral submissions in court,[1]

6. When authority is cited, whether in written or oral submissions, the following practice should be followed. Where a judgment is reported in the Official Law Reports (A.C., Q.B., Ch., Fam.) published by the Incorporated Council of Law Reporting for England and Wales, that report must be cited. These are the most authoritative reports; they contain a summary of the argument. Other series of reports and official transcripts of judgment may only be used when a case is not reported in the Official Law Reports.

7. If a judgment is not (or not yet) reported in the Official Law Reports but it is reported in the Weekly Law Reports (W.L.R.) or the All England Law Reports (All ER) that report should be cited. If the case is reported in both the W.L.R. and the All ER either report may properly be cited.

8. If a judgment is not reported in the Official Law Reports, the W.L.R, or the All ER, but it is reported in any of the authoritative specialist series of reports which contain a headnote and are made by individuals holding a Senior Courts qualification (for the purposes of section 115 of the Courts and Legal Services Act 1990), the specialist report should be cited.

9. Where a judgment is not reported in any of the reports referred to in paragraphs [6] to [8] above, but is reported in other reports, they may be cited.

10. Where a judgment has not been reported, reference may be made to the official transcript if that is available, not the handed-down text of the judgment, as this may have been subject to late revision after the text was handed down. Official transcripts may be obtained from, for instance, BAILLI (*http://www.bailii.org/*). An unreported case should not usually be cited unless it contains a relevant statement of legal principle not found in reported authority.

11. Occasions arise when one report is fuller than another, or when there are discrepancies between reports. On such occasions, the practice outlined above need not be followed, but the court should be given a brief explanation why this course is being taken, and the alternative references should be given.

12. If a judgment under appeal has been reported before the hearing but after

---

[1] *Practice Direction: Citation of Authorities* [2012] 1 W.L.R. 780 which was issued by the Lord Chief Justice and came into force on 24 March 2012 (*http://www.judiciary.gov.uk*).

skeleton arguments have been filed with the court, and counsel wish to argue from the published report rather than from the official transcript, the court should be provided with photocopies of the report for the use of the court.

13. Judgments reported in any series of reports, including those of the Incorporated Council of Law Reporting, should be provided either by way of a photocopy of the published report or by way of a copy of a reproduction of the judgment in electronic form that has been authorised by the publisher of the relevant series, but in any event (1) the report must be presented to the court in an easily legible form (a 12-point font is preferred but a 10 or 11-point font is acceptable) and (2) the advocate presenting the report is satisfied that it has not been reproduced in a garbled form from the data source. In any case of doubt the court will rely on the printed text of the report (unless the editor of the report has certified that an electronic version is more accurate because it corrects an error contained in an earlier printed text of the report).

There is a wide range of specialist law reports containing cases of relevance to judicial review. The following are among those referred to in this book.

Journal title	Abbreviation	Publisher
Administrative Court Digest (formerly Crown Office Digest)	A.C.D.	Sweet & Maxwell
Administrative Law Reports	Admin. L.R.	Barry Rose Law Periodicals from 1989 to 1998
Butterworths Human Rights Cases	B.H.R.C.	LexisNexis Butterworths
Butterworths Local Government Reports	B.L.G.R.	LexisNexis Butterworths
Common Market Law Review	C.M.L.R.	Kluwer Law International
Community Care Law Reports	C.C.L. Rep.	Legal Action Group
Crown Office Digest (now called Administrative Court Digest)	C.O.D.	Sweet & Maxwell
Education Law Reports	E.L.R.	Jordan Publishing
Entertainment and Media Law Reports	E.M.L.R.	Sweet & Maxwell
Environmental Law Reports	Env. L.R.	Sweet & Maxwell
European Human Rights Reports	E.H.R.R.	Sweet & Maxwell
Housing Law Reports	H.L.R.	Sweet & Maxwell
Immigration Appeal Reports	Imm. A.R.	
Journal of Planning and Environmental Law	J.P.L.	Sweet & Maxwell
New Property Cases	N.P.C.	

Journal title	Abbreviation	Publisher
Property and Compensation Law Reports	P. & C.R.	Sweet & Maxwell
United Kingdom Human Rights Reports	U.K.H.R.R.	Sweet & Maxwell

USE OF UNREPORTED JUDGMENTS

On occasion we have referred to unreported judgments. While for academic purposes the fact that a case has or has not been selected to be reported is of little importance, practitioners appearing in the courts of England and Wales have restrictions placed on their use of unreported decisions. Attention is drawn to paragraph 6 of the 2012 Practice Direction (above). Further, in 2001 the Lord Chief Justice (Lord Woolf) gave the following guidance in *Practice Direction (Citation of Authorities)* [2001] 1 W.L.R. 1001:

A-002

Categories of judgments that may only be cited if they fulfil specified requirements

6.1 A judgment falling into one of the categories referred to in paragraph 6.2 below may not in future be cited before any court unless it clearly indicates that it purports to establish a new principle or to extend the present law. In respect of judgments delivered after the date of this Direction [April 9, 2001], that indication must take the form of an express statement to that effect. In respect of judgments delivered before the date of this Direction that indication must be present in or clearly deducible from the language used in the judgment.

A-003

6.2 Paragraph 6.1 applies to the following categories of judgment:
- Applications attended by one party only
- Applications for permission to appeal
- Decisions on applications that only decide that the application is arguable
- County Court cases, unless (a) cited in order to illustrate the conventional measure of damages in a personal injury case; or (b) cited in a County Court in order to demonstrate current authority at that level on an issue in respect of which no decision at a higher level of authority is available.

6.3 These categories will be kept under review, such review to include consideration of adding to the categories."

Citation of other categories of judgment

7.1 Courts will in future pay particular attention, when it is sought to cite other categories of judgment, to any indication given by the court delivering the judgment that it was seen by that court as only applying decided law to the facts of the particular case; or otherwise as not extending or adding to the existing law.

A-004

7.2 Advocates who seek to cite a judgment that contains indications of the type referred to in paragraph 7.1 will be required to justify their decision to cite the case."

Methods of citation

A-005   8.1 Advocates will in future be required to state, in respect of each authority that they wish to cite, the proposition of law that the authority demonstrates, and the parts of the judgment that support that proposition. If it is sought to cite more than one authority in support of a given proposition, advocates must state the reason for taking that course.

8.2 The demonstration referred to in paragraph 8.1 will be required to be contained in any skeleton argument and in any appellant's or respondent's notice in respect of each authority referred to in that skeleton or notice.

8.3 Any bundle or list of authorities prepared for the use of any court must in future bear a certification by the advocate responsible for arguing the case that the requirements of this paragraph have been complied with in respect of each authority included.

8.4 The statements referred to in paragraph 8.1 should not materially add to the length of submissions or of skeleton arguments, but should be sufficient to demonstrate, in the context of the advocate's argument, the relevance of the authority or authorities to that argument and that the citation is necessary for a proper presentation of that argument."

Judgments given at the permission stage of a claim for judicial review will usually fall within the ambit of paragraph 6.2 and are in any event of only persuasive authority.[2]

Judgments from other jurisdictions

A-006   We draw on experiences from other legal systems,[3] in particular Australia, Canada, India, New Zealand and South Africa. Most citations are from the following sources.

Australia	
Commonwealth Law Reports	C.L.R. (authorised reports)
Australian Law Reports	A.L.R
Online resources	*http://www.austlii.edu.au/*
Canada	
Supreme Court Reports	S.C.R. (authorised reports)
Online resources	*http://www.lexum.umontreal.ca* *http://www.canlii.org/en*
India	
Supreme Court Reports	S.C.R. (official reports)
Supreme Court Cases	S.C.C.
Online resources	*http://judis.openarchive.in/* *http://www.judis.nic.in*
New Zealand	
New Zealand Law Reports	N.Z.L.R. (authorised reports)
New Zealand Administrative Reports	N.Z.A.R.

---

[2] *Clark v University of Lincolnshire and Humberside* [2000] 1 W.L.R. 1988 at [43].
[3] See Ch.1.

New Zealand Resource Management Appeals	N.Z.R.M.A.
Online resources	*http://www.waikato.ac.nz/library/ resources/law/* *http://www.nzlii.org/*
South Africa	
South African Law Reports	S.A.
Online resources	*http://www.saflii.org/*

Practitioners in England and Wales seeking to rely upon overseas case law in written or oral submissions in court must heed the guidance set out in *Practice Direction (Citation of Authorities)* [2001] 1 W.L.R. 1001:

Authorities decided in other jurisdictions

9.1 Cases decided in other jurisdictions can, if properly used, be a valuable source of law in this jurisdiction. At the same time, however, such authority should not be cited without proper consideration of whether it does indeed add to the existing body of law.   **A-007**

9.2 In future therefore, any advocate who seeks to cite an authority from another jurisdiction must

   i. comply, in respect of that authority, with the rules set out in paragraph 8 above [set out above in relation to unreported judgments];

   ii. indicate in respect of each authority what that authority adds that is not to be found in authority in this jurisdiction; or, if there is said to be justification for adding to domestic authority, what that justification is;

   iii. certify that there is no authority in this jurisdiction that precludes the acceptance by the court of the proposition that the foreign authority is said to establish.

9.3 For the avoidance of doubt, paragraphs 9.1 and 9.2 do not apply to cases decided in either the European Court of Justice or the organs of the European Convention of Human Rights. Because of the status in English law of such authority, as provided by, respectively, section 3 of the European Communities Act 1972 and section 2(1) of the Human Rights Act 1998, such cases are covered by the earlier paragraphs of this Direction."

New form of naming for judicial review cases

As part of the justice modernisation programme, the style of naming cases in judicial review changed. Up to 11 January, 2001, the format was *R. v Secretary of State for Administrative Affairs Ex p. Bloggs* ("Ex parte" in this context meaning "on behalf of the claimant Bloggs"). From 2001, claims for judicial review are cited as *R. (on the application of Bloggs) v Secretary of State for Administrative Affairs*.   **A-008**

Neutral citation system

Between 2001 and January 2002, a "media neutral" citation system was introduced in England and Wales, in which each judgment is given a unique reference number and paragraphs are numbered. This enables cases to be identified and   **A-009** pinpoint references to be given without reliance on a particular series of law reports or a page number of a particular report. The transitional arrangements mean that there are three ways in which a judgment may be cited, depending on when it was handed down.

- Before 11 January 2001: no neutral citations. Reported cases are known only by the law report citations; unreported decisions are referred to by the relevant date and the court.
- Between 11 January 2001 and 13 January 2002: neutral citations to Administrative Court decisions are in the format [2001] EWHC Admin 8. "Admin" is an essential part of the neutral citation because each division of the High Court was responsible for allocating sequential numbers to its cases.[4]
- After 14 January 2002: the current neutral citation system came into force.[5] The unique reference numbers are now allocated according across all divisions of the High Court. The format for Administrative Court decisions after this date is therefore [2002] EWHC 5 (Admin). The description "(Admin)" is not an essential part of the citation as no other case will in another division will have been allocated the number 5. "Under these arrangements, it will be unnecessary to include the descriptive word in brackets when citing the paragraph number of a judgment. Thus paragraph 59 of *Smith v Jones* [2002] EWHC 124 (QBD) would be cited: *Smith v Jones* [2002] EWHC 124 at [59]".[6]

---

[4] *Practice Direction (Judgments: Form and Citation)* [2001] 1 W.L.R. 194 (issued on 11 January 2001).
[5] *Practice Direction (Judgments: Neutral Citations)* [2002] 1 W.L.R. 346.
[6] *Practice Direction (Judgments: Neutral Citations)* [2002] 1 W.L.R. 346 at [3].

APPENDIX B

Classification of Functions

INTRODUCTION

As we have noted,[1] for many years the development of English administrative **B-001**
law was impeded by the distinctions made by the courts between functions which
were classified as "legislative", "administrative", "judicial", "quasi judicial" and
"ministerial". In particular, natural justice was reserved for decision-making which
was "judicial" or "quasi judicial" in nature and judicial review as a whole was not
considered appropriate for decisions which were of a "legislative" or "ministerial" character. In the last edition of this work which he edited (in 1973), de Smith
was highly critical of the "terminological contortions" produced by these
classifications. Although he thought that the conceptual problems associated with
the classifications still "appeared to be overwhelming", he regarded them as
"analytically erroneous" and detected some hope that "to an increasing extent courts
exercising powers of judicial review in administrative law are abandoning servitude
to their own concepts and asserting mastery over them" (p.77).

ABANDONMENT OF THESE CLASSIFICATIONS

Servitude to these classifications has now largely been abandoned. In regard to **B-002**
natural justice, the notion that a fair hearing is reserved to a "judicial" or "quasi-
judicial" situation has been firmly "scotched" as a "heresy".[2] The prerogative
remedies of certiorari and prohibition are no longer confined, as they once were,
to the "judicial" functions of public bodies. The sweeping away of this restriction
was helped by the common procedure established by RSC Ord.53 in 1978.[3] Today
both certiorari and prohibition (quashing and prohibiting orders) may be granted in
relation to functions which may be regarded as "administrative" or even as
"legislative".[4] In cases regarding prison discipline the House of Lords has
disregarded the "fancied distinctions"[5] between "administrative" and "judicial or
quasi judicial" distinctions by upholding the possibility of judicial review of the
decisions of prison governors. Lord Oliver held that "it is not the label ... that

---

[1]   See Chs 1 and 6.
[2]   *R. v Gaming Board Ex p. Benaim and Khaida* [1970] 2 Q.B. 417 at 430 (Lord Denning, in respect
      of the decision of the HL in *Ridge v Baldwin* [1964] A.C. 40) and *O'Reilly v Mackman* [1983] A.C.
      23 at 279 (Lord Diplock).
[3]   See Ch.15.
[4]   On review of legislation, see Ch.3.
[5]   *Leech v Parkhurst Prison Deputy Governor* [1988] A.C. 533.

determines the existence of [the court's] jurisdiction but the quality and attributes of the decision".[6]

B-003   The rejection of the classification of functions as determining the existence or scope of judicial review means it no longer has a place at the start of a book on judicial review. However, its relevance to the history of judicial review is considerable, and it still throws light on the "quality and attributes" of decisions which may render them more or less amenable to judicial review. On the whole the test of "public function"[7] and "justiciability"[8] has replaced that of classification of function as a determinant of the appropriateness of a decision for judicial review.[9] Yet some of the qualities of the old classifications contribute to the identification of a decision's justiciable features. For example, the question may be asked as to whether "managerial"-type decisions, or decisions involving the allocation of scarce resources, are amenable to control by the courts rather than the electorate.[10] Similarly, delegation of powers is less likely to be tolerated in relation to bodies performing judicial-type functions.[11] In some cases a statute may specifically draw a distinction between so-called administrative and judicial functions, for example, in relation to the functions of the ombudsmen.[12] Immunity in tort claims is granted by statute and the common law in respect of acts and omissions in the course of judicial proceedings.[13] To the extent therefore that the classifications are still useful and relevant (and their relevance should by no means be overrated),[14] what follows is an abridged version of Chapter 2 of the 4th edition (1979) of this work, edited by J. Evans.

DE SMITH ON CLASSIFICATION OF FUNCTIONS

B-004   "We class schools, you see, into four grades: Leading School, First-rate School, Good School, and School." (Evelyn Waugh, *Decline and Fall*.)

The functions of public authorities may be roughly classified as (a) legislative, (b) administrative (or executive), (c) judicial (or quasi-judicial) and (d) ministerial. In some countries classification raises constitutional issues connected with the separation of powers.

B-005   In the United Kingdom this kind of problem does not arise. Hence constitutional decisions by the Privy Council and Commonwealth courts on the nature and characteristics of judicial power are only of marginal interest in this country. Those

---

6   *R. v Deputy Governor of Parkhurst Prison Ex p. Leech* [1988] A.C. 533 at 579; and 566 (Lord Bridge).

7   See Ch.3.

8   See Chs 1, 5 and 11.

9   On justiciability, see Chs 1 and 5.

10 For example, the distinction between managerial and other functions drawn in *R. v Secretary of State for the Environment Ex. p. Hammersmith and Fulham LBC* [1991] A.C. 521.

11 See Ch.7.

12 See Ch.1; *R. v Local Commissioner Ex p. Croydon LBC* [1989] 1 All E.R. 1033 at 1043.

13 See Ch.1; e.g. (a) the Crown Proceedings Act 1947 provides the Crown with absolute immunity from primary or vicarious liability for its officers' wrongful exercise of judicial power; (b) words spoken in the course of "judicial proceedings" are absolutely privileged in the law of defamation, and (c) those carrying out judicial functions enjoy wide immunity from suit for otherwise tortious acts done within their jurisdiction.

14 As they were it is submitted, in *R. v Inland Revenue Commissioners Ex p. TC Coombs & Co* [1991] 2 A.C. 283 (Lord Lowry: a "judicial"-type decision could not be held Wednesbury unreasonable); cf. *R. v Legal Aid Board Ex p. Bateman* [1992] 1 W.L.R. 711 at 719 (Nolan LJ: *Wednesbury* was "equally appropriate no matter whether the role of the board is regarded as administrative or quasi judicial").

decisions[15] may indeed be positively misleading if taken too seriously; for a decision to the effect that, for constitutional purposes, a power vested in a tribunal is non judicial does not necessarily imply that the tribunal is exempt from a duty to "act judicially" in accordance with natural justice or is immune from control by certiorari and prohibition.[16] English lawyers already have enough to puzzle them as they observe the terminological contortions of courts deciding cases in the field of administrative law.

The meanings attributed by the courts to the terms "judicial", "quasi-judicial",   **B-006**
"administrative", "legislative" and "ministerial" for administrative law purposes have been inconsistent. Lawyers are, of course, quite familiar with the notion that a legal term may convey a range of meaning and that within that range the meaning appropriate for the resolution of a particular dispute may well depend upon the context which the term has to be applied. Nonetheless, when specific legal consequences flow from the manner of classifying a particular function, the use of the same word to denote different things and different words to denote the same thing is apt to generate confusion. The development of administrative law has provided ample proof of the truth of this proposition, although in recent years English judges have to a large extent succeeded in extricating the law from the state of confusion into which it appeared to have fallen. The statutory admonition that the purpose for which a function is being classified should never be forgotten may go some way at least towards the avoidance of the pitfalls inherent in the limitations of language. Rather than elaborating at great length the problems of classification, an attempt will be made here (a) to state briefly the legal situations in which classification of a function in one category or another may be of material importance; (b) to outline the main approaches to classification adopted by the courts; and (c) to indicate, where possible, why the courts have chosen one method of classification rather than another in individual contexts.

Certain preliminary points must be stated. First, it is sometimes impossible to   **B-007**
discern why a court has characterised a given function as judicial or administrative. Often, it is true, the method of characterisation can be seen as a contrivance to support a conclusion reached on non-conceptual grounds. But in many cases the terms seem to have been used loosely and without deliberation: and in some cases definitions propounded in earlier reported cases appear to have dominated the juristic analysis of the case in hand and indeed the conclusion reached by the court. Although in this "highly acrobatic part of the law"[17] an aptitude for verbal gymnastics is of advantage, a commentator endowed with this attribute is frequently left wondering whether Mr Justice Malaprop's formulation is really more dextrous, more fortuitous, more laboured or simply more ineffectual than his own would have been. Secondly, recent English case law has tended to blur rather than clarify the distinctions between the two most important classes of function, the judicial and the administrative. And thirdly, as distinctions have been blurred, so has their practical importance tended to dwindle. Seldom does the outcome of a case nowadays

---

[15]   Among the best-known cases are *Shell Oil Co of Australia Ltd v Federal Commissioner of Taxation* [1931] A.C. 275; and the following appeals from Ceylon (now the Republic of Sri Lanka) before the abolition of PC appeals and the adoption of a republican constitution: *Bribery Commissioner v Ranasinghe* [1965] A.C. 172; *United Engineering Workers' Union v Devanayagam* [1968] A.C. 356; *Ranaweera v Wickramasinghe* [1970] A.C. 951; *Ranaweera v Ramachandran* [1970] A.C. 962.

[16]   *Ranaweera v Wickramasinghe* [1970] A.C. 951 at 962; *R. v Trade Practices Tribunal* [1970] A.L.R. 499; cf. *Jayawardane v Silva* [1970] 1 W.L.R. 13651, PC; *Trapp v Mackie* [1979] 1 W.L.R. 377 at 388.

[17]   Willis, "Administrative Law and the British North America Act" (1940) 53 Harv L.R. 251. The tendency in recent years for courts in a number of areas to move away from a classifactory approach is discussed by K. Keith (1976-1977) 7 N.Z.U.L.R. 325.

turn purely on the mode of classifying a function vested in the competent authority. The intrinsic difficulties of the topic under consideration have not diminished, but they are no longer as oppressive as they once were.

MINISTERIAL

B-008   In politics "ministerial" is commonly used as an epithet appertaining to Ministers of the Crown, or, more broadly, to the party in office. We speak of ministerial responsibility, ministerial cheers. As a technical legal term it has no single fixed meaning.

(1)   It may describe any duty, the discharge of which involves no element of discretion or independent judgment. Since an order of mandamus will issue to compel the performance of a ministerial act, and since, moreover, wrongful refusal to carry out a ministerial duty may give rise to liability in tort, it is often of practical importance to determine whether discretion is present in the performance of a statutory function. The cases on mandamus show, however, that the presence of a minor discretionary element is not enough to deter the courts from characterising a function as ministerial. Thus although the issue of a warrant for non-payment of rates is usually said to be a ministerial act, the justices must first be satisfied that the rate was properly made, published and demanded, that it has not been paid and that the person on whom it was made was in truth the person rateable; but once satisfied on these points they have no discretion to extend the time for payment.[18] The issue of a warrant for the nonpayment of taxes has been held to be a ministerial act (and therefore not reviewable by certiorari) although the officer issuing the warrant had discretionary power to take proceedings in the courts for the recovery of the taxes.[19] Again, where an authority has erroneously declined jurisdiction over a matter or has failed to exercise a discretion according to proper legal principles, the issue of a mandamus to it has sometime been represented as a remedy for breach of a ministerial duty, although the determination of such questions may be far from a mechanical operation.[20]

(2)   It is often used, more narrowly, to describe the issue of a formal instruction, in consequence of a prior determination which may or may not be of a judicial character, that direct action be taken in relation to another's person or property.[21]

(3)   It may describe the execution of such an instruction by an inferior officer (who is sometimes called a ministerial officer).

(4)   It is sometimes used loosely to describe any act that is neither judicial nor legislative. In this sense the term is used interchangeably with "executive" or "administrative".[22] So, the function of an assessment committee,[23] the making of slum clearance and compulsory purchase orders under housing legisla-

---

[18]   "Discretion not Unlimited" (1949) 113 J.P.J. 566; *R. v Middlesex Justices* (1842) 6 J.P. 772 (distress warrant); and *R. v York Justices Ex p. York Corp* [1949] W.N. 72 (order for possession).

[19]   *Hetherington v Security Export Co* [1924] A.C. 988.

[20]   For an analysis of the senses in which the term "ministerial" may be used in different contexts, see A. Rubinstein, *Jurisdiction and Illegality*, (1965) pp.16-20, 98-101, 135-139, 150-159.

[21]   D. Gordon, "Administrative Tribunals and the Courts" (1933) 49 L.Q.R. 94 at 98.

[22]   *Haridas v Khan* [1971] 1 W.L.R. 507 at 512; *Dean v District Auditor for Ashton-in-Makerfield* [1960] 1 Q.B. 149 at 156.

[23]   *R. v Westminster (City of) Assessment Committee* [1941] 1 KB. 53.

tion,[24] and the assessment of charges to be imposed on the inhabitants of a district in a colony,[25] have all been called ministerial, although their most obvious characteristic is that they involve the exercise of wide discretionary powers. This use of the term is misleading. In the present work the term will be used to refer to the making of decisions, the issue of orders or the execution of acts in which the element of judgment or discretion is either absent or relatively very small.[26]

"ADMINISTRATIVE" AND "LEGISLATIVE"

The term "administrative" is capable of bearing a wide range of meanings, some of which are remote from the problems raised by the classification of statutory functions. In such phrases as "administrative law" "administrative tribunal" and "judicial review of administration action" it refers to broad areas of government activity in which the repositories of power may exercise every class of statutory function. We need not dwell upon these usages. Nor, at this point, shall we consider the analytical distinctions drawn between administrative and judicial functions; these can conveniently be postponed until we discuss the meanings of "judicial".   **B-009**

A distinction often made between legislative and administrative acts is that between the general and the particular. A legislative act is the creation and promulgation of a general rule of conduct without reference to particular cases: an administrative act cannot be exactly defined, but it includes the adoption of a policy, the making and issue of a specific direction, and the application of a general rule to a particular case in accordance with the requirements of policy of expediency or administrative practice. Legal consequences flow from this distinction.   **B-010**

Since the general shades off into the particular, to discriminate between the legislative and the administrative by reference to these criteria may be a peculiarly difficult task, and it is not surprising that the opinions of judges as to the proper characterisation of a statutory function is at variance. If a Minister has power to requisition houses and to delegate his power, and he proceeds to delegate his power to an individual clerk to a local authority, there can be no doubt that this delegation is an administrative act,[27] but if he delegates his power to all clerks to local authorities, is the instrument of delegation a legislative or an administrative order?[28] Fortunately decisions in the courts seldom turn on this type of question alone; and when it arises it is apt to be glossed over.   **B-011**

Other criteria for distinguishing legislative from administrative acts appear in ordinary linguistic usage. In the first place, every measure duly enacted by Parliament is regarded as legislation. If land is compulsorily acquired by means of a Private Act of Parliament or a Provisional Order Confirmation Act, the acquisition is deemed to be a legislative act; though if the acquisition is effected by means of a compulsory purchase order made under enabling legislation, it will usually be classified as an administrative act. Secondly, departmental instruments or announcements which, although general in application, normally neither create legally   **B-012**

---

[24] *Errington v Minister of Health* [1935] 1 K.B. 249 at 259; *Robins (E) & Son Ltd v Minister of Health* [1939] 1 K.B. 520 at 534, 535.

[25] *Patterson v District Commissioner of Accra* [1948] A. C. 341 at 349.

[26] *R. v Majewski* [1977] A.C. 443 at 451 (power of registrar to refer appeals to the Court of Appeal (Criminal Division) for summary determination when the point raised is frivolous or vexatious).

[27] *Lewisham LBC v Roberts* [1949] 2 K.B. 608.

[28] For conflicting views on this point, see *Blackpool Corp v Locker* [1948] K.B. 349 (Scott and Asquith LJJ); *Lewisham LBC v Roberts* [1949] 2 K.B. 608 621-622 (Denning LJ).

enforceable rights nor impose legally enforceable obligations since they are not made pursuant to express statutory authority. Rules of this kind are usually referred to as examples of "administrative action". Circulars issued by the Department of the Environment to local planning authorities on the manner in which they should exercise their statutory powers fall into this category,[29] as do the rules formulated by the Foreign and Commonwealth Office to govern the exercise of the prerogative power over the issue and withdrawal of passports.[30] And the same is true of an announced amnesty for illegal immigrants who satisfy certain criteria.[31] Just as the Crown is without authority to alter the general law of the land by prerogative,[32] so are its servants and other public authorities without inherent authority to impose legal duties or liabilities or to confer legally enforceable rights, privileges or immunities on the subject.[33] Hence, the extra-statutory concessions to taxpayers that the Inland Revenue and Customs and Excise authorities announce from time to time cannot be relied upon in any court of law,[34] although they have been styled "administrative quasi-legislation".[35] It must not be assumed, however, that departmental communications issued in the form of circulars, notes for guidance or letters to local and regional authorities, or press notices, are necessarily destitute of legal effect.[36] It is possible that in some circumstances, at least, the promulgation of informal rules or the announcement of a policy must give rise to procedural obligations,[37] or be used as evidence of the matters that may legitimately be considered in the exercise of discretion[38] or even create a form of estoppel. And it may not be totally fanciful to imagine that a public authority may be held to have abused its discretion by clearly misinterpreting its own rules that it purported to apply. In one instance the courts have given legislative effect to what is ostensibly a purely administrative announcement. The Criminal Injuries Compensation Board was created to administer a non-statutory scheme for compensating victims of crimes of violence by ex gratia payments out of funds authorised by Parliament. The Board was required to follow a judicial-type procedure and to apply the legal standards contained in the scheme. Although a claimant has no legally enforce-

---

29 See, e.g. *Bizony v Secretary of State for the Environment* (1976) 239 E.G. 281 at 283.

30 Hansard HC, Vol.881, col.265WA 15 November 1974.

31 *Birdi v Secretary of State for Home Affairs, The Times,* 12 February 1975; *Purewal v Entry Clearance Officer* [1977] Imm. A.R. 93 (Immigration Appeal Tribunal: amnesty provisions not within jurisdiction of immigration appellate authorities); cf. *Salemi v MacKellar (No.2)* (1977) 137 C.L.R. 396.

32 Case of Proclamations (1611) 12 Co. Rep. 74; cf. *R. v Criminal Injuries Compensation Board Ex p. Lain* [19671 2 Q.B. 864 at 886-889 (Diplock LJ, for certain qualifications of the general rule).

33 cf. *Earl Fitzwilliam's Wentworth Estate Ltd v Minister of Town and Country Planning* [1951] 2 K.B. 284 at 311-312 (Denning LJ); *M'Ara v Edinburgh Magistrates* 1913 S.C. 1059; *R. v Knuller (Publishing etc) Ltd* [1973] A.C. 435 at 456 (Lord Reid, remarks on an assurance by a Law Officer of the Crown in the House of Commons that a charge of conspiracy to corrupt public morals would not be used to circumvent the statutory defences contained in the Obscene Publications Act 1959).

34 *R. v Customs and Excise Commissioners Ex p. Cook* [1970] 1 W.L.R. 450 at 454-455.

35 R. Megarry, "Administrative Quasi-Legislation" (1944) 60 L.Q.R. 125, 218; *Vestey v Inland Revenue Commissioners (No.2)* [1979] Ch. 198 at 202-204 (ad hoc use of this "dispensing power" is strongly criticised).

36 Thus a decision made solely on the basis of such a rule or policy may be impugned on the ground that the authority had thereby fettered its discretion. A decision made in accordance with announced policy may also be held invalid if the policy included factors that the authority was not statutorily empowered to take into consideration on the proper interpretation of its power.

37 See, e.g. *R. v Liverpool Corp. Ex p. Liverpool Taxi Fleet Operators' Association* [1972] 2 Q.B. 299; *R. v Home Secretary Ex p. Hosenball* [1977] 1 W.L.R. 766 at 781, 788; *R. v Criminal Injuries Compensation Board Ex p. Ince* [1973] 1 W.L.R. 1334 at 1345; *Salemi v Mackellar (No.2)* (1977) 137 C.L.R. 396.

38 *Bristol DC v Clark* [1975] 1 W.L.R. 1443 at 1451.

able right to any compensation, he is entitled to obtain certiorari to quash a determination of the Board if the proceedings or determination are tainted by defects that would warrant the award of certiorari to quash a determination of a statutory tribunal.[39]

There are other acts which, though non-legislative in form, are cognisable by the courts and approximate to legislation in effect. Standard terms embodied in contracts between local authorities and council tenants, between government departments and manufacturers or suppliers[40] may not differ in substance from byelaws[41] or statutory instruments. A decision of the House of Lords overturning an established judge-made rule can sometimes fairly be represented as unavowed legislation with, moreover, a limited retroactive operation.[42]

B-013

"QUASI-JUDICIAL"

In administrative law this term may have any one of three meanings. It may describe a function that is partly judicial and partly administrative, e.g. the making of a compulsory purchase order (a discretionary or administrative act) preceded by the holding of a judicial-type local inquiry and the consideration of objections. It may, alternatively, describe the "judicial" element in a composite function; holding an inquiry and considering objections in respect of a compulsory purchase order are thus "quasi-judicial" acts. Or it may describe the nature of a discretionary act itself where the actor's discretion is not unfettered. Seldom is it essential to use this ambiguous term, and it will be avoided here as far as possible.

B-014

JUDICIAL

A judicial decision made within jurisdiction is binding and conclusive in so far as it cannot be impeached in collateral proceedings; and it cannot, in general, be rescinded by the tribunal itself.[43] Words spoken in the course of judicial proceedings are absolutely privileged in the law of defamation; so too, it appears, are fair and accurate newspaper reports of judicial proceedings.[44] On the other hand, it is a contempt to comment on proceedings pending before a court in circumstances that prejudice a fair trial of the issues. No civil liability is incurred in respect of erroneous or negligent judicial decisions and acts, provided that the officers concerned have acted in good faith and within their jurisdiction.[45] The Crown is immune from liability in tort in respect of anything done or omitted to be done by any person

B-015

---

[39] *R. v Criminal Injuries Compensation Board Ex p. Lain* [1967] 2 Q.B. 864.
[40] See C. Turpin (1972), *Government Contracts*, Ch.3. And see *Racal Communications Ltd v Pay Board* [1974] W.L.R. 1149 (interpretation of Fair Wages Resolution passed by House of Commons).
[41] Housing Act 1957 s.12(1) (as amended).
[42] The retroactive effects of judicial decisions have tended to inhibit "judicial law-making"; there have been hints that English courts should be empowered to overrule decisions prospectively: see *R. v National Insurance Commissioner Ex p. Hudson* 944 at 1015, 1026.
[43] See, e.g. *Punton v Ministry of Pensions and National Insurance (No.2)* [1964] 1 W.L.R. 226.
[44] But newspaper reports of proceedings before "any justice or justices of the peace acting otherwise than as a court exercising judicial authority" enjoy only qualified privilege (Defamation Act 1952 Sch. para.10(b)).
[45] A majority of the Court of Appeal in *Siros v Moore* [1975] Q.B. 118 stated that a judicial act or decision bona fide done or made in the purported exercise of jurisdiction was not actionable, even though it turned out to be one that was outside the jurisdiction of the tribunal. Judges of courts stricto sensu are immune from liability for all acts down within jurisdiction, even if they have acted maliciously.

while discharging or purporting to discharge "responsibilities of a judicial nature"[46] even if that person is individually liable. Only in very exceptional circumstances may judicial functions be sub-delegated in the absence of express authorisation. In a number of cases courts have refused to entertain appeals from decisions which are not of a judicial character.[47]

B-016 We have listed the main contexts in which the courts may have to determine whether to classify the functions of public authorities as judicial; the catalogue is not, however, exhaustive.[48] The meaning is apt to vary according to the purpose for which it has to be defined. For example, a function deemed to be judicial in so far as it is reviewable by certiorari may become "administrative" when an attempt is made to establish that it attracts absolute privilege in the law of defamation.[49] A Minister making a town planning decision may be required to act judicially in the sense of being obliged to observe the rules of natural justice, but if his decision is quashed he will not enjoy the immunity from liability to pay costs that is granted to members of judicial tribunals.[50] When it is said that mandamus will not issue in respect of judicial acts "judicial" is being contrasted with ministerial and includes discretionary acts which would ordinarily be called administrative. Similarly, the rules protecting judicial acts within jurisdiction from collateral impeachment and granting exemptions from tortious liability for judicial acts embrace some discretionary functions that are typically administrative.[51]

B-017 These illustrations of terminological vagaries could be multiplied. Some have been deliberately contrived by judges seeking to impose on their decisions a veneer of superficially persuasive legal reasoning. The difficulties posed by these verbal problems have been particularly perplexing in two sets of situations. How does one determine (i) whether a body is required to act in a judicial capacity for the purpose of ascertaining if its acts are reviewable by the orders of certiorari and prohibition and (ii) whether a body is under a duty to act judicially in the sense of being obliged to observe the rules of natural justice? Fortunately, however, recent developments in the law have reduced the importance that these two questions at one time had.

B-018 The two questions overlap, for among the grounds for which certiorari and prohibition will issue is breach of the rules of natural justice. But the questions are also partly distinct, since certiorari and prohibition will issue on other grounds

---

[46] Crown Proceedings Act 1947 s.2(5). The meaning of "judicial" for this purpose may well be held to be as wide as for the purpose of determining the immunity of persons in respect of non-malicious judicial acts.

[47] *Moses v Parker* [1896] A.C. 245; *Kaye v Hunter* 1958 S.C. 208; *Dean v District Auditor for Ashton-in-Makerfield* [1960] 1 Q.B. 149; *Attorney General of the Gambia v N'Jie* [1961] A.C. 617, 633; *R. v Cornwall Q. S. Ex p. Kerley* [1956] 1 W.L.R. 906.

[48] The phrase "judicial officer" has had to be interpreted for the purpose of s.3 of the Judicial Committee Act 1833 (*Lovibond v Governor General of Canada* [1930] A.C. 717), and the phrase "judicial proceedings" for the purpose of the Perjury Act 1911. See also *St Catherine's Flying School Ltd v Minister of National Revenue* [1956] 1 W.L.R. 1336. For the "non judicial" character of the functions exercised by inspectors conducting inquiries into proposals of the former Legal Government Commission, see *Wednesbury Corp v Ministry of Housing and Local Government (No.2)* [1966] 2 Q.B. 275. The provisions of the Tribunals and Inquiries Act 1971 were inapplicable to the exercise of "executive functions" by certain of the tribunals there specified (s.19(4)). The judicial functions of government departments are excluded from the terms of reference of the Parliamentary Commissioner for Administration (Parliamentary Commissioner Act 1967 s.5(1)).

[49] This emerges most clearly in the case on licensing tribunals: see *Royal Aquarium & Summer and Winter Gardens Society v Parkinson* [1892] 1 Q.B. 431; *Attwood v Chapman* [1914] 3 K.B. 275.

[50] *Tysons (Contractors) Ltd v Minister of Housing and Local Government* (1965) 63 L.G.R. 506. And in *R. v Secretary of State for the Environment Ex p. Ostler* [1977] 1 Q.B. 122, the administrative nature of the power to make a compulsory purchase order was one reason given for the court's adoption of a literal interpretation of the statutory limitation upon the availability of judicial review.

[51] A. Rubinstein, *Jurisdiction and Illegality* (1965), pp.137-139, 157-160.

(notably want or excess of jurisdiction) and a person aggrieved by a breach of natural justice may have recourse to other remedies, such as a declaratory order.

Until the 1960s it was generally assumed that certiorari and prohibition could not   **B-019**
issue to a body of persons acting in a purely administrative capacity[52] though in fact the orders had often issued in respect of acts and decisions bearing only a remote resemblance to the judicial. This assumption is now obsolete[53] and, in any event, the introduction of a single procedure an application for judicial review, in which any of the common law forms of relief may be sought, has further diminished the practical significance of having to characterise as judicial the order or decision impugned.

TESTS FOR IDENTIFYING JUDICIAL FUNCTIONS

The more closely a statutory body resembles a court in the strict sense, the more   **B-020**
likely is it that that body will be held to act in a judicial capacity. Indeed, the proceedings of a tribunal will not be held to be judicial for the purpose of attracting absolute privilege unless the tribunal resembles a court very closely. But it must not be assumed that because a body closely resembles a court, each and every one of its functions will be characterised as judicial. Even functions performed by courts are not necessarily characterised as judicial. Thus, it was recognised from early times that justices of the peace had ministerial duties and that their immunity from civil liability in respect of the erroneous performance of their judicial functions did not extend to their ministerial functions[54] and orders of mandamus frequently issue to compel inferior courts to carry out ministerial duties. Courts also exercise a wide variety of discretionary powers.[55] When exercised by courts, these powers are usually called judicial discretions; when exercised by bodies which are not courts they may possibly be called administrative acts.[56] And just as courts and bodies analogous to courts may be held to exercise non judicial functions, so may bodies that are not analogous to courts be held to exercise judicial functions. In short, the answer to the question whether a body is acting in a judicial capacity when performing a particular function does not necessarily depend upon the degree in which that body's general characteristics resemble those of an ordinary court, although the degree of resemblance may be a major factor influencing a decision that the function in question is judicial.

Conclusiveness

The first test that may be applied for distinguishing judicial functions from other   **B-021**
classes of functions turns upon whether the performance of the function terminates

---

52 See, e.g. *R. v Electricity Commissioners* [1924] 1 K.B. 171; *Nakkuda Ali v Jayaratne* [1951] A. C. 66; *R. v Manchester Legal Aid Committee Ex p. Brand (RA) & Co* [1952] 2 Q.B. 413.
53 See, e.g. *Ridge v Baldwin* [1964] A.C. 40 at 74-76; *R. v Birmingham City Justices Ex p. Chris Foreign Foods (Wholesalers) Ltd* [1970] 1 W.L.R. 1428: *R. v Liverpool Corp ex p. Liverpool Taxi Operators' Association* [1972] 2 Q.B. 299 at 308-309, 310; *R. v Hillingdon LBC Ex p. Royco Homes Ltd* [1947] Q.B. 720 at 728; *R. v Race Relations Board Ex p. Selvarajan* [1975] 1 W.L.R. 1686 at 1700. *R. v Barnsley MBC Ex p. Hook* [1976] 1 W.L.R. 1052. And in a case decided in part, at least, on the ground that certiorari was not available to impugn the proceedings in question, the old distinction was not revived: *R. v Hull Prison Board of Visitors Ex p. St Germain* [1978] Q.B. 678; rev'd [1979] Q.B. 425, CA.
54 *Green v Hundred of Bucclechurches* (1589) 1 Leon. 323 at 324; Justice Protection Act 1848 s.1.
55 I. Jennings, *The Law and the Constitution*, 5th edn (1959) App. I.
56 But a court may hold that it has no discretion when its exercise would require broad political considerations to be weighed: *Lord Advocate v Glasgow Corp*, 1973 S.L.T. 33 at 36.

in an order that has conclusive effect. The decisions of courts are binding and conclusive, inasmuch as they have the force of law without the need for confirmation or adoption by any other authority[57] and cannot be impeached (if the court has acted within its jurisdiction) indirectly in collateral proceedings. This characteristic is generally regarded as one of the essential features of judicial power.[58] And a body exercising powers which are of a merely advisory,[59] deliberative,[60] investigatory[61] or conciliatory[62] character, or which do not have legal effect until confirmed by another body,[63] or involve only the making of a preliminary decision,[64] will not normally be held to be acting in a judicial capacity. Nevertheless, the proceedings of bodies exercising functions of this type have sometimes been held to be judicial for the purpose of enjoying absolute privilege in the law of defamation; they are not invariably exempt from the duty to observe natural justice.[65] It must be added that where orders made by an administrative body are given finality by being exempted from judicial review, those orders do not thereby acquire a judicial quality if no other characteristic of judicial power is present. Power to make orders that are binding and conclusive is not, therefore, a decisive factor.

Trappings and procedure

B-022	A second test, or group test, for ascertaining whether statutory functions are of a judicial character turns primarily on the presence or absence of certain formal and procedural attributes. The manner in which courts proceed is distinguished by a number of special characteristics. They determine matters in cases initiated by parties; they must normally sit in public[66] they are empowered to compel the attendance of witnesses, who may be examined on oath; they are required to follow the

---

[57]	Where constitutional or statutory provision exists for courts to give advisory opinions, differences of opinion often arise as to whether the advisory jurisdiction is of a truly judicial character. The Judicial Committee of the PC has a special advisory jurisdiction under s.4 of the Judicial Committee Act 1833; its decision in other cases are in effect judgments, but take the form of advisory reports to Her Majesty, which are always promulgated by Order in Council: *Ibralebbe v R.* [1964] A.C. 900.

[58]	See, e.g. *Stow v Mineral Holdings (Australia) Pty Ltd* (1977) 51 A.L.J.R. 672, High Ct. Aust.

[59]	*Re Clifford and O'Sullivan* [1921] 2 A.C. 570; *R. v MacFarlane Ex p. O'Flanagan and O'Kelly* (1923) 32 C.L.R. 518; *R. v St Lawrence's Hospital. Caterham, Statutory Visitors Ex p. Pritchard* [1953] 1 W.L.R. 1158.

[60]	*R. v Legislative Committee of the Church Assembly Ex p. Haynes-Smith* [1928] 1K.B.411.

[61]	See, e.g. *Re Grosvenor & West-End Railway Terminus Hotel Co* (1897) 76 L.T. 337, *Hearts of Oak Assurance Co v Attorney General* [1932] A.C. 392; *O'Conner v Waldron* [1935] A.C. 76; *St John v Fraser* [1935] S.C.R. 441; *Lockwood v Commonwealth* (1954) 90 C.L.R. 177; *Ex p. Mineral Deposits Pty Ltd; re Claye and Lynch* (1959) S.R. (N.S.W.) 167; *R. v Fowler Ex p. McArthur* [1958] Qd.R 41; *R. v Coppel Ex p. Viney Industries Pty Ltd* [1962] V.R. 630; *Testro Bros Pty Ltd v Tait* (1963) 109 C.L.R. 353; *Guay v Lafleur* [1965] S.C.R. 12; *R. v Collins Ex p. ACTU-Solo Enterprises Pty Ltd* (1976) 8 A.L.R. 691, High Ct Aust.f. *Re Pergamon Press Ltd* [1971] Ch. 388: cf., however, the subsequent decision in *Maxwell v Department of Trade and Industry* [1974] Q.B. 523.

[62]	*Ayriss (FF) & Co v Alberta Labour Relations Board* (1960) 23 D.L.R. (2nd) 584; *R. v Clipsham Ex p. Basken* (1965) 49 D.L.R. (2nd) 747; *R. v Race Relations Board Ex p. Selvarajan* [1975] 1 W.L.R 1686.

[63]	*R. v Hastings Local Board of Health* (1865) 6B.& S. 401; *Re Local Government Board Ex p. Kingstown Commissioners* (1885)16 L.R.Ir.150; (1886)18 L.R.Ir. 509; *Re Zadrevec and Town of Brampton* (1973) 37 D.L.R. (3rd) 326.

[64]	*Jayawardane v Silva* [1970] 1 W.L.R. 1365: *Pearlberg v Varty* [1972] 1 W.L.R. 534 (cf. *Wiseman v Borneman* [1971] A.C. 297).

[65]	See e.g. *R. v Kent Police Authority Ex p. Godden* [1971] 2 Q.B. 662; *Committee for Justice and Liberty v National Energy Board* [1978] 1 S.C.R. 369. Alternatively, they may be held to be under a duty to "act fairly". And see generally, on the availability of certiorari to bodies which have no authority to make binding decisions, *R. v Criminal Injuries Compensation Board Ex p. Lain* [1967] 2 Q.B. 864.

[66]	*Scott v Scott* [1913] A.C. 417; *McPherson v McPherson* [1936] A.C. 177; *Stone v Stone* [1949] P.

rules of evidence; they are entitled to impose sanctions by way of imprisonment, fine, damages or mandatory or prohibitory orders, and to enforce obedience to their own commands. The fact that a body has been endowed with many of the "trappings of a court" may not always be sufficient to establish conclusively that it has been invested with judicial power[67] but the presence of such trappings tends to support that conclusion. Thus, in seeking to establish that the proceedings (or the functions) of a statutory body are to be classified as judicial for any given purpose, it maybe material to show that the body is called a "tribunal" which holds "sittings" and makes "decisions" in relation to "cases" before it,[68] that it is empowered to summon witnesses and administer oaths,[69] that it is normally required to sit in public,[70] that its members are debarred from sitting if personally interested in a matter before them,[71] that it has power to award costs[72] or to impose sanctions to enforce compliance with its orders.[73]

Perhaps the most obvious characteristic of ordinary courts is that they determine, on the basis of evidence and arguments submitted to them, disputes between two or more parties about their respective legal rights and duties, powers and liabilities, privileges and immunities. "It is a truism that the conception of the judicial function is inseparably bound up with the idea of a suit between parties, whether between Crown and subject or between subject and subject, and that it is the duty of the court to decide the issue between those parties".[74] If, then, the functions of a statutory body include the determination of issues that closely resemble jus inter partes, (rights as between parties) it is to be expected that for most if not all purposes those functions will be classified as judicial. **B-023**

First, when determining a lis inter partes (dispute between parties) a court gives a binding decision in relation to the dispute. A body that hears evidence in a dispute between parties will not normally be held to be acting in a judicial capacity unless it has power to give a binding decision. **B-024**

Secondly, in administrative law many of the issues that arise between contending parties are different in character from those typically determined by courts. An applicant may appear before a licensing tribunal to seek a legal privilege; a member of the public may appear to oppose the application. Superficially the tribunal seems to be deciding a lis inter partes; but if it decides to refuse the application it is not deciding only in favour of the objector; it is deciding that it is not in the public interest to grant the licence, and the decision may in effect be in favour of the public at **B-025**

165.

[67] cf. *Shell Co of Australia Ltd v Federal Commission of Taxation* [1931] A.C. 275 at 296-297 (dealing with judicial power under the Australian Constitution).

[68] *Jackson (FE) & Co v Price Tribunal (No.2)* [1950] N.Z.L.R 433 at 448-449; *New Zealand United Licensed Victuallers' Association of Employers v Price Tribunal* [1957] N.Z.L.R. 167 at 204, 207.

[69] And see *Attorney General v BBC* [1978] 1 W.L.R. 477 at 481.

[70] *Copartnership Farms v Harvey-Smith* [1918] 2 K.B. 405 at 411.

[71] *Copartnership Farms* [1918] 2 K.B. 405.

[72] *R. v Manchester Justices* [1899] 1 Q.B. 571; *R. v Sunderland Justices* [1901] 2 K.B. 357 at 369.

[73] The power of the Commonwealth Court of Conciliation and Arbitration to impose penalties for breaches or non-observance of its orders and awards was held by the PC in the Boilermakers' case to be "plainly judicial" ([1957] A.C. 288 at 322).

[74] *Labour Relations Board of Saskatchewan v John East Iron Works Ltd* [1949] A. C. 134 at 149. See also *Boulter v Kent Justices* [1897] A.C. 556 at 569; *Huddart Parker & Co Pty Ltd v Commonwealth* (1908) 8 C.L.R. 330 at 357 (Griffith CJ); Report of the Committee on Ministers' Powers (Cmd.4060 (1932), 73. cf. *Re Rubber Plastic and Cable Making Industry Award* (1963) 8 F.L.R. 396 (Commonwealth Industrial Court exercising judicial power of the commonwealth in interpreting award although no dispute between parties bound by the award).

large, who are not directly represented at the hearing.[75] In the context of inquiries relating to administrative orders which affect private interests in land, analogies with lis inter partes are also questionable. A local authority makes a compulsory purchase order: a property-owner lodges objections to the order; the Minister, who will have to decide whether or not to confirm the order, causes a local inquiry to be held; the local authority and the objector appear before the inspector who conducts the inquiry: the Minister considers the inspector's report and the objections, together with any other materials that appear to him to be relevant, and then makes his decision. He is entitled to disregard the weight of the evidence submitted at the inquiry and to found his decision on broad considerations of national policy. The procedural steps that have to be taken when an objection is lodged have therefore been described (perhaps too readily) as "merely a stage in the process of arriving at an administrative decision".[76]

B-026 These considerations have had some influence on the scope of judicial review. They help to explain why at one time licensing justices were held not to be a "court"[77] and why their proceedings have not been regarded as judicial for the purpose of attracting absolute privileged.[78] They also help to explain why a Minister who had to decide whether or not to confirm an order made by a local authority was not held to be under an obligation to observe the rules of natural justice at certain stages of his functions.[79]

B-027 Nevertheless, functions may become reviewable as "judicial" because of statutory interpolation of a procedure bearing a superficial resemblance to a lis inter partes. Thus, the proceedings of licensing bodies that are required to conduct hearings are sufficiently judicial to be amenable to review by certiorari and prohibition and must be conducted in conformity with natural justice. A Minister acting as confirming authority must act judicially in accordance with the rules of natural justice from the moment when objections are lodged against the local authority's order, although his functions have been characterised as "purely administrative" before objections have been lodged or if he himself is the initiating authority.[80] Indeed, preoccupation with the pseudo-concept of a lis, particularly in the latter class of situation, led to the development of a trend of opinion that a body could not be said to be acting in a judicial capacity unless it was expressly obliged to hold a hearing in respect of an issue between two or more contending parties. This heresy has been exposed, and the courts have conceded that in certain circumstances a body may be under an implied duty to act judicially in accordance with the rules of natural justice although not expressly required to determine a lis inter partes or anything resembling a lis.[81]

---

[75] *Boulter v Kent Justices* [1897] A.C. 556 at 569 (Lord Herschell); and *R. v Howard* [1902] 2 K.B. 363; *Tynemouth Corp v Attorney General* [1899] A.C. 293 at 307; *R. v Ashton Ex p. Walker* (1915) 85 L J.K.B. 27 at 30.

[76] *Johnson (B) & Co (Builders) Ltd v Minister of Health* [1947] 2 All E.R. 395 at 399 (Lord Greene MR); *R. v Canterbury (Archbishop) Ex p. Morant* [1944] K.B. 282 (observations on false analogies with lites inter partes); *Lithgow v Secretary of State for Scotland* 1973 S.L.T. 81; *R. v Medical Appeal Tribunal (Northern Region) Ex p. Hubble* [1958] 2 Q.B. 228 at 239-241; *R. v Deputy Industrial Injuries Commissioner Ex p. Moore* [1965] 1 Q.B. 456 at 472-474, 486, 489-491 (analyses of the inquisitional functions of tribunals involved in the administration of a social security scheme); *Bushell v Secretary of State for the Environment* [1981] A.C. 75.

[77] *Boulter v Kent Justices* [1897] A.C. 556; cf. *Jeffrey v Evans* [1964] 1 W.L.R. 505; *R. v East Riding of Yorkshire QS* [1968] 1 Q.B. 32.

[78] *Attwood v Chapman* [1914] 3 K.B. 275.

[79] *Johnson and Co (Builders) Ltd v Minister of Health* [1947] 2 All E.R. 395.

[80] *Johnson and Co (Builders) Ltd v Ministry of Health* [1947] 2 All E.R. 395.

[81] *Ridge v Baldwin* [1964] A.C. 40; *Maradana Mosque Trustees v Mahmud* [1967] 1 A.C. 13;

Interpretation and declaration

A typical lis inter partes culminates in a decision by a tribunal resolving any **B-028**
disputed questions of law or fact; the legal issues are determined by reference to
principles and rules already in being. A tribunal or other deciding body is therefore
likely to be held to be acting in a judicial capacity when, after investigation and
deliberation, it determines an issue conclusively by the application of a pre-
existing legal rule or another objective legal standard to the facts found by it. That
interpreting, declaring and applying the law are characteristic hallmarks of the
judicial function is too elementary a proposition to call for authoritative support.[82]
It would, of course, be absurd to insist that these are mechanical operations in which
an adjudicator has no freedom to choose between alternative rules or competing
interpretations, for judges can and do develop and modify the law when deciding
cases before them. And there is another reason why it would be inaccurate to
describe the judicial function as being merely to declare pre-existing rights or
obligations. P may be guilty of a crime; Q may be entitled to damages for breach
of contract; R may be entitled to social security benefit and S to compensation for
compulsory acquisition of his land: but until a competent tribunal has pronounced
on the law in relation to the facts of these cases, their liabilities and rights are incho-
ate; they acquire legal recognition by virtue of the judgment or order, which to this
extent has a "constitutive" effect.

There is, however, an obvious difference of substance and degree between a deci- **B-029**
sion that X is or is not liable to pay a certain tax in respect of a particular transaction, and a decision that it is in the public interest that Y should or should not be
granted an office development permit. In the first case the function is typically
judicial: in the second the function is typically administrative inasmuch as it entails
the exercise of almost unfettered discretionary power. The wider the "public policy"
content of an administrative discretion the more reluctant may the courts be to
require the repository of the direction, to "act judicially" according to natural
justice.[83]

Between clearly judicial acts and clearly administrative acts lies an awkward **B-030**
intermediate category, sometimes called judicial discretions. Judges exercise discretion in awarding costs, sentencing prisoners, removing arbitrators and trustees, varying the terms of a trust, permitting applications to be made out of time, and so on.
In exercising such powers they may create new rights and duties or otherwise vary
the status quo, but the powers are normally called "judicial" discretions, partly
because it is customary to call all the non-ministerial powers of courts judicial, and
partly because these discretionary powers have to be exercised according to reasonably well-settled principles, which are capable of being formulated and applied as
standards by higher courts when entertaining appeals against the manner in which
they have been exercised. The difference between a judicial discretion (which need
not necessarily be confided in a court stricto sensu) and an "administrative" discretion in which the subjective elements of policy and expediency loom large, is
seldom more than one of degree.[84] But, as has been indicated, the distinction is
sometimes of practical importance. If a court is prepared to review the factors on
which the exercise of a discretion has been founded, it is apt to label the discretion

---

Durayappah v Fernando [1967] 2 A.C. 337.
[82] *Moses v Parker* [1896] A. C. 245; *United Engineering Workers; Union v Devanayagam* [1968] A.C.
356.
[83] See, e.g. *R. v Brixton Prison Governor Ex p. Soblen* [1963] 2 Q.B. 243; *Essex CC v Ministry of Housing and Local Government* (1967) 66 L.G.R. 23; *Schmidt v Home Secretary* [1969] 2 Ch. 149.
[84] *R. v Manchester Legal Aid Committee Ex p. Brand (RA) & Co* [1952] 2 Q.B. 413.

"judicial"; if it feels that it would be inappropriate or impracticable to embark on review, it may observe that the discretionary power is purely administrative.[85] Although, as we shall see, courts in recent years have been much less reluctant to review the bases upon which administrative discretion has been exercised than they once were.

B-031 When certiorari and prohibition and the rules of natural justice were said to extend only to bodies performing judicial functions, courts were readier so to characterise them where the decisions or orders in question were made on the basis of fact-finding, rule-applying and the exercise of limited discretion. In a number of contexts, however, courts have been prepared to label as "judicial" discretionary acts that would seem more appropriately to be called administrative.

B-032 In addition "judicial" was given a wide meaning in some of the older cases on mandamus. A tribunal or other body may be under a ministerial duty, enforceable by mandamus, to determine a matter or exercise a discretion. But it is not normally under any duty to determine that matter or exercise its discretion in a particular way, and mandamus will not, therefore, issue to it for such a purpose. When explaining their inability to issue mandamus for these non-ministerial purposes the courts occasionally described the functions concerned as judicial, irrespective of whether they involved the determination of questions of legal right[86] or the exercise of wide discretionary powers.[87]

B-033 One may sum up by saying that the courts classified wide discretionary powers as judicial when they thought such a classification to be necessary or desirable in a particular situation; though power to alter existing rights and obligations is not at all characteristic of the archetypal judicial function. As long as the only alternatives were "ministerial" and "legislative" this latitudinarianism caused few difficulties. But once the distinct concept of "administrative" functions began to emerge, analytical and verbal problems proliferated, and they are likely to persist for some time despite the recent and welcome tendency to belittle the practical importance of classification of functions.

JUDICIAL PROCEEDINGS AND ABSOLUTE PRIVILEGE

B-034 A narrow conception of "judicial" has prevailed in cases where it has been sought to establish that the proceedings of administrative tribunals are judicial proceedings for the purpose of attracting absolute privilege in respect of defamatory statements and reports made to or by them. "The question ... in every case", it has been said, "is whether the tribunal in question has similar attributes to a court of justice or acts in a manner similar to that in which such courts act.[88] It may be sufficient, in order to establish the judicial character of the tribunal, to show either that it decides issues of a type normally decided by the ordinary courts[89] or that its

---

85 See, e.g. *Johnson (B) & Co (Builders) Ltd v Minister of Health* [1974] 2 All E.R. 395; *Attorney General v Bastow* [1957] 1 Q.B. 514. To this extent what is administrative is non-reviewable, whereas for certain purposes an act may be non-reviewable because it is "judicial".

86 See, e.g. *R. v Law* (1857) 7 E. & B. 366.

87 See, e.g. *R. v Lichfield (Bishop)* (1734) 7 Mod. 217 at 218; *Staverton v Ashburton* (1855) 4 E. & B. 526 at 531; *Ex p. Cook, re Dyson* (1869) 2 E. & B. 586; *R. v London Justices* [1895] 1 Q.B. 214 at 616.

88 *O'Connor v Waldron* [1935] A.C. 76 at 81 (Lord Atkin); *Royal Aquarium & Summer and Winter Gardens Society v Parkinson* [1892] 1 Q.B. 431 at 442 (Lord Esher MR).

89 *Keenan v Auckland Harbour Board* [1946] N.Z.L.R. 97 (where the authorities are fully reviewed);

constitution and procedure closely resemble those of ordinary courts.[90] But in this context it has been difficult to persuade the courts that administrative tribunals possess those characteristics,[91] even when they are determining questions of legal right. Thus, in one case it was held that a Court of Referees in determining whether claimants were legally entitled to unemployment benefit was "merely discharging administrative duties" because it was "not a body deciding between parties nor does its decision ... affect the status of an individuals".[92] In a more recent Australian case,[93] however, immunity was said to extend to the proceedings of a Board of Inquiry, even though its functions were to investigate and make recommendations to the Governor-in-Council. In general the courts have taken the view that it would be contrary to public policy to concede absolute privilege to the proceedings of such bodies and that they are adequately protected by qualified privilege.[94] It is significant that the only English case in which absolute privilege was held to attach to the proceedings of an administrative tribunal[95] concerned a local tribunal set up to determine claims to exemption from military service in wartime.[96] There is undoubtedly much to be said in favour of denying absolute privilege to parties and witnesses appearing before administrative tribunals, for the proceedings are usually lacking in the traditional formality that may tend to deter irresponsible persons from making maliciously untrue statements.[97] This factor does not necessarily apply with equal force to the members of the tribunal themselves, and it is arguable that where membership of a tribunal is deemed to require a degree of judicial detachment that is incompatible with membership of the House of Commons,[98] it ought to carry with it the same immunity from liability for words spoken in the course of proceedings

---

Atkins v Mays [1974] 2 N.Z.L.R. 459 (proceedings to hear objections to town planning scheme absolutely privileged).

[90] *Copartnership Farms v Harvey Smith* [1918] 2 K.B. 405 at 410.

[91] *Thompson v Turbott* [1962] N.Z.L.R. 298 at 308 (held that hearings before Public Service Board of Appeal were absolutely privileged).

[92] *Collins v Henry Whiteway & Co* [1927] 2 K.B. 378 at 383 (distinguished in *Keenan* [1946] N.Z.L.R. 97; *Mason v Brewis Bros Ltd* [1938] 2 All E.R. 420; *Smith v National Meter Co* [1945] K.B. 453).

[93] *Tampion v Anderson* [1973] V.R. 321 at 715.

[94] *Royal Aquarium, etc. Society v Parkinson* [1892] 1 Q.B. 431 at 447-448, 451; *Attwood v Chapman* [1914] 3 K.B. 275 at 285-286; *Collins v Henry Whiteway & Co* [1927] 2 K.B. 378 at 382-383. Fair and accurate newspaper reports of the proceedings of administrative tribunals held in public also enjoy qualified privilege (Defamation Act 1952 s.7 Sch. para.10(e)).

[95] The courts have been less reluctant to concede absolute privilege to the proceedings of tribunals which, although lacking some of the attributes of courts *stricto sensu*, have not been connected with the administrative process. See *Dawkins v Lord Rokeby* (1873) L.R. 8 Q.B. 225; (1875) L.R. 7 H.L. 744 (military court of inquiry); *Barratt v Kearns* [1905] 1 K.B. 504 (ecclesiastical commission of inquiry); *Bretherton v Kaye and Winneke* [1971] V.R. 111 (board of inquiry into police practices); *Lilley v Roney* (1892) 61 L.J.Q.B. 727; *Addis v Crocker* [1961] 1 Q.B. 11 (Disciplinary Committee of the Law Society); *Bottomley v Brougham* [1908] 1 K.B. 584; *Burr v Smith* [1909] 2 K.B. 306 (reports by official receivers); *Lincoln v Daniels* [1962] Q.B. 237 (cf. *Marrinan v Vibart* [1963] 1 Q.B. 234 at 528 (inquiry by Benchers of an Inn of Court into allegations of professional misconduct)); *Tampion v Anderson* [1973] V.R. 321 (inquiry into Scientology). cf. *O'Connor v Waldron* [1935] A.C. 76 (proceedings of Commission of Inquiry under Canadian Combines Investigation Act not protected by absolute privilege).

[96] *Copartnership Farms v Harvey-Smith* [1918] 2 K.B. 405: *Slack v Burr* (1918) 82 J.P. 91 (Scot.) (absolute privilege held to attach to statement by witness before wartime industrial arbitration tribunal); cf. *Keenan v Auckland Harbour Board* [1946] N.Z.L.R. 95; *Trapp v Mackie* [1979] 1 W.L.R. 377.

[97] For this reason the Council on Tribunals recommended that there should be no change in the law (Second Report, 14-15).

[98] House of Commons Disqualification Act 1975 s.1 and Sch.1.

and statements made in orders or judgments as is enjoyed by members of courts stricto sensu.[99]

CONCLUSIONS

B-035 Judicial acts may be identified by reference to their formal, procedural or substantive characteristics, or by a combination of any of them. An act may be judicial because it declares and interprets pre-existing rights, or because it changes those rights provided that the power to change them is not unfettered. A duty to act judicially in conformity with natural justice may be inferred from the impact of an administrative act or decision on individual rights. Although sometimes used in a narrow sense, the term "judicial" in cases involving review by certiorari and prohibition has generally been used in a very wide sense and has been dropped altogether as a requirement for the availability of these remedies. In natural justice cases, variations in linguistic usage have been particularly spectacular and frequently puzzling; but it is generally more profitable to concentrate on what the court has done than on what it has said. In cases where the absolute privilege accorded to judicial proceedings has been claimed in respect of proceedings before statutory tribunals, the courts have fairly consistently given a narrow interpretation to the term "judicial". Where the meaning of judicial has been brought into issue for other purposes (e.g. tort liability and collateral impeachment), the judgments have been singularly deficient in conceptual analysis, but it would seem that judicial acts are to be understood as including certain discretionary functions that could have been called administrative.

B-036 At this point terminological and conceptual problems may appear to be overwhelming. However, to an increasing extent courts exercising powers of judicial review in administrative law are abandoning servitude to their own concepts and asserting mastery over them.

---

[99] Absolute privilege has been conferred by statute upon reports made by the Parliamentary Ombudsman (Parliamentary Commissioner Act 1967 s.10(5)) as well as certain other communications made in connection with the performance of the Commissioner's functions.

APPENDIX C

Procedural Checklist

Issue	Outline	References
Has the claimant exhausted any alternative remedies?	Judicial review is generally a remedy of last resort and alternatives should be exhausted unless they are unsuitable.	16-014—16-021
Is the decision amenable to judicial review?	Is the decision taken by a public authority in relation to its public law powers?	Ch.3
If so, should judicial review be commenced in the Administrative Court or the Upper Tribunal?	Presently, Criminal Injuries Compensation Scheme cases, challenges to rejections of "fresh" asylum and human rights claims and determinations of the age of a minor from outside the UK may be reviewed in the Upper Tribunal.	1-100 17-006
Does the claimant have standing to bring judicial review proceedings?	Does the claimant have a sufficient interest in the matter to which the application relates (in general) or is the claimant a "victim" of the decision (under the HRA)?	Ch.2
Has the claim been brought in time?	Judicial review claims must be brought promptly and in any event within three months of the decision (in general) and within a year (under the HRA), subject to an extension of time being granted.	16-055—16-064
Pre-action steps by the claimant	The claimant should send a letter before action to the defendant in accordance with the Pre-Action Protocol for Judicial Review.	16-025
Funding	The claimant may need to seek public funding. Costs protection is available in public interest cases.	16-086—16-096
Pre-action steps by the defendant	The defendant should respond to the letter before action in accordance with the Pre-Action Protocol for Judicial Review, usually within 14 days.	16-025
Issuing the claim	The claim should be issued in the Administrative Court in accordance with CPR Part 54 and Practice Direction 54A or in accordance with the Upper Tribunal rules.	16-036—16-041

Issue	Outline	References
Where should the claim be issued?	The claimant should decide whether he wishes to issue the claim in London or at one of the regional centres (Practice Direction 54D).	16-003 and 16-040
Should the claimant apply for urgent consideration of the claim?	Where appropriate, the claimant may seek urgent consideration of the claim.	16-042
Should the parties seek expedition?	The parties should consider whether a "rolled-up" hearing is appropriate.	2-016 and 16-078
Should the claimant apply for interim relief?	Interim relief is available in appropriate cases.	16-075
Should the claimant seek a reference to the Court of Justice of the European Union (CJEU)?	Where a matter of EU law will be determinative and is unclear, a party may seek a reference to the CJEU.	14-108–14-110
How long does the defendant have to respond to the claim?	The defendant should file their Acknowledgement of Service (including their Summary Grounds of Defence) with the Administrative Court within 21 days and serve it on the other parties within 7 further days.	16-043
How is the claimant's application for judicial review determined?	The claimant's application is considered by a single judge on the papers. The judge will grant permission if he considers that the claim is arguable.	16-044—16-047
Should the defendant concede the claim if permission is granted?	Defendants often concede a claim which has been granted permission, rather than pursue a merits hearing.	16-077
What can the claimant do if permission is refused on the papers?	The claimant may renew their application within 7 days of the refusal of permission and the matter will then be determined at a (generally 30 minute) oral hearing in open court. If the Judge certifies the claim as totally without merit, there is no right to an oral renewal and the claimant will have to seek permission from the Court of Appeal.	16-066–16-069
Can the defendant attend the oral permission hearing?	The defendant may attend the oral permission hearing and make submissions. The defendant will usually not recover their costs of attending the oral permission hearing.	16-066 and 16-092

Issue	Outline	References
What happens if permission is refused after an oral hearing?	In a civil matter, the claimant may appeal to the Court of Appeal, but not generally from there to the Supreme Court.	16-067–16-069
What happens if permission is granted?	The judge granting permission (on the papers or orally) will determine what are the next steps. In general, the claimant will have to pay the relevant fee and the defendant will have to file and serve their Detailed Grounds of Defence and any evidence on which they propose to rely (generally within 35 days of the grant of permission).	16-078–16-082
What do the parties have to do before the hearing?	The claimant must file and serve their Skeleton Argument and the hearing bundle 21 days before the hearing. The defendant should file and serve their Skeleton Argument 14 days before the hearing. The parties should file and serve their Schedules of Costs at least a day before the hearing.	16-076
What remedies may be granted by the court?	The Administrative Court may quash the decision challenged, or prohibit the public authority from taking a step or require the public authority to fulfil its statutory duties. The Administrative Court may also grant a declaration or an injunction and award damages or a restitutionary remedy in appropriate cases. The court may make a declaration of incompatibility under the Human Rights Act. The court may withhold remedies at its discretion and is required to do so if the ground of review relied on would have made no difference to the outcome.	Ch.18 13-050
Can the parties apply for their costs?	The successful party will generally be entitled to their costs.	16-096
What can the losing party in the Administrative Court do?	In civil cases, the losing party may appeal to the Court of Appeal and should request permission initially from the judge in the Administrative Court. The losing party may also apply for permission to appeal to the Court of Appeal. In criminal cases, an appeal lies straight to the Supreme Court where the case raises a question of general public importance.	16-083–16-085

Issue	Outline	References
What can the losing party in the Court of Appeal do?	The losing party may appeal to the Supreme Court and should request permission initially form the Court of Appeal. The losing party may also apply to the Supreme Court for permission.	16-085

APPENDIX D

Extracts from the Senior Courts Act 1981 (formerly the Supreme Court Act 1981)

Other particular fields of jurisdiction D-001

[Mandatory, prohibiting and quashing orders.

29.— ¹]

[(1)   The orders of mandamus, prohibition and certiorari shall be known instead as mandatory, prohibiting and quashing orders respectively.

(1A)   The High Court shall have jurisdiction to make mandatory, prohibiting and quashing orders in those classes of case in which, immediately before 1st May 2004, it had jurisdiction to make orders of mandamus, prohibition and certiorari respectively.]²

(2)   Every such order shall be final, subject to any right of appeal therefrom.

(3)   In relation to the jurisdiction of the Crown Court, other than its jurisdiction in matters relating to trial on indictment, the High Court shall have all such jurisdiction to make [mandatory, prohibiting or quashing orders]³ as the High Court possesses in relation to the jurisdiction of an inferior court.

[(3A)   The High Court shall have no jurisdiction to make mandatory, prohibiting or quashing orders in relation to the jurisdiction of the Court Martial in matters relating to—

(a)   trial by the Court Martial for an offence; or

(b)   appeals from the Service Civilian Court.]⁴

(4)   The power of the High Court under any enactment to require justices of the peace or a judge or officer of a county court to do any act relating to the duties of their respective offices, or to require a magistrates' court to state a case for the opinion of the High Court, in any case where the High Court formerly had by virtue of any enactment jurisdiction to make a rule absolute, or an order, for any of those purposes, shall be exercisable by [mandatory order].⁵

[(5)   In any statutory provision—

(a)   references to mandamus or to a writ or order of mandamus shall be read as references to a mandatory order;

(b)   references to prohibition or to a writ or order of prohibition shall be read as references to a prohibiting order;

---

¹   Words substituted by Civil Procedure (Modification of Supreme Court Act 1981) Order 2004/1033 art.3(e) (May 1, 2004).

²   S.29(1)–(1A) substituted for s.29(1) by Civil Procedure (Modification of Supreme Court Act 1981) Order 2004/1033 art.3(a) (May 1, 2004).

³   Words substituted by Civil Procedure (Modification of Supreme Court Act 1981) Order 2004/1033 art.3(b) (May 1, 2004).

⁴   Substituted by Armed Forces Act 2006 c. 52 Sch.16 para.93 (October 31, 2009).

⁵   Words substituted by Civil Procedure (Modification of Supreme Court Act 1981) Order 2004/1033 art.3(c) (May 1, 2004).

(c)   references to certiorari or to a writ or order of certiorari shall be read
      as references to a quashing order; and
(d)   references to the issue or award of a writ of mandamus, prohibition or
      certiorari shall be read as references to the making of the correspond-
      ing mandatory, prohibiting or quashing order.]⁶

[(6)   In subsection (3) the reference to the Crown Court's jurisdiction in matters relating to trial on indictment does not include its jurisdiction relating to orders
under section 17 of the Access to Justice Act 1999.]⁷

Application for judicial review

31.—(1)   An application to the High Court for one or more of the following
forms of relief, namely—
[(a)   a mandatory, prohibiting or quashing order;]⁸
(b)   a declaration or injunction under subsection (2); or
(c)   an injunction under section 30 restraining a person not entitled to do
      so from acting in an office to which that section applies,
shall be made in accordance with rules of court by a procedure to be known as an
application for judicial review.

(2)   A declaration may be made or an injunction granted under this subsection
in any case where an application for judicial review, seeking that relief, has been
made and the High Court considers that, having regard to—
(a)   the nature of the matters in respect of which relief may be granted by
      [mandatory, prohibiting or quashing orders]⁹;
(b)   the nature of the persons and bodies against whom relief may be
      granted by such orders; and
(c)   all the circumstances of the case,
it would be just and convenient for the declaration to be made or the injunction to
be granted, as the case may be.

(3)   No application for judicial review shall be made unless the leave of the
High Court has been obtained in accordance with rules of court; and the court shall
not grant leave to make such an application unless it considers that the applicant
has a sufficient interest in the matter to which the application relates.

[(4)   On an application for judicial review the High Court may award to the applicant damages, restitution or the recovery of a sum due if—
(a)   the application includes a claim for such an award arising from any
      matter to which the application relates; and
(b)   the court is satisfied that such an award would have been made if the
      claim had been made in an action begun by the applicant at the time
      of making the application.]¹⁰

[(5)   If, on an application for judicial review, the High Court quashes the decision to which the application relates, it may in addition—
(a)   remit the matter to the court, tribunal or authority which made the deci-

---

⁶   Substituted by Civil Procedure (Modification of Supreme Court Act 1981) Order 2004/1033 art.3(d)
    (May 1, 2004).
⁷   Added by Access to Justice Act 1999 c. 22 Sch.4 para.23 (April 2, 2001 subject to transitional provi-
    sions specified in SI 2001/916 Sch.2 para.2).
⁸   Substituted by Civil Procedure (Modification of Supreme Court Act 1981) Order 2004/1033 art.4(a)
    (May 1, 2004).
⁹   Words substituted by Civil Procedure (Modification of Supreme Court Act 1981) Order 2004/1033
    art.4(b) (May 1, 2004).
¹⁰ Substituted by Civil Procedure (Modification of Supreme Court Act 1981) Order 2004/1033 art.4(c)
    (May 1, 2004).

sion, with a direction to reconsider the matter and reach a decision in accordance with the findings of the High Court, or

(b) substitute its own decision for the decision in question.

(5A) But the power conferred by subsection (5)(b) is exercisable only if—

(a) the decision in question was made by a court or tribunal,

(b) the decision is quashed on the ground that there has been an error of law, and

(c) without the error, there would have been only one decision which the court or tribunal could have reached.

(5B) Unless the High Court otherwise directs, a decision substituted by it under subsection (5)(b) has effect as if it were a decision of the relevant court or tribunal.][11]

(6) Where the High Court considers that there has been undue delay in making an application for judicial review, the court may refuse to grant—

(a) leave for the making of the application; or

(b) any relief sought on the application,

if it considers that the granting of the relief sought would be likely to cause substantial hardship to, or substantially prejudice the rights of, any person or would be detrimental to good administration.

(7) Subsection (6) is without prejudice to any enactment or rule of court which has the effect of limiting the time within which an application for judicial review may be made.

[Transfer of judicial review applications to Upper Tribunal

31A.—(1) This section applies where an application is made to the High Court—

(a) for judicial review, or

(b) for permission to apply for judicial review.

(2) If Conditions 1, 2, 3 and 4 are met, the High Court must by order transfer the application to the Upper Tribunal.

[(2A) If Conditions 1, 2, 3 and 5 are met, but Condition 4 is not, the High Court must by order transfer the application to the Upper Tribunal.][12]

(3) If Conditions 1, 2 and 4 are met, but Condition 3 is not, the High Court may by order transfer the application to the Upper Tribunal if it appears to the High Court to be just and convenient to do so.

(4) Condition 1 is that the application does not seek anything other than—

(a) relief under section 31(1)(a) and (b);

(b) permission to apply for relief under section 31(1)(a) and (b);

(c) an award under section 31(4);

(d) interest;

(e) costs.

(5) Condition 2 is that the application does not call into question anything done by the Crown Court.

(6) Condition 3 is that the application falls within a class specified under section 18(6) of the Tribunals, Courts and Enforcement Act 2007.

(7) Condition 4 is that the application does not call into question any decision made under—

---

[11] S.31(5)–(5B) substituted for s.31(5) by Tribunals, Courts and Enforcement Act 2007 c. 15 Pt 7 s.141 (April 6, 2008).

[12] Added by Borders, Citizenship and Immigration Act 2009 c. 11 Pt 4 s.53(1)(a) (August 8, 2011).

      (a)   the Immigration Acts,

      (b)   the British Nationality Act 1981 (c. 61),

      (c)   any instrument having effect under an enactment within paragraph (a) or (b), or

      (d)   any other provision of law for the time being in force which determines British citizenship, British overseas territories citizenship, the status of a British National (Overseas) or British Overseas citizenship.

[(8)   Condition 5 is that the application calls into question a decision of the Secretary of State not to treat submissions as an asylum claim or a human rights claim within the meaning of Part 5 of the Nationality, Immigration and Asylum Act 2002 wholly or partly on the basis that they are not significantly different from material that has previously been considered (whether or not it calls into question any other decision).[13]][14]]

---

[13]   Added by Borders, Citizenship and Immigration Act 2009 c. 11 Pt 4 s.53(1)(b) (August 8, 2011).

[14]   Added by Tribunals, Courts and Enforcement Act 2007 c. 15 Pt 1 c.2 s.19(1) (November 3, 2008).

APPENDIX E

Extracts from the Tribunals, Courts and Enforcement Act 2007

"Judicial review"

Upper Tribunal's "judicial review" jurisdiction

15.—(1) The Upper Tribunal has power, in cases arising under the law of **E-001** England and Wales or under the law of Northern Ireland, to grant the following kinds of relief-
- (a) a mandatory order;
- (b) a prohibiting order;
- (c) a quashing order;
- (d) a declaration;
- (e) an injunction.

(2) The power under subsection (1) may be exercised by the Upper Tribunal if-
- (a) certain conditions are met (see section 18), or
- (b) the tribunal is authorised to proceed even though not all of those conditions are met (see section 19(3) and (4)).

(3) Relief under subsection (1) granted by the Upper Tribunal-
- (a) has the same effect as the corresponding relief granted by the High Court on an application for judicial review, and
- (b) is enforceable as if it were relief granted by the High Court on an application for judicial review.

(4) In deciding whether to grant relief under subsection (l)(a), (b) or (c), the Upper Tribunal must apply the principles that the High Court would apply in deciding whether to grant that relief on an application for judicial review.

(5) In deciding whether to grant relief under subsection (l)(d) or (e), the Upper Tribunal must-
- (a) in cases arising under the law of England and Wales apply the principles that the High Court would apply in deciding whether to grant that relief under section 31(2) of the Supreme Court Act 1981 (c.54) on an application for judicial review, and
- (b) in cases arising under the law of Northern Ireland apply the principles that the High Court would apply in deciding whether to grant that relief on an application for judicial review.

(6) For the purposes of the application of subsection (3)(a) in relation to cases arising under the law of Northern Ireland-
- (a) a mandatory order under subsection (1)(a) shall be taken to correspond to an order of mandamus,
- (b) a prohibiting order under subsection (1)(b) shall be taken to correspond to an order of prohibition, and

(c)   a quashing order under subsection (l)(c) shall be taken to correspond to an order of certiorari.

Application for relief under section 15(1)

E-002   **16.**—(1)   This section applies in relation to an application to the Upper Tribunal for relief under section 15(1).

(2)   The application may be made only if permission (or, in a case arising under the law of Northern Ireland, leave) to make it has been obtained from the tribunal.

(3)   The tribunal may not grant permission (or leave) to make the application unless it considers that the applicant has a sufficient interest in the matter to which the application relates.

(4)   Subsection (5) applies where the tribunal considers_
  (a)   that there has been undue delay in making the application, and
  (b)   that granting the relief sought on the application would be likely to cause substantial hardship to, or substantially prejudice the rights of, any person or would be detrimental to good administration.

(5)   The tribunal may-
  (a)   refuse to grant permission (or leave) for the making of the application;
  (b)   refuse to grant any relief sought on the application.

(6)   The tribunal may award to the applicant damages, restitution or the recovery of a sum due if-
  (a)   the application includes a claim for such an award arising from any matter to which the application relates, and
  (b)   the tribunal is satisfied that such an award would have been made by the High Court if the claim had been made in an action begun in the High Court by the applicant at the time of making the application.

(7)   An award under subsection (6) maybe enforced as if it were an award of the High Court.

(8)   Where-
  (a)   the tribunal refuses to grant permission (or leave) to apply for relief under section 15(1),
  (b)   the applicant appeals against that refusal, and
  (c)   the Court of Appeal grants the permission (or leave),
the Court of Appeal may go on to decide the application for relief under section 15(1).

(9)   Subsections (4) and (5) do not prevent Tribunal Procedure Rules from limiting the time within which applications may be made.

Quashing orders under section 15(1): supplementary provision

E-003   **17.**—(1)   If the Upper Tribunal makes a quashing order under section 15(l)(c) in respect of a decision, it may in addition-
  (a)   remit the matter concerned to the court, tribunal or authority that made the decision, with a direction to reconsider the matter and reach a decision in accordance with the findings of the Upper Tribunal, or
  (b)   substitute its own decision for the decision in question.

(2)   The power conferred by subsection (l)(b) is exercisable only if-
  (a)   the decision in question was made by a court or tribunal,
  (b)   the decision is quashed on the ground that there has been an error of law, and
  (c)   without the error, there would have been only one decision that the court or tribunal could have reached.

(3)   Unless the Upper Tribunal otherwise directs, a decision substituted by it under subsection (1)(b) has effect as if it were a decision of the relevant court or tribunal.

Limits of jurisdiction under section 15(1)

18.—(1)   This section applies where an application made to the Upper Tribunal   **E-004**
seeks (whether or not alone)-
  (a)   relief under section 15(1), or
  (b)   permission (or, in a case arising under the law of Northern Ireland, leave) to apply for relief under section 15(1).
(2)   If Conditions 1 to 4 are met, the tribunal has the function of deciding the application.
(3)   If the tribunal does not have the function of deciding the application, it must by order transfer the application to the High Court.
(4)   Condition 1 is that the application does not seek anything other than-
  (a)   relief under section 15(1);
  (b)   permission (or, in a case arising under the law of Northern Ireland, leave) to apply for relief under section 15(1);
  (c)   an award under section 16(6);
  (d)   interest;
  (e)   costs.
(5)   Condition 2 is that the application does not call into question anything done by the Crown Court.
(6)   Condition 3 is that the application falls within a class specified for the purposes of this subsection in a direction given in accordance with Part 1 of Schedule 2 to the Constitutional Reform Act 2005 (c. 4).
(7)   The power to give directions under subsection (6) includes-
  (a)   power to vary or revoke directions made in exercise of the power, and
  (b)   power to make different provision for different purposes.
(8)   Condition 4 is that the judge presiding at the hearing of the application is either-
  (a)   a judge of the High Court or the Court of Appeal in England and Wales or Northern Ireland, or a judge of the Court of Session, or
  (b)   such other persons as may be agreed from time to time between the Lord Chief Justice, the Lord President, or the Lord Chief Justice of Northern Ireland, as the case may be, and the Senior President of Tribunals.
(9)   Where the application is transferred to the High Court under subsection (3)-
  (a)   the application is to be treated for all purposes as if it-
    (i)   had been made to the High Court, and
    (ii)   sought things corresponding to those sought from the tribunal, and
  (b)   any steps taken, permission (or leave) given or orders made by the tribunal in relation to the application are to be treated as taken, given or made by the High Court.
(10)   Rules of court may make provision for the purpose of supplementing subsection (9).
(11)   The provision that may be made by Tribunal Procedure Rules about amendment of an application for relief under section 15(1) includes, in particular, provision about amendments that would cause the application to become transferrable under subsection (3).
(12)   For the purposes of subsection (9)(a)(ii), in relation to an application transferred to the High Court in Northern Ireland-

    (a)   an order of mandamus shall be taken to correspond to a mandatory order under section 15(1)(a),

    (b)   an order of prohibition shall be taken to correspond to a prohibiting order under section 15(1)(b), and

    (c)   an order of certiorari shall be taken to correspond to a quashing order under section 15(1)(c).

APPENDIX F

Extracts from the Human Rights Act 1998

An Act to give further effect to rights and freedoms guaranteed under the **F-001**
European Convention on Human Rights; to make provision with respect to holders of certain judicial offices who become judges of the European Court of Human Rights; and for connected purposes.

[9th November 1998]

BE IT ENACTED by the Queen's most Excellent Majesty, by and with the
advice and consent of the Lords Spiritual and Temporal, and Commons, in this
present Parliament assembled, and by the authority of the same, as follows:

Introduction

The Convention Rights.

1.—(1)   In this Act "the Convention rights" means the rights and fundamental   **F-002**
freedoms set out in
(a)   Articles 2 to 12 and 14 of the Convention,
(b)   Articles 1 to 3 of the First Protocol, and
(c)   [Article 1 of the Thirteenth Protocol][1] as read with Articles 16 to 18
of the Convention.

(2)   Those Articles are to have effect for the purposes of this Act subject to any
designated derogation or reservation (as to which see sections 14 and 15).

(3)   The Articles are set out in Schedule 1.

(4)   The Secretary of State may by order make such amendments to this Act as
he considers appropriate to reflect the effect, in relation to the United Kingdom, of
a protocol.

(5)   In subsection (4) "protocol" means a protocol to the Convention
(a)   which the United Kingdom has ratified; or
(b)   which the United Kingdom has signed with a view to ratification.

(6)   No amendment may be made by an order under subsection (4) so as to come
into force before the protocol concerned is in force in relation to the United
Kingdom.

Interpretation of Convention rights.

2.—(1)   A court or tribunal determining a question which has arisen in connec-   **F-003**
tion with a Convention right must take into account any
(a)   judgment, decision, declaration or advisory opinion of the European
Court of Human Rights,
(b)   opinion of the Commission given in a report adopted under Article 31
of the Convention,

---

[1]   Words substituted by Human Rights Act 1998 (Amendment) Order 2004/1547 art.2(1).

    (c)   decision of the Commission in connection with Article 26 or 27(2) of the Convention, or

    (d)   decision of the Committee of Ministers taken under Article 46 ofthe Convention, whenever made or given, so far as, in the opinion of the court or tribunal, it is relevant to the proceedings in which that question has arisen.

(2)   Evidence of any judgment, decision, declaration or opinion of which account may have to be taken under this section is to be given in proceedings before any court or tribunal in such manner as may be provided by rules.

(3)   In this section "rules" means rules of court or, in the case of proceedings before a tribunal, rules made for the purposes of this section

    (a)   by [the Lord Chancellor or][2] the Secretary of State, in relation to any proceedings outside Scotland;

    (b)   by the Secretary of State, in relation to proceedings in Scotland; or

    (c)   by a Northern Ireland department, in relation to proceedings before a tribunal in Northern Ireland

        (i)   which deals with transferred mailers; and

        (ii)   for which no rules made under paragraph (a) are in force.

Legislation

Interpretation of legislation.

F-004   **3.**—(1)   So far as it is possible to do so, primary legislation and subordinate legislation must be read and given effect in a way which is compatible with the Convention rights.

(2)   This section

    (a)   applies to primary legislation and subordinate legislation whenever enacted;

    (b)   does not affect the validity, continuing operation or enforcement of any incompatible primary legislation; and

    (c)   does not affect the validity, continuing operation or enforcement of any incompatible subordinate legislation if (disregarding any possibility of revocation) primary legislation prevents removal of the incompatibility.

Declaration of incompatibility.

F-005   **4.**—(1)   Subsection (2) applies in any proceedings in which a court determines whether a provision of primary legislation is compatible with a Convention right.

(2)   If the court is satisfied that the provision is incompatible with a Convention right, it may make a declaration of that incompatibility.

(3)   Subsection (4) applies in any proceedings in which a court determines whether a provision of subordinate legislation, made in the exercise of a power conferred by primary legislation, is compatible with a Convention right.

(4)   If the court is satisfied—

    (a)   that the provision is incompatible with a Convention right, and

    (b)   that (disregarding any possibility of revocation) the primary legislation concerned prevents removal of the incompatibility,

it may make a declaration of that incompatibility.

(5)   In this section "court" means—

---

[2]   Words inserted by Transfer of Functions (Lord Chancellor and Secretary of State) Order 2005/3429 Sch.1 para.3

[(a)   the Supreme Court;][3]
(b)   the Judicial Committee of the Privy Council;
(c)   the [Court Martial Appeal Court][4];
(d)   in Scotland, the High Court of Justiciary sitting otherwise than as a trial court or the Court of Session;
(e)   in England and Wales or Northern Ireland, the High Court or the Court of Appeal [;][5]
[(f)   the Court of Protection, in any matter being dealt with by the President of the Family Division, the Vice-Chancellor or a puisne judge of the High Court.][6]

(6)   A declaration under this section ("a declaration of incompatibility")—
(a)   does not affect the validity, continuing operation or enforcement of the provision in respect of which it is given; and
(b)   is not binding on the parties to the proceedings in which it is made.

Right of Crown to intervene.

5.—(1)   Where a court is considering whether to make a declaration of incompatibility, the Crown is entitled to notice in accordance with rules of court.   **F-006**

(2)   In any case to which subsection (1) applies—
(a)   a Minister of the Crown (or a person nominated by him),
(b)   a member of the Scottish Executive,
(c)   a Northern Ireland Minister,
(d)   a Northern Ireland department,
is entitled, on giving notice in accordance with rules of court, to be joined as a party to the proceedings.

(3)   Notice under subsection (2) may be given at any time during the proceedings.

(4)   A person who has been made a party to criminal proceedings (other than in Scotland) as the result of a notice under subsection (2) may, with leave, appeal to the [Supreme Court][7] against any declaration of incompatibility made in the proceedings.

(5)   In subsection (4)—

"criminal proceedings" includes all proceedings before the [Court Martial Appeal Court][8]; and
"leave" means leave granted by the court making the declaration of incompatibility or by the [Supreme Court][9].

Public authorities

Acts of public authorities.

6.—(1)   It is unlawful for a public authority to act in a way which is incompatible with a Convention right.   **F-007**

(2)   Subsection (1) does not apply to an act if—

---

3   Substituted by Constitutional Reform Act 2005 c. 4 Sch.9(1) para.66(2) (October 1, 2009).
4   Words substituted by Armed Forces Act 2006 c. 52 Sch.16 para.156 (October 31, 2009).
5   Added by Mental Capacity Act 2005 c. 9 Sch.6 para.43 (October 1, 2007).
6   Added by Mental Capacity Act 2005 c. 9 Sch.6 para.43 (October 1, 2007).
7   Words substituted by Constitutional Reform Act 2005 c. 4 Sch.9(1) para.66(3) (October 1, 2009).
8   Words substituted by Armed Forces Act 2006 c. 52 Sch.16 para.157 (October 31, 2009).
9   Words substituted by Constitutional Reform Act 2005 c. 4 Sch.9(1) para.66(3) (October 1, 2009).

(a) as the result of one or more provisions of primary legislation, the authority could not have acted differently; or

(b) in the case of one or more provisions of, or made under, primary legislation which cannot be read or given effect in a way which is compatible with the Convention rights, the authority was acting so as to give effect to or enforce those provisions.

(3) In this section "public authority" includes—

(a) a court or tribunal, and

(b) any person certain of whose functions are functions of a public nature,

but does not include either House of Parliament or a person exercising functions in connection with proceedings in Parliament.

[...][10]

(5) In relation to a particular act, a person is not a public authority by virtue only of subsection (3)(b) if the nature of the act is private.

(6) "An act" includes a failure to act but does not include a failure to—

(a) introduce in, or lay before, Parliament a proposal for legislation; or

(b) make any primary legislation or remedial order.

Proceedings.

F-008

7.—(1) A person who claims that a public authority has acted (or proposes to act) in a way which is made unlawful by section 6(1) may

(a) bring proceedings against the authority under this Act in the appropriate court or tribunal, or

(b) rely on the Convention right or rights concerned in any legal proceedings, but only if he is (or would be) a victim of the unlawful act.

(2) In subsection (1)(a) "appropriate court or tribunal" means such court or tribunal as may be determined in accordance with rules; and proceedings against an authority include a counterclaim or similar proceedings.

(3) If the proceedings arc brought on an application for judicial review, the applicant is to be taken to have a sufficient interest in relation to the unlawful act only if he is, or would be, a victim of that act.

(4) If the proceedings are made by way of a petition for judicial review in Scotland, the applicant shall be taken to have title and interest to sue in relation to the unlawful act only if he is, or would be, a victim of that act.

(5) Proceedings under subsection (1)(a) must be brought before the end of

(a) the period of one year beginning with the date on which the act complained of took place; or

(b) such longer period as the court or tribunal considers equitable having regard to all the circumstances, but that is subject to any rule imposing a stricter time limit in relation to the procedure in question.

(6) In subsection (1)(b) "legal proceedings" includes

(a) proceedings brought by or at the instigation of a public authority; and

(b) an appeal against the decision of a court or tribunal.

(7) For the purposes of this section, a person is a victim of an unlawful act only if he would be a victim for the purposes of Article 34 of the Convention if proceedings were brought in the European Court of Human Rights in respect of that act.

(8) Nothing in this Act creates a criminal offence.

(9) In this section "rules" means

(a) in relation to proceedings before a court or tribunal outside Scotland,

---

[10] Repealed by Constitutional Reform Act 2005 c. 4 Sch.18(5) para.1 (October 1, 2009).

         rules made by the [the Lord Chancellor or][11] Secretary of State for the
         purposes of this section or rules of court,

   (b)   in relation to proceedings before a court or tribunal in Scotland, rules
         made by the Secretary of State for those purposes,

   (c)   in relation to proceedings before a tribunal in Northern Ireland

      (i)   which deals with transferred matters; and

     (ii)   for which no rules made under paragraph (a) are in force, rules
           made by a Northern Ireland department for those purposes, and
           includes provision made by order under section 1 of the Courts
           and Legal Services Act 1990.

  (10)   In making rules, regard must be had to section 9.

  (11)   The Minister who has power to make rules in relation to a particular tribunal may, to the extent he considers it necessary to ensure that the tribunal can provide an appropriate remedy in relation to an act (or proposed act) of a public authority which is (or would be) unlawful as a result of section 6(1), by order add to

   (a)   the relief or remedies which the tribunal may grant; or

   (b)   the grounds on which it may grant any of them.

  (12)   An order made under subsection (11) may contain such incidental, supplemental, consequential or transitional provision as the Minister making it considers appropriate.

  (13)   "The Minister" includes the Northern Ireland department concerned.

Judicial remedies.

  8.—(1)   In relation to any act (or proposed act) of a public authority which the court finds is (or would be) unlawful, it may grant such relief or remedy, or make such order, within its powers as it considers just and appropriate.   **F-009**

  (2)   But damages may be awarded only by a court which has power to award damages, or to order the payment of compensation, in civil proceedings.

  (3)   No award of damages is to be made unless, taking account of all the circumstances of the case, including

   (a)   any other relief or remedy granted, or order made, in relation to the act
         in question (by that or any other court), and

   (b)   the consequences of any decision (of that or any other court) in respect
         of that act, the court is satisfied that the award is necessary to afford
         just satisfaction to the person in whose favour it is made.

  (4)   In determining

   (a)   whether to award damages, or

   (b)   the amount of an award,

the court must take into account the principles applied by the European Court of Human Rights in relation to the award of compensation under Article 41 of the Convention.

  (5)   A public authority against which damages are awarded is to be treated

   (a)   in Scotland, for the purposes of section 3 of the Law Reform (Miscel-
         laneous Provisions) (Scotland) Act 1940 as if the award were made in
         an action of damages in which the authority has been found liable in
         respect of loss or damage to the person to whom the award is made;

   (b)   for the purposes of the Civil Liability (Contribution) Act 1978 as li-

---

[11] Words inserted by Transfer of Functions (Lord Chancellor and Secretary of State) Order 2005/ 3429 Sch. 1 para.3

able in respect of damage suffered by the person to whom the award is made.

(6)   In this section

"court" includes a tribunal;
"damages" means damages for an unlawful act of a public authority; and
"unlawful" means unlawful under section 6(1).

Judicial acts.

F-010   **9.**—(1)   Proceedings under section 7(1)(a) in respect of a judicial act may be brought only—

    (a)   by exercising a right of appeal;

    (b)   on an application (in Scotland a petition) for judicial review; or

    (c)   in such other forum as may be prescribed by rules.

(2)   That does not affect any rule of law which prevents a court from being the subject of judicial review.

(3)   In proceedings under this Act in respect of a judicial act done in good faith, damages may not be awarded otherwise than to compensate a person to the extent required by Article 5(5) of the Convention.

(4)   An award of damages permitted by subsection (3) is to be made against the Crown; but no award may be made unless the appropriate person, if not a party to the proceedings, is joined.

(5)   In this section—

"appropriate person" means the Minister responsible for the court concerned, or a person or government department nominated by him;

"court" includes a tribunal;

"judge" includes a member of a tribunal, a justice of the peace [(or, in Northern Ireland, a lay magistrate)][12] and a clerk or other officer entitled to exercise the jurisdiction of a court;

"judicial act" means a judicial act of a court and includes an act done on the instructions, or on behalf, of a judge; and

"rules" has the same meaning as in section 7(9).

Remedial action

Power to take remedial action.

F-011   **10.**—(1)   This section applies if

    (a)   a provision of legislation has been declared under section 4 to be incompatible with a Convention right and, if an appeal lies

       (i)   all persons who may appeal have stated in writing that they do not intend to do so;

      (ii)   the time for bringing an appeal has expired and no appeal has been brought within that time; or

     (iii)   an appeal brought within that time has been determined or abandoned; or

    (b)   it appears to a Minister of the Crown or Her Majesty in Council that, having regard to a finding of the European Court of Human Rights made after the coming into force of this section in proceedings against

---

[12]   Words inserted by Justice (Northern Ireland) Act 2002 c. 26 Sch.4 para.39 (April 1, 2005 subject to transitional provisions and savings specified in 2002 c.26 s.89)

the United Kingdom, a provision of legislation is incompatible with an obligation of the United Kingdom arising from the Convention.

(2)   If a Minister of the Crown considers that there arc compelling reasons for proceeding under this section, he may by order make such amendments to the legislation as he considers necessary to remove the incompatibility.

(3)   If, in the case of subordinate legislation, a Minister of the Crown considers

(a)   that it is necessary to amend the primary legislation under which the subordinate legislation in question was made, in order to enable the incompatibility to be removed, and

(b)   that there are compelling reasons for proceeding under this section, he may by order make such amendments to the primary legislation as he considers necessary.

(4)   This section also applies where the provision in question is in subordinate legislation and has been quashed, or declared invalid, by reason of incompatibility with a Convention right and the Minister proposes to proceed under paragraph 2(b) of Schedule 2.

(5)   If the legislation is an Order in Council, the power conferred by subsection (2) or (3) is exercisable by Her Majesty in Council.

(6)   In this section "legislation" does not include a Measure of the Church Assembly or of the General Synod of the Church of England.

(7)   Schedule 2 makes further provision about remedial orders.

Other rights and proceedings

Safeguard for existing human rights.

11.—(1)   A person's reliance on a Convention right does not restrict   **F-012**

(a)   any other right or freedom conferred on him by or under any law having effect in any part of the United Kingdom; or

(b)   his right to make any claim or bring any proceedings which he could make or bring apart from sections 7 to 9.

Freedom of expression.

12.—(1)   This section applies if a court is considering whether to grant any   **F-013**
relief which, if granted, might affect the exercise of the Convention right to freedom of expression.

(2)   If the person against whom the application for relief is made ("the respondent") is neither present nor represented, no such relief is to be granted unless the court is satisfied

(a)   that the applicant has taken all practicable steps to notify the respondent; or

(b)   that there are compelling reasons why the respondent should not be notified.

(3)   No such relief is to be granted so as to restrain publication before trial unless the court is satisfied that the applicant is likely to establish that publication should not be allowed.

(4)   The court must have particular regard to the importance of the Convention right to freedom of expression and, where the proceedings relate to material which the respondent claims, or which appears to the court, to be journalistic, literary or artistic material (or to conduct connected with such material), to

(a)   the extent to which

(i)   the material has, or is about to, become available to the public; or
(ii) it is, or would be, in the public interest for the material to be published;
(b) any relevant privacy code.

(5)   In this section

"court" includes a tribunal; and

"relief" includes any remedy or order (other than in criminal proceedings).

Freedom of thought, conscience and religion.

F-014   **13.**—(1)   If a court's determination of any question arising under this Act might affect the exercise by a religious organisation (itself or its members collectively) of the Convention right to freedom of thought, conscience and religion, it must have particular regard to the importance of that right.

(2)   In this section "court" includes a tribunal.

Derogations and reservations

Derogations.

F-015   **14.**—(1)   In this Act "designated derogation" means any derogation by the United Kingdom from an Article of the Convention, or of any protocol to the Convention, which is designated for the purposes of this Act in an order made by the [Secretary of State].[13]

(3)   If a designated derogation is amended or replaced it ceases to be a designated derogation.

(4)   But subsection (3) does not prevent the [Secretary of State][14] from exercising his power under subsection (1) to make a fresh designation order in respect of the Article concerned.

(5)   The [Secretary of State][15] must by order make such amendments to Schedule 3 as he considers appropriate to reflect

(a)   any designation order; or
(b)   the effect of subsection (3).

(6)   A designation order may be made in anticipation of the making by the United Kingdom of a proposed derogation.

Reservations.

F-016   **15.**—(1)   In this Act "designated reservation" means

(a)   the United Kingdom's reservation to Article 2 of the First Protocol to the Convention; and
(b)   any other reservation by the United Kingdom to an Article of the Convention, or of any protocol to the Convention, which is designated for the purposes of this Act in an order made by the [Secretary of State][16].

(2)   The text of the reservation referred to in subsection (1)(a) is set out in Part II of Schedule 3.

---

[13]   Words substituted by Secretary of State for Constitutional Affairs Order 2003/1887 Sch.2 para.10(1)
[14]   Words substituted by Secretary of State for Constitutional Affairs Order 2003/1887 Sch.2 para.10(1)
[15]   Words substituted by Secretary of State for Constitutional Affairs Order 2003/1887 Sch.2 para.10(1)
[16]   Words substituted by Secretary of State for Constitutional Affairs Order 2003/1887 Sch.2 para.10(1)

(3)   If a designated reservation is withdrawn wholly or in part it ceases to be a designated reservation.

(4)   But subsection (3) does not prevent the [Secretary of State][17] from exercising his power under subsection (1)(b) to make a fresh designation order in respect of the Article concerned.

(5)   The [Secretary of State][18] must by order make such amendments to this Act as he considers appropriate to reflect

(a)   any designation order; or

(b)   the effect of subsection (3).

Period for which designated derogations have effect.

16.—(1)   If it has not already been withdrawn by the United Kingdom, a.   **F-017**
designated derogation ceases to have effect for the purposes of this Act, at the end of the period of live years beginning with the date on which the order designating it was made.

(2)   At any time before the period

(a)   fixed by subsection (1), or

(b)   extended by an order under this subsection,

comes to an end, the [Secretary of State][19] may by order extend it by a further period of five years.

(3)   An order under section 14(1) ceases to have effect at the end of the period for consideration, unless a resolution has been passed by each House approving the order.

(4)   Subsection (3) does not affect

(a)   anything done in reliance on the order; or

(b)   the power to make a fresh order under section 14(1).

(5)   In subsection (3) "period for consideration" means the period of forty days beginning with the day on which the order was made.

(6)   In calculating the period for consideration, no account is to be taken of any time during which

(a)   Parliament is dissolved or prorogued; or

(b)   both Houses are adjourned for more than four days.

(7)   If a designated derogation is withdrawn by the United Kingdom, the [Secretary of State][20] must by order make such amendments to this Act as he considers are required to reflect that withdrawal.

Periodic review of designated reservations.

17.—(1)   The appropriate Minister must review the designated reservation   **F-018**
referred to in section 15(1)(a)

(a)   before the end of the period of five years beginning with the date on which section 1 (2) came into force; and

(b)   if that designation is still in force, before the end of the period of five years beginning with the date on which the last report relating to it was laid under subsection (3).

(2)   The appropriate Minister must review each of the other designated reservations (if any)

---

[17]   Words substituted by Secretary of State for Constitutional Affairs Order 2003/1887 Sch.2 para.10(1)
[18]   Words substituted by Secretary of State for Constitutional Affairs Order 2003/1887 Sch.2 para.10(1)
[19]   Words substituted by Secretary of State for Constitutional Affairs Order 2003/1887 Sch.2 para.10(1)
[20]   Words substituted by Secretary of State Constitution Affairs Order 2003/1887 Sch.2 para.10(1)

(a) before the end of the period of five years beginning with the date on which the order designating the reservation first came into force; and

(b) if the designation is still in force, before the end of the period of five years beginning with the date on which the last report relating to it was laid under subsection (3).

(3) The Minister conducting a review under this section must prepare a report on the result of the review and lay a copy of it before each House of Parliament.

Parliamentary procedure

Statements of compatibility.

F-019   **19.**—(1)   Minister of the Crown in charge of a Bill in either House of Parliament must, before Second Reading of the Bill

(a) make a statement to the effect that in his view the provisions of the Bill are compatible with the Convention rights ("a statement of compatibility"); or

(b) make a statement to the effect that although he is unable to make a statement of compatibility the government nevertheless wishes the House to proceed with the Bill.

(2)   The statement must be in writing and be published in such manner as the Minister making it considers appropriate.

F-020

SCHEDULE 1

THE ARTICLES

Section 1(3)

PART I

THE CONVENTION RIGHTS AND FREEDOMS

RIGHT TO LIFE

Article 2

1.   Everyone's right to life shall be protected by law. No one shall be deprived of his life intentionally save in the execution of a sentence of a court following his conviction of a crime for which this penalty is provided by law.

2.   Deprivation of life shall not be regarded as inflicted in contravention of this Article when it results from the use of force which is no more than absolutely necessary:

(a) in defence of any person from unlawful violence;

(b) in order to effect a lawful arrest or to prevent the escape of a person lawfully detained;

(c) in action lawfully taken for the purpose of quelling a riot or insurrection.

PROHIBITION OF TORTURE

Article 3

F-021   No one shall be subjected to torture or to inhuman or degrading treatment or punishment.

PROHIBITION OF SLAVERY AND FORCED LABOUR

Article 4

F-022   **1.**   No one shall be held in slavery or servitude.

2.   No one shall be required to perform forced or compulsory labour.

3.   For the purpose of this Article the term "forced or compulsory labour" shall not include:

(a) any work required to be done in the ordinary course of detention imposed according to the provisions of Article 5 of this Convention or during conditional release from such detention;

(b) any service of a military character or, in case of conscientious objectors in countries where they are recognised, service exacted instead of compulsory military service;

(c) any service exacted in case of an emergency or calamity threatening the life or well-being of the community;

(d)   any work or service which forms part of normal civic obligations.

RIGHT TO LIBERTY AND SECURITY

Article 5

1.   Everyone has the right to liberty and security of a person. No one shall be deprived of his liberty   **F-023**
save in the following cases and in accordance with a procedure prescribed by law:

(a)   the lawful detention of a person after conviction by a competent court;

(b)   the lawful arrest or detention of a person for non-compliance with the lawful order of a court or in order to secure the fulfilment of any obligation prescribed by law;

(c)   the lawful arrest or detention of a person effected for the purpose of bringing him before the competent legal authority on reasonable suspicion of having committed an offence or when it is reasonably considered necessary to prevent his committing an offence or fleeing after having done so;

(d)   the detention of a minor by lawful order for the purpose of educational supervision or his lawful detention for the purpose of bringing him before the competent legal authority;

(e)   the lawful detention of persons for the prevention of the spreading of infectious diseases, of persons of unsound mind, alcoholics or drug addicts or vagrants;

(f)   the lawful arrest or detention of a person to prevent his effecting an unauthorised entry into the country or of a person against whom action is being taken with a view to deportation or extradition.

2.   Everyone who is arrested shall be informed promptly, in a language which he understands, of the reasons for his arrest and of any charge against him.

3.   Everyone arrested or detained in accordance with the provisions of paragraph 1 (c) of this Article shall be brought promptly before a judge or other officer authorised by law to exercise judicial power and shall be entitled to trial within a reasonable time or to release pending trial. Release may be conditioned by guarantees to appear for trial.

4.   Everyone who is deprived of his liberty by arrest or detention shall be entitled to take proceedings by which the lawfulness of his detention shall be decided speedily by a court and his release ordered if the detention is not lawful.

5.   Everyone who has been the victim of arrest or detention in contravention of the provisions of this Article shall have an enforceable right to compensation.

RIGHT TO A FAIR TRIAL

Article 6

1.   In the determination of his civil rights and obligations or of any criminal charge against him,   **F-024**
everyone is entitled to a fair and public hearing within a reasonable time by an independent and impartial tribunal established by law. Judgment shall be pronounced publicly but the press and public may be excluded from all or part of the trial in the interest of morals, public order or national security in a democratic society, where the interests of juveniles or the protection of the private life of the parties so require, or to the extent strictly necessary in the opinion of the court in special circumstances where publicity would prejudice the interests of justice.

2.   Everyone charged with a criminal offence shall be presumed innocent until proved guilty according to law.

3.   Everyone charged with a criminal offence has the following minimum rights:

(a)   to be informed promptly, in a language which he understands and in detail, of the nature and cause of the accusation against him;

(b)   to have adequate time and facilities for the preparation of his defence;

(c)   to defend himself in person or through legal assistance of his own choosing or, if he has not sufficient means to pay for legal assistance, to be given it free when the interests of justice so require;

(d)   to examine or have examined witnesses against him and to obtain the attendance and examination of witnesses on his behalf under the same conditions as witnesses against him;

(e)   to have the free assistance of an interpreter if he cannot understand or speak the language used in court.

NO PUNISHMENT WITHOUT LAW

Article 7

1.   No one shall be held guilty of any criminal offence on account of any act or omission which did   **F-025**
not constitute a criminal offence under national or international law at the time when it was committed. Nor shall a heavier penalty be imposed than the one that was applicable at the time the criminal offence was committed.

2. This Article shall not prejudice the trial and punishment of any person for any act or omission which, at the time when it was committed, was criminal according to the general principles of law recognised by civilised nations.

RIGHT TO RESPECT FOR PRIVATE AND FAMILY LIFE

Article 8

F-026

1. Everyone has the right to respect for his private and family life, his home and his correspondence.

2. There shall be no interference by a public authority with the exercise of this right except such as is in accordance with the law and is necessary in a democratic society in the interests of national security, public safety or the economic well-being of the country, for the prevention of disorder or crime, for the protection of health or morals, or for the protection of the rights and freedoms of others.

FREEDOM OF THOUGHT, CONSCIENCE AND RELIGION

Article 9

F-027

1. Everyone has the right to freedom of thought, conscience and religion, this right includes freedom to change his religion or belief and freedom, either alone or in community with others and in public or private, to manifest his religion or belief, in worship, teaching, practice and observance.

2. Freedom to manifest one's religion or beliefs shall be subject only to such limitation as are prescribed by law and arc necessary in a democratic society in the interests of public safety, for the protection of public order, health or morals, or for the protection of the rights and freedoms of others.

FREEDOM OF EXPRESSION

Article 10

F-028

1. Everyone has the right to freedom of expression. This right shall include freedom to hold opinions and to receive and impart information and ideas without interference by public authority and regardless of frontiers. This Article shall not prevent States from requiring the licensing of broadcasting, television or cinema enterprises.

2. The exercise of these freedoms, since it carries with ii duties and responsibilities, may be subject to such formalities, conditions, restrictions or penalties as are prescribed by law and are necessary in a democratic society, in the interests of national security, territorial integrity or public safety, for the prevention of disorder or crime, for the protection of health or morals, for the protection of the reputation or rights of others, for preventing the disclosure of information received in confidence, or for maintaining the authority and impartiality of the judiciary.

FREEDOM OF ASSEMBLY AND ASSOCIATION

Article 11

F-029

1. Everyone has the right to freedom of peaceful assembly and to freedom of association with others, including the right to form and to join trade unions for the protection of his interests.

2. No restrictions shall be placed on the exercise of these rights other than such as are prescribed by law and are necessary in a democratic society in the interests of national security or public safety, for the prevention of disorder or crime, for the protection of health or morals or for the protection of the rights and freedoms of others. This Article shall not prevent the imposition of lawful restrictions on the exercise of these rights by members of the armed forces, of the police or of the administration of the State.

RIGHT TO MARRY

Article 12

F-030

Men and women of marriageable age have the right to marry and to found a family, according to the national laws governing the exercise of this right.

PROHIBITION OF DISCRIMINATION

Article 14

F-031

The enjoyment of the rights and freedoms set forth in this Convention shall be secured without discrimination on any ground such as sex, race, colour, language, religion, political or other opinion, national or social origin, association with a national minority, property, birth or other status.

RESTRICTIONS ON POLITICAL ACTIVITY OF ALIENS

Article 16

F-032

Nothing in Articles 10, 11 and 14 shall be regarded as preventing the High Contracting Parties from imposing restrictions on the political activity of aliens.

PROHIBITION OF ABUSE OF RIGHTS

Article 17

Nothing in this Convention may be interpreted as implying for any State, group or person any right to **F-033**
engage in any activity or perform any act aimed at the destruction of any of the rights and freedoms set
forth herein or at their limitation to a greater extent than is provided for in the Convention.

LIMITATION ON USE OF RESTRICTIONS ON RIGHTS

Article 18

The restrictions permitted under this Convention to the said rights and freedoms shall not be applied for **F-034**
any purpose other than those for which they have been prescribed.

PART II

THE FIRST PROTOCOL

PROTECTION OF PROPERTY

Article 1

Every natural or legal person is entitled to the peaceful enjoyment of his possessions. No one shall be **F-035**
deprived of his possessions except in the public interest and subject to the conditions provided for by
law and by the general principles of international law.

The preceding provisions shall not, however, in any way impair the right of a State to enforce such
laws as it deems necessary to control the use of property in accordance with the general interest or to
secure the payment of taxes or other contributions or penalties.

RIGHT TO EDUCATION

Article 2

No person shall be denied the right to education. In the exercise of any functions which it assumes in **F-036**
relation to education and to teaching, the State shall respect the right of parents to ensure such education and teaching in conformity with their own religious and philosophical convictions.

RIGHT TO FREE ELECTIONS

Article 3

The High Contracting Parties undertake to hold free elections at reasonable intervals by secret ballot, **F-037**
under conditions which will ensure the free expression of the opinion of the people in the choice of the
legislature.[21]

PART III

[ARTICLE 1 OF THE THIRTEENTH PROTOCOL]

ABOLITION OF THE DEATH PENALTY

The death penalty shall be abolished. No one shall be condemned to such penalty or executed.][22] **F-038**

---

[21] Substituted by Human Rights Act 1998 (Amendment) Order 2004/1574 art.2(3)
[22] Substituted by Human Rights Act 1998 (Amendment) Order 2004/1574 art.2(3)

APPENDIX G

Civil Procedure Rules Pt 54

I

Scope and interpretation

54.1—(1)   This Section of this Part contains rules about judicial review.   **G-001**

(2)   In this Section-
  (a)   a 'claim for judicial review' means a claim to review the lawfulness of-
    (i)   an enactment; or
    (ii)   a decision, action or failure to act in relation to the exercise of a public function.
  (b)   revoked
  (c)   revoked
  (d)   revoked
  (e)   'the judicial review procedure' means the Part 8 procedure as modified by this Section;
  (f)   'interested party' means any person (other than the claimant and defendant) who is directly affected by the claim; and
  (g)   'court' means the High Court, unless otherwise stated.
(Rule 8.1(6)(b) provides that a rule or practice direction may, in relation to a specified type of proceedings, disapply or modify any of the rules set out in Part 8 as they apply to those proceedings)

Who may exercise the powers of the High Court

54.1A—(1)   A court officer assigned to the Administrative Court office who is   **G-002**
-
  (a)   a barrister; or
  (b)   a solicitor,
may exercise the jurisdiction of the High Court with regard to the matters set out in paragraph (2) with the consent of the President of the Queen's Bench Division.
(2)   The matters referred to in paragraph (1) are -
  (a)   any matter incidental to any proceedings in the High Court;
  (b)   any other matter where there is no substantial dispute between the parties; and
  (c)   the dismissal of an appeal or application where a party has failed to comply with any order, rule or practice direction.
(3)   A court officer may not decide an application for -
  (a)   permission to bring judicial review proceedings;
  (b)   an injunction;
  (c)   a stay of any proceedings, other than a temporary stay of any order or

decision of the lower court over a period when the High Court is not sitting or cannot conveniently be convened, unless the parties seek a stay by consent.

(4) Decisions of a court officer may be made without a hearing.

(5) A party may request any decision of a court officer to be reviewed by a judge of the High Court.

(6) At the request of a party, a hearing will be held to reconsider a decision of a court officer, made without a hearing.

(7) A request under paragraph (5) or (6) must be filed within 7 days after the party is served with notice of the decision.

When this Section must be used

G-003
54.2 The judicial review procedure must be used in a claim for judicial review where the claimant is seeking-
- (a) a mandatory order;
- (b) a prohibiting order;
- (c) a quashing order; or
- (d) an injunction under section 30 of the Supreme Court Act 1981[1] (restraining a person from acting in any office in which he is not entitled to act).

When this Section may be used

G-004
54.3—(1) The judicial review procedure may be used in a claim for judicial review where the claimant is seeking-
- (a) a declaration; or
- (b) an injunction.

(Section 31(2) of the Supreme Court Act 1981 sets out the circumstances in which the court may grant a declaration or injunction in a claim for judicial review)

(Where the claimant is seeking a declaration or injunction in addition to one of the remedies listed in rule 54.2, the judicial review procedure must be used)

(2) A claim for judicial review may include a claim for damages, restitution or the recovery of a sum due but may not seek such a remedy alone.

(Section 31(4) of the Supreme Court Act sets out the circumstances in which the court may award damages, restitution or the recovery of a sum due on a claim for judicial review)

Permission required

G-005
54.4 The court's permission to proceed is required in a claim for judicial review whether started under this Section or transferred to the Administrative Court.

Time limit for filing claim form

G-006
54.5—(1) The claim form must be filed-
- (a) promptly; and
- (b) in any event not later than 3 months after the grounds to make the claim first arose.

(2) The time limit in this rule may not be extended by agreement between the parties.

---

[1] 1981 c.54.

(3)   This rule does not apply when any other enactment specifies a shorter time limit for making the claim for judicial review.

Claim form

54.6—(1)   In addition to the matters set out in rule 8.2 (contents of the claim   **G-007** form) the claimant must also state-
    (a)   the name and address of any person he considers to be an interested party;
    (b)   that he is requesting permission to proceed with a claim for judicial review; and
    (c)   any remedy (including any interim remedy) he is claiming.
(Part 25 sets out how to apply for an interim remedy)

(2)   The claim form must be accompanied by the documents required by Practice Direction 54A.

Service of claim form

54.7   The claim form must be served on-   **G-008**
    (a)   the defendant; and
    (b)   unless the court otherwise directs, any person the claimant considers to be an interested party,
within 7 days after the date of issue.

Judicial review of decisions of the Upper Tribunal

54.7A—(1)   This rule applies where an application is made, following refusal   **G-009** by the Upper Tribunal of permission to appeal against a decision of the First Tier Tribunal, for judicial review-
    (a)   of the decision of the Upper Tribunal refusing permission to appeal; or
    (b)   which relates to the decision of the First Tier Tribunal which was the subject of the application for permission to appeal.

(2)   Where this rule applies -
    (a)   the application may not include any other claim, whether against the Upper Tribunal or not; and
    (b)   any such other claim must be the subject of a separate application.

(3)   The claim form and the supporting documents required by paragraph (4) must be filed no later than 16 days after the date on which notice of the Upper Tribunal's decision was sent to the applicant.

(4)   The supporting documents are-
    (a)   the decision of the Upper Tribunal to which the application relates, and any document giving reasons for the decision;
    (b)   the grounds of appeal to the Upper Tribunal and any documents which were sent with them;
    (c)   the decision of the First Tier Tribunal, the application to that Tribunal for permission to appeal and its reasons for refusing permission; and
    (d)   any other documents essential to the claim.

(5)   The claim form and supporting documents must be served on the Upper Tribunal and any other interested party no later than 7 days after the date of issue.

(6)   The Upper Tribunal and any person served with the claim form who wishes to take part in the proceedings for judicial review must, no later than 21 days after service of the claim form, file and serve on the applicant and any other party an acknowledgment of service in the relevant practice form.

(7)   The court will give permission to proceed only if it considers -

(a) that there is an arguable case, which has a reasonable prospect of success, that both the decision of the Upper Tribunal refusing permission to appeal and the decision of the First Tier Tribunal against which permission to appeal was sought are wrong in law; and

(b) that either -
　　(i) the claim raises an important point of principle or practice; or
　　(ii) there is some other compelling reason to hear it.

(8) If the application for permission is refused on paper without an oral hearing, rule 54.12(3) (request for reconsideration at a hearing) does not apply.

(9) If permission to apply for judicial review is granted -

(a) if the Upper Tribunal or any interested party wishes there to be a hearing of the substantive application, it must make its request for such a hearing no later than 14 days after service of the order granting permission; and

(b) if no request for a hearing is made within that period, the court will make a final order quashing the refusal of permission without a further hearing.

(10) The power to make a final order under paragraph (9)(b) may be exercised by the Master of the Crown Office or a Master of the Administrative Court.

Acknowledgment of service

G-010　　**54.8**—(1) Any person served with the claim form who wishes to take part in the judicial review must file an acknowledgment of service in the relevant practice form in accordance with the following provisions of this rule.

(2) Any acknowledgment of service must be-

(a) filed not more than 21 days after service of the claim form; and

(b) served on-
　　(i) the claimant; and
　　(ii) subject to any direction under rule 54.7(b), any other person named in the claim form,

as soon as practicable and, in any event, not later than 7 days after it is filed.

(3) The time limits under this rule may not be extended by agreement between the parties.

(4) The acknowledgment of service-

(a) must-
　　(i) where the person filing it intends to contest the claim, set out a summary of his grounds for doing so; and
　　(ii) state the name and address of any person the person filing it considers to be an interested party; and

(b) may include or be accompanied by an application for directions.

(5) Rule 10.3(2) does not apply.

Failure to file acknowledgment of service

G-011　　**54.9**—(1) Where a person served with the claim form has failed to file an acknowledgment of service in accordance with rule 54.8, he-

(a) may not take part in a hearing to decide whether permission should be given unless the court allows him to do so; but

(b) provided he complies with rule 54.14 or any other direction of the court regarding the filing and service of-
　　(i) detailed grounds for contesting the claim or supporting it on additional grounds; and

(ii)   any written evidence,

may take part in the hearing of the judicial review.

(2)   Where that person takes part in the hearing of the judicial review, the court may take his failure to file an acknowledgment of service into account when deciding what order to make about costs.

(3)   Rule 8.4 does not apply.

Permission given

54.10—(1)   Where permission to proceed is given the court may also give directions.   **G-012**

(2)   Directions under paragraph (1) may include-
    (a)   a stay(GL) of proceedings to which the claim relates;
    (b)   directions requiring the proceedings to be heard by a Divisional Court.

Service of order giving or refusing permission

54.11   The court will serve-   **G-013**
    (a)   the order giving or refusing permission; and
    (b)   any directions, on-
        (i)   the claimant;
        (ii)   the defendant; and
        (iii)   any other person who filed an acknowledgment of service.

Permission decision without a hearing

54.12(1)   This rule applies where the court, without a hearing-   **G-014**
    (a)   refuses permission to proceed; or
    (b)   gives permission to proceed-
        (i)   subject to conditions; or
        (ii)   on certain grounds only.

(2)   The court will serve its reasons for making the decision when it serves the order giving or refusing permission in accordance with rule 54.11.

(3)   The claimant may not appeal but may request the decision to be reconsidered at a hearing.

(4)   A request under paragraph (3) must be filed within 7 days after service of the reasons under paragraph (2).

(5)   The claimant, defendant and any other person who has filed an acknowledgment of service will be given at least 2 days' notice of the hearing date.

(6)   The court may give directions requiring the proceedings to be heard by a Divisional Court.

Defendant etc. may not apply to set aside

54.13   Neither the defendant nor any other person served with the claim form may apply to set aside an order giving permission to proceed.   **G-015**

Response

54.14—(1)   A defendant and any other person served with the claim form who wishes to contest the claim or support it on additional grounds must file and serve   **G-016**
-
    (a)   detailed grounds for contesting the claim or supporting it on additional grounds; and

(b)   any written evidence,
within 35 days after service of the order giving permission.
(2)   The following rules do not apply-
    (a)   rule 8.5 (3) and 8.5 (4)(defendant to file and serve written evidence at the same time as acknowledgment of service); and
    (b)   rule 8.5 (5) and 8.5(6) (claimant to file and serve any reply within 14 days).

Where claimant seeks to rely on additional grounds

G-017   **54.15**   The court's permission is required if a claimant seeks to rely on grounds other than those for which he has been given permission to proceed.

Evidence

G-018   **54.16**—(1)   Rule 8.6 (1) does not apply.
(2)   No written evidence may be relied on unless-
    (a)   it has been served in accordance with any-
        (i)   rule under this Section; or
        (ii)   direction of the court; or
    (b)   the court gives permission.

Court's powers to hear any person

G-019   **54.17**—(1)   Any person may apply for permission-
    (a)   to file evidence; or
    (b)   make representations at the hearing of the judicial review.
(2)   An application under paragraph (1) should be made promptly.

Judicial review may be decided without a hearing

G-020   **54.18**   The court may decide the claim for judicial review without a hearing where all the parties agree.

Court's powers in respect of quashing orders

G-021   **54.19**—(1)   This rule applies where the court makes a quashing order in respect of the decision to which the claim relates.
(2)   The court may -
    (a)
        (i)   remit the matter to the decision-maker; and
        (ii)   direct it to reconsider the matter and reach a decision in accordance with the judgment of the court; or
    (b)   in so far as any enactment permits, substitute its own decision for the decision to which the claim relates.
(Section 31 of the Supreme Court Act 1981[2] enables the High Court, subject to certain conditions, to substitute its own decision for the decision in question.)

---

[2]   1981 c.54. Section 31 is amended by section 141 of the Tribunals, Courts and Enforcement Act 2007 (c. 15).

Transfer

54.20   The court may   **G-022**
   (a)   order a claim to continue as if it had not been started under this Sec-
          tion; and
   (b)   where it does so, give directions about the future management of the
          claim.
(Part 30 (transfer) applies to transfers to and from the Administrative Court)

APPENDIX H

Practice Direction 54A — Judicial Review

I - General Provisions Relating to Judicial Review

1.1 In addition to Part 54 and this practice direction attention is drawn to: **H-001**
- section 31 of the Senior Courts Act 1981; and
- the Human Rights Act 1998.

The Court

2.1 Part 54 claims for judicial review are dealt with in the Administrative Court.   **H-002**
(Practice Direction 54D) contains provisions about where a claim for judicial
review may be started, administered and heard.)

2.2 Omitted

2.3 Omitted

2.4 Omitted

3.1 Omitted

3.2 Omitted

Rule 54.5 — Time limit for filing claim form

4.1 Where the claim is for a quashing order in respect of a judgment, order or   **H-003**
conviction, the date when the grounds to make the claim first arose, for the purposes
of rule 54.5(1)(b), is the date of that judgment, order or conviction.

Rule 54.6 — Claim form

Interested parties

5.1 Where the claim for judicial review relates to proceedings in a court or   **H-004**
tribunal, any other parties to those proceedings must be named in the claim form
as interested parties under rule 54.6(1)(a) (and therefore served with the claim form
under rule 54.7(b)).

5.2 For example, in a claim by a defendant in a criminal case in the Magistrates
or Crown Court for judicial review of a decision in that case, the prosecution must
always be named as an interested party.

Human rights

H-005   **5.3**   Where the claimant is seeking to raise any issue under the Human Rights Act 1998, or seeks a remedy available under that Act, the claim form must include the information required by paragraph 15 of Practice Direction 16.

Devolution issues

H-006   **5.4**   Where the claimant intends to raise a devolution issue, the claim form must:
   (1)   specify that the applicant wishes to raise a devolution issue and identify the relevant provisions of the Government of Wales Act 2006, the Northern Ireland Act 1998 or the Scotland Act 1998; and
   (2)   contain a summary of the facts, circumstances and points of law on the basis of which it is alleged that a devolution issue arises.

5.5   In this practice direction "devolution issue" has the same meaning as in paragraph 1, Schedule 9 to the Government of Wales Act 2006, paragraph 1, Schedule 10 to the Northern Ireland Act 1998; and paragraph 1, Schedule 6 to the Scotland Act 1998.

Claim form

H-007   **5.6**   The claim form must include or be accompanied by -
   (1)   a detailed statement of the claimant's grounds for bringing the claim for judicial review;
   (2)   a statement of the facts relied on;
   (3)   any application to extend the time limit for filing the claim form;
   (4)   any application for directions.

5.7   In addition, the claim form must be accompanied by
   (1)   any written evidence in support of the claim or application to extend time;
   (2)   a copy of any order that the claimant seeks to have quashed;
   (3)   where the claim for judicial review relates to a decision of a court or tribunal, an approved copy of the reasons for reaching that decision;
   (4)   copies of any documents on which the claimant proposes to rely;
   (5)   copies of any relevant statutory material; and
   (6)   a list of essential documents for advance reading by the court (with page references to the passages relied on).

5.8   Where it is not possible to file all the above documents, the claimant must indicate which documents have not been filed and the reasons why they are not currently available.

Bundle of documents

H-008   **5.9**   The claimant must file two copies of a paginated and indexed bundle containing all the documents referred to in paragraphs 5.6 and 5.7.

5.10   Attention is drawn to rules 8.5(1) and 8.5(7).

Rule 54.7 — Service of claim form

6.1   Except as required by rules 54.11 or 54.12(2), the Administrative Court will   **H-009**
not serve documents and service must be effected by the parties.

6.2   Where the defendant or interested party to the claim for judicial review is -
(a)   the Immigration and Asylum Chamber of the First-tier Tribunal, the address
      for service of the claim form is Official Correspondence Unit, PO Box 6987,
      Leicester, LE1 6ZX or fax number 0116 249 4240;
(b)   the Crown, service of the claim form must be effected on the solicitor acting
      for the relevant government department as if the proceedings were civil
      proceedings as defined in the Crown Proceedings Act 1947.
(Practice Direction 66 gives the list published under section 17 of the Crown
Proceedings Act 1947 of the solicitors acting in civil proceedings (as defined in that
Act) for the different government departments on whom service is to be effected,
and of their addresses.)
(Part 6 contains provisions about the service of claim forms.)

Rule 54.8 — Acknowledgment of service

7.1   Attention is drawn to rule 8.3(2) and the relevant practice direction and to rule   **H-010**
10.5.

Rule 54.10 — Permission given

Directions

8.1   Case management directions under rule 54.10(1) may include directions about   **H-011**
serving the claim form and any evidence on other persons.

8.2   Where a claim is made under the Human Rights Act 1998, a direction may
be made for giving notice to the Crown or joining the Crown as a party. Attention
is drawn to rule 19.4A and paragraph 6 of Practice Direction 19A.

8.3   Omitted

Permission without a hearing

8.4   The court will generally, in the first instance, consider the question of permis-   **H-012**
sion without a hearing.

Permission hearing

8.5   Neither the defendant nor any other interested party need attend a hearing on   **H-013**
the question of permission unless the court directs otherwise.

8.6   Where the defendant or any party does attend a hearing, the court will not
generally make an order for costs against the claimant.

Rule 54.11 — Service of order giving or refusing permission

H-014   **9.1**   An order refusing permission or giving it subject to conditions or on certain grounds only must set out or be accompanied by the court's reasons for coming to that decision.

Rule 54.14 — Response

H-015   **10.1**   Where the party filing the detailed grounds intends to rely on documents not already filed, he must file a paginated bundle of those documents when he files the detailed grounds.

Rule 54.15 — Where claimant seeks to rely on additional grounds

H-016   **11.1**   Where the claimant intends to apply to rely on additional grounds at the hearing of the claim for judicial review, he must give notice to the court and to any other person served with the claim form no later than 7 clear days before the hearing (or the warned date where appropriate).

Rule 54.16 — Evidence

H-017   **12.1**   Disclosure is not required unless the court orders otherwise.

Rule 54.17 — Court's powers to hear any person

H-018   **13.1**   Where all the parties consent, the court may deal with an application under rule 54.17 without a hearing.

13.2   Where the court gives permission for a person to file evidence or make representations at the hearing of the claim for judicial review, it may do so on conditions and may give case management directions.

13.3   An application for permission should be made by letter to the Administrative Court office, identifying the claim, explaining who the applicant is and indicating why and in what form the applicant wants to participate in the hearing.

13.4   If the applicant is seeking a prospective order as to costs, the letter should say what kind of order and on what grounds.

13.5   Applications to intervene must be made at the earliest reasonable opportunity, since it will usually be essential not to delay the hearing.

Rule 54.20 — Transfer

H-019   **14.1**   Attention is drawn to rule 30.5.

14.2   In deciding whether a claim is suitable for transfer to the Administrative Court, the court will consider whether it raises issues of public law to which Part 54 should apply.

Skeleton arguments

15.1 The claimant must file and serve a skeleton argument not less than 21 work- **H-020**
ing days before the date of the hearing of the judicial review (or the warned date).

15.2 The defendant and any other party wishing to make representations at the
hearing of the judicial review must file and serve a skeleton argument not less than
14 working days before the date of the hearing of the judicial review (or the warned
date).

15.3 Skeleton arguments must contain:
(1) a time estimate for the complete hearing, including delivery of judgment;
(2) a list of issues;
(3) a list of the legal points to be taken (together with any relevant authorities with
     page references to the passages relied on);
(4) a chronology of events (with page references to the bundle of documents (see
     paragraph 16.1);
(5) a list of essential documents for the advance reading of the court (with page
     references to the passages relied on) (if different from that filed with the claim
     form) and a time estimate for that reading; and
(6) a list of persons referred to.

Bundle of documents to be filed

16.1 The claimant must file a paginated and indexed bundle of all relevant docu- **H-021**
ments required for the hearing of the judicial review when he files his skeleton
argument.

16.2 The bundle must also include those documents required by the defendant and
any other party who is to make representations at the hearing.

Agreed final order

17.1 If the parties agree about the final order to be made in a claim for judicial **H-022**
review, the claimant must file at the court a document (with 2 copies) signed by all
the parties setting out the terms of the proposed agreed order together with a short
statement of the matters relied on as justifying the proposed agreed order and copies of any authorities or statutory provisions relied on.

17.2 The court will consider the documents referred to in paragraph 17.1 and will
make the order if satisfied that the order should be made.

17.3 If the court is not satisfied that the order should be made, a hearing date will
be set.

17.4 Where the agreement relates to an order for costs only, the parties need only
file a document signed by all the parties setting out the terms of the proposed order.

**II - Applications for Permission to Apply for Judicial Review in
Immigration and Asylum Cases - Challenging Removal**

18.1(1) This Section applies where - **H-023**
     (a) a person has been served with a copy of directions for his removal from

the United Kingdom by the UK Border Agency of the Home Office and notified that this Section applies; and

(b) that person makes an application for permission to apply for judicial review before his removal takes effect.

(2) This Section does not prevent a person from applying for judicial review after he has been removed.

(3) The requirements contained in this Section of this Practice Direction are additional to those contained elsewhere in the Practice Direction.

18.2(1) A person who makes an application for permission to apply for judicial review must file a claim form and a copy at court, and the claim form must -

(a) indicate on its face that this Section of the Practice Direction applies; and

(b) be accompanied by -

(i) a copy of the removal directions and the decision to which the application relates; and

(ii) any document served with the removal directions including any document which contains the UK Border Agency's factual summary of the case; and

(c) contain or be accompanied by the detailed statement of the claimant's grounds for bringing the claim for judicial review; or

(d) if the claimant is unable to comply with paragraph (b) or (c), contain or be accompanied by a statement of the reasons why.

(2) The claimant must, immediately upon issue of the claim, send copies of the issued claim form and accompanying documents to the address specified by the UK Border Agency.

(Rule 54.7 also requires the defendant to be served with the claim form within 7 days of the date of issue. Rule 6.10 provides that service on a Government Department must be effected on the solicitor acting for that Department, which in the case of the UK Border Agency is the Treasury Solicitor. The address for the Treasury Solicitor may be found in the Annex to Part 66 of these Rules.)

18.3 Where the claimant has not complied with paragraph 18.2(1)(b) or (c) and has provided reasons why he is unable to comply, and the court has issued the claim form, the Administrative Court -

(a) will refer the matter to a Judge for consideration as soon as practicable; and

(b) will notify the parties that it has done so.

18.4 If, upon a refusal to grant permission to apply for judicial review, the Court indicates that the application is clearly without merit, that indication will be included in the order refusing permission.

III - Applications for Permission to Apply for Judicial Review of Decisions of the Upper Tribunal

H-024   **19.1** A person who makes an application for permission to apply for judicial review of the decision of the Upper Tribunal refusing permission to appeal must file a claim form which must -

(a) state on its face that the application is made under Rule 54. 7A;

(b) set out succinctly the grounds on which it is argued that the criteria in Rule 54.7A(7) are met; and

(c) be accompanied by the supporting documents required under Rule 54.7A(4).

19.2   If the Upper Tribunal or any interested party wishes there to be a hearing of the substantive application under Rule 54.7A(9), it must make its request in writing (by letter copied to the claimant) for such a hearing no later than 14 days after service of the order granting permission.

APPENDIX I

Practice Direction 54D—Administrative Court (Venue)

This Practice Direction supplements Part 54.   I-001

Scope and purpose

1.1 This Practice Direction concerns the place in which a claim before the   I-002
Administrative Court should be started and administered and the venue at which it
will be determined.

1.2 This Practice Direction is intended to facilitate access to justice by enabling
cases to be administered and determined in the most appropriate location. To
achieve this purpose it provides flexibility in relation to where claims are to be
administered and enables claims to be transferred to different venues.

Venue-general provisions

2.1 The claim form in proceedings in the Administrative Court may be issued at   I-003
the Administrative Court Office of the High Court at-
  (1) the Royal Courts of Justice in London; or
  (2) at the District Registry of the High Court at Birmingham, Cardiff, Leeds,
       or Manchester unless the claim is one of the excepted classes of claim set
       out in paragraph 3 of this Practice Direction which may only be started and
       determined at the Royal Courts of Justice in London.

2.2 Any claim started in Birmingham will normally be determined at a court in
the Midland region (geographically covering the area of the Midland Circuit); in
Cardiff in Wales; in Leeds in the North-Eastern Region (geographically covering
the area of the North Eastern Circuit); in London at the Royal Courts of Justice; and
in Manchester, in the North-Western Region (geographically covering the Northern
Circuit).

Excepted classes of claim

3.1 The excepted classes of claim referred to in paragraph 2.1(2) are -   I-004
  (1) proceedings to which Part 76 or Part 79 applies, and for the avoidance of
       doubt -
       (a) proceedings relating to control orders (within the meaning of Part
            76);
       (b) financial restrictions proceedings (within the meaning of Part 79);
       (c) proceedings relating to terrorism or alleged terrorists (where that is
            a relevant feature of the claim); and
       (d) proceedings in which a special advocate is or is to be instructed;

(2) proceedings to which RSC Order 115 applies;

(3) proceedings under the Proceeds of Crime Act 2002;

(4) appeals to the Administrative Court under the Extradition Act 2003;

(5) proceedings which must be heard by a Divisional Court; and

(6) proceedings relating to the discipline of solicitors.

3.2   If a claim form is issued at an Administrative Court office other than in London and includes one of the excepted classes of claim, the proceedings will be transferred to London.

Urgent applications

I-005   **4.1**   During the hours when the court is open, where an urgent application needs to be made to the Administrative Court outside London, the application must be made to the judge designated to deal with such applications in the relevant District Registry.

4.2   Any urgent application to the Administrative Court during the hours when the court is closed, must be made to the duty out of hours High Court judge by telephoning 020 7947 6000.

Assignment to another venue

I-006   **5.1**   The proceedings may be transferred from the office at which the claim form was issued to another office. Such transfer is a judicial act.

5.2   The general expectation is that proceedings will be administered and determined in the region with which the claimant has the closest connection, subject to the following considerations as applicable -

(1) any reason expressed by any party for preferring a particular venue;

(2) the region in which the defendant, or any relevant office or department of the defendant, is based;

(3) the region in which the claimant's legal representatives are based;

(4) the ease and cost of travel to a hearing;

(5) the availability and suitability of alternative means of attending a hearing (for example, by videolink);

(6) the extent and nature of media interest in the proceedings in any particular locality;

(7) the time within which it is appropriate for the proceedings to be determined;

(8) whether it is desirable to administer or determine the claim in another region in the light of the volume of claims issued at, and the capacity, resources and workload of, the court at which it is issued;

(9) whether the claim raises issues sufficiently similar to those in another outstanding claim to make it desirable that it should be determined together with, or immediately following, that other claim; and

(10) whether the claim raises devolution issues and for that reason whether it should more appropriately be determined in London or Cardiff.

5.3(1)   When an urgent application is made under paragraph 4.1 or 4.2, this will not by itself decide the venue for the further administration or determination of the claim.

(2) The court dealing with the urgent application may direct that the case be assigned to a particular venue.

(3) When an urgent application is made under paragraph 4.2, and the court does

not make a direction under sub-paragraph (2), the claim will be assigned in the first place to London but may be reassigned to another venue at a later date.

5.4   The court may on an application by a party or of its own initiative direct that the claim be determined in a region other than that of the venue in which the claim is currently assigned. The considerations in paragraph 5.2 apply.

5.5   Once assigned to a venue, the proceedings will be both administered from that venue and determined by a judge of the Administrative Court at a suitable court within that region, or, if the venue is in London, at the Royal Courts of Justice. The choice of which court (of those within the region which are identified by the Presiding Judge of the circuit suitable for such hearing) will be decided, subject to availability, by the considerations in paragraph 5.2.

5.6   When giving directions under rule 54.10, the court may direct that proceedings be reassigned to another region for hearing (applying the considerations in paragraph 5.2). If no such direction is given, the claim will be heard in the same region as that in which the permission application was determined (whether on paper or at a hearing).

APPENDIX J

Pre-Action Protocol for Judicial Review

Introduction

This protocol applies to proceedings within England and Wales only. It does not   **J-001**
*affect the time limit specified by Rule 54.5(1) of the Civil Procedure Rules which
requires that any claim form in an application for judicial review must be filed
promptly and in any event not later than 3 months after the grounds to make the
claim first arose.*[1]

1 Judicial review allows people with a sufficient interest in a decision or action
by a public body to ask a judge to review the lawfulness of:
- an enactment; or
- a decision, action or failure to act in relation to the exercise of a public
  function.[2]

2 Judicial review may be used where there is no right of appeal or where all
avenues of appeal have been exhausted.

Alternative Dispute Resolution

3.1 The parties should consider whether some form of alternative dispute resolution procedure would be more suitable than litigation, and if so, endeavour to agree
which form to adopt. Both the Claimant and Defendant may be required by the
Court to provide evidence that alternative means of resolving their dispute were
considered. The Courts take the view that litigation should be a last resort, and that
claims should not be issued prematurely when a settlement is still actively being
explored. Parties are warned that if the protocol is not followed (including this
paragraph) then the Court must have regard to such conduct when determining
costs. However, parties should also note that a claim for judicial review 'must be
filed promptly and in any event not later than 3 months after the grounds to make
the claim first arose'.

3.2 It is not practicable in this protocol to address in detail how the parties might
decide which method to adopt to resolve their particular dispute. However, summarised below are some of the options for resolving disputes without litigation:
- Discussion and negotiation.
- Ombudsmen - the Parliamentary and Health Service and the Local Government Ombudsmen have discretion to deal with complaints relating to
  maladministration. The British and Irish Ombudsman Association provide

---

[1] While the court does have the discretion under Rule 3.1(2)(a) of the Civil Procedure Rules to allow
a late claim, this is only used in exceptional circumstances. *Compliance with the protocol alone is
unlikely to be sufficient to persuade the court to allow a late claim.*

[2] Civil Procedure Rule 54.1(2).

information about Ombudsman schemes and other complaint handling bodies and this is available from their website at *www.bioa.org.uk*. Parties may wish to note that the Ombudsmen are not able to look into a complaint once court action has been commenced.

- Early neutral evaluation by an independent third party (for example, a lawyer experienced in the field of administrative law or an individual experienced in the subject matter of the claim).
- Mediation - a form of facilitated negotiation assisted by an independent neutral party.

3.3   The Legal Services Commission has published a booklet on 'Alternatives to Court', CLS Direct Information Leaflet 23 (*www.clsdirect.org.uk*), which lists a number of organisations that provide alternative dispute resolution services.

3.4   It is expressly recognised that no party can or should be forced to mediate or enter into any form of ADR.

4   *Judicial review may not be appropriate in every instance.*

Claimants are strongly advised to seek appropriate legal advice when considering such proceedings and, in particular, before adopting this protocol or making a claim. Although the Legal Services Commission will not normally grant full representation before a letter before claim has been sent and the proposed defendant given a reasonable time to respond, initial funding may be available, for eligible claimants, to cover the work necessary to write this. (See Annex C for more information.)

5   This protocol sets out a code of good practice and contains the steps which parties should generally follow before making a claim for judicial review.

6   This protocol does not impose a greater obligation on a public body to disclose documents or give reasons for its decision than that already provided for in statute or common law. However, where the court considers that a public body should have provided relevant documents and/or information, particularly where this failure is a breach of a statutory or common law requirement, it may impose sanctions.

This protocol will not be appropriate *where the defendant does not have the legal power to change the decision being challenged, for example decisions issued by tribunals such as the Asylum and Immigration Tribunal.*

This protocol will not be appropriate *in urgent cases, for example, when directions have been set, or are in force, for the claimant's removal from the UK, or where there is an urgent need for an interim order to compel a public body to act where it has unlawfully refused to do so (for example, the failure of a local housing authority to secure interim accommodation for a homeless claimant) a claim should be made immediately. A letter before claim will not stop the implementation of a disputed decision in all instances.*

7   All claimants will need to satisfy themselves whether they should follow the protocol, depending upon the circumstances of his or her case. Where the use of the protocol is appropriate, the court will normally expect all parties to have complied with it and will take into account compliance or non-compliance when giving directions for case management of proceedings or when making orders for costs.[3] However, even in emergency cases, it is good practice to fax to the defendant the draft Claim Form which the claimant intends to issue. A claimant is also normally required to notify a defendant when an interim mandatory order is being sought.

The letter before claim

8   Before making a claim, the claimant should send a letter to the defendant. The purpose of this letter is to identify the issues in dispute and establish whether litigation can be avoided.

9   Claimants should normally use the suggested *standard format* for the letter outlined at Annex A.

10   The letter should contain *the date and details of the decision, act or omission being challenged and a clear summary of the facts* on which the claim is based. It should also contain the *details of any relevant information* that the claimant is seeking and an explanation of why this is considered relevant.

11   The letter should normally contain the *details of any interested parties*[4] known to the claimant. They should be sent a copy of the letter before claim for information. *Claimants are* strongly advised to seek appropriate legal advice *when considering such proceedings and, in particular, before sending the letter before claim to other interested parties or making a claim.*

12   A claim should not normally be made until the proposed reply date given in the letter before claim has passed, unless the circumstances of the case require more immediate action to be taken.

The letter of response

13   Defendants should normally respond within 14 days using the *standard format* at Annex B. Failure to do so will be taken into account by the court and sanctions may be imposed unless there are good reasons.[5]

14   Where it is not possible to reply within the proposed time limit the defendant should send an interim reply and propose a reasonable extension. Where an extension is sought, reasons should be given and, where required, additional information requested. This will not affect the time limit for making a claim for judicial review[6] nor will it bind the claimant where he or she considers this to be unreasonable. However, where the court considers that a subsequent claim is made prematurely it may impose sanctions.

15   If the *claim is being conceded in full*, the reply should say so in clear and unambiguous terms.

16   If the *claim is being conceded in part or not being conceded at all*, the reply should say so in clear and unambiguous terms, and:

---

3   Civil Procedure Rules Costs Practice Direction.
4   See Civil Procedure Rule 54.1(2)(f).
5   See Civil Procedure Rules Pre-action Protocol Practice Direction paragraphs 2-3.
6   See Civil Procedure Rule 54.5(1).

    (a)   where appropriate, contain a new decision, clearly identifying what aspects of the claim are being conceded and what are not, or, give a clear timescale within which the new decision will be issued;

    (b)   provide a fuller explanation for the decision, if considered appropriate to do so;

    (c)   address any points of dispute, or explain why they cannot be addressed;

    (d)   enclose any *relevant* documentation requested by the claimant, or explain why the documents are not being enclosed; and

    (e)   where appropriate, confirm whether or not they will oppose any application for an interim remedy.

17   The response should be sent to *all interested parties*[7] identified by the claimant and contain details of any other parties who the defendant considers also have an interest.

A   Letter Before Claim

1.   Information required in a letter before claim

Proposed claim for judicial review

1   *To*
(Insert the name and address of the proposed defendant - see details in section 2)

2   *The claimant*
(Insert the title, first and last name and the address of the claimant)

3   *Reference details*
(When dealing with large organisations it is important to understand that the information relating to any particular individual's previous dealings with it may not be immediately available, therefore it is important to set out the relevant reference numbers for the matter in dispute and/or the identity of those within the public body who have been handling the particular matter in dispute - see details in section 3)

4   *The details of the matter being challenged*
(Set out clearly the matter being challenged, particularly if there has been more than one decision)

5   *The issue*
(Set out the date and details of the decision, or act or omission being challenged, a brief summary of the facts and why it is contented to be wrong)

6   *The details of the action that the defendant is expected to take*
(Set out the details of the remedy sought, including whether a review or any interim remedy are being requested)

7   *The details of the legal advisers, if any, dealing with this claim*
(Set out the name, address and reference details of any legal advisers dealing with the claim)

8   *The details of any interested parties*

---

[7]   See Civil Procedure Rule 54.1(2)(f).

(Set out the details of any interested parties and confirm that they have been sent a copy of this letter)

9   *The details of any information sought*
(Set out the details of any information that is sought. This may include a request for a fuller explanation of the reasons for the decision that is being challenged)

10   *The details of any documents that are considered relevant and necessary*
(Set out the details of any documentation or policy in respect of which the disclosure is sought and explain why these are relevant. If you rely on a statutory duty to disclose, this should be specified)

11   *The address for reply and service of court documents*
(Insert the address for the reply)

12   *Proposed reply date*
(The precise time will depend upon the circumstances of the individual case. However, although a shorter or longer time may be appropriate in a particular case, 14 days is a reasonable time to allow in most circumstances)

2.   Address for sending the letter before claim

Public bodies have requested that, for certain types of cases, in order to ensure a prompt response, letters before claim should be sent to specific addresses.
- *Where the claim concerns a decision in an Immigration, Asylum or Nationality case:*
  — The claim may be sent electronically to the following UK Border Agency email address: UKBAPAP@UKBA.gsi.gov.uk
  — Alternatively the claim may be sent by post to the following UK Border Agency postal address:

> Judicial Review Unit
> UK Border Agency
> Lunar House
> 40 Wellesley Rd
> Croydon CR9 2BY

- *Where the claim concerns a decision by the Legal Services Commission:*
  — The address on the decision letter/notification; and

> Legal Director
> Corporate Legal Team
> Legal Services Commission
> 4 Abbey Orchard Street
> London SW1P 2BS

- *Where the claim concerns a decision by a local authority:*
  — The address on the decision letter/notification; and
  — Their legal department[8]
- *Where the claim concerns a decision by a department or body for whom*

---

[8]   The relevant address should be available from a range of sources such as the Phone Book; Business and Services Directory, Thomson's Local Directory, CAB, etc.

Treasury Solicitor acts and Treasury Solicitor has already been involved in the case *a copy should also be sent, quoting the Treasury Solicitor's reference, to:*

The Treasury Solicitor,
One Kemble Street,
London WC2B 4TS

In all other circumstances, the letter should be sent to the address on the letter notifying the decision.

3.   *Specific reference details required*

Public bodies have requested that the following information should be provided in order to ensure prompt response.
- *Where the claim concerns an Immigration, Asylum or Nationality case, dependent upon the nature of the case:*
    — The Home Office reference number
    — The Port reference number
    — The Asylum and Immigration Tribunal reference number
    — The National Asylum Support Service reference number
    Or, if these are unavailable:
    — The full name, nationality and date of birth of the claimant.
- *Where the claim concerns a decision by the Legal Services Commission:*
    — The certificate reference number.

B   Response To A Letter Before Claim

Information Required In A Response To A Letter Before Claim

Proposed claim for judicial review

1 *The claimant*
(Insert the title, first and last names and the address to which any reply should be sent)

2 *From*
(Insert the name and address of the defendant)

3 *Reference details*
(Set out the relevant reference numbers for the matter in dispute and the identity of those within the public body who have been handling the issue)

4 *The details of the matter being challenged*
(Set out details of the matter being challenged, providing a fuller explanation of the decision, where this is considered appropriate)

5 *Response to the proposed claim*
(Set out whether the issue in question is conceded in part, or in full, or will be contested. Where it is not proposed to disclose any information that has been requested, explain the reason for this. Where an interim reply is being sent and there is a realistic prospect of settlement, details should be included)

6 *Details of any other interested parties*

(Identify any other parties who you consider have an interest who have not already been sent a letter by the claimant)

7 *Address for further correspondence and service of court documents*
(Set out the address for any future correspondence on this matter)

C   Notes On Public Funding For Legal Costs In Judicial Review

Public funding for legal costs in judicial review is available from legal professionals and advice agencies which have contracts with the Legal Services Commission as part of the Community Legal Service. Funding may be provided for:

- Legal Help to provide initial advice and assistance with any legal problem; or
- Legal Representation to allow you to be represented in court if you are taking or defending court proceedings. This is available in two forms:
  - Investigative Help is limited to funding to investigate the strength of the proposed claim. It includes the issue and conduct of proceedings only so far as is necessary to obtain disclosure of relevant information or to protect the client's position in relation to any urgent hearing or time limit for the issue of proceedings. This includes the work necessary to write a *letter before claim* to the body potentially under challenge, setting out the grounds of challenge, and giving that body a reasonable opportunity, typically 14 days, in which to respond.
  - Full Representation is provided to represent you in legal proceedings and includes litigation services, advocacy services, and all such help as is usually given by a person providing representation in proceedings, including steps preliminary or incidental to proceedings, and/or arriving at or giving effect to a compromise to avoid or bring to an end any proceedings. Except in emergency cases, a proper *letter before claim* must be sent and the other side must be given an opportunity to respond before Full Representation is granted.

Further information on the type(s) of help available and the criteria for receiving that help may be found in the Legal Service Manual Volume 3: "The Funding Code". This may be found on the Legal Services Commission website at:
www.legalservices.gov.uk
A list of contracted firms and Advice Agencies may be found on the Community Legal Services website at:
www.justask.org.uk

APPENDIX K

N461 Claim Form

The form reproduced overleaf is available to download from
http://hmctscourtfinder.justice.gov.uk/courtfinder/forms/n461-eng.pdf.

Judicial Review
Claim Form

| In the High Court of Justice |
| Administrative Court |

Notes for guidance are available which explain how to complete the judicial review claim form. Please read them carefully before you complete the form.

Seal

For Court use only	
Administrative Court Reference No.	
Date filed	

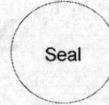

SECTION 1 Details of the claimant(s) and defendant(s)

Claimant(s) name and address(es)

name

address

Telephone no.   Fax no.

E-mail address

Claimant's or claimant's solicitors' address to which documents should be sent.

name

address

Telephone no.   Fax no.

E-mail address

Claimant's Counsel's details

name

address

Telephone no.   Fax no.

E-mail address

1st Defendant

name

Defendant's or (where known) Defendant's solicitors' address to which documents should be sent.

name

address

Telephone no.   Fax no.

E-mail address

2nd Defendant

name

Defendant's or (where known) Defendant's solicitors' address to which documents should be sent.

name

address

Telephone no.   Fax no.

E-mail address

SECTION 2 Details of other interested parties

Include name and address and, if appropriate, details of DX, telephone or fax numbers and e-mail

name

address

Telephone no.   Fax no.

E-mail address

name

address

Telephone no.   Fax no.

E-mail address

SECTION 3 Details of the decision to be judicially reviewed

Decision:

Date of decision:

Name and address of the court, tribunal, person or body who made the decision to be reviewed.

name

address

SECTION 4 Permission to proceed with a claim for judicial review

I am seeking permission to proceed with my claim for Judicial Review.

Is this application being made under the terms of Section 18 Practice Direction 54 (Challenging removal)? ☐ Yes ☐ No

Are you making any other applications? If Yes, complete Section 8. ☐ Yes ☐ No

Is the claimant in receipt of a Community Legal Service Fund (CLSF) certificate? ☐ Yes ☐ No

Are you claiming exceptional urgency, or do you need this application determined within a certain time scale? If Yes, complete Form N463 and file this with your application. ☐ Yes ☐ No

Have you complied with the pre-action protocol? If No, give reasons for non-compliance in the box below. ☐ Yes ☐ No

Have you issued this claim in the region with which you have the closest connection? (Give any additional reasons for wanting it to be dealt with in this region in the box below). If No, give reasons in the box below. ☐ Yes ☐ No

N461 CLAIM FORM

Does the claim include any issues arising from the Human Rights Act 1998?
If Yes, state the articles which you contend have been breached in the box below. ☐ Yes ☐ No

---

SECTION 5 Detailed statement of grounds

☐ set out below   ☐ attached

SECTION 6 Aarhus Convention claim

I contend that this claim is an Aarhus Convention claim ☐ Yes ☐ No

If Yes, indicate in the following box if you do not wish the costs limits
under CPR 45.43 to apply.

If you have indicated that the claim is an Aarhus claim set out the grounds below

---

SECTION 7 Details of remedy (including any interim remedy) being sought

---

SECTION 8 Other applications

I wish to make an application for:-

SECTION 9 Statement of facts relied on

Statement of Truth

I believe (The claimant believes) that the facts stated in this claim form are true.

Full name_____

Name of claimant's solicitor's firm _____

Signed_____ Position or office held_____

     Claimant ('s solicitor)   (if signing on behalf of firm or company)

SECTION 10   Supporting documents

If you do not have a document that you intend to use to support your claim, identify it, give the date when you expect it to be available and give reasons why it is not currently available in the box below.

Please tick the papers you are filing with this claim form and any you will be filing later.

☐ Statement of grounds   ☐ included   ☐ attached

☐ Statement of the facts relied on   ☐ included   ☐ attached

☐ Application to extend the time limit for filing the claim form   ☐ included   ☐ attached

☐ Application for directions   ☐ included   ☐ attached

☐ Any written evidence in support of the claim or
application to extend time

☐ Where the claim for judicial review relates to a decision of
a court or tribunal, an approved copy of the reasons for
reaching that decision

☐ Copies of any documents on which the claimant
proposes to rely

☐ A copy of the legal aid or CSLF certificate *(if legally represented)*

☐ Copies of any relevant statutory material

☐ A list of essential documents for advance reading by
the court *(with page references to the passages relied upon)*

If Section 18 Practice Direction 54 applies, please tick the relevant box(es) below to indicate which papers you are filing with this claim form:

☐ a copy of the removal directions and the decision to which
the application relates   ☐ included   ☐ attached

☐ a copy of the documents served with the removal directions
including any documents which contains the Immigration and
Nationality Directorate's factual summary of the case   ☐ included   ☐ attached

☐ a detailed statement of the grounds   ☐ included   ☐ attached

Reasons why you have not supplied a document and date when you expect it to be available:-

Signed _____ Claimant ('s Solicitor)_____

Click here to print form

APPENDIX L

N462 Acknowledgment of Service

The form reproduced overleaf is available to download from
http://hmctscourtfinder.justice.gov.uk/courtfinder/forms/n462-eng.pdf.

L-001

Judicial Review
Acknowledgment of Service

	In the High Court of Justice Administrative Court
Name and address of person to be served	

name

address

Claim No.	
Claimant(s) *(including ref.)*	
Defendant(s)	
Interested Parties	

SECTION A

Tick the appropriate box

1. I intend to contest all of the claim ☐ ⎫
2. I intend to contest part of the claim ☐ ⎬ complete sections B, C, D and F

3. I do not intend to contest the claim ☐ complete section F

4. The defendant (interested party) is a court or tribunal and **intends** to make a submission. ☐ complete sections B, C and F

5. The defendant (interested party) is a court or tribunal and **does not intend** to make a submission. ☐ complete sections B and F

6. The applicant has indicated that this is a claim to which the Aarhus Convention applies. ☐ complete sections E and F

Note: If the application seeks to judicially review the decision of a court or tribunal, the court or tribunal need only provide the Administrative Court with as much evidence as it can about the decision to help the Administrative Court perform its judicial function.

SECTION B

Insert the name and address of any person you consider should be added as an interested party.

name | name

address | address

Telephone no. | Fax no. | Telephone no. | Fax no.

E-mail address | E-mail address

SECTION C

Summary of grounds for contesting the claim. If you are contesting only part of the claim, set out which part before you give your grounds for contesting it. If you are a court or tribunal filing a submission, please indicate that this is the case.

SECTION D

Give details of any directions you will be asking the court to make, or tick the box to indicate that a separate application notice is attached.

If you are seeking a direction that this matter be heard at an Administrative Court venue other than that at which this claim was issued, you should complete, lodge and serve on all other parties Form N464 with this acknowledgment of service.

SECTION E

Response to the claimant's contention that the claim is an Aarhus claim

Do you deny that the claim is an Aarhus Convention claim?   ☐ Yes   ☐ No

If Yes, please set out your grounds for denial in the box below.

SECTION F

*delete as appropriate

*(I believe)(The defendant believes) that the facts stated in this form are true.

*I am duly authorised by the defendant to sign this statement.

(if signing on behalf of firm or company, court or tribunal)

Position or office held

(To be signed by you or by your solicitor or litigation friend)

Signed

Date

Give an address to which notices about this case can be sent to you

name

address

Telephone no.

Fax no.

E-mail address

If you have instructed counsel, please give their name address and contact details below.

name

address

Telephone no.

Fax no.

E-mail address

Completed forms, together with a copy, should be lodged with the Administrative Court Office (court address, over the page), at which this claim was issued within 21 days of service of the claim upon you, and further copies should be served on the Claimant(s), any other Defendant(s) and any interested parties within 7 days of lodgement with the Court.

| Click here to print form |

Administrative Court addresses

• Administrative Court in **London**

   Administrative Court Office, Room C315, Royal Courts of Justice, Strand, London, WC2A 2LL.

• Administrative Court in **Birmingham**

   Administrative Court Office, Birmingham Civil Justice Centre, Priory Courts, 33 Bull Street, Birmingham B4 6DS.

• Administrative Court in **Wales**

   Administrative Court Office, Cardiff Civil Justice Centre, 2 Park Street, Cardiff, CF10 1ET.

• Administrative Court in **Leeds**

   Administrative Court Office, Leeds Combined Court Centre, 1 Oxford Row, Leeds, LS1 3BG.

• Administrative Court in **Manchester**

   Administrative Court Office, Manchester Civil Justice Centre, 1 Bridge Street West, Manchester, M3 3FX.

APPENDIX M

N463 Application for Urgent Consideration

The form reproduced overleaf is available to download from *http://hmctscourtfinder.justice.gov.uk/courtfinder/forms/n463-eng.pdf.*

| | Click here to reset form | Click here to print form |

Judicial Review
Application for urgent consideration

| In the High Court of Justice |
| Administrative Court |

This form must be completed by the Claimant or the Claimant's advocate if exceptional urgency is being claimed and the application needs to be determined within a certain time scale.

The claimant, or the claimant's solicitors must serve this form on the defendant(s) and any interested parties with the N461 Judicial review claim form.

To the Defendant(s) and Interested Party(ies)
Representations as to the urgency of the claim may be made by defendants or interested parties to the relevant Administrative Court Office by fax or email:-

For cases proceeding in

Claim No.	
Claimant(s) *(including ref.)*	
Defendant(s)	
Interested Party(ies)	

London
Fax: 020 7947 6802   **email:** administrativecourtoffice.generaloffice@hmcts.x.gsi.gov.uk

Birmingham
Fax: 0121 250 6730   **email:** administrativecourtoffice.birmingham@hmcts.x.gsi.gov.uk

Cardiff
Fax: 02920 376461   **email:** administrativecourtoffice.cardiff@hmcts.x.gsi.gov.uk

Leeds
Fax: 0113 306 2581   **email:** administrativecourtoffice.leeds@hmcts.x.gsi.gov.uk

Manchester
Fax: 0161 240 5315   **email:** administrativecourtoffice.manchester@hmcts.x.gsi.gov.uk

SECTION 1 Reasons for urgency

SECTION 2 Proposed timetable *(tick the boxes and complete the following statements that apply)*

☐ a) The N461 application for permission should be considered within _____ hours/days

    If consideration is sought within 48 hours, you must complete Section 3 below

☐ b) Abridgement of time is sought for the lodging of acknowledgments of service

☐ c) If permission for judicial review is granted, a substantive hearing is sought by _____ (date)

SECTION 3 Justification for request for immediate consideration

Date and time when it was first appreciated that an immediate application might be necessary.

Date _____   Time _____

Please provide reasons for any delay in making the application.

What efforts have been made to put the defendant and any interested party on notice of the application?

SECTION 4 Interim relief *(state what interim relief is sought and why in the box below)*

A draft order must be attached.

SECTION 5 Service

A copy of this form of application was served on the defendant(s) and interested parties as follows:

Defendant

☐ by fax machine to   time sent
Fax no. _____   time _____

☐ by handing it to or leaving it with
name _____

☐ by e-mail to
e-mail address _____

Date served
Date _____

Interested party

☐ by fax machine to   time sent
Fax no. _____   time _____

☐ by handing it to or leaving it with
name _____

☐ by e-mail to
e-mail address _____

Date served
Date _____

I confirm that all relevant facts have been disclosed in this application

Name of claimant's advocate
name _____

Claimant (claimant's advocate)
Signed _____

APPENDIX N

N464 Application for Directions as to Venue for Administration and Determination

The form reproduced overleaf is available to download from
http://hmctscourtfinder.justice.gov.uk/courtfinder/forms/n464-eng.pdf.

N-001

Click here to reset form	Click here to print form

Application for directions as to venue for administration and determination

Name and address of party making application

name

address

In the High Court of Justice	
Administrative Court	
Claim No.	
Claimant(s)/ Appellant(s)	
Defendant(s)/ Respondent(s)	
Interested Party(ies)	

I/We apply to the court for a direction that this matter be administered and determined at the:

☐ Royal Courts of Justice in **London**

☐ District Registry of the High Court at **Birmingham**

☐ District Registry of the High Court at **Cardiff**

☐ District Registry of the High Court at **Leeds**

☐ District Registry of the High Court at **Manchester**

for the following reason(s): *(please refer to paragraph 5.2 of PD54D set out overleaf)*

(To be signed by you or by your solicitor or litigation friend)

Signed

Date

Name

(if signing on behalf of firm or company, court)

Position or office held

Please send your completed form to the Administrative Court Office which is currently administering this matter, within 21 days of service of the proceedings upon you. You must also serve copies of your completed application on all other parties.

N464 Application for directions as to venue for administration and determination (04.09)   © Crown copyright 2009

Practice Direction 54D 5.2

5.2 The general expectation is that proceedings will be administered and determined in the region with which the claimant/appellant has the closest connection, subject to the following considerations as applicable -

1) any reason expressed by any party for preferring a particular venue;

2) the region in which the defendant/respondent or any relevant office or department of the defendant/respondent is based;

3) the region in which the claimant's/appellant's legal representatives are based;

4) the ease and cost of travel to a hearing;

5) the availability and suitability of alternative means of attending a hearing (for example, by videolink);

6) the extent and nature of media interest in the proceedings in any particular locality;

7) the time within which it is appropriate for the proceedings to be determined;

8) whether it is desirable to administer or determine the claim in another region in the light of the volume of claims issued at, and the capacity, resources and workload of, the court at which it is issued;

9) whether the claim raises issues sufficiently similar to those in another outstanding claim to make it desirable that it should be determined together with, or immediately following, that other claim; and

10) whether the claim raises devolution issues and for that reason whether it should more appropriately be determined in London or Cardiff.

APPENDIX O

N465 Response to Application for Directions as to Venue for Administration and Determination

The form reproduced overleaf is available to download from
http://hmctscourtfinder.justice.gov.uk/courtfinder/forms/n465-eng.pdf.

O-001

Click here to reset form	Click here to print form

Response to application for directions as to venue for administration and determination

You must serve this form **within 7 days** of receiving form *N464 Application for directions as to venue for administration and determination.*

Name and address of party responding to application

name

address

In the High Court of Justice Administrative Court	
Claim No.	
Claimant(s)/ Appellant(s)	
Defendant(s)/ Respondent(s)	
Interested Party(ies)	

I/We oppose the application for directions as to the venue for administration and determination, for the following reason(s):-

(To be signed by you or by your solicitor or litigation friend)	Signed	Date
	Name	(if signing on behalf of firm or company, court)	Position or office held

Please send your completed form to the Administrative Court Office which is currently administering this matter, within 7 days of receiving form N464 Application for directions as to venue from administration and determination. You must also serve copies of your completed form on all other parties.

INDEX

LEGAL TAXONOMY
FROM SWEET & MAXWELL

This index has been prepared using Sweet and Maxwell's Legal Taxonomy. Main index entries conform to keywords provided by the Legal Taxonomy except where references to specific documents or non-standard terms (denoted by quotation marks) have been included. These keywords provide a means of identifying similar concepts in other Sweet & Maxwell publications and online services to which keywords from the Legal Taxonomy have been applied. Readers may find some minor differences between terms used in the text and those which appear in the index. Suggestions to *sweetandmaxwell.taxonomy@tr.com*.